Works	Year	Events
Parliament of Fowls (?) Boece Boethian balades Palamon and Arcite House of Fame (?)	1378	*January 16–March 9:* Chaucer in Frar ard to French king's daughter Mari replaced by annuity of 20 marks. *May 28–September 19:* Chaucer in Lombardy to treat with Barnabo Visconti (Gower given Chaucer's power of attorney).
	1380	*May 1:* Chaucer released from suit for "raptus" of Cecily Champain. (?) Birth of Lewis Chaucer.
	1381	Peasants' Revolt. *June 19:* deed of Geoffrey Chaucer, son of John Chaucer, vintner of London, quitclaiming his father's house.
Troylus and Criseyde Legend of Good Women	1382	Richard II marries Anne of Bohemia.
	1383	Chaucer obtains first loan against his annuity.
	1385	*October 12:* Chaucer appointed justice of the peace in Kent. Political struggle between Gaunt and his brother, Thomas of Woodstock. *September:* death of Joan of Kent.
Canterbury Prologue early Tales (Knight, Part VII)	1386	Justice of peace reaffirmed. *February 19:* Philippa admitted to fraternity of Lincoln Cathedral. *August:* Chaucer elected member of Parliament from Kent. *October 5:* Aldgate house rented to Richard Forester. *October 15:* Scrope-Grosvenor trial. *December 4:* Adam Yardley appointed controller of customs.
	1387	*June 18:* last payment of annuity of Philippa Chaucer.
Fabliaux (Miller, Reeve)	1388	*May 1:* Chaucer surrenders his royal annuities to John Scalby of Lincolnshire.
	1389	King Richard assumes power. Chaucer appointed clerk of the King's works (more than £30 a year).
Marriage group (Wife of Bath, Friar, Summoner, Merchant, Clerk, Franklin) Astrolabe Equatorie	1390	Commissions to repair St. George's Chapel, Windsor; to oversee repairs on the lower Thames sewers and conduits; to build bleachers for jousts at Smithfield, etc. Chaucer robbed three times. Chaucer appointed sub-forester of North Petherton, Somerset.
	1391	*June 17:* another clerk of the works appointed.
	1393	Chaucer granted a gift of £10 from Richard for services rendered "in this year now present."
	1394	Death of Queen Anne. Chaucer granted a new annuity of £20.
	1395	Richard marries Isabella of France. Thomas Chaucer marries heiress Maud Burghersh.
Balades to Scogan, Bukton	1396	John of Gaunt marries Katherine Swynford.
	1398	Chaucer borrows against his annuity; action for debt against Chaucer; letters of protection from the King.
	1399	Deposition of Richard II. Election of Henry IV. Death of John of Gaunt. *October 13:* on his coronation day, Henry doubles Chaucer's annuity. *December 24:* Chaucer signs 53-year lease for tenement in the garden of the Lady Chapel, Westminster Abbey.
	1400	*September 29:* last record of Chaucer: quittance given by him for a tun of wine received. *October 25:* date of Chaucer's death on tombstone in Westminster Abbey (erected in 1556).

The Complete Poetry and Prose of

Geoffrey Chaucer

Portrait of Chaucer, from the manuscript of Thomas Hoccleve's poem, "Regement of Princes", Harley MS 4866, folio 88r. © British Library Board. All Rights Reserved. The Bridgeman Art Library International

The Complete Poetry and Prose of Geoffrey Chaucer

Third Edition

Edited by
John H. Fisher

Revised by
Mark Allen

Australia • Brazil • Japan • Korea • Mexico • Singapore • Spain • United Kingdom • United States

The Complete Poetry and Prose of Geoffrey Chaucer, Third Edition
John H. Fisher, Mark Allen

Publisher: Michael Rosenberg

Development Editor: Megan Garvey

Assistant Editor: Erin Pass

Editorial Assistant: Rebecca Donahue

Marketing Manager: Melissa Holt

Marketing Communications Manager: Glenn McGibbon

Senior Content Project Manager: Lianne Ames

Art Director: Marissa Falco

Print Buyer: Susan Spencer

Rights Acquisition Specialist, Image: Jennifer Meyer Dare

Rights Acquisition Specialist, Text: Katie Huha

Production Service: S4Carlisle Publishing Services

Text Designer: S4Carlisle Publishing Services

Cover Designer: Marissa Falco

Compositor: S4Carlisle Publishing Services

Library of Congress Control Number: 2010929827

ISBN-13: 978-0-15-506041-8

ISBN-10: 0-15-506041-4

Wadsworth
20 Channel Center Street
Boston, MA 02210
USA

Printed in the United States of America
1 2 3 4 5 6 7 14 13 12 11 10

Contents

Preface vii

Canterbury Tales 1
Introduction 3

Part 1
Introduction 7
General Prologue 11
Knight's Tale 29
Miller's Tale 62
Reeve's Tale 74
Cook's Tale 82

Part 2
Introduction 85
Man of Law's Tale 87

Part 3
Introduction 109
Wife of Bath's Tale 112
Friar's Tale 132
Summoner's Tale 139

Part 4
Introduction 149
Clerk's Tale 151
Merchant's Tale 170

Part 5
Introduction 189
Squire's Tale 191
Franklin's Tale 203

Part 6
Introduction 217
Physician's Tale 219
Pardoner's Tale 224

Part 7
Introduction 237
Shipman's Tale 239
Prioress's Tale 247
Tale of Sir Thopas 252
Tale of Melibee 257
Monk's Tale 284
Nun's Priest's Tale 299

Part 8
Introduction 311
Second Nun's Tale 313
Canon's Yeoman's Tale 323

Part 9
Introduction 337
Manciple's Tale 339

Part 10
Introduction 345
Parson's Tale 347
Retraction 393

Troylus and Criseyde 395
Introduction 396

Book of the Duchess 535
Introduction 536

Parliament of Fowls 559
Introduction 560

House of Fame 577
Introduction 578

Legend of Good Women 617
Introduction 618
Prologue: Original Version (F) 621
Prologue: Revised Version (G) 631
I Legend of Cleopatra 641
II Legend of Thisbe 643
III Legend of Dido 646
IV Legend of Hypsipyle and Medea 653
V Legend of Lucrece 658
VI Legend of Ariadne 661
VII Legend of Philomela 667
VIII Legend of Phyllis 670
IX Legend of Hypermnestra 673

Short Poems 677
Introduction 678
1. Prier a Nostre Dame 684
2. Anelida and Arcite 687
3. Complaint of Mars 694
4. Complaint of Venus 699
5. A Complaint Unto Pity 701
6. A Balade of Pity 703
7. Womanly Noblesse 705
8. To Rosemounde 706
9. Proverbe of Chaucer 706
10. Fortune 707
11. Balade de Bon Conseil 708
12. Moral Balade of Gentilesse 709
13. The Former Age 710
14. Lack Of Steadfastnesse 711
15. To Adam Scryven 712
16. Lenvoy De Chaucer a Bukton 712
17. Lenvoy De Chaucer a Scogan 713
18. Complaint of Chaucer to his Purse 714
19. Merciless Beaute 715
20. Against Women Unconstant 716
21. A Balade of Complaint 716
22. An Amorous Complaint made at Windsor 717

Romaunt of the Rose 719
Introduction 720

Boece 821
Introduction 822

Treatise on the Astrolabe 911
Introduction 912

Equatorie of the Planetis 943
Introduction 944

Chaucer in His Time 960

Chaucer's Language and Versification 965

The Text of This Edition 970

Bibliography 977
Classifications 1024
Abbreviations 1026
Index of Authors in the Bibliography 1029
Glossary 1037

Preface

Following its predecessor, this edition is designed for student use and intended to make all of Chaucer's works accessible in a single volume, in Middle English, and in convenient format. The text closely follows John H. Fisher's edition of 1977 (see The Text of This Edition for changes), and, as in Fisher's edition, the *Equatorie of the Planetis* is included because it may well be Chaucer's work, because it supplements his *Treatise on the Astrolabe,* and because it is otherwise not readily available.

For the first time, both of Chaucer's versions of the Prologue to the *Legend of Good Women* are included because their relative chronology is not absolutely certain and because together they provide important perspective on Chaucer's practice of revision. *Canterbury Tales* and *Troylus and Criseyde* appear first in sequence because of their importance in the history of Chaucer's reputation. Other works follow in quasi-chronological order, even though the chronology of Chaucer's canon is impossible to determine; the lyrics and other short poems are grouped by genre and theme. Although Chaucer produced only some (if any) of the *Romaunt of the Rose* included here, it has traditionally been included in complete editions of his works.

Canterbury Tales is a corrected and updated version of the previously released *The Complete Canterbury Tales of Geoffrey Chaucer* (2006). Otherwise, the glosses, notes, introductory essays, and other apparatus are new to this edition. Because linguistic change has continued (perhaps accelerated) since 1977, the glossing throughout is extensive, gloss markers are provided, and glosses and notes are separated at the bottom of the page for ease of access. On the assumption that not all readers will read Chaucer's works in the order presented here, even common words are glossed recurrently. In awareness that individual words carry different connotations in various contexts, some glosses are repeated on the same page.

Selective rather than comprehensive, the notes explain unfamiliar concepts, identify sources and allusions, and illustrate textual variation. Textual comments are not intended for rigorous textual criticism, but rather to indicate that textual drift occurs in a manuscript environment, and to evince authorial, scribal, and editorial involvement in this drift. The fundamental practice is to depend on a reliable "best-text" manuscript, and then to correct it and illustrate variants from a "second-best" manuscript, with additional material where it may be of interest.

Explanatory notes, along with the introductory essays, are intended to aid modern readers and to direct them to the rich and various ways that Chaucer echoes literary tradition. Often prompted by Fisher's original notes, they also benefit from the scholarship and information published subsequently in *The Riverside Chaucer* and other editions, the Chaucer Variorum volumes, and a number of handbooks, reference works, and critical essays. The bibliography that concludes this volume is selective, intended to illustrate critical and scholarly trends from the latter portion of the twentieth century to the present.

Many readers have helped make this volume possible: Kenneth Bleeth, Mary Flowers Braswell, James M. Dean, Matthew Giancarlo, Daniel J. Ransom, Susan Yager, Mark Womack, and one reader who preferred to remain anonymous. My thanks to all of them and, for proof-reading of the Bibliography, to Laurel Boshoff, who was supported by the Department of English at the University of Texas at San Antonio. I also wish to thank the staffs of the following libraries that provided assistance and space to work during various phrases of the process of research and revision: Trinity University Library (San Antonio, Texas), the Huntington Library, the British Library, the Bodleian Library, and the National Library of Scotland. Special thanks to the staff of the John Peace Libraries at the University of Texas at San Antonio, particularly Sue McCray of the Interlibrary Loan service. Thanks also to Michael Rosenberg, Megan Garvey, and Lianne Ames of Cengage Learning, and to Norine Strang and her staff at S4Carlisle Publishing Services. Finally, and most gratefully, thanks to John Hurt Fisher and Judith Law Fisher, without whom this project would neither have begun nor ended.

Note on citation. Throughout this volume, Chaucer's works are cited parenthetically by line number or, where appropriate, by part or section and line number. For the prose *Tale of Melibee* and the prose *Parson's Tale,* the end of each line is indicated within the text by a slash (/). Bibliographical information for scholarly studies is also cited parenthetically, keyed to the numerical listing in the Bibliography at the end of the volume and often preceded by a date of publication; e.g., (1977; no. 37) indicates number 37 in the Bibliography, published in 1977.

Mark Allen
The University of Texas at San Antonio

Canterbury Tales

Introduction: Canterbury Tales

The *Canterbury Tales* is a collection of stories framed as a tale-telling contest. The contest begins as a means to pass time while a group of pilgrims journey to Canterbury, the holiest site in England. As a literary journey, the pilgrimage is metaphoric, a spiritual movement through life to death, passage beyond sin to salvation. As a form of competition, the contest is realistic, a record of the diversity of humanity and an enactment of the tensions that result from such variety and competition. Told by the various pilgrims, the tales themselves vary widely so that while Chaucer gives us an allegory of human life and a drama of social competition, he also gives us a tour-de-force exploration of the range and limits of literature at the time.

Eclectic in its various genres, verse forms, tones, and themes, the *Canterbury Tales* tests the potential of the English language against literary standards of its day. English was a provincial language at the time—hardly the international patois that it is today—and Chaucer adapts Latin, French, and Italian models to experiment, it seems, with how well such models might succeed in English. Of the twenty-four Canterbury tales, more or less complete, only one follows an English model, and that is a parody (the *Tale of Sir Thopas*). Other kinds of imitation, adaptation, and exploration characterize the tales, and in this respect, the *Canterbury Tales* is an *ars poetica* that teaches by example rather than by precept. The metafictional elements of the work—it is, after all, a story *about* storytelling—make it evident that Chaucer was self-conscious about the exploratory nature of his work and that he was deeply engaged with issues of how author, audience, and text collaborate to make meaning.

When Chaucer died in 1400, he left ten parts of the unfinished *Canterbury Tales*, some parts well polished and others less thoroughly integrated into the pilgrimage/contest frame. The outlines of his plan are clear enough, although many details are not. At one point, he envisioned thirty storytellers, each telling two tales on the trip to Canterbury and two tales on the return trip (see 1.792–94)—a total of 120. At some time, perhaps more than once, he altered his plan (see 5.698, 10.25), either expanding it to the ambitious 120 or scaling down from this initial idea. Several tales lack prologues or epilogues, and a few are fragmentary or interrupted. Some details indicate that Chaucer rearranged the sequence of his tales and reassigned some of the plots to different tellers (see, e.g., 7.19n). Parts 1 and 10 are clearly the opening and closing of the sequence, but the order of the parts within these twin peaks differs in some of the surviving manuscripts, with Parts 4 and 5 being particularly variable, perhaps indicating that Chaucer was rearranging or reconsidering them.

The order of the tales in this book is generally accepted as the best one, although it is in no way certain that it was Chaucer's. The order follows the lavish Ellesmere manuscript (Ellesmere 26.C.9 in the Huntington Library, San Marino, CA). Copied soon after Chaucer's death, the Ellesmere is one of the earliest and most authoritative of extant manuscripts, produced by the same scribe as the Hengwrt manuscript (National Library of Wales, MS Peniarth 392 D). Slightly earlier than the Ellesmere, the Hengwrt has a much less acceptable ordering of the parts, although individual words and spellings are often more authoritative than those in the Ellesmere.

At the 2004 meeting of the New Chaucer Society, Linne R. Mooney stunned and delighted the world of Chaucer scholarship by identifying the copyist of the two manuscripts as Adam Pinkhurst, someone who had been, Mooney shows, Chaucer's copyist for many years and, by extension, someone familiar with the poet's habits, perhaps his intentions. It is probable that Pinkhurst copied the workmanlike Hengwrt piecemeal, following Chaucer's linguistic habits as he gained access to the parts, perhaps late in Chaucer's lifetime or, more likely, soon after the poet's death. In the Ellesmere, Pinkhurst (or someone who guided him) imposed order on the relative chaos that Chaucer left behind in his working papers—making of them a work that is reflected in this volume, complete in design though lacking several portions.

The Ellesmere and the Hengwrt are two among more than fifty manuscripts of the *Canterbury Tales* that survive from the time before William Caxton first printed the work in 1476–77. Almost thirty more surviving manuscripts include selections from the work, often a single tale. None of the versions is exactly the same, so that the version you have in this book is an attempt to reconstruct the most probable readings. Because Chaucer himself was obviously not done with his work, this version (like all edited versions) is a reconstruction of a draft of an incomplete work—challenging in all its indeterminacies and rewarding for the ways that it engages us in the process of making meaning. The most complete information about the manuscripts and their variations is still the daunting eight-volume edition, *The Text of the Canterbury Tales* (1940, no. 43), edited by John M. Manly and Edith Rickert. Two more recent projects, however, are of value for textual questions: the Variorum edition, at present under the general editorship of Daniel J. Ransom (nos. 45, 47–48, 50, 52–55, 62–63, 67), and the electronic *Canterbury Tales* Project, spearheaded by Peter W. Robinson (nos. 46, 49, 51, 56). On the editorial tradition that has kept the *Canterbury Tales* steadily in print since Caxton, see Paul Ruggiers, *Editing Chaucer* (1984, no. 38).

The frame or organizing plot of a fictional pilgrimage was not new in Chaucer's time, nor was the idea of a literary contest. However, the incorporation of tale tellers from a variety of occupations and social ranks was unique in its time, and, despite the enormous influence of Chaucer's work, the superb fusion of journey, contest, and tellers from various social stations has not been duplicated in English literature. Early Chaucer scholars spent considerable effort identifying the sources and models for the frame and individual tales, and clarifying the literary debt of Chaucer's allusions to other works. Much of this work was published first by the Chaucer Society (1868–1925), usefully developed in *Sources and Analogues of Chaucer's Canterbury Tales* (1941, no. 233), edited by W. F. Bryan and Germaine Dempster, and brought up to date by the contributors to *Sources and Analogues of the Canterbury Tales* (2002–05, no. 234), edited by Robert M. Correale and Mary Hamel. Knowledge of Chaucer's sources continues to inform almost all critical approaches because it helps us understand how Chaucer shaped his materials.

Responding to Chaucer's realism, early critics identified real-life models for his pilgrims and mapped the day-by-day progress of the journey. Others examined the allegorical or symbolic import of the astrological references mentioned in the pilgrimage / contest frame or assessed Chaucer's imagery and characters for the ways they echo the Bible, the classics, and the vast medieval commentary on both. Still others treated the pilgrims as complex characters whose tales exist primarily to reflect the motives and desires of their tellers. This so-called dramatic school of criticism was inspired by George Lyman Kittredge's essay, "Chaucer's Discussion of Marriage" (1912, no. 660), and it dominated twentieth-century Chaucer studies, continuing to be influential today despite awareness that Chaucer's "drama" is more a matter of rhetoric than character. See C. David Benson, *Chaucer's Drama of Style* (1986, no. 640). Chaucer's long-lived reputation as the "father" of English poetry also encouraged scholars to assess his contributions to English vocabulary, prosody, and narrative traditions. More recently, the patriarchal assumptions in the term "father" have led critics to challenge the attitudes and biases that are embedded in various critical approaches themselves, as well as to direct attention to questions of gender and class that underlie almost all of Chaucer's tales.

One of the most striking features of recent criticism of the *Canterbury Tales* is the extent to which it is concerned with sociopolitical issues: not only gender and class, but also the Hundred Years' War, plague, Lollardy, the uprising of 1381 (Peasants' Revolt), acts of parliament, and the like. This would be no surprise at all if traditional Chaucer criticism had not been so adamant in its conviction that

Chaucer was unconcerned with such things in his fiction, despite his lifelong personal involvement with international trade and the affairs of court. Another recent critical trend has been to examine individual tales for the ways that they represent the late-medieval cultural forces at work in shaping nascent English nationalism and English notions of other peoples, places, and ideologies rather than the imagination or psychology of their teller. Many such analyses concentrate on particular tales instead of the work in general, because efforts to find unity in the *Canterbury Tales* as a whole strains against the incomplete state of the work. Donald R. Howard's the *Idea of* the *Canterbury Tales* (1976, no. 583) is perhaps still the most successful reading of the work as a structured, unified whole.

A number of valuable guides to Chaucer and his criticism ease the challenges of coming to grips with the complexities of the *Canterbury Tales* and the capacious scholarship and criticism that have accumulated over six hundred years. See the Bibliography at the end of this volume. The best of the guides is Helen Cooper's Oxford Guide, titled simply *The Canterbury Tales* (2d ed. 1996, no. 581). Among the others that are most useful and readable are Derek Pearsall's *The Canterbury Tales* (1985, no. 588) and Helen Phillips's *An Introduction to the Canterbury Tales* (2000, no. 589). The best one-volume encyclopedia of Chaucer is *The Oxford Companion to Chaucer* (2003, no. 100), by Douglas Gray, and the handiest glossaries are Norman Davis's *A Chaucer Glossary* (1979, no. 97) and the one included in *The Riverside Chaucer* (1987, no. 36), edited by Larry D. Benson. Neither of these glossaries, however, compares with the full lexical description of *The Middle English Dictionary* (no. 101), which we recommend to all readers of Chaucer.

Canterbury Tales, Part 1

Introduction

THE *GENERAL PROLOGUE* establishes the basic plot of the *Canterbury Tales*—the pilgrimage and the tale-telling contest. It introduces the pilgrim-tellers, the Host who conducts the contest, and the narrator who recounts the journey. Its springtime setting connotes renewal, and the opening of the poem aligns the pilgrims' journey with the revitalization of the created universe. The stars, the earth, animals, and plants—the entire "cheyne of love" as it is called in the *Knight's Tale* (2988)—participate in the annual cosmic cycle of rejuvenation. As part of this chain, human beings undertake the spiritual renewal of pilgrimage, a symbolic journey that mirrors the journey from life to death and from this world to the next.

Often called "sketches" or "portraits," the descriptions of the individual pilgrims are deeply influenced by traditional literary satires of the social and moral failings of various professions or occupations—the so-called estates satire of medieval society, not unlike modern complaints against doctors and lawyers. Chaucer enlivens and particularizes his descriptions by recording the successes of his characters as well as the failings that usually make up such satires. Friars were widely condemned for associating with the rich rather than the poor, a habit Chaucer's Friar shares; yet he is also the "beste beggere" in his house (252). The Miller overcharges his clients, a typical complaint against millers, but he is also a superb wrestler. Specific details counteract the stereotypical aspects of the descriptions, personalizing them and reminding the reader that generality and specificity are interdependent. The Friar is a generic friar, but he also has the unusual name Huberd. The Miller is a stereotype of millers, but his hairy wart, black nostrils, and bagpipes help to individuate him. Laura C. Lambdin and Robert T. Lambdin, editors of *Chaucer's Pilgrims* (1996, no. 741), provide background to each of the individual descriptions; Jill Mann discusses the tradition of estates satire in *Chaucer and Medieval Estates Satire* (1972, no. 742). Laura Hodges has published two book-length studies of the clothing worn by the pilgrims (2000 and 2005, nos. 738–39). For line-by-line discussion of the descriptions, see Malcolm Andrew's Variorum notes to *The General Prologue* (1993, no. 45).

The interplay between particular and universal within individual descriptions is magnified by connections among them that help to convey the distinct sense of a society. Some descriptions are clearly paired. The Knight and Squire are father and son, and they embody two aspects of chivalry. The Parson and Plowman are brothers and ideals of clerical and secular Christian labor. The pairing of the Sergeant at Law and the Franklin suggests financial collusion, and homosocial bonding is evident in the harmonious singing of the Summoner and Pardoner. On the other hand, the contrast in attitudes toward money in the descriptions of the Merchant and the Clerk (note the echoic verb *sownynge*, "suggesting," in 275 and 307) remind us that not all people pursue the same goals. Refusing to resolve themselves into a simple social formula, these and many more echoes among the descriptions communicate a rich variety of social relations.

The organization of the descriptions moves from the aristocratic Knight and his retinue to the socially pretentious Prioress and Monk down the social scale through the middle ranks to the churls and scalawags at the end. Yet this apparent hierarchy is disturbed or complicated by the recurrent presence of one character or another who seems out of order—the Physician or the Manciple, for example, or perhaps the Wife of Bath. The upshot is that even though the society depicted seems to have a shape or pattern, it is not a simple or placid one.

Through such techniques, Chaucer's society brings to literary life the affiliations and struggles of late-medieval English society. Much of the sense of vibrancy has to do with aspects of rank and finance—wealthy or impoverished attire, varying table manners, the relative excellence of the horses ridden by the pilgrims (horses were status symbols much as cars are today). Yet subtler reverberations are at work, too. It is startling, for example, to observe the varieties of meaning in words such as *worthy*, *good*, or *gentle* in the *General Prologue*. The Knight is resoundingly worthy, but when the word is applied to the Friar and the Franklin (269, 360) and to the townswomen with whom the Friar flirts (217), it has quite different nuances and compels consideration of what it really means to be "worthy." One learns quickly that the Wife of Bath is a "good" woman in a sense different from the Parson being a "good" man (445, 477), that the meaning of *gentle* must have had a wide semantic field to be applied to the Manciple and the Pardoner (567, 669). These linguistic reverberations between the descriptions lure readers, almost unaware, to feel the cohesion of the society, while they remind us that neither language nor society is altogether stable.

In *Chaucer and the Politics of Discourse* (1996, no. 361), Michaela Paasche Grudin tallies the variety of ways in which the pilgrims themselves speak—the professional bragging implicit in the Physician's description (429ff.), the laughing and joking of the Wife of Bath (474), the Summoner's rote Latin (646), the boldness of the Host (755), and so on—making clear how the society of the pilgrims is constituted in large part in, through, and by language. After all, the narrator describes the pilgrims only after he has spoken with each of them, "everichon" (31). This concern with language anticipates the variety of forms and genres in the Canterbury collection, although this plurality is here represented in indirect rather than direct speech. We seem to overhear snatches of the narrator's many conversations, and when the Host does propose the contest in direct discourse—the agreement or "foreward" (829) that brings this society into speaking life—the scene indicates that human society is fundamentally verbal and competitive, that language makes community.

Overarching all this is a narrator who reports from memory what he has seen and heard. He tells us that his own "wit is short" (746) and thereby raises questions about his reliability and about the reliability of literature. Critics have argued whether this narrator is better seen as a projection of Chaucer himself (a shrewd but disarming critic of others) or as a naïve persona (whose generosity of spirit enables us to take what he says ironically). He is perhaps both and more, a shifting perspective that compels us to make our own judgments and everywhere reminds us not to take things at face value. The classic discussion of the persona is E. Talbot Donaldson's "Chaucer the Pilgrim" (1954, no. 670), but see also H. Marshall Leicester's "The Art of Impersonation: A General Prologue to *The Canterbury Tales*" (1980, no. 674), and Barbara Nolan's "A Poet Ther Was: Chaucer's Voices in the *General Prologue*" (1986, no. 677).

There is evidence that, like the *Canterbury Tales* itself, the *General Prologue* is unfinished, that Chaucer was still adjusting it or intending to adjust it when he died in 1400. Thus, efforts to date it are futile, but it is likely that he had a notion of a prologue as he began to develop the collection of various tales sometime in the late 1380s. Quite possibly Chaucer intended to develop the description of the Second Nun with a description of the Nun's Priest to follow (see 164n). Certainly the plan for a two-way journey and four tales told by each pilgrim (792–94) was left in need of revision.

Coming first as it does in the Canterbury sequence, the *Knight's Tale* is the secular yardstick against which the tales to follow can be measured. Its epic setting and lofty tone, its concern with hierarchy and order, and its profound message have encouraged critics to regard the tale as the philosophical backbone of *The Canterbury Tales*, at least with regard to the major themes of love, order, and divine Providence. It can be described as a philosophical romance because it so successfully fuses weighty themes with the subjects of chivalry and aristocratic love.

The story of Palamon and Arcite's noble but destructive love for Emelye derives from Giovanni Boccaccio's *Il Teseida*. Chaucer compressed the plot and deepened it by increasing its concern for astrological determinism (represented in classical planetary gods) and by lending it a strong sense of organization and balance (see, e.g., 2051n, 2156n). Living under threat of violence, humans seek to restrain social chaos through law and reasoned pity. Hedged in by what appears to be unknowable fate or chance, humans must restrain their passions to avoid the emotional chaos of sorrow and despair. Similarly hedged in by history and literary tradition, storytelling must restrain digression through orderly narration. Thematically and stylistically the tale counsels restraint, suggesting that we not allow impulses to overwhelm order.

Expressed in Duke Theseus's speech at the end of the tale, this theme of orderly restraint derives from Boethius's *Consolation of Philosophy*, which Chaucer translated as his *Boece* and which deeply influenced many of his works. Theseus explains the influence of the planets as manifestations of omniscient Providence and counsels that humans make a "vertu of necessitee" (3042) by accepting what we cannot avoid. Set against love, battle, and death, this counsel leaves little space for human freedom beyond embracing the inevitable. It is freedom tinged with regret, but—to the extent that we assume a Boethian outlook—this freedom is made grand by the opportunity to participate willingly in providential order.

This rarefied idealism has been scrutinized from alternative points of view, often class or gender based. Feminist critics, for example, challenge the hierarchical assumptions taken for granted in Emelye's passivity and Theseus's defeat of "Femenye" (866). In "Chaucerian Ritual and Patriarchal Discourse" (1992, no. 761), John Ganim attributes this masculinist outlook to the Knight rather than to Chaucer; in *Gender and Romance in Chaucer's Canterbury Tales* (1994, no. 622), Susan Crane explores the unresolved "gendered oppositions" of the tale as an aspect of its romance genre. In *Feminizing Chaucer*, Jill Mann (2002, no. 475) argues that feminine pity is more strongly present in the tale than a masculinist warrior ethos. In *Philosophical Chaucer* (2004, no. 586), Mark Miller explores how gender, psychology, and the dialogic structure of the *Consolation* underlie the ways that the *Knight's Tale* prompts the audience to desire and to distrust normative ideals of gender and self-identity. Such readings often indict the political self-interest of Thesus in the tale, although in *Wisdom and Chivalry: Chaucer's* Knight's Tale *and Medieval Political Theory* (2009, no. 770b), Stephen H. Rigby argues that the duke embodies traditional political ideals

In a manner of speaking, the Miller is the first critic of the *Knight's Tale*, although he challenges not its depiction of sexuality but its high-mindedness and the limitations it sets on human self-determination. Chaucer composed his story of Palamon and Arcite before he conceived of the Canterbury pilgrimage, and by incorporating it into the frame (see 889–91n), he exposed it to competing points of view. The *Miller's Tale*, the *Reeve's Tale*, and the unfinished *Cook's Tale* are all fabliaux—humorous tales, usually indecent, about middle- or low-class characters and situations. One of the principal comic devices of the genre is burlesque of pretentious values and behaviors, and Chaucer's stacking of three sequential fabliaux enables him to explore and expose a range of outlooks.

The *Miller's Tale* ridicules the theological speculations and astrological learning of the *Knight's Tale* as well as its courtly idealism, and it does so with unrestrained vitality, even rebellion. Its comic outcome has a distinct air of inevitability about it, but it is the inevitability of poetic justice—if it is justice at all—rather than the astrological determinism of the opening tale. As Charles Muscatine discusses in *Chaucer and the French Tradition* (1957, no. 199), the interrelation of style and substance in the *Miller's Tale* is particularly successful, effectively communicating that character is fate. Arguably, each of the male characters gets his "just desserts," even though the question of justice for Alisoun goes unasked. In this respect, the Miller's Alisoun parallels the Knight's Emelye, prompting us to explore the range of striking similarities between the tales, as well as their overt and covert differences. In *Chaucer's Queer Nation* (2003, no. 461), Glenn Burger argues that both tales assert normative sexuality, but he also shows how the *Miller's Tale* disturbs sexual assumptions with a "a touch of the queer," as it disturbs so many of the Knight's ideals. Tison Pugh addresses queer approaches to fabliaux more generally in *Queering Medieval Genres* (2004, no. 466).

The *Reeve's Tale* is set in rural Trumpington (near Cambridge) instead of the court of Athens (*Knight's Tale*) or civic Oxford (*Miller's Tale*), and there is little cosmic inevitability or poetic justice in the plot. Chance, animal passion, and vengeance dominate. The two clerks, John and Aleyn (paralleling Palamon and Arcite and the Miller's Nicholas and Absolon), stumble into blunt sexual escapades and win their competition with Symkyn the miller by an accidental stroke in the dark. They are country bumblers whose lack of sophistication is marked by their northern dialect—the first time in English literature that dialect is used for characterization (see the glosses to 4022ff.). The Reeve tells the tale, he informs us, to punish the Miller for a perceived offense, an intensification of the Miller's claim that he will "quite" (repay, 3127) the *Knight's Tale* and an invitation that we consider the role of intention in storytelling. This concern with intention recurs throughout the *Canterbury Tales*, as do issues of competition among classes, professions, and individuals.

In these first three tales, Chaucer explores the social and stylistic implications of competing attitudes in what appears to be a descending sequence, but he seems unwilling to investigate a thoroughly debauched outlook. Breaking off just as it is getting underway, the *Cook's Tale* is set in the London underworld and populated by downright scoundrels, particularly the apprentice Perkyn, who steals, plays at dice, abuses the contract of his apprenticeship, and takes up residence with a prostitute. The major motifs of the tales of the Miller and the Reeve are found elsewhere in fabliau tradition, but the Cook's fragment seems to be based in contemporary reality. No single source is universally accepted for any of the three, but Carol Falvo Heffernan (2004, no. 792), and others argue for "memorial borrowing" from both French and Italian traditions. Similarly, dating these fabliaux is general rather than specific; they are usually ascribed to the late 1380s or early 1390s. Much or all of the *Knight's Tale* had been written earlier (Chaucer refers to the plot in his Prologue to the *Legend of Good Women* 420), but the formulation of part 1 as a whole almost certainly dates from this time.

We do not know whether Chaucer had more of a plot in mind, but the *Cook's Tale* is effective as it stands. In his first four tales, he establishes a range of values, classes, and styles. The vitality of the *Miller's Tale* successfully challenges the stoicism of the *Knight's Tale*, but it may be a step on a slippery slope to the relative rudeness of the *Reeve's Tale* and the debauchery of the *Cook's Tale*. In *Chaucer and the Subject of History* (1991, no. 442), Lee Patterson shows how conflicting assumptions about social control and human agency underlie various class-based outlooks and how Chaucer's depiction of these outlooks lays the assumptions bare. In "The Three Styles of Fragment I of the *Canterbury Tales*," (1973, no. 726), John H. Fisher argues that the *Knight's Tale* illustrates *high style*; the *Miller's Tale*, *middle style*; and the *Reeve's Tale*, *low style*. Thematically, ideologically, and stylistically, the variety of the *Canterbury Tales* begins to emerge, and each tale gains dimension through juxtaposition.

Canterbury Tales
Part 1

Woodcut from William Caxton's second edition of *The Canterbury Tales* published ca. 1484

General Prologue

Here bigynneth the Book of the Tales of Caunterbury.

When that Aprill with his shoures soote°
The droghte° of March hath perced° to the roote,
And bathed every veyne° in swich licour°
Of which vertu° engendred° is the flour°;
Whan Zephirus eek° with his sweete breeth°
Inspired hath in° every holt and heeth°
The tendre croppes°, and the yonge sonne°
Hath in the Ram his halfe cours yronne°,
And smale foweles° maken melodye,
That slepen° al the nyght with open eye—
So priketh hem nature° in hir corages°—
Thanne longen folk to goon° on pilgrimages,
And palmeres for to seken straunge strondes°
To ferne halwes°, kowthe° in sondry londes°;
And specially from every shires° ende
Of Engelond to Caunterbury they wende°

---

1 his shoures soote, *its sweet showers* **2 droghte,** *dryness,* **hath perced,** *has pierced* **3 veyne,** *vein* (of the plants), **swich licour,** *such liquid* **4 Of which vertu,** *by which potency,* **engendred,** *born,* **flour,** *flower* **5 eek,** *also,* **breeth,** *breath* **6 Inspired hath,** *has breathed into,* **holt and heeth,** *woodland and plain* **7 tendre croppes,** *new foliage,* **yonge sonne,** *young sun* **8 his halfe cours yronne,** *run his half-course* **9 smale foweles,** *small fowls* **10 slepen,** *sleep* **11 priketh hem nature,** *nature incites them,* **hir corages,** *their hearts* **12 Thanne longen folk to goon,** *then people yearn to go* **13 seken straunge strondes,** *seek foreign shores* **14 ferne halwes,** *faraway saints,* **kowthe,** *known,* **sondry londes,** *various lands* **15 shires,** *district's* **16 wende,** *travel*

Text based on Huntington Library, San Marino, CA, MS EL 26.C.9 (El), with select variants from National Library of Wales MS Hengwrt 392 D (Hg). **1 Aprill,** accented on the first syllable. The first two feet of the poem begin with accented beats. **2 droghte of March,** early spring is a relatively dry season in southern England. **5 Zephirus,** the west wind, associated with spring and renewal; in classical mythology, husband of Flora, goddess of flowers, and father of Carpus, god of fruit. **7 yonge sonne,** the sun is young because the poem is set soon after the springtime equinox, when the days begin to lengthen toward summer. **8 in the Ram,** Aries, the zodiacal sign of the Ram. **halfe cours,** in April the sun passes through the last half of Aries and first half of Taurus, so the sun has already passed Aries and entered Taurus. In Chaucer's time, the sun entered Taurus on April 12. At *MLP* 2.5–6 (perhaps the second day of the pilgrimage), April 18 is indicated, so the beginning of the pilgrimage may be set on April 17. **13 palmeres,** professional pilgrims whose emblem was a frond from a palm tree, a sign they had been to the Holy Land.

The hooly blisful martir for to seke°
That hem hath holpen° whan that they were seeke°.
Bifil° that in that seson° on a day
In Southwerk at the Tabard as I lay
Redy to wenden° on my pilgrymage
To Caunterbury with ful devout corage°,
At nyght was come into that hostelrye°
Wel nyne and twenty in a compaignye
Of sondry folk°, by aventure yfalle°
In felaweship°, and pilgrimes were they alle,
That toward Caunterbury wolden ryde°.
The chambres° and the stables weren wyde°,
And wel we weren esed atte beste°.
And shortly, whan the sonne was to reste,
So hadde I spoken with hem everichon°
That I was of hir felaweship anon°,
And made forward° erly° for to ryse,
To take oure wey ther as I yow devyse°.
But nathelees°, whil I have tyme and space,
Er° that I ferther in this tale pace°,
Me thynketh it° acordaunt to° resoun
To telle yow al the condicioun°
Of ech of hem°, so as it semed me,
And whiche° they weren, and of what degree°,
And eek° in what array° that they were inne,
And at a knyght than wol° I first bigynne.
A KNYGHT ther was, and that a worthy man,
That fro the tyme° that he first bigan
To riden out, he loved chivalrie,
Trouthe and honour, fredom and curteisie.
Ful worthy was he in his lordes werre°,
And therto hadde he riden, no man ferre°,
As wel in cristendom° as in hethenesse°,
And evere honoured for his worthynesse.
At Alisaundre he was whan it was wonne.
Ful ofte tyme° he hadde the bord bigonne°
Aboven alle nacions° in Pruce.
In Lettow hadde he reysed° and in Ruce,
No Cristen man so ofte° of his degree°.
In Gernade at the seege° eek hadde he be°
Of Algezir, and riden in Belmarye.
At Lyeys was he and at Satalye,
Whan they were wonne, and in the Grete See
At many a noble armee° hadde he be.
At mortal batailles hadde he been fiftene°,
And foughten for oure feith at Tramyssene
In lystes thries°, and ay slayn his foo°.
This ilke° worthy knyght hadde been also
Somtyme with the lord of Palatye
Agayn° another hethen in Turkye,
And everemoore he hadde a sovereyn prys°.
And though that he were worthy, he was wys,
And of his port° as meeke as is a mayde.
He nevere yet no vileynye ne sayde°
In al his lyf unto no maner wight°.

---

17 seke, *seek* **18 hem hath holpen,** *has helped them,* **seeke,** *sick* **19 Bifil,** *it happened,* **seson,** *season* **21 Redy to wenden,** *ready to travel* **22 ful devout corage,** *very devout spirit* **23 hostelrye,** *inn* **25 sondry folk,** *various people,* **by aventure yfalle,** *by chance fallen* **26 In felaweship,** *into fellowship* **27 wolden ryde,** *intended to ride* **28 chambres,** *bedrooms,* **weren wyde,** *were roomy* **29 esed atte beste,** *accommodated in the best manner* **31 hem everichon,** *every one of them* **32 anon,** *immediately* **33 made forward,** (we) *made agreement,* **erly,** *early* **34 I yow devyse,** *I* (will) *tell you* **35 nathelees,** *nonetheless* **36 Er,** *before,* **pace,** *go* **37 Me thynketh it,** *I think it,* **acordaunt to,** *in accord with* **38 condicioun,** *circumstances* **39 ech of hem,** *each of them* **40 whiche,** *what* **degree,** *social rank* **41 eek,** *also,* **array,** *clothing,* **42 wol,** *will* **44 fro the tyme,** *from the time* **47 lordes werre,** *lord's war* **48 ferre,** *further* **49 cristendom,** *Christian lands,* **hethenesse,** *heathen lands* **52 Ful ofte tyme,** *very often,* **bord bigonne,** *sat at the head of the table (board)* **53 nacions,** *nationalities* **54 reysed,** *campaigned* **55 so ofte,** *as often,* **degree,** *social rank* **56 seege,** *siege,* **eek hadde he be,** *also had he been* **60 armee,** *expedition* **61 mortal batailles . . . fiftene,** *fifteen mortal battles* **63 In lystes thries,** *thrice in duels,* **ay slayn his foo,** *always killed his foe* **64 ilke,** *same* **66 Agayn,** *against* **67 sovereyn prys,** *supreme reputation* **69 of his port,** *in his behavior* **70 no vileynye ne sayde,** *said nothing villainous* **71 no maner wight,** *any kind of person*

17 blisful martir, blessed martyr, St. Thomas Becket, martyred in Canterbury Cathedral in 1170, making it among the most popular pilgrimage sites in England. **20 In Southwerk at the Tabard,** in the area south of London Bridge at the Tabard Inn, identified by its sign shaped like a smock or sleeveless surcoat. The site of the inn is still identified on Borough High Street in modern Southwark. **24 nyne and twenty,** Chaucer evidently intended thirty pilgrims here (including the narrator), but the number does not fit the text (see 164n); the Host and later the Canon's Yeoman join this group. **43 KNYGHT . . . ,** the Knight is emphatically worthy and his virtues include a wide range—from integrity or fidelity (**Trouthe**) to generosity and good manners (**fredom and curteisie**). The wide-flung campaigns attributed to him—all against pagans at war with Christians—were fought over some forty years, unlikely for any real person. **51 Alisaundre,** Alexandria (in Egypt), won in 1365. **53–54 in Pruce,** fighting in Prussia (on the Baltic Sea), the Knights of the Teutonic Order were organized by nationality. The Teutonic Knights fought also in Lithuania (**Lettow**) and Russia (**Ruce**). **56–57 Gernade at . . . Algezir,** Algeciras, a port in Granada of southern Spain, taken in 1344. **57 Belmarye,** a fourteenth-century Moorish kingdom in modern Morocco, attacked by Christians in the 1360s. **58 Lyeys,** Ayash, a seaport in Turkey, captured in 1367. **Satalye,** Antalya, also in Turkey, was attacked in 1361. **59 Grete See,** Mediterranean Sea. **62 Tramyssene,** Tlemcen, in Algeria, is not known to have been attacked by Christians in the fourteenth century. **63 lystes,** lists were enclosures for battle in which single champions fought to decide the outcome of a larger battle; also used in tournaments. **65 lord of Palatye,** a title used by rulers of the Turkish city Balat (Byzantine Palation; Greek Miletus); it is uncertain who the other Turkish leader may be (line 66). **68 worthy . . . wys,** strength and wisdom were the most valued qualities of the hero from classical times onward.

He was a verray, parfit, gentil° knyght.
But for to tellen yow of his array°,
His hors° weren goode, but he was nat gay°.
Of fustian° he wered° a gypoun°
Al bismotered with° his habergeoun°,
For he was late ycome° from his viage°,
And wente for to doon° his pilgrymage.

With hym ther was his sone, a yong SQUIER,
A lovyere° and a lusty bacheler°,
With lokkes crulle° as they were leyd in presse°.
Of twenty yeer° of age he was, I gesse.
Of his stature he was of evene lengthe°,
And wonderly delyvere°, and of greet strengthe.
And he hadde been somtyme in chyvachie°
In Flaundres, in Artoys, and Pycardie,
And born hym weel°, as of so litel space°,
In hope to stonden in his lady grace°.
Embrouded was he, as it were a meede°
Al ful of fresshe floures, whyte and reede°.
Syngynge he was or floytynge° al the day.
He was as fressh as is the monthe of May.
Short was his gowne, with sleves longe and wyde.
Wel koude° he sitte on hors and faire ryde.
He koude songes make and wel endite°,
Juste° and eek° daunce, and weel purtreye° and write.
So hoote° he lovede that by nyghtertale°
He slepte namoore° than dooth a nyghtyngale.
Curteis° he was, lowely°, and servysable°,
And carf biforn° his fader at the table.

A YEMAN° hadde he and servantz namo°
At that tyme, for hym liste° ride so,
And he was clad in cote° and hood of grene°.
A sheef of pecok arwes°, bright and kene°,
Under his belt he bar ful thriftily°—
Wel koude he dresse his takel yemanly°;
His arwes drouped noght° with fetheres lowe—
And in his hand he baar° a myghty bowe.
A not-heed° hadde he, with a broun visage°.
Of wodecraft wel koude° he al the usage°.
Upon his arm he baar a gay bracer°,
And by his syde a swerd and a bokeler°,
And on that oother syde a gay daggere
Harneised° wel and sharp as point of spere;
A Cristophre on his brest° of silver sheene.
An horn he bar°, the bawdryk° was of grene;
A forster° was he, soothly°, as I gesse.

Ther was also a Nonne°, a PRIORESSE,
That of hir smylyng° was ful symple and coy°;
Hire gretteste ooth° was but by Seint Loy.

---

72 verray, parfit, gentle, *true, perfect, noble* **73 array,** *equipment* **74 hors,** *horses,* **gay,** *extravagant* **75 fustian,** *coarse, cloth,* **wered,** *wore,* **gypoun,** *tunic* **76 bismotered with,** *stained by,* **habergeoun,** *coat of mail* **77 late ycome,** *lately come,* **viage,** *journey* **78 to doon,** *to do* **80 lovyere,** *lover,* **lusty bacheler** *lively young man or aspirant to knighthood* **81 lokkes crulle,** *hair curled,* **leyd in presse,** *laid in a presss* **82 yeer,** *years* **83 evene lengthe,** *average height* **84 wonderly delyvere,** *wondrously agile* **85 chyvachie,** *cavalry action* **87 born hym weel,** *conducted himself well,* **litel space,** *short time* **88 stonden in his lady grace,** *stand in his lady's favor* **89 Embrouded . . . meede,** *embroidered . . . as if a meadow* **90 floures, whyte and reede,** *flowers, white and red* **91 floytynge,** *playing a flute or pipes* **94 koude,** *could* **95 songes make and wel endite,** *compose music and lyrics,* **96 Juste,** *joust,* **eek,** *also,* **weel purtreye,** *draw well* **97 hoote,** *hotly,* **by nyghtertale,** *at nighttime* **98 namoore,** *no more* **99 Curteis,** *courteous,* **lowely,** *humble,* **servysable,** *willing to serve* **100 carf biforn,** *carved in front of* **101 YEMAN,** *Yeoman (servant),* **namo,** *no more* **102 hym liste,** *(it) pleased him (to)* **103 cote,** *coat,* **grene,** *green* **104 sheef of pecok arwes,** *bundle of arrows with peacock feathers,* **kene,** *sharp* **105 bar ful thriftily,** *bore very appropriately* **106 Wel koude he dresse his takel yemanly,** *he knew how to care for his equipment as a yeoman should* **107 drouped noght,** *drooped not* **108 baar,** *carried* **109 not-heed,** *closely cropped head,* **broun visage,** *tanned face* **110 koude,** *knew,* **usage,** *practice* **111 gay bracer,** *fancy arm guard* **112 swerd and a bokeler,** *sword and a small shield* **114 Harneised,** *decorated* **115 brest,** *breast* **116 bar,** *bore,* **bawdryk,** *chest strap* **117 forster,** *forest keeper,* **soothly,** *truly* **118 Nonne,** *Nun,* **119 hir smylyng,** *her smiling,* **coy,** *reserved (Lat. quietus) or affecting reserve (see LGW 1548)* **120 Hire gretteste ooth,** *her greatest oath*

79 SQUIER, the rank of Squire is just below that of his father, the Knight, whom he serves humbly and properly. Yet the contrast of the two portraits is clear: the Knight battles for Christendom in faraway lands; the Squire for his lady's favor in familiar Flanders and France. Their clothes and their activities also contrast. **80 bacheler,** the term has a range of meaning from "young unmarried man" to "aspirant to knighthood" to "a rank of knighthood not qualified to carry his own banner." **82 of age he was,** Hg reads "he was of age." **86 Flaundres, in Artoys, and Pycardie,** apparently an allusion to the 1383 English "crusade" against Flanders and adjoining districts in northeastern France in support of Urban IV of Rome and against the French supporters of Clement VII of Avignon, two claimants to the papacy. The campaign was part of the Hundred Years' War. **93ff. gowne . . . sleves . . . ,** the short gown and long sleeves are very fashionable, and the Squire's skills in the following lines indicate his aristocratic accomplishments. **98 nyghtyngale,** it was thought that the nightingale sang all night long in the mating season. **100 carf . . . at the table,** a characteristic activity of squires. **101 YEMAN,** a freeborn servant, the well-equipped yeoman serves the Knight (the referent of **he** in this line), apparently as a huntsman and the keeper of his forests. Like the Squire and several other pilgrims, he is decked out in his finery. **108 myghty bowe,** the English longbow was the most effective weapon in the Hundred Years' War. **115 Cristophre,** a badge or metal of St. Christopher, who was the patron of travelers. **118 PRIORESSE,** a high-ranking nun, in this case probably the superior of an independent Benedictine convent. The Prioress's courtly demeanor is emphasized over her Christian piety, although she is in some ways also rather provincial. **120 ooth . . . Seint Loy,** strictly speaking, the Prioress should swear no oaths whatsoever, even one by the genteel French St. Eligius (Fr. *Eloi*).

And she was cleped° madame Eglentyne.
Ful weel° she soong the service dyvyne°,
Entuned° in hir nose ful semely°,
And Frenssh she spak ful faire and fetisly°,
After the scole° of Stratford atte Bowe,
For Frenssh of Parys was to hire unknowe°.
At mete° wel ytaught was she with-alle°:
She leet° no morsel from hir lippes falle,
Ne wette° hir fyngres in hir sauce depe°.
Wel koude she° carie a morsel and wel kepe°
That no drope ne fille° upon hire brest.
In curteisie was set ful muchel hir lest°.
Hir over-lippe° wyped° she so clene
That in hir coppe° ther was no ferthyng sene°
Of grece°, whan she dronken hadde hir draughte°.
Ful semely° after hir mete° she raughte°.
And sikerly° she was of greet desport°,
And ful plesaunt, and amyable of port°,
And peyned hire° to countrefete cheere°
Of court, and to been estatlich of manere°,
And to ben holden digne° of reverence.
But, for to speken of hire conscience,
She was so charitable and so pitous°
She wolde wepe°, if that she saugh° a mous
Kaught in a trappe, if it were deed or bledde°.
Of smale houndes° hadde she that she fedde°
With rosted flessh°, or milk and wastel-breed°.
But soore wepte she° if oon° of hem were deed,
Or if men smoot° it with a yerde smerte°—
And al was conscience and tendre herte.
Ful semyly° hir wympul pynched was°,
Hir nose tretys°, hir eyen° greye as glas,
Hir mouth ful smal, and therto softe and reed.
But sikerly° she hadde a fair forheed;
It was almoost a spanne brood°, I trowe°,
For, hardily°, she was nat undergrowe.
Ful fetys° was hir cloke°, as I was war°.
Of smal coral aboute hire arm she bar°
A peire of bedes°, gauded° al with grene,
And theron heng° a brooch of gold ful sheene°
On which ther was first write° a crowned A,
And after *Amor vincit omnia.*

Another NONNE with hir hadde she,
That was hir chapeleyne°, and preestes thre.

---

121 cleped, *named* **122 Ful weel,** *very well,* **service dyvyne,** *liturgy* (a cycle of prayers) **123 Entuned,** *intone,* **ful semely,** *very attractively* **124 fetisly,** *elegantly* **125 After the scole,** *in accord with the school* **126 unknowe,** *unknown* **127 mete,** *dining,* **with-alle,** *in addition* **128 leet,** *let* **129 Ne wette,** *nor wet,* **depe,** *deeply* **130 Wel koude she,** *she was well able to,* **kepe,** *take care* **131 fille,** *fell* **132 ful muchel hir lest,** *her greatest pleasure* **133 over-lippe,** *upper lip,* **wyped,** *wiped* **134 coppe,** *cup,* **no ferthyng sene,** *no spot seen (farthing = small coin)* **135 grece,** *grease* **draughte,** *drink* **136 Ful semely,** *very attractively,* **after hir mete,** *for her food,* **raughte,** *reached* **137 sikerly,** *certainly* **greet desport,** *excellent conduct* **138 amyable of port,** *agreeable in demeanor* **139 peyned hire,** *took pains,* **countrefete cheere,** *imitate the behavior* **140 to been estatlich of manere,** *to be stately in manner* **141 to ben holden digne,** *to be considered worthy* **143 pitous,** *tenderhearted* **144 wolde wepe,** *would weep,* **saugh,** *saw* **145 deed or bledde,** *dead or bleeding* **146 smale houndes,** *small dogs,* **fedde,** *fed* **147 rosted flessh,** *cooked meat,* **wastelbreed,** *high-quality bread* **148 soore wepte she,** *she wept sorely,* **oon,** *one* **149 smoot,** *hit,* **yerde smerte,** *stick smartly* **151 Ful semyly,** *very attractively,* **wympul pynched was,** *headdress was pleated* **152 tretys,** *well shaped,* **eyen,** *eyes* **154 sikerly,** *certainly* **155 spanne brood,** *hand-span broad,* **I trowe,** *I believe* **156 hardily,** *assuredly* **157 Ful fetys,** *very elegant,* **cloke,** *cloak,* **war,** *aware* **158 bar,** *bore* **159 peire of bedes,** *string of beads* (a rosary), **gauded,** *ornamented* **160 heng,** *hung,* **ful sheene,** *very shiny* **161 write,** *written* **164 chapeleyne,** *assistant*

121 Eglentyne, a typical romance heroine's name, meaning "briar rose," although there was a Madam Argentyn in St. Leonard's convent near Stratford-at-Bow (two miles from London; see *HF* 117), which Chaucer visited as a youth. She was not prioress. **123 Entuned in hir nose,** the appropriate way to sing or chant the long services. **125 scole of Stratford atte Bowe,** a convent school, located near London. **126 Frenssh of Parys,** the Parisian dialect was more prestigious than provincial Anglo-Norman. **127 At mete . . . ,** the Prioress's table manners follow proper etiquette, but they are modeled on the advice of La Vieille (Old Woman) of *RR* 13,374ff. on how to attract men. **131 ne,** omitted in Hg. **146–47 small houndes . . . fedde . . . ,** nuns were ordinarily forbidden lapdogs, popular among fashionable ladies. The food that the Prioress feeds to her dogs is also extraordinary, as meat was generally reserved for the ill in Benedictine convents and **wastel-breed** was vastly superior to the dark breads eaten by peasants. **148 oon,** El reads "any." **151 wympul,** the nun's wimple, or headdress, normally covered much of her face (including the forehead) and neck as well as the rest of her head. The pleating (**pynched was**) is a fashionable touch. **152 greye,** the precise color is uncertain (blue? gray?), although it is typical of the eyes of romance heroines. **155 spanne brood,** the breadth of a hand span, about seven to nine inches. A broad forehead was thought to be beautiful. **159–62 peire of bedes . . . ,** a rosary, i.e., a string of beads used to organize the recitation of prayers, although the rosary did not develop a standard form until the fifteenth century. Like much church equipment, the Prioress's rosary is splendid, the coral beads articulated (**gauded**) by green beads and hung with a pendant ornament (**brooch**) which is inscribed with a crowned letter *A* and the Latin phrase ***Amor vincit omnia***, "Love conquers all." Proverbial. **163 NONNE,** the most salient feature of the so-called Second Nun is the lack of description. As chaplain (**chapeleyne**), she was assistant secretary to the Prioress. **164 preestes thre,** the three priests bring the number of pilgrims in the *Prologue* to thirty-two (compare line 24), and only one priest appears later (at *CT* 7.2809). Chaucer may have left the line incomplete, intending to develop the portraits of the Second Nun and the Nun's Priest, providing opportunity for an early scribe to complete the rhyme, which is in all manuscripts.

A MONK ther was, a fair for the maistrie°,
An outridere, that lovede venerie,
A manly man, to been an abbot able°.
Ful many a deyntee° hors hadde he in stable.
And whan he rood, men myghte his brydel° heere
Gynglen in a whistlynge wynd als cleere°
And eek as loude as dooth the chapel belle
Ther as this lord° was kepere of the celle°.
The reule° of Seint Maure or of Seint Beneit,
By cause° that it was old and somdel streit°,
This ilke° Monk leet olde thynges pace°,
And heeld after the newe world the space°.
He yaf nat of that text a pulled hen°
That seith° that hunters been nat hooly men,
Ne that a monk, whan he is recchelees°,
Is likned til° a fissh that is waterlees°—
This is to seyn°, a monk out of his cloystre°.
But thilke° text heeld he nat worth an oystre°.
And I seyde° his opinioun was good.
What, sholde he studie and make hymselven wood°,
Upon a book in cloystre alwey to poure°,
Or swynken° with his handes, and laboure,
As Austyn bit?° How shal the world be served?
Lat° Austyn have his swynk to hym reserved!
Therfore he was a prikasour aright°.
Grehoundes° he hadde as swift as fowel° in flight.
Of prikyng° and of huntyng for the hare
Was al his lust°; for no cost wolde° he spare.
I seigh° his sleves ypurfiled° at the hond
With grys°, and that the fyneste° of a lond.
And, for to festne° his hood under his chyn,
He hadde of gold ywroght° a ful curious pyn°,
A love-knotte in the gretter° ende ther was.
His heed was balled°, that shoon as any glas,
And eek° his face, as° he hadde been enoynt°.
He was a lord ful fat and in good poynt°;
His eyen stepe° and rollynge in his heed,
That stemed as a forneys of a leed°;
His bootes souple°; his hors in greet estaat°.
Now certeinly he was a fair prelaat°.
He nas nat° pale as a forpyned goost°.
A fat swan loved he best of any roost.
His palfrey° was as broun as is a berye°.

---

165 a fair for the maistrie, *an extremely fine* (one) **167 to been an abbot able,** *able to be an abbot* (monastic superior) **168 deyntee,** *excellent* **169 brydel,** *bridle* **170 als cleere,** *as clearly* **172 Ther as this lord,** *where this lord* (i.e., the Monk), **celle,** *dependent monastery* **173 reule,** *rule* **174 By cause,** *because,* **somdel streit,** *somewhat strict* **175 ilke,** *same,* **leet . . . pace,** *let pass* **176 heeld after the newe world the space,** *held with the custom of the modern world* **177 yaf nat of that text a pulled hen,** *gave not a plucked chicken for that* (written) *text* **178 seith,** *says* **179 recchelees,** *disobedient* **180 likned til,** *likened to,* **waterlees,** *waterless* **181 seyn,** *say,* **cloystre,** *monastery* (cloister) **182 thilke,** *this,* **oystre,** *oyster* **183 seyde,** *said* **184 wood,** *crazy* **185 poure,** *pore over* **186 swynken,** *work* **187 Austyn bit,** *St. Augustine commands* **188 Lat,** *let* **189 prikasour aright,** *hunter on horseback truly* **190 Grehoundes,** *greyhounds,* **fowel,** *bird* **191 prikyng,** *riding* **192 lust,** *pleasure,* **wolde,** *would* **193 seigh,** *saw,* **ypurfiled,** *trimmed* **194 grys,** *gray fur,* **fyneste,** *finest* **195 festne,** *fasten* **196 of gold ywroght,** *made of gold,* **curious pyn,** *intricate pin* **197 gretter,** *larger* **198 balled,** *bald* **199 eek,** *also* **as,** *as if,* **enoynt,** *oiled* **200 in good poynt,** *stout* (French en bon poynt) **201 eyen stepe,** *eyes prominent* **202 stemed as a forneys of a leed,** *glowed like a furnace under a pot* **203 souple,** *supple,* **greet estaat,** *fine condition* **204 prelaat,** *churchman* **205 nas nat,** *was not,* **forpyned goost,** *tortured spirit* **207 palfrey,** *riding horse,* **berye,** *berry*

165 MONK, by definition, is a man who dedicates his life to work and prayer, generally expected to remain within the walls of his monastery ("cloistered") and obey its rules. Chaucer's Monk is commissioned to leave the monastery, and, rejecting regulations, he pursues his genteel interests in horses and hunting. **166 outridere,** an "agent of a monastery who rides out to administer to its affairs" (*MED*), overseeing its farms and manors (see *CT* 7.65–66). **venerie,** the primary meaning is "hunting," but there may be connotations of "sexual pursuit." This line clearly contrasts with *CT* 1.45. **170 Gynglen,** jingling; small bells were fashionable decorations for bridles; the flowers "Canterbury bells" later took their name from the clusters of bells adorning pilgrims' horses. **172 was,** Hg reads "is." **celle,** a monk's cell could be his own small enclosure, but here and elsewhere the term means a subordinate monastery. **173 reule of Seint Maure or of Seint Beneit,** a "rule" is a set of regulations for the goals and activities of a monastery—its hierarchy, schedule of prayers, organization of labor, etc. St. Benedict (480-ca. 550) wrote the influential *Benedictine Rule,* which according to legend was brought to France by his pupil St. Maurus. **178 hunters been nat hooly men,** hunters are criticized as unholy in a number of medieval texts, rooted perhaps in the Biblical story of Nimrod, Gen. 10.9. **179–80 monk . . . recchelees, / . . . fissh . . . waterlees,** a common comparison in medieval comments on monks who break the rules of their monasteries. **184–86 studie . . . laboure,** book learning and manual labor are, with prayer, the major monastic activities. **187 Austyn,** St. Augustine (354–430), one of the four Latin "fathers" of the Catholic Church, thought to have written a rule for monks, *De Opere Monachorum* ("Concerning the Work of Monks"). **world be served,** ideally, monks served the world by praying for the salvation of souls. **188 his,** El reads "his owene." **191–92 prikyng . . . hare . . . lust,** the language and imagery here may associate hunting with sexual pursuit (compare *CT* 1.4231 and Gower, *Mirour de l'omme* 21,053), although the hare was highly regarded as the object of sport hunting. **197 love-knotte,** an interlace design, but the term suggests amorousness. **201 eyen stepe,** bright, prominent eyes, often attributed to heroes in medieval romances. **207 as is a,** Hg reads "as any."

A FRERE° ther was, a wantowne and a merye°,
A lymytour°, a ful solempne° man.
In alle the ordres foure° is noon that kan°
So muchel of daliaunce° and fair langage°.
He hadde maad° ful many a mariage
Of yonge wommen at his owene cost°.
Unto his ordre he was a noble post°.
Ful wel biloved and famulier° was he
With frankeleyns° over al in his contree,
And eek° with worthy wommen of the toun,
For he hadde power of confessioun,
As seyde° hymself, moore than a curat°,
For of his ordre he was licenciat°.
Ful swetely herde he confessioun,
And plesaunt was his absolucioun°—
He was an esy° man to yeve penaunce°
Ther as he wiste° to have a good pitaunce°.
For unto a poure ordre for to yive°
Is signe° that a man is wel yshryve°,
For if he yaf°, he dorste make avaunt°,
He wiste° that a man was repentaunt;
For many a man so hard is of his herte,
He may nat wepe, althogh hym soore smerte°.
Therfore in stede of wepynge and preyeres
Men moote yeve° silver to the poure freres°.
His typet° was ay farsed° ful of knyves
And pynnes° for to yeven faire wyves.
And certeinly he hadde a murye note°:
Wel koude° he synge and pleyen on a rote°;
Of yeddynges he baar outrely the pris°.
His nekke whit was° as the flour delys°;
Therto he strong was as a champioun.
He knew the tavernes wel in every toun,
And everich hostiler° and tappestere°
Bet° than a lazar° or a beggestere°,
For unto swich° a worthy man as he
Acorded nat°, as by his facultee°,
To have with sike° lazars aqueyntaunce.
It is nat honeste°, it may nat avaunce°,
For to deelen° with no swich poraille°,
But al with riche and selleres of vitaille°.
And over al ther as° profit sholde arise
Curteis° he was and lowely° of servyse.
Ther nas no man nowher so vertuous.
He was the beste beggere in his hous,
And yaf° a certeyn ferme° for the graunt°—
Noon of his bretheren cam ther in his haunt°—
For thogh a wydwe° hadde noght a sho°,
So plesaunt was his "In principio,"
Yet wolde he have a ferthyng° er he wente°.
His purchas° was wel bettre than his rente.
And rage he koude°, as it were right a whelpe°.

---

208 FRERE, *Friar,* **a wantowne and a merye,** *a flirtatious and merry* (one) **209 lymytour,** *limiter* (see note) **ful solempne,** *very solemn* **210 ordres foure** *four orders of friars,* **kan,** *knows* **211 daliaunce,** *light talk,* **langage,** *language* **212 maad,** *arranged* **213 owene cost,** *own expense* **214 post,** *support* **215 famulier,** *familiar* **216 frankeleyns,** *independent landowners* **217 eek,** *also* **219 seyde,** *said* **curat,** *parish priest* **220 licenciat,** *licensed* **222 absolucioun,** *forgiving of sin* **223 esy,** *lenient,* **yeve penaunce,** *give penance* **224 Ther as he wiste,** *when he expected,* **good pitaunce,** *large donation* **225 yive,** *give* **226 signe,** *sign* **yshryve,** *forgiven* **227 he yaf,** *the penitent gave* **he dorst make avaunt,** *the Friar dared to boast* **228 He wiste,** *the Friar knew* **230 soore smerte,** *hurts sorely* **232 moote yeve,** *may give,* **freres,** *friars* **233 typet,** *end of his hood,* **ay farsed,** *always crammed* **234 pynnes,** *pins* **235 murye note,** *merry voice* **236 koude,** *could,* **rote,** *stringed instrument* **237 Of yeddynges he baar outrely the pris,** *for ballads he absolutely took the prize* **238 nekke whit was,** *neck was white* **flour delys,** *lily* **241 everich hostiler,** *every innkeeper,* **tappestere,** *barmaid* **242 Bet,** *better,* **lazar,** *leper,* **beggestere,** *beggarmaid* **243 swich,** *such* **244 Acorded nat,** *it was not suitable,* **facultee,** *ability* **245 sike,** *sick* **246 honeste,** *respectable* **avaunce,** *advance* **247 deelen** *deal,* **swich poraille,** *such poor folks* **248 vitaille,** *food* **249 over al ther as,** *everywhere where* **250 Curteis,** *courteous,* **lowely,** *humble* **252b yaf** *gave,* **ferme,** *fee,* **graunt,** *license* **252c haunt,** *locale* **253 wydwe,** *widow,* **sho,** *shoe* **255 ferthyng,** *farthing* (small coin), **er he wente,** *before he departed* **256 purchas,** *profits* **257 rage he koude,** *he could flirt,* **whelpe,** *puppy*

208 FRERE, friars were members of clerical orders, but they differed from monks insofar as they were not cloistered in monasteries but made their way in the world by begging, preaching, hearing confessions, administering to the poor, etc. Chaucer's Friar embodies many of the abuses satirized by critics of the friars. **209 lymytour,** "a friar whose begging, preaching, and hearing of confessions was limited" to a particular territory (*MED*). **210 ordres foure,** Franciscans (Gray Friars), Dominicans (Black Friars), Carmelites (White Friars), Augustinians (Austin Friars). Other orders were suppressed in 1274. The depiction of Chaucer's Friar does not specify a particular order. **212–13 maad . . . mariage . . . at his owene cost,** the friar paid for many marriages, perhaps generously, but perhaps to marry off his mistresses. **215 Ful,** El reads "And." **217 eek,** omitted in El. **218–20** a principal tension of the late-medieval church was the conflicting authority of friars and parish priests to hear confession and grant absolution of sins, especially since friars sometimes assumed special authority. The fact that pardoners could also absolve the guilt due to sins further complicated the situation; see lines 669–714 below. **licenciat,** licensed specifically to hear confessions, in contrast to parish priests who had additional spiritual responsibilities. **223–24 to yeve penaunce . . . pitaunce,** the sacrament of penance normally required that the penitent pray or do other acts of contrition (including giving alms—donations for the poor or support of the church) assigned by the confessor. This Friar assigns light punishments when he expects a sizable donation. **230 althogh him,** Hg reads "thogh that he." **234 faire,** El reads "yonge." **238 nekke whit,** a white neck was a sign of sensuality. **240 every,** El reads "al the." **241–42 tappestere . . . beggestere,** *-stere* is the OE feminine suffix. **251 nas,** Hg reads "was." **252b-c** This couplet is omitted in a large number of manuscripts, including El; Chaucer may have marked it for deletion. **254 "In principio,"** "In the beginning," the opening words of St. John's gospel (and of Genesis), the first fourteen lines of which were used by friars as a greeting, and perhaps as kind of incantation.

In love-dayes ther koude he muchel helpe°,
For ther he was nat lyk° a cloysterer°
With a thredbare cope°, as is a poure scoler°,
But he was lyk a maister or a pope.
Of double worstede° was his semycope°,
That rounded° as a belle out of the presse°.
Somwhat he lipsed° for his wantownesse°
To make his Englissh sweete upon his tonge.
And in his harpyng, whan that he hadde songe,
His eyen twynkled in his heed aryght°,
As doon the sterres in the frosty nyght.
This worthy lymytour was cleped° Huberd.

A MARCHANT was ther with a forked berd,
In mottelee°, and hye on horse° he sat,
Upon his heed a Flaundryssh bevere hat°,
His bootes clasped faire and fetisly°.
His resons° he spak ful solempnely°,
Sowny nge alwey° th'encrees° of his wynnyng°.
He wolde the see were kept for any thyng°
Bitwixe Middelburgh and Orewelle.
Wel koude° he in eschaunge sheeldes selle.
This worthy man ful wel his wit bisette°—
Ther wiste no wight° that he was in dette,
So estatly° was he of his governaunce°
With his bargaynes° and with his chevyssaunce°.
For sothe° he was a worthy man withalle°,
But, sooth to seyn°, I noot° how men hym calle.

A CLERK ther was of Oxenford also
That unto logyk hadde longe ygo°.
As leene° was his hors as is a rake,
And he nas nat° right fat, I undertake°,
But looked holwe°, and therto sobrely°.
Ful thredbare was his overeste courtepy°,
For he hadde geten hym yet no benefice°,
Ne was so worldly for to have office°.
For hym was levere° have at his beddes heed°
Twenty bookes, clad in blak or reed,
Of Aristotle and his philosophie,
Than robes riche, or fithele°, or gay sautrie°.
But al be that he was a philosophre,
Yet hadde he but litel gold in cofre.
But al that he myghte of his freendes hente°,
On bookes and on lernynge he it spente,
And bisily gan for the soules preye°
Of hem° that yaf hym wherwith to scoleye°.
Of studie took he moost cure° and moost heede°.

258 koude he muchel helpe, *he could do much good* **259 nat lyk,** *not like,* **cloysterer,** *monastic* **260 thredbare cope,** *worn-out cloak,* **poure scoler,** *poor scholar* **262 double worstede,** *high-quality wool,* **semycope,** *short cloak* **263 rounded,** *was round,* **presse,** *bell mold* **264 lipsed,** *lisped,* **wantownesse,** *affectation* **267 aryght,** *exactly* **269 cleped,** *named* **271 mottelee,** *cloth of mixed color,* **hye on horse,** *in a high saddle* **272 Flaundryssh bevere hat,** *beaverskin hat made in Flanders* **273 fetisly,** *elegantly* **274 resons,** *opinions,* **solempnely,** *solemnly* **275 Sowny nge alwey,** *indicating always,* **th'encrees,** *the increase,* **wynnyng,** *profit* **276 wolde the see were kept for any thyng,** *wanted the sea protected at any cost* **278 koude,** *could* **279 bisette,** *used* **280 Ther wiste no wight,** *no person knew* **281 estatly,** *dignified* **governaunce,** *management* **282 bargaynes,** *transactions,* **chevyssaunce,** *investments* **283 For sothe,** *in truth,* **withalle,** *indeed* **284 sooth to seyn,** *to tell the truth,* **noot,** *don't know* **286 unto logyk hadde longe ygo,** *had long studied logic* **287 leene,** *skinny* **288 nas nat,** *wasn't,* **undertake,** *declare* **289 holwe,** *emaciated,* **therto sobrely,** *therefore serious* **290 overeste courtepy,** *outermost jacket* **291 benefice,** *ecclesiastical or academic job* **292 office,** *secular job* **293 hym was levere,** *he would rather,* **beddes heed,** *bed's head* **296 fithele,** *fiddle,* **gay sautrie,** *fine psaltery* (harp) **299 hente,** *acquire* **301 bisily gan . . . preye,** *busily did pray* **302 hem,** *those,* **yaf hym wherwith to scoleye,** *gave him support to attend school* **303 cure,** *care,* **heede,** *attention*

258 love-dayes, days set apart for settlement of social or domestic disputes; Church officials often acted as arbiters. **ther,** omitted in Hg. **263 That,** Hg reads "And." **267 eyen twynkled,** contrast the flashing eyes of the Monk, line 201 above. **269 Huberd,** not a common name in the fourteenth century, but in *Roman de Renart,* the name of the kite, a bird of prey. **270 MARCHANT,** fourteenth-century merchants were traders in commodities, not small businessmen, and of considerable economic importance. The brief description of Chaucer's Merchant emphasizes the expense of his clothing, his commercial dealings, and little else. **forked berd,** high fashion for the time. **277 Middelburgh and Orewelle,** the Dutch port Middleburgh was licensed to import English wool 1384–88 and the center thereafter for the Merchant Adventurers, a commercial organization of growing influence. Middleburgh lies across the English Channel from the Orwell River, where the English wool-exporting port of Ipswich is located. **278 eschaunge sheeldes selle,** make money by trafficking in currencies; "shields" were French coins or Flemish money on account. **282 bargaynes . . . chevyssaunce,** may suggest shrewd or perhaps shady dealings. **284 noot how men hym calle,** contrast with the narrator's knowledge of the Friar's name, line 269. **285 CLERK,** student, although the term was coming to mean a man who was skilled in reading and writing or keeping accounts. It is related to "clergy" because medieval university curricula had as their goal the study of theology. In his disregard for money, the Clerk clearly contrasts several of the other pilgrims, most pointedly the Merchant. **Oxenford,** Oxford is home to the oldest university in England. **286 logyk,** logic, or dialectic, was the top of the undergraduate curriculum, the so-called trivium (grammar, rhetoric, logic). The quadrivium (arithmetic, geometry, astronomy, music) were studied by students seeking master of arts degrees before going on to study theology. Together, the trivium and quadrivium were the seven liberal arts. The Clerk's long study of logic may be humorous. **290 thredbare,** unlike the Friar's (line 260), the Clerk's clothing was well worn. **294 Twenty bookes,** a large library for a poor student, especially since books were very expensive. **295 Aristotle,** preeminent authority on logic in the Middle Ages, when he was known as "the Philosopher." **297 philosophre,** applied to alchemists as well as those who studied philosophy, because the goal of alchemy was to turn base metals to gold with the help of the "philosopher's stone." The wordplay underscores the Clerk's failure to make money. **301–2 soules . . . Of hem that yaf hym,** patrons often supported students who in turn were expected to pray for the souls of their benefactors.

Noght o° word spak he moore than was neede,
And that was seyd° in forme and reverence°,
And short and quyk and ful of hy sentence°.
Sownynge in° moral vertu was his speche,
And gladly wolde he lerne° and gladly teche°.

A SERGEANT OF THE LAWE, war° and wys°,
That often hadde been at the Parvys,
Ther was also, ful riche of° excellence.
Discreet° he was and of greet reverence°—
He semed swich°, his wordes weren so wise.
Justice he was ful often in assise,
By patente° and by pleyn commissioun°.
For his science° and for his heigh renoun°,
Of fees and robes hadde he many oon°.
So greet a purchasour° was nowher noon°:
Al was fee symple° to hym in effect,
His purchasyng myghte nat been infect°.
Nowher so bisy a man as he ther nas°,
And yet he semed bisier than he was.
In termes° hadde he caas° and doomes° alle
That from the tyme of Kyng William° were
yfalle°.
Therto he koude endite and make a thyng°,
Ther koude no wight pynche° at his writyng;
And every statut koude he pleyn by rote°.
He rood but hoomly° in a medlee cote°,
Girt° with a ceint° of silk, with barres° smale—
Of his array telle I no lenger tale.

A FRANKELEYN was in his compaignye.
Whit was his berd° as is the dayesye°;
Of his complexioun he was sangwyn°.
Wel loved he by the morwe° a sop in wyn°.
To lyven in delit was evere his wone°,
For he was Epicurus owene sone,
That heeld opinioun that pleyn delit°
Was verray felicitee parfit°.
An housholdere, and that a greet, was he;
Seint Julian he was in his contree.
His breed, his ale, was alweys after oon°.
A bettre envyned° man was nowher noon.
Withoute bake mete° was nevere his hous,
Of fissh and flessh°, and that so plenteuous,
It snewed° in his hous of mete and drynke,
Of alle deyntees° that men koude thynke.
After the sondry sesons° of the yeer,
So chaunged he his mete and his soper.

---

304 Noght o, *not one* **305 seyd,** *said,* **in forme and reverence,** *formally and respectfully* **306 hy sentence,** *lofty meaning* **307 Sownynge in,** *reflecting* **308 lerne,** *learn,* **teche,** *teach* **309 war,** *careful,* **wys,** *wise* **311 ful riche of,** *well endowed with* **312 Discreet,** *prudent,* **of greet reverence,** *highly dignified* **313 semed swich,** *seemed such* **315 patente,** *royal letter,* **pleyn commissioun,** *full commission* **316 science,** *knowledge,* **heigh renoun,** *high reputation* **317 many oon,** *many* (a one) **318 purchasour,** *land buyer,* **nowher noon,** *nowhere none* **319 fee symple,** *owned without restriction* **320 infect,** *invalidated* **321 nas,** *wasn't* **323 termes,** *legal language,* **caas,** *cases,* **doomes,** *decisions* **324 William,** *William the Conqueror,* **were yfalle,** *had happened* **325 Therto he koude endite and make a thyng,** *also he was able to compose and draw up a legal document* **326 Ther koude no wight pynche,** *where no one could find fault* **327 every statut koude he pleyn by rote,** *knew every statute fully by heart* **328 hoomly,** *informally* **medlee cote,** *multicolored coat* **329 Girt,** *belted* **ceint,** *sash,* **barres,** *stripes* **332 berd,** *beard* **dayesye,** *daisy* **333 sangwyn,** *reddish* **334 by the morwe,** *in the morning,* **sop in wyn,** *bread soaked in wine* **335 wone,** *habit* **337 pleyn delit,** *complete pleasure* **338 verray felicitee parfit,** *true perfect happiness* **341 after oon,** *uniformly good* **342 envyned,** *stocked with wine* **343 bake mete,** *dinner pies* **344 flessh,** *meat* **345 snewed,** *snowed* **346 deyntees,** *delicacies* **347 sondry sesons,** *various seasons*

307 Sownynge . . . , contrast line 275 above. **309 SERGEANT OF THE LAWE,** a small faction of high-ranking lawyers from whom all judges were chosen. Chaucer's Sergeant (later, "Man of Law") has the wealth and deep knowledge of the law required for the position, although he also seems concerned with appearances. **310 Parvys,** the porch before St. Paul's Cathedral in London, a traditional place for lawyers and clients to conduct legal business. **314 Justice . . . in assise,** sergeants of the law had exclusive rights to act as judge in courts of the assize, district courts originally concerned with questions of land rights. **315 patente . . . pleyn commissioun,** kings issued open or "patent" letters to appoint judges, and full commission enabled a judge to hear all cases. **317 robes,** fee payment was frequently in the form of clothing or jewelry, often an annual gift for life or a specified term. **318–19 purchasour . . . fee symple,** in the late fourteenth century, people began to be able to purchase real estate (etymologically, *royal estate,* because under William the Conqueror, all land belonged to the King); until that time, the only way to acquire land had been to inherit or receive by gift. The most desirable kind of purchase was "fee simple," without any restrictions on future sale or transfer. **326 pynche,** a possible play on the name of a sergeant of the law, Thomas Pynchbeck, whom Chaucer probably knew. **331 FRANKELEYN,** a country landowner, who traditionally served as justice of the peace and knight of the shire (representative to Parliament) for his locale. The Franklin rides with the Sergeant at Law, his social superior, with whom he shares interest in land ownership and district courts. This association and the Franklin's obsession with fine dining may indicate social climbing. **332 berd,** El reads "heed." **333 complexioun . . . sangwyn,** the physiological combination or "complexion" of four humors, or bodily fluids, was thought to influence or determine an individual's health and personality. The sanguine or hopeful person was dominated by blood; the phlegmatic or dull, by phlegm; the choleric or excitable, by yellow bile; the melancholic, by black bile. See 420–21n below. **336 Epicurus owene sone,** Epicurus's own son, an Epicurean, a pursuer of pleasure; Epicurus (341–270 BC) was a Greek philosopher whose name was attached (with little real justification) to a philosophy of pleasure. **340 Seint Julian,** the legendary patron saint of hospitality, here used metaphorically to indicate the Franklin's hospitality. **347–48 sondry sesons . . . chaunged,** changed his menu according to the climatic (summer, winter) and / or liturgical seasons (e.g., Lent, Christmas, etc.).

Ful many a fat partrich hadde he in muwe°,
And many a breem° and many a luce° in
stuwe°.
Wo° was his cook but if° his sauce were
Poynaunt° and sharp, and redy al his geere°.
His table dormant° in his halle alway
Stood redy covered al the longe day.
At sessiouns ther was he lord and sire.
Ful ofte tyme he was knyght of the shire.
An anlaas° and a gipser° al of silk
Heeng at his girdel, whit as morne° milk.
A shirreve° hadde he been, and a contour°.
Was nowher swich° a worthy vavasour°.

An HABERDASSHERE° and a CARPENTER,
A WEBBE°, a DYERE°, and a TAPYCER°,
And they were clothed alle in o lyveree°
Of a solempne° and a greet fraternitee.
Ful fressh and newe hir geere apiked was°:
Hir knyves were chaped noght° with bras
But al with silver; wroght° ful clene and weel
Hire girdles° and hir pouches everydeel°.
Wel semed ech of hem° a fair burgeys°
To sitten in a yeldehalle° on a deys°.
Everich°, for the wisdowm that he kan°,
Was shaply° for to been an alderman°.
For catel° hadde they ynogh° and rente,
And eek hir° wyves wolde it wel assente°;
And elles° certeyn were they to blame.
It is ful fair to been ycleped° "madame,"
And goon to vigilies al bifore°,
And have a mantel roialliche ybore°.

A COOK they hadde with hem for the nones°
To boille the chiknes° with the marybones°,
And poudre-marchant tart° and galyngale°.
Wel koude he knowe° a draughte° of Londoun ale.
He koude° rooste and sethe° and broille and
frye,
Maken mortreux°, and wel bake a pye.
But greet harm was it, as it thoughte me°,
That on his shyne° a mormal° hadde he.
For blankmanger°, that made he with the beste.

A SHIPMAN was ther, wonynge fer by weste°.
For aught I woot°, he was of Dertemouthe.
He rood upon a rouncy°, as he kouthe°,
In a gowne of faldyng° to the knee.

---

349 muwe, *coop* **350 breem,** *bream* (a fish), **luce,** *pike* (a fish), **stuwe,** *pond* **351 Wo,** *woeful* **but if,** *unless* **352 Poynaunt,** *spicy,* **geere,** *equipment* **353 table dormant** *removable table* **357 anlaas,** *dagger,* **gipser,** *purse* **358 morne,** *morning* **359 shirreve,** *sheriff,* **contour,** *tax collector* **360 swich,** *such,* **vavasour,** *feudal landowner* **361 HABERDASSHERE,** *dealer in men's clothing* **362 WEBBE,** *weaver,* **DYERE,** *one who dyes cloth,* **TAPYCER,** *tapestry maker* **363 o lyveree,** *one uniform* **364 solempne,** *solemn* **365 geere apiked was,** *equipment was adorned* **366 chaped noght,** *mounted not* **367 wroght,** *made* **368 Hire girdles,** *their belts* **everydeel,** *every part* **369 ech of hem,** *each of them,* **fair burgeys,** *impressive citizen* **370 yeldehalle,** *guildhall,* **deys,** *platform* **371 Everich,** *each one,* **kan,** *knew* **372 shaply,** *suitable,* **alderman,** *city or guild official* **373 catel,** *property,* **ynogh,** *enough* **374 eek hir,** *also their,* **wolde it wel assente,** *would well agree to it* **375 And elles,** *or else* **376 ycleped,** *called* **377 goon to vigilies al bifore,** *go to services in front of all* **378 mantel roialliche ybore,** *robe carried royally* **379 nones,** *occasion* **380 chiknes,** *chickens* **marybones,** *marrowbones* **381 poudre-marchant tart,** *pungent spice,* **galyngale,** *aromatic spice* **382 knowe,** *recognize,* **draughte,** *drink* **383 he koude,** *he knew how to,* **sethe,** *boil* **383 mortreux,** *stews* **385 as it thoughte me,** *as it seemed to me* **386 shyne,** *shin,* **mormal,** *scabby sore* **387 blankmanger,** *a spiced mousse* **388 wonynge fer by west,** *living far in the west* **389 For aught I woot,** *for all I know* **390 rouncy,** *workhorse,* **as he kouthe,** *as well as he could* **391 faldyng,** *coarse wool*

349–50 muwe . . . stuwe, bird coops and fish ponds were kept on manors to supply the household. **353 table dormant,** tables were normally removed from the hall after meals, although the Franklin keeps his set up. **355 sessiouns,** district courts at which the lord of the manor presided. **356 knyght of the shire,** member of Parliament for his district. **359 shirreve,** sheriff (from *shire-reeve*), the legal and administrative representative of the Crown in a given district. **361–62 HABERDASSHERE . . . CARPENTER . . . WEBBE . . . DYERE, . . . TAPYCER,** generally referred to as the "Guildsmen" because their common livery (a kind of uniform) indicates that they were members of a parish guild, a social and charitable organization influential because of its collective membership. None is assigned an extant tale. **363 lyveree,** as in modern fraternities and organizations, members of medieval guilds identified themselves by wearing distinctive dress, often a robe or hood. **364 fraternitee,** perhaps the fraternity or brotherhood of St. Fabian and St. Sebastian of St. Botolph's Church in Aldersgate Ward, a center of cloth trade. **367 silver,** silver ornamentation on knives was allowed by law only to citizens and others who had property worth five hundred pounds or more, a considerable amount. **370 sitten in yeldehalle on a deys,** sitting on the dais, or raised platform, in a guildhall was a sign of importance. **377 goon to vigilies al bifore,** to lead the congregation in a procession as part of a religious service. **378 mantel,** a ceremonial robe, perhaps a reference to some particular ritual, though none has been identified. **379 COOK,** a servant of the Guildsmen, who apparently preferred their food prepared specially for them. The Cook later names himself Roger, and it is suggested that he operates a shop or booth in London (*CT* 1.4325, 4336, 4346–47. Here the praise of his culinary skill is punctuated abruptly by mention of a disgusting sore. **for the nones,** a phrase often used as a line filler, it seems here to mean "for the occasion," i.e., for the pilgrimage. **383 broille,** El reads "boille." **386–87 mormal . . . blankmanger,** this juxtaposition of a sore and a soft gelatinous mousse or pudding is revolting. The "For" that links the two lines underscores the juxtaposition, especially in the manuscripts, which are largely unpunctuated; its primary meaning is "As for." **388 SHIPMAN,** a sailor, although this one owns his own vessel. His nautical skill is emphasized, along with indications of piracy. **389 Dertemouthe,** Dartmouth is a port in the west of England, notorious for smugglers and pirates. **390 as he kouthe,** implies that the Shipman does not ride well.

A daggere hangynge on a laas° hadde he
Aboute his nekke, under his arm adoun°.
The hoote somer hadde maad his hewe° al broun.
And certeinly he was a good felawe.
Ful many a draughte of wyn° had he ydrawe°
Fro Burdeux-ward, whil that the chapman sleepe°.
Of nyce° conscience took he no keepe°.
If that he faught, and hadde the hyer° hond,
By water he sente hem hoom° to every lond.
But of his craft to rekene° wel his tydes°,
His stremes, and his daungers hym bisides°,
His herberwe°, and his moone, his lodemenage°,
Ther nas noon swich° from Hulle to Cartage.
Hardy he was and wys to undertake°.
With many a tempest hadde his berd been shake°.
He knew alle the havenes°, as they were,
Fro Gootlond to the cape of Fynystere,
And every cryke° in Britaigne and in Spayne.
His barge ycleped was° the Maudelayne.

With us ther was a DOCTOUR OF PHISIK°;
In al this world ne was ther noon hym lik,
To speke of phisik and of surgerye,
For he was grounded in astronomye°.
He kepte° his pacient a ful greet deel
In houres° by his magyk natureel.
Wel koude he fortunen° the ascendent
Of his ymages for his pacient.
He knew the cause of everich° maladye,
Were it of hoot, or coold, or moyste, or drye,
And where engendred°, and of what humour°.
He was a verray, parfit praktisour°.
The cause yknowe°, and of his° harm the roote,
Anon he yaf° the sike man his boote°.
Ful redy hadde he his apothecaries°
To sende hym drogges° and his letuaries°,
For ech of hem° made oother for to wynne°—
Hir° frendshipe nas nat newe° to bigynne.
Wel knew he the olde Esculapius,
And Deyscorides, and eek Rufus,
Olde Ypocras, Haly, and Galyen,
Serapion, Razis, and Avycen,
Averrois, Damascien, and Constantyn,
Bernard, and Gatesden, and Gilbertyn.
Of his diete mesurable° was he,
For it was of no superfluitee°,
But of greet norissyng° and digestible.
His studie was but litel on the Bible.

---

392 laas, *cord* **393 under his arm adoun,** *below his arm* **394 hewe,** *color* **396 draughte of wyn,** *drink of wine,* **ydrawe,** *taken* **397 chapman sleepe,** *merchant slept* **398 nyce,** *scrupulous,* **keepe,** *notice* **399 hyer,** *upper* **400 sente hem hoom,** *sent them home* **401 craft to rekene,** *skill to calculate* **tydes,** *tides* **402 daungers hym bisides,** *dangers nearby* **403 herberwe,** *harbors,* **lodemenage,** *navigating* **404 nas noon swich,** *wasn't another such* **405 wys to undertake,** *wise in his management* **406 shake,** *shaken* **407 havenes,** *safe spots* **409 cryke,** *creek* **410 barge ycleped was,** *ship was called* **411 DOCTOUR OF PHISIK,** *Doctor of Medicine* **414 grounded in astronomye,** *learned in astrology* **415 kepte,** *took care of* **416 In houres,** *according to astrological times* **417 fortunen,** *determine* **419 everich,** *every* **421 engendred,** *generated,* **humour,** *bodily liquid* **422 verray, parfit praktisour,** *true perfect practitioner* **423 yknowe,** *known,* **his,** *its* **424 Anon he yaf,** *immediately he gave,* **boote,** *remedy* **425 apothecaries,** *pharmacists* **426 drogges,** *drugs,* **letuaries,** *mixtures* **427 hem,** *them,* **wynne,** *profit* **428 Hir,** *their,* **nas nat newe,** *wasn't new* **435 mesurable,** *moderate* **436 superfluitee,** *excess* **437 of greet norissyng,** *very nourishing*

396 ydrawe, El and Hg read "drawe." **397 Fro Burdeux-ward . . . ,** transporting from Bordeaux, renowned for its wine; the Shipman stole from the wine merchants. **399–400 faught . . . ,** those that the Shipman fought and defeated he threw overboard. **404 nas,** Hg reads "was." **Hulle to Cartage,** port cities, Hull in northern England; Carthage in North Africa, or Cartagena in southeastern Spain. **408 Gootlond,** Gotland, an island off Sweden. **cape of Fynystere,** Cape Finistere ("end of the earth") in western Spain. **409 Britaigne,** Brittany, in western France. **410 Maudelayne,** Peter Risshenden was in 1391 recorded as the master of a ship named the *Maudelеyne* out of Dartmouth. **411 DOCTOUR OF PHISIK,** doctors of medicine were learned in astrology, since it was believed that the configuration of the stars and planets interacted with the physiology of the human body. Like the stereotype of modern doctors, Chaucer's Physician (as he is generally called) is wealthy and concerned only with physical things. **413 phisik and surgerye,** physic (or medicine) and surgery were related though separate fields, the first concerned with treatment through diet, hygiene, and pharmaceuticals; the latter, with operations. **416 magyk natureel,** natural magic had no occult connotations; it meant the understanding of natural forces. **417 ascendent,** an astrological configuration at an important moment, such as the time of birth or illness. An ascendant is the point on the zodiacal circle (or path of a planet) that ascends above the horizon at the particular moment. **418 ymages,** doctors constructed images—graphic representations—of patients or their astrological configurations by which health could be studied and treated. The images were either drawn or molded of specific materials at specific times. **420 hoot, or coold, or moyste, or drye,** these four qualities, or contraries, were thought to define the four fluids (or humors; see 333n above) of the human body as well as the four elements of the physical cosmos. Combining hot and moist qualities, blood parallels air; cold and moist, phlegm parallels water; hot and dry, yellow bile is like fire; and cold and moist, black bile is like earth. Understanding these parallels and their appropriate hours and seasons enabled physicians to treat their patients according to ancient science, seeking to keep things in proper balance by administering medicines, heating or cooling the patient, letting blood, etc. **421 where,** El reads "where they"; Hg "where it." **422** This line echoes line 72. **425–28** The friendship and mutual profit making of the Physician and his **apothecaries** (pharmacists) reflect a traditional complaint that the two professions collaborated to take advantage of the ill. **429–34** Aescalapius, Dioscorides, Rufus, Hippocrates, and Galen were famous Greek medical authorities. Ali ibn Abbas or Ali ibn Ridwan (**Haly**), Serapion, Rhazes, Avicenna (**Avycen**), and Averroes, were Persian, Egyptian, and Arabic medical authorities. Pseudo-John of Damascus (**Damascien**) and Constantinus Africanus translated medical works into Latin. Bernard of Gordon lectured at the medical school at Montpelier. John Gaddesden (**Gatesden**) and Gilbertus Anglicanus were famous English physicians. **430 Rufus,** El reads "Risus."

In sangwyn° and in pers° he clad° was al,
Lyned° with taffata and with sendal°,
And yet he was but esy of dispence°.
He kepte that he wan in pestilence°,
For gold in phisik is a cordial°;
Therefore he lovede gold in special°.

A good WIF° was ther OF biside° BATHE,
But she was somdel deef°, and that was scathe°.
Of clooth makyng she hadde swich an haunt°,
She passed hem° of Ypres and of Gaunt.
In al the parisshe° wif ne was ther noon°
That to the offrynge° bifore hire sholde goon°;
And if ther dide, certeyn so wrooth° was she
That she was out of alle° charitee.
Hir coverchiefs° ful fyne weren of ground°.
I dorste swere° they weyeden° ten pound
That on a Sonday weren upon hir heed.
Hir hosen° weren of fyn scarlet reed,
Ful streite yteyd°, and shoes ful moyste° and newe.
Boold was hir face, and fair, and reed of hewe°.
She was a worthy womman al hir lyve.
Housbondes at chirche dore she hadde fyve,
Withouten° oother compaignye in youthe—
But therof nedeth nat to speke as nowthe°.
And thries° hadde she been at Jerusalem.
She hadde passed many a straunge strem°.
At Rome she hadde been, and at Boloigne,
In Galice at Seint-Jame, and at Coloigne.
She koude muchel° of wandrynge by the weye.
Gat-tothed° was she, soothly for to seye°.
Upon an amblere° esily she sat,
Ywympled wel°, and on hir heed an hat
As brood as is a bokeler or a targe°,
A foot-mantel° aboute hir hipes large,
And on hir feet a paire of spores° sharpe.
In felaweshipe wel koude she laughe and carpe°.
Of remedies of love she knew per chaunce°,
For she koude° of that art the olde daunce.

A good man was ther of religioun,
And was a poure PERSOUN of a toun,
But riche he was of hooly thoght and werk.
He was also a lerned man, a clerk,
That Cristes gospel trewely wolde preche.
His parisshens° devoutly wolde he teche.
Benygne° he was, and wonder° diligent,
And in adversitee ful pacient°,
And swich° he was preved° ofte sithes°.
Ful looth were hym° to cursen for his tithes,
But rather wolde he yeven°, out of doute°,
Unto his poure parisshens aboute

---

439 sangwyn, *red,* **pers,** *blue,* **clad,** *dressed* **440 Lyned,** *lined,* **taffata . . . sendal,** *taffeta . . . sendal* (kinds of rich cloth) **441 esy of dispence,** *moderate in spending* **442 that he wan in pestilence,** *what he acquired during plague* **443 cordial,** *heart medicine* **444 in special,** *especially* **445 WIF,** *wife or woman,* **biside,** *near* **446 somdel deef,** *somewhat deaf,* **scathe,** *unfortunate* **447 haunt,** *skill* **448 passed hem,** *surpassed them (clothmakers)* **449 parisshe,** *locale of a church,* **wif ne was ther noon,** *there was no woman* **450 offrynge,** *offering* **sholde goon,** *should go* **451 wrooth,** *angry* **452 out of alle,** *without any* **453 coverchiefs,** *headcloths or kerchiefs,* **ful fyne weren of ground,** *were very fine of texture* **454 dorste swere,** *dare say* **weyeden,** *weighed* **456 hosen,** *leggings* **457 streite yteyd,** *closely tied,* **moyste,** *supple* **458 reed of hewe,** *rosy in color* **461 Withouten,** *without counting* **462 as nowthe,** *now* **463 thries,** *three times* **464 straunge strem,** *foreign river* **467 koude muchel,** *knew much* **468 Gat-tothed,** *gap-toothed,* **soothly for to seye,** *to speak truly* **469 amblere,** *easy-gaited saddle horse* **470 Ywympled wel,** *wearing a large headdress that covered much of her face* **471 bokeler . . . targe,** *buckler . . . targe* (kinds of shields) **472 foot-mantel,** *protective outer skirt* **473 spores,** *spurs* **474 carpe,** *talk* **475 per chaunce,** *it so happened* **476 koude,** *knew* **482 His parisshens,** *members of his church* **483 Benygne,** *kind,* **wonder,** *wondrously* **484 ful pacient,** *completely patient* **485 swich,** *such,* **preved,** *proved,* **ofte sithes,** *oftentimes* **486 Ful looth were hym,** *very reluctant was he* **487 yeven,** *give,* **out of doute,** *no doubt*

443 gold . . . cordial, a play on words: gold was used in heart medicines and it was also dear to the Physician's heart. **445 WIF . . . OF . . . BATHE,** the association of the Wife with the city of Bath is appropriate because it was a center for cloth weaving, a skill traditionally associated with women. In the autobiographical prologue to the *Wife of Bath's Tale,* the Wife of Bath is depicted as profiting from her many marriages, putting to use her knowledge of love and sex, introduced here. **448 Ypres . . . Gaunt,** Ypres and Ghent, cities in Flanders, modern Belgium, famous for their cloth making. English cloth was widely regarded as inferior, so the praise of the Wife's weaving may be comic exaggeration. **450 offrynge,** the Offertory, part of the liturgy of the Mass, a procession in which bread, wine, and other offerings were brought to the priest by the faithful, among whom social precedence was evidently important. See line 377 above and *CT, ParsT* 10.407, where the desire to lead the procession indicates pride. **452 out of alle charitee,** ironic because Offertory gifts symbolize charity. **454 weyeden ten pound,** probably an exaggeration, although multiple coverchiefs were sometimes worn over wire frames. **460 chirche dore,** the marriage ceremony took place at the door, after which the couple entered the church for Mass. **463ff. Jerusalem . . . ,** on pilgrimages to Jerusalem, Rome, Boulogne (France), St. James de Compostela in Galicia (Spain), and Cologna (Germany), an impressive array. See *WBP* 3.555ff. **468 Gat-tothed,** gap-toothed, thought to indicate a bold, envious, and suspicious nature. The Wife later claims (*WBP* 3.603–05) that her spaced teeth help explain her sensuous nature. **475–76 remedies of love . . . that art,** remedies are cures for love, although the phrase translates the title of Ovid's *Remedia Amoris,* and "art of love" translates the title of his *Ars Amatoria,* both books of erotic verse. **olde daunce,** all the techniques, perhaps a euphemism for copulation. **478 PERSOUN,** parish priest, responsible for the spiritual welfare of his congregation. The Parson's description echoes scriptural and social ideals of a priest, and contradicts criticism leveled by contemporary satirists. **486 cursen for his tithes,** tithes equaled 10 per cent of a person's income, due for support of the Church. Failure to pay tithes could lead to being cursed or excommunicated, i.e., excluded from participation in the Church.

Of his offryng° and eek of his substaunce°.
He koude° in litel thyng have suffisaunce°.
Wyd° was his parisshe° and houses fer asonder°,
But he ne lefte nat°, for reyn ne thonder,
In siknesse nor in meschief° to visite
The ferreste° in his parisshe, muche and lite°,
Upon his feet, and in his hand a staf°.
This noble ensample° to his sheep he yaf°,
That first he wroghte°, and afterward he taughte.
Out of the gospel he tho wordes caughte°,
And this figure° he added eek° therto,
That if gold ruste, what shal iren° do?
For if a preest be foul, on whom we truste,
No wonder is a lewed° man to ruste.
And shame it is, if a preest take keep°,
A shiten° shepherde and a clene° sheep.
Wel oghte° a preest ensample for to yive,
By his clennesse°, how that his sheep sholde lyve.
He sette nat his benefice to hyre
And leet° his sheep encombred in the myre°
And ran to Londoun unto Seinte Poules
To seken hym° a chaunterie° for soules,
Or with a bretherhed° to been withholde°,
But dwelte at hoom, and kepte wel his folde°
So that the wolf ne made it nat myscarie°.
He was a shepherde and noght a mercenarie°.
And though he hooly were and vertuous,
He was nat to synful men despitous°,
Ne of his speche daungerous ne digne°,
But in his techyng discreet and benygne.
To drawen folk to hevene by fairnesse,
By good ensample, this was his bisynesse.
But it were any persone° obstinat,
What so° he were, of heigh or lough estat°,
Hym wolde he snybben° sharply for the nonys°.
A bettre preest I trowe° that nowher noon ys.
He waited after° no pompe and reverence
Ne maked hym a spiced° conscience,
But Cristes loore° and his apostles twelve
He taughte, but first he folwed it hymselve.

With hym ther was a PLOWMAN, was his brother,
That hadde ylad° of dong° ful many a fother°.
A trewe swynkere° and a good was he,
Lyvynge in pees° and parfit° charitee.
God loved he best with al his hoole herte
At alle tymes, thogh him gamed or smerte°,
And thanne° his neighebore right as° hymselve.
He wolde thresshe°, and therto° dyke° and delve°,
For Cristes sake, for every poure wight°,
Withouten hire°, if it lay in his myght.
His tithes payde° he ful faire and wel,

---

489 Of his offryng, *from his donations,* **substaunce,** *income* **490 koude,** *could,* **suffisaunce,** *sufficiency* **491 Wyd,** *large,* **parisshe,** *parish,* **fer asonder,** *far apart* **492 ne lefte nat,** *refrained not* **493 meschief,** *trouble* **494 ferreste,** *farthest,* **muche and lite,** *great and small* **495 staf,** *walking staff* **496 ensample,** *example* **yaf,** *gave* **497 wroghte,** *performed* **498 tho wordes caughte,** *those words took* **499 figure,** *metaphor,* **eek,** *also* **500 iren,** *iron* **502 lewed,** *unlearned* **503 keep,** *heed* **504 shiten,** *filthy,* **clene,** *clean* **505 oghte,** *ought* **506 clennesse,** *purity* **508 leet,** (did not) *leave,* **encombred in the myre,** *stuck in the mud* **510 seken hym,** *seek for himself,* **chaunterie,** *endowed chapel* **511 bretherhed,** *guild* **withholde,** *supported* **512 folde,** *flock* **513 ne made it nat myscarie,** *did not make it go wrong* **514 mercenarie,** *hired priest* **516 despitous,** *contemptuous* **517 daungerous ne digne,** *disdainful nor haughty* **521 But it were any persone,** *but if it happened that any person was* **522 What so,** *whatever,* **heigh or lough estat,** *high or low class* **523 snybben,** *scold,* **for the nonys,** *because of it* **524 trowe,** *believe* **525 waited after,** *expected* **526 Ne maked hym a spiced,** *nor made (of or for) himself a fussy* **527 loore,** *teachings* **530 ylad,** *hauled* **dong,** *dung* **fother,** *load* **531 trewe swynkere,** *true worker* **532 pees,** *peace,* **parfit,** *perfect* **534 thogh him gamed or smerte,** *whether it pleased or hurt him* **535 thanne,** *then,* **right as,** *just as* **536 thresshe,** *separate grain* **therto,** *also,* **dyke,** *make dikes,* **delve,** *dig* **537 poure wight,** *poor person* **538 hire,** *payment* **539 tithes payde,** *church dues paid*

495ff. staf . . . sheep . . . shepherde, the pastoral (from Lat. *pastor,* "shepherd") imagery throughout the description aligns the Parson with Christ as the Good Shepherd, an ancient ideal that in Christian tradition is rooted in John 10.11ff. **497** The Parson practices what he preaches, an echo of Matthew 5.19. **afterward he,** El reads "afterward that he." **500 gold . . . iren,** a proverbial notion. **507ff. benefice to hyre . . . ,** a benefice is a religious appointment that pays the priest an income, in this case his income for tending to his parish. It was a common complaint that parish priests rented their benefices to others (at less than the stipulated income) and, for additional profit, accepted positions as chaplains for guilds or at endowed chapels, known as "chantries." Chantries were endowed so that priests would pray for the souls of the endowers. **509 Seinte Poules,** St. Paul's Cathedral in London had a notorious number of chantries. **512 dwelte . . . kepte,** El reads "dwelleth . . . kepeth." **513–14** An echo of John 10.12–13. **519 by,** Hg reads "with." **523 for the nonys,** i.e., the Parson would scold obstinate or stubborn sinners (regardless of their class) for their obstinacy. **524 that,** Hg reads "ther." **525 waited,** El reads "waiteth." **528 taughte . . . folwed,** like line 497, an echo of Matthew 5.19, in which those who follow and teach the commandments of God are called great in the kingdom of heaven. **529 PLOWMAN,** a free laborer, here an idealized Christian worker. No tale is assigned to the Plowman. **brother,** the brotherhood of the Plowman and Parson is spiritual as well as by birth. **533–35** An echo of Matthew 22.27–29, Christ's commandments to love God and neighbor. **534 him,** El reads "he." **539–40** The plowman paid tithes on what he earned and what he owned; see 486n above.

Bothe of his propre swynk° and his catel°.
In a tabard° he rood upon a mere°.

Ther was also a REVE, and a MILLERE,
A SOMNOUR, and a PARDONER also,
A MAUNCIPLE, and myself—ther were namo°.

The MILLERE was a stout carl° for the nones;
Ful byg° he was of brawn°, and eek of bones.
That proved wel, for over al ther he cam°,
At wrastlynge he wolde have alwey the ram°.
He was short-sholdred, brood, a thikke knarre°;
Ther was no dore° that he nolde heve of harre°,
Or breke° it at a rennyng° with his heed.
His berd as any sowe or fox was reed°,
And therto brood, as though it were a spade.
Upon the cop right° of his nose he hade
A werte°, and theron stood a toft of herys°
Reed as the brustles° of a sowes erys°.
His nosethirles° blake were and wyde.
A swerd and bokeler° bar° he by his syde.
His mouth as greet was as a greet forneys°.
He was a janglere° and a goliardeys°,
And that was moost of synne° and harlotries°.
Wel koude he stelen° corn and tollen thries°.
And yet he hadde a thombe° of gold, pardee°.
A whit cote° and a blew° hood wered° he.
A baggepipe wel koude he blowe and sowne°,
And therwithal he broghte us out of towne.

A gentil MAUNCIPLE was ther of a temple°,
Of which achatours° myghte take exemple
For to be wise in byynge of vitaille°.
For wheither that he payde or took by taille°,
Algate° he wayted° so in his achaat°
That he was ay biforn° and in good staat°.
Now is nat that of God a ful fair grace°
That swich a lewed mannes wit° shal pace°
The wisdom of an heep° of lerned men?
Of maistres hadde he mo than thries ten°
That weren of lawe expert and curious°,
Of which ther were a duszeyne° in that hous
Worthy to been stywardes° of rente and lond
Of any lord that is in Engelond,
To maken hym lyve by his propre good°
In honour dettelees°, but if° he were wood°,
Or lyve as scarsly as hym list desire°;
And able for to helpen al a shire°
In any caas° that myghte falle or happe°—
And yet this Manciple sette hir aller cappe°.

---

540 propre swynk, *own work* **catel,** *possessions* **541 tabard,** *long sleeveless overshirt,* **mere,** *mare* **544 namo,** *no more* **545 carl,** *fellow* **546 byg,** *strong,* **brawn,** *muscle* **547 over al ther he cam,** *wherever he went* **548 wolde have alwey the ram,** *would always take the prize* **549 thikke knarre,** *broad fellow* **550 dore,** *door,* **nolde heve of harre,** *couldn't heave off hinges* **551 breke,** *break* **rennyng,** *butting* **552 reed,** *red* **554 Upon the cop right,** *right on the top of* **555 werte,** *wart,* **toft of herys,** *tuft of hair* **556 brustles,** *bristles,* **sowes erys,** *sow's ears* **557 nosethirles,** *nostrils* **558 bokeler,** *shield,* **bar,** *carried* **559 forneys,** *furnace* **560 janglere,** *constant talker,* **goliardeys,** *tale-teller* **561 synne,** *sin,* **harlotries,** *dirty stories* **562 koude he stelen,** *could he steal,* **tollen thries,** *take three times his due* **563 thombe,** *thumb,* **pardee,** *by God* **564 whit cote,** *white coat,* **blew,** *blue,* **wered,** *wore* **565 sowne,** *play* **566 therewithal,** *with that* **567 temple,** *law school* **568 achatours,** *purchasers* **569 byynge of vitaille,** *buying of food* **570 by taille,** *on credit* **571 Algate,** *always,* **wayted,** *watched,* **achaat,** *buying* **572 ay biforn,** *always ahead,* **in good staat,** *financially sound* **573 grace,** *favor* **574 swich a lewed mannes wit,** (the) *wit of such an unlearned man, pace, surpass* **575 heep,** *heap* **576 mo than thries ten,** *more than thirty* **577 curious,** *clever* **578 duszeyne,** *dozen* **579 stywardes,** *managers* **581 lyve by his propre good,** *live within his own means* **582 dettelees,** *debt-free,* **but if,** *unless,* **wood,** *crazy* **583 as scarsly as hym list desire,** *as economically as he wishes* **584 al a shire,** *an entire district* **585 caas,** *case,* **falle or happe,** *occur or happen* **586 sette hir aller cappe,** *deceived them all*

545 MILLERE, one who owns or operates a mill for grinding grain into flour, a crucial role in medieval rural economy. Chaucer's Miller, named Robin at *MilP* 1.3129, is notable for his physicality, his bawdy tongue, and his thievery. **for the nones,** the phrase could mean "for the occasion" (line 379 above) or "for this reason" (523 above), but here and elsewhere Chaucer used it (as did other writers) as a line filler, meaning something like "indeed" or "surely." **548 wrastlynge . . . the ram,** a ram was a traditional prize for wrestling matches. **550–51** Door heaving and door butting are evidently the Miller's idea of sport, although scholars have tallied a number of people who butted doors. Door heaving takes place in the *MilT* 1.3470. **559 mouth . . . forneys,** recalls medieval representations of the gaping mouth of hell. **560 goliardeys,** a rare word, meaning something like "windbag, teller of tales"; the phrase "goliardeis, a gloton of wordes" (goliard, glutton of words) occurs in *PP*, B. Pro. 139. **563 thombe of gold,** a metaphor (compare modern "green thumb"); it implies he kept his thumb on the scales. There was also a proverb "An honest miller has a golden thumb," meaning there is no such thing as an honest miller. **567 MAUNCIPLE,** a business agent, a buyer of provisions for an institution, in this case one of the Inns of Court, residences for lawyers and their apprentices during court sessions. As a bureaucratic official in London, Chaucer would have known these Inns. He may have known someone like the shrewd and deceptive Manciple. **temple,** two of the four Inns of Court were the Inner Temple and Middle Temple (with Lincoln's Inn and Gray's Inn) because they occupied land and buildings once owned by the Knights Templars. **586 sette hir aller cappe,** this idiom is similar to the modern expression "pulled the wool over their eyes."

The REVE° was a sclendre° colerik man.
His berd was shave as ny as ever he kan°.
His heer was by his erys° ful round yshorn°.
His top was dokked° lyk a preest biforn°.
Ful longe were his legges and ful lene°,
Ylyk° a staf: ther was no calf ysene°.
Wel koude he kepe° a gerner° and a bynne°.
Ther was noon auditour koude on him wynne°.
Wel wiste° he by the droghte and by the reyn°
The yeldynge of his seed° and of his greyn.
His lordes sheep, his neet°, his dayerye°,
His swyn°, his hors, his stoor°, and his pultrye°
Was hoolly° in this Reves governynge°,
And by his covenant° yaf the rekenynge°,
Syn that° his lord was twenty yeer of age.
Ther koude no man brynge hym in arrerage°.
Ther nas baillif°, ne hierde°, nor oother hyne°
That he ne knew his sleighte° and his covyne°;
They were adrad° of hym as of the deeth.
His wonyng° was ful faire upon an heeth°;
With grene trees shadwed° was his place.
He koude bettre than his lord purchace°;
Ful riche he was astored pryvely°.
His lord wel koude he plesen subtilly°,
To yeve and lene hym of his owene good°,
And have a thank°, and yet a cote and hood.
In youthe he hadde lerned a good myster°,
He was a wel good wrighte°, a carpenter.
This Reve sat upon a ful good stot°,
That was al pomely grey° and highte° Scot.
A long surcote of pers° upon he hade,
And by his syde he baar° a rusty blade.
Of Northfolk was this Reve of which I telle,
Biside a toun men clepen° Baldeswelle.
Tukked he was as is a frere aboute°,
And evere he rood the hyndreste° of oure route°.

A SOMONOUR was ther with us in that place
That hadde a fyr-reed cherubynnes° face,
For sawcefleem° he was, with eyen narwe°.
As hoot he was and lecherous as a sparwe°,
With scalled browes blake° and piled berd°.
Of his visage° children were aferd°.
Ther nas quyksilver°, lytarge°, ne brymstoon°,
Boras°, ceruce°, ne oille of tartre° noon,
Ne oynement that wolde clense and byte°,
That hym myghte helpen of his whelkes white°,
Nor of the knobbes sittynge on his chekes.
Wel loved he garleek°, oynons, and eek lekes°,
And for to drynken strong wyn, reed as blood.

---

587 REVE, *manager of a farm,* **sclendre,** *skinny* **588 ny as ever he kan,** *as close as he could* **589 erys,** *ears* **round yshorn,** *closely cut* **590 His top was dokked . . . biforn,** *the top of his head was cropped . . . in front* **591 lene,** *lean* **592 Ylyk,** *like,* **ysene,** *seen* **593 koude he kepe,** *could he manage,* **gerner,** *storehouse,* **bynne,** *storage bin* **594 noon auditour koude on him wynne,** *no accountant* (who) *could get the best of him* **595 wiste,** *knew,* **reyn,** *rain* **596 yeldynge of his seed,** *what his seed would produce* **597 neet,** *cattle,* **dayerye,** *dairy herd* **598 swyn,** *pigs,* **stoor,** *livestock,* **pultrye,** *poultry* **599 hoolly,** *completely,* **governynge,** *control* **600 covenant,** *contract,* **yaf the rekenynge,** *gave the reckoning* **601 Syn that,** *since* **602 Ther koude no man brynge hym in arrerage,** *no man knew how to find him behind in his accounts* **603 nas baillif,** *was no foreman,* **hierde,** *herdsman,* **hyne,** *peasant* **604 sleighte,** *tricks,* **covyne,** *dishonesty* **605 adrad,** *afraid* **605 wonyng,** *home,* **heeth,** *heath* **607 shadwed,** *shadowed* **608 He koude bettre . . . purchace,** *he could better . . . buy land* **609 astored pryvely,** *stocked up secretly* **610 His lord wel koude he plesen subtilly,** *he knew well how to please his lord craftily* **611 yeve and lene hym of his owene good,** *give and loan to his lord from his lord's own goods* **612 have a thank,** *have thanks* **613 myster,** *craft* **614 wrighte,** *wood-worker* **615 stot,** *farm horse* **616 pomely grey,** *dapple gray,* **highte,** *named* **617 surcote of pers,** *blue overcoat* **618 baar,** *carried* **620 clepen,** *call* **621 Tukked . . . as is a frere aboute,** *tucked up . . . like a friar* **622 hyndreste,** *furthest back,* **route,** *company* **624 fyr-reed cherubynnes,** *firered cherub's* **625 sawcefleem,** *inflamed with pustules,* **eyen narwe,** *narrow eyes* **626 sparwe,** *sparrow* **627 scalled browes blake,** *scabby black eyebrows,* **piled berd,** *mangy beard* **628 visage,** *face,* **aferd,** *afraid* **629 quyksilver,** *mercury,* **lytarge,** *lead oxide,* **byrmstoon,** *sulphur* **630 Boras,** *borax,* **ceruce,** *white lead,* **oille of tartre,** *cream of tartar* **631 clense and byte,** *cleanse and sting* **632 whelkes white,** *pus-filled pimples* **634 garleek,** *garlic,* **eek lekes,** *also leeks*

587 REVE, the term meant the manager or overseer of a farm or estate, a rural parallel to the Manciple's urban occupation. Chaucer's Reeve is a watchful, calculating man, thin and quick to anger, who uses his skills to his own advantage. Later named Oswald (*RvP* 1.3860), the Reeve is the physical opposite of the Miller, a contrast Chaucer develops in their tales. **colerik,** choleric or irritable, dominated by yellow bile. On the four humors, see 333n. **590 lyk a preest biforn,** a reference to the clerical tonsure, the shaving of the crown of the head; see 675–79n below. **603–05** The Reeve knew the secrets of his underlings and apparently used his knowledge to strike fear in them. **604 ne,** omitted in El. **609 astored,** wealth was reckoned in stored food and possessions rather than money in the bank. **612 cote and hood,** payment was frequently in clothing; see line 317 above. El reads "gowne" for "cote." **615 ful,** Hg reads "wel." **616 Scot,** a common name for a horse. **619–20 Northfolk . . . Baldeswelle,** modern Bawdeswell in Norfolk, eastern England. **622 hyndreste,** last in the group; if line 566 indicates that the Miller led the travelers, this underscores the opposition between Miller and Reeve. **623 SOMONOUR,** a summoner, or *apparitor,* was a subpoena server for an ecclesiastical court that oversaw moral and religious behavior—cases involving clerics, tithes, sexual conduct, etc. Chaucer's Summoner is physically and morally grotesque. **624–28** The Summoner's skin disease gives him a face swollen with pimply sores and knobs, and his facial hair is falling out. The disease is a form of leprosy, or perhaps syphilis, both thought to result from moral debauchery. **624 cherubynnes,** cherubim (sing., *cherub*) were the second of nine orders of angels, burning with divine love. **626 lecherous as a sparwe,** the association of the sparrow with lechery was traditional. **629–31** Unsuccessful remedies for the Summoner's condition. **632 his,** El read "the." **634–35** Strong food and drink were thought to promote lechery and skin disease. Such food and drink have negative moral connotations in Numbers 11.5 and Psalms 23.31–33.

Thanne° wolde he speke and crie as he were
wood°,
And whan that he wel dronken hadde the wyn,
Thanne wolde he speke no word but Latyn.
A fewe termes hadde he, two or thre,
That he had lerned out of som decree°—
No wonder is, he herde it al the day,
And eek ye° knowen wel how that a jay°
Kan clepen "Watte"° as wel as kan the pope.
But whoso koude° in oother thyng hym
grope°,
Thanne hadde he spent° al his philosophie.
Ay "Questio quid iuris"° wolde he crie.
He was a gentil harlot° and a kynde;
A bettre felawe sholde men noght fynde.
He wolde suffre° for a quart of wyn
A good felawe to have his concubyn°
A twelf-monthe°, and excuse hym atte fulle°.
Ful prively° a fynch° eek koude he pulle.
And if he foond owher° a good felawe,
He wolde techen° hym to have noon awe°
In swich caas of° the ercedekenes curs,
But if° a mannes soule were in his purs°,
For in his purs he sholde ypunysshed° be.
"Purs is the ercedekenes helle," seyde he.
But wel I woot° he lyed right in dede°.
Of cursyng oghte ech gilty man him drede°,
For curs wol slee right as assoillyng savith°,
And also war hym° of a *Significavit*°.
In daunger° hadde he at his owene gise°
The yonge girles° of the diocise°,
And knew hir conseil, and was al hir reed°.
A gerland° hadde he set upon his heed
As greet as it were for an alestake°.
A bokeleer° hadde he maad° hym of a cake°.

With hym ther rood a gentil PARDONER
Of Rouncivale, his freend and his compeer°,
That streight was comen fro the court of
Rome.
Ful loude° he soong "Com hider°, love, to me!"
This Somonour bar to hym a stif burdoun°.
Was nevere trompe° of half so greet a soun.
This Pardoner hadde heer° as yelow as wex°,
But smothe it heeng° as dooth a strike of flex°.
By ounces henge his lokkes° that he hadde,
And therwith he his shuldres overspradde°,
But thynne° it lay, by colpons oon and oon°.
But hood, for jolitee°, wered he noon°,
For it was trussed° up in his walet°.
Hym thoughte° he rood al of the newe jet°;
Dischevelee°, save his cappe, he rood al bare°.

---

636 Thanne, *then,* **wood,** *crazed* **640 lerned out of som decree,** *learned out of some legal decree* **642 eek ye,** *also you,* **jay,** *talking bird* **643 Kan clepen "Watte,"** *can say "Walter"* **644 whoso koude . . . hym grope,** *whoever could . . . test him* **645 spent,** *used up* **646 Ay "Questio quid iuris,"** *always "What point of law is the question"* **647 harlot,** *rascal* **649 suffre,** *allow* **650 have his concubyn,** *keep his whore* **651 A twelf-monthe,** *for a year,* **atte fulle,** *completely* **652 Ful prively,** *very secretively,* **fynch,** *finch* (see note) **653 owher,** *anywhere* **654 techen,** *teach,* **noon awe,** *no respect* **655 swich caas of,** *such cases as* **656 But if,** *unless,* **purs,** *purse* **657 ypunysshed,** *punished* **659 woot,** *know,* **lyed right in dede,** *lied indeed* **660 oghte,** *ought,* **him drede,** *be afraid* (for himself) **661 curs wol slee right as assoillyng savith,** *excommunication will slay just as absolution saves* **662 war hym,** (let) *him beware,* ***Significavit,*** *"Be it known . . ."* **663 daunger,** *power,* **owene gise,** *own pleasure* **664 girles,** *males and females,* **diocise,** *church territory* **665 hir reed,** *their counselor* **666 gerland,** *wreath* **667 alestake,** *tavern sign* **668 bokeleer,** *shield,* **maad,** *made,* **cake,** *round loaf* **670 compeer,** *companion* **672 Ful loude,** *very loudly,* **hider,** *hither* **673 bar to hym a stif burdoun,** *accompanied him in a strong bass* (voice) **674 trompe,** *trumpet* **675 heer,** *hair,* **wex,** *wax* **676 heeng,** *hung,* **strike of flex,** *length of flax* **677 By ounces henge his lokkes,** *in strings hung the hair* **678 shuldres overspradde,** *spread over his shoulders* **679 thynne,** *thin,* **colpons oon and oon,** *strands one by one* **680 jolitee,** *playfulness,* **wered he noon,** *he wore none* **681 trussed,** *tied,* **walet,** *pouch* **682 Hym thoughte,** *he thought* (that), **newe jet,** *new fashion* **683 Dischevelee,** *with loose hair,* **bare,** *bareheaded*

637–38 Lines omitted in Hg. **639ff.** The Summoner understands the few words of Latin he speaks no better than a trained bird understands what it says. **646 "Questio quid iuris,"** the equivalent of senselessly repeating "Point of order!" **650–51** Though it was the Summoner's responsibility to bring fornicators to ecclesiastical court, he accepts bribes instead. **652 a fynch . . . pulle,** to "pull a finch" or "pluck a bird" meant to trick or deceive, but it seems also to have had sexual overtones. **655 ercedekenes curs,** the archdeacon's curse, or excommunication, could exclude the sinner from all church activities, and hence from hope of salvation. The archdeacon, a bishop's representative, presided over church courts. **657 in his purs . . . ypunysshed,** to be punished in one's purse meant to pay fines. **658 "Purs is the ercedekenes helle,"** i.e., "the purse is the archdeacon's hell"; it's the only place he will (can?) punish you. **660 him,** omitted in El and Hg. **662 *Significavit,*** "Be it known," the opening phrase of the written order that authorized civil arrest if the excommunicated person did not fulfill the demands of the church court. **664 diocise,** diocese, the territory in which a bishop and his officials (including archdeacon and summoners) had jurisdiction. **669 PARDONER,** sins were forgiven by priests in the sacrament of confession, or penance, but the sinner's punishment (also commonly known as his penance) due for sinning could be alleviated or eliminated through pardons or indulgences, available from pardoners, or *questors.* The sale of pardons was a source of revenue for the Church, intended to support worthy causes. Chaucer's Pardoner traffics in relics as well as pardons for personal gain. His association with the Summoner implies financial and perhaps sexual collusion. **670 Rouncivale,** the Pardoner was a fundraiser for the chapel and hospital of St. Mary of Roncevalles, at Charing Cross just west of medieval London. **672 "Com hider . . . ,"** line from a popular song, now lost. **673 burdoun,** critics read homosexual connotations here, as the word could mean either "staff" or "the bass part of a melody." **675–79 heer . . . ,** the Pardoner's hair suggests extravagance; clerics cut their hair in a specified way (the tonsure) as a sign of their dedication to God.

Swiche glarynge eyen° hadde he as an hare.
A vernycle° hadde he sowed upon his cappe.
His walet lay biforn hym in his lappe,
Bretful of° pardoun, comen from Rome al hoot°.
A voys° he hadde as smal° as hath a goot°.
No berd hadde he, ne nevere sholde have.
As smothe it was as it were late shave.
I trowe° he were a geldyng or a mare.
But of his craft, fro Berwyk into Ware,
Ne was ther swich another° pardoner.
For in his male° he hadde a pilwe-beer°,
Which that he seyde° was Oure Lady veyl°.
He seyde he hadde a gobet° of the seyl°
That Seint Peter hadde, whan that he wente
Upon the see°, til Jhesu Crist hym hente°.
He hadde a croys of latoun° ful of stones,
And in a glas° he hadde pigges bones.
But with thise relikes°, whan that he fond°
A poure person dwellynge upon lond°,
Upon a day he gat hym° moore moneye
Than that the person gat in monthes tweye°.
And thus, with feyned flaterye° and japes°,
He made the person° and the peple his apes°.
But trewely° to tellen atte laste°,
He was in chirche a noble ecclesiaste°.
Wel koude he rede a lessoun° or a storie,
But alderbest° he song an offertorie,
For wel he wiste°, whan that song was songe,
He moste preche° and wel affile° his tonge
To wynne silver, as he ful wel koude;
Therefore he song the murierly° and loude.

Now have I toold you shortly, in a clause°,
Th'estaat°, th'array°, the nombre, and eek the cause°
Why that assembled was this compaignye
In Southwerk at this gentil hostelrye°
That highte° the Tabard, faste° by the Belle.
But now is tyme to yow for to telle
How that we baren° us that ilke° nyght,
Whan we were in that hostelrie alyght°.
And after wol I telle of oure viage°
And al the remenaunt of oure pilgrimage.
But first I pray yow°, of youre curteisye,
That ye n'arette it nat° my vileynye°
Thogh that I pleynly° speke in this mateere,
To telle yow hir wordes and hir cheere°,
Ne thogh I speke hir wordes proprely°.
For this ye knowen al so° wel as I,
Whoso shal telle a tale after a man,
He moot reherce as ny° as evere he kan
Everich a° word, if it be in his charge°,
Al° speke he never so rudeliche° and large°,
Or ellis° he moot° telle his tale untrewe,
Or feyne thyng°, or fynde wordes newe.
He may nat spare°, although he were his brother;

684 eyen, *eyes* **685 vernycle,** *veronica* (see note) **687 Bretful of,** *crammed with,* **al hoot,** *all hot* **688 voys,** *voice,* **smal,** *high-pitched,* **goot,** *goat* **691 trowe,** *believe* **693 Ne was ther swich another,** *there was no comparable* **694 male,** *sack,* **pilwe-beer,** *pillowcase* **695 seyde,** *said,* **Oure Lady veyl,** *our Lady's veil* **696 gobet,** *piece,* **seyl,** *sail* **698 see,** *sea,* **hente,** *grabbed* **699 croys of latoun,** *cross of copper alloy* **700 glas,** *jar* **701 relikes,** *relics,* **fond,** *found* **702 person dwellynge upon lond,** *peasant laborer* **703 gat hym,** *got himself* **704 monthes tweye,** *two months* **705 feyned flaterye,** *fake flattery,* **japes,** *tricks* **706 person,** *parson,* **apes,** *dupes* **707 trewely,** *truly,* **atte laste,** *finally* **708 ecclesiaste,** *churchman* **709 Wel koude he rede a lessoun,** *he knew well how to read a scripture* **710 alderbest,** *best of all* **711 wiste,** *knew* **712 preche,** *preach,* **affile,** *polish* **713 koude,** *was able to* **714 murierly,** *more merrily* **715 in a clause,** *briefly* **716 Th'estaat,** *the rank,* **th'array,** *the clothing,* **eek the cause,** *also the u son* **718 hostelrye,** *inn* **719 highte,** *is called,* **faste,** *near* **721 baren,** *conducted,* **ilke,** *same* **722 alyght,** *stopped* **723 viage,** *journey* **725 pray yow,** *ask you* **726 ye n'arette it nat,** *you blame not,* **vileynye,** *vulgarity* **727 pleynly,** *directly* **728 hir cheere,** *their attitudes* **729 proprely,** *exactly* **730 al so,** *as* **732 moot reherce as ny,** *must repeat as closely* **733 Everich a,** *every single,* **charge,** *responsibility* **734 Al,** *although,* **rudeliche,** *discourteously,* **large,** *freely* **735 ellis,** *else* **moot,** *may* **736 feyne thyng,** *invent something* **737 spare,** *refrain*

684 glarynge eyen . . . as an hare, glaring eyes were thought to be indications of folly and excess; the hare, to have characteristics of both sexes. **685 vernycle,** a badge or token named after St. Veronica, whose cloth was thought to have the miraculous imprint of Christ's face. Copies of the "vera icon" (true likeness) were sold to pilgrims who visited Rome. **686 lay,** omitted in El and Hg. **688–91** The Pardoner's high voice and beardlessness apparently lead the narrator to conclude that he is effeminate, or perhaps a eunuch or homosexual, notions reflected in metaphoric comparison with a **geldyng**, a castrated horse, and a mare. The suggestion of infertility or infertile behavior is underscored by the fact that he keeps his pardons and (if the **walet** [line 686] and **male** [line 694] are the same) his false relics in the sack on his lap. **692 fro Berwyk into Ware,** from Berwick-upon-Tweed in northernmost England to Ware in southern England, i.e., from one end of England to the other. **694–701** Relics are material remains of saints and other holy people, objects of veneration that were thought capable of producing miracles. Trafficking in false relics was criticized by satirists and condemned by the Church. **696–98** Matthew14.24–31 describes how Jesus grasped St. Peter on the water. **710 song an offertorie,** sang the prayers of the Offertory (see 450n above), followed soon after by the preaching of the sermon. **715 shortly,** Hg reads "soothly" (truly). **719 the Tabard . . . Belle,** no inn named the Bell has been identified near the Tabard (see 20n above), although the Bell was a licensed house of prostitution in Southwark in the sixteenth century. **725–42** This explanation or "apology" raises several literary and linguistic issues: Is it possible to retell a tale exactly in a new context? In what sense(s) can fiction be unfeigned or true? What is the relation between scripture and other literature? What is the relation between word and deed? **737 He . . . although he were his brother,** even if the original teller or speaker (i.e., the "man" of line 731) is his brother, the reteller must not refrain from his retelling. The pronouns reflect the complexities of literary responsibility.

He moot as wel seye o° word as another.
Crist spak hymself ful brode° in hooly writ,
And wel ye woot° no vileynye° is it.
Eek° Plato seith°, whoso kan hym rede°,
The wordes moote be cosyn° to the dede.
Also I prey yow to foryeve° it me,
Al have I nat° set folk in hir degree°
Heere in this tale, as that they sholde stonde.
My wit is short, ye may wel understonde.
  Greet chiere made oure Hoost us everichon°,
And to the soper° sette he us anon.
He served us with vitaille at the beste°.
Strong was the wyn, and wel to drynke us leste°.
A semely° man oure HOOSTE was withalle°
For to been a marchal in an halle°.
A large man he was with eyen stepe°—
A fairer burgeys° was ther noon in Chepe—
Boold of his speche, and wys, and wel ytaught,
And of manhod hym lakked right naught°.
Eek therto° he was right a myrie° man,
And after soper pleyen he bigan°,
And spak of myrthe° amonges othere thynges,
Whan that we hadde maad our rekenynges°,
And seyde thus: "Now, lordynges, trewely,
Ye been to me right welcome, hertely°;
For by my trouthe, if that I shal nat lye,
I saugh° nat this yeer so myrie a compaignye
Atones° in this herberwe° as is now.
Fayn wolde I doon yow myrthe°, wiste I° how.
And of a myrthe° I am right now bythoght°,
To doon yow ese°, and it shal coste noght.
  "Ye goon to Caunterbury—God yow speede!
The blisful martir quite° yow youre meede°!
And wel I woot°, as ye goon by the weye,
Ye shapen yow° to talen° and to pleye.
For trewely, confort ne myrthe is noon°
To ride by the weye doumb° as a stoon°.
And therfore wol I maken yow disport°,
As I seyde erst°, and doon yow som confort.
And if yow liketh alle by oon assent°
For to stonden at my juggement°,
And for to werken° as I shal yow seye°,
To-morwe, whan ye riden by the weye,
Now, by my fader° soule that is° deed,
But ye be° myrie, I wol yeve° yow myn heed!
Hoold up youre hondes, withouten moore speche."
  Oure conseil° was nat longe for to seche°.
Us thoughte° it was noght worth to make it wys°,
And graunted hym° withouten moore avys°,
And bad him seye his voirdit° as hym leste°.
  "Lordynges," quod° he, "now herkneth° for the beste,
But taak° it nought, I prey yow, in desdeyn°.
This is the poynt, to speken short and pleyn,
That ech of yow, to shorte with° oure weye,
In this viage° shal telle tales tweye°
To Caunterbury-ward, I mene it so,

---

738 o, *one* **739 brode,** *freely* **740 ye woot,** *you know,* **vileynye,** *vulgarity* **741 Eek,** *also,* **seith,** *says,* **whoso kan hym rede,** *whoever can read him* **742 moote be cosyn,** *must be related* **743 foryeve,** *forgive* **744 Al have I nat,** *although I have not,* **hir degree,** *their social order* **747 us everichon,** *to each one of us* **748 soper,** *supper* **749 vitaille at the beste,** *the best of food* **750 wel to drynke us leste,** *we were well pleased to drink* **751 semely,** *impressive,* **withalle,** *indeed* **752 marchal in an halle,** *master of ceremonies* **753 eyen stepe,** *prominent eyes* **754 burgeys,** *citizen* **756 right naught,** *nothing at all* **757 Eek therto,** *besides that,* **right a myrie,** *a very merry* **758 pleyen he bigan,** *began to entertain* **759 spak of myrthe,** *spoke of enjoyment* **760 maad our rekenynges,** *paid our bills* **762 hertely,** *sincerely* **764 saugh,** *saw* **765 Atones,** *at one time,* **herberwe,** *inn* **766 Fayn wolde I doon yow myrthe,** *I would gladly make you happy,* **wiste I,** *if I knew* **767 a myrthe,** *an entertainment,* **am . . . bythoght,** *have thought* **768 doon yow ese,** *give you pleasure* **770 quite,** *pay,* **meede,** *reward* **771 woot,** *know* **772 Ye shapen yow,** *you plan,* **talen,** *tell tales* **773 confort ne myrthe is noon,** *there is no comfort nor mirth* **774 doumb,** *silent,* **stoon,** *stone* **775 disport,** *a diversion* **776 seyde erst,** *said before* **777 yow liketh alle by oon assent,** (it) *pleases you all together* **778 stonden at my juggement,** *accept my direction* **779 to werken,** *act,* **seye,** *tell* **781, fader,** *father's,* **that is,** *who is* **782 But ye be,** *unless you are,* **yeve,** *give* **784 conseil,** *discussion,* **for to seche,** *in deliberation* **785 Us thoughte,** *it seemed to us that,* **worth to make it wys,** *worthwhile to make an issue of it* **786 graunted hym,** *agreed with him,* **avys,** *discussion* **787 seye his voirdit,** *give his verdict,* **as hym leste,** *as he wished* **788 quod,** *said,* **herkneth,** *listen* **789 But taak,** *and take,* **desdeyn,** *disdain* **791 shorte with,** *shorten* **792 viage,** *journey,* **tweye,** *two*

741–42 Plato seith . . . wordes moote be cosyn to the dede, the notion that words must relate ("be a cousin") to actuality is found in Plato's *Timaeus* 29, but Chaucer took it from Boethius; see his translation, *Bo* pr.3 pr.12.207. Like his contemporaries, Chaucer could not read Greek. The *MED* records *cosyn* as "fraud, trickery" as early as 1453. **743 foryeve,** the narrator, perhaps Chaucer himself, asks for a different forgiveness at the end of the Canterbury fiction; see *Ret* 10.1084. **751 HOOSTE,** the Host is an innkeeper, later named Harry Bailly (*CkP* 1.4358). A "Henri Bayliff" is recorded as an innkeeper in Southwark in 1380–81, perhaps Chaucer's inspiration and no doubt an inside joke for some of Chaucer's original audience. The Host is an impressive man, concerned with his accounts and with keeping his guests well entertained. His literary judgment (or lack of) is a theme that recurs throughout the work. Final *–e* added here and elsewhere for disyllabic pronunciation encouraged by the meter.**752 marchal in an halle,** an officer responsible for managing the arrangements and service in a royal or noble dining hall. **753 eyen stepe,** see 201n above. **754 Chepe,** Cheapside was an important commercial district in medieval London. **761 lordynges,** Hg reads "lordes." **774 a stoon,** El reads "the stoon"; Hg omits "a." **782 But ye,** El reads "But if ye." **792–94** This plan of four tales per pilgrim (two going and two returning) evidently changed as Chaucer developed his work; see *CT* 5.698 and 10.16.

And homward he shal tellen othere° two,
Of aventures that whilom han bifalle°.
And which of yow that bereth hym° best of alle,
That is to seyn, that telleth in this caas°
Tales of best sentence° and moost solaas°,
Shal have a soper at oure aller cost°
Heere in this place, sittynge by this post,
Whan that we come agayn fro Caunterbury.
And for to make yow the moore mury°,
I wol myselven goodly° with yow ryde,
Right at myn owene cost, and be youre gyde°.
And whoso° wole my juggement withseye°
Shal paye al that we spenden by the weye.
And if ye vouchesauf° that it be so,
Tel me anon° withouten wordes mo,
And I wol erly shape me° therfore."
This thyng was graunted, and oure othes° swore
With ful glad herte, and preyden° hym also
That he wolde vouchesauf for to do so,
And that he wolde been oure governour,
And of our tales juge and reportour°,
And sette a soper at a certeyn pris°,
And we wol reuled been° at his devys°
In heigh and lough°. And thus by oon assent°
We been acorded to his juggement.
And therupon the wyn was fet anon°.
We dronken, and to reste wente echon°
Withouten any lenger taryynge°.
Amorwe°, whan that day gan for to sprynge°,
Up roos oure Hoost, and was oure aller cok°,
And gadrede° us togidre alle in a flok,
And forth we riden a litel moore than paas°
Unto the wateryng of Seint Thomas.
And there oure Hoost bigan his hors areste°
And seyde, "Lordynges, herkneth°, if yow leste°.
Ye woot° youre foreward°, and it yow recorde°.
If even-song and morwe-song accorde,
Lat se now who shal telle the firste tale.
As evere mote° I drynke wyn or ale,
Whoso be rebel to my juggement
Shal paye for al that by the wey is spent.
Now draweth cut°, er° that we ferrer twynne°;
He which that hath the shorteste shal bigynne.
Sire Knyght," quod° he, "my mayster and my lord,
Now draweth cut, for that is myn accord.
Cometh neer," quod he, "my lady Prioresse.
And ye, sire Clerk, lat be youre shamefastnesse°,
Ne studieth noght; ley hond to°, every man!"
Anon to drawen every wight° bigan,
And shortly for to tellen as it was,
Were it by aventure, or sort, or cas°,
The sothe° is this, the cut fil to° the Knyght,
Of which ful blithe° and glad was every wyght,
And telle he moste° his tale, as was resoun,
By foreward° and by composicioun°,
As ye han herd. What nedeth wordes mo?
And whan this goode man saugh° that it was so,
As he that wys was and obedient
To kepe his foreward by his free assent,
He seyde, "Syn° I shal bigynne the game,
What, welcome be the cut, a Goddes name°!
Now lat us ryde, and herkneth what I seye."
And with that word we ryden forth oure weye,
And he bigan with right a myrie cheere°
His tale anon, and seyde in this manere.

---

794 othere, *another* **795 whilom han bifalle,** *once upon a time have happened* **796 bereth hym,** *conducts himself* **797 caas,** *case* **798 best sentence,** *highest wisdom,* **solaas,** *delight* **799 soper at oure aller cost,** *supper at the expense of all of us* **802 mury,** *merry* **803 goodly,** *gladly* **804 gyde,** *guide* **805 whoso,** *whoever,* **wole . . . withseye,** *contradicts* **807 vouchesauf,** *agree* **808 anon,** *immediately* **809 wol erly shape me,** *will prepare myself early* **810 othes,** *oaths* **811 preyden,** (we) *asked* **814 reportour,** *scorekeeper* **815 pris,** *price* **816 wol reuled been,** *will be ruled,* **at his devys,** *by his will* **817 In heigh and lough,** *in all ways,* **oon assent,** *common agreement* **819 fet anon,** *fetched quickly* **820 echon,** *each one* **821 taryynge,** *delay* **822 Amorwe,** *in the morning,* **gan . . . sprynge,** *did break* **823 oure aller cok,** *rooster for us all* **824 gadrede,** *gathered* **825 litel moore than paas,** *at a slow pace* **827 areste,** *stop* **828 herkneth,** *listen,* **leste,** *please* **829 woot,** *know,* **foreward,** *agreement,* **recorde,** *remember* **832 mote,** *may* **835 draweth cut,** *draw straws,* **er,** *before,* **ferrer twynne,** *depart further* **837 quod,** *said* **840 lat be youre shamefastnesse,** *give up your modesty* **841 ley hond to,** *pick one* **842 wight,** *person* **844 Were it by aventure, or sort, or cas,** *whether by chance, fate, or destiny* **845 sothe,** *truth,* **fil to,** *fell to* **846 blithe,** *happy* **847 moste,** *must* **848 foreward,** *promise,* **composicioun,** *agreement* **850 saugh,** *saw* **853 Syn,** *since* **854 a Goddes name,** *in God's name* **857 right a myrie cheere,** *a most happy expression*

798 sentence . . . solaas, a balance between meaning (sentence) and pleasure (solaas) is an aesthetic ideal rooted in Cicero's assertion that the goal of oratory is to teach, delight, and move (*De optimo genere oratorum* 16); both Horace (*Ars Poetica* 343) and Philip Sidney (*Defence of Poesy*) say that the dual aim of writing is to teach and to delight. **822 gan for to,** Hg reads "bigan to." **824 alle,** omitted in Hg. **826 wateryng of Seint Thomas,** a brook convenient for watering horses about a mile and a half from the Tabard Inn. **828 Lordynges,** Hg reads "Lordes." **835 draweth cut,** drawing straws or sticks, one of which is "cut" or shortened, was (and is) a familiar way of making a random selection in a competition; compare the "cut" of a deck of cards. Some critics have suggested that it is no luck or coincidence at all that when the Host offers first draw to the Knight, he is the one to whom the cut falls. **847 And telle,** El reads "A telle." **850 And whan,** El reads "An whan." **858 in this manere,** Hg reads "as ye may heere."

From woodcut made by W.H. Hooper and published by the Chaucer Society between 1868 and 1879

Knight's Tale

Heere bigynneth the Knyghtes Tale.

Iamque domos patrias Scithice post aspera gentis Prelia laurigero &c

Whilom°, as olde stories° tellen us,
Ther was a duc° that highte° Theseus.
Of Atthenes he was lord and governour,
And in his tyme swich° a conquerour,
That gretter was ther noon under the sonne.
Ful many a riche contree hadde he wonne,
What with° his wysdom and his chivalrie;
He conquered al the regne° of Femenye°,
That whilom was ycleped° Scithia,
And wedded the queene Ypolita,
And broghte hire hoom with hym in his contree
With muchel° glorie and greet solempnytee°,
And eek° hir yonge suster° Emelye.
And thus with victorie and with melodye
Lete I° this noble duc to Atthenes ryde,
And al his hoost° in armes hym bisyde.
And certes°, if it nere° to long to heere,
I wolde yow have toold fully the manere
How wonnen° was the regne of Femenye
By Theseus and by his chivalrye°,
And of the grete bataille° for the nones°
Bitwixen Atthenes and Amazones,
And how asseged° was Ypolita,
The faire, hardy queene of Scithia,
And of the feste° that was at hir° weddynge,
And of the tempest at hir hoom-comynge—
But al that thyng I moot as now forbere°.
I have, God woot°, a large feeld to ere°,
And wayke° been the oxen in my plough°.
The remenant° of the tale is long ynough.

859 Whilom, *once,* **stories,** *histories* **860 duc,** *duke,* **highte,** *was called* **862 swich,** *such* **865 What with,** *as a result of* **866 regne,** *realm,* **Femenye,** *land of women* **867 ycleped,** *called* **870 muchel,** *much,* **solempnytee,** *ceremony* **871 eek,** *also,* **suster,** *sister* **873 Lete I,** *I let* **874 hoost,** *army* **875 certes,** *certainly,* **nere,** *weren't* **877 wonnen,** *won* **878 chivalrye,** *knights* **879 grete bataille,** *great battle,* **for the nones,** *on that occasion* **881 asseged,** *besieged* **883 feste,** *festivities,* **hir,** *their* **885 moot as now forbere,** *must now forsake* **886 woot,** *knows,* **ere,** *plow* **887 wayke,** *weak,* **plough,** *plow* **888 remenant,** *rest*

Iamque domos . . . , "And now to his native land in a decorated chariot after fierce struggles with the Scithians, etc." This line and a half is from Statius, *Thebaid* 12.519–20, the ultimate source of the *KnT,* although Chaucer modeled his version on Boccaccio's *Teseida,* influenced by a glossed version of the *Thebaid* and twelfth-century French *Roman de Thèbes.* An expanded form of the motto is in Chaucer's short poem *Anelida and Arcite* (line 22), which appears to have been a trial run for some of the *KnT* material. **861 Atthenes,** Athens was regarded by medieval people as a social and political ideal. **866 Femenye,** derived from Lat. *femina,* "woman," Chaucer's name for the land of the Amazons. **867 Scithia,** Scythia, on the shores of the Black Sea. **867 Ypolita,** Hippolyta, queen of the Amazons. **871 yonge,** El reads "faire." **876 yow,** omitted in Hg. **884 tempest,** Chaucer invents the detail of the tempest, possibly an allusion to the storm that occurred just as Anne of Bohemia arrived in 1382 in England for her wedding to Richard II.

I wol nat letten eek° noon of this route°.
Lat every felawe telle his tale aboute°,
And lat se now who shal the soper wynne°;
And ther° I lefte, I wol ayeyn° bigynne.
  This duc, of whom I make mencioun,
Whan he was come almoost unto the toun,
In al his wele° and in his mooste° pride,
He was war°, as he caste his eye aside°,
Where that ther kneled° in the heighe weye°
A compaignye of ladyes, tweye° and tweye,
Ech after oother, clad in clothes blake.
But swich° a cry and swich a wo they make
That in this world nys° creature lyvynge
That herde swich another waymentynge°,
And of this cry they nolde nevere stenten°
Til they the reynes° of his brydel henten°.
  "What folk been ye, that at myn homcomynge
Perturben° so my feste° with criynge?"
Quod Theseus. "Have ye so greet envye
Of myn honour, that thus compleyne and crye?
Or who hath yow mysboden° or offended?
And telleth me if it may been amended,
And why that ye been clothed thus in blak."
  The eldeste lady of hem° alle spak,
Whan she hadde swowned° with a deedly cheere°,
That it was routhe° for to seen and heere,
And seyde: "Lord, to whom Fortune hath yeven°
Victorie, and as a conqueror to lyven°,
Nat greveth us youre glorie° and youre honour,
But we biseken° mercy and socour°.
Have mercy on oure wo and oure distresse!
Som drope of pitee, thurgh thy gentillesse°,
Upon us wrecched wommen lat° thou falle.
For, certes, lord, ther is noon of us alle,
That she ne hath been a duchesse or a queene.
Now be we caytyves°, as it is wel seene,
Thanked be Fortune and hire false wheel,
That noon estaat assureth° to be weel°.
And certes, lord, to abyden° youre presence,
Heere in this temple of the goddesse Clemence°
We han ben waitynge al this fourtenyght°.
Now help us, lord, sith° it is in thy myght.
"I, wrecche, which that wepe and wayle thus,
Was whilom° wyf to Kyng Cappaneus,
That starf° at Thebes—cursed be that day!
And alle we that been in this array
And maken al this lamentacioun,
We losten alle oure housbondes at that toun,
Whil that the seege° theraboute lay.
And yet now the olde Creon, weylaway°,
That lord is now of Thebes the citee,
Fulfild of ire° and of iniquitee°,
He, for despit° and for his tirannye,
To do the dede° bodyes vileynye°
Of alle oure lordes whiche that been yslawe°,
He hath alle the bodyes on an heep ydrawe°,
And wol nat suffren hem°, by noon assent,
Neither to been yburyed° nor ybrent°,
But maketh houndes ete hem° in despit°."
  And with that word, withouten moore respit°,
They fillen gruf° and criden pitously,
"Have on us wrecched wommen som mercy,
And lat oure sorwe synken in thyn herte."
  This gentil duc doun from his courser sterte°
With herte pitous°, whan he herde hem° speke.
Hym thoughte that his herte wolde breke

---

889 wol nat letten eek, *also will not hinder,* **route,** *company* **890 aboute,** *in turn* **891 the soper wynne,** *win the supper* **892 ther,** *where,* **wol ayeyn,** *will again* **895 wele,** *prosperity,* **mooste,** *greatest* **896 war,** *aware,* **caste . . . aside,** *looked around* **897 kneled,** *kneeled,* **heighe weye,** *main road* **898 tweye,** *two* **900 swich,** *such* **901 nys,** (there) *isn't* **902 waymentynge,** *lamenting* **903 nolde nevere stenten,** *would never stop* **904 reynes,** *reins,* **henten,** *grasped* **906 Perturben,** *disturb,* **feste,** *festivities* **909 mysboden,** *injured* **912 hem,** *them* **913 swowned,** *fainted,* **deedly cheere,** *deathly expression* **914 routhe,** *pity* **915 yeven,** *given* **916 lyven,** *live* **917 Nat greveth us youre glorie,** *your glory doesn't distress us* **918 biseken,** *request,* **socour,** *aid* **920 thurgh thy gentillesse,** *through your nobility* **921 lat,** *let* **924 caytyves,** *wretches* **926 noon estaat assureth,** *assures no class,* **weel,** *prosperous* **927 abyden,** *await* **928 Clemence,** *Pity* **929 fourtenyght,** *two weeks* **930 sith,** *since* **932 whilom,** *once* **933 starf,** *died* **937 seege,** *siege* **938 weylaway,** *alas* **940 ire,** *anger,* **iniquitee,** *wickedness* **941 for despit,** *because of spite* **942 dede,** *dead,* **vileynye,** *dishonor* **943 yslawe,** *slain* **944 on an heep ydrawe,** *pulled into a heap* **945 wol nat suffren hem,** *will not allow them* **946 yburyed,** *buried,* **ybrent,** *burned* **947 ete hem,** *eat them,* **despit,** *scorn* **948 respit,** *delay* **949 fillen gruf,** *fell groveling* **952 courser sterte,** *steed leapt* **953 pitous,** *compassionate,* **hem,** *them*

889–91 A reference in *LGW* (F420–21) indicates that Chaucer composed a version of the story of Palamon and Arcite before he had begun the *CT*, but these lines show that he adapted the material to some extent before incorporating it into *CT*. **915 And,** Hg reads "She." **925 Fortune and hire false wheel,** the wheel of the goddess Fortuna, described in *Bo* 2pr2, is an image of random fate. The theme of fortune and its relation to destiny and freedom are major concerns in *KnT* and elsewhere in Chaucer's works. **928 this,** El reads "the." **931 wayle,** El reads "crie." **932 Cappaneus,** Capaneus was one of the "seven against Thebes" in Greek legend. In the assault on the city, he was destroyed by Zeus for presuming to be invulnerable. His wife, Evadne, committed suicide. **933 that day,** Hg reads "the day." **938 olde Creon,** Creon, who became ruler of Thebes after the conclusion of the war with the seven, was the medieval stereotype of a tyrant. His fixed epithet in *Roman de Thèbes* is "Creon li Vieuz" (Creon the old). **943 yslawe,** El and Hg read "slawe." **944 He hath,** Hg omits "He."

Whan he saugh° hem so pitous° and so maat°,
That whilom weren of so greet estaat,
And in his armes he hem alle up hente°,
And hem conforteth in ful good entente°,
And swoor his ooth, as he was trewe knyght,
He wolde doon so ferforthly° his myght
Upon the tiraunt Creon hem to wreke°,
That al the peple of Grece sholde speke
How Creon was of Theseus yserved°
As he that hadde his deeth ful wel deserved.
  And right anoon°, withouten moore abood°,
His baner° he desplayeth, and forth rood
To Thebes-ward°, and al his hoost° biside.
No neer° Atthenes wolde° he go ne ride,
Ne take his ese fully half a day,
But onward on° his wey that nyght he lay°,
And sente anon Ypolita the queene,
And Emelye, hir yonge suster sheene°,
Unto the toun of Atthenes to dwelle,
And forth he rit°; ther is namoore to telle.
  The rede° statue of Mars, with spere and targe°,
So shyneth in his white baner large,
That alle the feeldes glyteren° up and doun,
And by° his baner° born is his penoun°
Of gold ful riche, in which ther was ybete°
The Mynotaur, which that he slough° in Crete.
  Thus rit° this due, thus rit this conquerour,
And in his hoost of chivalrie the flour°,
Til that he cam to Thebes and alighte°
Faire in a feeld, ther as° he thoughte to fighte.
But shortly for to speken of this thyng,
With Creon, which that was of Thebes kyng,
He faught, and slough hym manly as a knyght
In pleyn bataille°, and putte the folk to flyght.
And by assaut he wan° the citee after,
And rente adoun° bothe wall and sparre° and rafter.
And to the ladyes he restored agayn
The bones of hir housbondes that were slayn,
To doon obsequies°, as was tho the gyse°.
But it were al to longe for to devyse°
The grete clamour and the waymentynge°
That the ladyes made at the brennynge°
Of the bodies, and the grete honour
That Theseus, the noble conquerour,
Dooth to the ladyes, whan they from hym wente;
But shortly for to telle is myn entente.
  Whan that this worthy due, this Theseus,
Hath Creon slayn, and wonne Thebes thus,
Stille in that feeld he took al nyght his reste,
And dide with al the contree as hym leste°.
  To ransake° in the taas° of bodyes dede,
Hem° for to strepe° of harneys° and of wede°,
The pilours° diden bisynesse° and cure°
After the bataille and disconfiture°.
And so bifel° that in the taas they founde,
Thurgh-girt° with many a grevous blody wounde,
Two yonge knyghtes liggynge by and by°,
Bothe in oon armes°, wroght° ful richely,
Of whiche two Arcita highte that oon°,
And that oother knyght highte Palamon.
Nat fully quyke°, ne fully dede they were.
But by hir cote-armures° and by hir gere°
The heraudes° knewe hem best in special°
As they that weren of the blood roial°
Of Thebes, and of sustren° two yborn.
Out of the taas the pilours han hem torn°,
And han hem caried softe° unto the tente
Of Theseus, and he ful soone hem sente
To Atthenes, to dwellen in prisoun

---

955 saugh, *saw,* **pitous,** *pitiable,* **maat,** *defeated* **957 hente,** *took* **958 entente,** *intention* **960 wolde doon so ferforthly,** *would impose so thoroughly* **961 hem to wreke,** *to avenge them* **963 of Theseus yserved,** *treated by Theseus* **965 right anoon,** *immediately,* **abood,** *delay* **966 baner,** *banner* **967 To Thebes-ward,** *toward Thebes,* **hoost,** *army* **968 neer,** *nearer,* **wolde,** *would* **970 onward on,** *further on,* **that nyght he lay,** *he spent the night* **972 sheene,** *beautiful* **974 rit,** *rides* **975 rede,** *red,* **targe,** *shield* **977 feeldes glyteren,** *fields glittered* **978 by,** *near,* **born,** *carried,* **penoun,** *pennant* **979 ybete,** *embroidered* **980 slough,** *slew* **981 rit,** *rides* **982 of chivalrie the flour,** *the flower of chivalry* **983 alighte,** *dismounts* **984 ther as,** *where* **988 pleyn bataille,** *open combat* **989 wan,** *conquered* **990 rente adoun,** *tore down,* **sparre,** *beam* **993 obsequies,** *funeral services,* **tho the gyse,** *then the custom* **994 devyse,** *describe* **995 waymentynge,** *lamenting* **996 brennynge,** *burning* **1004 hym leste,** (it) *pleased him* **1005 ransake,** *search,* **taas,** *heap* **1006 Hem,** *them,* **strepe,** *strip,* **harneys,** *armor,* **wede,** *clothes* **1007 pilours,** *pillagers,* **diden bisynesse,** *did business,* **cure,** *care* **1008 disconfiture,** *defeat* **1009 bifel,** *it happened* **1010 Thurgh-girt,** *pierced through* **1011 liggynge by and by,** *lying side by side* **1012 oon armes,** *identical armor,* **wroght,** *made* **1013 highte that oon,** *one was named* **1015 quyke,** *alive* **1016 hir cote-armures,** *their coats of arms,* **gere,** *equipment* **1017 heraudes,** *heralds,* **best in special,** *especially well* **1018 roial,** *royal* **1019 sustren,** *sisters* **1020 han hem torn,** *have them pulled* **1021 softe,** *gently*

966 baner he desplayeth, displaying or unfurling the flags was a sign of going to battle. Theseus's military insignia included images of **Mars** (line 975), the red or bloody god of war, on his banner; and on his pennant, the **Mynotaur** (Minotaur, line 980), a half-man, half-bull figure of bestiality, defeated by Theseus in the labyrinth on Crete. **978 is,** Hg reads "was." **980 slough,** Hg reads "wan" (defeated). **992 housbondes,** Hg reads "freendes." **1005 To ransake . . . ,** ransacking or pillaging the bodies of the slain was normal medieval practice. **of,** El reads "of the." **1009 that,** omitted in Hg. **1019 of sustren two yborn,** Palamon and Arcite are first cousins.

Perpetuelly—he nolde no raunsoun°.
And whan this worthy duc hath thus ydon°,
He took his hoost, and hoom he rood anon
With laurer° crowned as a conquerour.
And ther he lyveth in joye and in honour
Terme° of his lyf; what nedeth wordes mo?
And in a tour°, in angwissh and in wo,
This Palamon and his felawe° Arcite
For everemoore; ther may no gold hem quite°.
This passeth yeer by yeer and day by day
Til it fil ones°, in a morwe° of May,
That Emelye, that fairer was to sene°
Than is the lylie upon his stalke grene,
And fressher than the May with floures newe—
For with the rose colour stroof hire hewe°,
I noot° which was the fyner of hem° two—
Er° it were day, as was hir wone° to do,
She was arisen and al redy dight°,
For May wole° have no slogardie a-nyght°.
The sesoun priketh° every gentil herte,
And maketh hym out of his slep to sterte°,
And seith, “Arys, and do thyn observaunce.”°
This maked Emelye have remembraunce
To doon honour to May, and for to ryse.
Yclothed was she fressh, for to devyse°.
Hir yelow heer was broyded° in a tresse
Bihynde hir bak, a yerde long, I gesse.
And in the gardyn, at the sonne upriste°,
She walketh up and doun, and as hire liste°
She gadereth floures°, party° white and rede,
To make a subtil gerland° for hire hede.
And as an aungel hevenysshly° she soong.
The grete tour that was so thikke and stroong,
Which of the castle was the chief dongeoun°—
Ther as° the knyghtes weren in prisoun
Of whiche I tolde yow and tellen shal—
Was evene joynant° to the gardyn wal
Ther as this Emelye hadde hir pleyynge°.
Bright was the sonne and cleer that morwenynge°,
And Palamoun, this woful prisoner,
As was his wone°, by leve° of his gayler°,
Was risen and romed° in a chambre an heigh°,
In which he al the noble citee seigh°,
And eek the gardyn, ful of braunches grene,
Ther as this fresshe Emelye the shene°
Was in hir walk, and romed up and doun.
This sorweful prisoner, this Palamoun,
Goth° in the chambre romynge to and fro,
And to hymself compleynynge of his wo.
That he was born, ful ofte he seyde, “Allas!”
And so bifel, by aventure or cas°,
That thurgh a wyndow, thikke of many a barre°
Of iren greet and square as any sparre°,
He cast his eye upon Emelya.
And therwithal he bleynte° and cride, “A!”
As though he stongen° were unto the herte.
And with that cry Arcite anon up sterte°,
And seyde, “Cosyn myn, what eyleth° thee,
That art so pale and deedly on to see°?
Why cridestow°? Who hath thee doon offence?
For Goddes love, taak° al in pacience
Oure prisoun, for it may noon oother be.
Fortune hath yeven° us this adversitee.
Som wikke° aspect or disposicioun
Of Saturne, by sum° constellacioun,
Hath yeven us this, although we hadde it sworn°.
So stood the hevene whan that we were born.
We moste endure; this is the short and playn.”

1024 nolde no raunsoun, *would accept no ransom* **1025 ydon,** *done* **1027 laurer,** *laurel wreath* **1029 Terme,** (for the) *duration,* **1030 tour,** *tower* **1031 felawe,** *companion* **1032 hem quite,** *pay for them* **1034 Til it fil ones,** *until it happened once,* **morwe,** *morning* **1035 to sene,** *to look at* **1038 stroof hire hewe,** *competed her complexion* **1039 noot,** *don't know,* **fyner of hem,** *finer of them* **1040 Er,** *before,* **wone,** *custom* **1041 dight,** *dressed* **1042 wole,** *will,* **slogardie a-nyght,** *laziness at night* **1043 sesoun priketh,** *season prods* **1044 sterte,** *awaken* **1048 devyse,** *describe* **1049 broyded,** *braided* **1051 upriste,** *rising* **1052 hire leste,** (it) *pleased her* **1053 gadereth floures,** *gathered flowers,* **party,** *of mixed colors* **1054 subtil gerland,** *skillful wreath* **1055 hevenysshly,** *in a heavenly way* **1057 dongeoun,** *fortification* **1058 Ther as,** *where* **1060 evene joynant,** *directly adjoining* **1061 pleyynge,** *entertainment* **1062 morwenynge,** *morning* **1064 wone,** *custom,* **leve,** *permission,* **gayler,** *jailer* **1065 romed,** *roamed,* **an heigh,** *high up* **1066 seigh,** *saw* **1068 shene,** *beautiful* **1071 Goth,** *goes* **1074 aventure or cas,** *accident or chance* **1075 thikke of many a barre,** *heavily barred* **1076 sparre,** *beam* **1078 bleynte,** *turned pale* **1079 stongen,** *stung* **1080 anon up sterte,** *leapt up immediately* **1081 eyleth,** *ails* **1082 on to see,** *to look at* **1083 cridestow,** *did you cry out* **1084 taak,** *take* **1086 yeven,** *given* **1087 Som wikke,** *some wicked* **1088 sum,** *some* **1089 hadde it sworn,** *had sworn the opposite*

1024 raunsoun, there is no concern with ransom in Chaucer's sources. Theseus seeks no ransom for Palamon and Arcite because, presumably, they have not surrendered and, if released, might seek revenge for the defeat of Thebes. Ransom was a source of income in medieval practice, but Theseus's interests are not financial. **1027 laurer,** the crown of laurel leaves was traditionally awarded to the hero (or the poet). **1029 his,** omitted in El. **1031** Hg reads "Dwellen this Palamon and eek Arcite." **1039 fyner,** Hg reads "fairer." **1044 hym,** Hg reads "it." **1047 honour to May,** May was celebrated as a time of rejuvenation and fertility. **1062 that morwenynge,** Hg reads "in that mornyng." **1063 And,** El reads "And this." **1068 this,** Hg reads "the." **1077 eye,** in courtly tradition, love enters through the eye and lodges in the heart. Arcite sees Emily first in Chaucer's source, and Emily, noticing the attention of the knight, sings coyly; *Teseida* 3.11ff. **1087–88 wikke aspect . . . Of Saturne . . . ,** Arcite equates Fortune with the astrological influence of Saturn, the most malevolent of the planets, blaming it for their imprisonment. **1091 moste endure,** Hg reads "mote endure it" (must).

This Palamon answerde and seyde agayn°,
"Cosyn, for sothe°, of this opinioun
Thow hast a veyn ymaginacioun°.
This prison caused me nat for to crye,
But I was hurt right now thurghout myn° eye
Into myn herte, that wol my bane° be.
The fairnesse of that lady that I see
Yond° in the gardyn romen to and fro
Is cause of al my criyng and my wo.
I noot wher° she be womman or goddesse,
But Venus is it soothly°, as I gesse."
And therwithal on knees doun he fil,
And seyde, "Venus, if it be thy wil
Yow in this gardyn thus to transfigure
Bifore me, sorweful, wrecched creature,
Out of this prisoun help that we may scapen°.
And if so be my destynee be shapen°
By eterne° word to dyen in prisoun,
Of oure lynage° have som compassioun,
That is so lowe ybroght by tirannye."
And with that word Arcite gan espye°
Wher as this lady romed to and fro,
And with that sighte hir beautee hurte hym so
That, if that Palamon was wounded soore,
Arcite is hurt as muche as he, or moore.
And with a sigh he seyde pitously,
"The fresshe beautee sleeth° me sodeynly°
Of hire that rometh in the yonder place,
And but° I have hir mercy and hir grace,
That I may seen° hire atte leeste weye°,
I nam° but deed; ther nis namoore to seye."
This Palamon, whan he tho° wordes herde,
Dispitously° he looked and answerde,
"Wheither seistow this° in ernest or in pley?"
"Nay," quod Arcite, "in ernest, by my fey°!
God helpe me so, me list ful yvele pleye°."
This Palamon gan knytte his browes tweye°.
"It nere°," quod he, "to thee no greet honour
For to be fals, ne for to be traitour
To me, that am thy cosyn and thy brother
Ysworn ful depe°, and ech of us til° oother,
That nevere, for to dyen in the peyne°
Til that deeth departe shal us tweyne°,
Neither of us in love to hyndre° oother,
Ne in noon oother cas°, my leeve° brother,
But that thou sholdest trewely forthren° me
In every cas, as I shal forthren thee:
This was thyn ooth, and myn also, certeyn.
I woot° right wel, thou darst it nat withseyn°.
Thus artow of my conseil°, out of doute,
And now thow woldest falsly been aboute
To love my lady, whom I love and serve,
And evere shal til that myn herte sterve°.
Nay, certes°, false Arcite, thow shalt nat so.
I loved hire first, and tolde thee my wo
As to my conseil° and to my brother sworn
To forthre° me, as I have toold biforn.
For which thou art ybounden as a knyght
To helpen me, if it lay in thy myght,
Or elles artow fals°, I dar wel seyn."
This Arcite ful proudly spak ageyn°:
"Thow shalt," quod he, "be rather fals than I,
And thou art fals, I telle thee outrely°,
For paramour I loved hire first er thow°.
What wiltow seyen°? Thou wistest° nat yet now
Wheither she be a womman or goddesse!
Thyn is affeccioun of hoolynesse°,
And myn is love as to a creature,
For which I tolde thee myn aventure°
As to my cosyn and my brother sworn.
I pose° that thow lovedest hire biforn:
Wostow nat° wel the olde clerkes sawe°,
That 'who shal yeve° a lovere any lawe?'
Love is a gretter lawe, by my pan°,
Than may be yeve to any erthely man.

1092 agayn, *in response* **1093 for sothe,** *truly* **1094 veyn ymaginacioun,** *foolish notion* **1096 thurghout myn,** *through my* **1097 bane,** *death* **1099 Yond,** *there* **1101 noot wher,** *don't know whether* **1102 soothly,** *truly* **1107 scapen,** *escape* **1108 shapen,** *predetermined* **1109 eterne,** *eternal* **1110 lynage,** *lineage* **1112 gan espye,** *did see* **1118 sleeth,** *slays,* **sodeynly,** *suddenly* **1120 but,** *unless* **1121 seen,** *see,* **atte leeste weye,** *at least* **1122 nam,** *am nothing* **1123 tho,** *those* **1124 Dispitously,** *scornfully* **1125 Wheither seistow this,** *do you say this* **1126 fey,** *faith* **1127 me list ful yvele pleye,** *play is very unpleasing to me* **1128 gan knytte his browes tweye,** *knitted his two eyebrows* (frowned) **1129 nere,** *would not be* **1132 ful depe,** *very deeply,* **til,** *to* **1133 for to dyen in the peyne,** *to the extent of dying by torture* **1134 departe shal us tweyne,** *shall separate the two of us* **1135 hyndre,** *hinder* **1136 cas,** *situation,* **leeve,** *dear* **1137 forthren,** *further* **1140 woot,** *know,* **darst it nat withseyn,** *dare not deny it* **1141 artow of my conseil,** *you are in my confidence* **1144 sterve,** *dies* **1145 certes,** *surely* **1147 conseil,** *confidant* **1148 forthre,** *further* **1151 elles artow fals,** *else you are false* **1152 spak ageyn,** *replied* **1154 outrely,** *utterly* **1155 For paramour,** *as a lover,* **er thow,** *before you* **1156 wiltow seyen,** *will you say,* **wistest,** *knew* **1158 affeccioun of hoolynesse,** *spiritual love* **1160 aventure,** *condition* **1162 pose,** *posit,* **biforn,** *earlier* **1163 Wostow nat,** *don't you know,* **clerkes sawe,** *scholarly saying* **1164 yeve,** *give* **1165 pan,** *head*

1106 wrecched, El reads "wrecche." **1107–08 scapen . . . shapen,** Hg reads "scape . . . shape." **1122 nis,** El reads "is." **1129 It nere quod he to thee,** Hg reads "It were to thee quod he." **1131 cosyn . . . brother,** Palamon and Arcite are first cousins (line 1019) and sworn brothers, joined by blood and by formal oath. These bonds, familiar in medieval romance, are disrupted by the sight of Emily. **1134 that,** Hg read "that the." **1145 Nay,** Hg reads "Now." **1147 and to my,** Hg omits "to." **1156 wistest,** Hg reads "woost." **1165** The line is nearly identical to Chaucer's translation in *Bo* 3m12, where passionate love is criticized.

And therfore positif lawe° and swich decree°
Is broken alday° for love in ech degree°.
A man moot nedes° love, maugree his heed°.
He may nat flee it, thogh he sholde be deed,
Al be she° mayde or wydwe° or elles wyf.
And eek° it is nat likly al thy lif
To stonden in hir grace. Namoore shal I.
For wel thou woost° thyselven, verraily°,
That thou and I be dampned° to prisoun
Perpetuelly—us gayneth no raunsoun°.
We stryven° as dide the houndes for the boon°.
They foughte al day, and yet hir part° was noon.
Ther cam a kyte°, whil that they weren so wrothe°,
And baar° awey the boon bitwixe hem° bothe.
And therfore, at the kynges court, my brother,
Ech man for hymself, ther is noon oother°.
Love, if thee list°, for I love and ay° shal.
And soothly°, leeve° brother, this is al.
Heere in this prisoun moote° we endure,
And everich° of us take his aventure°."
  Greet was the strif° and long bitwix hem tweye°,
If that I hadde leyser° for to seye,
But to th'effect°. It happed on a day,
To telle it yow as shortly as I may,
A worthy duc that highte° Perotheus,
That felawe° was unto Duc Theseus
Syn thilke day° that they were children lite°,
Was come to Atthenes his felawe to visite,
And for to pleye as he was wont° to do,
For in this world he loved no man so,
And he loved hym als° tendrely agayn°.
So wel they lovede, as olde bookes sayn,
That whan that oon was deed, soothly to telle,
His felawe wente and soughte hym doun in helle—
But of that storie list me nat° to write.
Duc Perotheus loved wel Arcite,
And hadde hym knowe° at Thebes yeer by yere°,
And finally at requeste and preyere
Of Perotheus, withouten any raunsoun,
Duc Theseus hym leet out of prisoun
Frely to goon wher that hym liste over al°,
In swich a gyse° as I you tellen shal.
  This was the forward°, pleynly for t'endite°,
Bitwixen Theseus and hym Arcite,
That if so were that Arcite were yfounde
Evere in his lif, by day or nyght or stounde°,
In any contree of this Theseus,
And he were caught, it was acorded° thus,
That with a swerd he sholde lese° his heed.
Ther nas noon° oother remedie ne reed°,
But taketh his leve, and homward he him spedde°.
Lat hym be war. His nekke° lith to wedde°.
  How greet a sorwe suffreth now Arcite!
The deeth he feeleth thurgh his herte smyte°.
He wepeth, wayleth, crieth pitously;
To sleen° hymself he waiteth prively°.
He seyde, "Allas that day that I was born!
Now is my prisoun worse than biforn.
Now is me shape° eternally to dwelle
Nat in purgatorie, but in helle.
Allas, that evere knew I Perotheus!
For elles hadde I dwelled with Theseus,
Yfetered° in his prisoun everemo.
Thanne hadde I been in blisse and nat in wo.
Oonly the sighte of hire whom that I serve,

1167 positif lawe, *man-made law,* **swich decree,** *similar rules* **1168 alday,** *always,* **degree,** *social class* **1169 moot nedes,** *must necessarily,* **maugree his heed,** *in spite of anything* **1171 Al be she,** *whether she is,* **wydwe,** *widow* **1172 eek,** *also* **1174 woost,** *know,* **verraily,** *truly* **1175 dampned,** *condemned* **1176 us gayneth no raunsoun,** *no ransom can help us* **1177 stryven,** *fight,* **boon,** *bone* **1178 hir part,** *their portion* **1179 kyte,** *bird of prey,* **wrothe,** *angry* **1180 baar,** *carried,* **bitwixe,** *from between* **1182 noon oother,** *no other* (way) **1183 thee list,** (it) *pleases you,* **ay,** *always* **1184 soothly,** *truly,* **leeve,** *dear* **1185 moote,** *must* **1186 everich,** *each,* **aventure,** *chance* **1187 strif,** *strife,* **hem tweye,** (the) *two of them* **1188 leyser,** *time* **1189 th'effect,** *the point* **1191 highte,** *was called* **1192 felawe,** *companion* **1193 Syn thilke day,** *since the time,* **lite,** *little* **1195 wont,** *accustomed* **1197 als,** *as,* **agayn,** *in return* **1201 list me nat,** *I wish not* **1203 knowe,** *known,* **yeer by yere,** *for years* **1207 hym liste over al,** *anywhere it pleased him* **1208 swich a gyse,** *such a manner* **1209 forward,** *agreement,* **t'endite,** *to write* **1212 stounde,** *moment* **1214 acorded,** *agreed* **1215 lese,** *lose* **1216 Ther nas noon,** *there was no,* **reed,** *help* **1217 him spedde,** *hurried himself* **1218 nekke,** *neck,* **lith to wedde,** *is pledged* **1220 smyte,** *strike* **1222 sleen,** *slay,* **waiteth prively,** *awaits* (a time) *secretly* **1225 is me shape,** *I am destined* **1229 Yfetered,** *shackled*

1167 positif lawe, Lat. *lex positiva,* or "placed" (rather than unchangeable), human law. **1171 or wydwe,** Hg omits "or." **1180 And,** Hg reads "That." **1182 Ech man for hymself,** the first recorded instance of this proverb. **1191 Perotheus,** the friendship of Pirithous and Theseus was legendary. Pirithous's suit in favor of Arcite was known to Chaucer from *Teseida* 3.47ff., but the story of Theseus's descent into hell to save Pirithous is from *RR* 8148ff. **1192 unto,** El reads "to." **1195 wont,** El reads "won." **1201 list me nat to write,** "it pleases me not to write," a break in literary decorum since the Knight is talking. Such breaks are not unusual in medieval literature, but this may be a vestige of Chaucer's story before he adapted it to the *CT.* **1223 that day that I,** El reads "that day that he"; Hg "the day that I." **1226 purgatorie,** purgatory, in Roman Catholic tradition, the place where souls suffer extended but not eternal punishment for their sins. El reads "my purgatorie."

Though that I nevere hir grace may deserve,
Wolde han° suffised right ynough for me.
O deere cosyn Palamon," quod he,
"Thyn is the victorie of this aventure.
Ful blisfully in prison maistow dure°—
In prison? Certes nay°, but in paradys!
Wel hath Fortune yturned thee the dys°,
That hast the sighte of hire, and I th'absence.
For possible is, syn° thou hast hire presence,
And art a knyght, a worthy and an able,
That by som cas°, syn Fortune is chaungeable,
Thow maist to thy desir somtyme atteyne°.
But I that am exiled and bareyne°
Of alle grace, and in so greet dispeir
That ther nys° erthe, water, fir, ne eir,
Ne creature that of hem maked is,
That may me helpe or doon confort in this,
Wel oughte I sterve° in wanhope° and distresse.
Farwel my lif, my lust°, and my gladnesse!
"Allas, why pleynen° folk so in commune°
On purveiaunce° of God, or of Fortune,
That yeveth° hem ful ofte in many a gyse°
Wel bettre than they kan hemself devyse°?
Som man desireth for to han° richesse,
That cause is of his moerdre° or greet siknesse.
And som man wolde out of his prisoun fayn°,
That in his hous is of his meynee° slayn.
Infinite harmes been in this mateere.
We witen° nat what thing we preyen° heere:
We faren° as he that dronke° is as a mous.
A dronke man woot° wel he hath an hous,
But he noot which the righte wey is thider°,
And to a dronke man the wey is slider°.
And certes, in this world so faren we.
We seken° faste after felicitee,
But we goon wrong ful often, trewely.
Thus may we seyen alle°, and namely I°,
That wende° and hadde a greet opinioun
That if I myghte escapen from prisoun,
Thanne hadde I been in joye and perfit heele°,
Ther° now I am exiled fro my wele°.
Syn that I may nat seen you, Emelye,
I nam° but deed; ther nys no° remedye."
Upon that oother syde Palamon,
Whan that he wiste° Arcite was agon°,
Swich sorwe he maketh that the grete tour
Resouneth of his youlyng° and clamour.
The pure fettres° on his shynes° grete
Weren of his bittre salte teeres wete.
"Allas," quod he, "Arcita, cosyn myn,
Of al oure strif, God woot°, the fruyt is thyn.
Thow walkest now in Thebes at thy large°,
And of my wo thow yevest litel charge°.
Thou mayst, syn° thou hast wisdom and man-hede,
Assemblen alle the folk of oure kynrede°,
And make a werre° so sharp on this citee
That by som aventure or som tretee
Thow mayst have hire to° lady and to wyf
For whom that I moste nedes lese° my lyf.
For, as by wey of possibilitee,
Sith° thou art at thy large, of prisoun free,
And art a lord, greet is thyn avauntage
Moore than is myn, that sterve° here in a cage.
For I moot° wepe and wayle, whil I lyve,
With al the wo that prison may me yeve°,
And eek with peyne that love me yeveth also
That doubleth al my torment and my wo."
Therwith° the fyr of jalousie up sterte
Withinne his brest, and hente° him by the herte
So woodly° that he lyk was to biholde°

1233 Wolde han, *would have* **1236 maistow dure,** *can you live* **1237 Certes nay,** *certainly no* **1238 yturned thee the dys,** *tossed the dice for you* **1240 syn,** *since* **1242 som cas,** *some chance* **1243 atteyne,** *achieve* **1244 bareyne,** *barren* **1246 nys,** *isn't* **1249 sterve,** *die,* **wanhope,** *despair* **1250 lust,** *desire* **1251 pleynen,** *complain,* **in commune,** *commonly* **1252 On purveiaunce,** *about the providence* **1253 yeveth hem,** *gives them,* **gyse,** *way* **1254 devyse,** *imagine* **1255 han,** *have* **1256 moerdre,** *murder* **1257 wolde . . . fayn,** *would like* **1258 of his meynee,** *by his servants* **1260 witen,** *know,* **preyen,** *pray for* **1261 faren,** *act,* **dronke,** *drunk* **1262 woot,** *knows* **1263 noot which the righte wey is thider,** *knows not which is the right way there* **1264 slider,** *slippery* **1266 seken,** *seek* **1268 seyen alle,** *all say,* **namely I,** *especially me* **1269 wende,** *thought* **1271 perfit heele,** *perfect well-being* **1272 Ther,** *whereas,* **wele,** *joy* **1274 nam,** *am nothing,* **nys no,** *isn't any* **1276 wiste,** *knew,* **agon,** *gone* **1278 youlyng,** *howling* **1279 pure fettres,** *very shackles,* **shynes,** *shins* **1282 woot,** *knows* **1283 at thy large,** *free* **1284 yevest litel charge,** *give little care* **1285 syn,** *since* **1286 kynrede,** *relatives* **1287 werre,** *war* **1289 to,** *as* **1290 moste nedes lese,** *must necessarily lose* **1292 Sith,** *since* **1294 sterve,** *die* **1295 moot,** *must* **1296 yeve,** *give* **1299 Therwith,** *with this* **1300 hente,** *grabbed* **1301 woodly,** *madly,* **lyk was to biholde,** *looked like*

1237 Certes nay, Hg reads "Nay certes." **1242 by,** omitted in El. **1248 helpe,** El reads "heele." **1252 purveiaunce of God, or of Fortune . . . ,** in Boethian thought, divine Providence or foresight is omniscient, atemporal awareness of all events; human beings know only sequentially in time and therefore mistakenly consider events to be the whims of fortune. Chaucer fashioned Arcite's speech from *Bo* 3pr2. Later in *Bo* the difference between Providence and fortune is made clear, so Arcite's speech reflects incomplete or erroneous understanding. **1256 is of,** Hg reads "is ofte of." **1260 We witen nat what thing we preyen,** we don't what it is that we pray for, an echo of Romans 8.26, which contrasts human desires and divine knowledge. El reads "We witen nat what we preyen"; Hg "We woot nat what thyng that we prayen." **1262–64** From *Bo* 3pr2.88, where the drunken man who cannot find his home exemplifies how improper desires confuse humans. **1262 wel he,** El reads "wel that he." **1272 Ther,** El reads "That." **1278 Resouneth,** El reads "Resouned."

The boxtree or the asshen° dede and colde.
Thanne seyde he, "O crueel goddes that governe
This world with byndyng of youre word eterne,
And writen in the table of atthamaunt°
Youre parlement° and youre eterne graunt°,
What is mankynde moore unto you holde°
Than is the sheep that rouketh° in the folde°?
For slayn is man right° as another beest,
And dwelleth eek in prison and arreest,
And hath siknesse and greet adversitee,
And ofte tymes giltelees, pardee°.
"What governance° is in this prescience°,
That giltelees tormenteth innocence?
And yet encresseth this al my penaunce,
That man is bounden to his observaunce°,
For Goddes sake, to letten of° his wille,
Ther as° a beest may al his lust fulfille.
And whan a beest is deed he hath no peyne,
But after his deeth man moot° wepe and pleyne°,
Though in this world he have care and wo.
Withouten doute it may stonden so.
The answere of this lete I° to dyvynys°,
But wel I woot° that in this world greet pyne ys°.
Allas, I se° a serpent or a theef,
That many a trewe man hath doon mescheef°,
Goon at his large°, and where hym list may turne°.
But I moot° been in prisoun thurgh° Saturne,
And eek thurgh Juno, jalous and eek wood°,
That hath destroyed wel ny al° the blood
Of Thebes with his waste° walles wyde.
And Venus sleeth me on that oother syde
For jalousie and fere° of hym Arcite."
Now wol I stynte of° Palamon a lite,
And lete hym in his prisoun stille dwelle,
And of Arcita forth I wol yow telle.
The somer passeth, and the nyghtes longe
Encressen double wise the peynes stronge
Bothe of the lovere and the prisoner.
I noot° which hath the wofuller mester°.
For, shortly for to seyn, this Palamoun
Perpetuelly is dampned° to prisoun,
In cheynes and in fettres to been deed.
And Arcite is exiled upon his heed°
For, evere mo, as out of that contree,
Ne nevere mo he shal his lady see.
Yow loveres axe° I now this questioun:
Who hath the worse, Arcite or Palamoun?
That oon may seen his lady day by day,
But in prison he moot° dwelle alway;
That oother wher hym list° may ride or go°,
But seen his lady shal he nevere mo.
Now demeth as yow liste°, ye that kan,
For I wol telle forth as I bigan.

Explicit prima pars. Sequitur pars secunda.

Whan that Arcite to Thebes comen was,
Ful ofte a day he swelte° and seyde "Allas!"
For seen his lady shal he nevere mo.
And shortly to concluden al his wo,
So muche sorwe hadde nevere creature
That is, or shal, whil that the world may dure°.
His slep, his mete°, his drynke, is hym biraft°,
That lene he wex° and drye as is a shaft°;

1302 asshen, *ashes* **1305 atthamaunt,** *adamant* **1306 parlement,** *decision,* **eterne graunt,** *eternal decree* **1307 holde,** *obliged* **1308 rouketh,** *cowers,* **folde,** *pen* **1309 right,** *just* **1312 pardee,** *by God* **1313 governance,** *caretaking,* **prescience,** *foreknowledge* **1316 observaunce,** *duty* **1317 letten of,** *refrain from* **1318 Ther as,** *whereas* **1320 moot,** *must,* **pleyne,** *complain* **1323 lete I,** *I let,* **dyvynys,** *theologians* **1324 woot,** *know,* **greet pyne ys,** *is great pain* **1325 se,** *see* **1326 doon mescheef,** *done wrong* (to) **1327 Goon at his large,** *go freely,* **where hym list may turne,** *and go where he likes* **1328 moot,** *must,* **thurgh,** *because of* **1329 wood,** *angry* **1330 wel ny al,** *almost all* **1331 his waste,** *its wasted* **1333 fere,** *fear* **1334 stynte of,** *stop* (talking) *about* **1340 noot,** *don't know,* **mester,** *occupation* **1342 dampned,** *condemned* **1344 upon his heed,** *on threat of death* **1347 axe,** *ask* **1350 moot,** *must* **1351 wher hym list,** *wherever he pleases,* **go,** *walk* **1353 demeth as yow liste,** *judge as you please* **1356 swelte,** *fainted* **1360 dure,** *endure* **1361 mete,** *food,* **is hym biraft,** *he is deprived* (of) **1362 lene he wex,** *he grew lean,* **shaft,** *stick*

1302 boxtree, the boxwood shrub has pale wood. **1303 crueel goddes,** Palamon's complaint against the gods resembles *Bo* 1m5, another instance where a prisoner mistakenly thinks that the suffering of the innocent evinces a breakdown in divine governance. **1320 after his deeth man,** Hg reads "man after his deeth." The word appears in the manuscripts in various places in the line, perhaps indicating late insertion or scribal efforts to smooth meter. **1322 may,** Hg reads "moot" (must). **1337 somer passeth,** El reads "sonne passeth"; Hg omits "passeth." **1329 Juno,** in the *Thebaid,* the goddess Juno hated Thebes because Zeus, her husband and king of the gods, loved Theban women. **1340 wofuller,** Hg reads "sorwefuller." **1341 shortly,** Hg reads "soothly." **1346 he shal,** Hg reads "ne shal." **1347 questioun,** a love question (*demande d'amour*), often included in courtly literature as an exercise or demonstration of refined speech and attitude. **1350 he moot,** Hg reads "moot he." **1354a *Explicit prima pars. Sequitur pars secunda.*** "Here ends part one. Here follows part two." Omitted in Hg; see 1881n. These and the other headings help give the *KnT* its formal atmosphere. **1361ff. His slep, his mete . . . ,** Arcite's symptoms are of lovesickness, a malady known as **hereos** (line 1374, from Gk. *eros*). In advanced stages it could produce mania (**manye,** line 1374), a disease of the front (**Biforen,** line 1376) cell of the brain (**celle fantastik,** line 1376). The brain was thought to be divided into three cells: rear (memory), middle (reason), front (image making). Mania could be caused by an influx of the **humour malencolik** (line 1375), i.e., black bile (see *GP* 1.333n), into the front cell, impairing the individual's ability to imagine anything new—a severe form of fixation that could be fatal. **1362 wex,** El reads "wexeth."

His eyen holwe° and grisly to biholde,
His hewe falow° and pale as asshen colde,
And solitarie he was and evere allone,
And waillynge al the nyght, makynge his mone°.
And if he herde song or instrument,
Thanne wolde he wepe, he myghte nat be stent°.
So feble eek were his spiritz, and so lowe,
And chaunged so, that no man koude knowe°
His speche nor his voys°, though men it herde.
And in his geere° for al the world he ferde°,
Nat oonly lik the loveris maladye
Of hereos°, but rather lyk manye°,
Engendred° of humour malencolik
Biforen, in his celle fantastik°.
And shortly°, turned was al up so doun°
Bothe habit and eek disposicioun
Of hym, this woful lovere daun° Arcite.
What sholde I al day of his wo endite°?
Whan he endured hadde a yeer or two
This crueel torment and this peyne and wo,
At Thebes, in his contree, as I seyde,
Upon a nyght in sleep as he hym leyde°,
Hym thoughte how that the wynged god
Mercurie
Biforn hym stood and bad hym to be murie°.
His slepy yerde° in hond he bar° uprighte,
An hat he werede upon his heris° brighte.
Arrayed was this god, as he took keep°,
As he was whan that Argus took his sleep.
And seyde hym thus, "To Atthenes shaltou
wende°,
Ther is thee shapen of° thy wo an ende."
And with that word Arcite wook and sterte.
"Now trewely, hou soore that me smerte°,"
Quod he, "to Atthenes right now wol I fare,
Ne for the drede of deeth shal I nat spare°
To se my lady that I love and serve.
In hire presence I recche nat to sterve°."
And with that word he caughte° a greet mirour
And saugh that chaunged was al his colour,
And saugh his visage° al in another kynde°.
And right anon° it ran hym in his mynde°
That, sith° his face was so disfigured
Of maladye the which he hadde endured,
He myghte wel, if that he bar hym lowe°,
Lyve in Atthenes everemoore unknowe
And seen his lady wel ny day by day°.
And right anon he chaunged his array,
And cladde hym° as a poure laborer,
And al allone, save oonly a squier
That knew his privetee° and al his cas°,
Which was disgised pourely° as he was,
To Atthenes is he goon the nexte° way.
And to the court he wente upon a day,
And at the gate he profreth° his servyse
To drugge and drawe°, what so° men wol devyse°.
And shortly of this matere for to seyn°,
He fil in office° with a chamberleyn°
The which that dwellynge was with Emelye,
For he was wys and koude soone espye°
Of every servaunt which that serveth here°.
Wel koude he hewen wode° and water bere,
For he was yong and myghty for the nones°
And therto he was long° and big° of bones
To doon that° any wight° kan hym devyse.
A yeer or two he was in this servyse,
Page° of the chambre of Emelye the brighte,
And Philostrate he seyde that he highte°.
But half so wel biloved a man as he
Ne was ther nevere in court of his degree°.
He was so gentil of condicioun°
That thurghout al the court was his renoun°.

1363 eyen holwe, *eyes hollow* **1364 hewe falow,** *complexion yellow* **1366 mone,** *moan* **1368 stent,** *stopped* **1370 koude knowe,** *could recognize* **1371 voys,** *voice* **1372 geere,** *manner,* **ferde,** *behaved* **1374 hereos,** *lovesickness* (see 1361n), **manye,** *mania* **1375 Engendred,** *born* **1376 Biforen . . . celle fantastik,** *in the frontal lobe of his imagination* **1377 shortly,** *in short,* **up so doun,** *upside down* **1379 daun,** *sir* **1380 endite,** *write* **1384 leyde,** *laid* **1386 murie,** *merry* **1387 slepy yerde,** *sleep stick,* **bar,** *bore* **1388 heris,** *hair* **1389 he took keep,** *he* (Arcite) *was aware* **1391 shaltou wende,** *you shall go* **1392 shapen of,** *destined for* **1394 hou . . . smerte,** *however sorely I suffer* **1396–97 spare / To se,** *refrain from seeing* **1398 recche . . . sterve,** *care not if I die* **1399 caughte,** *took* **1401 visage,** *face,* **in another kynde,** *of a different nature* **1402 right anon,** *immediately,* **ran hym in his mynde,** *ran through his mind* **1403 sith,** *since* **1405 bar hym lowe,** *acted humbly* **1407 wel ny day by day,** *nearly every day* **1409 cladde hym,** *dressed himself* **1411 privetee,** *secret,* **cas,** *situation* **1412 pourely,** *as a poor man* **1413 nexte,** *nearest* **1415 profreth,** *offers* **1416 drugge and drawe,** *drudge and pull,* **what so,** *whatever,* **devyse,** *command* **1417 seyn,** *say* **1418 fil in office,** *happened to be employed,* **chamberleyn,** *personal attendant* **1420 espye,** *make assessment* **1421 here,** *her* **1422 hewen wode,** *cut wood* **1423 for the nones,** *in this way* **1424 long,** *tall,* **big,** *strong* **1425 that,** *what,* **wight,** *person* **1427 Page,** *servant* **1428 highte,** *was named* **1430 degree,** *status* **1431 condicioun,** *manners* **1432 renoun,** *reputation*

1376 Biforen, in his, El reads "Biforn his owene"; Hg, "Biforn his." **1385 Mercurie,** Mercury, the divine messenger, bears the staff with which he put to sleep the hundred-eyed guardian, **Argus** (line 1390); Ovid, *Metamorphoses* 1.670ff. There is no parallel dream in Chaucer's sources; Chaucer's addition increases the influence of the planets (gods). **1388 upon,** El reads "up." **1424 long,** Hg reads "strong." **1428 Philostrate,** the name means "one vanquished by love." Chaucer borrowed it, not from the *Teseida* (where the assumed name is "Penteo"), but from the title of Boccaccio's *Il Filostrato,* the source of *TC.* In *Teseida,* Emelye recognizes Arcite but lets no one know.

They seyden that it were a charitee°
That Theseus wolde enhauncen his degree,
And putten hym in worshipful° servyse,
Ther as he myghte his vertu exercise.
And thus withinne a while his name is spronge°,
Bothe of his dedes and his goode tonge,
That° Theseus hath taken hym so neer
That of his chambre he made hym a squier,
And gaf° hym gold to mayntene his degree.
And eek men broghte hym out of his contree,
From yeer to yeer, ful pryvely° his rente°.
But honestly° and slyly he it spente,
That no man wondred how that he it hadde.
And thre yeer in this wise° his lif he ladde,
And bar hym so, in pees and eek in werre,
Ther was no man that Theseus hath derre°.
And in this blisse lete I now Arcite,
And speke I wole of Palamon a lite.
  In derknesse and horrible and strong prisoun
Thise seven yeer hath seten Palamoun
Forpyned°, what for wo and for distresse.
Who feeleth double soor° and hevynesse
But Palamon, that love destreyneth° so
That wood° out of his wit he goth for wo?
And eek therto° he is a prisoner
Perpetuelly, noght oonly for a yer.
  Who koude ryme in Englyssh proprely
His martirdom? For sothe° it am nat I.
Therfore I passe as lightly as I may.
  It fel that in the seventhe yer, of May
The thridde° nyght, as olde bookes seyn,
That al this storie tellen moore pleyn,
Were it by aventure° or destynee—
As whan a thyng is shapen it shal be—
That soone after the mydnyght Palamoun,
By helpyng of a freend, brak his prisoun
And fleeth the citee faste as he may go.
For he hadde yeve° his gayler° drynke so
Of a clarree° maad of a certeyn wyn,
With nercotikes and opie° of Thebes fyn°,
That al that nyght, thogh that men wolde him shake,
The gayler sleep—he myghte nat awake.
And thus he fleeth as faste as evere he may.
The nyght was short and faste by° the day
That nedes cost° he moot° hymselven hyde,
And til° a grove faste° ther bisyde
With dredeful° foot thanne stalketh Palamoun.
For, shortly, this was his opinioun,
That in that grove he wolde hym hyde al day,
And in the nyght thanne wolde he take his way
To Thebes-ward°, his freendes for to preye°
On Theseus to helpe hym to werreye°.
And shortly, outher° he wolde lese his lif,
Or wynnen Emelye unto his wyf.
This is th'effect° and his entente pleyn.
  Now wol I turne to Arcite ageyn,
That litel wiste° how ny° that was his care
Til that Fortune had broght him in the snare.
  The bisy larke, messager of day,
Salueth° in hir song the morwe° gray,
And firy Phebus° riseth up so brighte
That al the orient laugheth of the lighte,
And with his stremes° dryeth in the greves°
The silver dropes hangynge on the leves.
And Arcita, that in the court roial
With Theseus is squier principal,
Is risen and looketh on the myrie° day.
And for to doon his observaunce to May,
Remembrynge on the poynt° of his desir,
He on a courser°, startlynge° as the fir,
Is riden into the feeldes hym to pleye,
Out of the court were it a myle or tweye.
And to the grove of which that I yow tolde
By aventure his wey he gan to holde°,
To maken hym a gerland of the greves°
Were it of wodebynde° or hawethorn leves.
And loude he song ayeyn the sonne shene°,

1433 charitee, *kindness* **1435 worshipful,** *honorable* **1437 name is spronge,** *reputation spreads* **1439 That,** *so that* **1441 gaf,** *gave* **1443 pryvely,** *secretly,* **rente,** *income* **1444 honestly,** *fittingly* **1446 wise,** *manner* **1448 derre,** *more dear* **1453 Forpyned,** *agonized* **1454 soor,** *pain* **1455 destreyneth,** *afflicts* **1456 wood,** *crazed* **1457 eek therto,** *also* **1460 For sothe,** *in truth* **1463 thridde,** *third* **1465 aventure,** *chance* **1470 yeve,** *give,* **gayler,** *jailer* **1471 clarree,** *wine punch* **1472 opie,** *opium,* **fyn,** *special* **1476 faste by,** *so close* **1477 nedes cost,** *at any cost,* **moot,** *must* **1478 til,** *to,* **faste,** *near* **1479 dredeful,** *fearful* **1483 To Thebes-ward,** *toward Thebes,* **preye,** *beseech* **1484 werreye,** *make war* **1485 outher,** *either* **1487 th'effect,** *the point* **1489 wiste,** *knew,* **ny,** *near* **1492 Salueth,** *greets,* **morwe,** *morning* **1493 firy Phebus,** *the sun* **1495 stremes,** *beams,* **greves,** *branches* **1499 myrie,** *merry* **1501 Remembrynge on the poynt,** *thinking about the focus* **1502 courser,** *steed,* **startlynge,** *active* **1506 gan to holde,** *followed* **1507 greves,** *branches* **1508 wodebynde,** *woodbine* **1509 ayeyn the sonne shene,** *facing the bright sun*

1462 of May, El reads "in May." **1463 thridde,** May 3 is apparently an auspicious and perhaps an unlucky or unfortunate day, the date when the fox seizes Chanticleer (*NPT* 7.3190) and the night before Pandarus first approaches Criseyde on Troilus's behalf (*TC* 2.56). **1471 of a certeyn,** Hg omits "a." **1472 of Thebes,** the Egyptian city of Thebes was reputed for its exotic drugs. **1497 that in,** El reads "that is in." **1498 is,** El reads "his"; corrected in Hg from "his" to "is."

"May, with alle thy floures and thy grene,
Welcome be thou, faire, fresshe May,
In hope that I som grene gete may."
And from his courser, with a lusty herte,
Into the grove ful hastily he sterte,
And in a path he rometh up and doun
Theras by aventure this Palamoun
Was in a bussh, that no man myghte hym se,
For soore afered° of his deeth was he.
Nothyng ne knew he that it was Arcite,
God woot° he wolde have trowed° it ful lite°.
But sooth is seyd, gon sithen many yeres°,
That "feeld hath eyen and the wode hath eres."
It is ful fair° a man to bere hym evene°
For alday° meeteth men at unset stevene°.
Ful litel woot° Arcite of his felawe
That was so ny° to herknen al his sawe°,
For in the bussh he sitteth now ful stille.
  Whan that Arcite hadde romed al his fille°,
And songen al the roundel lustily°,
Into a studie° he fil sodeynly°,
As doon thise loveres in hir queynte geres°,
Now in the crope°, now doun in the breres°,
Now up, now doun, as boket° in a welle.
Right as° the Friday, soothly for to telle,
Now it shyneth°, now it reyneth° faste,
Right so kan geery° Venus overcaste
The hertes of hir folk. Right as hir day
Is gereful°, right so chaungeth she array.
Selde° is the Friday al the wowke° ylike.
  Whan that Arcite had songe, he gan to sike°,
And sette hym doun withouten any moore.
"Allas," quod he, "that day that I was bore!
How longe, Juno, thurgh thy crueltee,
Woltow werreyen° Thebes the citee?
Allas, ybroght is to confusioun
The blood roial of Cadme and Amphioun—
Of Cadmus, which that was the firste man
That Thebes bulte°, or first° the toun bigan,
And of the citee first was crouned kyng.
Of his lynage° am I and his ofspryng
By verray ligne°, as of the stok roial°,
And now I am so caytyf° and so thral°
That he that is my mortal enemy,
I serve hym as his squier pourely°.
And yet dooth Juno me wel moore shame,
For I dar noght biknowe° myn owene name,
But ther as I was wont to highte° Arcite
Now highte I Philostrate, noght worth a myte°.
Allas, thou felle° Mars! Allas, Juno!
Thus hath youre ire° oure lynage al fordo°,
Save oonly me and wrecched Palamoun,
That Theseus martireth° in prisoun.
And over al this, to sleen me outrely°,
Love hath his firy dart so brennyngly°
Ystiked° thurgh my trewe°, careful° herte,
That shapen° was my deeth erst° than my sherte°.
Ye sleen me with youre eyen, Emelye!
Ye been the cause wherfore that° I dye.
Of al the remenant of myn oother care
Ne sette I nat the montance° of a tare°,
So that° I koude doon aught° to youre plesaunce°."
And with that word he fil doun in a traunce
A longe tyme, and after he up sterte°.
  This Palamoun, that thoughte that thurgh his herte
He felte a coold swerd sodeynliche° glyde,
For ire he quook°, no lenger wolde he byde°.

1518 soore afered, *sorely afraid* **1520 woot,** *knows,* **trowed,** *believed,* **ful lite,** *very little* **1521 sooth is seyd, gon sithen many yeres,** *truly it is said for many years gone* **1523 ful fair,** *very good* (for), **evene,** *evenly* **1524 alday,** *always,* **unset stevene,** *unplanned appointments* **1525 woot,** *knows* **1526 ny,** *near,* **sawe,** *saying* **1528 romed al his fille,** *roamed as he wished* **1529 roundel lustily,** *song energetically* **1530 a studie,** *deep thought,* **sodeynly,** *suddenly* **1531 queynte geres,** *curious ways* **1532 crope,** *leaves,* **breres,** *briars* **1533 boket,** *bucket* **1534 Right as,** *just as* **1535 shyneth,** *shines,* **reyneth,** *rains* **1536 geery,** *variable* **1538 gereful,** *changeable* **1539 Selde,** *seldom,* **wowke,** *week* **1540 sike,** *sigh* **1544 Woltow werreyen,** *will you make war on* **1548 bulte,** *established,* **or first,** *before* **1550 lynage,** *lineage* **1551 verray ligne,** *true line,* **stok roial,** *royal stock* **1552 caytyf,** *wretched,* **thral,** *enslaved* **1554 pourely,** *humbly* **1556 biknowe,** *reveal* **1557 wont to highte,** *accustomed to being called* **1558 myte,** *tiny Flemish coin* **1559 felle,** *cruel* **1560 ire,** *anger,* **fordo,** *destroyed* **1562 martireth,** *torments* **1563 sleen me outrely,** *slay me utterly* **1564 brennyngly,** *burningly* **1565 Ystiked,** *stuck,* **trewe,** *sincere,* **careful,** *sorrowful* **1566 shapen,** *destined,* **erst,** *earlier,* **sherte,** *shirt* (see note) **1568 wherfore that,** *why* **1570 montance,** *value,* **tare,** *weed* **1571 So that,** *if only,* **aught,** *anything,* **plesaunce,** *pleasure* **1573 up sterte,** *leapt up* **1575 sodeynliche,** *suddenly* **1576 quook,** *quaked,* **byde,** *wait*

1512 I som grene gete may, "I may get some green," apparently an allusion to some sort of May custom. **1514 the grove,** El reads "a grove." **1516–20 by aventure . . . ,** Chaucer emphasizes the accidental nature (compare line 1506) of the meeting of Arcite and Palamon; in *Teseida,* Palamon plans the meeting and comes ready for battle. **1518 was,** El reads "thanne was." **1519 ne knew,** Hg reads "knew he." **1522** A common proverb, "Fields have eyes and woods have ears." **1524** Also proverbial. **1529 roundel,** a kind of French song sung as a round with a refrain; an example concludes some versions of *PF.* **1530 fil,** El reads "fil al." **1536–39 Venus . . . Friday,** Friday, legendary for its changeable weather, was Venus's day, named for Frigg, the Scandinavian goddess of fertility and love. **1546ff. Cadme and Amphioun,** Cadmus and Amphion were the legendary founders of Thebes. For Juno's animosity toward Thebes, see 1329n above. **1547 Of,** omitted in Hg. **1548 or first the toun bigan,** Hg reads "and first bigan." **1560 lynage,** El reads "kynrede." **1566** His fate was woven before his first shirt. **1573 after,** Hg reads "afterward."

And whan that he had herd Arcites tale,
As° he were wood°, with face deed and pale,
He stirte hym up out of the buskes° thikke,
And seide, "Arcite, false traytour wikke,
Now artow hent°, that lovest my lady so,
For whom that I have al this peyne and wo,
And art my blood, and to my conseil sworn,
As I ful ofte have told thee heerbiforn°,
And hast byjaped° heere Duc Theseus,
And falsly chaunged hast thy name thus!
I wol be deed, or elles thou shalt dye.
Thou shalt nat love my lady Emelye,
But I wol love hire oonly and namo°,
For I am Palamon, thy mortal foo.
And though that I no wepene° have in this place,
But out of prison am astert° by grace,
I drede° noght that outher° thow shalt dye,
Or thow ne shalt nat loven Emelye.
Chees° which thou wolt, or thou shalt nat asterte!"
  This Arcite, with ful despitous° herte,
Whan he hym knew and hadde his tale herd,
As fiers° as leon pulled out his swerd,
And seyde thus, "By God that sit above,
Nere it° that thou art sik° and wood for love,
And eek that thow no wepne° hast in this place,
Thou sholdest nevere out of this grove pace°,
That thou ne sholdest dyen of myn hond.
For I defye° the seurete° and the bond
Which that thou seist° that I have maad° to thee.
What, verray° fool, thynk wel that love is free,
And I wol love hire mawgree° al thy myght!
But for as muche thou art a worthy knyght,
And wilnest to darreyne° hire by bataille,
Have heer my trouthe°, tomorwe I wol nat faille,
Withoute wityng° of any oother wight°,
That heere I wol be founden as a knyght,
And bryngen harneys° right ynough for thee,
And ches° the beste, and leve the worste for me.
And mete and drynke this nyght wol I brynge
Ynough for thee, and clothes for thy beddynge.
And if so be that thou my lady wynne,
And sle° me in this wode ther° I am inne,
Thow mayst wel have thy lady as for me°."
  This Palamon answerde, "I graunte it thee."
And thus they been departed til amorwe°,
Whan ech of hem had leyd his feith to borwe°.
  O Cupide, out of alle° charitee!
O regne°, that wolt no felawe have with thee!
Ful sooth is seyd° that love ne lordshipe
Wol noght, his thankes°, have no felaweshipe.
Wel fynden that Arcite and Palamoun.
Arcite is riden anon unto the toun,
And on the morwe, er it were dayes light,
Ful prively two harneys° hath he dight°,
Bothe suffisaunt and mete to darreyne°
The bataille in the feeld bitwix hem tweyne°,
And on his hors, allone as he was born,
He carieth al the harneys hym biforn.
And in the grove, at tyme and place yset,
This Arcite and this Palamon ben met.
To chaungen gan° the colour in hir° face,
Right as the hunters in the regne of Trace,
That stondeth at the gappe° with a spere,
Whan hunted is the leon or the bere,
And hereth hym° come russhyng in the greves°,
And breketh bothe bowes and the leves,
And thynketh, "Heere cometh my mortal enemy!
Withoute faile, he moot° be deed, or I,
For outher° I moot sleen hym at the gappe,
Or he moot sleen me, if that me myshappe°."
So ferden° they in chaungyng of hir hewe,
As fer as everich° of hem oother knewe°.
  Ther nas no good day, ne no saluyng°,
But streight, withouten word or rehersyng,

1578 As, *as if,* **wood,** *crazed* **1579 buskes,** *bushes* **1581 artow hent,** *are you caught* **1584 heerbiforn,** *before this* **1585 byjaped,** *tricked* **1589 namo,** *no others* **1591 wepene,** *weapon* **1592 astert,** *escaped* **1593 drede,** *doubt,* **outher,** *either* **1595 Chees,** *choose* **1596 despitous,** *spiteful* **1598 fiers,** *fierce* **1600 Nere it,** *were it not,* **sik,** *sick* **1601 wepne,** *weapon* **1602 pace,** *pass* **1604 defye,** *renounce,* **seurete,** *pledge* **1605 seist,** *say,* **maad,** *made* **1606 verray,** *absolute* **1607 mawgree,** *despite* **1609 wilnest to darreyne,** *wish to decide the right to* **1610 trouthe,** *pledge* **1611 wityng,** *knowledge,* **wight,** *person* **1613 harneys,** *armor* **1614 ches,** (you can) *choose* **1618 sle,** *slay,* **ther,** *which* **1619 as for me,** *as far as I am concerned* **1621 til amorwe,** *until the next day* **1622 to borwe,** *as a pledge* **1623 out of alle,** *without any* **1624 regne,** *ruler* **1625 Ful sooth is seyd,** *very truly it is said* **1626 Wol nought, his thankes,** *will not, willingly* **1630 harneys,** *suits of armor,* **dight,** *prepared* **1631 mete to darreyne,** *fit to decide* **1632 tweyne,** *both* **1637 gan,** *began,* **hir face,** *their faces* **1639 gappe,** *gap* **1641 hereth hym,** *hears it,* **greves,** *brush* **1644 moot,** *must* **1645 outher,** *either* **1646 me myshappe,** *misfortune comes to me* **1647 ferden,** *seemed* **1648 As fer as everich,** *to the extent that each,* **knewe,** *understood* **1649 saluyng,** *greeting*

1584 toold, El reads "seyd." **1600–03** The syntax is strained, but the meaning clear: Arcite threatens Palamon, saying that if Palamon were not crazed with love and unarmed, Arcite would never let him leave the grove without killing him. **1624 with,** Hg reads "to." **1638 regne of Trace,** realm of Thrace, an area north of ancient Greece. **1639 gappe,** the space or opening to which the hunted animal is driven. **1640 or,** El reads "and." **1648 of hem oother,** Hg reads "oother of hem."

Everich of hem heelp for to armen oother
As freendly as he were his owene brother,
And after that, with sharpe speres stronge
They foynen° ech at oother wonder longe.
Thou myghtest wene° that this Palamoun
In his fightyng were as a wood leoun°,
And as a crueel tigre was Arcite.
As wilde bores° gonne they to smyte°,
That frothen° whit as foom° for ire wood.
Up to the ancle° foghte they in hir blood.
And in this wise I lete hem fightyng dwelle,
And forth I wole of Theseus yow telle.
  The destinee, ministre general,
That executeth° in the world over al
The purveiaunce° that God hath seyn biforn°,
So strong it is that, though the world had sworn
The contrarie of a thyng by ye or nay,
Yet somtyme it shal fallen on a day
That falleth nat eft° withinne a thousand yeere.
For certeinly, oure appetites° heere,
Be it of werre, or pees, or hate, or love,
Al is this reuled° by the sighte above.
  This mene° I now by myghty Theseus,
That for to hunten is so desirus°,
And namely at° the grete hert° in May,
That in his bed ther daweth° hym no day
That he nys clad°, and redy for to ryde
With hunte° and horn and houndes hym bisyde.
For in his huntyng hath he swich delit
That it is al his joye and appetit
To been hymself the grete hertes bane°,
For after Mars he serveth now Dyane.
  Cleer was the day, as I have toold er this,
And Theseus with alle joye and blis,
With his Ypolita, the faire queene,
And Emelye, clothed al in grene,
On huntyng be they riden roially.
And to the grove that stood ful faste° by,
In which ther was an hert, as men hym tolde,
Duc Theseus the streighte wey hath holde.
And to the launde° he rideth hym ful right,
For thider° was the hert wont° have his flight,
And over a brook, and so forth on his weye.
This duc wol han° a cours° at hym or tweye
With houndes swiche as that hym list
    comaunde°.
  And whan this duc was come unto the launde,
Under° the sonne he looketh, and anon
He was war° of Arcite and Palamon,
That foughten breme° as it were bores two.
The brighte swerdes wenten to and fro
So hidously that with the leeste strook
It semed as it wolde felle an ook.
But what° they were, nothyng he ne woot°.
This duc his courser with his spores° smoot,
And at a stert° he was bitwix hem two,
And pulled out a swerd and cride, "Hoo!
Namoore, up peyne° of lesynge of youre heed!
By myghty Mars, he shal anon be deed
That smyteth any strook that I may seen.
But telleth me what myster° men ye been
That been so hardy for to fighten heere
Withouten juge or oother officere,
As it were in a lystes roially°?"
  This Palamon answerde hastily,
And seyde, "Sire, what nedeth wordes mo?
We have the deeth disserved bothe two.
Two woful wrecches been we, two caytyves°,
That been encombred of° oure owene lyves.
And as thou art a rightful lord and juge,
Ne yeve° us neither mercy ne refuge.
But sle me first, for seinte° charitee!
But sle my felawe eek as wel as me,
Or sle hym first, for though thow knowest it lite°,
This is thy mortal foo, this is Arcite,
That fro thy lond is banysshed on his heed,
For which he hath deserved to be deed.
For this is he that cam unto thy gate

1654 foynen, *thrust* **1655 Thou myghtest wene,** *you might believe* **1656 wood leoun,** *mad lion* **1658 bores,** *boars,* **gonne . . . smyte,** *did they strike* **1659 frothen,** *slather,* **foom,** *foam* **1660 ancle,** *ankle* **1664 executeth,** *brings about* **1665 purveiaunce,** *providence,* **seyn biforn,** *foreseen* **1669 eft,** *again* **1670 appetites,** *desires* **1672 reuled,** *ruled* **1673 mene,** *mean* **1674 so desirus,** *full of desire* **1675 namely at,** *especially for,* **grete hert,** *stag* **1676 daweth,** *dawns* **1677 nys clad,** *isn't dressed* **1678 hunte,** *huntsman.* **1681 bane,** *slayer* **1688 faste,** *near* **1691 launde,** *clearing* **1692 thider,** *there,* **wont,** *accustomed to* **1694 wol han,** *would have,* **cours,** *chase* **1695 houndes . . . comaunde,** *hounds he selected for each chase* **1697 Under,** *toward* **1698 war,** *aware* **1699 breme,** *fiercely* **1703 what,** *what* (kind of men), **woot,** *knew* **1704 spores,** *spurs* **1705 at a stert,** *in a leap* **1707 up peyne,** *upon threat* **1710 myster,** *kind of* **1713 lystes roially,** *royal tournament* **1717 caytyves,** *wretches* **1718 encombred of,** *burdened with* **1720 Ne yeve,** *do not give* **1721 seinte,** *holy* **1723 lite,** *little*

1652 owene brother, it is ironic that the two are indeed sworn brothers. **1663 destinee, ministre general . . . ,** destiny, the general minister of Providence (**purveiaunce,** line 1665) or divine foresight (**seyn biforn,** line 1665), is the enactment in time of what Providence perceives from its supratemporal, omniscient vantage; from *Bo* 4pr6.108ff. **1673 This mene I now by myghty Theseus . . . ,** the statement associates Theseus with divine foresight. Also, his desire to hunt is equated with the human "appetites" of line 1670. **1682 Mars . . . Dyane,** god of war, goddess of hunting. **1693 on,** El reads "in." **1695 that,** omitted in El. **1698 He was war,** in the *Teseida* 5.80, it is Emily who finds the knights fighting. **1699 bores,** Hg reads "boles" (bulls). **1704 his spores,** Hg reads "the spores." **1707 up,** El and Hg read "upon." **1710 myster,** El reads "mystiers."

And seyde that he highte° Philostrate.
Thus hath he japed° thee ful many a yer,
And thou hast maked hym thy chief squier.
And this is he that loveth Emelye.
For sith° the day is come that I shal dye,
I make pleynly my confessioun
That I am thilke° woful Palamoun
That hath thy prisoun broken wikkedly.
I am thy mortal foo, and it am I
That loveth so hoote° Emelye the brighte
That I wol dye present in hir sighte.
Wherfore I axe° deeth and my juwise°;
But sle my felawe in the same wise°,
For bothe han° we deserved to be slayn."
  This worthy duc answerde anon agayn,
And seyde, "This is a short conclusioun.
Youre owene mouth, by youre confessioun,
Hath dampned° yow, and I wol it recorde°.
It nedeth noght to pyne° yow with the corde°.
Ye shal be deed, by myghty Mars the rede!"
  The queene anon, for verray wommanhede°,
Gan for to wepe, and so dide Emelye,
And alle the ladyes in the compaignye.
Greet pitee was it, as it thoughte hem alle°,
That evere swich a chaunce sholde falle°,
For gentil men they were of greet estaat,
And no thyng but for love was this debaat°;
And saugh hir blody woundes wyde and soore,
And alle crieden, bothe lasse and moore°,
"Have mercy, Lord, upon us wommen alle!"
And on hir bare knees adoun they falle,
And wolde have kist his feet ther as he stood,
Til at the laste aslaked° was his mood,
For pitee renneth soone in gentil herte.
And though he first for ire quook° and sterte°,
He hath considered shortly, in a clause°,
The trespas of hem bothe, and eek the cause,
And although that his ire hir gilt° accused,
Yet in his resoun he hem bothe excused,
As thus: he thoghte wel that every man
Wol helpe hymself in love, if that he kan,
And eek delivere hymself out of prisoun.
And eek his herte hadde compassioun
Of wommen, for they wepen evere in oon°,
And in his gentil herte he thoughte anon,
And softe unto hymself he seyde, "Fy°
Upon a lord that wol have no mercy,
But been a leon, bothe in word and dede,
To hem that been in repentaunce and drede,
As well as to a proud, despitous° man
That wol mayntene that° he first bigan.
That lord hath litel of discrecioun,
That in swich cas° kan no divisioun°,
But weyeth° pride and humblesse after oon°."
And shortly, whan his ire is thus agoon°,
He gan to looken up with eyen lighte,
And spak thise same wordes al on highte°:
  "The god of love, a, benedicite°!
How myghty and how greet a lord is he!
Ayeyns° his myght ther gayneth none obstacles°.
He may be cleped° a god for his myracles,
For he kan maken, at his owene gyse°,
Of everich° herte as that hym list divyse°.
Lo heere this Arcite and this Palamoun,
That quitly° weren out of my prisoun,
And myghte han lyved in Thebes roially,
And witen° I am hir mortal enemy,
And that hir deth lith in my myght also,
And yet hath love, maugree hir eyen° two,
Broght hem hyder bothe for to dye.
Now looketh, is nat that an heigh folye?
  "Who may been a fool but if° he love?
Bihoold, for Goddes sake that sit° above,
Se how they blede! Be they noght wel arrayed°?
Thus hath hir lord, the god of love, ypayed°

1728 highte, *is named* **1729 japed,** *fooled* **1732 sith,** *since* **1734 thilke,** *that* **1737 hoote,** *passionately* **1739 axe,** *ask,* **juwise,** *sentence* **1740 wise,** *way* **1741 han,** *have* **1745 dampned,** *condemned,* **recorde,** *confirm* **1746 pyne,** *torture,* **corde,** *rope* **1748 verray wommanhede,** *true womanhood* **1751 it thoughte hem alle,** *it seemed to them all* **1752 falle,** *occur* **1754 debaat,** *battle* **1756 lasse and moore,** *lesser and greater* (in rank) **1760 aslaked,** *diminished* **1762 for ire quook,** *quaked in anger,* **sterte,** *trembled* **1763 clause,** *moment* **1765 hir gilt,** *their guilt* **1771 evere in oon,** *continuously* **1773 Fy,** *shame* **1777 despitous,** *scornful* **1778 mayntene that,** *persist in what* **1780 swich cas,** *such situations,* **kan no divisioun,** *recognizes no distinctions* **1781 weyeth,** *weighs,* **after oon,** *the same* **1782 agoon,** *gone* **1784 on highte,** *aloud* **1785 a, benedicite,** *ah, bless us* **1787 Ayeyns,** *against,* **ther gayneth none obstacles,** *no barriers are effective* **1788 cleped,** *called* **1789 gyse,** *inclination* **1790 everich,** *each,* **as that hym list divyse,** *whatever it pleases him to create* **1792 quitly,** *freely* **1794 witen,** *know* **1796 maugree hir eyen,** *despite their eyes* **1799 but if,** *unless* **1800 sit,** *sits* **1801 arrayed,** *adorned* **1802 ypayed,** *paid*

1745 Hath dampned yow, the knights are not condemned in the *Teseida,* so the queen and her ladies have no cause to intercede. Scholars have suggested that actual intercessions by either Queen Philippa or Queen Anne inspired Chaucer's scene, although he may have invented it to parallel the weeping of the Theban women, lines 900ff. above. **1761** The statement recurs in *MLT* 2.660, *MerT* 4.1986, *SqT* 5.479, *TC* 3.5, and *LGW* F503, with parallels in a number of classical and medieval sources. **1785ff.** A familiar medieval sentiment, although not in the *Teseida* at this point; compare *RR* 4221ff. **1796 maugree hir eyen two,** an idiom meaning "despite their wishes or actions."

Hir° wages and hir fees for hir servyse!
And yet they wenen° for to been ful wyse
That serven love, for aught that may bifalle°.
But this is yet the beste game of alle,
That she for whom they han this jolitee°
Kan hem therfore° as muche thank° as me.
She woot° namoore of al this hoote fare°,
By God, than woot a cokkow° or an hare!
But all moot ben assayed°, hoot and coold.
A man moot ben a fool, or° yong or oold—
I woot it by myself ful yore agon°,
For in my tyme a servant was I oon°.
And therfore, syn I knowe of loves peyne,
And woot hou soore it kan a man distreyne°,
As he that hath ben caught ofte in his laas°,
I yow foryeve al hoolly this trespaas,
At requeste of the queene, that kneleth heere,
And eek of Emelye, my suster deere.
And ye shul bothe anon unto me swere
That nevere mo ye shal my contree dere°,
Ne make werre upon me nyght ne day,
But been my freendes in al that ye may.
I yow foryeve this trespas every deel°."
And they hym sworen his axyng° faire and weel,
And hym of lordshipe and of mercy preyde,
And he hem graunteth grace°, and thus he seyde,
"To speke of roial lynage° and richesse,
Though that she were a queene or a princesse,
Ech of you bothe is worthy, doutelees,
To wedden whan tyme is, but nathelees°—
I speke as for my suster Emelye,
For whom ye have this strif and jalousye—
Ye woot yourself she may nat wedden two
Atones°, though ye fighten everemo.
That oon of you, al be hym looth or lief°,
He moot go pipen° in an yvy leef.
This is to seyn, she may nat now han bothe,
Al be ye never° so jalouse ne so wrothe°.
And forthy° I yow putte in this degree°,
That ech of yow shal have his destynee
As hym is shape°, and herkneth° in what wyse°:
Lo heere youre ende of that° I shal devyse.
"My wyl is this, for plat° conclusioun,
Withouten any repplicacioun°—
If that you liketh, take it for the beste:
That everich° of you shal goon where hym leste°
Frely, withouten raunson or daunger,
And this day fifty wykes fer ne ner°,
Everich of you shal brynge an hundred knyghtes
Armed for lystes° up at alle rightes°,
Al redy to darreyne hire° by bataille.
And this bihote° I yow withouten faille,
Upon my trouthe, and as I am a knyght,
That wheither° of yow bothe that hath myght—
This is to seyn, that wheither he or thow
May with his hundred, as I spak of now,
Sleen his contrarie, or out of lystes dryve,
Thanne shal I yeve Emelya to wyve°
To whom that Fortune yeveth° so fair a grace.
The lystes shal I maken in this place.
And God so wisly on my soule rewe°,
As I shal evene° juge been and trewe,
Ye shul noon oother ende° with me maken
That oon of yow ne shal be deed or taken.
And if yow thynketh this is weel ysayd°,
Seyeth youre avys° and holdeth you apayd°.
This is youre ende and youre conclusioun."
Who looketh lightly° now but Palamoun?
Who spryngeth up for joye but Arcite?
Who kouthe° telle, or who kouthe endite°
The joye that is maked in the place
Whan Theseus hath doon so fair a grace?
But doun on knees wente every maner wight°,
And thonken hym with al hir herte and myght,
And namely the Thebans often sithe°.
And thus with good hope and with herte blithe

1803 Hir, *their* **1804 wenen,** *think* (themselves) **1805 for aught that may bifalle,** *whatever happens* **1807 jolitee,** *passion* **1808 Kan hem therfore,** *gives them for it,* **thank,** *thanks* **1809 woot,** *knows,* **hoote fare,** *hot business* **1810 cokkow,** *cuckoo* **1811 moot ben assayed,** *must be tested* **1812 or . . . or,** *either . . . or* **1813 yore agon,** *long ago* **1814 oon,** *one* (a servant of love) **1816 distreyne,** *afflict* **1817 laas,** *net* **1822 dere,** *harm* **1825 deel,** *part* **1826 axyng,** *request* **1828 grace,** *favor* **1829 lynage,** *lineage* **1832 nathelees,** *nonetheless* **1836 Atones,** *at the same time* **1837 al be hym looth or lief,** *whether he likes it or not* **1838 moot go pipen,** *may go whistle* **1840 Al be ye never,** *even if you weren't,* **wrothe,** *angry* **1841 forthy,** *therefore,* **degree,** *position* **1843 shape,** *foreordained,* **herkneth,** *listen,* **wyse,** *way* **1844 ende of that,** *outcome from what* **1845 plat,** *plain* **1846 Withouten any repplicacioun,** *allowing no argument* **1848 everich,** *each,* **hym leste,** *he wishes* **1850 wykes fer ne ner,** *weeks more or less* **1852 lystes,** *battle,* **up at alle rightes,** *in all respects* **1853 darreyne hire,** *lay claim to her* **1854 bihote,** *promise* **1856 wheither,** *whichever* **1860 to wyve,** *as wife* **1861 yeveth,** *gives* **1863 rewe,** *have pity* **1864 evene,** *impartial* **1865 ende,** *conclusion* **1867 weel ysayd,** *well said* **1868 avys,** *agreement,* **holdeth you apayd,** *consider yourself satisfied* **1870 lightly,** *delighted* **1872 kouthe,** *is able to,* **endite,** *write* **1875 maner wight,** *kind of person* **1877 sithe,** *times*

1810 or, El and Hg read "of." **1828 thus,** Hg reads "thanne." **1832 but nathelees,** El reads "is doutelees." **1838 go,** omitted in El. **1850 fifty wykes fer ne ner,** apparently a poetic expression for a full year. **1862 The,** El reads "Tho." **1872 endite,** Hg reads "it endite." **1878 with herte,** Hg omits "with."

They taken hir leve, and homward gonne they ride
To Thebes, with his olde walles wyde.

Explicit secunda pars. Sequitur pars tercia.

I trowe° men wolde deme° it necligence
If I foryete° to tellen the dispence°
Of Theseus, that gooth so bisily
To maken up the lystes° roially,
That swich° a noble theatre as it was,
I dar wel seyn in this world ther nas.
The circuit a myle was aboute,
Walled of stoon, and dyched al withoute°.
Round was the shape, in manere of compas°,
Ful of degrees°, the heighte of sixty pas°,
That whan a man was set on o degree,
He lette nat° his felawe for to see.
Estward ther stood a gate of marbul whit,
Westward right swich another in the opposit.
And shortly to concluden, swich a place
Was noon in erthe, as in so litel space.
For in the lond ther was no crafty° man
That geometrie or ars-metrik kan°,
Ne portreitour°, ne kervere° of ymages,
That Theseus ne yaf mete° and wages,
The theatre for to maken and devyse°.
And for to doon his ryte° and sacrifise,
He estward hath, upon the gate above,
In worshipe of Venus, goddesse of love,
Doon make an auter° and an oratorie°.
And on the gate westward, in memorie
Of Mars, he maked hath right swich another,
That coste largely° of gold a fother°.
And northward, in a touret° on the wal,
Of alabastre whit and reed coral,
An oratorie, riche for to see,
In worshipe of Dyane of chastitee°,
Hath Theseus doon wroght° in noble wyse°.
But yet hadde I foryeten to devyse
The noble kervyng and the portreitures,
The shape, the contenaunce°, and the figures,
That weren in thise oratories thre.
First in the temple of Venus maystow se°
Wroght on the wal, ful pitous to biholde,
The broken slepes and the sikes° colde,
The sacred teeris and the waymentynge°,
The firy strokes of the desirynge
That loves servantz in this lyf enduren,
The othes° that hir covenantz° assuren;
Plesaunce° and Hope, Desir, Foolhardynesse,
Beautee and Youthe, Bauderie°, Richesse,
Charmes and Force, Lesynges°, Flaterye,
Despense°, Bisynesse°, and Jalousye
That wered° of yelewe gooldes° a gerland
And a cokkow° sittynge on hir hand;
Festes°, instrumentz, caroles, daunces,
Lust° and array°, and alle the circumstaunces
Of love, whiche that I rekned° and rekne shal
By ordre, weren peynted on the wal,
And mo than I kan make of mencioun.
For soothly° al the mount of Citheroun,
Ther° Venus hath hir principal dwellynge,
Was shewed on the wal in portreyynge,
With al the gardyn and the lustynesse.
Nat was foryeten° the porter, Ydelnesse,
Ne Narcisus the faire of yore agon°,

1881 trowe, *believe,* **deme,** *judge* **1882 foryete,** *forget,* **dispence,** *expenditure* **1884 lystes,** *tournament yard* **1885 That swich,** *so that such* **1888 dyched al withoute,** *ditched all around* **1889 in manere of compas,** *circular* **1890 degrees,** *steps,* **pas,** *paces* **1892 lette nat,** *didn't hinder* **1897 crafty,** *skilled* **1898 ars-metrik kan,** *arithmetic knows* **1899 portreitour,** *painter,* **kervere,** *sculptor* **1900 yaf mete,** *gave food* **1901 devyse,** *design* **1902 ryte,** *rites* **1905 Doon make an auter,** *had an altar made,* **oratorie,** *place for praying* **1908 largely,** *nearly,* **fother,** *load* **1909 touret,** *small tower* **1912 of chastitee,** *the chaste* **1913 doon wroght,** *had made,* **wyse,** *fashion* **1916 contenaunce,** *appearance* **1918 maystow se,** *you can see* **1920 sikes,** *sighs* **1921 waymentynge,** *lamenting* **1924 othes,** *oaths,* **hir covenantz,** *their promises* **1925 Plesaunce,** *Pleasure* **1926 Bauderie,** *Pimping* **1927 Lesynges,** *Lies* **1928 Despence,** *Expenditure,* **Bisynesse,** *Preoccupation* **1929 wered,** *wore,* **yelewe gooldes,** *yellow marigolds* **1930 cokkow,** *cuckoo* **1931 Festes,** *festivities* **1932 Lust,** *desire,* **array,** *clothing* **1933 rekned,** *counted* **1936 soothly,** *truly* **1937 Ther,** *where* **1940 foryeten,** *forgotten* **1941 of yore agon,** *from long ago*

1880a *Explicit secunda pars. Sequitur pars tercia.* "Here ends part two. Here follows part three." Hg ends part one and begins part two at this point; see notes to 1354a and 2742. **1885 noble theatre,** Chaucer's description of the arena differs somewhat from Boccaccio's in *Teseida.* Most important, it is built especially for the battle, and in attaching the temples to the arena and equalizing the descriptions, Chaucer communicates a greater sense of unity and symmetry. Venus, Mars, and Diana are the deities of love, war, and chastity and hunting, respectively. **1896 litel,** Hg reads "lite a." **1906 gate,** omitted in El and Hg. **1918 temple of Venus,** the description is modeled on *Teseida* 7.53ff., although in this description and those of the temples of Mars and Diana below, Chaucer creates a sense of immediacy by direct address to the reader and by depicting the first-person narrator as present in the temples, a break in literary decorum. Chaucer also describes the temple of Venus in *HF* 119–39 and *PF* 211–94 (a close translation). **1928–29 Jalousye . . . ,** yellow is the traditional color of jealousy, and the cuckoo symbolizes adultery. **1933 rekned,** El reads "rekned have." **1936 mount of Citheroun,** the mountain of Cithaeron was often conflated with the island Cythera, where Venus rose from the sea. **1941 Narcisus,** the mythical Narcissus fell in love with his own reflection.

Ne yet the folye° of Kyng Salamon.
Ne yet the grete strengthe of Ercules,
Th'enchauntementz of Medea and Circes.
Ne of Turnus, with the hardy fiers corage,
The riche Cresus, kaytyf in servage°.
Thus may ye seen that wysdom ne richesse,
Beautee ne sleighte°, strengthe ne hardynesse,
Ne may with Venus holde champartie°,
For as hir list° the world than° may she gye°.
Lo, alle thise folk so caught were in hir las°,
Til they for wo ful ofte seyde allas.
Suffiseth heere ensamples oon or two.
And though I koude rekene° a thousand mo.
  The statue of Venus, glorious for to se,
Was naked, fletynge° in the large see,
And fro the navele doun al covered was
With wawes° grene, and brighte as any glas.
A citole° in hir right hand hadde she,
And on hir heed, ful semely for to se,
A rose gerland, fressh and wel smellynge;
Above hir heed hir dowves flikerynge°.
Biforn hire stood hir sone Cupido;
Upon his shuldres wynges hadde he two,
And blynd he was, as it is often seene;
A bowe he bar and arwes brighte and kene.
  Why sholde I noght as wel eek telle yow al
The portreiture that was upon the wal
Withinne the temple of myghty Mars the rede?
Al peynted was the wal, in lengthe and brede°,
Lyk to the estres° of the grisly place
That highte° the grete temple of Mars in Trace,
In thilke° colde, frosty regioun
Ther as Mars hath his sovereyn mansioun°.
  First on the wal was peynted a forest,
In which ther dwelleth neither man ne best,
With knotty, knarry°, bareyne° trees olde,
Of stubbes° sharpe and hidouse to biholde,
In which ther ran a rumbel and a swough°,
As though a storm sholde bresten° every bough.
And dounward from an hille, under a bente°,
Ther stood the temple of Mars armypotente°,
Wroght al of burned° steel, of which the entree°
Was long and streit° and gastly for to see.
And therout cam a rage° and swich a veze°
That it made al the gate for to rese°.
The northren lyght in at the dores shoon,
For wyndowe on the wal ne was ther noon,
Thurgh which men myghten any light discerne.
The dore was al of adamant° eterne,
Yclenched° overthwart and endelong°
With iren tough; and for to make it strong,
Every pyler°, the temple to sustene°,
Was tonne-greet°, of iren bright and shene.
  Ther saugh° I first the dirke ymaginyng°
Of Felonye, and al the compassyng°,
The crueel Ire°, reed as any gleede°;
The pykepurs°, and eek the pale Drede;
The smylere° with the knyfe under the cloke;
The shepne brennynge° with the blake smoke;
The tresoun of the mordrynge in the bedde;
The open werre°, with woundes al bibledde°;
Contek°, with blody knyf and sharp manace°.
Al ful of chirkyng° was that sory place.
  The sleere° of hymself yet saugh I ther—
His herte-blood hath bathed al his heer°;
The nayl ydryven in the shode a-nyght°;

1942 folye, *folly* **1946 kaytyf in servage,** *wretched in captivity* **1948 sleighte,** *trickery* **1949 holde champartie,** *compete successfully* **1950 hir list,** *she desires,* **than,** *so,* **gye,** *rule* **1951 las,** *snare* **1954 rekene,** *tally* **1956 fletynge,** *floating* **1958 wawes,** *waves* **1959 citole,** *stringed instrument* **1962 dowves flikerynge,** *doves fluttering* **1970 brede,** *breadth* **1971 estres,** *interior* **1972 highte,** *is called,* **Trace,** *Thrace* **1973 thilke,** *that same* **1974 sovereyn mansioun,** *highest dwelling* **1977 knarry,** *gnarled,* **bareyne,** *barren* **1978 stubbes,** *stumps* **1979 swough,** *sound of wind* **1980 bresten** *break* **1981 under a bente,** *near an open field* **1982 armypotente,** *potent in arms* **1983 burned,** *polished,* **entree,** *entrance* **1984 streit,** *narrow* **1985 rage,** *roar,* **veze,** *blast* **1986 rese,** *shake* **1990 adamant,** *indestructible stone* **1991 Yclenched,** *bound,* **overthwart and endelong,** *horizontally and vertically* **1993 pyler,** *pillar,* **sustene,** *support* **1994 tonne-greet,** *big around as a barrel* **1995 saugh,** *saw,* **dirke imaginyng,** *dark plans* **1996 compassyng,** *plotting* **1997 Ire,** *anger,* **gleede,** *glowing coal* **1998 pykepurs,** *pick-pocket* **1999 smylere,** *smiler* **2000 shepne brennynge,** *barn burning* **2002 werre,** *war,* **bibledde,** *bloodied* **2003 Contek,** *strife,* **manace,** *menace* **2004 chirkyng,** *creaking* **2005 sleere,** *slayer* **2006 heer,** *hair* **2007 shode a-nyght,** *head at night*

1942 Salamon, King Solomon had many wives, loves, and concubines who turned his heart from God; 1 Kings 11. **1942 Ne,** El reads "And." **1943 Ne yet,** El reads "And eek." **Ercules,** despite his great strength, Hercules was killed through the love and jealousy of his wife Deianira; see *MkT* 7.2119ff. **1944 Medea and Circes,** classical sorceresses who used magic on their lovers. **1945 Turnus,** killed by Aeneas, his opponent in love; *Aeneid* 12. **1946 Cresus,** Croesus, king of Lydia, was not known as a lover but was imprisoned after being defeated by Cyrus; see *MkT* 7.2727ff. **1949 holde,** Hg reads "maken." **1951 thise folk,** El reads "thise folkes"; Hg, "this folk." **1956 fletynge,** the traditional figure of Venus rising from the sea; doves and the citole are also familiar icons of Venus. **1963 Cupido,** son of Venus, Cupid was the blind (or blindfold) winged god whose arrows strike lovers. **1965 is,** El reads "was." **1969 temple . . . of Mars,** modeled on *Teseida* 7.30ff., preceding the temple of Venus. **1979 and,** Hg reads "in." **1981 from,** Hg reads "on." **1987 northren lyght,** light coming in from the north indicates that the temple is oriented toward the north, away from the sun, whereas most temples point east. **1996 al,** omitted in El. **2007** Scholars note similarities with Jael's killing of Sisera in Judges 4.21; see *WBP* 3.769.

The colde deeth, with mouth gapyng upright.
Amyddes° of the temple sat Meschaunce°,
With disconfort and sory contenaunce.
  Yet saugh I Woodnesse°, laughynge in his rage,
Armed Compleint, Outhees°, and fiers° Outrage;
The careyne° in the busk°, with throte ycorve°;
A thousand slayn, and nat of qualm ystorve°;
The tiraunt, with the pray° by force yraft°;
The toun destroyed, ther was nothyng laft.
  Yet saugh I brent° the shippes hoppesteres°;
The hunte° strangled with° the wilde beres;
The sowe freten° the child right in the cradel;
The cook yscalded, for al° his longe ladel°.
  Noght° was foryeten° by the infortune° of Marte
The cartere overryden with° his carte—
Under the wheel ful lowe he lay adoun.
  Ther were also, of Martes divisioun°,
The barbour, and the bocher°, and the smyth,
That forgeth sharpe swerdes on his styth°.
  And al above, depeynted° in a tour°,
Saugh I Conquest, sittynge in greet honour,
With the sharpe swerd over his heed
Hangynge by a soutil twynes threed°.
  Depeynted was the slaughtre of Julius,
Of grete Nero, and of Antonius—
Al be° that thilke° tyme they were unborn,
Yet was hir deth depeynted ther-biforn°
By manasynge° of Mars, right by figure°.
So was it shewed° in that portreiture
As is depeynted in the sterres above
Who shal be slayn or elles deed for love.
Suffiseth oon ensample° in stories olde;
I may nat rekene hem alle though I wolde.
  The statue of Mars upon a carte° stood
Armed, and looked grym as he were wood°,
And over his heed ther shynen° two figures
Of sterres°, that been cleped° in scriptures°
That oon Puella, that oother Rubeus.
This god of armes was arrayed thus.
A wolf ther stood biforn hym at his feet
With eyen rede, and of a man he eet°.
With soutil° pencel was depeynt this storie
In redoutynge° of Mars and of his glorie.
  Now to the temple of Dyane the chaste
As shortly as I kan I wol me haste,
To telle yow al the descripsioun.
Depeynted been the walles up and doun
Of huntyng and of shamefast° chastitee.
  Ther saugh I how woful Calistopee,
Whan that Diane agreved was° with here,
Was turned from a womman til a bere°,
And after was she maad the Ioode-sterre°,
Thus was it peynted, I kan sey yow no ferre°.
Hir sone is eek° a sterre, as men may see.
  Ther saugh I Dane, yturned til a tree—
I mene nat the goddesse Diane,
But Penneus doghter, which that highte° Dane.
  Ther saugh I Attheon an hert° ymaked,
For vengeaunce that he saugh Diane al naked.
I saugh how that his houndes have hym caught
And freeten° hym, for that they knewe hym
    naught.
  Yet peynted was a litel forther moor°
How Atthalante hunted the wilde boor,
And Meleagre, and many another mo,
For which Dyane wroghte hym care and wo.
Ther saugh I many another wonder storie,
The whiche me list nat° drawen to memorie.

2009 Amyddes, *in the middle,* **Meschaunce,** *Mischance* **2011 Woodnesse,** *Madness* **2012 Outhees,** *Outcry,* **fiers,** *fierce* **2013 careyne,** *corpse,* **busk,** *bush,* **throte ycorve,** *throat cut* **2014 of qualm ystorve,** *by plague killed* **2015 pray,** *prey,* **yraft,** *taken* **2017 brent,** *burned,* **hoppesteres,** *dancing* **2018 hunte,** *hunter,* **strangled with,** *killed by* **2019 freten,** *eat* **2020 for al,** *despite,* **ladel,** *ladle* **2021 Noght,** *nor,* **foryeten,** *neglected,* **infortune,** *evil influence* **2022 overryden with,** *run over by* **2024 Martes divisioun,** *Mars's numbers* **2025 bocher,** *butcher* **2026 styth,** *anvil* **2027 depeynted,** *depicted,* **tour,** *tower* **2030 soutil twynes threed,** *thin thread of twine* **2033 Al be,** *although,* **thilke,** *at that time* **2034 ther-biforn,** *before then* **2035 manasynge,** *menacing,* **right by figure,** *precisely in figures* **2036 shewed,** *shown* **2039 ensample,** *example* **2041 carte,** *chariot* **2042 wood,** *insane* **2043 shynen,** *shine* **2044 sterres,** *stars,* **cleped,** *called,* **scriptures,** *writings* **2048 eet,** *ate* **2049 soutil,** *subtle* **2050 redoutynge,** *honor* **2055 shamefast,** *modest* **2057 agreved was,** *was upset* **2058 til a bere,** *to a bear* **2059 Ioode-sterre,** *lodestar* (see note) **2060 ferre,** *further* **2061 eek,** *also* **2064 highte,** *is called* **2065 hert,** *stag* **2068 freeten,** *eaten* **2069 forther moor,** *further on* **2074 me list nat,** *I prefer not* (to)

2014 nat of, El reads "nat oon of." **2017 shippes hoppesteres,** apparently a misunderstanding of "navi ballatrici" (dancing ships) for *Teseida* 7.37 "navi bellatrici" (fighting ships). **2025 barbour,** El reads "laborer." **2031–32** Chaucer recounts the violent deaths of **Julius** (Caesar) in *MkT* 7.2695ff., **Nero** in *MkT* 7.2519ff., and Marc Antony (**Antonius**) in *LGW* 624ff. **2037 sterres,** El reads "Certres"; Hg, "Sertres." **2045 oon Puella . . . other Rubeus,** names for figures in geomancy, a form of divination that predicts the future by interpreting dots and lines thought to indicate astrological patterns. **2051 temple of Dyane,** there is no similar description in *Teseida*; Chaucer adds it for balance. **2056ff. Calistopee . . . ,** Callisto was transformed by Diana into the constellation of the Great Bear (Ursa Major) for surrendering her virginity to Jupiter; her son, Arcas, became the Lesser Bear (Ursa Minor). **2059 Ioode-sterre,** also known as the polestar or North Star, the lodestar is a single star in Ursa Minor, so there is some confusion in Chaucer's account. **2062 Dane,** Daphne was transformed by her father, Peneus (**Penneus,** line 2064) into a laurel tree to save her from Apollo. **2065 Attheon,** because he saw Diana naked, Acteon was transformed into a stag and killed by his own hounds. **2070–71 Atthalante . . . Meleagre,** Meleager killed the Caledonian boar, first wounded by Atalanta; the beast was sent by Diana.

This goddesse on an hert full hye seet°,
With smale houndes al aboute hir feet,
And undernethe hir feet she hadde a moone,
Wexynge° it was and sholde wanye° soone.
In gaude° grene hir statue clothed was,
With bowe in honde and arwes in a cas.
Hir eyen caste she ful lowe adoun,
Ther° Pluto hath his derke regioun.
A womman travaillynge° was hire biforn;
But for° hir child so longe was unborn,
Ful pitously Lucyna gan she calle,
And seyde, "Help, for thou mayst best of alle!"
Wel koude he peynten lifly° that it wroghte°;
With many a floryn° he the hewes° boghte.
Now been thise lystes maad°, and Theseus,
That at his grete cost arrayed thus
The temples and the theatre every deel°,
Whan it was doon, hym lyked wonder weel.
But stynte° I wole of Theseus a lite,
And speke of Palamon and of Arcite.
The day approcheth of hir retournynge,
That everich sholde an hundred knyghtes brynge
The bataille to darreyne°, as I yow tolde.
And til Atthenes, hir covenantz° for to holde,
Hath everich of hem broght an hundred knyghtes,
Wel armed for the werre at alle rightes°.
And sikerly° ther trowed° many a man
That nevere sithen° that the world bigan,
As for to speke of knyghthod of hir hond°,
As fer° as God hath maked see or lond,
Nas° of so fewe so noble a compaignye.
For every wight that lovede chivalrye,
And wolde, his thankes°, han° a passant° name,
Hath preyed that he myghte been of that game°;
And wel° was hym that therto chosen was.
For if ther fille° tomorwe swich a cas°,
Ye knowen wel that every lusty knyght
That loveth paramours° and hath his myght,
Were it in Engelond or elleswhere,
They wolde, hir thankes, wilnen° to be there—
To fighte for a lady, benedicitee°!
It were a lusty° sighte for to see.
And right so ferden° they with Palamon.
With hym ther wenten knyghtes many on°;
Som wol ben armed in an haubergeoun°,
And in a bristplate and a light gypoun°,
And somme woln° have a paire plates° large;
And somme woln have a Pruce° sheeld or a targe°;
Somme woln ben armed on hir legges weel,
And have an ax, and somme a mace° of steel—
Ther is no newe gyse° that it nas old.
Armed were they, as I have yow told,
Everych after his opinioun.
Ther maistow° seen comynge with Palamoun
Lygurge hymself, the grete kyng of Trace.
Blak was his berd and manly was his face;
The cercles of his eyen in his heed,
They gloweden bitwixen yelow and reed,
And lik a grifphon° looked he aboute,
With kempe heeris° on his browes stoute°,
His lymes grete°, his brawnes° harde and stronge,
His shuldres brode, his armes rounde and longe.
And as the gyse was in his contree,
Ful hye upon a chaar° of gold stood he,
With foure white boles° in the trays°.
Instede of cote-armure° over his harnays°,
With nayles yelewe° and brighte as any gold,
He hadde a beres skyn°, col-blak for old°.
His longe heer was kembd° bihynde his bak—
As any ravenes fethere it shoon for blak;
A wrethe of gold, arm-greet°, of huge wighte°,
Upon his heed, set ful of stones brighte,
Of fyne rubyes and of dyamauntz.
Aboute his chaar ther wenten white alauntz°,
Twenty and mo, as grete as any steer,

2075 ful hye seet, *sat very high* **2078 Wexynge,** *waxing,* **wanye,** *wane* **2079 gaude,** *yellowish* **2082 Ther,** *where* **2083 travaillynge,** *in labor* **2084 for,** *because* **2087 lifly,** *lifelike,* **wroghte,** *created* **2088 floryn,** *coin,* **hewes,** *paints* **2089 lystes maad,** *tournament yard made* **2091 deel,** *part* **2093 stynte,** *cease* **2097 darreyne,** *decide* **2098 covenantz,** *pledges* **2100 at alle rightes,** *in all ways* **2101 sikerly,** *surely,* **trowed,** *thought* **2102 sithen,** *since* **2103 knyghthod of hir hond,** *their knightly ability* **2104 fer,** *far* **2105 Nas** (there) *wasn't* **2107 his thankes,** *willingly,* **han,** *have,* **passant,** *outstanding* **2108 game,** *contest* **2109 wel,** *happy* **2110 fille,** *happened,* **cas,** *event* **2112 paramours,** *passionately* **2114 wilnen,** *crave* **2115 benedicitee,** *bless us* **2116 lusty,** *pleasurable* **2117 ferden,** *did* **2118 many on,** *many* **2119 haubergeoun,** *mail armor* **2120 gypoun,** *tunic* **2121 woln,** *will,* **paire plates,** *plate armor* **2122 Pruce,** *Prussian,* **targe,** *light shield* **2124 mace,** *war club* **2125 gyse,** *fashion* **2128 maistow,** *you may* **2133 grifphon,** *griffin* **2134 kempe heeris,** *shaggy hair,* **stoute,** *strong* **2135 lymes grete,** *large limbs,* **brawnes,** *muscles* **2138 chaar,** *chariot* **2139 boles,** *bulls,* **trays,** *harness* **2140 cote-armure,** *coat of arms,* **harnays,** *armor* **2141 nayles yelewe,** *claws yellow* **2142 beres skyn,** *bear-skin,* **for old,** *from age* **2143 kembd,** *combed* **2145 arm-greet,** *thick as an arm,* **wighte,** *weight* **2148 alauntz,** *wolfhounds*

2075–77 goddesse on an hert . . . moone, the stag and the moon are typical icons of Diana. **2082 Pluto,** classical god of the underworld. **2075 ful hye,** El reads "ful wel hye." **2085 Lucyna,** Lucina is another name for Diana in her manifestation as goddess of childbirth. **2089 thise,** El reads "the." **2120 a bristplate,** El omits "a." **and a,** El and Hg read "and in a." **2123 hir,** Hg reads "his." **2125 is,** Hg reads "nys." **2145 arm-greet,** Hg reads "greet." **2129 Lygurge,** Lycurgus of Nemea is mentioned in *Teseida* 6.14, although Chaucer conflates him with Lycurgus of Thrace and associates him with Saturn.

To hunten at the leoun or the deer,
And folwed hym with mosel° faste ybounde,
Colered of° gold, and tourettes fyled rounde°.
An hundred lordes hadde he in his route°,
Armed ful wel, with hertes stierne° and stoute.
  With Arcite, in stories as men fynde,
The grete Emetreus, the kyng of Inde,
Upon a steede bay° trapped in° steel,
Covered in clooth of gold, dyapred weel°,
Cam ridynge lyk the god of armes, Mars.
His cote-armure was of clooth of Tars
Couched° with perles white and rounde and grete;
His sadel was of brend° gold newe ybete°;
A mantel° upon his shulder hangynge,
Bratful° of rubyes rede as fyr sparklynge;
His crispe heer° lyk rynges was yronne°,
And that was yelow, and glytered as the sonne.
His nose was heigh°, his eyen bright citryn°,
His lippes rounde, his colour was sangwyn°;
A fewe frakenes° in his face yspreynd°,
Bitwixen yelow and somdel° blak ymeynd°;
And as a leoun he his lookyng caste°.
Of fyve and twenty yeer his age I caste°.
His berd was wel bigonne for to sprynge;
His voys was as a trompe° thonderynge.
Upon his heed he wered° of laurer° grene
A gerland, fressh and lusty° for to sene.
Upon his hand he bar for his deduyt°
An egle tame, as any lilye whyt.
An hundred lordes hadde he with hym there,
Al armed, save hir heddes, in al hir gere,
Ful richely in alle maner thynges.
For trusteth wel that dukes, erles, kynges
Were gadered° in this noble compaignye,
For love and for encrees° of chivalrye.
Aboute this kyng ther ran on every part°
Ful many a tame leoun and leopart.
And in this wise thise lordes, alle and some,
Been on the Sonday to the citee come
Aboute pryme°, and in the toun alight°.
  This Theseus, this duc, this worthy knyght,
Whan he had broght hem into his citee,
And inned hem°, everich at his degree°,
He festeth° hem, and dooth so greet labour
To esen hem° and doon hem al honour,
That yet men wenen° that no mannes wit
Of noon estaat ne koude amenden° it.
  The mynstralcye°, the service at the feeste,
The grete yiftes to the meeste° and leeste°,
The riche array of Theseus paleys°,
Ne who sat first ne last upon the deys°,
What ladyes fairest been or best daunsynge,
Or which of hem kan carole best and synge,
Ne who moost felyngly° speketh of love,
What haukes° sitten on the perche above,
What houndes liggen° on the floor adoun—
Of al this make I now no mencioun,
But al th'effect°, that thynketh me the beste.
Now cometh the point, and herkneth if yow leste.
  The Sonday nyght, er° day bigan to sprynge,
Whan Palamon the larke herde synge,
Although it nere nat° day by houres two,
Yet song the larke; and Palamon right tho°
With hooly herte and with an heigh corage°,
He roos to wenden on his pilgrymage
Unto the blisful Citherea benigne°,
I mene Venus, honurable and digne°.
And in hir houre he walketh forth a pas°
Unto the lystes ther hire° temple was,
And doun he kneleth, and with humble cheere

2151 mosel, *muzzle* **2152 Colered of,** *collared with,* **tourettes fyled rounde,** *leash rings filed smooth* **2153 route,** *company* **2154 stierne,** *stern* **2157 steede bay,** *red brown horse,* **trapped in,** *ornamented with* **2158 dyapred weel,** *well adorned with crisscross quilting* **2161 Couched,** *decorated* **2162 brend,** *refined,* **ybete,** *adorned* **2163 mantel,** *short robe* **2164 Bratful,** *brinful* **2165 crispe heer,** *curly hair,* **yronne,** *arranged* **2167 heigh,** *prominent,* **citryn,** *amber* **2168 sangwyn,** *reddish* **2169 frakenes,** *freckles,* **yspreyned,** *sprinkled* **2170 somdel,** *somewhat,* **ymeynd,** *mingled* **2171 his lookyng caste,** *set his gaze* **2172 caste,** *estimate* **2174 trompe,** *trumpet* **2175 wered,** *wore,* **laurer,** *laurel* **2176 lusty,** *attractive* **2177 deduyt,** *delight* **2183 gadered,** *gathered* **2184 encrees,** *increase* **2185 part,** *side* **2189 pryme,** *9 A.M.,* **alight,** *dismount* **2192 inned hem,** *housed them,* **degree,** *rank* **2193 festeth,** *feasts* **2194 esen hem,** *make, them comfortable* **2195 wenen,** *suppose* **2196 estaat,** *rank,* **koude amenden,** *could improve* **2197 mynstralcye,** *music* **2198 meeste,** *greatest,* **leeste,** *least* **2199 paleys,** *palace* **2200 deys,** *platform* **2203 felyngly,** *feelingly* **2204 haukes,** *hawks* **2205 liggen,** *lie* **2207 al th'effect,** *the total effect* **2209 er,** *before* **2211 nere nat,** *weren't* **2212 right tho,** *precisely then* **2213 heigh corage,** *high spirit* **2215 benigne,** *gracious* **2216 digne,** *worthy* **2217 a pas,** *quickly* **2218 ther hire,** *where her*

2156 Emetreus, king of India, not mentioned in *Teseida*; Chaucer makes him a martial figure, introducing him to balance Lycurgus. **2160 cote-armure was of clooth of Tars,** cloth vest bearing heraldic insignia, of silk from Tarsia in the Middle East. **2188 Sonday,** Chaucer is precise about day and time in *KnT*. Palmon breaks prison on May 3 "after the mydnyght" (line 1467). Hence it is Friday, May 4, when Arcite comes to the grove (line 1534), and they fight on Saturday, May 5 (line 1629). Theseus sets the tournament for one year later (line 1850), and the knights now assemble on Sunday. **2192 at,** El reads "in." **2200 sat . . . upon the deys,** sat on the dais, a raised platform in a position of prominence. **2202 carole,** El and Hg read "daunce(n)." **2205 on,** El reads "in." **2211 nere nat day by houres two,** two hours before sunrise on Monday, the twenty-third hour of Sunday, which belongs to Venus (**2217 hir houre**); Chaucer describes the assignment of hours to planets in *Astr* 2.12. **2212 right tho,** El reads "also." **2215 Citherea,** another name for Venus; see 1936n. **2219 and with,** El reads "with ful."

And herte soor, he seyde as ye shal heere:
  "Faireste of faire, O lady myn, Venus,
Doughter to Jove, and spouse of Vulcanus,
Thow gladere of° the mount of Citheron,
For thilke° love thow haddest to Adoon,
Have pitee of my bittre teeris smerte°,
And taak myn humble preyere at thyn herte.
Allas! I ne have no langage to telle
Th'effectes ne the tormentz of myn helle.
Myn herte may myne harmes° nat biwreye°.
I am so confus that I kan noght seye
But, 'Mercy, lady bright, that knowest weele
My thought, and seest what harmes that I feele!'
Considere al this and rewe° upon my soore°
As wisly° as I shal for everemoore,
Emforth° my myght, thy trewe servant be,
And holden werre° alwey with chastitee.
That make I myn avow°, so° ye me helpe.
I kepe° noght of armes for to yelpe°,
Ne I ne axe° nat tomorwe to have victorie,
Ne renoun in this cas, ne veyne glorie
Of pris of° armes blowen° up and doun.
But I wolde have fully possessioun
Of Emelye, and dye in thy servyse.
Fynd thow the manere hou°, and in what wyse.
I recche° nat, but° it may bettre be,
To have victorie of hem, or they of me,
So that° I have my lady in myne armes.
For though so be that Mars is god of armes,
Youre vertu° is so greet in hevene above
That if yow list°, I shal wel have my love.
  "Thy temple wol I worshipe everemo,
And on thyn auter°, where° I ride or go,
I wol doon sacrifice and fires beete°.
And if ye wol nat so, my lady sweete,
Thanne preye I thee, tomorwe with a spere
That Arcita me thurgh the herte bere°.
Thanne rekke° I noght, whan I have lost my lyf,
Though that Arcita wynne hire to his wyf.
This is th'effect and ende of my preyere:
Yif° me my love, thow blisful lady deere."
  Whan the orison° was doon of Palamon,
His sacrifice he dide and that anon,
Ful pitously° with alle circumstaunce°,
Al° telle I noght as now his observaunce.
But atte laste the statue of Venus shook,
And made a signe°, wherby that he took
That his preyere accepted was that day.
For thogh the signe shewed a delay,
Yet wiste he wel that graunted was his boone°;
And with glad herte he wente hym hoom ful soone.
  The thridde houre inequal that° Palamon
Bigan to Venus temple for to gon,
Up roos the sonne and up roos Emelye,
And to the temple of Dyane gan hye°.
Hir maydens, that she thider with hir ladde,
Ful redily° with hem the fyr they hadde,
Th'encens°, the clothes°, and the remenant al
That to the sacrifice longen shal°,
The hornes° fulle of meeth°, as was the gyse°—
Ther lakked noght to doon hir sacrifise.
  Smokynge° the temple, ful of clothes faire,
This Emelye, with herte debonaire°,
Hir body wessh with water of a welle.
But hou° she dide hir ryte° I dar nat telle,
But it be anything in general,
And yet it were a game° to heeren al.
To hym that meneth wel it were no charge°,
But it is good a man been at his large°.
  Hir brighte heer was kembd, untressed° al;
A coroune° of a grene ook cerial°
Upon hir heed was set ful fair and meete°.
Two fyres on the auter gan she beete°,
And dide hir thynges, as men may biholde
In Stace of Thebes and thise bookes olde.

2223 gladere of, *one who brings joy to* **2224 thilke,** *that* **2225 smerte,** *painful* **2229 harmes,** *pains,* **biwreye,** *reveal* **2233 rewe,** *have pity,* **soore,** *pain* **2234 wisly,** *surely* **2235 Emforth,** *to the extent of* **2236 holden werre,** *wage war* **2237 That make I myn avow,** *I make that my vow,* **so,** *if* **2238 kepe,** *care,* **yelpe,** *boast* **2239 axe,** *ask* **2241 pris of,** *praise of,* **blowen,** *announced* **2244 hou,** *how* **2245 recche,** *care,* **but,** *unless* **2247 So that,** *as long as* **2249 vertu,** *power* **2250 list,** *wish* **2252 auter,** *altar,* **where,** *wherever* **2253 beete,** *kindle* **2256 bere,** *pierce* **2257 rekke,** *care* **2260 Yif,** *give* **2261 orison,** *prayer* **2263 pitously,** *pitifully,* **alle circumstaunce,** *full ceremony* **2264 Al,** *although* **2266 signe,** *sign* **2268 boone,** *request* **2271 that,** *after* **2274 gan hye,** *did hurry* **2276 Ful redily,** *very properly* **2277 Th'encens,** *the incense,* **clothes,** *cloths* **2278 longen shal,** *were appropriate* **2279 hornes,** *drinking horns,* **meeth,** *mead,* **gyse,** *custom* **2281 Smokynge,** *increasing* **2282 debonaire,** *gentle* **2284 hou,** *how,* **ryte,** *rite* **2286 game,** *pleasure* **2287 charge,** *burden* **2288 at his large,** *at liberty* (to be selective) **2289 untressed,** *unbraided* **2290 coroune,** *crown,* **ook cerial,** *evergreen oak* **2291 meete,** *appropriate* **2292 beete,** *kindle*

2220 he seyde as ye shal heere, El reads "and seyde in this manere." **2222 to Jove,** Hg reads "of Jove." **of Vulcanus,** Hg reads "to Vulcanus." **2224 Adoon,** Adonis, beloved of Venus. **2271 thridde houre inequal that,** the calculation is in planetary hours (not clock hours), which are not equal because they are based upon the duration of daylight. Only at the equinoxes (when there are twelve hours of daylight and of darkness) are planetary hours and clock hours the same. This is the first hour of Monday (three hours after Palamon began), which was assigned to the moon, the planet of Diana. **2276 hadde,** El reads "ladde." **2294 In Stace of Thebes,** in Statius, concerning Thebes, i.e., the *Thebaid,* which does not include this scene. Chaucer obscures his debt to Boccaccio's *Teseida* here, as he obscures his debt to *Filostrato* in *TC* (1.394). **thise,** omitted in Hg.

Whan kyndled was the fyr, with pitous cheere
Unto Dyane she spak as ye may heere:
"O chaste goddesse of the wodes grene,
To whom bothe hevene and erthe and see is sene°,
Queene of the regne° of Pluto derk and lowe,
Goddesse of maydens, that myn herte hast knowe
Ful many a yeer, and woost° what I desire,
As keep° me fro thy vengeaunce and thyn ire,
That Attheon aboughte° cruelly.
Chaste goddesse, wel wostow° that I
Desire to ben a mayden al my lyf,
Ne nevere wol I be no love ne wyf.
I am, thow woost, yet of thy compaignye,
A mayde, and love huntynge and venerye°,
And for to walken in the wodes wilde,
And noght to ben a wyf and be with childe.
Noght wol I knowe the compaignye of man.
Now help me, lady, sith° ye may and kan,
For tho thre° formes that thou hast in thee.
And Palamon, that hath swich love to me,
And eek Arcite, that loveth me so soore—
This grace I preye thee withoute moore,
As sende love and pees bitwixe hem two,
And fro me turne awey hir hertes so
That al hire hoote love and hir desir,
And al hir bisy° torment and hir fir
Be queynt°, or turned in another place.
And if so be thou wolt do me no grace,
Or if my destynee be shapen so
That I shal nedes° have oon of hem two,
As sende° me hym that moost desireth me.
Bihoold, goddesse of clene chastitee,
The bittre teeris that on my chekes falle.
Syn° thou art mayde and kepere of us alle,
My maydenhede thou kepe and wel conserve,
And whil I lyve, a mayde I wol thee serve."
The fires brenne upon the auter cleere°,
Whil Emelye was thus in hir preyere.
But sodeynly she saugh a sighte queynte°,
For right anon oon of the fyres queynte°,
And quyked° agayn, and after that anon
That oother fyr was queynt and al agon°,
And as it queynte it made a whistelynge
As doon thise wete brondes° in hir brennynge°,
And at the brondes ende out ran anon
As it were blody dropes many oon.
For which so soore agast° was Emelye
That she was wel ny° mad, and gan to crye,
For she ne wiste° what is signyfied,
But oonly for the feere thus hath she cried,
And weep that it was pitee for to heere.
And therwithal° Dyane gan appeere,
With bowe in honde, right as an hunteresse,
And seyde, "Doghter, stynt° thyn hevynesse°.
Among the goddes hye it is affermed,
And by eterne word writen and confermed,
Thou shalt ben wedded unto oon of tho°
That han for thee so muchel care and wo,
But unto which of hem I may nat telle.
Farwel, for I ne may no lenger dwelle.
The fires whiche that on myn auter brenne
Shulle thee declaren, er that thou go henne°,
Thyn aventure of love, as in this cas."
And with that word, the arwes in the caas°
Of the goddesse clateren faste and rynge,
And forth she wente and made a vanysshynge
For which this Emelye astoned° was,
And seyde, "What amounteth° this, allas?
I putte me in thy proteccioun,
Dyane, and in thy disposicioun."
And hoom she goth anon the nexte° weye.
This is th'effect; ther is namoore to seye.
The nexte houre of Mars folwynge this,
Arcite unto the temple walked is
Of fierse Mars, to doon his sacrifise
With alle the rytes of his payen wyse°.
With pitous herte and heigh devocioun,
Right thus to Mars he seyde his orisoun°.
"O stronge god, that in the regnes° colde

2298 see is sene, *sea is seen* **2299 regne,** *realm* **2301 woost,** *know* **2302 As keep,** *keep* **2303 aboughte,** *paid for* **2304 wostow,** *you know* **2308 venerye,** *hunting* **2312 sith,** *since* **2313 tho thre,** *those three* (see note) **2320 bisy,** *intense* **2321 queynt,** *quenched* **2324 nedes,** *necessarily* **2325 As sende,** *send* **2328 Syn,** *since* **2331 cleere,** *brightly* **2333 queynte,** *strange* **2334 queynte,** *died out* **2335 quyked,** *came alive* **2336 agon,** *gone* **2338 wete brondes,** *damp logs,* **hir brennynge,** *their burning* **2341 agast,** *frightened* **2342 wel ny** *nearly* **2343 wiste,** *knew* **2346 therwithal,** *with that,* **gan appeere,** *did appear* **2348 stynt,** *stop,* **hevynesse,** *sorrow* **2351 tho,** *those* **2356 henne,** *hence* **2358 caas,** *quiver* **2361 astoned,** *astonished* **2362 amounteth,** *means* **2365 nexte,** *nearest* **2370 payen wyse,** *pagan ways* **2372 orisoun,** *prayer* **2373 regnes,** *regions*

2299 regne of Pluto derk and lowe, Pluto was god of the underworld. Diana, goddess of the moon, was sometimes identified with Greek Hecate and thus regarded also as goddess of the underworld. **2303 Attheon,** Acteon; see 2065n above. **2313 tho thre formes,** those three manifestions of the goddess: Luna in the heavens, Diana on earth, Hecate or Proserpina in the underworld. **2317 As,** El reads "And." **2321 or,** Hg reads "and." **2322 do me no,** Hg reads "noght do me." **2323 Or,** El reads "And." **2332 was,** Hg reads "is." **2366 is,** Hg reads "nys." **2367 nexte houre,** i.e., the fourth hour, belonging to Mars; see 2271n.

Of Trace honoured art° and lord yholde°,
And hast in every regne and every lond
Of armes al the brydel in thyn hond,
And hem fortunest° as thee lyst devyse°,
Accepte of me my pitous sacrifise.
If so be that my youthe may deserve,
And that my myght be worthy for to serve
Thy godhede, that I may been oon of thyne,
Thanne preye I thee to rewe° upon my pyne°.
For thilke° peyne and thilke hoote fir
In which thow whilom brendest° for desir,
Whan that thow usedest° the beautee
Of faire, yonge, fresshe Venus free°,
And haddest hire in armes at thy wille—
Although thee ones on a tyme mysfille°,
Whan Vulcanus hadde caught thee in his las°,
And foond thee liggynge° by his wyf, allas—
For thilke° sorwe that was in thyn herte,
Have routhe° as wel upon my peynes smerte.
I am yong and unkonnynge°, as thow woost°,
And, as I trowe°, with love offended moost°
That evere was any lyves° creature.
For she that dooth° me al this wo endure
Ne reccheth nevere wher° I synke or fleete°.
And wel I woot°, er she me mercy heete°,
I moot° with strengthe wynne hire in the place.
And wel I woot, withouten help or grace
Of thee, ne may my strengthe noght availle°.
Thanne help me, lord, tomorwe in my bataille
For thilke° fyr that whilom° brente thee
As wel as thilke fyr now brenneth me,
And do° that I tomorwe have victorie.
Myn be the travaille°, and thyn be the glorie!
Thy sovereyn temple wol I moost honouren
Of any place, and alwey moost labouren
In thy plesaunce° and in thy craftes stronge,
And in thy temple I wol my baner honge°
And alle the armes of my compaignye,
And everemo, unto that day I dye,
Eterne fir I wol biforn thee fynde°.
And eek to this avow° I wol me bynde:
My beerd, myn heer, that hongeth long adoun,
That nevere yet ne felte offensioun°
Of rasour° nor of shere°, I wol thee yeve,
And ben thy trewe servant whil I lyve.
Now, lord, have routhe upon my sorwes soore.
Yif me the victorie, I aske thee namoore.°
The preyere stynt° of Arcita the stronge,
The rynges on the temple dore that honge,
And eek the dores, clatereden ful faste,
Of which Arcita somwhat hym agaste°.
The fyres brenden upon the auter brighte,
That it gan al the temple for to lighte.
A sweete smel the ground anon up yaf°,
And Arcita anon his hand up haf°,
And moore encens° into the fyr he caste,
With othere rytes mo; and atte laste
The statue of Mars bigan his hauberk° rynge,
And with that soun he herde a murmurynge
Ful lowe and dym, and seyde thus, "Victorie!"
For which he yaf to Mars honour and glorie
And thus with joye and hope wel to fare
Arcite anon unto his in° is fare°,
As fayn as fowel° is of the brighte sonne.
And right anon swich strif ther is bigonne,
For thilke grauntyng°, in the hevene above,
Bitwixe Venus, the goddesse of love,
And Mars, the stierne° god armypotente°,
That Juppiter was bisy it to stente°,
Til that the pale Saturnus the colde,
That knew so manye of aventures olde,
Foond in his olde experience an art°
That he ful soone hath plesed every part.

2374 art, *are,* **lord yholde,** *treated as lord* **2377 hem fortunest,** *determines the fortune of them,* **thee lyst devyse,** *you choose to arrange* **2382 rewe,** *have pity,* **pyne,** *pain* **2383 thilke,** *that* **2384 whilom brendest,** *once burned* **2385 usedest,** *enjoyed* **2386 free,** *generous* **2388 thee . . . mysfille,** *for you at one time* (things) *went wrong* **2389 las,** *snare* **2390 liggynge,** *lying* **2391 thilke,** *that* **2392 routhe,** *pity* **2393 unkonnynge,** *inexperienced,* **woost,** *know* **2394 trowe,** *believe,* **with love offended moost,** *by love hurt most* **2395 lyves,** *living* **2396 dooth,** *makes* **2397 Ne reccheth nevere wher,** *cares not whether,* **fleete,** *float* **2398 woot,** *know,* **heete,** *promises* **2399 moot,** *must* **2401 availle,** *succeed* **2403 thilke,** *that,* **whilom,** *once* **2405 do,** *cause* **2406 travaille,** *suffering* **2409 In thy plesaunce,** *for your pleasure* **2410 my baner honge,** *hang my banner* **2413 fynde,** *provide for* **2414 avow,** *vow* **2416 offensioun,** *damage* **2417 rasour,** *razor,* **shere,** *scissors* **2421 stynt,** *stopped* **2424 hym agaste,** *was frightened* **2427 yaf,** *gave* **2428 haf,** *lifted* **2429 encens,** *incense* **2431 his hauberk,** *its mail armor* **2436 in,** *dwelling,* **is fare,** *goes* **2437 fayn as fowel,** *happy as a bird* **2439 thilke grauntyng,** *that promise* **2441 stierne,** *stern,* **armypotente,** *potent in arms* **2442 stente,** *stop* **2445 art,** *strategy*

2389 Vulcanus, Vulcan, husband of Venus, trapped Mars and Venus in bed together. **2400 or,** Hg reads "and." **2405 have,** Hg reads "may have." **2415–17 My beerd, myn heer . . . thee yeve,** dedication of beards and hair was an ancient custom among the Greeks and the Nazarites. **2427 A,** El reads "And." **the ground anon,** Hg reads "anon the ground." **2442–43 Juppiter . . . Saturnus,** throughout *KnT,* Chaucer blends notions of divine powers with notions of planetary influence. Jupiter (Jove) was the king of the gods, but Saturn was older. Jupiter was thought to be the largest of the planets, although the orbit of Saturn (**2454 cours . . . wyde**) was the largest known in the Middle Ages. Because of age and distance from earth, Saturn was thought to have malevolent influence on humankind. It is Chaucer's invention to include him in the plot.

As sooth is seyd, elde° hath greet avantage;
In elde is bothe wysdom and usage°;
Men may the olde atrenne°, and noght atrede°.
Saturne anon, to stynten° strif and drede,
Al be it that° it is agayn his kynde°,
Of al this strif he gan remedie fynde.
"My deere doghter Venus," quod Saturne,
"My cours°, that hath so wyde for to turne,
Hath moore power than woot° any man.
Myn is the drenchyng° in the see so wan°;
Myn is the prison in the derke cote°;
Myn is the stranglyng and hangyng by the throte;
The murmure and the cherles rebellyng;
The groynynge°, and the pryvee° empoysonyng.
I do vengeance and pleyn correccioun°,
Whil I dwelle in the signe of the leoun.
Myn is the ruyne° of the hye° halles;
The fallynge of the toures° and of the walles
Upon the mynour° or the carpenter.
I slow° Sampsoun, shakynge the piler;
And myne be the maladyes colde,
The derke tresons, and the castes° olde;
My lookyng is the fader° of pestilence.
Now weep namoore, I shal doon diligence°
That Palamon, that is thyn owene knyght,
Shal have his lady, as thou hast him hight°.
Though Mars shal helpe his knyght, yet nathelees°
Bitwixe yow ther moot° be som tyme pees,
Al be ye° noght of o compleccioun°,
That causeth al day swich divisioun.
I am thyn aiel°, redy at thy wille;
Weep now namoore, I wol thy lust° fulfille."
Now wol I stynten of the goddes above,
Of Mars and of Venus, goddesse of love,
And telle yow as pleynly as I kan
The grete effect for which that I bygan.

Explicit terica pars. Sequitur pars quarta.

Greet was the feeste in Atthenes that day,
And eek the lusty seson of that May
Made every wight to been in swich plesaunce
That al that Monday justen° they and daunce,
And spenden it in Venus heigh servyse.
But by the cause° that they sholde ryse
Eerly, for to seen the grete fight,
Unto hir reste wenten they at nyght.
And on the morwe, whan that day gan sprynge,
Of hors and harneys noyse and claterynge
Ther was in hostelryes° al aboute,
And to the paleys° rood ther many a route°
Of lordes upon steedes and palfreys°.
Ther maystow° seen devisynge° of harneys
So unkouth° and so riche, and wroght so weel
Of goldsmythrye, of browdynge°, and of steel,
The sheeldes brighte, testeres, and trappures°,
Gold-hewen helmes°, hauberkes°, cote-armures°,
Lordes in parementz° on hir courseres°,
Knyghtes of retenue°, and eek squieres
Nailynge° the speres, and helmes bokelynge°,
Giggynge° of sheeldes, with layneres lacynge°—
There as nede is they° weren nothyng ydel.
The fomy° steedes on the golden brydel
Gnawynge, and faste the armurers also
With fyle and hamer prikynge to and fro,
Yemen° on foote, and communes° many oon
With shorte staves°, thikke as they may goon;
Pypes, trompes°, nakers°, clariounes°,
That in the bataille blowen blody sounes;
The paleys ful of peple up and doun,
Heere thre, ther ten, holdynge hir questioun,
Dyvynynge of° thise Thebane knyghtes two.
Somme seyden thus, somme seyde, "It shal be so."

2447 elde, *age* **2448 usage,** *experience* **2449 atrenne,** *outrun,* **atrede,** *outwit* **2450 stynten,** *stop* **2451 Al be it that,** *although,* **agayn his kynde,** *against his nature* **2454 cours,** *orbit* **2455 woot,** *knows* **2456 drenchyng,** *drowning,* **wan,** *dark* **2457 cote,** *hut* **2460 groynynge,** *grumbling,* **pryvee,** *secret* **2461 pleyn correccioun,** *full punishment* **2463 ruyne,** *ruin,* **hye,** *high* **2464 toures,** *towers* **2465 mynour,** *miner* **2466 slow,** *slew* **2468 castes,** *plots* **2469 My lookyng is the fader,** *my influence is the cause* **2470 doon diligence,** *make sure* **2472 hight,** *promised* **2473 nathelees,** *nonetheless* **2474 moot,** *must* **2475 Al be ye,** *although you are,* **o compleccioun,** *the same temperament* **2477 aiel,** *grandfather* **2478 lust,** *desire* **2486 justen,** *joust* **2488 by the cause,** *because* **2493 hostelryes,** *lodgings* **2494 paleys,** *palace,* **route,** *company* **2495 palfreys,** *riding horses* **2496 maystow,** *you may,* **devisynge,** *preparation* **2497 unkouth,** *unfamiliar* **2498 browdynge,** *embroidering* **2499 testeres and trappures,** *horse armor* **2500 Gold-hewen helmes,** *gold-colored helmets,* **hauberkes,** *coats of mail,* **cote-armures,** *coats of arms* **2501 parementz,** *rich robes,* **hir courseres,** *their war horses* **2502 retenue,** *service* **2503 Nailynge,** *fastening* (heads on to), **bokelynge,** *buckling* **2504 Giggynge,** *filling out,* **layneres lacynge,** *lacing with straps* **2505 they,** i.e., *everyone* **2506 fomy,** *foamy* **2509 Yemen,** *yeomen,* **communes,** *commoners* **2510 staves,** *staffs* **2511 trompes,** *trumpets,* **nakers,** *kettledrums,* **clariounes,** *bugles* **2515 Dyvynynge of,** *speculating about*

2452 gan, Hg reads "kan." **2453 doghter,** granddaughter; Venus is daughter of Jupiter, who is son of Saturn. **2459 cherles rebellyng,** peasants' rebelling, perhaps one of Chaucer's few allusions to the Peasants' Revolt of 1381. **2462 signe of the leoun,** the influence of Saturn was most malevolent when the planet was aligned with the astrological sign of Leo, the lion. **2466 Sampsoun,** Samson died when he pulled the pillars and roof down on the heads of the Philistines; Judges. 16.25ff., retold in *MkT* 7.2079ff. **2482a *Explicit tercia pars. Sequitur pars quarta.*** "Here ends part three. Here follows part four." Omitted in Hg; see 2742n. **2489 fight,** Hg reads "sight." **2491 the morwe,** Tuesday, a day belonging to Mars, named after Tiw, a Scandanavian god of war. **2503 and,** Hg reads "and the."

Somme helden with hym with the blake berd,
Somme with the balled°, somme with the thikke herd°;
Somme seyde he° looked grymme, and he wolde fighte:
"He hath a sparth° of twenty pound of wighte."
Thus was the halle ful of divynynge°,
Longe after that the sonne gan to sprynge.
The grete Theseus, that of his sleep awaked
With mynstralcie and noyse that was maked,
Heeld yet° the chambre of his paleys riche
Til that the Thebane knyghtes, bothe yliche°
Honured, were into the paleys fet°.
Duc Theseus was at a wyndow set,
Arrayed right as he were a god in trone°.
The peple preesseth thiderward° ful soone
Hym for to seen, and doon heigh reverence,
And eek to herkne his heste° and his sentence°.
An heraud° on a scaffold made an "Oo!"
Til al the noyse of peple was ydo°,
And whan he saugh the peple of noyse al stille,
Tho shewed° he the myghty dukes wille.
"The lord hath of his heigh discrecioun
Considered that it were destruccioun
To gentil blood to fighten in the gyse°
Of mortal bataille now in this emprise°.
Wherfore, to shapen° that they shal nat dye,
He wol his firste purpos modifye.
No man therfore, up° peyne of los of lyf,
No maner shot°, ne polax°, ne short knyf
Into the lystes sende, or thider brynge,
Ne short swerd, for to stoke° with poynt bitynge,
No man ne drawe, ne bere it by his syde.
Ne no man shal unto° his felawe° ryde
But o cours°, with a sharpe ygrounde spere,
Foyne°, if hym list, on foote, hymself to were°.
And he that is at meschief° shal be take
And noght slayn, but be broght unto the stake
That shal ben ordeyned° on either syde;
But thider° he shal by force, and there abyde.
And if so falle° the chieftayn be take
On outher° syde, or elles sleen° his make°,
No lenger shal the turneiynge° laste.
God spede° you! Gooth forth, and ley on faste!
With long swerd and with maces° fighteth youre fille.
Gooth now youre wey, this is the lordes wille."
The voys of peple touchede the hevene,
So loude cride they with murie stevene°,
"God save swich a lord, that is so good!
He wilneth no destruccion of blood."
Up goon the trompes° and the melodye,
And to the lystes rit° the compaignye,
By ordinance°, thurghout the citee large,
Hanged with clooth of gold, and nat with sarge°.
Ful lik a lord this noble duc gan ryde,
Thise two Thebans upon either syde,
And after rood the queene, and Emelye,
And after that another compaignye
Of oon and oother, after hir degree°.
And thus they passen thurghout the citee,
And to the lystes come they by° tyme.
It nas nat of the day yet fully pryme°
Whan set was Theseus ful riche° and hye,
Ypolita the queene, and Emelye,
And othere ladys in degrees aboute.
Unto the seetes preesseth al the route°.
And westward, thurgh the gates under Marte°,
Arcite and eek the hondred of his parte°
With baner reed° is entred right anon.
And in that selve° moment Palamon
Is under Venus, estward in the place,
With baner whyt and hardy chiere° and face.
In al the world, to seken up and doun,
So evene°, withouten variacioun,
Ther nere swiche° compaignyes tweye,
For ther was noon so wys that koude seye
That any hadde of oother avauntage

2518 balled, *bald,* **thikke herd,** *thick haired* **2519 he,** *that one* **2520 sparth,** *battle-ax* **2521 divynynge,** *speculation* **2525 Heeld yet,** *stayed in* **2526 yliche,** *alike* **2527 fet,** *fetched* **2529 trone,** *throne* **2530 thiderward,** *toward this* **2532 herkne his heste,** *hear his command,* **sentence,** *judgment* **2533 heraud,** *herald* **2534 ydo,** *done* **2536 shewed,** *made clear* **2539 gyse,** *manner* **2540 emprise,** *undertaking* **2541 shapen,** *make sure* **2543 up,** *upon* **2544 maner shot,** *kind of arrow,* **polax,** *long battle-ax* **2546 stoke,** *stab* **2548 unto,** *against,* **felawe,** *opponent* **2549 But o cours,** *more than one charge* **2550 Foyne,** (let him) *thrust,* **were,** *defend* **2551 at meschief,** *in danger* **2553 ordeyned,** *established* **2554 thider** (brought) *there* **2555 if so falle,** *if it happens that* **2556 outher,** *either,* **sleen,** *slain,* **make,** *match* (the other leader) **2557 turneiynge,** *tournament* **2558 spede,** *assist* **2559 maces,** *war clubs* **2562 murie stevene,** *merry sound* **2565 trompes,** *trumpets* **2566 rit,** *rides* **2567 ordinance,** *proper order* **2568 sarge,** *wool* **2573 after hir degree,** *in order of their rank* **2575 by,** *in* **2576 fully pryme,** *9 a.m.* **2577 ful riche,** *very richly* **2580 preesseth,** *crowded,* **route,** *company* **2581 Marte,** *Mars* **2582 parte,** *group* **2583 baner reed,** *red banner* **2584 selve,** *same* **2586 chiere,** *expression* **2588 evene,** *equal* **2589 Ther nere swiche,** *there weren't such*

2541 that they shal nat dye, most of these humane restrictions on the use of deadly force were added to the story by Chaucer. **2544 ne polax,** El omits "ne." **2547 it,** omitted El. **2552 broght unto the stake,** yielding at the stake (a post or marker) was medieval tournament practice; such technicalities are not in *Teseida.* **2555 falle,** El reads "be." **2562 murie,** Hg reads "loude."

Of worthynesse, ne of estaat, ne age,
So evene were they chosen, for to gesse°.
And in two renges° faire they hem dresse°.
Whan that hir names rad° were everichon,
That in hir nombre gyle° were ther noon,
Tho were the gates shet, and cried was loude,
"Do now youre devoir°, yonge knyghtes proude!"
  The heraudes lefte hir prikyng° up and doun;
Now ryngen trompes loude and clarioun°.
Ther is namoore to seyn, but west and est
In goon the speres ful sadly in arrest°,
In gooth the sharpe spore° into the syde.
Ther seen° men who kan juste and who kan ryde.
Ther shyveren° shaftes upon sheeldes thikke;
He° feeleth thurgh the herte-spoon° the prikke;
Up spryngen speres twenty foot on highte;
Out goon the swerdes as the silver brighte;
The helmes they tohewen° and toshrede°;
Out brest° the blood with stierne° stremes rede;
With myghty maces the bones they tobreste°;
He thurgh the thikkeste of the throng gan threste°;
Ther stomblen steedes stronge, and doun gooth al;
He rolleth under foot as dooth a bal;
He foyneth° on his feet with his tronchoun°;
And he hym hurtleth with his hors adoun;
He thurgh the body is hurt and sithen ytake°,
Maugree his heed°, and broght unto the stake.
As forward° was, right ther he moste abyde°.
Another lad is° on that oother syde.
  And somtyme dooth hem° Theseus to reste,
Hem to fresshen and drynken, if hem leste.
Ful ofte a day° han thise Thebanes two
Togydre ymet and wroght his felawe wo;
Unhorsed hath ech oother of hem tweye°.
Ther nas no tygre in the vale of Galgopheye,
Whan that hir whelp° is stole° whan it is lite°,
So crueel on the hunte° as is Arcite
For jelous herte upon this Palamoun.
Ne in Belmarye ther nys so fel° leoun
That hunted is, or for his hunger wood°,
Ne of his praye° desireth so the blood,
As Palamon to sleen his foo Arcite.
The jelous strokes on hir helmes byte;
Out renneth blood on bothe hir sydes rede.
  Somtyme° an ende ther is of every dede.
For er the sonne unto the reste wente,
The stronge kyng Emetreus gan hente°
This Palamon, as he faught with Arcite,
And made his swerd depe in his flessh to byte,
And by the force of twenty is he take°,
Unyolden°, and ydrawe unto the stake.
And in the rescus° of this Palamoun
The stronge kyng Lygurge is born adoun°,
And Kyng Emetreus, for al his strengthe,
Is born out of his sadel a swerdes lengthe,
So hitte him Palamoun er he were take.
But al for noght—he was broght to the stake.
His hardy herte myghte hym helpe naught:
He most abyde°, whan that he was caught,
By force and eek by composicioun°.
  Who sorweth now but woful Palamoun,
That moot° namoore goon agayn to fighte?
And whan that Theseus hadde seyn this sighte,
Unto the folk that foghten thus echon°
He cryde, "Hoo! namoore, for it is doon!
I wol be trewe juge, and no partie°.
Arcite of Thebes shal have Emelie,
That by his fortune hath hire faire° ywonne."
Anon ther is a noyse of peple bigonne°
For joye of this, so loude and heighe withalle,
It semed that the lystes sholde falle.
  What kan now faire Venus doon above?

2593 for to gesse, *at an estimate* **2594 renges,** *lines,* **hem dresse,** *arrange themselves* **2595 rad,** *read* **2596 gyle,** *deceits* **2598 devoir,** *best* **2599 lefte hir prikyng,** *stopped their spurring* **2600 clarioun,** *clearly* **2602 ful sadly in arrest,** *very firmly against the breastplates* **2603 spore,** *spur* **2604 seen** (are) *seen,* **2605 shyveren,** *shatter* **2606 He,** *one,* **hertespoon,** *breastbone* **2609 tohewen,** *chop thoroughly,* **toshrede,** *shred thoroughly* **2610 brest,** *bursts,* **stierne,** *cruel* **2611 tobreste,** *break completely* **2612 threste,** *thrust* **2615 foyneth,** *stabs,* **tronchoun,** *spear shaft* **2617 sithen ytake,** *after taken* **2618 Maugree his heed,** *despite his wishes* **2619 forward,** *agreement,* **moste abyde,** *must remain* **2620 lad is,** *is led* **2621 dooth hem,** *compels them* **2623 a day,** *during the day* **2625 tweye,** *twice* **2627 whelp,** *cub,* **stole,** *stolen,* **lite,** *little* **2628 hunte,** *hunter* **2630 fel,** *cruel* **2631 wood,** *insane* **2632 praye,** *prey* **2636 Somtyme,** *eventually* **2638 gan hente,** *did seize* **2641 take,** *taken* **2642 Unyolden,** *unyielding* **2643 rescus,** *attempted rescue* **2644 born adoun,** *brought down* **2650 abyde,** *remain* **2651 composicioun,** *agreement* **2653 moot,** *might* **2655 echon,** *each one* **2557 partie,** *partisan* **2659 faire,** *fairly* **2660 bigonne,** *begun*

2605ff. shyveren shaftes upon sheeldes . . . , alliteration, present tense, and syntactic manipulation lend power to this battle scene; *LGW* 635ff. achieves the same effect, as does the alliteration in *TC* 4.38–42. **2613 stomblen,** El reads "semblen" (attack). **2622 fresshen,** Hg reads "refresshe." **2626 vale of Galgopheye,** the valley of Gargaphie, where Acteon, seeing Diana naked, was punished by being torn apart by his dogs; Ovid, *Metamorphoses* 3.155ff. **2630 Belmarye,** Benmarin, once a district in northwestern Africa; also cited in *GP* 1.57. **2655** This line is omitted in many MSS and a new line supplied before 2657: "Ne non shal lenger unto his felawe gon."

What seith she now? What dooth this queene of love,
But wepeth so, for wantynge° of hir wille,
Til that hir teeres in the lystes fille?
She seyde, "I am ashamed, doutelees°."
  Saturnus seyde, "Doghter, hoold thy pees!
Mars hath his wille, his knyght hath al his boone°,
And, by myn heed, thow shalt been esed° soone."
  The trompours° with the loude mynstralcie,
The heraudes that ful loude yolle° and crie,
Been in hire wele° for joye of daun° Arcite.
But herkneth me, and stynteth° noyse a lite°,
Which a° myracle ther bifel anon.
  This fierse Arcite hath of his helm ydon°,
And on a courser, for to shewe his face,
He priketh endelong° the large place,
Lokynge upward upon this Emelye,
And she agayn° hym caste a freendlich° eye—
For wommen, as to speken in comune,
Thei folwen alle the favour of Fortune—
And was al his chiere° as in his herte.
  Out of the ground a furie infernal sterte°,
From Pluto sent at requeste of Saturne,
For which his hors for fere gan to turne,
And leep aside, and foundred° as he leep;
And er that Arcite may taken keep°,
He pighte° hym on the pomel° of his heed,
That° in the place he lay as he were deed,
His brest tobrosten° with his sadel-bowe°.
As blak he lay as any cole° or crowe,
So was the blood yronnen in his face.
Anon° he was yborn° out of the place,
With herte soor, to Theseus paleys.
Tho was he korven° out of his harneys°,
And in a bed ybrought ful faire and blyve°,
For he was yet in memorie° and alyve,
And alwey criynge after Emelye.
  Duc Theseus, with al his compaignye,
Is comen hoom to Atthenes his citee,
With alle blisse° and greet solempnitee.
Al be it that this aventure was falle°,
He nolde noght disconforten° hem alle.
Men seyde eek that Arcite shal nat dye,
He shal been heeled of his maladye.
And of another thyng they weren as fayn°,
That of hem alle was ther noon yslayn,
Al° were they soore yhurt, and namely oon°
That with a spere was thirled° his brest-boon.
To othere woundes and to broken armes
Somme hadden salves, and somme hadden charmes.
Fermacies° of herbes and eek save°
They dronken, for they wolde hir lymes have°.
For which this noble duc, as he wel kan,
Conforteth and honoureth every man,
And made revel al the longe nyght
Unto the straunge° lordes, as was right.
Ne ther was holden no disconfitynge°,
But as a justes° or a tourneiynge,
For soothly° ther was no disconfiture°.
For fallyng nys nat but an aventure°,
Ne to be lad by force unto the stake
Unyolden°, and with° twenty knyghtes take,
O° persone allone, withouten mo°,
And haryed° forth by arme, foot, and too°,
And eke his steede dryven forth with staves°
With footmen, bothe yemen and eek knaves—
It nas arretted hym° no vileynye°,
Ther may no man clepen° it cowardye.
  For which anon Duc Theseus leet crye°,
To stynten° alle rancour° and envye°,
The gree° as wel of o syde as of oother,
And eyther syde ylik° as ootheres brother;

2665 wantynge, *lacking* **2667 doutelees,** *doubtless* **2669 boone,** *request* **2670 esed,** *satisfied* **2671 trompours** *trumpeters* **2672 yolle,** *yell* **2673 Been in hire wele,** *are in their happiness,* **daun,** *sir* **2674 stynteth,** *stop,* **lite,** *little* **2675 Which a,** *what a* **2676 of his helm ydon,** *taken off his helmet* **2678 endelong,** *the length of* **2680 agayn,** *upon,* freendlich, *friendly* **2683 chiere,** *appearance* **2684 furie infernal sterte,** *hellish spirit of anger leapt* **2687 foundred,** *stumbled* **2688 keep,** *care* **2689 pighte,** *threw,* **pomel,** *lop* **2690 That,** *so that* **2691 tobrosten,** *shattered,* **sadel-bowe,** *rigid front piece of the saddle* **2692 cole,** *coal* **2694 Anon,** *at once,* **yborn,** *carried* **2696 korven,** *cut,* **harneys,** *armor* **2697 blyve,** *quickly* **2698 in memorie,** *conscious* **2702 blisse,** *celebration* **2703 aventure was falle,** *accident had happened* **2704 disconforten,** *upset* **2707 fayn,** *glad* **2709 Al,** *although,* **namely oon,** *especially one* **2710 thirled,** *pierced* **2713 Fermacies,** *medicines,* **eek save,** *also sage* **2714 wolde hir lymes have,** *wished to save their limbs* **2718 straunge,** *foreign* **2719 holden no disconfitynge,** *thought to be no defeat* **2720 justes,** *joust* **2721 soothly,** *truly,* **disconfiture,** *defeat* **2722 aventure,** *accident* **2724 Unyolden,** *unyielded,* **with,** *by* **2725 O,** *one,* **mo,** *more* **2726 haryed,** *dragged,* **too,** *toe* **2727 staves,** *staffs* **2729 nas arretted hym,** *was not attributed to him,* **vileynye,** *shame* **2730 clepen,** *call* **2731 leet crye,** *had announced* **2732 stynten,** *stop,* **rancour,** *ill will,* **envye,** *hostility* **2733 gree,** *esteem* **2734 ylik,** *alike*

2668 Saturnus, Saturn's intervention is Chaucer's addition; in *Teseida,* Venus calls the fury (line 2685) herself. **2671 trompours,** El reads "trompes" (trumpets). **2674 noyse,** El reads "now." **2681–82** Lines omitted in El and Hg, but found in other manuscripts, perhaps indicating that Chaucer canceled them or that they are a later addition. **2683** The line can be paraphrased "And his expression mirrored the joy in his heart." **And was,** Hg reads "And she was." **2710 his,** Hg reads "the." **2723 lad,** Hg reads "had."

And yaf hem yiftes after hir degree,
And fully heeld a feeste dayes three,
And convoyed' the kynges worthily
Out of his toun a journee largely°.
And hoom wente every man the righte way.
Ther was namoore but “Farewel, have good day!”
Of this bataille I wol namoore endite°,
But speke of Palamon and of Arcite.
  Swelleth the brest of Arcite, and the soore°
Encreesseth at his herte moore and moore.
The clothered° blood, for any lechecraft°,
Corrupteth° and is in his bouk° ylaft°,
That neither veyne-blood°, ne ventusynge°,
Ne drynke of herbes may ben his helpynge.
The vertu expulsif, or animal°,
Fro thilke vertu cleped° natural
Ne may the venym voyden° ne expelle.
The pipes of his longes° gonne to swelle,
And every lacerte° in his brest adoun
Is shent° with venym and corrupcioun°.
Hym gayneth° neither, for to gete° his lif,
Vomyt upward, ne dounward laxatif°.
Al is tobrosten° thilke regioun°,
Nature hath now no dominacioun.
And certeinly, ther° Nature wol nat wirche°,
Farewel phisik°—go ber° the man to chirche!
This al and som°, that Arcita moot° dye;
For which he sendeth after Emelye,
And Palamon, that was his cosyn deere.
Thanne seyde he thus, as ye shal after heere:
  “Naught may the woful spirit in myn herte
Declare o point° of alle my sorwes smerte°
To yow, my lady, that I love moost,
But I biquethe the servyce of my goost°
To yow aboven every creature,
Syn° that my lyf may no lenger dure°.
Allas, the wo, allas, the peynes stronge
That I for yow have suffred, and so longe;
Allas, the deeth, allas, myn Emelye,
Allas, departynge° of oure compaignye;
Allas, myn hertes queene, allas, my wyf,
Myn hertes lady, endere of my lyf!
What is this world? What asketh men° to have?
Now with his love, now in his colde grave,
Allone, withouten any compaignye.
Farewel, my swete foo°, myn Emelye.
And softe° taak me in youre armes tweye°,
For love of God, and herkneth what I seye.
  “I have heer with my cosyn Palamon
Had strif and rancour many a day agon
For love of yow, and for my jalousye.
And Juppiter so wys° my soule gye°
To speken of a servaunt proprely,
With alle circumstances° trewely—
That is to seyn, trouthe, honour, knyghthede,
Wysdom, humblesse, estaat°, and heigh kynrede°,
Fredom°, and al that longeth to that art°—
So° Juppiter have of my soule part°,
As in this world right now ne knowe I non
So worthy to ben loved as Palamon,
That serveth yow, and wol doon al his lyf.
And if that evere ye shul ben a wyf,
Foryet nat Palamon, the gentil man.”
And with that word his speche faille gan°,
For from his feet up to his brest was come
The coold of deeth, that hadde hym overcome,
And yet moore over, for in his armes two

2737 convoyed, *accompanied* **2738 journee largely,** *a full day's journey* **2741 endite,** *write* **2743 soore,** *pain* **2745 clothered,** *clotted,* **for any lechecraft,** *despite any medical skill* **2746 Corrupteth,** *becomes infected,* **bouk,** *body,* **ylaft,** *left* **2747 That,** *so that,* **veyne-blood,** *bleeding,* **ventusynge,** *cupping* **2749 vertu expulsif, or animal,** *power to expel, also known as the animal power* **2750 Fro thilke vertu cleped,** *from that power called* **2751 voyden,** *remove* **2752 longes,** *lungs* **2753 lacerte,** *muscle* **2754 shent,** *destroyed,* **corrupcioun,** *infection* **2755 Hym gayneth,** *it helps him,* **gete,** *save* **2756 laxatif,** *to defecate* **2757 tobrosten,** *shattered,* **thilke regioun,** (in) *this area* (of his body). **2759 ther,** *where,* **wirche,** *work* **2760 phisik,** *medicine,* **ber,** *carry* **2761 This al and som,** *this is the extent of it,* **moot,** *must* **2766 o point,** *one bit,* **sorwes smerte,** *painful sorrows* **2768 goost,** *spirit* **2770 Syn,** *since,* **dure,** *last* **2774 departynge,** *the parting* **2777 asketh men,** *do men ask* **2780 swete foo,** *sweet enemy* **2781 softe,** *softly,* **tweye,** *two* **2786 wys,** *wise,* **gye,** *guide* **2788 circumstances,** *features* **2790 estaat,** *rank,* **heigh kynrede,** *high lineage* **2791 Fredom,** *generosity,* **art, i.e.,** *art of love* **2792 So,** *so that,* **have of my soule part,** (may) *have my spiritual portion* **2798 faille gan,** *did fail*

2742 Hg ends part two and begins part three at this point. It is divided into three parts; El, four. **2743ff.** This follows medical theory of the time. Because his internal organs have been severely damaged (**tobrosten,** line 2757) Arcite's thickened (**clothered,** line 2745) blood becomes infected (**Corrupteth,** line 2746) and produces poison (**venym,** line 2751). Bloodletting (**veyne-blood,** line 2747, release of “excess” blood), cupping (**ventusynge,** line 2747, extraction or suction by heating a glass cup applied to the skin), and medicines cannot remove the poison; Arcite's own **animal** (**2749**) and **natural** (**2750**) power of purgation is also ineffective. **2758 now,** omitted in Hg. **2776 endere of my lyf,** “one who ends my life”; like “swete foo” (line 2780), the phrase is a courtly oxymoron. **2775 wyf,** in *Teseida* 9.83, Arcite marries Emelye soon after the tournament; here the term is an acknowledgment of their betrothal or a term of endearment. **2787 speken of a servaunt,** the syntax is difficult, but the use of **serveth** below (line 2795) makes it clear that Arcite thinks of Palamon as a servant of love. **2788 alle circumstances,** Hg reads “circumstaunces alle.” **2799 For,** El reads “And.” **feet,** El reads “herte.”

The vital strengthe is lost and al ago°.
Oonly the intellect withouten moore,
That dwelled in his herte syk and soore,
Gan faillen whan the herte felte deeth.
Dusked° his eyen two, and failled breeth,
But on his lady yet caste he his eye;
His laste word was, "Mercy, Emelye!"
His spirit chaunged hous° and wente ther
As I cam nevere, I kan nat tellen wher.
Therfore I stynte°, I nam no divinistre°;
Of° soules fynde I nat in this registre°,
Ne me ne list thilke° opinions to telle
Of hem, though that they writen wher they dwelle.
Arcite is coold, ther° Mars his soule gye°.
Now wol I speken forth of Emelye.
  Shrighte° Emelye, and howleth Palamon,
And Theseus his suster took anon
Swownynge°, and baar hire fro the corps away.
What helpeth it to tarien forth the day°
To tellen how she weep bothe eve and morwe?
For in swich cas° wommen have swich sorwe,
Whan that hir housbondes ben from hem ago°,
That for the moore part they sorwen so,
Or ellis fallen in swich maladye
That at the laste certeinly they dye.
  Infinite been the sorwes and the teeres
Of olde folk and folk of tendre yeeres
In al the toun for deeth of this Theban.
For hym ther wepeth bothe child and man.
So greet wepyng was ther noon, certayn,
Whan Ector was ybroght, al fressh yslayn,
To Troye. Allas, the pitee that was ther,
Cracchynge° of chekes, rentynge° eek of heer.
"Why woldestow° be deed," thise wommen
    crye,
"And haddest gold ynough, and Emelye?"
  No man myghte gladen Theseus,
Savynge° his olde fader Egeus,
That knew this worldes transmutacioun,
As he hadde seyn it chaunge bothe up
    and doun,
Joye after wo, and wo after gladnesse,
And shewed hem ensamples° and liknesse°.
  "Right as ther dyed nevere man," quod he,
"That he ne lyvede in erthe in som degree,
Right so ther lyvede never man," he seyde,
"In al this world, that som tyme he ne deyde.
This world nys° but a thurghfare° ful of wo,
And we been pilgrymes, passynge to and fro.
Deeth is an ende of every worldly soore°."
And over al this yet seyde he muchel moore
To this effect, ful wisely to enhorte°
The peple that they sholde hem reconforte°.
  Duc Theseus, with al his bisy cure°,
Caste° now wher that the sepulture°
Of goode Arcite may best ymaked be,
And eek moost honurable in his degree.
And at the laste he took conclusioun°
That ther as first Arcite and Palamoun
Hadden for love the bataille hem bitwene,
That in that selve° grove, swoote° and grene,
Ther as he hadde his amorouse desires,
His compleynte°, and for love his hoote fires,
He wolde make a fyr in which the office
Funeral° he myghte al accomplice°.
And leet comande° anon to hakke and hewe
The okes° olde, and leye hem on a rewe°
In colpons° wel arrayed° for to brenne°.
His officers with swifte feet they renne
And ryden anon at his comandement.
And after this, Theseus hath ysent
After a beere°, and it al overspradde
With clooth of gold, the richeste that he hadde.
And of the same suyte° he cladde Arcite.
Upon his hondes hadde he gloves white,
Eek on his heed a coroune° of laurer° grene,
And in his hond a swerd ful bright and kene.
He leyde hym, bare the visage°, on the beere;

2802 ago, *gone* **2806 Dusked,** *darkened* **2809 hous,** *houses* **2811 stynte,** *stop,* **divinistre,** *theologian* **2812 Of,** *concerning,* **registre,** *book* **2813 Ne me ne list thilke,** *nor does it please me those* **2815 ther,** *where,* **gye,** *guides* **2817 Shrighte,** *shrieked* **2819 Swownynge,** *swooning* **2820 tarien forth the day,** *waste time* **2822 swich cas,** *such circumstances* **2823 ago,** *gone* **2834 Cracchynge,** *scratching,* **rentynge,** *tearing* **2835 woldestow,** *would you* **2838 Savynge,** *except* **2842 ensamples,** *examples,* **liknesse,** *analogies* **2847 nys,** *is nothing,* **thurghfare,** *road* **2849 soore,** *pain* **2851 enhorte,** *urge* **2852 hem reconforte,** *comfort themselves* **2853 cure,** *care* **2854 Caste,** *considered,* **sepulture,** *tomb* **2857 took conclusioun,** *concluded* **2860 selve,** *same,* **swoote,** *sweet* **2862 compleynte,** *lament* **2863–64 office / Funeral,** *funeral ceremony,* **accomplice,** *fulfill* **2865 leet comande,** *commanded* **2866 okes,** *oaks,* **on a rewe,** *in a row* **2867 colpons,** *piles,* **arrayed,** *arranged,* **brenne,** *burn* **2871 beere,** *bier* **2873 suyte,** *material* **2875 coroune,** *crown,* **laurer,** *laurel* **2877 bare the visage,** *with face uncovered*

2812 in this registre, Chaucer's source, *Teseida,* recounts that Arcite's spirit rose through the spheres, but Chaucer uses the scene elsewhere—as a model for the ascent of Troilus's soul in *TC* 5.1807ff. **2825 swich,** Hg reads "swich a." **2828 folk of,** El reads "eek of." **2830 and,** Hg reads "a." **2831 wepyng,** El reads "a wepyng." **2832 Ector,** Hector, hero of Troy, lamented by all after his defeat by Achilles; ultimate source, *Iliad* 22.405ff. **2840 chaunge bothe,** omitted in El. **2841 Joye after wo,** similar sentiments are expressed by the Knight when he interrupts the Monk in *NPP* 7.2767ff. **2849 worldly,** El reads "worldes." **2860 in that,** Hg reads "in the." **2865 comande anon,** Hg reads "anon comaunde." **2874 hadde he,** Hg reads "his." **gloves white,** funeral emblem for an unmarried person.

Therwith he weep that pitee was to heere.
And for the peple sholde seen hym alle,
Whan it was day, he broghte hym to the halle,
That roreth of the criyng and the soun,
  Tho came this woful Theban Palamoun,
With flotery° berd and ruggy°, asshy heeres°,
In clothes blake, ydropped al with teeres;
And, passynge othere of° wepynge, Emelye,
The rewefulleste° of al the compaignye.
In as muche as the servyce sholde be
The moore noble and riche in his degree,
Duc Theseus leet forth thre steedes brynge°,
That trapped° were in steel al gliterynge,
And covered with the armes of daun° Arcite.
Upon thise steedes grete and white
Ther sitten folk, of whiche oon baar° his sheeld,
Another his spere up on his hondes heeld,
The thridde baar with hym his bowe Turkeys°—
Of brend gold was the caas° and eek the harneys°—
And riden forth a paas° with sorweful cheere°
Toward the grove, as ye shul after heere.
The nobleste of the Grekes that ther were
Upon his shuldres caryeden the beere
With slak paas°, and eyen° rede and wete,
Thurghout the citee by the maister strete°,
That sprad was al° with blak, and wonder hye
Right of the same is the strete ywrye°.
Upon the right hond wente olde Egeus,
And on that oother syde Duc Theseus,
With vessels in hir hand of gold ful fyn,
Al ful of hony, milk, and blood, and wyn;
Eek Palamon, with ful greet compaignye;
And after that cam woful Emelye,
With fyr° in honde, as was that tyme the gyse°,
To do the office of funeral servyse.
  Heigh° labour and ful greet apparaillynge°
Was at the service and the fyr-makynge,
That with his° grene top the heven raughte°;
And twenty fadme of brede° the armes straughte°—
This is to seyn, the bowes weren so brode.
Of stree° first ther was leyd ful many a lode°.
But how the fyr was maked upon highte°,
Ne eek the names that the trees highte°,
As ook, firre, birch, asp°, alder, holm°, popler,
Wylugh°, elm, plane, assh, box, chasteyn°, lynde°, laurer,
Mapul, thorn, bech°, hasel, ew°, whippeltree°,
How they weren fild°, shal nat be toold for me;
Ne hou the goddes ronnen° up and doun,
Disherited° of hire habitacioun,
In which they woneden° in reste and pees,
Nymphus, fawnes, and amadrides;
Ne hou the beestes and the briddes alle
Fledden for fere, whan the wode was falle;
Ne how the ground agast° was of the light,
That was nat wont° to seen the sonne bright;
Ne how the fyr was couched° first with stree°,
And thanne with drye stikkes cloven a thre°,
And thanne with grene wode and spicerye°,
And thanne with clooth of gold and with perrye°,
And gerlandes, hangynge with ful many a flour;
The mirre°, th'encens, with al so greet odour;
Ne how Arcite lay among al this,
Ne what richesse aboute his body is;
Ne how that Emelye, as was the gyse°,
Putte in° the fyr of funeral servyse;
Ne how she swowned whan men made the fyr,
Ne what she spak, ne what was hir desir;
Ne what jeweles men in the fyre caste,
Whan that the fyr was greet and brente° faste;

2883 flotery, *fluttering,* **ruggy,** *shaggy,* **asshy heeres,** *ash-covered hair* **2885 passynge othere of,** *surpassing others in* **2886 rewefulleste,** *most sorrowful* **2889 leet forth . . . brynge,** *had brought forth* **2890 trapped,** *equipped* **2891 daun,** *sir* **2893 oon baar,** *one carried* **2895 bowe Turkeys,** *Turkish bow* **2896 caas,** *quiver,* **harneys,** *fittings* **2897 a paas,** *slowly,* **cheere,** *expression* **2901 slak paas,** *slow pace,* **eyen,** *eyes* **2902 maister strete,** *main street* **2903 That sprad was,** *the bier was covered* **2904 ywrye,** *draped* **2911 fyr,** *fire,* **gyse,** *custom* **2913 Heigh,** *great,* **apparaillynge,** *preparation* **2915 his,** *the woodpile's,* **raughte,** *reached to* **2916 twenty fadme of brede,** *120 feet across,* **armes straughte,** *cross pieces stretched* **2918 stree,** *straw,* **lode,** *load* **2919 highte,** *height* **2920 highte,** *were called* **2921 asp,** *aspen,* **holm,** *holly* **2922 Wylugh,** *willow,* **chasteyn,** *chestnut,* **lynde,** *linden* **2923 bech,** *beech,* **ew,** *yew,* **whippeltree,** *dogwood* **2924 fild,** *felled* **2925 ronnen,** *ran* **2926 Disherited,** *deprived* **2927 woneden,** *lived* **2931 agast,** *afraid* **2932 wont,** *accustomed* **2933 couched,** *laid,* **stree,** *straw* **2934 cloven a thre,** *split into three* **2935 spicerye,** *spices* **2936 perrye,** *gems* **2938 mirre,** *myrrh* **2941 gyse,** *custom* **2942 Putte in,** *lit* **2946 brente,** *burned*

2883 ruggy, El reads "rugged." **2892** An eight-syllable line. Later manuscripts emend variously, e.g., "steedes that weren." **2894 up on,** El reads "in." **2911 fyr in honde,** Emelye is prepared to light Arcite's funeral fire. **2913 ful,** omitted in Hg. **2915 raughte,** omitted in El. **2918 ful,** omitted in Hg. **2920 that,** Hg reads "how." **2924 shal nat be toold for me,** this description of what will *not* be described (what rhetoricians call *occupatio*) is the longest and clearest example of several in *KnT*; compare 875ff., 994ff., and 2197ff. **2925 the goddes,** in classical mythology minor deities inhabited forests and trees—nymphs (**nymphus,** line 2928) were nature spirits; fauns (**fawnes,** line 2928) were half-man and half-goat; hamadryads (**amadrides,** line 2928), spirits that lived in trees. **2930 for fere,** Hg reads "forferd" (frightened). **2934 stikkes,** El reads "stokkes." **2937 with ful many,** Hg reads "ful of many." **2940 his,** Hg reads "the." **2943 the,** omitted in Hg.

Ne how somme caste hir sheeld, and somme hir
spere,
And of hire vestimentz°, whiche that they were°,
And coppes° fulle of wyn, and milk, and blood,
Into the fyr, that brente as it were wood°;
Ne how the Grekes, with an huge route°,
Thries° riden al the fyr aboute
Upon the left hand, with a loud shoutynge,
And thries with hir speres claterynge;
And thries how the ladyes gonne crye;
Ne how that lad° was homward Emelye;
Ne how Arcite is brent to asshen colde;
Ne how that lyche-wake° was yholde
Al thilke nyght; ne how the Grekes pleye
The wake-pleyes°, ne kepe° I nat to seye;
Who wrastleth best naked with oille enoynt°,
Ne who that baar hym best, in no disjoynt°.
I wol nat tellen eek how that they goon
Hoom til Atthenes, whan the pley is doon;
But shortly to the point thanne wol I wende°,
And maken of my longe tale an ende.
By processe° and by lengthe of certeyn yeres,
Al stynted° is the moornynge and the teres
Of Grekes, by oon general assent.
Thanne semed me ther was a parlement°
At Atthenes, upon certein pointz and caas°,
Among the whiche pointz yspoken° was
To have with certein contrees alliaunce,
And have fully of Thebans obeisaunce°.
For which this noble Theseus anon
Leet senden after° gentil Palamon,
Unwist of° hym what was the cause and why,
But in his blake clothes sorwefully
He cam at his comandement in hye°.
Tho° sente Theseus for Emelye.
Whan they were set, and hust° was al the place,
And Theseus abiden° hadde a space
Er any word cam fram his wise brest,
His eyen sette he ther as was his lest°.
And with a sad visage° he siked stille°,
And after that right thus he seyde his wille°:
"The Firste Moevere of the cause above°,
Whan he first made the faire cheyne of love,
Greet was th'effect and heigh was his entente.
Wel wiste° he why and what therof he mente,
For with that faire cheyne of love he bond°
The fyr, the eyr, the water, and the lond
In certeyn° boundes, that they may nat flee.
That same Prince and that same Moevere," quod he,
"Hath stabilissed° in this wrecched world adoun°
Certeyn dayes and duracioun
To al that is engendred° in this place,
Over the whiche day they may nat pace°,
Al mowe they° yet tho dayes wel abregge°.
Ther nedeth noght noon auctoritee allegge°,
For it is preeved° by experience,
But that° me list declaren my sentence°.
Thanne may men by this ordre wel discerne
That thilke° Moevere stable is and eterne.
Wel may men knowe, but° it be a fool,
That every part dirryveth° from his hool°,
For nature hath nat taken his° bigynnyng
Of no partie° or cantel° of a thyng,
But of a thyng that parfit° is and stable,
Descendynge so til it be corrumpable°.
And therfore, of his wise purveiaunce°,

2948 hire vestimentz, *their clothing,* **were,** *wear* **2949 coppes,** *cups* **2950 wood,** *crazed* **2951 route,** *company* **2952 Thries,** *three times* **2956 lad,** *led* **2958 lyche-wake,** *body watch* **2960 wake-pleyes,** *funeral games,* **kepe,** *care* **2961 enoynt,** *anointed* **2962 in no disjoynt,** *without difficulty* **2965 wende,** *pass* **2967 processe,** *course of events* **2968 stynted,** *ceased* **2970 parlement,** *formal discussion* **2971 pointz and caas,** *issues and cases* **2972 yspoken,** *decided* **2974 obeisaunce,** *submission* **2976 Leet senden after,** *sent for* **2977 Unwist of,** *unknown to* **2979 in hye,** *in haste* **2980 Tho,** *then,* **2981 hust,** *hushed* **2982 abiden,** *waited* **2984 ther as was his lest,** *where it pleased him* **2985 sad visage,** *steady expression,* **siked stille,** *sighed quietly* **2986 seyde his wille,** *announced his decision* **2987 cause above,** *ultimate cause* **2990 wiste** *knew* **2991 bond,** *bound* **2993 certeyn,** *fixed* **2995 stabilissed,** *established,* **adoun,** *down here* **2997 engendred,** *born* **2998 pace,** *pass* **2999 Al mowe they,** *although they may,* **abregge,** *shorten* **3000 allegge,** *to call on* **3001 preeved,** *proved* **3002 But that,** *except,* **me list declaren,** *it pleases me to clarify,* **sentence,** *meaning* **3004 thilke,** *the same* **3005 but,** *unless* **3006 dirryveth,** *derives,* **hool,** *whole* **3007 his,** *its* **3008 partie,** *part,* **cantel,** *portion* **3009 parfit,** *perfect* **3010 corrumpable,** *able to decay* **3011 purveiaunce,** *providence*

2952 Thries, El reads "Tries." **fyr,** El reads "place." **2963 eek,** Hg reads "al." **how that they,** Hg reads "how they." **2967 certeyn yeres,** the passing of years is Chaucer's adjustment; in *Teseida,* the wedding takes place only days after the funeral. **2973–74 alliaunce . . . Thebans,** the political motivation for the marriage of Palamon and Emelye is not found in the *Teseida.* **2987 Firste Moevere,** the *primum mobile* (first mover; God) of *Bo* 1m5, 3pr12, etc., who sets all things in motion. **2988 faire cheyne of love,** the Platonic concept of a great ontological hierarchy descending from God through humans to other forms of animate and inanimate life, all held together by love, appears in *Bo* 2m8 and elsewhere. **2992 fyr . . . eyr . . . water . . . lond,** according to classical and medieval cosmology, all physical creation is composed of these four elements. **2994 same Moevere,** Hg omits "same." **2999 wel,** omitted in Hg. **3000 noght,** omitted in Hg. **3006 dirryveth . . . hool,** the Platonic notion that partiality derives from wholeness, as imperfection descends from perfection; *Bo* 3pr10. Hg reads "is diryved" for "dirryveth." **3007 nat,** omitted in El. **3008 or cantel,** El and Hg read "or of cantel." **3011 purveiaunce,** Chaucer's usual form for *providence,* i.e., foresight.

He hath so wel biset his ordinaunce°,
That speces° of thynges and progressiouns°
Shullen enduren by sucessiouns°,
And nat eterne°, withouten any lye°.
This maystow understonde and seen at eye°.
"Loo° the ook°, that hath so long a norisshynge
From tyme that it first bigynneth sprynge,
And hath so long a lif, as we may see,
Yet at the laste wasted is the tree.
"Considereth eek how that the harde stoon
Under oure feet, on which we trede and goon°,
Yet wasteth it as it lyth by the weye.
The brode ryver somtyme wexeth° dreye.
The grete tounes se we wane and wende°.
Thanne may ye se that al this thyng° hath ende.
"Of man and womman seen we wel also
That nedeth°, in oon of thise termes two°,
This is to seyn in youthe or elles age,
He moot be deed, the kyng as shal a page,
Som in his bed, som in the depe see,
Som in the large feeld, as men may see—
Ther helpeth noght, al goth that ilke° weye.
Thanne may I seyn that al this thyng moot deye°.
"What maketh this but Juppiter, the kyng,
That is prince and cause of alle thyng,
Convertynge° al unto his propre welle°
From which it is dirryved°, sooth° to telle?
And heer-agayns° no creature on lyve°,
Of no degree, availleth° for to stryve.
"Thanne is it wysdom, as it thynketh me,
To maken vertu of necessitee,
And take it weel° that we may nat eschue°,
And namely that° to us alle is due.
And whoso gruccheth ought°, he dooth folye,
And rebel is to hym that al may gye°.
And certeinly a man hath moost honour
To dyen in his excellence and flour°,
Whan he is siker° of his goode name;
Thanne hath he doon his freend, ne hym, no shame.
And gladder oghte his freend been of his deeth,
Whan with honour up yolden° is his breeth,
Than whan his name apalled° is for age,
For° al forgeten is his vassellage°.
Thanne is it best, as for a worthy fame,
To dyen whan that he is best of name.
"The contrarie of al this is wilfulnesse.
Why grucchen° we, why have we hevynesse,
That goode Arcite, of chivalrie flour°,
Departed is with duetee° and honour
Out of this foule prisoun of this lyf?
Why grucchen heere his cosyn and his wyf
Of his welfare, that loved hem° so weel?
Kan he hem° thank—nay, God woot°, never a deel°—
That bothe his soule and eek hemself offende°?
And yet they mowe hir lustes nat amende°.
What may I concluden of this longe serye°?
But after wo I rede° us to be merye,
And thanken Juppiter of al his grace.
And er that we departen from this place
I rede we make of sorwes two
O parfit joye, lastynge everemo.
And looketh now wher moost sorwe is herinne,
Ther wol we first amenden° and bigynne.
"Suster," quod he, "this is my fulle assent°,
With al th'avys° heere of my parlement,
That gentil Palamon, youre owene knyght,
That serveth yow with wille, herte, and myght,
And ever hath doon syn° ye first hym knewe,
That ye shul of youre grace upon hym rewe°,
And taken hym for housbonde and for lord.
Lene° me youre hond, for this is oure accord.
Lat se° now of youre wommanly pitee.
He is a kynges brother sone, pardee,
And though he were a poure bacheler°,

3012 ordinaunce, *hierarchy* **3013 speces,** *species,* **progressiouns,** *processes* **3014 by sucessiouns,** *in succession* **3015 eterne,** *eternally,* **lye,** *lie* **3016 at eye,** *plainly* **3017 Loo,** *behold,* **ook,** *oak* **3022 trede and goon,** *tread and walk* **3024 wexeth,** *becomes* **3025 wende,** *pass away* **3026 al this thyng,** *everything* **3028 nedeth,** *necessarily,* **termes two,** *two periods of life* **3033 ilke,** *same* **3034 moot deye,** *must die* **3037 Convertynge,** *returning,* **his propre welle,** *its own source* **3038 dirryved,** *derived,* **sooth,** *truth* **3039 heer-agayns,** *against this,* **on lyve,** *alive* **3040 availleth,** *benefits* **3043 weel,** *well,* **eschue,** *avoid* **3044 namely that,** *especially that which* **3045 whoso gruccheth ought,** *whoever grumbles at all* **3046 may gye,** *guides* **3048 flour,** *flower* **3049 siker,** *certain* **3052 up yolden,** *yielded up* **3053 apalled,** *grown pale* **3054 For,** *because,* **vassellage,** *service* **3058 grucchen,** *complain* **3059 of chivalrie flour,** *flower of chivalry* **3060 duetee,** *respect* **3063 hem,** *him* **3064 hem,** *them,* **woot,** *knows,* **never a deel,** *not a bit* **3065 offende,** *injure* **3066 mowe hir lustes nat amende,** *cannot resolve their desires* **3067 serye,** *series of points* **3068 rede,** *advise* **3074 amenden,** *make better* **3075 fulle assent,** *sincere desire* **3076 th'avys,** *the advice* **3079 syn,** *since* **3080 rewe,** *take pity* **3082 Lene,** *give* **3083 Lat se,** *show* **3085 bacheler,** *young knight*

3016 at eye, El reads "it eye." **3018 From tyme,** Hg reads "Fro the tyme." **bigynneth,** Hg reads "gynneth." **3019 we,** Hg reads "ye." **3022 trede,** Hg reads "ryde." **3023 Yet wasteth it,** Hg reads "It wasteth." **3025 tounes,** El reads "toures" (towers). **3026 may,** omitted in Hg. **3032 men,** Hg reads "ye." **3034 that,** omitted in El. **3042 maken vertu of necessitee,** the same proverbial phrase occurs in *SqT* 5.593 and *TC* 4.1586. **3052 up yolden is,** Hg reads "yolden is up." **3056 that,** omitted in Hg. **3060 and honour,** Hg reads "and with honour." **3063 loved,** Hg reads "loveth." **3070 that,** omitted in Hg. **3074 we,** Hg reads "I." **3077 youre,** El reads "thyn." **3078 herte and,** Hg reads "and herte." **3079 syn ye,** El reads "syn that ye."

Syn he hath served yow so many a yeer,
And had for yow so greet adversitee,
It moste been considered, leeveth° me,
For gentil mercy oghte to passen right°."
  Thanne seyde he thus to Palamon the knight,
"I trowe° ther nedeth litel sermonyng°
To make yow assente to this thyng.
Com neer, and taak youre lady by the hond."
  Bitwixen hem was maad anon the bond
That highte° matrimoigne or mariage,
By al the conseil and the baronage.
And thus with alle blisse and melodye
Hath Palamon ywedded Emelye.
And God, that al this wyde world hath wroght,
Sende hym his love that hath it deere aboght°,
For now is Palamon in alle wele°,
Lyvynge in blisse, in richesse, and in heele°,
And Emelye hym loveth so tendrely,
And he hire serveth also gentilly°,
That nevere was ther no word hem bitwene
Of jalousie or any oother teene°.
Thus endeth Palamon and Emelye,
And God save al this faire compaignye. Amen.

Heere is ended the Knyghtes Tale.

3088 leeveth, *believe* **3089 passen right,** *surpass prerogative* **3091 trowe,** *believe,* **sermonyng,** *preaching* **3095 highte,** *is called* **3100 deere aboght,** *dearly bought* **3101 alle wele,** *complete joy* **3102 heele,** *health* **3104 gentilly,** *nobly* **3106 teene,** *pain*

3090 the knight, El reads "ful right." **3099 wyde,** omitted in Hg. **3100 hath,** omitted in El. **3104 also,** El and Hg read "so." **3105 nevere,** omitted in Hg.

From woodcut made by W.H. Hooper and published by the Chaucer Society between 1868 and 1879

Miller's Tale

Prologue

Heere folwen the wordes bitwene the Hoost and the Millere.

Whan that the Knyght had thus his tale ytoold,
In al the route° ne was ther yong ne oold
That he ne seyde it was a noble storie
And worthy for to drawen to memorie°,
And namely the gentils everichon°.
Oure Hooste lough and swoor, "So moot° I gon°,
This gooth aright; unbokeled° is the male°.
Lat se° now who shal telle another tale.
For trewely the game is wel bigonne.
Now telleth ye, sire Monk, if that ye konne
Somwhat to quite with° the Knyghtes tale."
The Millere, that fordronken° was al pale
So that unnethe° upon his hors he sat,
He nolde avalen° neither hood ne hat,
Ne abyde° no man for his curteisie,
But in Pilates voys he gan to crie,
And swoor, "By armes and by blood and bones,
I kan° a noble tale for the nones°,
With which I wol now quite° the Knyghtes tale."
Oure Hooste saugh that he was dronke of ale,
And seyde, "Abyd°, Robyn, my leeve° brother,
Som bettre man shal telle us first another.
Abyd, and lat us werken thriftily°."
"By Goddes soule," quod he, "that wol nat I,
For I wol speke or elles go my wey."
Oure Hoost answerde, "Tel on, a devele wey°!
Thou art a fool; thy wit is overcome."
"Now herkneth°," quod the Millere, "alle and some°.
But first I make a protestacioun:
That I am dronke, I knowe it by my soun°.
And therfore if that I mysspeke or seye,
Wyte it° the ale of Southwerk, I you preye.
For I wol telle a legende and a lyf
Bothe of a carpenter and of his wyf,

3110 route, *company* **3112 drawen to memorie,** *remember* **3113 gentils everichon,** *each upper-class person* **3114 moot,** *might,* **gon,** *go* **3115 unbokeled,** *unbuckled,* **male,** *purse* **3116 Lat se,** *let's see* **3119 quite with,** *repay* **3120 fordronken,** *very drunk* **3121 unnethe,** *barely* **3122 nolde avalen,** *would not remove* **3123 abyde,** *wait for* **3126 kan,** *know,* **nones,** *occasion* **3127 quite,** *pay back* **3129 Abyd,** *wait,* **leeve,** *dear* **3131 thriftily,** *properly* **3134 a devele wey,** *by the devil's path* **3136 herkneth,** *listen,* **alle and some,** *everybody* **3138 soun,** *sound* **3140 Wyte it,** *blame.*

3110 route ne was, Hg reads "compaignie nas." **3114 So moot I gon,** an exclamation meaning something like "As I may walk" or "(I swear) by the fact that I am walking." **3118 ye,** Hg reads "on." **3120 al,** Hg reads "a." **3124 Pilates voys,** in popular religious plays, Pontius Pilate was a roaring loudmouth. **3125 By armes . . . ,** by God's arms and blood and bones, an extravagant oath. **3129 my,** omitted in Hg. **3140 you,** omitted in El and Hg.

How that a clerk hath set the wrightes° cappe."
The Reve answerde and seyde, "Stynt thy clappe°!
Lat be thy lewed° dronken harlotrye°.
It is a synne and eek a greet folye
To apeyren° any man, or hym defame,
And eek to bryngen wyves in swich fame°.
Thou mayst ynogh° of othere thynges seyn°."
This dronke Millere spak ful soone ageyn
And seyde, "Leve brother Osewold,
Who° hath no wyf, he is no cokewold°.
But I sey nat therfore that thou art oon°.
Ther been ful goode wyves many oon,
And evere a thousand goode ayeyns° oon badde.
That knowestow wel thyself, but° if thou madde°.
Why artow° angry with my tale now?
I have a wyf, pardee°, as wel as thow,
Yet nolde I°, for the oxen in my plogh,
Take upon me moore than ynogh,
As demen° of myself that I were oon.
I wol bileve wel that I am noon.
An housbonde shal nat been inquisityf
Of Goddes pryvetee°, nor of his wyf.
So° he may fynde Goddes foyson° there,
Of the remenant nedeth nat° enquere."
What sholde I moore seyn, but this Millere
He nolde° his wordes for no man forbere°,
But tolde his cherles° tale in his manere.
M'athynketh° that I shal reherce it heere.
And therfore every gentil wight° I preye,
For Goddes love, demeth° nat that I seye
Of yvel entente, but that I moot° reherce
Hir° tales alle, be they bettre or werse,
Or elles falsen° som of my mateere.
And therfore, whoso list° it nat yheere,
Turne over the leef° and chese° another tale;
For he shal fynde ynowe°, grete and smale,
Of storial° thyng that toucheth gentillesse°,
And eek moralitee and hoolynesse.
Blameth nat me if that ye chese amys°.
The Millere is a cherl°, ye knowe wel this,
So was the Reve and other manye mo,
And harlotrie° they tolden bothe two°.
Avyseth yow°, and put me out of blame;
And eek men shal nat maken ernest of game°.

Heere bigynneth the Millere his tale.

Whilom° ther was dwellynge at Oxenford°
A riche gnof° that gestes heeld to bord°,
And of his craft he was a carpenter.
With hym ther was dwellynge a poure scoler,
Hadde lerned art°, but al his fantasye°
Was turned for to lerne astrologye,
And koude° a certeyn° of conclusiouns°,
To demen° by interrogaciouns°,
If that men asked hym in certein houres
Whan that men sholde have droghte° or elles shoures°,
Or if men asked hym what sholde bifalle°
Of every thyng—I may nat rekene° hem alle.
This clerk was cleped hende° Nicholas.
Of deerne° love he koude° and of solas°,
And therto he was sleigh° and ful privee°,

3143 wrightes, *carpenter's* **3144 Stynt thy clappe,** *stop your chatter* **3145 lewed,** *ignorant,* **harlotrye,** *vulgarity* **3147 apeyren,** *injure* **3148 swich fame,** *such reputation* **3149 ynogh,** *enough,* **seyn,** *say* **3152 Who,** *who-ever,* **cokewold,** *cuckold* **3153 oon,** *one* **3155 ayeyns,** *compared with* **3156 but if,** *unless,* **madde** (are) *crazy* **3157 artow,** *are you* **3158 pardee,** *by God* **3159 nolde I,** *I wouldn't* **3161 demen,** *to consider* **3164 Goddes pryvetee,** *God's secrets* **3165 So,** *if,* **foyson,** *plenty* **3166 nedeth nat,** (he) *need not* **3168 nolde,** *wouldn't* **forbere,** *hold back* **3169 cherles,** *peasant's* **3170 M'athynketh,** *I regret* **3171 gentil wight,** *gentleperson* **3172 demeth,** *judge* **3173 moot,** *must* **3174 Hir,** *their* **3175 falsen,** *falsify* **3176 whoso list,** *whoever wants* **3177 leef,** *page,* **chese,** *choose* **3178 ynowe,** *enough* **3179 storial,** *narrative,* **gentillesse,** *gentility* **3181 amys,** *improperly* **3182 cherl,** *low-born fellow* **3184 harlotrie,** *vulgarity,* **bothe two,** *both of them* **3185 Avyseth yow,** *be advised* **3186 ernest of game,** *seriousness from play* **3187 Whilom,** *once,* **Oxenford,** *Oxford* **3188 gnof,** *oaf,* **gestes heeld to bord,** *took in guests as boarders* **3191 art,** *the liberal arts,* **fantasye,** *desire* **3193 koude,** (he) *knew,* **certeyn,** *number,* **conclusiouns,** *formulas* **3194 demen,** *assess,* **interrogaciouns,** *questions* **3196 droghte,** *drought,* **shoures,** *showers* **3197 sholde bifalle,** *might happen* **3198 rekene,** *tally* **3199 cleped hende,** *called handy* (see note) **3200 deerne,** *secret,* **koude,** *knew,* **solas,** *pleasure* **3201 sleigh,** *sly,* **ful privee,** *very secretive*

3143 set the . . . cappe, "set the cap," an idiom meaning "make a fool of him." The Reeve is a carpenter; see *RvP* 1.3861. **3155–56** Lines omitted in Hg and several other manuscripts. **3159 oxen in my plogh,** euphemism for genitalia, as plowing is a traditional sexual metaphor. This also seems to echo *KnT* 1.887. **3160–61 Take upon me . . . ,** assume more than is necessary and consider myself to be a cuckold. **3170–86** The epilogue to Boccaccio's *Decameron* includes an apology that is in some ways similar to Chaucer's. **3172** Hg reads "Demeth noght for Goddes love that I seye." **3173 that,** Hg reads "for." **3183 and other manye mo,** Hg reads "eek and othere mo". **3187 at,** Hg reads "in." **3195 certein houres,** astrological predictions depend on the positions of the stars at certain hours. **3199 hende,** consistently applied to Nicholas, the adjective means "handy" and "nearby" as well as "courteous." **3200 deerne love,** secret love, in the courtly tradition thought to intensify desire.

And lyk a mayden meke° for to see.
A chambre hadde he in that hostelrye
Allone, withouten any compaignye,
Ful fetisly ydight° with herbes swoote°,
And he hymself as sweete as is the roote
Of lycorys° or any cetewale°.
His Almageste° and bookes grete and smale,
His astrelabie° longynge for° his art,
His augrym° stones layen faire apart,
On shelves couched° at his beddes heed;
His presse° ycovered with a faldyng reed°;
And al above ther lay a gay sautrie°,
On which he made a-nyghtes melodie
So swetely that al the chambre rong,
And *Angelus ad virginem* he song,
And after that he song the Kynges Noote.
Ful often blessed was his myrie throte.
And thus this sweete clerk his tyme spente
After° his freendes fyndyng° and his rente°.
This carpenter hadde wedded newe° a wyf,
Which that he lovede moore than his lyf.
Of eighteteene yeer she was of age.
Jalous he was, and heeld hire narwe° in cage,
For she was yong and wylde, and he was old,
And demed° hymself been lik a cokewold.
He knew nat Catoun, for his wit was rude°,
That bad° man sholde wedde his simylitude°.
Men sholde wedden after hire estaat°,
For youthe and elde is often at debaat.
But sith° that he was fallen in the snare,
He moste° endure, as oother folk, his care.
Fair was this yonge wyf, and therwithal°
As any wezele° hir body gent° and smal°.
A ceynt° she werede°, ybarred° al of silk,
A barmclooth° eek as whit as morne° milk
Upon hir lendes°, ful of many a goore°;
Whit was hir smok°, and broyden° al bifoore
And eek bihynde, on hir coler° aboute,
Of col-blak silk, withinne and eek withoute;
The tapes° of hir white voluper°
Were of the same suyte of° hir coler;
Hir filet° brood of silk, and set ful hye.
And sikerly° she hadde a likerous° eye.
Ful smale ypulled° were hire browes° two,
And tho° were bent and blake as any sloo°.
She was ful moore blisful° on to see°
Than is the newe pere-jonette° tree,
And softer than the wolle is of a wether°.
And by hir girdel heeng° a purs of lether,
Tasseled with silk and perled° with latoun°.
In al this world, to seken up and doun,
Ther nys° no man so wys that koude thenche°
So gay a popelote° or swich° a wenche.
Ful brighter was the shynyng of hir hewe°
Than in the Tour the noble° yforged newe.
But of hir song, it was as loude and yerne°
As any swalwe° sittynge on a berne°.
Therto° she koude skippe and make game
As any kyde° or calf folwynge his dame°.
Hir mouth was sweete as bragot° or the meeth°,
Or hoord of apples leyd in hey° or heeth°.
Wynsynge° she was as is a joly colt,
Long as a mast, and upright° as a bolt°.
A brooch she baar° upon hir lowe coler
As brood as is the boos° of a bokeler°.
Hir shoes were laced on hir legges hye.

3202 meke, *meek* **3205 Ful fetisly ydight,** *very elegantly furnished,* **swoote,** *sweet* **3207 lycorys,** *licorice,* **cetewale,** *zedoary* (a spice) **3208 Almageste,** *astrology book* **3209 astrelabie,** *astrolabe,* **longynge for,** *belonging to* **3210 augrym,** *arithmetic* **3211 couched,** *arranged* **3212 presse,** *cupboard,* **faldyng reed,** *red coarse cloth* **3213 sautrie,** *harp* **3220 After,** *according to,* **freendes fyndyng,** *support from friends,* **rente,** *income* **3221 newe,** *recently* **3224 narwe,** *closely* **3226 demed,** *thought* **3227 rude,** *ignorant* **3228 That bad,** *who asserted,* **simylitude,** *equal* **3229 after hire estaat,** *according to their condition* **3231 sith,** *since* **3232 moste,** *must* **3233 therwithal,** *moreover* **3234 wezele,** *weasel,* **gent,** *delicate,* **smal,** *slender* **3235 ceynt,** *belt,* **werede,** *wore,* **ybarred,** *striped* **3236 barmclooth,** *apron,* **morne,** *morning* **3237 lendes,** *loins,* **goore,** *attached pleat* **3238 smok,** *dress,* **broyden,** *embroidered* **3239 coler,** *collar* **3241 tapes,** *ties,* **voluper,** *bonnet* **3242 suyte of,** *pattern as* **3243 filet,** *headband* **3244 sikerly,** *certainly,* **likerous,** *inviting* **3245 ypulled,** *plucked,* **browes,** *eyebrows* **3246 tho,** *those,* **sloo,** *blackthorn berry* **3247 blisful,** *splendid,* **on to see,** *to look at* **3248 pere-jonette,** *blossoming pear* **3249 wether,** *sheep* **3250 heeng,** *hung* **3251 perled,** *decorated,* **latoun,** *brass* **3253 nys,** *isn't,* **koude thenche,** *could imagine* **3254 popelote,** *doll,* **swich,** *such* **3255 hewe,** *complexion* **3256 noble,** *gold coin* **3257 yerne,** *lively* **3258 swalwe,** *swallow,* **berne,** *barn* **3259 Therto,** *also* **3260 kyde,** *kid,* **dame,** *mother* **3261 bragot,** *honey ale,* **meeth,** *mead* **3262 hey,** *hay,* **heeth,** *heather* **3263 Wynsynge,** *skittish* **3264 upright,** *straight,* **bolt,** *arrow* **3265 baar,** *wore* **3266 boos,** *central disk,* **bokeler,** *small shield*

3204 The line echoes *KnT* 1.2779. **3209 astrelabie,** astrolabe, a device for determining the position of the stars. **3210 augrym stones,** cubes marked with Arabic numerals for computation. **3216 *Angelus ad virginem*,** "The Angel to the Virgin," a hymn commemorating the angel Gabriel's Annunciation of the coming birth of Jesus to Mary (whose husband was a carpenter, as is Alisoun's). **3217 Kynges Noote,** an unidentified song, "The King's Tune." **3220 freendes fyndyng,** compare *GP* 1.299–302 and 301–02n. **3224 narwe in cage,** a metaphor for restricting her closely. **3225 yong and wilde,** Hg reads "wilde and yong." **3227 Catoun,** Dionysius Cato, supposed author of *Disticha Catonis* (Cato's Couplets), a collection of maxims used as a medieval schoolbook. **3236 eek,** omitted in El and Hg. **3246 any,** Hg reads "is a." **3248 pere-jonette tree,** pear trees were symbols of sexuality. **3251 silk,** El reads "grene." **3254 wenche,** the connotations ranged from "lass" to "prostitute." **3256 Tour,** Tower of London, site of the mint. **3258 swalwe,** the swallow was thought to be lascivious.

She was a prymerole°, a piggesnye°,
For any lord to leggen° in his bedde,
Or yet for any good yeman° to wedde.
Now sire, and eft° sire, so bifel the cas°
That on a day this hende Nicholas
Fil° with this yonge wyf to rage° and pleye,
Whil that hir housbonde was at Oseneye—
As clerkes ben ful subtile and ful queynte°—
And prively he caughte hire by the queynte°,
And seyde, "Ywis°, but if ich° have my wille,
For deerne° love of thee, lemman°, I spille°,"
And heeld hire harde by the haunche-bones°,
And seyde, "Lemman, love me al atones,
Or I wol dyen, also God me save!"
And she sproong as a colt dooth in the trave°,
And with hir heed she wryed° faste awey,
And seyde, "I wol nat kisse thee, by my fey°.
Why, lat be," quod she, "lat be, Nicholas,
Or I wol crie, 'out, harrow°' and 'allas'!
Do wey youre handes, for youre curteisye."
This Nicholas gan mercy for to crye,
And spak so faire, and profred him° so faste°,
That she hir love hym graunted atte laste,
And swoor hir ooth by Seint Thomas of Kent
That she wol been at his comandement,
Whan that she may hir leyser° wel espie°.
"Myn housbonde is so ful of jalousie
That but ye wayte wel and been privee°,
I woot° right wel I nam° but deed," quod she.
"Ye moste been ful deerne°, as in this cas."
"Nay, therof care° thee noght," quod Nicholas.
"A clerk hadde litherly biset° his whyle°,
But if he koude° a carpenter bigyle°."
And thus they been accorded and ysworn
To wayte a tyme, as I have told biforn.
Whan Nicholas had doon thus everideel°,
And thakked° hire aboute the lendes° weel,
He kist hire sweete and taketh his sawtrie°,
And pleyeth faste, and maketh melodie.
Thanne fil it thus, that to the paryssh chirche°,
Cristes owene werkes for to wirche°,
This goode wyf wente on an haliday°.
Hir forheed shoon as bright as any day,
So was it wasshen whan she leet° hir werk.
Now was ther of that chirche a parissh clerk°,
The which that° was ycleped° Absolon.
Crul° was his heer, and as the gold it shoon,
And strouted° as a fanne° large and brode—
Ful streight and evene lay his joly shode°.
His rode° was reed°, his eyen greye as goos°.
With Poules° wyndow corven° on his shoos,
In hoses rede° he wente fetisly°.
Yclad° he was ful smal° and proprely
Al in a kirtel° of a lyght waget°—
Ful faire and thikke been the poyntes° set—
And therupon he hadde a gay surplys°
As whit as is the blosme° upon the rys°.
A myrie child° he was, so God me save.
Wel koude he laten° blood, and clippe, and shave,
And maken a chartre of lond or acquitaunce°.
In twenty manere° koude he trippe° and daunce
After the scole° of Oxenforde tho°,
And with his legges casten° to and fro,
And pleyen songes on a smal rubible°,
Therto he song somtyme a loud quynyble°,
And as wel koude he pleye on a giterne°.
In al the toun nas° brewhous ne taverne

3268 prymerole, *primrose,* **piggesnye,** *pig's eye* **3269 leggen,** *lay* **3270 yeman,** *yeoman* **3271 eft,** *again,* **bifel the cas,** *happened the chance* **3273 Fil,** *happened,* **rage,** *romp* **3275 queynte,** *clever* **3276 queynte,** *crotch* **3277 Ywis,** *surely,* **but if ich,** *unless I* **3278 deeme,** *secret,* **lemman,** *beloved,* **spille,** *die* (with play on ejaculate?) **3279 haunchebones,** *thighs* **3280 atones,** *at once* **3282 trave,** *pen for shoeing unruly horses* **3283 wryed,** *twisted* **3284 fey,** *faith* **3286 harrow,** *help* **3289 profred him,** *urged himself* (on her), **faste,** *eagerly* **3293 leyser,** *opportunity,* **espie,** *spy* **3295 privee,** *cautious* **3296 woot,** *know,* **nam,** *am not* **3297 deerne,** *secretive* **3298 care,** *concern* **3299 litherly biset,** *badly used,* **whyle,** *time* **3300 But if he koude,** *unless he could,* **bigyle,** *trick* **3303 everideel,** *every bit* **3304 thakked,** *patted,* **lendes,** *loins* **3305 sawtrie,** *harp* **3307 paryssh chirche,** *parish church* **3308 wirche,** *perform* **3309 haliday,** *holy day* **3311 leet,** *left* **3312 parissh clerk,** *assistant to the priest* **3313 The which that,** *who,* **ycleped,** *named* **3314 Crul,** *curled* **3315 strouted,** *spread out,* **fanne,** *fan* **3316 joly shode,** *pretty part in his hair* **3317 rode,** *complexion,* **reed,** *rosy,* **goos,** *goose* **3318 Poules,** *Paul's,* **corven,** *cut* **3319 hoses rede,** *red stockings,* **fetisly,** *elegantly* **3320 Yclad,** *dressed,* **smal,** *daintily* **3321 kirtel,** *tunic,* **lyght waget,** *pale blue* **3322 poyntes,** *laces* **3323 surplys,** *outer gown* **3324 blosme,** *blossom,* **rys,** *branch* **3325 child,** *young man* **3326 laten,** *let* **3327 acquitaunce,** *legal release* **3328 manere,** *ways,* **trippe,** *cavort* **3329 scole,** *fashion,* **tho,** *then* **3330 casten,** *fling* **3331 rubible,** *fiddle* **3332 quynyble,** *high treble* **3333 giterne,** *guitar* **3334 nas,** (there) *was no*

3268 prymerole . . . piggesnye, flower names, and perhaps terms of endearment. **3274 Oseneye,** Osney, less than a mile from central Oxford and site of an abbey of Augustinian canons, at whose church carpenter John works; see lines 3659ff. below. **3285 she,** El and Hg read "Ich." **3289 him,** El reads "hire." **3291 Seint Thomas of Kent,** Thomas à Becket. **3304 aboute,** Hg reads "upon." **3313 Absolon,** recalls the Biblical Absolom, a beautiful man who was killed after his long hair tangled him in a tree; 2 Samuel 14.25,18.9ff. **3318 Poules wyndow,** the design of a window at St. Paul's Cathedral was cut into his shoes; very fashionable. **3322 set,** omitted here in Hg, but added to the end of the previous line. **3326 laten blood, and clippe, and shave,** the clerk Absolon was also a bloodletter (minor surgeon) and a barber, skilled with cutting instruments; see 3766n. On bloodletting, see *KnT* 1.2743n. **3328 In,** Hg reads "On." **3333 a,** El reads "his."

That he ne visited with his solas°
Ther° any gaylard tappestere° was.
But sooth° to seyn, he was somdeel squaymous°
Of fartyng, and of speche daungerous°.
  This Absolon, that jolif° was and gay,
Gooth with a sencer° on the haliday,
Sensynge° the wyves of the parisshe faste.
And many a lovely° look on hem he caste,
And namely on this carpenteris wyf.
To looke on hire hym thoughte a myrie lyf,
She was so propre and sweete and likerous°.
I dar wel seyn, if she hadde been a mous,
And he a cat, he wolde hire hente anon°.
This parissh clerk, this joly Absolon,
Hath in his herte swich a love-longynge
That of no wyf took he noon offrynge—
For curteisie, he seyde, he wolde noon.
  The moone, whan it was nyght, ful brighte shoon,
And Absolon his gyterne° hath ytake,
For paramours° he thoghte for to wake°.
And forth he gooth, jolif and amorous,
Til he cam to the carpenteres hous
A litel after cokkes hadde ycrowe°,
And dressed hym up° by a shot-wyndowe°
That was upon the carpenteris wal.
He syngeth in his voys gentil and smal,
"Now, deere lady, if thy wille be,
I praye yow that ye wole rewe° on me,"
Ful wel acordaunt° to his gyternynge.
This carpenter awook and herde him synge,
And spak unto his wyf and seyde anon,
"What, Alison, herestow nat° Absolon,
That chaunteth thus under oure boures° wal?"
And she answerde hir housbonde therwithal,
"Yis, God woot°, John, I heere it every deel°."
  This passeth forth; what wol ye bet° than weel°?
Fro day to day this joly Absolon
So woweth° hire that hym is wobigon°.
He waketh al the nyght and al the day;
He kembeth° his lokkes brode, and made hym gay;
He woweth hire by meenes° and brocage°,
And swoor he wolde been hir owene page;
He syngeth, brokkynge° as a nyghtyngale;
He sente hire pyment°, meeth°, and spiced ale,
And wafres°, pipyng hoot out of the gleede°;
And, for° she was of towne, he profreth meede°—
For som folk wol ben wonnen for richesse,
And somme for strokes°, and somme for gentillesse.
  Somtyme, to shewe° his lightnesse° and maistrye°,
He pleyeth Herodes upon a scaffold hye°.
But what availleth° hym as in this cas?
She loveth so this hende Nicholas
That Absolon may blowe the bukkes horn°;
He ne hadde for his labour but a scorn.
And thus she maketh Absolon hire ape,
And al his ernest turneth til a jape°.
Ful sooth° is this proverbe, it is no lye,
Men seyn right thus, "Alwey the nye slye°
Maketh the ferre leeve° to be looth°."
For though that Absolon be wood or wrooth°
By cause that he fer° was from hire sighte,
This nye° Nicholas stood in his lighte.
  Now bere thee wel, thou hende Nicholas,
For Absolon may waille and synge, "Allas!"
And so bifel it on a Saterday
This carpenter was goon til Osenay,
And hende Nicholas and Alisoun

3335 solas, *entertainment* **3336 Ther,** *where,* **gaylard tappestere,** *lively barmaid* **3337 sooth,** *true,* **somdeel squaymous,** *somewhat squeamish* **3338 daungerous,** *standoffish* **3339 jolif,** *merry* **3340 sencer,** *censer* **3341 Sensynge,** *incensing* **3342 lovely,** *amorous* **3345 likerous,** *desirable* **3347 hente anon,** *seize at once* **3353 gyterne,** *guitar* **3354 paramours,** *love,* **wake,** *stay up* **3357 ycrowe,** *crowed* **3358 dressed hym up,** *situated himself,* **shot-wyndowe,** *hinged window* **3362 rewe,** *have pity* **3363 acordaunt,** *harmonious* **3366 herestow nat,** *don't you hear* **3367 boures,** *bedroom's* **3368 therwithal,** *in that regard* **3369 woot,** *knows,* **deel,** *bit* **3370 bet,** *better,* **weel,** *well* **3372 woweth,** *woos,* **wobigon,** *woeful* **3374 kembeth,** *combs* **3375 meenes,** *go-betweens,* **brocage,** *use of agents* **3377 brokkynge,** *trilling* **3378 pyment,** *wine punch,* **meeth,** *mead* **3379 wafres,** *cakes,* **gleede,** *coals* **3380 for,** *because,* **profreth meede,** *offered money* **3382 for strokes,** *by force* **3383 shewe,** *show off,* **lightnesse,** *agility,* **maistrye,** *skill* **3384 scaffold hye,** *raised platform* (a stage) **3385 availleth,** *benefits* **3387 blowe the bukkes horn,** *go whistle* **3390 jape,** *joke* **3391 sooth,** *true* **3392 nye slye,** *sly one nearby* **3393 ferre leeve,** *distant lover,* **looth,** *loathed* **3394 wood or wrooth,** *crazy or angry* **3395 fer,** *far* **3396 nye,** *nearby*

3339 jolif, frequently applied to Absolon, the term meant "merry," even "frisky" or "amorous." **3340 sencer,** a portable incense burner used in church rituals. The aromatic smoke symbolized Christian zeal and the act of censing conveyed honor, although Absolon uses it otherwise. **3350 took,** Hg reads "ne took." **offrynge,** priests and their clerks usually accepted offerings to support themselves and the local church. **3362 rewe,** El reads "thynke." **3364 hym,** omitted in El. **3371 to day,** El reads "to day to day"; mistaken repetition. **3370 what wol ye bet than weel,** an idiom meaning "what more do you expect?" **3384 pleyeth Herodes,** played Herod, a raging bully in religious dramas. **3396 stood in his lighte,** i.e., got in his way.

Acorded been to this conclusioun,
That Nicholas shal shapen° hym a wyle°
This sely° jalous housbonde to bigyle°,
And if so be the game wente aright,
She sholde slepen in his arm al nyght,
For this was his desir and hire also.
And right anon, withouten wordes mo,
This Nicholas no lenger wolde tarie°,
But dooth ful softe° unto his chambre carie
Bothe mete and drynke for a day or tweye°,
And to hire housbonde bad hire for to seye,
If that he axed° after Nicholas,
She sholde seye she nyste° where he was,
Of al that day she saugh hym nat with eye;
She trowed° that he was in maladye,
For for no cry hir mayde koude hym calle,
He nolde answere for thyng° that myghte falle°.
  This passeth forth al thilke° Saterday,
That Nicholas stille in his chambre lay,
And eet° and sleep, or dide what hym leste°,
Til Sonday, that the sonne gooth to reste.
  This sely carpenter hath greet merveyle°
Of Nicholas, or what thyng myghte hym eyle°,
And seyde, "I am adrad°, by Seint Thomas,
It stondeth nat aright with Nicholas.
God shilde° that he deyde° sodeynly!
This world is now ful tikel°, sikerly°.
I saugh° today a cors° yborn to chirche
That now°, on Monday last, I saugh hym wirche.
  "Go up," quod he unto his knave° anoon,
"Clepe° at his dore, or knokke with a stoon.
Looke how it is, and tel me boldely."
  This knave gooth hym up ful sturdily°,
And at the chambre dore whil that he stood
He cride and knokked as that he were wood°,
"What? How? What do ye, maister Nicholay?
How may ye slepen al the longe day?"
  But al for noght; he herde nat a word.
An hole he foond, ful lowe upon a bord,
Ther as the cat was wont° in for to crepe,
And at that hole he looked in ful depe,
And at the laste he hadde of hym a sighte.
This Nicholas sat capyng° evere uprighte,
As he had kiked° on the newe moone.
Adoun he gooth and tolde his maister soone
In what array° he saugh this ilke° man.
  This carpenter to blessen hym bigan,
And seyde, "Help us, Seinte Frydeswyde!
A man woot° litel what hym shal bityde°.
This man is falle, with his astromye,
In som woodnesse° or in som agonye.
I thoghte ay° wel how that it sholde be—
Men sholde nat knowe of Goddes pryvetee°.
Ye°, blessed be alwey a lewed° man
That noght but oonly his bileve kan°!
So ferde° another clerk with astromye;
He walked in the feeldes for to prye°
Upon the sterres, what ther sholde bifalle°,
Til he was in a marle-put yfalle°—
He saugh nat that. But yet, by Seint Thomas,
Me reweth soore of° hende Nicholas.
He shal be rated of° his studiyng,
If that I may, by Jhesus, hevene kyng!
Get me a staf, that I may underspore°,
Whil that thou, Robyn, hevest up the dore.
He shal out° of his studiyng, as I gesse."
And to the chambre dore he gan hym dresse°.
His knave was a strong carl° for the nones°,
And by the haspe° he haaf it of° atones;
Into the floor the dore fil anon.
This Nicholas sat ay° as stille as stoon,
And evere caped° upward into the eir.
This carpenter wende° he were in despeir,
And hente° hym by the sholdres myghtily,

3403 shapen, *plan,* **wyle,** *scheme* **3404 sely,** *foolish* (see note), **bigyle,** *deceive* **3409 tarie,** *delay* **3410 softe,** *quietly* **3411 tweye,** *two* **3413 axed,** *asked* **3414 nyste,** *didn't know* **3416 trowed,** *believed* **3418 thyng,** *anything,* **falle,** *happen* **3419 passeth forth al thilke,** *goes on all that* **3421 eet,** *ate,* **hym leste,** *pleased him* **3423 merveyle,** *wonder* **3424 eyle,** *ail* **3425 adrad,** *afraid* **3427 shilde,** *forbid,* **deyde,** *should die* **3428 ful tikel,** *very uncertain,* **sikerly,** *certainly* **3429 saugh,** *saw,* **cors,** *corpse* **3430 now,** *now* (come to think of it) **3431 knave,** *servant* **3432 Clepe,** *call* **3434 sturdily,** *confidently* **3436 wood,** *crazed* **3441 was wont,** *was accustomed* **3444 capyng,** *gaping,* **uprighte,** *straight up* **3445 kiked,** *stared* **3447 array,** *condition,* **ilke,** *same* **3450 woot,** *knows,* **hym shal bityde,** *will happen to him* **3452 woodnesse,** *madness* **3453 ay,** *always* **3454 pryvetee,** *secrets* **3455 Ye,** *yes,* **lewed,** *ignorant* **3456 bileve kan,** *faith knows* **3457 ferde,** *fared* **3458 prye,** *study* **3459 what ther sholde bifalle,** *to predict the future* **3460 marle-put yfalle,** *day pit fallen* **3462 Me reweth soore of,** *I have much pity for* **3463 rated of,** *scolded for* **3465 underspore,** *pry up* **3467 shal out,** *shall come out* **3468 gan hym dresse,** *turned his attention* **3469 carl,** *fellow,* **for the nones,** *for the task* **3470 haspe,** *latch,* **haaf it of,** *heaved it off* **3472 ay,** *all this time* **3473 caped,** *gaped* **3474 wende,** *thought* **3475 hente,** *seized*

3404 sely, recurrently applied to John, the term is the ancestor of "silly," ranging in meaning from "innocent" or "simple" to "not shrewd, doltish." **3407 his . . . hire,** Hg reads "hir . . . his." **3418 for thyng,** Hg reads "for no thyng." **3422 the,** omitted in Hg. **3430 on,** Hg reads "a." **3444 capyng evere,** Hg reads "evere capyng." **3447 this,** El reads "that." **3449 Seinte Frydeswyde,** St. Frideswide was the patron saint of Oxford, known for her ability to heal the sick. **3465 underspore,** John pries the door up because medieval doors were hung on upright hinge pins. **3466 up,** El reads "of" (off). **3470 of,** Hg reads "up." **3473 upward,** Hg reads "up."

And shook hym harde and cride spitously°,
"What, Nicholay, what? How? What, looke adoun!
Awake and thenk on Cristes passioun!
I crouche° thee from elves and fro wightes°."
Therwith the nyght-spel° seyde he anon-rightes°
On foure halves° of the hous aboute,
And on the thresshfold° of the dore withoute:
"Jhesu Crist and Seint Benedight,
Blesse this hous from every wikked wight,
For nyghtes verye°, the White Pater Noster.
Where wentestow°, Seint Petres soster?"
And atte laste this hende Nicholas
Gan for to sike° soore, and seyde, "Allas,
Shal al the world be lost eftsoones° now?"
This carpenter answerde, "What seystow°?
What! Thynk on God, as we doon, men that swynke°."
This Nicholas answerde, "Fecche me drynke,
And after wol I speke in pryvetee
Of certeyn thyng that toucheth me and thee.
I wol telle it noon oother man, certeyn."
This carpenter goth doun and comth ageyn,
And broghte of myghty° ale a large quart.
And whan that ech of hem had dronke his part,
This Nicholas his dore faste shette°,
And doun the carpenter by hym he sette.
He seyde, "John, myn hooste, lief° and deere,
Thou shalt upon thy trouthe swere me heere
That to no wight° thou shalt this conseil wreye°,
For it is Cristes conseil that I seye.
And if thou telle it man, thou art forlore°,
For this vengeaunce thou shalt han therfore°,
That if thou wreye me, thou shalt be wood°."
"Nay, Crist forbede it, for his hooly blood,"
Quod tho° this sely man. "I nam no labbe°,
Ne, though I seye°, I nam nat lief to gabbe°.
Sey what thou wolt, I shal it nevere telle
To child ne wyf, by hym that harwed° helle!"
"Now, John," quod Nicholas, "I wol nat lye.
I have yfounde in myn astrologye,
As I have looked in the moone bright,
That now a Monday next, at quarter nyght°
Shal falle a reyn°, and that so wilde and wood°
That half so greet was nevere Noees flood.
This world," he seyde, "in lasse° than an hour
Shal al be dreynt°, so hidous is the shour.
Thus shal mankynde drenche°, and lese hir lyf°."
This carpenter answerde, "Allas, my wyf!
And shal she drenche? Allas, myn Alisoun!"
For sorwe of this he fil almoost adoun,
And seyde, "Is ther no remedie in this cas?"
"Why, yis, for Gode," quod hende Nicholas,
"If thou wolt werken after loore and reed°.
Thou mayst nat werken after thyn owene heed°,
For thus seith Salomon, that was ful trewe,
'Werk al by conseil, and thou shalt nat rewe°.'
And if thou werken wolt by good conseil,
I undertake°, withouten mast and seyl°,
Yet shal I saven hire and thee and me.
Hastow nat herd hou saved was Noe,
Whan that oure Lord hadde warned hym biforn
That al the world with water sholde be lorn°?"
"Yis," quod this Carpenter, "ful yoore° ago."
"Hastou nat herd," quod Nicholas, "also
The sorwe° of Noe with his felaweshipe,
Er° that he myghte gete his wyf to shipe?
Hym hadde be levere°, I dar wel undertake,
At thilke° tyme, than alle his wetheres blake°

3476 spitously, *roughly* **3479 crouche,** *bless,* **wightes,** *creatures* **3480 nyght-spel,** *nighttime charm,* **anon-rightes,** *immediately* **3481 halves,** *sides* **3482 thresshfold,** *threshold* **3485 For nyghtes verye,** *from night spirits* (?) **3486 wentestow,** *did you go* **3488 sike,** *sigh* **3489 eftsoones,** *again soon* **3490 seystow,** *say you* **3491 swynke,** *work* **3497 myghty,** *strong* **3499 shette,** *shut* **3501 lief,** *beloved* **3503 wight,** *person,* **wreye,** *reveal* **3505 forlore,** *lost* **3406 han therfore,** *have for this* **3407 be wood,** *go crazy* **3409 tho,** *then,* **labbe,** *blabbermouth* **3510 seye,** *speak,* **nam nat lief to gabbe,** *don't like to gab* **3512 harwed,** *broke open* **3516 quarter nyght,** *about 9 p.m.* **3517 reyn,** *rain,* **wood,** *violent* **3519 lasse,** *less* **3520 dreynt,** *drowned* **3521 drenche,** *drown,* **lese hir lyf,** *lose their lives* **3527 werken after loore and reed,** *follow learning and advice* **3528 heed,** *notions* **3530 rewe,** *regret* **3532 undertake,** *declare,* **seyl,** *sail* **3536 lorn,** *lost* **3537 yoore,** *long* **3539 sorwe,** *sorrow* **3540 Er,** *before* **3541 Hym hadde be levere,** *he would have rather* **3542 thilke,** *that,* **wetheres blake,** *black rams*

3477 What, look adoun, Hg omits "What." **3478 Cristes passioun,** the sufferings of Jesus that culminated in his crucifixion. **3482 of,** Hg reads "on." **3483 Seint Benedight,** St. Benedict, a convenient rhyme. **3485 White Pater Noster,** white Our Father, here a comic charm or incantation, indicating superstition. **3486 Seint Petres soster,** otherwise unknown, St. Peter's sister is cited in at least one English charm. **3501 He,** Hg reads "And." **3505 it,** omitted in El. **3510 Ne,** Hg reads "And." **3512 hym that harwed helle,** Jesus's breaking down the gates of hell is described in the popular though apocryphal Gospel of Nicodemus, 16–17. **3518 Noees flood,** recounted in Genesis 7.11ff., Noah's Flood was understood to separate the righteous from the sinful. The Flood began April 17 (Genesis 7.11), perhaps the first day of the Canterbury pilgrimage (see *GP* 1.8n). Hg reads "Nowels flood." **3529–30 Salomon . . . ,** the quotation is Ecclesiasticus 32.24, a book in the Catholic Bible often attributed to Solomon by confusion with Ecclesiastes. See *MerT* 4.1485–86 and *Mel* 7.1003. **3539 sorwe of Noe,** in popular religious dramas, the shrewish reluctance of Noah's wife to board the ark is a comic scene; the Bible has no parallel scene. **3540 gete,** El reads "brynge." **3541 be,** omitted in Hg.

That she hadde had a ship hirself allone.
And therfore, woostou° what is best to doone?
This asketh° haste, and of an hastif° thyng
Men may nat preche or maken tariyng°.
  "Anon go gete us faste into this in°
A knedyng trogh°, or ellis° a kymelyn°,
For ech of us, but looke that they be large,
In which we mowe swymme° as in a barge,
And han° therinne vitaille° suffisant
But for a day—fy on° the remenant°!
The water shal aslake° and goon away
Aboute pryme° upon the nexte day.
But Robyn may nat wite° of this, thy knave,
Ne eek thy mayde Gille I may nat save.
Axe° nat why, for though thou aske me,
I wol nat tellen Goddes pryvetee.
Suffiseth thee, but if thy wittes madde°,
To han as greet a grace° as Noe hadde.
Thy wyf shal I wel saven, out of doute.
Go now thy wey, and speed thee heer-aboute°.
  "But whan thou hast for hire and thee and me
Ygeten° us thise knedyng tubbes thre,
Thanne shaltow hange hem in the roof
    ful hye°,
That no man of oure purveiaunce° spye.
And whan thou thus hast doon as I have seyd,
And hast oure vitaille faire° in hem yleyd°,
And eek° an ax to smyte° the corde atwo°,
Whan that the water comth that we may go,
And breke an hole an heigh upon° the gable
Unto the gardyn-ward°, over the stable,
That we may frely passen forth oure way,
Whan that the grete shour is goon away,
Thanne shaltou swymme as myrie, I
    undertake,
As dooth the white doke after hire drake.
Thanne wol I clepe°, 'How, Alison! How, John!
Be myrie, for the flood wol passe anon.'
And thou wolt seyn, 'Hayl, maister Nicholay!
Good morwe, I se thee wel, for it is day.'
And thanne shul we be lordes al oure lyf
Of al the world, as Noe and his wyf.
  "But of o thyng I warne thee ful right:
Be wel avysed on that ilke° nyght
That we ben entred into shippes bord°,
That noon of us ne speke nat a word,
Ne clepe°, ne crie, but been in his preyere,
For it is Goddes owene heeste° deere.
  "Thy wyf and thou moote° hange fer atwynne°,
For° that bitwixe yow shal be no synne,
Namoore in lookyng than ther shal in deede.
This ordinance° is seyd. Go, God thee speede.
Tomorwe at nyght, whan folk ben alle aslepe,
Into oure knedyng tubbes wol we crepe,
And sitten there, abidyng° Goddes grace.
Go now thy wey, I have no lenger space°
To make of this no lenger sermonyng°.
Men seyn thus, 'sende the wise, and sey nothyng.'
Thou art so wys it needeth thee nat teche°.
Go, save oure lyf, and that I the biseche°."
  This sely carpenter goth forth his wey.
Ful ofte he seith "allas" and "weylawey,"
And to his wyf he tolde his pryveetee,
And she was war° and knew it bet° than he,
What al this queynte cast was for to seye°.
But nathelees she ferde° as she wolde deye,
And seyde, "Allas! go forth thy wey anon,
Help us to scape°, or we been dede echon!
I am thy trewe, verray° wedded wyf—
Go, deere spouse, and help to save oure lyf."
  Lo, which° a greet thyng is affeccioun°!
Men may dyen of ymaginacioun,
So depe may impressioun be take.
This sely carpenter bigynneth quake°.
Hym thynketh verraily that he may see
Noees flood come walwynge° as the see
To drenchen° Alisoun, his hony deere.
He wepeth, weyleth, maketh sory cheere°;
He siketh° with ful many a sory swogh°;
He gooth and geteth hym a knedyng trogh,
And after that a tubbe and a kymelyn,
And pryvely he sente hem° to his in°,

3544 woostou, *do you know* **3545 asketh,** *requires,* **hastif,** *hasty* **3546 maken tariyng,** *delay* **3547 in,** *house* **3548 knedyng trogh,** *kneading trough,* **ellis,** *else,* **kymelyn,** *brewing vat* **3550 mowe swymme,** *may float* **3551 han,** *have,* **vitaille,** *food* **3552 fy on,** *damn,* **remenant,** *rest* **3553 aslake,** *subside* **3554 pryme,** *9 a.m.* **3555 wite,** *know* **3557 Axe,** *ask* **3559 but if thy wittes madde,** *unless you are crazy* **3560 grace,** *favor* **3562 speed thee heer-aboute,** *hasten yourself in doing this* **3564 Ygeten,** *gotten* **3565 hye,** *high* **3566 purveiaunce,** *foresight* or *preparation* **3568 faire,** *duly,* **yleyd,** *laid* **3569 eek,** *also,* **smyte,** *cut,* **atwo,** *in two* **3571 an heigh upon,** *high up in* **3572 Unto the gardyn-ward,** *toward the garden* **3577 clepe,** *call* **3584 ilke,** *same* **3585 into shippes bord,** *aboard ship* **3587 clepe,** *call* **3588 heeste,** *command* **3589 moote,** *must,* **fer atwynne,** *far apart* **3590 For,** *so* **3592 ordinance,** *decree* **3595 abidyng,** *waiting for* **3596 space,** *time* **3597 sermonyng,** *preaching* **3599 teche,** *teach* **3600 the biseche,** *beg you* **3604 war,** *aware,* **bet,** *better* **3605 queynte cast was for to seye,** *clever plan meant* **3606 ferde,** *acted* **3608 scape,** *escape* **3609 verray,** *faithful* **3611 which,** *what,* **affeccioun,** *emotion* **3614 quake,** *to tremble* **3616 walwynge,** *billowing* **3617 drenchen,** *drown* **3618 sory cheere,** *sad faces* **3619 siketh,** *sighs,* **swogh,** *groan* **3622 hem,** *them,* **in,** *dwelling*

3575 shaltou, El reads "shal I." **3576 hire,** Hg reads "his" (its). **3577 wol I,** Hg reads "woltow." **3593 folk,** Hg reads "men." **3599 nat teche,** El reads "nat to preche." **3602 seith,** Hg reads "seyde." **3608 dede,** El reads "lost."

And heng hem in the roof in pryvetee.
His° owene hand he made laddres thre
To clymben by the ronges° and the stalkes°
Into the tubbes hangynge in the balkes°,
And hem vitailleth°, bothe trogh and tubbe,
With breed and chese and good ale in a jubbe°,
Suffisynge right ynogh as for a day.
But er that he hadde maad al this array,
He sente his knave and eek his wenche also
Upon his nede° to London for to go.
And on the Monday, whan it drow° to nyght,
He shette his dore withoute candel lyght,
And dresseth° alle thyng as it shal be.
And shortly, up they clomben° alle thre;
They seten° stille wel a furlong way.
"Now, Pater Noster°, clom°!" seyde Nicolay,
And "Clom," quod John, and "Clom," seyde
Alisoun.
This carpenter seyde his devocioun°,
And stille he sit and biddeth° his preyere,
Awaitynge on the reyn, if he it heere.
The dede sleep, for wery bisynesse,
Fil on this carpenter right as I gesse
Aboute corfew-tyme°, or litel moore.
For travaille° of his goost° he groneth soore,
And eft° he routeth°, for his heed myslay°.
Doun of the laddre stalketh Nicholay,
And Alisoun ful softe° adoun she spedde.
Withouten wordes mo they goon to bedde,
Ther as the carpenter is wont° to lye.
Ther was the revel and the melodye,
And thus lith° Alison and Nicholas,
In bisynesse of myrthe and of solas°,
Til that the belle of laudes° gan to rynge,
And freres° in the chauncel° gonne synge.
This parissh clerk, this amorous Absolon,
That is for love alwey so wobigon,
Upon the Monday was at Oseneye
With compaignye, hym to disporte°
and pleye,
And axed° upon cas° a cloisterer°
Ful prively after John the carpenter.
And he drough° hym apart out of the chirche
And seyde, "I noot°, I saugh hym heere nat wirche°
Syn° Saterday. I trowe° that he be went°
For tymber, ther° our abbot hath hym sent.
For he is wont° for tymber for to go
And dwellen at the grange° a day or two.
Or elles he is at his hous, certeyn.
Where that he be, I kan nat soothly seyn."
This Absolon ful joly was and light°,
And thoghte, "Now is tyme to wake al nyght,
For sikirly° I saugh hym nat stirynge
Aboute his dore syn day bigan to sprynge.
"So moot I thryve°, I shal at cokkes crowe
Ful pryvely knokke at his wyndowe
That stant° ful lowe upon his boures° wal.
To Alison now wol I tellen al
My love-longynge, for yet I shal nat mysse
That at the leeste wey° I shal hire kisse.
Som maner confort shal I have, parfay°.
My mouth hath icched° al this longe day—
That is a signe of kissyng atte leeste.
Al nyght me mette eek° I was at a feeste.
Therfore I wol go slepe an houre or tweye,
And al the nyght thanne wol I wake and pleye."
Whan that the firste cok hath crowe, anon
Up rist° this joly lovere Absolon,
And hym arraieth gay° at poynt devys°.
But first he cheweth greyn of lycorys°,
To smellen sweete, er he hadde kembd his heer.
Under his tonge a trewe-love° he beer,
For therby wende° he to ben gracious°.
He rometh° to the carpenteres hous,

3624 His, *by his* **3625 ronges,** *rungs,* **stalkes,** *poles* **3626 balkes,** *beams* **3627 hem vitailleth,** *supplies them with food* **3628 jubbe,** *jug* **3632 nede,** *errand* **3633 drow,** *drew* **3635 dresseth,** *organized* **3636 clomben,** *climbed* **3637 seten,** *sat* **3638 Pater Noster,** (by) *Our Father,* **clom,** *hush* **3640 devocioun,** *prayers* **3641 biddeth,** *prays* **3645 corfew-tyme,** *curfew* (see note) **3646 travaille,** *suffering,* **goost,** *spirit* **3647 eft,** *after,* **routeth,** *snores,* **myslay,** *lay wrong* **3649 softe,** *quietly* **3651 wont,** *accustomed* **3653 lith,** *lie* **3654 solas,** *enjoyment* **3655 of laudes,** *before dawn* **3656 freres,** *friars,* **chauncel,** *choir stalls* **3660 disporte,** *entertain* **3661 axed,** *asked,* **upon cas,** *by chance,* **cloisterer,** *member of the abbey* **3663 drough,** *drew* **3664 noot,** *don't know,* **wirche,** *work* **3665 Syn,** *since,* **trowe,** *believe,* **be went,** *has gone* **3666 ther,** *where* **3667 wont,** *accustomed* **3668 grange,** *farm* **3671 light,** *delighted* **3673 sikirly,** *certainly* **3675 moot I thryve,** *I might succeed* **3677 stant,** *stands,* **boures,** *bedroom's* **3680 at the leeste wey,** *at least* **3681 parfay,** *by faith* **3682 icched,** *itched* **3684 me mette eek,** *I dreamed also* **3688 rist,** *rises* **3689 hym arraieth gay,** *dresses himself gaily,* **at poynt devys,** *in every way* **3690 greyn of lycorys,** *cardamom seed* **3692 trewe-love,** *herb* **3693 wende,** *thought,* **gracious,** *favorable* **3694 rometh,** *walks*

3624 he, omitted in El. **3635 dresseth,** Hg reads "dressed." **shal,** Hg reads "sholde." **3637 a furlong way,** "a short while," an idiom derived from the time it takes to walk a furlong (220 yards). **3645 corfew-tyme,** about 9 p.m., when fires were to be covered. **3646 travaille,** Hg reads "travaillyng." **3653 lith,** omitted in El. **3654 of solas,** Hg reads "in solas." **3655 bell of laudes,** the bell rung to indicate that it is time for the morning prayers called lauds. Lauds follows matins (or are recited in conjunction with matins), followed later in the day by prime, terce, sext, none, vespers, and compline, known collectively as the canonical hours or the Divine Office, a cycle of prayer required of priests and other clerics. **3659 Oseneye,** see 3274n. **3660 With,** El reads "With a." **3672 to,** omitted in El. **3685 go,** El reads "goon." **3690 of,** Hg reads "and." **3692 trewe-love,** an herbal breath sweetener and love charm. **3694 rometh,** the same verb is used to describe romantic walking in *KnT* 1.1065, 1069, 1071, etc.

And stille he stant° under the shot-wyndowe°—
Unto his brest it raughte°, it was so lowe—
And softe he cougheth with a semy soun°:
"What do ye, honycomb, sweete Alisoun,
My faire bryd°, my sweete cynamome°?
Awaketh, lemman° myn, and speketh to me!
Wel litel thynken ye upon my wo,
That for youre love I swete ther° I go.
No wonder is thogh that I swelte° and swete;
I moorne° as dooth a lamb after the tete°.
Ywis°, lemman, I have swich love-longynge
That lik a turtel° trewe is my moornynge.
I may nat ete° na moore than a mayde."
  "Go fro the wyndow, Jakke° fool," she sayde.
"As help me God, it wol nat be 'com pa me°.'
I love another—and elles I were to blame—
Wel bet° than thee, by Jhesu, Absolon.
Go forth thy wey or I wol caste a ston,
And lat me slepe, a twenty devel wey°!"
  "Allas," quod Absolon, "and weylawey,
That trewe love was evere so yvel biset°!
Thanne kysse me, syn° it may be no bet°,
For Jhesus love and for the love of me."
  "Wiltow thanne go thy wey therwith°?" quod she.
  "Ye, certes, lemman," quod this Absolon.
  "Thanne make thee redy," quod she, "I come anon."
And unto Nicholas she seyde stille°,
"Now hust°, and thou shalt laughen al thy fille."
  This Absolon doun sette hym on his knees
And seyde, "I am a lord at alle degrees°,
For after this I hope ther cometh moore.
Lemman°, thy grace, and sweete bryd°, thyn oore°!"
  The wyndow she undoth° and that in haste.
"Have do°," quod she, "com of°, and speed the faste,
Lest that oure neighebores thee espie."
  This Absolon gan wype his mouth ful drie.
Dirk was the nyght as pich°, or as the cole°,
And at the wyndow out she putte hir hole,
And Absolon, hym fil° no bet ne wers°,
But with his mouth he kiste hir naked ers°
Ful savourly°, er he were war° of this.
  Abak he stirte, and thoughte it was amys,
For wel he wiste° a womman hath no berd°.
He felte a thyng al rough and long yherd°,
And seyde, "Fy! allas! what have I do°?"
  "Tehee," quod she and clapte the wyndow to.
And Absolon gooth forth a sory pas°.
  "A berd°, a berd!" quod hende Nicholas.
"By Goddes corpus°, this goth faire and weel."
  This sely Absolon herde every deel°,
And on his lippe he gan for anger byte,
And to hymself he seyde, "I shal thee quyte°,"
  Who rubbeth now, who froteth° now his lippes
With dust, with sond, with straw, with clooth, with chippes,
But Absolon, that seith ful ofte, "Allas."
"My soule bitake° I unto Sathanas°,
But me were levere than al this toun," quod he,
"Of this despit awroken for to be.
Allas," quod he, "allas, I ne hadde ybleynt°!"
His hoote love was coold and al yqueynt°,
For fro that tyme that he hadde kist hir ers
Of paramours° he sette nat a kers°,
For he was heeled of his maladie.
Ful ofte paramours he gan deffie°,
And weep as dooth a child that is ybete°.
A softe paas° he wente over the strete
Until° a smyth men cleped daun° Gerveys,

3695 stant, *stands,* **shot-wyndowe,** *hinged window* **3696 raughte,** *reached* **3697 a semy soun,** *half a sound* (cf. Lat. *semisonus)* **3699 bryd,** *bird* or *bride,* **cynamome,** *cinnamon* **3700 lemman,** *beloved* **3702 swete ther,** *sweat where* **3703 swelte,** *melt* **3704 moorne,** *yearn,* **tete,** *udder* **3705 Ywis,** *surely* **3706 turtel,** *turtledove* **3707 ete,** *eat* **3708 Jakke,** *Jack* **3709 'com pa me,'** *"come kiss me"* **3711 Wel bet,** *much better* **3713 a twenty devel wey,** *by twenty devils' ways* **3715 yvel biset,** *poorly treated* **3716 syn,** *since,* **bet,** *better* **3718 therwith,** *with that* **3721 stille,** *quietly* **3722 hust,** *hush* **3724 degrees,** *respects* **3726 Lemman,** *beloved,* **bryd,** *bird* or *bride,* **oore,** *merry* **3727 undoth,** *opens* **3728 Have do,** *get finished,* **com of,** *hurry* **3731 pich,** *pitch,* **cole,** *coal* **3733 hym fil,** *to him happened,* **wers,** *worse* **3734 ers,** *rump* **3735 Ful savourly,** *with great delight,* **war,** *aware* **3737 wiste,** *knew,* **berd,** *beard* **3738 yherd,** *haired* **3739 do,** *done* **3741 a sory pas,** *at sad pace* **3742 berd,** *trick* (with pun on *beard)* **3743 corpus,** *body* **3744 deel,** *bit* **3746 quyte,** *repay* **3747 froteth,** *scrubs* **3750 bitake,** *pledge,* **Sathanas,** *Satan* (see note) **3753 ybleynt,** *turned away* **3754 yqueynt,** *quenched* **3756 Of paramours,** *for amorousness,* **kers,** *watercress* (see note) **3758 gan deffie,** *did defy* **3759 ybete,** *beaten* **3760 softe paas,** *subdued pace* **3761 Until,** *unto,* **cleped daun,** *called master*

3697 softe he cougheth, El reads "softe he knokketh"; Hg, "ofte he cogheth." **3698–3707** The language is comically reminiscent of Songs of Songs (esp. 4.11–14) and perhaps Psalms 19.10, and an imitation (or parody) of courtly wooing. **3706 turtel,** the turtledove was thought to be the most loyal of lovebirds. **3716 syn it,** Hg reads "syn that it." **3718 therwith,** omitted in El. **3721–22** Lines omitted in Hg. In other versions of this plot, the successful male lover (not the woman) plans and enacts the trick. **3724 a,** omitted in El. **3735 were,** El reads "was." **3750–52** "Curse me, but I would rather be revenged for this insult than have the whole town." **3750 I,** omitted in Hg. **3756 sette nat a kers,** "set not (the value of) at a (water)cress," i.e., didn't value at all.

That in his forge smythed plough harneys°;
He sharpeth shaar° and kultour° bisily.
This Absolon knokketh al esily,
And seyde, "Undo°, Gerveys, and that anon."
"What, who artow?" "It am I, Absolon."
"What, Absolon, for Cristes sweete tree°,
Why rise ye so rathe°? Ey, benedicitee°,
What eyleth° yow? Som gay gerl°, God it woot°,
Hath broght yow thus upon the viritoot°.
By Seinte Note, ye woot wel what I mene."
This Absolon ne roghte° nat a bene°
Of° al his pley; no word agayn he yaf°.
He hadde moore tow° on his distaf
Than Gerveys knew, and seyde, "Freend so deere,
That hoote kultour in the chymenee° heere,
As lene° it me, I have therwith to doone,
And I wol brynge it thee agayn ful soone."
Gerveys answerde, "Certes, were it gold
Or in a poke° nobles alle untold°,
Thou sholdest have, as I am trewe smyth.
Ey, Cristes foo°, what wol ye do therwith?"
"Therof," quod Absolon, "be as be may°.
I shal wel telle it thee tomorwe day"—
And caughte the kultour by the colde stele°.
Ful softe out at the dore he gan to stele°,
And wente unto the carpenteris wal.
He cogheth first and knokketh therwithal
Upon the wyndowe, right as he dide er.
This Alison answerde, "Who is ther
That knokketh so? I warante° it a theef."
"Why, nay," quod he, "God woot°, my sweete leef°,
I am thyn Absolon, my deerelyng°.
Of gold," quod he, "I have thee broght a ryng.
My mooder yaf° it me, so God me save.
Ful fyn° it is and therto° wel ygrave°.
This wol I yeve thee, if thou me kisse."
This Nicholas was risen for to pisse,
And thoughte he wolde amenden al° the jape°;
He sholde kisse his ers er that he scape°.
And up the wyndowe dide he hastily,
And out his ers he putteth pryvely°
Over the buttok, to the haunche-bon°.
And therwith spak this clerk, this Absolon,
"Spek, sweete bryd, I noot nat° where thou art."
This Nicholas anon leet fle° a fart
As greet as it had been a thonder-dent°
That with the strook° he was almoost yblent°,
And he was redy with his iren hoot,
And Nicholas amydde° the ers he smoot°.
Of gooth° the skyn an hande-brede° aboute,
The hoote kultour brende° so his toute°,
And for the smert° he wende for to dye°.
As° he were wood°, for wo he gan to crye,
"Help! Water! Water! Help, for Goddes herte°!"
This carpenter out of his slomber sterte°,
And herde oon° crien° "water" as he were wood,
And thoughte, "Allas, now comth Nowelis flood!"
He sit hym up withouten wordes mo,
And with his ax he smoot the corde atwo,
And doun gooth al; he foond neither to selle°
Ne breed ne° ale til he cam to the celle°,
Upon the floor, and ther aswowne° he lay.

3762 smythed plough harneys, *made plowing equipment* **3763 sharpeth shaar,** *sharpened plow blades,* **kultour,** *turf cutters* **3765 Undo,** *open up* **3767 tree,** *cross* **3768 rathe,** *early,* **benedicitee,** *bless you* **3769 eyleth,** *ails,* **gerl,** *girl,* **woot,** *knows* **3770 viritoot,** *prowl* (?) **3772 roghte,** *cared,* **bene,** *bean* **3773 Of,** *for,* **agayn he yaf,** *gave he in response* **3774 tow,** *flax* (see note) **3776 chymenee,** *fireplace* **3777 As lene,** *lend* **3780 poke,** *sack,* **nobles alle untold,** *coins uncounted* **3782 Cristes foo,** (by) *Christ's foe* **3783 be as be may,** (it will) *be as it may be* (i.e., never mind) **3785 stele,** *handle* **3786 stele,** *sneak* **3791 warante,** *swear* **3792 woot,** *knows,* **leef,** *beloved* **3793 deerelyng,** *darling* **3795 yaf,** *gave* **3796 Ful fyn,** *excellent,* **therto,** *also,* **ygrave,** *engraved* **3799 amenden al,** *improve considerably,* **jape,** *joke* **3800 scape,** *escapes* **3802 pryvely,** *secretly* **3803 haunche-bon,** *thigh* **3805 noot nat,** *don't know* **3806 leet fle,** *let fly* **3807 thonder-dent,** *thunderclap* **3808 strook,** *blast,* **yblent,** *blinded* **3810 amydde,** *in the middle of,* **smoot,** *struck* **3811 Of gooth,** *off goes,* **hande-brede,** *hand's breadth* **3812 brende,** *burned,* **toute,** *rump* **3813 smert,** *pain,* **wende for to dye,** *thought he would die* **3814 As,** *as if,* **wood,** *crazed* **3815 herte,** *heart* **3816 sterte,** *jerked* **3817 oon,** *someone,* **crien,** *crying* **3821 foond neither to selle,** *didn't find for selling* **3822 Ne . . . ne,** *neither . . . nor,* **celle,** *floor* **3823 aswowne,** *unconscious*

3766 It am I, Absolon, their familiarity is understandable since Absolon, a bloodletter and barber (line 3326 above), would have known Gerveys, the smith who made and sharpened metal tools. Contemporary records show that smiths did work at night. El reads "I am heere, Absolon." **3770 viritoot,** the word is not found elsewhere; its meaning is uncertain. **3771 Seinte Note,** in legend St. Neot urged King Alfred to establish Oxford University. Musical notes are associated with the sound of anvils in Boethius *De Musica* 1.10. **3774 tow on his distaf,** flax on his distaff, i.e., raw material on the staff used to spin thread by hand. An idiom meaning "more on his mind." **3778 And,** omitted in Hg. **3784 tomorwe,** Hg reads "another." **3800 ers,** omitted in El. **3805 bryd,** Hg reads "herte." **3806 fart,** compare lines 3337–38 above. **3810 amydde the ers,** El reads "amydde ers"; Hg, "in the ers." **3811 hande-brede,** recalls "hende," the adjective used of Nicholas throughout; see line 3199 above. **3813 And,** Hg reads "That." **3818 Nowelis,** John's ignorant confusion of "Noel's" for "Noah's." It is repeated or mocked at line 3834 below. **3820** Compare line 3569 above. **3821–22** A French saying, meaning "he wasted no time": "Ainc tant come il mist à descendre, / Ne trouva pas point de pain a vendre" (When he began to fall, he found no bread to sell at all).

Up stirte hire° Alison and Nicholay,
And criden "out" and "harrow°" in the strete.
The neighebores, bothe smale and grete°,
In ronnen° for to gauren° on this man,
That aswowne lay bothe pale and wan,
For with the fal he brosten° hadde his arm.
But stonde he moste unto his owene harm°,
For whan he spak, he was anon bore doun°
With° hende Nicholas and Alisoun.
They tolden every man that he was wood,
He was agast° so of Nowelis flood
Thurgh fantasie°, that of his vanytee°
He hadde yboght° hym knedyng tubbes thre,
And hadde hem hanged in the roof above;
And that he preyed hem°, for Goddes love,
To sitten in the roof, *par compaignye*°.
The folk gan laughen at his fantasye.
Into the roof they kiken° and they cape°,
And turned al his harm° unto a jape°.
For what so° that this carpenter answerde,
It was for noght, no man his reson herde.
With othes° grete he was so sworn adoun°
That he was holde wood° in al the toun,
For every clerk anonright° heeld with other°.
They seyde, "The man is wood, my leeve brother,"
And every wight gan laughen° at this stryf°.
Thus swyved° was this carpenteris wyf,
For al his kepyng° and his jalousye,
And Absolon hath kist hir nether eye°,
And Nicholas is scalded° in the towte°.
This tale is doon, and God save al the rowte°!

Heere endeth the Millere his Tale.

3824 hire, *herself* **3825 out,** *come out,* **harrow,** *help* **3826 smale and grete,** *unimportant and important* **3827 In ronnen,** *ran in,* **gauren,** *stare* **3829 brosten,** *broken* **3830 unto his owene harm,** *to his own disadvantage* **3831 bore doun,** *brought down* **3832 With,** *by* **3834 agast,** *afraid* **3835 fantasie,** *delusion,* **vanytee,** *folly* **3836 yboght,** *bought* **3838 preyed hem,** *begged them* **3839 par compaignye,** *for companionship* **3841 kiken,** *gaze,* **cape,** *gape* **3842 harm,** *injury,* **jape,** *joke* **3843 what so,** *whatever* **3845 othes,** *oaths,* **sworn adoun,** *talked down* **3846 holde wood,** *thought crazy* **3847 anonright,** *immediately,* **heeld with other,** *sided with each other* **3849 wight gan laughen,** *person did laugh,* **stryf,** *disagreement* **3850 swyved,** *screwed* **3851 kepyng,** *guarding* **3852 nether eye,** *lower eye* **3853 scalded,** *burned,* **towte,** *rump* **3854 rowte,** *company*

3828 That aswowne lay, El reads "That yet aswowne he lay." **3837 roof,** El reads "rove." **3848 is,** El and Hg read "was."

From woodcut made by W.H. Hooper and published by the Chaucer Society between 1868 and 1879

Reeve's Tale

Prologue

The Prologe of the Reves Tale.

Whan folk hadde laughen at this nyce cas°
Of Absolon and hende Nicholas,
Diverse folk diversely they seyde,
But for the moore part they loughe and pleyde.
Ne at this tale I saugh no man hym greve°,
But it were° oonly Osewold the Reve.
By cause he was of carpenteris craft°,
A litel ire° is in his herte ylaft°.
He gan to grucche°, and blamed it a lite.
"So theek," quod he, "ful wel koude I yow quite°
With bleryng° of a proud milleres eye,
If that me liste° speke of ribaudye°.
But ik° am oold, me list no pley for age—
Gras tyme° is doon, my fodder° is now forage°;
This white top writeth° myne olde yeris;
Myn herte is mowled° also as myne heris°—
But if I fare° as dooth an open-ers°.
That ilke° fruyt is ever lenger the wers°,
Til it be roten in mullok° or in stree°.
We olde men, I drede°, so fare we:
Til we be roten, kan we nat be rype;
We hoppen ay whil° that the world wol pype°.
For in oure wyl° ther stiketh evere a nayl,
To have an hoor° heed and a grene tayl°,
As hath a leek; for thogh oure myght° be goon,
Oure wyl desireth folie evere in oon°.

3855 nyce cas, *silly incident* **3859 hym greve,** *trouble himself* **3860 But it were,** *unless it was* **3861 carpenteris craft,** *carpenter's training* **3862 ire,** *anger,* **is . . . ylaft,** *remains* **3863 grucche,** *complain* **3864 quite,** *repay* **3865 bleryng of . . . eye,** *tricking* **3866 me liste,** (it) *pleased me,* **ribaudye,** *vulgar things* **3867 ik,** *I* **3868 Gras tyme,** *fruitful time* (see note), **fodder,** *food,* **forage,** *grazing* **3869 white top writeth,** *white hair indicates* **3870 mowled,** *moldy,* **heris,** *hair* **3871 But if I fare,** *unless I do,* **open-ers,** *open arse* (see note) **3872 ilke,** *same,* **wers,** *worse* **3873 mullok,** *compost,* **stree,** *straw* **3874 drede,** *fear* **3876 hoppen ay whil,** *dance as long as,* **wol pype,** *plays a tune* **3877 wyl,** *will* **3878 hoor,** *white,* **tayl,** *tail* **3879 myght,** *potency* **3880 evere in oon,** *continually*

3860 Osewold, the name Oswald is common in the north of England. **3864 theek,** a dialect form from the north and east of England, a contraction of "thee ik" (might I prosper); Hg reads "the ik." East Anglian forms recur in the Reeve's speech, and northern forms characterize the speech of the two students in the *RvT.* Both dialects are provincial, perhaps satiric, the first sustained, self-conscious use of dialect in English literature. **yow,** Hg reads "thee." **3868 Gras tyme . . . ,** a livestock metaphor: "Good times are done; my food now is only what I can find in the fields after they have been harvested." **3870 mowled also,** Hg reads "also mowled." **3871 I,** Hg reads "ik," although the two forms vary inconsistently in the two manuscripts. **open-ers,** slang for medlar, an applelike fruit that must be stored a long time before it ripens. The slang term derives from its shape. **3872 lenger,** El reads "leng." **3876 hoppen ay . . . ,** recalls Luke 7.32. Hg reads "hoppe alwey." **3877 stiketh evere a nayl,** recalls the "thorn of the flesh" of sexual desire; see 2 Corinthians 12.7. **3878–79** The same (phallic?) comparison between old men and leeks is made by the old man in the introduction to book 4 of Boccaccio's *Decameron.* **3878 heed,** Hg reads "heer."

For whan we may nat doon, than wol we speke;
Yet in oure asshen° olde is fyr yreke°.
"Foure gleedes han° we, whiche I shal devyse°,
Avauntyng°, liyng, anger, coveitise°.
Thise foure sparkles longen unto eelde°.
Oure olde lemes° mowe° wel been unweelde°,
But wyl ne shal nat faillen, that is sooth.
And yet ik have alwey a coltes tooth,
As many a yeer as it is passed henne°
Syn° that my tappe of lif bigan to renne°.
For sikerly°, whan I was bore°, anon
Deeth drough° the tappe of lyf and leet it gon,
And ever sithe° hath so the tappe yronne°
Til that almoost al empty is the tonne°.
The streem of lyf now droppeth° on the chymbe°.
The sely tonge° may wel rynge and chymbe°
Of wrecchednesse° that passed is ful yoore°;
With olde folk, save dotage°, is namoore!"
Whan that our Hoost hadde herd this sermonyng°,
He gan to speke as lordly as a kyng.
He seide, "What amounteth° al this wit?
What° shul we speke alday° of hooly writ°?
The devel made a reve for to preche,
Or of a soutere° a shipman or a leche°.
Sey forth thy tale, and tarie° nat the tyme.
Lo Depeford, and it is half-wey pryme°.
Lo Grenewych, ther° many a shrewe° is inne.
It were al tyme thy tale to bigynne."
"Now, sires," quod this Osewold the Reve,
"I pray yow alle that ye nat yow greve
Thogh I answere and somdeel sette his howve°,
For leveful° is with force force of-showve°.
"This dronke Millere hath ytoold us heer
How that bigyled° was a carpenteer—
Peraventure° in scorn, for I am oon.
And, by youre leve, I shal hym quite° anoon.
Right in his cherles termes° wol I speke.
I pray to God his nekke mote tobreke°.
He kan wel in myn eye seen a stalke°,
But in his owene he kan nat seen a balke°."

Heere bigynneth the Reves Tale.

At Trumpyngtoun, nat fer fro Cantebrigge,
Ther gooth a brook, and over that a brigge°,
Upon the whiche brook ther stant° a melle°;
And this is verray sooth° that I yow telle.
A millere was ther dwellynge many a day;
As eny pecok° he was proud and gay.
Pipen° he koude, and fisshe, and nettes beete°,
And turne coppes°, and wel wrastle and sheete°.
Ay° by his belt he baar a long panade°,
And of° a swerd ful trenchant° was the blade.
A joly poppere° baar he in his pouche—
Ther was no man, for peril, dorste° hym touche.
A Sheffeld thwitel° baar he in his hose.
Round was his face, and camuse° was his nose;
As piled° as an ape was his skulle
He was a market-betere° atte fulle°—
Ther dorste no wight° hand upon hym legge°
That he ne swoor he sholde anon abegge°.

3882 asshen, *ashes,* **yreke,** *raked up* **3883 gleedes han,** *live coals have,* **devyse,** *describe* **3884 Avauntyng,** *boasting,* **coveitise,** *greed* **3885 sparkles longen unto eelde,** *sparks belong to old age* **3886 lemes,** *limbs,* **mowe,** *might,* **unweelde,** *weak* **3889 henne,** *by* **3890 Syn,** *since,* **tappe,** *spigol,* **renne,** *run* **3891 sikerly,** *certainly,* **bore,** *born* **3892 Deeth drough,** *death opened* **3893 sithe,** *since,* **yronne,** *run* **3894 tonne,** *barrel* **3895 droppeth,** *drips,* **chymbe,** *barrel rim* **3896 sely tonge,** *foolish tongue,* **chymbe,** *chime* **3897 Of wrecchednesse,** *about wickedness,* **ful yoore,** *long ago* **3898 save dotage,** *except senility* **3899 sermonyng,** *preaching* **3901 amounteth,** *value has* **3902 What,** *why,* **alday,** *always,* **hooly writ,** *scripture* **3904 soutere,** *shoemaker,* **leche,** *physician* **3905 tarie,** *delay* **3906 half-wey pryme,** *about 7:30* A.M. **3907 ther,** *where,* **shrewe,** *rascal* **3911 howve,** *hood* **3912 leveful,** *permissible,* **of-showve,** *to overthrow* **3914 bigyled,** *tricked* **3915 Peraventure,** *perhaps* **3916 quite,** *repay* **3917 cherles termes,** *low-life language* **3918 mote tobreke,** *might shatter* **3919 stalke,** *stem* **3920 balke,** *beam* **3922 brigge,** *bridge* **3923 stant,** *stands,* **melle,** *mill* **3924 verray sooth,** *absolute truth* **3926 eny pecok,** *any peacock* **3927 Pipen,** *play the pipes,* **beete,** *mend* **3928 coppes,** *cups,* **sheete,** *shoot a bow* **3929 Ay,** *always,* **panade,** *cutlass* **3930 of,** *as,* **trenchant,** *sharp* **3931 joly poppere,** *bright dagger* **3932 dorste,** *dared* **3932 thwitel,** *knife* **3934 camuse,** *snub* **3935 piled,** *bald* **3936 market-betere,** *market-beater, bully* (?), **atte fulle,** *complete* **3937 wight,** *person,* **legge,** *lay* **3938 abegge,** *pay for it*

3886 olde, omitted in Hg. **3888 coltes tooth,** an idiom meaning "youthful desire"; see *WBP* 3.602. **3904 Or,** El reads "And." **a shipman,** El omits "a." **3906–07 Depeford . . . Grenewych,** Deptford and Greenwich, villages on the Canterbury way, four to five miles from Southwark. Chaucer may have been living in Greenwich when he wrote this. **3911 sette his howve,** set his hood; an idiom meaning "to get the best of"; see *GP* 1.586 and *MilP* 1.3143. **3918 tobreke,** El reads "breke." **3919–20** Recalls Matthew 7.3. **3921 Trumpyngtoun,** Trumpington, about two miles south of central Cambridge (**Cantebrigge**), where the site of an old mill can still be located. **3928 turne coppes,** produce wooden cups on a lathe? play a drinking game? **3929 Ay,** El and Hg read "And." **3933 Sheffeld,** Sheffield, a city still famous for its knives.

A theef he was forsothe° of corn° and mele°,
And that a sly, and usaunt° for to stele.
His name was hoote deynous° Symkyn.
A wyf he hadde, ycomen of noble kyn—
The person° of the toun hir fader was.
With hire he yaf ful many a panne° of bras,
For° that Symkyn sholde in his blood allye°.
She was yfostred° in a nonnerye;
For Symkyn wolde no wyf, as he sayde,
But she were wel ynorissed° and a mayde°,
To saven his estaat of yomanrye°.
And she was proud, and peert° as is a pye°.
A ful fair sighte was it upon hem° two:
On halydayes biforn hire wolde he go
With his typet° bounde aboute his heed,
And she cam after in a gyte of reed°;
And Symkyn hadde hosen of the same.
Ther dorste° no wight clepen hire but° "dame";
Was noon so hardy that wente by the weye
That with hire dorste rage° or ones° pleye,
But if he wolde be slayn of Symkyn
With panade°, or with knyf, or boidekyn°.
For jalous folk ben perilous everemo—
Algate° they wolde hire wyves wenden° so.
And eek, for she was somdel smoterlich°,
She was as digne° as water in a dich°,
And ful of hoker° and of bisemare°.
Hir thoughte that a lady sholde hire spare°,
What for hire kynrede° and hir nortelrie°
That she hadde lerned in the nonnerie.
  A doghter hadde they bitwixe hem two
Of twenty yeer, withouten any mo,
Savynge a child that was of half yeer age;
In cradel it lay and was a propre page°.
This wenche thikke and wel ygrowen was,
With kamuse° nose and eyen greye as glas,
Buttokes brode and brestes rounde and hye,
But right fair was hire heer, I wol nat lye.
  This person° of the toun, for she was feir,
In purpos was° to maken hire his heir,
Bothe of his catel° and his mesuage°,
And straunge° he made it of hir mariage°.
His purpos was for to bistowe hire hye°
Into som worthy blood of auncetrye°,
For hooly chirches good° moot been despended°
On hooly chirches blood, that is descended.
Therfore he wolde his hooly blood honoure,
Though that he hooly chirche sholde devoure.
  Greet sokene° hath this millere, out of doute,
With whete and malt of al the land aboute;
And nameliche° ther was a greet collegge,
Men clepen° the Soler Halle at Cantebregge,
Ther was hir° whete and eek hir malt ygrounde.
And on a day it happed, in a stounde°,
Sik lay the maunciple° on a maladye.
Men wenden wisly° that he sholde dye,
For which this millere stal° bothe mele and corn
And hundred tyme moore than biforn;
For therbiforn° he stal but curteisly,
But now he was a theef outrageously,
For which the wardeyn° chidde and made fare°.
But therof sette the millere nat a tare°;
He craketh boost°, and swoor it was nat so.
  Thanne were ther yonge poure° clerkes two,
That dwelten in this halle, of which I seye.

3939 forsothe, *truly,* **corn,** *whole grain,* **mele,** *ground grain* **3940 usaunt,** *accustomed* **3941 hoote deynous,** *called proud* **3943 person,** *parson* **3944 panne,** *pan* (see note) **3945 For,** *so,* **in his blood allye,** *make an alliance into the family* **3946 yfostred,** *brought up* **3948 ynorissed,** *raised,* **mayde,** *virgin* **3949 saven his estaat of yomanrye,** *keep up his status as a freeholder* **3950 peert,** *saucy,* **pye,** *magpie* **3951 upon hem,** (to look) *at them* **3953 typet,** *long end of his hood* **3954 gyte of reed,** *red garment* **3956 dorste,** *dared,* **clepen hire but,** *call her* (anything) *but* **3958 rage,** *flirt,* **ones,** *once* **3960 panade,** *cutlass,* **boidekyn,** *dagger* **3962 Algate,** *at least,* **wenden,** *believed* **3963 somdel smoterlich,** *somewhat stained* (by illegitimacy) **3964 digne,** *proud,* **dich,** *ditch* **3965 hoker,** *scorn,* **bisemare,** *contempt* **3966 hire spare,** *be aloof* **3967 kynrede,** *kindred,* **nortelrie,** *nurture* **3972 page,** *boy* **3974 kamuse,** *snub* **3977 person,** *parson* **3978 In purpos was,** *intended* **3979 catel,** *possessions,* **mesuage,** *house* **3980 straunge,** *difficult,* **of hir mariage,** *for her to marry* **3981 hye,** *high* **3982 auncetrye,** *ancestry* **3983 good,** *goodness* or *goods,* **moot been despended,** *must be spent* **3987 Greet sokene,** *large monopoly* **3989 nameliche,** *especially* **3990 clepen,** *call* **3991 hir,** *their* **3992 in a stounde,** *at one time* **3993 maunciple,** *purchaser* **3994 wenden wisly,** *thought certainly* **3995 stal,** *stole* **3997 therbiforn,** *previously* **3999 wardeyn,** *head of the college,* **chidde and made fare,** *complained and fussed* **4000 tare,** *weed* **4001 craketh boost,** *exclaimed loudly* **4002 poure,** *poor*

3939 was forsothe of corn and mele, El reads "was of corn and eek of mele." **3941 hoote,** Hg reads "hoten" (called). **Symkyn,** familiar form of Symond or Simon. **3944 he yaf ful many a panne of bras,** the parson gave a dowry (to marry off his illegitimate daughter). Hg reads "a" for "of." **3948 But she,** El reads "But if she." **3949 estaat of yomanrye,** there were serfs, who were legally bound to the land they worked, and free peasants (the yeomanry), whose limited rights enabled them to work for their own profits as well as those they owed to lords of the manor. Symkyn has an exaggerated sense of his social class. **3953 bounde,** Hg reads "wounden." **3965 And,** El reads "As." **3973 wenche,** the connotations ranged from "lass" to "prostitute"; the following description is a comic mixture of stereotypic plebeian and aristocratic features. **3975 Buttokes,** Hg reads "With buttokes." **3977 This,** Hg reads "The." **was feir,** Hg reads "was so feir." **3987–88 Greet sokene . . . ,** Symkyn has exclusive legal rights to grind raw grain (for bread) and sprouted grain (**malt,** for beer) in the region. **3990 Soler Halle,** Solar Hall (having many windows to admit sunlight), also known as King's Hall, now part of Trinity College, Cambridge. **3993 lay the,** Hg reads "was this." **4002 clerkes,** Hg reads "scolers." **4003 this,** Hg reads "the."

Testif° they were, and lusty° for to pleye,
And, oonly for hire myrthe and reverye°,
Upon the wardeyn bisily they crye
To yeve° hem leve but a litel stounde°
To goon to mille and seen hir corn ygrounde;
And hardily° they dorste leye° hir nekke
The millere sholde nat stele hem° half a pekke
Of corn by sleighte, ne by force hem reve°;
And at the laste the wardeyn yaf hem leve.
John highte° that oon, and Aleyn highte that oother;
Of o° toun were they born, that highte Strother,
Fer in the north, I kan nat telle where.
  This Aleyn maketh redy al his gere,
And on an hors the sak he caste anon.
Forth goth Aleyn the clerk and also John
With good swerd and bokeler° by hir side.
John knew the wey—hem nedede no gyde—
And at the mille the sak adoun he layth.
Aleyn spak first, "Al hayl, Symond, y-fayth°!
Hou fares thy faire doghter and thy wyf?"
  "Aleyn, welcome," quod Symkyn, "by my lyf.
And John also, how now, what do ye heer°?"
  "Symond," quod John, "by God, nede has na° peer°.
Hym boes° serve hymselve that has na swayn°,
Or elles he is a fool, as clerkes sayn.
Oure manciple, I hope° he wil be deed,
Swa werkes° ay the wanges° in his heed;
And forthy is I° come, and eek Alayn,
To grynde oure corn and carie it ham° agayn.
I pray yow spede us heythen° that ye° may."
  "It shal be doon," quod Symkyn, "by my fay°!
What wol ye doon whil that it is in hande?"
  "By God, right by the hopur° wil I stande,"
Quod John, "and se how that the corn gas° in.
Yet saugh I nevere, by my fader kyn,
How that the hopur wagges° til and fra°."
  Aleyn answerde, "John, and wiltow swa°?
Thanne wil I be bynethe°, by my croun°,
And se how that the mele° falles doun
Into the trough; that sal° be my disport°.
For John, yfaith, I may been of youre sort;
I is° as ille° a millere as ar° ye."
  This millere smyled of hir nycetee°,
And thoghte, "Al this nys doon but for a wyle°.
They wene° that no man may hem bigyle°,
But by my thrift°, yet shal I blere hir eye°,
For al the sleighte° in hir philosophye°.
The moore queynte crekes° that they make,
The moore wol I stele whan I take.
Instide of flour yet wol I yeve hem bren°.
The gretteste clerkes been noght wisest men,
As whilom° to the wolf thus spak the mare.
Of al hir art° ne counte I noght a tare°."
  Out at the dore he gooth ful pryvely°,
Whan that he saugh his tyme, softely.
He looketh up and doun til he hath founde
The clerkes hors, ther as it stood ybounde
Bihynde the mille, under a lefesel°,
And to the hors he goth hym faire and wel;
He strepeth of° the brydel right anon.
And whan the hors was laus°, he gynneth gon°
Toward the fen ther° wilde mares renne°,
And forth with "wehee," thurgh thikke and thurgh thenne.
  This millere gooth agayn, no word he seyde,
But dooth his note° and with the clerkes pleyde
Til that hir corn was faire and weel ygrounde.
And whan the mele is sakked and ybounde°,
This John goth out and fynt° his hors away,
And gan to crie "Harrow°!" and "Weylaway!
Oure hors is lorn°, Alayn, for Goddes banes°,

4004 Testif, *willful,* **lusty,** *eager* **4005 reverye,** *wildness* **4007 yeve,** *give,* **stounde,** *time* **4009 hardily,** *confidently,* **dorste leye,** *dare bet* **4010 hem,** *from them* **4011 reve,** *rob* **4013 highte,** *was called* **4014 o,** *one* **4019 bokeler,** *small shield* **4022 *y-fayth,** *in faith* **4025 heer,** *here* **4026 *na,** *no,* **peer,** *equal* **4027 Hym *boes,** *it benefits him* (to), **swayn,** *servant* **4029 hope,** *expect* **4030 *Swa werkes,** *so aches,* ***wanges,** *teeth* **4031 forthy *is I,** *therefore am I* **4032 *ham,** *home* **4033 *heythen,** *hence,* **that ye,** *as fast as you* **4034 fay,** *faith* **4036 hopur,** *hopper* (intake bin) **4037 *gas,** *goes* **4039 wagges,** *shakes,* ***til and *fra,** *to and fro* **4040 wiltow *swa,** *will you so* **4041 bynethe,** *beneath,* **croun,** *head* **4042 mele,** *ground grain* **4043 *sal,** *shall,* **disport,** *entertainment* **4045 *is,** *am,* **ille,** *incompetent,* ***ar,** *are* **4046 of hir nycetee,** *at their simplemindedness* **4047 for a wyle,** *as a strategy* **4048 wene,** *think,* **hem bigyle,** *trick them* **4049 thrift,** *profit,* **blere hir eye,** *blur their eyes* **4050 sleighte,** *cleverness,* **philosophye,** *learning* **4051 queynte crekes,** *clever zigzags* **4053 bren,** *husks* (bran) **4055 whilom,** *once* **4056 hir art,** *their strategy,* **tare,** *weed* **4057 pryvely,** *secretly* **4061 under a lefesel,** *in the shade* **4063 strepeth of,** *strips off* **4064 laus,** *loose,* **gynneth gon,** *did go* **4065 fen ther,** *marsh where,* **renne,** *run* **4068 note,** *task* **4070 sakked and ybounde,** *put in a sack and tied* **4071 fynt,** *finds* **4072 Harrow,** *help* **4073 lorn,** *lost,* ***banes,** *bones*

4010 pekke, peck; a unit of measure, about one-quarter bushel. **4013 Aleyn highte,** El reads "Aleyn heet." **4014 Strother,** the town has not been identified. **4019 and,** Hg reads "and with." **4022ff.** Glosses marked with an asterisk (*) are northern words, forms, or constructions; they characterize the dialect of the students as provincial. **4026 Symond . . . by God,** Hg reads "By God . . . Symond." **4027 boes,** Hg reads "bihoves." **4031 forthy,** Hg reads "therfore." **4032 ham,** Hg reads "heem." **4033 that,** Hg reads "what." **4037 that,** omitted in Hg. **4040 and,** omitted in El and Hg. **4049 blere hir eye,** an idiom meaning "trick them." **4054 noght wisest,** Hg reads "noght the wisest." **4055 to the wolf . . . spak the mare,** in various traditional tales, a mare tells the wolf (or fox) who wants to buy her colt that the price is written on her back hoof. When the wolf goes to read it, she kicks him and, in the Reynard the fox story, comments on how clerks are not always wise. **4057 of,** Hg reads "of." **4066 thurgh thenne,** Hg omits "thurgh." **4070 is,** Hg reads "was." **4073 lorn,** Hg reads "lost."

Step on thy feet! Com of°, man, al at anes°!
Allas, oure wardeyn has his palfrey° lorn."
This Aleyn al forgat bothe mele and corn;
Al was out of his mynde his housbondrie°.
"What, whilk° way is he gane°?" he gan to crie.
The wyf cam lepynge inward with a ren.
She seyde, "Allas! youre hors goth to the fen
With wilde mares, as faste as he may go.
Unthank° come on his hand that boond hym so,
And he that bettre sholde han knyt° the reyne!"
"Allas," quod John, "Aleyn, for Cristes peyne,
Lay doun thy swerd, and I wil myn alswa°.
I is ful wight°, God waat°, as is a raa°;
By Goddes herte, he sal° nat scape us bathe°.
Why nadstow pit° the capul° in the lathe°?
Il-hayl°, by God, Alayn, thou is a fonne°!"
This sely° clerkes han ful faste yronne
Toward the fen, bothe Aleyn and eek John.
And whan the millere saugh that they were gon,
He half a busshel of hir flour hath take
And bad his wyf go knede it in a cake°.
He seyde, "I trowe° the clerkes were aferd°.
Yet kan a millere make a clerkes berd°
For al his art; now lat hem goon hir weye.
Lo, wher they goon! Ye, lat the children pleye.
They gete° hym nat so lightly°, by my croun."
Thise sely clerkes rennen up and doun
With "Keep°! Keep! Stand! Stand! Jossa°! Warderere°!
Ga° whistle thou, and I sal kepe hym heere!"
But shortly°, til that it was verray° nyght,
They koude nat°, though they dide al hir myght,
Hir capul cacche°, he ran alwey so faste,
Til in a dych they caughte hym atte laste.
Wery and weet, as beest° is in the reyn°,
Comth sely John, and with him comth Aleyn.
"Allas," quod John, "the day that I was born!
Now are we dryve til hethyng° and til scorn.
Oure corn is stoln, men wil us fooles calle,
Bathe° the wardeyn and oure felawes alle,
And namely the millere, weylaway!"
Thus pleyneth John as he gooth by the way
Toward the mille, and Bayard in his hond.
The millere sittynge by the fyr he fond,
For it was nyght, and forther° myghte they noght.
But for the love of God they hym bisoght°
Of herberwe° and of ese°, as for hir peny°.
The millere seyde agayn°, "If ther be eny,
Swich° as it is, yet shal ye have youre part.
Myn hous is streit°, but ye han lerned art.
Ye konne° by argumentes make a place
A myle brood of° twenty foot of space.
Lat se now if this place may suffise,
Or make it rowm° with speche as is your gise°."
"Now, Symond," seyde John, "by Seint Cutberd,
Ay is° thou myrie, and this is faire answered.
I have herd seyd, man sal taa° of twa thynges—
Slyk° as he fyndes, or taa slyk as he brynges.
But specially I pray thee, hooste deere,
Get us som mete° and drynke and make us cheere°,
And we wil payen trewely atte fulle.
With empty hand men may none haukes tulle°.
Loo, heere° oure silver, redy for to spende."
This millere into toun his doghter sende
For ale and breed, and rosted hem a goos,
And boond hire hors, it sholde namoore go loos,
And in his owene chambre hem made a bed
With sheetes and with chalons° faire yspred,
Noght from his owene bed ten foot or twelve.
His doghter hadde a bed al by hirselve
Right in the same chambre by and by°.
It myghte be no bet°, and cause why°?
Ther was no roumer herberwe° in the place.

4074 Com of, *hurry,* ***anes,** *once* **4075 palfrey,** *riding horse* **4077 housbondrie,** *responsible management* **4078 *whilk,** *which,* ***gane,** *gone* **4082 Unthank,** *bad luck* **4083 han knyt,** *have tied* **4085 *alswa,** *also* **4086 wight,** *swift,* ***waat,** *knows,* ***raa,** *deer* **4087 *sal,** *shall,* ***bathe,** *both* **4088 nadstow *pit,** *didn't you put,* **capul,** *horse,* ***lathe,** *barn* **4089 *Il-hayl,** *ill health,* **fonne,** *fool* **4090 This sely,** *these foolish* **4094 cake,** *loaf* **4095 trowe,** *believe,* **aferd,** *cautious* **4096 make a . . . berd,** *deceive* **4099 gete,** (will) *get,* **so lightly,** *very easily* **4101 Keep,** *stay,* **Jossa,** *whoa,* **Warderere,** *look out behind* **4102 *Ga,** *go* **4103 shortly,** *in short,* **verray,** *truly* **4104 koude nat,** *were not able to* **4105 Hir capul cacche,** *catch their horse* **4107 as beest,** *as an animal,* **reyn,** *rain* **4110 dryve *til *hethyng,** *driven to derision* **4112 *Bathe,** *both* **4117 forther,** (go) *further* **4118 bisoght,** *asked* **4119 Of herberwe,** *for lodging,* **ese,** *food,* **peny,** *money* **4120 agayn,** *in reply* **4121 Swich,** *such* **4122 streit,** *small* **4123 konne,** *are able to* **4124 of,** *from* **4126 rowm,** *roomy,* **gise,** *habit* **4128 Ay *is,** *always are* **4129 *sal *taa,** *shall take* **4130 *Slyk,** *such* **4132 mete,** *food,* **make us cheere,** *be friendly* **4134 tulle,** *lure* **4135 heere,** *here* (is) **4140 chalons,** *blankets* **4143 by and by,** *alongside* **4144 bet,** *better,* **cause why,** *why's that* **4145 roumer herberwe,** *roomier lodging*

4074 of, El reads "out." **4078 gane,** El reads "geen." **4084 John,** omitted in El. **4087 Goddes,** El and Hg read "God." **4088 nadstow,** El reads "nadtow"; Hg, "ne had thow." **4094 a,** omitted in El. **4097 now,** Hg reads "ye." **4102 sal,** El reads "shal." **4104 dide,** El reads "do." **4111 men,** El reads "me." **4112 Bathe,** Hg reads "Bothe." **4115 Bayard,** a conventional name for a horse. **4123 konne by argumentes,** Symkyn's satire of learned arguments was not uncommon. **4127 John,** Hg reads "this John." **Seint Cutberd,** Cuthbert was a famous monk and bishop of northern England. The pronunciation may play upon the meaning of "berd" in line 4096. **4129–30** The proverb means "One must put up with what is available." Later, the students do take both what they find in Symkyn's house and what they brought to it, at the expense of his pride in his lineage and in his cleverness. **4130 Slyk . . . slyk,** Hg reads "Swilk . . . swilk." Also at 4173. **4138 namoore go,** El reads "nat goon."

They soupen° and they speke, hem to solace°,
And drynken evere strong ale atte beste.
Aboute mydnyght wente they to reste.
Wel hath this millere vernysshed° his heed;
Ful pale he was fordronken and nat reed°.
He yexeth° and he speketh thurgh the nose
As° he were on the quakke° or on the pose°.
To bedde he goth, and with hym goth his wyf.
As any jay° she light was and jolyf,
So was hir joly whistle wel ywet°.
The cradel at hir beddes feet° is set,
To rokken, and to yeve the child to sowke°.
And whan that dronken al was in the crowke°,
To bedde wente the doghter right anon.
To bedde gooth Aleyn and also John—
Ther nas na° moore; hem nedede no dwale°.
This millere hath so wisly bibbed° ale
That as an hors he fnorteth° in his sleep,
Ne of his tayl bihynde he took no keep°.
His wyf bar hym a burdon°, a ful strong;
Men myghte hir rowtyng° heere two furlong°;
The wenche rowteth eek, *par*° *compaignye.*
Aleyn the clerk, that herde this melodye,
He poked John, and seyde, "Slepestow?
Herdestow evere slyk a sang° er now?
Lo, whilk° a complyn° is ymel° hem alle.
A wilde fyr upon thair bodyes falle!
Wha° herkned evere slyk a ferly° thyng?
Ye, they sal have the flour of il endyng°.
This lange° nyght ther tydes° me na reste;
But yet, na fors°, al sal° be for the beste.
For, John," seyde he, "als evere moot I thryve°,
If that I may, yon wenche wil I swyve°.
Som esement° has lawe yshapen° us,
For, John, ther is a lawe that says thus,
That gif° a man in a point be ygreved°,
That in another he sal be releved.
Oure corn is stoln, sothly, it is na nay°,
And we han had an il fit° al this day,
And syn° I sal have neen° amendement
Agayn my los, I wil have esement.
By Goddes saule°, it sal neen other bee°!"
This John answerde, "Alayn, avyse thee°.
The millere is a perilous man," he seyde,
"And gif that he out of his sleep abreyde°,
He myghte doon us bathe a vileynye°."
Aleyn answerde, "I counte hym nat a flye."
And up he rist, and by the wenche he crepte.
This wenche lay uprighte° and faste slepte,
Til he so ny° was er she myghte espie
That it had been to late for to crie,
And shortly for to seyn, they were aton°.
Now pley, Aleyn, for I wol speke of John.
This John lith° stille a furlong wey or two°,
And to hymself he maketh routhe° and wo.
"Allas," quod he, "this is a wikked jape°.
Now may I seyn° that I is but an ape°.
Yet has my felawe somwhat for his harm;
He has the milleris doghter in his arm.
He auntred hym°, and has his nedes sped°,
And I lye as a draf-sek° in my bed.
And when this jape is tald another day,
I sal been halde a daf°, a cokenay°.
I wil arise and auntre° it, by my fayth.
Unhardy° is unseely°, thus men sayth."
And up he roos, and softely he wente
Unto the cradel, and in his hand it hente°,
And baar° it softe° unto his beddes feet.
Soone after this the wyf hir rowtyng leet°,
And gan awake, and wente hire out to pisse,

4146 soupen, *ate,* **hem to solace,** *to satisfy themselves* **4149 vernysshed,** *polished* (see note) **4150 reed,** *red* **4151 yexeth,** *belches* **4152 As,** *as if,* **on the quakke,** *hoarse,* **on the pose,** *had a cold* **4154 jay,** *noisy bird* **4155 ywet,** *wet* (see note) **4156 hir beddes feet,** *foot of her bed* **4157 yeve . . . to sowke,** *breast-feed* **4158 crowke,** *crock* **4161 nas *na,** *wasn't any,* **dwale,** *sleeping potion* **4162 wisly bibbed,** *surely imbibed* **4163 fnorteth,** *snorts* **4164 keep,** *care* **4165 bar hym a burdon,** *accompanied him* **4166 rowtyng,** *snoring,* **furlong,** *220 yards* **4167 par,** *for* **4170 *slyk a *sang,** *such a song* **4171 *whilk,** *such,* **complyn,** *prayer* (see note), ***ymel,** *among* **4173 *Wha,** *who,* **ferly,** *strange* **4174 *sal,** *shall,* **flour of il endyng,** *result of bad outcome* **4175 *lange,** *long,* **tydes,** *comes to* **4176 *na fors,** *no matter* **4177 als evere moot I thryve,** *so may I ever succeed* **4178 swyve,** *screw* **4179 esement,** *compensation,* **yshapen,** *provided* **4181 gif,** *if,* **ygreved,** *injured* **4183 it is *na nay,** *there is no denying* **4184 il fit,** *bad time* **4185 syn,** *since,* ***neen,** *no* **4187 *saule,** *soul,* ***sal *neen other bee,** *shall not be otherwise* **4188 avyse thee,** *be careful* **4190 abreyde,** *awakes* **4191 *bathe a vileynye,** *both harm* **4194 uprighte,** *on her back* **4195 ny,** *close* **4197 aton,** *joined* **4199 lith,** *lies,* **furlong wey or two,** *about five minutes* **4200 routhe,** *pity* **4201 wikked jape,** *nasty trick* **4202 seyn,** *say,* **ape,** *monkey* **4205 auntred hym,** *chanced it,* **nedes sped,** *needs met* **4206 draf-sek,** *sack of chaff* **4208 halde a daf,** *thought a fool,* **cokenay,** *idiot* **4209 auntre,** *venture* **4210 Unhardy,** *unbrave,* **unseely,** *unlucky* **4212 hente,** *took* **4213 baar,** *carried,* **softe,** *quietly* **4214 hir rowtyng leet,** *stopped her snoring*

4149 vernysshed his heed, "polished his head," i.e., had a lot to drink. **4155 whistle wel ywet,** i.e., had a lot to drink. **4160 gooth,** El reads "wente." **4166 heere two furlong,** Hg reads "heren a furlong." **4170 Herdestow,** El reads "Herdtow"; Hg "Herd tow." **4171 complyn,** compline, the last in the daily cycle of prayers; see *MilT* 1.3655n. El and Hg read "couplyng," perhaps Aleyn's malapropism rather than a copying error. **4172 wilde fyr,** common name for erysipelas, a painful skin disease. **upon,** Hg reads "on." **4178** The form "if" is southern, a (scribal?) lapse in the representation of northern dialect that should have "gif," as in lines 4181 and 4190. **4181 ygreved,** Hg reads "agreved." **4183 sothly, it is na nay,** El reads "shortly is ne nay." **4184 il fit al this day,** Hg reads "ille fit today." **4185 neen,** Hg reads "naan." Also at 4187. **4187 Goddes saule,** El reads "god sale." **4192 counte hym nat a flye,** "consider him not (worth) a fly," i.e., don't consider him at all. **4213 his,** El reads "the."

And cam agayn, and gan hir cradel mysse,
And groped heer and ther, but she foond noon.
“Allas,” quod she, “I hadde almoost mysgoon°.
I hadde almoost goon to the clerkes bed.
Ey, benedicite°, thanne hadde I foule ysped°.”
And forth she gooth til she the cradel fond.
She gropeth alwey forther with hir hond,
And foond the bed, and thoghte noght but good,
By cause that the cradel by it stood,
And nyste° wher she was, for it was derk,
But faire and wel she creep° in to the clerk,
And lith° ful stille, and wolde han caught a sleep°.
Withinne a while this John the clerk up leep°,
And on this goode wyf he leith on soore°.
So myrie a fit° ne hadde she nat ful yoore°;
He priketh° harde and depe as he were mad.
This joly lyf han thise two clerkes lad°
Til that the thridde cok° bigan to synge.
  Aleyn wax wery° in the dawenynge,
For he had swonken° al the longe nyght,
And seyde, “Fareweel, Malyne, sweete wight°.
The day is come, I may no lenger byde°;
But everemo, wherso I go or ryde,
I is thyn awen° clerk, swa have I seel°!”
  “Now, deere lemman°,” quod she, “go, fareweel.
But er thow go, o thyng I wol thee telle:
Whan that thou wendest° homward by the melle°,
Right at the entree of the dore bihynde°
Thou shalt a cake of half a busshel fynde
That was ymaked of thyn owene mele°,
Which that I heelp° my fader for to stele.
And, goode lemman, God thee save and kepe.”
And with that word almoost she gan to wepe.
  Aleyn up rist, and thoughte, “Er that it dawe°,
I wol go crepen in by my felawe,”
And fond the cradel with his hand anon.
“By God,” thoughte he, “al wrang° I have mysgon°.
Myn heed is toty° of my swynk° tonyght;
That maketh me that I go nat aright.
I woot° wel by the cradel I have mysgo°;
Heere lith the millere and his wyf also.”
And forth he goth, a twenty devel way°,
Unto the bed ther as the millere lay.
He wende° have cropen° by his felawe John,
And by the millere in he creep anon,
And caughte hym by the nekke, and softe he spak.
He seyde, “Thou John, thou swynes-heed°, awak°,
For Cristes saule, and heer a noble game°.
For by that lord that called is Seint Jame,
As I have thries° in this shorte nyght
Swyved° the milleres doghter bolt upright°,
Whil thow hast°, as a coward, been agast°.”
  “Ye, false harlot°,” quod the millere, “hast?
A, false traitour, false clerk,” quod he,
“Thow shalt be deed°, by Goddes dignitee!
Who dorste° be so boold to disparage°
My doghter, that is come of swich lynage°?”
And by the throte-bolle° he caughte Alayn,
And he hente° hym despitously agayn°,
And on the nose he smoot hym with his fest;
Doun ran the blody streem upon his brest.
And in the floor, with nose and mouth tobroke°,
They walwe° as doon two pigges in a poke°,
And up they goon, and doun agayn anon,
Til that the millere sporned at° a stoon,
And doun he fil bakward upon his wyf
That wiste° nothyng of this nyce stryf°—
For she was falle° aslepe a lite wight°
With John the clerk, that waked hadde al nyght—
And with the fal out of hir sleep she breyde°.
“Help, hooly croys° of Bromeholm!” she seyde,

4218 mysgoon, *gone wrong* **4220 Ey, benedicite,** *whew, bless me,* **foule ysped,** *gone wrong* **4225 nyste,** *did not know* **4226 creep,** *crept* **4227 lith,** *lies,* **wolde han caught a sleep,** *would have fallen asleep* **4228 leep,** *leapt* **4229 leith on soore,** *attacks aggressively* **4230 So myrie a fit,** *such a good time,* **ful yoore,** *for a long time* **4231 priketh,** *pokes* **4232 lad,** *led* **4233 thridde cok,** *third rooster* **4234 wex wery,** *grew tired* **4235 swonken,** *worked* **4236 wight,** *creature* **4237 lenger byde,** *longer remain* **4239 I *is thyn *awen,** *I am your own,* ***swa have I seel,** *so I swear* **4240 lemman,** *beloved* **4242 wendest,** *go,* **melle,** *mill* **4243 of the dore bihynde,** *behind the door* **4245 mele,** *ground grain* **4246 heelp,** *helped* **4249 dawe,** *dawns* **4252 *wrang,** *wrong,* **mysgon,** *misgone* **4253 toty,** *dizzy,* **swynk,** *labor* **4255 woot,** *know,* **mysgo,** *gone wrong* **4257 a twenty devel wey,** *by twenty devils' ways* **4259 wende,** *thought,* **cropen,** *crept* **4262 swynes-heed,** *pig's head,* **awak,** *awake* **4263 game,** *joke* **4265 thries,** *three times* **4266 Swyved,** *screwed,* **bolt upright,** *lying flat* **4267 hast,** *have,* **agast,** *afraid* **4268 harlot,** *scoundrel* **4270 deed,** *dead* **4271 dorste,** *dares,* **disparage,** *dishonor* **4272 swich lynage,** *such lineage* **4273 throte-bolle,** *Adam's apple* **4274 hente,** *grabbed,* **despitously agayn,** *fiercely in return* **4277 tobroke,** *smashed* **4278 walwe,** *wallow,* **poke,** *sack* **4280 sporned at,** *tripped on* **4282 wiste,** *knew,* **nyce stryf,** *ridiculous struggle* **4283 was falle,** *had fallen,* **lite wight,** *little while* **4285 breyde,** *jerked* **4286 croys,** *cross*

4222–33 Changes in verb tense here help to create narrative pace. **4230 ne,** omitted in El. **4231 depe,** El reads “soore.” **4236 Fareweel, Malyne . . . ,** the following exchange is a burlesque of the courtly *alba* or *aube* (“dawn song”) in which lovers lament their parting. **4239 swa,** Hg reads “so.” **4246 fader,** Hg reads “sire.” **4248 she,** Hg reads “he.” **4255–56** The *o*-forms here (**mysgo**, **also**) and elsewhere are southern forms, lapses (scribal?) in the representation of a northern dialect that should have *a*-forms. **4262 swynes-heed,** i.e., you are drunk as a pig. **4264 Seint Jame,** St. James, a convenient rhyme. **4277 in,** Hg reads “on.” **4286 croys of Bromeholm,** a reputed piece of Christ's cross was kept at a religious institution at Bromholm, in Norfolk.

"*In manus tuas!* Lord, to thee I calle!
Awak, Symond, the feend is on us falle.
Myn herte is broken; help, I nam but deed°!
Ther lyth oon upon my wombe° and on myn heed.
Help, Symkyn, for the false clerkes fighte!"
This John stirte up as soone as ever he myghte,
And graspeth by° the walles to and fro
To fynde a staf; and she stirte up also,
And knew the estres bet° than dide this John,
And by the wal a staf she foond anon,
And saugh° a litel shymeryng of a light,
For at an hole in shoon the moone bright,
And by that light she saugh hem bothe two,
But sikerly° she nyste° who was who,
But as she saugh a whit thyng in° hir eye.
And whan she gan the white thyng espye,
She wende° the clerk hadde wered a volupeer°,
And with the staf she drow ay neer° and neer°,
And wende han hit this Aleyn at the fulle°,
And smoot the millere on the pyled° skulle
That doun he gooth, and cride, "Harrow°! I dye!"
Thise clerkes beete° hym weel and lete hym lye,
And greythen hem°, and tooke hir hors anon,
And eek hire mele°, and on hir wey they gon,
And at the mille yet they tooke hir cake°
Of half a busshel flour ful wel ybake.
Thus is the proude millere wel ybete°,
And hath ylost° the gryndynge of the whete,
And payed for the soper everideel°
Of Aleyn and of John, that bette° hym weel.
His wyf is swyved°, and his doghter als°.
Lo, swich° it is a millere to be fals!
And therfore this proverbe is seyd ful sooth°:
Hym thar nat wene wel that yvele dooth°.
A gylour° shal hymself bigyled be.
And God, that sitteth heighe in magestee,
Save al this compaignye, grete and smale.
Thus have I quyt° the Millere in my tale.

Heere is ended the Reves Tale.

4289 I nam but deed, *I'm all but dead* **4290 wombe,** *stomach* **4293 graspeth by,** *gropes around* **4295 estres bet,** *interior better* **4297 saugh,** *saw* **4300 sikerly,** *surely,* **nyste,** *knew not* **4301 in,** *with* **4303 wende,** *thought,* **volupeer,** *nightcap* **4304 drow ay neer,** *went always nearer* **4305 wende han . . . at the fulle,** *fully intended to have* **4306 pyled,** *bald* **4307 Harrow,** *help* **4308 beete,** *beat* **4309 greythen hem,** *dressed themselves* **4310 mele,** *ground grain* **4311 cake,** *loaf* **4313 ybete,** *beaten* **4314 hath ylost,** *has not been paid for* **4315 the soper everideel,** *every bit of the supper* **4316 bette,** *beat* **4317 swyved,** *screwed,* **als,** *also* **4318 swich,** *such* **4319 seyd ful sooth,** *said quite truly* **4320 Hym thar nat wene wel that yvele dooth,** *he should not expect good who does evil* **4321 gylour,** *deceiver* **4324 quyt,** *repaid*

4287 ***In manus tuas,*** "Into your hands"; from Luke 23.46; a prayer for protection. **4288 us,** Hg reads "me." **4290 on,** Hg reads "up." **4292 soone,** Hg reads "faste." **4302 the,** Hg reads "this." **4307 That,** El reads "And." **4318 swich,** Hg reads "which." **4322 magestee,** El reads "Trinitee."

From woodcut made by W.H. Hooper and published by the Chaucer Society between 1868 and 1879

Cook's Tale

Prologue

The Prologe of the Cokes Tale.

The Cook of Londoun, whil the Reve spak,
For joye him thoughte he clawed° him on the bak.
"Haha," quod he, "for Cristes passioun°,
This millere hadde a sharp° conclusioun
Upon° his argument of herbergage°!
Wel seyde Salomon in his langage,
"Ne brynge nat every man into thyn hous";
For herberwynge° by nyghte is perilous.
Wel oghte a man avysed for to be°
Whom that he broghte into his pryvetee.
I pray to God so yeve me sorwe and care
If evere, sitthe I highte° Hogge of Ware,
Herde I a millere bettre yset a werk°.
He hadde a jape of malice° in the derk.
But God forbede that we stynte° heere;
And therfore, if ye vouchesauf° to heere
A tale of me, that am a poure man,
I wol yow telle as wel as evere I kan
A litel jape that fil° in oure citee."
Oure Hoost answerde and seide, "I graunte it thee.
Now telle on, Roger, looke that it be good,
For many a pastee° hastow laten blood°,
And many a Jakke of Dovere hastow soold
That hath been twies hoot and twies coold.
Of many a pilgrym hastow Cristes curs
For of° thy percely° yet° they fare the wors,
That° they han eten with thy stubbel goos°,
For in thy shoppe is many a flye loos°.
Now telle on, gentil Roger by thy name.
But yet I pray thee, be nat wroth for game°:
A man may seye ful sooth in game and pley."

4326 clawed, *scratched* **4327 for Cristes passioun,** *by the suffering of Christ* **4328 sharp,** *painful* **4329 Upon,** *to,* **herbergage,** *lodging* **4332 herberwynge,** *giving shelter* **4333 avysed for to be,** *be careful* **4336 sitthe I highte,** *since I was named* **4337 yset a werk,** *put to work* **4338 jape of malice,** *spiteful joke* **4339 stynte,** *stop* **4340 vouchesauf,** *consent* **4343 fil,** *happened* **4346 pastee,** *meat pie,* **hastow laten blood,** *have you bled* (removed the filling) **4350 For of,** *because from,* **percely,** *parsley* (stuffing?), **yet,** *still* **4351 That,** *which,* **stubbel goos,** *stubble-fed goose* **4352 loos,** *loose* **4354 wroth for game,** *angry because of play*

4325 whil the, El reads "whil that the." **4326 For joye . . . ,** the Cook enjoyed the tale so much that it felt as if the Reeve scratched his back. **4328–29 conclusioun . . . ,** this recalls Symkyn's badgering of the clerks, *RvT* 1.4120–26. **4331** The saying is from Ecclesiasticus 11.29, traditionally ascribed to Solomon. **4336 Hogge of Ware,** Hodge is short for Roger; Ware is a small town near London. A "Roger Ware, Cook" has been found in London records, as has "Roger Knight de Ware of London, Cook." **4337 yset a werk,** an idiom meaning "had a job done on him." **4340 therfore,** omitted in Hg. **4347 Jakke of Dovere,** unidentified, but perhaps a fish or meat pie.

"Thou seist ful sooth," quod Roger, "by my fey°.
But sooth pley, quaad pley°, as the Flemyng°
seith.
And therfore, Herry Bailly, by thy feith,
Be thou nat wrooth°, er we departen° heer,
Though that my tale be of an hostileer°.
But nathelees I wol nat telle it yit,
But er we parte, ywis°, thou shalt be quit°."
And therwithal he lough° and made cheere°,
And seyde his tale as ye shul after heere.

Heere bigynneth the Cookes Tale.

A prentys whilom° dwelled in our citee,
And of a craft of vitailliers° was hee.
Gaillard° he was as goldfynch in the shawe°,
Broun as a berye, a propre° short felawe,
With lokkes blake, ykembd° ful fetisly°;
Dauncen he koude so wel and jolily
That he was cleped° Perkyn Revelour.
He was as ful of love and paramour°
As is the hyve ful of hony sweete—
Wel° was the wenche with hym myghte meete°.
At every bridale° wolde he synge and hoppe°.
He loved bet° the taverne than the shoppe,
For whan ther any ridyng° was in Chepe
Out of the shoppe thider° wolde he lepe—
Til that he hadde al the sighte yseyn,
And daunced wel, he wolde nat come
ayeyn°—
And gadered hym° a meynee° of his sort
To hoppe and synge and maken swich disport°.
And ther they setten stevene° for to meete
To pleyen at the dys° in swich a streete.
For in the toun nas ther no prentys
That fairer koude caste a paire of dys
Than Perkyn koude, and therto° he was free°
Of his dispense° in place of pryvetee°.
That fond° his maister° wel in his chaffare°,
For often tyme he foond his box ful bare.
For sikerly° a prentys revelour°
That haunteth dys°, riot°, or paramour,
His maister shal it in his shoppe abye°,
Al have he° no part of the mynstralcye.
For thefte and riot, they been convertible°,
Al konne he° pleye on gyterne° or ribible°.
Revel and trouthe, as in a lowe degree°,
They been ful wrothe al day°, as men may see.
This joly prentys with his maister bood°
Til he were ny° out of his prentishood°,
Al were he snybbed° bothe erly and late,
And somtyme lad° with revel to Newegate.
But atte laste his maister hym bithoghte°,
Upon a day, whan he his papir soghte°,
Of a proverbe that seith this same word:
Wel bet is° roten appul° out of hoord°
Than that it rotie° al the remenaunt.
So fareth it by° a riotous servaunt;
It is wel lasse° harm to lete hym pace°

4356 fey, *faith* **4357 sooth pley, quaad play,** *true play is no play,* **Flemyng,** *native of Flanders* (Belgium) **4359 wrooth,** *angry,* **departen,** *separate* **4360 hostileer,** *innkeeper* **4362 ywis,** *surely,* **quit,** *repaid* **4363 lough,** *laughed,* **made cheere,** *acted friendly* **4365 prentys whilom,** *apprentice once* **4366 vitailliers,** *food suppliers* **4367 Gaillard,** *lively,* **shawe,** *woods* **4368 propre,** *handsome* **4369 lokkes,** *hair,* **ykembd,** *combed,* **fetisly,** *elegantly* **4371 cleped,** *called* **4372 paramour,** *sexual desire* **4374 Wel,** *happy,* **hym myghte meete,** (that) *might meet him* **4375 bridale,** *wedding celebration,* **hoppe,** *dance* **4376 bet,** *better* **4377 ridyng,** *parade* **4378 thider,** *there* **4380 come ayeyn,** *return* (to the shop) **4381 gadered hym,** *he gathered,* **meynee,** *group* **4382 swich disport,** *such fun* **4383 setten stevene,** *made appointments* **4384 dys,** *dice* **4387 therto,** *also,* **free,** *generous* **4388 dispense,** *spending,* **place of pryvetee,** *a private place* **4389 fond,** *found,* **maister,** *master,* **chaffare,** *business* **4391 sikerly,** *surely,* **prentys revelour,** *party-going apprentice* **4392 haunteth dys,** *frequents dice,* **riot,** *debauchery* **4393 abye,** *pay for* **4394 Al have he,** *although he has* **4395 convertible,** *interchangeable* **4396 Al konne he,** *even though he can,* **gyterne,** *guitar,* **ribible,** *fiddle* **4397 as in a lowe degree,** *in a low-life person* **4398 been ful wrothe al day,** *are always in conflict* **4399 bood,** *lived* **4400 Til he were ny,** *until he was nearly,* **prentishood,** *apprenticeship* **4401 Al were he snybbed,** *even though he was scolded* **4402 lad,** *led* **4403 hym bithoghte,** *thought to himself* **4404 he his papir soghte,** *Perkyn sought his release from apprenticeship* **4406 Wel bet,** *much better,* **appul,** *apple,* **hoord,** *the pile* **4407 rotie,** *rots* **4408 So fareth it by,** *so it goes with* **4409 wel lasse,** *much less,* **pace,** *leave*

4358 Herry Bailly, the Host's name, here given for the first time. A "Henricus Bayliff, Ostyler" is listed in Southwark records of the 1380s. That the Cook apparently knows the Host (an innkeeper) may suggest professional rivalry, also reflected in their verbal sparring. **4359 nat,** El reads "na." **4365 prentys,** apprentices were legally contracted to work for their masters for a period of time in exchange for training in a particular skill or business. **4366 craft of vitailliers,** food suppliers' guild. In the 1380s, there were inflammatory struggles for political and economic power between the London guilds of food suppliers and those that supplied other commodities. **4371 Perkyn Revelour,** "Pete the Partier." **4374 wenche with,** Hg reads "wenche that with." **4377 Chepe,** Cheapside was an important commercial area in London. **4402 Newegate,** London's Newgate prison. When unruly persons were taken to prison, they were preceded by musicians to call attention to their disgrace. **4409 wel,** Hg reads "ful."

Than he shende° alle the servantz in
the place.
Therfore his maister yaf hym acquitance°,
And bad° hym go with sorwe and with meschance°.
And thus this joly prentys hadde his leve.
Now lat hym riote° al the nyght or leve°.
And for° ther is no theef withoute a lowke°
That helpeth hym to wasten and to sowke°
Of that he brybe° kan or borwe° may,
Anon he sente his bed and his array°
Unto a compier° of his owene sort,
That lovede dys and revel and disport,
And hadde a wyf that heeld for contenance°
A shoppe, and swyved° for hir sustenance° . . .

4410 shende, *ruin* **4411 yaf hym acquitance,** *released him from his contract of apprenticeship* **4412 bad,** *told,* **meschance,** *bad luck* **4414 riote,** *dissipate,* **leve,** *stop* (leave off) **4415 for,** *because,* **lowke,** *accomplice* **4416 sowke,** *suck* **4417 brybe,** *bribe,* **borwe,** *borrow* **4418 array,** *clothing* **4419 compier,** *companion* **4421 heeld for contenance,** *kept for appearance's sake* **4422 swyved,** *had sex,* **sustenance,** *living*

4420a A marginal comment aside a blank space in Hg reads: "Of this cokes tale maked Chaucer namoore." El has blank space but no comment.

Canterbury Tales, Part 2

Introduction

The Man of Law materials follow Part 1 in nearly all manuscripts. The *Man of Law's Prologue* sets the date of the pilgrimage as April 18, and in it—emulating or mocking lawyerly language—the Host restates the conditions of the storytelling contest (33ff.). The Man of Law's statement that he will tell a tale in "prose" (see 96n) and the references to law and philosophy in the *Epilogue* (see 1189n) suggest that the *Tale of Melibee* (now in Part 7) may have been originally assigned to the Man of Law. Chaucer apparently canceled the *Epilogue* when he rearranged the tales to follow it (see 1163–90n, 1179n), as it is omitted in twenty-two manuscripts, including the most reliable ones. It may be that in an earlier stage in the evolution of *The Canterbury Tales*, the Man of Law told the *Tale of Melibee*, which was then followed by the present *Shipman's Tale*, told by the Wife of Bath.

The source of the tale of Constance—Custance in Chaucer—is an episode in Nicholas Trivet's *Chronicle* (ca. 1335), an Anglo-Norman account of the history of the Western world. Trivet's episode has its roots in folklore, examined by Margaret Schlauch in *Constance and the Accused Queens* (1927, no. 843) and Nancy B. Black, *Medieval Narratives of Accused Queens* (2003, no. 822). Chaucer's friend, John Gower, also adapted Trivet's tale about the same time that Chaucer did (ca. 1390), but there is no convincing evidence that Chaucer relied upon Gower, or vice versa, although the former is more likely. Gower's version is closer to Trivet's and a straightforward exemplum of the wickedness of jealousy.

In contrast, Chaucer's tale is concerned with Christian Providence, and it achieves a high (some say too high) degree of pathos by incorporating a number of rhetorical apostrophes and exclamations not found in Trivet or Gower, heightened by the rhyme royal stanza form. The relation between Providence and pathos raises questions for many modern readers because it is difficult for us to see why a world governed by Providence should inspire such lamentation. The events of the plot are guided by the "wyl of Crist" (e.g., 511, 721, 825, etc.), and they are subject to the direct intervention of God and Mary (669, 920). Yet the narrator bewails the influence of the stars, the devil, and wicked mothers-in-law, and his references to divine assistance are cast as rhetorical questions (e.g., 473ff.) rather than confident assertions of faith. Divine aid seems not to respond directly to Custance's prayers, nor does it save her from floating at sea for years in a rudderless boat. Such aid arrives only sporadically, not easily explained by human reason.

This is consistent with late-medieval notions of the world as a place of misery. Several portions of the *Man of Law's Prologue* and *Tale* derive from the early thirteenth-century Latin treatise by Pope Innocent III, *On the Misery of the Human Condition*, which Chaucer says he translated (*LGWP* G414; see note to *MLT* 99–121), although no translation by him survives. The treatise epitomized for the Middle Ages the attitude of *contemptus mundi* (disdain for the world), which encouraged detachment from the world and its affairs on the logic that they cause only sorrow. In *Chaucer's Narrators* (1985, no. 376), David Lawton claims that the rhetoric of the *Man of Law's Tale* echoes Innocent's own rhetoric. The contributors to *Chaucer's Religious Tales*, edited by C. David Benson and Elizabeth Robertson (1990, no. 405), argue that the tale reflects late-medieval spirituality. Morton W. Bloomfield, "The *Man of Law's Tale*: A Tragedy of Victimization and Christian Comedy" (1972, no. 824), describes how the tale distances the audience while provoking deep pathos.

Not everyone agrees, of course. Some critics who regard the rhetoric of the tale as excessive rather than genuine rationalize it as characteristic of legal pleading—the Man of Law's attempt to convince the jury, as it were. In these readings, rhetorical excess and uncertain faith in Providence are blamed on the Man of Law, absolving Chaucer of responsibility for either. In his contribution to Benson and Robertson's collection of essays, A. S. G. Edwards (1990, no. 831) surveys such approaches, although he has little sympathy with them. In *Textual Subjectivities*, A. C. Spearing considers the question of the narrator's subjectivity more generally (2005, no. 678).

Custance's lack of agency in directing the events of her life has encouraged critics to read her as an emblem of women subordinated by patriarchy (God, her father, and her husbands) and the demands of lineage (her mothers-in-law). As such, her story can be seen as a transition between Part 1, where men are central and active in and out of marriage, to Part 3, where the Wife of Bath takes center stage as one who controls her own marital affairs. In "Worlds Apart: Orientalism, Antifeminism, and Heresy in Chaucer's *Man of Law's Tale*" (1996, no. 842), Susan Schibanoff argues that the Man of Law dehumanizes women and non-Christians alike to affirm male Christian control, but Elizabeth Robertson (2003, no. 841) reads Custance as an embodiment of powerful nonviolent Christianity. In "New Approaches to Chaucer" (in Boitani and Mann, 2003, no. 105), Carolyn Dinshaw surveys feminist, queer, and postcolonial studies of the *Man of Law's Tale.*

In *Chaucerian Polity* (1997, no. 311), David Wallace examines the shadowy presence of mercantilism in the tale as it correlates with the role of merchants in late-medieval English politics, and he explores similarities between the medieval legal profession and fiction making as a way of explaining Chaucer's references to his own poetry in the *Man of Law's Prologue* (47ff.). In his contribution to a collection of essays edited by Leonard Michael Koff and Brenda Deen Schildgen, *The Decameron and the Canterbury Tales* (2000, no. 295), Robert W. Hanning discusses mercantile exchange as one of the several forms of distorted mediation in the tale, a means to reveal the Man of Law's own distortion of the message intrinsic to the narrative. Joseph Hornsby, *Chaucer and the Law* (1988, no. 529), and Mary Flowers Braswell, *Chaucer's "Legal Fiction"* (2001, no. 525), explore law and legal notions in Chaucer's life and works.

Canterbury Tales
Part 2

From woodcut made by W.H. Hooper and published by the Chaucer Society between 1868 and 1879

Man of Law's Tale

Prologue

The wordes of the Hoost to the compaignye.

Oure Hooste saugh° wel that the brighte sonne
The ark of his artificial day hath ronne°
The ferthe part, and half an houre and moore,
And though he were nat depe ystert in loore°,
He wiste° it was the eightetethe day
Of Aprill, that is messager to May;
And saugh wel that the shadwe° of every tree
Was as in lengthe the same quantitee
That was the body erect that caused it.
And therfore by the shadwe he took his wit°
That Phebus°, which that shoon so clere and brighte,
Degrees was fyve and fourty clombe° on highte,
And for that day, as in that latitude,
It was ten at the clokke°, he gan conclude°;
And sodeynly he plighte° his hors aboute.
"Lordynges," quod he, "I warne yow, al this route°,
The fourthe party° of this day is gon.
Now, for the love of God and of Seint John,
Leseth° no tyme as ferforth° as ye may.
Lordynges, the tyme wasteth nyght and day,
And steleth° from us, what pryvely° slepynge,
And what thurgh necligence in oure wakynge,

1 saugh, *saw* **2 ronne,** *run* **4 depe ystert in loore,** *deeply advanced in learning* **5 wiste,** *knew* **7 shadwe,** *shadow* **10 took his wit,** *decided* **11 Phebus,** *the sun* **12 was . . . clombe,** *had climbed* **14 at the clokke,** *o'clock,* **gan conclude,** *did deduce* **15 plighte,** *pulled* **16 route,** *company* **17 party,** *part* **19 Leseth,** *lose,* **ferforth,** *far* **21 steleth,** *slips away,* **what pryvely,** *what with secretly*

2 ark of his artificial day, the arc of the sun moving across the sky. The artificial day is the time from sunrise to sunset, distinguished from the natural day of twenty-four hours. See *Astrolabe* 2.7. **3 ferthe part,** a quarter of the way through the sun's artificial day plus an hour and a half is somewhat earlier than ten o'clock on this date. **5–6 eightetethe day / Of Aprill,** the date and the following details of the tree's shadow, the angle of the sun, and the time align closely. They are documented in Nicholas of Lynn's *Kalendarium* as occurring April 18, 1386, discussed in Sigmund Eisner's edition of the *Kalendarium*, pp. 30–31. El reads "eighte and twentiethe." Here and elsewhere, misreading of Roman numerals is not uncommon. **20 tyme,** Hg reads "tyme it."

As dooth° the streem that turneth nevere agayn,
Descendynge fro° the montaigne into° playn.
Wel kan Senec and many a philosophre
Biwaillen° tyme moore than gold in cofre°,
For "los of catel° may recovered be,
But los of tyme shendeth° us," quod he.
It wol° nat come agayn, withouten drede°,
Namoore than wole° Malkynes maydenhede,
Whan she hath lost it in hir wantownesse.
Lat us nat mowlen° thus in ydelnesse.
"Sire Man of Lawe," quod he, "so have ye blis°,
Telle us a tale anon, as forward° is.
Ye been submytted, thurgh youre free assent,
To stonden° in this cas at my juggement.
Acquiteth yow° now of youre biheeste°;
Thanne have ye do° youre devoir° atte leeste°."
"Hooste," quod he, "depardieux°, ich assente°;
To breke forward is nat myn entente.
Biheste is dette°, and I wole holde fayn°
Al my biheste; I kan no bettre sayn.
For swich° lawe as a man yeveth° another wight°,
He sholde hymselven usen it, by right;
Thus wole° oure text. But nathelees, certeyn,
I kan right now no thrifty° tale seyn°
That Chaucer, thogh he kan but lewedly°
On° metres and on rymyng craftily°,
Hath seyd hem° in swich° Englissh as he kan
Of olde tyme°, as knoweth many a man.
And if he have noght seyd hem, leve brother,
In o book°, he hath seyd hem in another.
For he hath toold of loveris up and doun°
Mo° than Ovide made of mencioun
In his *Episteles* that been ful olde.
What sholde I tellen hem, syn° they ben
tolde?
"In youthe he made of° Ceys and Alcione,
And sitthen° hath he spoken of everichone°
Thise noble wyves and thise loveris eke°.
Whoso° that wole his large volume seke°
Cleped° the Seintes Legende of Cupide,
Ther may he seen° the large woundes wyde°
Of Lucresse, and of Babilan Tesbee;
The swerd° of Dido for the false Enee;
The tree of Phillis for hire Demophon;
The pleinte° of Dianire and of Hermyon,
Of Adriane, and of Isiphilee—
The bareyne yle° stondynge in the see—
The dreynte° Leandre for his Erro;
The teeris° of Eleyne, and eek the wo
Of Brixseyde, and the°, Ladomya;
The crueltee of the°, queene Medea,
Thy litel children hangynge by the hals°,
For thy Jason, that was in love so fals!
O Ypermystra, Penelopee, Alceste,

23 dooth, *does* **24 fro,** *from,* **montaigne into,** *mountain to* **26 Biwaillen,** *lament,* **cofre,** *chest* **27 catel,** *possessions* **28 shendeth,** *ruins* **29 wol,** *will,* **drede,** *doubt* **30 wole,** *will* **32 mowlen,** *get moldy* **33 so have ye blis,** *may you have happiness* **34 forward,** *promise* **36 stonden,** *stand* **37 Acquiteth yow,** *fulfill,* **biheeste,** *promise* **38 do,** *done,* **devoir,** *obligation,* **atte leeste,** *at the least* **39 depardieux,** *by God,* **ich assente,** *I agree* **41 Biheste is dette,** *promise is duty,* **wole holde fayn,** *will maintain gladly* **43 swich,** *such,* **yeveth,** *gives,* **wight,** *person* **45 wole,** *asserts* **46 thrifty,** *fitting,* **seyn,** *tell* **47 kan but lewedly,** *knows little* **48 On,** *about,* **rymyng craftily,** *skillful rhyming* **49 seyd hem,** *told them,* **swich,** *such* **50 Of olde tyme,** *in the past* **52 o book,** *one book* **53 loveris up and doun,** *lovers here and there* **54 Mo,** *more* **56 syn,** *since* **57 made of,** *wrote about* **58 sitthen,** *since then,* **everichone,** *every one* (of) **59 eke,** *also* **60 Whoso,** *whoever,* **wole . . . seke,** *will . . . seek* **61 Cleped,** *called* **62 seen,** *see,* **wyde,** *wide* **64 swerd,** *sword* **66 pleinte,** *lament* **68 bareyne yle,** *barren isle* **69 dreynte,** *drowned* **70 teeris,** *tears* **71 the,** *thee* **72 the,** *thee* **73 hals,** *neck*

25 Senec, Seneca the younger, a Roman philosopher in whose *Epistle* 1.3 a proverbial sentiment like that in lines 27–28 can be found. **30 Malkynes maydenhede,** Malkin's virginity; *Malkin* is a name for a rustic female. **35 Ye been submytted,** i.e., you have submitted yourself, the first in a series of legal phrases exchanged by the Host and Man of Law. **45 oure text,** the preceding statement is proverbial, but derives from a legal textbook, the *Digests* of Justinian, 2.2. **47 Chaucer,** this reference and the following metafictive references to some of Chaucer's actual poems simultaneously create and challenge the illusion that the fictional pilgrimage really happened. **51 he have noght,** Hg reads "he ne have nat." **55 *Episteles,*** Ovid's *Heroides,* presented as a series of letters, contains many of the stories listed below. **57 Ceys and Alcione,** Chaucer writes of the lovers Ceyx and Alcione at the beginning of *BD,* 62–220. **61 Seintes Legende of Cupide,** Lives of Cupid's Saints, a reference to *LGW,* which Chaucer calls the *Book of the XXV Ladies* in the *CT* 10.1086. The following list does not match the nineteen tales of the incomplete *LGW;* eight in the list are not found in *LGW,* and the list lacks two that are (Cleopatra, Philomela). Asterisks below indicate those found in *LGW.* **62 may he,** Hg reads "maystow." **63 *Lucresse,** the rape and suicide of Lucrece; Ovid's *Fasti* 2.685–852.***Babilan Tesbee,** Thisbe, a Babylonian, and her beloved Pyramus committed suicide; Ovid, *Metamorphoses* 4.55–166. **64 *Dido . . . Enee,** Dido killed herself with a sword because Aeneas abandoned her; Virgil, *Aeneid* 4, and Ovid, *Heroides* 7. **65 *Phillis,** in *LGW* 2484 and *HF* 394, Phyllis hangs herself because deserted by Demophon; the account in Ovid *Heroides* 2 does not include this detail. **66 Dianire,** Dianeira laments that she caused the death of Hercules, her husband, in *Heroides* 9. El reads "Diane." **Hermyon,** Hermione laments that Orestes is banished in *Heroides* 8. **67 *Adriane,** Ariadne laments that Theseus abandons her in *Heroides* 10. ***Isiphilee,** Hypsipile laments the falseness of Jason in *Heroides* 6; he left her on the isle of Naxos. **69 Leandre . . . Erro,** Leander drowned swimming across the Hellespont to visit Hero; *Heroides* 18. **70 Eleyne,** Helen's love of Paris caused the Trojan War; *Heroides* 16 and elsewhere. **eek,** omitted in El. **71 Brixseyde,** the original name of the lover of Troilus, changed by Boccaccio to Criseyde; *Heroides* 3. **the,** Hg reads "of the." **Ladomya,** Laodamia lamented the death of her husband, Protesilaus, the first man killed in the Trojan War; *Heroides* 13. **72 *Medea,** who killed their children when deserted by Jason; *Heroides* 6. **74 in,** Hg reads "of." **75 *Ypermystra,** Hypermnestra was killed by her father because she would not kill her husband; *Heroides* 14. **Penelopee,** Penelope long awaited the return of her husband, Ulysses; *Heroides* 14. **Alceste,** who was faithful to her husband, Admetus, and in his place; *LGW* F511ff.

Youre wifhede he comendeth° with the beste.
"But certeinly no word ne writeth he
Of thilke° wikke ensample° of Canacee,
That loved hir owene brother synfully—
Of swiche° cursed stories I sey fy°!
Or ellis° of Tyro Appollonius,
How that the cursed kyng Antiochus
Birafte° his doghter of hir maydenhede.
That is so horrible a tale for to rede—
Whan he hir threw upon the pavement.
And therfore he°, of ful avysement°,
Nolde nevere° write in none of his sermons°
Of swiche unkynde° abhomynacions,
Ne I wol noon reherce°, if that I may.
"But of my tale how shal I doon° this
day?
Me were looth be likned, doutelees°,
To muses that men clepe° Pierides—
Methamorphosios woot° what I mene°;
But nathelees, I recche noght a bene°
Though I come after hym with hawebake.
I speke in prose, and lat him rymes make."
And with that word he, with a sobre cheere°,
Bigan his tale, as ye shal after heere.

The Prologe of the Mannes Tale of Lawe.

O hateful harm°, condicion of poverte,
With thurst, with coold, with hunger so
confounded°!
To asken help thee shameth in thyn herte;
If thou noon aske°, so soore artow° ywounded
That verray nede unwrappeth° al thy wounde hid°.
Maugree thyn heed°, thou most° for indigence
Or stele°, or begge, or borwe thy despence°.

Thow blamest Crist and seist° ful bitterly
He mysdeparteth richesse temporal°;
Thy neighebore thou wytest° synfully
And seist° thou hast to lite° and he hath al.
"Parfay°," seistow°, "somtyme he rekene° shal,
Whan that his tayl° shal brennen° in the gleede°,
For he noght helpeth needfulle° in hir° neede."

Herke° what is the sentence° of the wise:
Bet is° to dyen than have indigence;
Thy selve° neighebor wol° thee despise.
If thou be poure, farwel thy reverence°.
Yet of the wise man take this sentence:
Alle the dayes of poure men been wikke°.
Bewar, therfore, er° thou come to that prikke°!

If thou be poure, thy brother hateth thee,
And alle thy freendes fleen° from thee, allas.
O riche marchauntz°, ful of wele been yee°;
O noble, O prudent folk, as in this cas°,
Youre bagges been nat fild° with ambes as
But with sys cynk that renneth° for youre chaunce°.
At Cristemasse myrie° may ye daunce!

---

76 comendeth, *praises* **78 thilke,** *that,* **ensample,** *example* **80 swiche,** *such,* **sey fy,** *say shame* **81 ellis,** *else* **83 Birafte,** *deprived* **86 he,** *i.e.,* "Chaucer," **of ful avysement,** *in wise consideration* **87 Nolde nevere,** *would never,* **sermons,** *discourses* **88 swiche unkynde,** *such unnatural* **89 noon reherce,** *none repeat* **90 doon,** *do* **91 Me were looth be likned, doutelees,** *I would hate to be compared, doubtless* **92 clepe,** *call* **93 woot,** *knows,* **mene,** *mean* **94 recche noght a bene,** *care not a bean* **97 cheere,** *expression* **99 harm,** *injury* **100 confounded,** *mixed* **102 noon aske,** *ask for none,* **soore artow,** *sorely are you* **103 verray nede unwrappeth,** *sheer need discloses,* **hid,** *hidden* **104 Maugree thyn heed,** *despite your head* (i.e., yourself), **most,** *must* **105 Or stele,** *either steal,* **despence,** *expenses* **106 seist,** *say* **107 mysdeparteth richesse temporal,** *unfairly divides worldly wealth* **108 wytest,** *blame* **109 seist,** *say,* **to lite,** *too little* **110 Parfay,** *by my faith,* **seistow,** *you say,* **rekene,** *account* (for it) **111 tayl,** *tail,* **brennen,** *burn,* **gleede,** *coals* **112 needfulle,** (the) *needy,* **hir,** *their* **113 Herke,** *hear,* **sentence,** *message* **114 Bet is,** *it is better* **115 Thy selve,** *your own,* **wol,** *will* **116 reverence,** *dignity* **118 wikke,** *wicked* **119 er,** *before,* **prikke,** *point* **121 fleen,** *flee* **122 marchauntz,** *merchants,* **wele been yee,** *prosperity are you* **123 cas,** *situation* **124 fild,** *filled* **125 renneth,** *runs,* **chaunce,** *luck* **126 myrie,** *merry*

78 Canacee, Canace; *Heroides* 11. Since Tyrwhitt, critics have taken the criticism of incest here and in the reference to Apollonius of Tyre (line 81) as Chaucer's jibes at his friend John Gower, who told both tales in *Confessio Amantis,* 3.143ff., 8.271ff. **81 Tyro Appollonius,** Apollonius of Tyre, hero of a medieval narrative of the same name, solved the riddle by which King **Antiochus** (line 82) sought to keep his daughter for his own pleasure. **92 muses . . . Pierides,** the nine daughters of Pierus who were changed into magpies for presuming to compete with the muses, goddesses of inspiration; Ovid's *Metamorphoses* 5.300ff. The Man of Law does not want to be compared with Chaucer. **men,** Hg reads "been." **95 come after hym with hawebake,** i.e., follow him with a hawthorn berry pie (inedible). **96 prose,** since *MLPT* are in poetry (seven-line rhyme royal stanzas), this is either a joke or indication that Chaucer once intended to have a prose tale follow, perhaps the present *Melibee.* The first stanza below is also found in the *Melibee* (7.1568–70), encouraging the connection. Yet it is hard to see how the "poverty prologue" below (99–121) is an appropriate introduction to either *MLT* or *Melibee.* **99–121** A paraphrase from *De Miseria Conditionis Humane* (*On the Misery of the Human Condition*) 1.14 of Pope Innocent III, which in *LGW* G414 Chaucer says he translated, although no complete Chaucerian translation has been found. Other echoes of the work are at lines 421–27, 771–77, 925–31, 1132–38 below, and elsewhere in *CT*; see *PardT* 6.484n. **102 so soore artow ywounded,** Hg reads "with nede artow so wounded." **118 the,** omitted in El. **124–25 ambes as . . . sys cynk,** two aces (snake eyes) . . . six and five (eleven), i.e., a losing throw versus a winning throw in dice.

Ye seken° lond and see for yowre wynnynges;
As wise folk ye known° al th'estaat°
Of regnes°; ye been fadres° of tidynges
And tales bothe of pees° and of debaat°.
I were° right now of tales desolaat°
Nere° that a marchant, goon is many a yeere°,
Me taughte° a tale which that ye shal heere.

Heere bigynneth the Man of Lawe his Tale.

In Surrye whilom° dwelte a compaignye
Of chapmen° riche, and therto sadde° and
trewe,
That wyde-where° senten hir spiceryе°,
Clothes of gold, and satyns riche of hewe°.
Hir chaffare° was so thrifty° and so newe
That every wight° hath deyntee to chaffare°
With hem°, and eek to sellen hem hire ware°.

Now fil it° that the maistres of that sort°
Han shapen hem° to Rome for to wende°,
Were it° for chapmanhode° or for disport°.
Noon oother message° wolde they thider° sende,
But comen hemself° to Rome, this is
the ende°,
And in swich° place as thoughte hem avantage°
For hire entente, they take hir herbergage°.

Sojourned han° thise marchantz in that toun
A certein tyme, as fil° to hire plesance°.
And so bifel that th'excellent renoun
Of the Emperoures doghter, dame Custance,
Reported was with every circumstance°
Unto thise Surryen marchantz in swich wyse°,
Fro day to day, as I shal yow devyse°.

This was the commune voys° of every man:
"Oure Emperour of Rome—God hym see°—
A doghter hath that syn° the world bigan,
To rekene° as wel hir goodnesse as beautee,
Nas nevere swich° another as is shee.
I prey to God in honour hire susteene,
And wolde° she were of al Europe the queene.

"In hire is heigh° beautee withoute pride,
Yowthe withoute grenehede° or folye°;
To alle hire werkes vertu is hir gyde°;
Humblesse hath slayn in hire al tirannye;
She is mirour of alle curteisye;
Hir herte is verray° chambre of hoolynesse;
Hir hand, ministre of fredam for almesse°."

And al this voys° was sooth°, as God is trewe.
But now to purpos lat us turne agayn.
Thise marchantz han doon fraught hir shippes
newe°,
And whan they han this blisful mayden sayn°,
Hoom° to Surrye been they went ful fayn°,
And doon hir nedes° as they han doon yoore°,
And lyven in wele°; I kan sey yow namoore.

Now fil it that thise marchantz stode° in grace°
Of hym that was the Sowdan° of Surrye,
For whan they cam from any strange° place
He wolde, of his benigne° curteisye,
Make hem good chiere°, and bisily espye°
Tidynges° of sondry regnes° for to leere°
The wondres that they myghte° seen or heere.

Amonges othere thynges, specially,
Thise marchantz han° hym toold of dame
Custance

---

127 seken, *search* **128 known,** *know,* **th'estaat,** *the condition* **129 regnes,** *kingdoms,* **been fadres,** *are fathers* **130 pees,** *peace,* **debaat,** *conflict* **131 were,** *would be,* **of tales desolaat,** *without tales* **132 Nere,** *were it not,* **goon is many a yeere,** *a long time ago* **133 Me taughte,** *taught me* **134 Surrye whilom,** *Syria once* **135 chapmen,** *merchants,* **therto sadde,** *also steady* **136 wyde-where,** *far and wide,* **hir spiceryе,** *their spices* **137 hewe,** *color* **138 chaffare,** *merchandise,* **thrifty,** *profitable* **139 wight,** *person,* **hath deyntee to chaffare,** *is pleased to trade* **140 hem,** *them,* **hire ware,** *their goods* **141 fil it,** *it happened,* **sort,** *company* **142 Han shapen hem,** *arranged* (for) *themselves,* **wende,** *travel* **143 Were it,** *either,* **chapmanhode,** *business,* **disport,** *pleasure* **144 message,** *messenger,* **thider,** *there* **145 hemself,** *themselves,* **ende,** *goal* **146 swich,** *such,* **avantage,** *advantageous* **147 hir herbergage,** *their lodging* **148 Sojourned han,** *stayed have* **149 fil,** *happened,* **plesance,** *pleasure* **152 circumstance,** *detail* **153 swich wyse,** *such a manner* **154 devyse,** *describe* **155 voys,** *voice* **156 see,** *watch over* **157 syn,** *since* **158 rekene,** *take into account* **159 Nas nevere swich,** *there was never such* **161 wolde,** *wish* **162 heigh,** *high* **163 grenehede,** *immaturity,* **folye,** *folly* **164 hir gyde,** *their guide* **167 verray,** *true* **168 fredam for almesse,** *generosity in giving alms* **169 voys,** *report,* **sooth,** *true* **171 han doon fraught hir shippes newe,** *have had their ships loaded again* **172 sayn,** *seen* **173 Hoom,** *home,* **fayn,** *pleased* **174 nedes,** *business,* **han doon yoore,** *had done before* **175 wele,** *prosperity* **176 stode,** *stood,* **grace,** *favor* **177 Sowdan,** *Sultan* **178 strange,** *foreign* **179 benigne,** *gentle* **180 Make hem good chiere,** *make them welcome,* **bisily espeye,** *eagerly seek* **181 Tidyngs,** *news,* **sondry regnes,** *various kingdoms,* **leere,** *learn* **182 myghte,** *might have* **184 han,** *have*

133a Rubric omitted in Hg. **150 And,** Hg reads "But." **152 Reported was,** in Trivet and Gower, the Syrian merchants are converted to Christianity when they meet and hear Custance. **153 swych wyse,** El reads "swich a wyse." **170 turne,** Hg reads "come."

So° greet noblesse, in ernest, ceriously°,
That this Sowdan hath caught so greet plesance°
To han hir figure in his remembrance
That al his lust° and al his bisy cure°
Was for to love hire whil his lyf may dure°.

Paraventure° in thilke° large book
Which that men clipe° the hevene ywriten was
With sterres°, whan that° he his birthe took°,
That he for love sholde han° his deeth, allas!
For in the sterres, clerer° than is glas,
Is writen, God woot°, whoso koude° it rede,
The deeth of every man, withouten drede°.

In sterres many a wynter therbiforn°
Was writen the deeth of Ector, Achilles,
Of Pompei, Julius, er° they were born;
The strif° of Thebes; and of Ercules,
Of Sampson, Turnus, and of Socrates
The deeth; but mennes wittes ben° so dulle
That no wight kan wel rede it atte fulle°.

This Sowdan for his privee conseil° sente,
And, shortly of this matiere° for to pace°,
He hath to hem declared his entente,
And seyde hem°, certein, but° he myghte have
grace°
To han° Custance withinne a litel space°
He nas but deed°; and charged hem in hye°
To shapen° for his lyf som remedye.

Diverse men diverse thynges seyden°.
They argumenten, casten° up and doun.
Many a subtil resoun forth they leyden°.
They speken° of magyk and abusioun°.
But finally, as in conclusioun,
They kan nat seen in that noon avantage°,
Ne in noon oother wey, save° mariage.

Thanne sawe they therinne swich° difficultee
By wey of reson, for to speke al playn,
By cause° that ther was swich diversitee
Bitwene hir bothe lawes°, that they sayn°
They trowe°, "that no Cristen prince wolde fayn°
Wedden his child under oure lawes sweete
That us° were taught by Mahoun, oure
prophete."

And he answerde, "Rather than I lese°
Custance, I wol be cristned°, doutelees.
I moot been hires°, I may noon oother chese°.
I prey yow hoold youre argumentz in pees.
Saveth° my lyf, and beth noght recchelees°
To geten hire that° hath my lyf in cure°;
For in this wo I may nat longe endure."

What nedeth gretter dilatacioun°?
I seye°, by tretys° and embassadrie°,
And by the popes mediacioun,
And al the chirche, and al the chivalrie°,
That in destruccioun of maumettrie°,
And in encrees° of Cristes lawe deere,
They been acorded°, so as ye shal heere:

How that the Sowdan and his baronage°
And alle his liges° sholde ycristned° be,
And he shal han Custance in mariage,
And certein gold, I noot° what quantitee;
And heer-to founden° sufficient suretee°.
This same accord was sworn on eyther syde.
Now, faire Custance, almyghty God thee gyde!

Now wolde som men waiten°, as I gesse,
That I sholde tellen al the purveiance°
That th'Emperour, of his grete noblesse,
Hath shapen° for his doghter, dame Custance.

---

185 So, *such,* **ceriously,** *in detail* **186 plesance,** *desire* **188 lust,** *pleasure,* **cure,** *care* **189 dure,** *last* **190 Paraventure,** *perhaps,* **thilke,** *that* **191 clipe,** *call* **192 sterres,** *stars,* **whan that,** *when,* **his birthe took,** *was born* **193 sholde han,** *should have* **194 clerer,** *clearer* **195 woot,** *knows,* **whoso koude,** *whoever could* **196 drede,** *doubt* **197 therbiforn,** *before that time* **199 er,** *before* **200 strif,** *strife* **202 ben,** *are* **203 wel rede it atte fulle,** *interpret it completely* **204 privee conseil,** *private advisers* **205 matiere,** *matter,* **pace,** *pass* **207 seyde hem,** *told them,* **but,** *unless,* **grace,** (the) *good fortune* **208 han,** *have,* **litel space,** *short time* **209 nas but deed,** *was nothing but dead,* **charged hem in hye,** *ordered them in haste* **210 shapen,** *arrange* **211 seyden,** *said* **212 casten,** *deliberated* **213 leyden,** *laid* **214 speken,** *speak,* **abusioun,** *deception* **216 noon avantage,** *no advantage* **217 save,** *except* **218 swich,** *such* **220 By cause,** *because* **221 hir bothe lawes,** *both their religions,* **sayn,** *said* **222 trowe,** *believe,* **wolde fayn,** *would willingly* **225 That us,** *which* (to) *us* **225 lese,** *lose* **226 cristned,** *baptized* **227 moot been hires,** *must be hers,* **chese,** *choose* **229 Saveth,** *preserve,* **beth noght recchelees,** *be not negligent* **230 geten hire that,** *win her who,* **cure,** *keeping* **232 gretter dilatacioun,** *more amplification* **233 seye,** *say,* **tretys,** *treaty,* **embassadrie,** *diplomacy* **235 chivalrie,** *knights* **236 destruccioun of maumettrie,** *defeat of idolatry* **237 encrees,** *increase* **238 been acorded,** *came to agreement* **239 baronage,** *barons* **240 liges,** *subjects,* **ycristned,** *baptized* **242 noot,** *know not* **243 heer-to founden,** *for this established,* **suretee,** *guaranty* **246 waiten,** *expect* **247 purveiance,** *preparation* **249 Hath shapen,** *has made*

188 That, Hg reads "And." **198 Ector,** Trojan hero of the Trojan War. **Achilles,** Greek hero of the Trojan War. **199 Pompei, Julius,** Pompey and Julius Caesar were rival Roman generals **200 Thebes,** city of turmoil in Greek legend and history. **Ercules,** Hercules, Greek hero and demigod. **201 Sampson,** biblical hero; Judges 13–16. **Turnus,** Aeneus's rival in Italy. **Socrates,** Greek philosopher. **224 were,** Hg reads "was." **Mahoun,** Mohammed, the prophet of Islam.

Wel may men knowen that so greet ordinance°
May no man tellen in a litel clause°
As was arrayed° for so heigh° a cause.

Bisshopes been shapen° with hire for to wende°,
Lordes, ladies, knyghtes of renoun,
And oother folk ynogh°, this is th'ende;
And notified is thurghout the toun
That every wight°, with greet devocioun,
Sholde preyen° Crist that he this mariage
Receyve in gree°, and spede this viage°.

The day is comen of hir° departynge—
I seye°, the woful day fatal is come,
That ther may be no lenger tariynge°,
But forthward they hem dressen°, alle and some°.
Custance, that was with sorwe al overcome,
Ful° pale arist°, and dresseth hire to wende°;
For wel she seeth° ther is noon oother ende.

Allas, what wonder is it thogh she wepte,
That shal be sent to strange nacioun°
Fro freendes that so tendrely hire kepte°,
And to be bounden under subjeccioun
Of oon° she knoweth nat his condicioun°?
Housbondes been° alle goode, and han ben yoore°.
That knowen wyves—I dar sey yow na moore.

"Fader," she seyde, "thy wrecched child Custance,
Thy yonge doghter fostred° up so softe°,
And ye, my mooder, my soverayn plesance°
Over alle thyng, out-taken° Crist on-lofte°,
Custance youre child hire recomandeth ofte°
Unto youre grace°, for I shal to Surrye,
Ne shal I nevere seen° yow moore with eye.

"Allas, unto the Barbre nacioun°
I moste goon°, syn° that it is youre wille;
But Crist, that starf° for our savacioun
So yeve° me grace his heestes° to fulfille!
I, wrecche° womman, no fors° though I spille°!
Wommen are born to thraldom° and penance,
And to been under mannes° governance."

I trowe° at Troye, whan Pirrus brak° the wal,
Or° Ilion brende°, at Thebes the citee,
N'at° Rome, for the harm thurgh° Hanybal
That Romayns hath venquysshed tymes thre,
Nas herd swich° tendre wepyng for pitee
As in the chambre was for hire departynge;
But forth she moot°, wher so° she wepe or synge.

O firste moevyng°, crueel firmament°,
With thy diurnal sweigh° that crowdest ay°
And hurlest° al from est til occident°
That naturelly wolde holde° another way,
Thy crowdyng° set the hevene in swich array°
At the bigynnyng of this fiers viage°
That crueel Mars hath slayn° this mariage.

Infortunat ascendent tortuous,
Of° which the lord° is helplees falle°, allas,
Out of his angle° into the derkeste hous°!
O Mars, o atazir°, as in this cas!

---

250 ordinance, *arrangements* **251 litel clause,** *short account* **252 arrayed,** *arranged,* **heigh,** *high* **253 been shapen,** *were prepared,* **wende,** *travel* **255 ynogh,** *enough* **257 wight,** *person* **258 preyen,** *beseech* **259 gree,** *favor,* **spede this viage,** *bring success to this journey* **260 hir,** *their* **261 seye,** *say* **262 tariynge,** *delaying* **263 hem dressen,** *prepare themselves,* **alle and some,** *everybody* **265 Ful,** *very,* **arist,** *arises,* **dresseth hire to wende,** *prepares herself to travel* **266 seeth,** *sees* **268 strange nacioun,** *foreign country* **269 hire kepte,** *cared for her* **271 oon,** *someone,* **condicioun,** *nature* **272 been,** *are,* **ben yoore,** *been for a long time* **275 fostred,** *raised,* **softe,** *gently* **276 soverayn plesance,** *supreme pleasure* **277 out-taken,** *excepting,* **on-lofte,** *above* **278 hire recomandeth ofte,** *commends herself often* **279 grace,** *favor* **280 seen,** *see* **281 Barbre nacioun,** *barbarous* (pagan) *country* **282 moste goon,** *must go,* **syn,** *since* **283 starf,** *died* **284 yeve,** *give,* **heestes,** *commands* **285 wrecche,** *wretched,* **no fors,** *no matter,* **spille,** *die* **286 thraldom,** *servitude* **287 mannes,** *man's* **288 trowe,** *believe,* **brak,** *broke* **289 Or,** *before,* **brende,** *burned* **290 N'at,** *nor at,* **for the harm thurgh,** *for the damage accomplished by* **291 venquysshed tymes thre,** *overcome three times* **292 Nas herd swich,** *was not heard such* **294 moot,** *must,* **wher so,** *whether* **295 moevyng,** *moving,* **firmament,** *sky* **296 diurnal sweigh,** *daily motion,* **crowdest ay,** *pushes always* **297 hurlest,** *forces,* **est til occident,** *east to west* **298 wolde holde,** *would hold (to)* **299 crowdyng,** *pushing,* **swich array,** *such* (an) *arrangement* **300 fiers viage,** *dangerous voyage* **301 slayn,** *destroyed* **303 Of,** *by,* **lord,** *i.e., the planet Mars,* **falle,** *fallen* **304 angle,** *beneficial position,* **derkeste hous,** *most malevolent position* **305 atazir,** *dominant influence*

274–87, lines not in Trivet or Gower. **282 goon,** Hg reads "anon." **283 savacioun,** Hg reads "redempcioun." **288 Pirrus,** Pyrrhus, son of Achilles, breached the walls of Troy. **289 Ilion,** citadel at Troy or Troy itself. **Thebes,** Greek city that was defeated by siege. **290 Hanybal,** Hannibal, general of Carthage, invaded Italy and threatened Rome in the Second Punic War. **291 tymes thre,** an allusion to the three Punic wars. **295–315,** lines not in Chaucer's source; they contribute a sense of astrological determinism. **295 firste moevyng,** *primum mobile,* first mover, the outermost sphere of the Ptolemaic universe that conveys east-to-west motion to the planets, despite the fact that their movement through the zodiac indicates a "natural" motion from west to east. The first mover was usually thought to be beneficial; see, e.g., *KnT* 1.2987ff. Hg reads "firste moever." **300 the,** omitted in Hg. **302 Infortunat ascendent tortuous,** unfortunate, inauspicious astrological arrangement. This stanza includes technical astrological terms, indicating a configuration that dooms Custance's marriage at the outset of her voyage.

O fieble° moone, unhappy been thy paas°.
Thou knyttest thee ther° thou art nat receyved°;
Ther° thou were weel°, fro thennes artow
weyved°.

Inprudent Emperour of Rome, allas,
Was ther no philosophre in al thy toun?
Is no tyme bet° than oother in swich cas°?
Of viage° is ther noon eleccioun°,
Namely° to folk of heigh condicioun°?
Noght whan a roote is of a burthe yknowe?
Allas, we been to lewed° or to slowe!

To ship is brought this woful faire mayde
Solempnely, with every circumstance°.
"Now Jhesu Crist be with yow alle!" she sayde.
Ther nys namoore° but "Farewel, faire Custance!"
She peyneth hire° to make good contenance°;
And forth I lete° hire saille in this manere,
And turne I wole° agayn to my matere.

The mooder° of the Sowdan, welle° of vices,
Espied° hath hir sones pleyn entente,
How he wol lete° his olde sacrifices;
And right anon° she for hir conseil sente,
And they been come° to knowe what she mente°.
And whan assembled was this folk in-feere°,
She sette hire° doun, and seyde as ye shal heere.

"Lordes," she said, "ye knowen everichon°,
How that my sone in point is for to lete°
The hooly lawes of oure Alkaron,
Yeven° by Goddes message Makomete°.
But oon avow° to grete God I heete°:
The lyf shall rather out of my body sterte°
Than Makometes lawe out of myn herte.
"What sholde us tyden of° this newe lawe
But thraldom° to oure bodies and penance,
And afterward in helle to be drawe°
For we reneyed Mahoun° oure creance°?
But, lordes, wol ye maken assurance°,
As I shal seyn, assentynge to my loore°,
And I shal make us sauf° for everemoore?"

They sworen and assenten, every man,
To lyve with hire and dye, and by hire stonde,
And everich°, in the beste wise° he kan,
To strengthen hire shal alle his frendes fonde°.
And she hath this emprise ytake on honde°
Which ye shal heren° that I shal devyse,
And to hem alle she spak° right in this wyse:

"We shul first feyne° us Cristendom to take—
Coold water shal nat greve° us but a lite°!
And I shal swich° a feeste° and revel make
That, as I trowe°, I shal the Sowdan quite°.
For thogh his wyf be cristned never so° white,
She shal have nede to wasshe awey the rede°,
Thogh she a font-ful° water with hire lede°."

O Sowdanesse°, roote of iniquitee!
Virago°, thou Semyrame the secounde!
O serpent under femynynytee,
Lik to the serpent depe in helle ybounde!
O feyned° womman, al that may confounde°
Vertu and innocence, thurgh thy malice,
Is bred in thee, as nest of every vice.

O Sathan°, envious syn thilke° day
That thou were chaced° from oure heritage°,

---

306 fieble, *weak,* **unhappy been thy paas,** *unfortunate was your passing* **307 knyttest thee ther,** *conjoined yourself where,* **receyved,** *welcome* **308 Ther,** *where,* **weel,** *well-positioned,* **fro thennes artow weyved,** *from there are you moved* **311 bet,** *better,* **swich cas,** *such a case* **312 Of viage,** *concerning the voyage,* **noon eleccioun,** *no selection of a beneficial time* **313 Namely,** *especially,* **heigh condicioun,** *high class* **315 lewed,** *ignorant* **317 circumstance,** *ceremony* **319 nys namoore,** *is no more* **320 peyneth hire,** *takes pains,* **make good contenance,** *appear happy* **321 lete,** *let* **322 wole,** *will* **323 mooder,** *mother,* **welle,** *source* **324 Espied,** *recognized* **325 wol lete,** *will abandon* **326 right anon,** *immediately* **327 been come,** *came,* **mente,** *intended* **328 in-feere,** *together* **329 hire,** *herself* **330 everichon,** *everyone* **331 in point is for to lete,** *is on the point of abandoning* **333 Yeven,** *given.* **Goddes message Makomete,** *God's messenger Mohammed* **334 oon avow,** *one vow,* **heete,** *promise* **335 sterte,** *leap* **337 us tyden of,** (for) *us result from* **338 thraldom,** *slavery* **339 drawe,** *pulled* **340 reneyed Mahoun,** *renounced Mohammed,* **creance,** *faith* **341 wol ye maken assurance,** *will you promise* **342 loore,** *advice* **343 sauf,** *safe* **346 everich,** *each one,* **wise,** *way* **347 fonde,** *test* **348 emprise ytake on honde,** *enterprise taken in hand* **349 heren,** *hear* **350 spak,** *spoke* **351 feyne,** *pretend* **352 greve,** *hurt,* **lite,** *little* **353 swich,** *such* **feeste,** *feast* **354 trowe,** *believe,* **Sowdan quite,** *Sultan repay* **355 cristned never so,** *baptized no matter how* **356 rede,** *red* (blood) **357 font-ful,** *baptismal font full of,* **lede,** *bring* **358 Sowdanesse,** *Sultaness* **359 Virago,** *mannish woman* **362 feyned,** *counterfeit,* **confounde,** *undermine* **365 Sathan,** *Satan,* **syn thilke,** *since that* **366 chaced,** *chased,* **heritage,** *salvation*

314 Noght whan a roote is of a burthe yknowe, not (even) when the basis for calculating the horoscope is known? **316 brought,** El reads "come." **330 she said,** Hg reads "quod she." **332 Alkaron,** the Koran, the sacred book of Islam. **352 Coold water,** disparaging reference to baptism, the sacrament whereby people become Christian, typically involving water administered from a receptacle known as a font (see lines 357 and 723) **359 Semyrame,** Semiramis, an Assyrian queen who usurped the throne from her son. **360 serpent under femynynytee,** in medieval art the serpent in Eden had the face of a woman. **361 depe in helle ybounde,** bound deep in hell; Satan is depicted so in much medieval art, following the apocryphal Gospel of Nicodemus.

Wel knowestow° to wommen the olde way.
Thou madest Eva brynge us in servage°;
Thou wolt fordoon° this Cristen mariage.
Thyn instrument so—weylawey the while°—
Makestow° of wommen, whan thou wolt bigile°.

This Sowdanesse, whom I thus blame and warye°,
Leet prively° hire conseil goon hire way°.
What sholde I in this tale lenger tarye?
She rydeth to the Sowdan on a day
And seyde° hym that she wolde reneye hir lay°,
And Cristendom of° preestes handes fonge°,
Repentynge hire she hethen was so longe;

Bisechynge hym° to doon hire that honour
That she moste han° the Cristen folk to feeste—
"To plesen hem I wol do my labour."
The Sowdan seith, "I wol doon at youre heeste°,"
And knelynge thanketh hire of° that requeste.
So glad he was he nyste° what to seye.
She kiste hir sone, and hoom she gooth hir weye.

Explicit prima pars. Sequitur pars secunda.

Arryved been° this Cristen folk to londe
In Surrye, with a greet solempne route°,
And hastifliche° this Sowdan sente his sonde°
First to his mooder, and al the regne° aboute,
And seyde his wyf was comen, out of doute°,
And preyde hire° for to ryde agayn° the queene,
The honour of his regne to susteene.

Greet was the prees° and riche was th'array
Of Surryens and Romayns met yfeere°.
The mooder of the Sowdan, riche and gay,
Receyveth hire with also° glad a cheere°
As any mooder myghte hir doghter deere,
And to the nexte° citee ther bisyde
A softe paas solempnely° they ryde.

Noght trowe I° the triumphe of Julius,
Of which that Lucan maketh swich a boost,
Was roialler° or moore curius°
Than was th'assemblee of this blisful hoost.
But this scorpioun, this wikked goost°,
The Sowdanesse, for al hire flaterynge
Caste under this° ful mortally to stynge.

The Sowdan comth° hymself soone after this
So roially that wonder is to telle,
And welcometh hire with alle joye and blis.
And thus in murthe and joye I lete hem dwelle;
The fruyt° of this matiere is that° I telle.
Whan tyme cam, men thoughte it for the beste;
The revel stynte° and men goon to hir reste.

The tyme cam° this olde Sowdanesse
Ordeyned° hath this feeste of which I tolde,
And to the feeste Cristen folk hem dresse°
In general, ye°, bothe yonge and olde.
Heere may men feeste and roialtee° biholde,
And deyntees mo° than I kan yow devyse°;
But al to deere° they boghte it er° they ryse.

O sodeyn° wo, that evere art successour
To worldly blisse, spreynd° with bitternesse,
The ende of the joye of oure worldly labour!
Wo occupieth the fyn° of oure gladnesse.
Herke° this conseil for thy sikernesse°:
Upon thy glade day have in thy mynde
The unwar° wo or harm that comth bihynde°.

For shortly for to tellen, at o° word,
The Sowdan and the Cristen everichone°

---

367 knowestow, *do you know* **368 in servage,** *into slavery* **369 wolt fordoon,** *will destroy* **370 weylawey the while,** *alas the time* **371 Makestow,** *do you make,* **wolt bigile,** *will mislead* **372 warye,** *curse* **373 Leet prively,** *let secretly,* **hire way,** *their way* **376 seyde,** *told,* **wolde reneye hir lay,** *would renounce her religion* **377 of,** *from,* **fonge,** *receive* **379 Bisechynge hym,** *requesting* (of) *him* **380 moste han,** *might have* **382 wol doon at youre heeste,** *will act as you request* **383 of,** *for* **384 nyste,** *knew not* **386 Arryved been,** *arrived have* **387 solempne route,** *impressive company* **388 hastifliche,** *hastily,* **sonde,** *message* **389 regne,** *kingdom* **390 doute,** *doubt* **391 preyde hire,** *asked her,* **ryde agayn,** *meet* **393 prees,** *crowd* **394 yfeere,** *together* **396 also,** *as,* **cheere,** *expression* **398 nexte,** *nearest* **399 softe paas solempnely,** *slow solemn pace* **400 Noght trowe I,** *I do not believe* **402 roialler,** *more royal,* **curius,** *elaborate* **404 goost,** *spirit* **406 Caste under this,** *planned under this* (deception) **407 comth,** *comes* **411 fruyt,** *outcome,* **that,** *what* **413 stynte,** *stopped* **414 cam,** *came* (when) **415 Ordeyned,** *ordered* **416 hem dresse,** *prepare themselves* **417 ye,** *yes* **418 roialtee,** *royalty* **419 deyntees mo,** *more delicacies,* **yow devyse,** *describe for you* **420 to deere,** *too dearly,* **er,** *before* **421 sodeyn,** *sudden* **422 spreyned,** *sprinkled* **424 fyn,** *end* **425 Herke,** *listen to,* **sikernesse,** *security* **427 unwar,** *unexpected,* **comth bihynde,** *comes afterward* **428 at o,** *in one* **429 everichone,** *every one*

373 hire way, Hg reads "his way." **381 wol,** Hg reads "shal." **385a *Explicit prima pars. Sequitur pars secunda.*** "Here ends part one. Here follows part two." Rubric omitted in Hg. **400 triumphe of Julius,** a great triumph, or victory procession, of Julius Caesar is mentioned in Lucan's *Pharsalia* 3.73–39 as something that may have occurred; it never takes place in the classical account, but French versions add them. **404 scorpioun,** the scorpion was a familiar symbol of treachery. **421–27** Not in Trivet or Gower; from Innocent *De Miseria* 1.23; see 99–121n above. **428 shortly,** El reads "soothly."

Been al tohewe° and stiked° at the bord°,
But it were° oonly dame Custance allone.
This olde Sowdanesse, cursed krone,
Hath with hir freendes doon this cursed dede,
For she hirself wolde° al the contree lede°.

Ne was ther Surryen noon that° was
converted,
That of the conseil of the Sowdan woot°,
That he nas al tohewe er he asterted°.
And Custance han they take anon°, foot-hoot°,
And in a ship al steerelees°, God woot°,
They han hir° set, and bidde hire lerne saille°
Out of Surrye agaynward to Ytaille°.

A certein tresor° that she with hire ladde°,
And, sooth to seyn°, vitaille° greet plentee
They han hire yeven°, and clothes eek she hadde,
And forth she sailleth in the salte see.
O my Custance, ful of benignytee°,
O Emperoures yonge doghter deere,
He that is Lord of Fortune be thy steere°!

She blesseth hire°, and with ful pitous voys
Unto the croys° of Crist thus seyde she,
"O cleere°, o welful auter°, hooly croys,
Reed of° the Lambes blood ful of pitee,
That wessh° the world fro the olde iniquitee°,
Me fro the feend and fro his clawes kepe,
That day° that I shal drenchen° in the depe.

Victorious tree, proteccioun of trewe°,
That oonly worthy were° for to bere
The Kyng of Hevene with his woundes newe,
The white Lamb, that hurt was with a spere°,
Flemere of feendes out° of hym° and here°
On which° thy lymes° feithfully extenden°,
Me helpe, and yif° me myght my lyf t'amenden°."

Yeres and dayes fleet° this creature
Thurghout the See of Grece unto the Strayte
Of Marrok, as it was hire aventure°;
On many a sory meel° now may she bayte°;
After° hir deeth ful often may she wayte°,
Er° that the wilde wawes° wol hire dryve
Unto the place ther° she shal arryve.

Men myghten asken why she was nat slayn
Eek° at the feeste? Who myghte hir body save?
And I answere to that demande agayn°,
Who saved Danyel in the horrible cave
Ther° every wight° save he, maister and knave,
Was with° the leon frete er° he asterte°?
No wight but God, that he bar° in his herte.

God liste to shewe° his wonderful myracle
In hire, for we sholde seen his myghty werkis°.
Crist, which that is to every harm triacle°,
By certeine meenes ofte°, as knowen clerkis,
Dooth thyng° for certein ende° that ful derk° is
To mannes wit, that for° oure ignorance
Ne konne noght knowe° his prudent
purveiance°.

Now sith° she was nat at the feeste yslawe°,
Who kepte hire fro° the drenchyng° in the see?
Who kepte Jonas in the fisshes mawe°
Til he was spouted up at Nynyvee°?
Wel may men knowe it was no wight° but he
That kepte the peple Ebrayk from hir
drenchynge°,
With drye feet thurghout the see passynge.

430 tohewe, *cut to pieces,* **stiked,** *stabbed,* **bord,** *table* **431 But it were,** *except* **434 wolde,** *wanted to,* **lede,** *rule* **435 Ne was ther Surryen noon that,** *nor was there any Syrian who* **436 woot,** *knew* **437 tohewe er he asterted,** *slaughtered before he escaped* **438 take anon,** *taken quickly,* **foot-hoot,** *immediately* **439 steerelees,** *rudderless,* **woot,** *knows* **440 han hir,** *have her,* **lerne saille,** *learn to sail* **441 agaynward to Ytaille,** *back to Italy* **442 tresor,** *treasure,* **ladde,** *brought* **443 sooth to seyn,** *truth to tell,* **vitaille,** *food* **444 han hire yeven,** *have given to her* **446 benignytee,** *goodness* **448 steere,** *rudder* **449 hire,** *herself* **450 croys,** *cross* **451 cleere,** *shining,* **welful auter,** *beneficial altar* **452 Reed of,** *red from* **453 wessh,** *washed,* **iniquitee,** *wickedness* **455 That day,** *on the day,* **drenchen,** *drown* **456 trewe,** *true* (ones) **457 That oonly worthy were,** *the only one that was worthy* **459 spere,** *spear* **460 Flemere of feendes out,** *one who drives fiends out,* **hym,** *him,* **here,** *her* **461 which,** *whom,* **lymes,** *arms,* **extenden,** *stretch* **462 yif,** *give,* **t'amenden,** *to correct* **463 fleet,** *floated* **465 aventure,** *fortune* **466 sory meel,** *miserable meal,* **bayte,** *eat* **467 After,** *for,* **wayte,** *wait* **468 Er,** *before,* **wawes,** *waves* **469 ther,** *where* **471 Eek,** *also* **472 agayn,** *in response* **474 Ther,** *where,* **wight,** *person* **475 with,** *by,* **frete er,** *eaten before,* **asterte,** *escaped* **476 bar,** *carried* **477 liste to shewe,** *was pleased to demonstrate* **478 werkis,** *works* **479 triacle,** *medicine* **480 meenes ofte,** *means often* **481 Dooth thyng,** *does something,* **ende,** *purpose,* **derk,** *mysterious* **482 for,** *because of* **483 Ne konne noght knowe,** *can not know,* **purveiance,** *providence* **484 sith,** *since,* **yslawe,** *slain* **485 fro,** *from,* **drenchyng,** *drowning* **486 fisshes mawe,** *fish's mouth* **487 Nynyvee,** *Nineveh* **488 wight,** *person* **489 hir drenchynge,** *their drowning*

435 Ne was ther, El omits "ther"; Hg reads "Ne ther nas." **442 with hire,** Hg reads "thider." **449–62** Not in Trivet or Gower. Addresses to Christ's cross occur in medieval lyrics and liturgy. **451 welful,** El reads "woful." **452 Lambes,** Jesus's; John 1.29. **459 a,** El reads "the." **462 helpe,** Hg reads "kepe." **yif,** Hg reads "yeve" (give). **464–65 See of Grece,** eastern Mediterranean Sea; **Strayte of Marrok,** Strait of Morocco (of Gibraltar). **470–504** Not in Trivet or Gower. **473 Danyel,** Daniel, through the power of God, survived being locked in a lion's den, where his accusers perished; Daniel 6.16–24. **486 Jonas,** Jonah, preserved by God, survived in a whale's belly for three days before being spewed up near Nineveh; Jonah 1.17–2.10. **489 the peple Ebrayk,** the Hebrew people were protected by God when they passed through the Red Sea; Exodus 14.21–22. El and Hg omit "the."

Who bad° the foure spirites of tempest
That power han t'anoyen° lond and see,
Bothe north and south and also west and est,
"Anoyeth, neither see, ne land, ne tree"?
Soothly°, the comandour of that was he
That fro the tempest ay° this womman kepte
As wel whan she wook as whan she slepte.

Where myghte this womman mete and drynke have
Thre yeer and moore? How lasteth hire vitaille°?
Who fedde the Egipcien Marie in the cave,
Or in desert? No wight but Crist, sanz faille°.
Fyve thousand folk it was as greet mervaille°
With loves fyve and fisshes two to feede.
God sente his foyson° at hir grete neede.

She dryveth forth° into oure occian°
Thurghout oure wilde see, til atte laste
Under an hoold° that nempnen° I ne kan
Fer° in Northhumberlond the wawe° hire caste,
And in the sond° hir ship stiked° so faste
That thennes wolde it noght of al a tyde°;
The wyl of Crist was that she sholde abyde°.

The constable of the castel doun is fare°
To seen this wrak, and al the ship° he soghte,
And foond this wery womman ful of care;
He foond also the tresor° that she broghte.
In hir langage mercy she bisoghte°,
The lyf out of hire body for to twynne°,
Hire to delivere of° wo that she was inne.

A maner Latyn corrupt was hir speche,
But algates° therby was she understonde.
The constable, whan hym lyst° no lenger seche°,
This woful womman broghte he to the londe.
She kneleth doun and thanketh Goddes sonde°;
But what she was she wolde no man seye°,
For foul ne fair, thogh that° she sholde deye°.

She seyde she was so mazed° in the see
That she forgat hir mynde, by hir trouthe°.
The constable hath of hire so greet pitee,
And eek his wyf, that they wepen for routhe°.
She was so diligent, withouten slouthe°,
To serve and plesen everich° in that place
That alle hir loven that looken in hir face.

This constable and dame Hermengyld, his wyf,
Were payens°, and that contree everywhere;
But Hermengyld loved hire right° as hir lyf,
And Custance hath so longe sojourned° there,
In orisons°, with many a bitter teere,
Til Jhesu hath converted thurgh his grace
Dame Hermengyld, constablesse of that place.

In al that lond no Cristen dorste route°;
Alle Cristen folk been fled fro that contree
Thurgh payens that conquereden al aboute
The plages° of the north by land and see.
To Walys° fledde the Cristyanytee°
Of olde Britons dwellynge in this ile°;
Ther was hir refut° for the meene while.

But yet nere° Cristene Britons so exiled
That ther nere somme that in hir privetee°
Honoured Crist and hethen folk bigiled°,
And ny° the castel swiche° ther dwelten three.
That oon° of hem was blynd and myghte nat see,
But° it were with thilke eyen° of his mynde

491 bad, *ordered* **492 han t'anoyen,** *have to damage* **495 Soothly,** *truly* **496 ay,** *always* **499 vitaille,** *food* **501 sanz faille,** *without doubt* **502 mervaille,** *marvel* **504 foyson,** *plenty* **505 dryveth forth,** *continues on,* **occian,** *ocean* **507 hoold,** *castle,* **nempnen,** *name* **508 Fer,** *far,* **wawe,** *waves* **509 sond,** *sand,* **stiked,** *stuck* **510 thennes wolde it noght of al a tyde,** *from there it would not move even at high tide* **511 abyde,** *remain* **512 doun is fare,** *goes down* **513 al the ship,** *the entire ship* **515 tresor,** *treasure* **516 bisoghte,** *requested* **517 twynne,** *separate* **518 of,** *from* **520 algates,** *nevertheless* **521 hym lyst,** *it pleased him,* **lenger seche,** *longer (to) search* **523 Goddes sonde,** *God's sending* **524 seye,** *tell* **525 thogh that,** *even if,* **deye,** *die* **526 mazed,** *dazed* **527 by hir trouthe,** *upon her word* **529 routhe,** *pity* **530 slouthe,** *laziness* **531 everich,** *everyone* **534 payens,** *pagans* **535 right,** *just* **536 sojourned,** *remained* **537 orisons,** *prayers* **540 dorste route,** *dared to assemble* **543 plages,** *coastal regions* **544 Walys,** *Wales,* **Christyanytee,** *Christian community* **545 ile,** *island* **546 refut,** *refuge* **547 nere,** *were not* **548 in hir privetee,** *in secrecy* **549 bigiled,** *deceived* **550 ny,** *near,* **swiche,** *such* **551 oon,** *one* **552 But,** *unless,* **eyen,** *eyes*

491 foure spirites of tempest, four angels, commanded by God, hold back the winds of destruction in Revelation 7.1–3. **500 Egipcien Marie,** St. Mary the Egyptian, a legendary hermit who survived forty-seven years in the desert. **503 loves . . . and fisshes,** Christ miraculously fed a crowd of five thousand with only five loaves and two fish; Matthew 14.16–21. **506 oure,** Hg reads "the." **508 Northhumberlond,** an area in northern England that eventually became a part of Northumbria. **512 constable,** the chief officer of the king's household or court. **513 this,** El reads "his." **519 maner Latyn corrupt,** a kind of mixed or popular Latin, a historically accurate dialect for a sixth-century Roman princess. Trivet says she spoke to the constable in Saxon; Gower does not specify. **525 For foul ne fair,** an idiom meaning "under no circumstances." **532 in,** Hg reads "on." **534 that contree everywhere,** i.e., the entire country was pagan. **539 that,** Hg reads "thilke."

With whiche men seen, whan that they ben
blynde.

Bright was the sonne as in that someres° day,
For° which the constable and his wyf also
And Custance han ytake° the righte° way
Toward the see a furlong wey° or two,
To pleyen and to romen° to and fro.
And in hir walk this blynde man they mette,
Croked° and oold, with eyen faste yshette°.

"In name of Crist," cride this blinde Britoun,
"Dame Hermengyld, yif° me my sighte agayn!"
This lady weex affrayed° of the soun,
Lest° that hir housbonde, shortly for to sayn,
Wolde hire for Jhesu Cristes love han slayn°,
Til Custance made hire boold, and bad hire
wirche°
The wyl of Crist, as doghter of his chirche.

The constable weex abasshed° of that sight,
And seyde, "What amounteth° al this fare°?"
Custance answerde, "Sire, it is Cristes myght,
That helpeth folk out of the feendes° snare."
And so ferforth° she gan oure lay° declare
That she the constable, er that° it was eve,
Converteth, and on Crist maketh hym bileve.

This constable was nothyng° lord of this place
Of which I speke, ther° he Custance fond,
But kepte° it strongly many wyntres space°
Under Alla, kyng of al Northhumbrelond,
That was ful wys and worthy of his hond
Agayn the Scottes, as men may wel heere.
But turne I wole° agayn to my mateere.

Sathan°, that evere us waiteth to bigile°,
Saugh of° Custance al hire perfeccioun,
And caste anon° how he myghte quite hir while°,
And made a yong knyght that dwelte in that
toun
Love hire so hoote of° foul affeccioun
That verraily hym thoughte° he sholde spille°
But° he of hire myghte ones° have his wille.

He woweth° hire, but it availleth noght°;
She wolde do no synne, by no weye.
And for despit° he compassed° in his thoght
To maken hire on shameful deeth to deye.
He wayteth° whan the constable was aweye,
And pryvely° upon a nyght he crepte
In Hermengyldes chambre, whil she slepte.

Wery, forwaked in hire orisouns°,
Slepeth Custance and Hermengyld also.
This knyght, thurgh Sathanas temptaciouns,
Al softely is to the bed ygo°,
And kitte the throte of Hermengyld atwo°,
And leyde° the blody knyf by dame Custance,
And wente his wey, ther God yeve hym
meschance°!

Soone after cometh this constable hoom
agayn,
And eek Alla, that kyng was of that lond,
And saugh his wyf despitously yslayn°,
For which ful ofte he weep and wroong his hond°.
And in the bed the blody knyf he fond
By dame Custance. Allas, what myghte she seye?
For verray wo hir wit was° al aweye.

To Kyng Alla was toold al this meschance°,
And eek the tyme, and where, and in what wise
That in a ship was founden dame Custance,
As heerbiforn° that ye han herd devyse°.
The kynges herte of pitee gan agryse°
Whan he saugh° so benigne° a creature
Falle in disese° and in mysaventure.

554 someres, *summer's* **555 For,** *on account of* **556 han ytake,** *have taken,* **righte,** *direct* **557 furlong wey,** *220 yards* **558 romen,** *roam* **560 Croked,** *bent,* **yshette,** *shut* **562 yif,** *give* **563 weex affrayed,** *grew frightened* **564 Lest,** *for fear* **565 han slayn,** *have slain* **566 bad hire wirche,** *urged her to work* **568 weex abasshed,** *grew amazed* **569 amounteth,** *means,* **fare,** *business* **571 feendes,** *devil's* **572 so ferforth,** *in such a manner,* **lay,** *law* **573 er that,** *before* **575 nothyng,** *not at all,* **576 ther,** *where* **577 kepte,** *defended,* **wyntres space,** *years* **581 wole,** *will* **582 Sathan,** *Satan,* **bigile,** *deceive* **583 Saugh of,** *saw in* **584 caste anon,** *soon plotted,* **quite hir while,** *repay her* **586 hoote of,** *hotly with* **587 verraily hym thoughte,** *truly he thought,* **spille,** *die* **588 But,** *unless,* **ones,** *once* **589 woweth,** *woos,* **availleth noght,** *has no effect* **591 for despit,** *out of spite,* **compassed,** *planned* **593 wayteth,** *sought a time* **594 pryvely,** *secretly* **596 forwaked in hire orisouns,** *from being awake in their prayers* **599 ygo,** *gone* **600 kitte . . . atwo,** *cut in two* **601 leyde,** *laid* **602 ther God yeve hym meschance,** *may God give him bad fortune* **605 despitously yslayn,** *cruelly slain* **606 wroong his hond,** *wrung his hands* **609 verry wo hir wit was,** *true sorrow her wits were* **610 meschance,** *disaster* **613 heerbiforn,** *before,* **herd devyse,** *heard described* **614 gan agryse,** *did shudder* **615 saugh,** *saw,* **benigne,** *good* **616 disese,** *distress*

553 whan, Hg reads "after." **558 to romen,** El repeats this phrase. **561 blinde,** El reads "olde." **578 Alla,** Aella, historical sixth-century king of Anglian Deira, an Anglo-Saxon kingdom. **579 worthy of his hond,** i.e., strong in battle. For the formula "wise and worthy," see *GP* 1.68. **580 Agayn the Scottes,** against the Scots, who threatened the northern kingdoms of England. **586 so,** omitted in Hg. **612 dame,** Hg reads "this."

For as the lomb° toward his deeth is broght,
So stant° this innocent bifore the kyng.
This false knyght, that hath this tresoun wroght°,
Berth hire on hond° that she hath doon thys thyng.
But nathelees, ther was greet moornyng
Among the peple, and seyn° they kan nat gesse°
That she had doon so greet a wikkednesse,

For they han seyn° hire evere so vertuous,
And lovynge Hermengyld right as° hir lyf.
Of this baar° witnesse everich° in that hous,
Save° he that Hermengyld slow° with his knyf.
This gentil kyng hath caught a greet motyf°
Of° this witnesse°, and thoghte he wolde enquere
Depper° in this, a trouthe for to lere°.

Allas, Custance, thou hast no champioun,
Ne fighte kanstow noght°, so weylaway°!
But he that starf° for oure redempcioun,
And boond° Sathan—and yet lith ther° he lay—
So be thy stronge champion this day.
For, but if° Crist open myracle kithe°,
Withouten gilt° thou shalt be slayn as swithe°.

She sette hire doun on knees, and thus she sayde,
"Immortal God, that savedest Susanne
Fro° false blame, and thou, merciful mayde,
Marie I meene, doghter of Seint Anne,
Bifore whos child angeles synge Osanne°,
If I be giltlees of this felonye,
My socour° be, for ellis° shal I dye!"

Have ye nat seyn° somtyme a pale face
Among a prees°, of hym that hath be lad°
Toward his deeth, wher as hym gat no grace,
And swich° a colour in his face hath had,
Men myghte knowe his face that was bistad°
Amonges alle the faces in that route°?
So stant° Custance, and looketh hire aboute.

O queenes, lyvynge in prosperitee,
Duchesses, and ye ladyes everichone°,
Haveth som routhe° on hire adversitee!
An Emperoures doghter stant allone;
She hath no wight° to whom to make hire mone°.
O blood roial, that stondest in this drede,
Fer been° thy freendes at thy grete nede!

This Alla kyng hath swich compassioun,
As gentil herte is fulfild° of pitee,
That from his eyen ran the water doun.
"Now hastily do fecche° a book," quod he,
"And if this knyght wol sweren° how that she
This womman slow°, yet wol we us avyse°
Whom that we wole° that shal been oure justise°."

A Britoun book written with Evaungiles
Was fet°, and on this book he swoor anoon
She gilty was. And in the meene whiles°,
An hand hym smoot° upon the nekke-boon,
That° doun he fil atones° as a stoon,
And bothe his eyen broste° out of his face
In sighte of everybody in that place.

A voys was herd in general audience°,
And seyde, "Thou hast desclaundred°, giltelees,
The doghter of hooly chirche in heigh presence°;
Thus hastou° doon, and yet holde I my pees°?"
Of this mervaille agast° was al the prees°;

---

617 lomb, *lamb* **618 stant,** *stands* **619 tresoun wroght,** *betrayal contrived* **620 Berth hire on hond,** *accuses her* **622 seyn,** (they) *say,* **gesse,** *imagine* **624 han seyn,** *have seen* **625 right as,** *as much as* **626 baar,** *bore,* **everich,** *everyone* **627 Save,** *except,* **slow,** *slew* **628 hath caught a greet motyf,** *was greatly moved* **629 Of,** *by,* **witnesse,** *witnessing* **630 Depper,** *deeper,* **lere,** *learn* **632 kanstow noght,** *can you not at all,* **weylaway,** *alas* **633 starf,** *died* **634 boond,** *bound,* **lith ther he,** *lies he* (Satan) *where* **636 but if,** *unless,* **kithe,** *shows* **637 Withouten gilt,** *guiltless,* **as swithe,** *quickly* **640 Fro,** *from* **642 angeles synge Osanne,** *angels sing Hosanna* **644 socour,** *help,* **ellis,** *else* **645 seyn,** *seen* **646 prees,** *crowd,* **be lad,** *been led* **648 swich,** *such* **649 bistad,** *under threat* **650 route,** *crowd* **651 stant,** *stands* **653 everichone,** *every one* **654 som routhe,** *some pity* **656 wight,** *person,* **mone,** *appeal* **658 Fer been,** *far* (away) *are* **660 fulfild,** *filled* **662 do fecche,** *bring* **663 wol sweren,** *will swear* **664 slow,** *slew,* **wol we us avyse,** *we will consider* **665 wole,** *choose,* **justise,** *judge* **667 fet,** *fetched* **668 in the meene whiles, i.e.,** *while he was doing this* **669 hym smoot,** *struck him* **670 That,** (so) *that,* **atones,** *at once* **671 broste,** *burst* **673 general audience,** *the hearing of all* **674 desclaundred,** *slandered* **675 in heigh presence,** *before God* **676 hastou,** *have you,* **yet holde I my pees,** *yet* (should) *I hold my peace* **677 mervaille agast,** *marvel frightened,* **prees,** *crowd*

631–58 Lines not in Trivet or Gower. **631 hast,** Hg reads "nast." **639 Susanne,** Susanna, who in the Apocryphal version of the book of Daniel (Ch. 13) is falsely accused of adultery by two lecherous elders and saved by the inspired wisdom of Daniel; the topic was popular in medieval and Renaissance art. **641 Marie,** Mary, mother of Jesus and daughter of St. Anne. **647 wher as hym gat no grace,** "it being the case that he got no reprieve"; seeing a condemned person conducted to public execution was not uncommon in the Middle Ages. **653 ye,** omitted in El. **660** A familiar chivalric sentiment; see *KnT* 1.1761n. **666 Britoun book written with Evaungiles,** i.e., a gospel book written in Briton; the specification is Chaucer's addition. Also, this formal judicial scene has been thought appropriate to the Man of Law. **676 holde I,** Hg reads "I holde."

As mazed° folk they stoden everichone°
For drede of wreche°, save Custance allone.

Greet was the drede and eek the repentance
Of hem that hadden wrong suspecioun
Upon this sely° innocent, Custance.
And for this miracle, in conclusioun°,
And by Custances mediacioun,
The kyng, and many another in that place,
Converted was, thanked be Cristes grace!

This false kynght was slayn for his untrouthe
By juggement of Alla hastifly°;
And yet Custance hadde of his deeth greet routhe°.
And after this Jhesus, of his mercy,
Made Alla wedden ful solempnely°
This hooly mayden, that is so bright and sheene°;
And thus hath Crist ymaad° Custance a queene.

But who was woful, if I shal nat lye,
Of this weddyng but Donegild, and namo°,
The kynges mooder, ful of tirannye?
Hir thoughte° hir cursed herte brast atwo°.
She wolde noght° hir sone had do° so;
Hir thoughte a despit° that he sholde take
So strange° a creature unto his make°.

Me list nat° of the chaf°, ne of the stree°,
Maken so long a tale as of the corn°.
What° sholde I tellen of the roialtee°
At mariage; or which cours goth biforn°;
Who bloweth in a trumpe° or in an horn?
The fruyt° of every tale is for to seye°:
They ete, and drynke, and daunce, and synge, and pleye.

They goon to bedde, as it was skile° and right;
For thogh that wyves be ful hooly thynges,
They moste° take in pacience at nyght
Swiche manere necessaries° as been plesynges°
To folk that han ywedded hem with rynges,
And leye a lite° hir hoolynesse aside,
As for the tyme—it may no bet bitide°.

On hire he gat° a knave child anon°,
And to a bisshop and his constable eke°
He took his wyf to kepe°, whan he is gon
To Scotlond-ward°, his foomen° for to seke.
Now faire Custance, that is so humble and meke,
So longe is goon with childe til that stille°
She halt° hire chambre, abidyng° Cristes wille.

The tyme is come a knave child she beer°;
Mauricius at the font-stoon they hym calle.
This constable dooth forth come° a messageer,
And wroot° unto his kyng, that cleped° was Alle,
How that this blisful tidyng is bifalle°,
And othere tidynges spedeful° for to seye.
He taketh the lettre, and forth he gooth his weye.

This messager, to doon his avantage°,
Unto the kynges mooder rideth swithe°,
And salueth° hire ful faire in his langage.
"Madame," quod he, "ye may be glad and blithe°,"
And thanketh God an hundred thousand sithe°.
My lady queene hath child, withouten doute°,
To joye and blisse to al this regne° aboute.

"Lo°, heere the lettres seled° of this thyng,
That I moot bere° with al the haste I may.

---

678 mazed, *stunned,* **stoden everichone,** *all stood* **679 drede of wreche,** *fear of vengeance* **682 sely,** *blessed* **683 in conclusioun,** *as a result* **688 hastifly,** *immediately* **689 routhe,** *pity* **691 ful solempnely,** *with all ceremony* **692 sheene,** *shining* **693 ymaad,** *made* **695 namo,** *no more* **697 Hir thoughte,** *she thought,* **brast atwo,** *burst in two* **698 wolde noght,** *did not at all wish,* **do,** *done* **699 Hir thoughte a despit,** *she thought* (it) *a disgrace* **700 strange,** *foreign,* **unto his make,** *as his mate* **701 Me list nat,** *I do not wish* (to), **chaf,** *chaff,* **stree,** *straw* **702 corn,** *grain* **703 What,** *why,* **roialtee,** *royalty* **704 cours goth biforn,** *course* (of the marriage feast) *goes first* **705 trumpe,** *trumpet* **706 fruyt,** *essence,* **for to seye,** *to be told* **708 skile,** *proper* **710 moste,** *must* **711 Swiche manere necessaries,** *such kinds of necessities,* **plesynges,** *pleasures* **713 leye a lite,** *lay a little* **714 no bet bitide,** *happen no better* **715 gat,** *begot,* **knave child anon,** *boy soon* **716 eke,** *also* **717 kepe,** *care for* **718 To Scotlond-ward,** *toward Scotland,* **foomen,** *enemies* **720 stille,** *constantly* **721 halt,** *stays* (in), **abidyng,** *awaiting* **722 beer,** *bears* **724 dooth forth come,** *summoned* **725 wroot,** *wrote,* **cleped,** *called* **726 blisful tidyng is bifalle,** *happy news has occurred* **727 spedeful,** *useful* **729 doon his avantage,** *gain himself an advantage* **730 swithe,** *quickly* **731 salueth,** *greets* **732 blithe,** *happy* **733 sithe,** *times* **734 doute,** *doubt* **735 regne,** *kingdom* **736 Lo,** *behold,* **seled,** *sealed* **737 moot bere,** *must bear*

701–02 chaf . . . corn, the image of chaff (husk) and grain (or shell and nut or rind and fruit) is traditional, conveying the contrast between vehicle and tenor or plot and meaning, although here it seems to contrast only details and major action; compare *NPT* 7.3443. **704 mariage,** El and Hg read "mariages." **705 in a trumpe,** El reads "in the trumpe"; Hg, "in trompe." **714 no bet,** Hg reads "noon other." **715 knave,** erased in El and changed to "man," here and at 722. Compare *ClT* 4.444n. **723 font-stoon they hym calle,** i.e., they call him at the baptismal font. The sacrament of baptism involves the giving of a name as well as blessing with water; see 352n above. **728 taketh,** Hg reads "tath." **731 hire,** omitted in Hg. **736 lettres seled,** letters were kept shut with wax seals of their senders in order to indicate authenticity.

If ye wol aught° unto youre sone the kyng,
I am youre servant, bothe nyght and day."
Donegild answerde, "As now at this tyme, nay;
But heere al nyght I wol° thou take thy reste.
Tomorwe wol° I seye° thee what me leste°."

This messager drank sadly° ale and wyn,
And stolen were his lettres pryvely°
Out of his box, whil he sleep as a swyn°;
And countrefeted was ful subtilly
Another lettre, wroght° ful synfully,
Unto the kyng direct, of° this mateere,
Fro his constable, as ye shal after heere.

The lettre spak° the queene delivered was
Of so horrible a feendly° creature
That in the castel noon° so hardy was
That any while dorste ther° endure.
The mooder° was an elf°, by aventure°
Ycomen°—by charmes or by sorcerie—
And everich wight° hateth hir compaignye.

Wo° was this kyng whan he this lettre had
sayn°,
But to no wight° he tolde his sorwes soore°,
But of° his owene hand he wroot agayn°,
"Welcome the sonde° of Crist for everemoore
To me that am now lerned in his loore°.
Lord, welcome be thy lust° and thy plesaunce°;
My lust I putte al in thyn ordinaunce°.

"Kepeth° this child, al be it foul or feir,
And eek° my wyf, unto myn hoom-comynge°.
Crist, whan hym list°, may sende me an heir
Moore agreable than this to my likynge."
This lettre he seleth, pryvely wepynge,
Which to the messager was take° soone,
And forth he gooth; ther is na moore
to doone.

O messager, fulfild° of dronkenesse,
Strong is thy breeth, thy lymes faltren ay°,
And thou biwreyest° alle secreenesse°.
Thy mynde is lorn°, thou janglest as° a jay°,
Thy face is turned in a newe array°.
Ther° dronkenesse regneth° in any route°,
Ther is no conseil hyd°, withouten doute.

O Donegild, I ne have noon Englissh digne°
Unto thy malice and thy tirannye!
And therfore to the feend I thee resigne°;
Lat hym enditen° of thy traitorie!
Fy, mannysh°, fy!—O nay, by God, I lye°—
Fy, feendlych° spirit, for I dar wel telle
Thogh thou heere walke thy spirit is in helle.

This messager comth fro° the kyng agayn,
And at the kynges moodres court he lighte°,
And she was of this messager ful fayn°,
And plesed hym in al that ever she myghte.
He drank and wel his girdel underpighte°;
He slepeth and he fnorteth° in his gyse°
Al nyght, til the sonne gan aryse°.

Eft° were his lettres stolen everychon°,
And countrefeted lettres in this wyse:
"The king comandeth his constable anon,
Up peyne° of hangyng, and on heigh juyse°,
That he ne sholde suffren° in no wyse
Custance in-with his reawme° for t'abyde
Thre dayes and o quarter of a tyde.

"But in the same ship as he hire fond°,
Hire, and hir yonge sone, and al hir geere,
He sholde putte, and croude° hire fro the lond,
And chargen hire that she never eft° coome
theere."
O my Custance, wel may thy goost° have feere,

---

738 ye wol aught, *you wish* (to send) *anything* **741 wol,** *wish* **742 seye,** *tell,* **me leste,** *pleases me* **743 sadly,** *constantly* **744 pryvely,** *secretly* **745 as a swyn,** *like a pig* **747 wroght,** *made* **748 of,** *concerning* **750 spak,** *said* **751 feendly,** *fiendlike* **752 noon,** *no one* **753 dorste ther,** *dared there* **754 mooder,** *mother,* **elf,** *wicked creature,* **aventure,** *misfortune* **755 Ycomen,** *come* **756 everich wight,** *every person* **757 Wo,** *woeful,* **sayn,** *seen* **758 wight,** *person,* **sorwes soore,** *painful sorrows* **759 of,** *by,* **wroot agayn,** *wrote in response* **760 sonde,** *sending* **761 loore,** *teachings* **762 lust,** *wishes,* **plesaunce,** *pleasure* **762 thyn ordinaunce,** *your control* **764 Kepeth,** *protect* **765 eek,** *also,* **unto myn hoom-comynge,** *until I return home* **766 whan hym list,** *when it pleases him* **769 take,** *taken* **771 fulfild,** *full* **772 lymes faltren ay,** *limbs always falter* **773 biwreyest,** *betrays,* **secreenesse,** *secrecy* **774 lorn,** *lost,* **janglest as,** *chatter like,* **jay,** *bird* **775 array,** *appearance* **776 Ther,** *where,* **regneth,** *rules,* **route,** *company* **777 hyd,** *hidden* **778 digne,** *suitable* **780 resigne,** *renounce* **781 enditen,** *write* **782 Fy, mannysh,** *shame, manlike,* **lye,** *lie* **783 feendlych,** *fiendlike* **785 comth fro,** *comes from* **786 lighte,** *arrives* **787 fayn,** *pleased* **789 his girdel underpighte,** *stuffed his belt* **790 fnorteth,** *snores,* **gyse,** *way* **791 gan aryse,** *did arise* **792 Eft,** *again,* **everychon,** *each one* **795 Up peyne,** *under pain,* **heigh juyse,** *high judgment* **796 ne sholde suffren,** *should not allow* **797 in-with his reawme,** *within his realm* **799 fond,** *found* **801 croude,** *push* **802 eft,** *again* **803 thy goost,** *your spirit*

756 wight, omitted in El and Hg. Various readings in other manuscripts indicate it may have been lacking in the original. **771–77** From Innocent, *De Miseria,* 2.19; see 99–121n above. **797 reawme,** Hg reads "regne." **798 o quarter of a tyde,** either one-quarter of a tide (a maritime calculation; see line 510 above) or, more loosely, a quarter of an hour. Hg transposes "o" and "a."

And slepynge, in thy dreem, been in penance°,
Whan Donegild cast° al this ordinance°.

This messager on morwe whan he wook
Unto the castel halt° the nexte° way,
And to the constable he the lettre took.
And whan that he this pitous lettre say°,
Ful ofte he seyde "allas" and "weylaway".
"Lord Crist," quod he, "how may this world endure,
So ful of synne is many a creature?

"O myghty God, if that it be thy wille,
Sith° thou art rightful juge, how may it be
That thou wolt suffren innocentz to spille°,
And wikked folk regnen° in prosperitee?
O goode Custance, allas, so wo is me
That I moot° be thy tormentour or deye
On shames deeth°; ther is noon oother weye."

Wepen° bothe yonge and olde in al that place
Whan that the kyng this cursed lettre sente,
And Custance, with a deedly pale face,
The ferthe° day toward hir ship she wente.
But nathelees she taketh in good entente
The wyl of Crist, and knelynge on the stronde°
She seyde, "Lord, ay° welcome be thy sonde°!

"He that me kepte fro the false blame
While I was on the lond amonges yow,
He kan me kepe from harm and eek fro shame
In salte see, althogh I se noght how.
As strong as evere he was, he is yet now.
In hym triste° I, and in his mooder deere°,
That is to me my seyl° and eek my steere°."

Hir litel child lay wepyng in hir arm,
And knelynge, pitously to hym she seyde,
"Pees°, litel sone, I wol do thee noon harm."
With that hir coverchief of° hir heed she breyde°,
And over his litel eyen° she it leyde,
And in hir arm she lulleth it° ful faste,
And into hevene hire eyen up she caste.

"Mooder," quod she, "and mayde bright°, Marie,
Sooth° is that thurgh wommanes eggement°
Mankynde was lorn°, and dampned ay° to dye,
For which thy child was on a croys yrent°.
Thy blisful eyen sawe al his torment.
Thanne is ther no comparison bitwene
Thy wo and any wo man may sustene°.

"Thow sawe thy child yslayn° bifore thyne eyen,
And yet now lyveth my litel child, parfay°.
Now, lady bright, to whom alle woful° cryen,
Thow glorie of wommanhede°, thow faire may°,
Thow haven of refut°, brighte sterre° of day,
Rewe° on my child, that° of thy gentillesse
Rewest on every reweful° in distresse.

"O litel child, allas, what is thy gilt,
That nevere wroghtest synne° as yet, pardee°?
Why wil thyn harde fader han thee spilt°?
O mercy, deere constable," quod she,
"As lat my litel child dwelle° heer with thee;
And if thou darst° nat saven hym, for blame°,
Yet kys° hym ones in his fadres° name."

Therwith° she looked bakward to the londe,
And seyde, "Farewel, housbonde routhelees°!"
And up she rist°, and walketh doun the stronde°
Toward the ship—hir folweth al the prees°.
And evere she preyeth° hire child to holde his pees;
And taketh hir leve, and with an hooly entente
She blissed hire°, and into ship she wente.

---

804 penance, *suffering* **805 cast,** *planned,* **ordinance,** *arrangement* **807 halt,** *took,* **nexte,** *nearest* **809 say,** *saw* **814 Sith,** *since* **815 spille,** *die* **816 regnen,** *rule* **818 moot,** *must* **819 On shames deeth,** *in a death of shame* **820 Wepen,** *weep* **823 ferthe,** *fourth* **825 stronde,** *shore* **826 ay,** *always,* **sonde,** *sending* **832 triste,** *trust,* **mooder deere,** *dear mother* **833 seyl,** *sail,* **steere,** *rudder* **836 Pees,** *peace* **837 coverchief of,** *kerchief from,* **breyde,** *removed* **838 eyen,** *eyes* **839 lulleth it,** *quieted him* **841 mayde bright,** *beautiful maiden* **842 Sooth,** *truth,* **eggement,** *encouragement* **843 lorn,** *lost,* **dampned ay,** *condemned always* **844 croys rent,** *cross torn* **847 sustene,** *endure* **848 yslayn,** *slain* **849 parfay,** *by my faith* **850 alle woful,** *all who suffer* **851 wommanhede,** *womanhood,* **may,** *maiden* **852 haven of refut,** *shelter for refuge,* **sterre,** *star* **853 Rewe,** *have pity,* **that,** *you who* **854 every reweful,** *everyone pitiable* **856 wroghtest synne,** *sinned,* **pardee,** *by God* (Fr.) **857 thyn hard fader han thee,** *your cruel father have you killed* **859 As lat . . . dwelle,** *and let . . . live* **860 darst,** *dare,* **blame,** *fear of blame* **861 kys,** *kiss,* **fadres,** *father's* **862 Therwith,** *with this* **863 routhelees,** *pitiless* **864 rist,** *rises,* **stronde,** *shore* **865 hir folweth al the prees,** *the whole crowd follows her* **866 preyeth,** *asks* **868 blissed hire,** *blessed herself*

813–19 Lines not in Trivet; compare Gower, *CA* 2.1057–61. The question raised in these lines is a common one in the face of trials; compare *Bo* 1m5.34ff. **834–75** Not in Trivet; compare Gower, *CA* 2.1064–83. **843 wommanes eggement,** the misogynist commonplace that a woman (Eve) was the cause of the fall of humankind is rooted in Genesis 3.6. It is often paired with the notion that salvation was achieved through Mary and her suffering. **849 litel,** omitted in El. **861 Yet,** Hg reads "So."

Vitailled° was the ship, it is no drede°,
Habundantly for hire ful longe space°,
And othere necessaries that sholde nede°
She hadde ynogh°, heryed° be Goddes grace.
For° wynd and weder°, almyghty God purchace°,
And brynge hire hoom! I kan no bettre seye,
But in the see she dryveth° forth hir weye.

Explicit secunda pars. Sequitur pars tercia.

Alla the kyng comth hoom° soone after this
Unto his castle, of the which I tolde,
And asketh where his wyf and his child is°.
The constable gan aboute his herte colde°,
And pleynly° al the manere° he hym tolde
As ye han herd—I kan telle it no bettre—
And sheweth° the kyng his seel and eek his lettre,

And seyde, "Lord, as ye comanded me
Up peyne° of deeth, so have I doon, certein."
This messager tormented° was til he
Moste biknowe° and tellen, plat° and pleyn,
Fro nyght to nyght, in what place he had leyn°.
And thus, by wit and sotil° enquerynge,
Ymagined° was by° whom this harm gan sprynge°,

The hand was knowe° that the lettre wroot,
And al the venym° of this cursed dede,
But in what wise°, certeinly, I noot°.
Th'effect is this, that Alla, out of drede°,
His mooder slow°—that may men pleynly rede—
For that she traitoure was to hire ligeance°.
Thus endeth olde Donegild, with meschance°.

The sorwe that this Alla nyght and day
Maketh for his wyf, and for his child also,
Ther is no tonge that it telle may.
But now wol I unto Custance go,
That fleteth° in the see, in peyne and wo,
Fyve yeer and moore, as liked Cristes sonde,
Er that° hir ship approched unto the londe.

Under° an hethen castel, atte laste,
Of which the name in my text noght I fynde°,
Custance, and eek hir child, the see up caste.
Almyghty God, that saved al mankynde,
Have on Custance and on hir child som mynde°,
That fallen is in hethen hand eftsoon°,
In point to spille°, as I shal telle yow soone.

Doun fro the castle comth ther many a wight°
To gauren° on this ship and on Custance.
But shortly, from the castle, on a nyght,
The lordes styward—God yeve° hym meschance°—
A theef that hadde reneyed oure creance°,
Cam into the ship allone, and seyde he sholde
Hir lemman be°, wher so she wolde or nolde°.

Wo was this wrecched womman tho bigon°;
Hir child cride, and she cride pitously.
But blisful Marie heelp° hire right anon°,
For with hir struglyng wel and myghtily
The theef fil overbord al sodeynly°,
And in the see he dreynte for vengeance°.
And thus hath Crist unwemmed° kept Custance.

O foule lust of luxurie°, lo, thyn ende°!
Nat oonly that thou feyntest° mannes mynde,
But verraily thou wolt his body shende°.
Th'ende of thy werk, or of thy lustes blynde°,
Is compleynyng°. Hou many oon° may men fynde
That noght for werk somtyme°, but for th'entente
To doon this synne, been outher slayn or shente°!

---

869 Vitailled, *stocked with food,* **drede,** *doubt* **870 space,** *time* **871 sholde nede,** (she) *would need* **872 ynogh,** *enough,* **heryed,** *praised* **873 For,** (as) *for,* **weder,** *weather,* **purchace,** *provide* **875 dryveth,** *goes* **876 comth hoom,** *comes home* **878 is,** *are* **879 gan . . . colde,** *did* (grow) *cold* **880 pleynly,** *clearly,* **al the manere,** *the whole proceeding* **882 sheweth,** *shows* **884 Up peyne,** *under pain* **885 tormented,** *tortured* **886 Moste biknowe,** *must reveal,* **plat,** *clear* **887 leyn,** *slept* **888 sotil,** *subtle* **889 Ymagined,** *deduced,* **by,** *from,* **gan sprynge,** *did originate* **890 knowe,** *ascertained* **891 venym,** *poison* **892 wise,** *way,* **noot,** *know not* **893 out of drede,** *without doubt* **894 slow,** *slew* **895 ligeance,** *allegiance* **896 meschance,** *bad fortune* **901 fleteth,** *floats* **903 Er that,** *before* **904 Under,** *near* **905 noght I fynde,** *I do not find* **908 som mynde,** *some attention* **909 eftsoone,** *again* **910 point to spille,** *danger of death* **911 comth,** *comes,* **many a wight,** *many people* **912 gauren,** *stare* **914 yeve,** *give,* **meschance,** *bad fortune* **915 reneyed oure creance,** *renounced our faith* **917 Hir lemman be,** *be her lover,* **wher so she wolde or nolde,** *whether she wished it or not* **918 Wo . . . tho bigon,** *miserable then* **920 heelp,** *helped,* **right anon,** *right away* **922 sodeynly,** *suddenly* **923 dreynte for vengeance,** *drowned as punishment* **924 unwemmed,** *untainted* **925 lust of luxurie,** *desire of lechery,* **ende,** *outcome* **926 feyntest,** *dims* **927 shende,** *destroy* **928 lustes blynde,** *blind desires* **929 compleynyng,** *lamenting,* **Hou many oon,** *how many* **930 werk somtyme,** (the) *deed sometimes* **931 been outher slayn or shente,** *are either killed or destroyed*

875a *Explicit secunda pars. Sequitur pars tercia.* "Here ends part two. Here follows part three." **882 seel,** wax seal; see 736n above. **902 as liked Cristes sonde,** so it pleased the sending of Christ, an idiom that means something like "as it accorded with the dispensation of Christ." **903 the,** omitted in Hg. **914 lordes styward,** the steward or manager of the castle who represented his lord. **916 the,** omitted in Hg. **922 theef fil,** villain fell; in Trivet's more elaborate account, she pushes him. **925–31** From Innocent, *De Miseria,* 2.21; see 99–121n above.

How may this wayke° womman han this strengthe
Hire to defende agayn° this renegat°?
O Golias, unmesurable of lengthe,
Hou myghte David make thee so maat°,
So yong and of armure so desolaat°?
Hou dorste° he looke upon thy dredful face?
Wel may men seen, it nas° but Goddes grace.

Who yaf° Judith corage or hardynesse°
To sleen° hym Oloferne in his tente,
And to deliveren out of wrecchednesse
The peple of God? I seye, for this entente°,
That right° as God spirit of vigour sente
To hem°, and saved hem out of meschance,
So sente he myght and vigour to Custance.

Forth gooth hir ship thurghout the narwe° mouth
Of Jubaltare and Septe, dryvynge ay°
Somtyme west and somtyme north and south
And somtyme est, ful many a wery day,
Til Cristes mooder—blessed be she ay—
Hath shapen°, thurgh hir endelees goodnesse,
To make an ende of al hir hevynesse°.

Now lat us stynte° of Custance but a throwe°,
And speke we of the Romayn Emperour,
That out of Surrye° hath by lettres knowe°
The slaughtre of Cristen folk, and dishonour
Doon to his doghter by a fals traytour,
I mene the cursed wikked Sowdanesse°
That at the feeste leet sleen° both moore and lesse°.

For which this Emperour hath sent anon
His senatour, with roial ordinance°,
And othere lordes, God woot°, many oon,
On Surryens to taken heigh° vengeance.
They brennen°, sleen°, and brynge hem to meschance°
Ful many a day; but shortly, this is th'ende,
Homward to Rome they shapen hem to wende°.

This senatour repaireth° with victorie
To Rome-ward°, saillynge ful roially°,
And mette° the ship dryvynge°, as seith the storie,
In which Custance sit ful pitously.
Nothyng° knew he what she was, ne why
She was in swich array°, ne she nyl seye°
Of hire estaat°, although° she sholde deye.

He bryngeth hire to Rome, and to his wyf
He yaf° hire and hir yonge sone also;
And with the senatour she ladde° hir lyf.
Thus kan Oure Lady bryngen out of wo
Woful Custance, and many another mo°.
And longe tyme dwelled she in that place,
In hooly werkes evere, as was hir grace°.

The senatoures wyf hir aunte was,
But for al that° she knew hire never the moore.
I wol no lenger tarien° in this cas,
But to Kyng Alla, which I spak of yoore°,
That wepeth for his wyf and siketh soore°,
I wol retourne°, and lete° I wol Custance
Under the senatoures governance.

Kyng Alla, which that hadde his mooder slayn,
Upon a day fil in swich repentance°
That, if I shortly tellen shal and playn,
To Rome he comth to receyven his penance,
And putte hym in° the Popes ordinance°
In heigh and logh°, and Jhesu Crist bisoghte°
Foryeve his wikked werkes° that he wroghte°.

The fame anon° thurghout the toun is born°,
How Alla kyng shal comen in pilgrymage,

932 wayke, *weak* **933 agayn,** *against,* **renegat,** *turncoat* (see line 915) **935 maat,** (check) *mated* **936 of armure so desolaat,** *without armor* **937 Hou dorste,** *how dares* **938 nas,** *is nothing* **939 yaf,** *gave,* **hardynesse,** *boldness* **940 sleen,** *slay* **942 entente,** *opinion* **943 right,** *just* **944 hem,** *them* **946 narwe,** *narrow* **947 dryvynge ay,** *moving always* **951 Hath shapen,** *has arranged* **952 hevynesse,** *sorrow* **953 stynte,** *pause,* **but a throwe,** *briefly* **955 Surrye,** *Syria,* **knowe,** *known* **958 Sowdanesse,** *Sultaness* **959 leet sleen,** *caused to be killed,* **moore and lesse,** *upper and lower* (classes) **961 roial ordinance,** *royal command* **962 woot,** *knows* **963 heigh,** *extreme* **964 brennen,** *burn,* **sleen,** *slay,* **meschance,** *ill fate* **966 shapen hem to wende,** *prepare themselves to travel* **967 repaireth,** *returns* **968 To Rome-ward,** *toward Rome,* **roially,** *royally* **969 mette,** *met,* **dryvynge,** *moving* **971 Nothyng,** *not at all* **972 swich array,** *such a condition,* **ne she nyl seye,** *nor will she speak* **973 estaat,** *social rank,* **althogh,** *even if* **975 yaf,** *gave* **976 ladde,** *led* **978 another mo,** *others more* **980 grace,** *good fortune* **982 for al that,** *even so* **983 tarien,** *delay* **984 yoore,** *earlier* **985 siketh soore,** *sighs sorely* **986 wol retourne,** *will return,* **lete,** *leave* **989 fil in swich repentance,** *fell into such remorse* **992 in,** *under,* **ordinance,** *orders* **993 In heigh and logh,** *in high and low* (i.e.. in all respects). **bisoghte,** *asked* **994 werkes,** *deeds,* **wroghte,** *worked* (i.e., had done) **995 fame anon,** *news quickly,* **born,** *carried*

934 Golias, Goliath, the gigantic warrior slain by David in 1 Samuel 17.4ff. **938 nas,** Hg reads "was." **939–40 Judith . . . hym Oloferne,** Judith saves the Israelites by killing Holofernes in the apocryphal book of Judith; compare *MkT* 7.2251ff. Redundant pronouns such as *hym* recur in Middle English. **947 Jubaltare and Septe,** Gibraltar and Ceuta, separated by the Strait of Gibraltar at the western end of the Mediterranean Sea. **ay,** El reads "alway." **971 thyng knew,** Hg reads "thyng ne knew." **973 althogh,** El and Hg read "thogh." **985 wepeth for his wyf,** Hg reads "for his wyf wepeth." **995 thurghout the toun,** Hg reads "thurgh Rome toun." **996 in,** El reads "on."

By herbergeours° that wenten hym biforn;
For which the senatour, as was usage°,
Rood hym agayns°, and many of his lynage°,
As wel to shewen his heighe magnificence
As to doon any kyng a reverence°.

Greet cheere dooth° this noble senatour
To Kyng Alla, and he to hym also;
Everich of hem° dooth oother greet honour.
And so bifel that inwith° a day or two
This senatour is to Kyng Alla go°
To feste°, and shortly, if I shal nat lye,
Custances sone° wente in his compaignye.

Som men wolde seyn° at requeste of Custance
This senatour hath lad this child to feeste;
I may nat tellen every circumstance:
Be as be may°, ther was he at the leeste°.
But sooth° is this, that at his moodres heeste°
Biforn° Alla, durynge the metes space°,
The child stood, lookyng in the kynges face.

This Alla kyng hath of this child greet wonder,
And to the senatour he seyde anon,
"Whos is that faire child that stondeth yonder?"
"I noot°," quod he, "by God, and by Seint John.
A mooder he hath, but fader hath he noon
That I of woot°"; but and shortly, in a stounde°,
He tolde Alla how that this child was founde.

"But God woot°," quod this senatour also,
"So vertuous a lyvere° in my lyf
Ne saugh I nevere° as she, ne herde of mo°,
Of worldly wommen, mayde, ne of wyf.
I dar wel seyn° hir hadde levere° a knyf
Thurghout hir brest than ben° a womman wikke;
There is no man koude° brynge hire to that prikke°."

Now was this child as lyk unto Custance
As possible is a creature to be.
This Alla hath the face in remembrance
Of dame Custance, and ther on mused° he
If that the childes mooder were aught° she
That is his wyf, and pryvely° he sighte°,
And spedde hym fro° the table that° he myghte.

"Parfay°," thoghte he, "fantome° is in myn heed.
I oghte deme°, of skilful° juggement,
That in the salte see my wyf is deed."
And afterward he made his argument:
"What woot I if that° Crist have hyder ysent°
My wyf by see, as wel as he hire sente
To my contree fro thennes that° she wente°?"

And after noon, hoom° with the senatour
Goth Alla, for to seen this wonder chaunce°.
This senatour dooth Alla greet honour,
And hastifly° he sente after Custaunce.
But trusteth weel, hire liste nat to daunce°
Whan that she wiste wherfore was that sonde°;
Unnethe° upon hir feet she myghte stonde.

Whan Alla saugh his wyf, faire° he hire grette°,
And weep that it was routhe° for to see;
For at the firste look he on hire sette,
He knew wel verraily° that it was she.
And she, for sorwe, as doumb stant° as a tree,
So was hir herte shet° in hir distresse,
Whan she remembred his unkyndenesse.

Twyes° she swowned° in his owene sighte.
He weep°, and hym excuseth° pitously.

997 herbergeours, *servants who arrange for lodgings* **998 usage,** *custom* **999 Rood hym agayns,** *rode to meet him,* **lynage,** *kindred* **1001 doon . . . a reverence,** *revere* **1002 Greet cheere dooth,** *great attention gives* **1004 Everich of hem,** *each of them* **1005 inwith,** *within* **1006 is . . . go,** *goes* **1007 To feste,** *for a feast* **1008 sone,** *son* **1009 wolde seyn,** *would say* **1012 Be as be may,** *whatever the case,* **leeste,** *least* **1013 sooth,** (the) *truth,* **moodres heeste,** *mother's request* **1014 Biforn,** *before,* **metes space,** *mealtime* **1019 noot,** *know not* **1021 woot,** *know,* **stounde,** *moment* **1023 woot,** *knows* **1024 lyvere,** *living person* **1025 Ne saugh I nevere,** *I never saw,* **herde of mo,** *heard of any* **1027 dar wel seyn,** *dare say,* **hir hadde levere,** *she would rather have* **1028 ben,** *be* **1029 koude,** (who) *could,* **prikke,** *point* **1033 ther on mused,** *considered* **1034 aught,** *none other than* **1035 pryvely,** *quietly,* **sighte,** *sighed* **1036 spedde hym fro,** *hurried himself from,* **that,** *as soon as* **1037 Parfay,** *by my faith,* **fantome,** *fantasy* **1038 deme,** *to accept,* **of skilful,** *by reasonable* **1041 woot I if that,** *do I know whether,* **have hyder ysent,** *has sent here* **1043 fro thennes that,** *from where,* **wente,** *traveled* **1044 hoom,** *home* **1045 wonder chaunce,** *wondrous possibility* **1047 hastifly,** *quickly* **1048 hire liste nat to daunce,** *she did not want to dance* (with joy) **1049 wiste wherfore was that sonde,** *knew the reason for the summons* **1050 Unnethe,** *scarcely* **1051 faire,** *fairly,* **grette,** *greeted* **1052 routhe,** *pity* **1054 verraily,** *truly* **1055 doumb stant,** *silent stands* **1056 shet,** *enclosed* **1058 Twyes,** *twice,* **swowned,** *fainted* **1059 weep,** *weeps,* **hym excuseth,** *excuses himself*

1000 As wel to shewen his, "Both to show his own"; the Roman senator meets King Aella as something of an equal, to show his own high station as well as to acknowledge the king's. **1005 inwith,** Hg reads "in." **1009 Som men,** Tyrwhitt and later editors have taken this and the reference at 1086 below as disparaging allusions to Gower's version of the story and indications that Chaucer thought it less decorous than his own. In Gower and Trivet, Custance instructs Maurice how to act at the meal. Generally, Chaucer's version is more compressed from the time that Constance returns to Rome.

"Now God," quod he, "and alle his halwes° brighte
So wisly° on my soule as have mercy,
That of youre harm as giltelees am I
As is Maurice my sone, so lyk youre face;
Elles° the feend me fecche out of this place!"

Long was the sobbyng and the bitter peyne,
Er that hir° woful hertes myghte cesse°;
Greet was the pitee for to heere hem pleyne°,
Thurgh whiche pleintes° gan hir° wo encresse.
I pray yow alle my labour to relesse°;
I may nat telle hir wo until tomorwe,
I am so wery for to speke° of sorwe.

But finally, whan that the sothe is wist°
That Alla giltelees was of hir wo,
I trowe° an hundred tymes been they kist°,
And swich° a blisse is ther bitwix hem° two
That, save° the joye that lasteth everemo°,
Ther is noon lyk that any creature
Hath seyn° or shal, whil that the world may dure°.

Tho preyde she° hir housbonde mekely,
In relief of hir longe, pitous pyne°,
That he wolde preye° hir fader specially
That of his magestee he wolde enclyne°
To vouchesauf° som day with hym to dyne°.
She preyde hym eek he sholde by no weye
Unto hir fader no word of hire seye°.

Som men wolde seyn° how that the child Maurice
Dooth° this message unto this Emperour;
But, as I guesse, Alla was nat so nyce°
To hym that was of so sovereyn° honour
As he that is of Cristen folk the flour,
Sente° any child, but it is bet to deeme°
He wente hymself, and so it may wel seeme.

This Emperour hath graunted° gentilly
To come to dyner, as he hym bisoughte°;
And wel rede I° he looked bisily°
Upon this child, and on his doghter thoghte.
Alla goth to his in°, and as hym oghte°,
Arrayed for this feste in every wise
As ferforth° as his konnyng° may suffise.

The morwe° cam, and Alla gan hym dresse°,
And eek his wyf, this Emperour to meete.
And forth they ryde in joye and in gladnesse.
And whan she saugh° hir fader in the strete,
She lighte doun and falleth hym to feete°.
"Fader," quod she, "youre yonge child Custance
Is now ful clene° out of youre remembrance.

"I am youre doghter Custance," quod she,
"That whilom° ye han sent unto Surrye.
It am I, fader, that in the salte see
Was put allone and dampned° for to dye.
Now, goode fader, mercy I yow crye!
Sende me namoore unto noon hethenesse°,
But thonketh my lord heere of his kyndenesse."

Who kan the pitous joye tellen al
Bitwixe hem thre°, syn° they been thus ymette°?
But of my tale make an ende I shal;
The day goth faste, I wol no lenger lette°.
This glade folk to dyner they hem sette°;
In joye and blisse at mete° I lete hem dwelle
A thousand foold° wel moore than I kan telle.

This child Maurice was sithen° Emperour
Maad° by the Pope, and lyved cristenly.
To Cristes chirche he dide greet honour.
But I lete al his storie passen by;
Of Custance is my tale specially.

1060 halwes, *saints* **1061 wisly,** *truly* **1064 Elles,** *or else* (may) **1066 Er that hir,** *before their,* **cesse,** *cease* **1067 hem pleyne,** *them lament* **1068 pleintes,** *lamentation,* **gan hir,** *did their* **1069 relesse,** *release* (me from) **1071 for to speke,** *of speaking* **1072 sothe is wist,** *truth is known* **1074 trowe,** *believe,* **been they kist,** *they kissed* **1075 swich,** *such,* **bitwix hem,** *between them* **1076 save,** *except for,* **everemo,** *eternally* **1078 seyn,** *seen,* **dure,** *last* **1079 Tho preyde she,** *then she asked* **1080 pyne,** *pain* **1081 preye,** *ask* **1082 enclyne,** *consent* **1083 vouchesauf,** *agree,* **dyne,** *dine* **1085 seye,** *speak* **1086 wolde seyn,** *would say* **1087 Dooth,** *conveys* **1088 nyce,** *insensitive* **1089 so sovereyn,** *such supreme* **1091 Sente,** (to) *send,* **bet to deeme,** *better to think* **1093 graunted,** *agreed* **1094 bisoughte,** *requested* **1095 wel rede I,** *I well read,* **bisily,** *intently* **1097 in,** *lodging* (inn), **hym oghte,** *he ought to* **1099 ferforth,** *far,* **konnyng,** *ability* **1100 morwe,** *morning,* **gan hym dresse,** *prepared himself* **1103 saugh,** *saw* **1104 hym to feete,** *at his feet* **1106 ful clene,** *completely* **1108 whilom,** *once* **1110 dampned,** *condemned* **1112 hethenesse,** *heathen land* **1115 Bitwixe hem thre,** *among the three of them,* **syn,** *since,* **ymette,** *met* **1117 lette,** *delay* **1118 hem sette,** *set themselves* **1119 mete,** (the) *meal* **1120 foold,** *times* **1121 sithen,** *afterward* **1122 Maad,** *made*

1060 alle, omitted in El and Hg. **1084 sholde,** El reads "wolde." **1086** See 1009n above. In Trivet and Gower, Maurice conveys the invitation. **1090 flour,** flower, i.e., the emperor is the apex of Christianity. **1124 his,** Hg reads "this."

In the olde Romayn geestes may men fynde
Maurices lyf; I bere it noght in mynde.

This Kyng Alla, whan he his tyme say°,
With his Custance, his hooly wyf so sweete,
To Engelond been they come the righte° way,
Wher as they lyve in joye and in quiete.
But litel while it lasteth, I yow heete°,
Joye of this world, for tyme wol nat abyde.
Fro day to nyght it changeth as the tyde.

Who lyved evere in swich delit o° day
That hym ne moeved outher° conscience,
Or ire°, or talent, or somkynnes affray°,
Envye, or pride, or passion, or offence?
I ne seye but for this ende this sentence°.
That litel while in joye or in plesance
Lasteth the blisse of Alla with Custance.

For deeth, that taketh of heigh and logh° his rente°,
Whan passed was a yeer, evene as I gesse,
Out of this world this Kyng Alla he hente°,
For whom Custance hath ful greet hevynesse°.
Now lat° us praye to God his soule blesse.
And dame Custance, finally to seye,
Toward the toun of Rome goth hire weye°.

To Rome is come this hooly creature,
And fyndeth hire freendes hoole° and sounde°.
Now is she scaped° al hire aventure.
And whan that she hir fader hath yfounde°,
Doun on hir knees falleth she to grounde;
Wepynge for tendrenesse in herte blithe°,
She heryeth° God an hundred thousand sithe°.

In vertu and in hooly almus-dede°
They lyven alle, and nevere asonder wende°;
Til deeth departed hem°, this lyf they lede.
And fareth now weel, my tale is at an ende.
Now Jhesu Crist, that of his myght may sende
Joy after wo, governe us in his grace,
And kepe° us alle that been in this place!

Amen.

Heere endeth the Tale of the Man of Lawe.

[EPILOGUE]

Owre Hoost upon his stiropes° stood anon°,
And seyde, "Goode men, herkeneth everych on°!
This was a thrifty° tale for the nones°!
Sir Parisshe Prest," quod he, "for Goddes bones,
Telle us a tale, as was thi forward yore°.
I se wel that ye lerned men in lore
Can moche° good, by Goddes dignite!"
The Parson him answerde, "Benedicite°!
What eyleth° the man, so synfully to swere°?"
Oure Host answerde, "O Jankin, be ye there?
I smelle a Lollere in the wynd," quod he.
"Now, goode men," quod oure Host, "herkeneth° me;
Abydeth°, for Goddes digne passioun°,

1128 say, *saw* **1130 righte,** *direct* **1132 yow heete,** *assure you* **1135 swich delit o,** *such delight one* **1136 hym ne moeved outher,** *disturbed him not either* **1137 ire,** *anger,* **somkynnes affray,** *some kind of fear* **1139 ne seye but for this ende this sentence,** *make this observation only for this purpose* **1142 heigh and logh,** *high and low,* **rente,** *payment* **1144 hente,** *snatched* **1145 hevynesse,** *sorrow* **1146 lat,** *let* **1148 goth hire weye,** *takes her way* **1150 hoole,** *undamaged,* **sounde,** *healthy* **1151 is . . . scaped,** *has escaped* **1152 hir fader hath yfounde,** *has found her father* **1154 blithe,** *happy* **1155 heryeth,** *praises,* **sithe,** *times* **1156 almus-dede,** *charitable deeds* **1157 asonder wende,** *traveled separately* **1158 departed hem,** *separated them* **1162 kepe,** *protect* **1163 stiropes,** *stirrups,* **anon,** *quickly* **1164 herkeneth everych on,** *listen everyone* **1165 thrifty,** *successful,* **nones,** *occasion* **1167 thi forward yore,** *your promise earlier* **1169 Can moche,** *know much* **1170 Benedicite,** *bless us* **1171 eyleth,** *ails,* **swere,** *utter oaths* **1174 herkeneth,** *listen to* **1175 Abydeth,** *wait,* **digne passioun,** *worthy suffering*

1126 olde Romayn geestes, old Roman stories or histories. The life of Maurice is found in Trivet's *Chronicle* along with that of Constance in the section titled "Les gestes des apostles, emperours, et rois" ("Accounts of Apostle, Emperors, and Kings"). **1132–38** Ecclesiasticus 18.26 and Job 21.12, both from Innocent, *De Miseria,* 1.20; see 99–121n above. **1146 praye to God,** Hg reads "prayen God." **1163–90** These lines are included in 35 manuscripts but omitted in El, Hg, and many others, perhaps canceled from Chaucer's original or circulating on a separate leaf. The text here is based on Corpus Christi College, Oxford, MS 198. **1172 Jankin,** familiar form of John (like *Johnny*), a traditional name for a priest. **1173 I smelle a Lollere in the wynd,** i.e., I think I detect a Lollard. The Lollards were followers of John Wycliffe, fourteenth-century Church reformer, who objected to swearing (and to pilgrimages) and promoted translation of the Bible into English. "Lollard" derives from Dutch for "mumbler" and was applied to many kinds of religious zealot.

For we schal han a predicacioun°;
This Lollere heer wil prechen° us somwhat."
"Nay, by my fader soule, that schal he nat!"
Seyde the Wif of Bath; "he schal nat preche;
He schal no gospel glosen° here ne teche°.
We leven alle° in the grete God," quod she;
"He wolde sowen° som difficulte,
Or springen cokkel° in our clene corn.
And therfore, Hoost, I warne thee biforn°,
My joly body schal a tale telle,
And I schal clynken° you so mery a belle,
That I schal waken al this compaignie.
But it schal not ben of philosophie,
Ne phislyas, ne termes queinte° of lawe.
Ther is but litel Latyn in my mawe°!"

1176 schal han a predicacioun, *shall have a sermon* **1177 prechen,** *preach* **1180 glosen,** *gloss* (comment on), **teche,** *teach* **1181 leven alle,** *all believe* **1182 wolde sowen,** *will plant* **1183 springen cokkel,** *raise weeds* **1184 biforn,** *in advance* **1186 clynken,** *jingle* **1189 termes queinte,** *curious words* **1190 mawe,** *mouth*

1179 Wif of Bath This reading is found in no MS; all read "Squyer," "Sumnour," or "Shipman," two-syllable words beginning with *S.* "Wife of Bath" is assumed to have been in Chaucer's original when this epilogue linked the present *ShT* (originally assigned to the Wife of Bath) to *MLT.* When Chaucer changed his plans and substituted another pilgrim name for "Wif of Bath," he had to supply a syllable; in the manuscripts "heer" is found in various positions, indicating that it may have been written with a caret in the margin of the original. **1185 joly body,** merry self; the same phrase occurs in *ShT* 7.423, referring to a woman. In both instances, Chaucer may have had the Wife of Bath in mind. **1189 phisylas,** uncertain meaning, but it may be a malapropism for "filace" (file of documents), some form of "physick" (medicine), or even the *Physics* of Aristotle. The original word confused the scribes, who provided a number of variants. This and the other terms of learning in lines 1188–89 may be seen as an appropriate response to *Mel,* which may once have stood in the place of *MLT*; see 96n above.

Canterbury Tales, Part 3

Introduction

IN 1908, ELEANOR PRESCOTT HAMMOND (1933, no. 86) heralded much modern Chaucer criticism when she labeled Parts 3, 4, and 5 of the *Canterbury Tales* the "marriage group," arguing that the sequence is the product of Chaucer's most mature art (after 1390?) and identifying a major source of the group: St. Jerome's *Epistola adversus Jovinianum* (Letter against Jovinian)—Jerome's tendentious argument that virginity is morally superior to marriage. Almost everyone agrees that among Chaucer's most remarkable achievements is the creation of the proto-feminist Wife of Bath out of Jerome's antimatrimonial, antifeminist material. Insofar as her strategies of argument can be seen to be similar to Jerome's own—interpreting authorities for one's own purposes—the Wife may be seen to "read like a man," to adapt Carolyn Dinshaw's felicitous phrase in *Chaucer's Sexual Poetics* (1989, no. 471).

Dinshaw focuses on how Jankyn (husband number five) treats (and beats!) the Wife, and identifies several correlations between the manipulation of texts and the treatment of women in Western tradition. In this line of thinking, Alison's uses and abuses of scripture and other written authorities parallel her manipulations of her husbands, an inversion of the traditional control of books and women by men, and an inversion of the traditional hierarchy of husband and wife in marriage.

In the Middle Ages, male control in marriage was a figure for the well-ordered hierarchical society, thought to parallel Christ's marriage to the Church, the king to the commonwealth, and reason to the senses. When the Wife of Bath asserts that her own experiences are equal or superior to the authority of Jerome and others, she verges on heresy; yet she does so with such gusto that it is difficult not to side with her. When we recognize that Chaucer constructs her experiences from the very authorities the Wife imitates and simultaneously rejects, we find ourselves in an interpretive circle from which escape is difficult: the Wife of Bath is a product of the very system she challenges.

The character of the Wife of Bath overshadows Part 3 and much of the marriage group. The acrimonious exchange of tales between the Friar and Summoner begins as an altercation that interrupts her prologue (829–56), following an earlier interruption by the Pardoner (163–92). Interruption occurs elsewhere in the Canterbury fiction, but only the Wife succeeds in quelling her interrupters. References to the Wife by the Clerk (4.1170) and in the *Merchant's Tale* (4.1685) contribute to her looming presence, but our sense of a real person speaking results largely from the confessional mode of her prologue, the tensions and contradictions in her claims, and the stylistic virtuosity through which Chaucer brings her to life.

Though Jerome is the major source for topics and arguments in the *Wife of Bath's Prologue*, La Vieille (Old Woman) of Jean de Meun's portion of the *Roman de la Rose* is the immediate model for her character, derived ultimately from the experienced old bawd found in Ovid. Works by Walter Map, Jehan LeFévre, Eustace Deschamps, and others contributed to the large antifeminist tradition from which the Wife of Bath arose, and they provide many echoes of details and diction. None of them achieves, however, as strong a sense of a living person speaking. In *The Disenchanted Self* (1990, no. 647), H. Marshall Leicester offers a feminist-psychoanalytical-deconstructive reading of the speaking voice in the *Wife of Bath's Prologue*. In *Chaucer and the Subject of History* (1991, no. 442), Lee Patterson examines the subjectivity of the Wife in light of the genre of *sermons joyeux* (parodic literary sermons), and he assesses her relation to La Vieille. In *Fallible Authors* (2008, no. 1044), A. J. Minnis examines the variety of ways that the Wife descends from La Vieille in her characteristic self-fashioning, while also embodying many of the restrictions placed on women in late-fourteenth-century England. Ralph Hanna III and Traugott Lawler collect materials for studying the tradition from which the *Wife of Bath's Prologue* arose—Jerome, Walter Map's *Dissuasio Valerii* (Dissuasion of Valerius), and Theophrastus's *Liber de Nuptiis* (Book of Marriage)—in *Jankyn's Book of Wikked Wyves* (1997, no. 869).

The *Wife of Bath's Tale* is a version of the "loathly lady" story that is also found in John Gower's "Tale of Florent" and in two fifteenth-century Arthurian tales, *The Weddynge of Sir Gawen and Dame Ragnell* (a romance) and *The Marriage of Sir Gawaine* (a ballad), all of them discussed as a group in a collection of essays, *The English "Loathly Lady" Tales*, edited by S Elizabeth Passmore and Susan Carter (2007, no. 880). Chaucer's version stands out for the ways it emphasizes female wisdom and female sovereignty, even though it ends in marital compromise (as does the *Wife of Bath's Prologue*). Among the changes Chaucer makes to the traditional tale (see, e.g., 889n, 1220n), the most apparent is the addition of the loathly lady's lecture on *gentillesse* (1109ff.), which converts the knight from rapist to compliant husband, a parallel to the lady's own transformation to youthful beauty. The lecture overturns traditional notions of class by suggesting that gentle deeds are more important than gentle birth, and, rooted in Dante's *Convivio*, it marks a stage in the slow growth of the ideal of human equality in Western thought. The topics of sovereignty in marriage and gentility are paired elsewhere in the marriage group, aligning issues of gender and class and cementing the cohesion of Parts 3, 4, and 5.

As much as the Wife's materials are about marital sovereignty and gentility, they are also concerned with texts and their meanings, orality in opposition to literacy, and, arguably, the role of *truth* in marriage be*troth*als. The *Friar's Tale* focuses more narrowly on what language does and under what conditions speech has real effects. It depicts a pledge of brotherhood between a demon and a summoner (a resounding slap at the pilgrim Summoner) and a pair of curses. The carter's curse produces no effect because he does not really intend to send his cart and horses to the devil, but the old lady's curse of the summoner is powerful and effective because she does intend it, because the summoner does not intend to repent, and because (as his questions to the demon show) he genuinely wants to know about hell. The speech acts of pledging, cursing, and questioning are brought together in this seemingly simple tale to explore the efficacy of language and its relation to the intentions of a speaker. See Daniel T. Kline, "'Myne By Right': Oath Making and Intent in *The Friar's Tale*" (1998, no. 895). No central pledge occurs in analogous accounts, and Penn R. Szittya, in "The Green Man as Loathly Lady" (1975, no. 849), shows how the pledge in the *Friar's Tale* links it with the pledge of marriage between knight and loathly lady in the *Wife of Bath's Tale* and how the pairing of the two tales recalls the echoic relation of the Knight's and Miller's tales in part 1 of the *Canterbury Tales*.

As the Reeve sought to outdo the Miller, his working-class rival, the Summoner goes after the Friar, his ecclesiastical rival—and (it is suggested) his equal in anger and avarice. Commissioned by the papacy, friars were outside the jurisdiction of the diocesan hierarchy of archbishops, bishops, and parish priests. Summoners were the subpoena servers of the judicial branch of this structure, notorious for using the office to bilk the poor, just as friars were notorious for currying favor with the rich. The vicious antagonism of Chaucer's Summoner and Friar embodies the social and spiritual upheavals latent in their greed and abuse of their respective offices. The *Summoner's Tale* is dominated by antifraternal satire through which the Summoner ridicules the claims of friars to be the new apostles (see e.g., 1737n, 2185–88n), and he undercuts these claims through scatology, recurrent puns (1707n), and a blasphemous parody of the Pentecost. The great wind of the Holy Spirit that brought the gift of speaking in tongues to Christ's apostles (Acts 2.1–6) is equated with the fart of an ailing man. Human speech, like all sound, is reduced to reverberating air (2234). We have no clear source for the plot of either the *Friar's Tale* or the *Summoner's Tale*, although parallels to many details can be found in sermon handbooks, anecdotes, and other popular materials. It is striking that Chaucer adapts medieval popular culture to create the tales of these two ecclesiastical officers when he uses more learned material to create the Wife of Bath.

On the treatment of antifraternalism and Pentecost in the tale, see Glending Olson, "The End of *The Summoner's Tale* and the Uses of Pentecost" (1999, no. 911); on clerical corruption and the *Friar's Tale*, see Brantley L. Bryant,

"'By Extorcions I Lyve': Chaucer's *Friar's Tale* and Corrupt Officials" (2007, no. 892). D. Thomas Hanks Jr. discusses puns in "Chaucer's *Summoner's Tale* and 'the first smel of fartes thre'" (1997, no. 905). In the Introduction to his Variorum edition of *The Summoner's Tale* (1995, no. 55), John F. Plummer III surveys the thematic and structural unity of Part 3 and its parallels with Part 1.

Canterbury Tales Part 3

From woodcut made by W.H. Hooper and published by the Chaucer Society between 1868 and 1879

Wife of Bath's Tale

Prologue

The Prologue of the Wyves Tale of Bathe.

Experience though noon auctoritee
Were in this world is right ynogh for me
To speke of wo that is in mariage.
For, lordynges, sith° I twelve yeer was of age,
Thonked be God that is eterne° on lyve,
Housbondes at chirche dore I have had fyve—
If I so ofte myghte have ywedded bee°—
And alle were worthy men in hir degree°.
But me was toold, certeyn, nat longe agoon is°,
That sith that Crist ne wente nevere but onis°
To weddyng in the Cane of Galilee,
That by the same ensample° taughte he me
That I ne sholde wedded be but ones°.
Herkne eek°, which a sharp word for the nones°:
Biside a welle, Jhesus, God and man,

---

4 sith, *since* **5 eterne,** *eternal* **7 ywedded bee,** *been married* **8 hir degree,** *their social standing* **9 nat longe agoon is,** (it) *is not long ago* **10 onis,** *once* **12 ensample,** *example* **13 ne . . . but ones,** *only once* **14 Herkne eek, which,** *listen also* (to this), *which* (is), **for the nones,** *indeed*

1 auctoritee, especially written authority, as the battle over Jankyn's book dramatizes in lines 788ff. below. The theme of experience and authority recurs throughout *CT.* **2 is right ynogh for,** El reads "were right ynogh to." **3 wo . . . in mariage,** the unhappiness of marriage was a standard argument in medieval antimatrimonial—often antifeminist—literature written to convince priests and nuns to remain celibate. These writings are the sources of the *WBP,* especially St. Jerome's *Epistola adversus Jovinianum* (Letter against Jovinian), although *WBP* confronts its antifeminist assumptions and arguments. **4 sith I,** Hg reads "sith that I." **twelve yeer was of age,** twelve years old, the age at which a girl could marry under Church law. **6 chirche dore,** the marriage ceremony was performed at the church door, after which the couple went inside for the nuptial mass; the line echoes *GP* 1.460. **7 If I so ofte myghte have,** El reads "For I so ofte have." **11 Cane of Galilee,** John 2.1–11 tells of Christ's going to a wedding in the town of Cana in Galilee. Jerome 1.40 asserts that Christ went to only one wedding in order to teach Christians to marry only once. **12 That,** omitted in El. **taughte he me,** El reads "thoughte me." **14 eek, which,** Hg reads "eek, lo, which."

Spak° in repreeve° of the Samaritan,
"Thou hast yhad° fyve housbondes," quod he,
"And that man the which that hath now thee
Is noght thyn housbonde." Thus seyde he certeyn.
What that he mente therby, I kan nat seyn°,
But that I axe° why that the fifthe man
Was noon° housbonde to the Samaritan?
How manye myghte she have in mariage?
Yet herde I nevere tellen in myn age
Upon this nombre diffinicioun.
Men may devyne° and glosen° up and doun,
But wel I woot°, expres°, withoute lye,
God bad° us for to wexe and multiplye;
That gentil text kan I wel understonde.
Eek wel I woot, he seyde° myn housbonde
Sholde lete° fader and mooder and take to me.
But of no nombre mencioun made he,
Of bigamye or of octogamye.
Why sholde men speke of it vileynye?
  Lo, heere the wise kyng, daun Salomon,
I trowe° he hadde wyves mo than oon°.
As wolde God° it were leveful unto° me
To be refresshed half so ofte as he.
Which yifte° of God hadde he for alle his wyvys°!
No man hath swich° that in this world alyve° is.
God woot°, this noble kyng, as to my wit°,
The firste nyght had many a myrie fit
With ech of hem°, so wel was hym on lyve°.
Yblessed° be God that I have wedded fyve,
Of whiche I have pyked° out the beste,
Bothe of here nether purs° and of here cheste°.
Diverse scoles° maken parfyt clerkes°,
And diverse practyk° in many sondry° werkes
Maketh the werkman parfit sekirly°;
Of fyve husbondes scoleiyng° am I.
Welcome the sixte, whan that evere he shal.
For sothe, I wol° nat kepe° me chaast° in al.
Whan myn housbonde is fro the world ygon°,
Som Cristen man shal wedde me anon°,
For thanne° th'apostle seith that I am free
To wedde, a Goddes half°, where it liketh me°.
He seith that to be wedded is no synne;
Bet° is to be wedded than to brynne°.
What rekketh me°, thogh folk seye vileynye°
Of shrewed° Lameth and his bigamye?
I woot° wel Abraham was an hooly man,
And Jacob eek, as ferforth° as I kan°,
And ech of hem hadde wyves mo° than two,
And many another holy man also.
Wher can ye seye, in any manere age°,
That hye° God defended° mariage
By expres° word? I pray yow, telleth me.
Or where comanded he virginitee?
I woot as wel as ye, it is no drede°,
Th'apostel, whan he speketh of maydenhede°,
He seyde that precept therof° hadde he noon.
Men may conseille° a womman to been oon°,
But conseillyng is nat comandement.
He putte it in oure owene juggement;
For hadde God comanded maydenhede,

16 Spak, *spoke,* **repreeve,** *criticism* **17 hast yhad,** *have had* **20 seyn,** *say* **21 axe,** *ask* **22 noon,** *no* **26 devyne,** *speculate,* **glosen,** *interpret* **27 woot,** *know,* **expres,** *clearly* **28 bad,** *commanded* **30 seyde,** *said* **31 lete,** *leave* **36 trowe,** *believe,* **mo than oon,** *more than one* **37 As wolde God,** *I wish to God,* **leveful unto,** *permitted for* **39 Which yifte,** *what a gift,* **wyvys,** *wives* **40 swich,** *such,* **alyve,** *alive* **41 woot,** *knows,* **wit,** *understanding* **43 ech of hem,** *each of them,* **wel was hym on lyve,** *lively was he* **44 Yblessed,** *blessed* **44a pyked,** *picked* **44b here nether purs,** *their lower purse,* **cheste,** *money box* **44c scoles,** *schools,* **parfyt clerkes,** *perfect students* **44d practyk,** *practice,* **sondry,** *various* **44e parfit sekirly,** *perfect certainly* **44f scoleiyng,** *schooling* **46 wol,** *will,* **kepe,** *keep,* **chaast,** *chaste* **47 ygon,** *gone* **48 anon,** *quickly* **49 thanne,** *then,* **50 a Goddes half,** *by God's flank,* **where it liketh me,** *whoever I want* **52 Bet,** *better,* **brynne,** *burn* **53 What rekketh me,** *what do I care,* **seye vileynye,** *speak ill* **54 shrewed,** *wicked* **55 woot,** *know* **56 ferforth,** *far,* **kan,** *know* **57 mo,** *more* **59 any manere age,** *any time period* **60 hye,** *high,* **defended,** *forbade* **61 expres,** *specific* **63 drede,** *doubt* **64 maydenhede,** *virginity* **65 precept therof,** *command concerning this* **66 conseille,** *counsel,* **been oon,** *be one* (a virgin)

16 Samaritan, Jesus's discussion with the Samaritan woman at the well is in John 4.5ff., interpreted by Jerome 1.14 as discouragement of remarriage after the death of a spouse. **18** Hg reads "And that ilke man which that now hath thee." **25 diffinicioun,** clear limit, echoing Jerome's Latin *definitum* (1.15). **28 wexe and multiplye,** increase and procreate; from Genesis 1.28, etc., quoted in Jerome 1.24. **29 wel,** omitted in El. **30 seyde myn,** Hg reads "seyde that myn." **31 lete fader and mooder,** from Matthew 1.5; Jerome 1.5. **to,** omitted in El. **33 bigamye or octogamye,** twice married or eight times married; Jerome 1.15 and other medieval thinkers used the terms for successive marriages. **34 men speke,** Hg reads "men thanne speke." **35 Lo, heere,** an idiom meaning "think for example of." **daun Salomon,** master Solomon, the biblical king who had seven hundred wives and three hundred concubines; 1 Kings 11.3; Jerome 1.24. **36 mo than,** Hg reads "many." **37 were leveful,** Hg reads "leveful were." **44a-f** Omitted in El and Hg; perhaps canceled by Chaucer or added later. Reading from Cambridge University Library MS Dd.4.24. See 575–84n. **46 For sothe,** Hg reads "For sith" (For since . . .), a reading that demands different punctuation. **49–52 th'apostle seith . . . ,** the apostle (St. Paul) says . . . ; from 1 Corinthians 7.9 and 39; Jerome 1.10. **54 Lameth,** Lamech. In Genesis 4.19, he takes two wives; Jerome 1.14. **his,** El reads "of." **55–56** Abraham and Jacob each had multiple wives (Genesis 25.1 and 35.22–26); Jerome 1.5. **56 as ferforth as,** Hg reads "as fer as evere." **59** El reads "Whanne saugh ye evere in manere age." **64–67** Paul in 1 Corinthians 7.25; Jerome 1.12, whose argument is echoed through line 76. **64 Th'apostle, whan he,** El reads "Whan th'apostle." **67 is nat,** Hg reads "nys no."

Thanne hadde he dampned° weddyng with the dede.
And certain, if ther were no seed ysowe°,
Virginitee wherof thanne° sholde it growe?
Poul dorste° nat comanden, atte leeste°,
A thyng of which his maister yaf noon heeste°.
The dart° is set up for virginitee:
Cacche whoso° may; who renneth best lat° see.
But this word° is nat taken of° every wight°,
But ther as God lust gyve it of his myght°.
I woot wel that th'apostel was a mayde°,
But nathelees, thogh that he wroot and sayde
He wolde° that every wight were swich° as he,
Al nys but° conseil° to virginitee.
And for to been a wyf he yaf me leve°
Of indulgence; so it is no repreve°
To wedde me if that my make° dye,
Withoute excepcioun of° bigamye.
Al were it° good no womman for to touche—
He mente as in his bed or in his couche—
For peril is bothe fyr and tow t'assemble°—
Ye knowe what this ensample may resemble.
This is al and som°: he heeld virginitee
Moore parfit° than weddyng in freletee°.
Freletee clepe I°, but if that° he and she
Wolde leden° al hir° lyf in chastitee.
I graunte it wel, I have noon envie,
Thogh maydenhede preferre bigamye°.
Hem liketh° to be clene, body and goost°.
Of myn estaat° I nyl nat° make no boost,
For wel ye knowe, a lord in his houshold
He nath nat° every vessel al of gold;
Somme been of tree°, and doon hir° lord servyse.
God clepeth° folk to hym in sondry wyse°,
And everich° hath of God a propre yifte,
Som this, som that, as hym liketh shifte°.
Virginitee is greet perfeccioun,
And continence° eek with devocioun,
But Crist, that of perfeccioun is welle°,
Bad nat° every wight° he sholde go selle
Al that he hadde and gyve it to the poore,
And in swich wise° folwe hym and his foore°.
He spak to hem that wolde lyve parfitly;
And lordynges, by youre leve°, that am nat I.
I wol bistowe° the flour° of al myn age°
In the actes and in fruyt of mariage.
Telle me also, to what conclusioun°
Were membres ymaad° of generacioun°,
And of so parfit wys a wight ywroght?
Trusteth right wel, they were nat maad for noght.
Glose whoso wole° and seye bothe up and doun°
That they were maked for purgacioun
Of uryne, and oure bothe thynges smale°
Were eek to knowe a femele from a male,
And for noon oother cause—say ye no?
The experience woot° wel it is noght so.
So that the clerkes be nat with me wrothe°,
I sey this, that they beth maked° for bothe,
This is to seye, for office° and for ese
Of engendrure°, ther° we nat God displese.
Why sholde men elles° in hir bookes sette
That a man shal yelde° to his wyf hire dette?

---

70 dampned, *condemned* **71 ysowe,** *planted* **72 wherof thanne,** *from where then* **73 Poul dorste,** *Paul dared,* **atte leeste,** *to say the least* **74 maister yaf noon heeste,** *master gave no commandment* **75 dart,** *prize* **76 Cacche whoso,** *catch* (it) *whoever,* **lat,** *let* (us) **77 word,** *advice,* **taken of,** *intended for,* **wight,** *person* **78 ther as God lust gyve it of his myght,** *only where God wants to give it through his strength* **79 mayde,** *virgin* **81 wolde,** *wants,* **swich,** *such* **82 Al nys but,** *it is nothing except,* **conseil,** *counsel* **83 yaf me leve,** *gave me permission* **84 repreve,** *disgrace* **85 make,** *mate* **86 excepcioun of,** *criticism for* **87 Al were it,** *although it is* **89 bothe fyr and tow t'assemble,** *bring together fire and tinder* **91 al and som,** *the sum total* **92 parfit,** *perfect,* **freletee,** *weakness* **93 clepe I,** *I call it,* **but if that,** *unless* **94 Wolde leden,** *would lead,* **hir,** *their* **96 preferre bigamye,** *be considered better than remarrying* **97 Hem liketh,** (it) *pleases them* (virgins), **goost,** *spirit* **98 estaat,** *status,* **nyl nat,** *will not* **100 nath nat,** *has not* **101 tree,** *wood,* **doon hir,** *do their* **102 clepeth,** *calls,* **sondry wyse,** *many ways* **103 everich,** *each one* **104 hym liketh shifte,** (it) *pleases God to ordain* **106 continence,** *self-restraint* **107 welle,** *the source* **108 Bad nat,** *did not command,* **wight,** *person* **110 swich wise,** *such a way,* **foore,** *footsteps* **112 by youre leve,** *with your permission* **113 wol bistowe,** *will give,* **flour,** *best part,* **age,** *life* **115 conclusioun,** *purpose* **116 membres ymaad of generacioun,** *sexual organs made* **119 Glose whoso wole,** *interpret whoever wants* (to), **bothe up and doun,** *in every way* **121 bothe thynges smale,** *the small things of both* (genders) **124 woot,** *knows* **125 wrothe,** *angry* **126 beth maked,** *were made* **127 office,** *service* (excretion) **128 engendrure,** *procreation,* **ther,** *where* **129 elles,** *otherwise* **130 yelde,** *yield*

72 wherof thanne, Hg reads "thanne wherof." **75 for,** El reads "of." **79 that,** omitted in El. **80 and,** Hg reads "or." **84 Of indulgence,** by concession; from 1 Corinthians 7.6 (*indulgentium*); Jerome 1.8. **85 that,** omitted in El. **87 womman . . . touche,** from 1 Corinthians 7.1; Jerome 1.7. **91 is,** omitted in Hg. **he heeld,** El reads "that." **92 parfit,** El reads "profiteth." **97** Hg reads "It liketh hem to be clene in body and soul." **100 He nath nat,** Hg reads "He hath nat." **every vessel . . . ,** Paul distinguishes between vessels of gold and wood in 2 Timothy 2.20; Jerome 1.40. **103 propre yifte,** special gift; from 1 Corinthians 7.7; Jerome 1.8. **107–11** From Matthew 19.21; Jerome 1.34. **108 he,** omitted in El. **113–14** Echoes *RR* 11,453–56. **117** "And by so wise a Being created," although the MSS have various readings. Jerome 1.36 asks the same question but argues that the topic is shameful and that the existence of sexual organs does not mean that we must use them for sex. **113 al,** omitted in El. **117** The line can mean either "And created by so wise a Being" or "And in such a perfect manner created a human being." El reads "And for what profit was a wight ywroght." **121** El reads "Of uryne bothe and thynges smale." **122 Were,** El reads "And"; Hg "Was." **126 this,** El reads "yis." **beth maked,** Hg reads "maked been." **127–28** Critics point out that we have no evidence whether or not the Wife has borne children. **130 a,** omitted in Hg. **hire dette,** the marital obligation (or debt) of intercourse. From Lat. *debitum,* 1 Corinthians 7.3; Jerome 1.7.

Now wherwith° sholde he make his paiement°,
If he ne used° his sely instrument?
Thanne were they maad upon a creature
To purge uryne, and eek for engendrure.
  But I seye noght that every wight is holde°,
That° hath swich harneys° as I to yow tolde,
To goon and usen hem in engendrure.
Thanne sholde men take of chastitee no cure°.
Crist was a mayde° and shapen as a man,
And many a seint° sith that the world bigan,
Yet lyved they evere in parfit chastitee.
I nyl nat° envye no virginitee.
Lat hem be breed° of pured whete seed°,
And lat us wyves hoten° barly-breed;
And yet with barly-breed, Mark telle kan,
Oure Lord Jhesu refresshed many a man.
In swich estaat° as God hath cleped° us
I wol persevere; I nam nat precius°.
In wyfhode I wol use myn instrument
As frely as my Makere hath it sent.
If I be daungerous°, God yeve° me sorwe.
Myn housbonde shal it have both eve and morwe°,
Whan that hym list° com forth and paye his dette°.
An housbonde I wol have, I nyl nat lette°,
Which° shal be bothe my dettour° and my thral°,
And have his tribulacioun withal°
Upon his flessh whil that I am his wyf.
I have the power durynge al my lyf
Upon his propre body, and noght he.
Right thus the Apostel° tolde it unto me,
And bad° oure housbondes for to love us weel°.
Al this sentence me liketh° every deel°—

  Up stirte° the Pardoner, and that anon°:
"Now, dame," quod he, "by God and by Seint John,
Ye been° a noble prechour° in this cas.
I was aboute to wedde a wyf. Allas,
What° sholde I bye° it on my flessh so deere°?
Yet hadde I levere° wedde no wyf to-yeere°."
  "Abyde," quod she, "my tale is nat bigonne.
Nay, thou shalt drynken of another tonne
Er° that I go, shal savoure wors° than ale.
And whan that I have toold thee forth my tale
Of tribulacioun in mariage,
Of which I am expert in al myn age—
This is to seyn, myself have been the whippe—
Than maystow chese° wheither thou wolt sippe
Of thilke tonne° that I shal abroche°.
Be war of it, er thou to ny° approche,
For I shal telle ensamples mo° than ten.
'Whoso that nyl be war by° othere men,
By hym shul othere men corrected be.'
The same wordes writeth Ptholomee;
Rede in his Almageste and take it there."
  "Dame, I wolde praye yow, if youre wyl it were,"
Seyde this Pardoner, "as ye bigan,
Telle forth youre tale; spareth° for no man,
And teche us yonge men of youre praktike°."
  "Gladly," quod she, "sith it may yow like°.
But yet I praye to al this compaignye
If that I speke after my fantasye°

131 wherwith, *with what,* **paiement,** *payment* **132 ne used,** *did not use* **135 holde,** *obligated* **136 That,** *who,* **swich harneys,** *such equipment* **138 cure,** *care* **139 mayde,** *virgin* **140 seint,** *saint* **142 nyl nat,** *will not* **143 breed,** *bread,* **pured whete seed,** *refined wheat grain* **144 hoten,** *be called* **147 swich estaat,** *such condition,* **cleped,** *called* **148 precius,** *valuable or fussy* **151 daungerous,** *standoffish,* **yeve,** *give* **152 morwe,** *morning* **153 hym list,** *it pleases him,* **dette,** *debt* **154 nyl nat lette,** *will not stop* **155 Which,** *who,* **dettour,** *debtor,* **thral,** *servant* **156 withal,** *as well* **160 the Apostel,** *St. Paul* **161 bad,** *ordered,* **weel,** *well* **162 sentence me liketh,** *message pleases me,* **deel,** *bit* **163 stirte,** *started,* **anon,** *quickly* **165 Ye been,** *you are,* **prechour,** *preacher* **167 What,** *why,* **bye,** *pay for,* **deere,** *dearly* **168 Yet hadde I levere,** *I would rather,* **to-yeere,** *this year* **171 Er,** *before,* **savoure wors,** *taste worse* **176 maystow chese,** *may you choose* **177 thilke tonne,** *that cask,* **abroche,** *tap* **178 to ny,** *too near* **179 mo,** *more* **180 Whoso that nyl be war by,** *whoever will not be made wary by* (the examples of) **186 spareth,** *stop* **187 praktike,** *practice* **188 sith it may yow like,** *since it may please you* **190 after my fantasye,** *in accord with my whims*

132 sely, triple meaning: "silly," "innocent," "blessed". **134 eek,** omitted in El. **136 to yow tolde,** El reads "of tolde." **138 Thanne sholde men take,** El reads "They shul nat take." **140 that,** omitted in El. **142 nat,** omitted in Hg. **144 barly-breed,** bread made from coarse rather than fine grain. The reference to **Mark** (line 145) is incorrect, as only John's gospel records how Jesus used barley loaves (and fishes) to feed the multitude. Comparison of wheat and barley as degrees of perfection echoes Jerome 1.7. **146 Jhesu,** omitted in El. **149 I wol,** Hg reads "wol I." **154 I wol,** Hg reads "wol I." **nyl nat,** Hg reads "wol nat." **156 tribulacioun,** tribulation; the word comes from 1 Corinthians 7.28; Jerome 1.13. **157 that,** omitted in El. **158–59** From 1 Corinthians 7.4; Jerome 1.7. **161 bad oure housbondes,** from Ephesians 5.25; Jerome 1.16. **170 drynken of another tonne,** drink from another wine cask; metaphor for "get worse treatment from me." The image is used of fortune in *RR* 6762ff. and elsewhere. **172 thee,** omitted in El. **173 tribulacioun in,** El reads "tribulacioun that is in." **175 is,** omitted in El. **176 wheither thou,** Hg reads "wheither that thow." **177 thilke,** El reads "that." **180 nyle,** El reads "wol nat." **182–83 Ptholomee . . . Almageste,** although not in the Greek original, this proverb and the one at line 326 are in the preface of the 1515 Venice edition of the *Almagest,* a treatise by the classical astrologer Ptolemy. **182 The,** Hg reads "Thise." **183 Rede in,** El reads "Rede it in." **188 quod she,** El reads "sires." **189 yet,** Hg reads "that."

As taketh not agrief of that° I seye,
For myn entente nys° but for to pleye."

Now sir, now wol I telle forth my tale:
As evere moote I° drynken wyn or ale,
I shal seye sooth°, of tho° housbondes that I hadde,
As thre of hem were goode, and two were badde.
The thre men were goode, and riche, and olde.
Unnethe° myghte they the statut holde
In which that they were bounden unto me.
Ye woot° wel what I meene of this, pardee°.
As help me God, I laughe whan I thynke
How pitously a-nyght° I made hem swynke°!
And, by my fey°, I tolde of it no stoor°;
They had me yeven hir° lond and hir tresoor.
Me neded nat do lenger diligence°
To wynne hir love, or doon hem° reverence.
They loved me so wel, by God above,
That I ne tolde no deyntee of° hir love.
A wys womman wol sette hire evere in oon°
To gete hire love, ye, ther as° she hath noon.
But sith° I hadde hem hoolly° in myn hond,
And sith they hadde me yeven al hir lond,
What° sholde I taken heede hem° for to plese
But° it were for my profit and myn ese?
I sette hem so a-werke°, by my fey,
That many a nyght they songen° "weilawey."
The bacon was nat fet for hem, I trowe°,
That som men han° in Essex at Dunmowe.
I governed hem so wel, after my lawe,
That ech of hem ful blisful was and fawe°
To brynge me gaye thynges fro the fayre°.
They were ful glad whan I spak to hem faire,
For, God it woot°, I chidde hem spitously°.
Now herkneth hou° I baar me° proprely,
Ye wise wyves, that kan understonde.
Thus shul ye speke and bere hem wrong on honde,
For half so boldely kan ther no man
Swere and lyen as a womman kan.
I sey nat this by° wyves that been wyse,
But° if it be whan they hem mysavyse°.
A wys wyf, if that she kan hir good°,
Shal beren hym on hond the cow is wood,
And take witnesse of hir owene mayde
Of hir assent°. But herkneth how I sayde:
Sire olde kaynard°, is this thyn array?
Why is my neighebores wyf so gay°?
She is honoured over al ther° she gooth;
I sitte at hoom; I have no thrifty clooth°.
What dostow° at my neighebores hous?
Is she so fair? Artow° so amorous?
What rowne° ye with oure mayde, benedicite°?
Sire olde lecchour, lat thy japes° be.
And if I have a gossib° or a freend
Withouten gilt, thou chidest as a feend
If that I walke or pleye unto his hous.
Thou comest hoom as dronken as a mous
And prechest on thy bench with yvel preef°.
Thou seist° to me it is a greet meschief
To wedde a poure womman for costage°;
And if that she be riche, of heigh parage°,
Thanne seistow that it is a tormentrie°
To suffren hire pride and hire malencolie°.
And if that she be fair, thou verray knave°,
Thou seyst° that every holour° wol hire have;
She may no while in chastitee abyde°
That is assailled upon ech a° syde.

---

191 As taketh not agrief of that, *don't be grieved by what* **192 nys,** *is not* **194 As evere moote I,** *as I might ever* **195 seye sooth,** *tell the truth,* **tho,** *those* **198 Unnethe,** *barely* **200 Ye woot,** *you know,* **pardee,** *by God* **202 a-nyght,** *at night,* **hem swynke,** *them work* **203 fey,** *faith,* **tolde . . . no stoor,** *took no account* **204 yeven hir,** *given their* **205 do lenger diligence,** *make more effort* **206 doon hem,** *show them* **208 tolde no deyntee of,** *placed no value on* **209 evere in oon,** *constantly* **210 ther as,** *where* **211 sith,** *since,* **hem hoolly,** *them completely* **213 What,** *why,* **taken heede hem,** *pay attention them* **214 But,** *unless* **215 a-werke,** *to working* **216 songen,** *sang* **217 trowe,** *trust* **218 han,** *have* **220 fawe,** *eager* **221 fro the fayre,** *from the fair* **223 woot,** *knows,* **chidde hem spitously,** *scolded them spitefully* **224 hou,** *how,* **baar me,** *bore myself* **229 by,** *about* **230 But,** *except,* **hem mysavyse,** *mistake themselves* **231 kan hir good,** *knows what's good for her* **234 hir assent,** (the maid's) *agreement* **235 kaynard,** *sluggard* **236 gay,** *gaily dressed* **237 over al ther,** *wherever* **238 thrifty clooth,** *appropriate clothes* **239 dostow,** *do you do* **240 Artow,** *are you* **241 rowne,** *whisper,* **benedicite,** *bless us* **242 japes,** *jokes* **243 gossib,** *confidant* **247 yvel preef,** *inaccurate evidence* **248 seist,** *say* **249 costage,** *expense* **250 heigh parage,** *high lineage* **251 tormentrie,** *torment* **252 malencolie,** *sullenness* **253 verray knave,** *absolute villain* **254 seyst,** *say,* **holour,** *lecher* **255 abyde,** *remain* **256 ech a,** *every*

191 nat agrief of that, El reads "it nat agrief that." **193 now wol I telle forth,** Hg reads "thanne wol I telle yow forth." **195 of,** omitted in Hg. **198 statut,** obligation; see marital debt at lines 130 and 153 above. **204 lond,** El reads "gold." **209 sette,** Hg reads "bisye." **212 sith,** Hg reads "sith that." **me yeven,** Hg reads "yeven me." **213 heede,** Hg reads "kepe" (care). **214 But it,** El reads "But if it." **215 so,** omitted in Hg. **217 bacon was nat fet,** bacon was not fetched; at Dunmow in Essex (southeastern England) and other places, a married couple who had not quarreled for a year could claim a side of bacon as reward. **220 ful blisful was,** El reads "was ful blisful." **226 bere hem wrong on honde,** an idiom meaning "accuse them wrongfully." El omits "wrong." **228 a womman kan,** El reads "kan a womman." **232 beren hym . . . cow is wood,** make him think the chough (a talking bird) is crazy, an allusion to a folk tale in which a bird tattles on his mistress—the plot of the *ManT.* **235–378** Most of the details here derive from well-known antifeminist material, based on Theophrastus, preserved in Jerome 1.47, and popularized by Matheolus, LeFèvre, *RR*, and Deschamps. **244 thou chidest,** Hg reads "ye chiden." **250 that,** omitted in El. **of,** El reads "and of." **251 that,** omitted in El. **253 that,** omitted in El.

Now wherwith° sholde he make his paiement°,
If he ne used° his sely instrument?
Thanne were they maad upon a creature
To purge uryne, and eek for engendrure.
 But I seye noght that every wight is holde°,
That° hath swich harneys° as I to yow tolde,
To goon and usen hem in engendrure.
Thanne sholde men take of chastitee no cure°.
Crist was a mayde° and shapen as a man,
And many a seint° sith that the world bigan,
Yet lyved they evere in parfit chastitee.
I nyl nat° envye no virginitee.
Lat hem be breed° of pured whete seed°,
And lat us wyves hoten° barly-breed;
And yet with barly-breed, Mark telle kan,
Oure Lord Jhesu refresshed many a man.
In swich estaat° as God hath cleped° us
I wol persevere; I nam nat precius°.
In wyfhode I wol use myn instrument
As frely as my Makere hath it sent.
If I be daungerous°, God yeve° me sorwe.
Myn housbonde shal it have both eve and morwe°,
Whan that hym list° com forth and paye his dette°.
An housbonde I wol have, I nyl nat lette°,
Which° shal be bothe my dettour° and my thral°,
And have his tribulacioun withal°
Upon his flessh whil that I am his wyf.
I have the power durynge al my lyf
Upon his propre body, and noght he.
Right thus the Apostel° tolde it unto me,
And bad° oure housbondes for to love us weel°.
Al this sentence me liketh° every deel°—

 Up stirte° the PARDONER, and that anon°:
"Now, dame," quod he, "by God and by Seint John,
Ye been° a noble prechour° in this cas.
I was aboute to wedde a wyf. Allas,
What° sholde I bye° it on my flessh so deere°?
Yet hadde I levere° wedde no wyf to-yeere°."
 "Abyde," quod she, "my tale is nat bigonne.
Nay, thou shalt drynken of another tonne
Er° that I go, shal savoure wors° than ale.
And whan that I have toold thee forth my tale
Of tribulacioun in mariage,
Of which I am expert in al myn age—
This is to seyn, myself have been the whippe—
Than maystow chese° wheither thou wolt sippe
Of thilke tonne° that I shal abroche°.
Be war of it, er thou to ny° approche,
For I shal telle ensamples mo° than ten.
'Whoso that nyl be war by° othere men,
By hym shul othere men corrected be.'
The same wordes writeth Ptholomee;
Rede in his Almageste and take it there."
 "Dame, I wolde praye yow, if youre wyl it were,"
Seyde this Pardoner, "as ye bigan,
Telle forth youre tale; spareth° for no man,
And teche us yonge men of youre praktike°."
 "Gladly," quod she, "sith it may yow like°.
But yet I praye to al this compaignye
If that I speke after my fantasye°

131 wherwith, *with what,* **paiement,** *payment* **132 ne used,** *did not use* **135 holde,** *obligated* **136 That,** *who,* **swich harneys,** *such equipment* **138 cure,** *care* **139 mayde,** *virgin* **140 seint,** *saint* **142 nyl nat,** *will not* **143 breed,** *bread,* **pured whete seed,** *refined wheat grain* **144 hoten,** *be called* **147 swich estaat,** *such condition,* **cleped,** *called* **148 precius,** *valuable or fussy* **151 daungerous,** *standoffish,* **yeve,** *give* **152 morwe,** *morning* **153 hym list,** *it pleases him,* **dette,** *debt* **154 nyl nat lette,** *will not stop* **155 Which,** *who,* **dettour,** *debtor,* **thral,** *servant* **156 withal,** *as well* **160 the Apostel,** *St. Paul* **161 bad,** *ordered,* **weel,** *well* **162 sentence me liketh,** *message pleases me,* **deel,** *bit* **163 stirte,** *started,* **anon,** *quickly* **165 Ye been,** *you are,* **prechour,** *preacher* **167 What,** *why,* **bye,** *pay for,* **deere,** *dearly* **168 Yet hadde I levere,** *I would rather,* **to-yeere,** *this year* **171 Er,** *before,* **savoure wors,** *taste worse* **176 maystow chese,** *may you choose* **177 thilke tonne,** *that cask,* **abroche,** *tap* **178 to ny,** *too near* **179 mo,** *more* **180 Whoso that nyl be war by,** *whoever will not be made wary by* (the examples of) **186 spareth,** *stop* **187 praktike,** *practice* **188 sith it may yow like,** *since it may please you* **190 after my fantasye,** *in accord with my whims*

132 sely, triple meaning: "silly," "innocent," "blessed". **134 eek,** omitted in El. **136 to yow tolde,** El reads "of tolde." **138 Thanne sholde men take,** El reads "They shul nat take." **140 that,** omitted in El. **142 nat,** omitted in Hg. **144 barly-breed,** bread made from coarse rather than fine grain. The reference to **Mark** (line 145) is incorrect, as only John's gospel records how Jesus used barley loaves (and fishes) to feed the multitude. Comparison of wheat and barley as degrees of perfection echoes Jerome 1.7. **146 Jhesu,** omitted in El. **149 I wol,** Hg reads "wol I." **154 I wol,** Hg reads "wol I." **nyl nat,** Hg reads "wol nat." **156 tribulacioun,** tribulation; the word comes from 1 Corinthians 7.28; Jerome 1.13. **157 that,** omitted in El. **158–59** From 1 Corinthians 7.4; Jerome 1.7. **161 bad oure housbondes,** from Ephesians 5.25; Jerome 1.16. **170 drynken of another tonne,** drink from another wine cask; metaphor for "get worse treatment from me." The image is used of fortune in *RR* 6762ff. and elsewhere. **172 thee,** omitted in El. **173 tribulacioun in,** El reads "tribulacioun that is in." **175 is,** omitted in El. **176 wheither thou,** Hg reads "wheither that thow." **177 thilke,** El reads "that." **180 nyle,** El reads "wol nat." **182–83 Ptholomee . . . Almageste,** although not in the Greek original, this proverb and the one at line 326 are in the preface of the 1515 Venice edition of the *Almagest,* a treatise by the classical astrologer Ptolemy. **182 The,** Hg reads "Thise." **183 Rede in,** El reads "Rede it in." **188 quod she,** El reads "sires." **189 yet,** Hg reads "that."

As taketh not agrief of that° I seye,
For myn entente nys° but for to pleye."

Now sir, now wol I telle forth my tale:
As evere moote I° drynken wyn or ale,
I shal seye sooth°, of tho° housbondes that I
hadde,
As thre of hem were goode, and two were badde.
The thre men were goode, and riche, and olde.
Unnethe° myghte they the statut holde
In which that they were bounden unto me.
Ye woot° wel what I meene of this, pardee°.
As help me God, I laughe whan I thynke
How pitously a-nyght° I made hem swynke°!
And, by my fey°, I tolde of it no stoor°;
They had me yeven hir° lond and hir tresoor.
Me neded nat do lenger diligence°
To wynne hir love, or doon hem° reverence.
They loved me so wel, by God above,
That I ne tolde no deyntee of° hir love.
A wys womman wol sette hire evere in oon°
To gete hire love, ye, ther as° she hath noon.
But sith° I hadde hem hoolly° in myn hond,
And sith they hadde me yeven al hir lond,
What° sholde I taken heede hem° for to plese
But° it were for my profit and myn ese?
I sette hem so a-werke°, by my fey,
That many a nyght they songen° "weilawey."
The bacon was nat fet for hem, I trowe°,
That som men han° in Essex at Dunmowe.
I governed hem so wel, after my lawe,
That ech of hem ful blisful was and fawe°
To brynge me gaye thynges fro the fayre°.
They were ful glad whan I spak to hem faire,
For, God it woot°, I chidde hem spitously°.
Now herkneth hou° I baar me° proprely,
Ye wise wyves, that kan understonde.
Thus shul ye speke and bere hem wrong on honde,
For half so boldely kan ther no man
Swere and lyen as a womman kan.
I sey nat this by° wyves that been wyse,
But° if it be whan they hem mysavyse°.
A wys wyf, if that she kan hir good°,
Shal beren hym on hond the cow is wood,
And take witnesse of hir owene mayde
Of hir assent°. But herkneth how I sayde:
Sire olde kaynard°, is this thyn array?
Why is my neighebores wyf so gay°?
She is honoured over al ther° she gooth;
I sitte at hoom; I have no thrifty clooth°.
What dostow° at my neighebores hous?
Is she so fair? Artow° so amorous?
What rowne° ye with oure mayde, benedicite°?
Sire olde lecchour, lat thy japes° be.
And if I have a gossib° or a freend
Withouten gilt, thou chidest as a feend
If that I walke or pleye unto his hous.
Thou comest hoom as dronken as a mous
And prechest on thy bench with yvel preef°.
Thou seist° to me it is a greet meschief
To wedde a poure womman for costage°;
And if that she be riche, of heigh parage°,
Thanne seistow that it is a tormentrie°
To suffren hire pride and hire malencolie°.
And if that she be fair, thou verray knave°,
Thou seyst° that every holour° wol hire have;
She may no while in chastitee abyde°
That is assailled upon ech a° syde.

---

191 **As taketh not agrief of that,** *don't be grieved by what* 192 **nys,** *is not* 194 **As evere moote I,** *as I might ever* 195 **seye sooth,** *tell the truth,* **tho,** *those* 198 **Unnethe,** *barely* 200 **Ye woot,** *you know,* **pardee,** *by God* 202 **a-nyght,** *at night,* **hem swynke,** *them work* 203 **fey,** *faith,* **tolde . . . no stoor,** *took no account* 204 **yeven hir,** *given their* 205 **do lenger diligence,** *make more effort* 206 **doon hem,** *show them* 208 **tolde no deyntee of,** *placed no value on* 209 **evere in oon,** *constantly* 210 **ther as,** *where* 211 **sith,** *since,* **hem hoolly,** *them completely* 213 **What,** *why,* **taken heede hem,** *pay attention them* 214 **But,** *unless* 215 **a-werke,** *to working* 216 **songen,** *sang* 217 **trowe,** *trust* 218 **han,** *have* 220 **fawe,** *eager* 221 **fro the fayre,** *from the fair* 223 **woot,** *knows,* **chidde hem spitously,** *scolded them spitefully* 224 **hou,** *how,* **baar me,** *bore myself* 229 **by,** *about* 230 **But,** *except,* **hem mysavyse,** *mistake themselves* 231 **kan hir good,** *knows what's good for her* 234 **hir assent,** (the maid's) *agreement* 235 **kaynard,** *sluggard* 236 **gay,** *gaily dressed* 237 **over al ther,** *wherever* 238 **thrifty clooth,** *appropriate clothes* 239 **dostow,** *do you do* 240 **Artow,** *are you* 241 **rowne,** *whisper,* **benedicite,** *bless us* 242 **japes,** *jokes* 243 **gossib,** *confidant* 247 **yvel preef,** *inaccurate evidence* 248 **seist,** *say* 249 **costage,** *expense* 250 **heigh parage,** *high lineage* 251 **tormentrie,** *torment* 252 **malencolie,** *sullenness* 253 **verray knave,** *absolute villain* 254 **seyst,** *say,* **holour,** *lecher* 255 **abyde,** *remain* 256 **ech a,** *every*

191 **nat agrief of that,** El reads "it nat agrief that." **193 now wol I telle forth,** Hg reads "thanne wol I telle yow forth." **195 of,** omitted in Hg. **198 statut,** obligation; see marital debt at lines 130 and 153 above. **204 lond,** El reads "gold." **209 sette,** Hg reads "bisye." **212 sith,** Hg reads "sith that." me **yeven,** Hg reads "yeven me." **213 heede,** Hg reads "kepe" (care). **214 But it,** El reads "But if it." **215 so,** omitted in Hg. **217 bacon was nat fet,** bacon was not fetched; at Dunmow in Essex (southeastern England) and other places, a married couple who had not quarreled for a year could claim a side of bacon as reward. **220 ful blisful was,** El reads "was ful blisful." **226 bere hem wrong on honde,** an idiom meaning "accuse them wrongfully." El omits "wrong." **228 a womman kan,** El reads "kan a womman." **232 beren hym . . . cow is wood,** make him think the chough (a talking bird) is crazy, an allusion to a folk tale in which a bird tattles on his mistress—the plot of the *ManT.* **235–378** Most of the details here derive from well-known antifeminist material, based on Theophrastus, preserved in Jerome 1.47, and popularized by Matheolus, LeFèvre, *RR,* and Deschamps. **244 thou chidest,** Hg reads "ye chiden." **250 that,** omitted in El. **of,** El reads "and of." **251 that,** omitted in El. **253 that,** omitted in El.

Now wherwith° sholde he make his paiement°,
If he ne used° his sely instrument?
Thanne were they maad upon a creature
To purge uryne, and eek for engendrure.
  But I seye noght that every wight is holde°,
That° hath swich harneys° as I to yow tolde,
To goon and usen hem in engendrure.
Thanne sholde men take of chastitee no cure°.
Crist was a mayde° and shapen as a man,
And many a seint° sith that the world bigan,
Yet lyved they evere in parfit chastitee.
I nyl nat° envye no virginitee.
Lat hem be breed° of pured whete seed°,
And lat us wyves hoten° barly-breed;
And yet with barly-breed, Mark telle kan,
Oure Lord Jhesu refresshed many a man.
In swich estaat° as God hath cleped° us
I wol persevere; I nam nat precius°.
In wyfhode I wol use myn instrument
As frely as my Makere hath it sent.
If I be daungerous°, God yeve° me sorwe.
Myn housbonde shal it have both eve and morwe°,
Whan that hym list° com forth and paye his dette°.
An housbonde I wol have, I nyl nat lette°,
Which° shal be bothe my dettour° and my thral°,
And have his tribulacioun withal°
Upon his flessh whil that I am his wyf.
I have the power durynge al my lyf
Upon his propre body, and noght he.
Right thus the Apostel° tolde it unto me,
And bad° oure housbondes for to love us weel°.
Al this sentence me liketh° every deel°—

  Up stirte° the PARDONER, and that anon°:
"Now, dame," quod he, "by God and by Seint John,
Ye been° a noble prechour° in this cas.
I was aboute to wedde a wyf. Allas,
What° sholde I bye° it on my flessh so deere°?
Yet hadde I levere° wedde no wyf to-yeere°."
  "Abyde," quod she, "my tale is nat bigonne.
Nay, thou shalt drynken of another tonne
Er° that I go, shal savoure wors° than ale.
And whan that I have toold thee forth my tale
Of tribulacioun in mariage,
Of which I am expert in al myn age—
This is to seyn, myself have been the whippe—
Than maystow chese° wheither thou wolt sippe
Of thilke tonne° that I shal abroche°.
Be war of it, er thou to ny° approche,
For I shal telle ensamples mo° than ten.
'Whoso that nyl be war by° othere men,
By hym shul othere men corrected be.'
The same wordes writeth Ptholomee;
Rede in his Almageste and take it there."
  "Dame, I wolde praye yow, if youre wyl it were,"
Seyde this Pardoner, "as ye bigan,
Telle forth youre tale; spareth° for no man,
And teche us yonge men of youre praktike°."
  "Gladly," quod she, "sith it may yow like°.
But yet I praye to al this compaignye
If that I speke after my fantasye°

131 wherwith, *with what,* **paiement,** *payment* **132 ne used,** *did not use* **135 holde,** *obligated* **136 That,** *who,* **swich harneys,** *such equipment* **138 cure,** *care* **139 mayde,** *virgin* **140 seint,** *saint* **142 nyl nat,** *will not* **143 breed,** *bread,* **pured whete seed,** *refined wheat grain* **144 hoten,** *be called* **147 swich estaat,** *such condition,* **cleped,** *called* **148 precius,** *valuable or fussy* **151 daungerous,** *standoffish,* **yeve,** *give* **152 morwe,** *morning* **153 hym list,** *it pleases him,* **dette,** *debt* **154 nyl nat lette,** *will not stop* **155 Which,** *who,* **dettour,** *debtor,* **thral,** *servant* **156 withal,** *as well* **160 the Apostel,** *St. Paul* **161 bad,** *ordered,* **weel,** *well* **162 sentence me liketh,** *message pleases me,* **deel,** *bit* **163 stirte,** *started,* **anon,** *quickly* **165 Ye been,** *you are,* **prechour,** *preacher* **167 What,** *why,* **bye,** *pay for,* **deere,** *dearly* **168 Yet hadde I levere,** *I would rather,* **to-yeere,** *this year* **171 Er,** *before,* **savoure wors,** *taste worse* **176 maystow chese,** *may you choose* **177 thilke tonne,** *that cask,* **abroche,** *tap* **178 to ny,** *too near* **179 mo,** *more* **180 Whoso that nyl be war by,** *whoever will not be made wary by* (the examples of) **186 spareth,** *stop* **187 praktike,** *practice* **188 sith it may yow like,** *since it may please you* **190 after my fantasye,** *in accord with my whims*

132 sely, triple meaning: "silly," "innocent," "blessed". **134 eek,** omitted in El. **136 to yow tolde,** El reads "of tolde." **138 Thanne sholde men take,** El reads "They shul nat take." **140 that,** omitted in El. **142 nat,** omitted in Hg. **144 barly-breed,** bread made from coarse rather than fine grain. The reference to **Mark** (line 145) is incorrect, as only John's gospel records how Jesus used barley loaves (and fishes) to feed the multitude. Comparison of wheat and barley as degrees of perfection echoes Jerome 1.7. **146 Jhesu,** omitted in El. **149 I wol,** Hg reads "wol I." **154 I wol,** Hg reads "wol I." **nyl nat,** Hg reads "wol nat." **156 tribulacioun,** tribulation; the word comes from 1 Corinthians 7.28; Jerome 1.13. **157 that,** omitted in El. **158–59** From 1 Corinthians 7.4; Jerome 1.7. **161 bad oure housbondes,** from Ephesians 5.25; Jerome 1.16. **170 drynken of another tonne,** drink from another wine cask; metaphor for "get worse treatment from me." The image is used of fortune in *RR* 6762ff. and elsewhere. **172 thee,** omitted in El. **173 tribulacioun in,** El reads "tribulacioun that is in." **175 is,** omitted in El. **176 wheither thou,** Hg reads "wheither that thow." **177 thilke,** El reads "that." **180 nyle,** El reads "wol nat." **182–83 Ptholomee . . . Almageste,** although not in the Greek original, this proverb and the one at line 326 are in the preface of the 1515 Venice edition of the *Almagest,* a treatise by the classical astrologer Ptolemy. **182 The,** Hg reads "Thise." **183 Rede in,** El reads "Rede it in." **188 quod she,** El reads "sires." **189 yet,** Hg reads "that."

As taketh not agrief of that° I seye,
For myn entente nys° but for to pleye."

Now sir, now wol I telle forth my tale:
As evere moote I° drynken wyn or ale,
I shal seye sooth°, of tho° housbondes that I hadde,
As thre of hem were goode, and two were badde.
The thre men were goode, and riche, and olde.
Unnethe° myghte they the statut holde
In which that they were bounden unto me.
Ye woot° wel what I meene of this, pardee°.
As help me God, I laughe whan I thynke
How pitously a-nyght° I made hem swynke°!
And, by my fey°, I tolde of it no stoor°;
They had me yeven hir° lond and hir tresoor.
Me neded nat do lenger diligence°
To wynne hir love, or doon hem° reverence.
They loved me so wel, by God above,
That I ne tolde no deyntee of° hir love.
A wys womman wol sette hire evere in oon°
To gete hire love, ye, ther as° she hath noon.
But sith° I hadde hem hoolly° in myn hond,
And sith they hadde me yeven al hir lond,
What° sholde I taken heede hem° for to plese
But° it were for my profit and myn ese?
I sette hem so a-werke°, by my fey,
That many a nyght they songen° "weilawey."
The bacon was nat fet for hem, I trowe°,
That som men han° in Essex at Dunmowe.
I governed hem so wel, after my lawe,
That ech of hem ful blisful was and fawe°
To brynge me gaye thynges fro the fayre°.
They were ful glad whan I spak to hem faire,
For, God it woot°, I chidde hem spitously°.

Now herkneth hou° I baar me° proprely,
Ye wise wyves, that kan understonde.
Thus shul ye speke and bere hem wrong on honde,
For half so boldely kan ther no man
Swere and lyen as a womman kan.
I sey nat this by° wyves that been wyse,
But° if it be whan they hem mysavyse°.
A wys wyf, if that she kan hir good°,
Shal beren hym on hond the cow is wood,
And take witnesse of hir owene mayde
Of hir assent°. But herkneth how I sayde:

Sire olde kaynard°, is this thyn array?
Why is my neighebores wyf so gay°?
She is honoured over al ther° she gooth;
I sitte at hoom; I have no thrifty clooth°.
What dostow° at my neighebores hous?
Is she so fair? Artow° so amorous?
What rowne° ye with oure mayde, benedicite°?
Sire olde lecchour, lat thy japes° be.
And if I have a gossib° or a freend
Withouten gilt, thou chidest as a feend
If that I walke or pleye unto his hous.
Thou comest hoom as dronken as a mous
And prechest on thy bench with yvel preef°.
Thou seist° to me it is a greet meschief
To wedde a poure womman for costage°;
And if that she be riche, of heigh parage°,
Thanne seistow that it is a tormentrie°
To suffren hire pride and hire malencolie°.
And if that she be fair, thou verray knave°,
Thou seyst° that every holour° wol hire have;
She may no while in chastitee abyde°
That is assailled upon ech a° syde.

191 As taketh not agrief of that, *don't be grieved by what* **192 nys,** *is not* **194 As evere moote I,** *as I might ever* **195 seye sooth,** *tell the truth,* **tho,** *those* **198 Unnethe,** *barely* **200 Ye woot,** *you know,* **pardee,** *by God* **202 a-nyght,** *at night,* **hem swynke,** *them work* **203 fey,** *faith,* **tolde . . . no stoor,** *took no account* **204 yeven hir,** *given their* **205 do lenger diligence,** *make more effort* **206 doon hem,** *show them* **208 tolde no deyntee of,** *placed no value on* **209 evere in oon,** *constantly* **210 ther as,** *where* **211 sith,** *since,* **hem hoolly,** *them completely* **213 What,** *why,* **taken heede hem,** *pay attention them* **214 But,** *unless* **215 a-werke,** *to working* **216 songen,** *sang* **217 trowe,** *trust* **218 han,** *have* **220 fawe,** *eager* **221 fro the fayre,** *from the fair* **223 woot,** *knows,* **chidde hem spitously,** *scolded them spitefully* **224 hou,** *how,* **baar me,** *bore myself* **229 by,** *about* **230 But,** *except,* **hem mysavyse,** *mistake themselves* **231 kan hir good,** *knows what's good for her* **234 hir assent,** (the maid's) *agreement* **235 kaynard,** *sluggard* **236 gay,** *gaily dressed* **237 over al ther,** *wherever* **238 thrifty clooth,** *appropriate clothes* **239 dostow,** *do you do* **240 Artow,** *are you* **241 rowne,** *whisper,* **benedicite,** *bless us* **242 japes,** *jokes* **243 gossib,** *confidant* **247 yvel preef,** *inaccurate evidence* **248 seist,** *say* **249 costage,** *expense* **250 heigh parage,** *high lineage* **251 tormentrie,** *torment* **252 malencolie,** *sullenness* **253 verray knave,** *absolute villain* **254 seyst,** *say,* **holour,** *lecher* **255 abyde,** *remain* **256 ech a,** *every*

191 nat agrief of that, El reads "it nat agrief that." **193 now wol I telle forth,** Hg reads "thanne wol I telle yow forth." **195 of,** omitted in Hg. **198 statut,** obligation; see marital debt at lines 130 and 153 above. **204 lond,** El reads "gold." **209 sette,** Hg reads "bisye." **212 sith,** Hg reads "sith that." **me yeven,** Hg reads "yeven me." **213 heede,** Hg reads "kepe" (care). **214 But it,** El reads "But if it." **215 so,** omitted in Hg. **217 bacon was nat fet,** bacon was not fetched; at Dunmow in Essex (southeastern England) and other places, a married couple who had not quarreled for a year could claim a side of bacon as reward. **220 ful blisful was,** El reads "was ful blisful." **226 bere hem wrong on honde,** an idiom meaning "accuse them wrongfully." El omits "wrong." **228 a womman kan,** El reads "kan a womman." **232 beren hym . . . cow is wood,** make him think the chough (a talking bird) is crazy, an allusion to a folk tale in which a bird tattles on his mistress—the plot of the *ManT.* **235–378** Most of the details here derive from well-known antifeminist material, based on Theophrastus, preserved in Jerome 1.47, and popularized by Matheolus, LeFèvre, *RR,* and Deschamps. **244 thou chidest,** Hg reads "ye chiden." **250 that,** omitted in El. **of,** El reads "and of." **251 that,** omitted in El. **253 that,** omitted in El.

Thou seyst som folk desire us for richesse,
Somme for oure shap, and somme for oure fairnesse,
And som for she kan synge and daunce,
And som for gentillesse° and daliaunce°,
Som for hir handes and hir armes smale°—
Thus goth al to the devel, by thy tale°.
Thou seyst men may nat kepe° a castel wal
It may so longe assailed been over al°.
And if that she be foul°, thou seist that she
Coveiteth° every man that she may se,
For as a spaynel° she wol on hym lepe
Til that she fynde som man hire to chepe°.
Ne noon so grey goos gooth° ther in the lake
As, seistow, wol been withoute make°.
And seyst it is an hard thyng for to welde°
A thyng that no man wole, his thankes, helde°.
Thus seistow, lorel°, whan thow goost to bedde,
And that no wys man nedeth for to wedde,
Ne no° man that entendeth unto° hevene—
With wilde thonder-dynt° and firy levene°
Moote° thy welked nekke° be tobroke°!
Thow seyst that droppyng° houses and eek smoke
And chidyng wyves maken men to flee
Out of hir owene° hous—a, benedicitee°!
What eyleth swich° an old man for to chide?
Thow seyst we wyves wol oure vices hide
Til we be fast°, and thanne we wol hem shewe°—
Wel may that be a proverbe of a shrewe°!
Thou seist that oxen, asses, hors°, and houndes,
They been assayed° at diverse stoundes°;
Bacyns°, lavours°, er° that men hem bye,
Spoones and stooles, and al swich housbondrye°,
And so been pottes, clothes, and array°;
But folk of wyves maken noon assay,
Til they be wedded—olde dotard shrewe°!
Thanne, seistow, we wol oure vices shewe.
Thou seist also that it displeseth me
But if that thou wolt preyse my beautee,
And but thou poure° alwey upon my face
And clepe° me "faire dame" in every place,
And but thou make a feeste° on thilke day
That I was born, and make me fressh and gay,
And but thou do to my norice° honour,
And to my chamberere° withinne my bour°,
And to my fadres° folk and his allyes°—
Thus seistow, olde barelful of lyes°!
And yet of oure apprentice Janekyn,
For° his crisp° heer, shynynge as gold so fyn,
And for he squiereth° me bothe up and doun,
Yet hastow° caught a fals suspecioun.
I wol° hym noght, thogh thou were deed tomorwe.
But tel me, why hydestow with sorwe°
The keyes of thy cheste awey fro me?
It is my good as wel as thyn, pardee°.
What, wenestow° to make an ydiot of oure dame?
Now by that lord that called is Seint Jame,
Thou shalt nat bothe, thogh that thou were wood°,
Be maister of my body and of my good°;
That oon° thou shalt forgo, maugree thyne eyen.
What needeth thee of me to enquere or spyen?
I trowe thou woldest loke° me in thy chiste°.
Thou sholdest seye, "Wyf, go where thee liste°;
Taak° youre disport°, I wol nat leve no talys°.

---

260 gentillesse, *courtesy,* **daliaunce,** *small talk* **261 smale,** *slender* **262 tale,** *account* **263 kepe,** *defend* **264 over al,** *in every way* **265 foul,** *ugly* **266 Coveiteth,** *lusts for* **267 spaynel,** *spaniel* **268 hire to chepe,** *to buy her* **269 Ne noon so grey goos gooth,** *nor is there any gray goose* (that) *goes* **270 make,** *mate* **271 welde,** *control* **272 wole, his thankes, helde** *wishes, willingly, to hold* **273 lorel,** *wretch* **275 Ne no,** *nor* (does any), **entendeth unto,** *intends to go to* **276 thonder-dynt,** *thunderclap,* **levene,** *lightning* **277 Moote,** *may,* **welked nekke,** *withered neck,* **tobroke,** *completely broken* **278 droppyng,** *leaking* **280 hir owene,** *their own,* **a, benedicitee,** *ah, bless us* **281 eyleth swich,** *ails such* **283 fast,** *secure* (married), **wol hem shewe,** *will reveal them* **284 shrewe,** *villain* **285 hors,** *horses* **286 assayed,** *tested,* **diverse stoundes,** *various times* **287 Bacyns,** *basins,* **lavours,** *washbowls,* **er,** *before* **288 swich housbondrye,** *such household items* **289 array,** *equipment* **291 dotard shrewe,** *senile villain* **295 poure,** *gaze* **296 clepe,** *call* **297 feeste,** *celebration,* **thilke,** *that* **299 norice,** *nurse* **300 chamberere,** *chambermaid,* **bour,** *bedroom* **301 fadres,** *father's,* **allyes,** *relatives* **302 lyes,** *dregs or lies* **304 For,** *because of,* **crisp,** *curled* **305 squiereth,** *accompanies* **306 hastow,** *have you* **307 wol,** *want* **308 hydestow with sorwe,** *do you hide with such great care* **310 pardee,** *by God* **311 wenestow,** *do you think* **313 wood,** *enraged* **314 good,** *possessions* **315 oon,** *one* **317 loke,** *lock,* **chiste,** *strongbox* **318 thee liste,** *you wish* **319 Taak,** *take,* **disport,** *pleasure,* **nat leve no talys,** *not believe any reports*

257 seyst som, El reads "seyst that som." **258 and,** omitted in El. **259 kan synge,** Hg reads "kan outher synge." **260 and daliaunce,** El reads "and som for daliaunce." **269 ther,** omitted in El. **271–72 welde . . . helde,** Hg reads "wolde . . . holde." **278–80** The often repeated comparison of wives and leaky houses derives from Proverbs 27.15; see *Mel* 7.1086 and *ParsT* 10.631. **282 seyst we,** El reads "seyst that we." **288 Spoones and,** Hg omits "and." **306 a,** omitted in Hg. **308 tel me, why,** Hg reads "tel me this, why." **309 thy,** El reads "my." **311 to,** omitted in Hg. **oure dame,** the Wife is referring to herself as the lady of the house. **312 Seint Jame,** St. James; two apostles were named James. **313 that,** omitted in El. **314 and of my,** Hg omits "of." **315 maugree thyne eyen,** despite your eyes; an idiom meaning something like "regardless of what you think." **316 needeth thee of me to enquere,** Hg reads "helpeth it of me enquere. **319 wol nat,** El omits "nat"; Hg reads "nyl."

I knowe yow for a trewe wyf, dame Alys°."
We love no man that taketh kepe° or charge°
Wher that we goon; we wol ben at oure large°.
  Of alle men yblessed moot° he be,
The wise astrologien°, daun Ptholome,
That seith this proverbe in his Almageste,
"Of alle men his wysdom is the hyeste°
That rekketh° nevere who hath the world in honde°."
By this proverbe thou shalt understonde,
Have thou ynogh°, what thar thee recche° or care
How myrily° that othere folkes fare?
For certeyn, olde dotard°, by youre leve,
Ye shul have queynte° right ynogh at eve.
He is to greet° a nygard° that wolde werne°
A man to lighte a candle at his lanterne;
He shal have never the lasse° light, pardee°.
Have thou ynogh, thee thar nat pleyne thee°.
Thou seyst also that if we make us gay
With clothyng and with precious array
That it is peril of° oure chastitee;
And yet with sorwe°, thou most enforce thee°,
And seye thise wordes in the Apostles name,
"In habit maad° with chastitee and shame
Ye wommen shul apparaille yow°," quod he,
"And noght in tressed° heer and gay perree°,
As° perles, ne with gold, ne clothes riche."
After thy text, ne after thy rubriche,
I wol nat wirche° as muchel° as a gnat.
  Thou seydest this, that I was lyk a cat;
For whoso° wolde senge° a cattes skyn
Thanne wolde the cat wel dwellen in his in°,
And if the cattes skyn be slyk° and gay
She wol nat dwelle in house half a day,
But forth she wole°, er° any day be dawed°,
To shewe hir skyn and goon a-caterwawed°.
This is to seye, if I be gay, sire shrewe°,
I wol renne° out my borel° for to shewe.
  Sire olde fool, what helpeth thee° to spyen?
Thogh thou preye° Argus with his hundred eyen
To be my warde-cors°, as he kan best,
In feith, he shal nat kepe° me but me lest°;
Yet koude I make his berd°, so moot I thee°!
  Thou seydest eek that ther been thynges thre
The whiche thynges troublen al this erthe,
And that no wight° may endure the ferthe°—
O leeve sire shrewe°, Jhesu shorte° thy lyf!
Yet prechestow° and seyst an hateful wyf
Yrekened is for oon° of thise meschances.
Been° ther none othere maner resemblances
That ye may likne° youre parables to,
But if° a sely° wyf be oon of tho°?
  Thou liknest° eek wommenes love to helle,
To bareyne lond°, ther° water may nat dwelle.
  Thou liknest it also to wilde fyr,
The moore it brenneth°, the moore it hath desir
To consume every thyng that brent wole be°.
Thou seyest, right as° wormes shende° a tree,
Right so a wyf destroyeth hire housbonde;
This knowe they that been to wyves bonde.
  Lordynges, right thus, as ye have understonde,
Baar I stifly myne olde housbondes on honde°
That thus they seyden in hir dronknesse—
And al was fals, but° that I took witnesse
On Janekyn and on my nece° also.
O Lord, the peyne I dide hem and the wo,
Ful giltelees, by Goddes° sweete pyne°!
For as an hors I koude byte° and whyne°.
I koude pleyne°, thogh I were in the gilt,

---

320 Alys, *Alice* **321 kepe,** *care,* **charge,** *responsibility* **322 wol ben at oure large,** *will be free* **323 yblessed moot,** *blessed may* **324 astrologien,** *astronomer* **326 hyeste,** *highest* **327 rekketh,** *cares,* **honde,** *control* **329 Have thou ynogh,** (if) *you have enough,* **what thar thee recche,** *why concern yourself* **330 myrily,** *happily* **331 dotard,** *fool* **332 queynte,** *vagina* **333 to greet,** *too great,* **nygard,** *miser,* **werne,** *refuse* **335 lasse,** *less,* **pardee,** *by God* **336 thee thar nat pleyne thee,** *you shouldn't complain* **339 peril of,** *a threat to* **340 sorwe,** *trouble,* **enforce thee,** *belabor yourself* **342 habit maad,** *clothes made* **343 apparaille yow,** *dress yourselves* **344 tressed,** *arranged,* **perree,** *jewels* **345 As,** (such) *as* **347 wirche,** *work,* **muchel,** *much* **349 whoso,** *whoever,* **senge,** *singe* **350 in his in,** *in his house* **351 slyk,** *sleek* **353 wole,** *will* (go), **er,** *before,* **dawed,** *dawned* **354 goon a-caterwawed,** *gone caterwauling* **355 sire shrewe,** *sir villain* **356 renne,** *run,* **borel,** *cloth* **357 helpeth thee,** *good does it do you* **358 preye,** *ask* **359 warde-cors,** *bodyguard* **360 kepe,** *guard,* **but me lest,** *unless I wish* **361 make his berd,** *deceive him,* **moot I thee,** *might I prosper* **364 wight,** *person,* **ferthe,** *fourth* **365 leeve sire shrewe,** *dear sir villain,* **shorte,** *shorten* **366 prechestow,** *you preach* **367 Yrekened is for oon,** *is considered one* **368 Been,** *are* **369 likne,** *compare* **370 But if,** *unless,* **sely,** *innocent,* **oon of those,** *one of them* **371 liknest,** *compare* **372 bareyne lond,** *barren land,* **ther,** *where* **374 brenneth,** *burns* **375 brent wole be,** *can be burned* **376 right as,** *just as,* **shende,** *destroys* **380 Baar I stifly . . . on honde,** *I strongly accused* **382 but,** *except* **383 nece,** *female relative* **385 Goddes,** *God's,* **pyne,** *pain* **386 koude byte,** *could bite,* **whyne,** *whinny* **387 pleyne,** *complain*

324–25 Ptholome . . . Almageste, see 182–83n above. **326 the,** omitted in Hg. **334 a,** El reads "his." **341 the Apostles name,** St. Paul's name; the quotation that follows is from 1 Timothy 2.9; Jerome 1.27. **346 After thy text . . . rubriche,** to follow neither your text nor your rubrics (words written in red for emphasis). **347 as a,** Hg reads "as is a." **349–54 cattes skyn . . . ,** cat's skin; a proverbial figure. **357 helpeth,** El reads "eyleth" (ails). **358 Argus,** mythic watchman who is deceived by Io despite his one hundred eyes; Ovid, *Metamorphoses* 1.625. **360 me but me lest,** El reads "me but lest." **362–64 thynges thre . . . ,** from Proverbs 30.21–23; Jerome 1.28. **366 an,** El reads "and." **371–78 wommenes love . . . ,** from Proverbs 30.16 and a version of Proverbs 25.20; Jerome 1.28. **371 eek,** omitted in El. **387 thogh I were,** Hg reads "and I was."

Or elles° often tyme hadde I been spilt°.
Whoso comth first to mille, first grynt°;
I pleyned first, so was oure werre ystynt°.
They were ful glad to excuse hem blyve°
Of thyng of which they nevere agilte hir lyve°.
  Of wenches wolde I beren hym on honde°,
Whan that for syk° unnethes° myghte he stonde.
Yet tikled it° his herte, for that he
Wende° that I hadde of hym so greet chiertee°.
I swoor that al my walkynge out by nyghte
Was for t'espye wenches that he dighte°.
Under that colour° hadde I many a myrthe°.
For al swich° wit is yeven us° in oure byrthe:
Deceite, wepyng, spynnyng God hath yeve
To wommen kyndely whil that they may lyve.
And thus of o° thyng I avaunte me°,
Atte° ende I hadde the bettre in ech degree°,
By sleighte° or force, or by som maner thyng,
As by continueel murmur or grucchyng°.
Namely abedde° hadden they meschaunce°.
Ther wolde I chide° and do hem no plesaunce;
I wolde no lenger in the bed abyde°
If that I felte his arm over my syde
Til he had maad his raunsoun unto me°;
Thanne wolde I suffre hym do° his nycetee°.
And therfore every man this tale I telle,
Wynne whoso° may, for al is for to selle;
With empty hand men may none haukes° lure.
For wynnyng wolde I° al his lust endure
And make me a feyned° appetit—
And yet in bacon° hadde I nevere delit.
That made me that evere I wolde hem chide;
For thogh the pope hadde seten hem biside°,
I wolde nat spare hem at hir owene bord°,
For, by my trouthe, I quitte° hem word for word.
As helpe me verray° God omnipotent,
Though I right now sholde make my testament°,
I ne owe hem nat a word that it nys quit°.
I broghte it so aboute by my wit
That they moste yeve° it up as for the beste,
Or elles hadde we nevere been in reste.
For thogh he looked as a wood leoun°,
Yet sholde he faille of his conclusioun°.
  Thanne wolde I seye, "Goode lief°, taak keep°,
How mekely° looketh Wilkyn°, oure sheep!
Com neer°, my spouse, lat me ba° thy cheke!
Ye sholde been al pacient and meke,
And han° a sweete spiced conscience,
Sith° ye so preche of Jobes pacience.
Suffreth alwey, syn° ye so wel kan preche;
And but° ye do, certein we shal yow teche
That it is fair° to have a wyf in pees°.
Oon of us two moste bowen°, douteless,
And sith a man is moore resonable
Than womman is, ye moste been suffrable°.
What eyleth° yow to grucche° thus and grone?
Is it for ye wolde have my queynte° allone?
Wy°, taak it al—lo, have it every deel°.
Peter, I shrewe° yow, but° ye love it weel.
For if I wolde selle my bele chose,
I koude walke as fressh as is a rose,
But I wol kepe it for youre owene tooth°.
Ye be to blame, by God, I sey yow sooth°."
  Swiche manere° wordes hadde we on honde.
Now wol I speken of my fourthe housbonde.
  My fourthe housbonde was a revelour°—
This is to seyn, he hadde a paramour°,
And I was yong and ful of ragerye°,
Stibourne° and strong, and joly as a pye°.
Wel koude I daunce to an harpe smale,

388 elles, *else,* **spilt,** *ruined* **389 grynt,** *grinds* **390 werre ystynt,** *war stopped* **391 blyve,** *quickly* **392 agilte hir lyve,** (were) *guilty in their lives* **393 beren hym on honde,** *accuse him* **394 syk,** *sickness,* **unnethes,** *barely* **395 tikled it,** *it pleased* **396 Wende,** *thought,* **chiertee,** *love* **398 dighte,** *had sex with* **399 colour,** *pretense,* **myrthe,** *happy time* **400 swich,** *such,* **yeven us,** *given us* (women) **402 kyndely,** *by nature* **403 o,** *one,* **avaunte me,** *boast* **404 Atte,** *at the,* **ech degree,** *each respect* **405 sleighte,** *trickery* **406 grucchyng,** *complaining* **407 abedde,** *in bed,* **meschaunce,** *bad luck* **408 chide,** *scold* **409 abyde,** *remain* **411 maad his raunsoun unto me,** *paid me* **412 suffre hym do,** *allow him to do,* **nycetee,** *foolishness* **414 whoso,** *whoever* **415 none haukes,** *no hawks* **416 For wynnyng wolde I,** *in order to profit I would* **417 feyned,** *pretended* **418 bacon,** *preserved meat* **420 seten hem biside,** *sat beside them* **421 hir owene bord,** *their own table* **422 quitte,** *repaid* **423 verray,** *true* **424 testament,** *will* **425 nys quit,** *isn't repaid* **427 yeve,** *give* **429 wood leoun,** *enraged lion* **430 faille of his conclusioun,** *fail to get his goal* **431 Goode lief,** *dearest,* **taak keep,** *take heed* **432 mekely,** *meekly,* **Wilkyn,** *Willie* **433 neer,** *nearer,* **ba,** *kiss* **435 han,** *have* **436 Sith,** *since* **437 syn,** *since* **438 but,** *unless* **439 fair,** *well,* **pees,** *peace* **440 moste bowen,** *must bend* **442 suffrable,** *accepting* **443 eyleth,** *ails,* **grucche,** *complain* **444 queynte,** *vagina* **445 Wy,** *why,* **every deel,** *completely* **446 Peter,** *by St. Peter,* **shrewe,** *curse,* **but,** *unless* **449 owene tooth,** *own taste* **450 sey yow sooth,** *tell you truly* **451 Swiche manere,** *such kinds of* **453 revelour,** *pleasure seeker* **454 paramour,** *mistress* **455 ragerye,** *high spirits* **456 Stibourne,** *stubborn,* **pye,** *magpie*

388 hadde I, Hg reads "I hadde." **389 comth first to mille,** Hg reads "that first to mille comth." **391 hem blyve,** Hg reads "hem ful blyve." **394 unnethes myghte he stonde,** Hg reads "they myghte unnethe stonde." **395 it,** Hg reads "I." **397 al,** omitted in Hg. **400 wit is yeven,** El reads "thyng was yeven." **402 that,** omitted in Hg. El and Hg vary much less frequently from this point on in *WBP*, indicating that the scribe must have changed his exemplar when copying one of them, almost certainly El. **424 Though,** Hg reads "Togh." **435 sweete spiced conscience,** a difficult phrase that seems to mean "tender adaptable sensibility." **436 Jobes pacience,** Job's patience is proverbial, deriving from the biblical book of Job. **447 bele chose,** French for "pretty thing," a sexual euphemism to match the English euphemism at line 444 and the Latin one at line 608. **457 Wel,** Hg reads "How."

And synge, ywis°, as any nyghtyngale,
Whan I had dronke a draughte of sweete wyn.
Metellius, the foule cherl°, the swyn°,
That with a staf birafte° his wyf hir lyf
For she drank wyn, thogh I hadde been his wyf,
He sholde nat han daunted° me fro drynke!
And after wyn on Venus moste° I thynke,
For al so siker° as cold engendreth hayl°,
A likerous mouth moste han a likerous tayl.
In wommen vinolent° is no defence—
This knowen lecchours by experience.
  But, Lord Crist, whan that it remembreth me°
Upon myyowthe and on my jolitee,
It tikleth° me about myn herte roote°.
Unto this day it dooth myn herte boote°
That I have had my world as in my tyme.
But age, allas, that al wole envenyme°,
Hath me biraft° my beautee and my pith°.
Lat go, farewel, the devel go therwith!
The flour is goon, ther is namoore to telle;
The bren°, as I best kan, now moste I selle;
But yet to be right myrie wol I fonde°.
Now wol I tellen of my fourthe housbonde.
  I seye, I hadde in herte greet despit°
That he of any oother had delit.
But he was quit°, by God and by Seint Joce.
I made hym of the same wode a croce°—
Nat of my body, in no foul manere,
But certeinly, I made folk swich cheere°
That in his owene grece° I made hym frye
For angre, and for verray jalousye.
By God, in erthe I was his purgatorie,
For which I hope his soule be in glorie.
For, God it woot°, he sat ful ofte and song°
Whan that his shoo ful bitterly hym wrong.
There was no wight save° God and he that wiste°,
In many wise°, how soore° I hym twiste°.
He deyde° whan I cam fro Jerusalem,
And lith ygrave° under the roode beem,
Al is his tombe° noght so curyus°
As was the sepulcre° of hym Daryus,
Which that Appelles wroghte subtilly;
It nys but wast° to burye hym preciously°.
Lat hym fare wel; God yeve° his soule reste.
He is now in his grave and in his cheste°.
  Now of my fifthe housbonde wol I telle.
God lete his soule nevere come in helle—
And yet was he to me the mooste shrewe°;
That feele I on my ribbes al by rewe°,
And evere shal unto myn endyng day.
But in oure bed he was so fresshe and gay,
And therwithal° so wel koude he me glose°,
Whan that he wolde han my bele chose°,
That thogh he hadde me bet° on every bon,
He koude wynne agayn my love anon°.
I trowe° I loved hym best for that he
Was of his love daungerous° to me.
We wommen han°, if that I shal nat lye,
In this matere a queynte fantasye°:
Wayte what° thyng we may nat lightly° have,
Therafter wol we crie al day and crave.
Forbede us thyng°, and that desiren we;
Preesse on° us faste, and thanne wol we fle°.
With daunger oute we° al oure chaffare°;
Greet prees° at market maketh deere ware°,
And to greet cheep° is holde at litel prys°.

---

458 ywis, *surely* **460 cherl,** *lowlifer,* **swyn,** *pig* **461 birafte,** *deprived* **463 han daunted,** *have scared* **464 moste,** *must* **465 al so siker,** *as certainly,* **engendreth hayl,** *produces hail* **467 vinolent,** *drunken* **469 it remembreth me,** *I remember* **471 tikleth,** *pleases,* **about myn herte roote,** *to the bottom of my heart* **472 boote,** *good* **474 al wole envenyme,** *will poison all* **475 me biraft,** *deprived me* (of), **pith,** *strength* **478 bren,** *bran* **479 fonde,** *strive* **481 despit,** *resentment* **483 quit,** *repaid* **484 croce,** *stick or cross* **486 folk swich cheere,** (to) *people such a welcoming disposition* **487 owene grece,** *own grease* **491 woot,** *knows,* **song,** *sang* **493 wight save,** *person except,* **wiste,** *knew* **494 wise,** *ways,* **soore,** *sorely,* **twiste,** *tormented* **495 deyde,** *died* **496 lith ygrave,** *lies buried* **497 Al is his tombe,** *although his tomb is,* **curyus,** *ornate* **498 sepulcre,** *sepulcher* **500 nys but wast,** *is nothing but waste,* **preciously,** *expensively* **501 yeve,** *give* **502 cheste,** *coffin* **505 mooste shrewe,** *greatest villain* **506 by rewe,** *in a row* **509 therwithal,** *with that,* **glose,** *coax or interpret* **510 bele chose,** *pretty thing* (vagina) **511 bet,** *beat* **512 anon,** *quickly* **513 trowe,** *believe* **514 daungerous,** *standoffish* **515 han,** *have* **516 queynte fantasye,** *strange desire* **517 Wayte what,** *observe whatever,* **lightly,** *easily* **519 Forbede us thyng,** *forbid us something* **520 Preesse on,** *pursue,* **fle,** *run* **521 daunger oute we,** *aloofness we put out,* **chaffare,** *merchandise* **522 prees,** *crowd,* **deere ware,** *expensive goods* **523 to greet cheep,** *too good a bargain,* **prys,** *value*

460 Metellius, killed his wife with his staff because she had been drinking; recorded in a medieval schoolbook, the *Memorabilium Exempla* of Valerius Maximus. Chaucer cites materials from the same chapter (6.3) at lines 643 and 647 below. **463 He,** Hg reads "Ne." **466 likerous mouth . . . likerous tayl,** gluttony produces lechery, with play on *liquorous* and *lecherous.* **483 Seint Joce,** St. Judocus, a Breton saint, whose emblem was a pilgrim's staff. **484 croce,** Hg reads "troce" (?). **489 purgatorie,** place of punishment for sin, but purgatory was a common image for the pains of marriage. **492 shoo . . . hym wrong,** shoe wrung (or pinched) him, another common image for the pains of marriage. **495 fro Jerusalem,** in *GP* 1.463, it is said that the Wife went to Jerusalem on pilgrimage three times. **496 roode beem,** crossbeam; a special place to be buried in a church, under the beam upon which the crucifix is hung. **498–99 Daryus . . . Appelles,** an account of the splendid tomb of Darius, built by Appelles, is in Gautier de Chatillon's *Alexandreis.* **508 so,** El reads "ful."

This knoweth every womman that is wys.
My fifthe housbonde—God his soule blesse—
Which that I took for love and no richesse,
He somtyme° was a clerk of Oxenford,
And hadde left scole°, and wente at hom to bord°
With my gossib°, dwellynge in oure toun—
God have hir soule—hir name was Alisoun;
She knew myn herte and eek my privetee°
Bet° than oure parisshe preest, so moot I thee°!
To hire biwreyed° I my conseil° al.
For hadde myn housbonde pissed on a wal,
Or doon a thyng that sholde han cost his lyf,
To hire, and to another worthy wyf,
And to my nece°, which that I loved weel,
I wolde han toold his conseil every deel°.
And so I dide ful often, God it woot°,
That made his face ful often reed and hoot
For verray shame, and blamed hymself for he
Had toold to me so greet a pryvetee.
And so bifel that ones in a Lente—
So often tymes I to my gossyb wente,
For evere yet I loved to be gay,
And for to walke in March, Averill, and May,
Fro hous to hous, to heere sondry talys°—
That Jankyn clerk and my gossyb dame Alys
And I myself into the feeldes wente.
Myn housbonde was at Londoun al the Lente;
I hadde the bettre leyser° for to pleye,
And for to se, and eek for to be seye°
Of lusty° folk. What wiste I° wher my grace°
Was shapen° for to be, or in what place?
Therfore I made my visitaciouns
To vigilies and to processiouns,
To prechyng eek, and to thise pilgrimages,
To pleyes of myracles, and to mariages,
And wered upon° my gaye scarlet gytes°—
Thise wormes, ne thise motthes°, ne thise
mytes°,
Upon my peril, frete° hem never a deel°;
And wostow° why? For they were used weel.
Now wol I tellen forth what happed me.
I seye° that in the feeldes walked we,
Til trewely we hadde swich daliance°,
This clerk and I, that of my purveiance°
I spak to hym and seyde hym how that he,
If I were wydwe°, sholde wedde me.
For certeinly, I sey for no bobance°,
Yet was I nevere withouten purveiance
Of mariage, n'of° othere thynges eek.
I holde a mouses herte nat worth a leek
That hath but oon hole for to sterte° to,
And if that faille°, thanne is al ydo°.
I bar hym on honde° he hadde enchanted
me—
My dame° taughte me that soutiltee°.
And eek I seyde I mette° of hym al nyght:
He wolde han slayn me as I lay upright°,
And al my bed was ful of verray° blood,
But yet I hope that he shal do me good,
For blood bitokeneth° gold, as me was taught—
And al was fals; I dremed of it right naught°,
But I folwed ay my dames loore°,
As wel of this as of othere thynges moore.
But now, sire, lat me se, what I shal seyn°?
Aha, by God, I have my tale ageyn°!
Whan that my fourthe housbonde was on beere°,
I weep algate° and made sory cheere°,
As wyves mooten° for it is usage°,
And with my coverchief covered my visage°;
But for that° I was purveyed of° a make°,
I wepte but smal°, and that I undertake°.
To chirche was myn housbonde born a-morwe°
With neighebores that for hym maden sorwe,
And Jankyn oure clerk was oon of tho°.
As help me God, whan that I saugh° hym go
After the beere°, me thoughte he hadde a paire

527 somtyme, *for a while* **528 scole,** *school,* **bord,** *board* **529 gossib,** *friend* **531 privetee,** *secrets* **532 Bet,** *better,* **moot I thee,** *might I prosper* **532 biwreyed,** *revealed,* **conseil,** *confidences* **537 nece,** *female relative* **538 conseil every deel,** *secrets completely* **539 woot,** *knows* **547 heere sondry talys,** *hear various stories* **551 leyser,** *opportunity* **552 be seye,** *be seen* **553 Of lusty,** *by pleasant,* **What wiste I,** *how did I know what,* **grace,** *fortune* **554 shapen,** *destined* **559 wered upon,** *wore,* **gytes,** *gowns* **560 motthes,** *moths,* **mytes,** *insects* **561 frete,** *ate,* **never a deel,** *not a bit* **562 wostow,** *do you know* **564 seye,** *say* **565 daliance,** *flirting* **566 purveiance,** *foresight* **568 wydwe,** *widow* **569 bobance,** *boast* **571 n'of,** *nor of* **573 sterte,** *escape* **574 faille,** *fail,* **ydo,** *done* **575 bar hym on honde,** *convinced him* **576 dame,** *mother,* **soutiltee,** *subtlety* **577 mette,** *dreamed* **578 upright,** *on my back* **579 verray,** *actual* **581 bitokeneth,** *signifies* **582 right naught,** *not at all* **583 dames loore,** *mother's advice* **585 seyn,** *say* **586 ageyn,** *again* **587 beere,** *bier* **588 algate,** *continuously,* **made sory cheere,** *acted sad* **589 mooten,** *must,* **usage,** *customary* **590 visage,** *face* **591 But for that,** *except because,* **purveyed of,** *provided with,* **make,** *mate* **592 smal,** *little,* **undertake,** *declare* **593 a-morwe,** *in the morning* **595 oon of tho,** *one of them* **596 saugh,** *saw* **597 After the beere,** *behind the bier*

530 Alisoun, a diminutive of Alice. The Wife (line 320) and her gossip have the same name, suggesting deep intimacy. **540 ful,** omitted in Hg. **543 Lente,** the liturgical season of repentance that precedes Easter. **550 the,** Hg reads "that." **556 vigilies,** vigils, services held before religious holidays. **558 pleyes of myracles,** popular religious dramas. **575–84** Lines lacking in Hg, usually considered to be added late by Chaucer, along with 605–12, 619–26, and 717–20. Lines 44[a-f] have a somewhat different status since they are lacking in El and Hg. **585 I shal,** Hg reads "shal I."

Of legges and of feet so clene° and faire
That al myn herte I yaf° unto his hoold°.
He was, I trowe°, a twenty wynter° oold,
And I was fourty, if I shal seye sooth;
But yet I hadde alwey a coltes tooth.
Gat-tothed I was, and that bicam° me weel;
I hadde the prente of Seinte Venus seel.
As help me God, I was a lusty oon,
And faire and riche and yong and wel bigon°,
And trewely, as myne housbondes tolde me,
I hadde the beste quonyam myghte be.
For certes, I am al Venerien
In feelynge, and myn herte is Marcien.
Venus me yaf° my lust, my likerousnesse°,
And Mars yaf me my sturdy hardynesse°.
Myn ascendent was Taur, and Mars therinne—
Allas, allas, that evere love was synne!
I folwed ay° myn inclinacioun
By vertu of my constellacioun,
That made me I koude noght withdrawe°
My chambre of Venus° from a goode felawe.
Yet have I Martes mark upon my face,
And also in another privee° place.
For God so wys be my savacioun°,
I ne loved nevere by no discrecioun°,
But evere folwede myn appetit,
Al were he° short, or long, or blak, or whit;
I took no kepe° so that° he liked° me,
How poore he was, ne eek° of what degree°.
What sholde I seye but at the monthes ende
This joly clerk Jankyn that was so hende°
Hath wedded me with greet solempnytee,
And to hym yaf° I al the lond and fee°
That evere was me yeven° therbifoore—
But afterward repented me ful soore.
He nolde suffre° nothyng of my list°;
By God, he smoot° me ones° on the lyst°,
For that° I rente° out of his book a leef°,
That of the strook myn ere wax al deef°.
Stibourne° I was as is a leonesse,
And of my tonge a verray jangleresse°,
And walke I wolde, as I had doon biforn°,
From hous to hous, although he had it sworn°;
For which he often tymes wolde preche°,
And me of olde Romayn geestes° teche:
How he Symplicius Gallus lefte his wyf,
And hire forsook for terme of al his lyf°,
Noght but for open-heveded° he hir say°
Lokynge out at° his dore upon a day.
Another Romayn tolde he me by name
That for° his wyf was at a someres game°
Withouten his wityng°, he forsook hire eke.
And thanne wolde he upon his Bible seke°
That ilke° proverbe of Ecclesiaste
Where he comandeth and forbedeth faste°
Man shal nat suffre° his wyf go roule° aboute.
Thanne wolde he seye right thus, withouten doute:
"Whoso that buyldeth his hous al of salwes°,
And priketh his blynde hors over the falwes°,
And suffreth° his wyf to go seken halwes°,
Is worthy to been hanged on the galwes°."
But al for noght; I sette° noght an hawe°
Of his proverbes n'of° his olde sawe°,
Ne I wolde nat of hym corrected be.
I hate hym that my vices telleth me,

---

598 clene, *trim* **599 yaf,** *gave,* **hoold,** *possession* **600 trowe,** *think,* **wynter,** *years* **603 bicam,** *suited* **606 wel bigon,** *well situated* **611 me yaf,** *gave me,* **likerousnesse,** *sexuality* **612 hardynesse,** *boldness* **615 ay,** *always* **617 withdrawe,** *withhold* **618 chambre of Venus,** *vagina* **620 privee,** *private* **621 so wys be my savacioun,** *so certainly be my salvation* **622 discrecioun,** *thoughtful decision* **624 Al were he,** *although he was* **625 kepe,** *notice,* **so that,** *as long as,* **liked,** *pleased* **626 ne eek,** *nor also,* **degree,** *class* **628 hende,** *courteous or handy* **630 yaf,** *gave,* **fee,** *wealth* **631 yeven,** *given* **633 nolde suffre,** *wouldn't allow,* **list,** *desire* **634 smoot,** *hit,* **ones,** *once,* **lyst,** *ear* **635 For that,** *because,* **rente,** *tore,* **leef,** *page* **636 ere wax al deef,** *ear became deaf* **637 Stibourne,** *stubborn* **638 verray jangleresse,** *true loudmouth* **639 biforn,** *before* **640 sworn,** *forbidden* **641 preche,** *lecture* **642 geestes,** *stories* **644 terme of al his lyf,** *his entire life* **645 open-heveded,** *bareheaded,* **hir say,** *saw her* **646 at,** *of* **648 for,** *because,* **someres game,** *summer clebration* **649 wityng,** *knowledge* **650 upon his Bible seke,** *look up in his Bible* **651 ilke,** *same* **652 faste,** *firmly* **653 suffre,** *allow,* **roule,** *roam* **655 salwes,** *willow sticks* **656 falwes,** *unused plowed fields* **657 suffreth,** *allows,* **seken halwes,** *seek shrines* **658 galwes,** *gallows* **659 sette,** *valued* (at), **hawe,** *hawthorn berry* **660 n'of,** *nor of,* **sawe,** *saying*

600 a, omitted in Hg. **602 But,** El reads "And." **coltes tooth,** an idiom meaning "youthful desire"; see *RvP* 1.3888. **603 Gat-tothed,** gap-toothed, thought to indicate a bold, envious, suspicious, and perhaps sensuous nature; see *GP* 1.468. **604 prente of Seinte Venus seel,** a birthmark associated with Venus and sensuality. **608 quonyam,** Latin, meaning "because" or "whereas," a euphemism for vagina; see 447n above. **609–12** Lines lacking in Hg. **609–10 Venerien . . . Marcien,** under the influence of Venus (planet of love) and Mars (planet of war). **613 ascendent . . . therinne,** the constellation of Taurus (the Bull) was rising with Mars within when the Wife was born. **616 vertu of my constellacioun,** the power of my constellation; i.e., the Wife blames her inclinations on her horoscope. **619–26** Lines lacking in Hg. **619 Martes mark,** a birthmark associated with Mars or boldness. **636 deef,** see *GP* 1.446. **643 Symplicius Gallus,** Sulpicius Gallus divorced his wife for appearing without her kerchief on; see 460n above. **647 Another Romayn,** Sempronius Sophus divorced his wife because she went to games; see 460n above. **651 Ecclesiaste,** Ecclesiasticus, a book in the Catholic Bible; see Ecclesiasticus 25.34–35. **655–58** A familiar saying. **660 sawe,** El reads "lawe."

And so doo mo°, God woot°, of us than I.
This made hym with me wood al outrely°.
I nolde noght forbere° hym in no cas.
  Now wol I seye yow sooth, by Seint Thomas,
Why that I rente° out of his book a leef°,
For which he smoot° me so that I was deef.
  He hadde a book that gladly, nyght and day,
For his desport° he wolde rede alway.
He cleped° it Valerie and Theofraste,
At which book he lough alwey ful faste°.
And eek ther was somtyme a clerk° at Rome,
A cardinal, that highte° Seint Jerome,
That made a book agayn Jovinian;
In which book eek ther was Tertulan,
Crisippus, Trotula, and Helowys,
That was abbesse nat fer fro Parys°;
And eek the Parables of Salomon,
Ovides Art, and bookes many on°.
And alle thise were bounden in o° volume,
And every nyght and day was his custume,
Whan he hadde leyser and vacacioun°
From oother worldly occupacioun,
To reden on this book of wikked wyves.
He knew of hem mo° legendes and lyves
Than been° of goode wyves in the Bible.
For trusteth wel, it is an inpossible°
That any clerk° wol speke good of wyves,
But if° it be of hooly seintes lyves,
Ne of noon oother womman never the mo.
Who peyntede the leon, tel me who?
By God, if wommen hadde writen stories,
As clerkes han withinne hire oratories°,
They wolde han writen of men moore wikkednesse
Than al the mark of Adam° may redresse°.
The children of Mercurie and of Venus
Been in hir wirkyng° ful contrarius°:
Mercurie loveth wysdam and science°,
And Venus loveth ryot° and dispence°,
And for hire° diverse disposicioun
Ech falleth in otheres exaltacioun.
And thus, God woot°, Mercurie is desolat
In Pisces wher Venus is exaltat,
And Venus falleth ther° Mercurie is reysed°.
Therfore no womman of° no clerk is preysed.
The clerk, whan he is oold and may noght do
Of Venus werkes worth his olde sho°,
Thanne sit he doun and writ in his dotage°
That wommen kan nat kepe hir mariage.
  But now to purpos°, why I tolde thee
That I was beten for a book, pardee°!
Upon a nyght Jankyn, that was oure sire°,
Redde on his book, as he sat by the fire,
Of Eva first, that for hir wikkednesse
Was al mankynde broght to wrecchednesse,
For which that° Jhesu Crist hymself was slayn
That boghte° us with his herte blood agayn—
Lo, heere expres° of womman may ye fynde
That womman was the los° of al mankynde.

663 mo, *more,* **woot,** *knows* **664 wood al outrely,** *utterly furious* **665 nolde noght forbere,** *would not put up with* **667 rente,** *tore,* **leef,** *page* **668 smoot,** *hit* **670 desport,** *enjoyment* **671 cleped,** *called* **672 ful faste,** *very loudly* **673 clerk,** *scholar* **674 highte,** *was called* **678 fer fro Parys,** *far from Paris* **680 bookes many on,** *many a book* **681 o,** *one* **683 leyser and vacacioun,** *leisure and spare time* **686 of hem mo,** *about them more* **687 been,** *are* **688 inpossible,** *impossibility* **689 clerk,** *scholar, member of the clergy* **690 But if,** *unless* **694 oratories,** *places for prayer* **696 mark of Adam,** *i.e., all men,* **redresse,** *amend* **698 hir wirkyng,** *their activities,* **ful contrarius,** *completely opposite* **699 science,** *knowledge* **700 ryot,** *partying,* **dispence,** *extravagance* **701 for hire,** *because of their* **703 woot,** *knows* **705 ther,** *when,* **reysed,** *raised* **706 of,** *by* **708 sho,** *shoe* **709 dotage,** *senility* **711 to purpos,** *to the point* **712 pardee,** *by God* **713 oure sire,** *master of the household* **717 For which that,** *on account of which* **718 That boghte,** *who redeemed* **719 expres,** *specifically* **720 los,** *loss*

671 Valerie and Theofraste, Walter Map's *Dissuasio Valerii ad Rufinum* (*Valerius's Dissuasion of Rufinus*) and Theophrastus's *Liber de Nuptiis* (*Book of Marriage*), the latter surviving in Jerome. More than sixty extant medieval manuscripts contain combinations of or selections from the antimatrimonial and antifeminist materials listed in lines 671–80. **674 cardinal,** an important Church official; historically, Jerome was not a cardinal but was often represented as such. **675 book agayn Jovinian,** Jerome's *Epistola adversus Jovinianum* (*Letter against Jovinian*). **676 Tertulan,** Tertullian, a classical writer mentioned in Jerome, although not quoted in *WBP.* **677 Crisippus,** mentioned by Jerome but otherwise obscure. **Trotula,** a female physician and writer on gynecology. **Helowys,** Heloise, whose *Letters* record why she chose not to marry Peter Abelard. **679 Parables of Salomon,** a medieval name for the Book of Proverbs. **680 Ovides Art,** Ovid's *Ars Amatoria* (*Art of Love*). **685 on,** Hg reads "in." **691 Ne of noon,** El reads "Ne noon"; Hg, N'of noon." **692 peyntede the leon,** an allusion to a fable in which a lion sees a picture of a man killing a lion and remarks that the picture would be different if a lion had painted it. **697 children of Mercurie and of Venus,** people associated with the planets Mercury (scholars) and Venus (lovers). El and Hg omit "of" before "Venus." **701–02 diverse disposicioun . . . exaltacioun,** semitechnical astronomical language, meaning that Mercury and Venus are so situated that when one exerts its strongest influence on the affairs of humans, the other exerts its least influence. A planet is at its exaltation when it is in the constellation of the zodiac thought to empower it; it is at its dejection (or desolation or declination) when in the constellation where it is weakest. **704 Pisces,** constellation of the Fish; the exaltation of Venus and dejection of Mars. **705 falleth,** Hg reads "failleth." **715 Eva,** Eve, blamed for causing the fall of humanity in Genesis. **717–20** Lines lacking in Hg.

Tho redde he me how Sampson loste his heres°.
Slepynge, his lemman kitte° it with hir sheres°,
Thurgh which treson loste he bothe his eyen.
  Tho redde he me, if that I shal nat lyen,
Of Hercules and of his Dianyre,
That caused hym to sette hymself afyre.
  Nothyng forgat he the sorwe and the wo
That Socrates hadde with his wyves two,
How Xantippa caste pisse upon his heed.
This sely° man sat stille as° he were deed;
He wiped his heed, namoore dorste° he seyn°
But "Er° that thonder stynte°, comth a reyn!"
  Of Phasifpha, that was the queene of Crete,
For shrewednesse° hym thoughte the tale swete.
Fy! Spek namoore—it is a grisly° thyng—
Of hire horrible lust and hir likyng.
  Of Clitermystra, for hire lecherye,
That falsly made hire housbonde for to dye,
He redde it with ful good devocioun.
  He tolde me eek for what occasioun
Amphiorax at Thebes loste his lyf.
Myn housbonde hadde a legende of his wyf
Eriphilem, that for an ouche° of gold
Hath prively° unto the Grekes told
Wher that hir housbonde hidde hym in a place
For which he hadde at Thebes sory grace°.
  Of Lyvia tolde he me, and of Lucye:
They bothe made hir housbondes for to dye,
That oon for love, that oother was for hate.
Lyvia hir housbonde, upon an even late°,
Empoysoned° hath for that she was his fo;
Lucia, likerous°, loved hire housbonde so
That for° he sholde alwey upon hire thynke,
She yaf° hym swich a manere love-drynke
That he was deed er it were by the morwe°—
And thus algates° housbondes han sorwe.
  Thanne tolde he me how that oon Latumyus
Compleyned unto his felawe Arrius
That in his gardyn growed° swich a tree
On which he seyde how that his wyves thre
Hanged hemself° for herte despitus°.
"O leeve° brother," quod this Arrius,
"Yif° me a plante of thilke° blissed tree,
And in my gardyn planted it shal bee."
  Of latter date°, of wyves hath he red°
That somme han slayn hir housbondes in hir bed
And lete hir lecchour° dighte hire° al the nyght,
Whan that the corps° lay in° the floor upright°.
And somme han dryve nayles° in hir brayn
Whil that they slepte, and thus they han hem slayn.
Somme han hem yeve° poysoun in hire drynke.
  He spak moore harm than herte may bithynke°,
And therwithal° he knew of mo° proverbes
Than in this world ther growen gras or herbes.
"Bet is°," quod he, "thyn habitacioun°
Be with a leoun or a foul dragoun
Than with a womman usynge for to chyde°."
"Bet is," quod he, "hye° in the roof abyde°
Than with an angry wyf doun in the hous;
They been so wikked and contrarious°,
They haten that° hir housbondes loveth ay°."
He seyde, "A womman cast hir shame away
Whan she cast of hir smok°," and forthermo,
"A fair womman, but° she be chaast also,
Is lyk a gold ryng in a sowes° nose."
Who wolde leeve° or who wolde suppose
The wo that in myn herte was, and pyne°?

---

721 heres, *hair* **722 lemman kitte,** *lover cut,* **hir sheres,** *her scissors* **730 sely,** *silly or innocent,* **as,** *as if* **731 namoore dorste,** *no more dared,* **seyn,** *say* **732 Er,** *before,* **stynte,** *stops* **734 shrewednesse,** *cursedness* **735 grisly,** *terrible* **743 ouche,** *jeweled ornament* **744 prively,** *secretly* **746 sory grace,** *bad fortune* **750 upon an even late,** *late one evening* **751 Empoysoned,** *poisoned* **752 likerous,** *lecherous* **753 for,** *so* **754 yaf,** *gave* **755 morwe,** *morning* **756 algates,** *always* **759 growed,** *grew* **761 hemself,** *themselves,* **for herte despitus,** *because of spiteful hearts* **762 leeve,** *dear* **763 Yif,** *give,* **thilke,** *that* **765 Of latter date,** *later on,* **red,** *read* **767 lecchour,** *lecher,* **dighte hire,** *have sex with her* **768 corps,** *dead body,* **in,** *on,* **upright,** *flat* **769 dryve nayles,** *driven nails* **771 han hem yeve,** *have given them* **772 bithynke,** *think of* **773 therwithal,** *further,* **mo,** *more* **775 Bet it,** *it is better,* **thyne habitacioun,** *your dwelling* **777 usynge for to chyde,** *accustomed to scold* **778 hye,** *high,* **abyde,** (to) *stay* **780 contrarious,** *quarrelsome* **781 that,** *what,* **ay,** *always* **783 smok,** *dress* **784 but,** *unless* **785 sowes,** *pig's* **786 leeve,** *believe* **787 pyne,** *pain*

721 Sampson, on Samson's haircut, loss of strength, and blindness, see Judges 16.15–21 and *MkT* 7.2015–94. This and most of the following antifeminist commonplaces are mentioned in Jerome, although some details come from elsewhere. **725 Hercules . . . Dianyre**, accidentally betrayed by his wife, Deianira, Hercules leapt into a burning fire; see *MkT* 7.2095–2142. **727 the wo,** El and Hg omit "the." **728–29 Socrates . . . Xantippa,** the account comes from Jerome 1.48. **733 Phasifpha,** Pasiphae's passion for a bull led to the birth of the Minotaur; Jerome 1.48. **737 Clitermystra,** Clytemnestra, committed adultery and helped kill her husband, Agamemnon; Jerome 1.48. **741 Amphiorax,** Amphiaraus died at Thebes after Eriphyle, his wife, disclosed his hiding place in exchange for a necklace; Jerome 1.48. **747–55 Lyvia . . . ,** the accounts come from Walter Map (see 671n); not in Jerome. Hg appears to read "Lyma" for "Lyvia," but the pen-stroke minims are hard to discriminate. **757–64 Latumyus . . . Arrius . . . ,** the story is found, with different names, in Walter Map. **764 it shal bee,** Hg reads "shal it be." **765–71** Similar stories are found together in John of Salisbury's *Policraticus* 8. **773 proverbes,** Jerome 1.28 and 48 quote most of the following proverbs from scriptural sources. **786 leeve,** Hg reads "wene" (think).

And whan I saugh he wolde nevere fyne°
To reden on this cursed book al nyght,
Al sodeynly thre leves° have I plyght°
Out of his book right as he radde°, and eke
I with my fest° so took° hym on the cheke
That in oure fyr he fil bakward adoun.
And he up stirte° as dooth a wood° leoun,
And with his fest he smoot° me on the heed
That in° the floor I lay as I were deed.
And whan he saugh° how stille that I lay,
He was agast and wolde han° fled his way,
Til atte lasted out of my swogh° I breyde°.
"O, hastow° slayn me, false theef?" I seyde,
"And for my land thus hastow mordred me?
Er° I be deed yet wol I kisse thee."
And neer he cam and kneled faire° adoun,
And seyde, "Deere suster° Alisoun,
As help me God, I shal thee nevere smyte°.
That° I have doon, it is thyself to wyte°,
Foryeve it me, and that I thee biseke°."
And yet eftsoones° I hitte hym on the cheke,
And seyde, "Theef, thus muchel° am I wreke°.
Now wol I dye; I may no lenger speke."
But atte laste with muchel care and wo
We fille acorded° by us selven° two.
He yaf° me al the bridel° in myn hond,
To han the governance of hous and lond,
And of his tonge, and of his hond also;
And made hym brenne° his book anon° right tho°.
And whan that I hadde geten° unto me
By maistrie° al the soveraynetee°,
And that he seyde, "Myn owene trewe wyf,
Do as thee lust° the terme° of al thy lyf;
Keep° thyn honour, and keep eek myn estaat°."
After that day we hadden never debaat.
God helpe me so, I was to hym as kynde
As any wyf from Denmark unto Ynde,
And also trewe, and so was he to me.
I prey to God that sit in magestee°
So blesse his soule for his mercy deere.
Now wol I seye my tale if ye wol heere.

Biholde the wordes bitwene the Somonour and the Frere.

The Frere lough° whan he hadde herd al this.
"Now dame," quod he, "so have I joye or blis,
This is a long preamble of a tale."
And whan the Somonour herde the Frere gale°,
"Lo," quod the Somonour, "Goddes armes two,
A frere wol entremette hym° everemo.
Lo, goode men, a flye and eek a frere
Wol falle in every dyssh and eek mateere.
What spekestow of preambulacioun?
What, amble° or trotte or pees° or go sit doun!
Thou lettest° oure disport° in this manere."
"Ye, woltow so, sire Somonour?" quod the Frere.
"Now, by my feith, I shal er° that I go
Telle of a somonour swich° a tale or two
That alle the folk shal laughen in this place."
"Now elles, Frere, I bishrewe° thy face,"
Quod this Somonour, "and I bishrewe me
But if° I telle tales two or thre
Of freres er I come to Sidyngborne,
That I shal make thyn herte for to morne,
For wel I woot° thy pacience is gon."
Oure Hoost cride, "Pees°, and that anon°!"
And seyde, "Lat the womman telle hire tale.
Ye fare as° folk that dronken ben° of ale.
Do, dame, telle forth youre tale, and that is best."
"Al redy, sire," quod she, "right as yow lest°,
If I have licence° of this worthy Frere."
"Yis, dame," quod he, "tel forth and I wol heere."

---

788 fyne, *cease* **790 leves,** *pages,* **plyght,** *snatched* **791 radde,** *read* **792 fest,** *fist,* **took,** *hit* **794 stirte,** *leaped,* **wood,** *enraged* **795 smoot,** *struck* **796 in,** *on* **797 saugh,** *saw* **798 wolde han,** *wished to have* **799 swogh,** *faint,* **breyde,** *awoke* **800 hastow,** *have you* **802 Er,** *before* **803 faire,** *gently* **804 suster,** *sweetheart* **805 smyte,** *hit* **806 That,** (for) *what,* **wyte** *blame* **807 thee biseke,** *plead of you* **808 efsoones,** *again* **809 muchel,** *much.* **wreke,** *avenged* **812 fille acorded,** *came to agreement,* **us selven,** *ourselves* **813 yaf,** *gave,* **bridel,** *bridle* **816 brenne,** *burn,* **anon,** *immediately,* **tho,** *then* **817 geten,** *gotten* **818 maistrie,** *mastery,* **soveraynetee,** *dominance* **820 lust,** *desire,* **terme,** *time* **821 Keep,** *protect,* **estaat,** *rank* **826 sit in magestee,** *sits in majesty* **829 Frere lough,** *Friar laughed* **832 gale,** *exclaim* **834 entremette hym,** *intrude himself* **838 amble,** *walk leisurely,* **pees,** *peace* (shut up!) **839 lettest,** *hinder,* **disport,** *fun* **841 er,** *before* **842 swich,** *such* **844 bishrewe,** *curse* **846 But if,** *unless* **849 woot,** *know* **850 Pees,** *peace,* **anon,** *immediately* **852 fare as,** *act like,* **ben,** *are* **854 lest,** *wish,* **855 licence,** *permission*

792 hym, omitted in Hg. **820 the terme,** El reads "to terme." **824 Denmark unto Ynde,** Denmark to India, i.e., in the whole world. **828a** Rubric lacking in Hg. **833 Goddes armes two,** by God's arms, a mild oath. **837 What spekestow of preambulacioun?** Why do you speak about making preambles? (line 831)—with a play on *perambulation,* which means "walking or traveling," echoed by *amble* in the next line. The Summoner and the Friar are professional antagonists because their religious offices (and abuses of these offices) led to conflicts or competition between them. **840 woltow so,** will you do so? i.e., are you trying to start something? **844 I beshrewe,** Hg reads "I wol bishrewe."

Heere endeth the Wyf of Bathe hir Prologe and bigynneth hir Tale.

In th'olde dayes of the Kyng Arthour,
Of which that Britons° speken greet honour,
Al was this land fulfild of fairye°.
The elf-queene with hir joly compaignye
Daunced ful ofte in many a grene mede°.
This was the olde opinion, as I rede—
I speke of manye hundred yeres ago.
But now kan no man se none elves mo°,
For now the grete charitee and prayeres
Of lymytours° and othere hooly freres,
That serchen° every lond and every streem
As thikke as motes° in the sonne-beem°,
Blessynge halles, chambres, kichenes, boures°,
Citees, burghes°, castels, hye toures°,
Thropes°, bernes°, shipnes°, dayeryes°—
This maketh that ther been no fairyes.
For ther as wont to walken was an elf°
Ther walketh now the lymytour hymself,
In undermeles° and in morwenynges°
And seyth his matyns° and his hooly thynges
As he gooth in his lymytacioun°.
Wommen may go now saufly° up and doun;
In every bussh or under every tree
Ther is noon oother incubus but he,
And he ne wol doon hem but° dishonour.
And so bifel that this Kyng Arthour
Hadde in his hous a lusty bacheler°
That on a day cam ridynge fro ryver,
And happed° that, allone as he was born,
He saugh° a mayde walkynge hym biforn°,
Of whiche mayde anon°, maugree hir heed°,
By verray° force he rafte hire maydenhed°;
For which oppressioun was swich clamour°
And swich pursute° unto the Kyng Arthour,
That dampned° was this knyght for to be deed,
By cours of lawe, and sholde han lost his heed—
Paraventure swich° was the statut tho°—
But° that the queene and othere ladyes mo
So longe preyeden° the kyng of° grace
Til he his lyf hym graunted in the place,
And yaf° hym to the queene, al at hir wille,
To chese° wheither she wolde hym save or spille°.
The queene thanketh the kyng with al hir myght,
And after this thus spak she to the knyght,
Whan that she saugh hir tyme upon a day,
"Thou standest yet," quod she, "in swich array°
That of thy lyf yet hastow no suretee°.
I grante thee lyf if thou kanst tellen me
What thyng is it that wommen moost desiren.
Bewar and keep thy nekke-boon from iren°.
And if thou kanst nat tellen it anon°,
Yet shal I yeve° thee leve° for to gon
A twelf-month and a day to seche and leere°
An answere suffisant in this mateere;
And suretee wol I han° er that thou pace,
Thy body for to yelden° in this place."
Wo° was this knyght and sorwefully he siketh°.
But what, he may nat do al as hym liketh;
And at the laste he chees hym for to wende°
And come agayn right at the yeres ende
With swich answere as God wolde hym purveye°,
And taketh his leve and wendeth° forth his weye.
He seketh every hous and every place
Where as he hopeth for to fynde grace°
To lerne what thyng wommen loven moost,
But he ne koude arryven° in no coost°
Wher as he myghte fynde in this mateere

---

857 the Kyng, El omits "the." **858 Britons,** *people from Celtic Britain* **859 fulfild of fairye,** *filled with fairy folk* **861 grene mede,** *green meadow* **864 se none elves mo,** *see any more elves* **866 lymytours,** *friars licensed to beg in a certain area* (limit) **867 serchen,** *seek out* **868 motes,** *dust specks,* **sonne-beam,** *sunbeam* **869 boures,** *bedrooms* **870 burghes,** *towns,* **hye toures,** *high towers* **871 Thropes,** *villages,* **bernes,** *barns,* **shipnes,** *animal pens,* **dayeryes,** *dairies* **873 ther as wont to walken was an elf,** *where an elf was accustomed to walk* **875 undermeles,** *afternoons,* **morwenynges,** *mornings* **876 seyth his matyns,** *says his morning prayers* **877 lymytacioun,** *licensed district* **878 saufly,** *safely* **881 ne wol doon hem but,** *will not do* (to) *them* (anything) *but* **883 bacheler,** *young knight* **885 happed,** (it) *happened* **886 saugh,** *saw,* **hym biforn,** *before him* **887 anon,** *soon,* **maugree hir heed,** *despite anything she could do* **888 verray,** *sheer,* **rafte hire maydenhed,** *stole her virginity* **889 swich clamour,** *such outcry* **890 swich pursute,** *such pleading* **891 dampned,** *condemned* **893 Paraventure swich,** *it happens* (that) *such,* **statut tho,** *law then* **894 But,** *except* **895 preyeden,** *pleaded with,* **of,** *for* **897 yaf,** *gave* **898 chese,** *choose,* **spille,** *kill* **902 swich array,** *such a condition* **903 hastow no suretee,** *you have no certainty* **906 iren,** *ax* (iron) **907 anon,** *immediately* **908 yeve,** *give,* **leve,** *permission* **909 seche and leere,** *seek and learn* **911 suretee wol I han,** *I will have a pledge* **912 yelden,** *yield* **913 Wo,** *woeful,* **siketh,** *sighs* **915 chees hym for to wende,** *chose to travel* **917 purveye,** *provide* **918 wendeth,** *goes* **920 grace,** *the good fortune* **922 ne koude arryven,** *could not arrive,* **coost,** *coast* (region)

847 Sidyngborne, Sittingbourne, about forty miles from London. **852 ben,** El reads "were." **857 the Kyng,** El omits "the." **878 now,** omitted in El and Hg. **880 incubus,** an evil spirit who had sex with humans. **883 his,** omitted in El. **888 he rafte,** El reads "birafte." **889 oppressioun,** rape; there is no rape in other versions of the story. **899** Line omitted in Hg. **907 it,** Hg reads "me." **908 shal,** Hg reads "wol." **909 twelf-month and a day,** a year and a day, a legal formula that occurs in other romances, e.g., *Sir Gawain and the Green Knight* 297. **914 what,** omitted in El.

Two creatures accordynge in-feere°.
Somme seyde wommen loven best richesse,
Somme seyde honour, somme seyde jolynesse,
Somme riche array, somme seyden lust a-bedde°,
And oftetyme to be wydwe° and wedde.
Somme seyde that oure hertes been moost esed°
Whan that we been yflatered and yplesed—
He gooth ful ny the sothe°, I wol nat lye.
A man shal wynne us best with flaterye,
And with attendance° and with bisynesse°
Been we ylymed°, bothe moore and lesse.
And somme seyn that we loven best
For to be free and do right° as us lest°,
And that no man repreve° us of oure vice,
But seye that we be wise and nothyng nyce°.
For trewely ther is noon of us alle,
If any wight wol clawe us on the galle°,
That we nel kike for° he seith us sooth°;
Assay°, and he shal fynde it that so dooth°,
For be we° never so vicious withinne,
We wol been holden° wise and clene of synne.
And somme seyn that greet delit han° we
For to been holden stable°, and eek secree°,
And in o purpos stedefastly to dwelle°,
And nat biwreye thyng° that men° us telle.
But that tale is nat worth a rake-stele°.
Pardee°, we wommen konne° nothyng hele°:
Witnesse on Myda—wol ye heere the tale?
Ovyde, amonges othere thynges smale,
Seyde Myda hadde under his longe heres°
Growynge upon his heed two asses eres°,
The which vice° he hydde as he best myghte
Ful subtilly from every mannes sighte,
That save° his wyf ther wiste° of it namo°.
He loved hire moost and trusted hire also.
He preyde hire that to no creature
She sholde tellen of his disfigure°.
She swoor him nay for al this world to wynne,
She nolde° do that vileynye or synne
To make hir housbonde han so foul a name;
She nolde nat telle it for hir owene shame.
But nathelees, hir thoughte° that she dyde°
That she so longe sholde a conseil° hyde;
Hir thoughte it swal° so soore° aboute hir herte
That nedely° som word hire moste asterte°.
And sith° she dorste° telle it to no man,
Doun to a mareys° faste° by she ran—
Til she cam there hir herte was afyre—
And as a bitore bombleth in the myre,
She leyde hir mouth unto the water doun:
"Biwreye° me nat, thou water, with thy soun°,"
Quod she; "to thee I telle it and namo°;
Myn housbonde hath longe asses erys two.
Now is myn herte al hool, now is it oute.
I myghte no lenger kepe° it, out of doute°."
Heere may ye se°, thogh we a tyme abyde°,
Yet out it moot°; we kan no conseil hyde.
The remenant° of the tale if ye wol heere,
Redeth Ovyde and ther ye may it leere°.
This knyght of which my tale is specially,
Whan that he saugh° he myghte nat come therby—
This is to seye, what wommen love moost—
Withinne his brest ful sorweful was the goost°.
But hoom he gooth, he myghte nat sojourne°;
The day was come that homward moste he tourne.
And in his wey it happed hym° to ryde
In al this care under° a forest syde,
Wher as° he saugh upon a daunce go°
Of ladyes foure and twenty° and yet mo;
Toward the whiche daunce he drow ful yerne°,
In hope that som wysdom sholde he lerne.
But certeinly, er° he cam fully there,

---

924 **accordynge in-feere,** *agreeing together* 927 **lust a-bedde,** *pleasure in bed* 928 **wydwe,** *widowed* 929 **esed,** *comforted* 931 **gooth ful ny the sothe,** *comes very near the truth* 933 **attendance,** *service,* **bisynesse,** *attention* 934 **ylymed,** *captured* (with birdlime) 936 **right,** *just,* **us lest,** *we please* 937 **repreve,** *accuse* 938 **nothyng nyce,** *not at all foolish* 940 **wight wol clawe us on the galle,** *person will hit us on a sore spot* 941 **nel kike for,** *will not kick because,* **seith us sooth,** *tells us truth* 942 **Assay,** *try it,* **so dooth,** *does so* 943 **be we,** *we are* 944 **wol been holden,** *would like to be considered* 945 **han,** *have* 946 **For to been holden stable,** *to be considered dependable,* **eek secree,** *also able to keep a secret* 947 **in o purpos stedefastly to dwelle,** *able to keep to one goal steadily* 948 **biwreye thyng,** *betray things,* **men,** *people* 949 **rake-stele,** *rake handle* 950 **Pardee,** *by God,* **konne,** *can,* **hele,** *hide* 953 **heres,** *hair* 954 **eres,** *ears* 955 **vice,** *flaw* 957 **save,** *except for,* **wiste,** *knew,* **namo,** *none more* 960 **disfigure,** *deformity* 962 **nolde,** *would not* 965 **hir thoughte,** *she thought,* **dyde,** *would die* 966 **conseil,** *secret* 967 **swal,** *swelled,* **soore,** *sorely* 968 **nedely,** *necessarily,* **hire moste asterte,** *from her must escape* 969 **sith,** *since,* **dorste,** *dared* 970 **mareys,** *marsh,* **faste,** *near* 974 **Biwreye,** *betray,* **soun,** *sound* 975 **namo,** *no more* 978 **kepe,** *contain,* **out of doute,** *without doubt* 979 **se,** *see,* **tyme abyde,** *wait awhile* 980 **moot,** *must* 981 **remenant,** *remainder* 982 **leere,** *learn* 984 **saugh,** *saw* 986 **goost,** *spirit* 987 **sojourne,** *stay* 989 **it happed hym,** *he happened* 990 **under,** *near* 991 **Wher as,** *where,* **saugh upon a daunce go,** *saw dancing* 992 **Of ladyes foure and twenty,** *twenty-four ladies* 993 **drow ful yerne,** *approached very eagerly* 995 **er,** *before*

927 **seyden,** omitted in Hg. 929 **been,** Hg reads "is." 951 **Myda,** Midas; from Ovid, *Metamorphoses* 11, where his secret is betrayed by his barber, not his wife. 958 **trusted,** El reads "triste." 972 **as a bitore bombleth in the myre,** as a bittern (a wading bird) burbles in the mud. 977 **is it,** Hg reads "it is."

Vanysshed was this daunce, he nyste° where.
Ne creature saugh he that bar lyf°
Save° on the grene° he saugh sittynge a wyf—
A fouler wight° ther may no man devyse°.
Agayn the knyght this olde wyf gan ryse°,
And seyde, "Sire knyght, heer forth ne lith° no wey.
Tel me what that ye seken, by youre fey°.
Paraventure° it may the bettre be;
Thise olde folk kan muchel° thyng," quod she.
"My leeve mooder°," quod this knyght, "certeyn
I nam° but deed but if° that I kan seyn
What thyng it is that wommen moost desire.
Koude ye me wisse°, I wolde wel quite youre hire°."
"Plight me thy trouthe° heere in myn hand," quod she,
"The nexte thyng that I requere° thee
Thou shalt it do, if it lye in thy myght,
And I wol telle it yow er it be nyght."
"Have heer my trouthe," quod the knyght. "I grante°."
"Thanne," quod she, "I dar me wel avante°
Thy lyf is sauf°, for I wol stonde therby.
Upon my lyf, the queene wol seye as I°.
Lat se which is the proudeste of hem alle
That wereth on° a coverchief or a calle°
That dar seye nat of that° I shal thee teche.
Lat us go forth withouten lenger speche."
Tho rowned° she a pistel° in his ere
And bad hym to be glad and have no fere.
Whan they be comen° to the court, this knyght
Seyde he had holde his day° as he hadde hight°,
And redy was his answere, as he sayde.
Ful many a noble wyf, and many a mayde,
And many a wydwe°—for that they been wise—
The queene hirself sittynge as justise,
Assembled been, his answere for to heere;
And afterward this knyght was bode appeere°.
To every wight° comanded was silence,
And that the knyght sholde telle in audience°
What thyng that worldly wommen loven best.
This knyght ne stood nat stille° as doth a best°,
But to his questioun anon° answerde
With manly voys that al the court it herde.
"My lige lady, generally," quod he,
"Wommen desiren to have sovereynetee
As wel over hir housbond as hir love,
And for to been in maistrie hym above.
This is youre mooste° desir thogh ye me kille.
Dooth as yow list°; I am heer at youre wille."
In al the court ne was ther wyf ne mayde
Ne wydwe that contraried° that he sayde,
But seyden he was worthy han his lyf.
And with that word up stirte° the olde wyf
Which that° the knyght saugh° sittynge on the grene°:
"Mercy," quod she, "my sovereyn lady queene!
Er that° youre court departe, do me right.
I taughte this answere unto the knyght,
For which he plighte me his trouthe° there
The firste thyng I wolde hym requere°
He wolde it do, if it lay in his myght.
Bifore the court thanne preye I thee, sir knyght,"
Quod she, "that thou me take unto thy wyf°,
For wel thou woost° that I have kept° thy lyf.
If I seye° fals, sey nat, upon thy fey°."
This knyght answerde, "Allas and weylawey!
I woot° right wel that swich° was my biheste°.
For Goddes love, as chees° a newe requeste;
Taak al my good° and lat my body go."
"Nay thanne," quod she, "I shrewe° us bothe two!

996 nyste, *knew not* **997 bar lyf,** *was alive* **998 Save,** *except,* **grene,** *grassy place,* **wyf,** *woman* **999 fouler wight,** *uglier creature,* **devyse,** *describe* **1000 Agayn . . . gan ryse,** *before . . . arose* **1001 heer forth ne lith,** *in this direction lies* **1002 fey,** *faith* **1003 Paraventure,** *perhaps* **1004 kan muchel,** *know many* **1005 leeve mooder,** *dear old lady* **1006 nam,** *am nothing,* **but if,** *unless* **1008 Koude ye me wisse,** *if you can instruct me,* **quite youre hire,** *repay your efforts* **1009 Plight me thy trouthe,** *pledge me your solemn promise* **1010 requere,** *demand of* **1013 grante,** *agree* **1014 dar me wel avante,** *I dare well boast* **1015 sauf,** *safe* **1016 seye as I,** *say as I say* **1018 wereth on,** *wears,* **calle,** *headdress* **1019 dar seye nat of that,** *dare deny what* **1021 rowned,** *whispered,* **pistel,** *message* **1023 be comen,** *are come* **1024 holde his day,** *returned on time,* **hight,** *promised* **1027 wydwe,** *widow* **1030 bode appeere,** *bidden to appear* **1031 wight,** *person* **1032 in audience,** *publicly* **1034 stille,** *quiet,* **best,** *beast* **1035 anon,** *immediately* **1041 mooste,** *greatest* **1042 list,** *please* **1044 contraried,** *contradicted* **1046 stirte,** *leapt* **1047 Which that,** *the one who,* **saugh,** *saw,* **grene,** *grassy place* **1049 Er that,** *before* **1051 plighte me his trouthe,** *pledged me his solemn promise* **1052 requere,** *demand* **1055 unto thy wyf,** *as your wife* **1056 woost,** *know,* **kept,** *saved* **1057 seye,** *speak,* **fey,** *faith* **1059 woot,** *know,* **swich,** *such,* **biheste,** *promise* **1060 as chees,** *choose* **1061 good,** *possessions* **1062 shrewe,** *curse*

1028 queene . . . as justise, the queen presides as judge, recalling the "courts of love" associated with Eleanor of Aquitaine and Marie de Champagne, and written about by Andreas Capellanus, *De Amore.* **1029 his,** Hg reads "this." **1038–40 sovereynetee . . . maistrie,** see line 818. **1103 So wolde God,** an idiom meaning something like "I wish to God." **1038 to,** omitted in El. **1042 heer,** omitted in El. **1046 the,** Hg reads "that." **1047 on,** El reads "in."

For thogh that I be foul and oold and poore,
I nolde° for all the metal ne for oore°
That under erthe is grave° or lith° above,
But if° thy wyf I were, and eek thy love."
"My love?" quod he, "nay, my dampnacioun!
Allas, that any of my nacioun°
Sholde evere so foule disparaged° be."
But al for noght; th'ende is this, that he
Constreyned was, he nedes moste° hire wedde;
And taketh his olde wyf and gooth to bedde.
Now wolden som men seye, paraventure°,
That for my necligence I do no cure°
To tellen yow the joye and al th'array°
That at the feeste° was that ilke° day.
To which thyng shortly answere I shal:
I seye ther nas no° joye ne feeste at al.
Ther nas° but hevynesse and muche sorwe.
For prively he wedded hire on morwe°,
And al day after hidde hym as an owle,
So wo was hym, his wyf looked so foule.
Greet was the wo the knyght hadde in his thoght.
Whan he was with his wyf abedde ybroght°
He walweth° and he turneth to and fro.
His olde wyf lay smylynge everemo,
And seyde, "O deere housbonde, benedicitee°,
Fareth° every knyght thus with his wyf as ye?
Is this the lawe of Kyng Arthures hous?
Is every knyght of his so dangerous°?
I am youre owene love and eek youre wyf;
I am she which that saved hath youre lyf,
And certes° yet ne dide I yow nevere unright°;
Why fare° ye thus with me this firste nyght?
Ye faren lyk a man had lost his wit°.
What is my gilt? For Goddes love, tel it,
And it shal been amended°, if I may."
"Amended?" quod this knyght, "allas, nay, nay,
It wol nat been amended nevere mo.
Thou art so loothly°, and so oold also,
And therto comen of so lough a kynde°,
That litel wonder is thogh I walwe and wynde°.
So wolde God myn herte wolde breste°!"
"Is this," quod she, "the cause of youre unreste?"
"Ye, certeinly," quod he, "no wonder is."
"Now sire," quod she, "I koude° amende al this,
If that me liste°, er° it were dayes thre,
So° wel ye myghte bere° yow unto me.
"But, for ye speken of swich gentillesse
As is descended out of old richesse,
That therfore sholden ye be gentil men,
Swich arrogance is nat worth an hen.
Looke who that° is moost vertuous alway,
Pryvee and apert°, and moost entendeth ay°
To do the gentil dedes that he kan,
Taak hym for the grettest gentil man.
Crist wole° we clayme of hym oure gentillesse,
Nat of oure eldres for hire old richesse.
For thogh they yeve° us al hir heritage,
For which we clayme to been of heigh parage°,
Yet may they nat biquethe° for no thyng
To noon of us hir vertuous lyvyng°,
That made hem gentil men ycalled be°,
And bad us folwen° hem in swich degree°.
"Wel kan the wise poete of Florence
That highte° Dant speken in this sentence.
Lo, in swich maner rym° is Dantes tale:
'Ful selde up riseth° by his branches smale
Prowesse° of man, for God of his goodnesse
Wole° that of hym we clayme oure gentillesse.'
For of oure eldres may we no thyng clayme
But temporel thyng that man may hurte and mayme°.
"Eek every wight woot° this as wel as I,
If gentillesse were planted natureelly

1064 nolde, *don't want,* **oore,** *ore* **1065 grave,** *buried,* **lith,** *lies* **1066 But if,** *unless* **1068 nacioun,** *kindred* **1069 disparaged,** *degraded* **1071 nedes moste,** *necessarily must* **1073 paraventure,** *perhaps* **1074 do no cure,** *take no care* **1075 th'array,** *the arrangements* **1076 feeste,** *celebration,* **ilke,** *same* **1078 nas no,** *was no* **1079 nas,** *was nothing* **1080 on morwe,** *in the morning* **1084 abedde ybroght,** *brought to bed* **1085 walweth,** *tosses* **1087 benedicitee,** *bless you* **1088 Fareth,** *acts* **1090 dangerous,** *standoffish* **1093 certes,** *certainly,* **unright,** *wrong* **1094 fare,** *act* **1095 had lost his wit,** (who) *has gone mad* **1097 been amended,** *be put right* **1100 loothly,** *hideous* **1101 therto comen of so lough a kynde,** *also come from so low a lineage* **1102 walwe and wynde,** *toss and turn* **1103 wolde brest,** *would burst* **1106 koude,** *could* **1107 me liste,** *it pleased me,* **er,** *before* **1108 So,** *so that,* **bere,** *behave* **1113 Looke who that,** *observe who* **1114 Pryvee and apert,** *in private and public,* **entendeth ay,** *tries always* **1117 Crist wole,** *Christ wishes that* **1119 yeve,** *give* **1120 heigh parage,** *upper-class birth* **1121 biquethe,** *hand down* **1122 hir vertuous lyvyng,** *their virtuous living* **1123 ycalled be,** *be called* **1124 bad us folwen,** *ordered us to follow,* **swich degree,** *same manner* **1126 highte,** *is named* **1127 swich maner rym,** *rhyme like this* **1128 Ful selde up riseth,** *very seldom rises up,* **branches smale,** *descendants* (branches of the family tree) **1129 Prowesse,** *worth* **1130 Wole,** *wishes* **1132 mayme,** *injure* **1133 wight woot,** *person knows*

1063 foul and, El and Hg omit "and." **1080 on morwe,** El reads "on a morwe." **1090 so,** Hg reads "thus." **1109 swich gentillesse,** such nobility. The idea that nobility depends on virtuous deeds rather than on lineage is commonplace, but the fourth tractate and the commentary on the third canzone of Dante's *Convivio* have the closest parallels; compare also *RR* 6579–92, 18607–946; *Bo* 3pr6, 3m6; Gower, *Mirour de l'omme* 17329–64, 17394–400. **1110 old richesse,** traditional wealth; Dante uses *antica ricchezza.* **1116 grettest gentil man,** Hg reads "gentileste man." **1120 heigh,** Hg reads "hir" (their). **1126 Dant,** Dante is the poet of Florence. **1128–30** From Dante's *Purgatorio* 7.121–23. **1129 goodnesse,** Hg reads "prowesse." **1133 as I,** Hg omits "as."

Unto a certeyn lynage doun the lyne,
Pryvee and apert, thanne wolde they nevere fyne°
To doon of gentillesse the faire office°—
They myghte do no vileynye or vice.
"Taak fyr° and ber° it in the derkeste hous
Bitwix this and the mount of Kaukasous,
And lat men shette° the dores and go thenne°,
Yet wole the fyr as faire lye° and brenne°
As twenty thousand men myghte it biholde;
His office° natureel ay° wol it holde,
Up peril of my lyf, til that it dye.
"Heere may ye se wel how that genterye°
Is nat annexed° to possessioun,
Sith° folk ne doon hir operacioun°
Alwey, as dooth the fyr, lo, in his kynde°.
For God it woot° men may wel often fynde
A lordes sone° do shame and vileynye;
And he that wole han pris° of his gentrye—
For he was born of a gentil hous
And hadde his eldres noble and vertuous—
And nel° hymselven do no gentil dedis
Ne folwen his gentil auncestre that deed° is,
He nys nat° gentil, be he due or erl,
For vileyns° synful dedes make a cherl.
For gentillesse nys° but renomee°
Of thyne auncestres for hire heigh bountee°,
Which is a strange thyng° to thy persone.
Thy gentillesse cometh fro God allone.
Thanne comth oure verray° gentillesse of grace;
It was no thyng° biquethe° us with oure place°.
"Thenketh hou° noble, as seith Valerius,
Was thilke° Tullius Hostillius
That out of poverte roos to heigh noblesse.
Reed° Senek, and redeth eek Boece;
Ther shul ye seen expres° that it no drede is°
That he is gentil that dooth gentil dedis.
And therfore, leeve° housbonde, I thus conclude:
Al were it that° myne auncestres were rude°,
Yet may the hye° God—and so hope I—
Grante me grace to lyven vertuously.
Thanne am I gentil whan that I bigynne
To lyven vertuously and weyve° synne.
"And there as ye of poverte me repreeve°,
The hye God, on whom that we bileeve,
In wilful° poverte chees° to lyve his lyf.
And certes every man, mayden, or wyf,
May understonde that Jhesus, hevene kyng,
Ne wolde nat chese a vicious lyvyng.
Glad poverte is an honeste° thyng, certeyn;
This wole Senec and othere clerkes seyn°.
Whoso that halt hym payd of° his poverte,
I holde hym riche al° hadde he nat a sherte.
He that coveiteth° is a poure wight°,
For he wolde han° that is nat in his myght;
But he that noght hath°, ne coveiteth have°,
Is riche, although ye holde hym but a knave°.
"Verray° poverte it syngeth proprely°.
Juvenal seith° of poverte myrily°,
'The poure man, whan he goth by the weye°,
Bifore the theves° he may synge and pleye.'
Poverte is hateful good and, as I gesse,
A ful greet bryngere out of bisynesse°;
A greet amendere eek° of sapience°
To hym that taketh it in pacience.
Poverte is this, although it seme alenge°,
Possessioun that no wight wol chalenge.
Poverte ful ofte, whan a man is lowe,
Maketh his God and eek hymself to knowe.
Poverte a spectacle° is, as thynketh me,
Thurgh which he may his verray° freendes see.
And therfore, sire, syn° that I noght yow
greve°,

1136 fyne, *cease* **1137 faire office,** *good actions* **1139 Taak fyr,** *take fire,* **ber,** *carry* **1140 Bitwix this,** *between here* **1141 shette,** *shut,* **thenne,** *from there* **1142 lye,** *blaze,* **brenne,** *burn* **1144 His office,** *its function,* **ay,** *always* **1146 genterye,** *gentility* **1147 annexed,** *attached* **1148 Sith,** *since,* **ne doon hir operacioun,** *do not operate* **1149 his kynde,** *its nature* **1150 woot,** *knows* **1151 sone,** *son* **1152 wol han pris,** *will have praise* **1155 nel,** *will not* **1156 deed,** *dead* **1157 nys nat,** *is not* **1158 vileyns,** *wicked* **1159 nys,** *is nothing,* **renomee,** *fame* **1160 hire heigh bountee,** *their high goodness* **1161 strange thyng,** *something alien* **1163 verray,** *true* **1164 no thyng,** *nothing,* **biquethe,** *passed on to,* **place,** *social rank* **1165 Thenketh hou,** *think how* **1166 thilke,** *that* **1168 Reed,** *read* **1169 expres,** *specifically,* **it no drede is,** *there is no doubt* **1171 leeve,** *dear* **1172 Al were it that,** *although,* **rude,** *of low class* **1173 hye,** *high* **1176 weyve,** *abandon* **1177 repreeve,** *accuse* **1179 wilful,** *voluntary,* **chees,** *chose* **1183 honeste,** *honorable* **1184 seyn,** *say* **1185 Whoso that halt hym payd of,** *whoever is content with* **1186 al,** *although* **1187 coveiteth,** *yearns for* (covets). **wight,** *person* **1188 wolde han,** *would have* **1189 noght hath,** *has nothing,* **ne coveiteth have,** *nor yearns to have* **1190 knave,** *servant* **1191 Verray,** *true,* **syngeth proprely,** *sings appropriately* **1192 seith,** *says,* **myrily,** *merrily* **1193 by the weye,** *on the road* **1194 theves,** *thieves* **1196 bryngere out of bisynesse,** *encourager of productive action* **1197 amendere eek,** *improver also,* **sapience,** *wisdom* **1199 seme alenge,** *seems wearisome* **1203 spectacle,** *lens* **1204 verray,** *true* **1205 syn,** *since,* **noght yow greve,** *don't injure you*

1136 and, El reads "nor." **1140 Kaukasous,** Caucasus, in Russia. **1145 Up peril of my lyf,** an idiom meaning "I assure you on my life." **1161 a,** omitted in Hg. **to,** Hg reads "for." **1165–67 Valerius . . . ,** Valerius Maximus 3.4 tells the legend of Tullius Hostilius, who rose from the peasantry to become third king of Rome. **1168 Senek,** Seneca, *Epistle* 44. **Boece,** Boethius, *Bo* 3pr6. **1169 it,** omitted in El and Hg. **1182 chese a,** El reads "chesen." **1184 Senec,** Seneca, *Epistle* 17. **1190 ye,** Hg reads "we." **1191 it syngeth proprely, it** sings appropriately or by its own nature. Hg reads "is synne properly," a misunderstanding. **1192 Juvenal,** *Satire* 10.21. **1199 this,** Hg reads "thyng." **1202 his God and eek hymself,** Hg reads "hymself and eek his God."

Of my poverte namoore ye me repreve°.
  "Now, sire, of elde° ye repreve me;
And certes°, sire, thogh noon auctoritee°
Were in no book, ye gentils of honour
Seyn° that men sholde an oold wight doon
    favour°
And clepe° hym fader for youre gentillesse—
And auctours° shal I fynden, as I gesse.
  "Now ther° ye seye that I am foul and old,
Than drede° you noght to been a cokewold°,
For filthe° and eelde°, also moot I thee°,
Been grete wardeyns° upon chastitee.
But nathelees, syn I knowe youre delit,
I shal fulfille youre worldly appetit.
  "Chese now," quod she, "oon of thise thynges
    tweye:
To han° me foul and old til that I deye°
And be to yow a trewe humble wyf,
And nevere yow displese in al my lyf,
Or elles° ye wol han° me yong and fair,
And take youre aventure° of the repair°
That shal be to youre hous by cause° of me,
Or in som oother place, may wel be.
Now chese yourselven, wheither° that yow liketh."
  This knyght avyseth hym° and sore siketh°,
But atte laste he seyde in this manere,
"My lady and my love, and wyf so deere,
I put me in youre wise governance;
Cheseth youreself which may be moost plesance°
And moost honour to yow and me also.
I do no fors the wheither° of the two,
For as yow liketh it suffiseth° me."
  "Thanne have I gete° of yow maistrie," quod she,
"Syn° I may chese and governe as me lest°?"
  "Ye, certes°, wyf," quod he. "I holde it best."
  "Kys me," quod she. "We be no lenger wrothe°,
For, by my trouthe, I wol be to yow bothe—
This is to seyn, ye°, bothe fair and good.
I prey to God that I moote sterven wood°
But° I to yow be also° good and trewe
As evere was wyf syn that the world was newe.
And but I be tomorn° as fair to seene°
As any lady, emperice, or queene,
That is bitwixe the est and eke the west,
Dooth with my lyf and deth right as yow lest°.
Cast up the curtyn, looke how that it is."
  And whan the knyght saugh verraily°
    al this,
That she so fair was, and so yong therto°,
For joye he hente° hire in his armes two.
His herte bathed in a bath of blisse,
A thousand tyme a-rewe° he gan hire kisse°,
And she obeyed hym in every thyng
That myghte doon hym plesance or likyng.
  And thus they lyve unto hir lyves ende
In parfit joye. And Jhesu Crist us sende
Housbondes meeke, yonge, and fressh abedde,
And grace t'overbyde hem° that we wedde.
And eek I pray Jhesu shorte hir° lyves
That wol nat be governed by hir wyves.
And olde and angry nygardes of dispence°,
God sende hem soone verray pestilence°!

Heere endeth the Wyves Tale of Bathe.

1206 repreve, *accuse* **1207 elde,** *old age* **1208 certes,** *certainly,* **auctoritee,** *authority* **1210 Seyn,** *say,* **an oold wight doon favour,** *respect an old person* **1211 clepe,** *call* **1212 auctours,** *authors* (who agree) **1213 ther,** *since* **1214 drede,** *fear,* **cokewold,** *cuckold* **1215 filthe,** *foulness,* **eelde,** *age,* **also moot I thee,** *so I may prosper* **1216 Been grete wardeyns,** *are great guardians* **1220 han,** *have,* **deye,** *die* **1223 elles,** *else,* **wol han,** *will have* **1224 aventure,** *chances,* **repair,** *visitors* **1225 by cause,** *because* **1227 wheither,** *whichever* **1228 avyseth hym,** *ponders,* **sore siketh,** *sighs painfully* **1232 plesance,** *happiness* **1234 do no fors the wheither,** *I don't care which* **1235 suffiseth,** *satisfies* **1236 gete,** *gotten* **1237 Syn,** *since,* **me lest,** *I please* **1238 Ye, certes,** *yes, certainly* **1239 lenger wrothe,** *longer at odds* **1241 seyn, ye,** *say, yes* **1242 moote sterven wood,** *might die insane* **1243 But,** *unless,* **also,** *as* **1245 tomorn,** *tomorrow,* **seene,** *see* **1248 yow lest,** *you wish* **1250 saugh verraily,** *saw truly* **1251 therto,** *also* **1252 hente,** *grasped* **1254 a-rewe,** *in a row,* **gan hire kisse,** *kissed her* **1260 t'overbyde hem,** *to outlive them* **1261 shorte hir,** *shorten their* **1263 nygardes of dispence,** *misers of money* **1264 verray pestilence,** *true plague*

1210 sholde an oold wight, Hg reads "an old wight sholde." **1219 Chese now . . . ,** in other versions of the tale, the loathly lady offers a different choice (fair by day and foul by night, or vice versa) and shows her beauty to the knight before he must choose. **1232 which may,** Hg reads "which that may." **1249 Cast up the curtyn,** the drapes of the canopy bed had been drawn for privacy.

From woodcut made by W.H. Hooper and published by the Chaucer Society between 1868 and 1879

Friar's Tale

Prologue

The Prologe of the Freres Tale.

This worthy lymytour, this noble Frere,
He made alwey a maner louryng chiere°
Upon the Somonour, but for honestee°
No vileyns° word as yet to hym spak he.
But atte laste he seyde unto the wyf,
"Dame," quod he, "God yeve° yow right good lyf.
Ye han heer° touched, also moot I thee,
In scole-matere greet difficultee.
Ye han seyd° muche thyng right wel, I seye.
But dame, heere as we ryde by the weye
Us nedeth nat to speken but of game°
And lete auctoritees°, on° Goddes name,
To prechyng and to scole° of clergye.
But if it lyke° to this compaignye,
I wol yow of a somonour telle a game.
Pardee°, ye may wel knowe by the name°
That of a somonour may no good be sayd;
I praye that noon of you be yvele apayd°.
A somonour is a rennere° up and doun
With mandementz° for fornicacioun,
And is ybet° at every townes ende."
Oure Hoost tho° spak, "A, sire, ye sholde be hende°
And curteys, as a man of youre estaat°;
In compaignye we wol have no debaat°.
Telleth youre tale and lat the Somonour be."
"Nay," quod the Somonour, "lat hym seye to me
Whatso hym list°. Whan it comth to my lot°,
By God, I shal hym quiten° every grot°.
I shal hym tellen which° a greet honour
It is to be a flaterynge lymytour,
And of many another manere° cryme

1266 maner louryng chiere, *kind of angry expression* **1267 for honestee,** *to keep his dignity* **1268 vileyns,** *rude* **1270 yeve,** *give* **1271 han heer,** *have here* **1273 han seyd,** *have said* **1275 of game,** *for entertainment* **1276 lete auctoritees,** *leave learned texts,* **on,** *in* **1277 scole,** *studies* **1278 lyke,** *is pleasing* **1280 Pardee,** *by God,* **the name,** *reputation* **1282 yvele apayd,** *displeased* **1283 rennere,** *runner* **1284 mandementz,** *summonses* **1285 ybet,** *beaten* **1286 tho,** *then,* **hende,** *gracious* **1287 estaat,** *status* **1288 debaat,** *quarreling* **1291 Whatso hym list,** *whatever he wishes,* **lot,** *turn* **1292 quiten,** *repay,* **grot,** *bit* (coin) **1293 hym tellen which,** *tell him what* **1295 another manere,** *more kinds of*

1265 lymytour, "a friar whose begging, preaching, and hearing of confessions was limited" to a particular territory (*MED*); see *GP* 1.208n and 209n. **1271 also moot I thee,** "as I may prosper," an idiom meaning something like "if I do say so myself." **1272 scole-matere,** school matter, i.e., intellectual things. **1278 But,** El reads "And." **1282 yvele,** omitted in Hg. **1283 somonour,** summoner, a subpoena server for an ecclesiastical court. **1288 have,** omitted in Hg.

Of my poverte namoore ye me repreve°.
"Now, sire, of elde° ye repreve me;
And certes°, sire, thogh noon auctoritee°
Were in no book, ye gentils of honour
Seyn° that men sholde an oold wight doon favour°
And clepe° hym fader for youre gentillesse—
And auctours° shal I fynden, as I gesse.
"Now ther° ye seye that I am foul and old,
Than drede° you noght to been a cokewold°,
For filthe° and eelde°, also moot I thee°,
Been grete wardeyns° upon chastitee.
But nathelees, syn I knowe youre delit,
I shal fulfille youre worldly appetit.
"Chese now," quod she, "oon of thise thynges tweye:
To han° me foul and old til that I deye°
And be to yow a trewe humble wyf,
And nevere yow displese in al my lyf,
Or elles° ye wol han° me yong and fair,
And take youre aventure° of the repair°
That shal be to youre hous by cause° of me,
Or in som oother place, may wel be.
Now chese yourselven, wheither° that yow liketh."
This knyght avyseth hym° and sore siketh°,
But atte laste he seyde in this manere,
"My lady and my love, and wyf so deere,
I put me in youre wise governance;
Cheseth youreself which may be moost plesance°
And moost honour to yow and me also.
I do no fors the wheither° of the two,
For as yow liketh it suffiseth° me."
"Thanne have I gete° of yow maistrie," quod she,
"Syn° I may chese and governe as me lest°?"
"Ye, certes°, wyf," quod he. "I holde it best."
"Kys me," quod she. "We be no lenger wrothe°,
For, by my trouthe, I wol be to yow bothe—
This is to seyn, ye°, bothe fair and good.
I prey to God that I moote sterven wood°
But° I to yow be also° good and trewe
As evere was wyf syn that the world was newe.
And but I be tomorn° as fair to seene°
As any lady, emperice, or queene,
That is bitwixe the est and eke the west,
Dooth with my lyf and deth right as yow lest°.
Cast up the curtyn, looke how that it is."
And whan the knyght saugh verraily° al this,
That she so fair was, and so yong therto°,
For joye he hente° hire in his armes two.
His herte bathed in a bath of blisse,
A thousand tyme a-rewe° he gan hire kisse°,
And she obeyed hym in every thyng
That myghte doon hym plesance or likyng.
And thus they lyve unto hir lyves ende
In parfit joye. And Jhesu Crist us sende
Housbondes meeke, yonge, and fressh abedde,
And grace t'overbyde hem° that we wedde.
And eek I pray Jhesu shorte hir° lyves
That wol nat be governed by hir wyves.
And olde and angry nygardes of dispence°,
God sende hem soone verray pestilence°!

Heere endeth the Wyves Tale of Bathe.

1206 repreve, *accuse* **1207 elde,** *old age* **1208 certes,** *certainly,* **auctoritee,** *authority* **1210 Seyn,** *say,* **an oold wight doon favour,** *respect an old person* **1211 clepe,** *call* **1212 auctours,** *authors* (who agree) **1213 ther,** *since* **1214 drede,** *fear,* **cokewold,** *cuckold* **1215 filthe,** *foulness,* **eelde,** *age,* **also moot I thee,** *so I may prosper* **1216 Been grete wardeyns,** *are great guardians* **1220 han,** *have,* **deye,** *die* **1223 elles,** *else,* **wol han,** *will have* **1224 aventure,** *chances,* **repair,** *visitors* **1225 by cause,** *because* **1227 wheither,** *whichever* **1228 avyseth hym,** *ponders,* **sore siketh,** *sighs painfully* **1232 plesance,** *happiness* **1234 do no fors the wheither,** *I don't care which* **1235 suffiseth,** *satisfies* **1236 gete,** *gotten* **1237 Syn,** *since,* **me lest,** *I please* **1238 Ye, certes,** *yes, certainly* **1239 lenger wrothe,** *longer at odds* **1241 seyn, ye,** *say, yes* **1242 moote sterven wood,** *might die insane* **1243 But,** *unless,* **also,** *as* **1245 tomorn,** *tomorrow,* **seene,** *see* **1248 yow lest,** *you wish* **1250 saugh verraily,** *saw truly* **1251 therto,** *also* **1252 hente,** *grasped* **1254 a-rewe,** *in a row,* **gan hire kisse,** *kissed her* **1260 t'overbyde hem,** *to outlive them* **1261 shorte hir,** *shorten their* **1263 nygardes of dispence,** *misers of money* **1264 verray pestilence,** *true plague*

1210 sholde an oold wight, Hg reads "an old wight sholde." **1219 Chese now . . . ,** in other versions of the tale, the loathly lady offers a different choice (fair by day and foul by night, or vice versa) and shows her beauty to the knight before he must choose. **1232 which may,** Hg reads "which that may." **1249 Cast up the curtyn,** the drapes of the canopy bed had been drawn for privacy.

From woodcut made by W.H. Hooper and published by the Chaucer Society between 1868 and 1879

Friar's Tale

Prologue

The Prologe of the Freres Tale.

This worthy lymytour, this noble Frere,
He made alwey a maner louryng chiere°
Upon the Somonour, but for honestee°
No vileyns° word as yet to hym spak he.
But atte laste he seyde unto the wyf,
"Dame," quod he, "God yeve° yow right good lyf.
Ye han heer° touched, also moot I thee,
In scole-matere greet difficultee.
Ye han seyd° muche thyng right wel, I seye.
But dame, heere as we ryde by the weye
Us nedeth nat to speken but of game°
And lete auctoritees°, on° Goddes name,
To prechyng and to scole° of clergye.
But if it lyke° to this compaignye,
I wol yow of a somonour telle a game.
Pardee°, ye may wel knowe by the name°
That of a somonour may no good be sayd;
I praye that noon of you be yvele apayd°.
A somonour is a rennere° up and doun
With mandementz° for fornicacioun,
And is ybet° at every townes ende."
Oure Hoost tho° spak, "A, sire, ye sholde be hende°
And curteys, as a man of youre estaat°;
In compaignye we wol have no debaat°.
Telleth youre tale and lat the Somonour be."
"Nay," quod the Somonour, "lat hym seye to me
Whatso hym list°. Whan it comth to my lot°,
By God, I shal hym quiten° every grot°.
I shal hym tellen which° a greet honour
It is to be a flaterynge lymytour,
And of many another manere° cryme

1266 maner louryng chiere, *kind of angry expression* **1267 for honestee,** *to keep his dignity* **1268 vileyns,** *rude* **1270 yeve,** *give* **1271 han heer,** *have here* **1273 han seyd,** *have said* **1275 of game,** *for entertainment* **1276 lete auctoritees,** *leave learned texts,* **on,** *in* **1277 scole,** *studies* **1278 lyke,** *is pleasing* **1280 Pardee,** *by God,* **the name,** *reputation* **1282 yvele apayd,** *displeased* **1283 rennere,** *runner* **1284 mandementz,** *summonses* **1285 ybet,** *beaten* **1286 tho,** *then,* **hende,** *gracious* **1287 estaat,** *status* **1288 debaat,** *quarreling* **1291 Whatso hym list,** *whatever he wishes,* **lot,** *turn* **1292 quiten,** *repay,* **grot,** *bit* (coin) **1293 hym tellen which,** *tell him what* **1295 another manere,** *more kinds of*

1265 lymytour, "a friar whose begging, preaching, and hearing of confessions was limited" to a particular territory (*MED*); see *GP* 1.208n and 209n. **1271 also moot I thee,** "as I may prosper," an idiom meaning something like "if I do say so myself." **1272 scole-matere,** school matter, i.e., intellectual things. **1278 But,** El reads "And." **1282 yvele,** omitted in Hg. **1283 somonour,** summoner, a subpoena server for an ecclesiastical court. **1288 have,** omitted in Hg.

Of my poverte namoore ye me repreve°.
"Now, sire, of elde° ye repreve me;
And certes°, sire, thogh noon auctoritee°
Were in no book, ye gentils of honour
Seyn° that men sholde an oold wight doon favour°
And clepe° hym fader for youre gentillesse—
And auctours° shal I fynden, as I gesse.
"Now ther° ye seye that I am foul and old,
Than drede° you noght to been a cokewold°,
For filthe° and eelde°, also moot I thee°,
Been grete wardeyns° upon chastitee.
But nathelees, syn I knowe youre delit,
I shal fulfille youre worldly appetit.
"Chese now," quod she, "oon of thise thynges tweye:
To han° me foul and old til that I deye°
And be to yow a trewe humble wyf,
And nevere yow displese in al my lyf,
Or elles° ye wol han° me yong and fair,
And take youre aventure° of the repair°
That shal be to youre hous by cause° of me,
Or in som oother place, may wel be.
Now chese yourselven, wheither° that yow liketh."
This knyght avyseth hym° and sore siketh°,
But atte laste he seyde in this manere,
"My lady and my love, and wyf so deere,
I put me in youre wise governance;
Cheseth youreself which may be moost plesance°
And moost honour to yow and me also.
I do no fors the wheither° of the two,
For as yow liketh it suffiseth° me."
"Thanne have I gete° of yow maistrie," quod she,
"Syn° I may chese and governe as me lest°?"
"Ye, certes°, wyf," quod he. "I holde it best."
"Kys me," quod she. "We be no lenger wrothe°,
For, by my trouthe, I wol be to yow bothe—
This is to seyn, ye°, bothe fair and good.
I prey to God that I moote sterven wood°
But° I to yow be also° good and trewe
As evere was wyf syn that the world was newe.
And but I be tomorn° as fair to seene°
As any lady, emperice, or queene,
That is bitwixe the est and eke the west,
Dooth with my lyf and deth right as yow lest°.
Cast up the curtyn, looke how that it is."
And whan the knyght saugh verraily° al this,
That she so fair was, and so yong therto°,
For joye he hente° hire in his armes two.
His herte bathed in a bath of blisse,
A thousand tyme a-rewe° he gan hire kisse°,
And she obeyed hym in every thyng
That myghte doon hym plesance or likyng.
And thus they lyve unto hir lyves ende
In parfit joye. And Jhesu Crist us sende
Housbondes meeke, yonge, and fressh abedde,
And grace t'overbyde hem° that we wedde.
And eek I pray Jhesu shorte hir° lyves
That wol nat be governed by hir wyves.
And olde and angry nygardes of dispence°,
God sende hem soone verray pestilence°!

Heere endeth the Wyves Tale of Bathe.

1206 repreve, *accuse* **1207 elde,** *old age* **1208 certes,** *certainly,* **auctoritee,** *authority* **1210 Seyn,** *say,* **an oold wight doon favour,** *respect an old person* **1211 clepe,** *call* **1212 auctours,** *authors* (who agree) **1213 ther,** *since* **1214 drede,** *fear,* **cokewold,** *cuckold* **1215 filthe,** *foulness,* **eelde,** *age,* **also moot I thee,** *so I may prosper* **1216 Been grete wardeyns,** *are great guardians* **1220 han,** *have,* **deye,** *die* **1223 elles,** *else,* **wol han,** *will have* **1224 aventure,** *chances,* **repair,** *visitors* **1225 by cause,** *because* **1227 wheither,** *whichever* **1228 avyseth hym,** *ponders,* **sore siketh,** *sighs painfully* **1232 plesance,** *happiness* **1234 do no fors the wheither,** *I don't care which* **1235 suffiseth,** *satisfies* **1236 gete,** *gotten* **1237 Syn,** *since,* **me lest,** *I please* **1238 Ye, certes,** *yes, certainly* **1239 lenger wrothe,** *longer at odds* **1241 seyn, ye,** *say, yes* **1242 moote sterven wood,** *might die insane* **1243 But,** *unless,* **also,** *as* **1245 tomorn,** *tomorrow,* **seene,** *see* **1248 yow lest,** *you wish* **1250 saugh verraily,** *saw truly* **1251 therto,** *also* **1252 hente,** *grasped* **1254 a-rewe,** *in a row,* **gan hire kisse,** *kissed her* **1260 t'overbyde hem,** *to outlive them* **1261 shorte hir,** *shorten their* **1263 nygardes of dispence,** *misers of money* **1264 verray pestilence,** *true plague*

1210 sholde an oold wight, Hg reads "an old wight sholde." **1219 Chese now . . . ,** in other versions of the tale, the loathly lady offers a different choice (fair by day and foul by night, or vice versa) and shows her beauty to the knight before he must choose. **1232 which may,** Hg reads "which that may." **1249 Cast up the curtyn,** the drapes of the canopy bed had been drawn for privacy.

From woodcut made by W.H. Hooper and published by the Chaucer Society between 1868 and 1879

Friar's Tale

Prologue

The Prologe of the Freres Tale.

This worthy lymytour, this noble Frere,
He made alwey a maner louryng chiere°
Upon the Somonour, but for honestee°
No vileyns° word as yet to hym spak he.
But atte laste he seyde unto the wyf,
“Dame,” quod he, “God yeve° yow right good lyf.
Ye han heer° touched, also moot I thee,
In scole-matere greet difficultee.
Ye han seyd° muche thyng right wel, I seye.
But dame, heere as we ryde by the weye
Us nedeth nat to speken but of game°
And lete auctoritees°, on° Goddes name,
To prechyng and to scole° of clergye.
But if it lyke° to this compaignye,
I wol yow of a somonour telle a game.
Pardee°, ye may wel knowe by the name°
That of a somonour may no good be sayd;
I praye that noon of you be yvele apayd°.
A somonour is a rennere° up and doun
With mandementz° for fornicacioun,
And is ybet° at every townes ende.”
Oure Hoost tho° spak, “A, sire, ye sholde be hende°
And curteys, as a man of youre estaat°;
In compaignye we wol have no debaat°.
Telleth youre tale and lat the Somonour be.”
“Nay,” quod the Somonour, “lat hym seye to me
Whatso hym list°. Whan it comth to my lot°,
By God, I shal hym quiten° every grot°.
I shal hym tellen which° a greet honour
It is to be a flaterynge lymytour,
And of many another manere° cryme

1266 maner louryng chiere, *kind of angry expression* **1267 for honestee,** *to keep his dignity* **1268 vileyns,** *rude* **1270 yeve,** *give* **1271 han heer,** *have here* **1273 han seyd,** *have said* **1275 of game,** *for entertainment* **1276 lete auctoritees,** *leave learned texts,* **on,** *in* **1277 scole,** *studies* **1278 lyke,** *is pleasing* **1280 Pardee,** *by God,* **the name,** *reputation* **1282 yvele apayd,** *displeased* **1283 rennere,** *runner* **1284 mandementz,** *summonses* **1285 ybet,** *beaten* **1286 tho,** *then,* **hende,** *gracious* **1287 estaat,** *status* **1288 debaat,** *quarreling* **1291 Whatso hym list,** *whatever he wishes,* **lot,** *turn* **1292 quiten,** *repay,* **grot,** *bit* (coin) **1293 hym tellen which,** *tell him what* **1295 another manere,** *more kinds of*

1265 lymytour, “a friar whose begging, preaching, and hearing of confessions was limited” to a particular territory (*MED*); see *GP* 1.208n and 209n. **1271 also moot I thee,** “as I may prosper,” an idiom meaning something like “if I do say so myself.” **1272 scole-matere,** school matter, i.e., intellectual things. **1278 But,** El reads “And.” **1282 yvele,** omitted in Hg. **1283 somonour,** summoner, a subpoena server for an ecclesiastical court. **1288 have,** omitted in Hg.

Which nedeth° nat rehercen for° this tyme.
And his office° I shal hym telle, ywis°."
  Oure Hoost answerde, "Pees, namoore of this."
And after this he seyde unto the Frere,
"Tel forth youre tale, leeve° maister deere."

Heere bigynneth the Freres Tale.

  Whilom° ther was dwellynge in my contree
An erchedekene, a man of heigh degree,
That boldely dide execucioun°
In punysshynge of fornicacioun,
Of wicchecraft, and eek of bawderye°,
Of diffamacioun°, and avowtrye°,
Of chirche reves°, and of testamentz°,
Of contractes°, and of lakke of° sacramentz,
Of usure°, and of symonye° also.
But certes, lecchours dide he grettest wo°—
They sholde syngen° if that they were hent°—
And smale tytheres° weren foule yshent°
If any persone° wolde upon hem pleyne°.
Ther myghte asterte hym no pecunyal peyne°.
For smale tithes and for smal offrynge°
He made the peple pitously to synge,
For er° the bisshop caughte hem° with his hook°,
They were in the erchedeknes° book.
And thanne hadde he, thurgh his jurisdiccioun,
Power to doon on hem correccioun.
He hadde a somonour redy to his hond—
A slyer boye nas noon° in Engelond,
For subtilly he hadde his espiaille°
That taughte hym wher that hym myghte availle°.
He koude spare of lecchours oon or two
To techen° hym to foure and twenty mo.
For thogh this somonour wood was as an hare,
To telle his harlotrye° I wol nat spare,
For we been out of his correccioun.
They han of us no jurisdiccioun,
Ne nevere shullen, terme° of alle hir lyves.
  "Peter°, so been° wommen of the styves°,"
Quod the Somonour, "yput out of my cure°!"
  "Pees, with myschance and with mysaventure,"
Thus seyde oure Hoost, "and lat hym telle his
    tale.
Now telleth forth, thogh that the Somonour
    gale°,
Ne spareth nat, myn owene maister deere."
  This false theef, this somonour, quod the Frere,
Hadde alwey bawdes° redy to his hond,
As any hauk to lure in Engelond,
That tolde hym al the secree° that they knewe,
For hire acqueyntance was nat come of newe.
They weren his approwours prively°.
He took hymself a greet profit therby;
His maister knew nat alwey what he wan°.
Withouten mandement° a lewed° man
He koude somne°, on peyne° of Cristes curs,
And they were glade for to fille his purs
And make hym grete feestes atte nale°.
And right as Judas hadde purses smale,
And was a theef, right swich a theef was he;
His maister hadde but half his duetee°.

1296 nedeth, (I) *need,* **for,** *at* **1297 office,** *function,* **ywis,** *surely* **1300 leeve,** *beloved* **1301 Whilom,** *once* **1303 dide execucioun,** *executed the laws* **1305 eek of bawderye,** *also of pimping* **1306 diffamacioun,** *slander,* **avowtrye,** *adultery* **1307 reves,** *robberies,* **of testamentz,** *pertaining to wills* **1308 contractes,** (marriage) *contracts,* **lakke of,** *failure to perform* **1309 usure,** *lending money for interest,* **symonye,** *buying or selling church offices* **1310 dide he grettest wo,** *he hurt most* **1311 syngen,** *wail,* **hent,** *caught* **1312 foule yshent,** *harshly punished* **1313 persone,** *parson* (parish priest), **upon hem pleyne,** *complain about them* **1314 Ther myghte asterte hym no pecunyal peyne,** *he would not escape financial suffering* **1315 offrynge,** *voluntary contribution* **1317 er,** *before,* **hem,** *them,* **hook,** *curved staff* **1318 erchedeknes,** *archdeacon's* **1322 A slyer boye nas noon,** *there was no slyer rascal* **1323 espiaille,** *spy network* **1324 availle,** *profit* **1326 techen,** *lead* **1328 harlotrye,** (sexual?) *wickedness* **1331 terme,** (for the) *time* **1332 Peter,** *by St. Peter,* **been,** *are,* **styves,** *brothels* **1333 cure,** *responsibility* **1336 gale,** *makes noise* **1339 bawdes,** *pimps* **1341 secree,** *secrets* **1343 approwours prively,** *undercover agents* **1345 wan,** *acquired* **1346 mandement,** *summons,* **lewed,** *ignorant* **1347 koude somne,** *could summon,* **on peyne,** *under threat* **1349 atte nale,** *at the alehouse* **1352 his duetee,** *amount due to him*

1302 erchedekene, archdeacon; in medieval church hierarchy, the officer just below the bishop, responsible for a subdivision of the diocese and the overseeing of its ecclesiastical court. **1308 and of,** El and Hg read "and eek of." **sacramentz,** church rites, including baptism, confirmation, Eucharist or communion, penance or confession, marriage, last rites, and ordination of priests. **1312 smale tytheres,** small tithers, those who fail to pay completes tithes, a ten percent income tax due the Church. **1315 and for,** El omits "for." **1327 wood was an hare,** proverbial: crazy as a (marsh or March) hare, i.e., out of control. **1329 we . . . correccioun,** we (friars) . . . authority. Friars were under the authority of their own orders rather than the diocesan courts. **1334 with myschance and with mysaventure,** an idiom meaning "bad luck to you." **1340 hauk to lure,** a hawk was trained to return to its handler when a "lure" (false bird on a rope) was swung. **1350 Judas . . . purses,** Judas Iscariot, who betrayed Jesus, was a thief and keeper of the disciples' money; John 12.4–6.

He was, if I shal yeven° hym his laude°,
A theef and eek a somnour and a baude°.
He hadde eek wenches at his retenue°.
That wheither that Sir Robert or Sir Huwe,
Or Jakke, or Rauf, or whoso that it were
That lay by hem°, they tolde it in his ere.
Thus was the wenche and he of oon assent°;
And he wolde fecche a feyned mandement°
And somne hem° to chapitre° bothe two,
And pile° the man and lete the wenche go.
  Thanne wolde he seye, "Freend, I shal for thy sake
Do striken hire out of° oure lettres blake.
Thee thar namoore, as in this cas, travaille°;
I am thy freend ther° I thee may availle°."
Certeyn he knew of briberyes mo
Than possible is to telle in yeres two.
For in this world nys dogge for the bowe°
That kan an hurt deer from an hool° knowe
Bet° than this somnour knew a sly lecchour
Or an avowtier° or a paramour°.
And for° that was the fruyt° of al his rente°,
Therfore on it he sette al his entente.
  And so bifel that ones° on a day
This somnour evere waityng on his pray°
Rood for to somne an old wydwe°, a ribibe,
Feynynge a cause, for he wolde brybe°.
And happed° that he saugh bifore hym ryde
A gay yeman° under a forest syde°.
A bowe he bar° and arwes° brighte and kene°;
He hadde upon a courtepy° of grene;
An hat upon his heed with frenges blake°.
  "Sire," quod this somnour, "hayl, and wel atake."
  "Welcome," quod he, "and every good felawe.
Wher rydestow°, under this grenewode shawe°?"
Seyde this yeman, "Wiltow fer° to day?"
  This somnour hym answerde and seyde, "Nay.
Heere faste° by," quod he, "is myn entente
To ryden for to reysen up° a rente
That longeth to my lordes duetee°."
  "Artow° thanne a bailly°?" "Ye," quod he.
He dorste° nat, for verray° filthe and shame
Seye that he was a somonour, for the name°.
  "Depardieux°," quod this yeman, "deere broother,
Thou art a bailly, and I am another.
I am unknowen as in this contree;
Of thyn aqueyntance I wolde praye thee°
And eek of bretherhede, if that yow leste°.
I have gold and silver in my cheste;
If that thee happe° to comen in oure shire°,
Al shal be thyn, right° as thou wolt desire."
  "Grantmercy°," quod this somonour, "by my feith!"
Everych° in ootheres hand his trouthe leith°,
For to be sworne bretheren til they deye.
In daliance° they ryden forth hir weye.
  This somonour, that was as ful of jangles°
As ful of venym been thise waryangles
And evere enqueryng upon everythyng,
"Brother," quod he, "where is now youre dwellyng
Another day if that I sholde yow seche°?"
This yeman hym answerde in softe speche,
  "Brother," quod he, "fer° in the north contree,
Where as° I hope som tyme I shal thee see.
Er° we departe I shal thee so wel wisse°
That of myn hous ne shaltow nevere° mysse."
  "Now, brother," quod this somonour, "I yow preye,

1353 yeven, *give,* **laude,** *proper praise* **1354 baude,** *pimp* **1355 at his retenue,** *in his service* **1358 hem,** *them* **1359 of oon assent,** *in agreement* **1360 feyned mandement,** *false document* **1361 somne hem,** *summon them,* **chapitre,** *court session* **1362 pile,** *rob* **1364 Do striken hire out of,** *erase her from* **1365 Thee thar . . . travaille,** *about this . . . trouble yourself* **1366 ther,** *where,* **thee may availle,** *may help you* **1369 nys dogge for the bowe,** *there is no hunting* (archery) *dog* **1370 hool,** *whole* (unwounded) *one* **1371 Bet,** *better* **1372 avowtier,** *adulterer,* **paramour,** *lover* **1373 for,** *because,* **fruyt,** *best part,* **rente,** *income* **1375 ones,** *once* **1376 pray,** *prey* **1377 wydwe,** *widow* **1378 brybe,** *blackmail* **1379 happed,** (it) *happened* **1380 gay yeman,** *well-dressed yeoman,* **under a forest syde,** *at the forest's edge* **1381 bar,** *carried,* **arwes,** *arrows,* **kene,** *sharp* **1382 courtepy,** *jacket* **1383 frenges blake,** *black fringe* **1386 rydestow,** *do you ride,* **shawe,** *grove* **1387 Wiltow fer,** *will you go far* **1389 faste,** *near* **1390 reysen up,** *collect* **1391 longeth to my lordes duetee,** *belongs to my lord* **1392 Artow,** *are you,* **bailly,** *bailiff* (agent or representative) **1393 dorste,** *dared,* **verray,** *true* **1394 for the name,** *because of the reputation* **1395 Depardieux,** *by God* **1398 wolde praye thee,** *would like to ask you* **1399 yow leste,** (it) *pleases you* **1401 happe,** *happen,* **shire,** *county* **1402 right,** *just* **1403 Grantmercy,** *thank you* **1404 Everych,** *each,* **his trouthe leith,** *laid his pledge* (i.e., they shook on it) **1405 deye,** *die* **1406 daliance,** *small talk* **1407 ful of jangles,** *talkative* **1411 seche,** *seek* **1413 fer,** *far* **1414 Where as,** *where* **1415 Er,** *before,* **wisse,** *teach* **1416 ne shaltow nevere,** *you shall never*

1374 entente, intention, a word that recurs throughout the tale. **1377 Rood,** omitted in El and Hg. **ribibe,** fiddle, slang term for an old woman, perhaps from a confusion of Lat. *vetula* (old woman) and *vitula* (viol). **1379 And,** omitted in El and Hg. **1384 hayl, and wel atake,** greetings, and I am happy I met (have overtaken) you. **1386 grenewode shawe,** Hg reads "grene shawe." **1406 hir weye,** Hg reads "and pleye." **1408 As ful of venym been thise waryangles,** as full of poison (as) are these butcher birds, or shrikes, who impaled their prey on thorns that were thought to be poisonous as a result. **1413 north contree,** hell was often located in the north; e.g., Isaiah 14.14 and Jeremiah 6.1.

Teche me whil that we ryden by the weye—
Syn that ye been a baillif as am I—
Som subtiltee, and tel me feithfully
In myn office how that I may moost wynne;
And spareth nat° for conscience ne synne,
But as my brother tel me how do ye°."
"Now by my trouthe, brother deere," seyde he,
"As I shal tellen thee a feithful tale:
My wages been ful streite° and ful smale.
My lord is hard to me and daungerous°,
And myn office is ful laborous,
And therfore by extorcions I lyve.
For sothe°, I take al that men wol me yeve°.
Algate°, by sleyghte° or by violence
Fro yeer to yeer I wynne° al my dispence°.
I kan no bettre telle°, feithfully."
"Now certes," quod this somonour, "so fare° I.
I spare nat° to taken, God it woot°,
But if° it be to hevy or to hoot.
What I may gete in conseil prively°,
No maner conscience of° that have I.
Nere myn° extorcioun, I myghte nat lyven,
Nor of swiche japes° wol I nat be shryven°.
Stomak ne conscience ne knowe I noon;
I shrewe° thise shrifte-fadres° everychoon°.
Wel be we met, by God and by Seint Jame!
But, leeve° brother, tel me thanne thy name,"
Quod this somonour. In this meene while
This yeman gan a litel for to smyle.
"Brother," quod he, "wiltow° that I thee telle?
I am a feend; my dwellyng is in helle.
And heere I ryde about my purchasyng°
To wite where° men wold me yeven° anythyng.
My purchas° is th'effect° of al my rente°.
Looke how thou rydest for the same entente—
To wynne good°, thou rekkest° nevere how.
Right so fare° I, for ryde I wold right now
Unto the worldes ende for a preye°."
"A," quod this somonour, "benedicite°, what sey ye?
I wende° ye were a yeman trewely.
Ye han° a mannes shap° as wel as I.
Han ye a figure thanne determinat
In helle, ther ye been in youre estat?"
"Nay, certeinly," quod he, "ther have we noon;
But whan us liketh° we kan take us oon°,
Or elles make yow seme° we been shape°.
Somtyme lyk a man, or lyk an ape,
Or lyk an angel kan I ryde or go.
It is no wonder thyng thogh it be so;
A lowsy jogelour° kan deceyve thee,
And pardee°, yet kan° I moore craft than he."
"Why," quod this somonour, "ryde ye thanne or goon
In sondry shap° and nat alwey in oon?"
"For° we," quod he, "wol° us swiche° formes make
As moost able° is oure preyes° for to take."
"What maketh yow to han° al this labour?"
"Ful many a cause, leeve° sire somonour,"
Seyde this feend, "but alle thyng hath tyme.
The day is short and it is passed pryme,
And yet ne wan I nothyng in this day.
I wol entende to wynnen, if I may,
And nat entende oure wittes to declare°.
For, brother myn, thy wit is al to bare°
To understonde althogh I tolde hem thee°.
But, for thou axest° why labouren we,
For somtyme we been Goddes instrumentz
And meenes to doon his comandementz,
Whan that hym list°, upon his creatures,
In divers art° and in diverse figures°.
Withouten hym we have no myght, certayn,
If that hym list to stonden ther-agayn°.

1422 spareth nat, *don't refrain* **1423 do ye,** *you operate* **1426 ful streite,** *very limited* **1427 daungerous,** *demanding* **1430 sothe,** *truth,* **yeve,** *give* **1431 Algate,** *always,* **sleyghte,** *trickery* **1432 wynne,** *acquire,* **dispence,** *money* **1433 telle,** *tally* **1434 fare,** *act* **1435 spare nat,** *don't refrain,* **woot,** *knows* **1436 But if,** *unless* **1437 conseil prively,** *secret counsel* **1438 No maner conscience of,** *no kind of moral concern about* **1439 Nere myn,** *if it were not for my* **1440 swiche japes,** *such tricks,* **shryven,** *confessed* **1442 shrewe,** *curse,* **shrifte-fadres,** *confessors,* **everychoon,** *every one* **1444 leeve,** *beloved* **1447 wiltow,** *do you wish* **1449 purchasyng,** *acquiring* **1450 wite where,** *know whether,* **yeven,** *give* **1451 purchas,** *acquisition,* **th'effect,** *the sum total,* **rente,** *income* **1453 wynne good,** *gain wealth,* **rekkest,** *care* **1454 fare,** *act* **1455 preye,** *victim* **1456 benedicite,** *bless you* **1457 wende,** *thought* **1458 han,** *have,* **shap,** *shape* **1462 us liketh,** *it pleases us,* **oon,** *one* (a shape) **1463 make yow seme,** *make it seem to you,* **been shape,** *are shaped* **1467 jogelour,** *conjurer* **1468 pardee,** *by God,* **kan,** *know* **1470 sondry shap,** *various shapes* **1471 For,** *because,* **wol,** *will,* **swiche,** *such* **1472 able,** *effective,* **preyes,** *victims* **1473 han,** *have* **1474 leeve,** *beloved* **1479 oure wittes to declare,** *to show off our* (demonic) *intellects* **1480 al to bare,** *altogether incapable* **1481 tolde hem thee,** *explained them to you* **1482 for thou axest,** *because you ask* **1485 hym list,** (it) *pleases him* **1486 divers art,** *various methods,* **figures,** *shapes* **1488 hym list to stonden ther-agayn,** (it) *pleases him to oppose* (what we do)

1421 that, omitted in El and Hg. **1436 if,** omitted in Hg. **1450 me yeven,** Hg reads "yeve me." **1454 I wold right now,** Hg reads "wold I now." **1459–60 Han ye . . . estat,** "Do you have, then, a definite or particular form when you are in hell, where you are in your (proper) condition?"—a debated metaphysical question. **1459 a,** omitted in El. **1475 alle thyng hath tyme,** the demon quotes Ecclesiastes 3.1. **1476 pryme,** one of medieval times of the day, about 9:00 A.M.; see *MilT* 1.3655n. **1478 wynnen,** Hg reads "wynnyng." **1479 oure,** El reads "hir."

And somtyme, at oure prayere°, han we leve°
Oonly the body and nat the soule greve°:
Witnesse on° Job, whom that we diden wo.
And somtyme han we myght of° bothe two,
This is to seyn, of soule and body eke.
And somtyme be we suffred for to seke
Upon° a man and doon his soule unreste,
And nat his body, and al is for the beste.
Whan he withstandeth oure temptacioun,
It is a cause of his savacioun,
Al be it that it was nat oure entente
He sholde be sauf but° that we wolde hym hente°.
And somtyme be we servant unto man,
As to the erchebisshop Seint Dunstan,
And to the apostles servant eek was I."
"Yet tel me," quod the somonour, "feithfully,
Make ye yow newe bodies thus alway
Of elementz?" The feend answerde, "Nay.
Somtyme we feyne°, and somtyme we aryse
With dede° bodyes in ful sondry wyse°,
And speke as renably° and faire and wel
As to the Phitonissa dide Samuel—
And yet wol som men seye it was nat he;
I do no fors of° youre dyvynytee°.
But o thyng warne I thee, I wol nat jape°:
Thou wolt algates wite° how we been shape;
Thou shalt herafterwardes°, my brother deere,
Come there° thee nedeth nat of me to leere°,
For thou shalt by thyn owene experience
Konne in a chayer rede° of this sentence°
Bet° than Virgile while he was on lyve,
Or Dant also. Now lat us ryde blyve°,
For I wole holde compaignye with thee
Til it be so that thou forsake me."
"Nay," quod this somonour, "that shal nat bityde°.
I am a yeman knowen is ful wyde°;
My trouthe° wol I holde, as in this cas.
For though thou were the devel Sathanas,
My trouthe wol I holde to thee my brother,
As I am sworn—and ech of us til° oother—
For to be trewe brother in this cas.
And bothe we goon abouten oure purchas°.
Taak thou thy part, what that° men wol thee yeve°,
And I shal myn; thus may we bothe lyve.
And if that any of us have moore than oother,
Lat hym be trewe and parte° it with his brother."
"I graunte," quod the devel, "by my fey°."
And with that word they ryden forth hir wey.
And right at the entryng of the townes ende°,
To which this somonour shoop hym for to wende°,
They saugh° a cart that charged° was with hey,
Which that a cartere° droof forth in his wey.
Deep° was the wey, for which the carte stood.
The cartere smoot° and cryde as he were wood°,
"Hayt°, Brok! Hayt, Scot! What, spare ye for° the stones?
The feend," quod he, "yow fecche°, body and bones,
As ferforthly° as evere were ye foled°,
So muche wo as I have with yow tholed°!
The devel have al, bothe hors and cart and hey."
This somonour seyde, "Heere shal we have a pley°."
And neer the feend he drough°, as noght ne were°,
Ful prively°, and rowned° in his ere,
"Herkne°, my brother, herkne, by thy feith!
Herestow nat how that° the cartere seith?

1489 prayere, *request,* **leve,** *permission* **1490 greve,** *afflict* **1491 Witnesse on,** *take as evidence* **1492 myght of,** *power over* **1494–95 suffred for to seke / Upon,** *allowed to attack* **1500 sauf but that,** *saved unless,* **hente,** *grab* **1507 feyne,** *create illusion* **1508 dede,** *dead,* **ful sondry wyse,** *very many ways* **1509 renably,** *reasonably* **1512 do no fors of,** *care not at all about,* **dyvynytee,** *theological dispute* **1513 jape,** *joke* **1514 wolt algates wite,** *will nevertheless know* **1515 herafterwardes,** *soon after this* **1516 there,** *where,* **leere,** *learn* **1518 Konne in a chayer rede,** *be able in a* (professor's) *chair to lecture,* **sentence,** *topic* **1519 Bet,** *better* **1520 blyve,** *quickly* **1523 bityde,** *happen* **1524 knowen is ful wyde,** (as) *is very widely known* **1525 trouthe,** *pledge* **1528 til,** *to* **1530 purchas,** *acquisition* **1531 what that,** *whatever,* **yeve,** *give* **1534 parte,** *divide* **1535 fey,** *faith* **1537 ende,** *edge* **1538 shoop . . . to wende,** *planned to go* **1539 saugh,** *saw,* **charged,** *loaded* **1540 cartere,** *cart driver* **1541 Deep,** *rutted,* **stood,** *was stuck* **1542 smoot,** *struck,* **wood,** *crazed* **1543 Hayt,** *giddy up,* **spare ye for,** *do you hold back because* (of) **1544 yow fecche,** *fetch you* **1545 ferforthly,** *surely,* **foled,** *foaled* (born) **1546 tholed,** *suffered* **1548 a pley,** *some fun* **1549 drough,** *approached,* **as noght ne were,** *as* (if it) *were nothing* **1550 Ful prively,** *very secretively,* **rowned,** *whispered* **1551 Herkne,** *listen* **1552 Herestow nat how that,** *don't you hear what*

1491 Job, God allowed Satan to afflict Job; Job 1.12, 2.6. **1496 body,** El reads "soule." **1498 a,** omitted in El. **1502 erchebisshop Seint Dunstan,** St. Dunstan, Archbishop of Canterbury (960–88), was reputed to have controlled demons. **1503 apostles servant,** in scripture (Acts 19.11–12) and saints' legends, the apostles had power over demons. **1506 elementz,** the four elements: fire, air, water, earth. **1510–11 Phitonissa . . . ,** in the Vulgate version of the biblical Chronicles (1 Paralipomenon 10.13), the Witch of Endor is called "pythonissam." In the Vulgate 1 Samuel 28.11 (1 Kings), she conjures the spirit of Samuel, who predicts to Saul the downfall of the Israelites. The spirit was later thought to be a demon, not Samuel's spirit. **1519–20, Virgile . . . Dant,** Virgil's *Aeneid* and Dante's *Inferno* include visits to hell or the underworld. **1532 thus,** El reads "and thus." **1543 Brok . . . Scot,** horse names.

Hent it anon°, for he hath yeve° it thee,
Bothe hey and cart, and eek his caples° thre."
"Nay," quod the devel, "God woot°, never a deel°.
It is nat his entente, trust thou me weel.
Axe° hym thyself, if thou nat trowest me°;
Or elles stynt° a while, and thou shalt see."
This cartere thakketh° his hors upon the croupe°,
And they bigonne drawen and to stoupe°.
"Heyt° now," quod he, "ther° Jhesu Crist yow blesse,
And al his handwerk°, bothe moore and lesse!
That was wel twight°, myn owene lyard° boy.
I pray God save thee, and Seinte Loy!
Now is my cart out of the slow°, pardee°."
"Lo, brother," quod the feend, "what tolde I thee?
Heere may ye se, myn owene deere brother,
The carl° spak oon°, but he thoghte another.
Lat us go forth abouten oure viage°;
Heere wynne I nothyng upon cariage."
Whan that they coomen somwhat out of towne,
This somonour to his brother gan to rowne°:
"Brother," quod he, "heere woneth° an old rebekke
That hadde almoost as lief to lese° hire nekke
As for to yeve a peny° of hir good°.
I wole han twelf pens°, though that she be wood°,
Or I wol sompne° hire unto oure office°;
And yet, God woot°, of hire knowe I no vice.
But for° thou kanst nat, as in this contree,
Wynne° thy cost°, taak heer ensample° of me."
This somonour clappeth° at the wydwes° gate.
"Com out," quod he, "thou olde virytrate°!
I trowe° thou hast som frere° or preest with thee."
"Who clappeth?" seyde this wyf, "Benedicitee°,
God save you, sire; what is youre sweete wille?"
"I have," quod he, "of somonce here a bille°.
Upon peyne of cursyng, looke that thou be
Tomorn° bifore the erchedeknes knee
T'answere to the court of certeyn thynges."
"Now, Lord," quod she, "Crist Jhesu, kyng of kynges,
So wisly° helpe me, as I ne may°.
I have been syk, and that ful many a day.
I may nat go so fer," quod she, "ne ryde,
But I be deed°, so priketh it in my syde.
May I nat axe a libel°, sire somonour,
And answere there by my procuratour°
To swich thyng as men wole opposen° me?"
"Yis," quod this somonour, "pay anon°—lat se—
Twelf pens to me, and I wol thee acquite.
I shal no profit han therby but lite;
My maister hath the profit and nat I.
Com of°, and lat me ryden hastily;
Yif° me twelf pens; I may no lenger tarye°."
"Twelf pens!" quod she, "Now, lady Seinte Marie
So wisly° help me out of care and synne,
This wyde world thogh that I sholde wynne,
Ne have I nat twelf pens withinne myn hoold°.
Ye knowen wel that I am poure and oold;
Kithe° youre almesse° on me, poure wrecche."
"Nay thanne," quod he, "the foule feend me fecche
If I th'excuse°, though° thou shul be spilt°!"
"Allas!" quod she, "God woot°, I have no gilt."
"Pay me," quod he, "or by the sweete Seinte Anne,
As I wol° bere awey thy newe panne
For dette° which that thou owest me of old.

1553 Hent it anon, *seize it now,* **yeve,** *given* **1554 caples,** *cart horses* **1555 woot,** *knows,* **never a deel,** *not at all* **1557 Axe,** *ask,* **nat trowest,** *don't believe* **1558 elles stynt,** *else wait* **1559 thakketh,** *pats,* **hors,** *horses,* **croupe,** *rump* **1560 stoupe,** *lean forward* **1561 Heyt,** *giddy up,* **ther,** *so that* **1562 handwerk,** *handiwork* **1563 twight,** *pulled,* **lyard,** *dappled* **1565 slow,** *mud,* **pardee,** *by God* **1568 carl,** *worker,* **oon,** *one* (thing) **1569 viage,** *journey* **1572 rowne,** *whisper* **1573 woneth,** *dwells* **1574 That hadde almoost as lief to lese,** *who would almost as willingly lose* **1575 yeve,** *give,* **good,** *property* **1576 wole han twelf pens,** *will have twelve pennies,* **wood,** *mad* **1577 sompne,** *summon,* **office,** *court* **1578 woot,** *knows* **1579 for,** *because* **1580 Wynne,** *earn,* **cost,** *expenses,* **taak heer ensample,** *take an example here* **1581 clappeth,** *knocks,* **wydwes,** *widow's* **1582 virytrate,** *hag* **1583 trowe,** *think,* **frere,** *friar* **1584 Benedicitee,** *bless you* **1586 of somonce . . . bille,** *a document of summons* **1588 Tomorn,** *in the morning* **1591 wisly,** *surely,* **ne may,** *cannot* **1594 But I be deed,** *or it will kill me* **1595 axe a libel,** *ask for a written copy* **1596 procuratour,** *representative* **1597 wole opposen,** *will bring against* **1598 anon,** *now* **1602 Com of,** *hurry* **1603 Yif,** *give,* **tarye,** *delay* **1605 wisly,** *surely* **1607 hoold,** *possession* **1609 Kithe,** *show,* **almesse,** *charity* **1611 th'excuse,** *excuse you,* **though,** *even if,* **spilt,** *ruined* **1612 woot,** *knows* **1614 As I wol,** *I will* **1615 dette,** *debt*

1559 thakketh, El and Hg read "taketh." **upon,** El reads "on." **1564 pray God,** El reads "pray to God." **Seinte Loy,** St. Eligius, patron saint of carters; see *GP* 1.120. **1568 oon,** Hg reads "o thyng." **1570 cariage,** a fee paid to a feudal lord in lieu of the lord's right to use his tenant's cart and horses; i.e., the devil knows he will profit nothing here. **1573 rebekke,** another term for fiddle, slang for "old woman"; see 1377n. **1587 Upon,** Hg reads "Up." **1596 procurator,** El and Hg read "procutour" (proctor). **1605 me out,** El and Hg read "me God out." **1613 Seinte Anne,** mother of Mary, grandmother of Jesus. **1615 that,** omitted in Hg.

Whan that thou madest thyn housbonde cokewold°,
I payde at hoom for thy correccioun°."
"Thou lixt°," quod she, "by my savacioun,
Ne was I nevere er° now, wydwe ne wyf,
Somoned unto youre court in al my lyf;
Ne nevere I nas but° of my body trewe°.
Unto the devel, blak and rough of hewe°,
Yeve° I thy body and my panne also!"
And whan the devel herde hire cursen so
Upon hir knees, he seyde in this manere,
"Now Mabely, myn owene moder deere,
Is this youre wyl in ernest that ye seye°?"
"The devel," quod she, "so fecche hym er he deye°,
And panne and al, but he wol hym° repente!"
"Nay, olde stot°, that is nat myn entente,"
Quod this somonour, "for to repente me
For any thyng that I have had of thee.
I wolde° I hadde thy smok and every clooth."
"Now brother," quod the devel, "be nat wrooth°;
Thy body and this panne been myne° by right.
Thou shalt° with me to helle yet tonyght,
Where thou shalt knowen of oure privetee°
Moore than a maister of dyvynytee°."
And with that word this foule feend hym hente°;
Body and soule he with the devel wente
Where as that somonours han hir° heritage.
And God, that maked after his ymage
Mankynde, save and gyde us alle and some,
And leve° thise somonours goode men bicome!

Lordynges, I koude han° toold yow, quod this Frere,
Hadde I had leyser° for this Somnour heere,
After the text of Crist, Poul, and John,
And of oure othere doctours many oon°,
Swiche peynes° that youre hertes myghte agryse°,
Al be it° so no tonge may it devyse°,
Thogh that I myghte a thousand wynter° telle,
The peynes of thilke cursed hous of helle.
But for to kepe us fro that cursed place,
Waketh and preyeth Jhesu for his grace
So kepe us fro the temptour Sathanas.
Herketh this word, beth war° as in this cas:
The leoun sit in his awayt alway
To sle° the innocent, if that he may.
Disposeth ay° youre hertes to withstonde
The feend that yow wolde make thral° and bonde°.
He may nat tempte yow over youre myght,
For Crist wol be youre champion and knyght.
And prayeth that thise somonours hem repente
Of hir mysdedes er° that the feend hem hente°!

Heere endeth the Freres Tale.

1616 madest . . . cokewold, *made your husband a victim of your adultery* **1617 correccioun,** *fine* **1618 Thou lixt,** *you lie* **1619 er,** *before* **1621 Ne nevere I nas but,** *nor was I ever* (anything) *but,* **trewe,** *faithful* (to my husband) **1622 hewe,** *appearance* **1623 Yeve,** *give* **1627 that ye seye,** *what you say* **1628 er he deye,** *before he dies* **1629 but he wol hym,** *unless he will* **1630 stot,** *cow* **1633 wolde,** *wish* **1634 wrooth,** *angry* **1635 been myne,** *are mine* **1636 shalt,** *shall* (go) **1637 privetee,** *secrets* **1638 dyvynytee,** *theology* **1639 hente,** *grabbed* **1641 han hir,** *have their* **1644 leve,** *let* **1645 koude han,** *could have* **1646 leyser,** *time* **1648 othere doctours many oon,** *many other theologians* **1649 Swiche peynes,** *such pains,* **agryse,** *terrify* **1650 Al be it so,** *even though,* **devyse,** *describe* **1651 wynter,** *years* **1656 beth war,** *be aware* **1658 sle,** *slay* **1659 Disposeth ay,** *prepare always* **1660 thral,** *slave,* **bonde,** *bound* **1664 mysdedes er,** *misdeeds before,* **hente,** *seizes*

1622 rough, Hg reads "row." **1636** A parody of Christ's words to the thief who repents; Luke 2343. **1644 bicome,** Hg reads "to bicome." **1647 After the text . . . ,** following scripture—the Gospels, Paul's letters, and John's Revelation. **1657 leoun . . . awayt,** lion sits waiting; Psalms 10.8–9. **1661** 1 Corinthians 10.13. **1663 thise,** Hg reads "this."

From woodcut made by W.H. Hooper and published by the Chaucer Society between 1868 and 1879

Summoner's Tale

Prologue

The Prologe of the Somonours Tale.

This Somonour in his styropes hye° stood;
Upon this Frere his herte was so wood°
That lyk an aspen leef he quook° for ire°.
"Lordynges," quod he, "but o° thyng I desire:
I yow biseke° that, of youre curteisye,
Syn° ye han herd this false Frere lye,
As suffreth me° I may my tale telle.
This Frere bosteth° that he knoweth helle,
And God it woot° that it is litel wonder—
Freres and feendes been but lyte asonder°.
For, pardee°, ye han ofte tyme herd telle
How that a frere ravysshed° was to helle
In spirit ones° by a visioun,
And as an angel ladde° hym up and doun
To shewen hym the peynes that ther were
In al the place saugh° he nat a frere;
Of oother folk he saugh ynowe° in wo.
Unto this angel spak the frere tho°,
'Now, sire,' quod he, 'han freres swich° a grace°
That noon of hem shal come to this place?'
'Yis,' quod this angel, 'many a millioun.'
And unto Sathanas° he ladde hym doun.
'And now hath Sathanas,' seith he, 'a tayl
Brodder than of a carryk° is the sayl.
Hold up thy tayl, thou Sathanas,' quod he.
'Shewe forth thyn ers°, and lat the frere se
Where is the nest of freres in this place!'
And er that half a furlong wey of space,
Right so° as bees out swarmen from an hyve,
Out of the develes ers ther gonne dryve
Twenty thousand freres in a route°,
And thurghout helle swarmeden aboute,
And comen agayn as faste as they may gon,
And in his ers they crepten everychon°.
He clapte° his tayl agayn and lay ful stille.
This frere, whan he hadde looke al his fille
Upon the tormentz of this sory place,
His spirit God restored, of his grace,

1665 styropes hye, *stirrups high* **1666 wood,** *angry* **1667 quook,** *trembled,* **ire,** *anger* **1668 but o,** *only one* **1669 biseke,** *request* **1670 Syn,** *since* **1671 As suffreth me,** *so allow me* **1672 bosteth,** *boasts* **1673 woot,** *knows* **1674 been but lyte asonder,** *are only a little different* **1675 pardee,** *by God* **1676 ravysshed,** *abducted* **1677 ones,** *once* **1678 ladde,** *led* **1680 saugh,** *saw* **1681 ynowe,** *enough* **1682 tho,** *then* **1683 swich,** *such,* **grace,** *favor* **1686 Sathanas,** *Satan* **1688 carryk,** *large ship* **1690 thyn ers,** *your arse* **1693 Right so,** *just* **1695 route,** *company* **1698 everychon,** *every one* **1699 clapte,** *closed*

1665 hye stood, Hg reads "hye he stood." **1676 ravysshed,** El reads "vanysshed." **1692 er that half a furlong wey of space,** before a minute or two (had passed). See *MilT* 1.3637n. **1695 in,** Hg reads "on." **1700 hadde looke al his,** Hg reads "looked hadde his."

Unto his body agayn, and he awook.
But natheles for fere° yet he quook°,
So was the develes ers ay in his mynde—
That is his heritage of verray kynde°.
God save yow alle, save this cursed Frere!
My prologe wol I ende in this manere."

Heere bigynneth the Somonour his Tale.

Lordynges, ther is in Yorkshire, as I gesse,
A mersshy° contree called Holdernesse
In which ther wente a lymytour aboute
To preche and eek to begge, it is no doute.
And so bifel that on a day this frere
Hadde preched at a chirche in his manere,
And specially, aboven every thyng,
Excited he the peple in his prechyng
To trentals, and to yeve° for Goddes sake
Wherwith men myghte hooly houses make°
Ther as divine servyce is honoured,
Nat ther as it is wasted and devoured,
Ne ther it nedeth nat for to be yeve°,
As to possessioners that mowen lyve°,
Thanked be God, in wele° and habundaunce.
"Trentals," seyde he, "deliveren fro penaunce
Hir° freendes soules, as wel olde as° yonge,
Ye°, whan that they been hastily ysonge,
Nat for to holde° a preest joly and gay—
He syngeth nat but o masse in a day.
Delivereth out," quod he, "anon° the soules.
Ful hard it is with flesshhook° or with oules°
To been yclawed°, or to brenne° or bake.
Now spede yow hastily, for Cristes sake!"
And whan this frere had seyd al his entente,
With *qui cum patre* forth his wey he wente.
Whan folk in chirche had yeve° him what hem leste°,
He wente his wey—no lenger wolde he reste—
With scrippe° and tipped staf°, ytukked hye°.
In every hous he gan to poure° and prye°,
And beggeth mele° and chese, or elles corn°.
His felawe hadde a staf tipped with horn,
A peyre of tables al of yvory,
And a poyntel° polysshed fetisly°,
And wroot the names alwey, as he stood,
Of alle folk that yaf° hym any good,
Ascaunces° that he wolde for hem preye.
"Yif° us a busshel whete, malt, or reye°,
A Goddes kechyl°, or a tryp° of chese,
Or elles what yow lyst°—we may nat cheese°—
A Goddes halfpeny, or a masse peny,
Or yif us of youre brawn°, if ye have eny,
A dagon° of youre blanket—leeve° dame,
Oure suster deere—lo, heere I write youre name—
Bacon or boef°, or swich thyng° as ye fynde."
A sturdy harlot° wente ay hem bihynde°,
That was hir hostes man°, and bar a sak°,
And what men yaf hem°, leyde it on his bak.
And whan that he was out at dore, anon
He planed° awey the names everichon°

1704 fere, *fear,* **quook,** *trembled* **1706 verray kynde,** *true nature* **1710 mersshy,** *marshy* **1717 yeve,** *give* **1718 make,** *build* **1721 yeve,** *given* **1722 mowen lyve,** *are able to live* **1723 wele,** *prosperity,* **1725 Hir,** *their,* **as wel . . . as,** *both . . . and* **1726 Ye,** *indeed* **1727 holde,** *keep* (support) **1729 anon,** *immediately* **1730 Ful hard,** *very painful,* **flesshhook,** *meat hook,* **oules,** *awls* **1731 been yclawed,** *be torn,* **brenne,** *burn* **1735 yeve,** *given,* **hem leste,** *pleased them* **1737 scrippe,** *bag,* **tipped staf,** *metal- or horn-tipped staff,* **ytukked hye,** (and cloak) *tucked up high* **1738 poure,** *examine,* **prye,** *peek* (into) **1739 mele,** *ground grain,* **elles corn,** *else whole grain* **1742 poyntel,** *stylus,* **fetisly,** *elegantly* **1744 yaf,** *gave* **1745 Ascaunces,** *as if to indicate* **1746 Yif,** *give,* **reye,** *rye* **1747 Goddes kechyl,** *small charity cake,* **tryp,** *bit* **1748 yow lyst,** *pleases you,* **cheese,** *choose* **1750 brawn,** *meat* **1751 dagon,** *piece,* **leeve,** *beloved* **1753 boef,** *beef,* **swich thyng,** *whatever* **1754 harlot,** *servant,* **wente ay hem bihynde,** *always traveled behind them* **1755 hir hostes man,** *their innkeeper's servant,* **bar,** *carried* **1756 yaf hem,** *gave them* **1758 planed,** *smoothed,* **everichon,** *every one*

1706 heritage, compare line 3.1641. **1707 save . . . save,** a powerful pun that initiates a series of word plays in *SumT*; see notes to lines 1793, 1877–78, 1916–17, 1934, 1967, 2148, 2185–87, and 2222. **1710 Holdernesse,** a district in Yorkshire, in northern England. Chaucer does not reproduce a northern accent here as he does in *RvT.* **1711 lymytour,** "a friar whose begging, preaching, and hearing of confessions was limited" to a particular territory (*MED*). See *GP* 1.209 and *FrT* 3.1265. **1717 trentals,** (the money paid for) thirty masses for the dead, conducted to release a soul from purgatory. **1721 for,** omitted in Hg. **1722 possessioners,** clergy (other than friars) who live on revenue from property or other endowments. **1726 hastily ysonge,** the friar recommends that the thirty masses be conducted (sung) simultaneously (by a group of friars rather than a single priest), presumably a quicker route to salvation than conducting one per day. **1734 *qui cum patre*,** "who with the father," a formula beginning for the closing of a prayer or sermon. **1737 scrippe and tipped staf,** satirizes friars' claims to be the new apostles, because Christ commanded his disciples to travel with neither sack nor staff (Luke 9.3). For other satiric details, see notes to lines 1740, 1770, 1820, and 2186–87. **1740 felawe,** friars were supposed to travel in pairs, in imitation of Christ's command to his disciples in Luke 10.1, but the "sturdy harlot" (line 1754) makes three. **1741 peyre of tables,** folding tablets, covered with wax for taking notes. **1746 us,** El reads "hym." **1749 Goddes halfpeny . . . masse peny,** money given as charity or as payment for a mass.

That he biforn had writen in his tables;
He served hem with nyfles° and with fables.
"Nay, ther thou lixt°, thou Somonour!" quod the Frere.
"Pees," quod oure Hoost, "for Cristes mooder deere.
Tel forth thy tale, and spare it nat at al°."
"So thryve I°," quod this Somonour, "so I shal."
So longe he wente, hous by hous, til he
Cam til° an hous ther he was wont° to be
Refresshed moore than in an hundred placis.
Syk° lay the goode man whos that the place is;
Bedrede° upon a couche lowe he lay.
"*Deus hic!*" quod he, "O Thomas, freend, good day,"
Seyde this frere, curteisly and softe.
"Thomas," quod he, "God yelde° yow. Ful ofte
Have I upon this bench faren ful weel°;
Heere have I eten many a myrie° meel."
And fro the bench he droof° awey the cat
And leyde adoun his potente° and his hat,
And eek his scrippe°, and sette hym softe adoun.
His felawe was go walked° into toun
Forth with his knave into that hostelrye
Where as he shoop° hym thilke° nyght to lye.
"O deere maister," quod this sike man,
"How han ye fare sith° that March bigan?
I saugh° yow noght this fourtenyght° or moore."
"God woot°," quod he, "laboured I have ful soore°,
And specially for thy savacioun
Have I seyd many a precious orisoun°,
And for oure othere freendes, God hem blesse!
I have to day been at youre chirche at messe,°
And seyd a sermon after my symple wit,
Nat al after the text of hooly writ;
For it is hard to° yow, as I suppose,
And therfore wol I teche° yow al the glose°.
Glosynge is a glorious thyng, certeyn,
For lettre sleeth, so as we clerkes seyn.
There° have I taught hem to be charitable,
And spende hir good ther° it is resonable;
And there I saugh oure dame—a, where is she?"
"Yond° in the yerd I trowe° that she be,"
Seyde this man, "and she wol come anon."
"Ey, maister, welcome be ye, by Seint John!"
Seyde this wyf, "How fare ye, hertely°?"
The frere ariseth up ful curteisly°
And hire embraceth in his armes narwe°,
And kiste hire sweete, and chirketh° as a sparwe
With his lyppes. "Dame," quod he, "right weel,
As he that is youre servant every deel°,
Thanked be God that yow yaf° soule and lyf.
Yet saugh I nat this day so fair a wyf
In al the chirche, God so save me!"
"Ye, God amende defautes°, sire," quod she.
"Algates°, welcome be ye, by my fey°!"
"Graunt mercy, dame, this have I founde alwey.
But of youre grete goodnesse, by youre leve,
I wolde prey yow that ye nat yow greve°,
I wole with Thomas speke a litel throwe°.
Thise curatz° been ful necligent and slowe
To grope° tendrely a conscience
In shrift; in prechyng is my diligence°,
And studie in Petres wordes and in Poules.
I walke and fisshe Cristen mennes soules
To yelden° Jhesu Crist his propre rente°;
To sprede his word is set al myn entente."
"Now, by your leve, O deere sire," quod she,
"Chideth° him weel, for seinte° Trinitee.
He is as angry as a pissemyre°
Though that he have al that he kan desire.
Though I hym wrye a-nyght° and make hym warm,

1760 nyfles, *trifles* **1761 lixt,** *lie* **1763 spare it nat at al,** *don't hold back* **1764 So thryve I,** *as I may prosper* **1766 til,** *to,* **wont,** *accustomed* **1768 Syk,** *sick* **1769 Bedrede,** *bedridden* **1772 yelde,** *reward* **1773 faren ful weel,** *done very well* **1774 myrie,** *merry* **1775 droof,** *drove* **1776 potente,** *staff* **1777 scrippe,** *bag* **1778 go walked,** *gone walking* **1780 shoop,** *planned,* **thilke,** *that* **1782 han ye fare sith,** *have you done since* **1783 saugh,** *saw,* **fourtenyght,** *fortnight* (two weeks) **1784 woot,** *knows,* **ful soore,** *very sorely* **1786 orisoun,** *prayer* **1788 messe,** *mass* **1791 hard to,** *difficult for* **1792 teche,** *teach,* **glose,** *interpretation* **1795 There,** *i.e., "in church"* **1796 hir good ther,** *their money where* **1798 Yond,** *over there,* **trowe,** *believe* **1801 hertely,** *with all my heart* **1802 curteisly,** *courteously* **1803 narwe,** *closely* **1804 chirketh,** *chirps* **1806 every deel,** *in every way* **1807 yow yaf,** *gave to you* **1810 amende defautes,** *repair* (my) *faults* **1811 Algates,** *always,* **fey,** *faith* **1814 yow greve,** *be upset* **1815 throwe,** *while* **1816 curatz,** *resident priests* **1817 grope,** *examine* **1818 diligence,** *concern* **1821 yelden,** *pay,* **propre rente,** *due income* **1824 Chideth,** *scold,* **seinte,** (the) *holy* **1825 pissemyre,** *ant* **1827 wrye a-nyght,** *cover at night*

1770 *Deus hic,* "God be here"; see Matthew 10.12. **1781 maister,** address of respect, accepted by the friar here and at lines 1800 and 1836, but see lines 2185–87 below. **1793 Glosynge . . . ,** "glossing" or interpreting (but also distorting or deceiving, a potent double entendre; see *MED* "gloze"). The friar defends his practice of interpreting scripture by alluding to St. Paul's assertion that the "letter slays" and the "spirit gives life" (2 Corinthians 3.6). The distinction recurs at 1919–20 below. **1794 we,** El reads "thise." **1804 sparwe,** sparrow, thought to be lecherous. **1818 shrift,** confession, the sacrament of the forgiveness of sins that involves a preparatory examination of conscience. **1820 fisshe . . . mennes soules,** the friar here claims to be a disciple of Christ; see Matthew 4.19.

And on hym leye my leg outher° myn arm;
He groneth lyk oure boor lith° in oure sty.
Oother desport° right noon of hym have I;
I may nat plese hym in no maner cas."
"O Thomas, *je vous dy,* Thomas! Thomas!
This maketh the feend; this moste ben amended.
Ire° is a thyng that hye° God defended°,
And therof wol I speke a word or two."
"Now, maister," quod the wyf, "er that I go,
What wol ye dyne°? I wol go theraboute."
"Now, dame," quod he, "now *je vous dy sanz doute,*
Have I nat of a capon° but the lyvere°,
And of youre softe breed nat but a shyvere°,
And after that a rosted pigges heed—
But° that I nolde no° beest for me were deed—
Thanne hadde I with yow hoomly suffisaunce°.
I am a man of litel sustenaunce°;
My spirit hath his fostryng° in the Bible.
The body is ay° so redy and penyble°
To wake° that my stomak° is destroyed.
I prey yow, dame, ye be nat anoyed,
Though I so freendly yow my conseil shewe°.
By God, I wolde nat telle it but a fewe."
"Now, sire," quod she, "but o word er I go.
My child is deed withinne thise wykes two,
Soone after that ye wente out of this toun."
"His deeth saugh° I by revelacioun,"
Seith this frere, "at hoom in oure dortour°.
I dar wel seyn that er that half an hour
After his deeth I saugh hym born° to blisse
In myn avisioun, so God me wisse°.
So dide oure sexteyn and oure fermerer,
That han been trewe freres fifty yeer;
They may now—God be thanked of his loone°—
Maken hir° jubilee and walke allone.
And up I roos, and al oure covent eke°,
With many a teere trillyng° on my cheke,
Withouten noyse or claterynge of belles;
Te Deum was oure song, and nothyng elles.
Save that to Crist I seyde an orisoun°,
Thankynge hym of° his revelacioun.
For, sire and dame, trusteth me right weel,
Oure orisons been moore effectueel°,
And moore we seen of Cristes secree° thynges,
Than burel° folk, although they weren kynges.
We lyve in poverte and in abstinence,
And burell folk in richesse and despence°
Of mete and drynke, and in hir foul delit.
We han this worldes lust al in despit°.
Lazar and Dives lyveden° diversly,
And diverse gerdon° hadden they therby.
Whoso wol preye, he moot° faste and be clene°,
And fatte° his soule, and make his body lene.
We fare as seith th'apostle; clooth° and foode
Suffisen us, though they be nat ful° goode.
The clennesse° and the fastynge of us freres
Maketh that Crist accepteth oure preyeres.
"Lo, Moyses fourty dayes and fourty nyght
Fasted er° that the heighe God of myght
Spak with hym in the Mount of Synay.
With empty wombe°, fastynge many a day,
Receyved he the lawe that was writen
With Goddes fynger; and Elye, wel ye witen°,
In Mount Oreb, er he hadde any speche
With hye God that is oure lyves leche°,
He fasted longe and was in contemplaunce°.
"Aaron, that hadde the temple in governaunce,

1828 outher, *or* **1829 lyk oure boor lith,** *like our* (male) *pig* (that) *lies* **1830 desport,** *entertainment* **1832 *je vous dy,*** *I say to you* **1834 Ire,** *anger,* **hye,** *high,* **defended,** *forbade* **1837 dyne,** *eat* **1839 capon,** *chicken,* **lyvere,** *liver* **1840 shyvere,** *sliver* **1842 But,** *except,* **nolde no,** *wish no* **1843 hoomly suffisaunce,** *family fare* **1844 of litel sustenaunce,** *who eats little* **1845 his fostryng,** *its nourishment* **1846 ay,** *always,* **penyble,** *painstaking* **1847 To wake,** *to stay awake,* **stomak,** *appetite* **1849 conseil shewe,** *secrets reveal* **1854 saugh,** *saw* **1855 dortour,** *dormitory* **1857 born,** *carried* **1858 wisse,** *instruct* **1861 loone,** *gift* **1862 hir,** *their* **1863 covent eke,** *assembly also* **1864 trillyng,** *trickling* **1867 orisoun,** *prayer* **1868 of,** *for* **1870 effectueel,** *effective* **1871 secree,** *secret* **1872 burel,** *nonreligious* **1874 despence,** *consumption* **1876 despit,** *scorn* **1877 lyveden,** *lived* **1878 gerdon,** *reward* **1879 moot,** *must,* **clene,** *pure* **1880 fatte,** *fatten* **1881 clooth,** *clothing* **1882 ful,** *very* **1883 clennesse,** *purity* **1886 er,** *before* **1888 wombe,** *stomach* **1890 witen,** *know* **1892 leche,** *physician* **1893 contemplaunce,** *contemplation*

1838 *je vous dy sanz doute,* "I say to you without doubt." The use of French and the repetition from line 1832 suggest affectation. **1859 sexteyn . . . fermerer,** two officers in the friar's convent, the first responsible for the sacred vessels and vestments, the second for the infirmary. **1862 jubilee and walke allone,** privileges such as walking without a companion (see 1740n above) were granted to friars at jubilee (fiftieth) anniversaries. **1864 trillyng,** El and Hg read "triklyng." **1866 *Te Deum,*** "To You O God," a hymn of praise, regularly sung to conclude matins (see *MilT* 1.3655n) but also sung to celebrate outstanding events or occasions. **1870 moore,** El and Hg read "wel moore." **1872 althogh they,** Hg reads "althogh that they." **1877 Lazar and Dives,** the biblical poor man and rich man; Luke 16.19–31. This and the other biblical allusions from here to line 1917 derive from St. Jerome's *Epistola adversus Jovinianum* (*Letter against Jovinian*), book 2, here 2.17. Also, note the play with "Dives," "diversly," and "diverse," lines 1877–78. **1881 th'apostle,** Paul, in 1 Timothy 6.8; Jerome 2.11. **1885–90 Moyses . . . ,** on Mt. Sinai, Moses fasted (Exodus 34.28) before he received for the second time the Ten Commandments written by God (see Exodus 31.18); Jerome 2.15. **1890–93 Elye . . . ,** Elijah fasted and spoke with God on Mount Horeb (1 Kings 19.8; Vulgate 3 Kings) Jerome 2.15. **1894–1901 Aaron . . . ,** Leviticus. 10.8–9; Jerome 2.15.

And eek the othere preestes everichon°
Into the temple whan they sholde gon
To preye for the peple and do servyse,
They nolden° drynken in no maner wyse
No drynke which that myghte hem dronke
make,
But there in abstinence preye and wake
Lest that they deyden°. Taak heede what I seye.
But° they be sobre that for the peple preye,
War° that I seye—namoore, for it suffiseth.
"Oure Lord Jhesu, as hooly writ devyseth°,
Yaf° us ensample of fastynge and preyeres.
Therfore we mendynantz°, we sely° freres,
Been wedded to poverte and continence°,
To charite, humblesse, and abstinence,
To persecucioun for rightwisnesse°,
To wepynge, misericorde°, and clennesse°.
And therfore may ye se that oure preyeres—
I speke of us, we mendynantz, we freres—
Been to the hye God moore acceptable
Than youres, with youre feestes at the table.
Fro Paradys first, if I shal nat lye,
Was man out chaced for his glotonye—
And chaast was man in Paradys, certeyn.
"But herkne° now, Thomas, what I shal seyn°.
I ne have no text of° it, as I suppose,
But I shal fynde it in a maner glose°
That specially oure sweete Lord Jhesus
Spak this by° freres whan he seyde thus,
'Blessed be they that povere° in spirit been.'
And so forth al the gospel may ye seen
Wher it be likker° oure professioun
Or hirs° that swymmen in possessioun.
Fy° on hire° pompe and on hire glotonye,
And for hir lewednesse I hem diffye°.
"Me thynketh they been lyk Jovinyan,
Fat as a whale and walkynge as a swan,
Al vinolent° as botel in the spence°.
Hir° preyere is of ful greet reverence
Whan they for soules seye the psalm of Davit:
Lo, 'buf°!' they seye, *'cor meum eructavit!'*
Who folweth Cristes gospel and his foore°
But we that humble been, and chaast, and poore,
Werkeris° of Goddes word, nat auditours°?
Therfore, right° as an hauk up at a sours°
Up springeth into th'eir, right so prayeres
Of charitable and chaste bisy freres
Maken hir sours° to Goddes eres two.
Thomas, Thomas, so moote I° ryde or go,
And by that lord that clepid° is Seint Yve,
Nere thou° oure brother, sholdestou° nat thryve.
In oure chapitre° praye we day and nyght
To Crist that he thee sende heele° and myght
Thy body for to weelden hastily°."
"God woot°," quod he, "nothyng therof feele I!
As help me Crist, as° I in a fewe yeres
Have spended upon diverse manere freres°
Ful many a pound, yet fare I never the bet°.
Certeyn, my good° I have almoost biset°.
Farwel, my gold, for it is al ago°."
The frere answerde, "O Thomas, dostow° so?
What nedeth yow diverse freres seche°?
What nedeth hym that hath a parfit leche°
To sechen othere leches in the toun?
Youre inconstance° is youre confusioun.
Holde ye thanne° me, or elles oure covent°,
To praye for yow been insufficient?
Thomas, that jape° nys nat worth a myte°.

1895 everichon, *each one* **1898 nolden,** *would not* **1901 Lest . . . deyden,** *in order that they would not die* **1902 But,** *unless* **1903 War,** *beware* **1904 devyseth,** *describes* **1905 Yaf,** *gave* **1906 mendynantz,** *begging friars* (mendicants), **sely,** *blessed* **1907 continence,** *restraint* **1909 for rightwisnesse,** *for the sake of righteousness* **1910 misericorde,** *mercy,* **clennesse,** *purity* **1918 herkne,** *listen,* **seyn,** *say* **1919 ne have no text of,** *have no biblical quotation for* **1920 maner glose,** *kind of interpretation* **1922 by,** *about* **1923 povere,** *poor* **1925 Wher it be likker,** *whether the gospel be closer to* **1926 hirs,** *theirs* **1927 Fy,** *fie,* **hire,** *their* **1928 diffye,** *defy* **1931 vinolent,** *full of wine,* **spence,** *storeroom* **1932 Hir,** *their* **1934 buf,** *burp* **1935 foore,** *footsteps* **1937 Werkeris,** *doers,* **auditours,** *listeners* **1938 right,** *just,* **up at a sours,** *soaring* **1941 hir sours,** *their soarings* **1942 so moote I,** *as I might* **1943 clepid,** *named* **1944 Nere thou,** (if) *you were not,* **sholdestou,** *you should* **1945 chapitre,** *assembly* **1946 heele,** *health* **1947 weelden hastily,** *use soon* **1948 woot,** *knows* **1949 as,** *though* **1950 diverse maner freres,** *various kinds of friars* **1951 bet,** *better* **1952 good,** *wealth,* **biset,** *spent* **1953 ago,** *gone* **1954 dostow,** *do you* **1955 What nedeth yow . . . seche,** *why do you need to seek* **1956 parfit leche,** *perfect physician* **1958 inconstance,** *inconsistency* **1959 Holde ye thanne,** *do you consider then,* **covent,** *assembly* **1961 jape,** *joke,* **myte,** *worthless coin*

1916–17 chaced . . . chaast, chased . . . chaste; the play links gluttony in Paradise (Adam's eating of the apple) and lechery (desire for Eve). Genesis 3.6–7; Jerome 2.15. **1918 now,** omitted in El and Hg. **1919–20 text . . . glose,** see 1793n above. **1923** Matthew 5.3. The claim is ironic since friars in the fourteenth century were notorious for self-indulgence. **1926 hirs,** Hg reads "hire." **1929 Jovinyan,** the target of St. Jerome's ascetic defense of celibacy and fasting, *Letter against Jovinian;* Jovinian is described in similar terms in the treatise, 1.40. See 1877n above. **1933 Davit,** King David, thought to be the composer of the biblical book of Psalms. **1934 buf,** El reads "but." ***cor meum eructavit,*** "my heart has uttered," the opening words of Psalm 45 (Vulgate 44), but a pun because *eructavit* also means "belched," as "buf" imitates the sound of a burp. **1935** Echoes Matthew 19.21, but also Jerome 2.6. **1937** James 1.22, but also Jerome 2.3. **1943 Seint Yve,** there were several saints named Ives, none clearly appropriate here. **1944 oure brother,** a lay member of the friar's convent. **1949 as I in a,** El omits "I"; Hg omits "a." **1950 Have,** El reads "I han."

Youre maladye is for° we han to lyte°.
A, yif° that covent half a quarter otes°!
A, yif that covent foure and twenty grotes°!
A, yif that frere a peny and lat hym go!
Nay, nay, Thomas, it may no thyng be so!
What is a ferthyng° worth parted in twelve?
Lo, ech thyng that is oned° in itselve
Is moore strong than whan it is toscatered°.
Thomas, of me thou shalt nat been yflatered;
Thou woldest han° oure labour al for noght.
The hye God, that al this world hath wroght,
Seith that the werkman worthy is his hyre°.
Thomas, noght of youre tresor I desire
As for myself, but that al oure covent
To preye for yow is ay° so diligent,
And for to buylden Cristes owene chirche.
Thomas, if ye wol lernen for to wirche°,
Of buyldynge up of chirches may ye fynde
If it be good in Thomas lyf of Inde.
Ye lye heere ful of anger and of ire,
With which the devel set youre herte afyre,
And chiden° heere the sely° innocent,
Youre wyf, that is so meke and pacient.
And therfore, Thomas, trowe° me if thee leste°,
Ne stryve nat with thy wyf, as for thy beste°.
And ber° this word awey now, by thy feith,
Touchynge this thyng, lo, what the wise seith:
'Withinne thyn hous ne be° thou no leoun;
To thy subgitz° do noon oppressioun;
Ne make thyne aqueyntance nat for to flee.'
And, Thomas, yet eftsoones° I charge° thee,
Bewar from° ire that in thy bosom slepeth,
Bewar fro the serpent that so slily crepeth
Under the gras and styngeth subtilly°.
Bewar, my sone, and herkne° paciently
That twenty thousand men han° lost hir lyves
For stryvyng with hir lemmans° and hir wyves.
Now sith° ye han so hooly meke° a wyf,
What nedeth yow, Thomas, to maken stryf?
Ther nys, ywys°, no serpent so cruel
Whan man tret° on his tayl, ne half so fel°
As womman is, whan she hath caught an ire;
Vengeance is thanne al that they desire.
Ire is a synne, oon of the grete of sevene,
Abhomynable unto the God of hevene;
And to hymself it is destruccioun.
This every lewed viker° or persoun°
Kan seye, how ire engendreth° homycide.
Ire is, in sooth°, executour of pryde°.
I koude° of ire seye so muche sorwe
My tale sholde laste til tomorwe.
And therfore preye I God bothe day and nyght
An irous° man, God sende hym litel myght!
It is greet harm and certes° greet pitee
To sette an irous man in heigh degree°.
"Whilom° ther was an irous potestat°,
As seith Senek, that durynge his estaat°
Upon a day out ryden knyghtes two,
And as Fortune wolde that it were so
That oon of hem° cam hoom that oother noght.
Anon the knyght bifore the juge is broght,
That seyde thus, 'Thou hast thy felawe slayn
For which I deme° thee to the deeth, certayn.'
And to another knyght comanded he,
'Go lede hym to the deeth, I charge° thee.'
And happed as they wente by the weye
Toward the place ther° he sholde deye,
The knyght cam which° men wenden° had be deed.
Thanne thoughte they it were the beste reed°
To lede hem bothe to the juge agayn.

1962 for, *because,* **to lyte,** *too little* **1963 yif,** *give,* **quarter otes,** *quarter* (measure of) *oats* **1964 grotes,** *silver coins* (worth four pennies) **1967 ferthyng,** *farthing* (coin worth a quarter penny) **1968 oned,** *united* **1969 toscatered,** *scattered around* **1971 woldest han,** *wish to have* **1973 hyre,** *pay* **1976 ay,** *always* **1978 for to wirche,** *to do good works* **1983 chiden,** *scold,* **sely,** *blessed* **1985 trowe,** *believe,* **leste,** *will* **1986 beste,** *benefit* **1987 ber,** *carry* **1989 ne be,** *do not be* **1990 subgitz,** *subjects* **1992 eftsoones,** *again,* **charge,** *order* **1993 Bewar from,** *beware of,* **1995 subtilly,** *stealthily* **1996 herkne,** *listen* **1997 han,** *have* **1998 lemmans,** *lovers* **1999 sith,** *since,* **hooly meke,** *wholly meek* **2001 ywys,** *certainly* **2002 tret,** *steps,* **fel,** *dangerous* **2008 lewed viker,** *unlearned vicar* (priest's representative), **persoun,** *parson* **2009 engendreth,** *produces* **2010 sooth,** *truth,* **executour of pryde,** *pride's representative* **2011 koude,** *could* **2014 irous,** *angry* **2015 certes,** *certainly* **2016 degree,** *rank* **2017 Whilom,** *once,* **potestat,** *ruler* **2018 estaat,** *time of rule* **2021 oon of hem,** *one of them* **2024 deme,** *judge* **2026 charge,** *order* **2028 ther,** *where* **2029 which,** *who,* **wenden,** *believed* **2030 reed,** *counsel*

1967 ferthyng . . . parted in twelve, this punningly anticipates lines 2253ff. below. **1968–69** Proverbial, but its application to "thyng" is unusual, emphasized here by repetition, lines 1966–68. **1968 itselve,** Hg reads "hymselve." **1973** Translates Luke 10.7, which continues, "Go not from house to house." **1980 Thomas lyf of Inde,** the life of Thomas of India; Thomas the Apostle was reputed to have traveled to India as a preacher and carpenter. **1981 and,** omitted in El. **1988 this,** Hg reads "swich." **1989–91** Ecclesiasticus 4.35. **1993 ire,** El and Hg read "hire." El and Hg vary more frequently from here to the end of *SumT,* indicating that the scribe changed exemplars at or near this point while copying one of them, probably El. **1994 Bewar,** Hg reads "War." **2002 Whan,** El reads "What." **2005 grete of sevene,** greatest of seven; Ire (Anger or Wrath) is one of the seven deadly sins, along with Pride, Envy, Sloth, Avarice, Gluttony, and Lechery. **2015 certes,** El reads "eek." **2018 Senek . . . ,** the following illustrations derive from Seneca's *De Ira* (first century CE), although Chaucer probably got them from a preachers' manual such as John of Wales's *Communiloquium* (*Common Sayings*) 1.4.4, 1.3.11, and 2.8.2–3. Such illustrations were common in sermons against Ire.

They seiden, 'Lord, the knyght ne hath nat slayn
His felawe; heere he standeth hool° alyve.'
'Ye shul be deed,' quod he, 'so moot I thryve°,
That is to seyn, bothe oon, and two, and thre.'
And to the firste knyght right thus spak he,
'I dampned° thee; thou most algate° be deed.
And thou also most nedes lese° thyn heed
For thou art cause why thy felawe deyth°.'
And to the thridde knyght right thus he seith,
'Thou hast nat doon that° I comanded thee.'
And thus he dide doon sleen hem° alle thre.
"Irous Cambises was eek dronkelewe°
And ay° delited hym to been a shrewe°.
And so bifel°, a lord of his meynee°
That loved vertuous moralitee
Seyde on a day bitwene hem two right thus,
'A lord is lost if he be vicius,
And dronkenesse is eek a foul record
Of any man, and namely° in a lord.
Ther is ful many an eye and many an ere
Awaityng on° a lord and he noot° where.
For Goddes love, drynk moore attemprely°!
Wyn maketh° man to lesen° wrecchedly
His mynde and eek his lymes° everichon.'
'The revers° shaltou se,' quod he, 'anon°,
And preve it by thyn owene experience,
That wyn ne dooth to folk no swich° offence.
Ther is no wyn bireveth me° my myght
Of hand ne foot, ne of myne eyen sight.'
And for despit° he drank ful muchel moore
An hondred part° than he hadde bifoore;
And right anon this irous, cursed wrecche
Leet this knyghtes sone bifore hym fecche°,
Comandynge hym he sholde bifore hym stonde.
And sodeynly he took his bowe in honde,
And up the streng he pulled to his ere,
And with an arwe he slow° the child right there.
'Now wheither° have I a siker° hand or noon?'
Quod he. 'Is al my myght and mynde agon?
Hath wyn byreved me° myn eyen sight?'
"What sholde I telle th'answere of the knyght?
His sone was slayn, ther is namoore to seye.
Beth war, therfore, with lordes how ye pleye.
Syngeth *Placebo* and 'I shal if I kan,'
But if° it be unto a poure man.
To a poure man men sholde his vices telle,
But nat to a lord thogh he sholde go to helle.
"Lo° irous Cirus, thilke Percien,
How he destroyed the ryver of Gysen
For that° an hors of his was dreynt° therinne
Whan that he wente Babiloigne to wynne°.
He made that the ryver was so smal
That wommen myghte wade it over al.
Lo, what seyde he that so wel teche kan:
Ne be no° felawe to an irous man,
Ne with no wood° man walke by the weye,
Lest thee repente—I wol no ferther seye.
"Now, Thomas, leeve° brother, lef thyn° ire;
Thou shalt me fynde as just as is a squyre°.
Hoold nat the develes knyf ay° at thyn herte—
Thyn angre dooth thee al to soore smerte°—
But shewe to me al thy confessioun."
"Nay," quod the sike man, "by Seint Symoun,
I have be shryven° this day at° my curat°.
I have hym toold hoolly al myn estat°.
Nedeth° namoore to speken of it," seith he,
"But if me list°, of myn humylitee."
"Yif° me thanne of thy gold, to make oure cloystre,"
Quod he, "for many a muscle° and many an oystre,

2033 hool, *wholly* **2034 so moot I thryve,** *as I may thrive* **2037 dampned,** *condemned,* **algate,** *surely* **2038 nedes lese,** *necessarily lose* **2039 deyth,** *dies* **2041 that,** *what* **2042 dide doon sleen hem,** *did have them slain* **2043 eek dronkelewe,** *also a drunkard* **2044 ay,** *always,* **shrewe,** *wicked person* **2045 bifel,** *it happened,* **meynee,** *household* **2050 namely,** *especially* **2052 Awaityng on,** *watching,* **noot,** *knows not* **2053 attemprely,** *temperately* **2054 Wyn maketh,** *wine causes,* **lesen,** *lose* **2055 lymes,** *limbs* **2056 revers,** *opposite,* **anon,** *immediately* **2058 swich,** *such* **2059 bireveth me,** (that) *deprives me of* **2061 despit,** *spite* **2062 part,** *times* **2064 Leet . . . fecche,** *had . . . brought* **2068 slow,** *slew* **2069 wheither,** (tell me) *whether,* **siker,** *steady* **2071 byreved me,** *deprived me of* **2076 But if,** *unless* **2079 Lo,** *consider* **2081 For that,** *because,* **dreynt,** *drowned* **2082 Babiloigne to wynne,** *to conquer Babylon* **2086 Ne be no,** *do not be a* **2087 wood,** *angry* **2089 leeve,** *dear,* **lef thyn,** *abandon your* **2090 squyre,** *carpenter's square* **2091 ay,** *always* **2092 to soore smerte,** *too much pain* **2095 be shryven,** *been absolved,* **at,** *by,* **curat,** *local priest* **2096 estat,** (spiritual) *condition* **2097 Nedeth,** *I need* **2098 list,** *wish* **2099 Yif,** *give* **2100 muscle,** *mussel*

2035 That, Hg reads "This." **2043 Cambises,** king of Persia. In Seneca's *De Ira*, but see 2018n above. **2052 noot where,** Hg reads "noot nat where." **2062 hadde bifoore,** Hg reads "hadde doon bifoore." **2075 *Placebo*,** "I will please"; Vulgate Psalms 114.9. The word came to imply subservient flattery; see *MerT* 4.1476ff. **2079 Cirus, thilke Percien,** Cyrus (the Great), the Persian. In Seneca's *De Ira*, but see 2018n above. **2080 ryver of Gysen,** Gyndes River, a tributary of the Tigris in southwestern Asia. **2085 he,** Solomon, author of Proverbs. **2086–87** Proverbs 22.24–25; John of Wales 2.8.2. See 2018n above. **2088 I wol no ferther seye,** El reads "ther is namoore to seye." **2094 Symoun,** St. Simon the disciple (Mark 3.18) or possibly Simon Magus, a sorcerer who competed with the apostles and sought to purchase their spiritual power (Acts 8.9ff.). **2099 cloystre,** cloister, the friars' place of residence.

Whan othere men han° ben ful wel at eyse,
Hath been oure foode, oure cloystre for to reyse°.
And yet, God woot°, unnethe° the fundement°
Parfourned° is, ne° of oure pavement°
Nys nat° a tyle° yet withinne oure wones°.
By God, we owen fourty pound for stones.
"Now help, Thomas, for hym that harwed helle!
For elles moste° we oure bookes selle.
And if yow lakke oure predicacioun°,
Thanne goth the world al to destruccioun.
For whoso wolde us fro this world bireve°,
So God me save, Thomas, by youre leve,
He wolde bireve out of this world the sonne°.
For who kan teche and werchen as we konne°?
And that is nat of litel tyme°," quod he,
"But syn° Elye was, or Elise,
Han° freres been, that fynde I of record,
In charitee, ythanked be oure Lord.
Now Thomas, help, for seinte° charitee!"
And doun anon he sette hym on his knee°.
This sike man wax wel ny wood° for ire;
He wolde that the frere had been on fire,
With his false dissymulacioun.
"Swich° thyng as is in my possessioun,"
Quod he, "that may I yeven°, and noon oother.
Ye sey° me thus, that I am youre brother?"
"Ye, certes," quod the frere, "trusteth weel.
I took oure dame oure lettre and oure seel."
"Now wel," quod he, "and somwhat shal I yeve
Unto youre hooly covent whil I lyve;
And in thyn hand thou shalt it have anon°
On this condicion and oother noon,
That thou departe° it so, my leeve brother,
That every frere have also muche as oother.
This shaltou° swere on thy professioun°,
Withouten fraude or cavillacioun°."
"I swere it," quod this frere, "by my feith!"
And therwithal his hand in his he leith°,
"Lo, heer° my feith°; in me shal be no lak."
"Now thanne, put in thyn hand doun by my bak,"
Seyde this man, "and grope wel bihynde.
Bynethe° my buttok ther shaltow° fynde
A thyng that I have hyd in pryvetee."
"A," thoghte this frere, "this shal go with me!"
And doun his hand he launcheth° to the clifte°
In hope for to fynde there a yifte.
And whan this sike man felte this frere
Aboute his tuwel° grope there and heere,
Amydde his hand he leet the frere a fart—
Ther nys no capul drawynge in° a cart
That myghte have lete a fart of swich° a soun.
The frere up stirte as dooth a wood leoun°,
"A, false cherl°," quod he, "for Goddes bones!
This hastow° for despit° doon for the nones°.
Thou shalt abye° this fart, if that I may."
His meynee°, whiche that herden this affray°,
Cam lepynge in and chaced out the frere.
And forth he gooth with a ful angry cheere°
And fette° his felawe, ther° as lay his stoor°.
He looked as it° were a wilde boor;
He grynte with his teeth, so was he wrooth°.
A sturdy paas° doun to the court he gooth
Wher as ther woned° a man of greet honour
To whom that he was alwey confessour.

2101 han, *have,* **eyse,** *ease* **2102 reyse,** *build* **2103 woot,** *knows,* **unnethe,** *scarcely,* **fundement,** *foundation* **2104 Parfourned,** *completed,* **ne,** *nor,* **pavement,** *flooring* **2105 Nys nat,** (there) *is not,* **tyle,** *tile,* **wones,** *dwelling* **2108 moste,** *must* **2109 predicacioun,** *preaching* **2111 us fro this world bireve,** *deprive the world of us* **2113 sonne,** *sun* **2114 konne,** *can* **2115 is nat of litel tyme,** *has not* (been true) *for only a short time* **2116 syn,** *since* **2117 Han,** *have* **2119 seinte,** *holy* **2120 sette hym on his knee,** *knelt* **2121 wax wel ny wood,** *grew nearly insane* **2124 Swich,** *such* **2125 yeven,** *give* **2126 sey,** *tell* **2131 anon,** *soon* **2133 departe,** *divide,* **leeve,** *beloved* **2135 shaltou,** *shall you,* **professioun,** *sacred vows* **2136 cavillacioun,** *quibbling* **2138 leith,** *lays* **2139 heer,** *here is,* **feith,** *pledge* **2142 Bynethe,** *beneath,* **shaltow,** *shall you* **2145 launcheth,** *thrusts,* **clifte,** *crack* (of the butt) **2148 tuwel,** *chimney* (anus) **2150 nys no capul drawynge in,** *is no horse pulling* **2151 swich,** *such* **2152 wood leoun,** *enraged lion* **2153 cherl,** *rascal* **2154 hastow,** *have you,* **despit,** *spite,* **for the nones,** *at this time* **2155 abye,** *pay for* **2156 meynee,** *household,* **affray,** *disruption* **2158 cheere,** *expression* **2159 fette,** *fetched,* **ther,** *where,* **stoor,** *loot* **2160 as it,** *as* (if) *he* **2161 wrooth,** *angered* **2162 sturdy paas,** *quick pace* **2163 woned,** *dwelled*

2107 hym that harwed helle, Christ, whose breaking down of the gates of hell to release meritorious souls ("harrowing of hell") is recounted in the apocryphal Gospel of Nicodemus. **2108 For elles moste,** Hg reads "Or ellis mote." **2111–13** Cicero, *De Amicitia* (On Friendship) 13.47; John of Wales 2.8.3. See 2018n above. **2111 wolde us fro this world bireve,** Hg reads "fro this world wolde us bireve." **2116 Elye . . . Elise,** Elijah . . . Elisha, who gathered the Israelites on Mt. Carmel; 1 Kings 18. Carmelite friars claimed that their order was founded by Elijah, but no orders of friars were created before the thirteenth century. El reads "Ennok" for "Elye." **2122 on fire,** Hg reads "afire." **2128 oure dame oure lettre and oure seel,** the friar has given to Thomas's wife a letter embossed with the convent's seal that confirms that Thomas and his wife are lay members of the convent; see 1944n above. Hg reads "lettre with" for "lettre and." **2133 leeve,** Hg reads "deere." **2134 also,** Hg reads "as." **2137 by,** Hg reads "upon." **2140 in,** omitted in Hg. **2144 this shal,** Hg reads "that shal." **2148 grope,** at line 1817, the friar says he has "groped" Thomas's conscience. **2158** In seven manuscripts the tale ends here with the following conclusion: "He had noght elles for his longe sermoun / To parte amonge his bredern when he come home / And thus is this tale of the Frere ydo, / For we were almost at the toune." **2160 it,** Hg reads "he." **2163 ther,** omitted in El.

This worthy man was lord of that village.
This frere cam as he were in a rage
Where as this lord sat etyng at his bord°.
Unnethes° myghte the frere speke a word,
Til atte laste he seyde, "God yow see°!"
  This lord gan looke°, and seide, "Benedicitee°,
What, Frere John, what maner world is this°?
I se wel that some thyng ther is amys°;
Ye looken as° the wode were ful of thevys°.
Sit doun anon and tel me what youre grief is,
And it shal been amended, if I may."
  "I have," quod he, "had a despit° this day,
God yelde° yow, adoun in youre village,
That in this world is noon so poure a page°
That he nolde° have abhomynacioun
Of that° I have receyved in youre toun.
And yet ne greveth me nothyng° so soore
As that this olde cherl with lokkes hoore°
Blasphemed hath oure hooly covent eke."
  "Now, maister," quod this lord, "I yow biseke°—"
  "No maister, sire," quod he, "but servitour°,
Thogh I have had in scole that honour.
God liketh nat that 'Raby' men us calle
Neither in market ne in youre large halle."
  "No fors°," quod he, "but tel me al youre grief."
  "Sire," quod this frere, "an odious meschief
This day bityd is° to myn ordre and me,
And so, *per consequens*°, to ech degree°
Of hooly chirche, God amende it soone."
  "Sire," quod the lord, "ye woot° what is to doone.
Distempre yow noght°; ye be my confessour;
Ye been the salt of the erthe and the savour°.
For Goddes love, youre pacience ye holde!
Tel me youre grief." And he anon hym tolde
As ye han herd biforn, ye woot wel what.
  The lady of the hous ay° stille sat
Til she had herd what the frere sayde.
  "Ey, Goddes mooder," quod she, "blisful mayde!
Is ther oght elles°? Telle me feithfully."
  "Madame," quod he, "how thynke ye herby°?"
  "How that me thynketh?" quod she. "So God me speede°,
I seye, a cherl° hath doon a cherles dede.
What shold I seye? God lat° hym nevere thee°.
His sike heed is ful of vanytee;
I holde hym in a manere frenesye°."
  "Madame," quod he, "by God, I shal nat lye,
But° I on hym oother weyes be wreke°,
I shal disclaundre° hym over al ther° I speke,
This false blasphemour that charged me
To parte° that wol nat departed be
To every man yliche°, with meschaunce°!"
  The lord sat stille as he were in a traunce,
And in his herte he rolled up and doun°:
How hadde the cherl this ymaginacioun
To shewe swich° a probleme to the frere?
Nevere erst er° now herde I of swich mateere.
I trowe° the devel putte it in his mynde.
In ars-metrik shal ther no man fynde
Biforn this day of swich a questioun°.
Who sholde make a demonstracioun°
That every man sholde have yliche his part
As of the soun or savour of a fart?
O nyce°, proude cherl, I shrewe° his face!
"Lo, sires," quod the lord, "with harde grace°,
Who herde evere of swich a thyng er now?

2167 bord, *table* **2168 Unnethes,** *scarcely* **2169 God yow see,** (may) *God watch over you* **2170 gan looke,** *looked,* **Benedicitee,** *bless you* **2171 what maner world is this,** *what in the world is wrong* **2172 amys,** *wrong* **2173 as,** *as if,* **thevys,** *thieves* **2176 despit,** *insult* **2177 yelde,** *reward* **2178 is noon so poure a page,** (there) *is no serving boy so lowly* **2179 nolde,** *would not* **2180 that,** *what* **2181 ne greveth me nothyng,** *nothing grieves me* **2182 lokkes hoore,** *white hair* **2184 biseke,** *request* **2185 servitour,** *servant* **2189 fors,** *matter* **2191 bityd is,** *has happened* **2192 *per consequens*,** *as a result,* **degree,** *rank* **2194 woot,** *know* **2195 Distempre yow noght,** *don't be angry* **2196 savour,** *flavoring* **2200 ay,** *completely* **2203 oght elles,** *nothing else* **2204 herby,** *by this* **2205 speede,** *help* **2206 cherl,** *rascal* **2207 lat,** *let,* **thee,** *prosper* **2209 manere frenesye,** *kind of madness* **2211 But,** *unless,* **be wreke,** *am avenged* **2212 disclaundre,** *slander,* **over al ther,** *everywhere* **2214 parte,** *divide* **2215 yliche,** *equally,* **meschaunce,** *bad fortune* **2217 rolled up and doun,** *contemplated* **2219 shewe swich,** *set such* **2220 erst er,** *before* **2221 trowe,** *believe* **2223 questioun,** *problem* **2224 demonstracioun,** *proof* **2227 nyce,** *foolish,* **shrewe,** *curse* **2228 with harde grace,** *curse it all*

2170 gan looke, El reads "bigan to looke." **2172 se wel that some thyng,** El reads "trowe som maner thyng." **2176 this day,** Hg reads "to day." **2181 ne,** omitted in El. **2185–88 maister . . . Raby,** the friar here refuses the religious title *rabbi* (Hebrew "my master"), purporting to follow Christ's commands that his disciples not accept the title (Matthew 23.7–8), even though he accepts the academic title "master of arts." See 1781n above. **2185 sire,** omitted in El. **2186 that,** El reads "swich." **2190 this frere,** El reads "he an." **2192 to,** El reads "in." **2196 salt of the erthe,** Christ addresses his disciples in this way in Matthew 5.13 **2200 ay,** El reads "al." **2204 thynke ye herby,** Hg reads "thynketh yow therby." **2211 on hym oother weyes be,** Hg reads "on oother wise may be." **2212 disclaundre,** Hg reads "diffame." **ther,** Hg reads "wher." **2213 This,** Hg reads "The." **2218 the cherl this ymaginacioun,** Hg reads "this cherl ymaginacioun." **2219 the,** El reads "a." **2220 of,** omitted in Hg. **2222 ars-metrik,** arithmetic, but also a pun on "arse-measurement." **2224** El reads "Certes it was a shrewed conclusioun." **2226 the,** Hg reads "a." **savour,** fragrance, but at line 2196 the word means "flavoring" when applied to the friar. **2227 nyce,** El reads "vile." **2229 herde evere,** Hg reads "evere herde."

To every man ylike, tel me how?
It is an inpossible, it may nat be.
Ey, nyce cherl, God lete him nevere thee°!
The rumblynge of a fart, and every soun,
Nis° but of eir reverberacioun,
And evere it wasteth litel and litel awey.
Ther is no man kan deemen°, by my fey°,
If that it were departed° equally.
What, lo, my cherl, lo, yet how shrewedly°
Unto my confessour today he spak.
I holde hym certeyn a demonyak°!
Now ete youre mete and lat the cherl go pleye;
Lat hym go honge° hymself a devel weye°."

The wordes of the lordes squier and his kervere for departynge of the fart on twelve.

Now stood the lordes squier at the bord,
That karf° his mete, and herde word by word
Of alle thynges whiche I have yow sayd.
"My lord," quod he, "beth nat yvele apayd°,
I koude° telle, for a gowne-clooth°,
To yow, sire frere, so ye be nat wrooth°,
How that this fart sholde evene ydeled° be
Among youre covent, if it lyked me."
"Tel," quod the lord, "and thou shalt have anon
A gowne-clooth, by God and by Seint John!"
"My lord," quod he, "whan that the weder° is fair,
Withouten wynd or perturbynge° of air,
Lat brynge a cartwheel heere into this halle—
But look that it have his° spokes alle;
Twelve spokes hath a cartwheel comunly°—
And bryng me thanne twelve freres, woot° ye why?
For thrittene is a covent, as I gesse.
Youre confessour heere, for his worthynesse,
Shal parfourne up° the nombre of his covent.
Thanne shal they knele doun by oon assent°
And to every spokes ende, in this manere,
Ful sadly leye° his nose shal a frere.
Youre noble confessour—there God hym save—
Shal holde his nose upright under the nave°.
Thanne shal this cherl, with bely stif and toght°
As any tabour°, been hyder ybroght°;
And sette hym on the wheel right of this cart,
Upon the nave, and make hym lete a fart.
And ye shul seen, up peril of my lyf°,
By preeve° which that is demonstratif°,
That equally the soun of it wol wende°,
And eke° the stynk, unto the spokes ende,
Save° that this worthy man, youre confessour,
By cause he is a man of greet honour,
Shal have the first fruyt, as resoun is.
As yet the noble usage° of freres is
The worthy men of hem shul first be served,
And certeinly he hath it weel disserved.
He hath today taught us so muche good
With prechyng in the pulpit ther° he stood
That I may vouchesauf°, I sey for me,
He hadde the firste smel of fartes thre;
And so wolde al his covent hardily,
He bereth hym so faire and hoolily."
The lord, the lady, and ech man save the frere
Seyde that Jankyn spak in this matere
As wel as Euclide or Protholomee.
Touchynge° this cherl°, they seyde, subtiltee
And heigh° wit made hym speke as he spak;
He nys no° fool, ne no demonyak°.
And Jankyn hath ywonne° a newe gowne—
My tale is doon; we been almoost at towne.

Heere endeth the Somonours Tale.

2232 thee, *prosper* **2234 Nis,** *is nothing* **2236 deemen,** *judge,* **fey,** *faith* **2237 departed,** *divided* **2238 shrewedly,** *evilly* **2240 a demonyak,** *one possessed by a demon* **2242 honge,** *hang,* **a devel weye,** *in the devil's name* **2244 karf,** *carved* **2246 yvele apayd,** *upset* **2247 koude,** *could,* **gowne-clooth,** *robe* (a reward) **2248 wrooth,** *angry* **2249 evene ydeled,** *evenly divided* **2253 weder,** *weather* **2254 perturbynge,** *disturbance* **2256 his,** *its* **2257 comunly,** *commonly* **2258 woot,** *know* **2261 parfourne up,** *complete* **2262 oon assent,** *unanimous agreement* **2264 Ful sadly leye,** *very steadily place* **2266 nave,** *hub* **2267 toght,** *tight* **2268 tabour,** *drum,* **been hyder ybroght,** *be brought here* **2271 up peril of my lyf,** *I bet my life* **2272 preeve,** *proof,* **demonstratif,** *demonstrable* **2273 wende,** *travel* **2274 eke,** *also* **2275 Save,** *except* **2278 usage,** *custom* **2282 ther,** *where* **2283 vouchesauf,** *grant* **2290 Touchynge,** *concerning,* **cherl,** *rascal* **2291 heigh,** *high* **2292 nys no,** *is no,* **demonyak,** *one possessed by a demon* **2293 ywonne,** *won*

2231 an inpossible, a textbook exercise in mathematics or logic. **2232 him,** El reads "thee." **2234 of eir reverberacioun,** vibration of air. In *HF* 765, Chaucer refers to speech as broken air. **2235 evere,** Hg reads "ther." **2240 certeyn a,** Hg reads "certeynly." **2242a-b** Lacking in Hg. ***kervere,*** carver; the squire cuts the lord's food; see *GP* 1.100. **2245 thynges which,** Hg reads "thynge of which." **whiche I have yow sayd,** El reads "whiche that I have sayd." **2249 sholde evene ydeled be,** El reads "evene delt shal be." **2255 heere,** omitted in El. **2259 thrittene is a covent,** in their aspirations to imitate the apostles and Christ, friars convened themselves in groups of twelve, plus a leader, to make thirteen. El reads "twelve." The scene of the friars around a cart wheel parodies visual representations of the first Pentecost (Acts 2), when the Holy Spirit visited the apostles in a great wind and tongues of fire, enabling the apostles to speak many languages and spread the Christian message. **2260 Youre,** El reads "The." **2261 his,** Hg reads "this." **2268 been hyder,** Hg reads "hider been." **2271 up,** Hg reads "on." **2278** Hg reads "The noble usage of freres yet is this." **2285 his,** El reads "the." **2287 and ech,** El reads "and alle"; Hg omits "and." **2289 Euclide or Protholomee,** Euclid or Ptolemy, classical mathematicians. **2290 this,** Hg reads "the."

Canterbury Tales, Part 4

Introduction

The Paired Tales of Part 4 are striking for their contrasts and for the ways they develop the connected concerns of gender and class initiated by the Wife of Bath: marital sovereignty and the nature of true gentility. The celibate Clerk tells an exemplum in which a well-loved aristocrat (Walter), who initially wishes not to marry, chooses a peasant woman (Griselda) and then tests her cruelly. The recently married Merchant tells a fabliau in which a doddering tyrant (January) selects with lascivious deliberation an attractive young wife (May) and then is cuckolded when she has sex in a pear tree with a squire (Damian). Christian allusions echo in the *Clerk's Tale* (see, e.g., 207n) and are brought to the foreground when the Clerk explains that his tale encourages not wifely submissiveness but human acceptance of God's will (1149–62). By contrast, fairy deities with classical names (Pluto and Proserpine, replacing Christ and St. Peter in some of the analogues) intervene directly in the action of the *Merchant's Tale*; in doing so, they show that the battle of the sexes extends beyond human affairs. In the *Clerk's Tale,* Walter's aristocratic lineage (gentility of blood) is in counterpoint to Griselda's extraordinary patience (gentility of action). The *Merchant's Tale* satirizes gentility of all sorts (1986) and exposes its delusions through January's blindness (both psychological and physical), May's outhouse disposal of Damian's love letter, and the absurdity of sex in a tree. Funny, though mordant in its criticism of human self-delusion, the *Merchant's Tale* is generalized through its use of allegorical names. Few have found humor in the tale of Griselda and Walter, and the tale both offers and resists allegorical interpretation.

Griselda's passivity and Walter's tyranny are offensive to modern sensibility, making it difficult for us to understand why the plot was so popular in the late Middle Ages and beyond. Of the many fourteenth- and early fifteenth-century versions, three were by the most famous authors of the age: Boccaccio, Petrarch, and Chaucer. Boccaccio first included it in the *Decameron* (1352); Petrarch translated it into Latin (1373), giving it wider currency; and Sercambi did another Italian version (after 1399). There is an anonymous Latin translation, at least four translations of Petrarch into French, and a dramatic adaptation of the tale. Chaucer worked from Petrarch (as he tells us through the Clerk) and an anonymous, updated French version, *Le Livre Griseldis*; he may also have been influenced by Philippe de Mézière's rendering (ca. 1385). In *Chaucerian Polity* (1997, no. 311), David Wallace argues that Chaucer's version critiques Petrarchan humanism for its collusion with tyranny. In *Faith, Ethics, and the Church* (2000, no. 401), David Aers thinks that it posits a Stoic alternative to dominant Catholic orthodoxy. In "T'assaye in thee thy wommanheede" (2005, no. 941), Tara Williamson explores how the tale shows late-medieval understanding of female power. Judith Bronfman documents the consistent popularity of the tale into the twentieth century in *Chaucer's Clerk's Tale* (1994, no. 918).

Chaucer's version is unique for the ways that it creates pathos through allusion and narrative perspective. The tale allows us to share Griselda's thoughts and increases the potential for regarding her as a figure of holy suffering (see, e.g., 281–94, 554–67). At times, the narrator laments her suffering (e.g., 460–62, 621–23); at others, he discloses the opinions of others (990–91, 995–1008). Yet Griselda's willingness to accept the cruelty of her husband and to give up her children opens her up to proto-feminist charges of collusion with her patriarchal tormentor, charges that Chaucer may well have had in mind since he has the Clerk address the Wife of Bath and "al hire secte" at the end of the tale (1163ff.).

The reference sharply recalls the Wife's claim that it is an "inpossible" (an impossibility) that any clerk "wol speke good of wyves" unless she be a saint (3.688–90), and the rapid shift from the Clerk's allegorical reading of the tale to his reference to the Wife makes it seem as if the tale can be read as personal rejoinder as well as a secular saint's life or a macabre fairy tale. If Chaucer composed his tale of Griselda with the Canterbury frame in mind, he must have shaped the material to produce the neck-whip reversals of the conclusion and the envoy. More likely, he assigned a previously written tale to the Clerk and sat back to watch the fun, if fun it is. Critical responses to the tale are intense in their castigations of Walter (and sometimes Griselda), and they often ignore the fact that gentility of deed overwhelms gentility of blood in both the *Clerk's Tale* and the *Wife of Bath's Tale*, even though the sexual politics of the two tales vary so widely. For a survey of criticism, see Charlotte C. Morse, "Critical Approaches to the *Clerk's Tale*" (1990, no. 936).

Tone and pace are crucial to understanding the *Merchant's Tale*. The opening praise of marriage (1267–1392) makes most sense in context if read as sarcastic, and the sexual efficiency of May and Damian in the tree (2353, "in he throng") is set provocatively against pages of January's rationalization about his choice of a wife; his self-justifying pseudo-debate with his counselors, Placebo and Justinus; and his sexual fantasies and delusions. The revolting description of January's lovemaking and the blunt irony of being told that we know not what May thinks of him (1851) clash with the idealized language of January's praise of May, drawn from the biblical Song of Songs (2138–48). The sardonic tone of the tale is palpable, though critics divide over whether we should attribute it to the bitterness of the narrator or to the traditional plot—the fabliau of the *senex amans* (old man) cuckolded by a young wife. Chaucer's use of a similar plot in the *Miller's Tale* is much less acerbic, but he treats aging sexuality with bitterness in the *Reeve's Prologue* and with a kind of nostalgia in the Wife of Bath's recollections (3.469–79).

No specific source of the pear-tree episode has been identified, although it is embellished here by some of the same sources found in the Wife of Bath's materials, particularly Jerome's *Epistola adversus Jovinianum* (*Letter against Jovinian*) and the *Roman de la Rose*. The intervention of the fairy gods recalls the planetary influences of the *Knight's Tale*. The *Merchant's Tale* also shares materials with the *Tale of Melibee*: much of the mock encomium of marriage (1311–88) derives ultimately from Albertano of Brescia, *Liber Consolationis et Consilii* (translated by Chaucer in *Melibee*), and *De Amore Dei*. The successful combination of such eclectic materials indicates that Chaucer shaped the Merchant about the same time as he did the Wife of Bath, probably late in his development of the *Canterbury Tales*.

A. S. G. Edwards, "The Merchant's Tale and Moral Chaucer" (1990, no. 948), assesses the thematic implications of perspective and tone in the tale, documenting how readers, from the earliest scribes to modern critics, have reacted to such shifts. In an illuminating essay that focuses on the *Clerk's Tale* and the Middle English *Pearl*, "Satisfaction and Payment in Middle English Literature" (1983, no. 935), Jill Mann explores the theme of sufficiency or "enoughness" in these works. The idea is reflected in the "suffisant answere" that the fairy goddess gives to May in order to sustain the deception of January in the *Merchant's Tale* (2266), an echo of the "answere suffisant" to the life question that the court demands of the rapist knight in the *Wife of Bath's Tale* (3.910). These and many more echoes among the tales of Parts 3 and 4—as well as Part 5—create a unity that is simultaneously thematic, dramatic, and rhetorical, encouraging us to read them as a single sequence, even though the manuscripts arrange them in different ways.

Canterbury Tales
Part 4

From woodcut made by W.H. Hooper and published by the Chaucer Society between 1868 and 1879

Clerk's Tale

Prologue

Heere folweth the Prologe of the Clerkes Tale of Oxenford.

"Sire Clerk of Oxenford°," oure Hooste sayde,
"Ye ryde as coy° and stille as dooth° a mayde
Were newe spoused°, sittynge at the bord°;
This day ne herde I of youre tonge a word.
I trowe° ye studie aboute som sophyme°,
But Salomon seith, everythyng hath tyme.
For Goddes sake, as beth° of bettre cheere°!
It is no tyme for to studien heere.
Telle us som myrie° tale, by youre fey°,
For what man that is entred in a pley°,
He nedes moot° unto the pley assente.
But precheth nat, as freres doon in Lente,
To make us for oure olde synnes wepe,
Ne that thy tale make us nat to slepe.
"Telle us som murie° thyng of aventures.
Youre termes, youre colours, and youre figures,
Keepe hem° in stoor° til so be that° ye endite°
Heigh style, as whan that men to kynges write.
Speketh so pleyn at this tyme, we yow preye,
That we may understonde what ye seye."
This worthy clerk benignely° answerde,
"Hooste," quod he, "I am under youre yerde°.
Ye han° of us as now the governance,
And therfore wol I do yow obeisance°
As fer as resoun axeth°, hardily°.
I wol yow telle a tale which that I

---

1 **Oxenford,** *Oxford* 2 **coy,** *quiet,* **dooth,** *does* 3 **Were newe spoused,** *who is newly married,* **bord,** *table* 5 **trowe,** *believe,* **sophyme,** *logical argument* 7 **as beth,** *be,* **cheere,** *mood* 9 **myrie,** *merry,* **fey,** *faith* 10 **pley,** *game* 11 **nedes moot,** *must necessarily* 15 **murie,** *merry* 17 **hem,** *them,* **stoor,** *reserve,* **til so be that,** *until,* **endite,** *compose* 21 **benignely,** *graciously* 22 **yerde,** *yardstick* (authority) 23 **han,** *have* 24 **do yow obeisance,** *obey you* 25 **axeth,** *asks,* **hardily,** *with all my heart*

6 Ecclesiastes 3.1, attributed to Solomon. 10–11 Proverbial. 12 **Lente,** a church season of repentance and fasting. 16 **termes . . . colours . . . figures,** technical terms, rhetorical flourishes, figures of speech—all part of academic training. 17 **that,** omitted in Hg. 18 **Heigh style,** elaborate rhetorical style suited to high purpose, as described in the medieval art of letter writing (*ars dictaminis*).

Lerned at Padwe of° a worthy clerk,
As preved° by his wordes and his werk.
He is now deed and nayled in his cheste°—
I prey to God so yeve his soule reste.
"Fraunceys Petrak, the lauriat poete,
Highte° this clerk, whos rethorike sweete
Enlumyned al Ytaille of° poetrie,
As Lynyan dide of philosophie,
Or lawe, or oother art particuler;
But deeth, that wol° nat suffre us dwellen° heer,
But as it were a twynklyng of an eye,
Hem bothe hath slayn, and alle shul we dye.
"But forth to tellen of this worthy man
That taughte me this tale, as I bigan
I seye that first with heigh stile he enditeth°,
Er° he the body of his tale writeth,
A prohemye, in the which discryveth° he
Pemond and of Saluces the contree,
And speketh of Apennyn, the hilles hye°,
That been the boundes of West Lumbardye,
And of Mount Vesulus in special
Where as the Poo out of a welle smal
Taketh his firste spryngyng and his sours°,
That estward ay° encresseth in his cours
To Emele-ward, to Ferrare, and Venyse,
The which a long thyng were to devyse°.
And trewely, as to my juggement,
Me thynketh it a thyng impertinent°,
Save that he wole convoyen° his mateere.
But this his tale, which that ye may heere."

Heere bigynneth the Tale of the Clerk of Oxenford.

Ther is at the west syde of Ytaille,
Doun at the roote of Vesulus the colde,
A lusty playne, habundant of vitaille°,
Where many a tour° and toun thou mayst biholde
That founded were in tyme of fadres olde°,
And many another delitable° sighte,
And Saluces this noble contree highte°.

A markys° whilom° lord was of that lond,
As were his worthy eldres° hym bifore;
And obeisant°, ay redy to his hond°,
Were alle his liges°, bothe lasse and moore.
Thus in delit he lyveth and hath doon yoore°,
Biloved and drad° thurgh favour of Fortune
Bothe of° his lordes and of his commune°.

Therwith he was, to speke as of lynage°,
The gentilleste yborn of Lumbardye:
A fair persone, and strong, and yong of age,
And ful of honour and of curteisye,
Discreet° ynogh his contree for to gye°—
Save in somme thynges that he was to blame.
And Walter was this yonge lordes name.

I blame hym thus, that he considered noght°
In tyme comynge what hym myghte bityde°,
But on his lust° present was al his thoght,
As for to hauke and hunte on every syde.
Wel ny° alle othere cures° leet he slyde°.
And eek° he nolde°—and that was worst of alle—
Wedde no wyf for noght that may bifalle°.

27 of, *from* **28 preved,** *proved* **29 cheste,** *coffin* **32 Highte,** *was named* **33 Enlumyned al Ytaille of,** *made famous all of Italy for* **36 wol,** *will,* **suffre us dwellen,** *allow us to remain* **41 enditeth,** *composed* **42 Er,** *before* **43 discryveth,** *describes* **45 hye,** *high* **49 sours,** *source* **50 ay,** *always* **52 devyse,** *describe* **54 impertinent,** *irrelevant* **55 wole convoyen,** *will introduce* **59 habundant of vitaille,** *rich in produce* **60 tour,** *tower* **61 fadres olde,** *ancient fathers* **62 delitable,** *delightful* **63 highte,** *was named* **64 markys,** *marquis (a noble rank),* **whilom,** *once* **65 eldres,** *ancestors* **66 obeisant,** *obedient,* **ay redy to his hond,** *always attentive to his rule* **67 liges,** *subjects* **68 hath doon yoore,** *has long done* **69 drad,** *respected* **70 of,** *by,* **commune,** *common people* **71 lynage,** *lineage* **75 Discreet,** *wise,* **gye,** *lead* **78 noght,** *not* **79 bityde,** *happen* (to) **80 lust,** *pleasure* **82 Wel ny,** *nearly,* **cures,** *cares,* **leet he slyde,** *he ignored* **83 eek,** *also,* **nolde,** *would not* **84 for noght that may bifalle,** *whatever might happen*

27 Padwe, Padua, city in northeastern Italy. **31 Fraunceys Petrak, the lauriat,** Francis Petrarch (d. 1374) was awarded the poet's crown of laurel leaves by the Roman Senate in 1341; Chaucer may have met him on his first visit to Italy, 1372–73. Petrarch translated into Latin Boccaccio's original Italian version of this story. Chaucer knew of both versions, as well as a French one, but he depends primarily on Petrarch's. **34 Lynyan,** Giovanni di Lignano (d. 1383), professor of canon law at Padua, visited England as papal legate. **36 suffre us,** omitted in El. **43 prohemye,** prologue; Petrarch added a prologue to Boccaccio's tale. **the,** omitted in Hg. **44 Pemond . . . Saluces,** Piedmont, Saluzzo. **45 Apennyn,** the Apennine hills. **46 Lumbardye,** Lombardy, a region of Italy. **47 Vesulus,** Monte Viso. **48 Poo,** River Po. **49 sours,** Hg reads "cours." **51 To Emele-ward . . . Ferrare . . . Venyse,** toward Emilia (region), Ferrara, Venice (cities). **56 may,** Hg reads "shal." **58 the colde,** Chaucer adds this adjective, line 61, and lines 64–70, emphasizing time and lineage in the tale. **66 ay,** El reads "and." **72 Lumbardye,** Lombardy, a region of Italy associated with tyranny. Chaucer added this detail here. **74 of honour,** El omits "of." **76 Save in,** El reads "Save that in." **79 hym myghte,** Hg reads "myghte hym." **81 hauke,** hunt with a hawk, a noble pastime.

Oonly that point his peple bar so soore°
That flokmeele° on a day they to hym wente,
And oon° of hem, that wisest was of loore,
Or elles° that the lord best wolde assente°
That he sholde telle hym what his peple mente,
Or elles koude° he shewe wel swich° mateere,
He to the markys seyde as ye shul heere:

"O noble markys, youre humanitee
Asseureth° us to yeve° us hardinesse°
As ofte as tyme is of necessitee°
That we to yow mowe° telle oure hevynesse°.
Accepteth, lord, now for youre gentillesse,
That we with pitous herte unto yow pleyne°,
And lat youre eres nat my voys° desdeyne°.

"Al have I noght to doone in this mateere
Moore than another man hath in this place,
Yet for as muche as° ye, my lord so deere,
Han° alwey shewed me favour and grace,
I dar the bettre aske of yow a space°
Of audience to shewen oure requeste,
And ye, my lord, to doon right as yow leste°.

"For certes°, lord, so wel us liketh yow°
And al youre werk, and evere han doon°, that we
Ne koude nat us self devysen how°
We myghte lyven in moore felicitee,
Save o thyng, lord, if it youre wille be,
That for to been a wedded man yow leste°—
Thanne were youre peple in sovereyn hertes reste°.

"Boweth youre nekke under that blisful yok°
Of soveraynetee, noght of servyse,
Which that men clepe° spousaille or wedlok.
And thenketh, lord, among youre thoghtes wyse
How that oure dayes passe in sondry wyse°,
For thogh we slepe, or wake, or rome°, or ryde,
Ay fleeth° the tyme; it nyl no man abyde°.

"And thogh youre grene youthe floure° as yit,
In crepeth age alwey as stille° as stoon,
And deeth manaceth° every age, and smyt°
In ech estaat°, for ther escapeth noon.
And also° certein as we knowe echoon°
That we shul deye, as uncerteyn we alle
Been of that day whan deeth shal on us falle.

"Accepteth thanne of us the trewe entente,
That nevere yet refuseden youre heeste°,
And we wol°, lord, if that ye wole assente,
Chese° yow a wyf in short tyme atte leeste,
Born of the gentilleste° and of the meeste°
Of al this land, so that it oghte seme
Honour to God and yow, as we kan deeme°.

"Delivere us out of al this bisy drede°
And taak a wyf, for hye Goddes° sake!
For if it so bifelle, as God forbede,
That thurgh youre deeth youre lyne sholde slake°,
And that a straunge° successour sholde take
Youre heritage, O wo were us alyve.
Wherfore we pray you hastily to wyve°."

Hir° meeke preyere and hir pitous cheere°
Made the markys herte° han pitee.
"Ye wol°," quod he, "myn owene peple deere,
To that° I nevere erst° thoughte streyne me°.
I me rejoysed of my liberte,
That seelde° tyme is founde in mariage.
Ther° I was free I moot° been in servage.

"But nathelees I se youre trewe entente,
And truste upon youre wit°, and have doon ay°;
Wherfore of my free wyl I wole assente
To wedde me as soone as evere I may.
But ther° as ye han profred° me today
To chese° me a wyf, I yow relesse°
That choys, and prey yow of that profre cesse°.

85 bar so soore, *took so badly* **86 flokmeele,** *in a group* **87 oon,** *one* **88 elles,** *else,* **best wolde assente,** *would most willingly agree* **90 koude,** *could,* **swich,** *such* **93 Asseureth,** *assures,* **yeve,** *give,* **hardinesse,** *courage* **94 As ofte as tyme is of necessitee,** *whenever it is necessary* **95 mowe,** *may,* **hevynesse,** *worry* **97 pleyne,** *lament* **98 voys,** *voice,* **desdeyne,** *disdain* **101 for as muche as,** *because* **102 Han,** *have* **103 space,** *moment* **105 leste,** *please* **106 certes,** *certainly,* **so wel us liketh yow,** *we like you so well* **107 han doon,** *have done* (so) **108 us self devysen,** *ourselves imagine* **111 leste,** *chose* **112 in sovereyn hertes reste,** *most perfectly content* **113 yok,** *yoke* **115 clepe,** *call* **117 sondry wyse,** *various ways* **118 rome,** *walk* **119 Ay fleeth,** *always flies,* **nyl no man abyde,** *will await no man* **120 floure,** *flourishes* **121 stille,** *quietly* **122 manaceth,** *menaces,* **smyt,** *strikes* **123 ech estaat,** *each social class* **124 also,** *as,* **echoon,** *each one* **128 heeste,** *command* **129 wol,** *will* **130 Chese,** *choose* **131 gentilleste,** *most noble,* **meeste,** *greatest* **133 deeme,** *judge* **134 bisy drede,** *constant fear* **135 hye Goddes,** *high God's* **137 lyne sholde slake,** *lineage should diminish* **138 straunge,** *foreign* **140 wyve,** *marry* **141 Hir,** *their,* **cheere,** *expression* **142 herte,** *heart* **143 wol,** *wish* **144 To that,** *for what,* **erst,** *before,* **streyne me,** (to) *constrain myself* **146 seelde,** *seldom* **147 Ther,** *there,* **moot,** *may* **149 wit,** *wisdom,* **doon ay,** *done always* **152 ther,** *where,* **profred,** *offered* **153 chese,** *choose,* **relesse,** *release* (from) **154 cesse,** *cease*

93 to yeve, Hg reads "and yeveth." **96 for,** Hg reads "of." **110 it,** omitted in El. **114 soveraynetee,** supremacy; see *WBP* 3.818. **119** Proverbial after Chaucer. **128 youre,** El and Hg read "thyn" (less formal). **136 it,** omitted in Hg. **152 today,** El reads "this day." **154 yow,** omitted in El.

"For God it woot° that children ofte been
Unlyk hir worthy eldres hem bifore;
Bountee° comth al of God, nat of the streen°
Of which they been engendred and ybore°.
I truste in Goddes bountee, and therfore
My mariage and myn estaat and reste
I hym bitake°; he may doon as hym leste°.

"Lat me allone in chesynge of my wyf.
That charge° upon my bak I wole endure.
But I yow preye, and charge° upon youre lyf,
What wyf that I take, ye me assure
To worshipe hire whil that hir lyf may dure°,
In word and werk, bothe heere and everywheere,
As° she an emperoures doghter weere.

"And forthermoore, this shal ye swere, that ye
Agayn my choys shul neither grucche ne stryve°.
For sith° I shal forgoon° my libertee
At youre requeste, as evere moot° I thryve,
Ther° as myn herte is set, ther wol I wyve°.
And but° ye wole assente in swich manere,
I prey yow speketh namoore of this matere."

With hertely wyl° they sworen and assenten
To al this thyng—ther seyde no wight° nay—
Bisekynge° hym of grace, er that they wenten,
That he wolde graunten hem a certein day°
Of his spousaille°, as soone as evere he may,
For yet alwey the peple somwhat dredde°,
Lest that° the markys no wyf wolde wedde.

He graunted hem a day swich° as hym leste°
On which he wolde be wedded sikerly°,
And seyde he dide al this at hir requeste.
And they with humble entente buxomly°,
Knelynge upon hir knees ful reverently,
Hym thonken alle°, and thus they han an ende°
Of hire entente and hoom agayn they wende°.

And heerupon° he to his officeres
Comaundeth for the feste to purveye°,
And to his privee° knyghtes and squieres
Swich charge yaf° as hym liste on hem leye;
And they to his comandement obeye,
And ech of hem dooth al his diligence
To doon unto the feeste reverence°.

Explicit prima pars. Incipit secunda pars.

Noght fer fro thilke paleys° honurable
Ther as° this markys shoop° his mariage
There stood a throop° of site delitable°,
In which that poure folk of that village
Hadden hir beestes and hir herbergage°,
And of hire labour tooke hir sustenance,
After° that the erthe yaf hem° habundance.

Amonges thise poure folk ther dwelte a man
Which that° was holden° pourest of hem alle,
But hye° God somtyme senden kan°
His grace into a litel oxes stalle.
Janicula men of that throop hym calle.
A doghter hadde he, fair ynogh to sighte,
And Grisildis this yonge mayden highte°.

But for to speke of vertuous beautee,
Thanne was she oon the faireste° under sonne.
For poureliche yfostred up° was she,
No likerous lust° was thurgh hire herte yronne°.
Wel ofter° of the welle than of the tonne°
She drank, and for° she wolde vertu plese
She knew wel labour but noon ydel ese.

But thogh this mayde tendre were of age,
Yet in the brest of hire virginitee
Ther was enclosed rype and sad corage°;
And in greet reverence and charitee
Hir olde poure fader fostred shee°.

---

155 woot, *knows* **157 Bountee,** *goodness,* **streen,** *family* **158 engendred and ybore,** *produced and born* **161 hym bitake,** *entrust* (to) *him,* **leste,** *pleases* **163 charge,** *burden* **164 charge,** *order* **166 dure,** *last* **168 As,** *as if* **170 grucche ne stryve,** *complain nor struggle* **171 sith,** *since,* **forgoon,** *give up* **172 moot,** *may* **173 Ther,** *where,* **wyve,** *marry* **174 but,** *unless* **176 hertely wyl,** *heartfelt will* **177 wight,** *person* **178 Bisekynge hym of grace,** *asking him by favor* **179 graunten hem a certein day,** *name for them the day* **180 spousaille,** *wedding* **181 dredde,** *feared* **182 Lest that,** *that* **183 swich,** *such,* **hym leste,** *it pleased him* **184 sikerly,** *certainly* **186 buxomly,** *humbly* **188 Hym thonken alle,** *all thanked him,* **han an ende,** *have a fulfillment* **189 wende,** *go* **190 heerupon,** *after this* **191 for the feste to purveye,** *to prepare for the feast* **192 privee,** *personal* **193 Swich charge yaf,** *such orders gave* **196 doon unto . . . reverence,** *make worthy* **197 Noght fer fro thilke paleys,** *not far from this palace* **198 Ther as,** *where,* **shoop,** *arranged* **199 throop,** *village,* **delitable,** *delightful* **201 herbergage,** *dwelling* **203 After,** *to the extent,* **yaf hem,** *gave them* **205 Which that,** *who,* **holden** *considered* **206 hye,** *high,* **senden kan,** *can send* **210 highte,** *was called* **212 oon the faireste,** *fairest of all* **213 poureliche yfostred up,** *raised in poverty* **214 likerous lust,** *sensual desire,* **was . . . yronne,** *ran* **215 Wel ofter,** *more often,* **tonne,** *wine cask* **216 for,** *because* **220 rype and sad corage,** *mature and steady spirit* **222 fostred shee,** *she took care of*

164 yow preye, Hg reads "preye yow." **165 What,** Hg reads "That what." **174 swich,** El reads "this." **180 he,** Hg reads "I." **196a *Explicit prima pars. Incipit secunda pars.*** "Here ends part one. Here begins part two." **198 Ther,** Hg reads "Wher." **204 thise,** Hg reads "this." **207 oxes stalle,** Chaucer added this image that recalls the humble birth of Christ; see 281–94n. **208 Janicula,** Latin word meaning "little gate." The name is in Boccaccio and Petrarch and may have suggested to Chaucer the themes of the Annunciation and Nativity. **211 beautee,** El reads "bountee." **215–17** Chaucer's addition.

A fewe sheep, spynnynge°, on feeld she kepte;
She wolde noght been ydel til she slepte.

And whan she homward cam, she wolde brynge
Wortes° or othere herbes tymes ofte,
The whiche she shredde and seeth° for hir lyvynge,
And made hir bed ful harde and nothyng softe;
And ay° she kepte hir fadres lyf on-lofte°
With everich° obeisaunce and diligence
That child may doon to fadres reverence.

Upon Grisilde, this poure creature,
Ful ofte sithe° this markys caste his eye
As he on huntyng rood, paraventure°;
And whan it fil° that he myghte hire espye,
He noght with wantowne lookyng of folye
His eyen caste on hire, but in sad wyse°
Upon hir chiere° he wolde hym ofte avyse°,

Commendynge in his herte hir wommanhede,
And eek hir vertu, passynge any wight°
Of so yong age, as wel in chiere as dede.
For thogh the peple° have no greet insight
In vertu, he considered ful right
Hir bountee, and disposed° that he wolde
Wedde hire oonly, if evere he wedde sholde.

The day of weddyng cam, but no wight° kan
Telle what womman that it sholde be.
For which merveille° wondred many a man,
And seyden whan they were in privetee,
"Wol nat oure lord yet leve his vanytee°?
Wol he nat wedde? Allas, allas, the while!
Why wole he thus hymself and us bigile?"

But natheless this markys hath doon make°,
Of gemmes set in gold and in asure°,
Brooches and rynges for Grisildis sake;
And of hir clothyng took he the mesure
By a mayde lyk to hire stature,
And eek of othere aornementes° alle
That unto swich a weddyng sholde falle°.

The time of undren of the same day
Approcheth that this weddyng sholde be,
And al the paleys° put was in array,
Bothe halle and chambres, ech in his° degree—
Houses of office° stuffed with plentee
Ther maystow seen°, of deynteuous vitaille°
That may be founde as fer as last Ytaille°.

This roial° markys richely arrayed,
Lordes and ladyes in his compaignye,
The whiche that to the feeste weren yprayed°,
And of his retenue° the bachelrye°,
With many a soun of sondry° melodye,
Unto the village of the which I tolde
In this array the righte° wey han holde°.

Grisilde of this, God woot°, ful innocent
That for hire shapen° was al this array,
To fecchen water at a welle is went°,
And comth hoom as soone as ever she may;
For wel she hadde herd seyd that thilke° day
The markys sholde wedde, and if she myghte
She wolde fayn han seyn° som of that sighte.

She thoghte, "I wole with othere maydens stonde,
That been my felawes, in oure dore and se
The markysesse°; and therfore wol I fonde°
To doon at hoom as soone as it may be
The labour which that longeth° unto me,
And thanne I may at leyser hire biholde
If she this wey unto the castel holde°."

And as she wolde over hir thresshfold° gon,
The markys cam and gan hire for to calle°,

223 spynnynge, *while spinning* **226 Wortes,** *plants* **227 shredde and seeth,** *chopped and cooked* **229 ay,** *always,* **kepte . . . on-lofte,** *maintained* **230 everich,** *every* **233 sithe,** *times* **234 paraventure,** *by chance* **235 fil,** *happened* **237 sad wyse,** *serious manner* **238 chiere,** *demeanor,* **avyse,** *consider* **240 passynge any wight,** *surpassing anyone* **242 peple,** *populace* **244 disposed,** *decided* **246 wight,** *person* **248 merveille,** *marvel* **250 leve his vanytee,** *abandon his foolishness* **253 hath doon make,** *has had made* **254 asure,** *lapis lazuli* **258 aornements,** *ornaments* **259 sholde falle,** *are appropriate* **262 paleys,** *palace* **263 his,** *its* **264 Houses of office,** *utility buildings* **265 maystow seen,** *may you see,* **deynteuous vitaille,** *delicious food* **266 last Ytaille,** *the ends of Italy* **267 roial,** *royal* **269 yprayed,** *invited* **270 retenue,** *service,* **bachelrye,** *young knights* **271 sondry,** *various* **273 righte,** *nearest,* **han holde,** *have taken* **274 woot,** *knows* **275 shapen,** *prepared* **276 is went,** *has gone* **278 thilke,** *this* **280 fayn han seyn,** *like to see* **283 markysesse,** *marquise* (wife of a marquis), **fonde,** *try* **285 longeth,** *belongs* **287 holde,** *takes* **288 thresshfold,** *threshold* **289 gan hire for to calle,** *called her*

227 hir, Hg reads "his." **233 caste,** Hg reads "sette." **235 whan that it,** Hg reads "whan it." **238 wolde,** El reads "gan." **242 have,** El reads "hadde"; Hg "hath." **249–52** Chaucer adds the subjects' questions. **249 whan they,** El reads "whan that they." **251 allas, allas,** Hg reads "allas." **260 undren,** midmorning, but also a time for auspicious encounters in romance tradition; Petrarch does not specify the hour, nor does he elaborate upon the household preparations. **281–94** Largely Chaucer's addition, including the description of Griselda's thoughts. The threshold and the mention of the Lord's will suggest the Annunciation, i.e., Mary's acceptance of God's will that she give birth to Jesus. The oxen's stall (also in line 207) recalls the scene of Jesus's birth, the Nativity. The water pot from the well (line 276) recalls the divine selection of Rebecca as wife for Isaac; Genesis 24. **288 hir,** Hg reads "the."

And she set doun hir water pot anon°,
Biside the thresshfold, in an oxes stalle,
And doun upon hir knes she gan to falle,
And with sad contenance° kneleth stille°
Til she had herd what was the lordes wille.

This thoghtful markys spak unto this mayde
Ful sobrely, and seyde in this manere,
"Where is youre fader, O Grisildis?" he sayde.
And she with reverence, in humble cheere,
Answerde, "Lord, he is al redy heere."
And in she gooth withouten lenger lette°,
And to the markys she hir fader fette°.

He by the hand thanne took this olde man
And seyde thus whan he hym hadde asyde°,
"Janicula, I neither may ne kan
Lenger the plesance° of myn herte hyde.
If that thou vouchesauf°, what so bityde°,
Thy doghter wol I take er that I wende°
As for my wyf, unto hir lyves ende.

"Thou lovest me, I woot° it wel certeyn,
And art my feithful lige man ybore°,
And al that liketh° me, I dar wel seyn
It liketh thee, and specially therfore
Tel me that poynt° that I have seyd bifore,
If that thou wolt unto that purpos drawe°
To take me as for thy sone-in-lawe."

The sodeyn cas° this man astonyed° so
That reed he wax°; abayst° and al quakynge
He stood. Unnethes° seyde he wordes mo
But oonly thus, "Lord," quod he, "my willynge
Is as ye wole°, ne ayeyns° youre likynge
I wol no thyng. Ye be my lord so deere,
Right° as yow lust°, governeth this mateere."

"Yet wol I," quod this markys softely,
"That in thy chambre I and thou and she
Have a collacioun°. And wostow° why?
For I wol axe° if it hire wille be
To be my wyf and reule hire after° me.
And al this shal be doon in thy presence;
I wol noght speke out of thyn audience°."

And in the chambre whil they were aboute
Hir tretys° which as ye shal after heere,
The peple cam unto the hous withoute°,
And wondred hem in how honeste° manere
And tentifly° she kepte hir fader deere.
But outrely° Grisildis wondre myghte,
For nevere erst° ne saugh she swich° a sighte.

No wonder is thogh she were astoned
To seen so greet a gest come in that place;
She nevere was to swiche gestes woned°,
For which she looked with ful pale face.
But shortly forth this matere for to chace°,
Thise arn° the wordes that the markys sayde
To this benigne°, verray°, feithful mayde.

"Grisilde," he seyde, "ye shal wel understonde
It liketh to° youre fader and to me
That I yow wedde, and eek° it may so stonde,
As I suppose, ye wol° that it so be.
But thise demandes axe° I first," quod he,
"That, sith° it shal be doon in hastif wyse°,
Wol ye assente, or elles yow avyse°?

"I seye this, be ye redy with good herte
To al my lust°, and that I frely may
As me best thynketh do yow° laughe or smerte°,
And nevere ye to grucche° it, nyght ne day?
And eek whan I sey 'ye' ne sey nat 'nay,'
Neither by word ne frownyng contenance?
Swere this, and heere I swere oure alliance."

Wondrynge upon this word, quakynge for drede,
She seyde, "Lord, undigne° and unworthy

---

290 anon, *immediately* **293 sad contenance,** *sober looks,* **stille,** *quietly* **300 lette,** *delay* **301 fette,** *fetched* **303 hadde asyde,** *had* (taken) *aside* **305 plesance,** *desire* **306 vouchesauf,** *agree,* **what so bityde,** *whatever happens* **307 wende,** *leave* **309 woot,** *know* **310 lige man ybore,** *subject born* **311 liketh,** *pleases* **313 Tel me that poynt,** *respond to the issue* **314 unto that purpos drawe,** *accept that plan* **316 sodeyn cas,** *sudden situation,* **astonyed,** *astonished* **317 reed he wax,** *he turned red,* **abayst,** *abashed* **318 Unnethes,** *scarcely* **320 wole,** *wish,* **ne ayeyns,** *nor against* **322 Right,** *just,* **lust,** *desire* **325 collacioun,** *discussion,* **wostow,** *do you know* **326 axe,** *ask* **327 reule hire after,** *obey* **329 audience,** *hearing* **331 Hir tretys,** *their negotiation* **332 cam unto . . . withoute,** *approached the outside* (of) **333 wondred hem in how honeste,** *they wondered at what an konorable* **334 tentifly,** *attentively* **335 outrely,** *utterly* **336 erst,** *before,* **swich,** *such* **339 to swiche gestes woned,** *accustomed to such guests* **341 chace,** *pursue* **342 arn,** *are* **343 benigne,** *good,* **verray,** *true* **345 It liketh to,** *it pleases* **346 eek,** *also* **347 wol,** *wish* **348 demandes axe,** *questions ask* **349 sith,** *since,* **hastif wyse,** *hurried manner* **350 elles yow avyse,** *else think about it* **352 lust,** *desire* **353 do yow,** *make you,* **smerte,** *hurt* **354 grucche,** *complain about* **359 undigne,** *undeserving*

300 in, omitted in Hg. **308 hir,** Hg reads "my." **319 thus,** Hg reads "this." **336 erst,** Hg reads "eft" (again). **338 that,** Hg reads "to." **341 tale,** El reads "matere." **342 the,** Hg reads "this." **357 oure,** El reads "yow." **359 and,** Hg reads "or."

Am I to thilke° honour that ye me beede°,
But as ye wole° yourself, right so wol I.
And heere I swere that nevere willyngly
In werk ne thoght I nyl° yow disobeye,
For to be deed°, though me were looth to deye."

"This is ynogh, Grisilde myn," quod he.
And forth he gooth with a ful sobre cheere°
Out at the dore, and after that cam she,
And to the peple he seyde in this manere,
"This is my wyf," quod he, "that standeth heere.
Honoureth hire and loveth hire, I preye,
Whoso me loveth; ther is namoore to seye."

And for° that nothyng of hir olde geere°
She sholde brynge into his hous, he bad°
That wommen sholde dispoillen° hire right theere;
Of which thise ladyes were nat right glad
To handle hir clothes wherinne she was clad.
But nathelees this mayde bright of hewe
Fro foot to heed they clothed han al newe.

Hir heris han they kembd°, that lay untressed°
Ful rudely°, and with hir° fyngres smale
A corone° on hire heed they han ydressed°,
And sette hire ful of nowches° grete and smale.
Of hire array what sholde I make a tale?
Unnethe° the peple hir knew for hire fairnesse
Whan she translated was in swich richesse.

This markys hath hire spoused with a ryng
Broght for the same cause°, and thanne hire sette
Upon an hors snow-whit and wel amblyng°,
And to his paleys er he lenger lette°
With joyful peple that hire ladde and mette
Convoyed hire, and thus the day they spende
In revel til the sonne gan descende°.

And shortly forth this tale for to chace°.
I seye that to this newe markysesse°
God hath swich favour sent hire of his grace
That it ne semed nat by liklynesse°
That she was born and fed in rudenesse°,
As in a cote° or in an oxe-stalle,
But norissed° in an emperoures halle.

To every wight° she woxen° is so deere
And worshipful that folk ther° she was bore°,
And from hire birthe knew hire yeer by yeere,
Unnethe trowed° they—but dorste han° swore—
That to Janicle, of which I spak bifore,
She doghter were, for as by conjecture
Hem thoughte she was another creature.

For though that evere vertuous was she,
She was encressed in swich excellence
Of thewes° goode, yset in heigh bountee°,
And so discreet and fair of eloquence,
So benigne° and so digne° of reverence,
And koude so the peples herte embrace,
That ech hire lovede that looked on hir face.

Noght oonly of Saluces in the toun
Publiced° was the bountee° of hir name,
But eek biside° in many a regioun,
If oon seide° wel, another seyde the same;
So spradde of hire heighe bountee the fame
That men and wommen, as wel yonge as olde,
Goon° to Saluce upon hire to biholde.

Thus Walter lowely—nay, but roially—
Wedded with fortunat honestetee°,
In Goddes pees lyveth ful esily
At hoom, and outward grace ynogh had he;
And for° he saugh that under low degree
Was ofte vertu hid, the peple hym heelde
A prudent man, and that is seyn° ful seelde°.

360 thilke, *this,* **beede,** *offer* **361 wole,** *wish* **363 nyl,** *will not* **364 For to be deed,** *upon pain of death* **366 cheere,** *expression* **372 for,** *so,* **geere,** *clothing* **373 bad,** *ordered* **374 dispoillen,** *undress* **379 han . . . kembd,** *have combed,* **untressed,** *unbraided* **380 Ful rudely,** *very disorderly,* **hir,** *their* **381 corone,** *nuptial garland,* **han ydressed,** *have placed* **382 nowches,** *brooches* **384 Unnethe,** *hardly* **387 cause,** *purpose* **388 wel amblyng,** *a gentle walker* **389 er he lenger lette,** *with no delay* **392 sonne gan descende,** *sun went down* **393 chace,** *follow* **394 markysesse,** *marquise* **396 nat by liklynesse,** *unlikely* **397 rudenesse,** *humbleness* **398 cote,** *pen* **399 norissed,** *raised* **400 wight,** *person,* **woxen,** *grown* **401 ther,** *where,* **bore,** *born* **403 Unnethe trowed,** *hardly believed,* **dorste han,** *necessarily* **409 thewes,** *qualities,* **heigh bountee,** *great generosity* **411 benigne,** *good,* **digne,** *worthy* **415 Publiced,** *made known,* **bountee,** *goodness* **416 eek biside,** *also nearby* **417 oon seide,** *one said* **420 Goon,** *went* **422 honestetee,** *virtue* **425 for,** *because* **427 seyn,** *seen,* **seelde,** *seldom*

365 Repeated at line 1051, framing the narrative and highlighting the theme of sufficiency. **375–76** Chaucer follows the French version rather than Petrarch here and develops its concern with clothing in greater detail elsewhere. **382 of,** omitted in Hg. **385 translated,** transformed; the term was used for various changes of state, including sanctification and deification. **404 That to,** El reads "That she to." **415 bountee,** El reads "beautee." **418 fame,** El reads "name." **425 low,** El reads "heigh." **426 ofte,** omitted in El.

Nat oonly this Grisildis thurgh hir wit
Koude° al the feet° of wyfly hoomlinesse°,
But eek, whan that the cas° required it,
The commune profit koude she redresse°.
Ther nas° discord, rancour, ne hevynesse°
In al that land that she ne koude apese°,
And wisely brynge hem alle in reste and ese.

Though that° hire housbonde absent were, anon
If gentil men or othere° of hire contree
Were wrothe°, she wolde bryngen hem aton°;
So wise and rype wordes hadde she,
And juggementz of so greet equitee°,
That she from hevene sent was, as men wende°,
Peple to save and every wrong t'amende.

Nat longe tyme after that this Grisild
Was wedded, she a doghter hath ybore,
Al had hire levere° have born a knave° child.
Glad was this markys and the folk therfore,
For though a mayde child coome al bifore,
She may unto a knave child atteyne°
By liklihede, syn° she nys nat bareyne°.

Explicit secunda pars. Incipit tercia pars.

Ther fil°, as it bifalleth tymes mo°,
Whan that this child had souked° but a throwe°,
This markys in his herte longeth so
To tempte his wyf, hir sadnesse° for to knowe,
That he ne myghte out of his herte throwe
This merveillous desir his wyf t'assaye—
Nedelees, God woot°, he thoghte hire for t'affraye°.

He hadde assayed hire ynogh bifore
And foond hire evere good. What neded it
Hire for to tempte, and alwey moore and moore,
Though som men preise it for a subtil wit°?
But as for me, I seye that yvele it sit°
To assaye a wyf whan that it is no nede,
And putten hire in angwyssh and in drede.

For which this markys wroghte° in this manere:
He cam allone a-nyght ther as she lay,
With stierne° face and with ful trouble cheere°,
And seyde thus, "Grisilde," quod he, "that day
That I yow took out of youre pouere° array
And putte yow in estaat of heigh noblesse—
Ye have nat that forgeten, as I gesse?

"I seye, Grisilde, this present dignitee°
In which that I have put yow, as I trowe°,
Maketh° yow nat foryetful for to be°
That I yow took in poure estaat ful lowe,
For any wele° ye moot yourselven knowe°.
Taak heede of every word that Y° yow seye;
Ther is no wight that hereth it but we tweye°,

"Ye woot° youreself wel how that ye cam heere
Into this hous, it is nat longe ago;
And though to me that ye be lief° and deere,
Unto my gentils° ye be no thyng so.
They seyn to hem° it is greet shame and wo
For to be subgetz° and been in servage°
To thee, that born art of a low lynage.

"And namely sith° thy doghter was ybore
Thise wordes han they spoken, doutelees.
But I desire, as I have doon bifore,

---

429 Koude, *knew,* **feet,** *feats,* **hoomlinesse,** *domesticity* **430 cas,** *situation* **431 koude she redresse,** *she was able to restore* **432 nas,** *was no,* **hevynesse,** *unhappiness* **433 apese,** *quell* **435 Though that,** *even if* **436 othere,** *others* **437 wrothe,** *angry,* **hem aton,** *them to accord* **439 equitee,** *fairness* **440 wende,** *believed* **444 Al had hire levere,** *though she would rather,* **knave,** *male* **447 unto . . . atteyne,** *achieve* **448 syn,** *since,* **baryene,** *barren* **449 Ther fil,** *it happened,* **tymes mo,** *often* **450 souked,** *breast-fed,* **throwe,** *short time* **452 sadnesse,** *steadfastness* **455 woot,** *knows,* **t'affraye,** *to frighten* **459 subtil wit,** *clever idea* **460 yvele it sit,** *it is evil* **463 wroghte,** *worked* **465 stierne,** *stern,* **trouble cheere,** *troubled expression* **467 pouere,** *poor* **470 dignitee,** *high rank* **471 trowe,** *trust* **472 Maketh,** *causes,* **foryetful for to be,** *to forget* **474 For any wele,** *despite any prosperity,* **knowe,** *experience* (now) **475 Y,** *I,* **476 tweye,** *two* **477 woot,** *know* **479 lief,** *beloved* **480 gentils,** *noble people* **481 to hem,** *among themselves* **482 subgetz,** *subject,* **servage,** *servitude* **484 sith,** *since*

429 hoomlinesse, El and Hg read "humblenesse," but the words in Petrarch and the French version suggest the household here. **431 commune profit,** public good; the medieval social ideal in which each class performed its proper function and individuals put the social good ahead of personal advantage. See *PF* 47n. **444 knave,** in El, erased and changed to "man" here and at lines 447 and 612. Some later manuscripts also have "man." Compare *MLT* 2.715n. **445 this,** Hg reads "the." **448a *Explicit secunda pars. Incipit tercia pars.*** "Here ends the second part. Here begins the third part." **452–54 To tempte . . . t'assaye,** both mean "to test," but *tempte* has more potential for negative connotations; *assaye* means "to gauge the perfection of." **456–70** Expanded by Chaucer. **482 and been,** El reads "and to been." **483 thee,** the uses of "thee" and "thy" here and in the next stanza are disrespectful, in contrast with Walter's respectful address in, for example, lines 491–97. Compare the more complex uses of second person pronouns in, for example, lines 890–91 and 963–73. **low lynage,** El and Hg read "smal village." The French is "basse lignie" (base lineage).

To lyve my lyf with hem in reste and pees.
I may nat in this caas° be recchelees°;
I moot doon° with thy doghter for the beste—
Nat as I wolde, but as my peple leste°.

"And yet, God woot°, this is ful looth° to me.
But nathelees withoute youre wityng°
I wol° nat doon. But this wol I," quod he,
"That ye to me assente as in this thyng.
Shewe now youre pacience in youre werkyng°
That° ye me highte° and swore in youre village
That day that maked was oure mariage."

When she had herd al this she noght ameved°
Neither in word or chiere or contenaunce°,
For, as it semed, she was nat agreved°.
She seyde, "Lord, al lyth° in your plesaunce°.
My child and I, with hertely obeisaunce°,
Been youres al, and ye mowe° save or spille°
Youre owene thyng; werketh after youre wille.

"Ther may nothyng, God so my soule save,
Liken to° yow that may displese me;
Ne I desire nothyng for to have,
Ne drede for to leese, save oonly yee.
This wyl is in myn herte and ay° shal be;
No lengthe of tyme or deeth may this deface°,
Ne chaunge my corage° to another place."

Glad was this markys of hire answeryng,
But yet he feyned° as he were nat so;
Al drery was his cheere° and his lookyng
Whan that he sholde out of the chambre go.
Soone after this, a furlong wey or two,
He prively hath toold al his entente
Unto a man, and to his wyf hym sente.

A maner sergeant° was this priyee° man,
The which that feithful ofte he founden hadde
In thynges grete, and eek swich folk° wel kan
Doon execucioun in thynges badde—
The lord knew wel that he hym loved and dradde°.
And whan this sergeant wiste° his lordes wille,
Into the chambre he stalked° hym ful stille°.

"Madame," he seyde, "ye moote foryeve it° me
Though I do thyng to which I am constreyned.
Ye been so wys° that ful wel knowe ye
That lordes heestes mowe° nat been yfeyned°;
They mowe° wel been biwailled and compleyned,
But men moote nede° unto hire lust° obeye,
And so wol I; ther is namoore to seye.

"This child I am comanded for to take—"
And spak namoore, but out the child he hente°
Despitously°, and gan a cheere make°
As though he wolde han slayn it er he wente.
Grisildis moot° al suffren and consente,
And as a lamb she sitteth meke and stille
And leet this crueel sergeant doon his wille.

Suspecious was the diffame° of this man,
Suspect his face, suspect his word also,
Suspect the tyme in which he this bigan.
Allas, hir doghter that she loved so,
She wende° he wolde han slawen° it right tho°.
But nathelees she neither weep ne syked°,
Conformynge hire to that° the markys lyked.

But atte laste to speken she bigan,
And mekely she to the sergeant preyde
So as he was a worthy gentilman
That she moste° kisse hire child er that° it deyde.
And in hir barm° this litel child she leyde°
With ful sad° face, and gan the child to blisse°,
And lulled it, and after gan it kisse.

And thus she seyde in hire benigne voys°,
"Fareweel, my child! I shal thee nevere see.

---

488 caas, *situation,* **be recchelees,** *pay no attention* **489 moot doon,** *must do* **490 leste,** *desire* **491 woot,** *knows,* **looth,** *hateful* **492 wityng,** *knowledge* **493 wol,** *will* **495 werkyng,** *actions* **496 That,** *what,* **highte,** *promised* **498 ameved,** *moved* **499 chiere or contenaunce,** *disposition or looks* **500 agreved,** *upset* **501 lyth,** *lies,* **plesaunce,** *pleasure* **502 hertely obeisaunce,** *sincere obedience* **503 mowe,** *may,* **spille,** *kill* **506 Liken to,** *be pleasing to* **509 ay,** *always* **510 deface,** *erase* **511 corage,** *heart* **513 feyned,** *pretended* **514 cheere,** *disposition* **519 A maner sergeant,** *a kind of agent,* **privee,** *confidential* **521 eek swich folk,** *also such persons* **523 dradde,** *revered* **524 wiste,** *knew* **525 stalked,** *crept,* **stille,** *quietly* **526 moote foryeve it,** *must forgive* **528 wys,** *wise* **529 lordes heestes mowe,** *lords' commands may,* **yfeyned,** *evaded* **530 mowe,** *may* **531 moote nede,** *necessarily,* **lust,** *desire* **534 hente,** *seized* **535 Despitously,** *pitilessly,* **gan a cheere make,** *made actions* **537 moot,** *must* **540 diffame,** *bad reputation* **544 wende,** *thought,* **han slawen,** *have killed,* **tho,** *then* **545 syked,** *sighed* **546 that,** *what* **550 moste,** *might,* **er that,** *before* **551 in hir barm,** *to her breast,* **leyde,** *laid* **552 sad,** *steady,* **blisse,** *bless* **554 benigne voys,** *kind voice*

503 or, El reads "and." **507 Ne I,** El and Hg read "Ne I ne." **508 yee,** El and Hg read "thee" (which is less respectful), but in each manuscript, "vel ye" is added in the margin; "vel" is Latin "or." **511 another,** Hg reads "oother." **516 furlong wey or two,** an idiom meaning the "time it takes to travel about 220 yards" (furlong), i.e., a short while. **522 in,** El reads "on." **524 his,** El reads "the." **530 and,** Hg reads "or." **537 and consente,** Hg reads "and al consente." **546 Conformynge,** El reads "Consentynge." **547 to,** omitted in Hg. **551 in,** Hg reads "on." **552–53 blisse . . . kisse,** El reads "kisse . . . blisse." **554–67** Chaucer's addition.

But sith° I thee have marked° with the croys°
Of thilke° Fader—blessed moote° he be—
That for us deyde upon a croys of tree°,
Thy soule, litel child, I hym bitake°,
For this nyght shaltow° dyen for my sake."

I trowe° that to a norice° in this cas°
It had been hard this reuthe° for to se°;
Wel myghte a mooder thanne han cryd "allas."
But nathelees so sad stidefast° was she
That she endured al adversitee,
And to the sergeant mekely she sayde,
"Have heer agayn youre litel yonge mayde.

"Gooth now," quod she, "and dooth my lordes heeste°.
But o thyng wol I prey yow of youre grace,
That, but° my lord forbad yow, atte leeste
Burieth this litel body in som place
That beestes ne no briddes° it torace°."
But he no word wol to that purpos° seye,
But took the child and wente upon his weye.

This sergeant cam unto his lord ageyn,
And of Grisildis wordes and hire cheere
He tolde hym point for point, in short and pleyn,
And hym presenteth with his doghter deere.
Somwhat this lord hath routhe° in his manere,
But nathelees his purpos heeld he stille,
As lordes doon whan they wol han hir° wille.

And bad° his sergeant that he pryvely°
Sholde this child softe wynde and wrappe°,
With alle circumstances° tendrely,
And carie it in a cofre° or in a lappe°
But upon peyne his heed of° for to swappe°
That no man sholde knowe of his entente,
Ne whenne° he cam, ne whider° that he wente;

But at Bologne to his suster deere,
That thilke° tyme of Panik was countesse,
He sholde it take and shewe hire° this mateere,
Bisekynge° hire to doon hire bisynesse°
This child to fostre in alle gentillesse;
And whos child that it was he bad° hire hyde
From every wight°, for oght that may bityde°.

The sergeant gooth and hath fulfild this thyng.
But to this markys now retourne we.
For now gooth he ful faste ymaginyng°
If by his wyves cheere° he myghte se,
Or by hire word aperceyve, that she
Were chaunged. But he nevere hire koude fynde
But evere in oon ylike sad° and kynde.

As glad, as humble, as bisy in servyse
And eek in love as she was wont° to be,
Was she to hym in every maner wyse,
Ne of hir doghter noght a word spak she.
Noon accident° for noon adversitee
Was seyn° in hire, ne nevere hir doghter name
Ne nempned° she, in ernest nor in game.

Explicit tercia pars. Sequitur pars quarta.

In this estaat° ther passed been foure yeer
Er° she with childe was, but as God wolde°
A knave° child she bar by this Walter,
Ful gracious and fair for to biholde.
And whan that folk it to his fader tolde,
Nat oonly he but al his contree merye°
Was for this child, and God they thanke and herye°.

Whan it was two yeer old, and fro the brest
Departed of° his norice°, on a day
This markys caughte yet another lest°
To tempte his wyf yet ofter° if he may.
O nedelees was she tempted in assay!
But wedded men ne knowe no mesure°
Whan that they fynde a pacient creature.

---

556 sith, *since,* **marked,** *signed,* **croys,** *cross* **557 thilke,** *that,* **moote,** *must* **558 tree,** *wood* **559 hym bitake,** *to him entrust* **560 shaltow,** *shall you* **561 trowe,** *believe,* **norice,** *nurse,* **cas,** *situation* **562 reuthe,** *pity,* **se,** *see* **564 sad stidefast,** *firmly steadfast* **568 lordes heeste,** *lord's command* **570 but,** *unless* **572 briddes,** *birds,* **torace,** *tear to pieces* **573 purpos,** *proposal* **579 routhe,** *pity* **581 wol han hir,** *will have their* **582 bad,** *ordered,* **pryvely,** *secretly* **583 softe wynde and wrappe,** *carefully clothe* **584 With alle circumstances,** *in all ways* **585 cofre,** *cradle,* **lappe,** *sling* **586 of,** *off,* **swappe,** *cut* **588 whenne,** *where from,* **whider,** *where to* **590 thilke,** *at this* **591 shewe hire,** *explain to her* **592 Bisekynge,** *requesting,* **doon hire bisynesse,** *undertake* **594 bad,** *ordered* **595 wight,** *person,* **for oght that may bityde,** *whatever might happen* **598 ful faste imaginyng,** *pondering very intensely* **599 wyves cheere,** *wife's behavior* **602 in oon ylike sad,** *constantly steadfast* **604 wont,** *accustomed* **607 Noon accident,** *no change* **608 seyn,** *seen* **609 nempned,** *named* **610 estaat,** *condition* **611 Er,** *before,* **wolde,** *wished* **612 knave,** *male* **615 merye,** *merry* **616 herye,** *praise* **618 Departed of,** *separated from,* **norice,** (wet) *nurse* **619 lest,** *desire* **620 ofter,** *again* **622 mesure,** *moderation*

563 mooder thanne han, Hg reads "mooder have." **564 sad stidefast,** El reads "sad and stidefast." **582 his,** Hg reads "this." **587 his,** Hg reads "this." **588 he cam,** omitted in El. **589–90 Bologne . . . of Panik,** perhaps the castle Panico, which is near the city of Bologna. **589 to his,** Hg reads "he to his." **594 hire,** El reads "hym." **609a *Explicit tercia pars. Sequitur pars quarta.*** "Here ends part three. Here follows part four." **621–23** Chaucer's addition; see 452–54n above.

"Wyf," quod this markys, "ye han herd er this
My peple sikly berth° oure mariage,
And namely sith° my sone yboren is,
Now is it worse than evere in al oure age°.
The murmur sleeth° myn herte and my corage°,
For to myne eres° comth the voys so smerte°
That it wel ny° destroyed hath myn herte.

"Now sey they thus, 'Whan Walter is agon,
Thanne shal the blood of Janicle succede
And been oure lord, for oother have we noon.'
Swiche° wordes seith my peple, out of drede°.
Wel oughte I of swich murmur taken heede,
For certeinly I drede° swich sentence°,
Though they nat pleyn° speke in myn audience°.

"I wolde lyve in pees, if that I myghte;
Wherfore I am disposed outrely°,
As I his suster servede° by nyghte
Right so thenke° I to serve hym pryvely.
This warne I yow that ye nat sodeynly
Out of youreself for no wo sholde outreye°;
Beth pacient, and therof I yow preye."

"I have," quod she, "seyd thus, and evere shal:
I wol no thyng, ne nyl no° thyng, certayn,
But as yow list°. Naught greveth me° at al
Though that my doughter and my sone be slayn—
At youre comandement, this is to sayn°.
I have noght had no part of children tweyne°
But first siknesse and after wo and peyne.

"Ye been oure lord—dooth with youre owene thyng
Right as yow list; axeth no reed at° me.
For as I lefte at hoom al my clothyng,
Whan I first cam to yow, right° so," quod she,
"Lefte I my wyl and al my libertee,
And took youre clothyng; wherfore° I yow preye,
Dooth youre plesaunce°; I wol youre lust° obeye.

"And certes°, if I hadde prescience°
Youre wyl to knowe er ye youre lust me tolde,
I wolde it doon withouten necligence.
But now I woot° youre lust and what ye wolde,
Al youre plesance ferme and stable° I holde.
For wiste I° that my deeth wolde do yow ese°,
Right gladly wolde I dyen yow to plese.

"Deth may noght make no comparisoun
Unto youre love." And whan this markys say°
The constance of his wyf, he caste adoun
His eyen two, and wondreth that she may
In pacience suffre al this array°.
And forth he goth with drery contenance,
But to his herte it was ful greet plesance.

This ugly sergeant in the same wyse
That he hire doghter caughte, right so he—
Or worse, if men worse kan devyse—
Hath hent° hire sone that ful was of beautee.
And evere in oon° so pacient was she
That she no chiere° maade of hevynesse°,
But kiste hir sone and after gan it blesse.

Save° this, she preyde° hym that if he myghte
Hir litel sone he wolde in erthe grave°,
His tendre lymes, delicaat to sighte°,
Fro foweles° and fro beestes for to save.
But she noon answere of hym myghte have.
He wente his wey as hym no thyng ne roghte°,
But to Boloigne he tendrely it broghte.

This markys wondred evere lenger the moore
Upon hir pacience, and if that he
Ne hadde soothly° knowen therbifoore
That parfitly° hir children loved she,
He wolde have wend° that of som subtiltee°,

625 sikly berth, *poorly accept* **626 namely sith,** *especially since* **627 age,** *time* **628 murmur sleeth,** *murmuring slays,* **corage,** *feelings* **629 myne eres,** *my ears,* **smerte,** *painful* **630 wel ny,** *nearly* **634 Swiche,** *such,* **out of drede,** *doubtless* **636 drede,** *fear,* **sentence,** *opinion* **637 pleyn,** *openly,* **audience,** *hearing* **639 disposed outrely,** *firmly decided* **640 servede,** *was treated* **641 thenke,** *think* **643 outreye,** *burst out* **646 wol . . . ne nyl no,** *desire . . . nor will not* (desire) *any* **647 list,** *wish,* **Naught greveth me,** *it grieves me not* **649 sayn,** *say* **650 tweyne,** *two* **653 axeth no reed at,** *ask no advice from* **655 right,** *just* **657 wherfore,** *therefore* **658 Dooth youre plesaunce,** *do as you please,* **lust,** *desire* **659 certes,** *surely,* **prescience,** *foreknowledge* **662 woot,** *know* **663 ferme and stable,** *firmly and solidly* **664 wiste I,** (if) *I knew,* **ese,** *ease* **667 say,** *saw* **670 array,** *condition* **676 Hath hent,** *has seized* **677 in oon,** *constantly* **678 chiere,** *expression,* **hevynesse,** *sorrow* **680 Save,** *except,* **preyde,** *pleaded with* **681 grave,** *bury* **682 delicaat to sighte,** *beautiful to see* **683 Fro foweles,** *from birds* **685 as hym no thyng ne roghte,** *as if he cared nothing* **689 Ne hadde soothly,** *had not truly* **690 parfitly,** *perfectly* **691 wend,** *thought,* **of som subtiltee,** *out of some treachery*

625 oure, Hg reads "this." **647–49** Chaucer's addition. **653 at,** Hg reads "of." **683 for,** Hg reads "hem" **685 ne,** omitted in Hg.

And of malice, or for crueel corage°,
That she hadde suffred° this with sad visage°.

But wel he knew that next hymself, certayn,
She loved hir children best in every wyse.
But now of wommen wolde I axen fayn°
If thise assayes° myghte nat suffise?
What koude a sturdy° housbonde moore devyse
To preeve° hir wyfhod and hir stedefastnesse,
And he continuynge evere in sturdinesse°?

But ther been° folk of swich° condicioun
That whan they have a certein purpos take°,
They kan nat stynte of° hire entencioun,
But right as° they were bounded° to that stake
They wol nat of that firste purpos slake°.
Right so this markys fulliche° hath purposed
To tempte his wyf as he was first disposed.

He waiteth if by word or contenance
That she to hym was changed of corage°,
But nevere koude he fynde variance.
She was ay oon° in herte and in visage,
And ay the forther° that she was in age,
The moore trewe—if that it were possible—
She was to hym in love, and moore penyble°.

For which it semed thus, that of hem two
Ther nas° but o wyl, for as Walter leste°
The same lust° was hire plesance° also.
And, God be thanked, al fil° for the beste.
She shewed wel° for no worldly unreste°
A wyf, as of hirself°, nothing ne sholde
Wille in effect, but as hir housbonde wolde.

The sclaundre° of Walter ofte and wyde spradde°
That of a crueel herte he wikkedly,
For he a poure womman wedded hadde,
Hath mordred bothe his children prively.
Swich murmur was among hem comunly°;
No wonder is, for to the peples ere
Ther cam no word but that they mordred were.

For which, where as his peple therbifore
Hadde loved hym wel, the sclaundre of his
diffame°
Made hem that they hym hatede therfore—
To been a mordrere is an hateful name.
But nathelees, for ernest ne for game,
He of his crueel purpos nolde stente°;
To tempte his wyf was set al his entente.

Whan that his doghter twelve yeer was of age,
He to the court of Rome, in subtil wyse
Enformed of his wyl, sente his message°,
Comaundynge hem swiche bulles to devyse°
As to his crueel purpos may suffyse—
How that the pope, as for his peples reste°,
Bad hym to wedde another if hym leste°.

I seye, he bad they sholde countrefete
The popes bulles, makynge mencioun
That he hath leve° his firste wyf to lete°
As by the popes dispensacioun°,
To stynte° rancour and dissencioun
Bitwixe his peple and hym; thus seyde the bulle,
The which they han publiced atte fulle°.

The rude° peple, as it no wonder is,
Wenden° ful wel that it hadde be right so;
But whan thise tidynges cam to Grisildis,
I deeme that hire herte was ful wo.
But she, ylike sad° for everemo,
Disposed was, this humble creature,
The adversitee of Fortune al t'endure,

Abidynge evere his lust and his plesance
To whom that she was yeven° herte and al
As to° hire verray° worldly suffisance°.
But shortly if this storie I tellen shal,
This markys writen hath in special

---

692 corage, *feelings* **693 suffred,** *allowed,* **sad visage,** *sober expression* **696 axen fayn,** *would like to ask* **697 assayes,** *tests* **698 sturdy,** *cruel* **699 preeve,** *test* **700 sturdinesse,** *cruelty* **701 been,** *are,* **swich,** *such* **702 take,** *taken* **703 stynte of,** *refrain from* **704 right as,** *just as* (if), **bounded,** *bound* **705 slake,** *stop* **706 fulliche,** *fully* **709 corage,** *heart* **711 ay oon,** *always one* **712 forther,** *more advanced* **714 penyble,** *painstaking* **716 nas,** *was not,* **leste,** *wanted* **717 lust,** *desire,* **plesance,** *wish* **718 fil,** *happened* **719 shewed wel,** *demonstrated well* (that), **for no worldly unreste,** *on account of no earthly distress* **720 as of hirself,** *in and of herself* **722 sclaundre,** *bad reputation,* **spradde,** *spread* **726 hem comunly,** *them* (the people) *generally* **730 diffame,** *ill repute* **734 nolde stente,** *would not stop* **738 message,** *messenger,* **devyse,** *compose* **741 peples reste,** *people's contentment* **742 leste,** *wished* **745 hath leve,** *has permission,* **lete,** *leave* **746 dispensacioun,** *allowance* **747 stynte,** *stop* **749 publiced atte fulle,** *made fully known* **750 rude,** *ignorant* **751 Wenden,** *believed* **754 ylike sad,** *constantly steadfast* **758 yeven,** *given* **759 As to,** *concerning,* **verray,** *complete,* **suffisance,** *satisfaction*

692 for, Hg reads "of." **699 and,** Hg reads "or." **712 in,** Hg reads "of." **736 his,** Hg reads "this"; **twelve yeer,** the legal age for a girl to marry. **739 bulles,** documents from the pope, so called because of their lead (Lat. *bulla*) seals.

A lettre in which he sheweth his entente,
And secreely he to Boloigne it sente.

To the Erl of Panyk, which that hadde tho°
Wedded his suster, preyde he specially
To bryngen hoom agayn his children two
In honourable estaat° al openly.
But o thyng he hym preyede outrely°,
That he to no wight°, though men wolde enquere,
Sholde nat telle whos children that they were,

But seye the mayden sholde ywedded be
Unto the Markys of Saluce anon.
And as this erl was preyed° so dide he;
For at day set° he on his wey is goon
Toward Saluce, and lordes many oon°
In riche array, this mayden for to gyde,
Hir yonge brother ridynge hire bisyde.

Arrayed was toward° hir mariage
This fresshe mayde, ful of gemmes cleere°;
Hir brother, which that seven yeer was of age,
Arrayed eek ful fressh in his manere.
And thus in greet noblesse and with glad cheere,
Toward Saluces shapynge hir° journey,
Fro day to day they ryden in hir wey.

Explicit quarta pars. Sequitur pars quinta.

Among al this after his wikke usage°,
This markys yet his wyf to tempte moore
To the outtreste preeve° of hir corage°,
Fully to han experience and loore°
If that she were as stidefast as bifoore,
He on a day in open audience°
Ful boistously° hath seyd hire this sentence:

"Certes°, Grisilde, I hadde ynogh plesance°
To han yow to° my wyf for youre goodnesse,
As for youre trouthe and for youre obeisance°,
Noght for youre lynage ne for youre richesse;
But now knowe I in verray soothfastnesse°
That in greet lordshipe, if I wel avyse°,
Ther is greet servitude in sondry wyse°.

"I may nat doon as every plowman may.
My peple me constreyneth for to take
Another wyf, and crien day by day;
And eek the pope, rancour for to slake°,
Consenteth it, that dar I undertake°.
And treweliche° thus muche I wol yow seye,
My newe wyf is comynge by the weye.

"Be strong of herte and voyde anon° hir place,
And thilke dowere that ye broghten me,
Taak it agayn°; I graunte it of my grace.
Retourneth to youre fadres hous," quod he.
"No man° may alwey han prosperitee.
With evene° herte I rede° yow t'endure
The strook of Fortune or of aventure°."

And she answerde agayn in pacience,
"My lord," quod she, "I woot°, and wiste° alway,
How that bitwixen youre magnificence
And my poverte no wight° kan ne may
Maken comparisoun; it is no nay°.
I ne heeld me nevere digne° in no manere
To be youre wyf, no, ne youre chamberere°.

"And in this hous, ther° ye me lady maade,
The heighe God take I for my witnesse,
And also wysly° he my soule glaade°,
I nevere heeld me° lady ne maistresse
But humble servant to youre worthynesse,
And evere shal whil that my lyf may dure°,
Aboven every worldly creature.

"That ye so longe of youre benignitee°
Han holden° me in honour and nobleye,
Where as I was noght worthy for to bee,
That thonke I God and yow, to whom I preye

764 tho, *then* **767 estaat,** *fashion* **768 outrely,** *utterly* **769 wight,** *person* **773 preyed,** *asked* **774 day set,** (the) *established day* **775 many oon,** *many* **778 toward,** *on the way to* **779 cleere,** *bright* **783 shapynge hir,** *taking their* **785 wikke usage,** *evil habit* **787 outtreste preeve,** *utmost test,* **corage,** *heart* **788 loore,** *knowledge* **790 audience,** *hearing* **791 boistously,** *roughly* **792 Certes,** *surely,* **plesance,** *pleasure* **793 han yow to,** *have you for* **794 obeisance,** *obedience* **796 verray soothfastnesse,** *full truth* **797 avyse,** *consider* **798 sondry wyse,** *many ways* **802 slake,** *quell* **803 dar I undertake,** *I dare claim* **804 treweliche,** *truly* **806 voyde anon,** *vacate immediately* **808 agayn,** *back* **810 man,** *person* **811 evene,** *steady,* **rede,** *advise* **812 aventure,** *chance* **814 woot,** *know,* **wiste,** *knew* **816 wight,** *person* **817 no nay,** *undeniable* **818 digne,** *worthy* **819 chamberere,** *chambermaid* **820 ther,** *where* **823 also wysly,** *as surely* (as), **glaade,** *may gladden* **823 me,** *myself* **825 dure,** *last* **827 benignitee,** *goodness* **828 Han holden,** *have held*

784a *Explicit quarta pars. Sequitur pars quinta.* "Here ends part four. Here follows part five." **807 thilke dowere,** that dowry, i.e., the property or money brought by a bride to her husband when they marry. **813 answerde agayn,** Hg reads "agayn answerde." **829 for to,** omitted in El.

Foryelde° it yow; ther is namoore to seye.
Unto my fader gladly wol I wende°,
And with hym dwelle unto my lyves ende.

"Ther° I was fostred of° a child ful smal,
Til I be deed my lyf ther wol I lede,
A wydwe° clene in body, herte, and al.
For sith I yaf° to yow my maydenhede,
And am youre trewe wyf, it is no drede°,
God shilde swich° a lordes wyf to take
Another man to housbonde or to make°.

"And of youre newe wyf God of his grace
So graunte yow wele° and prosperitee.
For I wol gladly yelden hire my place,
In which that I was blisful wont° to bee.
For sith it liketh° yow, my lord," quod shee,
"That whilom° weren al myn hertes reste,
That I shal goon, I wol goon whan yow leste°.

"But ther as ye me profre swich dowaire°
As I first broghte, it is wel in my mynde
It were my wrecched clothes nothyng faire°,
The whiche to me were hard now for to fynde—
O goode God, how gentil and how kynde
Ye semed by youre speche and youre visage
The day that maked was oure mariage!

"But sooth is seyd°—algate° I fynde it trewe,
For in effect it preeved is on me—
Love is noght oold° as whan that it is newe.
But certes°, lord, for noon adversitee,
To dyen in the cas°, it shal nat bee
That evere in word or werk I shal repente
That I yow yaf myn herte in hool entente°.

"My lord, ye woot° that in my fadres place
Ye dide me streepe° out of my poure weede°,
And richely me cladden of youre grace.
To yow broghte I noght elles, out of drede°,
But feith, and nakednesse, and maydenhede.
And heere agayn my clothyng I restoore,
And eek my weddyng ryng, for everemore.

"The remenant of youre jueles° redy be
Inwith° youre chambre, dar I saufly sayn°.
Naked out of my fadres hous," quod she,
"I cam, and naked moot I turne° agayn.
Al youre plesance° wol I folwen fayn°.
But yet I hope it be nat youre entente
That I smoklees° out of youre paleys wente°.

"Ye koude nat doon so dishonest° a thyng
That thilke° wombe in which youre children leye
Sholde biforn the peple in my walkyng
Be seyn al bare; wherfore I yow preye,
Lat me nat lyk a worm go by the weye.
Remembre yow, myn owene lord so deere,
I was youre wyf, though I unworthy weere.

"Wherfore, in gerdon of° my maydenhede,
Which that I broghte and noght agayn I bere,
As voucheth sauf to yeve me°, to my meede°,
But swich° a smok as I was wont° to were,
That I therwith may wrye° the wombe of here°
That was youre wyf. And heer take I my leeve
Of yow, myn owene lord, lest I yow greve."

"The smok," quod he, "that thou hast on
thy bak,
Lat it be stille and bere it forth with thee."
But wel unnethes thilke° word he spak,
But wente his wey, for routhe° and for pitee.
Biforn the folk hirselven strepeth° she,
And in hir smok, with heed and foot al bare,
Toward hir fader hous forth is she fare°.

The folk hire folwe, wepynge in hir weye,
And Fortune ay° they cursen as they goon.

---

831 Foryelde, *repay* **832 wende,** *go* **834 Ther,** *where,* **fostred of,** *raised as* **836 wydwe,** *widow* **837 sith I yaf,** *since I gave* **838 drede,** *doubt* **839 shilde swich,** *forbid such* **840 make,** *mate* **842 wele,** *happiness* **844 wont,** *accustomed* **845 sith it liketh,** *since it pleases* **846 whilom,** *once* **847 leste,** *wish* **848 profre swich dowaire,** *offer such dowry* **850 nothyng faire,** *not at all attractive* **855 sooth is seyd,** *truth is said,* **algate,** *always* **857 Love is noght oold,** *love is not* (the same when) *old* **858 certes,** *surely* **859 To dyen in the cas,** *upon my life* **861 in hool entente,** *in complete conviction* **862 woot,** *know* **863 dide me streepe,** *had me stripped,* **weede,** *clothing* **865 drede,** *doubt* **869 jueles,** *jewels* **870 Inwith,** *within,* **dar I saufly sayn,** *I safely dare say* **872 moot I turne,** *must I return* **873 plesance,** *pleasure,* **fayn,** *happily* **875 smoklees,** *without undergarments,* **paleys wente,** *palace go* **876 dishonest,** *dishonorable* **877 That thilke,** *that this* **883 gerdon of,** *return for* **885 As voucheth sauf to yeve me,** *so grant me,* **meede,** *reward* **886 But swich,** *only such,* **wont,** *accustomed* **887 wrye,** *cover,* **here,** *her* **892 wel unnethes thilke,** *barely this* **893 routhe,** *sympathy* **894 strepeth,** *strips* **896 is . . . fare,** *goes* **898 ay,** *always*

834–61 Expanded by Chaucer. **859 the,** Hg reads "this." **871–72** Similar to Job 1.21; see 932n. **880 lyk a worm,** Chaucer adds the proverbial comparison and lines 881–82. **888 take I,** Hg reads "I take." **890–91 thy . . . thee,** see 483n. **895 foot,** Hg reads "feet."

But she fro wepyng kepte hire eyen dreye,
Ne in this tyme word ne spak she noon.
Hir fader, that this tidynge herde anoon,
Curseth the day and tyme that Nature
Shoop° hym to been a lyves° creature.

For out of doute this olde poure man
Was evere in suspect° of hir mariage;
For evere he demed sith° that it bigan
That whan the lord fulfild hadde his corage°,
Hym wolde thynke it were a disparage°
To his estaat so lowe for t'alighte°,
And voyden° hire as soone as ever he myghte.

Agayns° his doghter hastiliche° goth he,
For he by noyse of folk knew hire comynge,
And with hire olde coote as it myghte be°
He covered hire, ful sorwefully wepynge.
But on° hire body myghte he it nat brynge,
For rude° was the clooth, and she moore of age°
By dayes fele° than at hire mariage.

Thus with hire fader for a certeyn space°
Dwelleth this flour° of wyfly pacience,
That neither by hire wordes ne hire face,
Biforn the folk, ne eek in hire° absence,
Ne shewed she that hire° was doon offence,
Ne of hire heighe estaat no remembraunce
Ne hadde she, as by hire contenaunce°.

No wonder is, for in hire grete estaat°
Hire goost° was evere in pleyn° humylitee;
No tendre mouth, noon herte delicaat°,
No pompe, no semblant° of roialtee,
But ful of pacient benyngnytee°,
Discreet and pridelees°, ay° honurable,
And to hire housbonde evere meke and stable°.

Men speke of Job, and moost° for his humblesse,
As clerkes whan hem list konne wel endite°,
Namely° of men, but as in soothfastnesse°,
Though clerkes preise wommen but a lite,
Ther kan no man in humblesse hym acquite°
As womman kan, ne kan been half so trewe
As wommen been, but it be falle of newe°.

[Pars sexta.]

Fro Boloigne is this Erl of Panyk come,
Of which the fame up sprang to moore and lesse°,
And in the peples eres° alle and some
Was kouth eek° that a newe markysesse
He with hym broghte, in swich pompe and richesse
That nevere was ther seyn with mannes eye
So noble array in al West Lumbardye.

The markys, which that shoop° and knew al this,
Er° that this erl was come sente his message
For thilke sely° poure Grisildis,
And she with humble herte and glad visage°,
Nat with no swollen thoght in hire corage°,
Cam at his heste° and on hire knees hire sette,
And reverently and wisely she hym grette°.

"Grisilde," quod he, "my wyl is outrely°
This mayden, that shal wedded been to me,
Received be tomorwe as roially
As it possible is in myn hous to be,
And eek that every wight° in his degree°
Have his estaat° in sittyng and servyse
And heigh plesaunce°, as I kan best devyse.

"I have no wommen suffisaunt°, certayn,
The chambres for t'arraye in ordinaunce°

903 Shoop, *created,* **lyves,** *living* **905 suspect,** *suspicion* **906 demed sith,** *judged since* **907 corage,** *feelings* **908 disparage,** *disgrace* **909 t'alighte,** *to descend* **910 voyden,** *dispense with* **911 Agayns,** *toward,* **hastiliche,** *hastily* **913 as it myghte be,** *as well as possible* **915 on,** *around* **916 rude,** *ragged,* **moore of age,** *older* **917 fele,** *many* **918 space,** *time* **919 flour,** *ideal* (flower) **921 ne eek in hire,** *nor also in their* **922 hire,** *to her* **924 contenaunce,** *behavior* **925 grete estaat,** *exalted status* **926 goost,** *spirit,* **pleyn,** *complete* **927 delicaat,** *fussy* **928 semblant,** *display* **929 benyngnytee,** *kindness* **930 pridelees,** *without pride,* **ay,** *always* **931 stable,** *faithful* **932 moost,** *mostly* **933 hem list konne wel endite,** *they wish can well write* **934 Namely,** *especially,* **soothfastnesse,** *truth* **936 hym acquite,** *behave themselves* **938 but it be falle of newe,** *unless it happened recently* **940 moore and lesse,** (people of) *greater and lesser* (class) **941 eres,** *ears* **942 kouth eek,** *known also* **946 which that shoop,** *who created* **947 Er,** *before* **948 thilke sely,** *this innocent* **949 visage,** *looks* **950 corage,** *heart* **951 heste,** *command* **952 grette,** *greeted* **953 outrely,** *utterly* (that) **957 wight,** *person,* **degree,** *rank* **958 estaat,** *proper due* **959 heigh plesaunce,** *lofty pleasures* **960 suffisaunt,** *satisfactory* **961 t'arraye in ordinaunce,** *to prepare in proper fashion*

902–03 Chaucer's addition, an echo of Job's curse of the day he was born; Job 3.1–3. **913 olde coote,** old coat; Petrarch and the French versions explain that her father kept the coat in anticipation of her disgrace. **916** Some manuscripts omit "she," which makes it the cloth that is older, as in Petrarch. **932 Job,** known for his patient suffering and the protagonist of the biblical Book of Job. **935** See *WBP* 3.688–91. **937 kan,** omitted in El. **938a [*Pars sexte.*],** part six. Omitted in El and Hg. **941 in,** Hg reads "to."

After my lust°, and therfore wolde I fayn°
That thyn were al swich manere governaunce,
Thou knowest eek of old al my plesaunce.
Thogh thyn array° be badde and yvel biseye°,
Do thou thy devoir° at the leeste weye°."

"Nat oonly, lord, that I am glad," quod she,
"To doon youre lust, but I desire also
Yow for to serve and plese in my degree°
Withouten feyntyng°, and shal everemo;
Ne nevere, for no wele° ne no wo,
Ne shal the goost° withinne myn herte stente°
To love yow best with al my trewe entente."

And with that word she gan the hous to dighte°,
And tables for to sette, and beddes make,
And peyned hire° to doon al that she myghte,
Preyynge° the chambereres°, for Goddes sake,
To hasten hem and faste swepe and shake,
And she, the mooste servysable° of alle,
Hath every chambre arrayed and his halle.

Abouten undren° gan this erl alighte°,
That with hym broghte thise noble children tweye,
For which the peple ran to seen the sighte
Of hire° array so richely biseye°;
And thanne at erst° amonges hem they seye
That Walter was no fool, thogh that hym leste°
To chaunge his wyf, for it was for the beste.

For she is fairer, as they deemen° alle,
Than is Grisilde, and moore tendre of age,
And fairer fruyt° bitwene hem sholde falle°,
And moore plesant, for hire heigh lynage°.
Hir brother eek so fair was of visage°
That hem to seen the peple hath caught plesaunce°,
Commendynge now the markys governaunce.

"O stormy peple, unsad° and evere untrewe!
Ay undiscreet° and chaungynge as a vane°,
Delitynge evere in rumbul° that is newe,
For lyk the moone ay wexe ye° and wane!
Ay ful of clappyng°, deere ynogh a jane,
Youre doom° is fals, youre constance yvele
preeveth°,
A ful greet fool is he that on yow leeveth°."

Thus seyden sadde° folk in that citee,
Whan that the peple gazed up and doun
For they were glad right for the noveltee
To han a newe lady of hir toun.
Namoore of this make I now mencioun,
But to Grisilde agayn wol I me dresse°,
And telle hir constance and hir bisynesse.

Ful bisy was Grisilde in everythyng
That to the feeste was apertinent°.
Right noght was she abayst° of hire clothyng,
Thogh it were rude° and somdeel eek torent°,
But with glad cheere to the yate is went°
With oother folk, to greete the markysesse,
And after that dooth forth° hire bisynesse°.

With so glad chiere his gestes she receyveth,
And konnyngly°, everich in his degree,
That no defaute° no man aperceyveth°,
But ay they wondren what she myghte bee
That in so poure array was for to see
And koude° swich honour and reverence,
And worthily they preisen° hire prudence.

In al this meenewhile she ne stente°
This mayde and eek hir brother to
commende
With al hir herte, in ful benyngne entente°,
So wel that no man koude hir pris amende°.
But atte laste, whan that thise lordes wende°
To sitten doun to mete°, he gan to calle
Grisilde as she was bisy in his halle.

---

962 lust, *wishes,* **fayn,** *wish* **965 array,** *clothing,* **yvel biseye,** *wretched to see* **966 devoir,** *duty,* **at the leeste weye,** *at least* **969 degree,** *place* **970 feyntyng,** *diminishing* **971 wele,** *prosperity* **972 goost,** *spirit,* **stente,** *cease* **974 dighte,** *prepare* **976 peyned hire,** *took pains* **977 Preyynge,** *asking,* **chambereres,** *chambermaids* **979 servysable,** *dedicated* **981 undren,** *midmorning,* **gan . . . alighte,** *arrived* **984 hire,** *their,* **richely biseye,** *rich to see* **985 at erst,** *for the first time* **986 leste,** *wished* **988 deemen,** *judge* **990 fruyt,** *offspring,* **falle,** *be born* **991 heigh lynage,** *high lineage* **992 visage,** *face* **993 hath caught plesaunce,** *were pleased* **995 unsad,** *inconstant* **996 Ay undiscreet,** *always thoughtless,* **vane,** *weather vane* **997 rumbul,** *rumor* **998 ay wexe ye,** *you always wax* **999 clappyng,** *chattering* **1000 doom,** *judgment,* **constance yvele preeveth,** *constancy tests poorly* **1001 leeveth,** *believes* **1002 sadde,** *steadfast* **1007 dresse,** *address* **1010 was apertinent,** *pertained* **1011 abayst,** *ashamed* **1012 rude,** *rough,* **somdeel eek torent,** *somewhat tattered too* **1013 yate is went,** *street goes* **1015 dooth forth,** *does more* (of), **bisynesse,** *tasks* **1017 konnyngly,** *skillfully* **1018 defaute,** *flaw,* **aperceyveth,** *perceives* **1021 koude,** *understood* **1022 preisen,** *praise* **1023 ne stente,** *never ceased* **1025 benyngne entente,** *kind intention* **1026 hir pris amende,** *improve her praise* **1027 wende,** *went* **1028 mete,** *dinner*

963–73 See 483n. **987 the,** Hg reads "his." **990–91** Chaucer's addition. **995–1008** Chaucer's addition. **999 deere ynogh a jane,** costly enough at a halfpenny, i.e., worth nothing. **1009–15** In Chaucer's sources, Griselda greets the new bride personally. **1013 is went,** El and Hg read "is she went." **1017 And,** El and Hg read "And so." **1028 gan to calle,** called; see line 289 above.

"Grisilde," quod he, as it were in his pley,
"How liketh thee my wyf, and hire beautee?"
"Right wel," quod she, "my lord, for in good fey°
A fairer saugh I nevere noon than she.
I prey to God yeve° hire prosperitee,
And so hope I that he wol to yow sende
Plesance ynogh unto youre lyves ende.

"O thyng biseke° I yow, and warne also,
That ye ne prikke with no tormentynge
This tendre mayden as ye han doon mo°,
For she is fostred in hire norissynge
Moore tendrely, and to my supposynge
She koude nat adversitee endure
As koude a poure fostred creature."

And whan this Walter saugh hire pacience,
Hir glade chiere, and no malice at al,
And he so ofte had doon to hire offence,
And she ay sad° and constant as a wal,
Continuynge evere hire innocence overal,
This sturdy° markys gan his herte dresse°
To rewen° upon hire wyfly stedfastnesse.

"This is ynogh, Grisilde myn," quod he.
"Be now namoore agast° ne yvele apayed°.
I have thy feith and thy benyngnytee°
As wel as evere womman was assayed°,
In greet estaat and poureliche arrayed.
Now knowe I, dere wyf, thy stedfastnesse"—
And hire in armes took and gan hire kesse°.

And she for wonder took of it no keep°;
She herde nat what thyng he to hire seyde;
She ferde as° she had stert° out of a sleep,
Til she out of hir mazednesse abreyde°.
"Grisilde," quod he, "by God that for us deyde°,
Thou art my wyf, ne noon oother I have,
Ne nevere hadde, as God my soule save.

"This is thy doghter, which thou hast supposed
To be my wyf; that oother feithfully°
Shal be myn heir, as I have ay disposed°—
Thou bare hym in thy body trewely.
At Boloigne have I kept hem prively°.
Taak hem agayn, for now maystow nat seye°
That thou hast lorn° noon of thy children tweye.

"And folk that ootherweys° han seyd of me,
I warne hem wel that I have doon this deede
For no malice ne for no crueltee,
But for t'assaye in thee thy wommanheede,
And nat to sleen my children—God forbeede°—
But for to kepe hem pryvely and stille°,
Til I thy purpos° knewe and al thy wille."

When she this herde, aswowne° doun she falleth
For pitous joye, and after hire swownynge
She bothe hire yonge children to° hire calleth,
And in hire armes, pitously wepynge,
Embraceth hem, and tendrely kissynge
Ful lyk a mooder, with hire salte teeres
She bathed bothe hire visage° and hire heeres°.

O which° a pitous thyng it was to se
Hir swownyng, and hire humble voys to heere!
"Grauntmercy, lord°, God thanke it yow," quod she,
"That ye han saved me my children deere.
Now rekke I nevere to been° deed right heere,
Sith° I stonde in youre love and in youre grace,
No fors of deeth ne° whan my spirit pace°.

"O tendre, O deere, O yonge children myne!
Youre woful mooder wende stedfastly°
That crueel houndes or som foul vermyne
Hadde eten yow; but God of his mercy,
And youre benyngne fader tendrely
Hath doon yow kept°"—and in that same stounde°
Al sodeynly she swapte° adoun to grounde.

1032 fey, *faith* **1034 yeve,** *give* **1037 biseke,** *beg* **1039 mo,** (to) *others* **1047 ay sad,** *always steady* **1049 sturdy,** *cruel,* **gan . . . dresse,** *arranged* **1050 rewen,** *take pity* **1052 agast,** *afraid,* **yvele apayed,** *treated evilly* **1053 benyngnytee,** *goodness* **1054 assayed,** *tested* **1057 gan hire kesse,** *kissed her* **1058 took . . . no keep,** *paid no attention* **1060 ferde as,** *acted as if,* **stert,** *started* **1061 mazednesse abreyde,** *dazedness awoke* **1062 deyde,** *died* **1066 feithfully,** *truly* **1067 ay disposed,** *always planned* **1069 prively,** *secretly* **1070 maystow nat seye,** *may you not say* **1071 lorn,** *lost* **1072 ootherweys,** *otherwise* **1076 sleen,** *slay,* **forbeede,** *forbid* **1077 pryvely and stille,** *secretly and quietly* **1078 purpos,** *intention* **1079 aswowne,** *fainting* **1085 hire visage,** *their faces,* **heeres,** *hair* **1086 which,** *what* **1090 rekke I nevere to been,** *don't care* (if I were to) *be* **1091 Sith,** *since* **1092 No fors of deeth ne,** *death does not matter,* **pace,** *passes* **1094 wende stedfastly,** *believed firmly* **1098 doon yow kept,** *protected you,* **stounde,** *moment* **1099 swapte,** *collapsed*

1051 See 365n. **1056 dere,** El reads "goode." **1063 ne,** omitted in El and Hg. **1067 disposed,** El and Hg read "supposed." **1075 wommanheede,** see line 239 above. **1079–1113** Chaucer's longest addition. **1081 to,** El and Hg read "unto." **1088 God thanke it yow,** El reads "that thanke I yow."

And in hire swough° so sadly° holdeth she
Hire children two whan she gan hem t'embrace
That with greet sleighte° and greet difficultee
The children from hire arm they gonne arace°.
O many a teere on many a pitous face
Doun ran of hem that stooden hire bisyde;
Unnethe abouten° hire myghte they abyde°.

Walter hire gladeth and hire sorwe slaketh°.
She riseth up abaysed° from hire traunce,
And every wight° hire joye and feeste maketh°
Til she hath caught agayn hire contenaunce°.
Walter hire dooth so feithfully plesaunce°
That it was deyntee° for to seen the cheere°
Bitwixe hem two, now they been met yfeere°.

Thise ladyes, whan that they hir tyme say°,
Han taken hire and into chambre gon,
And strepen hire out of hire rude array,
And in a clooth of gold that brighte shoon,
With a coroune of many a riche stoon
Upon hire heed, they into halle hire broghte,
And ther she was honured as hire oghte.

Thus hath this pitous day a blisful ende,
For every man and womman dooth his myght°
This day in murthe° and revel to dispende°
Til on the welkne° shoon the sterres lyght.
For moore solempne in every mannes syght
This feste° was, and gretter of costage°,
Than was the revel of hire mariage.

Ful many a yeer in heigh prosperitee
Lyven thise two in concord and in reste,
And richely his doghter maryed° he
Unto a lord, oon of the worthieste
Of al Ytaille; and thanne in pees and reste
His wyves fader in his court he kepeth
Til that the soule out of his body crepeth.

His sone succedeth in his heritage
In reste and pees after his fader° day,
And fortunat was eek in mariage,
Al° putte he nat his wyf in greet assay.
This world is nat so strong, it is no nay°,
As it hath been in olde tymes yoore°,
And herkneth° what this auctour° seith therfoore°.

This storie is seyd, nat for that wyves sholde
Folwen Grisilde as in humylitee,
For it were inportable° though they wolde°,
But for° that every wight° in his degree°
Sholde be constant in adversitee
As was Grisilde. Therfore Petrak writeth
This storie, which with heigh stile he enditeth°.

For sith° a womman was so pacient
Unto a mortal man, wel moore us oghte
Receyven al in gree° that God us sent°.
For greet skile is° he preeve° that he wroghte°.
But he ne tempteth no man that he boghte°
As seith Seint Jame, if ye his pistel° rede;
He preeveth folk al day°, it is no drede°,

And suffreth° us, as for oure exercise,
With sharpe scourges of adversitee
Ful ofte to be bete° in sondry wise°,
Nat for to knowe oure wyl, for certes° he
Er° we were born knew al oure freletee°,
And for oure beste is al his governaunce.
Lat us thanne lyve in vertuous suffraunce.

But o° word, lordynges, herkneth er I go:
It were ful hard to fynde now-a-dayes
In al a toun Grisildis thre or two,
For if that they were put to swiche assayes°,
The gold of hem hath now so badde alayes°
With bras°, that thogh the coyne be fair at eye,
It wolde rather breste a-two than plye.

1100 swough, *swoon,* **sadly,** *firmly* **1102 sleighte,** *skill* **1103 gonne arace,** *did separate* **1106 Unnethe abouten hire,** *scarcely nearby her,* **abyde,** *remain* **1107 slaketh,** *decreased* **1108 abaysed,** *disoriented* **1109 wight,** *person,* **hire joye and feeste maketh,** *celebrates and attends to her* **1110 caught agayn hire contenaunce,** *regained her composure* **1111 hire dooth . . . plesaunce,** *does her wishes* **1112 deyntee,** *a delight,* **cheere,** *joy* **1113 met yfeere,** *together* **1114 hir tyme say,** *saw their time* **1116 rude,** *rough* **1122 dooth his myght,** *does his best* **1123 murthe,** *mirth,* **dispende,** *spend* **1124 welkne,** *sky* **1126 feste,** *celebration,* **costage,** *expense* **1130 maryed,** *married* **1136 fader,** *father's* **1138 Al,** *although* **1139 no nay,** *undeniable* **1140 yoore,** *long ago* **1141 herkneth,** *listen,* **auctour,** *author,* **seith therfoore,** *says concerning this* **1144 inportable,** *unsustainable or intolerable,* **wolde,** *wished to* **1145 for,** *so,* **wight,** *person,* **degree,** *social position* **1148 enditeth,** *composed* **1149 sith,** *since* **1151 in gree that,** *happily what,* **sent,** *sends* **1152 greet skile is,** *it is very reasonable that,* **preeve,** *test,* **wroghte,** *made* **1153 boghte,** *redeemed* **1154 pistel,** *epistle* **1155 al day,** *always,* **drede,** *doubt* **1156 suffreth,** *allows* **1158 bete,** *beaten,* **sondry wise,** *various ways* **1159 certes,** *surely* **1160 Er,** *before,* **freletee,** *frailty* **1163 o,** *one* **1166 swiche assayes,** *such tests* **1167 alayes,** *alloys* **1168 bras,** *brass*

1133 in, Hg reads "and." **1137–41** Added by Chaucer. **1137 in,** Hg reads "his." **1140 in,** El reads "of." **1148 which with heigh stile he enditeth,** Hg reads "which he with heigh stile enditeth." See 18n above. **1154 Jame,** James 1.13. **1155 preeveth,** tests, but the connotations include "prove the quality of." See 452–54n. **1160 al,** omitted in El. **1162** Petrarch's and the French version end here. **1168–69 coyne . . . breste a-two than plye,** the coin . . . would break in two rather than bend; pliability is one test for the purity of gold.

For which, heere for the Wyves love of Bathe—
Whos lyf and al hire secte God mayntene
In heigh maistrie, and elles° were it scathe°—
I wol with lusty herte, fressh and grene,
Seyn yow a song to glade° yow, I wene°.
And lat us stynte of ernestful° matere.
Herkneth my song that seith in this manere:

Lenvoy de Chaucer.

Grisilde is deed, and eek hire pacience,
And bothe atones° buryed in Ytaille,
For which I crie in open audience°
No wedded man so hardy be t'assaille°
His wyves pacience in hope to fynde
Grisildis, for in certein he shal faille.

O noble wyves, ful of heigh prudence,
Lat noon humylitee youre tonge naille°,
Ne lat no clerk have cause or diligence°
To write of yow a storie of swich mervaille
As of Grisildis, pacient and kynde,
Lest Chichevache yow swelwe in hire entraille.

Folweth Ekko°, that holdeth no silence,
But evere answereth at the countretaille°.
Beth° nat bidaffed for° youre innocence,
But sharply taak on yow the governaille°.
Emprenteth wel this lessoun in youre mynde
For commune profit°, sith° it may availle°.

Ye archewyves, stondeth at defense,
Syn° ye be strong as is a greet camaille°;
Ne suffreth° nat that men yow doon offense.
And sklendre° wyves, fieble as in bataille,
Beth egre° as is a tygre yond in Ynde°;
Ay clappeth° as a mille, I yow consaille°.

Ne dreed hem nat; doth hem no reverence.
For though thyn housbonde armed be in maille°,
The arwes° of thy crabbed° eloquence
Shal perce his brest and eek his aventaille°.
In jalousie I rede eek° thou hym bynde,
And thou shalt make hym couche° as doth a quaille.

If thou be fair, ther° folk been in presence°,
Shewe thou thy visage and thyn apparaille;
If thou be foul, be fre° of thy dispence°;
To gete thee freendes ay° do thy travaille°;
Be ay of chiere as light as leef on lynde°,
And lat hym care and wepe and wrynge° and waille.

Bihoolde the murye wordes of the Hoost.

This worthy Clerk whan ended was his tale,
Oure Hoost seyde and swoor by Goddes bones,
"Me were levere than a barel ale°
My wyf at hoom had herd this legende ones°.
This is a gentil tale for the nones°
As to my purpos°, wiste° ye my wille.
But thyng that wol nat be, lat it be stille°."

Heere endeth the Tale of the Clerk of Oxenford.

1172 and elles, *or else,* **scathe,** *too bad* **1174 glade,** *gladden,* **wene,** *hope* **1175 stynte of ernestful,** *stop with serious* **1178 atones,** *together* **1179 open audience,** *public* **1180 t'assaille,** *to test* **1184 naille,** *nail* (stop) **1185 diligence,** *eagerness* **1189 Ekko,** *Echo* **1190 at the countretaille,** *in reply* **1191 Beth,** *be,* **bidaffed for,** *tricked because of* **1192 taak . . . governaille,** *take control* **1194 commune profit,** *general welfare,* **sith,** *since,* **availle,** *be useful* **1196 Syn,** *since,* **camaille,** *camel* **1197 suffreth,** *allow* **1198 sklendre,** *slender* **1999 Beth egre,** *be eager,* **tygre yond in Ynde,** *tiger yonder in India* **1200 Ay clappeth,** *always make noise,* **consaille,** *counsel* **1202 maille,** *chain mail* **1203 arwes,** *arrows,* **crabbed,** *angry* **1204 aventaille,** *neck protector* **1205 rede eek,** *advise also* **1206 couche,** *cower* **1207 ther,** *where,* **been in presence,** *are present* **1209 fre,** *generous,* **dispence,** *spending* **1210 ay,** *always,* **travaille,** *effort* **1211 leef on lynde,** *leaf on linden tree* **1212 wrynge,** *wring* (his hands) **1212c Me were levere than a barel ale,** *I would prefer to a barrel of ale* (that) **1212d legende ones,** *story once* **1212e nones,** *occasion* **1212f purpos,** *thinking,* **wiste,** (if you) *knew* **1212g stille,** *quiet*

1170 Wyves love of Bathe, love of the Wife of Bath, clear indication that the tale can be read as a response to *WBPT.* Yet this entire stanza is lacking in a number of manuscripts. The *Bathe-scathe* rhyme occurs also at *GP* 1.446. **1171 secte,** pun on sect (group of people) and sex. **1172 and,** Hg reads "or." **1176a Lenvoy de Chaucer,** "the envoy by Chaucer"; probably composed independently by Chaucer but appropriate to the Clerk as well. An envoy is a set of stanzas, often metrically ornate, that usually concludes a longer poem with a summary, directive, or message to a specific audience. **1181 hope,** Hg reads "trust." **1188 Lest Chichevache . . . swelwe,** so that Chichevache will not swallow you into her guts. A reference to a French fable of a very lean cow whose only food is patient wives; Bicorne, very fat, eats only patient husbands. **1195 archewyves,** leaders of the female sex (or sect); see 1171n above. Chaucer's coinage. **1200 as a mille,** like the waterwheel at a mill, which produces a repetitive noise. **1212a-g** In El, Hg, and twenty other manuscripts; but note that the rhyme scheme matches that of *ClT* rather than that of the envoy. Perhaps a canceled link. The concluding rubric occurs after this stanza in El; a similar one is found in Hg before the envoy.

From woodcut made by W.H. Hooper and published by the Chaucer Society between 1868 and 1879

Merchant's Tale

Prologue

The Prologe of the Marchantes Tale.

"Wepyng and waylyng, care and oother sorwe
I knowe ynogh, on even and a-morwe°,"
Quod the Marchant, "and so doon othere mo°
That wedded been. I trowe° that it be so,
For wel I woot° it fareth° so with me.
I have a wyf, the worste that may be;
For thogh the feend to hire ycoupled were,
She wolde hym overmacche, I dar wel swere.
What sholde I yow reherce in special
Hir hye° malice? She is a shrewe at al°.
Ther is a long and large difference
Bitwix Grisildis grete pacience
And of my wyf the passyng° crueltee.
Were I unbounden°, also moot I thee°,
I wolde nevere eft° comen in the snare.
We wedded men lyve in sorwe and care.
Assaye whoso wole° and he shal fynde
I seye sooth°, by Seint Thomas of Ynde,
As for the moore part°—I sey nat alle.
God shilde° that it sholde so bifalle°!
"A, goode sire Hoost, I have ywedded bee°
Thise monthes two, and moore nat, pardee°,
And yet, I trowe°, he that al his lyve°
Wyflees° hath been, though that men wolde him ryve°
Unto the herte, ne koude in no manere
Tellen so muchel sorwe as I now heere
Koude tellen of my wyves cursednesse."
"Now," quod oure Hoost, "Marchaunt, so God yow blesse,
Syn° ye so muchel knowen of that art,
Ful hertely° I pray yow telle us part."
"Gladly," quod he, "but of myn owene soore°
For soory herte I telle may namoore."

1214 on even and a-morwe, *in evenings and mornings* **1215 othere mo,** *others* **1216 trowe,** *believe* **1217 woot,** *know,* **fareth,** *goes* **1222 hye,** *high,* **at al,** *in every way* **1225 passyng,** *surpassing* **1226 unbounden,** *not bound,* **also moot I thee,** *as I may proser* **1227 eft,** *again* **1229 Assaye whoso wole,** *test it whoever will* **1230 seye sooth,** *speak truth* **1231 moore part,** *greater number* **1232 shilde,** *forbid,* **bifalle,** *happen* **1233 bee,** *been* **1234 pardee,** *by God* **1235 trowe,** *believe,* **lyve,** *life* **1236 Wyflees,** *wifeless,* **ryve,** *pierce* **1241 Syn,** *since* **1242 hertely,** *heartily* **1243 soore,** *suffering*

1213–44 Lacking in Hg, where *MerT* follows *SqT* and a version of its epilogue. **1213 Wepyng and waylyng . . . ,** echoes line 1212 above. **1219–20 feend . . . overmacche,** recalls the folk theme of the shrewish wife who defeats the devil after he carries her off. **1230 Thomas of Ynde,** cf. *SumT* 3.1980n. Perhaps merely a convenient rhyme. **1241 that art,** the art of marriage.

Heere bigynneth the Marchantes Tale.

Whilom° ther was dwellynge in Lumbardye
A worthy knyght that born was of Pavye,
In which he lyved in greet prosperitee;
And sixty yeer a wyflees° man was hee,
And folwed ay° his bodily delyt
On wommen ther as was his appetyt,
As doon thise fooles that been seculeer.
And whan that he was passed sixty yeer,
Were it for hoolynesse or for dotage°
I kan nat seye, but swich a greet corage°
Hadde this knyght to been a wedded man
That day and nyght he dooth al that he kan
T'espien where° he myghte wedded be,
Preyinge oure Lord to graunten him that he
Mighte ones knowe of thilke° blisful lyf
That is bitwixe an housbonde and his wyf,
And for to lyve under that hooly boond°
With which that first God man and womman bond°.
"Noon oother lyf," seyde he, "is worth a bene°,
For wedlok is so esy and so clene
That in this world it is a paradys."
Thus seyde this olde knyght, that was so wys.
And certeinly, as sooth° as God is kyng,
To take a wyf it is a glorious thyng,
And namely° whan a man is oold and hoor°;
Thanne is a wyf the fruyt° of his tresor.
Thanne sholde he take a yong wyf and a feir,
On which he myghte engendren hym an heir,
And lede his lyf in joye and in solas°,
Where as thise bacheleris synge allas,
Whan that they fynden any adversitee
In love, which nys° but childyssh vanytee.
And trewely it sit wel to be so°
That bacheleris have often peyne and wo.
On brotel° ground they buylde, and brotelnesse
They fynde whan they wene sikernesse°.
They lyve but as a bryd° or as a beest,
In libertee and under noon arreest°,
Ther as a wedded man in his estaat°
Lyveth a lyf blisful and ordinaat°
Under this yok of mariage ybounde.
Wel may his herte in joye and blisse habounde°.
For who kan be so buxom° as a wyf?
Who is so trewe and eek so ententyf°
To kepe° hym, syk and hool°, as is his make°?
For wele° or wo she wole hym nat forsake.
She nys nat wery° hym to love and serve
Thogh that he lye bedrede° til he sterve°.
And yet somme clerkes seyn it nys nat so,
Of whiche he Theofraste is oon of tho°.
What force° though Theofraste liste lye°?
"Ne take no wyf," quod he, "for housbondrye°,
As for to spare° in houshold thy dispence°.
A trewe servant dooth moore diligence
Thy good° to kepe than thyn owene wyf,
For she wol clayme half part al hir lyf.
And if that thou be syk°, so God me save,
Thy verray° freendes or a trewe knave°
Wol kepe thee bet° than she that waiteth ay
After° thy good and hath doon many a day.
And if thou take a wyf unto thyn hoold°,
Ful lightly maystow been a cokewold°."
This sentence° and an hundred thynges worse
Writeth this man, ther° God his bones corse°!
But take no kepe of al swich vanytee;
Deffie° Theofraste and herke° me.

1245 Whilom, *once* **1248 wyflees,** *wifeless* **1249 folwed ay,** *followed always* **1253 dotage,** *senility* **1254 corage,** *feeling* **1257 where,** *how* **1259 ones knowe of thilke,** *once experience that* **1261 boond,** *bond* **1262 bond,** *bonded* **1263 bene,** *bean* **1267 sooth,** *truly* **1269 namely,** *especially,* **hoor,** *gray* **1270 fruyt,** *fruit* **1273 solas,** *pleasure* **1276 nys,** *is nothing* **1277 sit wel to be so,** *is well fitting* **1279 brotel,** *insecure* **1280 wene sikernesse,** *expect security* **1281 bryd,** *bird* **1282 arreest,** *constraint* **1283 estaat,** *condition* **1284 ordinaat,** *regulated* **1286 habounde,** *abound* **1287 buxom,** *obedient* **1288 ententyf,** *attentive* **1289 kepe,** *care for,* **hool,** *healthy,* **make,** *mate* **1290 wele,** (in) *prosperity* **1291 nys nat wery,** *is not weary* **1292 lye bedrede,** *lie bedridden,* **sterve,** *dies* **1294 oon of tho,** *one of those* **1295 force,** (does it) *matter,* **liste lye,** *chooses to lie* **1296 housbondrye,** *domestic management* **1297 spare,** *reduce,* **dispence,** *spending* **1299 good,** *possessions* **1301 syk,** *ill* **1302 verray,** *true,* **knave,** *serving man* **1303 bet,** *better* **1303–4 waiteth ay/After,** *waits always for* **1305 hoold,** *keeping* **1306 Ful lightly maystow been a cokewold,** *very easily may you be a victim of adultery* **1307 sentence,** *message* **1308 ther,** *where,* **corse,** *curse* **1310 Deffie,** *defy,* **herke,** *listen to*

1245 Lumbardye, Lombardy; see *ClT* 4.72n. **1246 Pavye,** Pavia, near Milan. **1251 seculeer,** lay persons, or perhaps, worldly people; see lines 1322 and 1390. Chaucer may have originally intended the tale for a member of the clergy. **1266 so wys,** so wise; this is blunt sarcasm, as much of what follows may be. **1286–92** Echoes (mocks?) contemporary wedding vows. **1294 Theofraste,** Theophrastus, author of the lost antimatrimonial *Liber Aureolus de Nuptiis* (*Golden Book of Marriage*), part of which is preserved in Jerome's *Epistola adversus Jovinianum* (*Letter against Jovinian*) 1.47; see *WBP* 3.3n and 3.235–378n above. **1305–06** Reading found in El and one other manuscript. Hg reads "And if thow take a wyf," and then finishes the two lines into space originally left blank: "she wole destroye / Thy good substance and thy body annoye." The many variants in other manuscripts suggest Chaucer may not have completed the couplet.

A wyf is Goddes yifte verraily°;
Alle othere manere yiftes hardily°,
As londes, rentes, pasture, or commune,
Or moebles°, alle been yiftes° of Fortune,
That passen as a shadwe upon a wal.
But drede° nat, if pleynly speke I shal,
A wyf wol laste and in thyn hous endure
Wel lenger than thee list°, paraventure°.
Mariage is a ful greet sacrement.
He which that hath no wyf, I holde hym shent°.
He lyveth helplees and al desolat—
I speke of folk in seculer estaat°.
And herke° why, I sey nat this for noght,
That womman is for mannes help ywroght°.
The hye God, whan he hadde Adam maked.
And saugh him al allone, bely-naked,
God of his grete goodnesse seyde than,
"Lat us now make an help unto this man
Lyk to hymself," and thanne he made him Eve.
Heere may ye se, and heerby may ye preve°,
That wyf is mannes help and his confort,
His paradys terrestre° and his disport°.
So buxom° and so vertuous is she
They moste nedes° lyve in unitee.
O flessh they been, and o flessh, as I gesse,
Hath but oon herte in wele° and in distresse.
A wyf, a Seinte Marie°, benedicite°,
How myghte a man han any adversitee
That hath a wyf? Certes, I kan nat seye.
The blisse which that is bitwixe hem tweye°
Ther may no tonge telle or herte thynke.
If he be poure, she helpeth hym to swynke°;
She kepeth his good°, and wasteth never a deel°;
Al that hire housbonde lust°, hire liketh° weel;
She seith nat ones nay, whan he seith ye.
"Do this," seith he. "Al redy, sire," seith she.
O, blisful ordre of wedlok precious,
Thou art so murye° and eek so vertuous,
And so commended and appreved eek°
That every man that halt hym° worth a leek
Upon his bare knees oughte al his lyf
Thanken his God that hym hath sent a wyf,
Or elles preye to God hym for to sende
A wyf to laste unto his lyves ende,
For thanne his lyf is set in sikernesse°.
He may nat be deceyved, as I gesse,
So that° he werke after° his wyves reed°.
Thanne may he boldely beren up his heed—
They been so trewe and therwithal° so wyse.
For which, if thou wolt werken as the wyse,
Do alwey so as wommen wol thee rede°.
Lo how that Jacob, as thise clerkes rede°,
By good conseil of his mooder Rebekke
Boond° the kydes° skyn aboute his nekke,
Thurgh which his fadres benysoun° he wan.
Lo Judith, as the storie eek telle kan,
By wys conseil she Goddes peple kepte°,
And slow° hym Olofernus whil he slepte.
Lo Abigayl, by good conseil how she
Saved hir housbonde Nabal whan that he
Sholde han be slayn. And looke° Ester also
By good conseil delyvered out of wo
The peple of God, and made hym Mardochee
Of Assuere enhaunced° for to be.
Ther nys nothyng in gree superlatyf°,
As seith Senek, above an humble wyf.
Suffre° thy wyves tonge, as Catoun bit°;
She shal comande, and thou shalt suffren it,
And yet she wole obeye of curteisye°.
A wyf is kepere of thyn housbondrye°.

1311 verraily, *truly* **1312 hardily,** *certainly* **1314 moebles,** *movable possessions,* **been yiftes,** *are gifts* **1316 drede,** *doubt* **1318 list,** *wish,* **paraventure,** *perhaps* **1320 shent,** *lost* **1322 folk in seculer estaat,** *lay people* **1323 herke,** *listen* **1324 is . . . ywroght,** *is created* **1330 preve,** *prove* **1332 paradys terreste,** *worldly paradise,* **disport,** *entertainment* **1333 buxom,** *obedient* **1334 moste nedes,** *must necessarily* **1336 wele,** *happiness* **1337 Seinte Marie,** *Holy Mary,* **benedicite,** *bless us* **1340 tweye,** *two* **1342 swynke,** *work* **1343 good,** *goods,* **deel,** *bit* **1344 lust,** *desires,* **hire liketh,** (it) *pleases her* **1348 murye,** *merry* **1349 appreved eek,** *approved of too* **1350 halt hym,** *thinks himself* **1355 sikernesse,** *security* **1357 So that,** *as long as,* **werke after,** *follows,* **reed,** *advice* **1359 therwithal,** *also* **1361 rede,** *advise* **1362 rede,** *teach* **1364 Boond,** *tied,* **kydes,** *goat's* **1365 benysoun,** *blessing* **1367 kepte,** *protected* **1368 slow,** *slew* **1371 looke,** *consider* **1374 enhaunced,** *advanced* **1375 in gree superlatyf,** *in highest degree* **1377 Suffre,** *endure,* **bit,** *ordered* **1379 of curteisye,** *for proper manners* **1380 housbondrye,** *domestic arrangements*

1311–14 From Albertano of Brescia, *Liber de Amore Dei* (*Book of the Love of God*). **1313 commune,** rights to use common lands for grazing, woodcutting, etc. **1316 drede nat,** El reads "dredelees." **1325–35 Adam . . . O flessh,** one flesh; Genesis 2.18, 24; from Albertano of Brescia, *De Amore.* **1326 al,** omitted in Hg. **1330 heerby,** Hg reads "here." **1350 every,** Hg reads "any." **1362–88** These examples and sayings are all found in Albertano's *De Amore* or his *Liber Consolationis et Consilii* (*Book of Consolation and Counsel*). Chaucer uses the same biblical examples in *Mel* 7.1098–1101. **1362–63 Jacob . . . Rebekke,** Jacob is told by his mother Rebecca how to deceive his father Isaac with a goat's skin and gain Isaac's blessing; Genesis 27. **1365 Thurgh,** Hg reads "For." **1366–68 Judith . . . Olofernus,** in the apocryphal Book of Judith 12–13, Judith kills the intoxicated warrior Holofernes to protect the Israelites. **1367 wys,** Hg reads "good." **1369–70 Abigayl . . . Nabal,** Abigail convinces David not to seek revenge for the offense of her husband Nabal; David later marries Abigail; 1 Samuel 25.10–42. **1371–74 Ester . . . Mardochee . . . Assuere,** outfoxing the enemy of Mordecai, Esther convinces her husband, King Ahasuerus, to promote Mordecai and save the Jews; Esther 7–8. **1376 Senek,** not actually in Seneca; from Albertano *De Consolationis.* **1377 Catoun,** Cato, *Distiches,* but from Albertano, *De Amore.*

Wel may the sike man biwaille and wepe
Ther as ther nys no° wyf the hous to kepe.
I warne thee, if wisely thou wolt wirche°,
Love wel thy wyf as Crist loved his chirche.
If thou lovest thyself, thou lovest thy wyf.
No man hateth his flessh, but in his lyf
He fostreth it, and therfore bidde I thee
Cherisse° thy wyf or thou shalt nevere thee°.
Housbonde and wyf, whatso° men jape° or pleye,
Of worldly° folk holden the siker° weye.
They been so knyt° ther may noon harm bityde°,
And namely° upon the wyves syde.
For which this Januarie, of whom I tolde,
Considered hath, in with his dayes olde,
The lusty lyf, the vertuous quyete°
That is in mariage hony-sweete,
And for his freendes on a day he sente
To tellen hem th'effect° of his entente.
With face sad° his tale he hath hem toold.
He seyde, "Freendes, I am hoor° and oold,
And almoost, God woot°, on my pittes brynke°;
Upon my soule somwhat moste I thynke.
I have my body folily despended°.
Blessed be God that it shal been amended,
For I wol be, certeyn, a wedded man,
And that anoon° in al the haste I kan,
Unto som mayde fair and tendre of age.
I prey yow, shapeth° for my mariage
Al sodeynly°, for I wol nat abyde°;
And I wol fonde t'espien°, on my syde°,
To whom I may be wedded hastily.
But forasmuche as° ye been mo than I°,
Ye shullen rather swich° a thyng espyen
Than I, and where me best were to allyen°.
"But o thyng warne I yow, my freendes deere,
I wol noon oold wyf han° in no manere.
She shal nat passe twenty yeer, certayn.
Oold fissh and yong flessh wolde I have fayn°.
Bet° is," quod he, "a pyk than a pykerel°,
And bet than old boef° is the tendre veel.
I wol no womman thritty yeer of age;
It is but bene-straw° and greet forage°.
And eek thise olde wydwes°, God it woot°,
They konne so muchel craft on Wades boot,
So muchel broken harm° whan that hem leste°,
That with hem sholde I nevere lyve in reste.
For sondry scoles maken sotile° clerkis:
Womman of manye scoles half a clerk is.
But certeynly, a yong thyng may men gye°
Right as men may warm wex with handes plye°.
Wherfore I sey yow pleynly, in a clause,
I wol noon oold wyf han right for this cause.
For if so were° I hadde swich myschaunce
That I in hire ne koude han no plesaunce°,
Thanne sholde I lede my lyf in avoutrye°,
And streight° unto the devel whan I dye.
Ne children sholde I none upon hire geten°,
Yet were me levere° houndes had me eten
Than that myn heritage sholde falle
In straunge hand°. And this I telle yow alle:
I dote nat°, I woot° the cause why
Men sholde wedde, and forthermoore woot I
Ther speketh many a man of mariage
That woot namoore of it than woot my page°
For whiche causes man sholde take a wyf.
Siththe° he may nat lyven chaast° his lyf,
Take hym a wyf with greet devocioun
By cause of leveful° procreacioun
Of children, to th'onour of God above,
And nat oonly for paramour° or love;
And for° they sholde leccherye eschue°
And yelde hir dette whan that it is due;

1382 Ther as ther nys no, *where there is no* **1383 wirche,** *do* **1388 Cherisse,** *cherish,* **thee,** *prosper* **1389 whatso,** *however,* **jape,** *joke* **1390 Of worldly,** *among lay,* **siker,** *certain* **1391 knyt,** *tied,* **bityde,** *happen* **1392 namely,** *especially* **1395 quyete,** *quiet* **1398 hem th'effect,** *them the purpose* **1399 sad,** *sober* **1400 hoor,** *gray* **1401 woot,** *knows,* **pittes brynke,** *grave's edge* **1403 folily despended,** *foolishly spent* **1406 anoon,** *soon* **1408 shapeth,** *prepare* **1409 sodeynly,** *suddenly,* **abyde,** *wait* **1410 fonde t'espien,** *try to discover,* **syde,** *part* **1412 forasmuche as,** *because,* **been mo than I,** *outnumber me* **1413 rather swich,** *more readily such* **1414 allyen,** *ally* (myself) **1416 wol noon . . . han,** *will have no* **1418 wolde I have fayn,** *I prefer* **1419 Bet,** *better,* **pykerel,** *pickerel* (young pike) **1420 boef,** *beef* **1422 bene-straw,** *dried bean stalks,* **greet forage,** *coarse feed* **1423 wydwes,** *widows,* **woot,** *knows* **1425 So muchel broken harm,** *so much to cause damage,* **hem leste,** *it pleases them* **1427 sotile,** *subtle* **1429 gye,** *guide* **1430 plye,** *shape* **1433 if so were,** *if it happened* **1434 han no plesaunce,** *have no pleasure* **1435 avoutrye,** *adultery* **1436 streight,** (go) *straight* **1437 geten,** *beget* **1438 were me levere,** *I would rather that* **1440 In straunge hand,** *into the hands of someone unrelated to me* **1441 dote nat,** *am not senile,* **woot,** *know* **1444 page,** *servant* **1446 Siththe,** *since,* **chaast,** *chastely* **1448 By cause of leveful,** *for the purpose of lawful* **1450 paramour,** *passion* **1451 for,** *because,* **eschue,** *avoid*

1384–88 Ephesians 5.25, 28–29, 33, but from Albertano, *De Amore.* **1393 Januarie,** the suggestive name of the old knight contrasts with the youthful name of his future wife, May; see line 1693 below. **1399 his,** Hg reads "this." **1402 my,** El reads "the." **1424 konne so muchel craft on Wades boot,** know or can do so much cunning in Wade's boat, an obscure allusion to a mythical hero. The following lines suggest it means to cause sexual or domestic sorrow. **1425 that,** omitted in Hg. **1427 sondry scoles,** many schools; a clear echo of the Wife of Bath, *WBP* 3.44^{c-d}. **1433 were I,** El reads "were that I." **1436 unto,** Hg reads "to." **1438 levere houndes,** El reads "levere that houndes." **1446** Hg reads "If he ne may nat lyve chast his lyf." **1452 yelde hir dette,** pay their marital debt; *WBP* 3.130n. **it is,** El reads "they ben."

Or for that ech of hem sholde helpen oother
In meschief°, as a suster shal the brother,
And lyve in chastitee ful holily—
But sires, by youre leve, that am nat I.
For, God be thanked, I dar make avaunt°,
I feele my lymes stark° and suffisaunt
To do al that a man bilongeth to;
I woot myselven best what I may do.
Though I be hoor°, I fare° as dooth a tree
That blosmeth er that° fruyt ywoxen bee°,
And blosmy tree nys neither° drye ne deed.
I feele me nowhere hoor but on myn heed;
Myn herte and alle my lymes been as grene
As laurer° thurgh the yeer is for to sene°.
And syn that° ye han herd al myn entente,
I p ey yow to my wyl ye wole assente."
  Diverse men diversely hym tolde
Of mariage manye ensamples olde.
Somme blamed it, somme preysed it, certeyn,
But atte laste, shortly for to seyn,
As alday falleth° altercacioun
Bitwixen freendes in disputisoun,
Ther fil° a stryf bitwixe his bretheren two,
Of whiche that oon was cleped° Placebo.
Justinus soothly° called was that oother.
  Placebo seyde, "O Januarie, brother,
Ful litel nede hadde ye, my lord so deere,
Conseil to axe° of any that is heere,
But° that ye been so ful of sapience°
That yow ne liketh°, for youre heighe prudence,
To weyven fro° the word of Salomon.
This word seyde he unto us everychon:
'Wirk alle thyng by conseil,' thus seyde he,
'And thanne shaltow° nat repente thee.'
But though that Salomon spak swich° a word°,
Myn owene deere brother and my lord,
So wysly° God my soule brynge at reste,
I holde youre owene conseil is the beste.
For, brother myn, of me taak this motyf°,
I have now been a court-man al my lyf,
And God it woot°, though I unworthy be,
I have stonden° in ful greet degree°
Abouten lordes of ful heigh estaat;
Yet hadde I nevere with noon of hem debaat°.
I nevere hem contraried, trewely;
I woot wel that my lord kan° moore than I.
What that° he seith, I holde it ferme° and stable;
I seye the same or elles thyng semblable°.
A ful greet fool is any conseillour
That serveth any lord of heigh honour
That dar presume, or elles thenken it,
That his conseil sholde passe his lordes wit.
Nay, lordes been no fooles, by my fay°.
Ye han° youreselven shewed heer today
So heigh sentence°, so holily° and weel,
That I consente and conferme everydeel°
Youre wordes alle and youre opinioun.
By God, ther nys no° man in al this toun,
N'yn Ytaille°, that koude bet han sayd°!
Crist halt hym° of this conseil ful wel apayd°.
And trewely, it is an heigh corage°
Of any man that stapen° is in age
To take a yong wyf. By my fader kyn°,
Youre hert° hangeth on a joly pyn!
Dooth now in this matiere right as yow leste°,
For finally I holde it for the beste."
  Justinus that ay stille° sat and herde
Right in this wise° he to Placebo answerde:
"Now, brother myn, be pacient I preye,
Syn° ye han seyd°, and herkneth what I seye.
Senek among his othere wordes wyse
Seith° that a man oghte hym right wel avyse°
To whom he yeveth° his lond or his catel°.
And syn I oghte avyse me right wel
To whom I yeve my good awey fro me,
Wel muchel moore I oghte avysed be

1454 meschief, *misfortune* **1457 avaunt,** *boast* **1458 lymes stark,** *limbs strong* **1461 hoor,** *gray,* **fare,** *act* **1462 blosmeth er that,** *blossoms before,* **ywoxen bee,** *is grown* **1463 nys neither,** *is neither* **1466 laurer,** *laurel* (evergreen), **is for to sene,** *can be seen* **1467 syn that,** *since* **1473 alday falleth,** *always happens in* **1475 fil,** *occurred* **1476 cleped,** *called* **1477 soothly,** *truly* **1480 axe,** *ask* **1481 But,** *except,* **sapience,** *wisdom* **1482 ne liketh,** *don't like* **1483 weyven fro,** *deviate from* **1486 shaltow,** *you shall* **1487 swich,** *such,* **word,** *saying* **1489 wysly,** *surely* **1491 motyf,** *sentiment* **1493 woot,** *knows* **1494 stonden,** *stood,* **greet degree,** *high rank* **1496 debaat,** *disagreement* **1498 kan,** *knows* **1499 What that,** *whatever,* **holde it ferme,** *consider it solid* **1500 elles thyng semblable,** *else something similar* **1505 fay,** *faith* **1506 han,** *have* **1507 So heigh sentence,** *such noble judgment,* **holily,** *wholly* **1508 everydeel,** *completely* **1510 nys no,** *is no* **1511 N'yn Ytaille,** *nor in Italy,* **bet han sayd,** *have said better* **1512 halt hym,** *considers himself,* **ful wel apayd,** *very well satisfied* **1513 an heigh corage,** *grand impulse* **1514 stapen,** *advanced* **1515 fader kyn,** *father's relatives* **1517 leste,** *please* **1519 ay stille,** *completely still* **1520 wise,** *way* **1522 Syn,** *since,* **han seyd,** *have spoken* **1524 Seith,** *says,* **hym . . . avyse,** *consider* **1525 yeveth,** *gives,* **catel,** *possessions*

1456 Another echo of the Wife of Bath, *WBP* 3.112. **1462 that,** Hg reads "the." **1468 wyl,** Hg reads "conseil." **1476 Placebo,** "I will please." See *SumT* 3.2075n. **1477 Justinus,** "the just one." **1485–86** Ecclesiasticus 32.24, attributed to Solomon. **1495 of ful heigh,** Hg reads "in ful greet." **1506 shewed,** El reads "seyd." **1511 that,** omitted in Hg. **1516 hangeth on a joly pyn,** hangs on a jolly hinge, i.e., is merry. **1523 Senek,** Seneca, but the maxim recurs in antifeminist tradition. **among his,** Hg reads "amonges."

To whom I yeve my body for alwey.
I warne yow wel, it is no childes pley
To take a wyf withouten avysement°.
Men moste enquere°, this is myn assent°,
Wher she be wys, or sobre, or dronkelewe°,
Or proud, or elles ootherweys a shrewe,
A chidestere°, or wastour of thy good°
Or riche, or poore, or elles mannyssh wood°.
Al be it so that° no man fynden shal
Noon in this world that trotteth hool in al,
Ne man, ne beest, swich as men koude devyse°,
But nathelees it oghte ynough suffise
With any wyf, if so were° that she hadde
Mo° goode thewes° than hire vices badde.
And al this axeth leyser for t'enquere°.
For, God it woot°, I have wept many a teere
Ful pryvely syn° I have had a wyf.
Preyse whoso wole° a wedded mannes lyf,
Certein I fynde in it but° cost and care,
And observances° of alle blisses bare°.
And yet, God woot, my neighebores aboute,
And namely° of wommen many a route°,
Seyn° that I have the mooste stedefast wyf,
And eek the mekeste oon that bereth lyf°—
But I woot° best where wryngeth me my sho.
Ye mowe°, for me°, right as yow liketh do.
Avyseth yow—ye been a man of age—
How that ye entren into mariage,
And namely with a yong wyf and a fair.
By hym that made water, erthe, and air,
The yongeste man that is in al this route°
Is bisy ynough° to bryngen it aboute
To han his wyf allone°. Trusteth me,
Ye shul nat plesen hire fully yeres thre°—
This is to seyn, to doon hire ful plesaunce°.
A wyf axeth° ful many an observaunce°.
I prey yow that ye be nat yvele apayd°."
"Wel," quod this Januarie, "and hastow ysayd°?
Straw for thy Senek, and for thy proverbes.
I counte nat a panyer ful of herbes
Of scole-termes. Wyser men than thow,
As thou hast herd, assenteden right now
To my purpos. Placebo, what sey ye?"
"I seye it is a cursed man," quod he,
"That letteth° matrimoigne, sikerly°."
And with that word they rysen sodeynly
And been assented fully that he sholde
Be wedded whanne hym liste° and where he wolde°.
Heigh fantasye° and curious bisynesse°
Fro day to day gan in the soule impresse°
Of Januarie aboute his mariage.
Many fair shap and many a fair visage
Ther passeth thurgh his herte nyght by nyght.
As whoso° tooke a mirour, polisshed bryght,
And sette it in a commune market-place,
Thanne sholde he se ful many a figure pace
By his mirour, and in the same wyse
Gan Januarie inwith his thoght devyse°
Of maydens whiche that dwelten hym bisyde.
He wiste° nat wher that he myghte abyde°.
For if that oon have° beaute in hir face,
Another stant° so in the peples grace°
For hire sadnesse° and hire benyngnytee°
That of the peple grettest voys° hath she;
And somme were riche and hadden badde name.
But nathelees, bitwixe ernest and game°,
He atte laste apoynted hym° on oon,
And leet alle othere from his herte goon,
And chees° hire of his owene auctoritee—
For love is blynd alday° and may nat see.
And whan that he was in his bed ybroght,

1531 avysement, *consideration* **1532 moste enquere,** *must inquire,* **assent,** *opinion* **1533 dronkelewe,** *inclined to drink* **1535 chidestere,** *scolder,* **good,** *goods* **1536 mannyssh wood,** *crazy as a man or man crazy* **1537 Al be it so that,** *even though* **1539 devyse,** *imagine* **1541 if so were,** *if* (it) *were so* **1542 Mo,** *more,* **thewes,** *qualities* **1543 axeth leyser for t'enquere,** *takes time to investigate* **1544 woot,** *knows* **1545 Ful pryvely syn,** *in complete secrecy since* **1546 Preyse whoso wol,** (regardless of) *who will praise* **1547 but,** (nothing) *except* **1548 observances,** *duties,* **of alle blisses bare,** *without any joys* **1550 namely,** *especially,* **route,** *group* **1551 Seyn,** *say* **1552 bereth lyf,** *is alive* **1553 woot,** *know* **1554 mowe,** *may,* **for me,** *as far as I am concerned* **1559 route,** *company* **1560 bisy ynough,** *sufficiently occupied* **1561 allone,** *alone* (i.e., to himself) **1562 yeres thre,** (for) *three years* **1563 doon . . . plesaunce,** *give . . . pleasure* **1564 axeth,** *requires,* **observaunce,** *attention* **1565 yvele apayd,** *displeased* **1566 hastow ysayd,** *have you spoken* (i.e., are you done?) **1573 letteth,** *opposes,* **sikerly,** *surely* **1576 hym liste,** (it) *pleased him,* **wolde,** *wished* **1577 Heigh fantasye,** *intense imagining,* **curious bisynesse,** *complicated activity* **1578 gan in the soule impresse,** *impressed in the soul* **1582 As whoso,** *like someone who* **1586 Gan . . . devyse,** *did . . . fantasize* **1588 wiste,** *knew,* **abyde,** *stop* **1589 oon have,** *one has* **1590 stant,** *stands,* **grace,** *favor* **1591 sadnesse,** *seriousness,* **benyngnytee,** *goodness* **1592 voys,** *praise* **1594 game,** *play* **1595 apoynted hym,** *fixed himself* **1597 chees,** *chose* **1598 alday,** *always*

1530–36 Compare *WBP* 3.285–92. **1533 or sobre,** Hg reads "and sobre." **1538 trotteth hool in al,** an idiom that means "goes perfect in every respect." **1539 swich,** El reads "which." **1545 syn I have had,** Hg reads "syn that I hadde." **1552 oon,** omitted in Hg. **1553 where wryngeth me my sho,** where my shoe pinches me; see *WBP* 3.492n. **1567 Straw for,** an idiom meaning "I care nothing for." **1568–69 I counte . . . / Of scole termes,** I value school terms (i.e., educated talk) no more than a wicker basket full of herbs. **1582–83 mirour . . . market-place,** the image of the mirror of the mind is also used in *TC* 1.365 and *Bo* 5m4.27, but the mercantile comparison here makes January's fixation obnoxious.

He purtreyed° in his herte and in his thoght
Hir fresshe beautee and hir age tendre,
Hir myddel smal, hire armes longe and sklendre°,
Hir wise governaunce°, hir gentillesse,
Hir wommanly berynge, and hire sadnesse°.
And whan that he on hire was condescended°,
Hym thoughte his choys myghte nat ben amended.
For whan that he hymself concluded hadde,
Hym thoughte ech oother mannes wit so badde
That inpossible it were to repplye°
Agayn° his choys—this was his fantasye.
His freendes sente he to at his instaunce°,
And preyed hem° to doon hym that plesaunce
That hastily they wolden to hym come;
He wolde abregge hir° labour alle and some.
Nedeth namoore for hym to go ne ryde°;
He was apoynted ther° he wolde abyde°.
  Placebo cam and eek his freendes soone
And alderfirst° he bad hem° alle a boone°,
That noon of hem none argumentes make
Agayn° the purpos which that he hath take,
Which purpos was plesant to God, seyde he,
And verray ground° of his prosperitee.
  He seyde ther was a mayden in the toun,
Which that of beautee hadde greet renoun.
Al were it so° she were of smal degree°,
Suffiseth hym hir yowthe and hir beautee.
Which mayde, he seyde, he wolde han to his wyf,
To lede in ese and hoolynesse his lyf;
And thanked God that he myghte han hire al°,
That no wight° his blisse parten shal°.
And preyde hem to laboure in this nede°
And shapen° that he faille nat to spede°;
For thanne, he seyde, his spirit was at ese.
"Thanne is," quod he, "nothyng may me displese,
Save o thyng priketh in my conscience
The which° I wol reherce° in youre presence.
  "I have," quod he, "herd seyd ful yoore° ago,
Ther may no man han parfite° blisses two—
This is to seye, in erthe and eek in hevene.
For though he kepe hym fro the synnes sevene
And eek from every branche of thilke° tree,
Yet is ther so parfit felicitee
And so greet ese and lust° in mariage,
That evere I am agast° now in myn age
That I shal lede now so myrie a lyf,
So delicat°, withouten wo and stryf,
That I shal have myn hevene in erthe heere.
For sith that verray° hevene is boght so deere°
With tribulacioun and greet penaunce,
How sholde I thanne, that lyve° in swich plesaunce°,
As alle wedded men doon with hire wyvys,
Come to the blisse ther° Crist eterne on lyve ys°?
This is my drede, and ye, my bretheren tweye°,
Assoilleth° me this questioun, I preye."
  Justinus, which that° hated his folye,
Answerde anon right in his japerye°;
And for° he wolde his longe tale abregge°,
He wolde noon auctoritee allegge°,
But seyde, "Sire, so ther be° noon obstacle
Oother than this, God of his hygh myracle°
And of his mercy may so for yow wirche°
That er° ye have youre right of hooly chirche
Ye may repente of wedded mannes lyf,
In which ye seyn° ther is no wo ne stryf.
And elles°, God forbede but he sente°
A wedded man hym grace to repente
Wel ofte rather° than a sengle° man.
And therfore, sire, the beste reed I kan°:
Dispeire yow noght, but have in youre memorie
Paraunter° she may be youre purgatorie.
She may be Goddes meene° and Goddes whippe.
Thanne shal youre soule up to hevene skippe
Swifter than dooth an arwe out of the bowe.

1600 purtreyed, *portrayed* **1602 sklendre,** *slender* **1603 governaunce,** *behavior* **1604 sadnesse,** *seriousness* **1605 condescended,** *settled* **1609 repplye,** *argue* **1610 Agayn,** *against* **1611 instaunce,** *insistence* **1612 preyed hem,** *prayed them* **1614 abregge hir,** *shorten their* **1615 to go ne ryde,** *to walk nor ride* (i.e., to search) **1616 apoynted ther,** *fixed where* (i.e., with whom), **abyde,** *stay* **1618 alderfirst,** *first of all,* **bad hem,** *asked them,* **boone,** *request* **1620 Agayn,** *against* **1622 verray ground,** *true basis* **1625 Al were it so,** *even though,* **smal degree,** *humble class* **1629 han hire al,** *have her completely* **1630 wight,** *man,* **parten shal,** *shall share* **1631 nede,** *desire* **1632 shapen,** *arrange,* **spede,** *succeed* **1636 The which,** *which,* **reherce,** *describe* **1637 yoore,** *long* **1638 parfite,** *perfect* **1641 thilke,** *that* **1643 lust,** *pleasure* **1644 agast,** *terrified* **1646 delicat,** *delightful* **1648 sith that verray,** *since true,* **deere,** *dearly* **1650 that lyve,** *who lives,* **swich plesaunce,** *such pleasure* **1652 ther,** *where,* **on lyve ys,** *is alive* **1653 tweye,** *two* **1654 Assoilleth,** *solve* **1655 which that,** *who* **1656 japerye,** *mockery* **1657 for,** *because,* **abregge,** *shorten* **1658 allegge,** *appeal to* **1659 so ther be,** *as there is* **1660 myracle,** *power* **1661 wirche,** *bring about* **1662 er,** *before* **1664 seyn,** *say* **1665 And elles,** *or else,* **but he sente,** *unless he sends* **1667 Wel ofte rather,** *more often,* **sengle,** *single* **1668 the beste reed I kan,** (here is) *the best advice I know* **1670 Paraunter,** (that) *perhaps* **1671 Goddes meene,** *God's means*

1608 so, Hg reads "was." **1640–41 synnes sevene . . . tree,** the Seven Deadly Sins were represented as a tree with branches and twigs; see *ParsT* 10.388–90 and elsewhere. **1661 his mercy,** El reads "his hygh mercy." **1662 right of hooly chirche,** extreme unction, or the anointing of the sick, one of the seven sacraments. **1666 hym grace,** grace; "hym" is a reflexive reference to "wedded man." **1670–71 purgatorie . . . whippe,** these images of marital suffering echo *WBP* 3.175 and 489. **1673 the bowe,** Hg reads "a bowe."

I hope to God herafter shul ye knowe
That ther nys no so° greet felicitee
In mariage, ne nevere mo shal bee,
That yow shal lette of° youre savacioun,
So that ye° use, as skile° is and resoun°,
The lustes° of youre wyf attemprely°,
And that ye plese hire nat to° amorously,
And that ye kepe yow eek from oother synne.
My tale is doon for my wit is thynne.
Beth nat agast herof°, my brother deere,
But lat us waden° out of this mateere.
The Wyf of Bathe, if ye han understonde°,
Of mariage, which ye have on honde,
Declared hath ful wel in litel space.
Fareth now wel. God have yow in his grace."
  And with that word this Justyn and his brother
Han take hir leve°, and ech of hem of oother.
For whan they saugh that it moste nedes° be,
They wroghten° so, by sly° and wys tretee°,
That she, this mayden, which that Mayus highte°,
As hastily as evere that she myghte
Shal wedded be unto this Januarie.
I trowe° it were to longe yow to tarie°
If I yow tolde of every scrit° and bond
By which that she was feffed in° his lond,
Or for to herknen° of hir riche array°.
But finally ycomen° is the day
That to the chirche bothe be they went
For to receyve the hooly sacrement.
Forth comth° the preest, with stole aboute his nekke,
And bad hire be lyk Sarra and Rebekke
In wysdom and in trouthe of mariage,
And seyde his orisons°, as is usage°,
And croucheth hem°, and bad° God sholde hem blesse,
And made al siker° ynogh with hoolynesse.
  Thus been they wedded with solempnitee,
And at the feeste sitteth he and she
With othere worthy folk upon the deys°.
Al ful of joye and blisse is the paleys°,
And ful of instrumentz and of vitaille°,
The mooste deynteuous° of al Ytaille.
Biforn° hem stoode instrumentz of swich soun°
That Orpheus ne of Thebes Amphioun
Ne maden nevere swich a melodye.
At every cours thanne cam loud mynstralcye
That nevere tromped° Joab for to heere,
Nor he Theodomas yet half so cleere
At Thebes whan the citee was in doute.
Bacus the wyn hem skynketh° al aboute,
And Venus laugheth upon every wight°,
For Januarie was bicome hir knyght
And wolde bothe assayen° his corage°
In libertee and eek in mariage;
And with hire fyrbrond° in hire hand aboute
Daunceth biforn the bryde and al the route°.
And certeinly, I dar right wel seyn this,
Ymeneus that god of weddyng is
Saugh nevere his° lyf so myrie a wedded man.
Hoold thou thy pees°, thou poete Marcian,
That writest us that ilke° weddyng murie°
Of hire Philologie and hym Mercurie,
And of the songes that the Muses songe!

1675 nys no so, *is no such* **1677 yow shal lette of,** *shall keep you from* **1678 So that ye,** *as long as you,* **skile,** *proper,* **resoun,** *reasonable* **1679 lustes,** *pleasures,* **attemprely,** *moderately* **1680 to,** *too* **1683 Beth nat agast herof,** *be not frightened of this* **1684 waden,** *move* **1685 han understonde,** *have understood* **1690 Han take hir leve,** *take their leave* **1691 moste nedes,** *must necessarily* **1692 wroghten,** *worked* (it), **sly,** *skillful,* **tretee,** *negotiation* **1693 highte,** *was called* **1696 trowe,** *think,* **yow to tarie,** *to delay you* **1697 scrit,** *document* **1698 feffed in,** *endowed with* **1699 herknen,** *hear,* **array,** *clothing* **1700 ycomen,** *arrived* **1703 comth,** *comes* **1706 orisons,** *prayers,* **usage** *customary* **1707 croucheth hem,** *made the sign of the cross over them,* **bad,** *asked* **1708 siker,** *certain* **1711 deys,** *dais* (platform) **1712 paleys,** *palace* **1713 vitaille,** *food* **1714 deynteuous,** *extravagant* **1715 Biforn,** *before,* **swich soun,** *such sound* **1719 tromped,** *trumpeted* **1722 hem skynketh,** *pours for them* **1723 wight,** *person* **1725 assayen,** *test,* **corage,** *desire* **1727 hire fyrbrond,** *her torch* (Venus's) **1728 route,** *company* **1731 Saugh nevere his,** *saw never* (in) *his* **1732 pees,** *peace* **1733 us that ilke,** *for us that same,* **murie,** *merry*

1674 shul ye, Hg reads "ye shul." **1685–87 Wyf of Bathe . . . ,** this break in literary decorum has been thought Chaucer's mistake or the Merchant's, but it neatly compels the reader (or listener) to compare the sentiments of *MerT* with *WBPT.* **1686 ye have,** Hg reads "we han." **1689 that word,** El reads "this word." **1691 nedes,** omitted in El. **1693 Mayus,** May; see 1393n above. **1703 stole,** an ecclesiastical vestment like a long scarf, worn by priest or bishop when performing the sacraments, including marriage. **1700 the,** Hg reads "that." **1704 Sarra and Rebekke,** Sara and Rebecca, biblical figures of wise and faithful wives, referred to in the traditional marriage ceremony. This brisk summary of the ceremony is bitterly ironic, as is the following rhetorical excess. El reads "to Sarra and Rebekke." **1706 his,** El reads "hir." **1710 feeste,** Hg reads "laste." **1715 stoode, El reads "stooden";** Hg reads "stoode swiche." **1716 Orpheus,** mythic musician who freed his wife from Hades by music. **Amphioun,** mythic musician who built Thebes by charming stones to move. **1719 Joab,** King David's trumpeter; 2 Samuel 2.28. **1720 Theodomas,** seer in *Thebaid* (8.343) whose predictions of war came true when the trumpets of the armies sounded. **1722 Bacus,** Bacchus, god of wine. **skynketh,** Hg reads "shenketh." **1723 Venus,** goddess of love, whose laughter, phallic torch, and dance in the following lines are metaphoric and, given the unseemliness of January's desire, parodic. **1730 Ymeneus,** Hymen. **1732 Marcian,** Marcianus Capella, fifth-century author of *De Nuptiis Philologiae et Mercurii* (*Concerning the Marriage of Philology and Mercury*), an allegorical poem about the liberal arts that is antithetical to the libidinous marriage described here. **1734 hym,** Hg reads "he."

To° smal is bothe thy penne, and eek thy tonge
For to descryven of° this mariage
Whan tendre youthe hath wedded stoupyng age.
Ther is swich myrthe that it may nat be writen.
Assayeth° it youreself, thanne may ye witen°
If that I lye or noon° in this matiere.
Mayus, that sit° with so benyngne a chiere°,
Hire to biholde it semed fairye°.
Queene Ester looked nevere with swich an eye
On Assuer, so meke a look hath she.
I may yow nat devyse° al hir beautee,
But thus muche of hire beautee telle I may,
That she was lyk the brighte morwe° of May,
Fulfild of alle beautee and plesaunce.
This Januarie is ravysshed in a traunce
At every tyme he looked on hir face;
But in his herte he gan hire to manace°
That he that nyght in armes wolde hire streyne°
Harder than evere Parys dide Eleyne.
But nathelees yet hadde he greet pitee
That thilke° nyght offenden° hire moste° he,
And thoughte, "Allas, O tendre creature,
Now wolde God° ye myghte wel endure
Al my corage°, it is so sharp and keene!
I am agast° ye shul it nat susteene°—
But God forbede that I dide al my myght!
Now wolde God that it were woxen nyght°,
And that the nyght wolde lasten everemo.
I wolde that al this peple were ago°."
And finally he dooth al his labour°,
As he best myghte, savynge° his honour,
To haste hem fro the mete° in subtil wyse.
The tyme cam that resoun was° to ryse,
And after that men° daunce and drynken faste,
And spices al aboute the hous they caste,
And ful of joye and blisse is every man—
Al but a squyer highte° Damyan,
Which carf biforn the knyght ful many a day.
He was so ravysshed on his lady May
That for the verray peyne° he was ny wood°.
Almoost he swelte° and swowned ther° he stood,
So soore hath Venus hurt hym with hire brond°,
As that° she bar it daunsynge in hire hond,
And to his bed he wente hym hastily.
Namoore of hym at this tyme speke I,
But there I lete hym wepe ynogh and pleyne°,
Til fresshe May wol rewen° on his peyne.
O perilous fyr that in the bedstraw bredeth°!
O famulier foo° that his servyce bedeth°!
O servant traytour, false hoomly hewe°,
Lyk to the naddre° in bosom sly untrewe°!
God shilde° us alle from youre aqueyntaunce.
O Januarie, dronken in plesaunce
In mariage, se how thy Damyan,
Thyn owene squier and thy boren man°,
Entendeth for to do thee vileynye.
God graunte thee thy hoomly fo t'espye°!
For in this world nys° worse pestilence
Than hoomly foo al day° in thy presence.
Parfourned° hath the sonne his ark diurne;
No lenger may the body of hym sojurne°
On th'orisonte as in that latitude.
Night with his mantel° that is derk and rude°
Gan oversprede the hemysperie aboute,
For which departed is this lusty route°
Fro Januarie with thank° on every syde.
Hoom to hir houses lustily they ryde,
Where as they doon hir thynges as hem leste°,
And whan they sye° hir tyme goon to reste.
Soone after that, this hastif° Januarie
Wolde go to bedde, he wolde no lenger tarye.
He drynketh ypocras, clarree, and vernage

1736 To, *too* **1737 descryven of,** *describe* **1740 Assayeth,** *test,* **witen,** *know* **1741 noon,** *not* **1742 sit,** *sits,* **benyngne a chiere,** *serene an expression* **1743 fairye,** *enchanting* **1746 devyse,** *describe* **1748 morwe,** *morning* **1752 manace,** *threaten* **1753 streyne,** *bind* **1756 thilke,** *that,* **offenden,** *attack,* **moste,** *must* **1758 wolde God,** (I) *wish* (to) *God* **1759 corage,** *desire* **1760 I am agast,** *I fear,* **susteene,** *survive* **1762 it were woxen nyght,** *it would become night* **1764 ago,** *gone* **1765 dooth al his labour,** *does all he can* **1766 savynge,** *without compromising* **1767 mete,** *meal* **1768 resoun was,** (it) *was reasonable* **1769 men,** *people* **1772 highte,** *named* **1775 verray peyne,** *sheer pain,* **ny wood,** *nearly crazed* **1776 swelte,** *fainted,* **swowned ther,** *swooned where* **1777 brond,** *torch* **1778 As that,** *the one that* **1781 pleyne,** *lament* **1782 rewen,** *have pity* **1783 bedstraw bredeth,** *mattress begins* **1784 foo,** *foe,* **bedeth,** *offers* **1785 hoomly hewe,** *domestic pretense* **1786 naddre,** *snake,* **sly untrewe,** *secretly false* **1787 shilde,** *protect* **1790 boren man,** *servant since birth* **1792 hoomly fo t'espye,** *to see the enemy at home* **1793 nys,** *there is no* **1794 al day,** *always* **1795 Parfourned,** *performed* **1796 sojurne,** *remain* **1798 mantel,** *cloak,* **rude,** *rough* **1800 route,** *company* **1801 thank,** *thanks* **1803 as hem leste,** *as pleases them* **1804 sye,** *saw* **1805 hastif,** *eager*

1744–45 Ester . . . Assuer, Esther married King Ahasuerus to manipulate him and used her looks effectively; see Esther 2.15ff. and (in the Vulgate) 15.4–19. **1754 Parys . . . Eleyne,** Paris's abduction of Helen caused the Trojan War. **1773 Which carf biforn,** who carved before, i.e., Damian carved January's meat as his personal retainer; see *GP* 1.100. **1776 ther,** Hg reads "as." **1780 I,** omitted in El. **1786** In *Gesta Romanorum,* Tale 174, and elsewhere is found the story of the man who put the frozen serpent in his bosom to warm it only to have it bite him when it thawed. **1795–97 sonne his ark diurne . . . th'orisonte,** the diurnal or daily arc of the sun across the sky and its descent below the horizon, an elaborate way of saying that day is ending. **1799 hemysperie,** hemisphere, the half of the heavens seen from Earth. **1807 ypocras, clarree, and vernage,** three kinds of strong wine, sweetened and spiced, all thought to increase the lustiness and fertility of the drinker.

Of spices hoote t'encreessen his corage,
And many a letuarie° hath he ful fyn°,
Swiche° as the cursed monk daun° Constantyn
Hath writen in his book *De Coitu;*
To eten hem alle he nas no thyng eschu°.
And to his privee° freendes thus seyde he,
"For Goddes love, as soone as it may be,
Lat voyden° al this hous in curteys wyse°."
And they han doon right as he wol devyse°.
Men drynken and the travers drawe anon.
The bryde was broght abedde as stille as stoon;
And whan the bed was with° the preest yblessed,
Out of the chambre hath every wight hym dressed°.
And Januarie hath faste in armes take
His fresshe May, his paradys, his make°.
He lulleth hire, he kisseth hire ful ofte.
With thikke brustles of his berd unsofte—
Lyk to the skyn of houndfyssh, sharp as brere°,
For he was shave al newe in his manere—
He rubbeth hire aboute hir tendre face,
And seyde thus, "Allas, I moot trespace°
To yow, my spouse, and yow greetly offende°
Er tyme come° that I wil doun descende.
But nathelees, considereth this," quod he,
"Ther nys no° werkman, whatsoevere he be,
That may bothe werke wel and hastily.
This wol be doon at leyser parfitly°.
It is no fors° how longe that we pleye;
In trewe wedlok coupled be we tweye°,
And blessed be the yok° that we been° inne,
For in oure actes we mowe° do no synne.
A man may do no synne with his wyf,
Ne hurte hymselven with his owene knyf,
For we han leve to pleye us° by the lawe."
Thus laboureth he til that the day gan dawe°,
And thanne he taketh a soppe in fyn clarree°,
And upright in his bed thanne sitteth he,
And after that he sang ful loude an I cleere,
And kiste his wyf, and made wantown cheere°.
He was al coltissh°, ful of ragerye°,
And ful of jargon° as a flekked pye°.
The slakke skyn aboute his nekke shaketh
Whil that he sang, so chaunteth he and craketh°.
But God woot° what that May thoughte in hir herte
Whan she hym saugh up sittynge in his sherte,
In his nyght-cappe, and with his nekke lene.
She preyseth° nat his pleyyng worth a bene°.
Thanne seide he thus, "My reste wol I take.
Now day is come I may no lenger wake."
And doun he leyde his heed and sleep til pryme°.
And afterward whan that he saugh his tyme
Up ryseth Januarie. But fresshe May
Heeld hire chambre unto the fourthe day,
As us age° is of wyves for the beste,
For every labour° somtyme moot° han reste
Or elles longe may he nat endure,
This is to seyn, no lyves° creature
Be it of fyssh or bryd or beest or man.
  Now wol I speke of woful Damyan,
That langwissheth for love, as ye shul heere.
Therfore I speke to hym in this manere,
I seye, "O sely° Damyan, allas,
Andswere to my demaunde°, as in this cas°
How shaltow° to thy lady, fresshe May,
Telle thy wo? She wole alwey seye nay.
Eek° if thou speke, she wol thy wo biwreye°.
God be thyn help! I kan no bettre seye."
  This sike° Damyan in Venus fyr
So brenneth° that he dyeth for desyr,
For which he putte his lyf in aventure°.
No lenger myghte he in this wise° endure,
But prively a penner° gan he borwe°,
And in a lettre wroot he al his sorwe,
In manere of a compleynt or a lay,

1809 letuarie, *medicine,* **ful fyn,** *very fine* **1810 Swiche,** *such,* **daun,** *master* **1812 nas no thyng eschu,** *was not at all averse* **1813 privee,** *intimate* **1815 Lat voyden,** *empty out,* **curteys wyse,** *a courteous way* **1816 wol devyse,** *wished* **1819 with,** *by* **1820 wight hym dressed,** *man taken himself* **1822 make,** *mate* **1825 brere,** *a briar* **1828 moot trespace,** *must do wrong* **1829 offende,** *displease or injure* **1830 Er tyme come,** *before the time comes* **1832 nys no,** *is no* **1834 parfitly,** *perfectly* **1835 It is no fors,** *it doesn't matter* **1836 tweye,** *two* **1837 yok,** *yoke,* **been,** *are* **1838 mowe,** *are able to* **1841 pleye us,** *entertain ourselves* **1842 gan dawe,** *dawned* **1843 soppe in fyn clarree,** *bread soaked in wine* **1846 made wantown cheere,** *behaved lecherously* **1847 coltissh,** *frisky,* **rageryе,** *frolics* **1848 ful of jargon,** *talkative,* **flekked pye,** *spotted magpie* **1850 craketh,** *croaks* **1851 woot,** *knows* **1854 preyseth,** *praised,* **bene,** *bean* **1857 pryme,** *about 9 a.m.* **1861 usage,** *custom* **1862 labour,** *laborer,* **moot,** *must* **1864 lyves,** *living* **1869 sely,** *foolish* **1870 demaunde,** *question,* **cas,** *situation* **1871 shaltow,** *will you* **1873 Eek,** *and,* **biwreye,** *betray* **1875 sike,** *sick* **1876 brenneth,** *burns* **1877 aventure,** *jeopardy* **1878 wise,** *manner* **1879 penner,** *a case for pen and ink,* **gan he borwe,** *he borrowed*

1810 Constantyn, Constantinus Africanus, eleventh-century author of *De Coitu* (*On Intercourse*), which includes suggestions for virility and remedies for impotence. **1817 travers drawe anon,** the curtain is soon drawn, separating the bedchamber from the hall. **1824 thikke,** El and Hg read "thilke." **1825 houndfyssh,** dogfish, a small shark with rough skin. **1826 shave al newe,** recently shaven, even though older men usually wore beards in Chaucer's time. **1836 coupled,** El reads "wedded." **1839–40 wyf . . . owene knyf,** *ParsT* 10.859 gives the opposite, orthodox view. **1865 of,** omitted in Hg. **1881 compleynt or a lay,** complaint or song, both lyric forms.

Unto his faire, fresshe lady May;
And in a purs of sylk heng° on his sherte
He hath it put, and leyde it at his herte.
The moone, that at noon was thilke° day
That Januarie hath wedded fresshe May
In two of Tawr, was into Cancre glyden.
So longe hath Mayus in hir chambre byden°
As custume is unto thise nobles alle.
A bryde shal nat eten in the halle
Til dayes foure, or thre dayes atte leeste,
Ypassed been; thanne lat hire go to feeste.
The fourthe day compleet fro noon to noon,
Whan that the heighe masse was ydoon°,
In halle sit this Januarie and May
As fressh as is the brighte someres day.
And so bifel how that° this goode man
Remembred hym upon this Damyan,
And seyde, "Seynte° Marie, how may this be
That Damyan entendeth° nat to me?
Is he ay syk°, or how may this bityde°?"
His squieres whiche that stooden ther bisyde
Excused hym by cause of his siknesse,
Which letted hym to doon° his bisynesse;
Noon oother cause myghte make hym tarye.
"That me forthynketh°," quod this Januarie.
"He is a gentil squier, by my trouthe.
If that he deyde°, it were harm and routhe°.
He is as wys, discreet, and as secree°
As any man I woot° of his degree°,
And therto manly° and eek servysable°,
And for to been a thrifty° man right able.
But after mete° as soone as evere I may,
I wol myself visite hym, and eek May,
To doon hym al the confort that I kan."
And for that word hym blessed every man
That of his bountee° and his gentillesse
He wolde so conforten in siknesse
His squier, for it was a gentil dede.
"Dame," quod this Januarie, "taak good hede,
At after-mete ye° with youre wommen alle,
Whan ye han been in chambre out of this halle,
That alle ye go se this Damyan.
Dooth hym disport°—he is a gentil man;
And telleth hym that I wol hym visite,
Have I no thyng but° rested me a lite.
And spede yow faste, for I wole abyde°
Til that ye slepe faste° by my syde."
And with that worde he gan to hym to calle°
A squier that was marchal° of his halle
And tolde hym certeyn thynges what he wolde°.
This fresshe May hath streight hir wey yholde°
With alle hir wommen unto Damyan.
Doun by his beddes syde sit she than°,
Confortynge hym as goodly as she may.
This Damyan, whan that his tyme he say°,
In secree wise his purs and eek his bille°,
In which that he ywriten hadde his wille,
Hath put into hire hand withouten moore,
Save that he siketh° wonder depe and soore,
And softely to hire right thus seyde he,
"Mercy, and that° ye nat discovere° me,
For I am deed if that this thyng be kyd°."
This purs hath she in with hir bosom hyd
And wente hire wey—ye gete namoore of me.
But unto Januarie ycomen is she
That on his beddes syde sit ful softe.
He taketh hire and kisseth hire ful ofte,
And leyde hym doun to slepe, and that anon.
She feyned hire as° that she moste gon°
Ther as ye woot° that every wight° moot neede°,
And whan she of this bille hath taken heede,
She rente° it al to cloutes° atte laste,
And in the pryvee° softely° it caste.
Who studieth° now but faire fresshe May?
Adoun by olde Januarie she lay,
That sleep° til that the coughe hath hym awaked.
Anon he preyde hire strepen hire° al naked;
He wolde of hire, he seyde, han som plesaunce°,

1883 heng, *which hung* **1885 thilke,** *that same* **1888 byden,** *remained* **1894 ydoon,** *done* **1897 bifel how that,** *it happened that* **1899 Seynte,** *holy* **1900 entendeth,** *attends* **1901 ay syk,** *very sick,* **bityde,** *happen* **1904 letted hym to doon,** *prevented him from doing* **1906 That me forthynketh,** *I am sorry about that* **1908 deyde,** *died,* **routhe,** *pity* **1909 secree,** *confidential* **1910 woot,** *know,* **degree,** *rank* **1911 manly,** *reliable,* **eek servysable,** *also willing to serve* **1912 thrifty,** *accomplished* **1913 mete,** *dinner* **1917 bountee,** *goodness* **1921 At after-mete ye,** *after dinner you* **1924 Dooth hym disport,** *entertain him* **1926 Have I no thyng but,** *only after I have* **1927 abyde,** *wait* **1928 faste,** *close* **1929 gan . . . to calle,** *called* **1930 marchal,** *chief officer* **1931 wolde,** *wished* **1932 hath streight hir wey yholde,** *goes straight* **1934 than,** *then* **1936 say,** *saw* **1937 bille,** *plea* **1940 siketh,** *sighed* **1942 and that,** *and* (I ask) *that,* **discovere,** *betray* **1943 kyd,** *known* **1950 feyned hire as,** *pretended,* **moste gon,** *must go* **1951 woot,** *know,* **wight,** *person,* **moot neede,** *necessarily must* (go) **1953 rente,** *tears,* **cloutes,** *shreds* **1954 pryvee,** *toilet,* **softely,** *quietly* **1955 studieth,** *thinks* **1957 That sleep,** *who sleeps* **1958 preyde hire strepen hire,** *asked her to strip herself* **1959 plesaunce,** *pleasure*

1885–87 moone . . . / In two of Tawr . . . into Cancre glyden, the moon was in the second degree of Taurus, the zodiacal sign of the Bull, moving into Cancer, the sign of the Crab. This takes four days. **1894 heigh masse,** High Mass; an elaborate form of the daily liturgy. **1899 this,** Hg reads "it." **1909–12** Given Damian's passion for May, the sexual connotations of several of the adjectives here are ironic. **1909 as secree,** Hg reads "eek secree." **1921 after-mete,** El reads "after-noon." **1923 se,** Hg reads "to." **1958 preyde hire,** Hg omits "hire."

He seyde hir clothes dide hym encombraunce°,
And she obeyeth, be hire lief or looth°.
But lest that precious folk be° with me wrooth°,
How that he wroghte° I dar nat to yow telle,
Or wheither hire thoughte it° paradys or helle.
But heere I lete hem werken in hir wyse
Til evensong rong and that they moste aryse.
Were it by destynee or by aventure°,
Were it by influence° or by nature,
Or constellacioun°, that in swich estaat°
The hevene stood, that tyme fortunaat
Was for to putte a bille° of Venus werkes—
For alle thyng hath tyme, as seyn° thise clerkes—
To any womman for to gete hire love,
I kan nat seye, but grete God above
That knoweth that noon act is causelees,
He deme° of al, for I wole holde my pees°.
But sooth° is this, how that this fresshe May
Hath take swich impressioun that day
For pitee of this sike Damyan
That from hire herte she ne dryve kan°
The remembrance for to doon hym ese°.
"Certeyn," thoghte she, "whom that this thyng displese,
I rekke° noght, for heere I hym assure°
To love hym best of any creature,
Though he namoore hadde than his sherte."
Lo, pitee renneth° soone in gentil herte!
Heere may ye se how excellent franchise°
In wommen is whan they hem narwe avyse°.
Som tyrant is°, as ther be many oon,
That hath an herte as hard as any stoon,
Which wolde han let hym sterven° in the place
Wel rather than han graunted hym hire grace,
And hem rejoysen° in hire crueel pryde,
And rekke nat to been° an homycide.
This gentil May, fulfilled of pitee,
Right of° hire hand a lettre made she
In which she graunteth hym hire verray grace°.
Ther lakketh noght oonly but day and place
Wher that she myghte unto his lust suffise°,
For it shal be right as he wole devyse°.
And whan she saugh hir tyme upon a day,
To visite this Damyan gooth May,
And sotilly° this lettre doun she threste°
Under his pilwe: rede it if hym leste°.
She taketh hym by the hand and harde hym twiste
So secrely that no wight° of it wiste°,
And bad hym been al hool°, and forth she wente
To Januarie whan that he for hire sente.
Up riseth Damyan the nexte morwe.
Al passed was his siknesse and his sorwe.
He kembeth° hym, he preyneth° hym and pyketh°,
He dooth al that his lady lust° and lyketh,
And eek to Januarie he gooth as lowe°
As evere dide a dogge for the bowe°.
He is so plesant unto every man—
For craft is al, whoso that do it kan—
That every wight is fayn° to speke hym good,
And fully in his lady grace° he stood.
Thus lete I Damyan aboute his nede°,
And in my tale forth I wol procede.
Somme clerkes holden° that felicitee
Stant° in delit, and therfore certeyn he,
This noble Januarie, with al his myght
In honest wyse as longeth° to a kynght,
Shoop hym° to lyve ful deliciously.
His housynge, his array, as honestly
To his degree was maked as a kynges.
Amonges othere of his honeste thynges,
He made a gardyn walled al with stoon.
So fair a gardyn woot° I nowher noon,

1960 dide hym encombraunce, *encumbered him* **1961 be hire lief or looth,** *whether* (it was) *to her pleasing or offensive* **1962 lest that precious folk be,** *for fear that prudish people will be,* **wrooth,** *angry* **1963 wroghte,** *worked* **1964 hire thoughte it,** *it seemed to her* **1967 aventure,** *chance* **1968 influence,** *planetary influence* **1969 constellacioun,** *configuration of the stars,* **swich estaat,** *such arrangement* **1971 putte a bille,** *present a petition* **1972 seyn,** *say* **1976 He deme,** (may) *he judge,* **pees,** *peace* **1977 sooth,** *the truth* **1980 ne dryve kan,** *cannot drive* **1981 remembrance for to doon hym ease,** *thought of making him comfortable* **1983 rekke,** *care,* **assure,** *promise* **1986 renneth,** *runs* **1987 franchise,** *generosity* **1988 hem narwe avyse,** *consider carefully* **1989 Som tyrant is,** (perhaps) *there is some tyrant* **1991 sterven,** *die* **1993 hem rejoysen,** *take pleasure from him* **1994 rekke nat to been,** *not care about being* **1996 Right of,** *properly by* **1997 verray grace,** *complete favor* **1999 unto his lust suffise,** *satisfy his desire* **2000 wole devyse,** *will wish* **2003 sotilly,** *cleverly,* **threste,** *thrust* **2004 hym leste,** (it) *pleases him* **2006 wight,** *person,* **wiste,** *knew* **2007 hool,** *healthy* **2011 kembeth,** *combs,* **preyneth,** *preens,* **pyketh,** *cleans* **2012 lust,** *wants* **2013 lowe,** *lowly* (humbly) **2014 for the bowe,** *trained for hunting with a bow* **2017 fayn,** *pleased* **2018 lady grace,** *lady's grace* **2019 aboute his nede,** *pursuing his desire* **2021 holden,** *think* **2022 Stant,** *exists* **2024 longeth,** *pertains* **2025 Shoop hym,** *arranged* (for) *himself* **2030 woot,** *know*

1962 that, El reads "ye." **1966 evensong rong,** bells were rung to signal the beginning of evening religious service. **1979 For pitee of,** Hg reads "Of pitee on." **1986** The familiar chivalric sentiment is mocked here; for other occurrences see *KnT* 1.1761n. **1990 any,** Hg reads "is a." **1991 let hym sterven,** Hg reads "leten sterven." **2007 she,** El reads "he." **2008 hire,** El reads "hym." **2021 felicitee,** supreme happiness. The pursuit of worldly pleasure is attributed to Epicurus and condemned by Philosophy in *Bo* 3pr2.77ff. **2024–28 honest . . . honestly . . . honeste,** honorable / honorably, but the repetition three times in five lines mocks the meaning.

For out of doute I verraily° suppose
That he that wroot the *Romance of the Rose*
Ne koude° of it the beautee wel devyse°,
Ne Priapus ne myghte nat suffise°,
Though he be god of gardyns, for to telle
The beautee of the gardyn and the welle°
That stood under a laurer° alwey grene.
Ful ofte tyme he Pluto and his queene
Proserpina and al hire fairye°
Disporten hem° and maken melodye
Aboute that welle, and daunced, as men tolde.
  This noble knyght, this Januarie the olde,
Swich deyntee° hath in it to walke and pleye
That he wol no wight suffren bere° the keye
Save he hymself; for of the smale wyket°
He baar° alwey of silver a clyket°
With which, whan that hym leste°, he it unshette°.
And whan he wolde paye his wyf hir dette
In somer seson, thider wolde he go,
And May his wyf, and no wight but they two,
And thynges whiche that were nat doon abedde,
He in the gardyn parfourned hem° and spedde°.
And in this wyse many a murye day
Lyved this Januarie and fresshe May.
But worldly joye may nat alwey dure°
To Januarie, ne to no creature.
  O sodeyn hap°, O thou Fortune unstable,
Lyk to the scorpion so deceyvable°,
That flaterest with thyn heed whan thou wolt stynge!
Thy tayl is deeth, thurgh thyn envenymynge°.
O brotil° joye, O sweete venym queynte°,
O monstre that so subtilly kanst peynte°
Thy yiftes° under hewe° of stidefastnesse,
That° thou deceyvest bothe moore and lesse,
Why hastow Januarie thus deceyved,
That haddest hym for thy fulle freend receyved?
And now thou hast biraft hym° bothe his eyen
For sorwe of which desireth he to dyen.
  Allas, this noble Januarie free
Amydde his lust and his prosperitee
Is woxen° blynd, and that al sodeynly.
He wepeth and he wayleth pitously;
And therwithal the fyr of jalousie
Lest° that his wyf sholde falle in som folye
So brente° his herte that he wolde fayn°
That som man bothe hym and hire had slayn.
For neither after his deeth nor in his lyf
Ne wolde he that she were love° ne wyf,
But evere lyve as wydwe° in clothes blake
Soul° as the turtle that lost hath hire make°.
But atte laste, after a month or tweye,
His sorwe gan aswage°, sooth° to seye.
For whan he wiste° it may noon oother be,
He paciently took his adversitee
Save°, out of doute, he may nat forgoon°
That he nas jalous everemoore in oon°.
Which jalousye it was so outrageous
That neither in halle n'yn° noon oother hous,
N'yn noon oother place neverthemo,
He nolde suffre° hire for to ryde or go
But if that he had hond on hire alway;
For which ful ofte wepeth fresshe May
That loveth Damyan so benyngnely°
That she moot outher° dyen sodeynly
Or elles she moot han hym as hir leste°.
She wayteth whan° hir herte wolde breste°.
  Upon that oother syde Damyan
Bicomen is the sorwefulleste man
That evere was, for neither nyght ne day
Ne myghte he speke a word to fresshe May,
As to his purpos of no swich mateere,
But if that° Januarie moste it heere°,
That hadde an hand upon hire everemo.

2031 verraily, *truly* **2033 Ne koude,** *could not,* **devyse,** *describe* **2034 myghte nat suffise,** *might not be capable* **2036 welle,** *fountain* **2037 laurer,** *laurel tree* **2039 hire fairye,** *their fairies* **2040 Disporten hem,** *entertained themselves* **2043 Swich deyntee,** *such delight* **2044 no wight suffren bere,** *allow no one to carry* **2045 wyket,** *gate* **2046 baar,** *carried,* **clyket,** *key* **2047 hym leste,** (it) *pleased him,* **unshette,** *unlocked* **2052 parfourned hem,** *performed them,* **spedde,** *succeeded* **2055 alwey dure,** *forever sustain* **2057 sodeyn hap,** *sudden happening* **2058 deceyvable,** *able to deceive* **2060 envenymynge,** *poisoning* **2061 brotil,** *unstable,* **queynte,** *strange* **2062 kanst peynte,** *can disguise* **2063 yiftes,** *gifts,* **hewe,** *illusion* **2064 That,** (so) *that* **2067 biraft hym,** *deprived him* (of) **2071 woxen,** *become* **2074 Lest,** *for fear* **2075 brente,** *burned,* **wolde fayn,** *would have been happy* **2078 love,** *lover* **2079 wydwe,** *widow* **2080 Soul,** *solitary,* **make,** *mate* **2082 gan aswage,** *lessened,* **sooth,** *true* **2083 wiste,** *knew* **2085 Save,** *except that,* **forgoon,** *cease* **2086 nas jalous everemoore in oon,** *was jealous constantly* **2088 n'yn,** *nor in* **2090 nolde suffre,** *would not allow* **2093 benyngnely,** *graciously* **2094 moot outher,** *must either* **2095 hir leste,** *she desired* **2096 wayteth whan,** *expects the time,* **breste,** *burst* **2102 But if,** *except,* **moste it heere,** *would hear it*

2032 ***Romance of the Rose,*** the thirteenth-century allegory, *Roman de la Rose,* by Guillaume de Lorris and Jean de Meun, which opens in a garden of idleness and narcissistic love; translated by Chaucer, at least in part, as *Romaunt of the Rose.* **2034 Priapus,** Roman god of gardens and fertility, represented with an enormous phallus. **2038–39 Pluto . . . Proserpina,** traditionally, god and goddess of the underworld, but here king and queen, associated with fairies and later presented as comic. **2048 paye . . . hir dette,** see 1452n above. **2059 stynge,** El reads "synge." **2074 som,** El reads "swich." **2080 turtle,** turtledove, a bird fabled for its fidelity to its mate.

But nathelees, by writyng to and fro
And privee° signes wiste° he what she mente,
And she knew eek the fyn° of his entente.
O Januarie, what myghte it thee availle,
Thogh thou myghtest se as fer as shippes saille?
For as good is blynd deceyved be
As to be deceyved whan a man may se.
Lo Argus, which that hadde an hondred eyen,
For al that evere he koude poure or pryen,
Yet was he blent°, and God woot° so been mo°
That wenen wisly° that it be nat so.
Passe over is an ese, I sey namoore.
This fresshe May that I spak of so yoore°,
In warm wex hath emprented the clyket°
That Januarie bar of the smale wyket°,
By which into his gardyn ofte he wente;
And Damyan, that knew al hire entente,
The cliket countrefeted pryvely°.
Ther nys namoore to seye, but hastily°
Som wonder by this clyket shal bityde°,
Which ye shul heeren, if ye wole abyde.
O noble Ovyde, ful sooth seystou°, God woot°,
What sleighte° is it, thogh it be long and hoot°,
That he nyl° fynde it out in som manere?
By Piramus and Tesbee may men leere°,
Thogh they were kept ful longe streite overal°,
They been accorded rownynge° thurgh a wal,
Ther° no wight° koude han founde out swich a sleighte°.
But now to purpos: er that° dayes eighte
Were passed, er the month of Juyl, bifille°
That Januarie hath caught so greet a wille,
Thurgh eggyng° of his wyf, hym for to pleye
In his gardyn, and no wight but they tweye,
That in a morwe° unto his May seith he,
"Rys up, my wyf, my love, my lady free°;
The turtles voys° is herd, my dowve° sweete;
The wynter is goon with alle his reynes weete°.
Com forth now, with thyne eyen columbyn°.
How fairer been thy brestes than is wyn!
The gardyn is enclosed al aboute;
Com forth, my white spouse! Out of doute
Thou hast me wounded in myn herte, O wyf.
No spot of° thee ne knew I al my lyf.
Com forth and lat us taken oure disport°;
I chees° thee for my wyf and my confort."
Swiche olde lewed wordes used he.
On° Damyan a signe made she
That he sholde go biforn with his cliket.
This Damyan thanne hath opened the wyket
And in he stirte°, and that in swich manere
That no wight° myghte it se neither yheere,
And stille he sit under a bussh anon.
This Januarie, as blynd as is a stoon,
With Mayus in his hand, and no wight mo,
Into his fresshe gardyn is ago°,
And clapte to° the wyket sodeynly.
"Now wyf," quod he, "heere nys° but thou and I,
That art the creature that I best love.
For by that Lord that sit in hevene above
Levere ich hadde to° dyen on a kynf
Than thee offende, trewe deere wyf.
For Goddes° sake, thenk how I thee chees°,

2105 privee, *secret,* **wiste,** *knew* **2106 eek the fyn,** *also the goal* **2113 blent,** *blinded or deceived* **woot,** *knows,* **so been mo,** *so* (have) *more been* **2114 wenen wisly,** *think confidently* **2116 so yoore,** *such a while ago* **2117 clyket,** *key* **2118 wyket,** *gate* **2121 pryvely,** *secretly* **2122 hastily,** *soon* **2123 shal bityde,** *will happen* **2125 sooth seystou,** *truly you speak,* **woot,** *knows* **2126 sleighte,** *deception,* **long and hoot,** *long-lasting and impassioned* (?) **2127 nyl,** *will not* **2128 leere,** *learn* **2129 kept ful longe streite overal,** *separated for a long time strictly in every way* **2130 been accorded rownynge,** *came to an agreement whispering* **2131 Ther,** *where,* **wight,** *person,* **sleighte,** *deception* **2132 er that,** *before* **2133 bifille,** *it happened* **2135 eggyng,** *urging* **2137 morwe,** *morning* **2138 free,** *gracious* **2139 turtles voys,** *turtledove's song,* **dowve,** *dove* **2140 reynes weete,** *wet rains* **2141 eyen columbyn,** *dovelike eyes* **2146 spot of,** *blemish on* **2147 disport,** *pleasure* **2148 chees,** *chose* **2150 On,** *to* **2153 stirte,** *leapt* **2154 wight,** *person* **2158 ago,** *gone* **2159 clapte to,** *slammed* **2160 nys,** *no one is* **2163 Levere ich hadde to,** *I would rather* **2165 Goddes,** *God's,* **chees,** *chose*

2108 thou, omitted in Hg. **2109–10** i.e., it is no better to be deceived when you are blind as when you can see. **2111 Argus,** one-hundred-eyed guardian who is blinded and killed; Ovid *Metamorphoses* 1.625ff. **2115 Passe over is an ese,** proverbial, meaning something like "The easy way is to ignore it." **I sey,** Hg reads "and sey." **2117 warm wex . . . emprented the clyket,** ironic and suggestive. January had earlier thought to mold his young bride like warm wax (lines 1429–30), and the recurrent rhyme pair "clyket / wyket" (key / gate) suggests genitalia. Impressions and imprintings recur at lines 1578, 1978, and 2178. **2120 hire,** Hg reads "his." **2124–31 Ovyde . . . ,** in the story of Pyramus and Thisbe, two tragic lovers who communicate by whispering through a chink in a wall, the question is asked, "Quid non sentit amor?" (What does love not perceive?); Ovid *Metamorphoses* 4.55–166. **2127 he,** refers to personified Love. **2133 Juyl,** July; found in all manuscripts. The reference in line 2222 to Gemini (May 11-June 11) encourages many to take this as an error for June, but "er" (before) can well mean "*in the month before* the month of July." **2137 his,** El reads "this." **2138–48 Rys up . . . ,** January's speech echoes the biblical Song of Songs, borrowed via Jerome's *Epistola adversus Jovinianum* (see *WBP* 3.3n) and undercut by January's lasciviousness and several double entendres. **2140 with alle his,** El reads "with his"; Hg, "with." **2143 enclosed al aboute,** the enclosed garden (*hortus conclusus*) was a figure for Mary, mother of Jesus. **2147 oure,** El reads "som." **2149 lewed,** multiple meanings in this context—secular, lascivious, and unlearned—all in contrast to the scriptural source of January's words.

Noght for no coveitise°, doutelees,
But oonly for the love I had to thee.
And though that I be oold and may nat see,
Beth to me trewe, and I wol telle yow why:
Thre thynges, certes°, shal ye wynne therby.
First, love of Crist, and to yourself honour,
And al myn heritage, toun and tour—
I yeve° it yow, maketh chartres° as yow leste°;
This shal be doon tomorwe er sonne reste°,
So wisly° God my soule brynge in blisse.
I prey yow first, in covenant° ye me kisse,
And though that I be jalous, wyte° me noght.
Ye been so depe enprented in my thoght
That whan that I considere youre beautee
And therwithal° the unlikly elde° of me,
I may nat, certes°, though I sholde dye,
Forbere° to been out of youre compaignye
For verray° love. This is withouten doute.
Now kys me, wyf, and lat us rome° aboute."
  This fresshe May, whan she thise wordes herde,
Benyngnely° to Januarie answerde,
But first and forward° she bigan to wepe.
"I have," quod she, "a soule for to kepe
As wel as ye, and also myn honur,
And of my wyfhod thilke° tendre flour
Which that I have assured° in youre hond,
Whan that the preest to yow my body bond°.
Wherefore I wole answere in this manere,
By the leve° of yow, my lord so deere:
I prey to God that nevere dawe° the day
That I ne sterve°, as foule as womman may,
If evere I do unto my kyn° that shame,
Or elles I empeyre° so my name,
That I be fals; and if I do that lakke°,
Do strepe° me and put me in a sakke,
And in the nexte ryver do me drenche°.
I am a gentil womman and no wenche.
Why speke ye thus? But men been evere untrewe,
And wommen have repreve° of yow ay newe°.
Ye han noon oother contenance°, I leeve°,
But speke to us of untrust and repreeve°."
  And with that word she saugh wher Damyan
Sat in the bussh, and coughen she bigan,
And with hir fynger signes made she
That Damyan sholde clymbe upon a tree
That charged° was with fruyt, and up he wente.
For verraily° he knew al hire entente,
And every signe that she koude make,
Wel bet° than Januarie, hir owene make°,
For in a lettre she hadde toold hym al
Of this matere, how he werchen shal°.
And thus I lete hym sitte upon the pyrie°,
And Januarie and May romynge myrie.
  Bright was the day and blew° the firmament°.
Phebus hath of gold his stremes° doun ysent
To gladen every flour with his warmnesse.
He was that tyme in Geminis, as I gesse,
But litel fro his declynacion
Of Cancer, Jovis exaltacion.
And so bifel° that brighte morwe-tyde°
That in that gardyn in that ferther syde
Pluto, that is kyng of Fairye,
And many a lady in his compaignye,
Folwynge his wyf the queene Proserpyne,
Which that he ravysshed out of Ethna
Whil that she gadered floures in the mede°—
In Claudyan ye may the stories rede,
How in his grisely° carte he hire fette°—
This kyng of Fairye thanne adoun hym sette
Upon a bench of turves°, fressh and grene,
And right anon thus seyde he to his queene,

2166 coveitise, *greed* **2170 certes,** *certainly* **2173 yeve,** *give,* **chartres,** *documents,* **leste,** *please* **2174 er sonne reste,** *before sunset* **2175 wisly,** *surely* (may) **2176 covenant,** *pledge* **2177 wyte,** *blame* **2180 therwithal,** *moreover* **2180 unlikly elde,** *unsuitable age* **2181 certes,** *surely,* **2182 Forbere,** *endure* **2183 verray,** *true* **2184 rome,** *walk* **2186 Benyngnely,** *graciously* **2187 first and forward,** *first of all* **2190 thilke,** *that* **2191 assured,** *entrusted* **2192 bond,** *bonded* **2194 leve,** *permission* **2195 dawe,** *dawn* **2196 sterve,** *die* **2197 kyn,** *family* **2198 empeyre,** *damage* **2199 lakke,** *misdeed* **2200 strepe,** *strip* **2201 drenche,** *drown* **2204 repreve,** *blame,* **ay newe,** *always* **2205 contenance,** *attitude,* **leeve,** *believe* **2206 repreeve,** *blame* **2211 charged,** *heavy* **2212 verraily,** *truly* **2214 Wel bet,** *much better,* **make,** *mate* **2216 werchen shal,** *should act* **2217 pyrie,** *pear tree* **2219 blew,** *blue,* **firmament,** *sky* **2220 of gold his stremes,** *his golden rays* **2225 bifel,** *it happened,* **morwe-tyde,** *morning time* **2231 mede,** *meadow* **2233 grisely,** *horrifying,* **fette,** *fetched* **2235 of turves,** *made of turf*

2169 wol, El reads "shal." **2179 that,** omitted in El. **2220–24 Phebus . . . in Geminis . . . Jovis exaltacion,** i.e., the sun was in the sign of Gemini shortly before ("litel fro") entering into Cancer, over which Jupiter (Jove) exerted most influence. This perhaps indicates a date of June 8; see 2133n. On declination and exaltation, see *WBP* 3.701–02n. **2227–29 Pluto . . . Proserpyne,** see 2038–39n above. Contrast their intervention with that of the gods in *KnT.* **2230** This line seems to have been lacking in Chaucer's original. El reads "Ech after oother, right as a lyne"; Hg, "Whos answere hath doon many a man pyne." Both appear to have been added or completed in blank spaces. Other manuscripts read "Which that he ravysshed out of Proserpyna" with variants for the final word. The reading "Ethna" is no doubt scribal, found in two manuscripts only, supplied from Claudian (line 2232). **2232 Claudyan,** Claudian, author of fourth-century *De Raptu Proserpinae* (*The Abduction of Proserpine*). **2233 How,** El reads "And." **fette,** El and Hg read "sette."

"My wyf," quod he, "ther may no wight seye nay°,
Th'experience so preveth every day
The tresons whiche that wommen doon to man.
Ten hondred thousand stories tellen I kan
Notable of youre untrouthe and brotilnesse°.
O Salomon, wys and richest of richesse,
Fulfild of sapience° and of worldly glorie,
Ful worthy been thy wordes to memorie
To every wight that wit and reson kan°.
Thus preiseth he yet the bountee° of man:
'Amonges a thousand men yet foond I oon°,
But of wommen alle foond I noon.'
"Thus seith the kyng that knoweth youre wikkednesse.
And Jhesus filius Syrak, as I gesse,
Ne speketh of yow but seelde reverence°.
A wylde fyr° and corrupt° pestilence
So falle upon youre bodyes yet tonyght!
Ne se ye nat° this honurable knyght,
By cause, allas, that he is blynd and old,
His owene man shal make hym cokewold°.
Lo°, where he sit, the lechour in the tree!
Now wol I graunten, of my magestee,
Unto this olde, blynde, worthy knyght
That he shal have ayeyn° his eyen syght
Whan that his wyf wold doon hym vileynye,
Thanne shal he knowen al hire harlotrye,
Bothe in repreve° of hire and othere mo°."
"Ye shal?" quod Proserpyne, "Wol ye so?
Now by my moodres sires soule I swere
That I shal yeven° hire suffisant answere,
And alle wommen after, for hir sake,
That though they be in any gilt ytake°
With face boold they shulle hemself° excuse,
And bere hem doun° that wolden hem° accuse.
For lakke of answere noon of hem shal dyen.
Al° hadde man seyn a thyng with bothe his eyen,
Yit shul we wommen visage it hardily°,
And wepe, and swere, and visage it subtilly,
So that ye men shul been as lewed as gees°.
What rekketh me° of youre auctoritees?
"I woot° wel that this Jew, this Salomon,
Foond of° us wommen fooles many oon°.
But though that he ne foond no good womman,
Yet hath ther founde many another man
Wommen ful trewe, ful goode, and vertuous.
Witnesse on hem that dwelle in Cristes hous°;
With martirdom they preved hire constance°.
The Romayn geestes eek° maken remembrance
Of many a verray°, trewe wyf also.
But sire, ne be nat wrooth°, al be it so
Though that he seyde he foond no good womman;
I prey yow take the sentence° of the man;
He mente thus, that in sovereyn bontee°
Nis noon° but God that sit° in Trinitee.
Ey°, for verray God that nys but oon°.
"What make ye so muche of Salomon?
What though he made a temple, Goddes° hous?
What though he were riche and glorious?
So made he eek a temple of false goddis;
How myghte he do a thyng that moore forbode° is?
Pardee°, as faire as ye his name emplastre°,
He was a lecchour and an ydolastre°,
And in his elde° he verray God forsook;
And if that God ne hadde, as seith the book,
Yspared hym for his fadres sake, he sholde
Have lost his regne rather° than he wolde°.
I sette right noght of al the vileynye

2237 ther may no wight seye nay, *no one can deny* **2241 brotilnesse,** *untrustworthiness* **2242 Salomon,** *Solomon* **2243 sapience,** *wisdom* **2245 kan,** *knows* **2246 bountee,** *goodness* **2247 oon,** *one* (good man) **2251 seelde reverence,** *seldom honor* **2252 wylde fyr,** *itchy skin disease,* **corrupt,** *incurable* **2254 Ne se ye nat,** *don't you see* **2256 cokewold,** *victim of adultery* (cuckold) **2257 Lo,** *look* **2260 ayeyn,** *again* **2263 repreve,** *blame,* **othere mo,** *others more* **2266 yeven,** *give* **2268 ytake,** *taken* **2269 hemself,** *themselves* **2270 bere hem doun,** *defeat those,* **hem,** *them* **2272 Al,** *although* **2273 visage it hardily,** *face it out boldly* **2275 lewed as gees,** *ignorant as geese* **2276 rekketh me,** *do I care* **2277 woot,** *know* **2278 Foond of,** *found among,* **many oon,** *many* **2282 Cristes hous, i.e.,** *heaven* **2283 hire constance,** *their constancy* **2284 The Romayn geestes eek,** *Roman history also* **2285 verray,** *genuine* **2286 wrooth,** *angry* **2288 sentence,** *meaning* **2289 sovereyn bontee,** *supreme goodness* **2290 Nis noon,** *there is none,* **sit,** *sits* **2291 Ey,** *yes,* **nys but oon,** *there is only one* **2293 Goddes,** *God's* **2296 forbode,** *forbidden* **2297 Pardee,** *by God,* **emplastre,** *whitewash* **2298 ydolastre,** *idolater* **2299 elde,** *old age* **2302 rather,** *sooner,* **wolde,** *wanted* **2303–4 sette right noght . . . boterflye,** *don't care . . . a butterfly* (for)

2240 stories, this word is lacking in the best MSS, including El and Hg, evidently omitted in the original. Later scribes supply near-synonyms: "stories," "samples," "historyes," and "tales." **2247–48** Ecclesiastes 7.28. **2250 Jhesus filius Syrak,** Jesus, son of Sirach; supposed author of the apocryphal Book of Ecclesiasticus, which contributed to antifeminist tradition. **2257 where,** El reads "heere." **2265 moodres sires,** Persephone's grandfather is Saturn, father of Ceres; see *KnT* 1.2441–42n. **2266 suffisant answere,** compare *WBT* 3.910. **2274 visage it,** Hg reads "chide." **2277–90** The antifeminist sentiment from Solomon (i.e., Ecclesiastes 7.29, attributed to him in the Middle Ages) and Proserpina's interpretation of it parallel Prudence's argument in *Mel* 7.1076–79. **2290 but God that sit in Trinitee,** Hg reads "but god but neither he ne she." **2293–95 temple . . . temple of false goddis,** Solomon built the first temple to Yahweh in Jerusalem (1 Kings 5.3–18) and temples to foreign gods (1 Kings 11.7–8). **2298–2302** 1 Kings 11.1–3; God spared Solomon for the sake of his father, David. **2300 that,** omitted in El and Hg.

That ye of wommen write a boterflye°.
I am a womman, nedes moot I° speke
Or elles swelle til myn herte breke°.
For sithen° he seyde that we been jangleresses°,
As evere hool I moote brouke my tresses,
I shal nat spare for no curteisye
To speke hym harm that wolde° us vileynye."
"Dame," quod this Pluto, "be no lenger wrooth°.
I yeve it up! But sith° I swoor myn ooth
That I wolde graunten hym his sighte ageyn,
My word shal stonde, I warne yow certeyn.
I am a kyng; it sit° me noght to lye."
"And I," quod she, "a queene of Fairye.
Hir answere shal she have, I undertake.
Lat us namoore wordes heerof make.
For sothe°, I wol no lenger yow contrarie."
Now lat us turne agayn to Januarie
That in the gardyn with his faire May
Syngeth ful murier than the papejay°,
"Yow love I best, and shal, and oother noon."
So long aboute the aleyes° is he goon
Til he was come agayns thilke pyrie°
Where as this Damyan sitteth ful myrie
An heigh° among the fresshe leves grene.
This fresshe May, that is so bright and sheene°,
Gan for to syke° and seyde, "Allas, my syde!
Now sire," quod she, "for aught that may bityde°,
I moste han° of the peres that I see,
Or I moot dye°, so soore longeth me°
To eten of the smale peres grene.
Help, for hir love that is of hevene queene.
I telle yow wel, a womman in my plit
May han to° fruyt so greet an appetit
That she may dyen but she of it have."
"Allas," quod he, "that I ne had heer a knave°
That koude clymbe! Allas, allas," quod he,
"That I am blynd!" "Ye sire, no fors°," quod she,
"But wolde ye vouchesauf°, for Goddes sake,
The pyrie inwith youre armes for to take°—
For wel I woot° that ye mystruste me—
Thanne sholde I clymbe wel ynogh," quod she,
"So I my foot myghte sette upon youre bak."
"Certes," quod he, "theron shal be no lak,
Mighte I yow helpen with myn herte blood."
He stoupeth doun, and on his bak she stood,
And caughte hire by a twiste°, and up she gooth—
Ladyes, I prey yow that ye be nat wrooth°,
I kan nat glose°, I am a rude° man—
And sodeynly anon this Damyan
Gan pullen up the smok° and in he throng°.
And whan that Pluto saugh this grete wrong,
To Januarie he gaf° agayn his sighte,
And made hym se as wel as evere he myghte.
And whan that he hadde caught his sighte agayn
Ne was ther nevere man of thyng so fayn°
But on his wyf his thoght was everemo.
Up to the tree he caste his eyen two
And saugh that Damyan his wyf had dressed°
In swich manere it may nat been expressed,
But if I wolde speke uncurteisly;
And up he yaf° a roryng and a cry,
As dooth the mooder whan the child shal dye.
"Out! Help! Allas! Harrow!" he gan to crye,
"O stronge° lady stoore°, what dostow°?"
And she answerde, "Sire, what eyleth° yow?
Have pacience and resoun in youre mynde.
I have yow holpe on° bothe youre eyen blynde.
Up peril of my soule, I shal nat lyen,
As me was taught, to heele with youre eyen,
Was no thyng bet°, to make yow to see,
Than strugle with a man upon a tree.
God woot°, I dide it in ful good entente."
"Strugle!" quod he, "Ye, algate° in it wente!
God yeve° yow bothe on shames deth to dyen!
He swyved° thee; I saugh it with myne eyen;
And elles be I° hanged by the hals°."
"Thanne is," quod she, "my medicyne fals.

2305 nedes moot I, *necessarily I must* **2306 breke,** *breaks* **2307 sithen,** *since,* **jangleresses,** *chatterboxes* **2310 wolde,** *wishes* **2311 wrooth,** *angry* **2312 sith,** *since* **2315 sit,** *suits* **2319 sothe,** *truly* **2322 papejay,** *parrot* **2324 aleyes,** *paths* **2325 agayns thilke pyrie,** *up to that pear tree* **2327 An heigh,** *on high* **2328 sheene,** *radiant* **2329 syke,** *sigh* **2330 for aught that may bityde,** *whatever happens* **2331 moste han,** *must have* (some) **2332 moot dye,** *may die,* **soore longeth me,** *sorely I desire* **2336 han to,** *have for* **2338 knave,** *boy servant* **2340 no fors,** *no matter* **2341 vouchesauf,** *agree* **2342 The pyrie inwith youre armes for to take,** *to hug the pear tree* **2343 woot,** *know* **2349 twiste,** *branch* **2350 wrooth,** *angry* **2351 glose,** *gloss over,* **rude,** *uneducated* **2353 smok,** *dress,* **throng,** *thrust* **2355 gaf,** *gave* **2358 fayn,** *happy* **2361 dressed,** *treated* **2364 yaf,** *gave* **2367 stronge,** *bold,* **stoore,** *impudent,* **dostow,** *are you doing* **2368 eyleth,** *ails* **2370 holpe on,** *helped in* **2373 bet,** *better* **2375 woot,** *knows* **2376 algate,** *entirely* **2377 yeve,** *grant* **2378 swyved,** *screwed* **2379 And elles be I,** *and* (if it were) *otherwise may I be,* **hals,** *neck*

2308 Literally, "As always healthy I may use (or enjoy) my braids," meaning approximately "I swear by my gender." **2335 in my plit,** in my condition, i.e., pregnant. May never declares herself pregnant, but she alleges an intense craving for green pears. **2340 That,** Hg reads "For." **2351 am,** omitted in Hg. **2360 Up to,** Hg reads "Unto." **2364–65** Contrast with Griselda's thoughts of her children, *ClT* 4.543ff. and 677ff. **2376 Strugle,** Hg reads "Strugled." **2380 fals,** Hg reads "al fals."

For certeinly if that ye myghte° se,
Ye wolde nat seyn thise wordes unto me.
Ye han som glymsyng and no parfit sighte."
  "I se," quod he, "as wel as evere I myghte,
Thonked be God, with bothe myne eyen two,
And by my trouthe, me thoughte he dide thee so."
  "Ye maze°, maze, goode sire," quod she.
"This thank have I for I have maad yow see.
Allas," quod she, "that evere I was so kynde!"
  "Now, dame," quod he, "lat al passe out of mynde.
Com doun, my lief°, and if I have myssayd°,
God helpe me so as I am yvele apayd°.
But by my fader soule, I wende han seyn°
How that this Damyan hadde by thee leyn°,
And that thy smok hadde leyn upon his brest."
  "Ye, sire," quod she, "ye may wene° as yow lest°.
But, sire, a man that waketh out of his sleep
He may nat sodeynly wel taken keep°
Upon a thyng, ne seen it parfitly,
Til that he be adawed verraily°.
Right so a man that longe hath blynd ybe°
Ne may nat sodeynly so wel yse°
First whan his sighte is newe come ageyn
As he that hath a day or two yseyn°.
Til that youre sighte ysatled be° a while
Ther may ful many a sighte yow bigile°.
Beth war°, I prey yow, for by hevene kyng,
Ful many a man weneth° to seen a thyng,
And it is al another than it semeth.
He that mysconceyveth°, he mysdemeth°."
And with that word she leep doun fro the tree.
  This Januarie, who is glad but he?
He kisseth hire and clippeth° hire ful ofte,
And on hire wombe he stroketh hire ful softe,
And to his palays° hoom he hath hire lad°.
Now, goode men, I pray yow to be glad.
Thus endeth heere my tale of Januarie.
God blesse us, and his mooder Seinte Marie.

Heere is ended the Marchants Tale of Januarie.

[Epilogue]

  "Ey, Goddes mercy," seyde oure Hoost tho°,
"Now swich a wyf I pray God kepe me fro!
Lo whiche sleightes° and subtilitees
In wommen been, for ay° as bisy as bees
Been they us sely° men for to deceyve,
And from a sooth° evere wol they weyve°
By this Marchauntes tale it preveth weel.
But doutelees, as trewe as any steel
I have a wyf, though that she poure be,
But of hir tonge a labbyng° shrewe is she,
And yet she hath an heep of vices mo°—
Therof no fors°. Lat alle swiche° thynges go.
But wyte° ye what? In conseil° be it seyd,
Me reweth soore° I am unto hire teyd°.
For and° I sholde rekenen° every vice
Which that she hath, ywis° I were to nyce°.
And cause why? It sholde reported be
And toold to hire of somme° of this meynee°—
Of whom, it nedeth nat for to declare
Syn° wommen konnen outen swich chaffare°.
And eek my wit suffiseth nat therto
To tellen al, wherfore my tale is do°."

2381 myghte, *could* **2387 maze,** *are dazed* **2391 lief,** *beloved,* **myssayd,** *misspoken* **2392 yvele apayd,** *poorly rewarded* **2393 wende han seyn,** *thought to have seen* **2394 leyn,** *laid* **2396 wene,** *think,* **lest,** *please* **2398 keep,** *heed* **2400 adawed verraily,** *truly awake* **2401 ybe,** *been* **2402 yse,** *see* **2404 yseyn,** *seen* **2405 ysatled be,** *is settled* **2406 bigile,** *deceive* **2407 Beth war,** *be aware* **2408 weneth,** *thinks* **2410 mysconceyveth,** *misperceives,* **mysdemeth,** *misjudges* **2413 clippeth,** *embraces* **2415 palays,** *palace,* **lad,** *led* **2419 tho,** *then* **2421 whiche sleightes,** *what tricks* **2422 ay,** *always* **2423 sely,** *innocent* **2424 sooth,** *truth,* **weyve,** *deviate* **2428 labbyng,** *blabbing* **2429 mo,** *more* **2430 no fors,** *no matter,* **swiche,** *such* **2431 wyte,** *know,* **In conseil,** *confidentially* **2432 Me reweth soore,** *I sorely regret,* **teyd,** *tied* **2433 For and,** *and if,* **rekenen,** *tally* **2434 ywis,** *surely,* **to nyce,** *very foolish* **2436 somme,** *someone,* **meynee,** *company* **2438 Syn,** *since,* **konnen outen swich chaffare,** *know how to present such merchandise* **2440 do,** *done*

2416 to, omitted in El. **2419–40** These lines appear in El, Hg, and most other manuscripts, with an additional eight lines that are adjusted for context. See the note to *SqT* 5.1–8.

Canterbury Tales, Part 5

Introduction

PART 5 IS MADE up of two of Chaucer's most exotic tales. The first, the *Squire's Tale*, is a story of adventure and betrayed love set in the Tartar Empire; it introduces a brass horse that can transport a rider anywhere in the world, a sword that both cuts and heals, a seeing mirror, and a ring that allows its bearer to converse with birds. The narrative potential latent in these motifs is not realized, and although the ring does enable its wearer, Canacee, to understand the lament of a female falcon who has been abandoned by her lover, this subplot is left hanging. The fantasy of the tale is muted by rationalization of its magical phenomena (see, e.g., 229–30, 253–57) or juxtaposition with scientific explanation (263–74). As Vincent DiMarco shows in his contribution to *Sources and Analogues* (2002–05, no. 234, volume 1), the various explanations of the marvels in the *Squire's Tale* are consistent with medieval understanding of optics, chemistry, and automata. Even in his most magical tales, Chaucer shows a basic distrust of unexplained marvels.

The *Squire's Tale* was long criticized and even ignored for its halting self-consciousness about rhetoric and its agglomeration of motifs that refuse to resolve themselves into formal unity (see 667–68n). Critics wondered whether the Franklin's interruption of the Squire comes when it does because Chaucer (or, according to many critics, the narratively challenged Squire) could not control the story. Early critics found parallels for many of the motifs in the *Thousand and One Nights*, a collection of Eastern stories in Arabic, even though the collection was unavailable to Chaucer in the form we know it. No known tale has been identified as the primary source of the *Squire's Tale*.

Postcolonial studies have brought new perspective to these Eastern connections by assessing narrative digressiveness as part of the "orientalism" of the tale. Edward Said coined the term as the title of his ground-breaking study (1978, no. 545), and it has come to be used generally for the Western attitude toward Eastern culture that stigmatizes it as excessive, bizarre, and sensual—often particularly feminized and in need of restraint or containment. In this kind of reading, the Squire's apologies for his rhetoric (see e.g., 67, 105–06, 401–05), his rationalizations of the marvelous, and the unfulfilled promise to cover all bases at the end of the tale become, arguably, Chaucer's orientalist send-up of Eastern tales or his disclosure of the Squire's jingoism or self-interest. Other issues informed by orientalist concerns are the relation of the Squire to his (arguably imperialistic) father, the Knight, and the possibility that historical events underlie those of the tale. See the pertinent essays in *Chaucer's Cultural Geography*, edited by Kathryn L. Lynch (2002, no. 543), and for a reading that explores desire, the psychology of fascination, and the otherness of change, see Patricia Clare Ingham, "Little Nothings: *The Squire's Tale* and the Ambition of Gadgets" (2009, no. 973a).

Based ultimately in Arabic learning, the astronomical aspects of the *Squire's Tale* have also been closely interpreted. J. D. North, *Chaucer's Universe* (1990, no. 436), reads a complex structure in the tale's astronomical allusions; and Marijane Osborn, *Time and the Astrolabe in* The Canterbury Tales (2002, no. 437), equates the brass horse with a pointer on the astrolabe (a tool for reading the stars) and argues that the identification helps alert us to the allegory of an astronomical day that runs throughout the *Canterbury Tales*. Useful surveys of the critical reception of the tale are available in Donald C. Baker's Variorum edition (1990, no. 47) and David Lawton's *Chaucer's Narrators* (1985, no. 376).

The *Franklin's Tale* is a Breton lay, a brief form of the romance genre, set in Brittany, the land of enchantment in medieval romance. It starts where many romances leave off, with a happy marriage, and many consider this marriage to be Chaucer's idealistic alternative to the battles of the sexes depicted earlier in the marriage group. This view is rooted ultimately in George Lyman Kittredge's landmark study, "Chaucer's Discussion of Marriage" (1912, no. 660). In this view, Arveragus and Dorigen marry as equals, neither claiming sovereignty, and by the end of the tale, *gentillesse* is shared among social classes. Yet the magic of the tale is largely a matter of tides and astronomical study, creating illusion. The coastal rocks that endanger Arveragus's return home to his wife are not actually removed; they simply appear to be so, rendering them perhaps more dangerous than ever.

The final turns of the plot result from the sequential grand gestures by three men—Arveragus, Aurelius (a squire who loves Dorigen), and a clerk-magician who had promised to remove the rocks—and after everyone goes away happy, the Franklin closes the tale with a *demande d'amour*, a love question: "Who was most generous?" As a result, many critics read the tale as evidence that human generosity, or virtue more generally, is capable of producing human happiness. Others, however, argue that each of the promises made in the tale (including the marriage vows), the *gentillesse* of the characters, and even the very notion of "trouthe" are in some way dependent on illusion. This reading is usually connected with the epilogue to the *Squire's Tale*, where the Franklin is thought to reveal himself as something of a social climber, invested in the notion that the nouveaux riche are as capable of gentility as the traditional aristocracy. Here, as is often the case in Chaucer, critical disagreement may reveal much about the outlook of the individual critic. See David M. Seaman, "'As Thynketh Yow': Conflicting Evidence and the Interpretation of *The Franklin's Tale*" (1991, no. 997).

The same issues of promises, love, happiness, and *gentillesse* appear in the falcon's lament in the *Squire's Tale*, and they echo resoundingly in the earlier tales of the marriage group, including the *Friar's Tale* and the *Summoner's Tale*, where promising and intention are central. Richard Firth Green, *A Crisis of Truth* (1999, no. 528), and Carolyn P. Collette, *Species, Phantasms, and Images* (2001, no. 439a), clarify cultural and psychological aspects of intention and will in late-medieval understanding of promises and troth plighting, important to the *Franklin's Tale* and throughout the *Canterbury Tales*.

Apart from the rocks, the basic plot of the *Franklin's Tale* parallels the tale of Menedon in Boccaccio's *Filocolo*, perhaps known to Chaucer in a version that circulated separately in a collection of love-question narratives. He also probably knew the similar story in Boccaccio's *Decameron* (10.5). In both versions by Boccaccio, the magic is a good deal more magical and idealistic: The lover must create a May-like garden in the month of January, likely the source for Chaucer's use of these months as names in the *Merchant's Tale*. For the names in the *Franklin's Tale* and perhaps for the motif of removing rocks, Chaucer turned to Geoffrey of Monmouth's *History of the Kings of Britain* (ca. 1138). He used Boethius's *Consolation* (4.pr6) for Dorigen's complaint about the rocks, the *Roman de la Rose* for most of the defense of equality in marriage (761–98), and Jerome's *Epistola adversus Jovinianum* for much of Dorigen's contemplation against her fortune (1368–1456)—sources used with equal brilliance elsewhere in the marriage group. Indeed, the successful pastiche here juxtaposed with the potential for sprawl in the *Squire's Tale* may suggest that Chaucer consciously set in opposition two kinds of composite narrative.

Canterbury Tales
Part 5

From woodcut made by W.H. Hooper and published by the Chaucer Society between 1868 and 1879

Squire's Tale

Prologue

“Squier, com neer, if it youre wille be,
And sey somwhat of love, for certes ye
Konnen° theron as muche as any man.”
“Nay, sire,” quod he, “but I wol seye as I kan
With hertly° wyl, for I wol nat rebelle
Agayn your lust°. A tale wol I telle;
Have me excused° if I speke amys.
My wyl is good, and lo, my tale is this.”

Heere bigynneth the Squieres Tale.

At Sarray, in the land of Tartarye,
Ther dwelte a kyng that werreyed° Russye,
Thurgh which ther dyde many a doughty° man.
This noble kyng was cleped° Cambyuskan,
Which in his tyme was of so greet renoun
That ther was nowher in no regioun
So excellent a lord in alle thyng.
Hym lakked noght that longeth° to a kyng.
And of the secte° of which that he was born
He kepte his lay°, to which that he was sworn.
And therto he was hardy, wys, and riche,
And pitous and just, alwey yliche°;
Sooth° of his word, benigne°, and honurable;
Of his corage as any centre stable;

---

3 Konnen, *know* **5 hertly,** *hearty* **6 lust,** *desire* **7 Have me excused,** *excuse me* **10 werreyed,** *waged war on* **11 doughty,** *valiant* **12 cleped,** *named* **16 longeth,** *is appropriate* **17 secte,** *religion* **18 his lay,** *its law* **20 yliche,** *consistently* **21 Sooth,** *true,* **benigne,** *gracious*

1–8 These lines read continuously from *MerT* 4.2440. In various manuscripts the entire passage (4.2419-40 with 5.1-8) introduces other tales, and in those cases, “Squier” (line 1) is replaced (by, e.g., “Sire Frankeleyn” in Hg), and “sey somwhat of love” (line 2) reads “sey us a tale.” **9 Sarray . . . Tartarye,** Sarai (modern Tsarev), capital of the Mongol (Tartar) Empire. In the thirteenth century, the Mongols conquered Russia. **12 Cambyuskan,** Genghis Khan, 1162–1227, founder of the Mongol Empire. Historically, his grandson Batu Khan (1198–1255) conquered Russia. **17 And,** Hg reads “As.” **20 And,** omitted in El. **alwey,** Hg reads “everemoore.”

Yong, fressh, strong, and in armes desirous°
As any bacheler° of al his hous.
A fair persone he was and fortunat,
And kepte alwey so wel roial estat°
That there was nowher swich another man.
  This noble kyng, this Tartre Cambyuskan,
Hadde two sones on Elpheta his wyf,
Of whiche the eldeste highte° Algarsyf,
That oother sone was cleped° Cambalo.
A doghter hadde this worthy kyng also
That yongest was, and highte Canacee.
But for to telle yow al hir beautee,
It lyth° nat in my tonge n'yn° my konnyng°.
I dar nat undertake so heigh a thyng;
Myn Englissh eek° is insufficient.
It moste been a rethor° excellent
That koude his colours longynge for° that art
If he sholde hire discryven° every part.
I am noon swich; I moot speke as I kan.
  And so bifel° that whan this Cambyuskan
Hath twenty wynter born his diademe°,
As he was wont° fro yeer to yeer, I deme°,
He leet the feeste of his nativitee
Doon cryen° thurghout Sarray his citee,
The laste Idus of March°, after the yeer°.
Phebus the sonne ful joly was and cleer,
For he was neigh° his exaltacioun
In Martes face, and in his mansioun
In Aries, the colerik hoote signe.
Ful lusty° was the weder° and benigne°,
For which the foweles agayn° the sonne sheene°,
What for° the sesoun and the yonge grene,
Ful loude songen hire affeccioun.
Hem semed han geten hem° proteccioun
Agayn the swerd° of wynter, keene° and coold.
  This Cambyuskan, of which I have yow toold,
In roial vestiment sit° on his deys°,
With diademe°, ful heighe in his paleys,
And halt° his feeste so solempne° and so ryche
That in this world ne was ther noon it lyche°.
Of which if I shal tellen al th'array,
Thanne wolde it occupie a someres day,
And eek it nedeth nat° for to devyse°
At every cours the ordre of hire servyse.
I wol nat tellen of hir strange sewes°,
Ne of hir swannes°, ne of hire heronsewes°.
Eek in that lond, as tellen knyghtes olde,
Ther is som mete° that is ful deynte holde°
That in this lond men recche of it but smal°.
Ther nys no man that may reporten al.
  I wol nat taryen° yow for it is pryme°
And for it is no fruyt° but los° of tyme.
Unto my firste I wole have my recours°.
  And so bifel° that after the thridde cours,
Whil that this kyng sit thus in his nobleye°,
Herknynge° his mynstrales hir thynges pleye
Biforn hym at the bord deliciously°,
In at the halle dore al sodeynly
Ther cam a knyght upon a steede of bras,
And in his hand a brood mirour of glas,
Upon his thombe he hadde of gold a ryng,
And by his syde a naked swerd hangyng.
And up he rideth to the heighe bord°.
In al the halle ne was ther spoken a word
For merveille of this knyght; hym to biholde
Ful bisily ther wayten° yonge and olde.
  This strange knyght, that cam thus sodeynly,
Al armed save his heed ful richely,
Saleweth° kyng and queene and lordes alle,
By ordre as they seten in the halle,
With so heigh reverence and obeisaunce°,
As wel in speche as in contenaunce°,

23 armes desirous, *battle eager* **24 bacheler,** *young knight* **26 roial estat,** *royal status* **30 highte,** *was called* **31 cleped,** *named* **35 lyth,** *resides,* **n'yn,** *nor in,* **konnyng,** *understanding* **37 eek,** *also* **38 rethor,** *rhetorician* **39 koude his colours longynge for,** *knew his figures of speech belonging to* **40 discryven,** *describe* **42 bifel,** *it happened* **43 born his diademe,** *carried his crown* **44 wont,** *accustomed,* **deme,** *believe* **45–46 leet . . . / Doon cryen,** *proclaimed* **47 laste Idus of March,** *March 15,* **after the yeer,** *in accord with the calendar* **49 neigh,** *near* **52 Ful lusty,** *very stirring,* **weder,** *weather,* **benigne,** *inviting* **53 foweles agayn,** *birds in response to,* **sheene,** *shine* **54 What for,** *because of* **56 Hem semed han geten hem,** (it) *seemed to them that they had gotten themselves* **57 swerd,** *sword,* **keene,** *sharp* **59 sit,** *sits,* **deys,** *dais* (platform) **60 diademe,** *crown* **61 halt,** *holds,* **solempne,** *grand* **62 lyche,** *like* **65 eek it nedeth nat,** *also there is no need,* **devyse,** *describe* **67 strange sewes,** *exotic soups* **68 hir swannes,** *their swans,* **heronsewes,** *young herons* **70 mete,** *food,* **ful deynte holde,** *considered very delicious* **71 recche of it but smal,** *think little of it* **73 taryen,** *delay,* **pryme,** *9 a.m.* **74 no fruyt,** *not fruitful,* **los,** *loss* **75 wole have my recours,** *will return* **76 bifel,** *it happened* **77 nobleye,** *nobility* **78 Herknynge,** *listening to* **79 bord deliciously,** *table delightfully* **85 heighe bord,** *high table* **88 wayten,** *watched* **91 Saleweth,** *greets* **93 obeisaunce,** *deference* **94 contenaunce,** *demeanor*

22 as any centre stable, stable as the center of a circle; proverbial. **23 strong, and,** Hg reads "and stronge." **38 It,** El reads "I." **46 thurghout,** El reads "thurgh." **48–51 the sonne . . . exaltacioun . . . signe,** the sun (Phebus) was at the point of its greatest influence, which is in the **face** (one-third or 10 degrees, line 50) of Mars and the **mansioun** (line 50) or house of Aries (the Ram), a constellation associated with the hot (and dry) choleric humor. **50 in his,** Hg omits "in." **61 so solempne,** Hg omits "so." **62 ne,** omitted in El. **65 for,** omitted in Hg. **67 I wol nat tellen,** the "occupatio" (see *KnT* 1.2924n) in the following lines and elsewhere in the tale clashes with the claim of rhetorical inability at lines 38–42. **81 Ther cam a knyght,** in *Sir Gawain and the Green Knight* and other romances, the interruption of a feast and / or the arrival of an unknown knight on horseback begins the action. **88 ther,** Hg reads "they.' **94 in . . . in,** Hg reads "in his . . . in his."

That Gawayn with his olde° curteisye,
Though he were comen ayeyn out of Fairye,
Ne koude hym nat amende° with a word.
And after this, biforn the heighe bord,
He with a manly voys seith his message,
After the forme used in his langage,
Withouten vice° of silable° or of lettre,
And for° his tale sholde seme the bettre
Accordant to his wordes was his cheere°,
As techeth art of speche hem° that it leere°.
Al be that° I kan nat sowne his stile,
Ne kan nat clymben over so heigh a style,
Yet seye I this, as to commune° entente,
Thus muche amounteth° al that evere he mente,
If it so be that I have it in mynde.
He seyde, "The kyng of Arabe° and of Inde°,
My lige° lord, on this solempne day
Saleweth yow, as he best kan and may,
And sendeth yow, in honour of youre feeste,
By me that am al redy at youre heeste°,
This steede of bras, that esily and weel
Kan in the space of o day natureel—
This is to seyn, in foure and twenty houres—
Wher so yow lyst°, in droghte or elles shoures°,
Beren° youre body into every place
To which youre herte wilneth° for to pace°,
Withouten wem of° yow, thurgh foul or fair,
Or if yow lyst° to fleen° as hye in the air
As dooth an egle whan hym list° to soore,
This same steede shal bere yow evere moore,
Withouten harm, til ye be ther yow leste°,
Though that ye slepen on his bak or reste,
And turne ayeyn° with writhyng° of a pyn°.
He that it wroghte° koude° ful many a gyn°.
He wayted many a constellacioun
Er° he had doon this operacioun,
And knew ful many a seel and many a bond.
"This mirour eek, that I have in myn hond,
Hath swich a myght° that men may in it see
Whan ther shal fallen any adversitee
Unto youre regne° or to youreself also,
And openly who is youre freend or foo.
And over al this, if any lady bright°
Hath set hire herte on any maner wight°,
If he be fals, she shal his tresoun see,
His newe love, and al his subtiltee,
So openly that ther shal no thyng hyde.
Wherfore, ageyn° this lusty someres tyde,
This mirour and this ryng that ye may see,
He hath sent unto my lady Canacee,
Youre excellente doghter that is heere.
"The vertu° of the ryng, if ye wol heere,
Is this, that if hire lust° it for to were°
Upon hir thombe, or in hir purs it bere,
Ther is no fowel° that fleeth° under the hevene
That she ne shal wel understonde his stevene°,
And knowe his menyng openly and pleyn,
And answere hym in his langage ageyn;
And every gras° that groweth upon roote
She shal eek knowe, and whom it wol do boote°,
Al be his woundes never so depe and wyde.
"This naked swerd that hangeth by my syde
Swich vertu° hath that what° man so ye smyte°
Thurghout his armure it wole kerve° and byte,
Were it° as thikke as is a branched ook.
And what man that is wounded with the strook

95 olde, *venerable* **97 amende,** *improve* **101 vice,** *error,* **silable,** *syllable* **102 for,** *so that* **103 cheere,** *expression* **104 hem,** *to them,* **leere,** *learn* **105 Al be that,** *although* **107 commune,** *general* **108 Thus muche amounteth,** *to this much amounts* **110 Arabe,** *Arabia,* **Inde,** *India* **111 lige,** *liege* **114 heeste,** *command* **118 Wher so yow lyst,** *wherever you wish,* **elles shoures,** *else showers* **119 Beren,** *carry* **120 wilneth,** *wishes,* **pace,** *go* **121 wem of,** *harm to* **122 lyst,** *wish,* **fleen,** *fly* **123 hym list,** *he wishes* **125 ther yow leste,** *where you please* **127 turne ayeyn,** *return again,* **writhyng,** *the twisting,* **pyn,** *peg* **128 wroghte,** *made,* **koude,** *understands,* **gyn,** *clever device* **130 Er,** *before* **133 myght,** *power* **135 regne,** *kingdom* **137 bright,** *beautiful* **138 maner wight,** *sort of man* **142 ageyn,** *in response to* **146 vertu,** *power* **147 hire lust,** *she wishes,* **were,** *wear* **149 fowel,** *bird,* **fleeth,** *flies* **150 stevene,** *speech* **153 gras,** *plant* **154 eek,** *also,* **wol do boote,** *will benefit* **157 Swich vertu,** *such power,* **what,** *whatever,* **smyte,** *strike* **158 kerve,** *carve* **159 Were it,** (even if) *it were*

95–96 Gawayn . . . Fairye, Sir Gawain was known for his courtesy and thought to reside in the fairyland, although the latter notion is generally found in romance tradition outside that of English. **99–104** The visitor's etiquette and rhetorical propriety are consistent with medieval ideals and rhetorical handbooks. **105–06 sowne his stile . . . clymben . . . a style,** "reproduce his style . . . climb a stile" (to get over so high a fence). This claim of rhetorical incompetence is expressed, paradoxically, in elaborate verbal play. **107 this, as,** Hg reads "this, that as." **109 in mynde,** Hg reads "in my mynde." **115 steede of bras,** there are Eastern analogues to this mechanical flying horse, but the notion may be related ultimately to actual automata or to the indicator on the astrolabe (often brass), known as the "horse." **123 whan hym,** El reads "whan that hym." **128 ful,** omitted in Hg. **129 wayted many a constellacioun,** i.e., waited for the proper astrological configuration. **131 seel . . . bond,** occult means of security and secrecy, although precisely what is meant is unclear. **132 mirour . . .,** magic mirrors recur in medieval literature as a means to learn of enemies' movements; mirrors of love are less frequent. **138 on,** El reads "in." **142 lusty someres tyde,** pleasant summer season, but *lusty* may connote amorous; summer in Middle English included spring (as winter included fall). **144 unto,** Hg reads "to." **146 ryng,** no specific precedent has been found for this ring that conveys the ability to converse with birds and know the medicinal properties of plants; see 250n. **156 swerd,** see 238–39n. **158 wole kerve,** El reads "wole hym kerve." **160 the,** El reads "a."

Shal never be hool° til that yow list°, of grace°,
To stroke° hym with the plat° in thilke° place
Ther he is hurt; this is as muche to seyn,
Ye moote° with the platte swerd ageyn
Stroke hym in the wounde and it wol close;
This is a verray sooth°, withouten glose°.
It failleth nat whils it is in youre hoold."
And whan this knyght hath thus his tale toold,
He rideth out of halle and doun he lighte°.
His steede, which that shoon as sonne brighte,
Stant in the court stille as any stoon.
This knyght is to his chambre lad anoon°,
And is unarmed, and unto mete yset°.
The presentes been ful roially yfet°—
This is to seyn, the swerd and the mirour—
And born° anon into the heighe tour°
With certeine officers ordeyned therfore°;
And unto Canacee this ryng was bore
Solempnely°, ther° she sit at the table.
But sikerly°, withouten any fable,
The hors of bras that may nat be remewed°,
It stant as it were to the ground yglewed.
Ther may no man out of the place it dryve°
For noon engyn of wyndas° ne polyve°;
And cause why? For they kan° nat the craft°.
And therfore in the place they han it laft
Til that the knyght hath taught hem the manere
To voyden° hym, as ye shal after heere.
Greet was the prees° that swarmeth to and fro
To gauren° on this hors that stondeth so,
For it so heigh was, and so brood and long,
So wel proporcioned for to been strong,
Right as° it were a steede of Lumbardye;
Therwith° so horsly and so quyk° of eye,
As° it a gentil Poilleys courser° were.
For certes°, fro his tayl unto his ere,
Nature ne art ne koude hym nat amende°
In no degree, as al the peple wende°.
But everemoore hir mooste° wonder was
How that it koude gon°, and was of bras.
It was a fairye°, as the peple semed°.
Diverse folk diversely they demed°;
As many heddes as manye wittes° ther been.
They murmureden as dooth a swarm of been°
And maden skiles° after hir fantasies,
Rehersynge of° thise olde poetries°,
And seyde that it was lyk the Pegasee,
The hors that hadde wynges for to flee°,
Or elles it was the Grekes hors Synoun
That broghte Troie to destruccioun,
As men mowe° in thise olde geestes° rede.
"Myn herte," quod oon, "is everemoore in drede.
I trowe° som men of armes been therinne,
That shapen hem° this citee for to wynne.
It were right good that al swich thyng were knowe."
Another rowned° to his felawe lowe
And seyde, "He lyeth; it is rather lyk
An apparence ymaad° by som magyk,
As jogelours° pleyen at thise feestes grete."
Of sondry doutes° thus they jangle° and trete°.
As lewed° peple demeth comunly°
Of thynges that been maad moore subtilly
Than they kan in hir lewednesse comprehende,
They demen gladly° to the badder° ende.
And somme of hem wondred on the mirour
That born was up into the maister tour°,
Hou men myghte in it swiche° thynges se.
Another answerde and seyde it myghte wel be
Naturelly, by composiciouns
Of anglis° and of slye° reflexiouns,
And seyden that in Rome was swich oon°.

---

161 **hool,** *healed,* **yow list,** *you choose,* **of grace,** *graciously* 162 **stroke,** *strike,* **plat,** *flat of the sword,* **thilke,** *that* 164 **moote,** *must* 166 **verray sooth,** *absolute truth,* **glose,** *interpretation* 169 **lighte,** *alights* 172 **lad anoon,** *led immediately* 173 **unto mete yset,** *given a meal* 174 **roially yfet,** *royally brought* 176 **born,** *carried,* **tour,** *tower* 177 **ordeyned therfore,** *assigned for this* 179 **Solempnely,** *ceremoniously,* **ther,** *where* 180 **sikerly,** *certainly* 181 **remewed,** *moved* 183 **dryve,** *move* 184 **wyndas,** *winch,* **polyve,** *pulley* 185 **kan,** *understand,* **craft,** *technique* 188 **voyden,** *remove* 189 **prees,** *crowd* 190 **gauren,** *stare* 193 **Right as,** *just as* (if) 194 **Therwith,** *moreover,* **quyk,** *lively* 195 **As,** *as if,* **courser,** *steed* 196 **certes,** *certainly* 197 **amende,** *improve* 198 **wende,** *thought* 199 **hir mooste,** *their greatest* 200 **koude gon,** *could move* 201 **fairye,** *magical thing,* **semed,** *thought* 202 **demed,** *judged* 203 **wittes,** *opinions* 204 **been,** *bees* 205 **skiles,** *explanations* 206 **Rehersynge of,** *recalling from,* **poetries,** *poems* 208 **flee,** *fly* 211 **mowe,** *might,* **geestes,** *stories* 213 **trowe,** *believe* 214 **shapen hem,** *plan* 216 **rowned,** *whispered* 218 **apparence ymaad,** *apparition made* 219 **jogelours,** *conjurers* 220 **sondry doutes,** *various fears,* **jangle,** *chatter,* **trete,** *argue* 221 **lewed,** *unlearned,* **demeth comunly,** *generally judge* 224 **demen gladly,** *judge willingly,* **badder,** *worse* 226 **maister tour,** *principal tower* 227 **swiche,** *such* 230 **anglis,** *angles,* **slye,** *clever* 231 **swich oon,** *such a one*

162 **thilke,** El reads "that." 165 **Stroke,** El reads "Strike. 178 **was,** Hg reads "is. 184 **ne,** Hg reads "or." 193–95 **Lumbardye . . . Poilleys,** Lombardy in northern Italy and Apulia in the south were both famous for horses. 201 **as the,** El reads "as al the." 202 **they,** Hg reads "han." 203 Proverbial after Chaucer. 207 **seyde that,** Hg reads "seyden." **the Pegasee,** Pegasus, mythological winged horse. 209 **Grekes hors Synoun,** the horse of Sinon the Greek, i.e., the Trojan horse (brass in several accounts) involved in the fall of Troy. 211 **mowe,** omitted in El and Hg. 217 **it is,** Hg reads "for it is." 222 **maad moore,** Hg reads "moore maad." 226 **maister,** El reads "hye." 231 **in Rome,** an allusion to the mirror that Virgil (thought to be a magician as well as a poet) was reputed to have erected in Rome to warn of enemy approach.

They speken of Alocen, and Vitulon,
And Aristotle, that writen in hir lyves
Of queynte° mirours and of perspectives°,
As knowen they that han hir bookes herd.
  And oother folk han wondred on the swerd
That wolde percen thurghout everythyng,
And fille in speche of Thelophus the kyng,
And of Achilles with his queynte° spere,
For he koude with it bothe heele and dere°
Right in swich wise° as men may with the swerd
Of which right now ye han youreselven herd.
They speken of sondry hardyng° of metal,
And speke of medicynes therwithal°,
And how and whanne it sholde yharded be°,
Which is unknowe, algates° unto me.
  Tho° speeke they of Canacees ryng,
And seyden alle that swich a wonder thyng
Of craft° of rynges herde they nevere noon,
Save° that he Moyses and Kyng Salomon
Hadde a name of konnyng° in swich art.
Thus seyn the peple and drawen hem apart°.
  But natheless somme seiden that it was
Wonder° to maken of fern-asshen glas,
And yet nys glas nat° lyk asshen of fern.
But for° they han knowen it so fern°,
Therfore cesseth hir janglyng° and hir wonder.
  As soore° wondren somme on cause of
    thonder,
On ebbe°, on flood, on gossomer°, and on myst,
And on alle thyng, til that the cause is wyst°.
Thus jangle they, and demen°, and devyse°,
Til that the kyng gan fro the bord° aryse.
  Phebus hath laft° the angle meridional,
And yet ascendynge was the beest roial,
The gentil Leon, with his Aldrian,
Whan that this Tartre kyng, this Cambyuskan,
Roos fro his bord, ther as he sat ful hye°.
Toforn° hym gooth the loude mynstralcye,
Til he cam to his chambre of parementz°,
Ther as they sownen diverse° instrumentz
That it is lyk an hevene for to heere.
Now dauncen lusty Venus children deere,
For in the Fyssh hir lady sat ful hye,
And looketh on hem with a freendly eye.
  This noble kyng is set up in his trone°.
This strange knyght is fet° to hym ful soone,
And on the daunce he gooth with Canacee.
Heere is the revel and the jolitee
That is nat able a dul man to devyse°.
He most han° knowen love and his servyse,
And been a feestlych° man as fressh as May,
That sholde yow devysen swich array.
  Who koude telle yow the forme of daunces
So unkouthe°, and so fresshe contenaunces°,
Swich subtil° lookyng and dissymulynges°
For drede of jalouse mennes aperceyvynges°?
No man but Launcelot, and he is deed.
Therfore I passe of° al this lustiheed°;
I sey namoore, but in this jolynesse
I lete hem til men to the soper dresse°.
  The styward bit° the spices for to hye°,
And eek the wyn, in al this melodye.
The usshers and the squiers been ygoon,
The spices and the wyn is come anoon.
They ete and drynke, and whan this hadde an
    ende,

234 queynte, *ingenious,* **perspectives,** *lenses* **239 queynte,** *marvelous* **240 dere,** *injure* **241 Right in swich wise,** *just in the way* **243 sondry hardyng,** *various* (ways of) *hardening* **244 therwithal,** *also* **245 sholde yharded be,** *might be hardened* **246 algates,** *in all ways* **247 Tho,** *then* **249 craft,** *the making* **250 Save,** *except,* **he Moyses,** *that Moses* **251 name of konnyng,** *reputation for knowledge* **252 drawen hem apart,** *withdrew themselves* **254 Wonder,** *wondrous* **255 And yet nys glas nat,** *even though glass is not* **256 for,** *because,* **fern,** *long ago* **257 janglyng,** *chattering* **258 soore,** *intently* **259 ebbe,** *tides,* **gossomer,** *cobwebs* **260 wyst,** *known* **261 demen,** *judge,* **devyse,** *imagine* **262 bord,** *table* **263 laft,** *left* **267 ful hye,** *very high* **268 Toforn,** *before* **269 chambre of parementz,** *ornamented chamber* **270 sownen diverse,** *play various* **275 trone,** *throne* **276 fet,** *brought* **279 devyse,** *describe* **280 most han,** *must have* **281 feestlych,** *festive* **284 unkouthe,** *exotic,* **so fresshe contenaunces,** *such fresh expressions* **285 subtil,** *secretive,* **dissymulynges,** *pretendings* **286 jalouse mennes aperceyvynges,** *jealous men's perceptions* **288 of,** *over,* **lustiheed,** *pleasure* **290 dresse,** *approach* **291 styward bit,** *steward bid,* **for to hye,** *to be brought quickly*

232–33 Alocen . . . Vitulon . . . Aristotle, Alhazen, an Arabian author of a treatise on optics, adapted into Latin by Witelo, a Polish physicist. Aristotle was known as a scientist as well as a philosopher, hardly separable in the Middle Ages. **233 And,** Hg reads "Of." **235 herd,** books were often read aloud in the past. **238–39 Thelophus . . . Achilles,** Telephus, king of Mysia, was wounded and then healed by the weapon of Achilles, rationalized by the curative properties of rust in Pliny's *Natural History* 34.45. **239 with,** Hg reads "for." **250 Moyses . . . Salomon,** the association of wisdom and magic led to the popular belief that Moses and Solomon were magicians; in legend, each possessed a magic ring. **254 fern-asshen,** the ash of burned ferns was an ingredient in glassmaking. **259 on flood,** Hg reads "and flood." **263–65 Phebus . . . Aldrian,** i.e., it is afternoon, because the sun has passed through the tenth of twelve domiciles, called the "angle meridional" (i.e., 10 a.m. to noon), during which the constellation Leo (the Lion, or royal beast) begins to rise above the horizon; "Aldrian" may refer to Castor and Pollux, stars in Gemini. **264 was,** Hg reads "is." **266 this Cambyuskan,** El and Hg omit "this." **267 as,** El reads "that." **270 they,** Hg reads "ther." **272–73 Venus children . . . Fyssh,** Venus's children (i.e., lovers) dance at this time because their planet exerts its greatest influence on them while it is in the constellation Pisces, the Fish. **275 in,** Hg reads "on." **283 of,** omitted in Hg. **287 Launcelot,** epitome of chivalry and lover of Guinevere in Arthurian romances. **291 the,** omitted in El and Hg.

Unto the temple, as reson was, they wende°.
  The service doon, they soupen° al by day°.
What nedeth yow rehercen hire array?
Ech man woot° wel that a kynges feeste
Hath plentee to the mooste and to the leeste,
And deyntees mo° than been in my knowyng.
At after-soper gooth this noble kyng
To seen this hors of bras, with al the route°
Of lordes and of ladyes hym aboute.
  Swich wondryng was ther on this hors of bras
That syn° the grete sege of Troie was,
Theras° men wondreden on an hors also,
Ne was ther swich a wondryng as was tho°.
But fynally the kyng axeth° this knyght
The vertu° of this courser and the myght,
And preyde° hym to telle his governaunce°.
  This hors anoon bigan to trippe° and daunce
Whan that this knyght leyde hand upon his reyne,
And seyde, "Sire, ther is namoore to seyne°
But whan yow list° to ryden anywhere,
Ye mooten trille a pyn stant° in his ere,
Which I shal yow telle bitwix° us two.
Ye moote nempne hym° to what place also,
Or to what contree, that yow list to ryde.
And whan ye come ther as yow list abyde°,
Bidde hym descende and trille another pyn—
For therin lith th'effect° of al the gyn°—
And he wol doun descende and doon youre wille,
And in that place he wol abyden stille.
Though al the world the contrarie hadde yswore,
He shal nat thennes° been ydrawe ne ybore°.
Or if yow liste bidde° hym thennes goon,
Trille this pyn and he wol vanysshe anoon
Out of the sighte of every maner wight°,
And come agayn, be it by day or nyght,
Whan that yow list to clepen hym ageyn°
In swich a gyse° as I shal to yow seyn
Bitwixe yow and me and that ful soone.
Ride whan yow list, ther is namoore to doone."
  Enformed whan the kyng was of° that knyght,
And hath conceyved in his wit aright
The manere and the forme of al this thyng,
Ful glad and blithe° this noble doughty° kyng
Repeireth° to his revel as biforn°.
The brydel is unto the tour yborn°
And kept among his jueles leeve° and deere.
The hors vanysshed, I noot° in what manere,
Out of hir sighte; ye gete namoore of me.
But thus I lete° in lust° and jolitee
This Cambyuskan his lordes festeiynge°
Til wel ny° the day bigan to sprynge.

Explicit pars prima. Sequitur pars secunda.

  The norice° of digestioun, the sleep,
Gan on hem wynke° and bad hem taken keep°
That muchel drynke and labour wolde han reste,
And with a galpyng° mouth hem alle he keste°,
And seyde it was tyme to lye adoun,
For blood was in his domynacioun.
"Cherisseth° blood, natures freend," quod he.
They thanken hym galpynge, by two, by thre,
And every wight gan drawe hym° to his reste
As sleep hem bad°; they tooke it for the beste.
  Hire dremes shul nat been ytoold for° me;
Ful were hire heddes° of fumositee°
That causeth dreem of which ther nys no charge°.
They slepen til that it was pryme large°,
The mooste part, but it were° Canacee.
She was ful mesurable° as wommen be,

---

296 wende, *go* **297 soupen,** *eat,* **by day,** *in daylight* **299 woot,** *knows* **301 deyntees mo,** *more delicacies* **303 route,** *company* **306 syn,** *since* **307 Theras,** *where* **308 tho,** *then* **309 axeth,** *asks* **310 vertu,** *power* **311 preyde,** *requested,* **his governaunce,** *how it is controlled* **312 trippe,** *cavort* **314 seyne,** *say* **315 list,** *wish* **316 mooten trille a pyn stant,** *must turn a peg* (that) *stands* **317 bitwix,** *between* **318 moote nempne hym,** *must tell him* **320 list abyde,** *wish to remain* **322 lith th'effect,** *lies the result,* **gyn,** *device* **326 thennes,** *from there,* **ydrawe ne ybore,** *pulled nor carried* **327 liste bidde,** *wish to order* **329 maner wight,** *kind of person* **331 clepen hym ageyn,** *call him back* **332 gyse,** *manner* **335 of,** *by* **338 blithe,** *happy,* **doughty,** *valiant* **339 Repeireth,** *returns,* **biforn,** *before* **340 tour yborn,** *tower carried* **341 jueles leeve,** *jewels beloved* **342 noot,** *know not* **344 lete,** *leave,* **lust,** *pleasure* **345 his lordes festeiynge,** *entertaining his lords* **346 Til wel ny,** *until nearly* **347 norice,** *nurse* **348 Gan . . . wynke,** *winked,* **taken keep,** *pay attention* **350 galpyng,** *yawning,* **hem alle he keste,** *(sleep) kissed them all* **353 Cherisseth,** *cherish* **355 gan drawe hym,** *took himself* **356 bad,** *ordered* **357 for,** *by* **358 hire heddes,** *their heads,* **fumositee,** *alcoholic fumes* **359 nys no charge,** *is no significance* **360 pryme large,** *9 a.m.* **361 but it were,** *except for* **362 ful mesurable,** *very moderate*

298 yow, El reads "me." **299 that a,** Hg reads "that at a." **303 the,** Hg reads "a." **306 grete sege of Troie,** Trojan War; see 209n. **322 therin,** El reads "ther." **324 abyde,** El reads "stonde." **325 Though,** Hg reads "Theigh." **338 Ful,** El reads "Thus." **346a *Explicit pars prima. Sequitur pars secunda.*** "Here ends part one. Here follows part two." **352 blood was in his domynacioun,** blood was in his dominance; i.e., the humor of blood (see *GP* 1.333), important to good health, became dominant at night. Both Sleep and Blood are personified here. **357 nat been,** Hg reads "nat now be."

For of hir fader hadde she take leve°
To goon to reste soone after it was eve.
Hir liste nat appalled for to be°
Ne on the morwe unfeestlich° for to se°.
And slepte hire firste sleep and thanne awook,
For swich a joye she in hir herte took
Bothe of hir queynte° ryng and hire mirour
That twenty tyme she changed hir colour°,
And in hire sleep right for impressioun°
Of hire mirour, she hadde a visioun°.
Wherfore°, er that the sonne gan up glyde°
She cleped° on hir maistresse° hire bisyde,
And seyde that hire liste° for to ryse.
  Thise olde wommen that been gladly wyse°,
As is hire maistresse, answerde hire anon
And seyde, "Madame, whider° wil ye goon
Thus erly, for the folk been alle on reste?"
  "I wol," quod she, "arise, for me leste°
No lenger for to slepe, and walke aboute."
  Hire maistresse clepeth° wommen a greet route°,
And up they rysen, wel a° ten or twelve.
Up riseth fresshe Canacee hirselve,
As rody° and bright as dooth the yonge sonne
That in the Ram is foure degrees up ronne—
Noon hyer° was he whan she redy was—
And forth she walketh esily a pas°,
Arrayed after° the lusty° seson soote°
Lightly, for to pleye and walke on foote,
Nat but with° fyve or sixe of hir meynee°,
And in a trench° forth in the park gooth she.
  The vapour which that fro the erthe glood°
Made the sonne to seme rody° and brood°,
But nathelees it was so fair a sighte
That it made alle hire hertes for to lighte°,
What for the seson and the morwenynge,
And for the foweles° that she herde synge.
For right anon° she wiste° what they mente,
Right by hir song, and knew al hire entente.
  The knotte° why that every tale is toold,
If it be taried° til that lust be coold°
Of hem that han it after herkned yoore°,
The savour passeth ever lenger the moore°
For fulsomnesse° of his prolixitee°.
And by the same resoun, thynketh me,
I sholde to the knotte condescende°,
And maken of hir walkyng soone an ende.
  Amydde° a tree, fordrye° as whit as chalk,
As Canacee was pleyyng in hir walk,
Ther sat a faucon° over hire heed ful hye
That with a pitous voys so gan to crye
That all the wode resouned of hire cry.
Ybeten° hath she hirself so pitously
With bothe hir wynges til the rede blood
Ran endelong° the tree ther° as she stood.
And evere in oon° she cryde alwey and shrighte,
And with hir beek hirselven so she prighte°,
That ther nys° tygre ne noon so crueel beest
That dwelleth outher° in wode or in forest
That nolde han° wept, if that he wepe koude,
For sorwe of hire, she shrighte alwey so loude.
For ther nas nevere° man yet on lyve°—
If that I koude° a faucon wel discryve°—
That herde of swich another of fairnesse°
As wel of plumage as of gentillesse
Of shap, and al that myghte yrekened be°.
A faucon peregryn thanne semed she
Of fremde° land, and everemoore as she stood

---

363 take leve, *received permission* **365 Hir liste nat appalled for to be,** *she wished not to become pale* **366 unfeestlich,** *unfestive,* **for to se,** *to look at* **369 queynte,** *marvelous* **370 changed hir colour,** *blushed* **371 right for impression,** *because of the effect* **372 visioun,** *dream* **373 Wherfore,** *as a result,* **gan up glyde,** *rose* **374 cleped,** *called,* **maistresse,** *governess* **375 hire liste,** *she wished* **376 gladly wyse,** *fortunately wise* **378 whider,** *where* **380 me leste,** *I wish* **382 clepeth,** *called,* **greet route,** *large group* **383 wel a,** *about* **385 rody,** *rosy* **387 Noon hyer,** *no higher* **388 esily a pas,** *slowly* **389 Arrayed after,** *dressed in accord with,* **lusty,** *pleasant,* **soote,** *sweet* **391 Nat but with,** *with only,* **meynee,** *group of attendants* **392 trench,** *path* **393 glood,** *glided* **394 to seme rody,** *seem red,* **brood,** *large* **396 made alle hire hertes for to lighte,** *lightened all their hearts* **398 foweles,** *birds* **399 right anon,** *immediately,* **wiste,** *knew* **401 knotte,** *crux* **402 taried,** *delayed,* **lust be coold,** *pleasure is cold* **403 han it after herkned yoore,** *have listened to it for a time* **404 savour passeth ever lenger the moore,** *enjoyment disappears increasingly* **405 fulsomnesse,** *abundance,* **prolixitee,** *lengthiness* **407 condescende,** *give way* **409 Amydde,** *in the middle of,* **fordrye,** *dried out* **411 faucon,** *falcon* **414 Ybeten,** *beaten* **416 endelong,** *down the length of,* **ther,** *where* **417 evere in oon,** *continuously,* **shrighte,** *shrieked* **418 prighte,** *pricked* **419 ther nys,** *there is no* **420 outher,** *either* **421 nolde han,** *would not have* **423 ther nas nevere,** *there was never,* **on lyve,** *alive* **424 koude,** *were able to,* **discryve,** *describe* **425 swich another of fairnesse,** *of another so beautiful* **427 yrekened be,** *be considered* **429 fremde,** *foreign*

367 thanne, omitted in Hg. **377 is,** omitted in El. **385–86 as dooth the yonge sonne . . . up ronne,** Canace is compared to the early-morning sun, and simultaneously we are told that it is about 6 A.M. The sun is "yonge" in mid-March (see line 47 above) because it is early in the year; it is just rising (**foure degrees up ronne**) above the horizon into the zodiacal sign of Aries, the Ram. **401–05** An elaborate way of saying that a tale told too long loses the appreciation of its audience. **406 the,** Hg reads "this." **412 That,** Hg reads "And." **416 as,** omitted in El. **419 noon,** omitted in Hg. **421 he,** El reads "she." **427 and,** Hg reads "of." **428 peregryn,** a species of falcon, literally "pilgrim" because young peregrines were caught in passage from their breeding grounds rather than taken from the nest.

She swowneth now and now° for lakke of blood,
Til wel neigh° is she fallen fro the tree.
  This faire kynges doghter, Canacee,
That on hir fynger baar the queynte° ryng
Thurgh which she understood wel everythyng
That any fowel may in his leden seyn°,
And koude answeren hym in his ledene ageyn,
Hath understonde what this faucon seyde,
And wel neigh for the routhe° almoost she deyde.
And to the tree she gooth ful hastily,
And on this faukon looketh pitously,
And heeld hir lappe abrood°, for wel she wiste°
The faukon moste fallen fro the twiste°,
Whan that it swowned next, for lakke of blood.
A longe while to wayten° hire she stood
Til atte laste she spak in this manere
Unto the hauk, as ye shal after heere:
  "What is the cause, if it be for to telle,
That ye be in this furial pyne° of helle?"
Quod Canacee unto the hauk above.
"Is this for sorwe of deeth or los of love?
For as I trowe° thise been causes two
That causen moost a gentil herte wo;
Of oother harm it nedeth nat to speke.
For° ye youreself upon yourself yow wreke°,
Which proveth wel that outher ire° or drede°
Moot been enchesoun° of youre cruel dede,
Syn that° I see noon oother wight yow chace°.
For love of God, as dooth youreselven grace°,
Or what may been youre help? For west nor est
Ne saugh° I nevere er now no bryd° ne beest
That ferde with hymself° so pitously.
Ye sle° me with youre sorwe verraily°,
I have of yow so greet compassioun.
For Goddes love, com fro the tree adoun;
And as I am a kynges doghter trewe,
If that I verraily the cause knewe
Of youre disese°, if it lay in my myght,
I wolde amenden it er° that it were nyght,
As wisly° helpe me the grete God of kynde°!
And herbes shal I right ynowe yfynde°
To heele with youre hurtes hastily."
  Tho shrighte° this faucon yet moore pitously
Than ever she dide, and fil to grounde anon,
And lith aswowne°, deed and lyk a stoon,
Til Canacee hath in hire lappe hire take
Unto the tyme she gan of swough° awake.
  And after that° she of hir swough gan breyde°,
Right in hir haukes ledene° thus she seyde:
"That pitee renneth soone in gentil herte,
Feelynge his similitude in peynes smerte°,
Is preved alday°, as men may it see,
As wel by werk° as by auctoritee,
For gentil herte kitheth° gentillesse.
I se wel ye han of my distresse
Compassion, my faire Canacee,
Of verray° wommanly benignytee°
That Nature in youre principles° hath yset.
But for noon° hope for to fare the bet°,
But for° to obeye unto youre herte free°,
And for to maken othere° bewar by me,
As by the whelp chasted° is the leoun,
Right for that cause° and that conclusioun°,
Whil that I have a leyser and a space°,
Myn harm I wol confessen er I pace°."
  And evere, whil that oon hir sorwe tolde,
That oother weep° as she to water wolde°,
Til that the faucon bad hire to be stille,
And with a syk° right thus she seyde hir wille:
  "That I was bred°—allas, that ilke° day—
And fostred in a roche° of marbul gray
So tendrely that nothyng eyled° me,
I nyste nat° what was adversitee

---

430 swowneth now and now, *swoons recurrently* **431 wel neigh,** *nearly* **433 queynte,** *marvelous* **435 leden seyn,** *language say* **438 routhe,** *pity* **441 heeld hir lappe abrood,** *held out the lap of her dress,* **wiste,** *knew* **442 twiste,** *branch* **444 wayten,** *watch* **448 furial pyne,** *furious pain* **451 trowe,** *believe* **454 For,** *because,* **wreke,** *avenge* **455 outher ire,** *either anger,* **drede,** *fear* **456 Moot been enchesoun,** *must be the reason* **457 Syn that,** *since,* **wight yow chace,** *creature pursue you* **458 as dooth youreselven grace,** *have mercy on yourself* **460 saugh,** *saw,* **bryd,** *bird* **461 ferde with hymself,** *treated himself* **462 sle,** *slay,* **verraily,** *truly* **467 disese,** *distress* **468 amenden it er,** *remedy it before* **469 wisly,** *surely* (may), **kynde,** *nature* **470 right ynowe yfynde,** *find sufficient* **472 Tho shrighte,** *then shrieked* **474 lith aswowne,** *lies fainted* **476 of swough,** *from the faint* **477 after that,** *after,* **gan breyde,** *awakened with a start* **478 haukes ledene,** *hawk's language* **480 peynes smerte,** *the sting of pain* **481 preved alday,** *proved continually* **482 werk,** *actions* **483 kitheth,** *reveals* **486 verray,** *true,* **benignytee,** *goodness* **487 principles,** *innate disposition* **488 But for noon,** *not for any,* **fare the bet,** *to do any better* **489 But for,** *except,* **free,** *generous* **490 othere,** *others* **491 chasted,** *corrected* **492 Right for that cause,** *just for that purpose,* **conclusioun,** *outcome* **493 space,** *time* **494 pace,** *depart* **496 weep,** *wept,* **wolde,** *would* (turn) **498 syk,** *sigh* **499 bred,** *born,* **ilke,** *same* **500 roche,** *rock* **501 eyled,** *troubled* **502 nyste nat,** *knew not*

431 the, Hg reads "that." **449 the,** Hg reads "this." **455 ire,** El reads "love." **463 compassioun,** El reads "passioun." **469 the,** omitted in Hg. **472 yet moore,** El reads "moore yet." **476 the,** Hg reads "that." **477 hir,** omitted in Hg. **479** Familiar chivalric sentiment; see *KnT* 1.1761n. **481 it,** omitted in El. **484 wel ye,** Hg reads "wel that ye." **489 to,** omitted in El. **491 whelp . . . leoun,** from the proverbial notion that a lion can be taught a lesson by beating a dog. In this highly rhetorical sentence, the falcon says she will tell her story, not because she hopes things will improve, but because she wishes to obey Canacee's request and because she hopes she can be a model for others to learn from. **492 and that,** El and Hg read "and for that." **499ff.** The falcon's tale has many verbal and narrative resemblances to Chaucer's poem *Anelida and Arcite,* lines 105ff. **499 ilke,** El reads "harde."

Til I koude flee° ful hye under the sky.
Tho° dwelte a tercelet° me faste° by
That semed welle° of alle gentillesse.
Al were he° ful of treson and falsnesse,
It was so wrapped under humble cheere°,
And under hewe° of trouthe in swich manere,
Under plesance and under bisy peyne°,
That no wight° koude han wend° he koude feyne°,
So depe in greyn he dyed his coloures°.
Right° as a serpent hit hym° under floures
Til he may seen his tyme for to byte,
Right so this god of loves ypocryte°
Dooth so his cerymonyes and obeisaunces°,
And kepeth in semblaunt° alle his observaunces
That sownen into° gentillesse of love.
As in a toumbe° is al the faire above°
And under is the corps°, swich° as ye woot°,
Swich was the ypocrite, bothe coold and hoot.
And in this wise he served his entente,
That, save° the feend°, noon wiste° what he mente,
Til he so longe hadde wopen° and compleyned,
And many a yeer his service to me feyned°,
Til that myn herte, to pitous and to nyce°,
Al innocent of his corouned° malice,
For fered° of his deeth, as thoughte me,
Upon° his othes and his seuretee°,
Graunted hym love upon this condicioun,
That everemoore myn honour and renoun°
Were saved°, bothe privee and apert°;
This is to seyn, that after his desert
I yaf° hym al myn herte and al my thoght—
God woot° and he, that ootherwise noght°—
And took his herte in chaunge° of myn for ay°.
But sooth° is seyd°, goon sithen many a day°,
A trewe wight° and a theef thenken nat oon°.
And whan he saugh the thyng so fer ygoon
That I hadde graunted hym fully my love
In swich a gyse° as I have seyd above,
And yeven hym my trewe herte as free°
As he swoor he yaf his herte to me,
Anon this tigre, ful of doublenesse,
Fil on his knees with so devout humblesse,
With so heigh reverence, and as by his cheere°
So lyk a gentil lovere of manere,
So ravysshed, as it semed, for the joye
That nevere Jason ne Parys of Troye—
Jason? Certes°, ne noon° oother man
Syn° Lameth was, that alderfirst° bigan
To loven two, as writen folk biforn°—
Ne nevere, syn° the firste man was born,
Ne koude man° by twenty thousand part°
Countrefete° the sophymes° of his art,
Ne were worthy unbrokelen his galoche°
Ther° doublenesse or feynyng sholde approche°,
Ne so koude thonke a wight° as he dide me!
His manere was an hevene for to see
Til° any womman, were she never so wys,
So peynted° he and kembde at point-devys°,
As wel his wordes as his contenaunce°.
And I so loved hym for his obeisaunce°,
And for the trouthe I demed° in his herte,
That if so were that any thyng hym smerte°,
Al were it never so lite°, and I it wiste°,
Me thoughte I felte deeth myn herte twiste°.
And shortly so ferforth° this thyng is went
That my wyl was his willes instrument;
This is to seyn, my wyl obeyed his wyl

---

503 koude flee, *was able to fly* **504 Tho,** *then,* **tercelet,** *male falcon,* **faste,** *near* **505 welle,** (a) *source* **506 Al were he,** *although he was* **507 cheere,** *demeanor* **508 hewe,** *illusion* **509 bisy peyne,** *busy efforts* **510 wight,** *creature,* **koude han wend,** *could have believed,* **feyne,** *pretend* **511 depe in greyn he dyed his coloures,** *deeply ingrained* (i.e., successfully) *he painted his words* (or used his rhetoric) **512 Right,** *just,* **hit hym,** *hides himself* **514 ypocryte,** *hypocrite* **515 obeisaunces,** *acts of humility* **516 semblaunt,** *outward show* **517 sownen into,** *contribute to* **518 toumbe,** *tomb,* **faire above,** *beauty on the outside* **519 corps,** *corpse,* **swich,** *such,* **woot,** *know* **522 save,** *except,* **feend,** *devil,* **wiste,** *knew* **523 wopen,** *wept* **524 feyned,** *pretended* **525 to nyce,** *too foolish* **526 corouned,** *sovereyn* **527 For fered,** *because of fear* **528 Upon,** *based on,* **seuretee,** *assurance* **530 renoun,** *reputation* **531 saved,** *preserved,* **privee and apert,** *privately and publicly* **533 yaf,** *gave* **534 woot,** *knows,* **ootherwise noght,** *on any other terms I would not have* **535 chaunge,** *exchange,* **for ay,** *forever* **536 sooth,** *truth,* **seyd,** *said,* **goon sithen many a day,** *for a long time* **537 trewe wight,** *true person,* **thenken nat oon,** *think not alike* **540 gyse,** *way* **541 free,** *freely* **545 as by his cheere,** *to judge by his expression* **549 Certes,** *surely,* **ne noon,** *nor any* **550 Syn,** *since,* **that alderfirst,** *who first* **551 biforn,** *before* **552 syn,** *since* **553 Ne koude man,** *could* (any) *man,* **twenty thousand part,** *one twenty thousandth* **554 Countrefete,** *imitate,* **sophymes,** *deceptive arguments* **555 unbrokelen his galoche,** *to unbuckle his sandal* **556 Ther,** *where,* **sholde approche,** *is concerned* **557 so koude thonke a wight,** *could so thank* (i.e., treat) *a person* **559 Til,** *to* **560 peynted,** *painted* (i.e., pretended), **kembde at point-devys,** *combed* (i.e., arranged) *perfectly* **561 contenaunce,** *behavior* **562 obeisaunce,** *acts of humility* **563 demed,** *judged to be* **564 hym smerte,** *pained him* **565 Al were it never so lite,** *regardless how insignificant,* **wiste,** *knew* **566 twiste,** *wring* **567 ferforth,** *far*

509–10 Hg reverses the order of these lines. **514 loves ypocryte,** El reads "love this ypocryte." **520 the,** Hg reads "this." **524 And,** Hg reads "A." **535 of,** El reads "for." **543 tigre,** tiger, thought to be a deceptive animal. **548 Jason,** deserted Hypsipyle and Medea; *LGW* 1370ff. El reads "Troilus." **Parys,** deserted Oenome. **550 Lameth,** Lamech had two wives; Genesis 4.19. **562 so,** omitted in El.

In alle thyng as fer as reson fil°,
Kepynge the boundes of my worship evere.
Ne nevere hadde I thyng so lief°, ne levere°,
As hym, God woot°, ne nevere shal namo.
  "This lasteth lenger than a yeer or two
That I supposed of hym noght but good.
But finally, thus atte laste it stood,
That Fortune wolde that he moste twynne°
Out of that place which that I was inne.
Wher me° was wo, that is no questioun.
I kan nat make of it discripsioun;
For o thyng dar I tellen boldely,
I knowe what is the peyne of deeth therby.
Swich harm° I felte for he ne myghte bileve°.
So on a day of me he took his leve
So sorwefully eek that I wende verraily°
That he had felt as muche harm as I,
Whan that I herde hym speke, and saugh his hewe°.
But nathelees, I thoughte he was so trewe;
And eek that he repaire sholde° ageyn
Withinne a litel while, sooth° to seyn;
And resoun wolde° eek that he moste° go
For his honour, as ofte it happeth so;
That I made vertu of necessitee
And took it wel, syn° that it moste be.
As I best myghte, I hidde fro hym my sorwe,
And took hym by the hond, Seint John to borwe,
And seyde hym thus, 'Lo, I am youres al.
Beth swich° as I to yow have been and shal.'
What he answerde, it nedeth noght reherce°.
Who kan sey bet° than he, who kan do werse?
Whan he hath al wel seyd, thanne hath he doon°.
Therfore bihoveth hire° a ful long spoon
That shal ete with a feend, thus herde I seye.
So atte laste he moste° forth his weye,
And forth he fleeth° til he cam ther hym leste°.
  "Whan it cam hym to purpos° for to reste,
I trowe° he hadde thilke° text in mynde,
That alle thyng, repeirynge° to his kynde°;
Gladeth° hymself—thus seyn men, as I gesse.
Men loven of propre kynde° newefangelnesse°,
As briddes doon° that men in cages fede°.
For though thou nyght and day take of hem hede°,
And strawe° hir cage faire and softe as silk,
And yeve° hem sugre, hony, breed, and milk,
Yet right anon as that° his dore is uppe,
He with his feet wol spurne° adoun his cuppe,
And to the wode he wole° and wormes ete.
So newefangel been they of hire mete°,
And loven novelries of propre kynde°;
No gentillesse of blood ne may hem bynde°.
  "So ferde° this tercelet°, allas the day!
Though he were gentil born, and fressh and gay,
And goodlich for to seen°, humble and free°,
He saugh upon a tyme a kyte flee°,
And sodeynly he loved this kyte so
That al his love is clene fro° me ago,
And hath his trouthe falsed° in this wyse.
Thus hath the kyte my love in hire servyse,
And I am lorn° withouten remedie."
And with that word this faucon gan to crie
And swowned eft in Canacees barm°.
  Greet was the sorwe for the haukes harm
That Canacee and alle hir wommen made.
They nyste hou° they myghte the faucon glade°.
But Canacee hom bereth hire in hir lappe,
And softely in plastres° gan hire wrappe,
Ther as° she with hire beek hadde hurt hirselve.
Now kan nat° Canacee but herbes delve°
Out of the ground, and make salves newe
Of herbes preciouse and fyne of hewe°,
To heelen with this hauk. Fro day to nyght
She dooth hire bisynesse and al hire myght,
And by hire beddes heed she made a mewe°,

---

570 fil, *extended* **572 lief,** *dear,* **levere,** *dearer* **573 woot,** *knows* **577 twynne,** *depart* **579 Wher me,** *whether to me* **583 Swich harm,** *such pain,* **bileve,** *remain* **585 wende verraily,** *thought truly* **587 hewe,** *color* **589 repaire sholde,** *should return* **590 sooth,** *truth* **591 wolde,** *wished,* **moste,** *must* **594 syn,** *since* **598 Beth swich,** *be such* **599 it nedeth noght reherce,** *I need not retell* **600 say bet,** *speak better* **601 doon,** *finished* **602 bihoveth hire,** *she needs* **604 moste,** *must* (go) **605 fleeth,** *flies,* **ther hym leste,** *where* (it) *pleased him* **606 it cam hym to purpos,** *he decided* **607 trowe,** *think,* **thilke,** *that* **608 repeirynge,** *returning,* **kynde,** *nature* **609 Gladeth,** *pleases* **610 of proper kynde,** *by natural disposition,* **newefangelnesse,** *novelty* **611 briddes doon,** *birds do,* **fede,** *feed* **612 hede,** *care* **613 strawe,** *line with straw* **614 yeve,** *give* **615 right anon as that,** *just as soon as* **616 spurne,** *kick* **617 wole,** *will* (go) **618 mete,** *diet* **619 of propre kynde,** *by natural disposition* **620 hem bynde,** *restrain them* **621 ferde,** *acted,* **tercelet,** *male falcon* **623 goodlich for to seen,** *attractive,* **free,** *generous* **624 kyte flee,** *kite* (scavenger bird) *fly* **626 clene fro,** *completely from* **627 trouthe falsed,** *pledge falsified* **629 lorn,** *lost* **631 barm,** *lap* **634 nyste hou,** *knew not how,* **glade,** *gladden* **636 plastres,** *bandages* **637 Ther as,** *where* **638 kan nat,** *can do nothing,* **delve,** *dig* **640 fyne of hewe,** *of good color* (i.e., fresh) **643 mewe,** *birdhouse*

583 he, El reads "I." **592 it,** omitted in Hg. **593** Echoes *KnT* 1.3042. **596 Seint John to borwe,** to pledge by St. John, the Apostle of Truth. **597 hym,** omitted in Hg, **601 wel,** omitted in El. **602-03** Proverbial after Chaucer. **608-09** *Bo* 3m2.42. **610-20** *Bo* 3m2.21-31. This application of a bird analogy to a bird is incongruous. **621 this tercelet,** Hg reads "this gentil tercelet." **634 hou they,** Hg reads "how that they." **641 hauk,** omitted in El. **642 and al hire,** El reads "and hire fulle."

And covered° it with velvettes blewe
In signe of trouthe that is in wommen sene.
And al withoute°, the mewe is peynted grene,
In which were peynted alle thise false fowles
As beth thise tidyves, tercelettes, and owles;
Right for despit° were peynted hem bisyde
Pyes°, on hem for to crie and chyde°.
  Thus lete I Canacee hir hauk kepyng;
I wol namoore as now speke of hir ryng
Til it come eft° to purpos for to seyn
How that this faucon gat hire love ageyn
Repentant, as the storie telleth us,
By mediacioun of Cambalus,
The kynges sone, of which that I yow tolde.
But hennesforth I wol my proces holde°
To speke of aventures and of batailles
That nevere yet was herd so grete mervailles.
  First wol I telle yow of Cambyuskan,
That in his tyme many a citee wan;
And after wol I speke of Algarsif,
How that he wan° Theodera to his wif,
For whom ful ofte in greet peril he was,
Ne hadde he° been holpen° by the steede of bras;
And after wol I speke of Cambalo,
That faught in lystes° with the bretheren two
For Canacee er that he myghte hire wynne.
And ther I lefte I wol ayeyn bigynne.

Explicit secunda pars. Incipit pars tercia.

  Appollo whirleth up his chaar° so hye,
Til that the god Mercurius hous, the slye°—

Heere folwen the wordes of the Frankeleyn to the Squier, and the wordes of the Hoost to the Frankeleyn.

  "In feith, Squier, thow hast thee wel yquit°
And gentilly. I preise wel thy wit,"
Quod the Frankeleyn, "considerynge thy yowthe,
So feelyngly thou spekest, sire, I allow° the.
As to my doom°, ther is noon that is heere
Of eloquence that shal be thy peere°,
If that thou lyve—God yeve thee good chaunce°,
And in vertu sende thee continuaunce,°
For of thy speche I have greet deyntee°.
I have a sone, and by the Trinitee,
I hadde levere than twenty pound worth lond°,
Though it right now were fallen in myn hond,
He were a man of swich discrecioun
As that ye been. Fy on possessioun,
But if° a man be vertuous withal°!
I have my sone snybbed°, and yet shal,
For he to vertu listeth nat entende°,
But for to pleye at dees°, and to despende°
And lese° al that he hath is his usage°.
And he hath levere° talken with a page
Than to comune° with any gentil wight°
Where° he myghte lerne gentillesse aright."
  "Straw for youre gentillesse!" quod oure Hoost.
"What, Frankeleyn, pardee° sire, wel thou woost°
That ech of yow moot° tellen atte leste
A tale or two, or breken his biheste°."
  "That knowe I wel, sire," quod the Frankeleyn.
"I prey yow, haveth me nat in desdeyn°,

644 covered, *lined,* **646 al withoute,** *on the outside* **649 Right for despit,** *just for mockery* **650 Pyes,** *magpies,* **chyde,** *scold* **653 eft,** *again* **658 proces holde,** *story continue* **664 wan,** *won* **666 Ne hadde he,** (if) *he had not,* **holpen,** *helped* **668 lystes,** *single combat* **671 chaar,** *chariot* **672 slye,** *cunning* **673 thee wel yquit,** *accounted well for yourself* **676 allow,** *praise* **677 doom,** *judgment* **678 peere,** *equal* **679 chaunce,** *fortune* **681 deyntee,** *pleasure* **683 hadde levere than twenty pound worth lond,** *would rather* (have) *land generating twenty pounds* (income) *annually* **687 But if,** *unless,* **vertuous withal,** *talented also* **688 snybbed,** *scolded* **689 to vertu listeth nat entende,** *wishes not to attend to accomplishments* **690 dees,** *dice,* **despende,** *spend,* **691 lese,** *lose,* **in his usage,** *habitually* **692 hath levere,** *would rather* **693 comune,** *converse,* **gentil wight,** *gentleman* **694 There,** *where* **696 pardee,** *by God,* **woost,** *know* **697 moot,** *must* **698 beheste,** *promise* **700 desdeyn,** *scorn*

644–46 blewe . . . grene, blue is the color of constancy and green of inconstancy in the refrain of *Against Women Unconstant* (Short Poem 20), attributed to Chaucer. **647 which were,** El reads "which ther were." **648 tidyves,** an unidentified variety of bird, evidently reputed to be inconstant; cf. *LGW* 154. **657 of which that I yow,** El reads "of which I yow"; Hg, "of which I to yow." **663–64 Algarsif . . . Theodera,** nothing is known for certain of Algarsif (Cambyuskan's oldest son–line 30), nor of his wife. **667–68 Cambalo . . . bretheren two,** it is impossible to know if this is the younger son of Cambyuskan (line 31) or a suitor of Canace who fights her brothers. At this point, the many plots and magical devices seem to suggest that only a loose and very long narrative could bring them all together. **670a *Explicit secunda pars. Incipit pars tercia.*** "Here ends part two. Here begins part three." **671–72** Some later manuscripts omit these two lines, which set the time in mid-May when the sun (Apollo) enters Gemini, one of the houses or domiciles of Mercury, who is the clever or trickster god. The rest of the page in El is blank after the lines. **675 Frankelyn,** Hg reads "Marchant" here and at 696 and 699, as do other manuscripts in which *MerT* follows. **689 listeth,** El reads "listneth." **697–98 moot tellen atte lest / A tale or two,** must tell at least a tale or two. This suggests a less ambitious program of tales than the initial requirement of four tales per pilgrim; see *GP* 1.792-94n.

Though to this man I speke a word or two."
"Telle on thy tale withouten wordes mo."
"Gladly, sire Hoost," quod he, "I wole obeye
Unto your wyl. Now herkneth° what I seye.
I wol yow nat contrarien° in no wyse
As fer as that my wittes wol suffyse.
I prey to God that it may plesen yow;
Thanne woot° I wel that it is good ynow°,"

704 herkneth, *listen to* **705 contrarien,** *oppose* **708 woot,** *know,* **ynow,** *enough*

701 a word, omitted in El, but added later in the margin. **708a** El and Hg add ***Explicit*** "Here this ends."

From woodcut made by W.H. Hooper and published by the Chaucer Society between 1868 and 1879

Franklin's Tale

Prologue

The Prologe of the Frankeleyns Tale.

Thise olde gentil Britouns in hir dayes
Of diverse aventures maden layes,
Rymeyed° in hir firste° Briton tonge,
Whiche layes with hir instrumentz they songe
Or elles redden° hem for hir plesaunce°;
And oon of hem have I in remembraunce,
Which I shal seyn with good wyl as I kan.
But, sires, by cause I am a burel° man,
At my bigynnyng first I yow biseche,
Have me excused of my rude speche.
I lerned nevere rethorik, certeyn.
Thyng that I speke, it moot° be bare and pleyn.
I sleep nevere on the Mount of Pernaso,
Ne lerned Marcus Tullius Scithero.
Colours° ne knowe I none, withouten drede,
But swiche colours° as growen in the mede°,
Or elles swich as men dye or peynte.
Colours of rethoryk been to queynte°;
My spirit feeleth noght of swich mateere.
But if yow list, my tale shul ye heere.

Heere bigynneth the Frankeleyns Tale.

In Armorik, that called is Britayne,
Ther was a knyght that loved and dide his payne
To serve a lady in his beste wise;
And many a labour, many a greet emprise°
He for his lady wroghte° er she were wonne,
For she was oon the faireste under sonne,
And eek therto comen of so heigh kynrede°
That wel unnethes dorste° this knyght for drede
Telle hire his wo, his peyne, and his distresse.

---

711 Rymeyed, *composed in rhyme,* **hir firste,** *their original* **713 redden,** *read,* **plesaunce,** *pleasure* **716 burel,** *unlearned* **720 moot,** *must* **723 Colours,** *rhetorical devices* **724 colours,** *flowers,* **mede,** *meadow* **726 to queynte,** *too ingenious* **732 emprise,** *enterprise* **733 wroghte,** *undertook* **735 kynrede,** *lineage* **736 wel unnethes dorste,** *scarcely dared*

709 Britouns, Bretons, Celtic peoples of Brittany by whom the Arthurian legend and other Celtic stories are thought to have been conveyed to the French and English. **710 layes,** short romances; the tale fits in the subgenre of brief medieval romance, the Breton lay. **721 on,** Hg reads "in." **Pernaso,** Mt. Parnassus, sacred to the Muses. **722 Scithero,** Cicero, exemplary Latin rhetorician. **729 Armorik,** Armorica, ancient name of Brittany, in northwestern France.

But atte laste she for his worthynesse,
And namely° for his meke obeysaunce°,
Hath swich° a pitee caught of his penaunce°
That pryvely° she fil of his accord°
To take hym for hir housbonde and hir lord,
Of swich lordshipe as men han° over hir wyves.
And for to lede the moore in blisse hir lyves,
Of his free wyl he swoor hire° as a knyght
That nevere in al his lyf he day ne nyght
Ne sholde upon hym take no maistrie°
Agayn hir wyl, ne kithe° hire jalousie,
But hire obeye and folwe hir wyl in al,
As any lovere to his lady shal,
Save that the name of soveraynetee°,
That wolde he have for shame of his degree°.
  She thanked hym, and with ful greet humblesse
She seyde, "Sire, sith° of youre gentillesse
Ye profre° me to have so large a reyne°,
Ne wolde nevere God bitwixe us tweyne,
As in my gilt°, were outher werre° or stryf.
Sire, I wol be youre humble trewe wyf—
Have heer my trouthe°—til that myn herte breste°."
Thus been they bothe in quiete and in reste.
  For o thyng, sires, saufly° dar I seye,
That freendes everych° oother moot° obeye
If they wol longe holden compaignye.
Love wol nat been constreyned by maistrye.
Whan maistrie comth°, the God of Love anon°
Beteth his wynges and farewell, he is gon.
Love is a thyng as any spirit free.
Wommen, of kynde°, desiren libertee,
And nat to been constreyned as a thral°—
And so doon men, if I sooth° seyen shal.
Looke who that is moost pacient in love,
He is at his avantage° al above.
Pacience is an heigh vertu, certeyn,
For it venquysseth°, as thise clerkes seyn,
Thynges that rigour° sholde nevere atteyne°.
For° every word men may nat chide° or pleyne°.
Lerneth to suffer°, or elles so moot I goon,
Ye shul it lerne wher so ye wole or noon°.
For in this world, certain, ther no wight° is
That he ne dooth or seith somtyme amys°.
Ire°, siknesse, or constellacioun°,
Wyn°, wo, or chaungynge of complexioun
Causeth ful ofte to doon amys or speken.
On every wrong a man may nat be wreken°.
After° the tyme moste° be temperaunce°
To every wight that kan on° governaunce.
And therfore hath this wise, worthy knyght
To lyve in ese suffrance hire bihight°,
And she to hym ful wisly gan to swere
That nevere sholde ther be defaute in here°.
  Heere may men seen an humble, wys accord;
Thus hath she take hir servant and hir lord—
Servant in love and lord in mariage.
Thanne was he bothe in lordshipe and servage°.
Servage? Nay, but in lordshipe above°
Sith° he hath bothe his lady and his love;
His lady, certes°, and his wyf also,
The which that lawe of love acordeth to.
And whan he was in this prosperitee,
Hoom with his wyf he gooth to his contree,
Nat fer fro Pedmark ther his dwellyng was,
Where as he lyveth in blisse and in solas°.
  Who koude telle but° he hadde wedded be°
The joye, the ese, and the prosperitee
That is bitwixe an housbonde and his wyf?
A yeer and moore lasted this blisful lyf,
Til that the knyght of which I speke of thus,
That of Kayrrud was cleped° Arveragus,
Shoop hym° to goon and dwelle a yeer or tweyne
In Engelond, that cleped was eek° Briteyne,

---

739 namely, *especially,* **obeysaunce,** *submissiveness* **740 swich,** *such,* **penaunce,** *suffering* **741 pryvely,** *secretly,* **fil of his accord,** *agreed* **743 han,** *have* **745 hire,** *to her* **747 maistrie,** *control* **748 kithe,** *show* **751 soveraynetee,** *dominance* **752 for shame of his degree,** *in consideration of his social rank* **754 sith,** *since* **755 profre,** *offer,* **so large a reyne,** *such free rein* **757 As in my gilt,** *through my fault,* **outher werre,** *either war* **759 trouthe,** *pledge,* **breste,** *burst* **761 saufly,** *surely* **762 everych,** *each,* **moot,** *must* **765 comth,** *comes,* **anon,** *at once* **768 of kynde,** *by nature* **769 thral,** *slave* **770 sooth,** *truth* **772 at his avantage,** i.e., *has the advantage* **774 venquysseth,** *overcomes* **775 rigour,** *strictness,* **atteyne,** *achieve* **776 For,** *at,* **chide,** *scold,* **pleyne,** *complain* **777 suffre,** *tolerate* **778 wher so ye wole or noon,** *whether you want to or not* **779 wight,** *person* **780 amys,** *wrongly* **781 Ire,** *anger,* **constellacioun,** *astrological influence* **782 Wyn,** *wine* **784 wreken,** *avenged* **785 After,** *according to,* **moste,** (there) *must,* **temperaunce,** *tolerance* **786 kan on,** *knows about* **788 suffrance hire bihight,** *promised her patience* **790 defaute in here,** *flaws in her* **794 servage,** *servitude* **795 above,** *higher* **796 Sith,** *since* **797 certes,** *surely* **802 solas,** *pleasure* **803 but,** *unless,* **be,** *been* **808 cleped,** *called* **809 Shoop hym,** *prepared himself* **810 cleped was eek,** *also was called*

756–57 Ne wolde nevere God . . . were, i.e., may there never be, by God **764–67** Similar to *RR* 9440-42. **768–69** Similar to *RR* 13959-66. **771 is moost,** Hg reads "moost is." **772 avantage,** Hg reads "avantate." **773–74** Proverbial. **777 so moot I goon,** as I am able to walk; i.e., by my life. **782 complexioun,** balance of humors (see *GP* 1.333n). The list of causes here are commonplaces of medieval psychology and physiology. **793-98** See *RR* 9449-53. **801 Pedmark,** Penmarch, on the coast of Brittany. **808 of Kayrrud,** Kérity, a village near Penmarch.

To seke in armes worship° and honour—
For al his lust° he sette in swich° labour—
And dwelled there two yeer, the book seith thus.
  Now wol I stynten of° this Arveragus,
And speken I wole of Dorigen his wyf
That loveth hire housbonde as hire hertes lyf.
For his absence wepeth she and siketh°,
As doon thise noble wyves whan hem liketh°.
She moorneth, waketh°, wayleth, fasteth,
    pleyneth°.
Desir of his presence hire so destreyneth°
That al this wyde world she sette at noght.
Hire freendes, whiche that knewe hir hevy
    thoght,
Conforten hire in al that ever they may.
They prechen hire, they telle hire nyght and day
That causelees she sleeth hirself, allas,
And every confort possible in this cas°
They doon to hire with al hire bisynesse,
Al for to make hire leve hire hevynesse.
  By proces°, as ye knowen everichoon°,
Men may so longe graven° in a stoon
Til som figure therinne emprented be.
So longe han they conforted hire, til she
Receyved hath, by hope and by resoun,
The emprentyng° of hire consolacioun,
Thurgh which hir grete sorwe gan aswage°;
She may nat alwey duren° in swich rage°.
  And eek Arveragus in al this care
Hath sent hire lettres hoom of his welfare,
And that he wol come hastily agayn;
Or elles hadde this sorwe hir herte slayn.
  Hire freendes sawe hir sorwe gan to slake°,
And preyde hire on knees, for Goddes sake,
To come and romen hire° in compaignye,
Awey to dryve hire derke fantasye.
And finally she graunted that requeste,
For wel she saugh° that it was for the beste.
  Now stood hire castel faste° by the see,
And often with hire freendes walketh shee
Hire to disporte° upon the bank an heigh
Where as she many a ship and barge seigh°
Seillynge hir cours°, where as hem liste go°.
But thanne was that a parcel° of hire wo,
For to hirself ful ofte, "Allas," seith she,
"Is ther no ship of so manye as I se
Wol bryngen hom my lord? Thanne were myn
    herte
Al warisshed° of his° bittre peynes smerte."
  Another tyme ther wolde she sitte and thynke,
And caste hir eyen dounward fro the brynke.
But whan she saugh the grisly rokkes blake
For verray° feere so wolde hir herte quake
That on hire feet she myghte hire noght sustene.
Thanne wolde she sitte adoun upon the grene
And pitously into the see biholde,
And seyn right thus with sorweful sikes° colde:
  "Eterne God, that thurgh thy purveiaunce°
Ledest the world by certein governaunce,
In ydel°, as men seyn, ye no thyng make.
But, Lord, thise grisly, feendly° rokkes blake,
That semen rather a foul confusioun
Of werk than any fair creacioun
Of swich a parfit° wys God and a stable°,
Why han ye wroght° this werk unresonable?
For by this werk, south, north, ne west, ne eest,
Ther nys yfostred man°, ne bryd°, ne beest;
It dooth no good, to my wit, but anoyeth°.
Se ye nat, Lord, how mankynde it destroyeth?
An hundred thousand bodyes of mankynde
Han rokkes slayn, al be they nat in mynde°,
Which mankynde is so fair part of thy werk
That thou it madest lyk to thyn owene merk°.
  "Thanne semed it ye hadde a greet chiertee°
Toward mankynde; but how thanne may it bee
That ye swiche meenes° make it° to destroyen,
Whiche meenes do no good but evere anoyen°?
I woot° wel clerkes wol seyn as hem leste°,
By argumentz, that al is for the beste
Though I ne kan the causes nat yknowe.

811 worship, *reputation* **812 lust,** *desire,* **swich,** *such* **814 stynten of,** *stop about* **817 siketh,** *sighs* **818 hem liketh,** (it) *pleases them* **819 waketh,** *lies awake,* **pleyneth,** *laments* **820 destreyneth,** *torments* **826 cas,** *situation* **829 By proces,** *in time,* **everichoon,** *everyone* **830 graven,** *engrave* **834 emprentyng,** *impression* **835 gan aswage,** *diminished* **836 duren,** *endure,* **swich rage,** *such passion* **841 slake,** *subside* **843 romen hire,** *walk herself* **846 saugh,** *saw* **847 faste,** *near* **849 Hire to disporte,** *to entertain herself* **850 seigh,** *sees* **851 hir cours,** *their way,* **hem liste go,** *they wish to go* **852 parcel,** *portion* **856 warisshed,** *cured,* **his,** *its* **860 verray,** *genuine* **864 sikes,** *sighs* **865 purveiaunce,** *providence* **867 In ydel,** *to no purpose* **868 feendly,** *fiendish* **871 parfit,** *perfect,* **stable,** *stable one* **872 wroght,** *made* **874 Ther nys yfostred man,** *there is no man who benefits,* **ne bryd,** *nor bird* **875 anoyeth,** *afflicts* **878 al be they nat in mynde,** *although they are forgotten* **880 lyk to thyn owene merk,** *in your own image* **881 chiertee,** *charity* (love) **883 swiche meenes,** *such means,* **it,** i.e., *mankind* **884 anoyen,** *afflict* **885 woot,** *know,* **hem leste,** *they wish*

811 worship and honour, the tension between the pursuit of knightly honor and love of wife is a romance motif from Chrétien de Troyes (fl. 1160-90) onward. **853 to,** Hg reads "of." **865–93** This appeal to (questioning of?) Providence has its roots in Boethian thought (*Consolation* 4pr6) and recalls *KnT* 1.2986ff., although Dorigen fails to perceive or accept the wisdom of divine order. **887 ne,** omitted in El.

But thilke° God that made wynd to blowe
As kepe° my lord! This my conclusion.
To clerkes lete I al disputison.
But wolde° God that alle thise rokkes blake
Were sonken into helle for his sake!
Thise rokkes sleen myn herte for the feere."
Thus wolde she seyn, with many a pitous teere.
Hire freendes sawe that it was no disport°
To romen by the see, but disconfort,
And shopen° for to pleyen somwher elles.
They leden° hire by ryveres and by welles,
And eek in othere places delitables°;
They dauncen and they pleyen at ches and tables°.
So on a day, right in the morwetyde°,
Unto a gardyn that was ther bisyde,
In which that they hadde maad hir ordinaunce°
Of vitaille° and of oother purveiaunce°,
They goon and pleye hem al the longe day.
And this was on the sixte morwe of May,
Which May hadde peynted with his softe shoures°
This gardyn ful of leves and of floures;
And craft° of mannes hand so curiously°
Arrayed hadde this gardyn, trewely,
That nevere was ther gardyn of swich prys°
But if it were the verray° paradys.
The odour of floures and the fresshe sighte
Wolde han° maked any herte lighte
That evere was born but if to° greet siknesse
Or to greet sorwe helde it in distresse,
So ful it was of beautee with plesaunce°.
At after-dyner gonne they to daunce,
And synge also, save Dorigen allone,
Which made alwey hir compleint and hir moone°,
For she ne saugh hym on the daunce go
That was hir housbonde and hir love also.
But nathelees she moste° a tyme abyde°,
And with good hope lete hir sorwe slyde°.
Upon this daunce, amonges othere men,
Daunced a squier biforn Dorigen,
That fressher was and jolyer° of array,
As to my doom°, than is the monthe of May.
He syngeth, daunceth, passynge° any man
That is or was sith° that the world bigan.
Therwith he was, if men sholde hym discryve°,
Oon of the beste farynge° man on lyve:
Yong, strong, right vertuous, and riche, and wys,
And wel biloved, and holden in greet prys°.
And shortly, if the sothe I tellen shal,
Unwityng of° this Dorigen at al
This lusty squier, servant to Venus,
Which that ycleped° was Aurelius,
Hadde loved hire best of any creature
Two yeer and moore, as was his aventure°,
But nevere dorste° he tellen hire his grevaunce.
Withouten coppe he drank al his penaunce.
He was despeyred°; nothyng dorste he seye,
Save in his songes somwhat wolde he wreye°
His wo, as in a general compleynyng.
He seyde he lovede and was biloved no thyng°.
Of swich matere made he manye layes,
Songes, compleintes, roundels, virelayes,
How that he dorste° nat his sorwe telle,
But langwissheth° as a furye dooth in helle,
And dye he moste, he seyde, as dide Ekko
For Narcisus, that dorste nat telle hir wo.
In oother manere than ye heere me seye
Ne dorste he nat to hire his wo biwreye°,
Save that paraventure° somtyme at daunces,
Ther° yonge folk kepen hir observaunces°,
It may wel be he looked on hir face
In swich a wise° as man that asketh grace°;
But nothyng wiste° she of his entente.

888 thilke, *that* **889 As kepe,** *so protect* **891 wolde,** *I wish to* **895 disport,** *pleasure* **897 shopen,** *arranged* **898 leden,** *led* **899 delitables,** *delightful* **900 tables,** *backgammon* **901 morwetyde,** *morning* **903 hir ordinaunce,** *their arrangements* **904 vitaille,** *food,* **purveiaunce,** *provisions* **907 shoures,** *showers* **909 craft,** *skill,* **curiously,** *ingeniously* **911 swich prys,** *such excellence* **912 verray,** *true* **914 Wolde han,** *would have* **915 but if to,** *unless too* **917 plesaunce,** *pleasure* **920 Which,** *who,* **moone,** *moan* **923 moste,** *must,* **abyde,** *await* **924 slyde,** *pass* **927 jolyer,** *more attractive* **928 doom,** *judgment* **929 passynge,** *surpassing* **930 sith,** *since* **931 discryve,** *describe* **932 beste farynge,** *most handsome* **934 prys,** *honor* **936 Unwityng of,** *unknown to* **938 ycleped,** *named* **940 aventure,** *luck* **941 dorste,** *dared* **943 despeyred,** *in despair* **944 wreye,** *reveal* **946 no thyng,** *not at all* **949 dorste,** *dared* **950 langwissheth,** *suffers* **954 biwreye,** *betray* (reveal) **955 paraventure,** *perhaps* **956 Ther,** *where,* **observaunces,** *courtly rituals* **958 wise,** *manner,* **grace,** *favor* **959 wiste,** *knew*

890 al disputison, El reads "al this disputison." **906 on,** El reads "in." **937 Venus,** goddess of love. **942 Withouten coppe . . . his penaunce,** he drank all his sorrow without a cup, i.e., he did it the hard way, suffering extraordinarily. **947–48 layes / Songes, compleintes, roundels, virelayes,** lays (brief songs), songs, complaints (laments), roundels, virelayes. Several of Chaucer's short poems are cast as complaints; roundels and virelays are now verse forms, but originally were names for dance songs with refrains. **947 swich,** Hg reads "which." **950 furye dooth in hell,** typically, the classical Furies were figures of punishment, but Chaucer presents them as tormented, perhaps influenced by Dante, *Inferno* 9.37–51. **951–52 Ekko / For Narcisus,** refused love by Narcissus, the nymph Echo faded away to a mere voice; Ovid, *Metamorphoses* 3.353–400 and elsewhere.

Nathelees it happed°, er they thennes° wente,
By cause that he was hire neighebour,
And was a man of worship° and honour,
And hadde° yknowen hym of tyme yoore°,
They fille in speche; and forthe moore° and moore
Unto his purpos drough° Aurelius,
And whan he saugh his tyme, he seyde thus:
  "Madame," quod he, "by God that this world made,
So° that I wiste it myghte youre herte glade°,
I wolde° that day that youre Arveragus
Wente over the see, that I, Aurelius,
Hadde went ther° nevere I sholde have come agayn.
For wel I woot° my servyce is in vayn;
My gerdon° is but brestyng° of myn herte.
Madame, reweth° upon my peynes smerte°,
For with a word ye may me sleen° or save.
Heere at youre feet God wolde° that I were grave°!
I ne have as now no leyser° moore to seye;
Have mercy, sweete, or ye wol do me deye!"
  She gan to looke upon Aurelius:
"Is this youre wyl°," quod she, "and sey ye thus?
Nevere erst°," quod she, "ne wiste I what ye mente.
But now, Aurelie, I knowe youre entente,
By thilke° God that yaf° me soule and lyf
Ne shal I nevere been untrewe wyf
In word ne werk, as fer as I have wit.
I wol been his to whom that I am knyt°.
Taak this for fynal answere as of me."
But after that in pley thus seyde she:
  "Aurelie," quod she, "by heighe God above,
Yet wolde I graunte yow to been youre love,
Syn° I yow se° so pitously complayne°.
Looke° what day that endelong° Britayne
Ye remoeve alle the rokkes, stoon by stoon,
That they ne lette° ship ne boot to goon—
I seye, whan ye han maad the coost so clene
Of rokkes that ther nys no stoon ysene°,
Thanne wol I love yow best of any man.
Have heer my trouthe° in al that evere I kan°."
  "Is ther noon oother grace° in yow?" quod he.
  "No, by that Lord," quod she, "that maked me!
For wel I woot° that it shal never bityde°.
Lat swiche° folies out of youre herte slyde°.
What deyntee° sholde a man han in his lyf
For to go love another mannes wyf,
That hath hir body whan so that hym liketh?"
  Aurelius ful ofte soore siketh°;
Wo was Aurelie whan that he this herde,
And with a sorweful herte he thus answerde:
  "Madame," quod he, "this were an inpossible°.
Thanne moot I dye° of sodeyn deth horrible."
And with that word he turned hym anon°.
Tho° coome hir othere freendes many oon
And in the aleyes° romeden up and doun,
And nothyng wiste° of this conclusioun,
But sodeynly bigonne revel° newe
Til that the brighte sonne loste his hewe,
For th'orisonte hath reft° the sonne his lyght—
This is as muche to seye as it was nyght.
And hoom they goon in joye and in solas°,
Save° oonly wrecche Aurelius, allas!
He to his hous is goon with sorweful herte.
He seeth° he may nat fro his deeth asterte°;
Hym semed that he felte his herte colde°.
Up to the hevene his handes he gan holde,
And on his knowes° bare he sette hym doun,
And in his ravyng seyde his orisoun°.
For verray° wo out of his wit he breyde°.
He nyste° what he spak, but thus he seyde;
With pitous herte his pleynt° hath he bigonne
Unto the goddes, and first unto the sonne:
  He seyde, "Appollo, god and governour
Of every plaunte, herbe, tree, and flour,
That yevest after thy declinacioun°
To ech of hem his tyme and his sesoun,

960 happed, *happened,* **thennes,** *from there* **962 worship,** *reputation* **963 hadde,** (she) *had,* **of tyme yoore,** *for a long time* **964 moore,** *closer* **965 drough,** *drew* **968 So,** *if,* **glade,** *gladden* **969 wolde,** *wish* **971 went ther,** *gone where* **972 woot,** *know* **973 gerdon,** *reward,* **brestyng,** *bursting* **974 reweth,** *have pity,* **smerte,** *sore* **975 sleen,** *slay* **976 God wolde,** *I wish to God,* **grave,** *buried* **977 leyser,** *time* **980 wyl,** *desire* **981 erst,** *before* **983 thilke,** *that,* **yaf,** *gave* **986 knyt,** *wedded* (knitted) **991 Syn,** *since,* **se,** *see,* **complayne,** *lament* **992 Looke,** *consider,* **endelong,** *the entire length of* **994 lette,** *hinder* **996 ysene,** *seen* **998 trouthe,** *pledge,* **kan,** *am able* (to do) **999 grace,** *kindness* **1001 woot,** *know,* **bityde,** *happen* **1002 swiche,** *such,* **slyde,** *pass* **1003 deyntee,** *pleasure* **1006 soore siketh,** *sighs sorely* **1009 inpossible,** *impossibility* **1010 moot I dye,** *must I die* **1011 turned hym anon,** *turned himself away quickly* **1012 Tho,** *then* **1013 aleyes,** *paths* **1014 wiste,** *knew* **1015 bigonne revel,** *began revelry* **1017 orisonte hath reft,** *horizon has stolen* **1019 solas,** *pleasure* **1020 Save,** *except* **1022 seeth,** *sees that,* **asterte,** *escape* **1023 colde,** *turn cold* **1025 knowes,** *knees* **1026 orisoun,** *prayer* **1027 verray,** *true,* **breyde,** *leapt* **1028 nyste,** *knew not* **1029 pleynt,** *lament* **1033 yevest after thy declinacioun,** *give according to your angle above the equator*

987 answere, omitted in Hg. **988 in pley,** the phrase connotes much the same as in modern English, from "amiably" to "playfully" to "teasingly," all of which seem to qualify Dorigen's promise that follows. In romance tradition, rash promises usually come about when the promise-maker is tricked or deceived; the impossibility of a task is another folk motif. **1003 in,** omitted in Hg. **1004 go,** omitted in Hg. **1031 Appollo,** Phebus Apollo, god of the sun.

As thyn herberwe° chaungeth lowe or heighe,
Lord Phebus, cast thy merciable eighe°
On wrecche Aurelie which that am but lorn°.
Lo, lord, my lady hath my deeth ysworn
Withoute gilt, but thy benignytee°
Upon my dedly° herte have som pitee.
For wel I woot°, lord Phebus, if yow lest°,
Ye may me helpen, save° my lady, best.
Now voucheth sauf° that I may yow devyse°
How that I may been holpen° and in what wyse.
"Youre blisful suster, Lucina the sheene,
That of the see° is chief goddesse and queene—
Though Neptunus have deitee° in the see,
Yet emperisse° aboven hym is she—
Ye knowen wel, lord, that right° as hir desir
Is to be quyked° and lightned of youre fir,
For which she folweth yow ful bisily°,
Right° so the see desireth naturelly
To folwen hire, as she that is goddesse
Bothe in the see and ryveres moore and lesse°.
Wherfore, lord Phebus, this is my requeste—
Do this miracle, or do myn herte breste°—
That now next at this opposicioun
Which in the signe shal be of the Leoun,
As preieth hire° so greet a flood° to brynge
That fyve fadme° at the leeste it oversprynge°
The hyeste rokke in Armorik Briteyne;
And lat this flood endure yeres tweyne°.
Thanne certes to my lady may I seye,
'Holdeth° youre heste°, the rokkes been aweye.'
"Lord Phebus, dooth this miracle for me.
Preye° hire she go no faster cours than ye;
I seye, preyeth youre suster that she go
No faster cours than ye thise yeres two.
Thanne shal she been evene atte fulle alway,
And spryng flood laste bothe nyght and day.
And but° she vouchesauf° in swich manere
To graunte me my sovereyn lady deere,
Prey hire to synken every rok adoun
Into hir owene dirke regioun
Under the ground ther° Pluto dwelleth inne,
Or nevere mo shal I my lady wynne.
Thy temple in Delphos wol I barefoot seke°.
Lord Phebus, se the teeris on my cheke,
And of my peyne have som compassioun."
And with that word in swowne° he fil adoun,
And longe tyme he lay forth in a traunce.
His brother, which that knew of his penaunce°,
Up caughte hym, and to bedde he hath hym broght.
Dispeyred° in this torment and this thoght
Lete I this woful creature lye;
Chese he, for me°, wheither he wol lyve or dye.
Arveragus, with heele° and greet honour,
As he that was of chivalrie the flour°,
Is comen hoom, and othere worthy men.
O blisful artow° now, thou Dorigen,
That hast thy lusty housbonde in thyne armes,
The fresshe knyght, the worthy man of armes,
That loveth thee as his owene hertes lyf.
No thyng list hym to been ymaginatyf°
If any wight hadde spoke, whil he was oute,
To hire of love; he hadde of it no doute.
He noght entendeth° to no swich mateere,
But daunceth, justeth°, maketh hire good cheere.
And thus in joye and blisse I let hem dwelle,
And of the sike Aurelius I wol yow telle.
In langour° and in torment furyus
Two yeer and moore lay wrecche Aurelyus
Er any foot he myghte on erthe gon°;
Ne confort in this tyme hadde he noon
Save of his brother, which that was a clerk°.

1035 herberwe, *house* (in the zodiac) **1036 merciable eighe,** *merciful eye* **1037 lorn,** *lost* **1039 thy benignytee,** (may) *your goodness* **1040 dedly,** *deadlike* **1041 woot,** *know,* **lest,** *wish* **1042 save,** *besides* **1043 voucheth sauf,** *grant,* **yow devyse,** *explain to you* **1044 holpen,** *helped* **1046 see,** *sea* **1047 have deitee,** *has rule* **1048 emperisse,** *empress* **1049 right,** *just* **1050 quyked,** *brought to life* **1051 bisily,** *intently* **1052 Right,** *just* **1054 moore and lesse,** *greater and lesser* **1056 breste,** *burst* **1059 As preieth hire,** *so ask her,* **flood,** *tide* **1060 fadme,** *fathoms* (six feet), **oversprynge,** *rise above* **1062 yeres tweyne,** *two years* **1064 Holdeth,** *keep,* **heste,** *promise* **1066 Preye,** *ask* **1071 but,** *unless,* **vouchesauf,** *agrees* **1075 ther,** *where* **1077 seke,** *seek* **1080 swowne,** *a faint* **1082 penaunce,** *suffering* **1084 Dispeyred,** *hopeless* **1086 Chese he, for me,** *he can choose, as far as I'm concerned* **1087 heele,** *health* **1088 flour,** *flower* **1090 artow,** *are you* **1094 No thyng list hym to been ymaginatyf,** *he was not at all inclined to wonder* **1097 noght entendeth,** *pays no attention* **1098 justeth,** *jousts* **1101 langour,** *affliction* **1103 gon,** *walk* **1105 clerk,** *scholar*

1037 that, omitted in El. **1045 Lucina the sheene,** Luna the beautiful, goddess of the moon and controller of tides. **1047 Neptunus,** Neptune, god of the sea. **1050** The moon reflects the light of the sun. **1057–58 opposicioun . . . Leoun,** opposition of sun and moon, in the sign of Leo. Tides are highest when the gravity of sun and moon pull together (in conjunction) or against each other (opposition). **1066 no faster cours,** the moon appears to travel faster than the sun through the sky; Aurelius asks that they travel at the same speed to maintain their opposition, keep the moon full, and keep the tide high. **1067 seye, preyeth,** Hg reads "seye this, preyeth." **1074 hir owene dirke regioun,** her own dark region, the underworld. The moon goddess was recognized in two other manifestations: Diana, goddess of the hunt, and Hecate, goddess of the underworld. **1075 Pluto,** god of the underworld. **1077 Delphos,** Delphi, Apollo's most famous temple. **1086 wheither,** Hg reads "wher." **1096 he hadde,** Hg reads "he ne hadde." **1100 yow,** omitted in Hg.

He knew of al this wo and al this werk°,
For to noon oother creature, certeyn,
Of this matere he dorste° no word seyn.
Under his brest he baar it moore secree
Than evere dide Pamphilus for Galathee.
His brest was hool withoute° for to sene,
But in his herte ay° was the arwe kene°.
And wel ye knowe that of a sursanure°
In surgere is perilous the cure,
But° men myghte touche the arwe or come therby°.
His brother weep and wayled pryvely°
Til atte laste hym fil in remembraunce°
That whiles he was at Orliens in Fraunce,
As yonge clerkes that been lykerous°
To reden° artes that been curious°
Seken° in every halke° and every herne°
Particuler° sciences for to lerne,
He hym remembred that upon a day
At Orliens in studie a book he say°
Of magyk natureel°, which his felawe,
That was that tyme a bacheler of lawe—
Al were he° ther to lerne another craft—
Hadde prively upon his desk ylaft°.
Which book spak muchel° of the operaciouns
Touchynge the eighte and twenty mansiouns
That longen° to the moone, and swich folye°
As in oure dayes is nat worth a flye,
For hooly chirches feith in oure bileve°
Ne suffreth noon° illusioun us to greve°.
And whan this book was in his remembraunce,
Anon for joye his herte gan to daunce,
And to hymself he seyde pryvely:
"My brother shal be warisshed° hastily,
For I am siker° that ther be sciences
By whiche men make diverse apparences°
Swiche° as thise subtile tregetoures pleye°.
For ofte at feestes have I wel herd seye
That tregetours withinne an halle large
Have maad come in a water and a barge,
And in the halle rowen up and doun.
Somtyme hath semed come a grym leoun;
And somtyme floures sprynge as in a mede°;
Somtyme a vyne and grapes white and rede;
Somtyme a castel, al of lym° and stoon;
And whan hym lyked°, voyded it anon°.
Thus semed it to every mannes sighte.
  "Now thanne conclude I thus, that if I myghte
At Orliens som oold felawe° yfynde
That hadde thise moones mansions in mynde,
Or oother magyk natureel above,
He sholde wel make my brother han° his love.
For with an apparence° a clerk may make
To mannes sighte that alle the rokkes blake
Of Britaigne weren yvoyded everichon°,
And shippes by the brynke° comen and gon,
And in swich forme° enduren a wowke° or two.
Thanne were my brother warisshed° of his wo;
Thanne moste she nedes holden hire biheste°,
Or elles he shal shame hire atte leeste."
  What sholde I make a lenger tale of this?
Unto his brotheres bed he comen is,
And swich confort he yaf° hym for to gon
To Orliens that he up stirte° anon
And on his wey forthward thanne is he fare°
In hope for to been lissed° of his care.
  Whan they were come almoost to that citee,
But if it were a° two furlong° or thre,
A yong clerk romynge by hymself they mette,
Which that° in Latyn thriftily° hem grette°,
And after that he seyde a wonder thyng:
"I knowe," quod he, "the cause of youre comyng."
And er they ferther any foote wente,
He told hem al that was in hire entente.
  This Briton° clerk hym asked of felawes°
The whiche that he had knowe in olde dawes°,

1106 werk, *matter* **1108 dorste,** *dared* **1111 hool withoute,** *whole on the outside* **1112 ay,** *always,* **arwe keen,** *sharp arrow* **1113 sursanure,** *superficially healed wound* **1115 But,** *unless,* **arwe,** *arrowhead,* **come therby,** *get at it* **1116 pryvely,** *in secret* **1117 fil in remembraunce,** *recalled* **1119 lykerous,** *eager* **1120 reden,** *study,* **curious,** *arcane* **1121 Seken,** *seek,* **halke,** *nook,* **herne,** *corner* **1122 Particuler,** *specialized* **1124 say,** *saw* **1125 magyk natureel,** *astrology* **1127 Al were he,** *although he was* **1128 ylaft,** *left* **1129 spak muchel,** *said much* **1131 longen,** *pertain,* **swich folye,** *such folly* **1133 bileve,** *need* **1134 Ne suffreth noon,** *allows no,* **greve,** *afflict* **1138 warisshed,** *healed* **1139 siker,** *certain* **1140 apparences,** *apparitions* **1141 Swiche,** *such,* **tregetoures pleye,** *magicians produce* **1147 mede,** *meadow* **1149 lym,** *mortar* **1150 hym lyked,** (it) *pleased* (the magician), **voyded it anon,** (he) *sent it away at once* **1153 felawe,** *companion* **1156 han,** *have* **1157 apparence,** *illusion* **1159 yvoyded everichon,** *all removed* **1160 brynke,** *coast* **1161 swich forme,** *such appearance,* **wowke,** *week* **1162 warisshed,** *healed* **1163 biheste,** *promise* **1167 yaf,** *gave* **1168 up stirte,** *leapt up* **1169 fare,** *gone* **1170 lissed,** *relieved* **1172 But if it were a,** *except for,* **furlong,** *eighth of a mile* **1174 Which that,** *who,* **thriftily,** *suitably,* **grette,** *greeted* **1179 Briton,** *Breton,* **felawes,** *companions* **1180 dawes,** *days*

1110 Pamphilus for Galathee, Pamphilus yearns for and seduces Galatea in the popular thirteenth-century Latin poem *Pamphilus de Amore.* **1118 Orliens,** Orleans, site of a famous university in the Middle Ages. **1130 eighte and twenty mansiouns,** the twenty-eight positions in the lunar month. **1140 whiche,** El reads "whce." **1174 Latyn,** Latin, the international language of scholars and universities in medieval Europe.

And he answerde hym that they dede were,
For which he weep ful ofte many a teere.
Doun of his hors Aurelius lighte anon°,
And with this magicien forth is he gon
Hoom to his hous, and maden hem wel at ese.
Hem lakked° no vitaille° that myghte hem plese.
So wel arrayed hous as ther was oon°
Aurelius in his lyf saugh nevere noon.
He shewed hym, er he wente to sopeer°,
Forestes, parkes ful of wilde deer:
Ther saugh he hertes° with hir hornes hye°,
The gretteste that evere were seyn with eye.
He saugh of hem an hondred slayn with houndes,
And somme with arwes blede of bittre woundes.
He saugh, whan voyded° were thise wilde deer,
Thise fauconers upon° a fair ryver
That with hir haukes han the heron slayn.
Tho saugh° he knyghtes justyng in° a playn.
And after this he dide hym swich plesaunce°
That he hym shewed his lady on a daunce,
On which hymself he daunced, as hym thoughte.
And whan this maister that this magyk wroughte°
Saugh it was tyme, he clapte his handes two,
And farewel, al oure revel was ago°.
And yet remoeved they nevere out of the hous
Whil they saugh al this sighte merveillous,
But in his studie, ther as his bookes be,
They seten stille, and no wight° but they thre.
To hym this maister called his squier
And seyde hym thus: "Is redy oure soper?
Almoost an houre it is, I undertake°,
Sith° I yow bad oure soper for to make,
Whan that thise worthy men wenten with me
Into my studie, ther as my bookes be."
"Sire," quod this squier, "whan it liketh yow,
It is al redy, though ye wol right now."
"Go we thanne soupe°," quod he, "as for the beste.
Thise amorous folk somtyme moote han° hir reste."
At after-soper fille they in tretee°
What somme° sholde this maistres gerdon° be
To remoeven alle the rokkes of Britayne,
And eek from Gerounde to the mouth of Sayne.
He made it straunge°, and swoor, so God hym save,
Lasse than a thousand pound he wolde nat have,
Ne gladly for that somme he wolde nat goon°.
Aurelius, with blisful herte anoon,
Answerde thus: "Fy on a thousand pound!
This wyde world, which that men seye is round,
I wolde it yeve° if I were lord of it.
This bargayn is ful dryve°, for we been knyt°.
Ye shal be payed trewely, by my trouthe.
But looketh° now, for no necligence or slouthe°
Ye tarie° us heere no lenger than to-morwe."
"Nay," quod this clerk, "have heer my feith to borwe°."
To bedde is goon Aurelius whan hym leste°,
And wel ny° al that nyght he hadde his reste.
What for his labour and his hope of blisse,
His woful herte of penaunce° hadde a lisse°.
Upon the morwe whan that it was day
To Britaigne tooke they the righte° way,
Aurelius and this magicien bisyde,
And been descended ther° they wolde abyde.
And this was, as thise bookes me remembre°,
The colde, frosty seson of Decembre.
Phebus wax° old and hewed lyk latoun°,
That in his hoote declynacioun°
Shoon as the burned° gold with stremes brighte;
But now in Capricorn adoun he lighte°,
Where as he shoon ful pale, I dar wel seyn.
The bittre frostes, with the sleet and reyn,
Destroyed hath the grene in every yerd.

1183 lighte anon, *alighted soon* **1186 Hem lakked,** *they lacked,* **vitaille,** *food* **1187 as ther was oon,** i.e., *as this one* **1189 sopeer,** *supper* **1191 hertes,** *harts,* **hornes hye,** *tall antlers* **1195 voyded,** *removed* **1196 fauconers upon,** *falconers near* **1198 Tho saugh,** *then saw,* **justyng in,** *jousting on* **1199 swich plesaunce,** *such pleasure* **1202 wroughte,** *worked* **1204 ago,** *gone* **1208 wight,** *creature* **1211 undertake,** *declare* **1212 Sith,** *since* **1217 soupe,** *to dine* **1218 moote han,** *must have* **1219 tretee,** *negotiation* **1220 somme,** *sum,* **maistres gerdon,** *master's payment* **1223 straunge,** *difficult* **1225 goon,** *go* (with them) **1229 yeve,** *give* **1230 ful dryve,** *completed,* **knyt,** *agreed* **1232 looketh,** *make sure,* **slouthe,** *laziness* **1233 tarie,** *delay* **1234 to borwe,** *in pledge* **1235 hym leste,** *he pleases* **1236 wel ny,** *nearly* **1238 of penaunce,** *from sorrow,* **lisse,** *release* **1240 righte,** *most direct* **1242 been descended ther,** *dismounted where* **1243 me remembre,** *remind me* **1245 Phebus wax,** *the sun grew,* **hewed lyk latoun,** *colored like brass* **1246 hoote declynacioun,** *summertime position* **1247 burned,** *burnished* **1248 adoun he lighte,** *he descends*

1184 is he, Hg reads "he is." **1199 swich,** Hg reads "this." **1204 al oure revel was ago,** all our entertainment was gone; compare Shakespeare's *Tempest* 4.1.148. **1222 Gerounde . . . Sayne,** the rivers Gironde and Seine, marking a coastline that includes much of western France. **1224 thousand pound,** a very large sum of money. **1248 in Capricorn,** the sun descends into the zodiacal sign of Capricorn (the Goat) at the beginning of winter.

Janus sit by the fyr with double berd
And drynketh of his bugle horn° the wyn.
Biforn hym stant° brawen of the tusked swyn,
And "Nowel" crieth every lusty° man.
  Aurelius in al that evere he kan
Dooth to this maister chiere and reverence°,
And preyeth° hym to doon his diligence°
To bryngen hym out of his peynes smerte°,
Or with a swerd that he wolde slitte his herte°.
  This subtil clerk swich routhe° had of this man
That nyght and day he spedde hym that he kan°
To wayten° a tyme of his conclusioun°—
This is to seye, to maken illusioun
By swich an apparence of jogelrye°
(I ne kan no° termes of astrologye)
That she and every wight sholde wene° and seye
That of Britaigne the rokkes were aweye,
Or ellis they were sonken under grounde.
So atte laste he hath his tyme yfounde
To maken his japes° and his wrecchednesse
Of swich a supersticious cursednesse.
His tables Tolletanes forth he brought,
Ful wel corrected; ne ther lakked nought,
Neither his collect ne his expans yeeris,
Ne his rootes, ne his othere geeris°,
As been his centris and his argumentz,
And his proporcioneles convenientz
For his equaciouns in everythyng.
And by his eighte speere in his wirkyng°
He knew ful wel how fer Alnath was shove
Fro° the heed of thilke fixe° Aries above,
That in the ninthe speere considered is;
Ful subtilly he kalkuled° al this.
  Whan he hadde founde his firste mansioun°,
He knew the remenaunt° by proporcioun,
And knew the arisyng of his moone weel,
And in whos face°, and terme°, and everydeel°;
And knew ful weel the moones mansioun
Acordaunt to his° operacioun,
And knew also his° othere observaunces°
For° swiche illusiouns and swiche meschaunces°
As hethen folk useden° in thilke° dayes.
For which no lenger maked he delayes,
But thurgh his magik, for a wyke° or tweye°,
It semed that alle the rokkes were aweye.
  Aurelius, which that yet despeired is°
Wher° he shal han his love or fare amys°,
Awaiteth nyght and day on this myracle;
And whan he knew that ther was noon obstacle,
That voyded° were thise rokkes everychon,
Doun to his maistres° feet he fil anon
And seyde, "I woful wrecche, Aurelius,
Thanke yow, lord, and lady myn Venus,
That me han holpen° fro my cares colde."
And to the temple his wey forth hath he holde°,
Where as he knew he sholde his lady see.

1253 bugle horn, *drinking horn* **1254 stant,** *stands* **1255 lusty,** *cheerful* **1257 Dooth . . . chiere and reverence,** *entertains and honors* **1258 preyeth,** *asks,* **diligence,** *best* **1259 peynes smerte,** *sharp pains* **1260 slitte his herte,** *commit suicide* **1261 swich routhe,** *such pity* **1262 spedde hym that he kan,** *hastened so that he might be able* **1263 wayten,** *determine,* **conclusioun,** *calculations* **1265 apparence of jogelrye,** *apparition of conjuring* **1266 ne kan no,** *know no* **1267 wene,** *believe* **1271 japes,** *tricks* **1276 geeris,** *equipment* **1280 wirkyng,** *studying* **1282 Fro,** *by means of,* **thilke fixe,** *that fixed* **1284 kalkuled,** *calculated* **1285 mansioun,** *location* (of the moon) **1286 remenaunt,** *the other locations* **1288 whos face,** *the first third of which constellation,* **terme,** *which of five unequal divisions of the constellations,* **everydeel,** *everything* **1290 Acordaunt to his,** *in relation to its* **1291 his,** *its* (the moon's), **observaunces,** *regular movements* **1292 For,** *for the purpose of,* **swiche meschaunces,** *such misdoings* **1293 useden,** *were accustomed to,* **thilke,** *those* **1295 wyke,** *week,* **tweye,** *two* **1297 despeired is,** *is in despair* **1298 Wher,** *whether,* **fare amys,** *go wrong* **1301 voyded,** *removed* **1302 maistres,** *master's* **1305 han holpen,** *have helped* **1306 hath he holde,** *has he taken*

1252 Janus, god of gateways with two bearded faces, one looking inward and the other outward; source of the name "January". **1254–55 brawen of the tusked swyn . . . "Nowel,"** meat of the boar (the traditional Christmas feast features boar's head); "noel" is a traditional Christmas song. This portrait of the season has little to do with the plot; it may be a remnant of source material, most likely the narrative accompanying Menedon's fourth question in Boccaccio's *Filocolo,* where the magician makes a garden blossom in winter. **1257 this,** El reads "his." **1265 of,** Hg reads "or." **1273–74 tables Tolletanes . . . corrected,** astrological tables originally composed to be used in Toledo, Spain, but calibrated ("corrected") to other cities or locations. Chaucer's familiarity with astral science is evident in this passage, even though the Franklin protests that he knows nothing of the subject (line 1266). **1275 collect,** table recording the degrees of planetary motions in twenty-year periods. **expans yeeris,** table recording the degrees of planetary motions in a single year. **1276 rootes,** base locations and dates from which planetary motions are calculated, usually the position of the planet at the time of the birth of Christ. **1277 centris,** table recording positions of planetary centers by minutes, days, hours, and minutes; see *Equat* 120. **argumentz,** angles and arcs used in calculating planetary positions; see *Equat* 344-45. **1278 proporcioneles convenientz,** uncertain, but perhaps table recording the degrees of planetary motions by fractional parts of years. **1279 equaciouns,** method of dividing heavenly sphere into equal sections; see *Equat* 194, 348, etc. **1280-83 eighte speere . . . Alnath . . . Aries . . . ninthe speere,** i.e., he knew from its relation to the eighth sphere (fixed stars) how far the star Alnath had been moved in the head of the zodiacal sign of the Ram (Aries) that is thought to be in the ninth sphere (Primum Mobile). This movement marks the gradual westward shift of the equinoxes. **1284 he kalkuled,** El reads "he hadde kalkuled." **1288 whos face . . . terme . . . everydeel,** i.e., he knew when the moon would rise in the first third of which zodiacal sign, which division of those signs, and everything else.

And whan he saugh his tyme, anon-right° hee
With dredful° herte and with ful humble cheere°
Salewed hath° his sovereyn lady deere:
  "My righte° lady," quod this woful man,
"Whom I moost drede° and love as I best kan,
And lothest were of al this world displese°,
Nere it° that I for yow have swich disese°
That I moste dyen heere at youre foot anon
Noght wolde° I telle how me is wo bigon°.
But certes° outher° moste I dye or pleyne°;
Ye sle me giltelees for verray peyne°.
But of my deeth thogh that ye have no routhe°,
Avyseth yow er that° ye breke youre trouthe.
Repenteth yow, for thilke° God above,
Er ye me sleen by cause that I yow love.
For, madame, wel ye woot° what ye han hight°—
Nat that I chalange° any thyng of right°
Of yow, my sovereyn lady, but youre grace°—
But in a gardyn yond°, at swich a place,
Ye woot° right wel what ye bihighten° me,
And in myn hand youre trouthe plighten ye°
To love me best—God woot, ye seyde so,
Al be that° I unworthy am therto.
Madame, I speke it for the honour of yow
Moore than to save myn hertes lyf right now.
I have do° so as ye comanded me,
And if ye vouchesauf°, ye may go see.
Dooth as yow list; have youre biheste° in mynde;
For, quyk° or deed, right there ye shal me fynde.
In yow lith al to do° me lyve or deye—
But wel I woot° the rokkes been aweye."
  He taketh his leve, and she astoned° stood;
In al hir face nas a drope of blood.
She wende° nevere han° come in swich a trappe.
"Allas," quod she, "that evere this sholde happe°!
For wende I nevere by possibilitee
That swich a monstre° or merveille myghte be.
It is agayns the proces of nature."
And hoom she goth a sorweful creature.
For verray feere unnethe° may she go°.
She wepeth, wailleth, al a day or two,
And swowneth that° it routhe° was to see.
But why it was to no wight° tolde shee,
For° out of towne was goon Arveragus.
But to hirself she spak and seyde thus,
With face pale and with ful sorweful cheere°,
In hire compleynt°, as ye shal after heere:
  "Allas," quod she, "on thee, Fortune, I pleyne°,
That unwar° wrapped hast me in thy cheyne°,
Fro which t'escape woot° I no socour°
Save oonly deeth or elles dishonour;
Oon of thise two bihoveth° me to chese°.
But nathelees, yet have I levere° to lese
My lif than of my body to have a shame,
Or knowe myselven fals, or lese my name°;
And with my deth I may be quyt°, ywis°.
Hath ther nat many a noble wyf er this,
And many a mayde, yslayn hirself, allas,
Rather than with hir body doon trespas?
  "Yis, certes°, lo, thise stories beren witnesse.
Whan thritty tirauntz° ful of cursednesse
Hadde slayn Phidon in Atthenes atte feste°,
They comanded his doghtres for t'areste°,
And bryngen hem biforn hem in despit°,
Al naked, to fulfille hir foul delit,
And in hir fadres° blood they made hem daunce
Upon the pavement, God yeve° hem myschaunce°!
For which thise woful maydens, ful of drede,
Rather than they wolde lese hir maydenhede°,
They prively been stirt° into a welle
And dreynte° hemselven, as the bookes telle.

1308 anon-right, *at once* **1309 dredful,** *fearful,* **cheere,** *manner* **1310 Salewed hath,** *has greeted* **1311 righte,** *true* **1312 moost drede,** *must fear* **1313 lothest . . . displese,** *most reluctant to displease* **1314 Nere it,** *were it not,* **disese,** *pain* **1316 Noght wolde,** *not at all would,* **wo bigon,** *in such woe* **1317 certes,** *surely,* **outher,** *either,* **pleyne,** *lament* **1318 verray peyne,** *true pain* **1319 routhe,** *pity* **1320 Avyseth yow er that,** *consider before* **1321 thilke,** *that* **1323 woot,** *know,* **hight,** *promised* **1324 chalange,** *claim,* **of right,** *as a right* **1325 youre grace,** (by) *your favor* **1326 yond,** *yonder* **1327 woot,** *know,* **bihighten,** *promised* **1328 youre trouthe plighten ye,** *you pledged your truth* **1330 Al be that,** *even though* **1333 do,** *done* **1334 vouchesauf,** *consent* **1335 biheste,** *promise* **1336 quyk,** *alive* **1337 lith al to do,** *lies all to make* **1338 woot,** *know* **1339 astoned,** *astonished* **1341 wende,** *thought,* **han,** *to have* **1342 happe,** *happen* **1344 monstre,** *wonder* **1347 unnethe,** *hardly,* **go,** *walk* **1349 swowneth that,** *faints so that,* **routhe,** *pity* **1350 why . . . tolde shee,** (the reason) *why she told no one was* **1351 For,** *because* **1353 cheere,** *manner* **1354 compleynt,** *lament* **1355 pleyne,** *complain* **1356 unwar,** *unexpectedly,* **cheyne,** *chain* **1357 woot,** *know,* **socour,** *help* **1359 bihoveth,** *is necessary for,* **chese,** *choose* **1360 have I levere,** *I would prefer* **1362 name,** *reputation* **1363 quyt,** *free,* **ywis,** *surely* **1367 certes,** *surely* **1368 thritty tirauntz,** *thirty tyrants* **1369 feste,** *feast* **1370 for t'areste,** *to be arrested* **1371 despit,** *scorn* **1373 hir fadres,** *their father's* **1374 yeve,** *give,* **myschaunce,** *ill fate* **1376 Rather . . . maydenhede,** i.e., *to preserve their virginity* **1377 prively been stirt,** *secretly jumped* **1378 dreynte,** *drowned*

1357 Fro, El and Hg read "For." **1358 elles,** omitted in El and Hg. **1361 to,** omitted in El. **1369–78 Phidon . . . ,** this account and the twenty-two that follow are all from Jerome, *Epistola adversus Jovinianum* (here 1.41; see *WBP* 3.3n), although Chaucer rearranges the order. Some critics think the reordering and sheer number produce comedy or bathos, whereas others assess them as a reflection of Dorigen's psychology or as a rhetorical set piece.

"They of° Mecene leete enquere and seke°
Of Lacedomye fifty maydens eke°,
On whiche they wolden doon hir lecherye.
But was ther noon of al that compaignye
That she nas slayn°, and with a good entente
Chees° rather for to dye than assente
To been oppressed of hir maydenhede°.
Why sholde I thanne to dye been in drede?
"Lo, eek the tiraunt Aristoclides,
That loved a mayden heet° Stymphalides,
Whan that hir fader slayn was on a nyght,
Unto Dianes temple goth she right°
And hente the ymage° in hir handes two,
Fro which ymage wolde she nevere go.
No wight° ne myghte hir handes of it arace°
Til she was slayn right in the selve° place.
"Now sith° that maydens hadden swich despit°
To been defouled with mannes foul delit,
Wel oghte a wyf rather hirselven slee
Than be defouled, as it thynketh me.
"What shal I seyn of Hasdrubales wyf
That at Cartage birafte° hirself hir lyf?
For whan she saugh that Romayns wan the toun,
She took hir children alle and skipte° adoun
Into the fyr, and chees rather to dye
Than any Romayn dide° hire vileynye.
"Hath nat Lucresse yslayn hirself, allas,
At Rome whan that she oppressed° was
Of° Tarquyn, for hire thoughte it was a shame
To lyven whan that she had lost hir name°?
"The sevene maydens of Melesie also
Han slayn hemself for verrey drede° and wo
Rather than folk of Gawle hem sholde oppresse.
Mo° than a thousand stories as I gesse
Koude I now telle as touchynge this mateere.
"Whan Habradate was slayn, his wyf so deere
Hirselven slow° and leet hir blood to glyde
In Habradates woundes depe and wyde,
And seyde, 'My body, at the leeste way,
Ther shal no wight° defoulen, if I may.'
"What sholde I mo ensamples heerof sayn,
Sith that° so manye han hemselven slayn
Wel rather than they wolde defouled be?
I wol conclude that it is bet° for me
To sleen myself than been defouled thus.
I wol be trewe unto Arveragus,
Or rather sleen myself in som manere,
As dide Demociones doghter deere
By cause that she wolde nat defouled be.
"O Cedasus, it is ful greet pitee
To reden how thy doghtren° deyde, allas,
That slowe hemself° for swich a manere cas°.
"As greet a pitee was it, or wel moore,
The Theban mayden that for Nichanore
Hirselven slow right for swich manere wo.
"Another Theban mayden dide right so°
For oon of Macidonye hadde hire oppressed;
She with hire deeth hir maydenhede redressed°.
"What shal I seye of Nicerates wyf
That for swich cas birafte° hirself hir lyf?
How trewe eek was to Alcebiades
His love, that rather for to dyen chees°
Than for to suffre° his body unburyed be,

1379 They of, *the men of,* **leete enquere and seke,** *did request and select* **1380 eke,** *also* **1383 nas slayn,** *did not die* **1384 Chees,** *chose* **1385 oppressed of hir maydenhede,** *raped* **1388 heet,** *called* **1390 right,** *directly* **1391 hente the ymage,** *clung to the statue* **1393 wight,** *person,* **arace,** *tear away* **1394 selve,** *same* **1395 sith,** *since,* **swich despit,** *such scorn* **1400 birafte,** *deprived* **1402 skipte,** *leapt* **1404 Than . . . dide,** *than (let) . . . do* **1406 oppressed,** *raped* **1407 Of,** *by* **1408 name,** *reputation* **1410 verrey drede,** *true fear* **1412 Mo,** *more* **1415 slow,** *slew,* **1418 wight,** *man* **1420 Sith that,** *since* **1422 bet,** *better* **1429 doghtren,** *daughters* **1430 slowe hemself,** *slew themselves,* **swich a manere cas,** *this kind of situation* **1434 right so,** *the same* **1436 redressed,** *amended* **1438 swich cas birafte,** *such a situation deprived* **1440 chees,** *chose* **1441 suffre,** *allow*

1379–80 Mecene . . . Lacedomye, Jerome 1.41 reports that Messene and Sparta (Lacedaemonia) exchanged virgins in connection with religious ritual; one time, when the Spartans attempted rape, the Messenian virgins all committed suicide. **1387–94 Aristoclides . . . ,** follows the account in Jerome 1.41. **1390 Dianes temple,** Diana was goddess of virginity. **1399–1404 Hasdrubales wyf . . . ,** Jerome 1.43 reports that when the Roman Scipio conquered Carthage, the wife of King Hasdrubal burned herself and her children to escape capture; see *NPT* 7.3363-68. **1405–08 Lucresse,** unlike the preceding women, Lucretia killed herself after being raped (by Tarquinus); *LGW* 1680ff.; Jerome 1.46. **1409–11 Melesie . . . ,** Jerome 1.41 mentions the seven virgins of Melitus (Asia Minor), who commit suicide to escape the invading Galatians (**folk of Gawle,** line 1411); unattested elsewhere. **1410 verray,** omitted in El. **1414–18 Habradate . . . ,** Chaucer expands Jerome's account (1.45) by adding a quotation from Abradatas's wife (named Panthea). **1426 Demociones doghter,** the daughter of Demotion; Jerome 1.41. **1428 Cedasus,** Scedasus; Jerome 1.41. **1430 a,** omitted in El and Hg. **1432 Theban mayden,** unnamed suicide, lusted after by Nicanor; Jerome 1.41. **1434 Another Theban mayden,** unnamed in Jerome 1.41; killed her Macedonian rapist and herself. **1436 hire deeth,** Hg reads "hir owene deeth." **1437 Nicerates wyf,** wife of Niceratus, committed suicide to avoid rape; Jerome 1.44. **1439 Alcebiades,** after Alcibiades was killed, his concubine risked death to bury him; Jerome 1.44.

"Lo, which° a wyf was Alceste," quod she.
"What seith° Omer of goode Penalopee?
Al Grece knoweth of hire chastitee.
Pardee°, of Laodomya is writen thus,
That whan at Troie was slayn Protheselaus,
No lenger wolde she lyve after his day.
"The same of noble Porcia telle I may;
Withoute Brutus koude she nat lyve,
To whom she hadde al hool hir herte yeve°.
"The parfit wyf hod° of Arthemesie
Honured is thurgh al the barbarie°.
O Teuta, queene, thy wyfly chastitee
To alle wyves may a mirour bee.
The same thyng I seye of Bilyea,
Of Rodogone, and eek Valeria."
Thus pleyned° Dorigen a day or tweye,
Purposynge° evere that she wolde deye.
But nathelees, upon the thridde nyght
Hoom cam Arveragus, this worthy knyght,
And asked hire why that she weep so soore°,
And she gan wepen ever lenger the moore.
"Allas," quod she, "that evere I was born!
Thus have I seyd," quod she, "thus have I sworn—"
And toold hym al as ye han herd bifore°;
It nedeth nat reherce it yow namoore.
This housbonde with glad chiere° in freendly wyse
Answerde and seyde as I shal yow devyse°,
"Is ther oght elles°, Dorigen, but this?"
"Nay, nay," quod she, "God helpe me so as wys°!
This is to muche, and it were Goddes° wille."
"Ye, wyf," quod he, "lat slepen that is stille.
It may be wel, paraventure°, yet today.
Ye shul youre trouthe° holden, by my fay°,
For God so wisly° have mercy upon me,
I hadde wel levere ystiked for to be°,
For verray love which that I to yow have,
But if° ye sholde youre trouthe kepe and save.
Trouthe is the hyeste thyng that man may kepe."
But with that word he brast anon° to wepe,
And seyde, "I yow forbede°, up° peyne of deeth,
That nevere whil thee° lasteth lyf ne breeth
To no wight° telle thou of this aventure°.
As I may best I wol my wo endure,
Ne make no contenance of hevynesse°,
That folk of yow may demen° harm or gesse."
And forth he cleped° a squier and a mayde:
"Gooth forth anon with Dorigen," he sayde,
"And bryngeth hire to swich a place anon."
They take hir leve and on hir wey they gon,
But they ne wiste° why she thider° wente.
He nolde no wight tellen° his entente.
Paraventure° an heep° of yow, ywis°,
Wol holden hym a lewed° man in this,
That he wol putte his wyf in jupartie°.
Herkneth° the tale er ye upon hire crie°.
She may have bettre fortune than yow semeth°;
And whan that ye han herd the tale, demeth°.
This squier, which that highte° Aurelius,
On Dorigen that was so amorus,
Of aventure happed° hire to meete
Amydde° the toun, right in the quykkest strete°,
As she was bown° to goon the wey forth right
Toward the gardyn ther as she had hight°.
And he was to the gardyn-ward° also,
For wel he spyed° whan she wolde go

1442 which, *such* **1443 seith,** *says* **1445 Pardee,** *by God* **1450 yeve,** *given* **1451 parfit wyf hod,** *perfect fidelity* **1452 barbarie,** *heathen world* **1457 pleyned,** *lamented* **1458 Purposynge,** *intending* **1461 weep so soore,** *wept so bitterly* **1465 han herd biforn,** *have heard earlier* **1467 glad chiere,** *joyful expression* **1468 devyse,** *describe* **1469 oght elles,** *nothing else* **1470 so as wys,** *surely* **1471 and it were Goddes,** *even if it is God's* **1473 paraventure,** *perhaps* **1474 trouthe,** *pledge,* **fay,** *faith* **1475 God so wisly,** (may) *God surely* **1476 wel levere ystiked for to be,** *much prefer to be stabbed* **1478 But if,** *unless* **1480 brast anon,** *burst at once* **1481 forbede,** *forbid,* **up,** *upon* **1482 thee,** *to you* **1483 wight,** *person,* **aventure,** *incident* **1485 make no contenance of hevynesse,** *give no appearance of sorrow* **1486 demen,** *judge* **1487 cleped,** *called* **1491 ne wiste,** *did not know,* **thider,** *there* **1492 nolde no wight tellen,** *did not want to tell anyone* **1493 Paraventure,** *perhaps,* **an heep,** *many,* **ywis,** *surely* **1494 lewed,** *ignorant* **1495 jupartie,** *jeopardy* **1496 Herkneth,** *listen to,* **er,** *before,* **upon hire crie,** *lament her* **1497 yow semeth,** *seems to you* **1498 demeth,** *judge* **1499 highte,** *was called* **1501 Of aventure happed,** *by chance happened* **1502 Amydde,** *in the middle of,* **quykkest strete,** *liveliest street* **1503 bown,** *preparing* **1504 hight,** *promised* **1505 to the gardyn-ward,** (going) *to the garden* **1506 spyed,** *watched*

1442–45 Alceste . . . Penalopee . . . Laodomya, the three are mentioned together in Jerome 1.45: Alcestis offered her life for that of her husband, Admetus (see *LGWP* F510ff.); Penelope, loyal wife of Odysseus in Homer (**Omer**, line 1443); Laodamia wished not to outlive her husband, Protesilaus, when he was killed at Troy. **1443 seith,** omitted in Hg. **1448 Porcia,** Portia could not live without her husband, Brutus; Jerome 1.46. **1451–53 Arthemesie . . . Teuta,** mentioned together in Jerome 1.44. Artemesia, renowned for chastity, loved her husband even after he died. Teuta, queen of Illyrica, gained power through chastity. **1455–56** Omitted in Hg. Lines found only in El and one other manuscript, probably from the margin of Chaucer's original. **Bilyea,** Bilia, famed for chastity and for tolerating her husband's bad breath; Jerome 1.46. **Rodogone,** Rhodogune killed her maid for recommending that she remarry; Jerome 1.45. **Valeria,** refused to remarry; Jerome 1.46. **1481 of,** omitted in El. **1491 she,** Hg reads "they." **1493–98** Omitted in Hg. Lines found only in El and one other manuscript (same as 1455–56).

Out of hir hous to any maner place.
But thus they mette, of aventure or grace°,
And he saleweth° hire with glad entente,
And asked of hire whiderward° she wente.
  And she answerde, half as she were mad,
"Unto the gardyn, as myn housbonde bad°,
My trouthe° for to holde°, allas, allas!"
  Aurelius gan wondren on this cas°,
And in his herte hadde greet compassioun
Of hire and of hire lamentacioun,
And of Arveragus, the worthy knyght,
That bad hire holden al that she had hight°,
So looth hym was° his wyf sholde breke hir trouthe;
And in his herte he caughte of this greet routhe°,
Considerynge the beste on every syde,
That fro his lust° yet were hym levere abyde°
Than doon so heigh a cherlyssh° wrecchednesse
Agayns franchise° and alle gentillesse;
For which in fewe wordes seyde he thus:
  "Madame, seyth to° youre lord Arveragus
That sith° I se his grete gentillesse
To yow, and eek I se wel youre distresse,
That him were levere han shame°—and that were routhe—
Than ye to me sholde breke thus youre trouthe,
I have wel levere evere° to suffre wo
Than I departe° the love bitwix yow two.
I yow relesse°, madame, into youre hond
Quyt every serement° and every bond
That ye han maad to me as heerbiforn°,
Sith thilke° tyme which that ye were born.
My trouthe° I plighte°, I shal yow never repreve°
Of no biheste°, and heere I take my leve
As of the treweste and the beste wyf
That evere yet I knew in al my lyf.
But every wyf be war of hire biheeste;
On Dorigen remembreth atte leeste.
Thus kan a squier doon a gentil dede
As wel as kan a knyght, withouten drede°."
  She thonketh hym upon hir knees al bare,
And hoom unto hir housbonde is she fare°,
And tolde hym al, as ye han herd me sayd;
And be ye siker°, he was so weel apayd°
That it were inpossible me to wryte.
What sholde I lenger of this cas endyte°?
  Arveragus and Dorigen his wyf
In sovereyn blisse leden forth hir lyf.
Nevere eft° ne was ther angre hem bitwene.
He cherisseth hire as though she were a queene,
And she was to hym trewe for everemoore.
Of thise two folk ye gete of me namoore.
  Aurelius, that his cost° hath al forlorn°,
Curseth the tyme that evere he was born:
"Allas," quod he, "allas that I bihighte°
Of pured° gold a thousand pound of wighte°
Unto this philosophre. How shal I do?
I se namoore but that I am fordo°.
Myn heritage° moot I nedes° selle
And been a beggere. Heere may I nat dwelle
And shamen al my kynrede° in this place,
But° I of hym may gete bettre grace°.
But nathelees, I wole of hym assaye°,
At certeyn dayes, yeer by yeer, to paye,
And thanke hym of his grete curteisye.
My trouthe wol I kepe, I wol nat lye."
  With herte soor he gooth unto his cofre°,
And broghte gold unto this philosophre
The value of fyve hundred pound, I gesse,
And hym bisecheth of his gentillesse
To graunte hym dayes of the remenaunt°,
And seyde, "Maister, I dar° wel make avaunt°,
I failled nevere of my trouthe° as yit.
For sikerly° my dette shal be quyt°
Towardes yow, howevere that I fare
To goon a-begged° in my kirtle° bare.

1508 of aventure or grace, *by chance or providence* **1509 saleweth,** *greets* **1510 whiderward,** *where* **1512 bad,** *directed* **1513 trouthe,** *promise,* **holde,** *keep* **1514 cas,** *situation* **1518 hight,** *promised* **1519 So looth hym was,** *so hateful* (to) *him* (it) *was* (that) **1520 routhe,** *pity* **1522 lust,** *desire,* **yet were hym levere abyde,** *he would rather refrain* **1523 cherlyssh,** *churlish* **1524 franchise,** *liberality* **1526 seyth to,** *tell* **1527 sith,** *since* **1529 him were levere han shame,** *he would rather have shame* **1531 have wel levere evere,** *much prefer always* **1532 departe,** *separate* **1533 relesse,** *release* **1534 serement,** *oath* **1535 as heerbiforn,** *before this* **1536 Sith thilke,** *since that* **1537 trouthe,** *word,* **plighte,** *pledge,* **repreve,** *accuse* **1538 biheste,** *promise* **1544 drede,** *doubt* **1546 is she fare,** *she goes* **1548 siker,** *certain,* **apayd,** *pleased* **1550 cas endyte,** *situation compose* **1553 eft,** *after* **1557 cost,** *payment,* **forlorn,** *forfeited* **1559 bihighte,** *promised* **1560 pured,** *refined,* **wighte,** *weight* **1562 fordo,** *destroyed* **1563 heritage,** *inheritance,* **moot I nedes,** *I must necessarily* **1565 kynrede,** *kindred* **1566 But,** *unless,* **grace,** *favor* **1567 assaye,** *try* **1570 trouthe,** *pledge* **1571 cofre,** *money chest* **1575 dayes of the remenaunt,** *time to pay the remainder* **1576 dar,** *dare,* **avaunt,** *boast* **1577 trouthe,** *pledge* **1578 sikerly,** *certainly,* **quyt,** *repaid* **1579–80 howevere . . . a-begged,** i.e., *even if I have to go beg* **1580 kirtle,** *undergarments*

1541–44 In two late MSS, these lines follow line 1550. Placed there, they must be spoken by the narrator, as is also possible here.

But wolde ye vouchesauf°, upon seuretee°,
Two yeer or thre for to respiten me°,
Thanne were I wel, for elles moot° I selle
Myn heritage; ther is namoore to telle."
This philosophre sobrely answerde,
And seyde thus, whan he thise wordes herde,
"Have I nat holden covenant° unto thee?"
"Yes, certes, wel and trewely," quod he.
"Hastow nat had thy lady as thee liketh?"
"No, no," quod he, and sorwefully he siketh°.
"What was the cause? Tel me if thou kan."
Aurelius his tale anon bigan,
And tolde hym al as ye han herd bifoore;
It nedeth nat to yow reherce it moore.
He seide, "Arveragus, of gentillesse,
Hadde levere° dye in sorwe and in distresse
Than that his wyf were of hir trouthe fals."
The sorwe of Dorigen he tolde hym als°,
How looth hire was to been° a wikked wyf,
And that she levere had° lost that day hir lyf,
And that hir trouthe she swoor thurgh innocence,
She nevere erst° hadde herd speke of apparence°.
"That made me han of hire so greet pitee;
And right as frely as he sente hire me,
As frely sente I hire to hym ageyn.
This al and som°; ther is namoore to seyn."
This philosophre answerde, "Leeve° brother,
Everich° of yow dide gentilly til oother.
Thou art a squier, and he is a knyght;
But God forbede, for his blisful myght,
But if° a clerk koude° doon a gentil dede
As wel as any of yow, it is no drede°.
"Sire, I releesse thee thy thousand pound
As° thou right now were cropen° out of the ground
Ne nevere er now ne haddest knowen me.
For, sire, I wol nat taken a peny of thee
For al my craft°, ne noght for my travaille°.
Thou hast ypayed wel for my vitaille°.
It is ynogh, and farewel, have good day."
And took his hors, and forth he goth his way.
Lordynges, this question, thanne, wol I aske now,
Which was the mooste fre°, as thynketh yow?
Now telleth me, er that ye ferther wende°.
I kan° namoore; my tale is at an ende.

Heere is ended the Frankeleyns Tale.

1581 wolde ye vouchesauf, *if you would consent,* **seuretee,** *security* **1582 respiten me,** *grant me an extension* **1583 elles moot,** *otherwise must* **1587 holden covenant,** *kept my promise* **1590 siketh,** *sighs* **1596 Hadde levere,** *would rather* **1598 als,** *also* **1599 looth hire was to been,** *she would have hated to be* **1600 levere had,** *would rather have* **1602 erst,** *before,* **apparence,** *illusions* **1606 This al and som,** *this is all of it* **1607 Leeve,** *dear* **1608 Everich,** *each* **1611 But if,** *unless,* **koude,** *could* **1612 drede,** *doubt* **1614 As,** *as if,* **cropen,** *crept* **1617 craft,** *skill,* **travaille,** *labor* **1618 vitaille,** *food* **1622 fre,** *noble or generous* **1623 wende,** *travel* **1624 kan,** *know*

1584 Myn heritage, presumably Aurelius does not want to sell inherited property that is the source of an annual income. **1593 ye,** El reads "he."

Canterbury Tales, Part 6

Introduction

PART 6 OF THE *CANTERBURY TALES* focuses on death. The tellers of the paired tales are healers by profession: a physical healer, the Physician, and a spiritual healer, the Pardoner. There is, however, no healing in these tales, but death instead—not the deaths that result from epic battle, tragic misfortune, or ideological struggle found elsewhere in the *Canterbury Tales*, but deaths that result from relatively naked vices (lechery and greed), with little or no evidence of honor, reward, or salvation. The moral categories of the tales appear to be stark, and death dominates the plots, seeming to invite easy interpretation. The experience of reading the tales, however, belies this ease and raises questions about the relation of virtue to reward, about tale-telling as a form of moral discourse, and about the relationship between the material world and the spiritual realm.

Derived from the *Roman de la Rose*, ultimately from Livy's *History of Rome*, the *Physician's Tale* is more disturbing morally and aesthetically than its predecessors. Livy uses the story to exemplify degenerate justice in a straightforward exemplum. In the *Roman de la Rose*, the character Reason uses it to demonstrate that love is preferable to justice. In analogous versions by Gower and Boccaccio (of no apparent influence on Chaucer), the exemplum illustrates bad government. Chaucer suppresses the social and political concerns and heightens the contrast between virtue and the mortal power of vice. He adds prefatory material in praise of the protagonist's beauty and virginity, advises parental governance, and intensifies the personal relation of the father-daughter pair in the tale, Virginius and Virginia.

As a result, when Virginius slays Virginia to save her from the lechery of the judge, Appius, the act can be seen as more horrifying than exemplary or pathos-ridden. Then, when Appius commits suicide after his lechery is disclosed and his henchman Claudius is exiled instead of executed, the final message of the tale—forsake sin—seems only loosely applicable to these villains and not at all applicable to Virginius, much less Virginia. The tale is cast as an exemplum drawn from history (155–56), but its digressions threaten to overwhelm its plot, which itself seems unjust and unjustified by its moralization. By setting us such challenges, the tale can be seen to engage us in the process of seeking the purpose and efficacy of exemplary tales; see Anne Middleton, "The *Physician's Tale* and Love's Martyrs: 'Ensamples Mo Than Ten' as a Method in the *Canterbury Tales*" (1973, no. 1017). Various studies address the issues of virginity and violence in the tale, among them R. Howard Bloch's "Chaucer's Maiden's Head: *The Physician's Tale* and the Poetics of Virginity" (1989, no. 1008), Sandra Pierson Prior's "Virginity and Sacrifice in Chaucer's *Physician's Tale*" (1999, no. 1018), and Karma Lochrie's *Heterosyncrasies* (2005, no. 465), which considers virginity in light of late-medieval spirituality. The best available survey of critical approaches is in Helen Storm Corsa's Variorum edition of the tale (1987, no. 52).

Impersonal and dislocating, the *Physician's Tale* sets up various aspects of the Pardoner's stunningly personal performance: virginity is juxtaposed with suggestions of sterility, imitation of nature with hypocrisy, governance with unrestrained indulgence, physical with spiritual death. Both tales deal with the self-destructiveness of evil, but where the Physician asserts this as a moral platitude, the Pardoner effectively dramatizes the truism and embodies it himself.

Like the Wife of Bath, the Pardoner reveals his defects through a confessional mode in his *Prologue*. The inspiration is again the *Roman de la Rose*, this time Faus-Semblant (False Seeming or Hypocrisy, lines 11,065ff.), who proclaims his own avarice, hypocrisy, and disdain for those who fear God. Chaucer naturalizes these attitudes in action when the Pardoner tallies his past successes in selling relics, performs his sermon-like tale, and attempts to sell pardons to the pilgrim audience. Underlying such efforts is the Pardoner's willful, cynical disregard for the power of the spiritual gifts that he purveys. In Chaucer's time (and for believers today), relics mediate between the material and the spiritual realms; they embody holiness in material objects. Pardons (also called indulgences) remove the need for temporal punishment due for sin in order to pave the way to heavenly reward. In his knowing abuse of relics, preaching, and pardons, the Pardoner is on a headlong crash course with spiritual death.

Traffic in relics and pardons was a real danger to the Church because it had itself come to depend upon profits derived from them and because the essential connection between the material and the spiritual lay at the very core of its worldly mission. Through the Pardoner, Chaucer condemns the spiritual arrogance of refusing to acknowledge spiritual reality, and he explores how such transgression can threaten to corrupt the entire system. As Alan J. Fletcher has shown in "The Topical Hypocrisy of Chaucer's Pardoner" (1990, no. 1028a), Wycliffite concerns with religious hypocrisy lend considerable dimension to the Pardoner's performance, and A. L. Kellogg and L. A. Haselmayer, "Chaucer's Satire on the Pardoner" (1951, no. 1037), long ago documented that the orthodox Church was well aware of systemic dangers. In "Holy Duplicity: The Preacher's Two Faces" (2002, no. 1213), Claire M. Waters adds to the critical tradition that views the Pardoner as an antithesis to the Parson.

The rioters in the *Pardoner's Tale* believe that they can destroy death, a parody or perversion of Christian salvation by this unholy trinity. Unlike the Pardoner himself, they seem unaware of their blasphemy, and they fall easy and unwitting victims to their own greed. Along the way, they exemplify not only greed but also the so-called tavern vices against which the Pardoner preaches—oathtaking, gluttony, and gambling. The plot is stark, powerful, and disturbing, often regarded as Chaucer's greatest success in brief narration.

No clear source has been identified for the tale, but worldwide analogues ranging from the Far East to Africa and Hollywood (John Huston's *The Treasure of the Sierra Madre*) attest to the ironic power of the plot: we find death, or death finds us, when we least expect it, especially when distracted by vice. The Old Man is especially uncanny in Chaucer's version, elsewhere a more easily defined figure. Critics have read him as, among other suggestions, Death itself, Death's messenger, the Wandering Jew, a demon, and even a projection of the Pardoner's own soul or his psyche. The power of the Old Man to tug at the mind is perhaps best reflected in a pair of essays by Lee Patterson, who first assesses the Old Man as a psychological projection of the Pardoner and later retracts his own analysis. See "Chaucerian Confession: Penitential Literature and the Pardoner" (1976, no. 1046) and "Chaucer's Pardoner on the Couch: Psyche and Clio in Medieval Literary Studies" (2001, no. 1047). In *Literary Character* (2003, no. 1029), Elizabeth Fowler examines Chaucer's characterization of the Pardoner in light of the various kinds of intention that are evident in the *Prologue* and *Tale*.

Perhaps the most vigorously debated crux of the *Pardoner's Prologue* and *Tale* is the Pardoner's offer to sell his wares to the pilgrims after admitting his own avarice and hypocrisy. Some critics read a self-destructive impulse here, whereas others find sheer arrogance, cynicism, and even despair. The offer provokes the Host's brutal response to the Pardoner, which with its threat of castration recalls the narrator's comment in the *General Prologue* that he believes the Pardoner may be a gelding or a mare (1.691)—that he may be sterile, a eunuch, or homosexual. Many critics consider the Pardoner's sexuality or the Host's homophobia in the scene, although A. J. Minnis has argued against specifying this sexuality in "Chaucer and the Queering Eunuch" (2003, no. 1043), and he details the Pardoner's abuses of sacerdotal privileges in *Fallible Authors* (2008, no. 1044). Monica A. McAlpine surveys the topic of the Pardoner's homosexuality in "The Pardoner's Homosexuality and How It Matters" (1980, no. 1040). For theoretically charged approaches, see Robert S. Sturges's *Chaucer's Pardoner and Gender Theory* (2000, no. 1055) and Glenn Burger's *Chaucer's Queer Nation* (2003, no. 461).

Canterbury Tales
Part 6

From woodcut made by W.H. Hooper and published by the Chaucer Society between 1868 and 1879

Physician's Tale

Heere folweth the Phisiciens Tale.

Ther was, as telleth Titus Livius,
A knyght that called was Virginius,
Fulfild of honour and of worthynesse,
And strong of freendes and of greet richesse.
This knyght a doghter hadde by his wyf;
No children hadde he mo in al his lyf.
Fair was this mayde in excellent beautee
Aboven every wight° that man may see,
For Nature hath with sovereyn° diligence
Yformed hire in so greet excellence,
As though she wolde seyn, "Lo, I, Nature,
Thus kan I forme and peynte a creature
Whan that me list°. Who kan me countrefete°?
Pigmalion noght°, though he ay° forge° and bete°,
Or grave° or peynte, for I dar wel seyn
Apelles, Zanzis, sholde werche in veyn°
Outher° to grave or peynte or forge or bete,
If they presumed me to countrefete.
For He that is the formere principal°
Hath maked me his vicaire general,
To forme and peynten erthely creaturis
Right as me list°, and ech thyng in my cure° is
Under the moone that may wane and waxe°,
And for my werk right no thyng wol I axe°.
My lord and I been ful of oon accord°.
I made hire to the worship° of my lord.
So do I alle myne othere creatures,
What° colour that they han or what figures."
Thus semeth me that Nature wolde seye.
This mayde of age twelve yeer was and tweye°,

---

8 wight, *creature* **9 sovereyn,** *ultimate* **13 me list,** (it) *pleases me,* **countrefete,** *imitate* **14 noght,** (could) *not,* **ay,** *always,* **forge,** *shape in metal,* **bete,** *hammer* **15 grave,** *engrave* **16 werche in veyn,** *work in vain* **17 Outher,** *either* **19 formere principal,** *creator* **22 Right as me list,** *just as it pleases me,* **cure,** *care* **23 wane and waxe,** *decrease and increase* **24 axe,** *ask* **25 ful of oon accord,** *fully in agreement* **26 to the worship,** *in honor of* **28 What,** *whatever* **30 and tweye,** *plus two*

1 Titus Livius, Livy, Roman historian, the ultimate source of this story, although Chaucer adapted it from *RR* 5589ff. **2 called was,** El reads "was called." **14–16 Pigmalion . . . Apelles, Zanzis,** famous artists, mentioned together in a discussion of nature vs. art in *RR* 16177ff. **20 vicaire general,** general deputy, a common title for Nature, found, e.g., in *RR* 16782 and 19505 and elsewhere. **23 Under the moone,** below the moon, where all is natural, i.e., in the realm of Nature; above is the realm of the supernatural.

In which that° Nature hadde swich delit°.
For right as° she kan peynte a lilie whit
And reed a rose, right° with swich peynture°
She peynted hath this noble creature
Er she were born, upon hir lymes fre°,
Where as by right° swiche colours sholde be.
And Phebus° dyed hath hire tresses grete°
Lyk to the stremes° of his burned heete°.
And if that excellent was hire beautee,
A thousand foold moore vertuous was she.
In hire ne lakked no condicioun
That is to preyse, as by discrecioun°.
As wel in goost° as body chast was she,
For which she floured in virginitee
With alle humylitee and abstinence,
With alle attemperaunce° and pacience,
With mesure eek° of beryng° and array.
Discreet she was in answeryng alway,
Though° she were wis as Pallas, dar I seyn,
Hir facound° eek ful wommanly and pleyn.
No countrefeted° termes hadde she
To seme wys, but after° hir degree°
She spak, and alle hire wordes moore and lesse
Sownynge in° vertu and in gentillesse.
Shamefast° she was in maydens shamefastnesse,
Constant in herte, and evere in bisynesse
To dryve hire° out of ydel slogardye°.
Bacus hadde of hir mouth right no maistrie°;
For wyn and youthe dooth Venus° encresse
As° men in fyr wol casten oille or greesse°.
And of hir owene vertu, unconstreyned,
She hath ful ofte tyme syk hire feyned°
For that° she wolde fleen° the compaignye
Where likly was to treten of° folye,
As is at feestes, revels, and at daunces,
That been occasions of daliaunces°.
Swich thynges maken children for to be
To soone rype and boold, as men may se,
Which is ful perilous and hath been yoore°.
For al to soone may she lerne loore
Of booldnesse, whan she woxen is° a wyf.
And ye maistresses°, in youre olde lyf,
That lordes doghtres han° in governaunce,
Ne taketh of my wordes no displesaunce°.
Thenketh° that ye been set in governynges
Of lordes doghtres oonly for two thynges°,
Outher for° ye han kept youre honestee,
Or elles ye han falle in freletee°
And knowen wel ynough the olde daunce°,
And han forsaken fully swich meschaunce°
For everemo; therfore for Cristes sake,
To teche hem vertu looke that ye ne slake°.
A theef of venysoun° that hath forlaft°
His likerousnesse° and al his olde craft
Kan kepe a forest best of any man.
Now kepeth wel, for if ye wole°, ye kan.
Looke wel that ye unto no vice assente
Lest ye be dampned° for youre wikke entente,
For whoso dooth°, a traitour is certeyn.
And taketh kepe of° that that I shal seyn:
Of alle tresons sovereyn pestilence°
Is whan a wight bitrayseth° innocence.
Ye fadres and ye moodres eek also,
Though° ye han children, be it oon or mo,
Youre° is the charge of al hire surveiaunce°
Whil that they been under youre governaunce.
Beth war if by ensample of youre lyvynge
Or by youre necligence in chastisynge
That they perisse°; for I dar wel seye
If that they doon ye shul it deere abeye°.
Under a shepherde softe and necligent
The wolf hath many a sheep and lamb torent°.
Suffiseth oon ensample° now as heere,
For I moot° turne agayn to my matere.
This mayde, of which I wol this tale expresse,
So kepte hirself hir neded° no maistresse,

31 which that, *whom,* **swich delit,** *such delight* **32–33 right as . . . right,** *just as . . . so* **33 swich peynture,** *such painiting* **35 lymes fre,** *noble limbs* **36 by right,** *appropriately* **37 Phebus,** *the sun,* **tresses grete,** *long hair* **38 stremes,** *rays,* **burned heete,** *burnished heat* **42 discrecioun,** *discrimination* **43 goost,** *spirit* **46 attemperaunce,** *temperance* **47 mesure eek,** *moderation also,* **beryng,** *manners* **49 Though,** *as thought* **50 facound,** *way of speaking* **51 countrefeted,** *false* **52 after,** *in accord with,* **degree,** *social rank* **54 Sownynge in,** *resounding* **55 Shamefast,** *modest* **57 hire,** *herself,* **ydel slogardye,** *idle laziness* **58 right no maistrie,** *no dominance at all* **59 Venus,** i.e., *sexual desire* **60 As,** *as when,* **greesse,** *grease* **62 syk hire feyned,** *pretended illness* **63 For that,** *because,* **wolde fleen,** *wished to avoid* **64 treten of,** *deal with* **66 daliaunces,** *flirtation* **69 yoore,** *for a long time* **71 woxen is,** *has become* **72 maistresses,** *governesses* **73 han,** *have* **74 displesaunce,** *displeasure* **75 Thenketh,** *realize* **76 thynges,** *reasons* **77 Outher for,** *either because* **78 han falle in freletee,** *have fallen in frailty* **79 olde daunce,** i.e., *lovemaking* **80 meschaunce,** *misconduct* **82 ne slake,** *do not slacken* **83 theef of venysoun,** *deer poacher,* **forlaft,** *abandoned* **84 likerousnesse,** *evil hunger* **86 wole,** *wish to* **88 Lest ye be dampned,** *so you will not be damned* **89 whoso dooth,** *whoever does* **90 taketh kepe of,** *pay attention to* **91 sovereyn pestilence,** *the ultimate evil* **92 bitrayseth,** *betrays* **94 Though,** *since* **95 Youre,** *yours,* **surveiaunce,** *protection* **99 perisse,** *perish* **100 it deere abeye,** *pay for it dearly* **102 torent,** *torn to pieces* **103 Suffiseth oon ensample,** *one example suffices* **104 moot,** *must* **106 hir neded,** *for her* (was) *needed*

39–71 This idealized portrait of virtuous virginity reflects the tradition of the virgin martyr, here in implicit tension with the fecundity of Nature, as in *RR* 18999ff. **49 as,** omitted in El and Hg. **Pallas,** Pallas Athena, goddess of wisdom. **58 Bacus,** Bacchus, god of wine. **60 casten,** El reads “wasten.” **94 mo,** El reads “two.” **101–02** Proverbial. **103–04** Lines lacking in El.

For in hir lyvyng maydens myghten rede
As in a book every good word or dede
That longeth° to a mayden vertuous,
She was so prudent and so bounteuous°.
For which the fame out sprong on every syde
Bothe of hir beautee and hir bountee wyde,
That thurgh that land they preised hire echone°
That loved vertu, save Envye allone
That sory is of oother mennes wele°,
And glad is of his sorwe and his unheele°—
The doctour maketh this descripcioun.
  This mayde upon a day wente in the toun
Toward a temple, with hire mooder deere,
As is of yonge maydens the manere.
  Now was ther thanne a justice° in that toun
That governour was of that regioun.
And so bifel° this juge his eyen caste
Upon this mayde, avysynge hym ful faste°
As she cam forby ther as° this juge stood.
  Anon his herte chaunged and his mood,
So was he caught with beautee of this mayde,
And so hymself ful pryvely he sayde,
"This mayde shal be myn, for° any man!°
Anon the feend into his herte ran
And taughte hym sodeynly that he by slyghte°
The mayden to his purpos wynne myghte.
For certes°, by no force ne by no meede°,
Hym thoughte, he was nat able for to speede°.
For she was strong of freendes° and eek she
Confermed was in swich soverayn bountee°
That wel he wiste° he myghte hire nevere wynne
As for to make hire with hir body synne.
For which, by° greet deliberacioun,
He sente after a cherl, was in the toun,
Which that he knew for subtil and for boold.
This juge unto this cherl his tale hath toold
In secree wise, and made hym to ensure°
He sholde telle it to no creature,
And if he dide, he sholde lese his heed.
Whan that assented was this cursed reed°,
Glad was this juge, and maked him greet cheere°,
And yaf° hym yiftes preciouse and deere°.
  Whan shapen° was al hire° conspiracie
Fro point to point, how that his lecherie
Parfourned° sholde been ful subtilly°,
As ye shul heere it after openly,
Hoom gooth the cherl, that highte° Claudius.
This false juge, that highte Apius—
So was his name, for this is no fable°,
But knowen for historial° thyng notable;
The sentence° of it sooth° is out of doute—
This false juge gooth now faste aboute°
To hasten his delit al that he may.
And so bifel° soone after on a day
This false juge, as telleth us the storie,
As he was wont°, sat in his consistorie°,
And yaf° his doomes° upon sondry cas°.
This false cherl cam forth a ful greet pas°,
And seyde, "Lord, if that it be youre wille,
As dooth me right° upon this pitous bille°
In which I pleyne upon° Virginius;
And if that he wol seyn it is nat thus,
I wol it preeve° and fynde good witnesse
That sooth° is that° my bille wol expresse."
  The juge answerde, "Of this, in his absence,
I may nat yeve diffynytyve° sentence.
Lat do hym calle°, and I wol gladly heere.
Thou shalt have al right and no wrong heere."
  Virginius cam to wite° the juges wille,
And right anon was rad° this cursed bille.
The sentence of it was as ye shul heere:
  "To yow, my lord, sire Apius so deere,
Sheweth youre poure servant Claudius
How that a knyght, called Virginius,
Agayns the lawe, agayn al equitee°,
Holdeth, expres agayn° the wyl of me,
My servant, which that is my thral° by right,
Which fro myn hous was stole upon a nyght,

109 longeth, *pertains* **110 bounteuous,** *good* **113 echone,** *each one* **115 mennes wele,** *men's prosperity* **116 unheele,** *misfortune* **121 justice,** *judge* **123 bifel,** *it happened that* **124 avysynge hym ful faste,** *considering very intensely* **125 forby ther as,** *past where* **129 for,** *despite* **131 slyghte,** *deception* **133 certes,** *surely,* **meede,** *bribery* **134 speede,** *succeed* **135 strong of freendes,** i.e., *had powerful friends* **136 soverayn bountee,** *supreme goodness* **137 wiste,** *knew* **139 by,** *with* **143 made hym to ensure,** *made him promise* **146 reed,** *plan* **147 maked hym greet cheere,** i.e., *acted pleasantly toward him* **148 yaf,** *gave,* **deere,** *valuable* **149 shapen,** *planned,* **hire,** *their* **151 Parfourned,** *accomplished,* **subtilly,** *secretly* **153 highte,** *was named* **155 fable,** *fiction* **156 historial,** *historical,* **157 sentence,** *significance,* **sooth,** *true* **158 faste aboute,** *quickly all around* **160 bifel,** *it happened* **162 wont,** *accustomed,* **consistorie,** *court* **163 yaf,** *gave,* **doomes,** *judgments,* **sondry cas,** *various cases* **164 a ful greet pas,** *in a great hurry* **166 As dooth me right,** *do me justice,* **bille,** *formal complaint* **167 pleyne upon,** *accuse* **169 preeve,** *prove* **170 sooth,** *true,* **that,** *what* **172 yeve diffynytyve,** *give definitive* **173 Lat do hym calle,** *let him be summoned* **175 wite,** *know* **176 rad,** *read* **181 equitee,** *justice* **182 expres agayn,** *specifically against* **183 thral,** *slave*

117 the doctour, epithet of St. Augustine; the preceding sentiment about Envy is also attributed to Augustine in *ParsT* 10.484. **132 The,** Hg reads "This." **140 cherl,** low-class fellow or ruffian; some MSS have "clerk," but *RR* 5599 reads "Li ribauz" (the debauched one). **169 witnesse,** either "testimony" or "evidence." In medieval law, witnesses' testimony to the character or statements of the claimants was important. *RR* 5612–14. **172 diffynytyve,** El reads "diffynyve."

Whil that she was ful yong—this wol I preeve°
By witnesse, lord, so that it nat yow greeve°.
She nys° his doghter nat, what so° he seye.
Wherfore to yow, my lord the juge, I preye,
Yeld° me my thral, if that it be youre wille.°
Lo, this was al the sentence of his bille.
Virginius gan upon the cherl biholde°,
But hastily, er° he his tale° tolde
And wolde have preeved it as sholde a knyght°,
And eek by witnessyng of many a wight°,
That al was fals that seyde his adversarie,
This cursed juge wolde nothyng tarie°
Ne heere a word moore of Virginius,
But yaf° his juggement, and seyde thus:
"I deeme anon° this cherl his servant have;
Thou shalt no lenger in thyn hous hir save°.
Go bryng hire forth and put hire in oure warde°.
The cherl shal have his thral. This I awarde."
And whan this worthy knyght Virginius
Thurgh sentence of this justice Apius
Moste° by force his deere doghter yeven°
Unto the juge, in lecherie to lyven,
He gooth hym hoom and sette him in his halle,
And leet anon his deere doghter calle°,
And with a face deed as asshen colde
Upon hir humble face he gan biholde,
With fadres pitee stikynge thurgh his herte,
Al° wolde he from his purpos nat converte°.
"Doghter," quod he, "Virginia, by thy name,
Ther been two weyes, outher° deeth or shame,
That thou most suffre. Allas, that I was bore°!
For nevere thou deservedest wherfore°
To dyen with a swerd or with a knyf.
O deere doghter, endere° of my lyf,
Which° I have fostred up with swich plesaunce°
That thou were nevere out of my remembraunce!
O doghter, which that art my laste wo,
And in my lyf my laste joye also,
O gemme of chastitee, in pacience
Take thou thy deeth, for this is my sentence°.
For love, and nat for hate, thou most be deed°;
My pitous hand moot smyten of° thyn heed.
Allas, that evere Apius the say°!
Thus hath he falsly jugged the today."
And tolde hire al the cas, as ye bifore
Han herd; nat nedeth for to telle it moore.
"O mercy, deere fader!" quod this mayde,
And with that word she bothe hir armes layde
Aboute his nekke, as she was wont° to do.
The teeris bruste° out of hir eyen two,
And seyde, "Goode fader, shal I dye?
Is ther no grace, is ther no remedye?"
"No, certes°, deere doghter myn," quod he.
"Thanne yif me leyser°, fader myn," quod she,
"My deeth for to compleyne° a litel space°;
For, pardee°, Jepte yaf° his doghter grace
For to compleyne er he hir slow°, allas!
And God it woot°, nothyng was hir trespas°
But for° she ran hir fader first to see
To welcome hym with greet solempnitee."
And with that word she fil aswowne anon°,
And after whan hir swownyng is agon
She riseth up and to hir fader sayde,
"Blissed be God that I shal dye a mayde.
Yif° me my deeth er that I have a shame.
Dooth with youre child youre wyl, a Goddes° name!"
And with that word she preyed hym ful ofte
That with his swerd he wolde smyte softe°.
And with that word aswowne doun she fil.
Hir fader, with ful sorweful herte and wil,
Hir heed of smoot°, and by the top it hente°,
And to the juge he gan it to presente°
As he sat yet in doom° in consistorie°.
And whan the juge it saugh°, as seith the storie,

---

185 preeve, *prove* **186 greeve,** *displease* **187 nys,** *is not,* **what so,** *whatever* **189 Yeld,** *give* **191 gan . . . biholde,** *stared at* **192 er,** *before,* **tale,** *version* **193 as sholde a knyght,** i.e., *in trial by combat* **194 wight,** *person* **196 wolde nothyng tarie,** *would not delay* **198 yaf,** *gave* **199 deeme anon,** *judge at once* **200 save,** *keep* **201 warde,** *custody* **205 Moste,** *must,* **yeven,** *give* **208 leet anon . . . calle,** *at once summoned* **212 Al,** *although,* **converte,** *turn* **214 outher,** *either* **215 bore,** *born* **216 wherfore,** *for any reason* **218 endere,** *one who ends* **218 Which,** *who,* **swich plesaunce,** *such pleasure* **224 sentence,** *decision* **225 most be deed,** *must be dead* **226 moot smyten of,** *must strike off* **227 the say,** *saw you* **233 wont,** *accustomed* **234 teeris bruste,** *tears burst* **237 certes,** *certainly* **238 leyser,** *time* **239 compleyne,** *lament,* **space,** *while* **240 pardee,** *by God,* **yaf,** *gave* **241 slow,** *slew* **242 woot,** *knows,* **trespas,** *wrongdoing* **243 But for,** *except that* **245 fil aswowne anon,** *fainted at once* **249 Yif,** *give* **250 a Goddes,** *in God's* **252 smyte softe,** *strike softly* **255 of smoot,** *struck off,* **hente,** *grasped* **256 gan . . . presente,** *presented* **257 doom,** *judgment,* **consistorie,** *court* **258 saugh,** *saw*

187 Wherfore, Hg reads "Wher." **195 al,** El and Hg read "it." **207 his halle,** the great hall of his manor. In all other versions, Virginius executes Virginia without deliberation in a public act. From here to line 255, Chaucer reshapes his source. **240 Jepte,** in Judges 11.30ff., Jephthah vows to God, if given victory in battle, to sacrifice whoever comes out of the house first. His daughter is first, and he allows her two months to bewail the fact that she must die a virgin. Virginia, of course, wants to remain virginal. Chaucer's addition. **243 first to see,** El and Hg read "for to see."

He bad° to take hym and anhange° hym faste.
But right anon° a thousand peple in thraste°
To save the knyght, for routhe° and for pitee,
For knowen was the false iniquitee°.
The peple anon had suspect° in this thyng,
By manere of the cherles chalangyng°,
That it was by the assent of Apius;
They wisten° wel that he was lecherus.
For which unto this Apius they gon
And caste hym in a prisoun right anon,
Ther as° he slow° hymself; and Claudius,
That servant was unto this Apius,
Was demed° for to hange upon a tree,
But that Virginius of his pitee
So preyde for hym that he was exiled,
And elles°, certes°, he had been bigyled°.
The remenant° were anhanged, moore and
lesse,
That were consentant of° this cursednesse.
Heere may men seen how synne hath his
merite°.
Beth war°, for no man woot° whom God wol smyte
In no degree°, ne in which manere wyse
The worm of conscience may agryse
Of° wikked lyf, though it so pryvee° be
That no man woot° therof but God and he.
For be he lewed° man or ellis lered
He noot° how soone that he shal been afered°.
Therfore I rede° yow this conseil take:
Forsaketh° synne er synne yow forsake°.

Heere endeth the Phisiciens Tale.

---

259 bad, *ordered,* **anhange,** *hang* **260 right anon,** *immediately,* **in thraste,** *rushed in* **261 routhe,** *compassion* **262 iniquitee,** *wickedness* **263 suspect,** *suspicion* **264 chalangyng,** *accusation* **266 wisten,** *knew* **269 Ther as,** *where,* **slow,** *slew* **271 demed,** *judged* **274 elles,** *otherwise,* **certes,** *certainly,* **bigyled,** *tricked* (i.e., killed) **275 remenant,** *remainder* **276 consentant of,** *in support of* **277 his merite,** *its reward* **278 Beth war,** *beware,* **woot,** *knows* **279 In no degree,** *of any social rank* **280–81 agryse / Of,** *be terrified by* **281 pryvee,** *secret* **282 woot,** *knows* **283 lewed,** *uneducated* **284 noot,** *knows not,* **afered,** *frightened* (by death) **285 rede,** *advise* **286 Forsaketh,** *abandon,* **forsake,** *betrays*

263 in, El reads "of." **271 Was,** El reads "And." **286** This common proverb is echoed in *ParsT* 10.83; it here raises questions, as it applies to Appius and Claudius rather than Virginia.

From woodcut made by W.H. Hooper and published by the Chaucer Society between 1868 and 1879

Pardoner's Tale

Prologue

The wordes of the Hoost to the Phisicien and the Pardoner.

Oure Hooste gan to swere as he were wood°,
"Harrow°," quod he, "by nayles and by blood!
This was a fals cherl and a fals justise.
As shameful deeth as herte may devyse
Come to thise false juges and hire advocatz°.
Algate° this sely° mayde is slayn, allas!
Allas, to deere° boughte she beautee!
Wherfore I seye al day° as men may see
That yiftes° of Fortune and of Nature
Been cause of deeth to many a creature.
Of bothe yiftes that I speke of now
Men han ful ofte moore for harm than prow°.
"But trewely, myn owene maister deere,
This is a pitous tale for to heere.
But nathelees, passe over, is no fors°.
I pray to God so save thy gentil cors°,
And eek thyne urynals and thy jurdones,
Thyn ypocras, and eek thy galiones,
And every boyste° ful of thy letuarie°;
God blesse hem, and oure lady Seinte Marie.
"So moot I theen°, thou art a propre man,
And lyk a prelat°, by Seint Ronyan!
Seyde I nat wel? I kan nat speke in terme°;
But wel I woot° thou doost myn herte to erme°
That I almoost have caught a cardynacle.
By corpus bones, but° I have triacle°,
Or elles a draughte° of moyste° and corny° ale,
Or but I heere anon° a myrie tale,

---

287 wood, *crazed* **288 Harrow,** *alas* **291 hire advocatz,** *their lawyers* **292 Algate,** *at any rate,* **sely,** *innocent* **293 to deere,** *too dearly* **294 al day,** *always* **295 yiftes,** *gifts* **300 prow,** *profit* **303 no fors,** *no matter* **304 cors,** *body* **307 boyste,** *jar,* **letuarie,** *medicine* **309 So moote I theen,** *as I may thrive* **310 prelat,** *clergyman* **311 terme,** *in learned terms* **312 woot,** *know,* **erme,** *grieve* **314 but,** *unless,* **triacle,** *medicine* **315 draughte,** *drink,* **moyste,** *fresh,* **corny,** *malty* (?) **316 heere anon,** *hear soon*

287–328 Variants in the manuscripts suggest that Chaucer expanded and revised this link when he decided to place *PardT* after *PhyT*. See MR 2.325–28 and 4.78-81 for discussion and details. **288 by nayles and by blood,** by the nails and blood of Christ's crucifixion, a strong oath. **291 false,** omitted in Hg. **294 as,** Hg reads "that." [297–98] Most editors include two lines here not found in El or Hg: "Hir beaute was hir deth, I dar wel sayn. / Allas, so pitously as she was slayn." We follow the traditional line numbering throughout the prologue and tale. **305 urynals . . . jurdones,** chamber pots, but also vessels used for urinalysis. **306 ypocras . . . galiones,** concoctions named for the famous physicians Hippocrates and Galen, although the latter seems to have been invented by the Host, who (in this passage and elsewhere) imitates professional jargon. **310 Seint Ronyan,** a Scottish saint, Ronan, but with play upon *runnion,* "kidney, sexual organ." **313 cardynacle,** evidently the Host's error, corrected in many manuscripts to *cardiacle,* "heart attack." **314 By corpus bones,** a distortion of the oath *Corpus Dei* (By the Lord's Body). See 474n below.

Myn herte is lost for pitee of this mayde.
Thou beel amy, thou Pardoner," he sayde,
"Telle us som myrthe or japes° right anon."
"It shal be doon," quod he, "by Seint Ronyon.
But first," quod he, "heere at this ale stake
I wol bothe drynke and eten of a cake°."
And right anon thise gentils° gonne to crye,
"Nay, lat hym telle us of no ribaudye°!
Telle us som moral thyng that we may leere°
Som wit°, and thanne wol we gladly heere."
"I graunte, ywis°," quod he, "but I moot° thynke
Upon som honest° thyng while that I drynke."

Heere folweth the Prologe of the Pardoners Tale.

Lordynges, quod he, in chirches whan I preche,
I peyne me° to han an hauteyn° speche
And rynge it out as round° as gooth° a belle,
For I kan° al by rote° that I telle.
My theme is alwey oon°, and evere was:
Radix malorum est cupiditas.
First I pronounce whennes° that I come,
And thanne my bulles° shewe I, alle and some.
Oure lige lordes seel on my patente,
That shewe I first my body to warente°,
That no man be so boold, ne preest ne° clerk,
Me to destourbe of° Cristes hooly werk.
And after that thanne telle I forth my tales.
Bulles of popes and of cardynales,
Of patriarkes and bisshopes I shewe,
And in Latyn I speke a wordes fewe,
To saffron with° my predicacioun°,
And for to stire° hem to devocioun.
Thanne shewe I forth my longe cristal stones,
Ycrammed ful of cloutes° and of bones—
Relikes been they, as wenen they echoon°.
Thanne have I in latoun° a sholder-boon
Which that was of an hooly Jewes° sheep.
"Goode men," I seye, "taak of my wordes keep°;
If that this boon be wasshe° in any welle,
If cow, or calf, or sheep, or oxe swelle°
That any worm° hath ete° or worm ystonge,
Taak water of that welle and wassh his tonge,
And it is hool anon°; and forthermoor,
Of pokkes° and of scabbe° and every soor
Shal every sheep be hool that of this welle
Drynketh a draughte. Taak kepe eek° what I telle:
If that the goode man that the beestes oweth°
Wol° every wyke°, er that the cok hym croweth°,
Fastynge, drynken of this welle a draughte,
As thilke° hooly Jew oure eldres taughte,
His beestes and his stoor° shal multiplie.
"And, sires, also it heeleth jalousie;
For though a man be falle in jalous rage,
Lat maken with this water his potage°,
And nevere shal he moore his wyf mystriste°,
Though he the soothe of hir defaute wiste°,
Al° had she taken preestes two or thre.
"Heere is a miteyn eek°, that ye may se.
He that his hand wol putte in this mitayn,
He shal have multipliyng of his grayn,
Whan he hath sowen, be it whete or otes—
So that he offre° pens, or elles grotes.
"Goode men and wommen, o thyng warne I yow:
If any wight° be in this chirche now
That hath doon synne horrible, that he

---

319 japes, *jokes* **322 cake,** *loaf* **323 gentils,** *gentlefolk* **324 ribaudye,** *coarse humor* **325 leere,** *learn* **326 wit,** *wisdom* **327 ywis,** *certainly,* **moot,** *must* **328 honest,** *moral* **330 peyne me,** *take pains,* **hauteyn,** *loud* **331 round,** *resoundingly,* **gooth,** *goes* **332 kan,** *know,* **rote,** *repetition* **333 alwey oon,** *always the same* **335 pronounce whennes,** *proclaim whence* (i.e., from Rome) **336 bulles,** *official documents* **338 warente,** *protect* **339 ne . . . ne,** *neither . . . nor* **340 destourbe of,** *prevent from doing* **345 saffron with,** *i.e., add spice to,* **predicacioun,** *preaching* **346 stire,** *stir* **348 cloutes,** *rags* **349 wenen they echoon,** *they all believe* **350 latoun,** *brass* **351 Jewes,** *Jew's* **352 keep,** *heed* **353 wasshe,** *washed* **354 swelle,** *swells up* **355 worm,** *snake,* **ete,** *bitten* **357 hool anon,** *healed at once* **358 pokkes,** *pox,* **scabbe,** *scabs* **360 Taak kepe eek,** *take heed also* **361 oweth,** *owns* **362 Wol,** *will,* **wyke,** *week,* **er that the cok hym croweth,** i.e., *before dawn* **364 thilke,** *that* **365 stoor,** *livestock* **368 Lat maken . . . his potage,** *make his soup* **369 mystriste,** *mistrust* **370 soothe of hir defaute wiste,** *knew the truth of her fault* **371 Al,** *although* **372 miteyn eek,** *mitten also* **376 So that he offre,** *as long as he offers* **378 wight,** *person*

318 beel amy, French feminine *belle amie,* "pretty friend"; here derisive. **321 ale stake,** projecting pole hung with a garland or bush; sign of an alehouse. **323 thise,** El reads "the." **334 *Radix malorum est cupiditas,*** the root of all evil is greed; 1 Timothy 6.10. Cupidity is the opposite of charity. **337 lige lordes seel . . . patente,** the seal of the pope or bishop on the open (or "patent") letter that granted authority to the bearer. **342–43 popes . . . cardynales . . . patriarkes . . . bisshopes,** popes, cardinals, patriarchs, bishops—all high-ranking church officials. **349 Relikes,** relics, objects of religious veneration, often parts of the body of saints or material objects associated with the saints or Christ. The Pardoner traffics in false relics and false pardons, both growing problems in the late Middle Ages; see *GP* 1.669n. **350 have I in,** El reads "have in"; Hg, "have I in a." **351 hooly Jewes sheep,** reference uncertain, but probably related to line 364. **363 drynken,** El reads "drynke." **364 hooly Jew,** Genesis 30.32–43 recounts how Jacob multiplied the number of sheep he could claim from Laban. **366 sires,** El and Hg read "sire." **376 pens, or elles groats,** pennies or silver coins worth four pennies.

Dar nat for shame of it yshryven° be,
Or any womman, be she yong or old,
That hath ymaked hir housbonde cokewold°,
Swich° folk shal have no power ne no grace
To offren to° my relikes in this place.
And whoso fyndeth hym out of swich blame,
They wol come up and offre in Goddes name,
And I assoille hem° by the auctoritee
Which that by bulle° ygraunted was to me."
  By this gaude° have I wonne, yeer by yeer,
An hundred mark sith° I was pardoner.
I stonde lyk a clerk in my pulpet,
And whan the lewed° peple is doun yset,
I preche so as ye han herd bifoore,
And telle an hundred false japes° moore.
Thanne peyne I me° to strecche forth the nekke,
And est and west upon the peple I bekke°,
As dooth a dowve° sittynge on a berne°.
Myne handes and my tonge goon so yerne°
That it is joye to se my bisynesse°.
Of avarice° and of swich cursednesse
Is al my prechyng, for to make hem free°
To yeven hir pens°, and namely unto me,
For myn entente is nat but for to wynne°,
And nothyng for correccioun of synne.
I rekke° nevere, whan that they been beryed°,
Though that hir soules goon a-blakeberyed!
For certes°, many a predicacioun°
Comth ofte tyme of yvel entencioun;
Som for plesance° of folk and flaterye,
To been avaunced° by ypocrisye,
And som for veyne glorie°, and som for hate.
For whan I dar noon oother weyes debate°,
Thanne wol I stynge hym with my tonge smerte°
In prechyng, so that he shal nat asterte°
To been defamed° falsly, if that be
Hath trespased to° my bretheren or to me.
For though I telle noght his propre name,
Men shal wel knowe that it is the same
By signes and by othere circumstances.
Thus quyte° I folk that doon us displesances°;
Thus spitte I out my venym under hewe°
Of hoolynesse, to semen hooly and trewe.
  But shortly myn entente I wol devyse°:
I preche of nothyng but for coveityse°.
Therfore my theme is yet, and evere was,

Radix malorum est cupiditas.

Thus kan I preche agayn° that same vice
Which that I use, and that is avarice°.
But though myself be gilty in that synne,
Yet kan I maken oother folk to twynne°
From avarice, and soore to repente.
But that is nat my principal entente—
I preche nothyng but for coveitise.
Of this mateere it oghte ynogh suffise.
  Thanne telle I hem ensamples many oon°
Of olde stories longe tyme agoon.
For lewed° peple loven tales olde;
Swiche° thynges kan they wel reporte° and holde°
What, trowe ye the whiles° I may preche,
And wynne gold and silver for° I teche,
That I wol lyve in poverte wilfully°?
Nay, nay, I thoghte it nevere, trewely,
For I wol preche and begge in sondry° landes;
I wol nat do no laboure with myne handes,
Ne make baskettes and lyve therby,
By cause I wol nat beggen ydelly°.
I wol noon of the apostles countrefete°;
I wol have moneie°, wolle°, chese, and whete,
Al° were it yeven of° the povereste page°,
Or of the povereste wydwe° in a village,
Al° sholde hir children sterve° for famyne.
Nay, I wol drynke licour of the vyne

380 yshryven, *forgiven* **382 cokewold,** *a cuckold* **383 Swich,** *such* **384 offren to,** *make an offering for* **387 assoille hem,** *absolve them* **388 bulle,** *official document* **389 gaude,** *trick* **390 sith,** *since* **392 lewed,** *ignorant* **394 japes,** *tricks* **395 peyne I me,** *I take pains* **396 bekke,** *nod* **397 dowve,** *dove,* **on a berne,** *in a barn* **398 yerne,** *rapidly* **399 bisynesse,** *intensity* **400 avarice,** *greed* **401 free,** *generous* **402 yeven hir pens,** *give their pennies* **403 wynne,** *acquire* **405 rekke,** *care,* **beryed,** *buried* **407 certes,** *certainly,* **predicacioun,** *sermon* **409 plesance,** *pleasure* **410 avaunced,** *advanced* **411 veyne glorie,** *empty pride* **412 debate,** *dispute* **413 smerte,** *painfully* **414 asterte,** *escape* **415 defamed,** *slandered* **416 trepased to,** *offended* **420 quyte,** *repay,* **displesances,** *displeasure* **421 hewe,** *disguise* **423 devyse,** *describe* **424 coveityse,** *greed* **427 agayn,** *against* **428 avarice,** *greed* **430 twynne,** *turn away* **435 ensamples many oon,** *many examples* **437 lewed,** *ignorant* **438 Swiche,** *such,* **reporte,** *repeat,* **holde,** *remember* **439 trowe ye the whiles,** *do you think that while* **440 for,** *because* **441 wilfully,** *voluntarily* **443 sondry,** *various* **446 ydelly,** *idly* **447 countrefete,** *imitate* **448 moneie,** *money,* **wolle,** *wool* **449 Al,** *although,* **yeven of,** *given by,* **povereste page,** *poorest servant* **450 wydwe,** *widow* **451 Al,** *even if,* **sterve,** *die*

385 out of swich blame, not guilty of such offenses; the Pardoner's insidious implication is that anyone who does not offer money *is* guilty of such offenses. El reads "fame" for "blame." **386 They,** Hg reads "He." **in,** El reads "on"; Hg, "a." **387 hem,** Hg reads "hym." **390 mark,** coin worth two-thirds pound; one hundred marks was a healthy income. **392 the,** Hg reads "that." **405 that,** omitted in El. **406 goon a-blakeberyed,** pick blackberries; the precise meaning is uncertain, but it is clearly dismissive. **407–08** From *RR* 5113–14. **426** See 334n. **439 the whiles,** Hg reads "that whiles." **441–47** The ideals rejected here—voluntary poverty, manual labor, imitation of the apostles, and begging—underlie clerical vows.

And have a joly wenche in every toun.
  But herkneth°, lordynges, in conclusioun:
Youre likyng is that I shal telle a tale.
Now have I dronke a draughtte of corny° ale,
By God, I hope I shal yow telle a thyng
That shal by reson been at youre likyng.
For though myself be a ful vicious man,
A moral tale yet I yow telle kan,
Which I am wont° to preche for to wynne°.
Now hoold youre pees; my tale I wol bigynne.

Heere bigynneth the Pardoners Tale.

  In Flaundres whilom° was a compaignye
Of yonge folk that haunteden folye°,
As riot°, hasard°, stywes°, and tavernes,
Where as with harpes, lutes, and gyternes°
They daunce and pleyen at dees° bothe day and nyght,
And eten also and drynken over hir myght°,
Thurgh which they doon the devel sacrifise
Withinne that develes temple in cursed wise
By superfluytee° abhomynable.
Hir othes been° so grete and so dampnable
That it is grisly for to heere hem swere.
Oure blissed Lordes body they totere—
Hem thoughte° that Jewes rente° hym noght ynough—
And ech of hem at otheres synne lough°.
And right anon° thanne comen tombesteres°
Fetys° and smale°, and yonge frutesteres°,
Syngeres with harpes, baudes°, wafereres°,
Whiche been the verray° develes officeres
To kyndle and blowe the fyr of lecherye
That is annexed unto glotonye.
  The hooly writ° take I to my witnesse
That luxurie° is in wyn and dronkenesse.
Lo, how that dronken Looth, unkyndely°,
Lay by his doghtres two, unwitynglу°;
So dronke he was, he nyste° what he wroghte°.
Herodes, whoso wel the stories soghte°,
Whan he of wyn was repleet° at his feeste,
Right at his owene table he yaf° his heeste°
To sleen° the Baptist John, ful giltelees.
  Senec seith a good word doutelees;
He seith he kan no difference fynde
Bitwix a man that is out of his mynde
And a man which that is dronkelewe°
But that woodnesse°, fallen in a shrewe°,
Persevereth° lenger than dooth dronkenesse.
O glotonye, ful of cursednesse!
O cause first of oure confusioun!
O original of oure dampnacioun,
Til Crist hadde boght° us with his blood° agayn!
Lo, how deere°, shortly for to sayn,
Aboght° was thilke° cursed vileynye!
Corrupt° was al this world for glotonye.
  Adam oure fader and his wyf also
Fro Paradys to labour and to wo
Were dryven for that vice, it is no drede°.
For whil that Adam fasted, as I rede,

454 herkneth, *listen* **456 corny,** *malty* (?) **461 wont,** *accustomed,* **wynne,** *acquire* **463 whilom,** *once* **464 haunteden folye,** *lived in folly* **465 As riot,** *such as partying,* **hasard,** *gambling,* **stywes,** *brothels* **466 gyternes,** *guitars* **467 dees,** *dice* **468 myght,** *capacity* **471 superfluytee,** *overindulgence* **472 Hir othes been,** *their oaths are* **475 Hem thoughte,** (it was) *thought by them,* **rente,** *tore* **476 lough,** *laughed* **477 right anon,** *soon,* **tombesteres,** *female acrobats* **478 Fetys,** *shapely,* **smale,** *slim,* **frutesteres,** *female fruit sellers* **479 baudes,** *pimps,* **wafereres,** *cake sellers* **480 verray,** *actual* **483 hooly writ,** *Bible* **484 luxurie,** *lechery* **485 unkyndely,** *unnaturally* **486 unwityngly,** *unknowingly* **487 nyste,** *knew not,* **wroghte,** *did* **488 whoso . . . soghte,** *whoever . . .* (may) *investigate* **489 repleet,** *filled* **490 yaf,** *gave,* **heeste,** *order* **491 sleen,** *slay* **495 dronkelewe,** *regularly drunk* **496 woodnesse,** *madness,* **fallen in a shrewe,** *happening to a wretch* **497 Persevereth,** *lasts* **501 boght,** *redeemed,* **blood,** *i.e., death* **502 deere,** *expensively* **503 Aboght,** *redeemed,* **thilke,** *that* **504 Corrupt,** *corrupted* **507 drede,** *doubt*

463 Flaundres, Flanders, in modern Belgium. **470 develes temple,** devil's temple, i.e., tavern. **474 totere,** tear apart. Swearing was thought to tear the body of Christ, as many oaths cite parts of Christ's body or aspects of his crucifixion. See lines 651–64 below and *ParsT* 10.591. **484** 1 Ephesians 5.18, but Chaucer may have taken it from Pope Innocent III, *De Miseria Conditionis Humane* (*On the Misery of the Human Condition*) 2.19; see *MLT* 2.99-121n. Other materials below that may derive from *De Miseria*—all from sections 2.17-19—are at lines 488–91, 517–20, 521–23, 527–28, 535–36, 537–46, 549–50, 551–52, and 560–61. There is related material from St. Jerome, *Epistola adversus Jovinianum* 2.10–15 (*Letter against Jovinian*) at lines 508–11, 517–20, 527–28, and 549–50; see *WBP* 3.3n. **485 Looth,** Lot; Genesis 19.30-35. **488-91 Herodes . . . Baptist John,** at a meal Herod fulfilled an oath to a dancing girl by ordering the decapitation of John the Baptist; Mark 6.22-28 and Matthew 14.7-11. Drunkenness is not mentioned in the biblical accounts, although the association was common; see *PP* C.11.176-79. Alluded to in Innocent 2.18; see 484n above. **492–97 Senec . . . ,** Seneca, *Letters* 83.18-19. **499 cause first,** gluttony was commonly condemned as the primary reason why Adam and Eve ate the forbidden fruit and were expelled from Paradise. See *SumT* 3.1915-17; *ParsT* 10.819.

He was in Paradys; and whan that he
Eet° of the fruyt deffended° on the tree,
Anon° he was out cast to wo and peyne.
O glotonye, on thee° wel oghte us pleyne°!
O, wiste a man° how manye maladyes
Folwen of excesse and of glotonyes,
He wolde been the moore mesurable°
Of his diete, sittynge at his table.
Allas, the shorte throte, the tendre mouth,
Maketh that est and west and north and south,
In erthe, in eir, in water, men to swynke°
To gete a glotoun deyntee mete° and drynke.
Of this matiere, O Paul, wel kanstow trete°:
"Mete unto wombe°, and wombe eek unto mete,
Shal God destroyen bothe," as Paulus seith.
Allas, a foul thyng is it, by my feith,
To seye this word, and fouler is the dede,
Whan man so drynketh of the white and rede°
That of his throte he maketh his pryvee°
Thurgh thilke° cursed superfluitee°.
The apostel wepyng seith ful pitously,
"Ther walken manye of whiche yow toold have I—
I seye it now wepyng, with pitous voys—
They been enemys of Cristes croys°,
Of whiche the ende is deeth; wombe is hir god!"
O wombe, O bely, O stynkyng cod°,
Fulfilled of° donge and of corrupcioun!
At either ende of thee foul is the soun°.
How greet labour and cost is thee to fynde°!
Thise cookes, how they stampe and streyne and grynde
And turnen substaunce into accident
To fulfille al thy likerous talent°.
Out of the harde bones knokke they
The mary°, for they caste noght° awey
That may go thurgh the golet° softe and swoote°.
Of spicerie° of leef and bark and roote
Shal been his sauce ymaked by delit°,
To make hym yet a newer° appetit.
But certes°, he that haunteth swiche delices
Is deed whil that he lyveth in tho° vices.
A lecherous thyng is wyn, and dronkenesse
Is ful of stryvyng° and of wrecchednesse.
O dronke man, disfigured is thy face,
Sour is thy breeth, foul artow° to embrace,
And thurgh thy dronke nose semeth the soun
As though thou seydest ay° "Sampsoun, Sampsoun."
And yet, God woot°, Sampsoun drank nevere no wyn.
Thou fallest as it were a styked swyn°;
Thy tonge is lost, and al thyn honeste cure°;
For dronkenesse is verray sepulture°
Of mannes wit° and his discrecioun.
In whom that drynke hath dominacioun
He kan no conseil° kepe, it is no drede°.
Now kepe yow fro the white and fro the rede,
And namely° fro the white wyn of Lepe,
That is to selle° in Fysshstrete or in Chepe.
This wyn of Spaigne crepeth subtilly
In othere wynes, growynge faste by°,
Of which ther ryseth swich fumositee°
That whan a man hath dronken draughtes thre,
And weneth° that he be at hoom in Chepe,
He is in Spaigne right at the toune of Lepe—

---

510 Eet, *ate,* **deffended,** *forbidden* **511 Anon,** *soon* **512 on thee,** *against you,* **pleyne,** *lament* **513 wiste a man,** *if a person knew* **515 mesurable,** *moderate* **519 swynke,** *work* **520 mete,** *food* **521 kanstow trete,** *can you explain* **522 wombe,** *stomach* **526 the white and rede,** *wine* **527 pryvee,** *toilet* **528 thilke,** *this,* **superfluitee,** *overindulgence* **532 croys,** *cross* **534 cod,** *sack* **535 Fulfilled of,** *filled with* **536 soun,** *sound* **537 is thee to fynde,** *is it to provide for you* **540 likerous talent,** *greedy desire* **542 mary,** *marrow,* **noght,** *nothing* **543 golet,** *gullet,* **swoote,** *sweet* **544 spicerie,** *aromatic mixture* **545 by delit,** *for delight* **546 newer,** *renewed* **547 certes,** *surely,* **haunteth swiche delices,** *lives in such delicacies* **548 tho,** *those* **550 stryvyng,** *quarreling* **552 artow,** *are you* **554 ay,** *always* **555 woot,** *knows* **556 styked swyn,** *stuck pig* **557 honeste cure,** *noble concern* **558 verray sepulture,** *true burial* **559 wit,** *reason* **561 conseil,** *confidences,* **drede,** *doubt* **563 namely,** *especially* **564 to selle,** *for sale* **566 faste by,** *nearby* **567 fumositee,** *potency* **569 weneth,** *believes*

510 the tree, H reads "a tree." **517–20** Echoes Innocent 2.17 and Jerome 2.8; see 484n. **519 men,** El reads "man." **521–23 Paul . . . ,** 1 Corinthians 6.13, perhaps by way of Innocent 2.17; see 484n above. **527–28** Echoes Jerome 2.17; see 484n. **529 The apostel,** St. Paul. **530–33** Philippians 3.18-19; also *ParsT* 10.820. **532 They,** El and Hg read "Ther." **535–36** Echoes Innocent 2.18 and 2.17; see 484n. **539 substaunce into accident,** essential nature into outward appearance; a grim philosophical joke that claims culinary preparation to be deeply unnatural, even blasphemous. In Catholic doctrine, in the sacrament of the Eucharist, the substance of the bread and wine become the body and blood of Christ while the outward appearance remains the same. **543 swoote,** Hg reads "soote." **547–48** 1 Timothy 5.6; Jerome 2.9. **549-50** A version of Proverbs 20.1, in Innocent 2.19 and Jerome 2.10; see 484n. **551–52** Echoes Innocent 2.19; see 484n. **554–55 Sampsoun . . . ,** imitation of loud, nasal breathing. The biblical Samson was conceived by his mother while she abstained, and he lived as a Nazarite, in abstention; Judges 13.4-7. **560–61** The Vulgate version of Proverbs 31.4, in Innocent 2.19; see 484n above. Referred to again in 584n below. **563 Lepe,** in Spain. **564 Fysshstrete . . . Chepe,** commercial areas of medieval London. **565 crepeth subtilly,** sneaks slyly, a reference to the practice of adulterating expensive (usually French) wines with cheaper ones.

Nat at the Rochele, ne at Burdeux toun—
And thanne wol he seye "Sampsoun, Sampsoun!"
But herkneth, lordynges, o word I yow preye,
That alle the sovereyn° actes, dar I seye,
Of victories in the Olde Testament,
Thurgh verray° God that is omnipotent,
Were doon in abstinence and in preyere.
Looketh the Bible and ther ye may it leere°.
Looke° Attilla, the grete conquerour,
Deyde in his sleep with shame and dishonour,
Bledynge ay° at his nose in dronkenesse.
A capitayn sholde lyve in sobrenesse.
And over al this, avyseth yow right wel
What was comaunded unto Lamwel—
Nat Samuel, but Lamwel, seye I—
Redeth the Bible, and fynde it expresly°
Of wyn-yevyng° to hem that han justise°.
Namoore of this, for it may wel suffise.
And now that I have spoken of glotonye,
Now wol I yow deffenden hasardrye°.
Hasard is verray mooder° of lesynges°,
And of deceite, and cursed forswerynges°,
Blaspheme of° Crist, manslaughtre, and wast° also
Of catel° and of tyme; and forthermo,
It is repreeve° and contrarie of honour
For to ben holde° a commune hasardour°.
And ever the hyer° he is of estaat°,
The moore is he yholden desolaat°,
If that a prynce useth hasardrye,
In alle governaunce and policye
He is, as by commune opinioun,
Yholde the lasse in reputacioun.
Stilboun, that was a wys embassadour,
Was sent to Corynthe in ful greet honour
Fro Lacidomye to make hire alliaunce.
And whan he cam, hym happede par chaunce°
That alle the gretteste that were of that lond
Pleyynge atte hasard he hem fond°.
For which as soone as it myghte be
He stal hym hoom° agayn to his contree
And seyde, "Ther wol I nat lese° my name,
Ne I wol nat take on me so greet defame°
Yow for to allie° unto none hasardours.
Sendeth othere wise embassadours,
For by my trouthe me were levere dye°
Than I yow sholde to hasardours allye.
For ye that been so glorious in honours
Shul nat allyen yow with hasardours
As by my wyl, ne as by my tretee°."
This wise philosophre, thus seyde hee.
Looke eek° that to the kyng Demetrius
The kyng of Parthes, as the book seith us,
Sente him a paire of dees° of gold in scorn,
For he hadde used hasard ther-biforn°,
For which he heeld his glorie or his renoun
At no value or reputacioun.
Lordes may fynden oother maner° pley
Honeste° ynough to dryve the day awey.
Now wol I speke of othes° false and grete
A word or two, as olde bookes trete.
Gret sweryng is a thyng abhominable,
And fals sweryng is yet moore reprevable.
The heighe God forbad sweryng at al,
Witnesse on Mathew, but in special
Of sweryng seith the hooly Jeremye,
"Thou shalt swere sooth° thyne othes and nat lye,
And swere in doom° and eek in rightwisnesse°,
But ydel sweryng is a cursednesse."
Bihoold and se that in the firste table
Of heighe Goddes heestes° honurable

574 sovereyn, *supreme* **576 Thurgh verray,** *through true* **578 leere,** *learn* **579 Looke,** *consider* **581 ay,** *steadily* **586 expresly,** *specifically* **587 Of wyn-yevyng,** *about giving wine,* **han justise,** *dispense justice* **590 deffenden hasardye,** *speak against gambling* **591 verray mooder,** *true mother,* **lesynges,** *lies* **592 forswerynges,** *broken oaths* **593 Blaspheme of,** *blasphemy against,* **wast,** *waste* **594 catel,** *possessions* **595 repreeve,** *shame* **596 ben holde,** *be considered,* **hasardour,** *gambler* **597 hyer,** *higher,* **estaat,** *class* **598 yholden desolaat,** *considered wretched* **606 hym happede par chaunce,** *to him it happened by chance* **608 fond,** *found* **610 stal hym hoom,** *i.e., slipped home quietly* **611 lese,** *lose* **612 so greet defame,** *such great dishonor* **613 Yow for to allie,** *to ally you* **615 me were levere dye,** *I would rather die* **619 tretee,** *negotiation* **621 Looke eek,** *consider also* **623 dees,** *dice* **624 ther-biforn,** *before that* **627 oother maner,** *other kinds of* **628 Honeste,** *noble* **629 othes,** *oaths* **636 sooth,** *truly* **637 doom,** *judgment,* **rightwisnesse,** *righteousness* **640 Goddes heestes,** *God's commandments*

571 Rochele . . . Burdeux, La Rochelle . . . Bordeaux, regions that produce expensive French wines. **573 lordynges,** El reads "lordes." **579–81 Attilla . . . ,** the Hun, reported to have passed out and died from drink. **581 ay,** omitted in Hg. **584 What was comaunded unto Lamwel,** the command is in the Vulgate version of Proverbs 31.4: "Do not to kings, O Lamuel, do not to kings give wine, for there is no secret where drunkenness reigns." See 560–61n above. **589 that,** omitted in El. **591** From John of Salisbury *Policraticus* 1.5 [36], although Chaucer probably derived much of lines 591–626 from a preacher's manual such as that of John of Wales, *Communiloquium* 1.10.7. **593 Blaspheme,** El reads "Blasphemyng." **598 yholden,** El and Hg reads "holden." **603–20 Stilboun . . . Corynthe . . . Lacidomye,** an attempted alliance between Corinth and Sparta (Lacedaemon). John of Salisbury, *Policraticus* 1.5 [37] and John of Wales 1.10.7; the ambassador's name is *Chilon* in both. **612 Ne I,** Hg reads "Ny." **621 to,** omitted in El. **Demetrius,** is sent dice by the king of Parthia; John of Salisbury *Policraticus* 1.5 [38] and John of Wales 1.10.7. **631 Gret sweryng,** solemn oaths, i.e., those sworn by something holy or serious. **634 Mathew,** see Matthew 5.34-37, quoted in *ParsT* 10.589-90. **635 Jeremye,** Jeremiah 4.2 is adapted in lines 636-38, quoted in *ParsT* 10.592. **636 swere,** El reads "seye." **639 firste table,** first tablet; the Ten Commandments were given to Moses on two tablets; *MED* 1c.

Hou that the seconde heeste of hym is this,
"Take nat my name in ydel° or amys°."
Lo, rather he forbedeth swich sweryng
Than homycide or many a cursed thyng—
I seye that as by ordre° thus it stondeth,
This knoweth that his heestes understondeth
How that the seconde heeste of God is that.
And fortherover I wol thee telle al plat°
That vengeance shal nat parten° from his hous
That of his othes is to outrageous.
"By Goddes precious herte and by his nayles°,"
And "By the blood of Crist that is in Hayles,
Sevene is my chaunce and thyn is cynk and treye,"
"By Goddes armes, if thou falsly pleye
This daggere shal thurghout thyn herte go,"
This fruyt° cometh of the bicched bones° two—
Forsweryng°, ire°, falsnesse, homycide.
Now for the love of Crist, that for us dyde,
Lete° youre othes bothe grete and smale.
But, sires, now wol I telle forth my tale.
  Thise riotoures° thre of whiche I telle,
Longe erst er prime rong° of any belle,
Were set hem in a taverne for to drynke,
And as they sat they herde a belle clynke
Biforn a cors° was caried to his grave.
That oon of hem gan callen to his knave°,
"Go bet°," quod he, "and axe redily°
What cors is this that passeth heer forby°,
And looke that thou reporte his name weel."
  "Sire," quod this boy, "it nedeth never-a-deel°;
It was me toold er ye cam heer two houres.
He was, pardee°, an old felawe° of youres,
And sodeynly he was yslayn° tonyght,
Fordronke° as he sat on his bench upright.
Ther cam a privee° theef men clepeth° Deeth
That in this contree al the peple sleeth°,
And with his spere he smoot his herte atwo°
And wente his wey withouten wordes mo.
He hath a thousand slayn this pestilence°.
And, maister, er ye come in his presence,
Me thynketh that it were necessarie
For to be war of swich an adversarie.
Beth redy for to meete hym everemoore—
Thus taughte me my dame°. I sey namoore."
  "By Seinte Marie," seyde this taverner,
"Tile child seith sooth°, for he hath slayn this yeer
Henne° over a mile withinne a greet village
Bothe man and womman, child, and hyne°, and page°.
I trowe° his habitacioun be there.
To been avysed° greet wysdom it were
Er that° he dide a man a dishonour.°
  "Ye, Goddes armes," quod this riotour,
"Is it swich° peril with hym for to meete?
I shal hym seke by wey° and eek by strete,
I make avow to Goddes digne° bones!
Herkneth, felawes, we thre been al ones°;
Lat ech of us holde up his hand til° oother;
And ech of us bicomen otheres brother,
And we wol sleen this false traytour Deeth.
He shal be slayn, he that so manye sleeth,
By Goddes dignitee, er it be nyght."
  Togidres han thise thre hir trouthes plight°
To lyve and dyen ech of hem for oother
As though he were his owene ybore° brother.
And up they stirte°, al dronken in this rage,
And forth they goon towardes that village
Of which the taverner hadde spoke biforn.
And many a grisly ooth thanne han they sworn,
And Cristes blessed body they torente°—
Deeth shal be deed, if that they may hym hente°!
  Whan they han goon nat fully half a mile,
Right° as they wolde han troden over a stile,
An oold man and a poure with hem mette.

---

642 ydel, *vain,* **amys,** *wrongly* **645 by ordre,** *in order of occurrence* **648 al plat,** *plainly* **649 parten,** *depart* **651 nayles,** *nails* **656 fruyt,** *result,* **bicched bones,** *bitched* (i.e., cursed) *dice* **657 Forsweryng,** *breaking oaths,* **ire,** *anger* **659 Lete,** *abandon* **661 riotoures,** *villains* **662 Longe erst er prime rong,** *well before 9 a.m. was rung* **665 cors,** *corpse* (that) **666 knave,** *servant boy* **667 Go bet,** *go now,* **axe redily,** *ask quickly* **668 heer forby,** *by here* **670 it nedeth never-a-deel,** *it is not necessary at all* **672 pardee,** *by God,* **felawe,** *companion* **673 yslayn,** *killed* **674 Fordronke,** *completely drunk* **675 privee,** *stealthy,* **clepeth,** *call* **676 sleeth,** *slays* **677 smoot . . . atwo,** *struck in two* **679 this pestilence,** (during) *this outbreak of the plague* **684 dame,** *mother* **686 seith sooth,** *tells the truth* **687 Henne,** *from here* **688 hyne,** *farm worker,* **page,** *court servant* **689 trowe,** *believe* **690 avysed,** *prepared* **691 Er that,** *before* **693 swich,** *such* **694 wey,** *path* **695 digne,** *honored* **696 al ones,** *together* **697 til,** *to* **702 hir trouthes plight,** *pledged their words* **704 ybore,** *born* **705 stirte,** *leapt* **709 torente,** *tore* (see 474n) **710 hente,** *seize* **712 Right,** *just*

641 seconde heeste, second commandment in Vulgate Bible; third in King James version. **644 many a,** El reads "any." **646 knoweth,** El reads "knowen." **649–50** Echoes Ecclesiasticus 23.11, quoted in *ParsT* 10.593. **652 Hayles,** Hayles Abbey in Gloucestershire had a vial said to contain Christ's blood. **653 Sevene . . . cynk and treye,** seven . . . five and three (eight); combinations in a dice game. **663 for,** omitted in El and Hg. **664 belle clynke,** handbell ring before a funeral procession. **697 til,** Hg reads "to." **698 bicomen,** Hg reads "bicome." **700 he that,** El reads "which that." **703 for,** Hg reads "with." **705 al,** El reads "and." **710 that,** omitted in Hg. **712 wolde han troden over a stile,** would have crossed a fence by means of a stile, a low stone or wooden ladder on each side of the fence. **713 oold man,** this enigmatic figure who desires but cannot find death has been assessed as Old Age, Death, the Wandering Jew, and a projection of the Pardoner himself.

This olde man ful mekely hem grette°,
And seyde thus, "Now, lordes, God yow see!"
  The proudeste of thise riotoures three
Answerde agayn°, "What, carl with sory grace°,
Why artow° al forwrapped° save thy face?
Why lyvestow° so longe in so greet age?"
  This olde man gan looke in his visage°,
And seyde thus: "For° I ne kan nat fynde
A man, though that I walked into Ynde,
Neither in citee ne in no village,
That wolde chaunge° his youthe for myn age;
And therfore moot° I han myn age stille
As longe tyme as it is Goddes wille.
Ne Deeth, allas, ne wol nat han° my lyf.
Thus walke I lyk a restelees kaityf°,
And on the ground, which is my moodres gate,
I knokke with my staf bothe erly and late,
And seye, 'Leeve° mooder, leet me in!
Lo, how I vanysshe°, flessh and blood and skyn.
Allas, whan shul my bones been at reste?
Mooder, with yow wolde I chaunge my cheste°
That in my chambre longe tyme hath be,
Ye, for an heyre clowt° to wrappe me.'
But yet to me she wol nat do that grace°,
For which ful° pale and welked° is my face.
  "But, sires, to yow it is no curteisye
To speken to an old man vileynye
But he trespasse° in word or elles in dede.
In Hooly Writ ye may yourself wel rede,
'Agayns° an oold man, hoor° upon his heed,
Ye sholde arise.' Wherfore I yeve° yow reed°,
Ne dooth unto an oold man noon harm now
Namoore than that ye wolde men did to yow
In age, if that ye so longe abyde°.
And God be with yow, where ye go° or ryde.
I moot go thider as° I have to go."
  "Nay, olde cherl° by God thou shalt nat so,"
Seyde this oother hasardour anon.
"Thou partest nat so lightly, by Seint John!
Thou spak right now of thilke° traytour Deeth,
That in this contree alle oure freendes sleeth.
Have heer my trouthe, as thou art his espye°,
Telle where he is or thou shalt it abye°,
By God and by the hooly sacrement!
For soothly° thou art oon of his assent°
To sleen us yonge folk, thou false theef!"
  "Now, sires," quod he, "if that ye be so leef°
To fynde Deeth, turne up this croked wey,
For in that grove I lafte hym, by my fey°
Under a tree and there he wole abyde°.
Noght for youre boost he wole him nothyng° hyde.
Se ye that ook°? Right there ye shal hym fynde.
God save yow, that boghte agayn° mankynde,
And yow amende°." Thus seyde this olde man.
And everich° of thise riotoures ran
Til he cam to that tree, and ther they founde
Of floryns fyne° of gold ycoyned° rounde
Wel ny an° eighte busshels as hem thoughte.
No lenger thanne after Deeth they soughte,
But ech of hem so glad was of that sighte,
For that° the floryns been so faire and brighte,
That doun they sette hem by this precious hoord.
The worste of hem he spak the firste word.
  "Bretheren," quod he, "taak kepe° what I seye;
My wit is greet, though that I bourde° and pleye.
This tresor hath Fortune unto us yeven°
In myrthe and joliftee oure lyf to lyven,
And lightly° as it comth so wol we spende.
Ey, Goddes precious dignitee, who wende°
Today that we sholde han so fair a grace°?
But myghte this gold be caried fro this place
Hoom to myn hous—or elles unto youres—
For wel ye woot° that al this gold is oures,
Thanne were we in heigh felicitee°.

---

714 grette, *greeted* **717 agayn,** *in return,* **carl with sory grace,** *bad luck to you fellow* **718 artow,** *are you,* **al forwrapped,** *all wrapped up* **719 lyvestow,** *do you live* **720 gan looke in his visage,** *gazed into his face* **721 For,** *because* **724 chaunge,** *exchange* **725 moot,** *must* **727 ne wol nat han,** *will not have* **728 kaityf,** *wretch* **731 Leeve,** *dear* **732 vanysshe,** *waste away* **734 cheste,** *money chest* **736 heyre clowt,** *haircloth* (burial shroud) **737 grace,** *favor* **738 ful,** *very,* **welked,** *withered* **741 But he trespasse,** *unless he offends* **743 Agayns,** *in the presence of,* **hoor,** *white* **744 yeve,** *give,* **reed,** *advice* **747 abyde,** *live* **748 go,** *walk* **749 thider as,** *where* **750 cherl,** *peasant* **753 thilke,** *this* **755 espye,** *spy* **756 abye,** *pay for* **758 soothly,** *truly,* **oon of his assent,** *in agreement with him* **760 leef,** *eager* **762 fey,** *faith* **763 wole abyde,** *will remain* **764 nothyng,** *not at all* **765 ook,** *oak* **766 boghte agayn,** *redeemed* **767 amende,** *correct* **768 everich,** *each* **770 floryns fyne,** *coins pure,* **ycoyned,** *coined* **771 Wel ny an,** *nearly* **774 For that,** *because* **777 taak kepe,** *heed* **778 bourde,** *joke* **779 yeven,** *given* **781 lightly,** (as) *easily* **782 wende,** *thought* **783 han so fair a grace,** *have such luck* **786 woot,** *know* **787 heigh felicitee,** *high happiness*

715 God yow see, may God look over you; a blessing. **722 Ynde,** India, i.e., the end of the earth. **723 ne,** El reads "nor." **729 moodres gate,** mother's (and Mother Earth's) entrance; the image and the Old Man's desire for death, neither found in analogous tales, parallel Maximianus Etruscus *Elegies* 1.227-34. Rebirth and reentry into the womb are associated in John 3.4. **743–44** Leviticus 19.32. **744 sholde,** Hg reads "shal." **753 spak,** Hg reads "speeke." **757 hooly sacrement,** Eucharist, another blasphemous oath. **760 ye,** Hg reads "yow." **773 that,** Hg reads "the." **777 what I,** Hg reads "what that I." **786 this gold is oures,** in English law, found treasure was property of the monarch.

But trewely, by daye it may nat bee.
Men wolde seyn° that we were theves stronge°,
And for oure owene tresor doon us honge°.
This tresor moste ycaried be by nyghte
As wisely and as slyly as it myghte.
Wherfore I rede° that cut° among us alle
Be drawe°, and lat se wher the cut wol falle;
And he that hath the cut with herte blithe°
Shal renne° to towne, and that ful swithe°,
And brynge us breed and wyn ful prively°.
And two of us shul kepen subtilly°
This tresor wel. And if he wol nat tarie°,
Whan it is nyght we wol this tresor carie
By oon assent° where as us thynketh best."
That oon of hem the cut broghte in his fest
And bad hem° drawe and looke° where it wol falle,
And it fil on the yongeste of hem alle,
And forth toward the toun he wente anon.
  And also° soone as that he was gon
That oon of hem spak thus unto that oother,
"Thow knowest wel thou art my sworn brother;
Thy profit wol I telle thee anon.
Thou woost° wel that oure felawe is agon.
And heere is gold, and that ful greet plentee,
That shal departed° been among us thre.
But nathelees, if I kan shape° it so
That it departed were among us two,
Hadde I nat doon a freendes torn° to thee?"
  That oother answerde, "I noot hou° that may be.
He woot° wel that the gold is with us tweye°.
What shal we doon? What shal we to hym seye?"
  "Shal it be conseil°?" seyde the firste shrewe°,
"And I shal tellen in a wordes fewe
What we shal doon, and brynge it wel aboute."
  "I graunte," quod that oother, "out of doute,
That by my trouthe I shal thee nat biwreye°."
  "Now," quod the firste, "thou woost° wel we be tweye,
And two of us shul strenger be than oon.
Looke whan that° he is set that right anoon
Arys° as though thou woldest with hym pleye,
And I shal ryve° hym thurgh the sydes tweye
Whil that thou strogelest° with hym as in game,
And with thy daggere looke° thou do the same.
And thanne shal al this gold departed be,
My deere freend, bitwixen me and thee.
Thanne may we bothe oure lustes° all fulfille,
And pleye at dees° right° at oure owene wille."
And thus acorded been thise shrewes tweye°
To sleen the thridde, as ye han herd me seye.
  This yongeste, which that wente unto the toun,
Ful ofte in herte he rolleth up and doun°
The beautee of thise floryns° newe and brighte.
"O Lord," quod he, "if so were that I myghte
Have al this tresor to myself allone
Ther is no man that lyveth under the trone°
Of God that sholde lyve so murye° as I."
And atte laste the feend, oure enemy,
Putte in his thought that he sholde poyson beye°
With which he myghte sleen his felawes tweye—
Forwhy° the feend foond hym in swich lyvynge°
That he hadde leve° hem to sorwe brynge.
For this was outrely° his fulle entente,
To sleen hem bothe and nevere to repente.
And forth he gooth, no lenger wolde he tarie,
Into the toun unto a pothecarie°,
And preyde° hym that he hym wolde selle
Som poyson that he myghte his rattes quelle°,
And eek ther was a polcat° in his hawe°
That, as he seyde, his capouns° hadde yslawe°,
And fayn he wolde wreke hym°, if he myghte,
On vermyn that destroyed° hym by nyghte.
  The pothecarie answerde, "And thou shalt have
A thyng that, also° God my soule save,
In al this world ther is no creature
That eten or dronken hath of this confiture°
Noght but the montance° of a corn° of whete
That he ne shal his lif anon forlete°—

---

789 seyn, *say,* **theves stronge,** *a band of thieves* **790 doon us honge,** *hang us* **793 rede,** *advise,* **cut,** *straws* (i.e., drawing for the short straw) **793 drawe,** *drawn* **795 blithe,** *happy* **796 renne,** *run,* **ful swithe,** *very quickly* **797 prively,** *secretly* **798 kepen subtilly,** *protect carefully* **799 tarie,** *delay* **801 oon assent,** *mutual consent* **803 bad hem,** *told them,* **looke,** *consider* **806 also,** *as* **810 woost,** *know* **812 departed,** *divided* **813 shape,** *arrange* **815 freendes torn,** *friendly favor* **816 noot hou,** *don't know how* **817 woot,** *knows,* **tweye,** *two* **819 conseil,** *confidential,* **shrewe,** *villain* **823 biwreye,** *betray* **824 woost,** *know* **826 Looke whan that,** *see to it that when* **827 Arys,** *get up* **828 ryve,** *stab* **829 strogelest,** *struggle* **830 looke,** *make sure* **833 lustes,** *desires* **834 dees,** *dice,* **right,** *completely* **835 shrewes tewye,** *two villains* **838 rolleth up and doun,** *contemplates* **839 floryns,** *coins* **842 trone,** *throne* **843 murye,** *merrily* **845 beye,** *buy* **847 Forwhy,** *because,* **swich lyvynge,** *such a condition of life* **848 leve,** *permission* **849 outrely,** *utterly* **852 pothecarie,** *druggist* **853 preyde,** *asked* **854 quelle,** *kill* **855 polcat,** *weasel,* **hawe,** *yard* **856 capouns,** *chickens,* **yslawe,** *slain* **857 fayn he wolde wreke hym,** *he wished to have revenge* **858 destroyed,** *injured* **860 also,** *as* (may) **862 confiture,** *concoction* **863 Noght but the montance,** *nothing more than the size,* **corn,** *grain* **864 anon forlete,** *immediately lose*

793 Wherfore, Hg reads "Therfore." **803 hem,** El reads "hym." **806 gon,** Hg reads "agon." **807 of hem,** omitted in El. **817 woot wel that,** El reads "woot how that"; Hg, "woot that." **818 What shal,** El reads "Whal." **823 shal,** El reads "wol." **832 bitwixen me and thee,** Hg reads "bitwixe thee and me." **837 unto,** Hg reads "to." **848 hem,** Hg reads "hym." **862 eten or dronken,** Hg reads "ete or dronke."

Ye, sterve° he shal and that in lasse while°
Than thou wold goon a paas nat but° a mile,
The poysoun is so strong and violent."
  This cursed man hath in his hond yhent°
This poysoun in a box, and sith° he ran
Into the nexte strete unto a man
And borwed of hym large botels° thre,
And in the two his poyson poured he.
The thridde he kepte clene for his owene drynke
For al the nyght he shoop° hym for to swynke°
In cariynge of the gold out of that place.
And whan this riotour, with sory grace°,
Hadde filled with wyn his grete botels thre,
To his felawes agayn repaireth° he.
  What nedeth it to sermone° of it moore?
For right as they hadde cast° his deeth bifoore,
Right so they han hym slayn, and that anon.
And whan that this was doon, thus spak that oon,
"Now lat us sitte and drynke and make us merie,
And afterward we wol his body berie°."
And with that word it happed hym par cas°
To take the botel ther° the poyson was,
And drank, and yaf° his felawe drynke also,
For which anon they storven° bothe two.
  But certes, I suppose that Avycen
Wroot° nevere in no canon° ne in no fen°
Mo wonder signes° of empoisonyng
Than hadde thise wrecches two er hir° endyng.
Thus ended been thise homycides two
And eek the false empoysonere also.
  O cursed synne of alle cursednesse!
O traytours homycide, O wikkednesse!
O glotonye, luxurie°, and hasardrye°!
Thou blasphemour of Crist with vileynye
And othes° grete of usage° and of pride!
Allas, mankynde, how may it bitide°
That to thy creatour, which that the wroghte°
And with his precious herte-blood thee boghte°,
Thou art so fals and so unkynde°, allas?
  Now goode men, God foryeve yow youre trespas,
And ware yow fro° the synne of avarice.
Myn hooly pardoun may yow alle warice°—
So that° ye offre nobles° or sterlynges°
Or elles silver broches, spoones, rynges.
Boweth youre heed under this hooly bulle°!
Com up, ye wyves, offreth of youre wolle°!
Youre names I entre heer in my rolle anon°;
Into the blisse of hevene shul ye gon.
I yow assoille° by myn heigh power,
Yow that wol offre, as clene and eek as cleer
As ye were born.—And lo, sires, thus I preche.
And Jhesu Crist, that is oure soules leche°,
So graunte yow his pardoun to receyve,
For that is best—I wol yow nat deceyve.
  But, sires, o word forgat I in my tale:
I have relikes° and pardoun in my male°
As faire as any man in Engelond,
Whiche were me yeven° by the popes hond.
If any of yow wole° of devocioun
Offren, and han myn absolucioun,
Com forth anon and kneleth heere adoun
And mekely receyveth my pardoun,
Or elles taketh pardoun as ye wende°
Al newe and fressh at every miles ende—
So that ye offren, alwey newe and newe,
Nobles or pens° whiche that be goode and trewe.
It is an honour to everich° that is heer
That ye mowe° have a suffisant° pardoneer
T'assoille° yow in contree as ye ryde
For aventures° whiche that may bityde°.
Paraventure° ther may fallen oon or two
Doun of his hors and breke his nekke atwo.
Looke which a seuretee° is it to yow alle
That I am in youre felaweship yfalle°,
That may assoille yow bothe moore and lasse
Whan that the soule shal fro the body passe.
I rede° that oure Hoost heere shal bigynne,
For he is moost envoluped° in synne.

865 sterve, *die,* **lasse while,** *less time* **866 goon a paas nat but,** *go at a pace only* **868 yhent,** *seized* **869 sith,** *then* **871 botels,** *bottles* **874 shoop,** *planned,* **swynke,** *work* **876 sory grace,** *ill fate* **878 repaireth,** *returns* **879 sermone,** *preach* **880 cast,** *planned* **884 berie,** *bury* **885 it happed hym par cas,** *he happened by chance* **886 ther,** *where* **887 yaf,** *gave* **888 storven,** *died* **890 Wroot,** *wrote,* **canon,** *chart,* **fen,** *section* **891 Mo wonder signes,** *more extreme symptoms* **892 er hir,** *before their* **897 luxurie,** *lechery,* **hasardrye,** *gambling* **899 othes,** *oaths,* **usage,** *habit* **900 bitide,** *happen* **901 the wroghte,** *made you* **902 boghte,** *redeemed* **903 unkynde,** *unnatural* **905 ware yow fro,** *beware* **906 warice,** *save* **907 So that,** *as long as,* **nobles,** *gold coins,* **sterlynges,** *silver coins* **909 bulle,** *document* **910 wolle,** *wool* **911 rolle anon,** *records immediately* **913 assoille,** *absolve* **916 leche,** *physician* **920 relikes,** *relics,* **male,** *bag* **922 yeven,** *given* **923 wole,** *will* **927 wende,** *travel* **930 pens,** *pennies* **931 everich,** *everyone* **932 mowe,** *are able to,* **suffisant,** *capable* **933 T'assoille,** *to absolve* **934 aventures,** *accidents,* **bityde,** *happen* **935 Paraventure,** *perhaps* **937 which a seuretee,** *what an assurance* **938 am in youre felaweship yfalle,** *have happened into your company* **941 rede,** *advise* **942 envoluped,** *enveloped*

871 of, omitted in El and Hg, and all manuscripts. **873 owene,** omitted in Hg. **880 as,** El reads "so as." **882 whan that,** Hg omits "that." **889-90 Avycen . . . canon . . . fen,** Avicenna, medieval Islamic physician, whose famous treatise, *Liber Canonis Medicinae* (*Book of the Rules of Medicine*), is divided into fens (Arabic *fann,* a unit of technical discussion); *Liber* 4.6 discusses poisons. **910 Com,** Hg reads "Cometh." **914 Yow,** Hg reads "Ye." **929–30** Echoes lines 907–08. **941 heere,** omitted in Hg.

Com forth, sire Hoost, and offre first anon,
And thou shalt kisse my relikes everychon°—
Ye, for a grote°: unbokele anon° thy purs."
"Nay, nay," quod he, "thanne have I Cristes curs.
Lat be," quod he, "it shal nat be, so theech°
Thou woldest make me kisse thyn olde breech°
And swere it were a relyk of a seint,
Though it were with thy fundement depeint°.
But by the croys which that Seint Eleyne fond
I wolde I hadde thy coillons in myn hond
Instide of relikes or of seintuarie°.
Lat kutte hem of°, I wol thee helpe hem carie.
They shul be shryned° in an hogges toord°."
This Pardoner answerde nat a word.
So wrooth° he was, no word ne wolde he seye.
"Now," quod oure Hoost, "I wol no lenger pleye
With thee ne with noon oother angry man."
But right anon the worthy Knyght bigan,
Whan that he saugh that al the peple lough°,
"Namoore of this, for it is right ynough.
Sire Pardoner, be glad and myrie of cheere°;
And ye, sire Hoost, that been to me so deere,
I prey yow that ye kisse the Pardoner.
And Pardoner, I prey thee drawe thee neer,
And as we diden lat us laughe and pleye."
Anon they kiste and ryden° forth hir weye.

Heere is ended the Pardoners Tale.

---

944 everychon, *each one* **945 grote,** *four-penny silver coin,* **unbokele anon,** *unbuckle quickly* **947 theech,** *may I prosper* **948 breech,** *underpants* **950 fundement depeint,** *bottom stained* **953 seintuarie,** *sacred objects* **954 Lat kutte hem of,** *let them be cut off* **955 shryned,** *enshrined,* **hogges toord,** *hog's turd* **957 wrooth,** *enraged* **961 lough,** *laughed* **963 myrie of cheere,** *good humored* **968 ryden,** *rode*

944 my, Hg reads "the." **951 croys . . . Seint Eleyne,** St. Helen was thought to have found the cross of Christ's crucifixion. **952 coillons,** testicles, recalling the earlier suggestions of the Pardoner's castration or infertility, *GP* 1.688-91n. The association of relics and coillons was inspired by Reason's theory of names and allegory in *RR* 7081ff., especially 7108–09. **954 thee helpe hem,** El reads "with thee hem"; Hg, "thee hem." Other manuscripts read "helpe hem." **964 ye,** omitted in Hg.

Canterbury Tales, Part 7

Introduction

PART 7 IS THE MOST VARIED SECTION of the *Canterbury Tales*, with six tales of differing genre: one of them in prose, two in rhymed couplets, and the others in various verse forms. The pilgrim Chaucer tells two of the tales himself, and in the links among the tales, the Host comments recurrently on literature and its effects. Throughout the *Canterbury Tales*, Chaucer explores the commonplace that diverse people speak diversely (see, e.g., *KnT* 1.2516ff., *WBT* 3.925ff., *SqT* 5.202), and in Part 7 he experiments with literary form while exploring how and to what extent tales are appropriate to individual tellers and our expectations of them. The briefer sections of the *Canterbury Tales* often juxtapose two different or opposed literary genres or modes, but here the variety is greater and the complexity richer.

The teller's use of first-person female pronouns in the *Shipman's Tale* (see 11–19) indicates that the story was once intended by Chaucer to be told by the Wife of Bath. Its reassignment in unrevised form to the Shipman may be due to the mercantile concerns of the tale, as the Shipman makes a shady living in the business of nautical transport (*GP* 1.395ff.). The tale commodifies sex rather than celebrates it or moralizes about it, and the fabliau lacks the slapstick humor and bawdiness of Chaucer's other examples of the genre. In their place it offers restrained conversation and double entendre (see 36, 416). The sex-for-money device of the traditional plot—the "lover's gift regained"—does not rebound on the monk, who trades in sex with a merchant's wife and in money with the merchant. Nor does adultery negatively affect the married couple. Unlike in the closest analogues to the tale, Boccaccio's *Decameron* 8.1 and 8.2 and Sercambi's *Novelle*, the wife is not compelled to repay the money for which she prostitutes herself, perhaps a vestige of the Wife of Bath as original teller. Sex and money pay dividends in a world where everyone profits, so the class and gender inequalities of the fabliau are muted by urbanity, opportunism, and accommodation. Albert H. Silverman, "Sex and Money in Chaucer's *Shipman's Tale*" (1953, no. 1072) long ago identified the punning equation of sex and money in the tale. In "Thinking about Money in Chaucer's *Shipman's Tale*" (2003, no. 1069), William E. Rogers and Paul Dower survey subsequent criticism and argue that varying attitudes toward money produce varying interpretations of the tale.

The bourgeois urbanity of the *Shipman's Tale* is contrasted sharply by lofty idealism, bloody action, and heightened sentimentality in the *Prioress's Tale*. We leave a gray world for one that is black and white. Medieval miracles of the Virgin (the genre of the tale) promoted piety by depicting the rewards of steadfast devotion in the face of persecution. As are so many stereotyped "bad guys" of popular literature, the Jews in this tale are demonized, here quite literally (558–64), and the ending of the tale reminds us sharply that such demonizing occurs in history as well as literature, with brutal consequences. The devotion of the little choirboy slain by the Jews is emphasized by the fact that he does not understand the Latin words he sings, only that they praise Mary. The Prioress identifies with such innocent or unthinking devotion (481–87), encouraging many to blame her for the goriness and anti-Semitism of the tale. Others blame the genre itself, and still others argue that the anti-Semitism was Chaucer's own, unavoidable in his time. The Prioress's pity for mice and dogs (see *GP* 1.144–50) at a time when human beings were dying from plague and starvation encourages the first view. However we read the brutality of the tale, it confronts us with the powers of speech and narrative to affect human lives and with the dangers that lie in the gaps between intention, understanding, and language use. The essays edited by Sheila Delany in *Chaucer and the Jews* (2002, no. 537) explore Judaism in Chaucer's works and bring postcolonial perspective to bear on the issues surveyed by Florence Ridley in *The Prioress and the Critics* (1965, no. 1095) and Beverly Boyd in the Variorum edition of the tale (1987, no. 53). Henry Ansgar Kelly documents the likelihood of Chaucer's personal contact with Jews and other non-Christians in "Jews and Saracens in Chaucer's England" (2005, no. 541).

The rhyme royal stanza form of the *Prioress's Tale* heightens its emotional effects, and the verse form is tellingly sustained—and perhaps undercut—in the comic prologue that follows and sets up the *Tale of Sir Thopas.* Told by the pilgrim-narrator Chaucer at the invitation of the Host, the tale is a burlesque of tail-rhyme romances popular in late-medieval England. To appreciate the fun, we must recognize the brilliant clichés by which Chaucer systematically parodies every convention of the genre-verse form, setting, plot, character, diction, imagery, and so on. On the clichés, see Joanne A. Charbonneau's chapter in Correale and Hamel's *Sources and Analogues* (2002–05; no. 234, volume 2) and, for analysis of the verse, Alan T. Gaylord's "Chaucer's Dainty 'Dogerel'" (1979, no. 1100). Twenty-first century readers may be forgiven for missing some of the joke, but the Host is not let off so easily. His brusque interruption of Chaucer's parody exposes literary ignorance or insensitivity. As well, the plumpness and naïveté of the narrator-persona in the *Thopas* prologue make Chaucer himself a comic target. Nowhere is his humor more genial or inclusive, yet there is more here than literary fun. The contrast with the seriousness of the *Prioress's Tale* is emphatic, and *Thopas* touches on the aesthetic aspects of many issues from the previous tale: ignorance versus understanding, intention and effect, and the function of conventions and stereotypes.

The *Tale of Melibee* has also been read as something of a joke—a lengthy, sententious treatise that is introduced as a "litel thyng in prose" (937). Little it is not, and at the end the joke seems again to be on the Host, who misses the political and personal allegory of the tale and reveals himself to be intimidated by his wife. The very serious issues of the tale—the value of taking counsel and the desirability of peace—are appropriate to late fourteenth-century England, which was embroiled in the Hundred Years' War and the shifting power struggles of the minority of Richard II and his troubled reign. Chaucer may have written the work before Richard took full control of the kingdom (see 1199n), but the message of prudential restraint is apposite under almost any political conditions. As well, the allegory encourages individual self-reflection, as Prudence eventually convinces her husband, Melibee, to pursue the personal calm that parallels social peace. Female advice is a positive force, and marriage is a figure for moral or psychological balance as well as political stability. The tale translates Renaud de Louens's *Livre de Melibée et de Dame Prudence* (1336), itself a French translation of Albertanus of Brescia's Latin *Liber Consolationis et Consilii* (Book of Consolation and Counsel). On the moral allegory of the tale, see Richard L. Hoffman, "Chaucer's Melibee and Tales of Sondry Folk" (1969, no. 1115); and, for political concerns, Lynn Staley Johnson, "Inverse Counsel: Contexts for the *Melibee*" (1990, no. 1116), and Judith Ferster, "Chaucer's *Tale of Melibee*: Contradictions and Context" (2000, no. 1112).

The weightiness of *Melibee* contrasts the fun of *Thopas* as *sentence* contrasts *solaas*; and the message of *Melibee* can be seen as a secular complement to Chaucer's other prose tale, the *Parson's Tale,* and crucial to understanding the *Canterbury Tales* overall. In "Langland and Chaucer" (2007, no. 424), Nicholas Watson reads *Melibee* as central to Chaucer's theological concerns. The *Thopas/Melibee* pairing represent the poet's traditional roles of entertainer and adviser, and the Host's responses suggest Chaucer's concerns about audience reception and the role of the poet. See Alan T. Gaylord, "*Sentence* and *Solaas* in Fragment VII of the *Canterbury Tales*: Harry Bailly as Horseback Editor" (1967, no. 717), and Andrew James Johnston's discussion of the paired tales in *Clerks and Courtiers* (2001, no. 530). Peter Travis assesses the masculinist assumptions of the Host's aesthetic judgment in "The Body of the Nun's Priest, or Chaucer's Disseminal Genius" (2005, no. 725).

The *Monk's Tale* continues Chaucer's experimentation with form and genre. Its eight-line stanza is used elsewhere in Chaucer's poetry only in the *ABC,* and the tale is really an anthology of tales that mirrors Part 7 and the *Canterbury Tales* overall, though it tellingly lacks their variety. The

Monk labels his brief narratives "tragedies" (1971), defining them as stories of men who fall from prosperity, leaving aside concern with the cause(s) of the fall or the merit of the victim. This definition and the persistent lamenting of Fortune's effects in the tale encourage negative judgments of the Monk, who by vocation, the argument goes, ought to be more concerned with spiritual merit than the vagaries of fortune. The definition of *tragedy* has prompted commentary on Chaucer's medieval understanding of the term in contrast with Aristotle's classic definition in his *Poetics*, which better fits later works by Shakespeare and Arthur Miller, for example. For discussion of Chaucer's notion of tragedy and its legacy, see Henry Ansgar Kelly, *Chaucerian Tragedy* (1997, no. 627). *Studies in the Age of Chaucer* 22 (2000, no. 1131) includes a cluster of articles that discuss a range of issues that pertain to the *Monk's Tale*.

"De casibus" tragedy, as medieval tragedy is also called, derives from Boccaccio's collection *De Casibus Virorum Illustrium* (*On the Falls of Famous Men*). Chaucer took little or none of his material from Boccaccio's collection, although the rubric that opens the Monk's narrative borrows the Latin title. Chaucer's sources are eclectic, including the Bible, the *Romance of the Rose*, Boethius, Ovid, Dante, and others. Consistent with Chaucer's recurrent disguising of his debt to Boccaccio, the account of Zenobia, the only woman in this list, derives from Boccaccio's *De Claris Mulieribus* (*On Famous Women*) while suggesting that Petrarch is the source (2325). The four accounts about Chaucer's near contemporaries raise textual questions because they appear in two different places in the manuscripts (see 2375–2461n). These "modern instances" align ancient history with events of Chaucer's day, in two cases with the lives of men whom Chaucer met.

The Knight's interruption of the Monk comes as a relief to many readers since he suggests an alternative to a tragic view of life and a different kind of story. The Host agrees, and his responses to the Monk's performance are a comic screen through which Chaucer extends his concern with audience response to tales, setting up the literary tour de force that is the *Nun's Priest's Tale*. We arrive at this tale with barely any expectations because the teller is not introduced in the *General Prologue* and we have come to distrust the Host's evaluations of people and tales. The *Nun's Priest's Tale* returns to the rhymed couplets of the *Shipman's Tale* and fulfills the narrative and ethical potential in that earlier tale for tricking a trickster—in this case a rooster outdoing a fox. Within its beast-fable genre, it balances the mock heroism of *Thopas* and the sententiousness of *Melibee*, combining *solaas* and *sentence* as well as anywhere in the Canterbury fiction. It mentions the murder of a little boy (3110ff.), recalling the *Prioress's Tale*, and it echoes both the Prioress's table manners and at least one of her phrases (2834, 3052). Most emphatically, it counters the Monk's catastrophes with delight, renders absurd the self-seriousness that underlies them, and shows that though people (and chickens) may fall, they also can rise again. For a comprehensive description of studies that pertain to the tales of the Nun's Priest and the Monk, see *Chaucer's* Monk's Tale *and* Nun's Priest's Tale*: An Annotated Bibliography 1900–2000* (2009, no. 89a), edited by Peter Goodall.

The themes and digressions of the *Nun's Priest's Tale* are kaleidoscopic, shifting among serious concerns such as free will, dream psychology, gender relations, Adam's fall, the Uprising of 1381 (Peasants' Revolt), and the morality of fiction—all rendered comic by reminders that the tale is set in a barnyard. The widow's modest living in the narrative frame casts into relief the rooster's self-centeredness, which in turn occasions a number of exempla and rhetorical set pieces that offer contradictory proverbs and other kinds of wisdom literature. The effect is rather like a set of Chinese boxes or Russian dolls, so the serious concerns of the tale are constantly undercut but never disappear from view. When the rooster offers one moral at the end of the tale, the fox offers another. The narrator hints at a third in language that implies everything written must be taken seriously. These "nested" morals, like the narrative layers of the tale, challenge the reader to make sense of it all without losing awareness of the tale's playfulness.

The basic plot derives from Marie de France's "Del Coke del Gupil" (The Cock and the Fox), a beast fable in the tradition of Aesop, and from medieval beast epics that centered on the adventures of Reynard the fox, especially the *Roman de Renart* and perhaps the *Renart le Contrefait* (Reynard the Trickster). Robert A. Pratt (1972, no. 1148; 1977, no. 1149) has shown that Chaucer adapted these and fleshed them out with a variety of materials, particularly Robert Holcott's commentary of the biblical Book of Wisdom attributed to Solomon, *Super Sapientiam Salomonis.* Edward Wheatley summarizes Pratt's arguments in the recent *Sources and Analogues* (2002–05, no. 234). Derek Pearsall's Variorum edition (1984, no. 50) of the tale is thorough and judicious in its judgments, and his reading of the tale in his *The Canterbury Tales* (1985, no. 588) is a benchmark for other studies. See also John Finlayson, "Reading Chaucer's 'Nun's Priest's Tale': Mixed Genres and Multi-Layered Worlds of Illusion" (2005, no. 1140).

Two versions of the *Nun's Priest's Prologue* survive, and Chaucer evidently canceled the *Epilogue* (see 2767n, 3447–62n). These and other features of part 7 left unrevised or in process indicate that Chaucer's exploration of—perhaps anxiety about—poetics and literary reception was an ongoing concern.

Canterbury Tales Part 7

From woodcut made by W.H. Hooper and published by the Chaucer Society between 1868 and 1879

Shipman's Tale

Heere bigynneth the Shipmannes Tale.

A marchant whilom° dwelled at Seint Denys,
That riche was, for which men helde hym wys.
A wyf he hadde of excellent beautee,
And compaignable and revelous° was she,
Which is a thyng that causeth more dispence°
Than worth is al the chiere° and reverence°
That men hem doon° at festes and at daunces.
Swiche salutaciouns° and contenaunces°
Passen as dooth a shadwe upon the wal.
But wo is hym that payen moot° for al!
The sely° housbonde algate° he moot paye,
He moot us clothe, and he moot us arraye°,
Al for his owene worship°, richely—
In which array we daunce jolily.
And if that he noght may°, par aventure°,
Or ellis list no swich dispence endure°,
But thynketh it is wasted and ylost,
Thanne moot another payen for oure cost,
Or lene° us gold—and that is perilous.
This noble marchaunt heeld° a worthy hous,
For which he hadde alday° so greet repair°
For his largesse°, and for his wyf was fair,
That wonder is. But herkneth° to my tale:
Amonges alle his gestes grete and smale
Ther was a monk, a fair man and a boold—
I trowe a thritty wynter° he was oold—
That evere in oon° was drawynge to that place.
This yonge monk that was so fair of face

---

1 whilom, *once* **4 revelous,** *inclined to partying* **5 dispence,** *expense* **6 chiere,** *attention,* **reverence,** *respect* **7 hem doon,** *give them* **8 Swiche salutaciouns,** *such greetings,* **contenaunces,** *courtesies* **10 moot,** *must* **11 sely,** *innocent* or *foolish,* **algate,** *always* **12 arraye,** *adorn* **13 worship,** *esteem* **15 noght may,** *is unable to,* **par aventure,** *by chance* **16 ellis list no swich dispence endure,** *else does not wish to endure such expense* **19 lene,** *lend* **20 heeld,** *maintained* **21 alday,** *always,* **so greet repair,** *so many visitors* **22 largesse,** *generosity* **23 herkneth,** *listen* **26 trowe a thritty wynter,** *believe about thirty years* **27 evere in oon,** *constantly*

1 Seint Denys, town north of Paris, known in the Middle Ages for trade and a major abbey. **11–19 us . . . we . . . ,** the first-person pronouns in these lines require a female speaker, almost certainly the Wife of Bath before this tale was reassigned and left unrevised. **26 a,** El reads "of." **27 drawynge,** El reads "comynge."

Aqueynted was so with the goode man
Sith that hir° firste knoweliche° bigan,
That in his hous as famulier was he
As it is possible any freend to be.
And for as muchel as° this goode man
And eek this monk of which that I bigan
Were bothe two yborn in o° village,
The monk hym claymeth as for cosynage;
And he agayn°, he seith nat ones nay
But was as glad therof as fowel° of day,
For to his herte it was a greet plesaunce°.
Thus been they knyt with eterne alliaunce,
And ech of hem gan oother for t'assure°
Of bretherhede whil that hir lyf may dure°.
  Free° was daun John and namely° of dispence°
As in that hous, and ful of diligence
To doon plesaunce and also greet costage°.
He noght forgat to yeve° the leeste page°
In al the hous, but after hir degree°
He yaf° the lord and sitthe° al his meynee°,
Whan that he cam, som manere honest° thyng,
For which they were as glad of his comyng
As fowel° is fayn° whan that the sonne up riseth.
Namoore of this as now, for it suffiseth.
  But so bifel, this marchant on a day
Shoop hym° to make redy his array
Toward the toun of Brugges for to fare°
To byen° there a porcioun of ware°.
For which he hath to Parys° sent anon
A messager, and preyed hath° daun John
That he sholde come to Seint Denys to pleye
With hym and with his wyf a day or tweye,
Er° he to Brugges wente, in alle wise°.
  This noble monk of which I yow devyse°
Hath of his abbot as hym list licence°,
By cause he was a man of heigh prudence
And eek an officer, out for to ryde
To seen° hir graunges° and hire bernes° wyde°,
And unto Seinte Denys he comth anon.
Who was so welcome as my lord daun John,
Oure deere cosyn, ful of curteisye?
With hym broghte he a Jubbe° of malvesye°,
And eek another, ful of fyn vernage°,
And volatyl°, as ay° was his usage°.
And thus I lete hem ete and drynke and pleye,
This marchant and this monk, a day or tweye.
  The thridde day this marchant up ariseth
And on his nedes sadly hym avyseth°,
And up into his countour-hous° gooth he
To rekene with° hymself, wel may be,
Of thilke° yeer how that it with hym stood,
And how that he despended° hadde his good°,
And if that he encressed were or noon.
His bookes and his bagges many oon
He leith° biforn hym on his countyng-bord.
Ful riche was his tresor and his hord,
For which ful faste° his countour-dore he shette°;
And eek he nolde that no man° sholde hym lette°
Of his acountes for the meene tyme;
And thus he sit til it was passed pryme°.
  Daun John was rysen in the morwe° also
And in the gardyn walketh to and fro
And hath his thynges° seyd ful curteisly°.
  This goode wyf cam walkynge pryvely°
Into the gardyn there° he walketh softe°,
And hym saleweth° as she hath doon ofte.
A mayde child cam in hire compaignye
Which as hir list° she may governe and gye°

30 Sith that hir, *since their,* **knoweliche,** *acquaintance* **33 for as muchel as,** *on account of the fact that* **35 o,** *the same* **37 agayn,** *in return* **38 fowel,** *bird* **39 plesaunce,** *pleasure* **41 gan . . . for t'assure,** *did assure* **42 dure,** *last* **43 Free,** *generous,* **namely,** *especially,* **dispence,** *spending* **45 doon . . . costage,** *spend money* **46 yeve,** *give,* **page,** *servant boy* **47 after hir degree,** *in accord with their rank* **48 yaf,** *gave,* **sitthe,** *after,* **meynee,** *household* **49 manere honest,** *kind of appropriate* **51 fowel,** *bird,* **fayn,** *happy* **54 Shoop hym,** *prepared himself* **55 fare,** *go* **56 byen,** *buy,* **porcioun of ware,** *quantity of goods* **57 Parys,** *Paris* **58 preyed hath,** *has asked* **61 Er,** *before,* **wise,** *ways* **62 devyse,** *describe* **63 as hym list licence,** *permission as he wishes* **66 seen,** *oversee,* **graunges,** *farms,* **bernes,** *barns,* **wyde,** *widespread* **70 jubbe,** *jug,* **malvesye,** *sweet Greek wine* **71 vernage,** *sweet Italian wine* **72 volatyl,** *game fowl,* **ay,** *always,* **usage,** *habit* **76 his nedes sadly hym avyseth,** *thinks seriously about his business* **77 countour-hous,** *counting house* (office) **78 rekene with,** *reckon by* **79 thilke,** *that* **80 despended,** *spent,* **good,** *assets* **83 leith,** *lays* **85 ful faste,** *very tightly,* **shette,** *shut* **86 nolde that no man,** *wished that no one,* **lette,** *hinder* **88 pryme,** *about 9 a.m.* **89 morwe,** *morning* **91 thynges,** *prayers,* **ful curteisly,** *very courteously* **92 pryvely,** *secretly* **93 there,** *where,* **softe,** *softly* **94 saleweth,** *greets* **96 as hir list,** *as it pleases her,* **gye,** *guide*

29 goode man, the usual label for the head of a household. **36 cosynage,** kinship. The kinship terms *cosynage* and *cosyn* recur frequently throughout the tale, arguably punning with forms of *cosin* (trickery or deception), which the *MED* first records some fifty years after Chaucer's death. **43 daun,** master, a formulaic address of respect. **Namely,** Hg reads "manly." **47 the house,** Hg reads "that house." **55 Brugges,** Bruges in Flanders (modern Belgium), a mercantile city. **59 to pleye,** Hg reads "and pleye." **65 out for to ryde,** i.e., he is an "outrider," like the Monk in the *GP* 1.166. **73 ete and,** omitted in El.

For yet under the yerde° was the mayde.
"O deere cosyn myn, daun John," she sayde,
"What eyleth° yow so rathe° for to ryse?"
"Nece," quod he, "it oghte ynough suffise
Fyve houres for to slepe upon a nyght
But° it were for an old appalled wight°,
As been thise wedded men that lye and dare°
As in a fourme° sit a wery hare
Were° al forstraught° with houndes grete and smale.
But deere nece, why be ye so pale?
I trowe°, certes°, that oure goode man
Hath yow laboured sith° the nyght bigan
That yow were nede to resten hastily°."
And with that word he lough° ful murily,
And of his owene thought he wax al reed°.
This faire wyf gan for to shake hir heed
And seyde thus, "Ye, God woot° al," quod she.
"Nay, nay, cosyn myn, it stant° nat so with me;
For by that God that yaf° me soule and lyf,
In al the reawme° of France is ther no wyf
That lasse lust hath to° that sory pley.
For I may synge 'allas and weylawey
That I was born,' but to no wight°," quod she,
"Dar I nat telle how that it stant with me.
Wherfore I thynke out of this land to wende°,
Or elles of myself to make an ende,
So ful am I of drede and eek of care."
This monk bigan upon this wyf to stare,
And seyde, "Allas, my nece, God forbede
That ye for any sorwe or any drede
Fordo° youreself. But telleth me youre grief—
Paraventure° I may in youre meschief°
Conseille or helpe; and therfore telleth me
Al youre anoy°, for it shal been secree°.
For on my porthors° I make an ooth
That nevere in my lyf, for lief ne looth°,
Ne shal I of no conseil yow biwreye°."
"The same agayn to yow," quod she, "I seye.
By God and by this porthors I yow swere,
Though men me wolde al into pieces tere,
Ne shal I nevere, for to goon to helle,
Biwreye a word of thyng that ye me telle,
Nat for no cosynage° ne alliance
But verraily° for love and affiance°."
Thus been they sworn, and heerupon they kiste
And ech of hem tolde oother what hem liste°.
"Cosyn," quod she, "if that I hadde a space°,
As I have noon, and namely° in this place,
Thanne wolde I telle a legende of my lyf,
What I have suffred sith° I was a wyf
With myn housbonde, al be he youre cosyn."
"Nay," quod this monk, "by God and Seint Martyn,
He is na moore cosyn unto me
Than is this leef that hangeth on the tree.
I clepe° hym so, by Seint Denys of Fraunce,
To have the moore cause of aqueyntaunce
Of yow, which I have loved specially
Aboven alle wommen, sikerly°.
This swere I yow on my professioun°.
Telleth youre grief, lest that° he come adoun,
And hasteth yow, and gooth youre wey anon."
"My deere love," quod she, "O my daun John,
Ful lief were me° this conseil° for to hyde,
But out it moot°; I may namoore abyde°.
Myn housbonde is to me the worste man
That evere was sith° that the world bigan.
But sith I am a wyf, it sit° nat me
To tellen no wight of oure privetee,
Neither abedde ne in noon oother place;
God shilde° I sholde it tellen, for his grace!
A wyf ne shal nat seyn of hir housbonde
But al honour, as I kan understonde—
Save° unto yow thus muche I tellen shal:
As helpe me God, he is noght worth at al

97 the yerde, *supervision* **99 eyleth,** *ails,* **rathe,** *early* **102 But,** *unless,* **appalled wight,** *feeble person* **103 dare,** *cower* **104 fourme,** *burrow* **105 Were,** *when it is,* **forstraught,** *distraught* **107 trowe,** *think,* **certes,** *surely* **108 sith,** *since* **109 hastily,** *soon* **110 lough,** *laughed* **111 wax al reed,** i.e., *blushed* **113 woot,** *knows* **114 stant,** *stands* **115 yaf,** *gave* **116 reawme,** *realm* **117 lasse lust hath to,** *less pleasure has for* **119 wight,** *person* **121 wende,** *travel* **127 Fordo,** *kill* **128 Paraventure,** *perhaps,* **meschief,** *misfortune* **130 anoy,** *trouble,* **secree,** *secret* **131 porthors,** *breviary* (prayer book) **132 lief ne looth,** *love nor hate* **133 biwreye,** *betray* **139 cosynage,** *kinship* (see 36n) **140 verraily,** *truly,* **affiance,** *trust* **142 hem liste,** *they pleased* **143 space,** *while* **144 namely,** *especially* **146 sith,** *since* **151 clepe,** *call* **154 sikerly,** *certainly* **155 professioun,** *monastic vows* **156 lest that,** *before* **159 Ful lief were me,** *very much I would like,* **conseil,** *secret* **160 out it moot,** *it must come out,* **abyde,** *wait* **162 sith,** *since* **163 sit,** *suits* **166 shilde,** *forbid* **169 Save,** *except*

100 Nece, kinswoman; a term of address for a female relative. **114 Nay, nay,** Hg reads "nay." **127 telleth me,** El reads "telleth me of." **128 I may,** El reads "I yow may." **135 yow,** omitted in Hg. **147 youre cosyn,** El reads "of youre kyn." **148 Seint Martyn,** St. Martin of Tours, founded the first monastery in France. El reads "by Seint Martyn." **151 Seint Denys,** St. Denis, patron saint of France. **156 lest that he come adoun,** i.e., quickly before he comes down. As in modern usage, "lest that" is used to express fear or apprehension. **157 youre wey,** Hg reads "awey."

In no degree° the value of a flye.
But yet me greveth moost his nygardye°.
And wel ye woot° that wommen naturelly
Desiren thynges sixe as wel as I:
They wolde that hir housbondes sholde be
Hardy°, and wise, and riche, and therto free°,
And buxom° unto his wyf, and fressh abedde°.
But by that ilke° Lord that for us bledde,
For his honour myself for to arraye,
A° Sonday next I most nedes paye°
An hundred frankes, or ellis I am lorn°.
Yet were me levere° that I were unborn
Than me were doon a sclaundre or vileynye.
And if myn housbonde eek it myghte espye°,
I nere° but lost. And therfore I yow preye,
Lene° me this somme°, or ellis moot° I deye.
Daun John, I seye lene me thise hundred frankes.
Pardee°, I wol nat faille yow my thankes,
If that yow list° to doon that I yow praye.
For at a certeyn day I wol yow paye,
And doon to yow what plesance° and service
That I may doon, right° as yow list devise°.
And but° I do, God take on me vengeance
As foul as evere hadde Genylon of France."
   This gentil monk answerde in this manere,
"Now trewely, myn owene lady deere,
I have," quod he, "on yow so greet a routhe°
That I yow swere and plighte° yow my trouthe°
That whan youre housbonde is to Flaundres fare°,
I wol delyvere yow out of this care,
For I wol brynge yow an hundred frankes."
And with that word he caughte hire by the flankes,
And hire embraceth harde, and kiste hire ofte.
"Gooth now youre wey," quod he, "al stille and
      softe°,
And lat us dyne as soone as that ye may,
For by my chilyndre° it is pryme of day°,
Gooth now, and beeth as trewe as I shal be."
   "Now elles° God forbede, sire," quod she,
And forth she gooth as jolif as a pye,
And bad° the cookes that they sholde
      hem hye°
So that men myghte dyne, and that anon.
Up to hir housbonde is this wyf ygon,
And knokketh at his countour° boldely.
   "Qui la°?" quod he. "Peter, it am I,"
Quod she; "what sire, how longe wol ye faste?
How longe tyme wol ye rekene° and caste°
Youre sommes°, and youre bookes, and youre
      thynges?
The devel have part on° alle swiche rekenynges!
Ye have ynough, pardee, of Goddes sonde°.
Com doun today, and lat youre bagges
      stonde.
Ne be ye nat ashamed that daun John
Shal fasting al this day alenge goon°?
What, lat us heere a messe° and go we dyne."
   "Wyf," quod this man, "litel kanstow devyne°
The curious° bisynesse that we have.
For of us chapmen°, also° God me save,
And by that lord that clepid° is Seint Yve,
Scarsly amonges twelve tweye° shul thryve
Continuelly, lastynge unto oure age.
We may wel make chiere and good visage°,
And dryve forth° the world as it may be,
And kepen oure estaat in pryvetee°
Til we be deed, or elles that° we pleye°
A pilgrymage, or goon out of the weye°.
And therfore have I greet necessitee
Upon this queynte° world t'avyse me,

171 In no degree, *in no way* **172 nygardye,** *stinginess* **173 woot,** *know* **175 wolde,** *wish* **176 Hardy,** *bold,* **therto free,** *also generous* **177 buxom,** *obedient,* **fressh abedde,** *lively in bed* **178 ilke,** *same* **180 A,** *by,* **most nedes paye,** *need to pay* **181 lorn,** *lost* **182 were me levere,** *I would rather* **184 espye,** *discover* **185 nere,** *would be nothing* **186 Lene,** *loan,* **somme,** *sum,* **moot,** *must* **188 Pardee,** *by God* **189 list,** *choose* **191 plesance,** *pleasure* **192 right,** *just,* **list devise,** *wish to devise* **193 but,** *unless* **197 routhe,** *pity* **198 plighte,** *pledge,* **trouthe,** *word* **199 fare,** *gone* **204 al stille and softe,** i.e., *quietly* **206 chilyndre,** *pocket sundial,* **pryme of day,** *9 a.m.* **208 elles,** *otherwise* **210 bad,** *ordered,* **hem hye,** *hurry themselves* **213 countour,** *counting house* (see line 77) **214 Quila,** *who's there* (Fr.) **216 rekene,** *reckon,* **caste,** *project* **217 sommes,** *sums* **218 have part on,** *take a portion of* **219 sonde,** *gifts* **222 alenge goon,** *go unhappy* **223 messe,** *mass* **224 kanstow devyne,** *can you imagine* **225 curious,** *intricate* **226 chapmen,** *merchants,* **also,** *so* (may) **227 clepid,** *named* **228 tweye,** *two* **230 visage,** *face* **231 dryve forth,** *advance* **232 pryvetee,** *secrecy* **233 elles that,** *otherwise,* **pleye,** *perform* **234 goon out of the weye,** *go into hiding* **236 queynte,** *complicated*

180 most, Hg reads "moot." **181 hundred frankes,** one hundred gold coins, a sizable sum. **I am,** Hg reads "am I." **183 Than me were doon a sclaundre or vileynye,** than an embarrassment or dishonor were done to me. The wife fears that her debt (for clothing) will be made known, presumably jeopardizing future borrowing. **184 it myghte,** Hg reads "myghte it." **194 Genylon,** Ganelon, who betrayed Roland in *Chanson de Roland,* was torn to pieces by horses. **209 jolif as a pye,** jolly as a magpie, i.e., happy as a lark. **212 is this,** Hg reads "is his." **214 Qui la,** El and Hg read "Who ther," an English translation of the French; the French is in the margin. **Peter,** by St. Peter, keeper of the gates of heaven. **223 What,** omitted in El. **227 Seint Yve,** St. Ivo of Chartres? A convenient rhyme?

For everemoore we moote° stonde in drede
Of hap° and fortune in oure chapmanhede°.
"To Flaunders wol I go tomorwe at day,
And come agayn as soone as evere I may.
For which, my deere wyf, I thee biseke°
As be to every wight° buxom° and meke,
And for to kepe° oure good° be curious°,
And honestly governe wel oure hous.
Thou hast ynough, in every maner wise,
That to a thrifty houshold may suffise.
Thee lakketh noon array° ne no vitaille°;
Of silver in thy purs shaltow° nat faille°."
And with that word his countour-dore he shette,
And doun he gooth, no lenger wolde he lette°.
But hastily a messe° was ther seyd,
And spedily the tables were yleyd°,
And to the dyner faste they hem spedde,
And richely this monk the chapman fedde.
At after-dyner daun John sobrely
This chapman took apart, and prively
He seyde hym thus, "Cosyn, it standeth so
That wel I se to Brugges wol ye go.
God and Seint Austyn spede yow and gyde°!
I prey yow, cosyn, wisely that ye ryde.
Governeth yow also of youre diete
Atemprely°, and namely° in this hete°.
Bitwix us two nedeth no strange fare°.
Farewel, cosyn. God shilde° yow fro care.
And if that any thyng by day or nyght,
If it lye in my power and my myght,
That ye me wol comande in any wyse,
It shal be doon right° as ye wol devyse.
"O thyng, er that ye goon, if it may be:
I wolde prey yow for to lene° me
An hundred frankes for a wyke° or tweye,
For certein beestes that I moste beye
To stoore with° a place that is oures.
God helpe me so, I wolde it were youres!
I shal nat faille surely at my day,
Nat for a thousand frankes, a mile way.
But lat this thyng be secree°, I yow preye,
For yet tonyght thise beestes moot I beye.
And fare now wel, myn owene cosyn deere;
Graunt mercy of° youre cost and of youre cheere°."
This noble marchant gentilly anon
Answerde and seyde, "O cosyn myn, daun John,
Now sikerly° this is a smal requeste.
My gold is youres whan that it yow leste°,
And nat oonly my gold but my chaffare°.
Take what yow list°, God shilde° that ye spare°.
"But o thyng is, ye knowe it wel ynogh,
Of chapmen that hir moneie is hir plogh°,
We may creaunce° whil we have a name°,
But goldlees for to be it is no game.
Paye it agayn whan it lith° in youre ese;
After my myght° ful fayn° wolde I yow plese."
Thise hundred frankes he fette° forth anon,
And prively he took hem to daun John.
No wight° in al this world wiste° of this lone°
Savynge this marchant and daun John allone.
They drynke, and speke, and rome° a while and pleye,
Til that daun John rideth to his abbeye.
The morwe cam, and forth this marchant rideth
To Flaundres-ward; his prentys° wel hym gydeth°
Til he cam into Brugges murily.
Now gooth this marchant faste and bisily
Aboute his nede, and byeth° and creaunceth°.
He neither pleyeth at the dees° ne daunceth,
But as a marchaunt, shortly for to telle,
He let° his lyf, and there I lete hym dwelle.
The Sonday next° this marchant was agon,
To Seint Denys ycomen is daun John,
With crowne° and berd al fressh and newe yshave.

---

237 moote, *must* **238 hap,** *chance,* **chapmanhede,** *trading* **241 biseke,** *request* **242 wight,** *person,* **buxom,** *helpful* **243 kepe,** *protect,* **good,** *property,* **curious,** *careful* **247 array,** *clothing,* **vitaille,** *food* **248 shaltow,** *you shall,* **faille,** *lack* **250 lette,** *delay* **251 messe,** *mass* **252 yleyd,** *laid* **259 gyde,** *guide* **262 Atemprely,** *moderately,* **namely,** *especially,* **hete,** *heat* **263 nedeth no strange fare,** (there) *need be no elaborate parting* **264 shilde,** *protect* **268 right,** *just* **270 lene,** *loan* **271 wyke,** *week* **273 stoore with,** *stock* **277 secree,** *secret* **280 Graunt mercy of,** *many thanks for,* **cheere,** *hospitality* **283 sikerly,** *surely* **284 it yow leste,** *you want it* **285 chaffare,** *merchandise* **286 list,** *desire,* **shilde,** *forbid,* **spare,** *refrain* **288 plogh,** *plow* **289 creaunce,** *obtain credit,* **name,** *reputation* **291 lith,** *lies* **292 myght,** *ability,* **ful fayn,** *very gladly* **293 fette,** *fetched* **295 wight,** *person,* **wiste,** *knew,* **lone,** *loan* **297 rome,** *stroll* **300 prentys,** *apprentice,* **gydeth,** *leads* **303 byeth,** *purchases,* **creaunceth,** *buys on credit* **304 dees,** *dice* **306 let,** *leads* **307 next,** *after* **309 crowne,** *head*

259 Seint Austyn, St. Augustine of Hippo. **272 beestes that I moste beye,** animals that I must buy. The monk is responsible for his monastery's farms; see lines 62–66 above. **275 at my,** Hg reads "of my." **276 a mile way,** i.e., I won't be late by even the time it takes to walk a mile, about twenty minutes. **293 fette forth,** El reads "fette hym forth." **304 at the,** El omits "the." **307 this,** Hg reads "the."

In al the hous ther nas so litel a knave°,
Ne no wight elles°, that he nas ful fayn°
That my lord daun John was come agayn.
And shortly to the point right for to gon,
This faire wyf acorded° with daun John
That for thise hundred frankes he sholde al nyght
Have hire in his armes bolt upright°.
And this acord parfourned° was in dede;
In myrthe al nyght a bisy lyf they lede
Til it was day, that daun John wente his way,
And bad the meynee°, "Farewel, have good day,"
For noon of hem, ne no wight in the toun,
Hath of daun John right no° suspecioun.
And forth he rydeth hoom to his abbeye,
Or where hym list°; namoore of hym I seye.
This marchant, whan that ended was the faire,
To Seint Denys he gan for to repaire°,
And with his wyf he maketh feeste and cheere°,
And telleth hire that chaffare° is so deere°
That nedes moste he make a chevyssaunce°,
For he was bounded in a reconyssaunce°
To paye twenty thousand sheeld anon°.
For which this marchant is to Parys gon
To borwe of certeine freendes that he hadde
A certeyn frankes, and somme with him he ladde.
And whan that he was come into the toun,
For greet chiertee° and greet affeccioun,
Unto daun John he gooth hym first—to pleye,
Nat for to axe° or borwe of hym moneye,
But for to wite and seen of° his welfare,
And for to tellen hym of his chaffare°,
As freendes doon whan they been met yfeere°.
Daun John hym° maketh feeste and murye cheere,
And he hym tolde agayn°, ful specially,
How he hadde wel yboght and graciously°,
Thanked be God, al hool° his marchandise,
Save° that he moste, in alle maner wise,
Maken a chevyssaunce° as for his beste°,
And thanne he sholde been in joye and reste.
Daun John answerde, "Certes°, I am fayn°
That ye in heele° ar comen hom agayn.
And if that I were riche, as have I blisse,
Of twenty thousand sheeld sholde ye nat mysse°,
For ye so kyndely this oother day
Lente me gold; and as I kan and may,
I thanke yow, by God and by Seint Jame.
But nathelees, I took unto oure dame
Youre wyf at hom the same gold ageyn
Upon youre bench; she woot° it wel, certeyn,
By certeyn tokenes° that I kan yow telle.
Now, by youre leve, I may no lenger dwelle.
Oure abbot wole out of this toun anon,
And in his compaignye moot° I goon.
Grete° wel oure dame, myn owene nece sweete,
And fare wel, deere cosyn, til we meete."
This marchant, which that was ful war and wys,
Creanced° hath, and payd eek in Parys
To certeyn Lumbardes redy in hir hond
The somme of gold, and gat of hem his bond,
And hoom he gooth murie as a papejay°,
For wel he knew he stood in swich array°
That nedes moste he wynne° in that viage°
A thousand frankes aboven al his costage°.
His wyf ful redy mette hym atte gate,
As she was wont of oold usage algate°,
And al that nyght in myrthe they bisette°,
For he was riche and cleerly out of dette.
Whan it was day, this marchant gan embrace
His wyf al newe°, and kiste hire on hir face,

---

310 knave, *boy servant* **311 wight elles,** *other person,* **fayn,** *happy* **314 acorded,** *agreed* **316 bolt upright,** *flat on her back* **317 acord parfourned,** *agreement performed* **320 meynee,** *household* **322 right no,** *any* **324 hym list,** *it pleases him* **326 gan . . . to repaire,** *did return* **327 feeste and cheere,** *celebration and entertainment* **328 chaffare,** *merchandise,* **deere,** *expensive* **329 nedes moste he make a chevyssaunce,** *he must necessarily take a loan* **330 reconyssaunce,** *contract* **331 sheeld anon,** *units of credit immediately* **336 chiertee,** *friendship* **338 axe,** *ask* **339 for to wite and seen of,** *to know and look after* **340 chaffare,** *trading* **341 yfeere,** *together* **342 hym,** *for him* **343 agayn,** *in response* **344 graciously,** *favorably* **345 al hool,** *completely* **346 Save,** *except* **347 Maken a chevyssaunce,** *take out a loan,* **beste,** *advantage* **349 Certes,** *surely,* **fayn,** *happy* **350 in heele,** *in prosperity* **352 mysse,** *lack* **358 woot,** *knows* **359 tokenes,** *evidence* **362 moot,** *must* **363 Grete,** *greet* **366 Creanced,** *borrowed* **369 papejay,** *parrot* (see 209n) **370 swich array,** *such an arrangement* **371 wynne,** *profit,* **viage,** *venture* **372 costage,** *expenses* **374 wont of oold usage algate,** *accustomed to by regular habit always* **375 bisette,** *applied* (themselves) **378 al newe,** *anew*

313 to the point right, El reads "right to the point." **325 faire,** trade fair, where buyers and sellers come together for purchase and exchange. The merchant is evidently there to purchase on credit goods that he later expects to sell at a profit. **333–34 borwe . . . / A certeyn frankes, and somme with him he ladde,** borrow . . . some francs (French coins), and he took some with him. **337 gooth hym first,** Hg reads "first goth hym." **366–68 payd eek in Parys . . . Lumbardes redy in hir hond . . . his bond,** repaid in Paris to Lombard bankers the sum of gold (which he borrowed in Bruges, line 330) in return for the original promissory note (**bond,** line 368). Lombard bankers were well known for their international transactions. Nowhere in the tale is the buying or selling straightforward. **368 gat,** El reads "hadde."

And up he gooth° and maketh it ful tough°.
“Namoore,” quod she, “by God, ye have ynough!”
And wantownely agayn° with hym she pleyde,
Til atte laste thus this marchant seyde,
“By God,” quod he, “I am a litel wrooth°
With yow, my wyf, although it be me looth°.
And woote° ye why? By God, as that I gesse
That ye han maad a manere straungenesse°
Bitwixen me and my cosyn daun John.
Ye sholde han warned me, er I had gon,
That he yow hadde an hundred frankes payed
By redy tokene°; and heeld hym yvele apayed°
For that I to hym spak of chevyssaunce°—
Me semed so° as by his contenaunce.
But nathelees, by God oure hevene kyng,
I thoughte° nat to axen hym° no thyng.
I prey thee, wyf, as do namoore so;
Telle me alwey er that I fro thee go
If any dettour hath in myn absence
Ypayed thee, lest thurgh thy necligence
I myghte hym axe a thing that he hath payed.”
This wyf was nat afered° nor affrayed°,
But boldely she seyde, and that anon,
“Marie°, I deffie the false monk, daun John!
I kepe° nat of his tokenes° never a deel°.
He took° me certeyn° gold, that woot° I weel.
What, yvel thedam° on his monkes snowte°,
For, God it woot°, I wende° withouten doute
That he hadde yeve° it me bycause of yow,
To doon therwith myn honour and my prow°,
For cosynage°, and eek for beele° cheere
That he hath had ful ofte tymes heere.
But sith° I se I stonde in this disjoynt°,
I wol answere yow shortly to the poynt:
Ye han mo slakkere° dettours than am I!
For I wol paye yow wel and redily
Fro day to day, and if so be I faille,
I am youre wyf; score° it upon my taille
And I shal paye as soone as ever I may.
For by my trouthe, I have on myn array°,
And nat on wast°, bistowed° every deel°,
And for I have bistowed it so weel
For youre honour, for Goddes sake, I seye
As° be nat wrooth°, but lat us laughe and pleye.
Ye shal my joly body have to wedde°.
By God, I wol nat paye yow but a-bedde!
Forgyve it me, myn owene spouse deere;
Turne hiderward°, and maketh bettre cheere.”
This marchant saugh ther was no remedie,
And for to chide it nere° but greet folie
Sith that° the thyng may nat amended be.
“Now wyf,” he seyde, “and I foryeve it thee;
But by thy lyf, ne be namoore so large°.
Keep bet° oure good, that yeve° I thee in charge.”
Thus endeth now my tale, and God us sende
Taillynge ynough unto oure lyves ende.
Amen.

Heere endeth the Shipmannes Tale.

Bihoold the murie wordes of the Hoost to the Shipman and to the Lady Prioresse.

“Wel seyd, by corpus dominus,” quod oure Hoost,
“Now longe moote° thou saille by the cost°,
Sire gentil maister, gentil maryneer!
God yeve° this monk a thousand last quade yeer°.
Aha, felawes, beth war° of swich a jape°!

---

379 gooth, *rises,* **maketh it ful tough,** *acts proud* **381 wantownely agayn,** *lasciviously in return* **383 wrooth,** *peeved* **384 it be me looth,** *I hate to be* **385 woote,** *know* **386 manere straungenesse,** *a kind of distance* **390 By redy tokene,** *with clear evidence,* **heeld hym yvele apayed,** *he thought himself mistreated* **391 chevyssaunce,** *borrowing* **392 Me semed so,** *it seemed so to me* **394 thoughte,** *intended,* **axen hym,** *ask of him* **399 hym axe,** *ask him* (for) **400 afered,** *frightened,* **affrayed,** *afraid* **402 Marie,** *by Mary* **403 kepe,** *care,* **tokenes,** *evidence,* **never a deel,** *not at all* **404 took,** *gave,* **certeyn,** *some,* **woot,** *know* **405 yvel thedam,** *evil luck,* **snowte,** *snout* **406 woot,** *knows,* **wende,** *thought* **407 yeve,** *given* **408 prow,** *advantage* **409 cosynage,** *kinship* (see 36n above) **409 beele,** *good* **411 sith,** *since,* **disjoynt,** *difficulty* **413 mo slakkere,** *more unreliable* **416 score,** *record* **418 array,** *clothing* **419 on wast,** *in waste,* **bistowed,** *spent,* **deel,** *bit* **422 As,** *so,* **wrooth,** *angry* **423 to wedde,** *in pledge* **426 hiderward,** *this way* **428 for to chide it nere,** *to scold would be nothing* **429 Sith that,** *since* **430 large,** *unthrifty* **432 bet,** *better,* **yeve,** *give* **436 moote,** *may,* **cost,** *coast* **438 yeve,** *give,* **last quade yeer,** *cartloads of bad years* **439 beth war,** *beware,* **jape,** *trick*

384 be, El reads “were.” **389 an hundred,** Hg reads “a hundred.” **394 axen hym,** Hg reads “axe of hym.” **395 as do,** Hg reads “ne do.” **411 I stonde,** Hg reads “it stonde.” **416 taille,** pun on tally (account or tax) and tail (sexual sense). The pun occurs again at line 434. **419 on wast,** Hg reads “in wast.” **428 greet folie,** Hg omits “greet.” **432 oure,** Hg reads “thy.” **that yeve,** Hg reads “this yeve.” **435 corpus dominus,** the Host's mistake for *corpus domini,* the Lord's body. **437 Sire,** Hg reads “Thow.” **438 this monk,** Hg reads “the monk.”

The monk putte in the mannes hood an ape,
And in his wyves eek, by Seint Austyn.
Draweth no monkes moore unto youre in°.
"But now passe over and lat us seke° aboute:
Who shal now telle first of al this route°
Another tale?" And with that word he sayde,
As curteisly as it had been a mayde,
"My lady Prioresse, by youre leve°,
So that I wiste° I sholde yow nat greve°,
I wolde demen° that ye tellen sholde
A tale next, if so were that ye wolde.
Now wol ye vouchesauf°, my lady deere?"
"Gladly," quod she, and seyde as ye shal
heere.

Explicit.

442 in, *house* (inn) **443 seke,** *look* **444 route,** *company* **447 leve,** *permission*
448 wiste, *knew,* **greve,** *offend* **449 demen,** *judge* **451 vouchesauf,** *consent*

440 putte in the mannes hood an ape, put a monkey in the man's hood, i.e., made a monkey of him. **441 Seint Austyn,** St. Augustine of Hippo. **442 unto,** Hg reads "into."

From woodcut made by W.H. Hooper and published by the Chaucer Society between 1868 and 1879

Prioress's Tale

Prologue

The Prologe of the Prioresses Tale.

Domine dominus noster.

O Lord, oure Lord, thy name how merveillous
Is in this large world ysprad°, quod she,
For noght oonly thy laude° precious
Parfourned° is by men of dignitee,
But by the mouth of children thy bountee°
Parfourned is, for on the brest soukynge°
Somtyme shewen° they thyn heriynge°.

Wherfore in laude°, as I best kan or may,
Of thee and of the white lylye flour
Which that the bar°, and is a mayde alway,
To telle a storie I wol do my labour—
Nat that I may encreessen hir honour,
For she hirself is honour and the roote
Of bountee, next hir Sone, and soules boote°.

O mooder mayde, O mayde mooder free°!
O bussh unbrent, brennynge in Moyses sighte,
That ravysedest° doun fro the deitee,
Thurgh thyn humblesse, the goost° that in th'alighte°,
Of whos vertu° whan he thyn herte lighte°
Conceyved was the Fadres sapience,
Help me to telle it in thy reverence.

Lady, thy bountee, thy magnificence,
Thy vertu, and thy grete humylitee,

---

454 ysprad, *spread* **455 laude,** *praise* **456 Parfourned,** *performed* **457 bountee,** *goodness* **458 soukynge,** *sucking* **459 shewen,** *show,* **heriynge,** *praising* **460 laude,** *praise* **462 Which that the bar,** *she who bore you* (i.e., Mary) **466 boote,** *remedy* **467 free,** *bountiful* **469 ravysedest,** *ravished* **470 goost,** *Holy Spirit,* **th'alighte,** *alighted in you* **471 vertu,** *power,* **lighte,** *illuminated*

452a Domine dominus noster, Lord, our lord [how excellent is your name]; translated in line 453, a version of Psalms 8.1 (Vulgate 8.2), used in the liturgy of the Blessed Virgin and in the mass of the Holy Innocents (December 23). **454 quod she,** carries on without a break from epilogue of *ShT* (line 452), although the verse form shifts to rhyme royal. **461 white lylye flour,** the white lily is an emblem of Mary's purity. **468 bussh unbrent, brennynge in Moyses sighte,** bush unburned, burning, i.e., the burning bush that Moses saw (Exodus 3.2), a prefiguration of the Virgin Birth. **472 Fadres sapience,** Father's Wisdom, i.e., Christ; 1 Corinthians 1.24. **474–80** Echoes Dante's *Paradiso* 3.16–21.

Ther may no tonge expresse in no science°,
For somtyme, Lady, er° men praye to thee,
Thou goost biforn° of thy benyngnytee°,
And getest° us the lyght of thy preyere
To gyden° us unto thy Sone so deere.

My konnyng° is so wayk°, O blisful queene,
For to declare thy grete worthynesse
That I ne may the weighte nat susteene,
But as a child of twelf monthe oold or lesse
That kan unnethe° any word expresse,
Right so fare° I, and therfore I yow preye,
Gydeth° my song that I shal of yow seye.

Explicit.

Heere bigynneth the Prioresses Tale.

Ther was in Asye° in a greet citee
Amonges Cristene folk a Jewerye°
Sustened by a lord of that contree
For foul usure and lucre of vileynye°,
Hateful to Crist and to his compaignye;
And thurgh the strete° men myghte ride or wende°,
For it was free and open at eyther ende.

A litel scole° of Cristen folk ther stood
Doun at the ferther ende, in which ther were
Children an heep° ycomen of Cristen blood,
That lerned in that scole yeer by yere
Swich manere doctrine° as men used there,
This is to seyn, to syngen and to rede,
As smale children doon in hire childhede.

Among thise children was a wydwes° sone,
A litel clergeoun° seven yeer of age,
That day by day to scole was his wone°,
And eek also, where as° he saugh th'ymage
Of Cristes mooder, hadde he in usage°,
As hym was taught, to knele adoun and seye
His *Ave Marie* as he goth by the weye.

Thus hath this wydwe hir litel sone ytaught
Oure blisful Lady, Cristes mooder deere,
To worshipe ay°, and he forgat it naught,
For sely° child wol alday° soone leere°.
But ay whan I remembre on this mateere,
Seint Nicholas stant° evere in my presence,
For he so yong to Crist dide reverence.

This litel child his litel book lernynge,
As he sat in the scole at his prymer,
He *Alma redemptoris* herde synge,
As children lerned hire antiphoner°;
And as he dorste°, he drough° hym ner° and ner,
And herkned ay° the wordes and the noote,
Til he the firste vers koude al by rote°.

Noght wiste he° what this Latyn was to seye°,
For he so yong and tendre was of age.
But on a day his felawe gan he preye°
T'expounden° hym this song in his langage,
Or telle hym why this song was in usage°;
This preyde he hym to construe° and declare
Ful often tyme upon his knowes° bare.

---

476 science, *factual way* **477 er,** *before* **478 goost biforn,** *go before,* **benyngnytee,** *generosity* **479 getest,** *wins* **480 gyden,** *guide* **481 konnyng,** *understanding,* **wayk,** *feeble* **485 unnethe,** *scarcely* **486 Right so fare,** *just so do* **487 Gydeth,** *guide* **488 Asye,** *Asia* **489 Jewerye,** *Jewish ghetto* **491 lucre of vileynye,** *wicked profits* **493 strete,** *street,* **wende,** *walk* **495 scole,** *school* **497 Children an heep,** *a number of children* **499 Swich manere doctrine,** *such kind of teaching* **502 wydwes,** *widow's* **503 clergeoun,** *schoolboy,* **wone,** *custom* **505 where as,** *wherever* **506 hadde he in usage,** *he was accustomed* **511 ay,** *always* **512 sely,** (an) *innocent,* **alday,** *always,* **leere,** *learn* **514 stant,** *stands* **519 antiphoner,** *religious songbook* **520 dorste,** *dared,* **drough,** *drew,* **ner,** *nearer* **521 herkned ay,** *listened constantly to* **522 koude al by rote,** *knew by heart* **523 Noght wiste he,** *he knew not at all,* **was to seye,** i.e., *meant* **525 gan he preye,** *he asked* **526 T'expounden,** *to explain* **527 in usage,** *used* **528 construe,** *interpret* **529 knowes,** *knees*

479 the lyght, El reads "thurgh lyght." **491 usure,** usury, i.e., lending money for profit at excessive interest rates. Church law forbade usury, although there was no consistency concerning what rate constituted usury. Royalty often protected Jewish lenders to ensure tax revenue and access to loans. **503 seven yeer,** in analogous tales, he is ten. **506 hadde he,** El reads "he hadde." **508 *Ave Marie,*** Hail Mary, the most popular prayer to Mary, based on the Annunciation, the greeting of the angel Gabriel to Mary at the time that she conceived Jesus; Luke 1.28, 42. **512** Proverbial. **Alday,** Hg reads "alwey." **514 Seint Nicholas,** patron saint of schoolboys, known for his piety when an infant. **517 prymer,** first schoolbook, made up of alphabet, prayers, Ten Commandments, etc. **518 *Alma redemptoris,*** Mother of the Redeemer, a Latin song used in religious services from four weeks before Christmas until February 2.

His felawe, which that elder was than he,
Answerde hym thus, "This song, I have herd seye,
Was maked of oure blisful Lady free°,
Hire to salue°, and eek hire for to preye
To been oure help and socour° whan we deye°.
I kan° namoore expounde in this mateere;
I lerne song, I kan° but smal grammeere."

"And is this song maked in reverence
Of Cristes mooder?" seyde this innocent.
"Now, certes°, I wol do my diligence
To konne° it al er Cristemasse be went°—
Though that I for my prymer shal be shent°,
And shal be beten thries° in an houre,
I wol it konne° Oure Lady for to honoure."

His felawe taughte hym homward prively°,
Fro day to day, til he koude it by rote,
And thanne he song it wel and boldely.
Fro word to word, acordynge with the note.
Twies a day it passed thurgh his throte,
To scoleward and homward whan he wente;
On Cristes mooder set was his entente.

As I have seyd, thurghout the Juerie°
This litel child, as he cam to and fro,
Ful murily than wolde he synge and crie
O Alma redemptoris everemo.
The swetnesse his herte perced so
Of Cristes mooder that to hire to preye
He kan nat stynte° of syngyng by the weye.

Oure firste foo, the serpent Sathanas°,
That hath in Jues° herte his waspes nest,
Up swal° and seide, "O Hebrayk peple, allas,
Is this to yow a thyng that is honest°,
That swich a boy shal walken as hym lest°
In youre despit°, and synge of swich sentence°,
Which is agayn youre lawes reverence°?"

Fro thennes forth the Jues han conspired
This innocent out of this world to chace°.
An homycide° therto han they hyred
That in an aleye° hadde a privee° place;
And as the child gan forby for to pace°,
This cursed Jew hym hente° and heeld hym faste,
And kitte° his throte and in a pit hym caste.

I seye that in a wardrobe° they hym threwe
Where as thise Jewes purgen hire entraille°.
O cursed folk of Herodes al newe,
What may youre yvel entente yow availle°?
Mordre wol out, certeyn, it wol nat faille,
And namely ther° th'onour of God shal sprede;
The blood out crieth on youre cursed dede.

O martir sowded° to virginitee,
Now maystow° syngen, folwynge evere in oon°
The white Lamb celestial—quod she—
Of which the grete evaungelist Seint John
In Pathmos wroot, which seith that they that goon
Biforn this Lamb and synge a song al newe,
That nevere flesshly° wommen they ne knewe.

This poure wydwe awaiteth al that nyght
After hir litel child, but he cam noght;
For which, as soone as it was dayes lyght,
With face pale of drede and bisy thoght,
She hath at scole and elleswhere hym soght,
Til finally she gan so fer espie°
That he last seyn was in the Juerie.

532 free, *generous* **533 salue,** *greet* **534 socour,** *aid,* **deye,** *die* **535 kan,** *can* **536 kan,** *know* **539 certes,** *surely* **540 konne,** *know,* **be went,** *is gone* **541 shent,** *scolded* **542 beten thries,** *beaten three times* **543 konne,** *learn* **544 homward prively,** *on the way home secretly* **551 Juerie,** *ghetto* **557 stynte,** *stop* **558 Sathanas,** *Satan* **559 Jues,** *Jews'* **560 swal,** *swelled* **561 honest,** *honorable* **562 hym lest,** *he pleases* **563 despit,** *scorn,* **of swich sentence,** *with such a meaning* **564 reverence,** *honor* **566 chace,** *banish* **567 homycide,** *murderer* **568 aleye,** *alley,* **privee,** *secret* **569 gan forby to pace,** *did walk by* **570 hente,** *seized* **571 kitte,** *cut* **572 wardrobe,** *cesspit* **573 purgen hire entraille,** *empty their bowels* **575 availle,** *help* **577 namely ther,** *especially where* **579 sowded,** *joined* **580 maystow,** *may you,* **evere in oon,** *forever* **585 flesshly,** *sexually* **591 espie,** *discover*

536 I kan but smal grammeere, I know only a little grammar (i.e., Latin). The boy's older friend is not in the analogues, and the fact that neither boy understands the words of the song increases the distance between comprehension and faith. Compare with the Prioress's own lack of understanding, lines 481–85. **540 be,** El and Hg read "is." **545 koude it by rote,** knew it by heart; compare *PardT* 6.332. **547 word to word,** El reads "word to word to word." **564 youre,** El and Hg read "oure." **568 hadde a,** Hg reads "at a." **574 folk of Herodes al newe,** present-day people of Herod, the ruler of the Jews, who at Christ's birth ordered all newborn children killed; Matthew 2.16. **576** Proverbial. **577 ther,** Hg reads "theras." **581–83 white Lamb . . . Pathmos,** the vision of the Heavenly Lamb (Christ) in procession with 144,000 virgins is in Revelation 14.1ff, attributed in the Middle Ages to St. John the evangelist (gospel writer), written on the isle of Patmos. Children who died early were associated with virgins. **581 quod she,** evidently the Prioress (and a convenient rhyme).

With moodres pitee in hir brest enclosed,
She gooth, as she were half out of hir mynde,
To every place where she hath supposed
By liklihede hir litel child to fynde;
And evere on Cristes mooder meeke and kynde
She cride, and atte laste thus she wroghte°,
Among the cursed Jues she hym soghte.

She frayneth° and she preyeth pitously
To every Jew that dwelte in thilke° place
To telle hire if hir child wente oght forby°.
They seyde "nay"; but Jhesu of his grace
Yaf in hir thoght° in with a litel space°
That in that place after hir sone she cryde
Where he was casten in a pit bisyde.

O grete God, that parfournest thy laude°
By mouth of innocentz, lo heere thy myght!
This gemme of chastite, this emeraude°,
And eek of martirdom the ruby bright,
Ther° he with throte ykorven° lay upright°,
He *Alma redemptoris* gan to synge
So loude that al the place gan to rynge.

The Cristene folk that thurgh the strete wente
In coomen° for to wondre upon this thyng,
And hastily they for the provost° sente.
He cam anon withouten tariyng,
And herieth° Crist that is of hevene kyng,
And eek his mooder, honour of mankynde,
And after that the Jewes leet he bynde°.

This child with pitous lamentacioun
Up taken was, syngynge his song alway,
And with honour of greet processioun
They carien hym unto the nexte° abbay.
His mooder swownynge° by his beere° lay;
Unnethe° myghte the peple that was theere
This newe Rachel brynge fro his beere.

With torment and with shameful deeth echon°
This provost dooth the Jewes for to sterve°
That of this mordre wiste°, and that anon°.
He nolde no swich° cursednesse observe°.
Yvele shal he have that yvele wol deserve;
Therfore with wilde hors he dide hem drawe,
And after that he heng° hem by the lawe.

Upon this beere ay lith° this innocent
Biforn the chief auter°, whil the masse laste;
And after that the abbot with his covent°
Han sped hem° for to burien hym ful faste;
And whan they hooly water on hym caste,
Yet spak this child, whan spreynd° was hooly water,
And song *O Alma redemptoris mater.*

This abbot which that was an hooly man
As monkes been—or elles oghte be—
This yonge child to conjure° he bigan,
And seyde, "O deere child, I halse° thee,
In vertu° of the Hooly Trinitee,
Tel me what is thy cause for to synge,
Sith° that thy throte is kut to my semynge°?"

"My throte is kut unto my nekke-boon,"
Seyde this child, "and as by wey of kynde°
I sholde have dyed, ye, longe tyme agon.
But Jesu Crist, as ye in bookes fynde,
Wil° that his glorie laste and be in mynde;
And for the worship of his Mooder deere
Yet may I synge *O Alma* loude and cleere.

"This welle° of mercy, Cristes mooder sweete,
I loved alwey as after my konnynge°;
And whan that I my lyf sholde forlete°,
To me she cam, and bad me for to synge

---

598 wroghte, *worked* **600 frayneth,** *asks* **601 thilke,** *that* **602 wente oght forby,** *went by in any way* **604 Yaf in hir thoght,** *put it in her mind,* **in with a litel space,** *in a little while* **607 parfournest thy laude,** *performs your praise* **609 emeraude,** *emerald* **611 Ther,** *where,* **ykorven,** *carved,* **upright,** *on his back* **615 In coomen,** *came in* **616 provost,** *magistrate* **618 herieth,** *praises* **620 leet he bynde,** *he had tied up* **624 nexte,** *nearest* **625 swownynge,** *fainting* **625 beere,** *bier* **626 Unnethe,** *scarcely* **628 echon,** *each one* **629 dooth . . . for to sterve,** *has . . . put to death* **630 wiste,** *knew,* **anon,** *immediately* **631 nolde no swich,** *would no such,* **observe,** *overlook* **634 heng,** *hanged* **635 ay lith,** *always lies* **636 auter,** *altar* **637 covent,** *group of monks* **638 Han sped hem,** *hurried themselves* **640 spreynd,** *sprinkled* **644 conjure,** *plead with* **645 halse,** *entreat* **646 In vertu,** *by the power* **648 Sith,** *since,* **to my semynge,** *it seems to me* **650 as by wey of kynde,** *in the course of nature* **653 Wil,** *wishes* **656 welle,** *source* **657 konnynge,** *capability* **658 forlete,** *lose*

595 where, Hg reads "wheras" **627 newe Rachel,** Jewish mother who weeps inconsolably for her lost child; Jeremiah 31.15 and Matthew 2.18. The allusion complicates the anti-Semitism of the tale. **629 the Jewes,** Hg reads "thise Jewes." **632 Yvele shal he have . . . ,** evil shall he have who evil deserves. Proverbial; compare Exodus 21.23–25 and Matthew 5.38–39. Hg omits "he." **635 this,** Hg reads "his." **645 halse,** El and Hg read "halsen." **653 Wil,** Hg reads "Wol."

This anthem verraily° in my deyynge°,
As ye han herd, and whan that I hadde songe,
Me thoughte she leyde a greyn upon my
tonge.

"Wherfore I synge and synge I moot°, certeyn,
In honour of that blisful Mayden free°
Til fro my tonge of° taken is the greyn;
And afterward thus seyde she to me,
'My litel child, now wol I fecche thee
Whan that the greyn is fro thy tonge ytake°.
Be nat agast°, I wol thee nat forsake.'"

This hooly monk, this abbot, hym meene I,
His tonge out caughte and took awey the greyn,
And he yaf° up the goost ful softely.
And whan this abbot hadde this wonder seyn,
His salte teeris trikled doun as reyn,
And gruf° he fil al plat° upon the grounde,
And stille he lay as he had leyn ybounde.

The covent° eek lay on the pavement
Wepynge, and heryen° Cristes mooder deere,
And after that they ryse and forth been went,
And tooken awey this martir from his beere;
And in a tombe of marbul stones cleere°
Enclosen they his litel body sweete.
Ther he is now, God leve° us for to meete!

O yonge Hugh of Lyncoln, slayn also
With° cursed Jewes—as it is notable,
For it is but a litel while ago—
Preye eek for us, we synful folk unstable,
That of his mercy, God so merciable
On us his grete mercy multiplie,
For reverence of his mooder Marie. Amen.

Heere is ended the Prioresses Tale.

---

660 verraily, *truly,* **deyynge,** *dying* **663 I moot,** *I must* **664 free,** *generous* **665 of,** *off* **668 ytake,** *taken* **669 agast,** *frightened* **672 yaf,** *gave* **675 gruf,** *face down,* **plat,** *flat* **677 covent,** *group of monks* **678 heryen,** *they praise* **681 cleere,** *shining* **683 leve,** *grant* **685 With,** *by*

660 anthem, El reads "Anthephene." **662 greyn,** seed; in other versions of the story, a lily, a jewel, or a pebble. **663 I moot,** Hg omits "I." **666 afterward,** Hg reads "after that." **675 plat,** Hg reads "flat." **681 tombe,** El reads "temple." **683 us,** El reads "us alle." **684 Hugh of Lyncoln,** a supposed victim of child murder, for which nineteen Jews were executed by Henry III in 1255; accusations of ritual murder against Jews recur throughout European history.

From woodcut made by W.H. Hooper and published by the Chaucer Society between 1868 and 1879

Tale of Sir Thopas

Prologue

Bihoold the murye wordes of the Hoost to Chaucer.

Whan seyd was al this miracle, every man
As sobre was that wonder was to se,
Til that oure Hooste japen tho° bigan,
And thanne at erst° he looked upon me,
And seyde thus, "What man artow°?" quod he.
"Thou lookest as thou woldest fynde an hare,
For evere upon the ground I se thee stare.

"Approche neer and looke up murily.
Now war yow°, sires, and lat this man have place°—
He in the waast° is shape as wel as I!
This were a popet° in an arm t'enbrace
For any womman, smal and fair of face.
He semeth elvyssh° by his contenaunce,
For unto no wight° dooth he daliaunce°.

"Sey now somwhat, syn° oother folk han sayd.
Telle us a tale of myrthe, and that anon."
"Hooste," quod I, "ne beth nat yvele apayd°,
For oother tale certes kan° I noon,
But of a rym I lerned longe agoon."
"Ye, that is good," quod he. "Now shul we heere
Som deyntee° thyng, me thynketh by his cheere°."

Explicit.

693 japen tho, *to joke then* **694 at erst,** *for the first time* **695 artow,** *are you* **699 war you,** *beware,* **place,** *room* **700 waast,** *waist* **701 popet,** *doll* **703 elvyssh,** *otherworldly* **704 wight,** *person,* **daliaunce,** *pay attention* **705 syn,** *since* **707 yvele apayd,** *displeased* **708 kan,** *know* **711 deyntee,** *delightful,* **cheere,** *expression*

694–704 Chaucer's comic self-portrait here can be compared with that in his short poem, *Lenvoy to Scogan* (lines 27 and 31), and his *HF* 574 and 660 (plumpness), and *HF* 647–59 (bookish isolation). **707 apayd,** Hg reads "ypayd."

Heere bigynneth Chaucers Tale of Thopas.

Listeth, lordes, in good entent,
And I wol telle verrayment°
Of myrthe and of solas°;
Al of a knyght was fair and gent°
In bataille and in tourneyment—
His name was Sire Thopas.

Yborn he was in fer° contree,
In Flaundres al biyonde the see,
At Poperyng in the place°.
His fader was a man ful free°,
And lord he was of that contree,
As it was Goddes grace.

Sire Thopas wax° a doghty swayn°;
Whit was his face as payndemayn,
His lippes rede as rose;
His rode° is lyk scarlet in grayn°,
And I yow telle in good certayn,
He hadde a semely° nose.

His heer, his berd was lyk saffroun°,
That to his girdel raughte° adoun,
His shoon° of cordewane°.
Of Brugges were his hosen broun°,
His robe was of syklatoun°,
That coste many a jane°.

He koude hunte at wilde deer,
And ride an haukyng for river°
With grey goshauk° on honde;
Therto he was a good archeer,
Of wrastlyng was ther noon his peer,
Ther° any ram shal stonde°.

Ful many a mayde bright in bour°,
They moorne° for hym paramour°,
Whan hem were bet° to slepe.
But he was chaast and no lechour,
And sweete as is the brembul flour°
That bereth the rede hepe°.

And so bifel° upon a day,
Forsothe° as I yow telle may,
Sire Thopas wolde out ride.
He worth° upon his steede gray,
And in his hand a launcegay°,
A long swerd by his side.

He priketh° thurgh a fair forest
Therinne is many a wilde best,
Ye, bothe bukke and hare;
And as he priketh north and est,
I telle it yow, hym hadde almest
Bitidde° a sory care.

Ther spryngen° herbes grete and smale,
The lycorys° and cetewale°,
And many a clowe-gylofre°,
And notemuge° to putte in ale,
Wheither it be moyste° or stale,
Or for to leye in cofre°.

The briddes synge, it is no nay°,
The sparhauk and the papejay,
That joye it was to heere;
The thrustelcok made eek hir lay,
The wodedowve upon a spray°
She sang ful loude and cleere.

713 verrayment, *truly* **714 solas,** *pleasure* **715 gent,** *beautiful* **718 fer,** *distant* **720 place,** *plaza* **721 free,** *noble* **724 wax,** *grew* (up), **doghty swayn,** *brave squire* **727 rode,** *complexion,* **in grayn,** *deeply dyed* **729 semely,** *handsome* **730 saffroun,** *yellow orange spice* **731 raughte,** *reached* **732 shoon,** *shoes,* **cordewane,** *Spanish leather* **733 hosen broun,** *brown stockings* **734 syklatoun,** *costly silken fabric* **735 jane,** *cheap coin from Genoa* **737 haukyng for river,** *hawking for waterfowl* **738 goshauk,** *hunting bird* **741 Ther,** *where,* **stonde,** *stand* **742 bright in bour,** *beautiful in* (bed) *chamber* **743 moorne,** *yearn,* **paramour,** *sexually* **744 bet,** *better* **746 brembul flour,** *wild rose* **747 rede hepe,** *red* (rose) *hip* **748 bifel,** *happened* **749 Forsothe,** *truly* **751 worth,** *climbs* **752 launcegay,** *light lance* **754 priketh,** *spurs* **759 Bitidde,** *happened* **760 spryngen,** *grow* **761 lycorys,** *licorice,* **cetewale,** *zedoary* (a spice) **762 clowe-gylofre,** *clove* **763 notemuge,** *nutmeg* **764 moyste,** *fresh* **765 cofre,** *a chest* **766 it is no nay,** *it can't be denied* **770 spray,** *branch*

712 Listeth, lordes, a formulaic beginning of an oral performance; the tale is a parodic pastiche (in jog-trot verse) of absurdities juxtaposed with clichés and formulas from popular romances. **717 Thopas,** topaz, a yellow semiprecious stone. **719 Flaundres,** bourgeois trade nation, just across the English Channel. **720 Poperyng,** a Flemish market town, hardly aristocratic. **725 payndemayn,** white bread, with a possible play on "dough" from previous line? **728 And,** Hg reads "As." **733 Of Brugges,** from Bruges, center of Flemish trade. **739–40 archeer . . . wrastlyng,** archery and wrestling were distinctly nonaristocratic. A ram was the prize in wrestling contests. **742 many a,** Hg omits "a." **748 bifel,** Hg reads "it fel." **760 herbes,** plants, none of which are native to Flanders. **767 sparhauk . . . papejay,** the sparrow hawk and parrot are not songbirds. **769 thrustelcok . . . hir lay,** male thrush . . . her song; note the gender confusion. Hg reads "his." **770 wodedowve,** wood pigeon, not a songbird.

Sire Thopas fil in love-longynge,
Al whan he herde the thrustel synge,
  And pryked as he were wood°.
His faire steede in his prikynge
So swatte° that men myghte him wrynge;
  His sydes were al blood.

Sire Thopas eek so wery was
For prikyng on the softe gras,
  So fiers was his corage,
That doun he leyde him in that plas°
To make his steede som solas°,
  And yaf° hym good forage.

"O Seinte Marie, benedicite°,
What eyleth this love at me°
  To bynde me so soore?
Me dremed al this nyght, pardee°,
An elf-queene shal my lemman° be
  And slepe under my goore°.

"An elf-queene wol I love, ywis°,
For in this world no womman is
  Worthy to be my make°
        In towne;
Alle othere wommen I forsake,
And to an elf-queene I me take
  By dale° and eek by downe°."

Into his sadel he clamb° anon,
And priketh over stile and stoon
  An elf-queene for t'espye°,
Til he so longe hadde riden and goon
That he foond in a pryve woon°
  The contree of Fairye
        So wilde;
For in that contree was ther noon
That to him durste° ride or goon,
  Neither wyf ne childe.

Til that ther cam a greet geaunt°,
His name was Sire Olifaunt°,
  A perilous man of dede.
He seyde, "Child°, by Termagaunt,
But if° thou prike out of myn haunt°,
  Anon I sle thy steede
        With mace°.
Heere is the queene of Fairye,
With harpe and pipe and symphonye°,
  Dwellynge in this place."

The child seyde, "Also moote I thee°,
Tomorwe wol I meete with thee,
  Whan I have myn armoure;
And yet I hope, *par ma fay*°,
That thou shalt with this launcegay
  Abyen° it ful sowre°.
        Thy mawe°
Shal I percen if I may,
Er it be fully pryme of day°,
  For heere thow shalt be slawe°."

Sire Thopas drow abak° ful faste;
This geant at hym stones caste
  Out of a fel staf-slynge°;
But faire escapeth Sir Thopas,
And al it was thurgh Goddes gras,
  And thurgh his fair berynge°.

[The Second Fit]

Yet listeth, lordes, to my tale,
Murier° than the nightyngale,
  For now I wol yow rowne°

774 wood, *crazed* **776 swatte,** *sweated* **781 plas,** *place* **782 solas,** *relief* **783 yaf,** *gave* **784 benedicite,** *bless you* **785 eyleth this love at me,** *does love have against me* **787 pardee,** *by God* **788 lemman,** *lover* **789 goore,** *garment* **790 ywis,** *surely* **792 make,** *mate* **796 dale,** *valley,* **downe,** *hill* **797 clamb,** *climbed* **799 t'espye,** *to discover* **801 pryve woon,** *secret place* **805 durste,** *dared* **807 geaunt,** *giant* **808 Olifaunt,** *Elephant* **810 Child,** *knight* **811 But if,** *unless,* **haunt,** *area* **813 mace,** *a club* **815 symphonye,** *hurdy-gurdy* **817 Also moote I thee,** *as I may prosper* **820 par ma fay,** *by my faith* (Fr.) **822 Abyen,** *pay for,* **sowre,** *bitterly* **823 mawe,** *stomach* **825 pryme of day,** *9 a.m.* **826 slawe,** *killed* **827 drow abak,** *retreated* **829 fel staf-slynge,** *deadly slingshot* **832 fair berynge,** *good conduct* **834 Murier,** *merrier* **835 rowne,** *whisper*

774 pryked, spurred, but acquires absurd sexual connotations through repetition and context (lines 775, 779, and 798); see *RvT* 1.4231. **790 love,** Hg reads "have." **793 In towne,** one-foot metrical lines such as this (also at lines 803, 813, etc.) are part of English romance tradition, but here they ring falsely. **800 hadde,** Hg reads "hath." **805** This line is omitted in El and Hg, and may be a scribal addition. Reading from Cambridge University Library MS Dd.4.24. **810 Termagaunt,** a pagan god in fiction. **814 the queene,** Hg reads "this queene." **818 meete with,** Hg omits "with." **824** El reads "Thyn hauberk shal I percen, if I may," confusing both the syntax and the meter. Either "Thy mawe" (line 823) or "Thyn hauberk" can make sense, but not both. **826 thow shalt be,** Hg reads "shaltow ben." **830 Sir,** Hg reads "child." **832a Fit,** a section of a poem or song. El indicates section breaks at lines 833 and 891 with enlarged capitals, not in Hg. Neither has rubrics.

How Sir Thopas with sydes smale°,
Prikyng over hill and dale,
  Is comen agayn to towne.

His myrie men comanded he
To make hym bothe game° and glee°,
  For nedes moste he fighte°
With a geaunt with hevedes° three,
For paramour° and jolitee°
  Of oon that° shoon ful brighte.

"Do come°," he seyde, "my mynstrales,
And geestours° for to tellen tales,
  Anon° in myn armynge,
Of romances that been roiales°,
Of popes and of cardinales,
  And eek of love-likynge."

They fette° hym first the sweete wyn,
And mede° eek in a mazelyn°,
  And roial spicerye°
Of gyngebreed that was ful fyn,
And lycorys°, and eek comyn°,
  With sugre that is trye°.

He dide next° his white leere°
Of clooth of lake° fyn and cleere°,
  A breech° and eek a sherte,
And next his sherte an aketoun°,
And over that an haubergeoun°
  For percynge° of his herte.

And over that a fyn hawberk°,
Was al ywroght° of Jewes werk,
  Ful strong it was of plate;
And over that his cote-armour
As whit as is a lilye flour,
  In which he wol debate°.

His sheeld was al of gold so reed,
And therinne was a bores° heed,
  A charbocle bisyde.
And there he swoor on ale and breed
How that the geaunt shal be deed,
  Bityde° what bityde!

His jambeux° were of quyrboilly°,
His swerdes shethe of yvory,
  His helm of latoun° bright;
His sadel was of rewel-boon°,
His brydel as the sonne shoon,
  Or as the moone light.

His spere was of fyn ciprees,
That bodeth werre and nothyng pees,
  The heed ful sharpe ygrounde;
His steede was al dappull gray,
It gooth an ambil in the way
  Ful softely and rounde°
            In londe.
Loo, lordes myne, heere is a fit!
If ye wol any moore of it,
  To telle it wol I fonde°.

[The Third Fit]

Now holde youre mouth, *par charitee*,
Bothe knyght and lady free°,
  And herkneth to my spelle°.
Of bataille and of chivalry
And of ladyes love-drury°
  Anon I wol yow telle.

---

836 sydes smale, *slender waist* **840 game,** *entertainment,* **glee,** *song* **841 nedes moste he,** *he must necessarily* **842 hevedes,** *heads* **843 paramour,** *love,* **jolitee,** *pleasure* **844 Of oon that,** *for someone who* **845 Do come,** *summon* **846 geestours,** *tale-tellers* **847 Anon,** *soon* **848 roiales,** *royal* **851 fette,** *fetched* **852 mede,** *mead* (honey liquor), **mazelyn,** *wooden bowl* **853 roial spicerye,** *royal spice selection* **855 lycorys,** *licorice,* **comyn,** *cumin* **856 trye,** *excellent* **857 dide next,** *put on next to,* **leere,** *flesh* **858 clooth of lake,** *linen,* **cleere,** *bright* **859 A breech,** *pants* **860 aketoun,** *padded jacket* **861 haubergeoun,** *chain mail shirt* **862 For percynge,** *to prevent piercing* **863 hawberk,** *plate mail shirt* **864 ywroght,** *made* **868 debate,** *fight* **870 bores,** *boar's* **874 Bityde,** *happen* **875 jambeux,** *leg armor,* **quyrboilly,** *boiled leather* **877 latoun,** *brasslike alloy* **878 rewelboon,** *whalebone* **886 rounde,** *confidently* (?) **890 fonde,** *try* **892 free,** *generous* **893 spelle,** *story* **895 love-drury,** *service in love*

849 popes . . . cardinales, Church officials rather than members of royalty, and not usual subjects of romances. **856 is trye,** El reads "is so trye." **864 Jewes werk,** Jews were not known for making armor. **866 cote-armour,** surcoat (outer shirt) decorated with heraldic insignia, here either blank or not described. **871 charbocle,** carbuncle, a precious stone or the heraldic device that represents one. **bisyde,** Hg reads "by his syde." **881 spere was,** El reads "spere it was." **fyn ciprees,** fine cypress. Spears were traditionally made of ash; cypress was known for shipbuilding and fragrance, not weaponry. **884–85 dappull gray . . . ambil,** dapple gray . . . slow walk; neither the color nor the gait of a warhorse. **888 here is a fit,** here is a section; a formulaic transition in a number of metrical romances. **890a** No rubric in either El or Hg. El indicates a break here with a large capital in line 891; see note to 832a. **891 holde youre mouth, *par charitee*,** shut your mouth, for charity; a comic combination of rudeness and currying favor.

Men speken of romances of prys°,
Of Horn Child and of Ypotys,
Of Beves and of Sir Gy,
Of Sir Lybeux and Pleyndamour—
But Sir Thopas, he bereth the flour
Of roial chivalry!

His goode steede al he bistrood°,
And forth upon his wey he glood°
As sparcle° out of the bronde°;
Upon his creest° he bar a tour°,
And therinne stiked a lilie flour—
God shilde° his cors° fro shonde°!

And for° he was a knyght auntrous°,
He nolde° slepen in noon hous,
But liggen° in his hoode;
His brighte helm was his wonger°,
And by hym baiteth° his dextrer°
Of herbes fyne and goode.

Hymself drank water of the well,
As dide the knyght Sire Percyvell
So worthy under wede°,
Til on a day . . .

---

897 prys, *excellence* **903 al he bistrood,** *he completely mounted* **904 glood,** *glided* **905 sparcle,** *spark,* **bronde,** *torch* **906 creest,** *helmet top,* **tour,** *tower* **908 shilde,** *protect,* **cors,** *body,* **shonde,** *harm* **909 for,** *because,* **auntrous,** *adventurous* **910 nolde,** *would not* **911 liggen,** *lie* **912 wonger,** *pillow* **913 baiteth,** *grazes,* **dextrer,** *warhorse* **917 wede,** *clothing*

898–900 Horn Child, hero of the ME romance *King Horn.* **Ypotys,** central character in a verse dialogue (not a romance), *Ypotis,* in which a Christian child converts the pagan emperor of Rome. **Beves,** hero of *Bevis of Hampton.* **Sir Gy,** hero of *Guy of Warwick.* **Sir Lybeux,** pseudonym of Gawain's son, Guinglain, hero of *Libeaus Desconus* (*The Fair Unknown*). **Pleyndamour,** "Filled with Love." This romance has not been identified; perhaps facetious. Several of the ME romances cited here are found together in the Auchinleck MS, which suggests Chaucer may have known it or a similar anthology. **899 of Sir Gy,** Hg omits "of." **904 glood,** El reads "rood." **916 Sire Percyvell,** well-known character in Arthurian legends; the context here indicates the opening episode of the ME romance, *Sir Perceval de Galles.*

From woodcut made by W.H. Hooper and published by the Chaucer Society between 1868 and 1879

Tale of Melibee

Prologue

Heere the Hoost stynteth° Chaucer of his Tale of Thopas.

"Namoore of this, for Goddes dignitee,"
Quod oure Hooste, "for thou makest me
So wery of thy verray lewednesse°
That, also wisly° God my soule blesse,
Myne eres aken of° thy drasty° speche.
Now swich° a rym° the devel I biteche°!
This may wel be rym dogerel," quod he.
"Why so?" quod I, "why wiltow lette° me
Moore of my tale than another man,
Syn that° it is the beste rym I kan?"
"By God," quod he, "for pleynly, at o word,
Thy drasty rymyng is nat worth a toord°!
Thou doost noght elles but despendest tyme°.
Sire, at o word, thou shalt no lenger ryme.
Lat se wher° thou kanst tellen aught in geeste°,
Or telle in prose somwhat at the leeste,
In which ther be som murthe or som doctryne."
"Gladly," quod I, "by Goddes sweete pyne°,
I wol yow telle a litel thyng in prose
That oghte liken yow, as I suppose,
Or elles certes ye been to daungerous°.
It is a moral tale vertuous,
Al be it told somtyme in sondry wyse°
Of sondry folk as I shal yow devyse°.
"As thus: ye woot° that every Evaungelist°
That telleth us the peyne of Jhesu Crist
Ne seith nat alle thyng as his felawe dooth,
But nathelees hir sentence° is al sooth°,
And alle acorden as in hire sentence,
Al be ther in hir tellyng difference.
For somme of hem seyn moore and somme seyn lesse

918a stynteth, *stops* **921 verray lewednesse,** *genuine ignorance* **922 also wisly,** *as truly as* **923 Myne eres aken of,** *my ears ache from,* **drasty,** *worthless* **924 swich,** *such,* **rym,** *rhyme,* **biteche,** *give* **926 wiltow lette,** *will you hinder* **928 Syn that,** *since* **930 toord,** *turd* **931 despendest tyme,** *waste time* **933 wher,** *whether,* **aught in geeste,** *anything in alliterative verse* (?) **936 pyne,** *pain* **939 to daungerous,** *too hard to please* **941 sondry wyse,** *various ways* **942 devyse,** *describe* **943 woot,** *know.* **Evaungelist,** *gospel writer* **946 hir sentence,** *their meaning,* **sooth,** *truth*

925 rym dogerel, wretched verse; "doggerel" appears to be Chaucer's coinage. **928 rym,** El reads "tale." **929 o word,** El reads "a word." **935 murthe . . . doctryne,** entertainment . . . meaning; these parallel "solaas" and "sentence" in *GP* 1.798. The sheer delight of *Thopas* is matched with the sententiousness of *Melibee.* **941 told,** El reads "take."

Whan they his pitous passioun expresse—
I meene of Mark, Mathew, Luc, and John—
But doutelees hir sentence is al oon°.
"Therfore, lordynges alle, I yow biseche,
If that yow thynke I varie as° in my speche,
As thus, though that I telle somwhat moore
Of proverbes than ye han herd bifoore
Comprehended° in this litel tretys heere,
To enforce with° th'effect of my mateere,
And though I nat the same wordes seye
As ye han herd, yet to yow alle I preye
Blameth me nat, for as in my sentence
Shul ye nowher fynden difference
Fro the sentence of this tretys lyte°
After the which° this murye tale I write.
And therfore herkneth what that I shal seye
And lat me tellen al my tale I preye."

Explicit.

Here biginneth Chaucers Tale of Melibee.

A yong man called Melibeus, mighty and riche, bigat upon his wyf, that called was Prudence, a doghter which that called was Sophie. /

Upon a day bifel° that he for his desport° is went into the feeldes hym to pleye. / His wyf and eek his doghter hath he left inwith his hous of which the dores weren fast yshette°. / Thre of his olde foes han it espyed°, and setten laddres to the walles of his hous, and by the wyndowes been entred, / and betten his wyf, and wounded his doghter with fyve mortal woundes in fyve sondry places— / this is to seyn, in hir feet, in hire handes, in hir erys, in hir nose, and in hire mouth—and leften hire for deed, and wenten awey. /

Whan Melibeus retourned was into his hous and saugh al this meschief, he lyk a mad man, rentinge° his clothes, gan to wepe and crye. /

Prudence his wyf, as ferforth° as she dorste°, bisoghte° hym of his wepyng for to stynte°, / but nat forthy° he gan to crie and wepen ever lenger the moore./

This noble wyf Prudence remembered hire upon the sentence of Ovide, in his book that cleped° is *The Remedie of Love,* wher as he seith, / "He is a fool that destourbeth° the mooder to wepen in the deeth of hire child til she have wept hir fille as for a certein tyme, / and thanne shal man doon his diligence with amyable wordes hire to reconforte°, and preyen hire of hir weping for to stynte°." /

For which resoun this noble wyf Prudence suffred hir housbond for to wepe and crie as for a certein space, / and whan she saugh hir tyme she seyde hym in this wise, "Allas, my lord," quod she, "why make ye yourself for to be lyk a fool? / For sothe°, it aperteneth nat° to a wys man to maken swiche a sorwe. / Youre doghter, with the grace of God, shal warisshe° and escape. / And al were it so that° she right now were deed, ye ne oughte nat as for hir deeth yourself to destroye. / Senek seith, 'The wise man shal nat take to greet disconfort for the deeth of his children, / but certes he sholde suffren it in pacience, as wel as he abideth the deeth of his owene propre persone.'" /

This Melibeus answerde anon and seyde, "What man," quod he, "sholde of his wepyng stente° that hath so greet a cause for to wepe? / Jesu Crist oure lord hymself wepte for the deeth of Lazarus hys freend." /

---

952 al oon, *the same* **954 varie as,** *deviate* (from expectations) **957 Comprehended,** *included* **958 enforce with,** *reinforce,* **th'effect,** *impact* **963 lyte,** *little* **964 After the which,** *in imitation of which* **968 bifel,** *it happened,* **desport,** *recreation* **969 fast yshette,** *firmly shut* **970 espyed,** *discovered* **973 rentinge,** *tearing* **974 as ferforth,** *as far,* **dorste,** *dared,* **bisoghte,** *asked,* **stynte,** *stop* **975 nat forthy,** *nonetheless* **976 cleped,** *titled* **977 destourbeth,** *prevents* **978 reconforte,** *comfort,* **stynte,** *stop* **981 For sothe,** *truly,* **aperteneth nat,** *it is not appropriate* **982 warisshe,** *recover* **983 al were it so that,** *even if* **986 stente,** *stop*

967 man called, Hg reads "man whilom called." **Melibeus,** "one who drinks honey"; see line 1410 below. **Prudence,** "the ability to see what is virtuous." **Sophie,** "wisdom"; unnamed in Chaucer's source. The line numbers for this prose tale are conventional, for convenient reference. The numbers indicate the end of the respective lines. **970 Thre . . . foes,** identified at lines 1420–26 as the world, the flesh, and the devil—the traditional sources of temptation. **hous . . . wyndowes,** in the allegory, temptation enters the mind through the eyes. **972** Signifying the five senses: hand (touch), ears (hearing), nose (smell), mouth (taste), and eyes (seeing). Chaucer follows his French source in mistakenly substituting feet for eyes. **976 Ovide,** Ovid, *Remedia Amoris* (*Remedies for Love*) 127–30; note the reversal of gender roles when Prudence remembers the quotation. **984 Senek,** Seneca, *Letters* 74.30. **987 Lazarus,** John 11.35.

Prudence answerde, "Certes, wel I woot attempree° wepyng is nothing deffended° to hym that sorweful is, amonges folk in sorwe, but it is rather graunted hym to wepe. / The Apostle Paul unto the Romayns writeth, 'Man shal rejoyse with hem that maken joye, and wepen with swich folk as wepen.' / But though attempree wepyng be ygraunted, outrageous wepyng certes is deffended. / Mesure° of wepyng sholde be considered, after the loore that techeth us Senek. /

'Whan that thy frend is deed,' quod he, 'lat nat thyne eyen to moyste been of teeres, ne to muche drye. Although the teeres come to thyne eyen, lat hem nat falle.' / And whan thou hast forgoon° thy freend, do diligence to gete another freend; and this is moore wysdom than for to wepe for thy freend which that thou hast lorn°, for therinne is no boote°. / And therfore if ye governe yow by sapience° put awey sorwe out of your herte. / Remembre yow that Jesus Syrak seith, 'A man that is joyous and glad in herte, it hym conserveth florisshyng in his age°, but soothly sorweful herte maketh his bones drye.' / He seith eek thus, that sorwe in herte sleeth ful many a man. / Salomon seith that right as motthes in the shepes flees° anoyeth to° the clothes, and the smale wormes to the tree, right so anoyeth sorwe to the herte. / Wherfore us oghte as wel in the deeth of oure children as in the losse of oure goodes temporels have pacience. / Remembre yow upon the pacient Job. Whan he hadde lost his children and his temporel substance, and in his body endured and receyved ful many a grevous tribulacioun, yet seyde he thus, / 'Oure Lord hath yeven it me, our Lord hath biraft it me. Right as our Lord hath wold, right so it is doon. Blessed be the name of our Lord.'" /

To thise foreseide° thinges answerde Melibeus unto his wyf Prudence, "Alle thy wordes," quod he, "been sothe° and therwith profitable. But trewely myn herte is troubled with this sorwe so grevously that I noot° what to doone." /

"Lat calle," quod Prudence, "thy trewe freendes alle and thy lynage° whiche that been wise. Telleth your cas and herkneth what they seye in conseillyng, and yow governe° after hire sentence°. / Salomon seith, 'Werk alle thy thinges by conseil and thou shalt never repente.'" /

Thanne, by the conseil of his wyf Prudence, this Melibeus leet callen a greet congregacioun of folk, / as surgiens°, phisiciens, olde folk and yonge, and somme of his olde enemys reconsiled as by hir semblaunt° to his love and into his grace. / And ther with al° ther coomen somme of his neighebores that diden hym reverence more for drede than for love, as it happeth ofte. / Ther coomen also ful many subtille flatereres, and wise advocatz lerned in the lawe. /

And whan this folk togidre assembled weren, this Melibeus in sorweful wise shewed hem his cas, / and by the manere of his speche it semed wel that in herte he baar a crueel ire, redy to doon vengeaunce upon his foes, and sodeynly desired that the werre° sholde bigynne. / But nathelees yet axed° he hire conseil upon this matiere. / A surgien, by licence and assent of swiche as weren wise, up roos and to Melibeus seyde as ye may heere. /

"Sire," quod he, "as to us surgiens aperteneth° that we do to every wight° the beste that we kan, wher as° we been withholde° and to our pacientz that we do no damage, / wherfore it happeth many tyme and ofte that whan twey° men han everich° wounded oother, oon same surgien heleth hem bothe. / Wherfore unto our art it is nat pertinent° to norice° werre, ne parties to supporte°. / But certes, as to the warisshynge° of youre doghter, al be it so that she perilously be wounded, we shullen do so ententif° bisynesse fro day to nyght that with the grace of God she shal be hool and sound as soone as is possible." /

---

988 woot attempree, *know that temperate,* **nothing deffended,** *not at all forbidden* **991 Mesure,** *moderation* **993 forgoon,** *lost,* **lorn,** *lost,* **boote,** *remedy* **994 sapience,** *wisdom* **995 conserveth florisshyng in his age,** *preserves freshness in his old age* **997 shepes flees,** *wool* (sheep's fleece). **anoyeth to,** *damage* **1001 foreseide,** *previously stated,* **sothe,** *true,* **noot,** *don't know* **1002 lynage,** *relatives,* **yow governe,** *govern yourself,* **sentence,** *advice* **1005 surgiens,** *surgeons,* **as by hir semblaunt,** *apparently* **1006 ther with al,** *also* **1009 werre,** *war* **1010 axed,** *asked* **1012 aperteneth,** *it is appropriate,* **wight,** *person,* **wher as,** *wherever,* **withholde,** *retained* **1013 twey,** *two,* **everich,** *each* **1014 pertinent,** *appropriate,* **norice,** *encourage,* **parties to support,** *to support either party* **1015 warisshynge,** *healing,* **ententif,** *attentive*

989 Paul, Romans 12.15. **991–92 Senek . . . ,** Seneca, *Letters* 63.1. **995 Jesus Syrak,** Jesus, son of Sirach, author of Ecclesiasticus, but the passage is from Proverbs 17.22, an error in Chaucer's source. **996 He seith,** Ecclesiasticus 30.23 (Vulgate). **997 Salomon,** Proverbs 25.20 (Vulgate). **998 oure goodes temporels,** imitates French grammar, with adjective following noun and agreeing in number. El reads "othere goodes temporals." **999–1000** Job 1.21. **1003 Salomon,** Ecclesiasticus 32.24 (Vulgate); see *MilT* 1.3529–30n. **1000 Right as,** Hg reads "Right so as." **1001 therwith,** Hg reads "therto." **1009 wel,** omitted in Hg.

Almoost right in the same wise the phisiciens
answerden, save that they seyden a fewe woordes
moore, / that "right as maladies been cured by
hir contraries, right so shul men warisshe werre
by vengeaunce." / His neighebores ful of envye,
his feyned freendes that semeden reconsiled, and
his flatereres / maden semblant° of wepyng, and
empeireden° and agreggeden° muchel of this
matiere in preising greetly Melibee of myght°, of
power, of richesse, and of freendes, despisynge the
power of his adversaries, / and seiden outrely° that
he anon sholde wreken° hym on his foes and
bigynne werre. / 1020

Up roos thanne an advocat° that was wys, by
leve and by conseil of othere that were wise, and
seide, / "Lordynges, the nede for which we been
assembled in this place is a ful hevy° thyng and an
heigh° matiere, / by cause of the wrong and of the
wikkednesse that hath be doon, and eek by resoun
of the grete damages that in tyme comynge been
possible to fallen° for this same cause, / and eek
by resoun of the grete richesse and power of the
parties bothe, / for the whiche resouns it were
a ful greet peril to erren° in this matiere. / 1025
Wherfore, Melibeus, this is our sentenc°: we
conseille yow aboven alle thing that right anon
thou do thy diligence° in kepynge of° thy propre
persone° in swich a wise that thou wante° noon
espie° ne wacche° thy body for to save. / And
after that we conseille that in thyn hous thou sette
sufficeant garnisoun° so that they may as wel thy
body as thyn hous defende. / But certes°, for to
moeve werre°, or sodeynly for to doon vengeaunce,
we may nat demen° in so litel tyme that it were profitable. / Wherfore we axen leyser° and espace° to
have deliberacioun in this cas to deme°. / For the
commune proverbe seith thus, 'He that sone
deemeth, soone shal repente.' / And eek 1030
men seyn that thilke° juge is wys that soone
understondeth a matiere and juggeth by leyser°. /
For al be it so that° alle tariyng° be anoyful°,
algates° it is nat to repreve° in yevynge° of juggement, ne in vengeance-takyng, whan it is sufficeant
and resonable. / And that shewed oure lord Jesu
Crist by ensample, for whan that the womman
that was taken in avowtrie° was broght in his presence, to knowen what sholde be doon with hire
persone, al be it so that he wiste° wel hymself what
that he wolde answere, yet ne wolde he nat answere
sodeynly, but he wolde have deliberacioun, and in
the ground he wroot twies°. / And by thise causes°
we axen° deliberacioun, and we shal thanne, by
the grace of God, conseille thee thyng that shal be
profitable." /

Up stirten° thanne the yonge folk at ones, and
the mooste partie of that compainye scorned the
olde wise men, and bigonnen to make noyse,
and seyden that / right so as whil that° iren 1035
is hoot men sholden smyte°, right so men
sholde wreken° hir wronges while that they been
fresshe and newe. And with loud voys they criden,
'Werre! Werre!' /

Up roos tho° oon of thise olde wise, and with his
hand made contenaunce° that men sholde holden
hem stille and yeven° hym audience. / "Lordynges,"
quod he, "ther is ful many a man that crieth 'werre,
werre,' that woot° ful litel what werre amoun-
teth°. / Werre at his° bigynnyng hath so greet an
entryng° and so large that every wight° may entre
whan hym liketh, and lightly° fynde werre. / But
certes what ende that shal therof bifalle°, it is
nat light° to knowe. / For soothly°, whan 1040
that werre is ones° bigonne, ther is ful many
a child unborn of his mooder that shal sterve°
yong by cause of that ilke° werre, or elles lyve in
sorwe and dye in wrecchednesse. / And therfore,
er that° any werre bigynne, men moste have greet
conseil and greet deliberacioun." /

1019 semblant, *appearance,* **empeireden,** *made worse,* **agreggedden,** *aggravated,* **Melibee of myght,** *the might of Melibee* **1020 outrely,** *utterly,* **wreken,** *revenge* **1021 advocat,** *lawyer* **1022 hevy,** *serious,* **heigh,** *important* **1023 fallen,** *occur* **1025 to erren,** *to make an error* **1026 sentence,** *advice,* **do thy diligence,** *take care,* **kepynge of,** *protecting,* **thy propre persone,** *yourself,* **wante,** *lack,* **espie,** *spy,* **wacche,** *watchman* **1027 garnisoun,** *guards* **1028 certes,** *certainly,* **moeve werre,** *make war,* **demen,** *decide* **1029 axen leyser,** *ask time,* **espace,** *opportunity,* **deme,** *judge* **1031 thilke,** *that,* **by leyser,** *in time* **1032 al be it so that,** *even though,* **tariyng,** *delaying,* **anoyful,** *disturbing,* **algates,** *nevertheless,* **nat to repreve,** *not to be objected to,* **yevynge,** *giving* **1033 avowtrie,** *adultery,* **wiste,** *knew,* **wroot twies,** *wrote twice* **1034 by thise causes,** *for these reasons,* **axen,** *ask* **1035 stirten,** *leapt* **1036 right so as whil that,** *just as when* **smyten,** *strike,* **wreken,** *avenge* **1037 tho,** *then,* **made contenaunce,** *gestured,* **yeven,** *give* **1038 woot,** *knows,* **amounteth,** *amounts to* **1039 his,** *its,* **entryng,** *entry,* **wight,** *person,* **lightly,** *easily* **1040 that shal therof bifalle,** *will result from that,* **light,** *easy* **1041 soothly,** *truly,* **ones,** *once,* **sterve,** *die,* **ilke,** *same* **1042 er that,** *before*

1017 cured by hir contraries, the medieval belief that good health was a matter of balance among the humors; see *GP* 1.333n. Healing war with vengeance, however, is a non sequitur not found in the Latin original but added in Chaucer's French source. **1026 thou wante,** Hg reads "thou ne wante." **body,** El reads "persone." **1028 or sodeynly,** Hg reads "ne sodeynly." **1030 commune proverbe,** Publilius Syrus, first-century BCE dramatist, *Sententiae* 32. **1031–32** Also proverbial. **1033 Jesu Crist,** John 8.3–8. **1035 han,** omitted in El. **the olde,** Hg reads "thise olde." **1036 whil that iren is hoot men sholden smyte,** Proverbial. **1039 entryng,** Hg reads "entree." **1042 bigynne,** Hg reads "be bigonne."

And whan this olde man wende to enforcen° his tale by resons°, wel ny° alle at ones bigonne they to rise for to breken° his tale, and beden° hym ful ofte his wordes for to abregge°. / For soothly, he that precheth to hem that listen nat heeren° his wordes, his sermon hem anoieth°. / For Jesus Syrak seith that musik in wepynge is anoyous thing—this is to seyn, as muche availleth° to speken bifore folk to whiche his speche anoyeth, as it is to synge biforn hym that wepeth. / And whan this wyse man saugh that hym wanted° audience, alshamefast° he sette him doun agayn. / For Salomon seith, "Ther as thou ne mayst have noon audience, enforce thee nat to speke." / "I see wel," quod this wise man, "that the commune proverbe is sooth, that good conseil wanteth° whan it is most nede°." /

Yet hadde this Melibeus in his conseil many folk that prively in his eere conseilled hym certeyn thing and conseilled hym the contrarie in general audience°. /

Whan Melibeus hadde herd that the gretteste partie° of his conseil weren accorded° that he sholde maken werre, anoon he consented to hir conseilling and fully affermed hir sentence°. / Thanne dame Prudence, whan that she saugh how that hir housbonde shoop hym° for to wreken° hym on his foes and to bigynne werre, she in ful humble wise, when she saugh hir tyme, seide to hym thise wordes, / "My lord," quod she, "I yow biseche as hertely as I dar and kan, ne haste yow nat to faste, and for alle gerdons° as yeveth° me audience. / For Piers Alfonce seith, 'Whoso that dooth to thee oother° good or harm, haste thee nat to quiten° it; for in this wise thy freend wol abyde° and thyn enemy shal the lenger lyve in drede.' / The proverbe seith, 'He hasteth wel that wisely kan abyde,' and in wikked haste is no profit." /

This Melibee answerde unto his wyf Prudence, "I purpose nat," quod he, "to werke by thy conseil for many causes and resouns. For certes°, every wight° wolde holde me thanne a fool— / this is to seyn, if I for thy conseilling wolde chaungen thynges that been ordeyned and affermed by so manye wyse. / Secoundly, I seye that alle wommen been wikke and noon good of hem alle. For of a thousand men, seith Salomon, I foond o good man, but, certes, of alle wommen, good womman foond I never. / And also certes, if I governed me by thy conseil, it sholde seme that I hadde yeve° to thee over me the maistrie, and God forbede that it so weere. / For Jesus Syrak seith that if the wyf have maistrie, she is contrarious to hir housbonde. / And Salomon seith, 'Never in thy lyf to thy wyf ne to thy child ne to thy freend ne yeve° no power over thyself. For bettre it were that thy children aske of thy persone thynges that hem nedeth than thou be thyself in the handes of thy children.' / And if I wolde werke by thy conseilling, certes my conseilling moste somtyme° be secree til it were tyme that it moste be knowe, and this ne may noght be. / For it is writen that the janglerie° of wommen kan nat hyden thynges save that° they witen° noght. / Furthermore the philosophre seith, 'In wikked conseil wommen venquisshe° men.' And for thise resouns I ne owe nat usen° thy conseil." /

Whanne dame Prudence ful debonairly° and with greet pacience hadde herd al that hir housbonde lyked for to seye, thanne axed° she of hym licence for to speke, and seyde in this wyse. / "My lord," quod she, "as to your firste resoun, certes it may lightly° been answered. For I seye that it is no folie to chaunge conseil whan the thyng is chaunged, or elles whan the thyng semeth otherweyes than it was biforn. / And moore-over

1043 wende to enforcen, *thought to convey,* **resons,** *arguments,* **wel ny,** *nearly,* **breken,** *interrupt,* **beden,** *request,* **abregge,** *shorten* (it) **1044 listen nat heeren,** *don't wish to hear,* **hem anoieth,** *annoys them* **1045 as muche availleth,** *it accomplishes as much* **1046 hym wanted,** *he lacked,* **al shamefast,** *ashamed* **1048 wanteth,** *is lacking,* **nede,** *needed* **1049 in general audience,** i.e., *publicly* **1050 partie,** *portion,* **accorded,** *agreed,* **hir sentence,** *their advice* **1051 shoop hym,** *prepared himself,* **wreken,** *revenge* **1052 gerdons,** *benefits,* **as yeveth,** *so give* **1053 oother,** *either,* **quiten,** *repay,* **abyde,** *remain* **1055 certes,** *sure,* **wight,** *man* **1058 yeve,** *given* **1060 yeve,** *give* **1061 moste somtyme,** *must for a time* **1062 janglerie,** *blabbing,* **that,** *what,* **witen,** *know* **1063 venquisshe,** *vanquish,* **ne owe nat usen,** *ought not follow* **1064 debonairly,** *courteously,* **axed,** *asked* **1065 lightly,** *easily*

1045 Jesus Syrak, Ecclesiasticus 22.6 (Vulgate). **1046 whan,** omitted in El. **1047 Salomon,** Ecclesiasticus 32.6 (Vulgate); compare *NPP* 7.2801–02. **1048 commune proverbe,** Publilius, Syrus *Sententiae* 594. **1053 Piers Alfonce,** Petrus Alphonsus, author of a popular collection of exempla, *Disciplina Clericalis* (*Guide for Scholars*) 24.3. **thee oother good,** El reads "that oother good." **1054** Chaucer's addition; *TC* 1.956 and *ParsT* 10.1003. **1057 Salomon,** Ecclesiastes 7.28; *MerT* 4.2247–48. **o good,** El reads "a good." **1058 God forbede,** Hg reads "Goddes forbode" (God's prohibition). **1059** Ecclesiasticus 25.20; compare *WBP* 3.818 and *ParsT* 10.927. **1060 Salomon,** Ecclesiasticus 33.20–21 (Vulgate). **be thyself,** Hg reads "see thyself." **1062–63** Lines found in no manuscript. Probably not in Chaucer's immediate source, although in the extant Latin and French versions. Here emended slightly from Skeat's translation of the French. **1063 the philosophre,** Publilius Syrus, *Sententiae* 324.

I seye that though ye han sworn and bihight° to
parfourne° youre emprise°, and nathelees ye
weyve° to parfourne thilke same emprise by juste
cause, men sholde nat seyn therfore that ye were
a lier ne forsworn. / For the book seith that the
wise man maketh no lesyng° whan he turneth his
corage° to the bettre. / And al be it so that° your
emprise be establissed and ordeyned° by greet
multitude of folk, yet thar ye nat accomplice thilke
ordinaunce but yow lyke°. / For the trouthe of
thynges and the profit been rather founden in fewe
folk that been wise and ful of resoun than by greet
multitude of folk ther° every man crieth and clat-
ereth° what that hym liketh. Soothly swich° multitude is nat honeste°. / As to the seconde resoun,
where as ye seyn that alle wommen been wikke,
save your grace°, certes ye despisen° alle wommen
in this wyse; and he that alle despseth alle
displeseth, as seith the book. / And Senec 1070
seith that who so wole° have sapience° shal
no man dispreise°, but he shal gladly techen the
science° that he kan withouten presumpcioun
or pryde. / And swiche thynges as he nought ne
kan°, he shal nat been ashamed to lerne hem and
enquere of lasse° folk than hymself. / And sire,
that ther hath been many a good womman may
lightly° be preved°. / For certes, sire, oure lord
Jesu Crist wolde nevere have descended to be
born of a womman if alle wommen hadden ben
wikke. / And after that, for the grete bountee°
that is in wommen, our lord Jesu Crist, whan
he was risen fro deeth to lyve, appeered
rather to a womman than to his apostles. / 1075
And though that Salomon seith that he ne
fond never womman good, it folweth nat therfore that alle wommen ben wikke. / For though
that he ne fond no good womman, certes,
ful many another man hath founden many a
womman ful good and trewe. / Or elles peraventure the entente of Salomon was this, that as in
sovereyn bountee° he foond no womman— /
this is to seyn, that ther is no wight that hath
sovereyn bountee save God allone, as he hymself
recordeth in hys Evaungelie. / For ther nys no creature so good that hym ne wanteth° somwhat of the
perfeccioun of God that is his maker. / Your 1080
thridde resoun is this: ye seyn if ye governe yow by
my conseil, it sholde seme that ye hadde yeve me
the maistrie and the lordshipe over your persone. /
Sire, save your grace°, it is nat so. For if it were so,
that no man sholde be conseilled but oonly of hem
that hadden lordshipe and maistrie of his persone,
men wolden nat be conseilled so ofte. / For soothly,
thilke man that asketh conseil of a purpos°, yet hath
he free choys, wheither he wole werke by that conseil
or noon°. / And as to youre fourthe resoun, ther ye
seyn that the janglerie° of wommen kan nat hyd
thynges save that they wiste noght°, as who seith
that a womman kan nat hyde that she woot°, / sire,
thise wordes been understonde of wommen
that been jangleresses and wikked, / of 1085
whiche wommen men seyn that three thinges
dryven a man out of his hous, that is to seyn,
smoke, dropping of reyn, and wikked wyves. /
And of swiche wommen seith Salomon that it were
bettre dwelle in desert than with a womman that
is riotous°. / And sire, by youre leve, that am nat
I. / For ye haan° ful ofte assayed° my grete silence
and my gret pacience, and eek how wel that I kan
hyde and hele° thynges that men oghte secreely
to hyde. / And soothly°, as to youre fifthe resoun,
wher as ye seyn that in wikked conseil wommen
venquisshe° men, God woot thilke° resoun
stant heere in no stede°. / For understoond 1090

1066 bihight, *pledged,* **parfourne,** *perform,* **emprise,** *enterprise,* **nathelees ye weyve,** (if) *you nonetheless opt not* **1067 lesyng,** *lie,* **corage,** *heart* **1068 al be it so that,** *even if,* **ordeyned,** *planned,* **thar ye nat accomplice thilke ordinaunce but yow lyke,** *you need not fulfill this plan unless you wish* **1069 ther,** *where,* **clatereth,** *chatters,* **Soothly swich,** *truly such a,* **honeste,** *respectable* **1070 save your grace,** i.e., *with all due respect,* **despisen,** *insult* **1071 who so wole,** *whoever will,* **sapience,** *wisdom,* **dispreise,** *slander,* **science,** *knowledge* **1072 nought ne kan,** *does not know,* **lasse,** *lesser* **1073 lightly,** *easily,* **preved,** *proved* **1075 bountee,** *goodness* **1078 sovereyn bountee,** *supreme goodness* **1080 ne wanteth,** *lacks not* **1082 save your grace,** *with all due respect* **1083 of a purpos,** *about a plan,* **noon,** *not* **1084 janglerie,** *chatter,* **save that they wiste noght,** *except when they know nothing,* **woot,** *knows* **1087 riotous,** *contentious* **1088 haan,** *have,* **assayed,** *tested,* **hele,** *conceal* **1090 soothly,** *truly,* **venquisshe,** *overwhelm,* **woot thilke,** *knows this,* **stant . . . in no stede,** *is of no value*

1067 the book, Seneca, *De Beneficiis* (*On Benefits*) 4.38.1. **1070 As to,** Hg reads "And to." **and he that . . . book,** omitted in El (eyeskip). **1071 Senec,** not in Seneca, but Martinus Dumiensis, *Formula Honestae Vitae* (*Formula for a Noble Life*), chap. 3. **dispreise,** El reads "despisen." **1075** Matthew 28.9; Mark 16.9. **1076 Salomon,** Ecclesiastes 7.29, attributed to Solomon in the Middle Ages; see *MerT* 4.2277–79. **1077 ful many another,** Hg omits "ful." **1079 Evaungelie,** Gospel; Matthew 19.17; Luke 18.19. **1084 janglerie of wommn kan nat hyd thynges save that,** Hg omits "nat"; El reads "hath" for "nat hyd." All manuscripts omit "save." Women's inability to keep a secret is a common motif, e.g., in *WBT* 3.945–80, but, unemended, the meaning here may be that jangling is a form of hiding. This counters the French, however. **1086** Derives from Proverbs 27.15; see *WBP* 3.278–80 and *ParsT* 10.631. **1087 Salomon,** Proverbs 21.9; compare *WBP* 3.775–80. **1088 that am nat I,** see *WBP* 3.112 and *MerT* 4.1456. This and other echoes indicate connections between *Melibee* and the Marriage Group of parts 3–5.

now, ye asken conseil to do wikkednesse; / and if ye wole werken wikkednesse and your wyf restreyneth thilke° wikked purpos and overcometh yow by resoun and by good conseil, / certes, youre wyf oghte rather to be preised than yblamed. / Thus sholde ye understonde the philosophre that seith, 'In wikked conseil wommen venquisshen hir housbondes.' / And ther as ye blamen alle wommen and hir resouns°, I shal shewe yow by manye ensamples that many a womman hath ben ful good, and yet been°, and hir conseils ful hoolsome and profitable. / Eek som men han seyd that the conseillinge of wommen is outher to deere° or elles to litel of prys°. / But al be it so that ful many a womman is badde and hir conseil vile and noght worth, yet han men founde ful many a good womman and ful discrete and wise in conseillinge. / Loo Jacob by good conseil of his mooder Rebekka wan the benysoun° of Ysaak his fader and the lordshipe over alle his bretheren. / Judith by hire good conseil delivered the citee of Bethulie, in which she dwelled, out of the handes of Olofernus that hadde it biseged° and wolde have al destroyed it. / Abygail delivered Nabal hir housbonde fro David the kyng that wolde have slayn hym, and apaysed° the ire of the kyng by hir wit and by hir good conseillyng. / Hester enhaunced greetly by hir good conseil the peple of God in the regne of Assuerus the kyng. / And the same bountee° in good conseilling of many a good womman may men telle. / And mooreover, whan our Lord hadde creat Adam our formefader°, he seyde in this wyse, / 'It is nat good to been a man alloone. Make we to hym an help semblable° to hymself.' / Heere may ye se that if that wommen were nat goode, and hir conseils goode and profitable, / oure lord God of hevene wolde neither han wroght hem, ne called hem help of man, but rather confusioun of man. / And ther seyde oones a clerk in two vers: 'What is bettre than gold? Jaspre°. What is bettre than jaspre? Wisedoom. / And what is bettre than wisedoom? Womman. And what is bettre than a good womman? Nothyng.' / And sire, by manye of othre resons may ye seen that manye wommen been goode and hir conseils goode and profitable. / And therfore, sire, if ye wol triste to° my conseil, I shal restoore yow youre doghter hool and sound. / And eek I wol do to yow so muche that ye shul have honour in this cause." /

Whan Melibee hadde herd the wordes of his wyf Prudence he seyde thus, / "I se wel that the word of Salomon is sooth°. He seith that wordes that been spoken discreetly by ordinaunce° been honycombes, for they yeven° swetnesse to the soule and hoolsomnesse° to the body. / And wyf, by cause of thy swete wordes and eek for I have assayed and preved thy grete sapience° and thy grete trouthe, I wol governe me by thy conseil in alle thing." /

"Now sire," quod dame Prudence, "and syn ye vouchesauf° to been governed by my conseil, I wol enforme yow how ye shul governe yourself in chesynge of° your conseillours. / Ye shul first in alle youre werkes mekely biseken to° the heighe God that he wol be your conseillour; / and shapeth yow° to swich entente that he yeve yow conseil and confort, as taughte Thobie his sone: / 'At alle tymes thou shalt blesse God, and praye hym to dresse° thy weyes.' And looke that all thy conseils been in hym for evermoore. / Seint Jame eek seith, 'If any of yow have nede of sapience, axe it of God.' / And afterward thanne shul ye taken conseil of yourself and examyne wel your thoghtes of swich thyng as yow thynketh that is best for your profit. / And thanne shul ye dryve fro your herte thre thynges that been contrariouse to good conseil, / that is to seyn, ire°, coveitise°, and hastifnesse°. /

"First, he that axeth conseil of hymself, certes he moste been withouten ire, for manye causes. / The firste is this: he that hath greet ire and wratthe in hymself, he weneth° alwey that he may do thyng that he may nat do. / And secoundely, he that is irous and wrooth, he ne may nat

---

1092 thilke, *this* **1095 hir resouns,** *their arguments,* **yet been,** *still is* **1096 outher to deere,** *either too costly,* **prys,** *value* **1098 benysoun,** *blessing* **1099 biseged,** *besieged* **1100 apaysed,** *appeased* **1102 bountee,** *goodness* **1103 formefader,** *first father* **1104 semblable,** *similar* **1107 Jaspre,** *jasper* (semiprecious stone) **1110 triste to,** *trust* **1113 sooth,** *true,* **by ordinaunce,** *in due order,* **yeven,** *give,* **hoolsomnesse,** *health* **1114 sapience,** *wisdom* **1115 syn ye vouchesauf,** *since you consent,* **chesynge of,** *choosing* **1116 biseken to,** *ask* **1117 shapeth yow,** *bend yourself* **1118 dresse,** *prepare* **1122 ire,** *anger,* **coveitise,** *greed,* **hastifnesse,** *hastiness* **1124 weneth,** *thinks*

1094 See 1063n. **1098–1101** These examples are cited in the same order in *MerT* 4.1362–74. **Jacob . . . Rebekka,** Genesis 27. **Judith . . . Olofernus,** the apocryphal Book of Judith 12–13. **Abygail . . . Nabal,** Abigail convinces David not to seek revenge for the offense of her husband Nabal; 1 Samuel 25.10–42. **Hester . . . Assuerus,** Esther 7–8. **1104 Adam,** Genesis 2.18. **1106 confusioun of man,** see *NPT* 7.3164. **neither,** El reads "nevere." **1107 a clerk,** unidentified, but the saying was common. **1113 Salomon,** Proverbs 16.24. **1115** At this point, the French text followed by Chaucer omits about ten pages of the Latin original. **1117 Thobie,** Tobias 4.20 (Vulgate). **1119 Seint Jame,** James 1.5.

wel deme°; / and he that may nat wel deme may nat wel conseille. / The thridde is this, that he that is irous and wrooth, as seith Senec, ne may nat speke but blameful thynges; / and with his viciouse wordes he stireth oother folk to angre and to ire. / And eek, sire, ye moste° dryve coveitise out of youre herte. / For the apostle seith that coveitise is roote of alle harmes. / And trust wel that a coveitous man ne kan noght deme° ne thynke, but° oonly to fulfille the ende of his coveitise. / And certes°, that ne may never been accompliced, for ever the moore habundaunce that he hath of richesse, the moore he desireth. / And sire, ye moste also dryve out of youre herte hastifnesse, for certes, / ye may nat deeme° for the beste by a sodeyn thought that falleth in youre herte, but ye moste avyse yow° on it ful ofte. / For as ye herde biforn, the commune proverbe is this, that he that soone demeth, soone repenteth. /

"Sire, ye ne be nat alwey in lyke° disposicioun / for certes somthyng that somtyme semeth to yow that it is good for to do another tyme it semeth to yow the contrarie. /

"Whan ye han taken conseil of yourself, and han deemed by good deliberacion swich thyng as you list best°, / thanne rede° I yow that ye kepe it secree. / Biwrey° nat youre conseil° to no persone but if so be that ye wenen sikerly° that, thurgh your biwreying, your condicioun shal be to yow the moore profitable. / For Jesus Syrak seith, 'Neither to thy foe ne to thy frend discovere nat thy secree ne thy folie, / for they wol yeve° yow audience and looking° and supportacioun° in thy presence and scorne thee in thyn absence.' / Another clerk seith that scarsly shaltou° fynden any persone that may kepe conseil sikerly°. / The book seith, 'Whil that thou kepest thy conseil in thyn herte, thou kepest it in thy prisoun, / and whan thou biwreyest° thy conseil to any wight, he holdeth thee in his snare.' / And therfore yow is bettre to hyde your conseil in your herte than praye hem to whom he han biwreyed youre conseil that he wole kepen it cloos and stille. / For Seneca seith, 'If so be that thou ne mayst nat thyn owene conseil hyde, how darstou prayen any oother wight thy conseil sikerly to kepe?' / But nathelees, if thou wene sikerly° that the biwreiyng° of thy conseil to a persone wol make thy condicioun to stonden in the bettre plyt° thanne shaltou tellen hym thy conseil in this wise. / First, thou shalt make no semblant wheither thee were levere pees° or werre, or this or that, ne shewe hym nat thy wille and thyn entente. / For trust wel, that comenli° thise conseillours been flatereres, / namely° the conseillours of grete lordes, / for they enforcen hem° alwey rather to speken plesante wordes, enclynynge to the lordes lust°, than wordes that been trewe or profitable. / And therfore men seyn that the riche man hath seeld° good conseil but if he have it of hymself. / And after that, thou shalt considere thy freendes and thyne enemys. / And as touchynge thy freendes, thou shalt considere wiche of hem that been moost feithful and moost wise, and eldest and most approved in conseilling. / And of hem shalt thou aske thy conseil, as the caas requireth. /

"I seye that first ye shul clepe° to youre conseil your freendes that been trewe. / For Salomon seith that right as the herte of a man deliteth in savour° that is soote°, right so the conseil of trewe freendes yeveth° swetenesse to the soule. / He seith also, 'Ther may nothing be likned° to the trewe freend.' / For certes, gold ne silver beth nat so muche worth as the goode wyl of a trewe freend. / And eek he seith that a trewe freend is a strong deffense; whoso that hym fyndeth, certes he fyndeth a greet tresour. / Thanne shul ye eek considere if that° your trewe freendes been discrete and wyse. For the book seith, 'Axe° alwey

---

1125 deme, *judge* **1129 moste,** *must* **1131 deme,** *judge,* **but,** *except* **1132 certes,** *surely* **1134 deeme,** *judge,* **moste avyse yow,** *must deliberate* **1136 lyke,** *the same* **1138 you list best,** *best pleases you* **1139 rede,** *advise* **1140 Biwrey,** *reveal,* **conseil,** *decision,* **wenen sikerly,** *believe securely* **1142 yeve,** *give,* **looking,** *attention,* **supportacioun,** *support* **1143 shaltou,** *shall you,* **sikerly,** *securely* **1145 biwreyest,** *reveal* **1148 wene sikerly,** *think securely,* **biwreiyng,** *revealing,* **plyt,** *state* **1149 semblant wheither thee were levere pees,** *indication whether you prefer peace* **1150 comenli,** *commonly* **1151 namely,** *especially* **1152 enforcen hem,** *compel themselves,* **lust,** *wishes* **1153 seeld,** *seldom* **1157 clepe,** *summon* **1158 savour,** *taste,* **soote,** *sweet,* **yeveth,** *gives* **1159 likned,** *compared* **1162 if that,** *whether,* **Axe,** *ask*

1127 Senec, not in Seneca, but Publilius Syrus, *Sententiae* 281. **blameful thynges,** El reads "he blame thynges." **1130 the apostle,** Paul, 1 Timothy 6.10. See line 1840 below; *PardP* 6.334; and *ParsT* 10.739. **1134 beste by,** Hg omits "by." **1135 commune proverbe,** same proverb as line 1030 above. **1141 Jesus Syrak,** Ecclesiasticus 19.8–9 (Vulgate). **1143 Another clerk,** not identified. **sikerly,** Hg reads "secrely." **1144 The book,** not identified. **1147 Seneca,** not in Seneca, but Martinus Dumiensis, *De Moribus* (On Customs) 16. **sikerly,** Hg reads "secrely." **1158 Salomon,** Proverbs 27.9. **1159** Ecclesiasticus 6.15 (Vulgate). **1161** Ecclesiasticus 6.14 (Vulgate). **hym fyndeth,** Hg reads "it fyndeth." **1162 the book,** Tobias 4.19 (Vulgate).

thy conseil of hem that been wise.' / And by this same resoun shul ye clepen° to youre conseil of youre freendes that been of age°, swiche as han seyn° and been expert in manye thynges, and been approved in conseillinges. / For the book seith that in the olde men is the sapience° and in longe tyme the prudence. / And Tullius seith that grete thynges ne been nat ay° accompliced by strengthe, ne by delivernesse° of body, but by good conseil, by auctoritee of persones, and by science°, the whiche thre thynges ne been nat fieble by age, but certes they enforcen° and encreesen day by day. / And thanne shul ye kepe this for a general reule. First shul ye clepen° to your conseil a fewe of your freendes that been especiale, / for Salomon seith, 'Manye freendes have thou, but among a thousand chese° thee oon to be thy conseillour.' / For al be it so that thou first ne telle thy conseil but to a fewe, thou mayst afterward telle it to mo° folk if it be nede. / But looke° alwey that thy conseillours have thilke° thre condiciouns that I have seyd bifore, that is to seyn, that they be trewe, wise, and of oold experience. / And werke° nat alwey in every nede by oon counseillour allone, for somtyme bihooveth it to been conseilled by manye. / For Salomon seith, 'Salvacioun° of thynges is wher as ther been manye conseillours.' /

"Now sith° I have toold yow of which folk ye sholde been counseilled, now wol I teche yow which conseil ye oghte to eschewe°. / First ye shul escheue the conseillyng of fooles. For Salomon seith, 'Taak no conseil of a fool, for he ne kan noght conseille but after his owene lust° and his affeccioun°.' / The book seith that the propretee° of a fool is this: he troweth lightly° harm of every wight, and lightly troweth alle bountee° in hymself. / Thou shalt eek escheue the conseillyng of flatereres, swiche as enforcen hem° rather to preise your persone by flaterye than for to telle yow the sothfastnesse° of thinges. /

"Wherfore Tullius seith, 'Amonges alle the pestilences° that been in freendshipe, the gretteste is flaterie.' And therfore is it moore nede° that thou escheue and drede flatereres than any oother peple. / The book seith, 'Thou shalt rather drede and flee fro the sweete wordes of flaterynge preiseres° than fro the egre° wordes of thy freend that seith° thee thy sothes°.' / Salomon seith that the wordes of a flaterere is a snare to cacche with innocents. / He seith also that he that speketh to his freend wordes of swetnesse and of plesaunce setteth a net biforn his feet to cacche hym. / And therfore seith Tullius, 'Enclyne nat thyne eres to flatereres, ne taaketh no conseil of the wordes of flaterye.' / And Caton seith, 'Avyse thee° wel and escheue the wordes of swetnesse and of plesaunce.' / And eek thou shalt escheue the conseillyng of thyne olde enemys that been reconsiled. / The book seith that no wight° retourneth saufly° into the grace° of hys olde enemy. / And Isope seith, 'Ne trust nat to hem to whiche thou hast had somtyme werre or enemytee°, ne telle hem nat thy conseil.' / And Seneca telleth the cause why: 'It may nat be,' seith he, 'that where greet fyr hath longe tyme endured that ther ne dwelleth som vapour of warmnesse°.' / And therfore seith Salomon, 'In thyn olde foo trust nevere.' / For sikerly° though thyn enemy be reconsiled and maketh thee chiere° of humylitee and lowteth° to thee with his heed, ne trust him nevere. / For certes°, he maketh thilke feyned° humilitee moore for his profit than for any love of thy persone, by cause° that he deemeth° to have victorie over thy persone by swich feyned contenance°, the which

1163 clepen, *summon,* **of age,** *mature,* **swiche as han seyn,** *such as have seen* **1164 sapience,** *wisdom* **1165 ay,** *always,* **delivernesse,** *agility,* **science,** *knowledge,* **enforcen,** *grow stronger* **1166 clepen,** *summon* **1167 chese,** *choose* **1168 mo,** *more* **1169 looke,** *be sure,* **thilke,** *those* **1170 werke,** *act* **1171 Salvacioun,** *security* **1172 sith,** *since,* **eschewe,** *avoid* **1173 lust,** *desire,* **affeccioun,** *gratification* **1174 propretee,** *quality,* **troweth lightly,** *easily believes,* **bountee,** *goodness* **1175 enforcen hem,** *strive,* **sothfastnesse,** *truthfulness* **1176 pestilences,** *plagues,* **nede,** *necessary* **1177 preiseres,** *praisers,* **egre,** *painful,* **seith,** *tells,* **sothes,** *truths* **1181 Avyse thee,** *consider* **1183 wight,** *person,* **saufly,** *securely,* **grace,** *favor* **1184 enemytee,** *antagonism* **1185 vapour of warmnesse,** *warm air* **1187 sikerly,** *certainly,* **chiere,** *expressions,* **lowteth,** *bows* **1188 certes,** *surely,* **thilke feyned,** *this pretended,* **by cause,** *for the reason,* **deemeth,** *thinks,* **swich feyned contenance,** *such pretended behavior*

1165 Tullius, Cicero, *De Senectute* (*On Old Age*) 6.17. **1167 Salomon,** Ecclesiasticus 6.6 (Vulgate). **1171 Salomon,** Proverbs 11.14. **1173 Salomon,** Ecclesiasticus 8.20 (Vulgate). **1174 The book,** Cicero, *Disputationes Tusculanae* (*Tusculan Disputations*) 3.30.73. **1176 Tullius,** Cicero *De Amicitia* (*On Friendship*) 25.91. **1177 The book,** Martinus Dumiensis, *Formula Honestae Vitae* (*Formula for a Noble Life*), chap. 3. **1178** Caecilius Balbus, *De Nugis Philosophorum* (*On the Trifles of Philosophers*), 27. **to cacche with innocents,** Hg reads "to cacchen innocentz." **1179** Proverbs 29.5. **1180 Tullius,** Cicero *De Officiis* (*On Duties*) 1.91. **1181 Caton,** Dionysius Cato, supposed author of *Disticha Catonis* (*Cato's Couplets*) 3.4. **1183 The book,** Publilius Syrus, *Sententiae* 91. **1184 Isope,** Aesop's *Fables* and Caecilius Balbus *De Nugis Philosophorum* (*On the Trifles of Philosophers*), 25. **1185 Seneca,** not Seneca, but Publilius Syrus, *Sententiae* 389. **1186 Salomon,** Ecclesiasticus 12.10 (Vulgate).

victorie he mighte nat wynne by strif or werre. / And Peter Alfonce seith, 'Make no felawshipe with thyne olde enemys, for if thou do hem bountee°, they wol perverten it into wikkednesse.' / And eek thou most escheue° the conseilling of hem that been thy servants and beren thee greet reverence, for peraventure° they doon it moore for drede° than for love. / And therfore seith a philosophre in this wise, 'Ther is no wight parfitly° trewe to hym that he to soore dredeth°.' / And Tullius seith, 'Ther nys no myght so greet of any emperour that longe may endure but if° he have moore love of the peple than drede.' / Thou shalt also escheue the conseiling of folk that been dronkelewe°, for they kan no conseil hyde. / For Salomon seith, 'Ther is no privetee ther as regneth° dronkenesse.' / Ye shul also han in suspect the conseillyng of swich folk as conseille yow o thyng prively and conseille yow the contrarie openly. / For Cassidorie seith that it is a manere sleighte to hyndre° whan he sheweth to doon o thyng openly and werketh prively the contrarie. / Thou shalt also have in suspect the conseillyng of wikked folk. For the book seith, 'The conseillyng of wikked folk is alwey full of fraude.' / And David seith, 'Blisful is that man that hath nat folwed the conseilyng of shrewes°.' / Thou shalt also escheue the conseillyng of yong folk, for hir conseil is nat rype. /

"Now sire, sith I have shewed yow of which folk ye shul take your conseil, and of which folk ye shul folwe the conseil, / now wol I teche yow how ye shal examyne your conseil, after the doctrine of Tullius. / In the examynynge thanne of your conseillour, ye shul considere manye thynges. / Alderfirst° thou shalt considere that in thilke° thyng that thou purposest°, and upon what thyng thou wolt have conseil, that verray° trouthe be seyd and conserved°, this is to seyn, telle trewely thy tale. / For he that seith fals may nat wel be conseilled in that cas of which° he lieth. / And after this, thou shalt considere the thynges that acorden to that thou purposest° for to do by thy conseillours, if resoun accorde therto, / and eek if thy myght may atteine therto°, and if the moore part and the bettre part of thy conseillours accorde therto or noon°. / Thanne shaltou° considere what thyng shal folwe after hir conseillyng, as hate, pees, werre, grace°, profit, or damage, and manye othere thynges. / Thanne of alle thise thynges thou shalt chese° the beste and weyve° alle othere thynges. / Thanne shaltow considere of what roote° is engendred° the matiere of thy conseil and what fruyt it may conceyve and engendre. / Thou shalt eek considere alle thise causes fro whennes° they been sprongen°. / And whan ye han examyned youre conseil as I have seyd, and which partie° is the bettre and moore profitable, and hast approved it by manye wise folk and olde, / thanne shaltou considere if thou mayst parfourne° it and maken of it a good ende. / For certes, resoun wol nat that any man sholde bigynne a thyng but if he myghte parfourne it as hym oghte. / Ne no wight° sholde take upon hym so hevy a charge that he myghte nat bere it. / For the proverbe seith, he that to muche embraceth, distreyneth° litel. / And Catoun seith, 'Assay° to do swich° thing as thou hast power to doon lest that the charge° oppresse thee so soore° that thee bihoveth to weyve thyng° that

1189 bountee, *goodness* **1190 escheue,** *avoid,* **peraventure,** *perhaps,* **drede,** *fear* **1191 parfitly,** *perfectly,* **to soore dredeth,** *fears too much* **1192 but if,** *unless* **1193 dronkelewe,** *drunkards* **1194 ther as regneth,** *where reigns* **1196 a manere sleighte to hyndre,** *a kind of trick intended to do damage* **1198 shrewes,** *villains* **1203 Alderfirst,** *first of all,* **thilke,** *that,* **purposest,** *proposes,* **verray,** *genuine,* **conserved,** *preserved* **1204 cas of which,** *matter about which* **1205 acorden to that thou purposest,** *suit what you propose* **1206 atteine therto,** *achieve it,* **accorde therto or noon,** *agree with it or not* **1207 shaltou,** *you shall,* **grace,** *kindness* **1208 chese,** *choose,* **weyve,** *abandon* **1209 roote,** *source,* **engendred,** *produced* **1210 whennes,** *where,* **been sprongen,** *have arisen* **1211 partie,** *choice* **1212 parfourne,** *fulfill* **1214 wight,** *person* **1215 distreyneth,** *keeps* **1216 Assay,** *attempt,* **swich,** *such,* **lest that the charge,** *so that the weight will not,* **soore,** *painfully,* **thee bihoveth to weyve thyng,** *it requires you to abandon something*

1188 wynne, Hg reads "have." **1189 Peter Alfonce,** Petrus Alphonsus, *Disciplina Clericalis* (*Guide for Scholars*) 2.2. **1190 doon,** Hg reads "seyn" (see). **1191 a philosophre,** unidentified. **1192 Tullius,** Cicero, *De Officiis* (*On Duties*) 2.7.23. **1192 than drede,** El reads "than for drede." **1194 Salomon,** Proverbs 31.4 (Vulgate). **1195 o thyng,** El and Hg read "a thyng." **1196 Cassidorie,** Cassiodorus, sixth-century statesman and author who founded two monasteries, *Variae Epistolae* (*Various Letters*) 10.18. **1197 the book,** Publilius Syrus, *Sententiae* 354. **1198 David,** Psalms 1.1. **1199** Chaucer and his French source omit about two pages of the Latin original here; in addition, Chaucer omits a quotation from Ecclesiastes 10.16 that warns against childhood rulers, leading scholars to think he was translating while Richard II was in his minority. **1200–10 Tullius . . . ,** Cicero, *De Officiis* (*On Duties*) 2.18; a paraphrase. **1207 after hir,** Hg reads "of that." **1208 Thanne of,** Hg reads "And in." **1209 conceyve,** El reads "conserve." **1215 proverbe,** see Chaucer's short poem *Proverbe,* lines 7–8. **1216 Catoun,** Dionysius Cato, Roman moralist and supposed author of *Disticha Catonis* (*Cato's Couplets*) 3.14.

thou hast bigonne.' / And if so be that thou be in doute wheither thou mayst parfourne a thyng or noon, chese° rather to suffre° than bigynne. / And Piers Alphonce seith, 'If thou hast myght to doon a thyng of which thou most° repente thee, it is bettre nay than ye.' / This is to seyn that thee is bettre holde thy tonge stille than for to speke. / Thanne may ye understonde by strenger resons that if thou hast power to parfourne a werk of which thou shalt repente, thanne is it bettre that thou suffre than bigynne. / Wel seyn they° that defenden° every wight to assaye anything of which he is in doute, wheither he may parfourne it or noon. / And after, whan ye han examyned youre conseil as I have seyd biforn and knowen wel that ye may parfourne youre emprise°, conferme° it thanne sadly° til it be at an ende. /

"Now is it resoun and tyme that I shewe yow whanne and wherfore that ye may chaunge your conseil withouten youre repreve°. / Soothly° a man may chaungen his purpos and his conseil if the cause cesseth° or whan a newe caas bitydeth°. / For the lawe seith that upon thinges that newely bityden bihoveth° newe conseil. / And Senec seith, 'If thy conseil is comen to the eres of thyn enemy, change thy conseil.' / Thou mayst also chaunge thy conseil if so be that thou mayst fynde that by errour or by oother cause harm or damage may bityde. / Also, if thy conseil be dishonest or ellis cometh of dishoneste cause, chaunge thy conseil. / For the lawes seyn that alle bihestes° that been dishoneste been of no value. / And eek, if so be that it be inpossible or may nat goodly° be parfourned or kept. /

"And take this for a general reule that every conseil that is affermed so strongly that it may nat be chaunged for no condicioun that may bityde°, I seye that thilke° conseil is wikked." / This Melibeus, whanne he hadde herd the doctrine of his wyf dame Prudence, answerde in this wyse. /

"Dame," quod he, "as yet into this tyme ye han wel and convenably° taught me as in general how I shal governe me in the chesynge and in the withholdynge° of my conseillours. / But now wolde I fayn° that ye wolde condescende in especial° / and telle me how liketh yow°, or what semeth yow°, by° oure conseillours that we han chosen in oure present nede." /

"My lord," quod she, "I biseke° yow in al humblesse that ye wol nat wilfully replie° agayn my resouns, ne distempre° youre herte thogh I speke thyng that yow displese. / For God woot° that, as in myn entente, I speke it for your beste, for youre honour, and for youre profite eke. / And soothly°, I hope that youre benygnytee° wol taken it in pacience. / Trusteth me wel," quod she, "that your conseil as in this caas ne sholde nat, as to speke properly, be called a conseilling, but a mocioun° or a moevyng° of folye°, / in which conseil ye han erred in many a sondry wise°. /

"First and forward°, ye han erred in th'assemblynge of youre conseillours. / For ye sholde first have cleped° a fewe folk to your conseil, and after ye myghte han shewed° it to mo° folk, if it hadde been nede°. / But certes°, ye han sodeynly cleped to your conseil a greet multitude of peple ful chargeant° and ful anoyous° for to heere. / Also ye han erred for there as ye sholden oonly have cleped to youre conseil youre trewe frendes olde and wise, / ye han ycleped straunge° folk and yong folk, false flatereres and enemys reconsiled, and folk that doon yow reverence withouten love. / And eek also ye have erred for ye han broght with yow to youre conseil ire, coveitise, and hastifnesse, / the whiche thre thynges been contrariouse to every conseil honeste and profitable, / the whiche thre ye han nat anientissed° or destroyed hem, neither in yourself ne in your conseillours as yow oghte. / Ye han erred also for ye han shewed to your conseillours

1217 chese, *choose,* **suffre,** *be patient* **1218 most,** *must* **1221 Wel seyn they,** *they say well,* **defenden,** *forbid* **1222 emprise,** *enterprise,* **conferme,** *pursue,* **sadly,** *steadily* **1223 repreve,** *shame* **1224 Soothly,** *truly,* **cesseth,** *ceases,* **caas bitydeth,** *situation occurs* **1225 bihoveth,** *is necessary* **1229 bihestes,** *promises* **1230 goodly,** *well* **1231 may bityde,** *might happen,* **that thilke,** *that that* **1233 convenably,** *properly,* **withholdynge,** *retaining* **1234 wolde I fayn,** *I would like,* **condescende in especial,** *proceed to specifics* **1235 liketh yow,** *you like,* **seemeth yow,** *you think,* **by,** *about* **1236 biseke,** *ask,* **replie,** *object,* **distempre,** *upset* **1237 woot,** *knows* **1238 soothly,** *truly,* **benygnytee,** *goodness* **1239 mocioun,** *motion,* **moevyng,** *movement,* **folye,** *folly* **1240 sondry wise,** *various way* **1241 forward,** *foremost* **1242 cleped,** *summoned,* **shewed,** *revealed,* **mo,** *more,* **nede,** *necessary* **1243 certes,** *surely,* **ful chargeant,** *very burdensome,* **ful anoyous,** *very bothersome* **1245 ycleped straunge,** *summoned unfamiliar* **1248 anientissed,** *eliminated*

1218 Piers Alphonce, Petrus Alphonsus, *Disciplina Clericalis* (*Guide for Scholars*) 4.4. **1219** Proverbial. **1221 anything,** Hg reads "a thyng." **1225 the lawe,** Cicero, *Pro Lege Manilia* (*On the Manilian Law*) 20.60. **1226 Senec,** not identified in Seneca. **1246 ire, coveitise, and hastifnesse,** see line 1122 above. Such repetitions help organize the work as a scholastic treatise. **1248 whiche thre,** Hg reads "whiche thre thynges."

youre talent°, and youre affeccioun° to make werre an on and for to do vengeance. / They han espied by your wordes to what thyng ye been enclyned. / And therfore han they rather conseilled yow to your talent than to your profit. / Ye han erred also for it semeth that it suffiseth to han been conseilled by thise conseillours oonly and with litel avys°, / wher as in so greet and so heigh a nede it hadde been necessarie mo conseillours and moore deliberacioun to parfourne your emprise°. / Ye han erred also for ye ne han nat examyned youre conseil in the forseyde manere, ne in due manere as the caas requireth. / Ye han erred also, for ye han nat maked no divisioun bitwixe your conseillours—this is to seyn bitwixen your trewe freendes and your feyned° conseillours, / ne ye han nat knowe the wil of youre trewe freendes olde and wise, / but ye han cast alle hire wordes in an hochepot° and enclyned youre herte to the moore partie° and to the gretter nombre, and ther been ye condescended°. / And sith° ye woot° wel that men shal alwey fynde a gretter nombre of fooles than of wise men, / and therfore the conseils that been at° congragaciouns and multitudes of folk ther as men take moore reward° to the nombre than to the sapience° of persones, / ye se wel that in swiche° conseillynges fooles han the maistrie." /

Melibeus answerde agayn, and seyde, "I graunte wel that I have erred; / but ther as° thou hast toold me heerbiforn that he nys nat to blame that chaungeth his conseillours in certein caas and for certeine juste causes, / I am al redy to chaunge my conseillours, right as thow wolt devyse°. / The proverbe seith that for to do synne is mannyssh°, but certes° for to persevere longe in synne is werk of the devel." /

To this sentence° answerde anon dame Prudence and seyde, / "Examineth," quod she, "your conseil, and lat us see the whiche of hem han spoken most resonably and taught yow best conseil. / And for as muche as that the examynacioun is necessarie, lat us bigynne at the surgiens and at the phisiciens, that first speeken in this matiere. / I sey yow that the surgiens and phisiciens han seyd° yow in your conseil discreetly, as hem oughte, / and in hir speche seyd ful wisely, that to the office of hem aperteneth°, to doon to every wight honour and profit and no wight for to anoye, / and in hire craft°, to doon greet diligence unto the cure of hem whiche that they han in hire governaunce. / And sire, right as they han answered wisely and discreetly, / right so rede° I that they been heighly° and sovereynly gerdoned° for hir noble speche, / and eek for° they sholde do the moore ententif° bisynesse in the curacioun of your doghter deere. / For al be it so that° they been your freendes, therfore shal ye nat suffren° that they serve yow for noght, / but ye oghte the rather° gerdone hem° and shewe hem your largesse°. / And as touchynge the proposicioun which that the phisiciens encreesceden in this caas, this is to seyn, / that in maladies that oon contrarie is warisshed° by another contrarie, / I wolde fayn knowe hou ye understonde this text and what is youre sentence°." /

"Certes," quod Melibeus, "I understonde it in this wise: / that right as they han doon me a contrarie°, right so sholde I doon hem another. / For right as they han venged hem° on me and doon me wrong, right so shal I venge me upon hem and doon hem wrong, / and thanne have I cured oon contrarie by another." /

"Lo, lo," quod dame Prudence, "how lightly° is every man enclined to his owene desir and to his owene plesaunce! / Certes°," quod she, "the wordes of the phisiciens ne sholde nat han been understonden in thys wise. / For certes, wikkednesse is nat contrarie to wikkednesse, ne vengeaunce to vengeaunce, ne wrong to wrong, but they been semblable°. / And therfore, o vengeaunce is nat warisshed by another vengeaunce, ne o wrong by another wrong, / but everich° of hem encreesceth and aggreggeth°

1249 talent, *inclination,* **affeccioun,** *desire* **1252 avys,** *deliberation* **1253 emprise,** *enterprise* **1255 feyned,** *pretended* **1257 hochepot,** *hodgepodge,* **moore partie,** *larger group,* **condescended,** *settled* **1258 sith,** *since,* **woot,** *know* **1259 been at,** *are from,* **reward,** *regard,* **sapience,** *wisdom* **1260 swiche,** *such* **1262 ther as,** *since* **1263 devyse,** *advise* **1264 mannyssh,** *human,* **certes,** *surely* **1265 sentence,** *truism* **1268 seyd,** *spoken to* **1269 aperteneth,** *is appropriate* **1270 in hire craft,** *in accord with their profession* **1272 rede,** *advise,* **heighly,** *liberally,* **sovereynly gerdoned,** *supremely rewarded* **1273 eek for,** *also so,* **ententif,** *eager* **1274 al be it so that,** *even though,* **suffren,** *allow* **1275 the rather,** *instead,* **gerdone hem,** *reward them,* **largesse,** *generosity* **1277 warisshed,** *cured* **1278 sentence,** *interpretation* **1280 contrarie,** *offense* **1281 venged hem,** *avenged themselves* **1283 lightly,** *easily* **1284 Certes,** *certainly* **1285 semblable,** *alike* **1287 everich,** *each,* **aggreggeth,** *aggravates*

1249–51 In *MerT,* Placebo flatters January by echoing January's own opinions (see *MerT* 4.1467–68 and 1478ff.). **1252 that it,** Hg reads "that yow." **1276–77 proposicioun . . . phisiciens encreesceden in this caas . . . ,** first mentioned at 1016–17 above. **1276 encreesceden,** some manuscripts read "entreteden."

other. / But certes, the wordes of the phisiciens sholde been understonden in this wise: / for good and wikkednesse been two contraries, and pees and werre, vengeaunce and suffraunce°, discord and accord, and manye othere thynges. / But certes, wikkednesse shal be warisshed by goodnesse, discord by accord, werre by pees, and so forth of othere thinges. / And heerto accordeth° Seint Paul the apostle in manye places. / He seith, 'Ne yeldeth° nat harm for harm, ne wikked speche for wikked speche, / but do wel to hym that dooth thee harm, and blesse hym that seith to thee harm.' / And in manye othere places he amonesteth pees° and accord. / But now wol I speke to yow of the conseil which that was yeven° to yow by the men of lawe and the wise folk / that seyden alle by oon accord as ye han herd bifore, / that over alle thynges ye sholde doon youre diligence to kepen° youre persone and to warnestoore° youre hous. / And seyden also that in this caas yow oghten for to werken ful avysely° and with greet deliberacioun. / And sire, as to the firste point that toucheth to the kepyng° of youre persone, / ye shul understonde that he that hath werre shal evermore mekely and devoutly preyen biforn alle thynges / that Jesus Crist of his grete mercy wol han hym in his proteccioun and been his sovereyn° helpyng at his nede. / For certes, in this world ther is no wight that may be conseilled ne kept sufficeantly withouten the keping of oure lord Jesu Crist. / To this sentence accordeth° the prophete David that seith, / 'If God ne kepe the citee, in ydel waketh° he that it kepeth°.' / Now sire, thanne shul ye comitte the kepyng of youre persone to youre trewe freendes that been approved and yknowe°, / and of hem shul ye axen° help youre persone for to kepe. For Catoun seith, 'If thou hast nede of help, axe it of thy freendes, / for ther nys noon so good a phisicien as thy trewe freend.' / And after this, thanne shul ye kepe yow fro alle straunge folk° and fro lyeres°, and have alwey in suspect hir compaignye. / For Piers Alfonce seith, 'Ne taak no compaignye by the weye of straunge men but if so be that thou have knowe hym of a lenger tyme. / And if so be that he be falle into thy compaignye paraventure° withouten thyn assent, / enquere thanne as subtilly as thou mayst of his conversacioun° and of his lyf before, and feyne° thy wey. Seye that thou goost thider° as thou wolt not go. / And if he bereth° a spere, hoold° thee on the right syde, and if he bere a swerd, hoold thee on the lift syde.' / And after this, thanne shul ye kepe yow wisely from alle swich manere° peple as I have seyd bifore, and hem and hir conseil escheue°. / And after this, thanne shul ye kepe yow in swich manere / that for any presumpcioun of° youre strengthe that ye ne dispise nat, ne acounte nat the myght of your adversarie so litel that ye lete° the kepyng of youre persone for your presumpcioun, / for every wys man dredeth his enemy. / And Salomon seith, 'Weleful° is he that of alle hath drede, / for certes he that thurgh the hardynesse° of his herte and thurgh the hardynesse of hymself hath to greet presumpcioun, hym shal yvel bityde°.' / Thanne shul ye evermoore countrewayte° embusshementz° and alle espiaille°. / For Senec seith that the wyse man that dredeth harmes escheueth° harmes, / ne he ne falleth° into perils that perils escheueth. / And al be it so that it seme that thou art in siker° place, yet shaltow° alwey do thy diligence in kepynge of thy persone, / this is to seyn ne be nat necligent to kepe thy persone nat oonly fro thy gretteste enemys but fro thy leeste enemy. / Senek seith,

---

1289 suffraunce, *patient endurance* **1291 heerto accordeth,** *with this agrees* **1292 yeldeth,** *repay* **1294 amonesteth pees,** *encourages peace* **1295 yeven,** *given* **1297 kepen,** *protect,* **warnestoore,** *fortify* **1298 ful avysely,** *very thoughtfully* **1299 kepyng,** *protection* **1301 sovereyn,** *greatest* **1303 sentence accordeth,** *advice agrees* **1304 waketh,** *watches,* **it kepeth,** *protects it* **1305 yknowe,** *known* **1306 axen,** *ask* **1308 straunge folk,** *strangers,* **lyeres,** *liars* **1310 paraventure,** *perhaps* **1311 conversacioun,** *way of life,* **feyne,** *disguise,* **thider,** *where* **1312 bereth,** *carries,* **hoold,** *keep* **1313 swich manere,** *such kind of,* **escheue,** *avoid* **1315 presumpcioun of,** *overconfidence about,* **lete,** *neglect* **1317 Weleful,** *fortunate* **1318 hardynesse,** *boldness,* **hym shal yvel bityde,** *to him shall evil occur* **1319 countrewayte,** *watch for,* **embusshementz,** *ambushes,* **espiaille,** *spying* **1320 escheueth,** *avoids* **1321 ne he ne falleth,** *and he falls not* **1322 siker,** *a secure,* **shaltow,** *shall you*

1291 Seint Paul . . . manye places, Romans 12.17; 1 Thessalonians 5.15; 1 Corinthians 4.12–13; also 1 Peter 3.9. **1295 men of lawe . . . ,** see lines 1026ff. above. **1303–04 David,** Psalms 127.1 (Vulgate 126.1). **1306–07 Catoun,** Dionysius Cato, supposed author of *Distícha Catonis* (*Cato's Couplets*) 4.13. **1309–12 Piers Alfonce,** Petrus Alphonsus, *Disciplina Clericalis* (*Guide for Scholars*) 17.2. **1311 goost,** Hg reads "wolt go." **1312, the lift,** El reads "his lift." **1315 acounte,** Hg reads "attempte." **1317–18 Salomon,** Proverbs 28.14. **1320 Senec,** not in Seneca, but Publilius Syrus, *Sententiae* 607. **that dredeth harmes escheueth harmes,** El reads "he dredeth harmes." **1323 fro . . . fro,** El reads "for . . . for." **1324** Line lacking in El. **Senek,** not in Seneca, but from Publilius Syrus, *Sententiae* 255.

'A man that is wel avysed, he dredeth his leste enemy.' / Ovyde seith that the litel wesele wol slee the grete bole° and the wilde hert. / And the book seith, 'A litel thorn may prikke a greet kyng ful soore, and an hound wol holde the wilde boor.' / But nathelees, I sey nat thou shalt be so coward that thou doute° ther wher as is no drede. / The book seith that somme folk han greet lust° to deceyve, but yet they dreden hem to be deceyved. / Yet shaltou drede to been empoisoned and kepe yow from the compaignye of scorneres. / For the book seith, 'With scorneres make no compaignye, but flee hire wordes as venym.' /

"Now as to the seconde point, wher as youre wise conseillours conseilled yow to warnestoore° youre hous with gret diligence, / I wolde fayn° knowe how that ye understonde thilke° wordes and what is your sentence°." /

Melibeus answerde and seyde, "Certes I understande it in this wise, that I shal warnestoore myn hous with toures swiche° as han castelles and othere manere edifices, and armure, and artelries°, / by whiche thinges I may my persone and myn hous so kepen and deffenden that myne enemys shul been in drede myn hous for to approche." /

To this sentence answerde anon Prudence, "Warnestooryng°," quod she, "of heighe toures and of grete edifices apperteneth° somtyme to pryde, / and eek men make heighe toures and grete edifices with grete costages° and with greet travaille°, and whan that they been accompliced yet be they nat worth a stree° but if they be defended by trewe freendes that been olde and wise. / And understoond wel that the gretteste and the strongeste garnyson° that a riche man may have as wel to kepen his persone as his goodes is / that he be biloved amonges hys subgetz and with his neighebores. / For thus seith Tullius that ther is a manere° garnyson that no man may venquysse° ne disconfite° and that is / a lord to be biloved of his citezeins and of his peple. /

"Now sire, as to the thridde point: wher as your olde and wise conseillours seyden that yow ne oghte nat sodeynly ne hastily proceden in this nede°. / but that yow oghte purveyen° and apparaillen yow° in this caas with greet diligence and greet deliberacioun, / trewely I trowe° that they seyden right wisely and right sooth°. / For Tullius seith, 'In every nede er thou bigynne it, apparaille thee with greet diligence.' / Thanne seye I that in vengeance takyng, in werre, in bataille, and in warnestooryng, / er thow bigynne, I rede° that thou apparaille thee ther to, and do it with greet deliberacioun. / For Tullius seith that longe apparaillyng biforn the bataille maketh short victorie. / And Cassidorus seith, 'The garnyson is stronger whan it is longe tyme avysed°.' /

"But now lat us speken of the conseil that was accorded° by your neighebores swiche as doon yow reverence withouten love, / youre olde enemys reconsiled, your flatereres / that conseilled yow certeyne thynges prively°, and openly conseilleden yow the contrarie, / the yonge folk also that conseilleden yow to venge yow° and make werre anon. / And certes, sire, as I have seyd biforn, ye han greetly erred to han cleped° swich maner folk to youre conseil, / which conseillours been ynogh repreved by the resouns aforeseyd. / But nathelees lat us now descende to the special°. Ye shuln° first procede after the doctrine of Tullius. / Certes, the trouthe of this matiere or of this conseil nedeth nat diligently enquere°; / for it is wel wist whiche° they been that han doon to yow this trespas and vileynye, / and how manye trespassours, and in what manere they han to yow doon al this wrong and al this vileynye. / And after this thanne shul ye examyne the seconde condicioun, which that the same Tullius

1325 bole, *bull* **1327 doute,** *fear* **1328 lust,** *desire* **1331 warnestoore,** *fortify* **1332 fayn,** *like to,* **thilke,** *these,* **sentence,** *interpretation* **1333 toures swiche,** *towers such,* **artelries,** *artillery* **1335 Warnestooryng,** *fortifying,* **apperteneth,** *is related* **1336 costages,** *expense,* **travaille,** *effort,* **stree,** *straw* **1337 garnyson,** *garrison* **1339 manere,** *kind of* **venquysse,** *defeat,* **disconfite,** *overcome* **1341 nede,** *crisis* **1342 purveyen,** *provide for,* **apparaillen yow,** *prepare yourself* **1343 trowe,** *believe,* **sooth,** *truly* **1346 rede,** *advise* **1348 avysed,** *considered* **1349 accorded,** *agreed to* **1351 prively,** *in private* **1352 venge yow,** *avenge yourself* **1353 cleped,** *summoned* **1355 descende to the special,** *move to the specific,* **shuln,** *shall* **1356 nedeth nat diligently enquere,** *need not be methodically examined* **1357 wist whiche,** *known who*

1325 Ovyde, Ovid, *Remedia Amoris* (*Remedies of Love*) 421. **wesele** (weasel) is Chaucer's mistranslation of French *vivre* (viper) as Latin *viverra* (ferret). **1326** Chaucer's addition; note the rhyme. **1327 so coward,** El omits "so." **1328 The book,** Seneca, *Letters* 3.3. **1331 seconde point,** see line 1027 above. **1335–36 apperteneth . . . edifices,** omitted from El and Hg (eyeskip). **1339–40 Tullius,** not in Cicero, but Seneca, *De Clementia* (*On Mercy*) 1.19.6. **1341 thridde point,** see line 1028 above. **1344 Tullius,** Cicero, *De Officiis* (*On Duties*) 1.73. **1347 Tullius,** not found in Cicero. **seith that,** El reads "seith the." **1348 Cassidorus,** *Variae Epistolae* (*Various Letters*) 1.17. **1349–52** See lines 1035, 1049, and 1182. **1354 repreved by the resouns aforeseyd,** discredited by the arguments above; lines 1243ff. **1355 doctrine of Tullius,** Cicero, *De Officiis* (*On Duties*) 2.5; paraphrased in lines 1200–10.

addeth in this matiere. / For Tullius put a thing° which that he clepeth° 'consentynge'; this is to seyn, / who been they, and how manye, and whiche been they that consenteden to° thy conseil in thy wilfulnesse to doon hastif° vengeance. / And lat us considere also who been they, and how manye been they, and whiche been they that consenteden to your adversaries. / And certes, as to the firste poynt, it is wel knowen whiche folk been they that consenteden to youre hastif wilfulnesse, / for trewely alle tho that conseilleden yow to maken sodeyn werre ne been nat youre freendes. / Lat us now considere whiche been they° that ye holde so greetly youre freendes as to youre persone. / For al be it so that ye be mighty and riche, certes ye ne been but allone. / For certes, ye ne han no child but a doghter; / ne ye ne han bretheren ne cosyns germayns° ne noon oother neigh kynrede°, / wherfore that° youre enemys for drede sholde stinte° to plede° with yow or to destroye youre persone. / Ye knowen also that youre richesses mooten° been dispended° in diverse parties°; / and whan that every wight hath his part, they ne wollen taken but litel reward to venge thy deeth. / But thyne enemys been thre, and they han manie children, bretheren, cosyns, and oother ny kynrede. / And though so were° that thou haddest slayn of hem two or thre, yet dwellen ther ynowe° to wreken° hire deeth and to sle thy persone. / And though so be that° youre kynrede be moore siker° and stedefast than the kyn of youre adversarie, / yet nathelees youre kynrede nys° but a fer° kynrede; they been but litel syb° to yow, / and the kyn of your enemys been ny syb° to hem. And certes, as in that°, hire condicioun is bet than youres. / Thanne lat us considere also if the conseillyng of hem that conseilleden yow to taken sodeyn vengeaunce, wheither it accorde to resoun. / And certes, ye knowe wel nay. / For as by right and resoun, ther may no man taken vengeance on no wight but the juge that hath the jurisdiccioun of it, / whan it is graunted hym to take thilke° vengeance hastily or attemprely° as the lawe requireth. / And yet mooreover of thilke word that Tullius clepeth 'consentynge,' / thou shalt considere if thy might and thy power may consenten° and suffise to thy wilfulnesse and to thy conseillours. / And certes, thou mayst wel seyn that nay. / For sikerly°, as for to speke proprely, we may do nothing but oonly swich thyng as we may doon rightfully. / And certes, rightfully ne mowe ye° take no vengeance as of your propre auctoritee. / Thanne mowe° ye seen that youre power ne consenteth° nat ne accordeth nat with your wilfulnesse. / Lat us now examyne the thridde point that Tullius clepeth 'consequent°.' / Thou shalt understonde that the vengeance that thou purposest for to take is the consequent. / And therof folweth another vengeaunce, peril, and werre, and other damages withoute nombre of whiche we be nat war as at this tyme. / And as touchynge the fourthe point, that Tullius clepeth 'engendrynge°,' / thou shalt considere that this wrong which that is doon to thee is engendred of° the hate of thyne enemys; / and of the vengeance takinge upon that wolde engendre another vengeance and muchel° sorwe and wastinge of richesses, as I seyde. /

"Now sire, as to the point that Tullius clepeth 'causes,' which that is the laste point, / thou shalt understonde that the wrong that thou hast receyved hath certeine causes / whiche that clerkes clepen *oriens* and *efficiens*, and *causa longinqua* and *causa propinqua*, this is to seyn, the fer cause and the ny cause. / The fer cause is Almighty God, that is cause of alle thinges. / The neer cause is thy thre enemys. / The cause accidental was hate. / The cause material been the fyve woundes of thy doghter. / The cause formal is

1360 put a thing, *added a concern,* **clepeth,** *calls* **1361 consenteden to,** *agreed with,* **hastif,** *hasty* **1365 whiche been they,** *of what kind they are* **1368 cosyns germayns,** *first cousins,* **neigh kynrede,** *near relatives* **1369 wherfore that,** *because of whom,* **stinte,** *cease,* **plede,** *dispute* **1370 mooten,** *must,* **dispended,** *divided* (after death), **diverse parties,** *various parts* **1373 though so were,** *if it were,* **ynowe,** *enough,* **wreken,** *avenge* **1374 though so be that,** *even though,* **siker,** *dependable* **1375 nys,** *is nothing,* **fer,** *distant,* **syb,** *related* **1376 ny syb,** *closely related,* **as in that,** *in that respect* **1380 thilke,** *that,* **hastily or attemprely,** *swiftly or with care* **1382 consenten,** *accord with* **1384 sikerly,** *surely* **1385 ne mowe ye,** *you may not* **1386 mowe,** *may,* **consenteth,** *matches* **1387 clepeth 'consequent,'** *calls 'the consequence'* **1390 clepeth 'engendrynge,'** *calls 'the producing'* **1391 engendred of,** *produced by* **1392 muchel,** *much*

1361 and whiche been they, omitted in El. **1366 been but,** El reads "been nat but." **1372 enemys been thre,** see 970n above. **1395** ***oriens,*** rising. ***efficiens,*** efficient. ***causa longinqua,*** remote cause. ***causa propinqua,*** near cause. Chaucer seems to have added these Latin words to his French source. **1397–1401** These parallel three of the four Aristotelian categories of cause: *material,* i.e., in matter or material substance; *formal,* i.e., the shape or form; and *final,* i.e., the end or purpose. Aristotle's *efficient* cause is close to the modern notion of cause, and although *accidental* here may mean something similar, it is usually applied to nonessential features.

the manere of hire werkynge that° broghten laddres and cloumben° in at thy wyndowes. / The cause final was for to sle thy doghter; it letted° nat in as muche as in hem was. / But for to speken of the fer cause, as to what ende they shul come, or what shal finally bityde of° hem in this caas, ne kan I nat deme° but by conjectynge and by supposinge. / For we shul suppose that they shul come to a wikked ende, / by cause that the Book of Decrees seith, 'Seelden° or with greet peyne been causes ybroght to good ende whanne they been baddely bigonne.' /

"Now sire, if men wolde axe me, why that God suffred men to do yow this vileinye, certes I kan nat wel answere as for no sothfastnesse°. / For th'apostle seith that the sciences° and the juggementz of oure lord God Almighty been ful depe. / Ther may no man comprehende ne serchen hem suffisantly. / Nathelees, by certeyne presumpciouns and conjectynges I holde and bileeve / that God which that is ful of justice and of rightwisenesse° hath suffred° this bityde° by juste cause resonable. /

"Thy name is Melibee, this is to seyn, 'a man that drynketh hony.' / Thou hast ydronke so muchel hony of sweete temporeel richesses and delices° and honours of this world / that thou art dronken and hast forgeten Jesu Crist thy creatour. / Thou ne hast nat doon to hym swich honour and reverence as thee oughte. / Ne thou ne hast nat wel ytaken kepe° to the wordes of Ovide that seith, / 'Under the hony of the goodes of the body is hyd the venym that sleeth the soule.' / And Salomon seith, 'If thou hast founden hony, ete of it that suffiseth, / for if thou ete of it out of mesure° thou shalt spewe°,' and be nedy and poure. / And peraventure° Crist hath thee in despit° and hath turned awey fro thee his face and his eereis of misericorde°, / and also he hath suffred° that thou hast been punysshed in the manere that thow has ytrespassed°. / Thou has doon synne agayn our lord Crist, / for certes the thre enemys of mankynde, that is to seyn, the flessh, the feend, and the world, / thou hast suffred hem entre into thyn herte wilfully by the wyndowes of thy body, / and hast nat defended thyself suffisantly agayns hire assautes° and hire temptaciouns, so that they han wounded thy soule in fyve places, / this is to seyn, the deedly synnes that been entred into thyn herte by thy fyve wittes°. / And in the same manere our lord Crist hath woold° and suffred that thy three enemys been entred into thyn hous by the wyndowes / and han ywounded thy doghter in the forseyde manere." /

"Certes," quod Melibee, "I se wel that ye enforce yow muchel° by wordes to overcome me in swich manere that I shal nat venge me of myne enemys, / shewynge me the perils and the yveles that myghten falle of this vengeance. / But whoso wolde considere in alle vengeances the perils and yveles that myghte sewe of° vengeance takynge, / a man wolde never take vengeance, and that were harm°. / For by the vengeance takinge been the wikked men dissevered° fro the goode men. / And they that han wyl to do wikkednesse restreyne hir wikked purpos whan they seen the punyssynge and chastisynge of the trespassours." /

And to this answerde dame Prudence, "Certes," seyde she, "I graunte wel that of vengeaunce cometh muchel yvel and muchel good, / but vengeaunce taking aperteneth nat° unto everichoon° but only unto juges and unto hem that han jurisdiccioun upon the trespassours. / And yet seye I moore, that right as a singuler° persone synneth in takynge vengeance of another man, / right so synneth the juge if he do no vengeance of hem that it han disserved°. / For Senec seith thus, 'That maister,' he seith, 'is good that proveth shrewes°.' / And as Cassidore

---

1400 that, *who,* **cloumben,** *climbed* **1401 letted,** *lacked* (i.e., they succeeded as far as they were able) **1402 bityde of,** *happen to,* **deme,** *judge* **1404 Seelden,** *seldom* **1405 as for no sothfastnesse,** *i.e., with no certainty* **1406 sciences,** *wisdom* **1409 rightwisenesse,** *righteousness,* **suffred,** *allowed,* **bityde,** *to happen* **1411 delices,** *delights* **1414 ytaken kepe,** *paid attention* **1417 out of mesure,** *immoderately,* **spewe,** *vomit* **1418 peraventure,** *perhaps,* **despit,** *contempt,* **eereis of misericorde,** *ears of mercy* **1419 suffred,** *allowed,* **ytrespassed,** *sinned* **1423 hire assautes,** *their assaults* **1424 wittes,** *senses* **1425 woold,** *willed* **1427 enforce yow muchel,** *try hard* **1429 sewe of,** *result from* **1430 harm,** *wrong* **1431 dissevered,** *separated* **1434 aperteneth nat,** *is not appropriate,* **everichoon,** *everyone* **1435 singuler,** *individual* **1436 disserved,** *deserved* **1437 proveth shrewes,** *tests villains*

1404 Book of Decrees, *Decretum Gratiani* (*Gratian's Decrees*) 2.1.1.25, a twelfth-century compilation of canon law. **1406 th'apostle,** Paul, Romans 11.33. **1410 Melibee . . . ,** the etymology (Lat. *mel bibens,* honey drinking, i.e., living the good life) helps to make the tale a psychomachia, or internal allegory; see 967n above. **1414–15 Ovide,** Ovid, *Amores* 1.8.104. **1416–17 Salomon,** Proverbs 25.16. **1433–34** Lines found in no manuscript, apparently skipped by Chaucer; translated from the French source by Skeat in his edition. **1437 Senec,** not in Seneca, but Martinus Dumiensis, *De Moribus* (*On Customs*) 114. **1438 Cassidore,** Cassiodorus, *Variae Epistolae* (*Various Letters*) 1.4.

seith, 'A man dredeth to do outrages whan he woot° and knoweth that it displeseth to the juges and sovereyns°.' / Another seith, 'The juge that dredeth to do right maketh men shrewes.' / And Seint Paule the apostle seith in his Epistle, whan he wryteth unto the Romayns, that the juges beren nat the spere withouten cause, / but they beren it to punysse the shrewes and mysdoeres and to defende the goode men. / If ye wol thanne take vengeance of youre enemys, ye shul retourne or have your recours to the juge that hath the jurisdiccion upon hem, / and he shal punysse hem as the lawe axeth and requireth." /

"A," quod Melibee, "this vengeance liketh me nothyng°. / I bithenke me° now and take heede, how fortune hath norissed° me fro my childhede, and hath holpen° me to passe many a stroong paas°. / Now wol I assayen hir°, trowynge° with Goddes helpe, that she shal helpe me my shame for to venge." /

"Certes," quod Prudence, "if ye wol werke by my conseil, ye shul nat assaye fortune by no wey, / ne ye shul nat lene° or bowe unto hir after the word of Senec / for 'thynges that been folily° doon and that been in hope of fortune shullen never come to good ende.' / And as the same Senec seith, 'The moore cleer and the moore shynyng that fortune is, the moore brotil° and the sonner° broken she is.' / Trusteth nat in hire, for she nys nat stidefast ne stable, / for whan thow trowest° to be moost seur° and siker° of hire help, she wol faille thee and deceyve thee. / And where as ye seyn that fortune hath norissed yow fro youre childhede, / I seye that in so muchel° shul ye the lasse° truste in hire and in hir wit°. / For Senec seith, 'What man that is norissed by fortune, she maketh hym a greet fool.' / Now thanne, syn ye desire and axe° vengeance, and the vengeance that is doon after the lawe and bifore the juge ne liketh yow nat, / and the vengeance that is doon in hope of fortune is perilous and uncertein, / thanne have ye noon oother remedie but for to have youre recours unto the sovereyn juge° that vengeth° alle vileynyes and wronges, / and he shal venge yow after that° hymself witnesseth, where as he seith, / 'Leveth the vengeance to me and I shal do it.'" /

Melibee answerde, "If I ne venge me nat of the vileynye that men han doon to me, / I sompne° or warne° hem that han doon to me that vileynye and alle othere to do me another vileynye. / For it is writen, 'If thou take no vengeance of an oold vileynye, thou sompnest thyne adversaries to do thee a newe vileynye.' / And also, for my suffrance°, men wolden do to me so muchel vileynye that I myghte neither bere it ne susteene, / and so sholde I been put° and holden over lowe°. / For men seyn, 'In muchel suffrynge shul manye thynges falle unto thee whiche thou shalt nat mowe suffre°.'" /

"Certes," quod Prudence, "I graunte yow that over muchel suffraunce° nys nat good, / but yet ne folweth it nat therof that every persone to whom men doon vileynye take of it vengeance, / for that aperteneth° and longeth° al oonly to the juges, for they shul venge the vileynyes and injuries. / And therfore tho° two auctoritees that ye han seyd above been oonly understonden in the juges, / for whan they suffren° over muchel the wronges and the vileynyes to be doon withouten punysshynge, / they sompne nat a man al oonly° for to do newe wronges, but they comanden it. / Also a wys man seith that the juge that correcteth nat the synnere comandeth and biddeth hym do synne. / And the juges and sovereyns myghten in hire land so muchel suffre of° the shrewes° and mysdoeres, / that they sholden by swich suffrance°, by proces of tyme°, wexen of swich° power and myght that they sholden putte out the juges and the sovereyns from hire places /

1438 woot, *understands* **1438 sovereyns,** *monarchs* **1444 liketh me nothyng,** *pleases me not at all* **1445 bithenke me,** *recall,* **norissed,** *nourished,* **holpen,** *helped,* **stroong paas,** *difficult situation* **1446 assayen hir,** *test her,* **trowynge,** *believing* **1448 lene,** *bend* **1449 folily,** *foolishly* **1450 brotil,** *brittle,* **sonner,** *sooner* **1452 trowest,** *believe* (yourself), **seur,** *sure,* **siker,** *certain* **1454 in so muchel,** *for this reason,* **lasse,** *less,* **wit,** *cunning* **1456 axe,** *ask* **1458 sovereyn juge,** i.e., *God,* **vengeth,** *avenges* **1459 after that,** *as* **1462 sompne,** *summon,* **warne,** *inform* **1464 suffrance,** *patience* **1465 put,** *thrust,* **holden over lowe,** *held overly low* **1466 shalt nat mowe suffre,** i.e., *cannot endure* **1467 over muchel suffraunce,** *too much patient endurance* **1469 aperteneth,** *is appropriate,* **longeth,** *belongs* **1470 tho,** *those,* **auctoritees,** *writings* **1471 suffren,** *allow* **1472 sompne nat a man al oonly,** *not only summon a man* **1474 so muchel suffre of,** *allow so much from,* **shrewes,** *villains* **1475 swich suffrance,** *such allowance,* **by proces of tyme,** *eventually,* **wexen of swich,** *grow to such*

1439 Another seith, Publilius Syrus, *Sententiae* 528. **1440 Seint Paule . . . Romayns,** Romans 13.4; "spere" (spear) is an error for sword. **1448–49 Senec,** not Seneca, but Publilius Syrus, *Sententiae* 320. **1450 Senec,** Publilius Syrus, 189. **1455 Senec,** Publilius Syrus, 172. **1455 a greet,** Hg reads "to greet a." **1460** Romans 12.19. **1463 it is writen,** Publilius Syrus, 645. **1466 men seyn,** Publilius Syrus, 487. **1473 wys man,** Caecilius Balbus, *De Nugis Philosophorum* (*On the Trifles of Philosophers*) 41.4.

and atte laste maken hem lesen° hire lordshipes. /"But lat us now putte° that ye have leve° to venge yow. / I seye ye been nat of myght and power as now to venge yow. / For if ye wole maken comparisoun unto the myght of youre adversaries, ye shul fynde in manye thynges that I have shewed yow er this that hire condicioun is bettre than youres. / And therfore seye I that it is good as now that ye suffre and be pacient. /

"Forthermoore, ye knowen wel that, after the commune sawe°, it is a woodnesse° a man to stryve with a strenger° or a moore myghty man than he is hymself, / and for to stryve with a man of evene strengthe—that is to seyn, with as strong a man as he—it is peril, / and for to stryve with a weyker man it is folie. / And therfore sholde a man flee° stryvynge as muchel as he myghte. / For Salomon seith, 'It is a greet worship to a man to kepen him fro noyse and stryf.' / And if it so bifalle or happe° that a man of gretter myght and strengthe than thou art do thee grevaunce, / studie and bisye thee rather to stille° the same grevaunce than for to venge thee. / For Senec seith that he putteth hym in greet peril that stryveth with a gretter man than he is hymself. / And Catoun seith, 'If a man of hyer estaat or degree or moore myghty than thou do thee anoy or grevaunce°, suffre° hym, / for he that oones° hath greved thee another tyme may releeve thee and helpe.' / Yet sette I caas°, ye have bothe myght and licence for to venge yow. / I seye that ther be ful manye thynges that shul restreyne yow of vengeance takinge, / and make yow for to enclyne to suffre, and for to han pacience in the thynges that han been doon to yow. / First and foreward, if ye wole considere the defautes° that been in youre owene persone, / for whiche defautes God hath suffred yow have this tribulacioun°, as I have seyd yow heer biforn. / For the poete seith that we oghte paciently taken the tribulacions that comen to us, whan we thynken and consideren that we han disserved to have hem. / And Seint Gregorie seith that whan a man considereth wel the nombre of his defautes and of his synnes, / the peynes and the tribulaciouns that he suffreth semen the lesse unto hym; / and inasmuche as hym thynketh his synnes moore hevy and grevous, / insomuche semeth his peyne the lighter and the esier unto hym. / Also ye owen° for to enclyne and bowe youre herte to take the pacience of oure lord Jesu Crist, as seith Seint Peter in his Epistles. / 'Jesu Crist,' he seith, 'hath suffred for us and yeven° ensample to every man to folwe and sewe° him, / for he dide never synne, ne nevere cam ther a vileynous word out of his mouth. / Whan men cursed hym, he cursed hem noght, and whan men betten° hym, he manaced° hem noght.' / Also the grete pacience which the seintes that been in paradys han had in tribulaciouns that they han ysuffred withouten hir desert or gilt / oghte muchel stiren° yow to pacience. / Forthermoore, ye sholde enforce yow° to have pacience, / consideryinge that the tribulaciouns of this world but litel while endure and soone passed been and goone. / And the joye that a man seketh to have by pacience in tribulaciouns is perdurable°, after that the apostle seith in his Epistle. / 'The joye of God,' he seith, 'is perdurable,' that is to seyn, everlastinge. / Also troweth° and bileveth stedefastly that he nys nat wel ynorissed° ne wel ytaught that kan nat have pacience or wol nat receyve pacience. / For Salomon seith that the doctrine and the wit of a man is knowen by pacience. / And in another place he seith that he that is pacient governeth hym by greet prudence. / And the same Salomon seith, 'The angry and wrathful man maketh noyses, and the pacient man atempreth hym and stilleth°.' / He seith also, 'It is moore worth° to be pacient than for to be right strong; / and he that may have the lordshipe of his owene herte is moore to preyse than he that by his force or strengthe taketh grete citees.' / And therfore seith Seint Jame in

1476 lesen, *lose* **1477 putte,** *assume,* **leve,** *permission* **1481 sawe,** *proverb,* **woodnesse,** *madness* (for), **strenger,** *stronger* **1484 flee,** *avoid* **1486 happe,** *happen* **1487 stille,** *quiet* **1489 grevaunce,** *injure,* **suffre,** *endure* **1490 oones,** *once* **1491 sette I cas,** *let me assume* **1494 defautes,** *faults* **1495 tribulacioun,** *trouble* **1501 owen,** *ought* **1502 yeven,** *given,* **sewe,** *imitate* **1504 betten,** *beat,* **manaced,** *threatened* **1506 stiren,** *encourage* **1507 enforce yow,** *push yourself* **1509 perdurable,** *immortal* **1511 troweth,** *accept,* **nys nat wel ynorissed,** *is not well nourished* **1514 atempreth hym and stilleth,** *controls and quiets himself* **1515 moore worth,** *worth more*

1485 Salomon, Proverbs 20.3. **1488 Senec,** Publilius Syrus, *Sententiae* 483. **1489–90 Catoun,** Dionysius Cato, supposed author of *Disticha Catonis* (*Cato's Couplets*) 4.39. **1493 thynges,** Hg reads "wronges." **1496 the poet,** unidentified. **1497 Seint Gregorie . . . ,** unidentified passage. **1501–04 Seint Peter . . . ,** 1 Peter 2.21–23. **1509 the apostle,** Paul, 2 Corinthians 4.17. **1512 Salomon,** Proverbs 19.11 (Vulgate). **1513** Proverbs 14.29 (Vulgate). **1514** Proverbs 15.18. **hym,** El and Hg read "hem." **1515–16** Proverbs 16.32.

his Epistle that pacience is a greet vertu of perfeccioun." /

"Certes," quod Melibee, "I graunte yow, dame Prudence, that pacience is a greet vertu of perfeccioun. / But every man may nat have the perfeccioun that ye seken; / ne I nam nat° of the nombre of right parfite men, / for myn herte may never been in pees unto° the tyme it be venged. / And al be it so that it was greet peril to myne enemys to do me a vileynye in takinge vengeance upon me, / yet tooken they noon heede of the peril but fulfilleden hire wikked wyl and hir corage°. / And therfore methynketh° men oghten nat repreve° me though I putte me in a litel peril for to venge me, / and though I do a greet excesse, that is to seyn, that I venge oon outrage by another." /

"A," quod dame Prudence, "ye seyn youre wil and as yow lyketh°; / but in no caas of the world a man sholde nat doon outrage ne excesse for to vengen hym. / For Cassidore seith that as yvel° dooth he that vengeth hym by outrage as he that dooth the outrage. / And therfore ye shul venge yow after the ordre of right, that is to seyn by the lawe, and noght by excesse ne by outrage. / And also, if ye wol venge yow of the outrage of youre adversaries in oother manere than right comandeth, ye synnen. / And therfore seith Senec that a man shal nevere vengen shrewednesse° by shrewednesse. / And if ye seye that right axeth° a man to defenden violence by violence and fightyng by fightyng, / certes ye seye sooth° whan the defense is doon anon° withouten intervalle or withouten tariyng or delay / for to deffenden hym and nat for to vengen hym. / And it bihoveth° that a man putte swich attemperance° in his deffense, / that men have no cause ne matiere to repreven° hym that deffendeth hym of° excesse and outrage, for ellis were it agayn° resoun. / Pardee°, ye knowen wel that ye maken no deffense as now for to deffende yow, but for to venge yow, / and so seweth° it that ye han no wyl to do youre dede attemprely°. / And therfore, methynketh that pacience is good. For Salomon seith that he that is nat pacient shal have greet harm." /

"Certes," quod Melibee, "I graunte yow that whan a man is inpacient and wrooth of° that that toucheth° him noght and that aperteneth° nat unto hym though it harme him, it is no wonder. / For the lawe seith that he is coupable° that entremetteth° or medleth with swych thyng as aperteneth nat unto hym. / And Salomon seith that he that entremetteth hym of the noyse° or strif of another man is lyk to hym that taketh an hound by the eris. / For right as he that taketh a straunge hound by the eris is outherwhile° biten with° the hound, / right in the same wise is it resoun that he have harm that by his inpacience medleth hym of the noyse of another man wher as it aperteneth nat unto hym. / But ye knowen wel that this dede—that is to seyn, my grief and my disese°—toucheth me right ny°. / And therfore, though I be wrooth and inpacient, it is no merveille. / And savynge youre grace°, I kan nat seen that it mighte greetly harme me though I tooke vengeaunce, / for I am richer and moore myghty than myne enemys been. / And wel knowen ye that by moneye and by havynge grete possessions been all the thynges of this world governed. / And Salomon seith that alle thynges obeyen to moneye." /

Whan Prudence hadde herd hir housbonde avanten hym° of his richesse and of his moneye, dispreisynge° the power of his adversaries, she spak and seyde in this wise, / "Certes, dere sire, I graunte yow that ye been riche and myghty, / and that the richesses been goode to hem that han wel ygeten° hem and wel konne° usen hem. / For right as the body of a man may nat lyven withoute the soule, namore may it live withouten temporeel goodes. / And for richesses may a man gete

1520 ne I nam nat, *I am not* **1521 unto,** *until* **1523 hir corage,** *their desire* **1524 methynketh,** *it seems to me,* **repreve,** *blame* **1526 as yow lyketh,** *what pleases you* **1528 as yvel,** *as much evil* **1531 shrewednesse,** *wickedness* **1532 right axeth,** *justice demands* **1533 sooth,** *truth,* **anon,** *immediately* **1535 bihoveth,** *is appropriate,* **putte swich attemperance,** *use such moderation* **1536 repreven,** *blame,* **deffendeth hym of,** *defends himself against,* **agayn,** *against* **1537 Pardee,** *by God* **1538 seweth,** *follows,* **attemprely,** *temperately* **1540 wrooth of,** *angered by,* **toucheth,** *involves,* **aperteneth,** *pertains* **1541 coupable,** *culpable,* **entremetteth,** *interferes* **1542 noyse,** *uproar* **1543 outherwhile,** *sometimes,* **with,** *by* **1545 disese,** *distress,* **right ny,** *very closely* **1547 savynge youre grace,** *with all due respect* **1551 avanten hym,** *boast,* **dispreisynge,** *belittling* **1553 ygeten,** *acquire,* **konne,** *can*

1517 Seint Jame, adapted from James 1.4. **1528 Cassidore,** Cassiodorus; the following is posed as a question in *Variae Epistolae* 1.30. **1531 Senec,** not in Seneca, but Martinus Dumiensis, *De Moribus* (*On Customs*) 139. **1538 seweth,** El reads "sheweth." **1539 Salomon,** Proverbs 19.19. **1541 entremeteth,** this verb is used in the angry exchange between the Friar and the Summoner in *WBP* 3.834.**1542 Salomon,** Proverbs 26.17. **1550 Salomon,** Ecclesiastes 10.19.

hym grete freendes. / And therfore seith 1555
Pamphilles, 'If a netherdes° doghter,' seith
he, 'be riche, she may chesen of a thousand men
which she wol take to hir housbonde, / for of a
thousand men oon° wol nat forsaken hire ne
refusen hire.' / And this Pamphilles seith also,
'If thou be right happy (that is to seyn, if thou
be right riche) thou shalt fynd a greet nombre of
felawes° and freendes. / And if thy fortune change
that thou wexe° poure, farewel freendshipe
and felaweshipe, / for thou shalt be al alloone
withouten any compaignye, but if it be the
compaignye of poure folk.' / And yet seith 1560
this Pamphilles moreover that they that been
thralle and bonde of lynage° shullen been maad
worthy and noble by the richesses. / And right so
as by richesses ther comen manye goodes, right so
by poverte come ther manye harmes and yveles. /
For greet poverte constreyneth a man to do
manye yveles. / And therfore clepeth Cassidore
poverte 'the moder of ruyne°.' / that is to seyn
the mooder of overthrowynge or fallynge
doun. / And therfore seith Piers Alfonce, 1565
'Oon of the gretteste adversitees of this world
is / whan a free man by kynde or by burthe° is
constreyned by poverte to eten° the almesse° of
his enemy.' / And the same seith Innocent in
oon of his bookes. He seith that sorweful and
myshappy is the condicioun of a poure begger, /
for if he axe nat his mete° he dyeth for hunger, /
and if he axe he dyeth for shame; and algates°
necessitee constreyneth hym to axe. / And 1570
therfore seith Salomon that bet it is to dye
than for to have swich poverte. / And as the same
Salomon seith, 'Bettre it is to dye of bitter deeth
than for to lyven in swich wise.' / By thise resons that
I have seid unto yow, and by manye othere resons
that I koude seye, / I graunte yow that richesses
been goode to hem that geten hem wel, and to
hem that wel usen tho° richesses. / And therfore
wol I shewe yow hou ye shul have yow°, and how ye
shul bere yow in gaderynge° of richesses, and
in what manere ye shul usen hem. / 1575

"First, ye shul geten hem withouten greet
desir, by good leyser sokyngly°, and nat over
hastily. / For a man that is to desiryinge to gete
richesses abaundoneth hym first to thefte and to
alle otheryveles. / And therfore seith Salomon,
'He that hasteth hym to bisily to wexe riche shal be
noon innocent.' / He seith also that the richesse
that hastily cometh to a man soone and lightly
gooth and passeth fro a man, / but that richesse
that cometh litel and litel° wexeth° alwey
and multiplieth. / And sire, ye shul geten 1580
richesses by youre wit and by youre travaille°
unto youre profit, / and that withouten wrong or
harmdoinge to any oother persone. / For the lawe
seith that ther maketh no man himselven riche if
he do harm to another wight°, / this is to seyn that
nature deffendeth° and forbedeth by right that no
man make hymself riche unto the harm of another
persone. / And Tullius seith that no sorwe ne no
drede of deeth, ne nothing that may falle
unto a man / is so muchel agayns nature as a 1585
man to encressen his owene profit to the
harm of another man. / And though the grete
men and the myghty men geten richesses moore
lightly° than thou, / yet shaltou° nat been ydel ne
slow to do thy profit°, for thou shalt in alle wise
flee ydelnesse. / For Salomon seith that ydelnesse techeth a man to do manye yveles. / And
the same Salomon seith that he that travailleth°
and bisieth hym to tilien° his land shal eten
breed, / but he that is ydel and casteth hym° 1590
to no bisynesse ne occupacioun shal falle into
poverte and dye for hunger. / And he that is ydel
and slow kan never fynde covenable° tyme for to
doon his profit. / For ther is a versifiour° seith that

1556 netherdes, *cowherd's* **1557 oon,** *one* **1558 felawes,** *companions* **1559 wexe,** *become* **1561 thralle and bonde of lynage,** *slaves by birth* **1564 ruyne,** *ruin* **1567 free man by kynde or by burthe,** *a man free by nature or birth,* **eten,** *eat,* **almesse,** *charity* **1569 axe nat his mete,** *doesn't beg for food* **1570 algates,** *always* **1574 tho,** *those* **1575 have yow,** *behave yourself,* **gaderynge,** *gathering* **1576 leyser sokyngly,** *time gradually* **1580 litel and litel,** *little by little,* **wexeth,** *grows* **1581 travaille,** *labor* **1583 wight,** *person* **1584 deffendeth,** *prohibits* **1587 lightly,** *easily* **1588 shaltou,** *you should,* **to do thy profit,** *to make profit* **1590 travailleth,** *labors,* **tilien,** *cultivate* **1591 casteth hym,** *devotes himself*

1556–57 Pamphilles, hero of twelfth-century poetic dialogue *Pamphilus de Amore* (*Pamphilius on Love*), 53–54. **1556 seith he,** Hg reads "he seith." **which she . . . housbonde,** omitted in El. **1558** Not from *Pamphilus,* but Ovid *Tristia,* 1.9.5–6. **1560** Compare *KnT* 1.2779 and *MilT* 1.3204. **1561 Pamphilles,** not from *Pamphilus*; see Petrus Alphonsus, *Disciplina Clericalis* (*Guide for Scholars*) ex. 4.2. **1564 Cassidore,** Cassiodorus, *Variae Epistolae* 9.13. **1566–67 Piers Alfonce,** Petrus Alphonsus, *Disciplina Clericalis* (*Guide for Scholars*) 2.2. **1568–70 Innocent . . . ,** Pope Innocent III, *De Miseria Conditionis Humane* (*On the Misery of the Human Condition*) 1.16. **1571 Salomon,** Ecclesiasticus 40.29 (Vulgate). **1572 same Salomon,** Ecclesiasticus 30.17 (Vulgate). **1576 sokyngly,** El reads "sekyngly." **1578 Salomon,** Proverbs 28.20. **1579 seith also,** Proverbs 13.11. **1585–86 Tullius . . . ,** Cicero *De Officiis* (*On Duties*) 3.21. **1589 Salomon,** Ecclesiasticus 33.27 (Vulgate). **1590 Salomon,** Proverbs 28.19.

the ydel man excuseth hym in wynter by cause of the grete cold, and in somer by enchesoun° of the heete. / For thise causes seith Caton, 'Waketh° and enclyneth nat yow over muchel for to slepe, for over muchel reste norisseth and causeth manye vices.' / And therfore seith Seint Jerome, 'Dooth somme goode dedes that the devel which is oure enemy ne fynde yow nat unocupied.' / For the devel ne taketh nat lightly unto his werkynge swiche as he fyndeth occupied in goode werkes.' /

"Thanne thus in getynge richesses ye mosten° flee ydelnesse. / And afterward ye shul use the richesses whiche ye have geten by youre wit and by youre travaille / in swich a manere that men holde nat yow to scars°, ne to sparynge, ne to fool large°, that is to seyn over large a spender. / For right as men blamen an avaricious man by cause of his scarsetee° and chyncherye°, / in the same wise is he to blame that spendeth over largely. / And therfore seith Caton, 'Use,' he seith, 'thy richesses that thou hast geten / in swich a manere that men have no matiere ne cause to calle thee neither wrecche ne chynche°, / for it is a greet shame to a man to have a pouere° herte and a riche purs.' / He seith also, 'The goodes that thou hast ygeten, use hem by mesure°,' that is to seyn, spende hem mesurably. / For they that folily wasten and despenden the goodes that they han, / whan they han namore propre° of hire owene, they shapen hem° to take the goodes of another man. / I seye thanne that ye shul fleen avarice° / usynge youre richesses in swich manere that men seye nat that youre richesses been yburyed, / but that ye have hem in youre myght and in youre weeldynge°. / For a wys man repreveth° the avaricious man and seith thus in two vers: / 'Wherto and why burieth a man his goodes by his grete avarice, and knoweth wel that nedes moste he dye, / for deeth is the ende of every man as in this present lyf?' / And for what cause or enchesoun° joyneth° he hym or knytteth he hym so faste° unto his goodes, / that alle his wittes mowen nat disseveren° hym or departen hym from his goodes, / and knoweth wel, or oghte knowe, that whan he is deed he shal nothing bere with hym out of this world? / And therfore seith Seint Augustin that the avaricious man is likned° unto helle, / that the moore it swelweth°, the moore desir it hath to swelwe and devoure. / And as wel as ye wolde eschewe° to be called an avaricious man or chynche°, / as wel sholde ye kepe yow and governe yow in swich a wise that men calle yow nat fool large°. / Therfore seith Tullius, 'The goodes,' he seith, 'of thyn hous ne sholde nat been hyd, ne kept so cloos but that they mighte been opened by pitee and debonairetee°'— / that is to seyn, to yeven part to hem that han greet nede— / 'ne thy goodes shullen nat been so opene to been every mannes goodes.' /

"Afterward, in getynge of youre richesses and in usynge hem ye shul alwey have thre thynges in youre herte, / that is to seyn, our lord God, conscience, and good name. / First, ye shul have God in youre herte, / and for no richesse ye shullen do nothyng which may in any manere displese God that is youre creatour and maker. / For after the word of Salomon, 'It is bettre to have a litel good with the love of God / than to have muchel good and tresour and lese° the love of his lord God.' / And the prophete seith that bettre it is to been a good man and have litel good and tresour / than to been holden° a shrewe° and have grete richesses. / And yet seye I ferthermoore that ye sholde alwey doon your bisynesse to gete yow richesses, / so that ye gete hem with good conscience. / And th'apostle seith that ther nys thyng in this world of which we sholden have so greet joye as whan oure conscience bereth

1592 covenable, *convenient* **1593 versifiour,** *poet,* **enchesoun,** *reason* **1594 Waketh,** *be alert* **1597 mosten,** *must* **1599 to scars,** *too stingy,* **to fool large,** *too foolishly generous* **1600 scarsetee,** *stinginess,* **chyncherye,** *miserliness* **1603 chynche,** *miser* **1604 pouere,** *poor* **1605 by mesure,** *in moderation* **1607 propre,** *property,* **shapen hem,** *prepare themselves* **1608 fleen avarice,** *flee from greed* **1610 weeldynge,** *control* **1611 repreveth,** *blames* **1614 enchesoun,** *reason,* **joyneth,** *attaches,* **faste,** *tightly* **1615 mowen nat disseveren,** *may not separate* **1617 likned,** *compared* **1618 swelweth,** *swallows* **1619 eschewe,** *avoid,* **chynche,** *miser* **1620 fool large,** *foolishly generous* **1621 debonairetee,** *graciousness* **1629 lese,** *lose* **1631 holden,** *thought,* **shrewe,** *villain*

1593 Not identified, but see Proverbs 20.4. **1594 Caton,** Dionysius Cato, supposed author of *Disticha Catonis* (*Cato's Couplets*) 1.2. **1595 Seint Jerome,** see his *Epistles* 125.11. **goode dedes,** El reads "goodes." **1600 chyncherye,** El reads "chyngerie." **1602–03 Caton . . . ,** *Disticha* 4.16. **1605** *Disticha* 3.21. **1609 yburyed,** perhaps an allusion to the parable of buried talents; Matthew 25.14–30. **1612–13** Quotation not identified. **1617–18 Seint Augustin . . . ,** not identified in Augustine; see Proverbs 27.20. **1621–23 Tullius . . . ,** Cicero, *De Officiis* 2.55. **1628–29 Salomon,** Proverbs 15.16 has *fear* (Lat. *timore*) rather than *love.* **1630–31 prophete . . . ,** Psalms 36.16 (Vulgate). **1634 th'apostle,** Paul, 2 Corinthians 1.12.

us good witnesse. / And the wise man seith, 'The substance° of a man is ful good whan synne is nat in mannes conscience.' / Afterward in getynge of youre richesses and in usynge of hem, / yow moste have greet bisynesse° and greet diligence° that youre goode name be alwey kept° and conserved. / For Salomon seith that bettre it is and moore it availleth a man to have a good name than for to have grete richesses. / And therfore he seith in another place, 'Do greet diligence,' seith Salomon, 'in kepyng of thy freend and of thy goode name, / for it shal lenger abide with thee than any tresour be it never so precious.' / And certes he sholde nat be called a gentilman that° after God and good conscience, alle thynges left°, ne dooth his diligence and bisynesse to kepen his good name. / And Cassidore seith that it is signe of a gentil herte whan a man loveth and desireth to han a good name. / And therfore seith Seint Augustyn that ther been two thynges that arn necessarie and nedefulle, / and that is good conscience and good loos°— / that is to seyn, good conscience to thyn owene persone inward and good loos for thy neighebore outward. / And he that trusteth hym so muchel in his goode conscience / that he displeseth and setteth at noght his goode name or loos, and rekketh° noght though° he kepe nat his goode name, nys° but a crueel° cherl. /

"Sire, now have I shewed yow how ye shul do in getynge richesses, and how ye shullen usen hem, / and I se wel that for the trust that ye han in youre richesses ye wole moeve° werre and bataille. / I conseille yow that ye bigynne no werre in trust of youre richesses for they ne suffisen noght werres to mayntene. / And therfore seith a philosophre, 'That man that desireth and wole algates° han werre shal never have suffisaunce°, / for the richer that he is the gretter despenses° moste he make if he wole have worship and victorie.' / And Salomon seith that the gretter richesses that a man hath the mo despendours° he hath. / And deere sire, al be it so that° for youre richesses ye mowe° have muchel folk, / yet bihoveth it nat°, ne it is nat good, to bigynne werre where as ye mowe in oother manere have pees unto youre worship and profit. / For the victories of batailles that been in this world lyen nat in greet nombre or multitude of the peple ne in the vertu° of man, / but it lith° in the wyl and in the hand of oure lord God Almyghty. / And therfore Judas Machabeus, which was Goddes knight, / whan he sholde fighte agayn his adversarie that hadde a greet nombre and a gretter multitude of folk and strenger than was this peple of Machabee, / yet he reconforted° his litel compaignye, and seyde right in this wise: / 'Als lightly°,' quod he, 'may oure lord God Almighty yeve° victorie to a fewe folk as to many folk, / for the victorie of bataile comth nat by the grete nombre of peple / but it come from our lord God of Hevene.' / And deere sire, for as muchel as there is no man certein if he be worthy that God yeve hym victorie, namore than he is certein whether he be worthy of the love of God or naught, after that Salomon seith, / therfore every man sholde greetly drede werres to bigynne. / And by cause° that in batailles fallen° manye perils, / and happeth outher while° that as soone° is the grete man slayn as the litel man, / and as it is writen in the Seconde Book of Kynges, 'The dedes of batailles been aventurouse° and nothing certeyne,' / for as lightly° is oon hurt with a spere as another. / And for ther is gret peril in werre, therfore sholde a man flee° and escheue° werre in as muchel as a man may goodly. / For Salomon seith, 'He that loveth peril shal falle in peril.'" /

After that dame Prudence hadde spoken in this manere, Melibee answerde and seyde, / "I see wel,

---

1635 substance, *property* **1637 bisynesse,** *attention,* **diligence,** *effort,* **kept,** *protected* **1641 that,** *who,* **left,** *remaining* **1644 loos,** *reputation* **1647 rekketh,** *cares,* **though,** *if,* **nys,** *is nothing,* **crueel,** *crude* **1649 wole moeve,** *will begin* **1651 algates,** *always,* **suffisaunce,** *enough* **1652 despenses moste,** *spending must* **1653 mo despendours,** *more spenders* **1654 al be it so that,** *even though,* **mowe,** *may* **1655 bihoveth it nat,** *it is not appropriate* **1656 vertu,** *power* **1657 lith,** *lies* **1660 reconforted,** *encouraged* **1661 Als lightly,** *as easily,* **yeve,** *give* **1666 by cause,** *because,* **fallen,** *occur* **1667 outher while,** *sometimes,* **soone,** *readily* **1668 aventurouse,** *variable* **1669 lightly,** *easily* **1670 flee,** *shun,* **escheue,** *avoid*

1635 wise man, Ecclesiasticus 13.30 (Vulgate). **1638 Salomon,** Proverbs 22.1. **1639 another place,** Ecclesiasticus 41.15 (Vulgate). **freend,** the reading in all the manuscripts, although the French reads "fame." **1642 Cassidore,** Cassiodorus, a version of *Variae Epistolae* (*Various Letters*) 1.4. **1643 Seint Augustyn,** Sermon 355.1; this citation not in the Latin. **1644** Chaucer's addition. **1651 philosophre,** unidentified. **1653 Salomon,** Ecclesiastes 5.10 (Vulgate); the citation is not in the Latin original. **1658–63 Judas Machabeus . . . ,** 1 Maccabees 3.18–19. **1664 namore . . . God,** omitted in all manuscripts; translated from French by Skeat. **Salomon,** Ecclesiastes 9.1. **1668 Seconde Book of Kynges,** 2 Samuel 11.25 (Vulgate 2 Kings). **1671 Salomon,** Ecclesiasticus 3.27 (Vulgate).

dame Prudence, that by youre faire wordes and by youre resons that ye han shewed me, that the werre liketh yow nothing°. / But I have nat yet herd youre conseil, how I shal do in this nede." /

"Certes," quod she, "I conseille yow that ye accorde° with youre adversaries, and that ye have pees with hem. / For Seint Jame seith in his Epistles that by concord and pees the smale richesses wexen° grete, / and by debaat° and discord the grete richesses fallen doun. / And ye knowen wel that oon of the gretteste and moost sovereyn° thyng that is in this world is unytee° and pees. / And therfore seyde oure lord Jesu Crist to his apostles in this wise, / 'Wel, happy, and blessed been they that loven and purchacen° pees, for they been called children of God.'" /

"A," quod Melibee, "now se I wel that ye loven nat myn honour ne my worshipe. / Ye knowen wel that myne adversaries han bigonnen this debaat and bryge° by hire outrage; / and ye see wel that they ne requeren ne preyen me nat of pees, ne they asken nat to be reconsiled. / Wol ye thanne° that I go and meke me° and obeye me° to hem and crie hem mercy? / Forsothe, that were nat my worship°. / For right° as men seyn that over greet hoomlynesse engendreth dispreisynge°, so fareth it° by to greet humylitee or mekenesse." /

Thanne bigan dame Prudence to maken semblant° of wratthe° and seyde, / "Certes°, sire, sauf youre grace°, I love youre honour and youre profit as I do myn owene, and ever have doon; / ne ye ne noon oother syen nevere° the contrarie. / And yit, if I hadde seyd that ye sholde han purchaced the pees and the reconsiliacioun, I ne hadde nat muchel mystaken me ne seyd amys°. / For the wise man seith the dissensioun bygynneth by another man, and the reconsilyng bygynneth by thyself. / And the prophete seith, 'Flee shrewednesse° and do goodnesse; / seke pees and folwe it, as muchel as in thee is.' / Yet seye I nat that ye shul rather° pursue to youre adversaries for pees than they shuln° to yow, / for I knowe wel that ye been so hard herted, that ye wol do nothing for me. / And Salomon seith, 'He that hath over hard an herte, atte laste° he shal myshappe and mystyde°.'" /

Whanne Melibee hadde herd dame Prudence maken semblant of wratthe, he seyde in this wise, / "Dame, I prey yow that ye be nat displesed of thynges that I seye, / for ye knowe wel that I am angry and wrooth° and that is no wonder, / and they that been wrothe witen° nat wel what they don ne what they seyn°. / Therfore the prophete seith that troubled eyen han no cleer sighte. / But seyeth and conseileth me as yow liketh for I am redy to do right as ye wol desire, / and if ye repreve° me of my folye I am the moore holden° to love yow and preyse yow. / For Salomon seith that he that repreveth hym that dooth folye, / he shal fynde gretter grace° than he that deceyveth hym by sweete wordes." /

Thanne seide dame Prudence, "I make no semblant° of wratthe ne anger but for youre grete profit°. / For Salomon seith, 'He is moore worth° that repreveth or chideth a fool for his folye shewynge hym semblant of wratthe, / than he that supporteth hym and preyseth hym in his mysdoynge and laugheth at his folye.' / And this same Salomon seith afterward that by the sorweful visage° of a man—that is to seyn, by the sory and hevy countenaunce° of a man— / the fool correcteth and amendeth himself." /

Thanne seyde Melibee, "I shal nat konne° answere to so manye faire resouns as ye putten to me and shewen. / Seyeth shortly youre wyl and youre conseil, and I am al ready to fulfille and parfourne° it." /

Thanne dame Prudence discovered° al hir wyl to hym, and seyde, / "I conseille yow," quod she,

1673 liketh yow nothing, *pleases you not at all* **1675 accorde,** *come to agreement* **1676 wexen,** *grow* **1677 debaat,** *conflict* **1678 sovereyn,** *excellent* **1678 unytee,** *unity* **1680 purchacen,** *attain* **1682 bryge,** *trouble* **1684 Wol ye thanne,** *do you wish then,* **meke me,** *humble myself,* **obeye me,** *subject myself* **1685 worship,** *honor* **1686 right,** *just,* **hoomlynesse engendreth dispreisynge,** *familiarity breeds contempt,* **fareth it,** *it results* **1687 semblant,** *appearance,* **wratthe,** *anger* **1688 Certes,** *surely,* **sauf youre grace,** *with all due respect* **1689 ne ye ne noon oother syen nevere,** *and you never saw* **1690 seyd amys,** *misspoke* **1692 shrewednesse,** *evil* **1694 shul rather,** *should more readily,* **shuln,** *should* **1696 atte laste,** *ultimately,* **myshappe and mystyde,** *be unfortunate and unlucky* **1699 wrooth,** *wrathful* **1700 witen,** *know,* **seyn,** *say* **1703 repreve,** *blame,* **holden,** *compelled* **1705 grace,** *favor* **1706 semblant,** *appearance,* **profit,** *benefit* **1707 moore worth,** *worth more* **1709 visage,** *face,* **hevy countenaunce,** *serious expression* **1711 konne,** *be able to* **1712 parfourne,** *perform* **1713 discovered,** *revealed*

1676–77 Seint Jame . . . , mistake for *Seneque,* i.e., Seneca, *Letters* 94.46. **1679–80 Jesu Crist . . . ,** Matthew 5.9. **1691 wise man,** Martinus Dumiensis, *De Moribus* (*On Customs*) 49. **1692–93 prophete . . . ,** Psalms 33.15 (Vulgate). **1696 Salomon,** Proverbs 28.14. **1701 prophete,** unidentified. **1704–05 Salomon . . . ,** Proverbs 28.23. **1707–10 Salomon . . . ,** adapted from Ecclesiastes 7.4–6. **1708 preyseth,** El reads "peyseth."

"aboven alle thynges, that ye make pees bitwene God and yow, / and beth reconsiled unto hym and to his grace. / For as I have seyd yow heerbiforn°, God hath suffred° yow to have this tribulacioun° and disese° for youre synnes. / And if ye do as I sey yow, God wol sende youre adversaries unto yow, / and maken hem fallen at youre feet, redy to do youre wyl and youre comandementz. / For Salomon seith, 'Whan the condicioun of man is plesaunt° and likynge° to God, / he chaungeth the hertes of the mannes adversaries, and constreyneth hem to biseken hym of° pees and of grace.' / And I prey yow, lat me speke with youre adversaries in privee° place, / for they shul nat knowe that it be of youre wyl or of youre assent. / And thanne, whan I knowe hire wil and hire entente, I may conseille yow the moore seurely°." /

"Dame," quod Melibee, "dooth youre wil and youre likynge, / for I putte me hoolly in youre disposicioun° and ordinaunce°." /

Thanne dame Prudence, whan she saugh the goode wil of hire housbonde, delibered° and took avys° in hirself, / thinkynge how she myghte brynge this nede unto a good conclusioun and to a good ende. / And whan she saugh hire tyme, she sente for thise adversaries to come unto hire into a pryvee place, / and shewed wisely unto hem the grete goodes° that comen of pees, / and the grete harmes and perils that been in werre; / and seyde to hem in a goodly° manere, hou that hem oughten have greet repentaunce / of the injurie and wrong that they hadden doon to Melibee hire lord, and to hire, and to hire doghter. /

And whan they herden the goodliche° wordes of dame Prudence, / they weren so surpprised° and ravysshed°, and hadden so greet joye of hire, that wonder was to telle. / "A, lady," quod they, "ye han shewed unto us the blessynge of swetnesse, after the sawe° of David the prophete; / for the reconsilynge which we been nat worthy to have in no manere, / but we oghte requeren° it with greet contricioun and humylitee, / ye of youre grete goodnesse have presented unto us. / Now se we wel that the science° and the konnynge° of Salomon is ful trewe. / For he seith that sweete wordes multiplien and encreesen freendes, and maken shrewes° to be debonaire° and meeke. /

"Certes," quod they, "we putten oure dede° and al oure matere and cause al hoolly° in youre goode wyl, / and been redy to obeye to the speche and comandement of my lord Melibee. / And therfore, deere and benygne° lady, we preien° yow and biseke° yow as mekely as we konne° and mowen° / that it lyke unto° youre grete goodnesse to fulfillen in dede youre goodliche wordes, / for we consideren and knowlichen that we han offended and greved my lord Melibee out of mesure° / so ferforth° that we be nat of power to maken his amendes°. / And therfore we oblige° and bynden us and oure freendes to doon all his wyl and his comandementz. / But peraventure° he hath swich hevynesse° and swich wratthe° to us-ward° by cause of oure offense / that he wole enjoyne us° swich a peyne° as we mowe° nat bere ne susteene°. / And therfore, noble lady, we biseke° to youre wommanly pitee / to taken swich avysement in this nede° that we ne oure freendes be nat desherited° ne destroyed thurgh our folye." /

"Certes," quod Prudence, "it is an hard thyng and right perilous / that a man putte hym al outrely° in the arbitracioun and juggement and in the myght and power of his enemys. / For Salomon seith, 'Leeveth° me, and yeveth credence° to that I shal seyn. I seye,' quod he, 'ye peple, folk and governours of hooly chirche, / to thy sone, to thy wyf, to thy freend, ne to thy broother / ne yeve thou nevere myght ne maistrie° of thy body whil thou lyvest.' / Now sithen°

1716 heerbiforn, *before this,* **suffred,** *allowed,* **tribulacioun,** *trouble,* **disese,** *distress* **1719 plesaunt,** *pleasing,* **likynge,** *agreeable* **1720 biseken hym of,** *ask him for* **1721 privee,** *private* **1723 seurely,** *certainly* **1725 disposicioun,** *disposal,* **ordinaunce,** *command* **1726 delibered,** *deliberated,* **took avys,** *considered* **1729 goodes,** *benefits* **1731 goodly,** *pleasing* **1733 goodliche,** *excellent* **1734 surpprised,** *taken,* **ravysshed,** *overcome* **1735 sawe,** *saying* **1737 requeren,** *to request* **1739 science,** *wisdom,* **konnynge,** *understanding* **1740 shrewes,** *enemies,* **debonaire,** *compliant* **1741 dede,** *action,* **al hoolly,** *completely* **1743 benygne,** *gracious,* **preien,** *ask,* **biseke,** *beseech,* **konne,** *can,* **mowen,** *may* **1744 lyke unto,** *be pleasing to* **1745 out of mesure,** *immoderately* **1746 ferforth,** *far,* **maken his amendes,** *make it up to him* **1747 oblige,** *obligate* **1748 peraventure,** *perhaps,* **swiche hevynesse,** *such sternness,* **wratthe,** *anger,* **to us-ward,** *toward us* **1749 enjoyne,** *impose on,* **peyne,** *punishment,* **mowe,** *can,* **susteene,** *endure* **1750 biseke,** *plead* **1751 taken swich avysement in this nede,** *consider in this situation,* **desherited,** *impoverished* **1753 outrely,** *utterly* **1754 Leeveth,** *believe,* **yeveth credence,** *accept* **1756 maistrie,** *control*

1719 Salomon, Proverbs 16.7. **1735 David,** Psalms 20.4 (Vulgate). **1739–40 Salomon . . . ,** Ecclesiasticus 6.5 (Vulgate). **1754–56 Salomon . . . ,** Ecclesiasticus 33.19–20 (Vulgate).

he deffendeth° that man shal nat yeven to his broother ne to his freend the might of his body, / by strenger° resoun he deffendeth and forbedeth a man to yeven hymself to his enemy. / And nathelees I conseille you that ye mystruste nat my lord. / For I woot° wel and knowe verraily° that he is debonaire° and meeke, large°, curteys, / and nothing desyrous ne coveitous° of good ne richesse. / For ther nys nothing in this world that he desireth save° oonly worship° and honour. / Forthermoore I knowe wel and am right seur° that he shal nothyng doon in this nede withouten my conseil. / And I shal so werken in this cause that by grace of oure lord God ye shul been reconsiled unto us." /

Thanne seyden they with o voys, "Worshipful lady, we putten us and our goodes al fully in youre wil and disposicioun / and been redy to comen, what day that it lyke unto° youre noblesse to lymyte° us or assigne us, / for to maken oure obligacioun and boond as strong as it liketh unto youre goodnesse / that we mowe° fulfille the wille of yow and of my lord Melibee." /

Whan dame Prudence hadde herd the answeres of thise men, she bad hem goon agayn prively°, / and she retourned to hire lord Melibee and tolde hym how she foond his adversaries ful repentant, / knowlechynge° ful lowely hire synnes and trespas, and how they were redy to suffren all peyne, / requirynge° and preiynge hym of mercy and pitee. /

Thanne seyde Melibee, "He is wel worthy to have pardoun and foryifnesse of his synne that excuseth nat his synne / but knowlecheth it and repenteth hym, axinge indulgence°. / For Senec seith, 'Ther is the remissioun and foryifnesse where as confessioun is.' / For confessioun is neighebore to innocence. / And he seith in another place, 'He that hath shame for his synne and knowlecheth it is worthy remissioun.' And therfore I assente and conferme me° to have pees. / But it is good that we do it nat withouten the assent and wyl of oure freendes." /

Thanne was Prudence right glad and joyeful, and seyde, / "Certes, sire," quod she, "ye han wel and goodly answered. / For right as by the conseil, assent, and help of youre freendes ye han been stired° to venge yow and maken werre, / right so withouten hire conseil shul ye nat accorden yow, ne have pees with youre adversaries. / For the lawe seith, 'Ther nys nothing so good by wey of kynde° as a thyng to been unbounde° by hym that° it was ybounde.'" /

And thanne dame Prudence, withouten delay or tariynge, sente anon hire messages° for hire kyn°, and for hyr olde freendes whiche that were trewe and wyse, / and tolde hem by ordre°, in the presence of Melibee, al this mateere as it is aboven expressed and declared, / and preyden that they wolde yeven hire avys° and conseil what best were to doon in this nede. / And whan Melibees freendes hadde taken hire avys and deliberacioun of the forseide mateere, / and hadden examyned it by greet bisynesse° and greet diligence, / they yave ful conseil for to have pees and reste, / and that Melibee sholde receyve with good herte his adversaries to foryifnesse and mercy. /

And whan dame Prudence hadde herd the assent of hir lord Melibee and the conseil of his freendes / accorde with hire wille and hire entencioun, / she was wonderly° glad in hire herte, and seyde, / "Ther is an old proverbe," quod she, "seith that the goodnesse that thou mayst do this day, do it, / and abide° nat ne delaye it nat til tomorwe. / And therfore I conseille that ye sende youre messages, swiche as been discrete° and wise, / unto youre adversaries tellynge hem on youre bihalve / that if they wole trete of° pees and of accord, / that they shape° hem withouten delay or tariyng to comen unto us." /

Which thyng parfourned° was in dede. / And whanne thise trespassours and repentynge

1757 sithen, *since,* **deffendeth,** *forbids* **1758 strenger,** *stronger* **1760 woot,** *know,* **verraily,** *truly,* **debonaire,** *willing,* **large,** *generous* **1761 coveitous,** *greedy* **1762 save,** *except,* **worship,** *dignity* **1763 seur,** *certain* **1766 lyke unto,** *is pleasing to,* **lymyte,** *appoint* **1768 mowe,** *may* **1769 prively,** *privately* **1771 knowlechynge,** *acknowledging* **1772 requirynge,** *requesting* **1774 axinge indulgence,** *asking leniency* **1777 conferme me,** *resolve* **1781 stired,** *encouraged* **1783 by wey of kynde,** *in the course of nature,* **unbounde,** *released,* **that,** *by whom* **1784 messages,** *messengers,* **kin,** *relatives* **1785 by ordre,** *in order* **1786 yeven hire avys,** *given their advice* **1788 bisynesse,** *attention* **1793 wonderly,** *wonderfully* **1795 abide,** *wait* **1796 discrete,** *thoughtful* **1798 trete of,** *negotiate about* **1799 shape,** *prepare* **1800 parfourned,** *performed*

1775 Senec, not in Seneca, but Martinus Dumiensis, *De Moribus* (*On Customs*) 94. **1777** The Latin original follows Publilius Syrus, *Sententiae* 489, but the French differs somewhat. **And he seith . . . remissioun,** omitted in El, with variants in other manuscripts, including omissions and blank space in Hg. **conferme,** El reads "corforme." **1783 lawe seith,** Justinian, *Digesta* 1.17.35. **1794 old proverbe,** see *LGW* 452.

folk of hire folies—that is to seyn, the adversaries of Melibee— / hadden herd what thise messagers seyden unto hem / they weren right glad and joyeful, and answereden ful mekely and benignely°, / yeldynge graces° and thankynges to hire lord Melibee and to al his compaignye, / and shopen hem° withouten delay to go with the messagers and obeye to the comandement of hire lord Melibee. /

And right anon they tooken hire wey to the court of Melibee, / and tooken with hem somme of hire trewe freendes to maken feith° for hem and for to been hire borwes°. / And whan they were comen to the presence of Melibee, he seyde hem thise wordes, / "It standeth thus," quod Melibee, "and sooth° it is, that ye / causelees and withouten skile° and resoun / han doon grete injuries and wronges to me and to my wyf Prudence and to my doghter also. / For ye han entred into myn hous by violence, / and have doon swich outrage, that alle men knowen wel that ye have disserved the deeth. / And therfore wol I knowe and wite° of yow / wheither ye wol putte the punyssement and the chastisynge and the vengeance of this outrage in the wyl of me and of my wyf Prudence, or ye wol nat?" /

Thanne the wiseste of hem thre answerde for hem alle, and seyde, / "Sire," quod he, "we knowen wel that we been unworthy to comen unto the court of so greet a lord and so worthy as ye been. / For we han so greetly mystaken us and han offended and agilt in swich a wise agayn° youre heigh lordshipe / that trewely we han disserved the deeth. / But yet for the grete goodnesse and debonairetee° that al the world witnesseth in youre persone, / we submytten us to the excellence and benignitee° of youre gracious lordshipe, / and been redy to obeie to alle youre comandementz, / bisekynge yow that of youre merciable pitee ye wol considere oure grete repentaunce and lough° submyssioun, / and graunten us foryevenesse of oure outrageous trespas and offense. / For wel we knowe that youre liberal grace and mercy strecchen hem ferther into goodnesse than doon oure outrageouse giltes and trespas into wikkednesse, / al be it that cursedly and dampnably we han agilt agayn° your heigh lordshipe." /

Thanne Melibee took hem up fro the ground ful benignely, / and receyved hire obligaciouns° and hir boondes° by hire othes upon hire plegges° and borwes°, / and assigned hem a certeyn day to retourne unto his court / for to accepte and receyve the sentence and jugement that Melibee wolde comande to be doon on hem by the causes° aforeseyd; / whiche thynges ordeyned°, every man retourned to his hous. /

And whan that dame Prudence saugh hire tyme, she freyned° and axed hir lord Melibee / what vengeance he thoughte to taken of his adversaries. /

To which Melibee answerde and seyde, "Certes," quod he, "I thynke and purpose me fully / to desherite° hem of al that ever they han, and for to putte hem in exil forever." /

"Certes," quod dame Prudence, "this were a crueel sentence, and muchel agayn resoun. / For ye been riche ynough, and han no nede of oother mennes good°. / And ye mighte lightly° in this wise gete yow a coveitous name°, / which is a vicious thyng and oghte been escheued of° every good man. / For after the sawe° of the word of the apostle, 'Coveitise is roote of alle harmes.' / And therfore it were bettre for yow to lese° so muchel good of youre owene than for to taken of hire good in this manere. / For bettre it is to lesen good° with worshipe° than it is to wynne good with vileynye and shame. / And everi man oghte to doon his diligence and his bisynesse to geten hym a good name. / And yet shal he nat oonly bisie hym in kepynge of his good name, / but he shal also enforcen hym° alwey to do somthing by which he may renovelle° his good name. /

1803 benignely, *graciously* **1804 yeldynge graces,** *offering gratitude* **1805 shopen hem,** *prepared themselves* **1807 maken feith,** *bear witness,* **borwes,** *sureties* **1809 sooth,** *true* **1810 skile,** *justification* **1814 wite,** *learn* **1818 agilt in swiche a wise agayn,** *been guilty in such a way against* **1820 debonairetee,** *agreeableness* **1821 benignitee,** *goodness* **1823 lough,** *low* **1826 agilt agayn,** *been guilty against* **1828 obligaciouns,** *promises,* **boondes,** *guarantees,* **plegges,** *pledges,* **borwes,** *sureties* **1830 by the causes,** *for the reasons* **1831 ordeyned,** *established* **1832 freyned,** *inquired* **1835 desherite,** *deprive* **1837 good,** *possessions* **1838 lightly,** *easily,* **coveitous name,** *reputation for greed* **1839 escheued of,** *avoided by* **1840 sawe,** *saying* **1841 lese,** *lose* **1842 lesen good,** *lose possessions,* **worshipe,** *honor* **1845 enforcen hym,** *try,* **renovelle,** *renew*

1807 borwes, sureties, i.e., people who pledge to assume the responsibilities of others, especially in case of default on debts or obligations. **1825 hem,** omitted in Hg. **1832 freyned,** Hg reads "feyned." **1840 the apostle,** Paul, 1 Timothy 6.10; see *PardT* 6.334. **1842** Publilius Syrus *Sententiae* 479. El omits "good" and "good."

For it is writen that the olde° good loos° and good name of a man is soone goon and passed when it is nat newed ne renovelled. / And as touchynge° that ye seyn ye wole exile youre adversaries, / that thynketh me muchel agayn resoun and out of mesure°, / considered the power that they han yeve yow upon hemself. / And it is writen that he is worthy to lesen° his privilege that mysuseth the myght and the power that is yeven hym. / And I sette cas° ye myghte enjoyne° hem that peyne° by right and by lawe, / which I trowe° ye mowe° nat do; / I seye ye mighte nat putten it to execucioun peraventure°, / and thanne were it likly to retourne to the werre as it was biforn. / And therfore, if ye wole° that men do yow obeisance°, ye moste deemen° moore curteisly— / this is to seyn, ye moste yeven° moore esy sentences and juggementz. / For it is writen that he that moost curteisly comandeth, to hym men moost obeyen. / And therfore, I prey yow that in this necessitee and in this nede, ye caste yow° to overcome youre herte. / For Senec seith that he that overcometh his herte, overcometh twies°. / And Tullius seith, 'Ther is nothyng so comendable in a greet lord / as whan he is debonaire° and meeke, and appeseth hym lightly.°' / And I prey yow that ye wole forbere° now to do vengeance / in swich a manere that youre goode name may be kept and conserved; / and that men mowe° have cause and mateere° to preyse yow of° pitee and of mercy; / and that ye have no cause to repente yow of thyng that ye doon. / For Senec seith, 'He overcometh in an yvel manere that repenteth hym of his victorie.' / Wherfore I pray yow, lat mercy been in youre mynde and in your herte / to th'effect and entente that God Almyghty have mercy on yow in his laste juggement. / For Seint Jame seith in his Epistle, 'Juggement withouten mercy shall be doon to hym that hath no mercy of° another wight°.'" /

Whanne Melibee hadde herd the grete skiles° and resouns of dame Prudence, and hir wise informaciouns and techynges, / his herte gan enclyne to the wil of his wif, considerynge hire trewe entente, / and conformed hym anon, and assented fully to werken after hire conseil, / and thonked God of whom procedeth al vertu and alle goodnesse that hym sente a wif of so greet discrecioun. / And whan the day cam that his adversaries sholde appieren° in his presence, / he spak unto hem ful goodly°, and seyde in this wyse, / "Al be it so that° of youre pride and presumpcioun and folie and of youre necligence and unkonnynge°, / ye have mysborn yow° and trespassed unto me, / yet for as much as I see and biholde your grete humylitee, / and that ye been sory and repentant of youre giltes, / it constreyneth° me to doon yow grace and mercy. / Therfore I receyve yow to my grace / and foryeve yow outrely° alle the offenses, injuries, and wronges, that ye have doon agayn me and myne / to this effect and to this ende that God of his endelees mercy / wole at the tyme of oure dyinge foryeven us oure giltes that we han trespassed to hym in this wrecched world. / For doutelees, if we be sory and repentant of the synnes and giltes whiche we han trespassed in the sighte of oure lord God, / he is so free° and so merciable / that he wole foryeven us our giltes / and bryngen us to his blisse that never hath ende. Amen." /

Heere is ended Chaucers Tale of Melibee and of Dame Prudence.

1846 olde, *established,* **loos,** *reputation* **1847 touchynge,** *concerning* **1848 out of mesure,** *immoderate* **1850 lesen,** *lose* **1851 I sette cas,** *let me suppose,* **enjoyne,** *assign,* **peyne,** *punishment* **1852 trowe,** *believe,* **mowe,** *may* **1853 putten it to execucioun peraventure,** *enforce it perhaps* **1855 wole,** *want,* **do yow obeisance,** *respect you,* **deemen,** *judge* **1856 yeven,** *give* **1858 caste yow,** *try* **1859 twies,** *twice* **1861 debonaire,** *agreeable,* **appeseth hym lightly,** *soothes himself easily* **1862 forbere,** *refrain* **1864 mowe,** *may,* **mateere,** *reason,* **of,** *for* **1869 of,** *for,* **wight,** *person* **1870 skiles,** *arguments* **1874 appieren,** *appear* **1875 goodly,** *pleasantly* **1876 Al be it so that,** *even though,* **unkonnynge,** *ignorance* **1877 mysborn yow,** *acted wrongly* **1880 constreyneth,** *compels* **1881 outrely,** *completely* **1885 free,** *generous*

1846 it is writen, Publilius Syrus, *Sententiae* 293. **1850 it is writen,** Gregory, *Decretals* 3.31.18. **1857 it is writen,** Seneca, *De Clementia* (*On Mercy*) 1.24.1. **1859 Senec,** not in Seneca, but Publilius Syrus, *Sententiae* 64. **1860–61 Tullius . . . ,** Cicero, *De Officiis* (*On Duties*) 1.88. **1861 hym,** omitted in El. **1866 Senec,** not in Seneca, but Publilius Syrus, *Sententiae* 366. **1867 in youre mynde and,** omitted in Hg. **1869 Seint Jame,** James 2.13. **1871–72** Chaucer's addition. **1884–88** Chaucer's addition; see 1 John 1.9.

From woodcut made by W.H. Hooper and published by the Chaucer Society between 1868 and 1879

Monk's Tale

Prologue

The murye wordes of the Hoost to the Monk.

Whan ended was my tale of Melibee
And of Prudence and hire benignytee°,
Oure Hooste seyde, "As I am feithful man,
And by that precious corpus Madrian,
I hadde levere than a barel ale°
That Goodelief, my wyf, hadde herd this tale.
She nys nothyng° of swich pacience
As was this Melibeus wyf Prudence.
By Goddes bones, whan I bete my knaves°,
She bryngeth me forth the grete clobbed staves°,
And crieth, 'Slee° the dogges everichoon°,
And brek hem bothe bak and every boon!'
And if that any neighebore of myne
Wol nat in chirche to my wyf enclyne°,
Or be so hardy° to hire to trespace°,
Whan she comth hoom she rampeth° in my face,
And crieth, 'False coward, wrek° thy wyf!
By corpus bones, I wol have thy knyf,
And thou shalt have my distaf and go spynne!'
Fro day to nyght right thus she wol bigynne.
'Allas,' she seith, 'that evere I was shape°
To wedden a milksop, or a coward ape,
That wol been overlad with every wight°.
Thou darst° nat stonden by thy wyves right.'
"This is my lif but if that I wol fighte;
And out at dore anon° I moot me dighte°,
Or elles I am but lost but if that° I
Be lik a wilde leoun, fool-hardy.
I woot° wel she wol do° me slee somday
Som neighebore, and thanne go my way,

1890 benignytee, *graciousness* **1893 hadde levere than a barel ale,** *would rather than* (have) *a barrel of ale* **1895 nys nothyng,** *is nothing* **1897 knaves,** *boy servants* **1898 clobbed staves,** *knobby sticks* **1899 Slee,** *slay,* **everichoon,** *each one* **1902 enclyne,** *bow in respect* **1903 hardy,** *bold,* **trespace,** *do offense* **1904 rampeth,** *rages* **1905 wrek,** *avenge* **1909 shape,** *destined* **1911 overlad with every wight,** *pushed around by everybody* **1912 darst,** *dare* **1914 anon,** *immediately,* **moot me dighte,** *must take myself* **1915 but if that,** *unless* **1917 woot,** *know,* **do,** *make*

1892 corpus Madrian, body of Madrian. Because no St. Madrian is known, apparently the Host's malapropism. **1894 Goodelief,** a proper name; found in Kentish records, although some editors treat it as an epithet. The wife of the real Harry Bailly (see *GP* 1.751n) was named "Christian." **1898 forth,** omitted in Hg. **1904 hoom,** omitted in El and Hg. In MR 2.408–09 it is reported that the exemplar of the *MkT* for El and Hg was faulty. The notes that follow do not list the obvious errors in El and Hg, but see 2375–2462n. **1906 corpus bones,** a confusion of *corpus Dei* (God's body) and *God's bones.* **1907 distaf,** staff used in spinning thread and traditional symbol of female work.

For I am perilous with knyf in honde
Al be it that° I dar hire nat withstonde,
For she is byg° in armes, by my feith—
That shal he fynde that hire mysdooth or seith°.
But lat us passe awey fro this mateere.
  "My lord, the Monk," quod he, "be myrie of cheere,
For ye shul telle a tale trewely.
Loo, Rouchestre stant heer faste° by.
Ryde forth, myn owene lord, brek nat oure game.
But by my trouthe, I knowe nat youre name.
Wher° shal I calle yow my lord daun John,
Or daun Thomas, or elles daun Albon?
Of what hous be ye, by youre fader kyn?
I vowe to God, thou hast a ful fair skyn;
It is a gentil pasture ther° thow goost°.
Thou art nat lyk a penant° or a goost°.
Upon my feith, thou art som officer,
Som worthy sexteyn, or som celerer,
For by my fader soule, as to my doom°,
Thou art a maister whan thou art at hoom,
No poure cloysterer° ne no novys°,
But a governour, wily and wys,
And therwithal° of brawnes° and of bones,
A wel farynge° persone for the nones°.
I pray to God, yeve hym confusioun°
That first thee broghte unto religioun°!
Thou woldest han been a tredefowel aright°.
Haddestow° as greet a leeve° as thou hast myght
To parfourne° al thy lust in engendrure°,
Thou haddest bigeten ful many a creature.
Allas, why werestow° so wyd a cope°?
God yeve° me sorwe but°, and° I were a pope,
Nat oonly thou, but every myghty man,
Though he were shorn ful hye upon his pan,
Sholde have a wyf, for al the world is lorn°—
Religioun hath take up al the corn°
Of tredyng°, and we borel men° been shrympes.
Of fieble trees ther comen wrecched ympes°.
This maketh that oure heires been so sklendre°
And feble that they may nat wel engendre°.
This maketh that oure wyves wole assaye°
Religious folk, for ye mowe° bettre paye
Of Venus paiementz° than mowe we.
God woot°, no lussheburgh° payen ye!
But be nat wrooth°, my lord, though that I pleye.
Ful ofte in game a sooth° I have herd seye."
  This worthy Monk took al in pacience,
And seyde, "I wol doon al my diligence°—
As fer as sowneth into honestee°—
To telle yow a tale, or two, or three,
And if yow list° to herkne hyderward°,
I wol yow seyn° the lyf of Seint Edward—
Or ellis, first, tragedies wol I telle
Of whiche I have an hundred in my celle°.
  "Tragedie is to seyn a certeyn storie,
As olde bookes maken us memorie°,
Of hym that stood in greet prosperitee
And is yfallen out of heigh degree
Into myserie, and endeth wrecchedly.
And they ben versified communely
Of six feet which men clepen° exametron.
In prose eek been endited° many oon,

1920 Al be it that, *even though* **1921 byg,** *strong* **1922 mysdooth or seith,** *mistreats or misspeaks* **1926 faste,** *near* **1929 Wher,** *whether* **1933 a gentil pasture ther,** *highclass grazing where,* **goost,** *go* **1934 penant,** *penitent,* **goost,** *spirit* **1937 as to my doom,** *by my judgment* **1939 cloysterer,** *typical monk,* **novys,** *novice* **1941 therwithal,** *moreover,* **brawnes,** *muscles* **1942 wel farynge,** *good looking,* **nones,** *occasion* **1943 yeve hym confusioun,** *damn him* **1944 unto religioun,** *into the clergy* **1945 tredefowel aright,** *superb rooster* **1946 Haddestow,** *if you had,* **leeve,** *permission* **1947 parfourne,** *perform,* **engendrure,** *procreation* **1949 werestow,** *do you wear,* **cope,** *cape* **1950 yeve,** *give,* **but,** *unless,* **and,** *if* **1953 lorn,** *lost* **1954 corn,** *seed,* **1955 tredyng,** *copulating,* **borel men,** *laymen* **1956 wrecched ympes,** *weak branches* **1957 sklendre,** *skinny* **1958 engendre,** *procreate* **1959 assaye,** *try out* **1960 mowe,** *can* **1961 Venus paiementz,** *Venus's payments* (i.e., sexual performance) **1962 woot,** *knows,* **lussheburgh,** *counterfeit coins* (from Luxembourg) **1963 wrooth,** *angry* **1964 sooth,** *truth* **1966 diligence,** *effort* **1967 sowneth into honestee,** *contributes to decency* **1969 yow list,** *it pleases you,* **hyderward,** *in this direction* **1970 seyn,** *tell* **1972 celle,** *room* **1974 maken us memorie,** *remind us* **1979 clepen,** *call* **1980 eek been endited,** *also are composed*

1926 Rouchestre, Rochester, thirty miles from London and a little over halfway to Canterbury; Sittingbourne (mentioned in *WBP* 3.847) is ten miles beyond Rochester, prompting some editors to move Part 7 to precede Part 3, the so-called Bradshaw shift, after nineteenth-century critic, Henry Bradshaw, who first proposed this arrangement of the tales. **1929 daun John,** master John; the Host knows the Monk's name is "daun Piers" (master Peter) in *NPP* 7.2792. **1931 hous,** monastery, although in light of "fader kyn," it may here mean "noble family," of aristocratic blood. **1936 sexteyn . . . celerer,** monastic officials in charge of sacred vessels and garments (sexton) and of food and wine (cellarer). **1952 shorn ful hye upon his pan,** with hair trimmed full high upon his head (i.e., tonsured) as a sign of monastic vocation. **1957–58** Lines lacking in El. **1963 though,** El reads "for." **1970 yow,** omitted in El. **Seint Edward,** Edward I ("the Confessor"), king of England from 1043 to 1066. Richard II had a special regard for both Edward the Confessor and Edward II. **1973 Tragedie,** similar definitions of tragedy are found at lines 1991–94 and 2761–66 below, all echoing *Bo* 2pr2.69–74. Thus, the Boethian conception of tragedy frames *MkT,* but see also 2375–2462n. Chaucer was the first to treat tragedy as a narrative genre in English. **1979 exametron,** hexameters, six-foot meters used in Latin heroic poetry.

And eek in meetre, in many a sondry wyse°.
Lo, this declaryng° oghte ynogh suffise.
"Now herkneth, if yow liketh for to heere.
But first I yow biseeke° in this mateere,
Though I by ordre telle nat thise thynges,
Be it of popes, emperours, or kynges,
After hir ages°, as men writen fynde,
But tellen hem som before and som bihynde,
As it now comth unto my remembraunce,
Have me excused of myn ignoraunce."

Heere bigynneth the Monkes Tale De Casibus Virorum Illustrium.

I wol biwaille in manere of tragedie
The harm° of hem that stoode in heigh degree°,
And fillen° so that ther nas no remedie
To brynge hem out of hire adversitee.
For certein, whan that Fortune list° to flee.
Ther may no man the cours of hire withholde.
Lat no man truste on blynd prosperitee;
Be war by thise ensamples trewe and olde.

LUCIFER

At Lucifer, though he an angel were
And nat a man, at hym wol I bigynne.
For though Fortune may noon angel dere°,
From heigh degree yet fel he for his synne
Doun into helle where he yet is inne.
O Lucifer, brightest of angels alle,
Now artow Sathanas°, that mayst nat twynne°
Out of miserie, in which that thou art falle.

ADAM

Loo Adam, in the feeld of Damyssene
With Goddes owene fynger wroght was he,
And nat bigeten° of mannes sperme unclene,
And welte° al paradys savynge o° tree.
Hadde nevere worldly man so heigh degree
As Adam, til he for mysgovernaunce°
Was dryven out of hys hye prosperitee
To labour, and to helle, and to meschaunce°.

SAMPSON

Loo Sampsoun, which that was annunciat°
By the angel longe er° his nativitee,
And was to God Almyghty consecrat°,
And stood in noblesse whil° he myghte see.
Was nevere swich another as was hee,
To speke of strengthe and therwith hardynesse°;
But to his wyves toolde he his secree,
Thurgh which he slow° hymself for wrecchednesse.

Sampsoun, this noble almyghty champioun,
Withouten wepen save his handes tweye,
He slow and al torente° the leoun,
Toward his weddyng walkynge by the weye.
His false wyf koude° hym so plese and preye°
Til she his conseil knew; and she untrewe
Unto his foos° his conseil gan biwreye°,
And hym forsook and took another newe.

Thre hundred foxes took Sampson for ire°,
And alle hir tayles he togydre bond,
And sette the foxes tayles alle on fire,
For he on every tayl had knyt a brond°.
And they brende° alle the cornes° in that lond,
And alle hire olyveres°, and vynes eke°.

1981 sondry wyse, *various ways* **1982 declaryng,** *explanation* **1984 biseeke,** *request* **1987 After hir ages,** *chronologically* **1992 harm,** *sufferings,* **heigh degree,** *high rank* **1993 fillen,** *fell* **1995 list,** *chooses* **2001 dere,** *harm* **2005 artow Sathanas,** *are you Satan,* **twynne,** *escape* **2009 bigeten,** *begotten* **2010 welte,** *ruled,* **savynge o,** *except one* **2012 mysgovernaunce,** *lack of control* **2014 meschaunce,** *ill fate* **2015 which that was annunciat,** *who was foretold* **2016 er,** *before* **2017 consecrat,** *consecrated* **2018 whil,** *as long as* **2020 hardynesse,** *courage* **2022 slow,** *slew* **2025 al torente,** *completely tore apart* **2027 koude,** *could,* **preye,** *plead with* **2029 foos,** *foes,* **biwreye,** *betray* **2031 ire,** *anger* **2034 knyt a brond,** *attached a torch* **2035 brende,** *burned,* **cornes,** *grain crops* **2036 olyveres,** *olive trees,* **vynes eke,** *grapevines also*

1990a De Casibus Virorum Illustrium, "Concerning the Fall of Illustrious Men"; the same title as that of Boccaccio's famous collection, although Chaucer does not use it as a source. The phrase is lacking in the Hg rubric. **1998 by,** El reads "of." **1999 Lucifer,** a name for Satan that derives from Isaiah 14.12 and Luke 10.18; the account of the fall of Satan is Revelation 12.7–9. **2007–14** The account of the creation of Adam and the prohibition of eating from one tree are in Genesis 1.27–2.17. The stanza is omitted in Hg, although added in the margin. **Damyssene,** Damascus, city reputed to have been built on the site where Adam was created. **2015 Sampsoun,** the account of Samson follows mainly Judges 13ff. **2016, the,** omitted in El. **2023 almighty, a term usually reserved for God.** Some manuscripts read "and myghty"; see 2052n.

A thousand men he slow eek with his hond,
And hadde no wepen but an asses cheke°.

Whan they were slayn, so thursted hym that he
Was wel ny lorn°, for which he gan to preye
That God wolde on his peyne° han som pitee
And sende hym drynke or elles moste he deye,
And of this asses cheke that was dreye,
Out of a wang-tooth° sprang anon a welle°,
Of which he drank anon shortly to seye,
Thus heelp hym God, as Judicum can telle.

By verray° force at Gazan° on a nyght,
Maugree° Philistiens of that citee,
The gates of the toun he hath up plyght°
And on his bak ycaryed° hem hath hee
Hye° on an hill wher as men myghte hem see.
O noble, almyghty Sampsoun, lief° and deere,
Had thou nat toold to wommen thy secree,
In al this world ne hadde been thy peere°!

This Sampson nevere ciser° drank ne wyn,
Ne on his heed cam rasour° noon ne sheere°,
By precept° of the messager divyn°,
For alle his strengthes in his heeres weere.
And fully twenty wynter°, yeer by yeere,
He hadde of Israel the governaunce.
But soone shal he wepe many a teere,
For wommen shal hym bryngen to meschaunce°.

Unto his lemman° Dalida he tolde
That in his heeris al his strengthe lay,
And falsely to his foomen° she hym solde.
And slepynge in hir barm° upon a day,
She made to clippe or shere his heres away,
And made his foomen al this craft espyen°,
And whan that they hym foond in this array°,
They bounde hym faste and putten out his
eyen.

But er his heer were clipped or yshave,
Ther was no boond with which men myghte
him bynde.
But now is he in prison in a cave,
Where as they made hym at the queerne
grynde°.
O noble Sampsoun, strongest of mankynde,
O whilom° juge, in glorie and in richesse,
Now maystow° wepen with thyne eyen blynde,
Sith° thou fro wele° art falle in wrecchednesse.

The ende of this caytyf° was as I shal seye.
His foomen made a feeste upon a day,
And made hym as hire fool biforn hem pleye,
And this was in a temple of greet array°.
But atte laste he made a foul affray°,
For he two pilers° shook and made hem falle,
And doun fil temple and al, and ther it lay,
And slow° hymself, and eek his foomen alle.

This is to seyn, the prynces everichoon°
And eek thre thousand bodyes were ther slayn
With fallynge of the grete temple of stoon.
Of Sampson now wol I namoore sayn.
Beth war° by this ensample oold and playn
That no men telle hir conseil til° hir wyves
Of swich thyng as they wolde han secree fayn°,
If that it touche° hir lymes° or hir lyves.

HERCULES

Of Hercules, the sovereyn conquerour,
Syngen his werkes laude° and heigh renoun,
For in his tyme of strengthe he was the flour°.
He slow and rafte° the skyn fro the leoun;
He of centauros leyde the boost adoun°;
He arpies slow, the crueel bryddes felle°;

2038 cheke, *jawbone* **2040 wel ny lorn,** *nearly lost* **2041 peyne,** *pain* **2044 wang-tooth,** *molar,* **welle,** *spring* **2047 verray,** *sheer,* **Gazan,** *Gaza* **2048 Maugree,** *despite* **2049 up plyght,** *torn up* **2050 ycaryed,** *carried* **2051 Hye,** *high* **2052 lief,** *beloved* **2054 peere,** *equal* **2055 ciser,** *strong drink* **2056 rasour,** *razor,* **sheere,** *shears* **2057 precept,** *command,* **divyn,** *divine* **2059 wynter,** *years* **2062 meschaunce,** *ill fate* **2063 lemman,** *mistress* **2065 foomen,** *enemies* **2066 barm,** *lap* **2068 al this craft espyen,** *understand this secret* **2069 array,** *fashion* **2074 queerne grynde,** *mill grind* **2076 whilom,** *once* **2077 maystow,** *may you* **2078 Sith,** *since,* **wele,** *prosperity* **2079 caytyf,** *wretch* **2082 of greet array,** *ornately decorated* **2083 foul affray,** *horrible attack* **2084 pilers,** *pillars* **2086 slow,** *killed* **2087 everichoon,** *each one* **2091 Beth war,** *be warned,* **playn,** *clear* **2092 conseil til,** *secrets to* **2093 wolde han secree fayn,** *would want to have secret* **2094 touche,** *concerns,* **lymes,** *limbs* **2096 laude,** *praise* **2097 flour,** *apex* (flower) **2098 rafte,** *took away* **2099 leyde the boost adoun,** *laid to rest the boast* **2100 bryddes felle,** *fearsome birds*

2037 eek, omitted in Hg. **2045 anon,** Hg reads "ynogh." **2046 Judicum,** biblical Book of Judges (*Liber Judicum*). **2051 wher as,** El reads "that." **2052 almyghty,** some manuscripts read "o myghty"; see 2023n. **2063 Delida,** Delilah. **2081 hire,** El reads "a." **2084 two,** El reads "the." **2095 Hercules,** the account follows mainly *Bo* 4m7, mentioning only some of the twelve traditional labors of Hercules. **2098 fro,** El reads "of." **the leoun,** the first labor of Hercules was to slay the Nemean lion. **2099 centauros,** Hercules killed two centaurs (half-horse, half-man), but the reference is unclear. **2100 arpies,** Hercules destroyed the harpies (man-eating birds) as his sixth labor.

He golden apples rafte of° the dragoun;
He drow° out Cerberus, the hound of helle;

He slow the crueel tyrant Busirus,
And made his hors to frete° hym, flessh and boon;
He slow the firy serpent venymus°;
Of Acheloys hornes two he brak oon°;
And he slow Cacus in a cave of stoon;
He slow the geant Antheus the stronge;
He slow the grisly boor, and that anon;
And bar° the hevene on his nekke longe.

Was nevere wight° sith that° this world bigan
That slow so manye monstres as dide he.
Thurghout this wyde world his name ran°,
What for his strengthe and for his heigh bountee°,
And every reawme° wente he for to see.
He was so stroong that no man myghte hym lette°.
At bothe the worldes endes, seith Trophee,
In stide° of boundes° he a pileer° sette.

A lemman° hadde this noble champioun,
That highte° Dianira, fressh as May,
And as thise clerkes maken mencioun,
She hath hym sent a sherte, fressh and gay.
Allas, this sherte, allas and weylaway,
Envenymed° was so subtilly withalle°
That er that he had wered it half a day
It made his flessh al from his bones falle.
But nathelees somme clerkes hire excusen
By oon that highte° Nessus that it maked.
Be as be may, I wol hire noght accusen—
But on his bak this sherte he wered al naked
Til that his flessh was for the venym blaked°.
And whan he saugh° noon oother remedye,
In hoote coles he hath hymselven raked°,
For with no venym deigned hym to dye°.

Thus starf° this worthy, myghty Hercules.
Lo, who may truste on Fortune any throwe°?
For hym that folweth al this world of prees°
Er he be war is ofte yleyd° ful lowe.
Ful wys is he that kan hymselven knowe!
Beth war°, for whan that Fortune list to glose°,
Thanne wayteth° she her man to overthrowe
By swich a wey as he wolde leest suppose.

NABUGODONOSOR

The myghty trone°, the precious tresor,
The glorious ceptre, and roial magestee
That hadde the Kyng Nabugodonosor
With tonge unnethe° may discryved bee°.
He twyes wan° Jerusalem the citee;
The vessel° of the temple he with hym ladde°.
At Babiloigne° was his sovereyn see°,
In which his glorie and his delit he hadde.

The faireste children° of the blood roial
Of Israel he leet do gelde° anoon,
And maked ech of hem to been his thral°.

2101 rafte of, *took away from* **2102 drow,** *drew* **2104 frete,** *eat* **2105 venymus,** *poisonous* **2106 brak oon,** *broke one* **2110 bar,** *carried* **2111 wight,** *man,* **sith that,** *since* **2113 name ran,** *reputation spread* **2114 bountee,** *goodness* **2115 reawme,** *realm* **2116 lette,** *hinder* **2118 stide,** *stead,* **boundes,** *boundaries,* **pileer,** *pillar* **2119 lemman,** *lover* **2120 highte,** *was named* **2124 Envenymed,** *poisoned,* **withalle,** *as well* **2128 highte,** *was named* **2131 blaked,** *burned black* **2132 saugh,** *saw* **2133 hymselven raked,** *raked over himself* **2134 with no venym deigned hym to dye,** *he would not accept death by poison* **2135 starf,** *died* **2136 throwe,** *length of time* **2137 world of prees,** *crowded world* **2138 yleyd,** *laid* **2140 Beth war,** *be warned,* **list to glose,** *chooses to deceive* **2141 wayteth,** *watches* **2143 trone,** *throne* **2146 unnethe,** *hardly,* **discryved bee,** *be described* **2147 twyes wan,** *twice conquered* **2148 vessel,** *treasure,* **ladde,** *carried off* **2149 Babiloigne,** *Babylon,* **sovereyn see,** *imperial seat* **2151 children,** *young men* **2152 leet do gelde,** *had castrated* **2153 thral,** *slave*

2101 apples, a dragon guarded the golden apples of the Hesperides, Hercules' eleventh labor. **2102 Cerberus,** the three-headed guard dog of hell that Hercules brought up to earth as his twelfth labor. **2103 Busirus,** Chaucer conflates two stories from *Bo* 2pr6.68–70 and 4m7.40–41. **2105 firy serpent,** apparently the many-headed Hydra; even though it was not fiery, its poison did burn. Some manuscripts read "verray" (actual) for "firy." **2106 Acheloys,** a river god in the form of a horned bull who fought Hercules. **hornes two,** Hg reads "two hornes." **2107 Cacus,** gigantic, fire-breathing son of Vulcan who lived in a cave and beset the people of Evander. **2108 Antheus,** Antaeus, giant wrestler whose strength increased each time he touched the earth; throttled by Hercules as he held Antaeus off the ground. **2109 boor,** the Erymanthian boar, which Hercules captured (but did not slay) as his fourth labor. **2110 hevene,** heavens; in his eleventh labor, Hercules held up the heavens on his shoulders while Atlas took the golden apples from his daughters, the Hesperides. **2117 bothe the worldes endes,** it was commonplace that Hercules set pillars at the Strait of Gibraltar and the edge of the Far East. **Trophee,** unidentified. **2120 Dianira,** Deianira, second wife of Hercules, gave him a shirt poisoned with the blood of Nessus, a centaur slain by Hercules. Before dying, Nessus had convinced Deianira that the shirt would restore Hercules's love for her even though he had turned his attention to Iole. **2130 this,** Hg reads "the." **2145 Nabugodonosor,** Nebuchadnezzar; the account is mostly from Daniel 1–4, although there is no mention of castration (as in line 2152 below) in the Bible nor is Daniel one of the three who refuse to worship the idol (as in lines 2165–66).

Amonges othere Daniel was oon
That was the wiseste child of everychon°,
For he the dremes of the kyng expowned°,
Where as in Chaldeye clerk ne was ther noon
That wiste° to what fyn° his dremes sowned°.

This proude kyng leet maken° a statue of gold,
Sixty cubites long and sevene in brede°,
To which ymage bothe yong and oold
Comanded he to loute° and have in drede,
Or in a fourneys° ful of flambes rede
He shal be brent° that wolde noght obeye.
But nevere wolde assente to that dede
Daniel ne his yonge felawes tweye°.

This kyng of kynges proud was and elaat°.
He wende° that God that sit° in magestee
Ne myghte hym nat bireve° of his estaat.
But sodeynly he loste his dignytee,
And lyk a beest hym semed for to bee,
And eet hey° as an oxe, and lay theroute°
In reyn; with wilde beestes walked hee
Til certein tyme was ycome aboute.

And lik an egles fetheres wax° his heres;
His nayles lyk a briddes° clawes weere;
Til God relessed hym a certeyn yeres°,
And yaf hym wit°, and thanne with many a teere
He thanked God; and evere° his lyf in feere
Was he to doon amys° or moore trespace°;
And til that tyme he leyd was on his beere°,
He knew that God was ful of myght and grace.

BALTHASAR

His sone, which that highte° Balthasar,
That heeld the regne° after his fader° day,
He by his fader koude noght be war°,
For proud he was of herte and of array,
And eek an ydolastre° he was ay°.
His hye estaat assured hym in pryde°;
But Fortune caste hym doun, and ther he lay,
And sodeynly his regne gan divide°.

A feeste he made unto his lordes alle
Upon a tyme, and bad° hem blithe bee,
And thanne his officeres gan he calle.
"Gooth, bryngeth forth the vesseles," quod he,
"Whiche that my fader in his prosperitee
Out of the temple of Jerusalem birafte°;
And to oure hye goddes thanke we
Of° honour that oure eldres with us lafte."

Hys wyf, his lordes, and his concubynes
Ay° dronken whil hire appetites laste
Out of thise noble vessels sondry° wynes.
And on a wal this kyng his eyen caste,
And saugh an hand, armlees, that wroot ful faste,
For feere of which he quook° and siked soore°.
This hand that Balthasar so soore agaste°
Wroot *Mane, techel, phares* and namoore.

In al that land magicien was noon
That koude expoune° what this lettre° mente,
But Daniel expowned it anoon,
And seyde, "Kyng, God to thy fader lente
Glorie and honour, regne°, tresour, rente°,
And he was proud, and nothyng God ne dradde°,
And therfore God greet wreche° upon hym sente,
And hym birafte° the regne that he hadde.

"He was out cast of mannes compaignye—
With asses was his habitacioun,
And eet hey as a beest in weet and drye,
Til that he knew, by grace and by resoun,
That God of hevene hath domynacioun

2155 everychon, *everyone* **2156 expowned,** *explained* **2158 wiste,** *knew,* **fyn,** *end,* **sowned,** *indicated* **2159 leet maken,** *had made* **2160 brede,** *breadth* **2162 loute,** *bow* **2163 fourneys,** *furnace* **2164 brent,** *burned* **2166 tweye,** *two* **2167 elaat,** *arrogant* **2168 wende,** *thought,* **sit,** *sits* **2169 bireve,** *deprive* **2172 hey,** *hay,* **theroute,** *outside* **2175 wax,** *grew* **2176 briddes,** *bird's* **2177 a certeyn yeres,** *in a period of time* **2178 yaf hym wit,** *gave him reason* **2179 evere,** *i.e., for the rest of* **2180 doon amys,** *do wrong,* **trespace,** *sin* **2181 beere,** *funeral platform* **2183 highte,** *was named* **2184 heeld the regne,** *ruled,* **fader,** *father's* **2185 koude noght be war,** *could not be warned* **2187 ydolastre,** *idolater,* **ay,** *always* **2188 assured hym in pryde,** *confirmed his pride* **2190 regne gan divide,** *kingdom broke up* **2192 bad,** *commanded* **2196 birafte,** *carried off* **2198 Of,** *for the* **2200 Ay,** *continuously* **2201 sondry,** *various* **2204 quook,** *trembled,* **siked soore,** *sighed sorely* **2205 agaste,** *frightened* **2208 expoune,** *explain,* **lettre,** *writing* **2211 regne,** *kingdom,* **rente,** *profit* **2212 nothyng . . . ne dradde,** *dreaded not at all* **2213 wreche,** *misery* **2214 hym birafte,** *deprived him* (of)

2157 Where, Hg reads "Ther." **2157 Chaldeye,** Chaldea, often identified with Babylon and associated with occult learning. **2160 cubites,** measure of the length of a forearm, seventeen to twenty-two inches. **2161 To,** El reads "The." **2162 he,** omitted in El and Hg. **2166** In Daniel 3.20, the three are Shadrach, Meshach, and Abednego, but not Daniel. **2170 But,** El reads "And." **2183 Balthasar,** Belshazzar, son of Nebuchadnezzar; his story follows that of his father in Daniel 5. **2187 he was,** Hg reads "was he." **2192 bad,** Hg reads "made." **2206 *Mane, techel, phares,*** the handwriting on the wall of Daniel 5.25–28, there interpreted to mean "to number," "to weigh," and "to divide." **2208 this,** Hg reads "that." **2210 lente,** El reads "sente."

Over every regne° and every creature.
And thanne hadde God of hym compassioun,
And hym restored his regne and his figure°.

"Eek° thou that art his sone art proud also,
And knowest alle thise thynges verraily°,
And art rebel to God, and art his foo.
Thou drank eek of his vessels boldely;
Thy wyf eek, and thy wenches, synfully
Dronke of the same vessels sondry wynys°;
And heryest° false goddes cursedly.
Therfore to thee yshapen° ful greet pyne° ys.

"This hand was sent from God that on the wal
Wroot *Mane, techel, phares,* truste me.
Thy regne is doon, thou weyest noght° at al.
Dyvyded is thy regne°, and it shal be
To Medes and to Perses yeven°," quod he.
And thilke° same nyght this kyng was slawe°,
And Darius occupieth his degree°,
Thogh he therto hadde neither right ne lawe.

Lordynges, ensample heerby may ye take
How that in lordshipe is no sikernesse°,
For whan Fortune wole a man forsake,
She bereth awey his regne and his richesse,
And eek his freendes, bothe moore and lesse.
For what man that hath freendes thurgh Fortune,
Mishap wol maken hem° enemys as I gesse;
This proverbe is ful sooth° and ful commune°.

CENOBIA

Cenobia, of Palymerie queene,
As writen Persiens of hir noblesse,
So worthy was in armes and so keene°
That no wight° passed hire in hardynesse°,
Ne in lynage°, nor in oother gentillesse.
Of kynges blood of Perce is she descended—
I seye nat that she hadde moost fairnesse,
But of hir shape she myghte nat been amended°.

From hire childhede I fynde that she fledde
Office° of wommen, and to wode° she wente,
And many a wilde hertes° blood she shedde
With arwes brode that she to hem sente.
She was so swift that she anon° hem hente°.
And whan that she was elder, she wolde kille
Leouns, leopardes, and beres al torente°,
And in hir armes weelde° hem at hir wille.

She dorste° wilde beestes dennes seke°,
And rennen in the montaignes al the nyght,
And slepen under a bussh, and she koude eke°
Wrastlen by verray° force and verray myght
With any yong man, were he never so wight°.
Ther myghte no thyng in hir armes stonde.
She kepte hir maydenhod from every wight°;
To no man deigned hire for to be bonde°.

But atte laste hir freendes han hire maried°
To Odenake, a prynce of that contree,
Al were it so that° she hem longe taried°.
And ye shul understonde how that he
Hadde swiche fantasies° as hadde she.
But natheless, whan they were knyt in feere°,
They lyved in joye and in felicitee,
For ech of hem hadde oother lief° and deere.

Save o° thyng, that she wolde nevere assente
By no wey that he sholde by hire lye
But ones°, for it was hir pleyn° entente
To have a child the world to multiplye.
And also° soone as that she myghte espye

2220 regne, *kingdom* **2222 figure,** (human) *form* **2223 Eek,** *moreover* **2224 verraily,** *truly* **2228 sondry wynys,** *various wines* **2229 heryest,** *worship* **2230 to thee yshapen,** *to you destined,* **pyne,** *pain* **2233 regne,** *reign,* **weyest noght,** *weigh nothing* **2234 regne,** *kingdom* **2235 yeven,** *given* **2236 thilke,** *this,* **slawe,** *slain* **2237 degree,** *rank* **2240 sikernesse,** *certainty* **2245 hem,** *them* **2246 sooth,** *true,* **commune,** *widespread* **2249 keene,** *courageous* **2250 wight,** *person,* **hardynesse,** *boldness* **2251 lynage,** *lineage* **2254 amended,** *improved* **2256 Office,** *duties,* **wode,** *the forest* **2257 hertes,** *deer's* **2259 anon,** *soon,* **hente,** *caught* **2261 torente,** *torn to pieces* **2262 weelde,** *control* **2263 dorste,** *dared,* **seke,** *to seek* **2265 eke,** *also* **2266 verray,** *sheer* **2267 wight,** *strong* **2269 wight,** *man* **2270 deigned hire for to be bonde,** *did she condescend to be married* **2271 han hire maried,** *have married her* **2273 Al were it so that,** *even though,* **hem longe taried,** *long delayed them* **2275 swiche fantasies,** *such wishes* **2276 knyt in feere,** *joined together* **2278 lief,** *beloved* **2279 Save o,** *except one* **2281 ones,** *once,* **pleyn,** *simple* **2283 also,** *as*

2235 Medes . . . Perses, the Medes were a historical people absorbed by the Persians (Perses) before the fall of Babylon. **yeven,** omitted in El. **2237 Darius,** no historical person has been identified, although he is mentioned in Daniel 5.31. Historically Cyrus the Great of Persia defeated Babylonia. **2245 as,** omitted in Hg. **2246 This proverbe,** see *Bo* 3pr5.68–70. **2247 Cenobia . . . Palymerie,** Zenobia, queen of Palmyra, city-state in central Syria. Chaucer follows the account in Boccaccio's *De Claris Mulieribus* (*On Famous Women*) 98, which is odd, since he borrowed the title but no material from Boccaccio's *De Casibus*; see the note to 1990a above. **2251 nor in,** Hg reads "ne." **2252 Perce,** Persia, although Boccaccio says Egypt. **2272 Odenake,** Odenatus, prince of Palmyra. El and Hg read "Onedake" throughout this account.

That she was nat with childe with that dede,
Thanne wolde she suffre° hym doon his fantasye°
Eftsoone° and nat but oones, out of drede°.

And if she were with childe at thilke cast°,
Namoore sholde he pleyen thilke game
Til fully fourty wikes weren past.
Thanne wolde she ones suffre hym do the same.
Al were this Odenake wilde or tame,
He gat namoore of hire, for thus she seyde,
It was to wyves lecherie and shame,
In oother caas° if that men with hem pleyde.

Two sones by this Odenake hadde she
The whiche she kepte in vertu and lettrure°.
But now unto oure tale turne we:
I seye, so worshipful° a creature,
And wys therwith, and large with mesure°,
So penyble° in the werre, and curteis° eke,
Ne moore labour° myghte in werre° endure,
Was noon, though al this world men wolde seke.

Hir riche array° ne myghte nat be told,
As wel in vessel° as in hire clothyng.
She was al clad in perree° and in gold,
And eek she lafte° noght, for noon huntyng,
To have of sondry tonges° ful knowyng,
Whan that she leyser° hadde; and for to entende°
To lerne bookes was al hire likyng°,
How she in vertu myghte hir lyf dispende°.

And shortly of this proces° for to trete,
So doghty° was hir housbonde and eek she
That they conquered manye regnes° grete
In the orient, with many a fair citee
Apertenaunt° unto the magestee
Of Rome, and with strong hond held hem ful faste°,
Ne nevere myghte hir foomen° doon hem° flee
Ay whil° that Odenakes dayes laste.

Hir batailles, whoso list° hem for to rede,
Agayn Sapor the kyng and othere mo°,
And how that al this proces fil° in dede,
Why she conquered, and what title had therto°,
And after, of hir meschief° and hire wo,
How that she was biseged° and ytake;
Lat hym unto my maister Petrak go,
That writ ynough of this, I undertake°.

Whan Odenake was deed, she myghtily
The regnes° heeld, and with hire propre° hond
Agayn hir foos she faught so cruelly°
That ther nas kyng ne prynce in al that lond
That he nas glad, if he that grace fond,
That she ne wolde upon his lond werreye°.
With hire they maden alliance by bond
To been in pees, and lete hire ride and pleye.

The Emperour of Rome Claudius,
Ne hym bifore the Romayn Galien,
Ne dorste nevere been° so corageus,
Ne noon Ermyn°, ne noon Egipcien°,
Ne Surrien°, ne noon Arabyen,
Withinne the feeldes that dorste with hire fighte,
Lest° that she wolde hem with hir handes slen°,
Or with hir meignee° putten hem to flighte.

In kynges habit° wente hir sones two,
As heires of hir fadres regnes° alle,
And Hermanno and Thymalao
Hir names were, as Persiens hem calle.
But ay° Fortune hath in hire hony galle°:
This myghty queene may no while endure.

2285 suffre, *allow,* **fantasye,** *desire* **2286 Eftsoone,** *again,* **out of drede,** *without doubt* **2287 at thilke cast,** *in that attempt* **2294 caas,** *circumstances* **2296 lettrure,** *learning* **2298 worshipful,** *noble* **2299 large with mesure,** *appropriately generous* **2300 penyble,** *hardworking,* **curteis,** *courteous* **2301 labour,** *toil,* **werre,** *war* **2303 array,** *splendor* **2304 vessel,** *treasure* **2305 perree,** *jewels* **2306 lafte,** *neglected* **2307 sondry tonges,** *various languages* **2308 leyser,** *time,* **entende,** *strive* **2309 likyng,** *desire* **2310 dispende,** *spend* **2311 this proces,** *these events* **2312 doghty,** *brave* **2313 regnes,** *kingdoms* **2315 Apertenaunt,** *belonging* **2316 ful faste,** *very firmly* **2317 foomen,** *enemies,* **doon hem,** *make them* **2318 Aywhil,** *for the time* **2319 list,** *chooses* **2320 othere mo,** *many others* **2321 this proces fil,** *these events occurred* **2322 therto,** *as a result* **2323 meschief,** *misfortune* **2324 biseged,** *besieged* **2326 undertake,** *assert* **2328 regnes,** *kingdoms,* **propre,** *own* **2329 cruelly,** *fiercely* **2332 werreye,** *make war* **2337 Ne dorste nevere been,** *never dared to be* **2338 Ermyn,** *Armenian,* **Egipcien,** *Egyptian* **2339 Surrien,** *Syrian* **2341 Lest,** *for fear,* **slen,** *slay* **2342 meignee,** *army* **2343 habit,** *clothing* **2344 hir fadres regnes,** *their father's kingdoms* **2347 ay,** *always,* **galle,** *bitterness*

2289 fourty wikes, forty weeks or about nine months. El, Hg, and all but two manuscripts read "fourty days," but Boccaccio's "post partus purgationes" indicates the period of gestation. **2295 this,** omitted in El. **2302 wolde,** Hg reads "sholde."**2311 proces,** Hg reads "storie." **2320 Agayn Sapor,** against Shapur, king of Persia, third century BCE. **2321 that,** omitted in El. **2325 Petrak,** Petrarch, though Chaucer's source was Boccaccio, whom he never acknowledges. **2335–36 Claudius . . . Galien,** Roman emperors, Claudius (268–70 CE) and Gallienus (253–68 CE).

Fortune out of hir regne made hire falle
To wrecchednesse and to mysaventure.

Aurelian, whan that the governaunce
Of Rome cam into his handes tweye°,
He shoop° upon this queene to doon vengeaunce.
And with his legions he took his weye
Toward Cenobie, and shortly for to seye,
He made hire flee, and atte laste hire hente°,
And fettred° hire, and eek hire children tweye,
And wan the land, and hoom to Rome he wente.

Amonges othere thynges that he wan°,
Hir chaar° that was with gold wroght° and perree°.
This grete Romayn, this Aurelian,
Hath with hym lad, for that men sholde it see.
Biforen° his triumphe' walketh shee,
With gilte° cheynes on hire nekke hangynge.
Coroned° was she, as after° hir degree°,
And ful of perree charged° hire clothynge.

Allas, Fortune! She that whilom° was
Dredeful to kynges and to emperoures
Now gaureth° al the peple on hire, allas.
And she that helmed° was in starke stoures°,
And wan by force townes stronge and toures°,
Shal on hir heed now were° a vitremyte°
And she that bar the ceptre° ful of floures
Shal bere a distaf° hire costes for to quyte°.

DE PETRO REGE ISPANNIE°

O noble, O worthy Petro, glorie of Spayne,
Whom Fortune heeld so hye in magestee,
Wel oghten men thy pitous deeth complayne°.
Out of thy land thy brother made thee flee,
And after at a seege, by subtiltee°,
Thou were bitraysed° and lad unto his tente,
Where as he with his owene hand slow° thee,
Succedynge in thy regne and in thy rente°.

The feeld of snow, with th'egle of blak therinne,
Caught with the lymerod° coloured as the gleede°,
He brew° this cursednesse and al this synne.
The wikked nest was werkere of this nede°.
Noght Charles Olyver, that took ay heede°
Of trouthe and honour, but of Armorike
Genylon Olyver, corrupt for meede°,
Broghte this worthy kyng in swich a brike°.

DE PETRO REGE DE CIPRO

O worthy Petro, kyng of Cipre, also,
That Alisandre wan by heigh maistrie°,
Ful many an hethen wroghtestow ful wo°,
Of which thyne owene liges° hadde envie,
And for no thyng but for thy chivalrie
They in thy bed han slayn thee by the morwe.
Thus kan Fortune hir wheel governe and gye°,
And out of joye brynge men to sorwe.

2352 tweye, *two* **2353 shoop,** *prepared* **2356 hente,** *captured* **2357 fettred,** *chained* **2359 wan,** *won* **2360 chaar,** *chariot,* **wroght,** *made,* **perree,** *jewels* **2363 Biforen,** *in front of,* **triumphe,** *victory procession* **2364 gilte,** *gilded* **2365 Coroned,** *crowned,* **as after,** *in accord with,* **degree,** *rank* **2366 charged,** *weighted* **2367 whilom,** *once* **2369 gaureth,** *stare* **2370 helmed,** *helmeted,* **starke stoures,** *violent battles* **2371 toures,** *towers* **2372 were,** *wear,* **vitremyte,** *headdress* **2373 ceptre,** *scepter* **2374 distaf,** *stick for spinning,* **hire costes for to quyte,** *to pay for her upkeep* **2374a Rege Ispannie,** *king of Spain* **2377 complayne,** *lament* **2379 subtiltee,** *deception* **2380 bitraysed,** *betrayed* **2381 slow,** *slew* **2382 rente,** *income* **2384 lymerod,** *rod smeared with birdlime for trapping birds,* **gleede,** *glowing coal* (red) **2385 brew,** *brewed* **2386 nede,** *crisis* **2387 took ay heede,** *always paid attention* (to) **2389 corrupt for meede,** *corrupted by payment* **2390 brike,** *trap* **2392 heigh maistrie,** *grand victory* **2393 wroghtestow ful wo,** *you made very sorrowful* **2394 liges,** *followers* **2397 gye,** *guide*

2351 Aurelian, Roman emperor Aurelianus (270–75 CE). **2370 stoures,** El reads "shoures." **2375–2462** These medieval examples, often called the "modern instances," come at the end of *MkT* in El and Hg, although most manuscripts and modern editions place them here, with the result that attention is focused on tragedy at the beginning and end of *MkT*; see 1973n. As RI 1132 suggests, the modern instances may have been on loose sheets, able to be inserted in various places. More generally, the shared variants tallied in MR 2.404 indicate a flawed exemplar of El and Hg. **2375 Petro,** Pedro, king of Castile and León, was assassinated in 1369. His daughter married John of Gaunt in 1371. Chaucer's 1366 trip to Spain may have been an embassy to Pedro's court. **2378 thy brother,** Don Enrique of Trastamare, illegitimate half brother of Pedro who conspired in his defeat and death. In MR 4.511, it is suggested that Chaucer, politically motivated, emended "thy bastard brother," the reading in some manuscripts. **2383–84** Describes the coat of arms of Bertrand du Guesclin, conspirator in Pedro's overthrow. **2386 wikked nest,** Skeat 5.238–39 identifies as a play on the name of Olivier de Mauni (Fr. *mau ni,* i.e., *mal nid,* "bad nest"), another conspirator against Pedro. **2387 Charles Olyver,** Charlemagne's Oliver, loyal retainer and comrade of Roland in the *Chanson de Roland* (*Song of Roland*). **2388 Armorike,** Armorica, or Brittany, home of Oliver Mauny. **2389 Genylon Olyver,** i.e., traitor Oliver. Ganelon betrayed Roland in *Chanson de Roland.* **2391 Petro . . . Cipre,** Pierre de Lusignan, king of Cyprus, assassinated in 1369; he visited the English court in 1363. Chaucer's account follows Machaut's *La Prise d'Alexandrie* (*The Conquest of Alexandria*) rather than history.

DE BARNABO DE LUMBARDIA

Off° Melan grete Barnabo Viscounte,
God of delit and scourge of Lumbardye,
Why sholde I nat thyn infortune acounte°,
Sith° in estaat thow cloumbe° were so hye?
Thy brother sone, that was thy double allye,
For he thy nevew was and sone-in-lawe,
Withinne his prisoun made thee to dye—
But why ne how noot° I that thou were slawe°.

DE HUGELINO COMITE° DE PIZE

Off the Erl Hugelyn of Pyze the langour°
Ther may no tonge telle for pitee.
But litel out of° Pize stant a tour°
In which tour in prisoun put was he,
And with hym been his litel children thre—
The eldeste scarsly fyf yeer was of age.
Allas, Fortune, it was greet crueltee
Swiche briddes° for to putte in swich a cage!

Dampned° was he to dyen in that prisoun,
For Roger, which that bisshop was of Pize,
Hadde on hym maad a fals suggestioun°
Thurgh which the peple gan upon hym rise,
And putten hym to prisoun in swich wise°
As ye han herd, and mete° and drynke he hadde
So smal that wel unnethe° it may suffise,
And therwithal° it was ful poure and badde.

And on a day bifil° that in that hour
Whan that his mete wont° was to be broght,
The gayler° shette the dores of the tour.
He herde it wel, but he spak° right noght,
And in his herte anon° ther fil° a thoght
That they for hunger wolde doon° hym dyen.
"Allas," quod he, "allas, that I was wroght°!"
Therwith the teeres fillen from his eyen.

His yonge sone that thre yeer was of age
Unto hym seyde, "Fader, why do ye wepe?
Whanne wol the gayler bryngen oure potage°?
Is ther no morsel breed that ye do kepe?
I am so hungry that I may nat slepe.
Now wolde God that I myghte slepen evere!
Thanne sholde nat hunger in my wombe° crepe.
Ther is nothyng but breed that me were levere°."

Thus day by day this child bigan to crye,
Til in his fadres barm° adoun it lay
And seyde, "Farewel, fader, I moot° dye."
And kiste his fader, and dyde the same day.
And whan the woful fader deed it say°,
For wo his armes two he gan to byte.
And seyde, "Allas, Fortune, and weylaway!
Thy false wheel my wo al may I wyte°."

His children wende° that it for hunger was
That he his armes gnow°, and nat for wo,
And seyde, "Fader, do nat so, allas,
But rather ete the flessh upon us two.
Oure flessh thou yaf° us, take oure flessh us fro,
And ete ynogh°." Right thus they to hym seyde,
And after that, withinne a day or two,
They leyde hem in his lappe adoun and deyde.

Hymself, despeired, eek for hunger starf°.
Thus ended is this myghty Erl of Pize.
From heigh estaat Fortune awey hym carf°.
Of this tragedie it oghte ynough suffise;
Whoso wol here° it in a lenger wise,
Redeth the grete poete of Ytaille
That highte° Dant, for he kan al devyse°
Fro point to point, nat o word wol he faille.

2399 Off, *of* **2401 thyn infortune acounte,** *tell your misfortune* **2402 Sith,** *since,* **cloumbe,** *climbed* **2406 noot,** *know not,* **slawe,** *slain* **2406a Comite,** *count* **2407 langour,** *suffering* **2409 litel out of,** *a litile way from,* **tour,** *tower* **2414 Swiche briddes,** *such birds* **2415 Dampned,** *condemned* **2417 suggestioun,** *accusation* **2419 wise,** *manner* **2420 mete,** *food* **2421 unnethe,** *scarcely* **2422 therwithal,** *also* **2423 bifil,** *it happened* **2424 wont,** *usually* **2425 gayler,** *jailer* **2426 spak,** *spoke* **2427 anon,** *immediately,* **fil,** *came* **2428 doon,** *make* **2429 wroght,** *made* **2433 potage,** *soup* **2437 wombe,** *stomach* **2438 me were levere,** *to me is more desirable* **2440 fadres barm,** *father's lap* **2441 moot,** *must* **2443 deed it say,** *saw him dead* **2446 wyte,** *blame* **2447 wende,** *thought* **2448 gnow,** *gnawed* **2451 yaf,** *gave* **2452 ynogh,** *sufficiently* **2455 starf,** *died* **2457 carf,** *carved* **2459 here,** *hear* **2461 highte,** *is named,* **devyse,** *describe*

2399 Barnabo Viscounte, Bernabò Visconti, lord of Milan, with whom Chaucer did business on his 1378 trip to Italy. Visconti was arrested, imprisoned, and died under suspicious circumstances in 1385, evidently orchestrated by Gian Galeazzo Visconti, his nephew and son-in-law. **2407 Erl Hugelyn of Pyze,** Count Ugolino of Pisa. Chaucer cites Dante (line 2461), i.e., *Inferno* 33.1–90, but the accounts vary. Dante has Ugolino in the bottom of hell, among the treasonous, not worthy of pity. **2416 Roger,** Ruggiero, archbishop of Pisa, Ugolino's enemy, then collaborator; Dante does not mention that he accused Ugolino. **2421 wel,** omitted in El. **2432 Fader,** El and Hg read "Fader, fader." **2461 Dant,** Dante; see 2407n above.

NERO

Although that Nero were as vicius°
As any feend that lith in helle adoun,
Yet he, as telleth us Swetonius,
This wyde world hadde in subjeccioun,
Bothe est and west, south, and septemtrioun°.
Of rubies, saphires, and of peerles° white
Were alle his clothes brouded° up and doun,
For he in gemmes greetly gan delite.

Moore delicaat°, moore pompous of array,
Moore proud was nevere emperour than he.
That ilke clooth° that he hadde wered o day
After that tyme he nolde° it nevere see.
Nettes of gold threed hadde he greet plentee
To fisshe in Tybre whan hym liste° pleye.
His lustes° were al lawe in his decree
For Fortune as his freend hym wolde obeye.

He Rome brende° for his delicasie°;
The senatours he slow° upon a day
To heere how men wolde wepe and crie;
And slow his brother, and by his suster lay.
His mooder made° he in pitous array°,
For he hire wombe slitte to biholde
Where he conceyved was—so weilaway°,
That he so litel of his mooder tolde°!

No teere out of his eyen for that sighte
Ne cam, but seyde, "A fair womman was she."
Greet wonder is how that he koude or myghte
Be domesman° of hire dede beautee.
The wyn to bryngen hym comanded he,
And drank anon—noon oother wo he made.
Whan myght is joyned unto crueltee,
Allas, to depe° wol the venym wade°.

In yowthe a maister° hadde this emperour
To teche hym letterure° and curteisye,
For of moralitee he was the flour°,
As in his tyme, but if° bookes lye,
And whil this maister hadde of hym maistrye°,
He maked hym so konnyng° and so sowple°
That longe tyme it was er tirannye
Or any vice dorste° on hym uncowple°.

This Seneca, of which that I devyse°,
By cause Nero hadde of hym swich drede,
For he fro vices wolde hym ay chastise°
Discreetly, as by word and nat by dede:
"Sire," wolde he seyn, "an emperour moot nede°
Be vertuous and hate tirannye";
For which he in a bath made hym to blede
On bothe his armes, til he moste° dye.

This Nero hadde eek of acustumaunce°
In youthe agayns° his maister for to ryse°,
Which afterward hym thoughte greet
grevaunce;
Therfore he made hym dyen in this wise.
But natheless this Seneca the wise
Chees° in a bath to dye in this manere
Rather than han any oother tormentise°.
And thus hath Nero slayn his maister deere.

Now fil° it so that Fortune liste° no lenger
The hye pryde of Nero to cherice°,
For though that he was strong, yet was she
strenger.
She thoughte thus, "By God, I am to nyce°
To sette a man that is fulfild of vice
In heigh degree, and emperour hym calle.
By God, out of his sete° I wol hym trice°.
Whan he leest weneth°, sonnest shal he falle."

2463 vicius, *wicked* **2467 septemtrioun,** *north* **2468 peerles,** *pearls* **2469 brouded,** *embroidered* **2471 delicaat,** *fond of luxury* **2473 ilke clooth,** *same clothing* **2474 nolde,** *wished not* **2476 liste,** *wished to* **2477 lustes,** *desires* **2479 brende,** *burned,* **delicasie,** *pleasure* **2480 slow,** *killed* **2483 made,** *put,* **array,** *condition* **2485 weilaway,** *alas* **2486 tolde,** *thought* **2490 domesman,** *judge* **2494 to depe,** *too deep,* **wade,** *go* **2495 maister,** *teacher* **2496 letterure,** *literature* **2497 flour,** *apex* (flower) **2498 but if,** *unless* **2499 maistrye,** *control* **2500 konnyng,** *wise,* **sowple,** *compliant* **2502 dorste,** *dared,* **uncowple,** *attack* **2503 devyse,** *describe* **2505 ay chastise,** *always criticize* **2507 moot nede,** *must necessarily* **2510 moste,** *must* **2511 of acustumaunce,** *by custom* **2512 agayns,** *i.e., in deference to,* **ryse,** *stand up* **2516 Chees,** *chose* **2517 tormentise,** *torment* **2519 fil,** *happened,* **liste,** *wished* **2520 cherice,** *protect* **2522 to nyce,** *too foolish* **2525 sete,** *position,* **trice,** *snatch* **2526 weneth,** *expects*

2463–65 Nero . . . Swetonius, the Roman historian Suetonius records the life of Nero in *De Vita Caesarum* (*Lives of the Caesars*), Book 1, but Chaucer's details come from *RR* 6183ff., a section on Fortune, which influenced various parts of *MkT*; see, e.g., 2727n, 2758n, and also *NPT* 7.3370n. **2463 as,** omitted in El and Hg. **2464 in helle,** Hg reads "ful lowe." **2467 south,** El and Hg read "north," perhaps moved into the text from a marginal gloss on "septremtrioun." **2476 Tybre,** Tiber, river in Rome. **2481 how men,** Hg reads "how that men." **2483 made he,** Hg reads "he made."**2500 konnyng,** Hg reads "lovyng." **2502 on,** Hg reads "in." **2503 Seneca,** Stoic moral philosopher, dramatist, and tutor of Nero, who caused him to be bled to death (65 CE); Seneca was accused of conspiring against Nero; he selected his own manner of execution. **2505 ay,** omitted in El. **2513 greet,** Hg reads "a greet." **2517 any oother,** Hg reads "another."

The peple roos upon° hym on a nyght
For his defaute°, and whan he it espied
Out of his dores anon° he hath hym dight°
Allone, and ther° he wende° han been allied°
He knokked faste, and ay the moore he cried
The fastere shette° they the dores alle.
Tho wiste° he wel he hadde himself mysgyed°,
And wente his wey; no lenger dorste° he calle.

The peple cride and rombled° up and doun,
That with his erys° herde he how they seyde,
"Where is this false tiraunt, this Neroun?"
For fere almoost out of his wit he breyde°,
And to his goddes pitously he preyde
For socour°, but it myghte nat bityde°.
For drede of this, hym thoughte that he deyde,
And ran into a gardyn hym to hyde.

And in this gardyn foond he cherles tweye°
That seten by a fyr ful greet and reed.
And to thise cherles two he gan to preye
To sleen hym and to girden of° his heed,
That° to his body whan that he were deed
Were no despit° ydoon for his defame°.
Hymself he slow°, he koude° no bettre reed°,
Of which Fortune lough° and hadde a game.

DE OLOFERNO

Was nevere capitayn under a kyng
That regnes mo° putte in subjeccioun,
Ne strenger was in feeld of alle thyng°,
As in his tyme, ne gretter of renoun,
Ne moore pompous in heigh presumpcioun
Than Oloferne, which Fortune ay kiste°
So likerously°, and ladde hym up and doun
Til that his heed was of er° that he wiste°.

Nat oonly that this world hadde hym in awe
For lesynge of° richesse or libertee,
But he made every man reneyen his lawe°.
"Nabugodonosor was god," seyde hee.
"Noon oother god sholde adoured bee."
Agayns his heeste° no wight dorste° trespace
Save° in Bethulia, a strong citee,
Where Eliachim a preest was of that place.

But taak kepe of° the deeth of Oloferne:
Amydde° his hoost° he dronke lay a-nyght,
Withinne his tente, large as is a berne°,
And yet, for al his pompe and al his myght,
Judith, a womman, as he lay upright°
Slepynge, his heed of smoot° and from his tente
Ful pryvely° she stal° from every wight°,
And with his heed unto hir toun she wente.

DE REGE ANTHIOCHO ILLUSTRI

What nedeth it of Kyng Anthiochus
To telle his hye roial magestee,
His hye pride, his werkes venymus°?
For swich another was ther noon as he.
Rede which that° he was in Machabee,
And rede the proude wordes that he seyde,
And why he fil fro heigh prosperitee,
And in° an hill how wrecchedly he deyde.

Fortune hym hadde enhaunced so in pride
That verraily° he wende° he myghte attayne
Unto the sterres upon every syde,
And in balance weyen° ech montayne,
And alle the floodes of the see restrayne.

2527 roos upon, *rebelled against* **2528 defaute,** *wickedness* **2529 anon,** *soon,* **dight,** *gone* **2530 ther,** *where,* **wende,** *thought,* **han been allied,** *to have allies* **2532 fastere shette,** *more tightly shut* **2533 Tho wiste,** *then knew,* **mysgyed,** *misguided* **2534 dorste,** *dared* **2535 rombled,** *murmured* **2536 erys,** *ears* **2538 breyde,** *went* **2540 socour,** *help,* **bityde,** *happen* **2543 cherles tweye,** *two commoners* **2546 girden of,** *cut off* **2547 That,** *so that* **2548 despit,** *insult,* **defame,** *bad reputation* **2549 slow,** *killed,* **koude,** *knew,* **reed,** *plan* **2550 lough,** *laughed* **2552 regnes mo,** *more kingdoms* **2553 feeld of alle thyng,** *battlefield in any way* **2556 ay kiste,** *always kissed* **2557 likerously,** *wantonly* **2558 of er,** *off before,* **wiste,** *knew* **2560 lesynge of,** (fear of) *losing* **2561 reneyen his lawe,** *renounce his religion* **2564 heeste,** *command,* **wight dorste,** *person dared* **2565 Save,** *except* **2567 taak kepe of,** *pay attention to* **2568 Amydde,** *in the middle,* **hoost,** *army* **2569 berne,** *barn* **2571 upright,** *on his back* **2572 of smoot,** *cut off* **2573 Ful pryvely,** *very secretly,* **stal,** *slipped away,* **wight,** *person* **2577 venymus,** *poisonous* **2579 Rede which that,** *read what kind* **2582 in,** *on* **2584 verraily,** *truly,* **wende,** *thought* **2586 weyen,** *weigh*

2533 In El, Hg, and related manuscripts, line 2541 is here as well as in its proper place, a result of eyeskip between stanzas. The reading here is from British Library MS Harley 7334. **2556 Oloferne,** Holofernes served Nebuchadnezzar, king of Assyria, and was killed by Judith to protect the Jewish people. Chaucer's account is from the apocryphal Book of Judith, although he adds the concern with Fortune. **2561 he,** omitted in El and Hg. **2564 his,** Hg reads "this." **2565 Bethulia,** unidentified biblical city. **2566 Eliachim,** encourages resistance to Holofernes in Judith 4; sometimes thought to be author of the Book of Judith. **2575 Anthiochus,** Antiochus, king of Syria (175–63 BCE). **2579 Machabee,** Chaucer's account is from 2 Maccabees 9, where God punishes Antiochus for attacking the Jews. **2583 enhaunced,** Hg reads "enchaunted."

And Goddes peple hadde he moost in hate;
Hem wolde he sleen° in torment and in payne
Wenynge° that God ne myghte his pride abate°.

And for° that Nichanore and Thymothee
Of° Jewes weren venquysshed myghtily,
Unto the Jewes swich an hate hadde he
That he bad° greithen° his chaar° ful hastily,
And swoor and seyde ful despitously°
Unto Jerusalem he wolde eftsoone°
To wreken° his ire° on it ful cruelly,
But of his purpos he was let° ful soone.

God for his manace° hym so soore smoot°
With invisible wounde, ay° incurable,
That in his guttes carf° it so and boot°
That his peynes weren importable°.
And certeinly the wreche° was resonable
For many a mannes guttes dide he peyne.
But from his purpos cursed and dampnable,
For° al his smert°, he wolde hym nat restreyne,

But bad anon apparaillen° his hoost°;
And sodeynly, er he was of it war,
God daunted° al his pride and al his boost.
For he so soore fil° out of his char°
That it his limes° and his skyn to-tar°,
So that he neyther myghte go ne ryde,
But in a chayer° men aboute hym bar°
Al forbrused° bothe bak and syde.

The wreche° of God hym smoot° so cruelly
That thurgh his body wikked wormes crepte,
And therwithal° he stank so horribly
That noon of al his meynee° that hym kepte,
Wheither so he wook, or ellis slepte,
Ne myghte noght the stynk of hym endure.
In this meschief° he wayled and eek wepte,
And knew God lord of every creature.

To al his hoost and to hymself also
Ful wlatsom° was the stynk of his careyne°.
No man ne myghte hym bere° to ne fro.
And in this stynk and this horrible peyne
He starf° ful wrecchedly in° a monteyne.
Thus hath this robbour and this homycide°,
That many a man made to wepe and pleyne°,
Swich gerdoun° as bilongeth unto° pryde.

DE ALEXANDRO

The storie of Alisaundre is so commune°
That every wight° that hath discrecioun
Hath herd somwhat or al of his fortune.
This wyde world, as in conclusioun°,
He wan by strengthe, or for his hye renoun°
They weren glad for pees unto hym sende°.
The pride of man and beest he leyde adoun°
Wher so he cam unto the worldes ende.

Comparisoun myghte nevere yet been maked
Bitwixe hym and another conquerour
For al this world for drede of hym hath quaked°.
He was of knyghthod and of fredom° flour°.
Fortune hym made the heir of hire° honour.
Save° wyn and wommen, no thing myghte aswage°
His hye entente in armes and labour,
So was he ful of leonyn° corage.

What pris° were it to hym, though I yow tolde
Of Darius and an hundred thousand mo
Of kynges, princes, erles, dukes bolde
Which he conquered, and broghte hem into wo?

2589 Hem wolde he sleen, *he wished to slay them* **2590 Wenynge,** *believing,* **abate,** *lessen* **2591 for,** *because* **2592 Of,** *by* **2594 bad,** *commanded,* **greithen,** (to) *prepare,* **chaar,** *chariot* **2595 despitously,** *scornfully* **2596 eftsoone,** (go) *immediately* **2597 wreken,** *inflict,* **ire,** *anger* **2598 let,** *prevented* **2599 manace,** *threats,* **soore smoot,** *painfully struck* **2600 ay,** *forever* **2601 carf,** *cut,* **boot,** *bit* **2602 importable,** *intolerable* **2603 wreche,** *punishment* **2606 For,** *despite,* **smert,** *pain* **2607 bad anon apparaillen,** *ordered immediately to prepare,* **hoost,** *army* **2609 daunted,** *defeated* **2610 fil,** *fell,* **char,** *chariot* **2611 limes,** *limbs,* **to-tar,** *tore to shreds* **2613 chayer,** *chair,* **bar,** *bore* **2614 Al forbrused,** *completely bruised* **2615 wreche,** *vengeance,* **smoot,** *struck* **2617 therwithal,** *with that* **2618 meynee,** *household* **2621 meschief,** *bad fortune* **2624 wlatsom,** *loathsome,* **careyne,** *body* **2625 bere,** *carry* **2627 starf,** *died,* **in,** *on* **2628 homycide,** *murderer* **2629 pleyne,** *lament* **2630 Swich gerdoun,** *such reward,* **bilongeth unto,** *is appropriate to* **2631 commune,** *well known* **2632 wight,** *person* **2634 as in conclusioun,** *in sum* **2635 hye renoun,** *exalted fame* **2636 for pees unto hym sende,** *to send* (messages of) *peace to him* **2637 leyde adoun,** *put down* **2641 quaked,** *trembled* **2642 fredom,** *generosity,* **flour,** *the apex* (flower) **2643 hire,** *their* **2644 Save,** *except,* **aswage,** *reduce* **2646 leonyn,** *lionlike* **2647 pris,** *praise*

2591 Nichanore and Thymothee, Nicanor and Timothy, whose defeats by the Jews anger Antiochus; 2 Maccabees 9.3. **2617 so horribly,** El reads "horriblely. **2631 Alisaundre,** Alexander the Great (356–23 BCE), king of Macedon. No specific source for Chaucer's account has been identified. **2644 thing,** El reads "man." **2648 Darius,** Darius III of Persia, routed by Alexander in 333 and 331 BCE.

I seye, as fer as man may ryde or go
The world was his—what sholde I moore devyse°?
For though I write or tolde yow everemo
Of his knyghthode, it myghte nat suffise.

Twelf yeer he regned, as seith Machabee.
Philippes sone of Macidoyne he was,
That first was kyng in Grece the contree.
O worthy, gentil Alisandre, allas,
That evere sholde fallen swich a cas°!
Empoysoned of thyn owene folk thou weere;
Thy *sys* Fortune hath turned into *aas*,
And for thee ne weep she never a teere.

Who shal me yeven° teeris to compleyne°
The deeth of gentillesse° and of franchise°,
That al the world weelded° in his demeyne°,
And yet hym thoughte it myghte nat suffise?
So ful was his corage of heigh emprise°.
Allas, who shal me helpe to endite°
False Fortune, and poyson to despise,
The whiche two of al this wo I wyte°?

DE JULIO CESARE

By wisedom, manhede, and by greet labour,
From humble bed to roial magestee
Up roos he Julius, the conquerour,
That wan° al th'occident° by land and see,
By strengthe of hand, or elles by tretee°,
And unto Rome made hem tributarie.
And sitthe° of Rome the emperour was he
Til that Fortune weex° his adversarie.

O myghty Cesar, that in Thessalie
Agayn° Pompeus, fader thyn in lawe,
That of the orient hadde al the chivalrie°
As fer as that the day bigynneth dawe,
Thou thurgh thy knyghthod hast hem take
and slawe°,
Save° fewe folk that with Pompeus fledde,
Thurgh which thou puttest al th'orient° in
awe.
Thanke Fortune, that so wel thee spedde°.

But now a litel while I wol biwaille
This Pompeus, this noble governour
Of Rome, which that fleigh at° this bataille.
I seye, oon of his men, a fals traitour,
His heed of smoot, to wynnen hym favour
Of Julius, and hym the heed he broghte.
Allas, Pompeye, of th'orient conquerour,
That Fortune unto swich a fyn° thee broghte.

To Rome agayn repaireth° Julius
With his triumphe, lauriat ful hye;
But on a tyme Brutus Cassius,
That evere hadde of his hye estaat° envye,
Ful prively hath maad conspiracye
Agayns this Julius in subtil wise,
And caste° the place in which he sholde dye
With boydekyns°, as I shal yow devyse°.

This Julius to the Capitolie wente
Upon a day, as he was wont° to goon,
And in the Capitolie anon hym hente°
This false Brutus and his othere foon°,
And stiked hym with boydekyns anoon
With many a wounde, and thus they lete
hym lye;
But nevere gronte° he at no strook but oon,
Or elles at two, but if his storie lye.

2652 devyse, *describe* **2659 swich a cas,** *such a situation* **2663 yeven,** *give,* **compleyne,** *lament* **2664 gentillesse,** *nobility,* **franchise,** *magnanimity* **2665 weelded,** *controlled,* **demeyne,** *dominion* **2667 emprise,** *enterprise* **2668 endite,** *accuse* **2670 wyte,** *blame* **2674 wan,** *conquered,* **occident,** *Western world* **2675 tretee,** *treaty* **2677 sitthe,** *afterward* **2678 weex,** *became* **2680 Agayn,** *against* **2681 chivalrie,** *knights* **2683 take and slawe,** *taken and killed* **2684 Save,** *except* **2685 th'orient,** *the Eastern world* **2686 spedde,** *helped* **2689 fleigh at,** *fled from* **2694 fyn,** *end* **2695 repaireth,** *returns* **2698 estaat,** *rank* **2701 caste,** *planned* **2702 boydekyns,** *daggers,* **devyse,** *describe* **2704 wont,** *accustomed* **2705 anon hym hente,** *immediately seized him* **2706 foon,** *foes* **2709 gronte,** *groaned*

2655 Machabee, 1 Maccabees 1.1–7. **2656 Philippes sone,** Philip II of Macedon, Alexander's father, consolidated the Greek states through conquest. **2660 Empoysoned,** Alexander died of a fever, although poison is blamed in a number of literary accounts. **2661 *sys . . . aas,*** six . . . ace, highest and lowest dice throws. **2665 the world,** Hg reads "this world." **2671 greet,** omitted in El. **2673 Julius,** Julius Caesar (102?-44 BCE), Roman statesman and general. Chaucer's account is too general to indicate a specific source, and many of its inaccuracies were medieval commonplaces, e.g., Caesar was not humbly born (line 2672) and never became emperor (line 2677). **2679–80 Thessalie . . . Pompeus,** in 48 BCE, near the city of Pharsala in Thessaly, a region in Greece, Caesar defeated his longtime competitor, Pompey the Great, famous for his conquests in the East. He was Caesar's son-in-law, not father-in-law; this confusion predates Chaucer. **2682 bigynneth dawe,** begins to dawn, i.e., from where the sun rises. **2691 of smoot,** cut off; actually Pompey was stabbed in Egypt after fleeing Thessaly. **2696 lauriat,** crowned with laurel leaves, ancient symbol of victory. **2697 Brutus Cassius,** Brutus and Cassius were two of the conspirators who killed Caesar; here (and in other medieval accounts) they are conflated into one person. **2705 Capitolie,** Caesar was killed in the Curia, not the Capitoline Hill; another common medieval error.

So manly was this Julius of herte,
And so wel lovede estaatly honestee°,
That though his deedly woundes soore smerte°,
His mantel° over his hypes° castyth he
For no man sholde seen his privetee°,
And as he lay of diyng° in a traunce,
And wiste verraily° that deed was hee,
Of honestee° yet hadde he remembraunce.

Lucan, to thee this storie I recomende°,
And to Swetoun, and to Valerius also,
That of this storie writen word and ende°,
How that to thise grete conqueroures two
Fortune was first freend and sitthe° foo.
No man ne truste upon hire favour longe,
But have hire in awayt° for everemoo.
Witnesse on alle thise conqueroures stronge.

CRESUS

This riche Cresus, whilom° kyng of Lyde,
Of which Cresus Cirus soore hym dradde°,
Yet was he caught amyddes° al his pryde,
And to be brent° men to the fyr hym ladde°.
But swich a reyn doun fro the welkne shadde°
That slow° the fyr and made hym to escape;
But to be war° no grace° yet he hadde,
Til Fortune on the galwes° made hym gape°.

Whanne he escaped was, he kan nat stente°
For to bigynne a newe werre agayn.
He wende° wel, for that° Fortune hym sente
Swich hap° that he escaped thurgh the rayn,
That of° his foos he myghte nat be slayn,
And eek a swevene° upon a nyght he mette°
Of which he was so proud and eek so fayn°
That in vengeance he al his herte sette.

Upon a tree he was, as that hym thoughte,
Ther° Juppiter hym wessh°, bothe bak and syde,
And Phebus eek a fair towaille° hym broughte
To dryen hym with. And therfore wax° his pryde,
And to his doghter that stood hym bisyde,
Which that he knew in heigh sentence habounde°,
He bad hire telle hym what it signyfyde,
And she his dreem bigan right thus expounde:

"The tree," quod she, "the galwes° is to meene°,
And Juppiter bitokneth° snow and reyn,
And Phebus with his towaille so clene,
Tho been the sonne stremes for to seyn°.
Thou shalt anhanged° be, fader, certeyn;
Reyn shal thee wasshe, and sonne shal thee drye."
Thus warned hym ful plat° and eek ful pleyn
His doghter, which that called was Phanye.

Anhanged was Cresus, the proude kyng;
His roial trone° myghte hym nat availle°.
Tragedies noon oother maner° thyng
Ne kan° in syngyng crie ne biwaille
But that Fortune alwey wole assaille°
With unwar strook° the regnes° that been proude;
For whan men trusteth hire, thanne wol she faille,
And covere hire brighte face with a clowde.

Explicit Tragedia.

Heere stynteth the Knyght the Monk of his tale.

2712 estaatly honestee, *honorable decency* **2713 soore smerte,** *hurt grievously* **2714 mantel,** *cloak,* **hypes,** *hips* **2715 privetee,** *private parts* **2716 of diyng,** *dying* **2717 wiste verraily,** *knew truly* **2718 honestee,** *decency* **2719 recomende,** *submit* **2721 word and ende,** *beginning and end* **2723 sitthe,** *afterward* **2725 have hire in awayt,** *keep watch on her* **2727 whilom,** *once* **2728 dradde,** *feared* **2729 amyddes,** *in the middle of* **2730 brent,** *burned,* **ladde,** *led* **2731 welkne shadde,** *sky poured* **2732 slow,** *killed* **2733 war,** *warned,* **grace,** *favor* **2734 galwes,** *gallows,* **gape,** *stare* **2735 stente,** *stop* **2737 wende,** *believed,* **for that,** *because* **2738 Swich hap,** *such chance* **2739 of,** *by* **2740 swevene,** *dream,* **mette,** *dreamed* **2741 fayn,** *pleased* **2744 Ther,** *where,* **wessh,** *washed* **2745 towaille,** *towel* **2746 wax,** *grew* **2748 in heigh sentence habounde,** *abounded in high wisdom* **2751 galwes,** *gallows,* **is to meene,** *signifies* **2752 bitokneth,** *symbolizes* **2754 Tho** *then,* **been the sonne stremes for to seyn,** *stand for the sun rays* **2755 anhanged,** *hanged* **2757 plat,** *clearly* **2760 trone,** *throne,* **availle,** *help* **2761 maner,** *kind of* **2762 Ne kan,** *do not* **2763 assaille,** *attack* **2764 unwar strook,** *unexpected stroke,* **regnes,** *kingdoms*

2713 soore, Hg reads "so soore." **2719–20 Lucan . . . Swetoun . . . Valerius,** three who wrote about Caesar: Lucan, *Pharsalia* (*The Story of Pharsala*); Suetonius, *De Vita Caesarum* (*Lives of the Caesars*); Valerius Maximus, *Factorum ac Dictorum Memorabilium* (*Memorable Deeds and Sayings*). **2723 sitthe foo,** Hg reads "sitthe a foo." **2727 Cresus,** Croesus, king of Lydia. Chaucer's account comes from *Bo* 2pr2.60–65 and *RR* 6489ff. **2728 Cirus,** Cyrus the Great, king of Persia, was threatened by Croesus but defeated him in 546 BCE. **2744 Juppiter,** Jupiter was god of sky and rains. **2745 Phebus,** Phoebus Apollo, god of the sun. **2748 sentence,** El reads "science." **2758 Phanye,** Phania, Croesus's daughter in *RR* 6514. **2761–64** Tragedies cannot lament or bewail in singing any kind of thing except that Fortune will attack with unexpected stroke the reigns that are proud. Repeats the medieval definition of tragedy, introduced at lines 1973ff. and 1991–94 above, helping to frame *MkT*. **2766 clowde,** the image derives from *Bo* 1pr2.26, 3m11.10, etc. It is echoed at *NPT* 7.2782 below, and thereby helps to justify placing the "modern instances" at 2375ff. See 2375–2462n.

From woodcut made by W.H. Hooper and published by the Chaucer Society between 1868 and 1879

Nun's Priest's Tale

Prologue

The Prologe of the Nonnes Preestes Tale.

"Hoo," quod the Knyght, "good sire, namoore of this!
That° ye han seyd is right ynough°, ywis°,
And muchel moore, for litel hevynesse°
Is right ynough to muche° folk, I gesse.
I seye for me, it is a greet disese°,
Where as men han been in greet welthe and ese,
To heeren of hire sodeyn° fal, allas.
And the contrarie is joye and greet solas°,
As whan a man hath been in poure estaat°
And clymbeth up and wexeth° fortunat,
And there abideth° in prosperitee.
Swich° thyng is gladsom°, as it thynketh me,
And of swich thyng were goodly for to telle."
"Ye," quod oure Hooste, "by Seint Poules belle,
Ye seye right sooth°. This Monk he clappeth lowde°.
He spak how Fortune covered with a clowde
I noot° nevere what; and also of a tragedie
Right now ye herde; and pardee°, no remedie
It is for to biwaille ne compleyne°
That that° is doon, and als° it is a peyne,
As ye han seyd, to heere of hevynesse.
"Sire Monk, namoore of this, so God yow blesse!
Youre tale anoyeth al this compaignye.
Swich talkyng is nat worth a boterflye°,

2768 That, *what,* **right ynough,** *plenty,* **ywis,** *indeed* **2769 hevynesse,** *sadness* **2770 muche,** *many* **2771 disese,** *discomfort* **2773 hire sodeyn,** *their sudden* **2774 solas,** *pleasure* **2775 poure estaat,** *miserable condition* **2776 wexeth,** *grows* **2777 abideth,** *stays* **2778 Swich,** *such,* **gladsom,** *pleasing* **2781 right sooth,** *very truly,* **clappeth lowde,** *chatters loudly* **2783 noot,** *know not* **2784 pardee,** *by God* **2785 compleyne,** *lament* **2786 That that,** *that which,* **als,** *also* **2790 boterflye,** *butterfly*

2767 Knyght, a shorter, probably earlier version of the *NPP* (lacking lines 2771–90) exists in fourteen manuscripts, including Hg. In some of these (not Hg), the Host rather than the Knight interrupts the Monk. Chaucer's expansion emphasizes the one-sidedness of the Monk's tragedies. **of,** omitted in El. **2780 Seint Poules belle,** the bell of St. Paul's Cathedral, London. **2782 covered with a clowde,** this echoes *MkT* 7.2766.

For therinne is ther no desport° ne game.
Wherfore, sire Monk, daun Piers by youre name,
I pray° yow hertely° telle us somwhat elles;
For sikerly°, nere° clynkyng of youre belles
That on youre bridel hange on every syde,
By Hevene Kyng that for us alle dyde°,
I sholde er° this han fallen doun for sleep,
Althogh the slough° had never been so deep.
Thanne hadde youre tale al be toold in veyn,
For certeinly, as that thise clerkes seyn,
Where as a man may have noon audience,
Noght helpeth it° to tellen his sentence°.
And wel I woot° the substance° is in me,
If any thyng shal wel reported be.
Sire, sey somwhat of huntyng, I yow preye."
"Nay," quod this Monk, "I have no lust° to pleye.
Now lat another telle, as I have toold."
Thanne spak oure Hoost with rude speche and boold,
And seyde unto the Nonnes Preest anon°,
"Com neer, thou preest, com hyder°, thou sir John!
Telle us swich thyng as may oure hertes glade°.
Be blithe°, though thou ryde upon a jade°.
What thogh° thyn hors be bothe foul and lene?
If he wol serve thee, rekke° nat a bene°.
Looke that thyn herte be murie° everemo."
"Yis, sire," quod he, "yis, Hoost, so moot I go°.
But I be° myrie, ywis° I wol be blamed."
And right anon his tale he hath attamed°,
And thus he seyde unto us everichon°,
This sweete preest, this goodly man sir John.

Explicit.

Heere bigynneth the Nonnes Preestes Tale of the Cok and Hen, Chauntecleer and Pertelote.

A poure wydwe° somdeel stape° in age
Was whilom° dwellyng in a narwe° cotage,
Biside a grove, stondynge in a dale°.
This wydwe, of which I telle yow my tale,
Syn thilke° day that she was last a wyf,
In pacience ladde° a ful symple lyf.
For litel was hir catel° and hir rente°,
By housbondrie° of swich° as God hire sente
She foond° hirself and eek hir doghtren° two.
Thre large sowes hadde she and namo°,
Three keen°, and eek a sheep that highte° Malle.
Ful° sooty was hir bour and eek hir halle,
In which she eet° ful many a sklendre° meel.
Of poynaunt° sauce hir neded never a deel°—
No deyntee morsel passed thurgh hir throte.
Hir diete was accordant to hir cote°.
Repleccioun° ne made hire nevere sik;
Attempree° diete was al hir phisik°,
And exercise, and hertes suffisaunce°.
The goute lette hire nothyng for to daunce°,
N'apoplexie° shente° nat hir heed.
No wyn ne drank she, neither whit ne reed.
Hir bord° was served moost with whit and blak—
Milk and broun breed, in which she foond no lak°,

2791 desport, *entertainment* **2793 pray,** *ask,* **hertely,** *earnestly* **2794 sikerly,** *certainly,* **nere,** (if it) *were not for* **2796 dyde,** *died* **2797 er,** *before* **2798 slough,** *mud* **2802 Noght helpeth it,** *it accomplishes nothing,* **sentence,** *meaning* **2803 woot,** *know,* **substance,** *essential meaning* **2806 lust,** *desire* **2809 anon,** *immediately* **2810 hyder,** *here* **2811 glade,** *gladden* **2812 blithe,** *happy,* **jade,** *nag* **2813 What thogh,** *so what if* **2814 rekke,** *care,* **bene,** *bean* **2815 murie,** *merry* **2816 so moot I go,** *as I may prosper* **2817 But I be,** *unless I am,* **ywis,** *surely* **2818 attamed,** *begun* **2819 everichon,** *every one* **2821 wydwe,** *widow,* **somdeel stape,** *somewhat advanced* **2822 whilom,** *once,* **narwe,** *small* **2823 dale,** *valley* **2825 Syn thilke,** *since that* **2826 ladde,** *led* **2827 catel,** *possessions,* **rente,** *income* **2828 housbondrie,** *careful treatment,* **swich,** *such* **2829 foond,** *provided for,* **doghtren,** *daughters* **2830 namo,** *no more* **2831 keen,** *cows,* **highte,** *was named* **2832 Ful,** *very* **2833 eet,** *ate,* **sklendre,** *sparse* **2834 poynaunt,** *tangy,* **deel,** *bit* **2836 cote,** *cottage* **2837 Repleccioun,** *overeating* **2838 Attempree,** *moderate,* **al hir phisik,** *her only medical treatment* **2839 hertes suffisaunce,** *heart's content* **2840 lette hire nothyng for to daunce,** *hindered her not at all from dancing* **2841 N'apoplexie,** *nor apoplexy* (a stroke), **shente,** *injured* **2843 bord,** *table* **2844 lak,** *fault*

2791 Hg and the other manuscripts that have the short form of *NPP* read "Your tales doon us no desport ne game." **2792 daun Piers,** master Peter; why the Host did not know or did not use the Monk's name at *MkT* 7.1929–30 has never been satisfactorily explained. **2794–95 belles . . . bridel,** the jingling of the Monk's bridle is referred to in *GP* 1.169–70. **2832 bour . . . halle,** bedroom . . . main room; dignified terms for a humble dwelling, perhaps implying that such extravagances are unnecessary. **2834–35 sauce . . . morsel,** the widow's diet contrasts directly with the description of the Prioress at table, *GP* 1.128–29. **2840 goute,** gout is a disease characterized by inflammation of the joints (often the feet), once thought to result from dietary excess.

Seynd° bacoun, and somtyme an ey° or tweye°,
For she was, as it were, a maner deye°.
  A yeerd° she hadde enclosed al aboute
With stikkes, and a drye dych withoute,
In which she hadde a cok hight° Chauntecleer.
In al the land of crowyng nas° his peer.
His voys was murier than the murie orgon°
On messe-dayes that in the chirche gon.
Wel sikerer° was his crowyng in his logge°,
Than is a clokke or an abbey orlogge°.
By nature° he knew ech ascencioun
Of the equynoxial in thilke toun°;
For whan degrees fiftene weren ascended,
Thanne crew° he that it myghte nat been amended°.
His coomb was redder than the fyn° coral,
And batailled° as it were a castel wal;
His byle° was blak, and as the jeet° it shoon°;
Lyk asure° were his legges and his toon°;
His nayles whitter than the lylye flour;
And lyk the burned° gold was his colour.
This gentil cok hadde in his governaunce
Sevene hennes for to doon al his plesaunce°,
Whiche were his sustres° and his paramours°,
And wonder lyk° to hym as of colours;
Of whiche the faireste hewed° on hir throte
Was cleped° faire damoysele Pertelote.
Curteys° she was, discreet, and debonaire°,
And compaignable, and bar° hyrself so faire,
Syn thilke° day that she was seven nyght oold,
That trewely she hath the herte in hoold
Of Chauntecleer, loken° in every lith°.
He loved hire so that wel was hym therwith°.
But swich a joye was it to here hem synge,
Whan that the brighte sonne bigan to sprynge,
In sweete accord°, "My lief is faren in londe"—
For thilke° tyme, as I have understonde,
Beestes and briddes° koude speke and synge.
  And so bifel° that in a dawenynge,
As Chauntecleer among his wyves alle
Sat on his perche that was in the halle—
And next hym sat this faire Pertelote—
This Chauntecleer gan gronen° in his throte,
As man that in his dreem is drecched soore°.
And whan that Pertelote thus herde hym roore°,
She was agast° and seyde, "O herte deere,
What eyleth yow to grone in this manere?
Ye been a verray° sleper; fy, for shame!"
  And he answerde and seyde thus, "Madame,
I pray yow that ye take it nat agrief°.
By God, me mette° I was in swich meschief°
Right now that yet myn herte is soore afright.
Now God," quod he, "my swevene recche aright°,
And kepe my body out of foul prisoun!
Me mette how that I romed up and doun
Withinne our yeerd, wheer as I saugh a beest
Was lyk an hound, and wolde han° maad areest
Upon my body, and wolde han had me deed.
His colour was bitwixe yelow and reed,
And tipped was his tayl and bothe his eeris°
With blak, unlyk the remenant° of his heeris;
His snowte smal, with glowynge eyen tweye°.
Yet of his look for feere almoost I deye°;
This caused me my gronyng, doutelees."
  "Avoy°," quod she, "fy on yow, hertelees°!
Allas," quod she, "for by that God above,
Now han ye lost myn herte and al my love.

2845 Seynd, *smoked,* **ey,** *egg,* **tweye,** *two* **2846 maner deye,** *kind of dairywoman* **2847 yeerd,** *yard* **2849 hight,** *called* **2850 nas,** *none was* **2851 murie orgon,** *merry organ* **2853 sikerer,** *more reliable,* **logge,** *lodging* **2854 orlogge,** *chiming clock* **2855 By nature,** *instinctively* **2856 thilke toun,** *that town* **2858 crew,** *crowed,* **amended,** *improved upon* **2859 fyn,** *fine* **2860 batailled,** *notched like a battlement* **2861 byle,** *beak,* **jeet,** *dark black gem,* **shoon,** *shined* **2862 asure,** *blue gem,* **toon,** *toes* **2864 burned,** *polished* **2866 plesaunce,** *pleasure* **2867 sustres,** *sisters,* **paramours,** *mistresses* **2868 wonder lyk,** *wondrously like* **2869 hewed,** *colored* **2870 cleped,** *called* **2871 Curteys,** *courtly,* **debonaire,** *gracious* **2872 bar,** *carried* **2873 Syn thilke,** *since that* **2875 loken,** *locked,* **lith,** *limb* **2876 therwith,** *with that* **2879 accord,** *harmony* **2880 thilke,** *at that* **2881 briddes,** *birds* **2882 bifel,** *it happened* **2886 gan gronen,** *began to groan* **2887 drecched soore,** *deeply troubled* **2888 roore,** *cry out* **2889 agast,** *upset* **2891 verray,** *sound* **2893 take it nat agrief,** *be not upset* **2894 me mette,** *I dreamed,* **swich mischief,** *such misfortune* **2896 my swevene recche aright,** *interpret my dream correctly* **2900 wolde han,** *would have* **2903 eeris,** *ears* **2904 remenant,** *rest* **2905 glowynge eyen tweye,** *two glowing eyes* **2906 deye,** *die* **2908 Avoy,** *for shame,* **hertelees,** *coward*

2854 an, Hg reads "any." **2855–57 ech ascensioun / Of the equynoxial . . . degrees fiftene. . . ,** each time the sun ascended 15 degrees above the horizon in its imaginary circle around the Earth, Chauntecleer crowed the new hour; a 360-degree orbit divides into twenty-four equal units (hours) of 15 degrees. **2855 knew,** El and Hg read "crew." **2877 But,** El reads "And." **2878 bigan,** Hg reads "gan." **2879 My lief is faren in londe,** "My love is gone away," a popular song. **2882 in a dawenynge,** one morning; according to medieval dreamlore, the best time for premonition. El reads "in the dawenynge." **2889 O,** omitted in Hg. **2894 mette,** El reads "thoughte." **2900 maad areest,** a formal term for "seized"; like "prisoun" (line 2897), the physical description of Chantecleer (lines 2859–64), and the courtly description of Pertelote (lines 2870–75), this is the inflated language of the mock heroic. **2901 wolde,** omitted in El and Hg.

I kan nat love a coward, by my feith!
For certes°, what so° any womman seith,
We alle desiren, if it myghte bee,
To han housbondes hardy°, wise, and free°,
And secree°, and no nygard°, ne no fool,
Ne hym that is agast° of every tool°,
Ne noon avauntour°. By that God above,
How dorste ye seyn°, for shame, unto youre love
That any thyng myghte make yow aferd?
Have ye no mannes herte, and han a berd°?
"Allas, and konne° ye been agast of swevenys°?
Nothyng, God woot°, but vanitee° in swevene is.
Swevenes engendren° of replecciouns°,
And ofte of fume° and of complecciouns,
Whan humours been to habundant° in a wight°.
Certes° this dreem which ye han met° tonyght
Cometh of the greet superfluytee
Of youre rede colera°, pardee°,
Which causeth folk to dreden° in hir dremes
Of arwes°, and of fyr with rede lemes°,
Of rede beestes, that they wol hem byte,
Of contek°, and of whelpes° grete and lyte°;
Right° as the humour of malencolie°
Causeth ful many a man in sleep to crie
For feere of blake beres, or boles° blake,
Or elles blake develes wole hem take.
Of othere humours koude° I telle also
That werken many a man in sleep ful wo;
But I wol passe as lightly as I kan.
Lo° Catoun, which that was so wys a man,
Seyde he nat thus, 'Ne do no fors° of dremes'?
"Now, sire," quod she, "whan ye flee° fro the bemes°,
For Goddes love, as taak° som laxatyf.
Up° peril of my soule and of my lyf,
I conseille yow the beste, I wol nat lye,
That bothe of colere and of malencolye
Ye purge yow; and for° ye shal nat tarie,
Though in this toun is noon apothecarie,
I shal myself to herbes techen° yow
That shul been for youre heele and for youre prow°;
And in oure yeerd tho° herbes shal I fynde
The whiche han of hire propretee by kynde°
To purge yow bynethe° and eek above.
Foryet nat this, for Goddes owene love,
Ye been ful coleryk of compleccioun.
Ware° the sonne in his ascencioun°
Ne fynde yow nat repleet° of humours hoote°.
And if it do, I dar wel leye° a grote°
That ye shul have a fevere terciane,
Or an agu° that may be youre bane°.
A day or two ye shul have digestyves°
Of wormes, er° ye take youre laxatyves
Of lawriol, centaure, and fumetere,
Or elles of ellebor, that groweth there,
Of katapuece, or of gaitrys beryis,
Of herbe yve, growyng in oure yeerd ther mery is°—
Pekke hem up right as they growe and ete hem yn.
Be myrie, housbonde, for youre fader kyn°!
Dredeth no dreem; I kan sey yow namoore."
"Madame," quod he, "graunt mercy of° youre loore.
But nathelees, as touchyng daun° Catoun,
That hath of wysdom swich° a greet renoun,
Though that he bad° no dremes for to drede,
By God, men may in olde bookes rede

2912 certes, *certainly,* **what so,** *whatever* **2914 hardy,** *bold,* **free,** *generous* **2915 secree,** *discreet,* **nygard,** *miser* **2916 agast,** *afraid,* **tool,** *weapon* **2917 noon avauntour,** *no boaster* **2918 dorste ye seyn,** *dare you say* **2920 berd,** *beard* **2921 konne,** *can,* **swevenys,** *dreams* **2922 woot,** *knows,* **vanitee,** *foolishness* **2923 engendren,** *are bred,* **replecciouns,** *overeating* **2924 fume,** *gas* **2925 to habundant,** *too abundant,* **wight,** *person* **2926 Certes,** *surely,* **met,** *dreamed* **2928 rede colera,** *reddish bile,* **pardee,** *by God* **2929 dreden,** *fear* **2930 arwes,** *arrows,* **lemes,** *flames* **2932 contek,** *conflict,* **whelpes,** *dogs,* **lyte,** *little* **2933 Right,** *just,* **malencolie,** *black bile* **2935 boles,** *bulls* **2937 koude,** *could* **2940 Lo,** *consider* **2941 Ne do no fors of,** *make no matter of* **2942 flee,** *fly,* **bemes,** *rafters* **2943 as taak,** *take* **2944 Up,** *upon* **2947 for,** *so that* **2949 techen,** *show* **2950 prow,** *advantage* **2951 tho,** *those* **2952 propretee by kynde,** *natural properties* **2953 bynethe,** *below* **2956 Ware,** *beware that,* **in his ascencioun,** *when it rises high* **2957 repleet,** *full,* **hoote,** *hot* **2958 leye,** *bet,* **grote,** *silver coin* **2960 agu,** *sharp fever,* **bane,** *death* **2961 digestyves,** *digestive aids* **2962 er,** *before* **2966 ther mery is,** *where it is pleasant* **2968 fader kyn,** *father's kin* **2970 graunt mercy of,** *many thanks for* **2971 touchyng daun,** *regarding master* **2972 swich,** *such* **2973 bad,** *told* (us)

2913–17 Compare *WBT* 3.925–48 and *ShT* 7.172–77. **2924 complecciouns,** (im)balances among the humors (blood, phlegm, yellow or reddish bile [choler], black bile [melancholy]); see *GP* 1.333n. and 2984n. below. **2927 the,** omitted in El. **2931 rede,** El reads "grete." **2940 Caton,** Dionysius Cato, supposed author of *Disticha Catonis* (*Cato's Couplets*), a collection of maxims used as a medieval school textbook; see *Disticha* 2.3. **2942 ye,** Hg reads "we." **the,** Hg reads "thise." **2959 fevere terciane,** fever that recurs every other day, attributed to an excess of reddish bile, especially when combined with black bile. **2963–66 lawriol, centaure, and fumetere . . . ellebor . . . katapuece . . . gaitrys beryis** (berries) **. . . herbe yve** (ivy), all herbs used in medieval medicine, although the combination here is overwhelming and perhaps deadly.

Of many a man moore of auctorite
Than evere Caton was, so moot I thee°,
That al the revers seyn° of this sentence°,
And han wel founden by experience
That dremes been significaciouns
As wel of joye as of tribulaciouns
That folk enduren in this lif present.
Ther nedeth° make of this noon argument;
The verray preeve° sheweth it in dede.
"Oon of the gretteste auctour that men rede
Seith thus, that whilom° two felawes° wente
On pilgrimage in a ful good entente,
And happed so° they coomen in a toun
Wher as ther was swich congregacioun
Of peple, and eek so streit of herbergage°,
That they ne founde as muche as o cotage°
In which they bothe myghte logged° bee.
Wherfore they mosten° of necessitee,
As for that nyght, departen° compaignye.
And ech of hem gooth to his hostelrye°,
And took his loggyng as it wolde falle°.
That oon of hem was logged in a stalle,
Fer° in a yeerd, with oxen of the plough;
That oother man was logged wel ynough,
As was his aventure° or his fortune
That us governeth alle as in commune.
"And so bifel that longe er it were° day,
This man mette° in his bed, ther as he lay,
How that his felawe gan° upon hym calle,
And seyde, 'Allas, for in an oxes stalle
This nyght I shal be mordred ther° I lye.
Now help me, deere brother, or I dye!
In alle haste com to me!" he sayde.
"This man out of his sleep for feere abrayde°;
But whan that he was wakened of his sleep,
He turned hym°, and took of it no keep°.
Hym thoughte his dreem nas° but a vanitee°.
Thus twies in his slepyng dremed hee,
And atte thridde tyme yet his felawe
Cam, as hym thoughte, and seide, 'I am now slawe°.
Bihold my bloody woundes depe and wyde.
Arys up erly in the morwe tyde,
And at the west gate of the toun,' quod he,
'A carte ful of donge° ther shaltow° se,
In which my body is hid ful prively°.
Do thilke carte arresten° boldely.
My gold caused my mordre, sooth° to sayn.'
And tolde hym every point how he was slayn,
With a ful pitous face, pale of hewe.
And truste wel, his dreem he foond ful trewe,
For on the morwe as soone as it was day
To his felawes in° he took the way,
And whan that he cam to this oxes stalle,
After his felawe he bigan to calle.
"The hostiler° answerede hym anon,
And seyde, 'Sire, youre felawe is agon.
As soone as day he wente out of the toun.'
"This man gan fallen in suspecioun,
Remembrynge on his dremes that he mette°,
And forth he gooth—no lenger wolde he lette°—
Unto the west gate of the town, and fond
A dong-carte, wente° as it were to donge° lond,
That was arrayed° in that same wise
As ye han herd the dede man devyse°.
And with an hardy° herte he gan to crye
Vengeance and justice of this felonye.
'My felawe mordred is this same nyght,
And in this carte heere he lith gapyng upright°.
I crye out on the ministres,' quod he,
'That sholden kepe° and reulen° this citee.
Harrow°, allas, heere lith my felawe slayn!'

2976 so moot I thee, *as I may prosper* **2977 revers seyn,** *opposite say,* **sentence,** *advice* **2982 Ther nedeth,** *there is no need to* **2983 verray preeve,** *actual experience* **2985 whilom,** *once,* **felawes,** *friends* **2987 happed so,** (it) *happened that* **2989 eek so streit of herbergage,** *also shortage of lodging* **2990 o cotage,** *one cottage* **2991 logged,** *lodged* **2992 mosten,** *must* **2993 departen,** *separate* **2994 hostelrye,** *lodging* **2995 wolde falle,** *so happened* **2997 Fer,** *far* (away) **2999 aventure,** *chance* **3001 er it were,** *before it was* **3002 mette,** *dreamed* **3003 gan,** *did* **3005 ther,** *where* **3008 abrayde,** *started up* **3010 turned hym,** *turned over,* **keep,** *heed* **3011 nas,** *was nothing,* **vanitee,** *folly* **3014 slawe,** *slain* **3018 donge,** *manure,* **shaltow,** *you will* **3019 prively,** *secretly* **3020 Do thilke carte arresten,** *have this cart seized* **3021 sooth,** *truth* **3026 felawes in,** *friend's inn* **3029 hostiler,** *innkeeper* **3033 mette,** *dreamed* **3034 lette,** *hesitate* **3036 wente,** *going,* **donge,** *fertilize* **3037 arrayed,** *arranged* **3038 devyse,** *describe* **3039 hardy,** *bold* **3042 gapyng upright,** *face upward* **3044 kepe,** *protect,* **reulen,** *rule* **3045 Harrow,** *alack*

2977 this, Hg reads "his." **2978 And,** El reads "That." **2980 of,** omitted in Hg. **2984 Oon of the gretteste auctour,** one of the greatest authors. The stories that follow are adjacent but reversed in Cicero, *De Divinatione* (*On Prophecy*) 1.27, and reversed and separated in Valerius Maximus, *Facta et Dicta Memorabilia* (*Memorable Deeds and Sayings*) 1.7; neither has them in sequential chapters as asserted by "next chapitre" (line 3065). Chaucer probably knew these and other versions, especially those in Robert Holcot's fourteenth-century *Super Sapientiam Salomonis* (*Commentary on Solomon's Book of Wisdom*), which also influenced Chaucer's discussion of dreams and the humors in lines 2923–41, 2974–81, and 3130–35. **3010 of it,** Hg reads "of this." **3036 wente,** omitted in El.

What sholde I moore unto this tale sayn?
The peple out sterte° and caste the carte to grounde,
And in the myddel of the dong they founde
The dede man that mordred was al newe°.
"O blisful God, that art so just and trewe,
Lo°, how that thou biwreyest° mordre alway!
Mordre wol out, that se we day by day.
Mordre is so wlatsom° and abhomynable
To God, that is so just and resonable,
That he ne wol nat suffre it heled be°,
Though it abyde° a yeer, or two, or thre.
Mordre wol out, this my conclusioun.
And right anon, ministres of that toun
Han hent° the cartere and so soore° hym pyned°,
And eek the hostiler so soore engyned°,
That they biknewe° hire wikkednesse anon°,
And were anhanged by the nekke-bon.
Heere may men seen that dremes been to drede°.
"And certes in the same book I rede,
Right in the nexte chapitre after this—
I gabbe° nat, so have I joye or blis—
Two men that wolde han passed over see
For certeyn cause, into a fer contree,
If that the wynd ne hadde been contrarie
That made hem in a citee for to tarie
That stood ful myrie upon an haven-syde°.
But on a day, agayn° the eventyde,
The wynd gan chaunge and blew right as hem leste°.
Jolif° and glad they wente unto hir reste,
And casten hem° ful erly for to saille.
But, herkneth, to that o° man fil a greet mervaille:
That oon of hem, in slepyng as he lay,
Hym mette° a wonder dreem agayn° the day.
Hym thoughte a man stood by his beddes syde,
And hym comanded that he sholde abyde°,
And seyde hym thus, 'If thou tomorwe wende°,
Thow shalt be dreynt°; my tale is at an ende.'
"He wook and tolde his felawe what he mette,
And preyde° hym his viage° to lette°;
As for that day, he preyde hym to byde°.
His felawe that lay by his beddes syde
Gan for to laughe°, and scorned him ful faste°.
'No dreem,' quod he, 'may so myn herte agaste°
That I wol lette for to do my thynges.
I sette nat a straw by° thy dremynges,
For swevenes been but° vanytees° and japes°.
Men dreme alday° of owles and of apes,
And eek° of many a maze therwithal°;
Men dreme of thyng that nevere was ne shal.
But sith° I see that thou wolt heere abyde°,
And thus forslewthen wilfully° thy tyde°,
God woot°, it reweth° me; and have good day!'
And thus he took his leve and wente his way.
But er that he hadde half his cours yseyled°,
Noot I nat° why, ne what myschaunce it eyled°,
But casuelly° the shippes botme rente°,
And ship and man under the water wente
In sighte of othere shippes it bisyde,
That with hem seyled at the same tyde.
"And therfore, faire Pertelote so deere,
By swiche° ensamples olde yet maistow leere°
That no man sholde been to recchelees°
Of dremes; for I seye° thee, doutelees,
That many a dreem ful soore is for to drede°.
Lo°, in the lyf of Seint Kenelm I rede°,

3047 sterte, *leapt* **3049 al newe,** *just recently* **3051 Lo,** *behold,* **biwreyest,** *reveals* **3053 wlatsom,** *repulsive* **3055 suffre it heled be,** *allow it to be hidden* **3056 abyde,** *waits* **3059 Han hent,** *have seized,* **soore,** *painfully,* **pyned,** *tortured* **3060 engyned,** *tortured* **3061 biknewe,** *admitted,* **anon,** *immediately* **3063 been to drede,** *are to be feared* **3066 gabbe,** *lie* **3071 ful myrie upon an haven-syde,** *very pleasantly on a harbor* **3072 agayn,** *before* **3073 right as hem leste,** *just as they wished* **3074 Jolif,** *cheerful* **3075 casten hem,** *planned* **3076 o,** *one* **3078 Hym mette,** *he dreamed,* **agayn,** *before* **3080 abyde,** *wait* **3081 wende,** *travel* **3082 dreynt,** *drowned* **3084 preyde,** *asked,* **viage,** *journey,* **lette,** *delay* **3085 byde,** *wait* **3087 Gan for to laughe,** *laughed,* **ful faste,** *very much* **3088 agaste,** *frighten* **3090 sette nat a straw by,** *don't give a darn about* **3091 swevenes been but,** *dreams are only,* **vanytees,** *empty things,* **japes,** *jokes* **3092 alday,** *always* **3093 eek,** *also,* **a maze therwithal,** *amazements as well* **3095 sith,** *since,* **wolt heere abyde,** *will stay here* **3096 forslewthen wilfully,** *deliberately waste by idleness,* **tyde,** *time* **3097 woot,** *knows,* **reweth,** *saddens* **3099 yseyled,** *sailed* **3100 Noot I nat,** *I know not,* **myschaunce it eyled,** *misfortune afflicted it* **3101 casuelly,** *accidentally,* **botme rente,** *bottom split* **3106 swiche,** *such,* **maistow leere,** *may you learn* **3107 to recchelees,** *too dismissive* **3108 seye,** *tell* **3109 soore is for to drede,** *deeply to be feared* **3110 Lo,** *consider,* **rede,** *read*

3047 out, Hg reads "up."**3052 Mordre wol out,** echoes *PrT* 7.576. **3074 wente unto hir reste,** El reads "wente to hir reste"; Hg "wenten unto reste." **3076 herkneth,** listen! This hypermetrical word is omitted in a number of manuscripts, but it produces a dramatic or a colloquial effect. **3092 of owles and of apes,** i.e., of fanciful or ominous things. **and,** El and Hg read "or." **3093 eek,** omitted in El and Hg. **3106 yet,** omitted in Hg. **3110–17 Seint Kenelm . . . ,** according to legend, Cenhelm, the son of Cenwulf (**Kenulphus,** line 3111), succeeded his father to the throne of Mercia (**Mercenrike,** line 3112) at the age of seven in 821. Though forewarned in a dream, he was betrayed by his aunt, murdered, and concealed under a thorn tree; a miraculous ray of light revealed his body. The "litel clergeoun" is also age seven in *PrT* 7.503.

That was Kenulphus sone, the noble kyng
Of Mercenrike, how Kenelm mette° a thyng
A lite er° he was mordred. On a day
His mordre in his avysioun° he say°.
His norice hym expowned every deel°
His swevene°, and bad° hym for to kepe hym° weel
For° traisoun; but he nas but° seven yeer oold,
And therfore litel tale hath he toold°
Of any dreem, so hooly was his herte.
By God, I hadde levere than my sherte
That ye hadde rad° his legende, as have I.
Dame Pertelote, I sey yow trewely,
Macrobeus, that writ° the avisioun
In Affrike° of the worthy Cipioun,
Affermeth° dremes, and seith that they been
Warnynge of thynges that men after seen°.
"And forthermoore, I pray yow, looketh wel
In the Olde Testament of Daniel,
If he heeld° dremes any vanitee°.
Reed eek° of Joseph and ther shul ye see
Wher° dremes be somtyme—I sey nat alle—
Warnynge of thynges that shul after falle°.
Looke° of Egipte the kyng, daun° Pharao,
His bakere and his butiller° also,
Wher° they ne felte noon effect in° dremes.
Whoso wol seken actes° of sondry remes°
May rede of dremes many a wonder thyng.
"Lo° Cresus, which that was of Lyde kyng,
Mette° he nat that he sat upon a tree,
Which signified he sholde anhanged bee°?
Lo heere° Andromacha, Ectores wyf,
That day that Ector sholde lese° his lyf,
She dremed on the same nyght biforn
How that the lyf of Ector sholde be lorn°
If thilke° day he wente into bataille.
She warned hym but it myghte nat availle°.
He wente for to fighte natheles°,
But he was slayn anon of Achilles.
But thilke tale is al to longe to telle,
And eek it is ny° day, I may nat dwelle°.
Shortly I seye, as for conclusioun,
That I shal han of this avisioun
Adversitee—and I seye forthermoor
That I ne telle of laxatyves no stoor°,
For they been venymes°, I woot° it weel;
I hem diffye°, I love hem never a deel°!
"Now lat us speke of myrthe and stynte° al this.
Madame Pertelote, so have I blis°,
Of o thyng God hath sent me large grace°,
For whan I se the beautee of youre face—
Ye been so scarlet reed aboute youre eyen—
It maketh al my drede for to dyen.
For al so siker° as *In principio,*
Mulier est hominis confusio—
Madame, the sentence° of this Latyn is
'Womman is mannes joye and al his blis.'
For whan I feele a-nyght° youre softe syde—
Al be it that° I may nat on yow ryde
For that oure perche is maad so narwe°, allas—
I am so ful of joye and of solas°
That I diffye bothe swevene° and dreem."
And with that word he fley° doun fro the beem°,
For it was day, and eek his hennes alle,
And with a chuk° he gan hem for to calle,
For he hadde founde a corn lay° in the yerd.
Real° he was, he was namoore aferd.

3112 mette, *dreamed* **3113 lite er,** *little before* **3114 avysioun,** *prophetic dream,* **say,** *saw* **3115 norice hym expowned every deel,** *nurse explained to him completely* **3116 swevene,** *dream,* **bad,** *told,* **kepe hym,** *protect himself* **3117 For,** *against,* **nas but,** *was only* **3118 litel tale hath he toold,** *little attention did he pay* **3121 rad,** *read* **3123 writ,** *wrote* **3124 Affrike,** *Africa* **3125 Affermeth,** *confirms* **3126 after seen,** *see afterward* **3129 heeld,** *considered,* **vanitee,** *folly* **3130 Reed eek,** *read also* **3131 Wher,** *whether* **3132 falle,** *happen* **3133 Looke,** *read about,* **daun,** *master* **3134 butiller,** *steward* **3135 Wher,** *whether,* **in,** *from* **3136 seken actes,** *look up histories,* **sondry remes,** *various kingdoms* **3138 Lo,** *consider* **3139 Mette,** *dreamed* **3140 anhanged bee,** *be hanged* **3141 Lo heere,** *consider now* **3142 lese,** *lose* **3144 lorn,** *lost* **3145 thilke,** *that* **3146 myghte nat availle,** *did no good* **3147 natheles,** *nonetheless* **3150 ny,** *nearly,* **dwelle,** *delay* **3154 ne telle of laxatyves no stoor,** *don't consider laxatives to have value* **3155 venymes,** *poisons,* **woot,** *know* **3156 hem diffye,** *reject them,* **deel,** *bit* **3157 stynte,** *stop* **3158 so have I blis,** i.e., *I swear by heaven* **3159 large grace,** *generous favor* **3163 so siker,** *as certainly* **3165 sentence,** *meaning* **3167 a-nyght,** *at night* **3168 Al be it that,** *even though* **3169 narwe,** *narrow* **3170 solas,** *pleasure* **3171 swevene,** *vision* **3172 fley,** *flew,* **beem,** *rafters* **3174 chuk,** *cluck* **3175 lay,** *lying* **3176 Real,** *royal*

3119 was, El reads "is." **3120–21 hadde levere than my sherte / That ye hadde rad his legende,** idiomatic expression meaning roughly, "I'd give up my shirt to have you read his story." **3123 Macrobeus,** Macrobius, late-classical author of a commentary on Cicero's *Somnium Scipionis* (*The Dream of Scipio*) and medieval authority on dreams. Chaucer summarizes Macrobius's commentary in *PF* 31ff. **3128 Daniel,** Daniel 7–12 records his prophetic dreams. **3130–35 Joseph . . . ,** Joseph has prophetic dreams and interprets the dreams of Egypt's pharaoh and the pharaoh's baker and steward in Genesis 37, 40, 41; see 2984n above. **3138 Cresus . . . Lyde,** Croesus . . . Lydia; see *MkT* 7.2727–60 and notes. **3141 Andromacha,** Andromache, Hector's wife, who dreamed prophetically of his death. The story first appears in Dares Phrygius's sixth-century *De Excidio Troiae Historica* (*The History of the Destruction of Troy*) 25. **3149 tale,** omitted in El. **to telle,** El reads "for to telle." **3163 *In principio,*** "in the beginning"; the opening words of Genesis and of John's gospel. **3164 *Mulier est hominis confusio,*** "woman is man's destruction"; an echo of *Mel* 7.1106 and a medieval commonplace rooted in the story of Adam and Eve. Chantecleer's mistranslation is genuine ignorance, or it is intended to impress and seduce Pertelote–or both.

He fethered° Pertelote twenty tyme,
And trad° hire eke as ofte, er it was pryme°.
He looketh as it were a grym leoun°,
And on his toos he rometh up and doun;
Hym deigned nat° to sette his foot to grounde.
He chukketh° whan he hath a corn yfounde,
And to hym rennen thanne his wyves alle.
Thus roial, as a prince is in an halle,
Leve I this Chauntecleer in his pasture°,
And after wol I telle his aventure.
Whan that the monthe in which the world bigan,
That highte° March, whan God first maked man,
Was compleet, and passed were also
Syn° March bigan thritty dayes and two,
Bifel° that Chauntecleer in al his pryde,
His sevene wyves walkynge by his syde,
Caste up his eyen to the brighte sonne
That in the signe of Taurus hadde yronne°
Twenty degrees and oon° and somwhat moore,
And knew by kynde° and by noon oother loore
That it was pryme°, and crew° with blisful stevene°.
"The sonne," he seyde, "is clomben° up on hevene
Fourty degrees and oon, and moore ywis°.
Madame Pertelote, my worldes blis,
Herkneth° thise blisful briddes° how they synge,
And se the fresshe floures how they sprynge!
Ful is myn herte of revel° and solas°."
But sodeynly hym fil° a sorweful cas°,
For evere the latter ende° of joye is wo.
God woot° that worldly joye is soone ago°,
And if a rethor koude faire endite°
He in a cronycle saufly° myghte it write
As for a sovereyn notabilitee°.
Now every wys man, lat him herkne° me:
This storie is also° trewe, I undertake°,
As is the book of Launcelot de Lake,
That wommen holde in ful greet reverence.
Now wol I torne° agayn to my sentence°.
A colfox ful of sly iniquitee°,
That in the grove hadde woned° yeres three,
By heigh ymaginacioun forncast°,
The same nyght thurghout° the hegges brast°
Into the yerd ther° Chauntecleer the faire
Was wont°, and eek his wyves, to repaire°,
And in a bed of wortes° stille he lay
Til it was passed undren° of the day,
Waitynge his tyme on Chauntecleer to falle,
As gladly doon° thise homycides alle
That in await liggen° to mordre men.
O false mordrour, lurkynge in thy den!
O newe Scariot, newe Genylon,
False dissymulour°, O Greek Synon,
That broghtest Troye al outrely° to sorwe!
O Chauntecleer, acursed be that morwe°
That thou into that yerd flaugh° fro the bemes!
Thou were ful wel ywarned by thy dremes

3177 fethered, *embraced* **3178 trad,** *copulated with,* **pryme,** *9 a.m.* **3179 grym leoun,** *fierce lion* **3181 Hym deigned nat,** *he did not condescend* **3182 chukketh,** *clucks* **3185 pasture,** *enclosure* **3188 highte,** *called* **3190 Syn,** *since* **3191 Bifel,** *it happened* **3194 yronne,** *progressed* **3195 oon,** *one* **3196 by kynde,** *instinctively* **3197 pryme,** *9 a.m.,* **crew,** *crowed,* **stevene,** *voice* **3198 clomben,** *ascended* **3199 ywis,** *certainly* **3201 Herkneth,** *listen to,* **briddes,** *birds* **3203 revel,** *joy,* **solas,** *pleasure* **3204 hym fil,** *to him happened,* **cas,** *event* **3205 latter ende,** *eventual outcome* **3206 woot,** *knows,* **ago,** *gone* **3207 koude faire endite,** *could well compose* **3208 saufly,** *confidently* **3209 sovereyn notabilitee,** *notable fact* **3210 herkne,** *listen to* **3211 also,** *as,* **undertake,** *declare* **3214 torne,** *return,* **sentence,** *subject matter* **3215 iniquitee,** *wickedness* **3216 woned,** *lived* **3217 By heigh ymaginacioun forncast,** *planned or foreseen by exalted imagination* **3218 thurghout,** *through,* **hegges brast,** *hedges burst* **3219 ther,** *where,* **3220 wont,** *accustomed,* **repaire,** *go* **3221 wortes,** *vegetables* **3222 undren,** *mid-morning* (see ClT.4.260n) **3224 gladly doon,** *usually do* **3225 liggen,** *lie* **3228 dissymulour,** *deceiver* **3229 al outrely,** *utterly* **3230 morwe,** *morning* **3231 flaugh,** *flew*

3177 He, El reads "And." **3178 hire eke as ofte, er,** El and Hg read "as oft er." **3182 He,** Hg reads "And." **3184 an,** Hg reads "his."**3188 first maked man,** in medieval tradition, God created the earth and Adam and Eve in March (the spring equinox). **3190 thritty dayes and two,** thirty-two days after the end of March is May 3, the same day that Palamon escapes from prison in *KnT* 1.1462–63 and that Pandarus dreams in *TC* 2.56. When simplified, the elaborate syntax of the sentence means "When the entire month of March and thirty-two more days more have passed, it happened that. . . ." **3192 by his syde,** Hg reads "hym bisyde." **3194 signe of Taurus,** the zodiacal sign of the Bull; on Friday, May 3, 1392, the sun was 21°6 min into Taurus, and at the latitude of central England, 41°5 min above the horizon, as precisely indicated in lines 3194—99. **3204–05** These lines contrast the Knight's comments at lines 2773–74 above. Compare also *MLT* 2.423–24. **3207 rethor,** rhetorician; the sentiment in the preceding three lines is developed at length in the *Poetria Nova* of rhetorician Geoffrey of Vinsauf and, of course, belied by the outcome of Chaucer's tale. **3211–12 trewe . . . As is the book of Launcelot,** this seems to be a humorous critique of romances, such as tales of Lancelot and Guenivere. **3214 torne,** Hg reads "come." **3215 colfox,** fox with ears, tail, and feet tipped black; see lines 2903–4 above. **3227 Scariot,** Judas Iscariot betrayed Jesus; Matthew 26.48–50. **Genylon,** Ganelon betrayed Roland in *Song of Roland.* **3228 Synon,** betrayed the city of Troy by means of the Trojan horse. **3231 that,** Hg reads "the."

That thilke° day was perilous to thee;
But what that God forwoot° moot nedes bee,°
After the opinioun of certein clerkis.
Witnesse on° hym that any parfit clerk° is
That in scole° is greet altercacioun
In this mateere, and greet disputisoun,
And hath been of an hundred thousand men.
But I ne kan nat bulte it to the bren°,
As kan the hooly doctour Augustyn,
Or Boece, or the bisshop Bradwardyn,
Wheither that Goddes worthy forwityng°
Streyneth° me nedely° for to doon a thyng—
"Nedely" clepe° I symple necessitee—
Or elles if free choys be graunted me
To do that same thyng or do it noght
Though° God forwoot° it er° that it was wroght°;
Or if his wityng° streyneth never a deel°
But° by necessitee condicioneel.
I wol nat han to do of° swich mateere.
My tale is of a cok, as ye may heere,
That took his conseil of his wyf, with sorwe,
To walken in the yerd upon that morwe
That he hadde met° that dreem that I yow
    tolde.
Wommennes conseils been ful ofte colde°;
Wommannes conseil broghte us first to wo
And made Adam fro Paradys to go
Ther as° he was ful myrie and wel at ese.
But for I noot° to whom it myght displese
If I conseil of wommen wolde blame,
Passe over, for I seyde it in my game.
Rede auctours°, where they trete of swich mateere,
And what they seyn of wommen ye may heere.
Thise been the cokkes wordes and nat myne;
I kan noon harm of no womman divyne°.
  Faire in the soond° to bathe hire myrily
Lith° Pertelote, and alle hire sustres by,
Agayn° the sonne, and Chauntecleer so free°
Soong murier than the mermayde in the
    see—
For Phisiologus seith sikerly°
How that they syngen wel and myrily.
And so bifel that as he caste his eye
Among the wortes° on a boterflye,
He was war of this fox that lay ful lowe.
Nothyng ne liste hym° thanne for to crowe,
But cride anon, "Cok, cok!" and up he sterte
As man that was affrayed in his herte.
For natureelly a beest desireth flee
Fro his contrarie° if he may it see,
Though he never erst° hadde seyn it with his eye.
  This Chauntecleer whan he gan hym espye
He wolde han fled, but that the fox anon°
Seyde, "Gentil sire, allas, wher wol ye gon?
Be ye affrayed of me that am youre freend?
Now, certes, I were worse than a feend
If I to yow wolde harm or vileynye.
I am nat come youre conseil for t'espye°,
But trewely the cause of my comynge
Was oonly for to herkne° how that ye synge.

3233 thilke, *that* **3234 forwoot,** *foreknows,* **moot nedes bee,** *must necessarily be* **3236 Witnesse on,** *take the evidence of,* **parfit clerk,** *graduated student* **3237 scole,** *school* **3240 bulte it to the bren,** *sift out the bran (i.e., find the answer)* **3243 worthy forwityng,** *exalted foreknowledge* **3244 Streyneth,** *constrains,* **nedely,** *necessarily* **3245 clepe,** *call* **3248 Though,** *even though,* **forwoot,** *foreknows,* **er,** *before,* **wroght,** *enacted* **3249 wityng,** *knowing,* **never a deel,** *not at all* **3250 But,** *except* **3251 han to do of,** *pay attention to* **3255 met,** *dreamed* **3256 colde,** *fatal* **3259 Ther as,** *where* **3260 noot,** *know not* **3263 auctours,** *authors* **3266 divyne,** *suppose* **3267 soond,** *sand* **3268 Lith,** *lies* **3269 Agayn,** *facing,* **free,** *noble* **3271 seith sikerly,** *says certainly* **3274 wortes,** *vegetables* **3276 Nothyng ne liste hym,** *not at all did he wish* **3280 contrarie,** *opposite* **3281 erst,** *before* **3283 anon,** *quickly* **3288 conseil for t'espye,** *to seek your secrets* **3290 herkne,** *listen*

3241–42 Augustyn . . . Boece . . . Bradwardyn, St. Augustine of Hippo (fourth century), Boethius (sixth century), and Thomas of Bradwardine (Chaucer's near contemporary) were all authorities on the complex and controversial issue of the relation between divine knowledge of all things and human free will. Put briefly: Augustine emphasized God's gifts of grace and choice to humans; Bradwardine emphasized predestination. Boethius sought to explain free will and divine (fore) knowledge by distinguishing between divine and human knowledge and between simple and conditional necessity. **3244 nedely for,** El reads "nedefully." **3245–50 symple necessitee . . . necessitee condicioneel,** Boethius's distinction; see *Bo* 5pr6.183ff. It is simple necessity that all humans are mortal. It is conditional necessity that if we know someone is sitting, then the person must be sitting: the condition is that we know it, although this condition does not affect the person's freedom to sit. God knows all things in one eternal moment, and they must come about by the (conditional) necessity of His knowing them; His knowledge does not affect the free will of the people who are involved. From our perspective in time, what He (fore)knows must necessarily happen, but the necessity may be on the condition of human free choice. **3248 it was,** Hg reads "I was." **3252 tale is of a cok,** the juxtaposition of philosophical issues with chickens has comic parallels with Boethius's contrast between divine and human knowledge. As God does, we foreknow Chauntecleer's fate without causing it. **3255 that,** Hg reads "the." **yow tolde,** El reads "of tolde." **3256** Proverbial. **3258 fro,** El reads "out of." **3264 ye may,** omitted in Hg. **3266 of,** Hg reads "on." **3270 mermayde,** the mermaid (or siren) was thought to lure sailors to destruction by singing. **3271 Phisiologus,** the title (sometimes the author) of the bestiary, an ancient collection of animal descriptions (sometimes including the mermaid), moralized to reflect Christian truisms and principles.

For trewely, ye have as myrie a stevene°
As any aungel hath that is in hevene.
Therwith° ye han in musyk moore feelynge
Than hadde Boece, or any that kan synge.
My lord youre fader—God his soule blesse—
And eek youre mooder, of hire gentillesse,
Han in myn hous ybeen° to my greet ese.
And certes, sire, ful fayn° wolde I yow plese.
"But for men speke of syngyng, I wol seye,
So moote I brouke° wel myne eyen tweye°,
Save yow°, herde I nevere man so synge
As dide youre fader in the morwenynge.
Certes, it was of° herte al that he song.
And for to make his voys the moore strong,
He wolde so peyne hym° that with bothe his eyen
He moste wynke°, so loude he wolde cryen,
And stonden on his tiptoon therwithal°,
And strecche forth his nekke long and smal.
And eek he was of swich discrecioun
That ther nas no man in no regioun
That hym in song or wisedom myghte passe°.
I have wel rad° in *Daun Burnel the Asse*,
Among his vers, how that ther was a cok
For that° a preestes sone yaf° hym a knok
Upon his leg whil he was yong and nyce°,
He made hym for to lese° his benefice°.
But certeyn, ther nys no comparisoun
Bitwixe the wisedom and discrecioun
Of youre fader and of his subtiltee.
Now syngeth, sire, for seinte charitee°;
Lat se, konne° ye youre fader countrefete°?"
This Chauntecleer his wynges gan to bete,
As man that koude his traysoun° nat espie,
So was he ravysshed° with his flaterie.
Allas, ye lordes, many a fals flatour°
Is in youre courtes, and many a losengeour°,
That plesen yow wel moore, by my feith,
Than he that soothfastnesse° unto yow seith.
Redeth Ecclesiaste of flaterye;
Beth war, ye lordes, of hir trecherye.
This Chauntecleer stood hye upon his toos,
Strecchynge his nekke, and heeld his eyen cloos,
And gan to crowe loude for the nones°.
And daun Russell the fox stirte up atones°,
And by the gargat hente° Chauntecleer,
And on his bak toward the wode hym beer°,
For yet ne was ther no man that hym sewed°.
O destinee that mayst nat been eschewed°!
Allas that Chauntecleer fleigh° fro the bemes!
Allas his wyf ne roghte° nat of dremes!
And on a Friday fil al this meschaunce°.
O Venus, that art goddesse of plesaunce°,
Syn° that thy servant was this Chauntecleer,
And in thy servyce dide al his poweer,
Moore for delit than world to multiplye,
Why woldestow suffre° hym on thy day to dye?
O Gaufred, deere maister soverayn°,
That whan thy worthy Kyng Richard was slayn
With shot°, compleynedest° his deeth so soore,
Why ne hadde I now thy sentence° and thy loore°,
The Friday for to chide°, as diden ye?
For on a Friday, soothly°, slayn was he.
Thanne wolde I shewe yow how that I koude pleyne°
For Chauntecleres drede and for his peyne.
Certes°, swich cry ne lamentacioun

3291 stevene, *voice* **3293 Therwith,** *also* **3297 Han . . . ybeen,** *have been* **3298 ful fayn,** *very eagerly* **3300 So moote I brouke,** *as I may enjoy,* **even tweye,** *two eyes* **3301 Save yow,** *except for you* **3303 of,** *from the* **3305 peyne hym,** *exert himself* **3306 moste wynke,** *must close* **3307 therwithal,** *also* **3311 passe,** *surpass* **3312 rad,** *read* **3314 For that,** *because,* **yaf,** *gave* **3315 nyce,** *foolish* **3316 lese,** *lose,* **benefice,** *church appointment* **3320 seinte charitee,** *holy charity* **3321 konne,** *can,* **countrefete,** *imitate* **3323 traysoun,** *betrayal* **3324 ravysshed,** *carried away* **3325 flatour,** flatterer **3326 losengeour,** *one who praises falsely* **3328 soothfastnesse,** *truth* **3333 for the nones,** *on this occasion* **3334 stirte up atones,** *leapt up immediately* **3335 gargat hente,** *throat seized* **3336 beer,** *carried* **3337 sewed,** *pursued* **3338 eschewed,** *avoided* **3339 fleigh,** *flew* **3340 roghte,** *cared* **3341 meschaunce,** *misfortune* **3342 plesaunce,** *pleasure* **3343 Syn,** *since* **3346 woldestow suffre,** *would you allow* **3347 maister soverayn,** *master most excellent* **3349 shot,** *an arrow,* **compleynedest,** *lamented* **3350 sentence,** *meaningfulness,* **loore,** *learning* **3351 chide,** *accuse* **3352 soothly,** *truly* **3353 koude pleyne,** *could lament* **3355 Certes,** *surely*

3292 hath, omitted in El. **3294 Boece,** Boethius's *De Musica* was the standard medieval textbook on music as a mathematical science. **3299 I wol,** El reads "I wol yow." **3301 herde I,** Hg reads "I herde." **so,** El reads "yet." **3312 *Daun Burnel the Asse*,** a title (though usually called the *Speculum Stultorum [Mirror of Fools]*) of a twelfth-century beast fable by Nigel Wirecker that satirizes a donkey (Burnel) who was dissatisfied with the length of his tail. It includes an account of a boy who broke the leg of a rooster. Years later, when the boy was scheduled to be ordained a priest, the rooster failed to awaken him. **3314 that,** omitted in Hg. **3329 Ecclesiaste,** probably Ecclesiasticus 12.10–19. **3341–42 Friday . . . Venus,** Friday was the day of Venus, goddess of love, and the day was associated traditionally with bad luck and disaster—including the expulsion of Adam, the beginning of the flood, Christ's crucifixion, and the death of Richard I (Lion-Heart) of England. **3347–48 Gaufred . . . Richard,** Geoffrey (or Galfrid) of Vinsauf was the author of the *Poetria Nova,* a textbook on rhetoric. Chaucer burlesques his exemplary lamentation on the death of Richard I (the Lion-Heart) in lines 3347–73.

Was nevere of ladyes maad° whan Ylioun
Was wonne, and Pirrus with his streite° swerd
Whan he hadde hent° Kyng Priam by the berd
And slayn hym, as seith° us *Eneydos,*
As maden alle the hennes in the clos°,
Whan they had seyn of Chauntecleer the sighte.
But sovereynly° dame Pertelote shrighte°
Ful louder than dide Hasdrubales wyf
Whan that hir housbonde hadde lost his lyf,
And that the Romayns hadde brend° Cartage.
She was so ful of torment and of rage
That wilfully° into the fyr she sterte°
And brende hirselven with a stedefast herte.
O woful hennes°, right so criden ye
As whan that Nero brende the citee
Of Rome cryden senatoures wyves
For that hir husbondes losten alle hir lyves—
Withouten gilt this Nero hath hem slayn.
Now turne I wole to my tale agayn.
This sely wydwe° and eek hir doghtres two
Herden thise hennes crie and maken wo,
And out at dores stirten they anon
And syen° the fox toward the grove gon,
And bar upon his bak the cok away,
And cryden, "Out, harrow, and weylaway!
Haha, the fox!" and after hym they ran,
And eek with staves° many another man.
Ran Colle oure dogge, and Talbot and Gerland,
And Malkyn with a dystaf° in hir hand;
Ran cow and calf, and eek the verray° hogges,
So fered for° the berkyng of the dogges
And shoutyng of the men and wommen eke;
They ronne so hem thoughte hir herte breke.
They yolleden° as feendes doon in helle;
The dokes° cryden as men wolde hem
quelle°;
The gees for feere flowen° over the trees;
Out of the hyve cam the swarm of bees.
So hydous was the noyse, a benedicitee°,
Certes°, he° Jakke Straw and his meynee°
Ne made nevere shoutes half so shrille
Whan that they wolden any Flemyng kille
As thilke° day was maad upon the fox.
Of bras they broghten bemes°, and of box°,
Of horn, of boon°, in whiche they blewe and
powped°,
And therwithal° they skriked° and they
howped°.
It seemed as that hevene sholde falle.
Now, goode men, I prey yow herkneth° alle.
Lo, how Fortune turneth° sodeynly
The hope and pryde eek of hir enemy.
This cok that lay upon the foxes bak
In al his drede unto the fox he spak,
And seyde, "Sire, if that I were as ye,
Yet wolde I seyn, as wys God helpe me,
'Turneth agayn°, ye proude cherles° alle!
A verray° pestilence upon yow falle!
Now I am come unto the wodes syde.
Maugree youre heed, the cok shal heere abyde°.
I wol hym ete, in feith, and that anon!'"
The fox answerde, "In feith, it shal be don."
And as he spak that word, al sodeynly
This cok brak from his mouth delyverly°,
And heighe upon a tree he fleigh° anon.
And whan the fox saugh that the cok was gon,
"Allas," quod he, "O Chauntecleer, allas!
I have to yow," quod he, "ydoon trespas°,

3356 of ladyes maad, *made by ladies* **3357 streite,** *drawn* **3358 hent,** *seized* **3359 seith,** *tells* **3360 clos,** *enclosure* **3362 sovereynly,** *supremely,* **shrighte,** *shrieked* **3365 brend,** *burned* **3367 wilfully,** *deliberately,* **sterte,** *leapt* **3369 hennes,** *hens* **3375 sely wydwe,** *innocent widow* **3378 syen,** *saw* **3382 staves,** *staffs* **3384 dystaf,** *stick for spinning thread* **3385 verray,** *actual* **3386 fered for,** *frightened by* **3389 yolleden,** *yelled* **3390 dokes,** *ducks,* **quelle,** *kill* **3391 flowen,** *flew* **3393 a benedicitee,** *ah bless us* **3394 Certes,** *surely,* **he,** i.e., *the famous,* **meynee,** *company* **3397 thilke,** *that* **3398 bemes,** *trumpets,* **box,** *boxwood* **3399 boon,** *bone,* **powped,** *puffed* **3400 therwithal,** *also,* **skriked,** *shrieked,* **howped,** *whooped* **3402 herkneth,** *hear* **3403 turneth,** *reverses* **3409 Turneth agayn,** *go back,* **cherles,** *peasants* **3410 verray,** *genuine* **3412 abyde,** *remain* **3416 delyverly,** *cleverly* **3417 fleigh,** *flew* **3420 ydoon trespas,** *done offense*

3356 Ylioun, Ilium, the citadel of Troy. **3357–59 Pirrus . . . King Priam . . . *Eneydos*,** Pyrrhus, son of Achilles, seizes Priam, king of Troy, by the hair (not the beard) and slays him in Virgil's *Aeneid* 2.550–54, although the Trojan women lament before Priam is slain, 2.486–90. **3362 sovereynly,** El reads "sodeynly." **3363 Hasdrubales wyf,** mentioned also in *FranT* 5.1399–1404; see the note there. Chaucer here adds the emphasis on the wife's lament. **3370 Nero brende . . . ,** a short version of *MkT* 7.2463–550; both derive from *RR* 6183ff., although Chaucer adds the emphasis on sorrowing women here. **3374 turne I wole,** Hg reads "wol I turne." **3375 This,** Hg reads "The." **3383 Colle . . . Talbot . . . Gerland,** dog names. **3384 Malkyn,** a name for a rustic female. **3385 eek,** omitted in El. **3386 for the,** El and Hg omit "the." **3388 They,** El reads "The." **3389 yolleden,** Hg reads "yelleden." **3394–96 Jakke Straw . . . Flemyng,** Jack Straw is named as a leader of the uprising of 1381 (Peasants' Revolt) in historical records, but it may be a pseudonym or a representative name; many Flemish (Belgian) workers were murdered in the uprising because of their economic success in the wool trade. This is Chaucer's only direct reference to this momentous event of his lifetime. **3395 shrille,** El reads "shille." **3408 wolde,** Hg reads "sholde." **3411 the,** Hg reads "this." **3412 Maugree youre head,** in spite of your head, i.e., despite anything you do.

In as muche as I maked yow aferd
When I yow hente° and broghte out of the yerd.
But, sire, I dide it of no wikke entente.
Com doun, and I shal telle yow what I mente.
I shal seye sooth° to yow, God help me so."
"Nay thanne," quod he, "I shrewe° us bothe two.
And first I shrewe myself bothe blood and bones
If thou bigyle° me any ofter° than ones°.
Thou shalt namoore thurgh thy flaterye
Do° me to synge and wynke° with myn eye;
For he that wynketh whan he sholde see,
Al wilfully°, God lat him nevere thee°!"
"Nay," quod the fox, "but God yeve° hym meschaunce°
That is so undiscreet of governaunce°
That jangleth° whan he sholde holde his pees."
Lo, swich it is for to be recchelees°
And necligent, and truste on flaterye.
But ye that holden this tale a folye,
As of a fox, or of a cok and hen,
Taketh the moralite, goode men.
For Seint Paul seith that al that writen is,
To° oure doctrine it is ywrite°, ywis.°
Taketh the fruyt and lat the chaf be stille.
Now, goode God, if that it be thy wille,
As seith my Lord, so make us alle goode men,
And brynge us to his heighe bliss. Amen.

Heere is ended the Nonnes Preestes Tale.

[Epilogue]

"Sire Nonnes Preest," oure Hooste seide anoon,
"Iblessed° be thy breche°, and every stoon°!
This was a murie tale of Chauntecleer.
But by my trouthe, if thou were seculer°,
Thou woldest ben a trede-foul° aright°.
For if thou have corage° as thou hast myght,
Thee were nede of° hennes, as I wene°,
Ya, moo than seven tymes seventene.
See, which braunes° hath this gentil preest,
So gret a nekke, and swich a large breest!
He loketh as a sperhauk with his eyen;
Him nedeth nat his colour° for to dyen
With brasile°, ne with greyn of Portyngale°.
Now, sire, faire falle yow° for youre tale!"
And after that he, with ful merie chere,
Seide unto another, as ye shuln° heere.

3422 hente, *seized* **3425 sooth,** *truth* **3426 shrewe,** *curse* **3428 bigyle,** *trick,* **ofter,** *more often,* **ones,** *once* **3430 Do,** *make,* **wynke,** *blink* **3432 wilfully,** *intentionally,* **thee,** *prosper* **3433 yeve,** *give,* **meschaunce,** *misfortune* **3434 governaunce,** *control* **3435 jangleth,** *chatters* **3436 recchelees,** *careless* **3442 To,** *for,* **ywrite,** *written,* **ywis,** *surely* **3448 Iblessed,** *blessed,* **breche,** *buttocks,* **stoon,** *testicle* **3450 seculer,** *a layman* **3451 trede-foul,** *breeding bird* (rooster), **aright,** *true* **3452 corage,** *heart* **3453 Thee were need of,** *you need,* **wene,** *believe* **3455 braunes,** *muscles* **3458 colour,** *complexion* **3459 brasile,** *red dye,* **greyn of Portyngale,** *red dye* **3460 faire falle yow,** *good luck to you* **3462 shuln,** *shall*

3423 of, Hg reads "in." **3441 Seint Paul seith,** Romans 15.4. Compare *Ret* 10.1083. **3443 fruyt . . . chaf,** wheat and chaff. Like grain and husk or nut and shell, this is a traditional way of distinguishing between the saved and the damned and (clearly applicable here) between the spiritual meaning and the literal meaning of literature. The imagery derives from Matthew 3.12; it is developed in Paul's letters (e.g., 2 Corinthians 3.6) and Augustine's *De Doctrina Christiana* (*On Christian Teaching*) and is used widely in medieval literature. Compare *MLT* 2.701–02; *ParsP* 10.35–36. **3445 my Lord,** perhaps a reference to Jesus, St. Paul, or the Nun's Priest's bishop or archbishop. **3447–62** Lines found in ten manuscripts only (not El or Hg), perhaps cancelled by Chaucer when he developed the description of the Monk in *MkP*; note the general similarities with *MkP* 7.1943–64, and especially the clear echoes between 7.1945–46 and 3451–52. Text from Cambridge University Library MS Dd.4.24. **3457 as a sperhauk,** like a sparrow hawk, a bird of prey.

Canterbury Tales, Part 8

Introduction

In her Contribution to *Sources and Analogues* (2002–05, no. 234), Sherry L. Reames makes clear the likelihood that Chaucer translated the *Second Nun's Tale* from two different sources and combined them with materials from Dante's *Paradiso* 33 and Marian liturgy. It is evident that he translated it before he began the *Canterbury Tales* because he mentions a "lyf" of Saint Cecilia in his *Legend of Good Women* (Prologue 426), dated before the Canterbury fiction. The tale is indeed a saint's life, perhaps the most intellectually charged example of this popular genre in Middle English. Chaucer adapts the saint's-life genre elsewhere (*Legend of Good Women, Man of Law's Tale, Clerk's Tale*), but only here does he give us an example in all of its awe and austerity. When granted its assumptions about Christianity and about language (see the note to line 84a), the tale is powerful in its endorsement of virginity as a spiritual ideal and its belief that spiritual truth is knowable, even palpable, in this world. Presented as history rather than fiction, the tale conveys such intense religious conviction that it reflects either profound spirituality or nostalgia for bygone certainty, perhaps both. In "Chaucer's Tale of the Second Nun and the Strategies of Dissent" (1992, no. 1166), Lynn Staley Johnson argues that Wycliffite concerns with political authority lie close to the surface of the tale, and Catherine Sanok considers it in light of the female saints' life genre in *Her Life Historical: Exemplarity and Female Saints' Lives in Late Medieval England* (2007, no. 632).

In the context of the *Canterbury Tales,* the tale gains additional dimensions. The Second Nun is not described in the *General Prologue,* though, like the Nun's Priest, she is apparently a member of the retinue of the Prioress (1.163–64). Similarities between the tales of the Second Nun and her superior invite comparison—rhyme royal stanzas, martyrdom, gaping neck or throat wounds—and their differences produce striking contrasts. Unlike the Prioress's unlearned little choirboy, the Second Nun's St. Cecilia comprehends divine mysteries deeply, and her martyrdom is depicted as heroic rather than pathetic. She experiences spiritual reality directly and uses her knowledge to convert others to Christianity and defend herself against charges of false faith. Taken together, the two tales and their prologues pose two different kinds of faith, one rooted in knowledge and the other in devotion. Carolyn P. Collette considers these issues and surveys the criticism in "Critical Approaches to the 'Prioress's Tale' and the 'Second Nun's Tale'" (1990, no. 1078). In *Singing the New Song: Literacy and Liturgy in Late Medieval England* (2008, no. 425a), Katherine Zieman assesses how the two tales (and other works) reflect aspects of public performance and its relations with liturgy.

Linguistic realism, epistemological certainty, and sequential conversions characterize the *Second Nun's Prologue* and *Tale,* whereas jargon, confusion, and failure to achieve alchemical transmutation recur in the *Canon's Yeoman's Tale* that follows—arguably a juxtaposition of the idealized Christian past with a dystopic view of contemporary society. The Church had long condemned alchemy as chicanery, but Chaucer's tale is apparently the earliest fictional account of the science and its potential to frustrate its practitioners and mislead the unwary. The Canon's Yeoman's description of his experiences in the laboratory (part 1 of the tale) emphasizes the frustration that results from thwarted expectations and the limits of human knowledge. The narrative of the priest and the canon (part 2 of the tale) satirizes gullibility and condemns trickery, as do most exposés of con games.

It is clear that Chaucer knew something about the literature of alchemy, if not its practice. The tale reflects rudimentary knowledge of metals (relative melting temperatures, for example) and considerable familiarity with alchemical terminology, which Chaucer may have derived directly from any number of Latin treatises on the subject—those he actually mentions or quotes (1428–28, 1450) or perhaps the standard textbook in the field, Geber's (or Jabir's) thirteenth-century *Summa Perfectionis* (*Sum of Perfection*). Edgar H. Duncan, "The Literature of Alchemy and Chaucer's Canon's Yeoman's Tale" (1968, no. 1174), discusses sources and Chaucer's knowledge of the practice. In *Darke Hierogliphicks* (1996, no. 433), Stanton J. Linden traces depictions of alchemy in English literature from Chaucer forward, and Peggy A. Knapp, "The Work of Alchemy" (2000, no. 1176), observes connections between the practice and nascent capitalism.

Because the Canon's Yeoman has not heard the *Second Nun's Tale*—he rides up after she finishes—the echoes between the two tales of Part 8 are evidence that Chaucer is communicating to his audience above the heads of his characters. This fact, the reference to Boughton in the link between the paired tales (556), and the concern in the two tales with the theme of transformation have encouraged critics to regard the tales as preparation for closure in the Canterbury fiction. Boughton-under-Blean is about five miles from Canterbury, and the decision by the Canon's Yeoman to leave his past life and join the pilgrimage at the eleventh hour indicates his own willingness to change. The abrupt departure of his former boss, the Canon, has not been explained satisfactorily, although in "The Canon's Yeoman as Imperfect Paradigm" (1982, no. 1173), Jackson J. Campbell argues that the entire scene anticipates the penitential message of the *Parson's Tale.* Speech and speechlessness are the major focus of the paired tales in Alcuin Blamires, *Chaucer, Ethics, and Gender* (2006, no. 383), and John Fyler reads them as a reenactment of the fall of humanity in *Language and the Declining World in Chaucer, Dante, and Jean de Meun* (2007, no. 412).

Canterbury Tales
Part 8

From woodcut made by W.H. Hooper and published by the Chaucer Society between 1868 and 1879

Second Nun's Tale

Prologue

The Prologe of the Seconde Nonnes Tale.

The ministre° and the norice° unto vices,
Which that men clepe° in Englissh ydelnesse,
That porter of the gate is of delices°,
To eschue° and by hire contrarie° hire oppresse°—
That is to seyn, by leveful bisynesse°—
Wel oughten we to doon al oure entente
Lest° that the feend thurgh ydelnesse us hente°.

For he that with his thousand cordes slye°
Continuelly us waiteth to biclappe°,
Whan he may man in ydelnesse espye°,
He kan so lightly cacche° hym in his trappe—
Til that a man be hent° right by the lappe°
He nys nat war° the feend hath hym in honde.
Wel oghte us werche° and ydelnesse withstonde.

And though men dradden nevere for° to dye,
Yet seen men wel by resoun, doutelees,
That ydelnesse is roten slogardye°
Of which ther nevere comth no good n'encrees°;
And seen that slouthe hire holdeth° in a lees°
Oonly to slepe, and for to ete and drynke,
And to devouren al that othere swynke°.

And for to putte us fro swich° ydelnesse,
That cause is of so greet confusioun°,

---

1 ministre, *servant,* **norice,** *nurse* **2 clepe,** *call* **3 delices,** *delights* **4 eschue,** *avoid,* **contrarie,** *opposite,* **hire oppresse,** *overcome her* **5 leveful bisynesse,** *permitted activities* **7 Lest,** *for fear,* **hente,** *seize* **8 cordes slye,** *subtle traps* **9 biclappe,** *ensnare* **10 espye,** *see* **11 lightly cacche,** *easily catch* **12 hent,** *seized,* **lappe,** *hem* **13 nys nat war,** *is not aware* **14 werche,** *work* **15 dradden nevere for,** *never dread* **17 roten slogardye,** *rotten laziness* **18 n'encrees** *nor profit* **19 slouthe hire holdeth,** *sloth holds her* (idleness), **lees,** *leash* **21 othere swynke,** *others work for* **22 swich,** *such* **23 confusioun,** *destruction*

2–3 ydelnesse . . . porter of the gate, Lady Idleness is gatekeeper to the garden of pleasure in the allegorical *Roman de la Rose.* Cautions against idleness are commonplace in monastic literature, where the activities of copying and translating, as well as manual labor, are presented as alternatives to the spiritual dangers of idleness. **3 of the,** Hg reads "at the." **7 hente,** El reads "shente" (destroy). **19 hire,** El reads "it." **20 to slepe and for to ete,** Hg reads "for to slepe and ete."

I have heer doon my feithful bisynesse
After the legende in translacioun
Right of° thy glorious lif and passioun°—
Thou with thy gerland wroght° of rose and lilie,
Thee meene I°, mayde and martyr Seint Cecilie.

Invocacio ad Mariam.

And thow that flour of virgines art alle°,
Of whom that Bernard list° so wel to write,
To thee at my bigynnyng first I calle;
Thou confort of us wrecches, do me endite°
Thy maydens deeth, that wan° thurgh hire merite
The eterneel lyf, and of the feend° victorie,
As man may after reden° in hire storie.

Thow mayde and mooder, doghter of thy sone,
Thow welle of mercy, synful soules cure,
In whom that God for bountee° chees° to wone°,
Thow humble and heigh over every creature,
Thow nobledest° so ferforth° oure nature
That no desdeyn° the Makere hadde of kynde°
His sone in blood and flessh to clothe and wynde°.

Withinne the cloistre° blisful of thy sydis°
Took mannes shap the eterneel love and pees
That° of the tryne compas lord and gyde is,
Whom erthe and see and hevene out of relees°
Ay heryen°; and thou, virgine wemmelees°,
Baar° of thy body—and dweltest mayden pure—
The creatour of every creature.

Assembled is in thee magnificence
With mercy, goodnesse, and with swich pitee
That thou that art the sonne° of excellence
Nat oonly helpeth hem that preyen thee,
But often tyme of thy benygnytee°
Ful frely, er that° men thyn help biseche°,
Thou goost° biforn and art hir lyves leche°.

Now help, thow meeke and blisful faire mayde,
Me, flemed wrecche°, in this desert of galle°;
Thynk on the womman Cananee that sayde
That whelpes° eten somme of the crommes° alle
That from hir lordes table been yfalle;
And though that I, unworthy sone of Eve,
Be synful, yet accepte my bileve°.

And for that° feith is deed withouten werkis,
So for to werken yif° me wit and space°,
That I be quit fro thennes° that most derk is.
O thou that art so fair and ful of grace,
Be myn advocat in that heighe place
Theras° withouten ende is songe° Osanne,
Thow Cristes mooder, doghter deere of Anne.

And of thy light my soule in prison lighte,
That troubled is by the contagioun
Of my body, and also by the wighte°
Of erthely lust and fals affeccioun;
O havene of refut°, O salvacioun
Of hem that been in sorwe and in distresse,
Now help, for to my werk I wol me dresse°.

Yet preye I yow that reden that I write,
Foryeve me that I do no diligence°
This ilke° storie subtilly to endite°,

26 Right of, *true to,* **passioun,** *suffering* **27 wroght,** *made* **28 Thee meene I,** *I mean you* **29 that flour of virgines art alle,** *who are the apex* (flower) *of all virgins* **30 list,** *chose* **32 do me endite,** *cause me to write* **33 wan,** *won* **34 feend,** *fiend* **35 after reden,** *read below* **38 bountee,** *graciousness,* **chees,** *chose,* **wone,** *dwell* **40 nobledest,** *ennobled,* **ferforth,** *thoroughly* **41 desdeyn,** *disdain,* **kynde,** (human) *nature* **42 wynde,** *wrap* **43 cloistre,** *holy enclosure,* **sydis,** *sides* **45 That,** *he who* **46 out of relees,** *without cease* **47 Ay heryen,** *always praise,* **wemmelees,** *flawless* **48 Baar,** *bore* **52 sonne,** *sun* **54 benygnytee,** *graciousness* **55 er that,** *before,* **biseche,** *beg for* **56 goost,** *go,* **leche,** *physician* **58 flemed wrecche,** *banished exile,* **galle,** *bitterness* **60 whelpes,** *young dogs,* **crommes,** *crumbs* **63 bileve,** *faith* **64 for that,** *because* **65 yif,** *grant,* **space,** *time* **66 quit fro thennes,** *saved from the place* **69 Theras,** *where,* **songe,** *sung* **73 wighte,** *weight* **75 refut,** *refuge* **77 me dresse,** *address myself* **79 do no diligence,** *take no pains* **80 ilke,** *same,* **endite,** *write*

25 legende, biography, usually a saint's life. **27 of,** El reads "with." **28 martyr,** El reads "mooder." **28a Invocacio ad Mariam,** "Invocation to Mary." Compare with *PrT* 7.467–80; both echo St. Bernard's praise of Mary in Dante's *Paradiso* 33, the liturgy dedicated to Mary, and other poems in her praise. **30 Bernard,** St. Bernard of Clairvaux (ca. 1090–1153), a major advocate of veneration of the Virgin. **31 I first,** Hg reads "first I." **45 tryne compas,** threefold universe–the earth, sea, and heavens of the next line. **51 and with,** Hg omits "with." **59 womman Cananee,** Canaanite woman; Matthew 15.21–28. **62 sone of Eve,** son of Eve; indication that Chaucer may have composed this prologue for a male pilgrim or before he conceived of the Canterbury fiction. However, the phrase is used as self-reference in the *Salve Regina* (*Hail Queen*), sung by medieval nuns every day. **64** Echoes James 2.17 and parallels concern with spiritual labor and production elsewhere in *SNPT.* **69 Osanne,** Hosanna; an exclamation of spiritual triumph and praise. **70 Anne,** St. Anne, by tradition the mother of Mary, first mentioned in the apocryphal Gospel of the Birth of Mary. **72 contagioun,** diseased influence; the notion that the body infects the spirit. **75 of refut,** Hg reads "o refut" **78 reden that,** read what; like the reference to reading (rather than telling the tale orally) in line 35, evidence that Chaucer may have written this before conceiving of the Canterbury fiction.

For bothe have I the wordes and sentence°
Of hym that at the seintes reverence°
The storie wroot, and folwen hire legende,
And I pray yow that ye wole my werk amende°.

Interpretacio nominis Cecilie quam ponit Frater Jacobus Januensis in Legenda

First wolde I yow the name of Seinte Cecilie
Expowne°, as men may in hir storie see.
It is to seye in Englissh "hevenes lilie,"
For pure chaastnesse of virginitee;
Or for she whitnesse hadde of honestee°,
And grene of conscience, and of good fame
The soote savour°, "lilie" was hir name.

Or Cecilie is to seye "the wey to blynde,"
For she ensample was by good techynge.
Or elles Cecile, as I writen fynde,
Is joyned by a manere° conjoynynge
Of "hevene" and "Lia"; and heere in figurynge°
The "hevene" is set for thoght of hoolynesse,
And "Lia" for hire lastynge bisynesse.
Cecile may eek be seyd° in this manere,
"Wantynge of blyndnesse," for hir grete light
Of sapience°, and for hire thewes cleere°;
Or elles, loo, this maydens name bright
Of "hevene" and "leos" comth, for which by right
Men myghte hire wel "the hevene of peple" calle,
Ensample of goode and wise werkes alle.

For "leos" "peple" in Englissh is to seye,
And right° as men may in the hevene see
The sonne and moone and sterres every weye,
Right so men goostly° in this mayden free
Seyen° of feith the magnanymytee°,
And eek the cleernesse hool° of sapience°,
And sondry° werkes brighte of excellence.

And right so as° thise philosophres write
That hevene is swift and round and eek brennynge,
Right so was faire Cecilie the white
Ful swift and bisy evere in good werkynge,
And round and hool in good perseverynge°,
And brennynge° evere in charite ful brighte.
Now have I yow declared what she highte°.

Explicit

Here bigynneth the Seconde Nonnes Tale of the Lyf of Seinte Cecile.

This mayden bright Cecilie, as hir life
seith,
Was comen of Romayns and of noble kynde,
And from hir cradel up fostred in the feith
Of Crist, and bar° his gospel in hir mynde.
She nevere cessed°, as I writen fynde,
Of hir preyere, and God to love and
drede,
Bisekynge° hym to kepe° hir maydenhede.

And whan this mayden sholde unto a man
Ywedded be, that was ful yong of age,

---

81 sentence, *meaning* **82 at the seintes reverence,** *out of reverence for the saint* **84 amende,** *correct* **86 Expowne,** *explain* **89 honestee,** *virtue* **91 soote savour,** *sweet scent* **95 manere,** *kind of* **96 in figurynge,** *symbolically* **99 eek be seyd,** *also mean* **101 sapience,** *wisdom,* **thewes cleere,** *shining virtues* **107 right,** *just* **109 goostly,** *spiritually* **110 Seyen,** *saw,* **magnanymytee,** *generosity* **111 cleernesse hool,** *complete brightness,* **sapience,** *wisdom* **112 sondry,** *various* **113 right so as,** *just as* **117 perseverynge,** *constancy* **118 brennynge,** *burning* **119 highte,** *is called* **123 bar,** *kept* **124 cessed,** *ceased* **126 Bisekynge,** *asking,* **kepe,** *protect*

84 And I pray yow, El omits "And"; Hg omits "I." **84a Interpretacio . . . Legenda,** "Interpretation of the name *Cecilia* that brother Jacob of Genoa included in the *Legend.*" Hg reads "Legenda aurea" ("Golden Legend"). Jacobus of Voragine (ca. 1230–1298), archbishop of Genoa, wrote the most famous collection of saints' lives in the Middle Ages, *Legenda Aurea* (The Golden Legend). More than half of Jacobus's two hundred saints' lives begin with Latin name etymologies, now known to be inaccurate, that reflect the faith in language typical of much medieval thought. Chaucer draws on Jacobus for the Interpretation and the beginning of his tale to line 357; specific sources for the rest of his tale have not been established with certainty. **85 yow,** omitted in El. **87 in,** Hg reads "on." **hevenes lilie,** heaven's lily; Lat. *celi lilia.* **92 wey to blynde,** pathway for the blind; Lat. *cecis via.* **96 "hevene" and "Lia,"** Lat. *celo et Lia*; Leah symbolizes the active religious life in scriptural commentary. **100 Wantynge of blyndnesse,** lacking blindness; Lat. *cecitate carens.* **103 hevene and leos,** heaven and people; Lat. *celo*; Greek λαοσ (leos). **114 hevene is swift and round and eek brennynge,** in the medieval cosmos, the uppermost heavenly sphere of the fixed stars moved most swiftly and the Empyrean was the realm of pure fire. **114a Explicit.** "The end." Hg omits this rubric and the one following.

Which that ycleped was° Valerian,
And day was comen of hir° marriage,
She ful devout and humble in hir corage°,
Under hir robe of gold that sat ful faire,
Hadde next° hire flessh yclad hire in an haire°.

And whil the orgnes maden melodie,
To God allone in herte thus sang she,
"O Lord, my soule and eek my body gye°
Unwemmed°, lest° that it confounded° be."
And for his love that dyde upon a tree,
Every seconde and thridde day she faste°,
Ay biddynge° in hire orisons° ful faste°.

The nyght cam and to bedde moste she gon
With hire housbonde, as ofte is the manere,
And pryvely° to hym she seyde anon,
"O sweete and wel biloved spouse deere,
Ther is a conseil°, and ye wolde it heere,
Which that right fayn° I wolde unto yow seye,
So that° ye swere ye shul it nat biwreye°."

Valerian gan faste° unto hire swere
That for no cas°, ne thyng that myghte be,
He sholde nevere mo biwreyen here°.
And thanne at erst° to hym thus seyde she,
"I have an aungel which that loveth me,
That with greet love, wherso I wake or sleepe,
Is redy ay° my body for to keepe°.

"And if that he may feelen, out of drede°,
That ye me touche, or love in vileynye°,
He right anon wol sle yow with the dede,
And in youre yowthe thus ye shullen dye°,
And if that ye in clene° love me gye°,
He wol yow loven as me, for youre clennesse,
And shewen yow his joye and his brightnesse."

Valerian, corrected as God wolde°,
Answerde agayn°, "If I shal trusten thee,
Lat me that aungel se and hym biholde,
And if that it a verray° angel bee,
Thanne wol I doon as thou hast prayed me;
And if thou love another man, for sothe°,
Right with this swerd thanne wol I sle yow bothe."

Cecile answerde anon-right° in this wise,
"If that yow list° the angel shul ye see
So that ye trowe° in Crist and yow baptize.
Gooth forth to Via Apia," quod shee,
"That fro this toun ne stant but° miles three,
And to the poure folkes that ther dwelle
Sey hem° right thus as that I shal yow telle.

"Telle hem that I, Cecile, yow to hem sente
To shewen yow the goode Urban the olde
For secree nedes° and for good entente.
And whan that ye Seint Urban han biholde°,
Telle hym the wordes whiche that I to yow tolde.
And whan that he hath purged yow fro synne,
Thanne shul ye se that angel er° ye twynne°."

Valerian is to the place ygon°,
And right as hym was taught by his lernynge
He foond this hooly olde Urban anon
Among the seintes buryeles lotynge°.
And he anon withouten tariynge
Dide his message, and whan that he it tolde
Urban for joye his handes gan up holde.

The teeris from his eyen leet he falle.
"Almyghty Lord, O Jhesu Crist," quod he,
"Sowere of chaast conseil°, hierde° of us alle,
The fruyt of thilke° seed of chastitee
That thou hast sowe in Cecile, taak to thee!
Lo, lyk a bisy bee, withouten gile,

---

129 Which that ycleped was, *who was called* **130 hir,** *their* **131 corage,** *spirit* **133 next,** *next to,* **yclad hire in an haire,** *dressed herself in a hair shirt* **136 gye,** *direct* **137 Unwemmed,** *spotless,* **lest,** *for fear,* **confounded,** *condemned* **139 faste,** *fasted* **140 Ay biddynge,** *always praying,* **orisons,** *prayers,* **ful faste,** *very eagerly* **143 pryvely** *privately* **145 conseil,** *secret* **146 right fayn,** *very happily* **147 So that,** *if,* **biwreye,** *betray* **148 gan faste,** *did eagerly* **149 for no cas,** *under no circumstances* **150, here,** *her* **151 at erst,** *for the first time* **154 ay,** *always,* **keepe,** *protect* **155 out of drede,** *without doubt* **156 in vileynye,** *shamefully* **158 shullen dye,** *shall die* **159 clene,** *pure,* **gye,** *keep* **162 wolde,** *wished* **163 agayn,** *in return* **165 verray,** *true* **167 for sothe,** *in truth* **169 anon-right,** *immediately* **170 list,** *wish* **171 trowe,** *believe* **173 ne stant but,** *stands only* **175 Sey hem,** *say to them* **178 secree nedes,** *secret purpose* **179 han biholde,** *do see* **182 er,** *before,* **twynne,** *depart* **183 ygon,** *gone* **186 seintes buryeles lotynge,** *hiding among the saint's burial places* **192 chaast conseil,** *chaste counsel,* **hierde,** *shepherd* **193 thilke,** *that*

134 whil the, Hg reads "whil that the." **orgnes,** organs; Cecilia's associations with organ music evidently led to her becoming patron saint of music in the Renaissance. **135 in herte,** Hg reads "in hir herte." **137 it,** Hg reads "I." **138 a tree,** Hg reads "the tree." **147 it nat,** El reads "me nat." **151 thus,** omitted in Hg. **155 that,** omitted in El. **161 shewen,** Hg reads "shew to." **171 baptize,** receive baptism, the sacrament whereby someone becomes a Christian. **169 anon-right.** Hg reads "right." **170 If that,** El reads "That if." **171 in,** Hg reads "on." **172 Via Apia,** the Appian Way leads south from Rome past the catacombs (subterranean burial galleries) where Christians may have buried their dead and hid from Roman persecution. **177 Urban,** Pope Urban I, beheaded in 230 CE. **178 nedes,** El reads "thynges." **180 that,** omitted in Hg. **182 er ye,** Hg reads "er we." **183 Valerian,** Hg reads "This Valerian."

Thee serveth ay thyn owene thral° Cecile.
"For thilke spouse that she took riht now,
Ful lyk a fiers leoun, she sendeth heere,
As meke as evere was any lomb, to yow."
And with that word anon ther gan appeere
An oold man clad in white clothes cleere°
That hadde a book with lettre of gold in honde,
And gan bifore Valerian to stonde.

Valerian as deed fil doun for drede
Whan he hym saugh, and he up hente° hym tho°,
And on his book right thus he gan to rede,
"O° Lord, O feith, O God, withouten mo,
O Cristendom, and Fader of alle also,
Aboven alle and over alle everywhere."
Thise wordes al with gold ywriten were.

Whan this was rad°, thanne seyde this olde man,
"Leevestow° this thyng or no? Sey ye or nay."
"I leeve° al this thyng," quod Valerian,
"For sother° thyng than this, I dar wel say,
Under the hevene no wight° thynke may."
Tho vanysshed this olde man, he nyste° where,
And Pope Urban hym cristened° right there.

Valerian gooth hoom and fynt° Cecilie
Withinne his chambre with an angel stonde°.
This angel hadde of roses and of lilie
Corones° two, the whiche he bar in honde,
And first to Cecile, as I understonde,
He yaf° that oon, and after gan he take
That oother to Valerian hir make°.

"With body clene and with unwemmed° thoght
Kepeth ay° wel thise corones," quod he.
"Fro Paradys to yow have I hem broght,
Ne nevere mo ne shal they roten bee,
Ne lese° hir soote savour°, trusteth me;
Ne nevere wight° shal seen hem with his eye
But° he be chaast and hate vileynye.

"And thow, Valerian, for° thow so soone
Assentedest to good conseil also,
Sey what thee list°, and thou shalt han thy boone°.
"I have a brother," quod Valerian tho°,
"That in this world I love no man so.
I pray yow that my brother may han grace
To knowe the trouthe, as I do, in this place."

The angel seyde, "God liketh thy requeste,
And bothe with the palm° of martirdom
Ye shullen come unto his blisful feste°."
And with that word Tiburce his brother coom°.
And whan that he the savour undernoom°,
Which that the roses and the lilies caste,
Withinne his herte he gan to wondre faste,

And seyde, "I wondre, this tyme of the yeer,
Whennes° that soote° savour cometh so
Of rose and lilies that I smelle heer?
For though I hadde hem in myne handes two,
The savour myghte in me no depper° go.
The sweete smel that in myn herte I fynde
Hath chaunged me al in° another kynde."

Valerian seyde, "Two corones° han we,
Snow white and rose reed that shynen cleere,
Whiche that thyne eyen° han no myght to see;
And as thou smellest hem thurgh my preyere,
So shaltow seen° hem, leeve° brother deere,
If it so be thou wolt, withouten slouthe°,
Bileve aright and knowen verray° trouthe."

Tiburce answerde, "Seistow° this to me
In soothnesse°, or in dreem I herkne° this?"
"In dremes," quod Valerian, "han we be
Unto this tyme, brother myn, ywis°.
And now at erst° in trouthe oure dwellyng is."
"How woostow° this," quod Tiburce, "and in what wyse?"
Quod Valerian, "That shal I thee devyse°.

"The aungel of God hath me the trouthe ytaught
Which thou shalt seen if that thou wolt reneye°

196 thral, *servant* **201 cleere,** *bright* **205 hente,** *lifted,* **tho,** *then* **207 O,** *one* **211 rad,** *read* **212 Leevestow,** *do you believe* **213 leeve,** *believe* **214 sother,** *truer* **215 wight,** *person* **216 nyste,** *knew not* **217 cristened,** *baptized* **218 fynt,** *finds* **219 stonde,** *standing* **221 Corones,** *crowns* **223 yaf,** *gave* **224 make,** *spouse* **225 unwemmed,** *spotless* **226 Kepeth ay,** *protect always* **229 lese,** *lose,* **soote savour,** *sweet scent* **230 wight,** *person* **231 But,** *unless* **232 for,** *because* **234 thee list,** *you desire,* **boone,** *wish* **235 tho,** *then* **240 palm,** *reward* **241 feste,** *feast* **242 coom,** *came* **243 savour under-noom,** *odor perceived* **247 Whennes,** *from where,* **soote,** *sweet* **250 depper,** *deeper* **252 al in,** *completely into* **253 corones,** *crowns* **255 thyne eyen,** *your eyes* **257 shaltow seen,** *shall you see,* **leeve,** *beloved* **258 slouthe,** *delay through spiritual laziness* **259 verray,** *genuine* **260 Seistow,** *do you say* **261 soothnesse,** *reality,* **herkne,** (do I) *hear* **263 ywis,** *certainly* **264 at erst,** *for the first time* **265 woostow,** *do you know* **266 devyse,** *explain* **268 reneye,** *renounce*

197 riht, Hg reads "but." **201 oold man,** probably St. Paul, as lines 207–09 quote his letter to the Ephesians 4.5–6. **214 soother,** El reads "oother." **219 Withinne,** Hg reads "Inwith." **220 roses . . . lilie,** the crowns of roses and lilies symbolize martyrdom and purity. **226 quod he,** El reads "three." **267 the trouthe,** El omits "the."

The ydoles and be clene°, and elles naught."
And of the myracle of thise corones tweye
Seint Ambrose in his preface list to seye°;
Solempnely this noble doctour° deere
Commendeth it, and seith in this manere:

"The palm° of martirdom for to receyve,
Seinte Cecile, fulfild of Goddes yifte,
The world and eek hire chambre° gan she weyve°—
Witnesse Tyburces and Valerians shrifte°,
To whiche God of his bountee wolde shifte°
Corones two of floures wel smellynge,
And made his angel hem the corones brynge.

"The mayde hath broght thise men to blisse above;
The world hath wist° what it is worth, certeyn,
Devocioun of chastitee to love."
Tho shewed hym Cecile al open° and pleyn
That alle ydoles nys° but a thyng in veyn,
For they been dombe and therto they been deve°,
And charged hym his ydoles for to leve.

"Whoso that troweth nat° this, a beest he is,"
Quod tho Tiburce, "if that I shal nat lye."
And she gan kisse his brest, that herde this,
And was ful glad he koude° trouthe espye°.
"This day I take thee for myn allye°,"
Seyde this blisful faire mayde deere,
And after that she seyde as ye may heere:

"Lo, right so as the love of Crist," quod she,
"Made me thy brotheres wyf, right in that wise°
Anon for myn allye heer take I thee,
Syn that° thou wolt thyne ydoles despise.
Go with thy brother now and thee baptise,
And make thee clene so that thou mowe° biholde
The angeles face of which thy brother tolde."

Tiburce answerde and seyde, "Brother deere,
First tel me whider I shal° and to what man?"
"To whom?" quod he, "Com forth with right good cheere.
I wol thee lede unto the Pope Urban."
"Til Urban? Brother myn Valerian,"
Quod tho Tiburce, "woltow° me thider° lede?
Me thynketh that it were a wonder dede.

"Ne menestow nat° Urban," quod he tho,
"That is so ofte dampned° to be deed,
And woneth in halkes° alwey to and fro,
And dar nat ones putte forth his heed?
Men sholde hym brennen° in a fyr so reed
If he were founde, or that men myghte hym spye,
And we also, to bere° hym compaignye.

"And whil we seken thilke° divinitee
That is yhid in hevene pryvely°,
Algate ybrend° in this world shul we be!"
To whom Cecile answerde boldely,
"Men myghten dreden wel and skilfully°
This lyf to lese°, myn owene deere brother,
If this were lyvynge oonly° and noon oother,

"But ther is bettre lif in oother place
That nevere shal be lost, ne drede thee noght,
Which Goddes Sone us tolde thurgh his grace.
That Fadres Sone hath alle thyng ywroght°,
And al that wroght is with a skilful° thoght,
The Goost° that fro the Fader gan procede°
Hath sowled° hem, withouten any drede.

By word and by myracle Goddes Sone,
Whan he was in this world, declared heere
That ther was oother lyf ther° men may wone°."
To whom answerde Tiburce, "O suster deere,
Ne seydestow° right now in this manere,
Ther nys but o° God, lord in soothfastnesse°?
And now of three how maystow bere witnesse?"

---

269 clene, *pure* **271 list to seye,** *chose to tell* **272 doctour,** *teacher* **274 palm,** *reward* **276 chambre,** *bedchamber,* **weyve,** *give up* **277 shrifte,** *conversion* **278 shifte,** *assign* **282 wist,** *learned* **284 open,** *openly* **285 nys,** *is nothing* **286 deve,** *deaf* **288 Whoso that troweth nat,** *whoever does not believe* **291 koude,** *could,* **espye,** *see* **292 allye,** *relative* **296 wise,** *way* **298 Syn that,** *because* **300 mowe,** *might* **303 whider I shal,** *where I shall* (go) **307 woltow,** *will you,* **thider,** *there* **309 Ne menestow nat,** *you can't mean* **310 dampned,** *condemned* **311 woneth in halkes,** *lives in hidden places* **313 brennen,** *burn* **315 bere,** *keep* **316 thilke,** *that* **317 pryvely,** *secretly* **318 Algate ybrend,** *nevertheless burned* **320 skilfully,** *reasonably* **321 lese,** *lose* **322 lyvynge oonly,** *the only* (kind of) *life* **326 ywroght,** *created* **327 skilful,** *reasoned* **328 Goost,** (Holy) *Spirit,* **gan procede,** *did come forth* **329 sowled,** *given them souls* **332 ther,** *where,* **wone,** *dwell* **334 Ne seydestow,** *did n't you say* **335 nys but o,** *is only one,* **soothfastnesse,** *truth*

271 Ambrose in his preface, St. Ambrose (ca. 340–397); lines 274–83 derive from the preface to the Mass for St. Cecilia, attributed to Ambrose. **273 it,** El reads "hym." **277 Valerians,** El, Hg, and a number of manuscripts read "Cecilies," a mistake, probably in Chaucer's original. **303 whider,** El and Hg read "whider that." **330 Goddes Sone,** Hg reads "he Goddes Sone."

"That shal I telle," quod she, "er I go.
Right as a man hath sapiences° three,
Memorie, engyn°, and intellect also,
So in o beynge° of divinitee
Thre persones may ther right wel bee."
Tho gan she hym ful bisily to preche
Of Cristes come°, and of his peynes teche°,

And manye pointes of his passioun°:
How Goddes Sone in this world was withholde°
To doon mankynde pleyn° remissioun,
That was ybounde in synne and cares colde.
Al this thyng she unto Tiburce tolde.
And after this, Tiburce in good entente
With Valerian to Pope Urban he wente,

That thanked God, and with glad herte and light
He cristned hym and made hym in that place,
Parfit° in his lernynge, Goddes kynght.
And after this Tiburce gat swich° grace
That every day he saugh in tyme and space
The aungel of God; and every maner boone°
That he God axed°, it was sped° ful soone.

It were ful hard by ordre° for to seyn
How manye wondres Jhesus for hem wroghte,
But atte laste, to tellen short and pleyn,
The sergeantz° of the toun of Rome hem soghte,
And hem biforn Almache the prefect° broghte,
Which hem apposed°, and knew al hire entente,
And to the ymage° of Juppiter hem sente,

And seyde, "Whoso wol nat sacrifise,
Swap of° his heed; this° my sentence heer."
Anon thise martirs that I yow devyse°,
Oon Maximus, that was an officer
Of the prefectes and his corniculer°,
Hem hente°, and whan he forth the seintes ladde
Hymself he weep° for pitee that he hadde.

Whan Maximus had herd the seintes loore°,
He gat hym of the tormentoures leve°,
And ladde hem to his hous withoute moore;
And with hir prechyng er that it were eve
They gonnen fro the tormentours to reve°,
And fro Maxime, and fro his folk echone°,
The false feith, to trowe° in God allone.

Cecile cam, whan it was woxen° nyght,
With preestes that hem cristned alle yfeere°;
And afterward, whan day was woxen light,
Cecile hem seyde with a ful stedefast cheere°,
"Now, Cristes owene knyghtes leeve° and deere,
Cast alle awey the werkes of derknesse,
And armeth yow in armure of brightnesse.

"Ye han forsothe° ydoon a greet bataille,
Youre cours° is doon, youre feith han ye conserved.
Gooth to the corone° of lif that may nat faille;
The rightful Juge, which that ye han served,
Shal yeve° it yow as ye han it deserved."
And whan this thyng was seyd as I devyse°,
Men ledde hem forth to doon the sacrefise.

But whan they weren to the place broght,
To tellen shortly the conclusioun,
They nolde° encense ne sacrifise right noght,
But on hir knees they setten hem adoun
With humble herte and sad° devocioun,
And losten bothe hir hevedes° in the place.
Hir soules wenten to the Kyng of Grace.

This Maximus, that saugh° this thyng bityde°,
With pitous teeris tolde it anon-right°,

---

338 sapiences, *mental faculties* **339 engyn,** *imagination* **340 o beynge,** *one being* **343 come,** *coming,* **teche,** *teach* **344 passioun,** *suffering* **345 withholde,** *retained* **346 pleyn,** *complete* **353 Parfit,** *perfect* **354 swich,** *such* **356 boone,** *request* **357 axed,** *asked,* **sped,** *accomplished* **358 by ordre,** *in proper order* **361 sergeantz,** *officers* **362 prefect,** *chief officer* **363 apposed,** *questioned* **364 ymage,** *statue* **366 Swap of,** *strike off,* **this,** *this is* **367 devyse,** *describe* **369 corniculer,** *assistant* **370 Hem hente,** *seized them* **371 weep,** *wept* **372 loore,** *teaching* **373 gat hym . . . leve,** *obtained permission* **376 gonnen . . . to reve,** *did . . . remove* **377 echone,** *each one* **378 trowe,** *believe* **379 was woxen,** *had become* **380 yfeere,** *together* **382 ful stedefast cheere,** *very resolute expression* **383 leeve,** *beloved* **386 forsothe,** *truly* **387 cours,** *path* **388 corone,** *crown* **390 yeve,** *give* **391 devyse,** *describe* **395 nolde,** *would not* **397 sad,** *steadfast* **398 hevedes,** *heads* **400 that saugh,** *who saw,* **bityde,** *happen* **401 anon-right,** *immediately*

340 o beynge, El omits "o." **341 Thre persones,** the Trinity, three persons in one God, one of the central mysteries of Christianity, explained with apparent ease by Cecilia. **342–48** Chaucer here summarizes a portion of the account in the *Legenda Aurea* and begins to follow a liturgical version of Cecilia's life at line 349; see the note to 84a and the introduction to Part 8 above. **363 apposed,** El and Hg read "opposed." **366 this my,** Hg reads "this is my." **382 hem,** Hg reads "hym." **385 armeth yow,** arm yourselves; see Romans 13.12 and Ephesians 6.11–13. **387 cours,** El reads "feith." **386–90** See 2 Timothy 4.7–8. **395 encense,** worship by burning aromatic materials (incense). **398 losten bothe hir hevedes,** both Valerian and Tiburce lost their heads.

That he hir soules saugh° to hevene glyde
With aungels ful of cleernesse° and of light,
And with this word converted many a wight°;
For which Almachius dide hym so tobete°
With whippe of leed til he his lif gan lete°.

Cecile hym took and buryed hym anon
By Tiburce and Valerian softely°
Withinne hire° buriyng place under the stoon;
And after this Almachius hastily
Bad° his ministres fecchen° openly
Cecile, so that she myghte in his presence
Doon sacrifice and Juppiter encense.

But they, converted at° hir wise loore,
Wepten ful soore° and yaven ful credence°
Unto hire word, and cryden moore and moore,
"Crist, Goddes sone, withouten difference,
Is verray° God—this is al oure sentence°—
That hath so good a servant hym to serve.
This with o voys° we trowen°, thogh we sterve°."

Almachius, that herde of this doynge,
Bad fecchen° Cecile that he myghte hire see;
And alderfirst°, lo, this was his axynge,
"What maner womman artow°?" tho quod he.
"I am a gentil womman born," quod she.
"I axe° thee," quod he, "though it thee greeve,
Of thy religioun and of thy bileeve."

"Ye han bigonne youre questioun folily°,"
Quod she, "that wolden two answeres conclude°
In o demande; ye axed lewedly°."
Almache answerde unto that similitude°,
"Of whennes° comth thyn answeryng so rude?"
"Of whennes?" quod she whan that she was
freyned°,
"Of conscience and of good feith unfeyned°."

Almachius seyde, "Ne takestow noon heede°
Of my power?" And she answerde hym this:
"Youre myght," quod she, "ful litel is to dreede,
For every mortal mannes power nys°
But lyk a bladdre ful of wynd, ywys°.
For with a nedles poynt, whan it is blowe°,
May al the boost° of it be leyd ful lowe."

"Ful wrongfully bigonne thow," quod he,
"And yet in wrong is thy perseveraunce.
Wostow nat° how oure myghty princes free°
Han thus comanded and maad ordinaunce
That every Cristen wight° shal han penaunce°
But if that° he his Cristendom withseye°,
And goon al quit° if he wole it reneye°?°"

"Yowre princes erren°, as youre nobleye°
dooth,"
Quod tho Cecile, "and with a wood sentence°
Ye make us gilty, and it is nat sooth°.
For ye, that knowen wel oure innocence,
For as muche as we doon a reverence
To Crist, and for we bere a Cristen name,
Ye putte on us a cryme and eek a blame.

But we that knowen thilke° name so
For vertuous, we may it nat withseye°."
Almache answerde, "Chees° oon of thise two:
Do sacrifice, or Cristendom reneye°,
That thou mowe° now escapen by that weye."
At which the hooly blisful faire mayde
Gan for to laughe, and to the juge sayde:

"O juge, confus in thy nycetee°,
Woltow° that I reneye° innocence
To make me a wikked wight°?" quod shee.
"Lo°, he dissymuleth° heere in audience°;
He stareth and woodeth° in his advertence°."

---

402 hir soules saugh, *saw their souls* **403 cleernesse,** *brightness* **404 wight,** *person* **405 dide hym so tobete,** *had him so thoroughly beaten* **406 gan lete,** *did lose* **408 softely,** *secretly* **409 hire,** *their* **411 Bad,** *ordered,* **fecchen,** *to seize* **414 at,** *by* **415 ful soore,** *very intensely,* **yaven ful credence,** *gave complete belief* **418 verray,** *true,* **sentence,** *meaning* **420 o voys,** *a single voice,* **trowen,** *affirm,* **sterve,** *die* **422 Bad fecchen,** *ordered seized* **423 alderfirst,** *first of all* **424 artow,** *are you* **426 axe,** *ask* **428 folily,** *foolishly* **429 conclude,** *include* **430 axed lewedly,** *asked ignorantly* **431 similitude,** *comparison* **432 Of whennes,** *from where* **433 freyned,** *asked* **434 unfeyned,** *sincere* **435 Ne takestow noon heede,** *aren't you concerned* **438 nys,** *is nothing* **439 ywys,** *to be sure* **440 blowe,** *inflated* **441 boost,** *boast* **444 Wostow nat,** *don't you know,* **free,** *generous* **446 wight,** *person,* **penaunce,** *punishment* **447 But if that,** *unless,* **withseye,** *deny* **448 al quit,** *completely free,* **reneye,** *renounce* **449 erren,** *make mistakes,* **nobleye,** *nobility* **450 wood sentence,** *insane mandate* **451 sooth,** *true* **456 thilke,** *that,* **457 withseye,** *deny* **458 Chees,** *choose* **459 reneye,** *renounce* **460 mowe,** *might* **463 nycetee,** *folly* **464 Woltow,** *do you wish,* **reneye,** *renounce* **465 wight,** *creature* **466 Lo,** *behold,* **dissymuleth,** *pretends,* **in audience,** *in public* **467 woodeth,** *raves,* **advertence,** *attention*

405 tobete, El and Hg read "bete." **406 whippe of leed,** a flail with pieces of metal (lead) attached. **418 al,** omitted in El. **429–30 two answeres . . . o demande,** Cecilia gives Almachius a blunt lesson in argumentation. **451 it is,** El and Hg omit "it." **461 the,** Hg reads "this." **462 sayde,** Hg reads "she sayde." **467 woodeth,** El reads "he woodeth."

To whom Almachius, "Unsely° wrecche,
Ne woostow nat° how fer my myght may strecche?

"Han noght° oure myghty princes to me yiven°,
Ye, bothe power and auctoritee
To maken folk to dyen or to lyven?
Why spekestow° so proudly thanne to me?"
"I speke noght but stedfastly," quod she,
"Nat proudly, for I seye, as for my syde,
We haten deedly thilke° vice of pryde.

"And if thou drede nat a sooth° to heere,
Thanne wol I shewe al openly, by right,
That thou hast maad a ful gret lesyng° heere.
Thou seyst thy princes han thee yeven° myght
Bothe for to sleen and for to quyken° a wight,
Thou that ne mayst but oonly lyf bireve°;
Thou hast noon oother power ne no leve°.

"But thou mayst seyn thy princes han thee maked
Ministre of deeth, for if thou speke of mo°,
Thou lyest, for thy power is ful naked°."
"Do wey thy booldnesse," seyde Almachius tho,
"And sacrifice to oure goddes er thou go.
I recche° nat what wrong that thou me profre°,
For I kan suffre it as a philosophre,

"But thilke° wronges may I nat endure
That thou spekest of oure goddes heere," quod he.
Cecile answerde, "O nyce° creature!
Thou seydest no word syn° thou spak to me
That I ne knew therwith thy nycetee;
And that thou were, in every maner wise,
A lewed° officer and a veyn° justise.

"Ther lakketh no thyng to thyne outter eyen
That thou n'art blynd, for thyng that we seen alle
That it is stoon—than men may wel espyen"—
That ilke° stoon a god thow wolt it calle.
I rede° thee, lat thyn hand upon it falle
And taste it wel and stoon thou shalt it fynde,
Syn° that thou seest nat with thyne eyen blynde.

"It is a shame that the peple shal
So scorne thee and laughe at thy folye,
For communly men woot° it wel overal
That myghty God is in his hevenes hye°.
And thise ymages, wel thou mayst espye
To thee ne to hemself° ne mowen noght profite°,
For in effect they been nat worth a myte°."

Thise wordes and swiche° othere seyde she,
And he weex wrooth° and bad° men sholde hir lede
Hom til hir hous, and "In hire hous," quod he,
"Brenne° hire right in a bath of flambes rede."
And as he bad, right so was doon in dede;
For in a bath they gonne hire faste shetten°,
And nyght and day greet fyr they under betten°.

The longe nyght and eek a day also
For al the fyr and eek the bathes heete
She sat al coold and feelede no wo;
It made hire nat a drope for to sweete°.
But in that bath hir lyf she moste lete°,
For he Almachius, with ful wikke entente,
To sleen hire in the bath his sonde° sente.

Thre strokes in the nekke he smoot° hire tho°,
The tormentour, but for no maner chaunce
He myghte noght smyte al hir nekke atwo°.
And for ther was that tyme an ordinaunce

---

468 Unsely, *unfortunate* **469 Ne woostow nat,** *don't you know* **470 Han noght,** *have not,* **yiven,** *given* **473 spekestow,** *do you speak* **476 deedly thilke,** *that deadly* **477 sooth,** *truth* **479 lesyng,** *lying* **480 yeven,** *given* **481 quyken,** *bring to life* **482 bireve,** *deprive* **483 leve,** *permission* **485 mo,** *more* **486 ful naked,** *wholly deficient* **489 recche,** *care,* **profre,** *offer* **491 thilke,** *those* **493 nyce,** *foolish* **494 syn,** *since* **497 lewed,** *ignorant,* **veyn,** *ineffective* **500 espyen,** *perceive* **501 ilke,** *same* **502 rede,** *advise* **504 Syn,** *since* **507 woot,** *know* **508 hye,** *high* **510 hemself,** *themselves,* **ne mowen noght profite,** *might they not profit* **511 myte,** *tiny coin* **512 swiche,** *such* **513 weex wrooth,** *grew angry,* **bad,** *ordered* (that) **515 Brenne,** *burn* **517 gonne hire faste shetten,** *shut her up tightly* **518 betten,** *fed* **522 sweete,** *sweat* **523 moste lete,** *must give up* **525 sonde,** *emissary* **526 smoot,** *struck,* **tho,** *then* **528 atwo,** *in two*

475 seye, El reads "speke." **485 mo,** Hg reads "me." **490 philosophre,** i.e., Almachius claims he can bear it philosophically; the noun was also used of alchemists, a link to *CYT,* which follows. **497 and,** omitted in Hg. **498–99 Ther lakketh . . . blynd,** i.e., you are blind despite the fact that your physical eyes lack nothing. **500 That it is,** Hg reads "That is a." **510 ne mowen noght,** Hg reads "mowe noght." **512 wordes,** omitted in Hg. **515 bath of flambes rede,** bath of red flames; the flame bath was either a room heated from below in the Roman manner (a hypocaust) or a large pot. The manner of attempting to kill Cecilia is analogous to alchemists' attempts to refine or purify substances by sweating or distillation. Cecilia's lack of sweat (line 522) demonstrates her purity and contrasts the sweat of *CYP* 8.560ff. **516 in dede,** Hg reads "the dede." **522 a drope,** Hg reads "o drope."

That no man sholde doon man swich penaunce°
The ferthe strook to smyten, softe or soore,
This tormentour ne dorste° do namoore,

But half deed, with hir nekke ycorven there,
He lefte hir lye, and on his wey he went.
The Cristen folk which that aboute hire were
With sheetes han the blood ful faire yhent°.
Thre dayes lyved she in this torment,
And nevere cessed hem° the feith to teche
That she hadde fostred°. Hem she gan to preche,

And hem she yaf° hir moebles° and hir thyng°,
And to the Pope Urban bitook° hem tho,
And seyde, "I axed° this at Hevene Kyng,
To han respit° thre dayes and namo°,
To recomende to yow er that I go
Thise soules, lo, and that I myghte do werche°
Heere of myn hous perpetuelly a cherche."

Seint Urban with his deknes° prively°
The body fette° and buryed it by nyghte
Among his othere seintes honestly°.
Hir hous the chirche of Seinte Cecilie highte°.
Seint Urban halwed° it as he wel myghte,
In which into this day in noble wyse
Men doon to Crist and to his seinte servyse.

Heere is ended the Seconde Nonnes Tale.

---

530 swich penaunce, *such punishment* **532 ne dorste,** *dared not* **536 yhent,** *soaked up* **538 hem,** *to them* **539 fostred,** *instructed* **540 yaf,** *gave,* **moebles,** *portable possessions,* **thyng,** *things* **541 bitook,** *entrusted* **542 axed,** *asked* **543 han respit,** *have delay,* **namo,** *no more* **545 do werche,** *have made* **547 deknes,** *deacons,* **prively,** *secretly* **548 fette,** *brought* **549 honestly,** *honorably* **550 highte,** *is called* **551 halwed,** *blessed*

530 doon man, El reads "doon men." **533 nekke ycorven,** compare *PrT* 7.611, and contrast the little boy's continued singing with Cecilia's preaching. **542 at,** Hg reads "of." **548 The,** El reads "This." **553a Seconde,** omitted in Hg.

From woodcut made by W.H. Hooper and published by the Chaucer Society between 1868 and 1879

Canon's Yeoman's Tale

Prologue

The Prologe of the Chanouns Yemannes Tale.

Whan ended was the lyf of Seinte Cecile,
Er° we hadde riden fully fyve mile,
At Boghtoun-under-Blee us gan atake°
A man that clothed was in clothes blake,
And undernethe he hadde a whyt surplys.
His hakeney°, that was al pomely grys°,
So swatte° that it wonder was to see;
It semed as he had priked° miles three.
The hors eek that his yeman° rood upon
So swatte that unnethe° myghte it gon.
Aboute the peytrel° stood the foom° ful hye;
He was of foom al flekked as a pye°.
A male tweyfoold° upon his croper° lay.
It semed that he caried lite° array.
Al light for somer° rood this worthy man.
And in myn herte to wondren I bigan
What that he was til that I understood
How that his cloke was sowed° to his hood,
For which, whan I hadde longe avysed me°,
I demed° hym som chanoun for to be.
His hat heeng at his bak doun by a laas°,
For he hadde riden moore than trot or paas°;
He hadde ay priked° lik as he were wood°.
A clote-leef° he hadde under his hood
For swoot°, and for to kepe his heed from heete—
But it was joye for to seen hym swete!
His forheed dropped as° a stillatorie
Were ful of plantayne° and of paritorie°.
And whan that he was come he gan to crye,
"God save," quod he, "this joly compaignye!

555 Er, *before* **556 gan atake,** *overtook* **559 hakeney,** *riding horse,* **pomely grys,** *dappled gray* **560 swatte,** *sweated* **561 priked,** *spurred* **562 yeman,** *servant* **563 unnethe,** *scarcely* **564 peytrel,** *breast harness,* **foom,** *foam* **565 pye,** *magpie* **566 male tweyfoold,** *double bag,* **croper,** *harness behind the saddle* **567 lite,** *little* **568 Al light for somer,** *equipped lightly for summer* **571 sowed,** *sewn* **572 avysed me,** *reflected* **573 demed,** *judged* **574 laas,** *cord* **575 paas,** (walking) *pace* **576 ay priked,** *the whole way spurred,* **wood,** *crazed* **577 clote-leef,** *leaf of a large weed* **578 swoot,** *sweat* **580 dropped as,** *dripped as if* **581 plantayne,** *an herb,* **paritorie,** *an herb*

554 ended was, El reads "toold was al." Hg lacks the entire *CYPT* 8.554–1481. **556 Boghtoun-under-Blee,** Boughton, a town about five miles from Canterbury, in the Blean Forest. **558 hadde a whyt surplys,** El reads "wered a surplys." A surplice is an ecclesiastical garment, usually worn as an outer garment. **562 hors,** El reads "hakeney." **564–65** Lines omitted in El; they are transposed with 562–63 in some manuscripts. **573 chanoun,** canon; a clergyman who lives a communal life and helps administer a cathedral, college, or other ecclesiastical institution. This is probably a secular canon, one who lives under a lax rule (as opposed to a regular canon who lives under strict regulations), or perhaps he has abandoned his office. **580 stillatorie,** still, distiller; a heating vessel used in medicine, chemistry, and alchemy to extract or purify by distillation. See the note to *SNT* 8.515.

Faste have I priked," quod he, "for youre sake,
By cause that I wolde yow atake°,
To riden in som myrie° compaignye."
His yeman eek was ful of curteisye
And seyde, "Sires, now in the morwe-tyde°
Out of youre hostelrie° I saugh yow ryde,
And warned° heer my lord and my soverayn,
Which that° to ryden with yow is ful fayn°
For his desport°; he loveth daliaunce°."
  "Freend, for thy warnyng God yeve° thee good
    chaunce,°"
Thanne seyde oure Hoost, "for certein it wolde seme
Thy lord were wys, and so I may wel deme°.
He is ful jocunde° also, dar I leye°!
Can he oght° telle a myrie tale or tweye,
With which he glade° may this compaignye?"
  "Who, sire? My lord? Ye, ye withouten lye.
He kan° of murthe and eek of jolitee
Nat but ynough°; also, sire, trusteth me,
And ye hym knewe as wel as, do I,
Ye wolde wondre how wel and craftily
He koude werke, and that in sondry wise°.
He hath take on hym many a greet emprise°,
Which were ful hard for any that is heere
To brynge aboute, but° they of hym it leere°.
As hoomly° as he rit° amonges yow,
If ye hym knewe, it wolde be for youre prow°.
Ye wolde nat forgoon° his aqueyntaunce
For muchel good, I dar leye in balaunce°
Al that I have in my possessioun.
He is a man of heigh discrecioun;
I warne° yow wel, he is a passyng° man."
  "Wel," quod oure Hoost, "I pray thee, tel me
    than,
Is he a clerk or noon? Telle what he is."
  "Nay, he is gretter than a clerk, ywis°,"
Seyde this Yeman, "and in wordes fewe,
Hoost, of his craft somwhat I wol yow shewe.
  "I seye, my lord kan swich° subtilitee—
But al his craft ye may nat wite at° me,
And somwhat helpe I yet to his wirkyng—
That al this ground on which we been ridyng
Til that we come to Caunterbury toun,
He koude al clene° turnen up so doun°,
And pave it al of silver and of gold!"
  And whan this Yeman hadde this tale ytold
Unto oure Hoost, he seyde, "Benedicitee°,
This thyng is wonder° merveillous to me,
Syn that° thy lord is of so heigh prudence,
By cause of which men sholde hym reverence,
That of his worshipe° rekketh he° so lite.
His oversloppe° nys nat° worth a myte°,
As in effect°, to hym, so moot I go°.
It is al baudy° and totore° also.
Why is thy lord so sluttissh°, I the preye,
And is of power° bettre clooth to beye°,
If that his dede° accorde with thy speche?
Telle me that, and that I thee biseche°."
  "Why?" quod this Yeman, "Wherto axe
    ye me?
God help me so, for he shal nevere thee°—
But I wol nat avowe that° I seye,
And therfore keep it seeree, I yow preye—
He is to wys°, in feith, as I bileeve.
That that° is overdoon, it wol nat preeve°
Aright, as clerkes seyn; it is a vice.
Wherfore in that I holde hym lewed° and nyce°.
For whan a man hath over-greet° a wit,
Ful oft hym happeth to mysusen it.
So dooth my lord, and that me greveth soore.
God it amende°! I kan sey yow namoore."
  "Therof no fors°, good Yeman," quod oure Hoost;
"Syn° of the konnyng° of thy lord thow woost°,
Telle how he dooth, I pray thee hertely,
Syn that he is so crafty and so sly°.
Where dwelle ye, if it to telle be°?°
  "In the suburbes of a toun," quod he,
"Lurkynge in hernes° and in lanes blynde°,

---

585 atake, *overtake* **586 myrie,** *merry* **588 morwe-tyde,** *morning* **589 hostelrie,** *inn* **590 warned,** *advised* **591 Which that,** *who,* **ful fayn,** *very eager* **592 desport,** *entertainment,* **daliaunce,** *conversation* **593 yeve,** *give* **595 deme,** *judge* **596 jocunde,** *cheerful,* **dar I leye,** *I dare bet* **597 oght,** *at all* **598 glade,** *please* **600 kan,** *knows* **601 Nat but ynough,** *more than enough* **604 sondry wise,** *many ways* **605 emprise,** *enterprise* **607 but,** *unless,* **leere,** *learn* **608 hoomly,** *familiarly,* **rit,** *rides* **609 prow,** *profit* **610 forgoon,** *give up* **611 leye in balaunce,** *bet* **614 warne,** *advise.* **passyng,** *excellent* **617 ywis,** *certainly* **620 kan swich,** *knows such* **621 wite at,** *know from* **625 koude al clene,** *could completely,* **up so doun,** *upside down* **628 Benedicitee,** *bless you* **629 wonder,** *wonderfully* **630 Syn that,** *since* **632 worshipe,** *honor,* **rekketh he,** *he cares* **633 oversloppe,** *overshirt,* **nys nat,** *is not,* **myte,** *tiny coin* **634 As in effect,** *in fact,* **so moot I go,** *as far as I can tell* **635 baudy,** *dirty,* **totore,** *torn* **636 sluttissh,** *sloppy* **637 of power,** *able,* **beye,** *buy* **638 dede,** *actions* **639 biseche,** *ask* **641 thee,** *prosper* **642 avowe that,** *admit to what* **644 to wys,** *too smart* **645 That that,** *that which,* **preeve,** *turn out* **647 lewed,** *ignorant,* **nyce,** *foolish* **648 overgreet,** *too great* **651 amende,** *correct* **652 no fors,** *no matter* **653 Syn,** *since,* **konnyng,** *knowledge,* **woost,** *knows* **655 sly,** *clever* **656 to telle be,** *can be told* **658 hernes,** *hidden places,* **lanes blynde,** *dead ends*

589 hostelrie, hostelry or inn; no location is specified or need be, but SK observed that five miles before Boughten (see lines 555–56) lies Ospringe, a customary lodging place for pilgrims on the way from London to Canterbury. **591 that,** omitted in El. **621 at me,** El reads "for me." **625 turnen,** El reads "turn it."

Where as thise robbours and thise theves by kynde°
Holden hir pryvee°, fereful residence,
As they that dar nat shewen hir presence;
So faren we, if I shal seye the sothe°.°
"Now," quod oure Hoost, "yit lat me talke to the.
Why artow° so discoloured of thy face?"
"Peter°," quod he, "God yeve it harde grace°!
I am so used in the fyr to blowe
That it hath chaunged my colour, I trowe°.
I am nat wont° in no mirour to prie°,
But swynke soore° and lerne multiplie.
We blondren° evere and pouren° in the fir,
And for al that we faille of oure desir,
For evere we lakken oure conclusioun°.
To muchel° folk we doon illusioun,
And borwe gold, be it a pound or two,
Or ten, or twelve, or manye sommes mo°,
And make hem wenen° at the leeste weye
That of a pound we koude make tweye°.
Yet is it fals, but ay° we han good hope
It for to doon, and after it we grope.
But that science is so fer us biforn,
We mowen° nat, although we hadden sworn,
It overtake, it slit° awey so faste.
It wole us maken beggers atte laste."
Whil this Yeman was thus in his talkyng,
This Chanoun drough hym° neer and herde al thyng
Which this Yeman spak, for suspecioun
Of mennes speche evere hadde this Chanoun.
For Catoun seith that he that gilty is
Demeth° alle thyng be spoke of hym, ywis°.
That was the cause he gan so ny° hym drawe
To his Yeman, to herknen° al his sawe°.
And thus he seyde unto his Yeman tho°,
"Hoold thou thy pees and spek no wordes mo,
For if thou do, thou shalt it deere abye°.
Thou sclaundrest° me heere in this compaignye,
And eek discoverest° that thou sholdest hyde."
"Ye," quod oure Hoost, "telle on what so bityde°.
Of al his thretyng° rekke° nat a myte°."
"In feith," quod he, "namoore I do but lyte°."
And whan this Chanoun saugh it wolde nat bee,
But his Yeman wolde telle his pryvetee°,
He fledde awey for verray° sorwe and shame.
"A," quod the Yeman, "heere shal arise game;
Al that I kan° anon now wol I telle.
Syn° he is goon, the foule feend hym quelle°!
For nevere heerafter wol I with hym meete
For peny ne for pound, I yow biheete°.
He that me broghte first unto that game,
Er that he dye, sorwe have he and shame.
For it is ernest to me, by my feith;
That feele I wel, what so° any man seith.
And yet for al my smert° and al my grief,
For al my sorwe, labour, and meschief°,
I koude nevere leve it in no wise°.
Now wolde God° my wit myghte suffise
To tellen al that longeth° to that art.
And nathelees yow wol I tellen part.
Syn that my lord is goon, I wol nat spare°;
Swich thyng as that I knowe, I wol declare."

Heere endeth the Prologe of the Chanouns Yemannes Tale.

Heere bigynneth the Chanouns Yeman his Tale.

With this Chanoun I dwelt have seven yeer,
And of his science° am I never the neer°.
Al that I hadde I have lost therby,
And God woot° so hath many mo° than I.

---

659 by kynde, *naturally* **660 hir pryvee,** *their secret* **662 seye the sothe,** *tell you truth* **664 artow,** *are you* **665 Peter,** *by St. Peter,* **yeve it harde grace,** *give it bad luck* **667 trowe,** *believe* **668 wont,** *accustomed,* **prie,** *look* **669 swynke soore,** *work hard* **670 blondren,** *blunder,* **pouren,** *stare* **672 conclusioun,** *goal* **673 muchel,** *many* **675 sommes mo,** *more sums* **676 wenen,** *think* **677 tweye,** *two* **678 ay,** *always* **681 mowen,** *may* **682 slit,** *slides* **685 drough hym,** *drew himself* **689 Demeth,** *thinks,* **ywis,** *surely* **690 ny,** *near* **691 herknen,** *hear,* **sawe,** *saying* **692 tho,** *then* **694 deere abye,** *pay for it dearly* **695 sclaundrest,** *slander* **696 eek discoverest,** *also reveal* **697 what so bityde,** *whatever happens* **698 thretyng,** *threatening,* **rekke,** *care,* **myte,** *tiny coin* **699 lyte,** *little* **701 pryvetee,** *secrets* **702 verray,** *genuine* **704 kan,** *know* **705 Syn,** *since,* **quelle,** *kill* **707 biheete,** *promise* **711 what so,** *whatever* **712 smert,** *pain* **713 meschief,** *misfortune* **714 wise,** *way* **715 wolde God,** *may God grant* **716 longeth,** *pertains* **718 spare,** *refrain* **721 science,** *knowledge,* **neer,** *nearer* **723 woot,** *knows,* **mo,** *more* (people)

663 talke, El reads "telle." **669 multiplie,** to transmute; i.e., the alchemical transformation of base to precious metals. **674 borwe gold,** earnest alchemists borrowed gold on the theory that it was necessary to initiate the process of transforming base metals; con artists capitalized on this belief. **688 Catoun,** Dionysius Cato, supposed author of *Disticha Catonis* (*Cato's Couplets*) 1.7. **711 what so,** El reads "what that."

Ther° I was wont° to be right fressh and gay
Of clothyng and of oother good array,
Now may I were an hose° upon myn heed;
And wher my colour was bothe fressh and reed,
Now is it wan° and of a leden hewe—
Whoso it useth° soore shal he rewe°—
And of my swynk° yet blered is myn eye.
Lo, which° avantage is to multiplie°!
That slidyng° science hath me maad so bare
That I have no good° wher that evere I fare°;
And yet I am endetted° so therby
Of gold that I have borwed, trewely,
That whil I lyve I shal it quite° nevere.
Lat every man bewar by me forevere!
What maner° man that casteth hym° therto,
If he continue I holde his thrift ydo°.
For so helpe me God, therby shal he nat wynne,
But empte his purs and make his wittes thynne.
And whan he thurgh his madnesse and folye
Hath lost his owene good thurgh jupartye°,
Thanne he exciteth° oother folk therto
To lesen hir good°, as he hymself hath do.
For unto shrewes° joye it is and ese
To have hir felawes in peyne and disese°.
Thus was I ones lerned of° a clerk—
Of that no charge°, I wol speke of oure werk.
  Whan we been there as we shul exercise
Oure elvysshe° craft we semen wonder° wise,
Oure termes been so clergial° and so queynte°.
I blowe the fir til that myn herte feynte.
What° sholde I tellen ech proporcioun
Of thynges whiche that we werche° upon,
As on fyve or sixe ounces, may wel be,
Of silver, or som oother quantitee,
And bisye me to telle yow the names
Of orpyment°, brent° bones, iren squames°,
That into poudre grounden been ful smal;
And in an erthen pot how put is al,
And salt yput in, and also papeer,
Biforn thise poudres that I speke of heer;
And wel ycovered with a lampe° of glas;
And of muche oother thyng which that ther was;
And of the pot and glasses enlutyng°,
That of the eyr° myghte passe out nothyng;
And of the esy° fir, and smart° also,
Which that was maad; and of the care and wo
That we hadden in oure matires sublymyng°;
And in amalgamyng and calceniyng
Of quyksilver°, yclept° mercurie crude°?
For alle oure sleightes° we kan nat conclude°.
Oure orpyment° and sublymed° mercurie,
Oure grounden litarge° eek in the porfurie°,
Of ech of thise of ounces a certeyn°,
Noght helpeth us. Oure labour is in veyn.
Ne eek° oure spirites ascencioun°,
Ne oure matires° that lyen al fix adoun°,
Mowe° in oure werkyng nothyng us availle,
For lost is al oure labour and travaille°;
And al the cost, a twenty devel way,
Is lost also which we upon it lay°.
  Ther is also ful many another thyng
That is unto oure craft apertenyng°.
Though I by ordre hem nat reherce kan
By cause that I am a lewed° man,
Yet wol I telle hem as they come to mynde,
Thogh I ne kan nat sette hem in hir kynde°,
As boole armonyak°, vertgrees°, boras°,
And sondry° vessels maad of erthe and glas,

724 Ther, *where,* **wont,** *accustomed* **726 hose,** *stocking* **728 wan,** *pale* **729 it useth,** *practices it* (i.e., alchemy), **rewe,** *regret* **730 of my swynk,** *by my work* **731 which,** *what,* **to multiplie,** *to transmute* **732 slidyng,** *unreliable* **733 good,** *goods,* **fare,** *go* **734 endetted,** *in debt* **736 quite,** *repay* **738 What maner,** *whatever kind of,* **casteth hym,** *devotes himself* **739 thrift ydo,** *welfare destroyed* **743 jupartye,** *taking chances* **744 exciteth,** *incites* **745 lesen hir good,** *lose their goods* **746 shrewes,** *scoundrels* **747 disese,** *discomfort* **748 ones lerned of,** *once taught by* **749 no charge,** *no matter* **751 elvysshe,** *mysterious,* **semen wonder,** *seem wonderfully* **752 clergial,** *learned,* **queynte,** *intricate* **754 What,** *why* **755 werche,** *work* **759 orpyment,** *arsenic,* **brent,** *burned,* **squames,** *chips* **764 lampe,** *lamp-shaped lid* **766 enlutyng,** *sealing* **767 eyr,** *air* **768 esy,** *moderate,* **smart,** *brisk* **770 matires sublymyng,** *refining materials* **772 quyksilver,** *mercury,* **yclept,** *called,* **crude,** *unrefined* **773 sleightes,** *tricks,* **conclude,** *succeed* **774 orpyment,** *arsenic,* **sublymed,** *purified* **775 litarge,** *lead monoxide,* **porfurie,** *marble mortar* (grinding bowl) **776 certeyn,** *certain* (amount) **778 Ne eek,** *nor also,* **spirites ascencioun,** *vapors rising* **779 matires,** *solids,* **al flx adoun,** *remaining in the bottom* **780 Mowe,** *might* **781 travaille,** *effort* **783 lay,** *took a chance* **785 is unto . . . apertenyng,** *pertains to* **787 lewed,** *unlearned* **789 in hir kynde,** *their natures* **790 boole armonyak,** *Armenian clay,* **vertgrees,** *copper acetate,* **boras,** *borax* **791 sondry,** *various*

730 blered is myn eye, my eye is blinded; i.e., I have been cheated. **762 salt . . . papeer,** salt and pepper; the bizarre concoction is typical of actual alchemical writing, but also parodic. **765 of muche,** El reads "muchel." **771 amalgamyng and calceniyng,** amalgamating and calcining; i.e., alloying with mercury and reducing to powder by heating. **776 Of ech,** El reads "And ech." **782 a twenty devel way,** by twenty devils' paths; an exclamation of frustration or irritation. **786 by ordre hem nat reherce kan,** cannot relate them in an orderly way. The wrenched syntax contributes to the laboriousness of the Yeoman's disorderly and disconcerting tally of alchemical apparatus, terms, and processes.

Oure urynals° and oure descensories°,
Violes°, crosletz°, and sublymatories°,
Cucurbites° and alambikes° eek,
And othere swiche°, deere ynough a leek—
Nat nedeth it for to reherce hem alle—
Watres rubifiyng°, and boles galle°,
Arsenyk, sal armonyak°, and brymstoon°;
And herbes koude° I telle eek many oon,
As egremoyne°, valerian, and lunarie°,
And othere swiche, if that me liste tarie°;
Oure lampes brennyng bothe nyght and day,
To brynge aboute oure purpos, if we may;
Oure fourneys° eek of calcinacioun°,
And of watres albificacioun°;
Unslekked lym°, chalk, and gleyre of an ey°,
Poudres diverse, asshes, donge, pisse, and cley,
Cered° pottes, sal peter°, vitriole°,
And diverse fires maad of wode and cole;
Sal tartre°, alkaly°, and sal preparat°,
And combust matires° and coagulat°;
Cley maad with hors or mannes heer°, and oille
Of tartre°, alum glas°, berme°, wort°, and argoille°,
Resalgar°, and oure matires enbibyng°,
And eek of oure matires encorporyng°,
And of oure silver citrinacioun°,
Oure cementyng° and fermentacioun,
Oure yngottes°, testes°, and many mo.
  I wol yow telle, as was me taught also,
The foure spirites and the bodies sevene
By ordre, as ofte I herde my lord hem nevene°.
  The firste spirit quyksilver called is,
The seconde orpyment, the thridde, ywis,
Sal armonyak, and the ferthe brymstoon.
The bodyes sevene eek, lo, hem heere anoon:
Sol° gold is, and Luna° silver we threpe°,
Mars iren, Mercurie quyksilver we clepe°,
Saturnus leed, and Juppiter is tyn,
And Venus coper, by my fader kyn°.
  This cursed craft whoso wole exercise°,
He shal no good han° that hym may suffise,
For al the good he spendeth theraboute
He lese° shal, therof have I no doute.
Whoso that listeth outen° his folie,
Lat hym come forth and lerne multiplie.
And every man that oght° hath in his cofre°,
Lat hym appiere° and wexe° a philosophre.
Ascauns° that craft is so light° to leere°—
Nay, nay, God woot°, al be he° monk or frere,
Preest or chanoun, or any oother wyght°,
Though he sitte at his book bothe day and nyght
In lernyng of this elvysshe nyce loore°,
Al is veyn°, and parde°, muchel moore.
To lerne a lewed man this subtiltee—
Fy, spek nat therof, for it wol nat bee.
And konne he letterure° or konne he noon,
As in effect he shal fynde it al oon°.
For bothe two°, by my savacioun,
Concluden in multiplicacioun
Ylike° wel, whan they han al ydo°—
This is to seyn, they faillen bothe two.
  Yet forgat I to maken rehersaille
Of watres corosif°, and of lymaille°,
And of bodies mollificacioun°,
And also of hire induracioun°,
Oilles, ablucions°, and metal fusible°—
To tellen al wolde passen any bible°

---

792 urynals, *glass bottles,* **descensories,** *vessels for distilling* **793 Violes,** *small bottles,* **crosletz,** *crucibles,* **sublymatories,** *vessels for vaporizing solids* **794 Cucurbites,** *curved vessels,* **alambikes,** *vessels for distilling* **795 swiche,** *such* (things) **797 Watres rubifiyng,** *liquids that produce redness,* **boles gall,** *bull's bile* **798 sal armonyak,** *ammonium chloride,* **brymstoon,** *sulfur* **799 koude,** *could* **800 egremoyne,** *agrimony,* **lunarie,** *moomvort fern* **801 me liste tarie,** *I wished to delay* **804 fourneys,** *furnace,* **calcinacioun,** *reducing to powder* **805 watres albificacioun,** *whitening of liquids* **806 Unslekked lym,** *caustic lime,* **gleyre of an ey,** *egg white* **808 Cered,** *waxed,* **sal peter,** *saltpeter,* **vitriole,** *metal sulfate or sulfuric acid* **810 Sal tartre,** *potassium carbonate,* **alkaly,** *salt from boiled sea plants,* **sal preparat,** *purified salt* **811 combust matires,** *burned materials,* **coagulat,** *congealed* **812 heer,** *hair* **812–13 oille / Of tartre,** *cream of tartar,* **alum glas,** *rock alum,* **berme,** *yeast,* **wort,** *beer mash,* **argoille,** *wine-cast deposits* **814 Resalgar,** *red arsenic,* **matires enbibyng,** *absorbent materials* **815 matires encorporyng,** *alloying materials* **816 silver citrinacioun,** *turning silver a yellowish color* **817 cementyng,** *fusing by heat* **818 yngottes,** *molds for casting metal,* **testes,** *testing vessels* **821 nevene,** *name* **826 Sol,** *the sun,* **Luna,** *the moon,* **threpe,** *assert* **827 clepe,** *call* **829 fader kyn,** *father's family* **830 exercise,** *practice* (it) **831 han,** *have* **833 lese,** *lose* **834 listeth outen,** *wishes to reveal* **836 oght,** *anything,* **cofre,** *treasure chest* **837 appiere,** *appear,* **wexe,** *become* **838 Ascauns,** *as if,* **light,** *easy,* **leere,** *learn* **839 woot,** *knows,* **al be he,** *even if he is* **840 wyght,** *person* **842 elvysshe nyce loore,** *otherworldly foolish learning* **843 veyn,** *empty,* **parde,** *by God* **846 konne he letterure,** (if) *he knows book learning* **847 al oon,** *all the same* **848 bothe two,** i.e., *the learned and the unlearned* **850 Ylike,** *alike,* **ydo,** *done* **853 watres corosif,** *acids,* **lymaille,** *metal filings* **854 mollificacioun,** *being softened,* **855 induracioun,** *being hardened* **856 ablucions,** *rinses,* **fusible,** *meltable* **857 bible,** *book*

795 deere ynough a leek, worth as much as a leek; i.e., worthless. **800 valerian,** like the others mentioned in this line, valerian is a plant. The husband of Cecilia in *SNT* is also named Valerian. **812 or,** El reads "and." **817 Oure,** El reads "And of oure." **820 foure spirites . . . bodies sevene,** four substances that can be vaporized by heat: quicksilver (mercury), orpyment (arsenic), sal armonyak (ammonia), and brimstone (sulfur); seven metals that correspond to the seven planets. Variations on the classification are common in alchemy, and the lines describing the metals (826–29) have the appearance of a mnemonic jingle.

That owher is°. Wherfore, as for the beste,
Of alle thise names now wol I me reste.
For, as I trowe°, I have yow toold ynowe°
To reyse a feend°, al looke he° never so rowe°.
 A, nay, lat be! The philosophres stoon,
Elixer clept°, we sechen faste echoon°,
For hadde we hym°, thanne were we siker ynow°.
But unto God of hevene I make avow,
For al oure craft whan we han al ydo°,
With al oure sleighte° he° wol nat come us to.
He° hath ymaad us spenden muchel good
For sorwe of which almoost we wexen wood°,
But° that good hope crepeth in oure herte
Supposynge evere, though we sore smerte°,
To be releeved by hym afterward.
Swich supposyng and hope is sharp and hard.
I warne yow wel, it is to seken evere°,
That futur temps° hath maad men dissevere°
In trust therof from al that evere they hadde.
Yet of that art they kan nat wexen sadde°,
For unto hem it is a bitter sweete—
So semeth it—for nadde° they but a sheete
Which that they myghte wrappe hem inne a-nyght,
And a brat° to walken inne by daylyght,
They wolde hem selle and spenden on this craft.
They kan nat stynte° til nothyng be laft.
And everemoore where that evere they goon
Men may hem knowe by smel of brymstoon°.
For al the world they stynken as a goot;
Hir savour° is so rammyssh° and so hoot°
That though a man a mile from hem be,
The savour wole infecte hym, trusteth me.
And thus by smell and threedbare array°,
If that men liste° this folk they knowe may.
And if a man wole aske hem pryvely°
Why they been clothed so unthriftily°,
They right anon° wol rownen° in his ere
And seyn if that they espied° were
Men wolde hem slee by cause° of hir science°.
Lo, thus this folk bitrayen innocence!
 Passe over this; I go my tale unto.
Er that the pot be on the fir ydo°,
Of metals with a certeyn quantitee,
My lord hem tempreth°, and no man but he—
Now he is goon, I dar seyn° boldely—
For, as men seyn, he kan doon craftily.
Algate° I woot° wel he hath swich a name,
And yet ful ofte he renneth in a blame°.
And wite° ye how? Ful ofte it happeth so
The pot tobreketh°, and farewel, al is go°.
Thise metals been of so greet violence
Oure walles mowe° nat make hem resistence,
But if° they weren wroght of lym° and stoon;
They percen so, and thurgh the wal they goon.
And somme of hem synke into the ground—
Thus han we lost by tymes° many a pound—
And somme are scatered al the floor aboute;
Somme lepe into the roof. Withouten doute,
Though that the feend noght in oure sighte hym shewe°,
I trowe° he with us be, that ilke shrewe°!
In helle, where that he lord is and sire,
Nis ther° moore wo ne moore rancour ne ire.
Whan that oure pot is broke, as I have sayd,
Every man chit° and halt hym yvele apayd°.
 Somme seyde it was long on the fir makyng.
Somme seyde nay, it was on the blowyng—
Thanne was I fered°, for that was myn office°,
"Straw°," quod the thridde, "ye been lewed° and nyce°!
It was nat tempred° as it oghte be."
"Nay," quod the fourthe, "stynt° and herkne° me.
By cause oure fir ne was nat maad of beech,

858 owher, *anywhere* **860 trowe,** *believe,* **ynowe,** *enough* **861 reyse a feend,** *call up a demon,* **al looke he,** *although he looks,* **rowe,** *rough* **863 clept,** *called,* **sechen faste echoon,** *each* (of us) *seek zealously* **864 hym,** *it,* **siker ynow,** *certain enough* **866 ydo,** *done* **867 sleighte,** *cleverness,* **he,** *it* **868 He,** *it,* **ymaad,** *made* **869 wexen wood,** *go insane* **870 But,** *except* **871 sore smerte,** *hurt sorely* **874 evere,** *forever* **875 That futur temps,** *so that future times* (i.e., hopes for the future), **dissevere,** *separate* **877 wexen sadde,** *become satisfied* **879 nadde they,** *had they nothing* **881 brat,** *rough coat* **883 stynte,** *stop* **885 brymstoon,** *sulfur* **887 savour,** *smell,* **rammyssh,** *ramlike,* **hoot,** *intense* **890 array,** *clothing* **891 liste,** *wish* **892 pryvely,** *secretly* **893 unthriftily,** *poorly* **894 right anon,** *immediately,* **rownen,** *whisper* **895 espied,** *discovered* **896 by cause,** *because,* **science,** *knowledge* **899 ydo,** *placed* **901 tempreth,** *mixes* **902 dar seyn,** *dare speak* **904 Algate,** *even though,* **woot,** *know* **905 renneth in a blame,** *is disgraced* **906 wite,** *know* **907 tobreketh,** *shatters,* **go,** *gone* **909 mowe,** *might* **910 But if,** *unless,* **lym,** *mortar* **913 by tymes,** *in a moment* **916 hym shewe,** *shows himself* **917 trowe,** *believe,* **ilke shrewe,** *same wretch* **919 Nis ther,** *there is no* **921 chit,** *accuses* (others), **halt hym yvele apayd,** *considers himself badly treated* **924 fered,** *afraid,* **office,** *responsibility* **925 Straw,** *pshaw,* **lewed,** *ignorant,* **nyce,** *foolish* **926 tempred,** *mixed* **927 stynt,** *stop,* **herkne,** *hear*

862–63 philosophres stoon . . . / Elixer, elixir (Arabic, "the philosopher's stone"), a mythic substance (solid, powder, or liquid) thought to transform base to precious metal, or even to extend human life. Compare *SNT* 8.487ff., where Almachius, who calls himself a philosopher (line 490), commands Cecilia to worship a stone idol, although Cecilia and the Christian God bring about conversion—spiritual transformation. **871 evere,** omitted in El. **880 a-nyght,** El reads "at nyght." **882 this,** El reads "the." **890 And . . . smell,** manuscripts other than El read "Lo . . . smellyng." **895 if that,** El reads "that is that." **915 lepe,** El reads "lepte." **922 long,** El reads "along."

That is the cause and oother noon, so theech°!"
I kan nat telle wheron it was along°,
But wel I woot° greet strif us is among.
"What," quod my lord, "ther is namoore to doone.
Of thise perils I wol be war eftsoone°.
I am right siker° that the pot was crased°.
Be as be may, be ye nothyng amased°;
As usage° is, lat swepe° the floor as swithe°.
Plukke up youre hertes and beeth glad and blithe."
The mullok° on an heep ysweped was,
And on the floor ycast a canevas,
And al this mullok in a syve ythrowe°,
And sifted and ypiked many a throwe°.
"Pardee°," quod oon, "somwhat of oure metal
Yet is ther heere, though that we han nat al.
And though this thyng myshapped have° as now,
Another tyme it may be wel ynow°.
Us moste putte oure good in aventure°.
A marchant, pardee, may nat ay° endure,
Trusteth me wel, in his prosperitee.
Somtyme his good is drenched° in the see,
And somtyme comth it sauf° unto the londe."
"Pees," quod my lord, "the nexte tyme I wol fonde°
To bryngen oure craft al in another plite°,
And but° I do, sires, lat me han the wite°.
Ther was defaute in somwhat°, wel I woot°."
Another seyde the fir was over-hoot.
But be it hoot or coold, I dar seye this,
That we concluden everemoore amys°.
We faille of that which that we wolden have,
And in oure madnesse everemoore we rave.
And whan we been togidres everichoon°,
Every man semeth a Salomon.
But al thyng which that shyneth as the gold
Nis nat gold, as that I have herd told;
Ne every appul that is fair to eye
Nis nat good, what so men clappe° or crye.
Right so, lo, fareth it° amonges us;
He that semeth the wiseste, by Jhesus,
Is moost fool whan it cometh to the preef°,
And he that semeth trewest is a theef.
That shul ye knowe er that I fro yow wende°
By that I of my tale have maad an ende.

Explicit prima pars. Et sequitur pars secunda.

Ther is a chanoun of religioun
Amonges us wolde° infecte al a toun,
Thogh it as greet were as was Nynyvee,
Rome, Alisaundre, Troye, and othere three.
His sleightes° and his infinite falsenesse
Ther koude no man writen, as I gesse,
Though that he lyve myghte a thousand yeer.
In al this world of falshede nis° his peer,
For in his termes so he wole hym wynde°,
And speke his wordes in so sly a kynde°,
Whanne he commune° shal with any wight°,
That he wol make hym doten anon-right°,
But° it a feend be as hymselven is.
Ful many a man hath he bigiled er° this,
And wole° if that he lyve may a while.
And yet men ride and goon ful many a mile
Hym for to seke and have his aqueyntaunce,
Noght knowynge of his false governaunce°.
And if yow list to yeve me audience°,
I wol it tellen heere in youre presence.
But worshipful chanons religious,
Ne demeth nat° that I sclaundre youre hous,
Although that my tale of a chanoun bee.
Of every ordre som shrewe° is, pardee°,
And God forbede that al a compaignye
Sholde rewe° o singuleer° mannes folye.
To sclaundre yow is nothyng myn entente,
But to correcten that is mys° I mente.
This tale was nat oonly toold for yow,
But eek for othere mo°. Ye woot° wel how

929 theech, *may I prosper* **930 wheron it was along,** *what it resulted from* **931 woot,** *know* **933 war eftsoone,** *aware after this* **934 siker,** *certain,* **crased,** *cracked* **935 amased,** *dismayed* **936 usage,** *habit,* **lat swepe,** *sweep,* **as swithe,** *at once* **938 mullok,** *rubbish* **940 in a syve ythrowe,** *thrown in a sieve* **941 ypiked many a throwe,** *picked through repeatedly* **942 Pardee,** *by God* **944 myshapped have,** *has gone wrong* **945 ynow,** *enough* **946 Us moste putte . . . in aventure,** *we must risk* **947 ay,** *always* **949 drenched,** *drowned* **950 sauf,** *safe* **951 wol fonde,** *will try* **952 plite,** *condition* **953 but,** *unless,* **han the wite,** *have the blame* **954 defaute in somwhat,** *flaw in something,* **woot,** *know* **957 amys,** *wrongly* **960 togidres everichoon,** *all together* **965 what so men clappe,** *whatever men jabber* **966 fareth it,** *it goes* **968 preef,** *test* **970 wende,** *go* **973 wolde,** (who) *would* **976 sleightes,** *tricks* **979 nis,** *none is* **980 wole hym wynde,** *will wrap himself* **981 kynde,** *manner* **982 commune,** *converse,* **wight,** *person* **983 doten anon-right,** *soon behave foolishly* **984 But,** *unless* **985 er,** *before* **986 wole,** *will* **989 governaunce,** *behavior* **990 list to yeve me audience,** *choose to listen to me* **993 Ne demeth nat,** *don't think* **995 shrewe,** *wretch,* **pardee,** *by God* **997 rewe,** *regret,* **o singuleer,** *one individual* **999 that is mys,** *what is amiss* **1001 othere mo,** *others more,* **woot,** *know*

944 And, El reads "Al." **953 sires,** omitted in El. **961 semeth a Salomon,** seems a Solomon, who in scripture and legend was the ideal of a wise man. **962 al . . . shyneth,** El reads "every . . . seineth." **966 lo,** omitted in El. **971a Explicit prima pars. Et sequitur pars secunda.** "Here ends part one. And here follows part two." **972 is,** El reads "was." **974 Nynyvee,** Nineveh, capital of the Assyrian Empire. **992 chanons religious,** canons regular; see 573n. This address may be simply rhetorical or may date from a time when Chaucer composed this section to be read before an audience such as the canons of King's Chapel at Windsor. If the latter, the address to the Host at line 1089 is evidence of revision. **993 sclaundre,** El reads "desclaundre."

That among Cristes aposteles twelve
Ther nas no traytour but Judas hymselve.
Thanne why sholde al the remenant have a blame
That giltlees were? By° yow I seye the same,
Save oonly this, if ye wol herkne° me,
If any Judas in youre coven° be,
Remoeveth hym bitymes°, I yow rede°,
If shame or los° may causen any drede.
And beeth nothyng displesed, I yow preye,
But in this cas° herkeneth what I shal seye.
  In Londoun was a preest, an annueleer,
That therinne had dwelled many a yeer,
Which° was so plesaunt and so servysable
Unto the wyf, where as he was at table,
That she wolde suffre° hym no thyng for to paye
For bord ne clothyng, wente he never so gaye,
And spendyng silver hadde he right ynow°.
Therof no fors°, I wol procede as now,
And telle forth my tale of the chanoun
That broghte this preest to confusioun.
  This false chanoun cam upon a day
Unto this preestes chambre, wher he lay,
Bisechynge° hym to lene° hym a certeyn°
Of gold, and he wolde quite° it hym ageyn.
"Leene° me a marc°," quod he, "but dayes three,
And at my day I wol it quiten° thee.
And if so be that thow me fynde fals,
Another day do hange me by the hals°."
  This preest hym took° a marc, and that as swithe°,
And this chanoun hym thanked ofte sithe°,
And took his leve, and wente forth his weye,
And at the thridde day broghte his moneye,
And to the preest he took his gold agayn°
Wherof this preest was wonder glad and fayn°.
  "Certes°," quod he, "nothyng anoyeth me°
To lene a man a noble°, or two, or thre,
Or what thyng were in my possessioun,
Whan he so trewe is of condicioun
That in no wise he breke wole his day°.
To swich a man I kan never seye nay."
  "What," quod this chanoun, "sholde I be untrewe?
Nay, that were thyng yfallen al of newe°.
Trouthe is a thyng that I wol evere kepe
Unto that day in which that I shal crepe
Into my grave, and ellis God forbede.
Bileveth this as siker° as your Crede.
God thanke I, and in good tyme° be it sayd
That ther was nevere man yet yvele apayd°
For gold ne silver that he to me lente,
Ne nevere falshede in myn herte I mente.
And sire," quod he, "now of my pryvetee°,
Syn° ye so goodlich han been unto me,
And kithed° to me so greet gentillesse,
Somwhat to quyte with° youre kyndenesse
I wol yow shewe°, if that yow list to leere°,
I wol yow teche pleynly the manere
How I kan werken in philosophie°.
Taketh good heede, ye shul wel seen at eye°,
That I wol doon a maistrie° er I go."
  "Ye," quod the preest, "ye, sire, and wol ye so?
Marie°, therof° I pray yow hertely."
  "At youre comandement, sire, trewely,"
Quod the chanoun, "and ellis God forbeede."
  Loo, how this theef koude his service beede°!
Ful sooth it is that swich° profred servyse
Stynketh, as witnessen thise olde wyse°,
And that ful soone° I wol it verifie
In this chanoun, roote of al trecherie,
That everemoore delit hath and gladnesse—
Swiche feendly thoghtes in his herte impresse°—
How Cristes peple he may to meschief brynge.
God kepe us from his false dissymulynge°!
  Noght wiste° this preest with whom that he delte,
Ne of his harm comynge he nothyng felte.

1005 By, *concerning* **1006 herkne,** *hear* **1007 covent,** *religious house* **1008 bitymes,** *at once,* **rede,** *advise* **1009 los,** *reputation* **1011 cas,** *instance* **1014 Which,** *who* **1016 suffre,** *allow* **1018 ynow,** *enough* **1019 no fors,** *no matter* **1024 Bisechynge,** *asking,* **lene,** *loan,* **certeyn,** *amount* **1025 quite,** *repay* **1026 Leene,** *loan,* **marc,** *coin equal to two thirds pound* **1027 quiten,** *repay* **1029 hals,** *neck* **1030 took,** *gave,* **as swithe,** *quickly* **1031 ofte sithe,** *many times* **1034 took . . . agayn,** *returned* **1035 fayn,** *pleased* **1036 Certes,** *certainly,* **nothyng anoyeth me,** *it doesn't bother me* **1037 noble,** *coin equal to about one-third pound* **1040 breke wole his day,** *will fail to pay on the promised day* **1043 were thyng yfallen al of newe,** i.e., *would be the first time* **1047 siker,** *certain* **1048 in good tyme,** *fortunately* **1049 yvele apayd,** *dissatisfied* **1052 pryvetee,** *secrets* **1053 Syn,** *since* **1054 kithed,** *shown* **1055 Somwhat to quyte with,** *something to repay* **1056 shewe,** *show,* **list to leere,** *wish to learn* **1058 philosophie,** *alchemy* **1059 at eye,** *plainly* **1060 doon a maistrie,** *demonstrate something special* **1062 Marie,** *by Mary,* **therof,** *for that* **1065 beede,** *offer* **1066 swich,** *such* **1067 witnessen thise olde wyse,** *old wise people make clear* **1068 ful soone,** *very quickly* **1071 impresse,** *make an impression* **1073 dissymulynge,** *disguising* **1074 Noght wiste,** *did not know*

1004 al, omitted in El. **1002–03** Matthew 26.47–49. **1012 annueleer,** a priest paid for a specified number of years to celebrate masses for the dead. **1043 thyng,** El reads "a thyng." **1045 Unto,** El reads "Into." **1047 Crede,** Creed (Lat. *credo,* "I believe"); a formal profession of faith. **1061** El has a long line: "'Ye,' quod the preest, 'ye, sire,' quod he. 'And wol ye so?'" **1066–67 profred servyse / Stynketh,** proferred (unasked for) service stinks; proverbial.

O sely° preest, O sely innocent!
With coveitise anon thou shalt be blent°!
O gracelees, ful blynd is thy conceite°.
Nothyng ne artow war° of the deceite
Which that this fox yshapen° hath to thee.
His wily wrenches° thou ne mayst nat flee.
Wherfore to go to the conclusioun
That refereth° to thy confusioun,
Unhappy man, anon I wol me hye°,
To tellen thyn unwit° and thy folye,
And eek the falsnesse of that oother wrecche
As ferforth° as my konnyng° may strecche.
  This chanoun was my lord ye wolden weene°?
Sire hoost, in feith, and by the hevenes queene,
It was another chanoun and nat hee,
That kan° an hundred foold moore subtiltee.
He hath bitrayed folkes many tyme.
Of his falsnesse it dulleth° me to ryme.
Evere whan that I speke of his falshede,
For shame of hym my chekes wexen rede°—
Algates° they bigynnen for to glowe,
For reednesse have I noon right wel I knowe
In my visage; for fumes diverse
Of metals, which ye han herde me reherce,
Consumed and wasted han my reednesse.
Now taak heed of this chanons cursednesse.
  "Sire," quod he to the preest, "lat youre man gon°
For quyksilver, that we hadde it anon;
And lat hym bryngen ounces two or three;
And whan he comth°, as faste shal ye see
A wonder thyng, which ye saugh nevere er this."
  "Sire," quod the preest, "it shal be doon, ywis°."
He bad his servant fecchen hym this thyng;
And he al redy was at his biddyng
And wente hym forth and cam anon agayn
With this quyksilver, shortly for to sayn,
And took thise ounces thre to the chanoun.
And he hem leyde faire and wel adoun,
And bad the servant coles° for to brynge
That he anon myghte go to his werkynge.
  The coles right anon weren yfet°,
And this chanoun took out a crosselet°
Of his bosom and shewed it to the preest.
"This instrument," quod he, "which that thou seest,
Taak in thyn hand and put thyself therinn
Of this quyksilver an ounce, and heer bigynne,
In name of Crist, to wexe a philosofre°.
Ther been ful fewe to whiche I wolde profre
To shewen hem thus muche of my science.
For ye shul seen heer, by experience,
That this quyksilver I wol mortifye
Right in youre sighte anon, withouten lye,
And make it as good silver and as fyn
As ther is any in youre purs or myn,
Or elleswhere, and make it malliable,
And elles holdeth me fals and unable°
Amonges folk forevere to appeere.
I have a poudre heer that coste me deere
Shal make al good, for it is cause of al
My konnyng°, which that I to yow shewen shal.
Voyde° youre man and lat hym be theroute,
And shette the dore whils we been aboute
Oure pryvetee°, that no man us espie
Whils that we werke in this philosophie."
  Al as he bad fulfilled was in dede.
This ilke° servant anonright out yede°,
And his maister shette the dore anon,
And to hire labour spedily they gon.
  This preest at this cursed chanons biddyng
Upon the fir anon sette this thyng,
And blewe the fir, and bisyed hym ful faste°.
And this chanoun into the crosselet caste
A poudre, noot I° wherof that it was
Ymaad°, outher° of chalk, or of glas,
Or somwhat elles, was nat worth a flye,
To blynde with this preest, and bad hym hye°
The coles for to couchen° al above
The crosselet. "For in tokenyng° I thee love,"
Quod this chanoun, "thyne owene handes two
Shul werche al thyng which shal heer be do."
  "Graunt mercy°," quod the preest and was ful
    glad,
And couched coles as that the chanoun bad.
And while he bisy was, this feendly wrecche,

1076 sely, *foolish* **1077 blent,** *blinded* **1078 conceite,** *thought* **1079 Nothyng ne artow war,** *not at all are you aware* **1080 yshapen,** *planned* **1081 wrenches,** *tricks* **1083 refereth,** *applies* **1084 hye,** *hurry* **1085 unwit,** *stupidity* **1087 ferforth,** *far* **konnyng,** *ability* **1088 weene,** *think* **1091 kan,** *knows* **1093 dulleth,** *wearies* **1095 wexen rede,** *grow red* **1096 Algates,** *at least* **1102 lat youre man gon,** *send your servant* **1105 comth,** *comes* **1107 ywis,** *certainly* **1114 coles,** *coals* **1116 yfet,** *brought* **1117 crosselet,** *crucible* **1122 wexe a philosofre,** *become an alchemist* **1131 unable,** *unfit* **1135 konnyng,** *skill* **1136 Voyde,** *send out* **1138 pryvetee,** *secrets* **1141 ilke,** *same,* **yede,** *went* **1146 ful faste,** *very intensely* **1148 noot I,** *I don't know* **1149 Ymaad,** *made,* **outher,** *either* **1151 hye,** *pile* **1152 couchen,** *arrange* **1153 in tokenyng,** *as a sign that* **1156 Graunt mercy,** *thank you*

1080 to, El reads "for." **1085 thy,** El reads "his." **1093 falsnesse,** El reads "falshede." **1111 shortly,** El reads "soothly." **1126 quyksilver . . . mortifye,** to "mortify" or "kill" quicksilver–i.e., "live" silver–is the alchemical term for transforming it into solid silver. **1126 I wol,** El reads "wol I." **1127 withouten,** El reads "I wol nat." **1128 it,** omitted in El. **1157 coles as that the chanoun,** El reads "cole as that chanoun."

This false chanoun—the foule feend hym fecche—
Out of his bosom took a bechen cole°
In which ful subtilly was maad an hole,
And therinne put was of silver lemaille°
An ounce, and stopped was withouten faille,
This hole with wex, to kepe the lemaille in.
And understondeth that this false gyn°
Was nat maad ther, but it was maad bifore;
And othere thynges I shal tellen moore
Herafterward, whiche that he with hym broghte.
Er he cam there, hym to bigile he thoghte.
And so he dide, er that they wente atwynne°;
Til he had terved° hym, he koude nat blynne°.
It dulleth° me whan that I of hym speke.
On his falshede fayn° wolde I me wreke°
If I wiste° how, but he is heere and there;
He is so variaunt°, he abit° nowhere.
  But taketh heede now, sires, for Goddes love.
He took this cole of which I spak above,
And in his hand he baar° it pryvely.
And whiles the preest couched° bisily
The coles, as I tolde yow er this,
This chanoun seyde, "Freend, ye doon amys.
This is nat couched as it oghte be.
But soone I shal amenden it," quod he.
"Now lat me medle therwith but a while,
For of yow have I pitee, by Seint Gile.
Ye been right hoot°; I se wel how ye swete.
Have heere a clooth, and wipe awey the wete."
And whiles that the preest wiped his face,
This chanoun took his cole—with sory grace°—
And leyde it above upon the myddeward°
Of the crosselet, and blew wel afterward,
Til that the coles gonne faste brenne°.
  "Now yeve° us drynke," quod the chanoun thenne.
"As swithe° al shal be wel, I undertake°.
Sitte we doun and lat us myrie make."
And whan that this chanounes bechen cole°
Was brent°, al the lemaille° out of the hole
Into the crosselet fil anon adoun—
And so it moste nedes°, by resoun,
Syn° it so evene° aboven it couched was.
But therof wiste° the preest nothyng, alas.
He demed° alle the coles yliche° good,
For of that sleighte° he nothyng understood.
And whan this alkamystre° saugh° his tyme,
"Ris up," quod he, "sire preest, and stondeth by me;
And for I woot° wel ingot° have ye noon,
Gooth, walketh forth, and bryng us a chalk stoon.
For I wol make it of the same shap
That is an ingot, if I may han hap°.
And bryngeth eek° with yow a bolle° or a panne
Ful of water, and ye shul se wel thanne
How that oure bisynesse shal thryve and preeve°.
And yet, for ye shul han no mysbileeve
Ne wrong conceite° of me in youre absence,
I ne wol nat been out of youre presence,
But go with yow and come with yow ageyn."
The chambre dore, shortly for to seyn,
They opened and shette and wente hir weye.
And forth with hem they carieden the keye
And coome agayn withouten any delay.
What sholde I tarien° al the longe day?
He took the chalk and shoop° it in the wise°
Of an ingot as I shal yow devyse°.
  I seye, he took out of his owene sleeve
A teyne° of silver—yvele moot he cheeve°—
Which that ne was nat but an ounce of weighte.
And taaketh heede now of his cursed sleighte.
  He shoop his ingot in lengthe and in breede°
Of this teyne, withouten any drede°,
So slyly that the preest it nat espide,
And in his sleve agayn he gan it hide,
And fro the fir he took up his mateere,

1160 bechen cole, *beechwood charcoal* **1162 lemaille,** *filings* **1165 gyn,** *contrivance* **1170 wente atwynne,** *separated* **1171 terved,** *fleeced,* **blynne,** *stop* **1172 dulleth,** *numbs* **1173 fayn,** *happily,* **wreke,** *avenge* **1174 wiste,** *knew* **1175 variaunt,** *shifty,* **abit,** *stays* **1178 baar** *held* **1179 couched,** *arranged* **1186 right hoot,** *very hot* **1189 sory grace,** *bad luck* **1190 myddeward,** *middle* **1192 gonne faste brenne,** *burned intensely* **1193 yeve,** *give* **1194 As swithe,** *soon,* **undertake,** *declare* **1196 bechen cole,** *beechwood charcoal* **1197 brent,** *burned,* **lemaille,** *filings* **1199 moste nedes,** *must necessarily* **1200 Syn,** *since,* **evene,** *squarely* **1201 wiste,** *knew* **1202 demed,** *thought,* **yliche,** *alike* **1203 sleighte,** *trick* **1204 alkamystre,** *alchemist,* **saugh,** *saw* **1206 woot,** *know,* **ingot,** *mold* **1209 han hap,** *have luck* **1210 eek,** *also,* **bolle,** *bowl* **1212 preeve,** *succeed* **1214 conceite,** *thought* **1221 tarien,** *delay* **1222 shoop,** *shaped,* **wise,** *manner* **1223 devyse,** *describe* **1225 teyne,** *small bar,* **yvele moot he cheeve,** *may he achieve evil* **1228 breede,** *breadth* **1229 drede,** *doubt*

1160 took, El reads "he took." **1175 he abit,** El reads "that he abit." **1185 Seint Gile,** St. Giles, patron saint of beggars and people who are crippled, but here possibly play on *guile.* **1189 sory,** El reads "harde." **1205 stondeth,** El reads "sit." **1208 it of,** El reads "oon of." **1226 ne,** omitted in El. **1228 and in,** El reads "and eek in." **1231 in his sleve,** the small bar (only an ounce) hidden up his sleeve is in preparation for the third deception at lines 1317–18. In the first deception, the quicksilver evaporates and the silver filings melt from the hollow charcoal into the crucible, from which the canon fills the mold (ingot) he carved into the soft chalk. In the second deception, the silver filings melt from the hollow stick held by the canon. In all cases, the powder is a ruse.

And in th'yngot putte it with myrie cheere,
And in the water-vessel he it caste
Whan that hym luste°, and bad the preest as
faste,
"Loke what ther is; put in thyn hand and grope.
Thow fynde shalt ther silver, as I hope."
What, devel of helle, sholde it elles be?
Shaving of silver silver is, pardee°!
He putte his hand in and took up a teyne
Of silver fyn°, and glad in every veyne
Was this preest whan he saugh that it was so.
"Goddes blessyng, and his moodres also,
And alle halwes°, have ye, sire chanoun,"
Seyde the preest, "and I hir malisoun°,
But°, and° ye vouchesauf° to techen me
This noble craft and this subtilitee,
I wol be youre in al that evere I may."
Quod the chanoun, "Yet wol I make assay°
The seconde tyme that ye may taken heede
And been expert of this, and in youre neede
Another day assaye in myn absence
This disciplyne and this crafty science.
Lat take° another ounce," quod he tho,
"Of quyksilver, withouten wordes mo,
And do therwith as ye han doon er this
With that oother, which that now silver is."
This preest hym bisieth° in al that he kan
To doon as this chanoun, this cursed man,
Comanded hym, and faste he blew the fir
For to come to th'effect° of his desir.
And this chanoun right in the meene while
Al redy was the preest eft° to bigile,
And for a contenaunce° in his hand he bar
An holwe° stikke—taak kepe° and bewar—
In the ende of which an ounce, and namoore,
Of silver lemaille° put was, as bifore
Was in his cole, and stopped with wex weel
For to kepe in his lemaille every deel°.
And whil this preest was in his bisynesse,
This chanoun with his stikke gan hym dresse°
To hym anon, and his poudre caste in
As he dide er—the devel out of his skyn
Hym terve°, I pray to God, for his falshede!
For he was evere fals in thoght and dede—
And with this stikke, above the crosselet,
That was ordeyned° with that false jet°,
He stired the coles til relente gan°
The wex agayn° the fir, as every man
But it a fool be woot° wel it moot nede°,
And al that in the stikke was out yede°,
And in the crosselet hastily it fel.
Now, goode sires, what wol ye bet than wel°?
Whan that this preest thus was bigiled ageyn,
Supposynge noght but treuthe, sooth to seyn,
He was so glad that I ne kan nat expresse
In no manere his myrthe and his gladnesse;
And to the chanoun he profred eftsoone°
Body and good. "Ye," quod the chanoun soone,
"Though poure I be, crafty thou shalt me fynde.
I warne° thee, yet is ther moore bihynde.
Is ther any coper herinne°?" seyde he.
"Ye," quod the preest, "sire, I trowe° wel ther be."
"Elles° go bye us som, and that as swithe°.
Now, good sire, go forth thy wey and hy the°."
He wente his wey, and with the coper cam,
And this chanon it in his handes nam°,
And of that coper weyed out but an ounce.
Al to symple is my tonge to pronounce
As ministre of my wit the doublenesse
Of this chanoun, roote of alle cursednesse.
He semed freendly to hem that knewe hym noght,
But he was feendly bothe in werk and thoght.
It weerieth me to telle of his falsnesse,
And nathelees yet wol I it expresse,
To th'entente that men may bewar therby,
And for noon oother cause, trewely.
He putte the ounce of coper in the crosselet,
And on the fir as swithe he hath it set,
And caste in poudre, and made the preest to
blowe,
And in his werkyng for to stoupe lowe
As he dide er—and al nas° but a jape°.
Right as hym liste°, the preest he made his ape°.
And afterward in the ingot he it caste,
And in the panne putte it at the laste
Of water, and in he putte his owene hand,

1235 luste, *chose* **1239 pardee,** *by God* **1241 fyn,** *pure* **1244 halwes,** *saints'* **1245 I hir malisoun,** (may) *I* (have) *their curse* **1246 But,** *unless,* **and,** *if,* **vouchesauf,** *agree* **1249 assay,** *attempt* **1254 Lat take,** *take* **1258 hym bisieth,** *busies himself* **1261 th'effect,** *the outcome* **1263 eft,** *again* **1264 a contenaunce,** *appearances* **1265 holwe,** *hollow,* **taak kepe,** *pay attention* **1267 lemaille,** *filings* **1269 deel,** *bit* **1271 gan hym dresse,** *approached* **1274 terve,** *flay* **1277 ordeyned,** *prepared,* **jet,** *device* **1278 relente gan,** *melted* **1279 agayn,** *as a result of* **1280 woot,** *knows,* **moot nede,** *necessarily must* **1281 yede,** *went* **1283 wol ye bet than wel,** *what more do you want* **1288 profred eftsoone,** *offered at once* **1291 warne,** *tell* **1292 coper herinne,** *copper in here* **1293 trowe,** *believe* **1294 Elles,** *or else,* **as swithe,** *quickly* **1295 hy the,** *hurry yourself* **1297 nam,** *took* **1312 nas,** *was nothing,* **jape,** *trick* **1313 liste,** *wished,* **ape,** i.e., *he made a monkey of him*

1236 Look what ther is, El reads "What that heer is." **1238–39** Lines omitted in El. **1245 the preest,** El reads "this preest." **1249 chanoun,** El reads "preest." **1268 Was,** omitted in El. **1303 werk,** El reads "herte." **1316 Of water, and in he,** El reads "Of the water in he."

And in his sleve (as ye biforen-hand
Herde me telle) he hadde a silver teyne.
He slyly took it out, this cursed heyne°,
Unwityng° this preest of his false craft,
And in the pannes botme° he hath it laft;
And in the water rombled to and fro,
And wonder pryvely° took up also
The coper teyne, noght knowynge° this preest,
And hidde it, and hym hente° by the breest,
And to hym spak, and thus seyde in his game°:
"Stoupeth adoun, by God, ye be to blame°!
Helpeth me now, as I dide yow whileer°;
Putte in youre hand, and looketh what is theer."
This preest took up this silver teyne anon,
And thanne seyde the chanoun, "Lat us gon
With thise thre teynes whiche that we han wroght°
To som goldsmyth, and wite° if they been oght°.
For by my feith I nolde°, for myn hood,
But if that° they were silver fyn and good,
And that as swithe preeved° it shal bee."
Unto the goldsmyth with thise teynes three
They wente, and putte thise teynes in assay°
To fir and hamer. Myghte no man seye nay
But that they weren as hem oghte be.
This sotted° preest, who was gladder than he?
Was nevere brid° gladder agayn the day°,
Ne nyghtyngale in the sesoun of May.
Nas nevere° man that luste° bet° to synge,
Ne lady lustier in carolynge,
Or for to speke of love and wommanhede,
Ne knyght in armes to doon an hardy dede,
To stonden in grace of his lady deere,
Than hadde this preest this soory craft to leere°,
And to the chanoun thus he spak and seyde,
"For love of God, that for us alle deyde°,
And as I may deserve it unto° yow,
What shal this receite° coste? Telleth now!"
"By oure Lady," quod this chanon, "it is deere°,
I warne yow wel; for save° I and a frere°,
In Engelond ther kan no man it make."
"No fors°," quod he, "now, sire, for Goddes sake,
What shal I paye? Telleth me, I preye."
"Ywis°," quod he, "it is ful deere, I seye.
Sire, at o word, if that thee list° it have,
Ye shul paye fourty pound, so God me save.
And nere° the freendshipe that ye dide er this
To me, ye sholde paye moore, ywis."
This preest the somme of fourty pound anon
Of nobles fette°, and took hem everichon
To this chanoun for this ilke receit°.
Al his werkyng nas° but fraude and deceit.
"Sire preest," he seyde, "I kepe han no loos°
Of my craft, for I wolde it kept were cloos°;
And as ye love me kepeth it secree.
For and° men knewen al my soutiltee°,
By God they wolden han so greet envye
To me by cause of my philosophye
I sholde be deed—ther were noon oother weye."
"God it forbeede," quod the preest, "what sey ye?
Yet hadde I levere° spenden al the good
Which that I have, or elles wexe I wood°,
Than that ye sholden falle in swich mescheef°."
"For youre good wyl, sire, have ye right good preef°,"
Quod the chanoun, "and farwel, grant mercy°."
He wente his wey, and never the preest hym sy°
After that day. And whan that this preest shoolde
Maken assay° at swich tyme as he wolde
Of this receit, farwel, it wolde nat be.
Lo, thus byjaped° and bigiled was he.
Thus maketh he his introduccioun°
To brynge folk to hir destruccioun.
Considereth, sires, how that in ech estaat°
Bitwixe men and gold ther is debaat°
So ferforth° that unnethe° is ther noon.
This multiplying blent° so many oon
That in good feith I trowe° that it bee
The cause grettest of swich scarsetee.

1319 heyne, *wretch* **1320 Unwityng,** *unaware* **1321 botme,** *bottom* **1323 wonder pryvely,** *very secretly* **1324 noght knowynge,** *unknown to* **1325 hente,** *grabbed* **1326 in his game,** *as part of his scheme* **1327 to blame,** *at fault* **1328 whileer,** *just before* **1332 wroght,** *created* **1333 wite,** *learn,* **oght,** (worth) *anything* **1334 nolde,** *wish nothing* **1335 But if that,** *unless* **1336 as swithe preeved,** *quickly proved* **1338 assay,** *test of the purity of precious metals* **1341 sotted,** *besotted* **1342 brid,** *bird,* **agayn the day,** *as a result of dawn* **1344 Nas nevere,** *there was never,* **luste,** *yearned,* **bet,** *better* **1349 leere,** *learn* **1351 deyde,** *died* **1352 deserve it unto,** *earn it from* **1353 receite,** *formula* **1354 deere,** *costly* **1355 save,** *except for,* **frere,** *friar* **1357 No fors,** *no matter* **1359 Ywis,** *certainly* **1360 list,** *wish* (to) **1362 nere,** *were it not for* **1365 nobles fette,** *gold coins fetched* **1366 ilke receit,** *same formula* **1367 nas,** *was nothing* **1368 kepe han no loos,** *care to have no fame,* **1369 cloos,** *secret* **1371 and,** *if,* **soutiltee,** *skill* **1376 levere,** *rather* **1377 wexe I wood,** (may) *I go insane* **1378 mescheef,** *misfortune* **1379 preef,** *proof* **1380 grant mercy,** *thank you* **1381 sy,** *saw* **1383 assay,** *a test* **1385 byjaped,** *tricked* **1386 introduccioun,** *beginning* **1388 estaat,** *social rank* **1389 debaat,** *conflict* **1390 ferforth,** *completely,* **unnethe,** *scarcely* **1391 blent,** *has blinded* **1392 trowe,** *believe*

1318 he, omitted in El. **1334 for myn hood,** an idiom meaning "in exchange for my hood (or head)," i.e., "by all that's dear to me." **1387 hir,** omitted in El.

Philosophres speken so mystily°
In this craft that men kan nat come therby.
For any wit that men han now-a-dayes
They mowe wel chiteren° as doon thise jayes°,
And in hir termes° sette° hir lust° and peyne,
But to hir purpos shul they nevere atteyne.
A man may lightly lerne°, if he have aught°,
To multiplie and brynge his good to naught!
  Lo, swich° a lucre° is in this lusty° game.
A mannes myrthe it wol turne unto grame°,
And empten also grete and hevye purses,
And maken folk for to purchacen curses
Of hem that han hir good therto ylent°.
O, fy, for shame, they that han been brent°,
Allas, kan they nat flee the fires heete?
Ye° that it use°, I rede° ye it leete°
Lest ye lese° al, for bet than nevere is late.
Nevere to thryve were to long a date°.
Though ye prolle ay°, ye shul it nevere fynde.
Ye been as boold as is Bayard the blynde
That blondreth forth and peril casteth° noon.
He is as boold to renne agayn° a stoon
As for to goon bisides in the weye°.
So faren° ye that multiplie, I seye.
If that youre eyen kan nat seen aright,
Looke that youre mynde lakke noght his° sight.
For though ye looken never so brode and
    stare,
Ye shul nothyng wynne on that chaffare°,
But wasten al that ye may rape and renne.
Withdraweth the fir lest it to faste brenne;
Medleth° namoore with that art, I mene,
For if ye doon, youre thrift° is goon ful clene.
And right as swithe° I wol yow tellen heere
What philosophres seyn in this mateere.
  Lo, thus seith Arnold of the Newe Toun,
As his *Rosarie* maketh mencioun;
He seith right thus, withouten any lye:
"Ther may no man mercurie mortifie
But it be with his brother knowlechyng°."
How be that° he which that first seyde this thyng
Of philosophres fader was, Hermes.
He seith how that the dragon, doutelees,
Ne dyeth nat but if that he be slayn
With his brother; and that is for to sayn,
By the dragon, Mercurie, and noon oother
He understood, and brymstoon by his brother,
That out of Sol and Luna were ydrawe°.
"And therfore," seyde he—taak heede to my sawe°—
"Lat no man bisye hym this art for to seche°
But if that° he th'entencioun and speche
Of philosophres understonde kan.
And if he do, he is a lewed° man.
For this science° and this konnyng°," quod he,
"Is of the secree of secretes°, pardee°."
  Also ther was a disciple of Plato
That on a tyme seyde his maister to,
As his book *Senior* wol bere witnesse,
And this was his demande in soothfastnesse°,
"Telle me the name of the privee° stoon?"
  And Plato answerde unto hym anoon,
"Take the stoon that Titanos men name."

1394 mystily, *mysteriously* **1397 mowe wel chiteren,** *might as well chatter,* **jayes,** *noisy birds* **1398 termes,** *jargon,* **sette,** *place,* **lust,** *desire* **1400 lightly lerne,** *learn easily,* **aught,** *anything* **1402 swich,** *such,* **lucre,** *profit,* **lusty,** *greedy* **1403 grame,** *grief* **1406 that han hir good therto ylent,** *to whom they have lent their goods* **1407 brent,** *burned* **1409 Ye,** *you,* **use,** *practice,* **rede,** *advise,* **leete,** *abandon* **1410 lese,** *lose* **1411 date,** *time* **1412 prolle ay,** *prowl forever* **1414 casteth,** *considers* **1415 renne agayn,** *run into* **1416 goon bisides in the weye,** *go around on the path* **1417 faren,** *do* **1419 his,** *its* (the mind's) **1421 chaffare,** *exchange* **1424 Medleth,** *meddle* **1425 thrift,** *prosperity* **1426 right as swithe,** *as quickly as possible* **1432 brother knowlechyng,** *brother's help* **1433 How be that,** *however* **1440 ydrawe,** *drawn* **1441 sawe,** *saying* **1442 seche,** *seek* **1443 But if that,** *unless* **1445 lewed,** *stupid* **1446 science,** *knowledge,* **konnyng,** *skill* **1447 secree of secretes,** *the secret of all secrets,* **pardee,** *by God* **1451 in soothfastnesse,** *truly* **1452 privee,** *secret*

1397 as doon thise jayes, El reads "as that doon joyes." **1407 O,** omitted in El. **1413 Bayard,** a proverbial blind horse, brave because it could not see danger. **1422 rape and renne,** seize and run, a proverbial idiom meaning "acquire by any means." **1427 What,** El reads "What that the." **1428–32 Arnold of the Newe Toun . . . ,** Arnaldus of Villanova, thirteenth-century French alchemist, wrote the *Rosarium Philosophorum* (*The Philosopher's Rosary*), but the quotations in lines 1431–47 echo his *De Lapide Philosophorum* (*On the Philosopher's Stone*), where the "mortification" or solidification of mercury (quicksilver) into silver is said to require sulfur, the "brother" of mercury. **1433 How be that,** no manuscript includes "be," essential unless we construe "How that" as parallel to the same phrase in line 1435. **1434 philosophres fader was, Hermes,** Hermes Trismegistus was the legendary founding father of alchemy, the Greek equivalent of the Egyptian god of learning, Thoth. El reads "fader first was." **1435–40 dragon . . . ,** an alchemical metaphor for mercury, which was combined with its "brother," brimstone (sulfur), in efforts to transform the mercury into silver by "slaying" it. One or both derive in some mysterious way from gold and silver, the metals associated with the sun (**Sol,** line 1440) and moon (**Luna,** line 1440). Such occult combinations of metaphor, chemistry, and astrology are characteristic of alchemical treatises. **1447 of secretes,** El reads "of the secretes." **1448–71 disciple of Plato . . . *Senior* . . . ,** Plato and his disciple have a similar discussion in a Latin version of an Arabic alchemical treatise, *Epistola Solis ad Lunam Crescentem* (*The Sun's Letter to the Crescent Moon*), published in the seventeenth century under the title *Senioris Zadith fil. Hamuelis Tabulis Chemica* (*Chemical Table of Senior Zadith, Son of Hamuel*). **1454–55 Titanos . . . Magnasia,** occult names for some mineral or substance.

Which is that?" quod he. "Magnasia is the
same,"
Seyde Plato. "Ye sire, and is it thus?
This is *ignotum per ignocius*°.
What is Magnasia, good sire, I yow preye?"
"It is a water that is maad, I seye,
Of elementes foure," quod Plato.
"Telle me the roote°, good sire," quod he tho,
"Of that water, if it be youre wille."
"Nay, nay," quod Plato, "certein, that I nylle°.
The philosophres sworn were everychoon
That they sholden discovere it unto noon,
Ne in no book it write in no manere.
For unto Crist it is so lief° and deere
That he wol nat that it discovered bee
But where it liketh° to his deitee
Men for t'enspire, and eek for to deffende°
Whom that hym liketh—lo, this is the ende."
Thanne conclude I thus, sith° that God of
hevene
Ne wil nat that the philosophres nevene°
How that a man shal come unto this stoon,
I rede°, as for the beste, lete it goon.
For whoso maketh God his adversarie,
As for to werken anythyng in contrarie
Of his wil, certes° never shal he thryve,
Thogh that he multiplie terme° of his lyve.
And there a poynt°, for ended is my tale.
God sende every trewe man boote of his bale°.
Amen.

Heere is ended the Chanouns Yemannes Tale.

1457 ignotum per ignocius, *explaining the unknown by the more unknown* **1461 roote,** *essential nature* **1463 nylle,** *will not* **1467 lief,** *beloved* **1469 it liketh,** *it is pleasing* **1470 deffende,** *forbid* **1472 sith,** *since* **1473 nevene,** *reveal* **1475 rede,** *advise* **1478 certes,** *surely* **1479 terme,** *the time* **1480 poynt,** *period* (full stop) **1481 boote of his bale,** *remedy for his suffering*

1475 as, El reads "us." **1479 his,** omitted in El.

Canterbury Tales, Part 9

Introduction

IT IS CONVENTIONAL to let the *Manciple's Prologue* and *Tale* stand alone as Part 9, but there is no good textual reason to do so. It regularly precedes Part 10 in the reliable manuscripts, is explicitly referred to in the *Parson's Prologue* (10.1), and combines with Parts 8 and 10 to create a geographical sequence as the pilgrims approach their destination. The Canon and his Yeoman meet the pilgrimage at Boughton in the Blean Forest (8.556), and the *Manciple's Prologue* opens in Harbledown (2, "Bobbe-up-and-doun") at the far edge of the Blean and only two miles from Canterbury. In the *Parson's Prologue*, the pilgrims enter a town, presumably Canterbury itself (10.12).

Yet a temporal discrepancy undercuts this geographical sequence. The Host says it is morning in the *Manciple's Prologue* (16), but following the Manciple's brief tale, the afternoon shadows are already lengthening in the *Parson's Prologue* (10.6–9). The discrepancy has encouraged a few critics to read the *Parson's Tale* as one of the tales intended for a return journey, but the signals to completion and closure in Parts 8–10 suggest otherwise. The temporal leap is read allegorically by critics who consider the drunken Cook to be a figure of spiritual unpreparedness (8–17n); critics who argue that the *Manciple's Tale* sets up the Parson's rejection of fable for truth disregard the leap as an oversight left in need of revision.

Speech, language, and their consequences are dominant issues in the *Manciple's Prologue* and *Tale*. The altercation between the Manciple and the Cook in the prologue suggests professional competitiveness—a Londoner, the Cook prepares food, and the Manciple is responsible for supplying food to his employers, who live at the city's edge. Drunkenness and the Manciple's chiding render the Cook speechless and provide some of the most energetic drama in the entire Canterbury frame. No one has explained satisfactorily why the Host calls for a tale from the Cook, who has already told a tale, albeit a fragmentary one, although the Host's reference to the Cook's "penaunce" (12), sleeplessness, and morning drunkenness are central to arguments that the Cook is spiritually unprepared. See Michael Kensak, "What Ails Chaucer's Cook? Spiritual Alchemy and the Ending of *The Canterbury Tales*" (2001, no. 1193).

The tale lacks the charm or pathos characteristic of Chaucer's other bird stories–the *Parliament of Fowls*, the *Nun's Priest's Tale*, and the falcon's lament in the *Squire's Tale*. In Ovid's *Metamorphoses* 2.531–632, the ultimate source of the plot of the *Manciple's Tale*, the central concern is Phoebus Apollo's punishing transformation of the tattletale crow from white to black. Chaucer maintains the concern with transformation but emphasizes speech and speechlessness by adding moralization and commentary on natural behavior and language use (163–234). See Jamie C. Fumo, "Thinking Upon the Crow" (2004, no. 1189). Much of the material Chaucer adds is adapted from the *Roman de la Rose*, and most of it suggests caution if not cynicism. The largest single addition, the concluding moralization (309–62), is a kind of self-cancellation—a loquacious recommendation not to speak or tell tales, whether false or true. Pervaded by a sense of expediency, the *Manciple's Prologue* and *Tale* suggest that we ought to distrust language, including our own speech, because it can get us into trouble.

Louise Fradenburg, "The Manciple's Servant Tongue" (1985, no. 1188), suggests that the tale be considered in light of the tradition in which poetry was offered as advice to princes, and she argues that it reflects Chaucer's anxious position as a poet and bureaucrat in the court of Richard II. A number of critics suggest a more general examination of communication whereby the Manciple's cynical distrust of language anticipates the penitential use of language in the *Parson's Tale.* See, for example, Celeste A. Patton, "False 'Rekenynges': Sharp Practice and the Politics of Language in Chaucer's 'Manciple's Tale'" (1992, no. 1194).

Canterbury Tales
Part 9

From woodcut made by W.H. Hooper and published by the Chaucer Society between 1868 and 1879

Manciple's Tale

Prologue

Heere folweth the Prologe of the Mauncipels Tale.

Woot° ye nat where ther stant a litel toun
Which that ycleped is° Bobbe-up-and-doun,
Under the Blee, in° Caunterbury weye?
Ther gan oure Hooste for to jape° and pleye,
And seyde, "Sires, what, Dun is in the myre!
Is ther no man for preyere ne for hyre°
That wole awake oure felawe al bihynde?
A theef myghte hym ful lightly° robbe and bynde.
See how he nappeth°! See how, for cokkes bones,
That he wol falle fro his hors atones°!
Is that a cook of Londoun, with meschaunce°?
Do hym° come forth—he knoweth his penaunce—
For he shal telle a tale, by my fey°,
Although it be nat worth a botel hey°,
"Awake, thou Cook," quod he, "God yeve° thee sorwe!
What eyleth thee to slepe by the morwe°?
Hastow° had fleen° al nyght, or artow° dronke?
Or hastow with som quene° al nyght yswonke°,
So that thow mayst nat holden up thyn heed?"
This Cook, that was ful pale and nothyng reed,

1 Woot, *know* **2 Which that ycleped is,** *which is called* **3 in,** *on* **4 jape,** *joke* **6 preyere ne for hyre,** *request nor for pay* **8 lightly,** *easily* **9 nappeth,** *sleeps* **10 atones,** *soon* **11 with meschaunce,** *bad luck to him* **12 Do hym,** *have him* **13 fey,** *faith* **14 botel hey,** *bundle of hay* **15 yeve,** *give* **16 by the morwe,** *in the morning* **17 Hastow,** *have you,* **fleen,** *fleas,* **artow,** *are you* **18 quene,** *whore,* **yswonke,** *worked*

1–104 Lines lacking in several MSS, perhaps evidence of late composition; see MR 2.445. **2–3 Bobbe-up-and-doun . . . Blee,** Harbledown, on the edge of the Blean Forest and two miles from Canterbury. Compare 8.556n above. **5 Dun is in the myre,** Dun (a proverbial horse) is stuck in the mud; i.e., things have come to a halt. **8–17** Critics have read echoes of 1 Thessalonians 5.2–8, suggesting that Chaucer's imagery recalls St. Paul's comments on those who are spiritually unprepared. **9 cokkes bones,** cock's bones; euphemism for "God's bones," a mild oath.

Seyde to oure Hoost, "So God my soule blesse,
As ther is falle on me swich hevynesse—
Noot I nat° why—that me were levere° slepe
Than the best galon wyn° in Chepe."
"Wel," quod the Maunciple, "if it may doon ese
To thee, sire Cook, and to no wight° displese,
Which that heere rideth in this compaignye,
And that oure Hoost wole° of his curteisye,
I wol as now excuse thee of thy tale.
For in good feith thy visage is ful pale,
Thyne eyen daswen eek°, as that me thynketh,
And wel I woot° thy breeth ful soure stynketh—
That sheweth wel thou art nat wel disposed.
Of me, certeyn, thou shalt nat been yglosed°.
See how he ganeth°, lo, this dronken wight,
As though he wolde swolwe us anonright°.
Hoold cloos thy mouth, man, by thy fader kyn°!
The devel of helle sette his foot therin!
Thy cursed breeth infecte wole us alle.
Fy, stynkyng swyn°, fy, foule moote thee falle°!
A, taketh heede, sires, of this lusty man.
Now, sweete sire, wol ye justen atte fan?
Therto° me thynketh ye been wel yshape°!
I trowe° that ye dronken han wyn ape,
And that is whan men pleyen with a straw."
And with this speche the Cook wax wrooth and wraw°,
And on the Manciple he gan nodde faste
For lakke of speche, and doun the hors hym caste,
Where as he lay til that men up hym took.
This was a fair chyvachee of° a cook!
Allas, he nadde holde° hym by his ladel°!
And er that he agayn were in his sadel,
Ther was greet showvyng bothe to and fro
To lifte hym up, and muchel care and wo,
So unweeldy was this sory palled° goost.
And to the Manciple thanne spak oure Hoost:
"By cause drynke hath dominacioun
Upon this man, by my savacioun,
I trowe lewedly° he wolde telle his tale.
For were it wyn or oold or moysty° ale
That he hath dronke, he speketh in his nose,
And fneseth° faste, and eek he hath the pose°.
He hath also to do moore than ynough
To kepen hym and his capul° out of the slough°.
And if he falle from his capul eftsoone°,
Thanne shal we alle have ynogh to doone°
In liftyng up his hevy dronken cors°.
Telle on thy tale; of hym make I no fors°.
"But yet, Manciple, in feith thou art to nyce°,
Thus openly repreve° hym of his vice.
Another day he wole, peraventure°,
Reclayme thee and brynge thee to lure—
I meene, he speke wole of smale thynges,
As for to pynchen at thy rekenynges°
That were nat honeste, if it cam to preef°."
"No," quod the Manciple, "that were a greet mescheef!
So myghte he lightly° brynge me in the snare.
Yet hadde I levere° payen for the mare
Which he rit° on than he sholde with me stryve°.
I wol nat wratthen° hym, also moot I thryve°!
That that I spak, I seyde it in my bourde°.
And wite° ye what? I have heer in a gourde°
A draghte of wyn, ye, of a ripe grape,
And right anon° ye shul seen a good jape°.
This Cook shal drynke therof, if I that may.
Up° peyne of deeth, he wol nat seye me nay."
And certeynly, to tellen as it was,
Of this vessel the Cook drank faste, allas.
What neded hym? He drank ynough biforyn.
And whan he hadde pouped in this horn

---

23 Noot I nat, *I don't know,* **me were levere,** *I would rather* **24 Than the best galon wyn,** *than* (have) *the best gallon of wine* **26 wight,** *person* **28 wole,** *will* **31 eyen daswen eek,** *eyes are dazed also* **32 woot,** *know* **34 yglosed,** *flattered* **35 ganeth,** *yawns* **36 anonright,** *soon* **37 fader kyn,** *father's relatives* **40 swyn,** *pig,* **foule moote thee falle,** *may evil happen to you* **43 Therto,** *for that,* **been wel yshape,** *are in good shape* **44 trowe,** *believe* **46 wax wrooth and wraw,** *grew angry and peevish* **50 chyvachee of,** *display of horsemanship by* **51 nadde holde,** *had not held,* **ladel,** *cooking ladle* **55 palled,** *pale* **59 trowe lewedly,** *think ignorantly* **60 oold or moysty,** *old or fresh* **62 fneseth,** *sneezes,* **pose,** *head cold* **64 capul,** *horse,* **slough,** *mud* **65 eftsoone,** *again* **66 doone,** *do* **67 cors,** *body* **68 no fors,** *no matter* **69 to nyce,** *too foolish* **70 repreve,** (to) *accuse* **71 peraventure,** *perhaps* **74 pynchen at thy rekenynges,** *find errors in your accounts* **75 preef,** *proof* **77 lightly,** *easily* **78 hadde I levere,** *I would rather* **79 rit,** *rides,* **stryve,** *quarrel* **80 wratthen,** *anger,* **also may I thryve,** *as I may prosper* **81 bourde,** *joke* **82 wite,** *know,* **gourde,** *gourd-shaped bottle* **84 right anon,** *soon,* **jape,** *joke* **86 Up,** *upon*

24 Chepe, Cheapside, the market district of medieval London. **25 Maunciple,** as the purchaser of goods for a London law school, the Manciple was something of a professional rival of the Cook; see *GP* 1.567n. **40 thee,** El reads "thou." **42 justen atte fan,** joust at the quintain, a practice target that pivots and strikes the jousting knight (or the player of a derivative game) if he fails to avoid it. Apparently, the Cook is reeling in his saddle. **44 wyn ape,** the four traditional states of drunkenness are lamb-drunk (mild), lion-drunk (belligerent), ape-drunk (raucous), and pig-drunk (sloppy). **46 this,** Hg reads "his." **47 he gan nodde,** Hg reads "bigan he nodde." **59 lewedly he wolde telle,** Hg reads "he lewedly telle wolde." **72 Reclayme thee . . . to lure,** i.e., "get you back"; derives from the language of falconry, where the "lure" is used to recall a bird from flight. **79 Which he,** El reads "Which that he." **81 speke,** El reads "spak." **82 ye,** omitted in Hg. **85 that,** omitted in Hg. **89 hym,** Hg reads "it." **90 pouped in this horn,** blown in this horn, with double entendre: taken a drink and farted or vomited.

To the Manciple he took the gourde agayn°.
And of that drynke the Cook was wonder fayn°,
And thanked hym in swich wise as he koude.
Thanne gan oure Hoost to laughen wonder loude,
And seyde, "I se wel it is necessarie,
Where that we goon, good drynke we with us carie.
For that wol turne rancour and disese°
T'acord and love, and many a wrong apese°.
O Bacus, yblessed be thy name,
That so kanst turnen erest into game!
Worship and thank be to thy deitee!
Of that mateere ye gete namoore of me.
Telle on thy tale, Manciple, I thee preye."
"Wel, sire," quod he, "now herkneth what I seye."

Heere bigynneth the Maunciples Tale of the Crowe.

Whan Phebus dwelled heere in this erthe adoun,
As olde bookes maken mencioun,
He was the mooste lusty bachiler°
In al this world, and eek the beste archer.
He slow Phitoun the serpent as he lay
Slepynge agayn° the sonne upon a day,
And many another noble worthy dede
He with his bowe wroghte°, as men may rede.
Pleyen he koude° on every mynstralcie°,
And syngen that it was a melodie
To heeren of his cleere voys the soun.
Certes° the kyng of Thebes Amphioun,
That with his syngyng walled that citee,
Koude nevere syngen half so wel as hee.
Therto° he was the semelieste° man
That is or was sith° that the world bigan.
What nedeth it his fetures to discryve°?
For in this world was noon so fair on-lyve°.
He was therwith fulfild of gentillesse,
Of honour, and of parfit° worthynesse.
This Phebus that was flour of bachilrie,
As wel in fredom° as in chivalrie,
For his desport° in signe eek of victorie
Of° Phitoun, so as telleth us the storie,
Was wont° to beren in his hand a bowe.
Now hadde this Phebus in his hous a crowe
Which in a cage he fostred many a day,
And taughte it speke as men teche a jay.
Whit was this crowe as is a snowwhit swan,
And countrefet° the speche of every man
He koude whan he sholde telle a tale.
Therwith in al this world no nyghtyngale
Ne koude, by an hondred thousand deel°,
Syngen so wonder myrily and weel.
Now hadde this Phebus in his hous a wyf
Which that he lovede moore than his lyf,
And nyght and day dide evere his diligence
Hir for to plese, and doon hire reverence—
Save oonly, if I the sothe° shal sayn,
Jalous he was and wolde have kept hire fayn°.
For hym were looth byjaped° for to be,
And so is every wight° in swich degree°.
But al in ydel, for it availleth noght°.
A good wyf that is clene° of werk and thoght
Sholde nat been kept in noon awayt°, certayn,
And trewely the labour is in vayn
To kepe a shrewe, for it wol nat bee.
This holde I for a verray nycetee°
To spille° labour for to kepe wyves;
Thus writen olde clerkes in hir lyves.
But now to purpos as I first bigan:
This worthy Phebus dooth al that he kan
To plesen hire, wenynge° for swich plesaunce°,
And for his manhede and his governaunce°,
That no man sholde han put hym from hir grace°.

91 took . . . agayn, *returned* **92 wonder fayn,** *wonderfully glad* **97 disese,** *discomfort* **98 apese,** *appease* **107 lusty bachiler,** *vigorous knight* **110 agayn,** *in* **112 wroghte,** *accomplished* **113 Pleyen he koude,** *he could play,* **mynstralcie,** *musical instrument* **116 Certes,** *certainly* **119 Therto,** *also,* **semelieste,** *most handsome* **120 sith,** *since* **121 discryve,** *describe* **122 on-lyve,** *alive* **124 parfit,** *perfect* **126 fredom,** *generosity* **127 desport,** *entertainment* **128 Of,** *over* **129 wont,** *accustomed* **134 countrefete,** *imitate* **137 deel,** *part* **143 sothe,** *truth* **144 wolde have kept hire fayn,** *would gladly have guarded her* **145 byjaped,** *tricked* **146 wight,** *man,* **swich degree,** *such social class* **147 availleth noght,** *accomplishes nothing* **148 clene,** *pure* **149 awayt,** *surveillance* **152 verray nycetee,** *true foolishness* **153 spille,** *waste* **157 wenynge,** *thinking,* **swich plesaunce,** *such pleasantness* **158 governaunce,** *behavior* **159 grace,** *favor*

96 good, El reads "that." **98 and,** Hg reads "a." **99 Bacus,** Bacchus, god of wine. **102 of me,** Hg reads "for me." **105 Phebus,** Phoebus Apollo, god of music, poetry, and the sun. **erthe,** El reads "worlde." **109 Phitoun,** the Python, killed by Apollo in Ovid's *Metamorphosis* 1.438–51. **116 Amphioun,** played his lyre (not sang) so beautifully that walls built themselves around the city of Thebes. A familiar medieval figure; see *MerT* 4.1716. **133 is,** omitted in El. **143 if I the sothe,** El reads "the sothe that I": Hg, "that the sothe if I." **147 in ydel,** Hg reads "for naught." **148 of,** Hg reads "in." **157 for,** El reads "that."

But God it woot°, ther may no man embrace°
As to destreyne° a thyng which that nature
Hath natureelly set in a creature.
Taak any bryd° and put it in a cage,
And do al thyn entente and thy corage°
To fostre it tendrely with mete and drynke
Of alle deyntees that thou kanst bithynke°,
And keep it al so clenly as thou may,
Although his cage of gold be never so gay,
Yet hath this brid by twenty thousand foold
Levere° in a forest that is rude° and coold
Goon ete° wormes and swich wrecchednesse.
For evere this brid wol doon his bisynesse
To escape out of his cage, if he may.
His libertee this brid desireth ay°.
Lat take° a cat and fostre hym wel with milk
And tendre flessh, and make his couche of silk,
And lat hym seen a mous go by the wal,
Anon he weyveth° milk and flessh and al,
And every deyntee that is in that hous,
Swich appetit hath he to ete a mous.
Lo, heere hath lust his dominacioun,
And appetit fleemeth° discrecioun.
A she-wolf hath also a vileyns kynde°.
The lewedeste wolf that she may fynde,
Or leest of reputacioun, that wol she take
In tyme whan hir lust° to han a make°.
Alle thise ensamples speke I by° thise men
That been untrewe and nothyng by° wommen.
For men han evere a likerous° appetit
On lower thyng to parfourne hire° delit
Than on hire wyves, be they never so faire,
Ne never so trewe, ne so debonaire°.
Flessh is so newefangel°, with meschaunce°,
That we ne konne° in nothyng han plesaunce°
That sowneth into° vertu any while.
This Phebus, which that thoghte upon no gile,
Deceyved was for al his jolitee°.
For under hym another hadde shee,
A man of litel reputacioun,
Nat worth to Phebus in comparisoun.
The moore harm is, it happeth ofte so,
Of which ther cometh muchel harm and wo.
And so bifel, whan Phebus was absent,
His wyf anon hath for hir lemman° sent.
Hir lemman? Certes, this is a knavyssh speche°!
Foryeveth it me, and that I yow biseche°.
The wise Plato seith, as ye may rede,
The word moot nede° accorde with the dede.
If men shal telle proprely a thyng,
The word moost cosyn be to the werkyng.
I am a boystous° man, right thus seye I,
Ther nys no° difference, trewely,
Bitwixe a wyf that is of heigh degree,
If of hir body dishonest she bee,
And a poure wenche, oother than this—
If it so be they werke bothe amys°—
But that the gentile° in hire estaat above,
She shal be cleped° his lady, as in love;
And for that oother is a poure womman,
She shal be cleped his wenche or his lemman.
And, God it woot°, myn owene deere brother,
Men leyn that oon as lowe as lith° that oother.
Right so bitwixe a titelees tiraunt°
And an outlawe or a theef erraunt°
The same I seye—ther is no difference.
To Alisaundre was toold this sentence°,
That, for° the tirant is of gretter myght,
By force of meynee° for to sleen dounright°,
And brennen° hous and hoom, and make al playn°,
Lo, therfore is he cleped° a capitayn;
And for the outlawe hath but smal meynee,
And may nat doon so greet an harm as he,
Ne brynge a contree to so greet mescheef,
Men clepen hym an outlawe or a theef.
But for I am a man noght textueel°,

160 woot, *knows* **embrace,** *undertake* **161 destreyne,** *restrain* **163 bryd,** *bird* **164 corage,** *effort* **166 bithynke,** *think of* **170 Levere,** *rather,* **rude,** *rugged* **171 Goon ete,** *go eat* **174 ay,** *always* **175 Lat take,** *take for example* **178 weyveth,** *abandons* **182 fleemeth,** *drives out* **183 vileyns kynde,** *evil nature* **186 hir lust,** *it pleases her,* **make,** *mate* **187 by,** *about* **189 likerous,** *lecherous* **190 parfourne hire,** *perform their* **192 debonaire,** *meek* **193 newefangel,** *eager for newness.* **with meschaunce,** *bad luck to it* **194 konne,** *can,* **plesaunce,** *pleasure* **195 sowneth into,** *produces* **197 jolitee,** *attractiveness* **204 lemman,** *lover* **205 knavyssh speche,** *low way to speak* **206 biseche,** *request* **208 moot nede,** *must necessarily* **211 boystous,** *rough* **212 nys no,** *is no* **216 amys,** *wrongly* **217 gentile,** *aristocrat* **218 cleped,** *called* **221 woot,** *knows* **222 lith,** *lies* **223 titelees tiraunt,** *untitled usurper* **224 theef erraunt,** *roving robber* **226 sentence,** *meaningful saying* **227 for,** *because* **228 force of meynee,** *strength of his army,* **sleen dounright,** *slaughter* **229 brennen,** *burn,* **make al playn,** *flatten everything* **230 cleped,** *called* **235 noght textueel,** *not book learned*

160–62 This sentiment and the following examples of the natural inclinations of bird and cat are in *RR* 13941–14030 and elsewhere; the she-wolf (line 183), in *RR* 7763–66 and elsewhere. **180 hath he,** El reads "he hath." **185 Or,** Hg reads "And." **188 and,** Hg reads "but." **205 is,** omitted in Hg. **207–10 Plato . . . werkyng,** see *GP* 1.741–42n. **217 hire,** omitted in Hg. **222 leyn,** lay; double entendre: consider (lay a bet) and lay sexually. **226 Alisaundre,** Alexander the Great. The anecdote was familiar in political admonitions, going back to Cicero's *De Republica* 3.12.

I wol noght telle of textes never a deel°.
I wol go to my tale as I bigan.
Whan Phebus° wyf had sent for hir lemman
Anon° they wroghten al hire lust volage°.
  The white crowe that heeng ay° in the cage
Biheeld hire werk and seyde never a word.
And whan that hoom was come Phebus, the lord,
This crowe sang "Cokkow! Cokkow! Cokkow!"
  "What, bryd?" quod Phebus, "What song syngestow°?
Ne were thow wont° so myrily to synge
That to myn herte it was a rejoysynge
To heere thy voys? Allas, what song is this?"
  "By God," quod he, "I synge nat amys.
Phebus," quod he, "for al thy worthynesse,
For al thy beautee and thy gentilesse,
For al thy song and al thy mynstralcye,
For al thy waityng°, blered is thyn eye°
With oon of litel reputacioun,
Noght worth to thee as in comparisoun
The montance° of a gnat, so moote° I thryve°!
For on thy bed thy wyf I saugh° hym swyve°."
  What wol ye moore? The crowe anon hym tolde
By sadde tokenes° and by wordes bolde
How that his wyf had doon hire lecherye
Hym to° greet shame and to greet vileynye,
And tolde hym ofte he saugh it with his eyen.
  This Phebus gan aweyward for to wryen°.
Hym thoughte his sorweful herte brast atwo°.
His bowe he bente and sette therinne a flo°,
And in his ire his wyf thanne hath he slayn—
This is th'effect°, ther is namoore to sayn—
For sorwe of which he brak° his mynstralcie°,
Bothe harpe, and lute, and gyterne, and sautrie°,
And eek he brak his arwes and his bowe,
And after that thus spak he to the crowe:
  "Traitour," quod he, "with tonge of scorpioun,
Thou hast me broght to my confusioun°.
Allas, that I was wroght°! Why nere I° deed?
O deere wyf, O gemme° of lustiheed°,
That were to me so sad° and eek so trewe,
Now listow° deed with face pale of hewe
Ful giltelees, that dorste° I swere, ywys°!
O rakel° hand, to doon so foule amys!
O trouble° wit, O ire recchelees°,
That unavysed° smyteth° giltelees!
O wantrust°, ful of fals suspecioun,
Where was thy wit and thy discrecioun?
O every man, bewar of rakelnesse°!
Ne trowe° nothyng withouten strong witnesse.
Smyt° nat to soone er that ye witen° why,
And beeth avysed° wel and sobrely
Er ye doon any execucioun
Upon youre ire for suspecioun.
Allas, a thousand folk hath rakel ire
Fully fordoon° and broght hem in the mire°.
Allas, for sorwe I wol myselven slee°."
  And to the crowe, "O false theef," seyde he,
"I wol thee quite° anon thy false tale!
Thou songe whilom° lyk a nyghtyngale;
Now shaltow, false theef, thy song forgon°,
And eek thy white fetheres everichon°,
Ne nevere in al thy lif ne shaltou° speke.
Thus shal men on a traytour been awreke°;
Thou and thyn ofspryng evere shul be blake,
Ne nevere sweete noyse shul ye make,
But evere crie agayn° tempest and rayn,
In tokenynge° that thurgh thee my wyf is slayn."
And to the crowe he stirte° and that anon
And pulled his white fetheres everychon,
And made hym blak, and refte hym° al his song,
And eek his speche, and out at dore hym slong
Unto the devel, which° I hym bitake°—
And for this caas° been alle crowes blake.
  Lordynges, by this ensample I yow preye
Beth war and taketh kepe° what ye seye,

236 never a deel, *not a bit* **238 Phebus,** *Phebus's* **239 Anon,** *soon,* **hire lust volage,** *their passing pleasure* **240 heeng ay,** *hung always* **244 syngestow,** *do you sing* **245 Ne were thow wont,** *were you not accustomed* **252 waityng,** *watching,* **blered is thyn eye,** *you have been blinded* **255 montance,** *value,* **moote,** *might,* **thryve,** *prosper* **256 saugh,** *saw,* **swyve,** *screw* **258 sadde tokenes,** *strong evidence* **260 Hym to,** *to his* **262 wryen,** *turn* **263 brast atwo,** *burst apart* **264 flo,** *arrow* **266 th'effect,** *the outcome* **267 brak,** *broke,* **mynstralcie,** *musical instruments* **268 sautrie,** *dulcimer* **272 confusioun,** *ruin* **273 wroght,** *created,* **nere I,** *were I not* **274 gemme,** *jewel,* **lustiheed,** *delight* **275 sad,** *steadfast* **276 listow,** *you lie* **277 dorste,** *dare,* **ywys,** *for sure* **278 rakel,** *rash* **279 trouble,** *disturbed,* **ire recchelees,** *reckless anger* **280 unavysed,** *thoughtless,* **smyteth,** *strikes* **281 wantrust,** *distrust* **283 rakelnesse,** *rashness* **284 trowe,** *believe* **285 Smyt,** *strike,* **witen,** *know* **286 beeth avysed,** *consider* **290 fordoon,** *destroyed,* **mire,** *mud* **291 slee,** *slay* **293 quite,** *repay* **294 whilom,** *once* **295 forgon,** *lose* **296 everichon,** *everyone* **297 shaltou,** *shall you* **298 awreke,** *avenged* **301 agayn,** *at the approach of* **302 In tokenynge,** *as a sign* **303 stirte,** *went suddenly* **305 refte hym,** *deprived him of* **307 which,** *to whom,* **bitake,** *commit* **308 caas,** *reason* **310 kepe,** *care*

243 Cokkow, the crow speaks in bird talk and (in human speech) declares Phebus a cuckold at the same time. **251 and al,** El omits "al." **256 swyve,** El reads "swy&"; Hg "&." El has a Latin gloss "Nota malum quid" (Note this bad thing). **263 Hym,** El and Hg read "And." **271 scorpioun,** a common figure of treachery. **284 trowe nothyng,** Hg reads "trowe ye nothyng." **290 and,** Hg reads "or." **300 noyse,** El reads "voys."

Ne telleth nevere no man in youre lyf
How that another man hath dight° his wyf.
He wol yow haten mortally, certeyn.
Daun Salomon, as wise clerkes seyn,
Techeth a man to kepen his tonge weel.
But, as I seyde, I am noght textueel°,
But nathelees thus taughte me my dame:
"My sone, thenk on the crowe, a Goddes name!
My sone, keep° wel thy tonge, and keep thy freend.
A wikked tonge is worse than a feend,
My sone; from a feend men may hem blesse°.
My sone, God of his endelees goodnesse
Walled a tonge with teeth and lippes eke,
For man sholde hym avyse° what he speeke.
My sone, ful ofte for to muche speche
Hath many a man been spilt°, as clerkes teche,
But for litel speche avysely°
Is no man shent°, to speke generally.
My sone, thy tonge sholdestow° restreyne
At alle tymes but° whan thou doost thy peyne°
To speke of God in honour and preyere.
The firste vertu, sone, if thou wolt leere°,
Is to restreyne and kepe wel thy tonge;
Thus lerne children whan that they been yonge.
My sone, of muchel spekyng yvele avysed°,
Ther lasse° spekyng hadde ynough suffised,
Comth muchel harm; thus was me toold and taught.
In muchel speche synne wanteth naught°.
Wostow° wherof a rakel° tonge serveth?
Right° as a swerd forkutteth and forkerveth°
An arm a-two, my deere sone, right so
A tonge kutteth freendshipe al.a-two.
A janglere° is to God abhomynable.
Reed Salomon, so wys and honurable,
Reed David in his psalmes, reed Senekke.
My sone, spek nat, but with thyn heed thou bekke°.
Dissimule° as thou were deef if that thou heere
A janglere speke of perilous mateere.
The Flemyng seith, and lerne it if thee leste°,
That litel janglyng causeth muchel° reste.
My sone, if thou no wikked word hast seyd
Thee thar nat drede for to be biwreyd°
But he that hath mysseyd°, I dar wel sayn,
He may by no wey clepe° his word agayn.
Thyng that is seyd is seyd, and forth it gooth,
Though hym repente or be hym nevere so looth°.
He is his thral° to whom that he hath sayd
A tale of which he is now yvele apayd°.
My sone, bewar and be noon auctour° newe
Of tidynges, wheither they been false or trewe.
Wherso thou come, amonges hye or lowe°,
Kepe° wel thy tonge and thenk upon the crowe."

Heere is ended the Maunciples Tale of the Crowe.

312 dight, *had sex with* **316 noght textueel,** *not book learned* **319 keep,** *guard* **321 blesse,** *protect by a blessing* **324 hym avyse,** *consider* **326 spilt,** *destroyed* **327 avysely,** *thoughtfully* **328 shent,** *hurt* **329 sholdestow,** *you should* **330 but,** *except,* **doost thy peyne,** *make the effort* **332 leere,** *learn* **335 yvele avysed,** *poorly considered* **336 Ther lasse,** *where less* **338 wanteth naught,** *lacks nothing* **339 Wostow,** *do you know,* **rakel,** *rash* **340 Right,** *just,* **forkutteth and forkerveth,** *cuts and carves completely* **343 janglere,** *chatterer* **346 bekke,** *nod* **347 Dissimule,** *pretend* **349 if thee leste,** *if you please* **350 muchel,** *much* **352 biwreyd,** *betrayed* **353 mysseyd,** *misspoken* **354 clepe,** *call back* **356 looth,** *unwilling* **357 thral,** *slave* **358 yvele apayd,** *unhappy* **359 auctour,** *author* **361 hye or lowe,** *aristocracy or peasants* **362 Kepe,** *guard*

314 Daun Salomon, "master" Solomon, thought to be the author of the Book of Proverbs; see Proverbs 21.23. **318 a Goddes,** El reads "on Goddes." **321 My sone,** the advisory "my son" formula recurs in Proverbs 23 and in other wisdom literature generally. The various proverbs and apothegms that follow recur in various sources, including Proverbs, Psalms, the *Distichs* of Cato, *RR,* and Albertanus de Brescia's *De arte loquendi et tacendi.* None of them counsels silence in such a long-winded way, but compare *RR* 7037–57. **344–45** Proverbs (attributed to Solomon) and David's Psalms are ultimate sources of several of the sentiments expressed in the Manciple's tally, but Seneca's works do not seem to be. **349–50 Flemyng seith . . . reste,** a Flemish (Belgian) proverb. **356 nevere so,** El and Hg read "leef or."

Canterbury Tales, Part 10

Introduction

IN THE *PARSON'S PROLOGUE*, the descending sun, lengthening shadows, and the astrological sign of Libra (signifying the Scales or judgment) are clear signs of closure. As the pilgrims approach the outskirts of an unnamed village, the Host says that only one teller remains, signaling the end of the pilgrimage and the completion of the tale-telling contest. The Parson's rejection of fables for "Moralitee and vertuous mateere" (38) leads to his "meditacioun" (55) on the sacrament of confession or penance—the sacrament whereby sins are forgiven in medieval Christian tradition (and a number of Christian denominations today). When the Parson equates the pilgrimage to the spiritual journey to the heavenly Jerusalem (51), the entire Canterbury fiction becomes allegorical for a moment at least, and the moral seriousness of the pilgrimage overtakes the lively give-and-take of the tale-telling contest. In a complex move, Chaucer indicates that his fiction is coming to an end, asks us once again to consider the relation of fiction to truth, and prompts us to consider his work as a story of human progress toward death and perhaps salvation—movement from the city of man to the City of God.

The sacrament of penance—the topic of the *Parson's Tale*—was thought to be a necessary step in the progress toward salvation. Baptism was the means to remove the effects of Adam's original sin that descended to all human beings, but penance was the means to eradicate the sins that the individual committed on the journey through life. Sinfulness was understood to be a state of being, not merely an accumulation of improper actions or misguided thoughts, and the effect of proper penance was to transform the individual from the state of being sinful to sinless. The sacrament required that the penitents be contrite—truly sorrowful—and that they confess all their sins to a priest, whose words of forgiveness were necessary to the action of the sacrament and the absolution of the sins. Intention and speech—the words of the penitent and of the priest—are equally important.

As a handbook or manual on penance, the *Parson's Tale* defines the sacrament and its functions, and clarifies the variety of sins and their remedies under the conventional arrangement of the seven deadly sins (pride, envy, anger, sloth, avarice, gluttony, lechery). Such manuals were initially designed for confessors to help their penitents understand the sacrament, identify their sins systematically, and achieve contrition so that the sins could be purged. Over time, the Latin manuals were translated into the vernacular languages, becoming accessible to more people and, in the process more meditational and affective, focused on personal examination of conscience. Reading a confessional manual was preparation for and part of the process of spiritual renewal—a medieval equivalent to self-help. It was a means to identify one's failings and inspire sincere sorrow, and the goal was the forgiveness of sins through the spoken sacrament, "shrift of mouthe" (87), as penance was known.

It is appropriate that such a treatise be assigned to the Parson since the pastoral duties of parish priests included instruction of their congregations about penance and administration of the sacrament to them. It has long been thought that by assigning this last tale to the Parson, Chaucer was submitting the rest of his tales to a higher, spiritual standard—perhaps a balance to the secular, philosophical standard of the *Knight's Tale*. Such readings can still stand, but they can be modified by the complex attitudes towards the priesthood (and knighthood) in Chaucer's age. Robert W. Swanson clarifies medieval pastoral responsibilities in "Chaucer's Parson and Other Priests" (1991, no. 1212). In *Confession and Resistance: Defining the Self in Late Medieval England* (2006, no. 1207),

Katherine C. Little compares the *Parson's Tale* with its orthodox sources and contemporary vernacular material, showing how Chaucer's tale can be seen to emphasize reformed attitudes toward the priesthood, lay instruction, and the role of contrition in penance. See also Frances McCormack's *Chaucer and the Culture of Dissent: The Lollard Context and Subtext of the Parson's Tale* (2007, no. 1208).

The most important sources of *The Parson's Tale* are two Latin treatises that Chaucer may have combined himself or were available to him in some version undiscovered by modern scholars. Raymund of Pennaforte's *Summa de paenitentia* (*The Sum of Penance*) underlies the discussion of penance at the opening and closing of the tale, while a version of William Peraldus's *Summa de vitiis et virtutibus* (*The Sum of the Vices and Virtues*) underlies the intervening descriptions of the vices and their remedies. For details, see Richard Newhauser's contribution to *Sources and Analogues* (Correale and Hamel eds. 2002–05, no. 234).

Reading through the *Parson's Tale* can encourage us to consider our own failings, but the process also prompts recollection of the pilgrims and tales that have come earlier in the Canterbury sequence. In general terms, "pride of dress" (415ff.) suggests the Monk, Squire, and others; "pride of table" (444ff.) suggests the Prioress and Franklin. Placebo in the *Merchant's Tale* is mentioned in connection with flattery (617), and the "remedy" for lechery (930ff.) recalls issues in the marriage group. In "The *Parson's Tale* and the Quitting of the *Canterbury Tales*" (1978, no. 1209), Lee W. Patterson tallies some thirty-five instances where Chaucer's penitential treatise echoes preceding material. Many of them are conventional, found in Chaucer's sources, but several indicate that he may have been working on the *Parson's Tale* recurrently during the composition of the Canterbury fiction. Perhaps he adjusted the tale he had translated earlier to reflect the rest of the collection, or at times he may have composed later tales to anticipate this final one. Either way, the *Parson's Tale* invites readers to view the Canterbury pilgrims retrospectively from a penitential perspective, although this hindsight view does not obviate the vitality and variety of the *Canterbury Tales.* As readers, our affective involvement in the penitential process helps to identify the failings of the pilgrims with our own and to remind us that to be human is to err.

When Chaucer asks forgiveness for his literary sins in his Retraction and then revokes a series of his works (10.1084–87), the penitential unity of pilgrims, audience, and author is complete. Retraction or apologies are conventional in medieval literature but, typically, Chaucer puts his to great advantage, reminding us of his entire literary output at the same time that he retracts it and includes himself among those in need of penance. There is no Dantesque or Miltonic elevation of the poet here, but instead the acknowledgment that the lively variety the *Canterbury Tales* cannot go on forever. Critics have read deathbed sincerity in the Retraction and others have perceived wry ironies. Nothing is more Chaucerian than this combination of moral seriousness and artistic self-awareness.

For a series of essays that survey the scholarship and confront critical questions of Part 10, see David Raybin and Linda Tarte Holley, eds. *Closure in The Canterbury Tales: The Role of the Parson's Tale* (2000, no. 1211). Thomas Bestul, "Chaucer's Parson's Tale and the Late-Medieval Tradition of Religious Meditation" (1989, no. 1202), addresses Chaucer's use of meditational materials. On the conventional nature of the Retraction, see Anita Obermeier, *The History and Anatomy of Self-Criticism in the European Middle Ages* (1999, no. 1219).

Canterbury Tales Part 10

From woodcut made by W.H. Hooper and published by the Chaucer Society between 1868 and 1879

Parson's Tale

Prologue

Heere folweth the Prologe of the Persouns Tale.

By that° the Maunciple hadde his tale al ended,
The sonne fro the south lyne° was descended
So lowe that he nas nat° to my sighte
Degrees nyne and twenty as in highte.
Foure of the clokke it was tho°, as I gesse,
For ellevene foot, or litel moore or lesse,
My shadwe was at thilke° tyme, as there
Of swiche feet° as my lengthe parted° were
In sixe feet equal of proporcioun.
Therwith° the moones exaltacioun—
I meene Libra—alwey gan ascende
As we were entryng at a thropes ende°.
For which oure Hoost, as he was wont to gye°
As in this caas° oure joly compaignye,

1 By that, *by* (the time) *that* **2 south lyne,** *meridian* **3 nas nat,** *was not* **5 tho,** *then* **7 thilke,** *that* **8 swiche feet,** *such units,* **parted,** *divided* **10 Therwith,** *also* **12 thropes ende,** *edge of a village* **13 wont to gye,** *accustomed to direct* **14 caas,** *situation*

1 Hg writes "Maunciple" over an erasure; some late manuscripts have "Marchaunt" or "Yeman," depending on the order of the tales. **2 was,** Hg reads "is." **4–5 Degrees nyne and twenty . . . / Foure of the clokke,** these numbers vary in the manuscripts as a result of misreading the Roman numerals. But at 4 p.m. in mid-April, according to Nicholas of Lynn's *Kalendarium,* the sun is approximately 29 degrees below the meridian (the astronomical overhead circle that passes through the celestial poles). Chaucer's method of calculation here parallels his method in *MLT* 2.2–14, but the details are less precise than suggestive. Twenty-nine recalls *GP* 1.24, and 4 p.m. suggests the end of day and closure. **4 in,** Hg reads "of." **5 Foure,** El and Hg read "Ten." **tho,** Hg reads "so." **6 ellevene foot,** the angle of the sun at 4 p.m. casts shadows that are eleven units (feet) in length for every six units (feet) of the standing figure; see *MLT* 2.7–9. The narrator is not six feet tall, but the ratio of his height to his shadow is six to eleven. **10–11 moones exaltacioun . . . Libra,** an astronomical fiction or perhaps a reference to the impending rise of the moon. The exaltation (i.e., position of greatest influence) of the moon is in Taurus; the exaltation of Saturn is in Libra, the sign of the scales. Chaucer may have chosen Libra for the ways it suggests the Crucifixion (the shape of the scales), judgment (scales of justice), or freedom of choice (Lat. *liber*)—perhaps all of them. Libra is the sign of the fall equinox, as Aries (*GP* 1.8) is the sign of the spring equinox.

Seyde in this wise, "Lordynges everichoon°,
Now lakketh us no tales mo than oon.
Fulfilled is my sentence and my decree.
I trowe° that we han herd of ech degree°.
Almoost fulfild is al myn ordinaunce°.
I pray to God, so yeve° hym right good chaunce
That telleth this tale to us lustily°.
"Sire preest," quod he, "artow° a vicary,
Or arte a person? Sey sooth°, by thy fey°.
Be what thou be, ne breke thou nat oure pley°,
For every man save thou hath toold his tale.
Unbokele° and shewe us what is in thy male°,
For trewely me thynketh by thy cheere°
Thou sholdest knytte up° wel a greet mateere.
Telle us a fable anon, for cokkes bones!"
This Persoun answerde al atones°,
"Thou getest fable° noon ytoold for° me,
For Paul, that writeth unto Thymothee,
Repreveth hem° that weyven° soothfastnesse,
And tellen fables and swich wrecchednesse.
Why sholde I sowen draf° out of my fest°
Whan I may sowen whete°, if that me lest°?
For which I seye, if that yow list° to heere
Moralitee and vertuous mateere,
And thanne that° ye wol yeve° me audience,
I wol ful fayn° at Cristes reverence
Do yow plesaunce leefful°, as I kan.
But trusteth wel, I am a southren man°.
I kan nat geeste 'rum, ram, ruf,' by lettre,
Ne, God woot°, rym° holde I but litel bettre.
And therfore, if yow list°—I wol nat glose°—
I wol yow telle a myrie° tale in prose
To knytte up al this feeste and make an ende.
And Jhesu for his grace wit° me sende
To shewe yow the wey in this viage°
Of thilke parfit° glorious pilgrymage
That highte° Jerusalem celestial.
And if ye vouchesauf°, anon I shal
Bigynne upon my tale, for which I preye
Telle youre avys°; I kan no bettre seye.
"But nathelees, this meditacioun
I putte it ay° under correccioun
Of clerkes, for I am nat textueel°.
I take but the sentence°, trusteth weel.
Therfore I make protestacioun
That I wol stonde to correccioun."
Upon this word we han assented soone,
For as us seemed° it was for to doone°
To enden in som vertuous sentence,
And for to yeve hym space° and audience,
And bede° oure Hoost he sholde to hym seye
That alle we to telle his tale hym preye.
Oure Hoost hadde the wordes for us alle,
"Sire preest," quod he, "now faire yow bifalle°!
Telleth," quod he, "youre meditacioun.
But hasteth yow, the sonne wole adoun;
Beth fructuous° and that in litel space,
And to do wel God sende yow his grace.
Sey what yow list, and we wol gladly heere."
And with that word he seyde in this manere.

Explicit prohemium.

15 everichoon, *every one* **18 trowe,** *think,* **degree,** *social rank* **19 ordinaunce,** *plan* **20 yeve,** *give* **21 lustily,** *pleasingly* **22 artow,** *are you* **23 sooth,** *truth,* **fey,** *faith* **24 breke . . . oure pley,** *spoil our game* **26 Unbokele,** *unbuckle,* **male,** *purse* **27 cheere,** *disposition* **28 knytte up,** *conclude* **30 al atones,** *immediately* **31 fable,** *fiction,* **for,** *by* **33 Repreveth hem,** *blames them,* **weyven,** *turn from* **35 draf,** *chaff,* **fest,** *fist* **36 whete,** *wheat,* **me lest,** *it pleases me* **37 list,** *wish* **39 that,** *if,* **yeve,** *give* **40 ful fayn,** *very happily* **41 Do yow plesaunce leefful,** *give you legitimate pleasure* **42 southren man,** *from the south* **44 woot,** *knows,* **rym,** *rhyme* **45 list,** *wish,* **glose,** *lie* **46 myrie,** *merry* **48 wit,** *intelligence* **49 viage,** *journey* **50 thilke parfit,** *that perfect* **51 highte,** *is called* **52 vouchesauf,** *agree* **54 avys,** *opinion* **56 ay,** *always* **57 textueel,** *book learned* **58 sentence,** *meaning* **62 For as us seemed,** *because it seemed to us,* **for to doone,** *necessary* **64 space,** *time* **65 bede,** *asked* **68 faire yow bifalle,** *may good things happen to you* **71 fructuous,** *fruitful*

22–23 vicary . . . person, vicar or parson, i.e., a priest acting in the place of the holder of a benefice (Church appointment) or the benefice holder himself. **25 every man . . . hath toold his tale,** a sign of closure, although Chaucer evidently changed his mind about the number of tales each pilgrim would tell; see *GP* 1.792 and *SqT* 5.698. **29 cokkes bones,** cock's bones; euphemism for God's bones, a mild oath. See *ManP* 9.9. **32 Paul,** St. Paul rejects fiction and prefers truth in 1 Timothy 1.4, 4.7; 2 Timothy 4.4. **35–36 draf . . . whete,** see *NPT* 7.3443n. **40 ful,** omitted in El. **43 geeste 'rum, ram, ruf' by lettre,** "tell a story in alliterative verse," often associated with the north and west of England. **51 Jerusalem celestial,** heavenly Jerusalem; repeated at line 80 below. This allusion to Revelation 21.2 lends a clear allegorical dimension to the journey to Canterbury. **58 the,** omitted in El. **59 make,** El reads "make a." **62 us,** Hg reads "it." **73–74** These lines follow line 68 in El, Hg, and all other manuscripts, so that *ParsP* ends with the word "grace" (line 72), but most recent editors have moved the lines on the assumption that it makes better sense. **74a Explicit prohemium,** "Here ends the prologue."

Heere bigynneth the Persounes Tale.

Jer. 6. State super vias et videte et interrogate de viis antiquis, que sit via bona; et ambulate in ea, et invenietis refrigerium animabus vestris. &c.

Our sweete lord God of hevene, that wole° no man perisse° but wole that we comen alle to the knoweleche of hym and to the blissful lif that is perdurable°, / amonesteth° us by the prophete Jeremie and seith in thys wyse, / "Stondeth upon the weyes and seeth and axeth of° olde pathes (that is to seyn, of olde sentences°) which is the goode wey; / and walketh in that wey, and ye shal fynde refresshynge for youre soules, &c." / Manye been the weyes espirituels° that leden folk to oure lord Jesu Crist and to the regne of glorie. / Of whiche weyes, ther is a ful noble wey and a ful covenable°, which may nat fayle to no man ne to womman, that thurgh synne hath mysgoon° fro the righte wey of Jerusalem celestial. / And this wey is cleped° penitence, of which man sholde gladly herknen° and enquere with al his herte / to wyten° what is penitence, and whennes° it is cleped penitence, and in how manie maneres been the acciouns° or werkynges of penitence, / and how manie speces ther been of penitence, and whiche thynges apertenen° and bihouven° to penitence, and whiche thynges destourben° penitence. /

Seint Ambrose seith that penitence is the pleynynge° of man for the gilt that he hath doon, and namore to do anythyng for which hym oghte to pleyne. / And som doctour seith "Penitence is the waymentynge° of man that sorweth for his synne and pyneth hymself° for he hath mysdoon."/ Penitence, with certeyne circumstances, is verray° repentance of a man that halt° hymself in sorwe and oother peyne for his giltes. / And for he shal be verray penitent, he shal first biwaylen the synnes that he hath doon and stidefastly purposen in his herte to have shrift° of mouthe and to doon satisfaccioun°, / and never to doon thyng for which hym oghte moore to biwayle or to compleyne, and continue in goode werkes, or elles his repentance may nat availle°. / For as seith Seint Ysidre, "He is a japer° and a gabbere° and no verray repentant that eftsoone° dooth thyng for which hym oghte repente." / Wepynge and nat for to stynte° to synne may nat avaylle°. / But nathelees men shal hope that every tyme that man falleth, be it never so ofte, that he may arise thurgh penitence if he have grace—but certeinly it is greet doute. / For as seith Seint Gregorie, "Unnethe° ariseth he out of synne that is charged° with the charge of yvel usage°." / And therfore repentant folk that stynte° for to synne and forlete° synne er that synne forlete hem, Hooly Chirche holdeth hem siker° of hire savacioun. / And he that synneth and verraily repenteth hym in his laste, Hooly Chirche yet hopeth° his savacioun by the grete mercy of oure lord Jesu Crist, for his repentaunce—but taak the siker wey. /

And now sith° I have declared yow what thyng is penitence, now shul ye understonde that ther been three acciouns° of penitence. / The firste accioun of penitence is that a man be baptized after that he hath synned. / Seint Augustyn seith, "But he be penytent for his olde synful lyf, he may nat bigynne the newe clene lif." / For certes if he be baptized withouten penitence of his olde gilt, he receyveth the mark of baptesme but nat the grace ne the remission of his synnes, til he have repentance verray°. / Another defaute° is this, that men doon deedly synne after that they

75 wole, *wishes,* **perisse,** *perish,* **perdurable,** *everlasting* **76 amonesteth,** *advises* **77 axeth of,** *ask about,* **sentences,** *meanings* **79 weyes espirituels,** *spiritual ways* **80 ful covenable,** *very appropriate,* **mysgoon,** *strayed* **81 cleped,** *named,* **herknen,** *listen* **82 wyten,** *know,* **whennes,** *why,* **acciouns,** *activities* **83 apertenen,** *belong to,* **bihouven,** *are necessary,* **destourben,** *hinder* **84 pleynynge,** *lamenting* **85 waymentynge,** *lamenting,* **pyneth hymself,** *punishes himself* **86 verray,** *genuine,* **halt,** *holds* **87 shrift,** *confession,* **satisfaccioun,** *acts of reparation* **88 availle,** *be effective* **89 japer,** *jokester,* **gabbere,** *chatterer,* **eftsoone,** *again* **90 stynte,** *cease,* **avaylle,** *have effect* **92 Unnethe,** *scarcely,* **charged,** *burdened,* **usage,** *habit* **93 stynte,** *cease,* **forlete,** *abandon,* **siker,** *certain* **94 hopeth,** *hopes for* **95 sith,** *since,* **acciouns,** *activities* **98 verray,** *true* **99 defaute,** *fault*

74c–74e *Jer. 6 . . .* , from Jeremiah 6.16, translated in lines 77–78. The line numbers for this prose tale are conventional for convenient reference. The numbers indicate the end of the respective lines. **75 and to.** El omits "to." **80 ful convenable,** El omits "ful." **84 Ambrose,** Pseudo-Ambrose, *Sermon* 25.1. **85 som doctour,** some doctor of the Church, theologian; unidentified. **89 Ysidre,** Isidore of Seville, *Sententiae* 2.16.1. **92 Gregorie,** Gregory *Morals* 4.27.51–52. **93** compare the first half of this sentence with *PhyT* 6.286. **97 Augustyn,** Augustine *Sermon* 351.2. **98 mark of baptesme,** the spiritual sign or character received by the soul in baptism that enables the soul to receive the other sacraments.

han receyved baptesme. / The thridde defaute
is that men fallen in venial synnes after hir
baptesme fro day to day. / Therof seith Seint 100
Augustyn that penitence of goode and humble folk is the penitence of every day. /

The speces° of penitence been three. That oon
of hem is solempne°, another is commune°, and
the thridde is privee°. / Thilke penance that is
solempne is in two maneres, as to be put out of
Hooly Chirche in Lente for slaughtre of children,
and swich maner thyng. / Another thyng is whan a
man hath synned openly, of which synne the fame°
is openly spoken in the contree, and thanne Hooly
Chirche by juggement destreyneth° hym for to do
open° penaunce. / Commune penaunce is that
preestes enjoynen° men comunly° in certeyn caas,°
as for to goon, peraventure°, naked in pilgrimages, or barefoot. / Pryvee penaunce is thilke 105
that° men doon alday° for privee synnes, of
whiche they shryve° hem privinely and receyve privee penaunce. /

Now shaltow understande what is bihovely° and
necessarie to verray perfit penitence. And this
stant on° three thynges: / contricioun of herte,
confessioun of mouth, and satisfaccioun. / For
which seith Seint John Crisostom, "Penitence
destreyneth a man to accepte benygnely every
peyne that hym is enjoyned, with contricioun of
herte, and shrift of mouth, with satisfaccioun, and
in werkynge of alle maner humylitee." / And this
is fruytful penitence agayn three thynges in
whiche we wratthe° oure lord Jesu Crist, / this 110
is to seyn, by delit° in thynkynge, by rec-
chelesnesse° in spekynge, and by wikked synful
werkynge°. / And agayns thise wikkede giltes is
penitence, that may be likned unto a tree. /

The roote of this tree is contricioun, that hideth
hym° in the herte of hym that is verray repentaunt,
right as the roote of a tree hydeth hym in the
erthe. / Of the roote of contricion spryngeth a
stalke that bereth braunches and leves of confessioun, and fruyt of satisfaccioun. / For which Crist
seith in his gospel, "Dooth digne° fruyt of penitence." For by this fruyt may men knowe this tree,
and nat by the roote that is hyd in the herte of
man, ne by the braunches ne by the leves of
confessioun. / And therfore oure lord Jesu 115
Crist seith thus, "By the fruyt of hem ye shul
knowen hem." / Of this roote eek spryngeth°
a seed of grace, the which seed is mooder° of
sikernesse°, and this seed is egre° and hoot. / The
grace of this seed spryngeth of God thurgh remembrance of the day of doome and on the peynes
of helle. / Of this matere seith Salomon that in
the drede of God man forleteth° his synne. / The
heete of this seed is the love of God and the
desiryng of the joye perdurable°. / This heete 120
draweth the herte of a man to God and dooth
hym haten his synne. / For soothly, ther is nothing
that savoureth° so wel to a child as the milk of his
norice°, ne nothing is to him moore abhomynable
than thilke milk whan it is medled° with oother
mete°. / Right so the synful man that loveth his
synne, hym semeth that it is to him moost sweete
of anything. / But fro that tyme that he loveth
sadly° oure lord Jesu Crist, and desireth the lif
perdurable, ther nys to him nothing moore abhomynable. / For soothly, the lawe of God is the
love of God; for which David the prophete seith,
"I have loved thy lawe and hated wikkednesse and
hate." He that loveth God kepeth his lawe
and his word. / This tree saugh the prophete 125
Daniel in spirit upon the avysioun° of the
king Nabugodonosor, whan he conseiled hym
to do penitence. / Penaunce is the tree of lyf to
hem that it receyven, and he that holdeth hym in

102 speces, *species,* **solempne,** *serious,* **commune,** *communal,* **privee,** *private* **104 fame,** *reputation,* **destreyneth,** *compels,* **open,** *public* **105 enjoynen,** *command,* **comunly,** *in groups,* **caas,** *situations,* **peraventure,** *perhaps* **106 thilke that,** *that which,* **alday,** *regularly* **shryve,** *confess* **107 bihovely,** *required of,* **stant on,** *depends upon* **110 wratthe,** *make angry* **111 delit,** *illicit pleasures,* **recchelesnesse,** *carelessness,* **werkynge,** *action* **113 hym,** *itself* **115 Dooth digne,** *produce worthy* **117 spryngeth,** *grows,* **mooder,** *mother,* **sikernesse,** *certainty,* **egre,** *bitter* **119 forleteth,** *abandons* **120 perdurable,** *everlasting* **122 savoureth,** *tastes,* **norice,** *nurse,* **medled,** *mixed,* **mete,** *food* **124 sadly,** *firmly* **126 upon the avysioun,** *after the dream*

99–100 Sorrow for one's sins is active in conjunction with baptism in removing "olde gilt" (line 98), and against sins, either "deedly" (i.e., mortal) or "venial," committed after baptism. Mortal sin deprives the soul of its inherent holiness through the severity of the sin and the complete intention of the sinner; venial sin is less serious or not fully intentional. See also lines 358ff. below. **101 Augustyn,** *Epistles* 265.8. **103 as to be put out of Hooly Chirche in Lente . . . ,** heinous sins required particularly strict penance; in this case, the denial of any participation in the church (excommunication) during the season leading up to Easter. **105 communly,** omitted in El. **106 they shryve hem,** Hg reads "we shryve us." **107 verray perfit penitence,** genuine perfect penitence, i.e., the state or condition of the penitent person who is completely realigned with God. **109 John Crisostom,** *Sermon on Penance,* attributed to Chrysostom in manuscripts and early editions. **115 Crist seith,** spoken by John the Baptist in Matthew 3.8. **116 Jesu Crist seith,** Matthew 7.20. **117 of grace,** El reads "a grace." **119 Salomon,** Proverbs 16.6. **122 is to him,** omitted in El. **125 David,** Psalms 119.123. **126 Daniel,** Daniel 4.1–24.

verray penitence is blessed, after the sentence of Salomon. /

In this penitence or contricioun man shal understonde foure thinges, that is to seyn: what is contricioun; and whiche been the causes that moeven a man to contricioun; and how he sholde be contrit; and what contricioun availleth to° the soule. / Thanne is it thus, that contricioun is the verray sorwe that a man receyveth° in his herte for his synnes, with sad° purpos to shryve hym°, and to do penaunce and nevermoore to do synne. / And this sorwe shal been in this manere, as seith Seint Bernard, "It shal been hevy and grevous, and
ful sharpe and poynaunt in herte." / First, for 130
man hath agilt° his lord and hys creatour; and moore sharpe and poynaunt for he hath agilt hys fader celestial; / and yet moore sharpe and poynaunt for he hath wrathed° and agilt hym that boghte° hym, which with his precious blood hath delivered us fro the bondes of synne and fro the crueltee of the devel and fro the peynes of helle. /

The causes that oghte moeve a man to contricioun been six. First, a man shal remembre hym of his synnes. / But looke he that thilke° remembraunce ne be to hym no delit by no wey, but greet shame and sorwe for his gilt. For Job seith, "Synful men doon werkes worthy of confusion." / And therfore seith Ezechie, "I wol remembre me° alle the yeres of my lyf in bitternesse
of myn herte." / And God seith in the 135
Apocalips, "Remembreth yow fro whennes° that ye been falle°." For biforn that tyme that ye synned ye were the children of God and lymes° of the regne° of God, / but for youre synne ye been woxen thral° and foul, and membres of the feend, hate of aungels, sclaundre° of Hooly Chirche, and foode of the false serpent, perpetueel matere° of the fir of helle. / And yet moore foul and abhomynable, for ye trespassen° so ofte tyme as dooth the hound that retourneth to eten his spewyng°. / And yet be ye fouler for youre longe continuyng in synne and youre synful usage°, for which ye be roten in youre synne as a beest in his dong°. / Swiche manere of thoghtes maken a man to have shame of his synne and no delit, as God seith by
the prophete Ezechiel, / "Ye shal remembre 140
yow of youre weyes and they shuln° displese yow." Soothly, synnes been the weyes that leden folk to helle. /

The seconde cause that oghte make a man to have desdeyn of synne is this, that as seith Seint Peter, "Whoso that dooth synne is thral of synne," and synne put a man in greet thraldom°. / And therfore seith the prophete Ezechiel, "I wente sorweful in desdayn of myself." And certes, wel oghte a man have desdayn of synne, and withdrawe hym from that thraldom and vileynye. / And lo, what seith Seneca in this matere? He seith thus, "Though I wiste° that neither God ne man ne sholde nevere knowe it, yet wolde I have desdayn for to do synne." / And the same Seneca also seith, "I am born to gretter thynges than to be thral to my body, or
than for to maken of my body a thral." / Ne a 145
fouler thral may no man ne womman maken of his body than for to yeven° his body to synne. / Al° were it the fouleste cherl or the fouleste womman that lyveth, and leest of value, yet is he thanne moore foule and moore in servitute. / Evere fro the hyer degree that man falleth, the moore is he thral, and moore to God and to the world vile and abhomynable. / O goode God, wel oghte man have desdayn of synne sith° that thurgh synne ther° he was free, now is he maked bonde°. / And therfore seyth Seint Augustin, "If thou hast desdayn of thy servant, if he agilte° or synne, have thou thanne desdayn that thou thyself sholdest
do synne." / Take reward° of thy value, that thou 150
ne be to foul to thyself. / Allas, wel oghten they thanne have desdayn to been servauntz and thralles to synne, and soore been ashamed of hemself, / that God of his endelees goodnesse hath set hem in heigh estaat, or yeven hem wit, strengthe of body, heele°, beautee, prosperitee, / and boghte° hem fro the deeth with his herte blood, that they so

---

128 availleth to, *does for* **129 receyveth,** *accepts,* **sad,** *firm,* **shryve hym,** *confess himself* **131 agilt,** *sinned against* **132 wrathed,** *angered,* **boghte,** *redeemed* **134 looke he that thilke,** *he must beware that that* **135 wol remembre me,** *will remind myself* **136 whennes,** *where,* **been falle,** *are fallen,* **lymes,** *members,* **regne,** *kingdom* **137 been woxen thral,** *have become enslaved,* **sclaundre,** *scandal,* **matere,** *fuel* **138 trespassen,** *sin,* **spewyng,** *vomit* **139 synful usage,** *habitual sin,* **dong,** *dung* **141 shuln,** *shall* **142 thraldom,** *servitude* **144 wiste,** *know* **146 yeven,** *give* **147 Al,** *even though* **149 sith,** *since,* **ther,** *when,* **bonde,** *slave* **150 agilte,** *is guilty* **151 reward,** *regard* **153 heele,** *health* **154 boghte,** *redeemed*

127 Salomon, Proverbs 28.13. **130 Bernard,** Bernard of Clairvaux's associate, Nicholas of Clairvaux, *Sermon on the Feast of St. Andrew* 8. **134 Job,** not in Job. **confusion,** El and Hg read "confession," but other manuscripts agree with Pennaforte's Latin. **135 Ezechie,** Hezekiah, in Isaiah 38.15. **136 the Apocalips,** Revelation 2.5. **138 hound,** Proverbs 26.11. **140–41 Ezechiel,** Ezekiel 20.43. **142 Peter,** John 8.34; compare 2 Peter 2.19. **143 Ezechiel,** not in Ezekiel. **144–45 Seneca,** the first reference is not in Seneca; the second is Seneca's *Moral Epistles* 65.21. **148 vile and,** omitted in El. **150 Augustin,** *Sermons* 9.16.

unkyndely° agayns his gentilesse quiten° hym so vileynsly, to slaughtre of hir owene soules. / O goode
God, ye wommen that been of so greet beautee,
remembreth yow of the proverbe of Salomon,
that seith, / "Likneth a fair womman that is a 155
fool of hire body lyk to a ryng of gold that
were in the groyn° of a soughe°." / For right as a
soughe wroteth° in everich ordure°, so wroteth she
hire beautee in the stynkynge ordure of synne. /

The thridde cause that oghte moeve a man to
contricioun is drede of the Day of Doome and of
the horrible peynes of helle. / For as Seint Jerome
seith, "At every tyme that me remembreth of the
Day of Doome, I quake, / for whan I ete or drynke
or whatso that I do, evere semeth me that the
trompe° sowneth in myn ere: / 'Riseth up, ye 160
that been dede, and cometh to the juggement.'" / O goode God, muchel oghte a man to
drede swich a juggement, "ther as we shullen been
alle," as Seint Poul seith, "biforn the seete° of oure
lord Jesu Crist," / where as he shal make a general
congregacioun, where as no man may been absent. / For certes, there availleth noon essoyne° ne
excusacioun. / And nat oonly that oure defautes
shullen be jugged, but eek that alle oure
werkes shullen openly be knowe. / And as 165
seith Seint Bernard, "Ther ne shal no pledynge availle, ne sleighte°. We shullen yeven° rekeninge of everich ydel word." / Ther shul we han
a juge that may nat been deceyved ne corrupt. And
why? For certes, alle oure thoghtes been discovered as to hym, ne for preyere ne for meede° he
shal nat been corrupt. / And therfore seith Salomon, "The wratthe of God ne wol nat spare no
wight for preyere ne for yifte°." And therfore at
the Day of Doom ther nys noon hope to escape. /
Wherfore, as seith Seint Anselm, "Ful greet angwyssh shul the synful folk have at that tyme. /
Ther shal the stierne and wrothe° juge sitte
above, and under hym the horrible put° of helle
open to destroyen hym that noot biknowen° his
synnes, whiche synnes openly been shewed biforn
God and biforn every creature. / And in the 170
left syde, mo develes than herte may bithynke,
for to harye° and drawe the synful soules to the
peyne of helle. / And withinne the hertes of folk
shal be the bitynge conscience, and withoute
forth° shal be the world al brennynge°. / Whider
shal thanne the wrecched synful man flee to hiden
hym? Certes, he may nat hiden hym; he moste°
come forth and shewen hym." / For certes, as seith
Seint Jerome, "The erthe shal casten hym out of
hym, and the see also, and the eyr also, that shal
be ful of thonder clappes and lightnynges." /
Now soothly, whoso wel remembreth hym of thise
thynges, I gesse that his synne shal nat turne hym
in delit, but to greet sorwe for drede of the
peyne of helle. / And therfore seith Job to 175
God, "Suffre°, Lord, that I may a while biwaille
and wepe er I go withoute returning to the derke
lond covered with the derknesse of deeth, / to the
lond of mysese° and of derknesse where as is the
shadwe of deeth, where as ther is noon ordre or or-
dinaunce°, but grisly drede that evere shal laste."
/ Loo, heere may ye seen that Job preyde respit° a
while, to biwepe and waille his trespas°, for soothly
a day of respit is bettre than al the tresor of the
world. / And forasmuche as a man may acquiten
hymself biforn God by penitence in this world,
and nat by tresor, therfore sholde he preye to God
to yeve him respit a while, to biwepe and biwaillen
his trespas. / For certes, al the sorwe that a man
myghte make fro the bigynnyng of the world nys
but a litel thyng at regard of° the sorwe of
helle. / The cause why that Job clepeth° helle 180
"the lond of derknesse," / understondeth that
he clepeth it "londe" or erthe for it is stable and
nevere shal faille; "dirk," for he that is in helle
hath defaute of light material°. / For certes, the
derke light that shal come out of the fyr that evere
shal brenne shal turne hym al to peyne that is in
helle; for it sheweth hym to the horrible develes
that hym tormenten. / "Covered with the derknesse of deeth"—that is to seyn that he that is in

---

unkyndely, *unnaturally,* **quiten,** *repaid* **156 groyn,** *snout,* **soughe,** *sow* **157 wroteth,** *roots,* **everich ordure,** *every kind of filth* **160 trompe,** *trumpet* **162 seete,** *throne* **164 essoyne,** *excuse from appearing in court* **166 sleighte,** *deception,* **yeven,** *give* **167 meede,** *bribery* **168 yifte,** *gift* **170 wrothe,** *angry,* **put,** *pit,* **noot biknowen,** *will not acknowledge* **171 harye,** *pull* **172 withoute forth,** *outside,* **brennynge,** *burning* **173 moste,** *must* **176 Suffre,** *allow* **177 mysese,** *suffering,* **ordinaunce,** *organization* **178 preyde respit,** *requested relief,* **trespas,** *sin* **180 at regard of,** *compared with* **181 clepeth,** *calls* **182 hath defaute of light material,** *lacks physical light*

155–56 proverbe of Salomon . . . , Proverbs 11.22; cf. *WBP* 3. 784–85. **155 that seith,** El and Hg read "he seith." **159–61 Jerome,** *Letters* 66.10, and Pseudo-Jerome, *The Rule of Monarchy,* 30. **162 Poul,** Romans 14.10. **166 Bernard,** Pseudo-Bernard, *Sermon to the Prelates in Council* 5. **168 Salomon,** quotation not identified. **169–73 Anselm,** paraphrase of Anselm's *Meditation* 1: "On the Last Judgment" 78–79. **170 noot,** Hg reads "moot" (must). **174 Jerome,** quotation not identified. **176–77 Job,** Job 10.20–22.

helle shal have defaute of the sighte of God, for certes the sighte of God is the lyf perdurable°. / "The derknesse of deeth" been the synnes that the wrecched man hath doon whiche that destourben° hym to see the face of God, right as dooth a derk clowde bitwixe us and the sonne. / "Lond of misese°," by cause that ther been three maneres of defautes agayn° three thynges that folk of this world han in this present lyf, that is to seyn, honours, delices°, and richesses. / Agayns honour have they in helle shame and confusioun. / For wel ye woot° that men clepen° "honour" the reverence that man doth to man; but in helle is noon honour ne reverence. For certes, namoore reverence shal be doon there to a kyng than to a knave. / For which God seith by the prophete Jeremye, "Thilke folk that me despisen shul been in despit." / "Honour" is eek cleped° greet lordshipe; ther shal no man serven other but of° harm and torment. "Honour" is eek cleped greet dignitee and heighnesse, but in helle shul they been al fortroden of° develes. / And God seith, "The horrible develes shulle goon and comen upon the hevedes° of the dampned folk." And this is forasmuche as° the hyer° that they were in this present lyf the more shulle they been abated° and defouled in helle. / Agayns the richesses of this world shul they han mysese of poverte. And this poverte shal been in foure thinges: / in defaute of tresor, of which that David seith, "The riche folk that embraceden and oneden° al hire herte to tresor of this world shul slepe in the slepynge of deeth; and nothyng ne shal they fynden in hir handes of al hir tresor." / And mooreover the myseyse of helle shal been in defaute° of mete° and drinke. / For God seith thus by Moyses, "They shul been wasted with hunger, and the briddes° of helle shul devouren hem with the bitter deeth, and the galle of the dragon shal been hire drynke, and the venym of the dragon hire morsels." / And fortherover, hire myseyse shal been in defaute of clothyng, for they shulle be naked in body as of clothyng, save the fyr in which they brenne° and othere filthes. / And naked shul they been of soule as of alle manere vertues, which that is the clothyng of the soule. Where been thanne the gaye robes and the softe shetes and the smale° shertes? / Loo, what seith God of hem by the prophete Ysaye, that under hem shul been strawed° mothes, and hire covertures° shulle been of wormes of helle. / And fortherover, hir myseyse shal been in defaute of freendes, for he nys nat poure that hath goode freendes. But there is no frend, / for neither God ne no creature shal been freend to hem, and everich° of hem shall haten oother with deedly hate. / "The sones and the doghtren shullen rebellen agayns fader and mooder, and kynrede° agayns kynrede, and chiden° and despisen everich of hem oother," bothe day and nyght, as God seith by the prophete Michias. / And the lovynge children, that whilom° loveden so flesshly° everich oother, wolden everich of hem eten oother if they myghte. / For how sholden they love togidre in the peyne of helle, whan they hated ech of hem oother in the prosperitee of this lyf? / For truste wel, hir flesshly love was deedly hate, as seith the prophete David, "Whoso that loveth wikkednesse, he hateth his soule." / And whoso hateth his owene soule, certes he may love noon oother wight° in no manere. / And therfore in helle is no solas° ne no freendshipe, but evere the moore flesshly kynredes° that been in helle, the moore cursynges, the moore chidynges, and the moore deedly hate ther is among hem. / And fortherover, they shul have defaute of alle manere delices°. For certes, delices been after the appetites of the fyve wittes, as sighte, herynge, smellynge, savorynge, and touchynge. / But in helle hir sighte shal be ful of derknesse and of smoke, and therfore ful of teeres; and hir herynge ful of waymentynge and of gryntynge of teeth, as seith Jesu Crist; / hir nosethirles° shullen be ful of stynkynge stynk. And as seith Ysaye the prophete, "Hir savoryng shal be ful of bitter galle." / And touchynge of al hir body ycovered with "fir that nevere shal quenche and with wormes that nevere

184 perdurable, *everlasting* **185 destourben,** *prevent* **186 misese,** *suffering,* **defautes agayn,** *deprivations that parallel,* **delices,** *sensory pleasures* **188 woot,** *know,* **clepen,** *call* **190 cleped,** *called,* **other but of,** *another except in,* **fortroden of,** *trampled by* **191 hevedes,** *heads,* **forasmuche as,** *because,* **hyer,** *higher,* **abated,** *degraded* **193 oneden,** *united* **194 defaute,** *lack,* **mete,** *food* **195 briddes,** *birds* **196 brenne,** *burn* **197 smale,** *fine* **198 strawed,** *strewn,* **covertures,** *blankets* **200 everich,** *each* **201 kynrede,** *relative,* **chiden,** *accuse* **202 whilom,** *once,* **flesshly** *passionately* **205 wight,** *person* **206 solas,** *comfort,* **flesshly kynredes,** *worldly relatives* **207 delices,** *sensory pleasures* **209 nosethirles,** *nostrils*

189 Jeremye, 1 Samuel 2.30. **190 ther shal . . . dignitee,** omitted in El. **191 God seith,** Job 20.25. **193 David,** Psalms 75.6 (Vulgate). **195 Moyses,** Deuteronomy 32.24 and 33. **197 softe shetes,** El reads "smale shetes." **smale shertes,** El reads "softe shertes." **198 Ysaye,** Isaiah 14.11. **201 Michias,** Micah 7.6. **204 David,** Psalms 11.5 (Vulgate 10.6). **206 in helle,** omitted in El. **208 Jesu Crist,** Matthew 13.42, 25.30. **209–10 Ysaye,** Isaiah 24.9 and 66.24.

shul dyen," as God seith by the mouth of
Ysaye. / And for as muche as they shul nat 210
wene° that they may dyen for peyne, and by
hir deeth flee fro peyne, that may they understonden by the word of Job that seith, "Ther as
is the shadwe of deeth." / Certes° a shadwe hath
the liknesse of the thyng of which it is shadwe, but
shadwe is nat the same thyng of which it is shadwe.
/ Right so fareth the peyne of helle. It is lyk deeth
for the horrible anguissh, and why? For it peyneth
hem evere as though they sholde dye anon; but
certes they shal nat dye. / For as seith Seint Gregorie, "To wrecche caytyves° shal be deeth withoute
deeth, and ende withouten ende, and defaute
withoute failynge. / For hir deeth shal alwey lyven,
and hir ende shal everemo bigynne, and hir
defaute shal nat faille." / And therfore seith 215
Seint John the Evaungelist, "They shullen folwe deeth and they shul nat fynde hym, and they
shul desiren to dye and deeth shal flee fro hem." /
And eek Job seith that in helle is noon ordre of
rule. / And al be it so that God hath creat alle
thynges in right ordre, and nothing withouten
ordre, but alle thynges been ordeyned and nom-
bred, yet nathelees they that been dampned been
nothyng in the ordre, ne holden noon ordre, / for
the erthe ne shal bere hem no fruyt. / For as the
prophete David seith, "God shal destroie the fruyt
of the erthe as fro hem°," ne water ne shal yeve
hem no moisture, ne the eyr no refresshyng, ne
fyr no light. / For as seith Seint Basilie, "The 220
brennynge° of the fyr of this world shal God
yeven in helle to hem that been dampned, /
but the light and the cleernesse° shal be yeven
in hevene to his children," right° as the goode
man yeveth flessh° to his children and bones to
his houndes. / And for they shullen have noon
hope to escape, seith Seint Job atte laste that
ther shal horrour and grisly drede dwellen withouten ende. / Horrour is alwey drede of harm
that is to come, and this drede shal evere dwelle
in the hertes of hem that been dampned. And
therfore han they lorn° al hire hope for sevene
causes. / First, for God that is hir juge shal be withouten mercy to hem, and they may nat plese hym
ne noon of his halwes°; ne they ne may yeve
nothyng for hir raunsoun°; / ne they have no 225
voys to speke to hym; ne they may nat fle fro
peyne; ne they have no goodnesse in hem that
they mowe shewe° to delivere hem fro peyne. /
And therfore seith Salomon, "The wikked man
dyeth, and whan he is deed he shal have noon
hope to escape fro peyne." / Whoso thanne wolde
wel understande these peynes, and bithynke hym
weel° that he hath deserved thilke° peynes for his
synnes, certes, he sholde have moore talent° to sik-
en° and to wepe than for to syngen and to pleye. /
For as that seith Salomon, "Whoso that hadde the
science° to knowe the peynes° that been establissed
and ordeyned for synne, he wolde make sorwe."
/ "Thilke science," as seith Seint Augustyn,
"maketh a man to waymenten° in his herte." / 230

The fourthe point that oghte maken a man
to have contricioun is the sorweful remembraunce
of the good that he hath left to doon° heere in erthe,
and eek the good that he hath lorn°. / Soothly, the
goode werkes that he hath lost, outher° they been
the goode werkes that he hath wroght er he fel into
deedly synne, or elles the goode werkes that he
wroghte while he lay in synne. / Soothly, the goode
werkes that he dide biforn that he fil in synne
been al mortefied° and astoned° and dulled by
the ofte synnyng. / The othere goode werkes that
he wroghte whil he lay in deedly synne, thei been
outrely dede° as to the lyf perdurable° in hevene. /
Thanne thilke goode werkes that been mortefied
by ofte synnyng, whiche goode werkes he dide whil
he was in charitee°, ne mowe° nevere quyken°
agayn withouten verray penitence. / And 235
therof seith God by the mouth of Ezechiel
that if the rightful man returne agayn° from his
rightwisnesse° and werke wikkednesse, shal he

211 wene, *think* **212 Certes,** *certainly* **214 wrecche caytyves,** *wretched captives* **220 as fro hem,** *as far as they are concerned* **221 brennynge,** *burning* **222 cleernesse,** *brightness,* **right,** *just,* **flessh,** *meat* **224 lorn,** *lost* **225 halwes,** *saints,* **raunsoun,** *ransom* **226 mowe shewe,** *may use* **228 bithynke hym weel,** *consider well,* **thilke,** *those,* **talent,** *inclination,* **siken,** *sigh* **229 science,** *knowledge,* **peynes,** *punishments* **230 waymenten,** *lament* **231 left to doon,** *left undone,* **lorn,** *lost* **232 outher,** *either* **233 mortefied,** *destroyed,* **astoned,** *stunned* **234 outrely dede,** *utterly dead,* **perdurable,** *everlasting* **235 charitee,** *spiritual love,* **mowe,** *may,* **quyken,** *come to life* **236 returne agayn,** *turns away,* **rightwisnesse,** *goodness*

211 Job, 10.22. **214–15 Gregorie,** *Morals* 9.66.100. **216 John,** Revelation 9.6; the author of Revelation and the Gospel of John were thought to be the same. **217 Job,** see lines 176–77 above. **220 David,** Psalms 107.34–35 (Vulgate 106). **221 Basilie,** Basil, *Sermon on the Psalms* 28.7.6. **223 Job,** see lines 176–77 above. **227 Salomon,** Proverbs 11.7. **229 Salomon,** Ecclesiastes 1.17. **230 Augustyn,** quotation not identified. **232 lost,** El and Hg read "left." **236–37 Ezechiel,** Ezekiel 18.24. **238 Gregorie,** Gregory's *Sermon on Ezekiel* 1.11.21.

live? / Nay, for alle the goode werkes that he hath wroght ne shul nevere been in remembraunce, for he shal dyen in his synne. / And upon thilke chapitre° seith Seint Gregorie thus, that we shulle understonde this principally, / that whan we doon deedly synne, it is for noght thanne to rehercen° or drawen into memorie the goode werkes that we han wroght biforn. / For certes, in the werkynge of the deedly synne, ther is no trust to no good werk that we han doon biforn, that is for to seyn as for to have therby the lyf perdurable in hevene. / But nathelees, the goode werkes quyken° agayn, and comen agayn, and helpen, and availlen° to have the lyf perdurable in hevene whan we han contricioun. / But soothly, the goode werkes that men doon whil they been in deedly synne, for as muche as they were doon in deedly synne, they may nevere quyke agayn. / For certes, thyng that nevere hadde lyf may nevere quykene; and nathelees, al be it that they ne availle noght to han the lyf perdurable, yet availlen they to abregge° of the peyne of helle, or elles to geten temporal richesse, / or elles that God wole the rather° enlumyne and lightne the herte of the synful man to have repentance; / and eek they availlen for to usen° a man to doon goode werkes that the feend have the lasse power of his soule. / And thus the curteis lord Jesu Crist wole that no good werk be lost, for in somwhat it shal availle. / But for as muche as the goode werkes that men doon whil they been in good lyf been al mortified by synne folwynge, and eek sith° that alle the goode werkes that men doon whil they been in deedly synne been outrely° dede as for to have the lyf perdurable, / wel may that man that no good werke ne dooth° synge thilke newe Frenshe song, *Jay tout perdu mon temps et mon labour.* / For certes, synne bireveth° a man bothe goodnesse of nature and eek the goodnesse of grace. / For soothly, the grace of the Holy Goost fareth° lyk fyr that may nat been ydel; for fyr fayleth anoon° as it forleteth his° wirkynge, and right so grace fayleth anoon as it forleteth his werkynge. / Then leseth° the synful man the goodnesse of glorie, that oonly is bihight° to goode men that labouren and werken. / Wel may he be sory thanne that oweth al his lif to God as longe as he hath lyved, and eek as longe as he shal lyve, that no goodnesse ne hath to paye with his dette to God, to whom he oweth al his lyf. / For trust wel, "He shal yeven° acountes," as seith Seint Bernard, "of alle the goodes that han be yeven hym° in this present lyf, and how he hath hem despended°, / noght so muche that ther shal nat perisse° an heer of his heed, ne a moment of an houre ne shal nat perisse of his tyme, that he ne shal yeve of it a rekening." /

The fifthe thyng that oghte moeve a man to contricioun is remembrance of the passioun° that oure lord Jesu Crist suffred for oure synnes. / For as seith Seint Bernard, "Whil that I lyve I shal have remembrance of the travailles° that oure lord Crist suffred in prechyng, / his werynesse in travaillyng, his temptaciouns whan he fasted, his longe wakynges whan he preyde, his teeres whan that he weepe for pitee of good peple, / the wo and the shame and the filthe that men seyden to hym, of the foule spittyng that men spitte in his face, of the buffettes that men yaven° hym, of the foule mowes°, and of the repreves° that men to hym seyden, / of the nayles with whiche he was nayled to the croys, and of al the remenant of his passioun that he suffred for my synnes, and nothing for his gilt." / And ye shul understonde that in mannes synne is every manere of ordre or ordinaunce° turned upsodoun. / For it is sooth° that God and resoun and sensualitee° and the body of man been ordeyned that everich of thise foure thynges sholde have lordshipe over that oother. / As thus: God sholde have lordshipe over resoun, and resoun over sensualitee, and sensualitee over the body of man. / But soothly whan man synneth, al this ordre or ordinaunce is turned upsodoun. / And therfore thanne, for as muche as the resoun of man ne wol nat be subget ne obeisant° to God, that

---

238 thilke chapitre, *that passage* **239 rehercen,** *recall* **241 quyken,** *come to life,* **availlen,** *are effective* **243 abregge,** *shorten* **244 rather,** *sooner* **245 usen,** *accustom* **247 sith,** *since,* **outrely,** *utterly* **248 no good werke ne dooth,** *does no good works* **249 bireveth,** *robs* **250 fareth,** *goes,* **fayleth anoon,** *disappears as soon,* **forleteth his,** *ceases its* **251 leseth,** *loses,* **bihight,** *promised* **253 yeven,** *give,* **han be yeven hym,** *have been given him,* **hem despended,** *spent them* **254 perisse,** *perish* **255 passioun,** *sufferings* **256 travailles,** *troubles* **258 yaven,** *gave,* **mowes,** *scowls,* **repreves,** *accusations* **260 ordinaunce,** *plan* **261 sooth,** *true,* **sensualitee,** *sensory responses* **264 obeisant,** *obedient*

248 ***Jay tout perdu mon temps et mon labour,*** "I have completely lost my time and my work"; apparently the refrain from a popular French song, used also in Chaucer's "Fortune" (Short Poem 10, line 7). **253–54 Bernard,** quotation not identified. **256–59 Bernard,** *Sermon on Wednesday of Holy Week* (*Concerning the Lord's Passion*) 11. **261–63** These notions of hierarchy and inversion are commonplace.

is his lord by right, therfore leseth it the lordshipe that it sholde have over sensualitee. and eek over the body of man. / And why? For sensualitee rebelleth thanne agayns resoun, and by that wey leseth resoun the lordshipe over sensualitee and over the body. / For right° as resoun is rebel to God, right so is bothe sensualitee rebel to resoun and the body also. / And certes, this disordinaunce° and this rebellioun oure lord Jesu Crist aboghte° upon his precious body ful deere, and herkneth in which wise. / For as muche thanne as resoun is rebel to God, therfore is man worthy to have sorwe and to be deed. / This suffred oure lord Jesu Crist for man, after that he hadde be bitraysed° of his disciple, and distreyned° and bounde, so that his blood brast out at every nayle of his handes, as seith Seint Augustyn. / And forther over, for as muchel as resoun of man ne wol nat daunte° sensualitee whan it may, therfore is man worthy to have shame. And this suffred oure lord Jesu Crist for man whan they spetten in his visage. / And forther over, for as muchel thanne as the caytyf° body of man is rebel bothe to resoun and to sensualitee, therfore is it worthy the deeth. / And this suffred oure lord Jesu Crist for man upon the croys, where as ther was no part of his body free withouten greet peyne and bitter passioun. / And al this suffred Jesu Crist that nevere forfeted°. "To muchel am I peyned for the thynges that I nevere deserved, and to muche defouled for shendshipe° that man is worthy to have." / And therfore may the synful man wel seye, as seith Seint Bernard, "Acursed be the bitternesse of my synne, for which ther moste be suffred so muchel bitternesse." / For certes, after the diverse disordinaunces of oure wikkednesses was the passioun of Jesu Crist ordeyned in diverse thynges, / as thus. Certes, synful mannes soule is bitraysed of° the devel by coveitise of temporeel prosperitee, and scorned by deceite whan he cheseth flesshly delices°; and yet is it tormented by inpacience of° adversitee, and bispet° by servage° and subjeccioun of synne; and atte laste it is slayn fynally. / For this disordinaunce of synful man was Jesu Crist bitraysed, and after that was he bounde that cam for to unbynden us of synne and peyne. / Thanne was he byscorned, that oonly sholde han been honoured in alle thynges and of alle thynges. / Thanne was his visage, that oghte be desired to be seyn of al mankynde, in which visage aungels desiren to looke, vileynsly bispet. / Thanne was he scourged° that nothing hadde agilt°. And finally thanne was he crucified and slayn. / Thanne was acompliced° the word of Ysaye that seith that he was wounded for oure mysdedes and defouled for oure felonies. / Now sith that° Jesu Crist took upon hymself the peyne of alle oure wikkednesses, muchel oghte synful man wepen and biwayle that for his synnes Goddes sone of hevene sholde al this peyne endure. /

The sixte thyng that oghte moeve a man to contricioun is the hope of three thynges: that is to seyn, foryifnesse of synne, and the yifte of grace wel for to do, and the glorie of hevene with which God shal guerdone° a man for his goode dedes. / And for as muche as Jesu Crist yeveth us thise yiftes of his largesse° and of his sovereyn bountee, therfore is he cleped° *Iesus Nazarenus rex Iudeorum.* / *Iesus* is to seyn "saveour" or "salvacioun," on whom men shul hope to have foryifnesse of synnes, which that is proprely salvacioun of synnes. / And therfore seyde the aungel to Joseph, "Thou shalt clepen° his name Jesus, that shal saven his peple of hir synnes." / And heerof seith Seint Peter, "Ther is noon other name under hevene that is yeve° to any man by which a man may be saved, but only Jesus." / *Nazarenus* is as muche for to seye as "florisshynge," in which a man shal hope that he that yeveth hym remission of synnes shal yeve hym eek grace wel for to do. For in the flour is hope of fruit in tyme comynge, and in foryifnesse of synnes hope of grace wel for to do. / "I was atte dore of thyn herte," seith Jesus, "and

266 right, *just* **267 disordinaunce,** *disorder,* **aboghte,** *redeemed* **269 be bitraysed,** *been betrayed,* **distreyned,** *arrested* **270 daunte,** *subdue* **271 caytyf,** *wretched* **273 forfeted,** *sinned,* **shendshipe,** *disgrace* **276 bitraysed of,** *betrayed by,* **cheseth flesshly delices,** *chooses bodily pleasures,* **inpacience of,** *impatience with,* **bispet,** *spit upon,* **servage,** *service* **280 scourged,** *whipped,* **nothing hadde agilt,** *sinned not at all* **281 acompliced,** *fulfilled* **282 sith that,** *since* **283 guerdone,** *reward* **284 largesse,** *generosity,* **cleped,** *called* **287 yeve,** *given*

269 be bitraysed of his disciple, been betrayed by his disciple, i.e., Judas; see, e.g., Matthew 26.47–50. **Augustyn,** not identified. **270 spetten in his visage,** spit in his face; see, e.g., Matthew 27.30. **273** Quotation not identified. **274 Bernard,** identified by Jill Mann as from Bernard's second sermon on Palm Sunday. **275 disordinaunces,** the El reads "disconcordaunces"; Hg, "discordaunces." But see lines 267 and 277. The sentence means that through divine order the passion or sufferings of Jesus paralleled (and compensated for) the process of human sin. **276 bispet,** El reads "dispeir." **281 Ysaye,** Isaiah 53.5. **284** ***Iesus Nazarenus rex Iudeorum,*** Jesus of Nazareth, king of the Jews. **286 aungel,** Matthew 1.20–21. **289–90 Jesus,** Revelation 3.20.

cleped for to entre. He that openeth to me shal have foryifnesse of synne. / I wol entre into hym by my grace and soupe° with hym" by the goode werkes that he shal doon, whiche werkes been the foode of God, "and he shal soupe with me" by the grete joye that I shal yeven hym. / Thus shal man hope for° his werkes of penaunce that God shall yeven hym his regne°, as he bihooteth° hym in the gospel. /

Now shal a man understonde in which manere shal been his contricioun. I seye that it shal been universal and total, this is to seyn a man shal be verray° repentant for alle his synnes that he hath doon in delit of his thoght, for delit is ful perilous. / For ther been two manere of consentynges. That oon of hem is cleped consentynge of affeccioun°, whan a man is moeved to do synne and deliteth hym longe for to thynke on that synne, / and his reson aperceyveth° it wel that it is synne agayns the lawe of God, and yet his resoun refreyneth° nat his foul delit or talent°, though he se wel apertly° that it is agayns the reverence of God. Although his resoun ne consente noght to doon that synne in dede, / yet seyn somme doctours° that swich delit that dwelleth longe it is ful perilous al be it nevere so lite. / And also a man sholde sorwe, namely°, for al that evere he hath desired agayn the lawe of God with perfit consentynge of his resoun, for therof is no doute that it is deedly synne in consentynge. / For certes, ther is no deedly synne that it nas first in mannes thought and after that in his delit, and so forth into consentynge and into dede. / Wherfore I seye that many men ne repenten hem nevere of swiche thoghtes and delites, ne nevere shryven hem° of it, but oonly of the dede of grete synnes outward. / Wherfore I seye that swiche wikked delites and wikked thoghtes been subtile bigileres° of hem that shullen be dampned. / Mooreover man oghte to sorwe for his wikkede wordes as wel as for his wikkede dedes, for certes the repentaunce of a synguler synne and nat repente of alle his othere synnes, or elles repenten him of alle his othere synnes and nat of a synguler synne, may nat availle°. / For certes, God Almighty is al good, and therfore he foryeveth al or elles right noght. / And heerof seith Seint Augustyn, "I woot° certeinly / that God is enemy to everich synnere." And how thanne, he that observeth o° synne, shal he have foryifnesse of the remenaunt of his othere synnes? Nay. / And fortherover, contricioun sholde be wonder sorweful and angwissous°. And therfore yeveth hym God pleynly° his mercy. And therfore whan my soule was angwissous withinne me, I hadde remembrance of God that my preyere myghte come to hym. / Fortherover, contricioun moste be continueel, and that man have stedefast purpos to shriven hym, and for to amenden hym of his lyf. / For soothly, whil contricioun lasteth man may evere have hope of foryifnesse. And of this comth hate of synne that destroyeth synne bothe in himself and eek in oother folk, at his power. / For which seith David, "Ye that loven God hateth wikkednesse." For trusteth wel, to love God is for to love that he loveth and hate that he hateth. /

The laste thyng that man shal understonde in contricioun is this: wherof avayleth contricioun°? I seye that somtyme contricioun delivereth a man fro synne, / of which that David seith, "I seye," quod David, that is to seyn, "I purposed fermely° to shryve me and thow, Lord, relessedest my synne." / And right so° as contricion availleth noght withouten sad° purpos of shrifte°, if man have oportunitee, right so litel worth is shrifte° or satisfaccioun withouten contricioun. / And mooreover, contricion destroyeth the prisoun of helle; and maketh wayk° and fieble alle the strengthes of the develes; and restoreth the yiftes of the Hooly Goost and of alle goode vertues. / And it clenseth the soule of synne, and delivereth the soule fro the peyne of helle, and fro the compaignye of the devel, and fro the servage of synne, and restoreth it to alle goodes espirituels°, and to the compaignye and communyoun of Hooly Chirche. / And fortherover, it maketh hym that whilom° was sone of ire to be sone of grace. And

290 soupe, *dine* **291 for,** *because of,* **regne,** *kingdom,* **bihooteth,** *promises* **292 verray,** *truly* **293 affeccioun,** *emotion* **294 aperceyveth,** *perceives,* **refreyneth,** *restrains,* **talent,** *inclination,* **se wel apertly,** *sees clearly* **295 doctours,** *theologians* **296 namely,** *especially* **298 shryven hem,** *confess themselves* **299 bigileres,** *deceivers* **300 may nat availle,** *is not effective* **302 woot,** *know* **303 observeth o,** *acknowledges one* **304 angwissous,** *anguished,* **pleynly,** *fully,* **308 wherof avayleth contricioun,** *in what ways is contrition effective* **309 purposed fermely,** *intended firmly* **310 right so,** *just,* **sad,** *firm,* **shrifte,** *confession* **311 wayk,** *weak* **312 espirituels,** *spiritual* **313 whilom,** *formerly*

291 in the gospel, Luke 15.7. **302–03 Augustyn,** Pseudo-Augustine, *De Vera et Falsa Poenitentia* (*Concerning True and False Penance*) 1.9.24. **302 I woot certeinly,** omitted in El. **304** Jonah 2.8. **307 David,** Psalms 97.10 (Vulgate 96). **309 David,** Psalms 32.5 (Vulgate 31). **313 sone of ire,** son of anger; see Ephesians 2.3.

alle thise thynges been preved by hooly writ. / And
therfore, he that wolde sette his entente to thise
thynges, he were ful wys, for soothly he ne sholde
nat thanne in al his lyf have corage° to synne, but
yeven his body and al his herte to the service of
Jesu Crist, and therof doon hym hommage°. / For
soothly, oure sweete lord Jesu Crist hath spared us
so debonairly° in our folies that if he ne hadde
pitee of mannes soule, a sory song we mighten
alle singe. / 315

Explicit prima pars Penitentie et sequitur secunda pars eiusdem.

The seconde partie° of penitence is confessioun, that is signe° of contricioun. / Now shul ye
understonde what is confessioun, and wheither it
oghte nedes be doon or noon°, and whiche thynges been covenable° to verray° confessioun. /

First shaltow° understonde that confessioun is
verray shewinge° of synnes to the preest. / This is
to seyn "verray" for he moste confessen hym of alle
the condiciouns° that bilongen to his synne, as fer-
forth° as he kan. / Al moot° be seyd, and nothyng
excused ne hyd ne forwrapped°; and noght
avaunte° thee of thy goode werkes. / And 320
fortherover, it is necessarie to understonde
whennes that° synnes spryngen°, and how they
encreessen, and whiche they been. /

Of the spryngynge of synnes seith Seint Paul in
this wise, that right° as by a man synne entred first
into this world, and thurgh that synne deeth, right
so thilke deeth entred into alle men that synneden.
/ And this man was Adam, by whom synne entred into this world whan he brak the comaundementz of God. / And therfore he that first was so
mighty that he sholde nat have dyed bicam swich
oon that he moste nedes dye, wheither he wolde
or noon°, and all his progenye in this world that
in thilke man synneden. / Looke that in th'estaat
of innocence, whan Adam and Eve naked weren
in paradys, and nothing ne hadden shame
of hir nakednesse, / how that the serpent 325
that was moost wily of alle othere beestes that
God hadde maked seyde to the womman, "Why
comaunded God to yow, ye sholde nat eten of
every tree in paradys?" / The womman answerde,
"Of the fruyt," quod she, "of the trees in paradys
we feden us, but soothly of the fruyt of the tree
that is in the myddel of paradys God forbad us for
to ete, and nat touchen it, lest peraventure° we
should dyen." / The serpent seyde to the womman, "Nay, nay, ye shul nat dyen of deeth, for
sothe! God woot° that what day that ye eten therof,
youre eyen shul opene and ye shul been as goddes knowynge good and harm°." / The womman
thanne saugh that the tree was good to feedyng,
and fair to the eyen, and delitable to the sighte.
She took of the fruyt of the tree and eet it, and
yaf to hire housbonde and he eet, and anoon the
eyen of hem bothe openeden: / And whan that
they knewe that they were naked, they sowed of
figeleves a maner° of breches° to hiden hire
membres°. / There may ye seen that deedly 330
synne hath first suggestion of the feend, as
sheweth heere by the naddre°; and afterward, the
delit of the flessh, as sheweth heere by Eve; and
after that, the consentynge of resoun, as sheweth
heere by Adam. / For trust wel, though so were°
that the feend tempted Eve, that is to seyn the
flessh, and the flessh hadde delit in the beautee of
the fruyt defended°, yet certes, til that resoun, that
is to seyn Adam, consented to the etynge of the
fruyt, yet stood he in th'estaat of innocence. / Of
thilke° Adam tooke we° thilke synne original; for
of hym flesshly° descended be we alle, and engen-
dred° of vile and corrupt matiere. / And whan the
soule is put in oure body, right anon is contract°
original synne, and that that was erst° but oonly
peyne° of concupiscence° is afterward bothe peyne

---

314 corage, *desire,* **doon hym hommage,** *acknowledge his lordship* **315 debonairly,** *graciously* **316 partie,** *part,* **signe,** *evidence* **317 noon,** *not,* **convenable,** *appropriate,* **verray,** *genuine* **318 shaltow,** *you shall,* **shewinge,** *revealing* **319 condiciouns,** *circumstances,* **ferforth,** *far* **320 moot,** *must,* **forwrapped,** *disguised,* **avaunte,** *boast* **321 whennes that,** *from what,* **spryngen,** *originate* **322 right,** *just* **324 wolde or noon,** *wished to or not* **327 lest peraventure,** *for fear perhaps* **328 woot,** *knows,* **harm,** *evil* **330 maner,** *kind,* **breches,** *garment,* **membres,** *genitals* **331 naddre,** *serpent* **332 though so were,** *even though it was,* **fruyt defended,** *forbidden fruit* **333 thilke,** *that,* **tooke we,** *we received,* **flesshly,** *physically,* **engendred,** *born* **334 right anon is contract,** *immediately is incurred,* **that that was erst,** *that which was first,* **peyne,** *suffering,* **concupiscence,** *worldly desire*

315a Explicit prima pars Penitentie et sequitur secunda pars eiusdem, "Here ends the first part of Penance, and here follows the second part of the same." **320 thee of thy,** Hg reads "hym of hise." **322 Paul,** Romans 5.12. **325–30 Adam and Eve . . . ,** Genesis 3.1–7. **331–32** A common allegorization of the fall. **333 synne original,** in Church doctrine, original sin is a state of sinfulness rather than an act of sinning (actual sin, line 357).

and synne. / And therfore be we alle born sones
of wratthe and of dampnacioun perdurable°, if it
nere° baptesme that we receyven which bynymeth°
us the culpe°. But for sothe, the peyne dwelleth with
us as to temptacioun, which peyne highte° concupiscence. / And this concupiscence whan 335
it is wrongfully disposed or ordeyned in man, it
maketh hym coveite, by coveitise of flessh, flesshly
synne by sighte of his eyen as to erthely thynges,
and coveitise of hynesse by pride of herte. /

Now as for to speken of the firste coveitise°, that
is concupiscence after the lawe of oure membres°
that weren lawefulliche ymaked and by rightful
juggement of God, / I seye for as muche as man is
nat obeisaunt to God that is his lord, therfore is the
flessh to hym disobeisaunt thurgh concupiscence,
which yet is cleped norissynge° of synne and occasioun of synne. / Therfore, al the while that a
man hath in hym the peyne of concupiscence, it
is impossible but he be tempted somtime and moeved in his flessh to synne. / And this thyng may
nat faille as longe as he lyveth. It may wel wexe fie-
ble° and faille by vertu of baptesme and by the
grace of God thurgh penitence, / but fully 340
ne shal it nevere quenche that he ne shal
somtyme be moeved in hymself, but if he were al
refreyded° by siknesse, or by malefice° of sorcerie, or colde drynkes. / For lo, what seith Seint
Paul, "The flessh coveiteth agayn the spirit, and
the spirit agayn° the flessh; they been so contrarie
and so stryven that a man may nat alwey doon as
he wolde." / The same Seint Paul, after his grete
penaunce in water and in lond (in water by night
and by day in greet peril and in greet peyne, in lond
in famyne, in thurst, in coold and cloothlees, and
ones stoned almoost to the deeth), / yet seyde he,
"Allas, I, caytyf° man, who shal delivere me fro the
prisoun of my caytyf body?" / And Seint Jerome,
whan he longe tyme hadde woned° in desert where
as he hadde no compaignye but of wilde beestes,
where as he ne hadde no mete° but herbes and
water to his drynke, ne no bed but the naked erthe,
for which his flessh was blak as an Ethiopeen
for heete and ny° destroyed for coold, / yet 345
seyde he that the brennynge° of lecherie boyled
in al his body. / Wherfore I woot wel sykerly° that
they been deceyved that seyn that they ne be nat
tempted in hir body. / Witnesse on Seint Jame the
apostel that seith that every wight° is tempted in his
owene concupiscence, that is to seyn that everich
of us hath matere and occasioun to be tempted of
the norissynge° of synne that is in his body. / And
therfore seith Seint John the Evaungelist, "If that
we seyn that we beth withoute synne, we deceyve
us-selve and trouthe is nat in us." /

Now shal ye understonde in what manere that
synne wexeth or encreesseth in man. The firste
thyng is thilke norissynge of synne of which I
spak biforn, thilke flesshly concupiscence. / 350
And after that comth the subjeccioun° of
the devel, this is to seyn the develes bely°, with
which he bloweth in man the fir of flesshly concupiscence. / And after that, a man bithynketh
hym° wheither he wol doon or no thilke thing to
which he is tempted. / And thanne, if that a man
withstonde and weyve° the first entisynge of his
flessh and of the feend, thanne is it no synne. And
if it so be that he do nat so, thanne feeleth he
anoon a flambe° of delit. / And thanne is it good
to bewar and kepen hym° wel, or elles he wol
falle anon into consentynge of synne; and thanne
wol he do it if he may have tyme and place. /
And of this matere seith Moyses by° the devel in
this manere, "The feend seith. I wole chace and
pursue the man by wikked suggestioun, and I
wole hente° him by moevynge or stirynge of
synne. I wol departe° my prise or my praye° by
deliberacioun, and my lust° shal been accompliced in delit°. I wol drawe my swerd in consentynge." / For certes, right as a swerd departeth° 355
a thyng in two peces, right so consentynge
departeth God fro man. "And thanne wol I sleen
hym with myn hand in dede° of synne," thus
seith the feend. / For certes, thanne is a man

---

335 perdurable, *everlasting,* **if it nere,** *if it weren't for,* **bynymeth,** *removes from,* **culpe,** *guilt,* **highte,** *is called* **337 firste coveitise,** *the first kind of covetousness,* **after the lawe of oure membres,** *resulting from sexual drive* **338 cleped norissynge,** *called nourishment* **340 wexe fieble,** *grow weak* **341 refreyded,** *cooled,* **malefice,** *evil work* **342 agayn,** *against* **344 caytyf,** *captive* **345 woned,** *lived,* **mete,** *food,* **ny,** *nearly* **346 brennynge,** *burning* **347 woot wel sikerly,** *know certainly* **348 wight,** *person,* **norissynge,** *nourishment* **351 subjeccioun,** *suggestion,* **bely,** *bellows* **352 bithynketh hym,** *considers* **353 weyve,** *deflect,* **flambe,** *flame* **354 kepen hym,** *guard himself* **355 by,** *about,* **hente,** *seize,* **departe,** *single out,* **praye,** *prey,* **lust,** *desire,* **in delit,** *through pleasure* **356 departeth,** *divides,* **in dede,** *through the deed*

335 sones of wratthe, see 313n above. **concupiscence,** the love of or desire for any improper object; see lines 366–67. **336 And this concupisence,** omitted in El. **coveitise of hynesse,** desire for worldly status; see 1 John 2.16. **342 Paul,** Galatians 5.17. **343–44 Paul,** 2 Corinthians 11.25–27; Romans 7.24. **345–46 Jerome,** *Letters,* To Eustochium 22.7. **348 Jame,** James 1.14. **349 John,** 1 John 1.8. **355–56 Moyses,** Exodus 15.9.

al deed° in soule. And thus is synne accompliced by temptacioun, by delit, and by consentynge; and thanne is the synne cleped° actueel. /

For sothe, synne is in two maneres: outher° it is venial or deedly sinne. Soothly, whan man loveth any creature moore than Jesu Crist oure creatour, thanne is it deedly sinne. And venial synne is it if man love Jesu Crist lasse than hym oghte. / For sothe, the dede of this venial synne is ful perilous, for it amenuseth° the love that men sholde han to God moore and moore. / And therfore, if a man charge° hymself with manye swiche venial synnes, certes, but if so be that he somtyme descharge hym of hem by shrifte°, they mowe° ful lightly° amenuse in hym al the love that he hath to Jesu Crist. / And in this wise skippeth° venial into deedly synne. For certes, the moore that a man chargeth his soule with venial synnes, the moore is he enclyned to fallen into deedly synne. / And therfore, lat us nat be necligent to deschargen us of venial synnes. For the proverbe seith that manye smale maken a greet. / And herkne° this ensample. A greet wawe° of the see comth somtyme with so greet a violence that it drencheth° the shipe. And the same harm dooth somtyme the smale dropes of water that entren thurgh a litel crevace into the thurrok°, and into the botme of the shipe, if men be so necligent that they ne descharge hem nat bytyme°. / And therfore, althogh ther be a difference bitwixe thise two causes of drenchynge, algates° the shipe is dreynt°. / Right so fareth it somtyme of deedly synne, and of anoyouse° veniale synnes, whan they multiplie in a man so greetly that thilke worldly thynges that he loveth, thurgh whiche he synneth venyally, is as greet in his herte as the love of God, or moore. / And therfore, the love of everything that is nat biset in God ne doon principally for Goddes sake, although that a man love it lasse than God, yet is it venial synne. / And deedly synne whan the love of anything weyeth° in the herte of man as muchel as the love of God, or moore. / "Deedly synne," as seith Seint Augustyn, "is whan a man turneth his herte fro God, which that is verray sovereyn bountee° that may nat chaunge, and yeveth° his herte to thyng that may chaunge and flitte°." / And certes, that is everything save God of hevene. For sooth is that if a man yeve his love the which that he oweth al to God with al his herte unto a creature, certes, as muche as he yeveth of his love to thilke creature, so muche he bireveth° fro God; / and therfore doth he synne. For he that is dettour to God ne yeldeth nat to God al his dette, that is to seyn al the love of his herte. /

Now sith man understondeth generally which is venial synne, thanne is it covenable° to tellen specially of synnes whiche that many a man peraventure° ne demeth hem° nat synnes, and ne shryveth hym nat of the same thynges, and yet nathelees they been synnes / soothly, as thise clerkes writen. This is to seyn that at every tyme that a man eteth or drynketh moore than suffyseth to the sustenaunce of his body, in certein he dooth synne. / And eek, whan he speketh moore than nedeth, it is synne. Eke whan he herkneth nat benignely° the compleint of the poure. / Eke whan he is in heele° of body and wol nat faste whan hym oghte faste, withouten cause resonable. Eke whan he slepeth moore than nedeth, or whan he comth by thilke enchesoun° to late to chirche, or to othere werkes of charite. / Eke whan he useth° his wyf withouten sovereyn° desir of engendrure° to the honour of God, or for the entente to yelde to his wyf the dette of his body. / Eke whan he wol nat visite the sike and the prisoner, if he may. Eke if he love wyf or child or oother worldly thyng moore than resoun requireth. Eke if he flatere or blandishe° moore than hym oghte for any necessitee. / Eke if he amenuse° or withdrawe the almesse of° the poure. Eke if he apparailleth his mete° moore deliciously than nede is or ete to hastily by likerousnesse°. / Eke if he tale vanytees° at chirche or at Goddes service, or that he be a talkere of ydel wordes of folye or of vileynye, for he

---

357 al deed, *completely dead,* **cleped,** *called* **358 outher,** *either* **359 amenuseth,** *decreases* **360 charge,** *burdens,* **shrifte,** *confession,* **mowe,** *may,* **lightly,** *easily* **361 skippeth,** *passes quickly* **363 herkne,** *pay attention to,* **wawe,** *wave,* **drencheth,** *drowns,* **thurrok,** *hold,* **bytyme,** *in time* **364 algates,** *nevertheless,* **dreynt,** *drowned* **365 anoyouse,** *annoying* **367 weyeth,** *weighs* **368 sovereyn bountee,** *supreme goodness,* **yeveth,** *gives,* **flitte,** *pass quickly* **369 bireveth,** *steals* **371 covenable,** *appropriate,* **peraventure,** *perhaps,* **demeth hem,** *judges them* **373 benignely,** *kindly* **374 heele,** *health,* **thilke enchesoun,** *that reason* **375 useth,** *has sex with,* **sovereyn,** *ultimate,* **engendrure,** *begetting children* **376 blandishe,** *praise* **377 amenuse,** *reduce,* **almesse of,** *charity for,* **apparailleth his mete,** *prepare his food,* **likerousnesse,** *gluttony* **378 tale vanytees,** *speak foolishness*

358 venial . . . deedly, see 99–100n above. **362 the proverbe,** a common proverb. **367 weyeth,** El reads "wexeth." **368 Augustyn,** *De libero arbitrio* (*On Free Will*) 1.16, but widely quoted in various forms. **371 hym,** El reads "hem." **374 hym oghte,** Hg reads "oother folk." **375 dette of his body,** marital obligation to sexual intercourse, 1 Corinthians 7.3; see *WBP* 3.130.

shal yelden acountes of it at the day of doome. / Eke whan he biheteth° or assureth to do thynges that he may nat perfourne. Eke whan that he by lightnesse° or folie mysseyeth° or scorneth his neighebore. / Eke whan he hath any wikked suspecioun of thyng ther he ne woot° of it no soothfastnesse°. / Thise thynges and mo withoute nombre been synnes, as seith Seint Augustyn. /

Now shal men understonde, that al be it so that noon erthely man may eschue° alle venial synnes, yet may he restreyne hym by the brennynge° love that he hath to oure lord Jesu Crist, and by preyeres and confessioun and othere goode werkes, so that it shal but litel greve°. / For as seith Seint Augustyn, "If a man love God in swich manere that al that evere he dooth is in the love of God, and for the love of God verraily°, for he brenneth in the love of God, / looke° how muche that a drope of water that falleth in a fourneys° ful of fyr anoyeth or greveth, so muche anoyeth a venial synne unto a man that is parfit in the love of Jesu Crist." / Men may also refreyne° venial synne by receyvynge worthily of the precious body of Jesu Crist, / by receyvyng eek of hooly water, by almesdede°, by general confessioun of *Confiteor* at masse and at complyn, and by blessynge of bisshopes and of preestes and oothere goode werkes. /

Sequitur de Septem Peccatis Mortalibus et eorum dependenciis circumstanciis et speciebus.

De Superbia.

Now is it bihovely° thyng to telle whiche been the Deedly Synnes, this is to seyn chieftaynes of synnes. Alle they renne in o lees, but in diverse maneres. Now been they cleped° chieftaynes for as muche as they been chief, and spryngers° of alle othere synnes. / Of the roote of thise sevene synnes thanne is pride the general roote of alle harmes, for of this roote spryngen certein braunches, as ire, envye, accidie or slewthe°, avarice or coveitise (to commune understondynge), glotonye, and lecherye. / And everich of thise chief synnes hath his braunches and his twigges, as shal be declared in hire chapitres° folwinge. /

And thogh so be that no man kan outrely telle° the nombre of the twigges and of the harmes that cometh of pride, yet wol I shewe a partie° of hem, as ye shul understonde. / Ther is inobedience, avauntynge°, ypocrisie, despit°, arrogance, inpudence, swellynge of herte, insolence, elacioun°, inpacience, strif, contumacie°, presumpcioun, irreverence, pertinacie°, veyne glorie°, and many another twig that I kan nat declare. / Inobedient is he that disobeyeth for despit to the comandementz of God, and to his sovereyns, and to his goostly° fader. / Avauntour° is he that bosteth of the harm or of the bountee° that he hath doon. / Ypocrite is he that hideth to shewe° hym swich as he is and sheweth hym swiche as he noght is. / Despitous is he that hath desdeyn of his neighebore, that is to seyn of his evene-Cristene°, or hath despit to doon that hym oghte to do. / Arrogant is he that thynketh that he hath thilke bountees in hym that he hath noght, or weneth° that he sholde have hem by his desertes, or elles he demeth° that he be that he nys nat°. / Inpudent

379 biheteth, *promises,* **lightnesse,** *silliness,* **mysseyeth,** *speak wrongly of* **380 woot,** *knows,* **soothfastnesse,** *truth* **382 eschue,** *avoid,* **brennynge,** *burning,* **greve,** *damage* **383 verraily,** *truly* **384 looke,** *notice,* **fourneys,** *furnace* **385 refreyne,** *restrain* **386 almesdede,** *charitable giving* **387 bihovely,** *necessary,* **cleped,** *called,* **spryngers,** *originators* **388 accidie or slewthe,** *sloth* **389 hire chapitres,** *their sections* **390 outrely telle,** *completely count,* **partie,** *portion* **391 avauntynge,** *boasting,* **despit,** *disdain,* **elacioun,** *self-promotion,* **contumacie,** *insubordination,* **pertinacie,** *obstinacy,* **veyne glorie,** *pretentiousness* **392 goostly,** *spiritual* **393 Avauntour,** *braggart,* **bountee,** *good things* **394 hideth to shewe,** *disguises* **395 evene-Cristene,** *fellow Christian* **396 weneth,** *thinks,* **demeth,** *judges,* **that he nys nat,** *what he isn't*

381 Augustyn, a list similar to the preceding is in Pseudo-Augustine, *In Lectione Apostolica* 3. **382 restreyne,** Hg reads "refreyne." **383–84 Augustyn,** not identified in Augustine. **385 receyvynge . . . the precious body,** consuming the communion wafer, the Eucharist, which by the priest's words of consecration has become the body of Christ. **386 receyvynge . . . hooly water,** anointing with water blessed by a priest, a spiritual cleansing. ***Confiteor,*** (I confess) the opening words of a communal confession of sin that takes place at the beginning of the Mass and during compline (**complyn**), the last of the canonical hours, recited before going to bed. On the hours, see *MilT* 1.3655n. **386a Sequitur de Septem Peccatis Mortalibus et eorum dependenciis circumstanciis et speciebus,** "Here follow the Seven Deadly Sins and their subdivisions, and circumstances, and varieties." Hg reads more briefly "De Septem peccatis mortalibus." Before its rubric here, El mistakenly includes "Explicit secunda pars penitentie," but repeats it again after line 1027 where it appears in most manuscripts. **386b De Superbia,** "Concerning Pride." Hg identifies the sin and several subspecies in the margins of this and other sections. **387 Alle they renne in o lees,** they all run on one leash; the seven deadly (or capital) sins are sometimes also called the "dogs of hell," with which the devil hunts his prey. **spryngers,** El reads "spryngen"; Hg, "spring."

is he that for his pride hath no shame of his
synnes. / Swellynge of herte is whan a man rejoyseth hym of harm that he hath doon. / Insolent is
he that despiseth in his juggement alle othere folk
as to regard of his value, and of his konning°, and
of his spekyng, and of his beryng°. / Elacioun is
whan he ne may neither suffre to have maister
ne felawe. / Inpacient is he that wol nat been 400
ytaught ne undernome° of his vice, and by strif
werreieth° trouthe wityngly, and deffendeth his
folye. / *Contumax*° is he that thurgh his indigna-
cion is agayns everich auctoritee or power of hem
that been his sovereyns. / Presumpcioun is whan a
man undertaketh an emprise° that hym oghte nat
do, or elles that he may nat do, and this is called
surquidrie°. Irreverence is whan men do nat honour there as hem oghte to doon, and waiten to be
reverenced. / Pertinacie is whan man deffendeth
his folies, and trusteth to muchel in his owene wit.
/ Veyne glorie is for to have pompe and delit in
his temporeel hynesse, and glorifie hym° in
this worldly estaat. / Janglynge is whan men 405
speken to muche biforn folk, and clappen as a
mille°, and taken no kepe° what they seye. /

And yet is ther a privee spece° of pride that waiteth first for to be salewed° er he wole salewe, al be
he lasse worth than that oother is peraventure°;
and eek he waiteth or desireth to sitte, or elles to
goon above hym° in the wey, or kisse pax, or been
encensed, or goon to offryng biforn his neighebore, / and swiche semblable° thynges agayns his
duetee°, peraventure, but that he hath his herte
and his entente in swich a proud desir to be magnified and honoured biforn the peple. /

Now been ther two maneres of pride, that oon of
hem is withinne the herte of man and that oother
is withoute°. / Of whiche soothly thise forseyde
thynges, and mo than I have seyd, apertenen° to
pride that is in the herte of man; and that
othere speces of pride been withoute. / 410
But natheles that oon of thise speces of pride is
signe of that oother, right as the gaye leefsel° atte
taverne is signe of the wyn that is in the celer°. /
And this is in manye thynges, as in speche and con-
tenaunce°, and in outrageous array of clothyng. /
For certes, if ther ne hadde be no synne in clothyng, Crist wolde nat have noted and spoken of
the clothyng of thilke riche man in the gospel. /
And as seith Seint Gregorie that precious clothyng
is cowpable° for the derthe° of it, and for his softe-
nesse, and for his strangenesse° and degisynesse°,
and for the superfluitee, and for the inordinat
scantnesse of it. / Allas, may men nat seen, as in
oure dayes, the synful costlewe° array of clothynge,
and namely in to muche superfluitee°, or elles
in to desordinat° scantnesse? / 415

As to the firste sinne, that is in superfluitee
of clothynge which that maketh it so deere°, to
harm° of the peple, / nat oonly the cost of em-
browdynge°, the degise endentynge°, barrynge°,
owndynge°, palynge°, wyndynge°, or bendynge°,
and semblable° wast of clooth in vanitee, / but ther
is also costlewe furrynge in hir gownes, so muche
pownsonynge of chisels° to maken holes, so muche
daggynge of sheres°, / forthwith° the superfluitee
in lengthe of the forseide° gownes, trailynge in the
dong and in the mire, on horse and eek on foote,
as wel of men as of wommen, that al thilke trailyng
is verraily as in effect wasted, consumed, thredbare,
and roten with donge, rather than it is yeven to
the poure, to greet damage of the forseyde poure
folk. / And that in sondry wise°. This is to seyn that
the moore that clooth is wasted, the moore it
costeth to the peple for the scantnesse. / And 420
fortherover, if so be that they wolde yeven°
swich pownsoned and dagged clothyng to the

---

399 konning, *understanding,* **beryng,** *behavior* **401 undernome of,** *accused of,* **werreieth,** *battles against* **402 Contumax,** (Lat.) *obstinate* **403 emprise,** *enterprise,* **surquidrie,** *arrogance* **405 glorifie hym,** *take pride* **406 clappen as a mille,** *make noise constantly* (like a mill wheel), **kepe,** *care* **407 privee spece,** *secret species,* **salewed,** *greeted,* **peraventure,** *perhaps,* **sitte or . . . goon above hym,** *take precedence at table or in procession* **408 swiche semblable,** *other similar,* **agayns his duetee,** *beyond what is due him* **409 withoute,** *outside* **410 apertenen,** *pertain* **411 leefsel,** *bush used as a tavern sign,* **celer,** *storeroom* **412 contenaunce,** *behavior* **414 cowpable,** *blameworthy,* **derthe,** *high cost,* **strangenesse,** *unusualness,* **degisynesse,** *trendiness* **415 costlewe,** *costly,* **superfluitee,** *excessiveness,* **desordinat,** *inappropriate* **416 deere,** *expensive,* **harm,** *detriment* **417 embrowdynge,** *embroidering,* **degise endentynge,** *fashionable notching,* **barrynge,** *striping,* **owndynge,** *wavy striping,* **palynge,** *vertical striping,* **wyndynge,** *wrapping,* **bendynge,** *bordering,* **semblable,** *similar* **418 pownsonynge of chisels,** *perforation with punches,* **daggynge of sheres,** *slashing with scissors* **419 forthwith,** *as well as,* **forseide,** *previously mentioned* **420 sondry wise,** *many ways* **421 yeven,** *give*

406 men speken, Hg reads "a man speketh," with singular forms in the rest of the line. **407 kisse pax . . . been encensed . . . goon to offryng,** i.e., be the first to kiss the pax, a symbolic tablet or disk, be blessed with incense, or offer gifts at the altar—all public parts of the liturgy of the Mass. On the offering, see *GP* 1.450. **413 in the gospel,** Luke 16.19. **414 Gregorie,** *Sermons on the Gospels* 2.40.3.

poure folk, it is nat convenient° to were for hire estaat°, ne suffisant to beete° hire necessitee, to kepe hem fro the distemperance° of the firmament°. / Upon that oother side, to speken of the horrible disordinat scantnesse of clothyng, as been thise kutted sloppes° or haynselyns°, that thurgh hire shortnesse ne covere nat the shameful membres° of man, to wikked entente. / Allas, somme of hem shewen the boce° of hir shape and the horrible swollen membres that semeth lik the maladie of hirnia, in the wrappynge of hir hoses°, / and eek the buttokes of hem faren° as it were the hyndre part of a she-ape in the fulle of the mone. / And mooreover the wrecched swollen membres that they shewe thurgh the degisynge°, in departynge° of hire hoses in whit and reed semeth that half hir shameful privee membres weren flayne°. / And if so be that they departen hire hoses in othere colours, as is whit and blak, or whit and blew, or blak and reed, and so forth, / thanne semeth it as by variaunce of colour that half the partie° of hire privee membres were corrupt by the fir of Seint Antony, or by cancre, or by oother swich meschaunce°. / Of the hyndre part of hir buttokes, it is ful horrible for to see. For certes, in that partie of hir body ther as they purgen hir stynkynge ordure, / that foule partie shewe they to the peple prowdly in despit of honestitee, the which honestitee° that Jesu Crist and his freendes observede to shewen in hir lyve. / Now as of the outrageous array of wommen, God woot° that though the visages of somme of hem seme ful chaast and debonaire°, yet notifie° they in hire array of atyr° likerousnesse° and pride. / I sey nat that honestitee in clothynge of man or womman is uncovenable°, but certes the super fluitee or disordinat scantitee of clothynge is reprevable°. /

Also the synne of aornement° or of apparaille is in thynges that apertenen° to rydynge, as in to manye delicat° horses that been hoolden for delit, that beenso faire, fatte, and costlewe°; / and also to many a vicious knave that is sustened by cause of hem; in to curious° harneys, as in sadeles, in crouperes°, peytrels°, and bridles covered with precious clothyng and riche, barres and plates of gold and of silver. / For which God seith by Zakarie the prophete, "I wol confounde° the ryderes of swiche horses." / This folk taken litel reward° of the rydynge of Goddes sone of hevene, and of his harneys whan he rood upon the asse and ne hadde noon oother harneys but the poure clothes of his disciples; ne we ne rede nat that evere he rood on oother beest. / I speke this for the synne of superfluitee, and nat for reasonable honestitee° whan reson it requireth. / And forther, certes, pride is greetly notified° in holdynge° of greet meynee° whan they be of litel profit or of right no profit. / And namely°, whan that meynee is felonous and damageous° to the peple, by hardynesse° of heigh lordshipe or by wey of offices°. / For certes, swiche lordes sellen thanne hir lordshipe to the devel of helle whanne they sustenen° the wikkednesse of hir meynee. / Or elles whan this folk of lowe degree, as thilke° that holden hostelries°, sustenen the thefte of hire hostilers°, and that is in many manere of deceites. / Thilke manere° of folk been the flyes that folwen the hony, or elles the houndes that folwen the careyne°. Swiche forseyde folk stranglen spiritually hir lordshipes. / For which thus seith David the prophete, "Wikked deeth moote° come upon thilke lordshipes, and God yeve° that they moote descenden into helle al doun, for in hire houses been° iniquitees and shrewednesses°," and nat God of hevene. / And certes, but if° they doon amendement, right as God yaf his benisoun° to Laban by the service of Jacob, and to Pharao by the service of Joseph, right so God wol yeve his malisoun° to swiche lordshipes as sustenen the

---

convenient, *suitable,* **estaat,** *social class,* **beete,** *provide for,* **distemperance,** *i.e., bad weather,* **firmament,** *heavens* **422 kutted sloppes,** *shortcut coats,* **haynselyns,** *jackets,* **membres,** *genitals* **423 boce,** *bulge,* **hoses,** *leggings* **424 faren,** *seem* **425 degisynge,** *fashioning,* **departynge,** *separating* **flayne,** *skinned* **427 partie,** *portion,* **meschaunce,** *misfortune* **429 despit of honestitee,** *scorn of decency* **430 woot,** *knows,* **debonaire,** *meek,* **notifie,** *announce,* **array of atyr,** *display of dress,* **likerousnesse,** *lechery* **431 uncovenable,** *unsuitable,* **reprevable,** *blameworthy* **432 aornement,** *adornment,* **apertenen,** *pertain,* **delicat,** *elegant,* **costlewe,** *costly* **433 to curious,** *too ornate,* **crouperes,** *hindquarter straps,* **peytrels,** *chest straps* **434 confounde,** *destroy* **435 reward,** *regard* **436 honestitee,** *honor* **437 notified,** *made known,* **holdynge,** *keeping,* **meynee,** *entourage* **438 namely,** *especially,* **damageous,** *harmful,* **hardynesse,** *insolence,* **offices,** *official appointments* **439 sustenen,** *support* **440 thilke,** *those,* **holden hostelries,** *own inns,* **of hire hostilers,** *by their innkeepers* **441 Thilke manere,** *this kind,* **careyne,** *rolled flesh* **442 moote,** *must,* **yeve,** *grant,* **been,** *are,* **shrewednesses,** *wickednesses* **443 but if,** *unless,* **yaf his benisoun,** *gave his blessing,* **malisoun,** *curse*

423 boce of hir shape and the, Hg reads "shape and the boce of hire." **427 fir of Seint Antony,** erysipelas (St. Anthony's fire), which causes acute skin rash. **434 Zakarie,** Zechariah 10.5. **435 rydynge of Goddes sone,** Christ's entry into Jerusalem, e.g., Matthew 21.1–11. **442 David,** Psalms 55.15 (Vulgate 54.16). **al doun,** El reads "al doun al doun"; Hg, "adown adown." **443 Laban . . . Joseph,** Genesis 31 and 47.7. El and Hg transpose "Laban" and "Pharao."

wikkednesse of hir servauntz, but if they come to
amendement. /

Pride of the table appeereth eek ful ofte, for
certes riche men been cleped° to festes, and poure
folk been put awey° and rebuked. / Also in excesse
of diverse metes° and drynkes, and namely swiche
manere bake metes° and dissh metes°, brennynge
of° wilde fyr, and peynted and castelled with papir°,
and semblable wast° so that it is abusioun° for
to thynke. / And eek in to greet preciousnesse 445
of vessel and curiositee of mynstralcie°, by
whiche a man is stired the moore to delices° of
luxurie, / if so be that he sette his herte the lasse
upon oure lord Jesu Crist, certeyn it is a synne.
And certeinly the delices myghte been so grete
in this caas that man myghte lightly falle by hem
into deedly synne. / The especes° that sourden of°
pride, soothly whan they sourden of malice yma-
gined°, avised°, and forncast°, or elles of usage°,
been deedly synnes, it is no doute. / And whan
they sourden by freletee unavysed° sodeynly, and
sodeynly withdrawen ayeyn, al been they grevouse
synnes, I gesse that they ne been nat deedly. /

Now myghte men axe° wherof that pride sourdeth and spryngeth and I seye somtyme it spryngeth of the goodes° of nature, and somtyme of the
goodes of fortune, and somtyme of the goodes
of grace. / Certes, the goodes of nature stonden 450
outher° in goodes of body or in goodes of
soule. / Certes, goodes of body been heele° of
body, as strengthe, delivernesse°, beautee, gen-
tries°, franchise°. / Goodes of nature of the
soule been good wit, sharpe understondynge,
subtil engyn°, vertu natureel, good memorie. /
Goodes of fortune been richesses, highe degrees
of lordshipes, preisinges of the peple. / Goodes
of grace been science°, power to suffre spiritueel
travaille, benignitee°, vertuous contemplacion,
withstondynge of temptacion, and semblable°
thynges. / Of whiche forseyde goodes, certes 455
it is a ful greet folye a man to priden hym in any
of hem alle. / Now as for to speken of goodes of
nature, God woot° that somtyme we han hem in
nature as muche to oure damage as to oure profit. /
As for to speken of heele of body, certes it passeth ful lightly°, and eek it is ful ofte enchesoun°
of the siknesse of oure soule. For God woot, the
flessh is a ful greet enemy to the soule, and therfore the moore that the body is hool, the moore
be we in peril to falle. / Eke for to pride hym in
his strengthe of body it is an heigh folye, for certes
the flessh coveiteth agayn° the spirit, and ay the
moore strong that the flessh is the sorier may the
soule be. / And over al this, strengthe of body and
worldly hardynesse° causeth° ful ofte many a
man to peril and meschaunce°. / Eek for to 460
pride hym of his gentrie° is ful greet folie, for
oftetyme the gentrie of the body binymeth° the
gentrie of the soule. And eek we ben alle of o fader
and of o mooder, and alle we been of o nature
roten and corrupt, bothe riche and poure. / For
sothe, o manere gentrie is for to preise, that appa-
railleth° mannes corage° with vertues and morali-
tees and maketh hym Cristes child. / For truste wel
that over what man that synne hath maistrie, he is
a verray cherl° to synne. /

Now been ther generale signes of gentillesse°, as
eschewynge° of vice and ribaudye° and servage of°
synne, in word, in werk, and contenaunce°, / and
usynge vertu, curteisye, and clennesse, and to be
liberal—that is to seyn, large by mesure°, for
thilke that passeth° mesure is folie and synne. / 465
Another is to remembre hym of° bountee that
he of oother folk hath receyved. / Another is to
be benigne to his goode subgetis. Wherfore seith
Senek, "Ther is nothing moore covenable° to a
man of heigh estaat than debonairetee° and pitee.
/ And therfore thise flyes° that men clepeth° bees,
whan they maken hire kyng, they chesen oon
that hath no prikke° wherwith he may stynge." /

---

444 cleped, *called,* **put awey,** *turned away* **445 diverse metes,** *various foods,* **bake metes,** *meat pies,* **dissh metes,** *stews,* **brennynge of,** *flambéed with,* **castelled with papir,** *adorned with paper castles,* **semblable wast,** *similar waste,* **abusioun,** *outrage* **446 curiositee of mynstralcie,** *elaborateness of musical accompaniment,* **delices,** *the sensory delights* **448 especes,** *subcategories,* **sourden of,** *arise from,* **ymagined,** *devised,* **avised,** *considered,* **forncast,** *planned,* **usage,** *habit* **449 freletee unavysed,** *thoughtless weakness* **450 axe,** *ask,* **goodes,** *gifts* **451 outher,** *either* **452 heele,** *health,* **delivernesse,** *agility,* **gentries,** *aristocratic birth,* **franchise,** *freedom* **453 engyn,** *ingenuity* **455 science,** *knowledge,* **benignitee,** *kindness,* **semblable,** *similar* **457 woot,** *knows* **458 lightly,** *quickly,* **enchesoun,** *cause* **459 coveiteth agayn,** *desires in conflict with* **460 hardynesse,** *boldness,* **causeth,** *provokes,* **meschaunce,** *misfortune* **461 gentrie,** *noble birth,* **binymeth,** *takes away* **462 apparailleth,** *adorns,* **corage,** *heart* **463 verray cherl,** *true servant* **464 gentillesse,** *nobility,* **eschewynge,** *avoiding,* **ribaudye,** *debauchery,* **servage of,** *bondage to,* **contenaunce,** *attitude* **465 large by mesure,** *generous with discretion,* **thilke that passeth,** *that which surpasses* **466 remembre hym of,** *recall* **467 covenable,** *appropriate,* **debonairetee,** *kindness* **468 flyes,** *insects,* **clepeth,** *call,* **prikke,** *stinger*

467 Senek, Seneca, *On Pity* 1.3.3, 1.19.2.

Another is, a man to have a noble herte and a diligent, to attayne to heighe vertuouse thynges. / Now certes, a man to pride hym in the goodes of grace is eek an outrageous folie, for thilke yiftes of grace that sholde have turned hym to goodnesse and to medicine turneth hym to venym and to confusioun, as seith Seint Gregorie. / Certes also, whoso prideth hym in the goodes of fortune, he is a ful greet fool. For somtyme is a man a greet lord by the morwe that is a caytyf° and a wrecche er it be nyght. / And somtyme the richesse of a man is cause of his deth. Somtyme the delices° of a man is cause of the grevous maladye thurgh which he dyeth. / Certes, the commendacion of the peple is somtyme ful fals and ful brotel° for to triste°. This day they preyse, tomorwe they blame. / God woot°, desir to have commendacioun eek of the peple hath caused deeth to many a bisy man. /

Remedium contra peccatum Superbie.

Now sith° that so is, that ye han understonde what is pride, and whiche been the speces of it, and whennes pride sourdeth° and springeth, / now shul ye understonde which is the remedie agayns the synne of pride, and that is humylitee or mekenesse. / That is a vertu thurgh which a man hath verray° knoweleche of hymself, and holdeth of hymself no pris° ne deyntee° as in regard of his desertes, considerynge evere his freletee°. / Now been ther three maneres° of humylitee, as humylitee in herte, and another humylitee in his mouth, the thridde in his werkes. / The humilitee in herte is in foure maneres: that oon is whan a man holdeth hymself as noght worth° biforn God of hevene. Another is whan he ne despiseth noon oother man. / The thridde is whan he rekketh° nat though men holde him noght worth. The ferthe is whan he nys nat sory of his humiliacioun. / Also the humilitee of mouth is in foure thynges: in attempree° speche, and in humblesse of speche, and whan he biknoweth° with his owene mouth that he is swich as hym thynketh that he is in his herte. Another is whan he preiseth the bountee° of another man and nothyng therof amenuseth°. / Humilitee eek in werkes is in foure maneres: the firste is whan he putteth othere men biforn hym. The seconde is to chese the loweste place overal. The thridde is gladly to assente to good conseil. / The ferthe is to stonde gladly to the award° of his sovereyns° or of hym that is in hyer degree. Certein, this is a greet werk of humylitee. /

Sequitur de Invidia.

After pryde wol I speken of the foule synne of envye, which is, as by the word of the philosophre, sorwe of oother mennes prosperitee, and after the word of Seint Augustyn it is sorwe of° oother mennes wele°, and joye of othere mennes harm. / This foule synne is platly° agayns the Hooly Goost. Al be it so that every synne is agayns the Hooly Goost, yet nathelees for as muche as bountee aperteneth° proprely to the Hooly Goost, and envye comth proprely of malice, therfore it is proprely agayn the bountee of the Hooly Goost. / Now hath malice two speces, that is to seyn, hardnesse of herte in wikkednesse, or elles the flessh of man is so blynd that he considereth nat that he is in synne or rekketh° nat that he is in synne, which is the hardnesse of the devel. / That oother spece of malice is whan a man werreyeth° trouthe whan he woot° that it is trouthe, and eek whan he werreyeth the grace that God hath yeve° to his neighebore, and al this is by envye. / Certes, thanne is envye the worste synne that is. For soothly, alle othere synnes been somtyme oonly agayns o special vertu. / But certes, envye is agayns alle vertues and agayns alle goodnesses. For it is sory of° alle the bountees° of his neighebore, and in this manere it is divers° from alle othere synnes. / For wel unnethe° is ther any synne that it ne hath

471 caytyf, *captive* **472 delices,** *sensory delights* **473 brotel,** *brittle,* **triste,** *trust* **474 woot,** *knows* **475 sith,** *since,* **sourdeth,** *arises* **477 verray,** *true,* **pris,** *value,* **deyntee,** *worth,* **freletee,** *weakness* **478 maneres,** *kinds* **479 noght worth,** *worth nothing* **480 rekketh,** *cares* **481 attempree,** *temperate,* **biknoweth,** *acknowledges,* **bountee,** *goodness,* **amenuseth,** *detracts* **483 award,** *decision,* **sovereyns,** *rulers* **484 sorwe of,** *sorrow at,* **wele,** *good fortune* **485 platly,** *directly,* **bountee aperteneth,** *goodness belongs* **486 rekketh,** *cares* **487 werreyeth,** *battles,* **woot,** *knows,* **yeve,** *given* **489 sory of,** *sorry about,* **bountees,** *advantages,* **divers,** *different* **490 wel unnethe,** *scarcely*

470 Gregorie, *Morals* 33.12.25. **474a Remedium contra peccatum Superbie,** "Remedy for the Sin of Pride." El places this rubric mid-sentence, after "springeth." Hg does not include it or those for the other remedies. Chaucer's source for the remedies ("cures" or "corrections") of the sins is *Summa Virtutem de Remediis Anime* (*Treatise on the Virtues That Cure the Soul*), also known as *Postquam* (*After*), which often follows treatises on the sins in manuscripts. Chaucer seems to have invented the idea of following each sin with its own remedy. **482 good,** omitted in El. **483a Sequitur de Invidia,** "Here follows [the section] concerning Envy." Hg reads only "Invidia." **484 the philosophre,** i.e., Aristotle, but the reference is uncertain. **Augustyn,** *Enarrationes in Psalmos* (*Exposition of the Psalms*) 104.17 (Vulgate 105.25). **485 foule,** omitted in El. **487 malice,** Hg reads "envye."

som delit in itself, save only envye that evere hath
in itself angwissh and sorwe. / The speces of 490
envye been thise: there is first sorwe of other
mannes goodnesse and of his prosperitee. And
prosperitee is kyndely° matere of joye, thanne is
envye a synne agayns kynde. / The secounde spece
of envye is joye of oother mannes harm, and that is
proprely lyk to the devel that evere rejoyseth hym
of mannes harm. / Of thise two speces comth bak-
bityng°, and this synne of bakbityng or detraccion
hath certeine speces, as thus. Som man preiseth his
neighebore by a wikke entente, / for he maketh
alwey a wikked knotte atte laste ende. Alwey he
maketh a "but" atte laste ende, that is digne of°
moore blame than worth is al the preisynge°. / The
seconde spece is that if a man be good and dooth
or seith a thing to good entente, the bakbiter wol
turne all thilke goodnesse upsodoun° to his
shrewed° entente. / The thridde is to amenuse° 495
the bountee° of his neighebore. / The fourthe
spece of bakbityng is this, that if men speke goodnesse of a man thanne wol the bakbitere seyn,
"Pardee°, swich a man is yet bet than he," in dispreisynge of hym that men preise. / The fifte spece is
this, for to consente gladly and herkne° gladly to the
harm that men speke of oother folk. This synne is ful
greet and ay° encreeseth after the wikked entente of
the bakbiter. / After bakbityng cometh grucching°
or murmuracion°; and somtyme it spryngeth of
inpacience agayns God and somtyme agayns man. /
Agayns God it is whan a man gruccheth agayn
the peynes of helle, or agayns poverte, or los of
catel°, or agayn reyn or tempest, or elles gruccheth
that shrewes° han prosperitee, or elles for that
goode men han adversitee. / And alle thise 500
thynges sholde men suffre paciently, for they
comen by the rightful juggement and ordinaunce°
of God. / Somtyme comth grucching of avarice, as
Judas grucched agayns the Magdaleyne whan she
enoynte° the hevede° of oure lord Jesu Crist with hire
precious oynement. / This maner murmure is swich
as whan man gruccheth of goodnesse that hymself
dooth, or that oother folk doon of hir owene catel°. /
Somtyme comth murmure of pride, as whan Simon
the Pharisee grucched agayn the Magdaleyne whan
she approched to Jesu Crist and weep at his feet for
hire synnes. / And somtyme grucchyng sourdeth°
of envye, whan men discovereth° a mannes harm
that was pryvee°, or bereth hym on hond° thyng
that is fals. / Murmure eek is ofte amonges 505
servauntz, that grucchen whan hir sovereyns
bidden hem doon leveful° thynges, / and for as
muche as they dar nat openly withseye° the comaundementz of hir sovereyns yet wol they seyn
harm and grucche and murmure prively for verray
despit°, / whiche wordes men clepen° the develes
Pater Noster, though so be that the devel ne hadde
nevere Pater Noster, but that lewed° folk yeven° it
swich a name. / Somtyme grucchyng comth of ire°
or prive° hate that norisseth° rancour in herte, as
afterward I shal declare. / Thanne cometh eek bitternesse of herte, thurgh which bitternesse every
good dede of his neighebor semeth to hym bitter and unsavory. / Thanne cometh discord 510
that unbyndeth alle manere of freendshipe. Thanne comth scornynge of his neighebore, al do he°
never so weel. / Thanne comth accusynge, as whan
man seketh occasioun to anoyen° his neighebor,
which that is lyk to the craft of the devel that waiteth
bothe night and day to accusen us alle. / Thanne
comth malignitee, thurgh which a man anoyeth his
neighebor prively if he may, / and if he noght may,
algate° his wikked wil ne shal nat wante° as for to
brennen° his hous pryvely, or empoysone or sleen°
his bestes°, and semblable° thynges. /

Remedium contra peccatum Invidie.

Now wol I speken of the remedie agayns the foule
synne of envye. First is the love of God principal,

491 kyndely, *naturally* **493 bakbityng,** *secretive criticism of another* **494 digne of,** *deserving of,* **preisynge,** *praising* **495 upsodoun,** *upside down,* **shrewed,** *evil* **496 amenuse,** *diminish,* **bountee,** *goodness* **497 Pardee,** *by God* **498 herkne,** *listen,* **ay,** *always* **499 grucching,** *complaining,* **murmuracion,** *grumbling* **500 catel,** *property,* **shrewes,** *bad people* **501 ordinaunce,** *arrangement* **502 enoynte,** *anointed,* **hevede,** *head* **503 hir owene catel,** *their own property* **505 sourdeth,** *arises,* **discovereth,** *reveals,* **pryvee,** *secret,* **bereth hym on hond,** *accuses him of* **506 leveful,** *legitimate* **507 withseye,** *refuse,* **despit,** *spite* **508 clepen,** *call,* **lewed,** *ignorant,* **yeven,** *give* **509 ire,** *anger,* **prive,** *secret,* **norisseth,** *nourishes* **511 al do he,** *although he may do* **512 anoyen,** *harm* **514 algate,** *nevertheless,* **wante,** *lack,* **brennen,** *burn,* **sleen,** *slay,* **bestes,** *beasts,* **semblable,** *similar*

497 Pardee, Hg reads "Parfey." **502 Judas . . . Magdaleyne,** see John 12.3–5, where the greedy Judas accuses Mary, sister of Martha (not Mary Magdalen), of being a spendthrift when she anoints the feet of Jesus. The other gospels do not name Judas or Mary here: Matthew 26.6–13, Mark 14.3–9, Luke 7.37–38. In Matthew and Mark, the woman anoints the head of Jesus. **504 Simon,** Luke 7.37–40. **508 develes Pater Noster,** devil's "Our Father," i.e., the devil's prayer. **512** Revelation 12.10. **514a Remedium contra peccatum Invidie,** " Remedy for the sin of Envy." **515 love of God . . . neighebor,** Matthew 22.37–39.

and loving of his neighebor as hymself, for soothly
that oon ne may nat been withoute that
oother. / And truste wel that in the name 515
of thy neighebore thou shalt understonde the
name of thy brother; for certes alle we have o fader
flesshly° and o mooder, that is to seyn Adam and
Eve; and eek o fader espiritueel°, and that is God
of hevene. / Thy neighebore artow holden for° to
love and wilne° hym alle goodnesse. And therfore
seith God, "Love thy neighebore as thyselve," that
is to seyn, to salvacioun bothe of lyf and of soule. /
And mooreover thou shalt love hym in word and
in benigne amonestynge° and chastisynge, and
conforten hym in his anoyes°, and preye for hym
with al thyn herte. / And in dede thou shalt love
hym in swich wise that thou shalt doon to hym in
charitee as thou woldest that it were doon to thyn
owene persone. / And therfore thou ne shalt
doon hym no damage in wikked word, ne harm in
his body, ne in his catel°, ne in his soule, by
entissyng° of wikked ensample°. / Thou shalt 520
nat desiren his wyf ne none of his thynges.
Understoond eek that in the name of neighebor is
comprehended his enemy. / Certes man shal loven
his enemy by the comandement of God; and soothly
thy freend shaltow° love in God. / I seye, thyn enemy shaltow love for Goddes sake, by his comandement. For if it were reson° that a man sholde haten
his enemy, forsothe God nolde nat receyven us to
his love that been his enemys. / Agayns three manere of wronges that his enemy dooth to hym, he
shal doon three thynges, as thus. / Agayns hate
and rancour of herte, he shal love hym in herte.
Agayns chiding and wikkede wordes, he shal preye
for his enemy. And agayn the wikked dede of
his enemy, he shal doon hym bountee°. / For 525
Crist seith, "Loveth youre enemys, and preyeth
for hem that speke yow harm, and eek for hem that
yow chacen and pursewen°, and doth bountee to
hem that yow haten." Loo, thus comaundeth us oure
lord Jesu Crist to do to oure enemys. / For soothly,
nature dryveth us to loven oure freendes, and
parfey° oure enemys han moore nede to° love than
oure freendes. And they that moore nede have,
certes to hem shal men doon goodnesse, / and
certes in thilke dede have we remembraunce of the
love of Jesu Crist that deyde° for his enemys. / And
inasmuche as thilke love is the moore grevous° to
parfourne°, insomuche is the moore gretter the
merite, and therfore the lovynge of oure enemy
hath confounded the venym of the devel. / For right
as the devel is disconfited° by humylitee, right so is
he wounded to the deeth by love of oure
enemy. / Certes, thanne is love the medicine 530
that casteth out the venym of envye fro mannes herte. / The speces of this paas° shullen be
moore largely in hir chapitres folwynge declared. /

Sequitur de Ira.

After envye wol I discryven° the synne of ire.
For soothly, whoso hath envye upon his neighebor, anon he wole comunly fynde hym a matere of
wratthe, in word or in dede, agayns hym to whom
he hath envye. / And as wel comth ire of pryde as
of envye; for soothly, he that is proude or envyous
is lightly wrooth°. /

This synne of ire, after the discryvyng of Seint
Augustyn, is wikked wil to been avenged by
word or by dede. / Ire, after the philosophre, 535
is the fervent blood of man yquiked° in his herte
thurgh which he wole° harm to hym that he hateth.
/ For certes the herte of man by eschawfynge° and
moevynge of his blood wexeth so trouble° that he is
out of alle juggement of resoun. / But ye shal understonde that ire is in two maneres, that oon of hem
is good, and that oother is wikked. / The goode ire
is by jalousye of° goodnesse, thurgh which a man is
wrooth with wikkednesse and agayns wikkednesse;
and therfore seith a wys man that ire is bet than pley.
/ This ire is with debonairetee°, and it is wrooth withouten bitternesse; nat wrooth agayns the man, but
wrooth with the mysdede of the man, as seith the
prophete David, *Irascimini et nolite peccare.* / Now 540

---

516 o fader flesshly, *one physical father,* **espiritueel,** *spiritual* **517 artow holden for,** *are you required,* **wilne,** *wish* **518 benigne amonestynge,** *gentle admonishing,* **anoyes,** *troubles* **520 catel,** *possessions,* **entissyng,** *enticing,* **ensample,** *example* **522 shaltow,** *you shall* **523 reson,** *reasonable* **525 bountee,** *goodness* **526 yow . . . pursewen,** *persecute . . . you* **527 parfey,** *in faith,* **nede to,** *need of* **528 deyde,** *died* **529 grevous,** *difficult,* **parfourne,** *perform* **530 disconfited,** *defeated* **532 paas,** *step or section* **533 discryven,** *describe* **534 lightly wrooth,** *easily angered* **536 yquiked,** *awakened,* **wole,** *wishes* **537 eschawfynge,** *heating,* **wexeth so trouble,** *grows so disturbed* **539 jalousye of,** *zeal for* **540 debonairetee,** *humility*

517 seith God, Matthew 22.39. **bothe,** omitted in El. **519** Matthew 7.12. **521** Exodus 20.17. **524 wronges,** E reads "thynges." **526 Crist seith,** Matthew 5.44. **532a Sequitur de Ira,** Here follows [the section] concerning Anger. **535 Augustyn,** *City of God* 14.15. **536 after the philosophre,** according to Aristotle, *On the Soul* 1.1.24. **539 bet than pley,** better than laughter; Ecclesiastes 7.4. **540 David . . . ,** Psalms 4.5 (Vulgate): "Be angry and do not sin."

understondeth that wikked ire is in two maneres, that is to seyn, sodeyn ire or hastif ire, withouten avisement° and consentynge of resoun. / The menyng and the sens of this is that the resoun of man ne consente nat to thilke sodeyn ire and thanne it is venial. / Another ire is ful wikked that comth of felonie of herte avysed° and cast biforn°, with wikked wil to do vengeance; and therto his resoun consenteth, and soothly this is deedly synne. / This ire is so displesant to God that it troubleth his hous and chaceth the Hooly Goost out of mannes soule, and wasteth and destroyeth the liknesse of God—that is to seyn the vertu that is in mannes soule— / and put in hym the liknesse of the devel, and bynymeth° the man fro God that is his rightful lord. / This ire is a ful greet plesaunce to the devel, for it is the develes fourneys° that is eschawfed° with the fir of helle. / For certes, right so as fir is moore mighty to destroyen erthely thynges than any oother element, right so ire is mighty to destroyen alle spiritueel thynges. / Looke how that fir of smale gleedes° that been almoost dede under asshen° wollen quike° agayn whan they been touched with brymstoon°. Right so ire wol everemo quyken agayn whan it is touched by the pride that is covered in mannes herte. / For certes fir ne may nat comen out of nothing, but if it were first in the same thyng natureelly, as fir is drawen out of flyntes with steel. / And right so as pride is ofte tyme matere of ire, right so is rancour norice° and keper of ire. / Ther is a maner tree as seith Seint Ysidre that whan men maken fir of thilke tree, and covere the coles of it with asshen, soothly the fir of it wol lasten al a yeer° or moore. / And right so fareth it° of rancour. Whan it is ones° conceyved in the hertes of som men, certein it wol lasten peraventure° from oon Estre day unto another Estre day, and moore. / But certes thilke man is ful fer° fro the mercy of God al thilke while. /

In this forseyde develes fourneys ther forgen three shrewes°: pride that ay° bloweth and encreesseth the fir by chidynge and wikked wordes. / Thanne stant° envye and holdeth the hoote iren upon the herte of man with a peire of longe toonges of long rancour. / And thanne stant the synne of contumelie°, or strif and cheeste°, and batereth and forgeth by vileyns reprevynges°. / Certes, this cursed synne anoyeth bothe to the man hymself and eek to his neighebor. For soothly, almoost al the harm that any man dooth to his neighebore comth of wratthe. / For certes, outrageous wratthe dooth al that evere the devel hym comaundeth, for he ne spareth neither Crist ne his sweete mooder. / And in his outrageous anger and ire, allas, allas, ful many oon at that tyme feeleth in his herte ful wikkedly bothe of Crist° and of alle his halwes°. / Is nat this a cursed vice? Yis, certes. Allas, it bynymeth° from man his wit and his resoun, and al his debonaire lif espiritueel° that sholde kepen° his soule. / Certes, it bynymeth eek goddes° due lordshipe, and that is mannes soule and the love of his neighebores. It stryveth eek alday° agayn trouthe. It reveth hym° the quiete of his herte and subverteth his soule. /

Of ire comen thise stynkynge engendrures°: first hate that is oold wratthe; discord, thurgh which a man forsaketh his olde freend that he hath loved ful longe. / And thanne cometh werre°, and every manere of wrong that man dooth to his neighebore in body or in catel°. / Of this cursed synne of ire cometh eek manslaughtre. And understonde wel that homycide, that is manslaughtre, is in diverse wise°. Som manere of homycide is spiritueel, and som is bodily. / Spiritueel manslaughtre is in thre thynges. First, by hate, as Seint John seith, "He that hateth his brother is homycide." / Homycide is eek by bakbitynge°. Of whiche bakbiteres seith Salomon that they han two swerdes with whiche they sleen hire neighebores. For soothly, as wikke is to bynyme° his good name as his lyf. / Homycide is eek in yevynge° of wikked conseil by fraude, as for to yeven conseil to areysen°

---

541 avisement, *consideration* **543 avysed,** *considered,* **cast biforn,** *planned ahead* **545 bynymeth,** *takes* **546 fourneys,** *furnace,* **eschawfed,** *heated* **548 gleedes,** *coals,* **asshen,** *ashes,* **wollen quike,** *will come to life,* **brymstoon,** *sulfur* **550 norice,** *nurse* **551 al a yeer,** *a whole year* **552 fareth it,** *it happens,* **ones,** *once,* **peraventure,** *perhaps* **553 ful fer,** *very far* **554 forgen three shrewes,** *three villains work the forge,* **ay,** *always* **555 stant,** *stands* **556 contumelie,** *contentiousness,* **cheeste,** *quarreling,* **reprevynges,** *accusations* **559 of Crist,** *toward Christ,* **halwes,** *saints* **560 bynymeth,** *takes,* **debonaire lif espiritueel,** *gracious spiritual life,* **kepen,** *protect* **561 goddes,** *God's,* **alday,** *always,* **reveth hym,** *steals from him* **562 engendrures,** *offspring* **563 werre,** *war,* **catel,** *property* **564 in diverse wise,** *of many kinds* **566 bakbitynge,** *secretive accusation,* **as wikke is to bynyme,** *it is as wicked to take* **567 yevynge,** *giving,* **areysen,** *impose*

551 maner tree . . . Ysidre, kind of tree; *juniper* is derived from Greek for "fire" in Isidore of Seville, *Etymologies* 17.7.35. After the word *tree,* Hg breaks off; the rest of it is lost. **552 Estre,** Easter Sunday; on Easter eve, a fire representing Christ's resurrection is kindled. **565 John,** 1 John 3.15. **thre thynges,** El reads "vi" (six), apparently a misreading for "iii." Only three kinds of spiritual manslaughter are given. **566 Salomon,** Proverbs 25.18.

wrongful custumes and taillages°. / Of whiche
seith Salomon, "Leon rorynge and bere° hongry
been like to the crueel lordshipes°," in withholdynge or abreggynge° of the shepe°, or the hyre°,
or of the wages of servauntz, or elles in usures° or
in withdraynge of the almesse° of poure folk. / For
which the wise man seith, "Fedeth hym that almoost
dyeth for honger," for soothly but if thow feede
hym, thou sleest hym. And alle thise been deedly
synnes. / Bodily manslaughtre is whan thow sleest
him with thy tonge in oother manere, as whan thou
comandest to sleen a man, or elles yevest° hym
conseil to sleen a man. / Manslaughtre in 570
dede is in foure maneres. That oon is by lawe,
right° as a justice dampneth° hym that is coup-
able° to the deeth. But lat the justice bewar that
he do it rightfully, and that he do it nat for delit to
spille blood, but for kepynge of rightwisenesse°. /
Another homycide is that is doon for necessitee,
as whan o man sleeth another in his defendaunt°,
and that he ne may noon ootherwise escape from
his owene deeth. / But certeinly, if he may escape
withouten manslaughtre of his adversarie, and
sleeth hym, he doth synne, and he shal bere penance as for deedly synne. / Eek if a man by caas°
or aventure° shete° an arwe or caste a stoon with
which he sleeth a man, he is homycide. / Eek if a
womman by necligence overlyeth° hire child in
hir slepyng, it is homycide and deedly synne. / 575
Eek whan man destourbeth° concepcioun of
a child, and maketh a womman outher bareyne°
by drynkinge venemouse° herbes, thurgh which
she may nat conceyve, or sleeth a child by drynkes
wilfully, or elles putteth certeine material thynges
in hire secree places to slee the child, / or elles
doth unkyndely° synne by which man or womman
shedeth hire nature° in manere or in place ther
as a child may nat be conceived, or elles if a womman have conceyved and hurt hirself and sleeth
the child, yet is it homycide. / What seye we eek
of wommen that mordren hir children for drede
of worldly shame? Certes, an horrible homycide.
/ Homycide is eek if a man approcheth to a womman by desir of lecherye, thurgh which the child
is perissed°, or elles smyteth° a womman wityng-
ly°, thurgh which she leseth hir child. Alle thise
been homycides and horrible deedly synnes. / Yet
comen ther of ire manye mo synnes, as wel in word
as in thoght and in dede; as he that arretteth upon°
God, or blameth God of thyng of which he is hymself gilty; or despiseth God and alle his halwes°,
as doon thise cursede hasardours° in diverse
contrees. / This cursed synne doon they whan 580
they feelen in hir hertes ful wikkedly of God°
and of his halwes. / Also, whan they treten unrev-
erently the sacrement of the auter, thilke sinne is
so greet that unnethe° may it been releessed°, but
that the mercy of God passeth° alle his werkes; it is
so greet and he so benigne°. / Thanne comth of ire
attry° angre. Whan a man is sharply amonested° in
his shrifte° to forleten° his synne, / than wole he
be angry and answeren hokerly° and angrily, and
deffenden or excusen his synne by unstedefast-
nesse° of his flessh, or elles he dide it for to holde
compaignye with his felawes, or elles, he seith, the
feend enticed hym, / or elles he dide it for his
youthe, or elles his complecccioun is so corageous°
that he may nat forbere°, or elles it is his destinee,
as he seith, unto a certein age, or elles, he seith, it
cometh hym of gentillesse° of his auncestres,
and semblable° thynges. / Alle this manere of 585
folk so wrappen hem in hir synnes that they
ne wol nat delivere° hemself. For soothly, no
wight° that excuseth hym wilfully of his synne may
nat been delivered of his synne til that he mekely
biknoweth° his synne. / After this thanne cometh
sweryng that is expres° agayn the comandement
of God, and this bifalleth° ofte of anger and of ire.
/ God seith, "Thow shalt nat take the name of thy
lord God in veyn or in ydel°." Also oure lord Jesu

---

custumes and taillages, *duties and taxes* **568 bere,** *bear,* **lordshipes,** *authorities,* **abreggynge,** *reducing,* **shepe,** *reward,* **hyre,** *payment,* **usures,** *usury,* **almesse,** *alms* **570 yevest,** *gives* **571 right,** *just,* **dampneth,** *condemns,* **coupable,** *guilty,* **rightwisenesse,** *righteousness* **572 defendaunt,** *defense* **574 caas,** *chance,* **aventure,** *accident,* **shete,** *shoots* **575 overlyeth,** *lies upon* **576 destourbeth,** *prevents,* **outher bareyne,** *either barren,* **venemouse,** *poisonous* **577 unkyndely,** *unnatural,* **shedeth hir nature,** *emit their procreative fluids* **579 perissed,** *destroyed,* **smyteth,** *strikes,* **wityngly,** *knowingly* **580 arretteth upon,** *finds fault with,* **halwes,** *saints,* **hasardours,** *gamblers* **581 of God,** *against God* **582 unnethe,** *barely,* **releessed,** *forgiven,* **passeth,** *surpasses,* **benigne,** *gracious* **583 attry,** *poisonous,* **amonested,** *admonished,* **shrifte,** *confession,* **forleten,** *abandon* **584 hokerly,** *scornfully,* **unstedefastnesse,** *instability* **585 corageous,** *passionate,* **forbere,** *stop* (himself), **gentillesse,** *high birth,* **semblable,** *similar* **586 delivere,** *free,* **wight,** *person,* **biknoweth,** *acknowledges* **587 expres,** *specifically,* **bifalleth,** *happens* **588 in ydel,** *without purpose*

568 Salomon, Proverbs 28.15. **569** Proverbs 25.21. **577 hirself,** El reads "hir child." **582 sacrement of the auter,** the sacrament of the altar, the Eucharist. **585 complecccioun,** temperament. On medieval theory of the humors, see *GP* 1.333n. **588 God seith,** Exodus 20.7.

Crist seith by the word of Seint Mathew, / "Ne wol
ye nat swere in alle° manere, neither by hevene for
it is Goddes trone°, ne by erthe for it is the bench
of his feet, ne by Jerusalem for it is the citee of
a greet king, ne by thyn heed for thou mayst nat
make an heer whit ne blak. / But seyeth by youre
word, ye, ye, andnay, nay. And what that is
moore, it is of yvel," seith Crist. / For Cristes 590
sake, ne swereth nat so synfully in dismembrynge of Crist by soule, herte, bones, and body.
For certes, it semeth that ye thynke that the
cursede Jewes ne dismembred nat ynough the
preciouse persone of Crist, but ye dismembre
hym moore. / And if so be that the lawe com-
pelle yow to swere, thanne rule yow after the
lawe of God in youre sweryng, as seith Jeremye
4 capitulo, "Thou shalt kepe three condicions:
thou shalt swere in trouthe, in doom°, and in
rightwisnesse°." / This is to seyn, thou shalt swere
sooth°, for every lesynge° is agayns Crist, for Crist
is verray° trouthe. And thynk wel this, that every
greet swerere nat compelled lawefully to swere,
the wounde shal nat departe from his hous whil
he useth swich unleveful° sweryng. / Thou shalt
sweren eek in doom whan thou art constreyned
by thy domesman° to witnessen the trouthe. /
Eek thow shalt nat swere for envye, ne for favour,
ne for meede°, but for rightwisnesse and for
declaracioun of it to the worship of God and
helpyngof thyne evene-Cristene°. / And 595
therfore, every man that taketh Goddesname
in ydel°, or falsly swereth with his mouth, or elles
taketh on hym the name of Crist, to be called a
Cristene man, and lyveth agayns Cristes lyvynge
and his techynge, alle they taken Goddes name in
ydel. / Looke eek what Seint Peter seith, *Actuum
4 capitulo, Non est aliud nomen sub celo*, &c.: "Ther
nys noon oother name," seith Seint Peter, "under
hevene yeven° to men in which they mowe° be
saved." That is to seyn, but the name of Jesu Crist.
/ Take kepe° eek how that the precious name of
Crist, as seith Seint Paul *ad Philipenses 2, In nomine
Iesu*, &c.: that in the name of Jesu every knee of
hevenely creatures, or erthely, or of helle sholden
bowe, for it is so heigh° and so worshipful that the
cursede feend in helle sholde tremblen to heeren
it ynempned°. / Thanne semeth it that men that
sweren so horribly by his blessed name, that they
despise hym moore booldely than dide the cursede Jewes, or elles the devel that trembleth whan
he heereth his name. /

Now certes, sith that° sweryng, but if° it be lawefully doon, is so heighly deffended°, muche
worse is forsweryng° falsly and yet nedelees. / 600
What seye we eek of hem that deliten hem in
sweryng, and holden it a gentrie° or a manly dede
to swere grete othes? And what of hem that of verray
usage° ne cesse° nat to swere grete othes, al be the
cause nat worth a straw°? Certes, it is horrible synne.
/ Sweryng sodeynly withoute avysement° is eek a
synne. / But lat us go now to thilke horrible sweryng
of adjuracioun° and conjuracioun°, as doon thise
false enchauntours or nigromanciens° in bacyns°
ful of water, or in a bright swerd, in a cercle, or in a
fir, or in a shulder boon° of a sheep. / I kan nat seye
but that they doon cursedly and dampnably, agayns
Crist and al the feith of Hooly Chirche. /

What seye we of hem that bileeven in divynailes°,
as by flight or by noyse of briddes°, or of beestes, or
by sort°, by nygromancye, by dremes, by chirkynge°
of dores, or crakynge of houses, by gnawynge
of rattes, and swich manere wrecchednesse? / 605
Certes, al this thyng is deffended° by God and
by al Hooly Chirche. For which they been acursed
til they come to amendement that on swich filthe setten hire bileeve°. / Charmes for woundes
or maladie of men or of beestes, if they taken any
effect it may be peraventure° that God suffreth°
it, for folk° sholden yeve° the moore feith and
reverence to his name. /

---

589 alle, *any,* **trone,** *throne* **592 doom,** *court,* **rightwisnesse,** *righteousness* **593 sooth,** *truth,* **lesynge,** *lie,* **verray,** *pure,* **unleveful,** *unlawful* **594 domesman,** *judge* **595 meede,** *payment,* **evene-Cristene,** *fellow Christian* **596 in ydel,** *without purpose* **597 yeven,** *given,* **mowe,** *might* **598 kepe,** *care,* **heigh,** *high,* **ynempned,** *named* **600 sith that,** *since,* **but if,** *unless,* **deffended,** *forbidden,* **forsweryng,** *perjuring* **601 gentrie,** *fashionable thing,* **verray usage,** *simple habit,* **cesse,** *cease,* **nat worth a straw,** i.e., *worth nothing* **602 avysement,** *consideration* **603 adjuracioun,** *exorcism,* **conjuracioun,** *calling spirits,* **nigromanciens,** *necromancers,* **bacyns,** *basins,* **boon,** *bone* **605 divynailes,** *divination,* **briddes,** *birds,* **sort,** *drawing lots,* **chirkynge,** *creaking* **606 deffenden,** *forbidden,* **bileeve,** *faith* **607 peraventure,** *perhaps,* **suffreth,** *allows,* **for folk,** *so that people,* **yeve,** *give*

588–90 Crist seith, Matthew 5.34–37. **591 in dismembrynge,** swearing was thought to tear apart or dismember the body of Christ, since many oaths cite parts of Christ's body or aspects of his crucifixion. See *PardT* 6.474. **592 Jeremye *4 capitulo*,** Jeremiah, chapter 4 (4.2). **597 Peter . . . ,** Acts 4.12; the English translates and completes the Latin. **598 Paul . . . ,** Philippians 2.10; the English translates and completes the Latin. **603** Various kinds of divination and casting of spells were more often presented as sins of pride or avarice. **nigromanciens,** El reads "nigromanens." **605 nygromancye,** El reads "geomancie" (divination by patterns on the ground).

Now wol I speken of lesynges°, which generally is
fals significacioun of word in entente to deceyven
his evene-Cristene°. / Some lesynge is of which
ther comth noon avantage to no wight°, and som
lesynge turneth to the ese and profit of o man and
to disese and damage of another man. / Another
lesynge is for to saven his lyf or his catel°. Another
lesynge comth of delit for to lye, in which delit
they wol forge a long tale, and peynten it with alle
circumstaunces, where al the ground° of the
tale is fals. / Som lesynge comth for° he wole 610
sustene° his word; and som lesynge comth of
reccheleesnesse°, withouten avisement°; and sem-
blable° thynges. /

Lat us now touche the vice of flaterynge, which
ne comth nat gladly but for drede or for coveitise. /
Flaterye is generally wrongful preisynge°. Flatereres been the develes norices°, that norissen his
children with milk of losengerie°. / For sothe, Salomon seith that flaterie is wors than detraccioun°.
For somtyme detraccion maketh an hauteyn° man
be the moore humble, for he dredeth detraccion.
But certes flaterye, that maketh a man to enhaun-
cen° his herte and his contenaunce°. / Flatereres
been the develes enchauntours, for they make a
man to wene of° hymself be lyk that he nys nat
lyk. / They been lyk to Judas that bitraysen 615
a man to sellen hym to his enemy, that is to the
devel. / Flatereres been the develes chapelleyns,
that syngen evere *Placebo.* / I rekene flaterie in°
the vices of ire for ofte tyme if o man be wrooth
with another, thanne wol he flatere som wight° to
sustene hym in his querele°. /

Speke we now of swich cursynge as comth of ir-
ous° herte. Malisoun° generally may be seyd every
maner power or harm. Swich cursynge bireveth°
man fro the regne° of God, as seith Seint Paul. /
And ofte tyme swich cursynge wrongfully retor-
neth° agayn to hym that curseth, as a bryd that
retroneth agayn to his owene nest. / And over 620
alle thyngmen oghten eschewe° to cursen hire
children and yeven° to the devel hire engendrure°,
as ferforth° as in hem is. Certes, it is greet peril and
greet synne. /

Lat us thanne speken of chidynge and reproche,
whiche been ful grete woundes in mannes herte,
for they unsowen° the semes° of freendshipe in
mannes herte. / For certes, unnethes° may a man
pleynly° been accorded with hym that hath hym
openly revyled and repreved° in disclaundre°.
This is a ful grisly° synne, as Crist seith in the gospel. / And taak kepe now that he that repreveth
his neighebor outher° he repreveth hym by som
harm of peyne that he hath on his body, as "me-
sel°," "croked harlot°," or by som synne that he
dooth. / Now if he repreve hym by harm of peyne°,
thanne turneth the repreve to Jesu Crist, for peyne
is sent by the rightwys sonde° of God, and by his
suffrance°, be it meselrie°, or maheym°, or
maladie. / And if he repreve hym uncharitably 625
of synne, as "thou holour°," "thou dronkelewe
harlot°," and so forth, thanne aperteneth° that to
the rejoysynge of the devel that evere hath joye
that men doon synne. / And certes, chidynge may
nat come but out of a vileyns herte. For after the
habundance of the herte speketh the mouth ful
ofte. / And ye shul understonde that looke°, by
any wey, whan any man shal chastise another, that
he bewar from° chidynge and reprevynge. For
trewely, but° he bewar he may ful lightly quyken°
the fir of angre and of wratthe, which that he sholde
quenche, and peraventure sleeth hym which that
he myghte chastise with benignitee°. / For as
seith Salomon, "The amyable° tonge is the tree of
lyf," that is to seyn, of lyf espiritueel. And soothly,
a deslavee° tonge sleeth the spirites of hym that
repreveth and eek of hym that is repreved. / Loo,
what seith Seint Augustyn, "Ther is nothyng so lyk

608 lesynges, *lies,* **evene-Cristene,** *fellow Christian* **609 wight,** *person* **610 catel,** *property,* **ground,** *basis* **611 for,** *because,* **sustene,** *support,* **reccheleesnesse,** *thoughtlessness,* **avisement,** *consideration,* **semblable,** *similar* **613 preisynge,** *praising,* **norices,** *nurses,* **losengerie,** *deceit* **614 detraccioun,** *belittling,* **hauteyn,** *arrogant,* **enhauncen,** *puff up,* **contenaunce,** *behavior* **615 wene of,** *believe* **618 in,** *among,* **wight,** *person,* **querele,** *quarrel* **619 irous,** *angry,* **Malisoun,** *cursing someone,* **bireveth,** *removes,* **regne,** *kingdom* **620 retorneth,** *turns back* **621 eschewe,** *avoid,* **yeven,** *give,* **engendrure,** *offspring,* **ferforth,** *far* **622 unsowen,** *unstitch,* **semes,** *seams* **623 unnethes,** *hardly,* **pleynly,** *fully,* **repreved,** *accused,* **disclaundre,** *slander,* **grisly,** *hideous* **624 outher,** *either,* **mesel,** *leper,* **croked harlot,** *crippled scoundrel* **625 repreve hym by harm of peyne,** *blames him for his suffering,* **rightwys sonde,** *righteous sending,* **suffrance,** *allowance,* **meselrie,** *leprosy,* **maheym,** *maiming* **626 holour,** *lecher,* **dronkelewe harlot,** *drunken scoundrel,* **aperteneth,** *belongs* **628 ye . . . that looke,** *you who see,* **bewar from,** *be cautious of,* **but,** *unless,* **lightly quyken,** *easily enliven,* **benignitee,** *goodness* **629 amyable,** *friendly,* **deslavee,** *uncontrolled*

610 is, omitted in El. **Another lesynge comth,** El omits "Another lesynge." **614 Salomon seith,** unidentified. **616 Judas,** see 269n above. **617 syngen evere *Placebo*,** always sing "I will please," a metaphor for flattery. See *SumT* 3.2075 and *MerT* 4.1476. **619 Paul,** 1 Corinthians 6.10. **623 Crist seith,** Matthew 5.22. **626 thou holour,** omitted in El. **627 after the habundance,** from the abundance; Matthew 12.24. **629 Salomon,** Proverbs 15.4. **630 Augustyn,** identified by Jill Mann as Augustine's *Confessions* 3.3.6.

the develes child as he thatofte chideth." Seint Paul
seith eek, "The servant of God bihoveeth° nat to
chide." / And how that° chidynge be a vileyns 630
thyng bitwixe alle manere folk, yet is it certes
moost uncovenable° bitwixe a man and his wyf, for
there is nevere reste. And therfore seith Salomon,
"An hous that is uncovered° and droppynge°,
and a chidynge wyf been lyke°." / A man that is
in a droppynge hous in manye places, though he
eschewe° the droppynge in o place, it droppeth
on hym in another place; so fareth it by a chidynge
wyf. But° she chide hym in o place, she wol chide
hym in another. / And therfore, "Bettre is a morsel of breed with joye than an hous ful of delices
with chidynge," seith Salomon. / Seint Paul seith,
"O ye wommen, be ye subgetes° to youre housbondes as bihoveth° in God; and ye men, loveth
youre wyves." *Ad Colossenses 3.* /

Afterward speke we of scornynge, which is a
wikked synne, and namely whan he scorneth a
man for his goode werkes. / For certes, swiche 635
scorneres faren° lyk the foule tode° that may
nat endure to smelle the soote savour° of the vyne
whanne it florissheth. / Thise scorneres been partyng felawes° with the devel, for they han joye whan
the devel wynneth and sorwe whan he leseth°. /
They been adversaries of Jesu Crist, for they haten
that he loveth, that is to seyn salvacion of soule. /

Speke we now of wikked conseil, for he that
wikked conseil yeveth° is a traytour. He deceyveth
hym that trusteth in hym, *ut Achitofel ad Absolonem.*
But natheless, yet is his wikked conseil first agayn
hymself. / For as seith the wise man, every fals
lyvynge° hath this propertee in hymself, that he
that wole anoye° another man he anoyeth first
hymself. / And men shul understonde that 640
man shal nat taken his conseil of fals folk, nor
of angry folk, or grevous° folk, ne of folk that loven
specially to muchel hir owene profit, ne to muche
worldly folk, namely, in conseilynge of soules. /

Now comth the synne of hem that sowen and
maken discord amonges folk, which is a synne that
Crist hateth outrely°; and no wonder is. For he
deyde° for to make concord. / And moore shame
do they to Crist than dide they that hym crucifiede,
for God loveth bettre that freendshipe be amonges
folk than he dide his owene body, the which that
he yaf° for unitee. Therfore been they likned to the
devel, that evere been aboute° to maken discord. /

Now comth the synne of double tonge, swiche°
as speken faire byforn folk and wikkedly bihynde,
or elles they maken semblant° as though they
speeke of good entencioun, or elles in game and
pley, and yet they speke of wikked entente. /

Now comth biwreying° of conseil°, thurgh which
aman is defamed. Certes, unnethe° may he
restoore the damage. / 645

Now comth manace°, that is an open folye,
for he that ofte manaceth, he threteth moore than
he may parfourne° ful ofte tyme. /

Now cometh ydel wordes, that is withouten
profit of° hym that speketh tho wordes and eek
of hym that herkneth tho° wordes. Or elles ydel
wordes been tho that been nedelees or withouten
entente of natureel° profit. / And al be it that ydel
wordes been somtyme venial synne, yet sholde
men douten° hem, for we shul yeve rekenynge of
hem bifore God. /

Now comth janglynge°, that may nat been withoute synne. And as seith Salomon, "It is a synne
of apert folye°." / And therfore a philosophre
seyde, whan men axed hym how that men sholde
plese the peple, and he answerde, "Do manye
goode werkes, and spek fewe jangles." / 650

After this comth the synne of japeres°, that
been the develes apes, for they maken folk to
laughe at hire japerie, as folk doon at the gawdes°
of an ape. Swiche japeres deffendeth° Seint Paul. /
Looke how that vertuouse wordes and hooly
conforten hem that travaillen° in the service of

---

630 bihoveeth, *ought* **631 how that,** *even though,* **uncovenable,** *unfitting,* **uncovered,** *roofless,* **droppynge,** *dripping,* **lyke,** *the same* **632 eschewe,** *may avoid,* **But,** *unless* **634 subgetes,** *subjects,* **bihoveth,** *is required* **636 faren,** *act,* **tode,** *toad,* **soote savour,** *sweet smell* **637 partyng felawes,** *partners,* **leseth,** *loses* **639 yeveth,** *gives* **640 fals lyvynge,** *wicked action,* **anoye,** *damage* **641 grevous,** *malicious* **642 outrely,** *utterly,* **deyde,** *died* **643 yaf,** *gave,* **aboute,** *active* **644 swiche,** *such,* **maken semblant,** *pretend* **645 biwreying,** *betraying,* **conseil,** *confidences,* **unnethe,** *scarcely* **646 manace,** *threats,* **parfourne,** *perform* **647 profit of,** *benefit to,* **herkneth tho,** *listens to those,* **natureel,** *usual* **648 douten,** *distrust* **649 janglynge,** *chattering,* **apert folye,** *obvious folly* **651 japeres,** *jokesters,* **gawdes,** *tricks,* **deffendeth,** *forbids* **652 travaillen,** *labor*

630 Seint Paul seith, 2 Timothy 2.24. **631 Salomon,** Proverbs 27.5; also in *WBP* 3.278–80 and *Mel* 7.1086. **633 Salomon,** Proverbs 17.1 **634 Paul . . . *Ad Colossenses*,** Paul, [Epistle] to the Colossians 3.18–19. **as bihoveth in God,** omitted in El. **639 *ut Achitofel ad Absolonem*,** as Achitophel (did) to Absolom; 2 Samuel 17. **640 wise man,** unidentified. **641 ne of folk,** omitted in El. **648 yeve rekenynge of hem,** account for them; Matthew 12.36. **649 Salomon,** Ecclesiastes 5.2. **650 a philosophre,** Jill Mann explains that the anecdote is associated with Socrates in John of Salisbury's *Policraticus* 5.6 and mentioned elsewhere. **651 Paul,** Ephesians 5.4. **652 hooly,** El reads "hooly woordes."

Crist. Right so° conforten the vileyns wordes and knakkes° of japeris hem that travaillen in the service of the devel. / Thise been the synnes that comen of the tonge, that comen of ire, and of othere synnes mo°. /

Sequitur remedium contra peccatum Ire.

The remedie agayns ire is a vertu that men clepen mansuetude°, that is debonairetee°, and eek another vertu that men callen pacience or suffrance. /

Debonairetee withdraweth and refreyneth° the stirynges and the moevynges of mannes corage° in his herte in swich manere that they ne skippe
nat out by angre ne by ire. / Suffrance suffreth 655
swetely alle the anoyaunces and the wronges that men doon to man outward. / Seint Jerome seith thus of debonairetee that it dooth noon harm to no wight°, ne seith°; ne for noon harm that men doon or seyn, he ne eschawfeth° nat agayns his resoun. / This vertu somtyme comth of nature, for as seith the philosophre, a man is a quyk° thyng, by nature debonaire and tretable° to goodnesse, but whan debonairetee is enformed of° grace, thanne is it the moore worth. /

Pacience that is another remedie agayns ire is a vertu that suffreth swetely every mannes goodnesse, and is nat wrooth for noon harm that is doon to hym. / The philosophre seith that pacience is thilke vertu that suffreth debonairely alle the outrages of adversitee and every wikked word. / 660
This vertu maketh a man lyk to God, and maketh hym Goddes owene deere child, as seith Crist. This vertu disconfiteth° thyn enemy. And therfore seith the wise man, if thow wolt venquysse° thyn enemy, lerne to suffre°. / And thou shalt understonde that man suffreth foure manere° of grevances in outward thynges, agayns the whiche foure he moot have foure manere of paciences. /

The firste grevance is of wikkede wordes. Thilke° suffrede Jesu Crist withouten grucchyng°, ful paciently, whan the Jewes despised and repreved° hym ful ofte. / Suffre thou therfore paciently, for the wise man seith if thou stryve with a fool, though the fool be wrooth° or though he laughe, algate° thou shalt have no reste. / That oother grevance outward is to have damage of thy catel°. Theragayns° suffred Crist ful paciently, whan he was despoyled° of al that he hadde in this lyf, and that
nas° but his clothes. / The thridde grevance is 665
a man to have harm in his body. That suffred Crist ful paciently in al his passioun. / The fourthe grevance is in outrageous labour in werkes°. Wherfore I seye that folk that maken hir servantz to travaillen to grevously, or out of tyme as on haly° dayes, soothly they do greet synne. / Heer agayns° suffred Crist ful paciently, and taughte us pacience, whan he baar° upon his blissed shulder the croys upon which he sholde suffren despitous° deeth. / Heer may men lerne to be pacient, for certes noght only Cristen men been pacient for love of Jesu Crist, and for gerdoun° of the blisful lyf that is perdurable°, but certes the olde payens° that nevere were Cristene commendeden and useden the vertu of pacience. /

A philosophre upon a tyme, that wolde have beten his disciple for his grete trespas°, for which he was greetly amoeved° and broghte a yerde°
to scoure with° the child, / and whan this child 670
saugh the yerde, he seyde to his maister, "What thenke ye to do?" "I wol bete thee," quod the maister, "for thy correccioun." / "For sothe," quod the child, "ye oghten first correcte youreself, that han lost al youre pacience for the gilt of a child." / "For sothe," quod the maister al wepynge, "thow seyst sooth. Have thow the yerde, my deere sone, and correcte me for myn inpacience." / Of pacience comth obedience, thurgh which a man is obedient to Crist and to alle hem to whiche he oghte to been obedient in Crist. / And understond wel that

---

Right so, *similarly,* **knakkes,** *jokes* **653 mo,** *more* **654 clepen mansuetude,** *call meekness,* **debonairetee,** *humility* **655 refreyneth,** *restrains,* **corage,** *disposition* **657 wight,** *person,* **seith,** *speaks,* **eschawfeth,** *heats up* **658 quyk,** *living,* **tretable,** *inclined,* **enformed of,** *inspired by* **661 disconfiteth,** *disturbs,* **venquysse,** *defeat,* **suffre,** *endure* **662 manere,** *kinds* **663 Thilke,** *this,* **grucchyng,** *complaining,* **repreved,** *accused* **664 wrooth,** *angry,* **algate,** *nevertheless* **665 catel,** *property,* **Theragayns,** *against this,* **despoyled,** *robbed,* **nas,** *was nothing* **667 outrageous labour in werkes,** *excessive physical labor,* **haly,** *holy* **668 Heer agayns,** *against this,* **baar,** *carried,* **despitous,** *scornful* **669 gerdoun,** *reward,* **perdurable,** *everlasting,* **payens,** *pagans* **670 trespas,** *offense,* **amoeved,** *provoked,* **yerde,** *stick,* **scoure with,** *beat*

653a Sequitur remedium contra peccatum Ira, "Here follows the remedy against the sin of Anger." **657 Jerome seith,** not identified. **658 the philosophre,** Aristotle, *On Interpretation* 11. **660 The philosophre,** Aristotle, unidentified. **661 seith Crist,** Matthew 5.9. **wise man,** Dionysius Cato, supposed author of *Disticha Catonis* (*Cato's Couplets*) 1.38. **664 wise man,** Proverbs 29.9. **669–73 A philosophre . . . ,** the episode is unidentified.

obedience is perfit° whan that a man dooth gladly and hastily, with good herte entierly, al that he sholde do. / Obedience generally is to parfourne° the doctrine of God and of his sovereyns°, to whiche hym° oghte to ben obeisaunt° in alle rightwisnesse°. /

Sequitur de Accidia.

After the synne of envye and of ire, now wol I speken of the synne of accidie°. For envye blyndeth the herte of a man, and ire troubleth a man, and accidie maketh hym hevy, thoghtful°, and wrawful°. / Envye and ire maken bitternesse in herte, which bitternesse is mooder° of accidie, and bynymeth hym° the love of alle goodnesse. Thanne is accidie the angwissh of troubled herte. And Seint Augustyn seith, "It is anoy° of goodnesse and joye of harm." / Certes, this is a dampnable synne, for it dooth wrong to Jesu Crist inasmuche as it bynymeth the service that men oghte doon to Crist with alle diligence, as seith Salomon. / But accidie dooth no swich diligence; he dooth alle thyng with anoy, and with wrawnesse°, slaknesse, and excusacioun, and with ydelnesse and unlust°. For which the book seith, acursed be he that dooth the service of God necligently. / Thanne is accidie enemy to everich estaat° of man, for certes, the estaat of man is in three maneres. / Outher° it is th'estaat of innocence, as was th'estaat of Adam biforn that he fil into synne, in which estaat he was holden° to wirche°, as in heriynge° and adowrynge° of God. / Another estaat is the estaat of synful men, in which estaat men been holden to laboure in preiynge to God for amendement of hire synnes, and that he wole graunte hem to arysen out of hire synnes. / Another estaat is th'estaat of grace, in which estaat he is holden to werkes of penitence. And certes, to alle thise thynges is accidie enemy and contrarie. For he loveth no bisynesse at al. / Now certes, this foule swyn° accidie is eek a ful greet enemy to the lyflode° of the body, for it ne hath no purveaunce° agayn temporeel necessitee, for it forsleweth° and forsluggeth°, and destroyeth alle goodes temporeles° by reccheleesnesse°. /

The fourthe thynge is that accidie is lyk to hem that been in the peyne of helle, by cause of hir slouthe and of hire hevynesse, for they that been dampned been so bounde that they ne may neither wel do ne wel thynke. / Of accidie comth first that a man is anoyed° and encombred for° to doon any goodnesse, and maketh that God hath abhomynacion of swich accidie, as seith Seint Johan. /

Now comth slouthe that wol nat suffre noon hardnesse° ne no penaunce. For soothly, slouthe is so tendre and so delicaat, as seith Salomon, that he wol nat suffre noon hardnesse ne penaunce, and therfore he shendeth° al that he dooth. / Agayns this roten-herted synne of accidie and slouthe sholde men exercise hemself to doon goode werkes, and manly° and vertuously cacchen corage° wel to doon, thynkynge that oure lord Jesu Crist quiteth° every good dede be it never so lite°. / Usage° of labour is a greet thyng, for it maketh, as seith Seint Bernard, the laborer to have stronge armes and harde synwes°, and slouthe maketh hem feble and tendre. / Thanne comth drede to bigynne to werke anye goode werkes, for certes he that is enclyned to synne, hym thynketh it is so greet an emprise° for to undertake to doon werkes of goodnesse, / and casteth° in his herte that the circumstaunces of goodnesse been so grevouse and so chargeaunt° for to suffre that he dar nat undertake to do werkes of goodnesse, as seith Seint Gregorie. /

Now comth wanhope° that is despeir of the mercy of God, that comth somtyme of to muche outrageous sorwe, and somtyme of to muche drede, ymaginynge that he hath doon so muche synne that it wol nat availlen° hym, though

---

675 perfit, *perfect* **676 parfourne,** *perform,* **sovereyns,** *rulers,* **hym,** *i.e., the one who is ruled,* **obeisaunt,** *obedient,* **rightwisnesse,** *righteousness* **677 accidie,** *sloth,* **thoghtful,** *inactive,* **wrawful,** *peevish* **678 mooder,** *mother,* **bynymeth hym,** *deprives him of,* **anoy,** *annoyance* **680 wrawnesse,** *peevishness,* **unlust,** *lack of fervor* **681 everich estaat,** *every condition* **682 Outher,** *either,* **holden,** *obliged,* **wirche,** *work,* **heriynge,** *praising,* **adowrynge,** *adoring* **685 swyn,** *swine,* **lyflode,** *livelihood,* **purveaunce,** *provision,* **forsleweth,** *loses through delay,* **forsluggeth,** *neglects through sluggishness,* **goodes temporeles,** *worldly goods,* **reccheleesnesse,** *lack of concern* **687 anoyed,** *wearied,* **encombred for,** *impeded* **688 hardnesse,** *hardship,* **shendeth,** *destroys* **689 manly,** *manfully,* **cacchen corage,** *take heart,* **quiteth,** *rewards,* **lite,** *little* **690 Usage,** *habit,* **synwes,** *sinews* **691 emprise,** *enterprise* **692 casteth,** *thinks,* **chargeaunt,** *burdensome* **693 wanhope,** *hopelessness,* **availlen,** *be of use to*

676a Sequitur de Accidia, "Here follows [the section] concerning Sloth." **678 Augustyn,** see line 484 and note. **679 Salomon,** perhaps Ecclesiastes 9.10. **680 the book,** Jeremiah 48.10, with "negligently" replacing "fraudulently." **685 swyn,** other manuscripts read "synne," but the Deadly Sins were often depicted as animals or riding on symbolic animals. **687 Johan,** Revelation 3.16. **688 Salomon,** Proverbs 18.9. **690 Bernard,** not identified. **692 Gregorie,** not identified.

he wolde repenten hym and forsake synne, / thurgh which despeir or drede he abaundoneth al his herte to every maner synne, as seith Seint Augustyn. / Which dampnable synne, if that it continue unto his ende°, it is cleped° synnyng in° the Hooly Goost. / This horrible synne is so perilous that he that is despeired, ther nys no felonye ne no synne that he douteth° for to do, as sheweth wel by Judas. / Certes, aboven alle synnes thanne is this synne moost displesant to Crist, and moost adversarie. / Soothly, he that despeireth hym is lyk the coward champioun recreant° that seith creant° withoute nede. Allas, allas, nedelees is he recreant and nedelees despeired. / Certes, the mercy of God is evere redy to every penitent and is aboven alle his werkes. / Allas, kan a man nat bithynke hym on the gospel of Seint Luc, 15, where as Crist seith that as wel shal ther be joye in hevene upon a synful man that dooth penitence, as upon nynety and nyne rightful men that neden no penitence? / Looke forther° in the same gospel, the joye and the feeste of the goode man that hadde lost his sone, whan his sone with repentaunce was retourned to his fader. / Kan they nat remembren hem eek that, as seith Seint Luc 23, how that the theef that was hanged bisyde Jesu Crist seyde "Lord, remembre of me whan thow comest into thy regne°"? / "For sothe," seyde Crist, "I seye to thee, today shaltow° been with me in Paradys." / Certes, ther is noon so horrible synne of man that it ne may, in his lyf, be destroyed by penitence, thurgh vertu° of the passion and of the deeth of Crist. / Allas, what nedeth man thanne to been despeired, sith that his mercy so redy is and large°? Axe° and have. / Thanne cometh sompnolence°, that is sluggy° slombrynge, which maketh a man be hevy and dul in body and in soule, and this synne comth of slouthe. / And certes, the tyme that by wey of resoun men sholde nat slepe, that is by the morwe°, but if° ther were cause resonable. / For soothly, the morwetyde is moost covenable° a man to seye his preyeres, and for to thynken on God, and for to honoure God, and to yeven almesse to the poure, that first cometh in the name of Crist. / Lo, what seith Salomon, "Whoso wolde by the morwe awaken and seke me, he shal fynde." / Thanne cometh necligence or recchelesnesse° that rekketh° of nothyng. And how that ignoraunce be mooder of alle harm, certes, necligence is the norice°. / Necligence ne dooth no fors°, whan he shal doon a thyng, wheither he do it weel or baddely. /

Of the remedie of thise two synnes, as seith the wise man that he that dredeth God, he spareth nat to doon that hym oghte doon. / And he that loveth God, he wol doon diligence to plese God by his werkes and abaundone hymself with al his myght wel for to doon. / Thanne comth ydelnesse that is the yate° of alle harmes. An ydel man is lyk to a place that hath no walles; the develes may entre on every syde and sheten° at hym at discovert° by temptacion on every syde. / This ydelnesse is the thurrok° of alle wikked and vileyns thoghtes, and of alle jangles°, trufles°, and of alle ordure°. / Certes, the hevene is yeven to hem that wol labouren, and nat to ydel folk. Eek David seith that they ne been nat in the labour of men, ne they shul nat been whipped with men, that is to seyn, in purgatorie. / Certes, thanne semeth it they shul be tormented with the devel in helle, but if they doon penitence. /

Thanne comth the synne that men clepen *tarditas*°, as whan a man is to laterede° or tariynge er he wole turne to God, and certes that is a greet folie. He is lyk to him that falleth in the dych and wol nat arise. / And this vice comth of a fals hope, that he thynketh that he shal lyve longe, but that hope faileth ful ofte. /

Thanne comth lachesse°, that is he that whan he biginneth any good werk anon he shal forleten° it and stynten°, as doon they that han any wight to governe° and ne taken of hym namore kepe anon as° they fynden any contrarie or any anoy°. / Thise been the newe sheepherdes that

---

695 ende, *death,* **cleped,** *called,* **in,** *against* **696 douteth,** *fears* **698 recreant,** *fearful,* **seith creant,** *says "I give up"* **701 Looke forther,** *notice further* **702 regne,** *kingdom* **703 shaltow,** *you shall* **704 vertu,** *the power* **705 large,** *generous,* **Axe,** *ask* **706 sompnolence,** *sleepiness,* **sluggy,** *sluggish* **707 by the morwe,** *in the morning,* **but if,** *unless* **708 covenable,** *appropriate* (for) **710 recchelesnesse,** *lack of concern,* **rekketh,** *cares,* **norice,** *nurse* **711 ne dooth no fors,** *does not care* **714 yate,** *gate,* **sheten,** *shoot,* **at discovert,** *in the open* **715 thurrok,** *bilge,* **jangles,** *gossip,* **trufles,** *trifles,* **ordure,** *filth* **718 tarditas,** (Lat.) *slowness,* **to laterede,** *too lardy* **720 lachesse,** *laziness,* **forleten,** *abandon,* **stynten,** *stop,* **wight to governe,** *person to supervise,* **kepe anon as,** *care as soon as,* **anoy,** *trouble*

694 Augustyn, not identified in Augustine. **696 Judas,** after betraying Jesus, Judas hanged himself, epitomizing despair; Matthew 27.5. **698 that seith . . . recreant,** omitted in El. **700–03 Luc,** Luke 15.7, 11–24 and 23.42–43. **700 nyne,** El reads "nyneteen." **703 seyde,** omitted in El. **705 Axe and have,** echoes Matthew 7.7. **707 the morwe,** omitted in El. **709 Salomon,** Proverbs 8.17. **712** Ecclesiastes 7.19. **714 yate,** see *KnT* 1.1940 and *SNT* 8.2–3n. **716 David,** perhaps Psalms 73.5 (Vulgate 72.5). **721 newe sheepherdes,** i.e., newfangled shepherds; the shepherd metaphor is recurrently applied to pastors, bad and good, but it is not in Chaucer's source. It underlies the idealization of the Parson in *GP* 1.496–514.

leten hir sheep witynglyº go renne to the wolf that is in the breresº, or do no forsº of hir owene governaunce. / Of this comth poverte and destruccioun, bothe of spiritueel and temporeel thynges. Thanne comth a manere cooldnesse that fresethº al the herte of a man. / Thanne comth undevocioun, thurgh which a man is so blentº, as seith Seint Bernard, and hath swiche langour in soule, that he may neither rede ne singe in hooly chirche, ne heere ne thynke of no devocioun, ne travailleº with his handes in no good werk, that it nys hym unsavouryº and al apalledº. / Thanne wexethº he sloughº and slombry, and soone wol be wrooth, and soone is enclyned to hate and to envye. / Thanne comth the synne of worldly sorwe which as is cleped *tristicia*º that sleeth man, as Seint Paul seith. / For certes, swich sorwe werketh to the deeth ofthe soule and of the body also, for therof comth that a man is anoyed of his owene lif. / Wherfore swich sorwe shorteth ful ofte the lif of man, er that his tyme be come by wey of kyndeº. /

Remedium contra peccatum Accidie.

Agayns this horrible synne of accidie, and the branches of the same, ther is a vertu that is called *fortitudo* or strengthe, that is an affecciounº thurgh which a man despiseth anoyouseº thynges. / This vertu is so myghty and so vigorous that it dar withstonde myghtily, and wisely kepen hymself fro perils that been wikked, and wrastle agayn the assautes of the devel. / For it enhaunceth and enforcethº the soule, right as accidie abatethº it and maketh it fieble. For this *fortitudo* may endure by long suffraunce the travailles that been covenableº. /

This vertu hath manye speces, and the firste is clepedº magnanimitee, that is to seyn greet corage. For certes, ther bihovethº greet corage agains accidie lest that it ne swolwe the soule by the synne of sorwe, or destroye it by wanhopeº. / This vertu maketh folk to undertake harde thynges and grevouse thynges, by hir owene wil, wysely and resonably. / And for as muchel as the devel fighteth agayns a man moore by queyntiseº and by sleighte than by strengthe, therfore men shal withstonden hym by wit and by resoun and by discrecioun. / Thanne arn ther the vertues of feith and hope in God and in his seintes, to acheve and acomplice the goode werkes in the whiche he purposeth fermely to continue. / Thanne comth seureteeº or sikernesseº, and that is whan a man ne doutethº no travailleº in tyme comynge of the goode werkes that a man hath bigonne. / Thanne comth magnificence, that is to seyn, whan a man dooth and parfourneth grete werkes of goodnesse, and that is the ende why that men sholde do goode werkes. For in the acomplissynge of grete goode werkes lith the grete gerdounº. / Thanne is ther constaunce, that is stablenesse of corage, and this sholde been in herte by stedefast feith, and in mouth, and in berynge, and in chiereº, and in dede. / Eke ther been mo speciale remedies agains accidie in diverse werkes, and in consideracioun of the peynes of helle, and of the joyes of hevene, and in trust of the grace of the Hooly Goost, that wole yeveº hym myght to parfourne his goode entente. /

Sequitur de Avaricia.

After accidie wol I speke of avarice and of coveitiseº, of which synne seith Seint Paule that the roote of alle harmes is coveitise, *ad Timotheum 6*. / For soothly, whan the herte of a man is confounded in itself and troubled, and that the soule hath lost the confort of God, thanne seketh he an ydel solas of worldly thynges. /

Avarice, after the descripcion of Seint Augustyn, is likerousnesseº in herte to have erthely thynges. / Som oother folk seyn that avarice is for to purchacen manye erthely thynges, and nothyng yeve to hem that han nede. / And understond that avarice ne stant nat oonly in lond ne catelº,

---

721 wityngly, *knowingly,* **breres,** *briars,* **do no fors,** *do not care* **722 freseth,** *freezes* **723 blent,** *blinded,* **travaille,** *labor,* **unsavoury,** *unpleasant,* **apalled,** *pale* **724 wexeth,** *grows,* **slough,** *slow* **725 tristicia,** (Lat.) *depression* **727 kynde,** *nature* **728 affeccioun,** *inclination,* **anoyouse,** *harmful* **730 enforceth,** *strengthens,* **abateth,** *weakens,* **covenable,** *appropriate* **731 cleped,** *called,* **bihoveth,** *is needed,* **wanhope,** *despair* **733 queyntise,** *cleverness* **735 seuretee,** *security,* **sikernesse,** *certainly,* **douteth,** *fears,* **travaille,** *labor* **736 gerdoun,** *reward* **737 chiere,** *manner* **738 yeve,** *give* **739 coveitise,** *greed* **741 likerousnesse,** *desire* **743 catel,** *possessions*

723 Bernard, *Sermons concerning the Song of Songs* 54. **725 Paul,** 2 Corinthians 7.10. **727a Remedium contra peccatum Accidie,** "Remedy against the sin of Sloth." **738a Sequitur de Avaricia,** "Here follows [the section] concerning Avarice." **739 Paule,** 1 Timothy 6.10. The phrase recurs at *PardP* 6.334 and 426. **741 Augustyn,** *City of God* 14.15.

but somtyme in science° and in glorie, and in every manere of outrageous° thyng is avarice and coveitise. / And the difference bitwixe avarice and coveitise is this. Coveitise is for to coveite swiche thynges as thou hast nat, and avarice is for to withholde and kepe swiche thynges as thou hast withoute rightful nede. / Soothly, this avarice is a synne that is ful dampnable, for al hooly writ curseth it and speketh agayns that vice, for it dooth wrong to Jesu Crist. / For it bireveth° hym the love that men to hym owen, and turneth it bakward agayns alle resoun, / and maketh that the avaricious man hath moore hope in his catel° than in Jesu Crist, and dooth moore observance in° kepynge of his tresor than he dooth to service of Jesu Crist. / And therfore seith Seint Paul *ad Ephesios 5*, that an avaricious man is in the thraldom of ydolatrie. /

What difference is bitwixe an ydolastre° and an avaricious man, but that an ydolastre peraventure ne hath but o mawmet° or two and the avaricious man hath manye? For certes, every florin° in his cofre° is his mawmet. / And certes, the synne of mawmetrye is the firste thyng that God deffended° in the Ten Comaundmentz, as bereth witnesse *Exodi 20*, / "Thou shalt have no false goddes bifore me, ne thou shalt make to thee no grave° thyng." Thus is an avaricious man that loveth his tresor biforn God an ydolastre / thurgh this cursed synne of avarice. Of coveitise comen thise harde lordshipes°, thurgh whiche men been distreyned° by taylages°, custumes, and cariages°, moore than hire duetee° or resoun is. And eek they taken of hire bondemen° amercimentz°, whiche myghten moore resonably ben cleped° extorcions than amercimentz. / Of whiche amercimentz and raunsonynge of° bondemen, somme lordes stywardes seyn that it is rightful for as muche as a cherl hath no temporeel thyng that it ne is his lordes, as they seyn. / But certes, thise lordshipes doon wrong that bireven° hire bondefolk thynges that they nevere yave hem, *Augustinus de Civitate, libro 9*. / Sooth is that the condicioun of thraldom° and the firste cause of thraldom is for synne, *Genesis, 9*. /

Thus may ye seen that the gilt disserveth thraldom, but nat nature. / Wherfore thise lordes ne sholde nat muche glorifien hem in hir lordshipes, sith that° by natureel condicion they been nat lordes of thralles, but for that thraldom comth first by the desert of synne. / And fortherover, ther as the lawe seith that temporeel goodes of boondefolk been the goodes of hir lordshipes, ye° that is for to understonde the goodes of the emperour, to deffenden hem° in hir right, but nat for to robben hem ne reven° hem. / And therfore seith Seneca, "Thy prudence sholde lyve benignely with thy thralles." / Thilke° that thou clepest thy thralles been Goddes peple, for humble folk been Cristes freendes; they been contubernyal° with the Lord. /

Thynk eek that of swich seed as cherles° spryngeth°, of swich seed spryngen lordes. As wel may the cherl be saved as the lord. / The same deeth that taketh the cherl, swich deeth taketh the lord. Wherfore I rede°, do right so with thy cherl as thou woldest that thy lord dide with thee, if thou were in his plit°. / Every synful man is a cherl to synne. I rede thee, certes, that thou, lord, werke in swiche wise with thy cherles that they rather love thee than drede. / I woot° wel ther is degree above degree, as reson is; and skile° it is that men do hir devoir ther as° it is due; but certes, extorcions and despit° of youre underlynges is dampnable. /

And fortherover, understoond wel that thise conquerours or tirauntz maken ful ofte thralles of hem that been born of as roial blood as been they that hem conqueren. / This name of thraldom was nevere erst kowth° til that Noe seyde that his sone Canaan sholde be thral to his bretheren for his synne. / What seye we thanne of hem that pilen° and doon extorcions to Hooly Chirche? Certes, the swerd that men yeven first to a knyght whan he is newe dubbed signifieth that he sholde deffenden Hooly Chirche, and nat

---

science, *knowledge,* **outrageous,** *excessive* **746 bireveth,** *robs* **747 catel,** *possessions,* **dooth moore observance in,** *pays more attention to* **749 ydolastre,** *idolator,* **o mawmet,** *one idol,* **florin,** *coin,* **cofre,** *money chest* **750 deffended,** *forbade* **751 grave,** *carved* **752 harde lordshipes,** *harsh regimes,* **distreyned,** *overwhelmed,* **taylages,** *taxes,* **cariages,** *tolls,* **duetee,** *obligations,* **bondemen,** *serfs,* **amercimentz,** *fines,* **cleped,** *called* **753 raunsonynge of,** *payments from* **754 bireven,** *deprive* **755 thraldom,** *slavery* **757 sith that,** *since* **758 ye,** *yes,* **deffenden hem,** *protect them,* **reven,** *steal* **760 Thilke,** *those,* **been contubernyal,** *dwell* **761 cherles,** *servants,* **spryngeth,** *grow from* **762 rede,** *advise,* **plit,** *condition* **764 woot,** *know,* **skile,** *reasonable,* **hir devoir ther as,** *their duty where,* **despit,** *scorn* **766 erst kowth,** *before known* **767 pilen,** *pillage*

748 Seint Paul, Ephesians 5.5. **750 *Exodi*,** Exodus 20.3–4. **754 *Augustinus* . . . ,** Augustine, *City of God* 19.15. **755 *Genesis*,** 9.22–27. **759 Seneca,** *Moral Epistles* 47.1. **766 Noe . . . Canaan,** Genesis 9.25. **767 to Hooly Chirche,** El reads "in Hooly Chirche."

robben it ne pilen it. And whoso dooth is traitour to Crist. / And as seith Seint Augustyn, "They been the develes wolves that stranglen the sheepe of Jesu Crist"—and doon worse than wolves. / For soothly, whan the wolf hath ful his wombe°, he stynteth° to strangle sheepe. But soothly, the pilours° and destroyours of goodes of Hooly Chirche ne do nat so, for they ne stynte nevere to pile. / Now, as I have seyd, sith so is that synne was first cause of thraldom, thanne is it thus, that thilke tyme that al this world was in synne, thanne was al this world in thraldom and subjeccioun. / But certes, sith the time of grace cam, God ordeyned that som folk sholde be moore heigh in estaat and in degree, and some folk moore lough°, and that everich sholde be served in his estaat and in his degree. / And therfore, in somme contrees ther° they byen° thralles, whan they han turned hem to the feith they maken hire thralles free out of thraldom. And therfore, certes, the lord oweth to his man that the man oweth to his lord. / The Pope calleth hymself servant of the servauntz of God; but for as muche as the estaat° of Hooly Chirche ne myghte nat han be°, ne the commune profit myghte nat han be kept, ne pees and reste in erthe, but if God hadde ordeyned that som men hadde hyer degree and som men lower, / therfore was sovereyntee ordeyned to kepe and mayntene and deffenden° hire underlynges or hire subgetz in resoun, as ferforth° as it lith° in hire power, and nat to destroyen hem ne confounde. / Wherfore I seye that thilke lordes that been lyk wolves, that devouren the possessiouns or the catel of poure folk wrongfully, withouten mercy or mesure°, / they shul receyven by the same mesure that they han mesured to poure folk the mercy of Jesu Crist, but if it be amended. /

Now comth deceite bitwixe marchant and marchant. And thow shalt understonde that marchandise° is in manye maneres: that oon is bodily°, and that oother is goostly°. That oon is honeste and leveful°, and that oother is deshoneste and unleveful. / Of thilke bodily marchandise that is leveful and honeste is this, that there as God hath ordeyned that a regne or a contree is suffisaunt to hymself, thanne is it honeste and leveful that of habundaunce of this contree that men helpe another contree that is moore nedy. / And therfore, ther moote° been marchantz to bryngen fro that o contree to that oother hire marchandises. / That oother marchandise that men haunten° with fraude and trecherie and deceite, with lesynges° and false othes, is cursed and dampnable. / Espiritueel marchandise is proprely symonye°, thatis ententif° desir to byen thyng espiritueel, that is thyng that aperteneth° to the seintuarie° of God and to cure of the soule. / This desir, if so be that a man do his diligence° to parfournen it, al be it that his desir ne take noon effect, yet is it to hym a deedly synne; and if he be ordred°, he is irreguleer°. / Certes, symonye is cleped of° Symon Magus, that wolde han boght for temporeel catel° the yifte that God hadde yeven by the Hooly Goost to Seint Peter and to the apostles. / And therfore understoond that bothe he that selleth and he that beyeth thynges espirituels been cleped symonials, be it by catel, be it by procurynge°, or by flesshly preyere° of his freendes, flesshly freendes or espiritueel freendes. / Flesshly in two maneres, as by kynrede or othere freendes. Soothly, if they praye° for hym that is nat worthy and able°, it is symonye if he take the benefice°, and if he be worthy and able, ther nys noon. / That oother manere is whan a man or womman preyen for folk to avauncen hem oonly for wikked flesshly affeccioun that they han unto the persone, and that is foul symonye. / But certes, in service for which men yeven thynges espiritueels° unto hir servantz, it moot° been understonde that the service moot been honeste, and elles nat; and eek that it be withouten bargaynynge; and that the persone be able. / For as seith Seint Damasie, "Alle the synnes of the world at regard of this synne arn as thyng of noght," for it is the gretteste synne that may be, after the synne of Lucifer and Antecrist. / For by this

---

769 wombe, *stomach,* **stynteth,** *ceases,* **pilours,** *pillagers* **771 lough,** *low* **772 ther,** *where,* **byen,** *buy* **773 estaat,** *status,* **han be,** *have been* **774 deffenden,** *protect,* **ferforth,** *far,* **lith,** *lies* **775 mesure,** *measurement* **777 marchandise,** *trading,* **bodily,** *physical,* **goostly,** *spiritual,* **leveful,** *lawful* **779 moote,** *might* **780 haunten,** *practice,* **lesynges,** *lies* **781 proprely symonye,** *correctly* (called) *simony* (see 783n), **ententif,** *intentional,* **aperteneth,** *pertains,* **seintuarie,** *sacred things* **782 do his diligence,** *makes an effort,* **ordred,** *ordained,* **is irreguleer,** *may not perform or receive the sacraments* **783 cleped of,** *named after,* **for temporeel catel,** *with worldly goods* **784 procurynge,** *manipulating,* **flesshly preyere,** *worldly pleas* **785 praye,** *intercede,* **able,** *competent,* **benefice,** *clerical appointment* **787 thynges espiritueels,** *spiritual rewards,* **moot,** *must*

768 Augustyn, quotation not identified. **769 goodes of,** El reads "goddes" (God's). **771 and in his degree,** omitted in El. **772 byen,** some manuscripts read "ben." **773 servant of the servauntz of God,** a signatory phrase used by popes since Gregory the Great in 591; see *TC* 1.15. **783 Symon Magus,** a magician who sought to buy power from the apostles; Acts 8.18–20. Simony is the buying and selling of church offices.**788 Seint Damasie,** Pope Damasus I; the quotation is found in Gratian, *Decretals* 2.1.7.27.

synne, God forleseth° the chirche and the soule that he boghte with his precious blood by hem that yeven chirches to hem that been nat digne°. / For they putten in theves that stelen the soules of Jesu Crist and destroyen his patrimoyne. / By swiche undigne° preestes and curates han lewed° men the lasse° reverence of the sacramentz of Hooly Chirche. And swiche yeveres° of chirches putten out the children of Crist, and putten into the chirche the develes owene sone. / They sellen the soules that lambes sholde kepen to° the wolf that strangleth° hem. And therfore shul they nevere han part of the pasture of lambes, that is the blisse of hevene. /

Now comth hasardrie° with his apurtenaunces°, as tables° and rafles°, of which comth deceite, false othes, chidynges, and alle ravynes°, blasphemynge and reneiynge° of God, and hate of his neighebores, wast of goodes, mysspendynge of tyme, and somtyme manslaughtre. / Certes, hasardours ne mowe nat been° withouten greet synne whyles they haunte that craft. / Of avarice comen eek lesynges°, thefte, fals witnesse, and false othes. And ye shul understonde that thise been grete synnes, and expres° agayn the comaundementz of God, as I have seyd. / Fals witnesse is in word and eek in dede. In word, as for to bireve° thy neighebores goode name by thy fals witnessyng, or bireven hym his catel or his heritage by thy fals witnessyng, whan thou for ire, or for meede°, or for envye berest fals witnesse, or accusest hym, or excusest hym by thy fals witnesse, or elles excusest thyself falsly. / Ware yow°, questemongeres° and notaries! Certes, for fals witnessyng was Susanna in ful gret sorwe and peyne, and many another mo. / The synne of thefte is eek expres agayns Goodes heeste°, and that in two maneres, corporeel or espiritueel. / Corporeel, as for to take thy neighebores catel° agayn his wyl, be it by force or by sleighte, be it by met or by mesure°. / By stelyng eek of false enditementz° upon hym, and in borwynge of thy neighebores catel, in entente nevere to payen it agayn, and semblable° thynges. / Espiritueel thefte is sacrilege, that is to seyn hurtynge of hooly thynges or of thynges sacred to Crist in two maneres: by reson of° the hooly place, as chirches or chirche hawes°, / for which every vileyns synne that men doon in swiche places may be cleped° sacrilege, or every violence in the semblable places. Also they that withdrawen falsly the rightes that longen° to Hooly Chirche. / And pleynly and generally, sacrilege is to reven° hooly thyng fro hooly place, or unhooly thyng out of hooly place, or hooly thyng out of unhooly place. /

Relevacio contra peccatum Avaricie.

Now shul ye understonde that the releevynge° of avarice is misericorde° and pitee largely taken°. And men myghten axe, why that misericorde and pitee is releevinge of avarice? / Certes, the avaricious man sheweth no pitee ne misericorde to the nedeful man, for he deliteth hym in the kepynge of his tresor, and nat in the rescowynge° ne releevynge of his evene-Cristene°. And therfore speke I first of misericorde. / Thanne is misericorde, as seith the philosophre, a vertu by which the corage° of man is stired by the mysese° of hym that is mysesed°. / Upon which misericorde folweth pitee in parfournynge of charitable werkes of misericorde. / And certes, thise thynges moeven a man to misericorde of Jesu Crist: that he yaf hymself for oure gilt, and suffred deeth for misericorde, and forgaf us oure originale synnes, / and therby relessed us fro the peynes of helle, and amenused° the peynes of purgatorie by penitence, and yeveth grace wel to do, and atte laste the blisse of hevene. / The speces of misericorde been as for to lene°, and for to yeve, and to foryeven and relesse°, and for to han pitee in herte, and compassioun of the meschief of his evene Cristene, and eek to chastise there as nede is. /

---

789 forleseth, *completely loses,* **digne,** *worthy* **791 By swiche undigne,** *because of such unworthy,* **lewed,** *unlearned,* **lasse,** *less,* **yeveres,** *givers* **792 kepen to,** *protect from,* **strangleth,** *kills* **793 hasardrie,** *gambling,* **apurtenaunces,** *accessories,* **tables,** *backgammon,* **rafles,** *dice,* **ravynes,** *robberies,* **reneiynge,** *denying* **794 ne mowe nat been,** *cannot be* **795 lesynges,** *lies,* **expres,** *explicitly* **796 bireve,** *deprive,* **meede,** *payment* **797 Ware,** *beware,* **questemongeres,** *lawsuit seekers* **798 heeste,** *command* **799 catel,** *possessions,* **by met or by mesure,** *in whatever quantity* **800 eek of false enditementz,** *also* (by means) *of false documents,* **semblable,** *similar* **801 by reson of,** *as the result of,* **chirche hawes,** *churchyards* **802 cleped,** *called,* **longen,** *belong* **803 reven,** *steal* **804 releevynge,** *remedying,* **misericorde,** *compassion,* **largely taken,** *generously applied* **805 rescowynge,** *rescuing,* **evene-Cristene,** *fellow Christian* **806 corage,** *heart,* **mysese,** *distress,* **mysesed,** *distressed* **809 amenused,** *reduced* **810 lene,** *lend,* **relesse,** *release* (from obligations)

794 whyles . . . craft, omitted in El. **797 Susanna,** a beautiful woman, victim of lust and false accusation; Daniel 13. **799 Corporeel,** omitted in El. **803a Relevacio contra peccatum Avaricie,** "Relief against the sin of Avarice." **806 the philosophre,** *Moralium Dogma Philosophorum,* attributed to William of Conches (ed. John Holmberg) 27.

Another manere of remedie agayns avarice is
resonable largesse°. But soothly, heere bihoveth°
the consideracioun of the grace of Jesu Crist and
of his temporeel goodes, and eek of the goodes
perdurables° that Crist yaf to us; / and to han
remembrance of the deeth that he shal receyve,
he noot° whanne, where, ne how; and eek that he
shal forgon al that he hath save oonly that he hath
despended° in goode werkes. /

But for as muche as som folk been unmesurable°,
men oughten eschue fool largesse°, that men clepen
wast°. / Certes, he that is fool large ne yeveth nat his
catel°, but he leseth his catel. Soothly, what thyng
that he yeveth for veyne glorie, as to mynstrals and
to folk, for to beren his renoun in the world, he
hath synne therof and noon almesse°. / Certes,
he leseth foule° his good that ne seketh with
the yifte of his good° nothing but synne. / 815
He is lyk to an hors that seketh rather to drynken
drovy° or trouble water than for to drynken water of
the clere welle. / And for as muchel as they yeven
ther as they sholde nat yeven, to hem aperteneth
thilke malisoun° that Crist shal yeven at the day of
doome to hem that shullen been dampned. /

Sequitur de Gula.

After avarice comth glotonye, which is expres°
eek agayn the comandement of God. Glotonye is
unmesurable appetit to ete or to drynke, or elles
to doon ynogh to° the unmesurable appetit and
desordeynee° coveitise to eten or to drynke. / This
synne corrumped° al this world as is wel shewed in
the synne of Adam and of Eve. Looke eek what seith
Seint Paul of glotonye. / "Manye," seith Seint Paul,
"good°, of whiche I have ofte seyd to yow and now
I seye it wepynge that they been the enemys of the
croys° of Crist, of whiche the ende is deeth, and
of whiche hire wombe° is hire god, and hire glorie
in confusioun° of hem that so devouren erthely
thynges." / He that is usaunt° to this synne of 820
glotonye, he ne may no synne withstonde. He
moot been in servage° of alle vices, for it is the
develes hoord ther° he hideth hym and resteth. /
This synne hath manye speces. The firste is dronkenesse, that is the horrible sepulture° of mannes
resoun. And therfore whan a man is dronken,
he hath lost his resoun, and this is deedly synne.
/ But soothly, whan that a man is nat wont° to
strong drynke, and peraventure° ne knoweth nat
the strengthe of the drynke, or hath feblesse in his
heed, or hath travailed°, thurgh which he drynketh
the moore, al be he sodeynly caught with drynke,
it is no deedly synne, but venyal. / The seconde
spece of glotonye is that the spirit of a man wexeth
al trouble°, for dronkenesse bireveth hym the discrecioun of his wit. / The thridde spece of glotonye
is whan a man devoureth his mete° and hath
no rightful manere of etynge. / The fourthe is 825
whan thurgh the grete habundaunce of his
mete the humours in his body been destempred°. /
The fifthe is foryetelnesse° by to muchel drynkynge,
for which somtyme a man foryeteth er the morwe
what he dide at even or on the nyght biforn. /

In oother manere been° distinct the speces of
glotonye, after° Seint Gregorie. The firste is for
to ete biforn tyme to ete. The seconde is whan a
man get hym to delicaat° mete or drynke. / The
thridde is whan men taken to muche over mesure°.
The fourthe is curiositee° with greet entente to
maken and apparaillen° his mete. The fifthe is for
to eten to gredily. / Thise been the fyve fyngres of
the develes hand by whiche he draweth folk to
synne. / 830

Remedium contra peccatum Gule.

Agayns glotonye is the remedie abstinence, as
seith Galien, but that holde I nat meritorie° if
he do it oonly for the heele° of his body. Seint

---

811 resonable largesse, *moderate generosity,* **bihoveth,** *is needed,* **perdurables,** *everlasting* **812 noot,** *knows not,* **despended,** *spent* **813 unmesurable,** *immoderate,* **eschue fool largesse,** *avoid foolish generosity,* **clepen wast,** *call waste* **814 catel,** *possessions,* **almesse,** *charity* **815 leseth foule,** *loses foully,* **good,** *possessions* **816 drovy,** *dirty* **817 aperteneth thilke malisoun,** *belongs that curse* **818 expres,** *explicitly,* **doon ynogh to,** *satisfy,* **desordeynee,** *excessive* **819 corrumped,** *corrupted* **820 Manye . . . goon,** (there are) *many who walk about,* **croys,** *cross,* **wombe,** *stomach,* **confusioun,** *damnation* **821 usaunt,** *accustomed,* **servage,** *slavery,* **hoord ther,** *treasury where* **822 sepulture,** *tomb* **823 wont,** *accustomed,* **peraventure,** *perhaps,* **travailed,** *suffered* **824 wexeth al trouble,** *grows all troubled* **825 mete,** *food* **826 destempred,** *out of balance* **827 foryetelnesse,** *forgetfulness* **828 oother manere been,** *another way are,* **after,** *according to,* **to delicaat,** *too fancy* **829 over mesure,** *beyond moderation,* **curiositee,** *intricacy,* **apparaillen,** *adorn* **831 meritorie,** *meritorious,* **heele,** *health*

817a Sequitur de Gula, "Here follows [the section] concerning Gluttony." **820 Seint Paul,** Philippians 3.18–19; also in *PardT* 6.529–32. **826 humours,** see *GP* 1.333n. **828 Seint Gregorie,** *Morals* 30.18.60. **830 fyve fyngres,** the devil's five fingers is a commonplace in sermon literature. **830a Remedium contra peccatum Gule,** "Remedy against the sin of Gluttony." **831 Galien,** Galen, second-century Greek authority on medicine.

Augustyn wole that abstinence be doon for vertu and with pacience. / Abstinence, he seith, is litel worth but if a man have good wil therto, and but it be enforced by pacience and by charitee, and that men doon it for Godes sake, and in hope to have the blisse of hevene. /

The felawes of abstinence been attemperaunce that holdeth the meene° in alle thynges; eek shame that eschueth° alle deshonestee; suffisance° that seketh no riche metes ne drynkes, ne dooth no fors of° to outrageous apparailynge° of mete; / mesure° also that restreyneth by resoun the deslavee° appetit of etynge; sobrenesse also that restreyneth the outrage° of drynke; / sparynge° also that restreyneth the delicaat ese° to sitte longe at his mete and softely, wherfore som folk stonden
of hir owene wyl to eten at the lasse leyser°. / 835

Sequitur de Luxuria.

After glotonye thanne comth lecherie, for thise two synnes been so ny cosyns° that ofte tyme they wol nat departe°. / God woot°, this synne is ful displesaunt thyng to God, for he seyde hymself, "Do no lecherie." And therfore he putte grete peynes° agayns this synne in the olde lawe. / If womman thral° were taken in this synne, she sholde be beten with staves to the deeth. And if she were a gentil womman, she sholde be slayn with stones. And if she were a bisshoppes doghter, she sholde been brent by Goddes comandement. / Fortherover, by° the synne of lecherie God dreynte° al the world at the diluge. And after that, he brente° fyve citees with thonder-leyt°, and sank hem into helle. /

Now lat us speke thanne of thilke stynkynge synne of lecherie that men clepe avowtrie° of wedded folk, that is to seyn if that oon of hem be
wedded, or elles bothe. / Seint John seith that 840
avowtiers shullen been in helle in a stank° brennynge of fyr and of brymston—in fyr for the lecherie, in brymston for the stynk of hire ordure°. / Certes, the brekynge of this sacrement is an horrible thyng. It was maked of God hymself in paradys, and confermed by Jesu Crist, as witnesseth Seint Mathew in the gospel, "A man shal lete° fader and mooder, and taken hym to his wif, and they shullen be two in o flessh." / This sacrement bitokneth the knyttynge togidre of Crist and of Hooly Chirche. / And nat oonly that God forbad avowtrie in dede, but eek he comanded that thou sholdest nat coveite thy neighebores wyf. / In this heeste°, seith Seint Augustyn, is forboden alle manere coveitise to doon lecherie. Lo what seith Seint Mathew in the gospel, that whoso seeth° a womman to coveitise of his lust, he hath doon
lecherie with hire in his herte. / Heere may ye 845
seen that nat oonly the dede of this synne is forboden, but eek the desir to doon that synne. / This cursed synne anoyeth° grevousliche hem that it haunten°. And first to hire soule, for he obligeth° it to synne and to peyne of deeth that is perdurable°. / Unto the body anoyeth it grevously also, for it dreyeth° hym, and wasteth, and shent° hym, and of his blood he maketh sacrifice to the feend of helle; it wasteth his catel° and his substaunce°. / And certes, if it be a foul thyng a man to waste his catel on wommen, yet is it a fouler thyng whan that for swich ordure° wommen dispenden upon men hir catel and substaunce. / This synne, as seith the prophete, bireveth° man and womman hir goode fame and al hire honour, and it is ful pleasaunt to the devel, for therby wynneth he the mooste
partie° of this world. / And right° as a marchant 850
deliteth hym moost in chaffare° that he hath moost avantage of, right so deliteth the fend in this ordure. /

---

833 meene, *middle way,* **eschueth,** *avoids,* **suffisance,** *sufficiency,* **dooth no fors of,** *makes no effort,* **apparailynge,** *decoration* **834 mesure,** *moderation,* **deslavee,** *uncontrolled,* **outrage,** *excess* **835 sparynge,** *self-control,* **delicaat ese,** *extravagant ease,* **lasse leyser,** *less leisure* **836 ny cosyns,** *close cousins,* **departe,** *separate* **837 woot,** *knows,* **peynes,** *punishments* **838 thral,** *servant* **839 by,** *because of,* **dreynte,** *drowned,* **brente,** *burned,* **thonder-leyt,** *lightning* **840 clepe avowtrie,** *call adultery* **841 stank,** *pond,* **ordure,** *filth* **842 lete,** *leave* **845 heeste,** *command,* **seeth,** *looks upon* **847 anoyeth,** *damages,* **haunten,** *practices,* **obligeth,** *compels,* **perdurable,** *everlasting* **848 dreyeth,** *dries,* **shent,** *ruins,* **catel,** *property,* **substaunce,** *wealth* **849 ordure,** *filth* **850 bireveth,** *deprives,* **mooste partie,** *greatest part* **851 right,** *just,* **chaffare,** *trading*

Seint Augustyn, not identified. **835a Sequitur de Luxuria,** "Here follows [the section] concerning Lechery." **837 "Do no lecherie,"** perhaps Exodus 20.14 **838 beten . . . to the deeth,** beating a servant to death for lechery contradicts Leviticus 19.20; stoning and burning are punishments for lechery in Deuteronomy 22.21 and Leviticus 21.9. **839 diluge . . . fyve citees,** lechery is the reason for the deluge (flood) in Genesis 6.4–7. Five cities are grouped in Genesis 14.8: Sodom, Gomorrah, Admah, Zeboim, and Bela, although only the first two are specified in the account of their destruction in Genesis 19. **841 Seint John,** Revelation 21.8. **in fyr . . . brymston,** omitted in El. **842 maked of God,** Genesis 2.18–25. **Seint Mathew,** Matthew 19.5. **843** The comparison between marriage and Christ's relation to his Church is rooted in Ephesians 5.25. **844 coveite,** Exodus 20.17. **845 Seint Augustyn,** *Concerning the Sermon on the Mount* 1.36. **Seint Mathew,** Matthew 5.28. **850 the prophete,** reference unidentified.

This is that other hand of the devel, with fyve fyngres to cacche the peple to his vileynye. / The firste
fynger is the fool° lookynge of the fool womman
and of the fool man, that sleeth right as the basilicok sleeth folk by the venym of his sighte, for the
coveitise of eyen folweth the coveitise of the herte. /
The seconde fynger is the vileyns touchynge in
wikkede manere, and therfore seith Salomon
that whoso toucheth and handleth a womman, he
fareth lyk hym that handleth the scorpioun that
styngeth and sodeynly sleeth thurgh his envenymynge. As whoso toucheth warm pych° is shent°
his fyngres. / The thridde is foule wordes that
fareth° lyk fyr, that right anon brenneth° the
herte. / The fourthe fynger is the kyssinge, 855
and trewely he were a greet fool that wolde
kisse the mouth of a brennynge ovene or of a fourneys. / And moore fooles been they that kissen in
vileynye, for that mouth is the mouth of helle—and
namely, thise olde dotardes holours°, yet wol they
kisse though they may nat do, and smatre hem°. /
Certes, they been lyk to houndes, for an hound
whan he comth by the roser° or by othere beautees,
though he may nat pisse yet wole he heve up his leg
and make a contenaunce to pisse. / And for that
many man weneth° that he may nat synne for no
likerousnesse° that he dooth with his wyf, certes,
that opinion is fals. God woot, a man may sleen
hymself with his owene knyf, and make hymselven
dronken of his owene tonne°. / Certes, be it wyf, be
it child, or any worldlythyng that he loveth biforn
God, it is his mawmet° and he is an ydolastre.
/ Man sholdeloven hys wyf by discrecioun, 860
paciently and atemprely°, and thanne is she as
though it were his suster. / The fifthe fynger of the
develes hand is the stynkinge dede of leccherie. /
Certes, the fyve fyngres of glotonie the feend put in
the wombe° of a man, and with his fyve fyngres of
lecherie he gripeth hym by the reynes for to throwen
hym into the fourneys of helle / ther as they shul
han the fyr and the wormes that evere shul lasten,
and wepynge and wailynge, sharpe hunger and
thurst, and grymnesse of develes that shullen al to-
trede° hem, withouten respit° and withouten ende.
/ Of leccherie, as I seyde, sourden° diverse speces,
as fornicacioun that is bitwixe man and womman
that been nat maried, and this is deedly synne and
agayns nature. / Al that is enemy and destruccioun to nature is agayns nature. / Parfay°, 865
the resoun of a man telleth eek hym wel that
it is deedly synne for as muche as God forbad leccherie. And Seint Paul yeveth hem the regne°
that nys dewe° to no wight but to hem that doon
deedly synne. / Another synne of leccherie is to
bireve° a mayden of hir maydenhede°, for he that
so dooth, certes he casteth a mayden out of the hyeste degree° that is in this present lif / and bireveth
hire thilke precious fruyt that the book clepeth°
"the hundred fruyt." I ne kan seye it noon oother
weyes in Englissh, but in Latyn it highte *centesimus fructus.* / Certes, he that so dooth is cause of
manye damages and vileynyes, mo than any man
kan rekene°, right as he somtyme is cause of alle
damages that beestes don in the feeld that breketh
the hegge or the closure thurgh which he destroyeth that may nat been restoored. / For 870
certes, namore may maydenhede be restoored
than an arm that is smyten° fro the body may
retourne agayn to wexe°. / She may have mercy,
this woot° I wel, if she do penitence; but nevere
shal it be that she nas corrupt. / And al be it so
that I have spoken somwhat of avowtrie°, it is
good to shewen mo perils that longen to avowtrie, for to eschue that foule synne. / Avowtrie
in Latin is for to seyn approchynge of oother
mannes bed, thurgh which tho° that whilom°
weren o flessh abawndone° hir bodyes to othere persones. / Of this synne, as seith the wise
man, folwen manye harmes. First, brekynge of
feith; and certes, in feith is the keye of Cristendom. / And whan that feith is broken 875
and lorn°, soothly Cristendom stant veyn° and

---

853 fool, *foolish* **854 pych,** *pitch,* **is shent,** *are ruined* **855 fareth,** *act,* **brenneth,** *burns* **857 dotardes holours,** *doltish lechers,* **smatre hem,** *defile themselves* **858 roser,** *rosebush* **859 weneth,** *believes,* **likerousnesse,** *lechery,* **tonne,** *wine barrel* **860 mawmet,** *idol* **861 atemprely,** *temperately* **863 wombe,** *stomach* **864 to-trede,** *trample,* **respit,** *pause* **865 sourden,** *arise* **867 Parfay,** *by the faith,* **regne,** *kingdom* (reward). **nys dewe,** *is not due* **868 bireve,** *deprive,* **maydenhede,** *virginity,* **hyeste degree,** *most perfect condition* **869 clepeth,** *calls* **870 rekene,** *count up* **871 smyten,** *struck,* **wexe,** *grow* **872 woot,** *know* **873 avowtrie,** *adultery* **874 tho,** *then,* **whilom,** *once,* **abawndone,** *abandon* **876 lorn,** *last.* **veyn,** *empty*

852 fyve fyngres, see 830n. **853 basilicok,** basilisk, a mythical beast with the head of a cock and body of a serpent, supposed to kill with its glance or its breath. **854 Salomon,** Ecclesiasticus 26.10. **warm pych,** Ecclesiasticus 13.1. **859 with his owene knyf,** see *MerT* 5.1839–40. **867 Seint Paul,** Galatians 5.19–21. **869 highte *centesimus fructus*,** "is called the hundred fruit." The phrase is from Matthew 13.8, used as a metaphor for virginity by Jerome, *Letter Against Jovinian* 1.3, and others. **875 wise man . . . harmes,** Ecclesiasticus 23.33.

withouten fruyt. / This synne is eek a thefte, for thefte generally is for to reve° a wight his thyng agayns his wille. / Certes, this is the fouleste thefte that may be, whan a womman steleth hir body from hir housbonde and yeveth it to hire holour° to defoulen hire, and steleth hir soule fro Crist and yeveth it to the devel. / This is a fouler thefte than for to breke a chirche and stele the chalice, for thise avowtiers° breken the temple of God spiritually and stelen the vessel of grace, that is the body and the soule, for which Crist shal destroyen hem, as seith Seint Paul. / Soothly of this thefte douted° gretly Joseph, whan that his lordes wyf preyed hym of vileynye, whan he seyde, "Lo, my lady, how my lord hath take° to me under my warde° al that he hath in this world, ne nothyng of his
thynges is out of my power but oonly ye that
been his wyf. / And how sholde I thanne do 880
this wikkednesse and synne so horrible agayns
God and agayns my lord? God it forbeede." Allas, al to litel is swich trouthe now yfounde! / The thridde harm is the filthe thurgh which they breken the comandement of God and defoulen the auctour° of matrimoyne, that is Crist. / For certes, insomuche as the sacrement of mariage is so noble and so digne°, so muche is it gretter synne for to breken it. For God made mariage in paradys, in the estaat of innocence, to multiplye mankynde to the service of God. / And therfore is the brekynge moore grevous. Of which brekynge comen false heires ofte tyme, that wrongfully occupien folkes heritages. And therfore wol Crist putte hem out of the regne of hevene, that is heritage to goode folk. / Of this brekynge comth eek ofte tyme that folk unwar° wedden or synnen with hire owene kynrede, and namely thilke harlotes° that haunten bordels° of thise fool wommen that mowe° be likned to a
commune gonge° where as men purgen hire
ordure°. / What seye we eek of putours° that 885
lyven by the horrible synne of putrie°, and constreyne wommen to yelden to hem a certeyn rente of hire bodily puterie, ye somtyme of his owene wyf or his child, as doon this bawdes°? Certes, thise been cursede synnes. / Understoond eek that avowtrie is set gladly° in the Ten Comandementz bitwixe thefte and manslaughtre, for it is the gretteste thefte that may be, for it is thefte of body and of soule. / And it is lyk to homycide, for it kerveth a-two° and breketh a-two hem that first were maked o flessh, and therfore by the olde lawe of God they sholde be slayn. / But nathelees, by the lawe of Jesu Crist, that is lawe of pitee, whan he seyde to the womman that was founden in avowtrie and sholde han been slayn with stones after the wyl of the Jewes as was hir lawe, "Go," quod Jesu Crist, "and have namoore wyl to synne," or "wille namore to do synne." / Soothly, the vengeaunce of avowtrie
is awarded to the peynes of helle, but if so be°
that it be destourbed° by penitence. / Yet been 890
ther mo speces of this cursed synne, as whan
that oon of hem is religious, or elles bothe; or of folk that been entred into ordre°, as subdekne, or dekne, or preest, or hospitaliers. And evere the hyer that he is in ordre, the gretter is the synne. / The thynges that gretly agreggen° hire synne is the brekynge of hire avow of chastitee, whan they receyved the ordre. / And fortherover, sooth is that hooly ordre is chief of al the tresorie of God, and his especial signe and mark of chastitee, to shewe that they been joyned to chastitee, which that is moost precious lyf that is. / And thise ordred folk been specially titled° to God, and of the special meignee° of God, for which whan they doon deedly synne, they been the special traytours of God and of his peple; for they lyven of° the peple to preye for the peple, and whyle they been suche traitours hire preyers availen nat° to the peple. / Preestes been aungeles, as by the dignitee of hir mysterye°, but
for sothe, Seint Paul seith that Sathanas trans-
formeth hym in° an aungel of light. / Soothly, 895
the preest that haunteth° deedly synne, he may
be likned to the aungel of derknesse transformed in the aungel of light—he semeth aungel of light but for sothe he is aungel of derknesse. / Swiche

---

877 reve, *deprive* **878 holour,** *lecher* **879 avowtiers,** *adulterers* **880 douted,** *feared,* **take,** *given,* **warde,** *control* **882 auctour,** *author* **883 digne,** *worthy* **885 unwar,** *unaware,* **thilke harlotes,** *those lechers,* **bordels,** *brothels,* **mowe,** *may,* **commune gonge,** *public toilet,* **ordure,** *excrement* **886 putours,** *pimps,* **putrie,** *prostitution,* **bawdes,** *pimps* **887 gladly,** *appropriately* **888 a-two,** *in half* **890 but if so be,** *unless it happens,* **destourbed,** *prevented* **891 ordre,** *organized religious life* **892 agreggen,** *aggravate* **894 titled,** *dedicated,* **meignee,** *household,* **lyven of,** *are supported by,* **availen nat,** *are of no use* **895 mysterye,** *duties,* **transformeth hym in,** *transforms himself into* **896 haunteth,** *practices*

879 Seint Paul, 1 Corinthians 3.17. **880–81 Joseph,** Genesis 39.8–9; the story of Potiphar's wife. **889 quod Jesu Crist,** John 8.11. **891 subdekne, or dekne . . . or hospitaliers,** deacons and subdeacons are ordained Church officers who help the priest with daily and liturgical duties; Knights Hospitallers were organized to build and maintain hospitals. **or dekne,** omitted in El. **894 to preye . . . to the peple,** omitted in El. **895 Seint Paul,** 2 Corinthians 11.14.

preestes been the sones of Helie, as sheweth in the Book of Kynges that they weren the sones of Belial, that is the devel. / Belial is to seyn "withouten juge," and so faren they. Hem thynketh they been free and han no juge, namore than hath a free bole° that taketh which° cow that hym liketh in the town. / So faren they by wommen. For right as a free bole is ynough for al a town, right so is a wikked preest corrupcioun ynough for al a parisshe or for al a contree. / Thise preestes, as seith the book, ne konne° nat the mysterie° of preesthode to the peple, ne God ne knowe they nat. They ne holde hem nat apayd°, as seith the book, of soden flesh° that was to hem offred but they tooke by force the flessh that is rawe. / Certes, so thise shrewes° ne holden hem nat apayed° of roosted flessh and sode flessh° with which the peple fedden hem in greet reverence, but they wole have raw flessh of folkes wyves and hir doghtres. / And certes, thise wommen that consenten to hire harlotrie doon greet wrong to Crist and to Hooly Chirche and alle halwes° and to alle soules, for they bireven alle thise hym° that sholde worshipe Crist and Hooly Chirche and preye for Cristene soules. / And therfore han° swiche preestes, and hire lemmanes° eek that consenten to hir leccherie, the malisoun° of al the court Cristiene°, til they come to amendement. / The thridde spece of avowtrie is somtyme bitwixe a man and his wyf; and that is whan they take no reward° in hire assemblynge°, but oonly to hire flesshly delit, as seith Seint Jerome, / and ne rekken° of nothyng but that they been assembled. By cause that they been maried al is good ynough, as thynketh to hem. / But in swich° folk hath the devel power, as seyde the aungel Raphael to Thobie, for in hire assemblynge they putten Jesu Crist out of hire herte, and yeven hemself to alle ordure. / The fourthe spece is the assemblee of hem that been of hire kynrede°, or of hem that been of oon affynytee°, or elles with hem with whiche hir fadres or hir kynrede han deled in the synne of leccherie. This synne maketh hem lyk to houndes that taken no kepe° to kynrede. / And certes, parentele° is in two maneres, outher goostly° or flesshly. Goostly as for to deelen with his godsibbes, / for right so as he that engendreth° a child is his flesshly fader, right so is his godfader his fader espiritueel. For which a womman may in no lasse synne assemblen with hire godsib than with hir owene flesshly brother. / The fifthe spece is thilke abhomynable synne of which that no man unnethe° oghte speke ne write, natheless it is openly reherced° in hooly writ. / This cursednesse doon men and wommen in diverse entente and in diverse manere. But though that hooly writ speke of horrible synne, certes, hooly writ may nat been defouled namore than the sonne that shyneth on the mixne°. / Another synne aperteneth to leccherie that comth in slepynge, and this synne cometh ofte to hem that been maydenes°, and eek to hem that been corrupt, and this synne men clepen polucioun°, that comth in foure maneres. / Somtyme of langwissynge° of body, for the humours been to ranke° and habundaunt in the body of man. Somtyme of infermetee, for the fieblesse of the vertu retentif° as phisik° maketh mencioun. Somtyme for surfeet° of mete and drynke. / And somtyme of vileyns thoghtes that been enclosed in mannes mynde whan he gooth to slepe, which may nat been withoute synne. For which men moste kepen° hem wisely, or elles may men synnen ful grevously. /

Remedium contra peccatum Luxurie.

Now comth the remedie agayns leccherie, and that is, generally, chastitee and continence that restreyneth alle the desordeynee moevinges°

898 bole, *bull,* **which,** *whichever* **900 konne,** *know,* **mysterie,** *duties,* **apayd,** *satisfied,* **soden flesh,** *boiled meat* **901 shrewes,** *wretches* **902 halwes,** *saints,* **bireven alle thise hym,** *rob all these of him* **903 han,** *have,* **lemmanes,** *lovers,* **malisoun,** *curse,* **court Cristiene,** *ecclesiastical court* **904 reward,** *regard,* **assemblynge,** *sexual intercourse* **905 rekken,** *care* **906 swich,** *such* **907 kynrede,** *relatives,* **oon affynytee,** *related by marriage,* **taken no kepe,** *pay no attention* **908 parentele,** *kinship,* **goostly,** *spiritual* **909 engendreth,** *begets* **910 unnethe,** *hardly,* **reherced,** *discussed* **911 mixne,** *manure pile* **912 maydenes,** *virgins,* **clepen polucioun,** *call nocturnal emission* **913 langwissynge,** *weakness,* **to ranke,** *overripe,* **vertu retentif,** *power to retain fluids,* **phisik,** *medical science,* **surfeet,** *too much* **914 moste kepen,** *must guard* **915 desordeynee moevinges,** *inordinate impulses*

897 sones of Helie, sons of Eli; 1 Samuel 2.12 (1 Kings in the Vulgate). **898 withouten juge,** in Judges 19.22, "Belial" is interpreted as *absque iugo* (without a yoke); in French, *sans ioug* could easily be misread *sans iuge* (without judge). **900 the book,** 1 Samuel 2.13. **904 Jerome,** *Against Jovinian* 1.49. **906 Raphael to Thobie,** Tobias 6.17. **908 godsibbes,** god-siblings, a special spiritual relationship; the children of one's godparents or godchildren of one's parents. Godparents accept spiritual responsibility for the children they sponsor at baptism. **910 hooly writ,** Romans 1.26–27 speaks vehemently against homosexuality. **912 foure,** El reads "iii" (three). **914a Remedium contra peccatum Luxurie,** "Remedy against the sin of Lechery."

that comen of flesshly talentes°. / And evere the gretter merite shal he han that moost restreyneth the wikkede eschawfynges° of the ardour of this synne. And this is in two maneres, that is to seyn chastitee in mariage and chastitee of widwehode. / Now shaltow understonde that matrimoyne is leefful° assemblynge of man and of womman that receyven by vertu of the sacrement the boond thurgh which they may nat be departed in al hir lyf, that is to seyn whil that they lyven bothe. /

This, as seith the book, is a ful greet sacrement. God maked it, as I have seyd, in paradys, and wolde hymself be born in mariage. / And for to halwen mariage°, he was at a weddynge, where as he turned water into wyn, which was the firste miracle that he wroghte in erthe biforn his disciples. / Trewe effect of mariage clenseth fornicacioun and replenysseth Hooly Chirche of good lynage, for that is the ende° of mariage and it chaungeth deedly synne into venial synne bitwixe hem that been ywedded, and maketh the hertes al oon of hem that been ywedded, as wel as the bodies. / This is verray° mariage, that was establissed by God er that synne bigan, whan natureel lawe was in his right poynt° in paradys. And it was ordeyned that o man sholde have but o womman, and o womman but o man, as seith Seint Augustyn, by manye resouns. /

First, for° mariage is figured° bitwixe Crist and Hooly Chirche. And that oother is for a man is heved° of a womman, algate by ordinaunce° it sholde be so. / For if a womman hadde mo men than oon, thanne sholde she have moo hevedes than oon, and that were an horrible thyng biforn God, and eek a womman ne myghte nat plese to many folk at oones. And also ther ne sholde nevere be pees ne reste amonges hem, for everich wolde axen his owene thyng. / And fortherover, no man ne sholde knowe his owene engendrure°, ne who sholde have his heritage, and the womman sholde been the lasse biloved fro the tyme that she were conjoynt to many men. /

Now comth how that a man sholde bere hym with his wif, and namely in two thynges, that is to seyn in suffraunce and reverence, as shewed Crist whan he made first womman. / For he ne made hire nat of the heved of Adam, for she sholde nat clayme to greet lordshipe. / For ther as the womman hath the maistrie, she maketh to muche desray°. Ther neden none ensamples of this; the experience of day by day oghte suffise. / Also certes, God ne made nat womman of the foot of Adam for she ne sholde nat been holden to lowe, for she kan nat paciently suffre. But God made womman of the ryb of Adam, for womman sholde be felawe unto man. / Man sholde bere hym to° his wyf in feith, in trouthe, and in love, as seith Seint Paul, that a man sholde loven his wyf as Crist loved Hooly Chirche, that loved it so wel that he deyde for it. So sholde a man for his wyf if it were nede. /

Now how that a womman sholde be subget to hire housbonde, that telleth Seint Peter. First, in obedience. / And eek, as seith the decree, a womman that is wyf, as longe as she is a wyf, she hath noon auctoritee to swere ne bere witnesse withoute leve of hir housbonde that is hire lord, algate° he sholde be so by resoun. / She sholde eek serven hym in alle honestee and been attempree° of hire array. I woot° wel that they sholde setten hire entente to plesen hir housbondes, but nat by hire queyntise° of array. / Seint Jerome seith that wyves that been apparailled in silk and in precious purpre° ne mowe° nat clothen hem in Jesu Crist. What seith Seint John eek in thys matere? / Seint Gregorie eek seith that no wight seketh precious array but° oonly for veyne glorie° to been honoured the moore biforn the peple. / It is a greetfolye, a womman to have a fair array outward and in hirself be foul inward. / A wyf

---

talentes, *capabilities* **916 eschawfynges,** *inflamings* **917 leefful,** *lawful* **919 halwen mariage,** *make marriage holy* **920 ende,** *purpose* **921 verray,** *true,* **his right poynt,** *its proper state* **922 for,** *because,* **figured,** *symbolized,* **heved,** *head,* **algate by ordinaunce,** *at any rate by decree* **924 engendrure,** *offspring* **925 suffraunce,** *patience* **927 desray,** *disorder* **929 bere hym to,** *behave toward* **931 algate,** *at least* **932 attempree,** *moderate,* **woot,** *know,* **queyntise,** *cleverness* **933 purpre,** *purple,* **mowe,** *might* **934 but,** *except,* **veyne glorie,** *empty pomp*

916 ardour, El and most other manuscripts read "ordure," but the emendation has been accepted generally. **918 the book,** Ephesians 5.32. **God maked it,** Genesis 2.24. **919 at a weddynge,** the wedding at Cana; John 2.1–11. See *WBP* 3.11. **921 Augustyn,** *On Good Marriage,* 20–21. **922 Crist and Hooly Chirche . . . heved,** Ephesians 5.23–24. **927 womman hath the maistrie,** female control, a concern in *WBPT* 3.818 and 1038–40. **928 ryb of Adam,** the account of Eve made from Adam's rib is Genesis 2.22, traditionally interpreted to indicate male-female fellowship. **929 Seint Paul,** Ephesians 5.25. **930 Seint Peter,** 1 Peter 3.1. **931 the decree,** Gratian's *Decretals* 2.33.5.17. **933 Seint Jerome,** not found in Jerome; the claim is made of virgins rather than wives in St. Cyprian, *On the Clothing of Virgins,* 13. **Seint John,** Revelations 17.4, where purple is associated with the Whore of Babylon. **934 Seint Gregorie,** *Sermons on the Gospels* 2.40.3; see 414n above.

sholde eek be mesurable° in lookinge and in berynge and in lawghynge, and discreet in alle hire wordes and hire dedes. / And aboven alle worldly thyng she sholde loven hire housbonde with al hire herte, and to hym be trewe of hir body. / So sholde an housbonde eek be to his wyf. For sith that° al the body is the housbondes, so sholde hire herte been, or elles ther is bitwixe hem two as in that no parfit mariage. / Thanne shal men understonde that for thre thynges a man and his wyf flesshly mowen assemble°. The firste is in entente of engendrure of children to the service of God, for certes that is the cause final of matrimoyne. / Another cause is to yelden everich° of hem to oother the dette of hire bodies, for neither of hem hath power over his owene body. The thridde is for to eschewe° leccherye and vileynye. The ferthe is for sothe° deedly synne. / As to the firste, it is meritorie°. 940
The seconde also, for as seith the decree that she hath merite of chastitee that yeldeth to hire housbonde the dette of hir body, ye though it be agayn hir lykynge and the lust° of hire herte. / The thridde manere is venyal synne, and trewely scarsly may ther any of thise be withoute venial synne for the corrupcion and for the delit. / The fourthe manere is for to understonde, if they assemble oonly for amorous love and for noon of the forseyde causes, but for to accomplice thilke brennynge delit, they rekke° nevere how ofte, soothly it is deedly synne. And yet with sorwe° somme folk wol peynen hem° moore to doon than to hire appetit suffiseth. /

The seconde manere of chastitee is for to been a clene wydewe and eschue° the embracynges of man, and desiren the embracynge of Jesu Crist. / Thise been tho that han been wyves and han forgoon° hire housbondes, and eek wommen that han doon leccherie and been releeved by
penitence. / And certes, if that a wyf koude 945
kepen hire al chaast by licence° of hir housbonde so that she yeve° nevere noon occasion that he agilte°, it were to hire a greet merite. / Thise manere° wommen that observen chastitee moste° be clene in herte as well as in body and in thoght, and mesurable° in clothynge and in contenaunce, and been abstinent in etynge and drynkynge, in spekynge, and in dede. They been the vessel or the boyste° of the blissed Magdelene, that fulfilleth Hooly Chirche of good odour. / The thridde manere of chastitee is virginitee, and it bihoveth° that she be hooly in herte and clene of body; thanne is she spouse to Jesu Crist, and she is the lyf of angeles. / She is the preisynge of this world, and she is as thise martirs in egalitee°; she hath in hire that° tonge may nat telle ne herte thynke. / Virginitee baar° oure lord Jesu Crist,
and virgine was hymselve. / 950

Another remedie agayns leccherie is specially to withdrawen swiche thynges as yeve occasion to thilke vileynye, as ese°, etynge, and drynkynge, for certes whan the pot boyleth strongly, the beste remedie is to withdrawe the fyr. / Slepynge longe in greet quiete is eek a greet norice° to leccherie. /

Another remedie agayns leccherie is that a man or a womman eschue the compaignye of hem by whiche he douteth° to be tempted, for al be it so that the dede is withstonden, yet is ther greet temptacioun. / Soothly° a whit wal, although it ne brenne° noght fully by stikynge° of a candele, yet is the wal blak of the leyt°. / Ful ofte tyme I rede that no man truste in his owene perfeccioun but° he be stronger than Sampson, and hoolier than
Danyel, and wiser than Salomon. / 955

Now after that I have declared yow as I kan the Sevene Deedly Synnes, and somme of hire braunches and hire remedies, soothly, if I koude, I wolde telle yow the Ten Comandementz. / But so heigh a doctrine I lete to divines°. Nathelees, I hope to God they been touched° in this tretice, everich of hem alle. /

936 mesurable, *modest* **938 sith that,** *since* **939 mowen assemble,** *might copulate* **940 yelden everich,** *yield each,* **eschewe,** *avoid,* **for sothe,** *truly* **941 meritorie,** *meritorious,* **lust,** *desire* **943 rekke,** *care,* **with sorwe,** *alas,* **peynen hem,** *strive* **944 eschue,** *avoid* **945 forgoon,** *lost* **946 licence,** *permission,* **yeve,** *give,* **agilte,** *sinned* **947 manere,** *kind of,* **moste,** *must,* **mesurable,** *modest,* **boyste,** *container* **948 bihoveth,** *is necessary* **949 as thise martirs in egalitee,** *equal to the martyrs,* **that,** *what* **950 baar,** *bore* **951 ese,** *ease* **952 norice,** *nourishment* **953 douteth,** *fears* **954 Soothly,** *truly,* **brenne,** *burns,* **stikynge,** *attaching,* **leyt,** *flame* **955 but,** *unless* **957 divines,** *theologians,* **touched,** *touched upon*

940 dette, see 375n above. **941 the decree,** unidentified, but see 931n. **merite of chastitee,** omitted in El. **947 moste be . . . mesurable,** omitted in El. **Magdelene . . . odour,** Matthew 26.7 and John 12.3.

Sequitur secunda pars Penitencie.

Now for as muche as the second partie of penitence stant in confessioun of mouth, as I bigan in the firste chapitre, I seye, Seint Augustyn seith, / "Synne is every word and every dede and al that men coveiten agayn the lawe of Jesu Crist." And this is for to synne in herte, in mouth, and in dede, by thy five wittes, that been sighte, herynge, smellynge, tastynge or savourynge, and feelynge. / Now is it good to understonde that that agreggeth muchel° every synne. / Thow shalt considere what thow art that doost the synne, wheither thou be male or femele, yong or oold, gentil or thral°, free or servant, hool or syk, wedded or sengle, ordred or unordred°, wys or fool, clerk or seculeer°, / if she be of thy kynrede bodily or goostly° or noon, if any of thy kynrede have synned with hire or noon, and manye mo thynges. /

Another circumstaunce is this: wheither it be doon in fornicacioun or in avowtrie° or noon, incest or noon, mayden or noon, in manere of homicide or noon, horrible grete synnes or smale, and how longe thou hast continued in synne. / The thridde circumstaunce is the place ther thou hast do synne, wheither in oother mennes hous or in thyn owene, in feeld or in chirche or in chirche hawe°, in chirche dedicat° or noon. / For if the chirche be halwed° and man or womman spille his kynde° in with° that place by wey of synne, or by wikked temptacioun, the chirche is entredited° til it be reconciled° by the bishop; / and the preest that dide swich a vileynye, to terme of al his lif he sholde namore synge masse, and if he dide he sholde doon deedly synne at every tyme that he so songe masse. / The fourthe circumstaunce is by whiche mediatours or by whiche messagers as for enticement or for consentement to bere compaignye with felaweshipe, for many a wrecche for to bere compaignye shal go to the devel of helle. / Wherfore° they that eggen° or consenten to the synne been parteners of the synne, and of the dampnacioun of the synnere. / The fifthe circumstaunce is how manye tymes that he hath synned, if it be in his mynde, and how ofte that he hath falle. / For he that ofte falleth in synne, he despiseth the mercy of God, and encreesseth hys synne, and is unkynde to Crist; and he wexeth° the moore fieble to withstonde synne, and synneth the moore lightly°, / and the latter ariseth°, and is the moore eschew for to shryven hym°, namely, to hym that is his confessour. / For which that folk whan they falle agayn in hir olde folies, outher° they forleten° hir olde confessours al outrely°, or elles they departen hir shrift° in diverse places. But soothly, swich departed shrift deserveth no mercy of God of his synnes. / The sixte circumstaunce is why that a man synneth, as by whiche temptacioun, and if hymself procure thilke° temptacioun, or by the excitynge of oother folk; or if he synne with a womman by force, or by hire owene assent; / or if the womman, maugree hir heed°, hath been afforced, or noon. This shal she telle, for coveitise° or for poverte, and if it was hire procurynge or noon, and swiche manere harneys°. / The seventhe circumstaunce is in what manere he hath doon his synne, or how that she hath suffred that folk han doon to hire. / And the same shal the man telle pleynly° with alle circumstaunces, and wheither he hath synned with comune bordel° wommen or noon, / or doon his synne in hooly tymes or noon, in fastyng tymes or noon, or biforn his shrifte, or after his latter shrifte, / and hath peraventure° broken therfore his penance enjoyned°, by whos help and whos conseil, by sorcerie or craft, al moste be toold. / Alle

---

960 that that agreggeth muchel, *what it is that intensifies greatly* **961 gentil or thral,** *aristocrat or slave,* **ordred or unordred,** *in religions orders or not,* **clerk or seculeer,** *clergy or lay person* **962 kynrede bodily or goostly,** *physical or spiritual family* **963 avowtrie,** *adultery* **964 chirche hawe,** *churchyard,* **dedicat,** *consecrated* **965 halwed,** *blessed,* **kynde,** *procreative fluid,* **in with,** *within,* **entredited,** *under interdiction* (prohibited), **reconciled,** *reconsecrated* **968 Wherfore,** *for what reason,* **eggen,** *urge* **970 wexeth,** *grows,* **lightly,** *easily* **971 latter ariseth,** (more) *slowly rises,* **eschew for to shryven hym,** *likely to avoid confessing himself* **972 outher,** *either,* **forleten,** *abandon,* **al outrely,** *utterly,* **departen hir shrift,** *divide their confession* **973 thilke,** *that* **974 maugree hir heed,** *despite her efforts,* **for coveitise,** *out of acquisitiveness,* **swiche manere harneys,** *such kind of conditions* **976 pleynly,** *openly,* **bordel,** *brothel* **978 peraventure,** *perhaps,* **enjoyned,** *assigned*

957a Sequitur secunda pars Penitencie, "Here follows the second part of Penance." **958–59 firste chapitre,** see lines 107–08. **Seint Augustyn,** *In Reply to Faustus* 22.27. **965 til it . . . bishop,** omitted in El. **967** The syntax is elliptical, but the point is clear: the fourth circumstance of sin is what kind of go-between enticed or gained consent from the sinner to come together with others for the purpose or occasion of sinning.

thise thynges, after that° they been grete or smale, engreggen° the conscience of man, and eek the preest that is thy juge may the bettre been awysed of his juggement in yevynge° of thy penaunce, and that is after thy contricioun. / For understond wel that after tyme that a man hath defouled his baptesme by synne, if he wole come to salvacioun ther is noon other wey but by penitence and
shrifte and satisfaccioun, / and namely by the 980
two if ther be a confessour to which he may shriven hym, and the thridde if he have lyf to parfournen° it. /

Thanne shal man looke and considere that if he wole maken a trewe and a profitable confessioun ther moste° be foure condiciouns. / First, it moot° been in sorweful bitternesse of herte, as seyde the King Ezechye to God, "I wol remembre me alle the yeres of my lif in bitternesse of myn herte." / This condicioun of bitternesse hath fyve signes. The firste is that confessioun moste be shamefast°, nat for to covere ne hyden his synne, for he hath agilt° his God and defouled his soule. / And therof seith Seint Augustyn, "The herte travailleth° for shame of his synne." And for he hath greet shame fastnesse,
he is digne° to have greet mercy of God. / 985
Swich was the confessioun of the puplican° that wolde nat heven° up his eyen to hevene for he hadde offended God of hevene, for which shamefastnesse he hadde anon° the mercy of God. / And therof seith Seint Augustyn that swich shamefast folk been next° foryevenesse and remissioun. / Another signe is humylitee in confessioun. Of which seith Seint Peter, "Humbleth yow under the might of God." The hond of God is mighty in confessioun, for therby God foryeveth thee thy synnes, for he allone hath the power. / And this humylitee shal been in herte and in signe outward, for right° as he hath humylitee to God in his herte, right so sholde he humble his body outward to the preest that sit in Goddes place. / For which in no manere, sith° that Crist is sovereyn, and the preest meene° and mediatour bitwixe Crist and the synnere, and the synnere is the laste by wey of
resoun. / thanne sholde nat the synnere sitte 990
as heighe as his confessour, but knele biforn hym or at his feet but if maladie destourbe° it. For he shal nat taken kepe° who sit there, but in whos place that he sitteth. / A man that hath trespased to a lord, and comth for to axe° mercy and maken his accord, and set him doun anon by the lord, men wolde holden hym outrageous and nat worthy so soone for to have remissioun ne mercy. / The thridde signe is how that thy shrift sholde be ful of teeres, if man may, and if man may nat wepe with his bodily eyen, lat hym wepe in herte. / Swich was the confession of Seint Peter, for after that he hadde forsake Jesu Crist, he wente out and weepe ful bitterly. / The fourthe signe is that he ne lette° nat for shame to shewen his confessioun. / Swich was the confessioun of the 995
Magdelene that ne spared for no shame of hem that weren atte feeste for to go to oure lord Jesu Crist and biknowe° to hym hire synnes. / The fifthe signe is that a man or a womman be obeisant to receyven the penaunce that hym is enjoyned° for his synnes, for certes Jesu Crist, for the giltes of a man, was obedient to the deeth. /

The seconde condicion of verray° confession is that it be hastily doon°, for certes if a man hadde a deedly wounde, evere the lenger that he taried to warisshe° hymself, the moore wolde it corrupte and haste hym to his deeth, and eek the wounde wolde be the wors for to heele. / And right so fareth synne that longe tyme is in a man unshewed°. / Certes, a man oghte hastily shewen his synnes for manye causes, as for drede of deeth that cometh ofte sodenly and is in no certeyn what tyme it shal be, ne in what place. And eek the drecchynge°
of o synne draweth in another, / and eek the 1000
lenger that he tarieth, the ferther he is fro Crist. And if he abide to his laste day, scarsly may he shryven hym or remembre hym of his synnes or repenten hym for° the grevous maladie of his deeth. / And for as muche as he ne hath nat in his

---

979 after that, *to the extent that,* **engreggen,** *burden,* **yevynge,** *giving* **981 parfournen,** *perform* **982 moste,** *must* **983 moot,** *must* **984 shamefast,** *humble,* **agilt,** *sinned against* **985 travailleth,** *labors,* **digne,** *worthy* **986 puplican,** *tax collector* **heven,** *lift,* **anon,** *immediately* **987 next,** *nearest to* **989 right,** *just* **990 sith,** *since,* **meene,** *the means* **991 destourbe,** *prevent,* **taken kepe,** *consider* **992 axe,** *ask* **995 lette,** *refrain* **996 biknowe,** *make known* **997 enjoyned,** *assigned* **998 verray,** *true,* **hastily doon,** *not delayed,* **warisshe,** *heal* **999 unshewed,** *unrevealed* **1000 drecchynge,** *continuing* **1001 for,** *because of*

983 Ezechye, Hezekiah; Isaiah 38.15. El reads "Ezechiel." **985 Seint Augustyn,** *On True and False Confession* 1.10.25 (attributed to Augustine). **986** Luke 18.13. **987 Seint Augustyn,** not identified. **988 Seint Peter,** 1 Peter 5.6. **994 Seint Peter,** Matthew 26.75. **996 the Magdelene,** this name was mistakenly applied to the reformed sinner of Luke 7.37–38, 47 because she was often conflated with Mary Magdalen. In Luke, the public washing of Christ's feet is interpreted as an act of contrition.

lyf herkned° Jesu Crist whanne he hath spoken, he shal crie to Jesu Crist at his laste day and scarsly wol he herkne hym. / And understond that this condicioun moste han foure thynges. Thi shrift moste be purveyed° bifore and avysed°, for wikked haste dooth no profit. And that a man konne° shryve hym of his synnes, be it of pride, or of envye, and so forth of the speces and circumstances; / and that he have comprehended in hys mynde the nombre and the greetnesse of his synnes, and how longe that he hath leyn in synne; / and eek that he be contrit of his synnes and in stidefast purpos, by the grace of God, nevere eft° to falle in synne; and eek that he drede and countrewaite° hymself that he fie the occasiouns of synne to whiche he
is enclyned. / Also thou shalt shryve thee of 1005
alle thy synnes to o man, and nat a parcel° to o man and a parcel to another, that is to understonde, in entente to departe° thy confessioun as for shame or drede, for it nys but stranglynge of thy soule. / For certes, Jesu Crist is entierly al good; in hym nys noon inperfeccioun; and therfore outher he foryeveth al parfitly or never a deel°. / I seye nat that if thow be assigned to the penitauncer for certein synne that thow art bounde to shewen hym al the remenaunt of thy synnes, of whiche thow hast be shryven to thy curaat°, but if it like to thee of thyn° humylitee. This is no departynge of shrifte. / Ne I seye nat, theras I speke of divisioun of confessioun, that if thou have licence° for to shryve thee to a discreet and an honeste preest, where thee liketh, and by licence of thy curat, that thow ne mayst wel shryve thee to him of alle thy synnes. / But lat no blotte be bihynde°; lat no synne been untoold, as fer as thow hast remembraunce. / And whan thou shalt be shriven 1010
to thy curaat, telle hym eek alle the synnes that thow hast doon syn thou were last yshryven. This is no wikked entente of divisioun of shrifte. /

Also the verray° shrifte axeth° certeine condiciouns. First, that thow shryve thee by thy free wil, noght constreyned, ne for shame of folk, ne for maladie, ne swiche thynges. For it is resoun° that he that trespasseth by his free wyl, that by his free wyl he confesse his trespas, / and that noon oother man telle his synne but he hymself. Ne he shal nat nayte° ne denye his synne, ne wratthe hym° agayn the preest for his amonestynge° to leve synne. / The seconde condicioun is that thy shrift be laweful, that is to seyn, that thow that shryvest thee, and eek the preest that hereth thy confessioun, been verraily° in the feith of Hooly Chirche, / and that a man ne be nat despeired of the mercy of
Jesu Crist, as Caym or Judas. / And eek a man 1015
moot° accusen hymself of his owene trespas, and nat another; but he shal blame and wyten° hymself and his owene malice of his synne, and noon oother. / But nathelees, if that another man be occasioun or enticere of his synne, or the estaat of a persone be swich thurgh which his synne is agregged°, or elles that he may nat pleynly° shryven hym but he telle the persone with which he hath synned, thanne may he telle, / so that his entente ne be nat to bakbite the persone, but oonly to declaren his confessioun. /

Thou ne shalt nat eek make no lesynges° in thy confessioun, for humylitee peraventure° to seyn that thou hast doon synnes of whiche that thou were nevere gilty. / For Seint Augustyn seith if thou by cause of thyn humylitee makest lesynges on thyself, though thow ne were nat in synne biforn, yet artow° thanne in synne thurgh thy
lesynges. / Thou most eek shewe thy synne 1020
by thyn owene propre mouth, but thow° be woxe dowmb°, and nat by no lettre°; for thow that hast doon the synne, thou shalt have the shame therfore. / Thow shalt nat eek peynte° thy confessioun by faire subtile wordes, to covere the moore° thy synne, for thanne bigylestow° thyself and nat the preest. Thow most tellen it pleynly, be it nevere so foul ne so horrible. / Thow shalt eek shryve thee to a preest that is discreet to conseille thee, and eek thou shalt nat shryve thee for veyne glorie°, ne for ypocrisye, ne for no cause, but oonly for the doute°

1002 herkned, *listened to* **1003 purveyed,** *prepared for,* **avysed,** *considered,* **konne,** *knows how to* **1005 eft,** *again,* **countrewaite,** *watch* **1006 parcel,** *part,* **departe,** *portion out* **1007 deel,** *bit* **1008 curaat,** *local priest,* **but if it like to thee of thyn,** *unless it pleases you for your* **1009 licence,** *permission* **1010 bihynde,** *left behind* **1012 verray,** *genuine,* **axeth,** *requires,* **resoun,** *reasonable* **1013 nayte,** *disclaim,* **wratthe hym,** *anger himself,* **amonestynge,** *admonishing* **1014 verraily,** *truly* **1016 moot,** *must,* **wyten,** *accuse* **1017 agregged,** *increased,* **pleynly,** *fully* **1019 lesynges,** *lies,* **peraventure,** *perhaps* **1020 artow,** *are you* **1021 but thow,** *unless you,* **woxe dowmb,** *grown dumb,* **nat by no lettre,** *not in writing* **1022 peynte,** *disguise,* **moore,** *greater part of,* **bigylestow,** *you deceive* **1023 veyne glorie,** *empty vanity,* **doute,** *fear*

1008 penitauncer, a priest appointed by the Pope or a bishop to attend to special cases of penance. **1015 Caym or Judas,** Cain and Judas are two standard figures of despair, based in Genesis 4.14 and Matthew 27.5. **1020 Seint Augustyn,** Sermon 181.4.

of Jesu Crist and the heele° of thy soule. / Thow shalt nat eek renne° to the preest sodeynly to tellen hym lightly thy synne, as whoso° telleth a jape° or a tale, but avysely° and with greet devocioun. / And generally, shryve thee ofte. If thou ofte falle, ofte thou arise by confessioun. / And thogh thou shryve thee ofter than ones of synne of which thou hast be shryven, it is the moore merite. And, as seith Seint Augustyn, thow shalt have the moore lightly relessyng and grace of God, bothe of synne and of peyne°. / And certes, oones a yeere atte leeste wey it is laweful for to been housled°, for certes oones a yeere alle thynges renovellen°. /

Now have I toolde you of verray confessioun, that is the seconde partie of penitence. /

Explicit secunda pars Penitencie et sequitur tercia pars eiusdem de Satisfaccione.

The thridde partie of penitence is satisfaccioun, and that stant moost generally in almesse° and in bodily peyne. / Now been ther three manere of almesses: contricion of herte, where a man offreth hymself to God; another is to han pitee of defaute° of his neighebores; and the thridde is in yevynge of good conseil and comfort goostly° and bodily, where men han nede, and namely in sustenaunce of mannes foode. / And tak kepe° that a man hath nede of thise thinges generally: he hath nede of foode, he hath nede of clothyng and herberwe°, he hath nede of charitable conseil and visitynge in prisone and in maladie, and sepulture° of his dede body. / And if thow mayst nat visite the nedeful with thy persone, visite him by thy message and by thy yiftes. / Thise been generally almesses or werkes of charitee of hem that han temporeel richesses or discrecioun in conseilynge. Of thise werkes shaltow heren° at the day of doome. /

Thise almesses shaltow doon° of thyne owene propre thynges°, and hastily and prively if thow mayst; / but nathelees if thow mayst nat doon it prively, thow shalt nat forbere to doon almesse though men seen it; so that it be nat doon for thank of the world, but oonly for thank of Jesu Crist. / For as witnesseth Seint Mathew, *capitulo 5*, "A citee may nat been hyd that is set on a montayne. Ne men lighte nat a lanterne and put it under a busshel, but men sette it on a candlestikke to yeve light to the men in the hous. / Right so shal youre light lighten bifore men, that they may seen youre goode werkes, and glorifie youre fader that is in hevene." /

Now as to speken of bodily peyne°, it stant in preyeres, in wakynges°, in fastynges, in vertuouse techynges of orisouns°. / And ye shul understonde that orisouns or preyeres is for to seyn a pitous wyl of herte that redresseth it in° God, and expresseth it by word outward to remoeven harmes and to han thynges° espiritueel and durable, and somtyme temporele thynges. Of whiche orisouns, certes, in the orisoun of the Pater Noster hath Jesu Crist enclosed° moost thynges. / Certes, it is privyleged of° thre thynges in his dignytee° for which it is moore digne than any oother preyere: for that Jesu Crist hymself maked it; / and it is short for it sholde be koud° the moore lightly°, and for to withholden it the moore esily in herte, and helpen hymself the ofter° with the orisoun, / and for a man sholde be the lasse wery to seyen it, and for a man may nat excusen hym to lerne it, it is so short and so esy; and for it comprehendeth in itself alle goode preyeres. / The exposicioun of this hooly preyere, that is so excellent and digne°, I bitake° to thise maistres of theologie, save thus muchel wol I

---

heele, *health* **1024 renne,** *run,* **whoso,** *someone who,* **jape,** *joke,* **avysely,** *thoughtfully* **1026 peyne,** *punishment* **1027 to been housled,** *to receive communion,* **renovellen,** *renewed* **1029 almesse,** *charity* **1030 defaute,** *the lack,* **goostly,** *spiritually* **1031 tak kepe,** *take note,* **herberwe,** *shelter,* **sepulture,** *burial* **1033 heren,** *hear* **1034 shaltow doon,** *you shall do,* **propre thynges,** *personal property* **1038 bodily peyne,** *physical penance,* **wakynges,** *vigils,* **orisouns,** *prayers* **1039 redresseth it in,** *addresses itself to,* **han thynges,** *acquire things,* **enclosed,** *included* **1040 privyleged of,** *endowed with,* **his dignytee,** *its worthiness* **1041 koud,** *learned,* **lightly,** *easily,* **ofter,** *more often* **1043 digne,** *worthy,* **bitake,** *leave*

1026 Seint Augustyn, *On True and False Confession* 1.10.25 (attributed to Augustine). **1027 it is laweful,** it is required by law; the requirement to confess one's sins and receive Communion annually was established at the Fourth Lateran Council of 1215–16, which inspired penitential treatises such as those of Raymund of Pennafort and Guilielmus Peraldus from which *ParsT* derives. **1028a Explicit secunda pars Penitencie et sequitur tercia pars eiusdem de Satisfaccione,** "Here ends the second part of Penance and follows the third part of the same concerning Satisfaction." El omits "de Satisfaccione." **1036 Seint Mathew,** ***capitulo 5,*** chapter 5.14–16. **1039 Pater Noster,** Lord's Prayer; Matthew 6.9–13 and Luke 11.2–4.

seyn: that whan thou prayest that God sholde foryeve thee thy giltes as thow foryevest hem that agilten to thee, be ful wel war that thow ne be nat out of charitee. / This hooly orisoun amenuseth° eek venyal synne, and therfore it aperteneth° specially to penitence. /

This preyere moste be trewely° seyd and in verray° feith, and that men preye to God ordinatly° and discreetly and devoutly; and alwey a man shal
putten his wyl to be subget to the wille of God.
/ This orisoun moste eek been seyd with 1045
greet humblesse and ful pure, honestly and nat
to the anoyaunce of any man or womman. It moste eek been continued° with the werkes of charitee. / It avayleth eek agayn° the vices of the soule, for as seith Seint Jerome, "By fastynge been saved the vices of the flessh, and by preyere the vyces of the soule." /

After this thou shalt understonde that bodily peyne stant in wakynge°, for Jesu Crist seith, "Waketh and preyeth that ye ne entre in wikked temptacioun." / Ye shul understanden also that fastynge stant in thre thynges, in forberynge of° bodily mete and drynke, and in forberynge of worldly jolitee, and in forberynge of deedly synne. This is to seyn that a man shal kepen hym fro deedly synne with al his myght. /

And thou shalt understanden eek that God
ordeyned fastynge. And to fastynge appertenen
foure thinges: / largenesse° to poure folk, 1050
gladnesse of herte espiritueel, nat to been an-
gry ne anoyed, ne grucche° for he fasteth, and also resonable houre for to ete by mesure°. That is for to seyn, a man shal nat ete in untyme° ne sitte the lenger at his table to ete for° he fasteth. /

Thanne shaltow understonde that bodily peyne stant in disciplyne or techynge by word, or by writynge, or in ensample. Also in werynge of heyres°, or of stamyn°, or of haubergeons° on hir naked flessh, for Cristes sake, and swiche manere penances. / But war thee wel that swiche manere penaunces on thy flessh ne make thee nat bitter or angry or anoyed of thyself. For bettre is to caste awey thyn heyre than for to caste away the sikernesse° of Jesu Crist. / And therfore seith Seint Paul, "Clothe yow, as they that been chosen of God, in herte of misericorde°, debonairetee°, suffraunce°, and swich manere of clothynge"; of whiche Jesu Crist is moore apayed° than of heyres, or haubergeouns, or hauberkes°. /

Thanne is disciplyne eek in knokkynge° of thy
brest, in scourgynge with yerdes°, in knelyn-
ges, in tribulacions, / in suffrynge paciently 1055
wronges that been doon to thee, and eek in pa-
cient suffraunce of maladies, or lesynge° of worldly catel°, or of wyf, or of child, or othere freendes. /

Thanne shaltow understonde whiche thynges destourben° penaunce, and this is in foure maneres, that is, drede, shame, hope, and wanhope°, that is, desperacion. / And for to speke first of drede, for which he weneth° that he may suffre no penaunce, / ther agayns is remedie for to thynke that bodily penaunce is but short and litel at regard of the peynes of helle, that is so crueel and so long that it lasteth withouten ende. /

Now again the shame that a man hath to shryven
hym, and namely thise ypocrites that wolden been
holden so parfite that they han no nede to
shryven hem, / agayns that shame sholde a 1060
man thynke that by wey of resoun that he
that hath nat been shamed to doon foule thynges, certes hym oghte nat been ashamed to do faire thynges, and that is confessiouns. / A man sholde eek thynke that God seeth and woot° alle his thoghtes and alle his werkes. To hym may nothyng been hyd ne covered. / Men sholden eek remembren hem of the shame that is to come at the day of doome to hem that been nat penitent and shryven in this present lyf. / For alle the creatures in hevene, in erthe, and in helle shullen seen apertly° al that they hyden in this world. /

Now for to speken of the hope of hem that
been necligent and slowe to shryven hem,
that stant in two maneres: / that oon is 1065
that he hopeth for to lyve longe and for to

1044 amenuseth, *reduces,* **aperteneth,** *pertains* **1045 trewely,** *sincerely,* **verray,** *genuine,* **ordinatly,** *in an orderly way* **1046 continued,** *extended* **1047 avayleth eek agayn,** *is effective also against* **1048 wakynge,** *keeping vigils* **1049 forberynge of,** *abstaining from* **1051 largenesse,** *generosity,* **grucche,** *complain,* **by mesure,** *appropriately,* **untyme,** *inappropriate times,* **for,** *because* **1052 heyres,** *hair shirts,* **stamyn,** *coarse cloth,* **haubergeons,** *mail shirts* **1053 sikernesse,** *certainty* **1054 misericorde,** *mercy,* **debonairetee,** *graciousness,* **suffraunce,** *long-suffering,* **apayed,** *repaid,* **hauberkes,** *chain mail* **1055 knokkynge,** *beating,* **yerdes,** *yardsticks* **1056 lesynge,** *losing,* **catel,** *possessions* **1057 destourben,** *impede,* **wanhope,** *despair* **1058 weneth,** *thinks* **1062 woot,** *knows* **1064 apertly,** *openly*

1043 God sholde foryeve thee . . . to thee, from the Lord's Prayer; Matthew 6.12. **1047 Seint Jerome,** not found in Jerome, but attributed to him in Chaucer's source. **1047 vyces of the soule,** El reads "virtues of the soule." **1048 Jesu Crist,** Matthew 26.41. **1053 bitter,** omitted in El. **1054 Seint Paul,** Colossians 3.12. **1058 weneth,** El reads "demeth."

purchacen° muche richesse for his delit, and thanne he wol shryven hym, and as he seith, hym semeth° thanne tymely ynough to come to shrifte. / Another is surquidrie° that he hath in Cristes mercy. / Agayns the firste vice, he shal thynke that oure lif is in no sikernesse°, and eek that alle the richesses in this world ben in aventure° and passen as a shadwe on the wal. / And as seith Seint Gregorie that it aperteneth° to the grete rightwisnesse° of God, that nevere shal the peyne stynte° of hem that nevere wolde withdrawen hem fro synne hir thankes°, but ay continue in synne. For thilke° perpetueel wil to do synne shul they han perpetueel peyne. /

Wanhope° is in two maneres: the firste wanhope is in the mercy of Crist, that oother is that they thynken that they ne myghte nat longe persevere in goodnesse. / The firste wanhope comth of that he demeth that he hath synned so greetly and so ofte, and so longe leyn in synne that he shal nat be saved. / Certes, agayns that cursed wanhope sholde he thynke that the passion° of Jesu Crist is moore strong for to unbynde than synne is strong for to bynde. / Agayns the seconde wanhope, he shal thynke, that as ofte as he falleth he may arise agayn by penitence. And though he never so longe have leyn in synne, the mercy of Crist is alwey redy to receiven hym to mercy. / Agayns the wanhope that he demeth that he sholde nat longe persevere in goodnesse, he shal thynke that the feblesse of the devel may nothing doon but if men wol suffren° hym; / and eek he shal han strengthe of the helpe of God, and of al Hooly Chirche, and of the proteccioun of aungels, if hym list°. /

Thanne shal men understonde what is the fruyt of penaunce, and after the word of Jesu Crist it is the endelees blisse of hevene, / ther° joye hath no contrarioustee of wo ne grevaunce, ther alle harmes been passed of this present lyf, ther as is the sikernesse° fro the peyne of helle, ther as is the blisful compaignye that rejoysen hem everemo everich of otheres joye, / ther as the body of man that whilom° was foul and derk is moore cleer than the sonne, ther as the body that whilom was syk, freele°, and fieble, and mortal, is inmortal, and so strong and so hool that ther may nothing apeyren° it, / ther as ne is neither hunger, thurst, ne coold, but every soule replenyssed with the sighte of the parfit knowynge of God. / This blisful regne may men purchace by poverte espiritueel, and the glorie by lowenesse, the plentee of joye by hunger and thurst, and the reste by travaille, and the lyf by deeth and mortificacion° of synne. /

1066 purchacen, *acquire,* **hym semeth,** *it seems to him* **1067 surquidrie,** *overconfidence* **1068 sikernesse,** *certainty,* **in aventure,** *at risk* **1069 aperteneth,** *relates,* **rightwisnesse,** *righteousness,* **stynte,** *cease,* **hir thankes,** *voluntarily,* **thilke,** *this* **1070 Wanhope,** *despair* **1072 passion,** *suffering and death* **1074 suffren,** *allow* **1075 hym list,** *he chooses* **1077 ther,** *where,* **sikernesse,** *certainty* **1078 whilom,** *formerly,* **freele,** *frail,* **apeyren,** *harm* **1080 lowenesse,** *humility,* **mortificacion,** *destroying*

1064 in hevene, omitted in El. **1069 Seint Gregorie,** *Morals* 34.19.36.

Portrait of Chaucer, from the manuscript of Thomas Hoccleve's poem, "Regement of Princes," Harley MS 4866, folio 88r. The Bridgeman Art Library International

Retraction

Heere taketh the makere of this book his leve.

Now preye I to hem alle that herkne° this litel tretys or rede°, that if ther be anythyng in it that liketh° hem that therof they thanken oure lord Jhesu Crist, of whom procedeth al wit° and al goodnesse. / And if ther be anythyng that displese hem, I preye hem also that they arrette° it to the defaute° of myn unkonnynge°, and nat to my wyl that wolde ful fayn° have seyd bettre if I hadde had konnynge. / For oure book seith, "Al that is writen is writen for oure doctrine," and that is myn entente. / Wherfore I biseke yow mekely, for the mercy of God, that ye preye for me that Crist have mercy on me and foryeve me my giltes, / and namely° of my translacions and enditynges° of worldly vanitees, the whiche I revoke in my retraccions: / as is the Book of Troilus; the Book also of Fame; the Book of the xxv Ladies; the Book of the Duchesse; the Book of Seint Valentynes Day of the Parlement of Briddes; the Tales of Caunterbury, thilke that sownen into° synne; / the Book of the Leoun; and many another book, if they were in my remembrance, and many a song and many a leccherous lay°, that Crist for his grete mercy foryeve me the synne. / But of the translacioun of Boece de Consolacione and othere bookes of legendes° of seintes, and omelies°, and moralitee, and devocioun, / that thanke I oure lord Jhesu Crist and his blisful mooder, and alle the seintes of hevene, / bisekynge hem that they from hennes° forth unto my lyves ende sende me grace to biwayle my giltes and to studie to the salvacioun of my soule, and graunte me grace of verray° penitence, confessioun and satisfaccioun to doon in this present lyf, / thurgh the benigne°

1081 herkne, *listen to,* **rede,** *read,* **liketh,** *pleases,* **wit,** *capability* **1082 arrette,** *attribute,* **defaute,** *fault,* **unkonnynge,** *lack of ability,* **fayn,** *gladly* **1085 namely,** *particularly,* **enditynges,** *writing* **1086 sownen into,** *tend toward* **1087 lay,** *verse romance* **1088 legendes,** *lives,* **omelies,** *sermons* **1090 hennes,** *hence* **verray,** *genuine* **1091 benigne,** *goodly,* **boghte,** *redeemed*

1083 oure book, the Bible; Romans 15.4; also quoted in *NPT* 7.3441–42. **1085 revoke,** retract, but also rescue or restate; Chaucer's only other use of the verb is at *TC* 3.1118, where it means "to call back to consciousness." **1086–88** This list of Chaucer's writings may be compared with the lists in *LGWP* F329–34 and 417–30. **Book of the xxv Ladies,** *Legend of Good Women,* where nine tales are told. The Roman numerals vary in the manuscripts. **1087 Book of the Leoun,** a lost, unidentified, or yet-to-be written book by Chaucer, perhaps a translation of Machaut's *Dit dou Lyon* or Deschamps's *Dict du Lyon.*

grace of hym that is kyng of kynges and preest over alle preestes, that boghte° us with the precious blood of his herte, / so that I may been oon of hem at the day of doome that shulle be saved. *Qui cum patre* &c.

Heere is ended the book of The Tales of Caunterbury compiled by Geffrey Chaucer of whos soule Jhesu Christ have mercy. Amen.

1092 ***Qui cum patre,*** the beginning of a Latin formulaic prayer: He who with the Father and the Holy Spirit lives and reigns forever and ever. Amen.

Troylus and Criseyde

Troylus and Criseyde

Introduction

Troylus and Criseyde is the first great love poem in English. It casts the private emotions of love against the public sweep of the Trojan War and makes clear the complementary, archetypal drives toward sex and death, *eros* and *thanatos*. Although love is more emphatic than war in the poem, Troylus dies on the battlefield at the end, and the ancient siege of Thebes lies behind the impending fall of Troy (see 2.84n and 5.1485–1510n), reminding us how deeply the human impulses to destruction threaten our impulses to love and union. Troy had a particular resonance for late-medieval England because London was fashioning itself as the "New Troy," thereby claiming a place in the legacy of legendary greatness that began in Troy, passed to Rome via Aeneas, and came to England with the mythical Felix Brutus. Despite the grandeur of love in the poem, Troylus's death at the end of it, like his loss of Criseyde, is a reminder that, in this world, all things pass.

In neo-Platonic Christian terms, however, the loss of this world is no loss at all. When Troylus dies at the end of the poem, his spirit rises to a height (physically and metaphorically) that enables him to realize the triviality of all human affairs. He enters the poem laughing at the foolishness of lovers, is smitten by love, gains the love of Criseyde, loses her, and regains after death the laughter of cosmic distance—perhaps rewarded because he has been a true lover. In the poem love is, by turns, silly, painful, glorious, contemptible, and the driving force of the cosmos. On the latter, see especially the proem to Book 3 and Troylus's praise of love in the consummation scene (3.1254–74).

Earthly love, its consummation, and its demise are caused or influenced by a complex and wide-ranging combination of factors in the poem—astrology, the demands of war and politics, past events, circumstance, impulses and desires, dreams, and the artful machinations of Pandarus, who is Troylus's friend, Criseyde's uncle, and a go-between for the lovers. Interconnections and parallels among such conditioning factors make it difficult to determine simple cause-and-effect relations among external events and the thoughts, words, and deeds of the characters. Indeed, it is often only in hindsight, if at all, that words and actions are fully accepted or understood. Pandarus often speaks in fictions or with ironic implications that are disclosed only after readers and the other characters have assumed or struggled to guess his meaning or intention (see, e.g., 1.561ff. or 2.267–73); his motives are matter for ongoing critical debate. Criseyde's decision to go to bed with Troylus is a rich moment of hindsight when she tells Troylus—and perhaps realizes herself—that she had yielded long before (3.1210). Foresight also plays an important part in the story and in readers' perception of it, embodied in the narrator and in Calkas, Criseyde's father, whose prophetic foreknowledge of the fall of Troy launches the plot. The narrator, of course, knows the outcome of events, stating it in the opening five lines. He recurrently declares that his knowledge is limited, however, and he otherwise forestalls simple assessment of the characters by reminding readers of the limits of our knowledge as well as his. Foresight, hindsight, and the struggle to comprehend fully what we know or think we know are concerns of the characters, readers, and the narrator, who is both character and reader. Set against issues of love and war, truth and betrayal, such epistemological concerns lend the poem extraordinary philosophical depth.

Chaucer's source for the plot of *Troylus and Criseyde* is Giovanni Boccaccio's *Il Filostrato*, written about 1340, forty or forty-five years before Chaucer's poem. Behind Boccaccio lie works by Dictys Cretensis and Dares Phrygius, two purportedly eyewitness accounts of the Trojan War available in Latin from the fourth and sixth centuries respectively—Dictys's *Ephemeridos Belli Troiani Libri* (*Journal of the Trojan War*) and Dares's *De Excidio Troiae Historia* (*The History of the Fall of Troy*). In his twelfth-century French *Roman de Troie*, Benoît de

Ste. Maure adds love interest to these war chronicles, although he concentrates on the loss of love only. In 1287 Guido delle Colonne made Benoît's poem less exotic while translating it into Latin prose, *Historia Destructionis Troiae* (*The History of the Destruction of Troy*), making the story widely available to medieval Europe. The Middle Ages did not know Homer except by reputation.

Boccaccio added to this traditional material the story of Troiolo falling in love, and presents it as a commentary on his separation from his own beloved. Chaucer increased the length of Boccacio's poem by about one-third (5740 to 8239 lines), adding the latter quarter of Book 2, most of Book 3, the proems or prologues to the books, and a number of important speeches. He shaped a new structural design for the material by reducing the number of books from eight to five and by adding or moving individual speeches and scenes to create an overall sense of balance that is similar to the rising and falling action of Senecan and Renaissance drama. Troylus's laughter at the end of the poem (derived from Boccaccio's *Teseide* rather than the *Filostrato*; see 5.1807–27n) balances his mocking of lovers in the opening (1.190ff.); his song of woe near the end of the action (5.638–44) counterpoints his initial song of love (1.400–420). The consummation scene takes place very near the middle of the work in Book 3 (see also 3.1271n).

The structural design of Chaucer's poem reinforces its philosophical and psychological concerns in various ways, although only a few examples can be mentioned here. In *Filostrato,* Pandaro arranges that Troiolo ride past Criseida's window to help convince her to accept Troiolo as a lover. Chaucer introduces into his version an additional ride past Criseyde's window that results from complicated coincidences (2.610ff); it anticipates the ride arranged by Pandarus (2.1247ff.) and subsumes Pandarus's arrangements within a broader pattern of circumstances that shape the process of Criseyde's decision. Early in the poem, Troylus's conventional complaint about the overwhelming effects of love (1.507–39, also found in *Filostrato*) is echoed by his later, fatalistic complaint that divine foreknowledge obviates human free choice (4.953–1085). Chaucer also introduced Criseyde's dream of her heart being stolen by an eagle (2.925–31) to come before Troylus's dream of a boar stealing Criseyde from him (5.1233–43, also found in *Filostrato*). The characters' reactions to the dreams (and to love in general) are psychologically richer in Chaucer than in Boccaccio, and he connects Troylus's dream with the cycle of human failure through the explanation of the dream delivered to Troylus by his sister, the seer Cassandra (5.1450–1519), herself a structural and thematic parallel to the prophet Calkas found earlier in the work.

Critics have identified a number of influences on *Troylus and Criseyde* besides Boccaccio—Virgil, Statius, Lucan, Ovid, the *Roman de la Rose,* Petrarch, Dante, and, above all, *De Consolatione Philosophiae* (*The Consolation of Philosophy*) of Boethius. Chaucer translated Boethius's work into prose, *Boece,* and framed some of its sentiments and arguments in various lyrics and narratives—*Fortune, The Former Age,* the *Knight's Tale,* the *Nun's Priest's Tale,* and others. Several crucial aspects of *Troylus and Criseyde* derive from Boethius: five-book structure; ideas of love, fortune, and destiny; definitions of happiness; and even aspects of Pandarus's characterization as a counselor. Like a great number of medieval authors, Boccaccio had been influenced by Boethius as well, but Chaucer's increase in Boethian material makes his poem simultaneously more universal and more particular—more universal in his expanded attention to Boethian notions of cosmic love, fortune, and free will; more particular in the ways that attitudes and assertions of individual characters fall short of Boethian ideals. At times Pandarus does echo the counsel found in Boethius's work, but he does not move toward its rational conclusion of distancing oneself from the world. Criseyde's notion of felicity falls short of Boethian self-sufficiency (see 3.814n), and Troylus's thoughts on fatalism stop short of Boethian resolution of the apparent conflict between free will and foreknowledge. In many ways, omissions from ostensibly Boethian sentiments indicate the characters' limitations and anticipate the conclusion of the poem.

Chaucer's uses of other sources have as much to do with the nature of his poetic enterprise as with plot and theme, although the concerns are not wholly separable. Near the end of the poem, the narrator sends his poem to "kys the steppes" of his classical predecessors (5.1786–92), in this way bidding to join them. In the tradition of the *roman antique,* he uses ancient material to reflect contemporary concerns—combining the epic and heroic material of Homer and Statius with the love interests of Ovid, the courtliness of the

Roman de la Rose, the Christian allegory of Dante, even the nascent humanism of Petrarch. The tensions and continuities among these ideological frames are not so much resolved in the poem as they are posed as the condition of being human. In the Proem to Book 2, Chaucer aligns remarkable comments about linguistic change, the process of literary transmission, and the experience of love in one of the most powerful juxtapositions of the poem (2.12–49). In doing so, he asserts both the individuality of his work and its dependence on the past—a striking parallel with his theme of human choice and its conditioning factors. No one has explained completely Chaucer's assertion that "Lollius" was his source (see 1.394, 2.14, and 5.1653)—a mistake, a simple fiction, wry irony, or some combination—but the claim acknowledges that the poem depends on earlier literature while freeing it to be something quite unlike its claimed and its actual source, and something altogether new in English literature.

As with its sources and influences, the variety of genres and styles in *Troylus and Criseyde* is dazzling. Conventions of the classical epic combine with those of medieval romance, punctuated by letters, lyrics, dawn songs, dreams, and proverbial wisdom. The narrator twice refers to the poem as a "litel bok" (5. 1786 and 1789), a classical formula, and he calls the poem a "tragedye" (5.1786)—the first time this term is applied to a narrative in English, although Chaucer also used the term in *Boece.* An extraordinary percentage of the poem (about seven lines out of eight) is direct discourse—monologues (soliloquies?) and dialogues. The latter vary between rapid-fire stichomythia and more languorous exchanges, helping to create a complex texture in the poem. The pace of the narrative slows and quickens recurrently so that readers experience, for example, the contrast between the rapidity with which love's arrow strikes Troylus and the studied process whereby Criseyde considers her possible responses to his affection.

Subtle details of wording and emphasis, moreover, help to create rich psychological realism. Gestures and manners—a raised eyebrow, a cough, suppressed laughter—imply a great deal so that attentiveness to subtleties is one of the demands and rewards of the poem. Private thoughts, personal letters, and enclosed spaces create a strong sense of interiority, set against the poem's backdrop of public, political affairs. These extremes are mediated by small social gatherings—Criseyde's book club (2.81ff.), the family gathering at Deiphebus's house (2.1555ff.), the celebration of truce at Sarpedon's (5.435ff.). In their range and consequences, the interrelations between private self-awareness and public context in the poem are like that of a modern novel, despite being largely unconcerned with money or class distinction. Reputation—especially Criseyde's reputation—is a concern of the characters, and the related issue of secrecy may disturb modern readers by whom privacy is taken for granted. In the world of the poem, however, the necessity for secrecy is a reminder that private affairs are under constant pressure from external events and the interests of others.

The structural elements of the poem, its themes and genres, and summaries of the various medieval histories of Troy are discussed in Barry Windeatt's thorough Oxford Guide to the poem (1992, no. 1232). A. C. Spearing's introduction, *Troilus and Criseyde* (1976, no. 1231), has the advantages of brevity, and Allen J. Frantzen, *Troilus and Criseyde: The Poem and the Frame* (1993, no. 1226) is concerned with underlying ideologies. Windeatt's valuable edition (1984, no. 59) presents Chaucer's and Boccaccio's poems in parallel columns for convenient comparison; it also corrects the text and textual history hypothesized by Robert K. Root, *The Book of Troilus and Criseyde* (1926, no. 58), still useful for its notes. C. David Benson traces the development of the plot material in *The History of Troy in Middle English Literature* (1980, no. 1235), while Sylvia Federico, *New Troy* (2003, no. 1238), assesses the cultural value of Troy in medieval London. The various essays in Piero Boitani's *The European Tragedy of Troilus* (1989, no. 1236) clarify Chaucer's contributions to later Troy stories as well as his dependence on earlier ones. Barbara Nolan discusses the development of the *roman antique* in *Chaucer and the Tradition of the Roman Antique* (1992, no. 1243). Matthew Giancarlo explores the relationships the poem poses between history and freedom in "The Structure of Fate and the Devising of Freedom in Chaucer's *Troilus and Criseyde*" (2004, no. 1299).

Winthrop Wetherbee's *Chaucer and the Poets* (1984, no. 1247) is still the best single discussion of Chaucer's self-conscious use of classical and medieval predecessors, usefully supplemented by John V. Fleming, *Classical Imitation and Interpretation in Chaucer's Troilus* (1990, no. 1239). In *Chaucerian*

Tragedy (1997, no. 627), H. A. Kelly argues that Chaucer was the first vernacular poet to compose tragedies, particularly *Troylus and Criseyde.* Mark Lambert, "Telling the Story in *Troilus and Criseyde*" (2004, no. 1271), offers a useful explanation of the poem's stylistic and thematic texture; it can be supplemented with Howell Chickering's demonstration of Chaucer's dexterous use of rhyme royal stanzas, "The Poetry of Suffering in Book V of *Troilus*" (2000, no. 1264a). Marion Turner's "*Troilus and Criseyde* and the 'Treasonous Aldermen of 1382'" (2003, no. 1315), considers the theme of treason in the poem and offers new historical exploration of the plot's relation to contemporary events. The major characters of the poem continue to fascinate critics, with several critical and theoretical approaches collected in the essays edited by Cindy L. Vitto and Marcia Smith Marzec in *New Perspectives on Criseyde* (2004, no. 1373) and those edited by Tison Pugh and Marcia Smith Marzec in *Men and Masculinities in Chaucer's Troilus and Criseyde* (2008, no. 484). See also Gretchen Mieszkowski's *Medieval Go-Betweens and Chaucer's Pandarus* (2006, no. 1378).

Note: Throughout this edition, the spelling *Troylus* is preferred to *Troilus* because it is the spelling used in our base manuscript (Pierpont Morgan Library, New York, MS M.817) and because it reinforces the metonymic connection between Troylus and Troy.

Troylus and Criseyde

Book 1

Incipit liber primus.

The double sorwe of Troylus to tellen,
That was the Kyng Priamus sone of Troye,
In lovynge, how his aventures fellen
Fro wo to wele°, and after out of joye,
My purpos is, er° that I parte fro ye.
Thesiphone, thow help me for t'endite°
These woful vers°, that wepen as I write.

To the clepe° I, thow goddesse of torment,
Thow cruel Furie, sorwynge evere yn peyne,
Help me, that am the sorwful instrument
That helpeth loveres, as I kan, to pleyne°.
For wel sit it°, the sothe° for to seyne°,
A woful wight to han° a drery feere°,
And to a sorwful tale, a sory cheere°.

For I, that God of Loves servauntz serve,
Ne dar to Love, for myn unliklynesse,
Preyen for sped°, al° sholde I therfor sterve°,
So fer° am I fro his help in derknesse.
But natheles°, if this may don gladnesse
Unto ony lovere, and his cause avayle°,
Have he my thank, and myn be his travayle°.

But ye loveres, that bathen in gladnesse,
If ony drope of pite in yow be,
Remembreth yow on passed hevyness°
That ye han° felt, and on the adversite
Of othere folk, and thenketh how that ye
Han felt that Love dorste° yow displese,
Or° ye han wonne hym with to grete an ese°.

And preyeth for hem that ben yn the cas°
Of Troylus, as ye may after here,
That Love hem brynge° in hevene to solas°.
And ek° for me, preyeth to God so dere
That I have myght to shewe in som manere
Swych peyne° and wo as Loves folk endure,
In Troylus unsely° aventure.

And biddeth ek° for hem that ben despeyred°
In love, that nevere nyl° recovered be,
And ek for hem that falsly ben apeyred°
Thorugh wykked tonges, be it he or she;
Thus biddeth God, for his benignite°,
So graunte hem soone out of this world to pace°,
That ben despeyred out° of Loves grace.

4 wele, *happiness* **5 er,** *before* **6 endite,** *compose* **7 vers,** *verses* **8 clepe,** *call* **11 pleyne,** *lament* **12 sit it,** *it suits,* **sothe,** *truth,* **seyne,** *say* **13 wight to han,** *person to have,* **feere,** *companion* **14 sory cheere,** *sorrowful disposition* **17 sped,** *success,* **al,** *although,* **sterve,** *die* **18 fer,** *far* **19 natheles,** *nonetheless* **20 avayle,** *assist* **21 travayle,** *labor* **24 hevynesse,** *sadness* **25 han,** *have* **27 dorste,** *dared* **28 Or,** *or* (that), **to grete an ese,** *too easily* **29 cas,** *situation* **31 hem brynge,** *bring them,* **solas,** *joy* **32 ek,** *also* **34 Swych peyne,** *such pain* **35 Troylus unsely,** *Troylus's unfortunate* **36 biddeth ek,** *pray also,* **ben despeyred,** *have been* (made) *hopeless* **37 nevere nyl,** *will never* **38 apeyred,** *damaged* **40 benignite,** *graciousness* **41 pace,** *pass* **42 despeyred out,** *deprived*

Text based on Pierpont Morgan Library, New York, MS Morgan 817 (Cl), formerly known as the Campsall manuscript, with corrections and selected variants from Corpus Christi College, Cambridge, MS 61 (Cp). ***Incipit liber primus.*** "Here begins the first book." **1–21** This invocation is not in Boccaccio, and Chaucer omits his predecessor's opening address to his beloved Fiametta, picking up the translation at line 22. Chaucer evidently composed the proems to Books 2, 3, and 4 separately; they are omitted in some manuscripts and treated as conclusions to 1, 2, and 3 in others. The invocations in 1 and 5 are included in all the texts. **2 Kyng Priamus sone of Troye,** the son of King Priam of Troy. **5 er that I parte fro ye,** before I leave you. With *tellen* in line 1, this indicates an oral performance, or the illusion of one. **6 Thesiphone,** Tisiphone, one of the three Furies (or Erinyes), traditional goddesses of punishing vengeance, but here the emphasis is on the torment and sorrow shared by Fury and victim alike, as in *Bo* 3.m12.33–36. **15 servauntz serve,** adapts the papal title, "servus servorum dei," servant of the servants of God; compare *ParsT* 10.773. **16 myn unliklynesse,** my unsuitableness; Chaucer also represents himself as unsuitable to love at *HF* 613–40, *CT* 7.700–01, and *Envoy to Scogan* 27–32. **21 his,** Cp reads "this." **36 despeyred,** Cl and Cp read "desespeyred." **39 wykked tonges,** gossip, personified as an enemy to love in *Rom* 3257 and 3799ff.

And biddeth ek for hem that ben at ese,
That God hem graunte ay° good
perseveraunce°,
And sende hem myght hire° ladies so to plese
That it to Love be worship and plesaunce°.
For so hope I my soule best avaunce°,
To prey for hem that Loves servauntz be,
And write hire wo, and lyve in charite.

And for to have of hem compassioun,
As though I were hire° owne brother deere.
Now herkneth° with a good entencioun,
For now wol I gon streyght to my matere,
In which ye may the double sorwes here°
Of Troylus, in lovynge of Criseyde,
And how that she forsok hym er she deyde.

Yt is wel wyst° how that the Grekes stronge
In armes with a thousand shippes wente
To Troyewardes, and the cite longe
Assegeden°, neigh° ten yer er they stente°;
And in diverse wyse° and oon entente°,
The raveshyng to wreken of Eleyne,
By Paris don, thei wroughten al hire peyne°.

Now fil it so° that in the town ther was
Dwellyng a lord of gret auctorite,
A gret devyn°, that clepid° was Calkas,
That in science° so expert was that he
Knew wel that Troye sholde destroyed be,
By answere of his god that highte° thus
Daun Phebus or Appollo Delphicus.

So whan this Calkas knew by calkulynge°,
And ek by answer of this Appollo,
That Grekes sholden swych a peple° brynge
Thorugh which that Troye moste ben fordo°,
He caste anoon° out of the town to go.
For wel wyste° he by sort° that Troye sholde
Destroyed ben, ye°, wolde whoso nolde°.

For which for to departen softely°
Took purpos ful° this forknowyng wyse°,
And to the Grekes ost° ful pryvely°
He stal anoon°; and they in curteys wyse
Hym deden bothen worship° and servyse,
In trust that he hath konnyng hem to rede°
In every peril which that is to drede.

The noyse° up ros, whanne it was first aspied°,
Thorugh al the town, and generally was spoken
That Calkas, traitour fals, fled was and allyed
With hem of Grece; and casten to ben wroken°
On hym that falsly hadde his feith so broken,
And seyden he and al his kyn at onys°
Ben worthi for to brennen°, fel° and bones.

Now hadde Calkas left in this meschaunce°,
Al unwist° of this false and wikked dede,
His douhter, which that was in gret penaunce°,
For of hire lyf she was ful sore in drede°,
As she that nyste° what was best to rede°,
For bothe a wydewe° was she and allone
Of ony frend to whom she dorste hire mone°.

Criseyde was this lady name al right.
As to my dome°, in al Troyes cyte°
Nas non so fair, forpassyng° every wyght°
So angelik was hire natyf° beaute
That lyk a thing inmortal semed she,
As doth an hevenysh parfit creature
That down were sent in scornynge of nature.

---

44 **ay,** *always,* **perseveraunce,** *continuation* 45 **hem myght hire,** *to them the power their* 46 **plesaunce,** *pleasure* 47 **avaunce,** *advance* 51 **hire,** *their* 52 **herkneth,** *listen* 54 **here,** *hear* 57 **Yt is wel wyst,** *it is well known* 60 **Assegeden,** *besieged,* **neigh,** *nearly,* **stente,** *stopped* 61 **diverse wyse,** *various ways,* **oon entente,** *one intent* 63 **wroughten al hire peyne,** *undertook all their efforts* 64 **fil it so,** *it came about* 66 **devyn,** *soothsayer,* **clepid,** *named* 67 **science,** *knowledge* 69 **highte,** *was called* 71 **calkulynge,** (astrological) *calculating* 73 **swych a peple,** *such a company* 74 **moste ben fordo,** *must be destroyed* 75 **caste anoon,** *decided at once* 76 **wyste,** *knew,* **sort,** *casting lots* 77 **ye,** *yes,* **wolde whoso nolde,** *whether anyone wanted it or not* 78 **softely,** *quietly* 79 **Took purpos ful,** *decided,* **this forknowyng wyse,** *this foreknowing wise* (man) 80 **ost,** *host,* **ful pryvely,** *very secretly* 81 **stal anoon,** *stole away immediately* 82 **worship,** *honor* 83 **konnyng hem to rede,** *knowledge to advise them* 85 **noyse,** *disturbance,* **aspied,** *found out* 88 **casten to ben wroken,** (they) *planned to be avenged* 90 **kyn at onys,** *kindred at once* 91 **brennen,** *burn,* **fel,** *skin* 92 **meschaunce,** *unfortunate situation* 93 **unwist,** *unknowing* 94 **penaunce,** *distress* 95 **was ful sore in drede,** *feared very sorely* 96 **nyste,** *knew not,* **rede,** *think* 97 **wydewe,** *widow* 98 **dorste hire mone,** *dared* (to make) *her complaint* 100 **dome,** *judgment,* **Troyes cyte,** *city of Troy* 101 **forpassyng,** *surpassing,* **wyght,** *person* 102 **natyf,** *native*

43 **ladies,** Cl reads "loves." 62 **raveshyng to wreken of Eleyne,** to avenge the abduction of Helen. The Greeks attacked Troy to avenge the abduction, by Paris, of Helen, wife to Menelaus. 70 **Daun Phebus . . . ,** Master Phoebus or Apollo of Delphi, the location of a famous oracle (i.e., a shrine for asking questions of the god). Cl reads "Delphebus." 98 **dorste hire,** Cl reads "dorst make hire." 99 **al,** Cp reads "a."

This lady, which that alday herd at ere°
Hire fadres shame, his falsnesse and tresoun,
Wel nygh out of hire wit for sorwe and fere,
In widewes habit° large of samyt broun°,
On knees she fil byforn Ector adoun;
With pitous voys and tendrely wepynge,
His mercy bad°, hireselven excusynge.

Now was this Ector pitous of nature,
And saugh that she was sorwfully bigon°,
And that she was so fair a creature;
Of his goodnesse he gladed° hire anon,
And seyde, "Lat youre fadres° treson gon
Forth with mischaunce°, and ye youreself in joye
Dwelleth with us, whil yow good lyst°, in Troye.

"And al th'onour that men may don yow have°,
As ferforth as° youre fader dwelled here,
Ye shul han°, and youre body shal men save°
As fer as I may ought° enquere or here°."
And she hym thonked with ful humble chere°,
And ofter wolde and it hadde° ben his wylle,
And took hire leve home and held hire stille°.

And in hire hous she abod° with swych meyne°
As to hire honour nede was° to holde,
And whil she was dwelled yn that cyte
Kepte hire estat°, and bothe of° yong and olde
Ful wel beloved, and wel men of hire tolde—
But whether that she children hadde or noon,
I rede° it naught, therfore I late° it goon.

The thinges fellen as thei don of werre
Bitwixen hem of Troye and Grekes ofte,
For som day boughten they of Troye it derre°,
And eft° the Grekes founde nothing softe
The folk of Troye; and thus Fortune on lofte°
Now up, now down gan hem to whilen° bothe
After hire cours, ay whil° that thei were wrothe°.

But how this town com to destruccion
Ne falleth naught to purpos me° to telle,
For it were here a long digression
Fro my matere, and yow to long to dwelle.
But the Troian gestes° as thei felle°,
In Omer, or yn Dares, or in Dite,
Whoso that kan may rede hem as thei write.

But though that Grekes hem of Troye shetten°,
And hire cyte bisegede al aboute,
Hire olde usage° wolde thei not letten°
As for to honoure hire goddes ful devoute;
But aldermost° yn honour out of doute°,
Thei hadde a relyk hight Palladion
That was hire tryst° aboven everichon°.

And so bifell, whan comen was the tyme
Of Aperil, whan clothed is the mede°
With newe grene of lusti ver° the pryme°,
And swoote° smellen floures white and rede,
In sondry wyses° shewed, as I rede°,
The folk of Troye hire observaunces olde,
Palladiones feste° for to holde.

And to the temple yn al hire beste wyse,
In general there went many a wight°,

---

106 alday herd at ere, *always heard whispered* **109 habit,** *clothing,* **large of samyt broun,** *of ample dark silk* **112 bad,** *pleaded for* **114 bigon,** *beset* **116 gladed,** *cheered her up* **117 fadres,** *father's* **118 mischaunce,** *bad luck* **119 yow good lyst,** *it pleases you well* **120 don yow have,** *caused you to have* **121 As ferforth as,** *as much as when* **122 shul han,** *shall have,* **save,** *protect* **123 ought,** *anything,* **here,** *hear* **124 chere,** *expression* **125 ofter wolde and it hadde,** *would have more often if it had* **126 held hire stille,** *remained quietly* **127 abod,** *lived,* **swych meyne,** *such attendants* **128 nede was,** *it was necessary* **130 Kepte hire estat,** *maintained her status,* **of,** *by* **133 rede,** *read,* **late,** *let* **136 derre,** *dearly* **137 eft,** *again* (at other times) **138 lofte,** *high* **139 gan hem to whilen,** *did wheel* (spin) *them* **140 ay whil,** *all the time,* **wrothe,** *angry* (at war) **142 Ne falleth naught to purpos me,** *does not happen to be my purpose* **145 gestes,** *deeds,* **felle,** *occurred* **148 shetten,** *shut in* **150 usage,** *habits,* **letten,** *give up* **152 aldermost,** *most of all,* **out of doute,** *without a doubt* **154 was hire tryst,** i.e., *that they trusted,* **everichon,** *every other one* **156 mede,** *meadow* **157 lusti ver,** *pleasurable Spring,* **pryme,** *beginning* **158 swoote,** *sweet* **159 sondry wyses,** *various ways,* **rede,** *read* **161 Palladiones feste,** *the festival of the Palladium* **163 wight,** *person*

110 Ector, Hector, Troylus's brother, oldest son of Priam; hero of Troy. **128 to hire,** Cp reads "til hire." **132 children,** at precisely this point, *Filostrato* 1.15 specifies that she has no children. Cl reads "hadde children." **138–40 Fortune . . . ,** this Boethian image of the goddess Fortune and her wheel are added by Chaucer. The following stanza is not in *Filostrato* either. **139 Now up, now down,** Cl reads "And under eft." **143 here,** omitted in Cl and Cp. **146 Omer . . . Dares . . . Dite,** Homer, Dares of Phrygia, and Dictys of Crete, traditional sources of information about the Trojan War, although Chaucer uses none of them directly. **153 relyk hight Palladion,** a sacred object called Palladium, i.e., a statue or image of Pallas, companion of Athena (or of the goddess herself), which was understood to protect Troy from conquest. Cp reads "heet" for "hight." **162 hire beste,** Cl reads "here goodly beste."

To herknen of° Palladion the servyse,
And namely° so many a lusti° knyght,
So many a lady fresch, and mayden bright,
Ful wel arayed, bothe meste and leste°,
Ye, bothe for the seson and the feste.

Among these othere folk was Criseyda,
In widewes habit blak. But natheles°,
Right° as oure first lettre is now an A,
In beaute first so stod she makeles°.
Hire goodly lokyng gladede° al the prees°.
Nas nevere yet thing seyn° to ben preysed derre°,
Nor under cloude blak so bright a sterre°,

As was Criseyde, as folk seyde everichone
That hire behelden in hire blake wede°.
And yet she stod ful lowe° and stille° allone,
Byhynden other folk, in litel brede°,
And neigh the dore, ay° under shames drede,
Symple of atyre° and debonaire of chere°,
With ful assuryd° lokyng and manere.

This Troylus, as he was wont° to gyde
His yonge knyghtes, ladde hem up and doun
In thilke large temple on every syde,
Byholding ay the ladyes of the toun,
Now here, now there, for no devocioun
Hadde he to noon, to reven° hym his reste,
But gan to preyse and lakken° whom hym leste°.

And yn his walk ful faste° he gan to wayten°
If knyght or squyer of his compaignie
Gan for to sike°, or lete his eien beyten°
On any woman that he koude aspye,
He wolde smyle and holden it folye,
And sey hym thus, "God wot°, she slepeth
    softe°
For love of the, whan thou turnest ofte.

"I have herd told, pardieux°, of youre lyvynge,
Ye loveres, and youre lewede observaunces°,
And swich° labour as folk han yn wynnynge
Of love, and yn the kepyng° which doutaunces°,
And whan youre prey is lost, woo and penaunces.
O verray° fooles, nyce° and blynde be ye!
Ther nys not oon kan war by other be."

And with that word he gan caste up° the browe
Ascaunces°, "Lo, is this nought wysely spoken?"
At which the God of Love gan loken rowe°
Right for despit, and shop° for to ben wroken°,
And kyd anoon° his bowe nas not broken,
For sodeynly he hit hym at the fulle°—
And yet° as proud a pekok kan he pulle°.

O blynde world, O blynde entencioun!
How often falleth al th'effect contraire°
Of surquidrie° and foul presumpcioun;
For caught is proud, and caught is debonaire°.
This Troylus is clomben° on the staire,
And litel weneth° that he most descenden—
But alday° faileth thyng that foles wenden°.

As proude Bayard gynneth° for to skyppe
Out of the wey, so priketh° hym his corn°,
Til he a lasshe have of the longe whippe,

---

164 herknen of, *listen to* **165 namely,** *especially,* **lusti,** *gallant* **167 meste and leste,** *highest and lowest* (in rank) **170 natheles,** *nonetheless* **171 Right,** *just* **172 makeles,** *matchless* **173 goodly lokyng gladede,** *beautiful appearance made glad,* **prees,** *crowd* **174 seyn,** *seen,* **derre,** *more dearly* **175 sterre,** *star* **177 wede,** *clothing* **178 ful lowe,** *very humbly,* **stille,** *quietly* **179 in litel brede,** *in a small space* **180 ay,** *always* **181 atyre,** *attire,* **debonaire of chere,** *gentle of expression* **182 assuryd,** *confident* **183 wont,** *accustomed* **185 thilke,** *this same* **188 reven,** *deprive* **189 lakken,** *criticize,* **leste,** *pleased* **190 ful faste,** *very closely,* **gan to wayten,** *did watch* **192 sike,** *sigh,* **eien beyten,** *eyes feast* **195 wot,** *knows,* **softe,** *quietly* **197 pardieux,** *by God* **198 lewede observaunces,** *ignorant practices* **199 swich,** *such* **200 kepyng,** *keeping* (of love), **doutaunces,** *uncertainties* **202 verray,** *genuine,* **nyce,** *silly* **204 gan caste up,** *raised* **205 Ascaunces,** *as if to say* **206 rowe,** *roughly* **207 Right for despit,** *just for anger,* **shop,** *prepared,* **ben wroken,** *be avenged* **208 kyd anoon,** *showed immediately* **209 at the fulle,** *squarely* **210 yet,** *even now,* **pulle,** *pluck* **212 th'effect contraire,** *the opposite results* **213 surquidrie,** *pride* **214 debonaire,** *humble* **215 is clomben,** *has climbed* **216 weneth,** *supposes* **217 alday,** *always,* **foles wenden,** *fools believe* **218 gynneth,** *begins* **219 so priketh,** *as spurs* (prompts), **corn,** *food*

167 meste and leste, Cl and Cp read "meste, me(y)ne, and leste." **168 and,** Cl reads "and for." **171 Right as oure first lettre is now an A,** J. L. Lowes first suggested that this is Chaucer's compliment to Queen Anne; the phrase replaces a more conventional comparison of the beauty of a rose to that of a violet (*Filostrato* 1.19). **183 This Troylus,** demonstrative *this* is used recurrently with the names Troylus, Pandarus, and Diomede, but not Criseyde. **196 ofte,** Cp reads "ful ofte." **198 lewede,** omitted in Cl and Cp. **199 swich labour as,** Cp reads "which a labour as." **202 fooles,** Cl reads "loves." **203** The proverbial notion that in their blindness lovers fail to learn from the example of others. **210 pekok,** the peacock is a proverbial image of pride; Chaucer's addition, as is Love's vengeance in 206–09. **214–66** Chaucer's first lengthy addition; it includes a great deal of traditional imagery and proverbial, universalizing sentiment. **217 faileth thyng that foles,** Cl reads "falleth thyng that foles ne." **218 Bayard,** a common name for a horse.

Than thenketh he, "Though I praunce al byforn°,
First yn the trays°, ful fat and newe shorn,
Yet am I but an hors, and horses lawe
I moot° endure, and with my feres° drawe";

So ferde it by° this ferse° and proude knyght:
Though he a worthi kynges sone were,
And wende° nothing hadde had swych° myght
Ayens° his wil that shold his herte stere°,
Yet with a lok his herte wax afere°,
That he that now was most in pride above
Wax° sodeynly most subget° unto love.

Forthi° ensample taketh of this man,
Ye wyse, proude, and worthi folkes alle,
To scornen° Love, which that so soone kan
The fredom of youre hertes to hym thralle°;
For evere it was, and evere it shal bifalle
That Love is he that alle thing may bynde,
For may no man fordo° the lawe of kynde°.

That this be soth° hath preved° and doth yet,
For this trowe° I ye knowen alle or some°.
Men reden° nat that folk han° gretter wit
Than they that han be most with love ynome°,
And strengest folk ben therwith overcome,
The worthiest and grettest yn degre—
This was and is and yet men shal it se.

And trewelich° it sit wel° to be so,
For alderwisest° han therwith ben plesed,
And thei that han ben aldermost in wo
With love han ben comforted most and esed;
And ofte it hath the cruel herte apesed°,
And worthi folk maad worthier of name,
And causeth most to dreden vice and shame.

Now sith° it may not goodly° be withstonde,
And is a thyng so vertuous yn kynde°,
Refuseth not to Love for to be bonde,
Syn° as hymselven lyste° he may yow bynde.
The yerde° is bet° that bowen wole° and wynde°
Than that that brest°, and therfor I yow rede°
To folowen hym that so wel kan yow lede.

But for to tellen forth yn special
As of this kynges sone of which I tolde,
And letten° other thing collateral°,
Of hym thenk I my tale forth to holde,
Bothe of his joies and of his cares colde,
And al his werk, as touchyng this matere,
For I it gan°, I wil therto refere°.

Withinne the temple he went hym forth pleyinge°,
This Troylus, of every wyght° aboute,
On this lady and now on that lokynge,
Where so° she were of towne or of withoute;
And upon cas° bifel that thorugh a route°
His eye percede, and so depe it wente
Til on Criseyde it smot, and ther it stente°.

And sodeynly he wax° therwith astoned°,
And gan hire bet biholde° yn thrifty wyse°.
"O mercy God," thoughte he, "wher hastow woned°,
That art so fair and goodly to devyse°?"
Therwith his herte gan to sprede° and ryse,
And softe sighed lest° men myghte hym here°,
And caught ayen° his firste pleyinge chere°.

She nas not with the leste° of hire stature,
But alle hire lymes so wel answerynge
Weren to womanhode that creature
Was nevere lasse mannyssh in semynge.
And ek° the pure wyse° of hire mevynge°

---

221 al byforn, *in front of all* **222 trays,** *harness* **224 moot,** *must,* **feres,** *companions* **225 ferde it by,** *it happened with,* **ferse,** *bold* **227 wende,** *thought,* **swych,** *such* **228 Ayens,** *against,* **stere,** *steer* **229 wax afere,** *caught fire* **231 Wax,** *grew,* **subget,** *subject* **232 Forthi,** *therefore* **234 To scornen,** *about scorning* **235 thralle,** *enslave* **238 fordo,** *undo,* **kynde,** *nature* **239 soth,** *truth,* **hath preved,** *has proved so* **240 trowe,** *believe,* **alle or some,** *one and all* **241 reden,** *read,* **han,** *have* **242 ynome,** *captured* **246 twewelich,** *truly,* **sit wel,** *is appropriate* **247 alderwisest,** *the wisest of all* **250 apesed,** *cured* **253 sith,** *since,* **goodly,** *easily* **254 yn kynde,** *by nature* **256 Syn,** *since,* **lyste,** *wishes* **257 yerde,** *rod,* **bet,** *better,* **bowen wole,** *will bend,* **wynde,** *twist* **258 brest,** *breaks,* **rede,** *advise* **262 letten,** *leave aside,* **collateral,** *auxiliary* **266 gan,** *began,* **refere,** *return* **267 pleyinge,** *making fun* **268 wyght,** *person* **270 Where so,** *whether* **271 upon cas,** *by chance,* **route,** *crowd* **273 stente,** *stopped* **274 wax,** *grew,* **astoned,** *astonished* **275 gan . . . bet biholde,** *did better consider,* **thrifty wyse,** *careful manner* **276 hastow woned,** *have you lived* **277 devyse,** *look at* **278 sprede,** *swell* **279 lest,** *for fear* **here,** *hear* **280 ayen,** *again,* **chere,** *manner* **281 leste,** *shortest* **285 ek,** *also,* **pure wyse,** *very manner,* **mevynge,** *moving*

224 feres, Cl reads "felawes." **228 stere,** Cl reads "dere" (hurt). **234 scornen,** Cp reads "serven." **244 yn,** Cp reads "of." **250–52** It is a commonplace that love ennobles the lover, echoed at 1.1079–80, 3.22–26, 1718–24, 1776–1806. **261 As,** omitted in Cl and Cp. **263 forth,** Cl reads "for." **272 eye percede,** Cl reads "eye procede"; Cp "sighte procede."

Shewed wel that men myght in hire gesse
Honour, estat°, and wommanly noblesse.

To Troylus right wonder wel with alle
Gan for to lyke° hire mevynge and hire chere°,
Which somdel deynous° was, for she leet falle
Hire look a lite° aside in swych° manere,
Ascaunces°, "What, may I nat stonden here?"
And after that hire lokynge gan she lyghte°,
That nevere thought hym seen so fair a sighte.

And of hire look yn hym ther gan to quyken°
So gret desir and such affeccioun
That in his hertes botme° gan to stiken
Of hire his fixe° and depe impressioun.
And though he erst° hadde poured° up and doun,
He was to glad his hornes yn to shrynke—
Unnethes wyste° he how to loke or wynke°.

Lo, he that leet° hymselven so konnynge°,
And scorned hem that Loves peynes dryen°,
Was ful unwar that Love hadde his dwellynge
Withinne the subtile stremes° of hire eyen,
That sodeynly hym thoughte he felte dyen
Right with hire look the spirit in his herte.
Blyssyd be Love that kan thus folk converte!

She, this in blak, lykynge° to Troylus
Over al thyng, he stood for to byholde;
Ne° his desir, ne wherfor he stod thus,
He neither chere ne made°, ne worde tolde;
But from afer, his manere° for to holde°,
On other thing his look somtyme he caste,
And eft° on hire, while that the servise laste.

And after this, not fullych al awhaped°,
Out of the temple al esilych° he wente,
Repentynge hym that he hadde evere yjaped°
Of Loves folk, lest° fully the descente°
Of scorn fille on hymself. But what he mente°,
Lest it were wyst° on any maner side,
His wo he gan dissimulen° and hide.

Whan he was fro the temple thus departed,
He streyght anoon unto his paleys turneth°,
Right with hire look thorugh-shoten and thorugh-darted,
Al feyneth° he yn lust° that he sojorneth°,
And al his speche and cher° also he borneth°,
And ay° of Loves servantz every while,
Hymself to wrye°, at hem he gan to smyle,

And seyde, "Lord, so ye lyve al yn lest°,
Ye loveres, for the konnyngeste° of yow,
That serveth most ententiflych° and best,
Hym tyt° as often harm therof as prow°.
Youre hire° is quyt ayeyn°, ye° God wot° how—
Nought wel for wel, but scorn for good service.
In feith, youre ordre is ruled in good wyse!

"In nouncerteyn° ben alle youre observaunces,
But it a sely fewe poyntes be°.
Ne nothing asketh so grete attendaunces°
As doth youre lay°, and that knowe alle ye.
But that is not the worste, as mote I the°—
But tolde I° yow the worste point, I leve°,
Al° seyde I soth°, ye wolden at me greve°.

"But take this: that° ye loveres ofte eschuwe°,
Or elles doon of good entencioun,

287 estat, *rank* **289 Gan for to lyke,** *did like,* **chere,** *expression* **290 somdel deynous,** *somewhat disdainful* **291 lite,** *little,* **swych,** *such* **292 Ascaunces,** *as if to say* **293 lyghte,** *brighten* **295 quyken,** *come alive* **297 botme,** *bottom* **298 fixe,** *fixed* **299 erst,** *first,* **poured,** *gazed* **301 Unnethes wyste,** *hardly knew,* **wynke,** *blink* **302 leet,** *considered,* **konnynge,** *knowing* **303 dryen,** *suffer* **305 subtile stremes,** *secret beams* **309 lykynge,** *pleasing* **311 Ne,** *neither* **312 chere ne made,** *revealed by expression* **313 manere,** *usual behavior,* **holde,** *maintain* **315 eft,** *again* **316 fullych al awhaped,** *completely all stupefied* **317 esilych,** *casually* **318 yjaped,** *joked* **319 lest,** *for fear that,* **descente,** *weight* **320 mente,** *thought* **321 wyst,** *known* **322 dissimulen,** *disguise* **324 paleys turneth,** *palace returns* **326 Al feyneth,** *although he pretends,* **lust,** *pleasure,* **sojorneth,** *remains* **327 cher,** *expression,* **borneth,** *polishes* **328 ay,** *always* **329 wrye,** *conceal* **330 lest,** *pleasure* **331 konnyngeste,** *wisest* **332 ententiflych,** *attentively* **333 Hym tyt,** *to him happens,* **prow,** *profit* **334 hire,** *payment,* **quyt ayeyn,** *repaid,* **ye,** *yes,* **wot,** *knows* **337 nouncertayn,** *uncertainty* **338 But . . . be,** *except for a few foolish details* **339 attendaunces,** *attention* **340 lay,** *law* **341 as mote I the,** *as I may prosper* **342 tolde I,** (if) *I told,* **leve,** *believe* **343 Al,** *although,* **soth,** *truth,* **greve,** *complain* **344 that,** *that which,* **eschuwe,** *avoid*

294 fair, Cp reads "good." **300 hornes yn to shrynke,** the figure is comic—that of a snail retracting the horn-like protrusions to which its eyes are attached. **306 he felte dyen,** Cl reads "that he sholde dyen." **309–12** The wrenched word order and clustered negatives convey a sense of Troylus's agitation. **312 ne made,** Cp omits "ne." **315 eft,** Cp reads "oft." **the,** omitted in Cp. **336 ordre is ruled,** here and in the rules of the following stanzas, Troylus suggests sarcastically that lovers constitute their own religious order dedicated to the Lord of Love, a notion that recurs without sarcasm at 1.998–1001 and elsewhere in courtly tradition.

Ful ofte thi lady wole it mysconstrue,
And deme° it harm yn hire opinyoun;
And yet if she for other enchesoun°
Be wroth°, than shalt thou han a groyn° anoon.
Lord, wel is hym that may ben of yow oon!"

But for al this, whanne he say° his tyme,
He held his pes°, noon other bote° hym gayned.
For love bygan his fetheres so to lyme
That wel unnethe° unto his folk he feyned°
That other besy nedes hym destrayned°;
For wo was hym that what to doon he nyste°,
But bad° his folk to gon wher that hem lyste°.

And whan that he in chambre was allone,
He down upon his beddes feet hym sette,
And first he gan to syke° and eft to grone,
And thoughte ay on hire so withouten lette°,
That as he sat and wok° his spirit mette°
That he hire saw a-temple, and al the wyse°
Right of hire lok, and gan it newe avyse°.

Thus gan he make a myrrour of his mynde,
In which he saugh alle holly° hire figure,
And that he wel koude° yn his herte fynde.
It was to hym a right good aventure°
To love swych on°, and yf he dede his cure°
To serven hire yet myghte he falle in° grace,
Or elles for on° of hire servauntz pace°;

Ymagynge that travaylle nor grame°
Ne myghte for so goodly on be lorn°
As she, ne hym for his desir no shame°,
Al° were it wist°, but yn prys° and upborn
Of alle lovers wel more than byforn.
Thus argumented he yn his gynnynge°,
Ful unavysed° of his wo comynge.

Thus tok he purpos loves craft to suwe°,
And thoughte he wolde werken pryvely°,
First to hiden his desir in muwe°
From every wight° yborn, al outrely°,
But° he myghte ought recovered be° therby;
Remembryng hym that love to wyde yblowe°
Yelt° bittre fruyt, though swete seed be sowe°.

And over all this, yet muche more he thoughte
What for to speke and what to holden inne;
And what to arten° hire to love he soughte;
And on a song anoon right to bygynne,
And gan loude on his sorwe for to wynne°;
For with good hope he gan fully assente
Criseyde for to love, and nought repente.

And of his song nought only the sentence°,
As writ° myn auctour called Lollyus,
But pleynly, save oure tonge deference°,
I dar wel seyn yn al that Troylus
Seyde yn his song, lo every word right thus
As I shal seyn; and whoso lyst it here°,
Lo next this vers he may it fynden here.

Cantus Troili°

"If no love is, O God, what fele I so?
And if love is, what thyng and which° is he?
If love be good, from whenes° cometh my wo?

---

347 deme, *think* **348 enchesoun,** *reason* **349 wroth,** *angry,* **groyn,** *complaint* **351 say,** *saw* **352 pes,** *peace,* **bote,** *reward* **354 unnethe,** *hardly,* **feyned,** *pretended* **355 destrayned,** *preoccupied* **356 nyste,** *knew not* **357 bad,** *ordered,* **hem lyste,** *it pleased them* **360 syke,** *sigh* **361 lette,** *ceasing* **362 wok,** *remained awake,* **mette,** *dreamed* **363 wyse,** *manner* **364 avyse,** *consider* **366 holly,** *wholly/holy* **367 koude,** *could* **368 aventure,** *opportunity* **369 swych on,** *such* (a) *one,* **dede his cure,** *took care* **370, in,** *into* **371 on,** *one,* **pace,** *pass* **372 travaylle nor grame,** *labor nor pain* **373 lorn,** *lost* **374 ne hym . . . no shame,** *nor for him no shame because of his desire* **375 Al,** *although,* **wist,** *known,* **prys,** *honor* **377 gynnynge,** *beginning* **378 unavysed,** *unaware* **379 suwe,** *pursue* **380 pryvely,** *secretly* **381 muwe,** *cage* **382 wight,** *person,* **outrely,** *utterly* **383 But,** *unless,* **ought recovered be,** *gain any advantage* **384 to wyde yblowe,** *too widely made known* **385 Yelt,** *yields,* **sowe,** *sown* **388 arten,** *urge* **390 wynne,** *overcome* **393 sentence,** *meaning* **394 writ,** *writes* **395 save oure tonge deference,** *except for the differences of our languages* **398 lyst it here,** *wishes to hear it* **399a *Cantus Troili*,** *song of Troylus* **401 which,** *of what kind* **402 whenes,** *where*

353 fetheres so to lyme, to smear his feathers with birdlime, a sticky substance used to trap birds. **357 hem,** Cl reads "hym." **361 withouten,** Cl reads "withouten ony." **363 a-temple,** Cp reads "and temple." **365 myrrour of his mynde,** the figure is also used in *MerT* 4.1582, *Rom* 2806, and *Bo* 5.m4.27. **372 grame,** Cp reads "grace." **385 seed,** omitted in Cl. **387 What for,** Cl reads "For what." **394 Lollyus,** Lollius, Chaucer's fictional source, also mentioned at 5.1653 and *HF* 1468; he may have thought there was an ancient authority by this name, but nowhere in his works does Chaucer mention Boccaccio or his *Filostrato* (the primary source of *TC*)—an unexplained though apparently deliberate omission. Chaucer does use "Philostrate" as Arcite's pseudonym in *KnT* 1.1428. **399a Cantus Troili,** "The Song of Troylus." The rubric is omitted in Cl; Cp reads "Canticus Troili." **400–420** The song is a translation of Petrarch's Sonnet 88 (*Canzoniere* 132), an artful collection of commonplaces about the paradoxical nature of love. Chaucer's version uses the three-stanza structure of the French *ballade* rather than Petrarch's fourteen-line sonnet form. **400 no,** omitted in Cl.

If it be wykke°, a wonder thenketh me
Whenne every torment and adversite
That cometh of hym may to me savory thynke°,
For ay thurst° I, the more that ich° it drynke.

"And yf that at myn owene lust° I brenne°,
Fro whennes cometh my waylyng and my pleynte°?
If harm agree° me, wherto pleyne I thanne?—
I not°; ne whi unweri° that I feynte°.
O quyke° deth, O swete harm so queynte°,
How may of the° yn me swich quantite,
But if that I consente that it be?

"And if that I consente, I wrongfully
Compleyne, iwys°. Thus possed° to and fro,
Al sterles° withinne a bot am I
Amyd the see, bitwixen wyndes two
That in contrarye stonden evere mo.
Allas, what is this wondre° maladye?
For hete of cold, for cold of hete, I deye°."

And to the God of Love thus seyde he
With pitous vois, "O lord, now youres is
My spirit, which that aughte youre be°.
Yow thank I, lord, that han° me brought to this,
But whether goddesse or womman, iwys°,
She be, I not°, which that ye do° me serve;
But as hire man I wol ay leve and sterve°.

"Ye stonden yn hire eyen myghtily,
As yn a place unto your vertu digne°,
Wherfore, my lord, if my servyse or I
May lyke° yow, so beth° to me benygne°;
For myn estat royal here I resigne
Into hire hond, and with ful humble chere
Bycome hire man, as to my lady dere."

In hym ne deyned spare° blood royal
The fyr of love—the wherfro° God me blysse°—
Ne hym forbar° in no degre, for al
His vertu or his excellent prowesse,
But held hym as his thral° lowe yn distresse,
And brende° hym so in sondry wyse ay° newe,
That sixty tyme a day he loste his hewe.

So muche day by day his owene thought
For lust° to hire gan quyken° and encrese,
That every other charge° he sett at nought.
Forthi° ful ofte his hote fyr to cese°,
To seen hire goodly look° he gan to prese°,
For therby to ben esed wel he wende°—
And ay the ner° he was, the more he brende.

For ay the ner the fyr, the hotter is—
This, trowe° I, knoweth al this compaignye.
But were he fer or neer, I dar seye this,
By nyght or day, for wysdom or folye,
His herte, which that is his brestes eye,
Was ay on hire that fairer was to sene
Than evere was Eleyne or Polixene.

Ek° of the day ther passed nought an houre
That to hymself a thousand tymes he seyde,
"Good goodly, to whom serve I and laboure
As I best kan, now wolde God°, Criseyde,
Ye wolden on me rewe° er that I deyde!
My dere herte, allas, myn hele° and hewe°
And lyf is lost but° ye wole on me rewe."

Alle other dredes weren from hym fledde,
Bothe of th'assege° and his salvacioun;
Ne yn hym desir noon other fownes° bredde
But argumentes to this conclusioun,

---

403 wykke, *wicked* **405 savory thynke,** *seem sweet* **406 ay thurst,** *always thirst,* **ich,** *I* **407 lust,** *desire,* **brenne,** *burn* **408 pleynte,** *complaint* **409 agree,** *pleases* **410 not,** *know not,* **unweri,** *unweary,* **feynte,** *weaken* **411 quyke,** *living,* **queynte,** *strange* **412 may of the,** *may* (there be) *of you* **415 iwys,** *surely,* **possed,** *tossed* **416 sterles,** *rudderless* **419 wondre,** *marvelous* **420 deye,** *die* **423 aughte youre be,** *should be yours* **424 han,** *have* **425 iwys,** *surely* **426 not,** *know not,* **do,** *make* **427 leve and sterve,** *live and die* **429 vertu digne,** *power worthy* **431 lyke,** *please,* **beth,** *be,* **benygne,** *generous* **435 ne deyned spare,** *did not think it right to spare* **436 wherfro,** *from which,* **blysse,** *save* **437 hym forbar,** *spared him* **439 thral,** *captive* **440 brende,** *burned,* **ay,** *always* **443 lust,** *desire,* **gan quyken,** *did come alive* **444 charge,** *duty* **445 Forthi,** *therefore,* **cese,** *extinguish* **446 goodly look,** *lovely face,* **gan to prese,** *crowded* **447 wende,** *thought* **448 ay the ner,** *always the nearer* **450 trowe,** *believe* **456 Ek,** *also* **459 wolde God,** *I wish to God* **460 rewe,** (have) *pity* **461 hele,** *health,* **hewe,** *color* **462 but,** *unless* **464 th'assege,** *the siege* **465 fownes,** *offspring*

405 may to me savory, Cl reads "may me so goodly." **406 ich,** Cl reads "I." **417 bitwixen,** Cl reads "bytwen." **428 Ye stonden yn hire eyen,** the phrase means both "you are regarded highly by her" and "you exist in her eyes." **430 my lord,** Cp omits "my." **434 Bycome hire man,** in a form of feudal subordination, Troylus pledges to Love in order to serve Criseyde. **436 fyr of love,** the fire of love, which does not spare even royal blood, is in *Filostrato* 1.40, and it is also a concept found in medieval mystical tradition, including the *Incendium Amoris* (*Fire of Love*) of Richard Rolle. **441 loste his hewe,** growing pale is one of the typical symptoms of love sickness. **449** Proverbial. Compare *Rom* 2478. **453 brestes eye,** the figure of the heart as the eye of the breast is not in *Filostrato,* but does recur in courtly and contemplative literature. **455 Eleyne . . . Polixene,** Helen of Troy; Polyxena, Troylus's sister, loved by Achilles. **458 Good,** Cp reads "God." **and,** omitted in Cp.

That she of hym wolde han compassioun,
And he to be hire man while he may dure°.
Lo, here his lyf, and from the deth his cure.

The shoures sharpe felle° of armes preve°,
That Ector or his othere bretheren diden,
Ne made hym oonly therfore ones meve°;
And yet was he wherso° men wente or riden
Founde oon the beste°, and lengest tyme abyden°
Ther° peril was, and dide ek such travayle°
In armes, that to thenke it° was mervayle.

But for non hate he to the Grekes hadde,
Ne also for the rescous° of the town,
Ne made hym thus yn armes for to madde°,
But oonly, lo, for this conclusioun,
To lyken° hire the bet° for his renoun.
Fro day to day yn armes so he spedde°
That the Grekes as the deth hym dredde.

And fro this forth° tho refte° hym love his sleep,
And made his mete° his foo, and ek his sorwe
Gan multiplie, that whoso took keep°,
It shewed in his hewe bothe eve and morwe.
Therfor a title° he gan hym for to borwe
Of other syknesse, lest° of hym men wende°
That the hote° fyr of love hym brende,

And seyde he hadde a fevere and ferde amys°.
But how it was, certeyn, kan I not seye,
If that his lady understod not this,
Or feynede hire she nyste°, oon of the tweye.
But wel I rede that by no manere weye
Ne semed it as that she of hym roughte°,
Nor of his peyne, or whatsoevere he thoughte.

But thanne felt this Troylus such wo
That he was wel neigh wood°, for ay his drede
Was this, that she som wyght° hadde loved so
That nevere of hym she wolde han taken hede°.
For which hym thoughte he felt his herte blede,
Ne of his wo ne dorste° he nat bygynne
To tellen hir for al this world to wynne.

But whanne he hadde a space fro° his care,
Thus to hymself ful ofte he gan to pleyne°;
He seyde, "O fool, now art thow in the snare,
That whilom japedest° at loves peyne.
Now artow hent°, now gnaw thin owen cheyne.
Thow were ay wont° eche lovere reprehende°
Of thing fro which thow kanst the nought defende.

"What wol now every lovere seyn of the°
If this be wist°, but evere yn thyn absence
Laughen yn skorn, and seyn, "Lo, ther goth he
That is the man of so gret sapience°;
That held us loveres lest° yn reverence.
Now, thonked be God, he may goon in the daunce
Of hem that Love lyst febely° for to avaunce°.

"But O thow woful Troylus, God wolde°,
Syn° thow most° loven thurgh thy desteno°,
That thow beset were° on swych oon° that sholde
Know al thi wo, al lakked hire° pite.
But also° cold yn love towardes the°
Thi lady is as frost in wynter mone,
And thow fordon° as snow yn fyre is soone.

"God wolde I were aryved° in the port
Of deth, to which my sorwe wil me lede!
A, Lord, to me it were gret comfort.
Than° were I quyt° of langwysshyng in drede.

468 dure, *live* **470 shoures sharpe felle,** *sharp terrible assaults,* **of armes preve,** *feats of arms* **472 Ne made him . . . meve,** *did not motivate him at all* **473 wherso,** *wherever* **474 oon the beste,** *one of the best,* **abyden,** *stayed* **475 Ther,** *where,* **travayle,** *labor* **476 to thenke it,** *to think on it* **478 rescous,** *rescue* **479 madde,** *rage* **481 lyken,** *please,* **bet,** *better* **482 spedde,** *succeeded* **484 fro this forth,** *moreover,* **tho refte,** *then deprived* **485 mete,** *food* **486 took keep,** *paid attention* **488 a title,** *the name* **489 lest,** *for fear that,* **wende,** *think* **490 hote,** *hot* **491 ferde amys,** *felt ill* **494 feynede hire she nyste,** *acted as if she did not know* **496 roughte,** *cared* **499 wood,** *crazed* **500 wyght,** *person* **501 wolde han taken hede,** *would have paid attention* **503 dorste,** *dared* **505 space fro,** *break from* **506 pleyne,** *lament* **508 whilom japedest,** *once joked* **509 artow hent,** *are you captured* **510 ay wont,** *always accustomed,* **reprehende,** *to accuse* **512 seyn of the,** *say of you* **513 wist,** *known* **515 sapience,** *wisdom* **516 lest,** *least* **518 lyst febely,** *chooses feebly,* **avaunce,** *advance* **519 God wolde,** *I wish to God* **520 Syn,** *since,* **most,** *must,* **destene,** *destiny* **521 beset were,** *were fixed,* **swych oon,** *such a one* **522 al lakked hire,** *even if she lacked* **523 also,** *as,* **the,** *you* **525 fordon,** *destroyed* **526 aryved,** *arrived* **529 Than,** *then,* **quyt,** *free*

483 the deth, the use of the definite article has led some to read this as a reference to the plague, but see 469 and 536. **484–87** Commonplace symptoms of love-sickness; compare *KnT* 1.1359ff. **495–97** The indifference of the lady is commonplace of chivalric love. **502 which,** Cl reads "such." **504 hir,** Cl reads "it." **517–18** The dance of love here seems to mean courtship, although sexual connotations are apparent in *GP* 1.476. **519–20** *Filostrato* 1.53 suggests determinism here also; Chaucer enriches the suggestion through the reference to God, and he increases the emphasis on destiny throughout the poem.

For be myn hidde sorwe° iblowe on brede°,
I shal byjaped ben° a thousand tyme
More than that fol of whos folye men ryme.

"But now help, God, and ye°, swete for whom°
I pleyne°, icaught, ye°, nevere wyght so faste°!
O mercy, dere herte, and help me from
The deth, for I while that my lyf may laste,
More than myself, wol love yow to my laste.
And with som frendly look gladeth me°, swete,
Though nevere more thyng° ye me byhete°"

Thise wordes and ful many an other to°
He spak, and called evere yn his compleynte
Hire name, for to tellen hire his woo,
Til neigh° that he in salte teres dreynte°.
Al was for nought; she herde nought his pleynte.
And whan that he bithought° on that folye,
A thousandfold his wo gan multiplie.

Bywayling yn his chambre thus allone,
A frend of his that called was Pandare
Com onys° in unwar and herde hym grone,
And say° his frend in swych distresse and care.
"Allas," quod he, "who causeth al this fare°?
O mercy God, what unhap° may this mene°?
Han° now thus soone Grekes maad° yow lene°?

"Or hastow som remors of conscience,
And art now fallen yn som devocioun,
And waylest° for thi synne and thyn offence,
And hast for ferde° caught attricioun°?
God save hem° that byseged han oure toun,
That so kan leye oure jolyte on presse°,
And brynge oure lusty° folk to holynesse!"

These wordes seyde he for the nones alle°
That with swych° thing he myght hym angry maken,
And with an angre don his wo to falle
As for the tyme°, and his corage awaken.
But wel he wiste°, as fer as tonges spaken,
Ther nas a man of grettere hardinesse
Thanne he, ne more desirede worthinesse.

"What cas°," quod Troylus, "or what aventure°
Hath gided the to se me langwysshynge,
That am refus of° every creature?
But for the love of God, at my preyinge°,
Go hennes° awey, for certes° my deyinge
Wol the dishese°, and I mot nedes° deye.
Therfor go wey; ther is na more to seye.

"But if thou wene° I be thus sike for drede,
It is not so, and therfore scorne nought.
Ther is another thing I take of hede°
Wel more than ought° the Grekes han yet wrought°;
Which cause is of my deth for sorowe and thought.
But though that I now telle it the ne leste°,
Be thow naught wroth°; I hide it for the beste."

This Pandare, that neigh malt° for sorwe and
  routhe°,
Ful often seyde, "Allas, what may this be?
Now, frend," quod he, "yf evere love or trouthe
Hath ben, or is, bytwyxen° the and me,
Ne do thou nevere such a cruelte
To hide fro thi frend so gret a care.
Wostow° nought wel that it am I, Pandare?

"I wole parten° with the al thyn peyne—
If it be so I do the no comfort—
As it is frendes right, soth° for to seyne°,
To entreparten° wo as glad desport°.
I have and shal, for trewe or fals report,
In wrong and right iloved the al my lyve
Hyd not thi wo fro me, but telle it blyve°."

---

530 be myn hidde sorwe, *if my hidden sorrow were to be,* **iblowe on brede,** *announced widely* **531 byjaped ben,** *be mocked* **533 ye,** *you,* **for whom,** *because of whom* **534 pleyne,** *lament,* **ye,** *yes!* **wyght,** *person,* **faste,** *firmly* **538 gladeth me,** *make me glad* **539 more thyng,** *anything more,* **byhete,** *promise* **540 to,** *too* **543 neigh,** *nearly,* **dreynte,** *drowned* **545 bithought,** *reflected* **549 onys,** *once* **550 say,** *saw* **551 fare,** *commotion* **552 unhap,** *misfortune,* **mene,** *indicate* **553 Han,** *have,* **maad,** *made,* **lene,** *feeble* **556 waylest,** (do you) *wail* **557 ferde,** *fear,* **attricioun,** *sorrow* (see n.) **558 hem,** *them* **559 leye oure jolyte on presse,** *put our good spirits in storage* **560 lusty,** *vigorous* **561 for the nones alle,** *all for the purpose* **562 swych,** *such* **564 As for the tyme,** *for the time being* **465 wiste,** *knew* **568 cas,** *chance,* **aventure,** *accident* **570 refus of,** *rejected by* **571 preyinge,** *request* **572 hennes,** *hence,* **certes,** *surely* **573 the dishese,** *distress you,* **mot nedes,** *must necessarily* **575 wene,** *believe* **577 take of hede,** *care about* **578 ought,** *anything,* **wrought,** *accomplished* **580 telle it the ne leste,** *choose not to tell it to you* **581 wroth,** *angry* **582 neigh malt,** *nearly melted,* **routhe,** *pity* **585 bytwyxen,** *between* **588 Wostow,** *know you* **589 parten,** *share* **591 soth,** *truth,* **seyne,** *tell* **592 entreparten,** *share,* **desport,** *pleasure* **595 blyve,** *quickly*

530 be, Cl and Cp read "by." **hidde,** Cl reads "hed." **532 that fol,** that fool; if a specific literary referent is intended here, it remains unidentified. **534 ye,** Cp reads "yet"; Cl, "the." **536 may,** Cl reads "wole." **554 som,** omitted in Cl. **557 attricioun,** attrition is, technically, the imperfect sorrow for sin; contrition is the perfect form. **569 me,** Cl reads "my." **581 Be,** Cl reads "Ne be."

Than gan this Troylus sorwfully to syke°,
And seyde hym thus, "God leve° it be my beste
To telle it the; for sith° it may the lyke°,
Yet wol I telle it thowh myn herte breste°.
And wel wot° I thow mayst don me no reste,
But lest thow deme° I truste not to the,
Now herke°, frend, for thus it stant° with me.

"Love, ayens° the which whoso° defendeth
Hymselven most hym alderlest avayleth°,
With desespeir° so sorwfully me offendeth
That streyght unto the deth myn herte sayleth,
Therto desir so brennyngly° me assayleth,
That to ben slayn it were a gretter joye
To me than kyng of Grece ben° and Troye.

"Suffiseth this, my fulle frend Pandare,
That I have seyd, for now wostow° my wo.
And for the love of God, my colde care
So hyd° it wel, I telle it nevere to mo°.
For harmes myghte folwen mo than two
If it were wyst°, but be thou in gladnesse,
And lat me sterve° unknowe of° my distresse."

"How hastow thus unkyndely° and longe
Hid this fro me, thow fool?" quod Pandarus.
"Paraunter° thow myghte after swych on° longe
That myn avys anoon° may helpen us."
"This were° a wonder thyng," quod Troylus.
"Thow koudest° nevere yn love thynselven wysse°.
How devel maystow° bryngen me to blysse?"

"Ye, Troilus, now herke," quod Pandare,
"Though I be nyce°, it happeth ofte so
That on that excesse doth ful yvele fare°
By good counseyl kan kepe his frend therfro°.
I have myself ek seyn° a blynd man go
Ther as he fel that koude loke wyde°.
A fool may ek ofte a wys man gyde°.

"A wheston° is no kervyng° instrument,
But yet it maketh sharpe kervyng tolys°.
And there° thow wost° that I have ought myswent°,
Eschewe° thou that, for swych thyng to the
scole° is—
Thus ofte wyse men ben war° by folys°.
If thou do so, thi wit is wel bywared°.
By his contrari is everything declared°.

"For how myght evere swetnesse have be knowe
To hym that nevere tasted bitternesse?
Ne no man may be inly° glad, I trowe°,
That nevere was yn sorwe or som distresse.
Ek° whit by blak, by shame ek worthinesse,
Ech set by other, more for other° semeth,
As men may se, and so the wyse it demeth°.

"Sith° thus of two contraries is o lore°,
I, that have in love so ofte assayed°,
Grevaunces oughte konne°, and wel the more°
Counsayllen the of that thow art amayed°.
Ek the ne oughte not ben yvel apayed°,
Thowh I desire with the for to bere
Thyn hevy charge°—it shal the lasse dere°.

"I wot° wel that it fareth° thus by me
As to thi brother Parys: an hierdesse°
Which that icleped° was Oenone

596 syke, *sigh* **597 leve,** *grant* **598 sith,** *since,* **lyke,** *please* **599 breste,** *burst* **600 wot,** *know* **601 lest thow deme,** *for fear you think* **602 herke,** *listen,* **stant,** *stands* **603 ayens,** *against,* **whoso,** *whoever* **604 hym alderlest avayleth,** *it benefits him the least* **605 desespeir,** *despair* **607 brennyngly,** *burningly* **609 ben,** *to be* **611 wostow,** *you know* **613 hyd,** *hide,* **mo,** *more* (people) **615 wyst,** *known* **616 sterve,** *die,* **unknowe of,** *unknown for* **617 unkyndely,** *unnaturally* **619 Paraunter,** *perhaps,* **after swych on,** *for such one* (someone) **620 avys anoon,** *advice soon* **621 were,** *would be* **622 koudest,** *could,* **wysse,** *instruct* **623 How devel maystow,** *how the devil may you* **625 nyce,** *foolish* **626 on that excesse doth ful yvele fare,** *one who excess causes to do poorly* **627 therfro,** *from that* **628 ek seyn,** *also seen* **629 koude loke wyde,** *could see far* **630 gyde,** *guide* **631 wheston,** *sharpener* (whetstone), **kervyng,** *carving* **632 tolys,** *tools* **633 there,** *where,* **wost,** *believe,* **ought myswent,** *gone at all wrong* **634 Eschewe,** *abandon,* **scole,** *school* **635 ben war,** *are* (made) *aware,* **folys,** *fools* **636 bywared,** *put to use* **637 declared,** *revealed* **640 inly,** *wholly,* **trowe,** *believe* **642 Ek,** *also* **643 for other,** *by the other* **644 demeth,** *judges* **645 Sith,** *since,* **o lore,** *one learning* **646 assayed,** *attempted* **647 oughte konne,** *ought to understand,* **wel the more,** *all the better* **648 the of that thow art amayed,** *you concerning that* (about which) *you are distressed* **649 ben yvele apayed,** *be displeased* **651 charge,** *burden,* **the lasse dere,** *harm you less* **652 wot,** *know,* **fareth,** *happens* **653 hierdesse,** *shepherdess* **654 icleped,** *named*

596 this Troylus, Cp reads "sorwful Troylus." **600 And,** Cl reads "But." **606 sayleth,** Cp reads "fayleth." **614 folwen,** Cp reads "fallen." **628–30** Proverbial notions. **631** The whetstone image and much of the remainder of Book 1 are Chaucer's additions, as Pandarus's learning of Criseyde's identity is expanded from 200 lines in *Filostrato* to 500 in *TC.* Chaucer adds several classical allusions, much that is commonplace and proverbial, and the language and imagery of Boethian philosophy. **633 ought,** Cl reads "out." **637–44** Pandarus's view on contraries and the imagery that accompanies it echo *RR* 21559–82, where, with sexual overtones, the Lover reports that varied experiences can improve discernment. **645** Proverbial.

Wrot yn a compleynt of hire hevynesse°.
Ye say° the lettre that she wrot, I gesse?"
"Nay nevere yet, ywis°," quod Troylus.
"Now," quod Pandare, "herkene°, it was thus:

"'Phebus, that first fond° art of medecyne,'
Quod she, 'and koude in every wyghtes° care
Remede and red by erbess° he knew fyne°;
Yet to hymself his konnyng° was ful bare°,
For love hadde hym so bounden yn a snare,
Al for the doughter of the kyng Amete,
That al his craft ne koude° his sorwe bete°.'

"Ryght so fare I, unhappily for me.
I love oon best, and that me smerteth sore°;
And yet peraunter° kan I rede the°,
And not myself—repreve° me no more.
I have no cause, I wot° wel, for to sore°
As doth an hauk that lysteth° for to pleye.
But to thyn help yet somwhat kan I seye.

"And of o thyng right siker° maystow be,
That certayn, for to dyen in the peyne°,
That I shal nevere more discoveren the°.
Ne by my trouthe, I kepe not restreyne°
The fro thi love, they° that it were Eleyne
That is thi brotheres wif, if ich° it wyste°—
Be what she be, and love hire as the liste°!

"Therfore, as a frend, fullich yn me assure°,
And telle me plat° what is thyn enchesoun°
And final cause of wo that ye endure.
For douteth nothyng, myn entencioun
Nys nought to yow of reprehencioun°,
To speke as now, for no wyght may bireve°
A man to love tyl that hym lyst to leve°.

"And weteth° wel that bothe two ben vices:
Mystrusten alle, or elles alle leve°.
But wel I wot°, the meene° of it no vice is,
For for to trusten sum wight is a preve°
Of trouth; and forthi° wolde I fayn remeve°
Thy wrong conseyte°, and do the° som wyght tryste°
Thi wo to telle—and telle me, yf thow lyste°.

"Thise wyse° seyth, 'Wo hym that is allone,
For, and he falle, he hath noon helpe to ryse'.
And sith° thou hast a felawe°, tel thi moone°;
For this nys not, yn certeyn, the nexte wyse°
To wynnen love, as techen us the wyse—
To walwe° and wepe as Niobe the queene,
Whos terys yet yn marbel ben yseene°.

"Lat be thi wepyng and thi drerynesse,
And lat us lyssen° wo with other speche.
So may thy woful tyme seme lesse.
Delite not in wo thi wo for to seche°,
As doon these foles° that hire sorwes eche°
With sorwe when they han mysaventure,
And lysten° nought to sechen other cure.

"Men seyn, to wrecche° is consolacioun
To have another felawe yn his peyne.
That oughte wel ben oure opynyoun,
For bothe thow and I, of love we pleyne°.
So ful of sorwe am I, soth° for to seyne,
That certaynly no more harde grace°
May sitte on me, forwhi° ther is no space.

655 hevynesse, *sorrow* **656 say,** *saw* **657 ywis,** *surely* **658 herkene,** *listen* **659 fond,** *established* **660 koude in every wyghtes,** *knew in every person's* **661 red by erbess,** *advice about herbs,* **fyne,** *fully* **662 konnyng,** *knowledge,* **ful bare,** *completely useless* **665 koude,** *could,* **bete,** *heal* **667 me smerteth sore,** *pains me sorely* **668 peraunter,** *perhaps,* **rede the,** *advise you* **669 repreve,** *accuse* **670 wot,** *know,* **sore,** *soar* **671 lysteth,** *chooses* **673 right siker,** *very secure* **674 for to dyen in the peyne,** *though I might die during torture* **675 discoveren the,** *betray you* **676 kepe not restreyne,** *care not to restrain* **677 they,** *though* **678 ich,** *I,* **wyste,** *knew* **679 liste,** *wish* **680 assure,** *be assured* **681 plat,** *plainly,* **enchesoun,** *reason* **684 reprehencioun,** *accusation* **685 bireve,** *prevent* **686 lyst to leve,** *wishes to stop* **687 weteth,** *know* **688 leve,** *believe* **689 wot,** *know,* **meene,** *middle way* **690 preve,** *proof* **691 forthi,** *therefore,* **fayn remeve,** *gladly remove* **692 conseyte,** *idea,* **do the,** *make you,* **tryste,** *trust* **693 lyste,** *choose* **694 Thise wyse,** *wise* (people) **696 sith,** *since,* **felawe,** *conpanion,* **moone,** *grief* **697 nexte wyse,** *nearest way* **699 walwe,** *wallow* **700 ben yseene,** *are seen* **702 lyssen,** *lessen* **704 seche,** *seek* **705 foles,** *fools,* **eche,** *increase* **707 lysten,** *choose* **708 wrecche,** *a sorrowful person* **711 pleyne,** *complain* **712 soth,** *truth* **713 harde grace,** *misfortune* **714 forwhi,** *because*

658 Now, Cl reads "No." **659–65** In Ovid's *Heroides* 5, **Oenone** laments that Paris (**Parys**) has abandoned her for Helen, and complains that though she is skilled in medicine, she cannot soothe her own pain. In an interpolation added to Ovid's original (5.151–52), Oenone alludes to Phoebus Apollo (**Phebus**) as a lover of the daughter of King Admetus (**Amete**). Chaucer may have known a version of Ovid that explains and expands the allusion, but it is likely that this derives from Boccaccio's own gloss to his *Teseida* 4.46. **661 he,** Cl and Cp read "she." **682 final,** Cl and Cp read "finally." **690 For for,** Cl and Cp read "For." **694–95** Proverbial, from Ecclesiastes 4.10. **699 Niobe,** weeping for her seven sons and seven daughters, Niobe was turned to marble, which still sheds tears; Ovid, *Metamorphoses* 6.312. She was a stock example of bereavement in art and rhetoric. **703 thy,** Cl reads "this." **708–09** A version of the proverbial "Misery loves company."

"If God wol°, thou art not agast° of me
Lest° I wold of thi lady the bygyle°.
Thow wost° thiself whom that I love, parde°,
As I best kan, gon sithen longe while°.
And sith° thow wost I do it for no wyle°,
And sithen° I am he in whom thou tristest° most,
Tel me sumwhat syn° al my wo thow wost."

Yet Troylus for al this no word seyde,
But longe he lay as stylle as he ded were;
And after this with sikynge° he abreyde°,
And to Pandarus voys he lente his eere,
And up his eyen caste° he, that° in feere
Was Pandarus lest° that in frenesye°
He sholde falle or elles soone dye,

And cride, "Awake!" ful wonderly° and sharpe.
"What, slombrestow° as yn a lytargie°?
Or artow° lyk an asse to the harpe,
That hereth soun whan men the strenges° plye,
But yn his mynde of that no melodye
May synken hym to glade°, for that he
So dul is of his bestialite?"

And with that Pandare of his wordes stente°,
And Troylus yet hym nothyng answerde,
Forwhy° to telle nas not° his entente
To nevere° man for whom that he so ferde°.
For it is seyd, man maketh ofte a yerdo°
With which the makere is hymself ybeten
In sondry manere—as thise wyse treten°;

And namelich° yn his counseyl tellynge°
That toucheth love, that oughte ben secre°,
For of hymself° it wol ynough out sprynge
But yf that° it the bet° governed be.
Ek somtyme it is a craft° to seme fle°
Fro thyng which yn effect° men hunte faste—
Al this gan Troylus in his herte caste°.

But natheles°, whan he hadde herd hym crye
"Awake," he gan to syke° wonder sore,
And seyde, "Frend, though that I stille lye,
I am not def. Now pes° and cry no more,
For I have herd thi wordes and thi lore°,
But suffre° me my myschef° to bywayle,
For thi proverbes may me nought avayle°.

"Nor other cure canstow noon for me.
Eke° I nyl not be cured; I wol deye.
What knowe I of the queene Niobe?
Lat be thyne olde ensamples, I the preye."
"No," quod tho Pandarus, "therfore I seye,
Such is delit of foles to bywepe
Hire wo, but seken bote thei ne kepe°.

"Now knowe I that ther reson yn the fayleth°.
But telle me, yf I wyste what° she were
For whom that the al this mysaunter° ayleth
Dorstestow° that I telle in hire eere
Thi wo, sith° thow darst not thiself for feere,
And hire bysoughte° on the to han som routhe°?"
"Why, nay," quod he, "by God and by my trouthe!"

"What, nat as bisily°," quod Pandarus,
"As though myn owen lyf lay on this nede?"
"No, certes°, brother," quod this Troylus.
"And why?"—"For that thow sholdest nevere spede°."

---

715 If God wol, *God willing,* **agast,** *afraid* **716 Lest,** *for fear,* **the bygyle,** *deprive you* (by deception) **717 wost,** *know,* **parde,** *by God* **718 gon sithen longe while,** *since a long time ago* **719 sith,** *since,* **wyle,** *deception* **720 sithen,** *since,* **tristest,** *trusts* **721 syn,** *since* **724 sikynge,** *sighing,* **abreyde,** *rose up* **726 up his eyen caste,** *rolled his eyes,* **that,** *so that* **727 lest,** *for fear,* **frenesye,** *frenzy* **730 wonderly,** *amazedly* **730 slombrestow,** *do you sleep,* **lytargie,** *lethargy* **731 artow,** *are you* **732 strenges,** *strings* **735 glade,** *gladden* **736 stente,** *stopped* **738 Forwhy,** *because,* **nas not,** *was not* **739 nevere,** *no,* **so ferde,** *acted so* **740 yerde,** *stick* **742 thise wyse treten,** *wise people tell* **743 namelich,** *especially,* **his counseyl tellynge,** *telling his inner thoughts* **744 secre,** *secret* **745 hymself,** *itself* **746 But yf that,** *unless,* **bet,** *better* **747 craft,** *skill,* **to seme fle,** *to seem to flee* **748 yn effect,** *in fact* **749 gan . . . caste,** *did . . . ponder* **750 natheles,** *nonetheless* **751 syke,** *sigh* **753 pes,** *peace* **754 lore,** *lesson* **755 suffre,** *allow,* **myschef,** *misfortune* **756 may me nought avayle,** *will not aid me at all* **758 Eke,** *also* **763 seken bote thei ne kepe,** *they care not to seek a remedy* **764 yn the fayleth,** *fails in you* **765 wyste what,** *knew who* **766 mysaunter,** *misfortune* **767 Dorstestow,** *would you dare* **768 sith,** *since* **769 hire bysoughte,** *asked her,* **routhe,** *pity* **771 nat as bisily,** *not* (if I asked) *as diligently* **773 certes,** *surely* **774 spede,** *succeed*

720 in whom, Cp reads "that." **731–35 asse to the harpe . . . ,** the proverbial figure of the ass who is too dull to hear the harp's melody is in *Bo* 1.m4.2–3. **732 plye,** Cp reads "pleye." **734 synken,** Cl reads "synk in." **737 nothyng,** Cl reads "no word." **740–41** Proverbial. **744** Secrecy is a commonplace of courtly love. **745 wol ynough out,** Cl reads "wolde not ought." **747–48** This proverbial idea is in *RR* 7557–58. **764 ther,** omitted in Cl. **767 telle,** Cp reads "told."

"Wostow° that wel?"—"Ye, that is out of drede°,"
Quod Troylus. "For al that evere ye konne°,
She nyl° to no swych wrecche as I be wonne."

Quod Pandarus, "Allas, what may this be,
That thow despered art thus causeles?
What, lyveth not thi lady, bendiste°?
How wostow so that thow art graceles°?
Such yver° is not alwey boteles°.
Why, put not impossible thus thi cure,
Syn° thyng to come is oft yn aventure°.

"I graunte wel that thow endurest wo
As sharp as doth he Ticius yn helle,
Whos stomak foughles tiren° everemo,
That highte° volturis, as bokes telle.
But I may not endure that thow dwelle
In so unskilful° an opynyoun
That of thi wo is no curacioun.

"But ones nyltow for° thy coward herte,
And for thyn ire° and folessh wilfulnesse,
For wantrust°, tellen of thi sorwes smerte°,
Ne to thyn owen help do bysynesse
As muche as speke a resoun more or lesse,
But lyest° as he that lest of nothyng
recche°—
What womman koude loven such a wrecche?

"What may she demen° other of thi deth,
If thou thus deye and she not° whi it is,
But that for fere is yolden° up thi breth,
For Grekes han byseged us, ywys°?
Lord, which a thonk° then shaltow han of this!
Thus wol she seyn, and al the toun atones°,
'The wrecche is ded, the devil have his
bones!'

"Thow mayst allone here wepe and crie and knele,
But love a womman that she wot° it nought,
And she wole quyte° that thow shalt not fele—
Unknowe, unkyst, and lost, that is unsought.
What, many a man hath love ful dere ybought°
Twenty wynter that his lady wyste°,
That nevere yet his lady mouth he kyste.

"What, shulde he therfore fallen in despeyr,
Or be recreaunt° for his owene tene°,
Or slen° hymself, al be° his lady feyr?
Nay, nay, but evere yn oon° be fressh and greene
To serve and love hys dere hertes queene,
And thenk it is a guerdoun° hire to serve
A thowsandfold more than he kan deserve."

And of that word tok hede Troylus,
And thought anoon what folye he was inne,
And how that hym soth seyde° Pandarus,
That for to slen hymself myght he nat wynne°,
But bothe doon unmanhod and a synne,
And of his deth his lady nought to wyte°,
For of his wo, God woot°, she knew ful lyte°.

And with that thought he gan ful sore syke°,
And seyde, "Allas, what is me best to do?"
To whom Pandare answerde, "Yf the lyke°,
The beste is that thow telle me al thi wo.
And have my trowthe, but° thow it fynde so
I be thi bote or° that it be ful longe,
To pieces do me drawe° and sithen honge°."

"Ye, so thow seyst," quod Troylus tho, "allas,
But God wot°, it is not the rather° so.
Ful hard were it to helpen yn this cas,
For wel fynde I that Fortune is my fo,
Ne alle the men that riden konne or go°

---

775 Wostow, *do you know,* **drede,** *doubt* **776 konne,** *can do* **777 nyl,** *will not* **780 bendiste,** *bless us* **781 graceles,** *without favor* **782 yvel,** *trouble,* **boteles,** *hopeless* **784 Syn,** *since,* **yn aventure,** *subject to chance* **787 foughles tiren,** *birds tear* **788 highte,** *are called* **790 unskilful,** *unreasonable* **792 But ones nyltow for,** *but you will not once because of* **793 ire,** *anger* **794 wantrust,** *distrust,* **smerte,** *pain* **795 do bysynesse,** *take action* **797 lyest,** *lie down,* **lest of nothyng recche,** *wishes to care for nothing* **799 demen,** *conclude* **800 not,** *knows not* (ne wot) **801 yolden,** *yielded* **802 ywys,** *surely* **803 which a thonk,** *such thanks* **804 atones,** *at the same time* **807 wot,** *knows* **808 quyte,** *repay* **810 dere ybought,** *dearly bought* **811 wyste,** *knew of* **814 recreaunt,** *cowardly,* **tene,** *grief* **815 slen,** *kill,* **al be,** *despite* **816 evere yn oon,** *always* **818 guerdoun,** *reward* **822 soth seyde,** *truth told* **823 wynne,** *profit* **825 nought to wyte,** *would know nothing* **826 woot,** *knows,* **ful lyte,** *very little* **827 syke,** *sigh* **829 the lyke,** *you please* **831 but,** *unless* **832 bote or,** *remedy before* **833 do me drawe,** *have me drawn* (pulled apart), **sithen honge,** *after hanged* **835 wot,** *knows,* **835 rather,** *sooner* **838 riden konne or go,** *can ride or travel*

777 nyl to no swych wrecche as I be, Cl reads "nyl not to no swych wrecche be." **779–84 causeles . . . yn aventure,** the language of causation and chance is part of the poem's concern with Boethian philosophy. **779 despered,** Cl reads "desespered." **780 bendiste,** Cl reads "benedicite." **786 he,** Cl reads "the." **Ticius,** for attempting to rape Diana, Titius lay stretched out in Hades where two vultures perpetually tore at his liver. Compare *Bo* 3.m12.42 and see 4.791n. **797 lyest,** Cl reads "lyk"; Cp "list." **798 koude,** Cl reads "wolde." **812 he,** Cl reads "yet"; omitted in Cp **822 hym soth,** Cp reads "soth hym." **826 God woot, she knew,** Cl reads "God knoweth." **837–54 Fortune is my fo . . . ,** the language of Fortune and her wheel is part of the poem's concern with Boethian philosophy; see *Bo* 2.pr2.84–86; pr3.75–79; pr1.111–15; pr2.81–83.

May of hire cruel whiel° the harm wythstonde,
For as hire lyst° she pleyeth with free and
bonde°."

Quod Pandarus, "Than blamestow Fortune
For thow art wroth°? Ye, now at erst° I se.
Wostow not° wel that Fortune ys comune
To every maner wight° yn som degre?
And yet thow hast this comfort, lo, parde°,
That as hire joyes moten overgone°,
So mote hire sorwes passen everychone°.

"For yf hire whiel stynte anythyng to torne°,
Thanne cessed° she Fortune anoon° to be.
Now, sith° hire whiel by no wey may sojourne°,
What wostow° if hire mutabilite
Ryght as thiselven lyst° wol don by the°,
Or that she be not fer fro thyn helpynge?
Paraunter° thow hast cause for to synge.

"And therfore wostow what I the beseche°?
Lat be thi wo and turnyng to the grounde,
For whoso lyst° have helyng of his leche°,
To hym byhoveth° first unwrye° his wounde.
To Cerberus yn helle ay be I° bounde,
Were it for my suster, al thy sorwe,
By my wil she sholde al be thyn tomorwe.

"Lok up, I seye, and telle me what° she is,
Anoon° that I may goon aboute thin nede.
Knowe ich hire ought°? For my love, telle me
this.
Thenne wolde I hopen rather° for to
spede°."
Tho gan the veyne of Troylus to blede,
For he was hit and wax° al red for shame.
"Aha," quod Pandare, "here bygynneth game."

And with that word he gan hym for to shake,
And seyde, "Thef, thow shalt hire name telle."
But tho° gan sely° Troylus for to quake
As though men sholde han lad hym into helle,
And seyde, "Allas, of al my wo the welle°,
Than° is my swete fo called Criseyde."
And wel neygh° with the word for fere he deyde.

And whan that Pandare herd hire name nevene°,
Lord, he was glad, and seyde, "Frend so dere,
Now fare aright°, for Joves name yn hevene.
Love hath beset the° wel; be of good chere.
For of good name and wysdom and manere
She hath ynough, and ek of gentilesse°—
If she be fayr, thow wost° thyself, I gesse.

"Ne nevere saw I a more bounteuous°
Of hire estat, ne a gladden°, ne of speche
A frendliour, ne a more gracious
For to do wel, ne lasse hadde nede° to seche°
What for to doon; and al this bet° to eche°
In honour, to as fer as she may strecche,
A kynges herte semeth by hires a wrecche.

"And forthy loke° of good comfort° thou be,
For certainly, the firste poynt is this,
Of noble corage and wel ordayne°,
A man to have pees with himself, ywis°.
So oughtest thou, for nought but good it is
To loven wel and in a worthy place.
The oughte nat to clepe it hap°, but grace.

"And also thenk and therwith glade the°
That sith° thy lady vertuous is al,
So foloweth it that there is som pite
Amonges alle thyse other° in general;
And forthy° se that thow in special

---

839 whiel, *wheel* **840 hire lyst,** *it pleases her,* **free and bonde,** *everyone* (freemen and slaves) **842 wroth,** *upset,* **at erst,** *for the first time* **843 Wostow not,** *don't you know* **844 maner wight,** *kind of person* **845 parde,** *by God* **846 moten overgone,** *must pass away* **847 everychone,** *each one* **848 stynte anything to torne,** *stopped turning at all* **849 cessed,** *ceased,* **anoon,** *immediately* **850 sith,** *since,* **sojourne,** *rest* **851 What wostow,** *how do you know* **852 Ryght as thiselven lyst,** *just as you yourself wish,* **by the,** *for you* **854 Paraunter,** *perhaps* **855 the beseche,** *ask you* **857 whoso lyst,** *whoever wishes to,* **leche,** *doctor* **858 To hym byhoveth,** *it is to his advantage* (that he), **unwrye,** *uncover* **859 ay be I,** *may I always be* **862 what,** *who* **863 Anoon,** *immediately* **864 ought,** *at all* **865 rather,** *sooner,* **spede,** *succeed* **867 wax,** *grew* **871 tho,** *then,* **sely,** *silly* (?) *innocent* (?) **873 welle,** *source* **874 Than,** *then* **875 wel neygh,** *very nearly* **876 nevene,** *named* **878 fare aright,** *go well* **879 beset the,** *treated you* **881 gentilesse,** *nobleness* **882 wost,** *know* **883 bounteuous,** *generous* **884 gladder,** *more cheerful* **886 ne lasse hadde need,** *nor* (one who) *had less need,* **seche,** *seek* **887 bet,** *better,* **eche,** *increase* **890 forthy loke,** *therefore make sure,* **comfort,** *composure* **892 wel ordayne,** *very ordered* **893 ywis,** *surely* **896 hap,** *chance* **897 glade the,** *make yourself glad* **898 sith,** *since* **900 thyse other,** *these other* (virtues) **901 forthy,** *therefore*

842 Ye, omitted in Cl. **857 helyng,** Cl reads "helpyng." **859 Cerberus,** the three-headed watchdog at the gate of Hades. **865 rather,** Cl reads "the rather." **871 But tho gan,** Cl reads "And tho bigan." **883 I,** omitted in Cl and Cp. **890–96** This stanza is missing in Cl, Cp, and many manuscripts, and may have been marked for removal by Chaucer. **892 ordayne** is used as an adjective in *Bo* 3.pr12.40 and 4.pr1.42. **900–01** Lines reversed in Cl and corrected in the margin.

Requere° not that is ayen° hire name°,
For vertu streccheth not hymself to shame.

"But wel is me that evere I was born
That thou biset art° yn so good a place,
For by my trouthe, yn love I dorste° have sworn
The sholde nevere han tyd° so fayr a grace.
And wostow whi? For thow were wont to chace
At° Love yn scorn, and for despit° hym calle
Seynt Idyot, lord of these foles alle.

"How ofte hastow mad thi nyce japes°
And seyd that Loves servantz everychone°
Of nycete° ben verray° Goddes apes;
And some wole mucche° hire mete° allone,
Lyggyng abedde, and make hem for to grone;
And som, thow seydest, hadde a blaunche fevere°,
And preydest God he sholde nevere kevere°;

"And som of hem toke on hem° for the colde°,
More than ynough, so seydestow° ful ofte;
And som han feyned° ofte tyme and tolde
How that they wake whan thei slepen softe—
And thus thei wolde han brought hemself alofte°,
And natheles° were under at the laste.
Thus seidestow, and japedest° ful faste.

"Yet seidestow that for the more part
These loveres wolden speke in general,
And thoughte that it was a siker art°
For faylyng° for to assayn overal°.
Now may I jape of the° if that I shal°;
But natheles, though that I sholde deye°,
That thow art none of tho° I dorste saye°!

"Now beet thi brest and seye to God of Love,
'Thi grace°, lord, for now I me repente
If I mysspak, for now myself I° love.'
Thus sey with al thyn herte yn good entente."
Quod Troylus, "A, lord, I me consente,
And pray to the my japes° thow foryeve°,
And I shal nevere more whil I leve."

"Thow seyst wel," quod Pandarus, "and now I hope
That thow the goddes wrathe° hast al apesed;
And sithen° that thow hast wepen many a drope,
And seyd swych° thyng wherwith thi god is plesed,
Now wolde nevere god but° thow were esed°.
And thynk wel, she of whom rist° al thi wo
Hereafter may thy comfort be also.

"For thilke° ground that bereth the wedys wykke°
Bereth eke these holsome° herbes as ful ofte;
Next° the foule netle°, rough and thikke,
The rose waxeth swote° and smothe and softe;
And next the valey is the hil alofte;
And next the derke nyght the glade morwe°—
And also joye is next the fyn° of sorwe.

"Now loke that atempre° be thy brydel°,
And for the beste ay suffre to the tyde°,
Or elles alle oure labour is on ydel°.
He hasteth wel that wisely kan abyde°.
Be diligent and trewe, and ay wel hide°,
Be lusty°, fre°, persevere yn thyn servyce,
And al is wel if thou werk in this wyse.

---

902 Requere, *request,* **ayen,** *against,* **name,** *reputation* **905 biset art,** *are devoted* **906 dorste,** *dare to* **907 tyd,** *befallen* **908–09 wont to chace / At,** *accustomed to attack* **909 for despit,** *out of spite* **911 nyce japes,** *foolish jokes* **912 everychone,** *every one* **913 nycete,** *foolishness,* **verray,** *truly* **914 mucche,** *munch,* **mete,** *food* **916 blaunche fevere,** *lovesickness* (white fever or pale with love) **917 kevere,** *recover* **918 hem,** *themselves,* **colde,** *shivers* **919 seydestow,** *you said* **920 feyned,** *pretended* **922 brought himself alofte,** *raised themselves up* **923 natheles,** *nonetheless* **924 japedest,** *teased* **927 siker art,** *sure technique* **928 For faylyng,** *to avoid failure,* **assayn overall,** *try everywhere* (i.e., test out all the ladies) **929 jape of the,** *mock you,* **shal,** *would* **930 deye,** *die* **931 tho,** *those,* **dorste saye,** *dare say* **933 Thi grace,** *grant me your grace* **934 myself I,** *I myself* **937 japes,** *mockings,* **foryeve,** *forgive* **940 goddes wrathe,** *god's anger* **941 sithen,** *since* **942 swych,** *such* **943 wolde nevere god but,** *may God never wish anything except that,* **esed,** *eased* **944 rist,** *arises* **946 thilke,** *the same,* **wedys wykke,** *evil weeds* **947 holsome,** *healthy* **948 Next,** *next to,* **netle,** *stinging plant* (nettle) **949 swote,** *sweet* **951 morwe,** *morning* **952 fyn,** *end* **953 atempre,** *moderate,* **brydel,** *self-control* (bridle) **954 ay suffer to the tyde,** *always submit to the occasion* **955 on ydel,** *in vain* **956 abyde,** *wait* **957 hide,** *conceal* **958 lusty,** *happy,* **fre,** *generous*

904 that evere, Cp reads "that evere that." **907 han,** Cl reads "a." **so,** Cp reads "thus." **931 I dorste saye,** Cl reads "that dorste I seye." **941 wepen,** Cl and Cp read "wopen." **946–52** Such proverbial oppositions recur in courtly literature. **952 the fyn of,** Cl reads "after." **956** Proverbial; see *Mel* 7.1054.

"But he that departed° is yn every place
Is nowher hool, as writen clerkes wyse.
What wonder is though swich on° have no grace?
Ek wostow° how it fareth on° som service—
As plaunte a tre or herbe yn sondry wyse,
And on the morwe° pulle it up as blyve°—
No wonder is though it mow° nevere thrive.

"And sith° that God of Love hath the bystowed
In place digne° unto thi worthynesse,
Stond faste, for to good port hastow rowed.
And of thyself, for any hevynesse°,
Hope alwey wel; for but if drerynesse°
Or over-haste oure bothe labour shend°,
I hope of this to maken a good ende.

"And wostow whi° I am the lasse afered
Of this matere with my nece trete°?
For this have I herd seyd of wyse ylered°.
Was nevere man ne womman yet bygete°
That was unapt° to suffren loves hete,
Celestial°, or elles love of kynde°—
Forthi° som grace I hope in hire to fynde.

"And for to speke of hire in special,
Hire beaute to bythynke° and hire youthe,
It sit° hire nought to be celestial
As yet, though that hire lyste bothe and kouthe°;
But trewly, it sate° hire wel right nowthe°
A worthy knyght to loven and cherice—
And but she do I holde it for a vice°.

"Wherfore I am and wole ben ay° redy
To peyne me° to do yow this servyse.
For bothe yow° to plese thus hope I
Herafterward, for ye beth bothe wyse
And konne it counseyl° kepe in such a wyse
That no man shal of it the wiser be.
And so we may ben gladed° alle thre.

"For by my trowthe, I have right now of the
A good conceyte° yn my wit, as I gesse,
And what it is I wol now that thow se°.
I thenke, sith° that Love of his goodnesse
Hath the° converted out of wikkednesse,
That thow shalt ben the best post°, I leve°,
Of al his lay°, and most his foos° to greve.

"Ensample whi°, se now these wyse clerkes
That erren aldermost ayen° the lawe,
And ben converted from hire wikked werkes
Thorugh grace of God that lyst° hem to hym
drawe,
Than arn° thei folk that han most God in awe,
And strengest feythed ben°, I understonde,
And konne an errour alderbest withstonde°."

Whanne Troylus had herd Pandare assentyd
To ben his help yn lovyng of Cryseyde,
Wex° of his wo, as who seyth°, untormentyd,
But hotter weex his love, and thus he seyde
With sobre chere° although his herte pleyde,
"Now blyssful Venus, help er that I sterve°!
Of the, Pandare, I may som thank deserve.

"But, dere frend, how shal myn wo be lesse
Til this be don? And, good°, eke telle me thisse:
How wyltow seyn° of me and my destresse,
Lest° she be wroth°—this drede I most, iwysse°—
Or nyl nat heren° or trowen° how it ysse°?
Al this drede I, and ek for the manere
Of the, hire em°, she nyl no swych thyng here."

---

960 departed, *divided* **962 swich on,** *such a person* **963 Ek wostow,** *also you know,* **fareth on,** *happens with* **965 morwe,** *morning,* **blyve,** *quickly* **966 mow,** *might* **967 sith,** *since* **968 digne,** *fitting* **970 for any hevynesse,** *despite any grief* **971 but if drerynesse,** *unless hopelessness* **972 shende,** *spoil* **974 wostow whi,** *do you know why* **975 trete,** *to discuss* **976 of wyse ylered,** *by wise learned people* **977 bygete,** *born* **978 unapt,** *unsuited* **979 Celestial,** *heavenly,* **love of kynde,** *natural* (sexual) *love* **980 Forthi,** *therefore* **982 bythynke,** *think about* **983 sit,** *suits* **984 lyste bothe and kouthe,** *both wished to and could* **985 sate,** *would suit,* **nowthe,** *now* **987 vice,** *fault* **988 wole ben ay,** *will be always* **989 peyne me,** *take pains* **990 bothe yow,** *both of you* **992 counseyl,** *secret* **994 ben gladed,** *be made glad* **996 conceyte,** *notion* **997 wol now that thow se,** *I wish now you to understand* **998 sith,** *since* **999 the,** *you* **1000 post,** *support,* **leve,** *believe* **1001 lay,** *law,* **foos,** *foes* **1002 Ensample whi,** *for example* **1003 erren aldermost ayen,** *do wrong most of all against* **1005 lyst,** *wishes* **1006 Than arn,** *then are* **1007 strengest feythed ben,** *are strongest of faith* **1008 alderbest withstonde,** *best of all resist* **1010 Wex,** (he) *grew,* **as who seyth,** *as one might say* **1013 chere,** *expression* **1014 sterve,** *die* **1017 good,** *good friend* **1018 wyltow seyn,** *will you speak* **1019 Lest,** *to avoid that,* **wroth,** *angry,* **iwysse,** *certainly* **1020 nyl nat heren,** *will not listen,* **trowe,** *believe,* **ysse,** *is* **1021–22 for the manere / Of the, hire em,** *considering the fact that you are her uncle*

960–61 This sentiment is also found in *RR* 2245–46 and *Bo* 3.pr11.61ff. **962 though,** Cl reads "that." **no,** omitted in Cp. **966 though,** Cp reads "thought." **969** The nautical imagery here (and often elsewhere in *TC*) is Chaucer's addition, although with this stanza he returns to *Filostrato* for much of the remainder of this book. **976 ylered,** Cp reads "lered." **987** In *Filostrato,* Pandaro says flatly that Criseida has sexual desires, even if she might deny them. **997 it,** Cl reads "that." **1002 se now,** Cl reads "se ye." **1003 the,** Cp reads "a." **1014–15** Troylus asks that Venus grant him a chance to repay Pandarus before dying. **1015 may,** Cp reads "mowe."

Quod Pandarus, "Thou hast a ful grete care
Lest that the cherl may falle out of the mone!
Whi, Lord, I hate of the thi nyce fare°.
Whi, entremete of° that thow hast to done.
For Goddes love, I bydde° the a bone°:
So lat me allone, and it shal be thi beste°."
"Whi, frend," quod he, "now do right as the leste°.

"But herke, Pandare, o word, for I nolde°
That thow in me wendest° so gret folye
That to my lady I desiren sholde
That° toucheth harm or ony vilenye,
For dredles me were levere dye°
Than she of me ought° elles understode
But that that° myghte sownen ynto° gode."

Tho lough° this Pandare and anoon answerde,
"And I thi borwh°? Fy°, no wyght doth but so.
I roughte nought° though that she stod and herde
How that thow seyst. But farewel, I wol go.
Adieu. Be glad. God spede us bothe two.
Yeve° me this labour and this besynesse,
And of my spede° be thyn al that swetnesse."

Tho Troylus gan doun on knees to falle,
And Pandare yn his armes hente faste°,
And seyde, "Now fy° on the Grekes alle.
Yet, parde°, God shal helpe us atte° laste.
And dredeles°, yf that my lyf may laste,
And God toforn°, lo, som of hem shal smerte°,
And yet m'athynketh° that this avant° me
asterte°.

"Now, Pandare, I kan no more seye,
But thow wys°, thow wost°, thow mayst°, thow art al!
My lyf, my deth, hool° yn thyn hond I leye.
Help now!"—Quod he, "Yis, by my trouthe
I shal."
"God yelde the°, frend, and this yn
special°,"
Quod Troylus, "that thou me recomaunde°
To hire that to the deth me may comaunde."

This Pandarus, tho° desirous to serve
His fulle frend, thenne seyde yn this manere,
"Fairwel, and thenk I wole thi thank
deserve,
Have here my trouthe°, and that thou shalt
wel here."—
And went his wey, thenkyng on this matere,
And how he best myghte hire beseche of
grace°,
And fynde a tyme therto, and a place.

For every wyght that hath an hows to
founde°
Ne renneth nought° the werk for to bygynne
With rakel° hond, but he wol byde a stounde°,
And send his hertes lyne° out fro withinne
Alderfirst° his purpos for to wynne°.
Al this Pandare yn his herte thoughte,
And caste° his werk ful wysly or° he wroughte°.

But Troylus lay tho° no lengere down,
But up anoon upon his stede bay°,
And in the feld he pleyde tho lyoun°.
Wo was that Grek that with hym mette that day!
And yn the town his manere tho forth ay°
So goodly was, and gat hym so yn grace°,
That eche hym loved that loked on his face.

1025 nyce fare, *foolish behavior* **1026 entremete of,** *concern yourself with* **1027 bydde,** *ask,* **bone,** *favor* **1028 beste,** *advantage* **1029 leste,** *choose* **1030 nolde,** *wish not* **1031 wendest,** *thought* **1033 That,** (anything) *that* **1034 dredles me were levere dye,** *doubtless I would rather die* **1035 ought,** *anything* **1036 that that,** *that which,* **sownen ynto,** *contribute to* **1037 lough,** *laughed* **1038 thi borwh,** *your guarantee,* **Fy,** *shame!* (see n.) **1039 roughte nought,** *would not care* **1042 Yeve,** *give* **1043 spede,** *success* **1045 hente faste,** *clasped tightly* **1046 fy,** *curses* **1047 parde,** *by God,* **atte,** *at the* **1048 dredeles,** *doubtless* **1049 God toforn,** *before God,* **smerte,** *suffer* **1050 m'athynketh,** *I think,* **avant,** *boast,* **me asterte,** *leapt from me* **1052 wys,** (are) *wise,* **wost,** *know,* **mayst,** *can do* **1053 hool,** *completely* **1055 yelde the,** *reward you,* **this yn special,** *for this especially* **1056 recomaunde,** *commend* **1058 tho,** *then* **1061 trouthe,** *promise* **1063 hire besche of grace,** *request good will of her* **1065 hows to founde,** *house to build* **1066 Ne renneth nought,** *Hurries not* **1067 rakel,** *rash,* **byde a stounde,** *wait a while* **1068 hertes lyne,** *heart's line* (plan) **1069 Alderfirst,** *first of all,* **wynne,** *attain* **1071 caste,** *planned,* **or,** *before,* **wroughte,** *worked* **1072 tho,** *then* **1073 stede bay,** *reddish brown steed* **1074 lyoun,** *the lion* **1076 tho forth ay,** *afterwards always* **1077 grace,** *favor*

1023–24 "You are afraid that the man will fall out of the moon" (i.e., you fear the impossible). In medieval English folk tradition, the man in the moon was a peasant who carried a bundle of thorn branches. **1024 may,** Cl reads "wole." **1038 Fy,** the exclamation "fie" expresses disbelief or a mild curse. **1044 Tho,** Cl reads "But." **1050 m'athynketh,** Cl reads "me of thynketh." **1063 best,** omitted in Cl. **1065–69** This passage translates advice about rhetorical composition found in Geoffrey de Vinsauf's *Poetria Nova,* lines 43–45; it may derive from a collection that includes the passage or from Chaucer's study of Vinsauf in school. It associates Pandarus's planning with literary composition. **1075 that day,** Cp reads "a-day."

For he bycom the frendlyeste wyght°;
The gentileste, and ek the moste fre°,
The thriftieste° and oon the beste° knyght
That yn his tyme was or myghte be.
Dede° were his japes° and his cruelte,
His heighe port°, and his manere estraunge°—
And ech of tho° gan for a vertu chaunge°.

Now lat us stynte° of Troylus a stounde°,
That fareth lyk a man that hurt is sore,
And is somdel° of akynge° of his wounde
Ilissed° wel, but heled no deel moore°,
And as an esy° pacient the lore°
Abit of° hym that goth aboute his cure.
And thus he drieth forth° his aventure.

Explicit liber primus.

1079 wyght, *person* **1080 fre,** *generous* **1081 thriftieste,** *most effective,* **oon the beste,** *one of the best* **1083 Dede,** *dead,* **japes,** *jokes* **1084 heighe port,** *proud style,* **estraunge,** *aloof* **1085 tho,** *those,* **chaunge,** *exchange* **1086 stynte,** *stop,* **stounde,** *while* **1088 somdel,** *somewhat,* **akynge,** *aching* **1089 Ilissed,** *relieved,* **no deel moore,** *not at all* **1090 esy,** *comfortable,* **lore,** *advice* **1091 Abit of,** *waits for* **1092 drieth forth,** *endures* **1092a *Explicit liber primus,*** "Here ends the first book"

Book 2

Incipit prohemium secundi libri.

Owt of these blake wawes° for to sayle,
O wynd, O wynd, the weder gynneth clere°;
For in this see the bot° hath swych travaylle°
Of my connyng° that unneth° I it stere—
This see clepe I° the tempestous matere
Of disesper° that Troilus was inne—
But now of hope the kalendes° bygynne.

O lady myn, that called art Cleo,
Thow be my sped° fro this forth, and my muse,
To ryme wel this book til I have do°;
Me nedeth here noon other art to use.
Forwhi° to every lovere I me excuse
That of no sentement° I this endite°,
But out of Latyn in my tunge it write.

Wherfore I nel° have neyther thank ne blame
Of al this werk, but pray yow mekely,
Disblameth° me if ony word be lame,
For as myn auctour seyde, so sey I.
Ek° though I speke of love unfelyngly,
No wonder is, for it nothyng of newe is°;
A blynd man kan not juggen wel in hewys°.

Ye knowe ek that in forme° of speche is chaunge
Withinne a thousand yer, and wordes tho°
That hadden prys° now wonder nyce° and straunge
Us thenketh hem, and yet they spake hem so,
And sped° as wel in love as men now do.
Eke° for to wynnen love in sondry° ages,
In sondry londes, sondry ben usages.

And forthi° if it happe yn ony wyse
That here be ony lovere yn this place,
That herkneth as the story wol devyse°,
How Troylus com to hys lady grace°,
And thenketh, "So nold I nat° love purchace,"
Or wondreth on his speche or his doynge,
I not°, but it is me° no wonderynge;

For every wyght° which that to Rome went
Halt nat o° path, or alwey o manere.
Ek in some lond were al the game shent°
If that thei ferde° yn love as men don here,
As thus, in open doyng or in chere°,
In vysitynge, in forme°, or seyde hire sawes°;
Forthi° men seyn, ech contre hath his lawes.

Ek scarsly ben ther in this place thre
That han yn love seyd lyk° and don yn al°,
For to thi purpos this may lyken the°,
And the° right nought; yet al is seyd or shal.
Ek som men grave° in tre, some in ston wal,
As it bitit°. But syn° I have bigonne,
Myn auctour shal I folwe if I konne.

Explicit prohemium secundi libri.

---

1 wawes, *waves* **2 gynneth clere,** *begins to clear* **3 bot,** *boat,* **travaylle,** *difficulty* **4 connyng,** *skill,* **unneth,** *scarsely* **5 This see clepe I,** *I call this sea* **6 disesper,** *despair* **7 kalendes,** *first day* **9 sped,** *help* **10 do,** *done* **12 Forthi,** *therefore* **13 sentement,** *personal feeling,* **endite,** *compose* **15 nel,** *will not* **17 Disblameth,** *excuse* **19 Ek,** *also* **20 nothyng of newe is,** *is not original* **21 hewys,** *colors* **22 forme,** *essence* **23 tho,** *then* **24 prys,** *value,* **nyce,** *foolish* **26 sped,** *succeeded* **27 Eke,** *also,* **sondry,** *various* **29 forthi,** *therefore* **31 devyse,** *describe* **32 lady grace,** *lady's favor* **33 So nold I nat,** *I would not so* **35 not,** *do not know,* **me,** *to me* **36 wyght,** *person* **37 Halt nat o,** *holds not to one* **38 shent,** *ruined* **39 ferde,** *acted* **40 open doyng or in chere,** *public behavior or appearance* **41 in forme,** *formally,* **seyde hire sawes,** *said* (in) *their speeches* **42 Forthi,** *therefore* **44 lyk,** *alike,* **don yn al,** *done* (alike) *in everything* **45 lyken the,** *please you* **46 the,** *to you* **47 grave,** *carve* **48 bitit,** *happens,* **syn,** *since*

Incipit prohemium secundi libri, "Here begins the proem of the second book." **1–6** A sea voyage is a commonplace figure for poetic composition, but Dante's *Purgatorio* 1.103 is the likely source here. The invocations and proems to the five books of *TC* all treat the artist's problems in handling his material. **4 connyng,** Cl and Cp read "comyng." **6 disesper,** Cl reads "desper"; Cp, "disepeir." **8 Cleo,** the muse of history. **11 other,** omitted in Cl. **14 Latyn,** Chaucer's fictitious source, Lollius (see 1.394), is supposedly in Latin, while *Filostrato,* his actual source, is in Italian, and he may have consulted a French translation. **21** Proverbial. **22–28** Ultimately from Horace, *Ars Poetica* (*Art of Poetry*) 69–72, although probably by way of Dante's *Convivio* 1.5.55–66 or 2.14.83–89. **28** Proverbial. **36–37** Proverbial: "Many paths lead to Rome." Also found in Chaucer's *Astr,* Prologue, 43–44. **37 o,** Cl reads "al o."

Incipit liber secundus.

In May, that moder° is of monthes glade,
That fresshe floures blew and white and rede
Ben quike° agayn, that wynter dede made,
And ful of bawme° is fletyng° every mede°,
Whan Phebus doth his bryghte bemes sprede
Right in the white Bole, it so bytydde°,
As I shal synge, on Mayes day the thridde,

That Pandarus, for al his wyse speche,
Felt ek his part of loves shotes keene°,
That koude he nevere so wel of lovyng preche,
It made his hewe a-day ful ofte grene.
So shop it° that hym fil that day a tene°
In love, for which yn wo to bedde he wente,
And made er it was day ful many a wente°.

The swalwe° Proigne with a sorowful lay°,
Whan morwe com gan make hire waymentynge°,
Whi she forshapen° was; and ever lay
Pandare abedde, half yn a slomberynge,
Til she so neigh° hym made hire cheterynge°,
How Tireux gan forth hire suster take,
That with the noyse of hire he gan awake,

And gan to calle and dresse hym° up to ryse,
Remembryng hym his erand was to done
From Troylus, and ek his gret emprise°,
And cast° and knew yn good plyt° was the mone
To don viage°, and tok his weye ful sone
Unto his neces palays° ther bysyde°.
Now Janus, god of entre, thow hym gyde!

Whan he was come unto his neces place,
"Wher is my lady?" to hire folk seyde he.
And they hym tolde, and he yn forth gan pace°,
And fond two othere ladyes sette, and she,
Withinne a paved parlour, and thei thre
Herden a mayden reden hem the geste°
Of the sege of Thebes while hem leste°.

Quod Pandarus, "Madame, God yow see°,
With yowre faire book and al the compaignye."
"Ey°, uncle myn, welcome ywys°," quod she.
And up she ros, and by the hond in hye°
She tok hym faste, and seyde, "This nyght thrie°—
To goode mot° it turne—of yow I mette°."
And with that word she doun on bench hym sette.

"Ye, nece, ye shal fare wel the bet°,
If God wole°, al this yer," quod Pandarus.
"But I am sory that I have yow let°
To herken of youre book ye preysen thus.
For Goddes love, what seith it? Telle it us.
Is it of love? Som good ye me lere°!"
"Uncle," quod she, "youre maystresse is nat here."

---

50 moder, *mother* **52 quike,** *alive* **53 bawme,** *fragrance,* **fletyng,** *floating,* **mede,** *meadow* **55 bytydde,** *happened* **58 shotes keene,** *sharp shots* **61 shop it,** *it was destined,* **tene,** *pang* **63 wente,** *turn* **64 swalwe,** *swallow* **64 lay,** *song* **65 waymentynge,** *lamenting* **66 forshapen,** *transformed* **68 neigh,** *near,* **cheterynge,** *twittering* **71 dresse hym,** *prepared himself* **73 emprise,** *enterprise* **74 cast,** *made astrological calculations,* **plyt,** *position* **75 don viage,** *undertake a task* **76 neces palays,** *niece's palace,* **ther bysyde,** *nearby* **80 gan pace,** *did walk* **83 geste,** *story* **84 hem leste,** *it pleased them* **85 God yow see,** *may God watch over you* **87 Ey,** *oh,* **ywys,** *indeed* **88 in hye,** *quickly* **89 faste,** *firmly,* **This nyght thrie,** *three times last night* **90 mot,** *may,* **mette,** *dreamed* **92 the bet,** *better* **93 If God wole,** *God willing* **94 let,** *hindered* **97 lere,** *teach*

Explicit prohemium secundi libri, "Here ends the proem to the second book." ***Incipit liber secundus,*** "Here begins the second book." **54–56 Phebus . . . white Bole . . . Mayes day the thridde,** the sun (Phoebus) is in the astrological sign of Taurus (the Bull, often white) from mid-April to mid-May. Chaucer's affinity for May 3rd has never been explained satisfactorily, despite many attempts; he mentions it also at *KnT* 1.1462–63 and *NPT* 7.3189–90. The scene of Pandarus's awakening is not in *Filostrato.* **59 of lovyng,** omitted in Cl. **61 fil,** Cl reads "felt." **64–69 Proigne . . . hire suster,** Procne was changed into the swallow and her sister Philomela into the nightingale after taking revenge on Procne's husband Tereus (**Tireux**) for raping Philomela. Tereus was changed into the hoopoe; Ovid, *Metamorphoses* 6.412ff. **75 his weye ful sone,** Cl reads "weye sone." **77 Janus,** Roman god of doorways and beginnings, represented with two faces, looking in different directions. **80 yn forth,** Cp reads "forth in." **84 sege of Thebes,** Statius's *Siege of Thebes* (1st century C.E.), known to the Middle Ages through the French *Roman de Thèbes* (12th century), is summarized below and alluded to elsewhere in *TC* (5.602, 1457ff.); the story is ominous for those who will be the victims of the siege of Troy. This account of reading about Thebes is not found in *Filostrato,* where Pandaro moves directly to a private conversation with Criseida. **86 yowre,** Cl and Cp read "al yowre." **97 Som,** Cp reads "o som."

With that thei gonnen laughe, and tho she seyde,
"This romaunce is of Thebes that we rede;
And we han herd how that Kyng Layus deyde°
Thorugh Edyppus his sone, and al that dede;
And here we stenten° at these lettres rede°,
How the bisshop, as the book kan telle,
Amphiorax fil thorugh the ground to helle."

Quod Pandarus, "Al this knowe I myselve,
And al the assege of Thebes and al the care,
For herof ben there maked bokes twelve.
But lat be this and telle me how ye fare.
Do wey° youre barbe° and shewe youre face bare.
Do wey youre book, rys up, and lat us daunce,
And lat us don to May som observaunce."

"I? God forbede!" quod she. "Be ye mad?
Is that a wydewes° lyf, so God you save?
By God, ye maken me ryght sore adrad°.
Ye ben so wylde, it semeth that ye rave.
It sate° me wel bet ay° in a cave
To bydde° and rede on holy seyntes lyves.
Lat maydens gon to daunce, and yonge wyves."

"As evere thrive° I," quod this Pandarus,
"Yet kowde I telle a thyng to doon yow pleye."
"Now, uncle deere," quod she, "tel it us,
For Goddes love. Is than the assege° aweye?
I am of Grekes so fered that I deye."
"Nay, nay," quod he, "as evere mot° I thryve,
It is a thyng wel bet than swyche fyve°."

"Ye, holy God," quod she, "what thyng is that?
What? Bet than swyche fyve? I°, nay, iwys°!
For al this world ne kan I eden° what
It sholde ben. Som jape°, I trowe°, is this.
And but youreselven telle us what it is,
My wit is for to arede° it al to lene°.
As help me God, I not nat° what ye mene."

"And I youre borugh°, ne nevere shal for me
This thing be told to yow, as mote I thryve."
"And why so, uncle myn? Why so?" quod she.
"By God," quod he, "that wol I telle as blyve°.
For proudder womman were ther noon on lyve°,
And° ye it wyst°, yn al the toun of Troye.
I jape° nought, as evere have I joye."

Tho° gan she wondren more than byforn
A thousandfold, and doun hire eyen caste,
For nevere sith° the tyme that she was born
To knowe thyng desired she so faste°.
And with a syk° she seyde hym at the laste,
"Now, uncle myn, I nel° yow nowght displese,
Nor axen° more that may do yow disese°."

So after this, with many wordes glade,
And frendly tales, and with mery chere,
Of this and that they pleyde, and gunnen wade°
In many an unkouth°, glad°, and dep matere,
As frendes don whanne thei ben met yfere°,
Til she gan axen hym how Ector ferde°,
That was the townes wal° and Grekes yerde°.

"Ful wel, I thanke it God," quod Pandarus,
"Save° in his arm he hath a litel wownde—
And ek his fresshe° brother Troylus,
The wyse, worthi Ector the secounde,
In whom that alle vertu lyst° abounde,
As alle trowth and alle gentilesse°,
Wysdom, honour, fredom°, and worthinesse."

---

101 deyde, *died* **103 stenten,** *stop,* **letters rede,** *red letters* (rubrics) *indicating a section break* **110 Do wey,** *put away,* **barbe,** *widow's head-dress* **114 wydewes,** *widow's* **115 ryght sore adrad,** *very afraid* **117 sate,** *suits,* **bet ay,** *better always* **118 bydde,** *pray* **120 thrive,** *prosper* **123 assege,** *siege* **125 mot,** *may* **126 wel bet than swyche five,** *five times better* **128 I,** *oh,* **iwys,** *indeed* **129 reden,** *say* **130 jape,** *joke,* **trowe,** *think* **132 arede,** *explain,* **to lene,** *too weakly* **133 not nat,** *don't know* **134 borugh,** *guarantee* **137 as blyve,** *immediately* **138 on lyve,** *alive* **139 And,** *if,* **wyst,** *knew* **140 jape,** *joke* **141 Tho,** *then* **143 sith,** *since* **144 faste,** *eagerly* **145 syk,** *sigh* **146 nel,** *don't wish* **147 axen,** *ask,* **disese,** *discomfort* **150 gunnen wade,** *moved forward* **151 unkouth,** *unfamiliar,* **glad,** *joyous* **152 yfere,** *together* **153 ferde,** *fared* **154 wal,** *defense,* **yerde,** *scourge* **156 Save,** *except* **157 fresshe,** *vigorous* **159 lyst,** *chooses to* **160 gentilesse,** *nobility* **161 fredom,** *generosity*

100 romaunce, the term meant either a narrative of love and adventure or any narrative written in a Romance language (especially French). The twelve books mentioned by Pandarus at line 108 suggest Statius's epic; Chaucer's summary includes details from both the *Roman de Thèbes* and Statius. **101–02 Layus . . . Edyppus,** King Laius of Thebes was killed by his son Oedipus. **105 Amphiorax,** Amphiaranus, one of the seven who besieged Thebes and who in Statius, *Thebaid* 6, accurately predicts his own living descent into Hades; in *Roman de Thèbes,* Amphiorax is called archbishop and bishop. **112 don to May some observaunce,** celebrate the springtime rituals (often a prelude to love in literature). **113 I,** Cl reads "A." **126 wel bet than,** Cl reads "is worth." **131 us,** omitted in Cl. **133 what,** Cl reads "whan."

"In good feyth, em°," quod she, "that lyketh° me.
They faren wel, God save hem bothe two.
For trewely I holde it gret deynte°,
A kynges sone in armes wel to do,
And ben of goode condicions therto°.
For gret power and moral vertu here
Is seelde yseye° in o persone yfere°."

"In good fayth, that is soth°," quod Pandarus.
"But by my trouthe, the kyng hath sones tweye°—
That is to mene, Ector and Troylus—
That certeynly, though that I sholde deye,
They ben as voyde of vices, dar I seye,
As ony men that lyven under the sonne.
Hire myght is wyde yknowe, and what they konne°.

"Of Ector nedeth it no more for to telle:
In al this world ther nys a bettre knyght
Than he, that is of worthinesse welle°,
And he wel more vertu hath than myght.
This knoweth many a wis and worthi wyght°.
The same pris° of Troylus I seye—
God help me so, I knowe not swyche tweye°."

"Be God," quod she, "of Ector that is soth.
Of Troylus the same thing trowe° I;
For dredeles°, men tellen that he doth
In armes day by day so worthily,
And bereth hym here at hom so gentilly
To every wight, that alle prys hath he
Of hem that me were levest preysed be°."

"Ye sey right soth, ywys," quod Pandarus,
"For yesterday whoso° hadde with hym ben,
He myghte han wondred upon Troylus,
For nevere yet so thikke a swarm of ben°
Ne fleygh°, as Grekes gonne fro hym flen°,
And thorugh the feld in every wightes ere°
There nas no cry but 'Troylus is there!'

"Now here, now ther, he hunted hem so faste,
Ther nas but Grekes blood, and Troylus.
Now hym he hurte, and hym al down he caste;
Ay° wher he wente, it was arayed° thus:
He was hire deth, and lyf and sheld° for us;
That al that day ther dorste° noon withstonde,
Whil that he held his blody swerd in honde.

"Therto° he is the frendlyeste man
Of gret estat that evere I sawh° my lyve,
And wher hym lyst°, best felawshipe kan°
To suche as hym thenketh able for to thryve°."
And with that word tho° Pandarus as blyve°
He tok his leve and seyde, "I wol go henne°."
"Nay, blame have I, myn uncle," quod she thenne.

"What eyleth° yow to be thus wery soone,
And namelych° of womman? Wol° ye so?
Nay, sitteth down. By God, I have to done°
With yow, to speke of wysdom er ye go."
And every wight that was aboute hem tho°,
That herde that gan fer awey to stonde,
Whil they two hadde al that hem liste yn honde°.

Whan that hire tale° al brought was to an ende
Of hire estat and of hire governaunce°.
Quod Pandarus, "Now is it tyme I wende°.
But yet, I say, aryseth and lat us daunce,
And cast youre wydewes habit° to myschaunce°.
What lyst yow° thus youreself to disfigure,
Sith yow is tyd° thus faire an aventure?"

"A, wel bithought°, for love of God," quod she,
"Shal I nat wete° what ye mene of this?"
"No, this thyng axeth layser°," tho quod he,
"And eke me wolde muche greve°, iwys°,

---

162 em, *uncle,* **lyketh,** *pleases* **164 deynte,** *honor* **166 condicions therto,** *qualities also* **168 seelde yseye,** *seldom seen,* **yfere,** *combined* **169 soth,** *true* **170 tweye,** *two* **175 konne,** *can do* **178 welle,** *source* **180 wyght,** *person* **181 pris,** *praise* **182 swyche tweye,** *such a pair* **184 trowe,** *think* **185 dredeles,** *doubtless* **189 hem that me were levest preysed be,** *them by whom I would most like to be praised* **191 whoso,** *whoever* **193 ben,** *bees* **194 fleygh,** *flew,* **gonne fro hym flen,** *fled from him* **195 wightes ere,** *person's ear* **200 Ay,** *always,* **arayed,** *appointed* **201 sheld,** *shield* **202 dorste,** *dared* **204 Therto,** *also* **205 sawh,** *saw* **206 lyst,** *chooses,* **kan,** *can* (show) **207 able for to thryve,** *worthy* **208 tho,** *then,* **as blyve,** *quickly* **209 henne,** *from here* **211 eyleth,** *ails* **212 namelych,** *especially,* **Wol,** *will* **213 to done,** (something) *to do* **215 tho,** *then* **217 hadde al that hem liste yn honde,** *concerned themselves with what they wished* **218 tale,** *account* **219 governaunce,** (household) *management* **220 wende,** *go* **222 habit,** *clothing,* **cast . . . to myschaunce,** *do away with* **223 What lyst yow,** *why do you want* **224 Sith yow is tyd,** *since to you has happened* **225 wel bithought,** *well planned* **226 wete,** *know* **227 axeth layser,** *requires time* **228 eke me wolde muche greve,** *also would bother me much,* **iwys,** *indeed*

190–203 Chaucer adds Pandarus's description of Troylus as warrior. **199 hym . . . hym,** Cl and Cp read "hem . . . hem." **202 al,** Cp reads "as." **206 wher,** Cl reads "wher that." **212 womman,** Cp reads "wommen." **215 tho,** Cl reads "two."

If I it tolde, and ye it toke amys.
Yet were it bet° my tonge for to stille
Than sey a soth° that were ayeyns° youre wylle.

"For, nece, by the goddesse Mynerve,
And Juppiter that maketh the thonder rynge,
And by the blysful Venus that I serve,
Ye be the womman in this world lyvynge—
Withoute paramours° to my wyttynge°—
That I best love and lothest° am to greve,
And that ye wete° wel yourself, I leve°."

"Iwis°, myn uncle," quod she, "grant mercy,
Youre frendshipe have I founden evere yit.
I am to no man holden°, trewely,
So muche as yow, and have so litel quyt°,
And with the grace of God, emforth my wit°,
As in my gilt° I shal yow nevere offende,
And yf I have er this, I wol amende°.

"But, for the love of God, I yow biseche°,
As ye ben he that most I love and triste°,
Lat be° to me youre fremde° manere speche,
And sey to me, youre nece, what yow lyste°."
And with that word hire uncle anoon hire kiste,
And seyde, "Gladly, leve° nece dere;
Tak it for good that° I shal sey yow here."

With that she gan hire eyen down to caste,
And Pandarus to koghe gan a lyte°,
And seyde, "Nece, alwey, lo, to the laste°,
How so it be that som men hem delite
With subtil art hire tales for to endite°,
Yet for al that in hire entencioun
Hire tale is al for som conclusioun°.

"And sithen° the ende is every tales strengthe,
And this matere is so byhovely°,
What° sholde I poynte° or drawen it on lenghthe
To yow that ben my frend so feithfully?"
And with that word he gan right inwardly°
Byholden hire and loken on hire face,
And seyde, "On suche a mirour, goode grace!"

Thanne thought he thus: "Yf I my tale endite°
Ought° hard, or make a proces ony while°,
She shal no savour° han theryn but lite°,
And trowe° I wold hire in my wyl bygile,
For tendre wittes wenen al be wyle°
Thereas° they kan not pleynly understonde.
Forthi° hire wit to serven wol I fonde°."

And loked on hire yn a besy wyse°,
And she was war that he byheld hire so,
And seyde, "Lord, so faste° ye me avyse°!
Sey° ye me nevere er now? What, sey ye no?"
"Yes, yes," quod he, "and bet wole er° I go.
But be my trowthe, I thoughte now yf ye°
Be fortunat, for now men shal it se;

"For to every wight° som goodly aventure
Som tyme is shape°, if he it kan receyven.
And if that he wol take of it no cure°
Whan that it cometh, but wylfully it weyven°,
Lo, neyther cas° nor fortune hym deseyven°,
But right° his verray slouthe° and wrecched-
nesse—
And swich a wyght is for to blame, I gesse.

"Good aventure, O bele° nece, have ye
Ful lightly founden, and° ye konne it take;
And for the love of God, and ek of me,
Cache it anoon° lest aventure slake°.
What sholde I lenger proces of it make?
Yif me youre hond, for yn this world is noon—
If that yow lyst°—a wyght so wel bygon°.

---

230 bet, *better* **231 soth,** *truth,* **ayeyns,** *against* **236 paramours,** *lovers,* **wyttynge,** *knowledge* **237 lothest,** *most unwilling* **238 wete,** *know,* **leve,** *believe* **239 Iwis,** *indeed* **241 holden,** *beholden* **242 quyt,** *repaid* **243 emforth my wit,** *to the extent of my ability* **244 As in my gilt,** *on purpose* **245 amende,** *make amends* **246 biseche,** *request* **247 triste,** *trust* **248 Lat be,** *give up,* **fremde,** *strange* **249 liste,** *wish* **251 leve,** *beloved* **252 that,** *what* **254 to koghe gan a lyte,** *coughed a little* **255 to the laste,** *in the end* **257 endite,** *compose* **259 conclusioun,** *purpose* **260 sithen,** *since* **261 byhovely,** *beneficial* **262 What,** *why,* **poynte,** *go into details* **264 inwardly,** *intently* **267 endite,** *compose* **268 Ought,** *in any way,* **make a proces ony while,** *make a long process of it* **269 savour,** *pleasure,* **lite,** *little* **270 trowe,** *think* **271 wenen al be wyle,** *think all is deception* **272 Thereas,** *which* **273 Forthi,** *therefore,* **fonde,** *test* **274 besy wyse,** *intense way* **276 faste,** *eagerly,* **me avyse,** *consider me* **277 Sey,** *saw* **278 bet wole er,** *will better before* **279 thoughte now yf ye,** *wondered now whether you* **281 wight,** *person* **282 shape,** *designed* **283 cure,** *advantage* **284 weyven,** *ignore* **285 cas,** *luck,* **deseyven,** *deceives* **286 right,** *justly,* **verray slouthe,** *genuine sloth* **288 bele,** *beautiful* **289 and,** *if,* **291 anoon,** *immediately,* **slake,** *fades* **294 lyst,** *wish,* **wyght so wel bygon,** *person so fortunate*

232 Mynerve, Minerva, another name for Athena, goddess of wisdom. **233 Juppiter,** Jupiter, the supreme god. **234 Venus,** goddess of love. **239 myn,** omitted in Cp. **248 fremde,** Cl reads "frendly"; Cp, "frende." **255 alwey, lo,** Cl reads "lo, alwey." **260** Proverbial. **262 poynte,** Cl and Cp read "peynte." **271–72** Proverbial. **276 faste,** omitted in Cl. **283 And,** Cl and Cp read "But." **284 weyven,** Cl reads "weylen"; Cp, "weynen."

"And sith° I speke of° good entencioun,
As I to yow have told wel heretoforn,
And love as wel youre honour and renoun°
As creature yn al this world yborn,
By alle the othes that I have yow sworn,
And ye be wroth therfore, or wene° I lye,
Ne shal I nevere seen yow eft° with eye.

"Beth nought agast°, ne quaketh not. Wherto°?
Ne chaungeth not for fere so youre hewe.
For hardely° the werst of this is do°,
And though my tale as now° be to yow newe,
Yet trist° alwey ye shal me fynde trewe.
And were it thyng that me thoughte unsittynge°,
To yow nolde I no° such tales brynge."

"Now, good em°, for Goddes love, I prey,"
Quod she, "com of°, and telle me what it is.
For both I am agast what ye wol sey,
And ek me longeth it to wyte°, ywys°;
For whether it be wel or be amys,
Say on, lat me not yn this fere dwelle."
"So wol I don; now herkeneth. I shal yow telle:

"Now, nece myn, the kynges dere sone,
The goode, wyse, worthi, fresshe°, and fre°,
Which alwey for to don wel is his wone°,
The noble Troylus, so loveth the,
That, bot° ye helpe, it wol his bane° be.
Lo, here is al. What sholde I more seye?
Doth what yow lyst° to make hym lyve or deye.

"But if yow late° hym deye, I wol sterve°.
Have here my trouthe°, nece, I nel not° lyen,
Al sholde I° with this knyf my throte kerve."
With that the teres braste out of his eyen,
And seyde, "Yf that ye doon° us bothe dyen,
Thus gilteles, than have ye fysshed faire°.
What mende° ye though that we both apeyre°?

"Allas, he which that is my lord so dere,
That trewe man, that noble, gentil knyght,
That nought desireth but youre frendly chere,
I se hym deye ther he goth upright°,
And hasteth hym with al his fulle myght
For to be slayn, yf fortune wole assente.
Allas, that God yow swich° a beaute sente!

"If it be so that ye so cruel be
That of his deth yow lyst° nought to recche°—
That is so trewe and worthi, as ye se—
No more than of a japere° or a wrecche,
If it be swych°, youre beaute may nat strecche°
To make amendes of so cruel a dede.
Avysement° is good byfore the nede.

"Wo worth° the faire gemme vertules°!
Wo worth that herbe also that doth no bote°!
Wo worth that beaute that is routheles°!
Wo worth that wight° that tret ech° under fote!
And ye that ben of beaute crop and rote°,
If therwithal° in you there be no routhe°,
Than is it harm ye lyven, by my trouthe.

"And also thenk wel that this is no gaude°;
For me were levere° thow and I and he
Were hanged than I sholde be his baude°,
As heygh as men myghte on us alle yse°.
I am thyn em°; the shame were to me
As wel as the, yf that I sholde assente
Thorugh myn abet° that he thyn honour shente°.

"Now understonde, for I yow nought requere
To bynde yow to hym thorugh no beheste°,
But oonly that ye make hym bettre chere
Than ye han don er this, and more feste°,
So that his lyf be saved atte leste°—
This al and som° and playnly° oure entente.
God help me so, I nevere other mente!

---

295 sith, *since,* **of,** *from* **297 renoun,** *reputation* **300 wene,** *think* **301 eft,** *again* **302 agast,** *frightened,* **Wherto,** *what for* **304 hardely,** *certainly,* **do,** *done* **305 as now,** *just now* **306 trist,** *trust* **307 unsittynge,** *unsuitable* **308 nolde I no,** *I would not* **309 em,** *uncle* **310 com of,** *come on* **312 wyte,** *know,* **ywys,** *indeed* **317 fresshe,** *vigorous,* **fre,** *generous* **318 wone,** *habit* **320 bot,** *unless,* **bane,** *death* **322 lyst,** *wish* **323 late,** *let,* **sterve,** *die* **324 trouthe,** *promise,* **nel not,** *will not* **325 Al sholde I,** *even if I had to* **327 doon,** *make* **328 fysshed fair,** *fished well* **329 mende,** *profit,* **apeyre,** *perish* **333 ther he goth upright,** *where he walks erect* **336 swich,** *such* **338 lyst,** *choose,* **recche,** *care* **340 japere,** *jokester* **341 swych,** *such,* **strecche,** *extend* **343 Avysement,** *forethought* **344 Wo worth,** *woe be to,* **vertules,** *without power* **345 doth no bote,** *performs no cure* **346 routheles,** *pitiless* (ruthless) **347 wight,** *person,* **tret ech,** *walks everyone* **348 crop and rote,** *everything* (leaf and root) **349 therwithal,** *with that,* **routhe,** *pity* **351 gaude,** *trick* **352 me were levere,** *I would rather that* **353 baude,** *go-between* **354 yse,** *see* **355 thyn em,** *your uncle* **357 abet,** *help,* **shente,** *ruin* **359 beheste,** *promise* **361 feste,** *welcome* **362 atte leste,** *at the least* **363 al and som,** (is) *the entire sum,* **playnly,** *fully*

325 my throte, Cl reads "my owene throte." **335 yf fortune wole assente,** Cp reads "yf his fortune assente." **343** Proverbial. **344 gemme vertules,** gemstones were thought to have medicinal and sometimes magical powers. **350 ye,** Cl reads "that ye."

"Lo, this requeste is not but skyle°, ywys°,
Ne doute of reson, pardee°, is ther noon.
I sette° the worste that ye dredden this°:
Men wolden wondren to se hym come or goon.
Ther-ayens° answere I thus anoon,
That every wight°, but° he be fool of kynde°,
Wol deme° it love of frendshipe yn his
 mynde.

"What, who wol demen though he se a man
To temple go that he th'ymages eteth?
Thenk ek how wel and wysely that he kan
Governe hymself, that he nothyng foryeteth°,
That wher he cometh, he prys° and thank
 hym geteth°.
And ek therto he shal come here so selde°,
What fors° were it though al the town behelde?

"Swych love of frendes regneth° al this town!
And wre yow° yn that mantel° everemo,
And, God so wys be my salvacioun,
As I have seyd, youre beste° is to do so.
But alwey, goode nece, to stynte° his wo,
So lat youre daunger sucred ben° a lyte,
That of his deth ye be nought for to wyte°."

Criseyde, which that herd hym yn this wyse,
Thought, "I shal fele° what he meneth, ywis°."
"Now, em," quod she, "what wole ye devyse°?
What is youre red° I shal don of this?"
"That is wel seyd," quod he, "certayn, best is
That ye hym love ayen° for his lovynge,
As love for love is skylful guerdonynge°.

"Thenk ek° how elde wasteth° every houre
In eche of yow a partie° of beaute;
And therfore, er that age the devoure,
Go love; for olde, ther wil no wight of the°.
Lat this proverbe a lore° unto yow be:
To late ywar°, quod beaute whan it paste,
For elde daunteth daunger° at the laste.

"The kynges fool is wonted° to cryen lowde
Whan that hym thenketh a womman bereth
 hire heighe°,
'So longe mot° ye lyve, and alle prowde°,
Til crowes feet be growen under youre eye,
And sende yow thanne a myrrour yn to prye°
In which that ye may se youre face a-morwe°.'
Nece, I bidde°, wisshe yow° no more sorwe."

With this he stente°, and caste adown the hed,
And she bygan to breste a-wepe° anoon,
And seyde, "Allas for wo, why nere I ded°?
For of this world the feyth is al agoon.
Allas, what sholde straunge° to me doon,
Whan he that for my beste frend y wende°
Ret° me to love, and sholde it me defende°?

"Allas, I wolde han trusted, douteles,
That if that I thurgh my disaventure°
Had loved other° hym or Achilles,
Ector, or ony mannes creature,
Ye nolde han had no° mercy ne mesure°
On me, but alwey had me in repreve°.
This false world, allas, who may it leve°?

"What, is this al the joye and al the feste°?
Is this youre red°? Is thys my blyssful cas°?
Is this the verray mede° of youre byheste°?
Is al this peynted proces seyd°, allas,
Right for this fyn°? O lady myn, Pallas,
Thow in this dredful° cas for me purveye°,
For so astoned° am I that I deye."

---

365 skile, *reason,* **ywys,** *surely* **366 pardee,** *by God* **365 sette,** *posit,* **this,** *thus* **369 Ther-ayens,** *Against this* **370 wight,** *person,* **but,** *unless,* **fool of kynde,** *a natural fool* **371 deme,** *think* **375 foryeteth,** *forgets* **376 prys,** *praise,* **geteth,** *gets* **377 selde,** *seldom* **378 What fors,** *what matter* **379 regneth,** *rules in* **380 wre yow,** *conceal yourself,* **mantel,** *cloak* **382 beste,** *best course* **383 stynte,** *stop* **384 daunger sucred ben,** *aloofness sweetened be* **385 wyte,** *blame* **385 fele,** *explore,* **ywis,** *indeed* **388 devyse,** *suggest* **389 red,** *advice* **391 ayen,** *in return* **392 skylful guerdonynge,** *reasonable rewarding* **393 Thenk ek,** *consider also,* **elde wasteth,** *age destroys* **394 partie,** *portion* **396 ther wil no wight of the,** *no one will want you* **397 lore,** *lesson* **398 ywar,** *aware* **399 elde daunteth daunger,** *age overcomes aloofness* **400 wonted,** *accustomed* **401 bereth hire heighe,** *acts proudly* **402 mot,** *may,* **alle prowde,** *always proud* **404 yn to prye,** *to look into* **405 a-morwe,** *in the morning* **406 bidde,** *ask,* **wisshe yow,** *wish yourself* **407 stente,** *stopped* **408 breste a-wepe,** *burst into weeping* **409 nere I ded,** *were I not dead* **411 straunge,** *strangers* **412 y wende,** *I considered* **413 Ret,** *advises,* **defende,** *forbid* **415 disaventure,** *misfortune* **416 other,** *either* **418 nolde han had no,** *would have had no,* **mesure,** *moderation* **419 repreve,** *blame* **420 leve,** *believe* **421 feste,** *pleasure* **422 red,** *advice,* **cas,** *situation* **423 verray mede,** *real payment,* **byheste,** *promise* **424 peynted proces seyd,** *painted account said* **425 fyn,** *end* **426 dredful,** *frightening,* **purveye,** *provide* **427 astoned,** *astonished*

372 What, omitted in Cl. **393–405 elde wasteth . . . beaute. . . . Go love . . . ,** the perennial poetic argument that, because time is passing, we must hurry and fall in love; the *carpe diem* (seize the day) theme. **421 this,** Cl reads "that." **425 Pallas,** Athena, goddess of wisdom.

Wyth that she gan ful sorwfully to syke°.
"Ay, may it be no bet°?" quod Pandarus.
"By God, I shal no more come here this wyke°,
And God toforn°, that am mystrusted thus.
I se ful wel that ye sette lite° of us,
Or of oure deth. Allas, I, woful wrecche!
Might he yet lyve, of me is nought to recche°.

"O cruel god, O dispitouse° Marte,
O Furyes thre of helle, on yow I crye!
So lat me nevere out of this hous departe
If I mente harm or ony vilenye!
But sith° I se my lord mot nedes dye°,
And I with hym, here I me shryve°, and seye
That wikkedly ye don us bothe deye.

"But sith it lyketh° yow that I be ded,
By Neptunus, that god is of the se,
Fro this forth shal I nevere eten bred
Til I myn owen herte blood may se.
For certayn I wol deye as sone as he."
And up he sterte° and on his weye he raughte°
Til she hym agayn by the lappe° caughte.

Criseyde, which that wel neigh starf° for fere,
So as she was the ferfulleste wyght°
That myghte be, and herde ek with hire ere,
And saw the sorwful ernest° of the knyght,
And in his preyer eke saw noon unrigh°,
And for the harm that myghte ek fallen more,
She gan to rewe° and dradde hire wonder sore,

And thoughte thus, "Unhappes° fallen thikke
Alday° for love, and in such manere cas°
As men ben cruel yn hemself and wykke.
And yf this man sle here hymself, allas,
In my presence, it wyl be no solas°.
What men of hit wolde deme° I kan nat seye:
It nedeth me° ful sleyghly° for to pleye."

And with a sorowful syk° she sayde thrie°,
"A, Lord, what me is tyd a sory chaunce°!
For myn estat° now lyth in jupartie°,
And ek myn emes° lif lyth in balaunce.
But natheles°, with Goddes governaunce,
I shal don so myn honour shal I kepe,
And ek his lyf"—and stynte° for to wepe.

"Of harmes two, the lesse is for to chese.
Yet have I levere° maken hym good chere
In honour than myn emes lyf to lese—
Ye seyn ye nothyng elles me requere?"
"No, ywys°," quod he, "myn owene nece dere."
"Now wel," quod she, "and I wol don my
peyne°.
I shal myn herte ayens my lust° constreyne.

"But that I nyl not holden hym yn honde°,
Ne love a man ne kan I not ne may
Ayens° my wil; but elles° wol I fonde°,
Myn honour sauf°, plesen° hym fro day to day.
Therto nolde I° nought onys° have seyd nay
But that I drede, as yn my fantasye°.
But cesseth cause°, ay cesseth maladye.

"And here I make a protestacioun,
That yn this proces° yf ye depper go,
That certaynly for no salvacioun
Of yow, though that ye sterve° bothe two,
Though al the world on o day be my fo,
Ne shal I nevere on hym han other routhe°."
"I graunte wel," quod Pandare, "by my
trouthe.

"But may I truste wel therto°," quod he,
"That of this thyng that ye han hight° me here,
Ye wole it holden trewly unto me?"
"Ye, doutlees," quod she, "myn uncle dere."
"Ne that I shal han cause in this matere,"

428 syke, *sigh* **429 bet,** *better* (than this) **430 wyke,** *week* **431 God toforn,** *before God* **432 sette lite,** *think little* **434 recche,** *care* **435 dispitouse,** *spiteful* **439 sith,** *since,* **mot nedes dye,** *must necessarily die* **440 me shryve,** *confess myself* **442 sith it lyketh,** *since it pleases* **447 sterte,** *leapt,* **raughte,** *began* **448 lappe,** *hanging garment* **449 starf,** *died* **450 ferfulleste wyght,** *most fearful person* **452 ernest,** *seriousness* **453 noon unright,** *nothing wrong* **455 rewe,** *be sorry* **456 Unhappes,** *misfortunes* **457 Alday,** *all the time,* **manere cas,** *situations* **460 solas,** *comfort* **461 deme,** *think* **462 It nedeth me,** *I need to,* **ful sleyghly,** *very carefully* **463 syk,** *sigh,* **thrie,** *three times* **464 what me is tyd a sory chaunce,** *what a misfortune has befallen me* **465 estat,** *condition,* **jupartie,** *jeopardy* **466 emes,** *uncle's* **467 natheles,** *nonetheless* **469 stynte,** *stopped* **471 have I levere,** *would I rather* **474 ywys,** *surely* **475 don my peyne,** *make an effort* **476 ayens my lust,** *against my desire* **477 holden . . . yn honde,** *mislead* **479 Ayens,** *against,* **elles,** *otherwise,* **fonde,** *try* **480 sauf,** *safe,* **plesen,** *to please* **481 Therto nolde I,** *to that I would,* **onys,** *ever* **482 fantasye,** *imagination* **483 cesseth cause,** *when cause ceases* **485 proces,** *matter* **487 sterve,** *die* **489 routhe,** *pity* **491 therto,** *also* **492 han hight,** *have promised*

429 A, Cl reads "Ay." **435 Marte,** Mars, god of war. **438 If,** Cl and Cp read "If that." **465 estat,** Criseyde seems here to refer to her social status as a widow. **470** Proverbial. **483** Proverbial. **466 lyth,** Cp reads "is." **474 ywys,** Cp reads "wys."

Quod he, "to pleyne°, or ofter yow to preche?"
"Why no, parde°, what nedeth more speche?"

Tho fillen thei yn° other tales glade°,
Til at the laste, "O good em," quod she tho,
"For his love which that us bothe made,
Tel me how first ye wysten° of his wo.
Wot noon° of hit but ye?"—He seyde, "No."—
"Kan he wel speke of love?" quod she.
"I preye,
Tel me for I the bet° me shal purveye°."

Tho Pandarus a litel gan to smyle,
And seyde, "By my trouthe, I shal yow telle.
This other day nought go ful longe while°,
In-with° the paleys° gardyn by a welle,
Gan he and I wel half a day to dwelle,
Right for to speken of an ordinaunce°
How we the Grekes myghten disavaunce°.

"Soon after that bigonne we to lepe,
And casten with oure dartes° to and fro,
Tyl at the laste he seyde he wolde slepe,
And on the gres adoun he leyde hym tho°
And I afer° gan romen° to and fro,
Til that I herd, as that I welk allone,
How he bygan ful wofully to grone.

"Tho gan I stalke softly hym byhynde,
And sikerly°, the sothe for to seyne,
As I kan clepe ayen° now to my mynde,
Right thus to Love he gan hym for to pleyne:
He seyde, 'Lord, have routhe° upon my peyne,
Al° have I ben rebel yn myn entente.
Now, *mea culpa,* lord, I me repente.

"'O god, that at thi disposicioun°
Ledest the fyn°—by juste purveyaunce°—
Of every wyght°, my lowe° confessioun
Accepte in gre°, and sende me swych°
penaunce
As liketh the°, but from desesperaunce°
That may my gost° departe awey fro the,
Thow be my sheld for thy benignite°.

"'For certes°, lord, so sore hath she me
wounded,
That stod in blak, wyth lokyng of hire eyen,
That to myn hertes botme it is ysounded°,
Thorugh which I wot° that I mot nedes
deyen°.
This is the werste, I dar me not bywreyen°,
And wel the hotter ben the gledes rede°
That men hem wrien° with asshen pale and
dede.'

"Wyth that he smot adown° his hed anoon,
And gan to motre°, I not° what, trewly.
And I awey with that stille gan to goon°,
And let° therof as° nothyng wyst° hadde I,
And com ayen anoon, and stod hym by,
And seyde, 'Awake, ye slepen al to longe.
It semeth not that love doth yow longe°,

"'That slepen so that no man may yow wake.
Who sey evere er this° so dul a man?'
'Ye, frend,' quod he, 'do ye yowre° hedes ake
For love, and lat me lyven as I kan.'
But though that he for wo was pale and wan,
Yet made he tho° as fressh a countenaunce°
As though he shulde have led the newe daunce.

---

496 pleyne, *complain* **497 parde,** *by God* **498 Tho fillen thei yn,** *then they happened into,* **tales glade,** *cheerful topics* **501 wysten,** *learned* **502 Wot noon,** *knows anyone* **504 the bet,** *better,* **purveye,** *prepare* **507 nought go ful longe while,** *not a long time ago* **508 In-with,** *within,* **paleys,** *palace* **510 ordinaunce,** *plan* **511 disavaunce,** *repel* **513 darts,** *spears* **515 tho,** *then* **516 afer,** *afar,* **romen,** *roam* **520 sikerly,** *truly* **521 clepe ayen,** *recall* **523 routhe,** *pity* **524 Al,** *although* **526 disposicioun,** *disposal* **527 Ledest the fyn,** *determine the outcome,* **purveyaunce,** *providence* **528 wyght,** *person,* **lowe,** *humble* **529 in gre,** *graciously,* **swych,** *such* **530 liketh the,** *pleases you,* **desesperaunce,** *despair* **531 gost,** *spirit* **532 benignite,** *goodness* **533 certes,** *surely* **535 to myn hertes botme it is ysounded,** *the bottom of my heart is probed* **536 wot,** *know,* **mot nedes deyen,** *must necessarily die* **537 bywreyen,** *betray* **538 ben the gledes rede,** *are the red coals* **539 wrien,** *cover* **540 smot adown,** *hung down* **541 motre,** *mutter,* **not,** *know not* **542 stille gan to gone,** *quietly went* **543 let,** *pretended,* **as,** *as if,* **wyst,** *known* **546 doth yow longe,** *makes you yearn* **548 sey evere er this,** *saw ever before this* **549 do ye yowre,** *make you your* (own) **552 tho,** *then,* **countenaunce,** *expression*

505 a litel gan to, Cl reads "bygan for to." **508–53** This entire recollection seems to be Pandarus's fabrication, although it is just possible that the events occurred earlier, and that Pandarus never tells Troylus how he has overheard him. In *Filostrato* 56–61, Pandaro does overhear Troiolo, although they are not at the time in a garden (a conventional setting for the lover's complaint), there is no mention of the Greek enemies, and Pandaro does not stalk Troiolo. **516 afer,** Cl and Cp read "ther after." **525** ***mea culpa,*** "through my fault"; this is a stock phrase from a familiar confessional prayer known as the *Confiteor,* part of several Catholic liturgies. Troylus is "confessing" his love, part of the tradition that includes Nature speaking to Genius in *RR* and John Gower's *Confessio Amantis* (*Lover's Confession*). **542 awey with that stille gan,** Cp reads "with that gan stille awey."

"This passed forth til now this other day
It fel that I com romynge° al allone
Into his chaumbre, and fond how that he lay
Upon his bed; but man so sore grone
Ne herd I nevere, and what that was his mone
Ne wyst° I nought, for as I was comynge
Al sodeynly he lefte his compleynynge.

"Of which I tok somwhat suspecioun,
And ner I com, and fond he wepte sore;
And God so wys be my salvacioun,
As nevere of thyng hadde I no routhe more°.
For neither with engyn° ne with no lore°
Unnethes° myghte I fro the deth hym kepe,
That yet fele I myn herte for hym wepe.

"And God woot°, nevere sith° that I was born
Was I so bysy no man° for to preche,
Ne nevere to wyght so depe was isworn°,
Er he me tolde who myghte ben his leche°.
But now to yow rehersen al his speche,
Or alle his woful wordes for to sowne°,
Ne bid me not, but° ye wol se me swowne°.

"But for to save his lif, and elles nought°,
And to noon harm of yow, thus am I dreven.
And for the love of God, that us hath wrought°,
Swych cher hym doth° that he and I may lyven!
Now have I plat° to yow myn herte shryven°,
And syn ye wot° that myn entent is clene,
Take hede therof, for I noon yvel mene.

"And right good thryft° I pray to God have ye,
That han swych on° ycaught withoute net.
And be ye° wys as ye ben fair to se,
Wel yn the ryng than° is the ruby set.
There were nevere two so wel imet°,
Whanne ye ben his al hool° as he is youre—
Ther myghty God yet graunte° us se that houre!"

"Nay, therof spak° I not, ha, ha!" quod she.
"As helpe me God, ye shenden every deel°."
"O, mercy, dere nece," anoon quod he,
"What so I spak, I mente nought but wel,
By Mars, the god that helmed is° of stel,
Now beth nought wroth°, my blod, my nece dere."
"Now, wel," quod she, "foryeven be it here."

With this he tok his leve, and home he wente,
And, Lord so he was glad and wel bygon°.
Criseyde aros, no lenger she ne stente°,
But streght into hire closet° wente anoon,
And sette hire down as stille as ony ston,
And every word gan up and down to wynde°
That he hadde seyd, as it com hire to mynde;

And was somdel astonyed° in hire thought
Right for the newe cas°. But whanne that she
Was ful avised°, tho fond she right nought
Of peril why she ought afered be.
For a man may love of possibilite
A womman so his herte may tobreste°,
And she naught love ayen° but yf hire leste°.

But as she sat allone and thoughte thus,
Ascry° aros at skarmyssh° al withoute,
And men cryde in the strete, "Se, Troylus
Hath right now put to flighte the Grekes route°!"
With that gan al hire meyne° for to shoute,
"A, go we se! Cast up° the yates° wyde!
For thurgh this strete he mot° to palays ryde.

555 com romynge, *came roaming* **559 wyst,** *knew* **564 hadde I no routhe more,** *had I more pity* **565 engyn,** *tricks,* **lore,** *advice* **566 Unnethes,** *hardly* **568 woot,** *knows,* **sith,** *since* **569 no man,** *any man* **570 depe was isworn,** *deeply was pledged* **571 leche,** *doctor* **573 sowne,** *speak* **574 but,** *unless,* **swowne,** *faint* **575 elles nought,** *nothing else* **577 wrought,** *made* **578 Swych cher hym doth,** *such favor show him* **579 plat,** *plainly,* **shryven,** *confessed* **589 syn ye wot,** *since you know* **582 thryft,** *success* **583 han swych on,** *have such one* **584 be ye,** *if you are* (as) **585 than,** *then* **586 imet,** *matched* **587 al hool,** *completely* **588 Ther . . . God yet graunte,** *may God grant* **589 spak,** *spoke* **590 shenden every deel,** *spoil everything* **593 helmed is,** *wears a helmet* **594 wroth,** *angry* **597 wel bygon,** *happy* **598 stente,** *remained* **599 closet,** *private room* **601 wynde,** *turn* (over) **603 somdel astonyed,** *somewhat astonished* **604 cas,** *situation* **605 Was ful avised,** *had considered it fully* **608 tobreste,** *shatter* **609 ayen,** *in return,* **leste,** *it pleases* **611 Ascry,** *outcry,* **skarmyssh,** *skirmish* **613 route,** *army* **614 meyne,** *household* **615 Cast up,** *open,* **yates,** *gates* **616 mot,** *must*

556 his, Cl reads "a." **588 yet,** omitted in Cp. **589 ha, ha,** omitted in Cl. **597 so,** omitted in Cl and Cp. **607 a,** omitted in Cl and Cp. **611–93** The scene of Troylus's first ride by, including Criseyde's reaction, is Chaucer's addition.

"For other weye is fro the yate noon
Of Dardanus, there° opyn is the cheyne."
With that come he and al his folk anoon,
An esy pas° rydynge yn routes tweyne°,
Right as his happy° day was, soth to seyne°,
For which men sayn may nought disturbed be
That° shal bytyden° of necessitee.

This Troylus sat on his baye stede°,
Al armed, save° his hed, ful richely,
And wounded was his hors, and gan to blede,
On which he rod a pas° ful softely°.
But swich a knyghtly sighte trewely
As was on hym was nought, withouten faile°,
To loke on Mars that god is of bataile.

So lyk a man of armes and a knyght
He was to sen°, fulfild of heigh prowesse;
For bothe he hadde a body and a myght
To don that thing, as wel as hardynesse°,
And ek to sen hym yn his gere° hym dresse,
So fressh, so yong, so weldy° semed he,
It was an hevene upon hym for to se.

His helm tohewen° was yn twenty places,
That by a tissew° heng his bak byhynde;
His sheld todasshed° was with swerdes and maces,
In which men myghte many an arwe fynde
That thirlled° hadde horn and nerf° and rynde°,
And ay the peple cryde, "Here cometh oure joye,
And next his brother, holder up of Troye!"

For which he wex° a litel reed for shame°,
Whan he the peple upon hym herde cryen,
That to biholde it was a noble game,
How sobrelich he caste doun his eyen.
Cryseyde gan al his chere aspien,
And let it so softe yn hire herte synke,
That to hireself she seyde, "Who yaf° me drynke?"

For of hire owene thought she wex al red,
Remembryng hire right thus, "Lo, this is he
Which that myn uncle swereth he mot be ded°,
But° I on hym have mercy and pite."
And with that thought for pure ashamed° she
Gan in hire hed to pulle, and that as faste,
Whil he and al the peple forby paste°,

And gan to caste° and rollen up and down
Withinne hire thought his excellent prowesse,
And his estat, and also his renoun,
His wit, his shap, and ek his gentillesse°,
But most hir favour was for° his distresse
Was al for hire, and thoughte it was a routhe°
To slen swich oon°, yf that he mente trouthe.

Now myghte som envious jangle° thus,
"This was a sodeyn° love. How myght it be
That she so lightly° loved Troylus,
Right for the firste syghte, ye, parde°?"
Now whoso seith so, mot he nevere the°!
For everythyng a gynnyng hath it nede
Er al be wrought, withouten ony drede°.

For I sey nought that she so sodeynly
Yaf hym hire love, but that she gan enclyne
To lyke hym first, and I have told yow why.
And after that, his manhod and his pyne°
Made love withinne hire herte for to myne°,
For which by proces and by good servise
He gat hire love, and in no sodeyn wyse.

---

618 there, *where* **620 esy pas,** *easy pace,* **routes tweyne,** *two groups* **621 happy,** *fortunate,* **soth to seyne,** *truth to tell* **623 That,** *what,* **bytyden,** *occur* **624 bay stede,** *reddish horse* **625 save,** *except for* **627 a pas,** *walking,* **ful softely,** *very quietly* **629 withouten faile,** *certainly* **632 to sen,** *look upon* **634 hardynesse,** *bravery* **635 gere,** *armor* **636 weldy,** *vigorous* **638 tohewen,** *hacked open* **639 tissew,** *braided cord* **640 todasshed,** *battered* **642 thirlled,** *pierced,* **nerf,** *sinew,* **rind,** *skin* **645 wex,** *grew,* **shame,** *embarrassment* **651 yaf,** *gave* **654 mot be ded,** *must be dead* **655 But,** *unless* **656 for pure ashamed,** *because of pure shame* **658 forby paste,** *passed by* **659 caste,** *consider* **662 gentillesse,** *nobility* **663 for,** *because* **664 routhe,** *pity* **665 slen swich oon,** *slay such a one* **666 envious jangle,** *envious person chatter* **667 sodeyn,** *sudden* **668 lightly,** *easily* **669 parde,** *by God* **670 mot he nevere the,** *may he never prosper* **672 drede,** *doubt* **676 pyne,** *pain* **677 myne,** *burrow*

618 Dardanus, ancestor of Priam. The Dardanides, or gate of Dardanus, was one of the six entrances to Troy mentioned in both Benôit and Guido. Chains blocked the passage of horses, so, apparently, Troylus's troop could use only this gate at this time. Cl reads "Gardanus." **opyn,** Cl reads "upon." **622–23** The phrasing of this reference to necessity echoes *Bo* 5.pr6.167–71, where it introduces the distinction between simple and conditional necessity. **624 This,** Cl reads "Thus." **642 thirlled,** Cl reads "thrilled." **649 Cryseyde,** Cp reads "Criseyda." **658 forby,** Cl reads "forth by." **670 whoso,** Cp reads "who." **the,** Cp reads "y-the." **671–72** Proverbial: For everything needs a beginning before it is completed. **677 herte,** omitted in Cl and Cp.

And also blisful Venus wel arayed°
Sat in hire seventhe hows of hevene tho,
Disposed wel and with aspectes payed°,
To helpen sely° Troilus of his wo.
And soth to seyn she nas not al a fo°
To Troilus in his natyvite;
God wot° that wel the sonner spedde° he.

Now lat us stynte of Troylus a throwe°,
That rideth forth, and lat us tourne faste
Unto Criseyde that heng hire hed ful lowe
Ther as she sat allone, and gan to caste°
Whereon she wolde apoynte hire° atte laste,
If it so were hire em° ne wolde cesse°
For Troilus upon hire for to presse.

And Lord, so she gan in hire thought argue
In this matere of which I have yow told,
And what to done best were, and what eschue°,
That plited° she ful ofte in many folde;
Now was hire herte warm, now was it colde.
And what she thoughte, somwhat shal I write,
As to myn auctour lysteth° for to endite°.

She thoughte wel that Troylus° persone
She knew by sighte, and ek his gentilesse°,
And thus she seyde, "Al were it nat to done°
To graunte hym love, yet for his worthynesse
It were honour with pley and with gladnesse
In honeste° with swych a lord to dele,
For myn estat°, and also for his hele°.

"Ek wel wot° I my kynges sone is he;
And sith° he hath to se me swych delit,
If I wolde outreliche° his sighte flee,
Peraunter° he myghte have me in dispit°,
Thorugh which I myghte stonde in worse plyt°.
Now were I wys me hate to purchace
Withouten nede there° I may stonde in grace°?

"In everythyng I wot°, there lith mesure°.
For though a man forbede° dronkenesse,
He nought forbet° that every creature
Be drynkeles for alwey, as I gesse.
Ek sith I wot° for me is his distresse,
I ne oughte nat for that thyng hym despise,
Sith it is so he meneth in good wyse.

"And eke I knowe of longe tyme agon
His thewes° goode, and that he is nat nyse°,
Ne avaunter°, certeyn, seyth men, is he non;
To wys is he to doon so gret a vyse—
Ne als° I nel hym nevere so cherise°
That he may make avaunt° by juste cause.
He shal me nevere bynde in swich° a clause.

"Now sette a cas°: the hardest is, ywys°,
Men myghten demen° that he loveth me.
What dishonour were it unto me, this?
May ich hym lette of° that? Why, nay, parde!
I knowe also, and alday° heere and se,
Men loven women al byside hire leve°,
And whanne hem leste° no more, lat hem byleve°.

"I thenke ek how he able is for to have
Of al this noble town the thryftiest°
To ben his love, so° she hire honour save.
For out and out he is the worthyest,
Save only Ector which that is the best;

---

680 arayed, *situated* **682 payed,** *made favorable* **683 sely,** *blessed* or *foolish* **684 fo,** *foe* **686 wot,** *knows,* **sonner spedde,** *sooner succeeded* **687 stynte . . . a throwe,** *stop . . . a while* **690 caste,** *consider* **691 apoynte hire,** *decide* **692 em,** *uncle,* **cesse,** *cease* **696 eschue,** *avoid* **697 plited,** *folded* (pleated) **700 lysteth,** *chooses,* **endite,** *compose* **701 Troylus,** *Troylus's* **702 gentilesse,** *nobility* **703 Al were it nat to done,** *although it would not do* **706 In honeste,** *honorably* **707 estat,** *situation,* **hele,** *health* **708 wot,** *know* **709 sith,** *since* **710 outreliche,** *utterly* **711 Peraunter,** *perhaps,* **dispit,** *blame* **712 plit,** *plight* **714 there,** *where,* **grace,** *favor* **715 wot,** *know,* **lith mesure,** *lies moderation* **716 forbede,** *forbids* **717 forbet,** *assert* **719 Ek sith I wot,** *also since I know* **723 thewes,** *virtues,* **nyse,** *foolish* **724 avaunter,** *boaster* **726 also,** *also,* **cherise,** *favor* **727 avaunt,** *boast* **728 swich,** *such* **729 sette a cas,** *consider a possibility,* **ywys,** *surely* **730 demen,** *think* **732 ich hym lette of,** *I prevent him from* **733 alday,** *always* **734 byside hire leve,** *without their permission* **735 hem leste,** (it) *pleases them,* **lat hem byleve,** *abandon them* **737 thryftiest,** *most admirable* **738 so,** *as long as*

680–82 Venus . . . seventhe hows, the planet Venus is in her seventh house, i.e., just above the western horizon, thought to be a fortunate situation for love. Imagined circles passing through the north and south points of the horizon separated the sphere of the heavens into twelve houses or segments. The aspects of Venus are here Jupiter and Mercury; they increase Venus's propitious influence in this disposition. **685 natyvite,** birth; i.e., Venus's influence was was not a foe at the time Troylus was born. **694** Cl reads "And Lord, so she yn thoughte gan to argue." **700 myn auctour,** actually Chaucer adapts his source very freely here, expanding the 80 lines of Creseida's deliberation in *Filostrato* to 230 lines, adding the garden scene and Antigone's song (2.813ff.) and Criseyde's dream of the eagle (2.925ff.). **702 his,** Cl reads "by." **710 outreliche,** Cl reads "uttirly." **715** Proverbial. **716–18** Proverbial, and echoing Reason's argument in *RR* 5744–45. **719 sith I wot for me is his,** Cl reads "for me sith I wol is al his." **732 ich,** Cl reads "I." **736 for,** omitted in Cl.

And yet his lif al lyth now in my cure°
But swych is love, and ek myn aventure°.

"Ne me to love, a wonder is it nought,
For wel wot° I myself, so God me spede°—
Al° wolde I that noon wyste° of this thought—
I am oon the faireste, out of drede°,
And goodliest° whoso taketh hede—
And so men seyn—in al the town of Troye.
What wonder is though he of me have joye?

"I am myn owene womman, wel at ese—
I thank it God—as after myn estat°,
Right yong, and stonde untyd in lusty lese°,
Withouten jalousye or swich debat.
Shal non housbonde seyn to me "Chekmat."
For either they ben ful of jalousye,
Or maisterful°, or loven novelrie°.

"What shal I don? To what fyn° lyve I thus?
Shal I nat love in cas yf that me leste°?
What, pardieux°, I am not religious°!
And though that I myn herte sette at reste
Upon this knyght, that is the worthieste,
And kep alwey myn honour and my name,
By alle right, it may do me no shame."

But ryght as whanne the sonne shyneth bright
In March, that chaungeth ofte tyme his face,
And that a cloud is put with wynd to flyght,
Which oversprat° the sonne as for a space,
A cloudy thought gan thorugh hire soule pace,
That overspradde hire brighte thoughtes alle,
So that for fere almost she gan to falle.

That thought was this: "Allas, syn° I am fre,
Sholde I now love and put in jupartie
My sikernesse°, and thrallen° liberte?
Allas, how dorst° I thenken that folye?
May I naught wel in other folk aspie
Hire dredfull° joye, hire constreynte, and hire peyne?
Ther loveth noon, that she nath why° to pleyne°.

"For love is yet the mooste stormy lyf,
Right to hymself, that evere was bygonne;
For evere som mystrust or nyce stryf°
Ther is in love, som cloud is over that sonne.
Therto° we wrecched wommen nothyng konne°,
Whan us is wo, but wepe and sitte and thynke.
Oure wreche° is this, oure owen wo to drynke.

"Also these wikked tonges ben so prest°
To speke us harm; ek men ben so untrewe
That right anoon as sesed° is hire lest°,
So cesseth love, and forth to love an newe.
But harm idon is don, whoso it rewe°;
For though these men for love hem ferst torende°,
Ful sharp° bygynnyng breketh ofte at ende.

"How ofte tyme hath it yknowe be°
The treson that to wommen hath ben do°.
To what fyn° is swych love I kan nat se,
Or wher bycomth it° whenne it is ago°.
Ther is no wyght° that wot°, I trowe° so,
Where it bycometh. Lo, no wyght on it sporneth°!
That erst° was nothyng, into nought it torneth.

"How bysy, if I love, ek most I be
To plesen hem that jangle° of love and dremen°,
And coye° hem that they seye noon harm of me.
For though there be no cause, yet hem semen°
Al be for harm° that folk hire frendes quemen°.
And who may stoppen every wikked tungen—
Or sown of belles, whil that thei be rungen?"

And after that hire thought bygan for to clere,
And seyde, "He which that nothyng under-taketh,

---

741 cure, *care* **742 aventure,** *fortune* **744 wot,** *know,* **spede,** *help* **745 Al,** *although,* **wyste,** *knew* **746 drede,** *doubt* **747 goodliest,** *most attractive* **751 as after myn estat,** *as befits my status* **752 stonde untyd in lusty lese,** *stand untied in pleasant pasture* **756 maisterful,** *domineering* **novelrie,** *new things* (lovers) **757 fyn,** *end* **758 in cas yf that me leste,** *in the event that it pleases me* **759 pardieux,** *by God,* **religious,** *a nun* **767 oversprat,** *covers* **771 syn,** *since* **773 sikernesse,** *security,* **thrallen,** *enslave* **774 dorst,** *dare* **776 Hire dredfull,** *their fearful* **777 nath why,** *has no reason,* **pleyne,** *lament* **780 nyce stryf,** *foolish conflict* **782 Therto,** *and,* **konne,** *can do* **784 wreche,** *misery* **785 prest,** *ready* **787 anoon as sesed,** *as soon as ceased,* **lest,** *desire* **789 rewe,** *regrets* **790 hem ferst torende,** *first tear themselves apart* **791 Ful sharp,** *very eager* **792 yknowe be,** *been known* **793 do,** *done* **794 fyn,** *end* **795 wher bycomth it,** *what becomes of it,* **ago,** *gone* **796 wyght,** *person,* **wot,** *knows,* **trowe,** *believe* **797 on it sporneth,** *trips over it* **798 That erst,** *what first* **800 jangle,** *gossip,* **dremen,** *imagine* (things) **801 coye,** *soothe* **802 hem semen,** *to them it seems* (that) **803 Al be for harm,** *all is for some harmful purpose,* **quemen,** (do) *please*

749 is, Cl reads "is it." **777 why,** Cl and Cp read "weye." **778 mooste,** Cl reads "meste." **791** Proverbial. **805 whil,** Cl reads "whanne."

Nothyng n'acheveth, be hym loth or dere°."
And with another thought hire herte quaketh.
Than slepeth hope, and after drede awaketh,
Now hot, now cold; but thus, bytwyxen tweye,
She rist hire up° and went hire° for to pleye.

Adoun the steyre° anoon-right tho she wente
Into the gardeyn, with hire neces thre,
And up and doun ther made many a wente°,
Flexippe, she, Tharbe, and Antigone,
To pleyen, that it joye was to se;
And othere of hire wommen a gret rowte°
Hire foloweden in the gardeyn al abowte.

This yerd was large, and rayled° alle the
aleyes°,
And shadwed wel with blosmy bowes grene°,
And benched newe°, and sonded° alle the weyes,
In which she walketh arm yn arm bytwene,
Til at the laste Antigone the shene°
Gan on a Troian song to syngen clere,
That it an heven was hire voys to here.

She seyd, "O Love, to whom I have and shal
Ben humble subgit°, trewe yn myn entente,
As I best kan, to yow, lord, yeve ych al°,
For everemore, myn herte lust to rente°.
For nevere yet thi grace no wight° sente
So blyssful cause as me my lyf to lede
In alle joye and surete out of drede°.

"Ye°, blissful god, han me so wel beset°
In love, ywys°, that al that bereth lyf
Ymagynen ne kowde° how to ben bet°.
For, lord, withouten jalousye or stryf,
I love oon which that is most ententyf°
To serven wel, unwery or unfeyned°,
That evere was, and lest° with harm distreyned°.

"As he that is the welle° of worthinesse,
Of trouthe ground°, myrour of goodlyhed°,
Of wit Appollo, ston of sikernesse°,
Of vertu rote°, of lust fyndere and hed°,
Thurgh which is alle sorwe fro me ded.
Iwys°, I love hym best, so doth he me.
Now good thryft° have he, wherso that he be!

"Whom sholde I thanken but yow, God
of Love,
Of° al this blysse in which to bathe I gynne°?
And thonked be ye, lord, for that I love.
This is the righte lyf that I am inne,
To flemen° alle manere vice and synne;
This doth° me so to vertu for t'entende,
That day by day I in my wil amende°.

"And whoso seyth that for to love is vice
Or thraldom°, though he fele in it destresse,
He outher° is envyous or right nyce°,
Or is unmyghty° for his shrewednesse°
To loven. For swich manere° folk, I gesse,
Defamen Love as nothing of him knowe;
They speken, but they benten nevere° his bowe.

"What, is the sonne wers of kynde right°
Though that a man, for feeblesse of his eyen,
May nought endure on it to se for bryght°?
Or love the wers, though wrecches on it crien°?

---

808 be hym loth or dere, *whether he likes it or not* **812 rist hire up,** *picks herself up,* **went hire,** *takes herself* **813 steyre,** *stairs* **815 wente,** *turn* **818 gret rowte,** *large group* **820 rayled,** *bordered,* **aleyes,** *paths* **821 blosmy bowes grene,** *green blossoming branches* **822 benched newe,** *newly provided with turf-covered mounds to sit on,* **sonded,** *sanded* **824 shene,** *beautiful* **828 subgit,** *subject* **829 yeve ych al,** *I give all* **830 herte lust to rente,** *heart's desire as tribute* **831 wight,** *person* **833 surete out of drede,** *security without fear* **834 Ye,** *you,* **beset,** *established* **835 ywys,** *surely* **836 Ymagynen ne kowde,** *could not imagine,* **bet,** *better* **838 ententyf,** *eager* **839 or unfeyned,** *and not false* **840 lest,** *least,* **distreyned,** *misled* **841 welle,** *source* **842 ground,** (the) *foundation,* **goodlyhed,** *excellence* **843 ston of sikernesse,** *rock of security* **844 rote,** (the) *root,* **of lust fyndere and hed,** *discoverer and source of pleasure* **846 Iwys,** *truly* **847 thryft,** *success* **849 Of,** *for,* **gynne,** *begin* **852 flemen,** *banish* **853 doth,** *makes* **854 amende,** *improve* **856 thraldom,** *servitude* **857 outher,** *either,* **right nyce,** *very foolish* **858 unmyghty,** *unable,* **shrewednesse,** *wickedness* **859 swich manere,** *such kind of* **861 benten nevere,** *never bent* **862 wers of kynde right,** *worse in its proper nature* **864 se for bright,** *look because of brightness* **865 on it crien,** *accuse it*

808–09 Proverbial: "Nothing ventured, nothing gained." **816 Flexippe . . . Tharbe . . . Antigone,** the three women and their names are Chaucer's invention, although he may have derived Antigone from the Thebes story or from Ovid's *Metamorphoses* 6.93–97, where she is Priam's sister who is changed into a stork. **820 yerd,** Cl reads "gardeyn." **821 blosmy bowes grene,** Cl reads "bowes blosmy and grene." **827–75** Antigone's song, punctuating Criseyde's "consent" to love, parallels Troylus's song at 1.400ff. No source has been found for this song, although a number of similarities have been identified in poems by Guillaume de Machaut. **838 that,** omitted in Cl. **840 distreyned,** Cp reads "disteyned" (sullied). **843 sikernesse,** Cl reads "secrenesse." **860 him,** Cl and Cp read "it." **861** Proverbial: "Many speak of Robin Hood who never bent his bow." Several of the scribes indicate their awareness that the proverb is associated with Robin Hood, although here it refers to the God of Love.

No wele° is worth that may no sorwe dryen°.
And forthi°, who that hath an hed of verre°,
Fro caste of stones war° hym in the werre°!

"But I with al myn hert and al my myght,
As I have seyd, wole love unto my laste
My dere hert and al myn owen knyght,
In which myn herte growen is so faste°,
And his in me, that it shal evere laste.
Al dredde I° first to love hym to bygynne,
Now wot° I wel ther is no peril inne."

And of hire song right with that word she stynte°.
And therwithal°, "Now, nece," quod Criseyde,
"Who made this song now with so good entente?"
Antigone answerde anoon and seyde,
"Madame, iwys°, the goodlyeste mayde
Of gret estat in al the town of Troye,
And led hire lif in most honour and joye."

"Forsothe°, so it semeth by hire song,"
Quod tho° Criseyde, and gan therwith to syke°,
And seyde, "Lord, is ther such blysse among
These loveres as they konne faire endite°?"
"Ye, wys°," quod fresshe Antigone the white,
"For alle the folk that han or ben on lyve°
Ne konne wel the blysse of love dyscrive°.

"But wene° ye that every wrecche wot°
The parfite blysse of love? Whi, nay, ywys.
They wenen° al be love yf oon° be hot.
Do wey, do wey, they wot nothyng of this!
Men mosten axe at seyntes° if it is
Aught° faire yn hevene—why? for they kan telle—
And axen fendes is it foul yn helle."

Criseyde unto that purpos nought answerde,
But seyde, "Ywys, it wole be nyght as faste°."
But every word which that she of hire herde
She gan to prenten° in hire herte faste°,
And ay° gan love hire lasse for to agaste°
Than it dide erst°, and synken in hire herte,
That she wax° somwhat able to converte.

The dayes honour and the hevenes eye,
The nyghtes fo—al this clepe° I the sonne—
Gan westren° faste and downward for to wrye°
As he that hadde his dayes cours yronne°,
And white thynges wexen° dymme and donne°
For lak of lyght, and sterres for to appere,
That she and alle hire folk in went yfere°.

So whan it liked hire° to gon to reste,
And voyded° were they that voyden oughte,
She seyde that to slepe wel hire leste°.
Hire wommen soone til hire bed hire broughte.
Whan al was hust°, thanne lay she stille and thoughte
Of al this thyng the manere and the wyse—
Reherce° it nedeth nought for ye ben wyse.

A nyghtyngale upon a cedre grene
Under° the chambre wal there as she lay
Ful loude sang ayen° the mone shene°,
Peraunter°, yn his bryddes wyse°, a lay°
Of love, that made hire herte fressh and gay.
That herkened she so longe yn good entente,
Til at the laste the dede slep hire hente°.

And as she slep, anoon-right tho hire mette°
How that an egle, fethered whit as bon,
Under hire brest his longe clawes sette,
And out hire herte he rente°, and that anoon,
And dide° his herte into hire brest to goon—
Of which she nought agros°, ne nothing smerte°—
And forth he fleygh° with herte left for herte.

---

866 wele, *prosperity,* **dryen,** *endure* **867 forthi,** *therefore,* **verre,** *glass* **868 war,** *beware,* **werre,** *war* **872 faste,** *firmly* **874 Al dredde I,** *although I feared* **875 wot,** *know* **876 stynte,** *stopped* **877 therwithal,** *with that* **880 iwys,** *truly* **883 Forsothe,** *truly* **884 tho,** *then,* **syke,** *sigh* **886 endite,** *express* **887 wys,** *indeed* **888 on lyve,** *alive* **889 dyscrive,** *describe* **890 wene,** *think,* **wot,** *knows* **892 wenen,** *think,* **oon,** *someone* **894 axe at seyntes,** *ask of saints* **895 Aught,** *at all* **898 as faste,** *very soon* **900 prenten,** *imprint,* **faste,** *deeply* **901 ay,** *ever,* **agaste,** *frighten* **902 erst,** *first* **903 wax,** *grew* **905 clepe,** *call* **906 Gan westren,** *moved westward,* **wrye,** *turn* **907 yronne,** *run* **908 wexen,** *became,* **donne,** *dark* **910 yfere,** *together* **911 liked hire,** *pleased her* **912 voyded,** *departed* **913 wel hire leste,** *it pleased her well* **915 hust,** *hushed* **917 Reherce,** *repeat* **919 Under,** *next to* **920 ayen,** *before,* **shene,** *bright* **921 Peraunter,** *by chance,* **bryddes wyse,** *bird's way,* **lay,** *song* **924 hente,** *took* **925 anoon-right tho hire mette,** *immediately then she dreamed* **928 rente,** *tore* **929 dide,** *made* **930 agros,** *feared,* **smerte,** *felt pain* **931 fleygh,** *flew*

867–68 Proverbial: "He who has a glass head (or helmet, as in some manuscripts) should beware of casting stones in war." **878 now,** omitted in Cl. **880 goodlyeste mayde,** most excellent maiden. Not identified. **896 axen,** Cl reads "axen of." **903 wex,** Cl reads "was." **925–31** The dream is Chaucer's addition; an exchange of hearts is a courtly convention.

Now lat hire slepe, and we oure tales holde
Of Troylus, that is to palays ryden
Fro the skarmuch° of the which I tolde,
And yn his chaumbre sit° and hath abyden°
Til two or thre of his messages yeden°
For Pandarus, and soughten hym ful faste
Til they hym founde and broughte hym at the laste.

This Pandarus com lepyng in atones°,
And seide thus, "Who hath ben wel ybete°
Today with swerdes and with slynge-stones,
But Troylus that hath caught hym now an hete°?"
And gan to jape°, and seyde, "Lord, ye so swete°!
But rys, and late us soupe° and go to reste."
And he answerd hym, "Do we as the leste°."

With al the haste goodly that they myghte,
They spedde hem fro the soper unto bedde;
And every wyght out at the dore hym dyghte°,
And wher hym lyst° upon his wey he spedde.
But Troilus, that thoughte his herte bledde
For wo til that he herde som tydynge,
He seyde, "Frend, shal I now wepe or synge?"

Quod Pandarus, "Ly stylle and lat us slepe.
And don thyn hod°; thy nedes spedde be°.
And chese° if thow wolt synge or daunce or lepe.
At shorte wordes, thow shalt trowe° me:
Sire, my nece wol do wel by the,
And love the best, by God and by my trouthe,
But° lak of pursuyt make it° in thi slouthe°.

"For thus ferforth° I have thi werk bygonne,
Fro day to day, til this day by the morwe°
Hire love of frendshipe have I to the wonne,
And also hath she leyd hire feyth to borwe°.
Algate a fot° is hameled° of thi sorwe!"
What sholde I lenger sermon of it holde?
As ye han herd byfore, al he hym tolde.

But right as floures, thorugh the cold of nyght
Yclosed, stoupen° on hire stalkes lowe,
Redressen° hem ayen° the sonne bryght,
And spreden on hire kynde cours by rowe°,
Right so gan tho his eyghen° up to throwe
This Troylus, and seyde, "O Venus dere,
Thi myght, thi grace, yhered° be it here!"

And to Pandare he held up bothe his hondes,
And seyde, "Lord, al thyn be that I have!
For I am hol°; al brosten° ben my bondes.
A thousand Troyes whoso that me yave°,
Ech after other, God so wys me save,
Ne myghte me so gladen. Lo myn herte,
It spredeth so for joye it wol tosterte°.

"But, Lord, how shal I don? How shal I lyven?
Whanne shal I next my dere herte se?
How shal this longe tyme awey be dryven
Til that thow be ayen at° hire fro me?
Thow mayst answere, 'Abyd°, abyd,' but he
That hangeth by the nekke, soth to seyne°,
In grete dishese° abydeth for the peyne."

"Al esily now, for the love of Marte°,"
Quod Pandarus, "for everythyng hath tyme.
So longe abyd til that the nyght departe;
For al so syker° as thow lyst° here by me,
And God toforn°, I wol be there at pryme°.
And forthi°, werk° somwhat as I shal seye,
Or on som other wyght this charge° leye.

"For parde°, God wot I have evere yit
Ben redy the to serve, and to this nyght
Have I nought fayned°, but emforth° my wit

934 skarmuch, *skirmish* **935 sit,** *sits,* **abyden,** *awaited* **936 messages yeden,** *messengers went* **939 atones,** *at once* **940 ybete,** *beaten* **942 hete,** *fever* **943 jape,** *joke,* **swete,** *sweat* **944 soupe,** *dine* **945 the leste,** *you wish* **948 hym dyghte,** *departed* (took himself) **949 wher hym lyst,** *where he wished* **954 hod,** *hood,* **spedde be,** *have succeeded* **955 chese,** *choose* **956 trowe,** *believe* **959 But,** *unless,* **make it,** *turn it otherwise,* **slouthe,** *idleness* **960 ferforth,** *far* **961 morwe,** *morning* **963 to borwe,** *as promise* **964 Algate a fot,** *In any case one foot,* **hameled,** *damaged* **968 stoupen,** *droop* **969 Redressen,** *revive,* **ayen,** *in* **970 on hire kynde cours by rowe,** *in their natural manner in a row* **971 eyghen,** *eyes* **973 yhered,** *praised* **976 hol,** *whole,* **brosten,** *broken* **977 whoso that me yave,** *whoever gave them to me* **980 tosterte,** *burst* **984 ayen at,** *again with* **985 Abyd,** *wait* **986 soth to seyne,** *truth to tell* **987 dishese,** *discomfort* **998 Marte,** *Mars* **991 al so syker,** *as surely,* **lyst,** *lie* **992 God toforn,** *before God,* **pryme,** *ca. 9:00 a.m.* (see 5.472n) **993 forthi,** *therefore,* **werk,** *do* **994 charge,** *responsibility* **995 parde,** *by God* **997 fayned,** *pretended,* **emforth,** *to the extent of*

950 that, omitted in Cl and Cp. **953 us,** Cp reads "me." **954 don thyn hod,** an idiomatic expression of uncertain meaning: perhaps "Call it a day" or "Get ready" or "Don't be impatient." **964 a fot is hameled,** one foot (of your sorrow) is lame, i.e., it cannot pursue you as quickly. Dogs that lived near forest preserves were hameled to stop them from chasing game. **977 Troyes,** Cl and Cp read "Troians." **983 be dryven,** Cl reads "ben ydreven."**989 everythyng hath tyme,** proverbial; from Ecclesiastes 3.1.

Don al thi lust°, and shal with al my myght.
Do now as I shal seye and fare aryght°.
And if thow nylt°, wyte° al thiself thy care;
On me ys nought ylong° thyn yvel fare°.

"I wot wel that thow wyser art than I
A thousand fold, but yf I were as thow,
God help me so, as I wolde outrely°
Of myn owene hond write hire right now
A lettre in which I wolde hire telle how
I ferde amys°, and hire beseche of routhe°.
Now help thiself and leve° it not for slouthe°.

"And I mynself wil therwith to hire gon;
And whanne thow wost° that I am with hire
there,
Worth° thow upon a courser° right anon,
Ye, hardyly°, ryght in thi beste gere°,
And ryd forth by the place as nought ne were°
And thow shalt fynde us, if I may, sittynge
At som wyndowe ynto the strete lokynge.

"And yf the lyst°, than maystow° us saluwe°,
And upon me make thi contenaunce°.
But by thy lyf bewar and faste eschuwe°
To taryen ought°—God shilde° us fro
myschaunce—
Ride forth thi wey and hold thy governaunce°.
And we shal spek of the somwhat, I trowe°,
Whan thow art goon, to don° thyne eeres
glowe.

"Towchyng° thi lettre, thow art wys ynowh°:
I wot thow nylt° it digneliche endite°,
As make it with thise argumentez towh°;
Ne scryvenyssh° or craftyly° thow it wryte;
Biblotte° it with thi teeris eke a lyte°,
And yf thow write a goodly word al softe°,
Though it be good, reherce it not to ofte.

"For though the beste harpour upon lyve°
Wolde on the beste souned° joly harpe
That evere was, with alle his fyngres fyve
Touche ay o streng, or ay o werbul harpe°,
Were his nayles poynted nevere so sharpe,
It shulde maken every wyght to dulle°
To here his gle°, and of his strokes fulle°.

"Ne jompre° ek no discordant thyng yfere°,
As thus°, to usen termes of phisyk°
In loves termes; hold° of thy matere
The forme° alwey, and do that it be lyk°.
For if a peyntour wolde peynte a pyk°
With asses feet and hede it as° an ape,
It cordeth nought°, so were it° but a jape°."

This counseyl liked wel unto Troylus,
But, as a dredful° lovere, he seyde this,
"Allas, my dere brother Pandarus,
I am ashamed for to write, ywys°,
Lest of° myn innocence I seyde amys,
Or that she nolde° it for despit° receyve.
Thanne were I ded; ther myght it nothyng
weyve°."

To that Pandare answered, "Yf the lest°,
Do that° I seye, and lat me therwith gon;
For by that Lord that formede est and west,
I hope of it to brynge answere anon
Ryght of hire hond. And yf that thow nylt non°
Lat be, and sory mot he ben his lyve°
Ayens thi lust° that helpeth the to thryve."

---

998 lust, *desire* **999 fare aryght,** *succeed* **1000 nylt,** *will not,* **wyte,** *blame* **1001 ylong,** *dependent,* **yvel fare,** *misfortune* **1004 outrely,** *utterly* **1007 ferde amys,** *suffered,* **beseche of routhe,** *ask for pity* **1008 leve,** *neglect,* **slouthe,** *inaction* **1010 wost,** *know* **1011 Worth,** *get,* **courser,** *warhorse* **1012 hardyly,** *surely,* **gere,** *equipment* **1013 as nought ne were,** *as if it were nothing* **1016 lyst,** *wish,* **maystow,** *you may,* **saluwe,** *greet* **1017 upon me make thi contenaunce,** *pay attention to me* **1018 faste eschuwe,** *wholly avoid* **1019 taryen ought,** *linger at all,* **shilde,** *shield* **1020 governaunce,** *self-control* **1021 trowe,** *believe,* **don,** *make* **1023 Towchyng,** *concerning,* **wys ynowh,** *wise enough* **1024 nylt,** *will not,* **digneliche endite,** *loftily compose* **1025 towh,** *difficult* **1026 scryvenyssh,** *like a professional scribe,* **craftily,** *artfully* **1027 Biblotte,** *blot,* **eke a lyte,** *also a little* **1028 softe,** *tender* **1030 harpour upon lyve,** *harpist alive* **1031 souned,** *sounding* **1033 ay o werbul herpe,** *always play one tune* **1035 dulle,** *become bored* **1036 here his gle,** *hear his song,* **fulle,** *overfull* **1037 Ne jompre,** *do not jumble,* **yfere,** *together* **1038 As thus,** *for example,* **phisyk,** *medicine* **1039 hold,** *maintain* **1040 forme,** *appropriate style,* **do that it be lyk,** *make sure that it is consistent* **1041 pyk,** *pike* (fish) **1042 hede it as,** *give it a head like* **1043 cordeth nought,** *is not fitting,* **so were it,** *even if it were,* **jape,** *joke* **1045 dredful,** *fearful* **1047 ywys,** *truly* **1048 Lest of,** *for fear that because of* **1049 nolde,** *would not,* **despit,** *scorn* **1050 weyve,** *avoid* **1051 Yf the lest,** *if it pleases you* **1052 that,** *what* **1055 nylt non,** *will not* (write a letter) **1056 mot,** *must,* **his lyve,** *all his life* **1057 Ayens thi lust,** *against your wishes*

999 fare, Cl reads "do." **1011 thow,** omitted in Cl. **1017 thi,** Cp reads "thow thi." **1024–43** A letter is suggested in *Filostrato* 2.91ff., but Chaucer derives the advice on how to write it from classical rhetoric and the medieval tradition of *ars dictaminis,* the art of writing formal letters. **1053 that Lord,** Cl reads "hym." **1055 Ryght,** omitted in Cl and Cp.

Quod Troylus, "Depardieux°, ich assente.
Syn that the lyst°, I wyl aryse and wryte;
And blysful God I pray with good entente
The viage°, and the lettre I shal endite°
So spede° it; and thow, Mynerva the white,
Yef° thow me wit° my lettre to devyse."
And sette hym down and wrot ryght yn this wyse.

Fyrst he gan hire his righte° lady calle,
His hertes lyf, his lust°, his sorwes leche°,
His blysse, and ek this othere termes alle
That yn such cas alle these loveres seche°;
And yn ful humble wyse as in his speche
He gan hym recomaunde° unto hire grace—
To telle al how, it axeth° muche space.

And after this, ful lowely° he hire prayde
To be nought wroth° thogh he of his folye
So hardy° was to hire to write; and seyde
That love it made°, or elles most° he dye;
And pitously gan mercy for to crye;
And after that he seyde—and ley ful loude°—
Hymself was lytel worth, and lesse he koude°;

And that she sholde han his konnyng° excused,
That litel was; and ek he dredde hire so;
And his unworthynesse he ay acused°;
And after that than gan he telle his wo—
But that was endeles, withouten ho°—
And seyde he wolde yn trouthe alwey hym holde;
And radde° it over, and gan the lettre folde.

And with his salty terys gan he bathe
The ruby yn his signet°, and it sette
Upon the wex delyverlyche° and rathe°.
Therwith a thousand tymes er he lette°,
He cussed tho° the lettre that he shette°,
And seyde, "Lettre, a blysful destene°
The shapen is°; my lady shal the se."

This Pandare tok the lettre and that bytyme°
A-morwe°, and to his neces paleys sterte°,
And faste° he swor that it was passed pryme°,
And gan to jape°, and seyde, "Ywys°, myn herte
So fressh° it is, although it sore smerte,
I may not slepe nevere a Mayes morwe;
I have a joly wo, a lusty° sorwe."

Criseyde, whan that she hire uncle herde,
With dredful° herte and desirous to here
The cause of his comynge, thus answerde,
"Now, by youre feyth, myn uncle," quod she, "dere,
What manere wyndes gydeth yow now here?
Tel us youre joly wo and youre penaunce°.
How ferforth be put ye° in loves daunce?"

"By God," quod he, "I hoppe alwey byhynde!"
And she to-laugh, it thoughte hire herte breste°.
Quod Pandarus, "Lok° alwey that ye fynde
Game° in myn hod°. But herkneth, yf yow leste°,
There is right now ycome into towne a geste°,
A Griek espie°, and telleth newe thynges,
For which I come to telle yow new tidynges°.

"Into the gardyn go we and ye shal here
Al prevely° of this a long sermon."
With that they wenten arm in arm yfere°
Into the gardeyn from the chaumbre doun.
And whan that he so fer was that the soun
Of that they spoke no man here myghte,
He seyde hire thus, and out the lettre plighte°,

1058 ich, Cl reads "I." **1058 Depardieux,** *by God* **1059 the lyst,** *you wish* **1061 viage,** (I will make the) *attempt,* **endite,** *compose* **1062 spede,** *succeed* **1063 Yef,** *if,* **wit,** *inspire* **1065 righte,** *own* **1066 lust,** *desire,* **sorwes eche,** *sorrow's physician* **1068 seche,** *seek* **1070 hym recomaunde,** *commend himself* **1071 axeth,** *requires* **1072 lowely,** *humbly* **1073 wroth,** *angry* **1074 hardy,** *bold* **1075 it made,** i.e., *made it so,* **most,** *must* **1077 ley ful loude,** *lied very openly* **1078 lesse he koude,** *could do* (even) *less* **1079 konnyng,** *understanding* **1081 ay acused,** *thoroughly blamed* **1083 ho,** *halt* **1085 radde,** *read* **1087 signet,** *seal* **1088 delyverlyche,** *deftly,* **rathe,** *quickly* **1089 lette,** *stopped* **1090 cussed tho,** *kissed then,* **shette,** *sealed* **1091 destene,** *destiny* **1092 The shapen is,** *for you is prepared* **1093 bytyme,** *early* **1094 A-morwe,** *the next morning,* **sterte,** *hurried* **1095 faste,** *earnestly,* **passed pryme,** *after 9:00 a.m.* **1096 jape,** *joke,* **Ywys,** *surely* **1097 fressh,** *joyous* **1099 lusty,** *pleasant* **1101 dredful,** *fearful* **1105 penaunce,** *suffering* **1106 ferforth be put ye,** *far forward are you* **1108 breste,** *would break* **1109 Lok,** *see to it* **1110 Game,** *entertainment,* **hod,** *hood,* **leste,** *please* **1111 geste,** *guest* **1112 espie,** *spy* **1113 new tidynges,** *news* **1115 prevely,** *privately* **1116 yfere,** *together* **1120 plighte,** *plucked*

1062 Mynerva the white, Minerva the beautiful, Roman goddess of wisdom. **1079 sholde,** Cl reads "wolde." **1085** Chaucer here trims *Filostrato,* where Troiolo's letter is quoted in 88 lines. **1087 signet,** a small seal or insignia, often set in a ring and here carved in a ruby. Pressed into warm wax that sealed a given document, the signet authenticated the writer, much as a signature does today, and ensured privacy. **1103 feyth,** Cp reads "fey." **1109 that,** omitted in Cl and Cp. **1110–11 fynde / Game in myn hood,** proverbial, meaning something like "find me diverting or entertaining." **1112 Griek espie,** Pandarus's ruse is Chaucer's addition.

"Lo, he that is al holly° youres fre°,
Hym recomaundeth lowly° to youre grace,
And sent you this lettre here by me.
Aviseth° yow on it, whan ye han space°,
And of som goodly answere yow purchace°,
Or helpe me God, so pleynly for to seyne°,
He may nat longe lyven for° his peyne."

Ful dredfully tho gan° she stonde stille,
And tok it nought, but al hire humble chere°
Gan for to chaunge, and seyde, "Scrit ne bille°,
For love of God, that toucheth swich° matere,
Ne brynge me noon; and also, uncle dere,
To myn estat° have more rewarde°, I preye,
Than to his lust°. What sholde I more seye?

"And loketh° now yf this be resonable,
And letteth nought° for favour° ne for slouthe°
To seyn a soth°; now were it covenable°
To myn estat, by God and by youre trouthe,
To taken it, or to han of° hym routhe°,
In harmyng of myself, or in repreve°?
Ber it ayen°, for hym that ye on leve°!"

This Pandarus gan on hire for to stare,
And seyde, "Now is this the grettest wonder
That evere I sey°! Lat be° this nyce fare°.
To dethe mot° I be smet° with thonder
If for the cite whiche that stondeth yonder
Wold I a lettre unto yow brynge or take
To harm of yow! What lyst° yow thus to make°?

"But thus ye faren° wel nyh al and some°
That he that most desireth yow to serve,
Of hym ye recche lest° wher he bycome°,
And whether that he lyve or elles sterve°.
But for al that that ever I may deserve,
Refuse it nought," quod he, and hent° hire faste°,
And yn hire bosom the lettre doun he thraste°,

And seyde hire, "Now cast it awey anon,
That folk may sen° and gauren on° us tweye."
Quod she, "I kan abyde° til they be gon";
And gan to smyle, and seyde hym, "Em°, I preye,
Swych answere as yow lyst° youreself purveye°,
For trewely I wol no lettre write."
"No? Than wol I," quod he, "so ye endite°."

Therwith she lough°, and seyde, "Go we dyne°."
And he gan at hymself to jape° faste,
And seyde, "Nece, I have so gret a pyne°
For love that everich° other day I faste°—"
And gan his beste japes forth to caste,
And made hire so to laughe at his folye
That she for laughter wende° for to dye.

And whan that she was comen into halle,
"Now, em," quod she, "we wol go dyne anon°."
And gan som of hire wommen to hire calle,
And streyght into hire chaumbre gan she gon°;
But of hire byesynesses° this was on°,
Amonges othere thynges, out of drede°,
Ful prevyly° this lettre for to rede.

Avysed° word by word in every lyne
And fond° no lak, she thoughte he koude good°;
And up it putte, and went hire yn to dyne.
But Pandarus, that in a study stood°,
Or° he was war°, she took hym by the hood,
And seyde, "Ye were caught er° that ye wyste°."
"I vouchesauf°," quod he. "Do what yow lyste°."

1121 holly, *completely,* **fre,** *freely* **1122 lowly,** *humbly* **1124 Aviseth,** *think,* **space,** *time* **1125 yow purchace,** *provide yourself* **1126 seyne,** *say* **1127 for,** *because of* **1128 dredfully tho gan,** *fearfully then did* **1129 chere,** *manner* **1130 Scrit ne bille,** (neither) *writing nor letter* **1131 swich,** *such* **1133 estat,** *position,* **rewarde,** *regard* **1134 lust,** *wishes* **1135 loketh,** *see* **1136 letteth nought,** *do not hesitate,* **favour,** *preference,* **slouthe,** *slowness* **1137 seyn a soth,** *tell the truth,* **convenable,** *suitable* **1139 han of,** *have on,* **routhe,** *pity* **1140 repreve,** *reproach* (of myself) **1141 Ber it ayen,** *return it,* **on leve,** *believe in* (God) **1144 sey,** *saw,* **Lat be,** *give up,* **nyce fare,** *foolish behavior* **1145 mot,** *may,* **smet,** *smitten* **1148 What lyst,** *why choose,* **make,** *act* **1149 faren,** *act,* **wel nyh al and some,** *nearly one and all* (of you women) **1151 recche lest,** *care least,* **wher he bycome,** *what becomes of him* **1152 sterve,** *die* **1154 hent,** *grasped,* **faste,** *firmly* **1155 thraste,** *thrust* **1157 sen,** *see,* **gauren on,** *stare at* **1158 abyde,** *wait* **1159 Em,** *uncle* **1160 lyst,** *wish,* **purveye,** *provide* **1162 endite,** *compose* **1163 lough,** *laughed,* **Go we dyne,** *let's go to dinner* **1164 jape,** *joke* **1165 pyne,** *pain* **1166 everich,** *every,* **faste,** *do not eat* **1169 wende,** *thought* **1171 anon,** *soon* **1173 gan she gon,** *did she go* **1174 byesynesses,** *activities,* **on,** *one* **1175 out of drede,** *without doubt* **1176 prevyly,** *secretly* **1177 Ayvsed,** (having) *considered* **1178 fond,** (having) *found,* **koude good,** *knew well* (how to write) **1180 that in a study stood,** *who stood lost in thought* **1181 Or,** *before,* **war,** *aware* **1182 er,** *before,* **wyste,** *knew* **1183 vouchesauf,** *grant* (it), **lyste,** *please*

1145 be smet, Cp reads "smyten be." **1155 lettre doun he thraste,** in *Filostrato,* Criseida takes the letter herself and places it in her bosom, Pandaro leaves, and she resolves to accept Troiolo as a lover as soon as she reads the letter. Within 400 lines she arranges to have Troiolo come to her house for an assignation. **1156 anon,** Cl reads "or noon." **1159 hym,** omitted in Cl and Cp.

Tho wesshen° they, and sette hem doun, and ete;
And after noon ful sleyly° Pandarus
Gan drawe hym° to the wyndowe next the strete,
And seyde, "Nece, who hath arayed° thus
The yonder hous, that stont aforyeyn° us?"
"Which hous?" quod she, and gan for to byholde,
And knew it wel, and whos it was hym tolde;

And fillen forth yn speche° of thynges smale,
And seten° yn the wyndowe bothe tweye.
Whan Pandarus sawe tyme unto his tale°,
And sawh wel that hire folk were alle aweye,
"Now, nece myn, tel on," quod he. "I seye,
How liketh yow the lettre that ye wot°?
Kan he theron°? For by my trouthe, I not°."

Therwith al rosy hewed tho wax° she,
And gan to humme, and seyde, "So I trowe°."
"Aquyte° hym wel, for Goddes love," quod he;
"Myself to medes° wol the lettre sowe°."
And held his hondes up, and fel on knowe°.
"Now, goode nece, be it nevere so lyte°,
Yif° me the labour it to sowe and plyte°."

"Ye, for I kan so writen," quod she tho,
"And ek° I not° what I sholde to hym seye."
"Nay, nece," quod Pandare, "sey nat so.
Yet at the leste, thanketh hym, I preye,
Of his good wil, and doth° hym not to deye.
Now, for the love of me, my nece dere,
Refuseth not at this tyme my preyere!"

"Depardieux°," quod she, "God leve° al be wel.
God help me so, this is the firste lettre
That evere I wrot, ye°, al or ony del°."
And into a closet° for to avyse hire° bettre
She wente allone, and gan hire herte unfettre°
Out of disdaynes° prison but a lyte,
And sette hire doun, and gan a lettre write.

Of which to telle in short° is myn entente
Th' effect°, as fer as I kan understonde.
She thonked hym of al that he wel mente
Towardes hire, but holden hym in honde°
She wolde nought ne make hireselven bonde°
In love, but as his suster, hym to plese,
She wolde ay fayn° to don his herte an ese.

She shette it, and in to Pandarus gan gon°
Ther as he sat and loked into the strete,
And doun she sette hire by hym on a ston
Of jaspre, upon a quysshon gold-ybete°,
And seyde, "As wysly° help me God the grete,
I nevere dide thing with more peyne°
Than write this, to which ye me constreyne°,"

And tok it hym. He thonked hire and seyde,
"God wot°, of thing ful ofte loth° bygonne
Comth ende good. And nece myn, Criseyde,
That ye to hym of hard° now be ywonne
Oughte he be glad, by God and yonder sonne,
For-whi° men seyth, impressiones lyghte°
Ful lyghtly ben ay° redy to the flyghte.

"But ye han played tyrant neigh° to longe,
And hard was it youre herte for to grave°.
Now stynt that° ye no lengere on it honge°,
Al° wolde ye the forme of daunger° save;
But hasteth yow to don° hym joye have.
For trusteth wel, to longe ydon hardnesse°
Causeth despit° ful often for° distresse."

1184 wesshen, *washed* **1185 sleyly,** *slyly* **1186 Gan drawe hym,** *went* **1187 arayed,** *decorated* **1188 aforyeyn,** *opposite* **1191 fillen forth yn speche,** (they) *began to speak* **1192 seten,** *sat* **1193 sawe tyme unto his tale,** *recognized it was the right time to speak* **1196 wot,** *know* **1197 Kan he theron,** *does he know about such things,* **not,** *know not* **1198 tho wax,** *then grew* **1199 trowe,** *believe* **1200 Aquyte,** *repay* **1201 to medes,** *in return,* **sowe,** *sew shut* **1202 knowe,** *knees* **1203 lyte,** *little* **1204 Yif,** *give,* **plyte,** *fold* **1206 And ek,** *although,* **not,** *don't know* **1209 doth,** *cause* **1212 Depardieux,** *by God,* **leve,** *grant* **1214 ye,** *surely,* **ony del,** *any part* **1215 closet,** *private room,* **avyse hire,** *consider* **1216 unfettre,** *release* **1217 disdaynes,** *disdain's* **1219 in short,** *briefly* **1220 effect,** *essence* **1222 holden hym in honde,** *mislead him* **1223 bonde,** *bound* **1225 ay fayn,** *always be happy* **1226 gan gon,** *went* **1229 quysshon gold-ybete,** *cushion gold-embroidered* **1230 wysly,** *surely* **1231 peyne,** *effort* **1232 constreyne,** *compel* **1234 wot,** *knows,* **loth,** *reluctantly* **1236 of hard,** *with difficulty* **1238 For-whi,** *because,* **lyghte,** *superficial* **1239 Ful lightly ben ay,** *are always very easily* **1240 neigh,** *almost* **1241 grave,** *engrave* **1242 stynt that,** *stop so that,* **honge,** *hang* (remain undecided) **1243 Al,** *even though,* **forme of daunger,** *appearance of aloofness* **1244 don,** *cause* **1245 to longe ydon hardnesse,** *hardheartedness maintained too long* **1246 despit,** *resentment,* **for,** *because of*

1194 were alle aweye, Cl reads "weren awaye." **1201 lettre sowe,** sew shut. Before envelopes, letters were folded then stitched shut or sealed with wax. **1202 fel,** Cl and Cp read "sat." **1219 telle in short,** as at 2.1085ff. above, Chaucer here trims *Filostrato,* where the letter is quoted in full. **1225 ay,** omitted in Cl and Cp. **1228–29 ston / Of jasper,** a window-seat fashioned out of or adorned with the semiprecious stone jasper, a kind of quartz, often green.

And right° as they declamed° this matere,
Lo, Troylus, right at the stretes ende,
Com rydyng with his tenthe som yfere°,
Al softly°, and thederward gan bende°
There as they sete°, as was his way to wende
To palays-ward°. And Pandarus hym aspyde°
And seyde, "Nece, yse° who comth here ryde°.

"O fle naught in—he seeth° us, I suppose—
Lest° he may thynken that ye hym eschuwe°,"
"Nay, nay," quod she, and waxe° as red as rose.
With that he gan hire humbly to saluwe°
With dredful chere°, and oft his hewes muwe°,
And up his look debonairly° he caste,
And bekked on° Pandare, and forth he paste.

God wot° yf he sat on his hors aright,
Or goodly was beseyn°, that like° day!
God wot wher° he was lyk a manly knyght!
What sholde I drecche° or telle of his aray?
Criseyde, which that alle these thynges say°,
To telle in short, hire lyked al yfere°,
His person, his aray, his look, his chere,

His goodly manere, and his gentilesse°,
So wel that nevere sith° that she was born
Ne hadde she swych a routhe° of his destresse.
And how so° she hath hard ben here byforn,
To God hope I she hath now kaught a thorn,
She shal nat pulle it out this nexte wyke°.
God sende mo swich° thornes on to pyke°!

Pandare, which that stod hire faste° by,
Felt iren hot, and he bygan to smyte°
And seyde, "Nece, I pray yow hertely,
Telle me that° I shal axen° yow a lyte.
A womman that were of his deth to wyte°,
Withouten his gilt, but for° hire lakked routhe°,
Were it wel don?" Quod she, "Nay, by my
 trouthe!"

"God help me so," quod he, "ye sey me soth.
Ye felen wel youreself that I not lye.
Lo, yond he rit°." "Ye," quod she, "so he doth."
"Wel," quod Pandare, "as I have told yow
 thrye°,
Lat be youre nice° shame and youre folye,
And spek with hym in esyng of his herte.
Lat nicete° not do° yow bothe smerte°."

But theron was to heven and to done°.
Considered alle thyng°, it may not be.
And whi? For shame, and it were ek to° soone
To graunten hym so gret a liberte.
For playnly hire entente, as seyde she,
Was for to love hym unwist°, if she myghte,
And guerdone° hym with nothyng but with
 sighte.

But Pandarus thoughte, "It shal not be so.
Yf that I may, this nyce° opinioun
Shal not be holde° fully yeres two."
What sholde I make of this a long sermoun?
He moste assente on° that conclusioun,
As for the tyme; and whanne that it was eve°,
And al was wel, he ros and tok his leve.

And on his wey ful faste homward he spedde,
And right for joye he felte his herte daunce;
And Troylus he fond alone abedde,
That lay as doth these loveres in a traunce,
Bytwixen hope and derk desesperaunce°.
But Pandarus right° at his in-comynge,
He song°, as who seyth°, "Somwhat I brynge,"

1247 right, *just,* **declamed,** *discussed* **1249 tenthe som yfere,** *troop of ten together* **1250 softly,** *slowly,* **thederward gan bende,** *that way did turn* **1251 sete,** *sat* **1252 To palays-ward,** *toward the palace,* **aspyde,** *saw* **1253 yse,** *see,* **ryde,** *riding* **1254 seeth,** *sees* **1255 Lest,** *for fear,* **eschuwe,** *avoid* **1256 waxe,** *grew* **1257 saluwe,** *greet* **1258 dredful chere,** *timid expression,* **hewes muwe,** *colors change* **1259 debonairly,** *meekly* **1260 bekked on,** *nodded at* **1261 wot,** *knows* **1262 beseyn,** *to see,* **ilke,** *same* **1263 wher,** *whether* **1264 drecche,** *delay* **1265 say,** *saw* **1266 yfere,** *together* **1268 gentilesse,** *nobility* **1269 sith,** *since* **1270 routhe,** *pity* **1271 how so,** *even though* **1273 wyke,** *week* **1274 mo swich,** *more such or to others such,* **pyke,** *pull out* **1275 faste,** *near* **1276 smyte,** *strike* **1278 that,** *what,* **axen,** *ask* **1279 wyte,** *blame* **1280 for,** *because,* **routhe,** *pity* **1284 yond he rit,** *yonder he rides* **1285 thrye,** *three times* **1286 nice,** *foolish* **1288 nicete,** *shyness,* **do,** *cause,* **smerte,** *pain* **1289 theron was to heven and to done,** *concerning this* (there was much) *to heave and to do* **1290 Considered alle thyng,** *all things considered* **1291 it were ek to,** *it was also too* **1294 unwist,** *unknown* **1295 guerdone,** *reward* **1297 nyce,** *foolish* **1298 holde,** *held* **1300 moste assente on,** *must agree to* **1301 eve,** *evening* **1307 desesperaunce,** *despair* **1308 right,** *right away* **1309 song,** *sang,* **as who seyth,** *like one who says*

1272 kaught a thorn, caught (on a) a thorn; the figure suggests sexual desire in 2 Corinthians 12.7 and was common in art and literature. **1276** Proverbial: "Strike while the iron is hot." **1284 Ye, quod she,** Cp reads "quod she ye; Cl omits "ye." **1291 shame,** other manuscripts read *speche* (talk, gossip). **1298 yeres,** the time seems lengthy, but scholars point out that two years was considered the appropriate period for widowhood.

And seyde, "Who is in his bed so soone
Yburyed° thus?" "It am I, frend," quod he.
"Who, Troylus? Nay, help me so the mone°,"
Quod Pandarus, "thow shalt arise and se
A charme that was sent right now to the°,
The which kan helen the of thyn accesse°,
Yf thow do forthwith° al thi besynesse°."

"Ye, thorugh the myght of God," quod Troylus.
And Pandarus gan hym the lettre take,
And seyde, "Parde°, God hath holpen° us.
Have here a lyght and loke on al this blake°."
But ofte gan° the herte glade and quake°
Of Troylus whil that he gan it rede
So as the wordes yaf° hym hope or drede°.

But fynally, he tok al for the beste
That she hym wrot, for sumwhat he byheld
On which hym thoughte° he myghte his herte reste,
Al° covered she the wordes under sheld°.
Thus to the more worthi part he held,
That what for hope and Pandarus byheste°,
His grete wo foryede° he at the leste.

But as we may alday° oureselven se°,
Thorugh more wode or col° the more fyr,
Right so encrees of hope, of what it be°,
Therwith ful ofte encresseth ek desir;
Or as an ok cometh of a litel spir°,
So thorugh this lettre which that she hym sente
Encressen gan desir, of which he brente°.

Wherfore° I seye alwey that day and nyght
This Troylus gan to desiren more
Thanne he dide erst°, thorugh hope, and dide his myght°
To pressen on, as by Pandarus lore°,
And writen to hire of his sorwes sore.
Fro day to day he leet it nought refreyde°
That by Pandare he wrot somwhat or seyde;

And dide also his othere observaunces
That to a lovere longeth° yn this cas°.
And after that thise dees torned on chaunces°,
So was he outher° glad or seyde° allas,
And held after his gistes ay his pas°,
And after swyche° answeres as he hadde,
So were his dayes sory outher gladde.

But to Pandarus alwey was his recours°,
And pitously gan ay til° hym to pleyne°,
And hym bisoughte of red° and som socours°;
And Pandarus, that sey° his wode peyne°,
Wex wel neigh° ded for ruthe°, soth to seyne,
And bysily with al his herte caste°
Som of his wo to slen°, and that as faste°;

And seyde, "Lord, and frend, and brother dere,
God wot° that thi dishese doth° me wo.
But wiltow stynten° al this woful chere,
And, by my trouthe, er° it be dayes two,
And God toforn°, yet shal I shape° it so
That thou shalt come into a certeyn place
There as° thow mayst thiself hire preye of grace.

"And certeynly—I not° if thow it wost°,
But tho° that ben expert in love it seye—
It is oon of the thynges furthereth° most,
A man to have a leyser° for to preye°,
And syker° place his wo for to bywreye°.
For in good herte it mot som routhe° impresse
To here and se the giltlees in distresse.

1311 Yburyed, *buried* **1312 mone,** *moon* **1314 the,** *you* **1315 accesse,** *fever* **1316 forthwith,** *immediately,* **besynesse,** *duties* **1319 Parde,** *by God,* **holpen,** *helped* **1320 blake,** *writing* (black ink) **1321 gan,** *did,* **glade and quake,** *become glad and* (alternately) *tremble* **1323 yaf,** *gave,* **drede,** *fear* **1326 hym thoughte,** *it seemed to him* **1327 Al,** *even though,* **sheld,** *shield* **1329 Pandarus byheste,** *Pandarus's promise* **1330 foryede,** *put aside* **1331 alday,** *always,* **se,** *see* (for) **1332 col,** *coal* **1333 of what it be,** *whatever the source* **1335 spir,** *seedling* **1337 brente,** *burned* **1338 Wherfore,** *for this* **1340 erst,** *first,* **dide his myght,** *tried his hardest* **1341 lore,** *teaching* **1343 refreyde,** *grow cold* **1345 observaunces,** *rituals* **1346 longeth,** *belong,* **cas,** *situation* **1347 after that thise dees torned on chaunces,** *according to how the dice rolled* **1348 outher,** *either,* **seyde,** *said* **1349 held after his gistes ay his pas,** *always kept his pace according to his stopovers* **1350 swyche,** *such* **1352 recours,** *return* (for help) **1353 ay til,** *always to,* **pleyne,** *lament* **1354 of red,** *for advice,* **socours,** *aid* **1355 sey,** *saw,* **wode peyne,** *crazed pain* **1356 Wel wel neigh,** *grew nearly,* **ruthe,** *pity* **1357 caste,** *planned* **1358 slen,** *slay,* **as faste,** *as quickly as possible* **1360 wot,** *knows,* **dishese doth,** *distress causes* **1361 wiltow stynten,** *if you will stop* **1362 er,** *before* **1363 God toforn,** *before God,* **shape,** *arrange* **1365 There as,** *where* **1366 not,** *don't know,* **wost,** *know* **1367 tho,** *those* **1368 furthereth,** *that furthers one* **1369 a leyser,** *an opportunity,* **preye,** *plead* **1370 siker,** *secure,* **bywreye,** *reveal* **1371 mot,** *may,* **routhe,** *pity*

1327 the, Cp reads "tho" (then).

"Peraunter thynkestow°: though it be so
That Kynde° wolde don° hire to bygynne
To han a manere routhe° upon my wo,
Seyth Daunger°, 'Nay, thow shalt me nevere wynne.'
So reuleth hire hire hertes gost° withinne
That though she bende°, yet she stant on rote°.
What in effect is this unto my bote°?

"Thenk hereayens°, whan that the stordy ok°,
On which men hakketh° ofte for the nones°,
Receyved hath the happy fallying strok,
The grete sweigh° doth it come al at onys°,
As doth these rokkes or thise mylnestones°;
For swifter cours cometh thyng that is of wighte°,
Whan it descendeth, than don thynges lyghte.

"And ried° that boweth down° for every blast,
Ful lightly, cesse wynd°, it wol aryse;
But so nyl nought° an ok whan it is cast°.
It nedeth me nought the longe to forbyse°.
Men shal rejoyssen of a gret emprise°
Acheved wel, and stant withouten doute,
Al° han men ben the lenger theraboute.

"But, Troylus, yet telle me yf the lest°,
A thing now which that I shal axen the:
Which is thi brother that thou lovest best,
As yn thi verray hertes prevyte°?"
"Iwys°, my brother Deyphebus," quod he.
"Now," quod Pandare, "er owres° twyes twelve,
He shal the ese°, unwyst° of it hymselve.

"Now lat me alone, and werken as I may,"
Quod he. And to Deiphebus wente he tho°
Which° hadde his lord and grete frend ben ay°;
Save° Troylus, no man he loved so.
To telle in short, withouten wordes mo,
Quod Pandarus, "I pray yow that ye be
Frend to a cause which that toucheth° me."

"Yis, parde°," quod Deiphebus, "wel thow wost°,
In al that evere I may, and God tofore°,
Al nere it but for° man I love most,
My brother Troylus. But sey wherfore°
It is, for sith° that day that I was bore,
I nas°, ne nevere mo to ben° I thynke,
Ayens° a thyng that myghte the forthynke°."

Pandare gan hym thonke and to hym seyde,
"Lo, sire, I have a lady yn this town
That is my nece and called is Criseyde,
Which som men wolden don oppressioun°,
And wrongfully have hire possessioun.
Wherfore° I of youre lordship yow byseche°
To ben oure frend, withouten more speche."

Deiphebus hym answerde, "O, is not this
That thow spekest of to me so straungely°
Criseyda, my frend?" He seyde, "Yis."
"Than nedeth," quod Deiphebus, "hardely°,
No more to speke, for trusteth wel that I
Wol be hire chaumpioun with spore and yerde°;
I roughte nought though° alle hire foos° it herde.

"But telle me, thow that wost° alle this matere,
How I myght best avaylen°."—"Now lat se°,"
Quod Pandarus; "yf ye, my lord so dere,
Wolden as now do this honour to me,
To prayen° hire tomorwe, lo, that she

1373 Peraunter thynkestow, *perhaps you think* **1374 Kynde,** *Nature,* **don,** *cause* **1375 manere routhe,** *kind of pity* **1376 Seyth Daunger,** *Aloofness says* **1377 hertes gost,** *heart's spirit* **1378 bende,** *bends,* **stant on rote,** *stands firm* (rooted) **1379 bote,** *remedy* **1380 Thenk hereayens,** *Think in response to this,* **stordy ok,** *sturdy oak* **1381 hakketh,** *chop,* **nones,** *purpose* **1383 sweigh,** *falling,* **onys,** *once* **1384 mylnestones,** *mill stones* **1385 of wighte,** *heavy* **1387 ried,** *reed,* **boweth down,** *bends* **1388 cesse wynd,** *when the wind ceases* **1389 nyl nought,** *will not,* **cast,** *toppled* **1390 forbyse,** *give examples* **1391 emprise,** *enterprise* **1393 Al,** *even though* **1394 the lest,** *it pleases you* **1397 prevyte,** *secrecy* **1398 Iwys,** *surely* **1399 er owres,** *before hours* **1400 the ese,** *aid you,* **unwyst,** *unaware* **1402 tho,** *then* **1403 Which,** *who,* **ay,** *always* **1404 Save,** *except for* **1407 toucheth,** *concerns* **1408 parde,** *by God,* **wost,** *know* **1409 God tofore,** *before God* **1410 Al nere it but for man,** *even if it were not only for the man* **1411 wherfore,** *for what purpose* **1412 sith,** *since* **1413 nas,** *was not,* **to ben,** *will be* **1414 Ayens,** *against,* **the forthynke,** *displease you* **1418 don oppressioun,** *do wrong* **1420 Wherfore,** *for this,* **byseche,** *request* **1423 so straungely,** *with such distance* **1425 hardely,** *surely* **1427 spore and yerde,** *spur and stick* (i.e., eagerly) **1428 roughte nought though,** *care not if,* **foos,** *foes* **1429 wost,** *knows* **1430 avaylen,** *help,* **lat se,** *tell me* **1433 prayen,** *ask*

1374–76 The personifications of Kynde (natural impulse or inclination) and Daunger (restraint or standoffiness) are courtly commonplaces, known to Chaucer from the *Romance of the Rose* and elsewhere. **1377 hire hire,** Cl reads "hire." **1380–84** It is proverbial that through continued chopping a final stroke will fell the oak. **1385–86** Galileo disproved (c. 1600) the Aristotelian notion that heavy objects fall faster than light ones. **1394ff.** The remainder of Book 2 is Chaucer's invention, although it may have been suggested by a later scene in *Filostrato* (7.77ff.), where family members do visit the sick Troiolo. **1398** Deiphebus is the third son of Priam and Hecuba. **1420–21 lordship . . . frend,** in aristocratic society, these terms suggest social and economic protection.

Come unto yow hire pleyntes° to devyse°,
Hire adversaries wolde of it agryse°.

"And yf I more dorste preye yow° as now,
And chargen° yow to have so gret travayle°,
To han som of youre bretheren here with yow,
That myghten to hire cause bet avayle°,
Than wot° I wel she myghte nevere fayle
For to ben holpen°, what at° youre instaunce°,
What with hire other frendes governaunce°."

Deiphebus, which that comen was of kynde°
To al honour and bounte° to consente,
Answerd, "It shal be don; and I kan fynde
Yet grettere help to this yn myn entente.
What wiltow seyn yf I for Eleyne sente
To speke of this? I trowe° it be the beste,
For she may ledyn° Parys as hire leste°.

"Of Ector, which that is my lord my brother,
It nedeth nought to prey hym frend to be,
For I have herd hym o tyme ek and other°
Speke of Criseyde swich° honour that he
May seyn no bet, swich hap to° hym hath she.
It nedeth nought his helpes for to crave;
He shal be swych right° as we wol hym have.

"Spek thow thiself also to Troylus
On my byhalve, and pray hym with us dyne."
"Sire, al this shal be don," quod Pandarus,
And tok his leve; and nevere wold he fyne°,
But to his neces° hous, as streyht as lyne,
He com, and fond hire fro the mete aryse°,
And sette hym down, and spak right in this
wyse°.

He seyde, "O verray° God, so have I ronne°!
Lo, nece myn, se ye nought how I swete°?
I not° whether ye me the more thank konne°.
Be° ye nought war° how false Polyphete
Is now abowte eftsoones° for to plete°,
And brynge on yow advocacies° newe?"
"I? No," quod she, and chaunged al hire
hewe°.

"What is he more aboute me to drecche°
And don me wrong? What shal I do, allas?
Yet of hymself nothyng nolde I recche°
Nere it° for Antenor and Eneas
That ben his frendys yn swych manere cas°.
But for the love of God, myn uncle dere,
No fors° of that; lat hym han al yfere°;

"Withouten that° I have ynowh° for us."
"Nay," quod Pandare, "it shall nothynge be so,
For I have ben right now at Deiphebus,
At Ector, and myn other lordes mo,
And shortly maked eche of hem his fo,
That, by my thryft°, he shal it nevere wynne,
For ought he kan°, whan that so he bygynne."

And as they casten° what was best to done,
Deiphebus, of his owene curtasie°,
Com hire to preye° yn his propre persone,
To holde hym on the morwe compaignye°
At dyner; which she nolde not denye°,
But goodly° gan to his preyere obeye°.
He thonked hire, and wente upon his weye.

Whan this was don, this Pandare up anoon°,
To tellen in short, and forth gan for to wende°

1434 pleyntes, *grievances,* **devyse,** *describe* **1435 agryse,** *be frightened* **1436 more dorste preye yow,** *dare ask you more* **1437 chargen,** *burden,* **travayle,** *trouble* **1439 bet avayle,** *better help* **1440 wot,** *know* **1441 ben holpen,** *be helped,* **what at,** *what with,* **instaunce,** *urging* **1442 governance,** *guidance* **1443 of kynde,** *by nature* **1444 bounte,** *goodness* **1448 trowe,** *believe* **1449 ledyn,** *lead,* **hire leste,** *she pleases* **1452 o tyme ek and other,** *i.e., on more than one occasion* **1453 swich,** *such* **1454 hap to,** *favor with* **1456 right,** *exactly* **1460 fyne,** *stop* **1461 neces,** *niece's* **1462 fro the mete aryse,** *rising from a meal* **1463 wyse,** *way* **1464 verray,** *true,* **ronne,** *run* **1465 swete,** *sweat* **1466 not,** *don't know,* **ye me the more thank konne,** *you can be more grateful to me* **1467 Be,** *are,* **war,** *aware* **1468 eftsoones,** *immediately,* **plete,** *plead at court* **1469 advocacies,** *claims* **1470 hewe,** *color* **1471 drecche,** *harass* **1473 nolde I recche,** *I would not care* **1474 Nere it,** *were it not* **1475 swych manere cas,** *such kinds of situations* **1477 No fors,** *no matter,* **han al yfere,** *have all of it* **1478 Withouten that,** *with the exception that,* **ynowh,** *enough* **1483 thryft,** *success* **1484 ought he kan,** *anything he can do* **1485 casten,** *planned* **1486 curtasie,** *courtliness* **1487 preye,** *request* **1488 holde hym . . . compaignye,** *accompany him* **1489 denye,** *refuse* **1490 goodly,** *graciously,* **gan to his preyere obeye,** *complied with his request* **1492 up anoon,** *got up at once* **1493 wende,** *go*

1447–49 Eleyne . . . Parys, son of Priam, Paris brought the beautiful Helen to Troy, despite the fact that she was married to the Greek Menelaus. The abduction caused the Trojan War. **1460 wold he,** Cp reads "gan to." **1467 Polyphete** does not appear in *Filostrato.* Chaucer may have picked up the name from Virgil's *Aeneid* (6.484) where Polyphoetes is mentioned before Deiphebus tells how Helen betrayed him in the fall of Troy. There is no way to know whether or not Pandarus invents the threat of legal proceedings, although "newe" and "more" in lines 1469 and 1471 suggest something ongoing. **1474 Antenor and Eneas,** Trojans who in some accounts betray the city. An exchange for Antenor will later cause Troylus to lose Criseyde; 4.133ff.

To Troylus, as stille as ony ston.
And al this thing he tolde hym, word and ende°,
And how that he Deiphebus gan to blende°,
And seyde hym, "Now is tyme, if that thow konne,
To bere the° wel tomorwe, and al is wonne.

"Now spek, now prey, now pitously compleyne;
Lat not° for nice° shame, or drede, or slouthe,
Somtyme a man mot° telle his owen peyne.
Bileve it, and she shal han on the routhe°.
Thow shalt be saved, by thi feyth, in trouthe.
But wel wot I° thow art now yn drede,
And what it is I ley° I kan arede°.

"Thow thinkest now, 'How sholde I don al this?
For by my cheres° mosten folk aspye°
That for hire love is that I fare amys°;
Yet hadde I levere unwyst° for sorwe dye.'
Now thenk not so for thou dost gret folye,
For right now have I founden o manere°
Of sleyghte° for to coveren al thi chere.

"Thow shalt gon over° nyght, and that blyve°,
Unto Deiphebus hous, as the to pleye°,
Thi maladye awey the bet to dryve—
For-why° thou semest syk, soth for to seye.
Soone after that, doun in thi bed the leye°,
And sey thow mayst no lengere up endure,
And lye right there and byde thyn aventure°.

"Sey that thi fevre is wont° the for to take
The same tyme and lasten til amorwe°;
And lat se now how wel thow kanst it make,
For, parde°, syk is he that is in sorwe.
Go now, farewel, and Venus here to borwe°,
I hope and thow° this purpos holde ferme,
Thi grace she shal fully ther conferme."

Quod Troylus, "Ywys°, thow nedeles°
Conseylest me that syklych I me feyne°,
For I am syk yn ernest, douteles,
So that wel neygh° I sterve° for the peyne."
Quod Pandarus, "Thow shalt the bettre pleyne°,
And hast the lasse nede to countrefete,
For hym men demen hot that° men seen swete.

"Lo, hold the° at thi tryste° clos, and I
Shal wel the der° unto thi bowe dryve."
Therwith he tok his leve al softely°,
And Troylus to palays wente blyve°.
So glad ne was he nevere in al his lyve,
And to Pandarus reed° gan all assente,
And to Deiphebus hous at nyght he wente.

What nedeth yow to tellen al the chere
That Deiphebus unto his brother made,
Or his accesse°, or his sykliche manere—
How men gan hym with clothes° for to lade°
Whanne he was leyd°, and how men wolde hym glade°?
But al for nought; he held forth ay the wyse°
That ye han herd Pandare er this devyse.

But certayn is, er Troylus hym leyde°,
Deiphebus had hym prayed over-nyght°
To ben a frend and helpyng to Criseyde.
God wot° that he it graunted anoon right,
To ben hire fulle frend with al his myght—
But swych a nede was to prey° hym thenne,
As for to bydde a wood° man for to renne°.

The morwen com and neyhen gan° the tyme
Of meltid° that the faire queene Eleyne

1495 word and ende, *start to finish* **1496 gan to blende,** *tricked* **1498 bere the,** *conduct yourself* **1500 Lat not,** *don't stop,* **nice,** *foolish* **1501 mot,** *must* **1502 on the routhe,** *pity on you* **1504 wot I,** *I know* **1505 ley,** *bet,* **arede,** *guess* **1507 cheres,** *looks,* **mosten folk aspye,** *people must recognize* **1508 fare amys,** *do poorly* **1509 hadde I levere unwyst,** *I would rather undetected* **1511 o manere,** *one kind* **1512 sleyghte,** *trickery* **1513 over,** *before,* **blyve,** *quickly* **1514 as the to pleye,** *as if to divert yourself* **1516 For-why,** *because* **1517 the leye,** *lie yourself* **1519 byde thyn aventure,** *await your luck* **1520 wont,** *accustomed* **1521 amorwe,** *tomorrow* **1523 parde,** *by God* **1524 and Venus here to borwe,** *with Venus as a guarantee* **1525 and thow,** *if you* **1527 Ywys,** *surely,* **nedeles,** *needlessly* **1528 feyne,** *pretend* **1530 wel neygh,** *nearly,* **sterve,** *die* **1531 pleyne,** *complain* **1533 hym men demen hot that,** *people judge him hot who* **1534 hold the,** *keep yourself,* **tryste,** *hunting station* **1535 der,** *deer* **1536 softely,** *quietly* **1537 blyve,** *quickly* **1539 Pandarus reed,** *Pandarus's advice* **1543 accesse,** *fever* **1544 clothes,** *blankets,* **lade,** *cover* **1545 leyd,** *laid in bed,* **glade,** *gladden* **1546 ay the wyse,** *always the way* **1548 hym leyde,** *laid himself down* **1549 over-nyght,** *before night* **1551 wot,** *knows* **1553 swych a need was to prey,** *there was as much need to ask* **1554 wood,** *mad,* **renne,** *run* **1555 neyhen gan,** *grew near* **1556 meltid,** *mealtime*

1502–03 The religious language of belief, faith, and salvation is here strikingly applied to secular love. See Luke 8.48, 18.42. **1526 fully ther,** Cl reads "there fully."

Shoop hire° to ben, an owre after the pryme°,
With Deiphebus, to whom she nolde feyne°;
But as his suster, homly°, soth to seyne,
She com to dyner yn hire playne entente°—
But God and Pandare wyst° what al this mente.

Come ek Criseyde, al innocent of this,
Antigone, hire sister Tarbe also.
But fle we now prolixite best is°,
For love of God, and lat us faste go
Right to th'effect withoute tales mo,
Whi al this folk assembled in this place,
And lat us of hire saluynges pace°.

Gret honour dide hem Deiphebus, certeyn,
And fedde hem wel with al that myghte like°.
But evere more "Allas" was his refreyn,
"My goode brother Troylus the syke°
Lyth yet," and therwithal he gan to syke°,
And after that he peyned hym° to glade
Hem as he myghte, and chere good he made.

Compleyned ek Eleyne of his syknesse
So feythfully° that pite was to here;
And every wight gan waxen for accesse°
A leche° anon, and seyde, "In this manere
Men curen folk."—"This charme I wol yow lere°."
But ther sat oon°, al lyst hire nought° to teche,
That thoughte, "Best koude I° yet ben his leche."

After compleynt°, hym gonnen thei to preyse°,
As folk don yet whan som wyght hath bygonne
To preyse a man, and up with prys hym reyse°
A thousandfold yet hyer than the sonne:
"He is, he kan°, that° fewe lordes konne."
And Pandarus, of that they wolde afferme,
He naught forgat hire preysynge to conferme.

Herde al this thyng Criseyde wel ynowh°,
And every word gan for to notefye°;
For which with sobre chere° hire herte lowh°,
For who is that ne wolde° hire glorifye°,
To mowen swych a knyght don° lyve or dye?
But al passe I, lyst ye° to longe dwelle,
For for o fyn° is al that evere I telle.

The tyme com° fro dyner for to ryse,
And as hem oughte arysen everychon°,
And gonne a while of this and that devyse°.
But Pandarus brak° al this speche anoon,
And seide to Deiphebus, "Wol ye gon°,
If youre wille be, as I yow preyde°,
To speke here of the nedes of Criseyde?"

Eleyne, which that by the hond hire held,
Took first the tale° and seyde, "Go we blyve,"
And goodly° on Criseyde she byheld,
And seyde, "Joves° lat hym nevere thryve°
That doth yow harm, and brynge hym soone of lyve°,
And yeve° me sorwe but he shal it rewe°,
If that I may, and alle folk be trewe."

"Telle thow thi neces cas," quod Deiphebus
To Pandarus, "for thow kanst best it telle."
"My lordes and my ladyes, it stant° thus.
What° sholde I lengere°," quod he, "do° yow dwelle?"
He rong° hem out a proces° lyk a belle

1557 Shoop hire, *planned,* **owre after the pryme,** *10 a.m.* **1558 nolde feyne,** *would not pretend* **1559 homly,** *familiarly* **1560 yn hire playne entente,** *willingly* **1561 wyst,** *knew* **1564 fle we now prolixite best is,** (it) *is best* (that) *we avoid longwindedness* **1568 hire saluynges pace,** *their greetings pass over* **1570 like,** *please* **1572 syke,** *sick* **1573 Lyth yet,** *still lies* (in bed), **syke,** *sigh* **1574 peyned hym,** *took pains* **1577 feythfully,** *earnestly* **1578 gan waxen for accesse,** *became concerning fever* **1579 leche,** *physician* **1580 lere,** *teach* **1581 oon,** *one,* **al lyst hire nought,** *although it pleased her not* **1582 Best koude I,** *I could best* **1583 compleynt,** *lamenting* (his illness), **preyse,** *praise* **1585 reyse,** *raise* **1587 kan,** *can do,* **that,** *what* **1590 ynowh,** *enough* **1591 notefye,** *take note of* **1592 chere,** *expression,* **lowh,** *laughed* **1593 who is that ne wolde,** *who is* (it) *who would not,* **hire glorifye,** *be proud of herself* **1594 To mowen swych a knight don,** *to be able to make such a knight* **1595 lyst ye,** *so that you will not* **1596 o fyn,** *one goal* **1597 com,** *came* **1598 arysen everychon,** *everyone arose* **1599 devyse,** *discuss* **1600 brak,** *broke* **1601 gon,** *proceed* **1602 preyde,** *asked* **1605 Took first the tale,** *spoke first,* **Go we blyve,** *let us proceed quickly* **1606 goodly,** *graciously* **1607 Joves,** (may) *Jove,* **thryve,** *prosper* **1608 brynge . . . of lyve,** *kill* **1609 yeve,** *give,* **rewe,** *regret* **1613 stant,** *stands* **1614 What,** *why,* **lengere,** *longer,* **do,** *make* **1615 rong,** *rang,* **proces,** *exposition*

1557 Shoop, Cl and Cp read "Shapt." **1561 God and Pandare wyst,** the correlation of Pandarus's knowledge with God's is comic exaggeration, but it also engages serious questions of freedom and determinism engaged directly elsewhere in the poem. In some accounts, Deiphebus marries Helen after Paris dies, so that the preceding passage may be ripe with suggestiveness, as may be their private time in the garden at 3.1705ff. **1563 Antigone . . . Tarbe,** Criseyde's entourage, mentioned previously at 2.816ff. **1585 up,** omitted in Cl and Cp. **1594 don,** omitted in Cl. **1614 quod he,** omitted in Cp, making the line metrically defective and assigning the statement to the narrator. Compare 2.1622. **1615 rong . . . lyk a belle,** Chaucer's Pardoner uses similar language to describe his own extravagant rhetoric; *CT* 6.331.

Upon hire fo, that highte° Poliphete,
So heynous°, that men myghte on it spete°.

Answerde of° this ech worse of hem° than other,
And Poliphete they gonnen thus to waryen°:
“Anhonged be swych on°, were he° my brother!”
“And so he shal, for it ne may not varyen°!”
What° shold I lengere yn this tale taryen°?
Pleynly alle at ones° they hire hyghten°
To ben hire helpe in al that evere they myghten.

Spak than Eleyne, and seyde, “Pandarus,
Woot ought my lord°, my brother, this matere,
I mene Ector? Or wot° it Troylus?”
He seyde, “Ye, but wole ye now me here?
Me thenketh this, sith° that Troylus is here,
It were good, if that ye wolde assente,
She tolde hireself hym al this er she wente.

“For he wol have the more hir grief at herte,
By cause°, lo, that she a lady is.
And, by youre leve°, I wol but yn right sterte°
And do yow wete°, and that anoon, ywys°,
If that he slepe or wol ought here° of this.”
And yn he lepte, and seyde hym in his ere,
“God have thi soule, ibrought° have I thi bere°!”

To smylen of this gan tho° Troylus,
And Pandarus withoute rekenynge°
Out wente anoon to Eleyne and Deiphebus,
And seyde hem, “So° ther be no taryinge°,
Ne more pres°, he wol wel that ye brynge
Criseyda, my lady, that is here;
And as° he may enduren, he wol here°.

“But wel ye wot°, the chaumbre is but lite°,
And fewe folk may lightly° make it warm.
Now loketh ye°—for I wol have no wyter°
To brynge yn pres that myghte don hym harm,
Or hym dishesen°, for my bettre arm°—
Where° it be bet° she byde° til eftsonys°?
Now loketh ye that knowen what to don is.

“I sey for me, best is° as I kan knowe
That no wight yn ne wente but ye tweye,
But° it were I, for I kan in a throwe°
Reherece° hire cas unlyk that° she kan seye.
And after this, she may hym ones preye°
To ben good lord, yn short, and take hire leve.
This may not mechel° of his ese hym reve°.

“And ek for she is straunge° he wol forbere°
His ese, which that hym thar nought° for yow,
Ek other thing that toucheth not to here°,
He wol yow telle—I wot° it wel right now—
That secret is, and for the townes prow°.”
And they, that nothing knewe of this entent,
Withoute more to Troylus yn they went.

Eleyne in al hire goodly softe wyse°
Gan hym saluwe°, and wommanly to pleye°,
And seyde, “Ywis°, ye moste alweyes arise°;
Now, faire brother, beth al hool°, I preye!”
And gan hire arm right over his sholder leye,
And hym with al hire wit to reconforte°.
As she best kowde, she gan hym to disporte°.

So after this quod she, “We yow byseke°,
My dere brother Deiphebus and I,
For love of God—and so doth Pandare eke—
To ben good lord and frend right hertely°
Unto Criseyde, which that certeynly
Receyveth wrong—as wot° wel here Pandare,
That kan° hire cas wel bet than I declare.”

1616 highte, *was called* **1617 heynous,** *hateful,* **spete,** *spit* **1618 Answerde of,** *responded to,* **ech worse of hem,** *each of them worse* **1619 waryen,** *curse* **1620 Anhonged be swych on,** *hanged be such a one,* **were he,** *even if he were* **1621 varyen,** *be otherwise* **1622 What,** *why,* **taryen,** *delay* **1623 Pleynly alle at ones,** *openly all together,* **hyghten,** *promised* **1626 Woot ought my lord,** *does my lord know anything* (of) **1627 wot,** *knows* **1629 sith,** *since* **1633 By cause,** *because* **1634 by your leve,** *with your permission,* **but yn right sterte,** *just run into* (his room) **1635 do yow wete,** *let you know,* **ywys,** *indeed* **1636 wol ought here,** *will hear anything* **1638 ibrought,** *brought,* **thi bere,** *your coffin* **1639 tho,** *then* **1640 withoute rekenynge,** *without calculation* (immediately) **1642 So,** *provided that,* **taryinge,** *lingering* **1643 pres,** *crowd* **1645 as,** *as long as,* **here,** *listen* **1646 wot,** *know,* **lite,** *little* **1647 lightly,** *easily* **1647 loketh ye,** *consider,* **wyte,** *blame* **1650 dishesen,** *discomfort,* **bettre arm,** *right arm* (a mild expletive) **1651 Where,** *whether,* **bet,** *better,* **byde,** *wait,* **eftsonys,** *later* **1653 best is,** *it is best* **1655 But,** *unless,* **throwe,** *moment* **1656 Reherce,** *recount,* **unlyk that,** *better than* **1657 ones preye,** *once request* **1659 mechel,** *much,* **hym reve,** *deprive him* **1660 straunge,** *unfamiliar,* **forbere,** *give up* **1661 which that hym thar nought,** *which he need not do* **1662 toucheth nought to here,** *do not concern her* **1663 wot,** *know* **1664 prow,** *benefit* **1667 softe wyse,** *quiet way* **1668 saluwe,** *greet,* **pleye,** *be playful* **1669 Ywis,** *surely,* **moste alweyes arise,** *must by all means get up* **1670 beth al hool,** *get well* **1672 reconforte,** *comfort* **1673 disporte,** *cheer up* **1674 byseke,** *request* **1677 right hertely,** *very earnestly* **1679 wot,** *knows* **1680 That kan,** *who knows*

1634 yn right, Cl reads “right yn.” **1638 thi,** Cl reads “the.” **1663 yow,** Cl and Cp read “me.” **1669 arise,** Cl reads “avise.”

This Pandarus gan newe° his tong affyle°,
And al hire cas reherce°, and that anoon.
Whan it was seyd, soone after in a while,
Quod Troylus, "As sone as I may gon°,
I wol right fayn° with al my myght ben oon°—
Have God my trouthe°—hire cause to susteyne."
"Good thryft° have ye," quod Eleyne the queene.

Quod Pandarus, "And it youre wille be°,
That she may take hire leve, er that she go?"
"O, elles God forbede°," tho quod he,
"If that she vouchesauf° for to do so."
And with that word quod Troylus, "Ye two,
Deiphebus and my suster leef° and dere,
To yow have I to speke of o matere,

To ben avysed by youre red° the bettre."
And fond, as hap° was, at his beddes hed
The copye of a tretes° and a lettre
That Ector hade hym sent to axen red°
If swych a man° was worthi to ben ded—
Woot° I nought who; but in a grysly wyse°
He preyede hem anoon on it avyse°.

Deiphebus gan this lettre to unfolde
In ernest gret°; so did Eleyne the queene;
And romyng outward°, faste° it gonne byholde,
Downward a steyre, into an herber grene°.
This ilke° thing thei redden hem bytwene,
And largely the mountance° of an owre°,
Thei gon on it to reden and to powre°.

Now lat hem rede, and turne we anoon
To Pandarus, that gan ful faste prye°
That al was wel, and out he gan to gon
Into the grete chaumbre and that in hye°,
And seyde, "God save al this compaynye.
Come, nece myn, my lady queene Eleyne
Abydeth° yow, and ek my lordes tweyne.

"Rys, take with yow yowre nece Antigone,
Or whom yow list°—or no fors°, hardyly°,
The lasse pres°, the bet—com forth with me,
And loke that ye thonken humbely
Hem alle thre; and whan ye may goodly°
Youre tyme se, taketh of hem youre leve
Lest we to longe his reste hym byreve°."

Al innocent of Pandarus entente,
Quod tho Criseyde, "Go we, uncle dere."
And arm in arm inward with hym she wente,
Avysed° wel hire wordes and hire chere.
And Pandarus yn ernestful manere
Seyde, "Alle folk, for Goddes love, I preye,
Stynteth° right here, and softely yow pleye.

"Aviseth yow° what folk ben here withinne,
And in what plit° oon is, God hym amende°!"
And inward thus ful softely bygynne,
"Nece, I conjure°, and heighly° yow defende°,
On his byhalf which that us al sowle sende°,
And in the vertue of corounes tweyne°,
Sle° naught this man, that hath for yow this peyne.

"Fy on° the devel! Thenk which on° he is,
And in what plyt he lith. Com of° anoon!
Thenk al swych taried tid but lost it nys°;
That wol ye bothe seyn° whan ye ben oon.
Secoundelich°, ther yet devyneth noon°
Upon yow two. Com of now, if ye konne;
While folk is blent°, lo, al the tyme is wonne.

"In titeryng° and pursuyte and delayes
The folk devyne° at waggyng of a stre°.

1681 newe, *freshly,* **affyle,** (to) *smooth* **1682 reherce,** *repeated* **1684 gon,** *walk* **1685 right fayn,** *very happily,* **oon,** *one* **1686 trouthe,** *promise* **1687 thryft,** *success* **1688 And it youre wille be,** *is it your wish* **1690 elles God forbede,** *God forbid otherwise* **1691 vouchesauf,** *agree* **1693 leef,** *beloved* **1695 red,** *counsel* **1696 hap,** *luck* **1697 tretes,** *treatise* **1698 axen red,** *ask advice* **1699 swych a man,** *a certain man* **1700 Woot,** *know,* **grysly wyse,** *frightening way* **1701 avyse,** *ponder* **1703 ernest gret,** *great earnestness* **1704 romyng outward,** *wandering out* **1704 faste,** *intently* **1705 herber grene,** *green garden* **1706 ilke,** *same* **1707 mountance,** *extent,* **owre,** *hour* **1708 powre,** *pore* **1710 ful faste prye,** *very quickly to see* **1712 hye,** *haste* **1715 Abydeth,** *waits for* **1717 list,** *wish,* **no fors,** *no matter,* **hardyly,** *truly* **1718 lasse pres,** *less crowd* **1720 goodly,** *properly* **1722 hym byreve,** *deprive him of* **1726 Avysed,** *having considered* **1729 Stynteth,** *remain* **1730 Aviseth yow,** *consider* **1731 plit,** *plight,* **amende,** *heal* **1733 conjure,** *command,* **heighly,** *strictly,* **defende,** *forbid* **1734 us al sowle sende,** *sent us all souls* (God) **1735 corounes tweye,** *two crowns* **1736 Sle,** *slay* **1737 Fy on,** *curse,* **which on,** *what kind of man* **1738 Com of,** *hurry* **1739 Thenk al swych taried tid but lost it nys,** *Realize* (that) *all such delayed time is not but lost* **1740 seyn,** *see* **1741 Secoundelich,** *secondly,* **ther yet devyneth noon,** *no one yet suspects* **1743 blent,** *blinded* (deceived) **1744 titeryng,** *hesitation* **1745 The folk devyne,** *people suspect,* **waggyng of a stre,** *movement of a straw* (any insignificant thing)

1690 forbede, Cp reads "forbede it." **tho,** omitted in Cl. **1722 his,** Cl reads "of hise." **byreve,** Cl reads "reve." **1735 corounes tweye,** there is no agreed-upon explanation of this obscure allusion, but see the note in Windeatt's edition that suggests the crowns of mercy and bounty.

And though ye wolden han after° merye dayes,
Than° dar ye nought. And why? For she and she
Spak swych a word; thus loked he and he.
Allas tyme ylost! I dar not with yow dele°.
Com of, therfore, and bryngeth hym to hele°."

But now to yow, ye loveres that ben here,
Was Troylus nought in a kankedort°,
That lay and myghte whysprynge of hem here,
And thought, "O Lord, ryght now renneth° my sort°
Fully° to dye or han anoon comfort!"
And was the firste tyme he shulde hire preye
Of love: O myghti God, what shal he seye?

Explicit secundus liber.

1746 wolden han after, *would like to have afterwards* **1747 Than,** *then* **1749 dele,** *argue* **1750 hele,** *health* **1751 kankedort,** *predicament* **1754 renneth,** *runs,* **sort,** *fate* **1755 Fully,** *completely*

1752 kankedort, Chaucer seems to have invented this evocative word for this occasion—a nonce word. **1757a *Explicit secundus liber,*** "Here ends the second book."

Book 3

Incipit prohemium tercii libri.

O blysful light, of which the bemes clere°
Adorneth al the thridde heven faire,
O sonnes lyef°, O Joves doughter dere,
Plesaunce° of love, O goodly debonaire°,
In gentil hertes ay redy to repair°,
O verray° cause of hele° and of gladnesse,
Iheried° be thi myght and thi goodnesse.

In hevene and helle, in erthe and salte se,
Is felt thi myght, if that I wel descerne;
As man, bryd°, best°, fissh, herbe, and grene tree
The fele in tymes° with vapour° eterne.
God loveth, and to love wol nought werne°;
And in this world no lyves° creature
Withouten love is worth or may endure.

Ye Joves first to thilke effectes glade°,
Thorugh which that thinges lyven alle and be,
Comeveden°, and amorous hym made
On mortal thyng, and as yow lyst ay ye°
Yeve° hym in love ese or adversite,
And in a thousand formes doun hym sente
For love in erthe, and whom yow lyste° he hente°.

Ye fierse Mars apeysen° of his ire°,
And as yow lyst, ye maken hertes digne°;
Algates° hem that ye wol sette afyre,
Thei dreden shame and vices thei resigne;
Ye do° hem corteys° be, fresche° and benigne°;
And hye or lowe°, after° a wyght entendeth°,
The joyes that he hath, youre myght hym sendeth.

Ye holden regne° and hous° in unite;
Ye sothfast° cause of frendshipe ben also;
Ye knowe al thilke covered° qualite
Of thynges, which that folk on wondren so,
Whan they kan noght construe how it may jo°
She loveth hym, or whi he loveth here,
As whi this fissh and nought that comth to were°.

Ye folk° a lawe han sett° in universe,
And this knowe I by hem that loveres be,
That whoso° stryveth with yow hath the werse.
Now, lady bryght, for thi benignite°,
At° reverence of hem that serven the,
Whos clerc° I am, so techeth me devyse°
Som joye of that° is felt in thi servyse.

Ye in my naked herte sentement
Inhelde°; and do° me shewe of thy swetnesse.
Caliope, thi voys be now present,
For now is nede. Sestow not° my destresse,
How I mot° telle anon-right the gladnesse
Of Troylus, to Venus heriynge°?
To which gladnesse, who nede hath, God hym brynge!

---

1 bemes clere, *bright rays* **3 sonnes lyef,** *beloved of the sun* **4 Plesaunce,** *pleasure,* **debonaire,** *gracious* **5 repaire,** *arrive* **6 verray,** *true,* **hele,** *well-being* **7 Iheried,** *praised* **10 bryd,** *bird,* **best,** *beast* **11 The fele in tymes,** *Feel you at times,* **vapour,** *influence* **12 werne,** *refuse* **13 lyves,** *living* **15–17 Ye Joves first . . . Comeveden,** *you first moved Jove* **15 thilke effectes glade,** *those joyous effects* **18 as yow lyst ay ye,** *as you wish you always* **19 Yeve,** *gave* **21 lyste,** *wished,* **hente,** *seized* **22 apeysen,** *appease,* **ire,** *anger* **23 digne,** *worthy* **24 Algates,** *always* **26 do,** *cause,* **corteys,** *courteous,* **fresche,** *vigorous,* **benigne,** *gracious* **27 hye or lowe,** *upper or lower class,* **after,** *according to* (how), **wyght entendeth,** *person wishes* **29 regne,** *kingdom,* **hous,** *household* **30 sothfast,** *true* **31 thilke covered,** *the hidden* **33 jo,** *happen* (that) **35 were,** *weir* (fish trap) **36 Ye folk,** *you for people,* **han sett,** *have established* **38 whoso,** *whoever* **39 benignite,** *goodness* **40 At,** *in* **41 clerc,** *student,* **devyse,** *to narrate* **42 that,** *what* **43 Inhelde,** *pour in,* **do,** *make* **46 Sestow not,** *do you not see* **47 mot,** *must* **48 heriynge,** *praising*

Incipit prohemium tercii libri, "Here begins the proem of the third book." **1–38** These lines of the proem derive from *Fiostratol* 3.74–79, part of Troiolo's song of joy after he has won the love of Criseida, in turn based on Boethius; see *Bo* 2.m8. **2 thridde heven,** the third heaven is the sphere of Venus, goddess of love and daughter of Jove. In Ptolemaic cosmology, the sun, moon, planets, and stars revolve around the earth in vast concentric spheres, drawing motion from one another and influencing human beings. In the combination of mythology and astrology here, love is the unifying and motivating force of the entire universe. **9 wel,** Cl reads "wole." **11 The fele,** Cl reads "The feld"; Cp, "They fele." **17 Comeveden,** Cp reads "Comended." **20 thousand formes,** a reference to the many forms Jove assumed (bull, swan, etc.) when wooing women in mythology. **hym,** Cl reads "hem." **28 hym,** Cl and Cp read "it." **36 universe,** Cl reads "universite." **42 thi,** Cl reads "this." **45 Caliope,** muse of epic poetry. **49 gladnesse,** omitted in Cl and Cp. **49a *Explicit prohemium tercii libri,*** "Here ends the proem of the third book." **49b *Incipit liber tercius,*** "Here begins the third book."

Explicit prohemium tercii libri.

Incipit liber tercius.

Lay al this menewhile Troylus
Recordyng his lesson in this manere:
"Mafay°," thought he, "thus wole I sey, and thus;
Thus wole I pleyne° unto my lady dere;
That word is good, and this shal be my chere°;
This nyl I not foryeten° in no wyse."
God leve° hym werken as he kan devyse!

And Lord, so that° his herte gan to quappe°,
Heryng hire come, and shorte for to syke°!
And Pandarus, that lad hire by the lappe°,
Com ner and gan in at the curtyn pyke°,
And seyde, "God do bot° on all syke.
Se who is here yow comen to visite;
Lo, here is she that is youre deth to wyte°."

Therwith it semed as he wepte almost.
"A-ha°," quod Troylus so rufully°,
"Wher me be wo, O myghty God, thow woost°!
Who is al there? I se nought trewely."
"Sire," quod Criseyde, "it is Pandare and I."
"Ye°, swete herte? Allas, I may nought ryse
To knele and do yow honour in some wyse."

And dressed hym° upward, and she right tho°
Gan bothe hire hondes softe upon hym leye.
"O, for the love of God, do ye not so
To me," quod she, "I°, what is this to seye?
Sire, comen am I to yow for causes tweye°.
First, yow to thonke, and of youre lordshipe eke°
Continuance I wolde yow biseke°."

This Troylus, that herde his lady preye
Of lordship hym, wax° neyther quyk° ne ded,
Ne myghte o word for shame to it seye,
Although men sholde smyten of his hed.
But Lord, so he wex sodeynliche red°,
And sire, his lesson that he wende konne°
To preyen hire is thurgh his wit yronne°.

Cryseyde al this aspied° wel ynowgh,
For she was wys, and loved hym nevere the lasse
Al nere he malapert° or made it towgh°
Or° was to bold to synge a fol° a masse.
But whan his shame gan somwhat to passe,
His resons°, as I may my rymes holde°,
I yow wol telle as techen bokes olde.

In chaunged voys, right for° his verray drede°,
Which voys ek quook°, and therto° his manere
Goodly abayst°, and now his hewes rede°,
Now pale, unto Criseyde his lady dere,
With look douncast and humble yolden° chere,
Lo, the alderfirste° word that hym asterte°
Was twyes°, "Mercy, mercy, swete herte!"

And stynte° awhile, and whan he myghte outbrynge,
The nexte word was, "God wot° that I have,
As ferforthly° as I have had konnynge°,
Ben yowres al, God so my sowle save,
And shal til that I, woful wyght, be grave°.
And though I ne dar ne kan° unto yow pleyne°,
I wys°, I suffre nought the lasse peyne.

"Thus muche as now, O wommanlyche wyf°,
I may out-brynge, and yf this yow displese,
That shal I wreke° upon myn owen lyf
Right sone°, I trowe°, and don youre herte an ese,

52 Mafay, (by) *my faith* **53 pleyne,** *lament* **54 chere,** *expression* **55 foryeten,** *forget* **56 leve,** *permit* **57 so that,** *how,* **quappe,** *pound* **58 syke,** *breathe* **59 lappe,** *hanging garment* **60 pyke,** *peek* **61 do bot,** *make remedy* **63 wyte,** *blame* **65 A-ha,** *ah me,* **rufully,** *pitifully* **66 woost,** *know* **69 Ye,** *you* **71 dressed hym,** *raised himself,* **tho,** *then* **74 I,** *oh* **75 causes tweye,** *two reasons* **76 lordshipe ek,** *protection also* **77 biseke,** *request* **79 wax,** *became,* **quyk,** *alive* **82 wex sodenynliche red,** *blushed* **83 he wende konne,** *thought he knew* **84 yronne,** *run* **85 aspied,** *saw* **87 Al nere he malapert,** *because he wasn't presumptuous,* **made it towgh,** *aggressive* **88 Or,** *nor,* **fol,** *fool* **90 resons,** *speeches,* **holde,** *sustain* **92 right for,** *simply because of,* **verray drede,** *genuine fear* **93 quook,** *quivered,* **therto,** *also* **94 Goodly abayst,** *attractively bashful* **95 rede,** *red* **96 yolden,** *submissive* **97 alderfirste,** *very first,* **hym asterte,** *escaped him* **98 twyes,** *twice* **99 stynte,** *stopped* **100 wot,** *knows* **101 ferforthly,** *far,* **konnynge,** *ability* **103 grave,** *buried* **104 ne dar ne kan,** *neither dare to nor can,* **pleyne,** *lament* **105 Iwys,** *surely* **106 wommanlyche wyf,** *womanly woman* **108 wreke,** *avenge* **109 sone,** *soon,* **trowe,** *think* **109 don . . . an ese,** *ease*

56 kan, Cl reads "gan." **65 A-ha,** Cp reads "Ha, a." **76 lordshipe,** Cl reads "mercy." **88 to synge a fol a masse,** may mean "to mislead or flatter deceptively," but the phrase has not been explained authoritatively. **96 yolden,** Cp reads "iyolden." **100 that,** Cp reads "for." **101 ferforthly,** Cl and Cp read "feythfully." **102 al God so,** Cl reads "also God." **104 ne dar,** "ne" omitted in Cl and Cp.

If with my deth youre wreththe° I may apese.
But syn that° ye han herd me somwhat seye,
Now recche° I nevere how sone° that I deye."

Therwith his manly sorwe to byholde,
It myght han mad° an herte of ston to rewe°;
And Pandare wep as he to water wolde°,
And poked evere his nece newe and newe°,
And seyde, "Wobygon ben° hertes trewe!
For love of God, make of this thyng an ende,
Or sle us bothe at ones er that ye wende°."

"I, what?" quod she, "By God and by my trowthe,
I not nought what ye wille that I shol seye."
"I, what?" quod he. "That ye han on hym routhe°,
For Goddes love, and doth° hym nought to deye."
"Now thanne thus," quod she, "I wolde hym preye
To telle me the fyn° of his entente.
Yet wyst° I nevere wel what that he mente."

"What that I mene, O swete herte dere?"
Quod Troylus, "O goodly fresshe fre°,
That with the stremes° of youre eyen clere°
Ye wolde somtyme frendly on me se°,
And thanne agreen° that I may ben he,
Withoute braunche° of vyce on ony wyse,
In trowthe alwey to don yow my servyse,

"As to my lady right° and chief resort°,
With al my wit and al my deligence;
And I to han right as yow lyst° comfort,
Under yowre yerde° egal° to myn offence,
As deth, if that I breke youre defence°;
And that ye deigne° me so muche honoure
Me to comaunden ought° yn any owre°;

"And I to ben yowre verray°, humble, trewe,
Secret, and yn myn paynes pacient°,
And everemo desiren fresshly newe
To serven, and ben ay ilyke° diligent,
And with good herte al holly youre talent°
Receyven wel, how sore° that me smerte—
Lo, this mene I, myn owene swete herte."

Quod Pandarus, "Lo, here° an hard requeste,
A resonable lady for to werne°!
Now, nece myn, by natal Joves feste°,
Were I a god ye sholden sterve as yerne°,
That heren° wel this man wol nothyng yerne°
But youre honour, and sen° hym almost sterve,
And ben so loth° to suffren° hym yow serve."

With that she gan hire eyen on hym caste
Ful esyly° and ful debonairly°,
Avysyng hire°, and hied° not to faste
With nevere a word, but seyde hym softely,
"Myn honour sauf°, I wol wel trewely,
And in swych forme° as he gan now devyse°,
Receyven hym fully to my servyse,

"Bysechyng° hym for Goddes love that he
Wolde in honour of trouthe and gentilesse°,
As I wel mene, eke mene wel to me,
And myn honour with wit° and besynesse°
Ay kepe°. And yf I may don hym gladnesse,
From hennesforth, iwys°, I nyl not feyne°.
Now beth al hol°, no lenger ye ne pleyne.

"But nathelees, this warne I yow," quod she,
"A kynges sone although ye be, iwys,
Ye shul no more have soveraynete
Of me in love than right in that cas is;
Ne I nyl forbere°, yf that ye don amys°,
To wrathen° yow; and whil that ye me serve,
Cherycen° yow right after° ye deserve.

"And shortly, dere herte and al my knyght,
Beth glad and draweth° yow to lustynesse°,

110 wreththe, *distress* **111 syn that,** *since* **112 recche,** *care,* **sone,** *soon* **114 han mad,** *have made,* **rewe,** *pity* **115 to water wolde,** *would turn to water* **116 newe and newe,** *again and again* **117 Wobygon ben,** *woeful are* **119 wende,** *go* **122 routhe,** *pity* **123 doth,** *cause* **125 fyn,** *goal* **126 wyst,** *knew* **128 goodly fresshe fre,** *superb young generous* (person) **129 stremes,** *beams,* **clere,** *bright* **130 se,** *look* **131 agreen,** *consent* **132 braunche,** *any kind* **134 right,** *proper,* **resort,** *source of comfort* **135 lyst,** *wish* **137 yerde,** *rule,* **egal,** *equal* **138 defence,** *prohibition* **139 deigne,** *grant* **140 ought,** *anything,* **owre,** *hour* **141 verray,** *genuine* **142 yn myn paynes pacient,** *patient in my suffering* **144 ay ilyke,** *always alike* **145 talent,** *wish* **146 how sore,** *however sorely* **148 here,** *here is* **149 werne,** *refuse* **150 by natal Joves feste,** *by the feast of Jupiter who presides over birthdays* (beginnings) **151 sterve as yerne,** *die very quickly* **152 That heren,** *who hears,* **yerne,** *desire* **153 sen,** *see* **154 loth,** *reluctant,* **suffren,** *allow* **156 esyly,** *kindly,* **debonairly,** *favorably* **157 Avysyng hire,** *deliberating,* **hied,** *hurried* **159 sauf,** *safe* **160 forme,** *manner,* **devyse,** *describe* **162 Bysechyng,** *asking* **163 gentilesse,** *nobility* **165 wit,** *intelligence,* **besynesse,** *diligence* **166 Ay kepe,** *always protect* **167 iwys,** *indeed,* **nyl not feyne,** *will not refrain* **168 hol,** *whole* **173 Ne I nyl forbere,** *nor will I hold back,* **don amys,** *do wrong* **174 wrathen,** *be angry with* **175 Cherycen,** *cherish,* **right after,** *just as* **177 draweth,** *move,* **lustynesse,** *pleasure*

110 wreththe, Cl and Cp read "herte." **136 I,** omitted in Cl and Cp. **139 deigne,** Cl reads "digne." **149 A,** Cp reads "And." **160 And,** Cl reads "But." **gan,** Cl reads "can." **171 soveraynete,** women's desire for sovereignty in love and in marriage is the topic of the *Wife of Bath's Tale.* **176 dere,** Cl reads "my dere."

And I shal trewely with al my myght
Youre bittre° tornen al into swetnesse.
If I be she that may yow do° gladnesse,
For every wo ye shal recovere a blysse."
And hym in armes tok, and gan hym kysse.

Fil Pandarus on knees, and up his eyen
To hevene threw, and held his hondes hye,
"Inmortal god," quod he, "that mayst nought
dyen,
Cupide I mene, of this mayst glorifie°,
And Venus, thow mayst make melodie.
Withouten hond°, me semeth° in the towne,
For this merveyle° ich here ech belle sowne°.

"But ho°, no more as now of this matere,
Forwhl° this folk wol comen up anoon
That han the lettre red—lo, I hem here°.
But I conjure the°, Criseyde and oon°,
And two° thow Troylus, whan thow mayst goon,
That at myn hows ye ben at my warnynge°,
For I ful wel shal shape° youre comynge;

"And eseth there youre hertes right ynough,
And lat se which of yow shal bere the belle°
To speke of love aright"—therwith he lough—
"For ther have ye a layser° for to telle°."
Quod Troylus, "How longe shal y dwelle
Er this be don?" Quod he, "Whan thow mayst ryse,
This thing shal be right as I yow devyse."

With that Eleyne and also Deiphebus
Tho comen upward right at the steyres ende°.
And Lord, so thanne gan grone Troylus
His brother and his suster for to blende°.
Quod Pandarus, "It tyme is that we wende°.
Tak, nece myn, youre leve at° alle thre,
And lat hem speke, and cometh forth
with me."

She tok hire leve at hem ful thryftyly°,
As she wel koude, and they hire reverence
Unto the fulle deden° hardely°,
And wonder wel speken, in hire absence,
Of hire in preysing of hire excellence:
Hire governaunce°, hire wit, and hire manere
Comendeden° that it was joye to here.

Now lat hire wende unto hire owen place,
And torne we to Troylus ayen,
That gan ful lyghtly of the lettre pace°
That Deiphebus hadde yn the gardeyn seyn°;
And of Eleyne and hym he wolde feyn°
Delyvered ben, and seyde that hym leste°
To slepe and after tales have reste.

Eleyne hym kyste and tok hire leve blyve°,
Deiphebus ek, and hom wente every wyght°;
And Pandarus, as faste as he may dryve°,
To Troylus tho com as lyne right°,
And on a paillet° al that glade nyght
By Troylus he lay with mery chere
To tale°, and wel was hem° thei were yfere°.

Whan every wyght was voyded° but they two,
And alle the dores were faste yshette,
To telle in shorte withoute wordes mo,
This Pandarus withouten ony lette°
Up roos, and on his beddes side hym sette,
And gan to speken in a sobre wyse°
To Troylus, as I shal yow devyse:

"Myn alderlevest° lord and brother dere,
God wot°, and thow, that it sat° me so sore
When I the saw so langwysshyng to-yere°
For love, of which thi wo wax alwey more,
That I with al my myght and al my lore°
Have evere sethen° do my bysynesse°
To brynge the to joye out of distresse;

---

179 bittre, *bitter suffering* **180 do,** *cause* **186 mayst glorifie,** *you may take glory* **188 hond,** *hands,* **me semeth,** *it seems to me* **189 merveyle,** *marvel,* **sowne,** *sound* **190 ho,** *stop* **191 Forwhi,** *because* **192 here,** *hear* **193 conjure the,** *command you,* **and oon,** *for one* **195 warnynge,** *summons* **196 shape,** *arrange* **198 bere the belle,** *carry the bell* (be the leader) **199 lough,** *laughed* **200 a layser,** *time,* **telle,** *talk* **205 steyres ende,** *top of the stairs* **207 blende,** *deceive* **208 wende,** *go* **209 at,** *from* **211 thryftyly,** *properly* **212–13 hire reverence . . . Unto the fulle diden,** *paid* (their) *full respects to her,* **hardely,** *certainly* **216 governaunce,** *self composure* **217 Comendeden,** *commended* **220 pace,** *pass over* **221 seyn,** *seen,* **222 feyn,** *gladly* **223 leste,** *wished* **225 blyve,** *quickly* **226 wyght,** *person* **227 dryve,** *move* **228 as lyne right,** *like a straight line* **229 paillet,** *mattress* **231 tale,** *talk,* **wel was hem,** *they were happy,* **yfere,** *together* **232 voyded,** *departed* **235 lette,** *delay* **237 sobre wyse,** *serious way* **239 alderlevest,** *most beloved* **240 wot,** *knows,* **sat,** *affected* **241 to-yere,** *this year* **243 lore,** *knowledge* **244 sethen,** *since,* **do my bysynesse,** *made it my business*

180 yow, Cl reads "now." **188–89 Withouten hond . . . ech belle sowne,** instances of bells ringing miraculously without being rung by hand recur in ballads and saints' lives. **189 ich,** Cl reads "I." **190 as,** omitted in Cl. **193–94 and oon / And two,** on the one hand and on the other. Cp reads "anoon / And to," which would read "from now on . . . and also." **239–87** Chaucer follows *Filostrato* 3.5–10 for this portion of Pandarus's discussion, expanding it with 65 lines of his own (288–343) and interpolating it into his own episode.

"And have it brought to swich plit° as thow wost°,
So that thorugh me thow stondest now in weye°
To faren wel—I sey it for no bost—
And wostow° whi? For shame it is to seye,
For the have I a game bygonne to pleye
Which that I nevere don shal eft° for other,
Although he were a thousandfold my brother.

"That is to seye, for the am I becomen
Bytwixen game and ernest swych a mene°
As maken wommen unto men to comen—
Al° sey I nought, thow wost wel what I mene.
For the have I my nece of vices clene°
So fully mad thi gentilesse triste°,
That al shal ben right° as thiselve lyste°.

"But God that al wot° take I to wytnesse
That nevere I this for coveytise° wroughte°,
But oonly for t'abrygge° that destresse
For which wel nygh° thow deydest, as me thoughte.
But, gode brother, do now as the oughte,
For Goddes love, and kep hire out of blame,
Syn° thow art wys, and save alwey hire name°.

"For wel thow woost, the name as yet of hire
Among the peple, as who seyth°, halwed is°,
For that man is unbore°, dar I swere,
That evere wyste° that she dide amys°.
But wo is me that I, that cause al this,
May thenken that she is my nece dere,
And I hire em, and traytour eke yfere°!

"And were it wyst° that I thorugh myn engyn°
Hadde in my nece iput this fantasye°,
To do thi lust° and holly° to be thyn,
Why, al the world upon it wolde crye,
And seyn that I the worste trecherye
Dide yn this cas that evere was bygonne,
And she forlost°, and thow right nought ywonne°.

"Wherfore, er I wol ferther gon a pas°,
Yet eft° I the byseche° and fully seye
That prevete° go with us in this cas—
That is to seyn, that thow us nevere wreye°,
And be nought wroth° though I the ofte preye°
To holden secre° swych an heigh matere,
For skylful° is, thow wost° wel, my preyere.

"And thenk what wo ther hath bytyd er° this
For makyng of avauntes°, as men rede,
And what myschaunce° in this world yet is
Fro day to day right for that wykked dede°.
For which these wise clerkes that ben dede°
Han evere yet proverbed° to us yonge,
That first vertu is to kepe tonge.

"And nere it° that I wilne° as now t'abregge°
Diffusion of speche, I koude almost
A thousand olde storyes the alegge°
Of wommen lost through fals and foles bost°.
Proverbes kanst thyselve ynow° and wost°
Ayens° that vice for to ben a labbe°,
Al° seyde men soth as often as they gabbe.

"O tonge, allas, so often here byforn°
Hastow° made many a lady bright of hewe
Seyd° 'Welaway° the day that I was born!'
And manye a maydes sorwe for to newe°.
And for the more part, al is untrewe
That men of yelpe°, and° it were brought to preve°.
Of kynde° noon avauntours° is to leve°.

---

246 swich plit, *such a state,* **wost,** *know* **247 stondest now in weye,** *are now likely* **249 wostow,** *do you know* **251 eft,** *again* **254 mene,** *means* **256 Al,** *although* **257 clene,** *clean* **258 mad thi gentilesse triste,** *made to trust your nobility* **259 right,** *exactly,* **lyste,** *desire* **260 al wot,** *knows all* **261 coveytise,** *greed,* **wrought,** *brought about* **262 t'abrygge,** *to reduce* **263 wel nygh,** *nearly* **266 Syn,** *since,* **name,** *reputation* **268 as who seyth,** *so to speak,* **halwed is,** *is holy* **269 unbore,** *unborn* **270 wyste,** *knew,* **amys,** *wrong* **273 traytour eke yfere,** *betrayer at the same time* **274 wyst,** *known,* **engyn,** *contriving* **275 iput this fantasye,** *placed this notion* **276 lust,** *desire,* **holly,** *wholly* **280 forlost,** *ruined,* **right nought ywonne,** *won nothing at all* **281 ferther gon a pas,** *go a step further* **282 eft,** *again,* **the byseche,** *beseech you* **283 prevete,** *secrecy* **284 wreye,** *reveal* **285 wroth,** *angry,* **preye,** *ask* **286 secre,** *secret* **287 skylful,** *reasonable,* **wost,** *know* **288 bytyd er,** *happened before* **289 avauntes,** *boasts* **290 myschaunce,** *misfortune* **291 wykked dede,** *wicked deed* (boasting) **292 ded,** *dead* **293 proverbed,** *taught via proverbs* **295 nere it,** *were it not,* **wilne,** *wish,* **t'bregge,** *to reduce* **297 the alegge,** *cite for you* **298 foles bost,** *fool's boast* **299 kanst thyselve ynowe,** *you know enough yourself,* **wost,** *know* **300 Ayens,** *against,* **labbe,** *blabbermouth* **301 Al,** *even if* **302 here byforn,** *before this* **303 Hastow,** *you have* **304 Seyd,** (to have) *said,* **Welaway,** *alas* **305 newe,** *renew* **307 of yelpe,** *brag about,* **and,** *if,* **brought to preve,** *tested* **308 Of kynde,** *by nature,* **avauntours,** *braggart,* **is to leve,** *is to be believed*

250 a game bygonne to, Cp reads "bigonne a gamen." **273 traytour,** Boccaccio's "trattator" (*Filostratol* 3.8.8) means "procurer" or "pimp," so Chaucer either mistranslated or softened the term. **294 kepe tonge,** restrain your tongue (speech) is proverbial advice. See *ManT* 9.309–62 and *RR* 7037, 7041–45, 7055–57. **308 kyynde,** Cl reads "kyng."

"Avauntoure and a lyere al is on°,
As thus: I pose° a womman graunte me
Hire love, and seyth that other wol she non°,
And I am sworn to holden it secre,
And after I go telle it two or thre;
Iwys°, I am avauntour at the leste,
And a lyere, for I breke my biheste°.

"Now loke° thanne yf they be nought to blame,
Swych manere folk—what shal I clepe° hem? what?—
That hem avaunte of wommen, and by name,
That nevere yet byhyghte° hem this ne that,
Ne knewe hem more than myn olde hat!
No wonder is, so God me sende hele°,
Though wommen drede with us men to dele.

"I sey this not for no mystrust of yow,
Ne for no wyse men, but for foles nice°,
And for the harm that in the world is now,
As wel for folye ofte as for malice;
For wel wot I in wyse folk that vice°
No womman drat°, if she be wel avised,
For wyse ben° by foles° harm chastised°.

"But now to purpos: leve° brother dere,
Have al this thing that I have seyd in mynde,
And kep the clos°, and be now of good chere,
For at thi day thow shalt me trewe fynde.
I shal thi proces° sette yn swych a kynde°,
And God toforn°, that it shal the suffise,
For it shal ben right° as thow wolt devyse.

"For wel I wot thow menest wel, parde°;
Therfore I dar this fully undertake°.
Thow wost eke what thi lady graunted the;
And day is set the chartres up to make.
Have now good nyght, I may no lengere wake.
And byd° for me, syn° thow art now yn blysse°,
That God me sende deth or soone lysse°."

Who myghte telle half the joye or feste°
Whiche that the sowle of Troylus tho° felte
Herynge th'effect° of Pandarus byheste°?
His olde wo that made his herte swelte°
Gan tho for joye wasten° and tomelte°,
And al the richesse° of his sikes° sore
At ones° fledde; he felte of hem no more.

But right so as these holtes° and these hayis°,
That han in wynter dede ben and dreye°,
Revesten° hem in grene when that May is,
Whan every lusti° lyketh best to pleye,
Right in that selve wyse°, soth for to seye,
Wax sodeynlyche° his herte ful of joye,
That gladder was there nevere man in Troye.

And gan his lok on Pandarus up caste°,
Ful sobrely° and frendly for to se,
And seyde, "Frend, in Aperil the laste—
As wel thow wost, if it remembreth the°—
How neigh° the deth for wo thow founde me,
And how thow dedest al thi bysynesse
To knowe of me the cause of my distresse;

"Thow wost how longe ich it forbar to seye°
To the, that art the man that I best triste°;
And peril was it noon to the bywreye°,
That wyst° I wel; but telle me, yf the lyste,
Sith° I so loth° was that thiself it wyste°,
How dorst° I mo tellen of this matere,
That quake° now and no wyght° may us here?

"But natheles, by that God I the swere,
That as hym lyst° may al this world governe,

---

309 on, *one* (the same) **310 I pose,** (if I were to) *suppose* **311 other wol she non,** *she will have no other* **314 Iwys,** *surely* **315 biheste,** *promise* **316 loke,** *consider* **317 clepe,** *call* **319 byhyghte,** *promised* **321 hele,** *good health* **324 foles nice,** *silly fools* **327 that vice,** i.e., *boasting,* **drat,** *dreads* **329 wyse ben,** *wise people are,* **foles,** *fool's,* **chastised,** *taught a lesson* **330 leve,** *beloved* **332 the clos,** *yourself secretive* **334 proces,** *course,* **kynde,** *manner* **335 God toforn,** *before God* **336 right,** *exactly* **337 parde,** *by God* **338 dar this fully undertake,** *take full responsibility* **342 byd,** *pray,* **syn,** *since,* **blysse,** *heaven* **343 lysse,** *comfort* **344 feste,** *celebration* **345 tho,** *then* **346 th'effect,** *the gist,* **byheste,** *promise* **347 swelte,** *faint* **348 wasten,** *shrink,* **tomelte,** *melt away* **349 richesse,** *abundance,* **sikes,** *sighs* **350 ones,** *once* **351 holtes,** *forests,* **hayis,** *hedges* **352 dreye,** *dry* **353 Revesten,** *re-clothe* **354 lusti,** *joyful person* **355 selve wyse,** *same way* **356 Wax sodeynlyche,** *grew suddenly* **358 up caste,** *raise* **359 sobrely,** *seriously* **361 if it remembreth the,** *if you recall it* **362 neigh,** *near* **365 ich it forbar to seye,** *I refrained from saying it* **366 triste,** *trust* **367 the bywreye,** *reveal it to you* **368 wyst,** *know* **369 Sith,** *since,* **loth,** *reluctant,* **thiself it wyste,** (even) *you knew it* **370 dorst,** *dare* **371 quake,** *tremble,* **and no wyght,** *even if no person* **373 as hym lyst,** *so as he pleases*

315 my biheste, Cl reads "myn heste." **319 nevere yet byhyghte hem,** Cp reads "yet bibyghte hem nevere." **329** Proverbial. **340** "And the day is set to draw up the legal papers." Pandarus's language is figurative, but in medieval practice control of property was arranged through charters. **344 or,** Cl reads "and." **346 th'effect,** Cl reads "the feyth." **347 herte,** Cl reads "sorwe." **360 Aperil the laste,** it is uncertain whether the phrase means a year earlier or "last April." The events in Book 2 take place in May (see 2.56).

And, yf I lye, Achilles with his spere
Myn herte cleve al° were my lyf eterne,
As I am mortal, if I late or yerne°
Wolde it bywreye°, or dorst°, or sholde konne°,
For al the good that God made under sonne,

"That rather deye I wolde and determyne°,
As thenketh me, now stokked yn presoun°,
In wrecchednesse, in filthe, and yn vermine,
Caytif° to cruel Kyng Agamenoun—
And this yn all the temples of this town,
Upon the goddes alle, I wol the swere
Tomorwe day°, if that it lyketh the here°.

"And that thow hast so muche ido° for me
That I ne may it nevere more deserve,
This knowe I wel, al myghte I now for the
A thowsand tymes on a morwe sterve°.
I kan° no more but that I wol the serve
Right as thi sclave°, whider so thow wende,
For everemore, unto my lyves ende.

"But here with al myn herte I the byseche
That nevere in me thow deme swych folye
As I shal seyn; me thowghte by thi speche
That this which thow me dost° for compaignye°,
I sholde wene° it were a bauderye°.
I am nought wood°, al if° I lewed° be.
It is not so; that wot I wel, parde.

"But he that goth for gold or for richesse
On swych message°, calle hym what the lyst°;
And this that thow dost, calle it gentilesse°,
Compassioun, and felawship, and trist°.
Departe° it so, for wydewhere is wyst°
How that ther is dyversite° requered
Bytwyxen thynges lyk, as I have lered°.

"And that thow knowe I thenke nought, ne wene°;
That this servise a shame be or a jape°,
I have my faire suster Polixene,
Cassandre, Eleyne, or ony of the frape°,
Be she nevere so faire or wel ishape°,
Tel me which thow wylt of everychone°
To han for thyn, and lat me thanne allone.

"But sith° thow hast idon° me this servyse
My lyf to save, and for noon hope of mede°,
So for the love of God, this grete emprise°
Performe it out°; for now is moste nede.
For hygh and low°, withouten ony drede°,
I wol alwey thye hestes° alle kepe.
Have now good nyght, and lat us bothe slepe."

Thus held hym eche of other wel apayed°,
That al the world ne myghte it bet amende°.
And on the morwe, whan they were arayed,
Ech to his owen nedes gan entende°.
But Troylus, though as the fyr he brende°
For sharp desir of hope and of plesaunce,
He not forgat his gode governaunce°.

But in hymself with manhood gan restreyne
Ech rakel dede° and ech unbrydled chere°,
That alle tho° that lyven, soth to seyne,
Ne sholde han wyst by word or by manere
What that he mente, as towchyng° this matere.
From every wyght as fer° as is the clowde
He was, so wel dissimulen° he kowde.

And al the while which that I yow devyse°,
This was hys lyf: with al his fulle myght
By day he was in Martes° highe servyse—
This is to seyn, in armes as a kynght—
And for the more part, the longe nyght

---

375 and, *even if* **376 cleve,** (may) *split,* **al,** *even if* **376 late or yerne,** *late or early* **377 bywreye,** *reveal,* **dorst,** *dared to,* **konne,** *be able to* **379 determyne,** *come to an end* **380 now stokked yn presoun,** *while imprisoned in the stocks* **382 Caytif,** *captive* **385 Tomorwe day,** *tomorrow morning,* **lyketh the here,** *please you to hear it* **386 ido,** *done* **389 sterve,** *die* **390 kan,** *can do* **391 sclave,** *slave* **396 me dost,** *does for me,* **for compaignye,** *out of friendship* **397 sholde wene,** *might believe,* **a bauderye,** *pimping* **398 wood,** *crazy,* **al if,** *even if,* **lewed,** *ignorant* **401 swych message,** *such an errand* **401 the lyst,** *you wish* **402 gentilesse,** *nobility* **403 trist,** *trust* **404 Departe,** *distinguish,* **wydewhere is wyst,** *widely it is known* **405 dyversite,** *distinction* **406 lered,** *learned* **407 wene,** *believe* **408 jape,** *joke* **410 frape,** *group* **411 ishape,** *shaped* **412 everychone,** *all of them* **414 sith,** *since,* **idon,** *done* **415 mede,** *reward* **416 emprise,** *enterprise* **417 Performe it out,** *carry it out* **418 hygh and low,** *in all respects,* **drede,** *doubt* **419 hestes,** *commands* **421 apayed,** *pleased* **422 bet amende,** *improve* **424 entende,** *attend* **425 brende,** *burned* **427 governaunce,** *self-control* **429 rakel dede,** *rash action,* **unbrydled chere,** *unguarded expression* **430 tho,** *those* **432 towchyng,** *concerning* **433 fer,** *distant* **434 dissimulen,** *conceal* **435 devyse,** *describe* **437 Martes,** *Mars's*

374 Achilles, the hero of the Greeks, Achilles does eventually kill Troylus (5.1806). **382 Caytif,** Cl reads "Castif." **Kyng Agamenoun,** Agamemnon, leader of the Greek forces. **391 sclave,** Cl reads "knave" in a later correction. **404–06** Editors since Root point out that this is a standard scholastic notion, quoting Thomas Aquinas: "Diversitas requirit distinctionem" (*Summa Theologica* 1–1.3.31.2; diversity requires a distinction). **408 a jape,** Cl and Cp omit "a." **425 though,** Cl reads "thought."

He lay and thoughte how that he myghte serve
His lady best, hire thank for to deserve.

Nyl I nought° swere, although he lay ful softe°,
That in his thought he nas sumwhat dishesed°,
Ne that he torned on his pylwes° ofte,
And wold of that° hym myssed° han ben sesed°.
But yn swych cas man is nought alwey yplesed,
For ought I wot, no more than was he;
That kan I deme of° possibilite.

But certeyn is, to purpos° for to go,
That in this while°, as wreten° is in geste°,
He say° his lady somtyme, and also
She with hym spak whan that she dorst° and leste°;
And by hire bothe avys°, as was the beste,
Apoynteden° full warly° in this nede,
So as they dorste, how they wolde procede.

But it was spoken in so short a wyse,
In swych awayt° alwey, and in swych fere,
Lest ony wyght dyvynen° or devyse°
Wolde of hem two, or to it leye an eere,
That al this world so lef° to hem ne were
As that Cupido wolde hem grace sende
To maken of hire speche aryght an ende°.

But thilke lytel° that they spake or wroughte°;
His wyse gost° tok ay° of al swych hede,
It semed hire° he wyste what she thoughte
Withouten word, so that it was no nede
To bidde hym ought to don, or ought forbede°;
For which she thoughte that love, al coom it late,
Of alle joye hadde opned hire the yate°.

And shortly of this proces for to pace°,
So wel his werk and wordes he bysette°
That he so ful stod in his lady grace°
That twenty thousand tymes, er she lette°,
She thonked God she evere with hym mette.
So koude he hym governe° in swych servyse
That al the world ne myght it bet devyse°.

For whi° she fond hym so dyscret° in al,
So secret, and of swych obeysaunce°,
That wel she felte he was to hire a wal
Of stel, and sheld from every dysplesaunce;
That to ben in his goode governaunce,
So wys he was, she nas no more afered°—
I mene as fer as oughte ben requered°.

And Pandarus to quyke° alwey the fyr
Was evere ylyke prest° and dyligent;
To ese his frend was set al his desir.
He shof ay on°, he to and fro was sent,
He lettres bar° whan Troylus was absent,
That nevere man, as in his frendes nede,
Ne bar hym bet than he withouten drede°.

But now, paraunter°, som man wene° wolde
That every word, or sonde°, or lok, or chere°
Of Troylus that I rehersen sholde,
In al this while unto his lady dere:
I trowe° it were a long thing for to here,
Or of what wyght that stont° in swych disjoynte°,
His wordes alle, or every lok, to poynte°.

Forsothe°, I have not herd it don er this
In storye noon, ne no man here, I wene°.
And though I wolde, I koude not, iwysy°,
For ther was som epistel° hem bytwene
That wolde, as seyth myn autour, wel contene°
Neigh° half this book, of which hym lyste° not write.
How sholde I thanne a lyne of it endite°?

442 Nyl I nought, *I will not,* **softe,** *quiet* **443 dishesed,** *disturbed* **444 pylwes,** *pillows* **445 wold of that,** *wished that what,* **myssed,** *lacked,* **sesed,** *possessed* **448 deme of,** *think to be a* **449 purpos,** *the point* **450 while,** *time,* **wreten,** *written,* **geste,** *story* **451 say,** *saw* **452 dorst,** *dared,* **leste,** *wished* **453 hire bothe avys,** *their shared deliberation* **454 Apoynteden,** *arranged,* **warly,** *cautiously* **457 awayt,** *watchfulness* **458 dyvynen,** *suspect,* **devyse,** *conjecture* **460 lef,** *dear,* **ne were,** *was not* **462 maken . . . aryght an ende,** *bring . . . to conclusion quickly* **463 thilke lytel,** *this little,* **wroughte,** *did* **464 gost,** *spirit,* **ay,** *always* **465 hire,** *to her* **467 ought forbade,** *forbid anything* **469 yate,** *gate* **470 pace,** *pass over* **471 bysette,** *applied* **472 lady grace,** *lady's favor* **473 lette,** *stopped* **475 hym governe,** *control himself* **476 it bet devyse,** *better imagine it* **477 For whi,** *because,* **dyscret,** *prudent* **478 obeysaunce,** *obedience* **482 afered,** *afraid* **483 oughte ben requered,** *ought to be expected* **484 quyke,** *increase* **485 ylyke prest,** *equally ready* **487 shof ay on,** *pressed ever on* **488 bar,** *carried* **490 drede,** *doubt* **491 peraunter,** *perhaps,* **wene,** *think* **492 sonde,** *message,* **chere,** *expression* **495 trowe,** *think* **496 stont,** *stands,* **disjoynte,** *difficulty* **497 poynte,** *record* **498 Forsothe,** *truly* **499 wene,** *think* **500 iwys,** *surely* **501 epistel,** *letter* **502 contene,** *hold* **503 Neigh,** *nearly,* **hym lyste,** *it pleased him* (my author) **504 endite,** *write*

442 ful, omitted in Cl and Cp. **445 sesed,** Cl is corrected to "esed." **450** Chaucer alludes to source material here, despite the fact that from this scene until after the consummation scene (i.e., 3.428–1309), he does not follow *Filostrato.* He is self-conscious about expansiveness at 3.491–504, and also attributes his ignorance of Criseyde's thoughts to his source at 3.575–78 despite his independence. **461 Cupido,** Cp reads "Cupide." **491 wene,** Cp reads "wayten." **502 as seyth myn autour,** see the note to 3.450.

But to the grete effect°: Than sey I thus,
That stondyng in concord and in quiete,
Thise ilke° two, Criseyde and Troylus,
As I have told, and in this tyme swete°—
Save only often myghte they nought mete,
Ne layser° have hire speches to fulfille—
That it befel° right as I shal yow telle,

That Pandarus, that evere dide his myght°
Right for the fyn° that I shal speke of here,
As for to bryngen to his hous som nyght
His faire nece and Troylus yfere°,
Wher as° at leyser al this heigh matere
Towchyng hire love were° at the fulle upbounde°,
Hadde out of doute° a tyme to° it founde.

For he with gret deliberacioun
Hadde everything that herto° myghte avayle°
Forncast° and put in execucioun°,
And neither laft° for cost ne for travayle°.
Come yf hem lest°, hem sholde nothing fayle;
And for to ben in ought espied° there,
That, wyst he wel, an inpossible° were.

Dredeles° it clere was in the wynd°
From every pye° and every lette-game°.
Now al is wel, for al the world is blynd
In this matere, bothe fremed° and tame.
This tymbur° is al redy up to frame°;
Us lakketh nought° but that we weten° wolde
A certeyn houre in whiche she comen sholde.

And Troylus, that al this purvyaunce°
Knew at the fulle and waytede on it ay,
Hadde hereupon ek made gret ordinaunce°,
And found° his cause°, and therto his aray°,
Yf that he were myssed nyght or day,
Ther while° he was abowte this servyse,
That he was gon to don his sacrifise,
And most° at swych a temple alone wake°,
Answered of Apollo for to be,
And first to sen the holy laurer° quake,
Er that Apollo spake out of the tre
To telle hym next whan Grekes sholden fle—
And forthy° lette° hym no man, God forbede,
But prey Apollo helpen in this nede.

Now is ther litel more for to done,
But Pandare up, and shortly for to seyne,
Right soone upon the chaungyng of the
  moone°,
Whan lyghtles is the world a nyght or tweyne,
And that the wolken° shop hym° for to reyne,
He straught amorwe° unto his nece wente;
Ye han wel herd the fyn° of his entente.

Whanne he was come, he gan anoon to pleye
As he was woned°, and of hymself to jape°;
And fynally he swor and gan hire seye,
By this and that, she sholde hym not escape,
Ne lenger don° hym after hire to gape°,
But certeynly she moste, by hire leve,
Come soupen° in his hous with hym at eve.

At which she lough° and gan hire faste excuse,
And seyde, "It rayneth, lo. How sholde I gon?"
"Lat be°," quod he, "ne stond not thus
  to muse°.
This mot° be don. Ye shal be ther anoon."
So at the laste herof they felle atoon°,
Or elles, softe he swor hire in hire ere,
He nolde nevere comen ther she were.

Soone after this, she to hym gan to rowne°,
And axed hym yf Troylus were there.
He swor hire nay, for he was out of towne,
And seyde, "Nece, I pose° that he were°;
Yow thurste han° nevere the more fere;

505 grete effect, *main point* **507 ilke,** *same* **508 swete,** *sweet* **510 Ne layser,** *nor time* **511 befel,** *happened* **512 dide his myght,** *exerted himself* **513 fyn,** *outcome* **515 yfere,** *together* **516 Wher as,** *where* **517 were,** *might be* (*MED ben* 14.c), **at the fulle upbounde,** *wrapped up completely* **518 out of doute,** *without doubt,* **to,** *for* **520 herto,** *for this,* **avayle,** *help* **521 Forncast,** *planned,* **put in execucioun,** *set in motion* **522 laft,** *neglected* **travayle,** *effort* **523 hem lest,** *they wished* **524 in ought espied,** *at all discovered* **525 inpossible,** *impossibility* **526 Dredeles,** *doubtless,* **it clere was in the wynd,** *the sky was empty* **527 pye,** *magpie* (talking bird), **lette-game,** *spoilsport* **529 fremed,** *wild* **530 tymbur,** *timber,* **up to frame,** *to build* **531 Us lakketh nought,** *we lack nothing,* **weten,** *know* **533 purvyaunce,** *preparation* **534 at the fulle,** *completely* **535 ordinaunce,** *plans* **536 found,** *established,* **cause,** *excuse,* **aray,** *arrangements* **538 Ther while,** *during the time* **540 most,** *must,* **wake,** *keep a vigil* **542 laurer,** *laurel tree* **545 forthy,** *therefore,* **lette,** *hinder* **549 the chaungyng of the moone,** *the coming of the new moon* **551 wolken,** *sky,* **shop hym,** *prepares itself* **552 straught amorwe,** *early in the morning* **553 fyn,** *goal* **555 woned,** *accustomed to,* **jape,** *joke* **558 don,** *make,* **gape,** *pursue* **560 soupen,** *dine* **561 lough,** *laughed* **563 Lat be,** *stop it,* **muse,** *ponder* **564 mot,** *must* **565 atoon,** *in agreement* **568 rowne,** *whisper* **571 pose,** *suppose,* **he were,** *if he were* **572 thurste han,** *need have*

541–46 Apollo . . . holy laurer quake . . . , the laurel tree was sacred to Apollo and, presumably, shook before the god spoke. **558 gape,** Cp reads "cape." **560 soupen in his house,** there is no parallel in *Filostrato*; perhaps inspired by the 12th-c. Latin *Pamphilus de Amore,* where the woman is invited to dinner by the baud and surprised by the lover; see the notes to 3.797 and 1555–82. **572 thurste,** Cl reads "dorste"; Cp, "thruste."

For rather than men myghte hym ther aspie,
Me were levere° a thousand fold to dye."

Nought list° myn auctour fully to declare
What that she thoughte whan that he seyde so,
That Troylus was out of towne yfare°,
As yf° he seyde therof soth° or no;
But that withouten awayt° with hym to go
She graunted hym, sith° he hire that bisoughte°,
And, as his nece, obeyed as hire oughte.

But natheles yet gan she hym byseche°,
Although with hym to gon it was no fere°,
For to bewar of goosish° poeples speche,
That dremen° thynges whiche that nevere were,
And wel avyse hym° whom he broughte there;
And seyde hym, "Em, syn I moste° on yow triste°,
Loke al be wel, and do now as yow liste°."

He swor hire yis° by stokkes° and by stones,
And by the goddes that in hevene dwelle,
Or elles were hym levere°, fel° and bones,
With Pluto kyng as depe ben yn helle
As Tantalus. What sholde I more telle?
Whan al was wel, he ros and tok his leve,
And she to souper com whan it was eve,

With a certeyn of hire owene men,
And with hire faire nece Antigone,
And othere of hire wommen nyne or ten.
But who was glad now? Who, as trow° ye,
But Troylus, that stod and myght it se
Thorughout° a lytel wyndowe in a stuwe°,
Ther° he byshet syn° mydnyght was in mewe°,

Unwist of° every wight but of Pandare.
But to the poynt. Now whanne she was ycome,
With alle joye and alle frendes fare°,
Hire em anoon in armes hath hire nome°,
And after to the souper alle and some°,
Whan tyme was, ful softe° they hem sette.
God wot, ther was no deynte° for to fette°.

And after souper gonnen they to ryse,
At ese wel with hertes fresshe and glade,
And wel was hym that koude best devyse°
To liken° hire, or laughen that hire made.
He song, she pleyde, he tolde tales of Wade.
But at the laste, as everything hath ende,
She tok hire leve, and nedes wolde wende°.

But O Fortune, executrice of wyrdes°!
O influences° of thise hevenes hye!
Soth is that under God ye ben oure hierdes°,
Though to us bestez° ben the causes wrie°.
This mene I now for she gan homward hye°;
But execut° was al byside hire leve°
The goddes wil, for which she moste bleve°.

The bente mone° with hire hornes pale,
Saturne, and Jove in Cancro joyned were°,
That swych a rayn from heven gan avale°
That every maner womman that was there
Hadde of that smoky reyn a verray fere°,
At which Pandare tho lough° and seyde thenne,
"Now were it tyme a lady to go henne°!

"But goode nece, yf I myghte evere plese
Yow any thing, thanne prey ich yow," quod he,
"To don myn herte as now so grete an ese
As for to dwelle here al this nyght with me,
For whi° this is youre owene hous, parde°.
For, by my trouthe, I sey it for no game,
To wende° now it were to me a shame."

---

574 me were levere, *I would rather* **575 list,** *wishes* **577 yfare,** *gone* **578 As yf,** *whether,* **soth,** *the truth* **579 awayt,** *delay* **580 sith,** *since,* **bisoughte,** *asked* **582 byseche,** *request* **583 it was no fere,** *she was not afraid* **584 goosish,** *goose-like* (silly) **585 dremen,** *imagine* **586 avyse hym,** *consider* **587 moste,** *must,* **triste,** *trust* **588 liste,** *wish* **589 yis,** *yes* **589 stokkes,** *stumps* **591 were hym levere,** *he would rather,* **fel,** *skin* **599 trowe,** *think* **601 Thorughout,** *out through,* **stuwe,** *small room* **602 Ther,** *where,* **byshet syn,** *shut up since,* **mewe,** *coop* **603 Unwist of,** *unknown to* **605 frendes fare,** *friendly ceremony* **606 nome,** *taken* **607 alle and some,** *everyone* **608 softe,** *comfortably* **609 deynte,** *delicacy,* **for to fette,** *that needed to be fetched* **612 devyse,** *contrive,* **liken,** *please* **616 nedes wolde wende,** *necessarily wished to leave* **617 executrice of wyrdes,** *executor* (female) *of fates* **618 influences,** *astrological influences* **619 hierdes,** *herdsmen* **620 bestez,** *beasts,* **wrie,** *hidden* **621 hye,** *hurry* **622 execut,** *brought about,* **al byside hire leve,** *without her consent* **623 bleve,** *remain* **624 bente mone,** *crescent moon* **625 joyned were,** *were in conjunction* **626 avale,** *descend* **628 verray fere,** *genuine terror* **629 tho lough,** *then laughed* **630 henne,** *from here* **635 For whi,** *because,* **parde,** *by God* **637 wende,** *go*

575 myn auctour, see the note to 3.450. **584 goosish,** Cl reads "gosylyche." **589 swor . . . by stokkes . . . stones,** swearing by wooden and stone idols. **591 fel,** Cl and Cp read "soule." **593 Tantalus,** in classical mythology, condemned to punishment in Hell (realm of Pluto), starving and thirsty, with food and drink forever just out of reach, see 4.791n. **612 devyse,** Cl reads "avyse." **614 Wade,** a mythical hero in Germanic legend known only by allusions such as this; elsewhere cited by Chaucer in *MerT* 4.1424 with sexual overtones. **624–25 bente mone . . . ,** this rare conjunction of the new moon, Saturn, and Jupiter in the zodiacal sign of Cancer occurred in May (or perhaps June) of 1385 after a lapse of 600 years, helping us to date the composition of the poem. The conjunction was thought to portend great storms and events. **636 for no game,** Cp reads "nought a-game."

Criseyde, which that kowde as muche good°
As half a world, tok hede of his preyere,
And syn it ron° and al was on a flod,
She thoughte, "As good chep° may I dwellen here,
And graunte it gladly with a frendes chere,
And have a thank°, as grucche° and thanne
 abyde°—
For hom to gon, it may noght wel betyde°."

"I wol," quod she, "myn uncle lef° and dere.
Syn that yow lyst°, it skile° is to be so.
I am right glad with yow to dwellen here.
I seyde but a-game° I wolde go."
"Iwys, graunt mercy°, nece," quod he tho,
"Were it a-game or no, soth for to telle,
Now am I glad syn that yow lyst to dwelle."

Thus al is wel. But tho bygan aright°
The newe joye and al the feste agayn.
But Pandarus, yf goodly hadde he myght°,
He wolde han hyed° hire to bedde fayn°,
And seyde, "Lord, this is an huge rayn!
This were a weder for to slepen inne,
And that I rede° us soone to bygynne.

"And, nece, wot ye wher° I wol yow leye°,
For° that we shul nat lyggen fer asonder,
And for ye neither shullen, dar I seye,
Heren noyse of reynes nor of thonder?
By God, right in my litel closet yonder.
And I wole in that outer hous° allone
Be wardeyn° of youre wommen everychone.

"And in this myddel chaumbre that ye se
Shul youre wommen slepen wel and softe.
And there° I seyde shal youreselven be—
And yf ye liggen wel tonyght, com ofte°,
And careth not what weder is on lofte°.
The wyn anon°, and whan so that yow leste°,
So go we slepe; I trowe° it be the beste."

Ther nys no more, but hereafter soone,
The voyde° dronke and travers° drawe anoon,
Gan° every wight that hadde nought to done°
More in the place out of the chaumber gon°.
And evermo so sternelyche° it ron°,
And blew therwith so wondirliche° loude,
That wel neigh no man heren other koude.

Tho° Pandarus, hire em, right as hym oughte,
With women swyche as were hire most aboute°,
Ful glad unto hire beddes syde hire broughte,
And tok his leve, and gan ful lowe lowte°,
And seyde, "Here at this closet dore withoute,
Right overthwart°, youre wommen liggen alle,
That whom yow lyst of hem°, ye may hire calle."

So whan that she was yn the closet leyd,
And alle hire wommen forth by ordenaunce°
Abedde weren, ther as I have seyd,
There was nomore to skippen nor to traunce°,
But boden° go to bedde with myschaunce°,
If ony wight was steryng° onywhere,
And lat hem slepen that abedde were.

But Pandarus, that wel koude° eche a del°
The olde daunce and every poynt therinne,
Whan that he sey° that alle thyng was wel,
He thought he wolde upon his werk bygynne,
And gan the stewe° doore al softe unpynne°,
And stille as ston, withouten lenger lette°,
By Troylus adown right he hym sette.

And shortly to the poynt ryght for to gon,
Of alle this werk he told hym word and ende°,
And seyde, "Make the redy right anoon,

---

638 kowde as muche good, *was as practical* **640 ron,** *rained* **641 good chep,** *profitably* **643 a thank,** *thanks,* **grucche,** *complain,* **abyde,** *remain* **644 betyde,** *happen* **645 lef,** *beloved* **646 lyst,** *wish,* **skile,** *reasonable* **648 a-game,** *in play* **649 graunt mercy,** *thank you* **652 aright,** *immediately* **654 yf goodly hadde he might,** *if he had been able to gracefully* **655 hyed,** *hurried,* **fayn,** *happily* **658 rede,** *advise* **659 wot ye wher,** *do you know where,* **leye,** *put* **660 For,** *so,* **lyggen,** *sleep* **664 hous,** *room* **665 wardeyn,** *guardian* **668 there,** *where* **669 ofte,** *often* **670 weder is on lofte,** *weather is in the sky* **671 wyn anon,** *wine soon,* **leste,** *wish* **672 trowe,** *think* **674 voyde,** *final drink* **674 travers,** *partition* **675 Gan,** *did,* **done,** *do* **676 gon,** *goes* **677 sternelyche,** *violently,* **ron,** *rained* **678 wondirliche,** *amazingly* **680 Tho,** *then* **681 hire most aboute,** *closest to her* **683 lowte,** *bow* **684 Right overthwart,** *directly across* **686 whom yow lyst of hem,** *which of them you want* **688 forth by ordenaunce,** *outside as arranged* **690 traunce,** *tramp about* **691 boden,** *ordered,* **with myschaunce,** *with ill wishes* **692 steryng,** *stirring* **694 koude,** *understood,* **eche a del,** *every part* **696 sey,** *saw* **698 stewe,** *small room,* **unpynne,** *unfasten* **699 lette,** *delay* **702 word and ende,** *start to finish*

663 litel closet . . . , the arrangement here seems to be that of a small private room (Criseyde's) at the end of the long dining hall. The hall itself was divided by a curtain or partition (**travers** 674) into a middle chamber (for Criseyde's women 666) and an outer room (for Pandarus 664). The location of Troylus's hiding place (601) is not clear. **664 outer,** Cl reads "other." **690 skippen,** Cl reads "speken." **695 olde daunce,** i.e., the game of love and courtship; Chaucer also uses the phrase in *GP* 1.476 and *PhyT* 6.79

For thow shalt into hevene blysse wende°."
"Now blisful Venus, thow me grace sende,"
Quod Troylus, "for nevere yet no nede
Hadde ich er now, ne halvendel° the drede."

Quod Pandarus, "Ne drede the nevere a del°,
For it shal ben right as thow wylt desire.
So thrive I°, this nyght shal I make it wel,
Or casten al the gruwel° in the fyre."
"Yit, blisful Venus, this nyght thow me enspire°,"
Quod Troylus, "As wys° as I the serve,
And evere bet and bet shal til I sterve°.

"And yf ich hadde, O Venus ful of myrthe°,
Aspectes° badde of Mars or of Saturne,
Or thow combest° or let° were in my byrthe,
Thy fader prey° al thilke° harm disturne°
Of grace°, and that I glad ayen may turne°,
For love of hym thow lovedest yn the
shawe°—
I mene° Adoon, that with the bor was slawe°.

"Jove ek, for the love of faire Europe,
The whiche in forme of bole° awey thow fette°,
Now help! O Mars, thow with thi blody cope°,
For love of Cipris, thow me noght ne lette°!
O Phebus, thenk whan Dane hireselven shette°
Under the bark, and laurer wax° for drede°,
Yet for hire love, O help now at this nede!

"Mercurie, for the love of Hierse ek,
For which Pallas was with Aglawros wroth°,
Now help! And ek Diane, I the bysek°
That this viage° be not to the loth°.
O fatal sustren°, which er ony cloth°
Me shapen was°, my destene me sponne°,
So helpeth to this werk that is bygonne."

Quod Pandarus, "Thow wrecched mouses herte,
Artow agast so° that she wol the byte?
Why, don° this furred cloke above° thi sherte,
And folwe me, for I wol have the wyte°.
But byde°, and lat me go byforn a lyte."
And with that word he gan undon a trappe°,
And Troylus he brought in by the lappe°.

The sterne° wynd so lowde gan to route°
That no wight other noyse myghte here,
And they that layen at the dore withoute,
Ful sikerly° they slepten al yfere°.
And Pandarus, with a ful sobre chere,
Goth to the dore anoon withowten lette°,
There as they laye, and softely it shette°.

And as he come ayeynward prevely°,
His nece awook and axed, "Who goth there?"
"My dere nece," quod he, "it am I.
Ne wondreth not, ne have of it no fere."
And ner he com and seyde hire yn hire ere,
"No word, for love of God, I yow byseche°!
Lat no wight rysen and heren of oure speche."

"What? Which wey be ye comen, bendiste°?"
Quod she. "And how thus unwyst° of hem alle?"

704 wende, *go* **707 halvendel,** *half* **708 nevere a del,** *not a bit* **710 So thrive I,** *as I may prosper* **711 casten al the gruwel,** *throw all the porridge* **712 thow me enspire,** (may) *you inspire me* **713 wys,** *surely* **714 sterve,** *die* **715 myrthe,** *pleasure* **716 Apectes,** *positions* **717 combest,** *too hot,* **let,** *hindered* **718 Thy fader prey,** *ask your father,* **thilke,** *this,* **disturne,** *to deflect* **719 Of grace,** *in graciousness,* **turne,** *become* **720 shawe,** *forest* **721 mene,** *mean,* **slawe,** *slain* **723 bole,** *bull,* **fette,** *fetched* **724 blody cope,** *blood-stained cloak* **725 me noght ne lette,** *do not hinder me at all* **726 shette,** *was trapped* **727 laurer wax,** *became a laurel tree,* **for drede,** *out of fear* **730 wroth,** *angry* **731 bysek,** *pray* **732 viage,** *undertaking,* **to the loth,** *hateful to you* **733 sustren,** *sisters* (the three Fates), **which er ony cloth,** *who before any cloth* **734 Me shapen was,** *was cut for me* **734 my destene me sponne,** *spun me my destiny* **737 Artow agast so,** *Are you so afraid* **738 don,** *put on,* **above,** *over* **739 have the wyte,** *take the blame* **740 byde,** *wait* **741 trappe,** *trap door* **742 lappe,** *hanging garment* **743 sterne,** *violent,* **route,** *roar* **746 sikerly,** *soundly,* **yfere,** *together* **748 lette,** *delay* **749 shette,** *shut* **750 come ayenward prevely,** *returned secretively* **755 byseche,** *ask* **757 bendiste,** *bless us* **758 unwyst,** *unknown*

711 Proverbial, meaning "ruin everything." **715–19** Troylus prays that Venus will intercede for him with her father, hoping that Jupiter will deflect any negative influences in Troylus's horoscope that may result either from the positioning of Mars or Saturn or from the possibility that Venus's own positive influence may have been counteracted because she was too close to the heat of the sun or otherwise hindered at his birth. **717 combest,** Cp reads "combust." **721 Adoon,** Adonis, beloved of Venus, was killed by a boar. **722–23 Jove . . . Europe . . . ,** Jupiter carried off Europa after he had assumed the shape of a bull; Ovid *Metamorphoses* 2.847–75. Troylus invokes aid from the planets sequentially, from the outermost inward (omitting malevolent Saturn and sympathetic Venus); then he invokes the three Fates. **724–25 Mars . . . Cipris . . . ,** Mars loved Venus, known as Cypris because she was born from the sea near the isle of Cyprus. **726–27 Phebus . . . Dane . . . ,** Phoebus Apollo, god of the sun, pursued the nymph Daphne, who to escape him was transformed into a laurel tree; Ovid, *Metamorphoses* 1.452–567. **729–30 Mercurie . . . Hierse . . . Pallas . . . Aglawros . . . ,** Mercury loved Hierse, whose sister, Aglauros, was made envious of the love by Pallas Athena; when Aglauros tried to thwart the love, Mercury turned her to stone; Ovid, *Metamorphoses* 2.708–832. **731 Diane,** the moon and goddess of chastity. **733–34** The Fates spin the destiny of a newborn before any cloth is cut for its clothing. **738 don,** Cl reads "do on." **741** The trapdoor apparently connects Troylus's hiding place with Criseyde's bedroom, perhaps through a cellar. **757 bendiste,** Cl reads "benedicite." **758 thus,** omitted in Cl and Cp. **hem,** Cl reads "us."

"Here at this secre trappe dore," quod he.
Quod tho Criseyde, "Lat me som wight° calle."
"I°, God forbede that it sholde falle°,"
Quod Pandarus, "that ye swych folye wroughte°—
They myghte demen thyng° they nevere er thoughte.

"It is nought good a slepyng hound to wake,
Ne yeve° a wyght a cause to devyne°.
Youre wommen slepen alle, I undertake°,
So that for hem° the hous men myghte myne°,
And slepen wolen° til the sonne shyne.
And whan my tale al brought is to an ende,
Unwist°, right° as I com, so wol I wende°.

"Now, nece myn, ye shul wel understonde,"
Quod he, "so as ye wommen demen° alle,
That for to holde in love a man in honde°,
And hym hire lef° and dere herte calle,
And maken hym an howve° above a calle°—
I mene, as love another in this while°—
She doth hireself a shame and hym a gyle°.

"Now, wherby° that I telle yow al this:
Ye wot yourself as wel as ony wyght
How that youre love al fully graunted is
To Troylus, the worthieste kynght
On° of this world, and therto° trouthe yplight°,
That but° it were on hym along°, ye nolde
Hym nevere falsen° while ye lyven sholde.

"Now stant° it thus, that sith° I fro yow wente,
This Troylus, right platly° for to seyn,
Is thurgh a goter° by a prevy wente°
Into my chaumbre come in al this reyn,
Unwyst of every manere wyght, certeyn,
Save of° myself, as wysly° have I joye,
And by that feith I shal° Pryam of Troye.

"And he is come in swich peyne and distressed
That but he be° al fully wod by this°,
He sodeynly mot° falle into wodnesse°,
But yf God helpe—and cause whi is this°.
He seyth hym told is of° a frend of his
How that ye loven sholde° on hatte° Horaste,
For sorwe of which this nyght shal ben his laste."

Criseyde, which that al this wonder herde,
Gan sodeynly aboute hire herte colde°,
And with a syk° she sorwfully answerde,
"Allas, I wende° whoso° tales tolde,
My dere herte wolde me not holde
So lyghtly° fals! Allas, conseytes wronge°,
What harm they don, for now lyve I to longe!

"Horaste, allas, and falsen° Troylus?
I knowe hym not, God helpe me so," quod she.
"Allas, what wykked spirit tolde hym thus?
Now certes°, em, tomorwe and° I hym se,
I shal therof as fully excusen me°
As evere dide womman, yf hym lyke°."
And with that word she gan ful sore syke.

"O God," quod she, "so worldly selynesse°,
Which clerkes° callen fals felicite,
Ymedled° is with many a bitternesse.
Ful angwysshous than° is, God wot," quod she,
"Condicioun° of veyn° prosperite.

760 wight, *person* **761 I,** *ah!,* **falle,** *happen* **762 swych folye wroughte,** *did such folly* **763 demen thyng,** *think something* **765 yeve,** *give,* **devyne,** *suspect* **766 undertake,** *declare* **767 for hem,** *as far as they are concerned,* **myne,** *dig under* **768 slepen wolen,** *they will sleep* **770 Unwist,** *undetected,* **right,** *just,* **wende,** *go* **772 demen,** *think* **773 holde in love a man in honde,** *mislead a man in love* **774 lef,** *beloved* **775 howve,** *hood,* **calle,** *cap* **776 in this while,** *at the same time* **777 doth . . . a gyle,** *deceives* **778 wherby,** *the reason* **781–82 worthieste kyght / On,** *the most honorable* **782 therto,** *also,* **trouthe yplight,** *you pledged loyalty* **783 but,** *unless,* **on hym along,** *by his fault* **784 falsen,** *be unfaithful* **785 stant,** *stands,* **sith,** *since* **786 platly,** *plainly* **787 goter,** *gutter,* **prevy wente,** *secret passage* **790 Save of,** *except for,* **wysly,** *surely* **791 shal,** *owe* **793 but he be,** *unless he is,* **al fully wod by this,** *completely mad by this time* **794 mot,** *may,* **wodnesse,** *madness* **795 cause whi is this,** *the reason for this* **796 of,** *by* **797 loven sholde,** *are said to love,* **on hatte,** *someone called* **800 Gan . . . colde,** *grew cold* **801 syk,** *sigh* **802 wende,** *thought* (that), **whoso,** *whoever* **804 lyghtly,** *easily,* **conseytes wronge,** *misconceptions* **806 falsen,** *betray* **809 certes,** *certainly,* **and,** *if* **810 excusen me,** *clear myself of accusation* **811 hym lyke,** *it pleases him* **813 selynesse,** *happiness* **814 clerkes,** *scholars* **815 Ymedled,** *mingled* **816 Ful angwysshous than,** *very painful then* **817 Condicioun,** *the state,* **veyn,** *empty*

764 Proverbial: "Let sleeping dogs lie." **775** To make a hood above a cap means to deceive or hoodwink. **776 while,** Cl and Cp read "mene while." **797 Horaste,** a character added by Chaucer, perhaps influenced by *Pamphilus de Amore* where a go-between invents a tale of jealous rivalry; see the note to 3.560. This cause of Troylus's anxiety and his trip through the gutter at 787 are, of course, Pandarus's fabrications. **on hatte,** Cl and Cp read "on that hatte." **799 this wonder,** Cl reads "these thynges." **809 tomorwe and,** Cl reads "to more if." **811 hym,** Cl reads "he." **814 fals felicite,** false joy, the Boethian concept that happiness based on impermanent worldly pleasures is not happiness at all. Much of Criseyde's speech (3.813–33) echoes *Bo* 2.pr4, where Philosophy explains that worldly happiness is not true happiness.

For either joyes comen nought yfere°,
Or elles no wight hath hem alwey° here.

"O brotel wele° of mannes joye unstable,
With what wyght so thow be, or how thow pleye,
Either he wot° that thow, joye, art muable°,
Or wot it not; it mot° ben on of tweye.
Now yf he wot it not, how may he seye°
That he hath verray° joye and selynesse°,
That is of ignoraunce ay° in derknesse?

"Now yf he wot that joye is transitorie,
As every joye of worldly thyng mot fle°,
Than every tyme he that hath in memorie,
The drede of lesyng° maketh hym that he
May in no parfit° selynesse be.
And yf to lese his joye he set a myte°,
Than semeth it that joye is worth but lyte.

"Wherfore I wol deffyne° in this matere,
That trewely, for ought I kan espie,
Ther is no verray wele° in this world here.
But O thow wykked serpent jalousye,
Thow mysbeleveed° and envyous folye,
Whi hastow mad° Troylus to me untriste°,
That nevere yet agylt° hym that I wyste°?"

Quod Pandarus, "Thus fallen is° this cas—"
"Whi, uncle myn," quod she, "who tolde hym this?
Whi doth my dere herte thus, allas?"
"Ye wot, ye°, nece myn," quod he, "what is.
I hope al shal be wel that is amys.
For ye may quenche° al this yf that yow leste.
And doth right so, for I holde it the beste."

"So shal I do tomorwe, ywys°," quod she,
"And God toforn°, so that° it shal suffise."
"Tomorwe? Allas, that were a fayr°!" quod he.
"Nay, nay, it may nat stonden° yn this wyse.
For, nece myn, thus writen clerkes wyse,
That peril° is with drecchyng° in idrawe°.
Nay, swyche abodes° be nought worth an hawe°.

"Nece, alle thing hath tyme, I dar avowe°;
For whan a chaumbre afyre is°, or an halle,
More nede is it sodeynly to rescowe°
Than to dispute and axe° amonges alle
How this candele in the straw is falle.
A, bendiste°, for al among that fare°
The harm is don, and farewel feldefare°.

"And nece myn—ne take it not agref°—
If that ye suffre hym al nyght in this wo,
God help me so, ye hadde hym nevere lef°—
That dar I seyn, now there is but we two.
But wel I wot that ye wol nat do so;
Ye ben to wys to do so gret folye,
To putte his lyf al nyght in jupartie°."

"Hadde I hym nevere lef? By God, I wene°
Ye hadde nevere thing so lief°!" quod she.
"Now by my thryft°," quod he, "that shal be sene,
For syn° ye make this ensaumple° of me,
If ich al nyght wolde hym in sorwe se,
For al the tresour yn the town of Troye
I bidde° God I nevere mote° have joye.

"Now loke thanne°, if ye that ben his love
Shul putte al nyght his lyf in jupartie
For thing of nought, now by that God above,
Naught only this delay cometh of folye,
But of malis°, if that I shal nought lye.
What, platly°, and ye suffre hym° in distresse,
Ye neyther bounte don° ne gentilesse°."

---

818 yfere, *together* **819 alwey,** *continuously* **820 brotel wele,** *brittle pleasure* **822 wot,** *knows,* **muable,** *variable* **823 mot,** *must* **824 seye,** *say* **825 verray,** *true,* **selynesse,** *happiness* **826 ay,** *always* **828 mot fle,** *must fly* **830 lesyng,** *losing* **831 parfit,** *perfect* **832 set a myte,** *cares a bit* **834 deffyne,** *conclude* **836 verray wele,** *true joy* **838 mysbeleved,** *misbelieving* **839 hastow mad,** *have you made,* **untriste,** *distrustful* **840 agylt,** *wronged,* **wyste,** *knew about* **841 Thus fallen is this cas,** *that is what has happened* **844 Ye wot, ye,** *you know indeed* **846 quenche,** *extinguish* **848 ywys,** *surely* **849 God toforn,** *before God,* **so that,** *in such a way that* **850 were a fayr,** *would be a fine thing* **851 stonden,** *remain* **853 peril,** *danger,* **with drecchyng,** *by delay,* **in idrawe,** *brought in* **854 swyche abodes,** *such delays,* **hawe,** *hawthorn berry* (worthless) **855 avowe,** *vow* **856 afyre is,** *is on fire* **857 rescowe,** *rescue* **858 axe,** *inquire* **860 bendiste,** *bless us,* **fare,** *business* **861 farewel feldefare,** *good-by thrush* **862 agref,** *wrongly* **864 hadde hym nevere lef,** *had never loved him* **868 jupartie,** *jeopardy* **869 wene,** *think* **870 lief,** *beloved* **871 thryft,** *prosperity* **872 syn,** *since,* **ensaumple,** *comparison* **875 bidde,** *pray,* **mote,** *might* **876 loke thanne,** *recognize then* **880 malis,** *ill will* **881 platly,** *obviously,* **and ye suffer hym,** *if you allow him* (to go on) **882 bounte don,** *act generously,* **gentilesse,** *nobly*

818 either, Cl reads "other." **823 Or wot,** Cl reads "Other he wot." **829 that,** omitted in Cl. **842 hym,** Cl reads "yow." **853** Proverbial. **855 alle thing hath tyme,** proverbial; from Ecclesiastes 3.1. **857 More,** Cp reads "Wel more. **to,** omitted in Cp. **859 this,** Cp reads "the." **861 farewel feldefare,** "The bird has flown; it's all over." **869 Hadde I,** Cl reads "Hadde ye." **870 Ye,** Cl reads "I."

Quod tho Criseyde, "Wole ye don o thing,
And ye therwith° shal stynte° al his disese°?
Have here, and bereth° hym this blewe ryng,
For there is nothing myghte hym bettre plese,
Save° I myself, ne more his herte apese°.
And sey° my dere herte that his sorwe
Is causeles, that shal ben sene tomorwe."

"A ryng?" quod he. "Ye°, haselwodes shaken°!
Ye, nece myn, that ryng moste han° a ston°
That myhte a dede man alyve maken,
And swych a ryng I trowe° that ye have non.
Discrecioun out of youre hed is gon—
That fele I now," quod he, "and that is routhe°
O tyme ylost, wel maystow coursen slouthe°!

"Wot ye not wel that noble and heigh corage
Ne sorweth not—ne stenteth° ek—for lyte?
But yf a fol were in a jalous rage,
I nolde not sette at his sorwe a myte°,
But feffe° hym with a fewe wordes white°
Another day, whan that I myghte hym fynde—
But this thing stont° al in another kynde.

"This is so gentil and so tendre of herte
That with his deth he wole his sorwes wreke°.
For trusteth wel, how sore° that hym smerte°,
He wol to yow no jalous wordes speke.
And forthi°, nece, er that his herte breke,
So speke youreself to him of this matere,
For with o word ye may his herte stere.

"Now have I told what peril he is inne,
And his comyng unwyst° is to every wyght.
Ne, parde°, harm may ther be non, ne synne;
I wol myself be with yow al this nyght.
Ye knowe ek how it is youre owen knyght,
And that by right ye moste upon hym triste°,
And I al prest° to fecche hym whan yow liste°."

This accident° so petous° was to here,
And ek so lyke a soth at pryme face°,
And Troylus hire knyght to hire so dere,
His preve° comyng, and the siker° place,
That, though that she dide hym as thanne° a gracee°,
Considered alle thinges as they stode,
No wonder is, syn she dide al for gode.

Cryseyde answerde, "As wysly° God at° reste
My sowle brynge, as me is for hym wo°!
And, em, ywys, fayn° wolde I do the beste,
Yf that I hadde a grace° to do so.
But whether that ye dwelle or for hym go,
I am, til God me bettre mynde sende,
At dulcarnon°, right at my wittes ende."

Quod Pandarus, "Ye, nece, wol ye here?
Dulcarnon called is 'flemyng° of wrecches°'—
It semeth hard, for wrecches nel hit lere°
For verray slouthe° or other wilful tacches°;
This seyd by° hem that ben not worth two facches°.
But ye ben wys, and that° we han on honde
Nis neither hard ne skylful to withstonde."

"Thanne, em," quod she, "doth herof° as yow lyst.
But er he come I wil up first aryse,
And, for the love of God, syn al my trist°
Is on yow two, and ye ben bothe wyse,
So wyrcheth° now in so discret a wyse
That I honour may have, and he plesaunce°;
For I am here al yn youre governaunce°."

---

884 therewith, *with this,* **stynte,** *stop,* **disese,** *misery* **885 bereth hym,** *take to him* **887 Save,** *except* **887 apese,** *calm* **888 sey,** *tell* **890 Ye,** *sure!,* **haselwodes shaken,** *nuts to that!* **891 moste han,** *must have,* **ston,** (magic) *stone* **893 trowe,** *think* **895 routhe,** *a pity* **896 coursen slouthe,** *curse inaction* **898 stenteth,** *ceases* **900 sette at his sorwe a myte,** *value his sorrow a bit* **901 feffe,** *present* **901 white,** *empty* **903 this thing stont,** *this kind of passion stands* **905 wreke,** *repay* **906 how sore,** *however sorely,* **hym smerte,** *it pains him* **908 forthi,** *therefore* **910 stere,** *guide* **912 unwyst,** *unknown* **913 parde,** *by God* **916 triste,** *trust* **917 prest,** *ready,* **liste,** *wish* **918 accident,** *incident,* **petous,** *pitiable* **919 pryme face,** *first sight* **921 preve,** *secret,* **siker,** *secure* **922 as thanne,** *at that time,* **grace,** *favor* **925 wysly,** *surely,* **at,** *to* **926 me is . . . wo,** *I am sorry* **927 fayn,** *happily* **928 grace,** *opportunity* **931 At dulcarnon,** *without a solution* **933 flemyng,** *banishment,* **wrecches,** *bad students* **934 nel hit lere,** *will not learn it* **935 verray slouthe,** *genuine laziness,* **tacches,** *vices* **936 by,** *about,* **facches,** *beans* **937 that,** *what* **939 herof,** *concerning this* **941 trist,** *trust* **943 wyrcheth,** *act* **944 plesaunce,** *relief* (pleasure) **945 governaunce,** *control*

887 more, Cl reads "bettre." **890** The figure of shaking a hazelwood or hazelnut tree seems to indicate derision or disbelief, at least when Pandarus uses it; see 5.505, 1174. **931 Dulcarnon,** a dilemma; derives from Arabic "Dhu 'l Karnayn" (the two-horned), used to label a drawing that accompanied the 47th proposition in Euclid's geometry, the standard textbook in the field. **933 flemyng of wrecches,** banishment of wretches translates "fuga miserorum," the title of Euclid's 5th proposition, which is here confused with the 47th. **934 nel hit,** Cl and Cp read "wol noughtt."

"That is wel seyd," quod he, "my nece deere.
Ther good thryft on° that wyse gentil herte.
But liggeth° stille, and taketh° hym ryght here.
It nedeth not no ferther for hym sterte°.
And eche of yow ese otheres sorwes smerte,
For love of God. And Venus, I the herye°,
For soone, hope I, we shul ben alle merye."

This Troylus ful sone on knes hym sette°,
Ful sobrely°, ryght be hire beddes hed,
And yn his beste wyse his lady grette°.
But Lord, so she wax sodeynlyche red!
Ne though° men sholden smyten of° hire hed,
She kowde nought a word aryght out-brynge°
So sodeynly, for his sodeyn comynge.

But Pandarus, that so wel koude fele°
In everythyng, to pleye anoon bygan,
And seyde, "Nece, se how this lord kan knele!
Now, for youre trouthe, seth° this gentil man!"
And with that word he for a quysshon° ran,
And seyde, "Kneleth now, while that yow leste°,
There God youre hertes brynge soone at reste."

Kan I not seyn, for she bad hym not ryse,
If sorwe it put out of hire remembraunce,
Or elles if she tok it in the wyse°
Of deuete°, as for his observaunce°;
But wel fynde I she dide hym this pleasaunce,
That she hym kyste, although she siked° sore,
And bad° hym sytte adown withowten more.

Quod Pandarus, "Now wol ye wel bygynne.
Now doth hym sitte, gode nece dere,
Upon youre beddes side al there withinne,
That eche of yow the bet may other here."
And with that word he drow hym° to the fyre,
And tok a lyght, and fond his contenaunce°
As for to loke upon° an old romaunce.

Criseyde, that was Troylus lady right,
And cler° stod on a ground of sykernesse°,
Al° thoughte she hire servaunt and hire knyght
Ne sholde of right° noon untrouthe in hire gesse°,
Yet natheles, considered his distresse,
And that love is in cause of° swych folye,
Thus to hym spak she of his jelousye:

"Lo, herte myn, as wolde° the excellence
Of love ayeyns the which that° no man may—
Ne oughte ek—goudly° make resistence,
And ek bycause I felte wel and say°
Youre grete trouthe and servyse every day,
And that yowre herte al myn was, soth to seyne,
This drof° me first to rewe° upon yowre peyne.

"And youre goodnesse have I founde alwey yit,
Of° which, my dere herte and al my° knyght,
I thonke it yow as fer as° I have wit,
Al° kan I nought as muche as it were right;
And I emforth° my konnyng° and my myght
Have and ay shal, how° sore that me smerte,
Ben to yow trewe and hol° with al myn herte;

"And dredles° that shal be founde at preve°.
But, herte myn, what al this is to seyne°
Shal wel be told, so that ye yow not greve°,
Though I to yow right on° youreself compleyne.
For therwith° mene I fynally the peyne
That halt° youre herte and myn in hevynesse°
Fully to slen°, and every wrong redresse°.

"My goode myn°, not I for-whi° ne how
That jalousye, allas, that wikkede wyvere°,
Thus causeles is cropen° into yow,
The harm of which I wolde fayn delyvere°.
Allas, that he°, al hool or of hym slyvere°,
Shuld have his refuyt° in so digne° a place,
Ther° Jove soone out of youre herte hym race°.

947 Ther good thryft on, *may good come to* **948 liggeth,** *lie,* **taketh,** *receive* **949 sterte,** *go* **951 the herye,** *praise you* **953 on knes hym sette,** *knelt* **954 sobrely,** *solemnly* **955 grette,** *greeted* **957 Ne though,** *even though,* **of,** *off* **958 aryght out-brynge,** *properly speak* **960 fele,** *perceive* **963 seth,** *see* **964 quysshon,** *cushion* **965 leste,** *wish* **969 in the wyse,** *as a matter* **970 deuete,** *proper duty,* **observaunce,** *attentions* **972 syked,** *sighed* **973 bad,** *asked* **978 drow hym,** *withdrew himself* **979 fond his contenaunce,** *arranged himself* **980 loke upon,** *read* **982 cler,** *pure,* **sykernesse,** *certainty* **983 Al,** *although* **984 of right,** *rightfully,* **gesse,** *infer* **986 in cause of,** *the cause of* **988 wolde,** *wished* **989 ayeyns the which that,** *against which* **990 goudly,** *rightly* **991 say,** *saw* **994 drof,** *compelled,* **rewe,** *have pity* **996 Of,** *for,* **al my,** *my own* **997 as fer as,** *to the extent that* **998 Al,** *although* **999 emforth,** *to the extent of,* **konnyng,** *understanding* **1000 how,** *however* **1001 hol,** *complete* **1002 dredles,** *doubtless,* **at preve,** *when tested* **1003 seyne,** *say* **1004 so that ye yow not greve,** *as long as you don't upset yourself* **1005 right on,** *specifically about* **1006 therwith,** *thereby* **1007 halt,** *holds,* **hevynesse,** *grief* **1008 slen,** *destroy,* **redresse,** *correct* **1009 My goode myn,** *my own dear one,* **not I forwhi,** *I don't know why* **1010 wyvere,** *snake* **1011 is cropen,** *has crept* **1012 fayn delyvere,** *happily release* (you) **1013 he,** *it,* **slyvere,** *small portion* **1014 refuyt,** *refuge,* **digne,** *noble* **1015 Ther,** *where,* **race,** *uproot*

976 withinne, within the curtains that surround a four-poster bed. **978 fyre,** a false rhyme in Cl; Cp reads "fere." **994 first to,** Cl reads "forto." **1015 hym race,** Cp read "arace."

"But O, thow Jove, O auctor° of nature,
Is this an honour to thi deite°,
That folk ungiltyf° suffren hire injure°,
And who that gyltyf is, al quyt° goth he?
O were it leful° for to pleyn on the°
That undeserved suffrest° jalousie,
Of that I wolde upon the pleyne and crye!

"Ek al my wo is this, that folk now usen°
To seyn right thus, 'Ye°, jalousye is love!'
And wolde a busshel venym° al excusen
For that o greyn° of love is on it shove°.
But that wot heighe God that sit° above,
If it be likere° love or hate or grame°;
And after that° it oughte bere his° name.

"But certeyn is, som manere jalousye
Is excusable more than som, iwys,
As whanne cause is°; and som swych fantasye°
With pite so wel repressed is
That it unnethe° doth or seyth amys°,
But goodly° rynketh up al his distresse.
And that excuse I for° the gentilesse°.

"And som so ful of furye is and despit°
That it sourmounteth his° repressioun.
But, herte myn, ye be not in that plyt°,
That thanke I God, for which yowre passioun
I wol not calle it but illusioun
Of habundaunce of love and bysy cure°,
That doth° youre herte this disese endure,

"Of which I am right sory, but not wroth.
But for my devoir° and youre hertes reste,
Wherso yow lyste°, by ordal° or by oth°,
By sort° or in what wyse so yow leste,
For love of God, lat preve it° for the beste,
And yf that I be gyltyf, do me° deye!
Allas, what myght I more do or seye?"

With that a fewe brighte terys newe
Owt of hire eyen fille, and thus she seyde,
"Now God, thow wost°, in thought ne dede untrewe
To Troylus was nevere yet Criseyde."
With that hire hed into the bed down she leyde,
And with the shete it wreygh°, and sighed sore,
And held hire pes°; not o word spak she more.

But now help God to quenchen° al this sorwe—
So hope I that he shal, for he best may.
For I have seyn of a ful mysty morwe°
Folwen ful ofte a merye someres day;
And after wynter foloweth grene May;
Men sen alday°, and reden ek in storyes,
That after sharpe shoures° ben victories.

This Troylus, whan he hire wordes herde,
Have ye no care°, hym lyste° not to slepe,
For it thought hym° no strokes of a yerde°
To here or sen Criseyde his lady wepe.
But wel he felte aboute his herte crepe,
For every teere which that Criseyde asterte°,
The crampe of deth to streyne° hym by the herte.

And in his mynde he gan the tyme acorse°
That he cam there, and that he was born,
For now is wykke° iturned unto worse,
And al the labour he hath don byforn,
He wend° it lost; he thoughte he nas but lorn°.
"O Pandarus," thoughte he, "allas, thi wyle°
Serveth of° nought, so welaway° the while."

And therwithal he heng adown the hed,
And fil on knes, and sorwfully he sighte°.
What myghte he seyn? He felte he nas but ded,
For wroth was she that shulde his sorwes lyghte°.
But natheles, whenne that he speken myghte,
Than seyde he thus, "God wot that of this game,
Whan al is wyst°, than am I not to blame."

1016 auctor, *creator* **1017 deite,** *diety* **1018 ungiltyf,** *unguilty,* **injure,** *injury* **1019 al quyt,** *completely free* **1020 leful,** *lawful,* **pleyn on the,** *to accuse you* **1021 That undeserved suffrest jalousie,** *who permits undeserved jealousy* **1023 usen,** *are accustomed* **1024 Ye,** *yes!* **1025 busshel venym,** *bushel of venom* **1025 For that o greyn,** *because a single grain,* **shove,** *thrust* **1027 sit,** *sits* **1028 likere,** *more like,* **grame,** *anger* **1029 after that,** *accordingly,* **his,** *its* **1032 cause is,** *when there is cause* **1032 fantasye,** *imaginings* **1034 unnethe,** *hardly,* **seyth amys,** *says wrong* **1035 goodly,** *happily* **1036 that excuse I,** *that I excuse you because of,* **gentilesse,** *nobility* **1037 despit,** *scorn* **1038 sourmounteth his,** *overwhelms its* **1039 plyt,** *wretched condition* **1042 bysy cure,** *anxious care* **1043 doth,** *makes* **1045 my devoir,** *the duty due me* **1046 Wherso yow lyste,** *wherever you wish,* **ordal,** *ordeal,* **oth,** *oath* **1045 sort,** *drawing lots* **1048 lat preve it,** *let it be tested* **1049 do me,** *make me* **1053 wost,** *know* **1056 wreygh,** *covered* **1057 pes,** *peace* **1058 quenchen,** *extinguish* **1060 ful mysty morwe,** *very misty morning* **1063 sen alday,** *see always* **1064 shoures,** *battles* **1066 care,** *worry,* **hym lyste,** *he wished* **1067 it thought hym,** *he thought it,* **yerde,** *stick* **1070 asterte,** *escaped from* **1071 streyne,** *squeeze* **1072 acorse,** *curse* **1074 wykke,** *bad* **1076 wend,** *thought,* **lorn,** *lost* **1077 thi wyle,** *your trickery* **1078 of,** *for,* **welaway,** *alas* **1079 the,** *his* **1080 sighte,** *sighed* **1082 lyghte,** *lighten* **1085 wyst,** *known*

1020 for to pleyn on, Cl reads "that I pleyn of." **1067 no strokes of a yerde,** i.e., worse than being beaten with a stick.

Therwith the sorwe so his herte shette°
That from his eyen fil there not a tere,
And every spirit his vigour yn-knette°,
So they astoned° and oppressed were.
The felyng of his sorwe, or of his fere,
Or of ought elles, fled was out of towne,
And doun he fel al sodeynly aswowne°.

This was no litel sorwe for to se—
But al was hust°, and Pandare up as faste,
"O nece, pes°, or we be lost," quod he.
"Beth nought agast°." But certeyn, at the laste,
For this or that he into bedde hym caste,
And seyde, "O thef°, is this a mannes herte?"
And of he rente al° to his bare sherte,

And seyde, "Nece, but° ye helpe us now,
Allas, youre owen Troylus is lorn°."
"Iwys°, so wolde I and I wiste° how,
Ful fayn°," quod she. "Allas that I was born!"
"Ye, nece, wole ye pullen out the thorn
That stiketh in his herte?" quod Pandare.
"Sey 'al foryeve,' and stynt° is al this fare°."

"Ye, that to me," quod she, "ful levere° were
Than al the good the sonne aboute goth°."
And therwithal° she swor hym in his ere,
"Iwis, my dere herte, I am nought wroth,
Have here my trouthe," and many another oth.
"Now speke to me, for it am I, Cryseyde!"
But al for nought; yet myght he nought abreyde°.

Therwith his pows° and pawmes° of his hondes
They gan to frote°, and wete° his temples tweyne;
And for to delyveren hym fro bittre bondes
She ofte hym kyste; and shortly for to seyne,
Hym to revoken° she dide al hire peyne.
And at the laste, he gan his breth to drawe,
And of his swough° sone after that adawe°,

And bet° gan mynde and reson to hym take.
But wonder sore° he was abayst°, iwys,
And with a syk°, whan he gan bet awake,
He seyde, "O mercy, God, what thing is this?"
"Whi do ye with yowreselven thus amys°?"
Quod tho Criseyde. "Is this a mannes game?
What, Troylus, wol ye do thus for shame?"

And therwithal hire arm over hym she leyde,
And al foryaf°, and ofte tyme hym keste.
He thonked hire, and to hire spak and seyde
As fil to purpos for° his hertes reste,
And she to that answerde hym as hire leste,
And with hire goodly wordes hym disporte°
She gan, and ofte his sorwes to comforte.

Quod Pandarus, "For ought I kan espyen,
This lyght nor I ne serven here of nought°.
Lyght is not good for syke° folkes eyen!
And for the love of God, syn ye ben brought
In thus good plit°, lat now non hevy thought
Ben hangynge in the hertes of yow tweye"—
And bar° the candele to the chimeneye.

Soone after this, though it no nede were°,
Whan she swyche othes as hire lyste devyse°
Hadde of hym take°, hire thoughte tho° no fere,
Ne cause ek non to bidde hym thennes° ryse.
Yet lesse thyng than othes may suffise
In many a cas, for every wyght, I gesse,
That loveth wel, meneth but gentilesse°.

But in effect she wolde wite° anoon
Of what man, and ek wher, and also why
He jalous was, syn there was cause non;
And ek the signe° that he tok° it by,
She bad hym that to telle hire bysily°,
Or elles, certeyn, she bar hym on honde°
That this was don of malys°, hire to fonde°.

1086 shette, *closed* **1088 his vigour yn-knette,** *its strength restrained* **1089 astoned,** *stunned* **1092 aswowne,** *in a faint* **1094 hust,** *hushed* **1095 pes,** *quiet!* **1096 agast,** *frightened* **1098 thef,** *wretch* **1099 of he rente,** *he tore off everything* **1100 but,** *unless* **1101 lorn,** *lost* **1102 Iwys,** *surely,* **and I wiste,** *if I knew* **1103 Ful fayn,** *very gladly* **1106 stynt,** *stop,* **fare,** *business* **1107 levere,** *more desirable* **1108 aboute goth,** *revolves around* **1109 therwithal,** *then* **1113 abreyde,** *awaken* **1114 pows,** *pulse,* **pawmes,** *palms* **1115 frote,** *rub,* **wete,** *dampen* **1118 revoken,** *call back* **1120 swough,** *swoon,* **adawe,** *to awaken* **1121 bet,** *better* **1122 wonder sore,** *wondrously deeply,* **abayst,** *embarrassed* **1123 syk,** *sigh* **1125 do . . . thus amys,** *act wrongly in this way* **1129 foryaf,** *forgave* **1131 fil to purpos for,** *was pertinent to* **1133 hym disporte,** *cheer him up* **1136 ne serven here of nought,** *serve no purpose here* **1137 syke,** *sick* **1139 plit,** *situation* **1141 bar,** *carried* **1142 no nede were,** *was not necessary* **1143 hire lyste devyse,** *it pleased her to devise* **1144 take,** *taken,* **tho,** *then* **1145 thennes** *from there* **1148 meneth but gentilesse,** *intends only nobleness* **1149 wolde wite,** *wanted to know* **1152 signe,** *indication,* **tok,** *suspected* **1153 bysily,** *thoroughly* **1154 bar hym on honde,** *accused him* **1155 malys,** *malice,* **fonde,** *test*

1088 spirit, medieval physiology understood there to be three kinds of vapors or spirits involved in human behavior: vital (in the heart), natural (in the liver), and animal (in the brain). Here they all cease to operate, and Troylus collapses. **1104–05 thorn / That stiketh, perhaps** the thorn of sexual desire; see the note to 2.1272. **1137** Proverbial.

Withouten more, shortly for to seyne,
He most° obeye unto his lady heste°;
And for the lasse harm, he moste feyne°.
He seyde hire whanne she was at swyche a feste°,
She myght on hym han loked at the leste°—
Noot I not what°, al dere ynow a rysshe°,
As he that nedes most° a cause fysshe°.

And she answerde, "Swete, al° were it so,
What harm was that, syn I noon yvel mene?
For by that God that bought us bothe two°,
In alle thyng is myn entente clene.
Swyche argumentz ne ben not worth a bene.
Wol ye the chyldyssh jalous contrefete°?
Now were it worthy° that ye were ybete°."

Tho° Troylus gan sorwfully to syke°—
Lest she be wroth, hym thoughte his herte
deyde—
And seyde, "Allas, upon my sorwes syke°
Have mercy, swete herte myn Cryseyde!
And yf that in tho° wordes that I seyde
Be ony wrong, I wol no more trespace.
Doth what yow lyst, I am al in youre grace°."

And she answerde, "Of gilt mysericorde°.
That is to seyn that I foryeve al this.
And evere more on this nyght yow recorde°,
And beth wel war ye do no more amys."
"Nay, dere herte myn," quod he, "iwys°."
"And now," quod she, "that I have don yow
smerte°,
Foryeve it me, myn owene swete herte."

This Troylus, with blysse of that supprised°,
Put al in Goddes hand, as he that mente°
Nothyng but wel, and sodeynly avysed°
He hire in armes faste to hym hente°.
And Pandarus with a ful good entente
Leyd hym to slepe, and seyde, "If ye ben wyse,
Swowneth° not now, lest more folk aryse°!"

What myght or may the sely° larke seye
Whan that the sperhauk° hath it in his fot°?
I kan no more, but of thise ilke tweye°,
To whom this tale sucre be or sot°,
Though that I tarye° a yer, somtyme I mot°
After myn auctour tellen hire gladnesse,
As wel as I have told hire hevynesse°.

Criseyde, which that felte hire thus itake°,
As writen clerkes in hire bokes olde,
Right as an aspes lef° she gan to quake°
Whan she hym felte hire in his armes folde.
But Troylus, al hool of° cares colde,
Gan thanken tho the blysful goddes sevene.
Thus sondry peynes° bryngen folk to hevene.

This Troylus yn armes gan hire streyne°,
And seyde, "O swete, as evere mot I gon°,
Now be ye kaught, now is ther but we tweyne.
Now yeldeth° yow, for other bote° is non."
To that Criseyde answerde thus anon,
"Ne hadde I er now, my swete herte dere,
Ben yold°, ywys, I were now not here!"

O soth is seyd,° that heled for to be°
As of a fevre or other gret syknesse,
Men moste° drynke, as men may ofte se,
Ful bittre drynke; and for to han gladnesse,
Men drynken ofte peyne and gret distresse—
I mene it here, as for this aventure,
That thorugh a peyne hath founden al his° cure.

And now swetnesse semeth more swete
That bitternesse assayed° was byforn,

1157 most, *must,* **lady heste,** *lady's command* **1158 feyne,** *pretend* **1159 swyche a fest,** *a certain party* **1160 at the leste,** *at least* **1161 Noot I not what,** *I don't know what,* **al dere ynow a rysshe,** *although costly enough at the price of a reed* (i.e., worthless) **1162 nedes most a cause fyshe,** *out of necessity must fish for a reason* **1163 al,** *even if* **1165 bought us bothe two,** *redeemed both of us* **1168 contrefete,** *imitate* **1169 worthy,** *fitting,* **ybete,** *beaten* **1170 Tho,** *then,* **syke,** *sigh* **1172 syke,** *sick* **1174 tho,** *those* **1176 am al in youre grace,** *depend wholly on your favor* **1177 mysericorde,** *mercy* **1179 recorde,** *remember* **1181 iwys,** *surely* **1182 don yow smerte,** *caused you pain* **1184 supprised,** *seized* **1185 mente,** *intends* **1186 avysed,** *decided* **1187 hente,** *hugged* **1190 Swowneth,** *swoon,* **aryse,** *get up* **1191 sely,** *innocent* **1192 sperhauk,** *sparrowhawk,* **fot,** *talons* **1193 ilke tweye,** *same two* **1194 sucre be or sot,** *is sugar or soot* (sweet or bitter) **1195 tarye,** *delay* **1196 mot,** *must* **1197 hevynesse,** *sorrow* **1198 itake,** *taken* **1200 aspes lef,** *aspen leaf,* **quake,** *tremble* **1202 al hool of,** *completely healed of* **1204 sondry peynes,** *various pains* **1205 streyne,** *hold tightly* **1206 mot I gon,** *I may live* **1208 yeldeth,** *yield,* **bote,** *remedy* **1211 yold,** *yielded* **1212 soth is seyd,** *truth is told,* **heled for to be,** *in order to be healed* **1214 moste,** *must* **1218 his,** *its* **1220 assayed,** *tested*

1165 bought, other manuscripts read "wrought," avoiding the Christian anachronism in the pagan world of Troy. **1168 jalous,** Cl reads "jalousye." **1194 sucre be or sot,** Cl reads "sour be or sot" (sour or sweet). **1203 goddes sevene,** the seven planetary gods to whom Troylus prays in 3.715–32. **1219–20** Proverbial.

For out of wo in blysse now they flete°—
Non swych they felten sith that they were born.
Now is this bet° than bothe two be lorn°.
For love of God, take every womman hede
To werken thus, yf it come to the nede.

Criseyde, al quyt° from every drede and tene°,
As she that just cause hadde hym to tryste°,
Made hym swych feste° it joye was to sene,
Whan she his trowthe and clene entente wyste;
And as abowte a tre, with many a twyste,
Bytrent and wryth° the soote wodebynde°,
Gan eche of hem in armes other wynde.

And as the newe abayssed° nyghtyngale,
That stynteth° first whan she gynneth to synge,
Whan that she hereth any herde tale°,
Or in the hegges ony wight sterynge°,
And after siker° doth hire voys out rynge,
Right so Criseyde, whan hire drede stente°,
Opened hire herte and tolde hym hire entente.

And right as he that seth° his deth yshapen°,
And deye mot°, in ought that he may gesse°,
And sodeynly rescous° doth hym escapen°
And from his deth is brought in sykernesse°,
For al this world, yn swych present gladnesse
Was Troylus, and hath his lady swete.
With worse hap° God lat us nevere mete!

Hire armes smale, hire streyghte bak and softe,
Hire sydes longe, flesshly°, smothe, and white,
He gan to stroke, and good thryft bad° ful ofte
Hire snowysshe° throte, hire brestes rounde and lyte.

Thus in this hevene he gan hym to delyte,
And therwithal a thowsand tyme hire kyste,
That what to don for joye unnethe° he wyste.

Than seyde he thus, "O Love, O Charite,
Thi moder ek, Citherea the swete,
After thiself next heried° be she—
Venus mene I, the wel-willy° planete—
And next the, Imeneus, I the grete°,
For nevere man was to yow goddes holde°
As I, which ye han brought fro cares colde.

"Benygne° Love, thow holy bond of thynges,
Whoso wol grace° and lyst the nought honouren°,
Lo, his desir wol fle° withouten wynges.
For noldestow° of bounte° hem socouren°
That serven best and most alwey labouren,
Yet were al lost, that dar I wel seyn certes°,
But yf° thi grace passeed° oure desertes.

"And for thow° me, that lest kowde deserv°
Of hem that noumbred ben unto thi grace°,
Hast holpen°, ther° I lykly was to sterve°,
And me bistowed in so heygh a place
That thilke boundes° may no blysse pace°,
I kan° namore but laude° and reverence
Be to thy bounte and thyn excellence!"

And therwithal Criseyde anoon he kyste,
Of which, certeyn, she felte no dishese°.
And thus seyde he, "Now wolde God I wyste,
Myn herte swete, how I yow myght plese.
What man," quod he, "was evere thus at ese
As I, on° which the faireste and the beste
That evere I say° deyneth° hire herte reste°?

1221 flete, *float* **1223 bet,** *better,* **lorn,** *lost* **1226 quyt,** *free,* **tene,** *grief* **1227 tryste,** *trust* **1228 Made hym swich feste,** *made him such celebration* **1231 Bytrent and wryth,** *circles and twines,* **soote wodebynde,** *sweet honeysuckle* **1233 newe abayssed,** *suddenly startled* **1234 stynteth,** *stops* **1235 herde tale,** *shepherd talk* **1236 wight sterynge,** *person stirring* **1237 after siker,** *later secure* **1238 drede stente,** *fear ceased* **1240 seth,** *sees,* **yshapen,** *destined* **1241 deye mot,** *must die,* **in ought that he may gesse,** *as far as he can tell* **1242 rescous,** *rescue,* **escapen,** *allow to escape* **1243 in sykernesse,** *into security* **1246 hap,** *luck* **1248 flesshly,** *shapely* **1249 good thryft bad,** *bid good wishes to* **1250 snowysshe,** *snow-white* **1253 unnethe,** *barely* **1256 heried,** *praised* **1257 wel-willy,** *well willing* **1258 the grete,** *salute you* **1259 holde,** *indebted* **1261 Benygne,** *gracious* **1262 Whoso wol grace,** *whoever desires favor,* **lyst the nought honouren,** *chooses now to honor you* **1263 fle,** *fly* **1264 noldestow,** *if you did not wish,* **of bounte,** *from goodness,* **socouren,** *to aid* **1266 certes,** *certainly* **1267 But yf,** *unless,* **passed,** *surpassed* **1268 for thow,** *because you,* **lest kowde deserve,** *deserves least* **1269 noumbred ben unto thi grace,** *are numbered in your favor* **1270 holpen,** *helped,* **ther,** *where,* **sterve,** *die* **1272 thilke boundes,** (beyond) *these boundaries,* **pace,** *pass* **1273 kan,** *know,* **laude,** *praise* **1276 dishese,** *pain* **1280 on,** *upon* **1281 say,** *saw,* **deyneth,** *permits,* **reste,** *to rest*

1230–31 The intertwining of tree and vine was a common figure for love. **1240 yshapen,** Cl reads "is shapen." **1248 flesshly,** Cp reads "flesshy." **1251 hevene,** omitted in Cl. **1255 Citherea,** Venus, who is the mother of the god of love, Cupid, and is named after Cythera, where she rose from the seas. **1258 Imeneus,** Hymen, god of marriage. **1261–67** This echoes St. Bernard's praise of the Virgin Mary in Dante's *Paradiso* 33.14–18, although some of the language may have been conventional. **1261 bond of thynges,** the chain of love or chain of being that unifies the universe. **1271 heygh a place,** Windeatt notes that this high point is also the precise mid-point of the poem—the 4120th line of 8239.

"Here may men se that mercy passeth° ryght;
The experience of that is felt in me,
That am unworthi to° so swete a wyght.
But herte myn°, of youre benyngnite°,
So thynketh, thowgh that I unworthi be,
Yet mot° I nede amenden° in som wyse,
Right thorugh the vertu° of yowre heygh servyse.

"And for the love of God, my lady dere,
Syn God hath wrought° me for° I shal yow serve—
As thus I mene, that ye wol be my stere°,
To do me lyve°, if that yow lyste, or sterve°—
So techeth me how that I may deserve
Youre thank° so that I thorugh myn ignoraunce
Ne do nothing that yow be displesaunce°.

"For certes°, fresshe wommanliche wyf°,
This dar I seye, that trouthe and diligence,
That shal ye fynden in me al my lyf;
Ne I wol nat, certeyn, breken youre defence°;
And if I do, present or in absence,
For love of God, lat sle me° with the dede,
If that it lyke unto° youre wommanhede."

"Iwys," quod she, "myn owene hertes lyst°,
My ground° of ese, and al myn herte dere,
Gramercy°, for on that is al my trist°.
But lat us falle awey fro this matere,
For it suffisith this that seyd is here,
And at o word, withouten repentaunce°,
Welcome, my knyght, my pes°, my suffisaunce°."

Of hire delyt or joyes oon the leste°
Were impossible to my wyt to seye;
But juggeth, ye that han ben at the feste°
Of swych gladnesse, yf that hem lyste pleye.
I kan no more, but thus thise ilke tweye
That nyght, betwixen drede and sikernesse°,
Felten in love the grete worthynesse.

O blysful nyght, of° hem so longe ysought,
How blithe° unto hem bothe two thow were!
Why nad I° swych on° with my soule ybought,
Ye, or the leeste joye that was there?
Awey, thow fowle daunger° and thow fere,
And lat hem in this hevene blysse dwelle,
That is so heygh that al ne kan I telle.

But soth is, though I kan nat tellen al,
As kan myn auctour of his excellence,
Yet have I seyd, and God toforn°, and shal
In everythyng the grete° of his sentence°;
And yf that ich, at Loves reverence°,
Have ony word in eched° for the beste,
Doth therwithal right as youreselven leste.

For myne wordes, here and every part,
I speke hem alle under correccioun
Of yow that felyng han in loves art,
And putte it al in youre discrecioun°
T'encresse or maken dyminucioun°
Of my langage, and that I yow byseche.
But now to purpos° of my rather° speche.

Thise ilke two, that ben° in armes laft°,
So loth to hem asonder gon it were°,
That ech from other wenden ben byraft°,
Or elles, lo, this was hir moste fere,
That al this thyng but nyce dremes nere°;
For which ful ofte ech of hem seyde, "O swete,
Clippe° ich yow thus, or elles I it mete°?"

1282 passeth, *surpasses* **1284 to,** *of* **1285 herte myn,** *my heart,* **benyngnite,** *graciousness* **1287 mot,** *must,* **nede amenden,** *necessarily improve* **1288 vertu,** *power* **1290 wrought,** *created,* **for,** *so that* **1291 stere,** *guide* **1292 do me lyve,** *make me live,* **sterve,** *die* **1294 thank,** *thanks* **1295 displesaunce,** *unpleasant* **1296 certes,** *surely,* **wommanliche wyf,** *womanly woman* **1299 breken youre defence,** *disobey your prohibition* **1301 lat sle me,** *let me be slain* **1302 lyke unto,** *is pleasing to* **1303 lyst,** *desire* **1304 ground,** *foundation* **1305 Gramercy,** *thank you,* **trist,** *trust* **1308 repentaunce,** *regret* **1309 pes,** *peace,* **suffisaunce,** *source of satisfaction* **1310 oon the leste,** *the least of which* **1310 feste,** *celebration* **1315 sikernesse,** *security* **1317 of,** *by* **1318 blithe,** *joyous* **1319 nad I,** *hadn't I,* **swych on,** *such one* (a night) **1321 daunger,** *aloofness* **1326 God toforn,** *before God* **1327 grete,** *substance,* **sentence,** *meaning* **1328 at Loves reverence,** *out of reverence for Love* **1329 in eched,** *worked in* **1334 discrecioun,** *judgment* **1335 dyminucioun,** *reduction* **1337 purpos,** *the point,* **rather,** *earlier* **1338 ben,** *were,* **laft,** *left* **1339 So loth to hem asonder gon it were,** *it was so hateful to them to be separated* **1340 ech from other wenden ben byraft,** *each imagined that the other might be taken away* **1342 but nyce dremes nere,** *were nothing but foolish dreams* **1344 Clippe,** *embrace,* **I it mete,** *do I dream it*

1286 thynketh, Cl and Cp read "thenk." **1291 that ye wol,** Cp reads "ye wol ye." **1310ff.** Chaucer here returns to Boccaccio's *Filostrato* for his basic plot, although he makes changes and additions as he proceeds; see the note to 3.450 above. **1322 blysse,** Cl reads "blyssyd." **1324–37** In a group of manuscripts, these stanzas follow 3.1414; one manuscript has them in both places. The fact that the lines do not work well with 3.1415 indicates a scribal error in moving them there. Here, the stanzas effectively protract the love scene with a digression on Chaucer's process of composition. **1327 the grete,** Cl and Cp read "al wholly." **1332 under correcioun,** it was commonplace for writers to suggest that readers improve or correct their works.

And Lord, so he gan goodly° on hire se°
That nevere his lok ne blente° from hire face,
And seyde, "O dere herte, may it be
That it be soth that ye ben in this place?"
"Ye, herte myn, God thank I of his grace,"
Quod tho Criseyde, and therwithal° hym kyste,
That where his spirit was for joye he nyste°.

This Troylus ful ofte hire eyen two
Gan for to kysse, and seyde, "O eyen clere°,
It weren ye that wroughte° me swych wo,
Ye humble nettes° of my lady dere.
Though there by mercy wreten° yn youre chere,
God wot, the text ful hard is, soth, to fynde.
How koude ye withouten bond° me bynde?"

Therwith he gan hire faste in armes take,
And wel an hundred tymes gan he syke°—
Nought swyche sorwful sykes as men make
For wo, or elles whanne that folk ben syke°,
But esy sykes swyche as ben to lyke,
That shewed his affeccion withinne;
Of swyche sikes koude he nought blynne°.

Sone after this they speke of sondry° thynges,
As fil to purpos of this aventure,
And pleyinge entrechaungeden° hire rynges,
Of which I kan nought tellen no scripture°;
But wel I wot, a broche°, gold and asure°,
In whiche a ruby set was lyk an herte,
Criseyde hym yaf°, and stak° it on his sherte.

Lord, trowe ye° a coveytous° or a wrecche,
That blameth love and holt of it despit°,
That of the pens° that he kan mokre° and
  krecche°
Was evere yet yyeve° hym swych delyt
As ys in love, in oo poynt in som plyt°?
Nay, douteles, for also° God me save,
So perfit joye may no nygard° have.

They wol sey "yis," but, Lord, so° that they lye,
Tho° bysy wrecches ful of wo and drede!
They callen love a woodnesse° or folye,
But it shal falle° hem as I shal yow rede°:
They shul forgo the white and ek the rede,
And leve° in wo, there God yeve hem
  myschaunce°,
And every lovere yn his trouthe avaunce°.

As wolde God tho° wrecches that dispise
Servyse of love hadde eerys also° longe
As hadde Myda, ful of coveytise,
And therto° drenken hadde° as hoot and stronge
As Crassus dide for his affectis wronge°,
To techen hem that they ben in the vice,
And loveres nought° although they holde hem nyce°.

Thise ilke° two of whom that I yow seye°,
Whan that hire hertes wel assured were,
Tho gonne° they to speken and to pleye,
And ek rehercen° how and whanne and where
They knewe hem° first, and every wo and feere
That passed was; but al swych hevynesse,
I thank it God, was tourned to gladnesse.

And everemo, when that hem fille° to speke
Of onything of swych a tyme agoon,

1345 gan goodly, *did intently,* **se,** *look* **1346 blente,** *wavered* **1350 therwithal,** *with that* **1351 nyste,** *didn't know* **1353 clere,** *beautiful* **1354 wroughte,** *made for* **1355 humble nettes,** *modest snares* **1356 wreten,** *written* **1358 bond,** *bonds* **1360 syke,** *sigh* **1362 syke,** *sick* **1365 blynne,** *cease* **1366 sondry,** *various* **1368 pleyinge entrechaungeden,** *playfully exchanged* **1369 scripture,** *inscription* **1370 broche,** *brooch,* **asure,** *lapis lazuli* (semiprecious blue stone) **1372 yaf,** *gave,* **stak,** *pinned* **1373 trowe ye,** *can you imagine,* **coveytous,** *greedy person* **1374 holt of it despit,** *holds it in scorn* **1375 pens,** *pennies,* **mokre,** *hoard,* **krecche,** *scratch* **1376 yyeve,** *given* **1377 in oo poynt in some plyt,** *in any way under any circumstances* **1378 also,** *as* **1379 nygard,** *miser* **1380 so,** *how* **1381 Tho,** *those* **1382 woodnesse,** *madness* **1383 falle,** *happen to,* **rede,** *advise* **1385 leve,** *live,* **myschaunce,** *misfortune* **1386 avaunce,** *advance* **1387 As wolde God tho,** *may God make it so that those* **1388 eerys also,** *ears as* **1390 therto,** *also,* **drenken hadde,** *had drunk* **1391 affectis wronge,** *evil desires* **1393 loveres nought,** (that) *lovers* (are) *not,* **holde hem nyce,** *consider them foolish* **1394 ilke,** *same,* **seye,** *tell* **1396 Tho gonne,** *then began* **1397 rehercen,** *repeat* **1398 hem,** *each other* **1401 hem fille,** *they happened*

1345 And, Cl reads "A." **goodly,** Cl reads "gladly." **1368** Some critics have argued that the exchange of rings indicates a "clandestine marriage," but the playful informality—while it does raise the idea of marriage—suggests no legal or canonical pact. No exchange of rings is found in *Filostrato.* **1370 broche,** this is not the brooch later found on Diomedes's armor (5.1661; *Fil.* 8.9–10), but it foreshadows that fateful jewel and contributes to the symmetry of Chaucer's poem. **1375 the pens,** Cp reads "tho pans." **mokre and krecche,** Cl reads "moke and kecche"; Cp, "mokre and tecche." **1384 the white and ek the rede,** the two colors can be construed both as (white) silver and (red) gold and as white and red wines (the latter in *PardT* 6.526). Either way, it is clear that those who despise love (or love improper objects) will be unsatisfied and miserable. **1389 Myda,** Midas, who sought to satisfy his greed by requesting that everything he touched turned to gold; later he was given ass's ears for preferring the music of Pan to that of Apollo. Ovid, *Metamorphoses* 2.100–193; Chaucer's Wife of Bath retells part of the story, *CT* 3.952–82. **1391 Crassus,** like Midas, the Roman general Crassus was a figure of greed. After he was killed, molten gold was poured in his mouth.

With kyssing al that tale sholde breke°
And fallen in a newe joye anoon;
And deden al hire myght, syn they were oon,
For to recoveren blysse and ben at eyse,
And passed° woo with joye contrepeyse°.

Reson wol not° that I speke of slep,
For it accordeth nought to my matere.
God wot, they tok of that ful lytel kep°!
But lest this nyght, that was to hem so dere,
Ne sholde in veyn escape in no manere,
It was byset° in joye and bysynesse
Of al that sowneth into° gentilesse.

But whanne the kok°, comune° astrologer,
Gan on his brest to bete and after crowe,
And Lucifer, the dayes messager,
Gan for to ryse and out hire bemys throwe,
And estward ros (to hym that kowde it knowe)
Fortuna Major, that anoon Criseyde,
With herte sor°, to Troylus thus seyde:

"Myn hertes lyf, my tryst°, and my plesaunce,°
That I was born, allas, what me is wo,
That day of us mot make desseveraunce°.
For tyme it is to ryse and hens° to go,
Or ellys I am lost for everemo.
O nyght, allas, whi nyltow° over us hove°
As longe as whanne Almena lay by Jove?

"O blake nyght, as folk in bokes rede,
That shapen° art by God this world to hide
At certeyn tymes wyth thi derke wede°,
That under that men myghte in reste abyde,
Wel oughte bestes pleyne° and folk the chide°
That there as° day wyth labour wolde us breste°,
That thow thus flest°, and deynest° us nought reste.

"Thow dost, allas, to shortly thyn office°,
Thow rakle° nyght, there° God, maker of kynde°,
The for thyn hast° and thyn unkynde vice
So faste ay° to oure hemyspere bynde°
That neveremore under the ground thow wynde°!
For now, for° thow so hyest° out of Troye,
Have I forgon° thus hastely my joye."

This Troylus, that with tho° wordes felte,
As thoughte hym tho°, for pitous distresse
The blody teerys from his herte melte,
As he that nevere yet swych hevynesse
Assayed° hadde out of so gret gladnesse,
Gan therwithal° Criseyde, his lady dere,
In armes streyne°, and seyde in this manere:

"O cruel day, accusour° of the joye
That nyght and love han stole and faste ywryen°,
Acursed be thi comyng into Troye,
For every bore° hath oon of thi bryghte eyen.
Envyous day, what lyst the° so to spyen?
What hastow lost? Why sekestow this place?
Ther° God thi lyght so quenche°, for his grace!

"Allas, what° han these loveres the agilt°,
Dispitous° day? Thyn be the pyne° of helle!
For many a lovere hastow shent°, and wilt°;
Thi pouryng° in wol nowhere lat hem dwelle.
What profrestow° thi light here for to selle?

1403 breke, *be interrupted* **1407 passed,** *past,* **contrepeyse,** *to counterbalance* **1408 Reson wol not,** *there is no reason* **1410 kep,** *notice* **1413 byset,** *occupied* **1414 sowneth into,** *contributes to* **1415 kok,** *cock,* **comune,** *everybody's* **1421 sor,** *aching* **1422 tryst,** *trust,* **plesaunce,** *pleasure* **1424 of us mot make desseveraunce,** *must separate us* **1425 hens,** *hence* **1427 nyltow,** *will you not,* **hove,** *linger* **1430 shapen,** *created* **1431 wede,** *cloak* **1433 bestes pleyne,** *beasts lament,* **the chide,** *scold you* **1434 there as,** *while,* **breste,** *crush* **1435 flest,** *flee,* **deynest,** *allow* **1436 office,** *duty* **1437 rakle,** *rash,* **there,** *may,* **kynde,** *nature* **1438 hast,** *haste* **1439 faste ay,** *firmly always,* **bynde,** *attach* **1440 wynde,** *go* **1441 for,** *because,* **hyest,** *hurry* **1442 forgon,** *lost* **1443 tho,** *those* **1444 tho,** *then* **1447 Assayed,** *experienced* **1448 Gan therwithal,** *did then* **1449 streyne,** *clasp* **1450 accusour,** *revealer* **1451 faste ywryen,** *closely hidden* **1453 bore,** *opening* **1453 what lyst the,** *why do you choose* **1456 Ther,** *may,* **quenche,** *extinguish* **1457 what,** *how,* **the agilt,** *offended you* **1458 Dispitous,** *cruel,* **pyne,** *pain* **1459 hastow shent,** *have you ruined,* **wilt,** *will* (in the future) **1460 pouryng,** *staring* **1461 What profrestow,** *why offer you*

1415 comune astrologer, the rooster was thought to announce the coming of the morning. Marginal glosses in several manuscripts label him "*vulgaris astrologus,*" so this was evidently a familiar epithet. **1417 Lucifer,** another name for Venus as the morning star. **1419 estward,** Cl reads "afterward." **1420 *Fortuna Major*,** either the rising sun or a group of six stars in occult geomancy. Chaucer probably derived the reference from Dante, *Purgatorio* 19.4–5, and he may simply have associated it with sunrise. **1428 Almena . . . Jove,** when Jove lay with Almena and begot Hercules, he miraculously extended the night. **1427–42** This address to night is part of the tradition of the dawn-song (also called *aubade, aude,* or *alba*), a lyric form that derived from Ovid's *Amores* 1.13 and was made popular in courtly tradition. Not included in the parting lament in *Filostrato.* **1436 to,** Cp reads "so." **1450–70** Troylus's address to the day is also part of the dawn-song tradition, adapted from *Filostrato* 3.44–47. **1459 shent,** Cp reads "slayn."

Go selle it hem that smale selys graven°;
We wol the° nought; us nedeth no day haven."

And ek the sonne, Tytan, gan he chyde°,
And seyde, "O fol, wel may men the dispise,
That hast the Dawyng al nyght by thi syde,
And suffrest hire so soone up fro the ryse,
For to disesen° loveres yn this wyse.
What, hold youre bed ther, thow and ek thi Morwe°;
I bidde God so yeve yow bothe sorwe!"

Therwith ful sore he sighte°, and thus he seyde,
"My lady right, and of my wele° or wo
The welle° and rote°, O goodly myn Criseyde,
And shal I ryse, allas, and shal I go?
Now fele I that myn herte mot a-two°.
For how sholde I an houre my lyf save,
Syn that with yow is al the lyf ich have?

"What shal I don, for, certes, I not how,
Ne whanne, allas, I shal the tyme se
That yn this plit° I may ben eft° with yow?
And of my lyf, God wot how that shal be,
Syn that desir ryght now so brenneth° me
That I am ded anoon but° I retorne.
How shold I longe, allas, fro yow sojourne°?

"But natheles, myn owene lady bryght,
Yit were it so that I wiste outrely°
That I, youre humble servant and youre knyght,
Were in youre herte iset° so fermely
As ye in myn—the which thyng, trewely,
Me levere were° than these worldes tweyne°—
Yet sholde I bet° enduren al my peyne."

To that Cryseyde answerde right anoon,
And with a syk she seyde, "O herte dere,
The game, ywys, so ferforth° now is gon
That first shal Phebus falle fro his spere°,
And everich egle° ben the dowves fere°,
And every roche° out of his place sterte°,
Er Troylus out of Criseydes herte.

"Ye ben so depe in-with myn herte grave°,
That though I wolde it turne out of my thought,
As wysly verray° God my soule save,
To dyen in the peyne°, I kowde nowght.
And for the love of God that us hath wrought,
Lat in youre brayn noon other fantasye
So crepe that it cause me to dye.

"And that ye me wolde han as faste° in mynde
As I have yow, that wold I yow byseche;
And yf I wyste sothly° that to fynde°,
God myghte not a poynt° my joyes eche°.
But herte myn, withoute more speche,
Beth to me trewe, or elles were it routhe°—
For I am thyn, by God and by my trouthe!

"Beth glad, forthi°, and lyve in sykernesse°;
Thus seyde I nevere er this, ne shal to mo°.
And yf to yow it were a gret gladnesse
To turne ayen° soone after that ye go,
As fayn wolde I° as ye that it were so,
As wysly° God myn herte brynge at reste."
And hym in armes toke and ofte keste.

Agayns his wil, syn it mot nedes be°,
This Troylus up ros, and faste hym cledde°,
And in his armes tok his lady fre°
An hondred tyme, and on his wey hym spedde;
And with swyche voys as though his herte bledde,
He seyde, "Farewel, myn herte and dere swete,
There° God us graunte sounde° and soone to mete!"

1462 smale selys graven, *engrave small seals* (an activity needing good light) **1463 wol the,** *want you* **1464 chyde,** *scold* **1469 disesen,** *disturb* **1469 Morwe,** *Morning* **1471 sighte,** *sighed* **1472 wele,** *joy* **1473 welle,** *source,* **rote,** *root* **1475 mot a-two,** *must break* **1480 plit,** *situation,* **eft,** *again* **1482 brenneth,** *burns* **1483 but,** *unless* **1484 fro yow sojourne,** *remain away from you* **1486 wiste outrely,** *knew completely* **1488 iset,** *set* **1490 Me levere were,** *to me is more preferable,* **these worldes tweye,** *heaven and earth* (?) **1491 bet,** *better* **1494 ferforth,** *far* **1495 spere,** *orbit* **1496 everich egle,** *every eagle,* **dowves fere,** *dove's companion* **1497 roche,** *rock,* **sterte,** *leap* **1499 grave,** *carved* **1501 As wysly verray,** *as surely* (may) *the true* **1502 To dyen in the peyne,** *even if I were to die by torture* **1506 faste,** *firmly* **1508 wyste sothly,** *knew truly,* **that to fynde,** *that I would find that* **1509 a poynt,** *one bit,* **eche,** *increase* **1511 routhe,** *pity* **1513 forthi,** *therefore,* **sykernesse,** *confidence* **1514 mo,** *others* **1516 turne ayen,** *return* **1517 as fayn wolde I,** *as happy would I* (be) **1518 wysly,** *surely* **1520 syn it mot nedes be,** *since it must need be* **1521 hym cledde,** *clothed himself* **1522 fre,** *gracious* **1526 There,** *may,* **sounde,** *health*

1464 Tytan, Titan, the sun, often conflated with Tithonus, the mortal lover of Aurora (the dawn) who became immortal. **1474 go,** Cp reads "so." **1482 brenneth,** Cp reads "biteth" (bites). **1495–97** Such "impossibilia," as they were called, are conventionally proclaimed by the man in the love relationship, as is the following promise of faithfulness. **1495 Phebus,** the sun. **1524 voys as though,** Cl and Cp read "wordes as." **1525 myn herte and dere,** Cp reads "my dere herte."

To which no word for sorwe she answerde,
So sore gan his partyng hire destreyne°.
And Troylus unto his palays ferde°
As wobygon° as she was, soth to seyne.
So hard hym wrong of sharp desir the peyne°
For to ben eft there° he was in plesaunce°,
That it may nevere out of his remembraunce.

Retorned to his palais real° soone,
He softe into his bedde gan for to slynke,
To slepe longe, as he was woned° to done.
But al for nought; he may wel lygge° and wynke°,
But slep ne may ther in his herte synke
Thenkynge how she, for whom desir hym brende°,
A thousandfold was worth more than he wende°.

And in his thought gan up and doun to wynde°
Hire wordes alle, and every countenaunce°,
And fermely impressen yn his mynde
The leste poynt° that to hym was plesaunce°;
And verraylich° of thilke° remembraunce
Desir al newe hym brende, and lust° to brede°
Gan more than erst°, and yet tok he non hede°.

Criseyde also, right in the same wyse,
Of Troylus gan in hire herte shette°
His worthinesse, his lust°, his dedes wyse,
His gentilesse, and how she with hym mette,
Thonkynge Love he so wel hire bysette°,
Desirying eft° to have hire herte dere
In swych a plyt she dorste make hym chere°.

Pandare, a-morwe° which that° comen was
Unto his nece and gan hire fayre grete,
Seyde, "Al this nyght so reyned it, allas,
That al my drede is that ye, nece swete,
Han litel layser had to slepe and mete°.
Al nyght," quod he, "hath reyn so do me wake°,
That som of us, I trowe, hire hedes ake°."

And ner he come and seyde, "How stont° it now,
This murye° morwe? Nece, how kan ye fare?"
Criseyde answerde, "Nevere the bet° for yow,
Fox that ye ben°. God yeve youre herte care°!
God help me so, ye caused al this fare°,
Trow° I," quod she, "for alle youre wordes whyte°.
O, whoso seth° yow, he knoweth yow ful lite."

With that she gan hire face for to wrye°
With the shete°, and wax for shame al red;
And Pandarus gan under for to prye°,
And seyde, "Nece, yf that I shal be ded,
Have here a swerd and smyteth of myn hed!"
With that his arm al sodeynly he thriste°
Under hire nekke, and at the laste hire kyste.

I passe al that which chargeth nought° to seye.
What, God foryaf° his deth, and she also
Foryaf, and with hire uncle gan to pleye,
For other cause° was ther noon but so.
But of this thing right to the effect° to go,
Whan tyme was, hom til° hire hous she wente,
And Pandarus hath fully his entente°.

Now torne we ayen to Troylus,
That resteles ful longe abedde lay,
And prevely° sente after Pandarus,
To hym to com in al the haste he may.
He com anoon, nought onyes° seyde he nay,
And Troylus ful sobrely he grette°,
And doun upon his beddes syde hym sette.

This Troylus, with al th'affeccioun
Of frendes love that herte may devyse,

1528 destreyne, *distress* **1529 ferde,** *went* **1530 wobygon,** *sorrowful* **1531 hym wrong of sharp desir the peyne,** *the pain of sharp desire wrung him* **1532 eft there,** *again where,* **plesaunce,** *pleasure* **1534 palais real,** *royal palace* **1536 woned,** *accustomed* **1537 lygge,** *lie,* **wynke,** *close his eyes* **1539 brende,** *burned* **1540 wende,** *assumed* **1541 wynde,** *turn* **1542 countenaunce,** *look* **1544 leste poynt,** *smallest bit,* **plesaunce,** *pleasurable* **1545 verraylich,** *truly,* **thilke,** *that* **1546 lust,** *desire,* **brede,** *grow* **1547 erst,** *before* **1547 tok . . . non hede,** *paid no attention* **1549 shette,** *enclose* **1551 lust,** *vigor* **1552 hire bysette,** *bestowed on her* **1553 eft,** *again,* **swych a plyt she dorste make hym chere,** *such a situation* (that) *she might welcome him* **1555 a-morwe,** *in the morning,* **which that,** *who* **1559 mete,** *dream* **1560 do me wake,** *kept me awake* **1561 hire hedes ake,** *their heads ache* **1562 stont,** *stands* **1563 murye,** *pleasant* **1564 bet,** *better* **1565 ben,** *are,* **care,** *trouble* **1566 fare,** *business* **1567 Trow,** *think,* **whyte,** *pretty* **1568 seth,** *sees* **1569 wrye,** *cover* **1570 shete,** *sheet* **1571 prye,** *peek* **1574 thriste,** *thrust* **1576 chargeth nought,** (it) *matters not* **1577 foryaf,** *forgave* **1579 cause,** *reason* **1580 effect,** *point* **1581 til,** *to* **1582 hath fully his entente,** *has accomplished his goal* **1585 prevely,** *secretly* **1587 onyes,** *once* **1588 ful sobrely he grette,** *he greeted very solemnly*

1542 Hire, Cl reads "His." **1543 his,** Cl reads "hire." **1555–82** Chaucer's addition, perhaps inspired by a similar scene in *Pamphilus de Amore* 725ff.; see the note to 3.560. There is no parallel visit by Pandaro in *Filostrato* as the consummation there takes place at Criseide's home. **1573 smyteth,** Cl reads "smyte"; Cp, "smyten." **1577 his deth,** a reference to Christ's crucifixion.

To Pandarus on knees fil adown,
And er that he wolde of the place aryse,
He gan hym thonken in his beste wyse
An hondred sithe°, and gan the tyme blysse°
That he was born to brynge hym fro distresse.

He seyde, "O frend, of frendes the alderbeste°
That evere was, the sothe for to telle,
Thow hast in hevene ybrought my soule at reste
Fro Flegiton, the fery° flood of helle,
That though I myght a thousand tymes selle
Upon a day my lyf in thy servise,
It myght nought a mote° in that suffise.

"The sonne, which that al the world may se,
Sawh° nevere yet my lyf°, that dar I leye°,
So inly feyr° and goodly as is she,
Whos I am al, and shal til that I deye.
And that I thus am hires, dar I seye
That thanked be the heighe worthynesse
Of Love, and ek thi kynde bysynesse°.

"Thus hastow me no lytel thyng yyeve°,
For which to the obliged be for ay°
My lyf. And whi? For thorugh thyn help I leve°,
Or elles ded hadde I be many a day."
And with that word doun in his bed he lay.
And Pandarus ful sobrely hym herde
Til al was seyd, and thanne he hym answerde:

"My dere frend, yf I have don for the
In ony cas, God wot, it is me lief°,
And am as glad as man may of it be,
God help me so. But tak it not a-grief°
That° I shal seyn: bewar of this myschief°,
That there as° thow now brought art into thy blysse,
That thow thiself ne cause it nought to mysse°.

"For of Fortunes sharpe adversite
The worste kynde of infortune is this,
A man to have ben in prosperite,
And it remembren whan it passed is.
Thow art wys ynowh°, forthi° do nought amys;
Be not to rakel°, though thou sitte warme°,
For if thow be, certeyn, it wol the harme.

"Thow art at ese°, and hold the° wel therinne.
For also seur° as red is every fir°,
As gret a craft° is kepe wel as wynne.
Bridle° alwey wel thi speche and thi desir,
For worldly joye halt° not but by a wir°.
That preveth wel° it brest alday° so ofte;
Forthi° nede is to werke with it softe°."

Quod Troylus, "I hope, and God toforn°,
My dere frend, that I shal so me bere°
That in° my gilt° ther shal nothing be lorn°,
Ne I nyl not rakle° as for to greven° hire.
It nedeth not this matere ofte stere°,
For wistestow° myn herte wel, Pandare,
God wot of this thow woldest litel care°."

Tho gan he telle hym of his glade nyght,
And wherof° first his herte dredde, and how,
And seyde, "Frend, as I am trewe knyght,
And by that feyth I shal° to God and yow,
I hadde it never half so hote as now;
And ay the more that desir me biteth°,
To love hire best the more it me delyteth.

"I not° myself not wisly° what it is,
But now I fele a newe qualite,
Ye, al another° than I dede er this."
Pandare answered, and seyde thus, that "He
That onys° may in hevene° blysse be,
He feleth other weyes, dar I leye,
Than thilke° tyme he first herde of it seye°."

1595 sithe, *times,* **blysse,** *bless* **1597 alderbeste,** *very best* **1600 fery,** *fiery* **1603 mote,** *particle* **1605 Sawh,** *saw,* **my lyf,** *in my life,* **leye,** *bet* **1606 So inly feyr,** (one who is) *so thoroughly superb* **1610 bysynesse,** *activities* **1611 yyeve,** *given* **1612 for ay,** *forever* **1613 leve,** *live* **1619 me lief,** *pleasing to me* **1621 tak it not a-grief,** *take no offense at* **1622 That,** *what,* **myschief,** *misfortune* **1623 there as,** *whereas* **1624 mysse,** *fail* **1629 ynowh,** *enough,* **forthi,** *therefore* **1630 to rakel,** *too rash,* **sitte warme,** *are comfortable* **1632 at ease,** *in joy,* **hold the,** *keep yourself* **1633 also seur,** *as sure,* **fir,** *fire* **1634 craft,** *skill* **1635 Bridle,** *control* **1636 halt,** *hangs,* **wir,** *thread* **1637 preveth wel,** *is shown by the fact that,* **brest alday,** *breaks always* **1638 Forthi,** *therefore,* **softe,** *carefully* **1639 God toforn,** *before God* **1640 me bere,** *behave* **1641 in,** *through,* **gilt,** *fault,* **lorn,** *lost* **1642 Ne I nyl not rakle,** *nor will I act rashly,* **greven,** *upset* **1643 stere,** *bring up (stir)* **1644 For wistestow,** *if you knew* **1645 care,** *worry* **1647 wherof,** *about what* **1649 shal,** *owe* **1650 biteth,** *stings* **1653 not,** *don't know,* **wisly,** *surely* **1655 al another,** *completely different* **1657 onys,** *once,* **hevene,** *heaven's* **1659 thilke,** *that,* **seye,** *spoken*

1592 knees, Cp reads "knowes." **1600 Flegiton,** Phlegethon, the river of fire in Hades. **1625–28** A commonplace: "There is no sorrow like remembered pleasure." See *Bo* 2.pr4.7; Dante, *Inferno* 5.121–23; Augustine's *Confessions* 10.14; and elsewhere. **1634** Proverbial: "Keeping is as great a skill as winning." **1636–37** Commonplace. **1643 stere,** Cl and Cp read "tere" (tear, rip).

This is o word for al°. This Troylus
Was nevere ful to speke° of this matere,
And for to preysen unto Pandarus
The bounte° of his righte° lady dere,
And Pandarus to thanke and maken chere°.
This tale° was ay span-newe° to bygynne
Til that the nyght departed hem atwynne°.

Soone after this, for that Fortune it wolde°,
Icomen° was the blysful tyme swete
That Troylus was warned° that he sholde,
There° he was erst°, Criseyde his lady mete°,
For which he felt his herte in joye flete°,
And feythfully gan alle the goddes herye°.
And lat se now yf that he kan be merye.

And holden° was the forme° and al the wyse°
Of hire commynge, and ek of his also,
As it was erst, whych nedeth nought devyse.
But playnly° to the effect° right for to go,
In joye and seurte° Pandarus hem two
Abedde brought whan that hem bothe leste°,
And thus thei ben in quyete and yn reste.

Nought nedeth it to° yow, syn they ben met,
To axe at° me yf that they blythe° were.
For yf it erst was wel, tho° was it bet°
A thousandfold; this nedeth not enquere.
Agon° was every sorwe and every fere,
And bothe, ywys, they hadde, and so they wende°,
As muche joye as herte may comprende°.

This is no litel thyng of for to seye°,
This passeth° every wyt° for to devyse,
For eche of hem gan otheres lust° obeye.
Felicite, which that thise clerkes wyse°
Commenden so, ne may not here suffise.
This joye may not ywrete ben° with inke;
This passeth al that herte may bythenke.

But cruel day, so welawey° the stounde°,
Gan for to aproche, as they by synes° knewe,
For which hem thoughte felen° dethes wounde.
So wo was hem° that changen gan hire hewe°,
And day they gonnen to dispise° al newe,
Callyng it traytour, envyous, and worse,
And bitterly the dayes light they corse°.

Quod Troilus, "Allas, now am I war
That Piros and tho swyfte stedes° thre,
Which that drawen forth the sonnes char°,
Han gon som bypath° in despit° of me.
That maketh it so soone day to be.
And for the sonne hym hasteth thus to ryse,
Ne shal I nevere don hym sacrifise."

But nedes day departe° hem moste soone,
And whanne hire speche don was and hire chere°,
They twynne° anoon, as they were woned° to done,
And setten tyme of metyng eft yfere°.
And many a nyght they wrought° yn this manere.
And thus Fortune a tyme° ledde in joye
Criseyde and ek this kynges sone of Troye.

In suffisaunce°, in blisse, and in syngynges,
This Troylus gan al his lyf to lede.
He spendeth°, justeth°, maketh festeynynges°,
He yeveth frely° ofte, and chaungeth wede°,
And held aboute hym alwey, out of drede,
A world° of folk as kam hym wel° of kynde°,
The fresshest and the beste he koude fynde.

1660 is o word for al, *says it all* **1662 Was nevere ful to speke,** *never had his fill of speaking* **1663 bounte,** *goodness,* **righte,** *true* **1664 maken chere,** *treat well* **1665 tale,** *topic,* **span-newe,** *brand new* **1666 departed hem atwynne,** *separated them* **1667 wolde,** *wished* **1668 Icomen,** *arrived* **1669 warned,** *informed* **1670 There,** *where,* **erst,** *before,* **mete,** *meet* **1671 flete,** *float* **1672 herye,** *praise* **1674 holden,** *kept,* **forme,** *propriety,* **wyse,** *manner* **1677 playnly,** *directly,* **effect,** *point* **1678 seurte,** *security* **1679 leste,** *wished* **1681 to,** *for* **1682 axe at,** *ask of,* **blythe,** *happy* **1683 tho,** *then,* **bet,** *better* **1685 Agon,** *gone* **1686 wende,** *thought* **1687 comprende,** *contain* **1688 of for to seye,** *to speak about* **1689 passeth,** *surpasses,* **wyt,** *mind* **1690 lust,** *desire* **1691 clerkes wyse,** *wise scholars* **1693 ywrete ben,** *be written* **1695 welawey,** *alas,* **stounde,** *time* **1696 synes,** *signs* **1697 hem thoughte felen,** *they seem to feel* **1698 wo was hem,** *woeful were they,* **hewe,** *color* **1699 dispise,** *rebuke* **1701 corse,** *curse* **1703 stedes,** *horses* **1705 sonnes char,** *sun's chariot* **1705 Han gon som bypath,** *has taken a shortcut,* **in despit,** *for spite* **1709 departe,** *separate* **1710 chere,** *pleasure* **1711 twynne,** *separate,* **woned,** *accustomed* **1712 eft yfere,** *again together* **1713 wrought,** *arranged* **1714 a tyme,** *for a time* **1716 suffisaunce,** *satisfaction* **1718 spendeth,** *spends money,* **justeth,** *jousts,* **festeynynges,** *celebrations* **1719 yeveth frely,** *gives generously,* **wede,** *clothing* **1721 world,** *multitude,* **as kam hym wel,** *as suited him well,* **of kynde,** *by nature*

1670 There he was erst, i.e., at Pandarus's house. **1687 comprende,** Cl reads "complende." **1690 Felicite,** one of several Boethian terms (also *blisfulnesse, welefulness, suffisaunce*) for true happiness (*Bo* 3pr10.193–94), a concept fundamental to *TC.* For the opposed idea of false, mutable happiness, see the note at 3.814. **1703 Piros,** in classical myth, Pyrois was the name of one of the four horses that pulled the chariot of the sun; Ovid, *Metamorphoses* 2.153. **1718 festeynynges,** Cp reads "festeyinges."

That swych a voys° was of hym and a stevene°
Thorughout the world, of honour and largesse°,
That it up rong° unto the yate° of hevene.
And, as in love, he was in swych gladnesse,
That in his herte he demede° as I gesse
That ther nys lovere in this world at ese
So wel as he°; and thus gan love hym plese.

The goodlihede° or beaute which that Kynde°
In ony other lady hadde yset
Kan not the mountaunce of a knot unbynde°
Aboute his herte of al Criseydes net.
He was so narwe ymasked° and yknet°,
That it undon° on any manere syde°,
That nyl not ben, for ought that may betide°.

And by the hond ful ofte he wolde take
This Pandarus, and into garden lede,
And swych a feste° and swych a proces° make
Hym of Criseyde, and of hire womanhede,
And of hire beaute, that withouten drede°
It was an hevene his wordes for to here;
And thanne he wolde synge in this manere:

Canticus Troili

"Love, that of erthe and se° hath governaunce,
Love, that his hestes° hath in hevenes hye°,
Love, that with an holsom° alliaunce
Halt° peples joyned as hym lyst hem gye°,
Love, that knetteth° lawe of compaignye°,
And couples doth° in vertu for to dwelle,
Bynd this acord that I have told and telle.

"That that° the world with feyth, which that is stable,
Dyverseth° so his stoundes concordynge°,
That elementes that ben so discordable°
Holden a bond perpetuely durynge°,
That Phebus mote° his rosy day forth brynge,
And that the mone° hath lordshipe over the
nyghtes—
Al this doth Love, ay heryed° be his myghtes.

"That that° the se, that gredy° is to flowen,
Constreyneth to a certeyn ende° so
His flodes that so fiersly they ne growen°
To drenchen° erthe and al for everemo.
And yf that Love ought° lat his bridel go,
Al that now loveth asondre sholde lepe°,
And al were lost that Love halt° now to-hepe°.

"So wolde God°, that auctour is of Kynde°,
That with his bond Love of his vertu° liste
To cerclen hertes alle and faste° bynde,
That from his bond no wight the weye out wyste°.
And hertes colde, hem wolde I that he twyste°
To make hem love, and that hem leste ay
rewe°
On hertes sore, and kep° hem that ben trewe."

In alle nedes for the townes werre°
He was and ay the firste in armes dight°,
And certaynly, but if that° bokes erre°,
Save° Ector most ydrad° of ony wight.
And this encres of hardinesse° and myght
Cam hym of love, his ladyes thank° to wynne,
That altered his spirit so withinne.

In tyme of trewe°, on haukyng wolde he ride,
Or elles hunten bor, ber, or lyoun—
The smale bestes leet he gon bysyde°.
And whan that he com rydynge into town,

1723 voys, *report,* **stevene,** *reputation* **1724 largesse,** *generosity* **1725 rong,** *rang,* **yate,** *gate* **1727 demede,** *thought* **1728–29 at ese / So wel as he,** *as content as he* **1730 goodlihede,** *excellence,* **Kynde,** *Nature* **1732 the mountaunce of a knot unbynde,** *as much as a single knot untie* **1734 narwe ymasked,** *tightly enmeshed,* **yknet,** *tied* **1735 it undon,** *to undo to,* **any manere syde,** *any side whatever* **1736 betide,** *happen* **1739 feste,** *celebration,* **proces,** *description* **1741 drede,** *doubt* **1744 se,** *sea* **1745 hestes,** *commands,* **hye,** *high* **1746 holsom,** *beneficial* **1747 halt,** *holds,* **hym lyst hem gye,** *it pleases him to guide them* **1748 knetteth,** *weaves,* **compaignye,** *companionship* **1749 doth,** *causes* **1751 That that,** *This* (love) *that* **1752 Dyverseth,** *varies,* **stoundes concordynge,** *seasons harmoniously* **1753 discordable,** *inclined to discord* **1754 durynge,** *enduring* **1755 Phebus mote,** *the sun must* **1756 mone,** *moon* **1757 ay heryed,** *forever praised* **1758 That that,** *This* (love) *that,* **gredy,** *eager* **1759 Constreyneth to a certeyn ende,** *confines to a certain boundary* **1760 growen,** *rise* **1761 drenchen,** *drown* **1762 ought,** *at all* **1763 asondre . . . lepe,** *spring apart* **1764 halt,** *holds,* **to-hepe,** *together* **1765 So wolde God,** *God wills* (it) *so,* **Kynde,** *Nature* **1766 vertu,** *power* **1767 faste,** *tightly* **1768 wyste,** *knows* **1769 twyste,** *constrain* **1770 hem leste ay rewe,** *it please them always to have pity* **1771 kep,** *protect* **1772 werre,** *war* **1773 dight,** *ready* **1774 but if that,** *unless,* **bokes erre,** *books are wrong* **1775 Save,** *except for,* **ydrad,** *dreaded* **1776 hardinesse,** *boldness* **1777 thank,** *gratitude* **1779 trewe,** *truce* **1781 leet he gon bysyde,** *he allowed to escape*

1743a Canticus Troili, "Song of Troylus." The rubric is omitted in Cl. **1744–71** Troylus's song derives from *Bo* 2.m8, having used in Proem three (see 3.1–38) a portion of Troiolo's song that occurs here in *Fil.* The difficult syntax of lines 1751 and 1758 (*That that . . .*) makes sense when compared with line 1744 (*Love, that . . .*), binding together the stanzas and echoing their theme of unity. **1745 hestes,** Cl reads "heste"; Cp "hevene."**1753 elementes,** the four elements (earth, water, air, fire). **1760 fiersly,** Cl reads "freshly." **1767 cerclen,** Cl reads "cerchen." **1769 twyste,** Cl reads "it wyste."

Ful ofte his lady from hire wyndow down,
As freshe as fawkon° comen out of muwe°,
Ful redy was hym goodly to saluwe°

And most of love and vertu was his speche,
And in despit° hadde alle wrecchednesse.
And douteles, no nede was hym byseche°
To honouren hem that hadde worthynesse,
And esen° hem that weren in distresse.
And glad was he yf any wyght wel ferde°,
That lovere was, whan he it wyste or herde.

For soth to seyn, he lost held° every wyght
But yf° he were in Loves heyhe servyse—
I mene folk that oughte it ben° of right.
And over al this, so wel koude he devyse°
Of sentement°—and in so unkouth wyse°—
Al his aray°, that every lovere thoughte
That al was wel, whatso he seyde or wroughte°.

And though that he be come of blod royal,
Lyst° hym of pride at no wyght for to chase°.
Benygne° he was to ech yn general,
For which he gat hym thank° in every place.
Thus wolde Love—yheryed° be his grace—
That pride, envye, ire, and avaryce
He gan to fle, and everich other vice.

Thow lady bryght, the doughter to Dyone,
Thy blynde and wynged sone ek, daun°
Cupide,
Ye sustren° nyne ek that by Elycone
In hil Pernaso lysten° for to abide,
That ye thus fer° han deyned° me to gyde—
I kan no more, but syn that ye wol wende°,
Ye heryed° ben for ay withouten ende.

Thorugh yow have I seyd fully in my song
Th'effect and joye of Troylus servyse,
Al be° that there were som dishese among°,
As to° myn auctour listeth to devyse.
My thridde book now ende ich in this wyse°,
And Troylus, in lust° and in quiete,
Is with Criseyde, his owne herte swete.

Explicit liber tercius.

1784 fawcon, *falcon,* **muwe,** *coop* **1785 saluwe,** *greet* **1787 despit,** *contempt* **1788 hym byseche,** *to ask him* **1790 esen,** *comfort* **1791 wel ferde,** *did well* **1793 lost held,** *considered lost* **1794 But yf,** *unless* **1795 oughte it ben,** *ought to be* (in Love's service) **1796 devyse,** *arrange* **1797 Of sentement,** *with feeling,* **so unkouth wyse,** *such an unusual way* **1798 aray,** *demeanor* **1799 wroughte,** *did* **1801 Lyst,** *wished,* **chase,** *bother* **1802 Benygne,** *gracious* **1803 thank,** *gratitude* **1804 yheryed,** *praised* **1808 daun,** *lord* **1809 sustren,** *sisters* **1810 lysten,** *chose* **1811 fer,** *far,* **deyned,** *condescended* **1812 wende,** *depart* **1813 heryed,** *praised* **1815 Al be,** *even though,* **disese among,** *displeasure mixed in* **1817 As to,** *which* **1818 wyse,** *manner* **1819 lust,** *pleasure*

1807–20 Chaucer's addition. **1807 Dyone,** mother of Venus. **1808 blynde and wynged,** standard attributes of Cupid, god of love and son of Venus. **1809–10 sustren nyne . . . Elycone . . . Parnaso,** the nine Muses were thought to reside near a spring named Helicon on Mount Parnassus. Actually, Helicon was a mountain near Parnassus, but the mistake recurs in Chaucer and elsewhere. **1820a *Explicit liber tercius,*** "Here ends the third book." This rubric follows line 4.28 in Cl and Cp.

Book 4

Incipit prohemium quarti libri.

But al to litel, weylaway° the whyle°,
Lasteth swych joye, ythonked be° Fortune,
That semeth trewest whanne she wol bygyle°,
And kan to foles° so hire song entune°,
That she hem hent° and blent°, traytour
comune°.
And whan a wyght is from hire whiel ythrowe,
Than laugheth she and maketh hym the mowe°.

From Troylus she gan hire brighte face
Awey to writhe°, and tok of hym noon hede,
But caste hym clene° oute of his lady grace°,
And on hire whiel she sette up Diomede;
For which ryght now myn herte gynneth blede,
And now my penne, allas, with which I write,
Quaketh for drede of that I moste endite.

For how Criseyde Troylus forsook,
Or at the leste how that she was unkynde,
Mot° hennesforth ben matere of my book,
As writen folk thorugh which° it is in mynde°.
Allas, that they shulde evere cause fynde
To speke hire harm—and yf they on°
hire lye,
Ywys°, hemself sholde han the vilonye.

O ye Herynes, Nyghtes doughtren° thre,
That endeles compleygnen evere in pyne,
Megera, Alete, and ek Thesiphone,
Thow cruel Mars ek, fader to Quyryne,
This ilke° ferthe book me helpeth fyne°,
So that the losse of lyf and love yfere°
Of Troylus be fully shewed here.

Incipit quartus liber.

Liggyng yn ost°, as I have seyd er this,
The Grekys stronge aboute Troye town,
Byfel° that whanne that Phebus shynyng is
Upon the brest of Hercules lyoun°,
That Ector with many a bold baroun
Caste° on a day with Grekes for to fighte,
As he was woned°, to greve° hem what he
myghte.

Not I° how longe or short it was bytwene
This purpos° and that day they fighte mente,
But on a day, wel armed, bright and shene°,
Ector and many a worthi wight out wente,
With spere yn honde and bygge° bowes bente,
And in the berd°, withouten lenger lette°,
Hire fomen° in the feld anon hem mette.

The longe day, with speres sharpe ygrounde,
With arwes, dartes, swerdes, maces° felle°,
They fyghte and bryngen hors and man to
grounde,
And with hire axes out the braynes quelle°.
But in the laste shour°, soth for to telle,
The folk of Troye hemselven so mysledden°
That with the worse at nyght homward they
fledden.

---

1 weylaway, *alas,* **whyle,** *time* **2 thonked be,** *thanks to* **3 bygyle,** *deceive* **4 foles,** *fools,* **entune,** *sing* **5 hent,** *seizes,* **blent,** *blinds,* **commune,** *common to all* **7 mayketh hym the mowe,** *mocks him* **9 writhe,** *turn* **10 clene,** *completely,* **lady grace,** *lady's favor* **17 Mot,** *must* **18 thorugh which,** *by whom,* **in minde,** *known* **20 on,** *about* **21 Ywys,** *surely* **22 doughtren,** *daughters* **26 ilke,** *same,* **fyne,** *finish* **28 yfere,** *together* **29 Liggyng yn ost,** *besieging* **31 Byfel,** *it happened* **32 lyoun,** *lion* **34 Caste,** *decided* **35 woned,** *accustomed to,* **greve,** *hurt* **36 Not I,** *I don't know* **37 purpos,** *plan* **38 shene,** *shining* **40 bygge,** *strong* **41 in the berd,** i.e., *face to face,* **lette,** *delay* **42 fomen,** *enemies* **44 maces,** *spiked clubs,* **felle,** *lethal* **46 quelle,** *smash* **47 shour,** *assault* **48 hymselven so mysledden,** *managed so poorly*

Incipit Prohemium quarti libri, "Here begins the proem to the fourth book." **1–28** Cl and Cp present these lines as a conclusion to Book 3. **11–28** Chaucer's addition, after which he returns to follow *Filostrato* 4.1. **6 whiel,** the wheel of Fortune, a figure of the unreliable changeableness of life. Common in medieval art and literature, the figure derives from Boethius. **7 hym,** Cl reads "here." **11 Diomede,** the Greek warrior who is to become Criseyde's lover in Book 5. **22ff. Herynes . . . ,** Chaucer invokes the Erinyes, the Furies, named Megaera, Alecto, and Tisiphone (see 1.6 above), and then Mars, the god of war. **25 Quyryne,** Quirinus, a name of Romulus, mythic founder of Rome. **28a Incipit quartus liber,** "Here begins the fourth book." **31–32 Phebus . . . Hercules lyoun,** Phoebus, the sun, enters into the zodiacal sign of Leo (the Lion) in mid-July; Hercules slew the Nemean lion as one of his twelve labors. **38–42** Chaucer also uses alliteration to describe battle in *KnT* 1.2602–12 and *LGW* 635–49. **39–40** These lines are transposed in some manuscripts.

At whiche day was taken Antenor,
Maugre° Polydamas or Monesteo,
Santippe, Sarpedon, Polynestor,
Polyte, or eke the Trojian daun° Rupheo,
And other lasse° folk as Phebuseo;
So that for harm° that day the folk of Troye
Dredden to lese° a gret part of hire joye.

Of Pryamus was yeve° at Grekes requeste
A tyme of trewe°, and tho they gonnen trete°
Hire prisoners to chaungen°, moste and leste,
And for the surplus° yeven sommes grete°.
This thing anoon was kouth° in every strete,
Bothe in th'assege°, in town, and everywhere.
And with° the firste it com to Calkas ere.

Whan Calkas knew this tretys° sholde holde°,
In consistorie° among the Grekes soone
He gan in thrynge° forth with lordes olde,
And sette hym there as he was woned° to done;
And with a chaunged face hem bad a bone°,
For love of God, to don that reverence,
To stynte° noyse and yeve hym audyence°.

Thanne seyde he thus, “Lo, lordes myne, ich was
Troian, as it is knowen out of drede°,
And, if that yow remembre, I am Calkas,
That alderfirst° yaf comfort to youre nede
And tolde wel how that ye sholden spede°.
For dredeles thorugh yow shal in a stounde°
Ben Troye ybrend° and bete doun to grounde.

“And in what forme or in what manere wyse,
This town to shende° and al youre lust to acheve,
Ye han er this wel herd it me devyse.
This knowe ye, my lordes, as I leve°.
And for° the Grekes weren me so leve°,
I com myself, in my propre° persone,
To teche in this how yow was best to done,

“Havyng unto my tresour ne my rente°
Right no resport° to respect of° youre ese.
Thus al my good I lefte and to yow wente,
Wenyng° in this you, lordes, for to plese.
But al that losse ne doth me no dishese°.
I vouchesaf°, as wysly° have I joye,
For you to lese al that I have in Troye,

“Save of° a doughter that I lafte, allas,
Slepynge at hom whanne out of Troye I sterte°.
O sterne and cruwel fader that I was,
How myghte I have yn that so hard an herte?
Allas I ne hadde ybrought hire in hire sherte°!
For sorwe of which I wol not lyve tomorwe
But yf ye lordes rewe° upon my sorwe.

“For by that cause° I say° no tyme er now
Hire to delyvere°, ich holden have my pes°,
But now or nevere, yif that it lyke° yow,
I may hire have right sone, douteles.
O help and grace amonges al this pres°!
Rewe on this olde caytyf° in destresse,
Syn° I for yow have al this hevynesse°.

“Ye have now kaught and fetered° in preson
Troians ynowe°, and yf youre wille be,
My chyld with on° may have redempcion°.
Now, for the love of God and of bounte°,
On° of so fele°, allas, so yeve hym me!
What nede were it this preyere for to werne°,
Syn ye shul bothe han folk and town as yerne°?

51 Maugre, *despite* **53 daun,** *lord* **54 lasse,** *lesser* **55 for harm,** *because of the damage* **56 Dredden to lese,** *feared to lose* **57 yeven,** *given* **58, trewe,** *truce,* **trete,** *to negotiate* **59 chaungen,** *exchange* **60 surplus,** *remainder,* **yeven sommes grete,** *great sums were given* **61 kouth,** *known* **62 th'assege,** *the siege* **63 with,** *among* **64 tretys,** *negotiation,* **holde,** *be held* **65 consistorie,** *council* **66 in thrynge,** *to press* **67 woned,** *accustomed* **68 bad a bone,** *asked a favor* **70 stynte,** *stop,* **yeve hym audyence,** *allow him to speak* **72 drede,** *doubt* **74 alderfirst,** *first* **75 spede,** *succeed* **76 dredeles, stounde,** *time* **77 Ben . . . ybrend,** *will be burned* **79 shende,** *destroy* **81 leve,** *believe* **82 for,** *because,* **leve,** *beloved* **83 propre,** *own* **85 rente,** *income* **86 resport,** *regard,* **to respect of,** *with respect to* **88 Wenyng,** *believing* **89 dishese,** *distress* **90 vouchesaf,** *am willing,* **wysly,** *surely* **92 Save of,** *except for* **93 sterte,** *hurried* **96 sherte,** *nightshirt* **98 rewe,** *take pity* **99 by that cause,** *because,* **say,** *saw* **100 delyvere,** *release,* **pes,** *peace* **101 lyke,** *please* **103 pres,** *crowd* **104 caytyf,** *wretch* **105 Syn,** *since,* **hevynesse,** *sorrow* **106 fetered,** *chained* **107 ynowe,** *enough* **108 with on,** *for one,* **have redempcion,** *be redeemed* **109 bounte,** *goodness* **110 On,** *one,* **fele,** *many* **111 werne,** *refuse* **112 as yerne,** *soon*

50–54 Antenor . . . , in *Filostrato,* this group of Trojan warriors is captured. Chaucer follows instead the version of Benoît and Guido, where Antenor alone is captured, and he invents the name Phebuseo, apparently for meter and rhyme. **75ff. tolde wel how that ye sholden spede . . . ,** at 1.82–84, Calkas, a seer, tells the Greeks that Troy will fall, although we are given details here only in hindsight. **87 lefte,** Cl reads “loste”; Cp, “leeste.” **105 for,** Cp reads “thorugh.”

"On peril of my lyf, I shal not lye,
Appollo hath me told it feythfully;
I have ek founden be astronomye°,
By sort°, and by augurye° ek, trewely;
And dar wel seye the tyme is faste° by
That fir and flaumbe° on al the toun shal sprede,
And thus shal Troye turne to asshen dede°.

"For certeyn, Phebus and Neptainus bothe,
That makeden the walles of the toun,
Ben° with the folk of Troye alwey so wrothe°
That thei wol brynge it to confusioun°,
Right in despit of° Kyng Lameadoun—
By cause he nolde payen hem here hire°,
The town of Troye shal ben set on fire."

Tellyng his tale alwey, this olde greye°,
Humble in his speche and yn his lokyng eke,
The salte terys from his eyen tweye
Ful faste ronnen° doun by eyther cheke.
So longe he gan of socour° hem byseke
That for to hele hym of his sorwes sore,
They yaf° hym Antenor withoute more°.

But who was glad ynowh but Calkas tho?
And of this thing ful sone his nedes leyde°
On hem that sholden for the tretis° go,
And hem for Antenor ful ofte preyde°
To bryngen hom Kyng Toas and Criseyde.
And whan Pryam his savegarde° sente,
The ambassiatours to Troye streyght thei wente.

The cause ytold of hire comyng, the olde
Pryam the kyng ful soone in general
Let hereupon° his parlement to holde°,
Of which the effect° rehersen yow° I shal:
Th'embassadours ben answerd for fynal°,
Th'eschaunge of prisoners and al this nede°
Hem lyketh wel, and forth in they procede.

This Troylus was present in the place
Whan axed° was for Antenor Criseyde,
For which ful soone chaungen gan his face
As he that with tho wordes wel neygh deyde°.
But natheles he no word to it seyde,
Lest° men sholde his affeccioun espye°.
With mannes herte he gan his sorwes drye°,

And ful of angwyssh and of grysly° drede
Abod° what lordes wolde unto it seye.
And yf they wolde graunte—as God forbede—
Th'eschaunge of hire, than thoughte he thynges tweye,
First how to save hire honour, and what weye
He myghte best th'eschaunge of hire withstonde°.
Ful faste° he cast° how al this myghte stonde.

Love hym made al prest° to don° hire byde°,
And rather dye than she sholde go;
But resoun seyde° hym, on that other syde,
"Withoute assent of hire ne do not so,
Lest for thi werk she wolde be thi fo°,
And seyn° that thorugh thi medlyng is yblowe°
Yowre bothere love° there° it was erst° unknowe."

For which he gan deliberen for° the beste
That though the lordes wolde that she wente,
He wolde lat hem graunte what hem leste,
And telle his lady fyrst what that they mente;
And whanne that she hadde seyd° hym hire entente°,
Therafter° wolde he werken also blyve°,
Though al the world ayen° it wolde stryve.

---

115 be astronomye, *by astrology* **116 sort,** *casting of lots* **117 augurye,** *reading the signs* **117 faste,** *close* **118 flaumbe,** *flame* **119 asshen dede,** *dead ashes* **122 Ben,** *are,* **wrothe,** *angry* **123 confusioun,** *destruction* **124 despit of,** *anger toward* **125 hem here hire,** *them their payment* **127 greye,** *greybeard* **130 ronnen,** *ran* **131 socour,** *help* **133 yaf,** *gave,* **more,** *more discussion* **135 his nedes leyde,** *entrusted his needs* **136 tretis,** *negotiation* **137 preyde,** *asked* **139 savegarde,** *promise of safe conduct* **143 Let . . . to holde,** *held,* **hereupon,** *quickly* **144 effect,** *result,* **rehersen yow,** *retell you* **145 for fynal,** *conclusively* **146 this nede,** *that is necessary* **149 axed,** *asked* **151 wel neygh deyde,** *nearly died* **153 Lest,** *for fear that,* **espye,** *perceive* **154 drye,** *endure* **155 grysly,** *horrible* **156 Abod,** *awaited* **160 withstonde,** *oppose* **161 faste,** *deeply,* **cast,** *considered* **162 prest,** *eager,* **don,** *cause,* **byde,** *to remain* **164 seyde,** *told* **166 fo,** *foe* **167 seyn,** *say,* **yblowe,** *made known* **168 Yowre bothere love,** *the love of you both,* **there,** *where,* **erst,** *before* **169 gan deliberen for,** *decided that it was* **173 seyd,** *told,* **entente,** *wishes* **174 Therafter,** *to that effect,* **also blyve,** *very quickly* **175 ayen,** *against*

120–26 Phebus . . . Lameadoun . . . , Phoebus Apollo and Neptune were reputed to have built the walls of Troy and not been paid by King Laomedon, father of Priam; see Ovid, *Metamorphoses* 11.194–206. Chaucer's addition. **138 hom,** Cl reads "hem." **Toas,** Thoas. Chaucer conflates *Filostaro* (4.12ff.), where Antenore is exchanged for Criseida on equal terms, and Benoît (13079ff.), where he is exchanged for Thoas and Briseyde is sent to her father without exchange.

Ector, which that wel the Grekis herde,
For Antenor how they wolde han Criseyde,
Gan it withstonde°, and sobrely answerde,
"Sires, she nys no presoner," he seyde.
"I not° on yow who that this charge° leyde,
But on my part ye may eftsone° hym telle
We usen here no° wommen for to selle."

The noyse of peple up stirte° thanne at onys,
As breme° as blase° of straw yset on fyre;
For infortune it wolde°, for the nonys°,
They sholden hire confusioun° desire.
"Ector," quod they, "what gost° may yow enspire
This womman thus to shilde°, and don us lese°
Daun° Antenor? A wrong wey now ye chese!

"That is so wys and ek so bold baroun,
And we han nede to folk°, as men may se.
He is ek on the grettest° of this town.
O Ector, lat tho fantasyes be!
O Kyng Pryam," quod they, "thus seggen° we,
That al oure voys° is to forgon° Criseyde."
And to delyveren Antenor they preyde.

O Juvenal, lord, trewe is thi sentence°,
That litel wyten° folk what is to yerne°,
That they ne fynde in hire desir offence°,
For cloude of errour lat hem not descerne
What best is. And lo, here ensample as yerne°:
This folk desiren now delyveraunce
Of Antenor, that brought hem to myschaunce°.

For he was after° traytour to the town
Of Troye—allas, they quyt° hym out to rathe°!
O nyce° world, lo thy dyscressioun°!
Criseyde, which that nevere dede hem skathe°,
Shal now no lengere in hire blysse bathe;
But Antenor, he shal come hom to towne,
And she shal out°—thus seyden here and
howne°.

For which delibered° was by parlement
For Antenor to yelden° up Criseyde,
And it pronounced by the president°,
Althey° that Ector "nay" ful ofte preyede°.
And fynaly, what wyght° that it withseyde°,
It was for nought; it moste ben and sholde,
For substaunce° of the parlement it wolde°.

Departed out of parlement echone°,
This Troylus withoute wordes mo
Unto his chambre spede hym faste allone,
But yf° it were a man of his or two
The which he bad° out faste for to go
Bycause he wolde slepen, as he seyde;
And hastily upon his bed hym leyde.

And as yn wynter leves ben byraft°,
Eche after other, til the tre be bare,
So that ther nys° but bark and braunche ylaft°,
Lyth Troylus, byraft° of ech welfare°,
Ibounden° in the blake bark° of care,
Disposed° wod out of his wit° to breyde°,
So sore hym sat° the chaungynge of Criseyde.

He rist° hym up, and every dore he shette°,
And wyndow ek, and tho this sorwful man
Upon his beddes side adoun hym sette,
Ful lyk a ded ymage°, pale and wan.
And in his brest the heped° wo bygan

---

178 withstonde, *oppose* **180 not,** *don't know,* **charge,** *responsibility* **181 eftsone,** *in reply* **182 We usen here no,** *It is not our custom* **183 stirte,** *leapt* **184 breme,** *fiercely,* **blase,** *blaze* **185 infortune it wolde,** *it would be unfortunate that,* **for that nonys,** *on that occasion* **186 hire confusioun,** *their own destruction* **187 gost,** *spirit* **188 shilde,** *shield,* **don us lese,** *make us lose* **189 Daun,** *lord* **191 to folk,** *of citizens* **192 on the grettest,** *one of the greatest* **194 seggen,** *say* **195 voys,** *opinion,* **forgon,** *give up* **197 thi sentence,** *your saying* **198 wyten,** *know,* **to yerne,** *to be desired* **199 offence,** *injury* **201 as yerne,** *so appropriate* **203 myschaunce,** *misfortune* **204 after,** *afterwards* **205 quyt,** *purchased,* **to rathe,** *too soon* **206 nyce,** *foolish,* **dyscressioun,** *judgment* **207 skathe,** *harm* **210 shal out,** *must go,* **here and howne,** *one and all* (?) **211 delibered,** *decided* **212 yelden,** *yield* **213 president,** *speaker* **214 Althey,** *although,* **preyede,** *pleaded* **215 what wyght,** *whatever person,* **withseyde,** *opposed* **217 substaunce,** *majority,* **wolde,** *wished* **218 echone,** *everyone* **221 But yf,** *unless* **222 bad,** *ordered* **225 ben byraft,** *are torn* **227 nys,** *is nothing* **ylaft,** *remaining* **228 byraft,** *deprived,* **welfare,** *happiness* **229 Ibounden,** *bound up,* **bark,** *tree bark* **230 Disposed,** *inclined,* **wod out of his wit,** *mad out of his mind,* **breyde,** *rush* **231 sore hym sat,** *painfully beset him* **232 rist,** *rises,* **shette,** *shuts* **235 ded ymage,** *dead statue* **236 heped,** *piled*

181 hym, Cp reads "hem." **183–184** This has been interpreted as an allusion to the uprising of 1381 (Peasants' Revolt) because one of its leaders was named Jack Straw. **176–217** Ector's participation, the parliamentary response, and the narrator's comments are largely Chaucer's addition. **197–201 Juvenal . . . ,** from Juvenal, *Satires* 10.2–4: "Few can distinguish true blessings from ills, free from the cloud from the cloud of error." **200 not,** omitted in Cp. **204 traytour,** with Aeneas, Antenor contrived to deliver to the Greeks the Palladium on which the safety of Troy depended; see the note to 1.153. The reference is not in *Filostrato.* **210 here and howne,** the meaning and derivation of this phrase are not agreed upon. **225–27** The image of sorrow as a leafless tree derives from Virgil, *Aeneid* 6.309–12, by way of Dante, *Inferno* 3.112–14.

Out brest°, and he to werken° yn this wyse
In his woodnesse°, as I shal yow devyse.

Ryght as the wylde bole° bygynneth sprynge°,
Now her, now ther, idarted° to the herte,
And of his deth roreth yn compleynynge,
Right so gan he aboute the chaumbre sterte°,
Smytyng his brest ay with his festes smerte°;
His hed to the wal, his body to the grounde
Ful ofte he swapte°, himselven to confounde°.

Hys eyen two for pite of his herte
Out stremeden as swyfte welles tweye°.
The heyghe° sobbes of his sorwes smerte
His speche hym rafte°. Unnethes° myghte he seye,
"O deth, allas, whi nyltow do° me deye?
Acursed be the day which that Nature
Shop° me to ben a lyves° creature!"

But after, whan the furye and the rage,
Which that his herte twyste° and faste threste°,
By lengthe of tyme somwhat gan aswage°,
Upon his bed he leyde hym down to reste.
But tho bygonne his terys more out breste,
That wonder is° the body may suffise°
To half this wo which that I yow devyse.

Thanne seyde he thus, "Fortune, allas the while°!
What have I don? What have I thus agilt°?
How myghtestow° for reuthe° me bygyle°?
Is ther no grace, and shal I thus be spilt°?
Shal thus Criseyde awey, for° that thow wylt?
Allas, how maystow° in thyn herte fynde
To ben to me thus cruwel and unkynde?

"Have I the nought honoured al my lyve,
As thow wel wost°, above the goddes alle?
Why wiltow° me fro joye thus depryve?
O Troylus, what may men the now calle
But wrecche of wrecches, out of honour falle°
Into myserie, yn which I wol bywayle
Criseyde, allas, til that the breth me fayle?

"Allas, Fortune, yf that my lyf yn joye
Displesed hadde unto thi foule envye,
Why ne haddestow° my fader, kyng of Troye,
Byraft° the lyf, or don° my bretheren deye,
Or slayn myself that thus compleyne and crye—
I, combre-world°, that may of° nothing serve,
But evere dye, and nevere fully sterve°?

"Yf that Criseyde allone were me laft,
Nought roughte° I wheder thow woldest me stere°!
And hire, allas, than° hastow me byraft!
But everemore, lo, this is thi manere,
To reve° a wyght that° most is to hym dere,
To preve° yn that thi gerful° violence.
Thus am I lost; there helpeth no defence.

"O verrey° lord of love, O god, allas,
That knowest best myn herte and al my thought,
What shal my sorwful lyf don in this cas,
Yf I forgo that° I so dere° have bought?
Syn ye Cryseyde and me han fully brought.
Into youre grace, and bothe oure hertes seled°,
How may ye suffre, allas, it be repeled°?

"What may I don? I shal whil I may dure°,
On lyve° in torment and yn cruwel peyne,
This infortune° of this disaventure°,
Allone as I was born, ywys°, compleyne°;
Ne nevere wyl I seen it shyne or reyne,
But ende I wil, as Edippe, yn derknesse
My sorwful lyf, and dyen in dystresse.

---

237 brest, *burst,* **werken,** *act* **238 woodnesse,** *madness* **239 bole,** *bull,* **sprynge,** *to leap* **240 idarted,** *speared* **242 sterte,** *leap* **243 smerte,** *painfully* **245 swapte,** *dashed* **245 confounde,** *destroy* **247 as swyfte welles tweye,** *like two swift springs* **248 heyghe,** *loud* **249 hym rafte,** *deprived him of,* **Unnethes,** *barely* **250 nyltow do,** *will you not make* **252 Shop,** *created,* **lyves,** *living* **254 twyste,** *twisted,* **threste,** *pierced* **255 gan aswage,** *did abate* **259 wonder is,** *it is a wonder,* **suffise,** *be adequate* **260 while,** *time* **261 agilt,** *offended* **262 myghtestow,** *could you,* **reuthe,** *pity,* **bygyle,** *deceive* **263 spilt,** *destroyed* **264 for,** *because* **265 maystow,** *can you* **268 wost,** *know* **269 wiltow,** *will you* **271 falle,** *fallen* **276 ne haddestow,** *haven't you* **277 Byraft,** *deprived* **don,** *caused,* **combre-world,** *burden to the world* **279 of,** *for* **280 sterve,** *die* **282 Nought roughte,** *would care nothing,* **stere,** *steer* **283 than,** *then* **285 reve,** *take from,* **that,** *what* **286 preve,** *demonstrate,* **gerful,** *changeable* **288 verray,** *true* **291 forgo that,** *give up what,* **dere,** *costly* **293 seled,** *sealed* **294 repeled,** *repealed* **295 dure,** *endure* **296 On lyve,** *alive* **297 infortune,** *ill fortune,* **disaventure,** *disaster* **298 ywys,** *truly,* **compleyne,** *lament*

239–42 The comparison with the mad bull derives from *Filostrato* 4.27, Dante, *Inferno* 12.22–24, and, ultimately, Virgil, *Aeneid* 2.222–24; more generally, the lover's madness is a convention of courtly tradition. **246 his,** omitted in Cp. **295 may I,** Cl and Cp read "I may," which makes the whole line a declaration without a question. **298 Allone,** Cl reads "Allas." **300 Edippe,** Oedipus, who wandered in exile,blinded by his own hand, before dying. Chaucer's addition.

"O wery goost° that errest° to and fro,
Why nyltow fle° out of the wofulleste
Body that evere myghte on grounde go?
O soule, lurkynge in this wo, unneste°,
Fle forth out of myn herte and lat it breste°,
And folowe alwey Criseyde, thi lady dere.
Thi righte place is now no lenger here.

"O wofulle eyen two, syn° youre desport°
Was al to seen Criseydes eyen bryght,
What shal ye don but for my discomfort
Stonden for nought°, and wepen out youre sight,
Syn she is queynt° that wont° was yow to light?
In vayn fro this forth° have ich eyen tweye
Yformed°, syn youre vertu° is aweye.

"O my Criseyde, O lady sovereyne
Of thilke° woful soule that thus crieth,
Who shal now yeven° comfort to the peyne?
Allas, no wight; but whan myn herte dyeth,
My spirit, which that so unto yow hyeth°,
Receyve in gre°, for that shal ay yow serve;
Forthi no fors is°, though the body sterve°.

"O ye loveres, that heyhe° upon the whiel
Ben set of Fortune, yn good aventure,
God leve° that ye fynde ay love of stel°,
And longe mot° youre lyf yn joye endure!
But whanne ye comen by my sepulture°,
Remembreth that youre felawe resteth there—
For I loved ek, though ich unworthi were.

"O old, unholsom°, and myslyved° man,
Calkas I mene, allas, what eyleth the°
To ben a Grek syn thou art born Troian?
O Calkas, which that wilt my bane° be,
In cursed tyme was thow born for me!
As wolde blisful Jove° for his joye
That I the hadde° where as I wolde° in Troye!"

A thousand sykes° hottere than the glede°
Out of his brest eche after other wente,
Meddled° with pleyntes new his wo to fede°,
For which his woful terys nevere stente°.
And shortly, so his peynes hym torente°
And wex so mat° that joye nor penaunce
He feleth noon, but lyth forth° in a traunce.

Pandare, which that in the parlement
Hadde herd what every lord and burgeys° seyde,
And how ful graunted was by on assent
For Antenor to yelden° so Criseyde,
Gan wel neygh wod° out of his wit to breyde°,
So that for wo he nyste° what he mente,
But in a res° to Troylus he wente.

A certeyn knyght that for the tyme kepte°
The chaumbre door undede it hym° anoon;
And Pandare that ful tendreliche wepte
Into the derke chambre, as stille as ony ston,
Toward the bed gan softely° to gon,
So confus° that he nyste what to seye;
For verray wo his wit was neigh aweye°.

And with his chere° and lokyng al totorn°
For sorwe of this, and with his armes folden,
He stod this woful Troylus byforn,
And on his pitous face he gan byholden.
But Lord, so ofte gan his herte colden°,
Seyng° his frend in wo, whose hevynesse°
His herte slow°, as thought hym, for distresse.

This woful wight, this Troylus, that felte
His frend Pandare ycomen hym to se,
Gan as the snow ayen° the sonne melte,
For whych this sorwful Pandare of pyte
Gan for to wepe as tendrelyche as he,
And specheles thus ben this ilke tweye°,
That neyther myghte o word for sorwe seye.

---

302 goost, *spirit,* **that errest,** *who wanders* **303 nyltow fle,** *won't you flee* **305 unneste,** *leave the nest* **306 breste,** *burst* **309 syn,** *since,* **desport,** *pleasure* **312 Stonden for nought,** *be of no use* **313 queynt,** *extinguished,* **that wont,** *who was accustomed* **314 fro this forth,** *from this time forward* **315 Yformed,** *been created with,* **vertu,** *power* **317 thilke,** *this* **318 yeven,** *give* **320 hyeth,** *hastens* **321 gre,** *favor* **322 Forthi no fors is,** *therefore it is no matter,* **sterve,** *die* **323 heyhe,** *high* **325 leve,** *permit,* **of stel,** *durable as steel* **326 mot,** *may* **327 sepulture,** *tomb* **330 unholsom,** *corrupt,* **myslyved,** *evil-living* **331 eyleth the,** *ails you* **333 bane,** *death* **335 As wolde blisful Jove,** (I wish that) *blessed Jove would grant* **336 the hadde,** *had you,* **wolde,** *wish* **337 sykes,** *sighs,* **glede,** *glowing coal* **339 Meddled,** *mixed,* **fede,** *feed* **340 stente,** *ceased* **341 torente,** *tore apart* **342 wex so mat,** *grew so exhausted* **343 lyth forth,** *continues to lie* **345 burgeys,** *citizen* **347 yelden,** *hand over* **348 wel neygh wod,** *nearly mad,* **breyde,** *go* **349 nyste,** *knew not* **350 res,** *rush* **351 kepte,** *guarded* **352 undede it hym,** *undid it for him* **355 softely,** *quietly* **356 confus,** *confused* **357 neigh aweye,** *nearly gone* **358 chere,** *face,* **totorn,** *distorted* **362 colden,** *grow cold* **363 Seyng,** *seeing,* **hevynesse,** *sorrow* **364 slow,** *slew* **367 ayen,** *before* **370 ilke tweye,** *same pair*

302 wery, Cl reads "verray." **330 myslyved,** Cl reads "mysbyleved." **354 ony,** omitted in Cp.

But at the laste this woful Troylus,
Ney° ded for smert°, gan bresten° out to rore°,
And with a sorwful noyse he seyde thus,
Among his sobbes and his sikes° sore,
"Lo, Pandare, I am ded withouten more°.
Hastow nought herd at parlement," he seyde,
"For Antenor how lost is my Criseyde?"

This Pandarus, ful dede° and pale of hewe,
Ful pytously answerde and seyde, "Yis,
As wysly were it° fals as it is trewe,
That I have herd and wot° al how it is.
O mercy God, who wolde have trowed° this?
Who wolde have wend° that yn so lytel a throwe°
Fortune oure joye wolde han overthrowe?

"For yn this world there is no creature,
As to my dom°, that ever saw ruyne°
Straunger than this, thorugh cas° or aventure°.
But who may al eschewe° or al devyne°?
Swych is this world! Forthi° I thus defyne°:
Ne trust no wyght to fynden in Fortune
Ay proprete°—hire yeftes° ben comune°.

"But tel me this: whi thou art now so mad
To sorwen thus? Whi listow° in this wyse,
Syn thi desir al holly hastow° had,
So that by right it oughte ynow suffise?
But I, that nevere felte in my servyse°
A frendly chere°, or lokyng of an eye,
Lat me thus wepe and wailen til I dye.

"And over° al this, as thow wel wost° thiselve,
This town is ful of ladyes al aboute;
And, to my dom°, fairer than swyche twelve°
As evere she was shal I fynde yn som route°,
Ye° oon or two, withouten any doute.
Forthi° be glad, myn owen dere brother.
If she be lost, we shul recovere another.

"What, God forbede alwey that ech plesaunce°
In o thyng were and in noon other wyght.
Yf oon kan synge, another kan wel daunce;
Yf this be goodly, she is glad and lyght°;
And this is fayr, and that kan° good aright.
Ech for his vertu holden is for dere°,
Bothe heroner° and faukoun for ryvere°.

"And ek, as writ° Zanzis that was ful wys,
The newe love out chaceth ofte the olde,
And upon newe cas° lyth newe avys°.
Thenk ek, thi lif to saven thow art holde°.
Swych fyr by proces shal of kynde colde°;
For syn it is but casuel° plesaunce,
Som cas shal putte it out of remembraunce.

"For also seur° as day cometh after nyght,
The newe love, labour, or other wo,
Or ellys° selde seynge° of a wyght,
Don° olde affeccioun al overgo°.
And for thi part, thow shalt have one of tho°
To abrigge with° thi bittre peynes smerte;
Absence of hire shal dryve hire out of herte."

Thise wordes seyde he for the nones alle°,
To helpe his frend lest he for sorwe deyde.
For douteles, to don° his wo to falle°,
He roughte nought° what unthryft° that he seyde.
But Troylus, that neigh for sorwe deyde,
Tok litel hed° of al that evere he mente°;
Oon eere it herde, at the other out it wente.

---

373 Ney, *nearly,* **smert,** *pain,* **bresten,** *burst,* **rore,** *roar* **375 sikes,** *sighs* **375 withouten more,** *and nothing else* **379 ful dede,** *very deathly* **381 As wysly were it,** (I wish that) *it were as surely* **382 wot,** *know* **383 trowed,** *believed* **384 wend,** *thought* **384 throwe,** *time* **387 dom,** *judgment,* **ruyne,** *ruin* **388 cas,** *accident,* **aventure,** *chance* **389 eschewe,** *avoid,* **devyne,** *foresee* **390 Forthi,** *therefore,* **defyne,** *conclude* **392 Ay properte,** *permanent possessions,* **yeftes,** *gifts,* **ben comune,** *are shared by all* **394 listow,** *do you lie down* **395 hastow,** *have you* **397 servyse,** *love service* **398 chere,** *face* **400 over,** *above,* **wost,** *know* **402 dom,** *judgment,* **fairer than swyche twelve,** *twelve times fairer* **403 route,** *group* **404 Ye,** *yes* **405 Forthi,** *therefore* **407 plesaunce,** *pleasure* **410 lyght,** *cheerful* **411 kan,** *knows* **412 holden is for dere,** *is valued* **413 heroner,** *falcon for hunting herons,* **faukoun for ryvere,** *falcon for hunting waterfowl* **414 writ,** *wrote* **416 cas,** *situation,* **avys,** *consideration* **417 holde,** *responsible* **418 of kynde colde,** *naturally become cold* **419 casuel,** *accidental* **421 seur,** *surely* **423 ellys,** *else,* **selde seynge,** *seldom seeing* **424 Don,** *cause,* **overgo,** *to go away* **425 tho,** *those* (women or experiences) **426 abrigge with,** *reduce* **428 for the nones alle,** *completely for the purpose at hand* **430 don,** *cause,* **falle,** *decrease* **431 roughte nought,** *cared not,* **unthryft,** *nonsense* **433 hed,** *heed,* **mente,** *said*

392 hire, Cl reads "his." **407–13** Chaucer's addition. **413 heroner and faukoun,** two different kinds of hunting bird, valuable for similar purposes. **414 Zanzis,** unidentified; Cl reads "Zauzis." The commonplace statement in line 415 is from *Filostrato* 4.49. **417 lif,** Cl reads "self." **thow art,** Cp reads "artow." **419–20** This observation is not in Pandaro's speech in *Filostrato* 4.49. **430 wo,** Cl reads "sorwe." **428–34** Chaucer's addition. **434** Proverbial.

But at the laste he answerde and seyde, "Frend,
This lechecraft°, or heled° thus to be,
Were wel sittyng° if that I were a fend°—
To traysen° hire that trewe is unto me.
I pray to God lat this consayl nevere the°,
But do me rathere anon sterve° right here,
Er I thus do as thow me woldest lere°.

"She that I serve, ywys°, what so° thow seye,
To whom myn herte enhabyt° is by right,
Shal han me holly hires° til that I deye.
For, Pandarus, syn I have trouthe° hire hight°,
I wol nat ben untrewe for no wyght,
But as hire man I wole ay lyve and sterve°,
And nevere other creature serve.

"And ther° thow seyst thow shalt as faire fynde
As she, lat be°. Make no comparysoun
To creature yformed here by kynde°.
O leve° Pandare, in conclusion,
I wol nat ben of thyn opynyon
Towchyng° al this. For whiche I the byseche°,
So hold thi pes°; thow slest° me with thi
speche!

"Thow biddest° me I sholde love another
Al fresshly newe, and lat Criseyde go.
It lith nat in my power, leve brother;
And though I myght, I wolde not do so.
But kanstow° pleyen raket°, to and fro,
Nettle in, dokke out, now this, now that, Pandare?
Now fowle falle hire° that for thi wo hath care!

"Thow farest ek by me°, thow Pandarus,
As he that whan a wyght is wobygon°,
He cometh to hym a pas° and seyth right thus,
'Thenk not on smert, and thow shalt fele noon.'
Thow most me first transmewen in° a ston,
And reve me° my passiones alle,
Er thow so lightly do° my wo to falle°.

"The deth may wel out of my brest departe°
The lyf, so longe may this sorwe myne°;
But fro my sowle shal Criseydes darte
Out° neveremo. But down with Proserpyne,
Whan I am ded, I wol go wone° in pyne°,
And ther I wol eternally compleyne°
My wo, and how that twynned° be we tweyne.

"Thow hast here mad an argument for fyn°,
How that it sholde a lasse° peyne be
Criseyde to forgon for° she was myn
And lyved in ese and yn felicite.
Whi gabbestow° that seydest thus to me,
That 'hym is wors that is fro wele ythrowe°,
Than he hadde erst non of that wele yknowe?'

"But tel me now, syn that the thenketh° so lyght°
To chaungen so in love ay to and fro,
Whi hastow not don bysyly thi myght°
To chaungen hire that doth the al thi wo?
Why neltow° lete hire fro thyn herte go?
Whi neltow love another lady swete,
That may thin herte setten in quyete°?

"If thow hast had in love ay yet myschaunce°,
And kanst it not out of thyn herte dryve,
I that levede yn lust° and in plesaunce
With hire as muche as creature on lyve,
How sholde I that foryete, and that so blyve°?
O, where hastow ben hid so longe in muwe°,
That kanst so wel and formaly° arguwe?

---

436 lechecraft, *medicine,* **heled,** *healed* **437 wel sittyng,** *appropriate,* **fend,** *fiend* **438 traysen,** *betray* **439 the,** *succeed* **440 do me . . . sterve,** *kill me* **441 lere,** *teach* **442 ywys,** *surely,* **what so,** *whatever* **443 enhabyt,** *devoted* **444 holly hires,** *wholly hers* **445 trouthe,** *fidelity,* **hight,** *promised* **447 sterve,** *die* **449 ther,** *where* **450 lat be,** *give it up* **451 here by kynde,** *in this world by nature* **452 leve,** *dear* **454 Towchyng,** *concerning,* **the byseche,** *ask you* **455 hold thi pes,** *be quiet,* **slest,** *slay* **456 biddest,** *tell* **460 kanstow,** *can you,* **raket,** *tennis* **462 fowle falle hire,** *evil luck to her* **463 Thow farest ek by me,** *you treat me also* **464 wobygon,** *sorrowful* **465 a pas,** *quickly* **467 transmewen in,** *transform into* **468 reve me,** *strip me* (of) **469 do,** *cause,* **falle,** *decrease* **470 departe,** *drive* **471 myne,** *undermine* **473 Out,** *move out* **474 wone,** *live,* **pyne,** *pain* **475 compleyne,** *lament* **476 twynned,** *separated* **477 mad an argument for fyn,** *argued for a conclusion* **478 lasse,** *lesser* **479 forgon for,** *lose because* **481 gabbestow,** *do you jabber* **482 fro wele ythrowe,** *from happiness thrown* **484 the thenketh,** *you think* (it), **lyght,** *easy* **486 don bysyly thi myght,** *energetically done all you can* **488 neltow,** *won't you* **490 in quyete,** *at rest* **491 ay yet myschaunce,** *continuous bad luck* **493 levede yn lust,** *lived in joy* **495 blyve,** *quickly* **496 hid . . . in muwe,** *cooped up* **497 formaly,** *correctly*

439 the, Cp reads "ythe." **460 raket,** rackets was a predecessor of modern tennis, played off the walls of an enclosed court. **459 wolde,** Cl reads "wil"; Cp, "wol." **461 Nettle in, dokke out,** the first words of a charm recited to stop the stinging of nettles, spoken while rubbing the sting with dock leaves; a proverbial expression for inconstancy. **466** A commonplace notion. **473 Proserpyne,** Proserpina, queen of Hades. **480 lyved,** Cl reads "leve." **482–83** Recalls 3.1625–28. **491–532** Six stanzas lacking in Cp.

"Nay, God wot, nought worth is al thi red°.
For which, for what that evere may byfalle,
Withouten wordes mo, I wol be ded.
O deth, that endere art of sorwes alle,
Com now, syn I so ofte after the calle;
For sely° is that deth, soth for to seyne,
That, ofte ycleped°, cometh and endeth peyne.

"Wel wot I, whil my lyf was in quyete,
Er thow me slowe°, I wolde have yeven hire°;
But now thi comynge is to me so swete
That in this world I nothing so desire.
O deth, syn with this sorwe I am afyre,
Thou other do° me anoon yn teris drenche°,
Or with thi colde strok myn hete quenche.

"Syn that thou sleest so fele° in sondry wyse°,
Ayens hire wil, unpreyed°, day and nyght,
Do me at my requeste this servise:
Delyvere now the world, so dostow° right,
Of me that am the wofulleste wyght
That evere was, for tyme is that I sterve°,
Syn in this world of right nought may I serve."

This Troylus in teris° gan distille,
As licour° out of a lambyc° ful faste.
And Pandarus gan holde his tunge stille,
And to the ground his eyen doun he caste.
But natheles, thus thought he at the laste,
"What, parde°, rather than my felawe deye,
Yet shal I somwhat more unto hym seye."

And seyde, "Frend, syn thow hast swych distresse,
And syn thee list° myn argumentes blame,
Why nylt° thiself helpen don redresse°,
And with thy manhod letten° al this grame°?
To ravysshe° hire ne kanstow° not? For shame!
And other lat° hire out of towne fare°,
Or hold hire stille, and leve thi nyce fare°.

"Artow in Troye, and hast noon hardiment°
To take a womman which that loveth the,
And wolde hireselven ben of thyn assent°?
Now is nat this a nyce vanyte°?
Rys up anoon, and lat this wepyng be,
And kyth° thow art a man, for yn this owre°
I wil be ded or she shal bleven oure°."

To this answerde hym Troylus ful softe°,
And seyde, "Parde, leve° brother dere,
Al this have I myself yet thought ful ofte,
And more thyng than thow devysest° here.
But whi this thyng is laft° thow shalt wel here,
And whan thow me hast yeve° an audience,
Therafter maystow telle al thi sentence°.

"Fyrst, syn thow wost this town hath al this werre
For ravysshyng of womman so by myght°,
It sholde not be suffred me to erre°,
As it stant° now, ne don° so gret unright.
I sholde han also blame of every wyght
My fadres graunt° yf that I so withstode°,
Syn she is chaunged° for the townes goode.

"I have ek thought, so° it were hire assent,
To axe° hire at my fader, of his grace;
Than thenke I this were hire accusement°,
Syn wel I wot I may hire nought purchace°.
For syn my fader in so heigh a place
As parlement hath hire eschaunge enseled°,
He nyl for me his lettre° be repeled.

"Yet drede I moost hire herte to pertourbe°
With violence, yf I do swych a game°.

---

498 red, *advice* **503 sely,** *happy* **504 ycleped,** *called for* **506 slowe,** *killed,* **yeven hire,** *paid ransom* **510 other do,** *either cause,* **drenche,** *to drown* **512 fele,** *many,* **sondry wyse,** *various ways* **513 unpreyed,** *unasked* **515 so dostow,** *as you do* **517 sterve,** *die* **519 teris,** *tears* **520 licour,** *liquid,* **lambyc,** *alembic* **524 parde,** *by God* **527 thee list,** *you wish* **528 nylt,** *will you not,* **thiself helpen don redresse,** *help to relieve yourself* **529 letten,** *prevent,* **grame,** *grief* **530 ravysshe,** *abduct,* **kanstow,** *can you* **531 other lat,** *either let,* **fare,** *go* **532 nyce fare,** *silly behavior* **533 hardiment,** *courage* **535 ben of thyn assent,** *agree with you* **536 nyce vanyte,** *foolish thing* **538 kyth,** *show,* **owre,** *hour* **539 bleven oure,** *remain ours* **540 ful softe,** *very quietly* **541 leve,** *beloved* **543 devysest,** *describe* **543 laft,** *undone* **545 yeve,** *given* **546 sentence,** *opinion* **548 myght,** *force* **549 suffred me to erre,** *permitted me to break the law* **550 stant,** *stands,* **don,** *commit* **552 graunt,** *decree,* **withstode,** *opposed* **553 chaunged,** *to be exchanged* **554 so,** *if* **555 axe,** *ask* **556 were hire accusement,** *would be an accusation against her* **557 purchace,** *obtain* **559 enseled,** *approved formally* **560 lettre,** *decree* **561 pertourbe,** *upset* **562 do swych a game,** *make such a move*

503–04 Echoes *Bo* 1.m1.18–20. **510 yn teris,** Cl reads "yn this teris." **519–20** An alembic is a vessel used in distillation; the figure implies that Troylus's tears are pure. **548 ravysshing of womman,** the Trojan War was caused by the abduction of women: Telamon's abduction of Priam's sister, Hesione, and Paris's retaliatory abduction of Helen, wife of Menelaus, brother to Agammenon, leader of the Greeks (Benoît 2793ff., 3187ff, 4059ff.). **555 axe her at my fader,** Troylus apparently has thought of asking his father for permission to marry Criseyde.

For yf I wolde it openly distourbe°,
It moste ben disclaundre° to hire name,
And me were levere° ded than hire defame—
As nolde God but yf° I sholde have
Hire honour levere° than my lyf to save!

"Thus am I lost, for ought that I kan se.
For certeyn is, syn that I am hire knyght,
I moste hire honour levere han° than me
In every cas, as lovere ought of right.
Thus am I with desir and reson twyght°:
Desir for to destourben° hire me redeth°,
And reson nyl not, so myn herte dredeth°."

Thus wepyng that° he koude nevere cesse,
He seyde, "Allas, how shal I, wrecche, fare°?
For wel fele° I alwey my love encresse,
And hope is lasse and lasse alway, Pandare.
Encressen ek the causes of my care.
So welawey, whi nyl myn herte breste°?
For as in love ther is but litel reste."

Pandare answerde, "Frend, thow mayst, for me,
Don as the list; but hadde ich it so hote,
And thyn estat°, she sholde go with me,
Though al this town criede on this thyng by note°.
I nolde sette at al that noyse a grote°.
For when men han wel cried, than wol they rowne°—
A wonder last but° nyne nyght nevere yn towne.

"Devyne° not in reson ay so depe
Ne curteysly, but help thiself anoon.
Bet is° that othere than thiselven wepe,
And namly syn° ye two ben al oon°.
Rys up, for by myn hed she shal not goon!
And rather be in blame a lite yfounde
Than sterve here as a gnat°, withowten wounde.

"It is no shame unto yow, ne no vice,
Hire to withholden° that ye loveth most.
Peraunter°, she myghte holden the for nyce°
To late° hire go thus unto the Greke ost°.
Thenk ek Fortune, as wel thiselven wost°,
Helpeth hardy° man to his enprise°,
And weyveth° wrecches for hire cowardise.

"And though thi lady wolde a lite hire greve°,
Thow shalt thi pes ful wel hereafter make,
But as for me, certeyn, I kan not leve°
That she wolde it as now for yvel take°.
Whi sholde thanne of fered° thyn herte quake?
Thenk ek how Parys hath, that is thi brother,
A love; and whi shaltow nat have another?

"And Troylus, o thyng I dar the swere,
That if Criseyde, whiche that is thi lef°,
Now loveth the as wel as thow dost hire,
God helpe me so, she nyl not take a-gref°,
Theigh° thou do bote° anoon in this myschef°.
And yf she wilneth° fro the for to passe,
Thanne is she fals; so love hire wel the lasse.

"Forthi° tak herte, and thenk right as a knyght,
Thorugh love is broken alday° every lawe.
Kith° now somwhat thi corage and thi myght,
Have mercy on thiself for ony awe°.
Lat nat this wrecched wo thyn herte gnawe,
But manly set° the world on sixe and sevene,
And yf thow deye a martir, go to hevene.

"I wol myself ben with the at this dede,
Theygh° ich and al my kyn upon a stounde°

563 it openly distourbe, *publicly thwart the exchange* **564 disclaundre,** *slander* **565 me were levere,** *I would rather* (be) **566 As nolde God but yf,** *God forbid anything but that* **567 levere,** *rather* **570 levere han,** *rather have* **572 twyght,** *pulled* **573 destourben hire,** *prevent her* (going), **redeth,** *advises* **575 dredeth,** *is afraid* **575 that,** *as if* **576 fare,** *act* **577 fele,** *feel* **580 breste,** *burst* **584 estat,** *status* **585 by note,** *in unison* **586 grote,** *small coin* **587 rowne,** *whisper* (quiet down) **588 last but,** *lasts only* **589 Devyne,** *ponder* **591 Bet is,** *it is better* **592 namly syn,** *especially since,* **al oon,** *in agreement* **595 sterve as a gnat,** *die like an insect* **597 withholden,** *retain* **598 Peraunter,** *perhaps,* **nyce,** *foolish* **599 late,** *let,* **ost,** *army* **600 wost,** *know* **601 hardy,** *bold,* **enprise,** *enterprise* **602 weyveth,** *abandons* **604 hire greve,** *be offended* **605 leve,** *believe* **606 as now for yvel take,** *take is wrong at this time* **607 of fered,** *from fear* **611 lef,** *beloved* **613 take a-gref,** *be offended* **614 Theigh,** *though,* **do bote,** *make a remedy,* **myschef,** *bad situation* **615 wilneth,** *wishes* **617 Forthi,** *therefore* **618 alday,** *always* **619 Kith,** *show* **620 for ony awe,** *despite any fear* **622 manly set,** *like a man wager* **625 Theygh,** *though,* **stounde,** *time*

586 sette at al that noyse a grote, an idiom meaning, "consider that outcry worthless." **588** Proverbial. **A wonder,** Cp reads "Ek wonder." **594 lite,** Cl reads "litel." **600–01** Proverbial. **604 thi pes ful wel,** Cp reads "thi self thi pees." **608 Parys,** see 4.548n. **614 Theigh,** Cl reads "They." **618** Proverbial. **622 set the world on sixe and sevene,** bet the world on a dice throw, i.e., "take your chances." The derivation of the phrase is unknown. **623** To die a martyr's death is an anachronism in pagan Troy, but martyrdom for love is a medieval courtly convention. **624–30** Chaucer's addition. **624 dede,** Cl reads "nede."

Shulle° in a strete as dogges liggen dede,
Thorugh-girt° with many a wyd and blody wounde.
In every cas I wol a frend be founde.
And yf the lyst here sterven° as a wrecche,
Adieu—the devel spede° hym that it recche°."

This Troylus gan with tho wordes quyken°,
And seyde, "Frend, graunt mercy°, ich assente.
But certeynly thow mayst not me so priken°,
Ne peyne noon ne° may me so tormente,
That for no cas° it is not myn entente,
At shorte wordes, though I dyen sholde,
To ravysshen° hire but yf hireself it wolde°."

"Why, so mene I," quod Pandarus, "al this day.
But telle me thanne, hastow hire wil assayed,
That sorwest thus?" And he answerde hym, "Nay."
"Wherof artow°," quod Pandare, "than amayed°,
That nost not° that she wol ben evele apayed°
To ravysshen hire, syn thow hast not ben there,
But if° that Jove told it yn thyn eere?

"Forthi rys up as nought ne were°, anoon,
And wassh thi face, and to the kyng thow wende°,
Or he may wondren whider thow art goon.
Thow most° with wysdom hym and othere blende°,
Or, upon cas°, he may after the sende,
Er thow be war. And shortly, brother dere,
Be glad, and lat me werke in this matere.

"For I shal shappe° it so that sikerly°
Thow shalt this nyght somtyme in som manere
Com speke with thi lady prevely°,
And by hire wordes ek, and by hire chere°,
Thow shalt ful sone aparceyve° and wel here°
Al hire entente, and in this cas the beste.
And fare now wel, for in this point I reste."

The swyfte Fame°, which that false thynges
Egal° reporteth lyk the thynges trewe,
Was thorughout Troye yfled with preste° wynges
Fro man to man and made this tale al newe°,
How Calkas doughter with hire brighte hewe,
At parlement, withoute wordes more,
Igraunted was yn chaunge of° Antenore.

The whiche tale anoon-right° as Criseyde
Had herd, she which that of hire fader roughte°,
As in this cas, right nought, ne whanne he deyde,
Ful bysily to Juppiter bysoughte
Yeve hym myschaunce° that this tretis° broughte.
But shortly, lest this° tales sothe were,
She dorste at no wyght asken it for fere,

As she that hadde hire herte and al hire mynde
On Troilus yset so wonder faste°
That al the world ne koude hire love unbynde,
Ne Troylus out of hire herte caste—
She wol ben his, whil that hire lyf may laste.
And thus she brenneth° bothe in love and drede,
So that she nyste° what was best to rede°.

But as men sen in towne and al aboute
That wommen usen° frendes to visite,
So to Criseyde of wommen come a rowte°,
For pitous° joye, and wenden hire delite°.
And with hire tales, dere ynowh a myte°,
These wommen, whiche that yn the cite dwelle,
Thei sette hem doun and seyde as I shal telle.

---

626 Shulle, *shall* **627 Thorugh-girt,** *pierced through* **629 the lyst heresterven,** *you choose to die here* **630 spede,** *help,* **it recche,** *cares about it* **631 quyken,** *to revive* **632 graunt mercy,** *thank you* **633 priken,** *prod* **634 Ne peyne noon ne,** *no pain* **635 for no cas,** *under no circumstances* **637 ravysshen,** *abduct,* **wolde,** *wished* **641 Wherof artow,** *why are you,* **than amayed,** *then dismayed* **642 nost not,** *know not,* **evele apayed,** *displeased* **644 But if,** *unless* **645 as nought ne were,** *as if it were nothing* **646 wende,** *go* **648 most,** *must,* **blende,** *deceive* **649 upon cas,** *by chance* **652 shappe,** *arrange,* **sikerly,** *certainly* **654 prevely,** *secretly* **655 chere,** *manner* **656 aparceyve,** *perceive,* **here,** *hear* **659 Fame,** *rumor* **660 Egal,** *equally* **661 preste,** *swift* **662 al newe,** *told and retold* **665 chaunge of,** *exchange for* **666 anoon-right,** *as soon as* **667 roughte,** *cared* **670 Yeve hym myschaunce,** *to give him bad luck,* **tretis,** *negotiation* **671 lest this,** *apprehensive that these* **674 wonder faste,** *marvelously firmly* **678 brenneth,** *burns* **679 nyste,** *knew not,* **best to rede,** *best to consider* **681 usen,** *are accustomed* **682 rowte,** *group* **683 pitous,** *compassionate,* **wenden hire delite,** *thought to please her* **684 dere ynowh a myte,** i.e., *too costly*

638–44 Chaucer's addition. **639 wil,** Cl reads "wel." **659–60** A commonplace view of rumor.

Quod first that oon, "I am glad, trewely,
By cause of yow, that ye shal youre fader se."
Another seyde, "Iwys°, so am not I,
For al to litel hath she with us be."
Quod tho the thridde, "I hope, ywys, that she
Shal bryngen us the pes on every side,
That whanne she gooth, Almyghty God hire gide°."

Tho° wordes and tho wommanysshe thynges,
She herd hem ryght as though she thennes° were,
For God it wot°, hire herte on other thing is.
Although the body sat among hem there,
Hire advertence° is alwey ellyswhere,
For Troylus ful faste hire soule soughte.
Withouten word, alwey on hym she thoughte.

This wommen, that thus wenden° hire to plese,
Aboute nought° gonne alle hire tales spende°.
Swych vanite° ne kan don hire non ese,
As she that al this menewhile brende°
Of other passioun than that they wende°,
So that she felte almost hire herte deye
For wo and wery° of that companye.

For which no lenger myghte she restreyne
Hire teeris, so they gonnen up to welle,
That yaven° signes of the bittre peyne
In which hir spirit was, and moste° dwelle,
Remembryng hire fro heven into which helle
She fallen was syn she forgoth° the syghte
Of Troylus; and sorwfully she sighte°.

And thilke fooles sittynge hire aboute
Wenden° that she wepte and syked° sore
By cause that she sholde out of that route°
Departe, and nevere pleye° with hem more.
And they that hadde yknowen hire of yore°
Seygh° hire so wepe and thoughte it kyndenesse°,
And eche of hem wepte eke for hire distresse.

And bisily they gonnen hire comforten
Of thing, God wot, on which she litel thoughte,
And with hire tales wenden° hire disporten°,
And to be glad they often hire bysoughte°.
But swich an ese therwith° they hire wroughte°,
Right° as a man is esed for to fele°
For ache of hed to clawen° hym on his hele!

But after al this nyce vanyte
They tok hire leve and hom they wenten alle.
Cryseyde, ful of sorwful pite,
Into hire chaumbre up went out of the halle,
And on hire bed she gan for ded° to falle,
In purpos° nevere thennes for to ryse.
And thus she wroughte° as I shal yow devyse.

Hire ownded° heer that sonnyssh° was of hewe
She rente°, and ek hire fyngres longe and smale°
She wrong° ful ofte, and bad° God on hire rewe°,
And with the deth to don bote° on hire bale°.
Hire hewe, whilom° bryght that tho° was pale,
Bar° witnesse of hire wo and hire constreynte°.
And thus she spak, sobbynge in hire compleynte:

"Allas," quod she, "out of this regioun
I, woful wrecche and infortuned° wight,
And born in corsed° constellacioun,
Mot gon°, and thus departen fro my knyght.
Wo worth°, allas, that ilke° dayes lyght
On which I saw hym first with eyen tweyne,
That causeth me, and ich hym, al this peyne!"

Therwith the terys from hire eighen° two
Doun fille, as shour in Aperill ful swythe°.
Hire white brest she bet°, and for° the wo

---

689 Ywys, *indeed* **693 gide,** *guide* **694 Tho,** *those* **695 thennes,** *far away* **696 wot,** *knows* **698 advertence,** *attention* **701 wenden,** *thought* **702 Aboute nought,** *For nothing,* **gonne alle hire tales spende,** *spent all their talking* **703 vanite,** *idle talk* **704 brende,** *burned* **705 wende,** *thought* **707 wery,** (she was) *weary* **710 yaven,** *gave* **711 moste,** *must* **713 forgoth,** *is losing* **714 sighte,** *sighed* **716 Wenden,** *thought,* **syked,** *sighed* **717 route,** *company* **718 pleye,** *take pleasure* **719 of yore,** *for a long time* **720 Seygh,** *saw,* **kyndenesse,** *natural affection* **724 wenden,** *thought,* **disporten,** *to amuse* **725 bysoughte,** *asked* **726 therwith,** *from that,* **wroughte,** *caused* **727 Right,** *just,* **fele,** *feel* **728 clawen,** *scratch* **733 for ded,** *as if dead* **734 In purpos,** *intending* **735 wroughte,** *did* **736 ownded,** *wavy,* **sonnyssh,** *sunny* **737 rente,** *tore,* **smale,** *slender* **738 wrong,** *wrung,* **bad,** *asked,* **rewe,** *have pity* **739 don bote,** *cure,* **bale,** *wretched situation* **740 whilom,** *once,* **tho,** *then* **741 Bar,** *bore,* **constreynte,** *distress* **744 infortuned,** *unfortunate* **745 corsed,** *cursed* **746 Mot gon,** *must go* **747 worth,** *be to,* **ilke,** *same* **750 eighen,** *eyes* **751 swythe,** *swiftly* **752 bet,** *beat,* **for,** *because of*

688 ye, omitted in Cp. **689 seyde,** Cl reads "answered." **691 tho,** omitted in Cl. **699 soule,** Cl reads "herte." **701 thus,** omitted in Cl. **708–14** Stanza omitted in Cl and Cp; reading from St. John's College, Cambridge, MS J.1. **745 born in corsed constellacioun,** in astrology, the configuration of the planets at the time of one's birth was thought to influence or determine the person's life; Criseyde thinks that the need for her to leave Troy and her present pain were predetermined at her birth. **750–56** In several manuscripts, this stanza follows line 735. **751 ful,** omitted in Cl and Cp.

After the deth° she cried a thousand sithe°,
Syn he that wont hire wo was for to lythe°
She mot forgon°; for which disaventure°
She held hireself a forlost° creature.

She seyde, "How shal he don, and ich also?
How sholde I lyve, yf that I from hym twynne°?
O dere herte ek, that I love so,
Who shal that sorwe sleen° that ye ben
inne?
O Calkas, fader, thyn be al this synne!
O moder myn, that cleped were° Argyve,
Wo worth° that day that thow me bere on lyve°!

"To what fyn° sholde I lyve and sorwen thus?
How sholde a fyssh withoute water dure°?
What is Criseyde worth, from° Troylus?
How sholde a plaunte or lyves° creature
Lyve withouten his kynde noriture°?
For which ful oft a byword° here I seye,
That 'roteles° mot grene° sone deye.'

"I shal don thus, syn neyther swerd ne darte
Dar I noon handle for the cruweltee°:
That ilke° day that I from yow departe,
If sorwe of that nyl not my bane° be,
Than shal no mete° or drynke come in me
Til I my soule out of my breste unshethe°;
And thus myselven wil I don to dethe°.

"And, Troylus, my clothes everychon
Shul blake ben in tokenyng°, herte swete,
That I am as out of this world agon°,
That wont° was yow to setten in quiete°.
And of myn ordre°, ay til deth me mete,
The observance° evere, yn youre absence,
Shal sorwe ben, compleynte°, and abstinence.

"Myn herte and ek the woful gost° therinne
Biquethe I with youre spirit to compleyne
Eternally, for they shul nevere twynne°.
For though in erthe ytwynned be we tweyne,
Yet in the feld° of pite out of° peyne,
That hight° Elysos, shul we ben yfere°,
As Orpheus with Erudice his fere°.

"Thus, herte myn, for Antenor, allas,
I soone shal be chaunged, as I wene°.
But how shul ye don in this sorwful cas°?
How shal youre tendre herte this sustene?
But, herte myn, foryete° this sorwe and tene°,
And me also; for sothly for to seye,
So° ye wel fare, I recche not to° deye."

How myghte it evere yred° ben or ysonge
The pleynte° that she made in hire distresse,
I not°. But as for me, my litel tonge,
If I discreven° wolde hire hevynesse°,
It sholde make hire sorwe seme lesse
Than that it was, and chyldisshly deface°
Hire heyghe compleynte, and therfore ich it
pace°.

Pandare, which that sent from Troylus
Was to Criseyde—as ye han herd devyse
That for the beste it was acorded° thus,
And he ful glad to don hym that servise—
Unto Criseyde in a ful secree wyse°,
Ther as she lay in torment and in rage°,
Com hire to telle al hoolly° his message,

---

753 After the deth, *requesting death,* **sithe,** *times* **754 wont hire wo was for to lythe,** *was accustomed to relieve her woe* **755 forgon,** *give up,* **disaventure,** *misfortune* **756 forlost,** *completely lost* **758 twynne,** *separate* **760 sleen,** *slay* **762 cleped were,** *was called* **763 worth,** *be on,* **me bere on lyve,** *gave birth to me* **764 fyn,** *end* **765 dure,** *live* **766 from,** (separate) *from* **767 lyves,** *living* **768 kynde noriture,** *natural nourishment* **769 byword,** *proverb* **770 roteles,** *rootless,* **mot grene,** *greenery must* **772 cruweltee,** *violence* **773 ilke,** *same* **774 bane,** *killer* **775 mete,** *food* **776 unshethe,** *draw out* **777 don to dethe,** *cause to die* **779 in tokenyng,** *as a sign* **780 agon,** *gone* **781 wont,** *accustomed,* **setten in quiete,** *give peace* **782 ordre,** *religious order* **783 observaunce,** *rules* **784 compleynte,** *lament* **785 gost,** *spirit* **787 twynne,** *separate* **789 feld,** *field,* **out of,** *beyond* **790 hight,** *is called,* **yfere,** *together* **791 fere,** *companion* **793 wene,** *suppose* **795 cas,** *situation* **796 foryete,** *forget,* **tene,** *grief* **798 So,** *as long as,* **I recche not to,** *care not whether I* **799 yred,** *read* **800 pleynte,** *lament* **801 not,** *do not know* **802 discreven,** *describe,* **hevynesse,** *sorrow* **804 deface,** *spoil* **805 pace,** *pass over* **808 acorded,** *agreed* **810 ful secree wyse,** *very secret manner* **811 rage,** *passion* **812 al hoolly,** *completely*

762 Argyve, no name is given in Chaucer's sources. In Statius's *Thebaid* 2.297, Argia is the name of Polynices's wife, a separate character, although Chaucer calls her Argyve at 5.1509 below. **765** Proverbial. **770** Proverbial. **782–84 of myn ordre . . . ,** Criseyde proclaims that she will act as someone in a religious order, dressing in symbolic clothing (lines 778–79), and following a set of rules. **789–90 feld . . . Elysos,** not mentioned in *Filostrato,* the Elysian fields—the classical paradise—are not usually associated with pity. Scholars have suggested that Chaucer was influenced by Dante, *Inferno* 4; Ovid, *Metamorphosis* 11.62; and the verbal similarity with *eleison* (have mercy on us), a Greek word in the Latin liturgy. **791 Orpheus . . . Erudice,** not in *Filostrato.* Chaucer derives the reference from *Bo* 3.m12, which describes the pains of the lovers' separation, Orpheus's efforts to reclaim Eurydice, and their eventual reunion in hell. The passage in *Bo* is the source of nearly all of Chaucer's allusions to the classical underworld in *TC.*

And fond that she hireselven gan to trete°
Ful pitously, for with hire salte terys
Hire brest, hire face, ybathed was ful wete;
The myghty° tresses of hire sonnysshe herys°
Unbroyden° hangen al aboute hire eris°,
Which yaf° hym verray signal° of martire°
Of deth, which that hire herte gan desire.

Whan she hym saw, she gan for sorwe anoon
Hire tery face atwixe° hire armes hyde,
For which this Pandare is so wobygon°
That in the hous he myghte unnethe abyde°,
As he that pyte felte on every syde.
For yf Criseyde hadde erst° compleyned sore,
Tho° gan she pleyne a thousand tymes more.

And in hire aspre pleynt° thus she seyde,
"Pandare first of joyes mo than two
Was cause causyng° unto me, Criseyde,
That now transmewed° ben in cruel wo.
Wher° shal I seye to yow welcom or no,
That alderferst° me brought into servise
Of love, allas, that endeth in this wyse?

"Endeth thanne love in wo? Ye, or men lieth!
And alle worldly blysse, as thenketh me.
The ende° of blisse ay sorwe it occupieth;
And who that troweth° not that it so be,
Lat hym upon me, woful wrecche, yse°,
That myself hate and ay my birthe accorse°,
Felynge° alwey fro wikke° I go to worse.

"Whoso me seth°, he seth sorwe al atonys°,
Peyne, torment, pleynte, wo, and distresse.
Out of my woful body harm ther non is°,
As° angwyssh, langour°, cruel bitternesse,
Anoy°, smert°, drede, fury, and ek siknesse.
I trowe, iwys°, from hevene teris reyne°
For pite of myn aspre° and cruwel peyne."

"And thow, my suster, ful of discomfort,"
Quod Pandarus, "what thynkestow to do?
Whi ne hastow to thiselven som resport°?
Whi woltow thus thiselve, allas, fordo°?
Lef° al this werk°, and take now hede to
That I shal seyn, and herkene° of good entente
This which by me thi Troylus the sente."

Tornede hire tho° Criseyde, a wo° makynge
So gret that it a deth was for to se.
"Allas," quod she, "what wordes may ye brynge?
What wold my dere herte seyn to me,
Which that I drede° nevere mo to se?
Wol he han pleynte or terys er I wende°?
I have ynowe yf he therafter sende°!"

She was right swych to sen in hire visage°
As is that wight that men on bere bynde°;
Hire face, lyk of Paradys the ymage,
Was al ichaunged in another kynde;
The pleye, the laughtre, men was wont° to fynde
In hire, and ek hire joyes everychone,
Ben fled; and thus lith now Criseyde allone.

Aboute hire eyen two a purpre° ryng
Bytrent°, in sothfast tokenynge° of hire peyne,
That to byholde it was a dedly thing;
For which Pandare myght not restreyne
The terys from his eyen for to reyne.
But natheles as he best myghte he seyde
From Troilus thise wordes to Criseyde:

813 trete, *treat* **816 myghty,** *great,* **sonnysshe herys,** *sunny hair* **817 Unbroyden,** *unbraided,* **eris,** *ears* **818 yaf,** *gave,* **verray signal,** *true sign,* **martire,** *martyrdom* **821 atwixe,** *between* **822 wobygon,** *sorrowful* **823 myghte unnethe abyde,** *could barely remain* **825 erst,** *before* **826 Tho,** *then* **827 aspre pleynt,** *bitter lament* **829 cause causyng,** *primary cause* **829 transmewed,** *transformed* **831 Wher,** (I wonder) *whether* **832 alderferst,** *first of all* **836 ende,** *conclusion* **837 troweth,** *believes* **838 yse,** *look* **839 accorse,** *curse* **840 Felynge,** *suffering,* **fro wikke,** *from bad* **841 Whoso me seth,** *whoever sees me,* **atonys,** *together* **843 harm ther non is,** *there is no harm* **844 As,** *such as,* **langour,** *suffering* **845 Anoy,** *trouble,* **smert,** *pain* **847 iwys,** *truly,* **teris reyne,** *tears rain down* **847 aspre,** *bitter* **850 resport,** *regard* **851 fordo,** *destroy* **852 Lef,** *stop,* **werk,** *business* **853 herkene,** *listen* **855 Tornede hire tho,** *turned around then,* **wo,** *lament* **859 drede,** *fear* **860 wende,** *go* **861 therafter sende,** *sends for them* **862 visage,** *face* **863 on bere bynde,** *tie to a funeral bier* **864 was wont,** *were accustomed* **869 purpre,** *purple* **870 Bytrent,** *encircles,* **sothfast tokenynge,** *true sign*

818 martire, Cl and Cp read "matere." **827–47** Chaucer's addition here, although he adapts 841–47 from a speech of Pandaro in *Filostrato* 4.97. **829 cause causyng,** primary cause, distinct from a secondary cause (*causa causata,* "cause being caused") in scholastic logic. **836** Proverbial; see *MLT* 2.424. **840 wikke,** Cl reads "wo." **851 allas,** omitted in Cl. **854 which,** Cp reads "message which." **860 he,** Cl reads "ye."

"Lo, nece, I trowe wel ye han herd al° how
The kyng with othere lordes, for the beste,
Hath mad° eschaunge of Antenor and yow,
That cause is of this sorwe and this unreste.
But how this cas doth Troylus moleste°,
That may non erthely mannes tonge seye°;
For verray wo his wit is al aweye.

"For which we han so sorwed, he and I,
That into litel° bothe it hadde us slawe°;
But thurgh my conseyl this day fynally
He somwhat is fro wepyng now withdrawe.
It semeth me that he desireth fawe°
With yow to ben al nyght for to devyse
Remede in this yf ther were any wyse°.

"This, short and pleyn, th'effect° of my message,
As ferforth° as my wit may comprehende;
For ye that ben of torment in swych rage°
May to no long prologe as now entende°.
And herupon° ye may answere hym sende.
And for the love of God, my nece dere,
So lef° this wo er Troylus be here!"

"Gret is my wo," quod she, and sighed soore
As she that feleth dedly sharp distresse,
"But yet to me his sorwe is muche more,
That loveth hym bet° than he hymself, I gesse.
Allas, for me hath he swych hevynesse?
Kan he for me so pitously compleyne?
Iwis°, this sorwe doubleth al my peyne.

"Grevous to me, God wot°, is for to twynne°,"
Quod she, "but yet it harder is to me
To sen that sorwe which that he is inne,
For wel wot I it wol my bane° be,
And deye I wol in certeyn," tho quod she.
"But bidde hym come, er deth that thus me threteth°
Dryf° out the gost° which in myn herte beteth."

Thise wordes seyd, she on hire armes two
Fil gruf°, and gan to wepen pitously.
Quod Pandarus, "Allas, whi do ye so
Syn wel ye wot° the tyme is faste° by
That he shal come? Arys up hastely,
That he yow nat bywopen° thus ne fynde,
But° ye wol han hym wod° out of his mynde.

"For wist he° that ye ferde° in this manere,
He wolde hymselve sle. And yf I wende°
To han this fare°, he sholde nat come here
For al the good that Pryam may despende°.
For to what fyn° he wolde anoon pretende°,
That knowe ich wel; and forthi° yet I seye,
So lef° this sorwe or platly° he wol deye.

"And shappeth° yow his sorwe for to abregge°,
And nought encresse, leve° nece swete.
Beth rather to hym cause of flat than egge°,
And with som wysdom ye his sorwes bete°.
What helpeth it to wepen ful a strete°,
Or though ye bothe in salte teris dreynte°?
Bet° is a tyme of cure ay than of pleynte°.

"I mene thus: whan ich hym hider° brynge,
Syn ye ben wyse and bothe of on assent°,
So shappeth how distourbe° this goynge,
Or come ayen soone after ye be went.
Women ben wyse in short avysement°;
And lat sen° how youre wit shal now avayle°,
And what that I may helpe, it shal nat fayle."

"Go," quod Criseyde, "and uncle, trewely,
I shal don al my myght me to restreyne
From wepyng in his sighte, and bysily°
Hym for to glade° I shal don al my peyne,
And in myn herte seken every veyne°.
If to this sor° ther may be founden salve,
It shal nat lakken, certein, on myn halve°."

---

876 al, *all about* **878 mad,** *made* **880 doth Troylus moleste,** *afflicts Troylus* **881 seye,** *describe* **884 into litel,** *very nearly,* **slawe,** *slain* **887 fawe,** *eagerly* **889 wyse,** *way* **890 th'effect,** (is) *the upshot* **891 ferforth,** *far* **892 rage,** *frenzy* **893 entende,** *attend* **894 herupon,** *about this* **896 So lef,** *stop* **900 bet,** *better* **903 Iwis,** *truly* **904 wot,** *knows,* **twynne,** *separate* **907 bane,** *death* **909 threteth,** *threatens* **910 Dryf,** *drives,* **gost,** *spirit* **912 gruf,** *face down* **914 wot,** *know,* **faste,** *near* **916 bywopen,** *beweeped,* i.e., *tear-stained* **917 But,** *unless,* **wod,** *crazed* **918 wist he,** *if he knew,* **ferde,** *acted* **919 wende,** *thought,* **han this fare,** *to have this kind of behavior* **921 despende,** *spend* **922 fyn,** *end,* **pretende,** *pursue* **923 forthi,** *therefore* **924 lef,** *stop,* **platly,** *simply* **925 shappeth,** *prepare,* **abregge,** *reduce* **926 leve,** *dear* **927 flat than egge,** i.e., *healing rather than hurt* **928 bete,** *cure* **929 ful a strete,** *a streetful* **930 dreynte,** *drown* **931 Bet,** *better,* **pleynte,** *lament* **932 hider,** *here* **933 of on assent,** *in agreement* **934 distourbe,** *to prevent* **936 short avysement,** *quick decisions* **937 lat sen,** *show,* **avayle,** *help* **941 bysily,** *actively* **942 glade,** *gladden* **943 veyne,** *option* **944 to this sor,** *for this pain* **945 halve,** *part*

893 to, Cl reads "as to." **909 threteth,** Cl reads "treteth." **910 beteth,** Cl reads "he beteth." **927 cause,** omitted in Cl. **flat than egge,** the flat part of the sword instead of the edge; in myth and legend, the flats of special swords healed the wounds caused by their edges. **932 ich,** Cl reads "I." **hider,** Cl reads "here." **936** Proverbial, but not recorded before Chaucer. **937 sen how youre wit shal now,** Cl reads "sen now how youre wit shal."

Goth Pandarus and Troylus he soughte
Til in a temple he fond hym al allone,
As he that of his lyf no lenger roughte°,
But to the petouse° goddes everychone
Ful tendrely he preyed and made his mone°,
To don° hym sone out of this world to pace°,
For wel he thouhte ther was noon other grace°.

And shortly, al the sothe for to seye,
He was so fallen in despeyr that day
That outrely° he shop° hym for to deye,
For right thus was his argument alway.
He seyde, "I am but lorn°, so weylaway°!
For al that cometh, comth by necessite;
Thus to ben lorn, it is my destyne.

"For certeynly, this wot I wel," he seyde,
"That forsight° of dyvyne purveyaunce°
Hath seyn alwey me to forgon° Criseyde,
Syn God seth everything, out of doutaunce°,
And hem desponeth° thourgh his ordenaunce°,
In hire° merites sothly for to be,
As they shul comen by predestine°.

"But natheles, allas, whom shal I leve°?
For ther ben clerkes grete many on°
That destyne thorugh argumentez preve°;
And som men seyn that nedely ther is noon°,
But that fre choys is yeven us everychon.
O welaway, so sley° arn clerkes olde
That I not whos opynyoun I may holde.

"For som men seyn, yf God seth° al byforn—
Ne God may nat deceyved ben, parde—
Than mot it falle° theigh° men hadde it sworn°,
That purveyance° hath seighen byfore to be.
Wherfor I seye that from eterne° yf he
Hath wyst byforn oure thought ek as oure dede,
We have no fre choys, as these clerkes rede°.

"For other thought, nor other dede also,
Myghte nevere ben but swych as purveyaunce,
Which may nat ben deceyved nevere mo,
Hath feled° biforn withouten ignoraunce°.
For yf ther myghte ben a variaunce°
To writhen° out fro Goddes purveyinge,
Ther nere no prescience° of thyng comynge,

"But it were rathere an opynyoun
Uncerteyn, and no stedfast° forseynge.
And certes, that were an abusioun°
That God shulde han no parfit cler witynge°
More than we men that han doutous wenynge°.
But swych an errour upon God to gesse°
Were fals and foul and corsed wykkednesse.

"Ek this is an opynyoun of some
That han hire top ful heighe and smothe yshore°:
They seyn right thus, that thyng is nat to come
For that° the prescience hath seyghen byfore
That it shal come. But they seyn that therfore°
That it shal come, therfore° the purveyaunce
Wot° it byforn, withouten ignoraunce.

"And in this manere this necessite
Retorneth in his part contrarie agayn°.
For nedfully byhoveth it nat to be°
That thilke thinges fallen in certayn°
That ben purveyed; but nedely°, as they sayn,

---

948 roughte, *cared* **949 petouse,** *merciful* **950 mone,** *complaint* **951 don,** *cause,* **pace,** *pass* **952 grace,** *mercy* **955 outrely,** *utterly,* **shop,** *planned* **957 lorn,** *lost,* **welaway,** *alas* **961 forsight,** *foreknowledge,* **purveyaunce,** *providence* **962 seyn alwey me to forgon,** *always seen that I would lose* **963 out of doutaunce,** *without doubt* **964 desponeth,** *regulates,* **ordenaunce,** *decree* **965 In hire,** *according to their* **966 predestine,** *predestination* **967 leve,** *believe* **968 clerkes grete many on,** *many great scholars* **969 preve,** *prove* **970 nedely ther is noon,** *there is none by necessity* **972 sley,** *subtle* **974 seth,** *sees* **976 Than mot it falle,** *then it must happen,* **theigh,** *although,* **sworn,** *sworn it would not occur* **977 That purveyance,** *what providence* **978 eterne,** *eternity* **980 rede,** *advise* **984 feled,** *perceived,* **ignoraunce,** *error* **985 variaunce,** *variation* **986 writhen,** *twist* **987 prescience,** *foreknowledge* **989 stedfast,** *stable* **990 abusioun,** *falsehood* **991 witynge,** *knowing* **992 doutous wenynge,** *uncertain understanding* **993 gesse,** *infer* **996 top . . . smothe yshore,** *heads smoothly shaved* (see n.) **998 For that,** *because* **999 therfore,** *because,* **1000 therfore,** *for that reason* **1001 Wot,** *knows* **1003 Retorneth . . . contrarie agayn,** *turns back on itself* **1004 nedfully byhoveth it nat to be,** *it is not necessary by necessity* **1005 fallen in certayn,** *come about certainly* **1006 nedely,** *necessarily*

946–52 the temple setting is Chaucer's addition here, although he took the idea of Pandarus finding Troylus in a temple from *Filostrato* 3.4ff. **957–1078** This long speech on predestination, not found in *Filostrato* and lacking in several manuscripts of *TC,* paraphrases *Bo* 5.pr3. In *Bo* 5.pr4–6, Philosophy goes on to explain that, despite divine foreknowledge, human will is free by "conditional necessity." Troylus, however, stops short with a rigidly deterministic, fatalistic view. **957 I am,** Cl and Cp read "he nas," encouraging editors to begin the quotation at 958. **so,** omitted in Cl and Cp. **961 forsight . . . purveyaunce,** the etymological roots of the words mean much the same ("before" + "to see"); the same is true of "providence." **976 theigh,** Cl reads "they." **994 corsed wykkednesse,** Cp reads "wikked corsednesse." **996 top . . . smothe yshore,** throughout the Middle Ages, scholars were members of the clergy, who shaved the tops or crowns of their heads to signify religious commitment.

Byhoveth° it that thinges whiche that falle°,
That they in certayn ben purveyed° alle.

"I mene° as though I laboured me° in this,
To enqueren which thyng cause of which thing be,
As wheyther that the prescience of God is
The certeyn cause of the necessite
Of thinges that to comen ben°, parde,
Or yf necessite of thing comynge
Be cause certeyn° of the purveyinge°.

"But now n'enforce I me nought° in shewynge
How the ordre of causes stant°; but wel wot I
That it byhoveth° that the byfallynge°
Of thinges wyste° byforen certeynly
Be necessarie°, al seme it not° therby
That prescience put fallyng necessaire°
To thing to come, al falle it° foule or fayre.

"For if ther sit° a man yond° on a see°;
Than by necessite byhoveth it°
That, certes, thin opynyon soth be°
That wenest° or conjectest° that he sit°.
And ferther over° now ayeynward° yit,
Lo, right so is it of the part contrarie°
As thus—nowe herkne°, for I wol nat tarie°—

"I seye, that yf the opynion of the°
Be soth for that° he sit, than seye I this,
That he mot sitten° by necessite;
And thus necessite in eyther° is.
For yn hym nede of syttynge is, ywys,
And in the° nede of soth°. And thus, forsothe,
Ther mot necessite ben in yow bothe.

"But thow maist seyn the man sit not therfore°
That thyn opynyoun of his sittynge soth is,
But rather for° the man sit ther byfore°;
Therfore is thyn opynyoun soth, ywys.
And I seye, though the cause of soth of this
Comth of his sittyng, yet necessite
Is entrechaunged° both in hym and the.

"Thus on this same wyse, out of doutaunce°,
I may wel maken, as it semeth me,
My resonynge of Goddes purveyaunce
And of the thynges that to comen be.
By which resoun may men wel yse
That thilke thinges that in erthe falle°,
That by necessite they comen alle.

"For although that for thyng° shal come, ywys,
Therfore it is purveyed°, certaynly—
Nought that it comth for° it purveyed is.
Yet natheles, byhoveth it nedfully°
That thing to come be purveyed°, trewely,
Or elles thinges that purveyed be,
That they bytiden° by necessite.

"And this suffiseth right ynow, certeyn,
For to destroye oure fre choys every del°.
But now is this abusioun° to seyn
That fallynge° of the thinges temporel
Is cause of Godes prescience eternel.
Now trewely, that is a fals sentence,
That thyng to come sholde cause his prescience.

"What myght I wene°, and° ich hadde swych a thought,
But that God purveyeth° thyng that is to come
For° that it is to come, and ellis nought?

1007 Behoveth it, *it is necessary,* **falle,** *happen* **1008 ben purveyed,** *are foreseen* **1009 mene,** *intend,* **laboured me,** *belabored myself* **1013 to comen ben,** *are to come* **1015 Be cause certeyn,** *is the certain cause,* **purveyinge,** *foreknowing* **1016 n'enforce I me nought,** *I do not trouble myself* **1017 stant,** *stands* **1018 byhoveth,** *is necessary,* **byfallynge,** *occurring* **1019 wyste,** *known* **1020 Be necessarie,** *is necessary,* **al seme it not,** *although it seems not* **1021 put fallyng necessaire,** *makes occurring necessary* **1022 al falle it,** *whether it occurs* **1023 sit,** *sits,* **yond,** *yonder,* **see,** *seat* **1024 byhoveth it,** *it is necessary* **1025 soth be,** *must be true* **1026 wenest,** *thinks,* **conjectest,** *conjectures,* **sit,** *sits* **1027 ferther over,** *furthermore,* **ayeynward,** *on the other hand* **1028 part contrarie,** *antithetical view* **1029 herkne,** *listen,* **tarie,** *delay* **1030 of the,** *your* **1031 Be soth for that,** *is true because* **1032 mot sitten,** *must be sitting* **1033 eyther,** *either* **1035 the,** *you,* **soth,** *truth* **1037 therfore,** *because* **1039 for,** *because,* **byfore,** *already* **1043 entrechaunged,** *reciprocal* **1044 out of doutaunce,** *without doubt* **1049 falle,** *happen* **1051 for thyng,** *because something* **1052 Therfore it is purveyed,** *it is therefore foreknown* **1053 for,** *because* **1054 byhoveth it nedfully,** *it is necessarily necessary* **1055 be purveyed,** *are foreknown* **1057 bytiden,** *happen* **1059 every del,** *completely* **1060 abusioun,** *falsehood* **1061 fallynge,** *the occurrence* **1065 wene,** *think,* **and,** *if* **1066 purveyeth,** *foreknows* **1067 For,** *because*

1025 thin opynyon . . . , in this and the following two stanzas, Troylus speaks as if in dialogue, though he is alone, no doubt a result of the fact that Chaucer is following the debate technique in Boethius. Similar breaks in literary decorum occur elsewhere in Chaucer (e.g., *KnT* 1.1918 and *MerT* 4.1685), with notable rhetorical effects. **1036 yow bothe,** the man sitting and the man seeing him sit.

So myghte I wene that thynges alle and some,
That whylom ben byfalle° and overcome°,
Ben cause of thilke soveyren° purveyaunce
That forwot° al withouten ignoraunce°.

"And over al this, yet sey I more therto°,
That right° as whan I wot ther is a thing,
Iwys°, that thing mot° nedefully be so.
Ek right so°, whan I wot a thyng comyng,
So mot it come. And thus the byfallyng
Of thynges that ben wyst° byfore the tyde°,
They mowe° not ben eschewed° on no syde°."

Thanne seyde he thus, "Almyghty Jove in trone°,
That wost° of alle thyng the sothfastnesse°,
Rewe° on my sorwe, or do me deye sone,
Or bryng Criseyde and me fro this destresse!"
And whil he was in al this hevynesse,
Disputyng with hymself in this matere,
Com Pandare in, and seyde as ye may here.

"O myghti God," quod Pandarus, "in trone,
I°, who seygh° evere a wys man faren° so?
Whi, Troylus, what thenkestow to done?
Hastow swych lust° to ben thyn owen fo?
What, parde, yet is nat Criseyde ago°!
Whi lust the so thynself fordon° for drede,
That in thyn hed thyn eyghen semen° dede?

"Hastow not lyved many a yer byforn
Withouten hire, and ferd° ful wel at ese?
Artow for hire and for noon other born?
Hath Kynde the wrought° al oonly hire to plese?
Lat be°, and thenk right thus in thi disese°,
That in the des° right as there fallen chaunces°,
Right so in love ther com and gon plesaunces°.

"And yet this is a wonder most of alle,
Whi thow thus sorwest, syn thow nost not yit°,
Touchyng° hire goyng, how that it shal falle,
Ne yif she kan hireself destuorben° it.
Thow hast nat yet assayed al hire wit.
A man may al bytyme° his nekke bede°
Whan it shal of°, and sorwen at the nede.

"Forthi take hede of that that I shal the seye°:
I have with hire yspoke° and longe ybe°,
So as accorded was bytwyxe us tweye,
And everemo me thenketh thus, that she
Hath somwhat in hire hertes prevete°
Wherwith° she kan, if I shal right arede°,
Destorbe° al this of which thow art in drede.

"For which my counseyl is, whan it is nyght
Thow to hire go and make of this an ende.
And blisful Juno thorugh hire grete myght
Shal, as I hope, hire grace unto us sende.
Myn herte seyth, 'Certeyn, she shal not wende°.'
And forthi put thyn herte a whyle in reste,
And hold thi purpos, for it is the beste."

This Troylus answerde, and sighte° sore,
"Thow seyst right wel, and I wil do right so."
And what hym lyste° he seyde unto it more.
And whan that it was tyme for to go,
Ful prevely° hymself withouten mo°
Unto hire com, as he was wont° to done.
And how thei wroughte°, I shal yow telle sone.

Soth it is° whanne they gonne first to mete,
So gan the peynes hire hertes for to twyste
That neyther of hem other myghte grete,
But hem in armes tok and after kyste.
The lasse° wofulle of hem bothe nyste°

1069 whylom ben byfalle, *formerly occurred,* **overcome,** *happened* **1070 thilke sovereyn,** *this supreme* **1071 forwot,** *completely knows,* **ignoraunce,** *error* **1072 therto,** *also* **1073 right,** *just* **1074 Iwys,** *surely,* **mot,** *must* **1075 Ek right so,** *in the same way* **1077 ben wyst,** *are known,* **tyde,** *time* **1078 mowe,** *may,* **eschewed,** *escaped,* **on no syde,** *in any way* **1079 trone,** *throne* **1080 wost,** *knows,* **sothfastnesse,** *truth* **1081 Rewe,** *take pity* **1087 I,** *Oh,* **seygh,** *saw,* **faren,** *go on* **1089 lust,** *desire* **1090 ago,** *gon* **1091 fordon,** *to destroy* **1092 eyghen semen,** *eyes seem* **1094 ferd,** *gone* **1096 Kynde the wrought,** *Nature made you* **1097 Lat be,** *stop it,* **disese,** *distress* **1098 des,** *dice,* **fallen chaunces,** *occur various outcomes* **1099 plesaunces,** *pleasures* **1101 nost not yet,** *don't yet know* **1102 Touchyng,** *concerning* **1103 destuorben,** *prevent* **1105 al bytyme,** *soon enough,* **nekke bede,** *offer his neck* (to the executioner) **1106 shal of,** *must be* (cut) *off* **1107 the seye,** *tell you* **1108 yspoke,** *spoken,* **longe ybe,** *long been* (with her) **1111 hertes prevete,** *heart's secrets* **1112 Wherwith,** *by which,* **arede,** *interpret* **1113 Destorbe,** *prevent* **1118 wende,** *go* **1121 sighte,** *sighed* **1123 hym lyste,** *pleased him* **1125 prevely,** *secretly,* **mo,** *others* **1126 wont,** *accustomed* **1127 wroughte,** *acted* **1128 Soth it is,** *it is true* (that) **1132 lasse,** *less,* **nyste,** *knew not*

1073 That, omitted in Cl. **1079–82** Troylus's concluding prayer seems to indicate the possibility of divine intervention, although his philosophical discourse has been purely deterministic. **1086** A mocking(?) echo of line 1079. **1093** Chaucer here returns to *Filostrato,* at the same point that he left at 4.953. **1105–06** Proverbial. **1114 which,** Cl reads "swych." **1116 Juno,** wife of Jupiter, not mentioned in *Filostrato.*

Wher that he was, ne° myghte o word out brynge,
As I seyde erst°, for wo and for sobbynge.

Tho woful teris that they leten falle
As bittre weren out of teris kynde°,
For peyne, as is ligne aloes° or galle°—
So bittre teris weep nought, as I fynde,
The woful Myrra thorugh the bark and rynde—
That in this world ther nys so hard an herte
That nolde han rewed on° hire peynes smerte.

But whanne hire woful wery gostes tweyne°
Retorned ben ther as hem° oughte to dwelle,
And that somwhat to wayken° gan the peyne
By lengthe of pleynte, and ebben gan the welle
Of hire teris, and the herte unswelle,
With broken voys, al hoors forshright°, Criseyde
To Troylus thise ilke wordes seyde,

"O Jove, I deye, and mercy I beseche!
Help, Troylus!" And therwithal° hire face
Upon his brest she leyde and loste speche,
Hire woful spirit from his° propre place
Right with the word alwey o poynt to pace°.
And thus she lith with hewes° pale and grene,
That whilom° fressh and fairest was to sene.

This Troylus, that on hire gan byholde,
Clepynge° hire name—and she lay as for ded—
Withouten answere, and felte hir lymes° colde,
Hire eyen throwen° upward to hire hed,
This sorwful man kan° now noon other red°
But ofte tyme hire colde mouth he kyste.
Wher° hym was wo, God and hymself it wyste.

He rist° hym up and long streyght° he hire leyde,
For signe of lyf, for ought he kan or may°,
Kan° he non fynde in nothyng° on Criseyde,
For which his song ful ofte is "Weylaway!"
But whan he sawgh that specheles she lay,
With sorweful voys, and herte of blysse al bare,
He seyde how she was fro this world yfare°.

So after that he longe hadde hire compleyned,
His hondes wrong, and seyde that° was to seye,
And with his teris salte hire brest byreyned°,
He gan tho teris wypen of° ful dreye°,
And pitously gan for the soule preye,
And seyde, "O Lord, that set art in thy trone,
Rewe° ek on me, for I shal folwe hire sone."

She cold was and withouten sentement°,
For ought he wot°, for breth ne felte he non;
And this was hym a preignant° argument
That she was forth out of this world agon.
And whan he seygh ther was non other won°
He gan hire lymes dresse° in swych manere
As men don hem that shul be leyd on bere°.

And after this, with sterne and cruwel herte,
His swerd anoon out of his shethe he
twyghte°,
Hymself to slen, how sore° that hym smerte,
So that his sowle hire sowle folwen myghte
Ther as° the dom° of Mynos wolde it dyghte°,
Syn Love and cruwel Fortune it ne wolde
That in this world he lenger lyven sholde.

Thanne seyde he thus, "Fulfilled° of heigh
desdayn°,
O cruwel Jove, and thow, Fortune adverse,
This al and som°, that falsly have ye slayn
Criseyde. And syn ye may do me no werse,
Fy° on youre myght and werkes so diverse°!
Thus cowardly ye shul me nevere wynne°—
Ther shal no deth me fro my lady twynne°.

1133 ne, *nor* **1134 erst,** *before* **1135 out of teris kynde,** *beyond natural tears* **1137 ligne aloes,** *medicinal aloe,* **galle,** *gall* **1141 nolde han rewed on,** *would not have pitied* **1142 gostes tweyne,** *two spirits* **1143 ther as hem,** *where they* **1144 wayken,** *weaken* **1147 hoors forshright,** *hoarse from shrieking* **1150 therwithal,** *with that* **1152 his,** *its* **1153 o poynt to pace,** *on the point of leaving* **1154 hewes,** *colors* **1155 whilom,** *formerly* **1157 Clepynge,** *calling* **1158 lymes,** *limbs* **1159 throwen,** *rolled* **1160 kan,** *knows,* **red,** *thought* **1162 Wher,** *whether* **1163 rist,** *rises,* **long streyght,** *stretched out* **1164 kan or may,** *knows or can do* **1165 Kan,** *can,* **in nothyng,** *at all* **1169 yfare,** *gone* **1171 that,** *what* **1172 byreyned,** *rained upon* **1173 wypen of,** *wipe off,* **dreye,** *dry* **1176 Rewe,** *have pity* **1177 sentement,** *feeling* **1178 wot,** *knew* **1179 preignant,** *compelling* **1180 won,** *option* **1182 lymes dresse,** *limbs arrange* **1183 bere,** *funeral bier* **1185 twyghte,** *pulled* **1186 how sore,** *however painfully* **1188 Ther as,** *where,* **dom,** *judgment,* **dyghte,** *assign* **1191 Fulfilled,** *full,* **desdayn,** *scorn* **1193 al and som,** *is all I have to say* **1195 Fy,** *curses,* **diverse,** *contrary* **1196 wynne,** *defeat* **1197 twynne,** *separate*

1135–41 The description of the tears is Chaucer's;aloe and gall are proverbially bitter, the first being a nauseous bitter purgative, the latter, a secretion of the liver. **1139 Myrra,** Myrrha, was changed into a myrrh tree (because of incestuous love) that weeps tears aromatic gum through its bark; Ovid, *Metamorphoses* 10.298ff. **1147 forshright,** Cl reads "forbright." **1178 ought he,** Cl reads "I." **1188 Mynos,** Minos, the judge of spirits in Hades.

"For I this world, syn ye han slayn hire thus,
Wol lete° and folwe hire spirit lowe or hye.
Shal nevere lovere seyn° that Troylus
Dar nat for fere with his lady dye,
For certeyn I wol bere° hire companye.
But syn ye wol nat suffren° us lyven here,
Yet suffreth that oure soules ben yfere°.

"And thow, cite, whiche that I leve in wo;
And thow, Pryam, and bretheren al yfere;
And thow, my moder, farewel, for now I go.
And Attropos, make redy thow my bere.
And thow, Criseyde, O swete herte dere,
Receyve now my spirit," wold he seye,
With swerd at herte, al redy for to deye.

But as God wolde, of swough° therwith sh'abreyde°
And gan to syke°, and "Troylus" she cride.
And he answerde, "Lady myn, Cryseyde,
Lyve ye yet?" and let his swerd doun glide.
"Ye, herte myn, that thanked be Cipride,"
Quod she. And therwithal she sore syghte°,
And he bygan to glade° hire as he myghte,

Took hire in armes two, and kyste hire ofte,
And hire to glade he dide al his entente°,
For which hire gost°, that flikered° ay on lofte°,
Into hire woful herte ayeyn it wente.
But at the laste, as that hire eyen glente°
Asyde anoon she gan his swerd aspye,
As it lay bare, and gan for fere crie,

And asked hym whi he hadde it out drawe°.
And Troylus anoon the cause hire tolde,
And how hymself therwith he wolde han slawe°;
For which Criseyde upon hym gan byholde,
And gan hym in hire armes faste folde,
And seyde, "O mercy, God, lo swych a dede°!
Allas, how neigh° we were bothe dede!

"Thenne yf I nadde° spoken, as grace was,
Ye wolde han slayn youreself anoon?" quod she.
"Ye, douteles." And she answerde, "Allas,
For by that ilke° Lord that made me
I nolde a forlong wey° on lyve han be
After youre deth, to han be° crowned quene
Of al the londes the sonne on shyneth shene°.

"But with this selve° swerd whiche that here is
Myselve I wolde have slayn," quod she tho.
"But ho°, for we han right ynow° of this,
And lat us rise, and streyght to bedde go,
And there lat us speken of oure wo.
For by the morter° which that I se brenne°,
Knowe I right wel that day is not far henne°."

Whanne they were in hire bed, in armes folde°,
Nought was yt lyk the nyghtes herebyforn°.
For pitously eche other gan byholde,
As thei that hadden al hire blisse ylorn°,
Bywaylinge ay the day that they were born;
Til at the last this sorwful wyght° Criseyde
To Troylus these ilke° wordes seyde.

"Lo, herte myn, wel wot ye this," quod she,
"That yf a wyght alwey his wo compleyne,
And seketh nought how holpen° for to be,
It is but folye and encres° of peyne;
And syn that here assembled be we tweyne
To fynde bote° of wo that we ben inne,
It were al tyme° sone to bygynne.

"I am a womman, as ful wel ye wot,
And as I am avised sodeynly°,
So wole I telle yow whil it is hot.
Me thenketh thus, that neyther ye ne I

1199 lete, *leave* **1200 seyn,** *say* **1202 bere,** *keep* **1203 suffren,** *allow* **1204 yfere,** *together* **1212 swough,** *swoon,* **sh'abreyde,** *she awoke* **1213 syke,** *sigh* **1217 syghte,** *sighed* **1218 glade,** *comfort* **1220 al his entente,** *all he could think of* **1221 gost,** *spirit,* **flikered,** *hovered,* **on lofte,** *in the air* **1223 glente,** *glanced* **1226 drawe,** *drawn* **1228 slawe,** *slain* **1231 dede,** *deed* **1232 neigh,** *nearly* **1233 nadde,** *hadn't* **1236 ilke,** *same* **1237 nolde a forlong wey,** *would not for much time* **1238 to han be,** *even for the sake of being* **1239 shene,** *brightly* **1240 selve,** *same* **1242 ho,** *stop,* **ynow,** *enough* **1245 morter,** *lamp,* **brenne,** *burn* **1246 henne,** *from now* **1247 folde,** *embraced* **1248 herebyforn,** *before this* **1250 ylorn,** *lost* **1252 wyght,** *creature* **1253 ilke,** *very* **1256 holpen,** *helped* **1257 encres,** *increase* **1259 bote,** *remedy* **1260 al tyme,** *the right time* **1262 am avised sodeynly,** *have suddenly decided*

1205 leve, Cp reads "lyve" (live). **1208 Attropos,** Atropos, third of the three Fates, who cuts the thread and ends a person's life. **1215 Cipride,** Venus, so called because she was born from the sea near the island of Cyprus. **1237 forlong wey,** a short period of time; literally, the time it takes to travel 220 years (a furlong). **1245 morter,** a bowl filled with oil or wax with a wick, used as a night light and (indicated by quantity of fuel consumed) a timepiece. **1262** Cf. 4.936.

Ought° half this wo to maken, skilfully°.
For ther is art ynow° for to redresse°
That° yet is mys°, and slen this hevynesse°.

"Soth is, the wo the which that we ben inne,
For ought I wot, for nothyng elles is
But for the cause that we sholden twynne°.
Considered al°, ther nys no more amys.
But what is thanne a remede unto this,
But that we shape us° sone for to mete?
This al and som°, my dere herte swete.

"Now, that I shal wel bryngen it aboute
To come ayen°, soone after that I go,
Therof am I no manere thyng in doute.
For dredeles°, withinne a wowke° or two
I shal ben here; and that it may be so,
By alle right and in a wordes fewe°,
I shal yow wel an hep° of weyes shewe.

"For which I wol not make long sermon°,
For tyme ylost may not recovered be;
But I wol gon to my conclusyon,
And to° the beste, in ought that° I kan se.
And for the love of God, foryeve° it me
If I speke ought ayeyn youre hertes reste,
For trewely I speke it for the beste,

"Makyng alwey a protestacion
That now these wordes which that I shal seye
Nys but° to shewen yow my mocion°
To fynde unto oure help the beste weye;
And taketh it non other wyse, I preye.
For yn effect, what so° ye me comaunde,
That wol I don, for that is no demaunde°.

"Now herkneth this: ye han wel understonde
My goyng graunted is by parlement
So ferforth° that it may nat be withstonde
For al this world, as by my juggement.
And syn ther helpeth noon avisement°
To letten° it, lat it passe out of mynde,
And lat us shape a bettre wey to fynde.

"The soth is that the twynnyng of us tweyne
Wol us dishese° and cruweliche anoye°;
But hym byhoveth° somtyme han a peyne
That serveth Love, yf that he wol have joye.
And syn I shal° no ferther out of Troye
Than I may ride ayen° on half a morwe°,
It oughte the lasse causen us to sorwe.

"So as° I shal not so ben hid in muwe°,
That day by day, myn owne herte dere,
Syn wel ye wot that it is now a truwe°,
Ye shul ful wel al myn estat yhere°.
And er that truwe is don, I shal ben here.
And thanne have ye both Antenor ywonne
And me also. Beth glad now, yf ye konne°,

"And thenk right thus, 'Criseyde is now agon°.
But what, she shal come hastiliche ayen!'
And whanne, allas? By God, lo, right anoon°,
Er dayes ten, this dar I saufly° seyn.
And thanne at erst° shal we be so fayn°,
So as we shal togederes evere dwelle,
That al this world ne myghte oure blysse telle.

"I se° that ofte tyme, there as we ben now°,
That for the beste, oure counseyl° for to hide,
Ye speke not with me, nor I with yow,
In fourtenyght°, ne se° yow go ne ryde.
May ye not ten dayes thanne abyde
For myn honour, yn swych an aventure°?
Iwys, ye mowen ellys lite° endure.

1265 Ought, *should,* **skilfully,** *reasonably* **1266 art ynow,** *skill enough,* **redresse,** *correct* **1267 That,** *what,* **mys,** *amiss,* **slen this hevynesse,** *end this grief* **1270 twynne,** *separate* **1271 Considered al,** *all things considered* **1273 shape us,** *plan for ourselves* **1274 This al and som,** *that's all there is to it* **1276 come ayen,** *return* **1277 dredeles,** *doubtless,* **wowke,** *week* **1280 in a wordes fewe,** *said briefly* **1281 an hep,** *a lot,* **shewe,** *show* **1282 sermon,** *speech* **1285 to,** *for,* **in ought that,** *as far as* **1286 foryeve,** *forgive* **1291 Nys but,** *are intended only,* **mocion,** *proposal* **1294 what so,** *whatever* **1295 for that is no demaunde,** *for there is no question about that* **1298 So ferforth,** *so much so* **1300 syn ther helpeth no avisment,** *since no discussion helps* **1301 letten,** *prevent* **1304 dishese,** *distress,* **anoye,** *trouble* **1305 hym byhoveth,** *it is necessary that he* **1307 shal,** *shall go* **1308 ayen,** *back,* **morwe,** *morning* **1309 lasse,** *less* **1310 So as,** *as,* **hid in muwe,** *caged up* **1312 truwe,** *truce* **1313 myn estat yhere,** *hear about my status* **1316 konne,** *can* **1317 agon,** *gone* **1319 right anoon,** *very soon* **1320 saufly,** *safely* **1321 at erst,** *for the first time,* **fayn,** *happy* **1324 se,** *know,* **there as we ben now,** *as we are now* **1325 counseyl,** *secret* **1327 fourtenyght,** *two weeks,* **ne se,** *nor see* **1329 aventure,** *situation* **1330 mowen ellys lite,** *can otherwise little*

1283 Proverbial; cf. 3.893. **1303 that,** Cp reads "this."

"Ye knowe ek how that al my kyn° is here
But yf that onlyche it my fader be°,
And ek myn othere thinges alle yfere°,
And namelyche°, my dere herte, ye,
Whom that I nolde leven for to se°
For al this world, as wyd as it hath space°,
Or elles se ich nevere° Joves face!

"Whi trowe ye° my fader yn this wyse
Coveyteth° so to se me but for drede
Lest yn this town that folkes me despise
By cause of hym, for his unhappy° dede?
What wot° my fader what lyf that I lede?
For if he wyste in Troy how wel I fare,
Us neded for my wendyng° nought to care.

"Ye sen that every day ek, more and more,
Men trete of pees°, and it supposid is
That men the queene Eleyne shal restore,
And Grekes us restoren that is mys°.
So, though there nere comfort noon° but this,
That men purposen° pes on every syde,
Ye may the bettre at ese of herte abyde°.

"For yf that it be pes, myn herte dere,
The nature of the pes mot nedes dryve°
That men most entrecomunen yfere°,
And to and fro ek ryde and gon as blyve°
Alday° as thikke as ben flen° from an hyve,
And every wight han liberte to bleve°
Where as hym lyste the bet, withouten leve°.

"And though so be° that pes ther may be noon,
Yet hider°, though there nevere pes ne were,
I moste° come; for wheder° sholde I gon,
Or how, myschaunce°, sholde I dwellen there,
Among tho men of armes evere in fere?
For which, as wysly° God my soule rede°,
I kan nat sen wherof° ye sholden drede.

"Have here another wey, if it so be
That al this thing ne may yow not suffise:
My fader, as ye knowen wel, parde°,
Is old, and elde is ful of coveytise°,
And I right now have founden al the gyse°
Withoute net wherwith I shal hym hente°.
And herkeneth how, if that ye wol assente.

"Lo, Troylus, men seyn that hard it is
The wolf ful and the wether hol° to have;
This is to seyn, that men ful ofte, ywys°,
Mote° spenden part, the remnaunt for to save.
For ay with gold men may the herte grave°
Of hym that set is upon coveitise;
And how° I mene, I shal it yow devyse.

"The moeble° which that I have in this town
Unto my fader shal I take, and seye
That right for trust and for savacioun°
It sent is from a frend of his or tweye°;
The wheche° frendes ferventlyche hym preye
To senden after more, and that in hye°,
Whil that this town stant° thus in jupartie.

"And that shal ben an huge quantite—
Thus shal I seyn—but lest it folk aspide°,
This may be sent by no wyght but by me.
I shal ek shewen hym, yf pes bytyde°,
What frendes that ich have on every syde
Toward° the court, to don the wrathe pace°
Of Priamus, and don hym stonde in grace°.

1331 kyn, *family* **1332 But yf that onlyche it my fader be,** *excepting only my father* **1333 yfere,** *together* **1334 namelyche,** *especially* **1335 nolde leven for to se,** *would not stop seeing* **1336 as wyd as it hath space,** *as vast as it is* **1337 se ich nevere,** *may I never see* **1338 trowe ye,** *do you think* **1339 Coveyteth,** *wants* **1341 unhappy,** *unfortunate* **1342 wot,** *knows* **1344 Us neded for my wendyng,** *we would not need for my going* **1346 trete of pees,** *negotiate peace* **1348 that is mys,** *what is amiss* **1349 nere comfort none,** *were no comfort* **1350 purposen,** *intend* **1351 abyde,** *remain* **1353 mot nedes dryve,** *must compel* **1354 entrecomunen yfere,** *interact together* **1355 blyve,** *readily* **1356 Alday,** *always,* **ben flen,** *bees fly* **1357 bleve,** *remain* **1358 leve,** *permission* **1359 though so be,** *even if it happens* **1360 hider,** *here* **1361 moste,** *must,* **wheder,** *where* **1362 myschaunce,** *by bad luck* **1364 wysly,** *surely as,* **rede,** *may guide* **1365 wherof,** *of what* **1368 parde,** *by God* **1369 coveytise,** *greed* **1370 gyse,** *way* **1371 hente,** *trap* **1374 wether hol,** *sheep healthy* **1375 ywys,** *indeed* **1376 Mote,** *must* **1377 grave,** *make an impression on* **1379 how,** *what* **1380 moeble,** *personal possessions* **1382 savacioun,** *security* **1383 tweye,** *two* **1384 wheche,** *which* **1385 in hye,** *quickly* **1386 stant,** *stands* **1388 aspide,** *might notice* **1390 pes bytyde,** *peace should come* **1392 Toward,** *at,* **don the wrathe pace,** *cause the anger to pass away* **1393 don hym stonde in grace,** *enable him to regain favor*

1337 Combines the Christian notion of seeing God's face as a form of reward with the pagan diety Jove (Jupiter). **1369 elde is ful of coveytise,** Proverbial. **1373–74 men seyn . . . ,** unrecorded elsewhere as a proverb.

"So, what for o thyng and for other, swete,
I shal hym so enchaunten with my sawes°,
That right in hevene his sowle is shal he mete°.
For al Appollo, or his clerkes lawes°,
Or calkullyng° avayleth nought thre hawes°;
Desir of gold shal so his soule blende°
That as me lyst I shal wel make an ende.

"And yf he wolde aught° by hys sort° it preve°
If that I lye, in certayn I shal fonde°
Distourben° hym and plukke hym by the sleve,
Makynge his sort°, and beren hym on honde°
He hath not wel the goddes understonde—
For goddes speken in amphibologies°,
And for o soth they tellen twenty lyes.

"Eke drede fond first goddes°, I suppose—
Thus shal I seyn—and that his coward herte
Made hym amys° the goddes text to glose°,
Whan he for fered° out of Delphos sterte°.
And but° I make hym soone° to converte,
And don my red° withinne a day or tweye,
I wol to yow oblige° me to deye."

And trewelyche, as wreten wel I fynde,
That al this thyng was seyd of good entente,
And that hire herte trewe was and kynde
Towardes hym, and spak right as she mente,
And that she start° for wo neigh° whan she wente,
And was in purpos evere to be trewe:
Thus writen they that of hire werkes knewe.

This Troylus, with herte and eerys spradde°,
Herde al this thing devysen° to and fro.
And verraylich hym semed° that he hadde
The same wit°, but yet to lat hire go
His herte mysforyaf° hym everemo.
But fynally he gan his herte wreste°
To trusten hire, and tok it for the beste.

For which the grete fury of his penaunce°
Was queynt° with hope, and therwith hem bitwene
Bygan for joye the amorouse daunce°.
And as the briddes°, whanne the sonne is shene°,
Deliten in hire song yn leves grene,
Right so the wordes that they spake yfere°
Deliten hem and made hire hertes clere.

But natheles, the wendyng° of Criseyde
For al this world may nought out of° his mynde;
For which ful ofte he pitously hire preyde°
That of hire heste° he mighte hire trewe fynde,
And seyde hire, "Certes, yf ye be unkynde,
And but° ye come at day set° into Troye,
Ne shal I nevere have hele°, honour, ne joye.

"For also soth° as sonne uprist° on morwe,
And God, so wisly° thow me, woful wrecche,
To reste° brynge out of this cruwel sorwe,
I wol myselven sle yf that ye drecche°.
But of my deth though litel be to recche°,
Yet, er that ye me cause so to smerte,
Dwelle° rathere here, myn owene swete herte.

"For trewely, myn owne lady deere,
Tho sleyghtes° yet that I have herd yow stere°
Ful shaply° ben to fayllen alle yfere°.
For thus men seyn, 'that oon° thenketh the bere°,
But al another thenketh his ledere°.'
Youre sire° is wys; and seyd is°, out of drede,
'Men may the wyse at-renne°, but not at-rede°.'

1395 sawes, *speeches* **1396 his sowle is shal he mete,** *he shall dream his soul to be* **1397 clerkes lawes,** *scholarly ways* **1398 calkullyng,** *calculating,* **hawes,** *hawthorn berries* **1399 blende,** *blind* **1401 aught,** *at all,* **sort,** *divination,* **preve,** *test* **1402 fonde,** *arrange* **1403 Distourben,** *to prevent* **1404 Mayknge his sort,** (while he is) *casting his lots,* **beren hym on honde,** *lead him to think* **1406 amphibologies,** *ambiguities* **1408 drede fond first goddes,** *fear first invented the gods* **1410 amys,** *wrongly,* **glose,** *interpret* **1411 fered,** *fear,* **sterte,** *hurried* **1412 but,** *unless,* **soone,** *quickly* **1413 don my red,** *follow my advice* **1414 oblige,** *pledge* **1419 starf,** *died,* **neigh,** *nearly* **1422 eerys spradde,** *eyes wide open* **1423 devysen,** *described* **1424 verraylich hym semed,** *truly he thought* **1425 wit,** *idea* **1426 mysforyaf,** *thoroughly misgave* **1427 wreste,** *forced* **1429 penaunce,** *suffering* **1430 queynt,** *quenched* **1431 amorouse daunce,** *dance of love* **1432 briddes,** *birds,* **shene,** *bright* **1434 yfere,** *together* **1436 wendyng,** *leaving* **1437 out of,** *depart from* **1438 preyde,** *prayed* **1439 heste,** *promise* **1441 but,** *unless,* **day set,** *the set day* **1442 hele,** *health* **1443 also soth,** *as truly,* **uprist,** *rises* **1444 so wisly,** *so surely may* **1445 reste,** *comfort* **1446 drecche,** *delay* **1447 litel be to recche,** *it be of little concern* **1449 Dwelle,** *remain* **1451 Tho sleyghtes,** *those tricks,* **stere,** *devise* **1452 shaply,** *likely,* **yfere,** *together* **1453 oon,** *one way,* **bere,** *bear* **1454 ledere,** *trainer* **1455 sire,** *father,* **seyd is,** *it is said* **1456 at-renne,** *outrun,* **at-rede,** *outthink*

1398 avayleth nought thre hawes, an idiom meaning "helps not at all." Hawthorn berries are inedible. **1408** Proverbial. **1411 Delphos,** Delphi, where Calkas consulted Apollo; see 1.70n. **1453–54** Proverbial. Troylus's string of proverbs and proverbial material (1453–63) is not in *Filostrato.* **1456 but,** Cp reads "and"; **at-rede,"** Cl reads "arede" (redeem).

"It is ful hard to halten unespied°
Byfore a crepul°, for he kan° the craft.
Youre fader is in sleyght° as Argus eyed°;
For al be that his moeble is° hym byraft,
His olde sleyghte is yet so with hym laft
Ye shal nat blende° hym for youre womanhede°,
Ne feyne aright°; and that is alle my drede.

"I not° if pes shal evere mo bytyde°;
But pes or no, for ernest ne for game°,
I wot, syn Calkas on the Grekes syde
Hath ones° ben and lost so foule° his name°,
He dar no more come here ayen for shame;
For which that wey, for ought I kan espye,
To trusten on nys° but a fantasye.

"Ye shal ek sen, yowre fader shal yow glose°
To ben a wyf; and as he kan wel preche°,
He shal som Grek so preyse and wel alose°
That ravysshen° he shal yow with his speche,
Or do yow don° by force as he shal teche.
And Troylus, of whom ye nyl han routhe°,
Shal causeles so sterven° in his trouthe.

"And over al this°, youre fader shal despise°
Us alle and seyn this cite nys but lorn°,
And that th'assege nevere shal aryse,
For-why° the Grekes han it alle sworn,
Til we be slayn and doun oure walles torn.
And thus he shal you with his wordes fere°,
That ay drede I that ye wol bleven° there.

"Ye shul ek seen so mani a lusty knyght
Among the Grekes, ful of worthynesse,
And eche of hem with herte, wit, and myght
To plesen yow don al his besynesse°,
That ye shul dullen° of the rudenesse°
Of us sely° Troians, but yf routhe°
Remorde yow°, or vertue° of youre trouthe°.

"And this to me so grevous is to thenke
That fro my brest it wole my soule rende°.
Ne, dredles°, in me ther may not synke
A good opynyoun° yf that ye wende°;
For why° youre fadres sleyghte wole us shende°.
And yf ye gon, as I have told yow yore°,
So thenk I nam but ded, withoute more.

"For which with humble, trewe, and pitous herte,
A thousand tymes mercy I yow preye;
So reweth° on myn aspre° peynes smerte°,
And doth somwhat as that I shal yow seye,
And lat us stele awey bytwext us tweye.
And thenk that folye is°, whan man may chese°,
For accident° his substaunce° ay to lese°.

"I mene this, that syn we mowe° er day
Wel stele awey and ben togedere so,
What nede were it to putten in assay°,
In cas ye sholde to youre fader go,
If that ye myghte come ayen or no?
Thus mene I, that it were a gret folye
To putte that sikernesse° in jupartie.

"And vulgarly° to speken of substaunce,
Of tresour may we bothe with us lede°
Ynowh° to lyve in honour and plesaunce°
Til into tyme that we shul ben dede.
And thus we may eschewen° al this drede.
For everych° other wey ye kan recorde°,
Myn herte, ywys, may not therwith acorde°.

1457 halten unespied, *limp undetected* **1458 crepul,** *lame man* **1458 kan,** *knows* **1459 sleyght,** *trickery,* **as Argus eyed,** *very watchful* (see n.) **1460 moeble is,** *personal possessions are* **1462 blende,** *blind,* **for youre womanhede,** *despite your womanhood* **1463 feyne aright,** *pretend successfully* **1464 not,** *don't know,* **bytyde,** *happen* **1465 for ernest ne for game,** *in any case* **1467 ones,** *once,* **foule,** *foully,* **name,** *reputation* **1470 nys,** *is nothing* **1471 glose,** *persuade* **1473 preche,** *talk* **1473 alose,** *praise* **1474 ravysshen,** *overwhelm* **1475 do yow don,** *make you do* **1476 routhe,** *pity* **1477 sterven,** *die* **1478 over al this,** *moreover,* **despise,** *speak ill of* **1479 lorn,** *lost* **1481 For-why,** *because* **1483 fere,** *frighten* **1484 bleven,** *remain* **1488 don al his besynesse,** *makes great effort* **1489 dullen,** *grow weary,* **rudeness,** *boorishness* **1490 sely,** *foolish,* **but yf routhe,** *unless pity* **1491 Remorde yow,** *cause you regret,* **vertue,** *strength,* **trouthe,** *fidelity* **1493 rende,** *tear out* **1494 dredles,** *doubtless* **1495 good opynyoun,** *hopeful expectation,* **wende,** *depart* **1495 For why,** *because,* **shende,** *ruin* **1497 yore,** *earlier* **1501 reweth,** *have pity,* **aspre,** *bitter,* **smerte,** *sting* **1504 that folye is,** *what a folly it is,* **chese,** *choose* **1505 accident,** *something inessential,* **substaunce,** *something essential,* **lese,** *lose* **1506 mowe,** *may* **1509 in assay,** *to the test* **1512 sikernesse,** *certainly* **1513 vulgarly,** *in a non-technical way* **1514 lede,** *take* **1515 Ynowh,** *enough,* **plesaunce,** *pleasure* **1517 eschewen,** *avoid* **1518 everych,** *every,* **recorde,** *suggest* **1519 acorde,** *agree*

1459 Argus, the hundred-eyed watchman in Ovid, *Metamorphoses* 1.625. **1483 And,** Cl reads "Al." **1505 accident . . . substaunce,** scholastic language used to distinguish between superficial transient qualities (hair color, height, etc.) and essential permanent ones (being human, mortality). At 4.1513–14 Troylus refers to the common, nonscholastic sense of "substance." **1506 this,** Cp reads "thus." **1508 nede,** Cp reads "wit."

"And hardely°, ne dredeth no poverte,
For I have kyn and frendes elleswhere
That though we comen in oure bare sherte
Us sholde neyther lakke golde ne gere°,
But ben honured while we dwelten there.
And go we anoon°; for as yn myn entente°,
This is the beste, yf that ye wole assente."

Criseyde with a syk° right in this wyse
Answerde, "Ywys, my dere herte trewe,
We may wel stele awey as ye devyse,
And fynden swyche unthryfty° weyes newe;
But afterward ful sore it wole us rewe°.
And helpe me God° so at my moste nede,
As causeles ye suffren al this drede.

"For thilke° day that I for cherysshynge°
Or drede of fader, or for other wight,
Or for estat°, delit°, or for weddynge,
Be fals to yow, my Troylus, my knyght,
Saturnes doughter Juno, thorugh hire myght,
As wod° as Athamante do me° dwelle
Eternaly in Stix, the put° of helle!

"And this on every god celestial
I swere it yow, and ek on eche goddesse,
On every nymphe and diete° infernal,
On satiry° and fawny° more and lesse°
That halve-goddes ben of wildernesse.
And Attropos, my thred of lif thow breste°
If I be fals! Now trowe° me if ye leste°.

"And thow, Symoys, that as an arwe clere°
Thorugh Troye ay rennest° downward to the se,
Ber witnesse of this word that seyd is here:
That thilke° day that ich untrewe be
To Troylus, myn owene herte fre°,
That thow retorne bakwarde to thi welle°,
And I with body and soule synke in helle!

"But that ye speke° awey thus for to go
And leten° alle youre frendes, God forbede
For ony womman that ye sholden so,
And namly syn° Troye hath now swych nede
Of help. And ek of o thyng taketh hede:
If this were wist°, my lif lay in balaunce°,
And youre honour. God shilde° us fro
myschaunce!

"And if so be that pes hereafter take°,
As alday° happeth after anger game°,
Why, Lord, the sorwe and wo ye wolden make
That ye ne dorste° come ayen for shame.
And er that ye juparten° so youre name,
Beth nought to hastyf° in this hote fare°,
For hastyf man ne wanteth° nevere care°.

"What trowe ye° the peple ek al aboute
Wolde of it seye? It is ful light t'arede°.
They wolden seye, and swere it out of doute,
That love ne drof° yow nought to don this dede,
But lust voluptuous and coward° drede.
Thus were° al lost, ywys, myn herte dere,
Yowre honour, which that now shyneth so
clere.

"And also thenketh on myn honeste°,
That floureth° yet, how foule I sholde it
shende°,
And with what filthe it spotted sholde be,
If in this forme° I sholde with yow wende°.
Ne though I lyved unto the worldes ende,

1520 hardely, *surely* **1523 gere,** *possessions* **1525 go we anoon,** *let's go immediately,* **entente,** *opinion* **1527 syk,** *sigh* **1530 unthryfty,** *fruitless* **1531 it wole us rewe,** *we will regret it* **1532 helpe me God,** *as God may help me* **1534 thilke,** *that,* **cherysshynge,** *devotion to* **1536 estat,** *status,* **delit,** *pleasure* **1539 wod,** *mad,* **do me,** *cause me to* **1540 put,** *pit* **1543 diete,** *deity* **1544 satiry,** *satyrs,* **fawny,** *fauns,* **more and lesse,** *greater and lesser* **1546 breste,** *burst* **1547 trowe,** *believe,* **leste,** *wish* **1548 arwe clere,** *shining arrow* **1549 rennest,** *flows* **1551 thilke,** *same* **1552 fre,** *generous* **1553 welle,** *source* **1555 speke,** *propose* **1556 leten,** *leave* **1558 namly syn,** *especially since* **1560 wist,** *known* **1560 lay in balaunce,** *would lie at risk* **1561 shilde,** *shield* **1562 take,** *occurs* **1563 alday,** *always,* **after anger game,** *joy after conflict* **1565 That ye ne dorste,** *because you dare not* **1566 juparten,** *jeopardize* **1567 to hastyf,** *too hasty,* **hote fare,** *rash action* **1568 ne wanteth,** *never lacks,* **care,** *trouble* **1569 trowe ye,** *do you think* **1570 light t'arede,** *easy to predict* **1572 drof,** *drove* **1573 coward,** *cowardly* **1574 were,** *would be* **1576 honeste,** *honor* **1577 floureth,** *flourishes,* **shende,** *ruin* **1579 forme,** *manner,* **wende,** *go*

1535 for, Cl reads "of"; **other,** Cp reads "any other." **1538–40 Juno . . . Athamante . . . Stix,** Athamas, King of Thebes, was driven mad by Juno, daughter of Saturn; Ovid, *Metamorphoses* 4.416ff. In Dante, *Inferno* 30.1–12, Athamas is among the "falsifiers." In classical tradition, the Styx is the infernal river of fire. **1546 Attropos,** see 4.1208n. **thow breste,** Cp reads "to-breste." **1547 ye,** Cl reads "thow"; Cp, "yow." **1548 Symoys,** the Simois does not actually flow through Troy, but it is a river of the region that is associated with longevity in Ovid, *Amores* 1.15.10. **1555 awey,** Cl reads "alwey." **1568** Proverbial.

My name° sholde I nevere ayenward wynne°.
Thus were I lost, and that were routhe° and synne.

"And forthi sle° with reson al this hete°.
Men seyn 'the suffraunt° overcomith,' parde;
Ek 'whoso wol han leef°, he leef mot lete°.'
Thus maketh vertu of necessite
By pacience, and thenk that lord is he
Of Fortune ay, that nought wole of hire recche°;
And she ne daunteth° no wight but a wrecche.

"And trusteth this, that certes°, herte swete,
Er Phebus suster, Lucyna the shene°,
The Leoun passe° out of this Ariete,
I wol ben here withouten any wene°.
I mene, as° helpe me Juno, hevenes quene,
The tenthe day, but if that° deth me assayle°,
I wol yow sen withouten ony fayle."

"And now, so° this be soth," quod Troylus,
"I shal wel suffre° unto the tenthe day,
Syn that I se that nede it mot° be thus.
But for the love of God, yf it be may,
So late us stelen pryvely away;
For evere in oon°, as for to lyve in reste,
Myn herte seyth that it wol ben the beste."

"O mercy God, what lyf is this?" quod she.
"Allas, ye sle me thus for verray tene°!
I se wel now that ye mystrusten me,
For by youre wordes it is wel isene°.
Now for the love of Cynthia the shene°,
Mistrust me nought thus causeles, for routhe°,
Syn to be trewe I have yow plyght° my trouthe.

"And thenketh wel that somtyme it is wit°
To spende a tyme, a tyme for to wynne.
Ne, parde, lorn° am I nought fro yow yit,
Though that we ben a day or two atwynne°.
Dryf° out the fantasies yow withinne,
And trusteth me, and leveth° ek youre sorwe,
Or her° my trouthe, I wol not lyve til morwe.

"For if ye wiste how sore it doth me smerte°,
Ye wolde cesse of this; for God, thow wost,
The pure spirit wepeth in myn herte
To se yow wepen that I love most,
And that I mot° gon to the Grekes ost°.
Ye, nere it° that I wiste remedie°
To come ayeyn, right here I wolde dye.

"But certes, I am not so nyce° a wyght
That I ne kan ymagynen a weye
To come ayen that day that I have hight°.
For who may holde thing° that wole° awey?
My fader nought, for al his queynte° pley.
And by my thryft°, my wendyng° out of Troye
Another day shal torne us alle to joye.

"Forthy° with al myn herte I yow biseke°,
Yf that yow lyst don ought° for my preyere°,
And for the love which that I love yow eke,
That er that I departe fro yow here,
That of so good a confort and a chere
I may yow sen that ye may brynge at reste
Myn herte, which that is o poynt to breste°.

"And over° al this I pray yow," quod she tho,
"Myn owen hertes sothfast suffisaunce°,

1581 name, *good reputation,* **ayenward wynne,** *reclaim* **1582 routhe,** *pity* **1583 sle,** *kill,* **hete,** *passion* **1584 suffraunt,** *patient person* **1585 leef,** *something desired,* **mot lete,** *must give up* **1588 recche,** *care* **1589 daunteth,** *frightens* **1590 certes,** *surely* **1591 shene,** *shining* **1592 passe,** *passes through* **1593 wene,** *doubt* **1594 as,** *so* **1595 but if that,** *unless,* **me assayle,** *assaults me* **1597 so,** *as long as* **1598 suffre,** *be patient or suffer* **1599 nede it mot,** *it necessarily must* **1602 evere in oon,** *continually* **1605 verray tene,** *genuine pain* **1607 isene,** *seen* **1608 shene,** *shining* **1609 routhe,** *pity* **1610 plyght,** *pledged* **1611 wit,** *smart* **1613 lorn,** *lost* **1614 atwynne,** *apart* **1615 Dryf,** *drive* **1616 leveth,** *leave behind* **1617 her,** *have here* **1617 doth me smerte,** *pains me* **1622 mot,** *must,* **ost,** *army* **1623 Ye, nere it,** *indeed, were it not,* **remedie,** *a solution* **1625 nyce,** *foolish* **1627 hight,** *promised* **1628 thing,** *something,* **wole,** *wishes to be* **1629 queynte,** *clever* **1630 thryft,** *success,* **wendyng,** *going* **1632 Forthy,** *therefore,* **biseke,** *request* **1633 lyst don ought,** *choose to do anything,* **for my preyere,** *at my request* **1638 o poynt to breste,** *on the point of bursting* **1639 over,** *above* **1640 sothfast suffisaunce,** *true satisfaction*

1583–87 In *Filostrato,* Criseida argues that their passion will cool if they indulge it. Chaucer's Criseyde instead offers proverbial wisdom and the Boethian notion that Fortune cannot affect those who care not for her benefits. **1584** Proverbial. **1585** Proverbial. **1586** Proverbial; see *KnT* 1.3041 and *SqT* 5.593. **1587 By pacience,** Cl reads "Be pacient." **1591–92 Phebus suster . . . Ariete,** Lucina, the moon, is the sister of Phoebus, the sun. The moon will move beyond its present location in the zodiacal sign of Aries (the ram) and through that of Leo (the lion) in ten days, when the moon will be a new crescent. Chaucer's addition. **1608 Cynthia, another name for** the moon, a figure of changeableness. **1628** Proverbial.

Syn I am thyn al hool, withouten mo,
That whil that I am absent, no plesaunce°
Of other do° me fro youre remembraunce.
For I am evere agast°, forwhi° men rede°
That love is thing ay ful of bysy° drede.

"For yn this world ther lyveth lady noon,
If that ye were untrewe—as God defende°—
That so bytraysed were° or wobygon
As I, that al trouthe in yow entende°.
And douteles, yf that ych other wende°,
I nere but ded, and er ye cause fynde°,
For Goddes love, so beth me not unkynde."

To this answerde Troylus and seyde,
"Now God, to whom ther nys no cause ywrye°,
Me glade°, as wys° I nevere unto Criseyde,
Syn thilke day I saw hire first with eye,
Was fals, ne nevere shal til that I dye.
At shorte wordes, wel ye may me leve°:
I kan no more; it shal be founde at preve°."

"Graunt mercy°, goode myn, ywys," quod she,
"And blysful Venus lat me nevere sterve°,
Er I may stonde of plesaunce in degre°
To quyte° hym wel that so wel kan deserve.
And whil that God my wit wol me conserve°,
I shal so don—so trewe I have yow founde,
That ay honour to me-ward° shal rebounde°.

"For trusteth wel that youre estat° royal,
Ne veyn delit°, nor oonly worthinesse
Of yow in werre° or torney marcial°,
Ne pompe, array, nobley°, or ek richesse
Ne made me to rewe° on youre destresse.
But moral vertu, grounded upon trouthe,
That was the cause I first hadde on yow routhe°.

"Ek gentil herte and manhod that ye hadde;
And that ye hadde, as me thoughte, in despit°
Everythyng that souned into° badde,
As rudenesse and pepelyssh appetit°;
And that yowre reson brydled youre delit—
This made° aboven every creature
That I was youre, and shal while I may dure°.

"And this may lengthe of yeres not fordo°,
Ne remuable° Fortune deface°;
But Juppiter, that of his myght may do°
The sorwful to be glad, so yeve us grace
Er° nyghtes ten to meten in this place,
So that it may youre herte and myn suffise.
And fareth now wel, for tyme is that ye ryse."

And after that they longe ypleyned° hadde,
And ofte ikist, and streyght° in armes folde,
The day gan ryse, and Troylus hym cladde°,
And rewfullych° his lady gan byholde,
As he that felte dethes cares colde,
And to hire grace he gan hym recomaunde.
Wher° hym was wo, this holde I no demaunde°.

For mannes hed ymagynen ne kan,
N'entendement° considere, ne tonge telle
The cruwel peynes of this sorwful man
That passen° every torment doun in helle.
For whan he saugh that she ne myghte dwelle°,
Which that his soule out of his herte rente°,
Withouten more out of the chaumbre
he wente.

Explicit liber quartus.

1642 plesaunce, *pleasure* **1643 Of other do,** *from another put* **1644 agast,** *afraid,* **forwhi,** *because,* **rede,** *say* **1645 bysy,** *anxious* **1647 defende,** *forbid* **1648 so bytraysed were,** *would be so betrayed* **1649 entende,** *assume* **1650 other wende,** *thought otherwise* **1651 er ye cause fynde,** *before you could discover why* **1654 ywrye,** *hidden* **1655 Me glade,** *make me happy,* **wys,** *surely* **1658 leve,** *believe* **1659 at preve,** *through testing* **1660 Graunt mercy,** *thank you* **1661 sterve,** *die* **1662 stonde of plesaunce in degre,** *stand in comparable happiness* **1663 quyte,** *repay* **1664 conserve,** *preserve* **1666 to me-ward,** *toward me,* **rebounde,** *return* **1667 estat,** *rank* **1668 veyn delit,** *idle pleasure* **1669 werre,** *war,* **torney marcial,** *war-like tournaments* **1670 nobley,** *nobility* **1671 rewe,** *take pity* **1673 routhe,** *pity* **1675 despit,** *contempt* **1676 souned into,** *tended towards* **1677 pepelyssh appetit,** *vulgar desires* **1679 made,** *caused* **1680 dure,** *endure* **1681 fordo,** *destroy* **1682 remuable,** *mutable,* **deface,** *obliterate* **1683 do,** *cause* **1685 Er,** *before* **1688 ypleyned,** *lamented* **1689 streyght,** *tightly* **1690 cladde,** *dressed* **1691 rewfullych,** *sadly* **1694 Wher hym,** *whether to him,* **demaunde,** *question* **1696 N'entendement,** *nor intellect* **1698 passen,** *surpass* **1699 dwelle,** *remain* **1700 rente,** *tore*

1645 Proverbial. **1660–66** Chaucer's addition. **1664 God,** omitted in Cl. **1667–82** Follows *Filostrato* 4.164–66, but there it is Troiolo who expresses similar sentiments to Criseida. **1685 place,** Cp reads "pace." **1693 hire,** Cl reads "his." **1694 hym,** Cp reads "he." **1699 whan,** omitted in Cl. **1701a *Explicit liber quartus.*** "Here ends the fourth book."

Book 5

Incipit liber quintus.

Aprochen gan the fatal destyne
That Joves° hath in disposicioun°,
And to yow, angry Parcas, sustren° thre,
Comytteth to don execucioun°;
For which Criseyde moste out of the toun,
And Troylus shal dwellen forth yn pyne°
Til Lachesis his threed no lengere twyne°.

The gold-tressed° Phebus heighe on lofte
Thries hadde al with his bemes clene°
The snowes molte°, and Zephirus as ofte
Ybrought ayen the tendre leves grene,
Syn that the sone of Ecuba the queene
Bygan to love hire first for whom his sorwe
Was al that she departe sholde o-morwe°.

Ful redy was at pryme° Dyomede
Criseyde unto the Grekes ost° to lede,
For sorwe of which she felte hire herte blede
As she that nyste° what was best to rede°.
And trewely, as men in bokes rede,
Men wyste nevere° womman han the care°,
Ne was so loth° out of a town to fare.

This Troylus, withouten red° or lore,
As man that hath his joyes ek forlore°,
Was waytyng on his lady everemore
As she that was the sothfast crop° and more
Of al his lust° or joyes here-byfore.
But Troylus, now farwel al thi joye,
For shaltow nevere sen hire eft° in Troye.

Soth° is that while he bod° in this manere,
He gan his wo ful manly for to hyde,
That wel unnethe° it sene was in his
chere;
But at the yate there she sholde out ryde,
With certeyn folk he hovede° hire t'abyde°,
So wobygon al wolde he nought hym
pleyne°
That on his hors unnethe he sat for
peyne.

For ire he quok°, so gan his herte gnawe,
Whan Diomede on hors gan hym dresse°,
And seyde to hymself this ilke sawe°,
"Allas," quod he, "thus foul a wrecchednesse,
Why suffre ich it? Whi nyl ich it redresse°?
Were it not bet° at onys° for to dye
Than everemore in langour° thus to drye°?

"Whi nyl I° make at onys ryche and pore°
To have ynowh to done° er that she go?
Why nyl I brynge al Troye upon a rore°?
Whi nyl I slen° this Diomede also?
Why nyl I rathere with a man or two
Stele hire away? Whi wol° I this endure?
Whi nyl I helpen to myn owene cure?"

But why he nolde don° so fel° a dede,
That shal I seyn, and why hym lyst it spare°.
He hadde in herte alweys a manere° drede
Lest that Cryseyde, yn rumour° of this fare°,

---

2 Joves, *Jupiter,* **in disposicioun,** *under his control* **3 sustren,** *sisters* **4 don execucioun,** *bring about* **6 pyne,** *pain* **7 twyne,** *spin* **8 gold-tressed,** *golden haired* **9 bemes clene,** *clear beams* **10 molte,** *melted* **14 departe sholde o-morwe,** *was to depart in the morning* **15 pryme,** *about 9 a.m.* **16 ost,** *army* **18 nyste,** *didn't know,* **rede,** *think* **20 Men wyste nevere,** *no one ever knew,* **care,** *sorrow* **21 loth,** *unwilling* **22 red,** *advice* **23 forlore,** *lost* **25 sothfast crop,** *true fulfillment* **26 lust,** *desire* **28 sen hire eft,** *see her again* **29 Soth,** *truth,* **bod,** *waited* **31 wel unnethe,** *only barely* **33 hovede,** *lingered,* **t'abyde,** *to await* **34 al wolde he nought hym pleyne,** *although he would not lament* **36 quok,** *shook* **37 dresse,** *approach* **38 ilke sawe,** *same speech* **40 redresse,** *correct* **41 bet,** *better,* **onys,** *once* **42 langour,** *pain,* **drye,** *suffer* **43 nyl I,** *won't I,* **ryche and pore,** *everyone* **44 ynowh to done,** *enough to do* **45 rore,** *uproar* **46 slen,** *slay* **48 wol,** *will* **50 nolde don,** *wouldn't do,* **fel,** *fierce* **51 hym lyst it spare,** *he chose to refrain* **52 manere,** *kind of* **53 rumour,** *tumult,* **fare,** *action*

Incipit liber quintus. "Here begins the fifth book." **1–14** Chaucer's addition. **3 Parcas,** Parcae, the three Fates. **4 Comytteth,** Cl reads "Comytted." **7 Lachesis,** the Fate who measures the thread of human life before Atropos cuts it; see 4.1208 and 1546. Clotho is usually the one who spins. **8 Phebus,** the sun. **9–10 Thries . . . snowes molte,** three times the snows have melted, i.e., three years have passed. Although the detail is Chaucer's addition, the imagery through which he conveys the passing of time is commonplace. **9 clene,** Cl and Cp read "clere." **10 Zephirus,** the western wind of springtime. **13 Ecuba,** Hecuba, Troylus's mother, Priam's queen. **17 Dyomede,** see 4.11n. **27 now farwel,** Cl reads "farwel now."

Sholde han ben slayn; lo, this was al his care.
And elles, certeyn, as I seyde yore°,
He hadde° it don, withouten wordes more.

Criseyde, whan she redy was to ryde,
Ful sorwfully she sighte° and seyde allas.
But forth she mot°, for ought that may bytyde°,
And forth she rit° ful sorwfully a pas°.
Ther nys non other remedye yn this cas.
What wonder is, though that hire sore smerte,
Whan she forgoth° hire owene swete herte?

This Troylus, in wyse of curtasie°,
With hauke on honde and with an huge route°
Of knyghtes, rod and did° hire compaynye,
Passynge al the valey fer withoute,
And ferthere wold han ryden, out of doute,
Ful fayn°, and wo was hym to gon so sone;
But torne he moste°, and it was ek to done°.

And right with that was Antenor icome°
Out of the Grekes ost°, and every wyght
Was of it glad and seyde he was welcome.
And Troylus, al° nere° his herte lyght,
He peyned hym° with al his fulle myght
Hym to withholde of wepynge atte leste,
And Antenor he kyste and made feste°.

And therwithal he moste his leve take,
And caste his eye upon hire pitously,
And ner he rod his cause° for to make,
To take hire by the honde al sobrely.
And Lord, so she gan wepen tendrely!
And he ful softe and sleyghly° gan hire seye,
"Now holde yowre day°, and doth me not to deye."

With that his courser° torned he aboute,
With face pale, and unto Diomede
No word he spak, ne non of al his route°;
Of which the sone of Tydeus tok hede,
As he that koude° more than the crede°
In swych a craft°, and by the reyne° hire hente°.
And Troylus to Troye homward he wente.

This Diomede, that ladde hire by the bridel,
Whan that he saw the folk of Troye aweye,
Thoughte, "Al my labour shal nat ben on ydel,
If that I may, for somwhat shal I seye,
For at the worste it may yet shorte° oure weye.
I have herd seyd ek tymes twyes twelve°,
'He is a fool that wole foryete hymselve.'"

But natheles, this thoughte he wel ynowh,
That "Certaynlich I am aboute nought°
If that I speke of love or make it tough°,
For douteles, yf she have in hire thought
Hym that I gesse, he may nat ben ybrought
So son awey°. But I shal fynde a mene°
That she shal not as yet wete° what I mene."

This Diomede as he that koude his good°,
Whan this was don, gan fallen forth in° speche
Of this and that, and axed° whi she stood
In swych dishese°, and gan hire ek byseche°
That yf that he encrese myghte or eche°
With onythyng hire ese°, that she sholde
Comaunde it hym, and seyde he don it wolde.

For treweliche he swor hire as a knyght
That ther nas thyng° with whiche he myghte hire plese,
That he nolde don his peyne and al his myght
To don it, for to done hire herte an ese;
And preyede hire she wolde hire sorwe apese°,

---

55 yore, *earlier* **56 hadde,** *would have* **58 sighte,** *sighed* **59 mot,** *must* (go), **bytyde,** *happen* **60 rit,** *rides,* **a pas,** *at a slow walk* **63 forgoth,** *gives up* **64 in wyse of curtasie,** *in a courteous manner* **65 route,** *company* **66 did,** *kept* **69 Ful fayn,** *very happily* **70 moste,** *must,* **ek to done,** *must be done* **71 icome,** *arrived* **72 ost,** *army* **74 al,** *although,* **nere,** *wasn't* **75 peyned hym,** *made the effort* **77 made feste,** *showed respect* **80 cause,** *plea* **83 sleyghly,** *secretly* **84 holde yowre day,** *keep your* (promised) *day* **85 courser,** *warhorse* **87 route,** *company* **89 koude,** *knew,* **crede,** *basics* **90 a craft,** *an artl,* **reyne,** *reins,* **hente,** *grasped* **96 shorte,** *shorten* **97 tymes twyes twelve,** *twenty-four times* (i.e., many times) **100 aboute nought,** *wasting my time* **101 make it tough,** *move too fast* **103–04 ybrought / So son awey,** *so readily replaced* **104 mene,** *means* **105 wete,** *realize* **106 koude his good,** *knew his own best interests* **107 gan fallen forth in,** *fell into* **108 axed,** *asked* **109 swych dishese,** *such distress,* **gan hire ek byseche,** *also asked her* **110 eche,** *add to* **111 ese,** *comfort* **114 nas thyng,** *was nothing* **117 apese,** *calm*

60–61 A number of manuscripts transpose these lines. **65 hauke on honde,** bearing a hawk, a sign of aristocratic gentility. **82 she,** Cp reads "he." **88 sone of Tydeus,** i.e., Diomede. **89 crede,** the Christian creed is a basic statement of knowledge and belief; here used to mean fundamental knowledge. **98** Proverbial, though not recorded before Chaucer. **99–189** Chaucer's version of Diomede's immediate attempt to woo Criseyde follows (with adjustments) Benoît rather than *Filostrato,* in which Diomede waits four days before courting her after being initially smitten.

And seyde, "Ywys°, we Grekes kon have joye
To honouren yow as wel as folk of Troye."

He seyde ek thus, "I wot yow thenketh
straunge—
Ne wonder is, for it is to yow newe—
Th'aquayntaunce of these Troians to chaunge
For folk of Grece that ye nevere knewe.
But wolde nevere God but if° as trewe
A Grek ye shulde among us alle fynde
As ony Troian is, and ek as kynde.

"And by the cause° I swor yow right, lo, now,
To ben youre frend, and helply to° my myght,
And for° that more aquayntaunce ek of yow
Have ich had than another straunger wight,
So fro this° forth, I pray yow, day and nyght
Comaundeth me, how° sore that me smerte,
To don al that may like unto° youre herte;

"And that ye me wolde as youre brother trete°,
And taketh not my frendshipe in despit°.
And though youre sorwes be for thinges grete—
Not I not whi°—but out of more respit°
Myn herte hath for to amende it° gret delit.
And yf I may youre harmes nat redresse°,
I am right sory for youre hevynesse°.

"For though ye Troians with us Grekes wrothe°
Han many a day ben, alwey yet, parde°,
O god° of Love in soth° we serven bothe.
And for the love of God, my lady fre°,
Whomso° ye hate, as° beth not wroth with me,
For trewely, ther kan no wyght yow serve
That half so loth° yowre wraththe wold deserve.

"And nere it° that we been so neigh the tente
Of Calkas, which that sen us bothe may°,
I wolde of this yow telle al myn entente.
But this enseled° til another day—
Yeve° me youre hond. I am and shal ben ay,
God helpe me so, while that my lyf may dure,
Youre owene aboven every creature.

"Thus seyde I nevere er now to womman born,
For, God myn herte as wysly glade° so,
I loved never womman here-byforn
As paramours°, ne nevere shal no mo.
And for the love of God, beth not my fo,
Al° kan I not to yow, my lady dere,
Compleyne aryght°, for I am yet to lere.

"And wondreth not, myn owen lady bryght,
Though that I speke of love to you thus blyve°,
For I have herd er this of many a wyght
Hath loved thyng he nevere saugh his° lyve.
Ek I am not of power° for to stryve
Ayeyns the god of Love, but hym obeye
I wole alwey, and mercy I yow preye.

"Ther ben so° worthi knyghtes in this place,
And ye so feyr, that everich of hem alle
Wol peynen hym° to stonden in youre grace°.
But myghte me so faire a grace falle
That ye me for youre servant wolde calle.
So lowely ne so trewely yow serve
Nil noon of hem as I shal til I sterve°."

Criseyde unto that purpos° lite answerde,
As she that was with sorwe oppressed so
That in effect she nought his tales herde
But her and there, now here a word or two.
Hire thoughte hire sorwful herte brast a-two°,
For whan she gan hire fader fer aspye°
Wel neigh doun of hire hors she gan to sye°.

But natheles she thonked Diomede
Of al his travayle° and his goode chere,
And that hym lyst° his frendshipe hire to bede°.
And she accepteth it in goode manere,

118 Ywys, *surely* **124 wolde nevere God but if,** *God forbid but that* **127 by the cause,** *because* **128 helply to,** *helpful to the extent of* **129 for,** *so* **131 this,** *this time* **132 how,** *however* **133 like unto,** *please* **134 trete,** *treat* **135 despit,** *contempt* **137 Not I not whi,** *I do not know why,* **out of more respit,** *without delay* **138 amende it,** *relieve it* (i.e, them, her sorrows) **139 redresse,** *alleviate* **140 hevynesse,** *sorrow* **141 wrothe,** *angry* **142 parde,** *by God* **143 O god,** *one god,* **soth,** *truth* **144 fre,** *noble* **145 Whomso,** *whomever,* **as,** *so* **147 loth,** *unwillingly* **148 nere it,** *were it not* **149 sen us bothe may,** *we both can see* **151 this enseled,** *this* (matter) *is sealed* **152 Yeve,** *give* **156 so wysly glade,** *so surely gladden* **158 As paramours,** *passionately* **160 Al,** *although* **161 aryght,** *properly* **163 blyve,** *quickly* **165 saugh his,** *saw in his* **166 not of power,** *powerless* **169 so,** *such* **171 peynen hym,** *strive,* **grace,** *favor* **175 sterve,** *die* **176 purpos,** *propositiont* **180 brast a-two,** *burst apart* **181 fer aspye,** *see far away* **182 sye,** *sink* **184 travayle,** *effort* **185 lyst,** *wished,* **bede,** *offer*

176 lite, Cl reads "litel." **182 of,** Cl reads "on." **185–88** The repetition of *and* at the beginning of these lines (anaphora) and internally within the lines contributes to a sense of rapid pace.

And wold do fayn that° is hym lef° and dere,
And trusten hym she wolde, and wel she myghte,
As seyde she, and from hire hors sh'alighte.

Hire fader hath hire in his armes nome°,
And tweynty tyme he kyste his doughter swete,
And seyde, "O dere doughter myn, welcome."
She seyde ek she was fayn° with hym to mete,
And stod forth mewet°, mylde, and mansuete°.
But here I leve hire with hire fader dwelle,
And forth° I wole of Troylus yow telle.

To Troye is come this woful Troylus,
In sorwe aboven alle sorwes smerte°,
With felon° lok and face dispitous°.
Tho° sodeynly doun from his hors he sterte°,
And thorugh his paleys, with a swollen herte,
To chambre he wente. Of nothing tok he hede,
Ne noon to hym dar speke a word for drede.

And there his sorwes that he spared° hadde
He yaf an yssue large°, and "Deth" he cride;
And in his throwes frenetyk° and madde
He curssed Jove, Appollo, and ek Cupide,
He curssed Ceres, Bacus, and Cipryde,
His burthe, hymself, his fate, and ek nature,
And, save° his lady, every creature.

To bedde he goth and walwith° there and torneth
In furye, as doth he Ixion in helle.
And in this wyse he neigh til° day sojourneth°.
But tho bygan a lyte his herte unswelle
Thorugh teris which that gonnen up to welle.
And pitously he cride° upon Criseyde,
And to hymself right thus he spak and seyde:

"Wher is myn owene lady lief° and dere?
Wher is hire white brest? Wher is it? Where?
Wher ben hire armes and hire eyen clere
That yesternyght° this tyme with me were?
Now may I wepe allone many a tere,
And graspe aboute I may, but in this place
Save a pilwe° I fynde nought t'enbrace.

"How shal I do? Whan shal she come ayen?
I not°, allas! Whi let ich hire to go?
As wolde God° ich hadde as tho° be sleyn!
O herte myn, Criseyde, O swete fo!
O lady myn that I love and no mo°,
To whom for evermo myn herte I dowe°,
Se how I deye; ye nyl me not rescowe!

"Who seeth yow now, my righte lode-sterre°?
Who sit° right now, or stant in yowre presence?
Who kan conforten now youre hertes werre°?
Now I am gon, whom yeve° ye audience?
Who speketh for me right now in myn absence?
Allas, no wight, and that is al my care,
For wel I wot° as yvele as I ye fare°.

"How shulde I thus ten dayes ful endure,
Whan I the firste nyght have al this tene°?
How shal she don° ek, sorwful creature?
For tendernesse how shal she ek sustene
Swich wo for me? O pitous pale and grene
Shal ben youre fresshe wommanlyche face
For langour°, er ye torne° unto this place."

And whan he fil° in ony slomberynges,
Anoon bygonne he sholde for to grone°,
And dremen of the dredefulleste thinges
That myghte ben: as mete° he were allone
In place horrible, makyng ay his mone,
Or meten° that he was amonges alle
His enemys, and in hire hondes falle°.

And therwithal° his body sholde sterte°,
And with the stert al sodeynlich awake,
And swich a tremor° fele aboute his herte
That of the feere his body sholde quake,
And therwithal he sholde a noyse make,

187 wold do fayn that, *would happily do whatever,* **lef,** *desirable* **190 nome,** *taken* **193 fayn,** *pleased* **194 mewet,** *quiet,* **mansuete,** *meek* **196 forth,** *further* **198 smerte,** *painful* **199 felon,** *hostile,* **dispitous,** *angry* **200 Tho,** *then,* **sterte,** *leapt* **204 spared,** *withheld* **205 yaf an yssue large,** *gave full vent to* **206 throwes frenetyk,** *fits frantic* **210 save,** *except* **211 walwith,** *wallows* **213 neigh til,** *nearly until,* **sojourneth,** *remains* **216 cride,** *called* **218 lief,** *beloved* **221 yesternyght,** *last night* **224 Save a pilwe,** *except for a pillow* **226 not,** *don't know* **227 As wolde God,** *I wish to God,* **as tho,** *at that time* **229 mo,** *other* **230 dowe,** *give* **232 righte lode-sterre,** *true guiding star* **233 sit,** *sits* **234 youre hertes werre,** *the war in your heart* **235 yeve,** *give* **238 wot,** *know,* **as yvele as I ye fare,** *you suffer as much as I do* **240 tene,** *grief* **241 don,** *survive* **245 langour,** *suffering,* **torne,** *return* **246 fil,** *fell* **247 Anoon bygonne he sholde for to grone,** *immediately he began to groan* **249 as mete,** *such as to dream* **251 meten,** *dream* **252 falle,** *fallen* **253 therwithal,** *with that,* **sholde sterte,** *would jerk* **255 tremor,** *violent movement*

208 Ceres, goddess of food. **Bacus,** god of drink. **Cipryde,** another name for Venus. **211 walwith,** Cl and Cp read "weyleth." **212 Ixion,** chained in Hades to an ever-turning wheel, which was sometimes associated with Fortune's wheel; see 4.791n. **238 I wot,** Cl and Cp read "wot I." **242 tendernesse,** Cl reads "tendresse." **ek,** Cl and Cp read "this."

And seme as though he sholde falle depe
From heighe o-lofte°—and than he wolde wepe,

And rewen on° hymself so pytously
That wonder was to here his fantasye°.
Another tyme he sholde° myghtily
Conforte hymself, and seine° it was folye
So causeles swych drede for to drye°—
And eft° bygynne his aspre° sorwes newe,
That every man myghte on his sorwes rewe.

Who koude telle aright or ful discryve
His wo, his pleynt, his langour°, and his peyne?
Nought al the men that han or ben° on lyve.
Thow, redere°, mayst thyself ful wel devyne°
That swych a wo my wit kan nat defyne.
On° ydel for to write it sholde I swynke°,
Whan that my wit is wery it to thenke°.

On hevene yet the sterres weren sene,
Although ful pale ywoxen° was the moone;
And whiten gan the orisonte shene°
Al estward, as it woned° is to done;
And Phebus with his rosy carte° sone
Gan after that to dresse° hym up to fare°,
Whan Troylus hath sent after Pandare.

This Pandare, that of al the day biforn
Ne myghte have comen Troylus to se,
Although° he on his hed° it hadde isworn—
For with the kyng Pryam alday was he,
So that it lay not in his liberte
Nowher to gon—but on the morwe° he wente
To Troylus whan that he for hym sente.

For in his herte he koude wel devyne°
That Troylus al nyght for sorwe wook°,
And that he wolde telle hym of his peyne,
This knew he wel ynough withoute book.
For which to chaumbre streyght the wey he took,
And Troylus tho sobrelych he grette°,
And on the bed ful soone he gan hym sette.

"My Pandarus," quod Troilus, "the sorwe
Which that I drye° I may not longe endure.
I trowe° I shal nat lyven til tomorwe.
For whiche I wolde alwey, on aventure°,
To the devysen° of my sepulture
The forme°, and of my moeble° thow
dispone°
Right as the semeth best is for to done.

"But of the fyr and flaumbe° funeral
In whiche my body brenne° shal to glede°,
And of the feste° and pleyes palestral°
At my vigile, I pray the take good hede
That that be wel; and offre Mars my stede°,
My swerd, myn helm, and, leve° brother dere,
My sheld to Pallas yef°, that shyneth clere.

"The poudre in° which myn herte ybrend° shal
torne,
That prey I the thow take and it conserve
In a vessel that men clepeth° an urne
Of gold, and to my lady that I serve,
For love of whom thus pitously I sterve°,
So yeve it hire, and do me this plesaunce,
To preyen hire to kepe it for a remembraunce.

"For wele I fele by my maladye,
And by my dremes now and yore ago°,
Al certeynly that I mot nedes° dye.
The owle ek which that hatte° Escaphilo
Hath after me shright° alle thise nyghtes two.

---

259 o-lofte, *aloft* **260 rewen on,** *feel sorry for* **261 fantasye,** *imaginings* **262 sholde,** *would* **263 seine,** *say* **264 drye,** *suffer* **265 eft,** *after,* **aspre,** *bitter* **268 langour,** *suffering* **269 han or ben,** *have been or are* **270 redere,** *reader,* **devyne,** *suppose* **272 On,** *in,* **swynke,** *labor* **273 thenke,** *think* **275 ywoxen,** *become* **276 orisonte shene,** *bright horizon* **277 woned,** *accustomed* **278 carte,** *chariot* **279 dresse,** *prepare,* **fare,** *travel* **283 Although,** *even if,* **hed,** *head* **286 morwe,** *morning* **288 devyne,** *imagine* **289 wook,** *was awake* **293 grette,** *greeted* **296 drye,** *suffer* **297 trowe,** *think* **298 on aventure,** *should it happen* **299 the devysen,** *describe to you* **299–300 of my sepulture / The forme,** *the design of my tomb* **300 moeble,** *private possessions,* **thow dispone,** (ask) *you to dispose* **302 flaumbe,** *flame* **303 brenne,** *burn,* **glede,** *coals* **304 feste,** *ceremony,* **pleyes palestral,** *athletic events* **306 stede,** *horse* **307 leve,** *beloved* **308 yef,** *give* **309 poudre in,** *powder into,* **ybrend,** *burned* **311 clepeth,** *call* **313 sterve,** *die* **317 yore ago,** *in the past* **318 mot nedes,** *necessarily must* **319 hatte,** *is called* **320 shright,** *shrieked*

274–78 This conventional description of daybreak is not in *Filostrato,* but it is very similar to Boccaccio's *Teseida* 7.94. **278 Phebus . . . carte,** Phoebus, the sun, is often depicted as driving a chariot across the sky. **281–82** As usual, Chaucer keeps the political events of Troy and the Trojan War in the background. **295–315** Glosses in several manuscripts identify this passage as a formal testament, a last will. Many of the details derive from Boccaccio's *Teseida,* rather than his *Filostrato.* **304 palestral,** a *palaestra* was a stadium; athletic contests or games in honor of a funeral occur in Virgil's *Iliad* 23, Statius's *Thebaid* 6, etc. **306 That that,** Cl reads "That al." **308 sheld,** Cp reads "swerde." **Pallas,** the goddess Athena, guardian of Troy. **319 Escaphilo,** Ascalaphus was changed into an owl, an ominous bird; Ovid, *Metamorphoses* 5.533ff.

And god Mercurye, of me now, woful wrecche,
The soule gide°, and whan the lyste° it fecche!"

Pandare answerde and seyde, "Troylus,
My dere frend, as I have told the yore°,
That it is folye for to sorwen thus,
And causeles, for which I kan no more.
But whoso wole not trowen rede ne lore°,
I kan nat seen in hym no remedye,
But late hym worthen° with his fantasye.

"But, Troylus, I pray the telle me now
If that thow trowe°, er this, that ony wyght
Hath loved paramours° as wel as thow?
Ye, God wot°, and fro many a worthi knyght
Hath his lady gon a fourtenyght°,
And he nat yet made halvendel° the fare°.
What nede is the to maken al this care?

"Syn° day by day thow mayst thiselven se
That from his love, or elles from his wyf
A man mot twynnen° of necessite,
Ye, though he love hire as his owene lif,
Yet nyl he with hymself thus maken stryf°.
For wel thou wost°, my leve brother dere,
That alwey frendes may not ben yfere°.

"How don this folk that seen hire loves wedded
By frendes myght°, as it bytyt° ful ofte,
And sen hem in hire spouses bed ybedded?
God wot, they take it wysly°, faire and softe,
Forwhy° good hope halt° up hire herte o-lofte°.
And for they kan a tyme of sorwe endure,
As tyme hem hurt° a tyme doth hem cure.

"So sholdestow° endure, and late slyde
The tyme, and fonde° to ben glad and lyght.
Ten dayes nys not so longe to abyde.
And syn she the° to come hath byhyght°,
She nyl not hire hestes° breken for no wight.
For drede that not that she nyl fynden weye
To come ayen; my lyf that dorste I leye°.

"Thy swevenes° ek and al swich fantasye
Dryf° out, and lat hem faren to myschaunce°,
For thei proceden of° thi malencolye°,
That doth the fele° in slep al this penaunce°.
A straw for alle swevenes signifiaunce;
God helpe me so, I counte hem not a bene!
Ther wot° no man aright° what dremes mene.

"For prestes of the temple tellen this,
That dremes ben the revelacions
Of goddes, and as wel they telle, ywys°,
That they ben infernals° illusions;
And leches° seyn that of complexions°
Proceden thei, or fast°, or glotonye.
Who wot° in soth thus what thei signifie?

"Ek other seyn that thorugh impressions,
As yf a wight hath faste° a thing in mynde,
That therof cometh swich avysions°;
And othere seyn, as they in bokes fynde,
That after° tymes of the yer, by kynde°,
Men dreme, and that th'effect goth by° the mone°.
But lef° no drem, for it is nought to done°.

"Wel worth of dremes ay° these olde wyves!
And treweliche ek augurye° of these fowles°,
For fere of which men wenen lese° here lyves,
As° ravenes qualm°, or shrykyng° of these owles—
To trowen° on it bothe fals and foule is.
Allas, allas, so noble a creature
As is a man shal drede swich ordure°!

322 gide, *guide,* **the lyste,** *it pleases you* (to) **324 the yore,** *you before* **327 trowen rede or lore,** *believe advice nor teaching* **329 worthen,** *dwell* **331 trowe,** *believe* **332 paramours,** *passionately* **333 wot,** *knows* **334 fourtenyght,** *two weeks* **335 halvendel,** *half,* **fare,** *fuss* **337 Syn,** *since* **339 mot twynnen,** *must separate* **341 stryf,** *trouble* **342 wost,** *know,* **343 yfere,** *together* **345 frendes myght,** *power of others,* **bytyt,** *happens* **347 wysly,** *wisely* **348 Forwhy,** *because,* **halt,** *holds,* **o-lofte,** *aloft* **350 hem hurt,** *hurts them* **351 sholdestow,** *should you* **352 fonde,** *try* **354 the,** *to you,* **byhyght,** *promised* **355 hestes,** *promises* **357 dorste I leye,** *I dare to wager* **358 swevenes,** *dreams* **359 Dryf,** *drive,* **faren to myschaunce,** *go with bad luck* **360 of,** *from,* **malencolye,** *melancholy* **361 the fele,** *you feel,* **penaunce,** *suffering* **364 wot,** *knows,* **aright,** *rightly* **367 ywys,** *indeed* **368 infernals,** *from hell* **369 leches,** *doctors,* **complexions,** *temperaments* **370 fast,** *fasting* **371 wot,** *knows* **373 faste,** *firmly* **374 avysions,** *visions* **376 after,** *according to,* **by kynde,** *naturally* **377 th'effect goth by,** *the result comes from,* **mone,** *moon* **378 lef,** *believe,* **it is nought to done,** *it is nothing at alle* **379 Wel worth of dremes ay,** *may dreams always be good for* (see n.) **380 treweliche ek augurye,** *similarly also prediction,* **fowles,** *birds* **381 wenen lese,** *think to lose* **382 As,** *such as,* **qualm,** *croak,* **shrykyng,** *shrieking* **383 trowen,** *believe* **385 ordure,** *trash*

321 Mercurye, Mercury, in classical tradition, the god who guided souls to Hades. **343** Proverbial. **345 frendes myght,** medieval relatives and powerful friends often arranged marriages. **353 not so longe,** Cl and Cp read "so longe nought." **358–85** Chaucer expands much on *Filostrato* 5.32, adding commonplace arguments against believing in dreams; compare *HF* 1ff., *PF* 99–109, and *NPT* 7.2922ff. **379** The syntax of the line is elliptical, but the sense is clear: "Dreams are for old women." **380 augurye of these fowles,** the cries or flight patterns of birds were believed to indicate the will of the gods. Augury and dreams are linked in *ParsT* 10.605.

"For which with al myn herte I the beseche°,
Unto thiself that al this thow foryeve°.
And rys now up withoute more speche,
And lat us caste° how forth may best be dreve°
This tyme, and ek how fresshly° we may leve°
Whan that she cometh, the which shal be right sone.
God help me so, the beste is thus to done.

"Rys, lat us speke of lusti° lyf in Troye
That we han led, and forth the tyme dryve,
And ek of tyme comynge us rejoye°,
That bryngen shal oure blysse now so blyve°.
And langour° of these twyes dayes fyve°
We shal therwith so foryete° or oppresse°
That wel unneth° it don° shal us duresse°.

"This town is ful of lordes al aboute,
And trewes° lasten al this mene while.
Go we pleye us in som lusty route°—
To Sarpedon, not hennes° but a myle.
And thus thow shalt the tyme wel bygile°,
And dryve it forth unto that blisful morwe°
That thow hire se that cause is of thi sorwe.

"Now rys, my dere brother Troylus,
For certes, it noon honour is to the
To wepe and in thi bed to jowken° thus.
For trewely, of o thing thow trust to me:
If thow thus ligge° a day or two or thre,
The folk wol wene° that thou for cowardyse
The feynest syk°, and that thow darst° nat ryse."

This Troylus answerde, "O brother dere,
This knowen folk that han ysuffred peyne,
That though he wepe and make sorwful chere
That feleth harm and smert yn every veyne,
No wonder is. And though ich evere pleyne°,
Or alwey wepe, I am nothing to blame,
Syn° I have lost the cause of al my game°.

"But syn of fyne force° I mot° aryse,
I shal aryse as soone as evere I may—
And God, to whom myn herte I sacrifise,
So sende us hastely the tenthe day!
For was ther nevere foule° so fayn° of May
As I shal ben, whan that she comth in Troye,
That cause is of my torment and my joye.

"But whider is thi red°," quod Troylus,
"That we may pleye us° best in al this town?"
"By God, my conseyl is," quod Pandarus,
"To ryde and pley us with Kyng Sarpedoun."
So longe of this they speken up and doun
Til Troylus gan at the laste assente
To ryse, and forth to Sarpedoun they wente.

This Sarpedoun, as he that honourable
Was evere his lyve, and ful of heigh largesse°,
With al that myghte yserved ben on table
That deynte° was, al coste it° gret richesse,
He fedde hem day by day, that swich noblesse,
As seyden bothe the meste° and ek the leste°,
Was nevere er° that day wyst° at ony feste.

Nor in this world ther is noon instrument
Delicious, thorugh wynd or touche of corde°,
As fer as ony wyght hath evere ywent°,
That tonge telle or herte may recorde,
That at that feste it nas wel herd accorde°;
Ne of ladyes ek so fayr a companye
On daunce, er tho°, was nevere yseyn with eye.

But what avayleth° this to Troylus,
That for his sorwe nothing of it roughte°?
For evere in oon his herte pitous
Ful bysily Criseyde, his lady, soughte.
On hire was evere al that his herte thoughte,
Now this, now that, so faste ymagynynge,
That glad, ywys, kan hym no festeyinge°.

---

386 beseche, *request* **387 Unto thiself . . . foryeve,** *give up* **389 caste,** *plan,* **dreve,** *spent* **390 fresshly,** *joyously,* **leve,** *live* **393 lusti,** *pleasurable* **395 us rejoye,** *let us rejoice* **396 blyve,** *quickly* **397 langour,** *suffering,* **twyes dayes fyve,** *ten days* **398 foryete,** *forget,* **oppresse,** *suppress* **399 unneth,** *barely,* **don,** *cause,* **duresse,** *trouble* **401 trewes,** *truce* **402 lusty route,** *lively company* **403 hennes,** *from here* **404 bygile,** *wile away* **405 morwe,** *morning* **409 jowken,** *rest* **411 ligge,** *lie* **412 wene,** *think* **413 feynest syk,** *pretend illness,* **darst,** *dare* **418 pleyne,** *lament* **420 Syn,** *since,* **game,** *joy* **421 syn of fyne force,** *since by sheer necessity,* **mot,** *must* **425 foule,** *bird,* **fayn,** *happy* **428 whider is thi red,** *where is* (it) *your advice* (that we go) **429 pleye us,** *entertain ourselves* **436 heigh largesse,** *noble generosity* **438 deynte,** *delicious,* **al coste it,** *even though it cost* **440 meste,** *greatest,* **leste,** *least* **441 er,** *before,* **wyst,** *known* **443 corde,** *string* **444 ywent,** *imagined* **446 wel herd accorde,** *heard played superbly* **448 er tho,** *before then* **449 avayleth,** *use was* **450 roughte,** *cared* **455 glad, ywys, kan hym no festeyinge,** *truly no festivity can gladden him*

398 or, Cl and Cp read "oure." **403 Sarpedon,** king of Licia, kinsman of Priam and ally of Troy. **409 jowken,** from Fr. *jouquier* (to roost), used in falconry. **436 largesse,** Cl and Cp read "prowesse." **443 of,** Cl reads "or." **455 festeyinge,** Cl and Cp read "festenynge."

These ladyes ek that at this feste ben,
Syn that he saw his lady was aweye,
It was his sorwe upon hem for to sen°,
Or for to here on instruments so pleye.
For° she that of his herte berth° the keye
Was absent, lo, this was his fantasye,
That no wight° sholde make melodye.

Nor ther nas houre in al the day or nyght,
Whan he was there as no wight myghte hym here,
That he ne seyde, "O lufsom° lady bryght,
How have ye faren syn° that ye were here?
Welcome, ywys, myn owne lady dere!"
But weylaway°, al this nas but a maze°.
Fortune his howve entendeth bet to glaze°.

The lettres ek that she of olde tyme
Had hym ysent he wolde allone rede
An hondred sithe° atwixen noon and pryme°,
Refiguryng hire shap, hire wommanhede,
Withinne his herte, and every word and dede
That passed was. And thus he drof to an ende°
The ferthe day, and seyde he wolde wende°.

And seyde, "Leve° brother Pandarus,
Intendestow° that we shul here bleve°
Til Sarpedoun wol forth congeyen us°?
Yet were it fairer that we toke oure leve.
For Godes love, lat us now sone at eve
Oure leve take, and homward lat us torne°,
For trewely, I wol not thus sojourne°."

Pandare answerde, "Be we comen hider°
To fecchen fyr° and rennen° hom ayen?
God helpe me so, I kan nat tellen whider°
We myghten gon, yf I shal sothly seyn,
Ther° ony wyght is of us more fayn°
Than Sarpedoun; and if we hennes hye°
Thus sodeynly, I holde it vilanye°,

"Syn that we seyden that we wolde bleve°
With hym a wowke°; and now thus sodeynly
The ferthe day to take of hym oure leve,
He wolde wondren on it, trewely.
Lat us holde forth oure purpos fermely.
And syn that ye bihighten° hym to byde°,
Holde forward° now, and after lat us ryde."

Thus Pandarus with alle peyne and wo
Made hym to dwelle, and at the wykes° ende
Of Sarpedoun thei toke hire leve tho°,
And on hire wey they spedden° hem to wende°.
Quod Troylus, "Now God me grace sende
That I may fynden at myn hom-comynge
Criseyde comen," and therwith gan he synge.

"Ye, haselwode°," thoughte this Pandare,
And to hymself ful softelich° he seyde,
"God wot°, refreyden° may this hote fare°
Er Calkas sende Troylus Cryseyde!"
But natheles, he japed° thus and pleyde,
And swor, ywys, his herte hym wel byhighte°
She wolde come as soone as evere she myghte.

Whan they unto the paleys were ycomen
Of Troylus, thei down of hors alighte°,
And to the chambre hire wey than han they nomen°,
And into° tyme that it gan to nyghte°,
They spaken of Criseyde the brighte.
And after this, whan that hem bothe leste°,
Thei spedde° hem fro the soper unto reste.

O-morwe° as soone as day bygan to clere,
This Troylus gan of his slep t'abreyde°,

---

458 sen, *look* **460 For,** *because,* **berth,** *carries* **462 wight,** *person* **465 lufsom,** *lovely* **466 faren syn,** *done since* **468 weylaway,** *alas,* **maze,** *delusion* **469 his howve entendeth bet to glaze,** *intended to better make him a hood of glass* (see n.) **472 sithe,** *times,* **pryme,** *morning* **475 drof to an ende,** *sustained throughout* **476 wende,** *go* **477 Leve,** *dear* **478 Intendestow,** *do you intend,* **bleve,** *remain* **479 forth congeyen us,** *send us away* **482 torne,** *return* **483 sojourne,** *remain* **484 hider,** *here* **485 fecchen fyr,** *fetch fire,* **rennen,** *run* **486 whider,** *where* **488 Ther,** *where,* **fayn,** *glad* **489 hennes hye,** *from here hurry* **490 vilanye,** *discourteous* **491 bleve,** *stay* **492 wowke,** *week* **496 bihighten,** *promised,* **byde,** *remain* **497 Holde forward,** *keep the promise* **499 wykes,** *week's* **500 tho** *then* **501 spedden,** *hurried,* **wende,** *go* **505 haselwode,** i.e., *nuts!* (see 3.890n) **506 softelich,** *quietly* **507 wot,** *knows,* **refreyden,** *cooled,* **hote fare,** *passionate business* **509 japed,** *joked* **510 byhighte,** *promised* **513 alighte,** *dismounted* **514 nomen,** *taken* **515 into,** *until,* **nyghte,** *become night* **517 leste,** *wished* **518 spedde,** *hurried* **519 O-morwe,** *in the morning* **520 t'abreyde,** *to awaken*

466 here, Cl and Cp read "there." **469 his howve . . . to bet glaze,** an idiom meaning "to delude or deceive him." **472 noon and pryme,** medieval labels for portions of the day, rather than particular times. Noon extended from 12:00–3:00 p.m.; prime, from 6:00–9:00 a.m. **485** Proverbial. Before matches were invented, getting fire from a neighbor was common, and hurrying home was necessary before the fire or coals died. **506 softelich,** Cl reads "sobrelich." **509 pleyde,** Cl and Cp read "seyde." **513 of hors,** Cl reads "of here hors."

And to Pandare, his owen brother dere,
"For love of God," ful pitously he seyde,
"As go we seen° the paleys° of Criseyde;
For syn° we yet may have no more feste°,
So lat us seen hire paleys atte leste."

And therwithal, his meyne° for to blende°,
A cause he fond in towne for to go,
And to Criseyde hous thei gonnen wende°.
But Lord, this sely° Troylus was wo!
Hym thoughte his sorwful herte braste a-two°.
For whan he saugh hire dorres sperid° alle,
Wel neigh for sorwe adown he gan to falle.

Therwith° whan he was ware° and gan byholde
How shet° was-every wyndowe of the place,
As frost hym thoughte his herte gan to
colde°,
For which with chaunged deedlych° pale face,
Withouten word, he forthby gan to pace°,
And, as God wolde, he gan so faste ryde
That no wight of his contenaunce aspide°.

Than seyde he thus, "O paleys desolat,
O hous of houses whilom best yhight°,
O paleys empty and disconsolat°,
O thou lanterne of which queynt° is the light,
O paleys whilom day that now art nyght,
Wel oughtestow° to falle, and I to dye,
Syn she is went° that wont° was us to gye°.

"O paleys whilom crowne of houses alle,
Enlumyned° with the sonne of alle blysse,
O ryng fro which the ruby is out falle°,
O cause of wo that cause hast ben of lisse°,
Yet syn I may no bet°, fayn° wolde I kysse
Thy colde dores, dorste I for° this route°,
And farewel shryne°, of which the seynt° is
oute°!"

Therwith° he caste on Pandarus his eye,
With chaunged face, and pitous to byholde;
And whan he myght his tyme aright aspye,
Ay° as he rod, to Pandarus he tolde
His newe sorwe and ek his joyes olde,
So pitously and with so dede an hewe°
That every wight myghte on his sorwe rewe°.

Fro thennesforth° he rideth up and down,
And everything cam hym to remembraunce
As he rod forby° places of the toun
In whiche he whilom° hadde al his plesaunce.
"Lo, yende° saugh° I myn owene lady daunce,
And in that temple, with hire eyen clere°,
Me kaughte first my righte lady dere.

"And yender° have I herd ful lustily
Me dere herte laugh; and yender pleye
Saugh ich° hire ones° ek ful blysfully;
And yender ones to me gan she seye,
'Now goode swete, love me wel, I preye.'
And yond so goodly° gan she me byholde
That to the deth myn herte is to hire holde°.

"And at that corner in the yonder hous
Herde I myn alderlevest° lady dere,
So wommanly with vois melodious,
Syngen so wel, so goodly, and so clere,
That in my soule yet me thenketh ich here
The blisful sown°. And in that yonder place
My lady first me tok unto hire grace°."

Thanne thought he thus, "O blisful lord Cupide,
Whanne I the proces have in memorie,
How thow me hast waryed° on every syde,
Men myght a book mak of it lyk a storie.
What nede is the to seke on me victorie,
Syn I am thyn and holly at thi wille?
What joye hastow thyn owene folk to spille°?

---

523 As go we seen, *we must go see,* **paleys,** *palace* **524 syn,** *since,* **more feste,** *greater celebration* **526 meyne,** *household,* **blende,** *deceive* **528 gonnen wende,** *went* **529 sely,** *poor* **530 braste a-two,** *burst apart* **531 sperid,** *barred* **533 Therwith,** *also,* **ware,** *aware* **534 How shet,** *that shut* **535 colde,** *become cold* **536 deedlych,** *deathly* **537 forby . . . pace,** *passed by* **539 his countenaunce aspide,** *saw his face* **541 whilom best yhight,** *once called the best* **542 disconsolat,** *cheerless* **543 queynt,** *quenched* **545 oughtestow,** *ought you* **546 went,** *gone,* **wont,** *accustomed,* **gye,** *guide* **548 Enlumyned,** *illuminated* **549 falle,** *fallen* **550 lisse,** *joy* **551 no bet,** (do) *no better,* **fayn,** *happily* **552 dorste I for,** *if I dared to before,* **route,** *company* **553 shryne,** *shrine,* **seint,** *saint,* **oute,** *gone* **554 Therwith,** *with that* **557 Ay,** *always* **559 dede an hewe,** *dead a color* **560 rewe,** *take pity* **561 Fro thennesforth,** *afterwards* **563 forby,** *past* **564 whilom,** *formerly* **565 yende,** *there* (yonder), **saugh,** *saw* **566 clere,** *bright* **568 yender,** *there* **570 Saugh ich,** *I saw,* **ones,** *once* **573 goodly,** *graciously* **574 holde,** *bound* **576 alderlevest,** *most beloved* **580 soun,** *sound* **581 grace,** *favor* **584 me hast waryed,** *warred upon me* **588 spille,** *destroy*

540–53 Chaucer expands *Filostrato,* developing a device of classical rhetoric called *araclausithyron* (apostrophe to the door). **545 falle,** after the death of his wife, Anne of Bohemia, in 1394, Richard II ordered the destruction of Sheen Palace. **550 lisse,** Cl reads "blysse." **563 forby,** Cl reads "forth by." **565–81** Much different in *Filostrato* 5.55, where Troiolo recalls Criseida's moodiness.

"Wel hastow, lord, ywroke° on me thin ire°,
Thow myghty god and dredful° for to greve°.
Now mercy, lord, thow wost wel I desire
Thi grace most of alle lustes leeve°,
And leve and deye I wol in thy byleeve°,
For which I n'axe° in guerdoun° but o bone°—
That thow Criseyde ayen me sende soone.

"Distreyne° hire herte as faste to retorne
As thow dost myn to longen hire to se.
Than wot° I wel that she nyl not sojourne°.
Now blisful lorde, so cruwel thow ne be
Unto the blod of Troye, I preye the,
As Juno was unto the blood Thebane,
For which the folk of Thebes caughte
hire bane°."

And after this he to the yates° wente
There as Criseyde out rood a ful good paas°,
And up and doun ther made he many a
wente°,
And to hymself ful ofte he seyde, "Allas,
Fro hennes rood° my blysse and my solas;
As wolde blisful God° now for his joye,
I myghte hire seen ayen come into Troye!

"And to the yonder hill I gan hire gyde°,
Allas, and ther I tok of hire my leve.
And yond I saugh hire to hire fader ryde,
For sorwe of which myn herte shal tocleve°.
And heder° hom I com° whan it was eeve,
And here I dwelle outcast from alle joye,
And shal til I may sen hire eft° in Troye."

And of hymself ymagyned he ofte
To ben defet°, and pale, and woxen lesse°
Than he was wont°, and that men seyde softe,
"What may it be? Who kan the sothe gesse
Whi Troylus hath al this hevynesse°?"
And al this nas° but his malencolye,
That he hadde of hymself swich fantasye.

Another tyme ymagynen° he wolde
That every wight that wente by the weye
Had of hym routhe°, and that thei seyen sholde,
"I am right sory Troylus wol deye."
And thus he drof a day yet forth° or tweye,
As ye have herd. Swich lyf right gan he lede
As he that stood bitwixen hope and drede.

For which hym liked° in his songes shewe°
Th'encheson° of his wo, as he best myghte,
And make a song of wordes but a fewe,
Somwhat his woful herte for to lyghte°.
And whan he was from every mannes sighte,
With softe voys he of his lady dere,
That absent was, gan synge as ye may here.

Canticus Troili

"O sterre of which I lost have al the light,
With herte sor wel oughte I to bewayle
That evere derk° in torment, nyght by nyght,
Toward my deth with wynd in stere° I sayle;
For which the tenthe nyght, if that I fayle°
The gydyng of thi bemes bright an houre°,
My ship and me Carybdes wol devoure."

This song when he thus songen hadde,
soone
He fil ayen into his sikes° olde.
And every nyght, as was his wone° to done,
He stod the bryghte mone° to beholde,
And al his sorwe he to the mone tolde,
And seyde, "Iwis°, whan thow art horned newe°,
I shal be glad, if al the world be trewe.

589 ywroke, *wreaked,* **thin ire,** *your anger* **590 dredful,** *terrifying,* **greve,** *offend* **592 lustes leeve,** *dear delights* **593 byleeve,** *religion* **595 n'axe,** *ask nothing,* **guerdoun,** *reward,* **o bone,** *one request* (boon) **596 Distreyne,** *compel* **598 Than wot,** *then know,* **sojourne,** *stay away* **602 bane,** *destruction* **603 yates,** *gates* **604 a ful good paas,** *very quickly* **605 wente,** *turn* **607 Fro hennes rood,** *from here rode* **608 As wolde blisful God,** *I wish that heavenly God would grant that* **610 gyde,** *guide* **613 tocleve,** *split apart* **614 heder,** *this way,* **com,** *came* **616 eft,** *again* **618 defet,** *disfigured,* **woxen lesse,** *shrunken* **619 was wont,** *used to be* **621 hevynesse,** *sorrow* **622 nas,** *was nothing* **624 ymagynen,** *imagine* **626 routhe,** *pity* **628 drof a day yet forth,** *passed another day* **631 hym liked,** *it pleased him,* **shewe,** *to show* **632 Th'encheson,** *the reason* **634 lyghte,** *lighten* **640 derk,** *dark* **641 in stere,** *behind* (astern) **642 fayle,** *lose* **643 an houre,** *for an hour* **646 sikes,** *sighs* **647 wone,** *custom* **648 mone,** *moon* **650 Iwis,** *surely,* **horned newe,** *a new crescent moon*

601–02 Juno . . . Thebes, Juno's hostility, because of Jove's infidelities with Theban women, was one of the causes of the fall of Thebes. **633 make,** Cp reads "made." **637 absent was,** Cl reads "was absent." **637a Canticus Troili,** "The Song of Troylus." Rubric omitted in Cl. The song (lines 638–44) replaces Troiolo's much longer one (forty lines) in *Filostrato* 5.62–66. **643 The,** Cl reads "Thy." **644 Carybdes,** Charybdis was a whirlpool in classical mythology, off the Sicilian coast and opposite the rocks of Scylla. **650 horned newe,** see 4.1591–92n. The new crescent moon, shaped like a set of horns, will signal the passage of ten days since Criseyde's departure.

"I saugh thyn hornes olde ek by the morwe
Whan hennes rod° my ryghte lady dere,
That cause is of my torment and my sorwe,
For which, O brighte Lathona the clere,
For love of God, ren° faste aboute thy spere°!
For whanne thyne hornes newe gynne sprynge°,
Than shal she come that may me blisse brynge."

The dayes more and lengere every nyght
Than they ben wont° to be, hym thoughte tho,
And that the sonne wente his cours unright°
By lenger wey than it was wont to go;
And seyde, "Iwis, me dredeth everemo
The sonnes sone, Pheton, be on lyve°,
And that his fadres carte amys° he dryve."

Upon the walles faste ek wolde he walke,
And on the Grekes ost° he wolde se°,
And to hymself right thus he wolde talke,
"Lo, yender° is myn owene lady fre°,
Or elles yender, there tho tenten be°.
And thennes° comth this eyr° that is so soote°
That in my soule I fele it doth me boote°.

"And hardely°, this wynd that more and more
Thus stoundemele° encreseth in my face
Is of my ladyes depe sikes° sore.
I preve it thus: for in noon othere place
Of al this town save onlyche° in this space
Feele I no wynd that sowneth° so lik peyne—
It seyth, 'Allas, why twynned° be we tweyne?'"

This longe tyme he dryveth forth° right thus,
Til fully passed was the nynthe nyght.
And ay bisyde° hym was this Pandarus,
That bysily did alle his fulle myght
Hym to comforte, and make his herte lyght,
Yevyng° hym hope alwey the tenthe morwe
That she shal come and stynten° al his sorwe.

Upon the tother° side ek was Criseyde,
With wommen fewe, among the Grekes stronge,
For whiche ful ofte a day "Allas," she seyde,
"That I was born! Wel may myn herte longe°
After° my deth, for now lyve I to longe.
Allas, and I ne may it not amende°,
For now is wors than evere yet I wende°.

"My fader nyl for nothing do me grace°
To goon ayen for ought I kan hym queme°;
And yf so be that I my terme° passe,
My Troylus shal in his herte deme°
That I am fals, and so it may wel seme.
Thus shal ich have unthank° on every side.
That I was born so weylaway° the tyde°!

"And yf that I me put in jupartie
To stele awey by nyght, and it byfalle°
That I be caught, I shal be hold° a spie.
Or elles—lo, this drede I most of alle—
Yf in the hondes of som wreche° I falle,
I am but lost, al° be myn herte trewe.
Now, myghty God, thow on my sorwe rewe°!"

Ful pale ywoxen was° hire brighte face,
Hire lymes lene°, as she that al the day
Stod, whan she dorste°, and loked on the place
Ther° she was born and ther she dwelt hadde ay°,
And al the nyght wepyng, allas, she lay.
And thus despeired out of alle cure°
She ladde hire lif, this woful creature.

---

653 hennes rod, *from here rode* **656 ren,** *run,* **spere,** *orbit* **657 gynne sprynge,** *begin to grow* **660 ben wont,** *are accustomed* **661 unright,** *incorrectly* **664 on lyve,** *alive* **665 amys,** *wrongly* **667 ost,** *army,* **se,** *look* **669 yender,** *there,* **fre,** *noble* **670 there tho tentes be,** *where those tents are* **671 thennes,** *from there,* **eyr,** *air,* **soote,** *sweet* **672 boote,** *cure* **673 hardely,** *surely* **674 stoundemele,** *gradually* **675 sikes,** *sighs* **677 save onlyche,** *except only* **678 sowneth,** *sounds* **679 twynned,** *separated* **680 dryveth forth,** *suffers through* **682 ay bisyde,** *always with* **685 Yevyng,** *giving* **686 stynten,** *end* **687 tother,** *other* **690 longe,** *yearn* **691 After,** *for* **692 amende,** *correct* **693 wende,** *think* **694 do me grace,** *allow me* **695 hym queme,** *please him* **696 terme,** *promised time* **697 deme,** *think* **699 unthank,** *blame* **700 weylaway,** *alas,* **tyde,** *time* **702 byfalle,** *happens* **703 hold,** *thought* **705 wreche,** *wretch* **706 al,** *although* **707 rewe,** *take pity* **708 ywoxen was,** *had become* **709 lymes lene,** *limbs lean* **710 dorste,** *dared* **711 Ther,** *where,* **ay,** *always* **713 out of alle cure,** *beyond all remedy*

652 hornes olde, the last quarter of the old moon. Although nearly all of the astrological references are Chaucer's additions to *Filostrato,* the old moon is mentioned at *Filostrato* 5.69. **655 Lathona,** the moon; Latona was the mother of Diana, goddess of the moon, and Diana was therefore referred to as Latonia. **662 go,** Cp reads "do." **664–65 Pheton . . . amys he dryve,** Phaëton, son of Phoebus the sun, drove his father's chariot erratically, endangering the Earth; he was killed by Zeus. Ovid, *Metamorphoses* 2.31ff.; see *HF* 940–56. Troylus fears that Phaëton is again driving the sun awry, making the days longer than they should be. **675 Is of,** Cl reads "It is of." **689–707** Chaucer's expansion of *Filostrato* 6.1 here helps to justify Criseyde's failure to return to Troy. **711 and ther,** Cl and Cp omit "ther."

Ful ofte a day she syked° for destresse,
And in hireself she wente ay portraynge°
Of Troylus the grete worthinesse,
And alle his goodly wordes recordynge°
Syn first that day hire love bygan to sprynge.
And thus she sette hire woful herte afyre
Thorugh remembraunce of that she gan desire.

In al this world ther nys so cruwel herte°
That hire hadde herd compleynen° in hire sorwe,
That nolde han wopen° for hire peynes smerte,
So tendrely she wepte, both eve and morwe.
Hire nedede° no teris for to borwe°!
And this was yet the worste of al hire peyne,
Ther nas no wight to whom she dorste hire pleyne°.

Ful rewfully° she loked upon Troye,
Byheld the toures heygh° and ek the halles.
"Allas," quod she, "the plesaunce and the joye,
The whiche that now al torned into galle° is,
Have ich had ofte withinne tho yonder wallys°.
O Troylus, what dostow° now?" she seyde.
"Lord, wheyther° yet thow thenke upon Criseyde?

"Allas, I ne hadde trowed on° youre lore°,
And went with yow, as ye me redde° er this,
Thenne had I now not siked° half so sore.
Who myght have seyd that I had don amys°
To stele awey with swich on° as he is?
But al to late cometh the letuarye°
Whan men the cors° unto the grave carye.

"To late is now to speke of this matere.
Prudence, allas, oon of thyne eyen thre°
Me lakked alwey, er that I cam here!
On tyme ypassed wel remembred me,
And present tyme ek koud° ich wel yse°,
But futur tyme, er I was in the snare,
Koude I not seen—that causeth now my care.

"But natheles, bytyde what bityde°,
I shal tomorwe at nyght, by est or west,
Out of this ost stele° on som manere syde°,
And gon with Troylus where as hym lest°.
This purpos wol ich holde, and this is best.
No fors of° wykked tonges janglerye°,
For evere on love han wrecches had envye.

"For whoso wold° of every word take hede,
Or rewelyn hym° by every wightes wit,
Ne shal he nevere thryven°, out of drede°;
For that that° som men blamen evere yit,
Lo, other manere folk comenden° it.
And as for me, for al swych variaunce°,
Felicite clepe I my suffisaunce°.

"For which, withouten ony wordes mo,
To Troye I wole°, as for conclusion."
But God it wot°, er fully monthes two
She was ful fer° fro that entencion.
For bothe Troylus and Troye toun
Shal knotteles° thorughout hire herte slyde,
For she wol take a purpos° for t'abyde°.

This Diomede, of whom yow telle I gan,
Gooth now withinne hymself ay arguynge,
With al the sleighte° and al that evere he kan,
How he may best, with shortest taryinge°,
Into his net Criseydes herte brynge.
To this entent he koude nevere fyne°;
To fysshen hire he leyde out hook and lyne.

But natheles, wel in his herte he thoughte
That she nas nat withoute a love in Troye.
For nevere sythen° he hire thennes° broughte,
Ne koude he sen hire laughen or maken joie.

715 syked, *sighed* **716 in hireself . . . portraynge,** *remembering* **718 recordynge,** *recalling* **722 nys so cruwel herte,** *is not such a cruel-hearted person* **723 compleynen,** *lament* **724 nolde han wopen,** *would not have wept* **726 Hire nedede,** *she needed,* **borwe,** *borrow* **728 dorste hire pleyne,** *dared to confide* **729 rewfully,** *sorrowfully* **730 toures heygh,** *high towers* **732 galle,** *gall* (very bitter) **733 wallys,** *walls* **734 dostow,** *do you* (do) **735 wheyther,** (I wonder) *whether* **736 trowed on,** *believed in,* **lore,** *advice* **737 redde,** *advised* **738 siked,** *sighed* **739 amys,** *wrongly* **740 swich on,** *such a one* **741 letuarye,** *medicine* **742 cors,** *corpse* **744 thyne eyen thre,** *your three eyes* **747 koud,** *could,* **yse,** *see* **750 bytyde what bityde,** *come what may* **752 ost stele,** *host depart secretly,* **on som manere syde,** *in one way or another* **753 lest,** *wishes* **755 No fors of,** (I will pay) *no attention to,* **janglerye,** *gossip* **757 whoso wold,** *whoever would* **758 rewelyn hym,** *regulate himself* **759 thryven,** *prosper,* **out of drede,** *without doubt* **760 that that,** *that which* **761 comenden,** *praise* **762 for,** *despite,* **variaunce,** *varied opinion* **763 Felicite clepe I my suffisaunce,** *I call happiness my sufficiency* **765 wole,** *will* (go) **766 wot,** *knows* **767 ful fer,** *very far* **769 knotteles,** *knotless* (i.e., without a hitch) **770 take a purpos,** *decide,* **t'abyde,** *to remain* **773 sleighte,** *cleverness* **774 taryinge,** *delay* **776 fyne,** *cease* **780 sythen,** *since,* **thennes,** *from there*

720 woful, Cl reads "ful." **741–42** Proverbial. **744 Prudence . . . eyen thre,** the personified figure of Prudence was depicted with three eyes, looking to the past, present, and future. **748 futur,** the first two recorded instances of the word in English are here and *Bo* 5.pr6.19 (*MED*). **760 som men blamen,** Cl reads "somme han blamed." **763 Felicite . . . suffisaunce,** see 3.1690n. Criseyde here asserts that happiness is enough to satisfy her.

He nyst° how best hire herte for t'acoye°.
"But for to assaye°," he seyde, "it nought ne greveth°,
For he that nought n'assayeth, nought n'acheveth."

Yet seide he to hymself upon a nyght,
"Now am I not a fool that wot wel how°
Hire wo for love is of another wight,
And hereupon° to gon assaye hire now?
I may wel wite°, it nyl nat ben my prow°.
For wyse folk in bokes it expresse,
'Men shal nat wowe° a wight in hevynesse°.'

But whoso myghte wynnen swych a flour°
From hym for whom she morneth nyght and day,
He myghte seyn° he were a conquerour."
And right anoon, as he that bold was ay°,
Thoughte in his herte, "Happe° how happe may.
Al° sholde I deye, I wole hire herte seche°.
I shal no more lesen but my speche."

This Diomede, as bokes us declare,
Was in his nedes° prest° and corageous,
With sterne voys and myghty lymes square°,
Hardy°, testyf°, strong, and chevalrous
Of dedes, lyk his fader Tideus;
And som men seyn he was of tunge large°.
And heyr° he was of Calydoyne and Arge.

Criseyde mene° was of hire stature°;
Therto° of shap, of face, and ek of chere°,
Ther myghte ben no fayrer creature.
And ofte tyme this was hire manere,
To gon ytressed° with hire heerys clere°
Doun by hire coler° at hire bak byhynde,
Which with a thred of gold she wolde bynde.

And save° hire browes joyneden yfere°,
Ther nas no lak° in ought° I kan espyen.
But for to speken of hire eyen clere,
Lo, trewely, thei writen that hire syen°
That Paradys stood formed in hire eyen.
And with hire riche beaute everemore
Strof° love in hire ay° which of hem was more.

She sobre was, ek symple°, and wys withal°,
The beste ynorisshed° ek that myghte be,
And goodly° of hire speche in general;
Charitable, estatlych°, lusty°, and fre°,
Ne nevere mo ne lakkede hire pyte°;
Tendre-herted, slydynge of corage°;
But trewely, I kan nat telle hire age.

And Troylus wel woxen° was in highte,
And complet° formed by° proporcion
So wel that kynde° it not amenden° myghte;
Yong, fresch, strong, and hardy° as lyon;
Trewe as stel in ech condicion°;
On of the beste enteched° creature
That is or shal whil that the world may dure°.

And certeynly in storye it is founde
That Troylus was nevere unto no wight,
As in his tyme, in no degre° secounde
In dorryng don that° longeth° to a knyght.
Al° myghte a geaunt passen° hym of myght,
His herte ay with the ferste° and with the beste
Stod paregal°, to dorre don° that hym leste°.

---

782 He nyst, *nor knew he,* **t'acoye,** *to soothe* **783 assaye,** *try,* **nought ne greveth,** *hurts nothing* **786 wot wel how,** *knows well that* **788 hereupon,** *concerning this* **789 wite,** *know,* **prow,** *advantage* **791 wowe,** *woo,* **hevynesse,** *sorrow* **792 flour,** *flower* **794 seyn,** *say* **795 ay,** *always* **796 Happe,** *happen* **797 Al,** *even if,* **seche,** *seek* **800 nedes,** *dealings,* **prest,** *prompt* **801 limes square,** *solid limbs* **802 Hardy,** *brave,* **testyf,** *impetuous* **804 of tunge large,** *free of tongue* **805 heyr,** *heir* **806 mene,** *average,* **stature,** *height* **807 Therto,** *also,* **chere,** *humor* **810 ytressed,** *in braids,* **cleere,** *shining* **811 coler,** *collar* **813 save,** *except that,* **browes joyneden yfere,** *eyebrows were joined together* **814 lak,** *flaw,* **ought,** *anything* **816 that hire syen,** *who saw her* **819 Strof,** *competed,* **ay,** *always* **820 symple,** *modest,* **withal,** *as well* **821 ynorisshed,** *brought up* **822 goodly,** *gracious* **823 estatlych,** *dignified,* **lusty,** *lively,* **fre,** *generous* **824 pyte,** *compassion* **825 slydynge of corage,** *changeable of heart* **827 woxen,** *grown* **828 complet,** *wholly,* **by,** *in* **829 kynde,** *nature,* **amenden,** *improve* **830 hardy,** *brave* **831 ech condicion,** *every situation* **832 enteched,** *endowed* **833 dure,** *last* **834 in no degre,** *in no way* **837 dorryng do that,** *daring to do what,* **longeth,** *pertains* **838 Al,** *although,* **geaunt passen,** *giant surpass* **839 ferste,** *first* **840 Stod paregal,** *stood equal,* **dorre don,** *dare to do,* **leste,** *wished*

784 Proverbial; cf. 2.807–08. **791** Source unknown. **799–840** The portraits of Diomede, Criseyde, and Troylus are not found in *Filostrato,* but are included in earlier Troy narratives. Chaucer's versions are based on those in the twelfth-century Anglo-Latin *Frigii Daretis Ylias* (*The Iliad of Dares the Phrygian*) by Joseph of Exeter. Joseph expanded the sixth-century *De excidio Troiae historia* (*The History of the Fall of Troy*) by Dares, and the portraits excerpted from the *Ylias* circulated independently as examples of rhetorical description. **805 Calydoyne and Arge,** Chaucer adds the reference to Calydon and Argos, described further in Cassandra's explication of Troylus's dream at 4.1457ff. **806 mene,** an ideal; not too tall and not too short. **813 browes joyneden,** joined eyebrows were considered a mark of beauty in ancient Greece and the Near East, although in Western medieval tradition they were thought to be defects and perhaps to indicate undesirable qualities such as sadness, fickleness, and cruelty. **819 love,** Joseph of Exeter (see 799–840n), reads *morum* (of virtues) rather than *amorum* (of love).

But for to tellen forth of Diomede:
It fil° that after, on the tenthe day
Syn that Criseyde out of the cite yede°,
This Diomede, as fressh as braunche in May,
Com to the tente ther as° Calkas lay°,
And feyned° hym with Calkas han to doon°;
But what he mente, I shal yow telle soon.

Criseyde, at shorte wordes° for to telle,
Welcomed hym and doun hym by hire sette—
And he was ethe ynowh° to maken dwelle!
And after this, withouten more lette°,
The spices and the wyn men forth hem fette°,
And forth thei speke of this and that yfere°,
As frendes don, of which som shal ye here.

He gan first fallen of the werre in speche°
Bytwyxen hem and the folk of Troye toun,
And of th'assege° he gan hire ek byseche°
To telle hym what was hire opynyoun.
Fro that demaunde° he so descendeth doun°
To axen hire yf that hire straunge thoughte
The Grekes gyse° and werkes° that they wroughte°;

And whi hire fader tarieth° so longe
To wedden hire unto som worthi wight.
Criseyde, that was in hire peynes stronge
For love of Troylus, hire owene knyght,
As ferforth° as she konnyng° hadde or myght,
Answerde hym tho°; but, as of his entente,
It semed not she wiste° what he mente.

But natheles this ilke° Diomede
Gan in hymself assure°, and thus he seyde,
"If ich aright° have taken of yow hede°,
Me thenketh thus, O lady myn, Criseyde,
That syn I first hond on youre bridel leyde,
Whan ye out come of Troye by° the morwe,
Ne koude I nevere sen yow but in sorwe.

"Kan I nat seyn° what may the cause be
But if° for love of som Troian it were,
The which right sore wolde athynken° me
That ye for ony wight that dwelleth there
Sholden spille a quarter of a tere°,
Or pitously yourselven so bygile°,
For dredles°, it is nought worth the while.

"The folk of Troye, as who seyth°, alle and some
In preson° ben, as ye youreselven se;
Fro thennes° shal nat oon on-lyve° come
For al the gold bytwixen sonne and se°.
Trusteth wel and understondeth me:
Ther shal nat on° to mercy gon on-lyve,
Al° were he lord of worldes twyes° fyve.

"Swyche wreche° on hem for fecchyng° of Eleyne
Ther shal ben take°, er that we hennes wende°,
That Manes, which that goddes ben° of peyne,
Shul ben agast° that Grekes wol hem shende°.
And men shul drede° unto the worldes ende
From hennesforth the ravesshynge° of a queene,
So cruel shal oure wreche on hem be seene.

"And but if° Calkas lede us with ambages°—
That is to seyn, with dowble wordes sleye°,
Swich as men clepe° a word with two visages°—
Ye shul wel knowen that I nought ne lye,
And al this thing right sen it with youre eye,
And that anoon; ye nyl not trowe° how soone.
Now taketh hede, for it is for to doone°.

---

842 fil, *happened* **843 yede,** *went* **845 ther as,** *where,* **lay,** *lived* **846 feyned,** *pretended,* **han to doon,** *to have* (something) *to do* **848 at shorte wordes,** *briefly* **850 ethe ynowh,** *easy enough* **851 lette,** *delay* **852 fette,** *fetched* **853 yfere,** *together* **855 fallen . . . in speche,** *to talk* **857 th'assege,** *the siege,* **byseche,** *ask* **859 demaunde,** *question,* **descendeth doun,** *moves on* **861 Grekes gyse,** *Greeks' ways,* **werkes,** *things,* **wroughte,** *did* **862 tarieth,** *waited* **866 ferforth,** *far,* **konnyng,** *ability* **867 tho,** *then* **868 wiste,** *knew* **869 ilke,** *same* **870 Gan in hymself assure,** *grew assured* **871 aright,** *correctly,* **taken of yow hede,** *observed you* **874 by,** *in* **876 Kan I nat seyn,** *I cannot say* **877 But if,** *unless* **878 athynken,** *upset* **880 tere,** *tear* **881 bygile,** *mislead* **882 dredeles,** *doubtless* **883 as who seyth,** *so to speak* **884 preson,** *prison* **885 Fro thennes,** *from there,* **on-lyve,** *alive* **886 se,** *sea* **888 on,** *one* **889 Al,** *even if,* **twyes,** *twice* **890 wreche,** *revenge,* **fecchyng,** *the abduction* **891 take,** *taken,* **hennes wende,** *travel from here* **892 goddes ben,** *are gods* **893 agast,** *afraid,* **shende,** *ruin* **894 drede,** *fear* **895 ravesshynge,** *abducting* **897 but if,** *unless,* **ambages,** *ambiguities* **898 sleye,** *sly,* **899 clepe,** *call,* **visages,** *faces* **902 trowe,** *believe* **903 for to doone,** *going to happen*

842 In *Filostrato,* this episode takes place on the fourth day after Criseida's departure. **851 more,** Cp reads "longe." **892 Manes,** gods of the underworld. **895 the ravesshynge of a,** Cp reads "to ravysshen any." **897 ambages,** *MED* lists only this instance of the word, defined in the following two lines.

"What, wene° ye youre wyse fader wolde
Han yeven° Antenor for yow anoon°
If he ne wiste° that the cite sholde
Destroyed ben? Whi nay, so mote I gon°.
He knew ful wel ther shal not skapen on°
That Troian is; and for the grete fere,
He dorste° not ye dwelte lenger there.

"What wole° ye more, lufsom° lady dere?
Lat Troye and Troian fro youre herte pace°.
Dryf out that bittre hope, and make good chere,
And clepe ayen° the beaute of youre face,
That ye with salte terys so deface.
For Troye is brought in swych a jupartie°
That it to save is° now no remedye.

"And thenketh wel, ye shal in Grekes fynde
A more parfit° love er° it be nyght
Than ony Troian is, and more kynde,
And bet° to serven yow wol don his myght°.
And yf ye vouchesauf°, my lady bryght,
I wol ben he to serven yow myselve,
Ye, levere° than be lord of Greces twelve."

And with that word he gan to waxen red°,
And in his speche a litel wight° he quok°,
And caste asyde a litle wight his hed,
And stynte° a while, and afterward awok,
And sobrelych° on hire he threw his lok,
And seyde, "I am, al be it° yow no joye,
As gentil° man as ony wight° in Troye.

"For yf my fader Tideus," he seide,
"Ilyved hadde°, ich hadde ben er this
Of Calydoyne and Arge a kyng, Criseyde,
And so hope I that I shal yet, ywys°.
But he was slayn, allas, the more harm is°,
Unhappyly° at Thebes al to rathe°,
Polymyte and many a man to skathe°.

"But herte myn, syn that I am youre man—
And ben° the ferste of° whom I seche grace°—
To serven yow as hertely as I kan,
And evere shal whil I to lyve have space°,
So° er that I departe out of this place,
Ye wol me graunte that I may tomorwe,
At bettre leyser°, tellen yow my sorwe."

What° shold I telle his wordes that he seyde?
He spak ynow° for o day at the meste°.
It preveth° wel. He spak so that Criseyde
Graunted on the morwe at his requeste
For to speken with hym at the leste—
So that° he nolde speke of swych matere.
And thus she to hym seyde as ye may here,

As she that hadde hire herte on Troylus
So faste° that there may non it arace°,
And strangely° she spak and seyde thus,
"O Diomede, I love that ilke° place
Ther° I was born, and Joves°, for his grace,
Delivere it soone of al that doth it care.
God, for thi might, so leve° it wel to fare!

"That Grekes wolde hire wrath on Troye wreke°,
If that thi myghte, I knowe it wel, ywys.
But it shal not bifallen as ye speke.
And God toforn°, and ferther over this°,
I wot° my fader wys and redy is,
And that he me hath bought°, as ye me tolde,
So dere°; I am the more unto hym holde°.

"That Grekes ben of heigh condicion°
I wot ek wel; but certeyn, men shal fynde
As worthi folk withinne Troye town,
As konnyng°, and as parfit°, and as kynde
As ben bitwyxen Orcades and Inde.
And that ye koude wel youre lady serve,
I trowe° ek wel, hire thank° for to deserve.

---

904 wene, *think* **905 yeven,** *given,* **anoon,** *quickly* **907 wiste,** *knew* **907 so mote I gon,** *as I may live* **908 scapen on,** *escape one* **910 dorste,** *dared* **911 wole,** *wish,* **lufsom,** *lovely* **912 pace,** *pass* **914 clepe ayen,** *call back* **916 jupartie,** *danger* **917 is,** *there is* **919 parfit,** *perfect,* **er,** *before* **921 And bet,** *and* (one who) *better,* **myght,** *effort* **922 vouchesauf,** *grant* **924 levere,** *rather* **925 waxen red,** *blush* **926 litel wight,** *little bit,* **quok,** *trembled* **928 stynte,** *ceased* **929 sobrelych,** *solemnly* **930 al be it,** *even though it* (is to) **931 gentil,** *nobly born,* **wight,** *person* **933 Ilyved hadde,** *had lived* **935 ywys,** *indeed* **936 the more harm is,** *the more is the damage* **937 Unhappyly,** *unluckily,* **to rathe,** *too soon* **938 Polymyte and many a man to skathe,** *to the detriment of Polynices and many other men* **940 ben,** (you) *are,* **ferste of,** *first from,* **seche grace,** *seek favor* **942 space,** *time* **943 So,** *if* **945 leyser,** *leisure* **946 What,** *why* **947 ynow,** *enough,* **meste,** *most* **948 preveth,** *works* **951 So that,** *as long as* **954 faste,** *firmly,* **arace,** *uproot* **955 strangely,** *aloofly* **955 ilke,** *same* **957 Ther,** *where* **957 Joves,** *may Jove* **959 leve,** *permit* **960 wreke,** *avenge* **961 ywys,** *indeed* **963 God toforn,** *before God,* **ferther over this,** *moreover* **964 wot,** *know* **965 bought,** *paid for* **966 dere,** *dearly,* **holde,** *obliged* **967 condicion,** *quality* **970 konnyng,** *capable,* **parfit,** *perfect* **973 trowe,** *believe,* **thank,** *thanks*

928 awok, Cp reads "he woke." **934 Calydoyne and Arge,** see 5.805n. **938 Polymyte,** Polynices, Tydeus's ally in the war against Thebes; see 5.1488. **971 bitwyxen Orcades and Inde,** between the Orkney Islands and India, i.e., the ends of the Earth.

"But as to speke of love, ywys°," she seyde,
"I hadde a lord, to whom I wedded was,
The whos° myn herte al was, til that he deyde;
And other love, as help me here Pallas,
Ther in myn herte nys°, ne nevere was.
And that ye ben of noble and heigh kynrede°,
I have wel herd it tellen, out of drede°.

"And that doth° me to han so gret a wonder
That ye wol scornen° ony womman so.
Ek God wot, love and I ben fer asonder°!
I am disposed bet°, so mot I go°,
Unto my deth to pleyne and maken wo.
What I shal after don, I kan nat seye;
But trewelich, as yet me lyst° not pleye.

"Myn herte is now in tribulacion°,
And ye in armes bisy day by day.
Hereafter, whan ye wonnen han° the town,
Peraunter° thanne so it happen may
That whan I se that° nevere yit I say°,
Than wol I werke° that I nevere wroughte°.
This word to yow ynough suffisen oughte.

"Tomorwe ek wol I speke with yow feyn°—
So that° ye touchen nought of this matere.
And whan yow list°, ye may come here ayeyn—
And er ye gon, thus muche I sey yow here:
As helpe me Pallas with hire heres clere°,
If that I sholde of any Grek han routhe°,
It shulde be yourselven, by my trouthe.

"I sey not therfore that I wol yow love,
Ne sey not nay; but in conclusion,
I mene wel, by God that sit° above!"
And therwithal she cast hire eyen down,
And gan to syke°, and seyde, "O Troye town,
Yet bidde° I God in quiete and in reste
I may yow sen, or do° myn herte breste°."

But in effect, and shortly for to seye,
This Diomede al fresshly newe ayeyn
Gan pressen on, and faste° hire mercy preye;
And after this, the sothe for to seyn,
Hire glove he tok, of which he was ful feyn°.
And fynally, whan it was woxen eeve°,
And al was wel, he ros and tok his leeve.

The bryghte Venus folewede° and ay taughte°
The wey there° brode Phebus doun alighte°;
And Cynthea hire charhors° overraughte°
To whirle out of the Lyon yf she myghte;
And Sygnyfer his candels shewed bryghte,
When that Criseyde unto hire bedde wente
Inwith° hire fadres faire bryghte tente,

Retornyng° in hire soule ay up and doun
The wordes of this sodeyn° Diomede,
His grete estat, and peril of the toun,
And that she was allone and hadde nede
Of frendes help. And thus bygan to brede°
The cause whi, the sothe° for to telle,
That sche tok fully purpos° for to dwelle°.

The morwen come, and gostly° for to speke,
This Diomede is come unto Criseyde;
And shortly, lest that ye my tale breke°,
So wel for hymself he spak and seyde

974 ywys, *truly* **976 The whos,** *whose* **978 nys,** *is not* **979 kynrede,** *kindred* **980 out of drede,** *without doubt* **981 doth,** *makes* **982 scornen,** *mock* **983 asonder,** *apart* **984 disposed bet,** *more inclined,* **so mot I go,** *as I may live* **987 me lyst,** *pleases me* **988 tribulacion,** *anguish* **990 wonnen han,** *have won* **991 Peraunter,** *perhaps* **992 se that,** *see what,* **say,** *saw* **993 werke,** *do,* **wroughte,** *have done* **995 feyn,** *happily* **996 So that,** *if* **997 list,** *wish* **999 heres clere,** *shining hair* **1000 routhe,** *pity* **1004 sit,** *sits* **1006 syke,** *sigh* **1007 bidde,** *pray* **1008 do,** *make,* **breste,** *burst* **1011 faste,** *earnestly* **1013 ful feyn,** *very pleased* **1014 woxen eeve,** *become evening* **1016 folewede,** *followed,* **ay taughte,** *always indicated* **1017 there,** *where* **alighte,** *sets* **1018 charhors,** *chariot horses,* **overraughte,** *reached over* **1022 Inwith,** *within* **1023 Retornyng,** *reconsidering* **1024 sodeyn,** *impulsive* **1027 brede,** *develop* **1028 sothe,** *truth* **1029 tok fully purpos,** *decided,* **dwelle,** *remain* **1030 gostly,** *truly* **1032 breke,** *interrupt*

977 Pallas, Athena, patron goddess of Troy. **975** Criseyde's widowhood is established at 1.97. **987 pleye,** Cl reads "to pleye." **989 bisy,** Cl reads "ben." **992 nevere yit I,** Cl and Cp read "I never er." **995–1008** Chaucer's addition. **1006 O Troye town,** Cl reads "O Troylus and Troie town." **1013 glove,** this detail of the glove is not in *Filostrato,* but does occur when Diomede first delivers Briseide to her father's tent in Benoît and in Guido. **1016–17 Venus . . . Phebus doun alighte,** the evening star, Venus, sets after the sun (Phoebus) and indicates where it went down. **1018–19 Cynthea . . . Lyon,** the moon, Cynthia, encouraged (**overraughte**) the horses of her chariot to draw her through the zodiacal sign of Leo, the lion, at which point the ten days would be over. **1020 Sygnyfer his candels,** the Signifier's candles, i.e., the stars of the zodiac, shine brightly because the sun has set and the moon is not visible in Leo. **1026–27 nede / Of frendes,** Chaucer's emphasis, following Benoît; in *Filostrato,* Criseida considers Diomede's manly virtues.

That alle hire sore sykes° adoun he leyde°.
And finally, the sothe for to seyne,
He refte° hire of the grete° of al hire peyne.

And after this the story telleth us
That she hym yaf° the fayre baye stede°,
The which he onys wan° of Troylus;
And ek a broche—and that was litel nede—
That Troylus° was, she yaf this Diomede.
And ek, the bet from sorwe hym to releve,
She made hym were° a pencel° of hire sleve.

I fynde ek in storyes ellyswhere,
Whan thorugh the body hurt was Diomede
Of° Troylus, tho° wepte she many a tere,
Whan that she saugh his wyde wowndes blede;
And that she tok to kepen° hym good hede°;
And for to helen hym of his sorwes smerte,
Men seyn—I not°—that she yaf hym hire herte.

But trewely, the story telleth us,
Ther made nevere woman more wo
Than she whan that she falsed° Troylus.
She seyde, "Allas, for now is clene ago°
My name of° trouthe in love for everemo!
For I have falsed oon the gentileste°
That evere was, and oon the worthieste.

"Allas, of me unto the worldes ende
Shal neyther ben° ywriten nor isonge
No good word, for these bokes wol me shende°.
O, rolled shal I ben on many a tonge;
Thorughout the world my belle shal be ronge!
And wommen most wol hate me of alle.
Allas, that swych a cas° me sholde falle°!

"Thei wol seyn, inasmuche as in me is°,
I have hem don dishonour, weylaway!
Al be I° not the firste that dide amys°,
What helpeth that to don my blame awey°?
But syn I se ther is no bettre way,
And that to late is now for me to rewe°,
To Diomede algate° I wol be trewe.

"But, Troylus, syn I no beter may°,
And syn that thus departen° ye and I,
Yet preye I God so yeve yow right good day°
As for the gentileste, trewely,
That evere I say° to serven feythfully,
And best kan ay° his lady° honour kepe."
And with that word she brast anon° to wepe.

"And certes, yow ne haten° shal I nevere;
And frendes love, that shal ye han of me,
And my good word, al myght y lyven evere°.
And, trewely, I wolde sory be
For to sen yow in adversite;
And gilteles, I wot wel, I yow leve°.
But al shal passe; and thus take I my leve."

But trewely, how longe it was bytwene
That she forsok hym for this Diomede,
Ther is noon auctour telleth it, I wene°.
Tak every man now to his bokes hede°:
He shal no terme° fynden, out of drede°.
For though that he gan for to wowe° hire sone,
Er he hire wan yet was ther more to done.

Ne me ne lyst° this sely° womman chyde°
Ferther than this story wol devyse°.
Hire name, allas, is punysshed so wyde
That for hire gilt it oughte ynow suffise.
And yf I myghte excuse hire ony wyse°,

1034 sykes, *sighs,* **adoun he leyde,** *he alleviated* **1036 refte,** *relieved,* **grete,** *greater part* **1038 yaf,** *gave,* **stede,** *steed* **1039 onys wan,** *once won* **1041 Troylus,** *Troylus's* **1043 were,** *wear,* **pencel,** *love token* **1046 Of,** *by,* **tho,** *then* **1048 kepen,** *tend,* **hede,** *care* **1050 not,** *don't know* **1053 falsed,** *betrayed* **1054 clene ago,** *completely gone* **1055 name of,** *reputation for* **1056 oon the gentileste,** *the noblest* **1059 ben,** *be* **1060 shende,** *destroy* **1064 cas,** *situation,* **me sholde falle,** *should happen to me* **1065 inasmuche as in me is,** *insofar as it is my doing* **1067 Al be I,** *although I am,* **amys,** *wrongly* **1068 don . . . awey,** *eliminate* **1070 rewe,** *be sorry* **1071 algate,** *in any case* **1072 no beter may,** *may do no better* **1073 departen,** *separated are* **1074 right good day,** *very good life* **1076 say,** *saw* **1077 ay,** *always,* **lady,** *lady's* **1078 brast anon,** *burst immediately* **1079 haten,** *hate* **1081 al might y lyven evere,** *even if I live forever* **1084 leve,** *believe* **1088 wene,** *think* **1089 Tak . . . hede,** *pay attention* **1090 terme,** *specific period of time,* **out of drede,** *without doubt* **1091 wowe,** *woo* **1093 Ne me ne lyst,** *I do not wish,* **sely,** *poor,* **chyde,** *to accuse* **1094 devyse,** *describe* **1097 ony wyse,** *in any way*

1038–39 baye stede . . . onys wan of Troylus, this unexplained detail is not found in *Filostrato,* but is adopted from Benoît, where it is told at greater length (15079–186) **1040 broche,** discovered by Troylus at 1661 below. **1043 pencel,** attached to a lance as a pennon or small flag, a woman's sleeve is a typical lady's favor in romances. The detail is in Benoît (15176), but not *Filostrato.* **1044–85 in storyes ellyswhere . . . ,** for much of the narrator's explanation and most of Criseyde's speech, Chaucer adapts Benoît rather than *Filostrato.* **1070 for,** omitted in Cl. **1086–99** Chaucer's addition. His refusal to blame Criseyde (1097–99) is unique in the tradition. **1095 punysshed,** some manuscripts read "published."

For she so sory was for hire untrouthe°,
Iwys°, I wolde excuse hire yet for routhe°.

This Troylus, as I byforn have told,
Thus dryveth forth° as wel as he hath myght.
But often was his herte hot and cold,
And namely° that ilke° nynthe nyght
Which on the morwe she hadde hym byhight°
To come ayeyn. God wot°, ful litel reste
Hadde he that nyght—nothing° to slepe hym leste°.

The laurer-crowned° Phebus with his hete°
Gan in his course, ay upward as he wente,
To warmen of the Est See the wawes wete°,
And Nisus doughter song° with fressh entente,
Whan Troylus his Pandare after sente,
And on the walles of the toun they pleyde°,
To loke if they kan sen ought° of Criseyde.

Til it was noone thei stoden° for to se
Who that ther come, and every maner wight°
That kam fro fer°, thei seyden it was she
Til that thei koude knowen hym aright°.
Now was hire° herte dul, now was it light.
And thus byjaped° stonden for to stare
Aboute nought° this Troylus and Pandare.

To Pandarus this Troylus tho° seyde,
"For ought° I wot, byfor noon, sykerly°,
Into this town ne cometh nought Criseyde.
She hath ynow to done, hardyly°,
To twynnen° from hire fader, so trowe° I.
Hire olde fader wole yet make hire dyne
Er that she go—God yeve° hys herte pyne!"

Pandare answerde, "It may wel be, certeyn.
And forthi° lat us dyne, I the byseche°.
And after noon than maystow come ayeyn."
And hom thei go withoute more speche,
And comen ayen. But longe may they seche°
Er that they fynde that° they after gape—
Fortune hem bothe thenketh° for to jape°.

Quod Troylus, "I se wel now that she
Is taried° with hire olde fader so
That er she come it wol neygh even° be.
Com forth; I wole unto the yate go.
Thise porterys° ben unkonnynge° everemo,
And I wol don° hem holden up the yate
As nought ne were°, although she come late."

The day goth faste, and after that come eve,
And yet com nought to Troylus Criseyde.
He loketh forth by hegge°, by tree, by greve°,
And fer° his hed over the wal he leyde°,
And at the laste he torned hym and seyde,
"By God, I wot hire menyng° now, Pandare—
Almost, ywys°, al newe° was my care—

"Now douteles, this lady kan hire good°.
I wot she meneth ryden pryvely°.
I comende hire wysdom, by myn hood!
She wol not maken peple nicely°
Gaure° on hire whan she comth, but softely°
By nyghte into the toun she thenketh ryde°.
And, dere brother, thenk not to longe t'abyde°—

"We han not ellys° for to don, ywys.
And Pandarus, now woltow trowen° me?
Have here my trouthe, I se hire! Yond she is!
Heve° up thyn eyen, man! Maystow not se?"
Pandare answerede, "Nay, so mot I the°.
Al wrong, by Gode. What seystow, man, where arte°?
That I se yond nys° but a fare-carte°."

1098 untrouthe, *infidelity* **1099 Iwys,** *surely,* **routhe,** *pity* **1101 dryveth forth,** *continues on* **1103 namely,** *especially,* **ilke,** *very* **1104 byhight,** *promised* **1105 wot,** *knows* **1106 nothing,** *not at all,* **hym leste,** *pleased him* **1107 laurer-crowned,** *crowned with laurel leaves,* **hete,** *heat* **1109 wawes wete,** *wet waves* **1110 song,** *sang* **1112 pleyde,** *diverted themselves* **1113 sen ought,** *see anything* **1114 stoden,** *stood* **1115 maner wight,** *kind of person* **1116 kam fro fer,** *approached from far away* **1117 koude knowen hym aright,** *could recognize the person accurately* **1118 hire,** *their* **1119 byjaped,** *deceived* **1120 Aboute nought,** *for no reason* **1121 tho,** *then* **1122 ought,** *all,* **sykerly,** *certainly* **1124 hardyly,** *surely* **1125 twynnen,** *separate,* **trowe,** *believe* **1127 yeve,** *give* **1129 forthi,** *therefore,* **the byseche,** *ask of you* **1132 seche,** *seek* **1133 that,** *what* **1134 thenketh,** *thinks,* **jape,** *trick* **1136 taried,** *delayed* **1137 wol neygh even,** *will nearly evening* **1139 porterys,** *gatekeepers,* **unkonnynge,** *ignorant* **1140 don,** *ask* **1141 As nought ne were,** *as if it was nothing* **1144 hegge,** *hedge,* **greve,** *grove* **1145 fer,** *far,* **leyde,** *stretched* **1147 wot hire menyng,** *know her intention* **1148 ywys,** *truly,* **al newe,** *renewed* **1149 kan hire good,** *knows what's best for her* **1150 ryden pryvely,** *to ride secretly* **1152 nicely,** *foolishly* **1153 Gaure,** *stare,* **softely,** *secretly* **1154 thenketh ryde,** *plans to ride* **1155 t'abyde,** *to wait* **1156 ellys,** (anything) *else* **1157 woltow trowen,** *will you believe* **1159 Heve,** *lift* **1160 so mot I the,** *as I may prosper* **1161 arte,** *are* (you) **1162 nys,** *is not* **fare-carte,** *work cart*

1110 Nisus doughter, Scylla, who was changed into a bird; earlier, she betrayed her city for her lover, by whom she was in turn abandoned; Ovid, *Metamorphoses* 8.11ff. **1118 hire,** Cp reads "his." **1125 twynnen,** Cp reads "wynnen." **1133 gape,** Cl and Cp read "cape." **1140 holden up the yate,** Chaucer evidently thought of the gate as being a portcullis that was raised and lowered.

"Allas, thow seist right soth°," quod Troylus.
"But, hardely°, it is not all for nought
That in myn herte I now rejoyse thus.
It is ayen° som good I have a thought.
Not I not° how, but syn that° I was wrought
Ne felt I swich a confort, dar I seye.
She comth tonyght, my lyf that dorste
I leye°!"

Pandare answerde, "It may be, wel ynowh,"
And held° with hym of al that evere he seyde.
But in his herte he thoughte, and softe lough°,
And to hymself ful sobreliche° he seyde,
"From haselwode, there° joly Robyn pleyde,
Shal come al that that° thow abydest° here.
Ye, farewel al the snow of ferne yere°!"

The wardeyn° of the yates gan to calle
The folk which that withoute the yates were,
And bad° hem dryven in hire bestes alle,
Or al the nyght they moste bleven° there.
And fer withinne° the nyght, with many a tere,
This Troylus gan homward for to ryde,
For wel he seth° it helpeth nought t'abyde.

But natheles, he gladed° hym yn thys:
He thought he mysacounted hadde his day,
And seyde, "I understonde° have al amys°.
For thilke° nyght I last Criseyde say°,
She seyde, 'I shal ben here, yf that I may,
Er that the mone, O dere herte swete,
The Lyon passe out of this Ariete.'

"For which she may yet holde al° hire byheste°."
And on the morwe unto the yate he wente,
And up and down, by west and ek by este°,
Upon the walles made he many a wente°—
But al for nought; his hope alwey hym blente°.
For which at nyght yn sorwe and sykes° sore
He wente hym hom withouten ony° more.

His hope al clene° out of his herte is fledde,
He nath° wheron now lenger for to honge°,
But for° the peyne hym thoughte his herte
bledde,
So were his throwes° sharpe and wonder stronge.
For when he saugh that she abood° so longe,
He nyste° what he juggen° of it myghte,
Syn she hath broken that° she hym byhyghte°.

The thridde, ferthe, fifthe, sixte day
After tho° dayes ten of which I tolde,
Bytwyxen hope and drede his herte lay,
Yet somwhat trustyng on hire hestes° olde.
But whan he saugh she nolde hire terme° holde,
He kan now sen° noon other remedye
But for to shape° hym soone for to dye.

Therwith the wykked spyrit—God us blesse—
Which that men clepeth° the wode° jalousye,
Gan in hym crepe, in al this hevynesse,
For whiche, by cause he wold° soone dye,
He ne eet ne dronk, for his malencolye,
And ek from every compaignye he fledde—
This was the lyf that al the tyme he ledde.

He so defet° was that no manere man
Unneth° myghte hym knowe° ther he
wente;
So was he lene°, and therto° pale and wan°,
And feble, that he walketh by potente°;
And with his ire he thus hymselve shente°.
And whoso axed hym wherof hym smerte°,
He seyde his harm was al aboute his herte.

1163 seist right soth, *speak very truly* **1164 hardely,** *surely* **1166 ayen,** *in anticipation of* **1167 Not I not,** *I don't know,* **syn that,** *since* **1169 dorste I leye,** *I dare wager* **1171 held,** *agreed* **1172 lough,** *laughed* **1173 sobreliche,** *sincerely* **1174 there,** *where* **1175 that that,** *that which,* **abydest,** *awaits* **1176 ferne yere,** *past years* **1177 wardeyn,** *guard,* **yates,** *gates* **1179 bad,** *ordered* **1180 moste bleven,** *must remain* **1181 fer withinne,** *far into* **1183 seth,** *sees* **1184 gladed,** *comforted* **1186 understonde,** *understood,* **amys,** *wrongly* **1187 thilke,** *that,* **say,** *saw* **1191 al,** *completely,* **byheste,** *promise* **1193 este,** *east* **1194 wente,** *turn* **1195 blente,** *blinded* **1196 sykes,** *sighs* **1197 ony,** *anything* **1198 clene,** *completely* **1199 nath,** *has nothing,* **honge,** *hang on to* **1200 for,** *because of* **1201 throwes,** *agonies* **1202 abood,** *remained away* **1203 nyste,** *knew not,* **juggen,** *think* **1204 that,** *what,* **byhyghte,** *promised* **1206 tho,** *those* **209 hestes,** *promises* **1209 terme,** *agreed upon time* **1210 sen,** *see* **1211 shape,** *prepare* **1213 men clepeth,** *one calls,* **wode,** *insane* **1215 wold,** *wished to* **1219 defet,** *disfigured* **1220 Unneth,** *barely,* **knowe,** *recognize* **1221 lene,** *thin,* **therto,** *also,* **wan,** *sickly* **1222 potente,** *crutch* **1223 shente,** *ruined* **1224 wherof hym smerte,** *what pained him*

1174 From haselwode, there joly Robyn pleyde, i.e., from the land of make believe, where merry Robin played. This is not necessarily Robin Hood, though ballads pertaining to him were available in Chaucer's time. Robin and Marion were lovers (often failed) in the French *pastourelle* tradition, set in an idealized landscape. **1176 ferne yere,** recalls the refrain of François Villon's "Ballade des dames du temps jadis" ("Ballad of the Women of Times Past"): "Mais ou sont les neiges d'antan?" (But where are the snows of yesteryear?). **1189–90 mone . . . Ariete,** see 4.1591–92n. Troylus is trying to stretch time by including one more day.

Pryam ful ofte, and ek his moder dere,
His bretheren and his sustren, gonne hym freyne°
Why he so sorwful was in al his chere°,
And what thyng was the cause of al his peyne.
But al for nought: he nolde° his cause pleyne°,
But seyde he felte a grevous maledye
Aboute his herte, and fayn° he wolde dye.

So on a day he leyde hym doun to slepe,
And so byfel° that yn his slep hym thoughte
That in a forest faste° he welk° to wepe
For love of here that hym these peynes wroughte°,
And up and doun as he the forest soughte,
He mette° he saugh a bor° with tuskes grete,
That slepte ayeyn° the bryghte sonnes hete.

And by this bor, faste° in hir armes folde°,
Lay kyssyng ay his lady bryght Criseyde.
For sorwe of which, whan he it gan byholde,
And for despit°, out of his slep he breyde°,
And loude he cride on Pandarus and seyde,
"O Pandarus, now know I crop and rote°!
I n'am but ded; ther nys non other bote°!

"My lady bryght Criseyde hath me bytrayed,
In whom I trusted most of ony wight.
She elliswhere hath now here herte apayed°.
The blysful goddes thorugh here° grete myght
Han in my drem yshewed° it ful right.
Thus in my drem Criseyde I have byholde"—
And al this thing to Pandarus he tolde.

"O my Criseyde, allas, what subtilte°,
What newe lust°, what beaute, what science°,
What wratthe of juste cause° have ye to me?
What gilt of me°, what fel° experience,
Hath fro me raft°, allas, thyn advertence°?
O trust, O feyth, O depe aseuraunce°!
Who hath me reft° Criseyde, al my plesaunce?

"Allas, whi leet I° you from hennes° go,
For which wel neigh out of my wit I breyde°?
Who shal now trowe on° ony othes mo°?
God wot, I wende°, O lady bright Criseyde,
That every word was gospel° that ye seyde!
But who may bet bigile°, yf hym lyste°,
Than he on whom men wenen° best to triste°?

"What shal I don, my Pandarus? Allas,
I fele now so sharp a newe peyne,
Syn that ther is no remedye in this cas,
That bet were it° I with myn hondes tweyne°
Myselven slowh° alwey than thus compleyne.
For thorugh my deth my wo shal han an ende,
Ther every day with lyf myself I shende°."

Pandare answerde and seyde, "Allas the while°
That I was born. Have I not seyd er this
That dremes many a maner° man bygyle°?
And whi? For folk expounden° hem amys°.
How darstow seyn° that fals thi lady ys
For ony drem right for° thyn owene drede?
Lat be this thought; thow kanst no dremes rede.

"Peraunter°, there° thow dremest of this bor,
It may so be that it may signyfie
Hire fader, which that° old is and ek hor°,
Ayen the sonne° lith o poynt to dye°,
And she for sorwe gynneth° wepe and crye,
And kysseth hym, there° he lyth on the grounde—
Thus sholdestow thi drem aright expounde."

"How° myghte I thanne do," quod Troylus,
"To knowe° of this, ye°, were it nevere so lite°?"

1227 freyne, *ask* **1228 chere,** *behavior* **1230 nolde,** *would not,* **pleyne,** *express* **1232 fayn,** *gladly* **1234 byfel,** *it happened* **1235 faste,** *dense,* **welk,** *walked* **1237 wroughte,** *caused* **1238 mette,** *dreamed,* **bor,** *boar* **1239 ayeyn,** *in* **1240 faste,** *tightly,* **folde,** *embraced* **1243 despit,** *anger,* **breyde,** *started* **1245 crop and rote,** *top to bottom* **1246 bote,** *remedy* **1249 apayed,** *satisfied* **1250 here,** *their* **1251 yshewed,** *showed* **1254 subtilte,** *deception* **1255 lust,** *desire,* **science,** *knowledge* **1256 wratthe of juste cause,** *just cause of anger* **1257 gilt of me,** *guilt of mine,* **fel,** *fearsome* **1258 raft,** *deprived,* **advertence,** *attention* **1259 aseuraunce,** *assurance* **1260 me reft,** *from me deprived* **1261 leet I,** *did I let,* **hennes,** *here* **1262 out of my wit I breyde,** *I go mad* **1263 trowe on,** *believe in,* **mo,** *more* **1264 wende,** *thought* **1265 gospel,** *truth* **1266 bet bigile,** *better deceive,* **lyste,** *wishes* **1267 men wenen,** *one thinks,* **triste,** *trust* **1271 bet were it,** *it would be better,* **tweyne,** *two* **1272 slowh,** *should slay* **1274 shende,** *destroy* **1275 while,** *time* **1277 maner,** *kind of,* **bygyle,** *mislead* **1278 expounden,** *interpret,* **amys,** *incorrectly* **1279 darstow seyn,** *dare you say* **1280 right for,** *just because of* **1282 Peraunter,** *perhaps,* **there,** *when* **1284 which that,** *who,* **ek hor,** *also gray* **1285 Ayen the sonne,** *in the sunshine,* **lith o poynt to dye,** *lies on the point of dying* **1286 gynneth,** *does* **1287 there,** *where* **1289 How,** *what* **1290 knowe,** *be sure,* **ye,** *indeed,* **were it never so lite,** *even if it were so insignificant*

1240 hir, Cl reads "his." **1247 Criseyde hath me bytraysed,** in *Filostrato* (7.27), Troilo interprets his dream and understands immediately that Diomede is Criseida's lover; see 1450–51n below. **1276 seyd er this,** see 5.358–85. **1278 folk,** Cl reads "men."

"Now seystow° wysly," quod this Pandarus.
"My reede° is this: syn thow kanst wel endite°,
That hastely a lettre thow hire write,
Thorugh which thow shalt wel bryngen it aboute
To knowe a soth° of that° thow art in doute.

"And se now why: for this I dar wel seyn,
That if so is° that she untrewe be,
I kan nat trowen that she wol write ayeyn.
And yf she write, thow shalt ful soone se°
As wheyther she hath ony liberte
To come ayen; or ellys yn som clause,
If she be let°, she wol assigne a cause°.

"Thow hast nat wreten hire syn that she wente,
Nor she to the; and this I dorste leye°,
There may swych cause ben in hire entente
That, hardely°, thow wolt thiselven seye
That hire abod° the beste is for yow tweye°.
Now write hire thanne, and thow shalt fele sone°
A soth of al. Ther is no more to done."

Accorded ben to this conclusioun,
And that anoon, these ilke° lordes two;
And hastely sit° Troylus adoun,
And rolleth yn his herte to and fro
How he may best discryven hire° his wo.
And to Criseyde, his owene lady dere,
He wrot right thus, and seyde as ye may here.

Litera Troili

"Right fresshe flour°, whos I ben have and shal,
Withouten part of elliswhere servise°,
With herte, body, lyf, lust°, thought, and al,
I, woful wight, in everich° humble wyse
That tonge telle or herte may devyse,
As ofte° as matere occupieth place°,
Me recomaunde° unto youre noble grace.

"Liketh it yow to witen°, swete herte,
As ye wel knowe, how longe tyme agon
That ye me lafte° yn aspre° peynes smerte,
Whan that ye went, of which yet bote° non
Have I non had, but evere wors bygon°
Fro day to day am I, and so mot dwelle,
While it yow lyst°, of wele and wo my welle°.

"For which to yow with dredful° herte trewe
I wryte, as he that sorwe dryfth° to wryte,
My wo, that everich houre encreseth newe,
Compleynyng, as I dar or kan endite°.
And that defaced is°, that may ye wyte°
The terys which that fro myn eyen reyne°,
That wolde speke, yf that they koude, and pleyne°.

"Yow first biseche I that youre eyen clere
To look on this defouled ye not holde°,
And over al this, that ye, my lady dere,
Wol vouchesauf° this lettre to byholde.
And by the cause ek of my cares colde,
That sleth° my wit, if ought amys m'asterte°,
Foryeve it me, myn owene swete herte.

"Yf ony servant dorste° or oughte of ryght
Upon hys lady pytously compleyne,
Thanne wene° I that ich oughte be that wyght°,
Considered this°, that ye these monethes tweyne
Han taried there° ye seyden, soth to seyne,
But° dayes ten ye nolde in ost sojourne°—
But yn two monethes yet ye nat retourne.

"But for as muche as me mot nedes lyke°
Al that yow lyste°, I dar not pleyne more,
But humbely, with sorwful sykes syke°,
Yow wryte ich° myn unresty° sorwes sore,
Fro day to day desyryng everemore
To knowen fully, yf youre wil it were,
How ye han ferd° and don whyl ye be there;

1291 seystow, *you speak* **1292 reede,** *advice,* **endite,** *compose* **1295 soth,** *truth,* **that,** *that which* **1297 so is,** *it is so* **1299 se,** *see* **1302 let,** *detained,* **cause,** *reason* **1304 dorste leye,** *would dare wager* **1306 hardely,** *surely* **1307 abod,** *delay,* **tweye,** *two* **1308 fele sone,** *feel soon* **1311 ilke,** *same* **1312 sit,** *sits* **1314 discryven hire,** *describe to her* **1317 flour,** *flower* **1318 part of elliswhere servise,** *any portion of service* (given) *elsewhere* **1319 lust,** *desire* **1320 everich,** *every* **1322 ofte,** *long,* **matere occupieth place,** *matter occupies space* **1323 Me recomaunde,** *commend myself* **1324 Liketh it yow witen,** *may it please you to recall* **1326 lafte,** *left,* **aspre,** *bitter* **1327 bote,** *remedy* **1328 bygon,** *beset* **1330 yow lyst,** *it pleases you,* **of wele and wo my welle,** (who are) *the source of my joy and woe* **1331 dredful,** *fearful* **1332 dryfth,** *drives* **1334 endite,** *compose* **1335 that defaced is,** *that* (my writing) *is blotted,* **wyte,** *blame* **1336 reyne,** *rain down* **1337 pleyne,** *lament* **1339 defouled ye not holde,** *do not regard* (your eyes) *as tainted* **1341 Wol vouchesauf,** *will consent* **1343 sleth,** *slays,* **ought amys m'asterte,** *anything wrong escapes from me* **1345 dorste,** *dared* **1347 wene,** *think,* **wyght,** *person* **1348 Considered this,** *this being considered* **1349 there,** *when* **1350 But,** *only,* **in ost sojourne,** *remain with the army* **1352 me mot nedes lyke,** *it must necessarily please me* **1353 lyste,** *desire* **1354 sykes sike,** *sighs sick* **1355 Yow wryte I,** *I write to you,* **unresty,** *restless* **1358 ferd,** *gotten on*

1316a Litera Troili, "The Letter of Troylus." This lengthy letter differs considerably from the one in *Filostrato*; much of it derives from the rhetorical conventions of the *ars dictaminis* (art of letter writing). Rubric omitted in Cl. **1352 me,** Cl reads "I."

"The whos° welfare and hele° ek God encresse
In honour swych that upward in degre
It growe alwey, so that it nevere cesse.
Right as youre herte ay kan°, my lady fre,
Devyse°, I prey to God, so mot° it be,
And graunte it that ye soone upon me rewe°,
As wysly° as in al I am yow° trewe.

"And if yow lyketh knowen of the fare°
Of me, whos wo ther may no wit discryve,
I kan no more but, chyste° of every care,
At writyng of this letre I was on-lyve°,
Al redy out my woful gost° to dryve,
Which I delaye, and holde hym yet in honde,
Upon the sighte of matere° of youre sonde°.

"Myn eyen two, in veyn with which I se,
Of sorweful teres salte arn woxen wellys°;
My song yn pleynte° of myn adversite;
My good yn harme; myn ese° ek woxen
helle ys°;
My joye yn wo. I kan sey yow nought ellys,
But turned ys—for which my lyf I warye°—
Everych joye or ese in his contrarye.

"Which with youre comyng hom ayen to Troye
Ye may redresse°, and more a thousand sithe°
Than evere ych hadde° encressen yn me joye.
For was there nevere herte yet so blythe°
To han his lyf as I shal ben as swythe°
As I yow se. And though no manere routhe°
Commeve° yow, yet thynketh on youre trouthe°.

"And yf so be° my gilt hath deth deserved,
Or yf yow lyst° no more upon me se°,
In guerdoun° yet of that I have yow served,
Biseche I yow, myn hertes lady fre,
That hereupon° ye wolden wryte me,
For love of God, my righte lode-sterre°,
That deth may make an ende of al my werre°.

"If other cause aught dothe° yow for to dwelle,
That° with youre lettre ye me recomforte°,
For though to me youre absence is an helle,
With pacience I wol my wo comporte°,
And with youre lettre of hope I wol desporte°.
Now writeth, swete, and lat me thus not pleyne,
With hope or deth delyvereth me fro peyne.

"Ywys°, myn owene dere herte trewe,
I wot° that whan ye next upon me se,
So lost have I myn hele° and ek myn hewe°,
Criseyde shal nought konne knowen° me.
Iwys, myn hertes day, my lady fre,
So thursteth ay myn herte to biholde
Youre beaute that my lyf unnethe° I holde.

"I say no more, al have I° for to seye
To yow wel more than I telle may,
But whether that ye do me lyve or deye,
Yet pray I God, so yeve yow right good day.
And fareth wel°, goodly, fayre, fresshe may°,
As ye that lyf and deth me may comaunde.
And to youre trouthe ay° I me recomaunde°,

"With hele swych° but that° ye yeven° me
The same hele, I shal noon hele have.
In yow lyth°, whan yow lyst° that it so be,
The day yn which me clothen° shal my grave;
In yow my lyf, in yow myght° for to save
Me fro dyshese° of alle peynes smerte;
And fare now wel, myn owene swete herte.
le vostre T°."

This lettre forth was sent unto Criseyde,
Of which hire answere yn effect was this:

1359 The whos, *the one whose* (i.e., Criseyde's), **hele,** *well-being* **1362 ay kan,** *always can* **1363 Devyse,** *determine,* **mot,** *may* **1364 rewe,** *have pity* **1365 wysly,** *surely,* **yow,** *to you* **1366 knowen of the fare,** *to know of the condition* **1368 chyste,** *container* **1369 on-lyve,** *alive* **1370 gost,** *spirit* **1372 matere,** *the content,* **sonde,** *message* (return letter) **1374 arn woxen wellys,** *have become fountains* **1375 pleynte,** *lament* **1376 ese,** *comfort,* **woxen helle ys,** *has become hell* **1378 warye,** *curse* **1381 redresse,** *correct,* **sithe,** *times* **1382 ych hadde,** *I once had* **1383 blythe,** *happy* **1384 swythe,** *soon* **1385 routhe,** *pity* **1386 Commeve,** *moves,* **trouthe,** *promise* **1387 yf so be,** *if* (it) *be so that* **1388 lyst,** *wish,* **se,** (to) *look* **1389 guerdoun,** *reward* **1391 hereupon,** *concerning this* **1392 righte lode-sterre,** *true guiding star* **1393 werre,** (inner) *war* **1394 aught dothe,** *in any way compels* **1395 That,** (I beseech you) *that,* **recomforte,** *comfort* **1397 comporte,** *endure* **1398 desporte,** *find comfort* **1401 Ywys,** *truly* **1402 wot,** *know* **1403 hele,** *health,* **hewe,** *color* **1404 konne knowen,** *be able to recognize* **1407 unnethe,** *barely* **1408 al have I,** *although I have* **1412 fareth wel,** *farewell,* **may,** *maid* **1414 ay,** *always,* **recomaunde,** *commend* **1415 hele swych,** *such well-being,* **but,** *unless,* **yeven,** *have given* **1417 lyth,** *resides,* **lyst,** *wish* **1418 clothen,** *enclose* (clothe) **1419 myght,** *power* **1420 dyshese,** *distress* **1421a le vostre T,** *your Troylus*

1367 wit, Cl reads "wight" (person). **1375–77** These traditional oxymora of love are expressed in elliptical syntax: in each case, "yn" can be read as "has changed into." **1388 no more,** Cl reads "no manere." **1390 hertes,** Cp reads "owen." **1421a** Omitted in Cl.

Ful pytously she wrot ayen° and seyde
That also° soone as that she myghte, ywys,
She wolde come and mende al that was mys°;
And fynally she wrot and seyde hym thanne,
She wolde come, ye, but she nyste whanne°.

But yn hire lettre made she swyche festes°
That wonder was, and swereth she loveth hym best;
Of which he forid but botmeles byhestes°.
But Troylus, thow mayst now, est or west,
Pype yn an ivy lef°, yf that the lest°.
Thus goth the world, God shylde° us fro myschaunce,
And every wight that meneth° trouthe avaunce°!

Encressen gan the wo fro day to nyght
Of Troylus for taryinge of Criseyde,
And lessen gan his hope and ek his myght,
For which al doun he yn his bed hym leyde.
He ne eet, ne dronk, ne slep, ne word ne seyde,
Ymagynyng ay that she was unkynde,
For which wel neigh° he wax° out of his mynde.

This drem of which I told have ek byforn
May nevere come° out of his remembraunce.
He thought ay wel he hadde his lady lorn°,
And that Joves, of his purveyaunce°,
Hym shewed hadde in sleep the signyfyaunce
Of hire untrothe and his disaventure°,
And that the bor was shewed hym yn figure°.

For which he for Sibille his suster sente,
That called was Cassandre ek al aboute,
And al his drem he tolde hire er he stente°,
And hire bisoughte assoylen hym° the doute
Of the stronge bor with tuskes stoute;
And fynally, withinne a lytel stounde°,
Cassandre hym gan right thus hys drem expounde.

She gan first smyle, and seyde, "O brother dere,
If thow a soth° of this desirest knowe°,
Thow most° a fewe of olde storyes here,
To purpos° how that Fortune overthrowe°
Hath lordes olde, thorugh which, withinne a throwe°,
Thow wel this bor shalt knowe, and of what kynde°
He comen is, as men yn bokes fynde.

"Diane, which that wroth was and yn ire
For° Grekes nolde don° hire sacrifise,
Ne encens° upon hire auter° sette afyre,
She, for that Grekes gonne hire so dispise,
Wrak hire° in a wonder cruwel wyse:
For with a bor as grete as oxe in stalle
She made up frete° hire corn and vynes° alle.

"To sle this bor was al the contre reysed°,
Amonges which ther com this bor to se
A mayde, on° of this world the beste ypreysed°.
And Meleagre, lord of that contre,
He loved so this fresshe mayde fre°,
That with his manhod, er he wolde stente°,
This bor he slow°, and hire the hed he sente.

"Of which, as olde bokes tellen us,
Ther ros a contek° and a gret envye.
And of this lord descendede Tydeus
By ligne°, or ellys olde bokes lye.
But how this Meleagre gan to dye°

1424 ayen, *in return* **1425 also,** *as* **1426 mys,** *wrong* **1428 nyste whanne,** *knew not when* **1429 swyche festes,** *such endearments* **1431 botmeles byhestes,** *groundless promises* **1433 Pype yn an ivy lef,** *i.e., go whistle,* **the lest,** *you wish* **1434 shylde,** *shield* **1435 meneth,** *intends,* **avaunce,** *(to) promote* **1442 wel neigh,** *nearly,* **wax,** *went* **1444 come,** *go* **1445 lorn,** *lost* **1446 purveyaunce,** *foreknowledge* **1448 disaventure,** *misfortune* **1449 yn figure,** *symbolically* **1452 er he stente,** *before he stopped* **1453 bisoughte assoylen hym,** *asked to release him from* **1455 stounde,** *time* **1458 soth,** *truth,* **knowe,** *to know* **1459 most,** *must* **1460 To purpos,** *that pertain to,* **overthrowe,** *overthrown* **1461 throwe,** *short while* **1462 kynde,** *lineage* **1465 For,** *because,* **nolde don,** *would not do* **1466 Ne encens,** *nor incense,* **auter,** *altar* **1468 Wrak hire,** *avenged herself* **1470 made up frete,** *caused to be devoured,* **hire corn and vynes,** *their grain and vines* **1471 reysed,** *roused to arms* **1473 on,** *one,* **ypreysed,** *praised* **1475 fre,** *noble* **1476 stente,** *stop* **1477 slow,** *slew* **1479 a contek,** *strife* **1481 ligne,** *lineage* **1482 gan to dye,** *died*

1443 This drem, Troylus's dream at 5.1233ff. **1448 his,** Cl reads "here." **1450–51 Sibille . . . Cassandre,** *sibyl* means "female prophet," but medieval writers took it as an alternative name for Cassandra, daughter of Priam and traditional seer of doom. In *Filostrato,* after Troiolo interprets the dream for himself (7.27ff.) and writes a letter (7.49ff.), he unintentionally discloses his love for Criseida to Deifobo (7.77), and is subsequently mocked by Cassandra for loving inappropriately (7.86–87). **1464–84 Diane . . . bor . . . ,** the story of Diana, the Caledonian boar, Meleager, and Atalanta (the **mayde,** line 1473) is told in Ovid *Metamorphoses* 8.271ff. After he successfully kills the ravaging boar sent by Diana, Meleager gives its head to Atalanta, with whom he has fallen in love. In the protest that ensues among the hunters, Meleager kills his mother's brothers. His mother, in turn, destroys the piece of wood upon which Meleager's life depends. **1480 Tydeus,** father of Diomede; in classical tradition, Tydeus is Meleager's half-brother rather than his descendent, but Chaucer follows the error found in *Filostrato* 7.27.

Thorugh his moder wol I yow not telle,
For al to longe it were for to dwelle."

She tolde ek how Tydeus, er she stente°,
Unto the stronge cite of Thebes,
To cleymen kyngdom° of the cite, wente,
For his felawe daun° Polymytes,
Of° which the brother daun Ethyocles
Ful wrongfully of Thebes held the strengthe—
This tolde she by proces° al the lengthe.

She tolde ek how Hemonydes asterte°
Whan Tydeus slowh° fifty knyghtes stoute°;
She tolde ek alle the prophesies by herte,
And how that seven kynges with hire route°
Bysegeden the cite al aboute;
And of the holy serpent, and the welle,
And of the furyes, al she gan hym telle;

Of Archymoris burynge and the pleyes°,
And how Amphiorax fil thorugh the grounde;
How Tydeus was slayn, lord of Argeyes°,
And how Ypomedon y lytel stounde°
Was dreynt°, and ded° Parthonope of wounde;
And also how Cappaneus the proude
With thonder-dynt was slayn, that cryde° loude.

She gan ek telle hym how that eyther brother,
Ethyocles and Polymyte also,
At a scarmyche° eche of hem slowh other°,
And of Argyves wepynge and hire wo;
And how the town was brent, she tolde ek tho.
And so descendeth doun from gestes olde
To Diomede, and thus she spak and tolde:

"This ilke° bor bytokeneth° Diomede,
Tydeus sone, that down descended is
Fro Meleagre, that made the bor to blede.
And thy lady, where that° she be, ywis°,
This Dyomede hire herte hath and she his.
Wep if thow wolt, or leef°, for out of doute,
This Diomede is inne and thow art oute."

"Thow seyst nat soth," quod he, "thou sorceresse!
With al thi fals gost° of prophesie,
Thow wenest ben° a grete devyneresse°!
Now seystow not° this fol of fantasye°
Peyneth hire° on ladyes for to lye°?
Awey°," quod he, "ther° Joves yeve the sorwe!
Thow shalt be fals°, peraunter°, yet tomorwe!

1485 stente, *stopped* **1487 cleymen kyngdom,** *claim kingship* **1487 daun,** *master* **1489 Of,** *from* **1491 by proces,** *in sequence* **1492 asterte,** *escaped* **1493 slowh,** *slew,* **stoute,** *strong* **1495 route,** *company* **1499 pleyes,** *funeral games* (see 304n) **1501 Argeyes,** *the people of Argos* **1502 y lytel stounde,** *in little time* **1503 dreynt,** *drowned,* **ded,** *died* **1505 cryde,** *boasted* **1508 scarmyche,** *skirmish,* **slowh outher,** *slew the other* **1513 ilke,** *same,* **bytokeneth,** *symbolizes* **1516 where that,** *wherever,* **ywis,** *surely* **1518 leef,** *leave off* **1521 gost,** *spirit* **1522 wenest ben,** *think to be,* **devyneresse,** *seer* **1523 seystow not,** *don't you see,* **fol of fantasye,** *deluded fool* (Cassandra) **1524 Peyneth hire,** *takes pain,* **on ladyes for to lye,** *to lie about ladies* **1525 Awey,** *be gone,* **ther,** *where* **1526 fals,** (proved) *wrong,* **peraunter,** *perhaps*

1485–1510 Chaucer's addition. A summary of Statius's *Thebaid*: Polynices (**Polymytes,** line 1488) and Eteocles (**Ethyocles,** line 1489), sons of Oedipus, were to be alternate rulers of Thebes. But Eteocles would not relinquish the rule at the proper time, so Polynices gained the assistance of six allies (King Adrastus of Argos, Amphiaraus, Capaneus, Hippomedon, Parthenopaeus, and Tydeus)—the seven against Thebes. In the assault of the city, all but Adrastus died, and Creon of Thebes refused burial for the bodies of the besiegers. Chaucer elsewhere uses aspects of the story in *KnT* and *Anel.* **1491 the,** Cp reads "by." **1492 Hemonydes,** Maeon, son of Haemon, was the only one of fifty sent to ambush Tydeus who escaped death at Tydeus's hand: *Thebaid* 2. **1494 prophesies,** perhaps a reference to the prophesies at the end *Thebaid* 3. **1497 holy serpent . . . welle,** a serpent sent by Jove kills Archemorus, infant son of Lycurgus; the well apparently refers to a river in a related incident; *Thebaid* 5. **1498 furyes,** the Furies, goddesses of vengeance, prompt the women of Lemnos to kill the men of their island; *Thebaid* 5. After this line, Cl, Cp, and most other manuscripts include a twelve-line, book-by-book Latin outline of the *Thebaid*: "Asociat profugum Tideo primus Polimitem; / Tidea legatum doceat insideas que secundus; / Tercius Hemoduden canit et vates latitantes; / Quartus habet reges in euntes prelia septem; / Mox furie Lenne quinto narratur et aguis; / Archimori bustum sexto ludique leguntur; / Dat Graios Thebes et vatem septimus umbris; / Octavo cecidit Tideus spes vita Pelasgis; / Ypomedon nono moritur cum Parthonopea; / Flumine percussus decimo Capaneus superatur; /Undecimo sese perimunt per vulnera fratres; / Argina flentem narrat duodenus et ignem." (The first links Polynices with Tydeus; the second tells of Tydeus the legate and of ambush; the third sings of Haemon's son and the hidden seers; the fourth has the seven kings going to battle; in the fifth, the Furies of Lemnos and the serpent are told about; in the sixth, the grave of Archemorus and the games are surveyed; the seventh takes the Greeks to Thebes and the seer to the shadows; in the eighth, Tydeus fell—hope, life of the Pelasgians; in the ninth, Ypomedon dies with Parthenopeus; in the tenth, Capaneus is overcome, struck by lightning; in the eleventh, the brothers kill each other with wounds; the twelfth tells of the weeping Argia and the burning.) **1500 Amphiorax,** Amphiaraus was swallowed by the earth just as he was about to be made prisoner; *Thebaid* 6. See 2.105n above. **1501–05 Tydeus . . . Ypomedon . . . Parthonope . . . Cappaneus,** the deaths of Tydeus, Hippomedon, Parthenopaeus, and Capeneus are told in *Thebaid* 8–10. **1502 how,** omitted in Cl. **y lytel,** Cp reads "a lytel." **1507–08** *Thebaid* 11. **1509–10** *Thebaid* 12, although the burning of the town is not specified. **Argyves,** Argia, wife of Polynices; see 4.762n.

"As wel thow myghtest lyen on° Alceste,
That was of creatures—but° men lye—
That evere weren, kyndest and the beste.
For whanne hire housbonde was in jupartie
To dye hymself, but yf° she wolde dye,
She ches for hym° to dye and go to helle,
And starf° anoon, as us the bokes telle."

Cassandre goth, and he with cruwel herte
Foryat° his wo, for angre of hire speche,
And from his bed al sodeynly he sterte
As though al hol hym hadde ymade a leche°.
And day by day he gan enquere and seche
A sooth of this with al his fulle cure°;
And thus he drieth forth° his aventure.

Fortune, whiche that permutacioun°
Of thinges hath, as it is hire commytted°
Thorugh purveyaunce° and disposicioun°
Of heyghe Jove, as regnes° shal ben flytted°
Fro folk yn° folk, or when they shal ben smytted°,
Gan pulle awey the fetheres brighte of Troye
Fro day to day, til they ben bare of joye.

Among al this, the fyn° of the parodye°
Of Ector gan aprochen wonder blyve°.
The fate wolde° his soule sholde unbodye°,
And shapen° hadde a mene° it out to dryve,
Ayeyns which fate hym helpeth not to stryve;
But on a day to fyghten gan he wende°,
At which, allas, he caught his lyves ende.

For which methenketh every manere wight°
That haunteth armes° oughte to bywayle
The deth of hym that was so noble a knyght;
For as he drough° a kyng by th'aventayle°,
Unwar of this, Achilles thorugh the mayle°
And thorugh the body gan hym for to ryve°;
And thus this worthi knyght was brought° of lyve.

For whom, as olde bokes tellen us,
Was mad swych wo that tonge may it not telle,
And namely° the sorwe of Troylus,
That next° hym was of worthinesse welle°.
And yn this wo gan Troylus to dwelle,
That, what for sorwe, and love, and for unreste,
Ful ofte a day he bad° his herte breste°.

But natheles, though he gan hym dispeyre,
And dradde° ay that his lady was untrewe,
Yet ay on° hire his herte gan repeyre°.
And as thise loveres don, he soughte ay newe
To gete ayen Criseyde, bright of hewe;
And in his herte he wente° hire excusynge
That Calkas caused al hire taryinge.

And ofte tyme he was yn purpose grete°
Hymselven lyk a pylgrym to desgyse
To sen hire, but he may not contrefete
To ben unknowen of° folk that weren wyse,
Ne fynde excuse aright that may suffise,
Yf he among the Grekes knowen° were,
For which he wep ful ofte many a tere.

To hire he wrot yet ofte tyme al newe
Ful pitously—he lefte it nought for slouthe°—
Bisechyng hire, syn that he was trewe,
That she wolde come ayeyn and holde hire
    trowthe°;
For which Criseyde upon a day, for routhe°—
I take it so—towchyng this matere,
Wrot hym ayeyn°, and seyde as ye may here:

Litera Criseydis

"Cupides sone, ensample of goodlihede°,
O swerd of knyghthod, sours° of gentilesse°,
How myght a wyght in torment and in drede
And heeleles°, yow sende as yet gladnesse—

1527 lyen on, *lie about* **1528 but,** *unless* **1531 but yf,** *unless* **1532 for hym,** *in his place* **1533 starf,** *died* **1535 Foryat,** *forgot* **1537 leche,** *doctor* **1539 cure,** *attention* **1540 drieth forth,** *endures* **1541 permutacioun,** *change* **1542 hire commytted,** *to her conveyed* **1543 purveyaunce,** *foresight,* **disposicioun,** *arrangement* **1544 regnes,** *kingdoms,* **flytted,** *transferred* **1545 yn,** *to,* **smytted,** *disgraced* **1548 fyn,** *end,* **parodye,** *period* **1549 blyve,** *quickly* **1550 wolde,** *wanted,* **unbodye,** *depart the body* **1551 shapen,** *prepared,* **mene,** *means* **1553 gan he wende,** *he went* **1555 manere wight,** *kind of person* **1556 haunteth armes,** *is involved with fighting* **1558 drough,** *dragged,* **th'aventayle,** *the back of his helmet* **1559 mayle,** *chain mail* **1560 ryve,** *pierce* **1561 brought,** *deprived* **1564 namely,** *especially* **1565 next,** *next to,* **welle,** (the) *source* **1568 bad,** *prayed,* **breste,** *burst* **1570 dradde,** *dreaded* **1571 ay on,** *always to,* **gan repeyre,** *returned* **1574 wente,** *thought* **1576 yn purpose grete,** *in full intent* **1579 unknowen of,** *unrecognized by* **1581 knowen,** *recognized* **1584 slouthe,** *inaction* **1586 trowthe,** *promise* **1587 routhe,** *pity* **1589 ayeyn,** *in return* **1590 goodlihede,** *excellence* **1591 sours,** *source,* **gentilesse,** *gentility* **1593 heeleles,** *without well-being*

1528 Alceste, Alcestis, an idealized wife; she chose to die to save her husband, Admetus; Chaucer's addition. See *LGWP* F510ff. **1546 brighte,** Cl reads "out." **1557 deth of him,** Chaucer derives his account of Hector's death from Benoît 16007ff. **1589a Litera Criseydis,** "The Letter of Criseyde." Rubric omitted in Cl. **1590–1630** Chaucer's addition, although some details derive from letters that are included earlier in *Filostrato.*

I herteles°, I syke°, I yn distresse?
Syn ye with me nor I with yow may dele°,
Yow neyther sende ich herte may nor hele°.

"Youre lettres ful, the papir al ypleynted°,
Conseyved° hath myn hertes piete°.
I have ek seyn with terys al depeynted°
Youre lettre, and how that ye requeren me
To come ayen, which yet ne may not be.
But why, lest° that this lettre founden were,
No mencion ne make I now, for fere.

"Grevous to me, God wot, is youre unreste,
Youre haste°, and that the goddes ordenaunce°
It semeth not ye take it for the beste;
Nor other thyng nys in youre remembraunce,
As thenketh me°, but oonly youre plesaunce°.
But beth not wroth, and that I yow byseche°:
For that I tarye is al for wykked speche°.

"For I have herd wel more than I wende°
Towchynge us two, how thynges han ystonde°,
Which I shal with dissimulynge amende°.
And—beth nought wroth—I have eke
understonde
How ye ne don but holden me in honde°.
But now no fors°—I kan not in yow gesse°
But alle trouthe and alle gentilesse.

"Come I wole, but yet in swich disjoynte°
I stonde as now that what yer or what day
That this shal be that kan I not apoynte°.
But yn effect I pray yow as I may
Of youre good word and of yowre frendship ay°.
For trewely, while that my lyf may dure°,
As for a frend ye may in me assure°.

"Yet preye ich yow, on yvyl° ye ne take
That it is short which that I to yow write.
I dar nat ther° I am wel lettres make°,
Ne nevere yet ne koude I wel endite°.
Ek gret effect° men write yn place lite°:
Th'entente is al, and nought the lettres space°.
And fareth now wel, God have yow in his grace.
la vostre C°."

This lettre this Troylus thoughte al straunge,
Whan he it saugh, and sorwfullich he sighte°;
Hym thoughte it lyk a kalendes° of chaunge.
But fynally, he ful ne trowen° myghte
That she ne wolde hym holden that° she
highte°;
For with ful yvel wil° lyst hym to leve°
That loveth wel, yn swich cas, though hym greve°.

But natheles, men seyn° that at the laste,
For° ony thyng, men shal the sothe se.
And swych a cas bytidde°, and that as faste°,
That Troylus wel understod that she
Nas not so kynde as that hire oughte be.
And fynally, he wot° now out of doute
That al is lost that he hath ben aboute.

Stod on a day in his malencolye
This Troylus, and yn suspecioun
Of hire for whom he wende° for to dye,
And so bifel that thorughout Troye town,
As was the gyse°, yborn° was up and down
A manere cote-armure°, as seyth the storye,
Byforn Deiphebe yn signe of his victorye,

The whiche cote, as telleth Lollius,
Deiphebe it had yrent fro° Diomede
The same day. And whan this Troylus
It saugh, he gan to taken of it hede,
Avysyng of° the lengthe and of the brede°,
And al the werk; but as he gan byholde,
Ful sodeynly his herte gan to colde°,

1594 herteles, *disheartened,* **syke,** *sick* **1595 dele,** *meet* **1596 hele,** *well-being* **1597 ypleynted,** *covered with laments* **1598 Conseyved,** *understood,* **piete,** *pity* **1599 depeynted,** *stained* **1602 lest,** *on the chance* **1605 haste,** *impatience,* **ordenaunce,** *arrangement* **1608 thenketh me,** *it seems to me,* **plesaunce,** *pleasure* **1609 byseche,** *ask* **1610 for wykked speche,** *on account of gossip* **1611 wende,** *thought* **1612 han ystonde,** *have stood* **1613 with dissimulynge amende,** *correct by pretending* **1615 ye ne don but holden me in honde,** *you only deceive me* **1616 no fors,** *no matter,* **gesse,** *imagine* **1618 disjoynte,** *predicament* **1620 apoynte,** *specify* **1622 ay,** *always* **1623 dure,** *last* **1624 assure,** *be sure* **1625 on yvyl,** *wrongly* **1627 ther,** *where,* **wel lettres make,** *write clearly* **1628 endite,** *compose* **1629 gret effect,** *important substance,* **place lite,** *small space* **1630 space,** *length* **1631 la vostre C,** *your Criseyde* **1633 sighte,** *sighed* **1634 kalendes,** *beginning* **1635 trowen,** *believe* **1636 that,** *what,* **highte,** *promised* **1637 ful yvel wil,** *very reluctantly,* **lyst hym to leve,** *is he willing to believe* **1638 hym greve,** *it distresses him* **1639 seyn,** *say* **1640 For,** *despite* **1641 cas bytidde,** *situation occurred,* **faste,** *clearly* **1644 wot,** *knows* **1648 wende,** *thought* **1650 gyse,** *custom,* **yborn,** *carried* **1651 manere cote-armure,** *a kind of tunic emblazoned with a coat of arms* **1654 yrent fro,** *torn from* **1657 Avysyng of,** *studying,* **brede,** *breadth* **1659 gan to colde,** *grew cold*

1607 nys, Cl reads "nys not." **1631a** Omitted in Cl and Cp. **1634 kalendes,** literally, the first day of a month. **1643 kynde,** Cl reads "trewe." **1645 ben,** Cl reads "gon." **1653 Lollius,** see 1.394n.

As he that on the coler° fond withinne
A broch° that he Criseyde yaf° that morwe
That she from Troye moste nedes twynne°,
In remembraunce of hym and of his sorwe,
And she hym leyde ayen° hire feyth to borwe°
To kepe it ay! But now ful wel he wiste°
Hys lady nas no lengere on to tryste°.

He goth hym hom and gan ful soone sende
For Pandarus, and al this newe chaunce,
And of this broche, he told hym word and ende°,
Compleynynge of hire hertes variaunce,
His longe love, his trouthe, and his penaunce°;
And after deth°, withouten wordes more,
Ful faste he cride, his reste hym to restore.

Thanne spak he thus, "O lady myn Criseyde,
Wher is youre feyth°, and where is youre byheste°?
Where is youre love? Where is youre trouthe?" he seyde.
"Of Diomede have ye now al this feste°?
Allas, I wolde have trowed° atte leste
That syn ye nolde° in trouthe to me stonde,
That ye thus nolde han holden me in honde°.

"Who shal now trowe° on any othes° mo?
Allas, I nevere wolde han wend° er this
That ye, Criseyde, koude han chaunged so;
Ne, but I hadde agilt° or don amys,
So cruwel wende I not youre herte, ywys°,
To sle me thus! Allas, youre name of trouthe
Is now fordon°, and that is al my routhe°.

"Was there noon other broche yow lyste lete°
To feffe° with youre newe love," quod he,
"But thilke° broch that I, with terys wete°,
Yow yaf° as for a remembraunce of me?
Non other cause, allas, ne hadde ye
But for despit°, and ek for that ye mente
Al outrely° to shewe youre entente.

"Thorugh which I se that clene° out of youre mynde
Ye han me cast; and I ne kan nor may,
For al this world, withinne myn herte fynde
To unloven° yow a quarter of a day.
In cursed tyme I born was, weylaway,
That ye that do me° al this wo endure
Yet love I best of any creature!

"Now God," quod he, "me sende yet the grace
That I may meten with this Diomede.
And trewely, yf I have myght and space,
Yet shal I make, I hope, his sides blede.
O God," quod he, "that oughtest taken hede°
To fortheren trouthe° and wronges to punyce°,
Whi nyltow don a vengeaunce on this vice?

"O Pandarus, that in dremes for to triste°
Me blamed hast, and wont art° ofte upbreyde°,
Now maystow se thiself yf that thow lyste°
How trewe is now thi nece, bryght Cryseyde!
In sondry° formes, God it wot," he seyde,
"The goddes shewen° bothe joye and tene°
In slep, and by my drem it is now sene

"And certeynly, withoute more speche,
From hennesforth°, as ferforth° as I may,
Myn owene deth in armes wol I seche°.
I recche° nat how soone be the day.
But trewely, Criseyde, swete may°,
Whom I have ay with al my myght iserved,
That ye thus don, I have it nought deserved."

1660 coler, *collar* **1661 broch,** *brooch,* **yaf,** *gave* **1662 moste nedes twynne,** *must depart* **1664 leyde ayen,** *gave in return,* **to borwe,** *as pledge* **1665 wiste,** *knew* **1666 on to tryste,** *to be trusted* **1669 word and ende,** *start to finish* **1671 penaunce,** *suffering* **1672 after deth,** *for death* **1675 feyth,** *faithfulness,* **byheste,** *promise* **1677 feste,** *respect* **1678 trowed,** *believed* **1679 nolde,** *would not* **1680 han holden me in honde,** *misled me* **1681 trowe,** *believe,* **othes,** *oaths* **1682 wend,** *thought* **1684 agilt,** *offended* **1685 ywys,** *surely* **1687 fordon,** *destroyed,* **routhe,** *pity* **1688 yow lyste lete,** (that) *it pleased you to give up* **1689 feffe,** *endow* **1690 thilke,** *that,* **wete,** *wet* **1691 Yow yaf,** *gave you* **1693 despit,** *scorn* **1694 Al outrely,** *very clearly* **1695 clene,** *completely* **1698 unloven,** *stop loving* **1700 do me,** *make me* **1706 taken hede,** *to take care* **1707 fortheren trouthe,** *advance faithfulness,* **punyce,** *punish* **1708 nyltow don,** *won't you make* **1709 triste,** *trust* **1710 wont art,** *are accustomed,* **upbreyde,** *to blame* **1711 lyste,** *wish* **1713 sondry,** *various* **1714 shewen,** *reveal,* **tene,** *sorrow* **1717 hennesforth,** *now on,* **ferforth,** *far* **1718 seche,** *seek* **1719 recche,** *care* **1720 may,** *maid*

1660–61 coler . . . broch . . . yaf that morwe, in *Filostrato* 8.9–10, the brooch is used as a clasp instead of being hidden (as it is here), and is recognized by Troiolo as the one he had given Criseida on their last night together rather than at their departure. Chaucer's Criseyde gives the brooch to Diomede at 5.1040–41. **1681 othes,** Cl reads "other." **1700 Yet love I best . . . ,** at this juncture in in *Filostrato* (8.18), Troiolo calls down curses on Criseida, and then we are told that he loves her no more (8.28).

This Pandarus, that alle these thynges herde,
And wist° wel he seyde a soth° of this,
He nought a word ayen° to hym answerde,
For sory of his frendes sorwe he is,
And shamed for° his nece hath don amys,
And stant astoned° of these causes tweye
As stille as ston—a word ne koude he seye.

But at the laste thus he spak and seyde,
"My dere brother, I may the do° no more.
What shulde I seyen? I hate, ywys°, Criseyde,
And God wot I wol hate hire everemore.
And that° thow me bysoughtest don° of yore,
Havynge unto myn honour ne my reste
Right no reward°, I dede al that the leste°.

"If I dede ought that myghte lyken the°,
It is me lef°; and of this treson now,
God wot° that it a sorwe is unto me.
And dredles°, for hertes ese of yow,
Right fayn° wolde I amende° it, wist I° how.
And fro this world almyghti God I preye
Delyvere hire soon—I kan no more seye."

Gret was the sorwe and pleynte° of Troylus,
But forth hire cours Fortune ay gan to holde°:
Criseyde loveth the sone of Tydeus,
And Troylus mot wepe in cares colde.
Swich is this world, whoso it kan biholde°.
In ech estat is litel hertes reste.
God leve° us for to take it for the beste!

In many cruwel batayle out of drede°
Of Troylus, this ilke° noble knyght,
As men may in these olde bokes rede,
Was sen° his knyghthod and his grete myght.
And dredles°, his yre°, day and nyght,
Ful cruwely the Grekes ay aboughte°,
And alwey most this Diomede he soughte.

And ofte tyme I fynde that they mette
With blody strokes and with wordes grete,
Assayings° how hire speres weren whette°,
And God it wot, with many a cruwel hete°
Gan Troylus upon his helm to bete.
But natheles, Fortune it nought ne wolde°
Of others° hond that eyther deyen sholde.

And yf I hadde ytaken° for to writen
The armes° of this ilke° worthi man,
Than wolde ich of his batayles enditen°,
But for that I to writen first bygan
Of his love, I have seyd as I kan—
His worthi dedes, whoso list° hem here,
Red° Dares, he kan telle hem alle yfere°—

Bysechyng° every lady bryght of hewe
And every gentil womman, what° she be,
That al be° that Criseyde was untrewe,
That for that gylt she be nat wroth° with me—
Ye may hire gilte in other bokes se;
And gladlyer I wol write, yf yow leste°,
Penelopees trouthe and goode Alceste.

Ne I sey not this alonly for these men,
But most for wommen that bytraysed be°
Thorugh false folk—God yeve° hem sorwe,
amen!—
That with hire grete wit and subtilte
Bytrayse yow. And this commeveth° me
To speke, and yn effect yow alle I preye,
Beth war° of men, and herkneth what I seye.

1724 wist, *knew,* **soth,** *truth* **1725 ayen,** *in response* **1727 for,** *because* **1728 stant astoned,** *stands stunned* **1731 the do,** *do for you* **1732 ywys,** *truly* **1734 that,** *what,* **me bysoughtest don,** *asked me to do* **1736 reward,** *regard,* **the leste,** *you wished* **1737 lyken the,** *please you* **1738 me lef,** *dear to me* **1739 wot,** *knows* **1740 dredles,** *doubtless* **1741 Right fayn,** *very gladly,* **amende,** *correct,* **wist I,** *if I knew* **1744 pleynte,** *lament* **1745 ay gan to holde,** *always held* **1748 biholde,** *perceive* **1750 leve,** *grant* **1751 drede,** *doubt* **1752 ilke,** *same* **1754 sen,** *seen* **1755 dredles,** *doubtless,* **yre,** *anger* **1756 ay aboughte,** *paid for thoroughly* **1760 Assayinge,** *testing,* **whette,** *sharpened* **1761 hete,** *passion* **1763 wolde,** *wish* **1764 others,** *the other's* **1765 ytaken,** *undertaken* **1766 armes,** *deeds of war,* **ilke,** *same* **1767 enditen,** *write down* **1770 whoso list,** *whoever wishes* **1771 Red,** *read,* **yfere,** *together* **1772 Bysechyng,** *requesting* **1773 what,** *whoever* **1774 al be,** *even though* **1775 wroth,** *angry* **1777 leste,** *wish* **1779 alonly,** *only* **1780 bytraysed be,** *are betrayed* **1781 yeve,** *give* **1783 commeveth,** *motivates* **1785 Beth war,** *beware*

1732–33 I hate . . . / wol hate hire everemore, in *Filostrato* 8.24, Pandaro prays that God punish Criseida for her treason, but he expresses no hatred of her. **1766** Recalls the opening line of Virgil's *Aeneid*: "Arma virumque cano . . . " ("I will sing of the arms and the man"); compare *HF* 143–44. **1771 Dares,** Dares Phrygius, *De excidio Troiae historia* (*The History of the Fall of Troy*), although it is likely that Chaucer here refers to the *Frigii Daretis Ylias* (*The Iliad of Dares the Phrygian*) by Joseph of Exeter. From this point forward, Chaucer adds his own conclusion, although some details come from Boccaccio's *Il Teseida* as well as his *Filostrato*. **1777–78, I wol write . . . Penelopees trouthe . . . Alceste,** Penelope's loyalty to Ulysses is commonplace; Alceste is a figure of idealized wifehood and a major character in the Prologue to *LGW*, Chaucer's next major work. See 1528n above.

Go litel bok, go litel myn tragedye,
Ther God° thi makere° yet, er that he dye,
So sende myght to make yn° som comedye.
But litel bok, no makyng thow n'envye°,
But subgit° be to alle poesye,
And kys° the steppes° where as thow seest pace°
Virgile, Ovyde, Omer, Lukan, and Stace.

And for° ther is so gret dyversite
In Englyssh and yn wrytyng of oure tonge,
So prey I God that noon myswryte the°,
Ne the mysmetre° for defaute° of tonge.
And red wherso thow be°, or elles songe°,
That thow be understonde°, God I beseche—
But yet to purpos° of my rathere° speche:

The wraththe°, as I bigan yow for to seye,
Of Troylus the Grekes boughten dere°,
For thousandys his hondes maden° deye,
As he that was withouten any pere°
Save Ector, yn his tyme, as I kan here.
But weylawey, save only° Goddes wille,
Despitously° hym slowh the fiers Achille.

And whan that he was slayn yn this manere,
His lighte gost° ful blysfully is went°
Up to the holughnesse° of the eighte spere°,
In convers lettynge° everich° element;
And ther he saugh with ful avysement°
The erratyk sterres°, herkenynge armonye°
With sownes° ful of hevenyssh melodye.

And doun from thennes° faste° he gan avyse°
This litel spot of erthe, that with the se°
Enbraced is, and fully gan despise
This wrecched world, and held° al vanite
To respect of° the pleyn felicite°
That is yn hevene above; and at the laste,
Ther° he was slayn his lokyng down he caste.

And yn hymself he lough° right at the wo
Of hem that wepten for his deth so faste°,
And dampned° al oure werk that foloweth so
The blynde lust°, the which that may not laste,
And shulden al oure herte on heven caste.
And forth he wente, shortly for to telle,
Ther as° Mercurye sorted° hym to dwelle.

Swich fyn° hath, lo, this Troylus for love;
Swych fyn hath al his grete worthynesse;
Swich fyn hath his estat real° above;
Swich fyn his lust°, swich fyn hath his noblesse°;
Swych fyn hath false worldes brotelnesse°!
And thus bigan his lovyng of Criseyde,
As I have told, and yn this wyse he deyde°.

1787 Ther God, *may God,* **thi makere,** *your author* (Chaucer) **1788 make yn,** *compose* **1789 no makyng thow n'envie,** *don't envy any writing* **1790 subgit,** *servant* **1791 kys,** *kiss,* **steppes,** *footprints,* **pace,** *walk* **1793 for,** *because* **1795 myswryte the,** *miscopy you* **1796 the mysmetre,** *ruin your meter,* **for defaute,** *because of* (their) *defects* **1797 red wherso thow be,** *wherever you are read,* **songe,** *sung* **1798 understonde,** *understood* **1799 to purpos,** *to the point,* **rathere,** *earlier* **1800 wraththe,** *anger* **1801 boughten dere,** *paid for dearly* **1802 maden,** *caused* (to) **1803 pere,** *equal* **1805 save only,** *except that* (it was) **1806 Despitously,** *violently* **1808 lighte gost,** *weightless spirit,* **is went,** *has gone* **1809 holughnesse,** *hollowness,* **spere,** *sphere* **1810 In convers lettynge,** *leaving on the opposite side,* **everich,** *every* **1811 ful avysement,** *careful study* **1812 erratyk sterres,** *wandering stars,* **herkenynge armonye,** *listening to harmony* **1813 sownes,** *sounds* **1814 thennes,** *there,* **faste,** *intently,* **avyse,** *study* **1815 se,** *sea* **1816 held,** *thought* **1818 To respect of,** *in comparison with,* **pleyn felicite,** *pure happiness* **1820 Ther,** *to where* **1821 lough,** *laughed* **1822 faste,** *intensely* **1823 dampned,** *condemned* **1824 lust,** *desire* **1827 Ther as,** *where,* **sorted,** *assigned* **1828 Swich fyn,** *such* (an) *end* **1830 estat real,** *royal status* **1831 lust,** *desire,* **noblesse,** *nobility* **1832 brotelnesse,** *insecurity* **1834 deyde,** *died*

1786–88 tragedye . . . comedye, in medieval understanding, the opposition between tragedy and comedy was often a matter of a protagonist's fall from joy to sorrow or vice versa. **1786 Go litel bok . . . ,** a formula for bringing a narrative poem to conclusion. **1791 where,** Cl reads "there." **pace,** Cp reads "space" (measure by walking). **1792 Virgile . . . ,** Virgil, Ovid, Homer, Lucan, and Statius were the most highly respected authors of classical narrative poetry. Chaucer's list seems to have been inspired by a similar one in the envoy of Boccaccio's *Filocolo* 2.376–78. **1793–96** Chaucer's concern with accurate copying extends from the dialectical variety in written English at the time; scribes used their own dialects when copying, introducing variation in wording and rhythm. See Chaucer's poem to Adam Pinkhurst, *Adam.* **1807–27** Written in imitation of the death of Arcita in Boccaccio's *Teseida* 11.1–3, deriving from the classical tradition of noble souls ascending through the Ptolemaic universe. The lines are omitted in two manuscripts of *TC* and added into a third one. **1809 holughnesse of the eighte spere,** the concavity of the eighth sphere. Cp and Cl read "seventhe" instead of "eighth," although Boccaccio's *Teiseda* 11.1 has "ottava" (eighth). Either is complicated by uncertainty about numbering the spheres outward from the Earth (to the fixed stars, indicating constancy?) or inward toward the Earth (to the moon, indicating inconstancy?). The confusion extends into the next line (line 1810), where "lettynge everich element" can mean leaving behind "each of the planets" (hence rising to the fixed stars) or leaving behind "each of the four elements" (hence rising to the moon). **1812 erratyk stars,** as opposed to the fixed stars. **armonye,** the harmony of the spheres; analogous to the eight tones on a musical scale, the movement of the celestial spheres was thought to produce a sublime, macrocosmic octave normally unheard by human ears. **1816–17 despise / This wrecched world,** a clear instance of *contemptus mundi,* disdain for the Earth as insignificant, a commonplace of the Ptolemaic cosmology. **1818 pleyn felicite,** see 3.1690n. **1827 Mercurye,** see 5.321. It is left unclear where the soul of Troylus resides finally.

O yonge, fresshe folkes, he or she,
In which that love up groweth with youre age,
Repeyreth hom° fro worldly vanyte,
And of youre herte up casteth the visag°
To thilke° God that after his ymage
Yow made; and thynketh al nys but a fayre°
This world that passeth soone as floures fayre°.

And loveth hym, the which° that right for love
Upon a cros, oure soules for to beye°,
First starf°, and ros, and sit° yn hevene above;
For he nyl falsen° no wight, dar I seye,
That wole his herte al holly° on hym leye°.
And syn° he best to love is, and most meke,
What nedeth feyned° loves for to seke?

Lo here° of payens° corsed° olde rytes;
Lo here what alle hire goddes may avayle°;
Lo here these wrecched worldes appetites;
Lo here the fyn° and guerdon° for travayle°
Of Jove, Appollo, of Mars, of swich rascayle°!
Lo here the forme° of olde clerkes speche
In poetrie, if ye hire bokes seche°.

O moral Gower, this bok I directe
To the, and to the, philosophical Strode,
To vouchen sauf° ther° nede is to corecte
Of° youre benygnites° and zeles° goode.
And to that sothefast° Crist, that starf° on rode°,
With al myn herte of mercy evere I preye,
And to the Lord right thus I speke and seye:

Thow oon and two and thre eterne on lyve°,
That regnest ay yn thre and two and oon,
Uncircumscript° and al mayst circumscryve°,
Us from visible and invysible foon°
Defende°, and to thy mercy everychon
So make us, Jesus, for thi mercy digne°,
For love of mayde° and moder thyn benigne°.
Amen.

Explicit liber Troili et Criseide.

1837 Repeyreth hom, *return home* **1838 of youre herte up casteth the visage,** *direct your heart's face* **1839 thilke,** *that* **1840 al nys,** *all is nothing,* **fayre,** *temporary diversion* **1841 floures fayre,** *pretty flowers* **1842 the which,** *who* **1843 beye,** *redeem* **1844 starf,** *died,* **sit,** *sits* **1845 nyl falsen,** *will not betray* **1846 holly,** *wholly,* **leye,** *commit* **1847 syn,** *because* **1848 feyned,** *pretended* **1849 Lo here,** *see here,* **payens,** *pagans',* **corsed,** *cursed* **1850 avayle,** *accomplish* **1852 fyn,** *end,* **guerdon,** *reward,* **travayle,** *effort* **1853 rascayle,** *a worthless mob* **1854 forme,** *essence* **1855 seche,** *seek* **1858 vouchen sauf,** *consent,* **ther,** *where* **1859 Of,** *according to,* **benygnites,** *goodness,* **zeles,** *zeal* **1860 sothefast,** *true,* **starf,** *died,* **rode,** *cross* **1863 eterne on lyve,** *alive eternally* **1865 Uncircumscript,** *limitless,* **al mayst circumscryve,** *able to contain everything* **1866 foon,** *foes* **1867 Defende,** *protect* **1868 digne,** *worthy* **1869 mayde,** *virgin,* **moder thyn benigne,** *your gracious mother*

1839–40 God that after his ymage / Yow made, Genesis 1.26–27 **1856–57 moral Gower . . . philosophical Strode,** John Gower, poet, and Ralph Strode, lawyer, were personal friends of Chaucer and important people in London. Strode may also have been an Oxford philosopher. The adjectives used here to describe the men call attention to two concerns of the entire poem: morality (actions of the will) and philosophy (actions of the intellect). **1857 and to the,** Cl reads "and the"; Cp, "and to." **1863 Thow oon and two and thre,** the Trinity: Father, Son, and Holy Spirit. **1865 Uncircumscript . . . circumscryve,** the root of each word—*script* and *scryve*—relates to the act of writing. Lines 1863–65 are modeled on Dante's *Paradiso* 14.28–30. **1869b Explicit liber Troili et Criseide,** "Here ends the book of Troylus and Criseyde." Cp reads "Explicit liber Troily."

Book of the Duchess

Book of the Duchess

Introduction

The *Book of the Duchess* is a poem of commemoration, but an indirect one. The narrator of the poem suffers from melancholic insomnia and seeks to find sleep by reading in bed the Ovidian story of Ceyx and Alcyone (in Chaucer, Seys and Alcione), a deeply sad account of a woman who dies from grief over the loss of her husband. The story provokes the sleep sought by the narrator, who then dreams that he awakens in a room ornately decorated with literary scenes. He departs on horseback (from his room?) to join a hart-hunting party, and when the hunters lose their quarry, the dreamer is led by an otherwise unexplained puppy to a lone grieving knight dressed in black. The dreamer questions the knight about his grief and learns that the knight has lost a game of chess while playing against Fortune, that his white "queen" has been taken from him, and that he has been checkmated. Much of the poem is taken up with idealized description of the lady, made possible by rather obtuse questions on the part of the dreamer and the knight's painful recollection of his lost love. Once the knight states bluntly that the lady has died, however, the plot returns abruptly to the hunt, which awakens the narrator, who then decides to record his dream as a poem.

The poem's shifts in venue are often explained (or explained away) as authentic dream psychology, but the juxtapositions created by the shifts are more powerful than is the illusion of the dream. The narrator's unnamed sorrow anticipates Alcyone's loss of her husband and the black knight's loss of his white lady; the hunting (and loss) of the hart (a deer) capitalizes on the medieval association of hunting with pursuing love; the dreamer's awakening into a room decorated with scenes from the *Roman de la Rose* and stories of Troy establishes the poem's two great concerns with love and loss. The predominant sentiment of the poem is admiration for the lady, intensified by the grief engendered by loss. The atmosphere is distinctly courtly—lavish decor, hunting, chess, elegant emotion, and the knight's conventional subordination to his lady. The dreamer's deference to the knight is part of this courtly atmosphere, and several puns on names ("White" / "Blanche" in French, "longe castel" / "Lancaster," etc.; see 948n and 1318–19n), enable us to recognize that lady of the poem represents Blanche, Duchess of Lancaster, and first wife of John of Gaunt. Indeed, later in his career, Chaucer refers to his poem as the *Deeth of Blaunche the Duchesse* (Prologue to the *Legend of Good Women* 418). Gaunt was a patron of Chaucer, granting him an annuity in 1374, so that, almost certainly, the knight of the poem represents Gaunt in some way. However, just as the depiction of Blanche is idealized through conventional language and imagery, so the black knight is more a stylized embodiment of grief than a portrait of Gaunt (see 455n). The knight and his lady are not married in the poem, and their relationship is more aesthetically conceived than realistically depicted.

The historical Blanche died of plague on September 12, 1368, clearly the earliest possible date of the poem. But it seems unlikely that Chaucer wrote it as a consolation or elegy immediately upon Blanche's death. As many critics observe, the poem offers no Christian consolation of the kind that might be expected: There is no mention of salvation or heavenly reward. Arguments to read the poem as a Christian allegory are not persuasive, even though some of the conventional praise of the lady shares language and imagery with biblical praise of beauty and goodness (see, e.g., 945–46n, 971–74n, 987, etc.). Occasional touches of humor (see, e.g., lines 178–91) and the obtuseness of the narrator make little sense if the poem is intended to console the shock of a recent death. The poem is better regarded as a kind of a commemorative verbal monument, a point argued by Phillipa Hardman, "The *Book of the Duchess* as Memorial Monument" (1994, no. 1424), and reinforced by Mary Carruthers, "'The Mystery of the Bed Chamber': Mnemotechnique and Vision in Chaucer's *The Book of the Duchess*" (2000, no. 1412). Perhaps the poem was composed for one of the annual commemorations of Blanche's death that we know to have been commissioned by Gaunt. One of the name-puns ("ryche hille" / "Richmond"; line 1319) seems to indicate that the poem was completed before 1372, when Gaunt lost claim to the title of Earl of Richmond. Whatever its precise date, the *Book of the Duchess* is Chaucer's earliest extant narrative poem.

Chaucer's models for the poem are found in the *dits amoureux* of contemporary French tradition—frame-narrative poems (often dream visions) in a courtly milieu, with embedded lyrics of love and lament. In particular, Jean Froissart's *Paradis d'Amours* (*Paradise of Love*) provided details for the opening and perhaps the closing of Chaucer's poem, while Guillaume de Machaut's works deeply influence the *Book of the Duchess.* His *Fonteinne Amoureuse* (*Fountain of Love*) inspired Chaucer's rendering of Ovid's story of Ceyx and Alcyone, although Chaucer also used Ovid's *Metamorphoses* directly and perhaps knew a moralized version from the *Ovide Moralisé.* Four lines of Machaut's brief *Lay de Confort* are translated in *Book of the Duchess* 693–96, and his *Remede de Fortune* influenced a number of Chaucer's details and provided the model for including his patron in his poem as a lover. In its numerous parallels of detail and device, Machaut's *Jugement du Roy de Behaigne* (*Judgment of the King of Bohemia*) is the most important single source for *Book of the Duchess.* In their edition of *Behaigne* and the *Remede* for the Chaucer Library (1988, no. 264), James I. Wimsatt and William W. Kibler tally 157 parallels between the *Behaigne* and the *Book of the Duchess*; 103 between *Remede* and Chaucer's poem.

Such lists only begin to indicate the complex nature of Chaucer's debts, as crossing lines of influence and the rich legacy of courtly verse complicate the relations among the poems. Some of the shared conventions are rooted in twelfth-century troubadour poetry, Machaut influenced Chaucer *through* Froissart at times, and the *Roman de la Rose* (cited by Chaucer at 334) inspired the French poets and Chaucer alike. One particular case is intriguing. In an essay entitled "Froissart's *Dit dou Bleu Chevalier*" (1992, no. 1415), Susan Crane argues that Froissart's knight in blue inspired Chaucer's knight in black, while in *Chaucer and His French Contemporaries* (1991, no. 314), James I. Wimsatt says the influence flows the other direction. Without certain dates, it is impossible to resolve the issue, although the poems have much in common. What is clear, as Ardis Butterfield argues in "Chaucer's French Inheritance" (2003, no. 281), is that Chaucer developed as a poet and produced the *Book of the Duchess* while being very much a *part* of the French tradition. In "Chaucer as a European Writer" (2007, no. 306), James Simpson presents Chaucer as a sideline participant in this tradition, but the difference is largely a matter of emphasis.

The octosyllabic couplets of the *Book of the Duchess* were also part of the legacy of French poetry, though long modified by Middle English tetrameter. Chaucer had yet to develop the decasyllabic / pentameter line used in his later poetry, but it does threaten to break into the *Book of the Duchess* at times (see, e.g., lines 11, 76, 87, 329–30). Some critics see immaturity or lack of skill in the verse and varied style of the poem, while others observe in it colloquial and psychological virtuosity. On the stylistic virtuosity of the poem, see Charles W. Owen, "Chaucer: Beginnings" (2000, no. 1429), and Winthrop Wetherbee, "Theme, Prosody, and Mimesis in the *Book of the Duchess*" (2001, no. 1450). A number of critics see the narrator of *Book of the Duchess* as a prototype of Chaucer's later narrators, and many regard the poem as the beginning of Chaucer's career-long concern with language, epistemology, and the poet's anxious concern about meaning. In this vein, see Kathryn L. Lynch, *Chaucer's Philosophical Visions* (2000, no. 1399).

Other critical concerns include feminist questions about the representation (or obliteration) of Blanche. Her very absence enables male discourse in the reading of Elaine Hansen, *Chaucer and the Fictions of Gender* (1992, no. 474), while the elegiac qualities of the poem and Blanche's "whiteness" are kinds of annihilation in Maud Ellman's study, "Blanche" (1984, no. 1421). A. J. Minnis acknowledges the power of these (and other) feminist readings in his Oxford Guide to Chaucer, *The Shorter Poems* (1995, no. 1400), but he goes on to challenge the gender binaries that underlie them. Minnis's Guide is the most comprehensive reading of the poem available, although two psychoanalytic readings may be mentioned: Peter W. Travis's, "White" (2000, no. 1447) and L. O. Aranye Frandenburg's chapter in her *Sacrifice Your Love: Psychoanalysis, Historicism, Chaucer* (2002, no. 440). In *Chaucer's Queer Poetics* (2006, no. 1402), Susan Schibanoff reads the narrator of the *Book of the Duchess* as a queer poet, Chaucer's means to deflect moral censure from John of Gaunt.

Book of the Duchess

I have gret wonder, be° this lyghte,
How that I lyve, for day ne nyghte
I may° nat slepe wel nygh noght°.
I have so many an ydel thoght
Purely for defaute° of slepe
That, by my trouthe°, I take no kepe°
Of nothing, how hyt cometh or gooth,
Ne me nys nothyng leve° nor looth°.
Al is ylyche° good to me,
Joy or sorowe, wherso hyt be°,
For I have felynge in nothynge,
But as yt were a mased° thynge,
Alway in poynt to falle° adoun;
For sorwful ymagynacioun°
Ys alway hooly° in my mynde.
And wel ye woot°, agaynes kynde°
Hyt were to lyven in thys wyse°,
For nature wolde° nat suffyse
To noon erthly creature
Nat longe tyme to endure
Withoute slepe and be in sorwe.
And I ne may°, ne° nyght ne morwe°,
Slepe; and thus melancolye
And drede I have for to dye°.
Defaute° of slepe and hevynesse°
Hath sleyn° my spirit of quyknesse°
That I have lost al lustyhede°.
Suche fantasies ben° in myn hede
So I not° what is best to doo.
But men° myght axe° me why soo
I may not sleepe, and what me is.
But natheles, who° aske this
Leseth° his asking trewely.
Myselven can not telle why
The sothe°; but trewly, as I gesse,
I hold hit be° a sicknesse
That I have suffred this eight yeere—
And yet my boote° is never the nere°,
For there is phisicien but oon°
That may me hele. But that is don;
Passe we over untill efte°.
That° wil not be mot need° be lefte.
Our first mater is good to kepe.
 So when I saw I might not slepe
Til now late° this other night,
Upon my bedde I sat upright
And bad oon reche° me a booke,
A romaunce, and he it me toke°,
To rede and drive the night away,
For me thought° it beter play
Then play either at chesse or tables°.
And in this boke were written fables
That clerkes° had in olde tyme,
And other poets, put in rime

---

1 be, *by* **3 may,** *can,* **wel nygh noght,** *nearly not at all* **5 defaute,** *lack* **6 trouthe,** *pledge,* **take no kepe,** *do not care* **8 Ne me nys nothyng leve,** *nor is anything to me dear,* **looth,** *loathsome* **9 ylyche,** *alike* **10 wherso hyt be,** *wherever it may be* **12 mased,** *dazed* **13 in poynt to falle,** *at the point of falling* **14 ymagynacioun,** *mental images* **15 hooly,** *wholly* **16 woot,** *know,* **kynde,** *nature* **17 thys wyse,** *this way* **18 wolde,** *will* **22 ne may,** *may not,* **ne,** *neither,* **ne morwe,** *nor morning* **24 for to dye,** i.e., *so that I may die* **25 Defaute,** *lack,* **hevynesse,** *sorrow* **26 sleyn,** *slain,* **quyknesse,** *liveliness* **27 lustyhede,** *vigorousness* **28 ben,** *are* **29 not,** *don't know* **30 men,** *someone,* **axe,** *ask* **32 who,** *whoever* **33 Leseth,** *wastes* **35 sothe,** *truth* **36 hold hit be,** *consider it to be* **38 boote,** *cure,* **nere,** *nearer* **39 but oon,** *only one* **41 efte,** *another time* **42 That,** *that which,* **mot nede,** *must necessarily* **45 Til now late,** *until recently* **47 bad oon reche,** *asked a person to get* **48 it me toke,** *brought it to me* **50 me thought,** *I thought* **51 tables,** *backgammon* **53 clerkes,** *scholars*

Text based on Bodleian Library, Oxford, MS Fairfax 16 (F), corrected with selected variants from Thynne's edition of 1532 (Th). Th is also the base text for 31–96, lacking in F and the two other surviving manuscripts. **1–8** Modeled on Jean Froissart's *Paradis d'Amours,* 1–9. **5 defaute,** spelled "defaulte" throughout F. **23 thus,** F and the other witnesses read "this." **melancolye,** in medieval physiology and psychology, a condition caused by an excess of black bile. It is associated with dreams of black things in *NPT* 7.2933–36. Here it helps to rationalize the upcoming dream of the Man in Black; see 445. In *KnT* 1.1373–75, it is associated with lovesickness. **26 sleyn,** omitted in F. **31–96** Lines found first in Thynne's edition of 1532; copied into F in the seventeenth century; see also the notes to 288, 480, and 886. **36–37 sicknesse . . . eight yeere,** this is often claimed to be love sickness as referred to in Froissart (*Paradis d'Amours* 7–12) and other French poets, but Chaucer leaves it unspecified. Critics have pointed out the possible echo of Machaut, *Le Jugement du Roy de Behaigne,* 125, where the period of love sickness is seven or eight years, but other critics have suggested that the length of time is autobiographical. **39 phisicien,** left ambiguous by Chaucer, this may be a physical, emotional, or even a spiritual physician—maybe all of them. Inconclusively identified by critics as a personification of sleep, a patron of Chaucer, God, and other possibilities. **48 romaunce,** the term often refers to a book in French (or other vernacular) rather than Latin, perhaps a tale of love and adventure. Chaucer seems to have invented the narrative device of preceding a dream with the reading of a book. **52–55 in this boke . . . be in minde,** on books as aids to memory, compare *LGW* 17–18, 25–26, and *CT* 7.1974.

To rede and for to be° in minde,
While° men loved the lawe of kinde°.
This boke ne spak but of such thinges,
Of quenes lives and of kinges,
And many other thinges smale.
Amonge al this I fond a tale
That me thoughte a wonder° thing.
  This was the tale: There was a king
That hight° Seyes, and had a wife,
The beste that mighte bere lyfe,
And this quene hight Alcyone.
So it befil thereafter soone
This king wol wenden° over see°.
To tellen shortly, whan that he
Was in° the see, thus in this wise,
Suche a tempest gan to rise°
That brak her° maste and made it fal,
And clefte° her ship and dreinte° hem al,
That never was founde, as it telles,
Bord ne man ne nothing elles.
Right thus this king Seyes loste his life.
  Now for to speke of Alcyone his wife:
This lady that was left at home,
Hath wonder that the king ne come
Hom, for it was a longe terme°.
Anone° her herte began to erme°;
And for that her thoughte° evermo
It was not wele—her thoghte so—
She longed so after the king
That certes° it were a pitous thing
To tell her hertely° sorowfull life
That she had, this noble wife,
For him, alas, she loved alderbeste°.
Anon she sent bothe eeste and weste
To seke him, but they founde nought.
"Alas!" quoth° shee, "that I was wrought°!
And where° my lord, my love, be deed?
Certes, I nil never° eate breed—
I make avowe to my god here—
But I mowe° of my lord here°."
Such sorowe this lady to her took
That trewly I, which made this book,
Had such pittee and such rowthe°
To rede° hir sorwe, that by my trowthe
I ferde° the worse al the morwe°
Aftir, to thenken on hir sorwe.
  So whan this lady koude here° noo word
That no man myghte fynde hir lord,
Ful ofte she swouned° and sayed "Alas."
For sorwe ful nygh wood° she was,
Ne she koude° no rede° but oon,
But doun on knees she sat anoon
And wepte that pittee was to here.
  "A, mercy, swete lady dere,"
Quod she to Juno, hir goddesse,
"Helpe me out of thys distresse,
And yeve° me grace my lord to se
Soone, or wete° wher so he be,
Or how he fareth, or in what wise°,
And I shal make yow sacrifise,
And hooly° youres become I shal
With good wille, body, herte, and al.
And but° thow wilt° this, lady swete,
Send me grace to slepe, and mete°
In my slepe som certeyn sweven°
Wherthorgh that° I may knowe even°
Whether my lord be quyke° or ded."
With that word she henge doun the hed°
And felle aswowne° as colde as ston.
Hyr women kaught hir up anoon°,
And broghten hir in bed al naked,
And she, forweped° and forwaked°,
Was wery, and thus the dede slepe
Fil on hir or° she tooke kepe°,

55 for to be, *in order to* **56 While,** *as long as,* **the lawe of kinde,** *natural law* **61 wonder,** *marvelous* **63 hight,** *was named* **67 wol wenden,** *wished to travel,* **see,** *the sea* **69 in,** *on* **70 gan to rise,** *did rise* **71 her,** *their* **72 clefte,** *split,* **dreinte,** *drowned* **79 terme,** *time* **80 Anone,** *soon,* **erme,** *grieve* **81 for that her thoughte,** *because she thought* **84 certes,** *surely* **85 hertely,** *deeply* **87 alderbeste,** *best of all* **90 quoth,** *said,* **wrought,** *created* **91 where,** *whether* (i.e., is it true that?) **92 nil never,** *will never* **94 But I mowe,** *unless I may,* **here,** *hear* **97 rowthe,** *compassion* **98 rede,** *read of* **99 ferde,** *felt,* **morwe,** *morning* **101 koude here,** *could hear* **103 swouned,** *fainted* **104 ful nygh wood,** *very nearly crazed* **105 koude,** *knew,* **rede,** *course of action* **111 yeve,** *give* **112 wete,** *to know* **113 wise,** *manner* **115 hooly,** *wholly* **117 but,** *unless,* **wilt,** *will (do)* **118 mete,** *to dream* **119 certeyn sweven,** *true dream* **120 Wherthorgh that,** *through which,* **even,** *exactly* **121 quyke,** *alive* **122 the hed,** *her head* **123 aswowne,** *in a faint* **124 anoon,** *immediately* **126 forweped,** *worn out through weeping,* **forwaked,** *worn out through lack of sleep* **128 or,** *before,* **tooke kepe,** *was aware*

56 of, F reads "in." **63–214 Seyes . . . ,** the story of Ceyx and Alcyone is found in Ovid, *Metamorphoses* 11.410ff. and in Guillaume de Machaut, *Dit de la Fonteinne Amoureuse,* 543–698; Chaucer drew upon both as sources. **80 erme,** following Thynne (see 31–96n), F has "yerne" (yearn), which does not quite rhyme. **92 nil,** F reads "will." **100 Aftir,** F reads "And aftir." **109 to,** omitted in F. **Juno,** queen of the gods in Roman mythology and patron of marriage. **123 as colde,** F reads "and colde."

Throgh Juno, that had herd hir bone°,
That made hir to slepe sone.
For as° she prayede, ryght so was done
In dede, for Juno ryght anone°
Called thus hir messagere
To doo hir erande, and he come nere°.
Whan he was come, she bad° hym thus:
"Go bet,°" quod Juno, "to Morpheus—
Thou knowest hym wel, the god of slepe;
Now understond wel and tak kepe°—
Sey thus on my halfe°, that he
Go faste into the Grete Se,
And byd° hym that on alle thyng°
He take up Seyes body°, the kyng
That lyeth ful pale and nothyng rody°.
Bid hym crepe into the body
And doo hit goon° to Alcione
The quene, ther° she lyeth allone,
And shewe hir shortly, hit ys no nay°,
How hit was dreynt° thys other day;
And do° the body speke ryght soo,
Ryght as hyt was woned° to doo
The whiles° that hit was alyve.
Goo now faste, and hye the blyve.°"
This messager tok leve and went
Upon hys wey, and never ne stent°
Til he com to the derke valey
That stant° betwexe roches twey°
Ther° never yet grew corn° ne gras,
Ne tre, ne noght that oughte° was,
Beste°, ne man, ne noght elles,
Save ther were a fewe welles°
Came rennynge fro the clyffes adoun,
That made a dedely slepynge soun,
And ronnen doun ryght by a cave
That was under a rokke ygrave°
Amydde the valey, wonder° depe.
There these goddes lay and slepe,
Morpheus and Eclympasteyre,
That° was the god of slepes heyre°,
That slepe and did noon other werk.
This cave was also as derk
As helle pitte overall° aboute.
They had good leyser° for to route°,
To envye° who myght slepe beste.
Somme henge her chyn° upon hir breste
And slept upright°, hir hed yhedde°,
And somme lay naked in her bedde
And slepe whiles the dayes laste.
This messager come fleynge° faste
And cried, "O how, awake anoon!"
Hit was for noght; there herde hym non.
"Awake!" quod he. "Whoo ys lyth° there?"
And blew his horn ryght in here eere°,
And cried "Awaketh" wonder hye°.
This god of slep with hys oon eye
Caste° up and axed, "Who clepeth° there?"
"Hyt am I," quod this messager.
"Juno bad° thow shuldest goon"—
And tolde hym what he shulde doon,
As I have told yow here-to-fore°—
Hyt ys no nede reherse° hyt more—
And went hys wey, whan he had sayde.
Anoon this god of slepe abrayede°
Out of hys slepe, and gan to goon,
And dyd as he had bede° hym doon:
Tooke up the dreynt body sone
And bar hyt forth to Alcione,
Hys wif the quene, ther as she lay
Ryght even° a quarter° before day,
And stood ryght at hyr beddes fete°,
And called hir ryght° as she hete°

129 bone, *request* (boon) **131 as,** *just as* **132 ryght anone,** *immediately* **134 come nere,** *came near* **135 bad,** *commanded* **136 Go bet,** *go quickly* **138 tak kepe,** *take care* **139 halfe,** *behalf* **141 byd,** *command,* **on alle thyng,** *without fail* **142 Seyes body,** *the body of Ceyx* **143 nothyng rody,** *not at all ruddy* **145 doo hit goon,** *make it go* **146 ther,** *where* **147 hit ys no nay,** *it cannot be denied* **148 dreynt,** *drowned* **149 do,** *make* **150 woned,** *accustomed* **151 whiles,** *time* **152 hye the blyve,** *hurry yourself quickly* **154 stent,** *stopped* **156 stant,** *stands,* **roches twey,** *two rocks* **157 Ther,** *where,* **corn,** *grain* **158 oughte,** *worth anything* **159 Beste,** *beast* **160 welles,** *springs* **164 ygrave,** *carved out* **165 wonder,** *wondrously* **168 That,** *who,* **slepes heyre,** *sleep's heir* **171 overal,** *everywhere* **172 leyser,** *opportunity,* **route,** *snore* **173 envye,** *compete* **174 her chyn,** *their chins* **175 upryght,** *face up,* **yhedde,** *hidden* **178 fleynge,** *flying* **181 ys lyth,** *is it who lies* **182 here eere,** *their ears* **183 wonder hye,** *very loudly* **185 Caste,** *looked,* **clepeth,** *calls* **187 bad,** *ordered* **189 here-to-fore,** *before this* **190 reherse,** *repeat* **192 abrayede,** *rose up quickly* **194 bede,** *bid* **198 even,** *exactly,* **a quarter,** *three hours* **199 fete,** *feet* **200 ryght,** *just,* **hete,** *was called*

136 Morpheus, god of sleep and dreams. **140 Grete Se,** Mediterranean Sea. **142 He take,** F reads "That he take." **145 Alcione,** the manuscripts spell the name "Alchione," following Machaut's French rather than Ovid's Latin; see 63–214n above. **166 a and slepe,** Th reads "aslepe." **167 Eclympasteyre,** son of Morpheus, invented by Froissart, *Paradys d'Amour* 28; see 1–8n above. In Ovid, *Metamorphoses,* 11.634ff., Morpheus is himself one of the many sons of Somnus, god of sleep. **168 heyre,** F spells "eyre." **178–91** This scene of awakening has recurrent touches of humor—Morpheus's sluggishness, the messenger's aggressiveness, etc. **179 O how,** an exclamation to awaken and gain attention; see *MED* "hou" (interj. (1)). **182 eere,** F reads "heere." **184 eye,** F spells "ye." **195 dreynt,** Th reads "deed." **199 hyr,** F reads "hys."

By name, and sayede, "My swete wyfe,
Awake, let be your sorwful lyfe,
For in your sorwe there lyth no rede°,
For certes°, swete, I am but dede—
Ye shul me never on lyve yse°.
But good swete herte, that° ye
Bury my body, for suche a tyde°
Ye mowe hyt fynde° the see besyde.
And farewel, swete, my worldes blysse.
I pray God youre sorwe lyses°.
To° lytel while oure blysse lasteth!"
With that hir eyen up she casteth
And sawe noght°. "Allas," quod she for sorwe,
And deyde within the thridde morwe°.
But what she sayede more in that swow°
I may not telle yow as now—
Hyt were to longe for to dwelle.
My first matere I wil yow telle,
Wherfore° I have tolde this thynge
Of Alcione and Seys the kynge.
For thus moche° dar I say welle°,
I had be dolven° everydelle°,
And ded, ryght thorgh defaute° of slepe,
Yif I ne had redde° and take kepe°
Of this tale next before°.
And I wol telle yow wherefore°.
For I ne myght for bote ne bale°
Slepe or° I had redde thys tale
Of this dreynte° Seyes the kynge,
And of the goddes of slepynge.
  When I had redde thys tale wel
And overloked° hyt everydel°,
Me thoght wonder° yf hit were so.
For I had never herde speke or tho°
Of noo goddes that koude make
Men to slepe ne for to wake,
For I ne knew never god but oon.
And in my game° I sayede anoon—
And yet me lyst ryght evel° to pley—
"Rather then that y shulde dey°
Thorgh defaute of slepynge thus,
I wolde yive° thilke° Morpheus,
Or hys goddesse, dame Juno,
Or some wight elles°, I ne roghte° who,
To make me slepe and have som reste—
I wil yive hym the alderbeste°
Yifte° that ever he abode hys lyve°,
And here on warde°, ryght now as blyve°,
Yif° he wol make me slepe a lyte°,
Of down of pure dowves white
I wil yif hym a fether-bedde,
Rayed° with gold and ryght wel cledde°
In fyn° blak satyn doutremere°,
And many a pelowe, and every bere°
Of clothe of Reynes, to slepe softe—
Hym thar not nede° to turnen ofte.
And I wol yive hym al that falles°
To a chambre, and al hys halles
I wol do peynte° with pure gold
And tapite hem° ful many-fold
Of oo sute°. This shal he have—
Yf I wiste° where were hys cave—
Yf he kan make me slepe sone,
As did the goddesse quene Alcione.
And thus this ylke° god Morpheus
May wynne of me moo° fees thus
Than ever he wan; and to Juno,
That ys hys goddesse, I shal soo do
I trow° that she shal holde hir payede.°"
  I hadde unneth° that word ysayede°,

203 lyth no rede, *lies no solution* **204 certes,** *certainly* **205 on lyve yse,** *see alive* **206 that,** *be sure that* **207 for suche a tyde,** *at such time that* **208 mowe hyt fynde,** *may find it* **210 lysse,** *relieve* **211 To,** *too* **213 noght,** *nothing* **214 within the thridde morwe,** *within three days* **215 swow,** *swoon* **219 Wherfore,** *for which* **221 moche,** *much,* **welle,** *confidently* **222 had be dolven,** *would have been buried,* **everydelle,** *completely* **223 defaute,** *lack* **224 ne had redde,** *had not read,* **take kepe,** *paid attention* **225 next before,** (told) *just before* **226 wherfore,** *why* **227 bote ne bale,** *good nor bad* **228 or,** *before* **229 dreynte,** *drowned* **232 overloked,** *considered,* **everydel,** *thoroughly* **233 Me thoght wonder,** *I thought* (it) *marvelous* **234 or tho,** *before then* **238 game,** *play* (fulness) **239 me lyst ryght evel,** *I really did not wish* **240 dey,** *die* **242 yive,** *give,* **thilke,** *this* **244 wight elles,** *other creature,* **ne roughte,** *didn't care* **246 alderbeste,** *best of all* **247 Yifte,** *gift,* **abode hys lyve,** *hoped for in his life* **248 on warde,** *as a pledge,* **blyve,** *quickly* **249 Yif,** *if,* **lyte,** *little* **252 Rayed,** *striped,* **ryght wel cledde,** *very well covered* **253 fyn,** *fine,* **doutremere,** *from beyond the farthest sea* **254 bere,** *pillowcase* **256 thar not nede,** *will not need* **257 falles,** *is suitable* **259 do peynte,** *have painted* **260 tapite hem,** *cover them with tapestries* **261 oo sute,** *matching* **262 wiste,** *knew* **265 ylke,** *same* **266 moo,** *more* **269 trow,** *think,* **holde hir payede,** *consider herself satisfied* **270 unneth,** *barely,* **ysayede,** *said*

215 swow, F reads "sorowe." **216** Ovid's story goes on to describe how Ceyx and Alcione are transformed into seabirds; see the similar truncation of an Ovidian tale in *WBT* 3.981–82. **226 I,** omitted in F. **253 doutremere,** F reads "de owtre mer." **255 clothe of Reynes,** linen; Rennes, France, was known for its fine linen. **240–61** The narrator of Froissart's *Paradis d'Amours,* 15–22, prays to Morpheus and Juno for sleep, offering Juno a ring as a gift; in Machaut's *Fonteinne Amoureuse,* 807–10, the narrator seeks the favor of Morpheus by offering him a bed and a nightcap; cf. Sir Philip Sidney's *Astrophil and Stella,* 39.9–14.

Ryght thus as I have tolde hyt yow,
That sodeynly, I nyste° how,
Such a lust anoon° me tooke
To slepe that ryght upon my booke
Y fil aslepe; and therwith evene°
Me mette° so ynly° swete a swevene°,
So wonderful that never yitte
Y trowe° no man had the wytte°
To konne wel my sweven rede°—
No, not Joseph, withoute drede°,
Of Egipte, he that redde° so
The kynges metynge Pharao°,
No more than koude the lest° of us;
Ne nat skarsly° Macrobeus
(He that wrot al th'avysyoun°
That he mette°, Kyng Scipioun,
The noble man, the Affrikan—
Suche marvayles fortuned than°)
I trowe arede° my dremes even°.
Loo, thus hyt was, thys was my sweven.
  Me thoghte thus, that hyt was May,
And 'in the dawenynge I lay—
Me mette thus—in my bed al naked
And loked forth, for I was waked
With smale foules a gret hepe°
That had affrayed° me out of my slepe,
Thorgh noyse and swetnesse of her songe.
And as me mette, they sate amonge°
Upon my chambre roof wythoute,
Upon the tyles overal° aboute,
And songen everych in hys wyse°
The moste solempne servise
By noote° that ever man, y trowe,
Had herd; for some of hem song lowe,
Some high, and al of oon acorde.
To telle shortly att oo worde,
Was never herd so swete a steven°
But hyt° had be° a thyng of heven,
So mery a soun, so swete entewnes°,
That certes° for the toune of Tewnes
I nolde but I had herd° hem synge;
For al my chambre gan to rynge
Thurgh syngynge of her armonye;
For instrument nor melodye
Was nowhere herd yet half so swete,
Nor of acorde half so mete°;
For ther was noon of hem that feyned°
To synge, for ech of hem hym peyned°
To fynde out° mery crafty° notes.
They ne spared not her throtes.
And sooth° to seyn, my chambre was
Ful wel depeynted°, and with glas
Were al the wyndowes wel yglased
Ful clere, and nat an hoole ycrased°,
That to beholde hyt was grete joye.
For hoolly° al the story of Troye
Was in the glasynge° ywroght° thus,
Of Ector and of Kyng Priamus,
Of Achilles and Kyng Lamedon,
And eke° of Medea and of Jason,

---

272 nyste, *know not* **273 lust anoon,** *desire immediately* **275 therwith evene,** *immediately as a result* **276 Me mette,** *I dreamed,* **ynly,** *deeply,* **swevene,** *dream* **278 trowe,** *think,* **wytte,** *intelligence* **279 konne wel . . . rede,** *interpret* **280 drede,** *doubt* **281 redde,** *interpreted* **282 kynnes metynge Pharao,** *dreaming of King Pharaoh* **283 lest,** *least* **284 Ne nat skarsly,** *nor could scarcely* **285 th'avysyoun,** *the vision* **286 mette,** *dreamed* **288 fortuned than,** *happened then* **289 I trowe arede,** (could), *I believe interpret,* **even,** *precisely* **295 gret hepe,** *large number* **296 affrayed,** *startled* **298 sate amonge,** *sat here and there* **300 overal,** *everywhere* **301 everych in ys wyse,** *each in his manner* **303 By noote,** *in melody* **307 steven,** *sound* **308 But hyt,** *unless it,* **be,** *been* **309 entewnes,** *melodies* **310 certes,** *surely* **311 nolde but I had herd,** *would not have missed hearing* **316 mete,** *suitable* **317 feyned,** *pretended* **318 hym peyned,** *took pains* **319 fynde out,** *produce,* **crafty,** *skillful* **321 sooth,** *true* **322 depeynted,** *adorned* **324 ycrased,** *cracked* **326 hooly,** *wholly* **327 glasynge,** *glass,* **ywroght,** *made* **330 eke,** *also*

271 as, omitted in F. **280–82 Joseph . . . Pharao,** for Joseph's interpretations of the Pharaoh's dreams, see Genesis 41. **284–87 Macrobeus . . . Scipioun . . . Affrikan,** Macrobius (4th–5th century C.E.) wrote a commentary on Cicero's *Dream of Scipio,* explaining various kinds of dreams and commenting on Scipio's dream of his ancestor, Scipio Africanus. By the time he wrote *Parliament of Fowls,* Chaucer's knowledge of this commentary was more precise and extensive (see *PF* 31n), so the reference here may be secondhand, derived from the opening lines of the *Roman de la Rose,* which Chaucer translated as his *Romaunt.* **288** Line supplied from Th, copied into F in the seventeenth century; see also 31–96n. **291–343** The description of morning and birdsong is modeled on the opening of the *Roman de la Rose* (see 45ff., 484ff., and 661ff.), cited in line 334. **307 herd,** F reads "harde." **310 Tewnes,** Tunis (?), a convenient rhyme. **319 out,** F reads "out of." **326–31 the story of Troye . . . Medea and of Jason . . . Lavyne,** this list of names associated with Troy seems to emphasize the love interests of the medieval romances rather than the epic concerns of Homer and Virgil, especially clear in the mention of Medea and Jason (line 330) and Lavinia (line 331). The tragic love story of Medea and Jason opens the French *Roman de Troie* by Benoît de Sainte Maure (twelfth century), translated into Latin by Guido delle Colonne (thirteenth century); Achilles's love for Polyxena is a recurrent concern in the narrative as well. Lavinia (**Lavyne**), Italian wife of Aeneas, plays a larger role in the *Roman d'Éneas* (twelfth century) than in Virgil's *Aeneid.* **328 Ector . . . Priamus,** the principal Trojan hero, Hector, was the oldest son of Priam, king of Troy. **329 Kyng,** the manuscripts read hypermetrically "of Kyng," probably under the influence of the previous line. **Achilles . . . Lamedon,** Achilles was the principal Greek hero; Lamedon, father of Priam, built the first city of Troy.

Of Paris, Eleyne, and of Lavyne.
And alle the walles with colouris fine
Were peynted, bothe text and glose°,
Of al the *Romaunce of the Rose.*
My wyndowes were shette echon,
And throgh the glas the sonne shon
Upon my bed with bryghte bemes,
With many glade gilde° stremes;
And eke° the welken° was so faire—
Blew, bryght, clere was the ayre—
And ful attempre° for soothe° hyt was,
For nother to° cold nor hoot yt nas°,
Ne in al the welken was a clowde.
  And as I lay thus, wonder lowde
Me thoghte I herde an hunte° blowe
T'assay° hys horn, and for to knowe°
Whether hyt were clere or hors° of soune,
And I herde goynge bothe up and doune
Men, hors°, houndes, and other thynge;
And al men speken of huntynge,
How they wolde slee the hert° with strengthe,
And how the hert had upon° lengthe
So moche embosed°—y not now° what.
Anoon-ryght°, whan I herde that—
How that they wolde on-huntynge goon—
I was ryght glad, and up anoon
Took my hors, and forth I went
Out of my chambre. I never stent°
Til I com to the feld withoute.
Ther overtok y a grete route°
Of huntes° and eke of foresteres°,
With many relayes° and lymeres°,
And hyed° hem to the forest faste,
And I with hem. So at the laste
I asked oon, ladde° a lymere,
"Say, felowe, whoo shal hunte here?"
Quod I, and he answered ageyn°,
  "Syr, th'emperour Octovyen,"
Quod he, "and ys here faste° by."
  "A Goddes halfe°, in good tyme," quod I,
"Go we faste," and gan to ryde.
Whan we came to the forest syde,
Every man didde ryght anoon
As to huntynge fille to doon°.
The mayster-hunte°, anoon fot-hote°,
With a gret horn blewe thre mote°
At the uncouplynge of hys houndes.
Withynne a while the hert yfounde ys,
Yhalowed°, and rechased° faste
Longe tyme. And so at the laste
This hert rused° and staal° away
Fro alle the houndes a prevy° way.
The houndes had overshette° hym alle,
And were upon a defaute yfalle°.
Therwyth the hunte wonder faste
Blewe a forloyn° at the laste°.
  I was go walked° fro my tree,
And as I wente ther cam by mee
A whelp°, that fauned° me as I stoode,
That hadde yfolowed and koude no goode°.

---

333 glose, *commentary* **338 glade gilde,** *pleasing golden* **339 eke,** *also,* **welken,** *sky* **341 attempre,** *temperate,* **for sothe,** *in truth* **342 nother to,** *neither too,* **nas,** *wasn't* **345 hunte,** *hunter* **346 T'assay,** *to test,* **knowe,** *determine* **347 hors,** *hoarse* **349 hors,** *horses* **351 hert,** *male red deer* **352 upon,** *at* **353 embosed,** *exhausted* (itself), **y not now,** *I don't know* **354 Anoon-ryght,** *immediately* **358 stent,** *stopped* **360 grete route,** *large group* **361 huntes,** *hunters,* **foresteres,** *hunters' aides* **362 relayes,** *packs of fresh hounds,* **lymeres,** *hounds that track by scent* **363 hyed,** *hastened* **365 ladde,** *who led* **367 ageyn,** *in return* **369 faste,** *near* **370 A Goddes halfe,** *for God's sake* **374 fille to doon,** (what) *needed to be done* **375 mayster-hunte,** *master-hunter,* **anoon fot-hote,** *immediately with speed* **376 mote,** *notes* **379 Yhalowed,** *hallooed,* **rechased,** *headed off* **381 rused,** *eluded,* **staal,** *stole* **382 prevy,** *secret* **383 overshette,** *overshot* **384 were upon a defaute yfalle,** *missed the opportunity* **386 forloyn,** *a signal to return* (to the hunters and dogs), **laste,** *end* **387 was go walked,** *proceeded on, walking* **389 whelp,** *puppy or small dog,* **fauned,** *paid attention to* **390 koude no goode,** *didn't know what to do*

331 Paris, Eleyne, the elopement of Trojan Paris, son of Priam, and Helen, wife of Menelaus of Greece, caused the Trojan War. **334 Of,** F reads "And." ***Romaunce of the Rose,*** the most influential love allegory of the late Middle Ages in France and England, written in two parts by Guillaume de Lorris (c. 1230) and Jean de Meun (c. 1270). It is no more possible to depict the lengthy *Roman de la Rose* on chamber walls than it is to depict the entire story of Troy (lines 326–27) on chamber windows, but the scene powerfully conveys immersion in these narratives. **342 nas,** F reads "was." **344–86** Scholars have commented on the technical language of hunting, used here as a kind of authentication, and have read the passage as an allegory of the pursuit and loss of love, grounded in the conventional play of "hart" and "heart." **362 many,** F reads "may." **368 Octovyen,** Octavian, the original name of Augustus Caesar (63 B.C.E. –14 C.E.), adopted son of Julius Caesar and founder of imperial Roman government; also a central character in a group of late-medieval romances. No one has explained satisfactorily the use of the name here, though some have read it as a veiled compliment to Edward III or John of Gaunt. At line 1314, the emperor is referred to as "this kynge." **378 yfounde,** F reads "founde." **387 fro my tree,** from my station; hunters were stationed to surround the hart and drive it back into the central hunting area, or, if possible, to shoot it. **389 whelp,** no explanation or interpretation of the whelp (puppy) is generally agreed upon, but scholars have noted that elsewhere in romances animal guides lead to adventure and that there are precedents for some details of Chaucer's scene in Machaut's *Jugement du Roy de Behaigne* (43–46 and 1204–15) and his *Dit dou Lyon* (325–31).

Hyt come and crepte to me as lowe
Ryght as hyt hadde me yknowe°,
Held doun hys hede and joyned hys eres,
And leyde al smothe doun hys heres°.
I wolde have kaught hyt, and anoon
Hyt fled and was fro me goon;
And I hym folwed, and hyt forthe went
Doun by a floury grene went°
Ful thikke of gras, ful softe and swete,
With floures fele° faire under fete,
And litel used—hyt semed thus;
For both Flora and Zephirus,
They two that make floures growe,
Had mad her dwellynge ther, I trowe°.
For hit was, on to beholde,
As thogh the erthe envye wolde°
To be gayer than the heven,
To have moo floures swiche seven°
As in the welken° sterres bee;
Hyt had forgete the povertee
That wynter, thorgh hys colde morwes°,
Had mad hyt suffre, and his sorwes.
All was forgeten, and that was sene,
For al the woode was waxen° grene;
Swetnesse of dewe had mad hyt waxe.
Hyt ys no nede eke° for to axe
Wher° there were many grene greves°,
Or thikke of° trees so ful of leves;
And' every tree stood by hymselve
Fro other wel ten foot or twelve—
So grete trees, so huge of strengthe,
Of fourty or fifty fadme° lengthe,
Clene withoute bowgh or stikke,
With croppes° brode and eke as thikke—
They were nat an ynche asonder—
That hit was shadewe overal° under.
And many an hert° and many an hynde°
Was both before me and behynde.
Of founes°, sowres°, bukkes°, does
Was ful the woode, and many roes°,
And many sqwirelles that sete
Ful high upon the trees and ete,
And in hir maner made festes.
Shortly°, hyt was so ful of bestes,
That thogh Argus, the noble countour°,
Sete to rekene° in hys countour°,
And rekene with his figures ten°—
For by tho figures mowe al ken°,
Yf they be crafty, rekene and noumbre,
And tel° of everything the noumbre—
Yet shoulde he fayle to rekene evene°
The wondres me mette° in my swevene°.
But forth I romed ryght wonder faste
Doun the woode; so at the laste
I was war° of a man in blak
That sete and had yturned his bak
To an ooke, an huge tree.
"Lord," thoght I, "who may that be?
What ayleth hym to sitten here?"
Anoon-ryght° I wente nere;
Than found I sitte even upryght°
A wonder wel farynge° knyght—
By the maner me thoghte so—
Of good mochel°, and ryght yong therto°,
Of the age of foure and twenty yere,
Upon hys berde but lytel here,
And he was clothed al in blake°.
I stalked even unto hys bake,
And there I stood as stille as ought°
That, soth° to saye, he saw me nought,

---

392 yknowe, *known* **394 heres,** *fur* **398 went,** *path* **400 fele,** *many* **404 trowe,** *believe* **406 envye wolde,** *wanted to compete* **408 swiche seven,** *seven times,* **welken,** *sky* **411 morwes,** *mornings* **414 waxen,** *grown* **416 eke,** *also* **417 Wher,** *whether,* **greves,** *branches* **418 Or thikke of,** *or* (whether the branches were) *thick on* **422 fadme,** *fathom* (6 feet) **424 coppes,** *treetops* **426 overal,** *everywhere* **427 hert,** *male deer,* **hynde,** *female deer* **429 founes,** *fawns,* **sowres,** *four-year-old bucks,* **bukkes,** *six-year-old bucks* **430 roes,** *brown deer* **434 Shortly,** *in short* **435 countour,** *mathematician* **436 rekene,** *calculate,* **countour,** *counting-room* **437 figures tens,** *ten numerals* **438 mowe al ken,** *all may people* **440 tel,** *tally* **441 evene,** *accurately* **442 mette,** *dreamed,* **swevene,** *dream* **445 war,** *aware* **450 Anoon-ryght,** *immediately* **451 sitte even upryght,** *sitting straight up* **452 wel farynge,** *handsome* **454 good mochel,** *fine physique,* **therto,** *as well* **458 bake,** *back* **459 as stille as ought,** *quietly as possible* **460 soth,** *true*

402 Flora, goddess of flowers. **Zephirus,** personification of the west wind. The two are depicted together as wife and husband in *Roman de la Rose,* 8403–30, which is also the source of Chaucer's notion (lines 406–09) that the flower-covered earth competes with the star-studded heaven. **409 welken,** F reads "walkene." **410–15** Echoes *Roman de la Rose,* 53–58. **420 foot or,** F reads "fete fro other." **422 Of,** F reads "Or"; **or,** omitted in F,. **424 brode,** F reads "bothe." **435 Argus,** Mohammed ibn Mūsā al-Khwārizmī, known as Algus and mistakenly recorded as "Argus" in the *Roman de la Rose,* line 12,790; ninth-century Persian mathematician whose book introduced Hindu-Arabic numerals and decimals into Europe in the twelfth century. **443 I,** F reads"they." **445 man in blak,** generally agreed to represent John of Gaunt, bereaved at the loss of his first wife, Blanche of Lancaster; see the Introduction. **446 yturned,** F reads "turned." **448 thoght,** F reads "thogh." **455 foure and twenty yere,** a chronological puzzle, often explained as the result of a misreading of roman numerals at a crucial point in the textual tradition (perhaps *xxiiii* for *xxviii).* Gaunt was 28 when Blanche died in 1368, and the preceding line clearly describes the character as young, perhaps as a form of idealization.

For-why° he heng hys hed adoune,
And with a dedely sorwful soune°
He made of ryme ten vers or twelfe
Of a compleynt to hymselfe—
The moste pitee, the moste rowthe°,
That ever I herde; for by my trowthe,
Hit was gret wonder that nature
Myght suffre any creature
To have such sorwe and be not ded.
Ful petous° pale and nothyng red°,
He sayed a lay°, a maner songe°,
Withoute noote°, withoute songe°,
And was thys, for ful wel I kan
Reherse° hyt ryght. Thus hyt began:

I have of sorwe so grete wone°
That joye gete I never none
Now that I see my lady bryght,
Which I have loved with al my myght,
Is fro me ded, and ys agoon.
Allas, dethe, what ayleth the
That thou noldest° have taken me,
Whan thou toke my lady swete,
That was so faire, so freshe, so fre°,
So goode, that men may wel se
Of al goodnesse she had no mete°?

Whan he had mad thus his complaynt
Hys sorwful hert gan faste faynt,
And his spirites wexen° dede;
The blood was fled for pure drede
Doun to hys herte to make hym warme,
For wel hyt feled the herte had harme,
To wete eke° why hyt was adrad,
By kynde° and for to make hyt glad,
For hit ys membre principal
Of the body; and that made al
Hys hewe° chaunge and wexe grene
And pale, for ther noo blood ys sene
In no maner lym of hys°.
Anoon therwith° whan y sawgh this
He ferde thus evel there° he sete,
I went and stoode ryght at his fete
And grette° hym, but he spake noght,
But argued° with his oune thoght,
And in hys wytte disputed faste
Why and how hys lyfe myght laste—
Hym thought hys sorwes were so smerte°,
And lay so colde upon hys herte.
So° throgh hys sorwes and hevy thoght
Made hym that he herde me noght,
For he had wel nygh° lost hys mynde,
Thogh° Pan, that men clepe° God of Kynde°,
Were for hys sorwes never so wroth°.
But at the last, to sayn ryght soth°,
He was war° of me, how y stoode
Before hym and did of° myn hoode,
And had ygret° hym as I best koude,
Debonayrly° and nothyng lowde°.
He sayde, "I prey the, be not wroth.
I herde the not, to seyn the soth,
Ne I sawgh the not, syr, trewely."
"A, goode sire, no fors°, quod y,
"I am ryght sory yif I have oughte°
Destroubled yow out of your thoughte.
Foryive me yif I have mystake.°"
"Yis, th'amendes° is lyght° to make,"
Quod he, "for ther lyeth noon therto°.

461 For-why, *because* **462 soune,** *sound* **465 rowthe,** *sorrow* **470 petous,** *piteously,* **nothyng red,** *not at all ruddy* **471 lay,** *poem,* **maner songe,** *kind of song* **472 noote,** *music,* **songe,** *singing* **474 Reherse,** *repeat* **475 *wone*,** *plenty* **482 *noldest*,** *would not* **484 *fre*,** *gracious* **486 *mete*,** *equal* **489 wexen,** *became* **493 To wete eke,** *also to learn* **494 By kynde,** *by nature* (i.e., naturally) **497 hewe,** *color* **498 ther,** *where* **499 no maner lym of hys,** *none of his limbs* **500 Anoon therwith,** *immediately moreover* **501 He ferde thus evel there,** (that) *he fared so badly where* **503 grette,** *greeted* **504 argued,** *debated* **507 smerte,** *painful* **509 So,** *thus* **511 wel nygh,** *nearly* **512 Thogh,** *even though,* **clepe,** *call,* **Kynde,** *Nature* **513 wroth,** *angry* **514 soth,** *truly* **515 war,** *aware* **516 did of,** *took off* **517 ygret,** *greeted* **518 Debonayrly,** *politely,* **nothyng lowde,** *not at all loudly* **522 no fors,** *no matter* **523 oughte,** *in any way* **525 mystake,** *done wrong* **526 th'amendes,** *reparation,* **lyght,** *easy* **527 ther lyeth noon therto,** *none is needed*

466 ever I herde, the overhearing of grief or other emotions occurs in medieval romances in various ways, see, e.g., Machaut's *Le Jugement du Roy de Behaigne,* 54ff., and Chaucer's *TC* 2.517ff. **475–86** This embedded lyric is labeled a "complaint" at lines 464 and 487, and a "lay" at 471. The first term was used of amatory laments like this one (as well as of certain satiric and didactic poems); the second, of any short lyric or brief narrative poem. **475 *so*,** F reads "of so." **480** In his edition of 1532, Thynne adds a line: "And thus in sorwe lefte me alone." Found in no manuscript, the line is generally omitted as an unnecessary and unsuccessful attempt to fill out the rhyme scheme; see 31–96n. Also in Thynne, line 486 stands before 484, evidence of effort to regularize into couplets. **499 lym,** F reads "hym." **509 hevy,** Th reads "holy." **510 herde me noght,** compare Machaut, *Le Jugement du Roy de Behaigne* 70–71; Chaucer's wording and sentiments in 509–64 have many echoes of *Behaigne* 70–92. **512–13 Pan . . . never so wroth,** the god Pan (Greek "all") here represents universal nature, which is disturbed because sorrows have threatened the mind of the Black Knight. **512 god,** F reads "the god." **519 I preye the,** the Black Knight uses "thee" and "thou" throughout his conversation with the Dreamer, who uses "you" forms in return. The difference marks the separation in social rank between the two characters, but implies no condescension on the Knight's part.

There ys nothyng myssayd nor do.°"
Loo, how goodely spak thys knyghte,
As° hit had be another wyghte°:
He made hyt nouther towgh ne queynte°.
And I saw that and gan me aqueynte
With hym, and fonde hym so tretable°,
Ryght wonder skylful° and resonable,
As me thoght, for al hys bale°.
Anoon-ryght I gan fynde a tale°
To hym, to loke wher° I myght oughte°
Have more knowynge of hys thoughte.
"Sir," quod I, "this game° is doon.
I holde° that this hert be goon;
These huntes konne° hym nowher see."
"Y do no fors therof,°" quod he.
"My thought ys thereon never a dele.°"
"By oure Lorde," quod I, "y trow° yow wele;
Ryght so me thenketh by youre chere°.
But sir, oo thyng wol ye here°?
Me thynketh in gret sorowe I yow see,
But certes°, sir, yif that yee°
Wolde ought discure me° youre woo,
I wolde, as wys God helpe me soo,
Amende hyt, yif I kan or may.
Ye mowe preve° hyt be assay°.
For, by my trouthe, to make yow hool°
I wol do alle my power hool°.
And telleth me of your sorwes smerte°.
Paraunter° hyt may ese youre herte
That semeth ful seke° under your syde."
With that he loked on me asyde°,
As who sayth, "Nay, that wol not be."
"Graunt mercy°, goode frend," quod he,
"I thanke thee that thow woldest° soo,
But hyt may never the rather° be doo°.
No man may my sorwe glade°;
That maketh my hewe° to fal and fade,
And hath myn understondynge lorne°,
That me ys wo that I was borne.
May noght make my sorwes slyde°
Nought al the remedyes of Ovyde,
Ne Orpheus, god of melodye,
Ne Dedalus with his playes slye°;
Ne hele me may noo phisicien,
Noght Ypocras ne Galyen.
Me ys woo that I lyve oures° twelve.
But whooso wol assay hymselve
Whether his hert kan have pitee
Of any sorwe, lat hym see me—
Y wrechche°, that deth hath made al naked
Of alle blysse that ever was maked,
Yworthe° worste of alle wyghtes°,
That hate my dayes and my nyghtes.
My lyf, my lustes°, be me loothe°,
For al welfare° and I be wroothe°.
The pure deth° ys so ful° my foo
That I wolde deye—hyt wolde not soo,
For whan I folwe hyt, hit wol flee.
I wolde have hym, hyt nyl nat° me.
This ys my peyne, wythoute rede°,
Alway deynge and be not dede,
That Thesiphus that lyeth in helle
May not of more sorwe telle.
And whoso wiste° al, be my trouthe,
My sorwe, but° he hadde rowthe°
And pitee of my sorwes smerte°,

528 do, *done* **530 As,** *as if,* **be another wyghte,** *been a different person* **531 nouther towgh ne queynte,** *neither rude nor indirect* **533 tretable,** *receptive* **534 skylful,** *sensible* **535 bale,** *grief* **536 gan fynde a tale,** *found something to say* **537 to loke wher,** *to see whether,* **oughte,** *in any way* **539 game,** *hunt* **540 holde,** *think* **541 huntes konne,** *hunters can* **542 do no fors therof,** *don't care about that* **543 dele,** *bit* **544 trow,** *believe* **545 chere,** *demeanor* **546 here,** *hear* **548 certes,** *surely,* **yif that yee,** *if you* **549 Wolde ought discure me,** *would reveal to me anything* (of) **552 mowe preve,** *might gauge,* **be assay,** *by a test* **553 hool,** *healthy* **554 hool,** *completely* **555 smerte,** *painful* **556 Paraunter,** *perhaps* **557 seke,** *sick* **558 asyde,** *sideways* **560 Graunt mercy,** *thank you* **561 woldest,** *wish* **562 rather,** *sooner,* **doo,** *done* **563 glade,** *gladden* **564 hewe,** *color* **565 lorne,** *ruined* **567 slyde,** *go away* **570 playes slye,** *clever devices* **573 oures,** *hours* **577 wrechche,** *wretch* **579 Yworthe,** *have become,* **wyghtes,** *creatures* **581 lustes,** *pleasures,* **be me loothe,** *are loathsome to me* **582 welfare,** *happiness,* **be wroothe,** *are angry at each other* **583 The pure deth,** *death itself,* **ful,** *fully* **586 hyt nyl nat,** *it will not* (have) **587 rede,** *remedy* **591 wiste,** *knew* **592 but,** *unless,* **rowthe,** *compassion* **593 smerte,** *painful*

549 discure me youre woo, the Dreamer has overheard the reason for the Black Knight's grief (at lines 475–83), but his request here enables the Knight to talk about it—a step toward assuaging the grief. Pandarus uses this as a strategy to provoke Troylus to talk in *TC* 1.561–66. **556 Paraunter,** F reads "Peraventure." **568 remedyes of Ovyde,** Ovid's *Remedia Amoris* (*Remedies for Love*) includes advice on easing love sickness, although it is deeply ironic, even satiric. The reference indicates that Chaucer was aware that such works could be misunderstood—or, less likely, that he misunderstood this one himself. **569 Orpheus,** the demi-god whose music distracted from their pains those suffering in the Underworld; Ovid *Metamorphoses* 10.40–44. **570 Dedalus,** sought to escape from exile and cure his homesickness by contriving to make wings; Ovid, *Metamorphoses* 8.183ff. **572 Ypocras . . . Galyen,** Hippocrates and Galen were the most famous doctors from antiquity. **589 Thesiphus,** seemingly a conflation or confusion of Tityus, who lay spread out in hell with a vulture tearing at his liver, and Sisyphus, whose punishment was to roll uphill a stone that eternally rolled back down; Ovid *Metamorphoses* 4.457–60.

That man hath a fendely° herte.
For whoso seeth me first on morwe°
May seyn he hath mette with sorwe,
For y am sorwe and sorwe ys y.
"Allas, and I wol tel the why
My song ys turned to pleynynge°,
And al my lawghtre to wepynge,
My glade thoghtes to hevynesse°:
In travayle° ys myn ydelnesse
And eke° my reste; my wele° is woo,
My goode ys harme, and evermoo
In wrathe° ys turned my pleynge,
And my delyt into sorwynge.
Myn hele° ys turned into seknesse,
In drede° ys al my sykernesse°,
To derke ys turned al my lyghte,
My wytte ys foly, my day ys nyghte,
My love ys hate, my slepe wakynge,
My merthe and meles° ys fastynge,
My countenaunce° ys nycete°,
And al abawed° whereso I be
My pees, in pledynge° and in werre°.
Allas, how myghte I fare werre°?
My boldenesse ys turned to shame
For fals Fortune hath pleyde a game
Atte chesse with me, allas the while°!
The trayteresse fals and ful of gyle,
That al behoteth° and nothyng halte°,
She geth° upryght and yet she halte°,
That baggeth° foule and loketh faire,
The dispitouse debonaire°,
That skorneth many a creature.
An ydole of fals portrayture°
Ys she, for she wol sone wrien°.
She is the mowstres hed ywrien°,
As fylthe over-ystrawed° with floures.
Hir moste worshippe° and hir flour ys
To lyen, for that ys hyr nature,
Withoute feyth, lawe, or mesure°.
She ys fals and ever lawghynge
With one eye, and that other wepynge.
That° ys broght up, she sette al doun.
I lykne° hyr to the scorpioun
That ys a fals, flaterynge beste°,
For with his hede he maketh feste°,
But al amydde his flaterynge
With hys tayle he wol stynge
And envenyme°—and so wol she.
She ys th'envyouse charite
That ys ay° fals and seemeth wele°,
So turneth she hyr false whele
Aboute, for hyt ys nothyng° stable,
Now by the fire, now at table.
For many oon hath she thus yblent°;
She ys pley° of enchauntement,
That semeth oon and ys not soo.
The false thef, what hath she doo°,
Trowest thou°? By oure Lord, I wol the seye°.
At the chesse with me she gan to pleye;
With hir fals draughtes dyvers°
She staarl° on me and toke my fers°.
And whan I sawgh my fers away,
Allas, I kouthe no lenger play,
But seyde, 'Farewel, swete, ywys°,
And farewel al that ever ther ys!'
Therwith Fortune seyde, 'Chek here!'

---

594 fendely, *fiendish* **595 morwe,** *morning* **599 pleynynge,** *lamenting* **601 hevynesse,** *misery* **602 travayle,** *labor* **603 eke,** *also* **603 wele,** *happiness* **605 In wrathe,** *into anger* **607 hele,** *health* **608 In drede,** *into fear,* **sykernesse,** *security* **612 meles,** *meals* **613 countenaunce,** (proper) *behavior,* **nycete,** *foolishness* **614 abawed,** *disturbed* **615 pledynge,** *pleadings,* **werre,** *war* **616 werre,** *worse* **619 while,** *time* **621 behoteth,** *promises,* **halte,** *fulfills* **622 geth,** *goes,* **halte,** *limps* **623 baggeth,** *squints* **624 dispitouse debonaire,** *scornful gracious one* **626 portrayture,** *representation* **627 wrien,** *turn away* **628 mowstres hed ywrien,** *monster's head disguised* **629 over-ystrawed,** *covered* **630 moste worshippe,** *greatest renown* **632 mesure,** *balance* **635 That,** *that which* **636 likne,** *compare* **637 beste,** *animal* **638 maketh feste,** *shows respect* **641 envenyme,** *poison* **643 ay,** *always,* **wele,** *good* **645 nothyng,** *not at all* **647 oon,** *one (person),* **yblent,** *blinded* **648 pley,** *trick* **650 doo,** *done* **651 Trowest thou,** *do you think,* **the seye,** *tell you* **653 draughtes dyvers,** *various moves* **654 staal,** *crept up,* **fers,** *queen* **657 ywys,** *surely*

599–617 Critics have sought to identify a source for this list of the paradoxes or oxymora of love, but it is conventional; see *Roman de la Rose,* 4293ff., and Machaut, *Le Jugement du Roy de Behaigne,* 177ff. **599 song,** F and Th read "sorowe." **607 seknesse,** F reads "sekeeness." **618 Fortune,** the late-classical goddess Fortune represented randomness, instability, and often (as here) cruel disregard for human beings; a common medieval figure in art and literature. **622 halte,** F reads "is halte." **627 wrien,** F reads "varien." **640 he,** F reads "hyt." **644 false whele,** the most common emblem of Fortune, her wheel is a symbol of capricious instability in human affairs. **647 she thus,** F reads "thus she." **652–70 chesse . . . ,** several details and phrases of the chess game and its association with Fortune derive from the *Roman de la Rose* 6620–726. **654 fers,** the word derives ultimately from Persian *firzan,* meaning "counselor" or "companion," and in medieval French it referred to the chess piece that developed into the queen of modern chess. **659–60 Chek . . . mate,** in modern chess, *check* indicates threat to the king, while *mate* or *checkmate* indicates that the king cannot be defended in any way and the game is over; the phrase derives ultimately from Persian, "shah mat(a)" (the king is defeated). The rules and techniques of chess playing have changed over time, compelling scholars to various surmises about Chaucer's knowledge of the game and the moves indicated by his description. One thing is clear: the Black Knight loses his game against Fortune when he loses his "fers."

And mate in myd poynt of the chekkere°
With a poune errant°. Allas,
Ful craftier to pley she was
Than Athalus that made the game
First of the chesse—so was hys name.
But God wolde° I had oones or twyes
Ykoud° and knowe° the jeupardyes°
That kowde° the Greke Pictagores!
I shulde have pleyd the bet° at ches,
And kept° my fers° the bet° therby.
And thogh wherto°? For trewely,
I holde° that wyssh nat worth a stree°.
Hyt had be° never the bet for me.
For Fortune kan° so many a wyle°
Ther be but fewe kan° hir begile.
And eke she ys the lasse° to blame;
Myself I wolde have do° the same,
Before God, hadde I ben as she;
She oghte the more excused be.
For this I say yet more therto°,
Had I be God and myghte have do°
My wille, whan she my fers kaughte,
I wolde have drawe° the same draughte°.
For, also wys° God yive° me reste,
I dar wel swere she took the beste.
But through that draughte I have lorn°
My blysse. Allas that I was born,
For evermore, y trowe° trewly,
For al my wille, my lust holly°
Ys turned°. But yet what to doone?
Be° oure Lord, hyt ys to° deye soone—
For nothyng I leve° hyt noghte,
But lyve and deye ryght° in this thoghte.
For there nys° planete in firmament°,
Ne in ayr ne in erthe noon element,
That they ne yive me a yifte echone°
Of wepynge whan I am alone.
For whan that I avise me° wel,
And bethenke me every del°,
How that ther lyeth in rekenyng
Inne my sorwe for nothyng°,
And how ther leveth° no gladnesse
May glade° me of my distresse,
And how I have lost suffisance°,
And therto° I have no pleasance°,
Thanne may I say I have ryght noghte°.
And whan al this falleth in my thoghte,
Allas, than am I overcome,
For that° ys doon ys not to come.
I have more sorowe than Tantale."
  And whan I herde hym tel thys tale
Thus pitously, as I yow telle,
Unnethe° myght y lenger duelle°—
Hyt dyde myn hert so moche woo.
"A, goode sir," quod I, "say not soo.
Have some pitee on your nature
That formed yow to° creature.
Remembre yow of° Socrates,
For he ne counted° nat thre strees°
Of noght that Fortune koude doo."
  "No," quod he, "I kan not soo."
  "Why so, good syr, parde°?" quod y.
"Ne say noght soo, for trewely,
Thogh ye had lost the ferses twelve,
And° ye for sorwe mordred yourselve,
Ye sholde be dampned° in this cas°
By as goode ryght as Medea was,
That slowgh° hir children for Jason;
And Phyllis also for Demophon
Henge hirselfe, so weylaway°,

---

660 chekkere, *chessboard* **661 poune errant,** *traveling pawn* **665 God wolde,** *I wish to God that* **666 Ykoud,** *understood,* **knowe,** *known,* **jeupardyes,** *chess problems* **667 kowde,** *knew* **668 bet,** *better* **669 kept,** *protected,* **fers,** *queen,* **bet,** *better* **670 wherto,** *to what effect* **671 holde,** *consider,* **stree,** *straw* **672 had be,** *would have been* **673 kan,** *knows,* **wyle,** *trick* **674 kan,** (who) *are able to* **675 lasse,** *less* **676 do,** *done* **679 therto,** *also* **680 do,** *done* **682 drawe,** *made,* **draughte,** *move* **683 also wys,** *as surely as,* **yive,** *give* **685 lorn,** *lost* **687 y trowe,** *I believe* **688 lust holly,** *desire completely* **689 turned,** *reversed* **690 Be,** *by,* **hyt ys to,** *the only option is to* **691 leve,** *believe* **692 ryght,** *precisely* **693 nys,** *is no,* **firmament,** *heavens* **695 echone,** *each one* **697 avise me,** *consider* **698 bethenke me every del,** *think about every aspect* **699–700 lyeth in rekenyng . . . nothyng,** *no sorrow owed to my account* **701 leveth,** *remains* **702 May glade,** *that might gladden* **703 suffisance,** *contentment* **704 therto,** *also,* **plesance,** *pleasure* **705 ryght noghte,** *exactly nothing* **708 that,** *what* **712 Unnethe,** *scarcely,* **duelle,** *remain* **716 to,** i.e., *as a* **717 Remembre yow of,** *recall* **718 counted,** *cared,* **strees,** *straws* **721 parde,** *by God* **724 And,** *if* **725 dampned,** *condemned,* **cas,** *situation* **727 slowgh,** *slew* **729 weylaway,** *alas*

663 Athalus, cited in the *Roman de la Rose* 6691ff. as the inventor of chess. **667 Pictagores,** Pythagorus, Greek philosopher and mathematician (6th–5th c. B.C.E.) known for his wisdom but not usually associated with chess. **670 thogh,** F reads "thoght." **677 hadde,** F reads "as." **684 she,** F reads "he." **693–96** Translates Machaut, *Lay de Confort,* 10–13. **709 Tantale,** Tantalus, who hungers and thirsts in Hades for eternity, with food and drink just beyond his grasp; Ovid, *Metamorphoses* 4.458–59; 10.41. **711 Thus,** F reads "This." **717 Socrates,** the Greek philosopher exemplifies imperviousness to Fortune in *Roman de la Rose,* 5845–50. **721 parde,** F reads "yis, parde." **722 say,** omitted in F. **723 the ferses twelve,** the twelve queens (chess pieces); it is unknown why the number is twelve. **726–27 Medea . . . Jason,** Medea helped Jason to acquire the Golden Fleece, eloped with him, and killed their children when he deserted her; see *Roman de la Rose* 13229–264. **728–31 Phyllis . . . Demophon . . . ,** Phyllis killed herself when Demophon failed to return to her on time; see *Roman de la Rose* 13211–14.

For he had broke his terme-day°
To come to hir. Another rage
Had Dydo, the quene eke° of Cartage,
That slough hirself for° Eneas
Was fals—which a fool she was—
And Ecquo died for Narcisus
Nolde nat° love hir. And ryght thus
Hath many another foly doon;
And for Dalida died Sampson,
That slough hymself with a pilere°.
But ther is no man alyve here
Wolde for a fers make this woo."
"Why so?" quod he, "hyt ys nat soo.
Thou woste° ful lytel what thou menest°.
I have lost more than thow wenest.°"
"Loo, sey how that may be," quod y.
"Good sir, telle me al hooly°
In what wyse, how, why, and wherfore°
That ye have thus youre blysse lore.°"
"Blythely,°" quod he. "Come sytte adoun.
I telle hyt the° upon condicioun
That thou shalt hooly with all thy wytte°
Doo thyn entent° to herkene hitte.°"
"Yis, syr."—"Swere thy trouthe therto."
"Gladly."—"Do thanne holde hereto."
"I shal ryght blythely, so° God me save,
Hooly, with al the witte I have,
Here° yow as wel as I kan."
"A Goddes half,°" quod he, and began.
"Syr," quod he, "sith° firste I kouthe°
Have any maner wyt fro° youthe,
Or kyndely° understondynge
To comprehende in any thynge
What love was, in myn oune wytte,
Dredeles°, I have ever yitte°
Be tributarye° and yiven rente°
To Love, hooly with good entente,
And throgh plesaunce° become his thralle°,
With good wille, body, hert, and alle.
Al this I putte in his servage°,
As to my lord, and did homage°,
And ful devoutely I prayed hym to°
He shulde besette° myn herte so
That hyt plesance to hym were°,
And worship° to my lady dere.
And this was longe and many a yere
Or that° myn herte was set owhere°,
That I dide thus, and nyste° why;
I trowe° hit came me kyndely°.
Paraunter° I was therto most able°,
As a white walle or a table,
For hit ys redy to cachche and take
Al that men wil theryn make°,
Whethir so° men wil portreye° or peynt,
Be the werkes never so queynt°.
"And thilke° tyme I ferde ryght so°
I was able to have lerned tho°
And to have kende° as wel or better
Paraunter other° art or letre°,
But for° love came first in my thoghte,
Therfore I forgat hyt noghte.
I ches° love to° my firste crafte,
Therfore hit ys with me lafte°,
Forwhy° I tok hyt of so° yonge age
That malyce° hadde my corage°
Nat that° tyme turned to nothynge

730 terme-day, *agreed-upon day* **731 Another rage,** *a similar madness* **732 eke,** *also* **733 for,** *because* **736 Nolde nat,** *would not* **739 pilere,** *pillar* **743 woste,** *know,* **menest,** *say* **744 wenest,** *think* **746 al hooly,** *completely* **747 wherfore,** *for what reason* **748 lore,** *lost* **749 Blythely,** *happily* **750 hyt the,** *it to you* **751 wytte,** *mind* **752 Doo thyn entent,** *make all effort,* **herkene hitte,** *listen to it* **755 so,** *may* **757 Here,** *listen to* **758 A Goddes half,** i.e., *in God's name* **759 sith,** *since,* **kouthe,** *was able* (to) **760 maner wyt fro,** *kind of intelligence in* **761 kyndely,** *natural* **764 Dredeles,** *doubtless,* **yitte,** *yet* **765 Be tributarye,** *been a vassal,* **yiven rente,** *paid tribute* **767 throgh plesaunce,** *with pleasure,* **thralle,** *servant* **769 servage,** *service* **770 did homage,** *pledged feudal allegiance* **771 hym to,** *to him that* **772 besette,** *direct* **773 hyt plesance to hym were,** *it might be a pleasure to him* **774 worship,** *honor* **776 Or that,** *before,* **owhere,** *anywhere* **777 nyste,** *knew not* **778 trowe,** *think,* **me kyndely,** *to me naturally* **779 Paraunter,** *perhaps,* **able,** *suitable* **782 wil theryn make,** *want to compose on it* **783 Whethir so,** *whether,* **wil portreye,** *want to draw* **784 Be . . . never so queynt,** *regardless of how elaborate* **785 thilke,** *at that,* **ferde ryght so,** *continued just as if* **786 tho,** *then* **787 kende,** *understood* **788 Paraunter other,** *perhaps a different,* **letre,** *subject* **789 for,** *because* **791 ches,** *chose,* **to,** *as* **792 lafte,** *remaining* **793 Forwhy,** *because,* **of so,** *at such a* **794 That malyce,** *when ill will,* **corage,** *heart* **795 that,** *at that*

732–34 Dydo . . . Eneas . . . , Dido killed herself after Aeneas abandoned her; see *Roman de la Rose* 13173–210. **735–36 Ecquo . . . Narcisus . . . ,** Echo died of grief and anger when Narcissus did not reciprocate her love; see *Roman de la Rose* 1439–56. **738–39 Dalida . . . Sampson . . . ,** because Delilah betrayed Samson, he destroyed himself and his captors when he pulled down the pillars that held up the house of the Philistines; Judges 16. **743–44** Cf. 1137–38 and 1305–06. **745 Loo, sey how that may be,** F reads "Loo she that may be." **750 upon,** F reads "up a." **754 hereto,** F reads "here, lo." **759–76** Echoes Machaut, *Jugement du Roy de Behaigne,* 125–33 and 261–73. **779 Paraunter,** F reads "Peraventure." **780 white walle or a table,** This figure of receptivity—the white wall or blank slate (tablet)—is ultimately Aristotelian, available to Chaucer and the Middle Ages in Boethius, *Consolation of Philosophy,* 5m.4, and elsewhere. In Machaut, *Remede de Fortune,* 26–30, it is associated with a state of innocence. **788 art or letre,** echoes Machaut, *Remede de Fortune,* 40. **793–804** Echoes Machaut, *Remede de Fortune,* 24–25 and 45–50.

Thorgh to mochel° knowlechynge.
For that tyme Yowthe, my maistresse,
Governed me in ydelnesse,
For hyt was in my firste youthe,
And thoo° ful lytel good y couthe°,
For al my werkes were flyttynge°
That tyme, and al my thoght varyinge.
Al° were to me ylyche° goode
That I knew thoo. But thus hit stoode:
  "Hit happed that I came on a day
Into a place ther° that I say°
Trewly the fayrest companye
Of ladyes that evere man with eye
Had seen togedres in oo° place.
Shal I clepe° hyt happe other grace°
That broght me there? Nay, but Fortune,
That ys to lyen ful comune°,
The false trayteresse pervers!
God wolde° I koude clepe hir wers°,
For now she worcheth° me ful woo°,
And I wol telle sone why soo.
  "Among these ladyes thus echon°,
Soth° to seyen y sawgh oon°
That was lyk noon of the route°,
For I dar swere, withoute doute,
That as the someres sonne bryghte
Ys fairer, clere°, and hath more lyghte
Than any other planete in hevene,
The moone, or the sterres sevene,
For al the world so hadde she
Surmounted hem° al of° beaute,
Of maner and of comelynesse°,
Of stature° and of wel sette gladnesse°,
Of godlyhede° so wel besey°,
Shortly—what shal y more sey—
By God and by his halwes° twelve,
Hyt was my swete°, ryght al hirselve°.
She had so stedfast° countenaunce,
So noble port° and meyntenaunce°,
And Love, that had wel herd my boone°,
Had espyed° me thus soone,
That she ful sone° in my thoght,
As° helpe me God, so was ykaught°
So sodenly, that I ne tok
No maner counseyl but at° hir loke,
And at myn herte. Forwhy° hir eyen°
So gladly, I trow°, myn herte seyen°
That purely tho° myn oune thoghte
Seyde hit were beter serve° hir for noghte°
Than with another to be wel°.
And hyt was soth°, for everydel°
I wil anoon ryght telle thee why:
I sawgh hyr daunce so comelely°,
Carole° and synge so swetely,
Lawghe and pleye so womanly,
And loke so debonairly°,
So goodely speke and so frendly,
That certes y trowe° that evermore
Nas seyn° so blysful a tresore.
For every heer on hir hede,
Soth to seyne hyt was not rede,
Ne nouther° yelowe ne broune hyt nas;
Me thoghte most lyk gold hyt was.
And whiche eyen my lady hadde—
Debonair°, goode, glade, and sadde°,
Symple°, of good mochel°, noght to wyde°.
Therto° hir look nas not asyde°,
Ne overthwert°, but beset° so wele
Hyt drewh and took up everydele°
Al that on hir gan beholde°.

796 to mochel, *too much* **800 thoo,** *then,* **y couthe,** *I knew* **801 flyttynge,** *transitory* **803 Al,** *all* (things), **ylyche,** *equally* **806 ther,** *where,* **say,** *saw* **809 oo,** *one* **810 clepe,** *call,* **happe other grace,** *accident or favor* **812 to lyen ful comune,** *very accustomed to lie* **814 God wolde,** *I wish to God,* **clepe hir wers,** *call her worse* **815 worcheth,** *causes,* **ful woo,** *deep woe* **817 echon,** *each one* **818 Soth,** *truth,* **y sawgh oon,** *I saw one* **819 route,** *crowd* **822 clere,** *brighter* **826 Surmounted hem,** *surpassed them,* **of,** *in* **827 comelynesse,** *loveliness* **828 stature,** *form,* **wel sette gladnesse,** *fitting gaiety* **829 godlyhede,** *virtue,* **besey,** *endowed* **831 halwes,** *saints* (apostles) **832 swete,** *sweetheart,* **ryght al hirselve,** *herself indeed* **833 so stedfast,** *such steady* **834 So noble port,** *such noble bearing,* **meyntenaunce,** *demeanor* **835 boone,** *request* **836 espyed,** *ambushed* **837 ful sone,** *immediately* **838 As,** *so,* **ykaught,** *caught* **839–40 ne tok . . . No maner counseyl but at,** *thought about nothing except at* **841 Forwhy,** *because,* **eyen,** *eyes* **842 trow,** *believe,* **seyen,** *looked at* **843 purely tho,** *unreservedly then* **844 were beter serve,** *would be better to serve,* **noghte,** *nothing* **845 wel,** *well provided* **846 soth,** *true,* **everydel,** *completely* **848 comelely,** *attractively* **849 Carole,** *dance* **851 debonairly,** *graciously* **853 certes y trowe,** *truly I believe* **854 Nas seyn,** *was never seen* **857 Ne nouther,** *nor neither* **859 Debonair,** *gracious,* **sadde,** *steady* **861 Symple,** *modest,* **mochel,** *size,* **to wyde,** *too wide* **862 Therto,** *also,* **nas not asyde,** *was not sidelong* **863 overthwert,** *glancing,* **beset,** *directed* **864 everydele,** *completely* **865 that on hir gan beholde,** *who looked at her*

805–08 Echoes Machaut, *Jugement du Roy de Behaigne,* 281–82. **811–12 Fortune . . . lyen ful comune,** from Machaut, *Jugement du Roy de Behaigne,* 284–85. **817–1041** The elaborate but fairly conventional portrait of the lady is broadly influenced by Machaut: *Jugement du Roy de Behaigne,* 286–415 and 149–59; *Remede de Fortune,* 217–27. **828 wel,** F reads "so wel." **830 more,** omitted in F. **831 his,** omitted in F. **841 And,** F reads "But"; **herte,** F reads "hest." **849 Carole,** late-medieval caroling involved singing and dancing in a circle, and had nothing particular to do with Christmas. **858 gold,** omitted in F. **863 overthwert,** F reads "over twert."

Hir eyen semed anoon° she wolde
Have mercy—foolys wenden° soo—
But hyt was never the rather doo°.
Hyt nas no° countrefeted thynge,
Hyt was hir oune pure° lokynge
That the goddesse dame Nature
Had made hem opene by mesure°,
And cloos; for were she never so glad,
Hyr lokynge was not foly sprad°,
Ne wildely, thogh that she pleyde.
But ever me thoght hir eyen seyde,
'Be° God, my wrathe ys al foryive°.'
  "Therwith hir lyste so wel to lyve°
That dulnesse was of hir adrad°.
She nas to sobre ne to glad.
In alle thynges more mesure°
Had never, I trowe°, creature°.
But many oon° with hire loke she hert°,
And that sat hyr ful lytel at hert°,
For she knew nothynge of her° thoght.
But whither she knew or knew it nowght,
Algate° she ne rought° of hem a stree°.
To gete hyr love noo nerre° was he
That woned° at hom than he in Ynde°;
The formest° was alway behynde.
But goode folk over al other
She loved as man may do° hys brother,
Of whiche love she was wonder large°
In skilful° places that bere charge°.
  "But which a visage° had she thertoo°!
Allas, myn herte ys wonder woo°
That I ne kan discryven° hyt.
Me lakketh both Englyssh and wit
For to undo° hyt at the fulle,
And eke° my spirites be so dulle
So gret a thyng for to devyse.
I have no witte that kan suffise
To comprehenden hir beaute.
But thus moche° dar I sayn, that she
Was rody°, fressh, and lyvely hewed°,
And every day hir beaute newed°.
And negh° hir face was alderbest°,
For certes°, Nature had swich lest°
To make that faire that trewly she
Was hir chefe patron° of beaute,
And chefe ensample of al hir werke,
And moustre°; for be hyt never so derke,
Me thynketh I se hir evermoo.
And yet moreover, thogh alle thoo°
That ever levede were now alyve,
Ne sholde have founde to diskryve°
Yn al hir face a wikked sygne°,
For hit was sad°, symple, and benygne°.
  "And which° a goodely, softe speche
Had that swete, my lyves leche°!
So frendly, and so wel ygrounded,
Up° al resoun so wel yfounded,
And so tretable° to alle goode,
That I dar swere wel, by the roode°,
Of eloquence was never founde
So swete a sownynge facounde°,
Ne trewer tonged, ne skorned lasse°,
Ne bet koude hele°, that, by the masse,
I durste° swere, thogh the pope hit songe,
That ther was never yet throgh hir tonge
Man ne woman gretely harmed—
As for her°, was al harm hyd.
Ne lasse flaterynge in hir word,
That purely° hir symple record°
Was founde as trewe as any bonde,
Or trouthe° of any mannes honde,
Ne chyde she koude° never a dele°;

---

866 semed anoon, *indicated that soon* **867 wenden,** *thought* **868 the rather doo,** *readily granted* **869 Hyt nas no,** *it was no* **870 hir oune pure,** *their own perfect* **872 mesure,** *moderation* **874 foly sprad,** *foolishly spread* **877 Be,** *by,* **foryive,** *given up completely* **878 hir lyste so wel to lyve,** *she enjoyed life* **879 of hir adrad,** *afraid of her* **881 mesure,** *moderation* **882 trowe,** *believe,* **creature,** *any creature* **883 many oon,** *many people,* **hert,** *hurt* **884 sat hyr ful lytel at hert,** *weighed little on her heart* **885 her,** *their* (other peoples') **887 Algate,** *nevertheless,* **rought,** *cared,* **stree,** *straw* **888 nerre,** *nearer* **889 woned,** *dwelled* **889 Ynde,** *India* **890 formest,** *foremost* **892 do,** *i.e., love* **893 wonder large,** *wonderfully generous* **894 skilful,** *suitable,* **bere charge,** *bear the weight* (i.e., deserve it) **895 which a visage,** *such a face,* **thertoo,** *also* **896 wonder woo,** *very sorrowful* **897 discryven,** *describe* **899 undo,** *reveal* **900 eke,** *also* **904 moche,** *much* **905 rody,** *rosy,* **lyvely hewed,** *alive with color* **906 newed,** *became new again* **907 negh,** *nearly,* **alderbest,** *best of all* **908 certes,** *surely,* **swich lest,** *such desire* **910 patron,** *pattern* **912 moustre,** *model* **914 thoo,** *those* **916 diskryve,** *discern* **917 wikked sygne,** *sign of wickedness* **918 sad,** *steady,* **benygne,** *good* **919 which,** *such* **920 lyves leche,** *life's physician* **922 Up,** *upon* **923 tretable,** *receptive* **924 roode,** *Cross* **926 a sownynge facounde,** *an elegant speech* **927 skorned lasse,** *mocked less* **928 bet koude hele,** *could better heal* **929 durste,** *dare* **932 As for her,** *as far as she was concerned* **934 purely,** *completely,* **record,** *statement* **936 trouthe,** *pledge* **937 Ne chyde she koude,** *nor could she scold,* **dele,** *bit*

885 knew, F reads "knowe." **886** Line supplied from Th, copied into F in the seventeenth century; see also 31–96n. **905 Was rody,** F reads "Was white, rody." **928–29 by the masse . . . songe,** a mild vow. The Mass is the Roman Catholic celebration of sacred community; one sung or celebrated by the Pope was (and is) popularly regarded as especially holy. **932–33** Note the unusual rhyme: *harmed / harm hyd.* **932 her,** F reads "hit."

That knoweth al the world ful wele.
"But swiche a fairenesse of a nekke
Had that swete° that boon° nor brekke°
Nas ther non° seene that myssatte°.
Hyt was smothe, streght, and pure flatte°,
Wythouten hole°, or canel-boon°,
As be semynge°, had she noon.
Hyr throte, as I have now memoyre,
Semed a round tour of yvoyre°,
Of good gretenesse° and noght to grete.
"And goode faire White she hete°,
That was my lady name ryghte°.
She was bothe faire and bryghte;
She hadde not hir name wronge.
Ryght faire shuldres and body longe
She had, and armes, every lyth°
Fattyssh°, flesshy°, not grete therwith;
Ryght white handes and nalyes rede°,
Rounde brestes; and of good brede°
Hyr hippes were; a streight flat bakke.
I knewe on hir noon other lakke°
That al hir lymmes nere pure sywynge°
In as ferre° as I had knowynge.
"Therto° she koude so wel pley,
Whan that hir lyst°, that I dar sey
That she was lyk to torche bryghte
That every man may take of lyghte
Ynogh°, and hyt hath never the lesse.
Of° maner and of comlynesse°
Ryght so ferde° my lady dere,
For every wight° of hir manere
Myght cachche° ynogh, yif that he wolde,
Yif he had eyen hir to beholde.
For I dar swere wel yif that° she
Had amonge ten thousande be°,
She wolde have be, at the lest°,
A chef meroure° of al the fest°,
Thogh they had stonden in a rowe
To mennes eyen° koude have knowe°.
For wher so° men had pleyed or waked°,
Me thoghte the felawsshyppe as naked
Withouten hir, that sawgh I oones°,
As a corowne withoute stones°.
Trewly she was to myn eye
The soleyn fenix° of Arabye;
For ther levyth never but oon,
Ne swich as she ne knowe I noon.
"To speke of godenesse, trewly she
Had as moche debonairyte°
As ever had Hester in the Bible,
And more yif more were possyble.
And soth° to seyn, therwythalle°
She had a wytte so generalle°,
So hoole° enclyned to alle goode,
That al hir wytte was set, by the rode°,
Withoute malyce, upon gladnesse.
And therto° I sawgh never yet a lesse°
Harmful than she was in doynge—
I sey nat that she ne had knowynge
What harm was, or elles she
Had koude no good°, so thenketh me.
And trewly, for to speke of trouthe,
But° she had had°, hyt hadde be routhe°.
Therof she had so moche hyr dele°—
And I dar seyn and swere hyt wele—
That Trouthe hymselfe over al and alle°
Had chose hys maner° principalle
In hir, that was his restyng place.

940 swete, *sweet one,* **boon,** *bone,* **brekke,** *blemish* **941 Nas ther non,** *there was none,* **myssatte,** *was unbecoming* **942 pure flatte,** *perfectly smooth* **943 hole,** *hollow,* **canel-boon,** *collarbone* **944 As be semynge,** *as apparently* **946 tour of yvoyre,** *tower of ivory* **947 gretenesse,** *size* **948 hete,** *was called* **949 lady name ryghte,** *lady's appropriate name* **953 lyth,** *limb* **954 Fattyssh,** *shapely,* **flesshy,** *plump* **955 nalyes rede,** *red nails* **956 brede,** *breadth* **958 noon other lakke,** *no deficiency* **959 nere pure sywynge,** *were not perfectly proportioned* **960 ferre,** *far* **961 Therto,** *also* **962 hir lyst,** *it pleased her* **965 Ynogh,** *plenty* **966 Of,** *in,* **of comlynesse,** *in graciousness* **967 ferde,** *acted* **968 For every wight,** *that everybody* **969 cachche,** *catch* (i.e., learn) **971 yf that,** *if* **972 be,** *been* **973 at the lest,** *at least* **974 chef meroure,** *superior model,* **fest,** *company* **976 eyen,** *eyes,* **koude have knowe,** (that) *could discriminate* **977 wher so,** *wherever,* **waked,** *stayed awake into the night* **979 oones,** *once* **980 stones,** *gems* **982 soleyn fenix,** *unique phoenix* **986 debonairyte,** *graciousness* **989 soth,** *true,* **therwythalle,** *also* **990 wytte so generalle,** *mind so comprehensive* **991 hoole,** *wholly* **992 rode,** *Cross* **994 therto,** *also,* **yet a lesse,** *anyone less* **998 Had koude no good,** *could not have understood virtue* **1000 But,** *unless,* **had had,** *had had it* (truth, integrity), **be routhe,** *been a pity* **1001 dele,** *portion* **1003 over al and alle,** *over everything* **1004 maner,** *residence* (manor)

942 was smothe, F reads "was white, smothe." **945–46 throte . . . yvoyre,** the image is conventional, drawn ultimately from the biblical Song of Songs 7.4. **948 White,** in French, "Blanche." Blanche of Lancaster was the first wife of John of Gaunt; see lines 1318–19. **963–65** Chaucer's re-uses this common figure with similar language but radically different application in *WBP* 3.334–36. **972–74 amonge ten thousand . . . a chef meroure,** echoes the biblical Song of Songs 5.10, there spoken of a man. **982 soleyn fenix of Arabye,** in animal lore, only one phoenix exists at a time, in Arabia; at death it bursts into flames and then rises again from its own ashes. **987 Hester,** the biblical Esther was an idealized woman who saved her people from being persecuted.

Therto° she hadde the moste grace
To have stedefast perseveraunce,
And esy, attempry governaunce°,
That ever I knew or wyste yitte°,
So pure suffraunt° was hir wytte.
And reson gladly she understood—
Hyt folowed wel she koude° good;
She used° gladly to do wel.
These were hir maners everydel°.
  "Therwith° she loved so wel ryght°,
She wrong do wolde to no wyght°.
No wyght myght doo hir noo shame,
She loved so wel hir oune name.
Hyr lust to holde no wyght in honde°,
Ne, be thou siker°, she wolde not fonde°
To holde no wyght in balaunce°
By halfe word° ne by countenaunce°,
But yf° men wolde upon° hir lye;
Ne° sende men into Walakye,
To Pruyse, and into Tartarye,
To Alysaundre, ne into Turkye,
And byd hym faste anoon° that he
Goo hoodles° into the Drye Se
And come horn by the Carrenare,
And seye, 'Sir, be now ryght ware°
That I may of yow here seyn°
Worshyppe° or that° ye come ageyn.'
She ne used no suche knakkes smale°.
  "But wherfore that y° tel my tale?
Ryght on thys same°, as I have seyde,
Was hooly° al my love leyde.
For certes she was, that swete wife°,
My suffisaunce°, my luste°, my lyfe,
Myn happe°, myn hele°, and al my blysse,
My worldes welfare, and my goddysse,
And I hooly hires° and everydel.°"
  "By oure Lord," quod I, "y trowe° yow wel.
Hardely°, your love was wel besette°.
I not° how ye myght have doo bette.°"
  "Bette? Ne no wyght° so wel!" quod he.
  "Y trowe hyt, sir," quod I, "parde.°"
  "Nay, leve° hyt wel!"—"Sire, so do I;
I leve yow wel, that trewely
Yow thoghte that she was the best,
And to beholde the alderfayrest°,
Whosoo° had loked hir with your eyen."
  "With myn? Nay, alle that hir seyen°
Seyde and sworen hyt was soo.
And tbogh they ne hadde, I wolde thoo°
Have loved best my lady free.
Thogh I had hadde al the beaute
That ever had Alcipyades,
And al the strengthe of Ercules,
And therto had the worthynesse
Of Alysaunder, and al the rychesse
That ever was in Babyloyne,
In Cartage, or in Macedoyne,
Or in Rome, or in Nynyve;
And therto also as hardy° be
As was Ector, so have I° joye,
That Achilles slough° at Troye—
And therfore was he slayn alsoo
In a temple, for bothe twoo°
Were slayne, he and Antylegyus,

1006 Therto, *also* **1008 attempry governaunce,** *temperate self-control* **1009 wyste yitte,** *learned of since* **1010 pure suffraunt,** *wholly tolerant* **1012 koude,** *recognized* **1013 used,** *was accustomed* **1014 everydel,** *in every way* **1015 Therwith,** *also,* **ryght,** *righteousness* **1016 wyght,** *person* **1019 Hyr lust to holde ny wyght in honde,** *she desired to control no one* **1020 siker,** *certain,* **fonde,** *strive* **1021 balaunce,** *uncertainty* **1022 halfe word,** *innuendo,* **countenaunce,** *facial expression* **1023 But yf,** *unless,* **upon,** *to* **1024 Ne,** *nor* (did she) **1025 faste anoon,** *quickly* **1028 hoodles,** *hoodless* **1030 ware,** *careful* **1031 here seyn,** *hear said* **1032 Worshyppe,** *praise,* **or that,** *before* **1033 knakkes smale,** *petty tricks* **1034 wherfore that y,** *why do I* **1035 thys same,** *this very* (woman) **1036 hooly,** *completely* **1037 wife,** *woman* **1038 suffisaunce,** *sufficiency,* **luste,** *desire* **1039 happe,** *good fortune,* **hele,** *health* **1041 hires,** *hers,* **everydel,** *in every way* **1042 trowe,** *believe* **1043 Hardely,** *certainly,* **besette,** *placed* **1044 not,** *don't know,* **doo bette,** *done better* **1045 wyght,** *person* **1046 parde,** *by God* **1047 leve,** *believe* **1050 alderfayrest,** *fairest of all* **1051 Whosoo,** *whoever* **1052 seyen,** *saw* **1054 thoo,** *still* **1064 hardy,** *brave* **1065 so have I,** *may I have* **1066 slough,** *slew* **1068 bothe twoo,** *together*

1024–27 Walakye . . . Pruyse . . . Tartarye . . . Alysaundre . . . Turkye, Wallachia (in Romania), Prussia, Tartary (Mongolia), Alexandria (Egypt), and Turkey were all distant and exotic places where, in folk tales and romances, cruel mistresses might send their lovers to test their love. **1028 Drye Se,** the Gobi Desert (Mongolia). **1029 Carrenare,** Lake Kara-Nor (The Black Lake), east of the Gobi Desert and on the trade route from China to Europe. **1046 hyt,** F reads "hyt wol." **1056–72** Although the details vary, this commonplace list of admirable models was probably inspired by Machaut, Remede de Fortune 107ff. **1057 Alcipyades,** Alcibiades was an Athenian renowned for his beauty. **1058 Ercules,** Hercules, renowned for strength. **1060 Alysaunder,** Alexander the Great, renowned for his conquests. **1061–63 Babyloyne . . . Cartage . . . Macedoyne . . . Rome . . . Nynyve,** Babylon, Carthage, Macedonia, Rome, and Nineveh were ancient cities renowned for their wealth. **1063 therto,** F reads "to." **1065–66 Ector . . . Achilles,** Hector, hero of Troy, slain by Achilles, hero of the Greeks. **1069–71 Antylegyus . . . Dares Frygius . . . Polixena,** Archilochus (sometimes mistaken as Antilogus) was slain along with Achilles, who was about to marry Polyxena. A brief account of these events is in Dares Phrygius's De Excidio Troiae Historia (The History of the Fall of Troy; sixth century, Latin), although Chaucer probably knew them from the twelfth-century Roman de Troie of Benoît de Sainte-Maure.

And so seyth Dares Frygius,
For love of hir Polixena—
Or ben as wis as Mynerva,
I wolde ever, withoute drede°,
Have loved hir, for I moste nede°.
Nede! Nay, trewly, I gabbe° nowe.
Noght nede°, and I wol telle howe.
For of good wille myn herte hyt wolde°,
And eke to love hir I was holde°
As for the fairest and the beste.
She was as good, so° have I reste,
As ever was Penelopee of Grece,
Or as the noble wife Lucrece,
That was the best—he telleth thus,
The Romayn, Tytus Lyvyus—
She was as good, and nothyng lyke°,
Thogh hir stories be autentyke°;
Algate° she was as trewe as she—
But wherfore that° I telle the?
"Whan I first my lady say°,
I was ryght yong, soth° to say,
And ful gret need I nadde to lerne;
Whan my herte wolde yerne°
To love, hyt was a gret empryse°.
But as my wytte koude best suffise°,
After° my yonge childely wytte°,
Withoute drede°, I besette hytte°
To love hir in my beste wyse°,
To do hir worshippe and the servise
That I koude thoo°, be° my trouthe,
Withoute feynynge outher slouthe°,
For wonder feyn° I wolde° hir se.
So mochel hyt amended° me
That whan I saugh hir first a-morwe°
I was warysshed° of al my sorwe
Of al day after, til hyt were eve;
Me thoghte nothyng myghte me greve,
Were my sorwes never so smerte°.
And yet she syt° so in myn herte
That, by my trouthe°, y nolde noghte°,
For al thys worlde, out of my thoghte
Leve° my lady. Noo, trewely!"
"Now, by my trouthe, sir," quod I,
"Me thynketh ye have such a chaunce°
As shryfte° wythoute repentaunce."
"Repentaunce? Nay, fy°!" quod he,
"Shulde y now repente me
To love? Nay, certes°, than° were I wel
Wers° than was Achetofel,
Or Anthenor, so have I° joye,
The traytor that betraysed Troye,
Or the false Genelloun,
He that purchased the tresoun°
Of Rowlande and of Olyvere.
Nay, while I am alyve here,
I nyl foryete° hir nevermoo."
"Now, good syr," quod I thoo°,
"Ye han° wel told me herebefore—
Hyt ys° no nede to reherse° hit more—
How ye sawgh hir firste, and where.
But wolde ye° tel me the manere
To hire which was your firste speche°,
Therof I wolde yow beseche°;
And how she knewe first your thoghte,

1073 drede, *doubt* **1074 moste nede,** *necessarily must* **1075 gabbe,** *talk foolishly* **1076 Noght nede,** *not at all necessarily* **1077 hyt wolde,** *wanted it* **1078 holde,** *held* **1080 so,** *may* **1085 nothyng lyke,** *not at all like* (not like Lucretia, except in virtue) **1086 autentyke,** *authentic* **1087 Algate,** *nevertheless* **1088 wherfore that,** *why do* **1089 say,** *saw* **1090 soth,** *true* **1092 yerne,** *yearn* **1093 empryse,** *undertaking* **1094 wytte koude best suffise,** *mind was best able* **1095 After,** *in accord with,* **childely wytte,** *childlike understanding* **1096 drede,** *doubt,* **besette hytte,** *set it* **1097 wyse,** *way* **1099 thoo,** *then,* **be,** *by* **1100 feynynge outher slouthe,** *pretense or laziness* **1101 wonder feyn,** *wonderfully gladly,* **wolde,** *would* **1102 amended,** *improved* **1103 a-morwe,** *in the morning* **1104 warysshed,** *cured* **1107 Were . . . smerte,** *even if my sorrows hadn't been so painful* **1108 syt,** *sits* **1109 trouthe,** *word,* **y nolde noghte,** *I would not at all* **1111 Leve,** *leave* **1113 such a chaunce,** *about as much chance (of abandoning her)* **1114 shryfte,** *confession* **1115 fy,** *away with it (see n.)* **1117 certes,** *surely,* **than,** *then* **1118 Wers,** *worse* **1119 so have I,** *may I have* **1122 purchased the tresoun,** *arranged the betrayal* **1125 nyl foryete,** *will not forget* **1126 thoo,** *then* **1127 han,** *have* **1128 Hyt ys,** *there is,* **reherse,** *repeat* **1130 wolde ye,** *if you would* **1131 speche,** *conversation* **1132 beseche,** *request*

1071 hir, omitted in F. **1072 Mynerva,** Minerva, Roman goddess of wisdom. **1081 Penelopee of Grece,** Penelope, loyal wife of Odysseus who awaited his return from the Trojan War. **1082 Lucrece,** Lucretia; raped by Tarquinius, she chose suicide rather than to live in dishonor. See LGW 1680–1885. **1084 Tytus Lyvyus,** Livy (59 B.C.E.–C.E. 17) recounts the story of Lucretia in the first book of his History of Rome. **1104 warysshed,** F reads "warshed." **1108 in,** omitted in F. **1114 shryfte wythoute repentaunce,** repentance (or contrition) is a necessary condition for the sacrament of confession (or penance); the dreamer thinks the Black Knight will never abandon his love. **1115 fy,** an exclamation that means something like "I reject that as impossible or obnoxious." **1118 Achetofel,** the biblical Achitophel advised Absalom to rebel against his father, David (2 Samuel 17). **1119 Anthenor,** in several medieval versions of the fall of Troy, Antenor betrayed the city to save his own life; see *TC* 2.204. **1121–23 Genelloun . . . Rowlande . . . Olyvere,** in the *Song of Roland,* Ganelon conspired with the enemies of Charlemagne to ambush the rearguard of the Frankish army, betraying to their deaths Roland (Charlemagne's champion and Ganelon's kinsman) and Oliver, Roland's companion. **1128 it,** omitted in F.

Whether ye loved hir or noghte?
And telleth me eke what ye have lore°,
I herde yow telle herebefore."
  "Yee," seyde he, "thow nost° what thou menest°.
I have lost more than thou wenest.°"
  "What losse is that?" quod I thoo.
"Nyl she not° love yow? Ys hyt soo?
Or have ye oght doon amys°,
That she hath left yow? Ys hyt this?
For Goddes love, telle me alle."
  "Before God," quod he, "and I shalle.
I say ryght° as I have seyde,
On hir was al my love leyde,
And yet she nyste hyt nat° never a del°
Noght longe tyme, leve° hyt wel.
For be ryght siker°, I durste° noght,
For al this world tel hir my thoght,
Ne I wolde have wraththed° hir, trewely.
For wostow° why? She was lady
Of the body—she had the hert°,
And who hath that may not astert°.
But for to kepe me fro ydelnesse,
Trewly I did my besynesse
To make songes, as I best koude,
And ofte tyme I songe hem loude,
And made songes this a gret dele°—
Althogh I koude not make so wele°
Songes, ne knewe the art alle,
As koude Lamekes sone Tuballe
That founde out first the art of songe,
For as hys brothres° hamers ronge
Upon hys anvelt° up and doun,
Therof he took the firste soun—
But Grekes seyn° Pictagoras,
That he the firste fynder was
Of the art, *Aurora* telleth soo.
But therof no fors°, of hem twoo°.
Algates° songes thus I made
Of my felynge, myn herte to glade°;
And lo, this was the altherferst°—
I not wher° hyt were the werst:

  Lord, hyt maketh min herte lyght,
Whan I thenke on that swete wyght°
That is so semely on to see°;
And wisshe to God hit myght so bee
That she wolde holde me for hir knyght,
My lady, that is so fair and bryght!

  "Now have I told thee, soth° to say,
My firste song. Upon a day
I bethoghte me what woo
And sorwe that I suffred thoo°
For hir, and yet she wyste° hyt noght,
Ne telle hir durst° I nat my thoght.
'Allas,' thoghte I, 'y kan no rede°,
And but I telle hir, I nam° but dede;
And yif I telle hyr, to seye ryght sothe°,
I am adred° she wol be wrothe°.
Allas, what shal I thanne doo?'
  "In this debat I was so woo°
Me thoghte myn herte braste atweyne°.
So at the laste, soth to sayne,
I bethoghte me° that Nature
Ne formed never in creature
So moche° beaute, trewely,
And bounte°, wythoute mercy.
In hope of that my tale I tolde,
With sorwe, as that I never sholde°;
For nedes°, and mawgree my hede°,

1135 lore, *lost* **1137 nost,** *know not,* **menest,** *say* **1138 wenest,** *think* **1140 Nyl she not,** *will she not* **1141 oght doon amys,** *done anything wrong* **1145 ryght,** *just* **1147 nyste hyt nat,** *didn't know it,* **del,** *bit* **1148 leve,** *believe* **1149 ryght siker,** *very sure,* **durste,** *dared* **1151 wraththed,** *angered* **1152 wostow,** *do you know* **1153 hert,** *heart* **1154 may not astert,** *may not fail* **1159 dele,** *amount* **1160 wele,** *well* **1164 brothres,** *brother's* **1165 anvelt,** *anvil* **1167 seyn,** *say* **1170 fors,** *matter,* **hem twoo,** *them both* **1171 Algates,** *nevertheless* **1172 glade,** *gladden* **1173 altherferst,** *first of all* **1174 not wher,** *don't know whether* **1176 wyght,** *person* **1177 see,** *look* **1181 soth,** *truth* **1184 thoo,** *then* **1185 wyste,** *knew* **1186 durst,** *dared* **1187 y kan no rede,** *I know no remedy* **1188 nam,** *am not* **1189 ryght sothe,** *quite truly* **1190 adred,** *afraid,* **wrothe,** *angry* **1192 woo,** *upset* **1193 atweyne,** *in two* **1195 bethoghte me,** *recalled* **1197 moche,** *much* **1198 bounte,** *goodness* **1200 as that I never sholde,** *in such a way that I never should have* **1201 nedes,** *necessarily,* **mawgree my hede,** *despite myself* (my head)

1137–38 See 743–44 and 1305–06. **1137 seyde he,** F reads "he seyde." **1147–50** Echoes Machaut, *Remede de* Fortune, 359–64. **1149 by ryght,** F reads "ryght be." **1153–54** An echo of *Roman de la Rose* 1996–97. **1155 me fro,** F reads "me so fro." **1161 ne knewe,** F reads "the knowe," which makes the dreamer a poet in the opinion of the Black Knight. **1162 Lamekes sone Tuballe,** Tubal, Lamech's son. In Genesis 4.21–22, Jubal is the inventor of music, while his half-brother, Tubalcain, invented metalwork; both are sons of Lamech. The confusion of the names recurs in medieval accounts. **1167 Pictagoras,** Pythagoras (c. 582–c. 507 B.C.E), Greek philosopher credited with (among other things) first associating music and number theory. **1169 *Aurora*,** the *Aurora* of Peter of Riga, a twelfth-century Latin commentary on portions of the Bible. Like other medieval sources, the *Aurora* mentions both Tubal and Pythagoras when commenting on the invention of music. **1173 this,** F reads "thus." **the,** omitted in F. **1174 werst,** F reads "first." **1183–1295** Echoes Machaut, *Jugement du Roy de Behaigne*, 453–505, 596–98, 655–60, and 166–73; and *Remede de Fortune* 681–82, 132–34, 137–40, and 147–49. **1188 nam,** F reads "am."

I most° have told hir or be dede.
I not° wel how that I beganne—
Ful evel rehersen° hyt I kanne,
And eke°, as helpe me God withalle°,
I trowe° hyt was in the dismalle°
That was the ten woundes of Egipte—
For many a word I overskipte°
In my tale, for pure fere
Lest my wordes myssette° were.
With sorweful herte and woundes dede°,
Softe and quakynge for pure drede
And shame, and styntynge° in my tale°
For ferde°, and myn hewe° al pale,
Ful ofte I wex° bothe pale and rede.
Bowynge to hir, I heng the hede°,
I durste° nat ones° loke hir on,
For witte, maner, and al was goon.
I seyde 'Mercy,' and no more.
Hyt nas no game°, hyt sat me sore°.
"So at the laste, sothe to seyn,
Whan that myn herte was come ageyn,
To telle shortly al my speche,
With hool° herte I gan hir beseche°
That she wolde be my lady swete,
And swore, and gan hir hertely hete°
Ever to be stedfast and trewe,
And love hir alwey fresshly newe,
And never other lady have,
And al hir worship° for to save°
As I best koude—I swor hir this:
'For youres is alle that ever ther ys
For evermore, myn herte swete!
And never to false° yow, but I mete°,
I nyl°, as wys God helpe me soo.'
"And whan I had my tale ydoo°,
God wot°, she acounted nat a stree°
Of al my tale, so thoghte me.
To telle shortly ryght as hyt ys,
Trewly hir answere hyt was this—
I kan not now wel counterfete
Hyr wordes, but this was the grete°
Of hir answere: she sayde 'Nay,'
Alle outerly°: Allas, that day
The sorowe I suffred, and the woo,
That trewly Cassandra, that soo
Bewayled the destruccioun
Of Troye and of Ilyoun,
Had never swich sorwe as I thoo°.
I durste° no more say thertoo
For pure fere, but stal° away.
And thus I lyved ful many a day,
That trewely I hadde no nede
Ferther than my beddes hede
Never a day to seche° sorwe.
I fond hyt redy every morwe°
For-why° I loved hyr in no gere°.
"So hit befel, another yere
I thoughte ones° I wolde fonde°
To do° hir knowe and understonde
My woo; and she wel understode
That I ne wilned° nothyng but gode
And worshippe° and to kepe hir name
Over all thynges, and drede hir shame,
And was so besy hyr to serve,
And pitee were I shulde sterve°,
Syth that° I wilned noon harm, ywys°.
So whan my lady knewe al thys,
My lady yaf° me al hooly°
The noble yifte of hir mercy,
Savynge° hir worshippe, by al weyes—
Dredles°, I mene noon other weyes.
And therwith she yaf me a rynge;
I trowe° hyt was the firste thynge.
But yf myn herte was iwaxe°

1202 most, *must* **1203 not,** *don't know* **1204 Ful evel rehersen,** *very poorly repeat* **1205 eke,** *also,* **withalle,** *moreover* **1206 trowe,** *think,* **dismalle,** *dismal times* (see n.) **1208 overskipte,** *skipped over* **1210 myssette,** *misplaced* **1211 dede,** *deadly* **1213 styntynge,** *halting,* **tale,** *speech* **1214 For ferde,** *out of fear,* **hewe,** *complexion* **1215 wex,** *became* **1216 heng the hede,** *hung the* (my) *head* **1217 durste,** *dared,* **ones,** *once* **1220 Hyt nas no game,** *it was no joke,* **sat me sore,** *was painful to me* **1224 hool,** *entire,* **gan hir beseche,** *did plead with her* **1226 gan hir hertely hete,** *fervently promised her* **1230 worship,** *honor,* **save,** *protect* **1234 false,** *be false to,* **but I mete,** *unless I be dreaming* (i.e., unconsciously) **1235 nyl,** *will not* **1236 my tale ydoo,** *finished speaking* **1237 wot,** *knows,* **acounted nat a stree,** *valued less than a straw* (i.e., worthless) **1242 grete,** *gist* **1244 outerly,** *utterly* **1249 thoo,** *then* **1250 durste,** *dared* **1251 stal,** *stole* **1255 seche,** *seek* **1256 morwe,** *morning* **1257 For-why,** *because,* **in no gere,** *in no changeable way* **1259 ones,** *once,* **fonde,** *try* **1260 do,** *make* **1262 wilned,** *intended* **1263 worshippe,** *honor* **1266 sterve,** *die* **1267 Syth that,** *since,* **ywys,** *indeed* **1269 yaf,** *gave,* **hooly,** *completely* **1271 Savynge,** *preserving* **1272 Dredles,** *doubtless* **1274 trowe,** *think* **1275 iwaxe,** *grown*

1206–07 dismalle . . . ten woundes of Egipte, *dismalle* has a double etymology in medieval tradition, "evil days" (Latin *dies mali*) and "ten evils" (French *dix mals*), and in popular superstition, two evil days each month were associated with the ten plagues (Latin *plaga,* "wound") of Egypt (Exodus 7–12). The Black Knight is saying that he first professed his love on an unlucky day. **1223 al,** F reads "at." **1246 Cassandra,** daughter of Priam; in medieval versions of the Troy story, she foresaw the fall of the city and lamented its demise. **1248 Ilyoun,** Latin *Ilium,* the central fortress of ancient Troy.

Glad, that is no nede to axe°.
As° helpe me God, I was as blyve°
Reysed as fro deth to lyve,
Of al happes° the alderbeste°,
The gladdest, and the moste at reste°.
For trewely that swete wyght°,
Whan I had wrong and she the ryght,
She wolde alway so goodely
Foryeve me, so debonairly°.
In al my yowthe, in al chaunce°,
She took me in hir governaunce°.
Therwyth° she was alway so trewe,
Our joye was ever ylyche° newe.
Oure hertes wern° so evene a payre
That never nas that oon° contrayre
To that other for noo woo.
Forsothe°, ylyche they suffred thoo°
Oo° blysse, and eke oo sorwe bothe,
Ylyche they were bothe glad and wrothe°.
Al was us oon, withoute were°.
And thus we lyved ful many a yere
So wel I kan nat telle how."
  "Sir," quod I, "where is she now?"
"Now?" quod he, and stynte anoon°.
Therwith he waxe° as dede as stoon,
And seyde, "Allas that I was bore°,
That was the losse that here before
I tolde the that I hadde lorne°.
Bethenke° how I seyde herebeforne,
'Thow wost° ful lytel what thow menest°.
I have lost more than thow wenest°'—
God wot°, allas, ryght that was she!"
  "Allas, sir, how? What may that be?"
  "She ysded."—"Nay!"—"Yis, be my
    trouthe!"
  "Is that youre losse? Be God, hyt ys routhe.°"
And with that worde ryght anoon
They gan to strake forth°; al was doon,
For that tyme, the herte-huntynge.
With that me thoghte that this kynge
Gan homwarde for to ryde
Unto a place was there besyde°,
Which was from us but a lyte°,
A longe castel with walles white,
Be° Seynt Johan, on a ryche hille,
As me mette°. But thus hyt fille,
Ryght thus me mette, as I yow telle,
That in the castell ther was a belle,
As hyt hadde smyten oures twelve°.
Therwith° I awook myselve
And fonde me° lyinge in my bedde,
And the book that I hadde redde
Of Alcione and Seyes the kyng,
And of the goddes of slepynge,
I fond hyt in myn honde ful evene°.
Thoghte I, "Thys ys so queynt a swevene°
That I wol, be processe° of tyme,
Fonde° to put this swevene in ryme
As I kan best, and that anoon."
This was my swevene; now hit ys doon.

1276 axe, *ask* **1277 As,** *so,* **blyve,** *quickly* **1279 happes,** *occurrences,* **alderbeste,** *very best* **1280 at reste,** *satisfying* **1281 wyght,** *person* **1284 debonairly,** *graciously* **1285 chaunce,** *situations* **1286 governaunce,** *guidance* **1287 Therwyth,** *also* **1288 ylyche,** *equally* **1289 wern,** *were* **1290 oon,** *one* **1292 Forsothe,** *truly,* **thoo,** *then* **1293 Oo,** *one* **1294 wrothe,** *vexed* **1295 were,** *doubt* **1299 stynte anoon,** *stopped abruptly* **1300 waxe,** *became* **1301 bore,** *born* **1303 lorne,** *lost* **1304 Bethenke,** *consider* **1305 wost,** *know,* **menest,** *say* **1306 wenest,** *think* **1307 wot,** *knows* **1310 routhe,** *a pity* **1312 strake forth,** *blow the horn-call of conclusion* (see n.) **1316 was there besyde,** (that) *was near there* **1317 lyte,** *little way* **1319 Be,** *by* **1320 mette,** *dreamed* **1323 smyten oures twelve,** *struck twelve hours* **1324 Therwyth,** *with that* **1325 fonde me,** *found myself* **1329 ful evene,** *still* **1330 queynt,** *peculiar,* **swevene,** *dream* **1331 be processe,** *in the course* **1332 Fonde,** *attempt*

1282 the, omitted in F. **1305–06** See 743–44 and 1137–38. **1312 strake,** see *MED* "straken" (v. 2.1). The verb was used to describe various hunting calls on a horn, signaling the death of the quarry, the end of the hunt, or the journey homeward. Its abruptness here makes it unclear whether or not the hart was slain, with rich possibilities for verbal play on *heart.* **1314 this kynge,** i.e., Octavian; see 368n. John of Gaunt took the title King of Castile when he married Constance in 1371. **1318–19** Chaucer here alludes to John of Gaunt, who became Duke of Lancaster (punned upon in "longe castel") by marrying Blanche ("walles white"; see 948n), and was Earl of Richmond ("ryche hille," from French *riche mont*) from age two until 1372. "Seynt Johan" is Gaunt's name-saint, and St. John of Patmos is the author of Revelation, the biblical dream vision and the ultimate model of medieval dream poetry.

Parliament of Fowls

Parliament of Fowls

Introduction

In a mere 699 lines, *Parliament of Fowls* combines love, philosophy, cosmic travel, social criticism, and bird talk. The dream vision of the poem includes three set pieces: the *locus amoenus* ("lovely place") of the garden of Nature, the sensual temple of Venus that stands within the garden, and the parliament proper where three eagles sue unsuccessfully for the hand (talon?) of a formel (female eagle), and where socially inferior birds clamor to be about their springtime business. These juxtaposed set pieces survey the nature of love and many of its varieties—the orderly, idealized beauties of Nature's garden, the sighs and heavy breathing within Venus's temple, the comic tensions between the eagles' lengthy proclamations of courtly affection, and the fretful haste of the lower birds who urgently want to choose their mates.

Enriching the concern with love are social issues evident in the hierarchy of the birds (see 323–24n) and in the ideal of government ("comoun profyt" 47, 75) mentioned in the narrator's summary of the book that he reads before he falls asleep, i.e., Cicero's semi-allegorical *Somnium Scipionis* (*Dream of Scipio*). The *Somnium* concluded Cicero's (partially lost) *De Republica*, recorded for the Middle Ages in Macrobius's *Commentary on the Dream of Scipio*, itself a medieval key to dream interpretation and literary analysis. Chaucer's summary of the *Somnium* (36–84) emphasizes the idealized concord of the cosmos and the importance of human accord with cosmic harmony.

The motifs of individual desire, social responsibility, and cosmic order interact throughout the poem, reflected in analogies between birds and humans and between humans and the cosmos. The cyclic patterns of birds, of humans, and of the planets are all driven by some form of love, yet it is love that may be imperfect or delayed. The cosmos has not yet returned to its ideal original position (68–69), Priapus stands alone with his phallic "scepter" in his hand (256), and the eagles must wait another year before the female eagle chooses one of them. Even though the other birds do fly off with their mates, they abandon their harmonious song in order to do so. Paradoxically, love is one and many, individual and communal, sensual and suprasensual.

Less satisfied than the birds is the narrator, who seems not to learn the "certeyn thing" (20) he seeks in reading the *Somnium*, and who seems not to learn anything from his dream either. Yet as the stars and the birds continue in their cycles, so the narrator promises to continue his cycle, reading in hopes that he will learn something more certain. Here, as elsewhere in Chaucer, learning and loving are parallel processes, similar—even equivalent—in their compelling drives and in the uncertainties of their achievement.

Parliament of Fowls has long been treated as an occasional poem, one that depicts in an oblique way the betrothal of Richard II—either to Marie, daughter of Charles V of France, in 1377–78, or perhaps to Anne of Bohemia in 1380–81. In the first edition of the present text (1977, no. 37), John H. Fisher followed Haldeen Braddy and dated the poem 1377–78, arguing it was written before *House of Fame*, which he dates 1379–80. Most scholars reverse the two, making *Parliament* the later of the two poems, aligning it with negotiations for marriage between Richard and Anne, and arguing that the ten-syllable pentameter verse of *Parliament* (in rhyme royal stanzas) is more like Chaucer's later poetry than it is like the eight-syllable lines of *Book of the Duchess* and *House of Fame*. Even this is vexed, however, because Chaucer uses ten-syllable verse in his early poem *An ABC* (Short Poem 1). On the uncertainties of establishing the dates of Chaucer's poems or even their relative chronology, see Kathryn L. Lynch, "Dating Chaucer" (2007, no. 1684).

The dating of the poem cannot be clarified by the astrological reference to the location of Venus in the "north-north-west" (117), and its occasion cannot be pinned down by its reference to St. Valentine's Day (309). The evening star, Venus, never appears north-northwest of London, even though the planet was visible in a northwesterly position recurrently between 1374 and 1382. More than one St. Valentine was celebrated in the medieval liturgical calendar, so that the apparent conflict between the springtime setting of the poem and the now-traditional date of St. Valentine's Day, February 14, may be no conflict at all. It is even impossible to know whether or not Chaucer was the first to associate springtime love with St. Valentine, but if he was the first, contemporary poets Oton de Graunson, John Gower, and Sir John Clanvowe helped to perpetuate the tradition. Chaucer made the association again in the *Complaint of Mars* (Short Poem 3) and in the possibly spurious *An Amorous Complaint Made at Windsor* (Short Poem 22).

What seems certain is that *Parliament of Fowls* was written after Chaucer's first visit to Italy (1372–73) where he encountered the new humanist learning. Unlike *Book of the Duchess*, but like *House of Fame*, *Parliament of Fowls* shows distinct Italian influence. There are French models for the poem's concerns with gardens, questions of love (*demandes d'amour*), and bird debates (for example, the thirteenth-century *Fablel dou Dieu d'Amors*, John de Condé's *Messe des Oisiaus*, and versions of the story of Florence and Blancheflor), but a number of details of the *Parliament* derive from Dante's *Inferno* (see, e.g., 123n and 169n) and several from Boccaccio's *Teseida* (see 183–294n). This learning combines with the neo-Platonic cosmology of Macrobius (fifth century), and the notion of Nature as a semidivine vice regent and figure of plentitude that Chaucer derived from Alain de Lille's twelfth-century *De Planctu Naturae* (*The Complaint of Nature*). None of these sources have the witty combination of serious philosophy and comic delight that Chaucer's *Parliament* does, and by fusing philosophy, conventional imagery, social satire, and quizzical attitudes toward love, Chaucer makes the material fresh and wholly his own.

Two consistently insightful readings of the poem are J. A. W. Bennett's *The Parlement of Foules: An Interpretation* (1965, no. 1454) and Derek Brewer's "Introduction" to his edition *The Parlement of Foulys* (1972, no. 60). The edition of the poem in Helen Phillips and Nick Havely, *Chaucer's Dream Poetry* (1997, no. 69), also includes excellent notes and commentary. On the medieval tradition of St. Valentine, see H. A. Kelly, *Chaucer and the Cult of Saint Valentine* (1986, no. 1476). On the figure of Nature, see Hugh White's *Nature, Sex, and Goodness in a Medieval Literary Tradition* (2000, no. 1491), Theresa Tinkle's "The Case of the Variable Source" (2000, no. 1490), and Barbara Newman, "Did Goddesses Empower Women? The Case of Dame Nature" (2003, no. 1480). For an ecocritical reading of nature in the poem, see Lisa Kiser's "Chaucer and the Politics of Nature" (2001, no. 1477), and for studies of its relations with the English Parliament and class politics, see Matthew Giancarlo, *Parliament and Literature in Late Medieval England* (2007, no. 1470) and Andrew James Johnston, "Literary Politics in Debate: Chaucer's *Parliament of Fowls* and Clanvowe's *Book of Cupid*" (2007, no. 1472).

Parliament of Fowls

Here begynyth the Parleament of Foulys.

The lyf so short, the craft so long to lerne°,
Th'assay° so hard, so sharp the conquerynge,
The dredful° joye alwey that slit so yerne°—
Al this mene I be Love that my felynge
Astonyeth° with his wondyrful werkynge
So sore°, iwis°, that whan I on hym thynke,
Nat wot I wel° wher that° I flete° or synke.

For al be that° I knowe nat Love in dede°,
Ne wol° how that he quiteth folk her hyre°,
Yit happeth me° ful ofte in bokes rede
Of his myrakles° and his crewel yre°.
There rede I wel he wol° be lord and syre—
I dar nat seyn°, his strokes been so sore°,
But° "God save swich° a lord!" I can° no more.

Of usage°, what for lust° and what for lore°,
On bokes rede I ofte, as I yow tolde.
But wherfore that I speke al this? Nat yore°
Agon° it happede me for° to beholde
Upon a bok, was write with letteres olde;
And therupon, a certeyn thing to lerne,
The longe day ful faste I redde and yerne°.

For out of olde feldes°, as men seyth°,
Cometh al this newe corn° fro yer to yere,
And out of olde bokes, in good feyth,
Cometh al this newe science° that men lere°.
But now to purpos as of° this matere:
To rede forth hit gan me so delite°
That al that day me thoughte but a lyte°.

This bok of which I make of mencioun°
Entytled° was al thus as I shal telle:
"Tullyus of the Drem of Scipioun."
Chapitres sevene it hadde of hevene and helle
And erthe and soules that theryn dwelle,
Of whiche, as shortly as I can it trete°,
Of his sentence° I wol yow seyn the grete°.

Fyrst telleth it, whan Scipion was come
In Affrik°, how he meteth° Massynisse,
That hym for joie in armes hath inome°,
Thanne telleth it here speche° and al the blysse
That was betwix hem til the day gan mysse°;
And how his auncestre°, Affrycan so dere°,
Gan in his slep that nyght to hym apere°.

---

1 lerne, *learn* **2 Th'assay,** *the attempt* **3 dredful,** *timid or frightening,* **slit so yerne,** *slides away so quickly* **5 Astonyeth,** *is astonished* **6 sore,** *sorely,* **iwis,** *surely* **7 Nat wot I wel,** *I don't well know,* **wher that,** *whether,* **flete,** *float* **8 al be that,** *although,* **in dede,** *indeed or the deed of Love* **9 Ne wot,** *Nor know,* **quiteth folk her hyre,** *pays people their wages* **10 Yit happeth me,** (it) *happens* (to) *me* (that I) **11 myrakles,** *miracles,* **crewel yre,** *cruel anger* **12 wol,** *wil* **13 seyn,** *say,* **sore,** *painful* **14 But** (anything) *except,* **swich,** *such,* **can** *know* **15 usage,** *habit,* **what for lust,** *whether for pleasure,* **lore,** *knowledge* **17 yore,** *long* **18 Agon,** *ago,* **it happede me for,** *I happened* **21 yerne,** *eagerly* **22 feldes,** *fields,* **seyth,** *say* **23 corn,** *grain* **25 science,** *knowledge,* **lere,** *learn* **26 as of,** *concerning* **27 hit gan me so delite,** *it delighted me so* **28 a lyte,** *little* **29 make of mencioun,** *mentioned* **30 Entytled,** *titled* **34 trete,** *treat* **35 sentence,** *meaning,* **wol yow seyn the grete,** *will tell you the great part* **37 In Affrik,** *into Africa,* **meteth,** *meets* **38 inome,** *embraced* **39 here speche,** *their speech* **40 gan mysse,** *did end* **41 auncestre,** *ancestor,* **dere,** *dear* **42 Gan . . . apere,** *did . . . appear*

Text based on MS Cambridge Gg.4.27 (Gg), with variants from Fairfax 16 (F). Title in F: "The Parlement of Briddes"; the subtitle here is from Gg. **1** A proverb that goes back at least to Hippocrates. **2 hard . . . sharp,** Gg transposes these words. **3 dredful,** F reads "slyde." **5 with his wondyrful,** F reads "so with a dredeful." **7 flete or synke,** Gg reads "slete or synke"; F, "wake or wynke." **10 happeth me,** like "happede me" (l. 18) an impersonal construction, here in the present tense. **ful ofte in bokes,** F reads "in bookes ofte to." **12 There,** Gg reads "That." **13 I dar,** F reads "Dar I." Because medieval manuscripts do not regularly indicate quotations, it is difficult to tell whether or not "his strokes been so sore" should be treated as a quotation, like "God save swich a lord" in line 14. **14 can,** Gg reads "seye." **17 wherfore,** F reads "why that." **18 happede me,** past impersonal construction; see the note to line 10. **22 out,** Gg and F read "ofte." **25 newe science,** this may be Chaucer's tribute to the renaissance of learning he observed on his trips to Italy in 1372–73 and 1378. **26 as of this,** F reads "of my first." **27 hit gan me so,** Gg reads "so gan me to." **30 al thus as I shal,** F reads "there I shal yow telle." **31 Tullyus,** Marcus Tullius Cicero wrote *Somnium Scipionis* (*The Dream of Scipio*) as an epilogue to his *De Republica* (54 B.C.E.). Most of the latter has been lost, but the *Somnium* was preserved independently by Macrobius (fl. ca. 400) who added an extensive commentary. Earlier Chaucer knew it only by name from *RR* and mistook its nature in *BD* 284–87. But by this time he has clearly read it and summarizes it in detail. **32 sevene it hadde,** F reads "hyt had vii." **36 Scipion,** called Scipio Africanus Minor, destroyer of Carthage in the Third Punic War (149–46 B.C.E.). His dream is of his grandfather, Scipio Africanus Major, conqueror of Hannibal in the Second Punic War (218–01 B.C.E.). Cicero describes Scipio Minor as a great general, patriot, patron of letters, and exemplary friend. **37 Massynisse,** Masinissa, King of Numidia (now Libya), and long-time supporter of Scipio Major. **39 it,** Gg and F read "he." **41 Affrycan,** i.e., Scipio Major.

Thanne telleth it that from a sterry place°
How Affrycan hath hym Cartage shewed°,
And warnede hym beforn° of al his grace°,
And seyde what° man, lered other lewed°,
That lovede comoun profyt°, wel ithewed°,
He shulde into a blysful place wende°
There as joye is that last withouten ende.

Thanne axede° he if folk that here been dede°
Han lyf° and dwellynge in another place.
And African seyde, "Ye, withouten drede,°"
And that oure present worldes lyves space°
Nys° but a maner° deth, what wey we trace°.
And rightful folk shul gon after they deye
To hevene; and shewede hym the Galaxye.

Thanne shewede he hym the litel erthe that
here is,
At regard of° the hevenes quantite;
And after shewede he hym the nyne speris°;
And after that the melodye herde he
That cometh of thilke speres thryes thre°,
That welle° is of musik and melodye
In this world here, and cause of armonye°.

Than bad° he hym, syn° erthe was so lyte°,
And ful of torment and of harde grace°,
That he ne shulde hym in the world delyte.
Thanne tolde he hym, in certeyn yeres space°
That every sterre shulde come into his° place,
Ther° it was first, and al shulde out of mynde°
That in this world is don of al mankynde.

Thanne preyede hym Scypyon° to telle
hym al.
The wey to come into that hevene blysse.
And he seyde, "Know thyself first inmortal,
And loke ay besyly thow° werche and wysse°
To comoun profit, and thow shalt not mysse
To comen swiftly to that place deere
That ful of blysse is and of soules cleere°.

"But brekers of the lawe, soth to seyn°,
And lykerous° folk, after that they ben dede,
Shul whirle aboute th'erthe alwey° in peyn,
Tyl manye a world be passed°, out of drede°,
And than, foryeven° al her weked dede°,
Than shul they comen into that blysful place
To which to comen God the sende° his grace."

43 sterry place, *place among the stars* **44 shewed,** *showed* **45 warnede hym beforn,** *told him in advance,* **grace,** *good fortune* **46 what,** *whatever,* **lered other lewed,** *learned or unlearned* **47 comoun profyt,** *the common good,* **wel ithewed,** *endowed with virtues* **48 wende,** *go* **50 axede,** *asked,* **been dede,** *are dead* **51 Han lyf,** *have life* **52 Ye,** *yes,* **drede,** *doubt* **53 lyves space,** *time of life* **54 Nys,** *is not,* **maner,** *kind of,* **wey we trace,** *whatever way we go* **58 At regard of,** *in comparison with* **59 nyne speris,** *nine spheres* **61 thilke speres thryes thre,** *the same spheres thrice three* **62 welle,** *source* **63 armonye,** *harmony* **64 bad,** *urged,* **syn,** *since,* **lyte,** *little* **65 grace,** *favor* **67 space,** *time* **68 his,** *its* **69 Ther,** *where,* **shulde out of mynde,** *be forgotten* **71 preyede hym Scypyon,** *Scipio asked him* **74 loke ay besyly thow,** *make sure* (that) *you always intently,* **werche and wysse,** *work and lead* **77 cleere,** *shining* **78 soth to seyn,** *to say truth* **79 lykerous,** *lecherous* (sinful) **80 th'erthe alwey,** *the earth always* **81 Tyl manye a world be passed,** *until the world changes many times,* **out of drede,** *no doubt* **82 foryeven,** *forgiven,* **her weked dede,** *their wicked deeds* **84 God the sende,** *may God send you*

43 tellith it that, F reads "told he hym." **sterry place,** it is implicit that Scipio Major and Minor ascend to the stars from where they view Carthage. **46 what,** F reads "hym." **lered,** Gg reads "lernyd."**47 comoun profyt,** an important social and political concept as Europe near the end of the Middle Ages moved toward becoming a society in which more people participated in government. "Common profit" had formed the basis for the Roman concept of *res publica (public things, the republic),* and was coming to form the basis of the English notion of *commonwealth,* or government working for the good of the majority rather than a favored aristocratic minority. Here the term translates Macrobius's *patriam,* "native land," and at 75 below, *salute patriae,* "health of the nation." The conflict between the "common profit" and personal desire is a central theme in *PF.* **49 as joye is that last,** F reads "joy is that lasteth." **50 if folk,** F reads "if the folk." **here,** Gg reads "now." **been,** F reads "be." **56 Galaxye,** the Milky Way. Gg reads "Galylye." **57 litel,** omitted in Gg. **59 nyne speris,** nine concentric crystalline spheres constitute the classical and medieval universe. The first seven include the planets (in ascending order: moon, Mercury, Venus, sun, Mars, Jupiter, Saturn), the eighth contains the fixed stars, and the ninth is the Primum Mobile (Prime Mover) that sets the others in motion. **62 musik and melodye,** analogous to the eight tones on a musical scale, the movement of the celestial spheres was thought to produce a sublime, macrocosmic octave; Chaucer misses this subtlety by having all nine spheres produce tones. The theme of harmony (**armonye**, line 63) as an ideal recurs throughout *PF,* reaching a crescendo in the final song of the birds. **65** Gg reads "And was somedel disseyvable and ful of harde grace." **68 sterre . . . come into his place,** the so-called "great" or "mundane" year, the length of time it takes for all the heavenly bodies to return to where they first began. The *Somnium* (2.11.11) gives 15,000 years, although the period varies in other sources. **75 comoun profit,** see l. 47n.**76 that,** G reads "this." **79 lykerous,** *lecherous* does not here mean sexual immorality per se, but moral depravity—what St. Augustine and some critics have termed "cupidity" in contrast to spiritual "charity." **80 whirle,** this has sometimes been taken as an allusion to the punishment of Paolo and Francesca in Dante's *Inferno* 5, but the *Somnium* (2.9.2) has the same figure. **83 blysful place,** the suggestion is that all spirits will ultimately achieve bliss. F reads "alwey whirle" and omits "alwey" later in the line. **84 the sende his,** Gg reads "send us"; F, "sende ech lover."

The day gan faylen°, and the derke nyght,
That reveth bestes from her besynesse°,
Berafte° me myn bok for lak of lyght,
And to° my bed I gan° me for to dresse°,
Fulfyld of thought and busy hevynesse°;
For bothe I hadde thyng which that I nolde°,
And ek° I ne hadde that thyng that I wolde°.

But fynally, my spirit at the laste,
For-wery of° my labour al the day,
Tok reste, that made me to slepe faste;
And in my slep I mette° as that I lay
How African, ryght° in the selfe aray°
That Scipion hym say° byfore that tyde°;
Was come and stod right at myn bedes syde.

The wery huntere slepynge in his bed,
To wode ayen° his mynde goth anon;
The juge dremeth how his plees° been sped°;
The cartere dremeth how his carte is gon°;
The riche, of gold; the knyght fyght with his fon°;
The syke met° he drynketh of the tonne°;
The lovere met he hath his lady wonne.

Can I nat seyn yf° that the cause were
For° I hadde red of African byforn
That made me to mete° that he stod there,
But thus seyde he, "Thow hast the° so wel born°
In lokynge of° myn olde bok totorn°,
Of which Macrobye roughte° nat a lyte°,
That sumdel° of thy labour wolde I quyte.°"

Cytherea, thow blysful lady swete,
That with thy ferbrond° dauntest° whom
the lest°,
And madest me thys swevene° for to mete°,
Be thow myn helpe in this, for thow mayst best!
As wisly° as I seye the° north-north-west
Whan I began myn swevene for to write,
So yif° me myght to ryme and ek t'endyte°.

This forseyde° African me hente anon°,
And forth with hym unto a gate broughte
Ryght of° a park walled of grene ston,
And over the gate, with letteres large iwroughte°,
There were vers iwreten°, as me thoughte,
On eyther half° of ful gret difference,
Of which I shal now seyn the pleyn sentence°.

"Thorw° me men gon into that blysful place
Of hertes hele° and dedly woundes cure;
Thorw me men gon unto the welle° of grace,
There° grene and lusty May shal evere endure.
This is the wey to al good aventure.
Be glad, thow redere°, and thy sorwe of-caste°.
Al open am I; passe in, and sped the faste."

85 gan faylen, *did pass* **86 reveth bestes from her besynesse,** *deprives beasts of their concerns* **87 Berafte,** *deprived* **88 to,** *for,* **gan,** *began,* **dresse,** *prepare* **89 busy hevynesse,** *restless sadness* **90 nolde,** *did not want* **91 ek,** *also,* **wolde,** *did want* **93 For-wery of,** *completely exhausted from* **95 mette,** *dreamed* **96 ryght,** *exactly,* **selfe aray,** *same clothing* **97 hym say,** *saw him* (in), **tyde,** *time* **100 wode ayen,** *the woods again* **101 plees,** *cases,* **been sped,** *have proceeded* **102 gon,** *gone* **103 fon,** *foes* **104 syke met,** *ill* (person) *dreams,* **tonne,** *wine cask* **106 Can I nat seyn yf,** *I can not say if* **107 For,** *because* **108 mete,** *dream* **109 the,** *yourself,* **born,** *conducted* **110 lokynge of,** *looking at,* **totorn,** *tattered* **111 roughte,** *cared,* **lyte,** *little* **112 sumdel,** *somewhat,* **wolde I quyte,** *will I repay* **114 ferbrond,** *flaming torch,* **dauntest,** *overcomes,* **whom the lest,** *whom you wish to* **115 swevene,** *dream* (noun), **mete,** *dream* (verb) **117 wisly,** *surely,* **seye the,** *saw you* **119 yif,** *give,* **ek t'endyte,** *also to compose* **120 forseyde,** *previously mentioned,* **hente anon,** *grasped quickly* **122 Ryght of** (to the) *right* (side) *of* **123 iwroughte,** *worked* (inscribed) **124 vers iwreten,** *verses written* **125 eyther half,** *either side* **126 sentence,** *meaning* **127 Throw,** *through* **128 hertes hele,** *heart's well-being* **129 welle,** *source* **130 There,** *where* **132 redere,** *reader,* **thy sorwe of-caste,** *cast off your sorrow*

85 day gan faylen, similar to *Inferno* 2.1–3, but Dante was borrowing from the *Aeneid*, 4.522, 9.224, which Chaucer also knew. Gg reads "folwyn" for "faylen"; F, "faile." **90–91** A clear echo of Boethius, *Bo* 3 pr.3.33–36, where the sentiment indicates the narrator's unreasoning discontent; cf. *Complaint unto Pity* (Short Poem 5) 99–104 and *Balade of Pity* (Short Poem 6) 43–45. **91 that thyng that,** Gg and F read "thyng that." **96 selfe,** Gg reads "same." **99 wery huntere . . . ,** the narrator hypothesizes that we dream about what occupies us in our waking hours. This dream psychology (which has a bearing on the dreams of *BD*, *HF*, and *LGW* also) is familiar in classical and medieval discussions, including Macrobius's commentary on the *Somnium.* **110 totorn,** Gg reads "byforn"; F "al totorn." **111 Macrobye,** Macrobius; see 31n. **113 Cytherea,** Venus, the goddess and the planet. **114 ferbrond,** firebrand, or flaming torch, a traditional icon of Venus. **117 north-north-west,** the compass reading has been taken either as Chaucer's ironic comment on the whole poem (north-northwest being a deviant position; cf. Hamlet, "I am but mad north-north-west," 2.2.396), or else as a means of dating the poem. Venus was visible as an evening star in a north westerly position in 1374, 1377, 1380, and 1382. Of these, 1377 coincides with negotiations for Richard II's betrothal to Marie of France and 1380 negotiations for betrothal to Anne of Bohemia; see Introduction. The reading in Gg "north nor west" (i.e., south or east) opens up another series of possible dates. **123 gate,** Gg reads "gatis." This recalls the gate of Hell in *Inferno* 3. Also African is similar to Dante's Virgil as a guide who can read questions in the face (line 155) of the one he guides. Unlike the gate in *Inferno*, however, Chaucer's gate is ambiguous, perhaps symbolizing, as some critics have suggested, heavenly and earthly love, or Nature and Venus, or fertile married love and sterile eroticism. It is impossible to tell whether the dreamer's entry (line 154) places him in a garden of heavenly or earthly love, or whether the two kinds of love are separable. **125 half,** Gg reads "syde." **126 the,** F reads "yow." **132 of-caste,** Gg reads "over caste." **133 sped,** F reads "hye."

“Thorw me men gon,” than spak° that other side,
“Unto the mortal strokes of the spere°,
Of which Disdayn and Daunger is the gyde°,
There° nevere tre° shal fruyt ne leves bere.
This strem yow ledeth to the sorweful were°
There as the fish in prysoun is al drye—
Th’eschewyng° is only the remedye.”

These vers° of gold and blak iwreten° were,
Of whiche I gan astonyed° to beholde,
Forwhi° that oon encresede ay° my fere,
And with that other gan myn herte bolde°;
That oon me hette°, that other dede me colde.
No wit hadde I, for errour°, for to chese
To entre or flen°, or me to save or lese.

Right° as betwixen adamauntes° two°
Of evene myght, a pece of yren° set
Ne hath no myght to meve° to ne fro—
For what that on may hale°, that other let°—
Ferde° I; that nyste° whether me was bet°
To entre or leve, til Affrycan my gide°
Me hente° and shot° in at the gates wide,

And seyde, “It stondeth writen in thy face,
Thyn errour, though thow telle it not to me.
But dred the not° to come into this place,
For this writyng nys nothyng ment bi the°
Ne by non but° he Loves servaunt be.
For thow of love hast lost thy tast, I gesse,
As sek° man hath of swete° and bytternesse.

“But natheles°, althow that thow be dul°,
Yit that° thow canst not do, yit mayst thow se°.
For manye a man that may nat stonde a pul°,
It liketh hym atte wrastlyng for to be,
And demen° yit wher° he do bet° or he.
And if thow haddest cunnyng° for t’endite°,
I shal the shewe mater° for to wryte.”

With that myn hand he tok in his anon,
Of whiche I confort kaughte°, and went in faste.
But, Lord, so I was glad and wel begoon°,
For overal where that I myn eyen° caste
Were trees clad with leves that ay° shal laste,
Eche in his kynde, of colour fresh and greene
As emeroude, that joye was to seene.

The byldere ok°; and ek the hardy assh°;
The piler° elm, the cofere° unto carayne°;
The boxtre pipere°; holm° to whippes lasch;
The saylynge firre°; the cipresse, deth to pleyne°;
The shetere ew°; the asp° for shaftes pleyne°;
The olyve of pes°; and ek the dronke° vyne;
The victor° palm; the laurer to devyne°.

A gardyn saw I ful of blosmy bowes°
Upon a rever in a grene mede°,
There as° swetnesse everemore inow° is,
With floures white, blewe, yelwe, and rede,

134 spak, *spoke* **135 spere,** *spear* **136 gyde,** *guide* **137 There,** *where,* **tre,** *tree* **138 were,** *weir* (fish trap) **140 Th’eschewyng,** *the avoiding* **141 vers,** *verses,* **iwreten,** *written* **142 gan astonyed,** *was astonished* **143 Forwhi,** *Because,* **oon encresede ay,** *one increased always* **144 gan myn herte bolde,** *did embolden my heart* **145 hette,** *heated,* **146 errour,** *confusion* **147 flen,** *flee* **148 Right,** *just,* **adamauntes,** *magnets* **149 pece of yren,** *piece of iron* **150 meve,** *move* **151 on may hale,** *one may attract,* **let,** *repels* **152 Ferde,** *acted,* **nyste,** *knew not,* **bet,** *better* **153 gide,** *guide* **154 hente,** *seized,* **shof,** *shoved* **157 dred the not,** *do not dread* **158 nys nothyng ment bi the,** *is not meant for you* **159 Ne by non but,** *nor for anyone unless* **161 sek,** *sick,* **swete,** *sweetness* **162 natheles,** *nonetheless,* **dul,** *dull* **163 Yit that,** *yet that which,* **se,** *watch* **164 stonde a pul,** *survive a bout* **165 It liketh hym,** *he enjoys* **166 demen,** *judges,* **wher,** *whether,* **bet,** *better* **167 cunnyng,** *skill,* **t’endite,** *to compose* **168 the shewe mater,** *show you matter* **170 Of whiche I confort kaughte,** *from which I took comfort* **171 wel begoon,** *happy* **172 myn eyen,** *my eyes* **173 ay,** *always* **176 byldere ok,** *builder oak,* **hardy assh,** *enduring ash* **177 piler,** *vine prop,* **cofere,** *coffin,* **carayne,** *corpse* **178 boxtre pipere,** *piper boxtree,* **holm,** *holly* **179 saylynge firre,** *sailing fir,* **pleyne,** *complain* **180 shetere ew,** *shooter yew,* **asp,** *aspen,* **shaftes pleyne,** *straight arrows* **181 pes,** *peace,* **dronke,** *drunken* **182 victor,** *victory,* **to devyne,** *for prediction* **183 blosmy bowes,** *blossoming boughs* **184 mede,** *meadow* **185 There as,** *where,* **inow,** *enough*

136 Disdayn and Daunger, Scorn and Standoffishness, personifications that represent the pains of love. **137 There nevere tre shal fruyt,** Gg reads “That never yit shal freut”; F. “There tree shal never frute.” **142 astonyed,** F reads “a stounde” (a while). **150 Ne,** F reads “That.” **155 writen in thy face,** see l. 123n above. **160 tast,** Gg reads “stat.” **164–65 stonde a pul . . . atte wrastlyng . . . ,** the figure suggests that those who cannot wrestle can still enjoy watching and judging wrestlers. **167 And if thow,** Gg reads “And there it.” **169 hand he took,** at *Inferno* 3.19, Virgil places his hand on Dante’s, comforts him, and leads him through the gates of Hell. **170 went in,** Gg reads “that as.” **175 joye,** Gg reads “sothe.” **176–82** The catalog of trees with their epithets is a rhetorical showpiece, derived from epic tradition. There is such a list in Boccaccio’s *Teseida* (11.22ff.), which was Chaucer’s source for the temple of Venus (183–294), but this list is more like the one in Joseph of Exeter’s *Iliad* 1.505ff. **Oak** was used in building, **ash** for making spears, **elm** as a prop for vines and for making coffins, **boxtree** for making pipes and recorders, **holly** for carving (of whip handles?), **fir** for masts and spars, **cypress** was planted in cemeteries, **yew** was used to make bows, **aspen** to make arrows, **olive** branches were signs of peace, grape **vines** produced wine, **palms** signified victory, and **laurel** leaves were thought to induce oracular powers. **183–294** These lines are modeled on Boccaccio’s *Teseida* 7.51–66. **183 blosmy,** Gg reads “blospemy”; F, “blossomed.” **186 yelwe,** Gg reads “and yelwe.”

And colde welle-stremes°, nothyng dede°,
That swymmen ful of smale fisches lyghte°,
With fynnes rede and skales sylver bryghte.

On every bow° the briddes° herde I synge,
With voys of aungel in here armonye°,
Some besyede hem here bryddes forth to
brynge°.
The litele conyes° to here pley gunne hye°.
And ferther al aboute I gan aspye°
The dredful ro°, the buk, the hert and hynde°,
Squyreles, and bestes° smale of gentil kynde°.

Of instrumentes of strenges° in acord
Herde I so pleye a ravyshyng swetnesse,
That God that makere is of al and lord
Ne herde nevere beter, as I gesse.
Therwith a wynd, unnethe° it myghte be lesse,
Made in the leves grene a noyse softe
Acordaunt to° the foules song alofte.

The aire of that place so attempre° was
That nevere was ther grevaunce° of hot
ne cold.
Ther wex ek° every holsum° spice and gras°;
Ne no man may there waxe sek° ne old.
Yit was there joye more a thousentfold
Than man can telle; ne nevere wolde it nyghte°,
But ay cler° day to any manes syghte.

Under a tre besyde a welle I say°
Cupide oure lord his arwes° forge and file.
And at his fet° his bowe al redy lay,
And Wille his doughter temperede° al this whyle°
The hevedes° in the welle, and with hire wile°
She couchede hem after as° they shulde serve,
Some for to sle°, and some to wounde and kerve°.

Tho° was I war° of Plesaunce anon-ryght°,
And of Aray°, and Lust°, and Curteysie,
And of the Craft° that can and hath the myght
To don° by force a wight° to don folye°—
Disfigurat° was she, I nyl° nat lye.
And by hemself° under an ok, I gesse,
Saw I Delyt that stod with Gentilesse°.

I saw Beute withouten any atyr°,
And Youthe ful of game and jolyte,
Foolhardynesse and Flaterye and Desyr,
Messagerye° and Meede° and other thre—
Here° names shul° not here be told for° me.
And upon pileres° greete of jasper longe
I saw a temple of bras ifounded stronge°.

Aboute that temple daunseden° alwey
Wemen inowe°, of whiche some ther weere
Fayre of hemself, and some of hem were gay°;
In kerteles°, al dishevele° wente they there;
That was here offys° alwey, yer by yeere.

---

187 welle-stremes, *springs,* **nothing dede,** *not at all still* **188 lyghte,** *lively* **190 bow,** *bough,* **briddes,** *birds* **191 here armonye,** *their harmony* **192 besyede hem here bryddes forth to brynge,** *busied themselves to bring up their young* **193 litele conyes,** *little rabbits,* **to here pley gunne hye,** *hurried to their play* **194 gan aspye,** *saw* **195 dredful ro,** *fearful roe deer,* **hert and hynde,** *male and female* **196 bestes,** *beasts,* **kynde,** *nature* **197 instrumentes of strenges,** *stringed instruments* **201 unnethe,** *scarcely* **203 Acordaunt to,** *in harmony with* **204 attempre,** *temperate* **205 grevaunce,** *annoyance* **206 wex ek,** *grew also,* **holsum,** *wholesome,* **gras,** *herb* **207 waxe sek,** *grow sick* **209 wolde it nyghte,** *would it become night* **210 ay cler,** *always bright* **211 say,** *saw* **212 arwes,** *arrows* **213 fet,** *feet* **214 temperede,** *hardened,* **whyle,** *while* **215 hevedes,** (arrow) *heads,* **wile,** *skill* **216 couchede hem after as,** *arranged them according to how* **217 sle,** *slay,* **kerve,** *cut* **218 Tho,** *then,* **war,** *aware,* **anon-ryght,** *right away* **219 Aray,** *Clothing,* **Lust,** *Desire* **220 Craft,** *Artifice* **221 don,** *make,* **wight,** *person,* **don folye,** *do folly* **222 Disfigurat,** *disfigured,* **nyl,** *will not* **223 hemself,** *themselves* **224 Gentilesse,** *Nobility* **225 atyr,** *attire* **228 Messagerye,** *Messengerhood,* **Meede,** *Bribery* **229 Here,** *their,* **shul,** *shall,* **for,** *by* **230 pileres,** *pillars* **231 ifounded stronge,** *firmly established* **232 daunseden,** *danced* **233 Wemen inowe,** *women enough* **234 gay,** *gaily adorned* **235 kerteles,** *straight dresses,* **al dishevele,** *with hair unbound* **236 here offys,** *their function*

188 lyghte, Gg reads "lite." **190 briddes,** Gg reads "foules." **191 armonye,** the ideal of harmony is expressed here again, connecting the notion of cosmic harmony from l. 60 with the harmony of the birds that will be reinstated at the end of the poem. **192 Some,** Gg reads "So"; F, "That." **203 foules,** Gg reads "bryddes." **204 aire,** Gg reads "erthe." **207 Ne,** omitted in Gg and F. **212 Cupide,** the god of love; through line 294 Chaucer includes various traditional figures of chivalric love. Many of the personifications are from the *RR* tradition, although suggested by Boccaccio's *Teseida* 7.53ff., which lies behind *HF* 119–39 and *CT* 1.1918–66 also. **214 Wille,** perhaps a misreading of the name of Cupid's daughter as "Voluntade" for "Vollutade," sensual pleasure (from Lat. *voluptas*; *Teseida* 7.54). Gg reads "Welle" (Prosperity). **215 hire wile,** F reads "harde file." **221 don by force,** F reads "goo before." **224 Delyt . . . Gentilesse,** from *Teseida* 7.55: "Diletto con Gentilezza" ("Delight with Nobility"). **225 withouten any atyr,** Chaucer's own detail; in *Teseida* she is merely "*Sanz ornament*" ("without ornament"). **228 Messagerye,** the figure of a go-between in love affairs. **other thre,** Chaucer uses the number three to fill out a rhyme also at *CT* 1.164. **230 jasper,** a semiprecious green quartz. **231 bras,** a possible echo of 1 Cor. 1, where sensual love is equated with sounding brass or a tinkling cymbal. *Teseida* 7.57 has "rame" (copper); both metals were associated with Venus.

And on the temple, of doves white and fayre
Saw I syttynge manye an hunderede peyre.

Byfore the temple dore ful sobyrly
Dame Pes° sat with a curtyn° in hire hond,
And by hire syde, wonder° discretly,
Dame Pacience syttynge there I fond°,
With face pale, upon an hil of sond°,
And aldirnext°, withinne and ek withoute,
Byheste° and Art, and of here° folk a route°.

Withinne the temple, of sykes hoote° as fyr
I herde a swow° that gan aboute renne°.
Whiche slikes° were engendered° with desyr
That maden every auter° for to brenne°
Of newe flaume°; and wel espyed I thenne
That al the cause of sorwe that they drye°
Cam of the bittere goddesse Jelosye.

The god Priapus saw I, as I wente,
Withinne the temple in sovereyn° place
    stonde,
In swich aray° as whan the asse hym shente°
With cri by nyghte, and with sceptre° in his
    honde.
Ful besyly° men gunne assaye and fonde
Upon his hed to sette, of sundery hewe°,
Garlondes ful of freshe floures newe.

And in a prive° corner in desport°
Fond I Venus and hire porter Richesse,
That was ful noble and hautayn of hyre port°—
Derk was that place, but afterward lightnesse
I saw a lyte°; unnethe° it myghte be lesse—
And on a bed of gold she lay to reste
Tyl that the hote sunne gan to weste°.

Hyre gilte heres° with a goldene thred
Ibounden° were, untressed° as she lay;
And naked from the brest up to the hed
Men myghte hyre sen°—and sothly° for to say,
The remenaunt° was wel kevered° to myn pay°
Ryght with a subtyl covercheif of Valence°.
Ther nas no thikkere cloth of no defense°.

The place yaf° a thousand savouris sote°,
And Bachus, god of wyn, sat hire besyde,
And Ceres next, that doth of hunger boote°,
And as I seyde, amyddes° lay Cypride°,
To whom on knees two yonge folk there cryde
To ben here helpe°: But thus I let hir lye,
And ferthere° in the temple I gan espie

That, in dispit° of Dyane° the chaste,
Ful many a bowe ibroke heng° on the wal
Of maydenes swich as gunne here tymes waste°
In hyre servyse°. And peynted overal

240 Pes, *Peace,* **curtyn,** *curtain* **241 wonder,** *wondrously* **242 fond,** *found* **243 sond,** *sand* **244 aldirnext,** *closest of all* **245 Byheste,** *Promise,* **here,** *their,* **route,** *company* **246 sykes hoote,** *sighs hot* **247 swow,** *swooning sound,* **gan aboute renne,** *did run about* **248 sikes,** *sighs,* **engendered,** *begotten* **249 auter,** *altar,* **brenne,** *burn* **250 flaume,** *flame* **251 drye,** *suffer* **254 sovereyn,** *dominant* **255 swich aray,** *such clothing,* **hym shente,** *ruined him* **255 sceptre,** *royal staff* **257 Ful besyly,** *very intently,* **gunne assaye and fonde,** *assayed and attempted* **258 sundery hewe,** *various colors* **260 prive,** *private,* **in desport,** *enjoying herself (or themselves)* **261 porter,** *doorkeeper* **262 hautayn of hyre port,** *haughty in her manner* **264 lyte,** *little,* **unnethe,** *scarcely* **266 gan to weste,** *moved to the west* **267 gilte heres,** *gilded hair* **268 Ibounden,** *bound,* **untressed,** *unbraided* **269 sen,** *see,* **sothly,** *truly* **271 remenaunt,** *rest,* **kevered,** *covered,* **pay,** *satisfaction* **272 subtyl covercheif of Valence,** *subtle Valencian cloth* **273 of no defense,** *of no protection* **274 yaf,** *exuded,* **savouris sote,** *sweet odors* **276 boote,** (provide the) *remedy* **277 amyddes,** *in the middle,* **Cypride,** *Venus* **279 To ben here helpe,** (for her) *to help them* **280 ferthere,** *further* **281 dispit,** *defiance,* **Dyane,** *Diana* **282 bowe ibroke heng,** *broken bow hung* **283 maydenes swich as gunne here tymes waste,** *virgins such as did waste their time* **284 hyre servyse,** *Venus's service*

237 of doves, F reads "saugh I." **238 Saw I syttynge,** F reads "Of doves white." **240 curtyn . . . hond,** in *Teseida* 7.58, Peace holds up a curtain, but Chaucer's detail is obscure. **243 face pale . . . hil of sond,** the pale face is in *Teseida* 7.58, but Chaucer adds the hill of sand, which suggests sterility and instability and contrasts Nature's hill of flowers, l. 302 below. **253 Priapus,** Roman fertility god, represented with an enormous phallus. **255 asse hym shente,** the ass in Ovid's *Fasti,* 1.415ff., brayed just as the sexually aroused Priapus was about to grab the nymph Lotis, enabling her to escape and turn into a water flower; as a result, Priapus was subject to derision. **256 sceptre in his,** F reads "his sceptre in." **260 desport,** in *Teseida* 7.63–64, Richezza guards the door. **261 Venus,** Gg reads "febz" (?). **271 was,** omitted in F. **272 Valence,** city in France famous for weaving. Its name survives in the modern *valance,* a type of curtain. **273 nas . . . of no defense,** i.e., it was transparent. **275–76 Bachus . . . Ceres,** a traditional association of the deities of drink and food with the goddess of love. **276 Ceres,** Gg reads "Sereis." **277 Cypride,** another name for Venus because she was reputed to have been born of the waves near Cyprus. **279 hir,** Gg reads "hem." **281 Dyane,** Diana, Roman goddess of the moon and virginity. **282 bowe ibroke,** symbolizes lost virginity because the bow is associated with Diana as a virgin huntress. **284 And peynted,** Gg reads "ipeyntede were."

Ful many a story, of which I touche shal°
A fewe, as of Calyxte and Athalante,
And manye a mayde of whiche the name
I wante°.

Semyramis, Candace, and Hercules,
Biblis, Dido, Thisbe, and Piramus,
Tristram, Isaude, Paris, and Achilles,
Eleyne, Cliopatre, and Troylus,
Silla, and ek° the moder of Romulus—
Alle these were peynted on that other syde,
And al here love, and in what plyt° they deyde°.

Whan I was come ayen° unto the place
That I of spak, that was so sote° and grene,
Forth welk° I tho° myselven to solace.
Tho was I war wher° that ther sat a queene
That, as of lyght the someres sonne shene°
Passeth° the sterre°, right so over° mesure
She fayrer was than any creature.

And in a launde°, upon an hil of floures,
Was set this noble Goddesse of Nature.
Of braunches were hire halles and hire
boures°
Iwrought° after hire cast° and hire mesure°,
Ne there nas foul° that cometh of engendrure°
That they ne were prest° in hire presence
To take hire dom° and yeve° hire audyence.

For this was on Seynt Valentynes day,
Whan every foul cometh there to chese his
make°,
Of every kynde° that men thynke may;
And that so huge a noyse gan they make
That erthe and eyr° and tre and every lake
So ful was that unethe° was there space
For me to stonde, so ful was al the place.

And right° as Aleyn in the *Pleynt of Kynde*°
Devyseth° Nature of aray° and face,
In swich° aray men myghte hire there fynde.
This noble emperesse, ful of grace,
Bad° every foul to take his° owne place,
As they were woned alwey°, fro yer to yeere,
Seynt Valentynes day to stonden theere.

---

285 touche shal, *will touch* (on) **287 wante,** *lack* **292 ek,** *also* **294 plyt,** *plight,* **deyde,** *died* **295 ayen,** *again* **296 sote,** *sweet smelling* **297 welk,** *walked,* **tho,** *then* **298 war wher,** *aware where* **299 someres sonne shene,** *summer's bright sun* **300 Passeth,** *surpasses,* **sterre,** *star,* **over,** *beyond* **302 launde,** *clearing* **304 boures,** *chambers* **305 Iwrought,** *made,* **cast,** *design,* **mesure,** *proportion* **306 nas foul,** *was no bird,* **engendrure,** *procreation* **307 prest,** *ready* **308 dom,** *judgment,* **yeve,** *give* **310 chese his make,** *chose its mate* **311 kynde,** *species* **313 eyr,** *air* **314 unethe,** *scarcely* **316 right,** *just,* ***Pleynt of Kynde,*** *Complaint of Nature* **317 Devyseth,** *describes,* **aray,** *clothing* **318 swich,** *such* **320 Bad,** *ordered,* **his,** *its* **321 woned alwey,** *accustomed to always*

285–94 many a story, a conventional list of unhappy lovers that Chaucer develops beyond what he found in *Teseida* 7.61–62. **Calyxte,** Callisto was a nymph beloved of Jove and changed to a bear by his jealous wife, the goddess Juno; Ovid, *Metamorphoses* 2.401ff. **Athalante,** Atalanta sought to avoid would-be lovers by defeating them in footraces and was eventually changed to a lion for violating a sacred temple with her husband; Ovid, *Metamorphoses* 10.560ff. **Semyramis,** legendary queen of Assyria who committed incest with her son. **Candace,** Indian queen in Alexander romances who seduces the hero. **Hercules,** accidentally betrayed by his wife, dies a painful death; see *MkT* 7.2119–34. **Biblis,** because of incestuous love for her brother, changed into a fountain; Ovid, *Metamorphoses* 9.45ff. **Dido,** Carthaginian queen abandoned by Aeneas; *Aeneid* 4. **Thisbe and Piramus,** star-crossed lovers who both commit suicide; Ovid, *Metamorphoses* 4.55ff. **Tristram** and **Isaude,** desperate lovers associated with the Arthurian cycle, victimized by a love potion. **Paris, Achilles,** and **Eleyne,** three major characters in the story of the fall of Troy; each one loves inordinately. **Cliopatre,** Cleopatra killed herself for love of Marc Antony; see *LGW* 580ff. **Troylus,** the "double sorrow"—yearning for love and losing love—of Troylus's love for Criseyde is told in *TC.* **Silla,** for love of Minos, Scylla brought about her father's death; Ovid, *Metamorphoses* 8.8ff. **moder of Romulus,** Rhea Silvia, raped by Mars, was the mother of Romulus and Remus; Ovid, *Fasti* 3.9ff. **303 of,** omitted in Gg. **306–08 foul . . . they . . . yeve hire audyence,** as acknowledged in line 316 below, this tableau may have been suggested to Chaucer by Alain de Lille's (Alanus ab Insulis) *De Planctu Naturae* (c1180), where birds are depicted as decorations on Nature's robe and described with epithets somewhat like those in lines 337ff. The robe is so ethereal that the birds appear to move about as in a council of animals ("*animalium celebratur concilium*"), perhaps the inspiration for Chaucer's parliament. However, assemblies of birds are common in medieval poetry, e.g., the thirteenth-century *Fablel dou Dieu d'Amors,* Jean de Condé's *Messe des Oisiaus,* and versions of the story of Florence and Blancheflor. **305 cast,** F reads "crafte." **306 nas,** G reads "was." **307 they,** F reads "there." **309 Seynt Valentynes day,** poems celebrating the love of birds (representing humans) on St. Valentine's day developed as a genre in Chaucer's time. Chaucer's *Complaint of Mars* and his *Complaint Made at Windsor* (perhaps spurious) are Valentine poems, and in *LGW* small birds sing of love and St.Valentine (F 139–47). There are also examples by John Gower, Sir John Clanvowe, and Oton de Graunson, although *PF* may be earlier than these. Because there appears to have been more than one medieval St. Valentine, the feast day is difficult to determine. February 14 has come to be the traditional date, but this seems inconsistent with the springtime setting of the poem. **310 foul,** Gg reads "bryd." **313 eyr,** F reads "see." **316 Aleyn . . . *Kynde*,** see ll. 305–08n. **317 Devyseth,** a considerable truncation of Aleyn's detailed description of Nature, perhaps Chaucer's comic undercutting of the lengthy rhetoric. **320 his,** F reads "her" (their).

That is to seyn, the foules of ravyne°
Were heyest° set, and thanne the foules smale
That eten° as hem Nature wolde enclyne°—
As werm° or thyng of which I telle no tale;
And water-foul sat loueste° in the dale;
But foul that lyveth by sed° sat on the grene,
And that so fele° that wonder was to sene.

There myghte men the ryal egle° fynde,
That with his sharpe lok perseth the sunne°,
And othere egles of a lowere kynde,
Of whiche that clerkes wel devyse cunne°.
Ther was the tiraunt° with his federys dunne°
And grey, I mene the goshauk, that doth pyne°
To bryddes for his outrageous ravyne°.

The gentyl faucoun° that with his feet
    distrayneth°
The kynges hand; the hardy sperhauk eke°,
The quayles foo°; the merlioun° that payneth°
Hymself ful ofte the larke for to seke°,
There was the douve° with hire eyen meke°;
The jelous swan, ayens his deth that syngeth°,
The oule ek° that of deth the bode° bryngeth;
The crane, the geaunt° with his trompes soun°,
The thef°, the chough; and ek the
    jangelynge pye°;
The skornynge° jay; the eles fo°, heroun;
The false lapwynge°, ful of trecherye;
The stare° that the conseyl° can bewreye°,
The tame roddok°; and the coward kyte°,
The kok°, that orloge° is of thorpes lyte°,

The sparwe°, Venus sone°; the nyghtyngale
That clepeth° forth the grene ieves newe;
The swalwe°, mortherere° of the foules smale
That maken hony of floures freshe of hewe;
The wedded turtil° with hire herte trewe;
The pecok with his aungels fetheres bryghte°;
The fesaunt°, skornere° of the cok° by nyghte;

The waker goos°; the cokkow° ever unkynde°;
The popynjay° ful of delicasye°;
The drake, stroyere° of his owene kynde;
The stork, the wrekere of avouterye°;
The hote cormeraunt of glotenye°;
The raven wys°, the crowe with vois° of care;
The thrustil° old; the frosty feldefare°.

---

323 foules of ravyne, *birds of prey* **324 heyest,** *highest* **325 eten,** *ate,* **enclyne,** *incline* **326 As werm,** (such) *as worms* **327 loueste,** *lowest* **328 lyveth by sed,** *lived by* (eating) *seeds* **329 fele,** *many* **330 ryal egle,** *royal eagle* **331 lok perseth the sunne,** *look pierces the sun* **333 wel devyse cunne,** *can well describe* **334 tiraunt,** *tyrant,* **federys dunne,** *feathers brown* **335 pyne,** *injury* **336 ravyne,** *rapaciousness* **337 gentyl faucon,** *noble falcon,* **distrayneth,** *grasps* **338 sperhauk eke,** *sparrow hawk also* **339 quayles foo,** *quail's foe,* **merlioun,** *merlin* (small hawk), **payneth,** *exerts* **340 seke,** *seek* **341 douve,** *dove,* **eyen meke,** *meek eye* **342 ayens his deth that syngeth,** *that sings at the approach of his death,* **343 oule ek,** *owl also,* **bode,** *warning* **344 geaunt,** *giant,* **trompes soun,** *trumpet sound* **345 thef,** *thief,* **jangelynge pye,** *chattering magpie* **346 skornyge,** *scolding,* **eles fo,** *eel's foe* **347 lapwynge,** *lapwing* **348 stare,** *starling,* **conseyl,** *secrets,* **bewreye,** *betray* **349 roddok,** *ruddock,* **kyte,** *kite* **350 kok,** *cock,* **orloge,** *clock,* **thorpes lyte,** *villages small* **351 sparwe,** *sparrow,* **Venus sone,** *Venus's son* **352 clepeth,** *calls* **353 swalwe,** *swallow,* **mortherere,** *murderer* **355 turtil,** *turtledove* **356 aungels fetheres bryghte,** *bright angel's feathers* **357 fesaunt,** *pheasant,* **skornere,** *scorner,* **cok,** *cock* **358 waker goos,** *watchful goose,* **cokkow,** *cuckoo,* **unkynde,** *unnatural* **359 popynjay,** *parrot,* **delicasye,** *delicacy* **360 stroyere,** *destroyer* **361 wrekere of avouterye,** *avenger of adultery* **362 hote cormeraunt of glotenye,** *cormorant hot with gluttony* **363 wys,** *wise,* **vois,** *voice* **364 thrustil,** *thrush,* **feldefare,** *fieldfare*

324 heyest set, the places of the birds are strictly hierarchical, an ingredient in the debate that follows. Although various attempts to make the classes of birds precisely fit classes of human society have not been satisfactory, there is at least a loose paralleling. If birds of prey are nobility, water fowl merchants, and seed fowl agricultural workers, then worm fowl must be the bourgeoisie; the celibate clergy are presumably not included. **326 of which I telle no tale,** Gg reads "I telle myn tale." **331 perseth the sunne,** in the bestiary tradition, the eagle can looks straight into the sun, a sign of clear-sightedness. **335 goshauk,** the goshawk was often trained for hunting. **337 faucoun . . . distrayneth . . . ,** the hunting falcon perched on the hand or fist of the (often noble) hunter. **338–39 sperhauk . . . merlioun,** the sparrow hawk and the merlin were used to hunt other birds. **338 hardy,** omitted in F. **342 jelous swan,** the swan was thought to protect its nest and, upon approaching death, give forth with a "swan song," now synonymous with a final performance. **his,** Gg reads "hire." **343 oule,** the owl is still associated with fear and death. **345 chough . . . pye,** the chough, a kind of crow, was legendary for its thievery; the magpie, for garrulity. Gg reads "crow" for "chough." **346 eles,** F reads "egles." **heroun,** herons do eat eels. **347 lapwynge,** the lapwing's practice of distracting intruders who approach its nest by pretending to have a broken wing made it a figure for fraud. **348 stare,** Gg reads "starlyng." **349 roddok . . . kite,** the ruddock is a kind of robin; the kite, a kind of falcon. **350 kok,** roosters were thought to crow at regular intervals of time. **351 sparwe,** the sparrow, sacred to Venus, was a figure for sexual desire. **nyghtyngale,** the nightingale calls forth the new leaves by singing in the springtime. **352 grene,** F reads "fresshe." **353–54 swalwe . . . hony,** the swallow was thought to be an eater of bees, sometimes classified as small birds. **355 turtil,** the turtledove was reputed never to take a second mate. **356 pecok,** the peacock's feathers, like depictions of angel wings, were thought to have eyes on them. **356 fetheres,** Gg reads "clothis." **357 fesaunt,** the pheasant, or wild cock, was supposed to breed with domestic hens. **358 waker goos . . . cokkow ever unkynde,** geese are called more vigilant guardians even than dogs; the cuckoo was considered unnatural because it was thought to deposit its eggs in other birds' nests (cf. ll. 610–13 below and *King Lear* 1.4.205). Gg reads "most" for "ever." **359 popynjay,** the parrot was reputed to have a weakness for wine. **360 drake,** the male duck was supposed to kill ducklings. **361 stork,** the stork was supposed to kill its adulterous mate. **362 cormeraunt,** the cormorant was supposed to burn of its own gluttony. **363 raven . . . crowe,** the raven was thought to be prophetic; the crow, to cry out with sorrowful voice. **364 thrustil . . . feldefare,** the thrush was supposed to live to be very old; the fieldfare, another kind of thrush, may have been thought "frosty" because it wintered in England.

What shulde I seyn ? Of foules every kynde
That in this world hath federes and stature°,
Men myghten in that place assemblede fynde
Byfore the noble Goddesse of Nature,
And everiche° of hem ded his besy cure°
Benygnely° to chese° or for to take,
By hire acord°, his formel° or his make°.

But to the poynt: Nature held on hire hond
A formel egle, of shap° the gentilleste°
That evere she among hire werkes fond°,
The moste benygne° and the goodlieste°.
In hire was everi vertu at his reste°
So ferforth° that Nature hireself hadde blysse
To loke on hire and ofte hire bek to kysse°.

Nature, the vicarye° of the almyghty Lord,
That hot, cold, hevy, lyght, moyst, and dreye
Hath knyt° with evene noumberes of acord°,
In esy voys° began to speke and seye,
"Foules, tak hed of° my sentence°, I preye,
And for youre ese, in fortheryng° of youre nede,
As faste as I may speke, I wol yow speede°.

"Ye knowe wel how, Seynt Valentynes day,
By my statute and thorw° my governaunce,
Ye come for to cheese°—and fle youre wey—
Youre makes°, as I prike° yow with plesaunce°.
But natheles°, myn ryghtful ordenaunce°
May I nat lete° for al this world to wynne,
That he that most is worthi shal begynne.

"The tersel° egle, as that ye knowe ful wel,
The foul ryal°; above yow in degre°,
The wyse and worthi, secre°, trewe as stel,
Whiche I have formed, as ye may wel se,
In every part as it best liketh me—
It nedeth not° his shap yow to devyse°—
He shal ferst chese° and speken in his gyse°.

"And after hym by order shul ye chese,
After youre kynde, everiche° as yow lyketh,
And as youre hap is° shul ye wynne or lese°—
But which of yow that love most entriketh°,
God sende hym hire that sorest for hym syketh°
And therwithal° the tersel gan she calle,
And seyde, "My sone, the choys° is to the falle°.

"But natheles, in° this condicioun
Mot° be the choys of everich that is heere,
That she agre to his eleccioun°
Whatso° he be that shulde° be hire feere°.
This is oure usage° alwey, from yer to yeere,
And whoso° may at this tyme have his grace
In blisful tyme he cam into this place."

With hed enclyned° and with ful humble cheere°
This ryal tersel spak, and tariede noht°.
"Unto my sovereyn° lady, and not my fere°,
I chese, and chese with wil and hert and thought,
The formel on youre hond, so wel iwrought°,
Whos° I am al°, and evere wol hire serve,
Do what hire lest to do° me lyve or sterve°,

---

366 federes and stature, *feathers and form* **369 everiche,** *each,* **ded his besy cure,** *did his busy effort* **370 Benygnely,** *courteously,* **chese,** *choose* **371 acord,** *agreement,* **formel,** *female,* **make,** *mate* **373 shap,** *shape,* **gentilleste,** *most noble* **374 werkes fond,** *works found* **375 benygne,** *gracious,* **goodlieste,** *most beautiful* **376 at his reste,** *in its place* **377 So ferforth,** *to such an extent,* **378 bek to kysse,** *nodded* (in order) *to kiss* **379 vicarye,** *deputy* (vicar) **381 knyt,** *knit,* **evene noumberes of acord,** *proper proportions in agreement* **382 esy voys,** *easy voice* **383 tak hed of,** *pay attention to,* **sentence,** *message* **384 fortheryng,** *furthering* **385 speede,** *hasten* **387 thorw,** *through* **388 cheese,** *choose* **389 makes,** *mates,* **prike,** *incite,* **plesaunce,** *pleasure* **390 natheles,** *nonetheless,* **ordenaunce,** *ordering* **391 lete,** *abandon* **393 tersel,** *male* **394 foul ryal,** *royal bird,* **degre,** *status* **395 secre,** *discreet* **398 It nedeth not,** *there is no need,* **devyse,** *describe* **399 ferst chese,** *choose first,* **gyse,** *manner* **401 everiche,** *everyone* **402 as youre hap is,** *according to your luck,* **lese,** *lose* **403 entriketh,** *entraps* **404 syketh,** *sighs* **405 therwithal,** *with that* **406 choys,** *choice,* **to the falle,** *falls to you* **407 in,** *under* **408 Mot,** *must* **409 eleccioun,** *selection* **410 Whatso,** *whatsoever,* **shulde,** *would,* **feere,** *mate* **411 usage,** *custom* **412 whoso,** *whoever,* **grace,** *good fortune* **414 hed enclyned,** *bowed head,* **cheere,** *expression* **415 tariede noht,** *delayed not at all* **416 sovereyn,** *supreme,* **fere,** *equal* **418 iwrought,** *created* **419 Whos,** *whose,* **al,** *completely* **420 Do what hire lest to do,** *regardless of whether it pleases her to make,* **sterve** *die*

368 of, omitted in Gg. **379 vicarye of the almyghty Lord,** Nature's traditional role as God's deputy is also mentioned in *De Planctu Naturae* 13.224, *RR* 16782, *PhyT* 6.20, etc. **380–81 hot, cold . . . knyt with evene noumberes,** the proportional bonding of these characteristics underlies the theory of the four elements (earth, cold and dry; air, hot and moist; fire, hot and dry; water, cold and moist), explaining why fire, for example, rises through air. Traceable to Empedocles, the philosophical commonplace can be found in Macrobius's *Commentary* 1.6.4ff., *De Planctu Naturae* 6.46ff., *Bo* 3.m9, and elsewhere. The theory includes the notion that the bonding of the elements is analogous to ideal love and that this bonding establishes a cosmic harmony throughout the entire universe, except where disrupted by inordinate passion or sin. 381 with, **F reads "be." 382 esy voys,** Chaucer specifies the tone in which Nature addresses her unruly audience; see 521n. **began,** Gg reads "gan for." **385 yow,** F reads "me." **390 ordenaunce,** F reads "governaunce." **391 lete,** Gg reads "breke." **392 most is worthi shal begynne,** Nature asserts that aristocratic hierarchy is the law of nature. 393 ful, **omitted in F. 394 yow in,** Gg reads "every." **400 ye,** Gg reads "they." **404 sorest,** Gg reads "soryest." **406 to the,** Gg reads "to yow." **410 Whatso,** F reads "Who so." **411 oure usage,** Nature's concession of veto power to the lady was not the "usage" (custom) of the time. **414 ful,** omitted in Gg.

"Besekynge° hire of merci and of grace,
As she that is myn lady sovereyne;
Or let me deye present° in this place.
For certes°, longe I may nat lyve in payne,
For in myn herte is korven° every veyne.
And havynge reward° only to my trouthe°,
My deere herte, have of my wo sum routhe°.

"And if that I to hyre be founde untrewe,
Disobeysaunt°, or wilful° necligent,
Avauntour°, or in proces° love a newe,
I preye to yow this be my jugement:
That with° these foules be I al torent°
That ilke° day that evere she me fynde
To hire untrewe, or in my gilt° unkynde.

"And syn° that hire loveth non° so wel as I—
Al be° she nevere of love me behette°—
Thanne ouhte° she be myn thourh hire mercy,
For other bond° can I non on hire knette°.
Ne nevere for no wo ne shal I lette°
To serven hire, how fer so that she wende°,
Say what yow lest°, my tale is at an ende."

Ryght° as the freshe, rede rose newe
Ayen° the somer sunne coloured is,
Ryght so for shame al wexen gan the hewe°
Of this formel whan she herde al this;
She neyther answerde wel ne seyde amys°,
So sore abashed was she, tyl that Nature
Seyde, "Doughter, drede the nought°, I yow
assure."

Another tersel egle spak anon,
Of lower kynde, and seyde, "That shal nat be!
I love hire bet° than ye don, by Seynt John,
Or at the leste° I love as wel as ye,
And longer have served hire in my degre°,
And if she shulde have loved for° long lovynge,
To me ful longe hadde be° the gerdonynge°.

"I dar ek seyn°, if she me fynde fals,
Unkynde, janglere°, or rebel in any wyse,
Or jelous, do me hangen by the hals°.
And but° I bere me in hire servyse
As wel as that my wit can me suffyse°,
From poynt to poynt°, hyre honour for to save,
Take she my lif and al the good° I have!"

The thredde° tercel egle answerde tho,
"Now, sires, ye seen the lytel leyser heere°,
For every foul cryeth out to ben ago°
Forth with his mak°, or with his lady deere;
And ek° Nature hireself ne wol not heere°,
For tarying° here, not half that I wolde seye.
And but° I speke, I mot for sorwe deye°.

"Of long servyse avaunte° I me nothing—
But as possible is me° to deye today
For wo as he that hath ben languysshyng°
This twenty wynter; and wel happen may°
A man may serven bet°, and more to pay°,
In half a yer, althow it were no moore,
Than sum man doth that hath served ful yoore°.

"I sey not this by me, for I ne can
Don° no servyse that may my lady plese.
But I dar seyn°, I am hire treweste man,
As to my dom°, and faynest wolde hire ese°,
At shorte wordes°, til that deth me sese°.
I wol ben hires°, whether I wake or wynke°,
And trewe in al that herte may bethynke."

---

421 Besekynge, *beseeching* **423 present,** *now* **424 certes,** *certainly* **425 korven,** *cut* **426 reward,** *regard,* **trouthe,** *fidelity* **427 sum routhe,** *some pity* **429 Disobeysaunt,** *disobedient,* **wilful,** *willfully* **430 Avauntour,** *braggart* (about love), **proces,** *time* **432 with,** *by,* **torent,** *torn to pieces* **433 ilke,** *same* **434 in my gilt,** *by my fault* **435 syn,** *since,* **hire loveth non,** *none love her* **436 Al be,** *even though,* **behette,** *promised* **437 Thanne ouhte,** *then ought* **438 bond,** *claim,* **knette,** *attach* **439 lette,** *stop* **440 how fer so that she wende,** *however far she may travel* **441 lest,** *wish* **442 Ryght,** *just* **443 Ayen,** *before* **444 wexen gan the hewe,** *grew the color* (she blushes) **445 seyde amys,** *spoke poorly* **448 drede the nought,** *fear you not* **451 bet,** *better* **452 leste,** *least* **453 degre,** *condition* (of love or rank) **454 for,** *because of* **455 hadde be,** *had been* (due), **gerdonynge,** *reward,* **456 dar ek seyn,** *dare also say* **457 janglere,** *gossiper* **458 hals,** *neck* **459 but,** *unless* **460 can me suffyse,** *makes me able* **461 From poynt to poynt,** *in all respects* **462 good,** *goods* **463 thredde,** *third* **464 lytel leyser heere,** *little time to spare here* **465 ben ago,** *be gone* **466 mak,** *mate* **467 ek,** *also,* **wol not heere,** *will not hear* **468 For tarying,** *on account of delay* **469 but,** *unless,* **mot for sorwe deye,** *must die for sorrow* **470 avaunte,** *boast* **471 as possible is me,** (it is) *as possible for me* **472 languysshyng,** *suffering,* **473 wel happen may,** (it) *might well happen* (that) **474 bet,** *better,* **more to pay,** *more satisfactorily* **476 yoore,** *long* **478 Don,** *do* **479 dar seyn,** *dare say* **480 dom,** *judgment,* **faynest wolde hire ese,** *most eagerly would I please her* **481 At shorte wordes,** *speaking briefly,* **sese,** *seize* **482 wol ben hires,** *will be hers,* **wynke,** *sleep*

426 reward only, Gg reads "only reward." **436 she nevere of love me,** Gg reads "it that he me nevere of love." **438 knette,** Gg reads "areete" (attribute). **444 the,** Gg reads "hire." **447 abashed,** Gg reads "a bashat." **454 have,** Gg reads "a." **457 janglere,** Gg reads "or janglere." **in,** omitted in Gg and F. **462 she,** Gg reads "the." **471 But as,** Gg reads "That." **480 ese,** F reads "plese."

Of al my lyf, syn that day I was born,
So gentil ple° in love or other thyng
Ne herde nevere no man me beforn—
Who that hadde leyser and cunnyng°
For to reherse hyre cher° and hire spekyng.
And from the morwe° gan this speche laste
Tyl dounward drow° the sunne wonder faste.

The noyse of foules for to ben delyvered°
So loude ronge°, "Have don°, and lat us wende°!"
That wel wende° I the wode° hadde al toshyvered°.
"Cum of,°" they crieden, "alias, ye wol us shende°!
Whan shal youre cursede pletynge° have an ende?
How shulde a juge eyther partie leve°
For ye or nay withouten other preve°?"

The goos, the cokkow°, and the doke° also
So cryede, "Kek kek, kokkow, quek quek," hye°,
That thourw myne eres° the noyse wente tho°.
The goos seyde, "Al this nys not worth a flye.
But I can shappe herof° a remedie,
And I wol seye my verdit° fayre and swythe°
For water-foul, whoso be wroth or blythe°!"

"And I for werm-foul," quod the fol kokkow°,
"For I wol of myn owene autorite°
For comun spede° take on the charge° now,
For to delyvere° us is gret charite."
"Ye may onbyde° a while yit, parde,°"
Quod the turtil°, "if it be youre wille.
A wight° may speke hym° were as fayr be stylle.

"I am a sed-foul° oon° the unworthieste,
That wot° I wel, and litel of cunnynge°,
But bet° is that a wyghtes tunge° reste
Than entermeten hym of° such doinge
Of which he neyther rede can° ne synge;
And whoso it doth ful foule° hymself acloyeth°
For offys uncommytted° ofte anoyeth."

Nature, which that alwey hadde an ere°
To murmur of the lewedenesse° behynde,
With facound voys° seyde, "Hold youre tonges there!
And I shal sone°, I hope, a conseyl fynde
Yow to delyvere, and from this noyse unbynde°.
I juge, of every folk men shul oon° calle
To seyn the verdit for yow foules alle."

Assented° were to this conclusioun
The briddes alle; and foules of ravyne°
Han° chosen fyrst, by pleyn eleccioun,
The terselet° of the faucoun to diffyne°
Al here sentence°, as him lest to termyne°,

---

485 So gentil ple, *such a noble plea* **487 leyser and cunnyng,** *leisure and ability* **488 reherse hyre cher,** *describe their behavior* **489 morwe,** *morning* **490 dounward drow,** *downward went* **491 for to ben delyvered,** *in order to be released* **492 loude ronge,** *loudly rang,* **don,** *done,* **wende,** *go* **493 wende,** *thought,* **wode,** *woods,* **toshyvered,** *splintered* **494 Cum of,** *get on with it,* **wol us shende,** *will ruin us* **495 cursede pletynge,** *cursed pleading* **496 eyther partie leve,** *believe either party* **497 preve,** *proof* **498 cokkow,** *cuckoo,* **doke,** *duck* **499 hye,** *loudly* **500 thourw myne eres,** *through my ears,* **tho,** *then* **502 shappe herof,** *make for this* **503 verdit,** *verdict,* **swythe,** *quickly* **504 whoso be wroth or blythe,** (regardless of) *who is angry or happy* **505 fol kokkow,** *foul cuckoo* **506 owene autorite,** *own authority* **507 comun spede,** *benefit of all,* **charge,** *responsibility* **508 delyvere,** *release* **509 onbyde,** *wait,* **parde,** *by God (par Dieu)* **510 turtil,** *turtledove* **511 wight,** *person,* **hym,** *himself* **512 sed-foul,** *seed-bird,* **oon,** *one* (of) **513 wot,** *know,* **cunnynge,** *skill* **514 bet,** *better,* **wyghtes tunge,** *person's tongue* **515 entermeten hym of,** *involve himself in* **516 rede can,** *can interpret* **517 foule,** *badly,* **acloyeth,** *overburdens* **518 offys uncommytted,** *unrequested service* **519 hadde an ere,** *listened* **520 lewedenesse,** *foolishness* **521 facound voys,** *eloquent voice* **522 sone,** *soon* **523 unbynde,** *release* **524 oon,** *one* **525 verdit,** *verdict* **526 Assented,** *agreed* **527 foules of raveyne,** *birds of prey* **528 Han,** *have* **529 terselet,** *male,* **diffyne,** *express* **530 here sentence,** *their opinion,* **as him lest to termyne,** *as it pleased him to determine*

485 ple, a plea is technically an argument in court, and this legal diction continues in "delyvere" (release, lines 491 and 508), "pletynge" (pleading, 495), "verdit" (verdict, 503), and others below. **490 drow,** F reads "went." **493 toshyvered,** Gg reads "toshyvered." **498 cokkow . . . doke,** F transposes the two. **499 noyse,** the noise here clashes with the ideal of harmony expressed elsewhere in the poem, especially the ideal of cosmic harmony expressed in line 63 and the achievement of harmony in the rondel at the end of the poem, lines 680ff. **505 quod,** F reads "seyde." **507 comun spede,** this appears to echo *comoun profyt* of lines 47 and 75, but here it is put into the mouth of the foolish cuckoo, a challenge for those who would treat it as a significant philosophical concern of the poem. Gg reads "comun profit," and the line varies elsewhere in the Gg and F. **509–11** These difficult lines have been punctuated and interpreted variously by editors, but the upshot of the turtledove's statement is clear: "It is sometimes better to be patient and keep your mouth shut, if you don't mind." **509 onbyde,** F reads "abyde." **511 fayr,** F reads "good." **518 uncommytted,** Gg reads "onquit." **520 lewdedenesse,** the foolishness or ignorance of the lower birds appears to be taken for granted here. **behynde,** omitted in Gg. **521 facound voys,** Nature's eloquent (perhaps "authoritative") voice is further evidence of Chaucer's sensitivity to tone of voice; see line 382n. **524 of every folk men shul one calle,** the conflation of humans and birds in the poem is here overt. **529 terselet,** the male falcon was referred to in the diminutive form (*-let*) because it was smaller than its female counterpart, although the form may also imply youth.

And to Nature hym gunne to presente°,
And she accepteth hym with glad entente.

The terslet seyde thanne, "In this manere
Ful hard were it to prove by resoun
Who loveth best this gentil formel heere,
For everych° hath swich replicacioun°
That non by skilles° may be brought adoun°.
I can not se that argumentes avayle°:
Thanne semeth it there moste be batayle.°"

"Al redy!" quod these egles tercels tho°.
"Nay, sires," quod he, "if that I durste it seye°;
Ye don me wrong, my tale is not ido°.
For, sires, ne taketh not agref°, I preye,
It may not gon as ye wolde° in this weye.
Oure° is the voys that han the charge° on honde,
And to the juges dom° ye moten stondo°.

"And therfore, pes°. I seye, as to myn wit,
Me wolde thynke° now that the worthieste
Of knyghthod, and lengest had used° it,
Most° of estat, of blod the gentilleste°,
Were sittyngest° for hire, if that hir leste°,
And of these thre she wot° hireself, I trowe°,
Which that he be, for it is light° to knowe."

The water-foules han here hedes leid°
Togedere, and of a short avysement°,
Whan everych° hadde his large golee° seyd,
They seyden sothly°, al by oon assent,
How that the goos, with hire facounde gent°,
"That so desyreth° to pronounce oure nede°,
Shal telle oure tale," and preyede "God hir spede."

And for these water-foules tho began
The goos to speke, and in hir kakelynge°
She seyde, "Pes, now tak kep°, every man,
And herkeneth which a° resoun I shal forth brynge—
My wit is sharp, I love no taryinge°—
I seye I rede° hym, thow he were my brother,
But° she wol love hym, let hym love another."

"Lo, here a parfit° resoun of a goos,"
Quod the sperhauk. "Nevere mot she thee°!
Lo, siche° it is to have a tunge loos.
Now, parde, fol°, yit were it bet for the°
Han holde thy pes° than shewed thyn nycete°.
It lyth nat° in his wit ne in his wille,
But soth is seyd°, a fol can not ben stille."

The laughtere aros of° gentil foules alle,
And right anon° the sed-foul chosen hadde
The turtle trewe, and gunne hire to hem calle°,
And preyeden hire to seyn the sothe sadde°
"Of this matere, and axede° what she radde°.
And she answerde that pleynly hire entente
She wolde shewe°, and sothly what she mente.

"Nay, God forbede° a lovere shulde chaunge,"
The turtle seyde, and wex for shame al red.
"Thow° that his lady everemore be straunge°,
Yit lat hym serve hire til that he be ded.

---

531 hym gunne to presente, *presented him* **536 everych,** *each,* **swich replicacioun,** *such ability to reply* **537 skilles,** *disputation,* **brought adoun** *eliminated* **538 avayle,** *are useful* **539 batayle,** *battle* **540 tho,** *then* **541 durste it seye,** *dare say it* **542 ido,** *done* **543 taketh not agref,** *take no grief* **544 wolde,** *want* **545 Oure,** *ours* (the representatives'), **charge,** *responsibility* **546 dom,** *judgment,* **moten stonde,** *must stand* **547 pes,** *peace* **548 Me wolde thynke,** *it seems to me* **549 used,** *practiced* **550 Most,** *highest,* **gentilleste,** *most noble* **551 sittyngest,** *most suitable,* **hir leste,** *it pleases her* **552 wot,** *knows,* **trowe,** *believe* **553 light,** *easy* **554 han here hedes leid,** *had put their heads* **555 avysement,** *deliberation* **556 everych,** *each one,* **golee,** *mouthful* **557 sothly,** *truly* **558 facounde gent,** *noble eloquence* **559 desyreth,** *desires,* **nede,** *opinion* **562 kakelynge,** *cackling* **563 tak kep,** *pay attention* **564 herkeneth which a,** *hear what* **565 taryinge,** *delay* **566 rede,** *advise* **567 But,** *unless* **568 parfit,** *perfect* **569 sperhauk,** *sparrow hawk,* **Nevere mot she the,** *may she never prosper* **570, siche,** *such* **571 fol,** *fool,* **bet for the,** *better for you* **572 Han hold thy pes,** (to) *have held your peace,* **nycete,** *silliness* **573 lyth nat,** *lies not* **574 soth is seyd,** *truth be said* **575 aros of,** *arose from* **576 right anon,** *right away* **577 gunne hire to hem calle,** *called her to them* **578 sothe sadde,** *steady truth* **579 axede,** *asked,* **radde,** *advised* **581 shewe,** *show* **582 forbede,** *forbid* **584 Thow,** *though,* **straunge,** *aloof*

533 thanne, omitted in Gg. **537 non by skilles may be,** F reads "by skilles may non be." **540 Al redy,** seemingly Chaucer's indication of how willing some aristocrats are to go to war. **these egles tercels,** Gg reads "this eglis terslet." **551 hir,** Gg reads "he." **553 it,** Gg reads "here." **558 facounde gent,** apparently sarcastic; the goose is neither noble nor eloquent. Both the goose and the turtledove (lines 575ff.) are female spokesbirds, but see lines 587–88n. Gg reads "facounde so gent." **560 God,** F reads "to God." **hir,** Gg reads "hym." **562 hir,** Gg reads "his." **563 She,** Gg reads "He." **564 forth,** omitted in Gg. **565 love,** Gg reads "take." **569 she,** Gg reads "he." **571 yit,** Gg reads "now." **573 wit,** Gg reads "mygh[t]." **577 turtle,** Gg reads "tersel." **581 wolde,** Gg reads "wolde it." **583 turtle,** Gg reads "tersel."

Forsoth°, I preyse° nat the goses red°.
For thow she deyede°, I wolde° non other make;
I wol ben hire° til that the deth me take."

"Wel bourded,°" quod the doke, "by myn hat!
That men shulde loven alwey causeles°,
Who can a resoun fynde or wit in that?
Daunseth he murye° that is myrtheles°?
What shulde I rekke° of him that is recheles°?
Ye quek," yit seyde the doke, ful wel and fayre,
"There been mo sterres°, God wot, than a payre°!"

"Now fy°, cherl,°" quod the gentil terselet,
"Out of the donghil° cam that word° ful right!
Thow canst nat seen what thyng is wel beset°.
Thow farst by° love as oules° don by lyght:
The day hem blent°, but wel they sen by nyght.
Thy kynde is of so low a wrechednesse
That what love is thow canst nat seen ne gesse."

Tho gan° the kokkow putte hym forth in pres°
For foul that eteth werm, and seyde blyve°,
"So I," quod he, "may have my make in pes,
I reche° nat how longe that ye stryve.
Lat ech of hem° be soleyn° al here° lyve!
This is my red°, syn° they may nat acorde.
This shorte lessoun nedeth nat recorde."

"Ye, have the glotoun fild inow his paunche°,
Thanne are we wel" seyde the merlioun.
"Thow mortherere° of the heysoge° on the braunche
That broughte the forth°, thow rewful° glotoun,
Lyve thow soleyn, wermes corupcioun!
For no fors is of lak° of thy nature°.
Go, lewed° be thow whil the world may dure°!"

"Now pes," quod Nature, "I comaunde here;
For I have herd al youre opynyoun,
And in effect yit be we nevere the nere°.
But fynally, this is my conclusioun,
That she hireself shal han the eleccioun°
Of whom hire lest°, and who be wroth or blythe°,
Hym that she cheseth, he shal hire han as swithe°.

"For syn° it may not here discussed° be
Who loveth hire best, as seyth the terselet,
Thanne wol I don hire this favour, that she
Shal han right° hym on whom hire herte is set,
And he hire that his herte hath on hire knet°.
Thus juge I, Nature, for I may not lye;
To non estat I have non other eye°.

"But as for conseyl for to chese° a make,
If I were Resoun, certes°, thanne wolde I
Conseyle yow the ryal tersel take°—
As seyde the terselet ful skylfully°—
As for the° gentilleste and most worthi,
Which I have wrought° so wel to my plesaunce°,
That to yow oughte to been a suffisaunce°.

---

586 Forsoth, *truly,* **preyse,** *praise,* **goses red,** *goose's advice* **587 deyede,** *died,* **wolde,** *desire* **588 hire,** *hers* **589 bourded,** *joked* **590 causeles,** *without cause* **592 murye,** *merrily,* **myrtheles,** *mirthless* **593 rekke,** *care,* **recheles,** *without care* **595 sterres,** *stars,* **payre,** *pair* **596 fy,** *shame,* **cherl,** *peasant* **597 donghill,** *manure pile,* **word,** *saying* **598 wel beset,** *suitable* **599 farst by,** *goes about,* **oules,** *owls* **600 blent,** *blinds* **603 Tho gan,** *then did,* **putte hym forth in pres,** *put himself forward in the crowd* **604 blyve,** *hastily* **606 reche,** *care* **607 hem,** *them* (the eagles), **soleyn,** *single,* **here,** *their* **608 red,** *advice,* **syn,** *since* **610 have the glotoun fild inow his paunche,** (when) *the glutton has filled his paunch enough* **612 mortherere,** *murderer,* **heysoge,** *hedge-sparrow* **613 broughte the forth,** *hatched you,* **rewful,** *pitiable* **615 For no fors is of lak,** *no matter* (if there is) *lack,* **nature,** *species* **616 lewed,** *ignorant,* **dure,** *last* **619 nere,** *nearer* (to a solution) **621 eleccioun,** *choice* **622 hire lest,** *pleases her,* **who be wroth or blythe** (regardless of) *who is angry or happy* **623 swithe,** *quickly* **624 syn,** *since,* **discussed,** *decided* **627 Shal han right,** *shall have precisely* **628 knet,** *fastened* **630 eye,** *view* **631 chese,** *chose* **632 certes,** *certainly* **633 take,** *to take* **634 skylfully,** *reasonably* **635 As for the,** *as the* **636 wrought,** *made,* **plesaunce,** *pleasure* **637 been a suffisaunce,** *be sufficient*

587–88 The female turtledove here speaks as a male; perhaps a quotation from a familiar song or lyric. **593** F reads "Who shulde recche of that is recheles?" **594 Ye quek," seyde,** Gg reads "Kek, kek yit seith;" F, "Ye quek, quod." **596 fy,** Gg reads "sey." **602 nat,** F reads "nouther." **604 blyve,** G reads "blythe." **610–13** The merlin sarcastically claims that all will be well when gluttons like the cuckoo have their fill and then accuses the cuckoo of the perfidy traditionally ascribed to its species: laying eggs in the nest of another bird (here the hedge-sparrow) and then killing the bird that hatches them; cf. line 358. **611 the,** Gg reads "thanne a." **613 rewful,** Gg reads "reufulles." **616 whil the, Gg reads "whi that the." 619 nevere,** Gg reads "not." **622 and who,** F reads "who so." **623 cheseth,** F reads "cheest." **as,** Gg reads "a." **626 hire this favour,** F reads "this favour to hire." **627 right,** omitted in Gg. **629 Thus,** F reads "This." **630 I have non other eye,** an idiom that means something like "I give preference to no other condition." **632 Resoun,** a personification of reason, indicating that choosing the royal eagle would be reasonable. **certes,** omitted in F. **637 oughte,** F reads "it oughte."

With dredful vois° the formel tho° answerde,
"My rightful lady, Goddesse of Nature,
Soth is° that I am evere under youre yerde°,
As is another lyves° creature,
And mot ben youre whil° that my lyf may dure°,
And therfore graunteth me my ferste bone°,
And myn entent yow wol I sey right sone."

"I graunte it yow," quod she. And right anon
This formel egle spak in this degre°,
"Almyghty queen, unto° this yer be gon
I axe respit° for to avise me°,
And after that to have my choys al fre°—
This al and sum° that I wol speke and seye;
Ye gete no more, althow ye do me deye°.

"I wol nat serve Venus ne Cupide
Forsothe, as yit, by no manere weye."
"Now, syn° it may non otherwise betyde,°"
Quod tho Nature, "heere is no more to seye.
Thanne wolde I that these foules were aweye,
Eche with his make, for taryinge° lengere heere."
And seyde hem° thus, as ye shul after here.

"To yow speke I, ye terseletes," quod Nature,
"Beth° of good herte, and serveth alle thre.
A yer ne is nat so longe to endure,
And ech of yow peyne hym° in his degre
For to do wel, for, God wot°, quyt° is she
Fro yow this yer; what after so befalle,
This entremes° is dressed° for yow alle."

And whan this werk al brought was to an ende,
To every foul Nature yaf° his make
By evene acord, and on here wey they wende°.
But, Lord, the blisse and joye that they make!
For ech gan other in his wynges take,
And with here nekkes eche gan other wynde°,
Thankynge alwey the noble queen of Kynde°.

But fyrst were chosen foules for to synge,
As yer by yer was alwey hir usaunce°
To synge a roundel° at here departynge,
To don to Nature honour and plesaunce.
The note°, I trowe°, imaked° was in Fraunce;
The wordes were swich° as ye may here fynde,
The nexte vers as I now have in mynde.

Now welcome, somor°, with thy sonne softe,
That hast this wintres wedres overshake°,
And drevyne° away the longe nyghtes blake!
Saynt Valentyn, that art ful hye on-lofte,°
Thus syngen smale foules for thy sake:
Now welcome, somer, with thy sonne softe,
That hast this wintres wedres overshake.

Well han they cause for to gladen° ofte,
Sith ech° of hem recovered hath hys make,

---

638 dredful vois, *timid voice,* **tho,** *then* **640 Soth is,** *it is true,* **yerde,** *authority* **641 another lyves,** *every other living* **642 mot ben youre whil,** *must be yours while,* **dure,** *last* **643 ferste bone,** *first request* **646 degre,** *manner* **647 unto,** *until* **648 axe respit,** *ask some time,* **avise me,** *consider* **649 choys al fre,** *free choice* **650 This al and sum,** *this* (is) *everything* **651 do me deye,** *make me die* **654 syn,** *since,* **betyde,** *happen* **657 for taryinge,** *rather than delaying* **658 hem,** *to them* **660 Beth,** *be* **662 peyne hym,** *strive* **663 wot,** *knows,* **quyt,** *released* **665 entremes,** *intermission,* **dressed,** *arranged* **667 yaf,** *gave* **668 wende,** *went* **671 wynde,** *intertwine* **672 Kynde,** *Nature* **674 hir usaunce,** *their custom* **675 roundel,** *song* **677 note,** *music,* **trowe,** *believe,* **imaked,** *made* **678 swich,** *such* **680 somor,** *summer* **681 wintres wedres overshake,** *winter weather shaken off* **682 drevyne,** *driven* **683 on-lofte,** *aloft* **688 Sith ech,** *since each*

638 tho, F reads "hir." **641 another lyves,** F reads "everich other." **642 mot ben youre whil that,** F reads "moste be youres while." **644 yow wol I sey right,** Gg reads "that wele I seyn wol." **645 right,** Gg reads "that." **647 gon,** F reads "don." **652–53 nat serve Venus ne Cupid,** the formel says she will not be a lover yet. **655 tho,** omitted in F. **662 peyne hym,** Gg reads "peignynge." **666 brought,** F reads "wroght." **670 ech,** F reads "ech of hem," and omits "his." **671 nekkes . . . wynde,** "necking," a form of sexual play traditionally ascribed to birds. **672 queen,** F reads "goddesse." **674 hir,** Gg reads "the." **675 roundel,** i.e., rondel, originally a dance song with a repeated refrain; by Chaucer's time a French song with a refrain; also a kind of stanza. The communal participation of the birds in this harmonious song connects with the ideal of cosmic harmony expressed in line 63. **677 note . . . Fraunce,** the French music to which Chaucer seems to refer is unknown, although the rondel can be sung to Machaut's music. Some MSS have the French line *Que bien ayme a tarde oublie* ("Who loves well forgets slowly") in the margin, but no accompanying tune is known, and the line appears in a variety of other contexts. **678 here,** omitted in Gg. **680–92** Lines lacking in F and most MSS. The longest form of the addition is in a later hand in Gg, but it has only eight lines (680–84, 687–89). The repeated lines that serve as a kind of refrain (685–86, 691–92), added by Skeat in his edition, make a rondel, which is a conventional French verse form. **680 thy,** omitted in Gg. **682 longe,** Gg reads "large." **683 on-lofte,** Gg reads "olofte."

Ful blisseful mowe° they synge when they wake:
Now welcome, somer, with thy sonne softe,
That hast this wintres wedres overshake,
And driven away the longe nyghtes blake!

And with the shoutyng, whan the song was do°,
That foules maden at here° flyght awey,
I wok°, and othere bokes tok° me to,
To reede upon, and yit I rede alwey
In hope, iwis°, to rede so sum day
That I shal mete° sumthyng for to fare°
The bet°, and thus to rede I nel nat spare°.

Explicit Parliamentum avium in die Sancti Valentini tentum secundum Galfridum Chaucer. Deo gracias.

---

689 mowe, *may* **693 do,** *done* **694 here,** *their* **695 wok,** *woke up,* **tok,** *took* **697 iwis,** *surely* **698 mete,** *dream,* **fare,** *proceed* **699 bet,** *better,* **nel nat spare,** *will not refrain*

689 synge, Gg reads "ben." **699a–b Explicit Parliamentum . . . ,** The Latin rubric is from Gg: "Here ends the Parliament of Birds held on St. Valentine's Day, according to Geoffrey Chaucer. Thanks be to God."

House of Fame

House of Fame

Introduction

EVEN THOUGH RICH with ancient material, *House of Fame* is a work that we might well describe as "postmodern." Its wry self-consciousness, asymmetry and incongruities, allusiveness, and play with style and genre will make it feel postmodern to readers in the twenty-first century even though we may have trouble recognizing some of its details and nuances. The topic of the poem is fame, which here means both transient reputation and enduring renown, and both of these aspects of fame are depicted as matters of caprice rather than merit. In Book 3, we are shown Fame commanding her servant, Eolus, god of winds, to blare forth the fame of various petitioners on his trumpets of Praise and Slander. With no concern whatsoever for the worthiness of the petitioners, Fame grants that they be famous, infamous, or unknown, and in various ways the poem suggests that speech, writing, song, and visual representation all participate in Fame's caprice—that fame, infamy, and oblivion are all random.

The poet's role is most clearly evident in the fact that statues of the great writers and poets—Homer, Statius, Virgil, Ovid, and others—support the roof of Fame's "house" or palace. We are told, however, with incongruity typical of the poem, that the great Homer is untrustworthy because he is a maker of lies, a fabulator who tendentiously favored the Greeks. Moreover, the outside of Fame's palace is decorated with statues of mere minstrels, charmers, and sleight-of-hand artists. Apparently, poets are not to be trusted. There is no clear line between poets and tricksters, and in supporting Fame, poets support her indiscriminate judgments.

Self-conscious concern with the function of poetry appears earlier in the poem when the poet-narrator, Geffrey—Chaucer's most detailed autobiographical projection (see notes to lines 562, 653, and 729)—recounts the story of Aeneas's famous love affair with Dido. Geffrey sees the story depicted on the walls of the temple of Venus, but whether it is represented in words or pictures is hard for us to tell. The account both praises and blames Aeneas. On the one hand, he is a great hero, survivor of the Trojan War and founder of Rome; on the other, he is a cad whose callous treatment of Dido leads to her suicide. Chaucer follows Virgil's *Aeneid* for the heroic account of Aeneas and combines it with Ovid's *Heroides* for the tragedy of Dido's love, which he developed later as Dido's story in *Legend of Good Women* (legend 3); the incongruous fusion of the two accounts here indicates the instability of fame and the inconsistencies of poetry and literary tradition. Further, Chaucer's poet-narrator is on a frustrating and seemingly unsuccessful search for love tidings as the subject matter for his poetry, so the incongruity deepens: This is a poem about the unreliability of fame and poetry in which a poet fails to find what he seeks.

Bridging the two major locales of the poem—the temple of Venus and the palace of Fame—is Geffrey's ascent through the cosmos while in the clutches of a gigantic eagle sent by Jupiter to lead the poet to love tidings as subject matter for his poetry. The journey and other details of the poem clearly allude to Dante's ascent through the heavens in his *Divine Comedy*, and along the way the talkative eagle offers a theory of acoustics. The allusions encourage us to compare Fame's caprice with the system of merit that underlies Dante's depiction of Christian punishment and reward in the afterlife. Combining religion with medieval science and humorous fancy, the eagle's disquisition on sound explains how all human discourse rises to Fame's palace, a fanciful burlesque of the ascent of souls.

Love is a major theme of the work, but the theme recurs unevenly in the three parts of the poem. The Aeneas / Dido story is one of love lost, the poet seeks love tidings, and several of the petitioners who approach Fame claim that they want to be known as great lovers. This focus has encouraged critics to regard the poem as written for the occasion of an aristocratic betrothal or marriage, perhaps the betrothal in 1377 of Richard II to Marie, daughter of Charles V of France (a marriage that never took place), or of Richard to Anne of Bohemia in 1380. But others have pointed out that love in the poem is tragic or frustrating, not a matter for celebration. If there was an occasion that inspired the poem, Chaucer let his concern with poetry and poetic tradition overwhelm it. See the Introduction to *Parliament of Fowls* for difficulties in dating it and *House of Fame.*

Like the allusions to Dante mentioned above, the many other allusions in the poem—drawn from classical literature, the Bible, and contemporary French and Italian poetry—are marked by a mixture of genuine respect and comic irreverence that leaves us wondering whether Chaucer was seeking to emulate or parody his sources. Similarly, the poem is cast as a dream vision, but opens by questioning the truth of dreams. It moves swiftly from within the lavishly decorated temple of Venus to outside, where the poet finds himself in a desert wasteland, an image perhaps of spiritual, intellectual, or emotional deprivation—arguably all three. Later, the magnificent palace of Fame stands on an unstable block of ice, while in its shadow, the fragile and labyrinthine House of Rumor will endure as long as there are people who tell tales.

The poem challenges the reader to make sense of its many shifts and turns, and then, despite a growing sense of crescendo, comically deflects any final attempt at synthesis or resolution by leaving us hanging. It stops abruptly just as the final figure to be introduced—the "man of gret auctorite"—appears. The possible identity of this figure has been much debated—John of Gaunt, Boethius, Christ, Dante, and others have been suggested—but it is best to see his introduction as one more feint in the game of trying to determine the basis of truth. Authority and experience, science and poetry, speech, writing, and sculpture all crisscross in the poem, but none of them provides a stable or consistent basis for knowledge or the fame dispensed in this world.

Sheila Delany's *Chaucer's House of Fame: The Poetics of Skeptical Fideism* (1972, no. 1500) is an influential explanation of the many ways in which the poem poses ambivalences and leaves them unresolved; her reading underlies a number of later discussions of skepticism and uncertainty in the poem. In *Chaucer and the Imaginary World of Fame* (1984, no. 1496), Piero Boitani sets the work in the context of the medieval tradition of fame, and in *Virgil and Medieval England* (1995, no. 1494), Christopher Baswell situates *House of Fame* in the medieval reception of Virgil and literary authority. Laurel Amtower discusses other aspects of literary transmission in "Authorizing the Reader in Chaucer's *House of Fame*" (2000, no. 1492), and William Quinn considers distrust of speech in "Chaucer's Recital Presence in the *House of Fame* and the Embodiment of Authority" (2008, no. 1521). Ruth Evans assesses memory and cognition in the poem in "Chaucer in Cyberspace" (2001, no. 1503). For a survey of scholarly and critical topic and opinions, see A. J. Minnis's Oxford Guide to Chaucer, *The Shorter Poems* (1995, no. 1400), which is useful for all of Chaucer's dream visions.

House of Fame

Book 1

[Proem]

God turne us° every dreme to goode,
For hyt is° wonder, be° the roode°,
To my wytte°? what causeth swevenes°,
Eyther on morwes° or on evenes°;
And why th'effect° folweth of somme°,
And of somme hit° shal never come;
Why that is an avisioun°,
And this a revelacioun,
Why this a dreme, why that a swevene°,
And noght to every man lyche evene°;
Why this a fantome°, why these oracles,
I not°. But whoso° of these meracles
The causes knoweth bet° then I,
Devyne he°, for I certenly
Ne kan hem noght°, ne never thinke
To besely° my wytte to swinke°,
To knowe of hir signifiaunce°
The gendres°, neyther the distaunce°
Of tymes of hem, ne the causis,
Or why this more then° that cause is—
As yf folkys complexions°
Make hem dreme of reflexions°,
Or ellis thus, as other sayne°,
For to gret° feblenesse of her brayne,
By abstinence or by sekenesse,
Prison, stewe°, or gret distresse,
Or ellis° by dysordynaunce°
Of naturell acustumaunce°,
That somme man is to curiouse
In studye, or melancolyouse°,
Or thus so inly° ful of drede°
That no man may hym bote bede°;
Or ellis that devocion
Of somme, and contemplacion
Causen suche dremes ofte°;
Or that the cruelle lyfe° unsofte
Which these ilke° lovers leden°
That hopen° over muche or dreden°,
That purely her impressions°
Causen hem avisions°,
Or yf that spirites have the myght°
To make folk to dreme a-nyght°;
Or yf the soule, of propre kynde°
Be so parfit°, as men fynde,
That yt forwot that° ys to come,
And that hyt warneth° al and some°
Of everych° of her aventures°
Be avisions or be figures°,

---

1 God turne us, (may) *God direct* (for) *us* **2 hyt is,** *it is* (a), **be,** *by,* **roode,** *Cross* **3 wytte,** *understanding,* **swevenes,** *dreams* **4 on morwes,** *in mornings,* **evenes,** *evenings* **5 th'effect,** *predicted result,* **of somme,** *from some* **6 hit,** *it* **7 avisioun,** *delusion* **9 swevene,** *dream* **10 lyche evene,** *exactly the same* **11 fantome,** *phantom* **12 not,** *do not know,* **whoso,** *whoever* **13 bet,** *better* **14 Devyne he,** *let him explain* **15 Ne kan hem noght,** *understand them not* **16 To besely,** *too intensely,* **swinke,** *work* **17 hir signifiaunce,** *their significance* **18 gendres,** *varieties,* **distaunce,** *intervals* **20 then,** *than* **21 folkys complexions,** *people's temperaments* **22 reflexions,** (mental) *reflections* **23 other sayne,** *others say* **24 to gret,** *too great* **25 stewe,** *cell* **27 ellis,** *else,* **dysordynaunce,** *disordering* **28 acustumaunce,** *routine* **30 melancolyouse,** *melancholy* **31 inly,** *inwardly,* **drede,** *fear* **32 bote bede,** *offer help* **35 ofte,** *often* **36 lyfe,** *life* **37 ilke,** *same,* **leden,** *lead* **38 hopen,** *hope,* **dreden,** *fear* **39 her impressions,** *their mental images* **40 avisions,** *delusions* **41 myght,** *power* **42 a-nyght,** *at night* **43 of proper kynde,** *of its own nature* **44 parfit,** *perfect* **45 yt forwot that,** *it foreknows what* **46 warneth,** *foretells,* **al and some,** *everyone* **47 everych,** *each,* **her aventures,** *their fortunes* **48 be figures,** *by symbols*

Text based on Bodleian Library, Oxford, MS Fairfax 16 (F) with corrections and selected variants from Magdalene College, Cambridge, MS Pepys 2006 (P) through line 1843 and from Caxton's edition of 1483 (Cx) for the rest. The title is from F. **Book 1,** none of the manuscripts divides *HF* into books, but there are large capitals or spaces left for large capitals that coincide with the book divisions introduced by Cx at lines 509 and 1091; see also the note to line 1093. **1–52** This discussion has been compared with the discussion of dreams in *RR* 18287ff. The varieties of dreams may also owe something to Macrobius's *Commentary on the Dream of Scipio,* which Chaucer uses extensively in *PF* 31ff., although the parallels are not exact and the English terms are not precise; e.g., both **dreme** and **swevene** (line 9) mean "dream." Macrobius's types (Chapter 3) are *somnium,* the enigmatic dream; *visio,* the prophetic dream; *oraculum,* the revelatory dream; *insomnium,* the nightmare; and *phantasma* (*visum*), the apparition. Dreams and their causes are also discussed in *TC* 5.358–85 and *NPT* 7.2922–3156. **8 Why,** F and P read "And why." **20 Or,** F reads "For." **this,** F and P read "this is." **21 complexions,** see *GP* 1.333. **26 stewe,** Cx reads "stryf." **39 impressions,** lovers dwell on mental images of their beloved in *TC* 5.372, *MerT* 4.1578, and *FranT* 5.371.

But° that oure flessh ne hath no myght
To understonde hyt aryght°,
For hyt is warned to derkly°—
But why the cause is, noght wot I°.
Wel worth of this thyng° grete clerkes
That trete° of this and other werkes,
For I of noon opinion
Nyl° as now make mensyon°,
But oonly that the holy roode°
Turne us° every dreme to goode.
For never sith° that I was borne,
Ne no man elles me beforne,
Mette°, I trowe stedfastly°,
So wonderful a dreme as I,
The tenthe day now of Decembre,
The which° as I kan now remembre
I wol° yow tellen everydel°.
  But at my gynnynge°, trusteth wel,
I wol make invocacion,
With special devocion,
Unto the god of slepe° anoon°,
That duelleth° in a cave of stoon°
Upon a streme that cometh fro Lete°,
That is a floode° of helle unswete°,
Besyde a folke men clepeth Cymerie°.
There slepeth ay° this god unmerie°
With his slepy thousand sones°,
That alwey for to slepe hir wone° is.
And to this god that I of rede°
Prey I that he wol me spede°
My swevene° for to telle aryght,
Yf° every dreme stonde in his myght°.
And he that mover ys of alle,
That is and was and ever shalle,°
So yive hem° joye that hyt here°
Of alle that they dreme to-yere°,
And for to stonden al in grace°
Of her° loves, or in what place
That hem were levest° for to stonde,
And shelde hem fro° poverte and shonde°,
And fro unhappe° and eche disese°,
And sende hem alle° that may hem plese°,
That take hit wel and skorne hyt noghte,
Ne hyt mysdemen° in her thoghte
Thorgh° malicious entencion.
And whoso thorgh presumpcion,
Or hate, or skorne, or thorgh envye,
Dispit°, or jape°, or vilanye,
Mysdeme° hyt, pray I Jesus God,
That dreme he barefot°, dreme he shod°,
That every harm that any man
Hath had syth° the world began
Befalle° hym therof or he sterve°.
And graunte he mote° hit ful° deserve,
Loo, with suche a conclusion°
As had of his avision
Cresus that was kyng of Lyde,
That high upon a gebet dyde°.

---

49 But, *except* **50 hyt aryght,** *it correctly* **51 warned to derkly,** *foretold too obscurely* **52 noght wot I,** *I don't know* **53 Wel worth of this thyng,** *good luck on this account* (to) **54 trete,** *treat* **56 Nyl,** *will not,* **mensyon,** *mention* **57 roode,** *cross* **58 Turne us,** *direct* (for) *us* **59 sith,** *since* **61 Mette,** *dreamed,* **trowe stedfastly,** *firmly believe* **64 The which,** *of which* **65 wol,** *will,* **everydel,** *every bit* **66 gynnynge,** *beginning* **69 slepe,** *sleep,* **anoon,** *immediately* **70 duelleth,** *dwells,* **stoon,** *stone* **71 fro Lete,** *from the river Lethe* **72 floode,** *river,* **unswete,** *unpleasant* **73 clepeth Cymerie,** *call Cimmerians* **74 ay,** *always,* **unmerie,** *unpleasant* **75 sones,** *sons* (i.e., dreams) **76 hir wone,** *their custom* **77 of rede,** *read about* **78 wol me spede,** *will aid me* **79 swevene,** *dream* **80 Yf,** *if,* **stonde in his myght,** *is in his control* **82 shalle,** *shall* (be) **83 yive hem,** *give them,* **hyt here,** *hear it* (i.e., the invocation) **84 to-yere,** *this year* **85 grace,** *favor* **86 her,** *their* **87 hem were levest,** *they would most like* **88 shelde hem fro,** *shield them from,* **shonde,** *harm* **89 unhappe,** *misfortune,* **eche disese,** *each discomfort* **90 alle,** *everything,* **hem plese,** *please them* **92 mysdemen,** *misinterpret* **93 Thorgh,** *through* **96 Dispit,** *malice,* **jape,** *foolishness* **97 Mysdeme,** *misinterpret* **98 barefot,** *barefoot,* **shod,** *wearing shoes* **100 syth,** *since* **101 Befalle,** *happen to,* **or he sterve,** *before he dies* **102 mote,** *may,* **ful,** *fully* **103 conclusion,** *result* **106 gebet dyde,** *gallows died*

57–58, echoes lines 1–2, making a rhetorical "envelope" for the intervening lines and marking them as an introduction. **63 tenthe day . . . of Decembre,** the date has not been explained satisfactorily, and the various suggestions are not mutually exclusive. December 10 was just before the winter solstice in the (Julian) calendar of Chaucer's time, not adjusted until 1582 (the Gregorian calendar) and not adopted in England until 1752. Chaucer may have selected the beginning of winter as particularly inappropriate to the topic of love, or he may have been indicating the beginning of a new cycle, perhaps signaling his attempt to create a new kind of poetry. If *HF* is an occasional poem, the date may relate to the betrothal of Richard in 1381 or 1382, or to the betrothal of Phillipa, John of Gaunt's daughter, discussed in 1384. Giving a precise date in a poem is a convention used by Machaut and Froissart. **64 now,** F reads "yow." **65–66** Lines lacking in P and Cx. **69 god of slepe,** Morpheus, described in Ovid's *Metamorphoses* 11.592 ff. (cited in a gloss to F and P) as living in a cave (**70**) on a branch of the river Lethe (**71 Lete**), the river of forgetfulness and one of the four rivers of Hades (**72 helle**), and "under a Cimmerian mountain" (**73 Cymerie**). Chaucer also describes the cave and its location in *BD* 155–77. **81 mover ys of alle,** God, the Unmoved Mover of classical and Christian neo-Platonic traditions; cf. *KnT* 1.2987ff. **82** A portion of the prayer known as the lesser doxology, the *Gloria Patri* ("Glory be to the Father . . ."): *Sicut erat in principio et nunc et semper* . . . ("As it was in the beginning, is now, and ever shall be . . .); cf. *TC* 1.245. **98 barefot . . . shod,** barefoot . . . wearing shoes, i.e., at night or by day. **105 Cresus . . . of Lyde,** Croesus, historical king of Lydia, whose story is retold by Chaucer in *MkT* 7.2727ff., derived from *RR* 6489ff., where Croesus refuses to accept that a dream foretells his eventual death by hanging.

This prayer shal he have of me—
I am no bet° in charyte!
Now herkeneth°, as I have yow seyde°,
What that I mette or I abreyde°.

[The Dream]

Of Decembre the tenthe day,
Whan hit was nyght to slepe I lay
Ryght ther° as I was wont° to done,
And fille on slepe wonder sone°,
As he that wery° was forgoo°
On pilgrymage myles° two
To the corseynt° Leonard,
To make lythe° of that° was hard.
But as I slepte, me mette° I was
Withyn° a temple ymad° of glas,
In whiche ther were moo° ymages
Of golde, stondynge° in sondry stages°,
And moo ryche tabernacles°,
And with perre° moo pynacles°,
And moo curiouse° portreytures,
And queynte° maner of figures
Of olde werke then I sawgh° ever.
For certeynly, I nyste° never
Wher that I was. But wel wyste° I
Hyt was of Venus redely°,
The temple, for in portreyture
I sawgh anoon-ryght° hir figure
Naked fletynge° in a see,
And also on hir hed, pardee°,
Hir rose garlond white and rede,
And hir comb to kembe° hyr hede,
Hir dowves°, and daun Cupido°
Hir blynde° sone, and Vulcano°
That in his face was ful broune°.
But as I romed° up and doune,
I fond° that on a wall ther was
Thus writen on a table of bras°:
"I wol° now singen, yif I kan,
The armes° and also the man
That first came, thorgh° his destinee,
Fugityf of° Troy contree°,
In° Itayle, with ful moche pyne°,
Unto the strondes of Lavyne.°"
And tho° began the story anoon
As I shal telle yow echon°
First sawgh° I the destruction
Of Troy throgh the Greke Synon,
That with his false forswerynge,
And his chere° and his lesynge°,
Made the hors broght° into Troye

108 bet, *better* **109 herkeneth,** *listen,* **seyde,** *told* **110 or I abreyde,** *before I awoke* **113 ther,** *where,* **wont,** *accustomed* **114 wonder sone,** *wonderfully soon* **115 wery,** *weary,* **forgoo,** *completely* **116 myles,** *miles* **117 corseynt,** *shrine* (of) **118 lythe,** *light,* **that,** *that which* **119 mette,** *dreamed* **120 Withyn,** *within,* **ymad,** *made* **121 moo,** *more* **122 stondyge,** *standing,* **sondry stages,** *various niches* **123 tabernacles,** *enclosures* **124 perre,** *jewelry,* **pynacles,** *pinnacles* **125 curiouse,** *intricate* **126 queynte,** *elaborate* **127 then I sawgh,** *than I saw* **128 nyste,** *did not know* **129 wyste,** *knew* **130 redely,** *truly* **132 sawgh anoon-ryght,** *saw immediately* **133 fletynge,** *floating* **134 pardee,** *by God* (Fr. *par Dieu*) **136 kembe,** *comb* **137 dowves,** *doves,* **daun Cupido,** *master Cupid* **138 blynde sone** *blind son,* **Vulcano,** *Vulcan* **139 ful broune,** *very brown* **140 romed,** *wandered* **141 fond,** *found* **142 table of bras,** *tablet of brass* **143 wol,** *will* **144 armes,** *deeds* **145 thorgh,** *through* **146 Fugityf of,** *fleeing from,* **contree,** *country* **147 In,** *into,* **ful moche pyne,** *very much pain* **148 strondes of Lavyne,** *shores of Lavinium* **149 tho,** *then* **150 echon,** *everyone* **151 sawgh,** *saw* **153 forswerynge,** *perjury* **154 chere,** *behavior,* **lesynge,** *lies* **155 Made . . . broght,** *caused . . . to be brought*

117 corseynt Leonard, the shrine (**corseynt,** "body-blessed") of St. Leonard, patron saint of repentant prisoners. The joke about the exhausting nature of a two-mile pilgrimage is unexplained, although Chaucer lived about two miles from the St. Leonard's nunnery at Stratford-atte-Bowe. In *RR* 8833ff., St. Leonard is invoked for the sake of those imprisoned in marriage, so the joke may entail marital release. **120 temple ymad of glas,** a fragile edifice that has no identified literary source; it inspired Lydgate's title, *Temple of Glas.* Details of the temple and its ornamentation derive from a variety of sources that also influenced Chaucer's temples of Venus in *PF* 211ff. and *KnT* 1.1918ff. **130–39 Venus . . . ,** the classical goddess of love; her associations with the sea (**fletynge in a see**), a garland (**garlond**) of roses, and doves (**dowves**) are all conventional. **135–36** P reads "Her roos garland on her hede," followed by a gap; Cx reads "Rose garlondes smellynge as a mede/ And also fleyng aboute her hede." **137 daun Cupido,** i.e., Dan Cupid, son of Venus and the god of love. The term *daun* derives from Lat. *dominus,* master, a respectful form of address. **138 Volcano,** Vulcan, god of metal work and mythological husband of Venus; his face is brown from working at the forge. **142 bras,** brass is also associated with Venus in *PF* 231. **143–48,** a close translation of the famous opening lines of Virgil's *Aeneid,* although Chaucer's addition of "yif I kan" (l. 143) undermines the confidence of the Latin original. Chaucer is more concerned in *HF* with love than with war or the founding of Rome, Virgil's concern. Chaucer also summarizes events in sequential order rather than following Virgil's beginning *in medias res* ("in the middle of things") and use of flashback. Compare the account in *LGW* 930ff. **143 singen,** F reads "say." **148 Lavyne,** Lavinium; in Virgil, Aeneas's landing site in Italy. **151 sawgh I,** i.e., I saw, initiating the rhetorical device of *ekphrasis,* the verbal description of visual artwork. The narrator reads words on the tablet of brass, but subsequently describes in visual terms engraved (**grave** 157) events that seem to come alive. Chaucer uses a similar technique in the descriptions of the temples in *KnT* 1.1918ff. **152 Synon,** Sinon deceived the Trojans, convincing them to take into the city the hollow wooden horse, filled with Greek warriors. Troy fell as a consequence, leading to Aeneas's journey and the founding of Rome. **153 That,** omitted in F and P.

Thorgh which Troyens lost al her joye.
And aftir this was grave°, allas,
How Ilyon assayled° was,
And wonne, and Kyng Priam yslayne°,
And Polite his sone, certayne°,
Dispitously°, of daun° Pirrus.
And next that sawgh° I how Venus,
Whan that she sawgh the castel brende°,
Doun fro the hevene gan descende°,
And bad° hir sone Eneas flee;
And how he fled, and how that he
Escaped was from al the pres°,
And tooke his fader° Anchises,
And bar° hym on hys bakke° away,
Cryinge, "Allas, and welaway!"
The whiche Anchises in hys honde
Bar the goddes of the londe,
Thilke° that unbrende° were.
  And I saugh next in al thys fere°
How Creusa, daun Eneas wif°,
Which that he lovede as hys lyf,
And hir yonge sone Iulo,
And eke° Askanius also,
Fledden° eke with drery chere°,
That hyt was pitee for to here°,
And in a forest as they went,
At a turnynge of a went°,
How Creusa was ylost, allas,
That ded°—not° I how—she was;
How he hir soughte, and how hir goste°
Bad° hym to flee the Grekes oste°,
And seyde he most° unto Itayle,
As was hys destynee, sauns faille°;
That hyt was pitee for to here,
When hir spirite gan appere°,
The wordes that she to hym seyde,
And for to kepe° hir sone hym preyde°.
Ther sawgh I grave eke how he,
Hys fader eke, and his meynee°,
With hys shippes gan to saylle°
Towardes the contree of Itaylle
As streight as that they myghte goo.
Ther saugh I the°, cruel Junoo°,
That° art daun Jupiteres wife,
That hast yhated al thy lyfe
Alle the Troianysshe bloode,
Renne° and crye as thou were woode°
On Eolus the god of wyndes
To blowen out of alle kyndes°
So lowde° that he shulde drenche°
Lorde and lady, grome° and wenche°,
Of al the Troian nacion,
Withoute any savacion°.
  Ther saugh I such tempeste aryse°
That every herte myght agryse°
To see hyt peynted on the walle.
Ther saugh I graven eke withalle°
Venus, how ye, my lady dere,
Wepynge with ful woful chere°,
Prayen Jupiter on hye°
To save and kepe that navye°
Of the Troian Eneas
Syth° that he hir sone was.
Ther saugh I Joves Venus kysse°,

---

157 grave, *engraved* **158 assayled,** *attacked* **159 yslayne,** *slain* **160 certayne,** *certainly* **161 Dispitously,** *cruelly,* **of daun,** *by master* **162 sawgh,** *saw* **163 brende,** *burned* **164 gan descende,** *did descend* **165 bad,** *urged* **167 pres,** *crowd* **168 fader,** *father* **169 bar,** *bore,* **bakke,** *back* **173 Thilke,** *those,* **unbrende,** *unburned* **174 fere,** *peril* **175 daun Eneas wif,** *master Aeneas's wife* **178 eke,** *also* **179 Fledden,** *fled,* **drery chere,** *sorrowful countenance* **180 here,** *hear* **182 went,** *path* **184 That ded,** (so) *that dead,* **not,** *do not know* **185 goste,** *spirit* **186 Bad,** *urged,* **oste,** *army* **187 most,** *must* (go) **188 sauns faille,** *without* (Fr. *sans*) *fail* **190 gan appere,** *did appear* **192 kepe,** *care for,* **hym preyde,** *entreated him* **194 meynee,** *company* **195 gan to saylle,** *did sail* **198 the,** *thee,* **Junoo,** *Juno* **199 That,** *who* **202 Renne,** *run,* **woode,** *insane* **204 alle kyndes,** *all kinds* (of winds) **205 lowde,** *loudly,* **shulde drenche,** *should drown* **206 grome,** *boy,* **wenche,** *girl* **208 savacion,** *salvation* **209 aryse,** *arise* **210 agryse,** *shudder* **212 eke withalle,** *also as well* **214 chere,** *countenance* **215 hye,** *high* **216 navye,** *navy* **218 Syth,** *since* **219 Joves Venus kysse,** *Jupiter kiss Venus*

158 Ilyon, Ilium, i.e., Troy. **159 Priam,** ruler of Troy. **160 Polite,** Polites, son of Priam and Hecuba, was killed in front of his parents by Pyrrhus (**Pirrus**), son of the Greek hero, Achilles; *Aeneid* 2.530. **161 of,** F reads "and." **165 hir sone,** Aeneas was the son of Venus and Anchises. **169 on hys bakke,** Aeneas carried Anchises upon his back from burning Troy because Anchises's advanced age made it impossible for him to walk. Anchises carried the household gods (Lares and Penates); *Aeneid* 2.706ff. **174 thys,** F reads "hys." **177–78 Iulo . . . Askanius,** Julius and Ascanius, two names for the son of Aeneas and Creusa, although Chaucer treats them as two sons; he gets it right in *LGW* 941. **181 in a forest,** there is no forest in *Aeneid* 2.736ff., although Chaucer follows other details closely. Virgil does not explain how Creusa died, but her spirit urges Aeneas on his journey. **198 saugh I the, cruel Junoo,** the narrator's direct address to Juno produces rhetorical intensity. The goddess Juno was the wife of Jupiter (Jove) and the perpetual enemy of the Trojans because Paris, son of the king of Troy, had judged Venus more beautiful than Juno, and because it had been foretold that a Trojan would destroy Carthage, her favored city. The events from here to line 238 recount the beginning of Virgil's *Aeneid.* **203 Eolus,** Aeolus, the god of winds, whom Chaucer later depicts (1571ff. below) as the servant of Fame; from *Aeneid* 1.50ff. **213 Venus,** Chaucer increases her influence; in *Aeneid* she does not seek Jupiter's favor until after Neptune has calmed the storm. **219 Joves,** another name for Jupiter; the *-s* ending is an OF nominative form, not a possessive.

And graunted of the tempest lysse°.
Ther saugh I how the tempest stent°,
And how with alle pyne° he° went,
And prevely toke arryvage°
In the contree of Cartage°;
And on the morwe°, how that he
And a knyght highte Achate°
Mette° with Venus that day,
Goynge in° a queynt array°
As she had ben an hunteresse,
With wynde blowynge upon hir tresse°;
How Eneas gan hym to pleyne°,
When that he knew° hir, of his peyne°;
And how his shippes dreynte° were,
Or elles lost, he nyste° where;
How she gan hym comforte thoo°,
And bad° hym to Cartage goo,
And ther he shulde his folke fynde
That in the see° were left behynde.
  And, shortly of this thyng° to pace°,
She° made Eneas so in grace°
Of Dido quene of that contree
That, shortly for to tellen, she
Became hys love and let hym doo
Al that weddynge longeth too°.
What° shulde I speke more queynte°,
Or peyne me° my wordes peynte°
To speke of love? Hyt wol° not be;
I kan° not of that faculte°.
And eke° to telle the manere
How they aqueynteden in-fere°,
Hyt were a long proces to telle,
And over-long for yow to dwelle.
Ther sawgh I grave° how Eneas
Tolde Dido every caas°
That hym was tyd° upon the see.
And after grave was how shee
Made of hym shortly at oo° worde
Hyr lyf, hir love, hir luste°, hir lorde,
And did hym al the reverence
And leyde° on hym al the dispence°
That any woman myghte do,
Wenynge° hyt had al be° so
As he hir swor; and herby demed°
That he was good, for he suche semed.
Allas, what harm doth apparence°
Whan hit is fals in existence°!
For he to hir a traytour was;
Wherfore she slowe° hirself, allas.
Loo, how a woman dothe amys°
To love him that unknowe ys°.
For be Cryste°, lo, thus yt fareth°,
Hyt is not al gold that glareth°.
For also browke I° wel myn hed,
Ther may be under godlyhed°
Kevered° rnany a shrewed° vice.
Therfore be no wyght° so nyce°
To take a love oonly for chere°,
Or speche, or for frendly manere.
For this shal every woman fynde,
That some man, of his pure kynde°,
Wol shewen° outward the fayreste°,
Tyl he have caught that what him leste,
And thanne wol he causes° fynde,
And swere how that she ys unkynde,
Or fals, or prevy°, or double° was.

220 lysse, *relief* **221 stent,** *stopped* **222 pyne,** *pain,* **he,** *Aeneas* **223 prevely toke arryvage,** *secretly took landing* **224 Cartage,** *Carthage* **225 on the morwe,** *in the morning* **226 highte Achate,** *named Achates* **227 Mette,** *met* **228 Goynge in,** *wearing,* **queynt array,** *strange costume* **230 tresse,** *unbound hair* **231 pleyne,** *lament* **232 knew,** *recognized,* **peyne,** *sorrow* **233 dreynte,** *drowned* **234 nyste,** *knew not* **235 thoo,** *then* **236 bad,** *told* **238 see,** *sea* **239 of this thing,** *about this topic,* **pace,** *proceed* **240 She,** *Venus,* **grace,** *good favor* **244 weddynge longeth too,** *belongs to a marriage* **245 What,** *why,* **queynte,** *indirectly* **246 peyne me,** *take pains,* **peynte,** (to) *disguise* **247 Hyt wol,** *it will* **248 kan,** *know,* **faculte,** *talent* **249 eke,** *also* **250 aqueynteden in-fere,** (were) *acquainted together* **253 grave,** *engraved* **254 caas,** *adventure* **255 hym was tyd,** *happened to him* **257 oo,** *one* **258 luste,** *delight* **260 leyde,** *lavished,* **dispence,** *expenditure* **262 Wenynge,** *believing,* **be,** *been* **263 herby demed,** *by this judged* **265 apparence,** *appearance* **266 existence,** *reality* **268 slowe,** *slew* **269 dothe amys,** *does wrong* **270 unknowe ys,** *is unknown* **271 be Cryste,** *by Christ,* **fareth,** *goes* **272 glareth,** *shines* **273 also browke I,** *as I may keep* **274 godlyhed,** (the appearance of) *virtue* **275 Kevered,** *covered,* **shrewed,** *cursed* **276 wyght,** *person,* **nyce,** *foolish* **277 chere,** *looks* **280 pure kynde,** *essential nature* **281Wol shewen,** *will show,* **fayreste,** *fairest* **282 hym leste,** *he wants* **283 causes,** *reasons* **285 prevy,** *secretive,* **double,** *duplicitous*

220–21 F conflates these lines into one. **226 Achate,** Achates, Aeneas's devoted companion. **239 pace,** proceed or pass (over). From this point, the account abandons Virgil's *Aeneid,* which treats Aeneas as a hero, to follow the version of Ovid's *Heroides* 7 (cited in line 379 below), which depicts him abandoning Dido. A similar treatment is *LGW* 924ff. The use of both Virgil and Ovid as sources raises questions about the consistency and reliability of literary tradition as a means by which fame is conveyed. **244 Al that,** F reads "That that." **253–55** This summarizes the flashback in *Aeneid* 3 and 4, in which are recounted the fall of Troy and Aeneas's escape. **272** Chaucer uses this familiar proverb again in *CYT* 7.962–63. **278 Or,** F reads "Of for." **280–83** Found only in Th, these lines are omitted in the manuscripts and in Caxton's edition, perhaps the result of eyeskip from "fynde" at the end of line 279 to the end of 283. **285 prevy,** privy or secretive, although the word has sexual implications here and at *Rom* 5964. **or double,** F and P read omit "or."

Al this sey I be° Eneas,
And Dido and hir nyce lest°,
That loved al to sone° a gest°.
Therfore I wol seye a proverbe,
That he that fully knoweth th'erbe°
May savely ley hyt° to his eye—
Withoute drede, this ys no lye.
  But let us speke of Eneas,
How he betrayed hir, allas,
And lefte hir ful unkyndely°
So when she saw al-utterly°,
That he wolde hir of trouthe fayle°,
And wende° fro hir to Itayle,
She gan to wringe hir hondes two.
"Allas," quod she, "what me ys woo°!
Allas, is every man thus trewe,
That every yere wolde° have a newe°,
Yf hit so longe tyme dure°,
Or elles three, peraventure°?
As thus, of oon° he wolde have fame
In magnyfyinge of hys name;
Another for frendshippe, seyth° he;
And yet ther shal the thridde° be
That shal be take for delyte°,
Loo, or for synguler profite.°"
In suche wordes gan to pleyne°
Dydo of hir grete peyne°,
As me mette redely°—
Non other auctour alegge I°.
"Allas," quod she, "my swete hert,
Have pitee on my sorwes smert°,
And slee° mee not! Goo noght awey!
O woful Dido, welaway°,"
Quod she to hirselve thoo,
"O Eneas, what wol° ye doo?
O that your love, ne your bonde°
That ye have sworn with your ryght honde,
Ne my crewel deth,°" quod she,
"May holde yow stille here with me.
O haveth of my deth pitee!
Iwys°, my dere herte, ye
Knowen ful wel that never yit,
As ferforth° as I hadde wyt°,
Agylte° I yowe in thoght ne dede.
O men, have ye suche godlyhede°
In speche, and never a dele° of trouthe?
Allas, that ever hadde routhe°
Any woman on any man.
Now see I wel, and telle kan,
We wrechched wymmen konne noon arte°,
For certeyne, for the more parte,
Thus we be served everychon°.
How sore° that ye men konne groon°,
Anoon° as we have yow receyved°,
Certaynly we ben deceyvyd°.
For though your love laste a seson°,
Wayte upon° the conclusyon,
And eke° how that ye determynen°,
And for the more part diffynen°.
  "O welawey that I was borne,
For thorgh° yow is my name lorne°,
And al myn actes red° and songe
Over al thys londe, on every tonge.
O wikke Fame, for ther nys°
Nothing so swift, lo, as she is!
O, sothe° ys, everything ys wyste°,
Though hit be kevered° with the myste.
Eke, though I myghte duren° ever,
That° I have don rekever° I never,
That° I ne shal be seyd°, allas,

286 be, *about* **287 nyce lest,** *foolish affection* **288 to sone,** *too soon,* **gest,** *guest* **290 th'erbe,** *the medicine* (herb) **291 savely ley hyt,** *safely lay it* **295 unkyndely,** *unkindly* **296 al-utterly,** *completely* **297 trouthe fayle,** *loyalty fail* **298 wende,** *depart* **300 what me ys woo,** *woe is me* **302 wolde,** (he) *would,* **newe,** *new* (love) **303 so longe tyme dure,** *lasts as long as that* **304 peraventure,** *perhaps* **305 oon,** *one* **307 seyth,** *says* **308 thridde,** *third* **309 take for delyte,** *taken for pleasure* **310 synguler profite,** *personal advantage* **311 gan to pleyne,** *did lament* **312 peyne,** *pain* **313 mette redely,** *dreamed truly* **314 Non other auctour alegge I,** *I cite no other authority* **316 smert,** *painful* **317 slee,** *slay* **318 welaway,** *alas* **320 wol,** *will* **321 bonde,** *promise* **323 crewel deth,** *cruel death* **326 Iwys,** *surely* **328 ferforth,** *far,* **wyt,** *knowledge* **329 Agylte,** *wronged* **330 godlyhede,** (an appearance of) *virtue* **331 dele,** *bit* **332 routhe,** *pity* **335 konne noon arte,** *understand no art* (of love) **337 served everychon,** *treated each one* **338 How sore,** *however sorely,* **konne groon,** *can groan* **339 Anoon,** *as soon,* **receyved,** *accepted* **340 deceyvyd,** *deceived* **341 laste a seson,** *lasts for some time* (a season) **342 Wayte upon,** *watch for* **343 eke,** *also,* **determynen,** *will determine* (it) **344 diffynen,** *end up* **346 thorgh,** *through,* **name lorne,** *reputation lost* **347 red,** *read* **349 nys,** *is not* **351 sothe,** *truth,* **wyste,** *known* **352 kevered,** *covered* **353 duren,** *live* **354 That,** *that which,* **rekever,** *recover* **355 That,** (so) *that,* **seyd,** *said*

305 oon, F reads "love." **310 synguler profite,** personal or individual advantage, the antithesis of "comoun profyt" (communal advantage), an important notion in *PF* 47 and 75. **311–12 pleyne / peyne,** the same rhyme is used of Aeneas's lament at 231–32 above. **314 Non other auctour,** no other author. This claim calls attention to the fact that most of Dido's complaint is Chaucer's own invention, not dependent on Virgil or Ovid. **330 men, have ye,** F reads "have ye men." **340** Line lacking in F. **345–60** Compare *Aeneid* 4.304–30, where Dido's lament is more imperious and less plaintive. Presented here as someone who is famous because an undeserving victim, Dido anticipates the victims of Fame's capriciousness in Book III below. **347 myn,** F reads "youre."

Yshamed be° hourgh Eneas,
And that I shal thus juged be,
'Loo, ryght as she hath don, now she
Wol doo eftesones, hardely'°—
Thus seyth the peple prevely.°"
  But that° is don, is not to° done.
Al hir compleynt ne al hir mone°,
Certeyn, avayleth° hir not a stre°.
And when she wiste sothly° he
Was forthe unto his shippes goon,
She into hir chambre wente anoon
And called on hir suster Anne,
And gan hir to compleyne thanne;
And seyde that she cause was
That she first loved him, allas,
And thus counseylled hir thertoo.
But what, when this was seyde and doo°,
She rof° hirselve to the herte,
And deyde° thorgh the wounde smerte°.
And al the maner how she deyde,
And al the wordes that she seyde,
Whoso° to knowe hit hath purpos,
Rede° Virgile in *Eneydos*
Or the *Epistle* of Ovyde,
What that she wrot or° that she dyde,
And nere hyt were° to long t'endyte°,
Be° God, I wolde° hyt here write.
But welaway, the harm, the routhe°,
That hath betyd° for suche untrouthe,
As men may ofte in bokes rede,
And al day se° hyt yet in dede,
That for to thynk hyt, a tene° is.
  Loo Demophon, duk of Athenys°,
How he forswore hym° ful falsly,
And trayid° Phillis wikkidly,
That kynges doghtre was of Trace°,
And falsly gan hys terme pace°;
And when she wiste° that he was fals,
She heng° hirself ryght be the hals°,
For° he had doon hir suche untrouthe.
Loo, was not this a woo and routhe°?
Eke lo how fals and reccheles°
Was to Breseyda Achilles,
And Paris to Enone,
And Jason to Isiphile,
And eft° Jason to Medea,
And Ercules to Dyanira,
For he left hir for Yole,
That made hym cache his deth, parde°.
How fals eke° was he Theseus,
That as the story telleth us
How he betrayed Adriane—
The devel be hys soules bane°!
For had he lawghed, had he loured°,
He moste° have ben al devoured
Yf Adriane ne had ybe°.
And for° she had of hym pite,
She made hym fro the dethe escape,
And he made hir a ful fals jape°,
For aftir this, withyn a while,

---

356 Yshamed be, *put to shame* **359 Wol doo eftesones, hardely,** *will do again, assuredly* **360 prevely,** *in private* **361 that,** *what,* **is not to,** *is not yet to* (be) **362 mone,** *moan* **363 avayleth,** *helps,* **stre,** *straw* **364 wiste sothly,** *knew truly* **372 doo,** *done* **373 rof,** *pierced* **374 deyde,** *died,* **smerte,** *painful* **377 Whoso,** *whoever* **378 Rede,** *read* **380 or,** *before* **381 nere hyt were,** (if) *it weren't,* **t'endyte,** *to compose* **382 Be,** *by,* **wolde,** *would* **383 routhe,** *pity* **384 betyd,** *happened* **386 se,** *see* **387 tene,** *sorrow* **388 duk of Athenys,** *duke of Athens* **389 forswore hym,** *perjured himself* **390 trayid,** *betrayed* **391 Trace,** *Thrace* **392 gan hys terme pace,** *did pass his designated time* **393 wiste,** *knew* **394 heng,** *hanged,* **hals,** *neck* **395 For,** *because* **396 routhe,** *pity* **397 reccheles,** *uncaring* **401 eft,** *again* **404 parde,** *by God* (Fr. *par Dieu*) **405 eke,** *also* **408 bane,** *destroyer* **409 loured,** *scowled* **410 moste,** *would* **411 ybe,** *been* **412 for,** *because* **414 jape,** *trick*

361 Phillips and Havely are the only modern editors to end Dido's speech with this line. Other editors end it at 360 and omit initial "But" in line 362, which appears in all the manuscripts and early editions. **363 Certeyn,** F reads "Certeynly." **365 goon,** F reads "agoon." **367 Anne,** Anna, Dido's sister, whose questions in *Aeneid* 4.31–55 encourage Dido to love Aeneas; Dido complains to her in *Aeneid* 4.415–52. Chaucer has Anna discourage the love affair in *LGW* 1182–83. **370 him,** omitted in F and P. **378–79 Eneydos . . . *Epistle*,** these are Chaucer's major sources for this section of his poem: Virgil's *Aeneid* (in the possessive form often used in titles, i.e., *The Book of Aeneas*), and Ovid's Epistle 7 of the *Heroides*, cast as a letter from Dido to Aeneas. Chaucer mentions Virgil again at 1244 and 1483 below. **381 nere,** F reads "nor." **388 Demophon,** betrothed to Phyllis, daughter of the king of Thrace, Demophon failed to show up for his wedding, as is recounted in *LGW* 2394ff. This and the following list of false and unfortunate lovers are all in Ovid's *Heroides*, the story of Demophon and Phyllis in Epistle 2. Parallel lists are in *MLP* 2.57ff., *BD* 726ff., *PF* 285ff., and the tales of *LGW*. Chaucer uses the lists as a device of adornment and in imitation of classical literature. **398 Achilles,** in *Heroides* 3, Achilles captures Briseis (**Breseyda**), but when she is given to Agamemnon, he pouts instead of seeking to recover her. **399 Paris,** in *Heroides* 5, Paris deserts Oenone (**Enone**) when he goes to abduct Helen of Troy. **400–01 Jason,** in *Heroides* 6, Jason deserts Hypsipyle (**Isiphile**), and in *Heroides* 12, he abandons Medea; see *LGW* 1370ff. **402 And,** omitted in F. **Ercules,** in *Heroides* 9, Hercules turns his attention from his wife Deianira (**Dyanira**) to her maidservant, Iole (**Yole**), leading to his own death at Deianira's hands; see *MkT* 7.2119ff. **405 Theseus,** in *Heroides* 10, Theseus deserts Ariadne (**Adriane**), who had saved his life by helping him in his battle against the Minotaur, and took her sister Phaedra (**Phedra**) instead; see *LGW* 1886ff. **409 lawghed . . . loured,** an idiomatic phrase that means "in all circumstances." **410 al,** omitted in F.

He lefte hir slepynge in an ile°
Deserte° allone, ryght in the se,
And stale° away and let hir be,
And took hir suster Phedra thoo°
With him, and gan to shippe goo°.
And yet he had yswore° to hire°
On alle that ever he myghte swere,
That so° she saved hym hys lyfe,
He wolde have take° hir to° hys wife,
For she desired nothing ellis°,
In certeyne, as the book us tellis°
  But to excusen Eneas
Fullyche° of al his grete trespas,
The booke seyth Mercur°, sauns fayle°,
Bad° hym goo into Itayle,
And leve Auffrikes regioun°,
And Dido and hir faire toun.
Thoo sawgh I grave° how to Itayle
Daun Eneas is goo° to sayle°;
And how the tempest al began,
And how he lost hys sterisman°,
Which° that the stere°, or he tok kepe°,
Smote overbord, loo, as he slepe.
And also sawgh I how Sybile
And Eneas besyde an yle°
To helle went for to see
His fader°, Anchyses the free;
How he ther fond Palinurus,
And Dido, and eke Deiphebus;
And every turment eke° in helle
Saugh° he, which is longe to telle;
Which whoso willeth for to knowe,
He most rede° many a rowe°
On° Virgile or on Claudian,
Or Daunte, that hit telle kan.
Tho saugh I grave al the aryvayle°
That Eneas had in Itayle;
And with Kyng Latyne hys tretee,°
And alle the batayles that hee
Was at hymself, and eke hys knyghtis,
Or° he had al ywonne° hys ryghtis;
And how he Turnus reft his lyfe°,
And wan° Lavina to his wife,
And alle the mervelous signals°
Of the goddys celestials°—
How, mawgree° Juno, Eneas,
For al hir sleight° and hir compas°;
Acheved al his aventure°,
For Jupiter took of hym cure°
At the prayer of Venus—
The whiche° I preye alwey save us,
And us ay° of oure sorwes lyghte°.
  When I had seen al this syghte
In this noble temple thus,
"A, Lord," thought I, "that madest us,
Yet sawgh° I never such noblesse
Of ymages, ne such richesse,
As I saugh grave° in this chirche°;
But not wot° I whoo did hem wirche°,
Ne where I am, ne in what contree.
But now wol I goo out and see,
Ryght at the wiket°, yf y kan
See owhere° any stiryng° man,
That may me telle where I am."

416 in an ile, *on an island* **417 Deserte,** *deserted* **418 stale,** *stole* **419 thoo,** *then* **420 gan to shippe goo,** *went to* (his) *ship* **421 yswore,** *sworn,* **hire,** *her* (Ariadne) **423 so,** *if* **424 wolde have take,** *would take,* **to,** *as* **425 ellis,** *else* **426 tellis,** *tells* **428 Fullyche,** *fully* **429 seyth Mercur,** *says Mercury,* **sauns fayle,** *without* (Fr. *sans*) *doubt* **430 Bad,** *ordered* **431 leve Auffrikes regioun,** *leave the region of Africa* **433 Thoo sawgh I grave,** *then I saw engraved* **434 goo,** *gone,* **to sayle,** *by sail* **436 sterisman,** *steersman* **437 Which,** *who,* **stere,** *steering oar,* **or he tok kepe,** *before he took heed* **440 yle,** *island* **442 fader,** *father* **445 turment eke,** *torment also* **446 Saugh,** *saw* **448 most rede,** *must read,* **rowe,** *line* **449 On,** *in* **451 aryvayle,** *arrival* **453 tretee,** *agreement* **456 Or,** *before,* **ywonne,** *won* **457 Turnus reft hys lyfe,** *deprived Turnus of his life* **458 wan,** *won* **459 signals,** *signs* **460 goddys celestials,** *celestial gods* **461 mawgree,** *in spite of* **462 sleight,** *trickery,* **compas,** *contriving* **463 aventure,** *fortune* **464 cure,** *care* **466 The whiche,** *who* **467 ay,** *always,* **lyghte,** *lighten* **471 sawgh,** *saw* **473 grave,** *engraved,* **chirche,** *temple* (see 131 above) **474 wot,** *know,* **hem wirche,** *made them* **477 wiket,** *gate* **478 owhere,** *anywhere,* **stiryng,** *moving*

426 the book, apparently used here of books or literary authority generally; the source of the incident is the *Heroides,* whereas the *Aeneid* is the source of the following account where "the booke" is cited again (line 429). **428 al,** omitted in P. **grete,** omitted in F. **429 Mercur,** Mercury is sent by Jove to command Aeneas to leave Carthage for Italy in *Aeneid* 4.219ff. **434 goo to,** F reads "goo for to." **436 sterisman,** in *Aeneid* 5.835ff., Aeneas's steersman (**Palinurus**) is swept overboard while asleep, still grasping the steering oar which is lost with him. **439–46 Sybile,** in *Aeneid* 6, Aeneas and the Sybil, the priestess of Apollo at Cumae, descend from the isle (**yle**) of Crete into the Underworld (**helle**), where they meet Anchises, Palinurus, Dido, and **Deiphebus**, who is a son of Priam, brother of Paris, and husband to Helen after Paris dies; Helen betrays Deiphebus to his death at the fall of Troy. **449–50 Virgile . . . Daunte,** the *Aeneid* of Virgil (**Virgile**), the *De Raptu Preserpinae* (c400 C.E.) of Claudian, and the *Divine Comedy* (c1315) of Dante (**Daunte**) include descriptions of the underworld. **453 Latyne,** Latinus, legendary king of the Latin race, who in *Aeneid* 7.12 greets Aeneas upon his arrival in Italy. **457–58 Turnus . . . Lavina,** first betrothed to Turnus by her father Latinus, Lavinia was afterward given to Aeneas, enraging Turnus, whose battles against Aeneas are told in Bks. 9–12 of the *Aeneid.* With the support of Venus and Jupiter, and to the distress of Juno, Aeneas eventually kills Turnus.

When I out at the dores cam,
I faste aboute me behelde°.
Then sawgh I but° a large felde°,
As fer as that I myghte see,
Withouten toun, or hous, or tree,
Or bush, or grass, or eryd londe°,
For al the feld nas° but of sonde°
As smal° as man may se yet lye°
In the desert of Lybye°.
Ne no maner creature
That ys yformed be° Nature
Ne sawgh I, me to rede or wisse°.
"O Crist," thoughte I, "that art in
blysse,
Fro fantome° and illusion
Me save," and with devocion
Myn eyen° to the hevene I caste.
Thoo° was I war°, lo, at the laste
That faste be° the sonne, as hye°
As kenne myghte I° with myn eye,
Me thoughte I sawgh an egle sore°,
But that hit semed moche more°
Then I had any egle seyn°.
But this° as sooth° as deth, certeyn,
Hyt° was of gold and shone so bryghte
That never sawe men such a syghte,
But yf° the heven had ywonne°
Alle newe of gold another sonne°,
So shone the egles fethers bryghte,
And somwhat dounward gan hyt lyghte°.

Book 2

[Proem]

Now herkeneth°, every maner man
That Englissh understonde kan,
And listeneth of my dreme to lere°,
For now at erste° shul ye here
So sely° an avisyoun°
That Isaye, ne Scipioun,
Ne Kynge Nabugodonosor,
Pharoo, Turnus, ne Elcanor,
Ne mette° such a dreme as this.
Now faire blisfull, O Cipris°,
So be my favour° at this tyme!
And ye, me to endite° and ryme
Helpeth, that on Parnaso° duelle,

481 behelde, *looked* **482 but,** *nothing but,* **felde,** *expanse* **485 eryd londe,** *plowed land* **486 nas,** *was nothing,* **sonde,** *sand* **487 smal,** *fine,* **lye,** *lie* **488 Lybye,** *Libya* **490 be,** *by* **491 rede or wisse,** *advise or inform* **493 Fro fantome,** *from phantom* **495 eyen,** *eyes* **496 Thoo,** *then,* **war,** *aware* **497 faste be,** *near,* **hye,** *high* **498 As kenne myghte I,** *as I might perceive* **499 egle sore,** *eagle soar* **500 semed moche more,** *seemed much larger* **501 seyn,** *seen* **502 this,** *this is,* **sooth,** *true* **503 Hyt,** *it* (the eagle) **505 But yf,** *unless,* **ywonne,** *acquired* **506 sonne,** *sun* **508 gan hyt lyghte,** *it descended* **Book 2. 509 herkeneth,** *pay attention* **511 lere,** *learn* **512 at erste,** *for the first time* **513 sely,** *fortunate,* **avisyoun,** *dream* **517 Ne mette,** *dreamed not* **518 Cipris,** *Venus* **519 favour,** *helper* **520 endite,** *compose,* **ryme,** *rhyme* **521 Parnaso,** *Mt. Parnassus*

486 of, omitted in F. **488 desert of Lybye,** often referred to in the *Aeneid*, Libya was known as a desert. In both biblical and classical traditions, such a desert suggests spiritual or emotional wasteland, e.g., the temptation of Christ (Matt. 4.1; Luke 4.2) or Virgil's rescue of Dante from a kind of despair (*Inferno* 1.64). In French love poems, the wasteland represents the lover's superficiality or desolation. Here, the desert may also suggest an empty or unfulfilled understanding of the story engraved in the temple. **489 Ne no,** F and P read "Ne I no." **499 egle,** the description of the eagle recalls the golden eagle that carries Dante to the gate in *Purgatorio* 9.19ff. In the bestiary tradition, the eagle was associated with perceptiveness because it was thought to be able to stare into the sun without blinking; it was also the symbol of St. John, one of the four Gospel writers, and a symbol of contemplation. **504–07** Lines omitted in F due to eyeskip. **506 another sonne,** the mention of another sun recalls Dante's *Paradiso* 1.61ff. **Book 2. 513 avisyoun,** a kind of dream, although used at l. 7 to mean "delusion"; see 1–52n. The dreams cited here are prophetic. P reads "So sely and dredfull a vision." **514 Isaye,** Isaiah 1 recounts the vision of the prophet Isaiah. **Scipioun,** Cicero's *Dream of Scipio* tells of Scipio's dream about his future and the future of Rome; see *PF* 31ff. **515 Nabugodonosor,** in Daniel 4, Nebuchadnezzer has a God-given dream, interpreted by Daniel; see *MkT* 7.2143ff. **516 Pharoo,** Pharoah's dream in Genesis 41 is interpreted by Joseph. **Turnus,** in *Aeneid* 9.1ff., the goddess Iris predicts to Turnus the coming of Aeneas. **Elcanor,** not identified. **518 Cipris,** another name for Venus because she was reputed to have been born of the waves near Cyprus. **520–22 ye . . . that on Parnaso . . . Elicon,** direct address to the nine muses, who in classical literature were the inspiration of literature and who were thought to live on Mt. Parnassus (**Parnaso**). The form *Parnaso* shows the influence of Italian. Helicon (**Elicon**), a mountain near Parnassus, was often understood to be a well or spring on Parnassus. This is the first invocation of the muses in English literature.

Be Elicon°, the clere welle°.
  O Thought that wrot° al that I mette,
And in the tresorye° hyt shette°
Of my brayn, now shal men se
Yf any vertu° in the° be
To tel al my drem aryght.
Now kythe° thyn engyne° and myght.

[The Dream]

  This egle, of whiche I have yow tolde,
That shone with fethres as of golde,
Which that so high gan to sore°,
I gan beholde more and more,
To se the beaute and the wonder.
But never was ther dynt° of thonder,
Ne that thyng that men calle fouder°,
That smyte° somtyme a tour° to powder,
And in his° swifte comynge brende°,
That so swithe° gan descende
As this four°, when hyt behelde
That I a-roume° was in the felde.
And with hys grymme pawes stronge,
Withyn hys sharpe nayles° longe,
Me, fleynge°, in a swappe° he hente°,
And with hys sours ayen° up wente,
Me caryinge in his clawes starke°
As lyghtly as I were a larke,
How high I can not telle yow,
For I cam up y nyste° how.
For so astonyed° and asweved°
Was every vertu° in my heved°,
What with his sours° and with my drede,
That al my felynge gan to dede°,
For-whi° hit was to gret affray°.
  Thus I longe in hys clawes lay
Til at the last he to me spake
In mannes vois, and seyde, "Awake,
And be not agaste° so, for shame."
And called me tho° by my name,
And for° I shulde the bet abreyde°,
Me mette° "awake" to me he seyde,
Ryght° in the same vois° and stevene°
That useth oon° I koude nevene°.
And with that vois, soth° for to seyn°,
My mynde cam to me ageyn,
For hyt was goodely° seyd to me
So nas hyt never wont° to be.
And herewithalle I gan to stere°,
And he me in his fete to bere
Til that he felt that I had hete°,
And felte eke tho° myn herte bete.
And thoo° gan he me to disporte°,
And with wordes to comforte,
And sayde twyes°, "Seynte° Marye,
Thou art noyous° for to carye,
And nothyng nedeth it°, pardee°!
For, also wis° God helpe me,
As thou noon harme shalt have of this;
And this caas° that betydde the is°,
Is for thy lore° and for thy prowe°.
Let see! Darst° thou yet loke nowe°?
Be ful assured, boldely°,
I am thy frend." And therwith I

---

522 Be Elicon, *by Helicon,* **clere welle,** *clear spring* **523 wrot,** *wrote* **524 tresorye,** *treasury,* **shette,** *shut* **526 vertu,** *power,* **the,** *thee* **528 kythe,** *reveal,* **engyne,** *skill* **531 gan to sore,** *did soar* **534 dynt,** *force* **535 fouder,** *thunderbolt* **536 smyte,** *strikes,* **tour,** *tower* **537 his,** *the thunderbolt's,* **brende,** *burned* **538 swithe,** *swiftly* **539 foul,** *bird* **540 a-roume,** *roaming* **542 nayles,** *talons* **543 fleynge,** *fleeing,* **swappe,** *swoop,* **hente,** *grasped* **544 sours ayen,** *rising again* **545 starke,** *powerful* **548 y nyste,** *I know not* **549 astonyed,** *astonished,* **asweved,** *bewildered* **550 vertu,** *power,* **heved,** *head* **551 sours,** *rising* **552 gan to dede,** *did die* **553 For-whi,** *because,* **to gret affray,** *too great fright* **557 agaste,** *frightened* **558 tho,** *then* **559 for,** *so that,* **bet abreyde,** *better awaken* **560 Me mette,** *I dreamed* **561 Ryght,** *exactly,* **vois,** *voice,* **stevene,** *tone* **562 oon,** *someone,* **koude nevene,** *could name* **563 soth,** *truth,* **seyn,** *say* **565 goodely** *pleasantly* **566 So nas hyt never wont,** *as it was never accustomed* **567 stere,** *move* **569 hete,** *heat* (i.e., life) **570 eke tho,** *again then* **571 thoo,** *then,* **disporte,** *divert* **573 twyes,** *twice,* **Seynte,** *holy* **574 noyous,** *troublesome* **575 nothyng nedeth it,** *no need for it,* **pardee,** *by God* (Fr. *par Dieu*) **576 also wis,** *as certainly* **578 caas,** *adventure,* **betydde the is,** *is come to thee* **579 lore,** *learning,* **prowe,** *advantage* **580 Darst thou,** *dare you,* **loke nowe,** *look now,* **boldely,** *confidently*

523 O Thought, Dante invokes Thought or Memory ("mente") as well as the muses in *Inferno,* 2.7–8, an opening Chaucer also echoes in *PF* 85–86. **524 tresorye,** echoes the image of a mental treasury in *Paradiso* 1.10–11. **534–39** The descent of the eagle recalls *Purgatorio* 9.28ff., although the **fouder/powder** rhyme echoes Machaut's *Jugement du Roi de Navarre,* 301–02, and *Confort d'ami,* 1889–90; *Bo* 1 m4.11–12 also refers to a thunderbolt smiting a tower. **535 thyng,** F reads "kyng." **fouder,** F reads "founder." **536 smyte,** F reads "smote." **"to,** F reads "of." **537 brende,** F reads "beende." **552 gan to dede,** the narrator's feelings die here, i.e., he faints. At 564 he awakens from this faint within a dream. **557 be not agaste,** in *Purgatorio* 9.46, Virgil tells Dante not to fear after Dante has been frightened by an eagle. **so,** omitted in F. **558 tho,** omitted in F and P. **562 oon I koude nevene,** the eagle appears to imitate the voice of someone close to Chaucer. His wife and a servant have been suggested as possibilities, but no one knows for sure. Probably an "in joke" for the members of Chaucer's audience who knew him well. **566 nas,** F reads "was." **570 tho,** F reads "that." **574 noyous for to carye,** that Chaucer is troublesome to carry may allude to his plumpness; compare line 660 below, *Thop* 7.700, and *To Scogan* (short poem 17), lines 27 and 31.

Gan for to wondren in my mynde.
"O God," thoughte I, "that madest kynde°,
Shal I noon other weyes dye?
Wher° Joves wol me stellefye°,
Or what thing may this sygnifye?
I neyther am Ennok ne Elye,
Ne Romulus, ne Ganymede,
That was ybore° up, as men rede°,
To hevene with daun Jupiter,
And made the goddys botiller.°"
Loo, this was thoo° my fantasye.
But he that bare me gan espye°
That I so thoughte, and seyde this,
"Thow demest° of thyself amys°,
For Joves ys not theraboute°—
I dar wel put the° out of doute—
To make of the as yet a sterre°.
But er° I bere the moche ferre°,
I wol the telle what I am,
And whider thou shalt°, and why I cam
To do thys, so that thou take
Good herte, and not for fere quake.°"
"Gladly," quod I.—"Now wel," quod he,
"First, I that in my fete° have the°,
Of which thou hast a fere and wonder,
Am dwellynge with the god of thonder,
Whiche that men callen Jupiter,
That dooth° me flee° ful ofte fer°
To do al hys comaundement.
And for this cause° he hath me sent
To the. Now herke°, be thy trouthe:
Certeyn, he hath of the routhe°
That thou so longe trewely
Hast served so ententyfly°
Hys blynde neviwe° Cupido,
And faire Venus also,
Withoute guerdon° ever yitte°,
And neverthelesse has set thy witte—
Although that in thy hed ful lyte° is—
To make bookes, songes, dytees°
In ryme or elles in cadence°,
As thou best canst, in reverence
Of Love and of hys servantes eke°
That have hys servyse soght, and seke°,
And peynest the° to preyse° hys arte,
Although thou haddest never parte°.
Wherfore, also° God me blesse,
Joves halt hyt° grete humblesse,
And vertu eke, that thou wolt make
A-nyght° ful ofte thyn hede to ake°
In thy studye, so° thou writest
And evermo° of love enditest°,
In honour of hym and in preysynges°,
And in his folkes furtherynges°,
And in hir matere al devisest°,
And noght hym nor his folk dispisest°,
Although thou maist° goo in the daunce
Of hem° that hym lyst not avaunce°
"Wherfore, as I seyde, ywys°,
Jupiter considereth this,
And also, beau° sir, other thynges,
That is that thou hast no tydynges°
Of Loves folk yf they be glade°,
Ne of noght elles that God made.
And noght oonly fro fer contree°
That ther no tydynge cometh to thee,

584 maydest kynde, *made nature* **586 Wher,** (I wonder) *whether,* **stellefye,** *make me a constellation* **590 ybore,** *carried,* **rede,** *read* **592 goddes botiller,** *god's butler* **593 thoo,** *then* **594 gan espye,** *did see* **596 demest,** *judge,* **amys,** *wrongly* **597 ys not theraboute,** *has no intention* **598 the,** *you* **599 sterre,** *star* **600 er,** *before,* **moche ferre,** *much farther* **602 whider thou shalt,** *where you will go* **604 quake,** *tremble* **606 fete,** *feet,* **the,** *you* **610 dooth,** *causes,* **flee,** *fly,* **fer,** *far* **612 cause,** *purpose* **613 herke,** *listen* **614 of the routhe,** *pity for you* **616 ententyfly,** *attentively* **617 neviwe,** *grandson* **619 guerdon,** *reward,* **yitte,** *yet* **621 ful lyte,** *very little* **622 dytees,** *poems* **623 cadence,** *rhythm* **625 eke,** *also* **626 seke,** *seek* **627 peynest the,** *trouble yourself,* **preyse,** *praise* **628 parte,** *a role* (in the art of love) **629 also,** *as* **630 halt hyt,** *holds it* **632 A-nyght,** *at night,* **ake,** *ache* **633 so,** *as* **634 evermo,** *continuously,* **enditest,** *compose* **635 preysynges,** *praisings* **636 in his folkes furtherynges,** *in furthering his folk* **637 hir matere al devisest,** *arrange all their matters* **638 dispisest,** *despise* **639 maist,** *may* **640 hem,** *them,* **hym lyst not avaunce,** *he wishes not to advance* **641 ywys,** *surely* **643 beau,** *good* **644 tydynges,** *news* **645 glade,** *joyful* **647 fro fer contree,** *from far country*

588 Ennok ne Elye, Enoch (Gen. 5.24) and the prophet Elijah (2 Kings 2.11 and Hebrews 11.5) were both taken up into heaven. **589 Romulus,** one of the legendary founders of Rome, was taken to the home of the gods at the request of Mars; Ovid, *Metamorphoses* 14.816ff. **Ganymede,** a beautiful Trojan prince, was carried to Olympus by Jupiter in the form of an eagle to serve as his cupbearer; Ovid, *Metamorphoses* 10.155ff. Dante wonders in similar terms if he is worthy to go on his journey; *Inferno* 2.32. **595 I so thoughte,** the eagle reads Chaucer's thoughts as Virgil reads Dante's in *Inferno,* e.g., 12.31. **619 Withoute guerdon,** Chaucer also presents himself as a love poet who is an unrewarded or unsuccessful lover in *PF* 8, *TC* 1.16, and lines 628 and 639–40 below. **621 lyte,** F and P read "lytel." **622 bookes, songes, dytees,** F reads "songes, dytees, bookys." **623 cadence,** the denotations of this early use of this word are uncertain, but it appears to mean rhythm as opposed to rhyme. **639 daunce,** here *dance* implies "circle" or "in the company of," the opposite of the group who participate in the dance of love; compare *GP* 1.476, and *TC* 1.516–17.

But of thy verray neyghebores°,
That duellen° almost at thy dores,
Thou herist° neyther that ne this;
For when thy labour doon al ys
And hast° ymad thy rekenynges°,
Instede of reste and newe thynges,
Thou goost hom to thy hous anoon
And, also dombe° as any stoon,
Thou sittest at another book
Tyl° fully daswyd° ys thy look,
And lyvest thus as an heremyte°;
Although thyn abstynence ys lyte°.
"And therfore Joves, thorgh hys grace,
Wol° that I bere the° to a place
Which that hight° the Hous of Fame,
To do the° somme disport° and game,
In somme recompensacion
Of° labour and devocion
That thou hast had, loo°, causeles°,
To Cupido the rechcheles°.
And thus this god°, thorgh° his merite,
Wol with somme maner thing° the quyte°,
So that thou wolt° be of good chere.
For truste wel that thou shalt here°,
When we be come there° I seye,
Mo wonder° thynges, dar I leye°.
Of Loves folke moo tydynges°,
Both sothe sawes° and lesynges°,
And moo loves newe begonne°,
And longe yserved loves wonne°,
And moo loves casuelly°
That betyd° no man wot° why
But° as a blynd man stert an hare°,
And more jolytee and fare°
While that they fynde love of stele°,
As thinketh hem°, and over-al wele°,
Mo° discordes, moo jelousies,
Mo murmures°, and moo novelries°,
And moo dissymulacions°,
And feyned reparacions°,
And moo berdys° in two houres
Withoute rasour° or sisoures°
Ymad then° greynes° be of sondes°;
And eke moo° holdynge in hondes,
And also moo renovelaunces°
Of olde forleten aqueyntaunces°;
Mo love-dayes° and acordes
Then° on instrumentes be cordes°;
And eke of loves moo eschaunges°
Then ever cornes° were in graunges°—
Unnethe maistow trowen° this?"
Quod he. "Noo, helpe me God so wys°!"
Quod I. "Noo? Why?" quod he.—"For hytte°
Were impossible, to my wytte,
Though that Fame had al the pies°
In al a realme°, and al the spies,
How that yet she° shulde here al this,
Or they espie hyt."—"O yis°, yis,"
Quod he to me, "that kan I preve°
Be° reson worthy for to leve°,
So that° thou yeve thyn advertence°
To understonde my sentence°:

649 verray neyghebores, *actual neighbors* **650 duellen,** *dwell* **651 herist,** *hear* **653 hast,** (you) *have,* **ymad thy rekenynges,** *made your accounts* **656 also dombe,** *as dumb* **658 Tyl,** *until,* **daswyd,** *dazed* **659 heremyte,** *hermit* **660 lyte,** *little* **662 Wol,** *wishes,* **bere the,** *carry you* **663 hight,** *is called* **664 do the,** *give you,* **disport,** *diversion* **666 Of,** *for* **667 loo,** *pay attention,* **causeles,** *without reason* **668 rechcheles,** *heedless* **669 this god,** *Jove,* **thorgh,** *on account of* **670 Wol with somme maner thyng,** *will in some way,* **the quyte,** *repay you* **671 wolt,** *will* **672 here,** *hear* **673 there,** *where* **674 Mo wonder,** *more wonderful,* **dar I leye,** *I bet* **675 moo tydynges,** *more news* **676 sothe sawes,** *true sayings,* **lesynges,** *lies* **677 begonne,** *begun* **678 wonne,** *won* **679 casuelly,** *accidently* **680 betyd,** *happened,* **wot,** *knows* **681 But,** *except,* **stert an hare,** *startles a rabbit* **682 fare,** *goings on* **683 of stele,** (true as) *steel* **684 As thinketh hem,** *so they think,* **over-al wele,** *overall well-being* **685 Mo,** *more* **686 murmures,** *grumblings,* **novelries,** *gossipings* **687 dissymulacions,** *pretences* **688 feyned reparacions,** *pretended reconciliations* **689 berdys,** *deceptions* **690 rasour,** *razor,* **sisoures,** *scissors* **691 Ymad then,** *made than,* **greynes,** *grains,* **sondes,** *sand* **692 eke moo,** *also more* **693 renovelaunces,** *renewals* **694 forleten aqueyntaunces,** *abandoned acquaintances* **695 love-dayes,** *days of reconciliation* **696 Then,** *than,* **cordes,** *strings* **697 eschaunges,** *exchanges* **698 cornes,** *kernels* (of grain), **graunges,** *barns* **699 Unnethe maistow trowen,** *scarcely may you believe* **700 wys,** *wise* **701 hytte,** *it* **703 pies,** *magpies* **704 realme,** *kingdom* **705 she,** i.e., *Fame* **706 yis,** *yes* **707 preve,** *prove* **708 Be,** *by,* **leve,** *believe* **709 So that,** *as long as,* **yeve thyn advertence,** *give your attention* **710 sentence,** *message*

653 ymad thy rekenynges, as Controller of Wool Customs in the Port of London in 1374–86, Chaucer was directed to make his reckonings (keep his accounts) himself, "*manu sua propria*" (in his own hand). These lines are autobiographical or pseudo-autobiographical. **660 thyn abstinence ys lyte,** your abstinence is small, a second indication that Chaucer depicts himself as plump; see 574n above. **681 as a blynd man stert an hare,** proverbial, meaning "purely by accident." **689–91 berdys . . . Ymad,** to "make a beard" is an idiomatic expresssion meaning to trick or deceive; see *MilT* 1.3742, *RvT* 1.4096, and *WBP* 3.361. **692 holdynge in hondes,** to "hold" or "bear in hand" meant to deceive with false hopes or lies. **695 love-dayes,** originally, days or occasions set aside for settling disputes out of court; eventually the word came to mean the settlements themselves. **696 cordes,** the strings on a musical instrument rather than modern *chord;* see *TC* 5.443. F reads "acordes" (harmonies). **703 pies,** magpies, raucous birds, were popularly thought to be capable of speech and even gossip. **705 she,** F and P read "he."

"First shalt thou here° where she duelleth,
And so thyn oune boke° hyt tellith.
Hir paleys stant°, as I shal sey,
Ryght even° in myddes° of the wey
Betwexen hevene and erthe and see,
That whatsoever in al these three
Is spoken, either prevy or aperte°,
The way therto ys so overte°,
And stant eke° in so juste° a place,
That every soune mot° to hyt pace°,
Or what so cometh from any tonge,
Be hyt rouned°, red°, for songe,
Or spoke in suerte° or in drede°,
Certeyn, hyt most thider need°.
"Now herkene wel, for-why° I wille
Tellen the° a propre skille°
And a worthy demonstracioun
In myn ymagynacioun.
Geffrey, thou wost° ryght wel this,
That every kyndely° thyng that is
Hath a kyndely stede ther he°
May best in hyt conserved be,
Unto which place everythyng
Thorgh his kyndely enclynyng°
Moveth for to come to,
Whan that hyt is awey therfro°—
As thus: loo, thou maist alday se°
That anything that hevy be,
As stoon° or led° or thyng of wight°,
And bere hyt never so hye on hight°,
Lat goo thyn hand°, hit falleth doun.
Ryght so° seye I be° fire or soun°
Or smoke or other thynges lyght,
Alwey they seke° upward on hight.
While ech of hem is at his large°,
Lyght thing upward°, and dounward charge°.
And for this cause mayst thou see
That every ryver to the see°
Enclyned ys to goo by kynde°,
And by these skilles°, as I fynde,
Hath fyssh duellynge° in floode° and see,
And trees eke in erthe bee.
Thus everything, by thys reson,
Hath his propre mansyon°
To which hit seketh° to repaire°,
As there° hit shulde not apaire°.
Loo, this sentence° ys knowen kouthe°
Of every philosophres mouthe,
As° Aristotile and daun Platon
And other clerkys many oon°.
And to confirme my resoun,
Thou wost° wel this, that spech is soun°,
Or elles no man myght hyt here;
Now herke° what y wol the lere°.
"Soune ys noght° but eyr ybroken°,
And every spech that ys yspoken,
Lowde° or pryvee°, foule or faire,
In his substaunce° ys but° aire,
For as flaumbe° ys but lyghted smoke,
Ryght° soo soune ys aire ybroke.

---

711 here, *hear* **712 thyn oune boke,** *your own book* **713 paleys stant,** *palace stands* **714 Ryght even,** *exactly,* **myddes,** *the middle* **717 prevy or aperte,** *privately or openly* **718 overte,** *open* **719 stant eke,** *stands also,* **juste,** *precise* **720 soune mot,** *sound must,* **pace,** *travel* **722 Be hyt,** (whether) *it be,* **rouned,** *whispered,* **red,** *read* **723 suerte,** *certainty,* **drede,** *doubt* **724 most thider nede,** *must necessarily go there* **725 for-why,** *because* **726 the,** *you,* **propre skille,** *actual reason* **729 wost,** *know* **730 kyndely,** *natural* **731 kyndely stede ther he,** *natural place where it* **734 enclynyng,** *inclination* **736 therfro,** *from there* **737 maist alday se,** *may always see* **738 stoon,** *stone,* **led,** *lead,* **wight,** *weight* **740 hye on hight,** *high on height* **741 Lat goo,** *let* (it) *go* (from) **742 Ryght so,** *Jus sot,* **seye I be,** *say I about,* **soun,** *sound* **744 seke,** *seek* **745 is at his large,** *has freedom* **746 upward,** *upward* (moves), **charge,** *heavy* (thing) **748 see,** *sea* **749 kynde,** *nature* **750 skilles,** *reasons* **751 duellynge,** *habitation,* **floode,** *river* **754 his propre mansyon,** *its appropriate home* **755 seketh,** *seeks,* **repaire,** *return* **756 As there,** *as* (the place) *where,* **apaire,** *deteriorate* **757 sentence,** *wisdom,* **kouthe,** *clearly* **759 As,** *such as* **760 other clerkys many oon,** *many other scholars* **762 wost,** *know,* **spech is soun,** *speech is sound* **764 herke,** *listen to,* **the lere,** *teach you* **765 noght,** *nothing,* **eyr ybroken,** *broken air* **767 Lowde,** *aloud,* **pryvee,** *secretly* **768 his substaunce,** *its essence,* **but,** (nothing) *but* **769 flaumbe,** *flame* **770 Ryght,** *just*

712 thyn oune boke, Ovid's *Metamorphoses,* an acknowledgment of Chaucer's affection for the work, which he used often as a source. **714–24** This description derives directly from *Metamorphoses* 12.39ff., although Chaucer emphasizes that the precise location of the palace is the reason that all sound travels there. Chaucer's preciseness introduces the comedy of exaggerated realism into Ovid's essentially metaphoric or allegorical description. **718 way,** F reads "aire." **727 a worthy,** F reads "worthy a." **729 Geffrey,** Chaucer's use of his own name in a poem about fame indicates that he is laying some claim—comic or serious—to being or becoming famous. He may also be emulating *Purgatorio* 30.55, where Beatrice calls Dante by name. **730ff. kyndely thyng . . . ,** this explanation of how and why things move—or "incline"—to their appropriate places in nature is a precursor to the modern "law" of gravitation. Rooted in neo-Platonic ideas of order and hierarchy, the medieval notion assumes that even inanimate things have inclinations and seek their natural or proper places. Various writers used similar explanations to argue that it is natural for the human soul to desire, or move toward, heaven. For comparison, see St. Augustine's *Confessions* 13.9 and *City of God* 11.28, *Bo* 3 pr.11.136ff., Dante's *Paradiso* 1.109ff., and others. **745–46** Lines transposed in P. **765 Soune ys . . . eyr ybroken,** sound is broken air, a commonplace in medieval theories of music and grammar, recorded in Boethius *De Musica* 1.3, 14; Vincent of Beauvais, *Speculum Naturale* 4.14; and others.

But this may be in many wyse°,
Of which I wil the twoo devyse°,
As soune that cometh of pipe or harpe.
For whan a pipe is blowen sharpe,
The aire ys twyst° with violence
And rent°—loo, thys ys my sentence°—
Eke°, whan men harpe-strynges smyte°,
Whether hyt be moche or lyte°,
Loo, with the stroke the ayr tobreketh°;
And ryght so breketh it when men speketh.
Thus wost° thou wel what thinge is speche.
  "Now hennesforth° y wol the teche°
How every speche, or noyse, or soun,
Thurgh hys° multiplicacioun,
Thogh hyt were piped of a mous°,
Mote nede° come to Fames Hous.
I preve° hyt thus—take hede now—
Be° experience: for yf that thow
Throwe on° water now a stoon,
Wel wost° thou hyt wol make anoon
A litel roundell° as a sercle°,
Paraunter brod° as a covercle°;
And ryght anoon° thow shalt see wel
That whele° wol cause another whel,
And that the thridde, and so forth, brother,
Every sercle causynge other°
Wydder° than hymselfe was.
And thus fro roundel to compas°,
Eche aboute other goynge°,
Caused of othres sterynge°,
And multiplyinge evermoo°,
Til that hyt be so fer ygoo°
That hyt at bothe brynkes° bee.
Although thou mowe° hyt not ysee,
Above hyt gooth yet alway under,
Although thou thenke hyt a gret wonder.
And whoso seyth° of trouthe I varye°,
Bid hym proven the contrarye.
And ryght thus° every word, ywys,°
That lowde or pryvee° yspoken ys
Moveth first an ayre° aboute,
And of thys movynge, out of doute,
Another ayre anoon ys meved,°
As I have of the watir preved°
That every cercle causeth other.°
Ryght so of ayr, my leve° brother;
Everych° ayre in other stereth°
More and more, and speche up bereth,°
Or° voys, or noyse, or word, or soun,
Ay° through multiplicacioun,
Til hyt be atte° Hous of Fame.
Take yt in ernest° or in game°.
  "Now have I tolde, yf ye have in mynde°,
How speche or soun of pure kynde°
Enclyned ys° upward to meve°—
This mayst thou fele wel ipreve°.
And that same place, ywys°,
That everythynge enclyned to ys,
Hath his kyndelyche stede°.
That sheweth° hyt, withouten drede°,
That kyndely° the mansioun°
Of every speche, of every soun,
Be hyt eyther foule or faire,
Hath hys kynde place in ayre.
And syn° that everythyng that is
Out of hys kynde place, ywys,
Moveth thidder° for to goo
Yif hyt aweye be therfroo°,

---

771 wyse, *ways* **772 the twoo devyse,** *describe two* (for) *you* **775 twyst,** *twisted* **776 rent,** *ripped,* **sentence,** *meaning* **777 Eke,** *also,* **smyte,** *strike* **778 moche or lyte,** *much or little* **779 tobreketh,** *breaks apart* **781 wost,** *know* **782 hennesforth,** *henceforth,* **the teche,** *teach you* **784 hys,** *its* **785 mous,** *mouse* **786 Mote nede,** *must necessarily* **787 preve,** *prove* **788 Be,** *by* **789 on,** *in* **790 wost,** *know* **791 roundell,** *ring,* **as a sercle,** *like a circle* **792 Paraunter brod,** *perhaps broad,* **covercle,** *pot lid* **793 ryght anoon,** *immediately* **794 whele,** *wheel* **796 other,** *another* **797 Wydder,** *wider* **798 fro roundel to compas,** *from small ring to large circumference* **799 goynge,** *going* **800 sterynge,** *movement* **801 multiplyinge evermoo,** *increasing ever more* **802 fer ygoo,** *far gone* **803 brynkes,** *edges* **804 mowe,** *may* **807 seyth,** *says,* **of trouthe I varye,** *I deviate from the truth* **809 ryght thus,** *just this way,* **ywys,** *certainly* **810 lowde or pryvee,** *aloud or privately* **811 an ayre,** (a wave of) *air* **813 meved,** *moved* **814 preved,** *proved* **815 other,** *another* **816 leve,** *dear* **817 Everych,** *every,* **stereth,** *moves* **818 up bereth,** *carries up* **819 Or,** *either* **820 Ay,** *always* **821 atte,** *at the* **822 in ernest,** *seriously,* **in game,** *playfully* **823 yf ye have in mynde,** *if you recall* **824 of pure kynde,** *by* (its) *essential nature* **825 Enclyned ys,** *is inclined,* **meve,** *move* **826 fele wel ipreve,** *consider well proved* **827 ywys,** *surely* **829 his kyndelyche stede,** *its natural location* **830 sheweth,** *demonstrates,* **drede,** *doubt* **831 kyndely,** *naturally,* **mansioun,** *home* **835 syn,** *since* **837 thidder,** *there* (i.e., to its natural place) **838 therfroo,** *from there*

773 As, F reads "Of." **784 multiplicacioun,** multiplication, the ME word meant to increase in size or quality as well as in number or quantity. **780** Line lacking in F. **788ff.** Comparison between sound and ripples on the water accompanies the theories of sound in Boethius, *De Musica* 1.14; Vincent of Beauvais, *Speculum Naturale,* 4.15; and elsewhere. However, the eagle extends this science of acoustics to a pseudoscientific assertion that all speech drifts up to Fame's house. **794 That whele,** F and P read "That whele sercle." **803 That,** F reads "Til." **827–64** Lines lacking in P and Cx. **827 same place,** F reads "sum place stide." The meaning is not altogether clear, although the general sense seems to be that things are inclined to go to their proper locations in nature. The strained meaning and the repetition of **kynde** (**kyndelyche, kyndely**) and synonyms for *place* (**place, stede, mansioun**) in this passage indicate that sound and fame are more complicated than the eagle makes them out to be.

As I have before preved the°,
Hyt seweth°, every soun, parde°,
Moveth kyndely to pace°
Al up into his kyndely place.
And this place of which I telle,
Ther as Fame lyst to duelle°,
Ys set amyddys° of these three,
Heven, erthe, and eke the see
As most conservatyf° the soun.
Than ys this the conclusyoun,
That every speche of every man,
As y the telle first began°,
Moveth up on high to pace°
Kyndely° to Fames place.
  "Telle me this now feythfully,
Have y not preved thus symply,
Withouten any subtilite°
Of speche, or gret prolixite°
Of termes of philosophie,
Of figures of poetrie,
Or colours of rethorike°?
Pardee°, hit oughte the to lyke°,
For hard langage and hard matere
Ys encombrous° for to here°
Attones°: "Wost° thou not wel this?"
  And y answered and seyde, "Yis."
  "Aha" quod he, "lo, so I can
Lewedly° to a lewed° man
Speke, and shewe hym swyche skiles°
That he may shake hem be the biles°,
So palpable° they shulden be.
But telle me this, now pray y the°,
How thenketh the° my conclusyon?"
  "A good persuasion,"
Quod I, "hyt is, and lyke° to be
Ryght so as thou has preved me."
  "Be° God," quod he, "and as I leve°,
Thou shalt have yet, or hit be eve°,
Of every word of thys sentence
A preve° by experience,
And with thyn eres heren° wel
Toppe and taylle° and everydel°,
That every word that spoken ys
Cometh into Fames Hous, ywys°,
As I have seyd. What wilt° thou more?"
And with this word upper to sore°
He gan, and seyde, "Be Seynt Jame°,
Now wil we speken al of game°!
How farest thou?" quod he to me.
  "Wel," quod I.—"Now see," quod he,
"By thy trouthe, yonde adoun°,
Wher° that thou knowest any toun,
Or hous, or any other thinge.
And whan thou hast of ought° knowynge°,
Looke that thou warne° me,
And y anoon shal telle the
How fer that thou art now therfro.°"
  And y adoun to loken thoo°,
And beheld feldes° and playnes°,
And now hilles, and now mountaynes,
Now valeyes, now forestes,
And now unnethes° grete bestes°,
Now ryveres, now citees,
Now tounes°, and now grete trees,
Now shippes seyllynge° in the see.
But thus sone° in a while hee

839 the, (to) *you* **840 seweth,** *follows* (that), **parde,** *by God* (Fr. *par Dieu*) **841 pace,** *proceed* **844 lyst to duelle,** *is pleased to dwell* **845 Ys set amyddes,** *is set amidst* **847 conservatyf,** *preservative* (of) **850 As y the telle first began,** *as I first began to tell you* **851 pace,** *move* **852 Kyndely,** *naturally* **855 subtilite,** *cleverness* **856 prolixite,** *excessiveness* **859 colours of rethorike,** *rhetorical adornment* **860 Pardee,** *by God* (Fr. *par Dieu*), **the to lyke,** *to please you* **862 encombrous,** *troublesome,* **here,** *hear* **863 Attones,** *at the same time,* **Wost,** *know* **866 Lewedly,** *unlearnedly,* **lewed,** *unlearned* **867 swyche skiles,** *such reasons* **868 hem be the biles,** *them by the beaks* **869 papable,** *easily understood* **870 the,** *you* **871 How thenketh the,** *what do you think of* **873 lyke,** *likely* **875 Be,** *by,* **leve,** *believe* **876 or hit be eve,** *before it is evening* **878 preve,** *proof* **879 thyn eres heren,** *your ears hear* **880 Toppe and taylle,** *beginning and end,* **everydel,** *every part* **882 ywys,** *surely* **883 wilt,** *wish* **884 upper to sore,** *higher to soar* **885 Be Seynt Jame,** *by St. James* **886 al of game,** *playfully* **889 yonde adoun,** *down there* **890 Wher,** *whether* **892 ought,** *anything,* **knowynge,** *recognition* **893 warne,** *inform* **895 therfro,** *from it* **896 adoun to loken thoo,** *looked down then* **897 feldes,** *fields,* **playnes,** *plains* **900 unnethe,** *with difficulty,* **grete bestes,** *great beasts* **902 tounes,** *towns* **903 seyllynge,** *sailing* **904 sone,** *soon*

845–46 A near repetition of lines 714–15, and one of several instances of the eagle's comic talkativeness. **859 colours of rethorike,** the "colors" or devices of rhetoric are means of ornamenting speech or writing and not clearly distinguishable from **figures of poetrie**. The eagle here uses a rhetorical question (among the many other rhetorical devices, poetic figures, and philosophical terms he uses throughout his explanation of speech) to disclaim ornamentation and claim simplicity—indication that his wordy speech about language is comic, even absurd. **872** The line is metrically deficient in all the witnesses. Modern editors usually supply "Quod he" at the beginning of the line for smoothness, but the clipped meter here, and Geffrey's monosyllabllic **"Yis"** at line 864 are effective contrasts to the eagle's talkativeness. This is Chaucer's only use of the word **"persuasion,"** indicating that the eagle has not wholly convinced the narrator, who perhaps awaits the proof of experience promised by the eagle at 878.

Was flowen° fro the ground so hye°
That al the worlde, as to myn eye,
No more semed° than a prikke°,
Or elles° was the air so thikke
That y ne myghte not discerne°.
With that he spak° to me as yerne°,
And seyde, "Seest thou any token°
Or ought° that in the world is of spoken?"
I sayde, "Nay."—"No wonder nys,°"
Quod he, "for half so high as this
Nas° Alixandre of Macedo,
Kynge; ne° of Rome daun Scipio
That saw in dreme°, at poynt-devys,°
Helle and erthe and paradys;
Ne eke° the wrechche° Didalus;
Ne his child, nyce° Ykarus,
That fleegh° so highe that the hete°
Hys wynges malte°, and he fel wete°
In myd the see°, and ther he dreynt°,
For whom was maked moch compleynt°.
"Now turne upward," quod he, "thy face,
And behold this large space,
This eyr—but loke thou ne be
Adrad° of hem that thou shalt se,
For in this region, certeyn,
Duelleth many a citezeyn°,
Of which that speketh daun Plato.
These ben° the eyryssh bestes°, lo!"
And so saw y all that meynee°
Boothe goon° and also flee°.
"Now," quod he thoo, "cast up thyn eye.
Se yonder, loo, the Galaxie,
Which men clepeth° the Melky Wey°,
For hit ys whit°—and somme, parfey°,
Kallen° hyt Watlynge Strete—
That ones° was ybrent° with hete,
Whan the sonnes sone°, the rede°,
That highte° Pheton, wolde lede°
Algate° hys fader° carte, and gye°.
The carte-hors° gonne wel espye°
That he koude° no governaunce°,
And gonne° for to lepe and launce°,
And beren hym now up, now doun,
Til that he sey° the Scorpioun,
Which that in heven a sygne° is yit.
And he for ferde° loste hys wyt
Of° that, and lat the reynes gon°
Of his hors°, and they anoon°
Gonne up to mounte and doun descende,
Til bothe the eyre and erthe brende°,
Til Jupiter, loo, atte laste,
Hym slow°, and fro the carte caste.
Loo, ys it not a gret myschaunce°
To lat a fool han governaunce

905 Was flowen, *had flown,* **hye,** *high* **907 more semed,** *greater seemed,* **prikke,** *pinpoint* **908 elles,** *else* **909 discerne,** *see clearly* **910 spak,** *spoke,* **yerne,** *eagerly* **911 token,** *sign* **912 ought,** *anything* **913 No wonder nys,** *it is no wonder* **915 Nas,** *was not* **916 ne,** *nor* **917 dreme,** *dream,* **at poynt-devys,** *to the last detail* **919 Ne eke,** *nor also,* **wrechche,** *wretch* **920 nyce,** *foolish* **921 fleegh,** *flew,* **hete,** *heat* **922 malte,** *melted,* **wete,** *wet* **923 see,** *sea,* **dreynt,** *drowned* **924 moch compleynt,** *great lament* **928 Adrad,** *afraid* **930 citezeyn,** *citizen* **932 ben,** *are,* **eyryssh bestes,** *airish beasts* **933 meynee,** *company* **934 goon,** (those that) *walk,* **flee,** *fly* **937 clepeth,** *call,* **Melky Wey,** *Milky Way* **938 whit,** *white,* **parfey,** *by my faith* **939 Kallen,** *call* **940 ones,** *once,* **ybrent,** *burned* **941 sonnes sone,** *sun's son,* **rede,** *red* **942 highte,** *is called,* **wolde lede,** *wanted to take* **943 Algate,** *at any cost,* **fader,** *father's,* **gye,** *drive* **944 carte-hors,** *chariot horses,* **gonne wel espye,** *perceived well* **945 koude,** *understood,* **governaunce,** *control* **946 gonne,** *began,* **launce,** *lunge* **948 sey,** *saw* **949 sygne,** *sign* (of the Zodiac) **950 ferde,** *fear* **951 Of,** (because) *of,* **lat the reynes gon,** *let the reins go* **952 hors,** *horses,* **anoon,** *immediately* **954 brende,** *burned* **956 Hym slow,** *slew him* **957 myschaunce,** *disaster*

907 prikke, i.e., dot or pinpoint. The same word is used in *Bo* 2 pr.7.26 to contrast the insignificance of the earth with the vast sublimity of the heavens. **911–12** Lines lacking in F; reading from Cx. **913 I sayde,** omitted in F. **915–16** Reading from Cx. F reads "Nas Alixandre Macedo / Ne the kynge daun Cipio." **915 Alixandre of Macedo,** Alexander, king of Macedonia (356–323 B.C.E.), whose legends tell of his being carried to heaven in a chariot drawn by four griffins. **916 Scipio,** Scipio Africanus Minor. The account of Scipio in *PF* 31ff. follows Macrobius's *Commentary* on Cicero's *Somnium Scipionis* (*Dream of Scipio*). Scipio dreams of rising to heaven in both Cicero and *PF,* but only in *RR* 18368 is it said that he dreams of hell (**Helle**). **919–20 Didalus . . . Ykarus,** Daedalus made wings of wax and feathers for himself and his son, Icarus, to escape from Crete. Icarus flew too near the sun, his wings melted, and he plummeted to his death in the sea; Ovid's *Metamorphoses* 8.183ff. **919 wrechche,** P reads "wright." **926 space,** F reads "place." **932 eyryssh bestes,** these airish beasts can be taken to mean either the constellations of the zodiac, or *daemons,* creatures whose bodies were made of air and who were thought to be the natural inhabitants of the region between earth and the heavens. Mentioned at line 986 below, Alan of Lille, *Anticlaudianus* 4.274 talks of inhabitants of the air who deceive humankind. **937 Melky Wey,** in many medieval countries, the Milky Way was popularly referred to by the name of an important road—in England, **Watlynge Strete,** Watling Street, the name of a road built by the Romans that ran from Dover through Canterbury and London to Chester. Cicero, *Somnium Scipionis* 3.6, cites the Milky Way as the habitation of virtuous souls; in his *Commentary* on Cicero, Macbrobius 1.4.5 gives the Greek name *galaxias* (**Galaxie**) and 1.12.2 discusses the Milky Way as a route between heaven and earth. See *PF* 56. **942 Pheton,** Phaethon, son of Phoebus Apollo, the sun god, convinced his father to let him drive the chariot of the sun across the sky, with disastrous results. Unable to guide the horses and fearful of the constellation Scorpio (**Scorpioun**), Phaethon abandons control and much of the earth is scorched; Ovid, *Metamorphoses* 2.31ff. **946 launce,** P reads "daunce." **956 fro,** F reads "fer fro." **957 gret,** F reads "mochil."

Of thing that he can not demeyne°?"
And with this word, soth for to seyne°,
He gan upper alway to sore°,
And gladded me ay° more and more,
So feythfully° to me spak he.
  Tho gan y loken° under me
And beheld the ayerissh bestes,
Cloudes, mystes, and tempestes,
Snowes, hayles°, reynes°, wyndes,
And th'engendrynge° in hir kyndes°,
All the wey thrugh which I cam.
"O God," quod y, "that made Adam,
Moche° ys thy myght and thy noblesse°!"
And thoo° thoughte y upon Boece,
That writ°, "A thought may flee° so hye
Wyth fetheres of Philosophye
To passen everych° element,
And whan he hath so fer ywent°,
Than° may be seen behynde hys bak
Cloude"—and al that y of spak°.
Thoo gan y wexen in a were°,
And seyde, "Y wote° wel y am here;
But wher° in body or in gost°
I not°, ywys°; but, God, thou wost°!"
For more clere entendement°
Nas° me never yit ysent.
And than° thoughte y on Marcian,
And eke° on *Anteclaudian*,
That sooth° was her° descripsion
Of alle the hevenes region,
As fer as that y sey° the preve°.
Therfore y kan hem now beleve°.
  With that this egle gan to crye,
"Lat° be," quod he, "thy fantasye°.
Wilt thou lere° of sterres aught°?"
  "Nay, certeynly," quod y, "ryght naught."
  "And why?"—"For y am now to° olde."
  "Elles° I wolde the° have tolde,"
Quod he, "the sterres names, lo,
And al the hevens sygnes° therto,
And which they ben°."—"No fors°," quod y.
  "Yis, pardee," quod he. "Wostow° why?
For when thou redest° poetrie,
How goddes gonne stellifye°
Bridd°, fissh, best, or him or here°,
As the Ravene°, or eyther Bere°,
Or Arionis harpe fyn°,
Castor, Pollux, or Delphyn,
Or Athalantes doughtres° sevene,
How al these arn° set in hevene,
For though thou have hem ofte on honde,
Yet nostow° not wher that they stonde."
  "No fors,°" quod y, "hyt is no nede.
I leve° as wel, so God me spede°,
Hem° that write of this matere,
As though I knew her° places here;

---

959 demeyne, *control* **960 soth for to seyne,** *to tell the truth* **961 gan upper alway to sore,** *did soar ever higher* **962 gladded me ay,** *always cheered me up* **963 feythfully,** *reassuringly* **964 Tho gan y loken,** *then I looked* **967 hayles,** *hails,* **reynes,** *rains* **968 th'engendrynge,** *the origination,* **in hir kyndes,** *according to their natures* **969 thrugh,** *through* **971 Moche,** *great,* **noblesse,** *nobility* **972 thoo,** *then* **973 That writ,** *who writes,* **flee,** *fly* **975 passen everych,** *surpass every* **976 ywent,** *gone* **977 Than,** *then* **978 spak,** *spoke* **979 Thoo gan y wexen in a were,** *then did I grow uncertain* **980 wote,** *know* **981 wher,** *whether,* **gost,** *spirit* **982 not,** *know not,* **ywys,** *certainly,* **wost,** *know* **983 entendement,** *understanding* **984 Nas,** *was not* **985 than,** *then* **986 eke,** *also* **987 sooth,** *true,* **her,** *their* **989 sey,** *saw,* **preve,** *proof* **990 beleve,** *believe* **992 Lat,** *Let,* **fantasye,** *imaginings* **993 lere,** *learn,* **of sterres aught,** *anything about the stars* **995 to,** *too* **996 Elles,** *otherwise,* **the,** *you* **998 sygnes,** *signs* **999 which they be,** *what they are,* **No fors,** *no matter* **1000 Wostow,** *do you know* **1001 redest,** *read* **1002 gonne stellifye,** *made into constellations* **1003 Bridd,** *bird,* **here,** *her* **1004 Ravene,** *Raven,* **eyther Bere,** *either Bear* **1005 harpe fyn,** *excellent harp* **1007 doughtres,** *daughters* **1008 arn,** *are* **1010 nostow,** *you know not* **1011 No fors,** *no matter* **1012 leve,** *believe,* **so God me spede,** *so help me God* **1013 Hem,** *them* **1014 her,** *their* (the stars')

965–69 Commenting on creatures of the air (**ayerissh bestes**; and see 932n above), Alan of Lille, *Anticlaudianus* 4.332ff., mentions passing through the region where clouds, hail, winds, etc., originate. **972 Boece,** Boethius, quoted in lines 973–78, a truncated version of *Bo* 4 m.1.1ff., where Philosophy says that her feathers (**fetheres**) enable humans to go beyond the clouds to sublimity. Chaucer stops short of this ideal, indicating that his concern is less exalted. **975 element,** each of the four elements (earth, water, air, fire) was thought to have its proper physical location in the Ptolemaic universe. **978 Cloude,** F reads "Cloude and erthe." **981 in body or in gost . . . ,** in body or in spirit, an echo of St. Paul, 2 Cor. 12.2, although Chaucer emphasizes his lack of knowledge while St. Paul emphasizes the special knowledge of one who has a mystical vision of the third heaven. **985 Marcian,** i.e., Martianus Capella, author of the fifth-century *De Nuptiis Philologiae et Mercurii* (*Concerning the Marriage of Philology and Mercury*), a book about the Seven Liberal Arts (grammar, logic, rhetoric, arithmetic, geometry, astronomy, music) which opens with a flight to the heavens; Book 8 is on astronomy. **986 *Anteclaudian*,** *Anticlaudianus,* by Alan of Lille, is a twelfth-century cosmological work that includes a heavenly journey that inspired details of *HF* (see 930n and 965–69n above). **1004 Ravene,** the constellation Corvus. **eyther Bear,** either bear, i.e., the Great Bear (Ursa Major) or the Lesser Bear (Ursa Minor). **1005 Arionis harpe,** the harp of Arion, i.e., the constellation Lyra. Arion was legendary poet and musician of Lesbos. **1006 Castor, Pollux,** the constellation Gemini, named after two heroes of classical mythology. **Delphyn,** the constellation Delphinus, the Dolphin. **1007 Athalantes doughtres sevene,** the Pleiades, named for the seven daughters of Atlas. **1009 have hem oft in honde,** to have them often in hand can mean "to deal with them often," but here it may mean "hold them often in a book."

And eke° they shynen° here so bryght,
Hyt shulde shenden° al my syght
To loke on hem."—"That may wel be,"
Quod he. And so forth bare° he me
A while, and than he gan to crye
That never herd I thing so hye°,
"Now up the hed, for alle ys wel;
Seynt Julyan, loo, bon hostel°!
Se° here the Hous of Fame, lo!
Maistow not heren that° I do?"
"What?" quod I.—"The grete soun,"
Quod he, "that rumbleth up and doun
In Fames Hous, full of tydynges,
Bothe of feir speche° and chidynges°,
And of fals and soth° compouned°.
Herke° wel—hyt is not rouned°.
Herestow not° the grete swogh°?"
"Yis, parde,°" quod y, "wel ynogh."
"And what soun is it lyk?" quod hee.
"Peter, lyk betynge° of the see,°"
Quod y, "ayen° the roches holowe,°
When tempest doth the shippes swalowe°,
And lat a man stond°, out of doute°,
A myle thens° and here° hyt route°;
Or elles° lyk the last humblynge°
After a clappe of oo° thundringe,
Whan Joves° hath the aire ybete°.
But yt doth me for fere swete°!"
"Nay, dred the° not thereof," quod he.
"Hyt is nothing will byten the°.
Thou shalt non harme have trewely.°"
And with this word both he and y
As nygh° the place arryved° were
As men may casten with a spere°.
Y nyste° how, but in a street°
He sette me fair° on my fete°,
And seyde, "Walke forth a pas°,
And tak thyn aventure or cas°
That thou shalt fynde in Fames place."
"Now," quod I, "while we han space°
To speke, or° that I goo fro the,
For the love of God, telle me,
In sooth, that° wil I of the lere°,
Yf thys noyse that I here
Be as I have herd the° tellen
Of folk that doun in erthe duellen,
And cometh here in the same wyse
As I the herde or this devyse°,
And that there lives body nys°
In al that hous that yonder ys,
That maketh al this loude fare.°"
"Noo," quod he, "by Seynte Clare,
And also wis° God rede° me.
But o thing y will warne the°
Of the whiche° thou wolt° have wonder:
Loo, to the Hous of Fame yonder,
Thou wost° now how, cometh every speche—
Hyt nedeth noght eft the to teche°.
But understond now ryght wel this,
Whan any speche ycomen ys°
Up to the paleys°, anon-ryght°
Hyt wexeth° lyk the same wight°
Which° that the word in erthe spak°,
Be hyt clothed red or blak,

1015 eke, *also,* **shynen,** *shine* **1016 shenden,** *ruin* **1018 bare,** *carried* **1020 hye,** *loud* **1022 bon hostel,** *good lodging* **1023 Se,** *see* **1024 Maistow not heren that,** *can't you hear what* **1028 feir speche,** *fair speech,* **chidynges,** *scoldings* **1029 soth,** *truth,* **compouned,** *combined* **1030 Herke,** *listen,* **rouned,** *whispered* **1031 Herestow not,** *don't you hear,* **swogh,** *murmur* **1032 parde,** *by God* (Fr. *par Dieu*) **1034 betynge,** *beating,* **see,** *sea* **1035 ayen,** *against,* **roches holowe,** *hollow rocks* **1036 swalowe,** *swallow* **1037 stond,** *stand,* **out of doute,** *surely* **1038 thens,** *from there,* **here,** *hear,* **route,** *roar* **1039 elles,** *else,* **humblynge,** *rumbling* **1040 oo,** *a single* (one) **1041 Joves,** *Jupiter,* **ybete,** *beaten* **1042 doth me for fere swete,** *makes me sweat with fear* **1043 dred the,** *dread you* **1044 will byten the,** (that) *will bite you* **1045 trewely,** *truly* **1047 nygh,** *near,* **arryved,** *arrived* **1048 spere,** *spear* **1049 nyste,** *know not,* **strete,** *street* **1050 fair,** *nicely,* **fete,** *feet* **1051 pas,** *pace* **1052 cas,** *chance* **1054 han space,** *have time* **1055 or,** *before* **1057 that,** *what,* **of the lere,** *learn from you* **1059 the,** *you* **1062 the herde or this devyse,** *heard you describe before this* **1063 lives body nys,** *is no living body* **1065 loude fare,** *loud clamor* **1067 also wis,** *as surely,* **rede,** (may) *counsel* **1068 warne the,** *tell you* **1069 Of the whiche,** *of which,* **wolt,** *will* **1071 wost,** *know* **1072 Hyt nedeth noght eft the to teche,** *no need to teach you again* **1074 ycomen ys,** *is come* **1075 paleys,** *palace,* **anon-right,** *immediately* **1076 Hyt wexeth,** *it becomes,* **wight,** *person* **1077 Which that,** *who,* **in erthe spak,** *spoke* (it) *on earth*

1015 they shynen, F reads "thy selven." **1022 Seynt Julian,** St. Julian, patron saint of hospitality. **1025ff. grete soun . . . ,** comparisons of a great sound with the beating (**betynge**) of the sea and the rumbling (**humblynge**) of thunder, and the combination of false and truth (**fals and soth**) derive from Ovid, *Metamorphoses* 12.48ff. **1034 Peter,** a mild oath, referring to St. Peter. **lyk,** omitted in F. **1044 lyten,** F and P read "beten." **1063 And,** omitted in F. **1066 Seynte Clare,** a contemplative and a follower of St. Francis of Assisi. **1076 wexeth lyk the same wight,** Chaucer's fanciful idea that words transform into likenesses of the people who spoke them was probably inspired by the personification of rumors in Ovid, *Metamorphoses,* 12.52ff., although Ovid does not indicate that the personifications kept their genders as Chaucer does (line 1082). **1078 red or blak,** perhaps a reference to written language, which in medieval manuscripts was often in red ("rubrics") and black inks.

And hath so very° hys lyknesse°
That° spak the word that thou wilt gesse°
That it the same body be,
Man or woman, he or she.
And ys not this a wonder thynge?"
"Yis," quod I tho, "by heven kynge!"
And with this word, "Farewel," quod he,
"And here I wol abyden the°,
And God of heven sende the grace
Some good to lernen in this place."
And I of him tok leve° anon,
And gan forth to the paleys gon°.

Book 3

[Proem]

O God of science° and of lyght,
Appollo, thurgh thy grete myght,
This lytel laste bok thou gye°!
Nat° that I wilne° for maistrye°
Here art poetical be shewed°,
But for° the ryme ys lyght and lewed°,
Yit° make hyt sumwhat agreable,
Though somme vers° fayle in° a sillable,
And that I do no diligence°
To shewe craft°, but o sentence°.
And yif, devyne vertu°, thow
Wilt helpe me to shewe now
That° in myn hed ymarked ys°—
Loo, that is for to menen° this,
The Hous of Fame for to descryve°—
Thou shalt se° me go as blyve°
Unto the nexte laure° y see,
And kysse yt, for hyt is thy tree.
Now entreth° in my brest anoon!

[The Dream]

Whan I was fro thys egle goon,
I gan beholde upon this place.
And certein, or° I ferther pace°,
I wol yow al the shap devyse°
Of hous and site, and al the wyse°
How I gan to thys place aproche°,
That stood upon so hygh a roche°,
Hier stant° ther non in Spayne.
But up I clomb° with alle payne,
And though to clymbe greved me,
Yit I ententyf° was to see,
And for to powren wonder low°,
Yf I koude° any weyes know
What maner stoon° this roche was,
For hyt was lyk alum de glas°,
But that hyt shoon ful more clere°,
But of what congeled matere°
Hyt was, I nyste redely°.
But at the laste aspied I°,

1079 very, *truly,* **lyknesse,** *appearance* **1080 That,** *who,* **gesse,** *think* **1086 wol abyden the,** *wait for you* **1089 of him tok leve,** *from him departed* **1090 gan . . . gon,** *went* **1091 science,** *knowledge* **1093 gye,** *guide* **1094 Nat,** *not,* **wilne,** *wish,* **for maistrye,** *out of superiority* **1095 shewed,** *showed* **1096 for,** *because,* **lewed,** *unlearned* **1097 Yit,** *yet,* **1098 vers,** *verses,* **fayle in,** *lack* **1099 do no diligence,** *make no effort* **1100 shewe craft,** *demonstrate skill,* **o sentence,** *only meaning* **1101 devyne vertu,** *divine power* (i.e., Apollo) **1103 That,** *what,* **ymarked ys,** *is recorded* **1104 menen,** *mean* **1105 descryve,** *describe* **1106 se,** *see,* **blyve,** *quickly* **1107 laure,** *laurel tree* **1109 entreth,** *enter* **1112 or,** *before,* **ferther pace** *go further* **1113 shap devyse,** *shape describe* **1114 wyse,** *ways* **1115 gan . . . aproche,** *did approach* **1116 roche,** *rock* **1117 Hier stant,** *higher stands* **1118 clomb,** *climbed* **1120 ententyf,** *eager* **1121 powren,** *examine,* **wonder low,** *very closely* **1122 koude,** *could* **1123 maner stoon,** *kind of stone* **1124 alum de glas,** *crystallized alum* **1125 clere,** *brightly* **1126 congeled matere,** *solidified matter* **1127 nyste redely,** *knew not initially* **1128 aspied I,** *I looked*

1079 And hath so very, F reads "And so were." **1080 That,** F reads "And." **1092 Appollo,** Apollo, classical god of poetry, music, and the sun. The Invocation here imitates Dante, *Paradiso* 1:13ff., although the tone is more playful. **1093 laste bok,** indicates that division into several books was Chaucer's intention, although none of the extant manuscripts has the clear three-book division introduced by Caxton. **1096 ryme ys lyght and lewed,** this claim of poetic incompetence is an example of the medieval "modesty topos," and may also indicate Chaucer's awareness of the low status of English as a literary language. He is similarly modest about his verse in *MLP* 2.47–48 and *Thop* 7.919ff. **1098 fayle in a sillable,** "lack a syllable," evidence that Chaucer was aware that he did not maintain strict octosyllabic lines. **1101 thow,** F reads "nowe." **1102 now,** F reads "yowe." **1106 me,** F reads "men." **1107 laure,** Apollo was depicted wearing a wreath of leaves of the laurel tree, later the emblem of great poets, i.e., poets "laureate." **1114 site,** F and P reads "citee." **1115 thys,** F reads "hys"; P, "the." **1117 in Spayne,** Chaucer had traveled to Spain in 1366, so this may reflect his recollection of Spanish mountains or outcroppings. **1124 alum de glas,** translucent, astringent mineral salt, used to fix dyes. F reads "a thyng of glas"; P, "alymde glas." **1127 nyste redely,** F reads "nyst I never."

And found that hit was every dele°
A roche of yse°, and not of stele°.
Thoughte I, "By Seynt Thomas of Kent,
This were a feble fundament°
To bilden on a place hye°.
He ought him° lytel glorifye
That her-on bilt°, God so me save!"
  Tho sawgh° I the half ygrave°
With famous folkes names fele°,
That had iben° in mochel wele°,
And her fames wide yblowe°.
But wel unnethes° koude I knowe°
Any lettres for to rede
Hir° names by; for, out of drede°,
They were almost of-thowed° so
That of the lettres oon or two
Was molte° away of every name,
So unfamous was wox hir° fame.
But men seyn, "What may ever laste?"
Thoo° gan I in myn herte caste°
That they were molte awey with hete,
And not awey with stormes bete°,
For on that other syde I say°
Of this hille, that northward lay,
How hit was writen ful of names
Of folkes that hadden grete fames
Of olde tyme, and yet they were
As fressh as° men had writen hem here
The selfe° day, ryght or° that houre
That I upon hem gan to poure°.
But wel I wiste° what yt made°,
Hyt was conserved with the shade—
Al this writynge that I sigh°—
Of a castel that stood on high,
And stood eke° on so cold a place
That hete myghte hit° not deface.
  Thoo° gan I up the hille to goon°
And fond upon the cop° a woon°
That al the men that ben on lyve°
Ne han the kunnynge° to descrive°
The beaute of that ylke° place,
Ne coude casten no compace°
Swich° another for to make,
That myght of beaute ben hys make°,
Ne so wonderlych ywrought°,
That hit astonyeth yit° my thought,
And maketh al my wyt to swynke°,
On this castel to bethynke,
So that the grete beaute,
The cast°, craft, and curiosite°
Ne kan I not to yow devyse°—
My wit ne may me not suffise.
  But natheles alle the substance
I have yit in my remembrance,
For-whi° me thoughte, be Seynt Gyle,
Alle was of ston of beryle°,
Bothe the castel and the toure°,
And eke° the halle and every boure°,
Wythouten peces° or joynynges.
But many subtil compassinges°,
Babewynnes° and pynacles°,
Ymageries° and tabernacles°
I say°, and ful eke° of wyndowes
As flakes falle in grete snowes.
And eke in ech° of the pynacles
Weren sondry habitacles°,

1129 dele, *bit* **1130 yse,** *ice,* **stele,** *steel* **1132 fundament,** *foundation* **1133 hye,** *high* **1134 him,** *himself* **1135 her-on bilt,** *built on this* **1136 Tho sawgh,** *then saw,* **half ygrave,** *one side engraved* **1137 fele,** *many* **1138 iben,** *been,* **mochel wele,** *much good fortune* **1139 yblowe,** *spread* **1140 unnethes,** *scarcely,* **knowe,** *discern* **1142 Hir,** *their,* **out of drede,** *without doubt* **1143 of-thowed,** *thawed off* **1145 molte,** *melted* **1146 wox hir,** *grown their* **1148 Thoo,** *then,* **caste,** *searched* **1150 bete,** *beaten* **1151 say,** *saw* **1156 as,** *as if* **1157 selfe,** *same,* **or,** *before* **1158 poure,** *look* **1159 wiste,** *knew,* **yt made,** *caused it* **1161 sigh,** *saw* **1163 eke,** *also* **1164 hit,** *the writing* **1165 Thoo,** *then,* **goon,** *go* **1166 cop,** *top,* **woon,** *dwelling* **1167 ben on lyve,** *are alive* **1168 Ne han the kunnynge,** *have not the skill,* **descrive,** *describe* **1169 ylke,** *same* **1170 Ne coude casten no compace,** *nor could devise any plan* **1171 Swich,** *such* **1172 hys make,** *its match* **1173 wonderlych ywrought,** *wonderfully made* **1174 astonyeth yit,** *stuns yet* **1175 swynke,** *labor* **1178 cast,** *design,* **curiosite,** *complexity* **1179 devyse,** *describe* **1183 For-whi,** *why* **1184 beryle,** *beryl,* **1185 toure,** *tower* **1186 eke,** *also,* **boure,** *room* **1187 peces,** *pieces* **1188 compassinges,** *devices* **1189 Babewynnes,** *gargoyles,* **pynacles,** *pinnacles* **1190 Ymageries,** *carvings,* **tabernacles,** *canopied niches* **1191 say,** *saw* **1193 in ech,** *on each* **1194 sondry habitacles,** *various niches*

1130 roche of ise, a rock of ice is the foundation of the house of Fortune in Nicole de Margival, *La Panthère d'Amours,* 1963–75. **1131 Seynt Thomas of Kent,** i.e., St. Thomas Becket, whose shrine is the goal of the pilgrimage in *CT.* **1142 by; for,** F reads "before." **1160 Hyt was conserved,** i.e., the names on the northern side of the rock are preserved by the shadow of the House of Fame. **1161–62** Lines transposed in P. **1178 craft,** omitted in F. **1183 Seynt Gyle,** St. Giles (Aegidius), patron saint of lepers, beggars, and cripples. A medieval church of St. Giles was at Cripplegate in northeast London, and a hospital of St. Giles was west of the city. **1184 beryle,** in medieval tradition, the gemstone beryl was associated with love and magnification (see lines 1290ff. below). **1188–1200 subtil compassinges,** the ornamentation recalls the elaborate external adornments of gothic buildings, especially cathedrals and chapels. Several literary sources and particular buildings have been suggested as Chaucer's inspiration, but none is agreed upon.

In which stoden, al withoute°
Ful° the castel alle aboute,
Of alle maner° of mynstralles°
And gestiours° that tellen tales,
Both of wepinge° and of game°
Of al that longeth unto° Fame.
Ther herde° I pleye upon an harpe,
That sowned° bothe wel and sharpe,
Orpheus ful craftely,
And on his syde, faste by°,
Sat the harper Orion,
And Eaycedis Chiron,
And other harpers many oon°,
And the Bret Glascurion.
And smale harpers with her glees°
Sate° under hem in dyvers sees°,
And gunne on hem upward to gape°,
And countrefete hem° as an ape,
Or as craft° countrefeteth kynde°.
  Tho saugh° I stonden hem behynde°,
Afer fro° hem, al be hemselve,
Many thousand tymes twelve,
That maden lowde mynstralcyes°
In cornemuse° and shalemyes°,
And many other maner pipe,
That craftely begunne to pipe
Bothe in doucet° and in rede°,
That ben at festes with the brede°,
And many flowte° and liltyng-horne°,
And pipes made of grene corne°,
As han° thise lytel herde-gromes°
That kepen bestis° in the bromes°.
Ther saugh° I than Atiteris,
And of Athenes daun Pseustis,
And Marcia that loste her skyn,
Bothe in face, body, and chyn,
For that° she wolde envien°, loo,
To pipen bet° than Appolloo.
Ther saugh I famous, olde and yonge,
Pipers of the Duche tonge°,
To lerne° love-daunces, sprynges°,
Reyes°, and these straunge thynges.
Tho saugh I in another place
Stonden in a large space
Of hem that maken blody soun°
In trumpe°, beme°, and claryoun°,
For in fyght and blood-shedynges
Ys used gladly clarionynges.
Ther herde I trumpen Messenius,
Of whom that speketh Virgilius.

1195 withoute, *outside* **1196 Ful,** *completely* **1197 maner,** *kinds,* **mynstralles,** *minstrels* **1198 gestiours,** *storytellers* **1199 wepinge,** *weeping,* **game,** *play* **1200 longeth unto,** *belongs to* **1201 herde,** *heard* **1202 sowned,** *sounded* **1204 faste by,** *nearby* **1207 oon,** (a) *one* **1209 her glees,** *their instruments* **1210 Sate,** *were situated,* **dyvers sees,** *various seats* **1211 gunne on hem upward to gape,** *did gape upward at them* **1212 countrefete hem,** *imitate them* **1213 craft,** *art,* **kynde,** *nature* **1214 Tho saugh,** *then saw,* **hem behynde,** *behind them* **1215 Afer fro,** *far from* **1217 mynstralcyes,** *music* **1218 In coremuse,** *on bagpipes,* **shalemyes,** *reed pipes* **1221 doucet,** *on dulcet flutes,* **rede,** *reeds* **1222 brede,** *roast meat* **1223 flowte,** *flute,* **liltyng-horne,** *trumpet* **1224 grene corne,** *fresh reeds* **1225 han,** *have,* **herde-gromes,** *shepherd boys* **1226 bestis,** *beasts,* **bromes,** *wild shrubs* **1227 Ther saugh,** *there saw* **1231 For that,** *because,* **envien,** *strive* **1232 bet,** *better* **1234 Duche tonge,** *Dutch language* **1235 lerne,** *teach,* **sprynges,** *springs* (a kind of dance) **1236 Reyes,** *ring dance* (Fr. *Dutch*) **1239 blody soun,** *bloody sound* **1240 In trumpe,** *on trumpet,* **beme,** *bugle,* **claryoun,** *trumpet*

1195 stoden, omitted in F. **1201 herde I,** the narrator hears the harping of the statue, which is not realistic, but an effective means of communicating that the statue was lifelike. **1203 Orpheus,** the celebrated harpist of classical tradition; Ovid, *Metamorphoses* 10 and 11. **1205 Orion,** i.e., Arion; see 1005n above. **1206 Eaycedis Chiron,** i.e., Chiron who belongs to Aecaides, or Achilles (so-called for his grandfather Aeacus); Ovid, *Ars Amatoria,* 1.17. Chiron, a centaur, taught Achilles music and horsemanship. **1208 Bret Glascurion,** a British, or Welsh, semi-legendary bard. "Glascurion" is perhaps a variant of Gwydion, son of Don, or of the Blue Bard ("Bardd Glas") Keraint, although it is unclear how Chaucer may have known of either. F reads "gret Glascurion." **1210–14** F reads "hym" for "hem" in these lines. **1210 Sate under hem,** a precise architectural detail; medieval column statues were often juxtaposed with smaller figures carved on the protruding corbels or platforms which supported the larger figures. **divers,** omitted in F. **1211 gape,** F reads "jape." **1212 as an ape,** apes were known to imitate human behavior; "to ape" still means to imitate. **1213 art countrefeteth nature,** art counterfeiting nature is a familiar notion; cf. *RR* 16029ff. Chaucer uses the notion more extensively in *PhyT* 6.11ff. **1216 thousand tymes twelve,** repeated at line 2126 below; perhaps an allusion to Rev. 7.4–8, the inspiration of much medieval visionary literature. **1224 pipes made of grene corne,** Panpipe, made of hollow reeds or grass (**corne,** i.e., grain) of uneven length to produce different tones. **1227–28** Lines transposed in F. **1227 Atiteris,** most likely a corruption of "Tityrus," a musical shepherd in the first of Virgil's *Eclogues.* **1228 Pseustis,** a musical shepherd from Athens in Theodulus's *Ecloga,* which was used as a textbook in the Middle Ages. **1229 Marcia,** Marsyas, a satyr who was flayed for presuming to compete in a musical contest with Apollo; Ovid, *Metamorphoses,* 6.382ff. Chaucer may have been misled about the satyr's gender by the Italian form of the name (*Marsïa*) in Dante, *Paradiso* 1.20, a passage which influenced 1091–1109 above. **1234 Pipers of the Duche tonge,** Dutch, or perhaps German (Deutsch), musicians, who apparently had a reputation for music, although the reference has not been clearly explained. F reads "alle" for "the." **1236 Reyes,** F reads "Reus"; P "Reyths." **1243 Messenius,** Misenus, son of Aeolus, god of winds, was the trumpeter to Hector and later Aeneas; Virgil, *Aeneid,* 3.238–39 and 6.162ff.

There herde I trumpe Joab also,
Theodomas, and other mo°.
And alle that used clarion
In Cataloigne and Aragon,
That in her° tyme famous were
To lerne°, saugh° I trumpe there.
There saugh I sitte in other sees°,
Pleyinge upon sondry glees°,
Which that I kan not nevene°,
Moo° than sterres ben° in hevene,
Of whiche I nyl° as now not ryme,
For ese of yow°, and losse of tyme.
(For tyme ylost°, this knowen ye°,
Be° no way may recovered be.)
Ther saugh I pleye jugelours°,
Magiciens, and tregetours°,
And phitonesses°, charmeresses,
Olde wicches, sorceresses,
That usen exorsisacions°,
And eke these fumygacions°;
And clerkes° eke, which konne° wel
Alle this magik naturel,
That craftely doon her ententes°
To make, in certeyn ascendentes°,
Ymages, lo, thrugh which magike
To make a man ben hool or syke°.
Ther saugh I the quene Medea,
And Circes eke, and Calipsa.
Ther saugh I Hermes Ballenus,
Limete, and eke Symon Magus.
There saugh I, and knew hem by name,
That by such art don° men han° fame.
Ther saugh I Colle tregetour
Upon a table of sycamour
Pleye an uncouth° thyng to telle—
Y saugh him carien° a wyndmelle°
Under a walsh-note shale°.
  What° shuld I make lenger tale
Of alle the pepil y ther say°,
Fro hennes° into domes day°?
When I had al this folk beholde,
And fond me lous° and nought yholde°,
And eft° I mused longe while
Upon these walles of berile,
That shoone ful lyghter° than a glas°,
And made wel more than hit was
To semen° everything, ywis°,
As kynde thyng° of Fames is,
I gan forth romen° til I fond°
The castel yate° on my ryght hond,

1246 mo, *more* **1249 her,** *their* **1250 lerne,** *learn* (about), **saugh,** *saw* **1251 sees,** *seats* **1252 sondry glees,** *various instruments* **1253 nevene,** *name* **1254 Moo,** *more,* **sterres ben,** *stars are* **1255 nyl,** *will not* **1256 ese of yow,** *your ease,* **1257 ylost,** *lost,* **ye,** *you* **1258 Be,** *by* **1259 jugelours,** *entertainers* **1260 tregetours,** *illusionists* **1261 phitonesses,** *female conjurers* **1263 exorsisacions,** *spells* **1264 fumygacions,** *fumigations* (incantations using smoke) **1265 clerkes,** *scholars,* **which konne,** *who understand* **1267 craftely doon her ententes,** *skillfully perform their plans* **1268 ascendentes,** *astrological configurations* **1270 ben hoole or syke,** *be well or sick* **1276 don,** *make,* **han,** *have* **1279 uncouth,** *strange* **1280 carien,** *carry,* **wyndmelle,** *windmill* **1281 walsh-note shale,** *walnut shell* **1282 What,** *why* **1283 pepil y ther say,** *people I saw there* **1284 Fro hennes,** *from now,* **domes day,** *judgment day* **1286 lous,** *loose,* **nought yholde,** *not held* **1287 eft,** *after* **1289 ful lyghter,** *more brightly,* **glas,** *mirror* **1291 semen,** *seem,* **ywis,** *certainly* **1292 kynde thyng,** *a natural function* **1293 gan forth romen,** *roamed forth,* **fond,** *found* **1294 yate,** *gate*

1245 Joab, trumpeter of the biblical David; 2 Sam. 2.28, 18.16, and 20.22. **1246 Theodomas,** in Statius, *Thebaid* 8.342ff., trumpets blare before the walls of Thebes after Thiodamas foretells the downfall of the city. **1248 Cataloigne and Aragon,** Catalonia and Aragon, regions in Spain noted for ceremonial trumpeting. **1255 nyl as now,** F reads "nyl not now." **1257–58** This sentiment is found in various proverbial forms in Chaucer's works; see *TC* 3.896 and 4.1283, *MLP* 2.27–28, and *Rom* 5123–24. **1261 phitonesses,** in the Latin Vulgate Bible, 1 Sam. 28.7, the Witch of Endor is called "pythonissam." **1262 wicches,** F reads "wrecches." **1266 magik naturel,** i.e., natural or "white" magic, the understanding and manipulation of nature, especially through astrology. **1268 ascendentes,** astrological configurations at important moments, such as the moment of birth or marriage. The ascendant is the point on the zodiacal circle that ascends above the horizon at the particular moment and enables the medical astrologer to make an image **(Ymages)** through which a person's health could be affected. The images were either drawn or molded. **1271ff.** The list of magicians can be compared with that in *RR* 14397ff. (which includes Medea, Circe, and Balenus) and that in Ovid, *Ars Amatoria* 2.101ff. (Medea, Circe, and Calypso). **Medea,** Jason's wife, who magically restored her father's youth; Ovid, *Metamorphoses* 7.162ff. **1272 Circes,** Circe used her potion to trap Odysseus's followers; Homer, *Odyssey* 10–12. Spurned by Glaucus, she magically transformed Scylla into a monster; Ovid, *Metamorphoses* 14.8ff. F reads "Artes." **Calipsa,** the nymph Calypso, like Circe, sought to delay the journey of Odysseus/Ulysses; Ovid, *Ars Amatoria* 2.103ff. and 123ff. **1273 Hermes Ballenus**, Balenus (or Belinous) discovered beneath a statue of Hermes Trismegistus ("Thrice Great") a book reputed to contain all the secrets of the universe. **1274 Limete,** probably the biblical magician Elymas; Acts 13.8. **Symon Magus,** the biblical magician Simon Magus; Acts 8.9ff. **1275–76** Lines lacking in F. **1277 Colle tregetour,** probably an English necromancer contemporary with Chaucer, referred to in a 1396 French conversation book to as "Colin T." **1278 table of sycamour,** it is unclear why the table is made of sycamore. **1280–81 wyndmelle . . . walsh-note shale, it is unclear** what this means, but it seems to refer to some sort of sleight-of-hand shell game. **1286 yholde,** F reads "yeolde." **1287 eft,** F reads "oft." **1290–92** ". . . and (by magnification) made everything seem greater than it was, as is a natural function of Fame. . . ." **1291** Line lacking in P. **1293 forth,** F reads "to."

Which that so wel corven° was
That never such another nas°—
And yit it was be aventure°
Iwrought° as often as be cure°.
Hyt nedeth noght° yow more to tellen,
To make yow to longe duellen,
Of this yates florisshinges°,
Ne of compasses°, ne of kervynges°,
Ne how they hatte° in masoneries°,
As corbetz°, ful of ymageries°.
But, Lord, so fair yt was to shewe°,
For hit was alle with gold behewe°.
  But in I went, and that anoon.
Ther mette I cryinge many oon°,
"A larges°, larges, hold up wel!
God save the lady of thys pel°,
Our oune° gentil Lady Fame,
And hem° that wilnen° to have name°
Of° us!" Thus herde y crien alle,
And faste comen out of halle,
And shoon nobles and sterlynges°.
And somme corouned° were as kynges°,
With corounes wroght° ful of losenges°,
And many ryban° and many frenges°
Were on her clothes trewely.
Thoo° atte last aspyed° y
That pursevantes° and heraudes°,
That crien ryche folkes laudes°,
Hyt° weren alle; and every man
Of hem, as y yow tellen can,
Had on him throwen a vesture°
Which that men clepe° a cote-armure°,
Enbrowded° wonderliche ryche,
Although they nere nought ylyche°.
But noght nyl I°, so mote° y thryve,
Ben aboute° to dyscryve°
Al these armes° that ther weren,
That they thus on her cotes beren°,
For hyt to me were impossible.
Men myghte make of hem a bible°
Twenty foot thykke, as y trowe°
For certeyn, whoso koude iknowe°
Myghte ther alle the armes seen
Of famous folk that han ybeen
In Auffrike°, Europe, and Asye,
Syth° first began the chevalrie°.
  Loo, how shulde I now telle al thys?
Ne of the halle eke what nede is°
To tellen yow that every wal
Of hit, and flor, and roof, and al,
Was plated° half a foote thikke
Of gold, and that nas nothyng wikke°
But for to prove° in alle wyse
As fyne° as ducat° in Venyse°—
Of which to lite° al in my pouche is!
And they were set as thik of nouchis°,
Ful of the fynest° stones faire
That men rede° in the Lapidaire°

1295 corven, *carved* **1296 nas,** *was not* **1297 be aventure,** *by accident* **1298 Iwrought,** *wrought,* **be cure,** *by intention* **1299 Hyt nedeth noght,** *there's no need* **1301 florisshinges,** *adornments* **1302 compasses,** *clever designs,* **kervynges,** *carvings* **1303 hatte,** *are called* **1304 corbetz,** *corbels,* **ymageries,** *sculpture* **1305 to shewe,** *for display* **1306 behewe,** *colored* **1308 cryinge many oon,** *many who were exclaiming* **1309 larges,** *gift* **1310 pel,** *castle* **1311 oune,** *own* **1312 hem,** *those,* **wilnen,** *wish,* **name,** *a reputation* **1315 shoon nobles and sterlynges,** ***gleamed like*** *gold and silver coins* **1316 crouned,** *crowned,* **kynges,** *kings-at-arms* **1317 wroght,** *made,* **losenges,** *diamond-patterned ornaments* **1318 ryban,** *ribbons,* **frenges,** *fringes* **1320 Thoo,** *then,* **aspyed y,** *I recognized* **1321 pursevantes,** *lesser heralds,* **heraudes,** *heralds* **1322 laudes,** *praises* **1323 Hyt,** *they* **1325 vesture,** *garment* **1326 clepe,** *call,* **cote-armure,** *coat of arms* **1327 Enbrowded,** *embroidered* **1328 nere nought ylyche,** *were not alike* **1329 noght nyl I,** *I will not,* **mote,** *might* **1330 Ben aboute,** *attempt,* **dyscryve,** *describe* **1331 armes,** *heraldic emblems* **1332 beren,** *wear* **1334 bible,** *book* **1335 trowe,** *believe* **1336 whoso koude iknowe,** *whoever could identify* (them) **1339 Auffrike,** *Africa* **1340 Syth,** *since,* **the chevalrie,** *knighthood* **1342 what nede is,** *what need is there* **1345 plated,** *covered* **1346 wikke,** *inferior* **1347 for to prove,** *could be proofed* (i.e., tested for purity) **1348 fyne,** *pure,* **ducat in Venyse,** *coin in Venice* **1349 to lite,** *too little* **1350 of nouchis,** *with jeweled settings or clasps* **1351 fynest,** *finest* **1352 rede,** *read* (about)

1304 corbetz, corbels, i.e., protruding architectural supports, often elaborately carved. **ful of,** omitted in F. **1309 A larges,** the cries of musicians and entertainers asking for generosity from patrons. **1315 shoon,** other editors follow P and read some form of "shoke" (shook), but there is no real trouble with the sense here: "and gleamed like coins." **1321 pursevantes and heraudes,** pursuivants and heralds, with **kynges** (kings-at-arms, line 1316), were the three categories of chivalric messengers and officials who were responsible for identifying the insignia of the aristocracy and announcing their patrons. **1326 cote-armure,** the cloth tunic worn over knightly armor, embroidered with heraldic insignia, the rigidly codified symbols that displayed the lineage of the knight; heralds wore the insignia of their patrons. It was from *cote-armure* that heraldic insignia became known as *coats of arms.* **1328 Although,** F reads "As though." **1329 so mote y thryve,** i.e., "as I might thrive," a common interjection or ejaculation. **1334–35 bible / Twenty foot thykke,** compendia of heraldic devices are indeed large books, but Chaucer seems to have developed his exaggerated notion from *RR* 6738ff. **1335 as,** omitted in F. **1348 ducat,** a Venetian gold coin known for its purity. **1351 Ful,** F reads "Fyne." **1352 Lapidaire,** several treatises still known as *lapidaries* describe precious stones and their medical and magical properties, e.g., *De Lapidarus* by Marbodus, bishop of Rennes (c1035–1123).

As grasses growen in a mede.°
But hit were al to longe to rede°
The names, and therfore I pace°.
But in this lusty° and ryche place,
That Fames halle called was,
Ful moche prees° of folk ther nas°,
Ne° crowdyng for to mochil° prees.
But al on hye°, above a dees°,
Sit° in a see° imperiall,
That mad° was of a rubee° all,
Which that a carbuncle ys ycalled,
Y saugh°, perpetually ystalled°,
A femynyne creature,
That never formed by Nature
Nas° suche another thing yseye°.
For altherfirst°, soth° for to seye,
Me thoughte that she was so lyte°
That the lengthe of a cubite
Was lengere than she semed be.
But thus sone° in a whyle she
Hir tho° so wonderliche streighte°
That with hir fet° she th'erthe reighte°,
And with hir hed she touched hevene
Ther as shynen sterres° sevene.
And therto eke°, as to my wit,
I saugh a gretter wonder yit
Upon her eyen° to beholde;
But certeyn y hem° never tolde°,
For as feele eyen° hadde she
As fetheres upon foules° be,
Or weren° on the bestes° foure
That Goddis trone gunne honoure°,
As John writ° in th'Apocalips.
Hir heer, that oundy° was and crips°,
As burned° gold hyt shoon to see.
And soth to tellen, also she
Had also fele° upstondyng eres°
And tonges as on bestes heres°.
And on hir fet wexen° saugh y
Partriches wynges redely°.
 But, Lord, the perry° and the richesse°
I saugh sittyng on this godesse!
And, Lord, the hevenyssh° melodye
Of songes ful of armonye°
I herde aboute her trone ysonge°,
That al the paleys° walles ronge.
So song° the myghty Muse, she
That cleped ys° Caliope,
And hir eighte sustren eke°,
That in her face semen meke°,
And evermo eternally
They songe of Fame, as thoo herd y°:
"Heryed° be thou and thy name,
Goddesse of Renoun and of Fame!"
 Tho was I war°, loo, atte laste,
As I myne eyen gan up caste,
That thys ylke° noble quene
On her shuldres° gan sustene°
Bothe the armes° and the name
Of thoo° that hadde large° fame,

1353 mede, *meadow* **1354 rede,** *recount* **1355 pace,** *pass over* **1356 lusty,** *pleasing* **1358 Ful moche prees,** (a) *very great crowd,* **nas,** *was not* **1359 Ne,** *nor,* **to mochil,** *too much* **1360 hye,** *high,* **dees,** *raised platform* (dais) **1361 Sit,** *sitting,* **see,** *seat* **1362 mad,** *made,* **rubee,** *ruby* **1364 saugh,** *saw,* **ystalled,** *established* **1367 Nas,** *was not,* **yseye,** *seen* **1368 altherfirst,** *first of all,* **soth,** *truth* **1369 lyte,** *little* **1372 sone,** *soon* **1373 Hir tho,** *herself then,* **streighte,** *stretched* **1374 fet,** *feet,* **reighte,** *reached* **1376 shynen sterres,** *shine planets* **1377 therto eke,** *in this regard also* **1379 eyen,** *eyes* **1380 y hem,** *I them,* **tolde,** *counted* **1381 feele eyen,** *many eyes* **1382 foules,** *birds* **1383 weren,** (as) *were,* **bestes** *beasts* **1384 trone gunne honoure,** *throne did honor* **1385 writ,** *writes* **1386 oundy,** *wavy,* **crips,** *curly* **1387 burned,** *burnished* **1389 also fele,** *as many,* **upstondyng eres,** *upright ears* **1390 heres,** *hairs* **1391 fet wexen,** *feet growing* **1392 redely,** *truly* **1393 perry,** *jewelry,* **richesse,** *riches* **1395 hevenyssh,** *heavenly* **1396 armonye,** *harmony* **1397 trone ysonge,** *throne sung* **1398 paleys,** *palace* **1399 song,** *sang* **1400 cleped ys,** *is called* **1401 sustren eke,** *sisters also* **1402 in her face semen meke,** *before her seem meek* **1404 thoo herd y,** *I heard then* **1405 Heryed,** *praised* **1407 war,** *aware* **1409 ylke,** *same* **1410 shuldres,** *shoulders,* **gan sustene,** *did support* **1411 armes,** *insignia* **1412 thoo,** *those,* **large,** *great*

1363 carbuncle, *carbuncle* was the name for several kinds of precious or semiprecious red gems (including rubies) known for their brightness. **1370 cubite,** a cubit is an ancient form of measurement from the elbow to the fingertips, usually 17–22 inches. **1371 semed be,** omitted in F. **1372** F reads "This was gret marvaylle to me." **1373 wonderliche streighte,** Fame's changeable size recalls the description of Fame in Virgil's *Aeneid* 4.176–77 and that of Philosophy in *Bo* 1 pr.1.13ff. **1374 th'erthe,** F reads "erthe." **1381–1390 feele eyen . . . fele upstondyng eres . . . And tonges,** the many eyes, ears, and tongues of Fame are found in *Aeneid* 4.182–84. **1383–85 bestes foure . . . in th'Apocalips,** four animals (lion, ox, man, eagle), thought to be symbols of the gospel writers, are described as winged, many-eyed attendants upon the throne of God in Revelation 4.6–8, also known as the Apocalypse. **1392 Partriches wynges,** partridges' wings seems to be a misreading of Virgil's "swift wings" in *Aeneid* 4.180 (*perdicibus alis* for *pernicibus alis*); the error may be Chaucer's or it may have been in his manuscript source. Chaucer translates it correctly at *TC* 4.661. **1400–01 Caliope / And hir eighte sustren,** Calliope, the muse of epic poetry, and her sisters are the mythical nine muses or goddesses of the arts in classical traditional. The sisters are humble before Calliope because epic poetry was regarded as the highest of the arts. **1406 and,** F reads "or." **1410 On her shuldres,** Chaucer imagines that Fame and the great authors of antiquity support the reputation of epic heroes. **1411 the armes,** F and P omit "the."

Alexander and Hercules,
That with a sherte hys lyfe les°.
Thus fond y syttynge this goddesse
In nobley°, honour, and rychesse—
Of which I stynte° a while now,
Other thing to tellen yow.
Tho saugh I stonde on eyther syde,
Streight doun to the dores wide
Fro the dees°, many a peler°
Of metal that shoon not ful cler°.
But though they nere of no rychesse°,
Yet they were mad° for gret noblesse°,
And in hem hy° and gret sentence°,
And folk of digne° reverence,
Of whiche I wil yow telle fonde°,
Upon the piler° saugh I stonde.
Alderfirst°, loo, ther I sighe°
Upon a piler stonde on highe,
That was of led° and yren fyne°,
Hym of secte saturnyne°,
The Ebrayk° Josephus the olde,
That of Jewes gestes° tolde,
And he bare° on hys shuldres hye°
The fame up of the Jewerye.
And by hym stonden other° sevene,
Wise and worthy for to nevene°,
To helpen hym bere up the charge°,
Hyt was so hevy and so large.
And for° they writen of batayles°,
As wel as other olde mervayles°,
Therfor was, loo, thys piler
Of whiche that I yow telle her°,
Of led and yren bothe, ywys°,
For yren Martes° metal ys,
Which that° god is of bataylle,
And the led, withouten faille°,
Ys, loo, the metal of Saturne,
That hath a ful large whel° to turne.
Thoo stoden° forth on every rowe
Of hem° which that I koude knowe°,
Though I hem noght be ordre telle°
To make yow to longe° to duelle°,
These of whiche I gynne rede°.
There saugh I stonden, out of drede°,
Upon an yren piler stronge
That peynted was al endelonge°
With tigres blode in every place,
The Tholosan that highte° Stace,
That bar° of Thebes up the fame
Upon his shuldres, and the name
Also of cruel Achilles.
And by him stood, withouten les°,
Ful wonder hye on a piler
Of yren, he, the gret Omer,
And with him Dares and Tytus
Before, and eke he Lollius,

1414 sherte hys lyfe les, *shirt lost his life* **1416 nobley,** *nobility* **1417 stynte,** *pause* **1421 Fro the dees,** *from the platform,* **peler,** *pillar* **1422 ful cler,** *very brightly* **1423 nere of no rychesse,** *were not of rich material* **1424 mad,** *made,* **noblesse,** *splendor* **1425 in hem hy,** *in them* (was) *high,* **sentence,** *significance* **1426 digne,** *worthy* **1427 telle fonde,** *try to tell* **1428 piler,** *pillars* **1429 Alderfirst,** *first of all,* **sighe,** *saw* **1431 led,** *lead,* **yren fyne,** *iron pure* **1432 secte saturnyne,** *Saturnine sect* **1433 Ebrayk,** *Hebrew* **1434 gestes,** *deeds* **1435 bare,** *bore,* **hye,** *high* **1437 other,** *another* **1438 nevene,** *name* **1439 charge,** *weight* **1441 for,** *because,* **batayles,** *battles* **1442 mervayles,** *marvels* **1444 her,** *here* **1445 ywys,** *certainly* **1446 Martes,** *Mars's* **1447 Which that,** *who* **1448 withouten faille,** *without doubt* **1450 ful large whel,** *very large wheel* **1451 Thoo stoden,** *then stood* **1452 Of hem,** *of those,* **koude knowe,** *could recognize* **1453 hem noght be order telle,** *do not recount them in order* **1454 to longe,** *too long,* **duelle,** *stay* **1455 gynne rede,** *do describe* **1456 out of drede,** *without doubt* **1458 al endelonge,** *from end to end* **1460 highte,** *is called* **1461 bar,** *bore* **1464 les,** *lies*

1413 Alexander, Alexander the Great (356–323 B.C.E.), king of Macedon and great conqueror; see *MkT* 7.2631ff. **Hercules,** legendary Greek hero, famous for his strength, died when given a poisoned shirt by his wife, Deianira; see *MkT* 7.2095ff. **1425** All authorities have a metrically short line, lacking *hy and.* **1432 secte saturnyne,** Judaism, called the sect of Saturn either because it was the oldest of religions (Saturn was the oldest of the planets) or because it arose from a conjunction of Saturn and Jupiter. Line lacking in P. **1433 Ebrayk Josephus,** Jewish historian, Flavius Josephus (37–95? C.E.), author of *Bellum Judaicum* (*The Jewish War*) and *Antiquitates Judaicae* (*Antiquities of the Jews*). **1436 up,** omitted in F. **1437 other sevene,** these other seven have not been identified. **1445 led and yren,** the associations of iron with Mars and lead with Saturn were commonplace in the Middle Ages. **1450 ful large whel,** Saturn was thought to have the largest orbit of any planet known in the Middle Ages. **1459 tigres blood,** two wounded, rampaging tigers caused the renewal of the Theban war; Statius, *Thebaid* 7. **1460 Tholosan that highte Stace,** i.e., Statius (c40–96 C.E.), who was mistakenly thought to be from Toulouse, famous for his stories of the city of Thebes (the *Thebaid*) and of Achilles (the *Achilleid*), the most famous Greek hero in the Trojan War, known for his anger. **1466–72 gret Omer . . . to bere up Troye,** like Homer, Dares the Phrygian and Dictys of Crete (**Dares and Tytus**), Guido delle Colonne (**Guido de Columpnis**), and Geoffrey of Monmouth (**Englyssh Gaufride**) were authorities on the story of Troy. Homer's Greek *Iliad* was not known in medieval Europe, but his name was revered. Originally written in Greek, Latin versions of works by Dares (*Ephimeridos Belli Troiani Libra,* fourth century) and Dictys (*De Excidio Troiae Historia,* sixth century) were the major medieval accounts of Troy. Guido translated into Latin Benoît de Sainte Maure's French *Roman de Troie* (c1160) under the title *Historia Destructionis Troiae* (1287), and Geoffrey links the settlement of England with the fall of Troy in his *Historia Regum Britanniae* (c1135). **1468 Lollius,** apparently a fictitious name for Boccaccio, whose *Filostrato* Chaucer used as a source for his Troy story; see *TC* 1.394; 5.1653.

And Guydo eke de Columpnis,
And Englyssh Gaufride eke, ywis—
And eche° of these, as have I joye,
Was besy for° to bere up Troye.
So hevy therof was the fame
That for to bere hyt was no game.
But yet I gan ful wel espie°,
Betwex hem° was a litil envye.
Oon seyde° Omer was lyes°,
Feynynge° in hys poetries,
And was to Grekes favorable;
Therfor held he hyt but° fable.
Tho saugh I stonde on a piler
That was of tynned yren cler°
That Latyn poete Virgile,
That bore hath up a longe while
The fame of Pius Eneas.
And next hym° on a piler was,
Of coper, Venus clerk° Ovide,
That hath ysowen° wonder wide
The grete god of Loves name.
And ther he bar up wel hys fame
Upon this piler, also hye°
As I myghte see hyt with myn eye.
For-why° this halle, of which I rede°,
Was woxen on° highte, length, and brede,
Wel more be° a thousand del°
Than hyt was erst°, that saugh I wel.
Thoo saugh I on a piler by
Of yren wroght° ful sternely°,
The grete poete daun° Lucan,
And on hys shuldres bar up than°,
As high as that y myghte see,
The fame of Julius and Pompe.
And by him stoden alle these clerkes
That writen of Romes myghty werkes,
That yf y wolde her° names telle,
Al to longe most° I dwelle.
And next him on a piler stoode
Of soulfre°; lyke as° he were woode°,
Daun Claudian, the sothe° to telle,
That bar up al the fame of helle°,
Of Pluto, and of Proserpyne
That quene ys° of the derke pyne°.
What shulde y more telle of this?
The halle was al° ful, ywys°,
Of hem that writen olde gestes°
As ben on° trees rokes° nestes;
But hit a ful confus matere°
Were al the gestes for to here°
That they of write°, or how they highte°.
But while that y beheld thys syghte,
I herd a noyse aprochen blyve°
That ferde° as been don° in an hive

1471 eche, *each* **1472 besy for,** *occupied* **1475 gan ful wel espie,** *did see very well* **1476 Betwex hem,** *among them* **1477 Oon seyde,** *one said,* **lyes,** *lies* **1478 Feynynge,** *falsifying* **1480 hyt but,** *it* (i.e., Homer's work) *only a* **1482 tynned yren cler,** *tinned iron bright* **1486 next hym,** *next to him* **1487 clerk,** *scholar* **1488 ysowen,** *planted* **1491 also hye,** *as high* **1493 For-why,** *because,* **rede,** *tell* **1494 Was woxen on,** *had increased in* **1495 be,** *by,* **del,** *times* **1496 erst,** *first* **1498 wroght,** *made,* **sternely,** *grimly* **1499 daun,** *master* **1500 than,** *then* **1505 y wolde her,** *I would their* **1506 most,** *must* **1508 soulfre,** *sulfur,* **lyke as,** *as if,* **woode,** *crazed* **1509 sothe,** *truth* **1510 helle,** *the underworld* **1512 That quene ys,** *who is queen,* **derke pyne,** *dark pain* **1514 al,** *as,* **ywys,** *certainly* **1515 gestes,** *tales* **1516 ben on,** *are in,* **rokes,** *rooks'* **1517 ful confus matere,** *very confusing matter* **1518 for to here,** *to hear* **1519 of write,** *write about,* **highte,** *are titled* **1521 aprochen blyve,** *approach quickly* **1522 ferde,** *went,* **been don,** *bees do*

1477 Oon seyde, the ultimate source of distrust in Homer is the preface to Dares's *Ephimeridos Belli Troiani,* where he claims that his own account is more accurate. Later accounts echo it. **1479 Grekes favorable,** medieval accounts of the Troy story favor the Trojans rather than the Greeks. **1482 tynned yren,** i.e., iron made shiny by being coated with tin. The suggestion seems to be that Virgil made the Trojan story attractive in the *Aeneid,* which recounts Aeneas's departure from the fall of Troy to found Rome. Tin is also the metal associated in the Middle Ages with Jupiter, who controlled Mars (iron) in the *Aeneid.* **1485 Pius Eneas,** *pious* was the standard epithet for Aeneas in Virgil's *Aeneid* and in pre-Virgilian literature; the adjective has the broad sense of faithfulness to one's homeland, parents, friends, etc., as well as the gods. **1487 coper,** copper was traditionally associated with Venus. **Ovide,** Ovid was associated with Venus because of his poems about love: *Ars Amatoria, Remedia Amoris, Heroides,* etc. Chaucer identifies him as a love-poet in *MLP* 2.53–54. **1494 Was woxen,** i.e., the hall increased in size to accommodate the magnifying effects of love, poetry, and fame; compare lines 1290–91 and 1373 above. **highte, length,** F reads "high, the length." **1499 Lucan,** Lucan (39–65 C.E.) wrote the *Pharsalia* (*Bellum Civile*) about the Roman civil war between Julius Caesar (**Julius**) and Pompey (**Pompe**). **1508 soulfre,** sulphur, or brimstone, is associated with the underworld. **1509 Claudian,** Claudian (died c404 C.E.) wrote his *De Raptu Proserpinae* (*The Abduction of Persephone*) in a rhapsodic style and described his own poetic inspiration as fury (*furor*) (1.5); either may help explain why he is presented here as mad. *De Raptu* tells the story of how **Pluto**, god of the underworld, took Persephone (**Proserpyne**), goddess of fertility, into the underworld and made her queen. Her annual time in the underworld is a mythic representation of winter. **1515 olde,** F reads "al of the olde." **1516 rokes nests,** small raucous crows, rooks nest in large colonies. **1522 been . . . in an hive,** bees swarming in a hive is an image of noise and confusion that Chaucer uses also in *TC* 2.193 and 4.1356, *SumT* 3.1693, and *NPT* 7.3392. He may have found precedent in Virgil's *Aeneid* 6.706–07 or Dante's *Inferno* 16.3.

Ayen her tyme° of out-fleynge°—
Ryght° such a maner° murmurynge,
For al the world, hyt semed me°.
Tho gan I loke° aboute and see
That ther come entryng° into the halle
A ryght gret companye withalle°,
And that of sundry° regiouns,
Of alleskynnes° condiciouns
That duelle in erthe under the mone,
Pore and ryche. And also sone°
As they were come in to the halle,
They gonne doun on knees falle
Before this ilke° noble quene,
And seyde, "Graunte us, lady shene°,
Ech° of us of thy grace a bone°!"
And somme of hem she graunted sone,
And somme she werned° wel and faire,
And some she graunted the contraire
Of her axyng outterly°.
But thus I seye° yow, trewely,
What her cause° was y nyste°.
For of this folk ful wel y wiste°
They hadde good fame ech deserved
Although they were dyversly served
Ryght° as her suster°, dame Fortune,
Ys wont° to serven in comune°.
  Now herke° how she gan to paye°
That gonne her of her grace praye°,
And yit, lo, al this companye
Seyden sooth°, and noght a lye.
  "Madame," seyde they, "we be
Folk that here besechen the°
That thou graunte us now good fame,
And let our werkes han° that name.
In ful recompensacioun
Of good werkes, yive° us good renoun."
  "I werne° yow hit," quod she anon.
"Ye gete° of me good fame non°,
Be° God, and therfore goo your wey."
  "Allas," quod they, "and welaway!
Telle us what may your cause be.°"
  "For me lyst hyt noght,°" quod she.
"No wyght° shal speke of yow, ywis°,
Good ne° harm, ne° that ne° this."
And with that word she gan to calle°
Her messanger that was in halle,
And bad° that he shulde faste goon°,
Upon peyne to be blynd anon°,
For Eolus the god of wynde,
"In Trace, ther ye shal him fynde,
And bid him bring his clarioun°,
That is ful dyvers of his soun°,
And hyt is cleped Clere Laude°,
With which he wont is° to heraude°
Hem° that me list ypreised be°.
And also bid him how that he
Brynge his other clarioun,
That highte Sklaundre° in every toun,
With which he wont is° to diffame°
Hem that me liste°, and do hem shame."

1523 Ayen her tyme, *before their time,* **out-fleynge,** *flying out* **1524 Ryght,** *just,* **maner,** *kind of* **1525 hyt semed me,** *it seemed to me* **1526 Tho gan I loke,** *then I looked* **1527 come entryng,** *came entering* **1528 withalle,** *as well* **1529 sondry,** *various* **1530 alleskynnes,** *all kinds of* **1532 also sone,** *as soon* **1535 ilke,** *same* **1536 shene,** *bright* **1537 Ech,** *each,* **bone,** *request* (boon) **1539 werned,** *refused* **1541 her axyng outterly,** *their asking utterly* **1542 seye,** *tell* **1543 cause,** *reason,* **nyste,** *know not* **1544 wiste,** *knew* **1547 Ryght,** *just,* **suster,** *sister* **1548 Ys wont,** *is accustomed,* **serven in comune,** *treat similarly* **1549 herke,** *listen,* **gan to paye,** *did pay* **1550 That gonne . . . praye,** (those) *that did request* **1551 Seyden sooth,** *told the truth* **1554 besechen the,** *beseech you* **1556 werkes han,** *accomplishments have* **1558 yive,** *give,* **renoun,** *reputation* **1559 werne,** *refuse* **1560 gete,** *get,* **non,** *none* **1561 Be,** *by* **1563 cause be,** *reason is* **1564 For me lyst hyt noght,** *because it pleases me not* **1565 wyght,** *person,* **ywis,** *surely* **1566 ne,** *neither,* **ne,** *nor* **1567 gan to calle,** *did call* **1569 bad,** *ordered,* **goon,** *go* **1570 Upon peyne to be blynd anon,** *Under threat of being blinded immediately* **1573 clarioun,** *trumpet* **1574 ful dyvers,** *very diverse,* **his soun,** *its sound* **1575 cleped Clere Laude,** *named Shining Praise* **1576 wont is,** *is accustomed,* **heraude,** *proclaim* **1577 Hem,** *those,* **me list ypreised be,** *it pleases me to praise* **1580 highte Sklaundre,** *is called Slander* **1581 wont is,** *is accustomed,* **diffame,** *defame* **1582 Hem that me liste,** *those that it pleases me to* (defame)

1530 alleskynnes, from "alles kindes," i.e., "of all kinds." Compare "noskynnes" at line 1794 below. **1544 of,** omitted in F. **1546** Line lacking in F. **1547 suster, dame Fortune,** Chaucer conceives of Fame as the sister of Fortune and attributes to her Fortune's traditional capriciousness. F reads "daun" (master) for "dame." **1551 yit,** F reads "ryght." **1553 seyde,** F reads "quod." **1571 Eolus,** Aeolus, classical god of the winds, is here the servant of Fame, much as he is the servant of Juno earlier; see 203n above. **1572 Trace,** Thrace, a region of southeast Europe, not frequently associated with Aeolus, although scholars have noted the association in the first-century *Argonautica* of Valerius Flaccus (1.597–613) and in the fourth-century Commentary on Virgil's *Aeneid* by Servius (1.57), which refers to Horace's *Odes* 4.12.1–2. Found in no manuscript, the line was introduced in Cx. **1573–82 Clere Laude . . . Sklaundre,** Shining Praise and Slander parallel the trumpets of Fame in John Gower's *Mirour de l'Omme* 22129ff., Renoumée (Renown) and Desfame (Disfame). The poets may have a mutual source or one may be borrowing from the other; clearly Chaucer and his friend were pondering the nature of fame at about the same time. **1577 ypreised,** F reads "preised."

This messanger gan faste goon°,
And found where in a cave of ston,
In a contree that highte° Trace,
This Eolus, with harde grace°,
Held the wyndes in distresse°,
And gan hem under him to presse°,
That° they gonne as beres rore°,
He bond and pressed hem° so sore°.
  This messanger gan faste crie°,
"Ryse up," quod he, "and faste hye°,
Til thou at my lady be,
And tak thy clariouns eke with the,
And spede the forth." And he anon
Tok to° a man that highte° Triton
Hys clarions to bere thoo°,
And let a certeyn wynd to goo,
That blew so hydously° and hye°
That hyt ne lefte not a skye°
In alle the welken° longe and brode.
This Eolus nowhere abode°
Til he was come to Fames fete°,
And eke the man that Triton hete°,
And ther he stod as stille as stoon.
  And herwithal° ther come° anoon
Another huge companye
Of goode folk, and gunne crie°,
"Lady, graunte us now good fame,
And lat oure werkes han that name°
Now in honour of gentilesse°—
And also° God your soule blesse—
For° we han wel deserved hyt,
Therfore is ryght that we ben quyt.°"
  "As thryve I," quod she, "ye shal faylle!
Good werkes shal yow noght availle°
To have of me good fame as now.
But wete° ye what? Y graunte yow
That ye shal have a shrewde° fame,
And wikkyd loos°, and worse name,
Though ye good loos have wel deserved.
Now goo your wey for ye be served.
And thou, dan° Eolus, let see°,
Tak forth thy trumpe anon," quod she,
"That is ycleped Sklaundre lyghte°,
And blow her loos that° every wighte°
Speke° of hem harme and shrewednesse°
In stede of good and worthynesse.
For thou shalt trumpe alle the contrayre
Of that they han don° wel or fayre."
  "Allas," thoughte I, "what aventures°
Han° these sory creatures!
For they, amonges al the pres°,
Shul° thus be shamed, gilteles°.
But what, hyt moste nedes be°.
What did this Eolus, but he
Tok out hys blake trumpe of bras,
That fouler than the devel was,
And gan this trumpe for to blowe,
As° al the world shulde overthrowe°,
That thrughout every regioun
Went this foule trumpes soun,
As swifte as pelet° out of gonne°
Whan fyr° is in the poudre ronne°.
And suche a smoke gan out-wende°
Out of his foule trumpes ende,
Blak, bloo°, grenyssh°, swartish° red,
As doth° where that men melte led°,
Loo, alle on high fro° the tuelle°.
And therto oo° thing saugh I welle,

1583 gan faste goon, *did go quickly* **1585 highte,** *is called* **1586 harde grace,** *ill favor* **1587 distresse,** *constraint* **1588 gan hem . . . to presse,** *did press them* **1589 That,** (so) *that,* **gonne as beres rore,** *did roar like bears* **1590 hem,** *them,* **sore,** *sorely* **1591 gan faste crie,** *quickly did cry* **1592 hye,** *hurry* **1596 Tok to,** *gave to,* **highte,** *is called* **1597 bere thoo,** *carry then* **1599 hydously,** *hideously,* **hye,** *loudly* **1600 skye,** *cloud* **1601 welken,** *heavens* **1602 abode,** *paused* **1603 fete,** *feet* **1604 hete,** *is called* **1606 herwithal,** *along with them,* **come,** *comes* **1608 gunne crie,** *did exclaim* **1610 name,** *reputation* **1611 gentilesse,** *nobility* **1612 also,** *as* **1613 For,** *because* **1614 quyt,** *rewarded* **1616 availle,** *benefit* **1618 wete,** *know* **1619 shrewde,** *evil* **1620 wikkyd loos,** *wicked reputation* **1623 dan,** *master,* **let see,** *let* (it be) *seen* **1625 ycleped Sklaundre lyghte,** *called frivolous Slander* **1626 her loos that,** *their reputation* (so) *that,* **wighte,** *person* **1627 Speke,** *speak,* **shrewednesse,** *wickedness* **1630 that they han don,** *what they have done* **1631 aventures,** *luck* **1632 Han,** *have* **1633 pres,** *crowd* **1634 Shul,** *shall,* **gilteles,** *guiltless* **1635 hyt moste nedes be,** *it must necessarily be* **1640 As,** *as* (if he), **overthrowe,** *destroy* **1643 pelet,** *cannonball,* **gonne,** *gun* **1644 fyr,** *fire,* **poudre ronne,** *gunpowder introduced* **1645 gan out-wende,** *did launch* **1647 bloo,** *blue,* **grenyssh,** *greenish,* **swartish,** *darkish* **1648 doth,** *occurs,* **led,** *lead* **1649 fro,** *from,* **tuelle,** *chimney* **1650 therto oo,** *moreover one*

1586–90 Aeolus's struggle with the winds is described in *Aeneid* 1.53ff. **1594 clariouns,** F reads "clarioun." **1595 he,** F reads "hye." **1596 Triton,** a classical sea god, Triton is the trumpeter of Neptune in Ovid's *Metamorphoses* 1.347ff. In Virgil's *Aeneid* 6.173ff., he jealously drowns Aeneas's trumpeter, Misenus, mentioned at line1243 above. **1599 That,** F reads "And." **1600 skye,** *sky* originally meant "cloud." **1611 gentilesse,** the term meant either the worthiness due to high birth or that which results from virtuous actions. Chaucer emphasizes the latter sense in *WBT* 3.1109–76; *Bo* 3 pr.6; and *Gentilesse* (Short Poem 12). **1623 And thou, dan,** F reads "Have done." **1647 swartish,** F reads "swart." **1649 tuelle,** chimney or chimney-pipe, but Chaucer uses it in *SumT* 3.2148 to mean "anus." The figure here combines imagery of apocalypse, war, the laboratory, and the toilet.

That the ferther that hit ran°,
The gretter wexen° hit began,
As dooth the ryver from a welle°,
And hyt stank as the pit of helle.
Allas, thus was her shame yronge°,
And gilteles, on every tonge!
  Tho° come the thridde° companye,
And gunne up to the dees° to hye°,
And doun on knes they fille anon,
And seyde, "We ben everychon°
Folke that han ful trewely
Deserved fame ryghtfully,
And pray yow, hit mot° be knowe°,
Ryghte as hit is, and forth yblowe.°"
  "I graunte," quod she, "for me liste°
That now your goode werkes be wiste°,
And yet ye shul han better loos°,
Right° in dispit° of alle your foos°,
Than worthy° is, and that anoon.
Lat now," quod she, "thy trumpe goon,
Thou Eolus, that is so blake,
And out thyn other trumpe take
That highte Laude°, and blow yt soo
That thrugh the world her° fame goo°
Al esely°, and not to faste,
That hyt be knowen atte laste."
  "Ful gladly, lady myn," he seyde.
And out hys trumpe of golde he brayde°
Anon, and sette hyt to his mouthe,
And blew it est, and west, and southe,
And northe, as lowde as any thunder,
That every wight° hath of hit wonder,
So brode° hyt ran or than hit stent°.
And, certes, al the breth that went
Out of his trumpes mouthe smelde°
As° men a potful bawme° helde°
Among a basket ful of roses.
This favour dide he til her loses°.
  And ryght with this y gan aspye°,
Ther come the ferthe° companye—
But certeyn they were wonder fewe—
And gunne stonden° in a rewe°,
And seyden, "Certes°, lady bryght°,
We han don wel with al our myght,
But we ne kepen° have no fame.
Hide our werkes and our name,
For Goddys love, for certes we
Han certeyn doon hyt for bounte°,
And for no maner° other thinge.
  "I graunte yow alle your askynge,"
Quod she; "let your werkes be dede°"
  With that aboute y clywe° myn hede
And saugh anoon the fifte route
That to this lady gunne loute°.
And doun on knes anoon to falle,
And to° hir thoo besoughten alle°
To hyde her° goode werkes ek°,
And seyden they yeven noght a lek°
For no fame ne for suche renoun,
For° they for contemplacioun
And Goddes love hadde ywrought°,
Ne of fame wolde° they nought.
  "What?" quod she, "and be ye wood°?
And wene ye° for to doo good,
And for to have of that no fame?
Have ye dispit° to have my name?
Nay, ye shul lyven° everychon°!
Blow thy trumpes, and that anon,"
Quod she, "thou Eolus, y hote°,
And ryng° this folkes werk be° note,

1651 ran, *went* **1652 gretter wexen,** *greater to grow* **1653 welle,** *spring* **1655 yronge,** *sounded* **1657 Tho,** *then* **thridde,** *third* **1658 gunne . . . to hye,** *hastened,* **dees,** ***platform*** (dais) **1660 ben everychon,** *are all* **1663 hit mot,** (that) *it may,* **knowe,** *known* **1664 yblowe,** *blown* **1665 me liste,** *it pleases me* **1666 wiste,** *known* **1667 loos,** *reputation* **1668 Right,** *precisely,* **dispit,** *spite,* **foos,** *foes* **1669 worthy,** *deserved* **1673 highte Laude,** *is called Praise* **1674 her,** *their,* **goo,** *goes* **1675 esely,** *slowly* **1678 brayde,** *snatched* **1682 wight,** *person* **1683 brode,** *widely,* **or than hit stent,** *before it stopped* **1685 smelde,** *smelled* **1686 As,** *as if,* **potful bawme,** *pot full of balm,* **helde,** *poured* **1688 til her loses,** *to their reputations* **1689 y gan aspye,** *I did see* **1690 ferthe,** *fourth* **1692 gunne stonden,** *did stand,* **rewe,** *row* **1693 Certes,** *surely,* **bryght,** *radiant* **1694 han don,** *have done* **1695 ne kepen,** (do) *not care* (to) **1698 bounte,** *kindness* **1699 maner,** *kind of* **1701 dede,** *dead* **1702 y clywe,** *I scratched* **1704 gunne loute,** *did bow* **1706 to,** *of,* **besoughten alle,** (they) *all requested* **1707 hyde her,** *hide their,* **ek,** *also* **1708 yeven noght a lek,** *gave not a leek* **1710 For,** *because* **1711 ywrought,** *worked* **1712 wolde,** *wished* **1713 be ye wood,** *are you crazy* **1714 wene ye,** *do you think* **1716 dispit,** *scorn* **1717 lyven,** *live on,* **everychon,** *everyone* **1719 hote,** *command* **1720 ryng,** *proclaim,* **be,** *by*

1651–52 A description of how Slander magnifies, recalling the magnification of Fame at lines 1290–92 and 1494–95 above and the multiplication of sound at 784ff.; see also line 306. **1655 yronge,** perhaps a pun on the auditory and geometric meanings of *ring.* **1661 han ful trewely,** F reads "ben ful cruelly." **1662 ryghtfully,** breaking the word into two, the F scribe seems to have taken this as "very completely" rather than "by right." Here and at 1664 (**Ryghte**) and 1668 (**Right**) below, Chaucer seems to be exploring nuances of the word. **1668 Right,** omitted in F. **1675 Al,** omitted in F. **1685 helde,** "poured" rather than "held," derived from OE *hield.* **1686 potful,** F and P read "potful of." **1709 yeven noght a leek,** an idiomatic expression meaning they "cared nothing" for fame. **1717 lyven,** F reads "lyen." **1720 werk,** F and P read "werkes."

That al the world may of hyt here."
And he gan blowe her loos° so clere
In° his golden clarioun
That thrugh the world wente the soun
Also kenely° and eke so softe°,
But atte last hyt was on-lofte°.
  Thoo come the sextet° companye,
And gunne faste on Fame crie.
Ryght verraly° in this manere
They seyden: "Mercy, lady dere,
To tellen certeyn as hyt is,
We han don neither that ne this,
But ydel° al oure lyf ybe°.
But natheles° yet preye we
That we mowe han° as good a fame,
And gret renoun and knowen name,
As they that han doon noble gestes°,
And acheved alle her lestes°,
As wel of love as other thynge.
Al° was us° never broche° ne rynge,
Ne elles noght°, from wymmen° sent,
Ne ones in her herte yment°
To make us oonly frendly chere°,
But myghten temen us upon bere°.
Yet lat us to the peple seme°
Suche as the world may of us deme°
That wommen loven us for wode°—
Hyt shal doon us as moche goode,
And to oure herte as moche avaylle°,
To countrepese° ese° and travaylle°,
As° we had wonne hyt with labour,
For that is dere boght honour°
At regard of° oure grete ese.
And yet thou most° us more plese:
Let us be holden eke therto°
Worthy, wise, and goode also,
And riche, and happy unto love.
For Goddes love, that sit° above,
Thogh we may not the body have
Of wymmen, yet, so God yow save,
Leet° men gliwe° on us the name°—
Sufficeth° that we han the fame."
  "I graunte," quod she, "be° my trouthe!
Now, Eolus, withouten slouthe°.
Tak out thy trumpe of gold, let se,
And blow as they han axed° me,
That every man wene hem° at ese,
Though they goon in ful badde lese.°"
This Eolus gan hit so blowe
That thrugh the world hyt was yknowe.
  Thoo come the seventh route° anoon,
And fel on knees everychoon,
And seyde, "Lady, graunte us sone
The same thing, the same bone,°
That ye this nexte folk° han doon.°"
  "Fy° on yow," quod she, "everychon!
Ye masty swyn°, ye ydel wrechches,
Ful of rotten°, slowe techches°!
What, false theves, wher ye wolde°
Be famous° good, and nothing nolde°
Deserve why, ne never ye roughte°?
Men rather yow to hangen oughte°.
For ye be lyke the sweynte° cat
That wolde have fissh; but wostow° what?

1722 her loos, *their reputation* **1723 In,** *on* **1725 Also kenely,** *both very sharply, eke* **so softe,** *also very softly* **1726 on-lofte,** *in the air* **1727 sexte,** *sixth* **1729 Ryght verraly,** *very truly* **1732 han don,** *have done* **1733 ydel,** *idle,* **ybe,** (have) *been* **1734 natheles,** *nonetheless* **1735 mowe han,** *may have* **1737 gestes,** *deeds* **1738 her lestes,** *their desires* **1740 Al,** *although,* **us,** *to us,* **broche,** *brooch* **1741 Ne elles noght,** *nor anything else,* **wymmen,** *women* **1742 Ne ones in her herte yment,** *nor once in their hearts intended* **1743 us oonly frendly chere,** *friendly looks to us only* **1744 But myghten temen us upon bere,** *but* (would rather) *cause us to die* (be brought to our bier) **1745 seme,** *seem* **1746 deme,** *judge* **1747 for wode,** *madly* **1748 moche,** *much* **1749 avaylle,** *advantage* **1750 countrepose,** *balance,* **ese,** *ease,* **travaylle,** *trouble* **1751 As,** *as if* **1752 that is dere boght honour,** *that honor is dearly bought* **1753 At regard of,** *in comparison with* **1754 most,** *might* **1755 holden eke therto,** *considered also for this* **1758 sit,** *sits* **1761 Leet,** *let,* **gliwe,** *attach,* **name,** *reputation* **1762 Sufficeth,** *it is sufficient* **1763 be,** *by* **1764 slouthe,** *laziness* **1766 han axed,** *have asked* **1767 wene hem,** *thinks them* **1768 ful badde lese,** *very bad pasture* **1771 route,** *company* **1774 bone,** *request* (boon) **1775 nexte,** *previous,* **han doon,** *have done* **1776 Fy,** *shame* **1777 masty swyn,** *nut-fed pigs* **1778 roten,** *rotten,* **slowe techches,** *slothful defects* **1779 wher ye wolde,** *do you wish to* **1780 famous,** *famously,* **nothing nolde,** *not at all wish to* **1781 roughte,** *cared* **1782 yow to hangen oughte,** *ought to hang you* **1783 sweynte,** *lazy* **1784 wostow,** *do you know*

1726 But, F reads "So." **1734 But,** F reads "That." **1765 lat se,** F reads "now let se"; P, "quod she." **1768 ful badde lede,** Chaucer also uses the image of bad pasture to depict a condition of love at *TC* 2.752. **1775 ye,** omitted in F and P. **1777 masty swyn,** swine were fattened by being driven into the woods to feed on acorns. *Masty* derives from *mæst,* the OE word for *nuts.* **1779 Wher ye wolde . . . ,** the syntax and idiom here are difficult, apparently a result of the virulence of Fame's response to this seventh group of supplicants. The question or exclamation seems to mean something like "Where do you get off wanting good fame when you have neither deserved it nor cared about it?" **1781 roughte,** P reads "thought." **1782 to,** omitted in F. **1783 sweynte cat,** the lazy cat that would not wet his claws to catch fish is proverbial.

He wolde nothing wete° his clowes°.
Yvel thrift° come to your jowes°,
And eke° to myn, if I hit graunte,
Or do yow favour, yow to avaunte°!
Thou Eolus, thou kyng of Trace,
Goo blowe this folk a sory grace,°"
Quod she, "anon; and wostow° how?
As I shal telle thee ryght now.
Sey: 'These ben they° that wolde honour
Have, and do noskynnes° labour,
Ne doo no good, and yet han lawde°;
And that men wende° that bele Isawde°
Ne coude hem noght of love werne°,
And yet she that grynt° at a querne°
Ys al to good to ese her herte.°'"
This Eolus anon up sterte,
And with his blake clarioun
He gan to blasen° out a soun
As lowde as beloweth° wynd in helle.
And eke therwith°; soth° to telle,
This soun was so° ful of japes°,
As ever mowes° were in apes,
And that wente al the world about,
That every wight gan on hem shout°,
And for to lawghe° as they were wode°—
Such game° fonde they in her hode°.
  Tho come another companye,
That had ydoon° the trayterye°,
The harm, the grettest wikkednesse
That any herte kouthe gesse°,
And prayed her to han good fame,
And that she nolde doon hem° no shame,
But yeve hem loos° and good renoun,
And do hyt blowe in a clarioun.
"Nay, wis,°" quod she, "hyt were a vice.
Al be ther° in me no justice,
Me lyste not° to doo hyt now,
Ne this nyl° I not graunte yow."
  Tho come ther lepynge° in a route°,
And gunne choppen° al aboute
Every man upon the crowne°,
That° al the halle gan to sowne°,
And seyden, "Lady, leefe° and dere,
We ben suche folke as ye mowe here°.
To tellen al the tale aryght,
We ben shrewes°, every wyght°,
And han delyt° in wikkednesse,
As good folk han in godenesse,
And joy° to be knowen shrewes,
And ful of vices and wikked thewes°.
Wherfore we praye yow, a-rowe°,
That oure fame such be knowe°
In alle thing ryght° as hit ys."
  "Y graunte hyt yow," quod she, "ywis°.
But what art thow that seyst this tale,
That werest° on thy hose° a pale°,
And on thy tipet° such a belle?"
  "Madame," quod he, "soth to telle,
I am that ylke shrewe°, ywis°,
That brende° the temple of Ysidis°
In Athenes, loo, that citee."
  "And wherfor didest thou so?" quod she.

1785 wolde nothing wete, *wants not to wet,* **clowes,** *claws* **1786 Yvel thrift,** *evil luck,* **jowes,** *jaws* **1787 eke,** *also* **1788 avaunte,** *praise* **1790 sory grace,** *bad favor* **1791 wostow,** *do you know* **1793 ben they,** *are those* **1794 noskynnes,** *of no kind* **1795 han lawde,** *have praise* **1796 wende,** *would think,* **bele Isawde,** *beautiful Iseult* **1797 werne,** *refuse* **1798 grynt,** *grinds,* **querne,** *hand mill* **1799 ese her herte,** *ease their hearts* **1802 blasen,** *blast* **1803 beloweth,** *bellows* **1804 eke therwith,** *also with this,* **soth,** *truth* **1805 so,** *as,* **japes,** *deceptive tricks* **1806 mowes,** *grimaces* **1808 wight gan on hem shout,** *person did jeer at them* **1809 lawghe,** *laugh,* **wode,** *crazed* **1810 game,** *entertainment,* **her hode,** *their situation* **1812 ydoon,** *done,* **trayterye,** *treason* **1814 kouthe gesse,** *could imagine* **1816 nolde doon hem no,** *would not do them* **1817 yeve hem loos,** *give them reputation* **1819 wis,** *surely* **1820 Al be ther,** *even though there* (is) **1821 Me lyste not,** (it) *pleases me not* **1822 nyl,** *will not* **1823 lepynge,** *leaping,* **route,** *group* **1824 gunne choppen,** *hit* **1825 crowne,** *top of the head* **1826 That,** (so) *that,* **sowne,** *resound* **1827 leefe,** *beloved* **1828 mowe here,** *must hear* **1830 shrewes,** *villains,* **wight,** *person* **1831 han delyt,** *have delight* **1833 joy,** *enjoy* **1834 thewes,** *qualities* **1835 a-rowe,** *successively* **1836 knowe,** *known* **1837 ryght,** *just* **1838 ywis,** *certainly* **1840 werest,** *wears,* **hose,** *stockings,* **pale,** *stripe or decorative band* **1841 tipet,** *hanging part of hood or sleeve* **1843 ylke shrewe,** *same villain,* **ywys,** *truly* **1844 brende,** *burned,* **Ysidis,** *Isis*

1793 they, omitted in F, where "wolde" reads "wolden." **1794 noskynnes,** from "nones kindes," i.e., "of no kind." Compare "alleskynnes" at line 1530 above. F reads "no skynnes"; P, "no kynnes." **1796 bele Isawde,** beautiful Iseult, Tristram's lover. The sarcastic implication is that members of the seventh company wish it to be believed that not even Iseult could refuse to love them. **1798 she that grynt at a querne,** even she that grinds a hand mill, a peasant woman, deserves better than these would-be lovers. Chaucer elsewhere uses milling or grinding as a low euphemism for sexual activity; *WBP* 3.389 and 477–78. **1810 game . . . in her hode,** an idiomatic expression that means "reason to laugh at them," i.e., people had much entertainment at the expense of the would-be lovers. The figure is also used at *TC* 2.1110. **1821 to,** omitted in F. **1824–25** The head-slapping here is a form of foolery, perhaps done with inflated bladders, like balloons tied to sticks. **1840–41** The costume of a medieval court fool. **1843** The Pepys 2006 manuscript (P) breaks off here. **1844 brende the temple of Ysidis,** no account of the burning of a temple of Isis at Athens is known, but when a man burned the temple of Diana at Ephesus in an attempt to gain fame, he was punished with anonymity; John of Salisbury, *Policraticus* 8.5.

"By my thrift,°" quod he, "madame,
I wolde fayn han° had a fame,
As other folk hadde in the toune°
Although they were of gret renounce
For her vertu and for her thewes°.
Thoughte y, as gret a fame han shrewes,
Though hit be for shrewednesse°,
As good folk han for goodenesse;
And sith° y may not have that oon°,
That other nyl y noght forgoon°.
And for to gette of Fames hire°,
The temple sette y alle afire.
Now do our loos° be blowen swithe°,
As wisly° be thou ever blythe°!"
"Gladly," quod she; "thow Eolus,
Herestow not° what they prayen us°?"
"Madame, yis, ful wel," quod he,
And I wil trumpen it, parde°!"
And tok his blake trumpe faste,
And gan to puffen and to blaste,
Til hyt was at the worldes ende.
With that y gan aboute wende°,
For oon° that stood ryght at my bak
Me thoughte goodly° to me spak°,
And seyde, "Frend, what is thy name?
Artow° come hider° to han° fame?"
"Nay, for sothe, frend," quod y.
"I cam noght hyder°, graunt° mercy,
For no such cause, by my hede°.
Sufficeth me, as° I were dede°,
That no wight° have my name in honde°.
I wot° myself best how y stonde°,
For what I drye°, or what I thynke,
I wil myselfen al hyt drynke,
Certeyn, for the more° parte,
As ferforth° as I kan° myn arte."
"But what doost thou° here?" quod he.
Quod y, "That wyl y tellen the°,
The cause° why y stonde here:
Somme newe tydynges for to lere°,
Somme newe thinges, y not° what,
Tydynges other° this or that,
Of love or suche thynges glade.
For certeynly, he that me made
To comen hyder seyde° me,
Y shulde bothe here and se°
In this place wonder thynges.
But these be no suche tydynges
As I mene° of."—"Noo?" quod he.
And I answered, "Noo, parde!
For wel y wiste° ever yit,
Sith° that first y hadde wit,
That somme folk han° desired fame
Diversly, and loos°, and name.
But certeynly, y nyste° how
Ne where that Fame duelled, er° now,
And eke of her descripcioun,
Ne also her condicioun,
Ne the ordre° of her dome°,
Unto° the tyme y hidder come."
"Whych than be°, loo, these tydynges,
That thou now thus hider brynges,
That thou hast herd?" quod he to me.
"But now no fors°, for wel y se
What thou desirest for to here°.
Com forth and stond no lenger here,
And y wil thee, withouten drede°,
In° such another place lede°

1847 thrift, *luck* **1848 wolde fayn han,** *would like to have* **1849 toune,** *town* (i.e., Athens) **1851 her thewes,** *their qualities* **1853 shrewednesse,** *villainy* **1855 sith,** *since,* **oon,** *one* **1856 nyl y noght forgoon,** *I will not do without* **1857 hire,** *reward* **1859 do our loos,** *make our reputation,* **swithe,** *quickly* **1860 wisly,** *surely* (as), **blythe,** *happy* **1862 Herestow not,** *don't you hear,* **prayen us,** *request of us* **1864 parde,** *by God* **1868 gan aboute wende,** *did turn around* **1869 For oon,** *because* (some)*one* **1870 goodly,** *pleasantly* **spak,** *spoke* **1872 Artow,** *are you,* **hider,** *here,* **han,** *have* **1874 hyder,** *here,* **graunt,** (may God) *grant* **1875 hede,** *head* **1876 as,** *if,* **dede,** *dead* **1877 wight,** *person,* **honde,** *hand* **1878 wot,** *know,* **stonde,** *stand* **1879 drye,** *endure* **1881 more,** *greater* **1882 ferforth,** *far,* **kan,** *understand* **1883 doost thou,** *are you doing* **1884 the,** *you* **1885 cause,** *reason* **1886 lere,** *learn* **1887 not,** *know not* **1888 other,** *either* **1889 glade,** *glad* **1891 seyde,** *told* **1892 here and se,** *hear and see* **1895 mene,** *speak* **1897 wiste,** *knew* **1898 Sith,** *since* **1899 han,** *have* **1900 loos,** *reputation* **1901 nyste,** *knew not* **1902 er,** *before* **1905 ordre,** *manner,* **dome,** *judgment* **1906 Unto,** *until* **1907 Whych than be,** *what then are* **1910 no fors,** *no matter* **1911 here,** *hear* **1913 drede,** *doubt* **1914 In,** *into,* **lede,** *lead*

1847 thrift, Cx reads "trouthe." **1853 hit be,** F reads "hit be nought." **1862 they,** F reads "this folke." **1876 as I were dede,** this reminder that Chaucer is not dead (even though he is in the heavens) and the unnamed Friend's question above were apparently influenced by parallel reminders that Dante is not dead when he visits the afterlife, e.g., *Inferno* 8.33, 12.80ff., 15.46ff., and 27.61ff. **1877 that no wight have my name in honde,** i.e., that no one remembers me. **1880 al hyt drinke**, an echo of the proverb, "As I brew, so must I drink." **1883 But,** omitted in Cx; **here,** Cx reads "here than." **1887 thinges,** F and Cx read "thing." **1897 wiste,** F and Cx read "wote." **1907–09** The question makes little sense unless the Friend is asking it mockingly, i.e., "What tidings that you have heard do *you* bring?" Moreover *brynges* is an unusual (Northern) form, more familiarly *bryngest.* Perhaps corruption through transmission has obscured the meaning in ways impossible to sort out. **1907 Whych,** F and Cx read "Why." **1908 thus,** omitted in F and Cx.

Ther° thou shalt here many oon.°"
Tho gan I forth with hym to goon°
Out of the castel, soth to sey.
Tho saugh y° stonde in a valey,
Under° the castel, faste° by,
An hous that Domus Dedaly°,
That Laboryntus cleped ys°,
Nas° mad so wonderlych, ywis°,
Ne half so queyntelych ywrought°.
And evermo°, so° swyft as thought
This queynt° hous aboute went°,
That never mo stil hyt stent°,
And therout com so gret a noyse°
That had hyt stonden° upon Oyse°,
Men myghte hyt han herd esely°
To Rome, y trowe sikerly°.
And the noyse which that I herde,
For al the world ryght° so hyt ferde°
As dooth the rowtynge° the ston
That from th'engyn° ys leten gon°.
And al thys hous of which y rede°
Was mad° of twigges, falwe°, rede,
And grene eke°, and somme weren white,
Swiche° as men to these cages thwite°,
Or maken of these panyers°,
Or elles hottes° or dossers°,
That for the swough° and for the twygges,
This hous was also ful of gygges°,
And also ful eke of chirkynges°,
And of many other werkynges°.
And eke this hous hath of entrees°
As fele° as of leves ben in° trees
In somer whan they grene been°,
And on the roof men may yet seen
A thousand holes, and wel moo°,
To leten° wel the soun° out goo.
And be° day in every tyde°
Been al the dores opened wide,
And by nyght echon unshet°,
Ne porter° ther is noon to let°
No maner tydynges in to pace°.
Ne never rest° is in that place
That hit nys fild° ful of tydynges,
Other loude° or of whisprynges;
And over alle the houses angles°
Ys ful of rounynges° and of jangles°
Of werres°, of pes°, of mariages,
Of reste, of labour, of viages°,
Of abood°, of deeth, of lyfe,
Of love, of hate, acord, of stryfe,
Of loos°, of lore, and of wynnynges,
Of hele°, of seknesse°, of lesynges°,
Of faire wyndes, and of tempestes,
Of qwalme° of folk, and eke of bestes°;
Of dyvers transmutacions°
Of estats°, and eke of regions;
Of trust, of drede°, of jelousye,
Of wit, of wynnynge, of folye;
Of plente, and of gret famyne,
Of chepe°, of derthe°, and of ruyne°,

1915 Ther, *where,* **many oon,** *many* (a tiding) **1916 Tho gan . . . goon,** *then went* **1918 Tho saugh y,** *then I saw* **1919 Under,** *below,* **faste,** *near* **1920 Domus Dedaly,** *House of Daedalus* **1921 Laboryntus cleped ys,** *is called Labyrinth* **1922 Nas,** *was not,* **ywis,** *certainly* **1923 queyntelych ywrought,** *elaborately constructed* **1924 evermo,** *continually,* **so,** *as* **1925 queynt,** *unusual,* **aboute went,** *spun around* **1926 stent,** *stopped* **1927 noyse,** *noise* **1928 stonden,** *stood,* **Oyse,** ***the Oise*** **1929 han herd esely,** *have heard easily* **1930 trowe sikerly,** *believe surely* **1932 ryght,** *just,* **hyt ferde,** *it went* **1933 rowtynge,** *roaring* **1934 th'engyn,** *catapult,* **ys leten gon,** *is released* **1935 rede,** *explain* **1936 mad,** *made,* **falwe,** *yellow* **1937 eke,** *also* **1938 Swiche,** *such,* **to these cages thwite,** *fashion into cages* **1939 of these panyers,** *bread baskets from* **1940 hottes,** *wicker backpacks,* **dossers,** *wicker saddle baskets* **1941 for the swough,** *with the murmuring noise* **1942 gygges,** *scraping noises (?)* **1943 chirkynges,** *creakings* **1944 werkynges,** *workings* **1945 of entrees,** *entrances* **1946 fele,** *many,* **in,** *on* **1947 been,** *are* **1949 moo,** *more* **1950 leten,** *let,* **soun,** *sound* **1951 be,** *by,* **tyde,** *season* **1953 echon unshet,** *each one unshut* **1954 porter,** *doorman,* **let,** *hinder* **1955 pace,** *pass* **1956 rest,** *resting spot* **1957 nys fild,** *is not filled* **1958 Other loude,** *either loud* **1959 angles,** *corners* **1960 rounynges,** *whispers,* **jangles,** *gossip* **1961 werres,** *wars,* **pes,** *peace* **1962 viages,** *voyages* **1963 abood,** *waiting* **1965 loos,** *praise* **1966 hele,** *health,* **seknesse,** *sickness,* **lesynges,** *deceptions* **1968 qwalme,** *plague,* **bestes,** *beasts* **1969 dyvers transmutacions,** *diverse changes* **1970 estats,** *classes* **1971 drede,** *doubt* **1974 chepe,** *surplus,* **derthe,** *scarcity,* **ruyne,** *ruin*

1919 Under the castel, the location of the House of Rumor below the Castle of Fame suggests subordinate status. **1920–21 Domus Dedaly . . . Laboryntus,** Daedalus built the complicated maze known as the Labyrinth, in which the Minotaur was imprisoned; see, e.g., Ovid, *Metamorphoses* 8.157ff. Also referred to in *Bo* 3 pr.12.155ff. More generally, Chaucer's House of Rumor is modeled on the dwelling place of Rumor in *Metamorphoses* 12.42ff., which also has innumerable doors that stand open day and night and is filled with whisperings and taletellings. **1928 Oyse,** the Oise River flows into the Seine River near Paris. **1931 which that I,** F reads "whiche I have." **1938 Swiche,** F reads "Whiche." **these,** a generalizing pronoun that implies that the listener is familiar with the objects referred to, here cages and various baskets. **1940 hottes,** F and Cx read "hattes." Skeat provides evidence for the emendation. **1944** F is incomplete: "As ful this lo." From Cx. **1945 of,** a "partitive" genitive preposition, used with numbers or division into parts. **1962** F reads "Of restes and of labour of viages"; Cx, "Of restes, of labour and of viages." **1966 lesynges,** F reads "bildynges."

Of good or mys governement,
Of fyr°, and of dyvers° accident.
And loo, thys hous of which I write,
Syker be ye°, hit nas not lyte°,
For hyt was sixty myle of lengthe.
Alle° was the tymber of no strengthe,
Yet hit is founded° to endure
While that hit lyst to Aventure°,
That is the moder of tydynges,
As the see° of welles and of sprynges;
And hyt was shapen lyk° a cage.
"Certys," quod y, "in al myn age,
Ne saugh y suche an hous as this."
And as y wondred me, ywys,
Upon this hous, tho war was y°
How that myn egle° faste° by
Was perched hye° upon a stoon,
And I gan streghte to hym gon°,
And seyde thus, "Y preye the°
That thou a while abide me°,
For Goddis love, and lete me seen°
What wondres in this place been°,
For yit°, paraunter°, y may lere°
Somme good thereon°, or sumwhat here°
That leef me were°, or° that y wente.°"
"Petre°, that is myn entente,"
Quod he to me. "Therfore y duelle°.
But certeyn, oon thyng I the telle,
That but° I bringe the therinne°,
Ne shalt thou never kunne gynne°
To come into hyt, out of doute,
So faste hit whirleth, lo, aboute.
But sith that° Joves, of his grace,
As I have seyd, wol the solace°
Fynally with these thinges,
Unkouthe syghtes° and tydynges,
To passe with thyn hevynesse°,
Such routhe° hath he of thy distresse
That thou suffrest debonairly°,
And wost° thyselfen outtirly°
Disesperat° of alle blys°,
Syth° that Fortune hath mad amys°
The fruit° of al thyn hertys° reste
Languysshe° and eke in poynt to breste°,
That he thrugh hys myghty merite
Wol do the an ese°, al° be hyt lyte°,
And yaf expres° commaundement,
To which I am obedient,
To further the° with al my myght,
And wisse° and teche the aryght°
Where thou maist° most tidynges here°.
Shaltow here° anoon many oon lere°."
With this word he ryght anoon
Hente° me up bytweene hys toon°
And at° a wyndowe yn me broghte,
That in this hous was, as me thoghte—
And therwithalle°, me thoughte hit stent°,
And nothing° hyt aboute went—
And me sette in the flore° adoun.
But which° a congregacioun
Of folk, as I saugh rome° aboute,
Some wythin and some wythoute,
Nas° never seen, ne shal ben eft°,
That°, certys°, in the world nys° left
So many formed be° Nature,
Ne ded° so many a creature,
That wel unnethe° in that place
Hadde y a fote-brede° of space.

1976 fyr, *fire,* **dyvers,** *various* **1978 Syker be ye,** *be assured,* **nas not lyte,** *was not little* **1980 Alle,** *although* **1981 founded,** *built* **1982 lyst to Aventure,** *it is pleasing to Chance* **1984 see,** *sea* (is) **1985 shapen lyk,** *shaped like* **1989 tho war was y,** *then I was aware* **1990 egle,** *eagle,* **faste,** *near* **1991 hye,** *high* **1992 gan streghte . . . gon,** *went straight* **1993 Y preye the,** *I ask you* **1994 abide me,** *wait for me* **1995 lete me seen,** *let me see* **1996 been,** *are* **1997 yit,** *yet,* **paraunter,** *perhaps,* **lere,** *learn* **1998 thereon,** *in there,* **sumwhat here,** *hear something* **1999 leef me were,** *may be pleasing to me,* **or,** *before,* **wente,** *depart* **2000 Petre,** (by Saint) *Peter* **2001 duelle,** *stay* **2003 but,** *unless,* **the therinne,** *you in there* **2004 kunne gynne,** *know the trick* **2007 sith that,** *since* **2008 wol the solace,** *wants to comfort you* **2010 Unkouthe syghtes,** *unknown sights* **2011 passe with thyn hevynesse,** *overcome your dullness* **2012 routhe,** *pity* **2013 debonairly,** *meekly* **2014 wost,** *know,* **outtirly,** *utterly* **2015 Disesperat,** *desperate,* **blys,** *bliss* **2016 Syth,** *since,* **mad amys,** *wrongly made* **2017 fruit,** *outcome,* **thyn hertes,** *your heart's* **2018 Languysshe,** *weaken,* **eke in poynt to breste,** *also at the point of breaking* **2020 Wol do the an ese,** *will do you the favor,* **al,** *although,* **lyte,** *little* **2021 yaf expres,** *gave explicit* **2023 further the,** *help you* **2024 wisse,** *instruct,* **teche the aryght,** *teach you correctly* **2025 maist,** *may,* **here,** *hear* **2026 Shaltow here,** *you shall here,* **many oon lere,** *learn many* **2028 Hente,** *picked,* **toon,** *toes* **2029 at,** *through* **2031 therwithalle,** *with that,* **hit stent,** *it stopped* **2032 nothing,** *not at all* **2033 in the flore,** *on the floor* **2034 which,** *such* **2035 saugh rome,** *saw roam* **2037 Nas,** *was not,* **eft,** *again* **2038 That,** (so) *that,* **certys,** *certainly,* **nys,** (there) *is not* **2039 be,** *by* **2040 Ne ded,** *nor* (have) *died* **2041 wel unnethe,** *scarcely* **2042 fote-brede,** *square foot*

2010 syghtes, F and Cx read "sygh t." **2017 fruit,** F reads "frot"; Cx, "swote." **2018 Languysshe,** F reads "Laugh." **2019 he,** i.e., Jove, from line 2007. The complicated and extended syntax here is typical of the eagle's discourse. **2021 yaf,** F reads "yaf in." **2028** Line lacking in F; supplied from Cx. **2032 nothing hyt aboute went,** i.e., when Geffrey enters into the House of Rumor, it no longer seems to him to be spinning. **2036** Line lacking in F; supplied from Cx. **2040 ded so many a creature,** like the parallels noted at line 1876, the crowd here is reminiscent of Dante, *Inferno* 3.55ff.; see also the notes to 1920–21 above and 2074 and 2089 below.

And every wight° that I saugh there
Rouned everych° in others ere°
A newe tydynge prevely°,
Or elles tolde alle openly
Ryght thus, and seyde, "Nost not thou°
That ys betyd°, lo, late or now°?"
"No," quod he, "telle me what."
And than he tolde hym this and that,
And swor therto that hit was sothe°—
"Thus hath he sayd," and "Thus he dothe°,"
"Thus shal hit be," "Thus herde y seye,"
"That shal be founde," "That dar I leye°"—
That al the folk that ys alyve
Ne han the kunnynge° to discryve°
The thinges that I herde there,
What aloude, and what in ere.
But al the wonder most was this:
Whan oon had herd a thinge, ywis°,
He come forth ryght to another wight°,
And gan him tellen° anon-ryght
The same that to him was tolde,
Or hyt° a forlong way° was olde,
But gan somwhat for to eche°
To this tydynge in this speche
More than hit ever was.
And nat so sone departed nas°
Tho fro° him, that he ne mette°
With the thrid°, and or he lette°
Any stounde° he told him als°.
Were the tydynge sothe° or fals,
Yit wolde° he telle hyt natheles°,
And evermo with more encres°
Than yt was erst°. Thus north and south
Wente every tydyng fro mouth to mouth,
And that encresing evermoo
As fire ys wont to quyke° and goo°
From a sparke spronge amys°,
Til° alle a citee brent° up ys.
And whan that was ful ysprong°
And woxen more° on every tong°
Than ever hit was, hit went anoon°
Up to a wyndowe out to goon;
Or, but hit myght° out there pace°,
Hyt gan out crepe° at somme crevace°,
And flygh forth° faste for the nones°.
And somtyme saugh I thoo at ones°
A lesyng° and a sad soth sawe°,
That gonne of aventure drawe°
Out at a wyndowe for to pace,
And when they metten in that place,
They were acheked° bothe two,
And neyther of hem most° out goo
For other°; so they gonne crowde°
Til ech of hem gan crien lowed°,
"Lat me go first!"—"Nay, but let me!
And here I wol ensuren the°
Wyth the nones° that thou wolt do so,
That I shal never fro the° go,
But be thyn owne sworen° brother!
We wil medle° us eche with° other,
That no man, be they never so wroth°,
Shal han that oon° of us two, but both
At ones°, al besyde his leve°,
Come we a-morwe° or on eve,

2043 wight, *creature* **2044 Rouned everych,** *whispered every one,* **others ere,** *another's ear* **2045 prevely,** *privately* **2047 Nost not thou,** *don't you know* **2048 That ys betyd,** *what has happened,* **late or now,** *recently* **2051 sothe,** *truth* **2052 dothe,** *does* **2054 dar I leye,** *dare I wager* **2056 kunnynge,** *ability,* **discryve,** *describe* **2060 ywis,** *truly* **2061 wight,** *person* **2062 gan him tellen,** *did tell him* **2064 Or hyt,** *before it,* **forlong way,** *furlong's way* **2065 eche,** *add* **2068 nat so sone departed nas,** (it) *was not so soon departed* **2069 Tho fro,** *then from,* **mette,** *met* **2070 thrid,** *third* (person), **or he lette,** *before he hesitated* **2071 stounde,** *time,* **als,** *also* **2072 sothe,** *true* **2073 Yit wolde,** *yet would,* **natheles,** *nonetheless* **2074 encres,** *addition* **2075 erst,** *first* **2078 wont to quyke,** *accustomed to kindle,* **goo,** *spread* **2079 spronge amys,** *sprung by mistake* **2080 Til,** *until,* **brent,** *burned* **2081 ful ysprong,** *fully sprung* **2082 woxen more,** *grown greater,* **tong,** *tongue* **2083 anoon,** *immediately* **2085 but hit myght,** *if it might not,* **pace,** *pass* **2086 gan out crepe,** *crept out,* **crevace,** *crack* **2087 flygh,** *flew,* **for the nones,** *under the conditions* **2088 at ones,** *at the same time* **2089 lesyng,** *lie,* **sad soth sawe,** *sober true statement* **2090 gonne of aventure drawe,** *did by chance move* **2093 acheked,** *stopped* **2094 most,** *might* **2095 For other,** *because of the other,* **gonne crowde,** *crowded* **2096 gan crien lowde,** *cried loudly* **2098 wol ensuren the,** *will assure you* **2099 Wyth the nones,** *on the condition* **2100 fro the,** *from you* **2101 sworen,** *sworn* **2102 medle,** *mingle,* **eche with,** *with each* **2103 be they never so wroth,** *despite their anger* **2104 Shal han that oon,** *shall have either one* **2105 At ones,** *together,* **besyde of his leve,** *contrary to his desire* **2106 a-morwe,** *in the morning*

2044 everych, omitted in F. **2048** Line is short in F; Cx reads "That is betid, lo ryght now." **2053 Thus shal,** F reads "And thus shal"; Cx, "And this shal." **Thus herde,** F and Cx read "And thus herde." **2064 forlong way,** the (short) length of time it takes to go a furlong (220 yards); a couple of minutes. **2069 Tho from him, that,** F reads "That he fro him thoo." **2074 evermo with more encres,** the amplification of rumor derives from Ovid, *Metamorphoses* 12.46–47, 55ff. **2076 tydyng,** F reads "mouthe." **2083 hit went,** F and Cx read "and went." **2088 saugh I thoo,** F reads "saugh thoo"; Cx, "I sawe there." **2089 lesyng and a sad soth sawe,** the mingling of falsehood and truth is a detail from Ovid's *Metamorphoses,* 12.54ff., but the slapstick comedy of getting jammed in the doorway is Chaucer's. See also lines 1029 and 2108. **2094** Caxton abandons the text here (or perhaps his exemplar broke off), and adds a spurious twelve-line conclusion in which the narrator awakens from his dream in a way that is similar to the ending of *PF.* **2104 of us,** omitted in F.

Be we cried° or stille yrouned°."
Thus saugh I fals and soth compouned°
Togeder fle for oo° tydynge.
  Thus out at° holes gunne wringe°
Every tydynge streght° to Fame,
And she gan yeven ech° hys name,
After hir disposicioun,
And yaf hem eke duracioun°,
Somme to wexe and wane sone°,
As doth the faire, white mone°,
And lete hem goon. Ther myght y seen
Wenged° wondres faste fleen°,
Twenty thousand in a route°,
As Eolus hem blew aboute.
  And, Lord, this hous in alle tymes,
Was ful of shipmen° and pilgrimes,
With scrippes bret-ful° of lesynges°,
Entremedled° with tydynges.
And eke allone be hemselve°,
O many a thousand tymes twelve
Saugh I eke of these pardoners,
Currours°, and eke messangers,
With boystes° crammed ful of lyes°
As ever vessel was with lyes°.
And as I altherfastest° went
About, and dide al myn entent
Me for to pleye and for to lere°,
And eke a tydynge for to here,
That I had herd of somme contre°
That shal not now be told for° me—
For hit no nede is, redely°;
Folk kan synge° hit bet° than I;
For al mot out°, other° late or rathe°,
Alle the sheves° in the lathe°—
I herde a grete noyse withalle°
In a corner of the halle,
Ther° men of love-tydynges tolde.
And I gan thiderward beholde°,
For I saugh rennynge° every wight°,
As faste as that they hadden myght,
And everych° cried, "What thing is that?"
And somme sayde, "I not never° what."
And whan they were alle on an hepe°,
Tho behynde° begunne up lepe,
And clamben° up on other° fast,
And up the nose and eyen kast°,
And troden fast on others heles°,
And stampen as men doon aftir eles°.
Atte laste y saugh a man,
Which that y nevene nat ne kan°,
But he semed° for to be
A man of gret auctorite°. . . .

2107 cried, *proclaimed,* **stille yrouned,** *quietly whispered* **2108 compouned,** *combined* **2109 fle for oo,** *fly as one* **2110 at,** *from* **gunne wringe,** *did squeeze* **2111 streght,** *straight* **2112 gan yeven ech,** *did give each* **2114 eke duracioun,** *also duration* **2115 wexe and wane sone,** *grow and fade quickly* **2116 mone,** *moon* **2117 seen,** *see* **2118 Wenged,** *winged,* **fleen,** *fly* **2119 route,** *company* **2122 shipmen,** *sailors* **2123 scrippes bret-ful,** *sacks brimful,* **lesynges,** *lies* **2124 Entremedled,** *intermixed* **2125 eke,** *also,* **be hemselve,** *by themselves* **2128 Currours,** *couriers* **2129 boystes,** *containers,* **lyes,** *lies* **2130 lyes,** *dregs* **2131 altherfastest,** *fastest of all* **2133 lere,** *learn* **2135 contre,** *country* **2136 for,** *by* **2137 redely,** *truly* **2138 kan synge,** *can sing,* **bet,** *better* **2139 mot out,** *must* (come) *out,* **other,** *either,* **rathe,** *early* **2140 sheves,** *crops,* **lathe,** *barn* **2141 withalle,** *as well* **2143 Ther,** *where* **2144 gan thiderward beholde,** *did look in that direction* **2145 rennynge,** *running,* **wight,** *creature* **2147 everych,** *each one* **2148 not never,** *don't know* **2149 on an hepe,** *in a heap* **2150 Tho behynde,** *those in back* **2151 clamben,** *clamber,* **other,** *others* **2152 up the nose and eyen kast,** *looked upwards* (cast up their noses and eyes) **2153 others heles,** *others' heels* **2154 doon aftir eles,** *do* (when) *chasing eels* **2156 y nevene nat ne kan,** *I cannot name* **2157 semed,** *seemed* **2158 gret auctorite,** *great authority*

2122–27 shipmen and pilgrimes . . . pardoners, these various kinds of travelers are bearers of news, which is associated with lying and deception. In his *CT,* Chaucer associates them with tale-telling. Lines 1529–30 may also anticipate the *CT.* **2152 nose and eyen,** F reads "noyse on highen." **2153 others,** F reads "other." **2156 nevene,** omitted in F. **2158 man of gret auctorite,** the identity of the man of authority is a matter of much debate; critics have proposed various candidates, none of whom are widely accepted. Similarly, it is debated whether an original ending has been lost or if the poem is intentionally open-ended. F ends with twelve lines added in a much later hand, derived from Caxton's spurious conclusion; see 2094n.

Legend of Good Women

Legend of Good Women

Introduction

Like *Canterbury Tales*, *Legend of Good Women* is a collection of short narratives-preceded by an introductory prologue. Where the Canterbury stories vary widely in genre and style and the *General Prologue* is anchored in the civic world of London, the legends of good women are homogeneous—modeled on saints' lives—and the Prologue to these tales is a courtly dream vision. The narrator opens with an explanation that we need books in order to know many things that we cannot experience directly, but admits that his love for flowers—especially the daisy—draws him from his books in springtime. A dynamic between learning from books and knowing through experience runs throughout the work, established early on when the narrator admits his need for literary predecessors to praise the daisy adequately. Books are essential to what we know and to what we can express.

In the dream that ensues, the narrator witnesses a procession led by the God of Love and his queen, Alceste (who is pointedly daisy-like in dress), and a train of ladies. The God of Love threatens to punish the poet-narrator for the heresy of having written books that discourage love (specifying *Troylus and Criseyde* and *Romaunt of the Rose*), clearly indicating that the narrator is a projection of Chaucer himself. The queen intercedes, cautions the deity against tyranny, and defends Chaucer's literary output, listing the works that precede *Legend* in Chaucer's writing. Yet, as penance for his literary sins (a notion Chaucer returns to in his *Retraction* of *Canterbury Tales*), Alceste tells the narrator that he must for the rest of his life write stories about good women betrayed by men who seek to do them shame. The narrator recognizes that the good lady before him is his daisy transformed, and the Prologue closes with the God of Love praising Alceste's "pitee" and commanding the narrator to include her story in his "legende."

Following this command are nine discrete narratives of "good" women from classical tradition who are loyal in love or suicidal when betrayed or raped. Alceste is a classical figure of wifely loyalty (432n), but she is not among these women in the work as we have it. The "goodness" of the women who are included is not a matter of moral or Christian virtue, but a kind of grim steadfastness in the face of sorrow or treachery. Indeed, the sequence includes protagonists better known for voluptuousness (Cleopatra) or wickedness (Medea) than for self-sacrifice (Thisbe) or being abandoned (Dido), so that reading the individual tales compels us to adjust our idea of these women and their goodness as we go.

The narratives also compel us to adjust what we know of the men involved, as the women are victims of male abandonment, sexual assault, or both. In the story of Dido (legend 3), Aeneas is not the heroic founder of Rome, but a cad whose sneak-thief departure leaves the queen devastated. In the account of Hypsipyle and Medea (legend 4), Jason's finding of the Golden Fleece is all but ignored in favor of his duplicity; Hercules is a go-between rather than a strongman. The abandonment of Ariadne (legend 6) is more important than Theseus's defeat of the Minotaur or any of his other famous exploits. His son, Demophon, is as treacherous as his father when betraying Phyllis (legend 8). Even in Thisbe's story (legend 2), Pyramus is presented as an exception that proves the rule of male treachery (917–21).

The ultimate model for these narratives is Ovid's *Heroides*, a work presented as a series of first-person laments by classical heroines in which the voicing of female perspective allows us to see traditional narratives from a new perspective, generating sympathy for the female narrators as well as some recognition of the limits of these perspectives. Increasing our sense of perspective, and perhaps influenced by Boccaccio's *De Mulieribus Claris* (*On Famous Women*) as well as the saints' life genre, Chaucer's third-person narrator is very much present throughout his accounts. As he reflects on his source material and struggles with a growing sense that male infidelity is appalling (e.g., 917–21, 1002–03, 1254-63, 1552-58, 1679, 1692–93, 2239–40, 2454–58, 2490–95), we recognize how these versions are constructed from their sources in ways that emphasize male perfidy and homogenize female virtue. The pathos of the narratives is high and at times intense, but the selective appropriations from traditional stories remind us that this pathos depends on what one knows and from what point of view one knows it. Stories shape the way we think and what we can say, but at times we misunderstand or even resist what they mean.

Early study of *Legend* focused on identifying source material until Robert W. Frank, Jr., *Chaucer and the Legend of Good Women* (1972; no. 1536), examined the narrative qualities of the work and Lisa Kiser, *Telling Classical Tales* (1983, no. 1541), demonstrated that epistemology is a concern throughout. In recent decades the poem has justly attracted the attention of feminist critics for the ways it rewrites portions of western literary tradition. Many are disturbed by the passivity or abuse of the female protagonists, even as they acknowledge the revisionist perspective of the poem. The most sustained studies show how attention to gender is fundamental to the work's concerns with epistemology and literature. In *The Naked Text* (1994, no. 1534), Sheila Delany argues that the interrelation of gender and the making of meaning are the central to the poem. In *Chaucer's Legendary Good Women* (1998, no. 1546), Florence Percival shows that the poem is anchored in conventions and rituals that were important to the gendered identity roles in Chaucer's contemporary court culture. Court games and competitions underlie several motifs of the Prologue in particular, and the entry of the God of Love, the procession of ladies, and Alceste's intercession evoke rituals that took place in the court of Richard II. Just as reading conventional literature helps us to know ourselves, the court comes to define and know itself through its rituals.

There is much critical disagreement about the extent to which the Prologue records or even suggests an historical occasion or how distinctly the God of Love can be equated with Richard or Alceste with Richard's first wife, Anne of Bohemia (see 230n and 496–97n). The allusions to flower-and-leaf competition (72n), the abject status of the poet-narrator, and the relations of the God of Love to his entourage refract rather than record late-fourteenth century court life, and almost all such aspects of the poem are conventional, derived from contemporary French poetry, particularly Guillaume de Machaut's *Jugement dou Roy de Behaigne* and *Jugement dou Roy de Navarre.* Chaucer acknowledges his predecessors when casting himself as a gleaner in the fields that others have reaped (75), yet his adaptations and adjustments to the individual legends assert his creative independence as well as his borrowings.

Alceste's references in *Legend's* Prologue to previous works by Chaucer (417–20, 425–28, and 441) enable us to be certain that it postdates the early translations, dream visions, and *Troylus and Criseyde,* while mention of *Legend* in the *Man of Law's Prologue* (2.61–75) and in Chaucer's *Retraction* (10.1087) confirm that he wrote it before *Canterbury Tales.* Scholars date the work, therefore, between *Troylus* and *Canterbury Tales,* likely begun in or around 1386, with the possibility that he composed the individual legends over time. See below for the revision of the Prologue.

The verse form of *Legend*—iambic pentameter couplets—anticipates *Canterbury Tales* as the first use in English of this highly influential metrical form. Its dream-vision frame, however, hearkens back to *Book of the Duchess, House of Fame,* and *Parliament of Fowls.* In the *Retraction,* Chaucer refers to the work as "the Book of the xxv Ladies," so there is some confusion about how many stories he intended for *Legend.* We have nine in the work as it stands and the *Retraction* mentions 25. To make matters worse, 16 names are listed as the contents of the "Seintes Legende of Cupide" in the *Man of Law's Prologue* (including some but not all of the extant tales), and Canace and the daughter of Antiochus are there mentioned as victims of incest who are therefore specially excluded from the collection (*MLT* 2.61–89). In an anthology of essays focused on *Legend* edited by Carolyn P. Collette (2006, no. 1532), Joyce Coleman adds to arguments that the Man of Law's comments indicate a competition of some kind between Chaucer and his friend, John Gower. While the arguments do not account for the discrepancies in number, they do reinforce the idea that some kind (or kinds) of court game or literary competition underlies the work in a fundamental way.

Specific passages of literary dependency on are identified in the notes that accompany the text, and R. Barton Palmer discusses pervasive influence of Machaut on the Prologue in "Chaucer's *Legend of Good Women*: The Narrator's Tale" (2003, no. 1545). On court culture and the roles of Richard and Anne, see Joyce Coleman, "'A bok for king Richardes sake'" (2007, no. 1554), and Andrew Taylor, "Anne of Bohemia and the Making of Chaucer" (1997, no. 1551). Andrew Galloway explores political dimensions of the poem in contrast with Gower's *Confessio Amantis* in "Gower's Quarrel With Chaucer, and the Origins of Bourgeois Didacticism in Fourteenth-Century London Poetry" (2007, no. 1537). For a sense of Chaucer's kaleidoscopic uses of Ovid and other classical and post-classical narratives, see Suzanne C. Hagedorn, *Abandoned Women: Rewriting the Classics in Dante, Boccaccio, & Chaucer* (2004, no. 291). On several of these issues, including court culture, public performance, and gender, consult the essays in Collette's collection.

The Two Prologues

One remarkable feature of *Legend of Good Women* is that there are two different versions of the Prologue, generally designated F and G. The latter exists in one manuscript only (Cambridge University Library MS Gg.4.7), which is widely accepted to be Chaucer's revision of the F version found in the other 11 manuscripts. Apparently the legends circulated with the F Prologue and then were released again after Chaucer reworked it, offering us in the G Prologue a unique example of how he changed his own work. The most likely reason for the revision is the death of Queen Anne in 1394. She is alluded to in F (496–97) but not mentioned in G, while suggestions of the narrator's advancing age in G (261–62, 315, 400; not found in F) and an addition to Chaucer's list of works mentioned by Alceste (see G414–15n) seem to confirm that G follows F. The G revision is usually dated soon after Anne's death, although some critics question the date and the F–G sequence of revision. See, for example, Kathryn L. Lynch, *Chaucer's Philosophical Visions* (2000, no. 1399).

Major differences between the two Prologues include a good deal of rearranging of sections as well as rewriting to create a different tone or attitude, but there are few substantial differences in action. In F, the narrator himself sings the ballade in praise of the lady (249–69), although she is not named until later (432); in G, the lyric is sung by the procession of ladies who refer three times to Alceste (G203–23), earlier identified by the narrator (G179). F presents the tales as told by the narrator while in his dream state, while the tellings take place after he awakens in the G version. Otherwise, the differences include more lyrical praise for the daisy in F (see 84–96), an expansive general tally in G of worthy women found among the pages in the narrator's library (G267–312), and number of other shifts and adjustments that we tabulate in the notes to G. The overall difference is impossible to capture in tabulation, so we print the two versions separately to enable readers to experience it for themselves.

Legend of Good Women

Prologue: Original Version (F)

A thousand tymes have I herd men telle
That ther ys joy in hevene and peyne in helle,
And I acorde° wel that it ys so.
But natheles, yet wot° I wel also
That ther nis noon° duellyng in this contree
That eyther hath in hevene or helle ybe°,
Ne may of hit noon other weyes witen°,
But as he hath herd seyde, or founde it written—
For by assay° ther may no man it preve°.
But God forbede but° men shulde leve°
Wel more thing then men han seen with eye.
Men shal not wenen° everything a lye
But yf himself yt seeth, or elles dooth,
For, God wot°, thing is never the lasse sooth°
Thogh every wight° ne may it nat ysee°.
Bernard the monk ne saugh° nat all, pardee°!
Than mote we to bokes° that we fynde,
Thurgh which that olde thinges ben in mynde°,
And to the doctrine of these olde wyse°,
Yeve° credence, in every skylful wise°,
That tellen of these olde appreved° stories
Of holynesse, of regnes°, of victories,
Of love, of hate, of other sondry° thynges,
Of whiche I may not maken rehersynges.
And yf that olde bokes were awey°,
Yloren° were of remembraunce the key.
Wel ought us thanne° honouren and beleve
These bokes, there° we han noon other preve°.
And as for me, though that I konne° but lyte°,
On bokes for to rede I me delyte,
And to hem yive I feyth and ful credence,
And in myn herte have hem in reverence
So hertely that ther is game° noon
That fro my bokes maketh me to goon
But° yt be seldom on the holyday,
Save°, certeynly, whan that the month of May
Is comen, and that I here° the foules° synge,
And that the floures gynnen for to° sprynge.
Fairwel my bok and my devocioun!
Now have I thanne eek° this condicioun,
That of al the floures in the mede°,
Thanne love I most thise floures white and rede,
Suche as men callen daysyes in oure toun.
To hem have I so gret affeccioun,
As I seyde erst°, whanne comen is the May,
That in my bed ther daweth° me no day
That I nam° up and walkyng in the mede
To seen this flour ayein° the sonne sprede,
Whan it upryseth erly by the morwe°.
That blisful sight softneth al my sorwe,
So glad am I, whan that I have presence
Of it, to doon it alle reverence,
As she that is of alle floures flour,
Fulfilled of al vertu and honour,
And evere ilyke° faire and fressh of hewe,
And I love it, and ever ylike newe,
And evere shal, til that myn herte dye,
Al swere I nat°—of this I wol nat lye—
Ther loved no wight° hotter in his lyve.
And whan that hit ys eve, I renne blyve°,

3 acorde, *agree* **4 wot,** *know* **5 nis noon,** *is no one* **6 ybe,** *been* **7 witen,** *know* **9 assay,** *attempt,* **preve,** *prove* **10 God forbede but,** *may God forbid unless,* **leve,** *believe* **12 wenen,** *think* **14 wot,** *knows,* **lasse sooth,** *less true* **15 wight,** *person,* **ysee,** *see* **16 saugh,** *saw,* **pardee,** *by God* **17 Than mote we to bokes,** *then must we* (go) *to books* **18 ben in mynde,** *are remembered* **19 wyse,** *wise people* **20 Yeve,** *give,* **skyful wise,** *reasonable way* **21 appreved,** *trustworthy* **22 regnes,** *kingdoms* **23 sondry,** *various* **25 awey,** *gone* **26 Yloren,** *lost* **27 thanne,** *then* **28 there,** *where,* **preve,** *proof* **29 konne,** *know,* **lyte,** *little* **33 game,** *diversion* **35 But,** *unless* **36 Save,** *except* **37 here,** *hear,* **foules,** *birds* **38 gynnen for to,** *begin to* **40 thanne eek,** *then also* **41 mede,** *meadow* **43 daysyes,** *daisies* **45 erst,** *before* **46 daweth,** *dawns* **47 nam,** *am not* **48 ayein,** *toward* **49 by the morwe,** *in the morning* **55 ilyke,** *equally* **58 Al swere I nat,** *even if I swear not* **59 wight,** *person* **60 renne blyve,** *run quickly*

Text based on Bodleian Library, Oxford, MS Fairfax 16 (F), with corrections from Cambridge University Library MS Gg.4.7 (Gg) and Trinity College, Cambridge, MS R.3.17 (Tr). **1–6** Compare Froissart's *Le Joli Buisson de Jonece* (*The Fair Bush of Youth*) 786–92. **1 men,** omitted in F. **2 That,** omitted in F. **6 or,** F and reads "or in." **16 Bernard,** mystic and theologian, St. Bernard of Clairvaux (1091–1153) is Dante's guide in the highest circle of *Paradiso* 32–33, although the line is proverbial. **40–65** These lines echo a number of French poems in praise of the *marguerite,* the French word for daisy. **40 eek this,** F reads "suche a." **42–43 white and rede . . . daysyes,** the so-called "English daisy," is white, red, or white tinged with red; Chaucer's description is similar to those that recur in marguerite poetry. **43 oure,** F reads "her."

As sone as evere the Sonne gynneth weste°,
To seen this flour, how it wol go to reste,
For fere of nyght, so hateth she derknesse.
Hire chere° is pleynly sprad in the brightnesse
Of the sonne, for ther yt wol unclose.
Allas that I ne had Englyssh, ryme or prose,
Suffisant this flour to preyse aryght°!
But helpeth, ye that han konnyng° and myght,
Ye lovers that kan make° of sentement,
In this cas oghte ye be diligent
To forthren° me somwhat in my labour,
Whethir ye ben with the leef or with the flour.
For wel I wot° that ye han her-biforne°
Of makyng ropen°, and lad° awey the corne°,
And I come after, glenyng° here and there,
And am ful glad yf I may fynde an ere°
Of any goodly word that ye han left.
And thogh it happen me rehercen eft°
That° ye han in your fresshe songes sayde,
Forbereth° me, and beth° nat evele apayde°,
Syn that° ye see I do yt in the honour
Of love, and eke° in service of the flour
Whom that I serve as I have witte or myght°.
She is the clerenesse° and the verray° lyght
That in this derke world me wynt° and ledeth.
The hert in-with my sorwfull brest yow dredeth°
And loveth so sore that ye ben verrayly°
The maistresse of my witte, and nothing I.
My word, my werk ys knyt so in youre bond°
That, as an harpe obeieth to the hond,
And maketh it soune° after his fyngerynge,
Ryght so mowe ye° oute of myn herte bringe
Swich vois°, ryght as yow lyst°, to laughe or pleyne.
Be ye my gide° and lady sovereyne!
As to myn erthely god to yow I calle,
Bothe in this werk and in my sorwes alle.
  But wherfore° that I spak°, to yive credence
To olde stories and doon hem reverence,
And that° men mosten° more thyng beleve
Then° men may seen at eighe° or elles preve°—
That shal I seyn, whanne that I see my tyme.
I may not al attones° speke in ryme.
My besy gost° that thursteth° alwey newe
To seen this flour so yong, so fressh of hewe,
Constreyned me with so gledy° desire
That in myn herte I feele yet the fire
That made me to ryse er yt were° day—
And this was now the first morwe° of May—
With dredful° hert and glad devocioun,
For to ben at the resureccioun
Of this flour, whan that yt shulde unclose
Agayn° the sonne, that roos as red as rose,
That in the brest was of the beste° that day
That Agenores doghtre ladde° away.
And doun on knes anoon-ryght° I me sette,
And as I koude°, this fresshe flour I grette°,
Knelyng alwey, til it unclosed was,
Upon the smale, softe, swote° gras,
That was with floures swote enbrouded al°,
Of swich° swetnesse and swich odour overal,
That, for to speke of gomme°, or herbe, or tree,
Comparisoun may noon ymaked bee,
For yt surmounteth° pleynly alle odoures,
And of riche beaute alle floures.

---

61 gynneth weste, *begins to set* **64 chere,** *face* **67 aryght,** *properly* **68 han konnyng,** *have knowledge* **69 make,** *write* **71 forthren,** *advance* **73 wot,** *know,* **han her-biforne,** *have before this time* **74 Of makyng ropen,** *reaped the harvest of poetry,* **led,** *taken,* **corne,** *grain* **75 glenynge,** *gleaning* **76 ere,** *ear* (of grain) **78 it happen me rehercen eft,** *I may happen to repeat again* **79 That,** *what* **80 Forbereth,** *bear with,* **beth,** *be,* **evele apayde,** *displeased* **81 Syn that,** *since* **82 eke,** *also* **83 witte or myght,** *knowledge or ability* **84 clerenesse,** *brightness,* **verray,** *true* **85 wynt,** *turns* **86 yow dredeth,** *honors you* **87 verrayly,** *truly* **89 knyt so in youre bond,** *so tied up in your bonds* **91 soune,** *sound* **92 mowe ye,** *are you able to* **93 Swich vois,** *such voice,* **yow lyst,** *you desire,* **pleyne,** *lament* **94 gide,** *guide* **97 wherfore,** *the reason,* **spak,** *spoke* **98 doon hem,** *do them* **99 that,** *so that,* **mosten,** *must* **100 then,** *than,* **at eighe,** *with eyes,* **elles preve,** *otherwise prove* **102 attones,** *at once* **103 besy gost,** *eager spirit,* **thursteth,** *thirsts* **105 so gledy,** *such glowing* **107 er yt were,** *before it was* **108 morwe,** *morning* **109 dredful,** *fearful* **112 Agayn,** *toward* **113 beste,** *beast* **114 ladde,** *led* **115 anoon-ryght,** *quickly* **116 koude,** *could,* **grette,** *paid respect to* **118 swote,** *sweet* **119 swote enbrouded al,** *all sweetly embroidered* **120 swich,** *such* **121 gomme,** (aromatic) *gum* **123 surmounteth,** *surpasses*

62 wol go to reste, the inner petals of the English daisy close at night. **66–77** Generally regarded as Chaucer's tribute to the French poets who inspired him. **69 make,** to compose or write; see *MED* māken (v.) 1.5. **72 the leef or . . . the flour,** in court games and celebrations, participants divided into contesting or debating groups, one side associated with or defending the leaf; the other, the flower. **74–76 Of maykyng ropen . . . glenyng . . . ,** rooted in the biblical Book of Ruth, reaping or harvesting is here a conventional figure for poetic inspiration; gleaning suggests that the poet follows in the footsteps of his predecessors and, as in Ruth, benefits greatly in the process. Chaucer uses a similar figure at *PF* 22–25. **86–96** In these lines, the narrator shifts from addressing lovers in general to a direct address and invocation of the object of his affection—the flower, which is a figure for his lady. The shift may be due to the influence of Boccaccio's *Filostrato* 1.1–6, where there is some similar conventional imagery and a shift from direct to general address. **102 al,** omitted in F. **108 this,** omitted in F. **111 that,** omitted in F. **113–14 beste . . . Agenores doghtre,** the beast that ravished Europa, Agenor's daughter, was a bull, Zeus in disguise. Chaucer is saying that the sun was in the central portion (**brest**) of the zodiacal sign of Taurus the Bull on May 1, a loosely accurate astronomical reference. **120 odour,** the English daisy is not a particularly fragrant flower, but the praise is conventional. **124 alle,** F reads "of."

Forgeten° had the erthe his pore estat°
Of wynter, that hym naked made and mat°,
And with his swerd of cold so sore greved.
Now hath th'atempre° sonne all that releved,
That naked was, and clad him new agayn.
The smale foules°, of the sesoun fayn°,
That from the panter° and the net ben scaped,
Upon the foweler°, that hem made awhaped°
In wynter, and distroyed hadde hire broode°,
In his dispit hem thoghte° yt did hem goode
To synge of hym and in hir song despise
The foule cherl° that for his coveytise°
Had hem betrayed with his sophistrye°.
This was hire song, "The foweler we deffye°,
And al his craft." And somme songen° clere
Layes° of love, that joye it was to here,
In worshipynge and preysinge of hir make°.
And for the newe blisful somers° sake,
Upon the braunches ful of blosmes softe,
In hire delyte they turned hem ful ofte,
And songen, "Blessed be Seynt Valentyne,
For on his day I chees° yow to be myne,
Withouten repentyng, myn herte swete!"
And therwithalle° hire bekes° gonnen meete°,
Yeldyng° honour and humble obeysaunces°
To love, and diden hire other observaunces
That longeth onto° love and to nature—
Construeth that as yow lyst°, I do no cure°.
And thoo° that hadde doon unkyndenesse,
As dooth the tydif°, for newfangelnesse°,
Besoghte mercy of hir trespassynge,
And humblely songen° hire repentynge,
And sworen on the blosmes to be trewe,
So that hire makes° wolde upon hem rewe°,
And at the laste maden hire acord.
Al° founde they Daunger° for a tyme a lord,
Yet Pitee, thurgh his stronge gentil° myght,
Forgaf, and made Mercy passen Ryght°,
Thurgh Innocence and ruled° Curtesye.
But I ne clepe° nat innocence folye,
Ne fals pitee, for vertu is the mene°,
As *Etik* seith—in swich° maner I mene.
And thus thise foweles, voide of al° malice,
Acordeden to love, and laften vice°
Of hate, and songen alle of oon acorde,
"Welcome, somer, oure governour and lorde."
  And Zepherus and Flora gentilly
Yaf° to the floures softe and tenderly
Hire swoote° breth, and made hem for to sprede,
As god and goddesse of the floury mede°.
In which me thoghte I myghte, day by day,
Dwellen alwey, the joly month of May,
Withouten slep, withouten mete° or drynke.
Adoun ful softely I gan to synke°,
And lenynge on myn elbowe and my syde,
The longe day I shoop me° for t'abide
For nothing elles, and I shal nat lye,
But for to loke upon the dayesie°,
That wel by reson men it calle may
The "dayesye," or elles the "eye of day,"
The emperice° and flour of floures alle.
I praye to God that faire mote she falle°,
And alle that loven floures, for hire sake!
  But natheles, ne wene nat° that I make°
In preysing of the flour agayn° the leef,
No more than of the corn agayn the sheef,
For as° to me nys lever noon ne lother°.
I nam withholden° yit with never nother°,
Ne I not° who serveth leef, ne who the flour—
Wel browken they her° service or labour.

---

125 Forgeten, *forgotten,* **pore estat,** *poor condition* **126 mat,** *defeated* **128 th'atempre,** *the temperate* (warm) **130 foules,** *birds,* **fayn,** *joyous* **131 panter,** *snare* **132 Upon the foweler,** *about the bird hunter,* **awhaped,** *terrified* **133 hire broode,** *their offspring* **134 In his dispit hem thoghte,** *to scorn him they thought* **136 foule cherl,** *rotten villain,* **coveytise,** *greed* **137 sophistrye,** *trickery* **138 deffye,** *defy* **139 songen,** *sang* **140 Layes,** *songs* **141 hir make,** *their mates* **142 somers,** *summer's* **146 chees,** *choose* **148 therwithalle,** *with that,* **hire bekes,** *their beaks,* **gonnen meete,** *did meet* **149 Yeldyng,** *submitting,* **obeysaunces,** *services* **151 longeth onto,** *pertain to* **152 lyst,** *wish,* **do no cure,** *don't care* **153 thoo,** *those* **154 tydif,** *bird,* **newfangelnesse,** *fickleness* **156 songen,** *sang* **158 makes,** *mates,* **rewe,** *have pity* **160 Al,** *although,* **Daunger,** *Disdain* **161 gentil,** *noble* **162 passen Ryght,** *overcome Justice* **163 ruled,** *restrained* **164 clepe,** *call* **165 mene,** (golden) *mean* **166 swich,** *such* **167 voide of al,** *lacking any* **168 laften vice,** *abandoned the vice* **172 Yaf,** *gave* **173 Hire swoote,** *their sweet* **174 mede,** *meadow* **177 mete,** *food* **178 gan to synke,** *did sink* **180 shoop me,** *prepared myself* **182 dayesie,** *daisy* **185 emperice,** *empress* **186 faire mote she falle,** *good may befall her* **188 ne wene nat,** *don't think,* **make,** *compose* **189 agayn,** *against* **191 For as,** *because,* **nys lever noon ne lother,** *neither one is more pleasing nor displeasing* **192 nam withholden,** *am not committed,* **never nother,** *neither one nor the other* **193 Ne I not,** *nor do I know* **194 Wel browken they her,** *well may they enjoy their*

125–29 The figure of re-clothing the earth in springtime derives from *Roman de la Rose* 57–62. **141 and,** F reads "and in." **145 Seynt Valentyne,** see *PF* 309n. Poems celebrating St. Valentine's Day developed as a sub-genre in Chaucer's time. Because there appears to have been more than one medieval St. Valentine, there is no real discrepancy between the May setting here and the now traditional date of celebration, February 14. **154 tydif,** the species of bird is unidentified, although it was evidently reputed to be fickle; see *SqT* 5.648. **164 ne clepe,** F reads "ne it clepe." **166 Etik,** Aristotle's *Ethics.* **171–74 Zepherus and Flora,** the West Wind and the goddess of flowers, affiliated in *Roman de la Rose* 8411ff. Compare *BD* 402–04 and *CT* 1.5–6. **184 "eye of day,"** this etymology of *daisy* is correct.

For this thing is al of another tonne°,
Of olde storye, er swich stryf° was begonne.
  Whan that the sonne out of the south gan west°,
And that this flour gan close° and goon° to rest
For derknesse of the nyght, the which she dred°,
Hom to myn hous ful swiftly I me sped
To goon to reste, and erly for to ryse,
To seen this flour to sprede°, as I devyse°.
And in a litel herber° that I have,
Ibenched newe with turves fressh ygrave°,
I bad° men sholde me my couche make,
For deyntee° of the newe someres° sake—
I bad hem strawen° floures on my bed.
Whan I was leyd°, and had myn eyen hed°,
I fel on slepe in-with° an houre or twoo.
Me mette° how I lay in the medewe thoo°,
To seen this flour that I so love and drede;
And from afer come walkyng in the mede°
The God of Love, and in his hand° a quene,
And she was clad in real habit grene°.
A fret° of gold she hadde next her heer,
And upon that a whyt corowne she beer°
With flourouns° smale. And I shal nat lye,
For al the world, ryght° as a dayesye°
Ycorouned° ys with white leves lyte°,
So were the flowrouns of hire coroune white.
For of o perle fyne°, oriental,
Hire white coroune was ymaked al,
For which the white coroune above the grene
Made hire lyke a daysie for to sene°,
Considered eke° the fret of golde above.
  Yclothed was this myghty God of Love
In silk, enbrouded° ful of grene greves°,
In-with a fret° of rede rose-leves,
The fresshest syn° the world was first bygonne.
His gilte° heer was corowned with a sonne,
Instede of gold, for° hevynesse and wyghte°.
Therwith me thoghte his face shoon so bryghte
That wel unnethes° myghte I him beholde.
And in his hand me thoghte I saugh° nim holde
Twoo firy dartes, as the gledes° rede.
And aungelyke hys wynges saugh I sprede.
And al be that° men seyn that blynd ys he,
Algate° me thoghte that he myghte se,
For sternely on me he gan byholde°,
So that his loking dooth° myn herte colde.
And by the hand he held this noble quene,
Corowned with white, and clothed al in grene,
So womanly, so benigne°, and so meke,
That in this world, thogh that men wolde seke,
Half hire beaute shulde men nat fynde
In creature that formed ys by kynde°.
And therfore may I seyn°, as thynketh me°,
This song in preysyng of this lady fre°.

[Balade]

  Hyd°, Absolon, thy gilte tresses clere°;
Ester, ley thou thy mekenesse al adown°;
Hyd, Jonathas, al thy frendly manere;
Penalopee and Marcia Catoun,

---

195 al of another tonne, *wholly from a different barrel,* i.e., *of a completely different sort* **196 er swich stryf,** *before such conflict* **197 gan west,** *went west* **198 gan close,** *closed,* **goon,** *went* **199 dred,** *feared* **202 to sprede,** *open,* **devyse,** *describe* **203 herber,** *garden* **204 Ibenched newe with turves fressh ygrave,** *newly furnished with benches made of fresh turf* **205 bad,** *directed* **206 deyntee,** *delight,* **someres,** *summer's* **207 strawen,** *to scatter* (strew) **208 was leyd,** *had laid down,* **hed,** *closed* (hidden) **209 in-with,** *within* **210 Me mette,** *I dreamed,* **medewe thoo,** *meadow then* **212 mede,** *meadow* **213 in his hand,** *leading by the hand* **214 real habit grene,** *green royal clothing* **215 fret,** *decorative hairnet* **216 beer,** *wore* **217 flourouns,** *petals* (see n.) **218 ryght,** *just,* **dayesye,** *daisy* **219 Ycorouned,** *crowned,* **leves lyte,** *little petals* **221 o perle fyne,** *one superb pearl* **224 sene,** *see* **225 Considered eke,** *taking into account also* **227 enbrouded,** *embroidered,* **greves,** *branches* **228 In-with a fret,** *within* (wearing) *a net* **229 syn,** *since* **230 gilte,** *golden* **231 for,** *because of,* **wyghte,** *weight* **233 wel unnethes,** *scarcely* **234 saugh,** *saw* **235 gledes,** *live coals* **237 al be that,** *even though* **238 Algate,** *nevertheless* **239 gan beholde,** *did look* **240 dooth,** *makes* **243 benigne,** *gracious* **246 kynde,** *nature* **247 seyn,** *say,* **as thynketh me,** *so I think* **248 fre,** *noble* **249 Hyd,** *hide,* **gilte tresses clere,** *bright golden hair* **250 ley . . . adown,** *lay down*

196 stryf, F reads "thinge." **202 to sprede,** F omits "to." **214–25** Probably derived from Machaut, *Dit de la Fleur de Lis et de la Marguerite* (*Poem of the Lily and the Daisy*) 213ff. **211–12** F transposes these lines. **217 flourouns,** the *MED* lists this as the only instance of the word, meaning "petal," but the *OED* includes it as a variant of *fleuron,* defined as "flower-shaped ornament." Also at line 529. **230 corowned with a sonne,** at G160–61, the God of Love is crowned with a garland of rose leaves and lilies rather than this unusual sun-crown. Either may have suggested Richard II to Chaucer's audience, the latter especially. **231 Instede,** F reads "Istede." **244–45** The two lines are conflated in F: "That in this world thogh that men nat fynde." **249–69** This embedded lyric follows the strict form of the ballade, three stanzas (here rhyme royal) of through-rhyme with a refrain. Evidently Chaucer was inspired by one or more of several French ballades by Machaut, Froissart, and others that include related catalogs of names. In the *MLP* 2.60–89 a related list of names is given, there presented as the contents of a book by Chaucer called "The Seintes Legende of Cupide" (2.61), an alternate title for *LGW.* No satisfactory explanation has been given for discrepancies between the two lists and the actual contents of *LGW,* although there have been conjectures that *LGW* was a work in-progress or abandoned; 554–55n. **249** Line omitted in F. **Absolon,** biblical son of David, known for his beauty. **250 Ester,** biblical ideal of meekness. **251 Jonathas,** biblical friend of David. **252 Penalopee,** Penelope, faithful wife of Odysseus. **Marcia Catoun,** wife or daughter of Cato, both named Marcia, and both examples of fidelity.

Make of youre wifhod no comparysoun;
Hyde ye youre beautes, Ysoude and Eleyne:
My lady cometh, that al this may disteyne°.

Thy faire body, lat yt nat appere,
Lavyne; and thou, Lucresse of Rome toun,
And Polixene, that boghten love so dere,
And Cleopatre, with al thy passyoun°,
Hyde ye your trouthe° of love and your renoun;
And thou, Tesbe, that hast for love such peyne:
My lady cometh, that al this may disteyne.

Herro, Dido, Laudomia, alle yfere°,
And Phillis, hangyng for thy Demophoun,
And Canace, espied° by thy chere°,
Ysiphile, betraysed with Jasoun,
Maketh of your trouthe neythir boost° ne soun°;
Nor Ypermystre or Adriane, ye tweyne°:
My lady cometh that al this may dysteyne.

This balade may ful wel ysongen be,
As I have seyd erst°, by° my lady free°,
For certeynly al thise mowe° nat suffise
To apperen° wyth my lady in no wyse.
For as the sonne wole the fyr disteyne°,
So passeth° al my lady sovereyne,
That ys so good, so faire, so debonayre°—
I prey to God that ever falle hire faire°!
For nadde° comfort ben of hire presence,
I hadde ben ded, withouten any defence°,
For drede° of Loves wordes and his chere°,
As, when tyme ys, herafter ye shal here.

Behynde this God of Love, upon the grene
I saugh° comyng of ladyes nyntene°,
In real habit°, a ful esy paas°,
And after hem° coome of wymen swich a traas°
That syn° that God Adam hadde mad of erthe
The thridde part of mankynde, or the ferthe,
Ne wende° I not by possibilitee
Had ever in this wide world ybee°—
And trewe of love° thise women were echon°.
Now wheither was that a wonder thing or non,
That ryght anoon° as that they gonne espye°
Thys flour which that I clepe° the dayesie,
Ful sodeynly they stynten° al attones°,
And kneled doun, as it were for the nones°,
And songen with o vois° "Heel° and honour
To trouthe of womanhede, and to this flour
That bereth our alder pris in figurynge°.
Hire white corowne bereth the witnessynge."
And with that word, a-compas enviroun°,
They setten hem ful softely adoun.
First sat the God of Love, and syth° his quene
With the white corowne, clad in grene,
And sithen° al the remenaunt by and by°,
As they were of estaat°, ful curteysly.
Ne nat a word was spoken in the place
The mountaunce of a furlong wey of space°.
I, knelyng by this flour, in good entente,
Abood° to knowen what this peple mente°,
As stille as any ston, til at the last
This God of Love on me hys eyen° cast
And seyde, "Who kneleth there?" And I answerde
Unto his askynge, whan that I it herde,

---

255 disteyne, *outshine* **259 passyoun,** *suffering* **260 trouthe,** *faithfulness* **263 yfere,** *together* **265 espied,** *recognized,* **chere,** *demeanor* **267 boost,** *boast,* **soun,** *brag* **268 tweyne,** *two* **271 erst,** *before,* **by,** *about,* **free,** *noble* **272 mowe,** *might* **273 apperen,** *be equal* **274 disteyne,** *outshine* **275 passeth,** *surpasses* **276 debonayre,** *gracious* **277 ever falle hire faire,** *good may always happen to her* **278 nadde,** *had not* **279 withouten any defence,** *without any doubt* **280 drede,** *fear,* **chere,** *demeanor* **283 saugh,** *saw,* **of ladyes nyntene,** *nineteen ladies* **284 real habit,** *royal clothing,* **a ful esy paas,** (walking) *at a slow pace* **285 hem,** *them,* **swich a traas,** *such a procession* **286 syn,** *since* **288 wende,** *thought* **289 ybee,** *been* **290 trewe of love,** *faithful in love,* **echon,** *each one* **292 ryght anoon,** *as soon,* **gonne espye,** *saw* **293 clepe,** *call* **294 stynten,** *stopped,* **attones,** *at once* **295 nones,** *occasion* **296 o vois,** *one voice, prosperity* **298 bereth our alder pris in figurynge,** i.e., *represents the best of us* **300 a-compas enviroun,** *all around* **302 syth,** *after* **304 sithin,** *then,* **by and by,** *side by side* **305 As they were of estaat,** *according to their rank* **307 The mountaunce of a furlong wey of space,** *for the time it takes to walk an eighth of a mile* (i.e., for a short while) **309 Abood,** *waited,* **mente,** *intended* **311 eyen,** *eyes*

254 Ysoude, Iseult, whose beauty overwhelmed Tristan. **Eleyne,** Helen of Troy, whose beauty provoked the Trojan War. **257 Lavyne,** Lavinia, wife of Aeneas, founder of Rome. **Lucresse,** Lucretia; raped by Tarquinius, she chose suicide rather than to live in dishonor; see legend 5. **258 Polixene,** Polyxena, daughter of Priam of Troy and beloved of Achilles, was sacrificed on the tomb of Achilles to be reunited with him. **259 Cleopatre,** queen of Egypt and beloved of Julius Caesar and Marc Antony; see legend 1. **261 Tesbe,** Thisbe, committed suicide for love of Pyramus; see legend 2. **263-69** These lines are misplaced in F after line 277. **263 Herro,** Hero, beloved of Leander. **Dido,** died for love of Aeneas; see legend 3. **Laudomia,** Laodomya, beloved wife of Protesilaus. **264 Phillis . . . Demophoun,** see legend 8. **265 Canace,** loved her brother incestuously; specifically excluded from the list of Cupid's saints in *MLP* 2.77–80. **266 Ysiphile . . . Jasoun,** Jason's betrayal of Hypsipyle is part of legend 4. **268 Ypermystre,** Hypermnestra, punished because unwilling to kill her husband; see legend 9. **Adriane,** Ariadne was abandoned by Theseus after helping him to defeat the Minotaur; see legend 6. **283 ladyes nyntene,** the number has not been explained; 18 women are named in the ballade at 249–69, along with two men. **298 bereth our alder pris in figurynge,** complex syntax: represents (bears in figuring) the value or honor (pris) of all of us.

And seyde, "Sir, it am I," and com him nere°,
And salwed° him. Quod he, "What dostow° here
So nygh° myn oune floure, so boldely?
Yt were better worthy°, trewely,
A worm to neghen ner° my flour than thow."
"And why, sire," quod I, "and yt lyke yow°?"
"For thow," quod he, "art therto nothing able°.
Yt is my relyke°, digne° and delytable°,
And thow my foo, and al my folk werreyest°,
And of myn olde servauntes thow mysseyest°,
And hynderest hem with thy translacioun,
And lettest° folk from hire devocioun
To serve me, and holdest° it folye
To serve Love. Thou maist yt nat denye,
For in pleyn text, withouten nede of glose°,
Thou hast translated the *Romaunce of the Rose*
That is an heresye ayeins° my lawe,
And makest wise folk fro me withdrawe.
And of Crescyde thou hast seyde as the lyste°,
That maketh men to wommen lasse triste°,
That ben as trewe as ever was any steel.
Of thyn answere avise the° ryght weel,
For thogh thou reneyed° hast my lay°,
As other wrecches han doon many a day,
By Seynt Venus, that my moder ys,
If that thou lyve, thou shalt repenten this
So cruelly that it shal wel be sene!"
Thoo° spak this lady, clothed al in grene,
And seyde, "God, ryght of° youre curtesye,
Ye moten herken° yf he can replye
Agayns al this that ye have to him meved°.
A god ne sholde nat be thus agreved°,
But of hys deitee he shal be stable,
And therto gracious and merciable.
And yf ye nere° a god that knowen al,
Thanne myght yt be as I yow tellen shal:
This man to yow may falsly ben accused,
That as by right him oughte ben excused.
For in youre court ys many a losengeour°,
And many a queynte totelere accusour°,
That tabouren° in youre eres many a soun
Ryght after° hire ymagynacioun
To have youre daliance°, and for envie.
Thise ben the causes, and I shal not lye.
Envie ys lavendere° of the court alway,
For she ne parteth° neither nyght ne day
Out of the hous of Cesar—thus seith Dante.
Whoso that gooth°, algate° she wol nat wante°.
And eke°, peraunter°, for° this man ys nyce°,
He myghte doon yt gessyng° no malice,
But for he useth thynges for to make°—
Hym rekketh° noght of what matere he take—
Or him was boden maken thilke tweye°
Of somme persone, and durste° yt nat withseye°,
Or him repenteth outrely° of this.
He ne hath nat doon so grevously amys°,
To translaten that° olde clerkes° writen,
As thogh that° he of malice wolde enditen°
Despite° of love, and had himself yt wroght°.
This shoolde a ryghtwis° lord have in his thoght,

---

314 nere, *nearer* **315 salwed,** *greeted,* **dostow,** *are you doing* **316 nygh,** *near* **317 Yt were better worthy,** *it would be better* **318 neghen ner,** *approach near* **319 and yt lyke yow,** *if you please* **320 art therto nothyng able,** *are not worthy of it* **321 relyke,** *treasure* (relic), **digne,** *noble,* **delytable,** *delightful* **322 werreyest,** *wage war against* **323 mysseyest,** *slander* **325 lettest,** *impede* **326 holdest,** *consider* **328 glose,** *interpretation* **330 heresye ayeins,** *heresy against* **332 the lyste,** *you please* **333 lasse triste,** *trust less* **335 avise the,** *consider* **336 reneyed,** *denied,* **lay,** *law* **341 Thoo,** *then* **342 ryght of,** *in accord with* **343 moten herken,** *must hear* **344 to him meved,** *accused him of* **345 agreved,** *angry* **348 nere,** *weren't* **352 losengeour,** *liar* **353 queynte totelere accusour,** *clever, tattling accuser* **354 tabouren,** *drums* **355 Ryght after,** *wholly in accord with* **356 daliance,** *private attention* **358 lavendere,** *washer woman* **359 parteth,** *departs* **361 Whoso that gooth,** *regardless who leaves,* **algate,** *nevertheless,* **wante,** *lack* **362 eke,** *also,* **peraunter,** *perhaps,* **for,** *because,* **nyce,** *foolish* **363 gessyng,** *thinking* **364 for he useth thynges for to make,** *because he is accustomed to writing poetry* **365 rekketh,** *cares* **366 boden,** *commanded* (to), **thilke tweye,** *these two* **367 durste,** *dared,* **withseye,** *refuse* **368 outrely,** *utterly* **369 amys,** *wrong* **370 that,** *what,* **clerkes,** *scholars* **371 As thogh that,** *as if,* **wolde enditen,** *intended to compose* **372 Despite,** *scorn,* **wroght,** *invented* **373 ryghtwis,** *righteous*

314 Sir, omitted in F. **326** Line omitted in F. **329** ***Romaunce of the Rose,*** for Chaucer's translation of the *Roman de la Rose,* or part of it, see the Introduction to his *Romaunt of the Rose.* Portions of the *Roman* are anti-love and antifeminist, at least ironically, although the extant *Romaunt* does not contain these portions. **332 of Creseyde,** in Chaucer's *Troylus and Criseyde,* Criseyde decides to stay with Diomedes in the Greek camp rather than returning to Troylus as she promised. **338 Seynt Venus,** Holy Venus; the Wife of Bath uses the same label for Venus, *WBP* 3.604. **moder,** Venus is the mother of Cupid in classical mythology. **342–408** Critics have read this speech, in the tradition of "advice to princes," as addressed to Richard II, with the lady who speaks it representing either his wife, Anne, or his mother, Joan. **360 seith Dante,** from *Inferno* 13.64–65, where envy is called a whore who never turns her eyes from the house of Caesar, a figure for any ruler. In Dante, the claim is spoken by Pier delle Vigne who, like Chaucer, was both poet and court servant. Chaucer's replacement of *whore* with *washerwoman* (line 358) captures the notion that court gossip is "dirty laundry." **364 But,** omitted in F. **366 Or,** F reads "Of."

And nat be lyk tirauntez° of Lumbardye
That han no reward° but at° tyrannye,
For he that kynge or lord ys naturel,
Hym oghte nat be tiraunt ne crewel,
As is a fermour°, to doon the harm he kan.
He moste thinke° yt is his leege man°,
And° is his tresour, and his gold in cofre°.
This is the sentence° of the philosophre,
A kyng to kepe° his leeges in justice—
Withouten doute, that is his office°.
Al° wol he kepe his lordes hire degree°,
As it ys ryght and skilful° that they bee
Enhaunced and honoured and most dere—
For they ben half-goddes in this world here—
Yit mot° he doon bothe ryght to poore and ryche,
Al be that° hire estaat be nat yliche°,
And han of poore folk compassyoun.
For loo° the gentil kynde° of the lyoun°,
For whan a flye offendeth him or biteth,
He with his tayle awey the flye smyteth°
Al esely, for of hys genterye°
Hym deyneth not° to wreke hym° on a flye,
As dooth a curre° or elles another best°.
In noble corage oughte ben arest°,
And weyen° everything by equytee°,
And ever have reward° to his owen degree°.
For, syr, yt is no maistrye° for a lorde
To dampen° a man without answere of worde°,
And for a lord, that is ful foul to use°.
And if so be he may hym nat excuse,
But asketh mercy with a sorweful herte,
And profereth him° ryght in his bare sherte
To ben ryght at your owen jugement,
Than° oght a god, by short avysement°,
Consydre his owne° honour and hys trespas°.
"For syth° no cause of deth lyeth° in this caas°,
Yow oghte to ben the lighter° merciable—
Leteth° youre ire°, and beth° sumwhat tretable°.
The man hath served yow of his kunnyng°,
And furthred wel youre lawe in his makyng°.
Al be hit that° he kan nat wel endite°,
Yet hath he maked lewed° folk delyte
To serve yow, in preysing of your name.
He made the book that hight° the *Hous of Fame*,
And eke° the *Deeth of Blaunche the Duchesse*,
And the *Parlement of Foules*, as I gesse,
And al the love of *Palamon and Arcite*
Of Thebes, thogh the storye ys knowen lyte°;
And many an ympne° for your halydayes°,
That highten° balades, roundels, virelayes;
And for to speke of other holynesse°,
He hath in prose translated *Boece*,
And maad the lyf also of *Seynt Cecile*.
He made also, goon ys a gret while°,
Origenes upon the Maudeleyne.
Hym oughte now to have the lesse peyne;

---

374 tirauntez, *tyrants* **375 reward,** *esteem,* **at,** *through* **378 fermour,** *tax collector* **379 thinke,** *remember,* **leege man,** *sworn follower* (liege) **380 And,** *that,* **cofre,** *treasury* **381 sentence,** *message* **382 kepe,** *protect* **383 office,** *duty* **384 Al,** *although,* **kepe his lordes hire degree,** *protect the status of his lords* **385 skilful,** *reasonable* **388 Yit mot,** *yet must* **389 Al be that,** *even though,* **yliche,** *alike* **391 loo,** *consider,* **gentil kynde,** *noble nature,* **lyoun,** *lion* **393 smyteth,** *swats* **394 genterye,** *nobility* **395 Hym deyneth not,** *he does not lower himself,* **wreke hym,** *take revenge* **396 curre,** *mongrel dog,* **best,** *beast* **397 ben arest,** *to be restraint* **398 weyen,** *to weigh,* **equytee,** *fairness* **399 reward,** *regard,* **degree,** *rank* **400 maistrye,** *great accomplishment* **401 dampne,** *condemn,* **answere of worde,** *opportunity to reply* **402 ful foul to use,** *very bad practice* **405 profereth him,** *offers himself* **407 Than,** *then,* **short avysement,** *brief deliberation* **408 his owne,** i.e., *the lord's own,* **hys trepas,** i.e., *the offense of the accused* **409 For syth,** *because,* **lyeth,** *is involved,* **caas,** *case* **410 the lyghter,** *more easily* **411 Leteth,** *let go,* **ire,** *anger,* **beth,** *be,* **tretable,** *flexible* **412 of his kunnyng,** *according to his ability* **413 makyng,** *writing* **414 Al be hit that,** *even though,* **endite,** *write* **415 lewed,** *unlearned* **417 hight,** *is called* **418 eke,** *also* **421 lyte,** *little* **422 ympne,** *hymn,* **halydayes,** *holy days* **423 highten,** *are called* **424 other holynesse,** *other virtues* **427 goon ys a gret while,** *a long time ago*

374 tirauntez of Lumbardye, Lombardy is a region in Italy that Chaucer and his contemporaries associated with the tyrannical rule of despotic families, particularly the Visconti of Milan. Compare *ClT* 4.72 and John Gower, *Mirour de l'Omme* (*Mirror of Mankind*) 23233. **381 the philosophre,** a common way of referring to Aristotle. Proper royal government is a recurrent topic in the various versions of the *Secreta Secretorum,* attributed to Aristotle in the Middle Ages. There are also general similarities between Chaucer's comments (lines 376–90) and those in John Gower, *Vox Clamantis* (*Voice Crying*) 6.581 and 1001, and *Confessio Amantis* (*Confession of the Lover*) 7.2695–764. **388 poore and ryche,** a common topic in medieval discussions of kingship; see Gower, *Vox Clamantis* 6.741ff. and *Confessio Amantis* 7.2743. **418 *Deeth of Blaunche the Duchesse,*** i.e., Chaucer's *Book of the Duchess.* **399 to,** F reads "unto." **420 *Palamon and Arcite,*** Chaucer's story that he later incorporated into *CT* as the *Knight's Tale.* **423 balades, roundels, virelayes**, ballades, roundels, and virelays are three of the "fixed forms" (*forme fixes*) of French lyric. If Chaucer wrote many of them, few survive that are attributed with much confidence: two roundels (*PF* 680–92 and perhaps *Merciless Beaute*), several love ballades (see e.g., *To Rosemounde* and portions of *Complaint of Venus*), and two sections of *Anelida and Arcite* (lines 256–71 and 317–32) that reflect the influence of the virelay. See *Ret.* 10.1087 and the Introduction to Chaucer's short poems in this text. **425 *Boece,*** Chaucer's translation of Boethius's *Consolation of Philosophy.* **426 *Seynt Cecile,*** Chaucer later incorporated his version of the life of St. Cecilia into *CT* as the *Second Nun's Tale.* **428 *Origenes . . . Maudeleyne,*** Origen upon Magdalene. Most scholars agree that this refers to a lost translation by Chaucer of a popular Latin sermon of womanly virtue, *De Maria Magdalena* (*Concerning Mary Magdalene*), attributed to Origen, a third-century theologian and philosopher.

He hath maad many a lay° and many a thinge.
  "Now as ye be a god and eke° a kynge,
I, your Alceste, whilom° quene of Trace,
Y aske yow this man, ryght of° your grace,
That ye him never hurte in al his lyve.
And° he shal swere to yow, and that as blyve°,
He shal no more agilten° in this wyse,
But he shal maken° as ye wol devyse,
Of wommen trewe in lovyng al hire lyf,
Wher so ye wol°, of mayden or of wyf,
And forthren° yow as muche as he mysseyde°
Or° in the *Rose* or elles in *Creseyde*."
  The God of Love answerde hire thus anoon,
"Madame," quod he, "it is so long agoon°
That I yow knew° so charitable and trewe,
That never yit, syn that° the world was newe,
To me ne found y better noon than yee.
If that I wol save my degree°,
I may, ne wol°, nat werne° your requeste.
Al lyeth° in yow; dooth° wyth hym as yow leste°.
I al foryeve° withouten lenger space°—
For whoso° yeveth a yift, or dooth a grace°,
Do it bytyme°, his thank ys° wel the more.
And demeth ye° what he shal doo therfore.
Goo thanke now my lady here," quod he.
  I roos, and doun I sette me on my knee,
And seyde thus, "Madame, the God above
Foryelde° yow that ye the God of Love
Han maked me his wrathe to foryive°,
And yeve me grace so long for to lyve
That I may knowe soothly° what ye bee,
That han me holpe° and put in this degree°.
But trewely I wende°, as in this cas,
Naught have agilt°, ne doon to love trespas.
For-why° a trewe° man, withouten drede°,
Hath nat to parten with° a theves dede°;
Ne a trewe lover oght me not to blame,
Thogh that I speke a fals lovere som shame.
They oghte rather with me for to holde°
For that° I of Creseyde wroot or tolde,
Or of the Rose, what so° myn auctour mente.
Algate°, God woot°, yt was myn entente
To forthren° trouthe in love and yt cheryce°,
And to ben war fro° falsnesse and fro vice
By swich° ensample—this was my menynge."
  And she answerde, "Lat be° thyn arguynge,
For love ne wol nat countrepleted° be
In ryght ne wrong; and lerne that of me.
Thow hast thy grace°, and hold the° ryght therto.
Now wol I seyn° what penance thou shalt do
For thy trespas, and understonde yt here:
Thow shalt, while that thou lyvest, yer by yere,
The most partye° of thy tyme spende
In makyng of a glorious legende°
Of goode wymmen, maydenes and wyves,
That weren trewe in lovyng al hire lyves;
And telle of false men that hem bytraien°,

---

430 lay, *poem* **431 eke,** *also* **432 whilom,** *once* **433 ryght of,** *in accord with* **435 And,** *if,* **as blyve,** *eagerly* **436 agilten,** *offend* **437 maken,** *write* **439 Wher so ye wol,** *whichever you wish* **440 forthren,** *promote,* **mysseyde,** *insulted* **441 Or,** *either* **443 so long agoon,** *a very long time* **444 yow knew,** *have known you to be* **445 syn that,** *since* **447 save my degree,** *preserve my status* **448 wol,** *will,* **werne,** *refuse* **449 lyeth,** *lies,* **dooth,** *do,* **leste,** *please* **450 al foryeve,** *forgive everything,* **space,** *time* **451 whoso,** *whoever,* **dooth a grace,** *does a favor* **452 Do it bytyme,** *if he does it promptly,* **thank ys,** *thanks are* **453 demeth ye,** *you judge* **457 Foryelde,** *reward* **458 foryive,** *give up* **460 soothly,** *truly* **461 holpe,** *helped,* **degree,** *status* **462 wende,** *think* **463 agilt,** *offended* **464 For-why,** *because,* **trewe,** *honest,* **withouten drede,** *no doubt* **465 to parten with** *share,* **theves dede,** *thief's deed* **468 with me for to holde,** *to agree with me* **469 For that,** *because* **470 what so,** *whatever* **471 Algate,** *nevertheless,* **woot,** *knows* **472 forthren,** *advance,* **cheryce,** *cherish* **473 ben war fro,** *give warning against* **474 swich,** *such* **475 Lat be,** *stop* **476 countrepleted,** *contradicted* **478 grace,** *forgiveness,* **the,** *yourself* **479 seyn,** *say* **482 most partye,** *greater part* **483 legende,** *collection of stories* **486 hem bytraien,** *betray them*

432 Alceste of Trace, Alcestis, usually queen of Thessaly, not Thrace, was an ideal of wifely devotion in classical mythology; she gave her own life to retrieve her husband Admetus from death. In some versions, Hercules rescues her from the underworld, but in no version except Chaucer's is she turned into a daisy, a detail that Chaucer gives at 512. She is elsewhere mentioned in Chaucer's *TC* (5.1527–33, 1778), and his knowledge of the story could derive from several possible sources, including Jerome, *Adversus Jovinian* (*Against Jovinian*), 1.45, and Valerius Maximus, *Factorum ac Dictorum Memorabilia Libri IX* (*Nine Books of Memorable Deeds and Sayings*) 4.6.1. For John Gower's version, see *Confessio Amantis* (*Confession of the Lover*), 7.1917–43 and 8.2640–46. **433–41 Y aske yow . . . ,** aristocratic female intercession occurred in medieval literature and life. In Chaucer's works, see *KnT* 1.1748–61, *WBT* 3.894–98, and *TC* 2.1447–49. Most famously, and with considerable ritual, Queen Philippa interceded with Edward III on behalf of the burghers of Calais (1347), and Queen Anne is said to have interceded with Richard II on behalf of Londoners (individuals and groups) on several occasions (in 1382, 1384, 1388, and 1392). **435 swere,** F reads "sweren." **436 no,** F reads "never." **442 that,** omitted in F. **447 I wol,** F reads "ye wolde." **451–52** Proverbial; see *Mel* 7.1794–95. **459 yeve me,** omitted in F. **483 legende,** the term was applied to single stories or collections of stories, usually about saints, that served as models or examples of ideal behavior.

That al hir lyf do nat but assayen°
How many women they may doon a shame;
For in youre world that is now holde° a game.
And thogh the lyke nat a lovere bee°,
Speke wel of love; this penance yive I thee.
And to the God of Love I shal so preye
That he shal charge his servantz by any weye°
To forthren° thee, and wel thy labour quyte°.
Goo now thy wey; this penanuce ys but lyte.
And whan this book ys maad, yive it the quene,
On my byhalf, at Eltham or at Sheene."
The God of Love gan smyle°, and than he sayde:
"Wostow°," quod he, "wher° this be wyf or mayde,
Or queene, or countesse, or of what degre°,
That hath so lytel penance yiven° thee,
That hast deserved sorer° for to smerte°?
But pite renneth soone in gentil herte;
That maistow° seen—she kytheth° what she ys."
And I answerd, "Nay, sire, so have I blys,
No moore° but that I see wel she is good°."
"That is a trewe tale, by myn hood,°"
Quod Love, "and that thou knowest wel, pardee°,
If yt be so that thou avise the°.
Hastow nat° in a book, lyth° in thy cheste,
The grete goodnesse of the quene Alceste,
That turned was into a dayesye°—
She that for hire housbonde chees° to dye,
And eke° to goon to helle, rather than he,
And Ercules rescowed hire, parde°,
And broght hir out of helle agayn to blys?"
And I answerd ageyn, and sayde, "Yis,
Now knowe I hire. And is this good Alceste,
The dayesie, and myn owene hertes reste°?
Now fele° I weel the goodnesse of this wyf,
That both aftir hir deth and in hir lyf
Hir grete bounte° doubleth hire renoun.
Wel hath she quyt me° myn affeccioun,
That I have to hire flour, the dayesye.
No wonder ys thogh Jove hire stellyfye°,
As telleth Agaton, for hire goodnesse!
Hire white corowne berith of hyt witnesse;
For also° many vertues hadde shee
As smale florouns° in hire corowne bee.
In remembraunce of hire and in honour
Cibella maade the daysye and the flour
Ycrowned al with white as men may see;
And Mars yaf° to hire corowne reed°, pardee,
Instede of rubyes, sette among the white."
Therwith this queene wex reed° for shame° a lyte,
Whan she was preysed so in hire presence.
Thanne seyde Love, "A ful gret necligence
Was yt to the°, that ylke tyme° thou made
'Hyd, Absolon, thy tresses,' in balade,
That thou forgate° hire in this song to sette,
Syn thar° thou art so gretly in hire dette,
And wost° so wel that kalender° ys shee
To any woman that wol lover bee.
For she taught al the craft of fyn lovynge°,
And namely° of wyfhod the lyvynge°,

---

487 assayen, *test* **489 holde,** *considered* **490 the lyke nat a lovere bee,** *you do not want to be a lover* **493 be any weye,** *by any means* **494 forthren,** *advance,* **quyte,** *repay* **497 gan smyle,** *smiled* **499 Wostow,** *do you know,* **wher,** *whether* **500 degre,** *status* **501 yiven,** *given* **502 sorer,** *more sorely,* **smerte,** *suffer* **504 maistow,** *may you,* **kytheth,** *shows* **505 so have I blys,** *as I may have bliss* (a mild oath) **507 No moore,** i.e., *I know no more* **507 by myn hood,** (I swear) *by my hood* **508 pardee,** *by God* **509 avise the,** *think about it* **510 Hastow nat,** *don't you have,* **lyth,** (which) *lies* **512 dayesye,** *daisy* **513 chees,** *chose* **514 eke,** *also* **515 parde,** *by God* **519 hertes reste,** *heart's comfort* **520 fele,** *feel* **522 bounte,** *goodness* **523 quyt me,** *repaid to me* **525 hire stellyfye,** *changes her into a star* (or constellation) **528 also,** *as* **529 florouns,** *petals* **533 yaf,** *gave,* **reed,** *redness* **535 wex reed,** *blushed,* **shame,** *embarrassment* **538 to the,** *of you,* **ylke tyme,** i.e., *when* **540 forgate,** *forgot* **541 Syn that,** *since* **542 wost,** *know,* **kalendar,** *a model* **544 fyn lovynge,** *refined loving* (i.e., courtly love) **545 namely,** *especially,* **lyvynge,** *way to live*

487 Line lacking in F. 496–97 quene . . . at Eltham, or at Sheene, a reference to Anne of Bohemia, wife of Richard II. There was a royal manor at each location near London. It was reported that after Anne died in 1394, Richard refused to return to either manor and ordered Shene (or Sheen) House demolished. **500 queene . . . countesse,** Richard's mother, Joan of Kent, was both dowager queen (although her husband, Edward, the Black Prince, never ruled) and Countess of Kent. **502–03** Lines conflated in F: "That hast deserved soone in gentil herte." **503 pite renneth . . . herte,** the sentiment recurs elsewhere in Chaucer (*KnT* 1.1761, *MLT* 2.660, *MerT* 4.1986, *SqT* 5.479, and *TC* 3.5), and has parallels in a number of classical and medieval sources. **508 and that,** F omits "and." **511–16 Alceste . . . ,** see 432n. **515 Ercules,** Hercules. **518–19 is this Alceste . . . myn owene hertes reste?,** the dreamer's failure until this point to recognize the queen before him bothers many critics, especially because she declares herself at 432. It is best, perhaps, to read the question here as an epiphany of sorts, where the dreamer finally realizes that the lady before him is identical to the one to whom he has been devoted. Compare *BD* 1309-10, where the dreamer comes to a similar late realization. **525 Jove hire stellyfye,** in no known account does Jove, or Jupiter, turn Alcestis into a constellation. See *HF* 586. **526 Agaton,** Plato's *Symposium* is set as a banquet at the house of Agathon and it includes the story of Alcestis as an example of love (*Symposium* 179B). **529 florouns,** see 217n. **531 Cibella,** Cybele, goddess of fertility. **533 Mars,** god of war; red is his color. **539 Hyd, Absolon . . . ,** see lines 249–69.

And al the boundes° that she oghte kepe.
Thy litel wit was thilke° tyme aslepe.
But now I charge the, upon thy lyf,
That in thy legend thou make of thys wyf,
Whan thou hast other smale ymaad before°;
And fare now wel; I charge the namore.
But er° I goo, thus muche I wol the telle,
Ne° shal no trewe lover come in helle.
Thise other ladies sittynge here arowe°
Ben° in thy balade, yf thou kanst hem knowe,
And in thy bookes alle thou shalt hem fynde.
Have hem now in thy legende al in mynde°—
I mene of hem° that ben in thy knowynge.
For here ben twenty thousand moo° sittynge
Than thou knowest, goode wommen alle,
And trewe of love, for oght that may byfalle°.
Make the metres of° hem as the leste°.
"I mot° goon hom—the sonne draweth weste°—
To paradys, with al this companye,
And serve alwey the fresshe dayesye.
At Cleopatre I wol that thou° begynne,
And so forth, and my love so shalt thou wynne.
For lat see° now what man that lover be,
Wol doon so strong a peyne° for love as she.
I wot° wel that thou maist nat al yt ryme°
That swiche° lovers diden in hire tyme;
It were to long to reden and to here.
Suffiseth me° thou make in this manere,
That thou reherce° of al hir lyf the grete°,
After° thise olde auctours lysten° for to trete°.
For whoso° shal so many a storye telle,
Sey shortly° or he shal to° longe dwelle."
And with that word my bokes gan I take°,
And ryght thus° on my legende gan I make°.

---

546 boundes, *principles* **547 thilke,** *at that* **550 Whan thou hast other smale ymaad before,** *after you have written about less significant ones* **552 er,** *before* **553 Ne,** *never* **554 arowe,** *in order* **555 Ben,** *are* **557 Have . . . in mynde,** *commemorate* **558 of hem,** *those* **559 moo,** *more* **561 for oght that may byfalle,** *regardless of what happens* **562 metres of,** *verses about,* **the leste,** *you wish* **563 mot,** *must,* **sonne draweth weste,** *sun is setting* **566 wol that thou,** *want you to* **568 lat see,** *make clear* **569 Wol doon so strong a peyne,** *will suffer such pain* **570 wot,** *know,* **maist nat al yt ryme,** *can not write poetry about everything* **571 swiche,** *such* **573 Suffiseth me,** *it satisfies me* **574 reherce,** *repeat,* **grete,** *essential part* **575 After,** *following what,* **lysten,** *chose,* **trete,** *deal with* **576 whoso,** *whoever* **577 Sey shortly,** *must speak briefly,* **to,** *too* **578 gan to take,** *took* **579 ryght thus,** *just like this,* **gan I make,** *I wrote*

554–55 other ladies . . . in thy balade, apparently a reference to the ladies of line 301, here equated with those mentioned in the ballade. Evidently the initial idea was that the subjects of the individual stories were to be the women cited in the ballade. We have stories of Cleopatra, Thisbe, Dido, Hypsipyle and Medea, Lucrece, Ariadne, Philomena, Phyllis, and Hypermnestra; all except Philomena are mentioned in the ballade. Names mentioned in the ballade but for which we lack stories are (leaving aside the men) Penelope, Marcia, Iseult, Helen, Lavinia, Polyxena, Hero, Laodomia, and Canace. See the notes to lines 249–69. **557 now,** omitted in F. **564 this,** F reads "thise." **571 diden,** F reads "dide." **573 Suffiseth,** F reads "Suffich."

Prologue: Revised Version (G)

A thousent sythis° have I herd men telle
That there is joye in hevene and peyne in helle,
And I acorde° wel that it be so;
But natheles, this wot° I wel also,
That there ne is non° that dwellyth in this contre
That eyther hath in helle or hevene ibe°.
Ne may of it non othere weyis wytyn°
But as he hath herd seyd or founde it wrytyn°.
For by asay° there may no man it preve°.
But Goddis forbode° but men shulde leve°
Wel more thyng than men han seyn° with eye!
Men schal nat wenyn° every thyng a lye
For that° he say° it nat of yore ago°.
God wot° a thyng is nevere the lesse so
Thow every wyght° ne may it nat ise°.
Bernard the monk ne say nat al, parde°!
Thanne motyn we to bokys° that we fynde,
Thurow° whiche that olde thyngis ben in mynde°,
And to the doctryne of these olde wyse°
Yevyn° credence, in every skylful wyse°,
And trowyn on° these olde aprovede° storyis
Of holynesse, of regnys°, of victoryis,
Of love, of hate, of othere sundery° thyngis
Of whiche I may nat make rehersyngys.
And if that olde bokis weryn aweye°,
Iloryn° were of remembrance the keye.
Wel oughte us thanne° on olde bokys leve°,
Thereas° there is non othyr asay be preve°.
And, as for me, thow that myn wit be lite°,
On bokys for to rede I me delyte,
And in myn herte have hem in reverence,
And to hem yeve swich lust° and swich credence,
That there is wel onethe game non°
That from myne bokys make me to gon,
But° it be other upon the halyday°
Or ellis° in the joly tyme of May,
Whan that I here° the smale foulys° synge
And that the flouris gynne for to sprynge°.
Farewel myn stodye°, as lastynge° that sesoun!
Now have I therto° this condycyoun°,
That of alle the floris° in the mede°,
Thanne° love I most these flourys white and rede
Swyche° as men calle dayesyis° in oure toun.
To hem have I so gret affeccioun,
As I seyde erst°, whan comyn° is the May,
That in myn bed there dawith° me no day
That I ne am up and walkynge in the mede°
To sen° these floris agen° the sonne to sprede
Whan it upryseth be the morwe schene°—
The longe day thus walkynge in the grene.
And whan the sunne begynnys for to weste°,
Thanne closeth it and drawith it to reste,
So sore° it is aferid° of the nyght,
Til on the morwe that it is dayis lyght.
This dayeseye of alle flouris flour,
Fulfyld of vertu and of alle honour,
And evere ylike fayr° and frosch° of hewe,

---

1 thousent sythis, *thousand times* **3 acorde,** *agree* **4 wot,** *know* **5 ne is non,** *is no one* **6 ibe,** *been* **7 weyis wytyn,** *ways know* **8 wrytyn,** *written* **9 asay,** *experiment,* **preve,** *prove* **10 Goddis forbode,** *God forbade,* **leve,** *believe* **11 han seyn,** *has seen* **12 wenyn,** *think* **13 For that,** *because,* **say,** *saw,* **of yore ago,** *a long time ago* **14 wot,** *knows* **15 Thow every wyght,** *though every person,* **ise,** *see* **16 parde,** *by God* **17 Thanne motyn we to bokys,** *Then must we* (go) *to books* **18 Thurow,** *through,* **ben in mynde,** *are remembered* **19 wyse,** *wise people* **20 Yevyn,** *give,* **skylful wyse,** *reasonable way* **21 trowyn on,** *believe in,* **aprovede,** *confirmed* **22 regnys,** *kingdoms* **23 othere sundery,** *various other* **25 weryn aweye,** *were gone* **26 Iloryn,** *lost* **27 thanne,** *then,* **leve,** *believe* **28 Theras,** *whenever,* **non othyr asay be preve,** *no other test of proof* **29 lite,** *little* **32 yeve swich lust,** *give such dedication* **33 wel onethe game non,** *scarcely any pleasure* **35 But,** *unless,* **halyday,** *holy day* **36 ellis,** *else* **37 here,** *hear,* **foulys,** *birds* **38 gynne for to sprynge,** *spring up* **39 stodye,** *study,* **as lastynge,** *for the duration of* **40 therto,** *also,* **condycyoun,** *disposition* **41 floris,** *flowers,* **mede,** *meadow* **42 Thanne,** *then* **43 Swyche,** *such,* **dayesyis,** *daisies* **45 erst,** *before,* **comyn,** *come* **46 dawith,** *dawns* **47 mede,** *meadow* **48 sen,** *see,* **floris agen,** *flowers toward* **49 be the morwe schene,** *in the beautiful morning* **51 begynnys for to weste,** *begins to set* **53 sore,** *sorely,* **aferid,** *afraid* **57 evere ylike fayr,** *always the same in beauty,* **frosch,** *fresh*

Text based on Cambridge University Library MS Gg.4.27 (Gg), with indications of differences from the F Prologue in Bodleian Library, Oxford, MS Fairfax 16 (F). **1–30** The same as F1–30, except for revisions at 13–14 and 21. **1–6** Compare Froissart's *Le Joli Buisson de Jonece* (*The Fair Bush of Youth*) 786–92. **4 wot,** Gg reads "wit." **16 Bernard,** Cistercian monk, mystic, and theologian, St. Bernard of Clairvaux (1091–1153) is Dante's guide in the highest circle of *Paradiso* 32–33, although the line is proverbial as the gloss in Gg indicates: "*Bernardus non vidit omnia*" (Bernard does not see all). **31–40** Revises F31–40. **40–65** These lines echo a number of French poems that praise the *marguerite,* Latin (*margarita*) for "pearl" or "daisy," and French for "daisy." **41–48** Same as F41–48. **42–43 white and rede . . . daysyes,** the so-called "English daisy," is white, red, or white tinged with red; descriptions similar to Chaucer's recur in marguerite poetry. **49–60** Replaces F49–72. **52 closeth it,** the inner petals of the English daisy close at night. **55 of alle flouris flour,** flower of all flowers, a commonplace description of female beauty and virtue in religious and courtly poetry.

As wel in wyntyr as in somyr newe,
Fayn wolde I preysyn°, if I coude aryght.
But wo is me, it lyth° nat in myn myght;
For wel I wot° that folk han herebeforn°
Of makynge ropyn° and lad° awey the corn°.
I come aftyr, glenynge° here and ther,
And am ful glad if I may fynde an er°
Of ony goodly word that they han laft.
And if it happe me reherse eft°
That° they han in here frosche° songis said,
I hope that they wele nat ben evele apayed°,
Sithe° it is seyd in fortheryng° and honour
Of hem that eythir servyn° lef or flour.
  For trustyth wel, I ne have nat undyrtake°
As of the lef agayn° the flour to make°,
Ne of the flour to make ageyn the lef,
No more than of the corn agen the shef°.
For, as to me, is lefere non ne lothere°.
I am withholde yit° with never nothire°;
I not° who servyth lef ne who the flour.
That nys nothyng the entent of myn labour,
For this werk is al of anothyr tunne°—
Of old story, er swich strif° was begunne.
  But wherfore° that I spak, to yeve° credence
To bokys olde and don hem reverence,
Is for° men schulde autoriteis° beleve,
Thereas° there lyth° non othyr asay be preve°.
For myn entent is, or° I fro yow fare°,
The nakede° text in Englis to declare
Of manye a story or ellis° of manye a geste°,
As autourys seyn—and levyth° hem if yow leste°.

  Whan passed was almost the monyth of May,
And I hadde romed° al the somerys day
The grene medewe° of which that I yow tolde,
Upon the frosche dayseie° to beholde,
And that the sonne out of the south gan weste°
And closede was the flour and gon to reste,
For derknese of the nyght of which sche
    dradde°,
Hom to myn hous ful swiftly I me spadde°,
And in a lytyl erber° that I have,
Ibenchede newe with turwis frosche igrawe°,
I bad° men schulde me myn couche make;
For deynte° of the newe somerys° sake—
I bad hem strowe° flouris on myn bed.
Whan I was layd and hadde myn eyen hid°,
I fel aslepe withinne an our or two.
Me mette° how I was in the medewe tho°,
And that I romede° in that same gyse°
To sen° that flour, as ye han herd devyse°.
Fayr was this medewe as thoughte me overal—
With flouris sote enbroudit° was it al.
As for to speke of gomme° or erbe° or tre°,
Comparisoun may non ymakede be°,
For it surmountede° pleynly alle odours,
And of ryche beute, alle flourys.
Forgetyn° hadde the erthe° his pore estat°
Of wintyr that hym nakede made and mat°,
And with his swerd of cold so sore hadde
    grevyd°.
Now hadde the tempre° sonne al that relevyd
And clothede hym in grene al newe ageyn.

---

59 **Fayn wolde I preysyn,** *gladly I would praise* 60 **lyth,** *lies* 61 **wot,** *know,* **han herebeforn,** *have before this time* 62 **Of makynge ropyn,** *harvested the fruits of poetry,* **lad,** *taken,* **corn,** *grain* 63 **glenynge,** *gleaning* 64 **er,** *ear* (of grain) 66 **it happe me reherse eft,** *I may happen to repeat again* 67 **That,** *what,* **here frosche,** *their fresh* 68 **wele nat ben evele apayed,** *will not be displeased* 69 **Sithe,** *since,* **fortheryng,** *advancement* 70 **eythir servyn,** *serve either* 71 **ne have nat undyrtake,** *have not undertaken* 72 **As of the lef agayn,** *in favor of the leaf against,* **make,** *write* 74 **corn agen the shef,** *corn against the sheaf* 75 **is lefere non ne lothere,** *neither one is more pleasing nor displeasing* 76 **withholde yit,** *committed yet,* **never nothire,** *neither one nor the other* 77 **not,** *don't know* 79 **al of anothyr tunne,** i.e., *completely of a different sort* 80 **er swich strif,** *before such conflict* 81 **wherfore,** *the reason,* **yeve,** *give* 83 **for,** *because,* **autoriteis,** *authorities/authors* 84 **Thereas,** *where,* **lyth,** *lies,* **asay be preve,** *test of proof* 85 **or,** *before,* **fare,** *go* 86 **nakede,** *unadorned* 87 **ellis,** *else,* **geste,** *history* 88 **levyth,** *believe,* **leste,** *wish* 90 **romed,** *roamed* 91 **medewe,** *meadow* 92 **frosche dayseie,** *fresh daisy* 93 **gan weste,** *went west* 95 **dradde,** *feared* 96 **spadde,** *hurried* 97 **erber,** *garden* 98 **Ibenchede newe with turwis frosche igrawe,** *newly furnished with benches made of fresh turf* 99 **bad,** *directed* 100 **deynte,** *delight,* **somerys,** *summer's* 101 **strowe,** *scatter* (strew) 102 **eyen hid,** *eyes closed* 104 **Me mette,** *I dreamed,* **tho,** *then* 105 **romede,** *roamed,* **gyse,** *manner* 106 **sen,** *see,* **herd devyse,** *heard described* 108 **With flouris sote enbroudit,** *embroidered with sweet flowers* 109 **gomme,** (aromatic) *gum,* **erbe,** *herb,* **tre,** *tree* 110 **ymakede be,** *be made* 111 **surmountede,** *surpassed* 113 **Forgetyn,** *forgotten,* **erthe,** *earth,* **estat,** *condition* 114 **mat,** *defeated* 115 **sore hadde grevyd,** *sorely had afflicted* 116 **tempre,** *temperate* (warm)

58 Written at the bottom of the page, with indicators for insertion in proper sequence. **61–67** Revises F73–79 to eliminate the direct, second person address. **62–64 Of maykynge ropyen . . . glenynge . . . ,** reaping or harvesting is here a conventional figure for poetic inspiration; gleaning suggests that the poet follows in the footsteps of his predecessors. Chaucer uses a similar figure at *PF* 22–25. **68–71** Replaces F79–83; F84–95 excised, eliminating direct address. **70 servyn lef or flour,** in court games and celebrations, participants divided into contesting or debating groups, one side associated with or defending the leaf; the other, the flower. **72–80** Revises F188–96. **77 not who,** Gg reads "not ho." **81–82** Revises F97–98. **83–95** Replaces F99–118. The temporal setting is late May in G89; the first of May in F108. **86 text,** Gg reads "tixt." **93 south,** Gg reads "souht." **94 closede,** Gg reads "clothede." **96–104** Revises F200–10, with F201–02 excised. In F, the narrator observes the sights and sounds of the beautiful setting before he falls asleep; here in Gg, they are part of the dream. **98 frosche,** Gg reads "frorsche." **105–07** Not in F. **106** Gloss in margin: "daieseye." **108–38** Revises F119–51; F142–43 excised. **113–17** The figure of springtime re-clothing the earth derives from *Roman de la Rose* 57–62.

The smale foulis°, of the seson fayn°,
That from the panter° and the net ben skapid°,
Upon the foulere° that hem made awapid°
In wyntyr, and destroyed hadde hire brod°,
In his dispit hem thoughte° it dede hem good
To synge of hym, and in here song despise
The foule cherl° that for his coveytyse°
Hadde hem betrayed with his sophistrye°.
This was here song: "The foulere we defye."
Some songyn° on the braunchis clere°
Of love, and that joye it was to here,
In worschepe and in preysyng of hire make°
And of the newe blysful somerys° sake.
They sungyn: "Blyssede be Seynt Volentyn!
At his day I ches° yow to be myn
Withoute repentynge, myn herte swete."
And therwithal° here bekys gune mete°—
The honour and the humble obeysances°—
And after dedyn othere observancys°
Ryht onto° love and to nature,
That formed eche of hem to cryature°.
This song to herkenyn° I dede al myn entent°;
Forwhy I mette° I wiste° what they ment.
Tyl at the laste a larke song° above:
"I se, quod she, "the myghty God of Love!
Lo, yond he comyth°. I se hise wyngis sprede."
Tho gan I lok° endelong the mede°
And saw hym come, and in hys hond a quene°,
Clothid in ryal abyte° al of grene.
A frette° of goold sche hadde next hyre her°,
And upon that a whit corone° sche ber°,
With mane° flourys. And I schal nat lye,
For al the world, ryht as° the dayseye
Icorounede is° with white levys lite°,
Swiche° were the flourys of hire corene white.
For of o perle°, fyn and oryental°,
Hyre white coroun was imakyd al,
For whiche the white coroun above the grene,
Made hire lyk a dayseye for to sene°,
Considerede ek° the fret of gold above.
Iclothede was this myhty God of Love
Of silk, ibroudede° ful of grene grevys°,
A garlond on his hed of rose levys°,
Stekid al° with lylye° flourys newe.
But of his face I can not seyn the hewe°,
For sekyrly° his face schon so bryhte
That with the glem° astonede° was the syhte:
A furlongwey° I myhte hym not beholde°.
But at the laste in hande I saw hym holde
Two fery° darts, as the gleedys rede°,
And aungellych° hyse wengis gan he sprede.
And al be that° men seyn that blynd is he,
Algate° me thoughte he myghte wel ise°,
For sternely on me he gan beholde
So that his lokynge doth myn herte colde°.
And be the hond he held the noble quene
Corouned with whit, and clothede al in grene,
So womanly, so benygne°, and so meke,
That in this world thow° that men wolde seke,
Half hire beute schulde men nat fynde
In cryature that formede is be kynde°.
Hire name was Alceste the debonayre°.

118 foulis, *birds,* **fayn,** *joyous* **119 panter,** *snare,* **ben skapid,** *are escaped* **120 foulere,** *bird hunter,* **awapid,** *terrified* **121 hire brod,** *their offspring* **122 In his dispit hem thoughte,** *to scorn him they thought* **124 foule cherl,** *rotten villain,* **coveytyse,** *greed* **125 sophistrye,** *trickery* **127 songyn,** *sang,* **clere,** *clearly* **129 hire make,** *their mates* **130 somerys,** *summer's* **132 ches,** *choose* **134 therwithal,** *with that,* **here bekys gune mete,** *their beaks did meet* **135 obeysances,** *services* **136 observancys,** *activities* **137 Ryht onto,** *appropriate to* **138 to cryature,** *as creatures* **139 herkenyn,** *hear,* **dede al myn entent,** *gave all my attention* **140 Forwhy I mette,** *because I dreamed,* **wiste,** *knew* **141 song,** *sang* **143 Lo, yond he comyth,** *look, yonder he comes* **144 Tho gan I lok,** *then I looked,* **endelong the mede,** *the length of the meadow* **145 in hys hond a quene,** *by his hand* (he led) *a queen* **146 ryal abyte,** *royal clothing* **147 frette,** *decorative hairnet,* **next hyre her,** *upon her hair* **148 corone,** *crown,* **ber,** *wore* **149 mane,** *many* **150 ryht as,** *just as* **151 Icorounede is,** *is crowned,* **levys lite,** *little petals* **152 Swiche,** *such* **153 o perle,** *one pearl,* **fyn and oryental,** *excellent and oriental* **156 sene,** *see* **157 Considerede ek,** *taking into account also* **159 ibroudede,** *embroidered,* **grene grevys,** *green branches* **160 levys,** *petals* **161 Stekid al,** *all pierced,* **lylye,** *lily* **162 seyn the hewe,** *describe the color* **163 sekyrly,** *truly* **164 glem,** *gleam,* **astonede,** *dazed* **165 A furlongwey,** *for several moments,* **beholde,** *see* **167 fery,** *fiery,* **as the gleedys rede,** *red as hot coals* **168 aungellych,** *angel-like* **169 al be that,** *even though* **170 Algate,** *neverthless,* **ise,** *see* **172 doth . . . colde,** *makes cold* **175 benygne,** *gracious* **176 thow,** *though* **178 be kynde,** *by nature* **179 debonayre,** *gracious*

127–38 Scribal corruption rather than authorial revision seems to account for many of the differences between the Gg and F versions here; we have emended as little as possible for sense. **131 They,** Gg reads "That." **Seynt Volentyn,** see *PF* 309n. Poems celebrating St. Valentine's Day developed as a subgenre in Chaucer's time. Because there appears to have been more than one medieval St. Valentine, there is no real discrepancy between the May setting here and the now traditional date of celebration, February 14. **136 obeysances,** Gg reads "obeysance." **137 nature,** Gg reads "natures." **138** Gg reads "So eche of hem to cryaturys." **139–43** Not in F. **144–78** Revises F212–46. **145–57** Derives from Machaut, *Dit de la Fleur de Lis et de la Marguerite* (*Poem of the Lily and the Daisy*) 213ff. **161 lylye flourys,** lily flowers; the fleur-de-lis symbolizes France. In the F version (F230), the God of Love is crowned with the sun. Either description may have suggested Richard II to Chaucer's audience. **167 Two,** Gg reads "Tho." **179 Alceste,** in classical mythology, Alcestis was an ideal of wifely devotion who gave her own life to retrieve her husband Admetus from death. For John Gower's version, see *Confessio Amantis* (*Confession of the Lover*), 7.1917–43 and 8.2640–46. The name is not given in F until much later in the narrative, F432. **debonayre,** Gg reads "thebonoyre."

I preye to God that evere falle hire fayre°,
For ne hadde confort been° of hire presense,
I hadde be ded°, withoutyn ony defence,
For dred of Lovys wordys and his chere°,
As, whan tyme is, hereaftyr ye schal here.
  Byhynde this God of Love, upon this grene,
I saw comynge of ladyis nynetene°
In ryal abyte°, a ful esy pas°.
And aftyr hem° come of wemen swich a tras°
That syn° that God Adam made of erthe
The thredde part of wemen or the ferthe
Ne wende° I not by possibilite
Haddyn evere in this world ybe°—
And trewe of love° these wemen were echon°.
Now whether was that a wondyr thyng or non
That ryht anon° as that they gunne espye°
This flour whiche that I clepe° the dayseye,
Ful sodeynly they styntyn° alle atonys°
And knelede adoun, as it were for the nonys°.
And aftyr that they wentyn in cumpas°
Daunsynge aboute this flour an esy pas
And songyn° as it were in carole-wyse°
This balade whiche that I schal yow devyse°:

[Balade]

Hyd,° Absalon, thyne gilte tressis clere°;
Ester, ley thow thyn meknesse al adoun°;
Hyde, Jonathas, al thyn frendely manere;
Penolope and Marcia Catoun,
Mak of youre wyfhod no comparisoun;
Hyde ye youre beuteis°, Ysoude and Elene:
Alceste is here, that al that may destene°.

Thyn fayre body, lat it nat apeere,
Laveyne; and thow, Lucresse of Rome toun,
And Pollexene, that boughte love so dere,
Ek Cleopatre withal thy passioun°,
Hide ye youre trouth° in love and youre renoun;
And thow Tysbe, that hast for love swich peyne:
Alceste is here, that al that may desteyne.

Herro, Dido, Laodomya, alle in fere°,
Ek Phillis hangynge for thyn Demophoun,
And Canace, espied° by thyn chere°,
Ysiphile, bytrayed with Jasoun,
Mak of youre trouthe in love no bost ne soun°;
Nor Ypermystre or Adriane ne pleyne°:

---

180 evere falle hire fayre, *good may always happen to her* **181 ne hadde confort been,** *if not for the comfort* **182 hadde be ded,** *would have been dead* **183 chere,** *demeanor* **186 of ladyis nynetene,** *nineteen ladies* **187 ryal abyte,** *royal clothing,* **a ful esy pas,** (walking) *at a slow pace* **188 hem,** *them,* **swich a traas,** *such a procession* **189 syn,** *since* **191 wende,** *thought* **192 ybe,** *been* **193 trewe of love,** *faithful in love,* **echon,** *each one* **195 ryht anon,** *as soon,* **gunne espye,** *saw* **196 clepe,** *call* **197 styntyn,** *stopped,* **atonys,** *at once* **198 nonys,** *occasion* **199 wentyn in cumpas,** *moved in a circle* **201 songyn,** *sang,* **carole-wyse,** *the manner of a ring-dance* **202 devyse,** *present* **203 Hyd,** *hide,* **gilte tressis clere,** *bright golden hair* **205 ley . . . adoun,** *lay down* **208 beuteis,** *beauties* **209 destene,** *outshine* **213 passioun,** *suffering* **214 trouth,** *faithfulness* **217 in fere,** *together* **219 espied,** *recognized,* **chere,** *demeanor* **221 soun,** *brag* **222 pleyne,** *lament*

180–198 Same as F277–295. **180 hire,** Gg reads "sche." **186 ladyis nynetene,** the number has not been explained; nineteen women are named in the ballade at G203–23 (along with two men), but Alceste who walks ahead of this procession is one of the names. **190 or,** Gg reads "ne." **199–202** Replaces F247–48, transferring the recitation of the ballade from the dreamer in F to the ladies in Gg. **201 carole-wyse,** late-medieval carols involved singing and dancing in a circle. The term *carol* did not have associations with Christmas as it does in modern usage. **203–23** This embedded lyric follows the strict form of the ballade, three stanzas (here rhyme royal) of through-rhyme with a refrain. Evidently Chaucer was inspired by one or more of several French ballades by Machaut, Froissart, and others that include related catalogs of names. In the *MLP* 2.60–89 a related list of names is given, there presented as the contents of a book by Chaucer called "The Seintes Legende of Cupide" (2.61), an alternate title for *LGW*. No satisfactory explanation has been given for discrepancies between the two lists and the actual contents of *LGW*, although there have been conjectures that *LGW* was a work in-progress or abandoned. The text in Gg is much the same as in F249–69, except that in Gg the name *Alceste* is given three times (G209, 216, 223: "Alceste is here" F255, 262, 269: "My lady cometh"), and G221–22 revises F267–68. **203 Absalon,** biblical son of David, known for his beauty. **204 Ester,** biblical ideal of meekness. **205 Jonathas,** biblical friend of David. **206 Penolope,** Penelope, faithful wife of Odysseus. **Marcia Catoun,** wife or daughter of Cato, both named Marcia, and both examples of fidelity. **208 Ysoude,** Iseult, whose beauty overwhelmed Tristan. **Elene,** Helen of Troy, whose beauty provoked the Trojan War. **211 Laveyne,** Lavinia, wife of Aeneas, founder of Rome. **Lucresse,** Lucretia; raped by Tarquinius, she chose suicide rather than to live in dishonor; see legend 5. **212 Pollexene,** Polyxena, daughter of Priam of Troy and beloved of Achilles, was sacrificed on the tomb of Achilles to be reunited with him. **213 Cleopatre,** queen of Egypt and beloved of Julius Caesar and Marc Antony; see legend 1. **214 renoun,** Gg reads "ronoun." **215 Tysbe,** Thisbe, who committed suicide for love of Pyramus; see legend 2. **217 Herro,** Hero, beloved of Leander. **Dido,** died for love of Aeneas; see legend 3. **Laodomya,** beloved wife of Protesilaus. **218 Phillis . . . Demophoun,** see legend 8. **219 Canace,** loved her brother incestuously; specifically excluded from the list of Cupid's saints in *MLP* 2.77–80. **220 Ysiphile . . . Jasoun,** Jason's betrayal of Hypsipyle is part of legend 4. **222 Ypermystre,** Hypermnestra, punished because she was unwilling to kill her husband; see legend 9. **Adriane,** abandoned by Theseus; see legend 6.

Alceste is here, that al that may desteyne.
Whan that this balade al isongen was
Upon the softe and sote° grene gras,
They setten hem ful softely adoun
By ordere alle, in cumpas alle inveroun°.
Fyrst sat the God of Love and thanne this queene
With the white corone, clad in grene,
And sithyn° al the remenant, by and by°,
As they were of degre° ful curteysly.
Ne nat a word was spokyn in that place
The mountenaunce of a furlongwey of space°.
I, lenynge faste° by, undyr a bente°,
Abod° to knowe what this peple mente,
As stille as ony ston, til at the laste
The God of Love on me his eye caste
And seyde: "Who restith there?" And I answerde
Unto his axsynge° whan that I hym herde,
And seyde, "Sere°, it am I," and cam hym ner,
And salewede° hym. Quod he, "What dost thow her
In myn presence and that so boldely?
For it were bettere worth°, trewely,
A werm to come in myn syht than thow."
"And why, Sere," quod I, "and it lyke yow°?"
"For thow," quod he, "art therto nothyng able°.
Myne servauntis ben alle wyse and honorable;
Thow art myn mortal fo and me warreyest°,
And of myne olde servauntis thow mysseyst°,
And hynderyst hem with thyn translacyoun,
And lettist° folk to han devocyoun
To servyn me, and haldist° it folye
To troste on° me. Thow mayst it nat denye.
For in pleyn tixt°, it nedyth nat to glose°,
Thow hast translatid the *Romauns of the Rose*
That is an eresye ageyns° myn lawe,
And makyst wise folk fro me withdrawe,
And thynkist in thyn wit that is ful cole°
That he nys° but a verray propre° fole
That lovyth paramouris° to harde° and hote.
Wel wot° I therby thow begynnyst dote°
As olde folis° whan here spryt° faylyth;
Thanne blame they folk and wete° nat what hem ealyth°.
Hast thow nat mad° in Englys ek° the bok
How that Crisseyde Troylis forsok
In schewynge° how that wemen han don mis°?
But natheles° answere me now to this:
Why noldist° thow as wel a seyd° goodnes
Of wemen as thow hast seyd° wekedenes?
Was there no good matyr° in thyn mynde,
Ne in alle thyne bokys ne coudist° thow nat fynde
Sum story of wemen that were goode and trewe?
Yis, God wot°, sixty bokys olde and newe
Hast thow thyn self alle ful of storyis grete°
That bothe Romaynys and ek Grekis trete
Of sundery wemen, whiche lyf° that they ledde,
And evere an hunderede goode ageyn on° badde—
This knoweth God and alle clerkis ek°
That usyn sweche materis for to sek°.
What seith° Valerye, Titus, or Claudyan?

225 sote, *sweet* **227 in cumpas alle inveroun,** *in a circle all around* **230 sithyn,** *after,* **by and by,** *side by side* **231 As they were of degre,** *according to their rank* **233 The mountenaunce of a furlongwey of space,** *the time it takes to walk an eighth of a mile* (i.e., for a short while) **234 faste,** *near,* **undyr a bente,** *near a grassy area* **235 Abod,** *waited* **239 axsynge,** *asking* **240 Sere,** *Sire* **241 salewede,** *greeted* **243 it were bettere worth,** *it would be better* **245 and it lyke yow,** *if you please* **246 art therto nothyng able,** *are not worthy of it* **248 me warreyest,** *war against me* **249 mysseyst,** *slander* **251 lettist,** *impede* **252 haldist,** *consider* **253 troste on,** *trust in* **254 tixt,** *text,* **glose,** *interpret* **256 eresye ageyns,** *heresy against* **258 ful cole,** *very unsympathetic* **259 nys,** *is nothing,* **verray propre,** *perfect* **260 paramouris,** *romantically,* **to harde,** *too energetically* **261 wot,** *know,* **bygynnyst dote,** *begin to dote* **262 folis,** *fools,* **spryt,** *spirit* **263 wete,** *know,* **hem ealyth,** *ails them* **264 mad,** *written,* **ek,** *also* **266 in schewynge,** *to show,* **han don mis,** *have done wrong* **267 natheles,** *nonetheless* **268 noldist,** *wouldn't,* **a seyd,** *have declared* **269 seyd,** *declared* **270 matyr,** *subject matter* **271 coudist,** *could* **273 wot,** *knows* **274 grete,** *many* **276 whiche lyf,** *what kind of life* **277 ageyn on,** *against one* **278 clerkis ek,** *scholars also* **279 usyn sweche materis for to sek,** *are accustomed to pursue such matters* **280,** *says*

224–25 Replaces F270-99. **226–27** Transposes and revises F300–01. **228–57** Adapts F302–331, removing references to the daisy, changing the dreamer's posture from kneeling next to the flower to the more detached leaning nearby, and adjusting the comments about Chaucer's translations. **238 Who,** Gg reads "ho." **243 worth,** Gg reads "worthy." **255 *Romauns of the Rose*,** for Chaucer's translation of the *Roman de la Rose*, or part of it, see the Introduction to *Romaunt of the Rose*. Portions of the *Roman* are anti-love and anti-feminist, at least ironically, although the extant *Romaunt* does not contain these portions. **258–312** Not in F. This is the longest addition made in the revision of F to Gg. **264–65 the bok . . . Crisseyde Troylis forsook,** in Chaucer's *Troylus and Criseyde*, Criseyde decides to stay with Diomedes in the Greek camp rather than returning to Troylus as she promised. **267 But,** Gg reads "Bit." **280 Valerye,** probably Valerius Maximus, Roman writer, who mentions Alcestis in his chapter on conjugal love in *Factorum ac Dictorum Memorabilia Libri IX* (*Nine Books of Memorable Deeds and Sayings;* c.30 C.E.) 4.6.1. **Titus,** Roman historian, Titus Livius, or Livy (d. 17 C.E.), tells the story of the rape of Lucretia in his history of Rome, *Ab Urbe Condita* 1.57–60; see line 1683 below. **Claudyan,** Claudian, fourth-century Roman poet, praises many women in *Laus Serena* (*In Praise of Serena*), including Alcestis (lines 12–15), Penelope (25–31), and Helen, Dido, Laodomia, and Lucretia (148–57).

What seith Jerome agayns° Jovynyan?
How clene maydenys and how trewe wyvys,
How stedefast wedewys° durynge alle here lyvys°
Tellyth Jerome and that nat of a fewe
But, I dar seyn, an hunderede on a rewe°
That it is pete° for to rede, and routhe°
The wo that they endure for here trouthe°.
For to hyre° love were they so trewe
That, rathere than they wolde take anewe°,
They chose to be ded in sundery wyse°
And deiedyn° as the story wele devyse°—
And some were brend° and some were cut the hals°,
And some dreynkt° for they woldyn not be fals.
For alle kepid° they here maydynhed,
Or ellis wedlek° or here wedewehed°.
And this thing was nat kept for holynesse
But al for verray° vertu and clennesse
And for° men schulde sette on hem° no lak—
And yit they were hethene°, al the pak,
That were so sore adrad° of alle schame.
These olde wemen kepte so here name
That in this world I trowe° men schal nat fynde
A man that coude be so trowe° and kynde
As was the leste woman in that tyde°.
What seyth also the *Epistelle* of Ovyde
Of trewe wyvys and of here labour?
What Vincent in his *Estoryal Myrour*?
Ek° al te world of autourys° maysttow here°,
Cristene and hethene, trete of swich matere°;
It nedyth nat al day thus for to endite°.
But yit I seye what eyleth the to wryte
The draf° of storyis and forgete the corn°?
Be seynt Venus, of whom that I was born,
Althow thow reneyid hast myn lay°
As othere olde folys°, manye a day°,
Thow schalt repente it, so that it schal be sene°."
Thanne spak Alceste the worthyere° quene
And seyde: "God, ryght of° youre curteysye,
Ye motyn herkenyn° if he can replye
Ageyns these poyntys that ye han to hym mevid°.
A god ne schulde not thus been agrevyd°,
But of his deite he schal be stable,
And therto ryghtful and ek mercyable;
He schal nat ryghtfully his yre wreke°
Or° he have herd the tother° partye speke.
Al ne is nat gospel that is to yow pleynyd°;
The God of Love heryth° manye a tale ifeynyd°.
For in youre court is manye a losenger°,
And manye a queynte totulour acusour°,
That tabourryn° in youre eres manye a thyng
For hate or for jelous ymagynyng,
And for to han with you sum dalyaunce°.
Envye—I preye to God yeve hire myschaunce°—
Is lavender° in the grete court alway,
For she ne partyth° neythir nyght ne day

---

281 agayns, *against* **283 wedewys,** *widows,* **here lyvys,** *their lives* **285 on a rewe,** *in a row* **286 pete,** *pity,* **routhe,** *sorrow* **287 here trouthe,** *their fidelity* **288 hyre,** *their* **289 take anewe,** *take a new love* **290 sundery wyse,** *various ways* **291 deiedyn,** *died,* **wele devyse,** *will describe* **292 brend,** *burned,* **cut the hals,** *decapitated* (cut at the neck) **293 dreynkt,** *drowned* **294 kepid,** *preserved* **295 wedlek,** *marriage,* **wedewehed,** *widowhood* **297 verray,** *genuine* **298 for,** *so that,* **sette on hem,** *attribute to them* **299 hethene,** *pagan* **300 adrad,** *fearful* **302 trowe,** *believe* **303 trowe,** *true* **304 tyde,** *time* **308 Ek,** *also,* **autourys,** *authorities,* **maysttow here,** *you may hear* **309 swich matere,** *such subject matter* **310 endite,** *write it down* **312 draf,** *husks,* **corn,** *kernels* **313 Be,** *by* **314 reneyid hast myn lay,** *have forsaken my law* **315 folys,** *fools,* **manye a daye,** *many times* **316 sene,** *well known* **317 worthyere,** *worthiest* **318 ryght of,** *in accord with* **319 motyn herkenyn,** *must hear* **320 han to hym mevid,** *have accused him of* **321 agrevyd,** *angry* **324 yre wreke,** *anger avenge* **325 Or,** *before,* **tother,** *the other* **326 pleynyd,** *pleaded* **327 heryth,** *hears,* **ifeynyd,** *fabricated* **328 losenger,** *liar* **329 queynte totulour acusour,** *clever tattling accuser* **330 tabourryn,** *drum* **332 dalyaunce,** *private conversation* **333 yeve hire myschaunce,** *give her misfortune* **334 lavender,** *washer woman* **335 ne partyth,** *never departs*

281 Jerome agayns Jovynyan, in *Epistola Adversus Jovinianum* (*Letter Against Jovinian;* 393 C.E.) 1.41–46, St. Jerome catalogs virtuous pagan women of the ancient world, including Lucretia. Chaucer used his catalog also for Dorigen's lament in *FranT* 5.1355–1456. **289 wolde,** Gg reads "wole." **293 they,** Gg reads "thy." **296 nat kept for holynesse,** Jerome, *Adversus Jovinianum* 1.41, begins his catalog by clarifying that the women listed were not motivated by religion. **303 that,** Gg reads "tha." **305 *Epistelle* of Ovyde,** Ovid's *Heroides,* or *Epistulae Heroidum* (*Letters of Heroines*), is a set of imaginary letters written by famous women who have been abandoned by their lovers. **307 Vincent in his *Estoryal Myrour*,** Vincent of Beauvais (c. 1190–1264), *Speculum Historiale* (*Mirror of History*); it is a wide-ranging work of exempla and anecdotes, including an account of Cleopatra. **313–43** Revises F336–65. **312 draf . . . corn,** husks and grain; like chaff and wheat or shell and nut, this is a traditional way of distinguishing between the literal meaning and the spiritual meaning of literature. The imagery derives from Matthew 3.12; it is developed in Paul's letters (e.g., 2 Corinthians 3.6) and Augustine's *De Doctrina Christiana* (*On Christian Teaching*), and is used widely in medieval literature. Compare *MLT* 2.701–02, *NPT* 7.3443, and *ParsP* 10.35–36. Echoed at line 529. **313 seynt Venus,** Holy Venus; the Wife of Bath uses the same label for Venus, *WBP* 3.604. **of whom I was born,** Venus is the mother of Cupid in classical mythology. **314 reneyid,** Gg reads "reneyist." **318–94** Some critics have read this speech, in the tradition of "advice to princes," as addressed to Richard II, with Alceste who speaks it representing either his wife, Anne, or his mother, Joan. **322 deite,** Gg reads "dede." **333 preye,** Gg reads "prere." **335 nyght,** Gg reads "nygh."

Out of the hous of Cesar; thus seyth Dante.
Whoso that goth°, alwey sche wol nat wante°.
This man to yow may wrongly ben acused,
Thereas be° ryght hym oughte ben excusid,
   Or ellis, Sere°, for that° this man is nyce°,
He may translate a thyng in no malyce,
But for he usyth bokis for to make°
And takyth non hed of° what matere he take.
Therfore he wrot the *Rose* and ek *Crisseyde*
Of innocence and nyste° what he seyde.
Or hym was bodyn° make thilke tweye°
Of° sum persone and durste° it not withseye°,
For he hath wrete° manye a bok er° this.
He ne hath nat don so grevosly amys°
To translate that° olde clerkis° wryte,
As thow that° he of maleys wolde endyte°
Despit° of love, and hadde hymself ywrought°.
This schulde a ryghtwys° lord han in his thought,
And not ben lyk tyrauntis° of Lumbardye
That usyn wilfulhed° and tyrannye.
For he that kyng or lord is naturel
Hym oughte nat be tyraunt and crewel,
As is a fermour°, to don the harm he can.
He muste thynke° it is his lige man°,
And that hym owith o verry duetee°
Schewyn° his peple pleyn benygnete°,
And wel to heryn here excusacyouns°
And here conpleyntys° and petyciouns°
In duewe° tyme, whan they schal it profre°.
This is the sentens° of the philysophre:
A kyng to kepe° hise lygis° in justise—
Withoutyn doute that is his offise°.
And therto° is a kyng ful depe ysworn,
Ful manye an hunderede wyntyr herebeforn°,
And for to kepe his lordys hir degre°,
As it is ryght and skylful° that they be
Enhaunsede and honoured most dere—
For they ben half-goddys in this world here.
This schal be don bothe to pore and ryche,
Al be that° here stat° be nat alyche°,
And han of pore folk compassioun.
For lo° the gentyl kynde° of the lyoun,
For whan a flye offendyth hym or bytith,
He with his tayl awey the flye smytyth°
Al esyly, for of his genterye°
Hym deynyth nat° to wreke hym° on a flye,
As doth a curre° or ellis anothir beste°.
In noble corage oughte ben areste°,
And weyen° everything by equite°,
And evere han reward° to his owen degre°.
For, Sire, it is no maystrye° for a lord
To dampne° a man withoute answere or word,
And for a lord, that is wel foul to use°.
And if so be he may hym nat ascuse°,
But axith mercy with a sorweful herte,
And proferyth hym° ryght in his bare scherte,
To been ryght at youre owene jugement,

---

337 Whoso that goth, *regardless who leaves,* **wante,** *lack* **339 Theras be,** *whereas by* **340 Sere,** *Sire,* **for that,** *because,* **nyce,** *foolish* **342 for he usyth bokis for to make,** *because is accustomed to writing books* **343 takyth non hed of,** *pays no attention to* **345 nyste,** *didn't know* **346 hym was bodyn,** *he was directed to,* **thilke tweye,** *these two* **347 Of,** *by,* **durste,** *dared,* **withseye,** *refuse* **348 wrete,** *written,* **er,** *before* **349 amys,** *wrong* **350 that,** *what,* **clerkis,** *scholars* **351 As thow that,** *as if,* **wolde endyte,** *had intended to compose* **352 Despit,** *scorn,* **ywrought,** *invented* **353 ryghtwys,** *righteous* **354 lyk tyrauntis,** *like tyrants* **355 usyn wilfulhed,** *use willfulness* **358 fermour,** *tax collector* **359 thynke,** *remember,* **lige man,** *sworn follower* (liege) **360 hym owith o verry duetee,** *he has a genuine obligation* **361 Schewyn,** *to show,* **pleyn benygnete,** *full goodness* **362 excusacyouns,** *pleas in defense* **363 conpleyntys,** *accusations,* **petyciouns,** *legal requests* **364 duewe,** *due,* **profre,** *present* **365 sentens,** *opinion* **366 kepe,** *protect,* **lygis,** *followers* (lieges) **367 offise,** *duty* **368 therto,** *to this* **369 wyntyr herebeforn,** *years before this* **370 kepe his lordys hir degre,** *protect the status of his lords* **371 skylful,** *reasonable* **375 Al be that,** *even though,* **here stat,** *their status,* **alyche,** *alike* **377 lo,** *consider,* **gentyl kynde,** *noble nature* **379 smytyth,** *swats* **380 genterye,** *nobility* **381 Hym deynyth,** *he does not lower himself,* **wreke hym,** *take revenge* **382 curre,** *mongrel dog,* **beste,** *beast* **383 ben areste,** *to be restraint* **384 weyen,** *to weigh,* **equite,** *fairness* **385 han reward,** *have regard,* **degre,** *rank* **386 maystrye,** *great accomplishment* **387 dampne,** *condemn* **388 wel foul to use,** *very bad practice* **389 ascuse,** *excuse* **391 proferyth hym,** *offers himself*

336 seyth Dante, from *Inferno* 13.64–65, where envy is called a whore who never turns her eyes from the house of Caesar, a figure for any ruler. In Dante, the claim is spoken by Pier delle Vigne who, like Chaucer, was both poet and court servant. Chaucer's replacement of *whore* with *washerwoman* (line 334) captures the notion that court gossip is "dirty laundry." **337 wol nat,** Gg reads "mote." **344–45** Not in F. **346–59** Revises F366–79. **354 tyrauntis of Lumbardye,** Lombardy is a region in Italy that Chaucer and his contemporaries associated with the tyrannical rule of despotic families, particularly the Visconti of Milan. Compare *ClT* 4.72 and John Gower, *Mirour de l'Omme* (*Mirror of Mankind*) 23233. **358–93** In Gg, these lines are mistakenly transposed with 394–429, although corrected. **360–64** Not in F. Note the legal terminology. **365–67** Revises F380–83. **365 the philysophre,** a common way of referring to Aristotle. Proper royal government is a recurrent topic in the various versions of the *Secreta Secretorum,* attributed to Aristotle in the Middle Ages. There are also general similarities between Chaucer's comments (lines 356–76) and those in John Gower, *Vox Clamantis* (*Voice Crying*) 6.581 and 1001, and *Confessio Amantis* (*Confession of the Lover*) 2.695ff. **367 Withoutyn,** Gg reads "Which oughtyn." **368–69** Not in F. **370–99** Same as F384–413. **374 pore and ryche,** a common topic in medieval discussions of kingship; see Gower, *Vox Clamantis* 6.741ff. and *Confessio Amantis* 7.2743ff. **and,** omitted in Gg. **384 everything,** Gg reads "everyth." **388 wel,** Gg reads "wol." **390 But,** omitted in Gg. **392 ryght,** Gg reads "rygh."

Than° ought a god, by schort avisement°,
Considere his owene° honour and his trespace°.
For sythe° no cause of deth lyth° in this cace°
Yow oughte to ben the lyghtere° merciable—
Letith° youre yre° and beth sumwhat tretable°.
The man hath servyd yow of his konnyng°
And fortheryd° youre lawe with his makyng°.
Whil he was yong, he kepte youre estat°.
I not where° he now be renegat°,
But wel I wot° with that° he can endyte°
He hath makid lewede° folk to delyte
To servyn yow in preysynge of youre name.
He made the bok that highte° the *Hous of Fame*,
And ek° the *Deth of Blaunche the Duchesse*,
And the *Parlement of Foulis*, as I gesse,
And al the love of *Palamon and Arcite*
Of Thebes, thow° the storye is knowe lite°,
And manye an ympne° for your halydayis°,
That hightyn° baladis, roundelys, and vyrelayes;
And for to speke of othyr besynesse°,
He hath in prose translatid *Boece*,
And of the *Wrechede Engendrynge*° *of Mankynde*,
As man may in Pope Innocent ifynde°,
And made the lyf also of *Seynt Cecile*.
He made also, gon is a gret while°,
Orygenes upon the Maudeleyne.
Him ouughte now to have the lesse peyne;
He hath mad manye a lay° and manye a thyng.
"Now as ye ben a god and ek a kyng,
I, youre Alceste, whilom° quene of Trace,
I axe° yow this man, ryght of° youre grace,
That ye hym nevere hurte in al his lyve,
And° he schal swere to yow, and that as blyve°,
He schal no more agiltyn° in this wyse°,
But he schal makyn° as ye wele devyse,
Of wemen trewe in lovynge al here lyve,
Wherso ye wele°, of maydyn or of wyve,
And fortheryn° yow as meche° as he mysseyde°
Or° in the *Rose* of ellis in *Crisseyde*."
The God of Love answerede hire thus anon:
"Madame," quod he, "it is so longe agon°
That I yow knew° so charytable and trewe,
That nevere yit, sithe that° the world was newe,
To me ne fond I nevere non betere than ye.
If that I wele save myn degre°,
I may, ne wol°, not warne° youre requeste.
Al lyth° in yow; doth° with hym what yow leste°,
And al forgeve°, withoute lengere space°.
For whoso° yevyth a yifte or doth a grace°,

393 Than, *then,* **schort avisement,** *brief deliberation* **394 his owene,** i.e., *the god's own,* **his trespace,** i.e., *the offense of the accused* **395 For sythe,** *because,* **lyth,** *is involved,* **cace,** *case* **396 the lyghtere,** *more easily* **397 Letith,** *let go,* **yre,** *anger,* **tretable,** *flexible* **398 of his konnyng,** *according to his ability* **399 fortheryd,** *advanced,* **makyng,** *writing* **400 kepte youre estat,** *defended your honor* **401 not,** *don't know whether,* **renegat,** *a traitor* **402 wot,** *know,* **that,** *what,* **endyte,** *write* **403 lewede,** *unlearned* **405 highte,** *is called* **406 ek,** *also* **409 thow,** *though,* **knowe lite,** *little known* **410 ympne,** *hymn,* **halydayis,** *holydays* **411 hightyn,** *are called* **412 besynesse,** *activity* **414 *Engendrynge*,** *condition* **415 ifynde,** *find* **417 gon is a gret while,** *a long time ago* **420 lay,** *poem* **422 whilom,** *once* **423 axe,** *ask,* **ryght of,** *in accord with* **425 And,** *if,* **as blyve,** *eagerly* **426 agiltyn,** *offend,* **wyse,** *manner* **427 makyn,** *write* **429 Wherso ye wele,** *whichever you wish* **430 fortheryn,** *promote,* **meche,** *much,* **mysseyde,** *insulted* **431 Or,** *either* **433 so longe agon,** *a very long time* **434 yow knew,** *have known you to be* **435 sithe that,** *since* **437 wele save myn degre,** *will preserve my status* **438 wol,** *will,* **warne,** *refuse* **439 lyth,** *lies,* **doth,** *do,* **leste,** *please* **440 al forgeve,** *forgive everything,* **space,** *time* **441 whoso,** *whoever,* **doth a grace,** *does a favor*

398 konnyng, Gg reads "konnyg." **400–01** Not in F. **402–13** Revises F414–25. **406 Deth of Blaunche the Duchesse,** i.e., Chaucer's *Book of the Duchess.* **408 *Palamon and Arcite*,** Chaucer's story that he later incorporated into *CT* as the *Knight's Tale.* **410 your,** Gg reads "thour." **411 baladis, roundelys, and vyrelayes,** ballades, roundels and virelays are three of the "fixed forms" (*forme fixes*) of French lyric that Chaucer adapted in English. If he wrote many of them, few survive that are attributed with much confidence: two roundels (*PF* 680–92 and perhaps *Merciless Beaute*), several love ballades (see e.g., *To Rosemounde* and portions of *Complaint of Venus*), and two sections of *Anelida and Arcite* (lines 256–71 and 317–32) that reflect the influence of the virelay. See *Ret.* 10.1087 and the Introduction to Chaucer's short poems in this text. **412 besynesse,** replaces "holynesse" of F424. **414–15** Not in F. ***Wrechede* . . . Pope Innocent,** apparently a reference to Chaucer's lost translation of Pope Innocent's III's *De Miseria Conditionis Humanae* (*On the Misery of the Human Condition*), also known as *De Contemptu Mundi* (*Disdain for the World*). There are several echoes of Innocent's treatise in *CT*, especially *MLP* 2.99–121, but no complete translation by Chaucer has been found. **416–525** Same as F426–537, except F496–97 excised, eliminating a reference to Anne of Bohemia, wife of Richard II, who died in 1394. See F496–97n. **416 *Seynt Cecile*,** Chaucer later incorporated his version of the life of St. Cecilia into *CT* as the *Second Nun's Tale.* **418 *Orygenes* . . . *Maudeleyne*,** Origen upon Magdalene. Most scholars agree that this refers to a lost translation by Chaucer of a popular Latin sermon of womanly virtue, *De Maria Magdalena* (*Concerning Mary Magdalene*), attributed to Origen, a third-century theologian and philosopher. **421 quene of Trace,** in mythology, Alcestis is queen of Thessely, not Thrace. **423–31 I axe you . . . ,** aristocratic female intercession occurred in medieval literature and life. In Chaucer's works, see *KnT* 1.1748–61, *WBT* 3.894–98, and *TC* 2.1447–49. Most famously, and with considerable ritual, Queen Philippa interceded with Edward III on behalf of the burghers of Calais (1347), and Queen Anne is said to have interceded with Richard II on behalf of Londoners (individuals and groups) on several occasions (1382, 1384, 1388, and 1392). **423 ryght,** Gg reads "rygh." **436 ye,** Gg reads "the." **438 wol,** Gg reads "wel." **441–42** Proverbial; see *Mel* 7.1794–95.

Do it betyme°, his thank is° wel the more.
And demyth ye° what he shal don therfore.
Go, thanke now myn lady here," quod he.
  I rose and doun I sette me on myn kne,
And seyde thus, "Madame, the God above
Foryelde° yow that ye the God of Love
Han makyd me his wrethe° to foryeve°,
And yeve me grace so longe for to leve°
That I may knowe sothly° what ye be
That han me holpyn° and put me in swich degre°.
But trewely I wende°, as in this cas,
Naught have agilt° ne don to love trespass,
Forwhy° a trewe° man, withoute drede°,
Hath nat to parte with° a thevys dede°;
Ne a trewe lovere aughte me nat to blame
Thaw° that I speke a fals lovere sum schame.
They aughte rathere with me for to holde°
For that° I of Criseyde wrot or tolde,
Or of the Rose, whatso° myn aughtour° mente.
Algate°, God wot°, it was myn entente
To forthere° trouthe in love and it cheryse°,
And to be war from° falsenesse and from vice
By swich° ensaumple—this was my menynge."
  And sche answerde, "Lat be° thyn arguynge,
For love ne wele° nat countyrpletyd° be
In ryght ne wrong; and lerne this at° me.
Thow hast thyn grace°, and holde the° ryght therto.
Now wole I seyn° what penaunce thow schalt do
For thyn trespace, and undyrstonde it here:
Thow schalt whil thow levyst°, yer be yere,
The moste partye° of thyn lyf spende
In makynge of a gloryous legende°
Of goode wemen, maydenys and wyves,
That were trewe in lovynge al here lyvys°;
And telle of false men that hem betrayen,
That al here° lyf ne don nat but asayen°
How manye wemen they may don a schame;
For in youre world that is now holdyn game°.
And thow the lestyth nat° a lovere be,
Spek wel of love; this penaunce yeve I the°.
And to the God of Love I schal so preye
That he schal charge his servauntys by ony weye°
To fortheryn the°, and wel thyn labour quite°.
Go now thyn wey; this penaunce is but lyte."
  The God of Love gan smyle°, and thanne he seyde,
"Wostow°," quod he, "wher° this be wif or mayde,
Or queen, or cuntesse°, or of what degre°,
That hath so lytil penaunce gevyn the
That hast deservyd sorere° for to smerte°?
But pete° rennyth sone in gentil herte;
That mayst thow sen°; sche kytheth° what sche is."
And I answerde, "Nay, Sere°, so have I blys°,
No more but that I se wel sche is good."
"That is a trewe tale, by myn hod°,"
Quod Love, "and that thow knowist wel, parde°,
Yif it be so that thow avise the°.
Hast thow nat in a bok, lyth° in thyn cheste,
The grete goodnesse of the queene Alceste,
That turnede was into a dayesye°—
Sche that for hire husbonde ches° to deye,
And ek to gon to helle rathere than he,

---

442 Do it bytyme, *if he does it promptly,* **thank is,** *thanks are* **443 demyth ye,** *you judge* **447 Foryelde,** *reward* **448 wrethe,** *anger,* **foryeve,** *give up* **449 leve,** *live* **450 sothly,** *truly* **451 han me holpyn,** *have helped me,* **swich degre,** *such status* **452 wende,** *think* **453 agilt,** *offended* **454 Forwhy,** *because,* **trewe,** *honest,* **withoute drede,** *without doubt* **455 parte with,** *share,* **thevys dede,** *thief's deed* **457 Thaw,** *though* **458 with me for to holde,** *to agree with me* **459 For that,** *because* **460 whatso,** *whatever,* **aughtour,** *source* (author) **461 Algate,** *nevertheless,* **wot,** *knows* **462 forthere,** *advance,* **cheryse,** *cherish* **463 to be war from,** *give warning against* **464, swich,** *such* **465 Lat be,** *stop* **466 wele,** *will,* **countyrpletyd,** *contradicted* **467 at,** *from* **468 grace,** *forgiveness,* **the,** *yourself* **469 seyn,** *say* **471 levyst,** *live* **472 moste partye,** *greater part* **473 legende,** *collection of stories* **475 al here lyvys,** *all their lives* **477 here,** *their,* **ne don nat but asayen,** *did nothing but test* **479 holdyn game,** *considered sport* **480 thow the lestyth nat,** *though you choose not* **481 yeve I the,** *I give you* **483 by ony way,** *by any means* **484 fortheryn the,** *advance you,* **quite,** *repay* **486 gan smyle,** *smiled* **487 Wostow,** *do you know,* **wher,** *whether* **488 cuntesse,** *countess,* **degre,** *status* **490 sorere,** *more sorely,* **smerte,** *suffer* **491 pete,** *pity* **492 sen,** *see,* **kythyth,** *shows* **493 Sere,** *sire,* **so have I blys,** *as I may have bliss* (a mild oath) **495 by myn hod,** (I swear) *by my hood* **496 perde,** *by God* **497 avise the,** *consider* **498 lyth,** (which) *lies* **500 dayesye,** *daisy* **501 ches,** *chose*

442 the, Gg reads "te." **456 oughte me nat to blame,** Gg reads "may me nat blame," with "may" over an erasure (". . . hte" still visible). **469 schalt,** Gg reads "schat." **473 legende,** the term was applied to single stories or collections of stories, usually about saints, that served as models or examples of ideal behavior. **475 lovynge,** Gg reads "levynge." **485 this,** Gg reads "thyn." **486** Two additional lines occur at this point of the narrative in F (F496–97), which are taken as a reference to the wife of Richard of II, Anne of Bohemia. The excision of these lines is strong evidence that the Gg version is a revision of the F version, done after Anne's death in 1394. **488 queen . . . cuntesse,** Richard's mother, Joan of Kent, was both dowager queen, although her husband (Edward, the Black Prince) never ruled, and Countess of Kent. **491 pete rennyth . . . herte,** the sentiment recurs elsewhere in Chaucer (*KnT* 1.1761, *MLT* 2.660, *MerT* 4.1986, *SqT* 5.479, and *TC* 3.5), and has parallels in a number of classical and medieval sources. **499–504 Alceste . . . ,** see 179n. In some versions of the Alcestis myth, Hercules rescues her after she gives up her own life to save that of her husband, Admetus; in no version except Chaucer's is she turned into a daisy.

And Ercules rescued hire, parde°,
And broughte hyre out of helle ageyn to blys?"
  And I answerde agen and seyde, "Yis,
Now knowe I hire. And is this goode Alceste,
The dayeseye, and myn owene herteis° reste?
Now fele° I wel the goodnesse of this wif,
That bothe aftyr hire deth and ek hire lyf
Hire grete bounte° doubelyth hire renoun.
Wel hath sche quit me° myn affeccioun
That I have to hire flour the dayesye.
No wondyr is thow° Jove hire stellefye°,
As tellyth Agaton, for hyre goodnesse!
Hire white coroun beryth of it witnesse;
For al so manye vertuys hath sche
As smale flourys° in hyre coroun be.
Of remembraunce of hire and in honour,
Cibella made the dayesye and the flour
Icorouned° al with whit, as men ma° se;
And Mars gaf to hire corone red, parde°,
Instede of rubeis set among the white."
  Therwith the queene wex red° for schame°
    a lyte,
Whan sche was preysid so in hire presence.
"Thanne," seyde Love, "A ful gret
    neglygence
Was it to the to write onstedefastnesse°
Of women sithe° thow knowist here°
    goodnesse
By pref° and ek by storyis herebyforn.
Let be the chaf° and writ wel of the corn°.
Why noldist thow han° writyn of Alceste
And latyn° Criseide ben aslepe and reste?
For of Alceste schulde thyn wrytynge be,
Syn that° thow wist° that calandier° is she
Of goodnesse, for sche taughte of fyn lovynge°,
And namely° of wifhod the lyvynge°,
And alle the boundys° that sche aughte kepe.
Thyn lityl wit was thilke° tyme aslepe.
But now I charge the, upon the lyf,
That in thyn legende° thow make of this wif,
Whan thow hast othere smale mad byfore°.
And fare now wel; I charge the no more.
At Cliopatre I wele that thow° begynne,
And so forth, and myn love so shalttow° wynne."
And with that word, of slep I gan awake°,
And right thus on myn legende gan I make°.

Explicit prohemium°

503 parde, *by God* **507 herteis,** *heart's* **508 fele,** *feel* **510 bounte,** *goodness* **511 quit me,** *repaid to me* **513 thow,** *though,* **hire stellefye,** *changes her into a star* (or constellation) **517 flourys,** *flowers* **520 Icorouned,** *crowned,* **ma,** *can* **521 parde,** *by God* **523 wex red,** *blushed,* **schame,** *embarrassment* **526 onstedefastnesse,** (of the) *inconstancy* **527 sithe,** *since,* **here,** *their* **528 pref,** *experience* **529 chaf,** *husks,* **corn,** *grain* **530 noldist thow han,** *would you not have* **531 latyn,** *let* **533 Syn that,** *since,* **wist,** *know,* **calandier,** *the model* **534 fyn lovynge,** *refined loving* (i.e., courtly love) **535 namely,** *especially,* **the lyvynge,** *the way to live* **536 boundys,** *principles* **537 thilke,** *at that* **539 legende,** *collection* **540 Whan thow hast othere smale mad byfore,** *after you have written less significant ones* **542 wele that thow,** *want you to* **543 shalttow,** *shall you* **544 gan awake,** *woke up* **545 gan I make,** *did I write* **545a *Explicit prohemium,*** *Here ends the Prologue.*

503 Ercules, Hercules. **506–07 is this goode Alceste . . . myn owene herteis reste?,** the dreamer's failure until this point to recognize the queen before him bothers many critics, especially as her name is first stated in the Gg version at 179. It is best, perhaps, to read this question as an epiphany of sorts, where the dreamer finally realizes that the lady is identical to the one to whom he has been devoted. Compare *BD* 1309–10 where the dreamer comes to a similar late realization. **513 Jove hire stellefye,** in no known account does Jove, or Jupiter, turn Alcestis into a constellation. **514 Agaton,** Plato's *Symposium* is set as a banquet at the house of Agathon, and it includes the story of Alcestis as an example of love (*Symposium* 179B). **519 Cibella,** Cybele, goddess of fertility. **521 Mars,** god of war; red is his color. **526–34** Revises F538–44, where the God of Love chides the dreamer for failing to mention Alcestis in his ballade. The Gg version of the ballade (203–23) does mention her three times; hence the revision. **529 chaf . . . corn,** see 312n. **535–41** Same as F545–51. **542–43** Same as F566–67; F552–65 excised. The excision eliminates a reference to the "other ladies" (F554), apparently some indication of Chaucer's plan for his tales. Evidently the initial idea was that the subjects of the individual stories were to be the women cited in the ballade. We have stories of Cleopatra, Thisbe, Dido, Hypsipyle and Medea, Lucrece, Ariadne, Philomena, Phyllis, and Hypermnestra; all except Philomena are mentioned in the ballade. Names mentioned in the ballade but for which we lack stories are (leaving aside the men) Penelope, Marcia, Iseult, Helen, Lavinia, Polyxena, Hero, Laodomia, Canace, and Alcestis. **544–45** Revises F578–79, where the dreamer does not awaken before he begins to write; F568–77 excised.

I

Legend of Cleopatra

Incipit legenda Cleopatrie martiris, Egipti regine.

After the deth of Tholome the kyng,
That al Egipt hadde in his governyng,
Regned hys queene Cleopataras,
Til on a tyme befel ther swich a cas°
That out of Rome was sent a senatour
For to conqueren regnes° and honour
Unto the toun of Rome, as was usaunce°,
To have the world at hir obeysaunce°,
And sooth° to seye, Antonius was his name.
So fil it°, as Fortune hym ought ashame°,
Whanne he was fallen in prosperitee,
Rebel unto the toun of Rome is hee.
And over al this°, the suster of Cesar,
He lafte° hir falsly er° that she was war°,
And wolde algates° han another wyf,
For which he took with Rome and Cesar strif°.
Natheles°, forsooth°, this ylke° senatour
Was a ful worthy gentil werreyour°,
And of his deeth it was ful gret damage°.
But love had broght this man in swich a rage°,
And him so narwe° bounden in his laas°,
Alle for the love of Cleopataras,
That al the world he sette at no value.
Him thoghte ther nas nothing° to him so due°
As Cleopatras for to love and serve;
Him roghte nat in armes for to sterve°
In the defence of hir and of hir ryght.
This noble queene ek° lovede so this knyght,
Thurgh his desert and for his chivalrye,
As certeynly, but if that° bookes lye,
He was of persone and of gentillesse°
And of discrecioun° and hardynesse°,
Worthy to any wight° that lyven may—
And she was fair as is the rose in May.
And for° to maken shortly is the beste,
She wax° his wif and hadde him as hir leste°.
The weddyng and the feste to devyse°,
To me that have ytake swich empryse°
Of so many a story for to make°,
It were to° longe, lest that I sholde slake
Of thing that bereth° more effect° and charge°,
For men may overlade° a shippe or barge. 621
And forthy° to th'effect° than wol I skyppe,
And al the remenaunt, I wol lete it slyppe.
Octovyan, that woode° was of this dede,
Shoop hym an oost° on Antony to lede
Al outerly° for his destruccioun.
With stoute Romayns, crewel as lyoun°,

583 befel ther swich a cas, *such a situation occurred* **585 regnes,** *kingdoms* **586 usaunce,** *custom* **587 hir obeysaunce,** *their submission* **588 sooth,** *truth* **589 fil it,** *it happened* **hym ought ashame,** *owed him shame* **592 over al this,** *especially* **593 lafte,** *left,* **er,** *before,* **war,** *aware* **594 algates,** *at all costs* **595 took . . . strif,** *battled* **596 Natheles,** *nevertheless,* **forsooth,** *truly,* **ylke,** *same* **597 gentil werreyour,** *noble warrior* **598 damage,** *loss* **599 in swich a rage,** *into such a passion* **600 narwe,** *tightly,* **laas,** *net* **603 nas nothyng,** *was nothing,* **to him so due,** *so required of him* **605 Him roghte nat in armes for to sterve,** *he didn't care if he died in battle* **607 ek,** *also* **609 but if that,** *unless* **610 gentillesse,** *nobility* **611 discrecioun,** *good sense,* **hardynesse,** *bravery* **612 wight,** *person* **614 for,** *because* **615 wax,** *became,* **as hir leste,** *as she wanted* **616 devyse,** *describe* **617 ytake swich empryse,** *taken such an enterprise* **618 make,** *write* **619 were to,** *would be too* **619-20 lest that I sholde slake / Of thing that bereth,** *for fear that I might fail* (to write) *of things that carry* **620 effect,** *importance,* **charge,** *weight* **621 overlade,** *overload* **622 forthy,** *therefore,* **th'effect,** *the point* **624 woode,** *enraged* **625 Shoop hym an oost,** *prepared a military force* (host) **626 outerly,** *utterly* **627 crewel as lyoun,** *fierce as lions*

Text based on Bodleian Library, Oxford, MS Fairfax 16 (F), with corrections and select variants from Cambridge University Library MS Gg.4.7 (Gg) and Trinity College, Cambridge, MS R.3.17 (Tr). **579a *Incipit* . . . ,** Here begins the legend of Cleopatra the martyr, queen of Egypt. No source is universally accepted for Chaucer's version, although Vincent of Beauvais, *Speculum historiale* (*Mirror of History*) 6.5, is most often cited. See G307. **580 Tholome,** Ptolemy, the name of a number of Egyptian kings, including Cleopatra's father and her two younger brothers. She was first married to the older of the two as queen of Egypt and overshadowed his kingship; when he drowned, she married the younger one, whom she had murdered in order to rule in conjunction with Julius Caesar. Contact and collaboration between Egypt and Rome began with Cleopatra's father. **588 Antonius,** Mark Antony became Cleopatra's consort in Egypt after the death of Julius Caesar. **592 suster of Cesar,** Octavia, second wife of Mark Antony and sister of Octavius Caesar (later Augustus Caesar). **598 his,** F reads "this." **611 hardynesse,** F reads "of hardynesse." **614–15** See F576–77. **614 for,** omitted in F. **621** Proverbial. **624 Octovyan,** Octavius Caesar. **622 th'effect,** F and Tr read "effect."

To shippe they wente, and thus I lat hem sayle.
Antonius was war°, and wol nat fayle
To meten with thise Romayns—if he may—
Took eke his rede°, and both upon a day
His wyf and he and al his oost forth went
To shippe anon°, no lengere they ne stent°.
And in the see° hit happed hem to mete°.
Up gooth the trumpe°, and for to shoute and shete°,
And penyen hem° to sette on with the sonne°.
With grisly soun° out gooth the grete gonne°,
And heterly° they hurtelen al attones°,
And fro the top doun° cometh the grete stones.
In gooth the grapenel°, so ful of crokes°;
Among the ropes renne° the sheryng-hokes°.
In with the polax° preseth he and he°;
Byhynde the mast begyneth he to fle,
And out agayn, and dryveth hym overborde.
He styngeth hym upon hys speres orde°;
He rent° the sayl with hokes lyke a sithe°;
He bryngeth the cuppe, and biddeth hem be blithe°,
He poureth pesen° upon the hacches slidre°;
With pottes ful of lyme° they goon togidre.
And thus the longe day in fight they spende,
Til at the laste, as everything hath ende,
Antony is shent° and put hym to the flyght,
And al hys folk to-goo° that best goo myght.
Fleeth ek the queene, with al hir purpre° sayle,
For° strokes which that went as thik as hayle.
No wonder was she myghte it nat endure.
And whan that Antony saugh° that aventure°,
"Allas," quod he, "the day that I was borne!
My worshippe° in this day thus have I lorne°."
And for dispeyr out of his wytte° he sterte°,
And rof° hymself anoon° thurghout the herte,
Er that° he ferther wente out of the place.
Hys wyf, that koude of° Cesar have no grace°,
To Egipt is fled for drede and for distresse.
But herkeneth°, ye that speken of kyndenesse,
Ye men that falsiy sweren many an oothe
That ye wol dye° if that youre love be wroothe°,
Here may ye seen of women which a trouthe°.
This woful Cleopatre hath mad swich routhe°
That ther nys tonge noon° that may it telle.
But on the morwe° she wol no lenger dwelle°,
But made hir subtil werkmen make° a shryne
Of al the rubees and the stones fine
In al Egipte that she koude espye°,
And putte ful° the shryne of spicerye°,
And let the cors enbawme°, and forth she fette°
This dede cors, and in the shryne yt shette°.
And next° the shryne a pitte than dooth she grave°,
And al the serpents that she myghte have,
She put hem in that grave, and thus she sayde,
"Now, love, to whom my sorweful hert obeyde
So ferforthely° that fro° that blisful houre
That I yow swor to ben al frely youre°—
I mene yow, Antonius, my knight—
That never wakyng, in the day or nyght,
Ye nere° out of myn hertes remembraunce,
For wele° or woo, for carole° or for daunce;
And in myself this covenaunt made I thoo°,
That ryght swich as° ye felten, wel or woo,

629 war, *aware* **631 Took eke his rede,** *and he took counsel* **633 anon,** *immediately,* **stent,** *remained* **634 see,** *sea,* **hit happed hem to mete,** *it happened that they met* **635 trumpe,** *trumpet,* **shete,** *shoot* **636 peynen hem,** *strove* (pained themselves), **sette on with the sonne,** *attack with the sun at their back* **637 grisly soun,** *terrifying sound,* **gonne,** *cannon* **638 heterly,** *violently,* **hurtelen al attones,** *all crash together* **639 fro the top doun,** *from upper decks downwards* **640 grapenel,** *grappling hook* (to pull ships together), **crokes,** *hooks* **641 renne,** *run,* **sheryng-hokes,** *shearing blades* (to cut enemy ropes) **642 polax,** *battle axe,* **preseth he and he,** *presses this man and that man* **645 speres orde,** *spear's point* **646 rent,** *rips,* **sithe,** *scythe* **647 blithe,** *happy* **648 pesan,** *peas,* **hacches slidre,** *slippery deck-planks* **649 lyme,** *lime* (which burns the eyes) **652 shent,** *ruined* **653 to-goo,** *disperse* **654 purpre,** *purple* **655 For,** *because of* **657 saugh,** *saw,* **aventure,** *outcome* **659 worshippe,** *honor,* **lorne,** *lost* **660 wytte,** *wits,* **sterte,** *went suddenly* **661 rof,** *pierced,* **anoon,** *immediately* **662 Er that,** *before* **663 koude of,** *could from,* **grace,** *forgiveness* **665 herkeneth,** *listen* **667 dye,** *die,* **wroothe,** *angry* **668 which a trouthe,** *such fidelity* **669 mad swich routhe,** *made such mourning* **670 nys tonge noon,** *is no tongue* **671 morwe,** *morning,* **dwelle,** *delay* **672 made . . . make,** *ordered . . . to make* **674 koude espye,** *could find* **675 putte ful,** *filled,* **of spicerye,** *with spices* **676 let the cors enbawme,** *had the corpse embalmed,* **fette,** *brought* **677 shette,** *shut* **678 next,** *next to,* **than doth she grave,** *then she orders to be dug* **682 ferforthely,** *completely,* **fro,** *from* **683 frely youre,** *willingly yours* **686 Ye nere,** *you were not* **687 For wele,** *because of joy,* **carole,** *ring-dance* **688 thoo,** *then* **689 ryght swich as,** *just as*

635–49 The historical sea battle of Actium took place between the forces of Octavius and those of Cleopatra and Mark Antony in B.C.E. 31, but details here reflect late-medieval naval warfare. The powerful description is notable for its alliteration (unusual in Chaucer's verse) and elliptical syntax; compare *KnT* 1.2605ff. **638 heterly,** F reads "hertely." **641 renne,** F reads "and." **648 pesan,** peas, poured out to make the decks precarious. **661 rof hymself anoon,** historically, Antony committed suicide a year after the battle.

As ferforth° as it in my power lay,
Unreprovable° unto my wifhood ay°,
The same wolde I felen°, life or deeth—
And thilke° covenant, whil me lasteth breeth,
I wol fulfille; and that shal wel be seene,
Was never unto hir love a trewer queene."
And with that worde, naked, with ful good herte,
Among the serpents in the pit she sterte°,
And ther she chees° to han hir buryinge.
Anoon the neddres° gonne hir for to stynge,
And she hir deeth receveth with good chere
For love of Antony, that was hir so dere.
And this is storial sooth°, it is no fable.
Now, er° I fynde a man thus trewe and stable,
And wol for love his deeth so frely take,
I prey God let oure hedes nevere ake!

Explicit legenda Cleopatre martiris &c.

II

Legend of Thisbe

Incipit legenda Tesbe Babilonie, martiris.

At Babiloine° whilom fil it° thus,
The whiche toun the queen Semyramus
Leet dichen° al about, and walles make°
Ful hye° of harde tiles wel ybake°.
Ther were dwellinge in this noble toune
Two lordes, which that were of grete renoune,
And woneden° so neigh° upon a grene°
That ther nas° but a stoon wal hem bitwene,
As ofte in grette tounes is the wone°.
And sooth to seyn°, that o° man had a sone,
Of al that londe oon° of the lustieste°.
That other had a doghter, the faireste
That esteward in the world was tho° dwellinge.
The name of everych° gan to other sprynge°
By wommen that were neighbores aboute,
For in that contree yit°, withouten doute,
Maydens ben ykept°, for jelosye,
Ful streite° lest they diden somme folye.
This yonge man was cleped° Piramus,
And Tesbe hight° the maid, Naso seith thus.
And thus by report was hir name yshove°
That as they wex° in age, wex hir love,
And certein, as by reson of hir age,
Ther myghte have ben betwex hem mariage,
But that hir fadres nolde hit nat assente°.
And boothe in love ylike° soore° they brente°
That° noon of al her frendes myghte hit lette°,
But prevely° somtyme yit they mette

690 ferforth, *much* **691 Unreprovable,** *without blame,* **wifhood ay,** *womanhood always* **692 felen,** *feel* **693 thilke,** *that* **697 sterte,** *leapt* **698 chees,** *chose* **699 neddres,** *snakes* (adders) **702 storial sooth,** *historical truth* **703 er,** *until* **704 wol,** F reads "wolde." **705 ake,** F reads "take." **706 Babiloine,** *Babylon,* **whilom fil it,** *once it happened* **708 Leet dichen,** *had ditches dug,* **make,** *made* **709 Ful hye,** *very high,* **ybake,** *baked* **712 woneden,** *lived,* **neigh,** *near,* **grene,** *grassy plot* **713 nas,** *was nothing* **714 wone,** *custom* **715 sooth to seyn,** *to tell the truth,* **o,** *one* **716 oon,** *one,* **lustieste,** *most attractive* **718 tho,** *then* **719 everych,** *each of them,* **gan to other sprynge,** *spread to the other* **721 yit,** *yet* **722 ben ykept,** *were protected* **723 Ful streite,** *very closely* **724 cleped,** *called* **725 hight,** *was named* **726 was hir name yshove,** *were their names spread* **727 wex,** *grew* **730 nolde hit nat assente,** *would not agree to it* **731 ylike,** *alike,* **soore,** *sorely,* **brente,** *burned* **732 That,** *so that,* **lette,** *diminish* **733 prevely,** *secretly*

697 Among the serpents in the pit she sterte, this detail of the death of Cleopatra is peculiar to the versions by Chaucer and Gower, *Confessio Amantis* 8.2573–75; Gower apparently followed Chaucer. Death in a snake pit recurs in medieval literature, however, particularly in saints' lives. **705a *Explicit* . . . ,** Here ends the legend of Cleopatra, martyr, etc. **705b *Incipit* . . . ,** Here begins the legend of Thisbe of Babylon, martyr. Chaucer's version closely follows Ovid, *Metamorphoses* 4.55–163. **707 Semyramus,** Semiramis, legendary founder and queen of Babylon. **712 upon a grene,** Chaucer's addition. **716 oon of,** F reads "oon." **719–20** Chaucer's addition. **725 Naso,** Ovid, Publius Ovidius Naso; acknowledgment that he is Chaucer's source.

By sleight°, and speken° somme of hir desire—
As wry the glede° and hotter is the fire,
Forbede° a love, and it is ten so woode°.
This wal, which that bitwix hem bothe stoode,
Was cloven a-twoo° right fro the toppe adoune
Of olde tyme of his fundacioun°,
But yit this clyft° was so narwe and lyte
It was nat seene deere ynogh a myte°.
But what is that, that love can nat espye°?
Ye lovers twoo, if that I shal nat lye,
Ye founden first this litel narwe clyfte,
And with a soune as softe as any shryfte°,
They lete hir wordes through the clyfte pace°,
And tolden while that they stoden in the place
Al hir compleynt of love, and al hir woo,
At every tyme whan they dorste° so.
Upon that o° syde of the wal stood he,
And on that other syde stood Tesbe,
The swoote soun° of other° to receyve,
And thus her wardeyns° wolde they deceyve.
And every day this walle they wolde threte°,
And wisshe to God that it were doun ybete°.
Thus wolde they seyn°, "Allas, thou wikked walle,
Through thyn envye thou us lettest alle°!
Why nyltow cleve° or fallen al a-two?
Or at the leste, but° thow woldest so,
Yit woldestow but ones° let us meete,
Or ones that we mighte kissen sweete,
Than were we covered of° our cares colde.
But natheles°, yit be we to thee holde°
Inasmuche as thou suffrest° for to goon
Our wordes through thy lyme° and ek° thy stoon.
Yet oghte we with the ben wel apayde°."
And whan these idel wordes weren sayde,
The colde wal they wolden kysse of stoon,
And take hir leve, and foorth they wolden goon.
And this was gladly° in the evetyde°,
Or wonder° erly lest men it espyde°.
And longe tyme they wroght° in this manere
Til on a day, whan Phebus gan to clere,
Aurora with the stremes of hir hete
Had dried up the dewe of herbes wete,
Unto this clyfte, as it was wont° to be,
Come Pyramus, and after come Tesbe,
And plighten trouthe° fully in here faye°
That ilke same° night to steele aweye,
And to begyle here wardeyns everychone,
And forth out of the citee for to gone,
And for° the feeldes ben° so broode and wyde,
For to meete in o place at o tyde.
They sette mark° here metyng sholde be
Ther° King Nynus was graven° under a tree—
For olde payens° that ydoles heried°
Useden thoo° in feeldes to ben beried—
And faste° by this grave was a welle°.
And shortly of this tale for to telle,
This covenaunt was affermed wonder faste.
And longe hem thoughte that the sonne laste°,
That hit nere goon° under the see° adoune.
This Tesbe hath so greete affeccioun,
And so grete lykynge Piramus to see,
That whan she seigh° hir tyme mighte bee,
At night she stal awey ful prevely°
With her face ywimpled° subtilly,
For al hir frendes, for to save hir trouthe°,
She hath forsake. Allas, and that is routhe°
That ever woman wolde be so trewe
To trusten man but she the bet° him knewe!
And to the tree she gooth a ful goode paas°,
For love made her so hardy° in this caas,
And by the welle adown she gan hir dresse°.

734 sleight, *trickery,* **speken,** *spoke* **735 wry the glede,** *cover the coals* **736 Forbede,** *forbid,* **ten so woode,** *ten times as intense* **738 cloven a-twoo,** *split in two* **739 Of old tyme of his fundacioun,** *in ancient time when it was built* **740 clyft,** *crack* **741 deere ynogh a myte,** i.e., *even a little bit* **742 espye,** *discover* **745 schryfte,** *confession* **746 pace,** *pass* **749 durste,** *dared* **750 o,** *one* **752 swoote soun,** *sweet sound,* **other,** *each other* **753 her wardeyns,** *their guardians* **754 threte,** *threaten* **755 doun ybete,** *beaten down* **756 seyn,** *say* **757 us lettest alle,** *deters us from everything* **758 nyltow cleve,** *won't you split* **759 but,** *if* **760 but ones,** *only once* **762 Then were we covered of,** *then would we be recovered from* **763 natheles,** *nevertheless,* **holde,** *indebted* **764 suffrest,** *allow* **765 lyme,** *mortar,* **ek,** *also* **766 with the ben wel apayde,** *be well pleased with you* **770 gladly,** *usually,* **evetyde,** *evening* **771 wonder,** *extremely,* **lest men it espyde,** *for fear that someone might see it* **772 wroght,** *worked* **776 wont,** *accustomed* **778 plighten trouthe,** *pledged,* **here faye,** *their faith* **779 ilke same,** *very same* **782 for,** *because,* **ben,** *are* **784 sette mark,** *established that* **785 Ther,** *where,* **graven,** *buried* **786 payens,** *pagans,* **ydoles heried,** *praised idols* **787 Useden thoo,** *were customarily then* **788 faste,** *near,* **welle,** *spring* **791 laste,** *lasted* **792 hit nere goon,** *it never would be gone,* **see,** *sea* **795 seigh,** *saw* **796 prevely,** *secretly* **797 ywimpled,** *veiled* **798 save hir trouthe,** *keep her promise* **799 routhe,** *pity* **801 the bet,** *better* **802 a ful goode paas,** *very quickly* **803 hardy,** *brave* **804 adown she gan hir dresse,** *she settled herself down*

750 that, F reads "the." **765 Our,** F reads "Or." **768 kysse,** F reads "kyssen." **773 Phebus,** the sun. **774 Aurora,** the dawn. **776 clyfte,** F reads "olyfte." **785 King Nynus,** husband of Semiramis and legendary founder of Nineveh. **792 goon,** omitted in F. **793 hath,** omitted in F. **794 And,** F reads "Had." **798–801** Chaucer's addition.

Allas, than comith a wilde leonesse
Out of the woode, withouten more arreste°,
With blody mouthe of strangeling° of a beste,
To drynken of the welle ther as she sat.
And whan that Tesbe had espyed that,
She ryst hir° up with a ful drery° herte,
And in° a cave with dredful° foot she sterte°,
For by the moone she saugh° hit wel withalle°.
And as she ran, hir wimpel° leet she falle,
And tooke noon hede°, so soore she was awhaped°,
And eke so glad of that she was escaped.
And thus she sytte and darketh wonder stille°.
Whan that this leonesse hath dronke hir fille,
Aboute the welle gan she for to wynde°,
And ryght anoon the wimpel gan she fynde°,
And with hir blody mouth hit al to-rente°.
Whan this was don, no lenger she ne stente°,
But to the woode hir wey than hath she nome°.
  And at the laste, this Piramus is come;
But al to longe, allas, at home was hee.
The moone shoon; men mighte wel ysee;
And in his wey, as that he come ful faste,
His eighen° to the grounde adoun he caste,
And in the sonde, as he beheld° adoune,
He seigh the steppes broode of a leoune,
And in his herte he sodeinly agroos°,
And pale he wex°, therwith his heer aroos.
And neer he come and found the wimpel torne.
"Allas," quod he, "the day that I was borne!
This oo° nyght wole us lovers boothe sle°.
How shulde I axen° mercy of Tesbe
Whan I am he that have yow slain, allas?
My bydding° hath yow slain, as in this caas.
Allas, to bidde a woman goon by nyghte
In place theras° peril fallen myghte,
And I so slowe! Allas I ne hadde be°
Here in this place a furlongwey or° ye!
Now what° leoun that be in this foreste,
My body mote° he renden, or what beste
That wilde is, gnawen mote he now myn herte."
And with that worde he to the wimpel° sterte°,
And kyste hit ofte, and weep on it ful sore,
And seyde, "Wimpel, allas, ther nys no more°
But thou shalt feele as wel the blod of me,
As thou hast felt the bledyng of Tesbe."
And with that worde he smot him° to the herte.
The blood out of the wounde as brode sterte°
As water whan the conduyt broken is.
  Now Tesbe, which that wyste° nat of this,
But sytting in hir drede, she thoghte thus,
"If hit so falle° that my Piramus
Be comen hider°, and may me nat fynde,
He may me holden fals and ek unkynde."
And out she comith and after him gan espien°
Booth with hir hert and with hir eighen,
And thoghte, "I wol him tellen of my drede
Booth of the leonesse and al my dede°"
And at the laste hir love than hath she founde
Betyng° with his helis° on the grounde,
Al blody; and therwithal° abak she sterte,
And lyke the wawes° quappe gan° her herte,
And pale as box° she wex°, and in a throwe°
Avised hir°, and gan him wel to knowe,
That it was Piramus, hir herte dere.
Who koude write whiche° a dedely chere°
Hath Tesbe now, and how hir heer she rente,
And how she gan hirselve to turmente,
And how she lyth and swowneth on the grounde,
And how she wepe of teres ful his wounde,
How medeleth she his blood with hir compleynte,
And with his blood hirselven gan she peynte°,
How clippeth° she the dede cors°, allas!
How dooth this woful Tesbe in this cas;
How kysseth she his frosty mouth so colde!
"Who hath doon this, and who hath ben so bolde
To sleen my leef°? O spek, my Piramus!
I am thi Tesbe, that thee calleth thus!"
And therwithal she lyfteth up his heed.

---

806 arreste, *delay* **807 of strangeling,** *from the killing* **810 ryst hir,** *rises,* **drery,** *terrified* **811 in,** *into,* **dredful,** *fearful,* **sterte,** *hurries* **812 saugh,** *saw,* **withalle,** *indeed* **813 wimpel,** *head scarf* **814 tooke noon hede,** *paid no attention,* **awhaped,** *frightened* **816 darketh wonder stille,** *hides in the dark very quietly* **818 wynde,** *prowl* **819 gan she fynde,** *she found* **820 hit al to-rente,** *tore it all to pieces* **821 stente,** *stayed* **822 nome,** *taken* **827 eighen,** *eyes* **828 beheld,** *looked* **830 agroos,** *trembled* **831 wex,** *became* **834 oo,** *one,* **sle,** *slay* **835 axen,** *ask* **837 bydding,** *pleading* **839 theras,** *where* **840 ne hadde be,** *had not been* **841 furlongwey or,** *while before* **842 what,** *whatever* **843 mote,** *must* **845 wimpel,** *head scarf,* **sterte,** *went quickly* **847 ther nys no more,** *there is nothing more* **850 smot him,** *stabbed himself* **851 as brode sterte,** *gushed as widely* **853 wyste,** *knew* **855 falle,** *happen* **856 Be comen hider,** *comes here* **858 him gan espien,** *looked for him* **861 dede,** *actions* **863 Betyng,** *beating,* **helis,** *heels* **864 therwithal,** *with that* (i.e., as a result) **865 wawes,** *waves,* **quappe gan,** *pounded* **866 box,** *boxwood,* **wex,** *became,* **throwe,** *moment* **867 Avised hir,** *thought to herself* **869 whiche,** *what* **869 dedely chere,** *deathly face* **875 gan she peynte,** *she did smear* **876 clippeth,** *embraces,* **cors,** *corpse* **880 leef,** *beloved* **882 therwithal,** *with that*

837 as, from Gg; omitted in F and Tr. **839 theras,** F reads "there a." **843 mote he renden,** F reads "mote rente." **846** Line lacking in F. **855 hit,** omitted in F. **875 And,** Gg and Tr read "How."

This woful man, that was nat fully deed,
Whan that he herd the name of Tesbe crien,
On hir he caste his hevy dedely eyen°,
And doune agayn, and yeldeth up the gooste°.
Tesbe rist° uppe withouten noyse or booste°,
And saugh° hir wimpel and his empty shethe,
And eke his swerd that him hath doon to dethe.
Than spak she thus, "My woful hand," quod she,
"Is strong ynogh in swiche° a werk to me,
For love shal yive me strengthe and hardynesse
To make my wounde large ynogh, I gesse.
I wol the folowen deed°, and I wol be
Felawe° and cause eke of thy deeth," quod she.
"And thogh that nothing save the deth° oonly
Myghte the fro° me departe° trewely,
Thou shalt noo more now departe fro me
Than fro the deth, for I wol goo with the!
And now, ye wrecched jelous fadres oure°,
We that weren whilom° children youre,
We prayen yow, withouten more envye,
That in oo grave yfere° we moten° lye,
Syn love hath brought us to this pitous ende.
And ryghtwis° God to every lover sende,
That loveth trewely, more prosperite
Than ever hadde Piramus and Tesbe!
And lat noo gentil° woman hir assure°
To putten hir in swiche° an aventure°.
But God forbede but a woman kan
Ben as trewe and lovyng as a man!
And, for my part, I shal anoon it kythe°."
And with that worde, his swerd she took as swythe°,
That warme was of hir loves blood and hoote,
And to the herte she hirselven smoote.
And thus ar Tesbe and Piramus agoo°
Of trewe men I fynde but fewe moo
In al my bookes save this Piramus,
And therfor have I spoken of him thus.
For hit is deyntee° to us men to fynde
A man that kan in love be trewe and kynde.
Here may ye seen, what lover so he be,
A woman dar and kan° as wel as he.

Explicit legenda Tesbe &c.

III

Legend of Dido

Incipit legenda didonis martiris, Cartaginis regine.

Glorie and honour, Virgile Mantoan,
Be to thy name, and I shal, as I kan,
Folow thy lanterne, as thou gost byforn°,
How Eneas to Dido was forsworn°.
In thyne *Eneyd* and Naso wol I take
The tenour° and the grete effectes make°.

885 dedely eyen, *dying eyes* **886 the gooste,** *his spirit* **887 rist,** *rises,* **booste,** *outcry* **888 saugh,** *saw* **891 swiche,** *such* **894 the folowen deed,** *follow you in death* **895 Felawe,** *partner* **896 save the deth,** *except death* **897 the fro,** *you from,* **departe,** *separate* **900 fadres oure,** *fathers of us* **901 whilom,** *once* **903 yfere,** *together,* **moten,** *might* **905 ryghtwis,** *righteous* **908 gentil,** *noble,* **hir assure,** *risk herself* **909 swiche,** *such,* **aventure,** *chance* **912 kythe,** *show* **913 as swythe,** *quickly* **916 agoo,** *gone* **920 deyntee,** *valuable* **923 dar and kan,** *dares* (to be true and kind in love) *and can* (do so) **926 thou gost byforn,** *you go before* **927 was forsworn,** *broke his promise* **929 tenour,** *meaning,* **grete effectes make,** *write a poem about the main events*

887 Chaucer's addition. **890 My,** from Gg; F and Tr read "thy." **892 yive me,** F reads "me yive." **903 yfere,** omitted in F; Gg reads "that." **904 this,** omitted in F. **905–23** Chaucer's addition, although 913–15 follows Ovid, *Metamorphoses* 4.162–63. **923a *Explicit* . . . ,** Here ends the legend of Thisbe, etc. **923b *Incipit* . . . ,** Here begins the legend of Dido, the martyr, queen of Carthage. As he acknowledges in his opening lines, Chaucer follows Virgil's account, *Aeneid* 1–4, but he incorporates aspects of Dido's characterization from Ovid, *Heroides* 7; see also *HF* 151–382. **924 Virgile Mantoan,** Virgil, born in Mantua (in northern Italy). **928 *Eneyd*,** Virgil's *Aeneid.* **Naso,** Ovid, Publius Ovidius Naso.

When Troye broght was to destruccion
By Grekes sleight° and namely by Synon,
Feynyng° the hors offred unto Mynerve,
Thurgh which that many a Troian moste sterve°;
And Ector had after his deeth appered,
And fire so woode° it mighte nat ben stered°
In al the noble tour° of Ilion,
That of the citee was the cheef dungeon°;
And al the contree was so lowe ybroghte,
And Priamus the king fordoon° and noghte;
And Eneas was charged by Venus
To fleen° awey, he tooke Ascanius,
That was his sone, in his right hande and fledde,
And on his bakke he baar and with him ledde
His olde fader cleped° Anchises,
And by the weye his wyf Creusa be lees°.
And mochel° sorwe hadde he in his mynde
Er that° he koude his felawshippe fynde.
But at the last, whan he hadde hem founde,
He made him redy in a certeyn stounde°,
And to the see° ful faste he gan him hye°,
And sayleth forth with al his companye
Towarde Itayle, as wolde destenee°.
But of his aventures in the see
Nys nat to purpos° for to speke of here,
For hit acordeth nat to my matere.
But, as I seyde, of him and of Dydo
Shal be my tale, til that I have do°.
So longe he saylled in the salte see
Til in Lybye unnethe° arryved he
With shippes seven and with no more navye,
And glad was he to londe for to hye°,
So° was he with the tempest al to-shake°.
And whan that he the havene° had ytake,
He had a knight was called Achates,
And him of al his felawshippe he ches°
To goon with him the contree for t'espye°;
He toke with him na more companye.
But forth they goon, and lafte his shippes ride,
His fere° and he, withouten any gyde.
So longe he walketh in this wildernesse
Til at the laste he mette an hunteresse.
A bowe in honde and arwes hadde she,
Her clothes knytte° were unto the knee,
But she was yit the fairest creature
That ever was yformed by nature.
And Eneas and Achates she grette°,
And thus she to hem spak whan she hem mette:
"Sawe ye°," quod she, "as ye han walked wide,
Any of my sustren° walke yow besyde,
With any wilde boor or other beste
That they han hunted to in this foreste,
Ytukked up°, with arwes in here cas°?"
"Nay, smoothly°, lady," quod this Eneas,
"But by thy beaute, as hit thynketh me°,
Thou myghtest never erthely woman be,
But Phebus suster artow°, as I gesse.
And if so be that thou be a goddesse,
Have mercy on our labour and our woo."
"I nam no goddesse, soothely," quod she thoo°,
"For maydens walken in this contree here
With arwes and with bowe in this manere.
This is the regne° of Libie ther° ye been,
Of which that Dido lady is and queen"—
And shortly tolde al the occasioun
Why Dido come° into that regioun
Of which as now me lusteth nat to ryme°;
It nedeth nat°; it nere° but los of tyme.
For this is al and somme°, it was Venus,
His owene moder, that spake with him thus;
And to Cartage she bad he sholde him dighte°,

931 sleight, *trickery* **932 Feynyng,** *pretending* **933 moste sterve,** *must die* **935 woode,** *intense,* **stered,** *controlled* **936 tour,** *tower* **937 dungeon,** *fortification* (not necessarily a prison) **939 fordoon,** *killed* **941 fleen,** *flee* **944 cleped,** *named* **945 lees,** *lost* **946 mochel,** *much* **947 Er that,** *before* **949 stounde,** *time* **950 see,** *sea,* **hye,** *hurry* **952 wolde destenee,** *destiny wanted* **954 Nys nat to purpos,** *is not to the point* **957 do,** *done* **959 unnethe,** *scarcely* **961 hye,** *approach* **962 So,** *as,* **to-shake,** *buffeted* **963 havene,** *harbor* **965 ches,** *chose* **966 t'espye,** *to investigate* **969 fere,** *companion* **973 knytte,** *tied* **976 grette,** *greeted* **978 Sawe ye,** *did you see* **979 sustren,** *sisters* **982 Ytukked up,** *with clothing tucked up,* **here cas,** *their quivers* **983 soothly,** *truly* **984 thynketh me,** *seems to me* **986 Phebus suster artow,** *you are Phoebus's sister* **989 thoo,** *then* **992 regne,** *kingdom,* **ther,** *where* **995 come,** *came* **996 me lusteth nat to ryme,** *I choose not to write poetry about* **997 It nedeth not,** *there is no need,* **nere,** *would be nothing* **998 al and somme,** *the whole of it* **1000 dighte,** *direct himself*

930–47 A rapid summary of the *Aeneid,* book 2. **931–32 Synon . . . the hors offred unto Mynerve,** Sinon was the Greek who allowed himself to be captured and then persuaded the Trojans to accept the Trojan horse as atonement to Minerva (Athena, in Greek), goddess of wisdom and patron of Troy. The horse concealed the Greek warriors who sacked Troy. **934 Ector,** the ghost of Hector tells Aeneas to flee Troy to escape its destruction. **936 Ilion,** originally synonymous with Troy, but understood in the Middle Ages to refer to the Trojan citadel. **940–55 Eneas . . . ,** son of the goddess Venus and the mortal Anchises, Aeneas fled Troy with his father (Anchises), son (Ascanius), and wife (Creusa); Creusa was lost despite Aeneas' efforts to find her; his sea adventures are detailed in *Aeneid,* book 3. **958–1102** Generally follows *Aeneid* 1.305–642, although scholars have identified a number of changes in detail and emphasis. **959 Lybye,** Libya, North Africa. **960–61** Lines lacking in F; from Gg. **964 Achates,** Aeneas's companion. **966 t'espye,** F and Tr read "to spye." **986 Phebus suster,** Phoebus is Apollo, the sun god, and Diana is his sister, goddess of the moon and of hunting.

And vanyshed anoon out of his sighte.
  I koude folwe word for worde Virgile,
But it wolde lasten al to longe a while.
  This noble queen, that cleped° was Dido,
That whilom° was the wife of Sitheo,
That fairer was than the bryghte sonne,
This noble toun of Cartage hath begonne°,
In which she regneth° in so greete honoure,
That she was holde° of alle quenes floure,
Of gentilesse, of fredom°, of beautee,
That wel was him that might hir oones° see;
Of kynges and of lordes so desired
That al the world hir beaute hadde yfired°,
She stood so wel in every wyghtes grace°.
  Whan Eneas was come unto that place,
Unto the maister° temple of al the toun
Ther° Dido was in her devocioun,
Ful prively° his wey than° hath he nome°.
Whan he was in the large temple come,
I kan nat seyn if that hit be possible,
But° Venus hadde him maked invisible—
Thus seith the book, withouten any les°.
And whan this Eneas and Achates
Hadden in this temple been over alle,
Than founde they depeynted° on a walle,
How Troye and al the lond destrued° was.
"Allas that I was born," quod Eneas,
"Throughout the world our shame is kid° so wide,
Now it is peynted upon every side.
We that weren in prosperitee
Be now disclaundred°, and in swiche° degre!
No lenger for to lyven I ne kepe°."
And, with that worde, he braste° out for to wepe
So tendrely that routhe° hit was to seene.
This fresshe lady of the citee queene
Stoode in the temple in hir estaat royalle°,
So richely and eke so fair withalle,
So yong, so lusty°, with her eighen glade°,
That if that God that hevene and erthe made
Wolde han a love° for beaute and goodenesse,
And womanhode, and trouthe° and seemlynesse°,
Whom sholde he loven but this lady swete?
There nys no womman to him half so mete°.
  Fortune, that hath the worlde in governaunce,
Hath sodeynly broght in so newe a chaunce
That never was ther yit so fremd a cas°.
For al the companye of Eneas,
Which that he wende han loren° in the see,
Aryved is noght fer fro° that citee,
For which the grettest of his lordes some
By aventure ben° to the citee come,
Unto that same temple, for to seke°
The queene, and of hir socour hir beseke°,
Swich° renown was ther spronge of hir goodenesse.
And whan they had told al here distresse,
And al here tempest° and here harde cas°,
Unto the queene appered Eneas
And openly beknew° that hit was hee.
Who hadde joye thanne° but his menee°,
That hadden founde here lord, here governour?
  The queene saw they dide him swich honour,
And had herd ofte of Eneas er thoo°,
And in her herte she hadde routhe° and woo
That ever swich a noble man as hee
Shal been° dishereted in swich degree,
And sawgh° the man, that he was lyke a knyghte,
And suffisaunt of persone and of mighte,
And lyke° to ben a verray gentil° man,
And wel his wordes he besette kan°,
And hadde a noble visage for the nones°,

1004 cleped, *named* **1005 whilom,** *formerly* **1007 begonne,** *established* **1008 regneth,** *ruled* **1009 holde,** *considered* **1010 fredom,** *generosity* **1011 oones,** *once* **1013 yfired,** *aroused* **1014 wyghtes grace,** *person's favor* **1016 maister,** *principal* **1017 Ther,** *where* **1018 Ful prively,** *very secretly,* **than,** *then,* **nome,** *taken* **1021 But,** *unless* **1022 les,** *lies* **1025 depeynted,** *depicted* **1026 destrued,** *destroyed* **1028 kid,** *known* **1031 disclaundred,** *disgraced,* **in swiche,** *to such a* **1032 kepe,** *care* **1033 braste,** *burst* **1034 routhe,** *pity* **1036 estaat royalle,** *royal status* **1038 lusty,** *attractive,* **eighen glade,** *joyful eyes* **1040 Wolde han a love,** *wished to love* **1041 trouthe,** *faithfulness,* **seemlynesse,** *attractiveness* **1043 mete,** *suitable* **1046 fremd a cas,** *strange a coincidence* **1048 wende han loren,** *supposed to have lost* **1049 noght fer fro,** *not far from* **1051 By aventure ben,** *by chance are* **1052 seke,** *seek* **1053 of hir socour hir beseke,** *beseech her for her help* **1054 Swich,** *such* **1056 here tempest,** *their storm,* **here harde cas,** *their difficult circumstances* **1058 beknew,** *revealed* **1059 thanne,** *then,* **menee,** *retinue* **1062 er thoo,** *before then* **1063 routhe,** *pity* **1065 Shal been,** *should have been* **1066 sawgh,** *saw* **1068 lyke,** *likely,* **verray gentil,** *true noble* **1069 his wordes he besette kan,** *he can express himself* **1070 for the nones,** *indeed*

1002 for, F reads "by." **1005 Sitheo,** Sychaeus, Dido's husband; after he was murdered, Dido escaped from Phoenicia and established Carthage. **1019 large,** omitted in F. **1022 Thus seith the book,** at *Aeneid* 1.412, Venus covers Aeneas and Achate in a cloud of invisibility. Chaucer's skepticism is part of his diminution of the supernatural in his version. **1024 this,** F reads "the." **1044–46** Chaucer's addition. **1046 ther,** omitted in F. **a cas,** F reads "in cas." **1048 he,** F reads "we." **1063 she hadde,** F reads "and." **1066 that he,** omitted in F.

And formed wel of brawnes° and of bones—
For after Venus° hadde he swich fairnesse
That no man myght be half so fair, I gesse—
And wel a lorde him semed for to be.
And for° he was a straunger, somwhat she
Lyked him the bette, as God do boote°,
To somme folk ofte newe thing is swoote°.
Anoon° hir herte hath pitee of his woo,
And with that pitee love come in alsoo.
And thus for pitee and for gentilesse,
Refresshed mote he been of° his distresse.
She seyde, certes, that she sory was
That he hath had swich peril and swich cas,
And in hir frendely speche, in this manere
She to him spak, and seide as ye may here:
"Be ye nat Venus sone and Anchises°?
In good feyth, al the worshippe° and encres°
That I may goodly doon yow, ye shal have.
Youre shippes and your meynee° shal I save."
And many a gentil word she spak him to,
And comaunded hir messageres go
The same day, withouten any faylle,
His shippes for to seke, and hem vitaylle°.
Ful many a beste° she to the shippes sente,
And with the wyn she gan hem to presente°,
And to hir royall paleys° she hir spedde,
And Eneas alwey with hir she ledde.
What nedeth yow the feste to discryve°?
He never beter at ease was in his lyve.
Ful was the feste of deyntees° and richesse,
Of instruments, of song, and of gladnesse,
And many an amorous lokyng and devys°.
This Eneas is come to paradys
Out of the swolowe° of helle, and thus in joye
Remembreth him of° his estaat in Troye.
To daunsyng chambres ful of parements°,
Of riche beddes, and of ornaments,
This Eneas is ladde after the mete°.
And with the queene whan that he hadde sete°,
And spices parted°, and the wyn agon°,
Unto his chambres was he lad anon
To take his ease and for to have his reste,
With al his folk, to doon what so hem leste°.
Ther nas coursere° wel ybrydled noon,
Ne stede° for the justyng wel to goon°,
Ne large palfrey° esy for the nones°,
Ne juwel fretted° ful of riche stones,
Ne sakkes ful of gold, of large wyghte°,
Ne rubee° noon that shyneth by nyghte,
Ne gentil hawteyn faucon heroneer°,
Ne hound for hert or wilde boor or deer,
Ne coupe° of golde with floryns newe ybete°,
That in the lond of Lybye may ben gete°,
That Dido ne hath hit Eneas ysente.
And al is payed, what that° he hath spente.
Thus kan this honorable queene hir gestes calle°,
As she that kan in fredom° passen alle.
Eneas soothly eke°, withouten les°,
Hath sent unto his shippe by Achates
After his sone, and after ryche thynges,
Both ceptre°, clothes, broches°, and eke rynges,
Somme for to were, and somme for to presente
To hir that al thise noble thynges him sente;
And bad° his sone, how that he sholde make
The presentyng, and to the queene hit take.
Repeyred° is this Achates agayne,
And Eneas ful blysful is and fayne°
To seen his yonge sone Ascanius.
But natheles° our autour° telleth us
That Cupido, that is the god of love,
At preyere of° his moder, hye° above,
Hadde the liknes° of the childe ytake°,

1071 brawnes, *muscles* **1072 after Venus,** *taking after Venus* (his mother) **1075 for,** *because* **1076 as God do boote,** *God help us!* **1077 swoote,** *sweet* **1078 Anoon,** *soon* **1081 mote he been of,** *must he be from* **1086 Venus sone and Anchises,** *the son of Venus and Anchises* **1087 worshippe,** *honor,* **encres,** *assistance* **1089 meynee,** *retinue* **1093 vitaylle,** *stock with provisions* **1094 beste,** *animal* **1095 gan hem to presente,** *provided them* **1096 paleys,** *palace* **1098 What nedeth yow the feste to discryve,** *what need is there to describe the feast to you* **1100 deyntees,** *delights* **1102 devys,** *ploy* **1104 swolowe,** *mouth or gulf* **1105 Remembreth him of,** *he recalls* **1106 parements,** *tapestries* **1108 mete,** *food* **1109 sete,** *sat* **1110 parted,** *taken,* **agon,** *gone* **1113 hem leste,** *he pleased* **1114 nas coursere,** *was no charger* **1115 Ne stede,** *nor steed,* **justyng wel to goon,** *well suited for jousting* **1116 palfrey,** *riding horse,* **the nones,** *that purpose* **1117 fretted,** *adorned* **1118 large wyghte,** *great weight* **1119 rubee,** *ruby* **1120 gentil hawteyn faucon heroneer,** *noble proud falcon for hunting herons* **1122 coupe,** *cup,* **floryns newe ybete,** *newly minted gold coins* **1123 may ben gete,** *can be obtained* **1125 what that,** *that which* **1126 hir gestes calle,** *treat her guests* **1127 fredom,** *generosity* **1128 soothly eke,** *truly also,* **withouten les,** *without lies* (truly) **1131 ceptre,** *scepter,* **broches,** *brooches* **1134 bad,** *directed* **1136 Repeyred,** *returned* **1137 fayne,** *happy* **1139 natheles,** *nevertheless,* **autour,** *author* **1141 At preyere,** *at the request,* **hye,** *high* **1142 liknes,** *likeness,* **ytake,** *taken*

1072 he, omitted in F. **1079 that,** omitted in F. **in,** omitted in F. **1085 and seide as ye may here,** F reads "sayde in this manere." **1099 in,** omitted in F. **1107 ornaments,** F reads "pavements." **1103–27** Chaucer's addition. **1110 spices . . . wyn,** the wine may have been spiced, or perhaps served with spiced delicacies; see *SqT* 5.291–94. **1128–49** Compressed from *Aeneid* 1.643–722. **1139 From Gg.** F reads "For to him yt was reported thus;" Tr, "Had gret desyre and aftyr fell hit thus."

This noble queene enamoured to make
On Eneas—but as of that scripture°,
Be as be may; I make of hit no cure°.
But sooth is this, the queene hath mad swich chere°
Unto this child that wonder is to here,
And of the present that his fader sente
She thanked him ful ofte, in good entente.
Thus is this queene in plesaunce and in joye,
With al this newe lusty° folk of Troye.
And of the dedes hath she moore enquered
Of Eneas, and al the story lered°
Of Troye; and al the longe day they twey°
Entendeden° to speke and for to pley,
Of which ther gan to breden swich a fire
That sely° Dido hath now swich° desire
With Eneas, her newe gest, to dele°
That she hath loste hir hewe° and eke hir hele°.
Now to th'effect°, now to the fruyt of al,
Why I have told this story, and tellen shal.
Thus I bygynne: hit fil upon a nyght,
Whan that the mone up-reyseth hath hir light,
This noble queene unto hir reste wente.
She siketh soore°, and gan hirself turmente.
She waketh°, walweth°, maketh many a brayed°,
As doon thise loveres, as I have herd sayde.
And at the laste unto her suster Anne
She made her mone°, and ryght thus spak she thanne.
"Now, dere suster myn, what may it be
That me agasteth° in my dreme?" quod she.
"This ilke° Troian is so in my thoghte,
For that° me thinketh he is so wel ywroghte°,
And eke° so likly for to ben a man°,
And therwithal° soo mykel good he kan°,
That al my love and lyf lyth in his cure°.
Have ye nat herd him telle his aventure?
Now certes°, Anne, if that ye rede° it me,
I wolde fayn° to him ywedded be—
This is th'effect; what sholde I more seye?
In him lith alle to do° me lyve or deye."
Hir suster Anne, as she that kouth hir goode°,
Seyde as hir thought°, and somdel hit withstoode°.
But herof was so longe a sermonynge,
Hit were to long to make rehersynge°.
But finally hit may nat be withstonde.
Love wol love—for no wyght° wol hit wonde°.
The dawenyng upryst° out of the see;
This amorous queene chargeth° hir meynee°
The nettes dresse°, and speres brode and kene°.
An huntyng wol° this lusty° fresshe quene,
So priketh° hir this newe joly woo.
To hors° is al hir lusty folke ygoo°.
Unto the court the houndes ben ybroughte,
And upon coursers° swyfte as any thoughte
Hir yonge knyghtes hoven° al aboute,
And of hir women eke an huge route°.
Upon a thikke palfrey°, paper whyt,
With sadel rede° enbroudet with delyt°,
Of gold the barres up-enbossed heighe°,
Sitte° Dido al in gold and perrey wreighe°.
And she is faire as is the brighte morwe°
That heeleth seke° folk of nyghtes sorwe.
Upon a courser startlyng° as the fire—
Men mighte turne him with a lytel wire°
Sitte Eneas, lyke Phebus to devyse°
So was he fressh arayed in hys wyse°

1144 scripture, *writing* **1145 make of hit no cure,** *pay it no attention* **1146 mad swich chere,** *acted in such a way* **1151 lusty,** *gallant* **1153 lered,** *learned* **1154 they twey,** *the two of them* **1155 Entendeden,** *were attentive* **1156 gan to breden swich,** *developed such* **1157 sely,** *innocent* **1158 dele,** *be involved with* **1159 hewe,** *color,* **hele,** *health* **1160 th'effect,** *the point* **1165 siketh soore,** *sighs sorely* **1166 waketh,** *stays awake,* **walweth,** *tosses,* **brayde,** *sudden movement* **1169 mone,** *lament* **1171 me agasteth,** *frightens me* **1172 ilke,** *same* **1173 For that,** *because,* **ywroghte,** *made* **1174 eke,** *also,* **likly for to ben a man,** *like what a man should be* **1175 therwithal,** *moreover,* **soo mykel good he kan,** *he can do so much good* **1176 lyth in his cure,** *lies in his care* **1178 certes,** *surely,* **rede,** *advise* **1179 fayn,** *gladly* **1181 do,** *make* **1182 kouth hir goode,** *knew what was best* **1183 Seyde as hir thought,** *gave her opinion,* **somdel hit withstoode,** *to an extent opposed it* **1185 make rehersynge,** *repeat* **1187 wyght,** *person,* **wonde,** *cease* **1188 dawenyng upryst,** *dawn rises up* **1189 chargeth,** *orders,* **meynee,** *retainers* **1190 dresse,** *to prepare,* **kene,** *sharp* **1191 An huntyng wol,** *a hunting will go,* **lusty,** *energetic* **1192 priketh,** *urges* **1193 To hors,** *to their horses,* **ygoo,** *gone* **1195 coursers,** *hunting horses* **1196 hoven,** *wait* **1197 route,** *group* **1198 thikke palfrey,** *sturdy riding horse* **1199 rede,** *red,* **enbroudet with delyt,** *delightfully adorned* **1200 Of gold the barres,** *with gold bars,* **up-enbossed heighe,** *highly embossed* **1201 Sitte,** *sits,* **perrey wreighe,** *jewels covered* **1202 morwe,** *morning* **1203 heeleth seke,** *heals sick* **1204 startlyng,** *quick moving* **1205 lytel wire,** *delicate bridle* **1206 devyse,** *describe* **1207 wyse,** *manner*

1142 liknes of the childe, in the *Aeneid,* Cupid disguises himself as Ascanius. **1145 make,** G and Tr read "take." **1150–61** Largely Chaucer's addition; he omits books 2 and 3 of the *Aeneid,* where in flashback Aeneas tells Dido of the fall of Troy and his sea voyages. **1159** Growing pale and feeling ill are conventional symptoms of love-sickness, as are sighing and having trouble sleeping (lines 1165–66). **hath,** omitted in F. **1162–1351** Generally follows book 4 of the *Aeneid,* although scholars have identified a number of changes in detail and emphasis. **1174 for,** omitted in F. **1183 somdel hit withstode,** Chaucer cuts short 22 lines in the *Aeneid* 4.31–53 and changes Anna's role. In the *Aeneid* she encourages the marriage. **1206 Phebus,** the god of the sun.

The fomy bridel with the bitte of golde
Governeth he right as himself hath wolde°
And foorth this noble quene, this lady ryde
On hunting, with this Troian by hir syde.
The herd of hertes° founden is anoon,
With "Hey! Goo bet°! Prik thou°! Lat goon, lat goon!
Why nyl° the leoun comen, or the bere,
That I mighte him ones° meten with this spere?"
Thus seyn thise yonge folk, and up they kille
These hertes wilde, and han hem at here wille.
Among al this to romblen gan the hevene;
The thonder rored with a grisly stevene°;
Doune come the rain with haile and sleet so faste,
With hevenes fire, that hit so sore agaste°
This noble quene, and also hir meynee°,
That yche of hem was glad awey to flee.
And shortly, fro the tempest hir to save,
She fled hirself into a lytel cave—
And with hir went this Eneas also.
I not° with hem yf ther went any moo;
The auctour maketh of hit no mencioun.
And here began the depe affeccioun
Betwix hem two. This was the firste morwe°
Of here gladnesse, and gynnyng of hir sorwe.
For ther hath Eneas ykneled° soo,
And told hir al his herte and al his woo,
And swore so depe to hir to be trewe
For wele° or woo and chaunge for noo newe°,
And as a fals lover so wel kan pleyne°,
That sely° Dido rewed° on his peyne
And tok hym for housbond and became his wyf
For evermo while that hem laste lyf.
And after this, whan that the tempest stente°,
With myrth out as they comen, home they wente.
The wikked fame° up roos, and that anoon,
How Eneas hath with the queene ygoon
Into the cave; and demed as hem liste°.
And whan the kynge that Yarbas hight° hit wiste°,
As he that had hir loved ever his lyf,
And wowed° hir to have hir to his wyf,
Swich° sorowe as he hath maked, and swich chere°,
Hit is a rewthe° and pitee for to here.
But as in love al day hit happeth soo°,
That oon° shal lawghen at anothers woo,
Now lawgheth Eneas and is in joye,
And more riches than ever was in Troye.
O sely° wemen, ful of innocence,
Ful of pitee and trouthe and conscience,
What maked yow to men to trusten soo?
Have ye suche rewthe upon here feyned° woo,
And han suche ensamples olde yow biforne?
Se ye nat al how they ben forsworne°?
Where se ye oon that he ne hath laft his leef°,
Or ben unkynde, or don hir som myscheef,
Or pilled° hir, or bosted of his dede?
Ye may as wel hit seen as ye may rede°.
Tak hede now of this grete gentilman,
This Troian, that so wel hir plesen kan,
That feyneth him so trewe and obeysinge°,
So gentil and so privy° of his doynge,
And kan so wel doon al his obeysaunces°,
And waiten hir° at festes and at daunces,
And whan she gooth to temple and home agayne,
And fasten° til he hath his lady a sayne°,
And beren in his devyses° for hir sake—
Wot I nat° what—and songes wolde he make,
Justen°, and doon of armes many thynges,
Send hir lettres, tokens, broches°, rynges—

1209 hath wolde, *has desire* **1212 hertes,** *deer* **1213 Goo bet,** *hurry,* **Prik thou,** *spur on,* **Lat goon,** *release* (the dogs) **1214 nyl,** *won't* **1215 ones,** *once* **1219 grisly stevene,** *fearsome sound* **1221 sore agaste,** *sorely frightened* **1222 meynee,** *retainers* **1227 not,** *don't know* **1230 morwe,** *morning* **1232 kneled,** *kneeled* **1235 wele,** *joy,* **chaunge for noo newe,** *never give her up for a new lover* **1236 pleyne,** *protest* **1237 sely,** *innocent,* **rewed,** *took pity* **1240 stente,** *stopped* **1242 wikked fame,** *scandal* **1244 demed as hem liste,** (people) *judged as they pleased* **1245 hight,** *was named,* **wiste,** *knew* **1247 wowed,** *wooed* **1248 Swich,** *such,* **chere,** *expression* **1249 rewthe,** *sorrow* **1250 al day hit happeth soo,** *it always happens so* **1251 oon,** *one* **1254 sely,** *incautious* **1257 rewthe,** *pity,* **here feyned,** *their pretended* **1259 ben forsworne,** *break promises* **1260 leef,** *beloved* **1262 pilled,** *robbed* **1263 rede,** *read* **1266 obeysinge,** *obedient* **1267 privy,** *secret* **1268 obeysaunces,** *duties* **1269 waiten hir,** *attend to her* **1271 fasten,** *not eat,* **a sayne,** *seen* **1272 beren in his devyses,** *wear his ornaments* **1273 Wot I nat,** *I know not* **1274 Justen,** *joust* **1275 broches,** *brooches*

1210 noble, omitted in F. **1212 herd of hertes,** hart-hunting was a conventional figure for the amorous chase in medieval literature because of the verbal play on hart / heart. **1219 thonder rored,** in *Aeneid* 4.90–128, Juno and Venus conspire to cause the storm in order to compel the marriage of Aeneas and Dido. Chaucer reduces the role of the gods throughout his version. **1221 hyt,** reading from Gg. F reads "ys;" Tr, "they." **1232–37** Chaucer's addition. **1242 wikked fame,** in the *Aeneid* at this point (4.173–8), Virgil has a description of Fame that Chaucer omits; he had adapted it earlier in *HF* 1360–92. **1245 Yarbas,** Iarbas, a neighboring king, had wooed Dido unsuccessfully. **1247 hir,** omitted in F. **1254–84** Chaucer's addition. **1254 wemen,** F reads "woman." **1269 And waiten hir,** F reads "To hir."

Now herkneth° how he shal his lady serve!
Ther as° he was in peril for to sterve°
For hunger and for myscheef° in the see,
And desolat, and fledde fro his contree,
And al his folk with tempeste al to-driven°,
She hath hir body and eke hir reame° yiven
Into his hand, ther as she myghte have bene
Of other lond than of Cartage a quene,
And lyved in joye ynogh°. What wolde ye more°?
This Eneas that hath thus depe yswore°
Is wery of his craft within a throwe°,
The hoote ernest is al over-blowe°.
And prively° he dooth his shippes dyghte°,
And shapeth him° to steele awey by nighte.
  This Dido hath suspecioun of thys,
And thoughte wel that hit was al amys°,
For in his bed he lyth anyght and siketh°.
She asketh him anoon what him mysliketh°—
“My dere hert, which that I love mooste?”
  “Certes°,” quod he, “thys nyght my fadres gooste
Hath in my sleep so sore me turmented,
And eke° Mercure his message hath presented,
That nedes to° the conquest of Itayle
My destany is soone for to sayle—
For whiche, methinketh, brosten° is myn herte!”
Therwith his fals teeres out they sterte°,
And taketh hir within his armes twoo.
  “Is that in ernest?” quod she. “Wil ye soo?
Have ye nat sworn to wife me to take?
Alas, what womman wol ye of me make?
I am a gentilwoman and a queen!
Ye wol nat fro your wife thus foule fleen°!
That I was borne, allas, what shal I do?”
  To telle in short, this noble queen Dido,
She seketh halwes° and dooth sacrifice,
She kneleth, crieth that routhe° is to devyse°,
Conjureth him, and profreth° him to bee
His thrall°, his servant in the lest degree;
She falleth him to foote° and swowneth° there
Dischevely° with hir bryght gilte here°,
And seith, “Have mercy! Let me with yow ryde!
These lordes which that wonien° me besyde
Wol me destroien oonly for youre sake.
And° ye wol me now to wife take,
As ye han sworn, than wol I yive yow leve
To sleen me with your swerd now soone at eve!
For than shal I yet dien as your wife.
I am with childe, and yive my childe his lyfe!
Mercy, lord, have pitee in youre thought!”
But al this thing avayleth hir ryght nought°,
For on a nyght sleping he let hir lye,
And staal awey unto his companye,
And as a traytour forthe he gan to saile
Toward the large contree of Itayle.
And thus he lefte Dido in woo and pyne°,
And wedded ther a lady highte° Lavyne.
  A cloth he lefte, and eke his swerd stondyng,
Whan he fro Dido staal in her sleping,
Ryght at hir beddes hed, so gan he hye°,
Whan that he staal awey to his navye.
Which cloth, whan sely° Dido gan awake,
She hath hit kyst ful ofte for hys sake,
And seyde, “O cloth, while Jupiter hit leste°,
Take now my soule, unbind me of this unreste!
I have fulfilled of Fortune al the cours.”
And thus, allas, withouten hys socours°,
Twenty tyme yswowned° hath she thanne°.
And whan that she unto her suster Anne
Compleyned had, of which I may nat write—

1276 herkneth, *listen* **1277 Ther as,** *whereas,* **sterve,** *die* **1278 myscheef,** *misfortune* **1280 to-driven,** *scattered* **1281 reame,** *realm* **1284 ynogh,** *plenty* (enough) **What wolde ye more,** *what more do you want* **1285 depe yswore,** *deeply sworn* **1286 throwe,** *short time* **1287 over-blowe,** *blown over* **1288 prively,** *secretly,* **dooth . . . dighte,** *makes ready* **1289 shapeth him,** *prepares* **1291 amys,** *wrong* **1292 siketh,** *sighs* **1293 him mysliketh,** *displeases him* **1295 Certes,** *surely* **1297 eke,** *also* **1298 That nedes to,** *that requires* **1300 brosten,** *broken* **1301 sterte,** *pour* **1307 foule fleen,** *foully flee* **1310 halwes,** *shrines* **1311 routhe,** *pitiful,* **devyse,** *describe* **1312 profreth,** *offers* **1313 thral,** *slave* **1314 him to foote,** *to his feet,* **swowneth,** *swoons* **1315 Dischevely . . . gilte here,** *golden hair unbound* **1317 wonien,** *live* **1319 And,** *if* **1325 avayleth hir ryght nought,** *gains her nothing at all* **1330 pyne,** *pain* **1331 highte,** *named* **1334 so gan he hye,** *he hurried so* **1336 sely,** *innocent* **1338 Jupiter hit leste,** *it pleases Jupiter* **1341 hys socours,** *Aeneas' comfort* **1342 yswowned,** *fainted,* **thanne,** *then*

1295–98 my fadres gooste . . . Itayle, in *Aeneid* 4.351–61 Anchises' spirit and other supernatural omens urge Aeneas to depart for Italy; in Chaucer's version, they are the false excuses of a restless lover. **1296 so sore me,** F reads “me so sore.” **1297 Mercure,** Mercury, the messenger of the gods. **1298 to,** omitted in F. **1303–24** The pathos here is Chaucer's invention; in *Aeneid* 4.362–87, Dido responds to the suggestion of Aeneas's departure with royal fury. **1323 with childe,** in *Aeneid* 4.327–29, Dido is not pregnant. **1326 sleping he let her lye,** Chaucer's addition; in the *Aeneid* 4.393–96, Aeneas departs at the bidding of heaven. **1327 unto,** F reads “upon.” **unreste,** F reads “reste.” **1330 And thus he,** F reads “And thus hath he.” **1332 A cloth,** in *Aeneid* 4.648, Aeneas leaves behind his Trojan garments. **1337 hit,** omitted in F. **1339 now,** omitted in F.

So grete a routhe° I have hit for t'endite°—
And bad hir noryce° and hir suster goon
To fecchen fire and other thinges anoon,
And seyde that she wolde sacrifyee,
And whan she myght hir tyme wel espyee°,
Upon the fire of sacrifice she sterte°,
And with his swerd she roof° hir to the herte.
  But, as myn auctour seyth, yit thus she seyde,
Or° she was hurt, beforne or° she deyde,
She wroot a lettre anoon, that thus biganne:
"Ryght so," quod she, "as that the white
    swanne
Ayenst° his deeth begynneth for to synge,
Ryght so to yow make I my compleynynge.
Nat that I trowe° to geten yow agayn,
For wel I woot° that hit is al in vayn,
Syn that° the goddes ben contraire to me.
But syn my name is lost thurgh yow," quod she,
"I may wel lese° a word on yow, or letter,
Al be it that I shal be never the better—
For thilke° wynd that blew your shipe away,
The same wind hath blowe away your fay°."
  But whoso wol al this letter have in mynde,
Rede Ovyde, and in him he shal hit fynde.

Explicit legenda Didonis martiris, Cartaginis regine.

IV

Legend of Hypsipyle and Medea

Incipit legenda Ysiphile et Medee, martirum.

Legend of Hypsipyle

  Thou roote of fals lovers, Duke Jasoun,
Thou slye devourer and confusyoun
Of gentilwomen, tender creatures,
Thou madest thy reclaimyng° and thy lures
To ladies of thy staately aparaunce,
And of thy wordes farsed° with plesaunce,
And of thy feyned° trouthe and thy manere,
With thyne obeysaunce° and humble chere°,
And with thy counterfeted peyn and woo.
Ther oother° falsen oon, thow falsest twoo!
O, ofte swore thou that thou woldest deye
For love, whan thou ne feltest maladeye
Save foul delyt, which that thou callest love.
If that I lyve, thy name shal be shove°
In Englyssh, that thy sekte° shal be knowe!
Have at thee, Jasoun, now thyn horn is blowe!
But certes, it is both rowth° and woo
That love with fals lovers werketh soo,
For they shal have wel better and gretter chere°
Than he that hath bought love ful dere°,
Or had in armes° many a blody box°.

1345 routhe, *sorrow,* **t'endite,** *to record* **1346 noryce,** *nurse* **1349 espyee,** *see* **1350 sterte,** *leapt* **1351 roof,** *stabbed* **1353 Or,** *before,* **beforne or,** *before* **1356 Ayenst,** *confronting* **1358 trowe,** *expect* **1359 woot,** *know* **1360 Syn that,** *since* **1362 lese,** *lose* **1364 thilke,** *that* **1365 fay,** *faith* **1371 reclaimyng,** *enticement* **1373 farsed,** *stuffed* **1374 feyned,** *pretended* **1375 obeysaunce,** *submission,* **chere,** *demeanor* **1377 Ther oother,** *where others* **1381 shove,** *thrust forward* **1382 sekte,** *sect* **1384 rowth,** *pity* **1386 chere,** *reception* **1387 ful dere,** *very dearly* **1388 armes,** *battle,* **box,** *blow*

1355–65 This letter is based on Dido's letter in Ovid, *Heroides* 7.1–8. **1355 white swanne,** it was thought that swans were mute until the time of their death; the origin of *swan song.* **1359 that,** omitted in F. **1360 contraire,** F reads "contrariouse." **1366–67** Compare *WBT* 3.981–82. **1367a *Explicit* . . . ,** Here ends the legend of Dido, martyr, Queen of Carthage. **1367b *Incipit* . . . ,** Here begins the legend of Hypsipyle and Medea, martyrs. Chaucer's major source is Guido delle Colonne, *Historia Destructionis Troiae* (*History of the Fall of Troy*) books 1–3, and Ovid, *Heroides* 6 and 12. **1368–95** Chaucer's invention; not in his sources. **1370 gentilwomen,** Gg reads "tendere womyn." **tender,** from Tr; F and Gg reads "gentil." **1382 sekte,** F reads "sleighte." **1383 thyn horn is blowe,** perhaps an allusion to Dante's *Inferno* 19.5, where horns proclaim criminals' offences, or something similar to "the hunt is up." 1389-91 i.e., even though the fox is false and a thief, it eats capons (male castrated chickens) that are every bit as tender as those eaten by the owner who paid for them.

For ever as tendre a capoun° eteth the fox,
Though he be fals and hath the foule° betrayed,
As shal the goodman° that therfor hath payed—
Allethof° he have to the capoun skille° and ryghte,
The false fox wil have his part at nyght.
On Jasoun this ensample is wel yseene
By Isiphile and Medea the queene.
  In Tessalye, as Guido telleth us,
Ther was a kyng that highte° Pelleus,
That had a brother which that hight Eson,
And whan for age he myghte unnethes gon°,
He yaf° to Pelleus the governynge
Of al his regne°, and made him lorde and kynge,
Of which Eson this Jasoun geten was°,
That in his tyme in al that land ther nas
Nat suche a famous kynght of gentilesse°,
Of fredome°, and of strengthe and lustynesse°.
After his fader deeth, he bare him soo
That there nas noon° that lyste ben his foo°,
But dide him al honour and companye;
Of which this Pelleus hath grete envye,
Imagynyng that Jasoun myghte be
Enhaunced so and put in suche degre°
With love of lordes of his regioun,
That from his regne he may be put adoun.
And in his witte anyghte° compassed he°
How Jasoun myghte best destroyed be,
Withoute sclaunder° of his compassemente°.
And at the laste he took avysemente°
To senden him into some fer contree
Ther as° this Jasoun may distroyed be.
This was his witte°, al° made he to Jasoun
Grete chere° of love and of affeccioun,
For drede leste° his lordes hit espyede°.
  So felle hit° so, as fame renneth° wyde,
Ther was suche tidynge overalle and suche los°,
That in an ile° that called was Colcos,
Beyonde Troy, esteward in the see,
That therin was a ram that men myghte see
That had a flees° of gold that shoon so bryght
That nowher was ther suche another sight.
But hit was kept° alway with a dragoun,
And many other mervels up and doun,
And with twoo booles° maked al of bras,
That spitten fire, and muche thinge ther was.
But this was eke the tale°, nathelees,
That whoso wolde wynne thilke° flees,
He moste bothe of° he hit wynne myghte,
With the booles and the dragoun fyghte;
And King Oetes lord was of that ile.
  This Pelleus bethoughte upon this wyle,
That he his nevywe° Jasoun wolde enhorte°
To saylen to that londe him to disporte°,
And seyde, "Neviwe, if hit myghte be
That suche a worshippe° myghte falle the°
That thou this famous tresor myghte wynne,
And bryngen hit my regyoun wythinne,
Hit were to me grette plesaunce and honoure;
Thanne were I holde° to quyte° thy laboure.
And al the costes I wole myselfe make°;
And chese° what folke thou wilt wyth the take;
Let see now, darstow° taken this viage°?"
Jasoun was yonge and lusty of corage°
And undertook to doon this ilke empryse°.
  Anoon Argus his shippes gan devyse°.
With Jasoun went the strong Ercules,
And many another that he with him ches°.
But whoso axeth° who is with him gon,
Let him go reden *Argoniauticon,*

1389 capoun, *chicken* **1390 foule,** *bird* **1391 goodman,** *householder* **1392 Allethof,** *although,* **skille,** *reasonable claim* **1398 highte,** *was named* **1399 unnethes gon,** *barely walk* **1400 yaf,** *gave* **1401 regne,** *kingdom* **1402 getten was,** *was begotten* **1404 gentilesse,** *nobility* **1405 fredome,** *generosity,* **lustynesse,** *vigor* **1407 nas noon,** *was no one,* **lyste ben his foo,** *wanted to be his enemy* **1411 degre,** *status* **1414 witte anyghte,** *thoughts at night,* **compassed he,** *he schemed* **1416 sclaunder,** *accusation,* **compassemente,** *plotting* **1417 took avysemente,** *decided* **1419 Ther as,** *where* **1420 witte,** *thought,* **al,** *although* **1421 chere,** *display* **1422 For drede leste,** *out of fear that,* **espeyede,** *might discover* **1423 felle,** *happened,* **renneth,** *runs* **1424 los,** *rumor* **1425 ile,** *island* **1428 flees,** *fleece* **1430 kept,** *guarded* **1432 booles,** *bulls* **1434 eke the tale,** *also the report* **1435 whoso wolde wynne thilke,** *whoever wanted to win this* **1436 or,** *before* **1440 nevywe,** *nephew,* **enhorte,** *encourage* **1441 him to disporte,** *to entertain himself* **1443 worshippe,** *honor,* **falle the,** *happen to you* **1447 Thanne were I holde,** *then would I be required,* **quyte,** *reward* **1448 make,** *pay* **1449 chese,** (you) *choose* **1450 darstow,** *do you dare,* **viage,** *journey* **1451 lusty of corage,** *vigorous of heart* **1452 ilke empryse,** *same enterprise* **1453 devyse,** *arrange* **1455 ches,** *chose* **1456 axeth,** *asks*

1396–1461 Follows Guido's *Historia* 1. **1396 Tessalye,** Thessaly, east of the Black Sea. **Guido,** from Gg and Tr; F reads "Ovyde." See lines 1464-65. **1397 kyng,** F reads "knyght." **Pelleus,** Pelias in classical sources, but Guido spells it "Peleus." **1398 Eson,** Aeson, father of Jason. **1405 and,** omitted in F and Tr. **1418 To,** F reads "That to." **1425 Colcos,** Colchis, in the Black Sea. **1438 Oetes,** Aeëtes, king of Colchis and father of Medea. **1439 wyle,** F reads "while." **1453 Argus,** legendary builder of the ship Argo, after which were named the Argonauts, Jason's sailing companions. **1454 Ercules,** Hercules. **1457 go,** omitted in F. ***Argoniauticon,*** the *Argonautica* (c70 C.E.) of Gaius Valerius Flaccus contains a list of the Argonauts, although Chaucer may have known the work secondhand.

For he wol telle a tale long ynoughe.
Philotetes anoon° the sayle up droughe°,
Whan that the wynd was good, and gan him
hye°
Out of his contree called Tessalye.
So longe he sayled in the salte see
Til in the ile of Lemnoun arryved he—
Al be° this nat rehersed of Guydo,
Yet seyth Ovyde in his *Epistoles* so—
And of this ile lady was and queene
The faire yonge Ysiphile the shene°,
That whilom° Thoas doughter was, the kynge.
Ysiphile was goon in hir pleyinge°,
And romyng on the clyves° by the see,
Under a banke anoon espied° shee
Where that the shippe of Jasoun gan arryve.
Of hir goodnesse adoun she sendeth blyve°
To weten yif that° any straunge wyghte°
With tempest thider were yblowe anyghte°—
To doon him socour°; as was hir usaunce°
To forthren° every wyght, and don plesaunce°
Of veray bountee° and of curteysie.
This messagere adoun him gan to hye°,
And found Jasoun, and Ercules also,
That in a cogge° to londe were ygo°
Hem to refresshen and to take the eyre—
The morwenyng atempree° was and faire.
And in his wey this messagere hem mette.
Ful kunnyngely° these lordes two he grette°,
And did his message, axyng° hem anoon
If they were broken° or ought woo begoon°
Or hadde nede of lodesmen° or vitayle°,
For of socoure° they shulde nothing fayle,
For hit was outrely° the queues wille.
Jasoun ansuerde, mekely and stille°,
"My lady," quod he, "thanke I hertely
Of hir goodnesse. Us nedeth°, trewely,
Nothing as now, but that we wery bee,
And come for to pley° out of the see
Til that the wynd be better in oure wey."
This lady rometh by the clyffe to pley°,
With hir meynee°, endelong the stronde°,
And fyndeth this Jasoun and these other stonde,
In spekyng of this thinge as I yow tolde.
This Ercules and Jasoun gan beholde
How that the queene it was, and faire hir grette°
Anoon ryght as° they with this lady mette.
And she tooke hede°, and knew by here°
manere,
By here aray°, by wordes and by chere°,
That hit were gentilmen of grete degree.
And to the castel with hir ledeth she
These straunge folk°, and dooth hem grete honour,
And axeth° hem of travaylle° and labour
That they han suffred in the salte see,
So that, withynne a day, or two, or three,
She knew, by folk that in his shippes bee,
That hit was Jasoun, ful of renomee°,
And Ercules, that hadde the grete los°,
That soughten the aventures of Colcos,
And did hem honour more than before,
And with hem deled° ever lenger the more,
For they ben worthy folk, withouten les°.
And namely°, she spak most with Ercules;
To him hir herte bar° he shulde bee
Sad°, wise, and trewe, of wordes avysee°,
Withouten any other affeccioun
Of love or evyl ymaginacioun.
This Ercules hath so this Jasoun preysed
That to the sonne he hath him up areysed,

1459 anoon, *soon,* **droughe,** *drew* **1460 gan him hye,** *hurried* **1464 Al be,** *even though* **1467 shene,** *beautiful* **1468 whilom,** *once* **1469 was goon in hir pleyinge,** *enjoying herself* **1470 clyves,** *cliffs* **1471 anoon espied,** *suddenly noticed* **1473 blyve,** *quickly* **1474 weten yif that,** *learn whether,* **straunge wyghte,** *foreign person* **1475 anyghte,** *at night* **1476 doon him socour,** *give him comfort,* **usaunce,** *custom* **1477 forthren,** *aid,* **don plesaunce,** *spread happiness* **1478 Of veray bountee,** *out of true goodness* **1479 gan to hye,** *hurried* **1481 cogge,** *small boat,* **ygo,** *gone* **1483 atempree,** *mild* **1485 kunnyngely,** *skillfully,* **grette,** *greeted* **1486 axyng,** *asking* **1487 broken,** *damaged,* **ought woo begoon,** *in anyway distressed* **1488 lodesmen,** *pilots,* **vitayle,** *provisions* **1489 socoure,** *aid* **1490 outrely,** *utterly* **1491 stille,** *quietly* **1493 Us nedeth,** *we need* **1495 to pley,** *recreation* **1497 to pley,** *for recreation* **1498 meynee,** *company,* **endelong the stronde,** *along the shore* **1502 grette,** *greeted* **1503 Anoon ryght as,** *as soon as* **1504 tooke hede,** *paid attention,* **here,** *their* **1505 aray,** *clothing,* **chere,** *demeanor* **1508 straunge folk,** *foreign people* **1509 axeth,** *asks,* **travaylle,** *trouble* **1513 renomee,** *renown* **1514 los,** *reputation* **1517 deled,** *had dealings* **1518 withouten les,** *truly* **1519 namely,** *especially* **1520 bar,** *inclined* (that) **1521 Sad,** *steadfast,* **avysee,** *discreet*

1459 Philotetes, Philoctetes. **1460 that,** omitted in F. **1462–1579** Generally, Chaucer's source here is Ovid's *Heroides* (*Letters of Heroines*) 6, although scholars have noted several details that occur in no known source. **1463 Lemnoun,** Lemnos; F reads "Lenoun." **1464–65 nay rehersed of Guydo,** the story of Hypsipyle is not in the English manuscripts of Guido, although Skeat points out in his edition of Chaucer's works (3.326) that a Spanish version of Guido printed in 1587 does include the story of Hypsipyle at this point. **1471 banke,** F reads "brake." **1472 that the shippe of,** F reads "lay the shippe that." **1487 ought,** omitted in F. **1489 of,** omitted in F. **1490** Line omitted in F. **1496 that,** F reads "at." **1512 by folk,** F reads "by the folk." **1524 Ercules . . . this Jasoun preysed,** Chaucer invents this role for Hercules; in no other version does he conspire to promote the love affair between Jason and Hypsipyle. **so,** omitted in F. **1525 him,** F reads "it."

That half so trewe a man ther nas° of love
Under the cope° of hevene that is above;
And he was wys, hardy, secree, and ryche.
Of these thre poyntes ther nas noon hym liche°:
Of fredom passed° he and lustihede°,
Al thoo° that lyven or ben dede;
Ther to° so grete a gentilman was he,
And of Tessalye likly kyng to be.
Ther nas no lakke but that he was agaste°
To love, and for to speke shamefaste°;
He had lever° hymselfe to mordre and dye
Than that men shulde a lover him espye°:
"As wolde God° that I hadde yive°
My blood and flessh so that I myghte lyve
With the nones° that he hadde oghwher° a wyf
For his estaat, for suche a lusty lyf
She sholde lede with this lusty knyghte!"
And al this was compassed on° the nyghte
Betwix him Jasoun and this Ercules.
Of these twoo her was mad a shrewed les°
To come to hous upon° an innocent,
For to bedote° this queen was here entent.
This Jasoun is as coy as is a mayde;
He loketh pitously, but noght he sayde,
But freely yaf° he to hir counseileres
Yiftes grete, and to hir officeres.
As wolde God I leyser hadde, and tyme,
By processe° al his wowyng° for to ryme.
But in this hous any fals lover be,
Ryght as himself now doth, ryght so did he,
With feynyng° and with every sotil° dede.
Ye gete no more of me, but° ye wol rede°
The original, that telleth al the cas.
The sothe° is this, that Jasoun weddid was
Unto this queene, and toke of hir substaunce
Whatso him lystet°, unto his purveyaunce°.
And upon hir begat he children two,
And drough° his sayle, and saugh hir nevermo.
A letter sente she him certeyn,
Which were to long to written° and to seyn,
And him repreveth° of his grete untrouthe,
And prayeth him on hir to have some routhe.
And of his children two, she sayede him this,
That they be lyke, of alle thing, ywis°,
To Jasoun, save° they coude nat begile;
And prayed God, or° hit were longe while,
That she, that had his herte yreft hir fro°,
Most fynden° him to hir untrewe also,
And that she moste° bothe hir children spille°,
And al thoo° that suffreth° him his wille.
And trew to Jasoun was she al hir lyf,
And ever kepte hir chast, as for his wyf;
Ne never had she joye at hir herte,
But dyed for his love of sorwes smerte°.

Legend of Medea

To Colcos comen is this Duke Jasoun,
That is of love devourer and dragoun.
As matere appetyteth forme° alwey,
And from forme into forme hit passen may,
Or as a welle that were botomles,
Ryght so kan fals Jasoun have no pes°
For to desiren, thurgh his appetyte,
To doon with gentilwymmen hys delyte—
This is his luste° and his felicitee°.
Jasoun is romed° forth to the citee
That whilom cleped° was Jaconitos,
That was the maister° toune of al Colcos,
And hath ytold the cause of his comynge
Unto Oetes, of that contree kynge,
Praying him that he most doon his assay°

1526 a man ther nas, *there was no man* **1527 cope,** *canopy* **1528 hardy,** *brave* **1529 ther nas noon hym liche,** *there was no one like him* **1530 Of fredom passed he,** *he surpassed in generosity,* **lustihede,** *vigor* **1531 thoo,** *those* **1532 Ther to,** *moreover* **1534 agaste,** *afraid* **1535 shamefaste,** *bashful* **1536 lever,** *rather* **1537 espye,** *discover* (to be) **1538 As wolde God,** *I would to God,* **yive,** *given* **1540 With the nones,** i.e., *to see the time,* **oghwher,** *anywhere* **1543 compassed on,** *devised in* **1545 mad a shrewed les,** *made a cursed lie* **1546 come to hous upon,** *deceive* **1547 bedote,** *infatuate* **1550 yaf,** *gave* **1553 By processe,** *step by step,* **wowyng,** *wooing* **1556 feynyng,** *pretending,* **sotil,** *subtle* **1557 but,** *unless,* **rede,** *read* **1559 sothe,** *truth* **1561 Whatso him lyste,** *whatever he wanted,* **purveyaunce,** *provisioning* **1563 drough,** *hoisted* **1565 written,** *write* **1566 repreveth,** *accuses* **1569 ywis,** *truly* **1570 save,** *except that* **1571 or,** *before* **1572 That she, that had his herte yreft hir fro,** *that she, who had taken his heart from her* **1573 Most fynden,** *must learn* **1574 moste,** *must,* **spille,** *kill* **1576 al thoo,** *all those,* **suffreth,** *allow* **1579 smerte,** *pain* **1582 matere appetyteth forme,** *matter desires form* **1585 pes,** *peace* **1588 luste,** *desire,* **felicitee,** *happiness* **1589 is romed,** *has walked* **1590 whilom cleped,** *formerly named* **1591 maister,** *principal* **1594 most doon his assay,** *might make his attempt*

1550 he, omitted in F. **1552 wolde God I,** F reads "God wolde that I." **1559 sothe,** Gg and Tr read "somme." **1568–70** Follows Ovid, *Heroides* 6.121–24. **1571–74** Follows Ovid, *Heroides* 6.151–56, where Hypsipyle is cursing Medea who she knows to be Jason's new lover. **1580–1655** Generally follows Guido's *Historia* 2–3. **1580 Colcos,** Colchis. **1582 matere appetyteth forme,** Chaucer takes this from Guido, *Historia* 2 (page 17 in edition by Griffin), although there it is applied to women's desire for men. **matere,** F reads "nature." **1583** F reads "And forme to forme to forme a hit passen may." **1590 Jaconitos,** F reads "Jasonicos;" Guido has "Iaconites."

To gete the flees of gold, if that he may.
Of which the kynge assentith to hys bone°,
And doth him honour, as hit is to done°,
So ferforth° that his doghtre and his eyre°,
Medea, which that was so wise and feyre,
That feyrer saugh ther never man with eye,
He made her doon to Jasoun companye°
Atte mete, and sitte by him in the halle.
  Now was Jasoun a semly° man withalle,
And like a lorde, and had a grete renoun,
And of his loke as real° as leoun,
And goodly of his speche, and famulere°,
And koude° of love al craft and art plenere°
Withoute boke, with everyche observaunce.
And as fortune hir oughte° a foul meschaunce,
She wex° enamoured upon this man.
"Jasoun," quod she, "for oght° I se or kan°,
As of this thing the which ye ben aboute,
Ye han yourself iput in moche doute°.
For whoso wol this aventure acheve,
He may nat wel asterten° as I leve°,
Withouten deth, but° I his helpe be.
But nathelesse, hit is my wille," quod she,
"To furtheren yow, so that ye shal nat dye,
But turnen° sound home to your Thessalye."
  "My ryghte° lady," quod thys Jasoun thoo°,
"That ye han of my dethe or of my woo
Any rewarde°, and doon me this honour,
I wot° wel that my myght ne my labour
May nat deserve hit in my lyves day°.
God thanke yow, ther° I ne kan ne may.
Youre man am I, and louly° yow beseche
To ben my help, withoute more speech;
But certes°, for my dethe° shal I nat spare°."
  Thoo° gan this Medea to him declare
The peril of this cas, fro poynt to poynte,
And of his batayle, and in what dysjoynte°
He mote° stonde, of which no creature
Save° oonly she ne myght his lyfe assure°.
And shortely ryght to the point for to go,
They ben accorded° ful betwex hem two,
That Jasoun shal hir wedde, as trewe knyght,
And terme° ysette, to come soone at nyght
Unto hir chambre, and make ther his ooth
Upon the goddes, that he for leef no looth°
Ne shulde hir never falsen°, nyght ne day,
To ben hir husbond while he lyve may,
As she that from his dethe him saved there.
And herupon, anight° they mette yfere°,
And doth° his oothe, and gooth with hir to bed.
And on the morwe, upward he him sped.
For she hath taught him how he shal nat faile
The flees to wynne, and stynten° his batayle;
And saved him his lyf and his honour;
And gat him a name as a conquerour
Ryght through the sleyght of hir enchauntement.
  Now hath Jasoun the flees, and home is went
With Medea and tresoures ful gret woon°.
But unwiste of° hir fader she is goon
To Thessaly with Duke Jasoun, hir leef°,
That afterward hath broght hir to myscheef°.
For as a traytour he is from hir goo°,
And with hir lefte his yonge children twoo,
And falsly hath betrayed hir, allas—
And ever in love a cheef traytour he was—
And wedded yet the thirdde wife anon°,
That was the doghtre of King Creon.
This is the mede° of lovynge and guerdon°
That Medea receyved of Jasoun
Ryght for° hir trouthe and for hir kyndenesse,
That loved him better than hirselfe, I gesse,
And lefte hir fader and hir heritage°.
And of Jasoun this is the vassalage°,
That in his dayes nas never noon yfounde
So fals a lover goynge on the grounde°.
And therfor in hir letter thus she sayde,

1596 bone, *request* **1597 to done,** *customary* **1598 So ferforth,** *to such an extent,* **eyre,** *heir* **1601 doon . . . companye,** *accompany* **1603 semely,** *attractive* **1605 real,** *royal* **1606 famulere,** *sociable* **1607 koude,** *knew,* **plenere,** *fully* **1609 hir oughte,** *owed to her* **1610 wex,** *became* **1611 oght,** *all,* **kan,** *know* **1613 doute,** *danger* **1615 asterten,** *escape,* **leve,** *believe* **1616 but,** *unless* **1619 turnen,** *return* **1620 ryghte,** *true,* **thoo,** *then* **1622 rewarde,** *regard* **1623 wot,** *know* **1624 lyves day,** *life* **1625 ther,** *where* **1626 louly,** *humbly* **1628 But certes,** *assuredly,* **for my dethe,** *for fear of death,* **spare,** *hold back* **1629 Thoo,** *then* **1631 dysjoynte,** *peril* **1632 mote,** *must* **1633 Save,** *except,* **assure,** *preserve* **1636 accorded,** *agreed* **1637 terme,** *time* **1639 leef no looth,** *love nor hate* **1640 falsen,** *be false* **1643 anight,** *at night,* **yfere,** *together* **1644 doth,** *makes* **1647 stynten,** *end* **1652 woon,** *won* **1653 unwiste of,** *unknown to* **1654 leef,** *beloved* **1655 myscheef,** *misfortune* **1656 goo,** *gone* **1660 anon,** *soon* **1662 mede,** *payment,* **guerdon,** *reward* **1664 Ryght for,** *in response to* **1666 heritage,** *inheritance* **1667 vassalage,** *chivalric behavior* **1669 goynge on the grounde,** *walking the earth*

1599 and, F reads "and so." **1613 han,** F reads "and." **1631 And,** omitted in F. **and in,** F reads "and." **1643** Line omitted in F. **1649 him,** omitted in F. **1656–79** Chaucer here follows Ovid, *Heroides* 12. **1657 his, omitted in F; Gg reads "hyr." 1661 the,** omitted in F and Tr. **doghtre of King Creon,** Creusa; see *Heroides* 12.53–754. **1667 the,** omitted in F.

First whan she of his falsnesse him umbrayde°,
"Why lyked me° thy yelow heer to see
More then the boundes of myn honeste;
Why lyked me thy youthe and thy fairnesse,
And of thy tonge the infynyt graciousnesse?
O, haddest thou in thy conquest ded ybe°,
Ful mykel° untrouthe had ther dyed with the!"
Wel kan Ovyde hir letter in vers endyte,
Which were as now to long for me to wryte.

Explicit legenda Ysiphile et Medee, martirum.

V

Legend of Lucrece

Incipit legenda Lucrecie Rome, martiris.

Now mote I sayn° th'exilynge of kynges
Of Rome, for her horrible doynges,
And of the laste kyng, Tarquynius,
As saythe Ovyde and Titus Lyvius.
But for that cause° ne telle I nat thys storie,
But for to preyse and drawen to memorie
The verray° wife, the verray trewe Lucresse,
That for hir wyfehode and hir stidfastnesse,
Nat oonly that these payens hir comende°,
But he that cleped° is in our legende
The grete Austyne hath grete compassyoun
Of this Lucresse that starf° at Rome toun.
And in what wise°, I wol bot shortly trete;
And of this thing I touche but the grete°.
Whan Ardea beseged was aboute
With Romaynes that ful sterne° were and stoute°,
Ful longe lay the sege and lytel wroghte°,
So that they were half ydel, as hem thoghte.
And in his pley Tarquynius the yonge
Gan for to jape°, for he was lyght of tonge,
And sayde that hit was an ydel lyfe,
No man dide ther more than his wife:
"And lat us speke of wyves—that is best.
Preise every man his oune as him lest°,
And with oure speche let us ease oure hert."
A knyght that hyght° Colatyne up stert°
And sayde thus, "Nay, for hit is no nede°
To trowen on° the word, but on the dede.
I have a wife," quod he, "that, as I trowe,
Is holden° good of° al that ever hir knowe.
Go we tonight to Rome, and we shul se."
Tarquynius answerde, "That lyketh° me."
To Rome be they come, and faste hem dighte°

1671 umbrayde, *accused* **1672 lyked me,** *pleased me* **1676 ded ybe,** *been dead* **1677 mykel,** *great* **1680 mote I sayn,** *must I tell* **1684 cause,** *purpose* **1686 verray,** *true* **1688 payens hir comende,** *pagans praised her* **1689 cleped,** *called* **1691 starf,** *died* **1692 wise,** *manner* **1693 grete,** *essence* **1695 sterne,** *fierce,* **stoute,** *strong* **1696 wroghte,** *accomplished* **1699 jape,** *joke* **1703 him lest,** *he wishes* **1705 hyght,** *was named,* **stert,** *leapt* **1706 no nede,** *not necessary* **1707 trowen on,** *believe in* **1709 holden,** *considered,* **of,** *by* **1711 lyketh,** *pleases* **1712 hem dighte,** *directed themselves*

1672–77 Follows *Heroides* 12.11–719, although eliminating details of Jason's exploits. **1679a *Explicit* . . . ,** Here ends the legend of Hypsipyle and Medea, martyrs. **1679b *Incipit* . . . ,** Here begins the legend of Lucretia of Rome, martyr. Chaucer's version (except for lines 1812–26 and 1870–85) closely follows Ovid, *Fasti* 2.721–852. The story is also found in Gower, *Confessio Amantis* 7.4754–5130. **1683 Titus Lyvius,** Livy; Chaucer does not use him as a source for Lucretia, although Livy tells a famous version of the story in his history of Rome, *Ab Urbe Condita* 1.57–60. **1682 And,** omitted in F, Gg, and Tr. **1685 and,** F reads "to." **1686 verray trewe,** F reads "werray" and omits "trewe." **1689 he,** omitted in F. **1690 Austyne,** St. Augustine, in *De Civitate Dei* (*The City of God*) 1.19, praises the purity of Lucretia but condemns her suicide; Chaucer probably knew the passage secondhand through a medieval commentary. **1693** Line omitted in F. **1694 Ardea,** capital city of the Rutuli, opponents of the Romans. **1706 for,** Gg and Tr read "sir." **1710 tonight to Rome,** F reads "to Rome tonyght."

To Colatynes hous, and doun they lyghte°,
Tarquynius and eke this Colatyne.
The housbond knew the estres° wel and fyne,
And prevely° into the hous they goon,
Nor at the gate porter° was ther noon;
And at the chambre dore they abyde°.
This noble wyf sat by hir beddys syde
Dischevely°, for no malice she ne thoght,
And softe wolle° our boke sayeth that she wroght°
To kepen hir fro slouthe° and ydelnesse,
And bad° hir servantes doon her besynesse°,
And axeth° hem, "What tydynges heren ye?
How sayne° men of the sege°? How shal hit be?
God wolde° the walls werne fal adoune°!
Myn housbond is to longe out of this toune,
For which the drede° doth me so to smerte°.
Ryght° as a swerd hit styngeth to myn herte
Whan I thenk on the sege or of that place.
God save my lord. I pray him for his grace."
And therwithalle ful tendirly she wepe,
And of hir werk she toke no more kepe°,
But mekely she let hir eyen falle.
And thilke semblant° sat hir wel withalle°,
And eke° hir teeres, ful of honestee°,
Embelysshed hir wifely chastitee.
Hir countenaunce is to hir herte digne°,
For they acordeden° in dede and signe.
  And with that word hir husbond Colatyne,
Or° she of him was war, com stertyng ynne°,
And sayde, "Drede the noght, for I am here!"
And she anoon up roos, with blysful chere°,
And kyssed him, as of wyves is the wone°.
  Tarquynius, this prowde kynges sone,
Conceyved° hath hir beautee and hir chere,
Hir yelow heer, hir shap, and hir manere,
Hir hew°, hir wordes that she hath compleyned°—
And by no crafte hir beautee nas nat feyned°—
And kaughte to° this lady suche desire
That in his hert brent° as any fire
So wodely° that his witte was al foryeten°.
For wel, thoghte he, she shulde nat be geten°.
And ay° the more that he was in dispaire,
The more he coveteth hir and thoght hir faire.
His blynde lust was al his covetynge.
On morwe°, whan the bird began to synge,
Unto the sege he cometh ful pryvely°,
And by himself he walketh sobrely,
The ymage of hir recordyng° alwey newe:
"Thus lay hir heer° and thus fresh was hir hewe;
Thus sat, thus spak, thus sparn°; this was hir chere;
Thus fair she was, and thys was hir manere,"
Al thys conceyt° his herte hath now ytake°.
And as the see with tempest al toshake°,
That after whan the storm is al agoo°
Yet wol the water quappe° a day or twoo,
Ryght so, thogh that hir forme were absent,
The plesaunce° of hir forme was present.
But natheles nat plesaunce but delyte,
Or an unryghtful talent° with despyte°:
"For, mawgre° hir, she shal my lemman° be;
Happe° helpeth hardy° man alway," quod he.
"What ende° that I make, hit shal be soo."
And gyrt him with° his swerde, and gan to goo
And forth he rit° til he to Rome is come,
And al aloon his way than hath he nome°
Unto the house of Colatyne ful ryght°.
Doun was the sonne, and day hath lost his lyght;
And in he come unto a prevy halke°,

1713 lyghte, *alight* **1715 estres,** *interior* **1716 prevely,** *secretly* **1717 porter,** *door keeper* **1718 abyde,** *wait* **1720 Dischevely,** *with hair unbound* **1721 wolle,** *wool,* **wroght,** *spun* (worked) **1722 fro slouthe,** *from inactivity* **1723 bad,** *directed,* **doon her besynesse,** *do their tasks* **1724 axeth,** *asks* **1725 How sayne,** *what say,* **sege,** *siege* **1726 God wolde,** *I wish to God that,* **werne fal adoune,** *were fallen down* **1728 drede,** *fear,* **smerte,** *suffer* **1729 Ryght,** *just* **1733 kepe,** *attention* **1735 thilke semblant,** *that appearance,* **sat hir wel withalle,** *sat well on her indeed* **1736 eke,** *also,* **honestee,** *modesty* **1738 digne,** *suitable* **1739 acordeden,** *agree* **1741 Or,** *before,* **stertyng ynne,** *rushing in* **1743 blysful chere,** *joyous face* **1744 wone,** *custom* **1746 Conceyved,** *observed* **1748 hew,** *color,* **compleyned,** *lamented* **1749 nas nat feyned,** *was not artificial* **1750 to,** *from* **1751 brent,** *burned* **1752 wodely,** *madly,* **his witte was al foryeten,** *he lost his wits* **1753 geten,** *won* (gotten) **1754 ay,** *always* **1757 On morwe,** *in the morning* **1758 pryvely,** *secretly* **1760 recordyng,** *recalling* **1761 heer,** *hair* **1762 span,** *spun* **1764 conceyt,** *thought,* **ytake,** *taken* **1765 toshake,** *tossed about* **1766 agoo,** *gone* **1767 quappe,** *pound* **1769 plesaunce,** *pleasure* **1771 unryghtful talent,** *wicked desire,* **despyte,** *malice* **1772 mawgre,** *despite,* **lemman,** *lover* **1773 Happe,** *luck,* **hardy,** *brave* **1774 ende,** *outcome* **1775 gyrt him with,** *strapped on* **1776 rit,** *rides* **1777 nome,** *taken* **1778 ful ryght,** *directly* **1780 prevy halke,** *hidden corner*

1716 prevely, F and Gg read "ful prevely." **1721–22 softe wolle our boke sayeth . . . ,** Ovid, *Fasti* 2.741–42 mentions the soft wool but does not say that Lucretia spins to avoid idleness. **1730 the sege or on,** F reads "these of." **1731 his,** F reads "my." **1736 her,** F reads "the." **honestee,** F reads "hevytee." **1747 shap,** F reads "bounte." **1755 he,** omitted in F. **coveteth hir,** F reads "coveteth." **1758 Unto the sege he cometh,** in Ovid, *Fasti* 2.768, the two men return together to the siege. **1763 thus . . . thys,** transposed in F and Tr. **1764 now,** F reads "newe"; Tr omits. **1776 rit,** F and Tr read "right." **1780** In Ovid, *Fasti* 2.788–91, Tarquin is welcomed into the house as kinsman before assaulting Lucretia at night.

And in the nyght ful thefely° gan he stalke,
Whan every wight° was to his reste broght,
Ne no wight had of tresoun suche a thoght.
Whether by wyndow or by other gynne°,
With swerde ydraw, shortly he cometh ynne
Ther as° she lay, thys noble wife Lucresse.
And as she woke, her bed she felte presse.
"What beste° is that," quod she, "that weyeth° thus?"
"I am the kynges sone, Tarquynius,"
Quod he, "but and° thou crye, or noyse mak,
Or if thou any creature awak,
By thilke° God that formed man on lyve,
This swerde through thyn herte shal I ryve°."
And therwithal° unto hir throte he sterte°,
And sette the poynt al sharpe unto hir herte.
No word she spak; she hath no myght therto.
What shal she sayn? Hir wytte is al ago°,
Ryght as a wolf that fynt° a lomb allone.
To whom shal she compleyne or make mone?
What, shal she fyghte with an hardy° knyght?
Wel wot° men a woman hath no myght.
What, shal she crye, or how shal she asterte°
That hath hir by the throte, with swerde at herte?
She axeth° grace, and seith al that she kan.
"Ne wolt thou nat°," quod he, this cruelle man,
"As wisly° Jupiter my soule save,
As I shal in the stable slee thy knave°,
And lay him in thy bed, and lowde crye,
That I the finde° in suche avowterye°.
And thus thou shalt be ded, and also lese°
Thy name, for thou shalt non other chese°."
These Romayn wyves loveden so her name
At thilke° tyme, and dredden so the shame,
That, what for fere of sklaundre and drede of dethe,
She loste bothe atones° wytte and brethe,
And in a swowgh° she lay, and wex so ded°
Men myghte smyten of° hir arm or hed—
She feleth nothing, neither foul ne feyre.
Tarquynius, that art a kynges eyre°,
And sholdest, as by lynage and by ryght,
Doon as a- lord and as a verray° knight,
Why hastow doon dispit° to chevalrye?
Why hastow doon this lady vylanye?
Allas, of the thys° was a vileyn dede°!
But now to purpos. In the story I rede
Whan he was goon al this myschaunce is falle°.
Thys lady sent aftir hir frendes alle,
Fader, moder, husbond, al yfere°,
And al dyschevelee°, with her heres clere°,
In habyt° suche as wymmen used thoo°
Unto the buryinge of her frendes goo,
She sitte in halle with a sorwful syght.
Hir frendes axen° what aylen might°,
And who was dede? And she sytte ay° wepynge;
A word for shame ne may she forth out brynge,
Ne upon hem she durste nat beholde°.
But atte last of Tarquyny she hem tolde
This rewful cas°, and al thys thing horryble.
The woo to tellen hit were impossible,
That she and al hir frendes make attones°.
Al° had folkes hertes ben of stones,
Hit myghte have maked hem upon hir rewe°,
Hir herte was so wyfley and so trewe.
She sayde that for hir gilt ne for hir blame
Hir husbond shulde nat have the foule name—
That nolde she nat suffre°, by no wey.
And they answerden alle, upon her fey°,
That they forgaf hit hir, for hit was ryght;
Hit was no gilt; hit lay nat in hir myght.
And seyden hir ensamples many oon.
But al for noght, for thus she seyde anoon:
"Be as be may," quod she, "of forgyvinge,
I wol nat have no forgyft° for nothinge."
But pryvely° she kaughte forth a knyf,

1781 thefely, *thief-like* **1782 wight,** *person* **1784 gynne,** *method* **1786 Ther as,** *where* **1788 beste,** *beast,* **weyeth,** *weighs* **1790 and,** *if* **1792 thilke,** *that* **1793 ryve,** *pierce* **1794 therwithal,** *with that,* **sterte,** *leapt* **1797 ago,** *gone* **1798 fynt,** *finds* **1800 hardy,** *strong* **1801 wot,** *know* **1802 asterte,** *escape* **1804 axeth,** *asks* **1805 Ne wolt thou nat,** *you will not* (have what you ask) **1806 wisly,** *surely as* **1807 knave,** *servant* **1809 the finde,** *find you,* **avowterye,** *adultery* **1810 lese,** *lose* **1811 chese,** *choose* **1813 thilke,** *that* **1815 atones,** *at once* **1816 swowgh,** *swoon,* **wex so ded,** *became so deathlike* **1817 smyten of,** *strike off* **1819 eyre,** *heir* **1821 verray,** *true* **1822 dispit,** *scorn* **1824 of the thys,** *from you this,* **vileyn dede,** *villain's deed* **1826 is falle,** *has occurred* **1828 yfere,** *together* **1829 dyschevelee,** *disheveled,* **clere,** *shining* **1830 habyt,** *clothing,* **used thoo,** *were accustomed then* **1833 axen,** *ask,* **hir aylen might,** *might ail her* **1834 sytte ay,** *sits constantly* **1836 durste nat beholde,** *dared not look* **1838 rewful cas,** *pitiable situation* **1840 attones,** *at once* **1841 Al,** *even if* **1842 rewe,** *take pity* **1846 That nolde she nat suffre,** *she would not allow that* **1847 her fey,** *their faith* **1853 forgyft,** *forgiveness* **1854 pryvely,** *secretly*

1786–88 Chaucer's addition. **1791 thou,** Gg and Tr read "ther." **1795 poynt,** F reads "swerd." **1798 wolf that fynt a lomb allone,** F reads "wolf that fayneth a love." **1811 non other,** F reads "not." **1812–26** Chaucer's addition; Ovid, *Fasti* 2.810, says simply that she gave in to his threats. **1823 this,** F reads "thy." **1824 vileyn,** F reads "vilenouse." **1836–1907** Lines lacking in Gg.

And therwithalle she rafte hirself° her lyf;
And as she felle adoun, she caste her look,
And of hir clothes yet she hede toke°,
For in hir falling yet she hadde care
Lest that° her fete or suche thyng lay bare—
So wel she loved clennesse° and eke
trouthe.
Of hir had al the toun of Rome routhe°.
And Brutus hath by hir chaste bloode swore
That Tarquyn shulde ybanysshed be therfore,
And al his kynne°; and let the peple calle°,
And openly the tale he tolde hem alle,
And openly let cary hir° on a bere°
Thurgh al the toun, that men may see and here
The horryble dede of hir oppressyoun°.
Ne never was ther kyng in Rome toun
Syn thilke° day. And she was holden° there
A seynt, and ever hir day yhalwed derer°
As in her lawe. And thus endeth Lucresse,
The noble wife, as Tytus bereth wittnesse.
I telle hit for° she was of love so trewe°,
Ne in hir wille she chaunged for no newe,
And for the stable herte, sadde° and kynde,
That in these wymmen man may alday° fynde.
Ther as they kaste her hert, ther hit duelleth.
For wel I wot° that Crist himselve telleth
That in Israel, as wyde as is the londe,
That so gret feythe in al the lond he ne fonde
As in a woman, and this is no lye.
And as of men, loketh which° tirannye
They doon alday, assay hem whoso lyste°—
The trewest is ful brotel° for to triste°.

Explicit legenda Lucrecie Rome, martiris.

VI

Legend of Ariadne

Incipit legenda Adriane de Athenes.

Juge infernal°, Mynos, of Crete kynge,
Now cometh thy lot° now comestow° on the
rynge°.
Nat for thy sake oonly wryte I this storie,
But for to clepe° ageyn unto memorie
Of Theseus the grete untrouthe° of love,
For which the goddes of the heven above
Ben wrothe°, and wreche° han take for thy synne.

1855 rafte hirself, *took from herself* **1857 hede toke,** *paid attention* **1859 Lest that,** *for fear that* **1860 clennesse,** *purity* **1861 routhe,** *grief* **1864 kynne,** *family,* **let the peple calle,** *called the people* **1866 let cary hir,** *ordered that she be carried,* **bere,** *funeral platform* **1868 oppressyoun,** *rape* **1870 Syn thilke,** *since that,* **holden,** *considered* **1871 yhalwed dere,** *honored as very holy* **1874 for,** *because,* **trewe,** *true* **1876 sadde,** *steadfast* **1877 alday,** *always* **1879 wot,** *know* **1883 which,** *what* **1884 assay them whoso lyste,** *test them whoever wishes to* **1885 brotel,** *unreliable,* **triste,** *trust* **1886 Juge infernal,** *judge in the underworld* **1887 lot,** *chance,* **comestow,** *you come,* **on the rynge,** *into the circle* **1889 clepe,** *call* **1890 untrouthe,** *infidelity* **1892 Ben wrothe,** *are angry,* **wreche,** *vengeance*

1862 Brutus, Lucius Junius Brutus; he founded the Republic of Rome after banishing Tarquinius, the last king. See Ovid, *Fasti* 2.849–52. **1870–85** Chaucer's addition, although the idea that Lucretia became a saint with a holyday (lines 1870–72) may have been prompted by the fact that Ovid's *Fasti* is arranged as a calendar of days. **1873 Tytus,** Livy; see 1683n. **as,** omitted in F. **1876 for the,** F reads "in hir." **1879–82 Crist himselve telleth . . . ,** nowhere does Christ say quite this, although scholars cite Matthew 15.28, along with Matthew 8.10 and Luke 7.9. 1882 and, **omitted in F. 1883 men,** F reads "women." **1885a Explicit . . . ,** Here ends the legend of Lucretia of Rome, martyr. **1885b *Incipit* . . . ,** Here begins the legend of Ariadne of Athens. No source is known for Chaucer's version, but some details parallel Ovid, *Metamorphoses* 8.6–176, and *Heroides* 10. Scholars have shown that Chaucer was probably influenced by commentaries on Ovid or glossed versions, and a range of other materials. Gower's version of the story is *Confessio Amantis* 5.5231–495. **1886 Mynos,** Minos, king of Crete; in medieval sources, recurrently confused or conflated with Minos, judge of the underworld. **Crete,** F reads "Greece"; see line 1894. **1888 Nat for thy sake oonly,** F reads "Nat oonly for thy sake." **wryte I,** "writen ys." **1890 untrouthe,** F reads "untrewe." **1891 the,** omitted in F.

Be rede° for shame, now I thy lyf begynne.
  Mynos that was the myghty kyng of Crete,
That hadde an hundred citees stronge and
    grete,
To scole° hath sent his sone Androgius
To Athenes, of the which° hit happed thus,
That he was slayn, lernyng philosophye,
Ryght in that citee, nat but for° envye.
The grete Mynos, of the whiche I speke,
His sones dethe is comen for to wreke°.
Alcathoe he besegeth harde and longe,
But natheles° the walles be so stronge,
And Nysus that was kyng of that citee
So chevalrous that lytel dredeth he.
Of Mynos or his ost° toke he no cure°,
Til on a day befel° an aventure
That Nysus doghtre stode upon the walle
And of the sege saw the maner alle.
So happed hit that at a skarmysshynge
She caste hir herte upon Mynos the kynge,
For his beaute and for his chevalrye,
So sore° that she wende° for to dye.
And shortly of this processe for to pace°,
She made Mynos wynnen thilke° place,
So that the citee was al at his wille,
To saven whom him lysrt°, or elles spille°.
But wikkedly he quytte° hir kyndenesse,
And let hir drenche° in sorowe and distresse,
Ner° that the goddes hadde of hir pite—
But that tale were to longe as now for me.
  Athenes wanne° thys kyng Mynos also,
And Alcathoe, and other tounes mo,
And this th'effect, that Minos hath so dryven
Hem of Athenes that they mote him yiven°
Fro yere to yere hir oune° children dere
For to be slayn, as ye shal after here.
Thys Mynos hath a monstre, a wikked beste,
That was so cruelle that without areste°,
Whan that a man was broght in his presence,
He wolde him ete, ther helpeth no defence.
And every thridde yere, withouten doute,
They casten lot°, and as hit came aboute
On ryche, on pore, he moste° his sone take,
And of his child he moste present make
Unto Mynos, to save him or to spille,
Or lat his best° devoure him at his wille.
And this hath Mynos doon, ryght in despyt°.
To wreke° his sone was sette al his delyt,
And maken hem of Athenes his thralle°
Fro yere to yere, while he lyven shalle—
And home he saileth whan this toun is wonne.
  This wikked custom is so longe yronne°
Til that of Athenes Kyng Egeus
Moste sende his oune sone Theseus,
Sith that° the lotte is fallen him upon,
To be devoured, for gracer° is ther non,
And forth is lad thys woful yonge knyght
Unto the contree of Kyng Mynos ful of myght,
And in a prison, fetred°, caste is he
Til thilke° tyme he shulde yfreten° be.
Wel maystow° wepe, O woful Theseus,
That art a kynges sone, and dampned° thus.
Me thynketh this, that thow depe were yholde°
To whom that saved the fro° cares colde.
And now, if any woman helpe thee,
Wel oughtestow° hir servant for to be,
And ben her trewe lover yere by yere.
But now to come agayn to my matere.

1893 Be rede, *blush* **1896 scole,** *school* **1897 of the which,** *the result of which* **1899 nat but for,** *for nothing but* **1901 wreke,** *avenge* **1903 But natheles,** *however* **1906 ost,** *army,* **toke he no cure,** *he cared not* **1907 befel,** *occurred* **1913 sore,** *sorely,* **wende,** *thought* **1914 pace,** *pass by* **1915 made Mynos wynnen thilke,** *enabled Minos to conquer that* **1917 him lyst,** *he wished,* **spille,** *kill* **1918 quytte,** *repaid* **1919 drenche,** *drown* **1920 Ner,** *were it not* **1922 wanne,** *conquered* **1925 mote him yiven,** *must give to him* **1926 hir oune,** *their own* **1929 areste,** *pause* **1933 They casten lot,** *the Athenians held a lottery* **1934 moste,** *must* **1937 best,** *beast* **1938 despyt,** *malice* **1939 wreke,** *avenge* **1940 thralle,** *slaves* **1943 is so longe yronne,** *ran for so long* **1946 Sith that,** *because* **1947 grace,** *mercy* **1950 fetred,** *shackled* **1951 thilke,** *that,* **yfreten,** *eaten* **1952 maystow,** *may you* **1953 dampned,** *condemned* **1954 depe were holde,** *would be deeply indebted* **1955 the fro,** *you from* **1957 oughtestow,** *ought you*

1895 hadde, F reads "whan." **1896–98 Androgius . . ./ slayn, lernyng philosophye,** in Gower, *Confessio Amantis* 5.5237–45, pride in his lineage lead Androgeus to ignore his studies, fall into mischief, and die as a result; Chaucer is closer to the rhetorical school text of Geoffrey de Vinsauf, *Documentum de modo et arte dictandi et versificandi* (*Instruction in the Method and Art of Speaking and Versifying*) 2.3. **1901** Minos's desire to avenge his son is mentioned in Ovid, *Metamorphoses* 7.456–58. **1902–21** Generally follows Ovid *Metamorphoses* 8.6–151, although the details are compressed and Chaucer eliminates (as he usually does) the transformations. **1902 Alcathoe,** the stronghold in Megara, a city near Athens. F reads "And the citee." **1908 Nysus doghtre,** Scylla is daughter of Nysus. **1922–2185** Chaucer here leaves Ovid and begins adapting what might be thought of as a common medieval tradition; also found in Gower. **1923 And,** Tr reads "With." **Alcathoe,** F reads "Al cities." **1928 monstre,** the monster is the Minotaur, half-man and half-bull, begotten by Minos's wife, Pasiphaë, through intercourse with a bull. **1930 in,** F reads "into." **1932** The three-year cycle seems to be Chaucer's invention. **1933 and,** omitted in F. **1940 And maken,** F reads "To make."

The tour ther as° this Theseus is throwe°,
Doun in the bothome, derke, and wonder lowe°,
Was joynyng° to the walle of a foreyne°,
And hit was longyng° to the doghtren tweyne°
Of Kyng Mynos, that in her chambres grete
Dwelten above, toward° the mayster strete°,
In mochel° mirthe, in joye, and in solas°.
Wot° I nat how, hit happed° ther, par cas°,
As Theseus compleyned him by nyght,
The kynges doghtre that Adriane hyghte°,
And eke hir suster Phedra, herden alle
His compleynt as they stode on the walle
And lokeden upon the brighte mone;
Hem leste nat° to goo to bed so sone.
And of his woo they had compassyoun:
A kynges sone to be in swich prisoun,
And be devoured, thoughte hem gret pitee.
Than Adriane spak to hir suster free°,
And seyde, "Phedra, leve° suster dere,
This woful lordes sone may° ye nat here,
How pitousely compleyneth he his kin,
And eke° his pore estat° that he is in,
And gilteless? Certes now, hit is routhe°!
And if ye wol assenten, by my trouthe,
He shal be holpen°, how soo that we doo."
Phedra answerde, "Ywis° me is as woo°
For him as ever I was for any man.
And to his help, the best rede° I kan°
Is that we doon° the gayler° prively°
To come, and speke with us hastely,
And doon this woful man with him to come°.
For if he may the monstre overcome,
Than° were he quyt°; ther is noon other bote°.
Lat us wel taste° him at his herte-rote,
That if so be that he a wepne° have
Wher° that his lyf he dar° to kepe or save,
Fighten with this fend°, and him defende.
For in the prison ther° he shal descende,
Ye wite° wel that the beste is in a place
That nys nat derke, and hath roum° and eke space
To welde an ax or swerd or staf or knyf,
So that me thenketh he shulde save his lyf.
If that he be a man, he shal do soo!
And we shal make him balles eke alsoo°
Of wexe and towe°, that, whan he gapeth faste°,
Into the bestes throte he shal hem caste
To sleke° his hunger and encombre his teeth.
And ryght anoon, whan that Theseus seeth
The beste achoked, he shal on him lepe
To sleen him or° they comen more to hepe°.
This wepen shal the gayler or that tyds°
Ful prively within the prison hyde;
And for° the hous is crynkled° to and fro,
And hath so queynte° weyes for to go—
For hit is shapen as the mase° is wroght—
Therto° have I a remedy in my thoght,
That by a clewe of twine°, as he hath goon,
The same way he may returne anoon,
Folwyng alwey the threde as he hath come.
And whan that he this beste hath overcome,
Then may he fleen away out of this stede°,
And eke the gayler may he with him lede,
And him avaunce° at home in his contree,
Syn that° so gret a lordes sone is he.
Thys is my rede°, if that he dar hit take."

1960 tour ther as, *tower where,* **throwe,** *thrown* **1961 wonder lowe,** *amazingly deep* **1962 joynyng,** *adjoining,* **foreyne,** *toilet pit* **1963 hit was longyng,** *it belonged,* **doghtren tweyne,** *two daughters* **1965 toward,** *facing,* **mayster strete,** *main street* **1966 mochel,** *much,* **solas,** *comfort* **1967 Wot,** *know,* **happed,** *happened,* **par cas,** *by chance* **1969 hyghte,** *was named* **1973 Hem leste nat,** *they desired not* **1977 free,** *noble* **1978 leve,** *beloved* **1979 may,** *can* **1981 eke,** *also,* **estat,** *condition* **1982 routhe,** *pity* **1984 holpen,** *helped* **1985 Ywis,** *surely,* **woo,** *sorry* **1987 rede,** *advice,* **kan,** *know* **1988 doon,** *compel,* **gayler,** *jailer,* **prively,** *secretly* **1990 doon . . . with him to come,** i.e., *bring with him* **1992 Than,** *then,* **were he quyt,** *would his debt be paid,* **bote,** *remedy* **1993 taste,** *test* **1994 wepne,** *weapon* **1995 Wher,** *whether,* **dar,** *dares* **1996 fend,** *fiend* **1997 ther,** *where* **1998 wite,** *know* **1999 roum,** *room* **2003 eke alsoo,** *moreover* **2004 wexe and towe,** *wax and fiber,* **he gapeth faste,** *the monster opens wide his mouth* **2006 sleke,** *satisfy* **2009 or,** *before,* **more to hepe,** *closer* **2010 or that tyde,** *before that time* **2012 for,** *because,* **crynkled,** *full of turnings* **2013 so queynte,** *such intricate* **2014 mase,** *maze* **2015 Therto,** *for that* **2016 clewe of twyne,** *ball of twine* **2020 stede,** *place* **2022 avaunce,** *reward* (advance) **2023 Syn that,** *since* **2024 rede,** *advice*

1960–72 Critics have suggested that the motif of imprisonment in proximity to the ladies may have been inspired by Boccaccio, *Teseide* 3.8, 11, 17–19; see 2032–37n. **1965 toward,** omitted in F. **1966 In mochel mirthe,** from Tr; F reads "Of Athenes," but Minos ruled in Crete. See line 2306. **1967 ther,** omitted in F and Gg. **1980 he,** omitted in F. **1985–2024** Only in Chaucer's version is Phaedra the one who plans Theseus's defeat of the Minotaur and escape from the Labyrinth. **1987 I,** F reads "that I." **1988 gayler,** the jailer's role appears to be Chaucer's addition, here and throughout the narrative. **1993 at,** F reads "as." **1995** F reads "That his lyf he dar to kepe and save." **1998** Line omitted in F; from Tr. **2003–04 balles . . . of wexe and towe,** the detail is similar in Gower, *Confessio Amantis* 5.5349, and in medieval commentary on Ovid, but does not occur in classical sources. **2007 that,** omitted in F. **2008 achoked,** F read "alseked." **2009 they,** F reads "the." **2012 hous is crynkled,** the Labyrinth. Before Chaucer, *crinkle* was used primarily in place names, meaning "curve" or "circle." **2016 clewe,** the modern meaning of *clue* developed from this usage in early English versions of the Labyrinth plot. **2019 that he this beste hath,** F reads "this beste is."

What° shulde I lenger sermoun of hit make?
The gayler cometh, and with him Theseus.
And whan these thynges ben acorded° thus,
Adoun sytte° Theseus upon his knee,
"The ryghte° lady of my lyf," quod he,
"I, sorwful man, ydampned° to the deth,
Fro yow, whiles that me lasteth lyf or breth,
I wol nat twynne°, after this aventure,
But in your servise thus I wol endure,
That as a wrechche unknowe° I wol yow serve
For evermore, til that myn herte sterve°.
Forsake I wol at home myn herytage,
And, as I seyde, ben of your court a page,
If that ye vouchesauf° that in this place
Ye graunte me to have suche a grace°
That I may have nat but my mete and drinke.
And for my sustenance yet wol I swynke°
Ryght as yow lyst°, that Mynos ne no wyghf°—
Syn that° he sawe me never with eighen syght—
Ne no man elles shal me konne espye°.
So slyly and so wel I shal me gye°,
And me so wel disfigure° and so lowe°
That in this world ther shal no man me knowe,
To han my lyf, and for to han presence
Of yow that doon to me this excellence.
And to my fader shal I senden here
This worthy man that is your gaylere,
And him to guerdon° that he shal wel bee
Oon of the gretest men of my contree.
And yif I durste sayne°, my lady bryght,
I am a kynges sone, and eke a knyght,
As wolde God°; yif that hit myghte bee
Ye weren in my contree, alle three,
And I with yow, to bere yow companye,
Than shulde ye seen yif that I therof lye°!
And if I profre° yow in low manere
To ben your page and serven yow ryght here,
But° I yow serve as lowly in that place°,
I prey to Mars to yeve me suche grace°
That shames dethe° on me ther mote° falle,
And dethe and povert to my frendes alle,
And that my spirit by nyghte mote goo°
After my dethe, and walke to and froo,
That I mot of a traytour have a name,
For which my spirit mot go to do me shame!
And yif I ever yclaime other degre°,
But if° ye vouchesauf° to yeve hit me,
As I have seyde, of shames deth I deye!
And mercy, lady! I kan no more saye!"

A seemly° knyght was Theseus to see,
And yong, but of twenty yere and three;
But whoso hadde yseen his countenaunce,
He wolde have wept for routhe° of his penaunce°.
For which this Adriane in this manere
Answerde to his profre and to his chere°:

"A kynges sone and eke a knyght," quod she,
"To ben my servant in so low degre,
God shelde hit°, for the shame of wymmen alle,
And leve° me never suche a cas befalle°!
But sende yow grace, and sleyghte° of here also.
Yow to defende and knyghtly sleen° your fo,
And leve herafter that I may yow fynde
To me and to my suster here so kynde
That I repente nat to geve yow lyf!
Yet wer hit better that I were your wyf,
Syn that° ye ben as gentil borne as I,
And have a realme° nat but faste by°,
Then° that I suffred° your gentilesse to sterve°,
Or that I let yow as a page serve;
Hit is not profit°, as unto your kynrede°,
But what is that that man wol nat do for drede?
And to my suster, syn thaf° hit is so
That she mot goon° with me, if that I goo,
Or elles suffre deth as wel as I,
That ye unto your sone as trewely
Doon her be wedded° at your home comynge.

2025 What, *why* **2027 acorded,** *agreed* **2028 sytte,** *set* **2029 ryghte,** *true* **2030 ydampned,** *condemned* **2032 twynne,** *depart* **2034 wrechche unknowe,** *unknown wretch* **2035 sterve,** *dies* **2038 vouchesauf,** *consent* **2039 grace,** *favor* **2041 swynke,** *labor* **2042 Ryght as yow lyst,** *just as you wish,* **wyght,** *person* **2043 Syn that,** *since* **2044 konne espye,** *be able to recognize* **2045 gye,** *conduct* **2046 disfigure,** *disguise,* **lowe,** *humbly* **2052 guerdon,** *reward* **2054 durste sayne,** *dared to say* **2056 As wolde God,** *God willing* **2059 therof lye,** *lie about this* **2060 profre,** *offer* **2062 But,** *unless,* **that place,** i.e., *Athens* **2063 grace,** *fortune* **2064 shames dethe,** *a shameful death,* **mote,** *might* **2066 mote goo,** *might move* **2070 degre,** *rank* (besides page) **2071 But if,** *unless,* **vouchesauf,** *consent* **2074 semely,** *attractive* **2077 routhe,** *pity,* **penaunce,** *punishment* **2079 chere,** *demeanor* **2082 shelde hit,** *forbid it* **2083 leve,** *grant,* **cas befalle,** *situation occur* **2084 sleyghte,** *skill* **2085 sleen,** *slay* **2090 Syn that,** *since* **2091 realme,** *kingdom,* **faste by,** *nearby* **2092 Then,** *than,* **suffred,** *allowed,* **sterve,** *die* **2094 profit,** *advantage,* **kynrede,** *kindred* **2096 syn that,** *since* **2097 mot goon,** *must go* **2100 Doon her be wedded,** *arrange for her to wed*

2025 sermoun, omitted in F. **2031 lyf or,** omitted in F. **2033–37 in your servise,** critics have suggested that the motif of willingness to serve as a page in disguise was inspired by Boccaccio, *Teseide* 4.22; see 1960–72n. **2046 me so,** F reads "so me." **2053 the,** omitted in F. **2060 if,** F reads "if that." **2064 dethe,** F reads "deed." **2074 was,** F reads "was this." **2098 elles,** F reads "elles that." **2099 your sone,** Theseus's son is Hippolytus; in several medieval sources, a betrothal is arranged between Phaedra and him. For the better-known classical account of Phaedra's incestuous love of her stepson, Hippolytus, see Ovid, *Heroides* 4. **2100 be,** F reads "to be."

This is the fynal ende of al this thynge—
Ye swere hit here, on al that may be sworne,"
"Ye, lady myn," quod he, "or elles torne
Mote° I be with the Mynatour tomorwe!
And haveth herof° my herte-blood to borwe°,
Yif that ye wole°. If I had knyf or spere,
I wolde hit laten out° and ther-on swere,
For then at erst° I wot° ye wol me leve°.
By Mars, that is the chefe° of my beleve°,
So that I myghte lyven and nat fayle
Tomorwe for t'acheve my bataile,
I nolde never fro this place flee
Til that ye shuld the verray prefe° see.
For now if that the sothe° I shal yow say,
I have loved yow ful many a day,
Thogh ye ne wiste° hit nat, in my contree,
And aldermost° desired yow to see
Of any erthly lyvyng creature.
Upon my trouthe I swere, and yow assure,
These seven yere I have your servant be°;
Now have I yow, and also have ye me,
My dere hert, of Athenes duchesse!"
This lady smyleth at his stedfastnesse,
And at his hertly° wordes, and at his chere°,
And to hir suster sayde in this manere,
Al softely, "Now, suster myn," quod she,
"Now be we duchesses, bothe I and ye,
And sykered° to the regals° of Athenes,
And both herafter lykly to be queenes,
And saved fro his deth a kynges sone,
As ever of gentil wymmen is the wone°
To save a gentil man, enforth° her myght,
In honest cause, and namely° in his ryght.
Me thinketh no wyght° oughte us herof° blame,
Ne beren us therfor an evel name."
And shortely of this mate re for to make,
This Theseus of hir hath leve ytake°.
And every point performed was in dede
As ye have in this covenant herd me rede°.
His wepne°, his clew°, his thing that I have sayde,
Was by the gayler in the hous ylayde
Ther as° this Mynatour hath his duellinge,
Ryght faste° by the dore at his entringe.
And Theseus is ladde unto his dethe,
And forthe unto this Mynatour he gethe°,
And by the techyng of this Adriane
He overcome° this beste, and was his bane°;
And oute he cometh by the clewe agayne
Ful prevely°, whan he this beste hath slayne;
And by the gayler geten hath a barge°,
And of his wyves tresor gan hit charge°,
And tok his wife, and eke hir suster fre°,
And eke the gayler, and wyth hem alle thre
Is stole° away out of the lond by nyghte,
And to the contree of Eunopye him dyghte°
There as° he had a frende of his knowynge.
There festen° they, there dauncen they and synge;
And in his armes hath this Adriane,
That of the beste hath kepte him from his bane°;
And gat him ther a newe barge anoon°,
And of his contree folk° a grete woon°,
And taketh his leve, and homeward sayleth hee.
And in an yle, amydde the wilde see,
Ther as ther° dwelleth creature noon
Save wilde bestes, and that ful many oon°,
He made his shippe alonde° for to sette;
And in that yle half a day he lette°,
And sayde that on the lond he moste° him reste.
His maryners han don ryght as him leste°,
And for to telle schortly in this cas,
Whan Adriane his wyf aslepe was,
For that° her suster fairer was than she,
He taketh hir in his hond, and forth gooth he
To shippe, and as a traitour stal° his way
While that this Adriane aslepe lay,
And to his contree-ward he sayleth blyve°

2104 Mote, *may* **2105 herof,** *for this,* **to borwe,** *as a pledge* **2106 wole,** *want* **2107 hit laten out,** *let blood* **2108 then et erst,** *only then,* **wot,** *know,* **leve,** *believe* **2109 chefe,** *chief,* **beleve,** *belief* **2112 nolde never fro,** *would never from* **2113 verray prefe,** *proof positive* **2114 sothe,** *truth* **2116 wiste,** *knew* **2117 aldermost,** *most of all* **2120 be,** *been* **2124 hertly,** *earnest,* **chere,** *demeanor* **2128 sykered,** *promised,* **regals,** *royalty* **2131 wone,** *custom* **2132 enforth,** *to the extent of* **2133 namely,** *especially* **2134 wyght,** *person,* **herof,** *for this* **2137 leve ytake,** *taken leave* **2139 rede,** *report* **2140 wepne,** *weapon,* **clew,** *ball of twine* **2142 Ther as,** *where* **2143 Ryght faste,** *very near* **2145 gethe,** *goes* **2147 overcome,** *overcomes,* **bane,** *slayer* **2149 Ful prevely,** *very secretly* **2150 hath geten a barge,** *has gotten a ship* **2151 gan hit charge,** *loaded it* **2152 fre,** *noble* **2154 Is stole,** *has stolen* **2155 him dyghte,** *went* **2156 There as,** *where* **2157 festen,** *feast* **2159 bane,** *death* **2160 anoon,** *soon* **2161 contree folk,** *countrymen,* **woon,** *number* **2164 Ther as ther,** *there where* **2165 ful many oon,** *very many* **2166 alonde,** *on land* **2167 lette,** *paused* **2168 moste,** *must* **2169 han don ryght as him leste,** *did just as he wanted* **2172 For that,** *because* **2174 stal,** *stole* **2176 blyve,** *quickly*

2109 the, omitted in F. **2111 t'acheve my,** F reads "to taken by." **2139 this,** F reads "the." **2150–53** From Tr; F conflates 2150 and 2153 by eyeskip and omits 2151–52. **2155 Eunopye,** Oenopia. **2160 newe,** F reads "noble."

(A twenty devel way° the wynd him dryve!),
And fond° his fader drenched° in the see.
  Me list° no more to speke of him, pardee°.
These false lovers, poyson be her bane°!
But I wol turne ageyn to Adriane,
That is with slepe for werynesse ytake°.
Ful sorwefully hir herte may awake.
Allas, for the° myn herte hath now pitee!
Ryght in the dawnyng awaketh shee
And gropeth in the bed, and fond right noght°.
"Allas," quod she, "that ever I was wroght°!
I am betrayed!" and hir heer to-rent°
And to the stronde° barefot faste she went,
And cryed, "Theseus, myn herte swete,
Wher be ye, that I may nat wyth yow mete,
And myghte thus with bestes ben yslayn°?"
The holwe rokkes answerde hir agayn.
No man she saw, and yet shone the mone,
And hye° upon a rokke she wente sone,
And saw his barge saylyng in the see.
Cold wax° hir hert, and ryght thus sayde she,
"Meker° than ye fynde I the bestes wilde!"
Hadde he nat synne° that hir thus begylde?
She cried, "O turne agayn, for routhe° and synne!
Thy barge hath nat al his meyny° inne!"
Hir kerchef on a pole up styked° shee,
Ascaunce° that he shulde hit wel ysee,
And him remembre that she was behynde,
And turne agayne, and on the stronde hir fynde.
But al for noght; his wey he is ygoon.
And doun she felle aswown° upon a stoon,
And up she ryst, and kyssed in al hir care
The steppes of his fete ther he hath fare°,
And to hir bedde ryght thus she speketh thoo°:
"Thow bed," quod she, "that hast received twoo,
Thou shalt answere of twoo, and nat of oon!
Wher is thy gretter part away ygoon?
Allas, wher shal I, wreched wyght° become°?
For though so be that any bote° here come,
Home to my contree dar I nat for drede°.
I kan myselven in this cas nat rede°!"
  What shulde I telle more hir compleynynge?
Hit is so long, hit were an hevy° thynge.
In hir epistil° Naso telleth alle.
But shortly to the ende I telle shalle.
The goddes have hir holpen°, for pitee,
And in the signe of Taurus men may see
The stones of hir corown shyne clere.
I wol no more speke of this matere.
But thus this false lover kan begile
His trewe love—the devel quyte him his while°!

Explicit legenda Adriane de Athenes.

2177 A twenty devel way, *the way of twenty devils* (a curse) **2178 fond,** *found,* **drenched,** *drowned* **2179 Me list,** *I want,* **pardee,** *by God* **2180 her bane,** *their death* **2182 ytake,** *taken* **2184 the,** *you* **2186 ryght noght,** *absolutely nothing* **2187 wroght,** *created* **2188 to-rent,** *tore* **2189 stronde,** *shore* **2192 with bestes ben yslayn,** *be slain by beasts* **2195 hye,** *high* **2197 wax,** *became* **2198 Meker,** *more meek* **2199 Hadde he nat synne,** *did he not sin* **2200 routhe,** *pity* **2201 his meyny,** *its passengers* **2202 up styked,** *hoisted* **2203 Ascaunce,** *as if* (in hope) **2207 aswown,** *in a faint* **2209 ther he hath fare,** *where he has walked* **2210 thoo,** *then* **2214 wyght,** *person,* **wher shal I . . . become,** *what will become of me* **2215 bote,** *boat or remedy* **2217 rede,** *advise* **2219 hevy,** *sorrowful* **2220 hir epistil,** *her letter* **2222 holpen,** *helped* **2227 quyte him his while,** *repay him his time* (a curse)

2185–2217 Chaucer here follows Ovid, *Heroides* 10.1–65, although he compresses and rearranges some details. **2193** Line lacking in F. **2198** Ovid, *Heroides* 10.1. **2201 his,** F reads "thy." **2203 that,** omitted in F. **2211–13** Ovid, *Heroides* 10.56–58. **2213 thy,** F reads "the." **2215 that any bote here come,** F reads "that botte noon here come." **2220 Naso,** Ovid; Publius Ovidius Naso. **2222–24** Ovid, *Metamorphoses* 8.176–82 describes how Bacchus made of Ariadne's crown the constellation Corona Borealis, the Northern Crown, which is most visible when the sun is in the sign of Taurus. **2226 this false lover,** F reads "these false lovers." **2227 His,** F reads "Hyr." **2227a *Explicit* . . . ,** Here ends the legend of Ariadne of Athens.

VII

Legend of Philomela

Incipit legenda Philomene.

Deus dator formarum.

Thow yiver° of the formes that hast wroght°
The faire worlde, and bare° hit in thy thoght
Eternally, or° thow thy werk began,
Why madest thow, unto the sklaundre° of man,
Or—al be that° hit was not thy doynge,
As for that fyn° to make such a thynge—
Why suffrest thow° that Tereus was bore,
That is in love so fals and so forswore°,
That fro thys world up to the firste hevene
Corrumpeth° whan that folk his name nevene°?
And, as to me, so grisly° was his dede
That whan that I his foule story rede,
Myn eyen wexen° foule and sore also—
Yet laste° the venym of so longe ago,
That hit infecteth him that wol beholde
The story of Tereus, of which I tolde°.
Of Trase was he lorde, and kynne to Marte,
The cruelle god that stant° with blody darte,
And wedded had he with a blisful chere°
Kyng Pandyones faire doghter dere,
That hyghte° Proygne, floure of hir contree,
Thogh Juno list nat at the feste bee°,
Ne Ymeneus, that god of weddyng is;
But at the feste redy ben°, ywis°,
The furies thre with al her mortel brond°.
The owle al nyght about the balkes wond°,
That prophet is of woo and of myschaunce°.
This revel, ful of songe and ful of daunce,
Laste a fourtenyght° or lytel lasse.
But shortly of this story for to passe—
For I am wery of him for to telle—
Fyve yere his wyf and he togedir dwelle,
Til on a day she gan so sore longe°
To seen her suster that° she saugh nat longe°,
That for desire she nyste° what to sey.
But to hir husbond gan she for to prey,
For Goddys love, that she moste ones goon°
Hir suster for to seen, and come anoon,
Or elles but she moste to hir wende°,
She preyde him that he wolde after° hir sende;
And this was, day be day, al hir prayere
With al humblesse of wyfhod, worde and chere°.
This Tereus let° make his shippes yare°,
And into Grece himself is forth yfare°
Unto his fader-in-lawe, and gan him prey
To vouchesauf° that for a moneth or twey°,
That Philomene, his wyfes suster, myght
On Proigne his wyf but ones have a syght—
"And she shal come to yow agayne anoon.
Myself with hir I wil bothe come and goon,
And as myn hertes lyf I wol hir kepe°."
This olde Pandeon, this kyng, gan wepe
For tendernesse of herte for to leve°

2228 yiver, *giver,* **wroght,** *created* **2229 bare,** *bore* **2230 or,** *before* **2231 sklaundre,** *disgrace* **2232 al be that,** *even though* **2233 fyn,** *purpose* **2234 suffrest thow,** *do you allow* **2235 so forswore,** *so perjured* **2237 Corrumpeth,** *corrupts all,* **his name nevene,** *name his name* **2238 grisly,** *horrible* **2240 wexen,** *became* **2241 Yet laste,** *so long lasts* **2243 tolde,** *mentioned* **2245 stant,** *stands* **2246 blisful chere,** *happy demeanor* **2248 hyghte,** *was named* **2249 list nat at the feste bee,** *chose not to be at the celebration* **2251 redy ben,** *ready were,* **ywis,** *indeed* **2252 mortel brond,** *deadly torches* **2253 about the balkes wond,** *flew around the roof beams* **2254 myschaunce,** *misfortune* **2256 a fourtenyght,** *two weeks* **2260 gan so sore longe,** *yearned so sorely* **2261 that,** *who,* **longe,** *for a long time* **2262 nyste,** *knew not* **2264 moste ones goon,** *might go once* **2266 but,** *unless,* **moste to hir wende,** *she might go to her* **2267 after,** *for* **2269 chere,** *action* **2270 let,** *ordered,* **yare,** *ready* **2271 yfare,** *gone* **2273 vouchesauf,** *consent,* **twey,** *two* **2278 kepe,** *protect* **2280 leve,** *let*

2227b ***Incipit*** **. . . ,** Here begins the legend of Philomela. Chaucer's version is based on Ovid, *Metamorphoses* 6.424–605 and the expanded version in the *Ovide Moralisé.* **2227c** ***Deus dator formarum,*** God is the giver of forms. F reads "*formatorum.*" The quotation probably derives from Chaucer's source for his opening lines, although the idea is a Platonic commonplace, occurring in *Bo* 3.m9.11–14, *Roman de la Rose* 15995–16004, and several medieval commentaries on Ovid. **2233 fyn,** F reads "fende." **2236 firste hevene,** outermost sphere of the cosmos, i.e., to the edge of the created universe. **2239 his,** F reads "this." **2242 hit,** omitted in F. **2244 Trase,** Thrace. **Marte,** Mars, god of war. **2247 Pandyones faire doghter,** Procne, daughter of Pandion, king of Athens. **2249 Juno,** wife of Jupiter and goddess of marriage. **list,** F reads "baste." **2250 Ymeneus,** Hymen, god of marriage. **2252 furies three with al her mortel brond,** in Ovid, *Metamorphoses* 6.430, the Furies light the way with torches stolen from a funeral.

His doghter goon, and for to yive hir leve°.
Of al this world he loved nothing soo.
But at the laste leve hath she to goo,
For Philomene with salte teres eke°
Gan of her fader grace to beseke°
To seen her suster that hir longeth soo°,
And him enbraceth with hir armes twoo.
And therwithal°, so yong and fair was she
That whan that Tereus sawgh hir beautee,
And of array that ther was noon hir lyche°,
And yet of bountee° was she two so° ryche,
He caste his firy herte upon hir soo
That he wol have hir, how soo that hit goo,
And with his wiles kneled and so preyde°,
Til at the laste Pandeon thus seyde,
"Now, sone," quod he, "that art to me so dere,
I the betake° my yonge doghter here,
That bereth the key of al my hertes lyf.
And grete wel my doghter and thy wyf,
And yeve hir leve° somtyme for to pleye°,
That she may seen me oones or° I deye."
And sothly°, he hath made him ryche feste°,
And to his folk, the moste and eke the leste,
That with him com; and yaf him yiftes grete,
And him conveyeth thurgh the maister-strete°
Of Athenes, and to the see° him broghte,
And turneth° home—no malice he ne thoghte.
  The ores pulleth forth the vessel faste,
And into Trace arryveth at the laste,
And up into a forest he hir ledde,
And into a cave pryvyly him spedde°;
And in this derke cave, yif hir leste°,
Or leste noght°, he bad hir for to reste;
Of which hir hert agrose°, and seyde thus,
"Wher is my suster, brother Tereus?"
And therwithal she wepte tenderly,
And quoke° for fere, pale and pitously,
Ryght° as the lamb that of the wolf is byten,
Or as the colver° that of° the egle is smyten°,
And is out of his clawes forth escaped,
Yet hit is aferde and awhaped°
Lest° hit be hent eft-sones°, so sat she.
But utterly hit may non other be:
By force hath he, this traytour, done that dede,
That he hath reft° hir of hir maydenhede,
Maugree hir hede°, by strengthe and by his myght.
Loo°, here a dede of men, and that a ryght!
She crieth "Suster!" with ful loude stevene°,
And "Fader dere!" and "Help me, God in Hevene!"
Al helpeth nat; and yet this false thefe
Hath doon this lady yet a more myschefe°,
For fere lest° she sholde his shame crye°,
And done him° openly a vilanye,
And with his swerd hir tonge of kerveth° he,
And in a castel made hir for to be
Ful privily° in prison evermore,
And kept hir to his usage° and to his store°,
So that she myghte him nevermore asterte°.
O sely° Philomene, woo is in thyn herte;
God wreke° the, and send the thy bone°!
Now is hit tyme I make an ende sone.
  This Tereus is to his wyf ycome,
And in his armes hath his wyf ynome°,
And pitously he wepe, and shook his hede,
And swor hir that he fond hir suster dede,
For which the sely Proigne hath suche woo
That nygh° hir sorwful herte brak atwoo°.
And thus in teres lat I Proigne dwelle,
And of hir suster forth I wol yow telle.
  This woful lady ylerned° had in yowthe

2281 leve, *permission* **2284 eke,** *also* **2285 Gan . . . grace to beseke,** *requested the favor* **2286 that hir longeth so,** *who so longs for her* **2288 therwithal,** *with that* **2290 lyche,** *equal* **2291 bountee,** *goodness,* **two so,** *twice as* **2294 preyde,** *pleaded* **2297 the betake,** *entrust to you* **2300 yeve hir leve,** *give her permission,* **for to pleye,** i.e., *to be free from her duties* **2301 oones or,** *once before* **2302 sothly,** *truly,* **ryche feste,** *lavish celebration* **2305 maister-strete,** *main street* **2306 see,** *sea* **2307 turneth,** *returns* **2311 pryvyly him spedde,** *he hurried secretly* **2312 yif hir leste,** *if she wished* **2313 leste noght,** *wished not* **2314 agrose,** *was terrified* **2317 quoke,** *trembled* **2318 Ryght,** *just* **2319 colver,** *dove,* **of,** *by,* **smyten,** *struck* **2321 awhaped,** *terrified* **2322 Lest,** *for fear,* **hent eft-sones,** *seized again* **2325 reft,** *deprived* **2326 Maugre hir hede,** *in spite of her wishes* **2327 Loo,** *behold* **2328 stevene,** *voice* **2331 more myschefe,** *greater wrong* **2332 For fere lest,** *for fear that,* **crye,** *proclaim* **2333 done him,** *accuse him of* **2334 of kerveth,** *cuts out* **2336 Ful privily,** *very secretly* **2337 to his usage,** *for his use,* **to his store,** *as his possession* **2338 asterte,** *escape* **2339 sely,** *innocent* **2340 wreke,** *avenge,* **bone,** *request* **2343 ynome,** *taken* **2347 nygh,** *nearly,* **brak atwoo,** *broke in two* **2350 ylerned,** *learned*

2297 here, F reads "dere." **2307 no malice he ne thoughte,** from the medieval tradition of Ovidian commentary; in Ovid, *Metamorphoses* 6.510, Pandion has foreboding thoughts at Philomela's departure. **2319 as,** F reads "of." **2320 his,** omitted in F. **2325 of hir,** omitted in F. **2328 loude,** F reads "longe." **2338** Line lacking in F, replaced by a spurious line after 2339: "Huges ben thy sorwes, and wonder smert." **2350 ylerned had in yowthe,** mention of Philomela's youthful training in weaving is from the medieval tradition of Ovidian commentary.

So that she werken and enbrowden cowthe°,
And weven° in her stole° the radevore°
As hit of wymen° hath be woved yore°.
And, shortly for to seyn, she hath hir fille
Of mete and drynke, of clothing at hir wille,
And koude eke rede° wel ynogh and endyte°,
But with a penne koude she nat wryte;
But lettres kan she weven° to and froo,
So that by that° the yere was agoo
She had ywoven in a stamen large°
How she was broght from Athenes in a barge°,
And in a cave how that she was broght;
And al the thing that Tereus hath wroght°,
She wave° hit wel, and wrote the story above,
How she was served° for hir suster love°.
And to a knave° a ryng she yaf anoon°,
And prayed him, by sygnes°, for to goon
Unto the queene, and beren hir that clothe,
And by sygne sworne many an othe
She shulde him yeve what she geten myghte.
This knave anoon unto the queene him dyght°,
And toke hit hir, and al the maner tolde.
And whan that Proigne hath this thing beholde°,
No word she spak, for sorwe and eke for rage,
But feyned hir° to goon a pilgrimage
To Bachus temple, and in a lytel stounde°
Hir dombe suster sytting hath she founde,
Weping in the castel hirself aloon.
Allas, the woo, the compleint, and the moon°
That Proigne upon hir dombe suster maketh!
In armes everych° of hem other taketh,
And thus I lat hem in her sorwe duelle.
The remenant is no charge° for to telle,
For this is al and somme°, thus was she served
That never harm agylte° ne deserved
Unto this cruelle man that she of wyste°.
Ye may bewar of men, yif that yow lyste°.
For al be that he° wol nat, for his shame,
Doon so as Tereus, to lese° his name,
Ne serve yow as a morderere or a knave°,
Ful lytel while shul ye trewe hem have.
That wol I seyn°, al were he° now my brother,
But° hit so be that he may have non other°.

Explicit legenda Philomela.

2351 enbrowden cowthe, *knew how to embroider* **2352 weven,** *weave,* **stole,** *tapestry frame,* **radevore,** *cloth* (?) **2353 of wymen,** *by women,* **be woved yore,** *been woven for a long time* **2356 koude eke rede,** *could also read,* **endyte,** *compose* **2358 weven,** *weave* **2359 by that,** *by the time that* **2360 stamen large,** *broad cloth* (tapestry?) **2361 barge,** *ship* **2363 wroght,** *done* **2364 wave,** *wove* **2365 served,** *treated,* **hir suster love,** *for love of her sister* **2366 knave,** *servant,* **yaf anoon,** *soon gave* **2367 sygnes,** *signs* **2371 him dyght,** *went* **2373 beholde,** *beheld* **2375 feyned hir,** *pretended* **2376 stounde,** *while* **2379 moon,** *moan* **2381 everych,** *each* **2383 no charge,** *not important* **2384 al and somme,** *the sum total* **2385 agylte,** *committed* **2386 of wyste,** *was aware of* **2387 yow lyste,** *you wish* **2388 al be that he,** *even though some man* **2389 lese,** *lose* **2390 knave,** *villain* **2392 wol I seyn,** *I will say,* **al were he,** *even if he were* **2393 But,** *unless,* **may have non other,** *may have no other lover*

2353 yore, F reads "wore." **2357 with a penne koude she nat wryte,** the skills of reading and writing were often separate in western education until well into the nineteenth century. Skill with a pen was part of male, business training, while sewing letters (e.g., samplers) was part of female, domestic training. **2379–80 the woo . . ./ That Proigne . . . maketh,** In Ovid, *Metamorphoses* 6.609-74, Proce refuses to lament in order to plan her wrathful revenge on Tereus. With Philomela's help, she kills her son, Itys, and feeds his flesh to Tereus; when Tereus retaliates by attacking the sisters, all three are transformed into birds. **2379 compleint,** F reads "constreynt." **2384 is,** omitted in F. **2389 so,** omitted in F and Tr. **2393 non other,** F reads "another." **2393a *Explicit* . . . ,** Here ends the legend of Philomela.

VIII

Legend of Phyllis

Incipit legenda Phillis.

By preve° as wel as by auctoritee,
That wikked frute cometh of a wikked tree,
That may ye fynde, if that hit lyketh° yow.
But for this ende° I speke this as now,
To telle you of fals Demophon.
In love a falser herde° I never non,
But if° hit were his fader Theseus.
God, for his grace, fro suche oon kepe° us—
Thus may these wymen° prayen that hit here.
Now to th'effect° turne I of my matere.
Destroyed is of Troye the citee.
This Demophon come sayling in the see
Towarde Athenes, to his paleys° large.
With him come many a shippe and many a barge
Ful of his folk, of which ful many oon
Is wounded sore, and seke°, and woo begoon°,
And they han at the sege longe ylayne°.
Behynde come a wynde and eke a rayne
That shofe so sore° his saylle might not stonde.
Him were lever° than al the world alonde°,
So hunteth him the tempest to and fro.
So derk hit was, he kouth° nowher go,
And with a wawe brosten° was his stere°.
His shippe was rent° so lowe in suche manere
That carpenter ne koude hit nat amende.
The see by nyght as any torche brende°
For wode°, and posseth° him now up now doun,
Till Neptunius hath of him compassyoun—
And Thetis, Thorus, Triton, and they alle—
And maden him upon a lond to falle
Wherof that Phillis lady was and quene,
Ligurgus doghter, fayrer on to sene°
Than is the flour ageyn the bryghte sonne.
Unnethe° is Demophon to londe ywonne,
Wayk° and eke wery°, and his folk forpyned°
Of werynesse, and also enfamyned°,
And to the dethe he was almost ydreven°.
His wise folk to conseyl han him yeven°
To seken help and socour° of the quene,
And loken what his grace° myghte bene,
And maken in that lond somme chevissaunce°
To kepen him fro woo and fro myschaunce°.
For seke° he was, and almost at the dethe;
Unneth myghte he speke or drawe brethe;
And lyeth in Rodopeya him for to reste.
Whan he may walke, him thought hit was the beste
Unto the court to seken for socour.
Men knewe him wel, and diden him honour,
For at Athenes duke and lord was he,
As Theseus his fader hadde ybe°,

2394 preve, *experience* **2396 lyketh,** *pleases* **2397 ende,** *purpose* **2399 herde,** *heard* **2400 But if,** *unless* **2401 fro suche oon kepe,** *from such a person protect* **2402 wymen,** *women* **2403 th'effect,** *the point* **2306 paleys,** *palace* **2409 seke,** *sick,* **woo begoon,** *sorrowful* **2410 at the sege longe ylayne,** *long remained at the siege* (of Troy) **2112 shove so sore,** *blew so hard* **2413 Him were lever,** *he would rather,* **alonde,** *be on land* **2415 kouth,** *could* **2416 wawe brosten,** *wave broken,* **stere,** *rudder* **2417 rent,** *damaged* **2419 brende,** *burned* **2420 For wode,** *like mad,* **posseth,** *tossed* **2425 sene,** *look* **2427 Unnethe,** *scarcely* **2428 Wayk,** *weak,* **eke wery,** *also weary,* **forpyned,** *tormented* **2429 enfamyned,** *famished* **2430 ydreven,** *driven* **2431 yeven,** *given* **2432 socour,** *comfort* **2433 grace,** *favor* **2434 chevissaunce,** *negotiation* **2435 myschaunce,** *misfortune* **2436 seke,** *sick* **2443 ybe,** *been*

2393b *Incipit* . . . , Here begins the legend of Phyllis. Chaucer's version derives ultimately from Ovid, *Heroides* 2, modified by some source or sources unknown. Gower's version in *Confessio Amantis* 4.731–878 is similar. **2395** Matthew 7.17. **a,** omitted in F. **2398 Demophon,** Demphoon, son of Theseus and Phaedra. **2404 Troye the citee,** it is a medieval, not classical, tradition that Demophoon was returning from the Trojan War. **2404 is,** omitted in F. **2408 his,** omitted in F. **2420 now up now doun,** F reads "up and doun." **2421 Neptunius,** Neptune, god of the sea. **2422 Thetis,** a sea nymph; F reads "Tetes." **Thorus,** unidentified, but evidently a sea deity. **Triton,** a god of the sea; omitted in F. **2425 Ligurgus,** F reads "Bygurgys." Both Chaucer and Gower (*Confessio Amantis* 4.738) make Phyllis the daughter of Lycurgus, although earlier sources disagree. **2438 Rodopeya,** a mountain range in Thrace. **2440 court,** F reads "contre."

That in his tyme was of grete renoun,
No man so grete in al his regyoun,
And lyk his fader of face and of stature—
And fals of love. Hit came him of nature
As dooth the fox Renard, the foxes sone.
Of kynde° he koude° his olde fadres wone°
Withoute lore°, as kan a drake° swimme
Whan hit is kaught and caried to the brymme°.
  This honourable Phillis doth him chere°,
Hir lyketh° wel his porte° and his manere—
But for° I am agroted° here beforne
To write of hem that in love ben forsworne°,
And eke° to haste me in my legende,
Which to performe God me° grace sende,
Therfore I passe shortly in this wyse°:
Ye han wel herd of Theseus devyse°
In the betraysing of fair Adriane,
That of° hir pite kepte him fro his bane°.
At shorte wordes°, ryght° so Demophon
The same wey, the same path hath gon
That did his false fader Theseus.
For unto Phillis hath he sworne thus,
To wedden hir, and hir his trouthe plyght°,
And piked of° hir al the good he myght,
Whan he was hole° and sound and had his reste,
And doth with Phillis whatso that him leste°.
And wel kouth° I, yif that me lest soo°,
Tellen al his doing to and froo.
He sayde to his contree moste hym° saylle
For ther he wolde hir wedding apparayle°
As fille to° hir honour and his also.
And openly he took his leve tho°,
And to hir sworne he wolde nat sojourne°,
But in a moneth he wolde ageyn retourne.
And in that lond let make his ordynaunce°
As verray° lord, and toke the obeisaunce°
Wel and homely°, and let his shippes dyght°,
And home he gooth the nexte° wey he myght.
But unto Phillis yet ne come he noght°,
And that hath she so harde and sore yboght°,
Allas, that, as the storye us recorde,
She was hir owne dethe ryght with a corde°,
Whan that she segh° that Demophon hir trayed°.
  But to him first she wrote and faste° him prayed
He wolde come and delyver hir of peyne,
As I reherse shal oo word or tweyne°.
Me lyste nat vouchesauf° on him to swynke°,
Dispenden° on him a penne ful of ynke,
For fals in love was he, ryght as his syre°—
The devel set her soules both on fire!
But of the letter of Phillis wol I wryte
A word or tweyne, althogh hit be but lyte°.
"Thyn hostesse," quod she, "O Demophon,
Thi Phillis, which that is so woobegon°,
Of Rodopeye, upon yow mot° compleyne
Over the terme° sette betwix us tweyne,
That ye ne holden forward°, as ye seyde.
Your anker°, which ye in oure haven° leyde,
Hyghte° us that ye wolde comen, out of doute,
Or that° the mone ones° went aboute.
But tymes foure° the mone hath hid hir face
Syn thylke° day ye wente fro this place,
And foure tymes lyght° the world ageyn.
But for al that, yif I shal soothly seyn°,

2449 Of kynde, *by nature,* **koude,** *knew,* **wone,** *customs* **2450 lore,** *teaching,* **drake,** *male duck* **2451 brymme,** *bank* **2452 doth him chere,** *makes him welcome* **2453 Hir lyketh,** *she likes,* **porte,** *looks* **2454 for,** *because,* **agroted,** *fed up* **2455 ben forsworne,** *break their vows* **2456 eke,** *also* **2457 God me,** *may God to me* **2458 wyse,** *way* **2459 Theseus devyse,** *Theseus' scheme* **2461 of,** *because of,* **bane,** *death* **2462 At shorte wordes,** *in brief,* **ryght,** *just* **2466 his trouthe plyght,** *his faithfulness pledged* **2467 piked of,** *stolen from* **2468 hole,** *healthy* **2469 leste,** *pleases* **2470 kouth,** *could,* **me lest soo,** *it pleased me* **2472 moste hym,** *he must* **2473 apparayle,** *prepare for* **2474 fille to,** *befitted* **2475 tho,** *then* **2476 sojourne,** *delay* **2478 let make his ordynaunce,** *he ordered preparation* **2479 As verray,** *like a genuine,* **toke the obeisaunce,** *accepted the respect* **2480 homely,** *familiarly,* **dyght,** *be prepared* **2481 nexte,** *nearest* **2482 yet ne come he noght,** *he never returned* **2483 yboght,** *suffered* **2485 was her own deth ryght with a corde,** *commited suicide with a rope* **2486 segh,** *realized,* **trayed,** *betrayed* **2486 faste,** *earnestly* **2489 oo word or tweyne,** *a word or two* **2490 Me lyste nat vouchesauf,** *it doesn't please me to consent,* **swynke,** *labor* **2491 Dispenden,** *to waste* **2492 ryght as his syre,** *just like his father* **2495 lyte,** *little* **2497 woobegon,** *sorrowful* **2498 mot,** *must* **2499 terme,** *appointed time* **2500 ne holden forward,** *have not kept the promise* **2501 anker,** *anchor,* **haven,** *harbor* **2502 Hyghte,** *promised* **2503 Or that,** *before,* **ones,** *once* **2504 tymes foure,** *four times* **2505 thylke,** *that* **2506 lyght,** *lighted* **2507 soothly seye,** *speak truly*

2444 of grete, F reads "grete of." **2448 Reynard,** the commonplace name for a deceptive fox in beast fables. **2452 Phillis,** F reads "quene"; Tr, "quene Phillis." **2454–58** This passage and the incompleteness of the final tale lead some critics to think that Chaucer grew tired of writing the *LGW.* **2459 devyse,** F reads "the vyse." **2475** Line omitted in F. **2482 But,** from Tr; F and Gg read "For." **ne,** omitted in F. **2485 dethe . . . with a corde,** hanging is only one of the several forms of suicide Phyllis considers in Ovid *Heroides* 2.133–42; Chaucer also specifies that she hanged herself at *BD* 729 and *HF* 394. **ryght,** omitted in F. **2496–2512** Follows Ovid, *Heroides* 2.1–9. **2506–07** Lines lacking in Gg. **2507 yif,** F reads "yet."

Yet hath the streme° of Sitho nat ybroght
From Athenes the shippe; yet° cometh hit noght.
And yif that ye the terme rekne° wolde,
As I or other trewe lovers sholde,
I pleyne nat, God wot° beforn my day."
But al hir letter writen I ne may
By ordre°, for hit were to me a charge°.
Hir letter was ryght° long and therto large°.
But here and there in ryme I have hit layde,
Ther as me thoghte that she wel hath sayde.
She seyde, "Thy saylles comen nat ageyn,
Ne to thy word ther nys no fey° certeyn;
But I wot° why ye come nat," quod she,
"For° I was of my love to yow so fre°.
And of the goddes that ye han forswore°,
Yf that her vengeaunce fal on yow therfore,
Ye be nat suffisaunt to bere the peyne.
To moche° trusted I, wel may I pleyne°,
Upon youre lynage and youre faire tonge,
And on youre teres falsly out ywronge°.
How kouth° ye wepe soo be° craft?" quod she.
"May ther suche teres feyned° be?
Now certes°, yif ye wolde have in memorye,
Hit oghte be to yow but lytel glorye
To have a sely° mayde thus betrayed!
To God," quod she, "prey I, and ofte have prayed,
That hit be now the grettest prise° of alle,
And moste honour that ever yow shal befalle.
And when thyn olde auncestres peynted be,
In° which men may her worthynesse se,
Than°, pray I God, thow peynted be also,
That folk may reden°, forthby° as they go,
'Lo°, this is he, that with his flaterye
Betrayed hath and doon her vilanye
That was his trewe love in thoghte and dede.'
But sothely°, of oo poynt° yet may they rede,
That ye ben lyke youre fader as in this,
For he begiled Adriane, ywis°,
With suche an art and suche soteltee°
As thou thyselven hast begiled me.
As in that poynt, althogh hit be nat fayr°,
Thou folwest him, certeyn, and art his eyr°.
But syn° thus synfully ye me begile,
My body mote° ye seen within a while
Ryght in the haven° of Athenes fletinge°,
Withouten sepulture° and buryinge,
Thogh ye ben harder then° is any ston!"
And whan this letter was forth sent anon,
And knew how brotel° and how fals he was,
She for dispeyr fordide° hirself, allas.
Suche sorowe hath she for she beset hir° so.
Bewar, ye wymmen, of your sotil fo°,
Syn yet this day men° may ensample se—
And, as in love, trust no man but me.

Explicit legenda Phillis.

2508 streme, *current* **2509 yet,** *still* **2510 rekne,** *reckon* **2512 wot,** *knows* **2514 By ordre,** *in order,* **charge,** *burden* **2515 ryght,** *very,* **therto large,** *also detailed* **2519 nys no fey,** *is no faith* **2520 wot,** *know* **2521 For,** *because,* **fre,** *generous* **2522 han forswore,** *have sworn to falsely* **2525 To moche,** *too much,* **pleyne,** *lament* **2527 ywronge,** *wrung* **2528 kouth,** *could,* **be,** *by* **2529 feyned,** *pretended* **2530 certes,** *surely* **2532 sely,** *innocent* **2534 grettest prise,** *greatest reward* **2537 In,** *by* **2538 Than,** *then* **2539 rede,** *read,* **forthby,** *passing by* **2540 Lo,** *look* **2543 sothely,** *truly,* **of oo poynt,** *in one respect* **2545 ywis,** *certainly* **2546 soteltee,** *subtlety* **2548 fayr,** *good* **2549 eyr,** *heir* **2550 syn,** *since* **2551 mote,** *may* **2552 haven,** *harbor,* **fletinge,** *floating* **2553 sepulture,** *tomb* **2554 then,** *than* **2556 brotel,** *unreliable* **2557 fordide,** *killed* **2558 for she beset hir,** *because she bestowed herself* **2559 sotil fo,** *subtle foe* **2560 Syn yet this day men,** *since to this day people*

2508 streme of Sitho, the Thracian current, named Sithonian after Phyllis's father Sitho. F reads "Sitoio"; Gg, "Sitoye"; Tr, "Sitoy." Skeat's emendation. **2516 wel hath, F and Tr read "hath well." 2518–2529** Compresses Ovid, *Heroides* 2.26–51. **2518Thy,** F reads "the." **2519 they, F reads "the." 2533–49** Follows Ovid, *Heroides* 2.63–78, where Demophoon and his ancestors are sculpted (rather than painted) and a statement of his infidelity is inscribed. **2525 pleyne,** F reads "seyne." **2549 him,** omitted in F. **2550–54** Follows Ovid, *Heroides* 2.133–37. **2561a** ***Explicit*** . . . , Here ends the legend of Phyllis.

IX

Legend of Hypermnestra

Incipit legenda Ypermystre.

In Grece whilom° weren brethren two
Of whiche that oon was called Danao,
That many a sone hath of his body wonne°,
As suche false lovers ofte konne°.
Among his sones alle ther was oon
That aldermost° he loved of everychon°.
And whan this child was born, this Danao
Shope° him a name, and called him Lyno.
That other brother called was Egiste,
That was in love as fals as ever him lyste°,
And many a doghtre gat he in his lyve,
Of which he gat upon his righte° wyve
A doghter dere, and dide hir for to calle
Ypermystra, yongest of hem alle.
The whiche childe of hir natyvite°
To al good thewes° born was she,
As lyked to° the goddes or° she was borne
That of the shefe° she shulde be the corne.
The Wirdes°, that we clepen° Destanee,
Hath shapen hir that she most nedes° be
Pitouse°, sadde°, wise, trewe as stele,
And to this woman hit acordeth wele°.
For though that Venus yaf hir grete beaute,
With Jupiter compouned° so was she
That conscience, trouthe, and drede of shame,
And of her wyfehod for to kepe hir name,
This thoghte hir was felicite as here°.
And rede° Mars was that° tyme of the yere
So feble that his malice is him rafte°;
Repressed hath Venus his cruelle crafte.
What with Venus and other oppressyoun
Of houses, Mars his° venym is adoun
That° Ypermystra dar nat handel a knyf
In malyce thogh she shulde lese hir lyf°.
But natheles, as heven gan thoo turne°,
To badde aspectes hath she of° Saturne,
That maked her to deyen in prisoun,
As I shal after make mencioun.
To Danao and Egistes also—
Althogh so be that they were brethren two,
For thilke tyme° nas spared, no lynage°—
Hit lyketh° hem to maken mariage
Betwix Ypermystra and him Lyno,
And casten° suche a day hit shal be so.
And ful acorded was hit uttirly:
The array is wroght°, the tyme is faste° by.
And thus Lyno hath of his fadres brother

2562 whilom, *once* **2564 wonne,** *fathered* **2565 konne,** *can* **2567 aldermost,** *most of all,* **everychon,** *all of them* **2569 Shope,** *gave* **2571 him lyste,** *it pleased him* **2573 righte,** *lawful* **2576 of hir natyvite,** *as a result of her horoscope* **2577 thewes,** *qualities* **2578 lyked to,** *it pleased,* **or,** *before* **2579 shefe,** *sheaf* **2580 Wirdes,** *Fates,* **clepen,** *call* **2581 most nedes,** *must necessarily* **2582 Pitouse,** *compassionate,* **sadde,** *steadfast* **2583 hit acordeth wele,** *it was very suitable* **2585 compouned,** *tempered* **2588 felicite as here,** *happiness on earth* **2589 rede,** *red,* **that,** *at that* **2590 is him rafte,** *is taken from him* **2593 Mars his,** *Mars's* **2594 That,** *so that* **2595 though shulde lese hir lyf,** *even if she should lose her life* (i.e., even in in self defense) **2596 as heven gan thoo turne,** *when the heavens turned* **2597 hath she of,** *that she has from* **2602 thilke tyme,** *at that time,* **nas spared no lynage,** *kinship was not restricted* **2603 lyketh,** *pleased* **2605 casten,** *decided upon* **2607 array is wroght,** *preparations are made* **faste,** *close*

2561b *Incipit*. . . , Here begins the legend of Hypermnestra. Chaucer's source is unknown, although it derives ultimately from Ovid, *Heroides* 14, adapted in medieval commentary and translation and modified by his own additions at lines 2576–98 and 2705–22. **2567 Danao,** Danaus; spelled "Danoo" throughout F. **2569 Lyno,** Lynceus. **2570** Line lacking in TR. **Egiste,** Aegyptus. **2574 hir,** F reads "hyt." **2576–98** Hypermnestra's nativity horoscope may be Chaucer's invention. The influence of the planet Venus gave her beauty; Jupiter, goodness. The potentially malevolent influence of Mars was repressed by Venus and by other planetary arrangements (**houses, 2593**) until the influence of Saturn brought about her death in prison. **2578 goddes,** F reads "goddesses." **2592 What,** F reads "And"; Gg and Tr, "That what." **2599 As,** F reads "And."**2601 Althogh,** F and Tr read "And though." **that,** omitted in Tr. **2603–04 marriage/Betwix Ypermystra and him Lyno,** in Ovid, *Heroides* 14, the 50 daughters of Danaus all marry their first cousins, the 50 sons of Aegyptus, and only Hypermnestra refuses to kill her husband, Lynceus. Chaucer (or perhaps his source) switches the fathers and eliminates the 49 siblings. **2606 uttirly,** F reads "witterly" (completely).

The doghter wedded, and eche of hem hath other.
The torches brennen° and the lampes bryght,
The sacrifices ben ful redy dyght°,
Th'encence° out of the fire reketh sote°,
The flour, the lefe is rent° up by the rote
To maken garlands and corounes hye°,
Ful is the place of soun of mynstralcye,
Of songes amorouse° of mariage,
As thilke tyme was the pleyn usage°.
And this was in the paleys° of Egiste,
That in his hous was lord ryght as him liste°.
And thus the day they dreven° to an ende;
The frendes taken leve, and home they wende°.
The nyght is comen, the bride shal go to bed.
Egiste to his chambre fast him sped,
And privELY he let his doghter calle°.
Whan that the hous was voyded° of hem alle,
He loked on his doghter with glad chere°,
And to hir spak as ye shal after here.
"My righte doghter, tresour of myn hert,
Syn first that day° that shapen° was my shert,
Or by the fatal sustren° hadde my dom°,
So ny° myn herte never thing me com
As thou, myn Ypermystra, doghter dere!
Tak heed what I thy fader sey thee here,
And wirk aftir thy wiser° evermoo.
For alderfirste° doghter, I love thee soo
That al the world to me nys° halfe so lefe°,
Ne I nolde rede the° to thy myschefe°
For al the goode under the colde moone.
And what I mene, hit shal be seyd ryght soone,
With protestacioun°, as in this wyse°;
That but thou do as I shal the° devyse,
Thou shalt be ded, by Him that al hath wrought°!
At shorte wordes°, thow nescapest nought
Out of my paleys or that° thou be deed,
But° thou consente and werke after my rede°—
Tak this to the for ful conclusioun°."
This Ypermystra caste hir eyen doun,
And quoke° as dooth the lefe of aspe grene°.
Ded wex° hir hewe, and lyk as ash° to sene,
And seyde, "Lord and fader, al your wille
After my myght°, God wot°, I shal fulfille,
So° hit to me be no confusioun°."
"I nyl°," quod he, "have noon excepcioun."
And out he kaughte a knyf, as rasour kene°,
"Hyd this," quod he, "that hit be nat ysene,
And whan thyn housbond is to bed ygo°,
While that he slepeth, kut his throte atwo.
For in my dremes hit is warned me
How that my nevywe° shal my bane° be,
But which I not°, wherfor I wol be siker°.
Yif thou sey nay, we two shal have a biker°
As I have seyd, by Him that I have sworn."
This Ypermystra hath nygh° hir wytte forlorn°,
And for to passen harmelesse° of that place,
She graunted him°; ther was noon other grace°.
And therwythal a costrel° taketh he tho°
And seyde, "Herof a draught or two
Yif him to drynke whan he gooth to reste,
And he shal slepe as longe as ever the leste°,
The narcotiks and opies° been so stronge.
And goo thy wey, lest that him thynke longe°."
Out cometh the bride and with ful sobre chere°,
As is of maydens ofte the manere.

2610 brennen, *burn* **2611 dyght,** *prepared* **2612 Th'encence,** *the incense,* **reketh sote,** *smokes sweetly* **2613 rent,** *torn* **2614 corounes hye,** *high crowns* **2616 songes amorouse,** *love songs* **2617 pleyn usage,** *well-known custom* **2618 paleys,** *palace* **2619 ryght as him liste,** *just as he pleased* **2620 dreven,** *bring* **2621 wende,** *travel* **2624 let his doghter calle,** *had his daughter called* **2625 voyded,** *empty* **2626 chere,** *expression* **2629 Syn first that day,** *since the first day,* **shapen,** *woven* **2630 fatal sustren,** i.e., *Fates,* **dom,** *destiny* **2631 ny,** *near* **2634 wirk aftir thy wiser,** *do as the wiser person tells you* **2635 alderfirste,** *first of all* **2636 nys,** *is not,* **lefe,** *dear* **2637 Ne I nolde rede the,** *nor I would not advise you,* **myschefe,** *misfortune* **2640 protestacioun,** *qualification* **wyse,** *way* **2641 the,** *for you* **2642 wrought,** *created* **2643 At shorte wordes,** *in brief* **2644 or that,** *before* **2645 But,** *unless,* **rede,** *counsel* **2647 for ful conclusioun,** *as an absolute mandate* **2648 quoke,** *trembled,* **lefe of aspe grene,** *green leaf of the aspen tree* **2649 Ded wex,** *deadly became,* **ash,** *ashes* **2651 After my myght,** *in accord with my ability,* **wot,** *knows* **2652 So,** *as long as,* **confusioun,** *disgrace* **2653 nyl,** *will not* **2654 as rasour kene,** *sharp as a razor* **2656 ygo,** *gone* **2659 nevywe,** *nephew,* **bane,** *death* **2660 not,** *do not know,* **siker,** *certain* **2661 a biker,** *contention* **2663 nygh,** *nearly,* **forlorn,** *lost* **2664 harmelesse,** *without harm* **2665 graunted him,** *consented,* **grace,** *mercy* **2666 costrel,** *flask,* **tho,** *then* **2669 the leste,** *you wish* **2670 opies,** *opiates* **2671 lest that him thynke longe,** *so that he doesn't think there is some delay* **2672 chere,** *expression*

2619 ryght, omitted in F. **2620 the,** F reads "that." **2624 he,** omitted in F. **2625 voyded of hem alle,** F reads "voyded was of alle." **2726 after,** omitted in F. **2629 first that day,** F reads "firste day." **2632 myn,** omitted in F. **2633 I,** omitted in F **2640 in this,** F reads "seyn these." **2652 to me be,** F reads "be to me." **2658 in my dremes,** there is no dream in Ovid, *Heroides* 14, although it does occur in medieval versions of the story. **2661 have,** F reads "make." **2666 therwythal,** F reads "withal." **Tho,** omitted in G and Tr, where "or thre" ends the following line (for rhyme). **2668 him to drynke,** F read "him drynke." **2670 longe,** F reads "to longe."

To chambre is brought with revel and with
songe,
And shortly, lest this tale be to longe,
This Lyno and she ben broght to bedde,
And every wight° out at the dore him spedde.
The nyght is wasted°, and he felle aslepe.
Ful tenderly begynneth she to wepe.
She rist° her up, and dreadfully° she
quaketh°,
As doth the braunche that Zephirus shaketh,
And husht were al in Argon that citee.
As colde as any frost now wexeth° she,
For pite by the herte hir streyneth° so,
And drede of deth doth hir so moche° woo,
That thries° doun she fel in swich a were°.
She ryst hir up and stakeretn° here and there,
And on hir handes faste° loketh she.
"Allas, and shal myn handes blody be?
I am a mayd, and as by my nature,
And by my semblant°, and by my vesture°,
Myn handes ben nat shapen° for a knyf,
As for to reve° no man fro his lyf.
What devel° have I with the knyf to do?
And shal I have my throte korve atwo°?
Than shal I blede, allas, and me beshende°.
And nedes cost° this thing not have an ende;
Or° he or I mot nedes lese° oure lyf.
Now certes°," quod she, "syn° I am his wyf,
And hath my feyth, yet is hit bet° for me
For to be ded in wyfly honeste
Than be a traytour lyving in my shame.
Be as be may, for erneste or for game°,
He shal awake and ryse and go his way
Out at this goter° or that° hit be day!"—
And wept ful tenderly upon his face,
And in hir armes gan him to embrace,
And him she roggeth° and awaketh softe°.
And at the window lepe he fro the lofte°
Whan she hath warned him, and doon him
bote°.
This Lyno swyfte was, and lyght of fote,
And from his wyf he ran a ful good pas°.
This sely° woman is so wayk°, allas,
And helples so that or that° she fer° went,
Her crwel fader did hir for to hent°.
Allas, Lyno, why art thou so unkynde?
Why ne haddest thou remerabred in thy
mynde
And taken hir, and ledde hir forth with the?
For whan she saw that goon awey was he,
And that she myghte nat so faste go,
Ne folwen him, she sate her doun ryght tho°,
Til she was kaught and fetered in prisoun.
This tale is seid for this conclusion.

2677 wight, *person* **2678 wasted,** *used up* **2680 rist her,** *rises,* **dredefully,** *fearfully,* **quaketh,** *trembles* **2683 wexeth,** *becomes* **2684 streyneth,** *grips* **2685 moche,** *much* **2686 thries,** *three times,* **were,** *turmoil* **2687 stakereth,** *staggers* **2688 faste,** *closely* **2691 semblant,** *form,* **vesture,** *attire* **2692 ben nat shapen,** *are not designed* **2693 reve,** *steal* **2694 What devel,** *what the devil* **2695 korve atwo,** *cut in two* **2696 me beshende,** *be ruined* **2697 nedes cost,** *it is essential that* **2698 Or,** *either,* **mot nedes lese,** *must necessarily lose* **2699 certes,** *surely,* **syn,** *since* **2700 bet,** *better* **2703 for erneste or for game,** *in any case* **2705 goter,** *water channel,* **or that,** *before* **2708 roggeth,** *shakes,* **softe,** *gently* **2709 lofte,** *upper room* **2710 doon him bote,** *saved him* **2712 ful good pas,** *very good pace* **2713 sely,** *innocent,* **wayk,** *weak* **2714 or that,** *before,* **fer,** *far* **2715 did her for to hent,** *had her seized* **2721 tho,** *then*

2681 Zephirus, the West Wind. **2682 Argon,** Argos, a city in southeastern Greece." **2691–93** Similar to Ovid, *Heroides* 14.55–60. **2696 me,** omitted in F. **2697 And,** F reads "Or." **2709–22** Lynceus's escape by means of a water channel or downspout of some sort may be Chaucer's invention, as may the account of Lynceus's running away without Hypermnestra. **2712 his wyf he,** F reads "hir." **2721 her,** omitted in F. **2723** The story ends with this line in most complete manuscripts. Some modern critics consider it unfinished and assume that Chaucer would have added some sort of moralization, but many of the manucript scribes evidently considered this a satisfactory conclusion.

Short Poems

Short Poems

Introduction

JOHN GOWER, Chaucer's contemporary and friend, praised the lyric love poetry that Chaucer wrote in his youth (*Confessio Amantis* 8.2941–57), and Chaucer's disciple, John Lydgate, attests that his predecessor wrote "many a fresh dite [poem] / Complaintes, ballades, roundles, virelaies (*Fall of Princes* 1.352–53). Chaucer himself acknowledges his experiments in short verse on several occasions (*LGWP* F421–22, *MLP* 2.47ff., *Ret* 10.1087). So it is all but certain that Chaucer wrote more than the twenty-two short poems traditionally assigned to him and included here. Despite their small number, the lyrics (and perhaps others by Chaucer that have been lost) helped to shape English lyric tradition. According to Rossell Hope Robbins, Chaucer's lyrics are "not only the pacemakers" of the English lyric from about 1350 until the Renaissance, "they are the *only* specimens" of the second half of the fourteenth century (1979: 383; no. 1593) and the models for later English lyrics. French forms dominated the court poetry of the age, and it was Chaucer who adapted and in many ways re-made these forms for and in English.

Certainly, earlier Middle English lyrics had been influenced by French, but the fashion of French poetry took a turn in the early fourteenth century, at which time elaborate poetic musical compositions stabilized into a set of new stanzaic and metrical forms—*formes fixes* (fixed forms), as they were called, that depend heavily on the ease of rhyming inherent in the inflectional endings of the French language. Though the English of the day generally lacked such inflectional endings, borrowing from French vocabulary helped Chaucer to imitate these forms, especially the ballade form and the rhyme royal stanza, and his experiments sparked the English lyric tradition of the fifteenth and sixteenth centuries. Moreover, he imitated several French lyric genres—the complaint and the begging poem—so that he helped to define the subject matter of the English lyric tradition as well as the metrical forms.

Clarification of a few terms will help. Chaucer employed the seven-line rhyme royal stanza (*ababbcc*) throughout much of his career (*Parliament of Fowls, Troylus and Criseyde,* four of the *Canterbury Tales,* and many of the Short Poems), apparently imitating—or at the very least influenced by—similar stanzas in the lyrics of French poets, especially Guillaume de Machaut (1300–1377). Machaut was the premiere French musician and poet of his day, and his example did much to standardize the fixed forms, although court poetry soon separated from musical accompaniment. The ballade—not to be confused with the popular folksong ballad—was one of Machaut's favorite forms, highly artificial in sentiment and expression, and characterized by three stanzas held together with a strict rhyme scheme and a refrain. The number of lines per stanza varied between seven and twelve, with the same rhymes used throughout (through-rhymed); the refrain—often a single line—is a holdover from the musical roots of the form. Machaut's disciple, Eustace Deschamps (c. 1345–1406), popularized the use of an envoy to conclude the ballade—i.e., he added a stanza, often shortened, which serves as a commentary or postscript, sometimes addressing the poem to a patron or recipient, fictional or real. Such envoys may have developed under the influence of the puys—medieval literary societies that held poetic contests, judged by elected "princes" who presided over the contests and were often addressed in the envoys of the poems entered into competition. The contests themselves are also called *puys* at times. Records are rare and we have no evidence that Chaucer ever entered such a contest, but his models were shaped by their influence. On the English puys, see, "London and Southwark Poetic Companies," Helen Cooper's study in Ardis Butterfield's collection of essays, *Chaucer and the City* (2006, no. 502).

Fifteen of the twenty-two poems included here are either strict ballades (nos. 4, 8, 10–12, 14, 18, 20) or are clearly influenced by the ballade form (nos. 2, 3, 5, 7, 16, 17, 21), although the latter either lack a refrain or do not maintain through-rhyme. Eight of these poems end with an envoy (nos. 4, 7, 10, 11, 14, 16–18), and thirteen are, in part or whole, in rhyme royal stanzas (nos. 2, 3, 5, 6, 11, 12, 14, 15, 17, 18, 20–22). Little more need be said to demonstrate Chaucer's sustained exploration of French metrical forms. Yet it is also worthwhile noticing that *Merciless Beaute* (no. 19; attribution uncertain) is a triple rondel and two sections of *Anelida and Arcite* (no. 2, lines 271–80 and 317–32) may reflect the influence of the virelay—two more of the French fixed forms. Moreover, all but four (1, 9, 15, 16) of the twenty-two poems here are, part or whole, influenced by the genres of love complaint or complaint against the failures of the world, popular in French tradition.

Despite his borrowings, Chaucer's innovations in his Short Poems are as remarkable as his uses of conventions. Not content with metrical experimentation alone—although there is much of that in poems such as *Merciless Beaute, Anelida and Arcite,* and *Balade of Pity*—Chaucer gained rhetorical and thematic richness by setting his lyrics in narrative contexts and particularized situations, and, at times, more simply, by straining against conventions of diction and decorum. His most often copied short poem, *Balade de Bon Conseil* or *Truth* (no. 11), is an exquisite example of traditional sentiments captured in masterful verse. *To Adam Scriveyn* (no. 15) is a single rhyme royal stanza that achieves a very personal tone, perched between exasperation and affection. The ballade *To Rosemounde* (no. 8) and the *Complaint of Chaucer to His Purse* (no. 18) play wittily against conventions of their forms. The comments on individual poems below summarize briefly the conventionalities and innovations of Chaucer's Short Poems and survey topics of scholarship and criticism.

General critical appreciation of this poetry has been surveyed by John Scattergood in his section of A. J. Minnis's Oxford Guide, *The Shorter Poems* (1995, no. 1400). Scattergood acknowledges his debt to discussion of fourteen of the poems by George B. Pace and Alfred David, edited for the Chaucer Variorum project, *The Minor Poems, Part One* (1982, no. 67); part two has not been published. James I. Wimsatt has done the most to clarify Chaucer's debt to French tradition and the *formes fixes,* especially in *Chaucer and His French Contemporaries* (1991, no. 314). In *Chaucer and the Poems of "Ch" in University of Pennsylvania MS French 15* (1982/2009, no. 1596), Wimsatt edits and discusses a manuscript anthology of French verse that Chaucer almost certainly knew; some of the poems may even be his own experiments in French poetry. W. A. Davenport discusses Chaucer's use of the complaint genre in *Chaucer: Complaint and Narrative* (1988, no. 623), and Wendy Scase assesses nine of his short poems in *Literature and Complaint in England* (2007, no. 1615). Jay Ruud, *"Many a Song and Many a Leccherous Lay": Tradition and Individuality in Chaucer's Lyric Poetry* (1992, no. 1594) is the only book-length study of Chaucer's Short Poems to date. Julia Boffey, "The Reputation and Circulation of Chaucer's Lyrics in the Fifteenth Century" (1993, no. 1587), and Seth Lerer, *Chaucer and His Readers* (1993, no. 338), explore the reception of the lyrics in the fifteenth and sixteenth centuries. In *Chaucer's Lyrics and Anelida and Arcite* (1984, no. 92), Russell A. Peck provides a comprehensive, annotated bibliography for study of the Short Poems, 1900–1980, and Bruce Holsinger offers consistently insightful and provocative readings in "Lyrics and Short Poems," his contribution to *The Yale Companion to Chaucer* (2007, no. 111), edited by Seth Lerer.

1. *Prier a Nostre Dame* (also titled *An ABC*) is Chaucer's only stand-alone religious lyric, although the poet did set similar prayers to the Virgin Mary in broader narrative contexts, particularly in the prologues to the *Prioress's Tale* and the *Second Nun's Tale* (*CT* 7.453–87 and 8.29–77). *ABC* translates a French original, drawn from a lengthy narrative allegory, *Le Pélèrinage de la Vie Humaine* (c. 1330) by Guillaume Deguileville. Chaucer follows Deguileville's alphabetic format (note the first letter of each stanza), but changes the octosyllabic line to decasyllabic, and reduces the twelve-line stanzas to eight lines. He also adds familiar images and ideas and introduces a number of interjections, altering rhythms and making more personal the plea for aid toward salvation. In 1602 Thomas Speght stated that the poem was made "as some say, at the request of Blanche Duchess of Lancaster, as a praier for her private use." If Speght is right, the poem must predate the death of Blanche in 1368, making it one of Chaucer's earliest extant poems, perhaps an exercise in adapting French into English.

2. *Anelida and Arcite* is one of Chaucer's most experimental poems. Perhaps a composite work and perhaps incomplete, it combines an epic setting with the pathos of romance, incorporating a metrically intricate complaint (see the note to 211a) into a narrative context that is based on medievalized classical material (Statius's *Thebaid* via Boccaccio's *Teseide*). No source has been found for the particular sequence of events of the narrative, although generally similar material underlies the *Knight's Tale*, where Chaucer follows Boccaccio more closely. The highly emotional sentiments of the complaint sound much like those of the falcon in the *Squire's Tale* (5.477–629)—a female lament about male infidelity—but because Anelida's complaint is cast as a letter (209–10), her shifts between general apostrophe and direct address to Arcite achieve a kind of psychological realism. Letters are a concern in the frame as well (112), though the connection seems not to have drawn much critical attention, except for recognition that Dido's letter in Ovid's *Heroides* 7 may have inspired the epistolary form of Chaucer's complaint. If the final stanza of *Anelida* is authentic (see 351–57n), it reiterates the concern with letters (352) and suggests more epic plot, perhaps the intervention of the gods and questions about human freedom. A. S. G. Edwards, "The Unity and Authenticity of *Anelida and Arcite*" (1988, no. 1604), argues from manuscript evidence that the poem is composite, with only the Complaint (211–350) by Chaucer. In the first chapter of *Chaucer and the Subject of History* (1991, no. 442), Lee Patterson reads the poem as Chaucer's contemplation of literary origins and originality.
3. *Complaint of Mars* also sets in a narrative frame a love complaint, here a traditional dawn song in which the male lover bemoans his separation from his beloved as the morning arrives. In this case, however, the love and separation take on broad implications because the speaker is the god/planet Mars who must depart from his beloved Venus when they are interrupted by the Sun. The anthropomorphized planets move in accord with fixed astrological cycles (e.g., 111, 117, 145, etc.), raising questions about their freedom to do otherwise and posing a theme of philosophical determinism (reminiscent of *Troylus and Criseyde*) that is reinforced by extended allusion to the tragic story of Thebes (245–71). The introduction to the poem sets the occasion for telling the story on Valentine's Day, the annual celebration of love when birds chose their mates. The lightheartedness of the Valentine convention—one Chaucer may have helped to establish—darkens quickly in the narrative and the complaint proper. At the same time, the very inclusiveness of the poem (birds, humans, gods, and planets are in the same boat, as it were) makes the poem more thought provoking than somber. Less varied than in *Anelida*, the stanza forms of *Mars* still dazzle—rhyme royal in the introduction and narrative, shifting in the complaint to nine-line stanzas, arranged as five ballades. On agency and determinism in the poem, see the discussion in Carolynn Van Dyke, *Chaucer's Agents* (2005, no. 398); on St. Valentine, Henry A. Kelly, *Chaucer and the Cult of St. Valentine* (1986, no. 1476).
4. *Complaint of Venus* is given its title by convention only. The poem recurrently appears with *Mars* in the manuscripts, often continuing it without a break; the speaker is female, but there is no other reason to associate it with Venus. It translates three ballades by Oton de Granson (see 82n), following his form strictly—eight-line stanza with refrain (*a b a b b c c b*)—but reducing the poem from five to three stanzas and shifting the gender of the speaker from male to female. The shift requires that Chaucer adjust some of the conventional imagery and diction of the original, praising, for example, the wisdom and knighthood of the beloved rather than the traditional feminine ideals found in Granson. In this way, the poem is new wine corked in an old bottle. In a similar self-conscious vein, Chaucer adds an envoy (not in Granson) that bemoans his ineptitude as a poet because of advancing age, complains about the scarcity of rhyme-words in English, and goes on to praise Granson. Genuine as the praise seems, something playful (or showy) is afoot: in the ten-line envoy, Chaucer uses only two rhymes even while he laments the limits of English.
5. Personification was a favorite device in French lyrics and allegory, but *A Complaint unto Pity* is the only place where Chaucer uses it to any considerable degree. Combining a human speaker with allegorical abstractions, the poem elegantly conveys a sense of frustration. The speaker cannot deliver his complaint to Pity

because she is dead, her corpse surrounded by the confederates of Cruelty. In telling us "Th'effect" (56) of what he *would* have said, however, the speaker does convey his message to his beloved, the one in whose heart (line 14) Pity now lies dead. This conceit of the allegorical frame is made even more urbane by the fact that the triple ballade of the complaint proper is cast as a legal petition, touched with mild threats to the reputation of the beloved amidst the more prevalent praise. It concludes wittily with the suggestion that through his own death the speaker may yet find Pity.

6. The fifteenth-century attribution of *A Balade of Pity* (also called *A Complaint to His Lady*) to Chaucer by fifteenth-century scribe and collector John Shirley has been questioned. If authentic, lines 15–40 are the only extant attempt by Chaucer to imitate Italian *terza rima* (*aba bcb cdc* etc.), and there is no real reason to assume that they were composed at the same time as the other parts of the poem—the opening rhyme royal stanzas and the closing ten-lines ones, one of which is imperfect (see 51–58n). Some efforts at cohesion are evident (rhyme in 14 and 15), but there also are indications (see 128n) that the three parts may have been independent metrical experiments.
7. Found in one manuscript only and apparently missing a line (see the note to line 12a), *Womanly Noblesse* opens and closes similarly (lines 31–32 echo lines 1–2) and follows a strict ballade form, in nine-line stanzas, plus envoy, while using only two rhymes. These indications of a high degree of formal polish (despite the lack of a refrain) are no proof that the poem is by Chaucer, but critical opinion has generally accepted it as such. The speaker praises his beloved and also argues gently that his act of writing merits her attention to him.
8. A combination of formal polish (strict ballade form in eight-line stanzas with refrain; no envoy) and colloquial touches (e.g., the diction and imagery in 2, 9, 11, 16–17) makes it almost certain that *To Rosemounde* is Chaucer's although, again, there is no proof. Like *Womanly Noblesse, Rosemounde* is a praise poem distinct from Chaucer's more usual complaint genre; it is also found in only one manuscript. Each poem poses an argument of sorts, but here there is gentle teasing rather than subtle persuasion. This tone and several details have prompted critics to infer that the poem approaches parody, intended for a very young woman, perhaps the child-wife of Richard II, Isabella. If Isabella were intended, the date of the poem would be quite late, perhaps on the occasion of her London entry in 1396.
9. *Proverbe of Chaucer* is simply an attempt to write epigrams, unremarkable in most ways except that they are attributed to Chaucer in two of the four manuscripts that survive.
10. *Fortune* and the four poems following it are usually grouped as Chaucer's Boethian lyrics, all closely connected to Boethius's *Consolation of Philosophy*, which Chaucer translated as his *Boece* and which deeply influenced his *Troylus and Criseyde, Knight's Tale*, and other works. Like *Complaint of Venus, Fortune* is a strict triple ballade with refrain. It is in eight-line stanzas and cast as a quasilegal debate between a plaintiff and Fortune as defendant. This debate format is unique among Chaucer's Short Poems, even though debate poetry is found widely in Latin and the medieval vernaculars. The format may well have been inspired in this instance by Book 2 prose 2 of the *Consolation*, where Philosophy voices Fortune's case against Boethius. In any event, critics have used the direct address of the envoy (an additional rhyme royal stanza) to date the poem (see 76n), and the plea of this envoy has the broad effect of converting the poem from a general lament on the condition of the world to a request for patronage. Ballade, debate, and complaint, *Fortune* is also a begging poem. Perhaps the body of the poem and its envoy were composed at different times, also possibly true of Short Poems 11, 14, and 18.
11. *Truth*, as *Balade de Bon Conseil* is usually called, survives in more manuscript versions (twenty-four) than any other short poem by Chaucer, perhaps because popular sentiment is presented in such confident, memorable verse. It counsels distance from the entanglements of worldly affairs—a familiar theme of *contemptus mundi*—but the refrain is fundamentally hopeful: truth will deliver those who seek to achieve it rather than worldly success. The envoy of the ballade uses the same rhymes as are found in stanzas 1–3 (rhyme royal and through-rhymed) and it includes two hortatory command words in stressed initial position

(lines 24 and 26), a device characteristic of the poem. Yet the urgings of the envoy seem calmer than the preceding ones, and the fact that the envoy appears in only one manuscript may indicate that Chaucer added it late when he addressed the poem to his friend, Sir Philip de la Vache (see 22n).

12. Lacking an envoy, the ballade *Moral Balade of Gentilesse* addresses the commonplace notion that nobility is defined by virtuous deeds rather than lineage or appointment. The idea is found in Boethius, the *Roman de la Rose*, Dante, the *Wife of Bath's Tale* (3.1109ff.) and elsewhere (see 1n); nevertheless, many have wrongly considered the idea to be somehow modern. *Gentilesse* is perhaps best understood in the tradition of counsel or advice poetry, although it actually gives no direct advice. The through-rhymed rhyme royal stanzas are polished but without energetic exhortation or personal address.

13. *The Former Age* derives directly from the fifth meter in Book 2 of Boethius's *Consolation*, beginning as a relatively close translation and then dilating further on the Golden Age theme and critiquing the present-day world by contrast. The eight-line stanzas (one line missing in stanza seven) are most remarkable for sharing no rhymes across stanza boundaries, a clear break from French models and perhaps a case where form(lessness) reflects content. Hammer-blow negatives recur throughout the poem (13–24 and elsewhere), and at the end the idealization of the past breaks out into full-fledged condemnation of the present. Read outside the context of the *Consolation*, it stands as Chaucer's most pessimistic statement about the contemporary world.

14. *Lack of Steadfastnesse* also laments the present in light of the past, but it expresses hope that the stability of the past may be regained if the "prince" (see 22n) will serve as model for his people. Through-rhymed and complete with refrain and envoy, the ballade relies almost exclusively on multisyllabic, French-derived rhyme words (three rhymes only) set against monosyllabic words that prevail elsewhere in the poem. As a result, the generalized *contemptus mundi* complaint of the first three stanzas is elegant in form and powerful in impact, anticipating the combination of pleading and exhortation in the envoy.

15. Perhaps a one-time jotting, *To Adam Scriveyn* demonstrates Chaucer's facility with rhyme royal and, apparently, his irritation with his actual scribe, Adam Pinkhurst. The identification of Pinkhurst as Chaucer's scribe was established by Linne R. Mooney (2006, no. 30), who documents Pinkhurst's copying of several manuscripts of works by Chaucer and suggests the link with the Adam of this poem. Complaints against scribes are known elsewhere, but few are as personal or as exasperatedly jovial, so that the brief poem seems to give a glimpse of Chaucer's working relation with Pinkhurst. The linking of *Boece* and *Troylus* in the poem (line 2) indicates that Chaucer was working on these two at about the same time (c. 1380–1385), and we have a fragment of a manuscript for each of these works that may also be in Pinkhurst's hand (for *Boece*, National Library of Wales, Peniarth 393D; for *Troylus*, a single leaf only, Hatfield House, Cecil Papers, Box S/1). Chaucer's plea that his *Troylus* not be miswritten (*TC* 5.1795) also ties in with *Adam*. The poem exists in a single manuscript only.

16. *Lenvoy de Chaucer a Bukton* also exists in only one manuscript and it also refers to Chaucer's own literature—this time to the Wife of Bath. It is a ballade (with envoy) in eight-line stanzas, without through-rhyme or refrain, cast as a verse epistle or letter of advice. The anti-matrimonial message is softened by the in-house humor of the reference to the Wife (129) and the other echoes of the *Wife of Bath's Prologue* (6, 18–20). Colloquial rather than elegant, the poem is addressed to someone who is clearly of Chaucer's circle, a male companion who has not been identified surely (see 1n).

17. Another verse epistle addressed to one of Chaucer's friends (see 13n), *Lenvoy de Chaucer a Scogan*, is more obscure than *Bukton*, but no less personal. Its references to astrology and weather, Scogan's love life, and Chaucer's age and writing seem to indicate a particular time or occasion that has yet to be identified; the envoy renders it a begging poem. Confident in its enjambments and shifting caesuras, its purpose seems more earnest than that of *Bukton*—perhaps only because we do not know what the context is for the joke. It is double ballade (with envoy) in rhyme royal, without through-rhyme or refrain.

18. The playfulness in the *Complaint of Chaucer to His Purse* is as clear as its earnest request (in the envoy) for financial support from the recently crowned Henry IV. It is likely, then, that the envoy is the last thing we have that Chaucer wrote—sometime after September 30, 1399, when Henry was accepted as king. This begging poem mocks the conventions of the complaint genre, addressing a purse instead of a lady in conventional praise and playing on the sexual suggestiveness of "light" and "heavy" (see 3–4n). The poem also sends up the ballade form by maintaining through-rhyme and a refrain for three rhyme royal stanzas while using utterly conventional—even trite—rhyme words through most of the poem. The grander rhymes and the more formal syntax of the envoy ensure that Henry is not included in the mockery.

19–22. Poems not attributed to Chaucer in the manuscripts. It is conventional to include the following in collections of Chaucer's works, although their authenticity is not generally agreed upon. If *Merciless Beaute* is authentic, it is the closest thing we have to a song by Chaucer, comparable to the one that concludes *Parliament of Fowls.* A through-rhymed ballade with refrain (rhyme royal), *Against Women Unconstant* expresses conventional antifeminist sentiment. Conventional in many ways, *A Balade of Complaint* lacks the through-rhyme and refrain of a strict ballade; it is rarely attributed to Chaucer. *An Amorous Complaint Made at Windsor* (also titled *Complaynt d'Amours*) echoes a number of characteristic Chaucerian phrases and the Valentine's Day tradition; it may as well be thought a good imitation as authentic.

Short Poems

Poems Attributed to Chaucer in the Manuscripts

1 PRIER A NOSTRE DAME

Of Our Lady the ABC.

Incipit carmen secundum ordinem litterarum alphabeticum.

Almyghty and al mercyable quene,
To whom that al this world fleeth° for socour°,
To have relees° of synne, of sorwe, of tene°,
Gloriouse virgyne, of alle floures flour,
To the I flee, confounded° in errour.
Help and releve, thow myghty debonayre°,
Have mercy of° my perilouse langour°.
Venquysshed hath me my cruel adversayre.

Bountee° so fix hath° in thine hert his tent,
That wel I wot°, thow wolt° my socour bee.
Thow kanst not werne° him that with good entent
Axeth° thyn help, thine herte is ay° so free°.
Thow art largesse of pleyn felicitee°,
Haven of refut°, of quiete, and of reste.
Loo, how that theves° seven chasen me!
Help, lady bryght, er that° my shippe to-breste.

Comfort is noon but in yow, lady dere,
For loo, my synne and my confusioun,
Which oughte not in my presence appere,
Han take° on me a grevouse accioun
Of verray° ryght and desperacioun°,
And, as by ryght, they myghten wel sustene
That I were worthy° my dampnacioun,
Nere° mercy of yow, blysful hevenes quene.

Doute is ther noon, quene of misericorde°,
That thow nart cause of grace and mercy here.
God vouched sauf° thurgh the° with us t'acorde,
For certes°, Cristes blysful moder dere,
Were now the bowe ybent in swich manere
As hit° was first, of justice and of ire,
The ryghtful God nolde of no° mercy here°—
But thurgh thee han we grace, as we desire.

Ever hath myn hope of refut° in the be°,
For here-beforn, ful ofte, in many a wyse,
Unto mercy hastow° receyved me.
But mercy, lady, at the grete assise,
Whan we shul come before the hye° justise.

---

2 fleeth, *flies,* **socour,** *help* **3 relees,** *forgiveness,* **tene,** *trouble* **5 confounded,** *distressed* **6 debonayre,** *gracious one* **7 of,** *on,* **langour,** *weakness* **9 Bountee,** *goodness,* **so fix hath,** *has so fixed* **10 wot,** *know,* **wolt,** *will* **11 werne,** *refuse* **12 Axeth,** *asks,* **ay,** *always,* **free,** *generous* **13 largesse of pleyn felicitee,** *generosity of complete happiness* **14 refut,** *refuge* **15 theves,** *thieves* **16 er that,** *before,* **to-breste,** *breaks to pieces* **20 Han take,** *have taken* **21 verray,** *genuine,* **desperacioun,** *despair* **23 were worthy,** *am deserving of* **24 Nere,** *if it were not for* **25 misericorde,** *pity* **26 nart,** i.e., *are* **27 vouched sauf,** *granted,* **thurgh the,** *through you* **28 certes,** *surely* **30 hit,** *it* **31 nolde of no,** *would of no,* **here,** *hear* **33 refut,** *refuge,* **in the be,** *been in you* **35 hastow,** *have you* **37 hye,** *high*

Text based on Bodleian Library MS Fairfax 16 (F), with selected variants from Cambridge University Library MS Ff.5.30 (Ff [2]). **Prier a Nostre Dame,** A Prayer to Our Lady. Editors also title the poem "An ABC." ***Incipit carmen . . . ,*** Here begins a song that follows the order of the letters of the alphabet. **2 that,** omitted in F. **3 of sorwe, of tene,** Ff [2] reads "sorwe, tene." **4 floures flour,** this commonplace epithet for the Virgin Mary is not in Chaucer's source. **15 theves seven,** the Seven Deadly Sins: pride, envy, anger, sloth, avarice, gluttony, lechery. **20 grevouse accioun,** serious legal action; the idea is that sin and confusion are accusing the speaker in a criminal court, a common metaphor in penitential literature. **24 Nere,** F reads "ne." **25 quene,** Ff [2] reads "thou queen." **29 bowe ybent,** a bow ready to shoot is a figure of vengeance. **34 ofte, in many a wyse,** F reads "often, in many wyse." **35 Unto mercy hastow,** Ff [2] reads "Hast thou to misericorde." **36 grete assise,** great court, i.e., the Last Judgment.

So litel good shal thanne in me be founde
That but° thou er that day correcte me,
Of verrey ryght° my werk wol me confounde°.

Fleeing, I flee for socour° to thy tent,
Me for to hide fro tempest ful of drede,
Beseching yow that ye yow nat absent
Though I be wikke°. O help yet at this nede!
Al have I ben° a best° in wytte and dede,
Yet, lady, thow me clothe wyth thy grace.
Thyn enemy and myn—lady, tak hede—
Unto my deth in poynt is° me to chace.

Gloriouse mayde and moder, which that never
Were bitter, nor in erthe nor° in see,
But ful of swetnesse and of mercy ever,
Help that my Fader be nat wroth° with me.
Spek thow, for I ne dar nat him ysee°.
So have I doon in erthe, allas the while,
That certes° but that° thou my socour bee,
To stynke eterne he wol my goost° exile.

He vouched sauf°, telle him, as was his wille,
Become a man as for our alliaunce,
And with his blood he wroot° the blysful bille°
Upon the crois° as general acquytaunce°
To every penytent in ful creaunce°.
And therfor, lady bryght, thow for us pray.
Than shalt thou both stynte° al his grevaunce,
And make our foo° to faylen of his pray°.

I wot° hit wel, thow wolt ben° oure socour,
That art so ful of bountee°, in certeyne,
For whan a soule falleth in errour,
Thy pitee gooth and haleth him ageyne°.
Than makestow his pees with his sovereyn,
And bringest him out of the crooked strete.
Whoso the loveth°, he shal nat love in veyn—
That shal he fynde as° he the life shal lete°.

Kalenderes enlumyned° ben they
That in this world ben lyghted with thi name,
And whoso° gooth to yow the ryghte wey,
Him thar nat drede° in soule to be lame.
Now, quene of comfort, sith° thou art that
same
To whom I seche for my medycine,
Lat not my foo no more my wounde entame°.
Myn hele° into thyn hand alle I resygne.

Lady, thy sorwe kan I nat purtreye°
Under the crois, ne° His grevous penaunce°.
But for your bothe peynes, I yow preye,
Lat nat our aller foo° make his bobaunce°
That he hath in his lystes of meschaunce°
Convict that ye both han° boght so dere.
As I seyde erst°, thou grounde° of our
substaunce°,
Contynue on us thy pitous eyen clere°.

Moises that saugh° the bussh with flambes
rede
Brenninge° of which ther never a stikke brende,
Was signe of thyn unwemmed° maydenhede.
Thou art the bussh on which ther gan°
discende
The Holy Gost, the which that Moises wende°
Had ben afire, and this was in figure°.

---

39 but, *unless* **40 Of verrey ryght,** *by true justice* **40 confounde,** *destroy* **41 socour,** *help* **44 wikke,** *wicked* **45 Al have I ben,** *although I have been,* **best,** *beast* **48 in poynt is,** *is just about* **50 nor . . . nor,** *neither . . . nor* **52 wroth,** *angry* **53 ysee,** *approach* (see) **55 certes,** *surely,* **but that,** *unless* **56 goost,** *spirit* **57 vouched sauf,** *agreed* (to) **59 wroot,** *wrote,* **bille,** *legal document* **60 crois,** *cross,* **acquytaunce,** *pardon* **61 ful creaunce,** *complete faith* **63 stynte,** *end* **64 foo,** *foe,* **pray,** *prey* **65 wot,** *know,* **wolt ben,** *will be* **66 bountee,** *goodness* **68 haleth him ageyne,** *pulls him back* **71 the loveth,** *loves you* **72 as,** *when,* **lete,** *give up* **73 Kalenderes enlumyned,** *illuminated calendars* **75 whoso,** *whoever* **76 Him thar nat drede,** *he need not fear* **77 sith,** *because* **79 entame,** *open* **80 Myn hele,** *my health* **81 purtreye,** *portray* **82 ne,** *nor,* **penaunce,** *suffering* **84 our aller foo,** *the enemy of us all,* **bobaunce,** *boast* **85 lystes of meschaunce,** *tricks of destruction* **86 Convict that ye both han,** *convicted what you* (Mary and Jesus) *both have* **87 erst,** *first,* **grounde,** *foundation,* **substaunce,** *being* **88 pitous eyen clere,** *compassionate beautiful eyes* **89 Moises that saugh,** *Moses who saw* **90 Brenninge,** *burning* **91 unwemmed,** *unblemished* **92 gan,** *did* **93 wende,** *thought* **94 in figure,** *symbolic*

38 good, Ff[2] reads "fruit." **39 correcte me,** this alteration in the rhyme scheme is found in all manuscripts except Ff[2] which has "me chastyse" over an erasure. **43 Beseching,** F reads "Besekyng." **50 bitter,** a commonplace play on *Maria* (Mary) and Hebrew *marah,* which means "bitterness." **56 stynke eterne,** eternal stench; hell. Chaucer added this familiar notion when translating. **58 as for,** Ff[2] reads "to have our." **59 blood he wroot the blysful bille,** Ff[2] reads "precious blood he wroot the bille." **70 of the crooked strete,** omitted in F. **73** There is no stanza for the letter *j,* historically a graphic variant of *i,* nor for the letters *v* or *w,* historically variants of *u.* **Kalenderes enlumymed,** in church calendars, decorated or illuminated letters indicated special feast days. **84 aller,** Ff[2] reads "alder." **88 on,** F reads "in." **89 the bussh,** the bush that burns but remains unconsumed (Exodus 3.2) was a recognized symbol of Mary, who gave birth while remaining a virgin. **94 in figure,** in medieval interpretation, characters and events of the Hebrew testament were thought to prefigure characters and events in the Christian testament.

Now lady, fro the fire thou us defende
Which that in helle eternally shal dure°.

Noble princesse that never haddest pere°,
Certes° if any comfort in us bee
That cometh of the, Cristes moder dere,
We han noon other melodie or glee°
Us to rejoyse in our adversitee,
Ne advocat noon that wol and dar so prey°
For us, and that for litel hyre° as ye
That helpen for an Ave Marie or twey°.

O verray° light of eyen that ben blynde,
O verray lust of° labour and distresse,
O tresorere of bounte° to mankynde,
The° whom God chees to° moder for humblesse!
From his ancile° he made the maistresse
Of heven and erthe, our bille° up for to beede°.
This worlde awaiteth ever on thy godenesse,
For thou ne failest never wight° at neede.

Purpos I have sommetyme for t'enquere
Wherfore and why the Holy Goost the sought,
Whan Gabrieles voys cam to thyn ere.
He nat to werre° us swich° a wonder wrought,
But for to save us that he sithen bought°.
Than nedeth us no wepene° us for to save,
But oonly ther we did nat, as we ought,
Do penytence and mercy axe° and have.

Queen of comfort, yet whan I me bethynke°
That I agilt° have bothe him and thee,
And that my soule is worthy for to synke,
Allas, I katyf°, whider may I flee?
Who shal unto thy sone my mene° be?
Who but thyself that art of pitee welle°?
Thow hast more routhe° on oure adversite
Than in this world myghte any tonge telle.

Redresse° me, moder, and me chastise,
For certeynly my fadres chastisinge,
That dar I nat abiden° in no wise,
So hidouse is his ryghtful rekeninge°.
Moder, of whom our mercy gan to springe,
Beth ye my juge and eke° my soules leche°,
For ever in yow is pitee haboundinge°
To ech that wol of pitee yow beseche.

Soth° is that He ne graunteth noo pitee
Withoute the°. For God of his goodnesse
Foryeveth noon, but hit lyke° unto the.
He hath the maked vicaire° and maistresse
Of alle this worlde, and eke governeresse
Of hevene; and he represseth his justice
Aftir° thy wille, and therefore in witnesse
He hath the crowned in so riall wise°.

Temple devout, ther° God hath his woninge°,
Fro which these mysbeleved pryved been°,
To yow my soule penytent I brynge.
Receyve me; I kan no ferther fleen!
With thornes venymouse°, O hevene queen,
For which the erthe acursed was ful yore°,
I am so wounded, as ye may wel seen,
That I am lost almost, it smert° so sore.

Virgyne, that art so noble of apparayle,
That ledest us into the hye toure°
Of Paradys, thou me wysse° and counsayle,
How I may have thy grace and thy socoure°.
Al° have I ben in filthe and in erroure,
Lady, unto that court thou me adjourne°
That cleped is° thy bench, O fresshe floure,
Ther as that mercy ever shal sojourne°.

---

96 dure, *endure* **97 pere,** *equal* **98 Certes,** *surely* **100 glee,** *music* **102 dar so prey,** *dare so to pray* **103 hyre,** *payment* **104 twey,** *two* **105 verray,** *true* **106 lust of,** *joy to* **107 tresorere of bounte,** *treasurer of goodness* **108 The,** *you,* **chees to,** *chose as* **109 ancile,** *serving maid* **110 bille,** *petition,* **beede,** *offer* **112 wight,** *person* **116 werre,** *make war on,* **swich,** *such* **117 sithen bought,** *afterwards redeemed* **118 wepene,** *weapon* **120 axe,** *ask* **121 me bethynke,** *consider* **122 agilt,** *offended* **124 katyf,** *captive* **125 mene,** *mediator* **126 of pitee welle,** *the source of pity* **127 routhe,** *pity* **129 Redresse,** *correct* **131 abiden,** *await* **132 ryghtful rekeninge,** *just account-keeping* **134 eke,** *also,* **leche,** *physician* **135 haboundinge,** *abounding* **137 Soth,** *true* **138 the,** *you* **139 but hit lyke,** *unless it is pleasing* **140 the maked vicaire,** *made you vicar* **143 Aftir,** *in accord with* **144 so riall wise,** *such royal fashion* **145 ther,** *where,* **woninge,** *dwelling* **146 mysbeleved pryved been,** *unbelievers are excluded* **149 venymouse,** *poisonous* **150 ful yore,** *very long ago* **152 smert,** *hurts* **154 hye toure,** *high tower* **155 wysse,** *instruct* **156 socoure,** *help* **157 Al,** *although* **158 me adjourne,** *set for me the day of appearance* **159 cleped is,** *is called* **160 sojourne,** *remain*

99 Cristes, Ff² reads "thou Cristes." **104 Ave Marie,** a prayer of veneration to Mary that echoes and commemorates the angel Gabriel's announcement to her that she was to become the mother of God. **109 ancile,** from Luke 1.38: "*Ecce ancilla Domini*" ("Behold the handmaid of the Lord"), the words spoken by the angel Gabriel. **114–15** Chaucer's addition. **137 He,** Ff ² reads "God." **146 pryved,** F and Ff ² read "deprived." **149–50 With thornes . . . the erthe acursed was,** see Genesis 3.18. **153** On the lack of a stanza beginning with the letter *u*, see 73n. **159 bench,** the Middle English word for "court of law" (e.g. King's Bench), here introduced into the translation by Chaucer.

Xpūs°, thy sone, that in this world alyghte°
Upon the crois to suffre his passioun,
And eke° that Longius his herte pighte°
And made his herte blood to renne adoun,
And al was this for my salvacioun,
And I to him am fals and eke unkynde,
And yet he wol° not my dampnacioun—
This thanke I yow, socour° of al mankynde.

Ysaac was figure of His dethe, certeyne,
That so ferforth° his fader wolde obeye
That him ne rought° nothing to be sleyne,
Ryght so thy sone lyst°, as a lamb, to deye.
Now lady, ful of mercy, I yow preye,
Sith° he his mercy mesured so large,
Be ye nat skant°, for al we° synge and seye
That ye been fro vengeaunce ay° oure targe°.

Zakarye yow clepeth° the open welle
To wasshe synful soule out of his gilt.
Therfore this lessoun oughte I wel to telle
That nere° thy tender herte, we were spilt°.
Now lady bryght, sith thou kanst and wilt
Been to the sede of Adam mercyable°,
Bryng us to that palays that is bilt
To° penytents that been to mercy able. Amen.

Explicit

2 ANELIDA AND ARCITE

The Compleynt of Feire Anelida and Fals Arcite.

Invocation

Thou fers° god of armes, Mars the rede°,
That in the frosty countre called Trace,
Within thy grisly temples ful of drede,
Honoured art as patroun of that place,
With thy Bellona, Pallas, ful of grace,
Be present, and my song contynew and gye°.
At my begynning thus I to the crye.
For hit° ful depe is sonken in my mynde,
With pitous hert in Englyssh to endyte°
This olde storie in Latyn which I fynde,
Of Quene Anelida and fals Arcite,
That elde°, which al can frete° and bite,
As hit hath freten mony a noble storie,
Hath nygh° devoured out of oure memorie.

---

161 Xpūs, i.e., *Christ,* **alyghte,** *descended* **163 eke,** *also,* **pighte,** *pierced* **167 wol,** *wishes* **168 socour,** *aid* **170 ferforth,** *completely* **171 rought,** *cared* **172 thy sone lyst,** *it pleased your son* **174 Sith,** *since* **175 skant,** *ungenerous,* **al we,** *we all* **176 ay,** *always,* **targe,** *shield* **177 yow clepeth,** *called you* **180 nere,** *if it were not for,* **spilt,** *destroyed* **182 mercyable,** *merciful* **184 To,** *for* **Anelida and Arcite** **1 fers,** *fierce,* **rede,** *red* **6 gye,** *guide* **8 hit,** *it* **9 endyte,** *write* **12 elde,** *age,* **frete,** *eat* **14 nygh,** *nearly*

161 Xpūs, the Greek letter *chi* followed by *rho* plus indication of abbreviation over *u* was a common contraction for *Christus* in medieval manuscripts, the origin of "Xmas." On the lack of a stanza beginning with the letter *w,* see 73n. **163 Longius,** Longinus; Chaucer added this allusion to the blind Roman centurion. At the crucifixion, drops of Christ's blood restored Longinus's eyesight when his lance pierced Christ's side. The name (deriving from λόγχη, "lance") is first recorded in the non-canonical Gospel of Nicodemus 7.8; compare John 19.34. **169 Ysaac was figure,** Isaac's willingness to be sacrificed by his father, Abraham (Genesis 22; Hebrews 11.17–19), was thought to prefigure Christ's willingness to die. See 94n. **177 Zakarye . . . open welle,** Zechariah 13.1; usually applied to the blood of Christ. Here Mary is presented as the source from which redemption comes. **181 bryght,** omitted in F. **Anelida and Arcite.** Text based on Bodleian Library, Oxford, MS Fairfax 16 (F), with corrections and selected variants from Caxton's edition of 1477–78 (Cx) and Magdalene College, Cambridge University, Pepys 2006 (P) for portions of the poem: Cx 1–210 and 311–50, and P otherwise. In F, 211–350 precede 1–210. The first stanzas of the poem and the names *Arcite* and *Emelye* (10 and 38) derive from Boccaccio's *Teseida,* which Chaucer later adapted more fully as the *Knight's Tale.* Stanza one here derives from *Teseida* 1.3. **1 Mars the rede,** Mars is the bloody or red god of war. **2. Trace,** Thrace, near modern Bulgaria. **5 Bellona, Pallas,** Bellona, sister of Mars and goddess of war, is here conflated with Pallas Athena, sometimes also goddess of war. In *Thebaid* 7.73, Statius mentions Bellona after describing the temple of Mars. **10 olde storie in Latyn,** Chaucer's inspiration here is Boccaccio's Italian, which also mentions an old story as a source (*Teseida* 1.2). No source is known for Chaucer's plot, so his claim for a Latin source may well be a bid for classical authority, a medieval convention. **14 oure,** Cx reads "my."

Be favorable eke°, thou Polymya,
On Parnaso that with thy sustres glade°,
By Elycon, not fer from Cirrea,
Singest with vois memorial° in the shade,
Under the laurer° which that may not fade,
And do° that I my shippe to haven wynne°.
First folow I Stace, and after him Corynne.

Narrative

Iamque domos patrias, Cithice post aspera gentis, &c.

Whan Theseus with werres° longe and grete
The aspre° folke of Cithe° had overcome,
With laurer° crouned, in his char golde-bete°,
Home to his contre houses is ycome,
For which the peple blisful al and somme
So criden° that to the sterres hit went,
And him to honouren dide al her entent°.

Beforn this duke, in signe of victorie,
The trompes° come, and in his baner large
The ymage of Mars, and in token of glorie
Men myghte sene° of tresour many a charge°,
Many a bright helm, and many a spere and targe°,
Many a fresh knyght, and many a blysful route°,
On hors, on fote, in al the felde aboute.

Ipolita his wife, the hardy° quene
Of Cithia, that he conquered had,
With Emelye hir yonge suster shene°,
Faire in a char of golde he with him lad°,
That al the grounde about hir char she sprad
With brightnesse of the beaute in hir face,
Fulfilled of largesse° and of alle grace.

With his tryumphe and laurer corouned thus,
In al the floure of fortunes yeving°,
Let I this noble prince Theseus
Towarde Athenes in his wey ryding,
And founde° I wol in shortly for to bring
The sley° wey of that° I gan° to write—
Of Quene Anelida and fals Arcite.

Mars which that thro° his furiouse course of ire
The olde wrath of Juno to fulfille
Hath set the peples hertes bothe on fire
Of Thebes and Grece, everich° other to kille
With blody speres, ne rested never stille,
But throng° now her, now ther, among hern
bothe,
That everych other slough°, so wer they wrothe°.

For whan Amphiorax and Tydeus,
Ipomedon and Parthonope also,
Were ded, and slayn proud Campaneus,
And whan the wrecches Thebans, bretheren two,
Were slayn, and Kyng Adrastus home ago,
So desolat stode Thebes and so bare
That no wyght° coude remedie of his care.

And whan the olde Greon gan espye°
How that the blood roial was broght adoun,
He held the cite by his tyrannye,
And dyd° the gentils of that regioun
To ben his frendes, and duellen in the toun.

15 eke, *also* **16 glade,** *joyful* **18 vois memorial,** *memorable voice* **19 laurer,** *laurel tree* **20 do,** *make* (it), **to haven wynne,** *sail safely to harbor* **22 werres,** *wars* **23 aspre,** *fierce,* **Cithe,** *Scythia* **24 laurer,** *laurel leaves,* **char golde-bete,** *chariot adorned with beaten gold* **27 criden,** *cheered* **28 dide al her entent,** *did their utmost* **30 trompes,** *trumpets* **32 sene,** *see,* **charge,** *load* **33 targe,** *shield* **34 blysful route,** *joyous troop* **36 hardy,** *brave* **38 shene,** *beautiful* **39 lad,** *led* **42 largesse,** *generosity* **44 fortunes yeving,** *fortune's giving* **47 founde,** *try* **48 sley,** *deceitful,* **of that,** *about which,* **gan,** *began* **50 thro,** *through* **53 everich,** *each* **55 throng,** *pushed* **56 slough,** *slew,* **wrothe,** *furious* **63 wyght,** *person* **64 gan espye,** *did see* **67 dyd,** *caused*

15–17 Polymya . . . Parnaso . . . , Polymnia was the muse of hymns or sacred music, one of the nine mythic muses who resided on Mount Parnassus. As in *HF* 522, Chaucer here presents Helicon (**Elycon**) as an inspirational spring on Parnassus instead of as Mount Helicon, another home of the muses in tradition. Cirra (**Cirrea**) is the port of an ancient town near Parnassus. **20 my shippe to haven wynne,** sailing successfully to harbor is a common metaphor for poetic composition. **21 Stace,** Statius, whose *Thebaid* is the model for the next stanzas. **Corynne,** not identified with certainty, although some legendary classical writer or singer is intended. **21a *Iamque* . . . , *&c,*** And now [drawing near] to his homeland after a fierce battle against the Scythians, [Theseus], et cetera. From Statius's *Thebaid* 12.519–20, also quoted in the headnote to *KnT.* Lines 22–28 here translate *Thebaid* 12.519–21, which F quotes in Latin. **24 With,** F reads "The." **25 houses,** Cx reads "hool"; the Latin is *domos patria* (native homes). **36 Ipolita,** Hippolyta, the legendary warrior queen of the Scythians (or Amazons). **50–70** A summary of *Teseida* 2.10–12. **51 wrath of Juno,** Juno, wife of Jupiter, was angered by her husband's infidelities. **57ff.** A synopsis of the legendary siege of the seven against Thebes. Amphiaraus (**Amphiorax**),Tydeus, Hippomedon (**Ipomedon**), Parthenopaeus (**Parthonope**) Capaneus, and Adrastus of Argos assisted Polynices of Thebes against his brother Eteocles, who refused to share rule. Compare Chaucer's somewhat fuller version, *TC* 5.1485–1510. **58 and,** omitted in F. **63 care,** Cx reads "fare." **68 duellen,** Cx reads "women," and other manuscripts have "wonnen."

So what for love of him, and what for awe,
The noble folk wer to the toune idrawe°.

Among al these, Anelida the quene
Of Ermony was in that toun duelling,
That fairer was then° is the sunne shene°.
Throughout the world so gan° hir name spring,
That hir to seen had every wyght° lyking,
For as of trouthe is ther noon hir lyche°
Of al thes wymen° in this worlde riche.

Yong was this quene, of twenty yer of elde°,
Of mydel stature, and of suche fairenesse
That nature had a joye hir to behelde.
And for to speken of hir stidfastnesse°,
She passed bothe Penolope and Lucresse,
And shortly, if she shal be comprehended,
In hir ne myght nothing been amended°.

This Theban knyght Arcite eke°, sothe to seyne°,
Was yonge, and therwithal° a lusty° knyght,
But he was double° in love and nothing pleyne°,
And subtil in that crafte over any wyght,
And with his kunning wan this lady bryght,
For so ferforth° he gan hir trouthe assure,
That she him trusted over any creature.

What shuld I seyn? She loved Arcite so
That whan that he was absent any throw°,
Anon hir thoght hir herte brast atwo°;
For in hir sight to hir he bare him low°,
So that she wende have° al his herte yknow°.
But he was fals; hit nas° but feyned chere°,
As nedeth not to men such craft to lere°.

But nevertheles, ful mykel° besynesse
Had he er that he myght his lady wynne,
And sworne he wolde dyen for distresse,
Or from his wit he seyde he wolde twynne°—
Alas the whyle°, for hit was routhe° and synne
That she upon his sorowes wolde rewe°!
But nothing thinketh the fals as doth the trewe.

Hir fredom° fond Arcite in suche manere
That al was his that she hath, moche and lyte°,
Ne to no creature made she chere°
Ferther than that hit lyked° to Arcite.
Ther was no lak with which he myghte hir wite°,
She was so ferforth yeven° him to plese
That al that lyked him, hit did hir ese.

Ther nas to hir no maner° lettre isent
That touched love from any maner wyght°,
That she ne shewed hit him er° hit was brent°—
So pleyn° she was, and did hir fulle myght
That she nyl° hyden nothing from hir knyght
Lest he° of any untrouthe hir upbreyde°.
Withouten bode° his heste° she obeyed.

And eke° he made him jelous over hire
That what that any man had to hir seyd
Anoon° he wolde preyen hir to swere
What was that word, or make him evel apayd°.
Than wende° she out of hir wit have brayd°.
But al this nas but sleght° and flaterye—
Withoute love he feyned jelousye.

And al this toke she so debonerly°
That al his wil° hir thoghte hit skilful° thing,
And ever the lenger she loved him tendirly,
And did him honour as° he were a kyng.
Hir hert was wedded to him with a ring.
So ferforth° upon trouthe is hir entent
That wher he goth, hir herte with him went.

---

70 idrawe, *drawn* **73 then,** *than,* **shene,** *beautiful* **74 gan,** *did* **75 wyght,** *person* **76 lyche,** *like* **77 wymen,** *women* **78 elde,** *age* **81 stidfastnesse,** *constancy* **84 amended,** *improved* **85 eke,** *also,* **sothe to seyne,** *to speak truly* **86 therwithal,** *also,* **lusty,** *lively* **87 double,** *duplicitous,* **pleyne,** *straightforward* **90 ferforth,** *completely* **93 throw,** *length of time* **94 brast atwo,** *burst in two* **95 bare him low,** *humbled himself* **96 wende have,** *thought to have,* **yknow,** *known* **97 nas,** *was nothing,* **feyned chere,** *pretended behavior* **98 lere,** *learn* **99 ful mykel,** *very much* **102 from his wit . . . twynne,** *lose his mind* **103 Alas the whyle,** *alas the time,* **routhe,** *grief* **104 rewe,** *take pity* **106 fredom,** *generosity* **107 moche and lyte,** *great and small* **108 made she chere,** *was she friendly* **109 that hit lyked,** *what was pleasing* **110 wite,** *blame* **111 ferforth yeven,** *completely committed* **113 maner,** *kind of* **114 wyght,** *person* **115 er,** *before,* **brent,** *burned* **116 pleyn,** *straightforward* **117 she nyl,** *she did not wish to* **118 Lest he,** *so that he would not,* **upbreyde,** *scold* **119 bode,** *bidding,* **heste,** *command* **120 eke,** *also* **122 Anoon,** *immediately* **123 evel apayd,** *ill-pleased* **124 wende,** *thought,* **out of hir wit have brayd,** *had gone mad* **125 sleght,** *deceit* **127 debonerly,** *graciously* **128 wil,** *desire,* **skilful,** *reasonable* **130 as,** *as if* **132 ferforth,** *far*

71–72 Anelida . . . Of Ermony, Anelida of Armenia, but the character has not been identified with certainty and from here on no source has been discovered for the poem. **82 bothe,** Cx reads "hath." **Penolope and Lucresse,** Penelope and Lucretia are classical and medieval models of female constancy. **85 Arcite,** the name is omitted in F and Cx. **105ff.** The relationship between Anelida and Arcite recalls that of the falcon and the false male bird in *SqT* 7.499 ff., with several specific echoes of language and detail. **107 moche,** F reads "both moche." **112 hit did her ese,** F reads "hir her an ese." **119 heste,** F reads "hert." **125 this,** omitted in F. **132 So ferforth,** F reads "For so."

Whan she shal ete, on him is so hir thoght
That wel unnethe° of mete° toke she kepe°,
And whan that she was to hir rest ybroght,
On him she thoght alwey til that she slepe°.
Whan he was absent, prevely° she wepe.
Thus lyveth feir Anelida the quene
For fals Arcite that did° hir al this tene°.

This fals Arcite, of his newfangelnesse°,
For° she to him so lowly° was and trewe,
Toke lesse deyntee for° hir stidfastnesse,
And saw another lady, proud and newe,
And ryght anon he clad° him in hir hewe°,
Wot I not° whether in white, rede, or grene,
And falsed fair Anelida the quene.

But neverthelesse, gret wonder was hit noon
Thogh he wer fals, for hit is kynde° of man
Sith° Lamek was, that is so longe agoon,
To ben in love as fals as ever he can.
He was the first fader that began
To loven two, and was in bigamye—
And he found° tentes first, but if° men lye.

This fals Arcite, sumwhat most° he feyn°
Whan he wex° fals, to covere his traitorie,
Ryght as° an hors that can both bite and pleyn°,
For he bar hir on honde° of trecherie,
And swore he coude hir doublenesse espie,
And al was falsnes that she to him ment.
Thus swore this thefe, and forth his way he went.

Alas, what hert myght enduren hit,
For routhe° or wo, hir sorow for to telle?
Or what man hath the cunning or the wit?
Or what man myght within the chamber duelle
If I to him rehersen shal the helle
That suffreth feir Anelida the quene
For fals Arcite, that did hir al this tene°?

She wepith, waileth, swowneth° pitously;
To grounde dede she falleth as a ston;
Al crampyssheth° hir lymes crokedly;
She speketh as° hir wit were al agon;
Other colour then° asshen hath she non;
Ne non other word speketh she moche or lyte°
But, "Mercie, cruel herte myn, Arcite!"

And thus endureth til that she was so mate°
That she nad° foot on which she may sustene,
But forth languisshing ever in this estate,
Of whiche Arcite hath nouther routhe ne tene°.
His herte was elleswher, newe and grene,
That on hir wo ne deyneth him° not to thinke.
Him rekketh° never wher she flete or synke.

His new lady holdeth him so narowe°,
Up by the bridel, at the staves ende°,
That every word he dred hit as an arowe.
Hir daunger° made him bothe bowe and bende,
And as hir liste° made him turne or wende°,
For she ne graunted him in hir lyvinge
No grace why that he hath lust to singe°,

But drof° him forth. Unnethe list° hir knowe
That he was servaunt unto hir ladishippe;
But lest that he wer° proud she helde him lowe.

---

135 unnethe, *scarcely,* **mete,** *food,* **kepe,** *care* **137 slepe,** *slept* **138 prevely,** *privately* **140 did,** *caused,* **tene,** *grief* **141 newfangelnesse,** *fickleness* **142 For,** *because,* **lowly,** *humble* **143 Toke lesse deyntee for,** *valued less* **145 clad,** *dressed,* **hewe,** *color* **146 Wot I not,** *I don't know* **149 kinde,** *the nature* **150 Sith,** *since* **154 found,** *invented,* **but if,** *unless* **155 most,** *must,* **feyn,** *pretend* **156 wex,** *became* **157 Ryght as,** *just like,* **pleyn,** *snort* **158 bar hir on honde,** *accused her* **163 routhe,** *pity* **168 tene,** *grief* **169 swowneth,** *faints* **171 crampyssheth,** *cramp together* **172 as,** *as if* **173 then,** *than* **174 moche or lyte,** *much or little* **176 mate,** *exhausted* **177 nad,** *had no* **179 nouther routhe ne tene,** *neither pity nor grief* **181 deyneth him,** *he bothers* **182 rekketh,** *cares* **183 narowe,** *strictly* **184 staves ende,** *shaft's end* (i.e., tightly reined in between the shafts of a cart) **186 daunger,** *standoffishness* **187 hir liste,** *she wished,* **wende,** *go forward* **189 grace . . . singe,** *favor that gave him reason to want to sing* **190 drof,** *drove,* **Unnethe list hir,** *scarcely did it please her to* **192 lest that he wer,** *to avoid that he become*

137 alwey, F reads "ay." **145 clad him in hir hewe,** knights wore their ladies' colors. **146 white, rede, or grene,** notably blue, the color of constancy, is lacking. **150 Lamek,** Lamech, the first bigamist, takes a second wife in Genesis 4.19; see *WBP* 3.54 and *SqT* 5.550. **154 found tentes first,** in Genesis 4.20, it is Lamech's son, Jabal, who invented tents. **165 myght,** omitted in F. **171 Al,** omitted in F and Cx. **177 nad,** F reads "ne hath." **178 forth,** F reads "for." **183 holdeth him so,** F reads "holdeth him up."

Thus serveth he withouten fee or shippe°.
She sent him now to londe, now to shippe;
And for she yaf him daunger al his fille,
Therfor she had him at hir oune wille.

Ensample of° this, ye thrifty° wymmen alle,
Take here of Anelida and fals Arcite,
That for hir liste° him "der herte" calle,
And was so meke, therfor he loved hir lyte.
The kynde° of mannes hert is to delyte
In thing that straunge° is, also God me save!
For what he may not gete, that wolde he have.

Now turne we to Anelida ageyn,
That pyneth° day by day in langwisshinge,
But whan she saw that hir ne gat no geyn°,
Upon a day ful sorowfully wepinge
She caste hir° for to make a compleyninge,
And with hir owne honde she gan hit write,
And sente hit to hir Theban knyght Arcite.

The Compleynt of Anelida the Quene upon Fals Arcite.

Proem

So thirleth° with the poynt of remembraunce
The swerd of sorowe, ywhet° with fals
plesaunce°,
Myn herte bare of blis and blake of hewe,
That turned is to quaking al my daunce,
My surete° in awhaped° countenaunce,
Sith hit availeth not° for to ben trewe.
For whoso trewest is, hit shal hir rewe°,
That serveth love and doth hir observaunce
Alwey to oon, and chaungeth for no newe.

Strophe

I wot° myself as wel as any wight°,
For I loved oon with al my herte and myght
More then myself, an hundred thousand
sithe°,
And cleped° him my hertes life, my knyght,
And was al his, as fer as hit was ryght,
And whan that he was glad, than was
I blithe°,
And his disese° was my deth as swithe°,
And he ayen° his trouthe me had iplyght°
For evermore, his lady me to kythe°.

Alas, now hath he left me causeles°,
And of my wo he is so routheles°
That with oo° worde him list not ones deyne°
To bring ayen my sorowful hert in pes°,
For he is caught up in another les°.
Ryght as him list°, he laugheth at my peyne,
And I ne can myn herte not restreyne
That I ne love him alwey, nevertheles.
And of al this I not° to whom me pleyne°.

And shal I pleyne—alas, the harde stounde°—
Unto my foo that yaf° my hert a wounde,

193 fee or shippe, *payment or reward* **197 of,** *from,* **thrifty,** *careful* **199 for hir liste,** *because she wished* **201 kynde,** *nature* **202 straunge,** *aloof* **205 pyneth,** *yearns* **206 geyn,** *gain* **208 caste hir,** *decided* **211 thirleth,** *pierces* **212 ywhet,** *sharpened,* **pleasaunce,** *pleasure* **215 surete,** *security,* **in awhaped,** *into stunned* **216 Sith it availeth not,** *because it accomplishes nothing* **217 rewe,** *regret* **220 wot,** *know,* **wight,** *person* **222 sithe,** *times* **223 cleped,** *called* **225 blithe,** *joyful* **226 disese,** *discomfort,* **swithe,** *quickly* **227 ayen,** *again,* **iplyght,** *pledged* **228 kythe,** *acknowledge* **229 causeles,** *for no reason* **230 routheles,** *without pity* **231 oo,** *one,* **him list not ones deyne,** *it does not please him once to bother* **232 pes,** *peace* **233 les,** *leash* **234 him list,** *it pleases him* **237 not,** *know not,* **me pleyne,** *I lament* **238 stounde,** *time* **239 yaf,** *gave*

193 fee or shippe, Cx reads "mete or sype." **194 now to londe, now to shippe,** i.e., kept him off balance; see *BD* 1024–33. **198 hede,** Cx reads "hede." **of Anelida and fals Arcite,** F reads "Anelida and Arcite." **211a The Compleynt . . . ,** the structure and form of the complaint is very elaborate. The last line (350) echoes the first (211), and flanked by an opening stanza (the Proem, lines 211–19) and a conclusion (342–50), the central twelve stanzas break evenly into two matched groups of six, labeled the Strophe and Antistrophe by modern editor W. W. Skeat. Stanzas 6 (256–71) and 12 (317–32) are parallel, with sixteen lines rhyming *a a a b a a a b b b b a b b b a,* while the other stanzas are nine lines each, rhyming *a a b a a b b a b,* except for stanza 10 (299–307), which is monorhyme. Stanzas 7 (272–80) and 13 (299–307) are also parallel, notable for their internal rhymes and regulated caesuras, indicated here with slashes. These stanza forms are not used elsewhere by Chaucer, although his model for the sixteen-line stanza is evidently the French virelay, and several fifteenth-century Scots poets use the nine-line stanza. **211 poynt of remembraunce,** echoes Dante's *Purgatorio* 12.20. **214 quaking . . . daunce,** compare *Lady* 52. P reads "in quaking." **215 in awhaped,** F reads "into a whaped." **217 hir,** F reads "him." **222** Compare *Lady* 32. **234 him,** F reads "me." **237** Identical to *Lady* 47.

And yet desireth that myn harm be more?
Nay, certes°, ferther wol I never founde°
Non other help, my sores for to sounde°
My destany hath shap° hit so ful yore°;
I wil° non other medecyne ne lore°.
I wil ben ay ther I was ones° bounde;
That° I have seid, be seid for evermore.

Alas, wher is become youre gentilesse°,
Youre wordes ful of plesaunce and humblesse,
Youre observaunces° in soo low° manere,
And your awayting° and your besynesse
Upon me that ye calden your maistresse,
Your sovereigne lady in this worlde here?
Alas, and is ther nother° word ne chere°
Ye vouchesauf° upon myn hevynesse°?
Alas, youre love, I bye° hit al to dere°!

Now certes°, swete, thogh that ye
Thus causeles the causer be
Of my dedely adversyte,
Your manly resoun oghte it to respite°
To slene° your frend, and namely me,
That never yet in no degre°
Offended yow, as wisly° He
That al wot° out of wo my soule quyte°!
But for° I shewed yow, Arcite,
Al that men wolde to me write,
And was so besy yow to delyte—
My honor safe—meke, kynde, and fre°,
Therfor ye put on me the wite°,
And of me rekke° not a myte°,
Thogh the swerd of sorow byte
My woful herte thro your cruelte.

My swete foo, / why do ye so? / For shame!
And thenke ye° / that furthered be / your name,
To love a newe / and ben untrewe? / Nay!
And putte yow / in sclaunder now / and blame,
And do to me / adversite / and grame°,
That love° yow most, / God, wel thou wost°, / alway?
Yet turn ayein / and be al pleyn° / somme day,
And than shal this / that now is mis° / be game°,
And al foryive / while that I lyve / may.

Antistrophe

Loo, herte myn, al this is for to seyn°
As wheder shal I prey° or elles pleyn°?
Whiche is the wey to doon° yow to be trewe?
For either mot° I have yow in my cheyn,
Or with the dethe ye mot departe° us tweyn.
Ther ben non other mene° weyes newe;
For God so wisly° on my soule rewe°,
As verrely° ye sleen me with the peyn
That may ye se unfeyned of myn hewe.

For thus ferforth° have I my dethe soght;
Myself I mordre with my prevy° thoght.
For sorow and routhe° of your unkyndenesse
I wepe, I wake, I fast. Al helpeth noght.
I weyve° joy that is to speke of oght°,
I voyde° companye, I fle gladnesse.
Who may avaunte hir bet of hevynesse°
Then I? And to this plyte° have ye me broght
Withoute gilt. Me nedeth no witnesse.

And shal I preye° and weyve° womanhede?
Nay, rather deth then do so foul a dede!

---

241 certes, *surely,* **founde,** *seek* **242 sounde,** *heal* **243 shap,** *shaped,* **ful yore,** *very long ago* **244 wil,** *desire,* **lore,** *advice* **245 ones,** *once* **246 That,** *what* **247 gentilesse,** *nobleness* **249 observaunces,** *services,* **low,** *humble* **250 awayting,** *attentiveness* **253 nother,** *neither,* **chere,** *look* **254 vouchesauf,** *bestow,* **hevynesse,** *sadness* **255 bye,** *purchase,* **dere,** *dearly* **256 certes,** *surely* **259 respite,** *cease* **260 slene,** *slay* **261 in no degre,** *to no extent* **262 as wisly,** *as surely as* **263 wot,** *knows,* **quyte,** *redeemed* **264 for,** *because* **267 fre,** *generous* **268 wite,** *blame* **269 rekke,** *care,* **myte,** *bit* **273 thenke ye,** *do you think* **276 grame,** *grief* **277 That love,** *who loves,* **wost,** *know* **278 pleyn,** *open* **279 mis,** *wrong,* **game,** *joy* **281 seyn,** *mean* **282 prey,** *beg,* **pleyn,** *lament* **283 doon,** *make* **284 mot,** *must* **285 departe,** *separate* **286 mene,** *middle* **287 wisly,** *surely,* **rewe,** *have pity* **288 verrely,** *truly* **290 ferforth,** *far* **291 prevy,** *private* **292 routhe,** *distress* **295 weyve,** *give up,* **oght,** *anything* **295 voyde,** *avoid* **296 avaunte hir bet of hevynesse,** *boast more about her sorrow* **297 plyte,** *condition* **299 preye,** *beg,* **weyve,** *give up*

241 ferther wol I never founde, F reads "ferther wol I never be founde"; P, "for ther shall never be be founde." **243 shap hit so ful,** F reads "shapen it ful." **252 worlde here,** F reads "worlde ne here." **253 and,** omitted in F. **ther nother word,** P reads "ther now word." **257 causer,** P reads "cause." **264–65 shewed yow . . . that men wolde to me write,** see lines 113–15. P reads "But for I was so pleyn, Arcite, / In all my werkes, muche and lite." **269** P reads "And als ye rekke nat a myte." **272 swete foo,** also used in *Lady* 38. **274 Nay,** P reads "Ay." **278 turn,** F and P read "come." **be al,** P reads "yet be." **279** F reads "And turne al this / that hath be nys / to game." **286 ben,** P reads "lye." **290–98** Lines lacking in P. **299 shal,** P reads "sholde." **300 deth then do so foul,** P reads "die then do so cruell."

And axe° mercy giltles? What nede?
And if I pleyn° what lyf that I lede,
Yow rekketh° not; that know I, out of drede.
And if I unto yow myn othes bede°
For myn excuse, a skorn shal be my mede°.
Your chere floureth°; but hit wol not sede°.
Ful longe agoon I oght to have take hede.

For thogh I had yow tomorow ageyn,
I myght as wel holde Aprill fro reyn°
As holde yow, to make yow be stidfast°.
Almighty God, of trouthe sovereign,
Wher is the trouthe of man? Who hath hit sleyn?
Who that hem loveth, she shal hem fynde as fast°
As in a tempest is a roten mast.
Is that a tame best° that is ay feyn°
To renne away when he is lest agast°?

Now mercie, swete, if I missey°;
Have I seyde oght amys, I prey?
I not°; my wit is al awey.
I fare as doth the song of *Chaunte-pleure.*
For now I pleyne° and now I pley;
I am so mased° that I dey°;
Arcite hath born awey the key
Of al my worlde, and my good aventure°.
For in this worlde there is no creature
Wakinge in more discomfiture
Then I, ne more sorow endure.
And if I slepe a furlong-wey or twey°,
Then thenketh me that your figure
Before me stant°, clad in asure°,
To swere yet eft a newe assure°
For to be trewe, and mercie me to prey.

The longe nyght / this wonder sight / I drye°,
And on the day / for this afray°/ I dye,
And of al this / right noght, ywis°, / ye reche°.
Ne never mo / myn eyen two /be drye,
And to your routhe° / and to your trouthe° / I crye.
But welawey°, / to fer° be they / to feche.
Thus holdeth me / my destany / a wreche.
But me to rede° / out of this drede, / or gye°,
Ne may my wit, / so weyk is hit, / not streche.

Than ende I thus, sith° I may do no more.
I yeve hit up for now and evermore.
For I shal never eft° put in balaunce°
My sekernes°, ne lerne of love the lore.
But as the swan, I have herd seyd ful yore°,
Ayeins° his deth shal singe in his penaunce°,
So singe I here my destany or chaunce,
How that Arcite Anelida to sore
Hath thirled° with the poynt of remembraunce.

Narrative

Whan that Anelida this woful quene
Hath of hir hande writen in this wise,
With face dede°, betwixe pale and grene,
She fel a-swow°; and sith° she gan to rise,
And unto Mars avoweth° sacrifise
Within the temple, with a sorowful chere,
That shapen° was as ye shal after here. . . .

---

301 axe, *ask* **302 pleyn,** *lament* **303 rekketh,** *care* **304 myn othes bede,** *offer my oaths* **305 mede,** *reward* **306 chere floureth,** *manner flowers,* **sede,** *bear fruit* **309 holde Aprill fro reyn,** *keep April from raining* **310 stidfast,** *faithful* **313 fast,** *steady* **315 best,** *beast,* **ay feyn,** *always eager* **316 lest agast,** *least frightened* **317 missey,** *misspeak* **319 not,** *don't know* **321 pleyne,** *lament* **322 mased,** *dazed,* **dey,** *die* **324 aventure,** *fortune* **328 furlong-wey or twey,** *i.e., a few minutes* **330 stant,** *stands,* **asure,** *blue* **331 assure,** *promise* **333 drye,** *endure* **334 afray,** *fear* **335 ywis,** *surely,* **reche,** *care* **337 routhe,** *pity,* **trouthe,** *promise* **338 welawey,** *alas,* **to fer,** *too far* **340 rede,** *advise,* **gye,** *guide* **342 sith,** *since* **344 eft,** *again,* **in balaunce,** *at risk* **345 sekernes,** *security* **346 ful lore,** *long ago* **347 Ayeins,** *before,* **penaunce,** *suffering* **350 thirled,** *pierced* **353 dede,** *deathly* (pale) **354 fel a-swow,** *fainted,* **sith,** *after* **355 avoweth,** *promises* **357 shapen,** *happened*

301 giltles, P reads "causeles." **303** P reads "Than woll ye laugh, I know it, out of drede." **307 oght to,** P reads "ofte." **311** P lacks the following leaf. **315 Is that,** F reads "This that." **316 renne,** Cx reads "flen." **318** Cx reads "Have I ought seyd out of the weye." **319 al awey,** Cx reads "hald aweye." **320 *Chaunte-pleure,*** "Sing-lament," a French song about how those who sing in this world will lament in the next; it became a commonplace for the vacillation of joy and woe. **322 mased,** Cx reads "marred." **325 there is no,** Cx reads "nys." **328 or,** F reads "other." **furlong-wey,** the time it takes to walk a furlong (an eighth of a mile). **330 asure,** see 146n. **331 To swere yet,** Cx reads "To profren eft." **332 mercie me to prey,** Cx reads "love me til he deye." **334 this,** Cx reads "thilke." **346–47 swan . . . shal singe,** swans were thought be silent until just before dying when they sang their "swan songs." **350** Echoes line 211. **351–57** Omitted in F and Cx. The stanza may be scribal, or it may have been intended to introduce a description of the temple of Mars, like that in *KnT* 1.1970ff.

3 COMPLAINT OF MARS

The Brooch of Thebes.

Introduction

Gladeth°, ye foules°, of the morow° gray,
Loo°, Venus rysen among yon rowes rede°;
And floures fresshe, honouren ye this day,
For when the sunne uprist°, then wol ye sprede.
But ye lovers that lye in any drede,
Fleeth lest wikked tonges yow espye°.
Loo, yond° the sunne, the candel of jalosye!

Wyth teres blew°, and with a wounded hert,
Taketh your leve, and with Seynt John to borow°,
Apeseth° sumwhat of your sorowes smert°.
Tyme cometh eft° that cese shal your sorow.
The glade nyght ys worth an hevy° morow!—
Seynt Valentyne, a foule thus herd I synge
Upon your day, er° sunne gan up-sprynge.

Yet sang this foul: I rede° yow al awake.
And ye that han not chosen, in humble wyse
Without repenting cheseth yow your make°.
And ye that han ful chosen as I devyse°,
Yet at the leste renoveleth° your servyse.
Confermeth hit perpetuely to dure°,
And paciently taketh your aventure°.

And for the worship of this highe fest
Yet wol I in my briddes wise° synge
The sentence° of the compleynt at the lest°
That woful Mars made atte departynge
Fro fresshe Venus in a morwenynge°,
Whan Phebus with his firy torches rede
Ransaked° every lover in his drede.

Narrative

Whilom° the thridde hevenes lord above,
As wel by hevenysh revolucion
As by desert, hath wonne Venus his love,
And she hath take him in subjeccion,
And as a maistresse taught him his lesson,
Commaunding him that never in hir servise
He nere° so bold no lover to dispise.

For° she forbad him jelosye at alle,
And cruelte, and bost, and tyrannye.
She made him at hir lust° so humble and
talle°
That when hir deyned° to caste on him her eye,
He toke in pacience to lyve or dye.
And thus she brydeleth° him in hir manere
With nothing but with scourging° hir chere°.

Who regneth° now in blysse but Venus,
That hath thys worthy knyght in governaunce?
Who syngeth now but Mars, that serveth thus

---

1 Gladeth, *be glad,* **foules,** *birds,* **morow,** *morning* **2 Loo,** *see,* **yon rowes rede,** *the red rays there* **4 uprist,** *rises* **6 espye,** *discover* **7 yond,** *there* **8 blew,** *blue* **9 to borow,** *as a guarantee* **10 Apeseth,** *soothe,* **smert,** *pain* **11 eft,** *again* **12 hevy,** *sad* **14 er,** *before* **15 rede,** *advise* **17 make,** *mate* **18 devyse,** *describe* **19 renoveleth,** *renew* **20 dure,** *endure* **21 aventure,** *chances* **23 briddes wise,** *bird's way* **24 sentence,** *sense,* **lest,** *least* **26 morwenynge,** *morning* **28 Ransaked,** *searched out* **29 Whilom,** *once* **35 nere,** *should not be* **36 For,** *because* **38 lust,** *desire,* **talle,** *responsive* **39 hir deyned,** *she bothered* **41 brydeleth,** *bridled* **42 scourging,** *whipping,* **chere,** *look* **43 regneth,** *rules*

Text based on Bodleian Library MS Fairfax 16 (F), with corrections and selected variants from the complete version in Magdalene College, Cambridge University, Pepys 2006 (P); P includes another version of lines 1–84 only. The title is modern, although the subtitle (used in some modern scholarship) is a shortened form of the title given in British Library MS Harley 7333. **1–12** The speaker of these lines (and 15–28) is a bird on St. Valentine's Day (see line 13 and *PF* 307), announcing the coming of morning in a version of a conventional aubade or dawn song. **1 ye,** P reads "the." **foules, of the,** F reads "lovers, on the." **2 yon,** F reads "yow." **Venus,** the planet Venus is also the morning star. The myth of the adultery of Venus and Mars (Ovid, *Metamorphoses* 4.171ff; *Ars Amatoria* [*The Art of Love*] 2.561) is used in the poem to personify an astrological conjunction of the two planets as they move through the zodiacal sign of Taurus. According to medieval observation and calculation, the conjunction of Mars and Venus (called *platic*) occurs when their nimbuses touch. **3 ye,** F reads "the." **day,** P reads "May." **4 ye,** F and P read "they." **5 ye,** P reads "the." 7 **candel of jalosye,** the jealousy of the sun recurs at 26–27, 81–84, and 140. **8 teres blew,** blue tears; blue was the color of constancy. **9 Seynt John to borow,** to pledge by St. John, the Apostle of Truth. **17 yow,** omitted in F and P. **19 the leste,** F reads "this ferst" and misplaces the entire line after line 16. **28 Ransaked,** F reads "Ransaked hath." **29 thridde hevenes lord,** Mars; counting inward from the outermost sphere, it is the third planet. **38 him,** omitted in F. **talle,** F reads "calle." **42 scourging,** F reads "stering."

The faire Venus, causer of plesaunce°?
He bynt° him to perpetuall obeisaunce°,
And she bynt hir to loven him forever,
But so° be that his trespace hit desever°.

Thus be they knyt, and regnen as in heven
Be° loking moost, til hit fil on a tyde°
That by her° bothe assent was set a steven°
That Mars shal entre as faste as he may glyde
Into hir nexte paleys°, to abyde°
Walking his cours til she had him atake°.
And he preide° hir to haste hir for his sake.

Then seyde he thus, "Myn hertes lady swete,
Ye knowe wel my myschef in that place;
For sikerly° til that I with yow mete,
My lyf stant° ther in aventure and grace°.
But when I se the beaute of your face,
Ther ys no dred of deth may do me smert°,
For alle your lust° is ese to myn hert."

She hath so gret compassion on hir knyght,
That dwelleth in solitude til she come—
For hit stode so, that ylke° tyme no wight°
Counseyled him, ne seyde to him welcome—
That nygh° hir wit for woo was overcome.
Wherfore she sped hir as faste in hir wey
Almost in oon day as he dyd in twey.

The grete joye that was betwex hem two
When they be met ther may no tunge tel.
Ther is no more, but unto bed thei go,
And thus in joye and blisse I let hem dwel.
This worthi Mars, that is of knyghthod wel°,
The flour of feyrnes° lappeth° in his armes,
And Venus kysseth Mars, the god of armes.

Sojourned° hath this Mars, of which I rede,
In chambre amyd° the paleys prively
A certeyn tyme, til him fel° a drede
Throgh Phebus that was comen hastely
Within the paleys yates ful sturdely°,
With torche in honde of which the stremes
bryghte
On Venus chambre knokkeden ful lyghte.

The chambre ther as ley° this fresshe quene
Depeynted° was with white boles° grete,
And by the lyght she knew, that shone
so shene°,
That Phebus cam to bren° hem with his hete.
This sely° Venus, nygh dreynt° in teres wete,
Enbraceth Mars and seyde, "Alas, I dye!
The torch is come that al this world wol
wrye°."

Up stert Mars; him liste° not to slepe
When he his lady herde so compleyne.
But for his nature was not for to wepe,
Instid of teres fro his eyen tweyne°
The firy sparkes brosten° out for peyne;
And hente° his hauberk° that ley him
besyde.
Fie wolde he not, ne myghte himselven hyde.

He throweth on his helme of huge wyght°,
And girt him with° his swerde, and in
his honde
His myghty spere, as he was wont° to fyght,
He shaketh so that almost hit towonde°.
Ful hevy was he to walken over londe.
He may not holde with Venus companye,
But bad hir fleen lest° Phebus° hir espye.

---

46 plesaunce, *pleasure* **47 bynt,** *binds,* **obeisaunce,** *obedience* **47 But so,** *unless it* **49 desever,** *separate* **51 Be,** *by,* **tyde,** *time* **52 her,** *their,* **steven,** *appointed time* **54 paleys,** *palace and zodiacal sign* (in this case, Taurus), **abyde,** *wait* **55 atake,** *overtaken* **56 preide,** *begged* **59 sikerly,** *surely* **60 stant,** *stands,* **aventure and grace,** *chance and fortune* **62 smert,** *pain* **63 lust,** *desire* **66 ylke,** *same,* **wight,** *person* **68 nygh,** *nearly* **75 wel,** *the source* **76 feyrnes,** *beauty,* **lappeth,** *enfolds* **78 Sojourned,** *remained* **79 amyd,** *within* **80 him fel,** *to him befell* **82 sturdely,** *boldly* **85 ther as ley,** *where lay* **86 Depeynted,** *adorned,* **boles,** *bulls* **87 shene,** *brightly* **88 bren,** *burn* **89 sely,** *pitiable,* **nygh dreynt,** *nearly drowned* **91 wrye,** *reveal* **92 him liste,** *he wished* **95 eyen tweyne,** *two eyes* **96 brosten,** *burst* **97 hente,** (he) *seized,* **hauberk,** *coat of mail* **99 wyght,** *weight* **100 girt him with,** *strapped on* **101 wont,** *accustomed* **102 towonde,** *snapped* **104 holde . . . companye,** *remain* **105 lest,** *for fear that,* **Phebus,** *the Sun*

51 Be loking moost, mostly by looks, but "loking" translates the Latin astrological term *aspectus,* literally "look," meaning a configuration of planets. **54 to abyde,** P reads "and abide." **55 had him atake,** overtaken him. From the earth, Venus appears to travel faster than Mars (see 137n below) so that in the poem Venus joins Mars in the "palace" of Taurus and then moves on when the sun approaches them. **56 haste,** F reads "faste." **58 my myschef,** my misfortune; Taurus (see line 86) is not an auspicious sign for Mars. **61** Compare *NPT* 7.3160. **66–67** These lines have encouraged some scholars to think that the poem is an allegory of some scandal in the English court. **68 woo,** F reads "sorowe." **70** Venus moves about twice as fast as Mars through the zodiac. **82** In Chaucer's time the sun entered Taurus on April 12; see line 139. **ful,** omitted in P. **84 knokkeden,** F reads "knokken." **86 white boles,** the white bull is the symbol of Taurus; see *TC* 2.54–56n. **92 liste,** F reads "lust." **99 throweth,** F reads "thrwe"; P, "throw." **103–05** Mars moves slowly enough that the sun overtakes it, although Venus outpaces them both.

O woful Mars, alas, what maist thou seyn,
That in the paleys of thy disturbaunce°
Art left behynde in peril to be sleyn?
And yet therto° is double thy penaunce,
For she that hath thin hert in governaunce
Is passed halfe the stremes of thin eyen.
That thou nere° swift, wel maist thou wepe and cryen.

Now fleeth Venus into Cilinios toure°
With voide° cours, for fere of Phebus lyght.
Alas, and ther ne hath she no socoure°,
For she ne found ne saugh no maner wyght°,
And eke as ther she had but litil myght,
Wherfor hirselven for to hyde and save,
Within the gate she fledde into a cave.

Derk was this cave, and smoking as the hel;
Not but two pas° within the yate hit stode.
A naturel day in derk I let hir dwel.
Now wol I speke of Mars, furiouse and wode°.
For sorow he wolde have sene his herte blode
Sith that° he myghte do° hir no companye—
He ne roghte° not a myte° for to dye.

So feble he wex° for hete and for his wo
That nygh he swelt°; he myghte unnethe° endure.
He passeth but oo steyre° in dayes two,
But ner° the lesse, for al his hevy armure,
He foloweth hir that is his lyves cure,
For whos departing he toke gretter ire°
Then for al his brenning° in the fire.

After he walketh softely a pas°,
Compleyning that hit pite was to here.
He seyde, "O lady bryght, Venus, alas
That ever so wyde a compas° is my spere°!
Alas, when shal I mete yow, herte dere?
This twelfte day of Apprile I endure
Throgh jelous Phebus this mysaventure."

Now God helpe sely° Venus allone!
But, as God wolde, hit happed for to be
That, while that Venus weping made hir mone,
Cilinius ryding in his chevache°—
Fro Venus valaunce° mighte his paleys se—
And Venus he salueth° and maketh chere°,
And hir receyveth as his frend ful dere.

Mars dwelleth forth° in his adversyte,
Compleyning ever on hir departinge,
And what his compleynt was remembreth me;
And therfore in this lusty morweninge°,
As I best can, I wol hit seyn° and singe,
And after that I wol my leve take.
And God yif every wyght joye of his make°!

---

107 of thy disturbance, *where you were disturbed* **109 therto,** *also* **112 nere,** *weren't* **113 toure,** *tower* **114 voide,** *solitary* **115 socoure,** *aid* **116 no maner wyght,** *no kind of person* **121 pas,** *steps or degrees* **123 wode,** *mad* **125 Sith that,** *because,* **do,** *keep* **126 roghte,** *cared,* **myte,** *bit* **127 wex,** *became* **128 nygh he swelt,** *he nearly died,* **unnethe,** *scarcely* **129 oo steyre,** *one degree* **130 ner,** *never* **132 ire,** *pain* **133 brenning,** *burning* **134 softely a pas,** *slowly* **137 compas,** *circuit,* **spere,** *sphere* **141 sely,** *poor* **144 Cilinius,** *Mercury* (see 113n), **chevache,** *cavalry* **145 Venus valaunce,** *Aries* (see note) **146 salueth,** *greets,* **maketh chere,** *is pleasant to* **148 dwelleth forth,** *remains still* **151 lusty morweninge,** *pleasant morning* **152 seyn,** *say* **154 yif,** *give,* **make,** *mate*

108 Art, F reads "Art thou." **111 passed halfe the stremes of thin eyes,** i.e., Venus has passed through more than half of the nimbus emanating from Mars (see 2n), here represented as the rays of Mars's eyesight. **113 Cilinios toure,** the tower or mansion of Cyllenius (Mercury) is the sign Gemini. Mercury was born on Mount Cyllene. **115 ne,** omitted in F. **116** Venus is alone because no other planet is in Gemini at this time. **117 litil myght,** Gemini was not an auspicious sign for Venus; see line 58. **119 gate,** the pathway by which the planet enters the astrological sign. **cave,** Skeat takes this as a translation of the Latin astrological term *puteus,* literally "pit," but used to designate one of several specific degrees of a planet's progress through a sign, here the second degree of Venus's progress through Gemini. Chaucer capitalizes on the literal meaning of the term. **120 Derk . . . smoking,** *gradus tenebrosi* (degree of darkness) and *gradus fumosi* (degree of smoke); technically, these indicate degrees in which the light of the planet is obscured. The beginning of Gemini is actually *gradus lucidi* (degree of brightness), so Chaucer apparently took poetic license. **121 pas,** F reads "pales." **122 naturel day,** twenty-four hours, as opposed to the artificial day of sunrise to sunset. **124 have sene,** P reads "aseien." **125 do hir no,** F reads "have don her no." **126 roghte,** F reads "thoghte"; P, "right." **127 feble he wex,** the light of Mars diminishes as the sun approaches. **129 oo steyre,** F reads "a sterre." **137 wyde a compas,** the fact that the orbit of Mars is larger than that of Venus is what makes its motion apparently slower. **139 This twelfthe day of Apprille,** the day on which the sun enters Taurus while Mars is still there. F reads "This xij dayes . . . ." **144 chevache,** P reads "chyvalrie." **145 valaunce,** F reads "valaunses"; P, "balaunce." French *faillance* translates the Latin astrological term *detrimentum,* the zodiacal sign opposite to a planet's mansion. Mercury's mansion (**paleys**) is Gemini, which he can perhaps see from Venus's vallance, Aries. Another explanation offered is that Chaucer adapted French *vaillance,* from Latin *valentia* (power), to indicate Venus's power in her house of Taurus, from which Mercury sees his mansion.

Compleynt of Mars.

Introduction

The ordre of compleynt requireth skylfully°
That if a wight° shal pleyne° pitously,
There mot° be cause wherfore that men pleyne,
Or men may deme° he pleyneth folely°
And causeles—alas, that am not I!
Wherfore° the ground and cause of al my peyne,
So as my troubled wit may hit ateyne°,
I wol reherse, not for to have redresse°,
But to declare my ground of hevynesse°.

I

The firste tyme, alas, that I was wroght°,
And for certeyn effectes hider° broght
Be° Him that lordeth° ech intelligence,
I yaf° my trewe servise and my thoght,
For evermore—how dere° I have hit boght—
To hir that is of so gret excelence
That what wight° that first sheweth his presence°,
When she is wroth and taketh of him no cure°,
He may not longe in joye of love endure.

This is no feyned° mater that I telle;
My lady is the verrey sours° and welle
Of beaute, lust°, fredam°, and gentilnesse,
Of riche aray—how dere men hit selle—
Of al disport° in which men frendly dwelle,
Of love and pley, and of benigne humblesse,
Of soune° of instrumentes, of al swetnesse,
And therto so wel fortuned and thewed°
That throgh the world hir goodnesse is yshewed.
What wonder is then thogh that I beset°
My servise on suche oon that may me knet°
To wele° or wo, sith° hit lyth in, hir myght?
Therfore my hert forever I to hir het°.
Ne, treuly, for my dethe I shal not let°
To ben hir treuest servaunt and hir knyght.
I flater° noght; that may wete° every wyght.
For this day in hir servise shal I dye,
But grace be I° see hir oonce wyth eye.

II

To whom shal I than pleyn of my distresse?
Who may me help; who may my harm redresse°?
Shal I compleyn unto my lady fre?
Nay, certes, for she hath such hevynesse
For fere and eke for wo, that as I gesse
In lytil tyme hit wol hir bane° be.
But were she° safe, hit wer no fors of° me.
Alas, that ever lovers mote° endure
For love so many a perilous aventure!

For tho so be that lovers be as trewe
As any metal that is forged newe,
In many a cas hem tydeth° ofte sorowe.
Somtyme hir ladies wil not on hem rewe°;
Somtyme, if that jelosie hit knewe°,
They myghten lyghtly ley her hede to borowe°;
Somtyme envyous folk with tunges horowe°
Depraven° hem. Alas, whom may they plese?
But° he be fals, no lover hath his ese.

But what availeth° suche a long sermoun
Of aventures of love up and doun?
I wol returne and speken of my peyne.

---

155 skylfully, *reasonably* **156 wight,** *person,* **pleyne,** *lament* **157 mot,** *must* **158 deme,** *judge,* **folely,** *foolishly* **160 Wherfore,** *therefore* **161 ateyne,** *understand* **162 redresse,** *relief* **163 hevynesse,** *sorrow* **164 The first tyme,** i.e., *when first,* **wroght,** *created* **165 hider,** *here* **166 Be,** *by,* **lordeth,** *governs* **167 yaf,** *gave* **168 dere,** *dearly* **170 what wight,** *whatever person,* **sheweth his presence,** i.e., *approaches her* **171 cure,** *care* **173 feyned,** *pretended* **174 verrey sours,** *true source* **175 lust,** *desire,* **fredam,** *generosity* **177 disport,** *enjoyment* **179 soune,** *sound* **180 thewed,** *well mannered* **182 beset,** *fixed* **183 knet,** *knit* **184 wele,** *joy,* **sith,** *since* **185 het,** *promised* **186 let,** *cease* **188 flater,** *deceive,* **wete,** *know* **190 But grace be I,** *unless I be favored to* **192 redresse,** *relieve* **196 bane,** *death* **197 were she,** *if she were,* **hit were no fors of,** *it would not matter about* **198 mote,** *must* **202 hem tydeth,** *to them happens* **203 rewe,** *have pity* **204 hit knewe,** *knew about it* (their love) **205 lyghtly ley her hede to borowe,** *readily bet their lives as pledge* **206 horowe,** *filthy* **207 Depraven,** *slander* **208 But,** *unless* **209 availeth,** *is accomplished by*

158 Or, F reads "Other." **165** Line lacking in P. **166 Him that lordeth,** taken as the pagan god Mars speaking of the governance of God the Creator, this is an anachronism; as speech by the personification of the planet, it is not one. **168** Line lacking in P. **169 To hir that,** F reads "That her that." **185 het,** F and P read "hight." **201 metal,** P reads "mortal." **203 Somtyme,** F reads "Somme." **207 Depraven,** F reads "Departen."

The poynt is this of my distruccioun,
My righte° lady, my savacyoun,
Is in affray°, and not to whom to pleyne.
O herte swete, O lady sovereyne,
For your disese° wel oght I swoune°, and swelt°,
Thogh I non other harm ne drede felt!

III

To what fyn° made the God that sit so hye°
Benethen him love other companye°,
And streyneth° folk to love, malgre her hede°?
And then her joye, for oght I can espye,
Ne lasteth not the twynkeling of an eye,
And somme han never joye til they be dede.
What meneth this? What is this mystihede°?
Wherto° constreyneth he his folk so fast°
Thing to desyre, but hit° shulde last?

And thogh he made a lover love a thing,
And maketh hit seme stidfast and during°,
Yet putteth he in hit such mysaventure
That reste° nys ther noon in his yevinge°.
And that is wonder that so just a kynge
Doth such hardnesse to his creature.
Thus, whether love breke or elles dure,
Algates° he that hath with love to done
Hath ofter wo° then° changed is the mone°.

Hit semeth he hath to lovers enmyte°,
And lyk a fissher, as men alday° may se,
Bateth his angle-hoke° with summe plesaunce
Til mony a fissch is wode to that° he be
Sesed° therwith. And then at erst° hath he
Al his desire, and therwith al myschaunce°;
And thogh the lyne breke, he hath penaunce°.
For with the hoke he wounded is so sore
That he his wages° hath for evermore.

IV The Brooch of Thebes.

The broche of Thebes was of suche a kynde,
So ful of rubies and of stones of Ynde°,
That every wight° that set on hit an eye
He wend anon° to worthe° out of his mynde.
So sore° the beaute wold his herte bynde
Til he hit had, him thoght he moste dye°,
And whan that hit was his, than shulde he drye°
Such woo for drede, ay° while that he hit had,
That welnygh° for the fere he shulde mad°.

And whan hit was fro his possessioun,
Than had he double woo and passioun
For he so feir a tresor had forgo°.
But yet this broche, as in conclusioun,
Was not the cause of this confusioun,
But he that wroghte hit enfortune hit so°
That every wight that had hit shuld have wo.
And therfore in the worcher° was the vyce,
And in the covetour° that was so nyce°.

So fareth hit by lovers and by me,
For thogh my lady have so gret beaute
That I was mad til I had get° hir grace,
She was not cause of myn adversite,
But he that wroghte hir, also mot I thee°,
That put suche a beaute in hir face,
That made me coveten and purchace
Myn oune deth—him wyte° I that I dye,
And myn unwit° that ever I clomb° so hye.

---

213 righte, *true* **214 in affray,** *frightened* **216 disese,** *discomfort,* **swoune,** *faint,* **swelt,** *die* **218 fyn,** *end,* **sit so hye,** *sits so high* **219 other companye,** *or companionship* **220 streyneth,** *constrains,* **malgre her hede,** *despite their wishes* **224 mystihede,** *mystery* **225 Wherto,** *why,* **fast,** *firmly* **226 but hit,** *unless it* **228 during,** *enduring* **230 reste,** *peacefulness,* **yevinge,** *giving* **234 Algates,** *nevertheless* **235 ofter wo,** *woe more often,* **then,** *than,* **mone,** *moon* **236 enmyte,** *hostility* **237 alday,** *always* **238 angle-hoke,** *fishing hook* **239 wode to that,** *frenzied until* **240 Sesed,** *caught,* **erst,** *first* **241 myschaunce,** *misfortune* **242 penaunce,** *pain* **244 wages,** *payment* **246 Ynde,** *India* **247 wight,** *person* **248 wend anon,** *thought immediately,* **worthe,** *go* **249 sore,** *painfully* **250 moste dye,** *must die* **251 drye,** *suffer* **252 ay,** *always* **253 welnygh,** *nearly,* **mad,** *go mad* **256 forgo,** *given up* **259 enfortune hit so,** *gave it such power* **261 worcher,** *maker* **262 covetour,** *the one who wanted it,* **nyce,** *foolish* **265 get,** *gotten* **267 also mot I thee,** *as I may prosper* **270 wyte,** *blame* **271 unwit,** *foolishness,* **clomb,** *climbed*

216 wel oght I, F reads "I oght wel." **swoune,** F reads "sowne." **218 the God,** P reads "He." **219 him,** omitted in F. **230 noon,** omitted in F. **244a The Brooch of Thebes,** the following account derives from Statius, *Thebaid* 2.265ff., describing the fateful gift from vengeful Vulcan to Harmonia, daughter of Mars and Venus. **251 that hit was his,** F reads "hit was." **259 he that wroghte hit,** in Statius, the brooch was made by Vulcan because he was jealous of Mars and Venus. **267 also,** F reads "as." **271 unwit,** F reads "oune witte."

V

But to yow, hardy° knyghtes of renoun,
Syn that° ye be of my devisioun°,
Al be I° not worthy to so grete a name,
Yet seyn° these clerkes I am your patroun.
Therfore ye oghte have somme compassioun
Of my disese°, and take it not agame°.
The proudest of yow may be mad ful tame.
Wherfore I prey yow, of your gentilesse°,
That ye compleyne° for myn hevynesse°.

And ye, my ladyes, that ben treue and stable
By wey of kynde°, ye oghten to be able
To have pite of folk that be in peyne.
Now have ye cause to clothe yow in sable°,
Sith that° your emperice°, the honorable,
Is desolat; wel oght ye to pleyne.
Now shuld your holy teres falle and reyne.
Alas, your honour and your emperise
Negh° ded for drede ne can hir not chevise°.

Compleyneth eke° ye lovers al in fere°
For hir that with unfeyned humble chere
Was ever redy to do yow socour°;
Compleyneth hir that ever hath had yow dere;
Compleyneth beaute, fredom° and manere;
Compleyneth hir that endeth your labour;
Compleyneth thilke° ensample of al honour,
That never dide but al gentilesse;
Kytheth therfor on° hir summe kyndenesse.

4 COMPLAINT OF VENUS

I

Ther nys° so high comfort to my plesaunce°,
When that I am in any hevynesse°,
As for to have leyser of° remembraunce
Upon the manhod and the worthyness,
Upon the trouthe and on the stidfastnesse
Of him whos I am al whiles° I may dure°.
Ther oghte blame me no creature,
For every wight° preiseth his gentilesse°.

In him is bounte°, wysdom, governaunce°,
Wel more then any mannes witte can gesse,
For grace hath wold° so ferforth° him avaunce
That of knyghthode he is parfit richesse°.
Honour honoureth him for his noblesse.
Therto so well hath formed him Nature
That I am his for ever, I him assure,
For every wight preyseth his gentilesse.

And notwithstanding al his suffisaunce°,
His gentil hert is of so grete humblesse
To me in word, in werk, in contenaunce°,
And me to serve is al his besynesse,
That I am set in verrey sikernesse°.
Thus oght I blesse wel myn aventure°,
Sith that him list° me serven and honoure,
For every wight preiseth his gentilesse.

II

Now certes°, Love, hit is ryght covenable°
That men ful dere bye° thy nobil thinge,

272 hardy, *brave* **273 Syn that,** *since,* **devisioun,** *ranks* **274 Al be I,** *although I am* **275 seyn,** *say* **277 disese,** *distress,* **agame,** *in jest* **279 gentilesse,** *nobleness* **280 compleyne,** *lament,* **hevynesse,** *sorrow* **282 kynde,** *nature* **284 sable,** *black* **285 Sith that,** *since,* **emperice,** *empress* **289 Negh,** *nearly,* **hir not chevise,** *she not sustain herself* **290 Compleyneth eke,** *lament also,* **in fere,** *together* **292 socour,** *aid* **294 fredom,** *generosity* **296 thilke,** *this* **298 Kytheth . . . on,** *show to* Complaint of Venus. **1 nys,** *is not,* **plesaunce,** *pleasure* **2 hevynesse,** *sorrow* **3 leyser os,** *time for* **6 al whiles,** *all the while,* **dure,** *last* **8 wight,** *person,* **gentilesse,** *nobleness* **9 bounte,** *goodness,* **governaunce,** *self-control* **11 wold,** *willed,* **ferforth,** *far* **12 parfit richesse,** *perfect fulfillment* **17 suffisaunce,** *self-sufficiency* **19 contenaunce,** *expression* **21 verrey sikernesse,** *true security* **22 aventure,** *good fortune* **23 Sith that him list,** *since it pleases him* (to) **25 certes,** *surely,* **covenable,** *suitable* **26 men ful dere bye,** *people purchase very dearly*

286 desolat, disconsolate, but also the astrological sense of lacking strong influence at the time. **oght ye to pleyne,** P reads "myghten ye compleyn." **297 al,** omitted in F. Complaint of Venus. Text based on Bodleian Library MS Fairfax 16 (F), with selected variants from Bodleian Library, Oxford, MS Ashmole 59 (A) or Trinity College, Cambridge, R.3.20 (R^2) where A is lacking. The title is from F, but there is no other reason to assume that the speaker is Venus. In most manuscripts, this poem follows *The Complaint of Mars* without a break, even though it is an independent adaptation of a group of French ballades by Oton de Granson (see 82). Chaucer's translation of Granson is acknowledged in a rubric at the beginning of A. **8** A reads "Sith he is croppe and roote of gentylesse." **11 hath,** omitted in A. **15 assure,** A reads "ensure." **22–23 aventure / honoure,** the rhyming of *-ure* and *-oure* does not occur elsewhere in any poem certainly attributed to Chaucer; see line 80. **22 I blesse wel,** A reads "me wel to blesse." **26 dere,** A reads "sore."

As wake abed, and fasten° at the table,
Weping to laugh, and sing in compleyninge,
And doun to cast visage and lokinge,
Often to chaungen hewe and contenaunce,
Pleyne° in sleping, and dremen° at the daunce,
Al the revers of any glad felinge.

Jelousye be hanged by a cable!
She wold al knowe thro hir espyinge.
Ther doth no wyght nothing° so reasonable
That al nys harm in hir ymageninge.
Thus dere° abought is love in yevinge°,
Which ofte he yifeth withouten ordynaunce°,
As° sorow ynogh and litel of plesaunce,
Al the revers of any glad felinge.

A lytel tyme his yift is agreable,
But ful encomberouse° is the usinge;
For subtil jelosie, the deceivable°,
Ful oftentyme causeth destourbinge.
Thus be we ever in drede and sufferinge,
In nouncerteyn° we languisshe in penaunce,
And han ful often many an hard meschaunce°,
Al the revers of any glad felinge.

III

But certes, Love, I sey nat in such wise
That for t'escape out of youre lace° I ment,
For I so longe have be in your servise
That for to lete of wil° never assent.
No fors° thogh jelosye me turment.
Sufficeth me to se him when I may.
And therfore certes to myn ending day
To love him best ne shal I never repent.

And certes, Love, when I me wel avise°
On any estat° that man may represent,
Then have ye maked me, thro your fraunchise°,
Chese° the best that ever on erthe went.
Now love wel, hert, and loke° thou never stent°,
And let the jelouse put hit in assay°
That for no peyne wille I not sey nay.
To love him best ne schal I never repente.

Hert, to the° hit oght ynogh suffise
That Love so highe a grace to the sent
To chese the worthiest in alle wise
And most agreable unto myn entent°.
Seche no ferther neyther wey ne went°,
Sith I have suffisaunce° unto my pay°.
Thus wol I ende this compleynt or this lay.
To love him best ne shal I never repent.

Lenvoy

Princes, resseyveth this compleynt in gre°,
Unto your excelent benignite°.
Direct° after my litel suffisaunce°,
For eld° that in my spirit dulleth me
Hath of endyting° al the subtilite
Wel nyghe bereft° out of my remembraunce.
And eke° to me hit is a grete penaunce°,
Syth° ryme in Englissh hath such skarsite,
To folowe word by word the curiosite°
Of Graunson, floure° of hem that make° in Fraunce.

---

27 fasten, *refrain from eating* **31 Pleyne,** *lament,* **dremen,** *dream* **35 doth no wyght nothing,** *no one does anything* **37 dere,** *dearly,* **yevinge,** *giving* **38 ordynaunce,** *plan* **39 As,** *such as* **42 encomberouse,** *burdensome* **43 deceyvable,** *deceitful* **46 nouncerteyn,** *uncertainty* **47 meschaunce,** *misfortune* **50 lace,** *snare* **52 lete of wil,** *cease by choice* **53 No fors,** *no matter* **57 avise,** *consider* **58 estat,** *condition* **59 fraunchise,** *generosity* **60 Chese,** *chose* **61 loke,** *make sure,* **stent,** *cease* **62 put hit in assay,** *put it to the test* **65 the,** *you* **68 myn entent,** *my mind* **69 wey ne went,** *path nor passage* **70 suffisaunce,** *enough,* **pay,** *satisfaction* **73 in gre,** *with favor* **74 benignite,** *goodness* **75 Direct,** *guide* (it), **suffisaunce,** *ability* **76 eld,** *advancing age* **77 endyting,** *writing* **78 Wel nygh bereft,** *nearly stolen* **79 eke,** *also,* **penaunce,** *difficulty* **80 Syth,** *since* **81 curiosite,** *intricacy* **82 floure,** *flower,* **make,** *compose*

30 Often, A reads "Offt sythes." **chaungen hewe,** F reads "chaunge visage." The French is *souvent changier couleur.* **31 Pleyne,** F and A read "Pley," but the French is *Plaindre.* **32 any,** A reads "my." **33–40** omitted in A. **33 Jelousye be hanged,** R^2 reads "Thaughe jalousye were hanged." **43 the,** A reads "is ful." **47 meschaunce,** F reads "penaunce"; the French is *meschance.* **52 lete of wil,** A reads "leet off wol." **56 ne,** omitted in F. **62 jelouse,** F reads "jelousie." **64 him,** F reads "yow." **ne schal I never,** A reads "ne never to." **66 the,** F reads "yow." **to the,** A reads "hath to thee." **69 Seche,** A reads "Serche." **70 I,** F reads "ye." **72 ne,** omitted in F. **ne shal I never,** A reads "and never to." **73 Princes,** see *Fortune* 73n. A and R^2 read "Princesse," which if correct may help to explain why Chaucer chose to use female speaker. **82 Graunson,** Oton de Granson (also "Graunson"; d. 1397), French poet from Savoy and acquaintance of Chaucer. He served the English court from c. 1369–1387 (captive in Spain 1372–74) and again from 1392–96; his "Cinque Balades" ("Five Ballades"), specifically numbers 1, 4, and 5, is the source of Chaucer's poem, although Chaucer changes the gender of the speaker from male to female, necessitating other adjustments.

5 A COMPLAINT UNTO PITY

Pite, that I have sought so yore agoo°,
With herte soore and ful of besy peyne,
That in this world was never wight so woo°
Withoute dethe, and yf I shal not feyne°
My purpos was to Pite to compleyne°
Upon° the crueltee and tirannye
Of Love, that for my trouthe doth me° dye.

And when that I, by lengthe of certeyn yeres,
Had ever in oon° a tyme sought to speke,
To Pite ran I, al bespreynt° with teres,
To preyen° hir on Cruelte me awreke°.
But er I myght with any worde outbreke,
Or tellen any of my peynes smerte,
I fond hir dede and buried in an herte.

Adoun I fel, when that I saugh the herse°,
Dede as a stone while that the swogh° me
laste,
But up I roos, with colour ful diverse°,
And petously on hir myn eyen I caste,
And ner° the corps I gan to presen faste°,
And for the soule I shope me° for to prey.
I was but lorn°; ther was no more to sey.

Thus am I slayn, sith that° Pite is dede.
Alias that day that ever hit shulde falle!
What maner man dar now holde up his hede?
To whom shal now any sorwful herte calle?
Now Cruelte hath cast° to slee us alle
In ydel hope, folk redelees of° peyne,
Syth° she is dede to whom we shulde us pleyne°.

But yet encreseth me this wonder newe,
That no wight woot° that she is dede but I.
So many men as in her tyme hir knewe,
And yet she dyed not so sodeynly.
For I have sought hir ever ful besely°
Sith first I hadde witte or mannes mynde,
But she was dede er that I koude hir fynde.

Aboute hir herse ther stoden lustely°,
Withouten any woo, as thoughte me,
Bounte parfyt°, wel armed and richely,
And fresshe Beaute, Lust°, and Jolyte,
Assured Maner, Youthe, and Honeste°,
Wisdom, Estaat°, Drede°, and Governaunce°,
Confedred° bothe by bonde° and
alliaunce.

A compleynt had I, writen in myn honde,
For to have put to Pite as a bille°.
But whan I al this companye ther fonde,
That rather wolden al my cause spille°
Than do me help, I held my pleynte stille.
For to that folk, withouten any fayle,
Withoute Pite ther may no bille availe°.

Then leve I al vertues save° oonly Pite
Keping° the corps, as ye have herd me seyn,
Confedred alle by bonde of Cruelte,
And ben assented that I shal be sleyn.
And I have put my complaynt up ageyn°;
For to my foes my bille I dar not shewe,
Th'effect° of which seith thus in wordes fewe:

1 so yore agoo, *for such a long time* **3 wight so woo,** *person so sorrowful* **4 feyne,** *pretend* **5 compleyne,** *lament* **6 Upon,** *about* **7 trouthe doth me,** *faithfulness causes me to* **9 ever in oon,** *constantly* **10 bespreynt,** *sprinkled* **11 preyen,** *ask,* **awreke,** *to avenge* **15 herse,** *coffin frame* **16 swogh,** *swoon* **17 ful dyverse,** *very changeable* **19 ner,** *near,* **presen faste,** *approach eagerly* **20 shope me,** *prepared myself* **21 lorn,** *lost* **22 sith that,** *because* **26 hath cast,** *has planned* **27 redelees of,** *confused in* **28 Syth,** *since,* **pleyne,** *lament* **30 no wight woot,** *no one knows* **33 besely,** *intently* **36 lustely,** *happily* **38 Bounte parfyt,** *perfect Goodness* **39 Lust,** *Pleasure* **40 Honeste,** *Honor* **41 Estaat,** *Rank,* **Drede,** *Respect,* **Governaunce,** *Self-control* **42 Confedred,** *joined,* **bonde,** *oath* **44 bille,** *petition* **46 spille,** *destroy* **49 availe,** *be effective* **50 save,** *except* **51 Keping,** *guarding* **54 put . . . up ageyn,** *put away* **56 Th'effect,** *the substance*

Text based on Bodleian Library, Oxford, MS Fairfax 16 (F), with substantive variants from British Library MS Harley 78 (H[1]). The conventional title is adapted from a rubric in Bodleian Library MS Bodley 638. **1 Pite,** the personification of pity and other human characteristics in this poem have been compared with that in Statius's *Thebaid* 11, but it is a familiar convention of medieval courtly and religious literature, particularly *Roman de la Rose.* **9 a tyme sought,** F reads "soughte a tyme." **15 that,** omitted in F and H[1]. **herse,** although the ancestor of our word *hearse,* historically this is a frame used to hold candles and other adornments around the funeral coffin. **16 a,** omitted in F and H[1]. **21** H[1] reads "Me thought me lorn; there was noon other weye." **27** H[1] reads "In ydel hope, we lyve redlesse of peyne." **28 to whom we shulde us pleyne,** F reads "to whom shul we compleyne." **32 yet she dyed not so,** F reads "yet dyed not." **34** F reads "Sith I hadde firste witte or mynde." **37 sorrow,** H[1] reads "doel." **42 alliaunce,** H[1] reads "assurance." **44 For,** omitted in F. **50 I,** F reads "we." **al vertues save oonly,** H[1] reads "alle thees vertues sauf."

The Bill of Complaint.

I

Humblest of herte, highest of reverence,
Benygne flour°, coroune° of vertues alle,
Sheweth unto your rialle° excellence
Your servaunt° yf I durste° me so calle,
His mortal harm, in which he is yfalle°,
And noght° al oonly for his evel fare°,
But for your renoun, as he shal declare.

Hit stondeth thus: your contraire Cruelte
Allyed is ageynst your regalye°
Under colour° of womanly Beaute,
For° men shulde not knowe hir tirannye,
With Bounte°; Gentilesse, and Curtesye,
And hath depryved yow of your place
That hyght° Beaute, apertenant° to Grace.

For kyndly°, by your herytage ryght,
Ye be annexed ever unto Bounte,
And verrely° ye oughte do youre myght
To helpe Trouthe in his adversyte.
Ye be also the corowne of Beaute.
And certes, if ye wanten° in these tweyne°,
The worlde is lore°; ther nis no more to seyne.

II

Eke° what availeth° Maner and Gentilesse
Withoute yow, benygne creature?
Shal Cruelte be your governeresse?
Allas, what herte may hit longe endure?
Wherfor but° ye the rather° take cure°
To breke that perilous alliaunce,
Ye sleen hem that ben in your obeisaunce°.

And further over°, yf ye suffre° this,
Youre renoun is fordoo than° in a throwe°.
Ther shal no man wete° wel what Pite is.
Allas, that ever your renoun is fall so lowe!
Ye be also fro youre heritage ythrowe°
By Cruelte, that occupieth youre place.
And we despeyred° that seken to your grace.

Have mercy on me, thow Herenus quene,
That yow have sought so tendirly and yore°.
Let somme streme of your lyght on me be sene,
That love and drede yow ever lenger the more.
For sothely° for to seyne, I bere the soore°,
And though I be not kunning for to pleyne°,
For Goddes love, have mercy on my peyne!

III

My peyne is this, that whatso I desire,
That have I not, ne nothing lyk therto;
And ever set° Desire myn hert on fire.
Eke on that other syde, wherso I goo,
What maner thing that may encrese woo,
That have I redy°, unsought, everywhere;
Me lakketh but my deth, and than my bere°.

What nedeth° to shewe parcel° of my peyne
Sith° every woo that herte may bethynke
I suffre, and yet I dar not to yow pleyne?
For wel I wot°, although I wake or wynke°,
Ye rekke° not whether I flete or synke.
But natheles, my trouthe° I shal sustene
Unto my deth, and that shal wel be sene°.
This is to seyne, I wol be youres ever,

---

58 Benygne flour, *gentle flower,* **coroune,** *crown* **59-60 Sheweth . . . Your servaunt,** *your servant shows* **59 rialle,** *royal* **60 durst,** *dare* **61 yfalle,** *fallen* **62 noght,** *not,* **evel fare,** *bad situation* **65 regalye,** *authority* **66 colour,** *the appearance* **67 For,** *so that* **68 Bounte,** *Generosity* **70 hyght,** *is named,* **apertenant,** *belonging properly* **71 kyndly,** *by nature* **73 verrely,** *truly* **76 wanten,** *are lacking,* **tweyne,** *two* **77 lore,** *lost* **78 Eke,** *also,* **availeth,** *is accomplished by* **82 Wherfor but,** *therefore unless,* **the rather,** *sooner,* **cure,** *care* **84 obeisaunce,** *obedience* **85 further over,** *furthermore,* **suffre,** *allow* **86 fordoo than,** *destroyed then,* **throwe,** *instant* **87 wete,** *know* **89 ythrowe,** *thrown* **91 despeyred,** *in despair* **93 yore,** *long* **96 sothely,** *truly,* **soore,** *wound* **97 kunning for to pleyne,** *skillful in lamenting* **101 set,** *sets* **104 redy,** *close by* **105 bere,** *funeral bier* **106 What nedeth,** *why do I need,* **parcel,** *part* **107 Sith,** *since* **109 wot,** *know,* **wake or wynke,** *am awake or asleep* **110 rekke,** *care* **111 trouthe,** *faithfulness* **112 sene,** *seen*

59 Sheweth, a technical term used in petitions. **rialle,** H^1 reads "souvereyne." **63 he,** H^1 reads "I." **64 your contraire,** F reads "that your contrary." **70 Grace,** F reads "your grace." **79 benygne,** H^1 reads "benigne and feyre." **80 be your,** H^1 reads "be nowe our." **83** H^1 reads "To breke of thoo persones the allyaunce." **87 Pite,** H^1 reads "the peyne." **88 that ever your renoun is,** H^1 reads "that youre renoune shoulde be." **89 also,** H^1 reads "thanne." **91 seken,** F reads "speken." **92 Herenus quene,** F reads "Heremus quene"; H^1, "yee vertouse quene." Though generally agreed upon as the best reading, "queen of the Furies (Erinyes)" does not seem very suitable to Pity, unless it be because she now rules them in the underworld. **93 so tendirly and,** H^1 reads "so truwely and so." **94 somme,** H^1 reads "the." **95 ever,** H^1 reads "ay." **96 the soore,** F reads "so soore"; H^1, "the hevy sore." **100 ne nothing lyk,** H^1 reads "ne nought that lythe" **101 set,** F reads "setteth." **103 woo,** F reads "my woo."

Though ye me slee by Cruelte, your foo;
Algate° my spirit shal never dissever°
Fro youre servise for any peyne or woo.
Sith° ye be ded—allas that hit is soo—
Thus for your deth I may wel wepe and pleyne,
With herte sore and ful of besy peyne.

Explicit

6 A BALADE OF PITY

I (rhyme royal)

The longe nyght, whan every creature
Shuld have her rest in somwhat° as by kynde°,
Or elles ne may her lyf nought long endure,
Hit falleth most into my wooful mynde
How I so fer have brought myself behynde°,
That sauf the° deth ther may nothing me lisse°,
So desespaired° I am from alle blisse.

This same thought me lasteth til the morow°,
And from the morow forth til hit be eve;
Ther nedeth me no care for to borow,
For both I have gode leyser° and gode leve°;
Ther is no wight° that wil my wo bereve°
To wepe inough, and wailen al my fille;
The sore spark of peyne now doth me spille°.

II (terza rima)

The sore spark of peyne now doth me spille,
This Love that hath me set in suche a place
That my desire never wil fulfille;

For neither pite, mercy, neyther grace
Can I nat fynde; and yet my sorowful hert,
For to be dede, I can hit nat arace°.
The more I love, the more she doth me smert°,
Thurgh which I see withoute remedye
That from the dethe I may no wise astert°.

III (terza rima)

Now sothly°, what she hight° I wil reherse:

Hir name is Bounte° set in womanhede,
Sadnesse° in yowth, and Beaute prideles,
And Plesaunce° under governaunce° and drede°.

Hir surname is eke Faire Rewtheles°
The Wise, iknyt° unto Goode Aventure°,
That for° I love hir sleeth me gilteles.

Hir love I best, and shal while I may dure°,
Betthan myself an hundred thousand dele°,
Than al this worldes riches or creature.

Now hath nat Love me bestowed wele
To love ther° I never shal have part?
Allas, right thus is turned me the whele°!

Thus am I slayn with loves firy dart;
I can but love hir best, my swete foo;

---

115 Algate, *nevertheless,* **dissever,** *depart* **117 Sith,** *since* **A Balade of Pity. 2 in somwhat,** *to some extent,* **kynde,** *nature* **5 brought myself behynde,** *disadvantaged myself* **6 sauf the,** i.e., *except for,* **lisse,** *comfort* **7 desespaired,** *deprived of* **8 morow,** *morning* **11 leyser,** *opportunity,* **leve,** *permission* **12 wight,** *person,* **bereve,** *take away* **14 doth me spille,** *makes me perish* **20 arace,** *tear out* **21 doth me smert,** *makes me hurt* **23 no wise astert,** *in no way escape* **24 sothly,** *truly,* **hight,** *is called* **25 Bounte,** *Generosity* **26 Sadnesse,** *Seriousness* **27 Plesaunce,** *Pleasure,* **governaunce,** *self-control,* **drede,** *fear* (of scandal) **28 Rewtheles,** *Pitiless* **29 iknyt,** *joined,* **Aventure,** *Fortune* **30 for,** *because* **31 dure,** *live* **32 dele,** *times* **35 ther,** *where* **36 the whele,** *Fortune's wheel*

116 H[1] reads "How pitee, that I have sought so youre agoo." **119** Identical to line 2. **A Balade of Pity.** Text based on British Library MS Additional 34360 (A[5]), with selected variants from the only other surviving manuscript, British Library MS Harley 78 (H[1]). In both manuscripts the poem is a continuation of "A Complaint Unto Pity," labeled "the balade of Pytee by Chauciers." Following Skeat's edition of 1894–97, editors assign an alternate title, "A Complaint to His Lady." Because of the experimental nature of the poem, its limited witnesses, and the tradition of heavy emendation by editors, only the most important textual concerns are indicated. **15** This line is not in A[5] or H[1]; Skeat repeated line 14 to begin the *terza rima* pattern. As a result, the subsequent line numbers do not match in various editions. Skeat also added three lines between 23 and 24, which we do not include. **24** No break in the manuscripts between parts II and III. The *terza rima* pattern continues in this section except for the nonrhyme in the introductory line (24) and the additional rhyme in the last line (40). **32** Compare *Anel* 222.

Love hath me taught no more of his art
But serve alwey, and stynte° for no woo.

IV (ten-line stanzas)

In my trewe, careful° herte there is
So moche woo and eke so litel blisse
That woo is me that ever I was bore,
For al that thyng whiche I desire I misse°,
And al that ever I wolde° nat, iwisse°,
That fynde I redy° to me evermore.
And of al this I not° to whom me pleyne°,
For she that myghte me out of this bring
Ne reccheth° nought whether I wepe or sing,
So litel rewth° hath she upon my peyne.

Allas, whan sleping-time is, lo than I wake,
Whan I shuld daunce, for feere lo than I qwake;
This hevy liff° I leede lo for yowre sake,
Though ye therof in no wise heede take,
Myn hertes lady, and hoole° my lives quene!
For trewly durste° I sey as that I feele,
Me semeth that your swete herte of steele
Is whetted° now ayens° me to kene°.

My dere hert and best beloved foo,
Why liketh yow to do me al this woo?
What have I don that greveth yow, or sayde,
But for° I serve and love yow and no moo°?
And while I live, I wil do ever soo.
And therfor, swete, ne beth nat evil apayd°,
For so goode and so faire as that ye be,
Hit were a right grete wonder but ye had
Of al servauntes, both of goode and bad;
And lest worthy of al hem, I am he.

But nevertheles, my right° lady swete,
Though that I be unkonning° and unmete°
To serve as I best kowde ay° yowr hyenesse°,
Yet is ther non fayner°, that wolde I hete°,
Than I to do yow ease or elles bete°
Whatso I wist° were to yow hevynesse°.
And had I myght as goode as I have wil,
Than shuld ye fele wher° it wer so or non,
For in this world than living is ther non
That fayner wolde youre hertes wil fulfil.

For both I love and eke drede yow so sore°,
And algates mote°, and have yow don ful
yore°,
That better loved is non, ne never shal.
And yet I wolde besechen° yow of no more,
But leveth° wel and be nat wroth therfore°,
And let me serve yow forth°—lo, this is al.
For I am nat so hardy° ne so wood°
For to desire that ye shuld love me,
For wel I wot°, allas, that wil nat be,
I am so litel worthy, and ye so good.

For ye be oon the worthiest° on lyve°,
And I the most unlikly for to thryve.
Yet for al this, witeth° ye right wele
That ye ne shul me from youre service dryve,
That I nil ay with al my wittes fyve
Serve yow trewly, what wo so that I fele.
For I am sette on yow in suche manere
That though ye never wil upon me rewe°,
I muste yow love and ever been as trewe
As any man can or may on lyve here.

The more that I love yow, goodly free,
The lasse fynde I that ye loven me.
Allas, whan shal that hard witte amende°?
Wher is now al your wommanly pite,
Youre gentilnesse, and your debonarite°?
Wil ye nothing therof upon me spende?
And so holy, swete, as I am yowres al,
And so gret wil as I have yow to serve,
Now, certes, and° ye lete me thus sterve°,
Yet have ye wonne theron but a smal.

---

40 stynte, *cease* **41 careful,** *full of care* **44 misse,** *lack* **45 wolde,** *desire,* **iwisse,** *certainly* **46 redy,** *close by* **47 not,** *know not,* **pleyne,** *lament* **49 reccheth,** *cares* **50 rewth,** *pity* **53 hevy liff,** *sad life* **55 hoole,** *wholly* **56 durste,** *dare* **58 whetted,** *sharpened,* **ayens,** *against,* **to kene,** *too sharply* **62 But for,** *except that,* **moo,** *other* (more) **64 evil apayd,** *angry* **69 right,** *true* **70 unkonning,** *ignorant,* **unmete,** *unfit* **71 kowde ay,** *could always,* **hyenesse,** *highness* **72 fayner,** *more eager,* **hete,** *promise* **73 bete,** *make better* **74 Whatso I wist,** *whatever I knew,* **hevynesse,** *sorrow* **76 wher,** *whether* **79 sore,** *sorely* **80 algates mote,** *always must,* **don ful yore,** *done* (loved) *for a long time* **82 besechen,** *ask* **83 leveth,** *believe,* **wroth therfore,** *angry for this* **84 forth,** *continually* **85 hardy,** *brave,* **wood,** *crazy* **87 wot,** *know* **89 oon the worthiest,** *the most worthy,* **on lyve,** *alive* **91 witeth,** *know* **96 rewe,** *have pity* **101 hard witte amende,** *cruel mind improve* **103 debonarite,** *graciousness* **107 and,** *if,* **sterve,** *die*

47 Identical to *Anel* 237. **52** Compare *Anel* 214. **51–58** This eight-line stanza differs from the other, ten-line stanzas in part IV, lacking two lines of *b* rhyme: *a a [b] a a [b] c d d c.* **74 were to yow hevynesse,** A^5 and H^1 read "that were to youre hyenesse." **98 here,** omitted in A^5 and H^1.

For at my knowing°, I do nothing why°,
And this I wil beseche yow hertely,
That therever° ye finde, whiles ye live,
A trewer servaunt to yow than am I,
Leveth° thanne, and sle me hardely°,
And I my deth to yow wil al forgive.
And if ye finde no trewer, so verily°,
Will ye suffre than that I thus spille°,
And for no maner gilt but my good wille?
Als good wer thanne° untrewe as trewe to be.
But I my lyf and deth to yow obey°,
And with right buxom° hert holy I prey
As is youre most plesure, so doth by me;
For wel lever is me° liken yow° and dey
Than for to anything or thynke or° sey
That yow might offende in any tyme.
And therfor, swete, rewe° on my peynes smert,
And of your grace granteth me som drope;
For elles may me last° ne blisse ne° hope,
Ne dwelle within my trouble, careful° hert.

Explicit Pyte

Dan Chaucer l'auceire.

7 WOMANLY NOBLESSE

Balade That Chaucer Made.

So hath myn herte caught in remembraunce
Yowre beaute hoole°, and stidefast governaunce°,
Yowre vertues al, and yowre hie noblesse,
That yow to serve is sette al my plesaunce°.
So wel me liketh° youre womanly contenaunce,
Youre fresshe fetures, and youre comlynesse,
That whiles I live, myn hert to his maystresse
Yow hath ful chose in trewe perseveraunce,
Never to chaunge for no maner distresse.

And sith° I shal do yow this observaunce°
Al my lif, withouten displesaunce,
Yow for to serve with al my besynesse,
And have me somwhat in your souvenaunce°.
My woful herte suffreth grete duresse,
And loke how humbly, with al symplesse,
My wil I conforme to youre ordynaunce°
As yow best list°, my peynes for to redresse°.

Considryng eke° how I hange in balaunce
In yowre service, such, lo, is my chaunce,
Abidyng° grace, whan that yowr gentilnesse
Of my grete woo liste do allegeaunce°,
And with youre pite me som wise avaunce°,
In ful rebatyng° of myn hevynesse°,
And thynketh by raison° that womanly noblesse
Shuld nat desire for to do the outrance°
Ther as she fyndeth non unbuxumnesse°.

---

109 at my knowing, *to my knowledge,* **why,** *to cause this* **111 therever,** *wherever* **113 Leveth,** *depart,* **hardely,** *assuredly* **115 verily,** *truly* **116 spille,** *die* **118 Als good wer thanne,** *it would be as good then* **119 obey,** *submit* **120 right buxom,** *very obedient* **122 wel lever is me,** *I would much rather,* **liken yow,** *please you* **123 or . . . or,** *either . . . or* **125 rewe,** *have pity* **127 me last,** *to me remain,* **ne . . . ne,** *neither . . . nor* **128 careful,** *full of care* **Womanly Noblesse. 2 hoole,** *perfect,* **governaunce,** *self-composure* **4 plesaunce,** *pleasure* **5 me liketh,** *pleases me* **10 sith,** *since,* **observaunce,** *attention* **13 souvenaunce,** *memory* **16 ordynaunce,** *command* **17 list,** *desire,* **redresse,** *compensate* **18 eke,** *also* **20 Abidyng,** *awaiting* **21 liste do allegeaunce,** *wishes to alleviate* **22 me som wise avaunce,** *advance me in some way* **23 ful rebatyng,** *complete reducing,* **hevynesse,** *sorrow* **24 by raison,** *reasonably* **25 outrance,** *great injury* **26 unbuxumnesse,** *disobedience*

113 Leveth, A[5] reads "Loveth." **119–28** Lines lacking in H[1]. **128 trouble, careful heart,** perhaps an echo of line 41. **128a *Explicit Pyte,*** Here ends Pity. **128b *Dan Chaucer l'auceire,*** Master Chaucer, the author. **Womanly Noblesse** Text based on British Library MS Additional 34360 (A[5]), the only surviving manuscript. The title is from Skeat's edition, derived from line 24; the subtitle, from A[5]. **10 yow,** omitted in A[5]. **11 lif,** A[5] reads "live." **12a** Rhyme calls for another line here. The most popular suggestion was composed by Furnivall: "Taketh me, lady, in your obeisaunce." The Variorum edition numbers this line 13, altering traditional lineation for the reminder of the poem. **15 loke,** omitted A[5].

Lenvoye

Auctour° of norture°, lady of plesaunce,
Soveraigne of beaute, floure of wommanhede,
Take ye non hede unto myn ignoraunce,
But this° receyveth of yowre goodelyhede°,
Thynkyng that I have caught in remembraunce
Yowr beaute hole, your stidefast governaunce.

8 TO ROSEMOUNDE

Madame, ye ben of alle beaute shryne°
As fer as cercled is the mapamounde°,
For as the cristall glorious ye shyne,
And lyke ruby ben your chekes rounde.
Therwyth° ye ben so mery and so jocounde°
That at a revell° whan that I se you daunce,
It is an oynement unto my wounde,
Thogh ye to me ne do no daliaunce°.

For thogh I wepe of teres ful a tyne°,
Yet may that wo myn herte nat confounde°.
Your semy voys°, that ye so small out twyne°,
Maketh my thoght in joy and blys habounde°.
So curtaysly I go, with love bounde,
That to myself I sey, in my penaunce°,
"Suffyseth me to love you, Rosemounde,
Thogh ye to me ne do no daliaunce."

Nas never pyk° walwed° in galauntyne°
As I in love am walwed and iwounde,
For whych ful ofte I of myself devyne°
That I am trewe Tristam the secounde.
My love may not refreyde° nor affounde°;
I brenne ay° in an amorouse plesaunce°.
Do what you lyst°; I wyl your thral° be founde,
Thogh ye to me ne do no daliaunce.

TREGENTIL. CHAUCER.

9 PROVERBE OF CHAUCER

What shul° these clothes thus manyfolde,
Loo, this hoote somers day?

After grete hete cometh colde;
No man caste his pilch° away.

Of al this world the large compace°,
Yt wil not in° my armes tweyne°.

Whooso mochel wol embrace,
Litel therof he shal distreyne°.

---

27 Auctour, *originator,* **norture,** *good manners* **30 this,** i.e., *the poem,* **goodelyhede,** *excellence* **To Rosemounde. 1 shryne,** *the shrine* **2 mapamounde,** *map of the world* **5 Therwyth,** *moreover,* **jocounde,** *cheerful* **6 revell,** *celebration* **8 ne do no daliaunce,** *make no small talk* **9 tyne,** *tub* **10 confounde,** *destroy* **11 semy voys,** *high voice,* **out twyne,** *spin out* **12 habounde,** *abound* **14 penaunce,** *suffering* **17 pyk,** *pike* (a fish), **walwed,** *wallowed,* **galauntyne,** *thickened sauce* **19 devyne,** *consider* **21 refreyde,** *thicken,* **affounde,** *decline* **22 brenne ay,** *burn always,* **plesaunce,** *pleasure* **23 lyst,** *wish,* **thral,** *servant* **Proverbe of Chaucer. 1 shul,** *shall be done with* **4 pilch,** *fur garment* **5 compace,** *circumference* **6 in,** *fit in,* **armes tweyne,** *two arms* **8 distreyne,** *hold on to*

31–32 The lines echo lines 1–2. **To Rosemounde.** Text based on Bodleian Library MS Rawlinson Poetry 163 (R), the only surviving manuscript. Title from Skeat's edition, derived from line 15. **1 alle,** R reads "al." **2 cercled is the mapamounde,** i.e., to the edges of the earth, as medieval maps of the world were often loosely circular within a frame. **8 Thogh,** R reads "Thoght." **20 Tristam,** lover of Isolde, victim of a love potion, and famed as a minstrel. **24a Tregentil—Chaucer,** this colophon, in a later hand, is probably an imitation of the colophon of *Troylus and Criseyde* on the preceding page of the manuscript. It has been suggested that "Tregentil" is the name of the scribe, or a kind of compliment: *tres gentil* (very gentle). **Proverbe of Chaucer.** Text from Bodleian Library MS Fairfax 16 (F), with variants from British Library MS Additional 16165 (A^3). The title is in F. **1 grete,** omitted in A^3. **5–7 compace / embrace,** Chaucer's authorship has been doubted on the basis of this rhyme since "compace" is normally "compas." Others have pointed out, however, that Chaucer does something similar, though perhaps with comic effect, in *Thop* 7.779–82 and 830–31. **5** A^3 reads "Of this world the wyde compace." **7–8** Compare *Mel* 7.1215.

10 FORTUNE

Balade de visage sanz peinture.

I Le Pleintif countre Fortune

This wrechched worldes transmutacioun,
As wele° or woo, now poure° and now honour,
Withouten ordre or wise discrecioun°
Governed is by Fortunes errour°;
But natheles, the lakke of hir favour
Ne may nat don me° synge, though I dye,
Jay tout perdue mon temps et mon labour°,
For fynaly, Fortune, I the diffye!

Yet is me left the light of my resoun,
To knowen frend fro foo in thy mirour.
So moche hath yet thy whirling up and doun
Ytaught me for to knowen in an hour.
But trewely, noo fors of° thy reddour°
To him that over himself hath the maistrye.
My suffisaunce° shal be my socour°,
For fynaly, Fortune, I thee dyffye!

O Socrates, thou stedfast champioun,
She mighte never be thy tormentour.
Thou never dreddest hir oppressioun,
Ne in hir chere° founde thou noo savour°.
Thow knewe wel the deceit of hir colour°,
And that hir mooste worshipe° is to lye.
I knowe hir eke° a fals dissymulour,
For fynaly, Fortune, I thee diffye!

II La respons du Fortune au Pleintif

Noo man is wrechched but himself hit wene°,
And he that hath himself hath suffisaunce.
Why seystow° thanne I am to the so kene°,
That hast thyself out of my governaunce?
Sey thus, "Grauntmercy of° thyn habundaunce
That thou hast lent or° this." Why wolt thou strive?
What woose° thou yet how I the wol avaunce?
And eke thou hast thy beste frend alive.

I have the taught divisioun° bitwene
Frend of effect° and frend of countenaunce°.
The nedeth nat° the galle of noon hyene
That cureth eyen derke fro her penaunce°.
Now seestow cleer, that were° in ignoraunce.
Yet halt thin ankre° and yet thow mayst arrive
Ther bounte° berith the keye of my substaunce°—
And eke thow hast thy beste frend alive.

How many have I refused to sustene,
Sith° I the fostred have in thy plesaunce°.
Woltow than make a statut on° thy quene,
That I shal ben ay° at thyn ordinaunce°?
Thow borne art in my regne° of variaunce.
Aboute the whele° with other most° thou drive°.

2 As wele, *such as happiness,* **poure,** *poverty* **3 discrecioun,** *judgment* **4 errour,** *variableness* **6 don me,** *compel me to* **7 *Jay tout perdue mon temps et mon labour,*** *I have completely lost my time and labor.* **13 noo fors of,** *does not matter,* **reddour,** *violence* **15 suffisaunce,** *self-sufficiency,* **socour,** *help* **20 chere,** *behavior,* **savour,** *pleasure* **21 colour,** *disguise* **22 mooste worshipe,** *greatest honor* **23 eke,** *also* **25 but himself it wene,** *unless he thinks himself so* **27 seystow,** *do you say,* **kene,** *sharp* **29 Grauntmercy of,** *thank you for* **30 or,** *before* **31 woost,** *know* **33 divisioun,** (the) *difference* **34 of effect,** *in reality,* **of countenaunce,** *in appearance* **35 The nedeth nat,** *you don't need* **36 her penaunce,** *their misery* **37 that were,** *you who were* **38 halt thin ankre,** *hold your anchor* **39 Ther bounte,** *where goodness,* **substaunce,** *essence* **42 Sith,** *since,* **plesaunce,** *pleasure* **43 statut on,** *law for* **44 ay,** *always,* **ordinaunce,** *control* **45 regne,** *realm* **46 whele,** *wheel,* **most,** *must,* **drive,** *go*

Text based on Bodleian Library MS Fairfax 16 (F), with corrections and selected variants from Cambridge University Library MS Ii.3.21 (C^2) and Bodleian Library, Oxford, MS Ashmole 59 (A). The title is modern, but the subtitle is in F, C^2, and A (all with *vilage* for *visage*): ***Balade de visage sanz peinture,*** Ballade about the face without painting (covering); an allusion to *Bo* 2.pr1.58–61: "Thow has now knowen and ataynt [perceived] the dowtous or dowble vysage of thilke blynde goddesse Fortune. She that yit covereth and wympleth hir to oother foolkes hath shewed hir everydel [completely] to the." This is an acknowledgment of the Boethian inspiration for these three ballades; see especially *Bo* 2.pr.1–4 and pr8 and the specific echoes noted below. **I Le Pleintif countre Fortune,** the Plaintiff against Fortune; an echo of legal proceedings. **4 errour,** A reads "fals errour." **7** The same line is quoted from a "newe Frenshe song" in *ParsT* 10.248. **8** The reading here and at lines 16 and 24 is from C^2. **9 light,** F and A read "sight." **11 whirling,** F and A read "turnyng." **17 Socrates,** Greek philosopher noted for his wise patience; see *BD* 717–19. **18 mighte never,** C^2 reads "never myght." **19 hir,** A reads "Fortune's." **II La respons du Fortune au Pleintif,** the response of Fortune to the Plaintiff. **25–26** Echoes *Bo* 2.pr4.112–13 and *Rom* 5672. **30 Why wolt thou strive,** F and A read "Thou shalt not strive." **32 beste frend alive,** perhaps an allusion to a specific person (Richard II or some other patron has been proposed), but this may be a more general reference, as in *RR* 8019–22. See 76n. **34** Very similar to *Rom* 5486. **35 galle of . . . hyene,** classical and medieval medical manuals state that the gall or bile of a hyena restores keenness of eyesight. **38 ankre,** compare *Bo* 2.pr4.55. **43–44 a statut . . . thyn ordinaunce,** compare *Bo* 2.pr1.98–101. **46** Line lacking in A. **most thou,** F reads "maisthow."

My lore° is bet° than wikke° is thy grevaunce;
And eke thow hast thy beste frend alive.

III Le Pleintif encountre Fortune

Thy lore I dampne°; hit is adversite.
My frend maistow nat reve°, blynd goddesse!
That I thy frendes knowe, I thanke hit the°!
Tak hem ageyn; let hem goo lye on presse°.
The negardye° in keping her° richesse
Prenostik is° thow wolt her tour assayle°.
Wikke appetit cometh ay before seknesse;
In general, this rule may nat fayle.

Fortune encountre le Pleintif

Thow pynchest at° my mutabilite,
For° I the lent a drope of my rychesse,
And now me liketh° to withdrawe me.
Why shuldest thow my realte oppresse°?
The see may ebbe and flowe more or lesse;
The welkene° hath myght to shyne, reyn, or hayle.
Ryght so mot I kythe° my brotelnesse°;
In general, this rule may nat fayle.

Loo°, th'execucion of the mageste
That al purveyeth of° his rightwisnesse°,
That same thing "Fortune" clepen ye°,
Ye blynde bestes, ful of lewednesse°.
The hevene hath proprete° of sikernesse°,
This world hath ever restelesse travayle°.
Thi last day is ende of myn intresse°;
In general, this rule may nat fayle.

Lenvoy du Fortune

Princes, I pray yow of your gentilesse°,
Lat nat thys man on me° thus crie and pleyne°,
And I shal quyte° yow your besynesse
At my requeste, as three of you or tweyne.
And but you list° releve him of his peyne,
Preyeth his beste frend of his noblesse°
That to som beter estat he may atteyne.

11 BALADE DE BON CONSEIL

Truth.

Fle fro the prees° and dwell with sothfastnesse°,
Suffise unto° thy good°, though it be smal,
For hord° hath hate, and clymbyng tykelnesse°,
Prees hath envye, and wele blent overal°.

47 lore, *teaching,* **bet,** *better,* **wikke,** *harmful* **49 dampne,** *condemn* **50 reve,** *steal* **51 thanke hit the,** *thank you for it* **52 on presse,** *in a group* **53 negardye,** *miserliness,* **her,** *their* **54 Prenostik is,** *forecasts that,* **her tour assayle,** *assault their tower* **57 pynchest at,** *find fault with* **58 For,** *because* **59 me liketh,** *it pleases me* **60 my realte oppresse,** *suppress my royal power* **62 welkene,** *sky* **63 mot I kythe,** *must I show,* **brotelnesse,** *changeableness* **65 Loo,** *consider* **66 al purveyeth of,** *provides for everything through,* **rightwisness,** *righteousness* **67 clepen ye,** *you call* **68 lewednesse,** *ignorance* **69 proprete,** *quality,* **sikernesse,** *certainty* **70 travayle,** *suffering* **71 intresse,** *interest* **73 gentilesse,** *nobleness* **74 on me,** *about me,* **pleyne,** *complain* **75 quyte,** *repay* **77 but you list,** *unless you wish* (to) **78 noblesse,** *magnificence* **Balade de Bon Conseil. 1 prees,** *crowd,* **sothfastnesse,** *truth* **2 Suffise unto,** *be satisfied with,* **good,** *goods* **3 hord,** *hoarding,* **tykelnesse,** *insecurity* **4 wele blent overal,** *prosperity blinds completely*

III Le Pleintif encountre Fortune, the Plaintiff against Fortune. **51 frendes,** F and A read "frend." **52 on presse,** F reads "a presse" (a cupboard). **53 negardye,** F and A read "negardes." **56** Similar to *RR* 18979–80. **56a Fortune encountre le Pleintif,** Fortune against the Plaintiff. **59 me liketh to withdrawe me,** see *Bo* 2.pr2.23–24. **61 or,** F reads "and." **65–72** F, C², and A include rubrics that mistakenly attribute this stanza to the Plaintiff rather than to Fortune. **65–67** Compare *Bo* 4.pr6.50–56. **72a Lenvoy de Fortune,** the Envoy of Fortune. **73 Princes,** addresses or appeals to princes or other great men are conventional in envoys (as in *Complaint of Venus* 73 and *Lack of Steadfastness* 22), a remnant of their original function as dedications and perhaps encouraged by poetic contests in which the judge was addressed as "prince." But see 76n. **75 your,** F and other manuscripts read "this." **76** Line found only in C². It has been used to date the poem after the issue of a Privy Council ordinance of March 8, 1390, in which it was mandated that any royal gifts or grants had to be approved by two of the three Dukes of Lancaster, Gloucester, and York. If this is a specific contemporary allusion, then the "Princes" of line 73 refers to the three dukes and the "beste frend" of line 78 (and of 32, 40, and 48) is Richard II. **Balade de Bon Conseil.** Text based on Huntington Library MS Ellesmere 26.C.9 (El), variants from the first of two versions in Bodleian Library, Oxford, MS Fairfax 16 (F) and from British Library MS Additional 10340 (A¹), which is the only version to include the Envoy (22–28). The title derives from Cambridge University Library MS Gg 4.27. Some editors give it the modern title "Truth." **2 thy good,** A¹ reads "thin owen thing," meaning "your own possessions," an echo of a Latin proverb: *Si res tue tibi non sufficiant, fac ut rebus tuis sufficias* (If your things are not sufficient for you, make yourself sufficient for your things). Gower's *Confessio Amantis* 5.7735ff. provides a clear parallel to Chaucer's sentiment and he quotes the Latin in a gloss to his text. **4 blent,** El reads "blyndeth"; A¹, "is blent."

Savour° no more than the byhove shal°.
Reule wel thiself, that other folk canst rede°;
And trouthe the shal delivere°, it is no drede°.

Tempest the° noght al croked° to redresse°,
In trust of hir that turneth as a bal.
Gret reste stant in lytel bisynesse.
Bewar also to sporne ayeyns° an al°.
Stryve noght as doth the crokke° with the wal.
Daunte° thiself, that dauntest otheres dede°;
And trouthe the shal delivere, it is no drede.

That the° is sent, receyve in boxomnesse°.
The wrastling for this world axeth a fal°.
Here nis non home, here nis but wyldernesse:
Forth, pilgrym, forth! Forth, beste°, out of thi stal!
Know thi contree, lok up, thank God of al;
Hold the hye° wey, and lat thi gost° the lede;
And trouthe the shal delivere, it is no drede.

Envoy

Therfore, thou Vache, leve thine old wrechedenesse;
Unto the world leve° now to be thral°.
Crie Hym mercy, that of His hie godnesse
Made the of noght, and in especial
Draw unto Him, and pray in general
For the, and eke for other hevenlyche mede°;
And trouthe the shal delivere, it is no drede.

12 MORAL BALADE OF GENTILESSE

The firste stok, fader° of gentilesse—
What man that claymeth gentil for to be
Must folowe his trace°, and alle his wittes dresse°
Vertu to sewe°, and vices for to fle.
For unto vertu longeth° dignite,
And nought the revers, savely° dar I deme°,
Al were he° mytre°, coroune°, or dyademe°.

This firste stok was full of rightwisenesse°,
Trewe of his word, sobre, pitous, and fre°,
Clene of his goost°, and loved besynesse,
Ayenst° the vyce of slouthe°, in honeste°;
And but° his heir love vertu as did he,
He is nought gentil, though he riche seme,
Al were he mytre, coroune, or dyademe.

---

5 Savour, *enjoy,* **the byhove shal,** *will be appropriate to you* **6 rede,** *advise* **7 the shal delivere,** *will free you,* **drede,** *fear* **8 Tempest the,** *disturb yourself,* **croked,** *crooked* (things), **redresse,** *correct* **11 sporne ayeyns,** *kick against,* **al,** *spur* **12 crokke,** *crockery* **13 Daunte,** *govern,* **dede,** *deeds* **15 That the,** *whatever to you,* **boxomnesse,** *obedience* **16 axeth a fal,** *asks for a defeat* **18 beste,** *beast* **20 hye,** *high,* **gost,** *spirit* **23 leve,** *cease,* **thral,** *slave* **27 mede,** *reward* **Moral Balade of Gentilesse. 1 fader,** *father* **3 trace,** *footsteps,* **dresse,** *direct* **4 sewe,** *follow* **5 longeth,** *belongs* **6 savely,** *safely,* **deme,** *judge* **7 Al were he,** *although he may wear* **mytre,** *miter* (i.e., a bishop), **coroune,** *crown* (i.e., a king), **dyademe,** *diadem* (i.e., an emperor) **8 rightwisenesse,** *righteousness* **9 fre,** *generous* **10 goost,** *spirit* **11 Ayenst,** *against,* **slouthe,** *laziness,* **honeste,** *honor* **12 but,** *unless*

6 Reule, El reads "Werke"; A[1], "Do." **7** See John 8.32. **the,** omitted in El and A[1], here and at lines 14, 21, and 28. **8 Tempest the noght . . .** , similar advice is given in *Bo* 2.pr4.68–69. F reads "Peyne the noght." **9 hir that turneth as a bal,** i.e., Fortune and her ever-turning wheel. **10 Gret reste,** El reads "For gret reste"; A[1], "Myche wele." **11 Bewar also,** El reads "And ek bewar"; A[1] "Biwar therfore." **sporne ayeyns an al,** i.e., "kick against the pricks or goad," which occurs in some versions of Acts 9.5. **17–19** Reflects the commonplace idea that human life is a journey from this world to the true home (or country) of heaven, and the commonplace criticism that humans are in some ways comparable to beasts. **19 lok up,** compare *Bo* 5.m5.16–19. It is conventional to distinguish upward looking humans from downward looking beasts. For this line, F reads "Loke up on high and thonk God of al." **20 thi gost the lede,** see Romans 8.4. **22–28** This stanza is found only in A[1]. **22 Vache,** French "cow," perhaps a connection with "beste" of line 18. Since Edith Rickert identified him in 1913, generally regarded as a reference to Sir Philip de la Vache (1348–1408), who seems to have been out of political favor between 1386–90. The identification has been used to help date the poem, although the final stanza may have been added late. **Moral Balade of Gentilesse.** Text based on British Library MS Cotton Cleopatra D.7 (C), with corrections and variants from Bodleian Library, Oxford, MS Ashmole 59 (A). The title derives from British Library MS Harley 7333. Editors give it the modern title "Gentilesse." **1 firste stok, fader,** A reads "firste fader and foundour." The "first stock" is the original ancestor, i.e., God, the source of the human race, although the meaning narrows to Christ or even Adam as the poem proceeds. **gentilesse,** nobleness; the term applies to the quality of aristocratic birth and to the ideal of virtuous behavior. Chaucer's exploration of tensions between the two is rooted in *Bo* 3.pr6 and m6, influenced by the *Roman de la Rose* and Dante's *Convivio*, and similar concerns are found in *WBT* 1109ff., the tales of the Clerk, Merchant, and Franklin, and among Chaucer's contemporaries. **2 claymeth,** from A; C reads "desireth." **4 sewe,** from A; C reads "love." **7 mytre, coroune,** C reads "coroune, miter" here, but is correct at 14 and 21.

Vices may well be heir to old richesse,
But ther may no man—as men may well se—
Bequethe his heir his vertuous noblesse:
That is appropred unto° no degre°
But° to the firste fader in mageste,
That maketh his heires hem that him queme°,
Al were he mytre, coroune, or dyademe.

Explicit

13 THE FORMER AGE

Chawcer upon the fyfte metrum of the second book.

A blysful lyf, a paysyble° and a swete,
Ledden the poeples in the former° age.
They helde hem paied of° the fructes° that they ete,
Whiche that the feldes yave hem by usage°.
They ne were nat forpampred° with owtrage°.
Unknowen was the quyerne° and ek the melle°;
They eten mast°, hawes°, and swych pownage°,
And dronken water of the colde welle.

Yit° nas the grownd nat wownded with the plowh,
But corn° up-sprong, unsowe of° mannes hond,
The which they gnodded°, and eete nat half inowh°.
No man yit knew the forwes° of his lond;
No man the fyr owt of the flynt yit fond°;
Unkorven° and ungrobbed° lay the vyne;
No man yit in the morter spices grond°
To clarre°, ne to sawse of galentyne°.

No mader, welde, or wod° no litestere°
Ne knew; the fles° was of his former hewe°.
No flessh ne wyste° offence of egge° or spere;
No coyn ne knew man which was fals° or trewe;
No ship yit karl° the wawes grene and blewe;
No marchaunt yit ne fette owtlandissh ware°;
No batails trompes° for the werres folk ne knewe,
No towres heye°, and walles rownde or square.

What sholde it han avayled to werreye°?
Ther lay no profyt, ther was no rychesse.
But corsed° was the tyme, I dar wel seye,
That men fyrst dede her swety bysynesse
To grobbe° up metal, lurkinge in derknesse,
And in the ryveres fyrst gemmes sowhte°.
Allas, than sprong up al the cursednesse
Of covetyse, that fyrst owr sorwe browhte!

Thyse tyrauntz putte hem gladly nat in pres°
No places wyldnesse ne no busshes for to wynne
Ther° poverte is, as seith Diogenes,
Ther as vitayle° is ek so skars° and thinne
That noght but mast° or apples is therinne.

---

18 appropred unto, *exclusive to,* **degre,** *status* **19 But,** *except* **20 queme,** *please* **The Former Age.** **1 paysyble,** *peaceful* **2 former,** *first* **3 paied of,** *satisfied with,* **fructes,** *fruits* **4 by usage,** *by habit* (i.e., without cultivation) **5 forpampred,** *pampered,* **owtrage,** *excess* **6 quyerne,** *hand grinder,* **melle,** *mill* **7 mast,** *nuts,* **hawes,** *hawthorn berries,* **swych pownage,** *such food by grazing* **9 Yit,** *as of yet* **10 corn,** *grain,* **unsowe of,** *unsown by* **11 gnodded,** *rubbed* (husked), **inowh,** *enough* **12 forwes,** *furrows* **13 fond,** *found* **14 Unkorven,** *unpruned,* **ungrobbed,** *uncultivated* **15 grond,** *ground* **16 to clarre,** *for spiced wine,* **to sawse of galentyne,** *for thickened sauce* **17 mader, welde, or wod,** *madder, weld, or woad* (plants used to make red, yellow, and blue dyes), **litestere,** *dyer* **18 fles,** *fleece,* **former hewe,** *original color* **19 wyste,** *knew,* **egge,** *sword* **20 fals,** *counterfeit* **21 karf,** *carved* **22 fette owtlandissh ware,** *fetched foreign merchandise* **23 trompes,** *trumpets* **24 heye,** *high* **25 werreye,** *make war* **27 corsed,** *cursed* **29 grobbe,** *dig* **30 sowhte,** *sought* **33 putte hem gladly nat in pres,** *do not usually make an effort* **35 Ther,** *where* **36 vitayle,** *food,* **ek so skars,** *also so scarce* **37 mast,** *nuts*

15 Vices, C reads "Vycesse." **old richesse,** traditional wealth; also at *WBT* 1110 and 1118. Dante uses *antica richezza* several times in his *Convivio* (e.g., 4.3) and the *Roman de la Rose* (20313) has *richeces anciens.* **The Former Age.** Text based on Cambridge University Library MS Ii.3.21 (C[2]); with selected variants from the only other surviving manuscript, Cambridge University Library MS Hh.4.12 (Hh). The title is modern, supplied by Skeat. The subtitle is from C[2], where the poem is included as part of Chaucer's *Boece,* immediately following his English prose translation of Book 2, meter 5 of Boethius's *Consolation of Philosophy.* Chaucer's opening lines, especially 1–5, follow *Bo* 2m5.1–24 fairly closely, with several details and much of the remainder of the poem drawn from the broader "Golden Age" tradition that includes Ovid's *Metamorphoses* 1.88ff., Boethius, and *RR* 8355ff. **13 fyr owt of the flynt yit fonde,** sparks struck from steel on flint was an early way of igniting fire. Hh reads "yit fier owt of the flynt fond." **15 in the morter,** whole spices were crushed and ground to powder in stone vessels called *mortars.* **20 was,** C[2] reads "is." **31 al the,** Hh reads "al owre." **34 places,** Hh reads "place of." **35 Diogenes,** Greek philosopher c. 412–323 B.C.E; the sentiment of this stanza is attributed to him in John of Salisbury, *Policraticus* 8.6, and Jerome, *Letter against Jovinian* 2.11.

But ther as bagges° ben, and fat vitaile,
Ther wol they gon and spare for° no synne
With al hir ost° the cyte° for t'assayle°.

Yit were° no paleis° chaumbres, ne non halles;
In kaves and wodes softe and swete
Slepten this blyssed folk withowte walles,
On gras or leves in parfyt° joye and quiete.
No down of fetheres ne no bleched° shete
Was kyd° to hem, but in surte° they slepte.
Hir hertes were al oon° withowte galles°;
Everych of hem his feith° to oother kepte.

Unforged was the hawberk° and the plate°;
The lambyssh° poeple, voyd of alle vyce,
Hadden no fantasye° to debate,
But eche of hem wolde oother wel cheryce°.
No pryde, non envye, non avaryce,
No lord, no taylage° by no tyranye:
Umblesse° and pes°; good feith the emperice°.

Yit was nat Juppiter the lykerous°,
That fyrst was fader of delicacie°,
Come in this world; ne Nembrot, desyrous
To regne, had nat maad his towres hye°.
Allas, allas, now may men wepe and crye!
For in owr dayes nis° but covetyse,
Dowblenesse, and tresoun, and envye,
Poysoun, and manslawhtre, and mordre in
sondry wyse°.

Finit etas prima. Chaucers.

14 LACK OF STEADFASTNESSE

Envoy to King Richard.

Sumtyme° the world was so stedfast and stable
That mannes word was obligacioun°,
And now it is so fals and deceivable°
That word and dede, as in conclusioun,
Ben nothing lyk, for turned up so doun°
Is al this world for mede° and wilfulnesse,
That all is lost for lak of stedfastnesse.

What maketh this world to be so veriable
But lust° that folk have in discencioun?
For among us now a man is holde unable°,
But if° he can by som collusioun
Do his neyghburgh wrong or oppressioun.
What causeth this but wilfull wrecchednesse°,
That all is lost for lak of stedfastnesse?

Trouthe is putte doun, resoun is holden fable°,
Vertu hath now no domynacioun;
Pite exiled, no man is merciable;
Through covetise is blent° discrecioun.

---

38 bagges, *bags* (full of plenty) **39 spare for,** *refrain because of* **40 ost,** *army,* **cyte,** *city,* **t'assayle,** *to assault* **41 Yit were,** *as of yet* (there) *were,* **paleis,** *palace* **44 parfyt,** *perfect* **45 bleched,** *whitened* **46 kyd,** *known,* **surte,** *security* **47 al oon,** *completely,* **galles,** *bitterness* **48 feith,** *promise* **49 hawberk,** *mail armor,* **plate,** *plate armor* **50 lambyssh,** *lamb-like* **51 fantasye,** *desire* **52 cheryce,** *cherish* **54 taylage,** *taxation* **55 Umblesse,** *humbleness,* **pes,** *peace,* **emperice,** *empress* **56 lykerous,** *lecherous* **57 delicacie,** *sensuality* **59 towres hye,** *high towers* **61 nis,** (there) *is nothing* **63 sondry wyse,** *many ways* **Lack of Steadfastnesse.** **1 Somtyme,** *at one time* **2 obligacioun,** *bond* **3 deceivable,** *deceitful* **5 up so doun,** *upside down* **6 mede,** *payment* **9 lust,** *pleasure* **10 holde unable,** *considered incompetent* **11 But if,** *unless* **13 wrecchednesse,** *wickedness* **15 holden fable,** *considered fiction* **18 blent,** *blinded*

39–40 Lines transposed in C^2. **40 for t'assayle,** C^2 reads "forto asayle." **41 were,** C^2 reads "was." **48 his feith to oother,** Hh reads "to odyr hys feith." **49–55** The rhyme scheme of the other stanzas indicates that this stanza lacks a final line in both surviving manuscripts. **50 voyd,** C^2 reads "voyded." **56 Juppiter,** the Roman king of the gods, known for his seductions. **58 Nembrot,** Nimrod; see Genesis 10.8–10. In medieval tradition, he was thought to be the builder of the Tower of Babel, a symbol of human ambitiousness. **60 men,** omitted in C^2. **61 nis,** Hh reads "is not." **62 and tresoun,** Hh omits "and." **63 and manslawtre, and mordre,** Hh omits "and" twice. **63a Finit etas primas,** Here ends the First Age. **Lack of Steadfastnesse.** Text based on British Library MS Cotton Cleopatra D.7 (C), with corrections and variants from British Library Harley 7333 (H^4). The title is modern, often printed "Lak of Stedfastnesse," as is the subtitle. **2 obligacioun,** H^4 reads "holde obligacioun." **4 dede,** H^4 reads "werke." **5 Ben,** C reads "Is." **lyk,** H^4 "oon." **turned up so doun . . . this world,** a commonplace complaint about the world, rooted in classical tradition. **6 for,** H^4 reads "thorowe." **10 among us now,** H^4 reads "now adayes." **11 collusioun,** C reads "conclusion."

The world hath mad a permutacioun°
Fro right to wrong, fro trouthe to fikelnesse,
That all is lost for lak of stedfastnesse.

Lenvoy to King Richard

O prince, desire to be honourable;
Cherice thi folk and hate extorcioun.
Suffre° nothing that may be
 reprevable°
To thyn estaat° don in thi regioun.
Shew forth thy swerd of castigacioun.
Dred God, do law, love trouthe and
 worthynesse,
And wed thy folk ageyn to stedfastnesse.

Explicit

15 TO ADAM SCRYVEN

Geffrey unto Adame his owen scryvene.

Adam scryveyn°; if ever it thee byfalle°
Boece or *Troylus* for to wryten newe,
Under thy long lokkes thow most have the
 scalle°
But° after my makyng° thow wryte° more trewe!
So ofte a daye I mot° thy werk renewe
It to corecte and eke° to rubbe and scrape;
And al is thorugh thy neglygence and rape°!

16 LENVOY DE CHAUCER A BUKTON

My maister Bukton, whan of Criste our kyng
Was axed° what is trouthe or sothefastnesse°,
He nat a word answerde to that axing,
As who saith°, “Noo man is al trew,” I gesse.
And therfore, though I highte° to expresse
The sorwe and woo that is in mariage,
I dar not writen of hit noo wikkednesse,
Lest° I myself falle eft° in swich dotage°.

I wol nat seyn how that hit is the cheyne
Of Sathanas, on which he gnaweth evere;
But I dar seyn, were he out of his peyne,
As by his wille he wolde be bounde nevere.
But thilke° doted fool that eft hath levere°
Ycheyned be than out of prisoun crepe,
God lete him never fro his woo dissevere°;
Ne noo man him bewayle, though he wepe.

---

19 permutacioun, *change* **24 Suffre,** *allow,* **reprevable,** *deserving of blame* **25 estaat,** *status* **To Adam Scryven. 1 scryveyn,** *scribe,* **thee byfalle,** *happens to you* **3 scalle,** *parasitic skin disease* (dermatophytosis) **4 But,** *unless,* **makyng,** *composing,* **wryte,** *copy* **5 mot,** *must* **6 eke,** *also* **7 rape,** *haste* **Lenvoy de Chaucer a Bukton. 2 axed,** *asked,* **sothefastnesse,** *truthfulness* **4 As who saith,** *as if to say* **5 highte,** *promised* **8 Lest,** *for fear that,* **eft,** *again,* **dotage,** *foolishness* **13 thilke,** *that,* **levere,** *rather* **15 dissevere,** *be divided*

19 a, omitted in C. **22 prince,** evidently an address to Richard II, although the rubric that mentions him is scribal. Addresses or appeals to princes or other great men were conventional in envoys (see *Fortune* 73n), but the language and details here do suggest that Chaucer is addressing his monarch. The fact that Lydgate used this entire stanza in his “Prayer for England” indicates its conventionality. **to be,** H^4 reads “for to be.” **28 wed thy folk,** a group of manuscripts reads “dryve thy people.” **To Adam Scryven.** Text based on the only surviving manuscript, Trinity College, Cambridge University, MS R.3.20. Title and subtitle adapted from the manuscript. **1 Adam,** Adam Pinkhurst, a professional scribe in London and a longtime copyist of Chaucer’s works, responsible for a number of late-medieval manuscripts of works by Chaucer, Gower, Langland, and others. **6 rubbe and scrape,** parchment was corrected by scraping off the old ink and then rubbing the surface smooth again. **Lenvoy de Chaucer a Bukton.** Text based on Bodleian Library MS Fairfax 16 (F); the only other surviving manuscript is Coventry, City Record Office, MS Coventry. The title is from F. **1 maister Bukton,** probably Sir Peter Bukton of Holdernesse, Yorkshire, affiliated with the House of Lancaster and favorite of the future Henry IV. Another possibility is Sir Robert Bukton of Goosewold, Suffolk, squire in the royal household. The title *master* is the ancestor of modern *Mr.* **2–3** Pilate asks the question of Christ in John 18.38. **6 woo that is in mariage,** compare *WBP* 3.3. **8 myself falle eft,** Chaucer’s wife, Philippa, died in 1387. **9–10 cheyne / Of Sathanas, on which he gnaweth,** the image of Satan chained in hell is common in medieval art and literature; see *MLT* 2.361. Troylus refers to gnawing on the chains of love; *TC* 1.509. **13 eft,** F reads “ofte.”

But yet, lest thow doo worse, take a wyf!
Bet is° to wedde than brenne° in worse wise.
But thow shalt have sorwe on thy flessh thy lyf°,
And ben thy wifes thral°, as seyn these wise°.
And yf that hooly writte may nat suffyse,
Experience shal the teche, so may happe°,
That the were lever° to be take in Frise°
Than eft to falle of weddynge in the trappe.

Envoy

This lytel writte°, proverbes° or figure°,
I sende yow; take kepe of° hit, I rede°:
Unwise is he that kan noo wele° endure;
Yf thow be siker, put the nat in drede°,
The Wyf of Bathe I pray yow that ye rede
Of° this matere that we have on honde.
God graunte yow your lyf frely to lede
In fredam—for ful hard it is to be bonde.

Explicit

17 LENVOY DE CHAUCER A SCOGAN

I

Tobroken been° the statutez° hye in hevene
That creat° weren eternally to dure°,
Syth that° I see the bryghte goddis sevene
Mowe° wepe and wayle, and passioun endure,
As may in erthe a mortal creature.
Allas, fro whennes may thys thing procede,
Of which errour° I deye almost for drede?

By word eterne whilom° was yshape°
That fro the fyfte sercle, in no manere,
Ne myghte a drope of teeres doun eschape.
But now so wepith Venus in hir spere°
That with hir teeres she wol drenche° us here.
Allas, Scogan, this is for thyn offence;
Thow cawsest this diluge of pestilence.

Hastow not seyd°, in blaspheme of the goddes,
Thurgh pride, or thrugh thy grete rekelnesse°,
Swich° thing as in the lawe of love forbede° is,
That for° thy lady sawgh° nat thy distresse,
Therfore thow yave hir up at Mychelmesse?
Allas, Scogan, of olde folk ne yonge
Was never erst° Scogan blamed for his tonge!

II

Thow drowe in skorn Cupide eke to recorde°
Of thilke rebel° word that thow hast spoken,

---

18 Bet is, *it is better,* **brenne,** *burn* **19 thy lyf,** *all your life* **20 thral,** *slave,* **wise,** *wise people* **22 happe,** *happen* **23 the were lever,** *you would rather,* **take in Frise,** *taken prisoner in Frisia* **25 writte,** *writing,* **proverbes,** *set of proverbs,* **figure,** *metaphoric composition* **26 take kepe of,** *pay attention to,* **rede,** *advise* **27 wele,** *happiness* **28 siker,** *secure,* **drede,** *jeopardy* **30 Of,** *concerning* **Lenvoy de Chaucer a Scogan. 1 Tobroken been,** *shattered are,* **statutez,** *laws* **2 creat,** *created,* **dure,** *endure* **3 Syth that,** *because* **4 Mowe,** *must* **7 errour,** *confusion* **8 whilom,** *once,* **yshape,** *established* **11 spere,** *sphere* **12 drenche,** *drown* **15 Hastow not seyd,** *have you not said* **16 rekelnesse,** *rashness* **17 Swich,** *such,* **forbede,** *forbidden* **18 for,** *because,* **sawgh,** *saw* **21 erst,** *before* **22 drowe . . . to recorde,** *called as witness* **23 thilke rebel,** *that rebellious*

18 Bet is to wedde than brenne, from 1 Corinthians 7.9; compare *WBP* 3.52. **19–20** Compare *WBP* 3.154–60. **21–22 hooly writte . . . Experience,** *WBP* begins with an opposition of authority (including Scripture) and experience. **23 Frise,** Frisia, or Friesland, a region of the northwestern European lowlands. The Frisians were reported to execute their prisoners. **26 yow,** in the preceding stanza, the less formal singular *thow* forms are used; *you* forms are used in the envoy, except line 28. **29 Wyf of Bathe,** the only character from Chaucer's *Canterbury Tales* that he refers to outside the collection of tales; compare *MerT* 4.1685. **Lenvoy de Chaucer a Scogan.** Text based on Bodleian Library MS Fairfax 16 (F), with corrections and selected variants from Magdalene College, Cambridge University, MS Pepys 2006 (P) and Cambridge University Library MS Gg.4.7 (Gg). The title is modern. **1 hye,** omitted in Gg. **3–4 bryghte goddis sevene . . . wepe and wayle,** tempestuous weather caused by the influence of the seven planets, here given figurative emotions. Scholars have attempted to date the poem by treating this is a topical reference. **6 whennes,** P reads "hens." **8 yshape,** P and Gg read "it shape." **9 fyfte sercle,** the sphere of Venus (counting inward), associated with love and with rain. **13 Scogan,** Sir Henry Scogan (1361?–1407), a squire of the king's household who became tutor to the sons of Henry IV. In his "Moral Ballade," he quotes all of Chaucer's *Gentilesse.* **14 diluge of pestilence,** pestilential deluge; sustained wet weather was associated with outbreaks of plague. **15 the goddes,** F reads "this goddis," suggesting that Venus may be understood rather than all the gods. **17 forbede,** Gg reads "forbodyn." **19 Mychelmesse,** Michaelmas, September 29, the traditional date for the beginning of the fall business and social season, and a day when annuities were renewed and paid. F and P read "Mighelmesse."

For which he wol no lenger be thy lorde.
And, Scogan, though his bowe be nat broken,
He wol nat with his arwes been ywroken°
On the ne me ne noon of oure figure°;
We shul of him have neyther hurt ne cure.

Now certes, frend, I dreed of° thyn unhappe°,
Lest° for thy gilt the wreche° of Love procede
On alle hem that ben hoor° and rounde of shappe,
That ben so lykly folk in love to spede°.
Than shal we for oure labour han no mede°—
But wel I wot°, thow wolt answere and saye,
"Loo, th'olde Grisel° lyst° to ryme and playe!"

Nay, Scogan, say not soo, for I m'excuse°—
God helpe me soo—in no ryme, dowteles°,
Ne thynke I never of° slepe to wake my muse,
That rusteth in my shethe° stille in pees.
While I was yong, I put hir forth in prees°,
But alle shal passe that men prose or ryme°.
Take every man his turn, as for his tyme.

Envoy

Scogan, that knelest at the stremes hed°
Of grace, of alle honour and worthynesse,
In th'ende of which streme I am dul as ded,
Forgete° in solytarie wildernesse—
Yet, Scogan, thenke° on Tullius kyndenesse:
Mynne° thy frend, there° it may fructyfye°!
Farewel, and loke thow never eft° Love
dyffye.

18 COMPLAINT OF CHAUCER TO HIS PURSE

A Supplication to King Henry.

To yow, my purs, and to non othir wyght°
Complayne I, for ye ben my lady dere!
I am so sory, now that ye been lyght;
For certes°, but yf° ye make me hevy chere°,
Me were as leef be° leyd upon my bere°;
For which unto your mercy thus I crye,
Beth hevy ayeyn, or elles mot° I dye!

Now voucheth sauf° this day, or° hyt be nyght,
That I of yow the blisful soun° may here,
Or se your colour lyk the sonne bryght,
That of yelownesse had never pere.
Ye be my lyf, ye be myne hertes stere°,
Quene of comfort and of gode
companye;
Beth hevy ayeyn, or elles mot I dye!

Now purs, that ben to me my lyves lyght
And saveour, as° doun in this worlde
here,

26 ywroken, *avenged* **27 figure,** *shape* (see line 31) **29 dreed of,** *fear for,* **unhappe,** *misfortune* **30 Lest,** *for fear that,* **wreche,** *vengeance* **31 hoor,** *white-headed* **32 spede,** *assist* **33 mede,** *reward* **34 wot,** *know* **35 Grisel,** *Grayhead,* **lyst,** *wants* **36 m'excuse,** *beg pardon for myself* **37 dowteles,** *doubtless* **38 of,** *from* **39 shethe,** *sheath* **40 in prees,** *in public* **41 prose or ryme,** *write in prose or poetry* **43 stremes hed,** *stream's head* **46 Forgete,** *forgotten* **47 thenke,** *think* **48 Mynne,** *remember,* **there,** *where,* **fructyfye,** *be fruitful* **49 eft,** *again* **Complaint of Chaucer to His Purse. 1 wyght,** *creature* **4 certes,** *surely,* **but yf,** *unless,* **make me hevy chere,** *treat me seriously* **5 Me were as leef be,** *I would like to be,* **bere,** *funeral bier* **7 mot,** *must* **8 voucheth sauf,** *grant,* **or,** *before* **9 soun,** *sound* **12 stere,** *rudder* **16 as,** *while* (I am)

25 his, F reads "thy." **27 oure,** F reads "youre." **28 ne,** F reads "nor." **32 in love,** omitted in P. **35 th'olde,** P and Gg read "olde." **ryme,** Thynne's edition of 1532 reads "renne" (run) in which case "th'olde Grisel" would have as its primary meaning "the old gray horse." **40 hir,** i.e., his muse; F and Gg read "hyt." **43 stremes hed,** all three surviving manuscripts gloss this "i. a. Wyndesor," i.e., "at Windsor [Castle]," near the head of the Thames and a royal residence. They also gloss line 45 (or 46) "i. a. Grenewych," i.e., "at Greenwich," located downstream from Windsor (and London) on the Thames and where Chaucer may have been living at the time. Gg reads "wellis" for "stremes." **47 Tullius kyndenesse,** Tullius's kindness; a reference to Marcus Tullius Cicero's *De Amicitia* (*On Friendship*), as recalled in *Romaunt* 5285ff. **Complaint of Chaucer to His Purse.** Text based on Cambridge University Library MS Ff.1.6 (Ff[1]), with corrections from Bodleian Library, Oxford, MS Fairfax 16 (F). Title from F; subtitle modified from British Library MS Harley 7333, which reads "Richard" for "Henry," even though the manuscript includes the envoy that refers to the latter. The titles and rubrics in the manuscripts vary considerably. **3–4 lyght . . . hevy,** in addition to the weight of coins, in the mock love complaint "light" can mean "fickle," and "hevy" can mean "serious" or "constant." **11 yelowwnesse,** Ff reads "the lewdnesse." **13 Quene of comfort,** applied to the Virgin Mary in *ABC* 77 and 121.

Out of this towne helpe me thurgh your
myght,
Syn that° ye wylle nat ben my tresorere;
For I am shave as nye° as any frere°.
But yet I pray unto youre curtesye,
Beth hevy ayeyn, or elles mot I dye!

Lenvoy de Chaucer

O conquerour of Brutes Albyoun,
Which that by lyne° and fre eleccioun
Ben verray° kyng, this song to you I sende;
And ye, that mowen° alle oure harmes amende°,
Have mynde upon° my supplicacioun°.

Poems Not Attributed To Chaucer In The Manuscripts

19 MERCILESS BEAUTE

A triple roundel.

I

Yowr eyen two woll sle me sodenly;
I may the beaute of hem not sustene°,
So woundeth hit throughout my herte kene.

And but° your word woll helen hastely
My hertes wound, while that hit is grene°,
Your eyen &c.

Upon my trouth, I sey yow feithfully
That ye ben of my lyf and deth the quene;
For with my deth the trouthe shal be sene.
Your eyen &c.

II

So hath yowr beaute fro your herte chaced
Pitee, that me navailleth not° to pleyne°;
For Danger° halt your mercy in his cheyne.

Giltles my deth thus han ye me purchaced—
I sey yow soth; me nedeth not to feyne°.
So hath yowr beaute &c.

Allas that Nature hath in yow compassed°
So grete beaute that no man may atteyn
To mercy, though he sterve° for the peyn.
So hath yowr beaute &c.

---

18 Syn that, *since* **19 nye,** *close,* **frere,** *friar* **23 lyne,** *descent* **24 verray,** *true* **25 mowen,** *can,* **harmes amende,** *injuries put right* **26 Have mynde upon,** *give thought to,* **supplicacioun,** *petition* **Merciless Beaute.** **2 sustene,** *bear* **4 but,** *unless* **5 grene,** *fresh* **12 me navailleth not,** *it does me no good,* **pleyne,** *lament* **13 Danger,** *aloofness* **15 feyne,** *pretend* **17 compassed,** *enclosed* **19 sterve,** *die*

17 this towne, the allusion is uncertain, although it has been taken to refer to the Abbey precinct at Westminster where Chaucer had rented a house on December 24, 1399, perhaps because it offered sanctuary from creditors. **19 shave as nye as any frere,** shaved as closely as any friar is tonsured; a figure of financial insolvency, i.e., barely with any money at all. Ff reads "shave as ys any frere"; F "shave as nye as is a frere." **22–23 conquerour . . . lyne . . . fre eleccioun,** conquest, royal blood, and general acclamation; the three have been discussed in connection with reports of Henry's claim to throne before the Parliament of 30 September 1399. Some version of the three recur in literature and records, helping to solidify and legitimize the claim. **22 Brutes Albyoun,** Brutus's Albion; Britain. Felix Brutus was legendary descendant of Aeneas and founder of Britain, once called Albion. **Merciless Beaute.** Text based on Magdalene College, Cambridge University, MS Pepys Library 2006 (P), the only surviving manuscript. The title derives from the index to this manuscript; the subtitle is modern. **1 eyen two wol sle me,** the commonplace hyperbole that the eyes of the beloved will kill the lover; compare *KnT* 1.1567. **6 Yowr eyen two,** P reads "Yowr two eyen," but compare lines 6 and 10. Lines 1–3 are to be sung as a refrain. **8 lyf,** the manuscript reads "liffe." **16 So hath yowr beaute &c,** lines 11–13 are to be sung as a refrain.

III

Syn° I fro Love escaped am so fat,
I nevere thenk to ben in his prison lene;
Syn I am fre, I counte hym not a bene°.

He may answere, and sey this and that.
I do no fors°; I speke ryght as I mene.
Syn I fro Love &c.

Love hath my name istrike° out of his
sclat°,
And he is strike out of my bokes clene
For evermo; ther is non other mene°.
Syn I fro Love &c.

Explicit

20 AGAINST WOMEN UNCONSTANT

Madame, that throgh your newfangelnesse°
Many a servaunt have put out of your grace,
I take my leve of your unstedfastnesse,
For wel I woot°, while ye have lyves space°,
Ye kan not love ful half yere in a° place;
To newe thing your lust° is ay° so kene;
Instede of blew, ye may wel were° al grene.

Ryght° as in a merour nothing may impresse°,
But lyghtly as hit cometh, so mot° it pace°,
So fareth° your love, your werkes beren witnesse.
Ther is noo feyth that may your hert embrace;
But as a wedercok° that turneth ay his face
With every wynd ye fare, and that is sene;
Instede of blew, ye may wel were al grene.

Ye myght be shryned°, for your brotelnesse°,
Bet° than Dalyda, Creseyde, or Candace;
Forever in chaungyng stant° your sikernesse°,
That tache° may noo wyght° fro your herte
arace°;
Yf ye lese° oon, ye kan wel tweyn purchace.
Al lyght for somer°—ye woot° wel what I mene—
Insted of blew, ye may wel were al grene.

21 A BALADE OF COMPLAINT

Compleyne ne koude ne might myn herte never
My peynes halve° ne what turment I have,
Though that I shoulde in youre presence ben ever,
My hertes lady, as wisely He° me save
That bounte° made, and beaute list to grave°
In youre persone, and bad° hem bothe in-fere°
Ever t'awayte, and ay° be wher ye were.

As wisely He gye° alle my joyes here
As I am youres, and to yow sadde° and trewe,

---

21 Syn, *since* **23 bene,** *bean* **25 do no fors,** *don't care* **27 istrike,** *erased,* **sclat,** *slate* **29 mene,** *course* **Against Women Unconstant. 1 newfangelnesse,** *fickleness* **4 woot,** *know,* **while ye have lyves space,** *while you live* **5 a,** *one* **6 lust,** *desire,* **ay,** *always* **7 were,** *wear* **8 Ryght,** *just,* **impresse,** *make a mark* **9 mot,** *must,* **pace,** *go* **10 fareth,** *goes* **12 wedercok,** *weathervane* **15 shryned,** *enshrined,* **brotelnesse,** *changeableness* **16 Bet,** *better* **17 stant,** *stands,* **sikernesse,** *security* **18 tache,** *defect,* **wyght,** *person,* **arace,** *tear out* **19 lese,** *lose* **20 lyght for somer,** *lightly dressed for summer,* **woot,** *know* **A Balade of Complaint. 2 My peynes halve,** *half of my pain* **4 wisely He,** *surely may he* (God) **5 bounte,** *goodness,* **list to grave,** *chose to engrave* **6 bad,** *commanded,* **in-fere,** *together* **7 ay,** *always* **8 gye,** *guide* **9 sadde,** *constant*

21 so fat, a play on the courtly commonplace that unrequited love makes one grow thin, and perhaps humorous treatment of Chaucer's own portliness. However, the line is closely paralleled by the opening line of the Jean Duc de Berry's Response to *Les Cent Ballades* (edited by Gaston Raynaud, Société des Anciens Textes Français. Paris: Firmin-Didot, 1905, 213): "Puiz qu'a Amours suis si gras eschapé." **23 counte hym not a bene,** an idiom meaning "consider him worthless." **26 Syn I fro Love &c.,** lines 21–23 are to be sung as a refrain. **29 ther,** P reads "this." **Against Women Unconstant.** Text based on Bodleian Library MS Fairfax 16 (F), corrected from British Library MS Harley 7578 and British Library MS Cotton Cleopatra D.7. **7 blew . . . grene,** blue, the color of constancy; green, of infidelity. **16 Bet,** F reads "Better." **Dalyda, . . . Creseyde . . . Candace,** types of faithless women: Delilah betrayed Samson; Criseyde was unfaithful to Troylus, and Candace deceived Alexander. **17 stant,** F reads "stondeth." **20 lyght for somer,** compare *CYT* 8.568, where the phrase seems to imply "ready for rapid travel." **A Balade of Complaint.** Text based on British Library MS Additional 16165, the only surviving manuscript.

And ye, my lyf and cause of my gode chere,
And dethe also, whan ye my peynes newe°,
My worldes joye, whom I wol serve and sewe°,
My heven hole°, and al my souffisaunce,
Whom for to serve is sette al my plesaunce°.

Beseching yow in my most humble wyse
T'accepte in worth this lytel pore dyte°,
And for my trouthe° my service nat despyse,
Myn observaunce eke° have nat in despyte°,
Ne yit to long to suffren in this plyte°,
I yow beseche, myn hertes lady dere,
Sith° I yow serve, and so wil yere by yere.

22 AN AMOROUS COMPLAINT MADE AT WINDSOR

Complaynt Damours.

I, which that am the sorwefullest man
That in this world was ever yet lyvinge,
And lest recoverer of himselven kan°,
Begynne right thus my dedely° compleyninge
On hir that may to lyf and deth me bringe,
Which hath on me no mercy ne noo routhe°,
That love hir best, but sleeth° me for my trouthe°.

Can I noght doon to seyn that° yow may lyke,
Ne certes°, now, allas, allas, the while°!
Your plesaunce° is to lawghen whan I syke°,
And thus ye me from al my blisse exile.
Ye han me cast in thilke spitous yle°
Ther° never man on lyve° myghte asterte°;
This have I for I love yow, swete herte.

Sothe is° that wel I wot°, by lyklynesse°,
Yf that it were a thing possible to doo,
T'acompte° youre beute and goodenesse.
I have no wonder thogh ye do me woo,
Sith° I, the unworthiest that may ryde or goo°,
Dorste° never thynken in so high a place;
What wonder is, though ye do me noo grace?

Allas, thus is my lyf brought to an ende;
My deth I se is my conclusioun.
I may wel singe, "In sory tyme I spende
My lyf"—that song may have confusioun°!
For mercy, pitee, and deep affeccioun,
I sey for me, for al my deedly chere°,
Alle thise diden in that me° love yow dere°.

And in this wise° and in dispeyre I lyve:
In love, nay, but in dispeyre I dye!
But shal I thanne my deth foryive,
That causeles doth me this sorwe drye?
Ye, certes°, I! For she of my folye
Hath noght to doone, although she do me sterve°.
Hit is nat with hir wil that I hir serve!

---

11 newe, *renew* **12 sewe,** *follow* **13 hole,** *whole,* **souffisaunce,** *sufficiency* **14 plesaunce,** *pleasure* **16 pore dyte,** *poor song* **17 trouthe,** *loyalty* **18 observaunce eke,** *dedication also,* **despyte,** *scorn* **19 plyte,** *sorrowful condition* **21 Sith,** *since* **An Amorous Complaint. 3 lest recoverer of himselven kan,** *is least able to cure himself* **4 dedely,** *deathly* **6 routhe,** *pity* **5 sleeth,** *slays,* **trouthe,** *loyalty* **8 doon to seyn that,** *cause* (myself) *to speak what* **9 Ne certes,** *certainly not,* **while,** *time* **10 plesaunce,** *pleasure,* **syke,** *sigh* **12 in thilke spitous yle,** *on this hateful isle* **13 Ther,** *where,* **on lyve,** *alive,* **asterte,** *escape* **15 Sothe is,** *it is true,* **wot,** *know,* **lyklynesse,** *probability* **17 T'acompte,** *to describe* **19 Sith,** *since,* **goo,** *walk* **20 Dorste,** *dare* **25 have confusioun,** *be damned* **27 dedely chere,** *deathly expression* **28 diden in that me,** *caused me to,* **dere,** *dearly* **29 wise,** *way* **32 drye,** *suffer* **33 certes,** *surely* **34 do me sterve,** *makes me die*

11 newe, corrected from "rewe" in manuscript. **20 dere,** the manuscript reads "here." **An Amorous Complaint.** Text based on Bodleian Library MS Fairfax 16 (F), with corrections from British Library MS Harley 7333 (Ha^3). **Complaynt Damours,** the French title, used by some editors, is in F; the English title derives from Ha^3. **22 my lyf,** F reads "mis[c]hefe." **24–28** Line ends are missing in F. **24–25 "In sory tyme . . . lyf,"** an allusion to (and near quotation of) a contemporary lyric.

And sithen° I am of my sorwe the cause
And sithen I have this withoute hir rede°,
Than may I seyn ryght shortely in a clause°
Hit is no blame unto hir womanhede
Though suche a wrecche as I be for hir dede.
Yet alwey two thinges doon° me dye,
That is to seyn, hir beute and myn eye.

So that, algates°, she is verray roote°
Of my disese, and of my dethe alsoo;
For wyth a word she myghte be my boote°,
Yf that she vouched sauf° for to do soo.
But than° is hir gladnesse at my woo;
Hit is hir wone° plesaunce° for to take
To seen hir servaunts dyen for hir sake.

But certes, than is al my wondering:
Sithen she is the fairest creature
As to my doome° that ever was lyving,
The benygnest° and best eke that Nature
Hath wrought or shal while that the world
may dure°,
Why that she lefte pitee all behinde?
Hit was, ywis°, a grete defaute in kynde°.

Yet is this no lakke to hir, pardee°,
But God or Nature, hem wolde I blame.
For though she shew no pitee unto me,
Sythen that° she dooth other men the same
I ne oughte to despyse° my ladies° game.
Hit is hir pley to lawghen whan men syketh°,
And I assente al that hir list and lyketh°.

Yet wolde I, as I dar, with sorwful hert,
Beseche unto your meke womanhede
That I dorste° my sharpe sorwes smerte°
Shewe° by word, that ye wolde ones rede°
Compleynte of me, which ful sore I drede
That I have seid through myn unkonninge°
In any worde to your displesinge°.

Lothest° of anything that ever was loothe
Were me, as wisly° God my soule save,
To seyn a thing thorgh which ye myght be
wroothe°;
And to that day that I be leyd in grave,
A trewer servaunt shul ye never have.
And though that I on yow have pleyned here,
Foryiveth it me, myn owne lady dere.

Ever have I ben, and shal howso I wende°,
Outher° to lyve or dye your humble trewe°;
Ye been to me my gynning and myn ende,
Sonne of the sterre, bryght and clere of hewe.
Alwey in oon°, to love yow freshly newe,
By God and by my trouthe, is myn entente;
To lyve or dye, I wol it never repente.

This compleynt on Seint Valentynes day,
Whan every foul chesen shal° his make°,
To hir whos I am hool° and shal alway,
This woful song and this compleynt I make,
That never yet wolde me to mercy take.
And yet wol I evermore hir serve
And love hir best although she do me sterve°:

Explicit

36 sithen, *since* **37 rede,** *encouragement* **38 ryght shortely in a clause,** *very briefly* **41 doon,** *make* **43 algates,** *neverthless,* **roote,** *root* **45 boote,** *remedy* **46 vouched sauf,** *consented* **47 than,** *then* **48 wone,** *custom,* **plesaunce,** *pleasure* **52 doome,** *judgment* **53 benygnest,** *most gracious* **54 dure,** *last* **56 ywis,** *surely,* **defaute in kynde,** *omission in nature* **57 pardee,** *by God* **60 Sythen that,** *since* **61 despyse,** *speak poorly of,* **ladies,** *lady's* **62 syketh,** *sigh* **63 hir list and lyketh,** *to her* (is) *pleasing and enjoyable* **66 dorste,** *dare,* **smerte,** *pain* **67 Shewe,** *show,* **ones rede,** *once read* **69 unkonninge,** *ignorance* **70 displesinge,** *displeasure* **71 Lothest,** *most hateful* **72 as wisly,** *surely may* **73 wroothe,** *angry* **78 howso I wende,** *however I travel* **79 Outher,** *either,* **trewe,** *true servant* **82 in oon,** *the same* **86 foul chesen shal,** *bird shall choose,* **make,** *mate* **87 hool,** *wholly* **91 do me sterve,** *causes me to die*

42 hir beute and myn hert, the commonplace notion that the lover is wounded when the arrows of love, including beauty, enter his heart through his eyes. **48 wone,** F reads "wone to." **69 myn,** Omitted in F. **70** Line lacking in F. **77 lady,** F reads "hert." Compare *TC* 3.1183 and 5.1344. **81** F reads "Sonne over sterre, bryght of hewe." **83 is myn,** F reads "this is myn." **85–86 Seint Valentynes day . . . ,** poems commemorating Valentine's Day developed in Chaucer's time, including the convention that it is the day on which birds choose their mates; examples include his *Parliament of Fowls* (line 309) and *Complaint of Mars* (line 13), as well as works by John Gower, Sir John Clanvowe, and Oton de Granson. **87 hool,** omitted in F.

Romaunt of the Rose

Romaunt of the Rose

Introduction

THE *ROMAUNT OF THE ROSE* translates into Middle English portions of the most influential French poem of the Middle Ages, the *Roman de la Rose,* a handbook of courtly sentiment and an exploration of human erotic psychology. Guillaume de Lorris wrote the beginning of the French *Roman* (4058 lines) ca.1230, and Jean de Meun completed it some fifty years later to a total of nearly 22,000 lines. The narrator—Amans (the Lover)—dreams of an idealized garden in which courtly figures, led by the God of Love, dance and sport amorously. The Lover joins the group, falls in love with a rosebud, and seeks to possess this blossom. The sexual allegory is clear but gentle throughout Guillaume's section, while Jean's section is much more expansive and hard edged. Sometimes cynical, sometimes academic, and everywhere syncretic, it includes a variety of characters who seek to aid or thwart the pursuit of the Rose. Reason dissuades the Lover; Fear, Shame, and Resistance try to protect the Rose; Friendship, Fair Welcome, the Old Woman, False Seeming, and Nature encourage the Lover's cause in diverse ways. Ranging digressions enable Jean to align a good deal of philosophy, psychology, science, and social criticism with the fundamental allegory of love: he includes an influential presentation of Fortune and her Wheel, literary and linguistic theory, some strident antifeminism, satire of friars, cosmology, mythology, and even an explanation of rainbows and how mirrors work. Construed very widely, love connects everything in the *Roman de la Rose.*

The poem inspired Chaucer throughout his career, from his early *Book of the Duchess* to several of the plots and characters of the *Canterbury Tales,* most notably the Wife of Bath (the Old Woman) and the Pardoner (False Seeming), perhaps even the Host (Diversion or Myrthe, the keeper of the garden). The combination of first-person narration within a dream-vision frame influenced all of Chaucer's dream-vision poems; echoes of the *Roman* recur throughout Chaucer's *Troylus and Criseyde.* The descriptions in *Roman* of figures lining the walls of the Garden of Love inspired Chaucer's descriptions of the pilgrims in his *General Prologue.* Familiarity with the French *Roman de la Rose* is fundamental to understanding Chaucer.

It seems that Chaucer must have translated the French *Roman* because in the *Legend of Good Women* the God of Love chides Chaucer's persona-narrator, exclaiming, "Thou hast translated the *Romaunce of the Rose* / That is an heresye ayeins my lawe" (*LGWP* 329–30). As part of a fiction, this claim is not proof that Chaucer did undertake such a translation, but it certainly suggests that he did. The suggestion is corroborated by the French poet, Eustace Deschamps, in his balade to Chaucer (ca.1386) where he praises the Englishman's translation of the *Roman* "En bon Anglés" (into good English; see Murray Brown 1999, no. 280). Unfortunately, there is little evidence that our extant Middle English *Romaunt* is Chaucer's own. His translation of the French poem may be lost, and the *Romaunt* may be by someone else. Nevertheless, most scholars agree that the opening portion of the Middle English version presented here is very likely by Chaucer and the rest by others, perhaps compiled by yet a third party in its present form, a pastiche of three sections.

Part A (1–1705; the description of the garden and the Rose) is generally agreed to be by Chaucer because its language and style are consistent with his other works. Part B (1706–5810; falling in love and Reason's discourse) is a less literal translation, marked by northern dialectic forms (e.g., 1928), distinct diction (e.g., 1721), and rhymes not found in Chaucer (e.g. 1853–54); scholars generally agree that this is not Chaucer's. Part C (5811–7696; False Seeming) has some troublesome rhymes (see 5869–70n), but is more like A than B, so perhaps by Chaucer. Parts A and B follow closely the narrative sequence of the French original but, complicating things, C continues from where B stops only after skipping some 5,500 lines of the French original. Clearly, the work is composite, with the likelihood that Chaucer did write A, may have written C, and most likely did not write B—or so goes the traditional scenario. In *The Language of the Chaucer Tradition* (2003; no. 162), Simon Horobin shows that Chaucer's eclectic London dialect includes some northern forms and he questions some of the traditional assumptions about rhymes, calling for a renewed consideration of the authorship of both B and C on the grounds of recent advances in dialect study and our understanding of the habits of scribes.

Horobin also enriched the textual tradition of the *Romaunt* when he announced the discovery of a newly found fragment of the poem in the National Library of Scotland. For generations, the only known manuscript of the *Romaunt* was Glasgow University Library Hunter 409 (formerly Hunterian V.3.7). This early fifteenth-century manuscript lacks 524 lines of the poem through loss of leaves (plus several other dropped lines), so that the earliest complete version of the poem is the first printed edition, William Thynne's of 1532. For electronic facsimiles of both the Hunter manuscript and Thynne's edition, along with transcription of the manuscript, see Graham D. Caie, "The Romaunt of the Rose" (no. 22). Horobin transcribes the fragment (2006; no. 1648).

Because Part A follows the French closely, including its octosyllabic verse form, most scholars date this portion of the *Romaunt* to very early in Chaucer's career, the late 1360s. There has been little study of the relative chronology of the three parts of the work, although the presence of the northern forms and rhymes in B and C may also indicate a similar date of translation if these parts were produced in London, as seems likely. The most extensive summary of these and other critical and textual aspects of the poem is in the Variorum edition by Charles Dahlberg (1999; no. 62). Ronald Sutherland has reconstructed a version of the French *Roman de la Rose* as it is likely to have been known to the translators of the *Romaunt* (1968, no. 1650), presenting it side-by-side with the Middle English. Walter W. Skeat also provides parallel texts for part A (1894-97, no. 39, vol. 1). Mark Miller, in *Philosophical Chaucer* (2004, no. 586), argues that the French poem inhabits Chaucer's imagination in a deep psychological way that goes well beyond simple borrowing and further shows how the poem anticipates many modern formulations of the interdependency of identity and desire.

Romaunt of the Rose

FRAGMENT A

Many men sayn that in sweveninges°
Ther nys° but fables and lesinges°,
But men may some swevenes sene
Which hardely° that false ne bene,
But afterward ben apparaunt°.
This maye I drawe to warraunt°
An authour that hight° Macrobes,
That halt° nat dremes false ne lees°,
But undothe° us the avysioun
That whilom mette Kyng Cipioun°.
And whoso saith or weneth° it be
A jape° or eles a nycete
To wene that dremes after fal°,
Lette whoso lyste° a fole me cal°.
For this trowe° I, and say for me,
That dremes signifiaunce be
Of good and harme to many wightes°
That dremen in her slepe anyghtes°
Ful many thynges covertly°
That fallen after al openly.

THE DREAM

Within my twenty yere of age,
Whan that Love taketh his carriage°
Of yonge folke, I went sone
To bedde, as I was wont to done°,
And faste I slept; and in slepyng,
Me mette° suche a swevenyng
That lyked° me wonders wel.
But in that sweven is never a del°
That it nys afterward befal,
Right° as this dreme wol tel us al.
Now this dreme wol I ryme aright°
To make your hertes gaye and lyght,
For Love it prayeth and also
Commaundeth me that it be so.
And if there any aske me,
Whether that it be he or she,
How this book whiche is here
Shal hatte°, that I rede° you here,
It is the *Romance of the Rose,*
In whiche al the arte of love I close°.
The mater fayre is of to make;
God graunte me in gree° that she it take
For whom that it begonnen is!
And that is she that hath, ywis°,
So mochel prise°, and therto she
So worthy is beloved to be
That she well ought, of prise and right,
Be cleped° Rose of° every wight°.
That it was May me thought tho°—
It is fyve yere or more ago—
That it was May thus dremed me
In tyme of love and jolyte,
That al thyng gynneth waxen° gay,
For ther is neyther busk° nor hay°
In May that it nyl shrouded bene°,
And it with newe leves wrene°.
These woddes eke° recoveren grene
That drie in wynter ben to sene°,
And the erthe wexeth° proud withall°
For swote° dewes that on it fall,
And the poore estate° forgette°
In which that wynter had it sette.
And than becometh the grounde so proude
That it wol have a newe shroude°,

---

1 sweveninges, *dreamings* **2 nys,** *isn't,* **lesinges,** *lies* **4 hardely,** *surely* **5 ben apparaunt,** *are apparent* (when they come to pass) **6 to warraunt,** *as a guarantee* **7 hight,** *is called* **8 halt,** *holds,* **lees,** *lies* **9 undothe,** *explains* **10 whilom mette Kyng Cipioun,** *King Scipio once dreamed* **11 weneth,** *thinks* **12 jape,** *joke,* **nycete,** *folly* **13 fal,** *happen* **14 lyste,** *wishes,* **a fole me cal,** *call me a fool* **15 trowe,** *believe* **17 wightes,** *people* **18 anyghtes,** *at night* **19 covertly,** *secretly* **22 cariage,** *toll* **24 wont to done,** *accustomed to do* **26 Me mette,** *I dreamed* **27 lyked,** *pleased* **28 del,** *part* **30 Right,** *just* **31 ryme aright,** *make properly into poetry* **38 hatte,** *be named,* **rede,** *advise* **40 close,** *enclose* **42 gree,** *good will* **44 ywis,** *truly* **45 mochel prise,** *much worth* **48 cleped,** *called,* **of,** *by,* **wight,** *person* **49 tho,** *then* **53 gynneth waxen,** *began to grow* **54 busk,** *bush,* **hay,** *hedge* **55 nyl shrouded bene,** *will not be clothed* **56 wrene,** *covered* **57 eke,** *also* **58 ben to sene,** *are to see* **59 wexeth,** *swells,* **withall,** *as well* **60 swote,** *sweet* **61 estate,** *condition,* **forgette,** *forgets* **64 shroude,** *garment*

The text is based on Thynne's edition (Th), with variants from Glasgow University Library, Hunter 409 (G). See also 2403–50n. **1–44** G lacks lines 1–44. **3 swevenes,** Th reads "sweven." **7 Macrobes,** Macrobius, author of the fifth-century commentary on Cicero's *Somnium Scipionis* (*Dream of Scipio*); the commentary was a major source of dream lore and dream psychology in the Middle Ages. See the notes to *BD* 284–87 and *PF* 31. **10 Kyng Cipioun,** Scipio is not a king in Cicero or Macrobius, but is given the title in *RR.* **12 a nycete,** G and Th omit "a." **22 cariage,** T reads "corage"; the French is *paage* (toll). **31 Now,** Th reads "Howe." **45 mochel,** T reads "mokel."

And maketh so queynt° his robe and fayre°
That it hath hewes° an hundred payre
Of grasse and floures, ynde° and pers°,
And many hewes ful dyvers—
That is the robe I mene, iwys°,
Through which the ground to praysen is°.
The byrdes, that han left her songe
Whyl they han suffred cold ful stronge
In wethers grille° and derke to sight,
Ben in May for the sonne bright
So gladde that they shewe in syngyng
That in her herte is suche lyking°
That they mote° syngen and be lyght°.
Than° doth the nightyngale hir myght°
To maken noyse and syngen blythe°.
Than is blysful many a sythe°
The chelaundre° and the popyngay°.
Than yonge folke entenden ay°
For to ben gay and amorous,
The tyme is than so savorous°.
Harde is his herte that loveth nought
In May, whan al this myrthe is wrought,
Whan he may on these braunches here
The smale byrdes syngen clere
Her blysful swet song pytous°.
And in this seson delytous°,
Whan love affraieth° alle thyng,
Me thought one night in my slepyng,
Right in my bedde, ful redyly,
That it was by the morowe erly,
And up I rose and gan me clothe°.
Anon° I wyssh° myn hondes bothe.
A sylver nedyl for the I drowe°
Out of an aguyler° queynt ynowe°,
And gan this nedyl threde° anon,
For out of town me lyst to gon°
The sowne° of briddes for to here
That on these buskes° syngen clere.
And in the swete seson that lefe° is,
With a threde bastyng° my slevys,
Alone I wente in my playing,
The smale foules song harkening
That payned hem° ful many a payre
To synge on bowes blossomed fayre.
Jolyf° and gay, ful of gladnesse,
Towarde a ryver gan I me dresse°
That I herde renne faste° by,
For fayrer playing non saugh I
Than playen° me by that ryvere,
For from an hyl that stode ther nere,
Come down the streme full styffe° and bold.
Clere was the water, and as cold
As any welle° is, sothe to sayne°;
And somdele lasse° it was than Sayne,
But it was strayter wel away°.
And never saugh I, er that day,
The water that so wel lyked me.
And wonder° glad was I to se
That lusty° place, and that ryvere.
And with that water that ran so clere
My face I wyssh. Tho° sawe I wel
The botme ypaved everydel
With gravel, ful of stones shene°.
The medowes softe, sote°, and grene,
Beet° right on the watersyde.
Ful clere was than the morow-tyde°,
And ful attempre°, out of drede°.
Tho° gan I walken thorowe the mede°,
Downward aye° in my playing,
The rivers side costeiyng°.
And whan I had a while ygone,
I sawe a garden right anone°, THE GARDEN

65 queynt, *elegant,* **fayre,** *attractive* **66 hewes,** *colors* **67 ynde,** *indigo blue,* **pers,** *bluish purple* **69 iwys,** *indeed* **70 to praysen is,** *is to be praised* **73 grille,** *harsh* **76 lyking,** *pleasure* **77 mote,** *must,* **lyght,** *happy* **78 Than,** *then,* **doth...hir myght,** *exerts herself* **79 blythe,** *happily* **80 sythe,** *time* **81 chelaundre,** *lark,* **popygnay,** *parrot* **82 entenden ay,** *are inclined always* **84 savorous,** *pleasing* **86 wrought,** *made* **89 pytous,** *compassionate* **90 delytous,** *delightful* **91 affraieth,** *arouses* **95 gan me clothe,** *clothed myself* **96 Anon,** *immediately,* **wyssh,** *wash* **97 drowe,** *draw* **98 aguyler,** *needle case* **queynt ynowe,** *quite elegant* **99 gan...threde,** *threaded* **100 me lyst to gon,** *it pleased me to go* **101 sowne,** *sound* **102 buskes,** *bushes* **103 lefe,** *beloved* **104 bastyng,** *attaching* **107 payned hem,** *exerted themselves* **109 Jolyf,** *joyful* **110 gan I me dresse,** *I took my way* **111 faste,** *near* **113 playen me,** *to amuse myself* **115 styffe,** *strong* **117 welle,** *spring,* **sothe to sayne,** *to speak truly* **118 somdele lasse,** *somewhat smaller* **119 strayter wel away,** *very much narrower* **122 wonder,** *very* **123 lusty,** *pleasant* **125 Tho,** *then* **126 everydel,** *completely* **127 shene,** *glistening* **128 sote,** *sweet* **129 Beet,** *bordered* **130 morow-tyde,** *morning* **131 attempre,** *mild,* **out of drede,** *without doubt* **132 Tho,** *then,* **mede,** *meadow* **133 Downward aye,** *downstream always* **134 costeiyng,** *following* **136 right anone,** *very soon*

66 hath, G and Th read "had." **69–72** Beginnings of lines torn off in G. **72 ful,** G reads "so." **78 Than,** Th reads "that." **85 his,** G reads "the." **91 affraieth,** Th reads "affirmeth"; the French is *s'esfroie.* **92 one night,** G reads "anyght." **101 sowne,** G reads "song"; the French is *les sons.* **102 on,** G reads "in." **104 bastyng my slevys,** sleeves were laced on to the body of the shirt or blouse in the fourteenth century. **107 That,** G reads "They." **117–20** Lines torn in G. **118 Sayne,** Seine River, in France. **136 THE GARDEN,** the shoulder notes here and elsewhere in the margins derive from Skeat's edition.

Ful longe and brode, and everydel°
Enclosed it was, and walled wel,
With hye° walles enbatayled°,
Portrayed° without and wel entayled°
With many riche portreytures.
And bothe the ymages and peyntures
Gan I beholde besely°.
And I wol tel you redely
Of thilke° ymages the semblaunce,
As ferre° as I have remembraunce.
  Amydde° sawe I Hate stonde, HATE
That for hir wrathe and yre and onde°
Semed to been a mynoresse°,
An angry wight°, a chideresse°;
And ful of gyle and fel corage°
By semblaunt° was that ylke° ymage.
And she was nothyng° wel arayde°,
But lyk a wode° woman afrayde;
Yfrounced foule was hir visage,
And grynnyng for dispitous° rage;
Hir nose snorted up for tene°.
Ful hydous was she for to sene;
Ful foule and rusty was she, this;
Hir heed ywrithen° was, ywis°,
Ful grymly with a great towayle.
  An ymage of another entayle° FELONY
A lyft half° was hir faste° by.
Hir name above hir heed sawe I,
And she was called Felonye.
  Another ymage that Villanye VILLAINY
Ycleped was° sawe I and fond
Upon the wall on hir right hond.
Vyllanye was lyk somdel°
That other ymage, and trusteth wel,
She semed a wicked creature.
By countenaunce, in portreyture,
She semed be ful dispytous°,
And eke° ful proude and outragious.
Wel coude he paynt, I undertake°,
That suche an ymage coude make.
Ful foule and cherlish° semed she,
And eke vileynous for to be,
And lytel coude of norture°
To worshippe° any creature.
  And next was paynted Covetyse,
That eggeth° folk in many a gyse° COVETOUSNESS
To take and yeve right° nought agayn,
And gret tresours up to layn°.
And that is she that for usure°
Leneth° to many a creature
The lasse° for the more wynnyng,
So covetous is her brennyng°.
And that is she, for pennes feele°,
That techeth for to robbe and steele
These theves and these smale harlotes°;
And that is routhe°, for by her throtes°
Ful many one hongeth at the last.
She maketh folk compasse° and cast°
To taken other folkes thynge
Through robberye or myscountyng.
And that is she that maketh trechours°.
And she maketh false pledours°,
That with her termes and her domes°
Done° maydens, children, and eke gromes°
Her heritage to forgo.
Ful croked were hir hondes two,
For Covetyse is ever wode°
To grypen° other folkes gode.
Covetyse for hir wynnyng°
Ful lefe hath° other mennes thyng.
  Another ymage set sawe I AVARICE
Next Covetyse faste° by,
And she was cleped° Avarice.
Ful foul in payntyng was that vice;

137 everydel, *completely* **139 hye,** *high,* **enbatayled,** *battlemented* **140 Portrayed,** *painted,* **entayled,** *carved* **143 besely,** *intently* **145 thilke,** *those* **146 ferre,** *far* **147 Amydde,** *in the middle* **148 onde,** *envy* **149 mynoresse,** *Franciscan nun* **150 wight,** *person,* **chideresse,** *scolder* **151 fel corage,** *evil spirit* **152 semblaunt,** *appearance,* **ylke,** *same* **153 nothyng,** *not at all,* **arayde,** *dressed* **154 wode,** *mad* **155 Yfrounced,** *wrinkled* **156 dispitous,** *spiteful* **157 tene,** *anger* **160 ywrithen,** *wrapped,* **ywis,** *truly* **162 entayle,** *shape* **163 A lyft half,** *on the left side,* **faste,** *near* **167 Ycleped was,** *was named* **169 somdel,** *somewhat* **173 ful dispytous,** *very spiteful* **174 eke,** *also* **175 undertake,** *assert* **177 cherlish,** *churlish* **179 coude of norture,** *knew of good manners* **180 worshippe,** *honor* **182 eggeth,** *urges,* **gyse,** *manner* **183 yeve right,** *give back* **184 up to layn,** *to store up* **185 usure,** *usury* **186 Leneth,** *loans* **187 lasse,** *less* **188 brennyng,** *burning* **189 pennes feele,** *many pennies* **191 smale harlotes,** *petty scoundrels* **192 routhe,** *a pity,* **her throtes,** *their throats* **194 compasse,** *scheme,* **cast,** *plan* **197 trechours,** *traitors* **198 pledours,** *lawyers* **199 her domes,** *their judgments* **200 Done,** *make,* **gromes,** *young men* **203 wode,** *mad* **204 grypen,** *grasp* **205 wynnyng,** *gain* **206 Ful lefe hath,** *very dear holds* **208 faste,** *near* **209 cleped,** *named*

141 riche portreytures, the carved and painted images depict principles that are antithetical to courtly virtues—hence their placement outside the garden. **142 peyntures,** G reads "the peyntures." **148 and yre,** G reads "yre." **149 mynoresse,** many editors following Skeat emend to "moveress" (agitator), but the reading is clear; anti-Franciscan sentiment and contention in convents were familiar notions. **163 faste,** omitted in G. **176 an,** omitted in G. **182 a,** omitted in G. **185 she,** omitted in G. **189 she, for,** G reads "that." **196 myscountyng,** G and Th read "myscoveytyng."

Ful fadde° and caytif° was she eke°,
And also grene as any leke°.
So yvel hewed was hir colour,
Hir semed to have lyved in langour°.
She was lyk thyng° for hungre deed,
That ladde hir lyf onely by breed
Kneden° with eysel° strong and egre°;
And therto° she was leane and megre.
And she was cladde° ful pourely
Al in an old torn courtepy°,
As° she were al with dogges torne;
And bothe behynde and eke beforne
Clouted° was she beggarly.
A mantel hong hir faste by,
Upon a perche°, weyke and smal;
A burnette° cote hong therwithal
Furred with no menyvere°,
But with a furre rough of here°,
Of lambe-skynnes hevy and blake—
It was ful old, I undertake°.
For Avarice to clothe hir wel
Ne hasteth hir never a del°,
For certainly it were hir lothe°
To wearen ofte that ilke° clothe.
And if it were forweared°, she
Wolde have ful great necessite
Of clothyng er° she boughte hir newe,
Al were it° bad of wol and hewe.
This Avarice held in hir hande
A purs, that hong by a bande;
And that she hydde and bond so stronge°,
Menne must abyde° wonder longe
Out of the purs er ther come ought°,
For that ne cometh in hir thought.
It was not, certayn, hir entente
That fro that purs a peny wente.

ENVY

And by that ymage, nygh° ynough,
Was paynted Envye, that never lough°
Nor never wel in herte ferde°
But if° she eyther sawe or herde
Som great mischaunce° or greet disese°.
Nothyng may so moch hir plese
As mischef and misaventure,
Or whan she seeth discomfyture
Upon any worthy man fall,
Than lyketh hir° ful wel withall.
She is ful glad in hir corage°,
If she se any gret linage
Be brought to naught in shamful wyse.
And if a man in honour ryse,
Or° by his wytte, or by his prowesse,
Of that hath she gret hevynesse°,
For trusteth wel, she goth nye wood°
Whan any chaunce happeth good.
Envye is of suche cruelte
That fayth ne trouthe° holdeth she
To frend ne felawe, badde or good.
Ne she hath kyn none° of hir blood
That she nys ful her° enemy.
She nolde°, I dar sayn hardely°,
Hir owne fader ferde wel°.
And sore abyeth° she everydel°
Hir malyce and hir maletalent°,
For she is in so great turment
And hath such wo whan folk doth good,
That nygh° she melteth for pure wood°.
Hir herte kerveth° and so breketh
That God the people wel awreketh°.
Envye, iwys°, shal never let°
Som blame upon the folk to set.
I trowe° that if Envye, iwys,
Knewe the best man that is
On this syde or beyond the see,
Yet somwhat lacken° him wolde she.
And if he were so hende° and wyse
That she ne mighte al abate his pryse°,
Yet wolde she blame his worthynesse,
Or by hir wordes make it lesse.

---

211 fadde, *wasted,* **caytif,** *wretched,* **eke,** *also* **212 leke,** *leek* **214 langour,** *wretchedness* **215 thyng,** *something* **217 Kneded,** *kneaded,* **eysel,** *vinegar,* **egre,** *bitter* **218 therto,** *also* **219 cladde,** *clothed* **220 courtepy,** *short coat* **221 As,** *as if* **223 Clouted,** *patched* **225 perche,** *peg* **226 burnette,** *coarse brown* **227 menyvere,** *fine fur* **228 here,** *hair* **230 undertake,** *declare* **232 never a del,** *not a bit* **233 hir lothe,** *to her offensive* **234 ilke,** *same* **235 forweared,** *worn out* **237 er,** *before* **238 Al were it,** *even if it were* **241 bond so stronge,** *tied so strongly* **242 abyde,** *wait* **243 come ought,** *comes anything* **247 nygh,** *near* **248 lough,** *laughed* **248 ferde,** *went* **250 But if,** *unless* **251 mischaunce,** *misfortune,* **disese,** *discomfort* **256 Than lyketh hir,** *then she is pleased* **257 corage,** *heart* **261 Or,** *either* **262 hevynesse,** *sorrow* **263 nye wood,** *nearly insane* **266 trouthe,** *promise* **268 kyn none,** *no kin* **269 nys ful her,** *isn't fully their* **270 nolde,** *doesn't wish,* **hardely,** *surely* **271 ferde wel,** *fared well* **272 sore abyeth,** *sorely pays for,* **everydel,** *every bit of* **273 maletalent,** *evil will* **276 nygh,** *nearly,* **wood,** *madness* **277 kerveth,** *cuts* **278 awreketh,** *avenges* **279 iwys,** *truly,* **let,** *cease* **281 trowe,** *believe* **284 lacken,** *degrade* **285 hende,** *attractive* **286 abate his pryse,** *lessen his worth*

211 fadde, Th reads "sadde"; the French is *meigre.* **225 perche,** Th reads "benche"; the French is *perche.* **236 necessite,** Th reads "nycete" (foolishness). **256 ful wel,** G and Th read "wel"; the French is *plet mout.* **264 chaunce,** G reads "chaunge." **275 hath,** Th reads "hate." **wo,** omitted in G and Th.

I sawe Envye in that payntyng
Had a wonderful lokyng°,
For she ne loked but awrie°,
Or overthwarte° al baggyngly°.
And she had a foule usage°,
She mighte loke in no visage°
Of man or womman forthright playn,
But shette one eye for disdayn°,
So for envye brenned° she
Whan she might any man yse°,
That fayre or worthy were, or wyse,
Or elles stood in folkes pryse°.
Sorowe was paynted next Envye SORROW
Upon that wal of masonrye.
But wel was sene in hir colour
That she had lyved in langour°;
Hir semed to have the jaunyce.
Not half so pale was Avaryce,
Nor nothyng lyk, as of leanesse;
For sorowe, thought, and great distresse,
That she had suffred day and nyght
Made hir ful yelowe and nothyng bryght,
Ful fade°, pale, and megre° also.
Was never wight° yet half so wo°
As that hir semed for to be,
Nor so fulfylled of yre° as she.
I trowe° that no wight mighte hir plese,
Nor do that thyng that mighte hir ese;
Nor she ne wolde° hir sorowe slake°,
Nor comfort none unto hir take,
So depe was hir wo begonne°,
And eke hir herte in angre ronne°—
A sorouful thyng wel semed she.
Nor she had nothyng slowe be°
For to cracchen° al hir face,
And for to rent° in many place
Hir clothes, and for to teare hir swyre°,
As she that was fulfylled of yre;
And al to-torn° lay eke hir here
Aboute hir shuldres, here and there,
As she that hadde it al to-rent
For angre and for maletalent°.
And eke I tel you certaynly
How that she wept ful tenderly.
In world nys wyght° so harde of herte
That had sene hir sorowes smerte°,
That nolde° have had of° hir pyte,
So wobegon° a thyng was she.
She al to-dassht° hirself for wo,
And smot° togyder hir hondes two.
To sorowe was she ful ententyf°,
That woful recheless caytyf°.
Hir rought° lytel of° playing,
Or of clypping° or kissing;
For whoso° soroweful is in herte,
Him luste not° to play ne sterte°,
Ne for to dauncen, ne to synge,
Ne may his herte in temper° bringe
To make joye on even° or morowe,
For joye is contrarie unto sorowe.
Elde was paynted after this, OLD AGE
That shorter was a foote, ywis°,
Than she was wonte° in hir yonghede°.
Unneth° hirself she mighte fede.
So feble and eke so old was she
That faded was al hir beaute.
Ful salowe° was waxen° hir colour,
Hir heed forhor° was, whyte as flour.
Iwys, great qualm° ne were it none,
Ne synne, although hir lyf were gone.
Al wòxen was hir body unwelde°,
And drie, and dwyned° al for elde°.
A foul forwelked° thyng was she
That whylom° rounde and softe had be.
Hir eeres shoken° fast withall°,
As from her heed they wolde fall.
Hir face frounced° and forpyned°,
And bothe hir hondes lorne°, fordwyned°.

290 wonderful lokyng, *strange appearance* **291 awrie,** *crookedly* **292 overthwarte,** *sideways,* **baggyngly,** *leeringly* **293 usage,** *habit* **294 visage,** *face* **296 disdayn,** *scorn* **297 brenned,** *burned* **298 yse,** *see* **300 pryse,** *esteem* **304 langour,** *wretchedness* **305 jaunyce,** *jaundice* **311 fade,** *faded,* **megre,** *skinny* **312 wight,** *person,* **wo,** *sorrowful* **314 fulfylled of yre,** *full of anger* **315 trowe,** *believe* **317 ne wolde,** *did not want,* **slake,** *to lessen* **319 begonne,** *established* **320 angre ronne,** *anger ran* **322 nothyng slowe be,** *not at all been slow* **323 cracchen,** *scratch* **324 rent,** *tear* **325 swyre,** *throat* **327 to-torn,** *torn out* **330 maletalent,** *evil will* **333 nys wyght,** *there is no person* **334 smerte,** *pain* **335 nolde,** *wouldn't,* **of,** *for* **336 wobegon,** *sorrowful* **337 to-dassht,** *beat* **338 smot,** *struck* **339 ententyf,** *devoted* **340 recheless caytyf,** *reckless wretch* **341 rought,** *cared,* **of,** *for* **342 clypping,** *hugging* **343 whoso,** *whoever* **344 Him luste not,** *he doesn't want,* **sterte,** *skip* **346 temper,** *moderation* **347 on even,** *in evening,* **morowe,** *morning* **350 ywis,** *truly* **351 wonte,** *formerly,* **yonghede,** *youth* **352 Unneth,** *scarcely* **355 salowe,** *pale,* **waxen,** *grown* **356 forhor,** *completely whitened* **357 qualm,** *pity* **359 Al woxen was hir body unwelde,** *her body had become thoroughly feeble* **360 dwyned,** *dwindled,* **for elde,** *because of age* **361 forwelked,** *much wrinkled* **362 whylom,** *once* **363 shoken,** *flapped,* **withall,** *as well* **365 frounced,** *wrinkled,* **forpyned,** *wasted with pain* **366 lorne,** *lost,* **fordwyned,** *shrunken*

295 or, T reads "ne." **296 one eye,** G reads "her eien"; Th, "her one eye"; the French is *i oil.* **299 fayre or worthy,** G reads " fayrer or worthier." **307 as,** omitted in G and Th. **310 ful,** omitted in Th. **314 of,** Th reads "with." **323 cracchen,** G reads "forcracchen." **333–80** Lines lacking in G.

So old she was that she ne wente
A foote, but° it were by potente°.
The Tyme, that passeth nyght and day, TIME
And restelees travayleth ay°,
And steleth from us so prively°,
That to us seemeth sykerly°
That it in one point dwelleth ever,
And certes, it ne resteth never,
But goth so faste, and passeth ay,
That ther nys man that thynke may
What tyme that now present is—
Asketh at these clerkes this;
For er° men thynke it redily°,
Thre tymes ben ypassed by.
The Tyme, that may not sojourne°,
But goth and may never retourne,
As water that downe renneth ay,
But never droppe retourne may.
Ther may nothyng as Tyme endure,
Metal nor erthely creature,
For al thing it fret° and shal.
The Tyme, eke, that chaungeth al,
And al doth waxe° and fostred be°,
And al thyng distroyeth he.
The Tyme that eldeth° our auncestours
And eldeth kynges and emperours,
And that us al shal overcomen
Er that Dethe us shal have nomen°.
The Tyme that hath al in welde°
To elden folk had maad hir elde°
So inly° that, to my wetyng°,
She might helpe hirself nothyng,
But turned ayen° unto childhede;
She had nothing° hirself to lede,
Ne wyt ne pyth° in hir holde
More than a chyld of two yere olde.
But nathelesse, I trowe° that she
Was fayr sumtyme°, and fressh to se,
Whan she was in hir rightful age.
But she was past al that passage
And was a doted° thyng becomen.
A furred cope° on had she nomen°;
Wel had she clad hirself and warme,
For colde might els done hir harme.
These olde folke have alway colde,
Hir kynde° is suche, whan they ben olde.
Another thyng was don ther writ°
That semede lyk an ipocryt°, POPE-HOLY
And it was cleped° Pope-Holy.
That ilke° is she that prively°
Ne spareth never a wicked dede,
Whan men of hir taken non hede;
And maketh hir outward precious,
With pale vysage and pytous°,
And semeth a symple creature;
But ther nys no misaventure°
That she ne thynketh in hir corage°.
Ful lyk to hir was thilke° ymage
That maked was lyk hir semblaunce°.
She was ful symple of countenaunce,
And she was clothed and eke shod
As she were, for the love of God,
Yolden° to relygion—
Suche semed hir devocion.
A psauter° held she faste in honde,
And besyly she gan to fonde°
To make many a feynt prayere
To God and to his payntes dere.
Ne she was gaye, fresshe, ne jolyf°,
But semed to be ful ententyf°
To good werkes and to fayre°,
And therto she had on an hayre°.
Ne certes, she was fatte nothyng°,
But semed wery for fastyng;
Of colour pale and dede° was she.
From hir the gates aye werned be°
Of paradyse, that blysful place.
For suche folk maken leane her face°,
As Christ sayth in his Evangyle,
To gette hem prise in town a whyle,

---

368 but, *unless,* **potente,** *crutch* **370 travayleth ay,** *labors always* **371 privKely,** *secretly* **372 sykerly,** *certainly* **379 er,** *before,* **redily,** *carefully* **381 sojourne,** *remain* **387 fret,** *devours* **389 al doth waxe,** *makes all grow,* **fostred be,** *be nourished* **391 eldeth,** *makes old* **394 nomen,** *taken* **395 in welde,** *in its control* **396 hir elde,** *her own old age* (i.e., Old Age had aged so) **397 inly,** *deeply,* **wetyng,** *knowledge* **399 ayen,** *again* **400 nothing,** *no capacity* **401 Ne wyt ne pyth,** *neither wit nor vigor* **403 trowe,** *believe* **404 sumtyme,** *once* **407 doted,** *feeble-minded* **408 cope,** *cloak,* **nomen,** *taken* **412 kynde,** *nature* **413 don ther writ,** *written* (carved) *there* **414 ipocryt,** *hypocrite* **415 cleped,** *named* **416 ilke,** *same,* **prively,** *secretly* **420 pytous,** *pitiable* **422 misaventure,** *misfortune* **423 corage,** *heart* **424 thilke,** *that* **425 semblaunce,** *appearance* **429 Yolden,** *given* **431 psauter,** *psalter* (Book of Psalms) **432 gan to fonde,** *began* **435 ne jolyf,** *nor happy* **436 ententyf,** *devoted* **437 fayre,** *fair* (deeds) **438 hayre,** *hair shirt* **439 fatte nothyng,** *not at all fat* **441 dede,** *deathly* **442 aye werned be,** *were always forbidden* **444 leane her face,** *their faces lean*

379 er, omitted in G and Th. **408 cope,** Th reads "cappe." **421 symple,** G reads "semely." **424 thilke,** G reads "that." **435 fresshe,** G reads "ne fresshe." **429 Yolden to relygion,** i.e., she was dressed as if a nun. **438 hayre,** hair shirts were worn as a form of penance. **444 face,** G and Th read "grace"; the French is *vis.* **445 Christ sayth,** Matthew 6.16. **446 hem,** omitted in G.

And for a lytel glory veine°
They lesen° God and eke his reigne°.
  And alderlast° of everychone
POVERTY
Was paynted Povert al alone,
That not a peny had in holde
Although she hir clothes solde,
And though° she shulde anhonged° be;
For naked as a worm was she.
And if the wether stormy were,
For colde she shulde have dyed there.
She nadde on° but a strayt° olde sacke,
And many a cloute° on it ther stacke°—
This was hir cote and hir mantel°.
No more was there never a del°
To clothe hir with, I undertake°.
Great leyser° had she to quake.
And she was put, that I of talke,
Ferre fro° these other, up in an halke°.
Ther lurked and ther coured° she,
For poore thyng°, wherso it be°,
Is shamfaste° and dispysed ay°.
Acursed may wel be that day
That poore man conceyved is,
For God wot°, al to selde°, iwys°,
Is any poore man wel yfedde,
Or wel arayed, or wel ycledde°,
Or wel beloved, in suche wyse°
In honour that he may aryse.
  Al these thinges, wel avysed°,
As I have you er this devysed°,
With golde and asure° over all
Depaynted were upon the wall.
Squar was the wall and hygh somdel°;
Enclosed and ybarred wel
In stede of hegge° was that gardyn;
Com never shepherde therin.
Into that gardyn, wel ywrought°,
Whoso that me coude have brought,
By laddre or elles by degre°,
It wolde wel have lyked° me.
For suche solace, suche joy and pley,
I trowe° that never man ne sey°
As was in that place delycious.
The gardyn was not daungerous°
To herberowe° byrddes many one;
So ryche a yerd was never none
Of byrdes songe and braunches grene.
Therin were byrdes mo, I wene°,
Than ben in al the realme of Fraunce.
Ful blysful was the accordaunce°
Of swete and pytous songe they mad,
For al this worlde it ought glad°.
And I myselfe so mery ferde°,
Whan I her blysful songes herde,
That for an hundred pound nolde° I—
If that the passage openly
Had be unto me fre—
That I nolde entren for to se
Th'assemblee—God kepe it fro care—
Of byrdes whiche therein ware°,
That songen through her mery throtes
Daunces of love and mery notes.
  Whan I thus herde foules synge,
I fel faste in a waymentynge°
By whiche art or by what engyn°
I might come into that gardyn.
But way I couthe° fynde none
Into that gardyn for to gone,
Ne nought wyst° I if that ther were
Eyther hole or place owhere°
By whiche I might have entre.
Ne ther was none to teche me,
For I was al alone, iwys°,
Ful wo° and anguissous° of this.
Til atte laste bethoughte I me
That by no way ne might it be
That ther nas ladder or way to pace°,
Or hole, into so fayre a place.

---

447 glory veine, *empty glory* **448 lesen,** *lose,* **reigne,** *kingdom* **449 alderlast,** *the very last* **453 And though,** *even if,* **anhonged,** *hanged* **457 nadde on,** *had nothing on,* **strayt,** *thin* **458 cloute,** *patch,* **stacke,** *stuck* **459 mantel,** *cloak* **460 never a del,** *not a bit* **461 undertake,** *declare* **462 leyser,** *opportunity* **464 Ferre fro,** *far from,* **halke,** *corner* **465 coured,** *cowered* **466 poore thyng,** *any poor thing,* **wherso it be,** *wherever it is* **467 shamfaste,** *shamed,* **ay,** *always* **470 wot,** *knows,* **to selde,** *too seldom,* **iwys,** *truly* **472 ycledde,** *dressed* **473 wyse,** *a way* **475 avysed,** *considered* **476 er this devysed,** *described before* **477 asure,** *azure* **479 somdel,** *somewhat* **481 In stede of hegge,** *instead of being surrounded by hedges* **483 ywrought,** *made* **485 degre,** *steps* **486 lyked,** *pleased* **488 trowe,** *think,* **sey,** *saw* **490 daungerous,** *reluctant* **491 herberowe,** *harbor* **494 wene,** *think* **496 accordaunce,** *harmony* **498 glad,** *to make happy* **499 ferde,** *went* **501 nolde,** *would not* **506 ware,** *were* **510 waymentynge,** *lamenting* **511 engin,** *ingenuity* **513 couthe,** *could* **515 wyst,** *knew* **526 owhere,** *anywhere* **519 iwys,** *truly* **520 Ful wo,** *woeful,* **anguissous,** *anguished* **523 pace,** *pass*

448 eke, omitted in G. **451 holde,** G reads "wolde" (possession). **457 nadde,** Th reads "ne hadde." **471 yfedde,** G reads "fedde." **472 wel ycledde,** G and Th omit "wel"; G reads "cled." **477 asure,** azure is a semiprecious blue stone; lapis lazuli. **478 were,** G reads "newe." **483 ywrought,** G and Th read "wrought." **492 yerd,** G reads "yere." **497 and,** omitted in Th. **501 nolde,** G reads "wolde." **516 owhere,** G and Th read "where." **520 Ful,** G and Th read "For"; the French is *mout engoiseus.* **521 atte,** Th reads "at."

Tho° gan I go a ful great paas°
Envyroning even in compas°
The closyng° of the square wall,
Tyl that I fonde a wyket° small
So shette° that I ne mighte in gone,
And other entre was ther none.

THE GATE

  Upon this dore I gan to smyte,
That was fetys° and so lyte°,
For other way coude I not seke.
Ful longe I shof°, and knocked eke,
And stode ful longe and oft herkenyng
If that I herde a wight° comyng,
Tyl that the dore of thylke° entre
A mayden curteys opened me.

IDLENESS

Hir heer was as yelowe of hewe
As any basen scoured° newe.
Hir flesh tender as is a chyke°,
With bent browes°, smothe and slyke°;
And by mesure large were
The openyng of hir eyen clere.
Hir nose of good proporcion;
Hir eyen gray as is a faucon°;
With swete brethe and wel savoured°.
Hir face whyt and wel coloured,
With lytel mouth, and round to se;
A clove° chynne eke hadde she.
Hir necke was of good fassyon°
In length and gretnesse°, by reson°,
Without bleyne°, scabbe, or royne°.
Fro Hierusalem unto Burgoyne
Ther nys a fayrer necke, iwys°,
To fele how smothe and softe it is.
Hir throte also whyte of hewe
As snowe on braunche snowed newe.
Of body ful wel wrought° was she;
Men neden not in no cuntre
A fayrer body for to seke.
And of fyne orfrays° had she eke
A chapelet°; so semly oon°
Ne wered never° mayde upon.
And fayre above that chapelet
A rose gerlande had she set.
She had in honde a gay mirrour,
And with a ryche gold tressour°
Hir heed was tressed queyntely°;
Hir sleves sewed fetisly°.
And for to kepe hir hondes fayre,
Of gloves whyte she had a payre.
And she had on a cote of grene
Of cloth of Gaunt; withouten wene°,
Wel semed by hir apparayle
She was not wont° to great travayle°.
For whan she kempt° was fetisly,
And wel arayed and richely,
Than had she done al hir journee°,
For mery and wel bigon° was she.
She ladde a lusty° lyf in May;
She had no thought, by night ne day,
Of nothing but it were onely
To grayth° hir wel and uncouthly°.
  Whan that this dore had opened me
This mayden semely for to se,
I thonked hir as I best myght,
And asked hir how that she hyght°,
And what she was I asked eke°.
And she to me was nought unmeke,
Ne of hir answer daungerous°,
But fayre answerde, and sayde thus:
"Lo, sir, my name is Idelnesse;
So clepe° men me, more and lesse.
Ful mighty and ful ryche am I,
And that of one thyng, namely°,
For I entende° to nothing
But to my joye and my playing,
And for to kembe and tresse me.
Acquaynted am I, and prive°,
With Myrthe, lorde of this gardyn,
That fro the lande of Alexandryn

525 Tho, *then,* **paas,** *distance* **526 Envyroning even in compas,** *circling completely around* **527 closyng,** *enclosure* **528 wyket,** *doorway* **529 shette,** *shut* **532 fetys,** *well made,* **lyte,** *little* **534 shof,** *pushed* **536 a wight,** *anyone* **537 thylke,** *that* **540 basen scoured,** *basin polished* **541 chyke,** *chick* **542 bent browes,** *arched eyebrows,* **slyke,** *sleek* **546 as is a faucon,** *as a falcon's* **547 wel savoured,** i.e., *smelling good* **550 clove,** *cleft* **551 fassyon,** *shape* **552 gretnesse,** *thickness,* **by reson,** *reasonable* **553 bleyne,** *blemish,* **royne,** *roughness* **555 iwys,** *truly* **559 wrought,** *made* **562 orfrays,** *gold embroidery* **563 chapelet,** *head cloth,* **so semly oon,** *such an attractive one* **564 Ne wered never,** *was never worn* **568 tressour,** *braiding thread of ribbon* **569 queyntely,** *elegantly* **570 sewed fetisly,** *neatly laced* **574 wene,** *doubt* **576 wont,** *accustomed,* **travayle,** *effort* **577 kempt,** *combed* **579 journee,** *day's work* **580 wel bigon,** *carefree* **581 lusty,** *pleasurable* **584 grayth,** *adorn,* **uncouthly,** *strikingly* **588 hyght,** *was named* **589 eke,** *also* **591 daungerous,** *aloof* **594 clepe,** *call* **596 namely,** *especially* **597 entende,** *attend* **600 prive,** *intimate*

535 oft, G reads "of"; Th, "al." **537 the,** omitted in G. **554 Hierusalem,** Jerusalem. **Burgoyne,** Burgundy in modern France. **560 neden,** G reads "neded." **567 in honde,** omitted in G and Th; the French is *En sa main.* **570 fetisly,** Th reads "fetously." **574 Gaunt,** Ghent, in modern Belgium, was known for its fine weaving. **586 mayden,** G and Th read "may." **601 Myrthe,** the French is *Deduit* (Diversion), so there are no doubt some negative connotations of "departing from the path" as well as the positive ones of "pleasing entertainment." **602 Alexandryn,** Alexandria (Egypt); a touch of orientalism.

Made the trees hyther be fette°
That in this garden ben ysette.
And whan the trees were woxen on hyght°,
This wal that stant here in thy syght
Dyde Myrthe enclosen al aboute.
And these ymages al without,
He dyd hem bothe entayle° and peynte
That neyther ben jolyf ne queynte°;
But they ben ful of sorowe and wo,
As thou hast sene a whyle ago.
"And ofte tyme, him to solace°,
Sir Myrthe cometh into this place,
And eke with him cometh his meyne°,
That lyven in luste° and jolyte.
And now is Myrthe therin, to here
The byrdes how they syngen clere,
The mavys° and the nyghtyngale,
And other joly byrdes smale.
And thus he walketh to solace
Hym and his folk, for swetter place
To playen in he may not fynde
Although he sought one intyl Inde°.
The alther-fayrest° folk to se
That in this world may founde be
Hath Myrthe with him in his route°,
That folowen him alwayes aboute."
Whan Idelnesse had told al this,
And I had herkned° wel, iwys°,
Than sayde I to Dame Idelnesse,
"Now also wisly° God me blesse,
Syth° Myrthe that is so fayre and fre°
Is in this yerde with his meyne,
Fro thylke° assemble if I may
Shal no man werne° me today,
That I this nyght ne mote° it se.
For wel wene° I, ther with him be
A fayre and joly companye
Fulfylled of al curtesye."
And forth without wordes mo
In at the wiket° went I tho°,
That Idelnesse had opened me,
Into that garden fayr to se.
And whan I was therin, iwys,
Myn herte was ful glad of this. THE GARDEN
For wel wende° I ful sykerly°
Have been in paradys erthly.
So fayre it was that, trusteth well,
It semed a place espyrituell°.
For certes, as at my devyse°,
Ther is no place in paradyse
So good in for to dwell or be
As in that garden, thoughte me.
For ther was many a byrd singyng
Throughout the yerde al thringing°.
In many places were nightyngales,
Alpes°, fynches, and wodewales°,
That in her swete song delyten
In thilke° places as they habyten°.
Ther might men se many flockes
Of turtles° and laverokkes°.
Chalaundres fele° sawe I there,
That wery nigh forsongen° were.
And thrustels°, teryns°, and mavise°,
That songen for to wynne hem prise°,
And eke to surmounte in her songe
That other byrdes hem amonge.
By note made fayr servyse
These byrdes that I you devyse°;
They songe her songe as fayre and well
As angels doon espirituell.
And trusteth wel, whan I hem herde,
Full lustily° and wel I ferde°,
For never yet suche melodye
Was herd of man that mighte dye°.
Suche swete song was hem amonge
That me thought it no byrdes songe,
But it was wonder lyk to be
Song of meermaydens of the see,
That for her synging is so clere,
Though we meermaydens clepe° hem here
In Englisshe, as in our usaunce°,
Men clepe hem sereyns° in Fraunce.

---

603 fette, *brought* (fetched) **605 were woxen on hyght,** *had grown tall* **609 dyd hem . . . entayle,** *had them carved* **610 jolyf ne queynte,** *pleasant nor elegant* **613 him to solace,** *to please himself* **615 meyne,** *company* **616 luste,** *pleasure* **619 mavys,** *song thrush* **624 intyl Inde,** *until India* **625 alther-fayrest,** *fairest of all* **628 route,** *company* **630 herkned,** *listened,* **iwys,** *truly* **632 also wisly,** *as surely as* **633 Syth,** *since,* **fre,** *gracious* **635 Fro thylke,** *from that* **636 werne,** *forbid* **637 ne mote,** *might not* **638 wene,** *believe* **642 wiket,** *gate,* **tho,** *then* **647 wende,** *thought,* **sykerly,** *certainly* **650 espyrituell,** *spiritual* **651 as at my devyse,** *to my mind* **656 thringing,** *thronging* **658 Alpes,** *bullfinches,* **wodewales,** *woodpeckers* (?) **660 thilke,** *those,* **habyten,** *dwell* **662 turtles,** *turtledoves,* **laverokkes,** *larks* **662 Chalaundres fele,** *many larks* **664 nigh forsongen,** *nearly "sung out"* **665 thrustels,** *thrushes,* **teryns,** *siskins* (?), **mavise,** *song thrushes* **666 prise,** *praise* **670 devyse,** *describe* **674 Full lustily,** *very happily,* **ferde,** *went* **676 man that mighte dye,** *mortal man* **682 clepe,** *call* **683 usaunce,** *custom* **684 sereyns,** *sirens*

604 ysette, G reads "sette." **645 therin,** G and Th read "in." **673 wel,** Th reads "me." **whan,** G reads "that." **674 lustily,** Th reads "lusty."

  Ententyf° weren for to syng
These byrdes that not unkonnyng°
Were of her craft, and aprentys°,
But of her song subtyl and wys.
And certes, whan I herde her songe,
And saw the grene place amonge,
In herte I wext° so wonder° gay
That I was never erst°, er° that day,
So jolyf nor so wel bygo°,
Ne mery in herte, as I was tho°.
And than wyste°, I and saw ful wel,
That Ydelnesse me served wel,
That me putte in suche jolyte.
Hir frend wel oughte I for to be
Syth° she the dore of that gardyn
Had opened and me lette in.
  From henceforth how that I wrought°,
I shall you tellen, as me thought.
First, whereof° Myrthe served there,
And eke what folk ther with him were,
Without fable I wol discryve°.
And of that garden eke as blyve°
I wol you tellen after this.
The fayre fassyon° al, iwys°,
That wel ywrought° was for the nones°,
I may not tel you al at ones,
But as I may and can, I shal
By ordre tellen you it al.
  Ful fayre servyce and eke ful swete
These byrdes maden as they sete°.
Layes° of love ful wel sowning°
They songen in her jargoning°.
Some hye° and some eke lowe songe
Upon the braunches grene isponge°.
The swetnesse of her melodye
Made al myn herte in revelrye°.
And whan that I had herd, I trowe°,
These byrdes synging on a rowe,
Than might I not withholde me°
That I ne went in for to se
Sir Myrthe; for my desyring
Was him to sene, over al thing—
His countenaunce and his manere.
That syghte was to me ful dere.
  Tho° went I forthe on my right honde,
Down by a lytel path I fonde,
Of myntes ful and fenell° grene,
And faste° by, withoute wene°,
Syr Myrthe I founde; and right anon
Unto Sir Myrthe gan I gon°, SIRMIRTH
Ther as he was, him to solace°.
And with him, in that lusty° place,
So fayre folk and so fresshe had he
That whan I sawe I wondred me
Fro whence suche folk might come,
So fayre they weren, al and some.
For they were lyk, as to my syght,
To angels that been fethered bright.
  These folke, of whiche I tel you so,
Upon a karole° wenten tho.
A lady karoled° hem that hyght°
Gladnes, the blysful and the lyght. GLADNESS
Wel coude she synge and lustely,
Non half so wel and semely°,
And make in song suche refraynynge°,
It sat° hir wonder wel to synge.
Hir voyce ful clere was and ful swete.
She was not rude ne unmete°,
But couthe° ynough of suche doyng
As longeth unto° karolyng,
For she was wont° in every place
To syngen fyrst folk to solace°,
For synging moste she gave hir to;
No crafte had she so lefe° to do.
  Tho mightest thou° karolles sene,
And folke daunce and mery bene°,
And make many a fayr tourning
Upon the grene gras springing.

---

685 Ententyf, *dedicated* **686 unkonnyng,** *ignorant* **687 aprentys,** *beginners* **691 wext,** *grew,* **wonder,** *very* **692 erst,** *before,* **er,** *before* **693 wel bygo,** *happy* **694 tho,** *then* **695 wyste,** *knew* **699 Syth,** *since* **701 wrought,** *acted* **703 whereof,** *how* **705 discryve,** *describe* **706 eke as blyve,** *also as quickly* **708 fassyon,** *appearance,* **iwys,** *truly* **709 ywrought,** *made,* **nones,** *conditions* **714 sete,** *sat* **715 Layes,** *songs,* **sowning,** *sounding* **716 jargoning,** *chirping* **717 hye,** *high* **718 grene isponge,** *sprouted green* **720 revelrye,** *celebration* **721 trowe,** *believe* **723 withholde me,** *restrain myself* **729 Tho,** *then* **731 fenell,** *fennel* (an aromatic) **732 faste,** *near,* **wene,** *doubt* **734 gan I gon,** *I went* **735 him to solace,** *to please himself* **736 lusty,** *pleasant* **744 karole,** *ring dance* **745 karoled,** *led,* **hyght,** *was named* **748 semely,** *pleasingly* **749 refraynynge,** *singing of refrains* **750 sat,** *suited* **752 unmete,** *discordant* **753 couthe,** *knew* **754 longeth unto,** *pertains to* **755 wont,** *accustomed* **756 solace,** *please* **758 so lefe,** *such pleasure* **759 Tho mightest thou,** *then might you* **760 mery bene,** *be merry*

688 But, G reads "For." **her,** omitted in G and Th. **716 her jargoning,** G reads " their yarkonyng." **720 revelrye,** G reads "reverye." The French is *reverdie* (joy in the return of spring). **743 These,** G reads "this." **744 karole,** a circle or ring dance that includes accompanying singing, also called "caroling"; not originally associated with Christmas. **746 the blysful,** G and Th omit "the." **the lyght,** Th omits "the." **749 make,** G and Th read "couthe make." **761 make,** G and Th read "made."

Ther mightest thou se these flutours°,
Mynstrales°, and eke joglours°,
That wel to synge dyd her payne°.
Som songe songes of Lorayne,
For in Lorayne her notes be
Ful swetter° than in this countre.
Ther was many a tymbestere°,
And saylours° that I dar wel swere
Couthe° her craft ful parfetly°.
The tymbres° up ful subtelly°
They caste, and hente° ful ofte
Upon a fynger fayre and softe,
That they ne fayled° nevermo.
Ful fetys° damosels two,
Right yonge and ful of semelyhede°,
In kyrtles° and none other wede°,
And fayre tressed every tresse°,
Had Myrthe done° for his noblesse
Amydde the carole for to daunce.
But herof lyeth no remembraunce,
How that they daunsed queyntely°.
That one wolde come al prively°
Agayn° that other, and whan they were
Togythre almost, they threwe yfere°
Her mouthes so that through her play
It semed as they kyste alway.
To dauncen wel couthe° they the gyse°;
What shulde I more to you devyse?
Ne bede° I never thence go,
Whyles that I saw hem daunce so.
  Upon the karol wonder faste°
I gan beholde°, tyl atte laste
A lady gan me for to espye,
And she was cleped° Curtesye, COURTESY
The worshypful°, the debonayre°—
I pray to God ever fall hir fayre°!
Ful curteysly she called me,
"What do ye there, beau sire°?" quod she,
"Come, and if it lyke° you
To daunsen, daunseth with us now."
And I, without tarying,
Went into the karolling.
I was abasshed never a del°,
But it me lykede right wel
That Curtesye me cleped° so,
And bade° me on the daunce go.
For if I had durst°, certayne
I wolde have karoled right fayne°,
As man that was to daunce right blythe°.
Than gan I loken ofte sythe°
The shap, the bodyes, and the cheres°,
The countenaunce, and the maneres
Of al the folk that daunsed there,
And I shal telle what they were.
  Ful fayr was Myrthe, ful longe° and hygh°;
A fayrer man I never sygh°. MIRTH
As rounde as appel was his face,
Ful roddy° and whyte in every place.
Fetys° he was and wel besey°,
With metely° mouth and eyen° grey;
His nose by mesure wrought° ful right;
Crysp° was his heer, and eke ful bright.
His shuldres of a large brede°,
And smallysshe in the gyrdelstede°.
He semed lyke a purtreyture,
So noble he was of his stature,
So fayr, so joly, and so fetyse,
With lymmes° wrought at poynt devyse°,
Delyver°, smerte°, and of great myght;
Ne sawe thou never man so lyght.
Of berde unnethe° had he nothyng,
For it was in the firste spring;
Ful yong he was, and mery of thought.
And in samyt°, with byrdes wrought°,
And with gold beten ful fetysly,
His body was clad ful richely.
Wrought was his robe in straunge gyse°,
And al to-slyttered° for queyntyse°

---

763 flutours, *flute players* **764 Mynstales,** *minstrels,* **eke joglours,** *also entertainers* **765 dyd her payne,** *made their efforts* **768 swetter,** *sweeter* **769 tymbestere,** *female tambourine player* **770 saylours,** *dancers* **771 Couthe,** *knew,* **parfetly,** *perfectly* **772 tymbres,** *tambourines,* **subtelly,** *skillfully* **773 hente,** *caught* **775 fayled,** *missed* **776 Ful fetys,** *very shapely* **777 semelyhede,** *prettiness* **778 kyrtles,** *smocks,* **wede,** *garment* **779 tressed every tresse,** *braided every hair* **780 Had...done,** *directed* **783 queyntely,** *skillfully* **784 prively,** *slyly* **785 Agayn,** *toward* **786 yfere,** *together* **789 couthe,** *knew,* **gyse,** *manner* **791 bede,** *asked* **793 wonder faste,** *very eagerly* **795 gan beholde,** *gazed* **796 cleped,** *named* **797 worshypful,** *honorable,* **debonayre,** *gracious* **798 ever fall hir fayre,** *may good things always happen to her* **800 beau sire,** *good sir* **801 lyke,** *pleases* **805 never a del,** *not a bit* **807 cleped,** *called* **808 bade,** *told* **809 durst,** *dared* **810 right fayne,** *very gladly* **811 blythe,** *happy* **812 gan I loken ofte sythe,** *I looked many times on* **813 cheres,** *expressions* **817 longe,** *tall,* **hygh,** *upright* **818 sygh,** *saw* **820 roddy,** *ruddy* **821 Fetys,** *well-made,* **wel besey,** *good-looking* **822 metely,** *well-proportioned,* **eyen,** *eyes* **823 by mesure wrought,** *made in proportion* **824 Crysp,** *curled* **825 brede,** *breadth* **826 gyrdelstede,** *waistline* **830 lymmes,** *limbs,* **at poynt devyse,** *to perfection* **831 Delyver,** *agile,* **smerte,** *quick* **833 unnethe,** *scarcely* **836 samyt,** *rich silk,* **wrought,** *worked* (adorned) **839 straunge gyse,** *unusual fashion* **840 to-slyttered,** *slashed* (to revel the decorative lining), **queyntyse,** *elegance*

766 Lorayne, Lorraine, in northeastern France. **775 ne,** omitted in Th. **791 bede,** G and Th read "bode." **836 samyt,** G and Th read "samette."

In many a place, lowe and hye.
And shod he was with great maystrye°,
With shoon decoped°, and with lace.
By druerye° and by solace°
His leefe° a rosen chapelet°
Had maad and on his heed it set.
  And wete ye° who was his leefe?
Dame Gladnes ther was him so lefe°, GLADNESS
That syngeth so wel with glad corage°
That from she was twelve yere of age
She of hir love graunt him made.
Sir Myrthe hir by the fynger hadde
In daunsyng, and she him also;
Great love was atwyxt° hem two.
Bothe were they fayre and brighte of hewe.
She semed lyke a rose newe
Of colours, and hir flesshe so tendre
That with a brere° smale and slendre
Mon° mighte it cleve°, I dar wel seyn.
Hir forheed, frounceles° al pleyn°;
Bent° were hir browes° two;
Hir eyen gray, and glad also,
That laugheden aye° in hir semblaunt°,
First or° the mouth, by covenaunt.
I not° what of hir nose descryve°;
So fayre hath no woman alyve.
Hir heer was yelowe° and clere shyning;
I wot° no lady so lyking°.
Of orfrayes° fresshe° was hir garlande;
I, whiche sene have a thousande,
Sawe never, iwys°, no garland yet
So wel ywrought° of sylke as it.
And in an overgylt samyte°
Cladde she was by great delyte—
Of whiche hir leefe° a robe werde°,
The meryer she in hir herte ferde°.
  And next hir wente, on hir other syde,
The God of Love, that can devyde° CUPID
Love, and as him lyketh it° be.
But he can cherles daunten°, he,
And maken folkes pride fallen.
And he can wel these lordes thrallen°,
And ladyes put at lowe degre,
Whan he may hem to proude se.
  This God of Love of his fascioun°
Was lyk no knave° ne quystroun°.
His beutie greatly was to prise°.
But of his robe to devyse°
I drede encombred° for to be.
For not yclad in sylk was he,
But al in floures and flourettes°,
Ypaynted al with amorettes°,
And with losenges° and scochons°,
With byrddes, lyberdes°, and lyons,
And other beestes wrought ful wel.
His garnement° was everydel
Ypurtrayed° and ywrought° with flours,
By dyvers medeling° of colours.
Floures ther were of many gyse
Yset by compas in assyse°.
Ther lacked no floure, to my dome°,
Ne not so moche as floure of brome°,
Ne vyolet, ne eke pervynke°,
Ne floure non that man can on thynke.
And many a rose-lefe ful longe
Was entermedled° ther amonge,
And also on his heed was set
Of roses reed a chapelet.
But nightyngales, a ful great route°,
That flyen over his heed aboute,
The leves felden° as they flyen.
And he was al with byrdes wryen°,

---

842 maystrye, *skill* **843 shoon decoped,** *shoes cut with decorative slashes* **845 By druerye,** *for love,* **solace,** *pleasure* **846 leefe,** *beloved,* **chapelet,** *garland* **847 wete ye,** *do you know* **848 lefe,** *dear* **849 corage,** *spirits* **854 atwyxt,** *between* **858 brere,** *briar* **859 Mon,** *anyone,* **cleve,** *cut* **860 frounceles,** *without wrinkles,* **pleyn,** *smooth* **861 Bent,** *arched,* **browes,** *eyebrows* **863 aye,** *always,* **semblaunt,** *appearance* **864 or,** *before* **865 not,** *don't know,* **decryve,** *to describe* **867 yelowe,** *blonde* **868 wot,** *know,* **lyking,** *pleasing* **869 orfrayes,** *gold embroidery,* **fresshe,** *new-made* **871 iwys,** *truly* **872 ywrought,** *made* **873 overgylt samyte,** *gold-adorned rich silk* **875 leefe,** *beloved,* **werde,** *wore* **876 ferde,** i.e., *felt* **878 devyde,** *distribute* **879 him lyketh it,** *it pleases him* **880 cherles daunten,** *churls subdue* **882 thrallen,** *enthrall* **885 fascioun,** *appearance* **886 knave,** *servant,* **quystroun,** *kitchen boy* **887 prise,** *value highly* **888 devyse,** *describe* **889 drede encombred,** *fear burdened* **891 flourettes,** *petals* **892 amorettes,** *love knots* **losenges,** *diamond shapes,* **scochons,** *heraldic devices* **894 lyberdes,** *leopards* **896 garnement,** *garment* **897 Ypurtrayd,** *adorned,* **ywrought,** *worked* **898 dyvers medeling,** *various mixing* **900 compas in assyse,** *design in position* **901 dome,** *judgment* **902 brome,** *broom* (a flowering shrub) **903 pervynke,** *periwinkle* **906 entermedled,** *intermixed* **909 route,** *company* **911 felden,** *knocked down* **912 wryen,** *covered*

847 leefe, Th reads "sefe." **853 In,** omitted in G and Th. **858 slendre,** Th reads "tendre," a repetition. **859 seyn,** Th reads "sey." **860 pleyn,** Th reads "pley." **865 not,** G and Th read "wot not." **nose descryve,** G and Th read "nose I shal descryve." **875–76** The sense is that Gladness took special joy in the fact that Mirth wears clothing that match hers. **884 proude,** G reads "poude." **891 and,** G reads "and in." **892** Line lacking in G. **897 Ypurtrayed . . . ywrought,** G reads "portraied . . . wrought." **904 man,** Th reads "men."

With popingay°, with nightyngale,
With chalaundre°, and with wodewale°,
With fynch, with lark, and with archangell°.
He semed as he were an angell
That down were comen fro heven clere.
  Love had with him a bachelere°,
That he made alwayes with him be;
Swete-Loking cleped° was he.
This bachelere stod beholding SWEET-
The daunce; and in his honde holding LOOKING
Turke° bowes two had he.
That one of hem was of a tree
That bereth a fruit of savour wicke°.
Ful croked was that foule stycke,
And knotty here and there also,
And blacke as bery or any slo°.
That other bowe was of a plante
Withoute wemme°, I dar warante°,
Ful° even, and by proporcioun
Treitys° and longe, of good facyoun°.
And it was paynted wel and twhitten°,
And over-al diapred° and written°
With ladyes and with bacheleres
Ful lyghtsom° and glad of cheres°.
These bowes two held Swete-Loking,
That semed lyk no gadeling°.
And ten brode arowes held he there,
Of whiche fyve in his right hond were.
But they were shaven wel and dyght°,
Nocked° and fethered aryght°,
And al they were with gold begon°,
And stronge° poynted everychon,
And sharpe for to kerven° wel.
But yron was ther noon, ne steel,
For al was gold, men mighte it se,
Outtake° the fethers and the tree°.
  The swyftest of these arowes fyve
Out of a bowe for to dryve,
And best yfethered for to flye,
And fayrest eke°, was cleped Beautie. BEAUTY
That other arowe, that hurteth lesse,
Was cleped, as I trowe°, Symplesse. SIMPLICITY
The thyrde cleped was Fraunchyse
That fethered was in noble wyse CANDOR
With valour° and with curtesye.
The fourthe was cleped Companye COMPANY
That hevy for to shoten is;
But whoso° shoteth right, iwys°,
May therwith don great harme and wo.
The fyfte of these and laste also
Fayr-Semblaunt men that arowe call, FAIR-
The leest grevous of hem all; APPEARANCE
Yet can it make a full great wounde.
But he may hope his sores sounde°
That hurt is with that arowe, iwys.
His wo the bette bestowed is;
For° he may soner have gladnesse,
His langour° ought be the lesse.
  Five arowes were of other gyse°,
That been ful foule to devyse°,
For shafte and ende, soth° for to tell,
Were also° blacke as fende in hell.
  The first of hem is called Pride. PRIDE
That other arowe next hym besyde,
It was cleped Vylanye. VILLAINY
That arowe was al with felonye
Envenymed, and with spytous° blame.
The thyrde of hem was cleped Shame. SHAME
The fourthe, Wanhope cleped is; DESPAIR
The fyfte, the Newe-Thought, iwys. FICKLENESS
  These arowes that I speke of here
Were al fyve on one manere°,
And al were they resemblable°.
To hem was wel sytting° and able
The foule croked bowe hydous,
That knotty was and al roynous°.
That bowe semed wel to shete°
These arowes fyve that ben unmete°,

913 popingay, *parrot* **914 chalaundre,** *lark,* **wodewale,** *woodpecker* **915 archangell,** *titmouse* (see n.) **918 bachelere,** *young man* **920 cleped,** *named* **923 Turke,** *Turkish* **925 savour wicke,** *evil taste* **928 slo,** *blackthorn fruit* **930 wemme,** *blemish,* **warante,** *swear* **931 Ful,** *very* **932 Treitys,** *graceful,* **facyoun,** *fashion* **933 twhitten,** *carved* **934 diapred,** *decorated with patterns,* **written,** *inscribed* **936 lyghtsom,** *happy,* **cheres,** *expressions* **938 gadeling,** *low-class fellow* **941 dyght,** *prepared* **942 Nocked,** *notched,* **aryght,** *properly* **943 begon,** *decorated* **944 stronge,** *powerfully* **945 kerven,** *cut* **948 Outtake,** *except,* **tree,** *wood* **952 eke,** *also* **954 trowe,** *believe* **957 valour,** *value* **960 whoso,** *whoever,* **iwys,** *truly* **966 sounde,** *healed* **969 For,** *because* **970 langour,** *suffering* **971 gyse,** *manner* **972 devyse,** *describe* **973 soth,** *truth* **974 also,** *as* **979 spytous,** *malicious* **984 on one manere,** *of one style* **985 resemblable,** *similar* **986 well sytting,** *well suited* **988 roynous,** *rough* **989 wel to shete,** *appropriate to shoot* **990 unmete,** *unpleasant*

915 archangell, translates the French *mesanges* (titmouse?); not found elsewhere in ME with this sense. **920 Swete-Loking,** alluring glances; the French is *Douz Regart.* **923 bowes two,** the two aspects of love, pain and joy, are commonly represented as the two bows of Cupid or his two sets of arrows. See Ovid, *Metamorphoses* 1.468–71. **had he,** G and Th read "ful wel devysed had he." **932 good,** G and Th read "ful good." **933 twhitten,** G reads "twythen." **942 aryght,** G reads "right." **944 poynted,** G reads "peynted." **947 it,** omitted in Th. **970 His,** G reads "Hir." **978 al,** G and Th read "as."

And contrarye to that other fyve.
But though I telle not as blyve°
Of her power, ne of her myght,
Herafter shal I tellen right
The sothe° and eke signyfyaunce
As ferre° as I have remembraunce.
Al shal be sayd, I undertake°,
Er° of this booke an ende I make.
  Now come I to my tale agayne.
But alderfirst° I wol you sayne
The fassyoun and the countenaunces
Of al the folk that on the daunce is.
The God of Love, jolyf and lyght,
Ladde on his honde a lady bright,
Of hygh prise° and of great degre°.
This lady called was Beaute— BEAUTY
As an° arowe, of which I tolde.
Ful wel thewed° was she holde°.
Ne she was derk ne° brown but bright
And clere as is the moonelyght,
Agayn° whom al the sterres° semen
But smale candels, as we demen°.
Hir flesshe was tendre as dewe of flour,
Hir chere° was symple as byrde in bour°,
As whyte as lylye or rose in ryse°,
Hir face, gentyl and tretyse°.
Fetys° she was and smal to see;
No wyndred° browes hadde she,
Ne popped hir°, for it neded nought
To wyndre hir or to paynte hir ought°.
Hir tresses yelowe and longe straughten°,
Unto hir heles down they raughten°.
Hir nose, hir mouthe, and eye, and cheke
Wel wrought°, and al the remenaunt eke°.
A ful gret savour° and a swote°
Me toucheth in myn herte rote°,
As helpe me God, whan I remembre
Of the fassyoun° of every membre!
In worlde is none so fayre a wight°,
For yonge she was and hewed bright,
Sote°, plesaunt, and fetys° withall,
Gent°, and in hir myddell small.
  Bisyde Beaute yede° Rychesse, RICHES
An hygh lady of great noblesse,
And great of prys° in every place.
But whoso durste° to hir trespace°,
Or tyl° hir folke, in word or dede,
He were ful hardy°, out of drede°,
For bothe she helpe and hyndre° may;
And that is not of yesterday°
That ryche folke have ful great myght
To helpe and eke to greve° a wight.
The best and greattest of valour
Dydden° Richesse ful great honour,
And besy weren hir to serve.
For that° they wolde hir love deserve,
They cleped° hir "Lady," greate and smal.
This wyde worlde hir dredeth al°;
This worlde is al in hir daungere°.
Hir courte hath many a losengere°,
And many a traytour envyous,
That ben ful besy and curious°
For to dispreysen° and to blame
That° best deserven love and name°.
Toforne° the folk, hem to begylen,
These losyngeours hem preyse and smylen,
And thus the world with worde anoynten°.
But afterwarde they pricke and poynten°
The folk right to the bare bone,
Behynde her back whan they ben gone,
And foule abaten° the folkes pris°.
Ful many a worthy man and wys
Han hyndred and ydon° to dye
These losyngeours° with her flaterye,

992 blyve, *eagerly* **995 sothe,** *truth* **996 ferre,** *far* **997 undertake,** *declare* **998 Er,** *before* **1000 alderfirst,** *first of all* **1005 prise,** *worth,* **degre,** *social rank* **1007 As an,** *like an* **1008 Ful wel thewed,** *very virtuous,* **holde,** *considered* **1009 Ne . . . ne,** *neither . . . nor* **1011 Agayn,** *against,* **sterres,** *stars* **1012 demen,** *judge* **1014 chere,** *face,* **byrde in bour,** *bride in bedchamber* **1015 in ryse,** *on stem* **1016 tretyse,** *well-formed* **1017 Fetys,** *pretty* **1018 wyndred,** *plucked* (?) **1019 popped hir,** *did she apply makeup* **1020 ought,** *at all* **1021 straughten,** *hung* **1022 raughten,** *reached* **1024 wrought,** *formed,* **remenaunt eke,** *rest also* **1025 savour,** *odor,* **swote,** *sweet* **1026 herte rote,** *heart's root* **1028 fassyoun,** *nature,* **membre,** *limb* **1029 wight,** *person* **1031 Sote,** *sweet,* **fetys,** *young* **1032 Gent,** *graceful* **1033 yede,** *went* **1035 prys,** *reputation* **1036 durste,** *would dare,* **trespace,** *do wrong to* **1037 tyl,** *to* **1038 hardy,** *brave,* **out of drede,** *without doubt* **1039 hyndre,** *hinder* **1040 of yesterday,** i.e., *just recently* **1042 greve,** *injure* **1044 Dydden,** *did to* **1046 For that,** *because* **1047 cleped,** *called* **1048 hir dredeth al,** *fears her entirely* **1049 daungere,** *power* **1050 losengere,** *flatterer* **1052 curious,** *eager* **1053 dispreysen,** *criticize* **1054 That,** *those who,* **name,** (good) *reputation* **1055 Toforne,** *before* **1057 anoynten,** *apply oil* **1058 poynten,** *stab* **1061 foule abaten,** *foully reduce,* **pris,** *reputation* **1063 ydon,** *caused* **1064 losyngeours,** *liars*

1007 As, G and Th read "And." **1010 is,** omitted in G and Th. **1018 wyndred,** G and Th read "wyntred." **1026 toucheth,** G and Th read "thought"; the French is *me touche.* **1031 Sote,** G and Th read "Sore"; the French is *Sade.* **1034 An hygh,** G and Th read "And." **1037 word,** G and Th read "werke"; the French is *diz.* **1043 greattest,** G reads "the grettest." **1055 Toforne,** G reads "Bifore." **1058 But,** G reads "And." **pricke,** G reads "prile"; Th reads "prill." **1061 abaten the,** G reads "abate the"; Th, "abaten." **1062 and wys,** G reads "ywys." **1063** G reads "An hundrid have to do to dye." **1064 with her,** G reads "thorough."

And maketh folk ful straunge° be
Ther as hem ought ben pryve°.
Wel yvel mote° they thryve and thee°,
And yvel aryved° mote they be,
These losyngeours, ful of envy!
No good man loveth her company.
Rychesse a robe of purple on hadde—
Ne trowe° nat that I lye or madde°,
For in this worlde is none it lyche°,
Ne by a thousand dele° so riche,
Ne non so fayr. For it ful wel
With orfreys° leyd was everydel°,
And purtrayed in the rybanynges°
Of dukes stories and of kynges,
And with a bend° of gold tassyled,
And knoppes° fyne of gold amyled°.
About hir necke of gentyl entayle°
Was shette° the riche chevesayle°,
In whiche ther was ful great plente
Of stones clere and fayr to se.
Richesse a gyrdel had upon,
The bokell° of it was of a ston
Of vertue great, and mokel° of myght.
For whoso bar° the ston so bright,
Of venym durst him nothyng dout°
While he the ston had him about.
That ston was greatly for to love,
And tyl° a riche mannes behove°
Worthe al the golde in Rome and Fryse.
The mourdant°, wrought in noble gyse°,
Was of a ston ful precious,
That was so fyne and vertuous
That whole a man it couthe° make
Of palsye and of tothe-ake°.
And yet the ston had suche a grace
That he was seker° in every place
Al thylke° day not blynde to bene°
That fastyng° might that ston sene°.
The barres° were of gold ful fyne
Upon a tyssu° of satyne,
Ful hevy, great, and nothyng° lyght;
In everych° was a besaunt-wyght°.
Upon the tresses° of Rychesse
Was set a cercle°, for noblesse,
Of brende° gold that ful lyght shone;
So fayr, trowe° I, was never none.
But he were konnyng°, for the nones°,
That coude devysen° al the stones
That in that cercle shewen clere;
It is a wonder thyng to here.
For no man coude preyse or gesse
Of hem the value or richesse.
Rubyes there were, saphirs, iagounces°,
And emeraudes more than two ounces.
But al before, ful subtelly°,
A fyn charboncle° set sawe I.
The stone so clere was and so bright
That also sone° as it was nyght
Men myghte sene to go, for nede,
A myle or two in length and brede°.
Suche lyght sprange out of the stone
That Richesse wonder brighte shone,
Bothe hir heed and al hir face,
And eke° aboute hir al the place.
Dame Richesse on hir hond gan lede°
A yonge man ful of semelyhede°,
That she best loved of any thyng.
His lust° was moche in housholdyng°;
In clothing was he ful fetys°,
And lovede wel to have hors of prys°.
He wende° to have reproved be°
Of thefte or murdre if that he

1065 straunge, *hostile* **1066 pryve,** *intimate* **1067 mote,** *may,* **thee,** *prosper* **1068 yvel aryved,** *evil arrived* (ill-fated) **1072 trowe,** *believe,* **madde,** *rave* **1073 lyche,** *like* **1074 thousand dele,** *thousandth part* **1076 orfreys,** *gold embroidery,* **everydel,** *completely* **1077 rybanynges,** *borders* **1079 bend,** *band* **1080 knoppes,** *decorative buttons,* **amyled,** *enameled* **1081 entayle,** *shape* **1082 shette,** *clasped,* **chevesayle,** *collar* **1086 bokell,** *buckle* **1087 mokel,** *great* **1088 whoso bar,** *whoever bore* **1089 durst him nothyng dout,** *he need fear not at all* **1092 tyl,** *for,* **behove,** *profit* **1094 mourdant,** *trimming at the end of the belt,* **gyse,** *fashion* **1097 couthe,** *could* **1098 tothe-ake,** *toothache* **1100 seker,** *certain* **1101 thylke,** *that,* **bene,** *be* **1102 fastyng,** *while fasting* (not eating), **sene,** *look upon* **1103 barres,** *decorative strips* **1104 tyssu,** *fabric* **1105 nothyng,** *not at all* **1106 everych,** *each one,* **besaunt-wyght,** *the weight of a bezant* (a Byzantine gold coin) **1107 tresses,** *hairdo* **1108 cercle,** *crown* **1109 brende,** *polished* **1110 trowe,** *believe* **1111 were konnyng,** *would be clever,* **nones,** *occasion* **1112 devysen,** *describe* **1117 iagounces,** *jacinths* (an orange-red gem) **1119 subtelly,** *skillfully* **1120 charboncle,** *carbuncle* (ruby or red gem) **1122 also sone,** *as soon* **1124 brede,** *breadth* **1128 eke,** *also* **1129 gan lede,** *led* **1130 semelyhede,** *attractiveness* **1132 lust,** *pleasure,* **housholdyng,** *mansion living* **1133 fetys,** *handsome* **1134 hors of prys,** *valuable horses* **1135 wende,** *thought,* **reproved be,** *been accused*

1065 And maketh, G reads "Have maad." **1066 as,** omitted in G. **1068 aryved,** G reads "achyved." **1073 it,** G reads "hir." **1080 amyled,** G reads "enameled." **1084 fayr,** G reads "bright." **1086–87 a ston . . . / Of vertue great,** precious and semiprecious stones were thought to have various medicinal or magical capabilities, described in books called *lapidaries.* **1092 mannes,** G reads "man." **1093 Fryse,** Frisia or Friesland, a part of modern Holland; not in the French and probably a convenient rhyme. **1094 gyse,** G reads "wyse." **1098 of tothe,** G reads "tothe." **1111 he,** G reads "she." **1117 iagounces,** G and Th read "ragounces"; the French is *iagonces.* **1134 well to have,** G reads "to have well."

Had in his stable an hakeney°.
And therfore he desyred ay°
To ben aqueynted with Richesse.
For al his purpos, as I gesse,
Was for to make great dispence°
Withouten warning° or defence°.
And Richesse myghte it wel sustene,
And hir dispences wel mayntene,
And hym alway suche plentie sende
Of golde and sylver for to spende
Without lacking or daungere°,
As it° were pourde in a garnere°.
 And after on the daunce went LARGESS
Largesse°, that sette al hir entent
For to be honorable and free°.
Of Alexanders kynne was she.
Hir moste joye was, iwys°,
Whan that she yaf°, and seide, "Have this."
Nat Avarice, the foule caytif°,
Was half to grype° so ententyf°
As Largesse is to yeve and spende.
And God alway ynowe° hire sende°
So that the more she yave away,
The more, ywis, she had alwey.
Gret loos° hath Largesse, and gret prys°,
For bothe wys folk and unwys
Were wholy to hir bandon° brought,
So wel with yeftes° hath she wrought°.
And if she hadde an enemy,
I trowe° that she couth° craftely
Make hym ful sone hir freend to be,
So large° of yeftes and free was she.
Therfore she stode in love and grace
Of riche and poore in every place.
A ful gret foole is he, ywis,
That bothe riche and nygarde° is.
A lord may have no maner° vyce
That greveth more° than avarice.
For nygard never with strength of hande
May wynne hym great lordship or lande,
For frendes al to fewe hath he
To done° his wyl performed be.
And whoso wol have frendes here,
He maye nat holde his tresour dere.
For by ensample tel I this:
Right° as an adamant°, ywis,
Can drawen to hym subtelly
The yron that is layd therby,
So draweth folkes hertes, ywis,
Sylver and gold that yeven° is.
 Largesse hadde on a robe fresshe
Of riche purpure Sarsynysshe°.
Wel fourmed was hir face and clere,
And opened had she hir colere°,
For she right there had, in present°,
Unto a lady mad present
Of a gold broche ful wel wrought°.
And certes°, it missat° hir nought,
For through hir smocke, wrought with sylke,
The flessh was sene as whyte as mylke.
Largesse, that worthy was and wys,
Held by the honde a knight of prys°,
Was sybbe° to Arthour of Breteigne.
And that was he that bar the enseigne°
Of worshyp°, and the gounfanoun°.
And yet he is of suche renoun
That men of hym say fayre thynges
Before barons, erles, and kynges.
This knyght was comen al newely°
Fro tourneyinge faste° by.
There had he done great chyvalrye
Through his vertu° and his maystrye°,
And for the love of his lemman°
He cast down many a doughty° man.

1137 hakeney, *small horse* **1138 ay,** *always* **1141 dispence,** *spending* **1142 warning,** *hindrance,* **defence,** *refusal* **1147 daungere,** *restraint* **1148 As it,** *as if it,* **in a garnere,** *into a barn* (granary) **1150 Largesse,** *Generosity* **1151 free,** *open handed* **1153 iwys,** *truly* **1154 yaf,** *gave* **1155 caytif,** *wretch* **1156 grype,** *grasp,* **ententyf,** *devoted* **1158 ynowe,** *enough,* **sende,** *sent* **1161 loos,** *praise,* **prys,** *reputation* **1163 bandon,** *control* **1164 yeftes,** *gifts,* **wrought,** *worked* **1166 trowe,** *believe,* **couth,** *could* **1168 large,** *lavish* **1172 nygarde,** *ungenerous* (niggardly) **1173 maner,** *kind of* **1174 greveth more,** *does more harm* **1178 done,** *cause* **1182 Right,** *just,* **adamant,** *magnet* **1186 yeven,** *given* **1188 Sarsynysshe,** *eastern cloth* (Saracenish) **1190 colere,** *collar* **1191 in present,** *at this time* **1193 wrought,** *made* **1194 certes,** *certainly,* **missat,** *ill-suited* **1198 prys,** *renown* **1199 sybbe,** *kin* **1200 enseigne,** *insignia* **1201 worshyp,** *honor,* **gounfanoun,** *banner* **1205 newely,** *recently* **1206 faste,** *near* **1208 vertu,** *strength,* **maystrye,** *skill* **1209 lemman,** *sweetheart* **1210 doughty,** *valiant*

1137 an, G reads "ony." **1141 For,** G reads "And." **1142 or,** G reads "of." **1146 spende,** G reads "dispende." **1147 lacking,** G reads "lakke." **1150 sette,** G reads "settith." **1152 Alexanders kynne,** the kin of Alexander the Great, who was the medieval model of liberality. **1158 alway ynowe,** G reads "ynough alwey." **1162 wys,** omitted in G. **1166 craftely,** G reads "tristely." **1168 free,** Th reads "wyse." **1172 riche and nygarde,** Th reads "riche and poore and nygarde." **1176 hym,** omitted in G. **1188 Sarsynysshe,** G and Th read "Sarlynysshe." **1199 Arthour of Breteigne,** King Arthur of Britain, the medieval model of magnificence. **1201 gounfanoun,** G and Th read "gousfaucon" (goshawk?); the French is *ganfanon.* **1207 There,** G reads "The."

And next hym daunced Dame Fraunchyse°,
Arayed in ful noble gyse. CANDOR
She nas not° browne ne dunne° of hewe,
But white as snowe yfallen newe.
Hir nose was wrought at poynt devyse°,
For it was gentyl° and tretyse°,
With eyen° glade and browes bente°.
Hir heer doun to hir heles wente.
And she was symple as dowve on tree.
Ful debonayre° of hert was she;
She durste° never saye ne do
But that that hyr longeth to°.
And if a man were in distresse,
And for hir love in hevynesse°,
Hir herte wolde have ful great pitee,
She was so amiable and free°.
For were a man for hir bistadde°,
She wolde ben right sore adradde°
That she dyd over great outrage°
But° she hym holpe° his harm t'aswage;
Hir thoughte it elles° a vylanye.
And she hadde on a suckenye°
That nat of hempen herdes° was;
So fayr was none in al Arras.
Lorde, it was ryddeled fetysly°!
Ther nas nat a poynt, trewely,
That it nas in his right assyse°.
Ful wel yclothed was Fraunchyse,
For ther nys no clothe sytteth bette°
On damosel than doth rokette°.
A womman wel more fetys is
In rokette than in cote, ywis.
The white rokette, ryddeled fayre,
Betokeneth° that ful debonayre
And swete was she that it bere.
By hir daunced a bachelere;
I can nat tellen you what he hyght°,
But fayr he was and of good hyght,
Al° had he ben—I say no more—
The lordes sone of Wyndesore.
And next that daunced Curtesye, COURTESY
That preysed was of° lowe and hye,
For neither proud ne fole° was she.
She for to daunce called me—
I pray God gyve hir right good grace!—
Whan I come first into the place.
She nas not nyce° ne outrageous°,
But wys and war° and vertuous,
Of fayre speche and fayre answere;
Was never wight° myssayd of here°;
She bar no rancour to no wight.
Clere brown° she was, and therto bright
Of face; of body avenaunt°.
I wot no lady so plesaunt.
She were worthy for to bene
An emperesse or crowned quene.
And by hir went a knyght dauncing
That worthy was and wel speking,
And ful wel coude he done honour.
The knyght was fayre and styf in stour°,
And in armure a semely° man,
And wel beloved of his lemman°.
Fair Idelnesse than saugh° I IDLENESS
That alway was me faste° by.
Of hir have I, withouten fayle,
Told you the shappe and appareyle,
For, as I sayde, lo, that was she
That dyd to me so great bounte°,
That she the gate of that gardyn
Undid and let me passen in.
And after daunced, as I gesse, YOUTH
Youthe, fulfyld of lustynesse°,
That has not yet twelve yere of age,
With herte wylde and thought volage°.
Nyce° she was, but she ne mente
None harm ne sleight in hir entente,

1211 Fraunchyse, *Openness* **1213 nas not,** *was not,* **dunne,** *dark* **1215 wrought at poynt devyse,** *shaped excellently* **1216 gentyl,** *aristocratic,* **tretyse,** *well-formed* **1217 eyen,** *eyes,* **bente,** *arched* **1220 debonayre,** *gracious* **1221 durste,** *dared* **1222 hyr longeth to,** *is suitable to her* **1224 hevynesse,** *sorrow* **1226 free,** *generous* **1227 bistadde,** *distressed* **1228 adradde,** *frightened* **1229 over great outrage,** *too much wrong* **1230 But,** *unless,* **holpe,** *helped* **1231 elles,** *otherwise* **1232 suckenye,** *loose dress* **1233 hempen herdes,** *coarse flax* **1235 ryddeled fetysly,** *pleated attractively* **1237 assyse,** *position* **1239 bette,** *better* **1240 rokette,** *a loose dress* **1244 Betokeneth,** *signifies* **1247 hyght,** *was called* **1249 Al,** *as if* **1252 of,** *by* **1253 fole,** *foolish* **1257 nyce,** *silly,* **outrageous,** *hostile* **1258 war,** *prudent* **1260 wight,** *a person,* **myssayd of here,** *spoken ill of her* **1262 Clere brown,** *shining brunette* **1263 avenaunt,** *attractive* **1270 styf in stour,** *strong in battle* **1271 semely,** *handsome* **1272 lemman,** *sweetheart* **1273 than saugh,** *then saw* **1274 faste,** *close* **1278 bounte,** *kindness* **1282 lustynesse,** *vigor* **1283 volage,** *flighty* **1285 Nyce,** *silly*

1219 on, G reads "of." **1221 never,** Th reads "neither."**1231 elles,** G reads "ell"; Th "al." **1234 Arras,** French city known for its fine cloth. **1236 nat,** omitted in G. **1250 lordes sone of Wyndesore,** the lord of Windsor's son, i.e., the prince of England. The site of Windsor, west of London, was a residence of the English monarchs from the Anglo-Saxon period onward, and the phrase "lord of Windsor" has been shown to be associated with King Arthur. It is best to regard this as a conventional reference rather than a specific one. **1255 right,** omitted in Th. **1256 Whan,** Th reads "For whan." **1257 nas,** G reads "was." **1261 no,** omitted in G. **1263 of body,** Th reads "and body." **avenaunt,** G reads "wenaunt." **1265 were,** omitted in G. **1279 that,** G reads "the." **1282 Youthe,** G and Th read "And she"; the French is *Joinece.*

But onely lust° and jolyte.
For yonge folk, wel weten ye°,
Have lytel thought but on her play.
Hir lemman° was besyde alway,
In suche a gyse° that he hir kyste°
At al tymes that him lyste°,
That al the daunce myghte it se;
They make no force of prevyte°.
For whoso spak of hem yvel or wel,
They were ashamed never-a-del°,
But men mighte sene hem kysse there,
As it two yonge dowves° were.
For yong was thylke bachelere°;
Of beaute wot° I non his pere°;
And he was right of suche an age
As Youthe his lefe°, and suche corage°.
  The lusty° folk thus daunced there,
And also other that with hem were,
That weren al of her meyne°;
Ful hende° folk, wys and fre°,
And folk of fayr port°, truely,
Ther weren al comenly°.
Whan I had sene the countenaunces
Of hem that ladden thus these daunces,
Than had I wyl to gon and se
The gardyn that so lyked° me,
And loken on these fayre laureres°,
On pyne-trees, cedres, and olmeres°.
For daunces than ended were;
For many of hem that daunced there
Were with her loves went away
Under the trees to have her play.
  A, lord, they lyved lustely!
A great fole° were he, sykerly°,
That nolde°, his thankes°, suche lyf lede!
For this dare I sayn, out of drede°,
That whoso myght so wel fare,
For better lyf durst him° not care.
For ther nys so good paradyse
As to have a love at his devyse°.
  Out of that place went I tho°,
And in that gardyn gan I go,
Playing along ful merily.
The God of Love ful hastely
Unto him Swete-Lokyng clepte°;
No lenger wolde° he that he kepte°
His bowe of golde, that shone so bright.
He bad° him bende it anon right°;
And he ful sone it sette anende°,
And at a brayd° he gan it bende,
And toke him of his arowes fyve
Ful sharpe and redy for to dryve.
Now God that syt° in magiste,
Fro deedly woundes he kepe° me,
If so be that he had me shete°,
For if I with his arowe mete,
It had me greved sore, ywis°!
But I, that nothing wyste° of this,
Went up and downe ful many a way,
And he me folowed faste alway,
But nowher wolde I reste me
Tyll I had in al the gardyn be.
  The gardyn was by mesuryng
Right even and square in compasyng°;
It as long was as it was large°.
Of fruit hadde every tree his charge°, TREES
But it were° any hydous° tre
Of whiche ther were two or thre.
Ther were, and that wot° I ful wel,
Of pomegarnettes a ful great del;
That is a frute ful wel to lyke,
Namely° to folk whan they ben syke.
And trees ther were, gret foysoun°,
That baren nuttes in her sesoun
Suche as men notemygges° call,
That swote of savour° ben withall°.
And almandres° great plente,
Fygges, and many a date tre

1287 lust, *pleasure* **1288 weten ye,** *you know* **1290 lemman,** *sweetheart* **1291 gyse,** *manner,* **kyste,** *kissed* **1292 him lyste,** *it pleased him* **1294 make no force of prevyte,** *don't care about privacy* **1296 never-a-del,** *not a bit* **1298 dowves,** *doves* **1299 thylke bachelere,** *that young man* **1300 wot,** *know,* **pere,** *equal* **1301 right,** *just* **1302 lefe,** *beloved,* **corage,** *spirits* **1303 lusty,** *pleasant* **1305 meyne,** *company* **1306 hende,** *courteous,* **fre,** *generous* **1307 port,** *behavior* **1308 comenly,** *in a group* **1312 lyked,** *pleased* **1313 laureres,** *laurel trees* **1314 olmeres,** *elms* **1320 fole,** *fool,* **sykerly,** *certainly* **1321 nolde,** *wouldn't,* **his thankes,** *in thanks* **1322 out of drede,** *without doubt* **1324 durst him,** *he dare* **1326 at his devyse,** *for his desire* **1327 tho,** *then* **1331 clepte,** *called* **1332 wolde,** *wanted,* **kepte,** *withheld* **1334 bad,** *directed,* **anon right,** *right away* **1335 anende,** *upright* **1336 at a brayd,** *suddenly* **1339 syt,** *sits* **1340 he kepe,** *may he protect* **1341 shete,** *shot* **1343 ywis,** *indeed* **1344 wyste,** *knew* **1350 compasyng,** *design* **1351 large,** *wide* **1352 charge,** *burden* **1353 But it were,** *except for,* **hydous,** *hideous* **1355 wot,** *know* **1358 Namely,** *especially* **1359 foysoun,** *abundance* **1361 notemygges,** *nutmegs* **1362 swote of savour,** *sweet of taste,* **withall,** *indeed* **1363 almandres,** *almond tress*

1288 wel, G reads "wole." **1295 whoso,** G reads "who." **1303 thus,** G and Th read "that"; the French is *Ensi.* **1306 wys,** G reads "and wys." **1313 laureres,** G reads "loreyes"; Th "laurelles." The French is *loriers.* **1314 olmeres,** G reads "oliveris." **1332 he kepte,** G and Th read "she kepte." **1334 bad him bende it anon,** G and Th read "had him bent anon." **1335 it,** omitted in G and Th. **1339 syt,** Th reads "sytteth." **1359 gret,** G reads "of gret."

Ther weren, if men hadde nede,
Through the gardyn in length and brede°.
Ther was eke wexyng° many a spyce,
As clow-gylofre° and lycoryce,
Gingere and greyn de paradys°,
Canell° and setewale° of prys°,
And many a spyce delytable
To eeten whan men ryse fro table.
  And many homely° trees ther were
That peches°, coynes°, and apples bere,
Medlers°, plommes, peeres, chesteynis°,
Cheryse°, of whiche many one fayn is°,
Notes°, aleys°, and bolas°,
That for to sene it was solas°;
With many hygh laurer° and pyne
Was renged clene° al that gardyne;
With cipres° and with olyveris°,
Of which that nygh no plente° here is.
Ther were elmes greate and stronge,
Maples, asshe, oke, asp°, planes longe°,
Fyne ewe°, popler, and lindes° fayre,
And othere trees ful many a payre.
  What° shulde I tel you more of it?
Ther were so many trees yit,
That I shulde al encombred be
Er I had rekened every tree.
  These trees were set, that I devyse°,
One from another in assyse°
Fyve fadome° or sixe, I trowe so°.
But they were hye° and great also,
And for to kepe out wel the sonne
The croppes were° so thicke yronne°,
And every braunche in other knytte,
And ful of grene leves sytte°,
That sonne myght there none descende
Lest it° the tendre grasses shende°.
Ther myghte men does and roes yse°,
And of squyrels ful great plente ANIMALS
From bowe to bowe alway lepynge.
Conies° ther were also playynge,
That comyn out of her claperes°,
Of sondrie° colours and maneres,
And maden many a tourneying°
Upon the fresshe grasse sprynging.
  In places sawe I welles° there, SPRINGS
In whiche ther no frogges were,
And fayre in shadowe was every wel.
But I ne can the nombre tel
Of stremys smal that by devyse°
Myrthe had don° come through condyse°,
Of which the water in renning
Gan make a noyse ful lyking°.
  About the brinkes of these welles,
And by the stremes over al elles,
Sprange up the grasse as thicke yset
And softe as any velvet,
On which men myghte his lemman° ley
As on a fetherbed to pley,
For the erthe was ful softe and swete.
Through moisture of the welle wete
Spronge up the sote° grene gras
As fayre, as thicke, as myster was°.
But moche amended° it the place
That th'erthe was of suche a grace
That it of floures hath plente,
That both in somer and wynter be.
  Ther sprang the violet al newe, FLOWERS
And fresshe pervynke°, riche of hewe,
And floures yelowe, white, and rede;
Suche plente grewe there never in mede°.
Ful gaye was al the grounde, and queynt°,
And poudred as° men had it peynt°
With many a fresshe and sondrie° flour,
That casten up ful good savour°.
  I wol nat longe holde you in fable°
Of al this garden dilitable.
I mote my tonge stynten nede°,
For I ne maye, withouten drede°,

1366 brede, *breadth* **1367 eke wexyng,** *also growing* **1368 clow-gylofre,** *clove* **1369 greyn de paradys,** *cardamom* **1370 Canell,** *cinnamon,* **setewale,** *zedoary,* **prys,** *value* **1373 homely,** *familiar* **1374 peches,** *peaches,* **coynes,** *quinces* **1375 Medlars,** *pears,* **chesteynis,** *chestnuts* **1376 Cheryse,** *cherries,* **many one fayn is,** *many* (people) *are pleased* **1377 Notes,** *nuts,* **aleys,** *serviceberries,* **bolas,** *plums* **1378 solas,** *pleasure* **1378 laurer,** *laurel* **1380 renged clene,** *completely surrounded* **1381 cipres,** *cypress,* **olyveris,** *olive trees* **1382 nygh no plente,** *nearly no abundance* **1384 asp,** *aspen,* **planes longe,** *tall plane trees* **1385 ewe,** *yew,* **lindes,** *lindens* **1387 What,** *why* **1391 devyse,** *describe* **1392 assyse,** *position* **1393 fadome,** *fathoms* (about six feet each), **I trowe so,** *so I believe* **1394 hye,** *high* **1396 croppes were,** *foliage was,* **yronne,** *grown* **1398 sytte,** *set* **1400 Lest it,** *so that it would not,* **shende,** *destroy* **1401 does and roes yse,** *see female deer* (two kinds) **1404 Conies,** *rabbits* **1405 claperes,** *warrens* **1406 sondrie,** *various* **1407 tourneying,** *tournament* **1409 welles,** *springs* **1413 devyse,** *design* **1414 had don,** *caused to,* **condyse,** *conduits* **1416 lyking,** *pleasing* **1421 lemman,** *sweetheart* **1425 sote,** *sweet* **1426 myster was,** *was necessary* **1427 moche amended,** *much improved* **1432 pervynke,** *periwinkle* **1434 mede,** *meadow* **1435 queynt,** *pleasing* **1436 poudred as,** *adorned as if,* **peynt,** *painted* **1437 sondrie,** *various* **1438 savour,** *smell* **1439 holde you in fable,** i.e., *detain you with description* **1441 mote . . . stynten nede,** *must necessarily stop* **1442 withouten drede,** *without doubt*

1365 weren, G reads "wexen." **1369 paradys,** G and Th read "parys"; the French is *paradis.* **1387–1422** Lines lacking in G; two leaves missing. **1400 it,** omitted in Th.

Naught tellen you the beaute al,
Ne halfe the bounte° therewithal.
  I went on right honde and on lefte
About the place; it was nat lefte°,
Tyl I had al the garden bene,
In the estres° that men myght sene.
And thus while I wente in my playe,
The God of Love me folowed aye°,
Right° as an hunter can abyde°
The beest, tyl he seeth his tyde°
To shoten at good mes° to the dere,
Whan that hym nedeth go no nere°.
  And so befyl°, I rested me
Besydes a wel, under a tree,
Whiche tree in Fraunce men cal a pyne.
But sithe° the tyme of Kyng Pepyne,
Ne grewe there tree in mannes syght
So fayre, ne so wel woxe° in hight;
In al that yarde so high was none.
And springyng in° a marble stone
Had Nature set, the sothe° to tel,
Under that pyne tree a wel°.
And on the border al without
Was written in the stone about
Letters smal that sayden thus,
"Here starf° the fayre Narcisus."
  Narcisus was a bachelere° NARCISUS
That Love had caught in his dangere°,
And in his nette gan hym so strayne°,
And dyd° him so to wepe and playne°,
That nede him must° his lyfe forgo.
For a fayre lady that hight° Echo
Him loved over any creature,
And gan for hym suche payne endure
That on a tyme she him tolde
That if he her loven nolde°,
That her behoved nedes dye°;
There laye none other remedy.
  But nathelesse for his beaute
So feirs° and daungerous° was he
That he nolde graunten her askyng,
For wepyng ne for fayre prayeng.
And whan she herde hym werne° her so,
She had in herte so great wo,
And toke it in so great dispyte°,
That she withoute more respyte°
Was deed anon. But er she deyde,
Ful pitously to God she prayde
That proude herted Narcisus,
That was in love so daungerous,
Mighte on a day ben hampred° so
For love, and ben so hot for wo,
That never he myghte to joye attayne;
Than shulde he fele in every vayne
What sorowe trewe lovers maken
That ben so vilaynously° forsaken.
  This prayer was but resonable;
Therefor God held it ferme and stable.
For Narcisus, shortly to tel,
By aventure° came to that wel
To rest him in the shadowing°,
A day whan he come from hunting.
This Narcisus had suffred paynes
For renning al day in the playnes,
And was for thurst in great distresse,
Of hete and of his werynesse
That had his brethe almost benomen°.
Whan he was to that wel ycomen,
That shadowed was with braunches grene,
He thoughte of thilke° water shene°
To drinke and fresshe° him wel withal.
And downe on knees he gan to fal°,
And forth his necke and heed outstraught
To drynke of that wel a draught.
And in the water anon was sene
His nose, his mouth, his eyen shene.
And he therof was al abasshed°;
His owne shadowe had him betrasshed°.
For wel wende° he the forme se
Of a chyld of great beaute.

1444 bounte, *graciousness* **1446 it was nat lefte,** i.e., *I did not cease* **1448 estres,** *inner parts* **1450 aye,** *constantly* **1452 Right,** *just,* **abyde,** *await* **1452 tyde,** *time* **1453 at good mes,** *from a good position* **1454 nere,** *nearer* **1455 befyl,** *it happened* **1458 sithe,** *since* **1460 woxe,** *grown* **1462 in,** *from* **1463 sothe,** *truth* **1464 wel,** *spring* **1468 starf,** *died* **1469 bachelere,** *young man* **1470 dangere,** *power* **1471 strayne,** *constrain* **1472 dyd,** *made,* **playne,** *lament* **1473 nede him must,** *he necessarily had to* **1474 hight,** *was named* **1478 nolde,** *would not* **1479 her behoved nedes dye,** *she necessarily had to die* **1482 feirs,** *cruel,* **daungerous,** *disdainful* **1485 werne,** *reject* **1487 dispyte,** *offense* **1488 respyte,** *delay* **1493 hampred,** *captivated* **1498 vilaynously,** *basely* **1502 aventure,** *chance* **1503 shadowing,** *shade* **1509 benomen,** *taken away* **1512 of thilke,** *from that,* **shene,** *shining* **1513 fresshe,** *refresh* **1514 gan to fal,** *fell* **1519 abasshed,** *disconcerted* **1520 betrasshed,** *betrayed* **1521 wende,** *thought*

1447 al, G reads "in al." **1458 Kyng Pepyne,** Pepin (714–68 C.E.); father of Charlemagne. **1468 Narcisus,** Narcissus fell in love with his own reflection; Ovid, *Metamorphoses* 3.356–503, summarized here. **1485 her,** omitted in G. **1496 Than shulde he,** G reads "And that he shulde." **1503 the,** G reads "that." **1508 hete,** Th reads "herte"; the French in *chaut.* **1515 outstraught,** G reads "he straught." **1520 had,** G reads "was."

Wel couthe° Love him wreke tho°
Of daunger° and of pride also,
That Narcisus somtyme him bere.
He quytte° him wel his guerdon° there.
For he musede° so in the well,
That shortely the sothe° to tell,
He loved his owne shadowe° so
That at laste he starf° for wo.
For whan he sawe that he his wyll°
Might in no maner way fulfyll,
And that he was so faste caught
That he him couthe° comfort naught,
He loste his wytte right in that place
And deyde within a lytell space.
And thus his warysoun° he toke
For the lady that he forsoke.
Ladyes, I praye ensample taketh,
Ye that ayenst your love mistaketh°,
For if her dethe be you to wyte°,
God can ful wel your whyle quyte°.
Whan that this lettre of whiche I tell
Had taught me that it was the well
Of Narcisus in his beaute,
I gan anon withdrawe me,
Whan it fell in my remembraunce
That him betyd° suche mischaunce°.
But at the laste than thoughte I
That scatheles°, ful sykerly°,
I myghte unto the welle go. HER EYES
Wherof° shulde I abasshen° so?
Unto the welle than went I me,
And down I louted° for to se
The clere water in the stone,
And eke° the gravel which that shone
Downe in the botome as sylver fyne,
For of the welle this is the fyne°:
In world is none so clere of hewe.
The water is ever fresshe and newe
That welmeth° up with wawes° bright
The mountenaunce° of two fynger hight°.
Abouten it is grasse springing,
For moyste° so thycke and wel lyking
That it ne may in wynter dye
No more than may the see be drye.
Down at the botome set sawe I
Two cristall stones craftely°
In thilke° fresshe and fayre well.
But o thyng sothly dar I tell,
That ye wol holde a great mervayle
Whan it is told, withouten fayle.
For whan the sonne clere in syght
Cast in that welle his bemes bright,
And that the heet discended is,
Than taketh° the Cristall stone, ywis°,
Agayne° the sonne an hundred hewes,
Blewe, yelowe, and reed, that fressh and newe is.
Yet hath the mervaylous cristall
Suche strength that the place over all,
Bothe flour and tree and leves grene
And al the yerd in it is sene.
And for to don° you to understonde,
To make ensample wol I fonde°:
Right° as a myrrour openly
Sheweth al thyng that stant therby,
As wel the colour as the fygure°,
Withouten any coverture°,
Right so the cristal stone shyning,
Withouten any disceyving,
The estrees° of the yerde accuseth°
To him that in° the water museth°;
For ever°, in whiche° half that he be,
He may wel half the gardyn se,
And if he turne, he may right wel
Sen° the remenaunt everydel.
For ther is none so lytel thing
So hydde°, ne closed with shytting°,
That it ne is sen as though it were
Paynted in the cristall there.
This is the myrrour perilous
In which the proude Narcisus

1523 couthe, *could,* **him wreke tho,** *avenge himself then* **1524 Of daunger,** *for disdain* **1526 quytte,** *repaid,* **guerdon,** *reward* **1527 musede,** *pondered* **1528 sothe,** *truth* **1529 shadowe,** *reflection* **1530 starf,** *died* **1531 wyll,** *desire* **1534 couthe,** *could* **1537 warysoun,** *payment* **1540 mistaketh,** *do wrong* **1541 wyte,** *blame* **1542 your whyle quyte,** *repay you* **1548 him betyd,** *to him happened,* **mischaunce,** *misfortune* **1550 scatheles,** *without harm,* **sykerly,** *certainly* **1552 Wherof,** *why,* **abasshen,** *be upset* **1554 louted,** *bent* **1556 eke,** *also* **1558 fyne,** *point* **1561 welmeth,** *swells,* **wawes,** *waves* **1562 mountenaunce,** *amount,* **hight,** *height* **1564 For moyste,** *because of moisture* **1568 craftely,** *skillfully* **1569 thilke,** *that* **1576 taketh,** *reflect,* **ywis,** *truly* **1577 Agayne,** *toward* **1583 don,** *help* **1584 fonde,** *try* **1585 Right,** *just* **1587 fygure,** *form* **1588 coverture,** *concealment* **1591 estrees,** *interior,* **accuseth,** *reveals* **1592 in,** *into,* **museth,** *stares* **1593 ever,** *always,* **whiche,** *whichever* **1596 Sen,** *see* **1598 hydde,** *hidden,* **shytting,** *shutting*

1528 the sothe, G reads "all the sothe." **1553** Line lacking in G. **1568 Two cristall stones,** these have been taken to be the eyes of the beloved (and/or of the lover), the means whereby love (and/or self-love) enters the heart. **1581 flour,** G and Th read "foule"; the French is *flors.* **1586 stant,** G and Th read "stondeth." **1591 estrees,** G and Th read "entrees"; the French is *l'estre.* **1593–94 he . . . / He,** G and Th read "ye . . . / Ye."

Sey° al his fayre face bright,
That made him sith° to lye upright°.
For whoso loke in that myrrour,
There may nothyng ben his socour°
That he ne shal there se somthing
That shal him lede into loving.
Ful many a worthy man hath it
Yblent°, for folke of greatest wyt
Ben soone caught here and awayted°;
Withouten respyt° ben they bayted°.
Here cometh to folk of newe rage°;
Here chaungeth many wight corage°;
Here lyth no rede° ne wytte° therto;
For Venus sone°, Daun Cupido°,
Hath sowen there of love the sede°,
That help ne lyth° there none, ne rede,
So cercleth it the welle aboute.
His gynnes° hath he set withoute
Right for to cacche in his panteres°
These damosels and bacheleres;
Love wyl none other byrde catche
Though he set eyther nette or latche°.
And for° the sede that here was sowen,
This welle is cleped°, as wel is knowen,
The Welle of Love, of verray right°,
Of which ther hath ful many a wight°
Spoke in bokes dyversely.
But they shul never so verily°
Discripcion of the welle here°,
Ne eke the sothe° of this matere,
As ye shul, whan I have undo°
The crafte that hir bylongeth to°.
  Allway me lyked for to dwell
To sene the christall in the well
That shewed me ful openly
A thousand thynges faste° by.
But I may say, in sory houre
Stod I to loken or to powre°,
For sythen° have I sore syked°;
That myrrour hath me nowe entryked°.
But had I first knowen in my wyt
The vertue and the strengthe of it,
I nolde not° have mused there;
Me hadde bet° ben elleswhere.
For in the snare I fell anone
That hath bytraisshed° many one.
  In thylke° myrrour sawe I tho°,
Amonge a thousand thynges mo,
A roser° charged° ful of roses,
That with an hedge aboute enclos is.

THE ROSE GARDEN

Tho had I suche lust° and envye,
That for Parys° ne for Pavye°
Nolde I have left to gone and se
Ther° greatest heape° of roses be.
When I was with this rage hent°,
That caught hath many a man and shent°,
Toward the roser gan I go.
And whan I was not ferre therfro,
The savour of the roses swote°
Me smote right to the herte rote,
As° I had al enbaumed° be.
And if I ne had endouted me°
To have ben hated or assayled°,
My thankes°, wol I not have fayled
To pull a rose of al that route°
To beren in myn honde aboute,
And smellen to it wher° I wente,
But ever I dredde me° to repente°
And leste it° greved° or forthought°
The lorde that thilke° gardyn wrought°.
Of roses ther were great wone°,
So fayre ware° never in rone°.
Of knoppes clos° some sawe I there;

1603 Sey, *saw* **1604 sith,** *after,* **lye upright,** *lie face upwards* (i.e., dead) **1606 socour,** *aid* **1610 Yblent,** *blinded* **1611 awayted,** *ambushed* **1612 respyt,** *relief,* **bayted,** *tormented* **1613 of newe rage,** *previously unknown passion* **1614 many wight corage,** *the hearts of many people* **1615 rede,** *wisdom,* **wytte,** *reason* **1616 Venus sone,** *Venus' son,* **Daun Cupido,** *Master Cupid* **1617 sede,** *seed* **1618 help ne lyth,** *no help lies* **1620 gynnes,** *traps* **1621 panteres,** *nets* **1624 latche,** *snare* **1625 for,** *because of* **1625 cleped,** *called* **1627 of verray right,** *quite rightly* **1628 wight,** *person* **1630 verily,** *truly* **1631 here,** *hear* **1632 eke the sothe,** *also the truth* **1633 undo,** *revealed* **1634 bylongeth to,** *pertains* **1638 faste,** *near* **1640 powre,** *pore* **1641 sythen,** *since then,* **sore syked,** *sighed sorely* **1642 entrycked,** *entrapped* **1645 nolde not,** *would never* **1646 Me hadde bet,** *I had better* **1648 bytraisshed,** *betrayed* **1649 thylke,** *that,* **tho,** *then* **1651 roser,** *rosebush,* **charged,** *loaded* **1653 lust,** *desire* **1654 Parys,** *Paris,* **Pavye,** *Pavia* (north Italy) **1656 Ther,** *where,* **heape,** *quantity* **1657 rage hent,** *passion seized* **1658 shent,** *destroyed* **1661 savour,** *smell,* **swote,** *sweet* **1663 As,** *as if,* **enbaumed,** *embalmed* **1664 endouted me,** *feared* **1665 assayled,** *attacked* **1666 My thankes,** *thankfully* **1667 route,** *group* **1669 wher,** *wherever* **1670 dredde me,** *feared,* **repente,** *to regret* (it) **1671 And leste it,** *for fear that it* **greved,** *offended,* **forthought,** *displeased* **1672 thilke,** *that,* **wrought,** *made* **1673 wone,** *quantity* **1674 ware,** *were,* **rone,** *bush* **1675 knoppes clos,** *closed buds*

1603 fayre face, G reads "face fayre and." **1608 loving,** G and Th read "laughyng"; the French is *d'amors.* **1609 a,** omitted in G. **1611 awayted,** Th reads "wayted." **1641 have,** omitted in G and Th. **1644 vertue,** G reads "vertues." **and the strengthe,** G and Th read "and the strengthes" **1652 enclos,** G reads "enclosed." **1655 and,** G reads "att." **1663 be,** G and Th read "me." **1666 My,** G reads "Me." **1674 ware,** G reads "waxe." **1675 knoppes,** see 1721n.

And some wel better woxen° were;
And some ther been of other moyson°
That drowe nygh° to her seson,
And spedde hem faste for to sprede°.
I love wel suche roses rede,
For brode roses, and open also,
Ben passed° in a day or two,
But knoppes° wyl al fresshe be
Two dayes at leest, or els thre.
The knoppes greatly lyked° me,
For fayrer may ther no man se.
Whoso mighte have one of all,
It oughte him ben ful leef withall°.
Mighte I a gerlond of hem geten,
For no richesse I wold it leten°.

THE ROSEBUD

Among the knoppes I chese° one
So fayr that of the remenaunt none
Ne preyse I half so wel as it,
Whan I avyse° it in my wyt.
For it so wel was enlumyned°
With colour reed, as wel yfyned°
As Nature couthe° it make fayre.
And it hath leves wel foure payre
That Kynde° hath set through his knowing
Aboute the redde roses sprynging.
The stalke was as rysshe right°,
And theron stode the knoppe upright
That it ne bowed upon no syde.
The swote° smell sprong so wyde
That it dyed° al the place aboute...

FRAGMENT B

When I had smelled the savour° swote,
No wyl had I fro thence yet go,
But somdele nere° it went I tho°
To take it; but myn honde, for drede,
Ne durste° I to the rose bede°,
For thystels sharpe, of many maners,
Netles, thornes, and hoked briers;
For moche they distourbled me,
For sore I dradde to harmed be.
The God of Love, with bowe bent,
That al day set had his talent°
To pursuen and to spyen me,
Was stondyng by a fygge-tree.
And whan he sawe howe that I
Had chosen so ententifly°
The bothum°, more unto my paye°
Than any other that I say°,

THE DREAMER PIERCED BY BEAUTY

He toke an arowe ful sharply whette°,
And in his bowe whan it was sette,
He streight up to his eere drough°
The stronge bowe, that was so tough,
And shotte at me so wonder smerte°
That through myn eye unto myn herte
The takel° smote, and depe it wente.
And therwithal° suche colde me hente°
That under clothes warme and softe
Sythen° that day I have chyvered° ofte.
When I was hurte thus in a stounde°,
I fell downe platte° unto the grounde.
Myn herte fayled and faynted aye°,
And longe tyme aswoune° I laye.
But whan I came out of swounyng,
And had wytte, and my felyng,
I was al mate°, and wende° ful wele
Of bloode have lorne° a ful great dele.

1676 woxen, *grown* **1677 moyson,** size **1678 drowe nygh,** *drew close* **1679 sprede,** *open* **1682 Ben passed,** *are gone* **1683 knoppes,** *buds* **1685 lyked,** *pleased* **1688 him ben ful leef withall,** *to him be very dear indeed* **1690 leten,** *give up* **1691 chese,** *chose* **1694 avyse,** *consider* **1695 enlumyned,** *illuminated* **1696 yfyned,** *finished* **1697 couthe,** *could* **1699 Kynde,** *Nature* **1701 as rysshe right,** *straight as a rush* **1704 swote,** *sweet* **1705 dyed,** *infused* **1706 savour,** *odor* **1708 somdele nere,** *somewhat nearer,* **tho,** *then* **1710 durste,** *dared,* **bede,** *offer* **1716 talent,** *desire* **1720 ententifly,** *attentively* **1721 bothum** *bud,* **paye,** *liking* **1722 say,** *saw* **1723 whette** *whetted* **1725 drough,** *drew* **1727 smerte,** *briskly* **1729 takel,** *arrow* **1730 therwithal,** *as a result,* **me hente,** *seized me* **1732 Sythen,** *since,* **chyvered,** *shivered* **1733 stounde,** *moment* **1734 platte,** *flat* **1735 aye,** *forever* **1736 aswoune,** *in a swoon* **1739 mate,** *exhausted,* **wende,** *thought* **1740 have lorne,** *to have lost*

1683 al, omitted in G and Th; the French has *tuit.* **1684 at,** G reads "atte." **1689 a,** omitted in G and Th. **1694 it,** omitted in G and Th. **1696 yfyned,** G and Th read "fyned." **1705 dyed,** G reads "dide." **1705a Fragment B,** there is no rubric and no indication of a change in translator or copy text in G or in Th. For discussion of the fragments, see the Introduction. **1717 pursuen,** Th reads "pursue." **1721 bothum,** G reads "botoun" with variant spellings throughout. One principal evidence of different translators for parts A and B is that B uses *bothum* forms to translate the French *bouton,* while A uses *knoppe;* see 1675, 1685, and 1702. **1727 shotte,** G reads "shette" throughout. **1728 through myn eye,** the passing of Love's arrow through the eye to the heart of the lover is a common figure. G reads "through me nye." **1733 a,** omitted in G and Th. **1736 aswoune,** Th reads "in swoune."

But certes, the arowe that in me stoode
Of me ne drewe no droppe of bloode,
For-why° I founde my woundes al drey.
Than toke I with myn hondes twey°
The arrowe, and ful faste it out-plyght°,
And in the pullyng sore I syght°.
So at the laste the shafte of tree°
I drough° out with the fethers thre,
But yet the hoked heed, ywis°,
The whiche Beaute called is,
Gan so depe in myn herte pace°
That I it might not arace°;
But in myn hert styl it stoode,
Al° bledde I not a droppe of bloode.
I was bothe anguysshous° and trouble°
For the peryll that I sawe double:
I nyste° what to say or do,
Ne get a leche° my woundes to;
For neyther through grasse ne rote°
Ne had I helpe of hope ne bote°.
But to the bothum° evermo
Myn herte drewe; for al my wo,
My thought was in none other thyng.
For had it ben in my kepyng°,
It wolde have brought my lyfe agayne.
For certes evenly°, I dare wel sayne°,
The sight onely, and the savoure,
Alegged° moche of my langoure°.
  Than gan I for to drawe me
Towarde the bothom fayre to se;
And Love had get him, in his throwe°,
Another arowe into his bowe,
And for to shote gan hym dresse°—
The arowes name was THE ARROW
  Symplesse. SIMPLICITY
And whan that Love gan nygh me nere°,
He drowe it up, withouten were°,
And shotte at me with al his myght,
So that this arowe anon right°
Throughout myn eygh°, as it was founde°
Into myn herte hath made a wounde.
Than I anon dyd al my crafte
For to drawen out the shafte,
And therewithal I syghed efte°,
But in myn herte the heed was lefte,
Whiche aye° encresed my desyre.
Unto the bothom drowe I nere;
And evermo that me was wo,
The more desyre had I to go
Unto the roser°, where that grewe
The fresshe bothom so bright of hewe.
Better me were to have letten be,
But it behoved nede° me
To don right as myn herte badde:
For ever the body muste be ladde
After the herte; in wele° and wo,
Of force° togyder they muste go.
But never this archer wolde fyne°
To shote at me with al his pyne°,
And for to make me to him mete°.
The thirde arowe he gan to shete°,
Whan best his tyme he myght espye,
The whiche was named THE ARROW
  Curtesye, COURTESY
Into myn herte it dyd avale°;
Aswoune° I fel, bothe deed° and pale;
Longe tyme I lay and styrred nought,
Tyl I abrayde° out of my thought.
And faste than° I avysed me°
To drawe out the shafte of tree°,
But ever the heed was lefte behynde
For aught I couthe° pull or wynde°.
  So sore it stycked whan I was hytte
That by no crafte I myght it flytte°,
But anguysshous and ful of thought,
I felte suche wo my wounde aye wrought,
That somoned° me alway to go
Towarde the rose that plesed me so;
But I ne durste° in no manere,
Bycause the archer was so nere.

1743 For-why, *because,* **drey,** *dry* **1744 twey,** *two* **1745 out-plyght,** *plucked out* **1746 syght,** *sighed* **1747 tree,** *wood* **1748 drough,** *drew* **1749 ywis,** *truly* **1751 Gan . . . pace,** *did pass* **1752 arace,** *pull out* **1754 Al,** *although* **1755 anguysshous,** *anxious,* **trouble,** *disturbed* **1757 nyste,** *didn't know* **1758 leche,** *doctor* **1759 grasse ne rote,** *grass nor root* (medicinal herbs) **1760 bote,** *remedy* **1761 bothum,** *bud* **1764 kepyng,** *possession* **1766 For certes evenly,** *surely even,* **sayne,** *say* **1768 Alleged,** *relieved,* **langoure,** *suffering* **1771 throwe,** *moment* **1773 gan hym dresse,** *prepared himself* **1775 gan nygh me nere,** *approached near to me* **1776 were,** *doubt* **1778 anon right,** *immediately* **1779 eygh,** *eye,* **founde,** *fixed* **1783 efte,** *again* **1785 aye,** *constantly* **1789 roser,** *rosebush* **1792 behoved nede,** *required* **1795 wele,** *joy* **1796 Of force,** *necessarily* **1797 fyne,** *cease* **1798 pyne,** *pain* **1799 mete,** *succumb* **1800 shete,** *shoot* **1803 avale,** *penetrate* **1804 Aswoune,** *in a faint,* **deed,** *deathly* **1806 abrayde,** *awakened* **1807 than,** *then,* **avysed me,** *thought* **1808 tree,** *wood* **1810 For aught I couthe,** *despite anything I could do to,* **wynde,** *twist* **1812 flytte,** *escape* **1815 somoned,** *summoned* **1817 ne durste,** *didn't dare*

1749 yet, G reads "atte." **1750 whiche,** G reads "which it." **1757 do,** G reads "to do." **1758 to,** G reads "two." **1779 myn,** omitted in G and Th. **1786 I,** omitted in G. **1806 of,** G reads "on." **1814 felte,** G and Th read "lefte." **1816 plesed me,** the phrase is used in the B and C fragments of *Rom* instead of "lyked me," which recurs in A; see, for example, lines 27, 486, 1312, and 1685.

For evermore gladly, as I rede°,
Brent chylde° of fyre hath moche drede.
And certes yet, for al my peyne,
Though that I sygh° yet arowes reyne°,
And grounde quarels° sharpe of steele,
Ne for no payne that I might fele,
Yet might I not myselfe withholde
The fayre roser to beholde;
For Love me yave° suche hardyment°
For to fulfyll his commaundement.
Upon my fete I rose up than
Feble as a forwounded° man,
And forthe to gon my might I sette°,
And for the archer nolde I lette°.
Towarde the roser faste I drowe°;
But thornes sharpe mo than ynowe°
There were, and also thystels thicke,
And breres°, brimme° for to pricke,
That I ne myght get grace
The roughe thornes for to pace°,
To sene the roses fresshe of hewe.
I muste abyde°, though it me rewe°,
The hedge aboute so thycke was,
That closed the roses in compas°.
But o thyng lyked° me right wele:
I was so nyghe°, I myght fele°
Of the bothom the swote° odoure,
And also se the fresshe coloure;
And that right greatly lyked me,
That I so nere might it se.
Suche joye anon thereof had I,
That I forgate my maladye.
To sene I had suche delyte,
Of sorowe and angre I was al quyte°,
And of my woundes that I had thore°.
For nothyng lyken me myght more
Than dwellen by the roser aye°,
And thence never to passe awaye.
But whan a whyle I had be thare°,
The God of Love, whiche al toshare°
Myn herte with his arowes kene,
Casteth him° to yeve me woundes grene°.
He shotte at me ful hastely°
An arowe named Company,
The whiche takell° is ful able
To make these ladyes merciable.

THE ARROW COMPANY

Than I anon gan chaungen hewe
For grevaunce of my wounde newe,
That I agayne fel in swounyng°,
And syghed sore in complaynyng.
Sore° I complayned that my sore
On me gan greven° more and more.
I had non hope of allegeaunce°,
So nygh I drowe to disperaunce°.
I rought of° dethe ne of lyfe,
Whether° that Love wolde me drife°,
If me a martyr wolde he make.
I myght his power not forsake.
And whyle for anger thus
I woke,

THE ARROW FAIR APPEARANCE

The God of Love an arowe toke;
Ful sharpe it was and pugnaunt°,
And it was called Fayre-Semblaunt,
The whiche in no wyse wol consent°
That any lover hym repente°
To serve his love with herte and all,
For any peryll that may befall.
But though this arowe was kene grounde°
As any rasour that is founde,
To cutte and kerve°, at the poynte
The God of Love it had anoynt°
With a precious oyntment,
Somdele to yeve alegement°
Upon the woundes that he hade
Through the body in my herte made,
To helpe her° sores, and to cure,
And that they may the bette endure.
But yet this arowe, without more,
Made in myn herte a large sore,
That in ful great payne I abode°.

1819 rede, *understand* **1820 Brent chylde,** (the) *burned child* **1822 Though that I sygh,** *even if I saw,* **reyne,** *rain down* **1823 grounde quarels,** *sharpened crossbow bolts* **1827 yave,** *gave,* **hardyment,** *courage* **1830 forwounded,** *seriously wounded* **1831 my might I sette,** *I made an effort* **1832 nolde I lette,** *I would not hesitate* **1833 faste I drowe,** *I drew near* **1834 ynowe,** *enough* **1836 breres,** *briars,* **brimme,** *cruel* **1838 pace,** *pass* **1840 abyde,** *wait,* **it me rewe,** *I regretted it* **1842 in compas,** *all around* **1843 lyked,** *pleased* **1844 nyghe,** *near,* **fele,** *perceive* **1845 swote,** *sweet* **1852 quyte,** *repaid* **1853 thore,** *there* **1855 aye,** *forever* **1857 be thare,** *been there* **1858 toshare,** *sliced* **1860 Casteth him,** *prepared himself,* **grene,** *fresh* **1861 hastely,** *quickly* **1863 The whiche takell,** *the arrow which* **1867 swounyng,** *fainting* **1869 Sore,** *sorely* **1870 gan greven,** *did hurt* **1871 allegeaunce,** *alleviation* **1872 disperaunce,** *despair* **1873 rought of,** *cared for* **1874 Whether,** *wherever,* **drife,** *drive* **1880 pugnaunt,** *piercing* **1881 consent,** *allow* **1882 hym repente,** *regret* **1885 kene grounde,** *keenly sharpened* **1887 kerve,** *pierce* **1888 anoynt,** *anointed* **1890 Somdele,** *somewhat,* **alegement,** *alleviation* **1893 her,** *their* **1897 abode,** *remained*

1820 Proverbial; RR has a related proverb about scalding water. **1831 my,** omitted in G and Th. **1853-54 thore...more,** the rhyme is not found in Chaucer, and *thore* is very unusual, perhaps a corruption or a forced rhyme. **1857 thare,** a northern dialect form of *there.* **1892** Line lacking in G, although space is left where a later hand added "That he hadde the body hole made"; see 1984n.

But aye the oyntement went abrode°;
Throughout my wounds large and wyde
It spredde aboute in every syde,
Thorough whose vertue and whose myght
Myn herte joyful was and lyght.
I had ben° deed and al toshent°
But° for the precious oyntment.
The shafte I drowe out of the arowe,
Rokyng for wo right wonder narowe°,
But the heed, whiche made me smerte,
Lefte behynde in myn herte
With other foure, I dare wel say,
That never wol be take° away.
But the oyntment halpe° me wele.
And yet suche sorowe dyd I fele
That al day I chaunged hewe°,
Of my woundes fresshe and newe,
As men might se in my vysage.
The arowes were so ful of rage°,
So varyaunt of diversyte°
That men in everyche might se
Bothe great anoye° and eke swetnesse,
And joye meynt° with bytternesse.
Nowe were they easy, nowe were they wood°.
In hem I felte bothe harme and good.
Nowe sore without aleggement°,
Nowe softyng with oyntment;
It softned here, and pricketh there.
Thus ease and anger togyther were.

LOVE CLAIMS HIS VICTIM

The God of Love delyverly°
Come lepande° to me hastely,
And sayd to me, in great rape°,
"Yelde the, for thou may not escape!
May no defence avayle the here°;
Therfore I rede° make no daungere°.
If thou wolte yelde the hastely,
Thou shalt the rather have mercy.
He is a foole in sykernesse°
That with daunger or stoutnesse°
Rebelleth there° that he shulde plese;
In suche folye is lytel ese.
Be meke where thou muste nedes bowe;
To stryve ayen is nought thy prowe°.
Come at ones, and have ydo°,
For I wol that it be so.
Than yelde the here debonairly°."

And I answered ful humbly,
"Gladly, sir, at your byddyng.
I wol me yelde in al thyng.
To your servyce I wol me take.
For God defende that I shulde make
Ayen° your byddyng resystence;
I wol not don so great offence,
For if I dyd, it were no skyll°.
Ye may do with me what ye wyll,
Save or spyll°, and also slo°,
Fro° you in no wyse may I go.
My lyfe, my dethe, is in your honde;
I may not laste out of your bonde°.
Playne° at your lyste° I yelde me,
Hopyng in herte that somtyme ye
Comforte and ese shul me sende,
Or els, shortly, this is the ende.
Withouten helthe I mote aye dure°,
But if° ye take me to your cure°.
Comforte or helthe howe shulde I have,
Sythe° ye me hurte, but° ye me save?
The helthe of lovers mote be founde
Where as they token first her wounde.
And if ye lyst of me to make
Your prisoner, I wol it take
Of herte and wyll, fully at gre°.
Holy and playne° I yelde me,
Without feynyng or feyntyse°,
To be governed by your emprise°.
Of you I here so moche price°,
I wol ben hole at your devyce°
For to fulfyll your lykyng
And repente° for nothyng,
Hopyng to have yet in some tyde°

1898 aye, *constantly,* **went abrode,** *spread* **1903 had ben,** *would have been,* **toshent,** *destroyed* **1904 But,** *except* **1906 Rokyng for wo right wonder narowe,** *rocking it very slightly because of the pain* **1910 take,** *taken* **1911 halpe,** *helped* **1913 hewe,** *color* **1916 rage,** *intensity* **1917 varyaunt of diversyte,** *changeable of kind* **1919 anoye,** *affliction* **1920 meynt,** *mixed* **1921 wood,** *mad* **1923 aleggement,** *alleviation* **1927 delyverly,** *nimbly* **1928 lepande,** *leaping* **1929 rape,** *haste* **1931 avayle the here,** *help you here* **1932 rede,** *advise,* **daungere,** *resistance* **1935 in sykernesse,** *surely* **1936 stoutnesse,** *pride* **1937 there,** *where* **1940 ayen is nought thy prowe,** *against* (love) *is not to your advantage* **1941 have ydo,** *have done* (i.e., hurry) **1943 debonairly,** *meekly* **1949 Ayen,** *against* **1951 no skyll,** *not appropriate* **1953 spyll,** *destroy,* **slo,** *slay* **1954 Fro,** *from* **1956 bonde,** *control* **1957 Playne,** *openly,* **lyste,** *desire* **1961 mote aye dure,** *must always endure* **1962 But if,** *unless,* **cure,** *care* **1964 Sythe,** *since,* **but,** *unless* **1969 at gre,** *willingly* **1970 Holy and playne,** *completely and openly* **1971 feynyng or feyntyse,** *pretence or delay* **1972 emprise,** *purpose* **1973 price,** *renown* **1974 hole,** *wholly,* **devyce,** *discretion* **1976 repente,** *regret* **1977 tyde,** *time*

1928 lepande, the *-ande* ending is a northern form, also found at 2263, 2708–09, 3138, 5363. **1929 rape,** Th reads "jape" (joke). **1934 the,** omitted in G and Th. **1965 lovers,** G and Th read "love."

Mercy; of that I abyde°."
And with that covenaunt yelde° I me
Anon°, downe knelyng upon my kne,
Proferyng° for to kysse his fete.
  But for nothyng he wolde me lete,
And sayd, "I love the bothe and preise,
Sens° that thyn answer dothe me ese,
For thou answered so curtesly.
For nowe I wote° wel utterly
That thou arte gentyl, by thy speche.
For though a man ferre wolde seche,
He shulde not fynden, in certayne,
No suche answere of no vilayne°.
For suche a worde ne myght nought
Isse out of a vylayns thought.
Thou shalt not lesen of° thy speche,
For to thy helpyng woll I eche°,
And eke encresen that I maye.
But first I wol that thou obaye
Fully, for thyn avauntage,
Anon to do me here homage.
And sythe° kysse thou shalte my mouthe,
Whiche to no vilayne was never couthe°
For to aproche it, ne for to touche;
For saufe of cherles I ne vouche°
That they shal never neigh it nere°.
For curteys, and of fayre manere,
Wel taught, and ful of gentylnysse
He muste ben that shal me kysse,
And also of ful hygh fraunchyse°,
That shal atteyne to that emprise°.
And first of o thyng warne I the,
That payne and great adversyte
He mote° endure, and eke travayle°,
That shal me serve, without fayle.
But there agaynst, the to comforte,
And with thy servyce to disporte°,
Thou mayst ful glad and joyful be
So good a mayster to have as me,
And lorde of so hygh renoun.
I beare of Love the gonfenoun°,
Of Curtesy the banere.
For I am of the selfe° manere,
Gentyll, curteys, meke, and fre°,
That whoever ententyfe° be
Me to honoure, doute°, and serve,
And also that he hym observe
Fro° trespace and fro vilanye,
And hym governe in curtesye
With wyll and with entencion.
For whan he first in my prison
Is caught, than muste he utterly,
Fro thence forthe ful besyly,
Caste hym gentyll for to be,
If he desyre helpe of me."
  Anon without more delay,
Withouten daunger or affray°,
I become his man anone,
And gave hym thankes many a one,
And kneled downe with hondes joynt°,
And made it in my port ful queynt°;
The joye went to my hert rote°.
Whan I had kyssed his mouthe so
    swote°,
I had suche myrthe and suche lykyng,
It cured me of languysshyng°.
He asked of me than° hostages:
"I have," he sayd, "taken fele° homages
Of one and other, where I have bene
Disceyved ofte, withouten wene°.
These felons, ful of falsyte,
Have many sythes° begyled me,
And through falshede her luste acheved,
Whereof I repent and am agreved.
And° I hem get in my daungere°,
Her falshede shul they bye° ful dere.
But for° I love the, I say° the playne,
I wol of the be more certayne;
For the so sore I wol nowe bynde
That thou away ne shalt not wynde°
For to denyen the covenaunt,
Or done that° is not avenaunt°.

THE DREAMER BECOMES A LOVER

1978 abyde, *await* **1979 yelde,** *yielded* **1980 Anon,** *immediately* **1981 Proferyng,** *stretching* **1984 Sens,** *since* **1986 wote,** *know* **1990 vilayne,** *lowborn person* **1993 lesen of,** *lose by* **1994 eche,** *add* **1999 sythe,** *after* **2000 couthe,** *known* **2002 saufe of cherles I ne vouche,** *I do not allow churls* **2003 neigh it nere,** *approach near it* **2007 fraunchyse,** *nobility* **2008 emprise,** *purpose* **2011 mote,** *must,* **eke travayle,** *also suffering* **2014 disporte,** *pleasure* **2018 gonfenoun,** *banner* **2020 selfe,** *same* **2021 fre,** *generous* **2022 ententyfe,** *devoted* **2023 doute,** *respect* **2024-25 hym observe . . . Fro,** *guard against* **2034 daunger or affray,** *delay or fear* **2037 joynt,** *joined* **2038 made it in my port ful queynt,** i.e., *acted with elaborate ceremony* **2039 rote,** *root* **2040 swote,** *sweet* **2042 languysshyng,** *sufferings* **2043 than,** *then* **2044 fele,** *many* **2046 wene,** *doubt* **2048 sythes,** *times* **2051 And,** *and if,* **daungere,** *control* **2052 bye,** *pay for* **2053 for,** *because,* **say,** *tell* **2056 wynde,** *turn* **2058 done that,** *do what,* **avenaunt,** *appropriate*

1982 me, omitted in G. **1984** In G this line is added in a later hand, filling a space; same hand as 1892, 2036, and 3490. **1994 to,** omitted in G and Th. **2036** In G this line is added in a later hand, filling a space; see 1984n. **2037 kneled . . . with hondes joynt,** the traditional posture of homage (and of prayer), kneeling with the hands joined. **2046 Disceyved,** G and Th read "Disteyned"; the French is *deceu* (deceive).

That° thou were false it were great ruthe°,
Sythe° thou semest so ful of truthe."
"Sir, if the lyst° to understande,
I mervayle° the askyng this demande.
For why or wherfore shulde ye
Hostages or borowes° aske of me,
Or any other sykernesse°,
Sythe ye wot, in sothfastnesse°,
That ye me have susprised° so,
And hole° myn herte taken me fro,
That it wol do for me nothyng
But if it be at your byddyng?
Myn herte is yours, and myn right nought,
As it behoveth°, in dede and thought,
Redy in al to worche your wyll,
Whether so it turne to good or yll.
So sore it lusteth° you to plese,
No man thereof may you disese°.
Ye have theron sette such justyse°
That it is werreyed° in many wyse;
And if ye doute it nolde obey,
Ye may therof do make a key°,
And holde it with you for hostage."
"Nowe certes, this is none outrage,"
Quod Love, "and fully I accorde,
For of the body he is ful lorde
That hath the herte in his tresore;
Outrage it were to asken more."
Thann of his aumener° he drough°
A lytel key, fetise° ynough,
Whiche was of golde polysshed clere°,
And sayd to me, "With this key here
Thyne herte to me nowe wol I shette,

THE LOVER'S HEART LOCKED

For al my jowels loke° and knette°
I bynde under this lytel key,
That no wight maye cary awey;
This key is ful of great poeste°."
With whiche anon he touched me
Under the syde ful softely,
That he myne herte sodainly
Without anoye° hadde speered°,
That yet right nought it hath me deered°.
Whan he hadde done his wyl al out,
And I had putte hym out of dout,
"Sir," I sayd, "I have right great wyl
Your luste and pleasure to fulfyl.
Loke ye° my servyce take at gree°,
By thilke° faythe ye owe to me.
I saye nought for recreaundyse°,
For I nought doute° of your servyce;
But the servaunt traveyleth° vayne
That for to serven doth his payne
Unto that lorde whiche in no wyse
Conne° hym no thanke for his servyce."
Love sayde, "Dismay the nought,
Syth° thou for socour° hast me sought.
In thanke thy servyce wol I take,
And highe of degree I wol the make,
If wyckednesse ne hynder the.
But as I hoope, it shal nought be:
To worshyppe° no wight by aventure°
Maye come but if he payne endure.
Abyde and suffre thy distresse
That hurteth nowe. It shal be lesse.
I wotte° myselfe what maye the save,
What medicyne thou woldest have.
And if thy trouthe to me thou kepe,
I shal unto thyne helpyng eke°,
To cure thy woundes and make hem clene
Whereso° they be olde or grene°;
Thou shalte be holpen, at wordes fewe.
For certainly thou shalte wel shewe
Where that thou servest with good wyl
For to accomplysshen and fulfyl
My commaundements, daye and nyght,
Whiche I to lovers yeve of right."
"Ah, sir, for Goddes love," sayd I,
"Er ye passe hens°, ententyfely°
Your commaundements to me ye say,
And I shal kepe hem, if I may,
For hem to kepen is al my thought,

2059 That, *if,* **ruthe,** *pity* **2060 Sythe,** *since* **2061 lyst,** *desire* **2062 mervayle,** *wonder about* **2064 borowes,** *pledges* **2065 sykernesse,** *security* **2066 sothfastnesse,** *truth* **2067 susprised,** *captured* **2068 hole,** *wholly* **2072 behoveth,** *is fitting* **2075 lusteth,** *desires* **2076 disese,** *dispossess* **2077 justyse,** *control* **2078 werreyed,** *beset* **2080 do make a key,** *have a key made* **2087 aumener,** *purse* (alms bag), **drough,** *drew* **2088 fetise,** *elegant* **2089 clere,** *brightly* **2092 loke,** *locked,* **knette,** *knitted up* **2095 poeste,** *power* **2099 anoye,** *pain,* **speered,** *locked* **2100 deered,** *injured* **2105 Loke ye,** *be sure to,* **at gree,** *in pleasure* **2106 thilke,** *that* **2107 recreaundyse,** *cowardice* **2108 nought doute,** *fear nothing* **2109 traveyleth,** *labors* **2112 Conne,** *acknowledges* **2114 Syth,** *since,* **socour,** *aid* **2119 worshyppe,** *honor,* **aventure,** *chance* **2123 wotte,** *know* **2126 eke,** *increase* **2128 Whereso,** *whether,* **grene,** *fresh* **2136 passe hens,** *go from here,* **ententyfely,** *specifically*

2066 wot, G reads "wole." **2074 it,** omitted in G and Th. **2092 jowels,** Th reads "iowel." **2132 accomplysshen,** G reads "compleysshen" (achieve).

And if so be I wote° hem nought,
Than maye I erre unwyttingly.
Wherfore I praye you entierly,
With al myne herte, me to lere°,
That I trespace in no manere."
  The God of Love than charged° me
Anon as ye shal here and se,
Worde by worde, by right emprise°,
So as the *Romaunt* shal devyse.
  The maister leseth his tyme to lere°
When the disciple wol nat here°
It is but vayne on hym to swynke°,
That on his lernynge wol nat thynke.
Whoso luste° love, lette him entende°,
For nowe the romance begynneth to amende°.
Nowe is good to here, in faye°,
If any be that canne it saye,
And poynt° it as the reason is
Sette; for other gate°, ywis°,
It shal nat wel in al thyng
Be brought to good understondyng.
For a reder that poynteth yl°
A good sentence maye ofte spyl°.
The boke is good at the endyng,
Made of newe and lusty thyng;
For whoso wol the endyng here,
The crafte of Love he shal mowe lere°,
If that he wol so longe abyde,
Tyl I this romance maye unhyde,
And undo the signyfiaunce
Of this dreme into romaunce.
The sothfastnesse° that nowe is hydde

LOVER'S COMMANDMENTS

Without coverture shal be
    kydde°
When I undone° have this dremyng,
Wherein no worde is of leasyng°.
  "Villany, at the begynnyng,
I wol°," sayde Love, "over al thyng,

AVOID VILLAINY

Thou leave, if thou wolte not be
False and trespace ayenst me.
I curse and blame generally
Al hem that loven villany;
For villany maketh villayne°;
And by his dedes a chorle° is seyne°.
These vilayns arne° without pyte,
Frendshyp, love, and al bounte°.
I nyl° receyve unto my servyce
Hem that ben vilayns of emprise°.
But understond in thyn entent
That this is not myn entendement,
To clepe° no wight in no ages
Onely gentyl for his lynages°.
But whoso° is vertuous,
And in his porte° not outragyous.
Whan suche one thou seest the beforne,
Though he be not gentyl borne,
Thou mayste wel seyne, this is in sothe,
That he is gentyl by cause he dothe

NATURAL GENTILESSE

As longeth° a gentylman;
Of hem none other deme I can.
For certaynly, withouten drede,
A chorle is demed by his dede,
Of hye or lowe, as ye may se,
Or of what kynrede that he be.
  "Ne say nought, for none yvel wyll,
Thyng that is to holden styll°,
It is no worshyp to missey°.
Thou mayste ensample take of Key,
That was somtyme for missayeng
Hated bothe of olde and yonge.
As ferre as Gaweyn the worthy
Was praysed for his curtesye,
Kaye was hated, for he was fell°
Of worde, dispytous° and cruell.
  "Wherfore be wyse and aqueyntable°,
Goodly of worde, and reasonable

2140 wote, *know* **2143 lere,** *teach* **2145 charged,** *instructed* **2147 by right emprise,** *in proper fashion* **2149 lere,** *teach* **2150 here,** *listen* **2151 swynke,** *expend effort* **2153 luste,** *desires,* **entende,** *attend* **2154 amende,** *improve* **2155 faye,** *faith* **2157 poynt,** *punctuate* (emphasize) **2159 other gate,** *otherwise,* **ywis,** *truly* **2161 yl,** *poorly* **2162 spyl,** *destroy* **2166 mowe lere,** *be able to learn* **2171 sothfastnesse,** *truth* **2172 kydde,** *known* **2173 undone,** *explained* **2174 leasyng,** *lying* **2176 wol,** *desire* **2181 villayne,** *a villain* **2182 chorle,** *churl,* **seyne,** *known* **2183 arne,** *are* **2184 bounte,** *goodness* **2185 nyl,** *will not* **2187 emprise,** *behavior* **2189 clepe,** *call* **2190 lynages,** *lineages* **2191 whoso,** *whoever* **2192 porte,** *behavior* **2197 longeth,** *is appropriate* **2198 deme,** *judge* **2204 to holden styll,** *should be kept quiet* **2205 missey,** *slander* **2011 fell,** *fierce* **2112 dispytous,** *spiteful* **2213 aqueyntable,** *affable*

2141 erre, omitted in G and Th. **2148 *Romaunt,*** G reads "Romance." **2149–52** In the French, these lines follow 2144 and are spoken by the God of Love. **2150 Whan the,** G reads "Whan that the." **2157–62** These comments about proper emphasis are not in the French, and may pertain to oral delivery. **2167 he,** G reads "ye." **2168–70 romance . . . romance,** the term was understood to mean the narrative form as well the Romance language, French. **2176 sayde,** G and Th read "say." **2177 not,** omitted in G and Th. **2191–2202** Lines not here in the French; the commonplace sentiments parallel *WBT* 3.1109ff., *Bo* 3m6, and *RR*18607ff. **2206 Key,** Sir Kay, who speaks rudely and out of turn in many Arthurian romances. **2209 Gaweyn,** Sir Gawain, who is noted for speaking courteously in many Arthurian romances.

Bothe to lesse and eke to mare.
And whan thou comest there° men are,
Loke that thou have in custome aye°
First to salue° hem, if thou may;
And if it fall that of hem somme
Salue the first, be not domme°,
But quyte° hem curtesly anon
Without abydyng°, er they gon.
"For nothyng eke thy tonge applye
To speke wordes of rybaudye°.
To vilayne speche in no degre°
Late° never thy lyppe unbounden be;
For I nought holde him, in good faythe,
Curteys that foule wordes saythe.
"And al women serve and preyse,
And to° thy power her honour reyse.
And if that any missayere°
Dispyse women, that thou mayste here,
Blame° him, and bydde him holde him styll.
And sette thy might and al thy wyll
Women and ladyes for to plese,
And to do thyng that may hem ese,
That they ever speke good of the;
For so thou mayste best praysed be.

AVOID PRIDE

"Loke fro pride thou kepe the wele°;
For thou mayste bothe parceyve and fele
That pride is bothe foly and synne;
And he that pride hath him within,
Ne may his herte in no wyse
Meken ne souplen° to servyce,
For pride is founde in every parte
Contrarye unto loves arte.
"And he that loveth trewly
Shulde him conteyne° jolyly,
Without pride, in sondrie wyse,
And him disgysen° in queyntyse°.
For queynte aray, without drede,
Is nothyng proude, who taketh hede;
For fresshe aray, as men may se,
Without pride may ofte be.
Mayntayne thyselfe after thy rent°
Of robe and eke of garnement°;
For many sythe° fayre clothyng
A man amendeth in moche thyng.
And loke alwaye that they be shape°—
What garnement that thou shalte make—
Of him that can best do
With al that parteyneth therto.
Poyntes° and sleves be wel syttande°,
Right and streight on the hande.
Of shone° and bootes, newe and fayre,
Loke at the leest thou have a payre,
And that they sytte so fetously°,
That these rude° may utterly
Mervayle, sythe that they sytte so playne°,
Howe they come on or of agayne.
Weare strayte° gloves, with aumenere°
Of sylke; and alway with good chere
Thou yeve, if thou have rychesse;
And if thou have naught, spende the lesse.
Alway be mery, if thou may,
But waste not thy good° alway.
Have hatte of floures as fresshe as May,
Chapelet of roses of Whitsonday;
For suche araye ne costneth but lyte.
Thyne hondes wasshe, thy tethe make white,
And lette no fylthe upon the be.
Thy nayles blacke if thou mayst se,
Voyde° it away delyverly°.
And kembe° thyne heed right jolyly.
Farce nat° thy visage in no wyse,
For that of love is nat th'emprise°,
For love dothe haten, as I fynde,
A beaute that cometh nat of
Kynde°.

BE GRACIOUS AND MERRY

"Alwaye in hert I rede the°
Gladde and mery for to be,
And be as joyful as thou canne;
Love hath no joye of sorouful manne.
That yvel° is ful of curtesy
That laugheth in his malady.
For ever of love the sicknesse

2216 there, *where* **2217 aye,** *always* **2218 salue,** *greet* **2220 domme,** *dumb* **2221 quyte,** *repay* **2222 abydyng,** *hesitation* **2224 rybaudye,** *rudeness* **2225 degre,** *situation* **2226 Late,** *let* **2230 to,** *according to* **2231 missayre,** *evil-speaker* **2233 Blame,** *accuse* **2239 kepe the wele,** *protect yourself well* **2244 Meken ne souplen,** *make meek or compliant* **2248 him conteyne,** *restrain himself* **2250 disgysen,** *dress,* **queyntyse,** *finery* **2255 after thy rent,** *in accord with your income* **2256 garnement,** *garment* **2257 sythe,** *times* **2259 shape,** *shaped* **2263 Poyntes,** *laces,* **syttande,** *fitting* **2265 shone,** *shoes* **2267 fetously,** *neatly* **2268 rude,** *uncultured people* **2269 sytte so playne,** *fit so smoothly* **2271 strayte,** *tight,* **aumenere,** *purse* **2276 good,** *goods* **2283 Voyde,** *clean,* **delyverly,** *quickly* **2284 kembe,** *comb* **2285 Farce nat,** *don't use makeup on* **2286 th'emprise,** *the intention* **2288 Kynde,** *nature* **2289 rede the,** *advise you* **2293 yvel,** *sickness*

2215 mare, the form is northern; G reads "more." **2234 sette,** omitted in G. **2270 on,** G and Th reads "an." **2271 aumenere,** G and Th read "aumere." **2278 Whitsonday,** Whitsunday, an English name for Pentecost, the Christian feast of the coming of the Holy Spirit, celebrated seven Sundays after Easter. **2294 laugheth,** G and Th read "knoweth."

Is meynte° with swete and bytternesse.
The sore° of love is mervaylous,
For now the lover is joyous,
Nowe can he playne°, nowe can he grone,
Now can he syngen, nowe maken mone;
Today he playneth for hevynesse,
Tomorowe he pleyeth for jolynesse.
The lyfe of love is ful contrarye,
Whiche stoundemeale° can ofte varye,
But if thou canste myrthes make,
That men in gre° wol gladly take,
Do it goodly, I commaunde the.
For men shulde, wheresoever they be,
Do thynge that hem best syttyng° is,
For therof cometh good loos° and pris°.
Wherof that° thou be vertuous°;
Ne be not straung° ne daungerous°.
For if that thou good ryder be,
Pricke° gladly, that men may se.
In armes also if thou conne,
Pursue tyl thou a name hast wonne.
And if thy voyce be fayre and clere,
Thou shalt maken no great daungere°
Whan to synge they goodly pray;
It is thy worshyp° for to obey.
Also to you it longeth aye°
To harpe and gyterne°, daunce and playe;
For if he can wel flute and daunce,
It may him greatly do avaunce°.
Amonge° eke for thy lady sake
Songes and complayntes that thou make°,
For that wol meven in her herte
Whan they reden of° thy smerte.

AVOID MISERLINESS

"Loke that no man for scare°
the holde,
For that may greve the many folde°;
Reson wol° that a lover be
In his yeftes more large° and fre°
Than chorles that ben not of lovyng.
For who thereof can° anythyng,
He shal be lefe° aye for to yeve—
In Loves lore whoso wolde leve°.
For he that through a sodayne syght,
Or for a kyssyng anon ryght°
Yave hole his herte in wyl and thought,
And to hymselfe kepeth right nought,
After so riche gift it is good reson
He yeve his good in abandon°.
"Nowe wol I shortly here reherce°
Of that I have sayd in verce,
Al the sentence° by and by,
In wordes fewe compendously°,
That thou the better mayste on hem thynke,
Whether so it be thou wake or wynke°;
For the wordes lytel greve
A man to kepe whan it is breve°.
Whoso with Love wol gon or ryde,
He mote° be curteyes and voyde of pride,
Mery and ful of jolyte,
And of largesse alosed° be.

RECAPITULATION OF LOVE'S COMMANDS

"First I joyne° the here in penaunce
That ever without
repentaunce,
Thou set thy thought in thy lovyng,
To laste without repentyng;
And thinke upon thy myrthes swete
That shal folowe after whan ye mete.
"And for° thou trewe to love shalt be,
I wyl and commaunde the
That in one place thou set, al hole,
Thyn herte, without halfen dole°,
For trecherye and sykernesse°,
For I loved never doublenesse.
To many his herte that wol departe°,
Everyche shal have but lytel parte;
But of him drede I me right nought
That in one place setteth his thought.
Therfore in o place it sette,

2296 meynte, *mixed* **2297 sore,** *pain* **2299 playne,** *lament* **2304 stoundemeale,** *from time to time* **2306 in gre,** *agreeably* **2309 best syttyng,** *most suitable* **2310 loos,** *praise,* **pris,** *esteem* **2311 Wherof that,** *regarding that which,* **vertuous,** *skillful* **2312 straunge,** *distant,* **daungerous,** *aloof* **2314 Pricke,** *spur* **2315 conne,** *are able* **2318 daungere,** *resistance* **2320 worshyp,** *honor* **2321 longeth aye,** *is always suitable* **2322 gyterne,** *play the guitar* **2324 him . . . do avaunce,** *advance him* **2325 Amonge,** *from time to time* **2326 that thou make,** (be sure) *that you make them* **2328 reden of,** *explain about* **2329 for scarce,** *as a miser,* **the holde,** *consider you* **2330 many folde,** *often times* **2331 Reson wol,** *it is reasonable* **2332 large,** *open,* **fre,** *generous* **2334 can,** *knows* **2335 lefe,** *happy* **2336 leve,** *live* **2338 anon ryght,** *immediately* **2342 in abandon,** *without restraint* **2343 reherce,** *repeat* **2345 sentence,** *substance* **2346 compendously,** *concisely* **2348 wynke,** *sleep* **2350 breve,** *brief* **2352 mote,** *must* **2354 of largesse alosed,** *for generosity praised* **2355 joyne,** *command* **2361 for,** *in order that* **2364 halfen dole,** *half portions* **2365 For trecherye and sykernesse,** *because of treachery and faithfulness* **2367 departe,** *divide*

2298 is, omitted in G and Th. **2302 pleyeth,** G and Th read "pleyneth." **2309 best,** omitted in G and Th; the French has *mieuz.* **2316 tyl,** G reads "to." **2318 no,** omitted in G. **2323 flute,** G and Th read "fote" (dance), but the French is *fleuter.* **2336 Loves,** G and Th read "londes"; the French is *d'amors.* **2341 so riche gift,** G and Th read "this swifte"; the French is *Après si riche don.* **2355 the,** G reads "the that." **2371–72 sette . . . flette,** G reads "sitte . . . flitte."

And lette it never thens flette°.
For if thou yevest it in lenyng°,
I holde it but a wretched thyng.
Therfore yeve it hole and quyte°,
And thou shalte have the more meryte.
If it be lent, than after soone
The bounte° and the thanke is done;
But in love free yeven thyng
Requyreth a great guerdonyng°.
Yeve it in yefte° al quyte fully,
And make thy gifte debonairly°;
For men that yefte holde more dere
That yeven is with gladsome° chere;
That gifte nought to praysen is
That man yeveth maugre his°.
"Whan thou hast yeven thyne hert, as I
Have sayde the° here openly,
Than aventures shul the fal,
Whiche harde and hevy ben withal.
For ofte whan thou bethynkest the
Of thy lovyng, whereso° thou be,
Fro folke thou must departe in hye°,
That none perceyve thy malady;
But hyde thyne harme thou must alone,
And go forthe sole°, and make thy mone.
Thou shalte no whyle be in o state,
But whylom° colde and whilom hate°,
Nowe reed as rose, nowe yelowe and fade;
Such sorowe, I trowe, thou never hade;
Cotidien° ne quarteyne°,
It is nat so ful of peyne.
For often tymes it shal fal
In love, among thy paynes al,
That thou thyselfe, al holy°,
Foryeten shalte so utterly,
That many tymes thou shalte be
Styl as an ymage of tree,
Domme as a stone, without steryng
Of fote or honde, without spekyng.
Than, soone after al thy payne,
To memorye shalte thou come agayne,
As man abasshed° wonder sore°,
And after syghen more and more.
For wytte° thou wele, withouten wene°,
In suche astate ful ofte have bene
That have the yvel° of love assayde,
Wherthrough° thou arte so dismayde.

MISERY OF ABSENOE

"After, a thought shal take the so
That thy love is to ferre the fro°,
Thou shalte saye, 'God, what may this be,
That I ne maye my lady se?
Myne herte alone is to her go,
And I abyde al sole in wo,
Departed fro myne owne thought,
And with myne eyen se right nought.
Alas, myne eyen sende I ne may,
My careful° hert to convay°!
Myne hertes gyde but they be,
I prayse nothyng whatever they se.
Shul they abyde than? Nay,
But gone and visyten without delay
That° myne herte desyreth so.
For certainly, but if they go,
A foole myselfe I maye wel holde,
Whan I ne se what myne hert wolde°.
Wherfore° I wol gone her to sene,
Or eased shal I never bene
But° I have some tokenyng.'
"Than gost thou forthe without dwellyng;
But ofte thou faylest of thy desyre,
Er thou mayst come her any nere°,
And wastest in vayne thy passage.
Than fallest thou in a newe rage°;
For want of syght thou gynnest murne,
And homwarde pensyfe thou dost returne.
In great myschefe° than shalte thou be,
For than agayne shal come to the
Sighes and playntes°, with newe wo,
That no itchyng pricketh° so.
Who wote° it nought, he maye go lere°

2372 flette, *depart* **2373 lenyng,** *lending* **2375 quyte,** *completely* **2378 bounte,** *goodness* **2380 guerdonyng,** *rewarding* **2381 in yefte,** *as a gift* **2382 debonairly,** *graciously* **2384 gladsome,** *cheerful* **2386 maugre his,** *in spite of himself* **2388 the,** *to you* **2392 whereso,** *wherever* **2393 hye,** *haste* **2396 sole,** *alone* **2398 whylom,** *sometimes,* **hate,** *hot* **2401 Cotidien,** *daily fever,* **quarteyne,** *fever recurring every third day* **2405 holy,** *wholly* **2413 abasshed,** *surprised,* **wonder sore,** *very painfully* **2415 wytte,** *know,* **wene,** *doubt* **2417 yvel,** *pain* **2418 Wherthrough,** *through which* **2420 ferre the fro,** *far from you* **2428 careful,** *woeful,* **convay,** *guide* **2433 That,** *what* **2436 wolde,** *desires* **2437 Wherfore,** *for this reason* **2439 But,** *unless* **2442 nere,** *nearer* **2444 rage,** *passion* **2447 myschefe,** *misfortune* **2449 playntes,** *laments* **2450 pricketh,** *stings* **2451 wote,** *knows,* **lere,** *learn*

2395–2442 Leaf missing in G. **2403–50** Lines included on mid-fifteenth-century manuscript leaf, among the papers of Reverend Joass, Sutherland Collection, National Library of Scotland (NLS). **2413 As,** from NLS; Th reads "A." The French is *Ausi.* **2427 sende,** from NLS; Th reads "sene." The French is *envoier.* **2436 what,** NLS reads "that." **2439 But,** NLS reads "But if." **2446 thou dost,** NLS reads "dost thou." **2450 itchyng,** the NLS reading "yrchon" (hedgehog) is probably correct; the French is *heriçons.*

Of hem that byen° love so dere°.
Nothynge thyne herte appesen maye
That ofte thou wolte gone and assaye
If thou mayst sene, by aventure,
Thy lyves joye, thyne hertes cure;
So that by grace if thou myght
Attayne of her to have a syght,
Than shalte thou done none other dede
But with that syght thyne eyen fede°.
That fayre fresshe° whan thou mayst se,
Thyne hert shal so ravysshed be,
That never thou woldest, thy thankes°, lete°
Ne remove for to se that swete.
The more thou seest in sothfastnesse°,
The more thou covytest° of that swetnesse;
The more thyn herte brenneth in fyre,
The more thyn herte is in desyre.
For who consydreth every dele°,
It may be lykened wonder wele,
The payne of love, unto a fere°.
For evermore thou neyghest nere°
That, or whoso that it be,
For very soth I tel it the,
The hotter ever shal thou brenne,
As experyence shal the kenne°.
Whereso comest in any coste°
Who is next fyre, he brenneth moste.
"And yet forsothe°, for al thyn hete,
Though thou for love swelte° and swete,
Ne for nothyng thou felen may,
Thou shalt not wyllen to passe away°.
And though thou go, yet muste the nede
Thynke al day on her fayre hede°,
Whom thou behelde with so good wyll,
And holde thyselfe begyled yll°
That thou ne haddest none hardyment°
To shewe her aught° of thyn entent.
Thyn herte ful sore thou wolte dispyse,
And eke repreve° of cowardyse,
That thou, so dull in everythyng,
Were domme° for drede, without spekyng.
Thou shalt eke thynke thou dyddest folye
That thou were her so faste° bye,
And durste not auntre the° to say
Somethyng er thou came away.
For thou haddest no more wonne°,
To speke of her whan thou begonne,
But yif° she wolde, for thy sake,
In armes goodly the have take—
It shulde have be more worthe to the
Than of tresour great plente.
"Thus shalte thou morne and eke complayne,
And get encheson° to gon agayne
Unto thy walke, or to thy place,
Where thou behelde her flesshly face.
And never, for false suspection,
Thou woldest fynde occasyon
For to gone unto her house.
So arte thou than desyrouse
A syght of her for to have,
If thou thyn honour myghtest save,
Or any erande mightest make
Thyder for thy loves sake;
Ful fayne° thou woldest°, but for drede
Thou goest not, leest that men take hede.
Wherfore I rede° in thy goynge,
And also in thyn agayne-commynge,
Thou be wel ware that men ne wyt°.
Feyne the° other cause than it
To go that waye, or faste° bye;
To heale° wel is no folye°.
"And if so be it happe the
That thou thy love there mayste se,
In syker° wyse thou her salewe°,
Wherwith thy coloure wol transmewe°,
And eke thy bloode shal al to-quake,
Thy hewe eke chaungen for her sake.
But worde and wytte, with chere ful pale,
Shul wante for to tel thy tale;
And if thou mayste so fer forthe wynne,
That thou reson° durste° begynne,
And woldest sayne thre thynges or mo,
Thou shalte ful scarsly sayne the two.
Though thou bethynke the° never so wele,

LOVE'S TORMENTS

2452 byen, *pay for,* **dere,** *dearly* **2460 fede,** *feed* **2461 fresshe,** *fresh* (person) **2463 thy thankes,** *willingly,* **lete,** *give up* **2465 sothfastnesse,** *truth* **2466 covytest,** *desires* **2469 dele,** *aspect* **2471 fere,** *fire* **2472 neyghest nere,** *approaches nearer* **2476 kenne,** *teach* **2477 coste,** *situation* (coast) **2479 forsothe,** *truly* **2480 swelte,** *swoon* **2482 passe away,** *depart* (from her) **2484 fayre hede,** *beauty* **2486 begyled yll,** *poorly misled* **2487 hardyment,** *courage* **2488 aught,** *anything* **2490 repreve,** *scold* **2492 domme,** *dumb* **2494 faste,** *near* **2495 durste not auntre the,** *dared not venture yourself* **2497 wonne,** *opportunity* **2499 But yif,** *unless* **2504 encheson,** *opportunity* **2515 fayne,** *gladly,* **woldest,** *would* (go) **2517 rede,** *advise* **2519 ne wyt,** *know not* **2520 Feyne the,** *pretend* **2521 faste,** *near* **2522 heale,** *conceal* **2525 syker,** *secure* (i.e., secret), **salewe,** *greet* **2526 transmewe,** *change* **2532 reson,** *speech,* **durste,** *dare* **2535 bethynke the,** *ponder*

2472 thou, G reads "tho." **2473 That,** G and Th read "Thought." **2499 yif,** G and Th read "yet."

Thou shalt foryete yet somdele°,
But if° thou deale° with trecherye.
For false lovers mowe° al folye
Sayne, what hem luste, withouten drede;
They be so double in her falshede,
For they in herte can thynke o thynge
And sayne another in her spekynge.
"And whan thy speche is ended all,
Right thus to the it shal befall,
If any worde than come to mynde,
That thou to saye haste° lefte behynde,
Than thou shalt brenne° in great martyre°,
For thou shalt brenne as any fyre.
This is the stryfe and eke the affraye°,
And the batell that lasteth aye.
This batell ende may never take
But if that she thy peace wyl make.
"And whan the nyght is comen anon,
A thousande angres° shal come upon.
To bedde as faste thou wolte the dyght°,
Where thou shalt have but smal delyght.
For whan thou wenest° for to slepe,
So ful of payne shalt thou crepe,
Sterte° in thy bedde aboute ful wyde,
And turne ful ofte on every syde,
Nowe downwarde groffe°, and nowe upright°,
And walowe in wo the longe nyght;
Thyn armes shalt thou sprede abrede
As man in werre were forwerede°.
Than shal the come a remembraunce
Of her shappe and her semblaunce,
Wherto non other may be pere°.
And wete° thou wel, without were°,
That the shal seme, somtyme that nyght,
That thou haste her that is so bright
Naked bytwene thyn armes there,
Al sothfastnesse° as though it were.
Thou shalte make castels than in Spayne,
And dreme of joy, al but in vayne,
And the delyten of right nought°,
Whyle thou so slombrest in that thought
That is so swete and delytable,
The whiche, in sothe, nys but a fable,
For it ne shal no whyle laste.
Than shalte thou syghe and wepe faste,
And say, 'Dere God, what thyng is this?
My dreme is turned al amys,
Which was ful swete and apparent°,
But nowe I wake; it is al shent°!
Nowe yede° this mery thought away.
Twenty tymes upon a day
I wolde this thought wolde come agayne,
For it alegeth° wel my payne;
It maketh me ful of joyfull thought;
It sleeth me that it lasteth nought.
Ah, Lorde, why nyl ye me socoure°
The joye, I trowe, that I langoure?
The dethe I wolde me shulde slo°
Whyle I lye in her armes two.
Myne harme is harde, withouten wene°;
My great unease ful ofte I mene°.
But wolde Love do so I might
Have fully joye of her so bright,
My payne were quytte me° rychely.
Alas, to great a thyng aske I!
It is but foly and wronge wenyng°
To aske so outragyous a thyng.
And whoso asketh folily,
He mote° be warned hastely.
And I ne wote° what I may say,
I am so ferre out of the way.
For I wolde have ful great lykyng
And ful great joy of lasse° thyng:
For wolde she, of her gentylnesse,
Withouten more, me ones kesse°,
It were to me a great guerdon°,
Relece of al my passyon.
But it is harde to come therto;
Al is but foly that I do,
So hygh. I have myn herte sette,
Where I may no comforte gette.
I not where° I say wel or nought.
But this I wote° wel in my thought,
That it were better of her alone°,

2536 somdele, *something* **2537 But if,** *unless,* **deale,** *behave* **2538 mowe,** *can* **2539 what hem luste,** *whatever they wish* **2546 haste,** *have* **2547 brenne,** *burn,* **martyre,** *torment* **2549 affraye,** *assault* **2554 angres,** *torments* **2555 as faste,** *quickly,* **the dyght,** *take yourself* **2557 wenest,** *intend* **2559 Sterte,** *toss* **2561 groffe,** *lie facing,* **upright,** *upwards* **2564 forwerede,** *defeated* **2567 pere,** *equal* **2568 wete,** *know,* **were,** *doubt* **2572 sothfastnesse,** *reality* **2575 right nought,** *absolutely nothing* **2583 apparent,** *evident* **2584 shent,** *ruined* **2585 yede,** *goes* **2588 alegeth,** *alleviates* **2591 socoure,** *provide* **2592 langoure,** *suffer* (for) **2593 slo,** *slay* **2595 wene,** *doubt* **2596 mene,** *bemoan* **2599 were quytte me,** *would be repaid to me* **2601 wenyng,** *thinking* **2604 mote,** *must* **2605 wote,** *know* **2608 lasse,** *a lesser* **2610 ones kesse,** *kiss once* **2611 guerdon,** *reward* **2617 not where,** *don't know whether* **2618 wote,** *know* **2619 of her alone,** *from her only*

2541 o, G reads "a." **2551 batell,** G and Th read "bargeyn"; the French is *guerre.* **2569 seme,** G and Th read "se"; the French is *avis* (seem). **2573 make castels . . . in Spayne,** equivalent to the modern idiom "build castles in the air." **2574 in,** Th reads "it." **2578 a,** omitted in G. **2617 not,** G and Th read "wote not."

For to stynte° my wo and mone,
A loke of her ycaste goodly,
Than for to have al utterly
Of another al hole the play.
Ah, Lorde, where° I shal byde° the day
That ever she shal my lady be?
He is ful cured that may her se.
A, God, whan shal the dawnyng spring?
To lyggen° thus is an angry thyng;
I have no joy thus here to lye
Whan that my love is not me bye.
A man to lyen hath great disese,
Whiche may not slepe ne rest in ese.
I wolde it dawed°, and were nowe day,
And that the nyght were went away;
For were it day, I wolde upryse.
Ah, slowe sonne, shewe thyne enprise°!
Spede the to sprede thy beemes bright,
And chace the derknesse of the nyght
To put away the stoundes° stronge
Whiche in me lasten al to longe.'
"The nyght shalt thou contynue so,
Without rest, in payne and wo.
If ever thou knewe of love distresse,
Thou shal mowe° lerne in that sicknesse.
And thus enduryng shalt thou lye,
And ryse on morowe up erly
Out of thy bedde, and harneys the°
Er° ever dawnyng thou mayst se.
Al prively than shalt thou gone,
What weder° it be, thyselfe alone,
For reyne or hayle, for snowe, for slete,
Thyder° she dwelleth that is so swete—
The whiche° may fall° aslepe be,
And thynketh but lytel upon the.
Than shalt thou go ful foule aferde°;
Loke if the gate be unsperde°,
And wayte without in wo and payne,
Ful yvel acolde° in wynde and rayne.
Than shalt thou go the dore before;
If thou mayste fynde any score°,
Or hole, or refte, whatever it were,
Than shalte thou stoupe and lay to eere°,
If they within aslepe be—
I mene al save° thy lady free,
Whom wakyng if thou mayst aspye,
Go put thyselfe in jupardye
To aske grace, and the bymene°,
That she may wete°, without wene°,
That thou anyght no rest hast had,
So sore for her thou were bestad°.
Women wel ought pyte to take
Of hem that sorowen for her sake.
"And loke°, for love of that relyke°,
That thou thynke none other lyke,
For whom thou haste so great annoy°,
Shal kysse the er thou go awey;
And holde that in ful great deynte°,
And, for that no man shal the se
Before the house, ne in the way,
Loke° thou be gon agayne er day.
Suche commyng, and suche goyng,
Suche hevynesse°, and suche wakyng,
Maketh lovers, withouten any wene°,
Under her clothes pale and lene.
For love leveth colour ne cleernesse°;
Who loveth trewe hath no fatnesse.

DISMAL EFFECTS OF LOVE

Thou shalte wel by thyselfe se
That thou must nedes assayed° be.
For men that shape hem° other way
Falsely her ladyes for to betray,
It is no wonder though they be fatte;
With false othes her loves they gatte°;
For ofte I se suche losengeours°
Fatter than abottes° or priours°.
"Yet with o thynge I the charge,
That is to saye, that thou be large°
Unto the mayde that her dothe serve,
So best her thanke° thou shalt deserve;

2620 stynte, *stop* **2624 where,** *how,* **byde,** *await* **2628 lyggen,** *lie* **2633 dawed,** *dawned* **2636 enprise,** *power* **2639 stoundes,** *hours* **2644 mowe,** *be able to* **2647 harneys the,** *dress yourself* **2648 Er,** *before* **2650 What weder,** *whatever weather* **2652 Thyder,** *to that place where* **2653 The whiche,** *the one who,* **fall,** *fallen* **2655 ful foule aferde,** *very wretchedly afraid* **2656 unsperde,** *unlocked* **2658 yvel acolde,** *painfully chilled* **2660 score,** *crack* **2662 lay to eere,** *listen* (at the opening) **2664 save,** *except* **2667 bymene,** *bemoan* **2668 wete,** *know,* **wene,** *doubt* **2670 bestad,** *afflicted* **2673 loke,** *consider* **relyke,** *treasure* **2675 annoy,** *pain* **2677 deynte,** *esteem* **2680 Loke,** *make sure* **2682 hevynesse,** *sorrow* **2683 wene,** *doubt* **2685 cleernesse,** *brightness* **2688 must nedes assayed be,** *must necessarily be tested* **2689 shape hem,** *contrive* **2692 gatte,** *got* **2693 losengeours,** *liars* **2694 abottes,** *abbots,* **priours,** *priors* (religious officials) **2696 large,** *generous* **2698 thanke,** *gratitude*

2621 A loke of her ycaste, G and Th read "A loke on hir I caste"; the French is *de li uns regarz* (from her a look). **2622 Than,** G and Th read "That." **2641 contynue,** G reads "contene" (endure). **2650 weder,** G and Th read "whider." **2660 score,** Th reads "shore." **2664 thy,** G reads "the." **2669 anyght,** G and Th read "nyght." **2673–76** In the French, the suggestion is that the lover should kiss the door before he departs. **2675 whom,** G and Th read "whanne." **2682 wakyng,** G and Th read "walkyng." **2693 ofte,** G reads "of." **2695–2709** This advice follows Ovid, *Ars Amatoria* (*Art of Love*) 2.251-60, a work echoed recurrently in this section of the poem. **2696 is,** G reads "it."

Yeve her yeftes, and get her grace°,
For so thou may thanke purchace,
That she the worthy holde and fre°,
Thy lady, and al that may the se.
Also her servauntes worshyp° aye,
And please as moche as thou may.
Great good through hem may come to the
Bycause with her they ben prive;
They shal her tel howe they the fande°
Curteys and wyse and wel doande°,
And she shal preyse wel the more.
Loke out of londe thou be not fore°;
And if suche cause thou have, that the
Behoveth° to gone out of countre,
Leave hole° thyn herte in hostage,
Tyl thou agayne make thy passage.
Thynke longe° to se the swete thyng
That hath thyn herte in her kepyng.
Nowe have I tolde the in what wise
A lover shal do me servyce.
Do it than, if thou wolte have
The mede° that thou after crave."

END OF LOVE'S COMMANDMENTS

  When Love al this had
    boden° me,
I sayd him: "Sir, howe may it be
That lovers may in suche manere
Endure the payn ye have said here?
I mervayle me wonder faste°
Howe any man may lyve or laste
In suche payne and suche brennyng,
In sorowe and thought and suche sighyng,
Aye° unrelesed wo to make,
Whether so it be they slepe or wake,
In suche anoy° contynuelly.
As helpe me God, this mervayle I
Howe man, but he were made of stele,
Might lyve a monthe suche paynes to fele."
  The God of Love than sayd me:
"Frende, by the faythe I owe to the,
May no man have good, but he it bye°.

LOVE CONTINUES

A man loveth more tenderlye
The thyng that he hath bought most dere.
For wete thou wel, without were°,
In thanke° that thynge is taken more
For whiche a man hath suffred sore,

VIRTUES OF HOPE

Certes, no wo ne may attayne
Unto the sore° of loves payne;
None yvel° therto ne may amounte,
No more than a man may counte
The droppes that of the water be.
For drie as wel the great see
Thou myghtest as the harmes tell
Of hem that with Love dwell
In servyce, for peyne hem sleeth°.
And yet eche man wolde flye° the dethe,
And trowe° they shulde never escape,
Nere° that Hoope couth° hem make
Gladde as man in prison sete,
And maye nat getten° for to ete
But barlye breed and water pure,
And lyeth in vermyn and in ordure;
With al this, yet canne he lyve,
Good Hope suche comforte hath hym
    yeve,
Whiche maketh wene° that he shal be
Delyvered and come to lyberte;
In fortune is his ful trust.
Though he lye in strawe or dust,
In Hoope is al his systaynyng.
And so for lovers, in her wenyng°,
Whiche Love hath shytte in his prisoun,
Good Hope is her salvatioun.
Good Hope, howe° sore that they smerte,
Yeveth hem bothe wyl and herte
To profer her body to martyre;
For Hope so sore dothe° hem desyre
To suffre eche harm that men devyse
For joye that afterwarde shal aryse.
Hoope in desyre catcheth victorie.
In Hoope, of love is al the glorie,
For Hoope is al that love maye yeve;
Nere° Hoope, there shulde no lover lyve.
Blessed be Hoope, whiche with desyre
Avaunceth lovers in suche manyre!

2699 grace, *favor* **2701 the worthy holde and fre,** *consider you worthy and generous* **2703 worshyp,** *honor* **2707 the fande,** *found you* **2708 wel doande,** *acting well* **2710 fore,** *gone* **2712 Bevoveth,** *requires* **2713 hole,** *completely* **2715 Thynke longe,** *yearn* **2720 mede,** *reward* **2721 boden,** *commanded* **2725 wonder faste,** *very earnestly* **2729 Aye,** *always* **2731 anoy,** *pain* **2737 bye,** *pay for* **2740 were,** *doubt* **2741 In thanke,** *with thanks* **2744 sore,** *soreness* **2745 None yvel,** *no* (other) *suffering* **2751 hem sleeth,** *slays them* **2752 flye,** *flee from* **2753 trowe,** *believe* **2754 Nere,** *were it not,* **couth,** *could* **2756 getten,** *get* (anything) **2761 wene,** (him) *think* **2766 her wenyng,** *their thinking* **2769 howe,** *however* **2772 sore dothe,** *sorely makes* **2778 Nere,** *were it not for*

2707–08 fande . . . doande, northern forms. **2709–10** the rhyme words were probably originally northern forms: "mare" and "fare." **2709 the,** G reads "thee." **2746 may,** omitted in G and Th. **2752 yet,** G and Th read "that." **2763 his,** omitted in G and Th. **2775 catcheth,** G and Th read "catche." **2778 lover,** Th reads "lenger"; the French is *amant.*

Good Hope is curteyse for to please,
To kepe lovers from al disease°.
Hoope kepeth his bonde, and wol abyde
For any peryll that may betyde°,
For Hoope to lovers, as most chefe°,
Dothe hem endure al myschefe.
LOVE'S THREE GIFTS
Hoope is her helpe, whan
   myster is°.
  "And I shal yeve the eke°, ywis°,
Thre other thynges that great solace
Dothe to hem that be in my lace°.
  "The first good that maye be founde
To hem that in my lace be bounde
SWEET-THOUGHT
Is Swete-Thought, for to recorde°
Thyng wherwith thou canst accorde°
Best in thyne herte where she be°;
Thynkyng in absence is good to the.
Whan any lover dothe complayne,
And lyveth in distresse and in payne,
Than Swete-Thought shal come as blyve°
Awaye his angre for to dryve.
It maketh lovers to have remembraunce
Of comforte, and of highe plesaunce,
That Hoope hath hight° hym for to wynne.
For Thought anone° than shal begynne,
As ferre, God wotte°, as he can fynde,
To make a myrrour of his mynde;
For to beholde he wol nat lette°.
Her persone he shal afore hym sette,
Her laughyng eyen, persaunt° and clere,
Her shappe, her forme, her goodly chere,
Her mouthe that is so gratious,
So swete, and eke so saverous.
Of al her feyters° he shal take hede,
His eyen with al her lymmes° fede.
Thus Swete-Thynkyng shal aswage
The payne of lovers and her rage°.
The joye shal double, without gesse,
Whan thou thynkest on her semelynesse°,
Or of her laughyng, or of her chere,
That to the made thy lady dere.
This comforte wol I that thou take;
And if the nexte° thou wolte forsake
Which is nat lesse saverous°,
Thou shuldest ben to daungerous°.
SWEET-SPEECH
  "The seconde shal be Swete-Speche,
That hath to many one be leche°,
To bringe hem out of wo and were°,
And helpe many a bachelere.
And many a lady sent socour°,
That have loved paramour°,
Through spekyng whan they might here
Of her lovers, to hem so dere.
To hem it voydeth° al her smerte,
The whiche is closed in her herte.
In herte it maketh hem glad and lyght,
Speche, when they ne mowe° have syght.
And therfore nowe it cometh to mynde,
In olde dawes°, as I fynde,
That clerkes writen that her knewe
There was a lady fresshe of hewe,
Whiche of her love made a songe
On him for to remembre amonge°,
In whiche she sayd, 'Whan that I here
Speken of him that is so dere,
To me it voydeth al smerte,
Iwys°, he sytteth so nere myn herte.
To speke of hem at eve or morowe,
It cureth me of al my sorowe.
To me is none so hygh plesaunce
As of° his person dalyaunce°.'
She wyste° ful wel that Swete-Spekyng
Comforteth in ful moche thyng.
Her love she had ful wel assayde°;
Of him she was ful wel apayde°;
To speke of him her joye was set.
  "Therfore I rede° the that thou get
A felowe° that can wel concele
And kepe thy counsayle, and wel hele°,
To whom go shewe holly° thyn herte,
Bothe wel° and wo, joye and smerte;
To gette comforte to him thou go,

2782 disease, *discomfort* **2784 betyde,** *occur* **2785 most chefe,** *greatest leader* **2787 myster is,** (there) *is need* **2788 eke,** *also,* **ywis,** *truly* **2790 lace,** *net* **2793 recorde,** *remember* **2794 accorde,** *reconcile* **2795 where she be,** *wherever she is* **2799 blyve,** *quickly* **2803 hight,** *promised* **2804 anone,** *immediately* **2805 wotte,** *knows* **2807 lette,** *stop* **2809 persaunt,** *piercing* **2813 feyters,** *features* **2814 lymmes,** *limbs* **2815 rage,** *passion* **2818 semelynesse,** *beauty* **2822 nexte,** *next* (comfort) **2823 saverous,** *agreeable* **2824 shuldest ben to daungerous,** *would be too aloof* **2826 be leche,** *been a physician* **2827 were,** *doubt* **2829 socour,** *aid* **2830 paramour,** *passionately* **2833 voydeth,** *relieves* **2836 mowe,** *may* **2838 dawes,** *days* **2842 amonge,** *always* **2846 Iwys,** *truly* **2850 of,** *with,* **dalyaunce,** *conversation* **2851 wyste,** *knew* **2853 assayde,** *tested* **2854 apayde,** *contented* **2856 rede,** *advise* **2857 felowe,** *companion* **2858 hele,** *hide* **2859 shew holly,** *show entirely* **2860 wel,** *prosperity*

2783 bonde, G and Th read "londe." **2793 Swete-Thought,** French, *Douz Penser.* **2806 myrrour of his mynde,** not in the French; compare *TC* 1.365 and *FranT* 4.1582–85. **2824 ben,** G and Th read "nat ben." **2825 Swete-Speche,** French, *Douz Parlers.* **2833 hem,** G and Th read "me." **2836 ne,** omitted in G and Th. **2840–50 lady . . . made a songe. . . ,** the lady and her song are unidentified.

And prively, bytwene you two,
Ye shal speke of that goodly thyng
That hath thyn herte in her kepyng,
Of her beaute and her semblaunce°,
And of her goodly countenaunce.
Of al thy state thou shalt him say°,
And aske him counsayle howe thou may
Do anythyng that may her plese.
For it to the shal do great ese,
That he may wete° thou truste him so,
Bothe of thy wele° and of thy wo.
And if his herte to love be sette,
His companye is moche the bette°,
For reson° wol he shewe to the
Al utterly his privyte°,
And what she is he loveth so
To the playnly he shal undo°,
Without drede of any shame
Bothe tel her renoune and her name.
Than shal he forther°, ferre and nere,
And namely° to thy lady dere,
In syker wyse°. Ye, every other°
Shal helpen as his owne brother,
In trouthe without doublenesse°,
And kepen close in sykernesse.
For it is noble thyng, in fay°,
To have a man thou darste say°
Thy prive counsayle every dele°;
For that wol comforte the right wele;
And thou shalt holde the wel apayed°,
Whan suche a frende thou haste assayed.
"The thirde good of great comforte
That yeveth to lovers moste disporte°
Cometh of syght and beholdyng,
That cleped° is Swete-Lokyng, SWEET-LOOKING
The whiche may none ese do
Whan thou arte ferre° thy lady fro;
Wherfore thou prese alway to be
In place where thou mayst her se.
For it is thyng moste amerous,
Moste delytable and saverous°,
For to aswage a mannes sorowe
To sene his lady by the morowe°,
For it is a ful noble thyng
Whan thyn eyen have metyng
With that relyke° precious,
Whereof they be so desyrous.
But al day after, sothe° it is,
They have no drede to faren amys°.
They dreden neyther wynde ne rayne,
Ne non other maner° payne.
For whan thyn eyen were thus in blysse,
Yet of her curtesye, ywysse°,
Alone they can not have her joye,
But to the herte they it convoye°;
Parte of her blysse to him they sende
Of al this harme° to make an ende.
The eye is a good messangere,
Whiche can to the herte in suche manere
Tydynges sende that he hath sene,
To voyde° him of his paynes clene°.
Whereof the herte rejoyseth so
That a great partye° of his wo
Is voyded and put away to flyght.
Right as the derknesse of the nyght
Is chased with clerenesse° of the moone,
Right so is al his wo ful soone
Devoyded clene, whan that the syght
Beholden may that fresshe wight°
That the herte desyreth so,
That al his derknesse is ago;
For than the herte al at ese,
Whan the eyen sene that may hem plese.
"Nowe have I declared the al out
Of that thou were in drede and doute;
For I have tolde the faithfully
What the may curen utterly,
And al lovers that wol be
Faythful, and ful of stabylite.
Good-Hope alwaye kepe by thy syde,
And Swete-Thought; make eke abyde°
Swete-Lokynge and Swete-Speche—
Of al thyne harmes they shal be leche°,
Of every° thou shalte have great plesaunce.

2865 semblaunce, *appearance* **2867 say,** *tell* **2871 wete,** *know* **2872 wele,** *prosperity* **2874 bette,** *better* **2875 For reson,** *because* **2876 privyte,** *secrets* **2878 undo,** *reveal* **2881 forther,** *advance* (you) **2882 namely,** *especially* **2883 syker wyse,** *sure way,* **every other,** *each of you* **2885 doubleness,** *deceit* **2886 sykernesse,** *secrecy* **2887 in fay,** *in faith* (a mild oath) **2888 say,** *tell* **2889 dele,** *part* **2891 apayed,** *repaid* **2895 disporte,** *pleasure* **2896 cleped,** *named* **2898 ferre,** *far* **2902 saverous,** *pleasant* **2904 by the morowe,** *the next day* **2907 relyke,** *treasure* **2909 sothe,** *true* **2910 faren amys,** *go wrong* **2912 maner,** *kind of* **2914 ywysse,** *truly* **2916 convoye,** *convey* **2918 harme,** *pain* **2922 voyde,** *relieve,* **clene,** *completely* **2924 partye,** *portion* **2927 clerenesse,** *brightness* **2930 wight,** *person* **2942 make eke abyde,** *also make stay* (with you) **2944 leche,** *physician* **2945 every,** *each*

2895 beholdyng, G reads "of biholdyng." **2896 Swete-Lokyng,** French, *Douz Regart.* **2916 it,** omitted in G and Th. **2917 they,** G and Th read "thou." **2921 he,** omitted in G and Th. **2934 the eyen sene,** G and Th read "they sene"; the French is *li oil.*

If thou canst byde in sufferaunce,
And serve wel without fayntise°,
Thou shalte be quyte° of thyne emprise°
With more guerdoun°, if that thou lyve;
But at this tyme this I the yeve."

LOVE DEPARTS

The God of Love whan al the day
Had taught me, as ye have herd say,
And enformed compendously,
He vanysshed awaye al sodainly,
And I alone lefte, al soole°,
So ful of complaynt and of doole°,
For I sawe no man there me by.
My woundes me greved wondersly;
Me for to curen nothyng I knewe,
Save the bothon° bright of hewe,
Whereon was sette hooly° my thought;
Of other comforte knewe I nought,
But° it were through the God of Love.
I knewe nat els to my behove°
That myght me ease or conforte gete,
But if he wolde hym entermete°.
The roser° was, withouten dout,
Closed° with an hedge without,
As ye toforne have herde me sayne;
And fast I besyed°, and wolde fayne°
Have passed the haye°, if I myght
Have getten in by any sleyght
Unto the bothom so fayre to se.
But ever I dradde° blamed to be,
If men wolde have suspectioun
That I wolde of ententioun
Have stole the roses that there were;
Therfore to entre I was in fere.
But at the laste, as I bethought
Wheder I shulde passe or nought,

FAIR-WELCOME APPEARS

I sawe come with a gladde chere
To me, a lusty bachelere°,
Of good stature, and of good height,
And Bialacoil forsoth he height°.
Sonne he was to Curtesy,
And he me graunted ful gladly
The passage of the utter° hay,
And sayd, "Sir, nowe that ye may
Passe, if your wyl be,
The fresshe roser for to se,
And ye the swete savour fele°.
You warrant° may I right wele;
So° thou the kepe fro folye,
Shal no man do the vylanye.
If I may helpe you in ought,
I shal not fayne°, dredeth nought;
For I am bounde to your servyse,
Fully devoyde of feyntyse°."
Than unto Bialacoyl sayd I,
"I thanke you, sir, ful hertely,
And your beheste take at gre°,
That ye so goodly profer me;
To you it cometh of great fraunchyse°,
That ye me profer your servyse."
Than after, ful delyverly°,
Through the breres° anon went I,
Whereof encombred° was the haye.
I was wel plesed, the sothe to saye,
To se the bothom fayre and swote°,
So fresshe spronge out of the rote.
And Bialacoyle me served wele,
Whan I so nyghe° me myght fele°
Of the bothon the swete odour,
And so lusty° hewed of colour.
But than a chorle°—foule him betyde°—

DANGER LIES HIDDEN

Besyde the roses gan him, hyde°
To kepe the roses of that rosere,
Of whom the name was Daungere.
This chorle was hyd there in the greves°,
Covered with grasse and with leves,
To spye and take whom° that he fonde
Unto that roser put an honde.
He was not soole°, for there was mo,
For with him were other two
Of wicked maners and yvel fame.
That one was cleped, by his name,

2947 fayntise, *weakening* **2948 quyte,** *repaid,* **emprise,** *effort* **2949 guerdoun,** *reward* **2955 al soole,** *all alone* **2956 doole,** *sorrow* **2960 bothon,** *rosebud* **2961 hooly,** *wholly* **2963 But,** *unless* **2964 behove,** *advantage* **2966 entermete,** *intercede* **2967 roser,** *rosebush* **2968 Closed,** *enclosed* **2970 besyed,** *busied* (myself), **fayne,** *gladly* **2971 haye,** *hedge* **2974 dradde,** *feared* **2982 lusty bachelere,** *lively young man* **2984 height,** *was called* **2987 utter,** *outer* **2991 fele,** *perceive* **2992 warrant,** *guarantee* **2993 So,** *as long as* **2996 fayne,** *pretend* **2998 feyntyse,** *deceit* **3001 at gre,** *with pleasure* **3003 fraunchyse,** *generosity* **3005 delyverly,** *quickly* **3006 breres,** *briars* **3007 Whereof encombred,** *by which encumbered* **3009 swote,** *sweet* **3012 nyghe,** *near,* **fele,** *perceive* **3014 lusty,** *pleasingly* **3015 chorle,** *churl,* **foule him betyde,** *may bad things happen to him* **3016 gan him hyde,** *hid himself* **3019 greves,** *branches* **3021 whom,** *whomever* **3023 soole,** *alone*

2950 at, G and Th read "all." **2964 els,** Th reads "ele." **2984 Bialacoil,** Fair Welcome, from French *Bel Acueil*; in fragment C, the character is called "Fayre-Welcomyng" (e.g., 5856). **2988 nowe,** G and Th read "howe." **2992 You warrant may I right wele,** G and Th read "Youre warrans may right wele." **3018 Daungere,** Standoffishness, aloofness; the quality of resistance and/or restraint on the part of the beloved.

WICKED-TONGUE

Wicked-Tonge, God yeve him sorowe!
For neyther at eve ne at morowe
He can of no man good speke;
On many a juste man dothe he wreke°.
There was a woman eke that hyght°
Shame, that who° can reken ryght.

SHAME

Trespace was her fathers name,
Her mother Reson; and thus was Shame
Brought of these ylke° two.
And yet had Trespasse never ado°
With Reason, ne never ley her by,
He was so hydous and so ugly—
I meane this° that Trespasse hight.
But Reason conceyveth of a sight
Shame, of that I spake aforne°.
And whan that Shame was thus borne,
It was ordayned that Chastite
Shulde of the roser° lady° be,
Whiche of° the bothoms° more and las,
With sondrie folke assayled was,
That she ne wyste° what to do.
For Venus her assayleth so
That nyght and day from her she stal°
Bothoms and roses over al.
To Reason than prayeth Chastyte,
Whom Venus hath flemed° over the see,
That she her doughter wolde her lene°
To kepe° the roser fresshe and grene.
Anone° Reason to Chastyte
Is fully assented that it be,
And graunted her, at her request,
That Shame, bycause she is honest,
Shal keper of the roser be.
  And thus to kepe it there were thre,
That none shulde hardy be ne bolde—
Were he yonge, or were he olde—
Agayne her wyl awaye to bere
Bothoms ne roses that there were.
I hadde wel spedde° had I nat bene
Awayted with° these thre and sene.
For Bialacoil, that was so fayre,
So gratious and debonayre,
Quytte hym° to me ful curtesly,
And, me to please, badde that I
Shulde drawe me to the bothom nere;
Prese° in to touche the rosere
Whiche bare the roses, he yafe° me leve°;
This graunt ne myght but lytel greve.
And for° he sawe it lyked° me,

THE LOVER APPROACHES THE ROSE

Right nygh° the bothom pulled he
A leafe al grene, and yave me that,
The whiche ful nyghe the bothom sat.
I made me of that leafe ful queynt°,
And whan I felte I was aqueynt
With Bialacoil, and so pryve,
I wende° all at my wyl hadde be°.
Than wext° I hardy° for to tel
To Bialocoil howe me befel
Of Love, that toke and wounded me,
And sayd, "Sir, so mote I the°,
I maye no joye have in no wyse,
Upon no syde, but it ryse°;
For sithe° (if I shal nat feyne°)
In herte I have had so great peyne,
So great annoye and suche affraye°,
That I ne wotte° what I shal saye;
I drede your wrathe to deserve.
Lever me were° that knyves kerve
My body shulde in peces smal,
Than in any wyse it shulde fal
That ye wrathed° shulde ben with me."
  "Saye boldely thy wyl," quod he,
"I nyl be wrothe if that I maye,
For nought that thou shalte to me saye."
  Than sayd I, "Sir, not you displease
To knowen of my great unese,
In whiche only Love hath me brought;
For paynes great, disese, and thought
Fro day to day he dothe me drie°.
Supposeth not, sir, that I lye.
In me fyve woundes dyd he make,
The sore of whiche shal never slake
But° ye the bothom graunt me,
Whiche is moste passaunt° of beaute—

3030 wreke, *take vengeance* **3031 hyght,** *was called* **3032 that who,** *the one who* **3035 ylke,** *same* **3036 ado,** *to do* **3039 this,** *this person* **3041 aforne,** *before* **3044 roser,** *rosebush,* **lady,** *guardian* **3045 of,** *because of,* **bothoms,** *rosebuds* **3047 wyste,** *knew* **3049 stal,** *stole* **3052 flemed,** *banished* **3053 lene,** *loan* **3054 kepe,** *protect* **3055 Anone,** *immediately* **3065 wel spedde,** *succeeded well* **3066 Awayted with,** *waylaid by* **3069 Quytte hym,** *did his part* **3072 Prese,** *push* **3073 yafe,** *gave,* **leve,** *permission* **3075 for,** *because,* **lyked,** *pleased* **3076 Right nygh,** *very near* **3079 made me . . . ful queynt,** *took great pride in* **3082 wende,** *thought,* **hadde be,** *had been* (fulfilled) **3083 wext,** *grew,* **hardy,** *bold* **3086 so mote I the,** *as I may prosper* **3088 but it ryse,** *unless it comes about* **3089 sithe,** *since,* **feyne,** *pretend* **3091 affraye,** *fear* **3092 wotte,** *know* **3094 Lever me were,** *I would rather* **3097 wrathed,** *angered* **3105 dothe me drie,** *makes me suffer* **3109 But,** *unless* **3110 passaunt,** *surpassing*

3027 Wicked-Tonge, evil-speaking or gossip; French *Male Bouche.* **3058 is,** omitted in G. **3079 me,** omitted in G and Th.

My lyfe, my dethe, and my martyre°,
And tresour that I most desyre."
Than Bialacoil, affrayde all°,
Sayd, "Sir, it may not fall;°
That ye desyre, it may not aryse°.
What, wolde ye shende° me in this wyse?
A mokel° foole than I were,
If I suffred you away to bere
The fresshe bothom, so fayre of syght.
For it were neyther skyll° ne right
Of the roser ye broke the rynde°,
Or take the rose aforne his kynde°.
Ye are not courteys to aske it;
Let it stylle on the roser syt,
And growe tyl it amended° be,
And parfetly come to beaute.
I nolde not that it pulled were
Fro the roser that it bere;
To me it is so lefe° and dere."
With that anon sterte° out Daungere,
Out of the place where he was hydde.
His malyce in his chere was kydde°; DANGER
Ful great he was and blacke of hewe, AWAKENS
Sturdy and hydous, whoso him knewe;
Lyke sharpe urchons° his heer was growe,
His eyes reed sparclyng as the fyre-glowe;
His nose frounced°, ful kyrked° stode,
He come cryande° as he were woode°,
And sayd, "Bialacoyl, tel me why
Thou bringest hyder so boldely
Him that so nyghe is the rosere?
Thou worchest in a wronge manere;
He thynketh to dishonour the.
Thou arte wel worthy to have maugre°
To lette hym of the rosere wytte°!
Who serveth a felonne is yvel quytte°.
Thou woldest have done great bounte°,
And he with shame wolde quyte the.
Flye hence, felowe! I rede° the go!
It wanteth lytel° I wol the slo°;
For Bialacoyl ne Knewe me nought,
Whan the to serve he sette his thought;
For thou wolte shame him, if thou myght,
Bothe agayne reason and right.
I wol no more in the affye°,
That comest so slyghrly° for t'espy;
For it proveth wonder wele,
Thy sleight° and trayson every dele°."
I durst no more make there abode,
For the chorle he was so wode;
So ganne he thrette and manace,
And through the haye° he dyd me chace.
For feare of him I trymbled and quoke,
So chorlisshly his heed he shoke,
And sayd if efte° he myght me take,
I shulde nat from his hondes scape.
Than Bialacoil is fledde and mate°, THE LOVER
And I al soole°, disconsolate, REPULSED
Was lefte alone in payne and thought.
For shame to dethe I was nygh brought.
Than thought I on my highe foly,
Howe that my body utterly
Was yeve° to payne and to martyre;
And therto hadde I so great yre°
That I ne durst° the hayes passe;
There was no hoope, there was no grace.
I trowe° never man wyste° of payne,
But he were laced° in Loves chayne;
Ne no man wot°, and sothe it is,
But if he love, what anger is.
Love holdeth his heest° to me right wele
Whan payne he sayd I shulde fele.
No herte maye thynke, no tonge sayne,
A quarter of my wo and payne
I myght nat with the angre last;
Myne herte in poynt° was for to brast
Whan I thought on the rose that so
Was through Daunger caste me fro.
A longe whyle stoode I in that state,
Tyl that me sawe, so madde and mate°,
The lady of the highe warde°,
Which from her towre loked thiderwarde.

3111 martyre, *martyrdom* **3113 affrayde all,** *very upset* **3114 fall,** *happen* **3115 aryse,** *occur* **3116 shende,** *destroy* **3117 mokel,** *great* **3120 skyll,** *reasonable* **3121 rynde,** *bark* **3122 aforne his kynde,** *before its nature* (maturity) **3125 amended,** *improved* **3129 lefe,** *beloved* **3130 anon sterte,** *immediately leapt* **3132 kydde,** *evident* **3135 urchons,** *hedgehogs* **3137 frounced,** *wrinkled,* **kyrked,** *crooked* **3138 cryande,** *yelling,* **woode,** *insane* **3144 maugre,** *reproach* **3145 wytte,** *know* **3146 yvel quytte,** *badly rewarded* **3147 bounte,** *goodness* **3149 rede,** *advise* **3150 It wanted lytel,** *i.e., it won't take much,* **slo,** *slay* **3155 affye,** *trust* **3156 slyghly,** *slyly* **3158 sleight,** *cunning,* **every dele,** *completely* **3162 haye,** *hedge* **3165 efte,** *again* **3167 mate,** *defeated* **3168 soole,** *alone* **3173 yeve,** *given* **3174 yre,** *anger* **3175 durste,** *dared* **3177 trowe,** *think,* **wyste,** *knew* **3178 laced,** *caught* **3179 wot,** *knows* **3181 heest,** *promise* **3186 in poynt,** *at the point* **3190 mate,** *defeated* **3191 warde,** *watchtower*

3125 And growe, G and Th read "And let it growe." **3130 anon sterte out,** G reads "sterte out anon." **Daungere,** see 3018n. **3136** Line omitted in G. **3141 is,** omitted in G and Th. **3150 I,** G reads "it"; Th, "he"; the French is *je.* **3159 make there,** G reads "there make." **3164 he,** G reads "it." **3179 wot,** omitted in G and Th. **3188 Was,** G reads "That was."

Reason men clepe° that lady,
Whiche from her toure delyverly°
Come downe to me without more.
But she was neyther yonge ne hore°,
Ne hygh ne lowe, ne fatte ne lene,
But best as it were in a mene°.
Her eyen two were clere and lyght
As any candell that brenneth bright,
And on her heed she had a crowne.
Her semed wel an hygh person,
For rounde envyron° her crownet
Was ful of ryche stones fret°.
Her goodly semblant°, by devyse°,
I trowe° was made in paradyse,
For Nature had never suche a grace
To forge a werke of suche compace°.
For certeyne, but if trie letter lye,
God himselfe, that is so hye,
Made her after his ymage,
And yafe her sythe° suche avauntage
That she hath might and seignorie°
To kepe men from al folye.
Whoso wol trowe her lore°
Ne may offenden nevermore.
  And whyle I stode thus derke and pale,
Reson began to me her tale.
She sayde: "Al hayle, my swete frende!
Foly and childhode° wol the shende°,
Whiche the have put in great affray°.
Thou haste bought dere the tyme of May
That made thyn herte mery to be.
In yvel tyme thou wentest to se
The gardyn, wherof Ydelnesse
Bare the keye and was maistresse,
Whan thou yedest° in the daunce
With her, and had aqueyntaunce.
Her aqueyntaunce is peryllous,
First softe°, and after noyous°;
She hath the trashed°, of without wene°.
The God of Love hadde the nat sene°,
Ne had Idelnesse the conveyde
In the verger° where Myrthe him pleyde.
If folly have supprised the,
Do so that it recovered be,
And be wel ware to take no more
Counsayle that greveth after sore°.
He is wyse that wol hymselfe chastyse.
And though a yonge man in any wyse
Trespasse amonge°, and do folly,
Lette hym nat tary, but hastely
Lette hym amende what so be mys.
And eke I counsayle the, ywis°,
The God of Love holly foryete°,
That hath the in suche payne sette,
And the in herte tourmented so.
I can nat sene howe thou maist go
Other wayes to garysoun°;
For Daunger, that is so feloun°,
Felly° purposeth the to werrey°,
Whiche is ful cruel, the sothe to sey.
  "And yet of Dangere cometh no blame,
In rewarde of° my doughter Shame,
Whiche hath the roses in her warde°,
As she that may be no musarde°.
And Wicked-Tonge is with these two,
That suffreth no man thyder go°,
For er a thynge be do°, he shal,
Where that he cometh, over al,
In fourty places, if it be sought,
Say thyng that never was don ne wrought;
So moche trayson° is in his male°,
Of falsnesse for to sayne a tale.
Thou delest with angry folke, ywis;
Wherfore to the better is
From these folke awaye to fare,
For they wol make the lyve in care.
This is the yvel that love they cal,
Wherein there is but foly al,
For love is folly everydell°.
Who loveth, in no wyse maye do wel,

3193 clepe, *call* **3194 delyverly,** *quickly* **3196 hore,** *old* **3198 mene,** *average,* i.e., *golden mean* **3203 rounde envyron,** *all around* **3204 fret,** *adorned* **3205 semblant,** *face,* **devyse,** *careful arrangement* **3206 trowe,** *believe* **3208 compace,** *craft* **3212 sythe,** *after* **3213 seignorie,** *authority* **3215 lore,** *teaching* **3220 childhode,** *childishness,* **shende,** *ruin* **3221 affray,** *distress* **3227 yedest,** *went* **3230 softe,** *gentle,* **noyous,** *troubling* **3231 trasshed,** *betrayed,* **wene,** *doubt* **3232 hadde the nat sene,** *would not have seen you* **3234 verger,** *orchard* **3238 after sore,** *afterward sorely* **3241 amonge,** *at times* **3244 ywis,** *truly* **3245 holly foryete,** *to forget completely* **3249 garysoun,** *protection* **3250 feloun,** *malicious* **3251 Felly,** *cruelly,* **werrey,** *make war upon* **3254 rewarde to,** *comparison with* **3255 warde,** *protection* **3256 musarde,** *sluggard* **3258 thyder go,** *go there* **3259 do,** *done* **3263 trayson,** *slander,* **male,** *pouch* **3271 everydell,** *completely*

3193ff. Reason, descending from on high to console the narrator and an idealized beauty, Lady Reason is related to biblical Wisdom (Proverbs 7–8 and Wisdom 6–8) and Boethius's Philosophy (*Consolation of Philosophy* 1pr.1ff.). **3206 was,** G reads "were." **3217 thus,** Th reads "this." **3227 yedest,** G reads "didest." **3231 the,** omitted in G and Th. **3248 nat,** omitted in G.

Ne sette his thought on no good werke;
His schole° he leseth°, if he be a clerke,
Or other crafte eke if that he be;
He shal nat thryve therin, for he
In love shal have more passyoun°
Than monke, hermyte, or chanoun.
This payne is herde°, out of measure,
The joye maye eke no whyle endure;
And in the. possessyoun
Is moche trybulatioun;
The joye it is so shorte lastynge,
And but in happe° is the gettyng;
For I se there many in travayle,
That at laste foule° fayle.
I was nothyng° thy counsayler,
Whan thou were made the homager°
Of God of Love to hastely;
There was no wysdom, but foly.
Thyn herte was joly but not sage°
Whan thou were brought in suche a rage
To yelde the° so redily,
And to love of his great maystry°.
I rede the° love away to drive,
That maketh the retche° not of thy lyve.
The foly more fro day to day
Shal growe but° thou it put away.
Take with thy tethe° the bridel faste°,
To daunte° thyn herte; and eke the caste°,
If that thou mayst, to get the defence
For to redresse thy first offence.
Whoso his herte alway wol leve°,
Shal fynde amonge° that shal him greve."
  When I her herde thus me chastyse,
I answerde in ful angry wyse. THE LOVER'S REPLY
I prayde her cesse° of her speche,
Eyther to chastyse me or teche,
To bydde me my thought refreyne,
Whiche Love hath caught in his demeyne°:
"What, wene ye° Love wol consente,
That me assayleth with bowe bente,
To drawe myn herte out of his honde,
Which is so quickly in his bonde?
That° ye counsayle may never be;
For whan he first arested° me,
He toke myne herte so sore him tyll°
That it is nothyng at my wyll.
He taught it so him for to obey
That he it sparred° with a key.
I pray you let me be al styll°,
For ye may wel, if that ye wyll,
Your wordes waste in ydelnesse;
For utterly, withouten gesse°,
Al that ye sayne is but in vayne.
Me were lever° dye in the payne,
Than Love to me-warde shulde arette°
Falshede, or treson on me sette.
I wol me get pris° or blame,
And love trewe, to save my name;
Who that me chastyseth°, I him hate."
  With that worde Reson went her gate°,
Whan she saw for no sermonyng
She myght me fro my foly bring.
Than° dismayed, I lefte al soole°,
Forwery°, forwandred° as a foole,
For I ne knewe no chevysaunce°.
Than I fel into my remembraunce
Howe Love bade me to purvey°
A felowe to whom I might sey
My counsell and my privyte,
For that shulde moche avayle me.
With that bethought I me that I
Had a felowe fast° by,
Trewe and syker°, curteys and hende°,
And he was called by name a Frende; THE FRIEND
A trewer felowe was nowhere non.
In haste to him I went anon,
And to him al my wo I tolde;
Fro him right nought I wolde witholde.
I tolde him al without were°,
And made my compleynt on Daungere,
Howe for to se he was hydous,
And to me-warde contraryous;

3274 schole, *education,* **leseth,** *loses* **3277 passyoun,** *suffering* **3279 herde,** *hard* **3284 but in happe,** *only by chance* **3286 foule,** *miserably* **3287 nothyng,** *not at all* **3288 homager,** *vassal, feudal subordinate* **3291 sage,** *wise* **3293 yelde the,** *yield yourself* **3294 maystry,** *dominion* **3295 rede the,** *advise you* **3296 retche,** *care* **3298 but,** *unless* **3299 tethe,** *teeth,* **faste,** *firmly* **3300 daunte,** *subdue,* **the caste,** *apply yourself* **3303 wol leve,** *will allow to leave* **3304 amonge,** *from time to time* **3307 cesse,** *stop* **3310 demeyne,** *power* **3311 wene ye,** *do you think* **3314 That,** *what* **3316 arested,** *captured* **3317 so sore him tyll,** *so forcefully to him* **3320 sparred,** *locked* **3321 al styll,** *in quiet* **3324 gesse,** *doubt* **3326 Me were lever,** *I would rather* **3327 arette,** *impute* **3329 pris,** *praise* **3331 chastyseth,** *reprimands* **3332 gate,** *way* **3335 Than,** *then,* **soole,** *alone* **3336 Forwery,** *very weary,* **forwandred,** *worn out with wandering* **3337 chevysaunce,** *relief* **3339 purvey,** *seek* **3343 fast,** *close* **3345 syker,** *reliable,* **hende,** *competent* **3351 were,** *doubt*

3275 Or...if that..., G reads "Of...if...." **3278 chanoun,** canon; a clergyman who lives a communal life and helps to administer a cathedral, college, or other ecclesiastical institution. **3279 This,** G reads "The." **of,** omitted in G. **3319 taught,** G and Th read "thought." **3337 chevysaunce,** G and Th read "cherysaunce." **3338 Than I,** G and Th read "Thanne."

The whiche through his cruelte
Was in poynte° to have meymed° me,
With Bialacoil whan he me sey°
Within the gardyn walke and pley.
Fro me he made him for to go,
And I belefte alone in wo;
I durste° no lenger with him speke,
For Daunger says he wolde be wreke°,
Whan that he sawe howe I wente
The fresshe bothom° for to hente°,
If I were hardy° to come nere
Bytwene the hay° and the rosere°.
 This Frende, whan he wyst° of my thought,
He discomforted me right nought,
But sayd, "Felowe, be not so madde,
Ne so abasshed° nor bestadde°.
Myselfe I knowe ful wel Daungere,
And howe he is fiers of his chere°
At prime temps° love to manace;
Ful ofte I have ben in his case°.
A felon first though that he be,
After thou shalt him souple° se.
Of longe passed I knew him wele;
Ungoodly first though men him fele,
He wol meke after in his bearynge
Ben, for servyce and obeyssynge°.
I shal the tel what thou shalt do:
Mekely I rede° thou go him to;
Of herte pray him specially
Of thy trespace to have mercy;
And hote° him wel, here to plese,
That thou shalte nevermore him displese,
Who can best serve of flatery
Shal plese Daunger moste utterly."
My Frende hath sayd to me so wele
That he me eased hath somdele°,
And eke alegged° of my turment;
For through him had I hardement°
Agayne to Daunger for to go,
To preve if I might meke° him so.
 To Daunger came I al ashamed,
The whiche aforne° me had blamed,
Desyring for to pese° my wo—
But over hedge durste I not go,
For he forbode me the passage.
I founde him cruel in his rage,
And in his honde a great burdown°.
To him I kneled lowe adown,
Ful meke of porte, and symple of chere,
And sayd, "Sir I am comen here
Onely to aske of you mercy.
That greveth me ful greatly
That ever my lyfe I wrathed° you.
But for to amenden I am come now,
With al my might, bothe loude and styll,
To done right at your owne wyl;
For Love made me for to do
That I have trespassed hiderto°;
Fro whom I ne maye withdrawe myne hert.
Yet shal I never, for joye ne smert°;
What so befal°, good or il,
Offende more agayne your wyl;
Lever I have° endure disease
Than do that shulde you displease.
 "I you requyre and praye that ye
Of me have mercy and pyte,
To stynt° your yre° that greveth so,
That I wol swere for evermo
To be redressed° at your lykyng,
Yf I trespasse in anythyng—
Save° that I praye the graunt me
A thynge that maye nat warned° be,
That I maye love, al onely°;
None other thynge of you aske I.
I shal done al wel, ywis°,
Yf of your grace ye graunt me this;
And ye maye nat letten° me,
For wel wote° ye that love is free,
And I shal loven, sith that° I wyl,
Whoever lyke it wel or yl;
And yet ne wolde I, for al Fraunce,
Do thynge to do you displesaunce."
 Than Daungere fyl in his entent°
For to foryeve° his maletalent°;

3356 in poynte, *ready,* **meymed,** *injured* **3357 sey,** *saw* **3361 durste,** *dared* **3362 wreke,** *avenged* **3364 bothom,** *bud,* **hente,** *seize* **3365 hardy,** *bold* **3366 hay,** *hedge,* **rosere,** *rosebush* **3367 wyst,** *knew* **3370 abasshed,** *confused,* **bestadde,** *beset* **3372 chere,** *expression* **3373 At prime temps,** *at the start* **3374 case,** *snare* **3376 souple,** *flexible* **3380 obeyssynge,** *obedience* **3382 rede,** *advise* **3385 hote,** *promise* **3390 somdele,** *somewhat* **3391 eke alegged,** *also allayed* **3392 hardement,** *courage* **3394 meke,** *soften* **3396 aforne,** *before* **3397 pese,** *appease* **3401 burdown,** *club* **3407 wrathed,** *angered* **3412 hiderto,** *until now* **3414 smert,** *pain* **3415 befal,** *happens* **3417 Lever I have,** *I would rather* **3421 stynt,** *cease,* **yre,** *anger* **3423 redressed,** *repaid* **3425 Save,** *except* **3426 warned,** *refused* **3427 al onely,** *simply* **3429 ywis,** *truly* **3431 letten,** *hinder* **3432 wote,** *know* **3433 sith that,** *since* **3437 fyl in his entent,** *decided* **3438 foryeve,** *give up,* **maletalent,** *malevolence*

3356 have meymed, G reads "meygned." **3372 his,** omitted in Th. **3379 meke,** G reads "make." **3414 I,** omitted in G. **3418 shulde you,** G reads "you shulde." **3429 al,** G reads "elles." **3433 sith,** G reads "sichen"; Th, "suche."

But al his wrathe yet. at last
He hath released, I prayde so fast.
Shortely he sayd, "Thy request
Is nat to mokel dishonest°;
Ne I wol nat werne° it the,
For yet nothynge engreveth° me.
For though thou love thus evermore,
To me is neither softe ne sore.
Love where that the lyst°: what retcheth me°,
So° thou ferre fro my roses be?
Trust nat on me, for none assaye°,
If any tyme thou passe the haye°."
Thus hath he graunted my prayere.
Than went I forthe, withouten were°
Unto my Frende, and tolde hym al,
Whiche was right joyful of my tale.
He sayd, "Nowe go the wel thyne affayre.
He shal to the be debonayre°
Though he aforne was dispitous°,
He shal herafter be gratious.
If he were touched on some good veyne,
He shulde yet rewern° on thy peyne.
Suffre, I rede°, and no boost make,
Tyl thou at good mes° mayst him take.
By sufferaunce and wordes softe,
A man maye overcome ofte
Him that aforne he had in drede,
In bokes sothely° as I rede."
Thus hath my Frende with great comforte
Avaunced me with high disporte°,
Whiche wolde° me good as moche as I.
And than anone ful sodainly
I toke my leave, and streight I went
Unto the haye; for great talent°
I hadde to sene the fresshe bothom°,
Wherein laye my salvatioun.
And Daungere toke kepe°, if that° I
Kepe him covenaunt trewly.
So sore I dradde his manasyng°,
I durste nat breke his byddyng;
For lest° that I were of him shent°,
I brake nat his commaundement,
For to purchase° good wyl.
It was hard for to come there-tyl°,
His mercy was to ferre° behynde.
I wepte for I ne myght it fynde,
I complayned and sighed sore,
And languysshed evermore,
For I durst nat over go
Unto the rose I loved so.
Throughout my demyng° utterly,
Tyl he had knowlege certainly,
That Love me ladde in suche a wyse,
That in me there was no feyntise°,
Falsheed, ne mo trechery.
And yet he, ful of villany,
Of disdayne, and cruelte,
On me ne wolde have pyte,
His cruel wyl for to refrayne°,
Tho I wepte alwaye, and me complayne.
And while I was in this tourment
Were come of grace, by God sent,
Fraunchise°, and with her
Pyte,
CANDOR AND PITY INTERCEDE
Fulfylde the bothen° of bounte.
They go to Daungere anon-ryght
To forther me with al her myght,
And helpe in worde and in dede,
For wel they sawe that it was nede.
First, of her grace, Dame Fraunchise
Hath taken word° of this emprise°.
She sayd, "Daungere, great wronge ye do
To worche this man so moche wo,
Or pynen° him so angerly;
It is to you great villany.
I canne nat se why, ne how,
That he hath trespassed agayne you,
Save that he loveth; wherfore ye shulde
The more in cherete of him holde°.
The force of Love maketh hym do this;
Who wolde him blame he dyd amys?
He leseth more than ye maye do;

3442 to mokel dishonest, *too much dishonorable* **3443 werne,** *refuse* **3444 engreveth,** *displeases* **3447 the lyst,** *it pleases you,* **retcheth me,** *do I care* **3448 So,** *as long as* **3449 assaye,** *attempt* **3450 haye,** *hedge* **3452 were,** *hesitation* **3456 debonayre,** *gentle* **3457 dispitous,** *scornful* **3460 rewen,** *have pity* **3461 rede,** *advise* **3462 at good mes,** *in good position* **3466 sothely,** *truly* **3468 disporte,** *solace* **3469 Whiche wolde,** *who wished* **3472 talent,** *desire* **3473 bothom,** *bud* **3475 kepe,** *care,* **if that,** *to determine if* **3477 manasyng,** *menacing* **3479 lest,** *fear,* **shent,** *destroyed* **3481 purchase,** *acquire* **3482 there-tyl,** *to that* **3483 to ferre,** *too far* **3489 demyng,** *consideration* **3491 Than,** *then* **3492 feyntise,** *deception* **3497 refrayne,** *restrain* **3501 Fraunchise,** *Frankness* **3502 the bothen,** *both of them* **3508 Hath taken word,** *spoke,* **emprise,** *undertaking* **3511 pynen,** *pain* **3516 in cherete of him holde,** *hold him in affection*

3448 thou, omitted in G and Th. **3450 If any tyme thou,** G reads "I ony tyme to"; Th, "In any tyme to." **3552 he,** G reads "ye." **3468 me,** omitted in G. **3482 hard,** omitted in G and Th. **3484 wepte,** Th reads "kepte." **3490** In G this line is added in a later hand, filling a space; see1984n. **3502 bothen,** G and Th read "bothom." **3508 word,** omitted in G and Th.

His payne is harde, ye maye se, lo!
And Love in no wyse wolde consent
That he have power to repent;
For though that quicke° ye wolde him slo°,
Fro Love his herte may nat go.
Nowe, swete sir, is it your ease
Him for to angre or disease°?
Alas, what maye it you avaunce
To done to him so great grevaunce?
What worshippe° is it agayne him take°,
Or on your man a werre make,
Sithe° he so lowly every wyse°
Is redy, as ye luste° devyse?
If Love hath caught him in his lace°,
You for t'obey in every caas,
And ben your subjecte at your wyl,
Shulde ye therfore wyllen him yl?
Ye shulde him spare more, al out°,
Than him that is bothe proude and stout°.
Curtesy wol° that ye socure°
Hem that ben meke under your cure°.
His hert is harde that wol nat meke°,
Whan men of mekenesse him beseke."
"This is certayne," sayd Pyte
"We se ofte that humylyte
Bothe yre° and also felony°
Venquyssheth, and also melancoly.
To stonde forthe in suche duresse°,
Th'is° cruelte and wickednesse.
Wherfore I pray you, Sir Daungere,
For to mayntene no lenger here
Suche cruel werre agayne your man,
As holly° yours as ever he can;
Nor that ye worchen no more wo
Upon this caytife° that languyssheth so,
Whiche wol no more to you trespace,
But put him holly in your grace;
His offence ne was but lyte.
The God of Love it was to wyte°,
That he your thrall so greatly is,
And if ye harme him, ye done amys,
For he hath had ful harde penaunce,
Syth that° ye refte° him th'aqueyntaunce
Of Bialacoil°, his moste joye,
Whiche al his paynes might acoye°.
He was before anoyed sore,
But than ye doubled him wel more;
For he of blysse hath ben ful bare
Sythe Bialacoil was fro hym fare°.
Love hath to hym do° great distresse;
He hath no nede of more duresse.
Voydeth° from him your yre, I rede°;
Ye may not wynnen in this dede.
Maketh Bialacoil repayre° agayne,
And haveth pyte upon his payne;
For Fraynchyse wol°, and I, Pyte,
That mercyful to him ye be.
And sythe that she and I accorde,
Have upon him misericorde°,
For I you pray, and eke moneste°,
Nought to refusen our requeste;
For he is harde and fel° of thought,
That for us two wol do right nought."
Daunger ne might no more endure;
He meked him° unto measure°.
"I wol in no wyse," sayth Daungere,
"Deny that ye have asked here;
It were to great uncurtesye.
I wol he have the companye
Of Bialacoil, as ye devyse;
I wol him let in no wyse."
To Bialacoil than went in hye°
Fraunchise, and sayd ful curteslye,
"Ye have to longe be deignous°
Unto this lover, and daungerous°,
Fro him to withdrawe your presence,
Whiche hath do to him great offence,
That ye not wolde upon him se°,
Wherfore a sorouful man is he.
Shape° ye to paye him, and to please,
Of° my love if ye wol have ease.

3523 quicke, *alive,* **slo,** *slay* **3526 disease,** *discomfort* **3529 worshippe,** *honor,* **agayne him taken,** *to take* (sides) *against him* **3531 Sithe,** *since,* **every wyse,** *in every way* **3532 ye luste,** *it pleases you to* **3533 lace,** *snare* **3537 al out,** *everything considered* **3538 stout,** *hostile* **3439 wol,** *demands,* **socure,** *comfort* **3540 cure,** *care* **3541 meke,** *be meek* **3545 yre,** *anger,* **felony,** *ill will* **3547 duresse,** *hardness* **3548 Th'is,** *this is* **3552 holly,** *wholly* **3554 caytife,** *captive* **3558 wyte,** *blame* **3562 Syth that,** *since,* **reft,** *deprived* (of) **3563 Bialacoil,** *Fair Welcome* **3564 acoye,** *quiet* **3568 fare,** *gone* **3569 do,** *done* **3571 Voydeth,** *remove,* **rede,** *advise* **3573 repayre,** *return* **3575 wol,** *wishes* **3578 misericorde,** *pity* **3579 eke moneste,** *also admonish* **3581 fel,** *evil* **3584 meked him,** *humbled himself,* **measure,** *moderation* **3591 hye,** *haste* **3593 deignous,** *disdainful* **3594 daungerous,** *aloof* **3597 se,** *look* **3599 Shape,** *plan* **3600 Of,** *for*

3522 he, G and Th read "he." **3525 is it,** G and Th read "it is." **3533 hath,** Th reads "have." **3543 This,** G reads "That." **3552 he,** G reads "ye." **3569 do,** omitted in Th. **3588 he,** G and Th read "ye." **3595–3690** Lines lacking in G; two pages missing.

RETURN OF FAIR-WELCOME

Fulfyl his wyl°, sithe that°
ye knowe
Daunger is daunted° and brought lowe
Through helpe of me and of Pyte;
You dare° no more aferde be."
"I shal do right as ye wyl,"
Saith Bialacoil, "for it is skyl°,
Sithe Daunger wol that it so be."
Than Fraunchise hath him sent to me.
Byalacoil at the begynnyng
Salued° me in his commyng;
No straungenesse° was in him sene,
No more than he ne had wrathed bene.
As fayre semblaunt° than shewed he me,
And goodly, as aforne° dyd he;
And by the honde, without dout,
Within, the haye° right al about
He ladde me, with right good chere,
Al envyron° the vergere°
That Daunger hadde me chased fro.
Nowe have I leave over al to go;
Nowe am I raysed, at my devyse°,
Fro hel unto paradyse.
Thus Bialacoil, of gentylnesse,
With al his payne and besynesse,
Hath shewed me onely of grace
The estres° of the swote° place.
I sawe the rose, whan I was nygh°,
Was greatter woxen°, and more high,
Fresshe, roddy°, and fayre of hewe,
Of coloure ever yliche° newe.
And when I hadde it longe sene,
I sawe that through the leves grene
The rose spredde to spaunysshinge°;
To sene it was a goodly thynge.
But it ne was so sprede on brede°
That men within myght knowe the sede;
For it covert was and close
Bothe with the leves and with the rose.
The stalke was even and grene upright;
It was theron a goodly syght,
And wel the better, without wene°,
For the seed was nat sene.
Ful fayre it spradde, God it blesse,
For suche another, as I gesse,
Aforne ne was, ne more vermayle°.
I was abawed° for marveyle,
For ever the fayrer that it was,
The more I am bounden in Loves laas°.
Longe I abode there, sothe to saye,
Tyl Bialacoil I ganne to praye,
Whan that I sawe him in no wyse
To me warnen° his servyce,
That he me wolde graunt a thynge,
Whiche to remembre is wel syttynge°—
This is to sayne that of his grace
He wolde me yeve leysar° and space,
To me that was so desyrous
To have a kyssynge precious
Of the goodly fresshe rose,
That so swetely smelleth in my nose:
"For if it you displeased nought,
I wolde gladly, as I have sought,
Have a cosse° therof freely
Of your yefte°; for certainly
I wol none have but by your leve,
So lothe me were you for to greve."
He sayd, "Frende, so God me spede,
Of Chastite I have suche drede;
Thou shuldest nat warned° be for me,
But I dare nat, for Chastyte.
Agayne her dare I nat mysdo,
For alwaye byddeth she me so
To yeve no lover leave to kysse.
For who therto maye wynnen, ywisse°,
He of the surplus° of the praye°
May live in hoope to gette some daye.
For whoso kyssynge maye attayne
Of loves payne hath, sothe to sayne,
The best and most avenaunt°,
And ernest° of the remenaunt."
Of his answere I sighed sore;
I durst assaye° him tho° no more,
I hadde suche drede to greve him aye°.
A man shulde nat to moche assaye
To chafe his frende out of measure°,

3601 wyl, *desire,* **sithe that,** *since* **3602 daunted,** *defeated* **3604 You dare,** *you need* **3606 skyl,** *reasonable* **3610 Salued,** *greeted* **3611 straungeness,** *aloofness* **3613 semblaunt,** *appearance* **3614 aforne,** *before* **3616 haye,** *hedge* **3618 Al envyron,** *all around,* **vergere,** *orchard* **3621 devyse,** *desire* **3626 estres,** *interior,* **swote,** *sweet* **3627 nygh,** *near* **3628 woxen,** *grown* **3629 roddy,** *red* **3630 yliche,** *like* **3634 spaunysshinge,** *full expansion* (blossom) **3635 on brede,** *in breadth* **3641 wene,** *doubt* **3645 vermayle,** *vermilion* **3646 abawed,** *amazed* **3648 laas,** *net* **3652 warnen,** *refuse* **3654 wel syttynge,** *appropriate* **3656 me yeve leysar,** *give me time* **3663 cosse,** *kiss* **3664 yefte,** *gift* **3669 warned,** *refused* **3674 ywisse,** *truly* **3675 surplus,** *remainder,* **praye,** *request* **3679 avenaunt,** *pleasing* **3680 ernest,** *promise* **3682 durst assaye,** *dared try,* **tho,** *then* **3683 aye,** *constantly* **3685 out of measure,** *inordinately*

3643 God it, Th reads "the god of." **3676 May live,** Th reads "My lyfe."

Nor putte his lyfe in aventure°;
For no man at the first stroke
Ne maye nat fel downe an oke,
Nor of the reysyns° have the wyne
Tyl grapes be rype and wel afyne°
Be sore empressed, I you ensure,
And drawn out of the pressure°.
But I, forpeyned° wonder stronge,
Thought that I abode° right longe
After° the kysse, in payne and wo,
Sithe° I to kysse desyred so;
Tyl that, rewyng° on my distresse,
There to me Venus the goddesse,
Whiche aye werryeth° Chastite,
Came of her grace to socour° me,
Whose myght is knowe° ferre and wyde,

VENUS ASSISTS THE LOVER

For she is mother of Cupyde,
The God of Love, blynde as stone,
That helpeth lovers many one.
This lady brought in her right honde
Of brennynge fyre a blasyng bronde°,
Wherof the flame and hote fyre
Hath many a lady in° desyre
Of love brought, and sore hette°,
And in her servyce her° hertes sette.
This lady was of good entayle°,
Right wonderful of apparayle;
By her atyre° so bright and shene,
Men myght perceyve wel and sene
She was nat of relygioun°.
Nor I nyl° make mencioun
Nor of robe, nor of tresour,
Of broche, neither of her riche attour°,
Ne of her gyrdel about her syde,
For that I nyl nat longe abyde;
But knoweth wel that certainly
She was arrayed richely.
Devoyde of pride certayne she was.
To Bialacoil she went a paas°,
And to hym shortely, in a clause,
She sayd: "Sir, what is the cause
Ye ben of porte so daungerous°
Unto this lover, and daynous°,
To graunt him nothyng but a kysse?
To warne° it him ye done amysse,
Sithe wel ye wotte° howe that he
Is Loves servant, as ye maye se,
And hath beaute, wherthrough he is
Worthy of love to have the blys.
Howe he is semely°, beholde and se,
Howe he is fayre, howe he is free°,
Howe he is swote° and debonayre,
Of age yonge, lusty°, and fayre.
There is no lady so hawtayne°,
Duchesse, countesse, ne chastelayne°,
That I nolde holde her ungoodly
For to refuce him utterly.
His brethe is also good and swete,
And eke his lyppes roddy°, and mete°
Onely to playne° and to kysse.
Graunt him a kysse of gentylnysse°!
His teth arne° also white and clene.
Me thynketh wronge, withouten wene°,
If ye nowe warne° him, trusteth me,
To graunt that a kysse have he.
The lasse to helpe him that ye haste,
The more tyme shul ye waste."
When the flame of the very° bronde

THE KISS GRANTED

That Venus brought in her right honde
Hadde Bialacoil with hete smete°,
Anone he badde°, withouten lete°,
Graunt° to me the rose kysse.
Than of my payne I ganne to lysse°,
And to the rose anone went I,
And kyssed it ful faithfully.
There no man° aske if I was blythe

3686 aventure, *hazard* **3689 reysyns,** *grapes* **3690 wel afyne,** *thoroughly* **3692 pressure,** *wine press* **3693 forpeyned,** *tormented* **3694 abode,** *waited* **3695 After,** *for* **3696 Sithe,** *since* **3697 rewyng,** *taking pity* **3699 werryeth,** *makes war upon* **3700 socour,** *aid* **3701 knowe,** *known* **3706 blasyng bronde,** *blazing torch* **3708 in,** *into* **3709 sore hette,** *intensely heated* **3710 her,** *their* **3711 entayle,** *shape* **3713 atyre,** *clothing* **3715 of relygioun,** *of a religious order* **3716 Nor I nyl,** *I will not* **3718 attour,** *dress* **3724 a paas,** *quickly* **3727 of porte so daungerous,** *so aloof in behavior* **3728 daynous,** *disdainful* **3730 warne,** *refuse* **3731 wotte,** *know* **3735 semely,** *handsome* **3736 free,** *generous* **3737 swote,** *pleasant* **3738 lusty,** *lively* **3739 hawtayne,** *haughty* **3740 chastelayne,** *lady of a castle* **3744 roddy,** *red,* **mete,** *suitable* **3745 playne,** *lament* **3746 gentylnysse,** *nobility* **3747 teth arne,** *teeth are* **3748 wene,** *doubt* **3749 warne,** *refuse* **3753 very,** *same* **3755 smete,** *struck* **3756 badde,** *ordered,* **lete,** *hesitation* **3757 Graunt,** *permission* **3758 lysse,** *be relieved* **3761 There no man,** *it is not necessary for any man to* (see *MED* "thurven" v.2b)

3694 Thought, G and Th read "Though." **3697 rewyng,** G and Th read "rennyng." **3698 to me,** G and Th read "come." **3710 hertes,** G and Th read "herte is." **3733 he,** omitted in G and Th. **3740 countesse,** G reads "ne countesse." **3751 to,** G and Th read "ye." **3752 The,** Th reads "And the." **3755 with hete,** Th reads "with his hete." **3756 bade,** G and Th read "bade me." **3761 There no,** Th reads "There nede no."

When the savour° softe and lythe°
Stroke° to myne hert without more,
And me alleged° of my sore,
So was I ful of joye and blysse.
It is fayre suche a floure to kysse,
It was so swote° and saverous.
I myght nat be so anguysshous°,
That I ne mote° gladde and joly be,
Whan that I remembre me.
Yet ever amonge°, sothly to sayne,
I suffre noye° and moche payne.
The see° may never be so styl,
That with a litel winde it wyl
Overwhelme and tourne also,
As it were woode°, in wawes go.
After the calme the trouble sonne
Mote° folowe and chaunge as the moone.
Right so fareth Love, that selde in one°
Holdeth his ancre°; for right anone
Whan they in ease wene° best to lyve,
They ben with tempest al fordryve°.
Who serveth Love canne tel of wo;
The stoundmele° joye mote overgo.
Nowe he hurteth, and nowe he cureth,
For selde in o poynte Love endureth.
  Nowe is it right me to procede, DEFENSE OF
Howe Shame gan medle and take hede, THE ROSE
Through whom fel angres° I have hade;
And howe the stronge wall was made,
And the castell of brede and length, SHAME
That God of Love wan with his strength.
Al this in romance wyll I sette,
And for nothyng ne wyll I lette°,
So that it lykyng° to her be,
That is the flour of beaute;
For she may best my labour quyte°,
That I for her love shal endyte°.
  Wicked-Tonge, that the covyne°
Of every lover can devyne°
Worste, and addeth more somdele°— WICKED-
For Wicked-Tonge saythe never wele— TONGUE
To me-warde bare he right great hate,
Espyeng me erly and late,
Tyl he hath sene the great chere°
Of Bialacoil and me yfere°.
He might not his tonge withstonde
Worse to reporte than he fonde,
He was so ful of cursed rage;
It satte him wel of° his lynage°,
For him an Irisshe° woman bare.
His tongue was fyled sharpe and square°,
Poignaunt° and right kervyng°,
And wonder bytter in spekyng.
For whan that he me gan espye°,
He swore affirmyng sykerly°
Bytwene Bialacoil and me
Was yvel aquayntaunce and prive°.
He spake thereof so folilye
That he awaked Jelousye, JEALOUSY
Whiche, al afrayde° in his risyng,
Whan that he herde janglyng°,
He ran anon as he were wode
To Bialacoil there that he stode,
Whiche had lever° in this caas°
Have ben at Reynes or Amyas.
For foote-hote°, in his felonye°,
To hym thus sayd Jelousye:
"Why haste thou ben so neglygent,
To kepen°, whan I was absent,
This verger° here left in thy warde°?
To me thou haddest no regarde,
To truste—to thy confusyon—
Him thus, to whom suspection
I have right great; for it is nede°,
It is wel shewed by the dede.
Great faute° in the nowe have I founde;
By God, anone thou shalte be bounde,
And faste loken° in a toure,

3762 savour, *taste,* **lythe,** *smooth* **3763 Stroke,** *struck* **3764 allegged,** *alleviated* **3767 swote,** *sweet* **3768 anguysshous,** *tormented* **3769 mote,** *may* **3771 ever amonge,** *now and then* **3772 noye,** *distress* **3773 see,** *sea* **3776 woode,** *mad* **3778 Mote,** *must* **3779 selde in one,** *seldom in one* (place) **3780 ancre,** *anchor* **3781 wene,** *think* **3782 fordryve,** *driven about* **3784 stoundmele,** *momentary* **3789 fel angres,** *cruel agonies* **3794 lette,** *stop* **3795 lykyng,** *pleasing* **3797 quyte,** *repay* **3798 endyte,** *write poetry* **3799 covyne,** *secret plans* **3800 devyne,** *discover* **3801 somdele,** *somewhat* **3805 chere,** *happiness* **3806 yfere,** *together* **3810 satte him wel of,** *was fitting to,* **lynage,** *lineage* **3811 Irisshe,** *Irish* (but perhaps also *angry, full of ire*) **3812 square,** *whetted* **3813 Poignaunt,** *piercing,* **kervyng,** *cutting* **3815 gan espye,** *did see* **3816 affirmyng sykerly,** (that) *secure agreement* **3818 prive,** *secret* **3821 afrayde,** *aroused* **3822 janglyng,** *argument* **3825 had lever,** *would rather,* **in this caas,** *at this time* **3827 foote-hoote,** *hot-footed* (in a hurry), **felonye,** *malice* **3830 kepen,** *protect* **3831 verger,** *orchard,* **warde,** *protection* **3835 nede,** *necessary* **3837 faute,** *fault* **3839 loken,** *locked*

3769 ne, omitted in G and Th. **3774 it wyl,** Th reads "at wyl." **3779 selde,** G reads "yelde." **3786 selde,** G reads "elde." **3826 Reynes or Amyas,** Rennes, in Brittany, and perhaps Meaux (near Paris). The French has *Estampes ou a Mieuz* (Etampes or Meaux), both near Paris. **3832 regarde,** G reads "rewarde."

Without refuyte° or socoure°.
For Shame to longe hath be the fro°;
Over soone she was ago°.
Whan thou hast lost bothe drede and fere,
It semed wel she was nat here.
She was besy in no wyse,
To kepe the and to chastice,
And for to helpen Chastite
To kepe the roser°, as thynketh me.
For than this boye-knave° so boldly
Ne shulde nat have be hardy°,
Ne in this verger hadde suche game,
Whiche nowe me tourneth to great shame."
  Bialacoil nyst° what to saye;
Ful fayne° he wolde have fledde away,
For feare have hydde, nere that he°
Al sodainly toke° him with me.
And whan I sawe he had so—
This Jelousye—take us two,
I was astoned and knewe no rede°,
But fledde away for very drede.
  Than Shame came forthe ful symply—
She wende have° trespaced ful greatly—
Humble of her porte, and made it symple°,
Wearyng a vayle° in stede of wymple°,
As nonnes done in her abbey.
Bycause her herte was in affray°,
She gan to speke within a throwe°
To Jelousye, right wonder lowe.
First of his grace she besought,
And sayd, "Sir, ne leveth° nought
Wicked-Tonge, that false espye°,
Whiche is so glad to fayne° and lye.
He hath you made, through flateryng,
On Bialacoil a false leasing°.
His falsnesse is not nowe anewe;
It is to longe that he him knewe.
This is not the first daye,
For Wicked-Tonge hath custome aye°
Yonge folkes to bewrye°,
And false lesynges on hem lye.
Yet neverthelesse I se amonge°
That the loigne° it is so longe
Of Bialacoil, hertes to lure,
In Loves servyce for to endure,
Drawyng suche folke him to
That he hath nothyng with to do°.
But in sothnesse° I trowe° nought
That Bialacoil had ever in thought
To do trespace or vilanye,
But for his mother Curtesye
Hath taught him ever to be
Good of acqueyntaunce° and prive°.
For he loveth none hevynesse°,
But myrthe and play and al gladnesse.
He hateth al trecherous,
Soleyne° folke and envyous,
For ye weten° howe that he
Wol ever glad and joyful be
Honestly with folke to pley.
I have be neglygent, in good fey°,
To chastyse him; therfore nowe I,
Of herte I crye you here mercy,
That I have ben so recheles°
To tamen hym withouten lees°.
Of my foly I me repente;
Nowe wol I hole° set myn entente
To kepe°, bothe lowde and styll°,
Bialacoil to do your wyll."
  "Shame, shame," sayd Jelousy;
"To be bytrasshed° great drede have I.
Lecherye hath clombe° so hye
That almoste blered° is myn eye.
No wonder is if that drede have I;
Over al reigneth Lechery,
Whose myght groweth nyght and dey.
Bothe in cloystre and in abbey

3840 refuyte, *refuge,* **socoure,** *aid* **3841 the fro,** *from you* **3842 ago,** *gone* **3848 roser,** *rosebush* **3849 boye-knave,** *scoundrel* **3850 hardy,** *bold* **3853 nyst,** *didn't know* **3854 ful fayne,** *very gladly* **3855 nere that he,** *if it had not been that he* (Jealousy) **3856 toke,** *caught* **3859 knewe no rede,** *knew not what to do* **3862 wende have,** *thought to have* **3863 made it symple,** *acted innocently* **3864 vayle,** *veil,* **wymple,** *pleated head-dress* **3866 affray,** *fear* **3867 throwe,** *moment* **3870 leveth,** *believe* **3871 espye,** *spy* **3872 fayne,** *pretend* **3874 leasyng,** *lie* **3878 aye,** *always* **3879 bewrye,** *betray* **3881 amonge,** *from time to time* **3882 loigne,** *leash* **3886 hath nothyng with to do,** *is not even aware of* **3887 sothnesse,** *truth,* **trowe,** *believe* **3892 Good of acqueyntaunce,** *companionable,* **prive,** *intimate* **3893 hevynesse,** *sadness* **3896 Soleyne,** *solitary* **3897 weten,** *know* **3900 fey,** *faith* **3903 recheles,** *careless* **3904 lees,** *lies* (or leash?) **3906 hole,** *wholly* **3905 kepe,** *compel,* **bothe lowde and styll,** *both loudly and quietly* (i.e., under all circumstances) **3910 bytrasshed,** *betrayed* **3911 clombe,** *climbed* **3912 blered,** *blinded* (deceived)

3846 to chastice, G and Th omit "to." **3851 Ne,** omitted in G and Th. **verger,** G and Th read "verge." **3895 trecherous,** G and Th read "trechours." **3902 I,** omitted in G and Th. **3907 lowde,** G and Th read "lowe." **3912 blered is myn eye,** blinded is my eye; I am deceived. Chaucer uses the image recurrently to indicate cuckolding, e.g., *CT* 1.3865, 9.252, etc.

Chastyte is werreyed° over all.
Therfore I wol with syker° wall
Close bothe roses and rosere°.
I have to long in this manere
Left hem unclosed wylfully;
Wherfore I am right inwardly
Sorouful, and repente me.
But nowe they shal no lenger be
Unclosed; and yet I drede sore,
I shal repent ferthermore,
For the game gothe al amys.
Counsayle I must newe°, iwys°.
I have to longe trusted the,
But nowe it shal no lenger be;
For he may best, in every coste°,
Disceyve, that men trusten moste.
I se wol that I am nyghe shent°,
But if° I sette my ful entent
Remedye to purvey°.
Wherfore close I shal the wey
Fro hem that wol the rose espye°,
And come to wayte me vilonye°.
For in good faythe and in trouthe,
I wol not let°, for no slouthe,
To lyve the more in sykernesse°,
To make anon a fortresse,
T'enclose the roses of good savour.
In myddes shall I make a tour°
To put Bialacoil in prison,
For ever I drede me of treson.
I trowe° I shal hym kepe so
That he shal have no might to go
Aboute to make companye
To hem that thynke of vilanye;
Ne to no suche as hath ben here
Aforne, and founde in him good chere,
Whiche han assayled° him to shende°,
And with her trowandyse° to blende°.
A foole is eyth° to begyle;
But may I lyve a lytel while,
He shal forthynke° his fayre semblaunt."
  And with that worde came Drede avaunt°, DREAD
Whiche was abasshed, and in great fere.
Whan he wyste° Jelousye was there,
He was for drede in suche affray°
That not a worde durste° he saye,
But quakyng stode ful styl alone
Tyl Jelousye his way was gone,
Save° Shame, that him not forsoke.
Bothe Drede and she ful sore quoke,
That at laste Drede abrayde°,
And to his cosyn Shame sayde:
"Shame," he sayd, "in sothfastnesse,
To me it is great hevynesse
That the noyse so ferre is go°,
And the sclaunder of us two.
But sythe° that it is befall°,
We may it not agayne call°,
Whan ones spronge is a fame°.
For many a yere withouten blame
We have ben, and many a day;
For many an Aprill and many a May
We han passed not shamed
Tyl Jelousye hath us blamed
Of mystrust and suspection
Causelesse, without encheson°.
Go we to Daunger hastely,
And let us shewe hym openly
That he hath not aright wrought°,
Whan that he set not his thought
To kepe° better the purprise°;
In his doyng he is not wyse.
He hath to us do great wronge,
That hath suffred nowe so longe
Bialacoil to have his wyll,
Al his lustes to fulfyll.
He muste amende it utterly,
Or els shal he vilaynously
Exyled be out of this londe,
For he the werre may not withstonde
Of Jelousye, nor the grefe,
Sythe° Bialacoil is at mischefe°."
  To Daunger, Shame and Drede anon
The righte° way ben gon. DANGER

3917 werreyed, *warred upon* **3918 syker,** *secure* **3919 rosere,** *rose bush* **3928 Counsayle...newe,** *I must have new advice,* **iwys,** *truly* **3931 coste,** *situation* **3933 nyghe shent,** *nearly ruined* **3934 But if,** *unless* **3935 purvey,** *arrange* **3937 espye,** *look upon* **3938 wayte me vilonye,** *plot villainy against me* **3940 let,** *hesitate* **3941 sykernesse,** *security* **3944 tour,** *tower* **3947 trowe,** *think* **3953 assayled,** *attempted,* **shende,** *destroy* **3954 trowandyse,** *fakery,* **blende,** *blind* **3955 eyth,** *easy* **3957 forthynke,** *regret* **3958 avaunt,** *forward* **3960 wyste,** *knew* **3961 affray,** *fear* **3962 durste,** *dared* **3965 Save,** *except* **3967 abrayde,** *burst out* **3971 so ferre is go,** *has gone so far* **3973 sythe,** *since,* **is befall,** *has happened* **3974 it...agayne call,** *call it back* **3975 fame,** *rumor* **3982 encheson,** *reason* **3985 aright wrought,** *acted properly* **3987 kepe,** *protect,* **purprise,** *enclosure* **3998 Sythe,** *since,* **at mischefe,** *in trouble* **4000 righte,** *direct*

3936 Wherfore, G reads "Therfore." **3942 To,** G and Th read "Do." **3943 T'enclose,** G and Th read "Thanne close." **3985 he,** omitted in G. **3986 he,** omitted in G. **3999 Daunger,** see 3018n.

The chorle° they founde hem aforne°,
Lyggyng under an hawethorne.
Under his heed no pylowe was,
But in the stede a trusse° of gras.
He slombred and a nappe he toke
Tyl Shame pitously him shoke,
And great manace° on him gan make.
"Why slepest thou whan thou shulde wake?"
Quod Shame. "Thou doest us vilanye!
Who trusteth the, he dothe folye,
To kepe roses or bothoms°
Whan they ben fayre in her sesons.
Thou arte woxe° to famyliere°
Where thou shulde be straunge of chere,
Stoute° of thy porte°, redy to greve.
Thou doest great folye for to leve
Bialacoil here-inne to call
The yonder man° to shenden° us all.
Though that thou slepe, we may here
Of Jelousye great noyse here.
Arte thou nowe late? Ryse up in hye°
And stoppe sone and delyverly°
Al the gappes of the hay°.
Do no favour, I the pray.
It falleth nothyng° to thy name
To make fayre semblant where thou mayste blame.
If Bialacoil be swete and free°,
Dogged° and fel° thou shuldest be;
Frowarde° and outragyous, iwys°.
A chorle chaungeth that curteys is—
This have I herde ofte in sayeng,
That man ne may, for no dauntyng°,
Make a sperhauke° of a bosarde°.
Al men wol holde the for musarde°,
That debonayre° have founden the;
It sytteth° the nought curteys to be.
To do men plesaunce or servyse.
In the it is recreaundyse°.
Let thy werkes, ferre and nere,
Be lyke thy name, whiche is Daungere."
  Than al abawed° in shewyng°,
Anon spake Drede, right thus sayeng,
And said, "Daunger, I drede me
That thou ne wolte besy be
To kepe that thou hast to kepe;
Whan thou shuldest wake, thou art aslepe.
Thou shalte be greved certainly
If the aspye Jelousye°,
Of if he fynde the in blame.
He hath today assayled° Shame,
And chased away with great manace
Bialacoil out of this place,
And swereth shortly that he shall
Enclose him in a sturdy wall;
And al is for thy wickydnesse,
For that the fayleth straungenesse°.
Thyn herte, I trowe, be fayled all;
Thou shalte repent in speciall,
If Jelousye the soth° knewe;
Thou shalte forthynke° and sore rewe°."
  With that the chorle his clubbe gan shake,
Frownyng his eyen gan to make,
And hydous chere, as man in rage.
For yre° he brent° in his visage
Whan that he herde him blamed so.
He said, "Out of my wytte I go!
To be discomfyte° I have great wronge.
Certes, I have nowe lyved to longe
Sithe° I maye nat this closer° kepe.
Al quycke° I wolde be dolven° depe
If any man shal more repayre°
Into this gardyn, for foule or fayre.
Myne herte for yre gothe afere°,
That I lette any entre here.
Lever I had° with swerdes twayne
Throughout myn herte, in every vayne
Perced to be, with many a wounde,
Than slouthe° shulde in me be founde.
I have do° folly, nowe I se,
But nowe it shal amended be.

4001 chorle, *churl or peasant,* **hem aforne,** *ahead of them* **4004 trusse,** *bundle* **4007 manace,** *menace* **4011 bothoms,** *rosebuds* **4013 woxe,** *grown,* **to famyliere,** *too friendly* **4015 Stoute,** *fierce,* **porte,** *demeanor* **4018 yonder man,** *man over there,* **shenden,** *ruin* **4021 in hye,** *in haste* **4022 delyverly,** *quickly* **4023 hay,** *hedge* **4025 falleth nothyng,** *suits not at all* **4027 free,** *generous* **4028 Dogged,** *surly,* **fel,** *malicious* **4029 Frowarde,** *obstinate,* **iwys,** *truly* **4032 dauntyng,** *threatening* **4033 sperhauke,** *sparrow hawk,* **bosarde,** *buzzard* **4034 musarde,** *sluggard* **4035 debonayre,** *gentle* **4036 sytteth,** *suits* **4038 recreaundyse,** *cowardice* **4041 abawed,** *abashed,* **shewyng,** *appearance* **4048 the aspye Jelousye,** *Jealousy sees you* **4050 assayled,** *attacked* **4056 straungenesse,** *aloofness* **4059 soth,** *truth* **4060 forthynke,** *repent,* **rewe,** *regret* **4064 yre,** *rage,* **brent,** *burned* **4067 discomfyte,** *defeated* **4069 Sithe,** *since,* **closer,** *enclosure* **4070 quycke,** *alive,* **dolven,** *buried* **4071 repayre,** *return* **4073 afere,** *on fire* **4075 Lever I had,** *I would rather* **4078 slouthe,** *sloth* **4079 do,** *done*

4002 hawethorne, a thorny shrub of the rose family often used for hedges. **4021 in hye,** G and Th read "an hye." **4032 ne,** omitted in G and Th. **4059 knewe,** G reads "knowe." **4065 he,** omitted in G. **4075–78** These lines follow line **4085** in G, Th, and most editions.

Who setteth fote here any more,
Truly he shal repent it sore;
For no man more into this place
Of me to entre shal have grace.
From hensforthe, by nyght or day,
I shal defende it, if I may,
Withouten any excepcion
Of eche maner condycion°;
And if I it any man graunte,
Holdeth me for recreaunte°."
   Than Daunger on his fete gan stonde,
And hente° a burdon° in his honde.
Wrothe in his ire, ne lefte he nought,
But through the verger° he hath sought
If he myght fynde hole or trace°
Where through that me mote fortheby pace°,
Or any gappe, he dyd it close,
That no man might touche a rose
Of the roser° all aboute;
He shytteth every man withoute.
Thus day by day Daunger is wers,
More wonderfull° and more dyvers°,
And feller eke° than ever he was.
For hym ful ofte I synge "Alas!"
For I ne may nought, through his yre,
Recover that I moste desyre.
Myn herte, alas, wol brest atwo,
For Bialacoil I wrathed° so;
For certaynly, in every membre
I quake, whan I me remembre
Of the bothom°, whiche I wolde
Ful ofte a day sene and beholde.
And whan I thynke upon the kysse,
And howe moche joye and blysse
I had through the savour swete,
For wante of it I grone and grete°.
Me thynketh I fele yet in my nose
The swete savour of the rose.
And nowe I wote° that I mote° go
So ferre the fresshe floures fro,
To me ful welcome were the dethe!
Absence therof, alas, me slethe°!
For whylom° with this rose, alas,
I touched nose, mouthe, and face;
But nowe the dethe I must abyde.
But° Love consent another tyde°
That ones I touche may and kysse,
I trowe my payne shal never lysse°.
Theron is al my covetyse°,
Whiche brent myn herte in many wyse.
Nowe shal repayre° agayne syghyng
Longe watche on nyghtes, and no slepyng,
Thought in wysshyng, turment, and wo,
With many a turnyng to and fro,
That halfe my payne I cannot tell,
For I am fallen into hell
From paradyse and welthe°. The more
My turment greveth, more and more
Anoyeth nowe the bytternesse,
That I toforne have felte swetnesse.
And Wicked-Tonge, through his falshede,
Causeth al my wo and drede;
On me he leyeth a pytous charge°,
Bycause his tonge was to large°.
   Nowe it is tyme, shortly, that I
Tell you somthyng of Jelousy,
That was in great suspection°.

THE TOWER OF JEALOUSY

Aboute him lefte he no mason
That stone coulde laye, ne querrour°;
He hyred hem to make a tour°.
And first, the roses for to kepe°,
Aboute hem made he a diche depe,
Right wonder large, and also brode;
Upon the whiche also stode
Of squared stone a sturdy wall,
Whiche on a cragge was founded all;
And right great thicknesse eke it bare.
About it was founded° square,
An hundred fadome° on every syde;
It was al lyche° longe and wyde.
Lest° any tyme it were assayled°,
Ful wel about it was batayled°,
And rounde envyron° eke were sette
Ful many a riche and fayre tourette.
At every corner of this wall
Was sette a toure ful principall;

4088 Of eche maner condycion, *from every rank or class* **4090 recreaunte,** *coward* **4092 hente,** *seized,* **burdon,** *club* **4094 verger,** *orchard* **4095 trace,** *path* **4096 mote fortheby pace,** *might pass alongside of* **4099 roser,** *rosebush* **4102 wonderfull,** *awful,* **dyvers,** *antagonistic* **4103 feller eke,** *also more fierce* **4108 wrathed,** *angered* **4111 bothom,** *rosebud* **4116 grete,** *lament* **4119 wote,** *know,* **mote,** *must* **4122 slethe,** *slays* **4123 whylom,** *once* **4126 But,** *unless,* **tyde,** *time* **4128 lysse,** *lessen* **4129 covetyse,** *desire* **4131 repayre,** *return* **4137 welthe,** *happiness* **4140 felte,** *felt* (to be) **4143 pytous charge,** *pitiable burden* **4144 to large,** *too unrestrained* **4147 suspection,** *suspicion* **4149 querrour,** *stonecutter* **4150 tour,** *tower* **4151 kepe,** *protect* **4158 founded,** *built* **4159 fadome,** *fathoms* (six-foot lengths) **4160 al lyche,** *equally* **4161 Lest,** *for fear that,* **were assayled,** *would be attacked* **4162 batayled,** *made with battlements* (crenellations) **4163 rounde envyron,** *all around*

And everiche hadde, without fable,
A port-colyse° defensable,
To kepe of° enemyes and to greve
That there her° force wolde preve°.
And eke amydde this purprise°
Was made a toure of great maistryse;
A fayrer saugh no man with syght,
Large and wyde and of great hyght.
They dradde none assaut
Of gynne°, gonne°, nor skaffaut°,
For the temprure° of the mortere
Was made of lycour° wonder dere°:
Of quicke lyme°, persaunt° and egre°,
The whiche was tempred with vynegre.
The stone was harde as adamant°,
Wherof they made the foundemant°.
The toure was rounde made in compas;
In al this worlde no richer was,
Ne better ordayned therewithal°.
About the toure was made a wal,
So that betwixt that and the toure
Rosers° were sette of swete savour,
With many roses that they bere.
And eke within the castel were
Springoldes°, gonnes, bowes and archers;
And eke above, at corners,
Men seyne over the wal stonde
Great engyns who were nere honde°.
And in the kernels°, here and there,
Of arblasters° great plentie were.
None armure myght her strok withstonde,
It were foly to preace to honde°.
Without the dytche were lystes° made,
With wal batayled large and brade,
For men and horse shulde not attayne
To nyghe° the dyche over the playne.

THE GARRISON OF THE TOWER

Thus Jelousye hath envyron°
Sette aboute his garnyson°
With walles rounde, and dyche depe,
Onely the roser for to kepe.
And Daunger erly and late
The keyes kepte of the utter° gate,
The whiche openeth towarde the eest;
And he had with him at leest
Thurty servauntes, echone by name°.
That other gate kept Shame,
Whiche opened, as it was couthe°,
Towarde the partie of the southe.
Sergeauntes° assigned were her to
Ful many, her wyl for to do.
Than Drede had in her baillye°
The kepyng of the conestablerye°
Towarde the northe, I understonde,
That opened upon the lyfte honde;
The whiche for° nothyng may be sure,
But if° she do besy cure°
Erly on morowe and also late
Strongly to shette and barre the gate.
Of every thyng that she may se
Drede is aferde, whereso she be;
For with a puffe of lytel wynde
Drede is astonyed in her mynde.
Therfore, for stealyng° of the rose,
I rede° her not the yate unclose.
A foules flyght wol make her fle,
And eke a shadowe, if she it se.
Than Wicked-Tonge, full of envye,
With soudyours° of Normandye,
As he that causeth al the bate°,
Was keper of the fourthe gate;
And also to the tother thre
He went ful ofte, for to se.
Whan his lotte° was to wake anyght°,
His instrumentes wolde he dyght°,
For to blowe and make sowne,
Ofter than he hath enchesoun°;
And walken ofte upon the wall,

4168 port-colyse, *portcullis* **4169 kepe of,** *protect against* **4170 That there her,** *those who there their,* **preve,** *test* **4171 purprise,** *enclosure* **4176 gynne,** *catapult,* **gonne,** *cannon,* **skaffaut,** *scaffold* **4177 temprure,** *mixture* **4178 lycour,** *liquid,* **wonder dere,** *very valuable* **4179 quicke lyme,** *caustic lime,* **persaunt,** *corrosive,* **egre,** *sharp* **4181 adamant,** *diamond* **4182 foundemant,** *foundation* **4185 ordayned therewithal,** *arranged also* **4188 Rosers,** *rosebushes* **4191 Springoldes,** *catapults* **4194 nere honde,** *near by* **4195 kernels,** *battlements* **4196 arblasters,** *large crossbows* **4198 preace to honde,** *press too close* **4199 lystes,** *barriers* **4202 To nyghe,** *too close* **4203 envyron,** *surrounding* **4204 garnyson,** *defense* **4208 utter,** *outer* **4211 by name,** *in order?* (convenient rhyme) **4213 couthe,** *known* **4215 Sergeauntes,** *soldiers* **4217 baillye,** *command* **4218 conestablerye,** *chief officer's quarters* **4221 The whiche for,** *for whom* **4222 But if,** *unless,* **cure,** *care* **4229 for stealyng,** *to prevent stealing* **4230 rede,** *advise* **4234 soudyours,** *paid soldiers* **4235 bate,** *strife* **4239 lotte,** *turn,* **to wake anyght,** *to serve as night watch* **4240 dyght,** *prepare* **4242 enchesoun,** *reason*

4174 hyght, G and Th read "myght"; the French is *haute.* **4177–80 temprure of the mortere . . . ,** mortar was mixed with various substances to give it consistency and hardness; quicklime (or unslaked lime) can burn badly; vinegar was not a common additive. **4177 For,** omitted in G and Th; the French is *Car.* **4188 Rosers,** G and Th read "Roses." **4191 bowes and,** G reads "and bow." **4192 above,** Th reads "about." **4194 nere,** G reads "nygh." **4208 kepte,** omitted in G. **4242 Ofter,** G reads "Ofte."

Corners and wickettes° over all
Ful narowe° serchen and espye;
Though he naught fonde, yet wolde he lye.
Discordaunt ever fro armony°,
And distoned from° melodye,
Controve° he wolde, and foule fayle°,
With hornepypes° of Cornewayle.
In floytes° made he discordaunce,
And in his musyke, with mischaunce°,
He wolde seyne, with notes newe,
That he fonde no woman trewe,
Ne that he sawe never in his lyfe
Unto her husbonde a trewe wyfe,
Ne none so ful of honeste,
That she nyl° laughe and mery be
Whan that she hereth or may espye
A man speken of lecherye.
Everyche of hem° hath some vyce;
One is dishonest, another is nyce°;
If one be ful of vilanye,
Another hath a lykerous° eye;
If one be ful of wantonnesse,
Another is a chyderesse°.
Thus Wicked-Tonge—God yeve him shame—
Can put hem everychone in blame
Without deserte and causelesse;
He lyeth, though they ben gyltlesse.
I have pyte to sene the sorowe
That waketh bothe eve and morowe,
To innocentes dothe suche grevaunce.
I pray God yeve him yvel chaunce°,
That he ever so besye is
Of any woman to seyne amys°!
Eke Jelousye God confounde,
That hath made a toure so rounde,
And made aboute a garyson
To sette Bealacoil in prison,
The whiche° is shette there in the tour,
Ful longe to holde there sojour°,
There for to lyve in penaunce,
And for to do him more grevaunce—
There hath ordayned Jelousye

THE DUENNA

And olde vecke° for to espye
The maner of his governaunce,
The whiche dyvel, in her enfaunce°,
Had lerned of Loves arte,
And of his pleys toke her parte.
She was expert in his servyse,
She knewe eche wrenche° and every gyse°
Of Love, and every wyle°;
It was harde her to begyle.
Of Bealacoil she toke aye hede°,
That ever he lyveth in wo and drede.
He kepte him koye° and eke prive°,
Leest° in him she had° se
Any foly countenaunce°,
For she knewe al the olde daunce.
And after this, whan Jelousye
Had Bealacoil in his baillie°,
And shette him up that was so fre°,
For sure of him he wolde be,
He trusteth sore° in his castell;
The stronge werke° him lyketh well.
He dradde not that no glotons
Shulde steale his roses or bothoms°—
The roses weren assured all,
Defenced with the stronge wall.
Nowe Jelousye ful wel may be
Of drede devoyde° in lyberte,
Whether that he slepe or wake;
For of his roses may none be take.
But I, alas, nowe morne shal,

COMPLAINT OF THE LOVER

Bycause I was without° the wal.
Ful moche doole° and mone I made.
Who had wyste° what wo I hade,
I trowe° he wolde have had pyte.
Love to dere° had solde me
The good that of his love had I.

4244 wickettes, *gates* **4245 Ful narowe,** *very carefully* **4247 fro armony,** *from harmony* **4248 distoned from,** *out of tune with* **4249 Controve,** *compose,* **foule fayle,** *fail miserably* **4250 hornepypes,** *pipes made of horn* **4251 floytes,** *flutes* **4252 mischaunce,** *malice* **4258 nyl,** *will not* **4261 Everyche of hem,** *each of them* **4262 nyce,** *foolish* **4264 lykerous,** *lecherous* **4266 chyderesse,** *scolder* **4274 yvel chaunce,** *bad luck* **4276 seyne amys,** *slander* **4281 The whiche,** *whom* **4282 sojour,** *in residence* **4286 vecke,** *hag* **4288 enfaunce,** *youth* **4292 wrenche,** *trick,* **gyse,** *practice* **4293 wyle,** *device* **4295 toke aye hede,** *paid every attention* **4297 koye,** *quiet,* **prive,** *secret* **4298 Leest,** *for fear that,* **had,** *would* **4299 foly countenaunce,** *foolish behavior* **4302 baillie,** *power* **4303 fre,** *generous* **4305 sore,** *completely* **4306 werke,** *fortification* **4308 bothoms,** *rosebuds* **4312 Of drede devoyde,** *without dread* **4316 without,** *outside* **4317 doole,** *lament* **4318 wyste,** *known* **4319 trowe,** *think* **4320 to dere,** *too expensively*

4246 wolde, G reads "wole." **4269 deserte,** G reads "disseit." **4272 waketh,** G and Th read "walketh." **4285 There,** G and Th read "Which." **4286 olde vecke,** this old woman, *Vieille* in French or *Duenna* in Spanish, is a stock character developed by Jean de Meun and the model for Chaucer's Wife of Bath. **4291 expert,** G and Th read "except." **4294 harde,** G reads "harder." **4300 olde daunce,** euphemism for shrewdness, perhaps seduction and copulation; cf. *GP* 1.475–76n. **4320 solde,** G reads "solde to."

I wende a bought° it al queyntly°,
But nowe, through doublyng of my payne,
I see he wolde it sell agayne,
And me a newe bargayne lere°,
The whiche al out° the more is dere°,
For the solace that I have lorne°,
Than° I had it never aforne°.
Certayne I am ful lyke, indede,
To him that caste in erthe his sede,
And hath joye of the newe spring,
When it greneth in the gynnyng,
And is also fayre and fresshe of floure,
Lusty° to sene, swote° of odoure;
But er he it in sheves shere°,
May fall a wether that shal it dere°,
And make it to fade and fall,
The stalke, the greyne, and floures all,
That to the tyllers° is fordone°
The hope that he had to sone.
I drede, certayne, that so fare I,
For hope and travayle sykerly°
Ben me byrafte° al with a storme;
The floure nyl seden of° my corne°.
For Love hath so avaunced me,
When I began my privyte°
To Bailacoil al for to tel,
Whom I ne founde frowarde° ne fel°,
But toke a gree° al hole° my play.
But Love is of so harde assaye°
That al at ones he reved° me,
When I wende° best aboven to have be.
It is of Love, as of Fortune,
That chaungeth ofte, and nyl contune°;
Whiche whilom° wol on folke smyle,
And glombe° on hem another while;
Nowe frende, nowe foe, shaltow° her fele.
For in a twynclynge tourneth her whele.
She canne writhe° her heed awaye;
This is the concourse° of her playe.
She canne areyse° that doth mourne,
And whirle adowne, and overtourne
Who sytteth hyghest, but as her lust°;
A foole is he that wol her trust.
For it is I that am come downe
Through change and revolutioun!
Sithe° Bialacoil mote° fro me twynne°,
Shette in the prison yonde° withinne,
His absence at myne herte I fele,
For al my joye and al myne hele°
Was in him and in the rose,
That but° yon wal, whiche him dothe close°,
Openne, that I maye him se,
Love wol nat that I cured be
Of the paynes that I endure,
Nor of my cruel aventure.
Ah, Bialacoil, myne owne dere!
Though thou be nowe a prisonere,
Kepe at leest thyne herte to° me,
And suffre° nat that it daunted° be,
Ne lette nat Jelousy in his rage
Putten thyne herte in no servage.
Although he chastice the without,
And make thy body unto him lout°,
Have herte as harde as diamaunt,
Stedfast, and naught plyaunt.
In prison though thy body be,
At large° kepe thyne herte free:
A trewe herte wol nat plye°
For no manace that it maye drye°.
If Jelousye doth the payne,
Quyte° him his while thus agayne,
To venge the°, at leest in thought,
If other waye thou mayst nought.
And in this wyse subtelly
Worche, and wynne the maistry.
But yet I am in great affraye°
Lest thou do nat as I saye;
I drede thou canst° me great maugre°,
That thou enprisoned arte for me.
But that is nat for my trespas,

4322 wende a bought, *thought to have bought,* **queyntly,** *cleverly* **4325 lere,** *teach* **4326 al out,** *thoroughly,* **dere,** *costly* **4327 lorne,** *lost* **4328 Than,** *than if,* **aforne,** *before* **4334 Lusty,** *pleasant,* **swote,** *sweet* **4335 it in sheves shere,** *harvests it in sheaves* **4336 dere,** *harm* **4339 tyllers,** *farmers,* **fordone,** *destroyed* **4342 travayle sykerly,** *labor surely* **4343 Ben me byrafte,** *I have been deprived of* **4344 nyl seden of,** *will not seed from,* **corne,** *grain* **4346 privyte,** *private counsel* **4348 frowarde,** *obstinate,* **fel,** *cruel* **4349 a gree,** *kindly,* **hole,** *wholly* **4350 assaye,** *trial* **4351 reved,** *robbed* **4352 wende,** *thought* **4354 nyl contune,** *won't continue* **4355 whilom,** *for a time* **4356 glombe,** *frown* **4357 shaltow,** *you will* **4359 writhe,** *turn* **4360 concourse,** *manner* **4361 areyse,** *lift up* **4363 her lust,** *it pleases her* **4367 Sithe,** *since,* **mote,** *must,* **twynne,** (be) *separate* **4368 yonde,** *over there* **4370 hele,** *health* **4372 but,** *unless,* **close,** *enclose* **4379 to,** *for* **4380 suffre,** *allow,* **daunted,** *defeated* **4384 lout,** *bow* **4388 At large,** *in liberty* **4389 plye,** *bend* **4390 drye,** *endure* **4392 Quyte,** *repay* **4393 venge the,** *avenge yourself* **4397 affraye,** *fear* **4399 canst,** *may bear,* **maugre,** *ill will*

4322 wende a bought, G and Th read "wente aboute." **4357 shaltow,** G and Th read "shalt." **4358 in,** omitted in G and Th. **tourneth,** G reads "turne." **4361 areyse,** G reads "arise." **4366 change,** G and Th read "charge." **4372 yon wal,** G reads "yone wole"; Th, "you wol." **4374 wol,** G reads "nyl." **4401 is,** omitted in G and Th.

For through me never discovered° was
Yet thynge that ought be secree.
Wel more annoye is in me
Than is in the of this myschaunce,
For I endure more harde penaunce
Than any canne sayne or thynke,
That for the sorowe almost I synke.
Whan I remembre me of my wo,
Ful nyghe out of my wytte I go.
Inwarde myne herte I fele blede,
For comfortlesse the dethe I drede.
Owe° I nat wel to have dystresse,
Whan false°, through her° wickednesse,
And traytours, that arne envyous,
To noyen° me be so curious°?
Ah, Bialacoile, ful wel I se
That they hem shape° to disceyve the,
To make the buxome° to her lawe,
And with her corde the to drawe
Wherso hem lust°, right at her wyl;
I drede they have the brought thertyl.
Without comforte, thought me slethe;
This game wol bringe me to my dethe.
For if your good wyl I lese°,
I mote° be deed; I maye nat chese.
And if that thou foryete me,
Myne hert shal never in lykynge° be;
Nor elsewhere fynde solace,
If I be putte out of your grace,

Jean de Meun's Continuation.

As it shal never ben, I hoope;
Than shulde I fal in wanhope°.
 Alas, in wanhope? Naye, parde°!
For I wol never dispeyred be.
If Hope me fayle, than am I
Ungratious and unworthy.
In Hoope I wol conforted be,
For Love, whan he betaught her me,
Sayde that Hoope, whereso I go,
Shulde aye be relees° to my wo.
But what and° she my bales bete°,
And be to me curteis and swete?
She is in nothynge ful certayne.
Lovers she putte in ful great payne.
And maketh hem with wo to dele.
Her fayre behest° disceyveth fele°,
For she wol behote°, sykerly°,
And faylen after utterly.
Ah, that is a ful noyous thyng!
For many a lover, in lovyng,
Hangeth upon her, and trusteth fast°,
Whiche lese her traveyle° at the last.
Of thyng to commen she wotte° right nought;
Therfore, if it be wisely sought,
Her counsayle foly is to take.
For many tymes, whan she wol make
A ful good sylogisme, I drede
That afterwarde there shal in dede
Folowe an yvel conclusyoun;
This putte me in confusyoun.
For many tymes I have it sene,
That many have begyled bene,
For truste that they have sette in Hoope,
Whiche fel hem afterwards aslope°.
But nathelesse yet, gladly she wolde°
That he that wol him with her holde,
Hadde al tymes his purpose clere,
Without disceyte or any were°.
That she desyreth sykerly°.
Whan I her blamed, I dyd foly.
But what avayleth° her good wyl,
Whan she ne maye staunche° my stounde yl°?

COMPLAINT OF THE LOVER

4402 discovered, *revealed* **4413 Owe,** *ought* **4414 false,** *false people,* **her,** *their* **4416 noyen,** *harm,* **curious,** *eager* **4418 shape,** *intend* **4419 buxome,** *obedient* **4421 hem lust,** *it pleases them* **4425 lese,** *lose* **4426 mote,** *must* **4428 lykynge,** *pleasure* **4432 wanhope,** *despair* **4433 parde,** *by God* **4440 relees,** *relief* **4441 what and,** *what if,* **my bales bete,** *amends my pains* **4446 behest,** *promise,* **fele,** *many* (people) **4447 behote,** *promise,* **sykerly,** *surely* **4451 fast,** *firmly* **4452 her traveyle,** *their effort* **4453 wotte,** *knows* **4464 aslope,** *askew* **4465 wolde,** *wished* **4468 were,** *uncertainty* **4469 sykerly,** *surely* **4470 avayleth,** *is the advantage of* **4472 staunche,** *heal,* **stounde yl,** *bad time*

4416 curious, G and Th read "coraious" or "coragious." **4430a Jean de Meun's Continuation,** this rubric is not in G or Th, but indicates where Guillaume de Lorris's portion ends of the French original ends and where Jean de Meun began his continuation. **4457 sylogisme,** syllogism, a form of argument in logic, and indication of Jean de Meun's involvement with higher education. He was associated with the University of Paris and includes in his expansion of Guillaume's courtly poem a wide range of the social, philosophical, and scientific ideas of his age. **4467 his,** G and Th read "her."

That helpeth lytel that she maye do,
Outtake beheest° unto my wo.
And heest° certayne, in no wyse,
Without yefte°, is nat to pryse°.
Whan heest and dede asondre vary,
They done me° have a great contrary.
Thus am I possed° up and downe
With doole°, thought, and confusyoune;
Of my disease° there is no nombre.
Daungere and Shame me encombre,
Drede also, and Jelousye,
And Wicked-Tonge, ful of envye,
Of whiche the sharpe and cruel ire
Ful ofte me putte in great martyre°.
They have my joye fully lette°,
Sithe° Bialacoil they have beshette
Fro me in prison wickedly,
Whome I love so entierly,
That it wol my bane° be,
But° I the sooner maye him se.
And yet moreover, worste of al,
There is sette to kepe—foule her befal°—
A rympled vecke°, ferre ronne in age,
Frownyng and yelowe in her visage,
Whiche in awayte° lyeth day and nyght,
That none of hem may have a syght.
  Nowe mote° my sorowe enforced° be;
Ful sothe° it is that Love yafe me
Thre wonder yeftes of his grace,
Whiche I have lorne° nowe in this place,
Sithe they ne maye, without drede
Helpen but lytel, who taketh hede.
For here aveyleth no Swete-Thought,
And Swete-Speche helpeth right nought.
The thirde was called Swete-Lokyng,
That nowe is lorne, without lesyng°.
Yeftes were fayre, but nat forthy°
They helpe me but symply°
But° Bialacoil loosed be,
To gone at large and to be free.
For him my lyfe lyeth al in dout,
But if he come the rather° out.
Alas, I trowe° it wol nat bene,
For howe shulde I evermore him sene?
He maye nat out, and that is wronge,
Bycause the toure is so stronge.
Howe shulde he out, or by whose prowesse,
Of so stronge a forteresse?
By me, certayne, it nyl° be do;
God wotte°, I have no wytte therto!
But wel I wotte I was in rage,
Whan I to Love dydde homage.
Who was in cause°, in sothfastnesse,
But herselfe, Dame Idelnesse,
Which me conveyde°, through my prayere°,
To entre into that fayre vergere°?
She was to° blame me to leve,
The whiche nowe dothe me sore greve.
A fooles worde is nought to trowe°,
Ne worthe an apple for to lowe°;
Menne shulde him snybbe° bitterly,
At prime temps° of his foly.
I was a foole, and she me leved°,
Through whom I am right nought releved;
She accomplysshed al my wyll,
That nowe me greveth wonder yll.
Reason me sayde° what shulde fall.
A foole myselfe I may wel call
That love asyde I had nat layde,
And trowed that° Dame Reson sayde.
Reson had bothe skyll° and ryght
Whan she me blamed with al her myght
To medle of° love, that hath me shent°;
But certayne nowe I wol repent.
  And shulde I repent? Nay, parde°!
A false traytour than shulde I be.
The dyvels engyns wolde me take
If I my lorde wolde forsake,
Or Bialacoil falsly betraye.
Shulde I at mischefe° hate him? Naye,
Sythe° he nowe, for his curtesye,
Is in prison of Jelousye.

4474 Outtake beheest, *except promise* **4475 heest,** *promise* **4476 yefte,** *gift,* **nat to pryse,** *of no value* **4478 done me,** *cause me to* **4479 possed,** *tossed* **4480 doole,** *sorrow* **4481 disease,** *discomforts* **4486 martyre,** *torment* **4487 lette,** *prevented* **4488 Sithe,** *since* **4491 bane,** *death* **4492 But,** *unless* **4494 foule her befal,** *may evil befall her* **4495 vecke,** *old woman* **4497 awayte,** *ambush* **4499 mote,** *must,* **enforced,** *reinforced* **4500 Ful sothe,** *very true* **4502 lorne,** *lost* **4508 lesyng,** *lying* **4509 nat forthy,** *nevertheless* **4510 but symply,** *only little* **4511 But,** *unless* **4514 rather,** *sooner* **4515 trowe,** *believe* **4521 nyl,** *won't* **4522 wotte,** *knows* **4525 in cause,** *the cause* **4527 conveyde,** *led,* **prayere,** *request* **4528 vergere,** *orchard* **4529 to,** *at* **4531 trowe,** *believe* **4532 lowe,** *value* **4533 snybbe,** *scold* **4534 prime temps,** *the start* **4535 leved,** *believed* **4539 sayde,** *told* **4542 that,** *what* **4543 skyll,** *reason* **4545 of,** *with,* **shent,** *ruined* **4547 parde,** *by God* **4552 mischefe,** *misfortune* **4553 Sythe,** *since*

4476 pryse, G and Th read "preyse." **4477 asondre,** G reads "asundry." **4478 me have,** omitted in G and Th. **4483 Drede,** G reads "Dre." **4495 age,** Th reads "rage." **4519 or by,** G reads "By." **4520 Of so,** G reads "Out of so." **4527 my,** G and Th read "fayre." **4541 asyde I had nat,** G reads "assayde I hadde." **4550 lorde,** G and Th read "love."

Curtesye certayne dyd he me,
So moche that it may not yolden° be,
Whan he the hay° passen me lete,
To kysse the rose, fayre and swete.
Shulde I therfore conne him maugre°?
Nay, certaynly, it shal not be;
For Love shal never, if God wyll,
Here of° me, through worde or wyll,
Offence or complaynt, more or lesse,
Neyther of Hope nor Idelnesse.
For certes, it were wronge that I
Hated hem for her curtesye.
There is not els° but suffre and thynke,
And waken whan I shulde wynke°,
Abyde in hope tyl Love, through chaunce,
Sende me socour° or allegeaunce°,
Expectant aye tyl I may mete°
To getten mercy of that swete.
  Whylom° I thynke howe Love to me
Sayd he wolde take at gre°
My servyce, if unpacience
Ne caused me to done offence.
He sayd, "In thanke I shal it take,
And hygh mayster° eke the make°,
If wickednesse ne reve° it the;
But sone, I trowe°, that shal not be."
These were his wordes by and by—
It semed he loved me trewly.
Nowe is there not° but serve him wele,
If that I thynke his thanke to fele.
My good, myn harme, lythe hole° in me;
In Love may no defaute° be.
For trewe Love ne fayled never man;
Sothly, the faute mote nedes than°—
As God forbyd—be founde in me,
And howe it commeth, I cannot se.
Nowe let it gone as it may go;
Whether Love wol socoure me or slo°,
He may do hole on me his wyll.
I am so sore bounde hym tyll,
From his servyce I may not flene°;
For lyfe and dethe, withouten wene°,
Is in his hande; I may not chese;
He may me do bothe wynne and lese.
And sythe so sore he dothe me greve,
Yet if my luste° he wolde acheve°,
To Bialacoil goodly to be,
I yeve no force° what fel on° me.
For though I dye, as I mote nede°,
I pray Love, of his goodlyhede,
To Bialacoil do gentylnesse,
For whom I lyve in suche distresse
That I mote° dyen for penaunce.
But first, without repentaunce,
I wol me confesse in god entent,
And make in haste my testament,
As lovers done that felen smerte°:
To Bialacoil leave I myn herte
Al hole, without departyng,
Or doublenesse° of repentyng.

Comment Raison vient a l'Amant

  Thus as I made my passage°
In compleynt, and in cruel rage,
And I not° where to fynde a leche°
That couthe° unto myn helpyng eche°.
Sodainly agayne comen doun
Out of her tour I sawe Reasoun,
Discrete, and wyse, and ful plesaunt,
And of her porte ful avenaunt°.
The right° way she toke to me,
Whiche° stode in great perplexite,
That was posshed° in every syde,
That I nyst° where I myght abyde,
Tyl she, demurely sadde° of chere,
Sayd to me, as she came nere:
  "Myne owne frende, arte thou yet greved?
Howe is this quarel° yet atcheved°
Of Loves syde? Anone° me tel.
Hast thou nat yet of love thy fyl?
Arte thou nat wery of thy servyce

REASON REAPPEARS

4556 yolden, *repaid* **4557 hay,** *hedge* **4559 conne him maugre,** *show him spite* **4562 Here of,** *hear from* **4567 not els,** *nothing else* **4568 wynke,** *close my eyes* **4570 socour,** *aid,* **allegeaunce,** *alleviation* **4571 mete,** *happen* **4573 Whylom,** *at times* **4574 at gre,** *with favor* **4578 mayster,** *master,* **eke the make,** *make you also* **4579 reve,** *deprive* **4580 trowe,** *believe* **4583 not,** *no option* **4585 lythe hole,** *lies wholly* **4586 defaute,** *fault* **4588 mote nedes than,** *must necessarily then* **4592 slo,** *slay* **4595 flene,** *flee* **4596 wene,** *doubt* **4600 luste,** *desire,* **wolde acheve,** *will bring about* **4602 yeve no force,** i.e., *care not,* **fel on,** *might happen to* **4603 mote nede,** *necessarily must* **4607 mote,** *must* **4611 felen smerte,** *feel pain* **4614 doublenesse,** *duplicity* **4615 passage,** *way* **4617 not,** *knew not,* **leche,** *physician* **4618 couthe,** *could,* **eche,** (give) *aid* **4622 porte ful avenaunt,** *demeanor very attractive* **4623 right,** *direct* **4624 Whiche,** *who* **4625 posshed,** *tossed* **4626 nyst,** *didn't know* **4627 sadde,** *serious* **4630 quarel,** *dispute,* **yet atcheved,** *still settled* **4631 Anone,** *quickly*

4556 it, omitted in G. **4561 if God,** G and Th read "yeve good." **4576 Ne,** omitted in G and Th. **4614 Or,** omitted in G. **4614a Comment Raison vient a l'Amant,** How Reason comes to the Lover. This rubric is in G and Th. **4629 yet,** omitted in Th. **4631 me tel,** Th reads "tel me."

That the° hath pyned° in suche wyse?
What joye haste thou in thy lovyng?
Is it swete or bytter thyng?
Canst thou yet chese, lette me se,
What best thy socour° myght be?
Thou servest a ful noble lorde,
That maketh the thral° for thy rewarde,
Whiche aye reneweth thy tourment,
With foly so he hath the blent°;
Thou fel in myschefe thylke° daye,
Whan thou dyddest, the sothe° to saye,
Obeysaunce and eke homage;
Thou wroughtest° nothyng as the sage.
Whan thou became his liege man,
Thou dyddest a great foly than;
Thou wystest° nat what fel therto,
With what lorde thou haddest to do°.
If thou haddest him wel knowe,
Thou haddest nought be brought so lowe.
For if thou wystest what it were,
Thou noldest serve him halfe a yere,
Nat a weke, nor halfe a daye,
Ne yet an hour without delaye,
Ne never yloved paramours°,
His lordshyppe is so ful of shours°.
Knowest him ought?"
L'AMAUNT: "Ye, dame, parde!"
RAYSOUN: "Nay, nay."
L'AMAUNT: "Yes, I."
RAYSOUN: "Wherfore, lette se?"
L'AMAUNT: "Of that° he sayd I shulde be
Gladde to have suche lorde as he,
And maister of suche seignorie°."
RAYSOUN: "Knowest him no more?"
L'AMAUNT: "Naye, certes, I,
Save° that he yafe me rules there,
And went his waye, I nyst° where,
And I abode bounde in balaunce."
RAYSOUN: "Lo, there a noble conysaunce°!
But I wol° that thou knowe him nowe,
Gynnynge and ende, sithe that thou
Arte so anguysshous and mate°,
Disfygured out of astate°;
There maye no wretche have more of wo,
Ne caytife° none enduren so.
It were to every manne syttyng°
Of his lorde have knowlegyng.
For if thou knewe him, out of dout,
Lightly° thou shuldest escapen out
Of thy prysone that marreth the°."
L'AMAUNT: "Ye, dame, sithe my lorde is he,
And I his manne, made with rnyne honde,
I wolde ryght fayne understonde°
To knowe of what kynde he be,
If any wolde enforme me."
RAYSOUN: "I wolde," sayd Reason, "the lere°,
Sithe thou to lerne hast suche desyre,
And shewe the, withouten fable,
A thynge that is nat demonstrable:
Thou shalte wite° withouten science°,
And knowe withouten experience,
The thyng that may nat knowen be,
Ne wyst°, ne shewed, in no degree.
Thou mayst the sothe° of it nat wytten,
Though in the it were written.
Thou shalte nat knowe therof more
Whyle thou arte ruled by his lore;
But unto him that love wol flye
The knotte may unclosed be,
Whiche hath to the, as it is founde,
So longe be° knytte and nat unbounde.
Now sette wel thyne ententioun,
To here of love discriptioun:

REASON'S LECTURE

"Love, it is an hateful pees,
A free acquytaunce° without relees,
A trouthe frette° ful of falshede,
A sickernesse° al sette in drede;
In herte is a dispeyryng hoope,
And ful of hoope, it is wanhoope°;
Wyse woodnesse°, and wode° reasoun,

4634 the, *you,* **pyned,** *pained* **4638 socour,** *comfort* **4640 thral,** *slave* **4642 the blent,** *blinded you* **4643 thylke,** *that same* **4644 sothe,** *truth* **4646 wroughtest,** *accomplished* **4649 wystest,** *know* **4650 haddest to do,** *were involved* **4657 paramours,** *passionately* **4658 shours,** *storms* **4661 Of that,** *on the basis of what* **4663 seignorie,** *authority* **4665 Save,** *except* **4666 nyst,** *don't know* **4668 conysaunce,** *relationship* **4669 wol,** *desire* **4671 mate,** *exhausted* **4672 astate,** *condition* **4674 caytife,** *captive* **4675 syttyng,** *suitable* **4678 Lightly,** *easily* **4679 marreth the,** *hinders you* **4682 ryght fayne understonde,** *very happily learn* **4685 the lere,** *teach you* **4689 wite,** *know,* **science,** *knowledge* **4692 wyst,** *understood* **4693 sothe,** *truth* **4700 be,** *been* **4704 acquytaunce,** *acquittal* **4705 frette,** *adorned* **4706 sickernesse,** *certainty* **4708 wanhoope,** *despair* **4709 woodnesse,** *madness,* **wode,** *mad*

4634 pyned, omitted in G and Th. **4660 Wherfore,** G reads "Wherof." **4672 Disfygured,** G reads "diffigured." **4679 thy,** G reads "the." **4689 wite,** omitted in G and Th. **4700 be,** Th reads "to." **4703–85** The contradictory or oxymoronic nature of Love is commonplace; Jean de Meun modeled his list on that of Alanus de Insulis (Alain de Lille) *De Planctu Naturae* (*Complaint of Nature*). Reason's speech in Jean (here lines 4685–4784) follows that of Alanus's Nature. **4705 A trouthe,** G and Th read "And through the." **4709 wode,** G and Th read "vo(y)de."

A swete peryl in to drowne,
An hevy burthen lyght to beare,
A wicked wawe° awaye to weare°.
It is Carybdes perilous,
Disagreable and gratious°.
It is descordaunce that can accorde,
And accordaunce to discorde.
It is connynge° without science,
Wysedom without sapyence°,
Wytte without discretioun,
Havoyre° without possessyoun.
It is syke hele° and hole sickenesse,
A thruste° drowned in dronknesse,
An helthe ful of maladye,
And charyte ful of envye,
An hunger ful of habundaunce,
And a gredy suffysaunce°;
Delyte right ful of hevynesse°,
And dreryhed° ful of gladnesse;
Bytter swetnesse and swete errour,
Right yvel savoured good savour;
Sen° that pardone hath withinne,
And pardone spotted without with synne;
A payne also it is, joyous,
And felonye ryght pytous°;
Also playe that selde° is stable,
And stedfast stat°, right mevable;
A strength weyked° to stonde upright,
And feblenesse ful of myght;
Wytte unavysed, sage folye,
And joye ful of tourmentrye;
A laughter it is, wepynge aye°,
Rest that traveyleth° nyght and daye.
Also a swete helle it is,
And a sorouful paradys;
A pleasaunt gayle° and easy prisoun,
And, ful of frost, somer seasoun;
Pryme temps° ful of frostes whyte,
And Maye devoyde of al delyte,
With seer° braunches, blossoms ungrene;
And newe° frute, fylled with wynter tene°.
It is a slowe°, maye nat forbeare
Ragges rybaned° with golde to weare;
For also° wel wol love be sette
Under ragges as riche rochette;
And eke° as wel be amorettes°
In mournyng blacke° as bright burnettes°.
For none is of so mokel prise°,
Ne no manne founden so wyse,
Ne none so highe is of parage°,
Ne no manne founde of wytte so sage,
No manne so hardy ne so wight°,
Ne no manne of so mokel° myght,
None so fulfylled of bounte°,
That ne with Love maye daunted° be.
Al the worlde holdeth this waye;
Love maketh al to gone myswaye°,
But° it be they of yvel lyfe,
Whome Genius cursed, man and wyfe°,
That wrongly werke agayne Nature.
None suche I love, ne have no cure°
Of suche as Loves servauntes bene,
And wol nat by my counsayle flene°.
For I ne preyse that lovynge
Wher-through men, at the laste endynge,
Shal cal hem° wretches ful of wo.
Love greveth hem and shendeth° so.
But if thou wolte wel Love eschewe°,
For to escape out of his mewe°,
And make al hoole thy sorowe to slake°,
No better counsayle mayst thou take
Than thynke to fleen wel, ywis°;
Maye nought helpe els, for wytte° thou this:
If thou flye it, it shal flye the;

4712 wawe, *wave,* **awaye to weare,** *wearing away* (?) **4714 gratious,** *attractive* **4717 connynge,** *knowing* **4718 sapyence,** *sapience* (Latin sapientia, i.e., knowledge) **4720 Havoyre,** *having* (French *avoir*) **4721 hele,** *health* **4722 thruste,** *thirst* **4726 suffysaunce,** *sufficiency* **4727 hevynesse,** *sadness* **4728 dreryhed,** *dreariness* **4731 Sen,** *sin* **4734 pytous,** *pitiable* **4735 selde,** *seldom* **4736 stat,** *state* **4737 weyked,** *too weak* **4741 aye,** *always* **4742 traveyleth,** *labors* **4745 gayle,** *jail* **4747 Pryme temps,** *spring* **4749 seer,** *withered* **4750 newe,** *fresh,* **tene,** *bitterness* **4751 slowe,** *sluggard,* **forbeare,** *give up* **4752 rybaned,** *ribboned* **4753 also,** *as* **4754 rochette,** *cloak* **4755 eke,** *also,* **amorettes,** *sweethearts* **4756 mournyng blacke,** *black mourning clothes,* **burnettes,** *garments* **4757 mokel prise,** *much value* **4759 parage,** *parentage* **4761 wight,** *active* **4762 mokel,** *much* **4763 bounte,** *goodness* **4764 daunted,** *overcome* **4766 myswaye,** *astray* **4767 But,** *unless* **4768 wyfe,** *woman* **4770 cure,** *concern* **4772 flene,** *flee* **4775 hem,** *themselves* **4776 shendeth,** *ruins* **4777 eschewe,** *avoid* **4778 mewe,** *cage* **4779 slake,** *diminish* **4781 ywis,** *truly* **4782 wytte,** *know*

4713 Carybdes, Charybdis, the threatening whirlpool of classical tradition. **4721 syke,** G and Th read "lyke." **4722 thruste,** G and Th read "trust." **in,** G and Th read "and." **4723 An,** G and Th read "And." **4725 An hunger,** G and Th read "And anger." **4728 dreryhed,** G and Th read "dreryed." **4732 with,** omitted in G and Th. **4736 stat,** omitted in G and Th. **4755 be,** G and Th read "by." **4764 ne,** G and Th read "he." **4768 Genius,** an allegorical character who stands for the natural desire or inclination that leads to procreation, developed at length later as the priest of Nature in *Roman de la Rose* 16,242ff. and as the priest of Venus in Gower's *Confessio Amantis* 1.190ff. At the end of Alanus (see 4703–85n), Genius curses unnatural love, understood to be homosexuality.

Folowe it, and folowen shal it the."
L'AMAUNT: Whan I hadde herde al
 Reason sayne,
Whiche° had spilte° her speche in vayne,
"Dame," sayd I, "I dare wel saye
Of this avaunt° me wel I maye
That from your schole so deviaunt
I am that never the more avaunt°
Right nought am I, through your doctryne;
I dulle° under your disciplyne;
I wotte° no more than wyste° I er,
To me so contrary and so fer
Is everythynge that ye me lere°.
And yet I canne° it al par cuere°;
Myne herte foryeteth therof right nought,
It is so written in my thought;
And depe graven° it is so tender
That al by herte I can it render,
And rede it over communely°;
But to myselfe lewdest° am I.
But sithe° ye love discryven° so,
And lacke° and preise it bothe two,
Defyneth it into this letter°
That I maye thynke on it the better.
For I herde never diffyne it ere,
And wylfully I'wolde it lere°."
 "If love be serched well and sought,
It is a sickenesse of the thought
Annexed and knedde° betwixt
 tweyne,

REASON DESCRIBES LOVE

Which male and female with o° cheyne
So frely byndeth that they nyl twynne°,
Wheder so therof they lese or wynne.
The rote spryngeth° through hoote brennynge
Into disordynate desyringe
For to kyssen and enbrace,
And at her luste them to solace.
Of other thynge love retcheth° nought,
But setteth her herte and al her thought
More for delectatioun
Than any procreatioun
Of other fruite by engendrure°,
Whiche love to God is nat pleasure.
For of her body fruyte to gette
They yeve no force°, they are so sette
Upon delyte, to playe in-fere°.
And some have also this manere,
To faynen° hem for love seke°;
Suche love I preyse nat at a leke°.
For paramours° they do but fayne;
To love trewly they disdayne.
They falsen ladyes traytoursly,
And swerne hem othes utterly
With many a leasyng° and many a fable,
And al they fynden disceyvable;
And whan they han her luste getten,
The hoote ernes° they al foryetten.
Women the harme byen° ful sore;
But menne this thynken evermore
That lasse harme is, so mote I thee°,
Disceyve them than disceyved be;
And namely°, where they ne maye
Fynde none other meane waye°.
For I wotte° wel, in sothfastnesse°,
That who dothe nowe his besynesse
With any woman for to dele,
For any luste that he may fele,
But if° it be for engendrure°,
He dothe trespasse, I you ensure;
For he shulde setten al his wyl
To getten° a lykely thynge him tyl°,
And to sustayne, if he myght,
And kepe for the°, by Kyndes° ryght,
His owne lykenesse and semblable°,
For because al is corrumpable,
And fayle shulde successyoun,

4786 Whiche, *who,* **spilte,** *wasted* **4788 avaunt,** *boast* **4790 avaunt,** *advanced* **4792 dulle,** *grow dull* **4793 wotte,** *know,* **wyste,** *knew* **4795 lere,** *teach* **4796 canne,** *know,* **par cuere,** *by heart* **4799 greven,** *engraved* **4801 communely,** *frequently* **4802 lewdest,** *most ignorant* **4803 sithe,** *since,* **discryven,** *describe* **4804 lacke,** *criticize* **4805 letter,** *description* **4808 lere,** *learn* **4811 knedde,** *knit* **4812 o,** *one* **4813 twynne,** *separate* **4815 rote spryngeth,** *root grows* **4819 retcheth,** *cares* **4823 engendrure,** *procreation* **4826 yeve no force,** *pay no attention* **4827 in-fere,** *together* **4829 faynen,** *pretend,* **seke,** *to seek* **4830 preyse nat at a leke,** *value less than a leek* **4831 paramours,** *passionate love* **4835 leasyng,** *lying* **4838 ernes,** *passion* **4839 byen,** *pay for* **4841 mote I thee,** *may I prosper* **4843 namely,** *especially* **4844 meane way,** *middle road* **4845 wotte,** *know,* **sothfastnesse,** *truth* **4849 But if,** *unless,* **engendrure,** *procreation* **4852 getten,** *beget,* **a lykely thynge him tyl,** *something alike to himself* **4854 kepe forthe,** *preserve,* **Kyndes,** *Nature's* **4855 semblable,** *similarity*

4793 wyste I er, G and Th read "wist euer." **4796 pare cuere,** G and Th read "by partuere." **4800 by,** Th reads "myne." **4807 diffyne it ere,** G and Th read "diffyned he(e)re." **4809–27** Critics have shown that Jean de Meun here echoes Andreas Capellanus, *De Amore* 1.1-2. **4812 Whiche,** G and Th read "With." **4813 frely,** G and Th read "frely that." **4839 byen,** G reads "they byen." **4846 who,** G and Th read "what." **4856** Line omitted in G.

Ne were their° generatioun
Our sectes sterne° for to save.
Whan father or mother arne° in grave,
Her chyldren shulde, whan they ben dede,
Ful dilygent bene in her stede
To use that warke on suche a wyse
That one may through another ryse.
Therfore sette Kynde therin delyte,
For men therin shulde hem delyte,
And of that dede be nat erke°,
But ofte sythes° haunt° that werke;
For none wolde drawe therof a draught°
Ne were delyte whiche hath him
    caught.
"Thus hath subtylled° Dame Nature;
For none gothe right, I the ensure,
Ne hath entent hoole ne parfyte°;
For her° desyre is for delyte,
The whiche fortened crease° and eke
The playe of love for-ofte° seke,
And thrall° hemselfe, they be so nyce°,
Unto the prynce of every vyce.
For of eche synne it is the rote,
Unleful° luste, though it be sote°,
And of all yvel the racyne°,
As Tullyus canne determyne,
Whiche in his tyme was ful sage,
In a booke he made *Of Age*,
Where that more he prayseth Elde,
Though he be croked and unwelde°,
And more of commendatioun°,
Than Youthe in his discriptioun;
For Youthe sette bothe man and wyfe
In al parel° of soule and lyfe;
And parel is, but men have grace,
The tyme of youthe for to pace°
Without any dethe or distresse,
It is so ful of wyldnesse;
So ofte it dothe shame or damage
To him or to his lynage.
It ledeth man nowe up, nowe downe,
In mokel° dissolutioun,
And maketh him love yvel company,
And lede his lyfe disrulyly°,
And halte hym payde° with none estate°.
Within hymselfe is suche debate,
He chaungeth purpose and entent;
And yalte° him into some covent°,
To lyven after her emprise°,
And leseth fredom and fraunchyse°
That Nature in him had sette,
The whiche agayne he may not gette,
If he there make his mansyon°
For to abyde professyon°.
Though for a tyme his herte absente°,
It may not fayle, he shal repente,
And eke abyde thilke° day
To leave his abyte° and gon his way,
And leseth his worshyp° and his name,
And dare not come agayne for shame.
But al his lyfe he dothe so mourne,
Bycause he dare nat home retourne.
Fredom of kynde° so loste hath he
That never may recured° be,
But if that God him graunte grace
That he may, er he hence pace°,
Conteyne° under obedyence
Through the vertue of pacience.
For Youthe set° man in al folye,
In unthrifte° and in ribaudye°,
In lechery and in outrage,
So ofte it chaungeth of corage°.
Youthe gynneth ofte suche bargayne
That may not ende without payne.
In great parell° is set youth-hede,
Delyte so doth his bridell lede.
Delyte thus hangeth, drede the° nought,
Bothe mans body and his thought,

4858 Ne were their, *if there were no* **4859 sectes sterne,** *species' offspring* **4860 arne,** *are* **4867 erke,** *weary* **4768 ofte sythes,** *frequently,* **haunt,** *engage in* **4869 drawe therof a daught,** i.e., *take a sip of that* **4871 subtylled,** *subtly established* **4873 parfyte,** *perfect* **4874 her,** *their* **4875 fortened crease,** *stimulated procreation* **4876 for-ofte,** *very often* **4877 thral,** *enslave,* **nyce,** *foolish* **4880 Unleful,** *unlawful,* **sote,** *sweet* **4881 racyne,** *root* **4886 unwelde,** *feeble* **4887 of commendatioun,** *praiseworthy* **4890 parel,** *peril* **4892 pace,** *pass* **4898 mokel,** *great* **4900 disrulyly,** *disruptively* **4901 halte hym payde,** *considers himself satisfied,* **none estate,** *no situation* **4904 yalte,** *yields,* **covent,** *monastery* **4905 emprise,** *rule* **4906 fraunchyse,** *right* **4909 mansyon,** *residence* **4910 abyde professyon,** *await the speaking of vows* **4911 absente,** *is absent* (from love) **4913 thilke,** *that* **4914 abyte,** *religious clothing* **4915 worshyp,** *reputation* **4919 Fredom of kynde,** *natural freedom* **4920 recured,** *recovered* **4922 pace,** *pass* **4923 Conteyne,** *keep (him)* **4925 set,** *sets* **4926 unthrifte,** *vice,* **ribaudye,** *debauchery* **4928 of corage,** *in spirit* **4931 parell,** *peril* **4933 drede the,** *doubt you*

4859 sterne, G reads "strene"; probably correct. **4861 dede,** Th reads "bede." **4871 Thus hath subtylled,** G and Th read "This had subtyl." **4878 vyce,** G reads "wise." **4882 Tullyus,** (Marcus Tullius) Cicero, author of *De Senectute* (*Concerning Old Age*); see book 12. **4892 tyme,** G and Th read "parel." **4904 him,** omitted in G and Th. **4921 if that,** G and Th read "that if." **4926 ribaudye,** Th reads "ribandrie." **4933 thus,** G and Th read "this."

Onely through Youthe, his chamberere°,
That to done yvell is customere°,
And of naught els taketh hede
But onely folkes for to lede
Into disporte° and wyldenesse,
So is she frowarde° from sadnesse°.
"But Elde draweth hem therfro.
Who wote° it not, he may wel go
Demand of hem that nowe arne olde,
That whylom° Youthe had in holde,
Whiche yet remembre of tender age,
Howe it hem brought in many a rage,
And many a foly therein wrought.
But nowe that Elde hath hem through sought°,
They repent hem of her folye,
That Youthe hem put in jeopardye,
In parell and in moche wo,
And made hem ofte amysse to do,
And sewen° yvell companye,
Ryot and avoutrye°.
But Elde can agayne restrayne°
From suche foly, and refrayne°
And set men by her ordynaunce°
In good rule and in governaunce.
But yvel° she spendeth° her servyse,
For no man wol her love ne preyse;
She is hated, this wote° I wele.
Her acqueyntaunce wolde° no man fele,
Ne han of Elde companye,
Men hate to be of her alye°.
For no man wolde becomen olde,
Ne dye whan he is yonge and bolde.
And Elde merveyleth right greatly,
Whan they remembre hem inwardly
Of many a perillous emprise°,
Whiche that they wrought in sondrie wyse,
However they might, without blame,
Escape away without shame,
In Youthe, without damage
Or reprefe° of her lynage,
Losse of membre°, shedyng of blood,
Parell of dethe, or losse of good.
"Woste° thou not where Youthe abyt°,
That men so preysen in her wyt?
With Delyte she halte sojour°,
For bothe they dwellen in o tour.
As longe as Youthe is in season,
They dwellen in one mansyon.
Delyte of Youthe wol have servyce
To do what so he wol devyse;
And Youthe is redy evermore
For to obeye, for smerte of soore,
Unto Delyte, and him to yeve
Her servyce whyle that she may lyve.
"Where Elde abytte I wol the tel
Shortly, and no while dwel,
For thyder behoveth the° to go,
If dethe in youthe the nat slo°;
Of this journey thou mayst nat fayle.
With her Labour and Travayle°
Lodged ben, with Sorowe and Wo,
That never out of her courte go.
Payne and Dystresse, Syckenesse and Yre.
And Melancoly, that angry syre°,
Bene of her paleys senatours°;
Gronyng and Grutchyng°, her
herbegeours°,
The daye and nyght, her to tourment,
With cruel Dethe they her present,
And tellen her, erlyche and late,
That Dethe stondeth armed at her gate.
Than brynge they to her remembraunce
The foly° dedes of her enfaunce°,
Whiche causen her to mourne in wo
That Youthe hath her begyled so,
Whiche sodainly awaye is hasted.
She wepeth the tyme that she hath wasted,
Complaynynge of the preterytte°,
And the present that nat abytte°,
And of her olde vanyte,
That but aforne° her she maye se
In the future some socoure°,

4935 chamberere, *household servant* **4936 customere,** *accustomed* **4939 disporte,** *frivolity* **4940 frowarde,** *opposite,* **sadnesse,** *seriousness* **4942 wote,** *knows* **4944 whylom,** *formerly* **4948 through sought,** *examined* (?) **4953 sewen,** *pursue* **4954 avoutrye,** *adultery* **4955 restrayne,** *hold back* **4956 refrayne,** *prevent* **4957 ordynaunce,** *arrangement* **4959 yvel,** *unsuccessfully,* **spendeth,** *expends* **4961 wote,** *know* **4962 wolde,** *desires* (to) **4964 of her alye,** *of her alliance* **4969 emprise,** *undertaking* **4974 reprefe,** *blame* **4975 membre,** *limb* **4977 Woste,** *know,* **abyt,** *lives* **4979 halte sojour,** *hold residence* **4991 thyder behoveth the,** *there it is necessary for you* **4992 slo,** *slay* **4994 Travayle,** *Affliction* **4998 syre,** *lord* **4999 senatours,** *officials* **5000 Grutchyng,** *Complaining,* **herbegeours,** *harbingers* (who go ahead and prepare lodgings) **5006 foly,** *foolish,* **enfaunce,** *youth* **5011 preterytte,** *time past* **5012 abytte,** *waits* **5014 aforne,** *before* **5015 socoure,** *comfort*

4935 Youthe, his chamberere, G and Th read "youthes chamb(e)re." **4940 she,** omitted in G and Th. **4943 Demand,** G and Th read "And mo(o)." **4945 remembre,** G and Th read "remembreth." **4948 hem,** G and Th read "him" **4952 to do,** G reads "do to." **4955 can,** G and Th read "gan." **4960 ne,** G and Th read "neither." **4995–5000** The personifications in these lines are not in the French. **5010 wepeth,** G and Th read "weped."

To leggen° her of her doloure°,
To graunt her tyme of repentaunce,
For her synnes to do penaunce,
And at the laste so her governe
To wynne the joye that is eterne.
Fro whiche go° backwarde Youthe her made,
In vanyte to drowne and wade,
For present tyme abydeth nought.
It is more swyfte than any thought;
So lytel whyle it dothe endure
That there nys compte° ne measure.
"But howe that ever the game go,
Who lyst° to have joye and myrthe also
Of love, be it he or she,
Hye, or lowe, who it be,
In fruyte° they shulde hem delyte.
Her parte° they maye nat els quyte°
To save hemselfe in honeste°.
And yet ful many one I se
Of women, sothly for to sayne,
That desyre and wolde fayne°
The playe of love, they be so wylde,
And nat coveyte° to go with chylde.
And if with chylde they be perchaunce,
They wol it holde a great myschaunce;
But whatsoever wo they fele,
They wol nat playne°, but concele,
But if° it be any foole or nyce°,
In whome that shame hath no justyce°.
For to delyte echone° they drawe,
That haunt° this worke, bothe hye and lawe,
Save° suche that arne worthe right nought,
That for money wol be bought.
Suche love I preyse in no wyse,
Whan it is goven° for covetyse.
I preyse no woman, though she be woode°,
That yeveth herselfe for any goode.
For lytel shulde a man telle°
Of her that wol her body selle,
Be she mayde, be she wyfe,
That quycke° wol selle her by her lyfe.
Howe fayre chere° that ever she make,
He is a wretch, I undertake,
That loveth suche one, for swete or soure,
Though she hym called her paramoure°,
And laugheth on him, and maketh him feest°.
For certainly no suche beest°
To be loved is nat worthy,
Or beare the name of drury°.
None shulde her please but° he were woode°,
That wol dispoyle° him of his goode.
Yet nathelesse, I wol nat saye
But she for solace and for playe
Maye a jewel or other thynge
Take of her loves free yevynge—
But° that she aske it in no wyse,
For drede of shame or covetyse.
And she of hers maye him, certayne,
Without sclaunder, yeven agayne°,
And joyne her hertes togyder so
In love, and take and yeve also.
Trowe° nat that I wol hem twynne°
Whan in her love there is no synne;
I wol that they togyder go,
And done al that they hanne ado°,
As curteys shulde and debonayre°,
And in her love beren hem fayre,
Without vyce, bothe he and she;
So that alwaye, in honeste°,
Fro folly love they kepe hem clere
That brenneth hertes with his fere;
And that her love in any wyse
Be devoyde of covetyse.
"Good love shulde engendred° be
Of trewe hert, juste and secree°,
And nat of suche as sette her thought
To have her luste and els nought;
So are they caught in Loves lace°,
Trewly, for bodily solace.
Flesshely delyte is so present
With the, that set al thyn entent,
Without more (what shulde I glose°?)

5016 leggen, *alleviate,* **doloure,** *sorrow* **5021 go,** *to go* **5026 compte,** *count* **5028 Who lyst,** *whoever desires* **5031 fruyte,** i.e., *children* **5032 Her parte,** *their portion,* **quyte,** *pay* **5033 honeste,** *virtue* **5036 wolde fayne,** *eagerly want* **5038 coveyte,** *desire* **5042 playne,** *lament* **5043 But if,** *unless,* **nyce,** *lascivious person* **5044 justyce,** *power* **5045 echone,** *each one* **5046 haunt,** *engage in* **5047 Save,** *except* **5050 goven,** *given* **5051 woode,** *crazy* **5053 telle,** *count* **5056 quycke,** *readily* **5057 chere,** *appearance* **5060 paramoure,** *beloved* **5061 maketh him feest,** *entertains him* **5062 beest,** *beast* **5064 drury,** *lover* **5065 but,** *unless,* **woode,** *insane* **5066 dispoyle,** *rob* **5071 But,** *except* **5074 yeven agayne,** *give in return* **5077 Trowe,** *think,* **twynne,** *separate* **5080 hanne ado,** *have to do* **5081 debonayre,** *gracious* **5084 honeste,** *honor* **5089 engendred,** *born* **5090 secree,** *private* **5093 lace,** *net* **5097 what shulde I glose,** *why should I paraphrase*

5021 her, G and Th read "he." **5028 have,** G and Th read "love." **5051 she,** G and Th read "so." **5054 wol,** Th reads "wel." **5059 loveth,** G and Th read "loved." **5060 called,** G reads calle." **5067 nathelesse,** G reads "nevertheles." **5072 or,** G reads "of." **5077 wol,** G reads "wolde." **5085 they,** G and Th read "to."

For to get and have the rose,
Whiche maketh the so mate° and wood°
That thou desyrest none other good.
But thou arte not an ynche the nerre°,
But ever abydest in sorowe and werre°,
As in thy face it is sene.
It maketh the bothe pale and lene;
Thy might, thy vertue° gothe away.
A sory gest°, in good fay°,
Thou herborest° hem in thyn inne°,
The God of Love whan thou let inne!
Wherfore I rede° thou shette him oute,
Or he shal greve the, out of doute;
For to thy profyte it wol turne,
If he nomore with the sojourne°.
In great mischefe and sorowe sonken
Ben hertes that of love arne dronken,
As thou peraventure° knowen shall,
Whan thou hast lost thy tyme all,
And spent thy youthe in ydelnesse,
In waste and woful lustynesse.
If thou mayst lyve the tyme to se
Of Love for to delyvered° be,
Thy tyme thou shalte bewepe sore
The whiche never thou mayst restore.
For tyme loste, as men may se,
For nothyng may recovered be.
And if thou scape yet, at laste,
Fro Love, that hath the so faste
Knytte and bounden in his lace,
Certayne I holde it but a grace°.
For many one, as it is seyne°,
Have loste and spent also in veyne
In his servyce, without socour,
Body and soule, good and treasour,
Wytte and strength and eke rychesse,
Of whiche they had never redresse°."
L'AMANT: Thus taught and preched hath Reason,
But Love spylte° her sermon,
That was so imped° in my thought,
That her doctryne I set at nought.
And yet ne sayd she never a dele°,
That I ne understode it wele,
Worde by worde, the mater all.
But unto Love I was so thrall°,
Whiche calleth over al his praye°;
He chaseth so my thought aye°,
And holdeth myne herte under his sele°
As trusty and trewe as any stele,
So that no devocion
Ne had I in the sermon
Of Dame Reason, ne of her rede;
It toke no sojour° in myn heede.
For al yede° out at one ere
That in that other she dyd lere°.
Fully on me she lost her lore;
Her speche me greved wonder sore.
  Than unto her for ire I sayde,
For anger, as I dyd abrayde°:
"Dame, and is it your wyl algate°
That I not love, but that I hate
Al men, as ye me teche?
For if I do after your speche,
Sythe that° ye seyne love is not good,
Than must I nedes say with mode,
If I it leve°, in hatred aye
Lyven; and voyde° love awaye
From me wole I, a synful wretche,
Hated of al that vertu tetche°.
I may not go none other gate°,
For eyther muste I love or hate.
And if I hate men of-newe°,
More than love it wol me rewe°,
As by your prechyng semeth me,
For love nothyng ne prayseth the.
Ye yeve good counsayle, sykerly°,
That precheth me al day° that I
Shulde not Loves lore alowe°—
He were a foole, wolde you not trowe°!

5099 mate, *confused,* **wood,** *mad* **5101 nerre,** *nearer* **5102 werre,** *strife* **5105 vertue,** *strength* **5106 gest,** *guest,* **fay,** *faith* **5107 herborest,** *shelters,* **inne,** *inn* **5109 rede,** *advise* **5112 sojourne,** *dwells* **5115 peraventure,** *perhaps* **5120 Of...delyvered,** *released from* **5128 but a grace,** *nothing but good luck* **5129 seyne,** *seen* **5134 redresse,** *compensation* **5136 spylte,** *spoiled* **5137 imped,** *planted* **5139 dele,** *bit* **5142 thrall,** *enslaved* **5143 praye,** *prey* **5144 aye,** *continuously* **5145 sele,** *seal* (i.e., control) **5150 sojour,** *lodging* **5151 yede,** *went* **5152 lere,** *teach* **5156 abrayde,** *scold* **5157 algate,** *thoroughly* **5161 Sythe that,** *since* **5162 mode,** *anger* **5163 leve,** *leave* **5164 voyde,** *repel* **5166 tetche,** *disposition* **5167 gate,** *way* **5169 of-newe,** *newly* **5170 rewe,** *distress* **5173 sykerly,** *truly* **5174 al day,** *constantly* **5175 alowe,** *approve of* **5176 wolde you not trowe,** *if he would not believe you* (sarcastic)

5099 the, omitted in G. **5107 hem,** omitted in Th. **5116 thy,** G and Th read "the." **5117 thy youthe,** G and Th read "by thought"; the French is *ta jenesce.* **5123–24** Commonplace; compare *HF* 1.1257–58. **5124 recovered,** G reads "recured." **5165–66** Editors have attempted various emendations of these lines, none wholly satisfactory. The text here follows G and Th, even though the meter is deficient. **5168 eyther,** G reads "other." **5165–66** Editors have attempted various emendations of these lines, none wholly satisfactory. The text here follows G and Th, even though the meter is deficient. **5168 eyther,** G reads "other."

In speche also ye han me taught
Another love that knowen is naught,
Whiche I have herde you not repreve°,
To love eche other. By your leve,
If ye wolde diffyne it me,
I wolde gladly here, to se,
At the leest, if I may lere°
Of sondrie loves the manere.
RAISON: "Certes, frende, a foole arte thou
Whan that thou nothyng wolte alow
That I for thy profyte saye.
Yet wol I saye the more, in faye°;
For I am redy, at the leest,
To accomplysshe thy request.
But I not where° it wol aveyle°;
In vayne, pareventure°, I shale traveyle°.
Love there is in sondrye wyse°,
As I shal the here devyse°.
For some love leful° is and goode—
I meane nat that whiche maketh the woode°,
And bringeth the in many a fytte,
And ravyssheth° fro the al thy wytte,
It is so marveylous and queynt°;
With suche love be no more aqueynt.

Comment Raison diffinist amitie

"Love of frendshippe also there is, VARIOUS KINDS OF LOVE
Whiche maketh no man done amys,
Of wyl knytte betwixte two,
That wol nat breke for wele° he wo;
Whiche longe is lykely to contune°,
Whan wyl and goodes ben in commune;
Grounded° by Goddes ordynaunce,
Hoole° without discordaunce;
With hem holdynge communte°
Of al her good in charyte,
That there be none exceptioun
Through chaungynge of ententioun;
That eche helpe other at her nede,
And wisely hele° bothe worde and dede;
Trewe of meanyng, devoyde of slouthe°,
For wytte is nought without trouthe;
So that the tone° dare al his thought
Sayne to his frende, and spare nought,
As to himselfe, without dredynge
To be discovered by wreying°.
For gladde is that conjunctioun
Whan there is none suspectioun
Ne lak° in hem whome they wolde prove
That trewe and parfyte weren in love.
For no man maye be amyable,
But if he be so ferme and stable
That Fortune chaunge him nat, ne blynde,
But that his frende alwaye him fynde,
Bothe poore and ryche, in o state.
For if his frende, through any gate°,
Wol complayne of his poverte,
He shulde nat byde° so longe tyl he
Of his helpynge him requyre°;
For good dede done through prayere°
Is solde and bought to dere, ywis°,
To hert that of great valor is.
For herte fulfylled of gentylnesse
Canne yvel demeane° his distresse.
And man that worthy is of name
To askenne° often hath great shame;
A good manne brenneth° in his thought
For shame, whan he asketh ought°.
He hath great thought and dredeth aye
For his disease°, whan he shal praye°
His frende, lest° that he warned° be,
Tyl that he preve his stabilyte.
But whan that he hath founden one
That trusty is and trewe as stone,
And assayed him at al,
And founde him stedfast as a wal,
And of his frendshippe be certayne,
He shal him shewe bothe joye and payne,
And al that he dare thynke or saye,
Without shame, as he wel maye.
For howe shulde he ashamed be
Of suche one as I told the?

5179 **repreve,** *blame* 5183 **lere,** *learn* 5188 **faye,** *faith* 5191 **not where,** *don't know whether,* **aveyle,** *do any good* 5192 **pareventure,** *perhaps,* **traveyle,** *work* 5193 **sondrye wyse,** *various ways* 5194 **the here devyse,** *describe to you here* 5195 **leful,** *lawful* 5196 **woode,** *insane* 5198 **ravyssheth,** *robs* 5199 **queynt,** *peculiar* 5204 **wele,** *happiness* 5205 **contune,** *continue* 5207 **Grounded,** *established* 5208 **Hoole,** *whole* 5209 **communte,** *community* 5214 **hele,** *conceal* 5215 **slouthe,** *laziness* 5217 **the tone,** *the one* 5220 **discovered by wreying,** *revealed by betrayal* 5223 **Ne lak,** *nor failure* 5230 **gate,** *circumstance* 5232 **byde,** *wait* 5233 **requyre,** *request* 5234 **prayere,** *asking* 5235 **ywis,** *surely* 5238 **yvel demeane,** *poorly control* 5240 **askenne,** *request* 5241 **brenneth,** *burns* 5242 **ought,** (for) *anything* 5244 **disease,** *distress,* **praye,** *ask* 5245 **lest,** *for fear,* **warned,** *refused*

5200a Comment Raison diffinist amitie, How Reason defines friendship. G and Th read "aunsete" instead of "amitie." **5223 Ne lak in hem,** omitted in G and Th. **5253 he,** omitted in G and Th.

For whan he wotte° his secree thought,
The thirde shal knowe therof right nought;
For twey in nombre is bette than thre
In every counsayle and secree.
Repreve° he dredeth never a dele,
Who that° besette his wordes wele,
For every wyse manne, out of drede°,
Canne kepe his tonge tyl he se nede.
And fooles cannenat holde her tonge;
A fooles belle is soone ronge.
Yet shal a trewe frende do more
To helpe his felowe of his sore,
And socour him whan he hath nede
In al that he maye done in dede,
And gladder be that he him pleaseth
Than his felowe that he easeth.
And if he do nat his request,
He shal as moche him molest°
As his felowe, for that he
Maye nat fulfyl his volunte°
Fully, as he hath requyred°.
If bothe the hertes Love hath fyred,
Joye and wo they shal departe°,
And take evenly eche his parte.
Halfe his anoye° he shal have aye,
And comforte him what that he maye;
And of his blysse parte shal he°,
If Love wel departed be.
"And whylom° of of this amyte°
Spake Tullius in a dyte°:
'A man shulde maken his request
Unto his frende that is honest,
And he goodly shulde it fulfyll
But° it the more were out of skyll°,
And otherwyse not graunte therto
Except only in cases two:
If men his frende to dethe wolde drive,
Let him be besy to save his lyve
Also if men wollen him assayle°
Of his worshyp° to make him fayle,
And hyndren him of his renoun,
Let him with ful entencioun,
His dever done° in eche degre
That his frende ne shamed be.
In this two cases with his might,
Takyng no kepe° to skyll° nor right,
As ferre as love may him excuse,
This ought no man to refuse.'
This love that I have tolde to the
Is nothyng contrarye to me;
This wol I° that thou folowe wele,
And leave the tother everydele°.
This love to vertue al attendith,
The tother fooles blent° and shendeth°.
"Another love also there is,
That is contrarye unto this,
Whiche desyre is so constrayned
That it is but wyl fayned°.
Away fro trouthe it dothe so varye°,
That to good love it is contrarye;
For it maymeth° in many wyse
Syke hertes with covetyse.
Al in wynnyng and in profyte
Suche love setteth his delyte.
This love so hangeth in balaunce
That if it lese° his hope parchaunce
Of lucre° that he is set upon,
It wol fayle and quench anon.
For no man may be amorous,
Ne in his lyvyng vertuous,
But° he love more, in moode°,
Men for hemselfe° than for her goode.
For love that profyte dothe abyde°
Is false, and bydeth° not in no tyde°.
This love cometh of Dame Fortune,
That lytel whyle wol contune°,
For it shal chaungen wonder soone,
And take eclyps right as the moone
Whan she is from us lette°
Through° erthe, that betwixt is sette

5257 wotte, *knows* **5261 Repreve,** *blame* **5262 Who that,** *he who* **5263 out of drede,** *without doubt* **5274 him molest,** *harm himself* **5276 volunte,** *desire* **5277 requyred,** *asked* **5279 departe,** *divide* **5281 anoye,** *pain* **5283 parte shal he,** *he shall have part* **5285 whylom,** *formerly,* **amyte,** *friendship* **5286 dyte,** *writing* **5290 But,** *unless,* **out of skyll,** *unreasonable* **5295 assayle,** *attack* **5296 worshyp,** *honor* **5299 His dever done,** *do his duty* **5302 Takyng no kepe,** *paying no attention,* **skyll,** *reason* **5307 wol I,** *I desire* **5308 tother everydele,** *the other completely* **5310 blent,** *blinds,* **shendeth,** *ruins* **5314 wyl fayned,** *pretended desire* **5315 varye,** *deviate* **5317 maymeth,** *harms* **5322 lese,** *lose* **5323 lucre,** *money* **5327 But,** *unless,* **moode,** *spirit* **5328 hemselfe,** *themselves* **5329 dothe abyde,** *expects* **5330 bydeth,** *lasts,* **tyde,** *time* **5332 contune,** *continue* **5335 lette,** *hidden* **5336 Through,** *by*

5259 in, G reads "of." **5271 be,** omitted in G and Th. **5282 him,** omitted in G and Th. **5383 his,** G and Th read "this." **5284 wel,** G and Th read "wol." **5285 amyte,** G and Th read "unyte." **5286 Tullius,** (Marcus Tullius) Cicero; the quotation (5287–5304) derives from his *De Amicitia* (*Concerning Friendship*), 17. **5287 A man,** G and Th read "And." **5292 cases,** G and Th read "cause." **5301 cases,** G and Th read "caas" (situation). **5309 attendith,** G and Th read "entendith." **5314 it,** omitted in G and Th. **5331 This,** omitted in G and Th. **5335 she,** G and Th read "he."

The sonne and her, as it may fall,
Be it in partie° or in all;
The shadowe maketh her bemes merke°,
And her hornes to shewe derke,
That parte where she hath loste her lyght
Of Phebus° fully, and the syght,
Tyl whan the shadowe is overpaste°,
She is enlumyned° ageyn as faste,
Through the brightnesse of the sonne bemes
That yeveth to her agayne her lemes°.
That love is right° of suche nature;
Nowe is fayre, and nowe obscure,
Nowe bright, nowe clipsy° of manere,
And whilom° dymme and whylom clere.
As soone as Poverte gynneth take°
With mantel° and weedes° blake
It hydeth of Love the light away,
That into nyght it turneth day;
It may not se Richesse shyne
Tyl the blacke shadowes fyne°.
For whan Rychesse shyneth bright,
Love recovereth ayen his lyght;
And whan it fayleth, he wol flyt°,
And as she groweth, so groweth it.
 “Of this love, here what I saye:
The ryche men are loved aye°,
And namely tho° that sparande° bene,
That wol not wasshe her hertes clene
Of the fylthe nor of the vyce
Of gredy brennyng Avaryce.
The ryche man ful fonde° is, ywis°,
That weneth° that he loved is.
If that his herte it understode,
It is not he, it is his good;
He may wel weten° in his thought,
His good is loved, and he right nought.
For if he be a nygarde eke°,
Men wol nat set by him a leke°,
But haten him; this is the sothe°.
Lo°, what profyte his catel dothe°!
Of every man that may him se,
It getteth him nought but enmyte.
But he amende hym of that vyce,
And knowe himselfe, he is not wyse.
 “Certes, he shulde aye frendly be,
To get hym love also ben fre°;
Or els he is not wyse ne sage
No more than is a gote ramage°.
That he not loveth, his dede proveth,
Whan he his richesse so wel loveth,
That he wol hyde it aye and spare°,
His poore frendes sene forfare°,
To kepen aye his purpose
Tyl for drede his eyen close,
And tyl a wicked dethe him take.
Hym had lever° asondre shake°
And let al his lymmes asondre ryve°,
Than leave his richesse in his lyve.
He thenketh parte° it with no man;
Certayne no love is in him than.
Howe shulde love within hym be,
Whan in his herte is no pyte?
That he trespaseth, wel I wate°;
For eche man knoweth his estate°;
For wel him ought to be reproved°
That loveth nought, ne is not loved.
 “But sithe° we arne to Fortune comen
And have our sermon of her nomen°, FORTUNE
A wonder wyll I tel the nowe,
Thou herdest never suche one, I trowe°.
I not where° thou me leven° shall,
Though sothfastnesse° it be all.
As it is written and is sothe°
That unto men more profyte° dothe
The frowarde° Fortune and contraire
Than the swote° and debonaire°.
And if the thynke it is doutable,
It is through argument provable,

5338 in partie, *partial* (eclipse) **5339 merke,** *dim* **5342 Of Phebus,** *from the sun* **5343 overpaste,** *passed by* **5344 enlumyned,** *illuminated* **5346 lemes,** *rays* **5347 right,** *just* **5349 clipsy,** *changeable* (?) **5350 whilom,** *at times* **5351 gynneth take,** *begins to prevail* **5352 mantel,** *cloak,* **weedes,** *clothing* **5356 fyne,** *end* **5359 flyt,** *fly away* **5362 aye,** *always* **5363 namely tho,** *especially those,* **sparande,** *miserly* **5367 fonde,** *foolish,* **ywis,** *surely* **5368 weneth,** *thinks* **5371 weten,** *know* **5373 nygarde eke,** *miser also* **5374 set by him a leke,** *consider him worth a leek* **5375 sothe,** *truth* **5376 Lo,** *behold,* **catel dothe,** *wealth accomplishes* **5382 ben fre,** *be generous* **5384 gote ramage,** *wild goat* **5387 spare,** *hoard* **5388 sene forfare,** *see perish* **5392 lever,** *rather,* **asondre shake,** *be shaken apart* **5393, ryve,** *be torn* **5395 parte,** *to divide* **5399 wate,** *know* **5400 estate,** *condition* **5401 reproved,** *blamed* **5403 sithe,** *since* **5404 nomen,** *undertaken* **5406 trowe,** *think* **5407 not where,** *don't know whether,* **leven,** *believe* **5408 sothfastnesse,** *truth* **5409 sothe,** *true* **5410 profyte,** *good* **5411 frowarde,** *adverse* **5412 swote,** *sweet,* **debonaire,** *pleasant*

5353 It, omitted in G and Th. **5360 growth so groweth,** G and Th read “greveth so greveth”; the French has *resaillent* (spout forth). **5379 hym,** G and Th read “hymselfe.” **5395 thenketh,** Th reads “thenketh to.” **5403 sithe,** G reads “se.” **5404 have,** G and Th read “hath.” **5408 it be all,** G reads “it be it all.” **5409–5560** Compare *Bo* 2.pr8, where fortune and friendship are discussed in a similar way, though more briefly. Jean de Meun translated Boethius, as did Chaucer.

For the debonayre and softe
Falseth and begyleth ofte.
For lyche° a mother she can cherishe
And mylken° as dothe a norice°;
And of her good to hem deles°,
And yeveth hem parte of her joweles°,
With great rychesse and dignite.
And hem she hoteth° stabylite
In a state that is not stable,
But chaungyng aye and variable;
And fedeth hem with glorie veyne
And worldly blysse noncertayne,
Whan she hem setteth on her whele.
Than wene° they to be right wele,
And in so stable state withall,
That never they wene for to fall.
And whan they sette so hygh be,
They wene to have in certeynte
Of hertly° frendes so great nombre
That nothyng might her state encombre.
They truste hem so on every syde,
Wenyng with hem they wolde abyde
In every parel° and mischaunce°,
Without chaunge or variaunce,
Bothe of catel° and of good;
And also for to spende° her blood
And al her membres° for to spyll°
Onely to fulfyll her wyll.
They maken it hole° in many wyse,
And hoten° hem her ful servyse,
Howe sore° that it do hem smerte
Into her very naked sherte!
Herte and al so hole they yeve
For the tyme that they may lyve
So that with her flaterye
They maken fooles glorifye°
Of her wordes spekyng,
And han therof a rejoysyng,
And trowe° hem as the Evangyle°,
And it is al falshede and gyle,
As they shal afterwarde se,
Whan they arne fall° in poverte
And ben of good and catell° bare;
Than shul they sene who frendes ware°.
For of an hundred, certaynly,
Nor of a thousande ful scarsly,
Ne shal they fynde unnethes° one,
Whan poverte is comen upon.
For this Fortune that I of tell,
With men whan her lust° to dwell,
Maketh hem to lese her conysaunce°,
And norissheth hem in ignoraunce.
"But frowarde° Fortune and perverse°,
Whan high estates she dothe reverse,
And maketh hem to tomble doune
Of her whele, with sodayne tourne,
And from her rychesse dothe hem° flye,
And plongeth hem in poverte,
As a stepmother envyous,
And layeth a playstre dolorous°
Unto her hertes, wounded egre°,
Whiche is not tempred with vynegre,
But with poverte and indygence,
For to shewe, by experience,
That she is Fortune verilye°
In whom no man shulde affye°,
Nor in her yeftes have fyaunce°,
She is so ful of varyaunce.
Thus can she maken hye and lowe,
Whan they from rychesse arne throwe°,
Fully to knowen, without were°,
Frende of affecte° and frende of chere°;
And whiche in love weren trewe and stable,
And whiche also weren varyable,
After Fortune, her goddesse,
In poverte, either in rychesse,
For al she yeveth here, out of drede°,
Unhappe bereveth° it in dede.
For Infortune lette° not one
Of frendes whan Fortune is gone—
I meane tho frendes that wol fle
Anon° as entreth poverte.

5417 lyche, *like* **5418 mylken,** *provide milk,* **norice,** *nurse* **5419 deles,** *gives a portion* **5420 joweles,** *jewels* **5422 hoteth,** *promises* **5428 wene,** *think* **5433 hertly,** *close* **5437 parel,** *peril,* **mischaunce,** *misfortune* **5439 catel,** *property* **5440 spende,** *spill* **5441 membres,** *limbs,* **spyll,** *destroy* **5443 maken it hole,** *affirm completely* **5444 hoten,** *promise* **5445 Howe sore,** *however painfully* **5450 maken fooles glorifye,** *cause fools to be glorified* **5453 trowe,** *believe,* **Evangyle,** *Gospel* **5456 arne fall,** *are fallen* **5457 catell,** *property* **5458 ware,** *were* **5461 unnethes,** *barely* **5464 her lust,** *it pleases her* **5465 conysaunce,** *understanding* **5467 frowarde,** *adverse,* **perverse,** *contrary* **5471 dothe hem,** *causes them to* **5474 playstre dolorous,** *painful medicinal plaster* **5475 egre,** *bitterly* **5479 verilye,** *truly* **5480 affye,** *trust* **5481 fyaunce,** *faith* **5484 arne throwe,** *are thrown* **5485 were,** *doubt* **5486 affecte,** *affection,* **chere,** *appearance* **5491 out of drede,** *without doubt* **5492 Uphappe bereveth,** *misfortune steals* **5493 lette,** *leaves* **5496 Anon,** *as soon*

5419–36 The various uses of *hem* in these lines appear in G and Th as *hym* or *him,* less familiar plural forms. **5425 glorie veyne,** G reads "glorie and veyne." **5433 so,** G and Th read "to." **5446 very,** omitted in G. **5452 therof,** G and Th read "chere of." **5463 this,** G and Th read "thus." **5465 hem,** G reads "men." **5470 Of,** G reads "Or with." **5490 either,** G reads "outher." **5491 she,** G and Th read "that."

And yet they wol not leave hem so,
But in eche place where they go
They cal hem 'wretche', scorne and blame,
And of her mishappe hem diffame;
And namely° suche as in rychesse
Pretendeth moste of stablenesse,
Whan that they sawe hem set onlofte,
And weren of hem socoured° ofte,
And moste yholpe° in al her nede.
But nowe they take no maner hede,
But seyne° in voyce of flaterye
That nowe appereth her folye
Over al where so they fare,
And synge, 'Go, farewel feldefare°!'
Al suche frendes I beshrewe°,
For of trewe there be to fewe;
But sothfaste frendes, what so betyde,
In every fortune wollen abyde°.
They han her hertes in suche noblesse
That they nyl° love for no rychesse,
Nor for that° Fortune may hem sende
They wollen hem socour and defende,
And chaunge for softe ne for sore,
For who is frende, loveth evermore.
Though men drawe swerde his frende to slo°,
He may not hewe her love atwo,
But in case that I shal say,
For pride and ire lese it° he may,
And for reprove by nycete°,
And discoveryng of privyte°,
With tonge woundyng, as felon,
Through venemous detraction.
Frende in this case wol gon his way,
For nothyng greve him more ne may;
And for nought els wol he fle,
If that he love in stabylite.
And certayne he is wel begone°
Amonge a thousande that fyndeth one.
For there may be no rychesse,
Ayenst° frendshyp of worthynesse;
For it ne may so hygh attayne
As may the valoure, sothe to sayne°,
Of him that loveth trewe and well.
Frendshyp is more than is catell°.
For frende in courte aye° better is
Than peny in purse, certis°;
And Fortune, mishappyng°,
Whan upon men she is fallyng,
Through misturnyng of her chaunce,
And caste hem out of balaunce,
She maketh, through her adversyte,
Men ful clerely for to se
Hym that is frende in existence°
From hym that is by apparence.
For infortune maketh anone°
To knowe thy frendes fro thy fone°,
By experyence, right as it is;
The whiche is more to prayse, ywis°,
Than is moche rychesse and tresour.
For more doth° profyte and valour
Povertie and suche adversyte
Before than dothe prosperyte;
For that one yeveth conysaunce°,
And the tother ignoraunce.
"And thus in poverte is in dede
Trouthe declared fro falshede,
For faynte° frendes it wol declare,
And trewe also, what way° they fare.
For whan he was in his rychesse,
These frendes, ful of doublenesse,
Offred him in many wyse
Herte and body and servyce.
What wolde he than have yove° to have bought
To knowen openly her thought,
That he nowe hath so clerely sene?
The lasse° begyled he shulde have bene
And° he hadde than° parceyved it,
But richesse nolde nat lette him wytte°.
Wel more avauntage dothe him than,
Sithe that° it maketh him a wyse man,

5501 namely, *especially* **5504 socoured,** *aided* **5505 yholpe,** *helped* **5507 seyne,** *say* **5510 feldefare,** *a kind of thrush* (see n.) **5511 beshrewe,** *curse* **5514 abyde,** *remain* **5516 nyl,** *will not* **5517 that,** *what* **5521 slo,** *slay* **5524 lese it,** i.e., *lose true friendship* **5525 reprove by nycete,** *foolish blame* **5526 discoveryng of privyte,** *revealing confidences* **5533 wel begone,** *fortunate* **5536 Ayenst,** *against* **5538 sothe to sayne,** *to tell the truth* **5540 catell,** *possessions* **5541 aye,** *always* **5542 certis,** *surely* **5543 mishappyng,** *going wrong* **5549 existence,** *reality* **5551 anone,** *quickly* **5552 fone,** *foes* **5554 ywis,** *truly* **5556 doth,** *bring about* (see n.) **5559 conysaunce,** *understanding* **5563 faynte,** *false* **5564 what way,** *by the way* **5569 yove,** *given* **5572 lasse,** *less* **5573 And,** *if,* **than,** *then* **5574 wytte,** *understand* **5576 Sithe that,** *because*

5503 they, G reads "the." **hem,** G and Th read "him." **5504 hem,** G and Th read "him." **5505 yholpe,** G reads "I hope." **5510 farewel feldefare,** good-bye birdie; i.e., the time is past. For the same phrase, see *TC* 3.861. **5544 fallyng,** G and Th read "fablyng"; the French is *cheanz* (falling). **5555 is,** G and Th read "in." **5556–58** For poverty and such adversity bring about profit and honor more than does prosperity. **5556 doth,** G and Th read "depe." **5569 yove,** G and Th read "yow."

The great myschefe° that he receyveth
Than dothe richesse that him disceyveth.
"Richesse riche ne maketh nought
Him that on treasour sette his thought;
For richesse stonte in suffysaunce° DECEPTION OF RICHES
And nothynge in habundaunce;
For suffysaunce al onely°
Maketh menne to lyve richely.
For he that at mytches tweyne°
Ne valued is in his demayne°
Lyveth more at ease, and more is riche,
Than dothe he that is chiche°,
And in his berne° hath, sothe to sayne,
An hundred mauys° of whete grayne,
Though he be chapman° or marchaunt,
And have of golde many besaunt°.
For in the gettyng he hath suche wo,
And in the kepyng drede also,
And sette evermore his besynesse
For to encrease, and nat to lesse,
For to augment and multiplye.
And though on heapes it lye him by,
Yet never shal make his richesse
Asseth° unto his gredynesse.
But the poore that retcheth° nought,
Save of his lyvelode°, in his thought,
Whiche that he getteth with his traveyle°,
He dredeth naught that it shal feyle,
Though he have lytel worldes goode,
Meate and drynke and easy° foode,
Upon° his traveyle and lyvyng,
And also suffysaunt clothyng.
Or if in syckenesse that he fal,
And lothe meate and drynke withal°,
Though he have nat° his meate to bye°,
He shal bethynke him hastely,
To putte him out of al daungere,
That he of meate hath no mystere°;
Or that he maye with lytel eke
Be founden°, whyle that he is seke;
Or that men shul hym berne° in haste
To lyve tyl his syckenesse be paste°,
To some maysondewe° besyde.
He caste° nought what shal him betyde.
He thynketh nought that ever he shal
Into any syckenesse fal.
And though it fal, as it maye be,
That al betyme° spare shal he°,
As mokel° as shal to hym suffyce,
Whyle he is sycke in any wyse,
He dothe° for that he wol be
Content with his poverte
Without nede of any manne.
So moche in lytel have he canne;
He is apayde° with his fortune.
And for° he nyl be importune°
Unto no wyght°, ne onerous,
Nor of her goodesse coveytous,
Therfore he spareth°, it maye wel bene,
His poore estate for to sustene.
"Or if hym luste° nat for to spare,
But suffreth forth as nought ne ware°,
At laste it hapneth, as it maye,
Right unto his laste daye,
And take the worlde as it wolde be.
For ever in herte thynketh he,
The sooner that dethe hym slo°,
To paradyse the sooner go
He shal, there for to lyve in blysse,
Where that he shal no good mysse.
Thyder he hoopeth God shal him sende
After his wretched lyves ende.
Pythagoras himselfe reherses,
In a booke that *The Golden Verses*
Is cleped°, for the nobilyte
Of the honorable dyte°:
'Than, whan thou gost thy body fro,
Free in the heyre° thou shalte up go,
And leaven al humanyte,

5577 myschefe, *misfortune* **5581 stonte in suffysaunce,** *consists of sufficiency* **5583 al onely,** *alone* **5585 mytches tweyne,** *two loaves of bread* **5586 demayne,** *possession* **5588 chiche,** *miserly* **5589 berne,** *barn* **5590 mauys,** *bushels* (?) **5591 chapman,** *seller* **5592 besaunt,** *gold coins* **5600 Asseth,** *enough* **5601 retcheth,** *cares* **5602 lyvelode,** *livelihood* **5603 traveyle,** *efforts* **5606 easy,** *light* **5607 Upon,** *as a result of* **5610 withal,** *completely* **5611 nat,** *nothing,* **bye,** *buy* **5614 mystere,** *need* **5616 founden,** *supported* **5617 berne,** *take* **5618 paste,** *past* **5619 maysondewe,** *hospital* (French maison-Dieu, house of God) **5620 caste,** *considers* **5624 al betyme,** *in plenty of time,* **spare shal he,** *he will save* **5625 mokel,** *much* **5627 dothe,** *acts* **5631 apayde,** *satisfied* **5632 for,** *because,* **nyl be importune,** *does not wish to be troublesome* **5633 wyght,** *person* **5635 spareth,** *saves* **5637 hym luste,** *it pleases him* **5638 as nought ne ware,** *as if it were nothing* **5643 slo,** *slays* **5651 cleped,** *called* **5652 dyte,** *writing* **5654 heyre,** *air*

5577 receyveth, G and Th read "parceyveth." **5585 at,** G and Th read "hath." **5586 valued is,** G and Th read "value." **5598 it,** G and Th read "that." **5633 wyght,** G reads "witte." **5649–50 Pythagoras . . . *The Golden Verses*,** a Greek philosopher of the sixth century B.C.E., whose works are lost. The *Golden Verses* are summary of his ideas on the transmigration of souls, written in the fifth century C.E.

And purely lyve in deite.'
He is a foole, withouten were°,
That troweth° have his countrey here:
'In erthe is nat our countre,'
That may these clerkes seyne and se
In Boece *Of Consolation,*
Where it is maked mention
Of our countre playne at° the eye,
By techyng of phylosophye,
Where leude° men might lere wyt°,
Whoso that wolde translaten it.
If he be suche that can wel lyve
After his rent° may him yeve,
And not desyreth more to have,
Than may fro poverte him save.
A wyse man sayd, as we may sene,
Is no man wretched but he it wene°,
Be he kyng, knyght, or rybaude°.
And many a rybaude is mery and baude°,
That swynketh° and bereth°, bothe day and nyght,
Many a burthen of great myght,
The whiche dothe him lasse offence
For he suffreth in patience.
They laugh and daunce, tryppe and synge,
And lay nought up for her lyvynge,
But in the taverne al dispendeth°
The wynnyng that God hem sendeth.
Than gothe he fardels° for to bere
With as good chere as he dyd ere°.
To swynke and travayle° he not fayneth°,
For to robben he disdayneth;
But right anon°, after his swynke,
He gothe to taverne for to drinke.
Al these are ryche in habundaunce
That can thus have suffysaunce°
Wel more than can an usurere°,
As God wel knoweth, without were°.
For an usurer, so God me se,
Shal never for rychesse ryche be,
But evermore poore and indygent,
Scarce and gredy in his entent.
"For sothe° it is, whom it° displese,
There may no marchaunt lyve at ese,
His herte in suche a were° is set,
That it quycke brenneth more to get;
Ne never shal enough have geten;
Though he have golde in garners yeten;°
For to be nedy he dredeth sore.
Wherfore to getten more and more
He set his herte and his desyre;
So hote he brenneth in the fyre
Of covetyse that maketh him wood°
To purchace other mennes good.
He underfongeth° a great payne
That undertaketh to drinke up Sayne°,
For the more he drinketh, aye°
The more he leaveth, the sothe° to saye.
Thus is thurst of false gettyng,
That laste ever in coveyting,
And the anguysshe and distresse
With the fyre of gredynesse.
She fyghteth with hym aye and stryveth
That his herte asonder ryveth°.
Suche gredynesse him assayleth
That whan he moste hath, moste he fayleth.
"Physiciens and advocates
Gone° right by the same yates°;
They sell her science° for wynnyng,
And haunte° her crafte for great gettyng.
Her wynnyng is of suche swetnesse
That if a man fall in sicknesse
They are ful glad for her encrese;
For by her wyll, without lese°,
Everyche man shulde be seke,
And though they dye, they set not a leke°.
After, whan they the golde have take,
Ful lytel care for hem they make.
They wolde that fourty were sicke at ones,
Ye, two hundred, in flesshe and bones,

5657 were, *doubt* **5658 troweth,** *thinks to* **5663 playne at,** *clear to* **5665 leude,** *unlearned,* **lere wyt,** *learn understanding* **5668 After his rent,** *according to what his income* **5672 wene,** *thinks* (so) **5673 rybaude,** *churl* **5674 baude,** *cheerful* **5675 swynketh,** *works,* **bereth,** *hauls* **5681 dispendeth,** *spends* **5683 fardels,** *loads* **5684 ere,** *before* **5685 travayle,** *labors* **fayneth,** *pretends* **5687 right anon,** *very soon* **5690 suffysaunce,** *sufficiency* **5691 usurere,** *money lender* **5692 were,** *doubt* **5697 sothe,** *true,* **whom it,** *whomever it may* **5699 were,** *war* **5702 in garners yeten,** *poured into storerooms* **5707 wood,** *frantic* **5709 underfongeth,** *undertakes* **5710 Sayne,** *the river Seine* (in France) **5711 aye,** *always* **5712 sothe,** *truth* **5718 ryveth,** *rips* **5722 Gone,** *travel,* **yates,** *routes* **5723 science,** *knowledge* **5724 haunte,** *pursue* **5728 lese,** *lie* **5730 set not a leke,** *care not a leek*

5659 nat our countre, see *Bo* 1.pr5.9ff. and 5.pr1.15. **5661 Boece *Of Consolation*,** Boethius wrote his *De Consolatione Philosophiae* in the sixth century C.E. Chaucer's translation is *Boece.* **5672** Compare *Bo* 2.pr4.112–13 and *For* 25. **5675 swynketh,** G reads "wynkith." **5680 nought,** G reads "not." **5685 fayneth,** G reads "feyntith." **5686 For,** Th read "For for." **disdayneth,** G reads "disdeyntith." **5699 were,** G and Th read "where." **5700 more,** omitted in G and Th; the French has *plus.* **5701 enough have,** G and Th read "though he hath."

And yet two thousande, as I gesse,
For to encresen her rychesse.
They wol not worchen, in no wyse,
But for lucre° and covetyse.
For physicke° gynneth first by *phy*°—
The phisycien also sothely°;
And sythen° it gothe fro *phy* to *sy*°—
To truste on hem, it is folye.
For they nyl°, in no maner gre°,
Do right nought for charyte.
"Eke in the same secte are sette
Al tho that prechen for to gette
Worshyps, honour, and rychesse.
Her hertes arne in great distresse
That folke lyve not holily.
But aboven al, specially,
Suche as prechen for veynglorie°,
And towarde God have no memorie,
But forthe as ypocrites trace°,
And to her soules dethe° purchace,
And outwarde shewen holynesse,
Though they be ful of cursednesse.
Nat lyche° to the apostels twelve,
They disceyve other and hemselve;
Begyled is the gyler than.
For preachyng of a cursed man,
Though it to other maye profyte,
Himselfe aveyleth° nat a myte°,
For ofte good predicatioun°
Cometh of yvel ententioun.
To him nat vayleth° his prechyng,
Al° helpe he other with his teachyng;
For where they good ensample take,
There is he with vaynglorie shake°.

MISERS

"But lette us leven these prechours,
And speke of hem that in her tours°
Heape up her golde, and faste shette°,
And sore° theron her herte sette.
They neyther love God, ne drede;
They kepe more than it is nede,
And in her bagges sore it bynde,
Out of the sonne and of the wynde;
They putte up more than nede ware°,
Whan they sene poore folke forfare°,
For hungre dye, and for colde quake—
God can wel vengeaunce therof take.
Thre great mischeves° hem assayleth,
And thus in gadring aye travayleth°:
With moche payne they wynne rychesse;
And drede hem holdeth in distresse,
To kepe that they gather faste;
With sorowe they leave it at the laste.
With sorowe they bothe dye and lyve
That° unto rychesse her hertes yeve°;
And in defaute° of love it is,
As it sheweth ful wel, ywis°.
For if these gredy, the sothe to sayne°,
Loveden°, and were loved agayne°,
And good love reigned over all,
Suche wickednesse ne shulde fall°.
But he shulde yeve that moste good had
To hem that weren in nede bestad°,
And lyve without false usure°,
For charyte ful clene and pure.
If they hem yeve to goodnesse,
Defendyng hem from ydelnesse,
In al this worlde than poore none
We shulde fynde, I trowe°, not one.
But chaunged is this worlde unstable,
For love is over al vendable;
We se that no man loveth nowe,
But for wynnyng and for prowe°;
And love is thralled° in servage
Whan it is solde for avauntage;
Yet women wol her bodyes sell;
Suche soules gothe to the dyvel of hell."

5738 lucre, *money* **5739 physicke,** *medicine,* **phy,** *"trusting"* **5740 sothely,** *truly* **5741 sythen,** *after,* **sy,** *"sighing"* **5743 nyl,** *will not,* **no maner gre,** *no kind of pleasure* **5751 veynglorie,** *empty pride* **5753 trace,** *proceed* **5754 dethe,** *death* **5757 lyche,** *like* **5762 aveyleth,** *benefits,* **myte,** *bit* **5763 predicatioun,** *sermon* **5765 vayleth,** *benefits* **5766 Al,** *although* **5768 shake,** *shaken* **5770 her tours,** *their towers* **5771 shette,** *lock* **5772 sore,** *intently* **5777 nede ware,** *need be* **5778 forfare,** *perish* **5781 mischeves,** *afflictions* **5782 in gadring aye travayleth,** *together always beset* (them) **5788 That,** *who,* **yeve,** *give* **5789 in defaute,** *instead* **5790 ywis,** *indeed* **5791 sothe to sayne,** *to tell the truth* **5792 Loveden,** *loved,* **agayne,** *in return* **5794 fall,** *happen* **5796 in nede bestad,** *afflicted in need* **5797 usure,** *usury* **5802 trowe,** *believe* **5804 vendable,** *for sale* **5806 prowe,** *profit* **5807 thralled,** *enslaved*

5739–42 This satirical etymological play is not in the French. The *phy* part is found in *La Bible Guiot de Provins,* line 2582, but no source has been found for the other. **5741** G reads "fy to fy"; Th "fye to fye." **5742 it,** omitted in G. **5751 for,** omitted in G and Th. **5761 it,** omitted in G and Th. **5763–64** See *PardP* 6.407–08. **5781 Thre,** G and Th read "The"; the French is *Treis.*

FRAGMENT C

When Love had tolde hem his entent,
The baronage° to counsayle went.
In many sentences° they fyll°,
And dyversly they sayde her wyll;
But after discorde they accorded,
And her acorde to Love recorded:
LOVE'S BARONS PLAN THE ASSAULT
"Sir," sayden they, "we ben at one,
By even accorde of everychone,
Out-take° Rychesse al-onely°,
That sworne hath ful hauteynly°
That she the castell nyl not assayle°,
Ne smyte a stroke in this batayle
With darte ne mace, speare ne knyfe,
For man° that speketh or bereth the lyfe°,
And blameth your emprise°, ywis°,
And from our hoste° departed is,
At leest way, as in this plyte°,
So hath she this man in dispyte°.
For she saythe he ne loved her never,
And therfore she wol hate him ever.
For he wol gather no tresore,
He hath her wrathe for evermore.
He agylte° her never in other caas°;
Lo, here al holy° his trepas!
She saythe wel that this other day
He asked her leave to gone the way
That is cleped° To-Moche-Yevyng,
And spak ful fayre in his prayeng;
But whan he prayed her, poore was he,
Therfore she warned° him the entre°.
Ne yet is he not thriven° so
That he hath getten a peny or two
That quytely° is his owne in holde.
Thus hath Rychese us all tolde;
And whan Rychesse us this recorded°,
Withouten her we ben accorded.
"And we fynde in our accordaunce,
That False-Semblant° and Abstynaunce,
With al the folke of her batayle°,
Shul at the hynder° gate assayle,
That Wicked-Tonge hath in kepyng,
With his Normans, ful of janglyng°.
And with hem Curtesy and Largesse°,
That shul shewe her hardynesse°
To the olde wyfe that kepte so harde
Fayre-Welcomyng within her warde.
Than shal Delyte and Wel-Helyng°
Fonde° Shame adowne to bring;
With al her hoost, early and late,
They shul assaylen that ylke° gate.
Agaynst Drede shal Hardynesse
Assayle, and also Sykernesse°,
With al the folke of her leadyng,
That never wyst° what was fleyng°.
Fraunchise° shal fyght, and eke Pyte,
With Daungere°, ful of cruelte.
Thus is your hoost ordayned wele;
Downe° shal the castel every dele°,
If everyche do his entent,
So that° Venus be present,
Your mother, ful of vesselage°,
That canne° ynough of such usage.
Withouten her maye no wight spede°
This werke, neither for worde ne dede.
Therfore is good ye for her sende,
For through her maye this worke amende."
"Lordynges, my mother, the goddesse, NATURE OF VENUS
That is my lady and my maistresse,

5812 baronage, *group of nobles* **5813 sentences,** *opinions,* **fyll,** *fell* **5819 Out-take,** *except,* **al-onely,** *alone* **5820 hauteynly,** *solemnly* **5821 nyl not assayle,** *will not attack* **5824 man,** *any man,* **bereth the lyfe,** *is alive* **5825 emprise,** *undertaking,* **ywis,** *indeed* **5826 hoste,** *army* **5827 At leest . . . plyte,** *at least in this situation* **5828 dispyte,** *contempt* **5833 agylte,** *offended,* **caas,** *manner* **5834 holy,** *wholly* **5837 cleped,** *called* **5840 warned,** *forbade,* **entre,** *entry* **5841 thriven,** *succeeded* **5843 quytely,** *freely* **5845 recorded,** *reported* **5848 False-Semblant,** *False-Seeming* (see n.) **5849 batayle,** *army* **5850 hynder,** *rear* **5852 janglyng,** *chatter* **5853 Largesse,** *Generosity* **5854 hardynesse,** *boldness* **5857 Wel-Helyng,** *Well-Hiding* (Secrecy) **5858 Fonde,** *attempt* **5860 ylke,** *same* **5862 Sykernesse,** *Certainty* **5864 wyst,** *knew,* **fleyng,** *fleeing* **5865 Fraunchise,** *Frankness* **5866 With Daungere,** *against Aloofness* **5868 Downe,** *fall,* **every dele,** *completely* **5870 So that,** *as long as* **5871 vesselage,** *noble skill* **5872 canne,** *knows* **5873 wight spede,** *person advance*

5810a Fragment C, this rubric is not in G and Th. The translation picks up at *Roman de la Rose* 10681, skipping some 5,500 lines of the French original. Evidently this resulted from fragments being drawn together. **5814 wyll,** G reads "till." **5821 That,** G reads "The." **5837 To-Moche-Yevyng,** French *Trop Doner.* **5848 False-Semblant,** False-Seeming or Hypocrisy and his companion Enforced Abstinence are introduced as part the God of Love's company in the portion that is omitted between fragments B and C. **5856 Fayre-Welcomyng,** the same character as Bialacoil in fragment B; see 2984. Here the French personifying name is translated into English. **5869–70 entent . . . present,** RI notes that this rhyme pair is "un-Chaucerian" and lists similar examples from Part C: 6105–06, 6565–66, 6111–12, 6301–02, 6339–40, 6373–74, 6875–76, 7317–18; also gives other examples from C in the note to 5919–20: 6429–30, 6469–70, 6717–18, 7481–82.

Nys nat at al at my wyllyng,
Ne dothe nat al my desyringe.
Yet canne she somtyme done labour,
Whan that her luste°, in my socour°,
Al my nedis for to atcheve,
But nowe I thynke her nat to greve°.
My mother is she, and of° childehede
I bothe worshippe her and eke drede;
For who that dredeth sire ne dame
Shal it abye° in body or name.
And, natheles, yet conne we
Sende after her, if nede be;
And were she nygh°, she commen wolde,
I trowe° that nothynge myght her holde.
My mother is of great prowesse;
She hath tane° many a forteresse,
That coste hath many a pounde er this,
There° I nas not present, ywis°;
And yet men sayd it was my dede;
But I come never in that stede.
Ne me ne lyketh°, so mote I the°,
That suche toures ben take withoute me.
For-why° me thynketh that in no wyse
It maye be cleped by marchaundyse°.
Go bye a courser°, blacke or white,
And paye therfore; than arte thou quite°.
The marchaunt oweth the right nought,
Ne thou him, whan thou it bought.
I wol nat sellyng clepe yevyng,
For sellyng asketh no guerdonyng°,
Here lythe no thanke, ne no meryte,
That one gothe from that other al quyte°.
But this sellyng is nat semblable°;
For whan his horse is in the stable,
He maye it selle agayne, parde°,
And wynnen° on it, suche happe maye be;
Al maye the manne nat lese, ywis,
For at the leest the skynne° is his.
Or els, if it so betyde
That he wol kepe his horse to ryde,
Yet is he lorde aye of his horse.
But thylke chaffare° is welle worse
There° Venus entremeteth ought°;
For whoso suche chaffare hath bought,
He shal not worchyn so wysely
That he ne shal lese° al utterly
Bothe his money and his chaffare°.
But the seller of the ware
The prise° and profyte have shal.
Certayne, the byer shal lese al
For he ne canne so dere it bye
To have lordshippe and ful maistry,
Ne have power to make lettyng°
Neyther for yefte° ne for preachyng,
That of his chaffare, maugre his°,
Another shal have as moche, ywis°,
If he wol yeve as moche as he,
Of what° countrey so that he be;
Or for right nought°, so happe maye,
If he canne flatter her to her paye°.
Bene than suche marchauntes wyse?
No, but fooles in every wyse,
Whan they bye suche thynge wylfully,
There as they lese her good fully.
But nathelesse, this dare I saye,
My mother is nat wonte° to paye,
For she is neither so foole ne nyce°,
To entremete her of suche vyce.
But truste wel, he shal paye al
That repent of his bargayne shal,
Whan Poverte putte him in distresse,
Al° were he scholer to° Rychesse,
That is for° me in great yernyng,
Whan she assenteth to my wyllyng.
"But by my mother Saynt Venus,
And by her father Saturnus,
That her engendred° by his lyfe—
But nat upon his wedded wyfe!—
Yet wol I more unto you swere,
To make this thyng the sikerere°.
Nowe by that faithe and that leaute°
That I owe to al my bretherne free,

5882 her luste, *it pleases her,* **socour,** *support* **5884 greve,** *bother* **5885 of,** *from* **5888 abye,** *pay for* **5891 nygh,** *near* **5892 trowe,** *believe* **5894 tane,** *taken* **5896 There,** *where,* **ywis,** *truly* **5899 Ne me ne lyketh,** *it pleases me not,* **so mote I the,** *as I may prosper* **5901 For-why,** *therefore* **5902 cleped by merchaundyse,** *called buying love* **5903 courser,** *steed* **5904 quite,** *paid up* **5908 guerdonyng,** *reward* **5910 al quyte,** *completely paid* **5911 semblable,** *similar* **5913 parde,** *by God* **5914 wynnen,** *make a profit* **5916 skynne,** *horsehide* **5920 thylke chaffare,** *that bargain* **5821 There,** *where,* **entremeteth ought,** *interferes at all* **5924 lese,** *lose* **5925 chaffare,** *property* **5927 prise,** *value* **5931 to make lettyng,** *to prevent* **5932 yefte,** *gift* **5933 maugre his,** *despite himself* **5934 ywis,** *indeed* **5936 Of what,** *from whatever* **5937 right nought,** *absolutely nothing* **5938 paye,** *satisfaction* **5944 wonte,** *accustomed* **5945 nyce,** *silly* **5950 Al,** *even if,* **scholer to,** *student of* **5951 That is for,** *whoever is because of* **5955 engendred,** *conceived* **5958 sikerere,** *more certain* **5959 leaute,** *loyalty*

5879 at, omitted in G and Th. **5883 Al my nedis,** G and Th read "As my nede is." **5900 withoute,** Th reads "with." **5942 fully,** G and Th read "folyly"; the French is *ou tout.* **5846 vyce,** G reads "wise." **5953 by,** omitted in G and Th. **5955–56 by her father Saturnus . . . engendred,** earlier in the French (5536ff.), Venus is born when Jupiter defeats Saturn, cuts off his testicles, and throws them into the sea. **5958 sikerere,** G and Th read "seurere." **5959 leaute,** G and Th read "beaute."

Of whiche there nys wight° under hevyn
That canne her fathers names nevyn°,
So dyvers° and so many there be
That with my mother have be pryvee°!
Yet wolde I swere, for sickernesse°,
The pole° of helle to my wytnesse,
Nowe drynke I nat this yere clarre°,
If that I lye, or forsworne be°!
(For of the goddes the usage° is
That whoso him forswereth amys
Shal that yere drynke no clarre.)
Nowe have I sworne ynough, parde.
If I forswere me, than am I lorne°;
But I wol never be forsworne.
Sithe° Rychesse hath me fayled here,
She shal abye° that trespas ful dere,
Atte leest ways, but° she her arme°
With swerde, or sparth°, or gysarme°.
For certes, sythe she loveth nat me,
Fro thylke° tyme that she maye se
The castel and the toure toshake°,
In sorye tyme she shal awake.
If I maye grype° a ryche manne,
I shal so pulle° him, if I canne,
That he shal in a fewe stoundes°
Lese al his markes and his poundes.
I shal him make his pens outslynge°,
But° they in his garner° sprynge°;
Our maydens shal eke plucke him so
That him shal neden fethers mo;
And make him selle his londe to spende,
But he the bette conne° him defende.
"Poore men han made her lorde of me,
Although they nat so mightye be,
That they maye fede me in delyte.
I wol nat have hem in dispyte°:
No good man hateth hem, as I gesse,
For chynche° and feloun is Richesse,
That so canne chase hem and dispsye,
And hem defoule in sondrye° wyse.
They loven ful bette, so God me spede,
Than dothe the riche, chynchy gnede°,
And bene, in good faythe, more stable
And trewer and more servyable.
And therfore it suffyseth me
Her good herte and her leaute°.
They han on me sette al her thought,
And therfore I foryet hem nought.
I wol hem bringe in° great noblesse,
If that I were god of rychesse,
As I am god of love, sothely°,
Suche routhe° upon her playnt° have I.
Therfore I muste his socour° be,
That payneth him to serven me,
For if he deyde for love of this,
Than semeth in me no love there is,"
"Sir," sayde they, "sothe is everydele°
That ye reherce, and we wote° wele
Thylke othe° to holde is resonable;
For it is good and covenable°
That ye on riche men han sworne.
For sir, this wote° we wel beforne:
If riche men done you homage,
That is as fooles done outrage;
But ye shul nat forsworne be°,
Ne lette° therfore to drynke clarre°,
Or pyment° maked fresshe and newe.
Ladyes shul hem suche pepyr brewe°
If that they fal into her laas°,
That they for wo mowe sayne° 'Alas!'
Ladyes shullen ever so curteis be
That they shal quyte° your othe al free.
Ne seketh never other vicayre°,
For they shal speke with hem so fayre
That ye shal holde ye° payde ful wele,
Though ye you medle° never a dele°.
Lat ladyes worche with her thynges,
They shal hem tel so fele° tydinges,
And move hem eke so many requestes
By flatery, that not honest is,

5961 nys wight, *is no person* **5962 nevyn,** *name* **5963 dyvers,** *various* **5964 be pryvee,** *been confidential* (i.e., had sex) **5965 sickernesse,** *certainty* **5966 pole,** *pool* **5967 this yere clarre,** *claret* (sweetened wine) *all this year* **5968 forsworne be,** *break my word* **5969 usage,** *custom* **5973 lorne,** *lost* **5975 Sithe,** *because* **5976 abye,** *pay for* **5977 but,** *unless,* **her arme,** *arm herself* **5978 sparth,** *battle axe,* **gysarme,** *halberd* **5980 thylke,** *that* **5981 toshake,** *destroyed* **5983 grype,** *seize* **5984 pulle,** *pluck* **5985 stoundes,** *moments* **5987 outslynge,** *throw away* **5988 But,** *unless,* **garner,** *barn,* **sprynge,** *grow* **5992 the bette conne,** *can very well* **5996 dispyte,** *contempt* **5998 chynche,** *miser* **6000 sondrye,** *various* **6002 chynchy gnede,** *miserly tightwad* **6006 leaute,** *loyalty* **6009 in,** *into* **6011 sothely,** *truly* **6012 routhe,** *pity,* **playnt,** *lament* **6013 socour,** *comfort* **6017 everydele,** *everything* **6018 wote,** *know* **6019 Thylke othe,** *that pledge* **6020 covenable,** *suitable* **6022 wote,** *know* **6025 forsworne be,** *swear in vain* **6026 Ne lette,** *nor cease,* **clarre,** *claret* **6027 pyment,** *sweetened wine* **6028 suche pepyr brewe,** *concoct such pepper* (trouble) **6029 laas,** *net* **6030 mowe sayne,** *must say* **6032 quyte,** *repay* **6033 vicarye,** *deputy* **6035 holde ye,** *consider yourself* **6036 you medle,** *involve yourself,* **dele,** *bit* **6038 fele,** *many*

5977 she, omitted in G and Th. **6002 gnede,** G and Th read "grede." **6006 leaute,** G and Th read "beaute." **6019 Thylke,** G reads "Tilk." **6035 holde ye,** G reads "holde you." **6037 worche,** G reads "worthe."

And therto yeve hem suche thankynges,
What with kyssyng, and with talkynges,
That certes, if they trowed° be,
Shal never leave hem° londe ne fee°
That it nyll° as the moeble fare°,
Of whiche they first delyvered are°.
Nowe may ye tell us al your wyll,
And we your hestes° shal fulfyll.
"But False-Semblant dare not, for drede
Of you, sir, medle him of this dede,
For he saythe that ye ben his fo;

FALSE-SEMBLANT (HYPOCRISY)

He not° if ye wol worche him wo.
Wherfore we praye you al, beau° sire,
That ye forgyve him nowe your ire,
And that he may dwell, as your man,
With Abstynence, his dere lemman°;
This our acorde and our wyll nowe."
"Parfey°," sayd Love, "I graunt it you;
I wol wel holde him for my man;
Nowe let him come."—And he for the ran.
"False-Semblant," quod Love, "in this wyse
I take the here to my servyce,
That thou our frendes helpe alway,
And hyndre hem neyther nyght ne day,
But do thy myght hem to releve,
And eke our enemyes that thou greve°.
Thyne be this might, I graunt it the:
My kyng of harlotes shalte thou be;
We wol° that thou have suche honour.
Certayne, thou arte a false traytour,
And eke a thefe; sythe° thou were borne,
A thousande tymes thou arte forsworne°.
But nathelesse, in our heryng,
To put our folke out of doutyng,
I bydde the teche hem, wost° thou howe,
By some general signe nowe,
In what place thou shalt founden be,
If that men had myster° of the,
And howe men shal the best espye,
For the to knowe is great maistrye;
Tel in what place is thyn hauntyng."
"Sir, I have ful dyvers wonnyng°,
That I kepe not rehersed be°,
So that° ye wolde respyten me°.
For if that I tell you the sothe,
I may have harme and shame bothe;
If that my felowes wysten° it,
My tales shulden me be quyt°.
For certayne, they wolde hate me
If ever I knewe° her cruelte,
For they wolde over al° holde hem styll
Of trouthe that is agayne her wyll;
Suche tales kepen they not here.
I myght eftsone° bye° it ful dere,
If I sayd of hem anythyng
That aught° displeaseth to her heryng;
For what° worde that hem pricke or byteth,
In that worde none of hem delyteth,
Al° were it gospel, the evangyle,
That wolde reprove° hem of her gyle,
For they are cruell and hautayne°.
And this thyng wote° I wel, certayne,
If I speke aught to payre her loos°,
Your courte shal not so wel be cloos°
That they ne shal wyte° it at last.
Of good men am I nought agast°,
For they wol taken on hem° nothyng
Whan that they knowe al my meanyng:
But he that wol it on him take,
He wol himselfe suspecious make,
That he his lyfe let° covertly,
In Gyle and in Ipocrisy,
That° me engendred and yave fostryng."
"They made a ful good engendring,"
Quod Love, "for whoso sothly tell,
They engendred the dyvel of hell.
But nedely°; howesoever it be,"
Quod Love, "I wyl and charge the,
To tell anon thy wonnyng° places,

6043 trowed, *believed* **6044 leave hem,** *depart from them,* **fee,** *property* **6045 nyll,** *will not,* **as the moeble fare,** *go* (be depleted) *like the movable property* **6046 delyvered are,** *are deprived* **6048 hestes,** *orders* **6052 not,** *doesn't know* **6053 beau,** *good* **6056 lemman,** *lover* **6058 Parfey,** *certainly* (from French, "by my faith") **6066 greve,** *afflict* **6069 wol,** *desire* **6071 sythe,** *since* **6072 forsworne,** *perjured* **6075 wost,** *know* **6078 myster,** *need* **6082 ful dyvers wonnyng,** *very many dwellings* **6083 kepe not rehersed be,** *care not to tally* **6084 So that,** *if,* **respyten me,** *excuse me* **6087 wysten,** *were to know* **6088 me be quyt,** *paid back to me* **6090 knewe,** *make known* **6091 over al,** *rather* **6094 eftsone,** *later,* **bye,** *pay for* **6096 aught,** *at all* **6097 what,** *whatever* **6099 Al,** *even if* **6100 reprove,** *rebuke* **6101 hautayne,** *haughty* **6102 wote,** *know* **6103 payre her loos,** *impair their reputation* **6104 cloos,** *discrete* **6105 wyte,** *know* **6106 agast,** *apprehensive* **6107 taken on hem,** *take personally* **6111 let,** *leads* **6113 That,** *who* **6117 nedely,** *necessarily* **6119 wonnyng,** *dwelling*

6063 alway, G reads "away." **6064 hyndre,** G and Th read "hyndreth." **6068 kyng of harlotes,** a minor officer (*roi de ribauds*) in the French royal household, responsible for dealing justice to members of the court, especially dissolute people in times of misrule. **6072 tymes,** G reads "tyme." **6082 ful,** G reads "fele."

Heryng° eche wight° that in this place is,
And what lyfe that thou lyvest also.
Hyde it no lenger nowe; wherto?
Thou must discover al thy wurchyng,
Howe thou servest, and of what thyng,
Though that thou shuldest for thy sothesawe°
Ben al tobeaten and todrawe°—
And yet arte thou not wont°, parde°.
But nathelesse, though thou beten be,
Thou shalt not be the first that so
Hath for soth-sawe suffred wo."
"Sir, sythe that° it may lyken° you,
Though that I shulde be slayne right nowe,
I shal done your commaundement,
For therto have I great talent°."
Withouten wordes mo, right than,
False-Semblant his sermon began,
And sayd hem thus in audyence:
"Barons, take hede of my sentence.
That wight° that lyste° to have knowyng
Of False-Semblant, ful of flateryng,
He must in worldly folke° him seke,
And certes in the cloysters eke.
I won° nowhere but in hem twey,
But not lyke even°; sothe to say.
Shortly, I wol herberowe° me
There I hope best to hulstred° be;
And certainly, sykerest° hydyng
Is underneth humblest clothyng.
Relygious folke ben ful coverte°;
Seculer folke ben more apperte°.
But nathelesse I wol not blame
Religyous folke, ne hem diffame,
In what habyte that ever they go.
Religyon humble and trewe also
Wol I not blame ne dispyse—
But I nyl° loove it in no wyse.
I meane of false relygious,
That stoute° ben, and malycious;
That wollen in an habyte go,
And setten not her herte therto.
"Relygious folke ben al pytous°;
Thou shalt not sene one dispytous°;
They loven no pride ne no stryfe,
But humbly they wol lede her lyfe.
With suche folke wol I never be,
And if I dwell, I fayne me°.
I may wel in her habyt go;
But me were lever° my necke atwo°,
Than lette° a purpose that I take,
What covenaunt° that ever I make.
"I dwell with hem that proude be,
And ful of wyles and subtelte;
That worshyp° of this worlde coveyten,
And great nede connen expleyten°,
And gon and gadren great pytaunces°,
And purchace hem the acqueyntaunces
Of men that mighty lyfe may leden;
And fayne hem poore, and hemselfe feden
With good morcels delycious,
And drinken good wyne precyous;
And preche us povert and distresse,
And fysshen° hemselfe great rychesse
With wyly nettes that they caste.
It wol come foule out at the laste.
They ben fro clene relygion went°;
They make the worlde an argument
That hath a foule conclusyon:
'I have a robe of religyon,
Than am I al religyous.'
This argument is al roignous°;
It is not worthe a croked brere°.
Habyt ne maketh neyther monke ne frere,
But clene lyfe and devocion
Maketh good men of religyon.
Nathelesse, there can none answere,
Howe hygh that ever his heed he shere°
With resour° whetted never so kene,
That Gyle in braunches cutte thurtene.
There can no wight distyncte° it so,
That he dare say a worde therto.

6120 Heryng, *in the hearing of,* **wight,** *person* **6125 sothesawe,** *truth telling* **6126 todrawe,** *pulled to pieces* **6127 wont,** *accustomed* (to speak truth), **parde,** *by God* **6131 sythe that,** *because,* **lyken,** *please* **6134 talent,** *urge* **6139 wight,** *person,* **lyste,** *wishes* **6141 in worldly folk,** *among secular people* **6143 won,** *dwell* **6144 lyke even,** *equally* **6145 herberowe,** *lodge* **6146 hulstred,** *hidden* **6147 sykerest,** *most secure* **6149 coverte,** *secretive* **6150 apperte,** *open* **6156 nyl,** *won't* **6158 stoute,** *arrogant* **6161 pytous,** *compassionate* **6162 dispytous,** *scornful* **6166 fayne me,** *pretend* **6168 me were lever,** *I would rather,* **atwo,** *severed* **6169 lette,** *give up* **6170 What covenaunt,** *whatever vow* **6173 That worshyp,** *those that the honor* **6174 expleyten,** *satisfy* **6175 pytaunces,** *contributions* **6182 fysshen,** *fish for* **6185 went,** *gone* **6190 roignous,** *scabby* **6191 brere,** *briar* **6196 shere,** *shaves* **6197 rasour,** *razor* **6199 distyncte,** *discern*

6165 suche, G and Th read "which." **6187 hath,** omitted in G. **6197 resour,** G reads "resoun"; the French is *rasoir* (razor). Monastic tonsure and scholastic disputation underlie the image, where precision in shaving is associated with skill in argument, and where the thirteen members of a convent (modeled on Christ and the twelve apostles) are aligned with thirteen categories of scholastic reasoning. The sardonic upshot is that no one—no matter how clever or holy—can answer the claim.

"But what herberowe° that ever I take,
Or what semblant° that ever I make,
I meane but° gyle, and folowe that;
For right no more than Gybbe our cat
That awayteth myce and rattes to kyllen,
Ne entende I but to begylen.
Ne no wight may, by my clothyng,
Wete° with what folke is my dwellyng;
Ne by my wordes yet, parde°,
So softe and so plesaunt they be.
Beholde the dedes that I do;
But thou be blynde, thou oughtest so.
For, varye her wordes fro her dede,
They thynke on gyle, without drede,
What maner clothyng that they were,
Or what estate that ever they bere,
Lered° or leude°, lorde or lady,
Knyght, squyer, burgeys°, or bayly°."
Right thus whyle False-Semblant sermoneth,
Eftesones° Love him aresoneth°,
And brake his tale in his speakyng
As though he had him tolde leasyng°,
And sayd, "What, dyvel, is that I here?
What folke haste thou us nempned° here?
Maye men fynde relygioun
In worldly habytatioun?"
"Ye, sir; it foloweth nat that they
Shulde lede a wicked lyfe, parfey°,
Ne nat therfore her soules lese°
That hem to worldly clothes chese,
For certes it were great pyte.
Menne maye in seculer clothes se
Florisshen hooly relygioun.
Ful many a saynt in felde and towne,
With many a virgyn glorious,
Devoute, and ful relygious,
Han dyed°, that commen° clothe aye beren°,
Yet sayntes neverthelesse they weren.
I coude recken you many a ten.
Ye, wel nygh al these holy women
That menne in churches herry° and seke,
Bothe maydens, and these wyves eke
That baren ful many a fayre chylde here,
Weared alwaye clothes seculere,
And in the same dieden° they
That sayntes weren, and ben alwaye.
The .xi. thousande maydens dere
That beren in heven her cierges clere°,
Of whiche men rede in churche and syng,
Were take in seculer clothyng
Whan they receyved martyrdome,
And wonnen heven unto her° home.
Good herte maketh the good thought;
The clothynge yeveth ne reveth° nought;
The good thought and the worchyng
That maketh the relygion flouryng°—
There lyeth the good relygioun
After the right ententioun.
"Whoso tooke a wethers° skynne,
And wrapped a gredy wolfe therinne,
For he shulde go with lambes white,
Wenest thou nat° he wolde hem byte?
Yes, neverthelesse, as he were wode°,
He wolde hem wirry° and drinke the blode,
And wel the rather° hem disceyve;
For sithe they coude nat perceyve
His tregette° and his cruelte,
They wolde him folowe, altho he flye.
If there be wolves of suche hewe
Amonges these apostles newe,
Thou, Holy Churche, thou mayste be wayled°!
Sythe that° thy cyte is assayled
Through knyghtes of thyn owne table,
God wot thy lordshyp is doutable°!
If they enforce hem° it to wyn°
That shulde defende it fro within,
Who myght defence ayenst hem make?
Without stroke it mote be take
Of trepeget° or mangonel°,
Without displayeng of pensel°.
And if God nyl done it socour°,
But let hem renne in this colour°,

6201 herberowe, *lodging* **6202 semblant,** *appearance* **6203 meane but,** *intend only* **6208 Wete,** *know* **6209 parde,** *by God* **6217 Lered,** *learned,* **leude,** *unlearned* **6218 burgeys,** *citizen,* **bayly,** *officer* **6220 Eftesones,** *immediately,* **aresoneth,** *disputes* **6222 leasyng,** *lies* **6224 nempned,** *named* **6228 parfey,** *indeed* **6229 lese,** *lose* **6237 Han dyed,** *have died,* **commen,** *ordinary,* **beren,** *worn* **6241 herry,** *harass* **6245 in the same dieden,** *died in the same* (clothes?) **6248 cierges clere,** *bright candles* **6252 unto her,** *as their* **6254 yeveth ne reveth,** *gives nor takes* **6256 flouryng,** *flourish* **6259 wethers,** *sheep's* **6262 Wenest thou nat,** *don't you think* **6263 wode,** *enraged* **6264 wirry,** *kill* **6265 rather,** *sooner* **6267 tregette,** *trickery* **6271 wayled,** *lamented* **6272 Sythe that,** *because* **6274 doutable,** *in doubt* **6275 enforce hem,** *attempt,* **wyn,** *conquer* **6279 trepeget,** *catapult* (trebuchet), **mangonel,** *catapult* **6280 pensel,** *war banner* **6281 nyl done it socour,** *will not aid it* **6282 colour,** *manner*

6204 Gybbe, a common English name for a cat; *Tiberz* in the French. **6205** Line lacking in G. **6206 begylen,** G reads "bigilyng." **6240 al,** omitted in G. **6247 .xi. thousande maydens,** St. Ursula and 11,000 virgins were legendary martyrs of fifth-century Cologne. **6268 altho,** G reads "al wolde." **flye,** G reads "fle." **6275 hem,** omitted in G and Th. **6282 hem,** omitted in G and Th.

Thou must thy heestes° letten be.
Than is there nought, but yelde the°,
Or yeve hem trybute, doutles,
And holde it of hem to have pees—
But greater harme betyde° the,
That they al maister of it be.
Wel conne they scorne the withall°.
By day stuffen° they the wall,
And al the nyght they mynen° there.
Nay, thou planten muste elsewhere
Thyn ympes°, if thou wolt fruite have;
Abyde not there thyselfe to save.
"But nowe pees! Here I turne agayne;
I wol no more of this thyng sayne
If I may passen me hereby;
I might maken you wery.
But I wol heten° you alway
To helpe your frendes what I may,
So they wollen° my company;
For they be shent° al utterly
But if so fall that I be
Ofte with hem, and they with me.
And eke my lemman° mote° they serve,
Or they shul not my love deserve.
Forsothe°, I am a false traytour;
God juged me for a thefe trechour°;
Forsworne° I am, but wel nygh none
Wote° of my gyle tyl it be done.
"Through me hath many one° deth receyved
That my treget° never aperceyved;
And yet receyveth, and shal receyve,
That my falsenesse shal never aperceyve.
But whoso dothe, if he wyse be,
Him is ryght good be ware of me.
But so slyghe° is the deceyving
That to hard is the aperceyvyng;
For Protheus, that coude him chaunge
In every shappe, homely° and straunge,
Coude° never suche gyle ne treasoune
As I; for I come never in towne
Ther as I myght knowen be,
Though men me bothe myght here and se.
Ful wel I canne my clothes chaunge,
Take one, and make another straunge.
Nowe am I knyght, nowe chastelayne°;
Nowe prelate°, and nowe chapelayne;
Nowe preest, nowe clerke°, and nowe forstere°;
Nowe am I maister, nowe scholere;
Nowe monke, nowe chanon°, nowe bayly°—
Whatever myster° manne am I.
Nowe am I prince, nowe am I page,
And canne° by herte every langage.
Somtyme am I hoore° and olde;
Nowe am I yonge, stoute°, and bolde.
Nowe am I Robert, nowe Robyn;
Nowe frere Mynor°, nowe Jacobyn°.
And with me foloweth my loteby°;
To done me solace and company,
That hight° dame Abstynence-Straigned°,
In many a queynt arraye fayned°.
Ryght as it cometh to her lykyng,
I fulfyl al her desyringe.
Somtyme a wommans clothe take I:
Nowe am I a mayde, nowe lady.
Somtyme I am relygious;
Nowe lyke an anker° in an hous.
Somtyme am I prioresse,
And nowe a nonne, and nowe abbesse;
And go through al regiouns,
Sekynge al relygiouns.
But to what° order that I am sworne,
I take the strawe and lete° the corne°.
To gyle° folke I enhabyte°;
I aske no more but her habite.
What wol ye more? In every wyse,
Ryght as me lyste°, I me disgyse.
Wel canne I beare me under wede°;
Unlyke is my worde to my dede.

6283 heestes, *promises* **6284 yelde the,** *give yourself up* **6287 betyde,** *comes to* **6289 withall,** *completely* **6290 stuffen,** *strengthen* **6291 mynen,** *undermine* **6293 ympes,** *seedlings* **6299 heten,** *promise* **6301 So,** *if,* **wollen,** *wish* **6302 shent,** *ruined* **6305 lemman,** *lover,* **mote,** *must* **6307 Forsothe,** *truly* **6308 trechour,** *treacherous* **6309 Forsworne,** *perjured* **6310 Wote,** *knows* **6311 many one,** *many a person* **6312 treget,** *trickery* **6317 slyghe,** *sly* **6320 homely,** *familiar* **6321 Coude,** *knew* **6327 chastelayne,** *keeper of a castle* **6328 prelate,** *church official* **6329 clerke,** *student,* **forstere,** *forest keeper* **6331 chanon,** *clerical officer,* **bayly,** *civil officer* **6332 Whatever myster,** *of any occupation* **6334 canne,** *know* **6335 hoore,** *gray* **6336 stoute,** *proud* **6338 frere Mynor,** *Franciscan friar,* **Jacobyn,** *Dominican friar* **6339 loteby,** *lover* **6341 hight,** *is called,* **Abstynence-Straigned,** *Enforced Abstinence* **6342 queynt arraye fayned,** *clever disguise* **6348 anker,** *recluse* (anchorite) **6353 what,** *whatever* **6354 lete,** *leave,* **corne,** *grain* **6355 gyle,** *deceive,* **enhabyte,** *dwell* (with them) **6358 me lyste,** *it pleases me* **6359 beare me under wede,** *act in clothes*

6296 sayne, G and Th read "feyne." **6317 deceyving,** G and Th read "aperceyvyng." **6318** Line lacking in G; Th reads "That al to late cometh knowynge." Text from Kaluza's edition (1891). **6319 Protheus,** Proteus, the shape-shifting Greek sea god. **6329 forstere,** Th reads "fostere." **6340 solace,** G reads "salas." **6341 Straigned,** G and Th read "and raigned." **6354 lete,** G and Th read "be(a)te." **6355 gyle,** G and Th read "jolye"; the French is *enbascler* (deceive). **6359 beare,** G reads "were."

Thus make I into my trappes fal
The people through my privyleges°, al
That bene in Christendome alyve.
I may assoyle°, and I maye shryve°,
That no prelate maye lette° me,
Al folke, whereever they founde be;
I not no° prelat may done so,
But° it the pope be, and no mo,
That made thilke establisshyng°.
Nowe is not this a propre thyng?
But were my sleightes aperceyved,
Ne shulde I ben so receyved
As I was wonte°; and woste° thou why?
For I dyd hem a tregetry°.
But thereof yeve I lytel tale°;
I have the sylver and the male°.
So have I preched and eke shriven,
So have I take, so have me yeven
Through her foly husbonde and wyfe,
That I lede right a joly lyfe,
Through symplesse° of the prelacye°—
They knowe not al my tregettrye.
"But forasmoche as man and wyfe
Shulde shewe her parisshe preest her lyfe°
Ones a yere, as saythe the boke,
Er° any wight° his housel° toke,
Than have I privyleges large°
That may of moche thyng discharge;
For he may say right thus, parde°:
'Sir Preest, in shrifte I tel it the,
That he to whom that I am shriven°
Hath me assoyled°, and me yeven
Penaunce, sothlye, for my syn,
Whiche that I fonde me gilty in;
Ne I ne have never entencion
To make double confession,
Ne reherce efte° my shrift to the.
O shrift° is right ynough to me.
This ought the suffyse wele°;
Ne be not rebell never a dele°.
For certes, though thou haddest it sworne,
I wote° no preest ne prelate borne
That may to shrift efte me constrayne.
And if they done, I wol me playne°;
For I wote where to playne wele.
Thou shalt not streyne me a dele,
Ne enforce me, ne not me trouble,
To make my confessyon double.
Ne I have none affection
To have double absolution.
The first is right ynough to me;
This latter assoyling quyte I the°.
I am unbounde°; what mayst thou fynde
More of my synnes me to unbynde?
For he that might° hath in his honde
Of al my synnes me unbonde.
And if thou wolte me thus constrayne,
That me mote nedes° on the playne,
There shal no juge imperyall,
Ne bysshop, ne offyciall,
Done jugement on me; for I
Shal gone and playne me openly
Unto my shrift-father newe°—
That hyght not° Frere° Wolfe untrewe—
And he shal cheveyse him for me°,
For I trowe° he can hamper the.
But, lorde, he wolde be wrothe withall°
If men him wolde Frere Wolfe call!
For he wolde have no pacience,
But done al cruell vengience.

6362 privyleges, *license* **6364 assoyle,** *absolve,* **shryve,** *hear confession* **6365 lette,** *prevent* **6367 not no,** *know that no* **6368 But,** *unless* **6369 thilke establisshyng,** *that rule* **6373 wonte,** *accustomed to,* **woste,** *know* **6374 tregetry,** *trickery* **6375 tale,** *account* **6376 male,** *purse* **6381 symplesse,** *ignorance,* **prelacye,** *church officials* **6384 shewe...her lyfe,** i.e., *confess their sins* **6386 Er,** *before,* **wight,** *person,* **housel,** *Communion* **6387 privyleges large,** *extensive license* **6389 parde,** *by God* **6391 shriven,** *confessed* **6392 assoyled** *absolved* **6397 reherce efte,** *repeat again* **6398 O shrift,** *one confession* **6399 the suffyse wele,** *suffice you well* **6400 dele,** *bit* **6402 wote,** *know* **6404 me playne,** *lodge a complaint* **6412 quyte I the,** *I give back to you* **6413 unbounde,** *absolved* **6415 might,** *power* **6418 me mote nedes,** *I must necessarily* **6423 shrift-father newe,** *new confessor* **6424 hyght not,** *is not called,* **Frere,** *Friar* **6425 cheveyse him for me,** *assert himself on my behalf* **6426 trowe,** *think* **6427 wrothe withall,** *thoroughly enraged*

6361–6472 This translates a passage in the French *Roman* that most scholars consider spurious, available only in select manuscripts. Echoes of detail and diction in Chaucer's Pardoner and Friar materials indicate that he knew a version of the *Roman* that included this passage. **6361 Thus make I into,** G reads "Make into." **6362 The people,** omitted in G. **6365 no prelate maye lette me,** friars were empowered to hear confessions by papal license, independent of the diocesan authority. Peoples' option to confess to (and receive Communion from) itinerant friars rather than local priests caused contention, even competition, between these kinds of clergy. **6372** Line omitted in G and line left blank in Th. Text from Sutherland's edition (1968). **6374 tregetry,** G reads "tegetry." **6375 lytel,** G and Th read "a lytel." **6378 me,** G and Th read "I." **6385 Ones a yere,** once a year; annual confession was mandated by the Fourth Lateran Council (1215–16), often undertaken in preparation to receive Communion on Easter Sunday. Communion could be withheld from parishioners who had not confessed. **the boke,** often a reference to the Bible, but here a more general reference to authority. **6392 assoyled,** G reads "assailed." **6393 Penaunce,** G reads "For penaunce." **6413 unbounde,** see Matthew 16.19 and 18.18. **6424** The assertion is ironic, as the name is so appropriate; see John 10.12ff. **not,** omitted in Th. **6425 cheveyse,** Th reads "chuse."

He wolde his myght done at the leest,
Nothyng spare for Goddes heest°.
And, God so wyse be my socour°,
But° thou yeve me my Savyour°
At Easter, whan it lyketh me,
Without preasyng° more on the,
I wol forthe, and to him gone,
And he shal housell° me anon,
For I am out of thy grutchyng°;
I kepe not deale° with the nothyng!'
  Thus may he shrive him° that forsaketh
His parysshe-preest and to me taketh.
And if the preest wol him refuse,
I am ful redy him to accuse,
And him punisshe and hamper so,
That he his churche shal forgo°.
But whoso hath in his felyng
The consequence° of suche shrivyng
Shal sene that preest may never have might
To knowe the conscience aright
Of him that is under his cure°.
And this is ayenst holy scripture,
That byddeth every heerd° honest
Have very° knowyng of his beest.
But poore folke that gon by strete°,
That have no golde, ne sommes grete,
Hem wolde I let to her prelates,
Or let her preestes knowe her states,
For to me right nought yeve they.
And why? It is for° they ne may;
They ben so bare, I take no kepe°.
But I wol have the fatte shepe;
Let parisshe preestes have the lene.
I yeve not of her harme a bene°!
And if that prelates grutchen° it,
That oughten wroth be in her wyt,
To lese her° fatte beestes so,
I shal yeve hem a stroke or two,
That they shal lesen with force°,
Ye, bothe her mytre° and her croce°.
Thus jape° I hem, and have do° longe,
My privileges° ben so stronge."
  False-Semblant wolde have stynted° here,
But Love ne made him no suche chere°
That he was wery of his sawe°;
But for to make him glad and fawe°,
He said: "Tel on more specially,
Howe that thou servest untruely.
Tel forthe and shame the never a dele°,
For as thyn habyt sheweth wele,
Thou semest an holy heremyte."
  "Sothe° is, but I am but an ypocryte."
  "Thou gost° and prechest poverte?"
  "Ye, sir; but rychesse hath poste°."
  "Thou prechest abstynence also?"
  "Sir, I wol fyllen, so mote I go°,
My paunche° of good meate and wyne,
As shulde a maister of divyne°;
For huwe° that I me poore fayne°,
Yet al poore folke I disdayne.
I love better the acqueyntaunce
Ten tymes of the kyng of Fraunce,
Than of a poore man of mylde mode°,
Though that his soule be also good.
For whan I se beggers quakyng
Naked on myxins° al stynkyng,
For hongre crye, and eke for care,
I entremet° not of her fare°.
They ben so poore and ful of pyne,
They might not ones yeve me dyne°,
For they have nothyng but her lyfe.
What shulde he yeve that lycketh his knyfe?
It is but folly to entremete,
To seke in houndes nest fatte mete.
Lette beare hem° to the spyttle° anone,
But for me, comforte gette they none.
But a riche sicke usurere°
Wolde I visyte and drawe nere;
Him wol I comforte and rehete°,
For I hope of his golde to gete;

6432 heest, *command* **6433 socour,** *aid* **6434 But,** *unless,* **Savyour,** i.e., *Communion* (see 6385n.) **6436 preasyng,** *urging* **6438 housell,** *give communion to* **6439 grutchyng,** *criticizing* **6440 kepe not deale,** *care not to deal* **6441 he shrive him,** *someone confess himself* **6446 forgo,** *lose* **6448 consequence,** *effects* **6451 cure,** *care* **6453 heerd,** *shepherd* **6454 very,** *true* **6455 gon by strete,** *travel about* **6460 for,** *because* **6461 take no kepe,** *pay no attention* **6464 yeve not of...a bene,** *don't give a bean for* **6465 grutchen,** *complain of* **6467 lese her,** *lose their* **6469 with force,** *necessarily* **6470 mytre,** *miter,* **croce,** *crozier* **6471 jape,** *trick,* **do,** *done* **6472 privileges,** *license* **6473 stynted,** *stopped* **6474 no suche chere,** *no indication* **6475 sawe,** *speaking* **6476 fawe,** *pleased* **6479 dele,** *bit* **6482 Sothe,** *truth* **6483 gost,** *travel about* **6484 poste,** *power* **6486 so mote I go,** i.e., *whatever happens* **6487 paunche,** *belly* **6488 divyne,** *theology* **6489 huwe,** *howsoever,* **fayne,** *pretend* **6493 mylde mode,** *gentle spirit* **6496 myxins,** *dung hills* **6498 entremet,** *interfere,* **of her fare,** *in their affairs* **6500 dyne,** *food* **6505 Lette beare hem,** *let them be taken,* **spyttle,** *hospital* **6507 userere,** *money lender* **6509 rehete,** *console*

6434 Savyour, Savior, i.e., Christ. In the Catholic sacrament of Communion, the body of Christ is received. **6452 is,** omitted in G. **6453–54** Proverbs 27.23. **6466 wroth,** G and Th read "woth." **6470 mytre...crose,** the miter (a tall, shovel-shaped headdress) and crozier (a hook-topped staff), symbols of the authority of a bishop. **6481 semest,** G and Th read "servest." **6491 the acqueyntaunce,** G reads "that queytaunce." **6492 tymes,** G reads "tyme." **6500 dyne,** G and Th read "a dyne."

And if that wicked dethe him have,
I wol go with him to his grave.
And if there any reprove° me,
Why that I lette the poore be,
Wost thou° howe I mot ascape?
I saye and swere him ful rape°
That riche menne han more tetches°
Of synne than han poore wretches,
And hanne of counsayle more myster°;
And therfore I wolde drawe hem ner.
"But as great hurte, it maye so be,
Hath a soule in right great poverte,
As soule in great richesse, forsothe,
Al-be-it that they hurten bothe.
For richesse and mendicitees°
Bene cleped° two extremytees;
The meane° is cleped suffysaunce°:
There lyeth of vertue the aboundaunce.
For Salomon, ful wel I wote°,
In his Parables us wrote,
As it is knowe of many a wight°,
In his thrittene° chapiter right,
'God, thou me kepe°, for thy poste°,
Fro richesse and mendycite;
For if a riche manne him dresse°
To thynke to moche on richesse,
His herte on that so ferre is sette
That he his creatour dothe foryette.
And him that begging wol aye greve°,
Howe shulde I by his worde him leve°?
Unneth° that he nys° a mycher°,
Forsworne°, or els God is lyer.'
Thus saithe Salomon sawes°.
Ne we fynde written in no lawes,
And namely in our Christen laye°—
Whoso saithe 'ye', I dare say 'naye'—
That Christ ne° his apostels dere,
While that they walked in erthe here,
Were never seen her bred beggyng,
For they nolden° beggen for nothyng.
And right thus were men wont° to teche;
And in this wyse wolde it preche
The maisters of dyvinyte
Somtyme in Parys the cyte.
And if men wolde theregayne° appose
The naked° texte, and lette° the glose°,
It myght soone assoyled° be.
For menne maye wel the sothe se,
That, pardie°, they myght aske° a thynge
Plainly forthe, without beggynge;
For they weren Goddes heerdes° dere,
And cure° of soules hadden here.
They nolde nothyng begge her foode;
For after Christ was done° on rodde°,
With their proper° hondes they wrought°;
And with traveyle°, and els nought,
They wonnen° al her sustenaunce,
And lyveden forthe in her penaunce;
And the remenaunt yaf° awaye
To other poore folkes alwaye.
They neither bylden towre ne halle,
But leye in houses smal withalle.
"A mighty° man, that canne and maye,
Shulde wyth his honde and body alwaye
Wynne him his foode in laboring,
If he ne have rent° or suche a thyng,
Although he be relygious,
And God to serven curyous°.
Thus mote° he done, or do trespas,
But if it be in certayne caas°,

6513 reprove, *accuse* **6515 Wost thou,** *do you know* **6516 rape,** *quickly* **6517 tetches,** *flaws* **6519 myster,** *need* **6525 mendicitees,** *begging* **6526 Bene cleped,** *are called* **6527 meane,** *middle ground* (golden mean), **suffysaunce,** *sufficiency* **6529 wote,** *know* **6531 wight,** *person* **6532 thrittene,** *thirteenth* (see n.) **6533 kepe,** *protect,* **poste,** *power* **6536 him dresse,** *makes himself* **6539 aye greve,** *constantly afflict* **6540 leve,** *believe* **6541 Unneth,** *scarcely* (is it possible), **nys,** *isn't,* **mycher,** *thief* **6542 Forsworne,** *perjured* **6543 Salomon sawes,** *Solomon's sayings* (Proverbs) **6545 laye,** *law* **6547 ne,** *nor* **6550 nolde,** *wouldn't* **6551 wont,** *accustomed* **6555 thereagayn,** *against that* **6556 naked,** *literal,* **lette,** *ignore,* **glose,** *interpretation* **6557 assoyled,** *disproved* **6559 pardie,** *by God,* **aske,** *ask for* **6561 heerdes,** *shepherds* **6562 cure,** *care* **6564 done,** *put,* **rodde,** *cross* **6565 proper,** *own,* **wrought,** *worked* **6566 traveyle,** *labor* **6567 wonnen,** *earned* **6569 yaf,** *gave* **6573 mighty,** *strong* **6576 rent,** *income* **6578 curyous,** *eager* **6579 mote,** *must* **6580 caas,** *cases*

6515 mot, G and Th read "not." **6529-43 Salomon . . . Parables . . . thrittene,** the book of Proverbs (often synonymous with *Parables* in Middle English) was attributed to King Solomon. The quotation echoes Proverbs 30.8–9, and the confusion of "thrittene" for thirty may be due to the French original, *triseme.* **6531 of,** G reads "to." **6538 dothe,** omitted in G. **6539 begging,** G and Th read "beggith." **6542 God is,** G and Th read "goddes." **6551 were,** G reads "was." **6553–54 maisters of dyvinyte . . . in Parys,** University of Paris professor Guillaume de Saint Amour was among a group of university clerics who opposed the friars and denied their claim that imitation of Christ and his apostles justified their mendicancy (begging). Guillaume is named at 6763, 6778, and 6781 below, and his polemical treatise, *Tractatus Brevis de Periculis Novissiorum Temporum* (*Brief Treatise on the Perils of the Most Recent Times*), is referred to at 6785. The treatise is dated 1255, and in 1256 the friars persuaded the pope to condemn it, resulting in Guillaume's banishment from Paris and what was then France. The treatise inspired much of Jean de Meun's antifraternalism and is the ultimate source of *Rom* 6544–7696. **6571 towre ne halle,** the friars were accused of building extravagant institutions. **6572 leye,** G and Th read "they."

That I can reherce, if myster° be,
Right wel, whan the tyme I se.
Seke the boke of Saynt Austyne,
Be it in paper or perchmyne°,
There-as he writte of these worchynges,
Thou shalt sene that none excusynges
A parfyte man ne shulde seke
By wordes, ne by dedes eke,
Although he be religyous,
And God to serven curyous,
That he ne shal, so mote I go°,
With propre hondes and body also,
Get his fode in laboring,
If he ne have proprete° of thyng.
Yet shulde he sell al his substaunce,
And with his swynke° have sustenaunce,
If he be parfyte° in bounte°.
Thus han the bookes tolde me.
For he that wol gone ydelly,
And useth it aye° besyly
To haunten° other mennes table,
He is a trechour°, ful of fable°;
Ne he ne may, by good reason,
Escuse him by his orison°.
For men behoveth°, in some gyse,
Somtyme leven Goddes servyse
To gone and purchasen her nede°.
Men mote° eaten, that is no drede°,
And slepe, and eke do other thyng;
So longe may they leave prayeng.
So may they eke her prayer blynne°
Whyle that they werke, her meate to wynne.
Seynt Austyn wol therto accorde,
In thilke boke that I recorde.
Justinian eke, that made lawes,
Hath thus forboden, by olde sawes°,
'No man, up° payne to be deed,
Mighty of body, to begge his breed,
If he may swynke° it for to gete;
Men shulde him rather mayme or bete,
Or done of him aperte° justyce,
Than suffren him in suche malyce.'
They done not wel, so mote I go°,
That taken suche almesse° so,
But if° they have somme privilege
That of the payne° hem wol alege°.
But howe that is can I not se,
But if the prince disceyved be,
Ne I ne wene° not, sykerly°,
That they may have it rightfully.
But I wol not determyne
Of princes power, ne defyne,
Ne by my worde comprehende, iwys°,
If it so ferre° may stretche in this;
I wol not entremete a dele°.
But I trowe° that the boke saythe wele,
Who that taketh almesses that be
Dewe° to folke that men may se
Lame, feble, wery, and bare,
Poore, or in suche maner care
(That conne wynne° hem nevermo,
For they have no power therto),
He eateth° his owne dampnyng°
But if he lye that made al thyng°.
And if ye suche a truaunt° fynde,
Chastyse him wel, if ye be kynde.
But they wolde hate you, par caas°,
And if ye fyllen in her laas°,
They wolde eftsones° do you scathe°,
If that they might, late or rathe°.
For they be not ful pacient,
That han the worlde thus foule blent°.
And weteth° wel that wher° God bad°
The good man sell al that he had,

6581 myster, *need* **6586 perchmyne,** *parchment* **6592 so mote I do,** i.e., *by my life* **6594 proprete,** *ownership* **6596 swynke,** *work* **6597 parfyte,** *perfect,* **bounte,** *goodness* **6600 useth it aye,** *is accustomed always* **6601 haunten,** *visit* **6602 trechour,** *cheat,* **fable,** *untruth* **6604 orison,** *prayer* **6605 behoveth,** *it is necessary* **6607 purchasen her nede,** *earn what they need* **6608 mote,** *must,* **drede,** *doubt* **6611 blynne,** *stop* **6616 sawes,** *sayings* **6617 up,** *upon* **6619 swynke,** *work* **6621 aperte,** *obvious* **6623 so mote I go,** i.e., *by my life* **6624 almesse,** *alms* **6625 But if,** *unless* **6626 payne,** *punishment,* **alege,** *exempt* **6629 wene,** *think,* **sykerly,** *surely* **6633 iwys,** *indeed* **6634 so ferre,** *this far* **6635 entremete a dele,** *interfere a bit* **6636 trowe,** *believe* **6638 Dewe,** *due* **6641 wynne,** *earn* **6643 eateth,** *feeds on,* **dampnyng,** *damnation* **6644 But if he lye that made al thyng,** i.e., *unless God lies* **6645 truant,** *beggar* **6647 par caas,** *perhaps* **6648 laas,** *net* **6649 eftsones,** *soon,* **scathe,** *harm* **6650 rathe,** *early* **6652 foule blent,** *foully blinded* **6653 weteth,** *understand,* **wher,** *where,* **bad,** *commanded*

6583–94 This translates a passage in the French that most scholars consider spurious, available only in select manuscripts. See 6361–6472n above. **6583 Seke,** the *S* is cut out in G. **boke of Saynt Austyne,** St. Augustine's *De Opere Monachorum* (*On the Labor of Monks*). **6598 the,** G reads "tho." **6600 besyly,** G reads "desily." **6601 To,** G reads "Go." **mennes,** G reads "mennens." **6606 Somtyme leven,** G and Th read "Ben somtyme in." **6615 Justinian,** the sixth-century Emperor at Constantinople whose codification of Roman law became the basis of medieval civil and canon law. Lines 6617–22 derive from the eleventh book of the *Justinian Code,* "De Mendicantibus Validus" (*On Healthy Beggers*); section numbering of the Code varies, so that the quotation can be found in 24, 25, or 26. **6616 sawes,** G reads "dawes" (days). **6633 comprehende,** G reads "comprende." **6648 And,** omitted in Th. **6653 wher,** omitted in G and Th. **6654–55 sell al . . . and to poore it yeve,** Luke 18.22.

And folowe him, and to poore it yeve,
He wolde not therfore that he lyve
To serven him in mendience°,
For it was never his sentence°.
But he bad werken whan that nede is,
And folowe him in good dedes.
Saynt Poule, that loved al holy churche,
He bade the apostels for to wurche,
And wynnen her lyvelode in that wyse,
And hem defended truandyse°,
And sayd, 'Werketh with your honden.'
Thus shulde the thyng be understonden.
He nolde, iwys°, have byd hem beggyng,
Ne sellen gospel, ne prechyng,
Lest they berafte°, with her askyng,
Folke of her catel° or of her thyng.
For in this worlde is many a man
That yeveth his good, for he ne can
Werne° it for shame, or els he
Wolde° of the asker delyvered be°.
And for° he him encombreth° so,
He yeveth him good to late him go.
But it can him nothyng profyte;
They lese the yefte and the meryte.
The good folke that Poule to preched
Profred° him ofte, whan he hem teched,
Some of her good in charyte;
But therof right nothyng toke he;
But of his hondewerke wolde he gete
Clothes to wryne° him, and his mete."
"Tell me than howe a man may lyven
That al his good to poore hath yeven,
And wol but onely bydde his bedes°,
And never with hondes labour his nedes.
Maye he do so?" "Ye, sir," "And howe?"
"Sir, I wol gladly tell you:
Seynt Austen saythe, a man may be
In houses that han properte,
As Templers and Hospytelers,
And as these chanons regulers,
Or whyte monkes, or these blake—
I wol no mo ensamples make—
And take therof his susteynyng°,
For therin lythe° no beggyng.
But otherwayes not, ywys°,
If Austyn gabbeth° not of this.
And yet ful many a monke laboureth
That God in holy churche honoureth;
For whan her swynkyng is agon°,
They rede and synge in churche anon.
"And for there hath ben great discorde,
As many a wight° may beare recorde,
Upon the estate° of mendicience°,
I wol shortly, in your presence,
Tel howe a man may begge at nede,
That hath not wherwith him to fede,
Maugre° his felones jangelynges°,
For sothfastnesse wol° none hydynges;
And yet, par case°, I may abey°,
That I to you sothly thus sey.
"Lo, here the case especial:
If a man be so bestyal°
That he of no crafte hath science°,
And nought desyreth° ignorence,
Than may he go a-beggyng yerne°,
Tyl he some maner crafte can lerne,
Through whiche without truandyng°,
He may in trouthe have his lyvyng.
Or if he may done no labour,
For elde, or sicknesse, or langour°,
Or for his tendre age also,
Than may he yet a-beggyng go.
Or if he have, peraventure,
Through usage° of his noriture°,
Lyved over delyciously°,
Than oughten good folke comenly

6657 mendience, *begging* **6658 sentence,** *meaning* **6664 defended truandyse,** *forbade begging* **6667 nolde, iwys,** *would not, surely* **6669 Lest they berafte,** *so that they would not deprive* **6670 catel,** *possessions* **6673 Werne,** *refuse* **6674 Wolde,** *wished to,* **delyvered be,** *be relieved* **6675 for,** *because,* **encombreth,** *troubles* **6680 Profred,** *offered* (to) **6684 wryne,** *cover* **6687 bydde his bedes,** *say his prayers* **6697 susteynyng,** *sustenance* **6698 lythe,** *lies* **6699 ywys,** *truly* **6700 gabbeth,** *lies* **6703 agon,** *done* **6706 wight,** *person* **6707 estate,** *condition,* **mendicience,** *begging* **6711 Maugre,** *despite,* **felones jangelynges,** *evil quarrellings* **6712 sothfastnesse wol,** *truthfulness desires* **6713 par case,** *perhaps,* **abey,** *suffer* **6716 bestyal,** *beast-like* **6717 science,** *knowledge* **6718 nought desyreth,** *does not desire* (this) **6719 yerne,** *validly* **6721 truandyng,** *begging* **6724 langour,** *weakness* **6728 usage,** *habit,* **noriture,** *upbringing* **6729 delyciously,** *delicately*

6661–65 Poule . . . Werken with your honden, Paul, 1 Thessalonians 4.11. **6682 therof,** G and Th read "therfore." **6688** Line lacking in G. **6693–95 Templers and Hospytelers . . . ,** the Knights Templar and Knights Hospitallers were military religious orders, formed in connection with the Crusades, making the citation to Augustine (354–430 C.E.) at line 6691, strictly speaking, anachronistic. But Guillaume de Saint Amour (see 6553–54n) and others applied Augustine's comments to all who lived by a religious rule or *regula,* including **chanouns regulers** (Church officers who lived in communities like monks), **whyte monkes** (Cistercians), **blake** monks (Benedictines), and others. Communal possession of even vast properties was permitted such orders, while the ideal of the mendicant friars was to live on charity, holding neither communal nor personal property. **6700 If,** G and Th read "Yit." **6711 felones,** T reads "felowes." **6728 noriture,** G reads "norture."

Han of his mischefe° some pyte,
And suffren° him also that he
May gon aboute and begge his breed,
That he be not for honger deed.
Or if he have of crafte connyng°,
And strength also, and desyring
To worchen, as he had what°,
But he fynde neyther this ne that,
Than may he begge tyl that he
Have geten his necessyte.
Or if his wynnyng be so lyte,
That his labour wol not acquyte
Suffyciantly al his lyvyng,
Yet may he go his breed beggyng;
Fro doore to doore he may go trace°,
Tyl he the remenaunt may purchace°.
Or if a man wolde undertake
Any emprise° for to make,
In the rescous of our lay°,
And it defenden as he may,
Be it with armes or lettrure°,
Or other covenable cure°,
If it be so he poore be,
Than may he begge, tyll that he
May fynde in trouthe for to swynke,
And get him clothes, meate, and drinke.
Swynke he with hondes corporell°,
And not with hondes espyrituell.
"In al this case, and in semblables°,
If that there ben mo resonables,
He may begge, as I tell you here,
And els not, in no manere—
As Willyam Seynt Amour wolde preche,
And ofte wolde dispute and teche
Of this mater al openly
At Parys ful solemply.
And also God my soule blesse,
As he had in this stedfastnesse°
The accorde° of the universite,
And of the people, as semeth me.
No good man ought it to refuse,
Ne ought° him therof to excuse,
Be wrothe° or blythe° whoso be;
For I wol speke and tell it the,
Al° shulde I dye and be put doun,
As was Seynt Poule, in derke prisoun,
Or be exiled in this caas
With wronge, as mayster William was,
That my mother Hypocrise
Banysshed for her great envye.
My mother flemed° him, Seynt Amour:
This noble dyd suche labour
To susteyne ever the loyalte,
That he to moche agylte° me.
He made a boke, and let it write°,
Wherein his lyfe he dyd al write,
And wolde yche renyed° beggyng,
And lyved by my traveylyng°,
If I ne had rent° ne other good.
What, weneth° he that I were wood°?
For labour might me never plese;
I have more wyl to ben at ese,
And have wel lever°, sothe° to say,
Before the people pattre° and pray,
And wrie° me in my foxerie°
Under a cope of papelardie°."
Quod Love, "What, dyvel, is this that I here?
What wordes tellest thou me here?"
"What, sir?" "Falsnesse, that apert° is.
Than dredest thou not God?" "No, certis,
For selde° in great thyng shal he spede
In this worlde that God wol drede.
For folke that hem to vertue yeven,
And truely on her owne lyven,
And hem in goodnesse aye contene°,
On hem is lytel thrifte ysene°.
Suche folke drinken great misese°.
That lyfe may me never plese.
But se what golde han usurers°,
And sylver eke in her garners°;

6731 mischefe, *misfortune* **6732 suffren,** *allow* **6735 connyng,** *knowledge* **6737 as he had what,** *for which he had the means* **6745 go trace,** *travel* **6746 purchace,** *acquire* **6748 emprise,** *enterprise* **6749 rescous of our lay,** *defense of our law* (religion) **6751 lettrure,** *education* **6752 covenable cure,** *appropriate duty* **6757 corporell,** *bodily* **6759 semblables,** *similar cases* **6768 stedfastnesse,** *firmness of purpose* **6769 accorde,** *agreement* **6772 ought,** *anything* **6773 wrothe,** *angry,* **blythe,** *happy* **6775 Al,** *even if* **6781 flemed,** *expelled* **6784 agylte,** *blamed* **6785 let it write,** *had it copied* (?) **6787 wolde yche renyed,** *desired that I renounced* **6788 traveylyng,** *working* **6789 rent,** *income* **6790 weneth,** *thinks,* **wood,** *crazy* **6793 have wel lever,** *would much rather,* **sothe,** *truth* **6794 pattre,** *recite the Pater Noster* (Our Father) **6795 wrie,** *hide,* **foxerie,** *cleverness* **6795 papelardie,** *hypocrisy* **6799 apert,** *overt* **6801 selde,** *seldom* **6805 aye contene,** *constantly hold* **6806 thrifte ysene,** *success seen* **6807 misese,** *discomfort* **6809 han usurers,** *money lenders have* **6810 garners,** *storerooms*

6756 clothes, G and Th read "clothe." **6757 hondes,** G and Th read "his hondes." **6763 Willyam Seynt Amour,** see 6553–54n. **6776 Seynt Poule . . . prisoun,** see Acts 21.30ff. **6778 mayster William,** see 6553-54n. **6782 This,** G reads "The." **6786** Line lacking in G. **6796 papelardie,** G reads "paperlardie." **6810 her,** omitted in G and Th.

Taylagiers°, and these monyours°,
Bayliffes°, bedels°, provost°, countours°;
These lyven wel nygh by ravyne°;
The smale people hem mote enclyne°,
And they as wolves wol hem eten.
Upon the poore folke they geten
Ful moche of that they spende or kepe;
Nys none of hem that he nyl strepe°,
And wrine° himselfe wel at full;
Without scaldyng they hem pull°.
The stronge the feble overgothe°,
But I, that weare my symple clothe,
Robbe bothe robbed and robbours,
And gyle gyled and gylours.
"By my treget° I gather and threst
The great tresour into my chest,
That lyeth with me so faste bounde.
Myn hygh paleys do I founde°,
And my delytes I fulfyll
With wyne at feestes at my wyll,
And tables ful of entremees°;
I wol no lyfe but ease and pees,
And wynne golde to spende also.
For whan the great bagge is go°,
It cometh right° with my japis°.
Make I not wel tomble myn apes°?
To wynnen is alway myn entent;
My purchace° is better than my rent°.
For though I shulde beten be,
Over al I entremet° me;
Without me may no wight dure°.
I walke soules for to cure°—
Of al the worlde cure° have I
In brede and length. Boldly
I wol bothe preche and eke counsaylen.
With hondes wyl I not travaylen°,
For of the pope I have the bull°;
I ne holde not my wyttes dull.
I wol not stynten° in my lyve
These emperours for to shrive°,
Or kynges, dukes, and lordes grete.
But poore folke al quyte I lete°;
I love no suche shrivyng, parde°,
But° it for other cause be.
I recke° not of poore men:
Her astate° is not worthe an hen.
Where fyndest thou a swynker° of labour
Have me unto his confessour?
"But empresses and duchesses,
These quenes and eke countesses,
These abbesses and eke bygyns°,
These great ladyes palasyns°,
These jolye knyghtes and baylives°,
These nonnes, and these burgeys° wyves
That ryche ben and eke plesyng,
And these maydens welfaryng°,
Whereso they clad or naked be,
Uncounsayled gothe there none fro me.
And, for her soules savete°,
At lorde and lady and her meyne°,
I aske, whan they hem to me shrive°,
The properte of al her lyve,
And make hem trowe°, bothe moste and leest,
Her parysshe-preest nys but a beest
Ayens° me and my company,
That shrewes° ben as great as I.
For whiche I wol not hyde in holde°
No pryvite° that me is tolde,
That I by worde or signe, ywis°,
Ne wol make hem knowe what it is,
And they wollen also tellen me;
They hele° fro me no pryvite.
"And for to make you hem parceyven,
That usen° folke thus to disceyven,

6811 Taylagiers, *tax collectors,* **monyours,** *money dealers* **6812 Bayliffes,** *civil officers,* **bedels,** *lesser officers,* **provost,** *magistrate,* **countours,** *accountants* **6813 ravyne,** *plunder* **6814 hem mote enclyne,** *must bow to them* **6818 strepe,** *strip* **6819 wrine,** *cover* **6820 hem pull,** *skin them* **6821 overgothe,** *overcome* **6825 treget,** *deception* **6828 do I founde,** *I establish* **6831 entremees,** *delicacies* **6834 go,** *empty* **6835 cometh right,** i.e., *fills up,* **japis,** *tricks* **6836 Make I . . . myn apes,** *don't I make my apes tumble well* **6838 purchase,** *booty,* **rent,** *income* **6840 entremet,** *intrude* **6841 wight dure,** *person endure* **6842 cure,** *care for* **6843 cure,** *care* **6846 travaylen,** *work* **6847 bull,** *written license* **6849 stynten,** *cease* **6850 shrive,** *confess* **6852 al quyte I lete,** *I abandon completely* **6853 parde,** *by God* **6854 But,** *unless* **6855 recke,** *care* **6856 astate,** *estate* **6857 swynker,** *worker* **6861 begyns,** *beguines* (see n.) **6862 palasyns,** *of the palace* (or court) **6863 baylives,** *bailiffs* (officers) **6864 burgeys,** *citizens'* **6866 welfaryng,** *prosperous* **6869 savete,** *safety* **6870 meyne,** *retinue* **6872 shrive,** *confess* **6873 trowe,** *believe* **6875 Ayens,** *compared with* **6876 shrewes,** *villains* **6877 holde,** *safekeeping* **6878 pryvite,** (confessional) *secrets* **6879 ywis,** *surely* **6882 hele,** *hide* **6884 usen,** *are accustomed*

6820 Without scaldyng . . . hem pull, animal carcasses were scalded to remove hair before skinning. **6823 robbed,** G and Th read "robbyng." **6824 gyled,** G and Th read "gyling." **6837** See *PardP* 6.403. **6838** See *GP* 1.256. **6841–48** This translates a passage in the French that most scholars consider spurious, available only in select manuscripts. See 6361–6472n and 6583–94n. **6851 Or,** G and Th read "Of." **and,** omitted in G. **6861 begyns,** beguines, members of lay sisterhoods, often including noblewomen who took vows of chastity and devoted themselves to charity. **6874 Her,** G reads "His." **6877 For,** G reads "Fro." **6880 Ne,** omitted in G.

I wol you sayne, withouten drede°,
What menne maye in the gospel rede
Of Saynt Mathue, the gospelere,
That saythe as I shal you saye here:
'Upon the chayre of Moyses'—
Thus it is glosed°, doutlees,
That is the Olde Testament,
For therby is the chayre ment—
'Sytte Scribes and Pharysen'—
That is to sayne, the cursed men
Whiche that we hypocrites call.
'Dothe that they preche, I rede° you all,
But dothe nat as they done a dele°,
That bene nat wery to saye wele°,
But to do wel no wyl have they.
And they wolde bynde on folke alwaye,
That bene to be gyled° able,
Burdons that ben importable°;
On folkes shulders thynges they couchen°
That they nyl with her fyngers touchen.'"
"And why wol they nat touche it?" "Why?
For hem ne lyste nat°, sykerly°;
For sadde° burdons that men taken
Make folkes shulders aken.
And if they do ought° that good be,
That is for° folke it shulde se.
Her bordurs° larger maken they,
And make her hemmes wyde alwaye,
And loven seates at the table
The fyrste and most honorable.
And for to hanne° the firste chayris
In synagogges to hem ful dere is;
And wyllen that folke hem loute° and grete
Whan that they passen through the strete;
And wollen be cleped° 'maister' also.
But they ne shulde nat wyllen so—
The gospel is there-agaynst, I gesse.
That sheweth wel her wickednesse.
"Another custome use we
Of hem that wol ayenst us be:
We hate hem deedly everychone,
And we wol werrey° hem as one.
Him that one hateth, hate we al,
And conjecte° howe to done° him fal.
And if we sene him wynne honour,
Rychesse or preyse, through his valour,
Provende°, rente, or dignyte,
Ful faste, ywis°, compassen° we
By what ladder he is clomben so;
And for to maken him downe to go,
With trayson we wol hym defame,
And done him lese° his good name.
Thus from his ladder we him take,
And thus his frendes foes we make.
But worde ne wete° shal he noon,
Tyl al his frendes bene his foon°,
For if we dyd it openly,
We myght have blame redily.
For hadde he wyste° of our malyce,
He hadde him kepte°, but° he were nyce°.
"Another is this, that if so fall°
That there be one amonge us all
That dothe a good tourne, out of drede°,
We sayne it is our alder dede°.
Ye, sykerly°, though he it fayned°,
Or that him lyste°, or that him dayned°
A manne through him avaunced° be,
Therof al parceners° be we,
And tellen folke, whereso we go,
That manne through us is sprongen° so.
And for to have of menne preysyng,
We purchace, through our flatterynge,
Of riche menne of great poste°,
Letters to wytnesse our bounte°,
So that manne weneth°, that maye us se,
That al vertue in us be.
And alwaye poore we us fayne°;
But howe so that we begge or playne,
We bene the folke, without leasyng°,
That al thynge have without havyng.
Thus be we dradde of° people, ywis°.

6885 drede, *doubt* **6890 glosed,** *interpreted* **6896 rede,** *advise* **6897 dele,** *bit* **6898 saye wele,** *speak well* **6901 gyled,** *beguiled* **6902 importable,** *unbearable* **6903 couchen,** *lay* **6906 ne lyste nat,** *don't want to,* **sykerly,** *certainly* **6907 sadde,** *serious* **6909 ought,** *anything* **6910 for,** *so that* **6911 bordurs,** *ornamental borders* **6915 hanne,** *have* **6917 loute,** *bow to* **6919 wollen be cleped,** *want to be called* **6926 werrey,** *wage war upon* **6928 conjecte,** *plan,* **done,** *make* **6931 Provende,** *stipend* **6932 ywis,** *indeed,* **compassen,** *determine* **6936 done him lese,** *make him lose* **6939 wete,** *understanding* **6940 foon,** *foes* **6943 wyste,** *known* **6944 kepte,** *protected,* **but,** *unless,* **nyce,** *foolish* **6945 if so fall,** *if it happens* **6947 drede,** *doubt* **6948 our alder dede,** *the deed of all of us* **6949 sykerly,** *certainly,* **fayned,** *pretended* **6950 him lyste,** *it pleased him,* **him dayned,** *he allowed that* **6951 avaunced,** *assisted* **6952 parceners,** *partners* **6954 sprongen,** *advanced* **6957 poste,** *power* **6958 bounte,** *goodness* **6959 weneth,** *believes* **6961 fayne,** *pretend* **6963 leasyng,** *lying* **6965 dradde of,** *feared by,* **ywis,** *indeed*

6887 Mathue, Matthew 23.1–8, 13–15. **6890 it is,** G reads "is it." **6911 bordurs,** G and Th read "burdons"; the French is *filatieres* (weavings). **6921 gospel,** Matthew 23.7–10.

And gladly my purpose is this:
I deale with no wight but° he
Have golde and treasour great plente.
Her acqueyntaunce wel love I;
This is moche my desyre, shortely.
I entremete me° of brocages°,
I make peace and mariages,
I am gladly executour,
And many tymes a procuratour°;
I am somtyme messagere—
That falleth nat to my mystere°.
And many tymes I make enqueste°—
For me that offyce is nat honest°.
To deale with other mennes thynge,
That is to me a great lykynge.
And if that ye have ought° to do
In place that I repeyre° to,
I shal it speden° through my wyt,
As soone as ye have tolde me it.
So that° ye serve me to paye,
My servyce shal be yours alwaye.
But whoso wol chastyce me,
Anone° my love loste hath he,
For I love no manne in no gyse
That wol me repreve or chastice.
But I wolde al folke undertake°,
And of no wight no teachynge take;
For I, that other folke chastye,
Wol nat be taught fro my folye.
  "I love none hermytage more°;
Al desertes and holtes hoore°,
And great woodes everychone,
I lette hem to the Baptyst John.
I queth him quyte°, and him relesse°
Of Egipte al the wyldernesse.
To ferre were° al my mansyons°
Fro al cytees and good towns.
My paleys and myne house make I
There° menne maye renne° in openly,
And saye that I the worlde forsake.
But al amydde° I bylde and make
My house, and swymme and playe therinne
Bette° than a fysshe dothe with his fynne.
  "Of Antechristes menne am I,
Of whiche that Christ sayth openly,
They have habyte° of holynesse,
And lyven in suche wickednesse.
Outwarde, lamben semen we°,
Ful of goodnesse and of pyte,
And inwarde we, withouten fable°,
Bene gredy wolves ravysable°.
We envyroun° bothe londe and see;
With al the worlde werryen° we;
We wol ordayne° of al thynge,
Of folkes good and her lyvyng.
  "If there be castell or cytee
Wherin that any bougerons° be,
Although that they of Myllayne° were—
For therof bene they blamed there;
Or if a wyght°, out of measure°,
Wolde leane° his golde and take usure°,
For that he is so coveytous,
Or if he be to lecherous,
Or thefe, or haunten simonye°,
Or provost° ful of trechery,
Or prelate° lyveng jolylye,
Or preest that halte his queyn° him by,
Or olde hoores hostylers°,
Or other baudes° or bordellers°,
Or els blamed of any vyce,

6967 wight but, *person unless* **6971 entremete me,** *involve myself,* **of brocages,** *in making deals* **6974 procuratour,** *agent* **6976 mystere,** *occupation* **6977 enqueste,** *legal inquiry* **6978 honest,** *honorable* **6981 ought,** *anything* **6982 repeyre,** *journey* **6983 speden,** *accomplish* **6985 So that,** *as long as* **6988 Anone,** *immediately* **6991 undertake,** *rebuke* **6995 none . . . more,** *not at all* **6996 holtes hoore,** *gloomy forests* **6999 queth him quyte,** *declare acquitted to him* (i.e., legally transferred), **relesse,** *remit* **7001 To ferre were,** *too far would be,* **mansyons,** *dwellings* **7004 There,** *where,* **renne,** *run* **7006 al amydde,** *in the midst of all* **7008 Bette,** *better* **7011 habyte,** *the clothing* **7013 lamben semen we,** *we seem to be lambs* **7015 withouten fable,** *to tell the truth* **7016 ravysable,** *predatory* **7017 envyroun,** *surround* **7018 werryen,** *wage war* **7019 ordayne,** *dispose* **7022 bougerons,** *heretics* **7023 Myllayne,** *Milan* **7025 wyght,** *person,* **out of measure,** *immoderately* **7026 leane,** *loan,* **usure,** *immoral profit* **7029 haunten simonye,** *is accustomed to sell church offices* **7030 provost,** *magistrate* **7031 prelate,** *church official* **7032 halte,** *keeps,* **queyn,** *harlot* **7033 hoores hostylers,** *innkeepers for whores* **7034 baudes,** *go-betweens,* **bordellers,** *brothel keepers*

6977 enqueste, G reads "enquestes." **6978 is nat honest,** G reads "not honest is." **6986 yours,** G reads "youre." **6998 Baptyst John,** John the Baptist lived a life of deprivation in the wilderness (Luke 3.2) that became the model for the ascetic life of monks and hermits. **7000 Egipte,** Christian monasticism began in the fourth century in the Egyptian desert; not mentioned in the French. **7002 al,** omitted in G. **7007 swymme,** G reads swmme." **7009 Antechristes menne,** the men of Antichrist, the chief antagonist of Christ whose arrival, it is believed, will signal Christ's second coming, the end of the world, and the destruction of many souls; see, e.g., 1 John 2.18. **7010 Christ sayth . . . ,** see Matthew 7.15. **7012** Lines 7109–58 are misplaced after this line in G and Th, evidently because a leaf was misplaced in the exemplar; another leaf, lines 7159–206, is misplaced after 7302. **7022 bougerons,** G reads "begger." **7025 if,** Th reads "of." **7026 his,** Th reads "her." **7029 thefe, or,** G and Th read "these that."

Of whiche men shulden done justyce:
By al the sayntes that we pray,
But° they defende them with lamprey°,
With luce°, with elys°, with samons°,
With tendre gees, and with capons°,
With tartes, or with chesses fatte,
With deyntie flaunes°, brode and flatte,
With caleweys°, or with pullayle°,
With conynges°, or with fyne vitayle°,
That we, under our clothes wyde,
Maken through our golet° glyde;
Or but he wol do come° in haste
Roe-venyson°, bake in paste°,
Whether so that he loure° or groyne°,
He shal have of a corde a loygne°,
With whiche men shal him bynde and lede,
To brenne° him for his synful dede,
That men shul here him crye and rore
A myle-way aboute, and more.
Or els he shal in prison dye,
But if° he wol our frendshyp bye,
Or smerten that that° he hath do,
More than his gylte amounteth to.
"But and° he couthe through his sleight
Do maken up° a toure of heyght,
Nought rought I° wheder of stone or tre°,
Or erthe, or turves° though it be,
Though it were of no vounde° stone,
Wrought with squyre and scantilone°,
So that° the tour were stuffed well
With al rychesse temporell;
And than, that he wolde updresse°
Engyns°, bothe more and lesse,
To caste at us, by every syde—
To bere his goode name wyde—
Suche sleightes° as I shal you neven°,
Barels of wyne, by syxe or seven,
Or golde in sackes great plente,
He shulde soone delyvered be.
And if he have no suche pytences°,
Let him study in equipolences°,
And lette° lyes and fallaces°,
If that he wolde deserve our graces;
Or we shal beare him such wytnesse
Of synne, and of his wretchydnesse,
And done his lose° so wyde renne°,
That al quicke° we shulde him brenne°,
Or els yeve him such penaunce,
That is wel worse than the pytaunce.
"For thou shalte never, for nothyng,
Con knowen° aright by her clothyng
The traitours ful of trecherye,
But° thou her werkes can aspye°.
And ne had the good kepyng be°
Whylom° of the Universyte,
That kepeth the key of Cristendome,
We had ben turmented al and some.
Suche ben the stynkyng prophetis.
Nys none of hem that good prophete is;
For they, through wicked entencion,
The yere of the Incarnacion
A thousande and two hundred yere,
Fyve and fyfty, ferther ne nere°,
Broughten° a boke, with sory grace,
To yeven ensample in commune place,
That sayd thus, though it were fable:
'This is the Gospel Perdurable°,
That fro the Holy Goost is sent.'
Wel were it worthe to ben brent.
Entytled was in suche manere

7038 But, *unless,* **lamprey,** *eatable eel* **7039 luce,** *pike,* **elys,** *eels,* **samons,** *salmon* **7040 capons,** *fattened roosters* **7042 flaunes,** *pies* **7043 caleweys,** *pears,* **pullayle,** *poultry* **7044 conynges,** *rabbits,* **fyne vitayle,** *fine food* **7046 golet,** *gullet* (throat) **7047 but he wol do come,** *unless he will provide* **7048 Roe-venyson,** *meat of a red deer,* **paste,** *pastry* **7049 loure,** *scowl,* **groyne,** *groan* **7050 loygne,** *length* **7052 brenne,** *burn* **7056 But if,** *unless* **7057 smerten that that,** *suffer for that which* **7059 But and,** *unless* **7060 Do maken up,** *raise* **7061 Nought rought I,** *I care not,* **tre,** *wood* **7062 turves,** *sod* **7063 vounde,** *found* (?) **7064 squyre and scantilone,** *builder's square and measure* **7065 So that,** *as long as* **7067 updresse,** *construct* **7068 Engyns,** *catapults* **7071 sleightes,** *tricks,* **neven,** *name* **7075 pytences,** *charitable gifts* **7076 equipolences,** *equivalent arguments,* i.e., *other effective bribes* **7077 lette,** *abandon,* **fallaces,** *deceits* **7081 done his lose,** *make his* (bad) *reputation,* **renne,** *spread* **7082 quicke,** *alive,* **brenne,** *roast* **7086 Con knowen,** *be able to know* **7088 But,** *unless,* **aspye,** *recognize* **7089 ne had the good kepyng be,** *if it had not been for the protection* **7090 Whylom,** *formerly* **7098 ferther ne nere,** *no later or sooner* **7099 Broughten,** *produced* **7102 Perdurable,** *eternal*

7037 we, G reads "me." **7041 chesses,** G and Th read "cheffis." **7047 he,** G reads "we." **7056 our,** G and Th read "his." **7071 Suche sleightes,** the "tricks" or "devices" that the rich man launches at the friars are the payments that they desire and the reason that they do not defame him. **as,** omitted in G and Th. **7075 he have,** omitted in G. **7090 Universyte,** the University of Paris; see 6553-54n. **7092** Line missing in G. **7098 ne nere,** G reads "neuer." **7099 a boke,** in 1254 (not 1255 as stated here and in the French), the Franciscan friar Gérard de Borgo San Donnino published the now-lost *Introductorius in Evangelium Eternum sive Spiritus Sancti (Introduction to the Eternal Gospel of the Holy Spirit)* in which he claimed that apocalyptic writings of Joachim de Fiore would supersede the New Testament (Gospel of the Son) as it had replaced the Old Testament (Gospel of the Father). In response, opponents of the friars sought and gained swift condemnation from Pope Alexander IV in 1255.

This boke, of whiche I telle here.
There nas no wight° in al Parys,
Beforne Our Lady, at parvys°,
That he ne myght bye the book,
To copy, if him talent° took.
There myght he se, by great traysoun,
Ful many false comparysoun:
'As moche as through his great myght,
Be it of heate, or of lyght,
The sonne surmounteth the moone,
That troubler° is, and chaungeth soone,
And the nutte-kyrnel° the shelle—
I skorne nat that I you telle—
Right so, withouten any gyle,
Surmounteth this noble Evangyle°
The worde of any evangelyst°.'
And to her tytell° they token Christ;
And many suche comparysoun,
Of whiche I make no mencioun,
Myght menne in that booke fynde,
Whoso coude of hem have mynde.
 "The Unyversyte, that tho° was aslepe,
Gan for to brayde° and taken kepe°,
And at the noyse the heed upcast°,
Ne never sythen° slepte it fast°;
But up it sterte and armes tooke
Ayenst this false, horryble booke,
Al redy batayle for to make,
And to the juge the booke they take.
But they that broughten the boke there
Hent° it anone awaye for fere;
They nolde shewe it no more a dele°,
But than it kepte°, and kepen wele,
Tyll such a tyme that they maye se
That they so stronge woxen be°
That no wight maye hem wel withstonde;
For by that boke they durst° nat stonde.
Awaye they gonne it for to bere,
For they ne durste nat answere
By exposytioun ne gloose°
To that that° clerkes wol appose
Ayenst the cursednesse, ywis°,
That in that booke written is.
Nowe wotte° I nat, ne I can nat se
What maner ende that there shal be
Of al this boke that they hyde.
But yet algate° they shal abyde
Tyl that they maye it bette defende;
This trowe° I best wol be her ende.
 "Thus Antechrist abyden° we,
For we bene al of his meyne°;
And what manne that wol nat be so,
Right soone he shal his lyfe forgo°.
We wol a people upon him areyse,
And through our gyle done him seise°,
And him on sharpe speares ryve°,
Or otherways bringe him fro lyve,
But-if° that he wol folowe, ywis,
That° in our booke written is.
Thus moche wol our booke signifye,
That whyle Peter hath maistrye,
May never Johan shewe wel his might.
 "Nowe have I you declared right
The meanyng of the barke and rynde°
That maketh the entencions blynde°.
But nowe at erst° I wol begyn
To expowne you the pythe° within,
And the seculers comprehende°,
That Christes lawe wol defende,
And shulde it kepen and mayntenen
Ayenst hem that al sustenen°,
And falsly to the people techen.

7107 wight, *person* **7108 Our Lady . . . parvys,** *the porch of the cathedral of Notre Dame* (Our Lady) **7110 talent,** *inclination* **7116 troubler,** *dimmer* **7117 nutte-kyrnel,** *nutmeat* (surpasses) **7120 Evangyle,** *Gospel* **7121 evangelyst,** *gospel-writer* **7122 her tytell,** *their title* **7127 tho,** *then* **7128 brayde,** *wake up,* **taken kepe,** *pay attention* **7129 the heed upcast,** *lifted its head* **7130 sythen,** *since,* **fast,** *soundly* **7136 Hent,** *grabbed* **7137 dele,** *bit* **7138 kepte,** *guarded* **7140 woxen be,** *are grown* **7142 durst,** *dare* **7145 gloose,** *commentary* **7146 that that,** *that which* **7147 ywis,** *truly* **7149 wotte,** *know* **7152 algate,** *nevertheless* **7154 trowe,** *think* **7155 abyden,** *await* **7156 meyne,** *company* **7158 forgo,** *lose* **7160 done him seise,** *have him seized* **7161 ryve,** *pierce* **7163 But-if,** *unless* **7164 That,** *what* **7169 rynde,** *shell* (outer meaning) **7170 maketh . . . blynde,** *disguises* **7171 at erst,** *for the first time* **7172 pythe,** *marrow* (inner meaning) **7173 the seculers comprehende,** *includes the seculars* (see 7172n.) **7176 sustenen,** *withstand*

7109–10 G is missing 7109, and Th has four lines in contorted sequence. These two lines are constructed from the first line in Th and the one in G, emended from the French. For detailed explanation, see the note in Dahlberg's Variorum edition. **7115 sonne,** G reads "same." **7123 suche,** G reads "a suche." **7133 for,** omitted in G. **7134 they take,** G reads "to take." **7137 it no,** omitted in G. **7142 they,** omitted in G. **7143 Awaye,** G reads "Alway." **7145 ne,** G and The read "no." **7151 boke,** omitted in G and Th. **7159–7206** Lines misplaced after 7302 in G and Th, evidently because of misplaced leaf in the exemplar; see 7012n. **7166–67 Peter . . . Johan,** i.e., St. Peter who here stands for the Pope and the secular clergy; St. John, for the friars. **7172** As other editors have indicated, material from the French is omitted after this line, perhaps through loss of a couplet. What is lacking is that the figure of Peter signifies or betokens the Pope (and, as line 7173 asserts, includes the secular clergy). **7173 seculers,** i.e., the secular clergy—those not under monastic or fraternal vows—who were locked in dispute with the friars.

For Johan betoketh° hem that prechen
That there nys lawe covenable°
But thilke° Gospel pardurable°
That fro the Holy Goste was sent
To turne folke that ben miswent.
The strength of Johan they understonde,
The grace in whiche they say they stonde,
That dothe the synful folke converte,
And hem to Jesu Christ reverte°.
Ful many another horriblete°
May men in that booke se,
That ben commaunded doutelesse
Ayenst the lawe of Rome expresse°.
And al with Antechrist they holden,
As men may in the boke beholden.
And then commaunden they to sleen°
Al tho that with Peter been;
But they shal never have that myght,
And God toforne°, for stryfe to fyght,
That they ne shal ynough fynde°
That Peters lawe shal have in mynde,
And ever holde, and so mayntene,
That at the laste it shal be sene
That they shal al come therto°,
For aught° that they can speke or do.
And thilke° lawe shal not stonde
That they by Johan have understonde;
But maugre° hem, it shal adoun°,
And ben brought to confusyoun.
But I wol stynte° of this matere,
For it is wonder longe to here;
But hadde that ylke boke endured°,
Of better estate I were ensured;
And frendes have I yet, parde,
That han me set in great degre.
"Of al this worlde is emperour
Gyle my father, the trechour,
And emperesse my mother° is,
Maugre the Holy Goste, iwys.
Our mighty lynage and our route°
Reigneth in every reigne° aboute.
And wel is worthy we maistres be,
For al this worlde governe we,
And can the folke so wel disceyve
That none our gyle can perceyve.
And though they done, they dare not say;
The sothe° dare no wight bewray°.
But he in Christes wrathe him ledeth°,
That more than Christ my bretherne dredeth.
He nys no ful good champion,
That dredeth suche similacion°,
Nor that for payne wol refusen
Us to correcte and accusen.
He wol not entremete° by right,
Ne have God in his eyesight,
And therfore God shal him punyce.
But me ne recketh° of no vyce,
Sythen° men us loven comunably°,
And holden us for so worthy
That we may folke repreve echone°,
And we nyll have reprefe of none.
Whom shulden folke worshypen so
But us, that stynten° never mo
To patren° whyle that folke may us se,
Though it not so behynde hem be?
"And where is more woode° folye,
Than to enhaunce° chivalrye,
And love noble men and gay,
That joly clothes weren alway?
If they be suche folke as they semen,
So clene, as men her clothes demen°,
And that her wordes folowe her dede,
It is great pyte, out of drede°,
For they wol be non hypocritis!
Of hem, me thynketh, great spyte° is;
I canne nat love hem on no syde.
But beggers with these hoodes wyde,
With sleighe° and pale faces leane,
And graye clothes nat ful cleane,
But fretted° ful of tatarwagges°,

7178 betoketh, *signifies* **7179 covenable,** *suitable* **7180 thilke,** *that,* **pardurable,** *eternal* **7186 reverte,** *return* **7187 horriblete,** *horrible thing* **7190 expresse,** *plainly* **7193 sleen,** *slay* **7196 God toforne,** *before God* **7197 ne shal ynough fynde,** *shall not discover enough people* **7201 al come therto,** *all come to that* (the law of Peter) **7202 For aught,** *regardless of anything* **7203 thilke,** *that* **7205 maugre,** *despite,* **adoun,** *fall down* **7207 stynte,** *cease* **7209 ylke boke endured,** *same book survived* **7215 mother,** i.e., *Hypocrisy* **7217 route,** *company* **7218 reigne,** *kingdom* **7223 sothe,** *truth,* **bewray,** *reveal* **7225 in . . . him ledeth,** *leads himself into* **7228 similacion,** *pretence* **7231 entremete,** *interfere* **7234 me ne recketh,** *I don't take account* **7235 Sythen,** *since,* **comunably,** *commonly* **7237 repreve echone,** *blame each one* **7240 stynten,** *cease* **7241 patren,** *recite Paternosters* (Our Fathers) **7243 woode,** *insane* **7244 enhaunce,** *encourage* **7248 demen,** *judge* **7250 out of drede,** *no doubt* **7252 spyte,** *envy* **7255 sleighe,** *sly* **7257 fretted,** *adorned,* **tatarwagges,** *tatters*

7178 For, G and Th read "That"; **betoketh,** G reads "bitokeneth." **that,** G and Th read "to." **7219 maistres,** G and Th read "mynistres." **7234 recketh,** G reads "rekke." **7242 hem,** omitted in G. **7254 beggers,** the modern sense is appropriate, hence "begging friars," although the word translates French *beguins,* i.e., members of lay brotherhoods (like the female *beguines*). **7255 sleighe,** G reads "steight."

And highe shoes, knopped° with dagges°,
That frouncen° lyke a quayle pype°,
Or bootes ryvelyng° as a gype°.
To suche folke, as I you devyse°,
Shulde princes and these lordes wyse
Take° al her londes and her thynges,
Bothe warre and pees in governynges—
To suche folke shulde a prince hym yeve
That wolde his lyfe in honour lyve.
And if they be nat as they seme,
That serven thus the worlde to queme°,
There wolde I dwelle, to disceyve
The folke, for they shal nat parceyve.
"But I ne speke in no suche wyse,
That men shulde humble habytte dispyse,
So that no pride there-under be;
No manne shulde hate, as thynketh me,
The poore man in such clothynge.
But God ne preyseth him nothynge
That saith he hath the worlde forsake°,
And hath to worldly glorie hym take,
And wol of suche delyces° use.
Who maye that begger wel excuse?
That papelarde° that him yeldeth° so,
And wol to worldly ease go,
And saith that he the worlde hath lefte,
And gredily it grypeth efte°,
He is the hounde, shame is to sayne,
That to his castynge° gothe agayne.
But unto you dare I nat lye.
But myght I felen or espy°,
That ye parceyved it nothynge°,
Ye shulde have a starke leasynge°
Right in your honde thus to begynne;
I nolde it lette° for no synne."
The god loughe at the wonder tho°,
And every wyght° gan laughe also,
And sayd, "Lo here a manne aright°
For to be trusty to every wight!
False-Semblant," quod Love, "say to me,
Sythe° I thus have avaunced the,
That in my courte is thy dwellyng,
And of rybaudes° shalt be my kyng,
Wolt thou wel holden my forwardes°?"
"Ye, sir, from hence forwardes.
Had never your father here beforne
Servaunt so trewe, sythe he was borne."
"That is ayenst al nature."
"Sir, put you in that aventure°;
For though ye borowes° take of me,
The sykerer° shal ye never be
For hostages, ne sykernesse,
Or chartres, for to beare wytnesse.
I take yourselfe to recorde° here,
That men ne may, in no manere,
Teren the wolfe out of his hyde
Tyl he be flayne°, backe and syde,
Though men him beate and al defyle.
What? Wene ye° that I ne wol begyle,
For I am clothed mekely?
There-under is al my trechery;
Myn herte chaungeth never the mo
For none habyt in whiche I go.
Though I have chere° of symplenesse,
I am not wery of shreudnesse.
My lemman°, Strayned°-Abstenaunce,
Hath myster of my purveyaunce°.
She had ful longe ago be dede°,
Nere° my counsayle and my rede°.
Let her alone, and you and me."
And Love answerde, "I truste the
Without borowe, for I wol none."
And False-Semblant, the thefe, anone,
Right in that ilke same° place,
That had of treson al his face,
Right blacke within and whyte without,
Thankyng him gan on his knees loute°.
Than was there nought but, "Every man
Nowe to assaute, that saylen° can," ASSAULT
Quod Love, "and that ful hardely." ON THE TOWER

7258 knopped, *studded,* **dagges,** *shreds* **7259 frouncen,** *wrinkle,* **quayle pype,** *quail net* (?) **7260 ryvelyng,** *creasing,* **gype,** *smock* **7261 devyse,** *describe* **7263 Take,** *entrust* **7268 queme,** *please* **7277 forsake,** *forsaken* **7279 delyces,** *pleasures* **7281 papelarde,** *hypocrite,* **him yeldeth,** *gives himself up* **7284 grypeth efte,** *grabs again* **7286 castynge,** *vomit* **7288 espy,** *see* **7289 parceyved it nothinge,** *perceived it not at all* **7290 leasynge,** *lying* **7292 lette,** *hesitate* **7293 tho,** *then* **7294 wyght,** *person* **7295 aright,** *indeed* **7298 Sythe,** *since* **7300 rybaudes,** *servants* **7301 forwardes,** *agreements* **7306 put you in that aventure,** i.e., *take that chance* **7307 borowes,** *pledges* **7308 sykerer,** *more certain* **7311 I take yourselfe to recorde,** *I call you to witness* **7314 flayne,** *skinned* **7315 Wene ye,** *do you think* **7321 chere,** *appearance* **7323 lemman,** *lover,* **Strayned,** *enforced* **7324 myster,** *need,* **purveyaunce,** *prudence* **7325 be dede,** *been dead* **7326 Nere,** *were it not for,* **rede,** *advice* **7331 ilke same,** *very same* **7334 loute,** *bow down* **7337 saylen,** *assail*

7270 The, G reads "To." **7286 to his castynge,** 2 Peter 2.22 and Proverbs 2.11. **7300 of rybaudes...kyng,** see 6068n. **7302** Lines 7159–7206 occur after 7302 in G and Th, evidently because a leaf was misplaced in the exemplar; see 7012n. **7314 flayne,** G and Th read "slayn." **7315 al,** G reads "alto." **7316 ne,** omitted in G and Th. **7323 Strayned,** G reads "Streyneth." **7334 Thankyng,** G reads "Thankith."

Than armed they hem comenly°
Of suche armour as to hem fell.
Whan they were armed, fiers and fell°,
They went hem forthe, al in a route°,
And set° the castel al aboute;
They wyl not away for no drede
Tyl it so be that they ben dede,
Or tyl they have the castel take.
And four batels° they gan make,
And parted hem° in four anon,
And toke her way, and forthe they gone
The foure gates for to assayle,
Of whiche the kepers wol not fayle,
For they ben neyther sicke ne dede,
But hardy folke, and stronge in dede.
  Nowe wol I sayne° the countenaunce°
Of False-Semblant and Abstynaunce,
That ben to Wicked-Tonge went.
But first they helde her parlyment°,
Whether it to done were
To maken hem be knowen° there,
Or els walken forthe disgysed.
But at the laste they devysed
That they wolde gone in tapynage°,
As it were in a pilgrymage,
Lyke good and holy folke unfeyned°.
And Dame Abstynence-Streyned
Toke on a robe of camelyne°,
And gan her graithe° as a bygyne°.
A large coverchiefe of threde
She wrapped al aboute her hede,
But she forgate not her psaltere°.
A payre of beedes° eke she bere
Upon a lace°, al of whyte threde,
On whiche that she her beades bede°;
But she ne bought hem never a dele°,
For they were gyven her, I wote° wele,
God wote, of a ful holy frere,
That sayd he was her father dere,
To whom she had ofter went°
Than any frere of his covent.
And he visyted her also,
And many a sermon sayd her to.
He nolde let°, for man on lyve,
That he ne wolde her ofte shrive°.
And with so great devocion
They made her confession
That they had ofte, for the nones°,
Two hedes in one hoode at ones.
Of fayre shappe I devyse her the°,
But pale of face somtyme was she;
That false traytouresse untrewe
Was lyke that salowe° horse of hewe,
That in the Apocalips is shewed°,
That signifyeth tho folke beshrewed°,
That ben al ful of trecherye,
And pale, through hypocrisye;
For on that horse no colour is,
But onely deed and pale, ywis°.
Of suche a colour enlangoured°
Was Abstynence, iwys, coloured.
Of her estate she her repented,
As her visage represented.
She had a burdowne° al of thefte
That Gyle had yeve her of his yefte°;
And a skryppe° of faynte° distresse
That ful was of elengenesse°;
And forthe she walked sobrely.
  And False-Semblant saynt°, je vous die°,
Had, as it were for suche mistere°,
Done° on the cope° of a frere,
With chere symple and ful pytous;
His lokyng was not disdeynous,
Ne proude, but meke and ful pesyble°.
About his necke he bare a Byble,
And squierly° forthe gan he gon.
And for to rest his lymmes upon,
He had of Treason a potent°;

7338 comenly, *generally* **7340 fell,** *bold* **7341 route,** *company* **7342 set,** *beset* **7346 batels,** *battalions* **7347 parted hem,** *divided themselves* **7353 sayne,** *describe,* **countenaunce,** *behavior* **7356 her parlyment,** *their discussion* **7355-56 it to done were / To maken hem be known,** *they should make themselves known* **7361 tapynage,** *disguise* **7363 unfeyned,** *sincere* **7365 camelyne,** *fabric of wool mixed with silk and other fibers* **7366 gan her graithe,** *dressed herself,* **bygyne,** *beguine* (see 6861n.) **7369 psaltere,** *book of Psalms* **7370 payre of beedes,** *set of beads* (rosary) **7371 lace,** *string* **7372 beades bede,** *said her prayers* **7373 never a dele,** *not at all* **7374 wote,** *know* **7377 ofter went,** *more often gone* **7381 nolde let,** *wouldn't refrain* **7382 her ofte shrive,** *hear her confession often* **7385 for the nones,** i.e., *in such a situation* **7387 devyse her the,** *describe her to you* **7390 salowe,** *pale* **7391 shewed,** *revealed* **7392 beshrewed,** *cursed* **7396 ywis,** *truly* **7397 enlangoured,** i.e., *sickly* **7401 burdowne,** *staff* **7402 yeve her of his yefte,** *given her of his property* **7403 skryppe,** *sack,* **faynte,** *pretended* **7404 elengenesse,** *sadness* **7406 saynt,** *girded* (?), **je vous die,** *I tell you* **7407 mistere,** *need* **7408 Done,** *put,* **cope,** *robe* **7411 pesyble,** *calm* **7413 squierly,** *like a squire* (?) **7415 potent,** *crutch*

7340 they, G reads "the." **7366 graithe,** G and Th read "gracche." **7369 psaltere,** G reads "sawter." **7383–7574** Lines lacking in G. **7386 two hedes in one hoode,** suggests collusion; sexual intimacy. **7387 devyse,** Th reads "devysed." **7390–91 salowe horse . . . Apocalips,** the pale horse of Revelation 6.8 is ridden by Death. **7392 tho,** Th reads "to." **7407 Had,** Th reads "And."

As he were feble, his way he went.
But in his sleve he gan to thring°
A rasour sharpe and wel bytyng,
That was forged in a forge
Whiche that men clepen Coupe-Gorge°.
So longe forthe her waye they nomen°,
Tyl they to Wicked-Tonge comen,
That at his gate was syttyng,
And sawe folke in the way passyng.
The pilgrymes sawe he faste by,
That beren hem ful mekely,
And humbly they with him mette.
Dame Abstynence first him grette,
And sythe° him False-Semblant salued°,
And he hem; but he not remeued°,
For he ne dredde° hem not a dele°.
For whan he sawe her faces wele,
Alway in herte him thought so,
He shulde knowe hem bothe two.
For wel he knewe Dame Abstynaunce,
But he ne knewe not constreynaunce°.
He knewe nat that she was constrayned,
Ne of her theves lyfe fayned°,
But wende° she come of wyl al free.
But she come in another degree;
And if of good wyl she beganne,
That wyl was fayled her thanne°.
And False-Semblant had he sayne° alse,
But he knewe nat that he was false.
Yet false was he, but his falsnesse
Ne coude he nat espye nor gesse;
For semblant was so slye wrought
That falsenesse he ne espyed nought.
But° haddest thou knowen hym beforne,
Thou woldest on a boke have sworne,
Whan thou him saugh in thylke° araye,
That he that whilome° was so gaye
And of the daunce joly Robyn
Was tho° become a Jacobyn°.
But sothely°, what so° menne hem cal,
Frere-prechours bene good menne al.
Her order wickedly they beren°,
Suche mynstrelles if they weren.
So bene Augustyns° and Cordylers°,
And Carmes°, and eke Sacked Freers°,
And al freres, shodde and bare
(Though some of hem ben great and square°),
Ful hooly men, as I hem deme°;
Everyche of hem wolde good man seme.
But shalte thou never of apparence
Sene conclude° good consequence°
In none argument, ywis°,
If existens° al fayled is.
For menne maye fynde alwaye sopheme°
The consequence to enveneme°,
Whoso that hath° the subtelte
The double sentence° for to se.
Whan the pylgrymes commen were
To Wicked-Tonge, that dwelled there,
Her harneys° nygh° hem was algate°.
By Wicked-Tonge adowne they sate,
That badde hem nere him for to come,
And of tidynges telle him some,
And sayd hem, "What case maketh you
To come into this place now?"
"Sir," sayd Strayned-Abstynaunce,
"We, for to drye° our penaunce,
With hertes pytous and devoute,
Are commen, as pylgrimes gon aboute.
Wel nygh on fote alway we go;
Ful dusty ben our heeles two.
And thus bothe we ben sent
Throughout this worlde that is miswent°
To yeve ensample, and preche also.
To fysshen° synful menne we go,
For other fysshynge ne fysshe we.
And, sir, for that charyte
As we be wonte°, herborowe° we crave,
Your lyfe to amende; Christ it save!
And, so it shulde you nat displease,

7417 gan to thring, *did thrust* **7420 Coupe-Gorge,** *Cut-Throat* **7421 nomen,** *took* **7429 sythe,** *after,* **salued,** *greeted* **7430 not remeued,** *did not depart* **7431 dredde,** *feared,* **dele,** *bit* **7436 knewe not constreynaunce,** *did not recognize constraint* **7439 fayned,** *hypocritical* **7440 wende,** *thought* **7442 was fayled her thanne,** *was ineffective afterward* **7443 sayne,** *seen* **7449 But,** *unless* **7451 thylke,** *that* **7452 whilome,** *formerly* **7454 tho,** *then,* **Jacobyn,** *Dominican friar* **7455 sothely,** *truly,* **what so,** *whatever* **7457 they beren,** *would they represent* **7459 Augustyns,** *Augustinian friars,* **Cordylers,** *Franciscan friars* **7460 Carmes,** *Carmelite friars,* **Sacked Freers,** *penitential friars* **7462 square,** *sturdy* **7463 deme,** *judge* **7466 Sene conclude,** *see concluded,* **consequence,** *conclusion* **7467 ywis,** *surely* **7468 existens,** *reality* **7469 sopheme,** *subtle fallacy* **7470 enveneme,** *poison* **7471 Whoso that hath,** *whoever has* **7472 sentence,** *meaning* **7475 harneys,** (war) *gear,* **nygh,** *near,* **algate,** *nevertheless* **7482 drye,** *endure* **7488 is miswent,** *has gone wrong* **7490 fysshen,** *fish for* **7493 wonte,** *accustomed to,* **herborowe,** *shelter*

7453 Robyn, a gallant figure from the pastourelle tradition and/or a figure in rustic dances. **7471 hath,** Th reads "hath hadde." **7485 nygh,** Th reads "nyght." **7486 dusty,** Th reads "doughty"; the French is *poudreus* (dusty). **7490 fysshen . . . menne,** friars claimed to be fishers of men as the new apostles; see Matthew 4.19 and compare *SumT* 3.1820.

We wolden, if it were your ease,
A shorte sermon unto you sayne°."
  And Wicked-Tonge answered agayne,
"The house," quod he, "such as ye se,
Shal nat be warned° you for° me,
Say what you lyst°, and I wol here."
  "Graunt mercy°, swete sir, dere!"

ABSTINENCE'S SPEECH TO WICKED-TONGUE

Quod alderfirst° Dame Abstynence,
And thus began she her sentence°:
  "Sir, the firste vertue, certayne,
The greatest and moste soverayne
That may be founde in any man,
For havynge° or for wytte he can°,
That is his tonge to refrayne°;
Therto ought every wight him payne°.
For it is better styll be
Than for to speken harme, parde°!
And he that herkeneth° it gladly,
He is no good man, sykerly°.
And, sir, aboven al other synne,
In that arte thou moste gilty inne:
Thou spake a jape° not longe ago—
And, sir, that was right yvel do°—
Of a yonge man that here repayred°,
And never yet this place apayred°.
Thou saydest he awayted° nothyng
But to disceyve Fayre-Welcomyng.
Ye sayd nothyng sothe° of that,
But, sir, ye lye, I tel you plat°.
He ne cometh no more, ne gothe, parde!
I trowe° ye shal him never se.
Fayre-Welcomyng in prison is,
That ofte hath played with you er this,
The fayrest games that he coude,
Without fylthe°, styl° or loude;
Nowe dare he nat himselfe solace°.
Ye han also the manne° do chace,
That he dare neyther come ne go.
What meveth you to hate him so
But properly your wicked thought
That many a false leasyng° hath thought?
That meveth° your foole° eloquence
That jangleth° ever in audyence°,
And on the folke areyseth blame,
And dothe hem dishonour and shame
For thynge that maye have no prevyng°,
But lykelynesse° and contryvyng°.
For I dare sayne that Reason demeth°
It is nat al sothe° thynge that semeth;
And it is synne to controve°
Thynge that is to reprove°.
This wote° ye wele, and sir, therfore
Ye arne to blame the more.
And nathelesse, he recketh lyte°;
He yeveth nat nowe therof a myte°.
For if he thought° harme, parfaye°,
He wolde come and gone al daye;
He coude himselfe nat abstene.
Nowe cometh he nat, and that is sene,
For he ne taketh of it no cure°,
But if° it be through aventure°,
And lasse than other folke, algate°.
And thou her watchest at the gate,
With speare in thyne arest° alwaye,
There muse°, musarde°, al the daye.
Thou wakest night and day for thought;
I wis°, thy traveyle° is for nought.
And Jelousye, withouten fayle,
Shal never quyte° the thy traveyle.
And skathe is° that Fayre-Welcomyng,
Without any trespassyng,
Shal wrongfully in prison be,
There wepeth and languyssheth° he.
And though thou never yet, ywis,
Agyltest° manne no more but this—
Take nat agrefe°—it were worthy
To putte the out of this bayly°,
And afterwarde in prison lye,
And fettre the tyl that thou dye.

7497 sayne, *speak* **7500 warned,** *denied,* **for,** *by* **7501 you lyst,** *pleases you* **7502 Graunt mercy,** *thank you* **7503 alderfirst,** *first of all* **7504 sentence,** *statement* **7508 havynge,** *possession,* **wytte he can,** *understanding* **7509 refrayne,** *restrain* **7510 wight him payne,** *person exert himself* **7512 parde,** *by God* **7513 herkeneth,** *listens to* **7514 sykerly,** *certainly* **7517 jape,** *falsehood* **7518 right yvel do,** *very wickedly done* **7519 repayred,** *came* **7520 apayred,** *harmed* **7521 awayted,** *planned* **7523 sothe,** *truthful* **7524 plat,** *openly* **7526 trowe,** *think* **7530 fylthe,** *foulness,* **styl,** *quietly* **7531 solace,** *please* **7532 the manne,** i.e., *the Lover* **7536 leasyng,** *lie* **7537 That meveth,** *that* (is what) *moves,* **foole,** *foolish* **7538 jangleth,** *chatters,* **audyence,** *public* **7541 prevyng,** *proof* **7542 lykelynesse,** *probability,* **contryvyng,** *fabrication* **7543 demeth,** *judges* **7544 sothe,** *true* **7545 controve,** *fabricate* **7546 to reprove,** *for blame* **7547 wote,** *know* **7549 recketh lyte,** *cares little* **7550 myte,** *smallest coin* **7551 thought,** *intended,* **parfaye,** *truly* **7555 cure,** *care* **7556 But if,** *unless,* **aventure,** *accident* **7557 algate,** *entirely* **7559 in thyne arest,** *in your holder* (i.e., ready for use) **7560 There muse,** *think on that,* **musarde,** *fool* **7562 Iwis,** *truly,* **traveyle,** *labor* **7564 quyte,** *repay* **7565 skathe is,** *it is too bad* **7568 languyssheth,** *weakens* **7570 Agyltest,** *sinned against* **7571 Take nat agrefe,** *don't resent it* **7572 bayly,** *responsibility*

7505–09 Compare *ManT* 9.332–33. **7531 he nat himselfe,** Th reads "she nat herselfe."

For thou shalte for this synne dwelle
Right in the dyvels arse of helle,
But if that thou repent the."
"Ma faye°, thou lyest falsely!" quod he.
"What, welcome with myschaunce° now?
Have I therfore herbered° you
To saye me shame, and eke reprove°?
With sorye happe°, to your behove°,
Am I today your herbegere!
Go herber you elswhere than here,
That han a lyer called me!
Two tregetours° arte thou and he,
That in myn house do me this shame,
And for my sothesawe° ye me blame.
Is this the sermon that ye make?
To al the dyvels I me take,
Or els°, God, thou me confounde!
But er° men dydden this castel founde°,
It passeth not ten dayes or twelve,
But it was tolde right to myselve,
And as they sayd, right so tolde I:
He kyste the rose prively!
Thus sayd I nowe, and have sayd yore°;
I not where° he dyd any more.
Why shulde men say me suche a thyng,
If it had been gabbyng°?
Right so sayd I, and wol saye yet;
I trowe, I lyed not of it;
And with my bemes° I wol blowe
To al neyghbours arowe°,
Howe he hath bothe comen and gone."
Tho° spake False-Semblant right anone,
"Al is not gospel, out of doute,
That men sayne in the towne aboute;
Lay no deefe eere to my spekyng;
I swere you, sir, it is gabbyng.
I trowe ye wote° wel certaynly
That no man loveth him tenderly
That saythe him harme, if he wote it,
Al be he never so poore of wyt°.
And sothe° is also, sykerly°—
This knowe ye, sir, as wel as I—
That lovers gladly wol visyten
The places there her loves habyten.
This man you loveth and eke honoureth,
This man to serve you laboureth,
And clepeth° you his frende so dere;
And this man maketh you good chere,
And everywhere that he you meteth,
He you saleweth°, and he you greteth.
He preseth° nat so ofte that ye
Ought of his comyng encombred° be;
There presen other folke on you
Ful ofter than he dothe nowe.
And if his herte him strayned so
Unto the rose for to go,
Ye shulde hym sene so ofte nede°,
That ye shulde take him with the dede.
He coude his comynge nat forbeare,
Though men him thrilled° with a speare;
It nere nat° than as it is now.
But trusteth wel, I swere it you,
That it is clene out of his thought.
Sir, certes, he ne thynketh it nought;
No more ne dothe Fayre-Welcomyng
That sore abyeth° al this thyng.
And if they were of one assent,
Ful soone were the rose hent°,
The maugre° yours wolde be.
And sir, of o thyng herkeneth me:
Sith° ye this man that loveth you
Han sayd suche harme and shame now,
Wytteth° wel, if he gessed it,
Ye maye wel demen° in your wyt
He nolde nothynge love you so,
Ne callen you his frende also,
But nyght and daye he wol wake,
The castel to destroye and take,
If it were sothe as ye devys°.
Or some manne in some maner wyse
Might it warne° him everydele°,
Or by himselfe parceyve wele,
For sithe° he myght nat come and gone
As he was whylome wonte° to done,

7578 Ma faye, *by my faith* **7579 myschaunce,** *bad luck* **7580 herbered,** *lodged* **7581 reprove,** *blame* **7582 sorye happe,** *bad luck,* **behove,** *benefit* **7586 tregetours,** *deceivers* **7588 sothesawe,** *truth telling* **7591 els,** *otherwise* **7592 er,** *before,* **founde,** *build* **7597 yore,** *earlier* **7598 not where,** *don't know whether* **7600 gabbyng,** *blather* **7603 bemes,** *trumpets* **7604 arowe,** *in order* **7606 Tho,** *then* **7611 trowe ye wote,** *think you know* **7614 Al be he never so poore of wyt,** *even if he is very stupid* **7615 sothe,** *true,* **sykerly,** *certainly* **7621 clepeth,** *calls* **7624 saleweth,** *greets* **7625 preseth,** *intrudes* **7626 encombred,** *bothered* **7631 hym sene so ofte nede,** *necessarily see him so often* **7634 thrilled,** *pierced* **7635 nere nat,** *would not be other* **7640 sore abyeth,** *sorely pays for* **7642 hent,** *seized* **7643 maugre,** *blame* **7645 Sith,** *since* **7647 Wytteth,** *know* **7648 demen,** *think* **7653 devys,** *describe* **7655 warne,** *inform,* **everydele,** *thoroughly* **7657 sithe,** *since* **7658 whylome wonte,** *once accustomed*

7623 he, omitted in G and Th. **7626 comyng,** G reads "come." **7634 men,** G and Th read "he." **7635 It nere,** G reads "I nerer."

He myght it soone wyte and se.
But nowe al otherwyse doth he.
Than have ye, sir, al utterly
Deserved helle, and jolyly
The dethe of helle, doutlesse,
That thrallen° folke so gyltlesse."
  False-Semblant so proveth this thyng
That he canne none answeryng,
And seeth alwaye suche apparaunce°
That nygh° he fel in repentaunce,
And sayd him, "Sir, it maye wel be.
Semblant, a good manne semen ye;
And, Abstynence, ful wyse ye seme;
Of o talent° you bothe I deme°.
What counsayle wol ye to me yeven?"
  "Right here anon thou shalt be shriven°,
And say thy synne without more;
Of this shalte thou repent sore,
For I am preest and have poste°
To shrive folke of most dignyte
That ben, as wyde as worlde may dure°.
Of al this worlde I have the cure°,
And that had never yet persoun°,
Ne vycarie° of no maner toun;
And, God wotte°, I have of the
A thousande tymes more pyte
Than hath thy preest parochial°,
Though he thy frende be special.
I have avauntage, in o wyse°,
That your prelates ben not so wyse
Ne halfe so lettred° as am I.
I am lycensed boldely
In divynite for to rede°,
And to confessen°, out of drede°.
If ye wol you nowe confesse,
And leave your synnes more and less,
Without abode°, knele downe anon,
And you shal have absolucion."

Here endeth the Romaunt of the Rose.

7664 thrallen, *enslave* **7667 apparaunce,** *spurious evidence* **7668 nygh,** *nearly* **7672 o talent,** *one desire,* **deme,** *consider* **7674 shriven,** *confessed* **7677 poste,** *power* **7679 dure,** *extend* **7680 cure,** *care* **7681 persoun,** *parson* **7682 vycarie,** *vicar* **7683 wotte,** *knows* **7685 preest parochial,** *parish priest* **7687 o wyse,** *one way* **7689 lettred,** *educated* **7691 rede,** *study* **7692 confessen,** *hear confession,* **out of drede,** *without doubt* **7695 abode,** *delay*

7660 doth, G and Th read "wote." **7661 ye,** omitted in G; Th reads "we." **7665 so proveth,** G reads "proveth so." **7684 tymes,** G reads "tyme." **7691** G reads "To reden in divinite." **7692** G reads "And long have red. Explicit." **7693–96** Not in G, and perhaps inauthentic. In the French the scene ends with False-Seeming cutting out the tongue of Wicked-Tongue.

Boece

Boece

Introduction

B*OECE* IS CHAUCER'S literal translation of the Latin *Consolation of Philosophy* by the late Roman philosopher-politician Anicius Manlius Severinus Boethius (d. 525 C.E.). Students of the Middle Ages read Boethius's work because it so profoundly influenced the philosophy and art of the era as well as its literature. The work includes details of Boethius's life but is cast as a Socratic dialogue between a fictional projection of Boethius and an allegorical personification of Philosophy. As a literary model, it helped to shape the medieval dream vision, the debate genre, ideas of tragedy, and the use of ironic first-person narration. In art, it inspired the ubiquitous imagery of Fortune and her wheel; in philosophy, it helped to establish a basic distinction between perpetuity and eternality, and contributed to discussions of epistemology and freewill. King Alfred the Great translated it into English, as did Queen Elizabeth I. Jean de Meun and others translated it into medieval French; Notker of St. Gall and others, into medieval German. There are medieval translations extant in Italian, Spanish, and Greek, and an impressive tradition of commentaries. With typical eloquence, C. S. Lewis said of the *Consolation* that "to acquire a taste for it is almost to become naturalised in the Middle Ages" (1967:75, no. 296).

Allusions to or echoes of the *Consolation* characterize nearly all of Chaucer's works, and in some works the pervasiveness of the influence reflects his deep absorption of a Boethian worldview. Concern with freewill and determinism, the existence of evil within divine order, the imagery and evanescent nature of fortune, disdain for the world, the hierarchies of ways of knowing and degrees of perfection—these and other topics are drawn together in Boethius's *Consolation* and they recur in Chaucer's works. His brief poem *To Adam Scryven* links *Boece* with *Troylus and Criseyde*, and the sustained Boethian passages and echoes in the *Troylus* indicate that Chaucer may have been working on the translation and his love epic about the same time (between 1380 and 1385). The laments of the lovers, the concern with destiny, and Theseus's consolation at the end of the *Knight's Tale* (1.2987ff.) all derive from Boethius's treatise, while the narrator of the *Nun's Priest's Tale* (7.3234–50) toys comically with Boethian ideas of necessity. The imagery of Fortune and notions of noble sufferance recur in the *Man of Law's Tale*, the *Clerk's Tale*, the *Franklin's Tale*, the *Monk's Tale*, and elsewhere. Chaucer's short poem, "The Former Age," is a polished verse translation of Book 2, meter 5, of the *Consolation*, and a number of Chaucer's other short poems are fundamentally Boethian in theme: "Fortune," "Balade de Bon Conseil (Truth)," and "Lack of Steadfastnesse." If further evidence of influence were needed, Chaucer tells us that he translated Boethius in both the Prologue to the *Legend of Good Women* (425) and in the *Retraction* of *Canterbury Tales* (10.1088).

Chaucer's elegant renderings and adaptations of portions of the *Consolation* in his poetry are justly regarded more highly than the prose style of his *Boece*. Boethius wrote his treatise in alternating passages of prose and poetry, but *Boece* is prose only—perhaps because Chaucer sought to be as literal as possible or to master the meaning of the original, suggestions made respectively by Caroline Eckhardt, "The Medieval *Prosimetrum* Genre from Boethius to *Boece*" (1982, no. 1652), and Tim William Machan, *Techniques of Translation: Chaucer's Boece* (1985, no. 1657). Refining the work of earlier scholars who tended to criticize Chaucer as a poor Latinist, Machan and A. J. Minnis approach the *Boece* as a product of complex textual transmission, exploring its relations with not only versions of the Latin original, but also the French translation by Jean de Meun and a series of glosses, most notably those by Nicholas Trivet, which helped to shape Chaucer's version. Machan brings these together in an effort to reconstruct as closely as possible Chaucer's source text or texts: *Sources of the Boece* (2005, no. 1658). See also the collections of essays edited by Minnis: *The Medieval Boethius: Studies in the Vernacular Translations of De Consolatione Philosophiae* (1987; no. 1662) and *Chaucer's Boece and the Medieval Tradition of Boethius* (1993, no. 1661).

Russell A. Peck surveys critical trends and provides extensive bibliography for *Boece* in *Chaucer's Romaunt of the Rose and Boece, Treatise on the Astrolabe, Equatorie of the Planetis, Lost Works, and Chaucerian Apocrypha: An Annotated Bibliography, 1900 to 1985* (1988, no. 93), usefully augmented by Noel Harold Kaylor, Jr., *The Medieval Consolation of Philosophy: An Annotated Bibliography* (1992, no. 1654). Still useful is Bernard L. Jefferson, *Chaucer and the Consolation of Philosophy* (1917, no. 294). The standard edition and modern translation of Boethius's *Consolation* is in the Loeb Classical Library (2d ed., 1973, no. 248).

Boece

Book 1

Incipit Liber Boecii de Consolacione Philosophic.

Metre 1. Carmina qui quondam.

Allas, I, weping, am constreyned to bygynnen vers of sorwful matere, that whilom° in floryssinge studie made delitable ditees°. For lo, rendinge° Muses of poetes enditen° to me thinges to ben writen, and drery vers of wrecchednesse weten° my face with verray° teres.

At the leeste, no drede ne myhte overcomen° tho° Muses, that they ne weren felawes° and foleweden my wey *(that is to seyn, whan I was exiled).* Thei that weren glorye of my yowthe, whilom weleful° and grene°, conforten now the sorwful wierdes° of me, olde man. For elde° is comen unwarly° upon me, hasted by the harmes that I have, and sorwe hath comaunded his age to ben in me. Heres hoore° arn shad overtymeliche° upon myn heved°, and the slake skyn trembleth of myn empted° body.

Thilke° deth of men is weleful° that ne cometh not in yeres that ben° swete, but cometh to wrecches often ycleped°. Allas, allas, with how def an ere deth, cruwel, torneth° awey fro wrecches, and nayteth° to closen wepinge eyen! Whil Fortune, unfeithful, favorede me with lyghte goodes°, the sorwful howre° *(that is to seyn, the deth),* hadde almost dreynt° myn heved°. But now for° Fortune, clowdy, hath chaunged hir deceyvable chere° to me-ward, myn unpitous° lyf draweth along° unagreable dwellings° in me. O ye, my frendes, what or wherto avauntede ye me° to ben weleful? For he that hath fallen stood nat in stidefast degree°.

Prose 1. Hec dum mecum tacitus.

While that I stille recordede° thise thinges with myself, and markede my weply° compleynte with office of poyntel°, I sawh°, stondinge aboven the heyhte° of myn heved° a womman of ful gret reverence by semblaunt°, hir eyen brenninge° and cleerseinge° over the comune myht° of men; with a lyfly° colour and with swych° vigour and strengthe that it myhte nat ben empted°, alle were it so that° she was ful of so

---

1 Meter 1. **2 that whilom,** *who once* **3 delitable ditees,** *pleasant poems,* **rendinge,** *tearing* **4 enditen,** *dictate* **6 weten,** *dampen,* **verray,** *genuine* **7 overcomen,** *overwhelm* **8 tho,** *those,* **felawes,** (my) *companions* **11 whilom weleful,** *formerly happy,* **grene,** *fresh* **12 wierdes,** *fates* **13 elde,** *old age,* **unwarly,** *unexpectedly* **15–16 Heres hoore,** *white hairs* **16 arn shad overtymeliche,** *are scattered prematurely* **17 heved,** *head* **18 empted,** *exhausted* **19 Thilke,** *that,* **weleful,** *happy* **20 ben,** *are* **21 ycleped,** *called* (for) **22 torneth,** *turns* **23 nayteth,** *refuses* **25 lyghte goodes,** *easy benefits* **26 howre,** *hour* **27 dreynt,** *drowned,* **heved,** *head,* **for,** *because* **28 deceyvable chere,** *deceitful face* **29 unpitous,** *miserable,* **draweth along,** *drags forward* **30 unagreable dwellinges,** *disagreeable delays* **31 what or wherto avauntede ye me,** *why or for what reason did you encourage me* **33 stidefast degree,** *stable position* 1 Prose 1. **1 recordede,** *called to mind* **2 weply,** *weeping* **3 with office of poyntel,** *by using a stylus to write in wax,* **sawh,** *saw* **4 heyhte,** *height,* **heved,** *head* **5–6 by semblaunt,** *in appearance* **6 brenninge,** *burning* **7 cleerseinge,** *clear-sighted,* **myht,** *power* **8 lyfly,** *lively,* **swych,** *such* **9 empted,** *exhausted* **10 alle were it so that,** *even though*

Text based on Cambridge University Library MS Ii.3.21 (C^2), with select corrections and variants from Cambridge University Library MS Ii.1.38 (C^1) and National Library of Wales, Peniarth 393D (Hn). ***Incipit Liber Boecii de Consolacione Philosophie,*** Here begins Boethius's Book of the Consolation of Philosophy. **Meter 1.** ***Carmina qui quondam,*** the Latin phrases at the beginning of each section of *Bo* are the opening words of the Latin text that is found with the English translation in C^2. **4 Muses,** in classical tradition, the minor deities who inspired writers. **9–10** ***that is to seyn . . . ,*** this and other italicized glosses or commentary are not in Boethius's original, although many of them are in the French translation used by Chaucer. **24 Fortune,** originally a minor Italian goddess, Fortuna was affiliated with Tyche, the Greek goddess of chance, and became a popular figure of prosperity, destiny, and uncertainty. Her familiarity in medieval literature is due largely to the influence of Boethius. **30 in me,** omitted in C^2, C^1, and Hn. **1 Prose 1. 3 sawh,** this spelling indicates that the palatal sound *gh* or *h* was silent to the scribe who copied this manuscript, resulting in its omission in some words (*through–thorw*) and its introduction in some words where there is no historical justification (*sawh*).

gret age that men ne wolden nat trowen in no manere that she were of owre elde°. The stature° of hir was of a dowtows° juggement, for somtyme she constreynede° and shronk hirselven lyk to the comune mesure of men, and sumtyme it semede that she towchede the hevene with the heyhte of hir heved; and whan she hef° hir heved hyer, she percede the selve hevene° so that the syhte of men looking was in ydel°.

Hir clothes weren maked of riht delye° thredes and subtil craft of perdurable° matere, the whiche clothes she hadde woven with hir owene handes, as I knewh° wel after by hirself declaringe and shewinge to me the beaute. The whiche clothes a dirknesse of a forleten° and despised elde° hadde dusked° and derked, as it is wont° to dyrken bismokede° ymages°. In the nethereste° hem or bordure of thise clothes, men redden° ywoven in a Grekyssh P *(that signifyeth the lyf actyf)*, and aboven that lettre, in the heyeste° bordure, a Grekyssh T *(that signifyeth the lyf contemplatyf)*. And bytwixen thise two lettres ther weren seyn degrees° nobely ywroght° in manere of laddres, by whiche degrees men myhten clymben fro the nethereste lettre to the uppereste. Natheles°, handes of some men hadden korven° that cloth by vyolence and by strengthe, and everyche man of hem hadde born° awey swiche peeces° as he myhte geten. And forsothe°, this forseide° woman bar° smale bookes in hir ryht hand, and in hir left hand she baar a ceptre°.

And whan she say° thise poetical Muses aprochen abowte my bed, and enditinge° wordes to my wepinges, she was a lytel amoved°, and glowede° with cruwel eyen°. "Who," quod she, "hath suffred° aprochen to this sike man thise comune strompeters° of swich° a place that men clepen° the theatre? The whiche nat oonly ne asswagen° nat his sorwes with none remedies, but they wolden feeden and noryssen hym with swete venym. Forsothe, thise ben tho° that with thornes and prykkinges of talentes° or affeccyouns, whiche that ne ben nothing fructefiinge° nor profytable, destroyen the corn plentyuous° of fruites of resoun. For they holden the hertes of men in usage°, but they ne delyvere nat foolkes fro maledye. But yif° ye Muses hadden withdrawen fro me with yowre flateryes any unkunninge and unprofitable° man, as men ben wont to° fynde comunly amonges the poeple, I wolde wene suffre° the lasse° grevously, for whi° in swiche° an unprofitable man myn ententes° ne weren nothing endamaged°. But ye withdrawen° me this man that hath be norysshed in the studies or schooles of Eliaticis and of Achademicis in Grece. But goth° now rather° awey, ye mermaydenes°, whiche that ben swete til it be at the laste° and, suffreth° this man to be cured and heeled by myne Muses" *(that is to seyn, by noteful sciences°)*.

---

11 ne wolden nat trowen, *would not believe* **12 elde,** *era* **13 stature,** *height,* **dowtows,** *uncertain* **14 constreynede,** *compressed* **18 hef,** *raised* **19–20 selve hevene,** *same heaven* **21 in ydel,** *in vain* **22 riht delye,** *very delicate* **23 perdurable,** *everlasting* **25 knewh,** *knew* **28 forleten,** *neglected,* **elde,** *oldness,* **dusked,** *dimmed* **29 wont,** *accustomed,* **bismokede,** *sooty* **30 ymages,** *statues,* **nethereste,** *lowest* **31 redden,** *read* **33 heyeste,** *uppermost* **36 seyn degrees,** *seen steps,* **nobely ywroght,** *handsomely made* **39 Natheles,** *nonetheless* **40 korven,** *slashed* **42 born,** *carried,* **swiche peeces,** *such pieces* **43 forsothe,** *truly,* **forseide,** *previously mentioned,* **bar,** *carried* **45 ceptre,** *scepter* **46 say,** *saw* **47 enditinge,** *dictating* **48 lytel amoved,** *momentarily upset* **49 glowede,** *glared,* **cruwel eyen,** *stern eyes* **50 suffred,** *allowed* **51 strompetes,** *prostitutes,* **swich,** *such* **52 clepen,** *call* **53 asswagen,** *soothe* **56 tho,** *those* **57 talentes,** *desires* **58 ne ben nothing fructefiinge,** *are not at all fruitful* **59 corn plentyous,** *plentiful grain* **61 in habit,** *habitually* **62 yif,** *if* **64 unkunninge and unprofitable,** *ignorant and useless* **65 ben wont to,** *usually* **66 wolde wene suffre,** *would think to suffer,* **lasse,** *less* **67 for whi,** *because,* **swiche,** *such* **68 ententes,** *purposes,* **endamaged,** *injured* **69 withdrawen,** *hold back from* **72 goth,** *go,* **rather,** *quickly,* **mermaydenes,** *mermaids* **73 at the laste,** *at the end,* i.e., death, **suffreth,** *allow* **75 noteful sciences,** *useful ways of learning*

26 herself declaringe, Philosophy describes her clothes further at 1.pr3.40–45, where their allegorical meaning becomes even clearer. **29 bismokede,** C[2] reads "the smokede." **32 Grekyssh P,** Greek π, *pi,* for practical knowledge; glossed "practik" in C[2]. **34 Grekyssh T,** Greek, Θ, *theta,* for theoretical or speculative knowledge; glossed "theorik" in C[2]. **49–75** This condemnation of the Muses was cited by medieval moralists as an argument against poetry. Because much of the *Consolation* is itself in verse, it is apparent that Philosophy was not condemning all poetry, but a certain kind (nonphilosophical, escapist). **52 nat,** omitted in C[1]. **61 ne,** omitted in C[2]. **62 fro,** omitted in C[2]. **71 Eliaticis . . . Achademicis,** Eleatics (philosophical school of Elia in Italy, founded by Zeno, regarded as the inventor of dialectics); Academics (followers of Plato). **72 mermaydenes,** mermaids were equated with the sirens who lured sailors to their deaths with enchanting songs. **74 *by,*** Hn begins here; the manuscript is missing an initial leaf.

And thus this companye of Muses, yblamed°, casten wrothly° the cheere° downward to the erthe, and shewinge by rednesse her° shame, they passeden sorwfully the thressh-fold. And I, of whom the syhte°, plownged° in teres, was dyrked° so that I ne myghte not knowen what that womman was of so imperial auctorite, I wax° al abaysshed and astoned°, and cast my syht down to the erthe, and bygan stille° for to abyde° what she wolde don afterward. Tho° com she ner, and sette hir doun upon the uttereste° corner of my bed; and she, byholdinge my cheere° that was cast to the erthe, hevy and grevous of wepinge, compleynede° with thise wordes that I shal seyen the perturbacyoun° of my thowht.

Metre 2. Heu quam precipiti mersa profundo.

"Allas, how the thowt of man, dreynt° in overthrowinge depnesse, dulleth°, and forleteth° his propre cleernesse°, myntinge° to goon into foreyne° dyrknesses as ofte as his anoyous° bysynesse wexeth° withowte mesure, that is dryven to and fro with worldly wyndes! This man, that whilom° was free, to whom the hevene was open and knowen, and was wont° to goon in hevenelyche paathes, and sawh° the lyhtnesse of the rede sonne, and sawh the sterres of the colde moone, and whiche sterre in hevene useth wandringe recourses°, iflyt° by diverse speeres°—this man, overcomer°, hadde comprehended al this by nowmbre of acountinge° in astronomie. And over this, he was wont to seken the causes whennes° the sowninge° wyndes moeven and bysien° the smothe water of the see; and what spiryt torneth° the stable hevene; and whi the sterre aryseth owt of the rede est° to fallen in the westrene wawes°; and what atempreth° the lusty° howres of the fyrst somer sesoun, that hyhteth° and aparaileth° the erthe with rosene flowres; and who maketh the plentyuos autompne° in fulle yeres fleteth° with hevy grapes. And ek° this man was wont to telle the diverse cawses of nature that weren ihydde°. Allas, now lieth he empted° of lyht of his thowht, and his nekke is pressed with hevy cheynes, and bereth his cheere° enclyned adown for° the grete weyhte, and is constreyned to looken on the fool° erthe.

Prose 2. Set medicine inquit tempus est.

"But tyme is now," quod she, "of medicine moore than of compleynte." Forsothe than° she, entendinge° to me-ward with alle the lookinge of hir eyen, seyde: "Art nat thow he," quod she, "that whilom ynoryssed° with my mylk and fostered with myne metes°, were escaped° and comen to corage° of a parfit man? Certes°, I yaf the° swiche armures° that yif° thow thyself ne haddest fyrst cast hem awey, they shulden han defended the in sikernesse° that may nat ben overcomen. Knowestow° me nat? Why artow° stille? Is it for shame or for astoninge°? It were me lever° that it were for shame; but it semeth me that astoninge hath oppressed the." And

---

76 yblamed, *scolded* **77 wrothly,** *sadly,* **cheere,** *faces* **78 her,** *their* **80 of whom the syhte,** *whose sight,* **plownged,** *plunged* **81 dyrked,** *darkened* **83 wax,** *became,* **abaysshed and astoned,** *abashed and astonished* **85 stille,** *quietly,* **abyde,** *await* **86 Tho,** *then* **87 uttereste,** *furthest* **88 cheere,** *face* **90 compleynede,** *lamente,* **91 perturbacyoun,** *disturbed state* <u>1 Meter 2.</u> **1 dreynt,** *drowned* **2 dulleth,** *grows dull,* **forleteth,** *abandons* **3 propre cleernesse,** *appropriate clarity,* **myntinge,** *intending* **4 foreyne,** *alien,* **anoyous,** *anxious* **5 wexeth,** *grows* **7 whilom,** *once* **8 wont,** *accustomed* **9 sawh,** *saw* **12 wandringe recourses,** *irregular orbits* **13 iflyt,** *moved* **speeres,** *spheres,* **overcomer,** *winner* **14–15 nowmbre of acountinge,** *computation* **16 whennes,** *from which* **17 sowninge,** *sounding,* **bysien,** *disturb* **19 torneth,** *turns* **20 rede est,** *red east* **21 wawes,** *waves,* **atempreth,** *makes mild* **22 lusty,** *pleasant* **23 hyhteth,** *adorns,* **aparaileth,** *apparels* **25 autompne,** *autumn,* **fleteth,** *flow* **26 ek,** *also* **27 ihydde,** *hidden* **28 empted,** *emptied* **30 cheere,** *face,* **for,** *because of* **32 fool,** *senseless* <u>1 Prose 2.</u> **2 than,** *then* **3 entendinge,** *looking* **5 whilom ynoryssed,** *formerly nourished* **6 myne metes,** *my foods* **7 escaped,** *free,* **corage,** *spirit* **8 Certes,** *surely,* **yaf the,** *gave to you,* **swiche armures,** *such armor* **9 yif,** *if* **11 sikernesse,** *security* **12 Knowestow,** *do you know,* **artow,** *are you* **13 astoninge,** *astonishment* **13–14 It were me levere,** *I would rather*

<u>1 Meter 2.</u> **6 to and fro,** omitted in C^1 and Hn. **worldly,** C^2 reads "wordly." **9 hevenlyche,** Hn is damaged here through the end of m2 and at pr3.1–2. **11–13 whiche sterre . . . by diverse speeres,** in the medieval understanding of the cosmos, the planets were thought to be stars different from the other, fixed stars because they followed individual orbits ("wandringe recourses"), each attached to one of the invisible concentric spheres that encompass the earth. **14 comprehended,** C^2 reads "comprendyd." <u>1 Prose 2.</u> **1 medicine,** the figure of rhetoric or argument as medicine recurs throughout Books 1–3; Philosophy here promises mild treatments and then stronger ones; see, for example, 1.pr5.73–75, 2.pr5.3, and 3.pr1.14–18.

whan she say° me nat oonly stille, but withowten office of tunge° and al dowmb°, she leyde hir hand softely upon my brest and seyde: "Her nis no° peril," quod she. "He is fallen into a litargie°, whiche that is a comune sykenesse to hertes that ben deceyved. He hath a litel foryeten° hymself, but certes° he shal lyhtly° remembren hymself yif so be that he hath knowen me or° now. And that he may so doon, I wol wypen° a litel his eyen, that ben derked by the clowde of mortal thinges." Thise wordes seyde she, and with the lappe° of hir garment, iplited° in a frounce°, she dryede myn eyen, that weren fulle of the wawes° of my wepinges.

Metre 3. Tunc me discussa liquerunt nocte tenebre.

Thus whan that nyht was discussed° and chased awey, dirknesses forleften° me, and to myn eyen repeyrede ayein° her fyrste° strength. And ryht by ensaumple as the sonne is hid whan the sterres ben clustred° *(that is to seyn, whan sterres ben covered with clowdes)* by a swifte wynde that heyhte° Chorus, and that the fyrmament stant° dirked° by wete plowngy° clowdes, and that the sterres nat apperen upon hevene, so that the nyht semeth sprad upon erthe, yif thanne the wind that hyhte° Boryas, isent° owt of the kaves° of the contre of Trace, beteth this night *(that is to seyn, chaseth it awey),* and descovereth° the closed° day, thanne shyneth Phebus° yshaken° with sodeyn lyht, and smyteth° with his bemes in merveylinge° eyen.

Prose 3. Haut aliter tristicie.

Riht so° and non oother wyse, the clowdes of sorwe dissolved and don awey, I took° hevene and receivede mynde to knowen the face of my fysicien°, so that I sette myn eyen on hir and fastnede my lookinge. I behoolde my noryse° Philosophie, in whos howses I hadde conversed and haunted° fro my yowthe, and I seide thus: "O thow maystresse° of alle vertuus, descended from the soverein sete°, whi artow° comen into this solitarie place of myn exil? Artow comen for° thou art maked coupable° with me of false blames?"

"O," quod she, "my norry°, sholde I forsaken the° now, and sholde I nat parten° with the, by comune travayle°, the charge° that thow hast suffred for envye of my name? Certes, it nere nat leveful° ne sittinge° thing to philosophie to leten° withowten compaygnye the wey of him that is innocent. Sholde I thanne redowte° my blame, and agrysen° as thowh ther were byfallen a newe thing? For trowestow° that philosophie be now alderfirst° assailed in perils by foolk of wikkede manneres? Have I nat striven with ful gret strif, in olde tyme, byfore the age of my Plato, ayenes° the foolhardinesse of folie? And ek°, the same Plato lyvinge°, his mayster° Socrates deservede° victorie of unryhtful deth in my presence. The heritage of the which Socrates *(the heritage is to seyn, the doctrine of the whiche Socrates in his opinioun of felicite°, that I clepe welefulnesse°),* whan that

---

16 say, *saw* **17 office of tunge,** *ability to speak,* **dowmb,** *mute* **19 nis no,** *is no* **20 litargie,** *stupor* **22 foryeten,** *forgotten,* **certes,** *surely,* **lyhtly,** *easily* **24 or,** *before* **25 wypen,** *wipe* **27 lappe,** *hem* **28 iplited,** *pleated,* **frounce,** *fold* **30 wawes,** *waves* <u>1 Meter 3.</u> **1 discussed,** *driven away* **2 forleften,** *left* **3 repeyrede ayein,** *returned again,* **her fyrste,** *their former* **5 clustred,** *covered by clusters* **7 heyhte,** *is called* **8 fyrmament stant,** *heavens stand,* **dirked,** *darkened,* **plowngy,** *stormy* **11 hyhte,** *is called* **12 isent,** *sent,* **kaves,** *caves* **14 descovereth,** *reveals,* **closed,** *hidden* **15 Phebus,** *the sun,* **yshaken,** *sparkling* **16 smyteth,** *strikes* **17 merveylinge,** *astonished* <u>1 Prose 3.</u> **1 Riht so,** *in this way* **2 took,** *perceived* **4 fysicien,** *physician* **6 noryyse,** *nurse* **7 haunted,** *lived* **8 maystresse,** *mistress* **10 soverein sete,** *highest location,* **artow,** *are you* **12 for,** *because,* **maked coupable,** *accused* **14 norry,** *pupil* **15 the,** *you* **16 parten,** *share,* **comune travayle,** *shared effort* **17 charge,** *burden* **18 leveful,** *lawful* **19 sittinge,** *suitable,* **leten,** *leave* **22 redowte,** *fear,* **agrysen,** *shudder* **23 trowestow,** *do you think* **25 alderfirst,** *for the first time* **28 ayenes,** *against* **29 ek,** *also,* **lyvinge,** (while he was) *living* **30 mayster,** *master,* **deservede,** *was rewarded with* **33–34 *opinioun of felicite*,** *understanding of happiness* **34 *clepe welefulnesse*,** *call well-being*

21 deceyved, C[2] reads "desseyvyd," here and elsewhere. <u>1 Meter 3.</u> **3 ayein,** omitted in C[2]. **7 Chorus,** Corus, the northwest wind. **8 by,** C[1] and Hn read "with." **12 Boryas,** Boreas, the north wind. **13 Trace,** Thrace, a region in southeastern Europe. <u>1 Prose 3.</u> **3 receivede,** C[2] reads "resseyvede," here and elsewhere. **4 fysicien,** C[2] reads "feissien." **34 *felicite . . . welefulnesse*,** these two terms for happiness reflect the effort to express precisely the Platonic notion of the ultimate good.

the poeple of Epicuriens and Stoyciens and many oothre enforseden hem° to gon ravysse° everich man for his part *(that is to seyn, that everich of hem wolde drawen to the defence of his opinioun the wordes of Socrates)*, they as in partye° of hir preye todrowen° me, cryinge and debatinge ther-ayeins, and korven° and torenten° my clothes that I hadde woven with myn handes; and with tho clowtes° that they hadden arraced° owt of my clothes they wenten awey, weninge° that I hadde gon with hem everydel°. In° whiche Epicuriens and Stoyciens for as moche° as ther semede some traces or steppes° of myn habite°, the folie of men, weninge tho Epicuriens and Stoiciens my famuleres, perverted some thorwh the errour of the wikkede or unkunninge° multitude of hem. *(This is to seyn, that for° thei semede philosophres they weren pursued to the deth and slayn.)* So yif° thow hast nat knowen the exilinge of Anaxogore, ne the enpoysoninge of Socrates, ne the tormentes of Zeno, for they weren straungeres°, yit mightestow han knowen° the Senecciens and the Canyos and the Sorans, of whiche foolk the renoun is neyther over-olde° ne unsolempne°. The whiche° men nothing elles ne browhte hem to the deth but oonly for they weren enformed of myne maneres°, and semeden most unlyk° to the studies° of wikkede foolk. And forthi° thow owhtest° nat to wondren thowh that I, in the bittre see° of this lyf, be fordryven with tempestes blowinge abowte, in the whiche tempestes this is my moost purpos, that is to seyn, to displesen to wikkede men. Of whiche shrewes°, al be° the oost° never so greet, it is to despise°, for it nis governed with no leder of resoun, but it is ravyssed° only by fleetinge° errour folyly° and lyhtly°. And yif they somtyme, makinge an oost° ayeins us, assayle us as strenger°, owr leder draweth togydere his rychesses into his towr, and they ben ententyf° abowte sarpuleres° or sachels° unprofitable for to taken. But we that ben heye° aboven, syker° fro alle tumolte and woode noyse, warnestored° and enclosed in swich a palis°, whider° as chateringe or anoyinge folye ne may nat atayne°, we scorne swiche ravyneres° and henteres° of fowleste thinges.

Metre 4. Quisquis composito.

"Whoso it be that is cleer of° vertu, sad°, and wel ordinat° of levinge°, that hath put under foot the prowde wierdes°, and looketh upriht° upon eyther° fortune, he may his cheere° holde undescounfited°. The rage ne the manaces° of the see, commoevinge° or chasinge upward heete fro the botme, ne shal nat moeve that man; ne the unstable mountaygne that hihte° Vesevus, that writheth° owt thorwh his brokene chymynees

36 oothre enforseden hem, *others labored* **36–37 gon ravysse,** *abduct* **40 in partye,** *a portion,* **todrowen,** *pulled at* **42 korven,** *slashed,* **torenten,** *tore apart* **44 tho clowtes,** *those pieces,* **arraced,** *torn* **46 weninge,** *thinking* **47 everydel,** *completely,* **In,** *among* **48 moche,** *much* **49 steppes,** *remnants,* **habite,** *clothing* **52 unkunninge,** *ignorant* **53 for,** *because* **55 yif,** *if* **58 straungeres,** *foreigners* (not Roman) **59 mightestow han knowen,** *you might have known* **61 over-olde,** *outdated,* **unsolempne,** *uncelebrated* **62 The whiche,** *these* **64 myne maneres,** *my* (Philosophy's) *methods* **65 unlyk,** *unfit,* **studies,** *inclinations* **66 forthi,** *therefore,* **owhtest,** *ought* **67 see,** *sea* **71 shrewes,** *wretches,* **al be,** *even though,* **oost,** *multitude* **72 to despise,** *to be despised* **73 ravyssed,** *carried way,* **fleetinge,** *transitory* **74 folyly,** *foolishly,* **lyhtly,** *easily* **75 oost,** *multitude* **76 as strenger,** *as if stronger* **77 ben ententyf,** *concern themselves* **78 sarpuleres,** *canvas sacks,* **sachels,** *satchels* **79 heye,** *high,* **syker,** *secure* **80 woode noyse,** *senseless noise* **81 warnestored,** *protected* **81 palis,** *fortified enclosure* **81 whider,** *where* **83 atayne,** *attain,* **ravyneres,** *thieves,* **henteres,** *seizers* **1 Meter 4. 1 cleer of,** *shining with,* **sad,** *steadfast* **2 ordinat,** *ordered,* **of levinge,** *in living* **3 prowde wierdes,** *proud fates,* **upriht,** *straight* **4 eyther,** *either* (good or bad), **cheere,** *demeanor* **5 descounfited,** *undisturbed* **6 manaces,** *menaces,* **commoevinge,** *causing commotion* **9 hihte,** *is called,* **writheth,** *spirals*

35ff. Epicuriens . . . Stoyciens, Epicureans (who taught that the good is pleasure) and Stoics (who taught that the good is self-control). Lady Philosophy represents Epicureanism and Stoicism as stealing portions of the totality of true philosophy—tearing her clothing—and using the words of Socrates to justify their arguments. **56 Anaxogore,** Anaxagoras, Greek philosopher (c.500–c.428 B.C.E.), exiled for theories of astronomy. **57 Socrates,** Greek philosopher (469–399 B.C.E.); his execution was the classic example of dying for the principles of true philosophy. **58 Zeno,** Greek philosopher (fifth century B.C.E.), tortured for seeking to defend his countrymen. **59 Senecciens,** followers of Seneca (c.3 B.C.E. –65 C.E.), the Roman teacher of Nero who was forced by his pupil to commit suicide. **60 Canyos,** Julius Canius (d. 40 C.E.), condemned by Caligula, who thought Canius shielded a plot against his life; see 1.pr4.183ff. **Sorans,** Barea Soranus (d. 66 C.E.), Roman senator, condemned to death by Nero for refusing to punish a provincial city. **1 Meter 4. 9 Vesevus,** Mount Vesuvius, Italian volcano, famous for burying Pompeii and other cities in 79 C.E.

smokinge fyres; ne the wey of thonder-lyht° that is wont° to smyten heye towres° ne shal nat moeve that man. Wharto thanne°, o wrechches, drede ye° tyrauntes that ben woode° and felonous° withowte any strengthe? Hope after nothing, ne drede nat, and so shaltow desarmen° the ire of thilke° unmyhty tyraunt. But whoso that, quakinge, dredeth or desireth thyng that nis nat stable of his ryht°, that man that so doth hath cast awey his sheld, and is remoeved from his place, and enlaceth him° in the cheyne with the which he may ben drawen.

Prose 4. Sentisne hec inquit.

"Felistow°," quod she, "thise thinges, and entren thei awht° in thi corage°? Artow° lik an asse to the harpe? Whi wepistow°, whi spillestow teeres? Yif thow abydest after° help of thi leche°, the byhoveth discovere° thi wownde."

Tho° I, that hadde gadered strengthe in my corage, answerede and seyde: "And nedeth it yit°," quod I, "of rehersinge° or of amonicioun°? And sheweth it nat inowh° by hymself° the sharpnesse of Fortune, that wexeth wood ayeins° me? Ne moeveth it nat the° to sen the face or the manere of this place? Is this the librarye which that thou haddest chosen for° a ryht certeyn sete to the° in myn hows, theras° thow desputedest ofte with me of the sciences of thinges towchinge devynyte° and mankynde? Was thanne myn habite swich° as now? Was my face or my cheere° swich as now, whan I sowhte° with the the secretes of nature, whan thou enformedest° my maneres and the resoun of alle my lyf to the ensaumple° of the ordre of hevene? Is nat this the gerdoun° that I referre° to the, to whom I have be obeysaunt?° Certes, thow confermedest by the mouth of Plato this sentence°, that is to seyn, that comune thinges or comunalitees weren blysful yif they that hadden studied al fully to wysdom governeden thilke thinges°, or elles yif it so byfille that the governoures of comunalites studieden to geten wysdom.

"Thow seydest ek by the mowth of the same Plato that it was a necessarye cause wise men to taken and desire the governaunce of comune thinges, for that° the governementes of citees yleft in the handes of felonous tormentours citesenes° ne sholde nat bryngen in pestelence and destruccioun to goode foolk. And therfor I, folwinge thilke° autorite, desired to putten forth in execucioun and in acte of comune° administracioun thilke° thinges that I hadde lerned of the° among my secre restingwhiles°. Thow and God that putte the in the thowhtes of wise foolk ben knowinge with me that nothing ne browhte me to maystrye or dignyte but the comune studie° of alle goodnesse. And therof comth it that bytwixen wikked foolkes and me han ben grevous descordes that ne myhten nat ben relesed by preyeres°; for this liberte hath the freedom of conscience, that the wraththe of moore myhty foolkes hath alwey ben despysed of me for° savacioun of ryht.

"How ofte have I resisted and withstonde thilke man that hyhte° Conigaste, that maade

11 thonder-lyht, *lightning* **12 wont,** *accustomed,* **heye towres,** *high towers* **13 Wharto thanne,** *why then* **14 drede ye,** *do you fear,* **woode,** *mad* **15 felonous,** *wicked* **17 shaltow desarmen,** *you will disarm,* **thilke,** *that* **20 stable of his ryht,** *properly steady* **22 enlaced him,** *binds himself* **1 Prose 4. 1 Felistow,** *do you feel* **2 thei awht,** *they at all,* **corage,** *spirit,* **Artow,** *are you* **3 wepistow,** *do you weep* **4 abydest after,** *wait for* **5 leche,** *physician,* **the byhoveth discovere,** *it is necessary for you to disclose* **7 Tho,** *then* **9 nedeth it yit,** *is it still in need,* **rehersinge,** *retelling* **10 amonicioun,** *reminding,* **inowh,** *enough* **11 hymself,** *itself,* **12 wexeth wood ayeins,** *grows furious against* **12–13 Ne moeveth it nat the,** *doesn't it compel you* **15 for,** *as* **16 sete to the,** *seat for you,* **theras,** *where* **18 towchinge devynyte,** *concerning divinity* **19 habite swich,** *clothing such* **20 cheere,** *disposition* **21 sowhte,** *sought* **22 enformedest,** *formed* **24 ensaumple,** *model* **25 gerdoun,** *reward,* **referre,** *attribute* **26 be obeysaunt,** *been obedient* **27 sentence,** *meaning* **28 commune thinges or communalitees,** *commonwealths* (Latin *res publicas*) **29–31 yif they . . . thilke thinges,** if those who had completely studied philosophy governed these commonwealths. **37 for that,** *so that* **38–39 felonous tormentours citesenes,** *wicked torturing inhabitants* **41 thilke,** *that* **43 comune,** *public,* **thilke,** *those* **44 of the,** *from you* **44–45 secre restingwhiles,** *private leisure* **48 comune studie,** *public pursuit* **52 relesed by preyeres,** *reconciled by pleading* **55 despysed of me for,** *rejected by me for the sake of* **57 hyghte,** *is named*

17 desarmen, C[2] reads "deserven." **1 Prose 4. 3 asse to the harpe,** an ass listening to a harp is a proverbial figure of dull insensitivity; see *TC* 1.731–35. **22–24 enformedest . . . of the ordre of hevene,** Boethius here refers to the time when Philosophy taught him to act in accord with the order of the heavens, a fundamental principle of neo-Platonic thought: man (the microcosm) must learn how to imitate the perfect order of the universe (macrocosm). **27–33 mouth of Plato . . . ,** *Republic* 5.473d. **34–41 same Plato . . . ,** *Republic* 1.347d. **57 Conigaste,** Cunigastus, a Goth, cited in Cassiodorus, *Variae* 8.28. C[2] spells "Coniugaste."

alwey assawtes° ayeins the prospre fortunes of poore feeble foolkes! How ofte ek have I put of° or cast owt him Trygwille, provost° of the kynges hows, bothe of the wronges that he hadde bygunne to don, and ek fully performed! How ofte have I covered and defended by the autorite of me put ayeins perils *(that is to seyn, put myn autorite in peril for)* the wrechched poore foolkes that the covetyse of straungeres, unpunysshed, tormented alwey with myseyses° and grevaunces owt of nowmbre! Never man ne drowh° me yit fro ryht to wronge. Whan I say° the fortunes and the richesses of the poeple of the provinces ben harmed or amenused° owther° by pryve raveynes° or by comune tributes° or cariages°, as sory was I as they that suffreden the harm. *(Glosa. Whan that Theodoric, the king of Gothes, in a dere yer° hadde his gerneres° ful of corn, and comaundede that no man ne sholde byen no corn tyl his corn were solde, and that at a grevous deere prys°, Boece withstood that ordinaunce and overcom it, knowinge al this the kyng hymself.)* Textus. Whan it was in the sowre° hungry tyme, ther was establisshed or cryed grevous and inplitable co-empcioun°, that men sayen wel it sholde gretly turmenten and endamagen al the province of Campaygne, I took stryf ayeins° the provost of the pretorie° for comune profit. And, the kyng knowinge of it, I overcom it, so that the co-empcioun ne was nat axed° ne tok effect. *(Co-empcioun is to seyn, comune achat° or byinge togidere, that were establyssed upon the poeple by swiche a manere imposiscioun, as who so bowhte a busshel corn, he moste yeve the kyng the fifte part.)*

"Paulyn, a counseiller° of Rome, the rychesses of the which Paulyn the howndes of the palays *(that is to seyn, the officeres)* wolden han devowred by hope and covetise, yit drowh° I him owt of the jowwes° of hem that gapeden. And forasmoche as° the peyne of the accusacioun ajuged byforn° ne sholde nat sodeynly henten° ne punisse wrongfully Albyn, a conseyler of Rome, I putte me ayeins the hates and indignaciouns of the accusor Cyprian. Is it nat thanne inowh isene° that I have purchased grete discordes ayeins myself? But I owhte be the moore assured° ayeins alle oothre foolk, that for the love of ryhtwisnesse° I ne reserved never° nothing to myself to hem-ward° of the kynges halle, by which I were moore siker°. But thorwh tho° same accusors acusinge I am condempned. Of the nowmbyr of the whiche acusors, oon Basilicis, that whilom° was chased owt of the kynges servise, is now compelled in accusinge of my name for nede of foreyne moneye°. Also Opylion and Gaudencius han° accused me, al be it so that° the justice regal° hadde whilom demed° hem bothe to go into exil for her° trecheryes and fraudes withowte nowmbyr. To whiche jugement they nolden nat° obeye, but defendeden hem by the sikernesse° of holy howses *(that is to seyn, fledden into sentuarye)*. And whan this was aperceyved to° the king, he comaundede that but° they voidede the cite of Ravenne by

---

58 assawtes, *assaults* **60 put of,** *thwarted,* **provost,** *chief officer* **68 myseyss,** *discomforts* **69 drowh,** *drew* **70 say,** *saw* **72 amenused,** *diminished,* **owther,** *either,* **pryve raveynes,** *private thefts* **73 comune tributes,** *public levies,* **cariages,** *taxes* **76 *dere yer*,** *lean harvest year,* ***gerneres*,** *storage bins* **78 *deere prys*,** *expensive cost* **81 sowre,** *bitter* **83 inplitable co-empcioun,** *unreasonable manipulation* **85–86 took stryf ayeins,** *challenged* **86 pretorie,** *Pretorian guard* **88 axed,** *required* **90 *achat*,** *purchase* **94 counseiller,** *consul* (elected official) **98 drowh,** *drew,* **jowwes,** *jaws* **99 forasmoche as,** *so that* **100 ajuged byforn,** *prejudged* (to be guilty) **101 henten,** *seize* **104 inowh isene,** *sufficiently seen* (apparent) **106 assured,** *secure* **108 ryhtwisnesse,** *justice,* **ne reserved never,** *never kept* **109 to hem-ward,** *against those* **110 siker,** *secure,* **thorwh tho,** *through those* **113 whilom,** *formerly* **115–16 for nede of foreyne money,** *because he is in debt* **116 han,** *have* **117 al be it so that,** *even though,* **regal,** *royal* **118 demed,** *judged* **119 her,** *their* **121 nolden nat,** *would not* **122 sikernesse,** *security* **124 aperceyved to,** *realized by* **125 but,** *unless*

60 Trygwille, Triguilla, known only from this reference. **74–80 *Glosa* . . . Textus,** indicates an inserted explanation or comment (i.e., a gloss) and then a return to the text itself. Not all glosses are so indicated in the manuscripts of *Bo,* but throughout this edition, they are in italics within parentheses. **75 *Theodoric*,** Theodoric the Great (c.454–526), Ostrogothic king who conquered much of Italy, although he maintained many Roman laws under his rule. He commanded the execution of Boethius. **85 Campaygne,** Campagna di Roma, a district around Rome. **89ff.** In the manuscripts, this gloss is misplaced to follow line 80. **94 Paulyn,** Paulinus, consul in 498; mentioned in Cassiodorus, *Variae* 1.23. **102–04 Albyn . . . Cyprian,** Boethius defended the senator Albinus against charges of treason made by Cyprian, a Roman official mentioned in Cassiodorus *Variae* 5.40–41. **113 Basilicis,** Basil; known with certainty only from this account, although perhaps the same Basil as in Cassiodorus *Variae* 4.22–23. **116 Opylion and Gaudencius,** Opilio, brother of Cyprian (see 102–04n above and Cassiodorus *Variae* 8.16); Gaudentius is otherwise unknown. C^2 spells "Caudensius." **123 *sentuarye*,** the ancient right of sanctuary, or protection in a holy place from criminal pursuit, was extended into late antiquity and the Middle Ages by Emperor Constantine I. **124 the king,** Theodoric, see 1.pr4.75n. **125 Ravenne,** Theodoric ruled from Ravenna.

certeyn day assigned, that men sholde merke hem on the forheved° with an hoot yren and chasen hem owt of the towne. Now what thing, semeth the°, myhte ben lykned° to this crwelte, for certes thilke° same day was received the accusinge of my name by thilke° same accusors. What may ben seid herto? Hath my studie and my kunninge° deserved thus, or elles the forseyde° dampnacioun of me made that hem° ryhtful acusors or no? Was not Fortune asshamed of this? Certes°, alle hadde nat Fortune° ben asshamed that innocens was accused, yit owte° she han had shame of the fylthe of myne accusours.

"But axestow in somme°, of what gylt I am accused? Men seyn that I wolde° save the compaygnye of the senatours. And desirest thow to heren in what manere? I am accused that I sholde han destorbed° the accusor to beren lettres, by whiche he sholde han maked° the senatoures gylty ayeins the kynges real° majeste. O Maysteresse°, what demestow° of this? Shal I forsake this blame°, that I ne be no shame to the°? Certes, I have wold° it *(that is to seyn, the savacioun of the senat),* ne I shal never leten to wilne° it; and that I confesse and I am aknowe°. But the entente of the accusor to be destorbed shal cese. For shal I clepe° it thanne a felonye or a synne that I have desired the savacioun of the ordre of the senat? And certes yit hadde thilke° same senat don by° me, thorw her decretes° and her jugementes, as thowh it were a synne or a felonye *(that is to seyn, to wilne the savacioun of hem).* But folye, that lieth° alwey to hymself, may not chaunge the merite of thinges. Ne I trowe° nat, by the jugement of Socrates, that it were leveful° to me to hide the sothe° ne assente to leesinges°. But certes, howsoever it be of this, I put it to gessen° or preisen° to the jugement of the and of wise foolk. Of whiche thing al the ordinaunce° and the sothe°, for as moche as foolk that ben to comen after owre dayes shullen knowen it, I have put it in scripture° and in remembraunce. For towching° the lettres falsly maked, by whiche lettres I am accused to han hoped the fredom of Roome, what aperteneth° me to speke therof? Of whiche lettres the fraude hadde ben shewed apertly°, yif I hadde had liberte for to han used° and ben at the confessioun of myne accusours, the whiche thing in alle needes hath gret strengthe. For what other fredom may men hopen? Certes, I wolde that som other freedom myhte ben hoped. I wolde thanne han answered by the wordes of a man that hyhte° Canyus; for whan he was accused by Gayus Cesar, Germeynes sone, that he (Canius) was knowinge and consentinge of a conjuracioun° ymaked ayeins him (Gayus), this Canyus answerede thus: 'Yif I hadde wist it, thou haddest nat wist° it.' In which thing sorwe hath nat so dulled my wit that I pleyne° oonly that shrewede° folk apareylen° felonies ayeins vertu, but I wondre gretly how that they may parforme° thinges that they han hoped for to don. For-whi°, to wilne° shrewednesse, that comth peraventure° of owre defaute°. But it is lyk a monstre° and a mervayle, how that in the present syhte of God may ben acheved and performed swiche° thinges as every felonous man hath conceyved in his thowht ayeins innocentes. For which

127 forheved, *forehead* **129 semeth the,** *seems to you,* **lykned,** *compared* **130 certes thilke,** *surely that* **132 thilke,** *these* **133 kunninge,** *knowledge* **134 elles the forseyde,** *else* (did) *the prior* **135 made that hem,** *make it so that they are* **136 Certes,** *certainly* **137 alle hadde nat Fortune,** *even if Fortune had not* **138 yit owte,** *yet ought* **140 axestow in summe,** *do you ask in sum* **141 wolde,** *wish to* **144 destorbed,** *hindered* **146 maked,** *proved* **147 real,** *royal,* **Maysteresse,** *mistress* **148 demestow,** *do you judge,* **forsake this blame,** *deny the charge* **149 the,** *you* **150 wold,** *wished* **151 leten to wilne,** *cease to desire* **152 am aknowe,** *do acknowledge* **154 clepe,** *call* **157 thilke,** *that,* **don by,** *done to* (i.e., condemned), **her decretes,** *their rulings* **160 lieth,** *lies* (deceives) **162 trowe,** *think* **163 leveful,** *lawful* **164 sothe,** *truth,* **leesinges,** *lies* **165 gessen,** (the) *evaluation* **166 preisen,** *appraisal* **167 ordinaunce,** *arrangement* **168 sothe,** *truth* **170 scripture,** *writing* **171 towching,** *concerning* **173 aperteneth,** *concerns* **175 apertly,** *openly* **176 for to han used,** *to use* (the confession) **182 hyhte,** *is named* **185 conjuracioun,** *conspiracy* **188 wist,** *known* **189 pleyne,** *lament* **190 shrewede,** *wicked,* **apareylen,** *prepare* **192 parforme,** *accomplish* **193 For-whi,** *because,* **wilne,** *desire* **194 peraventure,** *perhaps* **195 defaute,** *flaw,* **monstre,** *monstrosity* **197 swiche,** *such*

128 the towne, Hn reads "towne." **142 compaygnye of the senatours,** the Roman Senate ceased to exist in the sixth century, after having faded in effective power under imperial and then monarchial control. **152 I confesse . . . ,** in the original, Boethius questions his guilt rhetorically rather than asserting and acknowledging it. **159 or,** C² reads "and." **163–64 Socrates . . . ,** in Plato's *Republic,* 6.485c. **174 Of whiche lettres,** omitted in C². **183ff. whan he was accused . . . ,** see 1.pr3.60n. In Seneca, *De Tranquillitate Animi* (*On Tranquility of the Mind*), 14.4–10, Canus **(Canyus)** is nobly tranquil in the face of condemnation and death commanded by Emperor Caligula (**Gayus Cesar**); Seneca does not, however, include the quotation attributed here to Canus.

thing oon° of thy famyleres° nat unskylfully° axed thus: 'Yif God is, whennes comen wikkede thinges? And yif God ne is, whennes comen goode thinges?' But al° hadde it ben leveful° that felonous folk that now desiren the blod and the deth of alle goode men, and ek° of alle the senat, han willned° to gon and destroyen me, whom they han seyen° alwey bataylen and defenden goode men and ek al the senat, yit had I nat desserved of the faderes *(that is to seyn, of the senatoures)* that they sholden willne my destruccioun.

"Thow remembrest wel, as I gesse, that whan I wolde doon or seyen anything, thow thyself, alwey present, rewledest° me. At the cite of Verone, whan that the kyng, gredy of° comune slawhtre, caste him° to transporten° upon al the ordre of the senat the gylt of his real majeste°, of the whiche gylt that Albyn was accused, with how gret sykernesse° of peril to me deffendede I al the senat. Thow woost° wel that I seye soth°, ne I ne avauntede me° never in preysinge of myself. For alwey, whan any wyht° receyveth precious renoun in avauntinge himself of his werkes, he amenuseth° the secre° of his conscience. But now thou mayst wel seen to what ende I am comen for myne innocence: I receyve peyne of fals felonye for guerdon° of verray° vertu. And what open confessioun of felonye hadde ever juges so acordaunt° in crwelte *(that is to seyn, as myn accusinge hath)* that eyther errour of mannes wit or elles condicioun of fortune, that is uncerteyn to alle mortal folk, ne submittede° some of hem *(that is to seyn, that it ne enclinede som juge to han pite or compassioun)*? For althogh I hadde ben accused that I wolde brenne° holy howses and strangle° preestes with wykkede swerde, or that I hadde greythed° deth to alle goode men, algates° the sentence sholde han punysshed me present°, confessed or convict°. But now I am remewed° fro the cite of Roome almest fyve hundred thowsand paas°, I am withowte deffence dampned° to proscripcioun° and to the deth for the studie° and bowntes° that I have doon to the senat. But O wel ben they worthi of merite *(as who seyth, nay)*; ther myhte never yit non of hem be convict° of swich a blame as myne is! Of whiche trespas, myne accusours sayen° ful wel the dignite°, the whiche dignite, for° they wolden dirken° it with medlinge° of som felonye, they baren me on hand°, and lyeden° that I hadde polut° and defowled my conscience with sacrilege for coveytise of° dignete. And certes, thow thyself that are plaunted in me chasedest owt of the sege° of my corage alle coveytyse of mortal thinges; ne sacrelege ne hadde no leeve° to han a place in me byforn thyne eyen. For thow droppedest every day in myne eres and my thowt thilke° comaundement of Pictagoras, that is to seyn, men shal serve to Godde and not to goddes. Ne it was nat convenient ne no nede to taken help of the fowlest spirites—I, that thow has ordeyned and set in swiche excellence that thow makedest me lyk to God. And over this, the ryht clene secre chaumbre of myne hows° *(that is to seyn, my wyf)*, and the compaygnye of myn honest freendes, and my wyves fader, as wel holy as worthi to ben reverenced thorwh his owne dedes, deffenden me from alle suspecioun of swich blame. But O

---

200 oon, *one,* **famyleres,** *companions,* **unskylfully,** *unreasonably* **203 al,** *even if* **204 leveful,** *lawful* **206 ek,** *also,* **willned,** *desired* **207 seyen,** *seen* **214 rewledest,** *guided* **216 gredy of,** *eager for,* **caste him,** *decided* **217 transporten,** *impose* **218 gylt of his real majeste,** i.e., *guilt for treason against the king* **220 sykernesse,** *certainty* **221 woost,** *know,* **seye soth,** *speak truth* **222 avauntede me,** *boasted about myself* **223 wyht,** *person* **225 amenuseth,** *diminishes,* **secre,** *privacy* **228 for guerdon,** *as reward,* **verray,** *true* **230 acordaunt,** *unanimous* **234 submittede,** *restrained* **237 brenne,** *burn* **238 strangle,** *kill* **239 greythed,** *planned* **240 algates,** *nevertheless* **241 punysshed me present,** *sentenced me when I was present,* **convict,** *convicted* **242 remewed,** *removed* **243 paas,** *paces* **244 dampned,** *condemned* **245 proscripcioun,** *being an outlaw,* **studie,** *devotion* **246 bowntes,** *contributions* **249 convict,** *convicted* **250 sayen,** *see* **251 dignite,** *worth,* **for,** *because* **252 dirken,** *tarnish,* **medlinge,** *mixing* **253 baren me on hand,** i.e., accuse me, **lyeden,** *lied* **254 polut,** *polluted* **255 coveytise of,** *desire for* **257 sege,** *seat* **258–59 ne sacrelege ne hadde no leeve,** *nor did sacrilege have permission* **261 thilke,** *that* **269 hows,** *house*

201–03 Yf God is . . . , quotation not identified. The questions have been attributed to Epicurus in Lactantius's *De Ira Dei* (*Concerning God's Anger*), 13.21, but there the issue involves divine will and evil, not divine existence and evil, as here. **241 convict,** C^2 reads "committ." **243 fyve hundred thowsand paas,** five hundred miles; not literal. **246–47 But O wel ben they worthi of merite,** intended ironically. **262ff. Pictagoras . . . ,** Pythagorus (c.582–c.507), pre-Socratic Greek philosopher; the command to serve God is commonplace, although not attributable to Pythagorus specifically. Chaucer follows the French in adding the concern with polytheism. **264 was,** omitted in C^2. **269** ***my wyf,*** not in the Latin, where the meaning is private life. **271 wyves fader,** Symmachus, Boethius's father-in-law, was an accomplished builder and intellectual; like Boethius, he was executed by Theodoric.

malice, for° they that accusen me taken of° the, Philosophie, feyth of° so gret blame°! For they trowen° that I have had affinite to malefice° or enchauntement, by cause that I am replenysshed and fulfylled with thy techinges and enformed of thy maneres. And thus it suffiseth not oonly that thy reverence ne avayle° me nat, but that thow of thy fre wille rather be blemished with myn offencioun°. But certes, to the harmes that I have ther bytydeth° yit this encres of harm, that the gessinge° and the jugement of moche folk ne looken nothing to the desertes of thinges°, but oonly to the aventure° of fortune, and jugen that oonly swiche thinges ben purveyed of° God whiche that temporel welefulnesse° commendeth. *(Glose. As thus, that yif a wyht° have prosperite, he is a good man and worthi to han that prosperite; and who hath adversite, he is a wikked man and God hath forsake him, and he is worthi to han that adversite. This is the opinioun of some folk.)*

"And therof comth° that good gessinge° fyrst of alle thing forsaketh° wrechches. Certes, it greveth me to thinke riht now the diverse sentenses that the poeple seyth of me. And thus moche I seye, that the laste charge of contrarious fortune is this, that, whan that any blame is leyd upon a caytyf°, men wenen° that he hath desserved that° he suffreth. And I that am put awey fro goode men, and despoyled of dignitees, and defowled of my name by gessinge, have suffred torment for my goode dedes. Certes, me semeth° that I se the felonous covynes° of wikked men habownden° in joye and in gladnesse. And I se that every lorel° shapeth him° to fynde owt newe fraudes for to accuse goode foolk. And I se that goode men beth overthrowen° for drede° of my peril. And every luxurious° tourmentour dar doon° all felonye unpunysshed and ben excited° therto by yiftes. And innocentes ne ben not oonly despoyled of sikernesse° but of defence. And therfore me lyst° to cryen to God in this wyse:

Metre 5. O stelliferi conditor orbis.

"O thow makere of the whel that bereth the sterres, which that art° yfastned to thy perdurable chayer°, and tornest the hevene with a ravessing sweyh°, and constreynest the sterres to suffren° thi lawe so that the mone somtyme shyning wyth hir ful hornes°, meting with° alle the beemes of the sonne hir brother, hydeth the sterres that ben lesse, and somtyme whan the moone paale with hir derke hornes° aprocheth the sonne, leeseth hir lyhtes; and that the eve° sterre Hesperus, which that in the fyrste tyme of the nyht bryngeth forth hir colde arysinges, cometh eft ayein hir used° cours, and is paale by the morwe at the rysing of the sonne, and is thanne cleped° Lucyfer. Thow restreynest the day by shorter dwelling in the tyme of colde wynter that maketh the leeves falle. Thow dividest the swyft tydes° of the nyht whan the hoote somer ys comen. Thy myht atempreth° the varyauntes° sesons of the yer so that Zephirus the deboneyre° wynd brengeth ayein in the first somer sesoun the leeves that the wynd that hihte° Borias hath reft° away in autumpne *(that is to seyn, in the laste ende of somer)*, and the sedes° that the

274 for, *because,* **of,** *from* **275 feyth of,** *support through,* **blame,** *accusation* **276 trowen,** *think* **277 malefice,** *witchery* **281 avayle,** *helps* **282 offencioun,** *offense* **283 bytydeth,** *endured* **284 gessinge,** *opinion* **286 desertes of thinges,** *what is deserved* **287 aventure,** *chances* **288 ben purveyed of,** (that) *are foreknown* **289 welefulnesse,** *happiness* **290 wyht,** *person* **295 comth,** *it happens,* **gessinge,** *opinion* (of others) **296 forsaketh,** *abandons* **301 caytyf,** *wretch,* **wenen,** *believe* **302 that,** *what* **306 me semeth,** *it seems to me* **307 felonous covynes,** *evil bands,* **habownden,** *abound* **309 lorel,** *scoundrel,* **shapeth him,** *contrives* **311 overthrowen,** *overcome,* **drede,** *fear* **312 luxurious,** *wanton* **312–13 dar doon,** *dares to do* **313 excited,** *incited* **315 despoyled of sikernesse,** *deprived of security* **316 me lyst,** *I wish* **1 Meter 5. 2 art,** *is* **3 perdurable chayer,** *eternal throne* **4 ravessing sweyh,** *irresistible motion* **5 suffren,** *obey* **6–7 wyth hir ful hornes,** i.e., *full moon* (with her horns full) **7 meting with,** *reflecting* **10 derke hornes,** i.e., *crescent moon* (with her horns darkened) **12 eve,** *evening* **14–15 eft ayein hir used,** *again against her former* **17 cleped,** *called* **20 swift tydes,** *short hours* **22 atempreth,** *moderates,* **varyauntes,** *changing* **23 deboneyre,** *gentle* **25 hihte,** *is called,* **reft,** *ripped* **27 sedes,** *seeds*

275 Philosophie, C^2 reads "philosophre." **281 but that,** C^2 reads "but yf that." **1 Meter 5. 1–2 whel . . . sterres,** the orb to which the fixed stars are attached in the Ptolemaic universe. In the Latin original, the creator moves the stars directly, without the mediating sphere. **12 Hesperus,** the planet Venus, the evening star. **17 Lucyfer,** the planet Venus, the morning star. **23 Zephirus,** the west wind. **25 Borias,** Boreas, the north wind. **26–27 autumpne . . . ,** Chaucer may have added the gloss here and the one at 1.m6.17 because the word *autumn* was a borrowing from Latin and only coming into use at this time.

sterre° that hihte Arcturus sawgh° ben waxen° hyye cornes° whan the sterre Syryus eschaufeth° hem. Ther nis nothing unbownde fram his oolde° lawe, ne forleteth° the werke of his propre estat.

"O thow governour, governinge alle thinges by certeyn ende, whi refuses tow oonly to governe the werkes of men by dewe manere°? Whi suffresthow° that slydinge° fortune torneth so grete entrechaunginges of thynges, so that anoyous peyne° that sholde dewelly° punysshe felouns, punyssheth innocentes? And foolk of wykkede maneres sytten in heye chayres? And anoyinge foolk treden, and that unryhtfully, on the nekkes of holy men? And vertu, clere shyninge naturely, is hid in dirke derkenesses? And the ryhtful man bereth the blame and the peyne of the feloun. Ne the forsweringe° ne the fraude, covered and kembd° with a fals colour, ne anoyeth nat° to shrews°, the whiche shrewes, whan hem lyst° to usen her strengthe, they rejoysen hem to putten under hem the sovereyne kynges, whiche that poeple withowten nowmbre dreden?

"O thow, whatsoever thow be that knyttest alle bondes of thynges, looke on thise wrecchede erthes! We men that ben nat a fowle partye° but a fay re partye of so grete werk, we ben tormented in this see° of fortune. Thow governour, withdrawn and restreyne the ravessinge° floodes, and fastne and ferme° thise erthes stable with thilke° bonde by whiche thow governest the hevene that is so large."

Prose 5. Hic ubi continuato dolore delatraui.

Whan I hadde with a continuel sorwe sobbed or borken° owt thise thinges, she with hir chere pesyble° and nothing amoeved with my compleyntes seyde thus: "Whan I say the°," quod she, "soruful and wepinge, I wyste anon° that thow were a wrechche° and exiled, but I wyste never how ferre thine exil was yif thi tale nadde shewed° it me. But certes, al° be thow fer fro thy contre, thow nart nat° put owt of it, but thow hast fayled of thi wey and gon amys°. And yif thow hast levere° for to wene° that thow be put owt of thi contree, than hast thow put owt thyself rather than any other wyht° hath. For no wyht but thyself ne myhte never han don that to the. For yif thow remenbre of what contre thow art born, it nis nat governed by emperours, ne by governement of multitude, as weren the contres of hem of Athenes; but oo° lord and oo kynge *(and that is God that is lord of thy contre)* whiche that rejoyseth him of the dwelling of his cytesenes°, and nat for to put hem° in exil; of the whiche lord it is a soverayne° fredom to ben governed by the brydel of him and obeye to his justyce. Hastow foryeten thylke° ryht olde lawe of thi cite, in the whiche cyte it is ordeyned and establysshed, that for what wyht that hath lever fownden° therein his sete or his hows than elleswher he may nat be exiled by no ryht from that place? For whoso that is contened inwith° the palys° and the clos° of thilke cite, ther nis no drede that he may desserve to ben exiled. But whoso that leteth° the wyl for to enhabyte there, he forleteth° also to deserve to ben cytesein of thilke cyte. So that I sey that the face° of this place ne moveth me nat so mochel° as thine owne face, ne I axe° nat rather the walles of thi lybrarye, aparayled° and

---

28 **sterre,** *star,* **sawgh,** *saw,* **ben waxen,** *are grown into* 29 **hyye cornes,** *tall grains* 30 **eschaufeth,** *warms* 31 **olde,** *ancient,* **forleteth,** *escapes* 35 **by dew manere,** *in proper fashion* 36 **suffresthow,** *do you allow* (it), **slydinge,** *changeable* 38 **anoyous peyne,** *offensive pain,* **dewelly,** *properly* 46 **forsweringe,** *perjury* 47 **kembd,** *dressed up* 48 **anoyeth nat,** *is not offensive,* **shrewes,** *wicked people* 49 **hem lyst,** *they wish* 56 **partye,** *portion* 57 **see,** *sea* 59 **ravessinge,** *overwhelming,* **fastne and ferme,** *attach and make firm* 60 **thilke,** *that* 1 Prose 5. 2 **borken,** *barked* 3 **cheere pesyble,** *peaceful expression* 5 **say the,** *saw you* 6 **wyste anon,** *knew immediately,* **a wrechche,** *wretched* 8 **nadde shewed,** *had not showed* 9 **al,** *although* 10 **nart nat,** *aren't* 11 **amys,** *astray* 12 **thow hast levere,** *you prefer,* **wene,** *think* 15 **wyht,** *person* 20 **oo,** *one* 23 **cytesenes,** *citizens* 24 **hem,** *them* 25 **soverayne,** *highest* 27 **foryeten thylke,** *forgotten that* 29–30 **what wyht that hath lever fownden,** *whatever person who would rather establish* 33 **contened inwith,** *contained within,* **palys,** *fortifications* 34 **clos,** *enclosure* 36 **leteth,** *neglects* 37 **forleteth,** *abandons* 39 **face,** *appearance* 40 **mochel,** *much,* **axe,** *ask* 41 **aparayled,** *adorned*

28 **Arcturus,** a bright star in the constellation Boötes, especially noticeable in spring. 29 **Syryus,** Sirius, or Dog Star, the brightest star from earth, thought to indicate summer heat. 31 **elleswher,** C^2 reads "ellys were." 34 **and the clos,** omitted in C^1 and Hn.

wrowht° with yvory and with glas, than after the sete° of thy thowht, in whiche I put nat whilom° bookes, but I put that that° maketh bokes worthi of prys° or precyous, that is to seyn the sentense° of my bookes.

"And certeynly of thy desertes, bystowed in comune good, thow hast seyde soth°, but after° the multitude of thi goode dedes, thow hast seyd fewe. And of the honeste or of the falsnesse of thinges that ben aposed ayeins° the, thow hast remembred thinges that ben knowen to alle foolk. And of the felonyes and fraudes of thine acusours, it semeth the° have itowched° it forsothe ryhtfully and shortly, al myhten tho same thinges betere and moore plenteuousely ben cowth° in the mowthe of the poeple that knoweth al this. Thow hast ek blamed° gretly and compleyned of the wrongful dede of the senat, and thow hast sorwed for my blame, and thow hast wopen° for the damage of thi renoun° that is apayred°, and thy laste sorwe eschaufede° ayeins fortune and compleynest that gerdouns° ne ben evenlyche yolden° to the desertes of foolkes. And in the latere ende of thi woode muse°, thow preyedest that thilke pees° that governeth the hevene sholde governe the erthe. But for that° manye trybulacyouns° of affeccyouns° han assayled the, and sorwe and ire and wepinge to-drawen the° diversely, as thow art now feeble of thowht, myhtier° remedies ne shullen nat yit towchen the, for whiche we wol usen somdel lyhter medycynes, so that thilke° passyouns that ben woxen° harde in swellinge, by perturbacyouns° flowing into thi thowht, mowen wexen° esy and softe to receyven the strengthe of a more myhty and moore egre° medycene, by an esyer towchinge.

Metre 6. Cum Phebi radiis graue.

"Whan that the hevy sterre of the Cankyr eschaufeth° by the beemes of Phebus *(that is to seyn, whan that Phebus the sonne is in the sygne of the Cankyr)*, whoso yeveth thanne largely° his seedes to the feeldes that refusen to receive hem, lat him gon bygyled of trust that he hadde to his corn° to accornes of° okes. Yif thou wolt gadre vyolettes°, ne go thow nat to the purpure wode° whan the feeld, chyrkinge°, agryseth of° coolde by the felnesse° of the wynde that hyghte° Aquylon. Yif thow desyrest or wolt usen grapes, ne seke thow nat, with a glotonous hond, to streyne and presse the stalkes of the vyne in the ferst somer sesoun, for Bachus, the god of wyne, hath rather yeven his yiftes to autumpne *(the later ende of somer)*. God tokneth° and assygneth the tymes°, ablinge° hem to her propres offices°, ne he ne suffreth° nat the stowndes° whiche that himself hath devyded and constreyned to ben imedled° togydere. And forthy° he that forleteth° certeyn ordinaunce of doinge by overthrowinge wey° he ne hath no glade isswe° or ende of his werkes.

Prose 6. Primum igitur paterisne me pauculis.

"Fyrst woltow suffre° me to towche and assaye the estat of thi thowht by a fewe demaundes°, so that I may understonde what be the manere of thi curacioun°?"

"Axe° me," quod I, "at thi wille what thou wolt, and I shal answere."

42 wrowht, *made* **43 sete,** *seat* **44 whilom,** *formerly,* **that that,** *that which* **45 prys,** *value* **46 sentense,** *meaning* **48 soth,** *truth,* **after,** *concerning* **51 ben aposed ayeins,** *are brought against* **54 the,** *you* **55 itowched,** *considered* **57 cowth,** *known* **59 ek blamed,** *also accused* **62 wopen,** *wept,* **renoun,** *reputation* **63 apayred,** *slandered,* **eschaufede,** *heated up* **65 gerdouns,** *rewards,* **ne ben evenlyche yolden,** *are not evenly granted* **67 woode muse,** *passionate poem* **67–68 thilke pees,** *that peace* **69 for that,** *because,* **trybulacyouns,** *troublings* **70 affeccyouns,** *emotions* **71 to-drawen the,** *pull you apart* **73 myhtier,** *stronger* **75 thilke,** *these* **76 ben woxen,** *are grown* **77–78 perturbacyouns,** *disturbances* **78 mowen wexen,** *may grow* **79 egre,** *bitter* **1 Meter 6. 2 eschaufeth,** *grows warm* **4 largely,** *generously* **6–7 bygyled of trust that he hadde to his corn,** *cheated of the trust he put in his grain* **7 of,** *from* **8 wolt gadre vyolettes,** *wish to gather violets* **9 purpure wode,** *purple wood* **10 chyrkinge,** *rustling,* **agryseth of,** *trembles from* **11 felnesse,** *cruelty,* **hyghte,** *is called* **18 tokneth,** *distinguishes,* **tymes,** *seasons,* **ablinge,** *enabling* **19 propres offices,** *appropriate capacities,* **suffreth,** *allows* **20 stowndes,** *times* **21 imedled,** *mixed* **22 forthy,** *therefore,* **forleteth,** *abandons* **23 overthrowinge wey,** *rash action* **24 glade isswe,** *happy outcome* **1 Prose 6. 1 suffre,** *allow* **2 demaundes,** *questions* **4 curacioun,** *cure* **5 Axe,** *ask*

50 honeste, C[1] and Hn read "honestete." **1 Meter 6. Cankyr,** Cancer, the zodiacal sign of the Crab. The "heavy star" of Cancer may be the star cluster Praesepe. The sun is in Cancer in June. **6–7 lat . . . okes,** i.e., it is proper that he who unwisely puts faith in his seeds should have to eat acorns. **11 Aquylon,** Aquilo, the north wind.

Tho° seyde she thus: "Wheyther wenestow°," quod she, "that this world be governed by foolyssh happes° and fortunows° or elles that ther be in it any governement of resoun?"

"Certes," quod I, "I ne trowe nat in no manere that so certeyn thinges° sholden be moeved by fortunows folie, but I woot° wel that God, maker and mayster, is governour of his werk, ne never nas yit day that myhte put me owt of the sothnesse° of that sentence°."

"So is it," quod she, "for the same thing songe° thow a lytel her-byforn, and byweyledest° and byweptest that oonly men weren put owt of the cure° of God. For of alle oether thinges thou ne dowtedest nat that they nere governed by resoun. But owh°, I wondre gretly, certes°, why that thow art syk°, syn°, that thow art put in so holsom° a sentence. But lat us seken depper°: I conjecte° that ther laketh I not nere what°. But sey° me this: syn that thow ne dowtest nat that this world be governed by God, with which governayles° takestow heede° that it is governed?"

"Unnethe°," quod I, "knowe I the sentense° of thi questioun, so that I ne may yit answeren to thi demaundes."

"I nas nat deceyved," quod she, "that ther ne fayleth somwhat°, by whiche the maladye of thi perturbacyoun° is krept into thy thowt°, so as° the strengthe of the palys chyning° is open. But sey me this: remenbrest thow what is the ende° of thinges, and whider° that the entencioun° of alle kynde° tendeth?"

"I have herd it toold somtyme," quod I, "but drerynesse hath dulled my memorye."

"Certes°," quod she, "thow woost° wel whennes° that alle thinges ben comen and procedeth?"

"I woot wel," quod I, and answerede that God is bygynning of alle.

"And how may this be," quod she, "that syn° thow knowest the bygynninge of thinges, that thow ne knowest nat what is the ende of thinges? But swiche ben the customes of perturbacyouns, and this power they han, that they may moeve a man owt of his place *(that is to seyn, fro the stablenes and perfeccyoun of his knowinge).* But certes thei may nat al arace° him, ne alyene° him in al. But I wolde that thow woldest answere to this: remenbrestow that thou art a man?"

"Whi sholde I nat remenbre that?" quod I.

"Maystow nat telle me thanne," quod she, "what thinge is a man?"

"Axestow me nat," quod I, "wheither that I be a resonable mortal beest? I woot wel and I confesse wel that I am it."

"Wystestow° never yit that thow were any other thinge?" quod she.

"No," quod I.

"Now woot I," quod she, "oother° cause of thy maledye, and that ryht grete°. Thow hast left for° to knowen thiself, what thow art; thorwh whiche I have pleynly fownde the cause of thi maledye, or elles the entre° of recoeveringe of thin heele°. For-whi for° thow art confownded with foryeting° of thiself, forthy° sorwistow° that thow art exiled of thi propre goodes. And for thow ne wost° what is the ende of thinges, forthy demestow° that felonous and wykked men ben myhty and weleful°. And for thow hast foryeten by whiche governementes the world is governed, forthy wenestow° that thise mutacyouns° of fortune fleten° withowte governour. Thise ben grete

---

7 Tho, *then,* **Wheyther wenestow,** *do you believe* **9 foolyssh happes,** *silly occurrences,* **fortunows,** *accidental* **13 certeyn thinges,** *specific events* **14 woot,** *know* **17 sothnesse,** *certainty* **18 sentence,** *conviction* **20 songe,** *sang* **21 byweyledest,** *bewailed* **22 cure,** *care* **24 owh,** *oh!* **25 certes,** *indeed* **26 syk,** *sick,* **syn,** *since* **27 holsom,** *healthy,* **seken depper,** *seek deeper* **28 conjecte,** *suspect,* **not nere what,** *know not what* **29 sey,** *tell* **31 governayles,** *kind of control,* **takestow heede,** *do you consider* **33 Unnethe,** *scarcely,* **sentense,** *meaning* **37 ne fayleth somwhat,** *something is lacking* **38 perturbacyoun,** *disturbance* **39 thowt,** *thoughts,* **so as,** *just as* (when) **40 palys chyning,** *gap in the fort* **41 ende,** *purpose* **42 whider,** *where,* **entencioun,** *instinct* **43 kynde,** *nature* **46 Certes,** *surely,* **woost,** *know* **47 whennes,** *from where* **52 syn,** *since* **59 al arace,** *completely uproot,* **alyene,** *alienate* **68 Wystestow,** *don't you know* **71 oother,** *another* **72 ryht grete,** *quite serious* **73 left for,** *ceased* **75 entre,** *beginning* **76 thin heele,** *your health,* **For-whi for,** *because* **77 foryeting,** *forgetting* **78 forthy,** *therefore,* **sorwistow,** *you complain* **79 wost,** *know* **80 demestow,** *you think* **82 weleful,** *happy* **84 wenestow,** *you believe,* **mutacyouns,** *changes* **85 fleten,** *float*

1 Prose 6. **14 folie,** C^2, C^1, and Hn read "fortune," but the Latin is *temerita* and the French *folie.* **28 conjecte . . . not nere what,** the syntax here is quite unusual, but seems to be an attempt to render the sense of the Latin: *nescio quid abesse coniecto* (I think something is missing), with *nere* (weren't) emphasizing absence. **83 governementes,** C^2 reads "governement."

causes nat oonly to maledye, but certes° grete causes to deth. But I thanke the auctor and the makere of heele° that nature hath nat alle forleten the°. I have grete noryssinges of thin heele, and that is the sothe sentense° of governaunce of the worlde; that thow bylevest that the governinge of it nis nat subject ne underput° to the folie of thise happes aventurous°, but to the resoun of God. And therfor dowte the nothinge, for of this lytel sparke thin hete of lyf shal shyne°.

"But forasmeche as° it is nat tyme yit of fastere° remedies, and the nature of thowhtes deceyved° is this, that as ofte as they casten awey sothe opiniouns, thei clothen hem in false opynyouns, of which false opyniouns the dirkenesse of perturbacioun wexeth up° that confowndeth the verray° insyhte. And that dirkenesse shal I assaye° somwhat to maken thinne and wayk° by lyhte and menelyche° remedyes, so that after that the dirkenesse of deceyvinge desiringes is don awey, thow mowe° knowe the shyninge of verray lyht.

Metre 7. Nubibus atris condita.

"The sterres covered with blake clowdes ne mowen yeten° adoun no lyht. Yif the trowble wynde that hyht° Auster, turning and waluinge° the see°, medleth° the hete *(that is to seyn, the boylinge up fro the botme),* the wawes° that whilom° weren cleere as glas and lyk to the faire cleere dayes and brihte withstand anon° the syhtes° of men by the fylthe and ordure that is resolved°. And the fletinge° strem that royleth° down diversly fro hy mountaygnes is arested and resisted ofte tyme by the encountringe of a stoon that is departed° and fallen fram som roche. And forthy°, yif thow wolt looken and demen soth° with cleer lyht, and holden the wey with a ryht paath, weyve° thow joye, dryf fro the° drede, fleme° thow hope, ne lat no sorwe aproche *(that is to seyn, lat non of thise four passyouns overcomen the or blende° the),* for clowdy and dirke is thilke thowt°, and bownde with brydles, whereas° thise thinges reygnen."

Explicit liber primus.

BOOK 2

Incipit liber secundus.

Prose 1. Post hec paulisper obticuit.

Aftyr thys she stinte° a lytul; and, after that she hadde gadered by atempre° stillenesse myn atencioun, she seyde thus *(as who myhte seyn thus: after thise thinges she stynte a lytul; and whan she aperceyved° by atempre styllenesse that I was ententyf° to herkene° hir, she bygan to speke in this wise):* "Yif I," quod she, "have undyrstonden and knowen owtrely° the causes and the habyt° of thi maledye, thow languyssest and art defeted° for desire and talent of thi rather° fortune. She—that ilke° Fortune—oonly, that is changed, as thow feynest°, to the-ward°, hath perverted

86 certes, *truly* **88 heele,** *health* **89 forleten the,** *abandoned you* **90 sothe sentense,** *true meaning* **93 underput,** *subordinate* **93–94 happes aventurous,** *haphazard events* **96 shal shyne,** *will burn* **97 forasmeche as,** *because* **98 fastere,** *stronger,* **thowhtes deceyved,** *deluded thoughts* **102 wexeth up,** *increases* **103 verray,** *true* **104 assaye,** *attempt* **105 wayk,** *weak* **106 menelyche,** *moderate* **108 mowe,** *may* <u>1 Meter 7.</u> **2 ne mowen yeten,** *may not pour* **3 hyht,** *is called,* **waluinge,** *tossing* **4 see,** *sea,* **medleth,** *mixes* **5 wawes,** *waves* **6 whilom,** *once* **7–8 withstand anon,** *soon prevent* **8 syhtes,** *vision* **9 resolved,** *dissolved* **10 fletinge,** *flowing,* **royleth,** *rolls* **13 departed,** *separated* **14 forthy,** *therefore* **15 demen soth,** *judge truth* **16 weyve,** *abandon* **17 dryf fro the,** *drive from yourself,* **fleme,** *chase away* **19 blende,** *blind* **20 thilke thowt,** *that thought* **21 whereas,** *where* <u>2 Prose 1.</u> **1 stinte,** *paused* **2 atempre,** *temperate* **5 aperceyved,** *perceived* **6 ententyf,** *eager,* **herkene,** *listen to* **8 owtrely,** *utterly* **9 habyt,** *condition* **10 languyssest,** *weaken,* **art defeted,** *are overcome* **11 talent of thi rather,** *yearning for your earlier* **12 ilke,** *same* **13 feynest,** *pretend,* **to the-ward,** *toward you*

87 deth, C² reads "thi deth." <u>1 Meter 7.</u> **3 Auster,** the south wind. **22a *Explicit liber primus,*** Here ends Book One. <u>Book 2.</u> ***Incipit liber secundus,*** Here begins Book Two. **2 she,** C² reads "I."

the clernesse and the estat of thy corage. I understonde the feele-folde° colours and deceytes of thilke mervayles° monstre Fortune, and how she useth ful flateringe famylaryte with hem that she enforseth° to bygyle°, so longe tyl that she confounde with onsufferabele° sorwe hem that she hath left in dyspeyre unpurveyed°. And yif thow remenbrest wel the kynde, the maneres, and the desert° of thilke Fortune, thow shalt wel knowe that, as in hir°, thow nevere ne haddest ne hast ylost any fayr thinge. But, as I trowe°, I shal nat gretly travaylen to do the° remenbre on thise thinges. For thow were wont° to hurtelen° and despysen hir with manly wordes, whan she was blawndyssinge° and present, and purswedest hir with sentenses° that weren drawen owt of myn entre° *(that is to sayn, of myn enformacyoun)*. But no sodeyn mutacyoun ne bytydeth° nat withowte a manere° chaunginge of corages°, and so is it byfallen that thow art a lytel departed fro the pes of thi thowght.

"But now is tyme that thow drynke and ataaste° some softe and delitable° thinges, so that whan they ben entred within the, it mowe° maken wey to strengere drynkes of medicines. Com now forth therfore the suasioun° of swetenesse rethoryen°, whiche that goth oonly the ryht wey whil she forsaketh nat myne estatutes°. And with Rhetorice com forth Musyce, a damysel of owre hows, that syngeth now lyhter moedes° or prolacyouns°, now hevyere°. What eyleth the°, man? What is it that hath cast the into morninge and into wepinge? I trowe° that thow hast seyn som newe thinge and unkowth°. Thow wenest° that Fortune be chaunged ayein the°; but thow wenest wrong, yif thow that wene. Alwey tho° ben hir maneres; she hath rather kept, as to the-ward°, hir propre stabylnesse in the chaunginge of hirself. Ryht swich° was she whan she flatered the and deceyved the with unleffeful lykinges° of fals welfulnesse°. Thow hast now knowen and ataynt° the dowtous° or dowble vysage of thilke° blynde goddesse Fortune. She that yit covereth and wympleth hir° to oother foolkes hath shewed hir everydel° to the. Yif thow aprovest hir and thinkest that she is god°, use hir maneres° and pleyne the nat°. And yif thow agrysest° hir false trecherye, despyse and cast awey hir that pleyeth so harmfully. For she that is now cause of so mochel sorwe to the sholde ben cause to the of pes and of joye. She hath forsaken the, forsothe°, the whiche that never man may ben syker° that she ne shal forsake hym. *(Glose. But natheles, some bookes han the texte thus: Forsothe, she hath forsaken the, ne ther nis no man syker that she ne hath nat forsake.)*

"Holdestow° thanne thilke welefulnesse precyous to the, that shal passen? And is present Fortune dereworthe° to the, which that nis nat feythfulle for to dwelle; and whan she goth awey, that she bryngeth a wiht in° sorwe? For syn she may nat ben withholden° at a mannes wille, she maketh him a wrecche whan she departeth fro him. What oother thing is flyttinge Fortune but a maner° shewinge of wrecchednesse that is to comen? Ne it ne suffiseth nat oonly to loken on thynge that is present byforn the eyen of a man. But wysdom loeketh and amesureth° the ende of thinges; and the same chaunginge fram oon into another *(that is to seyn, from adversite into prosperite)* maketh that the manasses°

---

15 feele-folde, *many* **16 thilke mervayles,** *that marvelous* **18 enforseth,** *undertakes* **19 bygyle,** *deceive* **20 onsufferabele,** *insufferable* **21 dyspeyre unpurveyed,** *unprepared for despair* **23 desert,** *worth* **24 as in hir,** *with respect to her* **26 trowe,** *think* **27 travaylen to do the,** *work to make you* **28 wont,** *accustomed,* **hurtelen,** *attack* **30 blawndyssinge,** *flattering* **31 sentenses,** *opinions* **32 entre,** *beginning* **34 bytydeth,** *happens* **35 manere,** *kind of,* **corages,** *spirits* **39 ataaste,** *taste,* **delitable,** *pleasing* **41 mowe,** *might* **42 suasion,** *persuasion* **43 swetenesse rethoryen,** *rhetorical sweetness* **45 estatutes,** *statutes* **47 moedes,** *modes,* **prolacyouns,** *melodies* **48 hevyere,** *more somber,* **eyleth the,** *ails you* **50 trowe,** *think* **51 unkowth,** *unknown,* **wenest,** *believe* **52 ayein the,** *against you* **53 tho,** *those* **55 to the-ward,** *toward you* **56 Ryht swich,** *just so* **58 unleffeful lykinges,** *illegitimate pleasure,* **welfulnesse,** *happiness* **59 ataynt,** *attained,* **dowtous,** *unreliable* **60 thilke,** *that* **62 wympleth hir,** *hides her face in a wimple* (headcloth) **63 everydel,** *every part* **64 god,** *good,* **use hir maneres,** *be accustomed to her habits* **65 pleyne the nat,** *don't complain,* **agrysest,** *tremble at* **70 forsothe,** *truly* **71 syker,** *secure* **76 Holdestow,** *do you consider* **78 dereworthe,** *valuable* **80 wiht in,** *person into* **81 withholden,** *held firmly* **84 maner,** *kind of* **88 amesureth,** *gauges*

47 prolacyouns, C[2] reads "probasyons." **55 stabylnesse in,** C[2] reads "stabylnesse standeth in." **72 Glose,** see 1.pr4.74–80n.

of Fortune ne ben nat for to dreden, ne the flateringes of hir to ben desired. Thus, at the laste, it byhoveth the° to suffren with evene° wylle in paciense al that is don in-with° the floor of Fortune *(that is to seyn, in this world)*, syn thow hast ones° put thi necke under the yok of hir. For yif thow welt wryten° a lawe of wendinge° and of dwellinge° to Fortune, whiche that thow hast chosen freely to ben thi ladye, artow nat° wrongful in that, and makest Fortune wroth° and aspere° by thine inpacience, and yit thou mayst nat chaunge hir?

"Yif thow commyttest and bytakest° thi sayles° to the wynde, thow shalt be shoven° nat theder° that thou woldest°, but wheder that the wynde showveth the. Yif thow castest thi sedes into the feeldes, thow sholdest han in mynde that the yeres ben amonges° otherwhyle° plenteuous and otherwhile barayne. Thow hast bytaken° thiself to the governaunce of Fortune, and forthi° it bihoveth the to ben obeysaunt° the maneres of thi lady. Enforcest thow the° to aresten or withholden the swyftnesse and the sweyh° of hir turninge wheel? O thow fool of alle mortal fooles, yif Fortune bygan to dwelle stable, she cesede° thanne to ben Fortune!

Metre 1. Hec cum superba.

"Whan that Fortune with a prowd ryht hand hath torned hir chaunginge stowndes°, she fareth° lik the maneres of the boylinge Euripe. *(Glosa. Euripe is an arm of the see that ebbeth and floweth, and somtyme the strem is on o syde, and somtyme on the other.)* Text. She, crwel Fortune, casteth adown kynges that whilom weren ydrad; and she, deceyvable, enhanseth up the umble cheere of him that is descounfited°. Ne she neyther hereth ne rekketh of° wrecchede wepinges, and she is so hard that she laugheth and scorneth the wepinges of hem the whiche she hath maked wepe with hir free wille. Thus she pleyeth, and thus she proeveth hir strengthes, and sheweth a grete wonder to alle hir servauntes, yif that a wiht° is seyn weleful° and overthrowe° in an houre.

Prose 2. Vellem quidem pauca.

"Certes, I wolde pleten° with the a fewe thynges, usinge the wordes of Fortune. Tak hede now thyself, yif that she axeth° ryht. 'O thow man, wherfore° makest thow me gylty by thyne every dayes playninges°? What wronge have I don the? What goodes have I byreft the° that weren thyne? Stryf° or pleten wyth me byforn what juge that thow wolt of the possessyoun of rychesses or of dignitees, and yif thow mayst shewen me that evere any mortal man hath receyved any of tho thinges to ben his in propre°, than wol I graunte frely that alle thylke° thynges weren thyne whiche that thow axest. Whan that nature browht the forth owt of thi moder wombe, I receyved the naked and nedy of alle thinges, and I noryssede° the with my rychesses, and was redy and ententyf throw° my favour to susteyne the—and that maketh the now inpacyent ayeins me; and I envyrounde° the with alle the aboundance and shyninge of alle goodes that ben in my ryht°. Now it lyketh° me to withdrawen myn hand. Thow hast had grace as he that used of° foreyne° goodes; thow hast no ryht to pleyne the° as thowh thow haddest outrely° forlorn° alle thi thinges. Why pleynesthow thanne? I have don the no wrong.

91 manasses, *threats* **94 byhoveth the,** *is fitting for you,* **evene,** *steady* **95 in-with,** *within* **97 ones,** *once* **98 welt wryten,** *wish to write* **99 wendinge,** *traveling,* **dwellinge,** *remaining* **101 artow nat,** *aren't you* **102 wroth,** *angry,* **aspre,** *bitter* **104 bytakest,** *submits* **105 sayles,** *sails,* **shoven,** *pushed* **106 theder,** *where,* **woldest,** *wish* **109 ben amonges,** *are at times* **110 otherwhyle,** *sometimes* **111 bytaken,** *submitted* **112 forthi,** *therefore* **113 obeysaunt,** *obedient* **114 Enforcest thow the,** *do you strive* **115 sweyh,** *movement* **117 cesede,** *ceased* **2 Meter 1. 2 stowndes,** *hours* **3 fareth,** *acts* **10 descounfited,** *defeated* **11 rekketh of,** *cares about* **17 wiht,** *person,* **weleful,** *happy* **18 overthrowe,** *overthrown* **2 Prose 2. 1 pleten,** *debate* **3 axeth,** *asks* **4 wherfore,** *why* **5 every dayes playninges,** *daily complaints* **7 byreft the,** *taken from you* **8 Stryf,** *contend* **13 in propre,** *in personal possession* **14 thylke,** *those* **18 noryssede,** *nursed* **19 ententyf throw,** *attentive through* **21 envyrounde,** *surrounded* **23 ryht,** *control* **24 lyketh,** *pleases* **25 used of,** *made use of* **26 foreyne,** *external* **27 pleyne the,** *lament for yourself,* **outrely,** *utterly* **28 forlorn,** *lost*

4 Euripe, Euripus, a strait of sea between Boeotia (on the Greek mainland) and Euboea (a Greek island) where the currents change with the tides. **4–7** ***Glosa* . . . Text,** see 1.pr4.74–80n. **12 laugheth,** C^2 reads "lysseth." **2 Prose 2. 5 gylty,** C^2, C^1, and Hn read "gyltyf."

Rychesses, honours, and swyche° other thinges ben of my ryht. My servauntes knowen me for her° lady; they comen with me, and departen when I wende°. I dar wel affermen hardyly° that yif tho thinges of whiche thow pleynest that thow hast forlorn hadde ben thyne, thow ne haddest not lorn hem°. Shal I thanne, oonly, ben deffended° to usen my ryht?

'Certes, it is leveful to° the hevene to make cleere dayes, and after that to coeveren tho same dayes with dirke nyghtes. The yer hath ek leve to apayrelen° the visage of the erthe now with flowres and now with frut, and to confownden hem somtyme with reynes and with coldes. The see° hath ek his ryht to ben somtyme kalm and blawndyssinge° with smothe water, and somtyme to ben horible with wawes and tempestes. But the covetyse° of men, that may nat ben stanched°, shal It bynde me to ben stidefast°, syn that stide-fastnesse is unkowth° to my maneres? Swych is my strengthe, and this pley I pleye continuely. I torne the whirlinge wheel with the torninge cercle. I am glad to chaungen the lowest to the heyest, and the heyest to the lowest. Worth up°, yif thow wolt°, so it be° by this lawe, that thow ne holde nat that I do the wronge thogh thow dessende adoun whan the resoun° of my pley axeth it.

'Wistestow° nat how Cresus, the kyng of Lydyens, of whiche Kyng Cyrus was ful sore° agast° a lytel byforn, that this rewlyche° Cresus was kawht of Cyrus and lad to the fyr to ben brent°, but that a rayn dessendede down fro hevene that rescowede him? And is it owt of thy minde how that Pawlus, consul of Rome, whan he hadde taken the kyng of Percyens, weep pitowsly for the kaptivite of the self° kcynge? What other thing bywaylen the cryinges of tragedyes but oonly the dedes of Fortune, that with an unwar° stroke overtorneth realmes of grete noblye? *(Glose. Tragedye is to seyn, a dite° of a prosperite for a tyme that endeth in wrecchednesse.)*

'Lernedest nat thow in Greke, whan thow were yonge, that in the entre° or in the celere° of Jupyter ther ben cowched° two tonnes°, that on° is ful of good, that oother is ful of harm? What ryht hastow to pleyne, yif thow hast taken more plenteously of the goode syde *(that is to seyn, of my rychesses and prosperites)*, and what ek yif I ne be nat al departed fro the? What ek yif my mutabylyte yeveth the ryhtful cause of hope to han yit° beter thinges? Natheles dysmaye the nat in thi thowght; and thow that art put in the comune realme° of alle, ne desire nat to lyven by thin oonly propre ryht°.

Metre 2. Si quantas rapidis.

'Thowgh Plentee *(that is goddesse of rychesses)* hielde° adown with ful horn, and withdraweth nat hir hand, as many richesses as the see torneth upward sandes whan it is moeved with ravyssinge blastes, or elles as many rychesses as ther shynen bryhte sterres on hevene on the sterry nyhtes, yit for al that, mankynde nolde nat cese° to wepe wrecchede pleyntes°. And al be it so that God receyveth gladly her° preyers, and yeveth° them, as fool-large°, meche° gold, and aparayleth coveytous men with noble or cleere honours, yit semeth hem haven ygeten nothinge; but alwey her crewel ravyne°; devowringe al that thei han geten, sheweth oother gapinges *(that is to seyn, gapen and desyren*

30 swyche, *such* **32 her,** *their* **33 wende,** *go* **34 hardyly,** *surely* **37 lorn hem,** *lost them,* **ben deffended,** *be prevented* **39 leveful to,** *permissible for* **42 apayrelen,** *adorn* **45 see,** *sea* **46 blawndyssinge,** *favorable* **48 covetyse,** *greed* **49 stanched,** *stopped* **50 stidefast,** *unchanging* **51 unkowth,** *unknown* **56 Worth up,** *ascend,* **wolt,** *wish,* **so be it,** *as long as it is* **59 resoun,** *logic* **60 Wistestow,** *do you know* **61 ful sore,** *very sorely* **62 agast,** *frightened,* **rewlyche,** *pitiable* **64 brent,** *burned* **69 the self,** *that same* **71 unwar,** *unexpected* **73 dite,** *poem* **76 entre,** *threshold,* **celere,** *cellar* **77 cowched,** *stored,* **tonnes,** *wine casks* **78 on,** *one* **84 han yit,** *have again* **86 comune realme,** *universal realm* **87–88 thin oonly propre ryht,** *your own particular privilege* **2 Meter 2. 2 hielde,** *poured* **8 nolde nat cese,** *will not cease* **9 pleyntes,** *complaints* **10 her,** *their,* **yeveth,** *gives* **11 fool-large,** *overly generous,* **meche,** *much* **14 her crewel ravyne,** *their fierce greed*

37 Shal I thanne, C^2 reads "I shall thanne." **60 Cresus,** Croesus, king of Lydia (560–c. 546 B.C.E.) and fabled for his wealth, was defeated by Cyrus the Great of Persia; see *MkT* 7.2727ff. **66–69 Pawlus . . . ,** in Boethius's original, the reference is to King Perseus of the Macedonians, but Chaucer follows Trivet and the French version in this misunderstanding. **70–74 tragedyes . . . ,** compare *MkT* 7.1973. This is the earliest definition of *tragedy* in English. **77 Jupyter . . . two tonnes, a commonplace that derives ultimately from** Homer's *Iliad* 24.527–28. **2 Meter 2. 1–2 Plentee . . . with ful horn,** the figure is of the cornucopia, or horn of plenty, found in Greek mythology.

yit after mo rychesses). What brydles myhten wytholden, to any certeyn ende, the desordene° covetyse of men, whan ever the rather° that it fleteth° in large yiftes, the more ay° brenneth° in hem the thurst of havinge? Certes he that, quakinge and dredful, weneth° himselven nedy°, he ne leveth° nevermore ryche.'

Prose 3. Hiis igitur verbis si pro se.

"Therfor yif that Fortune spake with the for hirself in this manere, forsothe° thow ne haddest nat° what thow myhtest answere. And yif thow hast anythinge wherwith thow mayst ryhtfully defenden thy compleynt, it byhoveth the° to shewen it, and I wol yeven thee spase° to tellen it."

"Certeinly," quod I thanne, "thise beth fayre thinges, and enoynted with hony swetenesse of rethorike and musyke; and oonly whil thei ben herd° they ben dylycious, but to wreches° is a depper° feelinge of harm *(this is to seyn, that wrecches feelen the harmes that they suffren more grevously than the remedies or the delytes of thise wordes mowen° gladen or comforten hem)* so that whan thise thinges stynten° for to sowne° in eres, the sorwe that is inset greveth the thowght,"

"Ryht so is it," quod she. "For thise ne ben yit none remedyes of thi maledye, but they ben a maner noryssinges° of thi sorwes yit rebel° ayein° thi curacioun. For whan that tyme is, I shal moeve° swych thinges that percen° hemself depe. But natheles°, that° thow shalt nat wylne° to leten° thiself a wrecche, hastow foryeten the nowmber and the manere of thi welefulnesse°? I hoolde me° stylle how that the soverane° men of the cyte token the in cure° and kepinge, whan thow were orphelin of° fader and moder, and were chosen in affynite° of prinses of the cyte. And thow begunne rather to be leef° and deere than forto ben a neysshebour°, the whiche thing is the moost precyous kynde of any propinquite° or alyaunce° that may ben. Who is it that ne seyde tho° that thow were ryht weleful°, with so grete a nobleye° of thi fadyres-in-lawe, and with the chastete of thi wyf, and with the oportunite and noblesse of thi masculyn chyldren *(that is to seyn, thy sones)*? And over al this—me lyste° to passen° the comune thinges—how thow haddest in thi yowthe dygnites that weren werned° to oolde men. But it delyteth me to comen now to the singuler° uphepinge° of thi welfulnesse. Yif any frute of mortal thinges may han any weyhte or pris° of welfulnesse, myhtestow ever foryeten, for any charge° of harm that myhte befalle, the. remembraunce of thilke° day that thow saye° thy two sones maked conseileres, and ilad° togedere fro thin howse under so greet asemble of senatoures and under the blythenesse° of peeple, and whan thow saye hem set in the court in here chayeres of dignitees? Thow, rethoryen° or pronouncere of kynges preysinges, desservedest glorye of° wit and of eloquence whan thow, syttinge bitwyen thy two sones conseyleres, in the place that hihte circo°, fulfyldest° the abydinge° of the multitude of poeple that was sprad abowten the with so large preysinge and laude° as men syngen in victories. Tho yave° thow wordes to Fortune, as I trowe° *(that is to seyn, tho feffedest thow° Fortune with glosinge° wordes and deceyvedest hir)* whan she acoyede° the and noryssede the as hir owne delyces°.

---

18 desordene, *immoderate* **19 rather,** *more* **20 fleteth,** *floats,* **ay,** *always* **21 brenneth,** *burns* **22 weneth,** *believes* **23 nedy,** *needy,* **ne leveth,** *lives not* **2 Prose 3. 2 forsothe,** *truly* **3 nat,** *nothing* **6 it byhoveth the,** *it is necessary for you* **7 spase,** *space* **11 ben herd,** *are heard* **12 wreches,** *sorrowful people,* **depper,** *deeper* **15 mowen,** *may* **17 stynten,** *cease,* **sowne,** *sound* **21 maner noryssinges,** *kind of nursing* **22 yit rebel,** *still rebellious,* **ayein,** *against* **23 moeve,** *encourage* **24 percen,** *penetrate* **25 natheles,** *nonetheless,* **that,** *so that,* **wylne,** *wish* **26 leten,** *consider* **28 welefulnesse,** *happiness,* **hoolde me,** *remember,* **soverane,** *principal* **29 cure,** *care* **30 orphelin of,** *deprived of* **31–32 chosen in affynite,** *allied by marriage* **33 leef,** *beloved* **34 neysshebour,** *neighbor* **36 propinquite,** *relationship,* **alyaunce,** *alliance* **37 tho,** *then* **38 ryht weleful,** *truly happy,* **nobleye,** *nobility* **42–43 me lyste,** *I want* **43 passen,** *bypass* **45 werned,** *denied* **46 singuler,** *special* **47 uphepinge,** *culmination* **48 pris,** *value* **50 charge,** *burden* **51 thilke,** *that* **52 saye,** *saw* **53 ilad,** *led* **55 blythenesse,** *celebration* **57 rethoryen,** *orator* **59 of,** *for* **61 highte circo,** *is called the Circus,* **fulfyldest,** *satisfied* **62 abydinge,** *expectations* **64 laude,** *praise* **64 Tho yave,** *then gave* **65 trowe,** *believe* **66 *feffedest thow,*** *you endowed,* **glosinge,** *deceiving* **67 acoyede,** *soothed* **68 delyces,** *favorite*

2 Prose 3. **23 moeve,** C[1] reads "moeve and ajuste." **61 circo,** the Roman Circus, usually associated with sports, here means the Senate House. The reading is from Hn; other manuscripts read "circo and."

Thow bar away of° Fortune a yifte *(that is to seyn, swiche gerdoun°)* that she never yaf to pryve man°. Wilt thow therfor lye a rekeninge° with Fortune? She hath now twyncled° fyrst upon the with wyckede eye. Yif thow consydere the nowmbre and the manere of thy blysses and of thy sorwes, thow mayst nat forsaken that thow art yit blysseful. For yif thow therfor wenest° thiself nat weleful°, for° thynges that tho° semeden joyful ben passed, ther nis nat whr° thow sholdest wene thyself a wrecche, for thinges that semen now sorye passen° also.

"Art thow now comen fyrst°, a sodeyn gest°, into the shadwe or tabernacle° of this lyf? Or trowestow° that any stedefastnesse° be in mannes thinges, whan ofte a swyft howre dyssolvede the same man *(that is to seyn, whan the sowle departeth fro the body)*? For althowgh that selde° is ther any feith that fortunous° thinges wolen dwellen°, yit natheles the laste day. of a mannes lyf is a manere° deth to Fortune, and also to thilke that° hath dwelt. And therfor what wenestow that recke°, yif thow forlete° hir in deyinge°, or elles that she *(Fortune)* forlete the in fleinge awey?

Metre 3. Cum polo Phebus.

"Whan Phebus *(the sonne)* bygynneth to spreden his cleernesse° with rosene charyettes°, thanne the sterre, ydymmed, paleth hir white cheeres° by the flambes of the sonne that overcometh the sterre-lyght. *(This is to seyn, whan the sonne is rysen the day-sterre° wexeth° paale, and leseth hir lyht for the grete bryhtnesse of the sonne.)* Whan the wode wexeth rody° of rosen flowres in the fyrst somer sesoun thorwh the brethe of the wynde Zepherus that wexeth warm, yif the clowdy wynde Auster blowe fellyche°, than goth awey the fairenesse of thornesse°. Ofte the see is cleer and kalm, withowte moevinge floedes; and ofte the horyble wynd Aquilon moeveth boylinge tempestes and over-whelveth° the see. Yif the forme of this worlde is so selde° stable, and yif it turneth by so many entrechaunginges, woltow° thanne trusten in the towmblinge fortunes of men? Woltow trowen° on flettinge° goodes? It is certeyn and establyssed by lawe perdurable° that nothinge that is engendred° nys stedefast ne estable°."

Prose 4. Tum ego vera inquam.

Thanne seyde I thus: "O norice° of alle vertuus, thow seyst ful soth°; ne I may nat forsake° the ryht swyfte cours of my prosperiten *(that is to seyn, that prosperite ne be comen to me wonder swyftly and sone)*. But this is a thinge that gretely smerteth° me whan it remembreth me°. For in alle adversyte of fortune, the moost unsely° kynde of contrarious fortune is to han ben weleful°."

"But that thow," quod she, "abyest° thus the tormentes of thy false opynioun, that maystow nat ryhtfully blamen ne aretten° to thinges *(as who seyth, for thow hast yit many habundaunce of thinges)*. Text. For al be it so that the ydel name of aventurous welefulnesse° moeveth° the now, it is leefful° that thow rekne° with me of how manye grete thinges thow hast yit plente. And therfor, yif that thilke° thinge that thow haddest for° moost precyous in al thi rychesse of fortune be kept to the yit, by the grace of God, unwemmed° and undefowled, maystow thanne pleyne° ryhtfully upon the meschef of Fortune, syn° thow hast yit thy beste thinges? Certes, yit leveth° in good poynt° thilke° precious

69 of, *from* **70 swiche gerdoun,** *such reward* **71 pryve man,** *private citizen* **71–72 lye a rekeninge,** *claim a debt* **72 twyncled,** *winked* **77 wenest,** *think,* **weleful,** *happy* **78 for,** *because,* **tho,** *then* **79 whi,** *reason* **81 passen,** *will pass* **82 fyrst,** *for the first time,* **sodeyn gest,** *sudden guest* **83 tabernacle,** *canopy* **84 trowestow,** *do you think,* **stedefastenesse,** *stability* **88 selde,** *seldom,* **fortunous,** *fortuitous* **89 dwellen,** *remain* **90 manere,** *kind of* **91 thilke that,** *that which* **92 wenestow that recke,** *do you think it matters* **93 forlete** *abandon,* **deyinge,** *dying* 2 Meter 3. **2 cleernesse,** *brightness,* **rosene charyettes,** *rosy chariots* **4 cheeres,** *faces* **6 day-sterre,** *Venus* (the morning star) **7 wexeth,** *becomes* **8 rody,** *reddish* **12 fellyche,** *fiercely* **13 thornesse,** *hawthorns* **16 over-whelveth,** *turns over* **17 selde,** *seldom* **19 woltow,** *will you* **21 trowen,** *trust,* **flettinge,** *fleeting* **22 perdurable,** *eternal* **23 engendred,** *born,* **estable,** *stable* 2 Prose 4. **1 norice,** *nurse* **2 soth,** *truly* **3 forsake,** *deny* **6 smerteth,** *pains* **6–7 it remembreth me,** *I recall it* **8 unsely,** *unfortunate* **9 weleful,** *happy* **10 abyest,** *suffers* **12 aretten,** *attribute* **15 aventurous welefulnesse,** *accidental happiness* **16 moeveth,** *encourages,* **leefful,** *appropriate* **17 rekne,** *count* **19 thilke,** *those,* **haddest for,** *enjoyed as* **22 unwemmed,** *unblemished* **23 pleyne,** *complain* **24 syn,** *since* **25 yit leveth,** *still lives,* **poynt,** *condition,* **thilke,** *that*

87–88 althowgh that, C^2 reads "al that thowgh that." **88 fortunous,** C^2 reads fortune; C^2, "fortunes." **10 Zepherus,** the west wind. **12 Auster,** the south wind. **15 Aquilon,** the north wind. 2 Prose 4. **5–9** This sentiment is echoed in *TC* 3.1625–26 and in Dante's *Inferno* 5.121–23. **14 Text,** see 1.pr4.74–80n. **17 grete,** omitted in C^1.

honour of mankynde, Symacus, thy wyves fader, which that is a man maked alle of sapyence° and vertu, the whiche man thow woldest byen° redely with the pris° of thin owne lyf. He bewayleth the wronges that men don to the, and nat for hymself, for he leveth° in sykernesse° of any sentences put ayeins him. And yit lyveth thy wyf, that is atempre° of wyt°, and passinge° oother wymmen in clennesse of chastete; and for I wol closen° shortely hir bownte°, she is lik to hir fader. I telle the° wel that she lyveth loth° of this lyf, and keepeth to the oonly hir goost°, and is al maat° and overkomen by wepinge and sorwe for desyr of the, in the wheche, thing oonly I moot° graunten that thi welefulnesse is amenyssed°. What shal I seyn ek of thi two sones conseylours, of whiche, as of chyldren of her age, ther shyneth the lykenesse of the wyt of her fader or of her eldefader°? And syn° the sovereyn cure° of alle mortel folk is to saven hir owen lyves, O how weleful art thow yif thow knowe thy goodes! For yit ben ther thinges dwelled to the-ward° that no man dowteth that they ne ben more dereworthe° to the than thin owen lyf. And forthy° drye thy teeres, for yit nis nat everych fortune al hateful to the-ward, ne over gret tempest hath nat yit fallen upon the, whan that thyn ancres eleven faste°, that neyther wolen suffren the counfort of this tyme present ne the hope of tyme cominge to passen ne to faylen."

"And I preye," quod I, "that faste moten° they halden; for whyles that they halden, howsoever that thinges ben, I shal wel fleeten° forth and escapen. But thow mayste wel sen how grete aparayles° and aray that me lakketh, that ben passed away fro me."

"I have somwhat avaunsed° and forthered the," quod she, "yif that thow anoye° nat, or forthinke° nat of al thi fortune *(as who seyth, I have somwhat conforted the, so that thow tempest° the nat thus with al thi fortune, syn° thow hast yit thi beste thinges).* But I may nat suffren° thi delices°, that pleynest so wepinge and angwissous°, for that° ther lacketh somewhat to thi welefulnesse°. For what man is so sad°, or of so parfyt° welefulnesse, that he ne stryveth and pleyneth on som halve° ayen° the qualite of his estat? Forwhy° ful angwissous thing is the condysyoun of mannes goodes, for eyther it comth nat altogydere to a wyht° or elles it last nat perpetuel. For sum man hath grete rychesses, but he is ashamed of his ungentel lynage°, and som is renowned of noblesse of kynrede°, but he is enclosed in so grete angwysshe of nede of thinges that him were levere° that he were unknowe. And som man haboundeth° bothe in rychesse and noblesse, but yit he bewayleth his chaste lyf for he ne hath no wyf. And som man is wel and selyly ymaryed°, but he hath no chyldren and noriseth° his rychesses to the eyres° of strange foolkes. And som man is gladed with chyldren, but he weepeth ful sory for the trespace° of his sone or of his dowter. And for this ther ne acordeth no wyht lyhtly° to the condycioun of his fortune; for alwey to every man ther is in somwhat that, unassaied°, he ne wot° nat, or elles he dredeth that° he hath asayed. And adde this also, that every weleful° man hath a ful delycat° feelinge so that but yif alle thinges byfalle at his owne wyl, for he is inpacyent or is nat used to han non adversyte, anon° he is throwen adoun for every litul thinge. And ful litul thinges ben tho that withdrawen the somme° or the perfeccyoun of blysfulnesse fro hem that ben moost fortunat. How many men, trowestow°, wolden demen° hemself to ben almoost in hevene yif they myhten atayne to the leest party° of the

28 sapyence, *wisdom* **29 byen,** *pay for,* **pris,** *cost* **32 leveth,** *lives,* **sykernesse,** *safety* **34 atempre,** *temperate,* **wyt,** *mind,* **passinge,** *surpassing* **36 closen,** *summarize,* **bownte,** *goodness* **37 the,** *you,* **loth,** *displeased* **38 keepeth to the oonly hir goost,** *keeps her spirit only for you* **39 maat,** *miserable* **41 moot,** *may* **42 amenyssed,** *diminished* **46 eldefader,** *grandfather,* **syn,** *since,* **sovereyn cure,** *principal cares* **49–50 dwelled to the-ward,** *remaining to you* **51 dereworthe,** *precious* **52 forthy,** *therefore* **55 ancres eleven faste,** *anchors hold tightly* **59 moten,** *may* **61 fleeten,** *float* **63 aparayles,** *belongings* **65 avaunsed,** *advanced* **66 anoye,** *trouble* **67 forthinke,** *regret* **68 *tempest*,** *disturb* **69 *syn*,** *since* **70 suffren,** *allow* **71 delices,** *self-indulgence* **72 angwissous,** *anxiety ridden,* **for that,** *because* **73 welefulnesse,** *happiness,* **sad,** *stable* **74 parfyt,** *perfect* **75 halve,** *side,* **ayen,** *against* **76 Forthy,** *therefore* **78 wyht,** *person* **81 lynage,** *lineage* **82 kynrede,** *kindred* **83 him were levere,** *he would rather* **85 haboundeth,** *abounds* **87 selyly ymaryed,** *happily married* **88 noriseth,** *increases* **89 eyres,** *heirs* **91 trespace,** *offenses* **93 wyht lyhtly,** *person easily* **95 unassaied,** *untried,* **wot,** *knows* **96 that,** *what* **97 weleful,** *happy* **98 delycat,** *sensitive* **101 anon,** *soon* **103 somme,** *sum* **105 trowestow,** *do you believe,* **demen,** *think* **107 party,** *portion*

26 Symacus, Symmachus; see 1.pr4.271n.

remnaunt of thi fortune? This same place that thow clepest° exil is contre° to hem that enhabyten heere, and forthi° nothing is wrecched but whan thow wenest° hit *(as who seyth, thow thyself, ne no wyht elles°, nis a wrechche, but whan he weneth hymself a wrechche by reputacoun° of his corage°).* And ayeinward°, alle fortune is blisful to a man by the egreablete° or by the egalyte° of him that suffreth° hit.

"What man is that that is so weleful that nolde changen his estat whan he hath lost pacience? The swetnesse of mannes welefulnesse is sprayned° with many beternesses°; the whiche welefulnesse, althowgh it seme swete and joyful to hem that useth hit, yit may it nat ben withholden° that it ne goth away whan it woole°. Thanne is it wel sene how wrecched is the blysfulnesse of mortal thinges, that neyther it dureth perpetuel° with hem that every fortune receiven agreabley or egaly, ne it delyteth nat in al° to hem that ben angwissous°. O ye mortal folk, what° seke ye thanne blysfulnesse owt of yowrself whiche that is put in yourself? Erroure and folye confowndeth yow.

"I shal shewe the shortely the poynt° of sovereyne° blysfulnesse. Is ther anythinge more precyous to the than thiself? Thow wolt answere nay. Thanne yif hit so be that thow art myhty over thiself *(that is to seyn, by tranquillite of thy sowle),* than hast thow thinge° in thi power that thow noldest never leesen°, ne Fortune ne may nat beneme it the°. And that thow mayst knowe that blyssefulnesse ne may nat standen in thinges that ben fortunous° and temporel, now understonde and gadere it togidere thus: yif blisfulnesse be the sovereyn good of nature that lyveth by resoun, ne thilke thinge nis nat° sovereyn good that may be taken awey in any wyse, for more worthi thinge and more digne° is thilke° thinge that may nat ben take awey—than sheweth it wel, that the unstablenesse of fortune may nat atayne° to receyven verray° blysfulnesse. And yit moreover, what° man that this towmbling welefulnesse ledeth°, eyther he woot° that it is chaungeable or elles he woot hit nat. And yif he woot it nat, what blysful fortune may ther ben in the blyndnesse of ignorance? And yif he wot that it is chaungeable, he moot° alwey ben adrad° that he ne lese that thinge that he ne dowteth nat but that he may leesen hit *(as who seyth, he mot ben alway agast lest he leese that he wot wel he may leese it°);* for which the continuel drede that he hath ne suffreth° him nat to ben weleful, or elles yif he leese it, he weneth° to be dyspysed° and forleten°. Certes ek°, that is a ful lytul° good that is born with evene herte° whan it is lost *(that is to seyn, that men do no more fors of° the lost than of the havinge).* And for as meche° as thow thiself art he to whom it hath ben shewed and proved by ful manye demonstracyouns, as I wot° wel, that the sowles of men ne mowe° nat deyen in no wise, and ek syn° it is cleer and certeyn that fortunous welefulnesse° endeth by the deth of the body, it may nat ben dowted that yif that deth may take awey blysfulnesse, that alle the kynde of mortal thinges ne dessendeth into wrecchednesse by the ende of the deth°. And syn we knowen wel that many a man hath sowht° the frut of blysfulnesse nat oonly with suffringe of deth but ek with suffringe of peynes and tormentes, how myhte thanne this present lyf maken men blysful, syn that whan thilke selve° lyf is ended it ne maketh foolkes no wrecches?

---

109 clepest, *call,* **contre,** *native country* **110 forthi,** *therefore* **111 wenest,** *think* **112 *wyht elles,*** *other person* **114 *reputacoun,*** *opinion,* ***corage,*** *spirit,* **ayeinward,** *conversely* **115 egreablete,** *agreeableness* **116 egalyte,** *equanimity,* **suffreth,** *endures* **120 sprayned,** *sprinkled,* **beternesses,** *bitternesses* **123 withholden,** *preserved* **124 woole,** *wishes* **126 dureth perpetuel,** *remains perpetually* **128 in al,** *completely* **129 angwissous,** *anxiety ridden,* **what,** *why* **133 poynt,** *apex* **134 sovereyne,** *ultimate* **138 thinge,** *something* **139 leesen,** *lose* **140 beneme it the,** *take it from you* **143 fortunous,** *fortuitous* **146 ne thilke nis nat,** *no thing is* (the) **148 digne,** *noble,* **thilke,** *that* **151 atayne,** *be sufficient,* **receyven verray,** *achieve genuine* **152 what,** *whatever* **153 ledeth,** *leads* **154 woot,** *knows* **158 moot,** *must,* **adrad,** *fearful* **161–62 *lest he leese . . . he may leese it,*** *for fear that he will lose what he knows well he can lose* **163 suffreth,** *allows* **164 weneth,** *thinks,* **dyspysed,** *scorned* **165 forleten,** *deserted,* **Certes ek,** *certainly also,* **ful lytul,** *very minor* **166 born with evene herte,** *treated with steady heart* **167 *do no more fors of,*** *care no more for* **168 meche,** *much* **171 wot,** *know* **172 mowe,** *might* **173 syn,** *since* **173–74 fortunous welenesse,** *transitory happiness* **177–78 the kynde of mortal thinges . . . of the dethe,** *the species of mortal things will fall into misery through death* **180 sowht,** *sought* **184 thilke selve,** *that same*

110 is, omitted in C^2, C^1, and Hn, but the Latin is *est.* **113 reputacoun,** C^2 reads "reputasyn."

Metre 4. Quisquis volet perhennem cautus.

"What maner° man, stable and waar°, that wole° fownden him° a perdurable sete°, and ne wole nat ben cast down with the lowde blastes of the wynd Eurus, and wole despyse the see manasinge° with floodes, lat him eschewen° to bylde on the cop° of the mountaygne or in the moyste sandes. For the felle° wynd Auster tormenteth the cop of the montaygne with alle his strengthes, and the lause° sandes refusen to beren the hevy wyhte°. And forthy°, if thow wolt fleen the perylous aventure *(that is to seyn, of the worlde)*, have mynde certeynly to fychchen thin hows° of a merye° site in° a lowh stoon°. For althowgh the wynde, trowblinge the see, thondre with overthrowinges, thow that art put in quiete, and weleful° by strengthe of thi palis°, shalt leden a cler age, scorninge the woodnesses° and the ires of the eyr°.

Prose 5. Set quidem raciormm in te iam.

"But for as moche as the noryssinges° of my resouns° dessenden now into the, I trowe° it were tyme to usen a lytel strengere° medycynes. Now understond heere, al were it so° that the yiftes of Fortune ne were nat brutel° ne transitorye, what is ther in hem that may be thyn in any tyme, or elles that it nis fowl, yif that it be consydered and loked perfytly°? Rychesses, ben° they precyous by the nature of hemself, or elles by the nature of the? What is most worth of rychesses? Is it nat gold or myht of moneye assembled? Certes°, thilke° gold and thilke moneye shyneth and yeveth betere renoun to hem that despenden° it thanne to thilke folk that mokeren° it; for avarice maketh alwey mokereres to ben hated, and largesse° maketh folk cler° of renoun. For syn that swich thinge as is transferred fram o man to another ne may nat dwellen° with no man, certes thanne is thilke moneye precyous whan it is translated into° oother folkes and stenteth° to ben had by usage° of large yevinge of him that hath yeven it. And also yif al the moneye that is over al in the worlde were gadered toward o° man, it sholde maken alle oother men to ben nedy as of that. And certes a voys al hool° *(that is to seyn, withowte amenusinge°)*, fulfylleth togydere the hering of moche folk. But certes, yowre richesses ne mowen nat° passen into moche folke withowte amenusinge, and whan they ben apassed, nedes° they maken hem pore° that forgon° the rychesses. O streyte° and nedy° clepe° I this rychesse syn that many folk ne may nat han it al, ne al may it nat comen to o man withowten poverte of alle other folk!

"And the shyninge of gemmes *(that I clepe precyous stoones)* draweth it nat the eyen of folk to hem-ward° *(that is to seyn, for the beautes)*? But certes, yif ther were beaute or bounte° in the shyninge of stones, thilke° clernesse is of the stones hemself, and nat of men, for whiche I wondre gretely that men mervaylen on swyche thynges. For-why°, what thing is it that, yif it wanteth moeving° and joynture of sowle and body, that by ryht myhte semen a fayr creature to him that hath a sowle of resoun? For al be it so that gemmes drawen to hemself a lytel of the last° beaute of the world thorw the entente of her creatour and thorw the distinccioun of hemself°, yit for as mochel° as they ben put under° yowre excellense, they ne han nat desserved by no wey that ye sholden mervaylen on hem.

---

2 Meter 4. 1 **What maner,** *whatever kind of,* **waar,** *prudent* 2 **wole,** *wishes,* **fownden him,** *to establish for himself,* **perdurable sete,** *permanent seat* 5 **manasinge,** *threatening,* **eschewen,** *avoid* 6 **cop,** *tip* 7 **felle,** *fierce* 9 **lause,** *loose* 10 **wyhte,** *weight,* **forthy,** *therefore* 13 **fychchen thin hows,** *fix your house,* **merye,** *hospitable* 14 **in,** *within,* **lowh stoon,** *low stone* (wall) 17 **weleful,** *happy,* **thi palis,** *your enclosure* 18 **cler age,** *serene life,* **woodnesses,** *madnesses* 19 **ires of the eyr,** *angers of the air* (weather) 2 Prose 5. 1 **noryssinges,** *nursings* 2 **resouns,** *arguments,* **trowe,** *think* 3 **strengere,** *stronger* 4 **al were it so,** *even if it were so* 5 **brutel,** *brittle* 8 **loked perfytly,** *perceived perfectly* 9 **ben,** *are* 12 **Certes,** *certainly* 13 **thilke,** *that same* 15 **despenden,** *spends,* **mokeren,** *hoard* 17 **largesse,** *generosity,* **cler,** *shining* 20 **dwellen,** *remain* 21 **translated into,** *passed on to* 22 **stenteth,** *ceases* 23 **usage,** *habit* 25 **gadered toward o,** *accumulated by one* 27 **voys al hool,** *voice spoken out loud* 28 **amenusinge,** *diminishing* 30 **ne mowen nat,** *may not* 32 **nedes,** *necessarily* 33 **hem pore,** *them poor,* **forgon,** *give up,* **streyte,** *limited* 34 **nedy,** *poor,* **clepe,** *call* 40 **to hem-ward,** *towards them* 42 **bounte,** *value,* **thilke,** *that* 45 **For-why,** *why* 46 **wanteth moeving,** *lacks movement* (life) 50 **last,** *lowest* 52 **distinccioun of hemself,** *particularities of themselves* 53 **mochel,** *much,* **ben put under,** *are placed below*

4 **Eurus,** the southeast wind. 7 **Auster,** the south wind. 2 Prose 5. 3 **medycynes,** the figure of medicinal rhetoric was introduced at 1.pr2.1. 27 **al hool,** omitted in C^2.

"And the beaute of feldes, delyteth it nat mochel unto yow?"

Boece. "Why sholde it nat delyten us, syn that it is a ryht fayr porsyoun° of the ryht fayre werke *(that is to seyn, of this world)*? And ryht so ben we gladed° somtyme of the face of the see° whan it is cler; and also merveyllen we on the hevene, and on the sterres, and on the sonne, and on the moone."

Philosophie. "Aperteneth°," quod she, "any of thilke thinges to the? Why darstow gloryfyen the in the shyninge° of any swyche thinges? Artow distingwed° and embelysed be° the sprynginge flowres of the fyrst somer sesoun, or swelleth thy plente in the fructes of somer? Whi artow ravyssed with ydel joyes? Whi enbracest thow straunge goedes° as they weren thyne? Fortune ne shal never maken that swyche thynges ben thyne, that nature of thinges hath maked foreyne fro° the. Soth° is that withowten dowte the frutes of the erthe owen° to ben to the noryssinge of bestes. And yif thou wolt fulfylle thy nede after that° it suffiseth to nature, than is it no nede that thow seke after the superflwite of fortune. For with ful fewe thinges and with ful lytel thinges nature halt hir apayed°; and yif thou wolt achoken° the fulfyllinge of nature with superflwites, certes thilke thinges that thou wolt thresten° or powren° into nature shullen ben unjoyful to the, or elles anoyous°.

"Wenest° thow ek that it be a fayre thing to shyne with diverse clothinge? Of which klothinge yif the beaute be agreable to loken upon, I wol mervaylen on the nature of the matere of thilke klothes, or elles on the werkman that wrowht hem. But also a longe rowte of meyne°, maketh that a blysful man? The whiche servantes, yif they ben vicious of condiciouns°, it is a gret charge° and a distrucsyoun to the hows, and a gret enemy to the lord himself. And yif they ben goode men, how shal straunge or foreyne goodnesse° ben put in the nowmbre of thi rychesse? So that by all thyse forseide thinges, it is cleerly ishewed° that never oon of thilke thinges that thow acountedest for thine goodes nas nat thi good. In the whyche thinges, yif ther be no beaute to ben desyred, why sholdestow ben sory yif thow leese hem, or why sholdestow rejoysen the to holden hem? For yif they ben fayre of her owne kynde°, what aperteneth that to the? For al so wel° sholden they han ben fayre by hemselve, thowgh they weren departed° fram alle thyne rychesses. For-why° fayre ne precyous ne weren they nat for that they comen amonge thy rychesses, but for they semeden fayre and precyous, therfor thow haddest lever rekne° hem amonges thy rychesses.

"But what desirest thow of Fortune with so grete a noyse and with so gret a fare°? I trowe° thow seke to dryve awey nede with habundaunce of thinges; but certes it torneth to yow al in the contrarye. For-why° certes it nedeth of ful manye helpinges to kepen° the diversite of precyous ostelementes°. And soth it is that of manye thinges han they nede that many thinges han; and ayeinward°, of lytul nedeth hem that mesuren her fille after° the nede of kynde° and nat after the owtrage° of coveytyse. Is it thanne so that ye men ne han no proper goode iset in° yow, for whiche ye moten° seken owtward yowre goodes in foreyne and subgyt° thinges? So is thanne the condicyoun of thinges torned up-so-down°, that a man, that is a devine beest by meryte of his resoun, thinketh that himself nis neyther fayre ne noble but yif it be thorw possessyoun of ostelmentes that ne han no sowles. And certes, al oother thinges ben apayed° of hir owne beautes; but ye men,

---

59 porsyoun, *portion* **61 gladed,** *pleased* **62 see,** *sea* **65 Aperteneth,** *belong* **67 shyninge,** *beauty* **68 Artow distingwed,** *are you distinguished,* **embelysed be,** *embellished by* **72 straunge goedes,** *goods that are not your own* **75 foreyne fro,** *external to* **76 Soth,** *true* **77 owen,** *ought* **78–79 after that,** *to the extent that* **82 halt hir apayed,** *holds herself satisfied* **83 achoken,** *choke* **85 thresten,** *thrust,* **powren,** *pour* **86 anoyous,** *troubling* **87 Wenest,** *think* **93 rowte of meyne,** *string of servants* **94–95 vicious of conditions,** *wicked by character,* **charge,** *burden* **98 straunge or foreyne goodnesse,** i.e., *the goodness of other people* **101 ishewed,** *showed* **107 of her owne kynde,** *by their own nature* **108 as so wel,** *just as well* **110 departed,** *separated,* **For-why,** *for this reason* **114 haddest lever rekne,** *would rather count* **117 fare,** *disturbance* **118 trowe,** *think* **120 For-why,** *because* **122 kepen,** *protect,* **ostelementes,** *household goods* **125 ayeinward,** *conversely* **126 after,** *in accord with,* **kynde,** *nature* **127 owtrage,** *excess* **128 iset in,** *set within* **129 moten,** *must* **130 sybgyt,** *inferior* **132 up-so-doun,** *upside down* **137 apayed,** *satisfied*

58–64 Boece . . . , in the Latin original, this is part of Philosophy's speech.

that ben semblable° to God by yowr reasonable thowght, desyren to apayrelen° yowr excellent kynde of° the lowest thinges. Ne ye understonden nat how gret a wrong ye don to yowre creatour. For he wolde° that mankynde were most worthy and noble of any oothre worldly thinges, and ye threste° adown yowre dignitees bynethe the lowest thinges. For yif that al the good of every thinge be more precyous than is thilke thing whos that the good is, syn ye demen that the fowlest thinges ben yowre goodes, thanne submitten ye and putten yowrselven under the fowleste thinges by yowre estimacioun. And certes, this tydeth° nat withowte yowre desertes°, for certes, swyche is the condysyoun of alle mankynde, that oonly whan it hath knowinge of itselve, than passeth° it in noblesse alle oother thinges; and whan it forleteth° the knowinge of itself, than is it browht bynethen alle beestes. For-why° al oother levinge° bestes han of kynde° to knowe nat hemself; but whan men leten° the knowinge of hemself, it comth hem of vice. But how brode sheweth the erroure and the folye of yow men, that wenen° that any thinge may ben aparayled with straunge aparaylementes°! But forsothe, that may nat ben doon. For yif a wyht° shyneth with thinges that ben put to° him *(as thus, if thilke° thinges schynen with which a man is aparayled)*, certes thilke thinges ben comended and preysed with whych he is aparaled; but natheles, the thinge that is covered and wrapped under that dwelleth in his felthe°.

"And I denye that thilke thinge be good that anoyeth° him that hath it. Gabbe° I of this? Thow wolt seye nay. Certes, rychesses han anoyed ful ofte hem that han tho° rychesses syn° that every wycked shrewe°—and for his wyckednesse the more gredy after oother folkes rychesses, whersoever it be in any place, be it gold or precious stones—weneth° him only most worthi that hath hem. Thow thanne, that so bysy° dredest now the swerd and now the spere, yif thow haddest entred in the path of this lyf a voyde° wayferinge man, than woldest thow synge byforn the thef *(as who seyth, a pore man that berth no rychesse on him by the weye may boldely synge byforn theves, for he hath nat wherof to ben robbed)*. O precyous and ryht cler° is the blysfulnesse of mortal rychesses that whan thou hast geten it, than hast thow lorn° thi sikernesse°!

Metre 5. Felix nimium prior etas.

"Blysful was the fyrst age of men. They helden hem apayed° with the metes° that the trewe feeldes browhten forth. They ne dystroyede nor deceivede nat hemself with owtrage°. They weren wont lyhtly° to slaken her hunger at even° with accornes of okes. They ne cowde nat medly° the yifte of Bachus to the cleer hony *(that is to seyn, they cowed make no pyment° nor clarree°)*, ne they cowde nat medle° the bryhte fleeses° of the contre of Seryens with the venym° of Tyrye *(this is to seyn, they cowde nat deyen white fleses of Syryen contre with the bloode of a manere shyllefyssh° that men fynden in Tyrye, with whiche blood men deyen purpur°)*. They slepen holsom slepes upon the gras, and dronken of the renninge wateres, and layen under the shadwes of the heye pyn° trees. Ne no gest ne straungere ne karf yit the heye see with oores or with shippes, ne they ne hadde seyn yit none newe strondes° to leden marchaundyse into diverse contres. Tho° weren the crwel claryouns° ful hust°

138 semblable, *similar* **139 apayrelen,** *decorate* **140 of,** *with* **142 wolde,** *wishes* **144 threste,** *thrust* **152 tydeth,** *happens,* **desertes,** *deserving* (it) **155 passeth,** *surpasses* **156 forleteth,** *abandons* **158 For-why,** *because,* **levinge,** *living* **159 of kynde,** *by nature* **160 leten,** *abandons* **163 wenen,** *think* **164 aparaylementes,** *adornments* **165 wyht,** *person* **166 to,** *on* **167 *thilke*,** *those* **171 felthe,** *filth* **173 anoyeth,** *disturbs,* **Gabbe,** *lie* **175 tho,** *those* **176 syn,** *since,* **shrewe,** *villain* **179 weneth,** *thinks* **181 bysy,** *anxious* **183 voyde,** *poor* **188 ryht cler,** *very bright* **190 lorn,** *lost,* **sikernesse,** *security* **2 Meter 5. 2 apayed,** *satisfied,* **metes,** *foods* **5 owtrage,** *excess,* **wont lyhtly,** *accustomed easily* **6 at even,** *calmly* **7 medly,** *mix* **9 *pyment*,** *spiced wine,* ***clarree*,** *sweetened wine* **10 medle,** *mix,* **fleeses,** *wool* **11 venym,** *poison* **13 *manere shyllefyssh*,** *kind of shellfish* **15 *deyen purpur*,** *dye purple* **18 heye pin,** *high pine* **21 strondes,** *shores* **22 Tho,** *then,* **crwel claryouns,** *fierce bugles,* **hust,** *hushed*

184 synge byforn the thef, the image of idealized poverty, singing before thieves, comes from Juvenal, *Satire* 10.20–22; Chaucer uses it again in *WBT* 3.1191–94. **2 Meter 5.** Chaucer adapted much of this into the lyric known as "The Former Age" (Short Poem 13), lines 1–32, which accompanies 2.m5 in C^2. **7 yifte of Bachus,** gift of Bacchus, god of wine. **10–11 fleeses . . . of Seryens . . . venym of Tyrye,** the wool of the Syrians . . . the poison or dye (Latin *veneno*) of Tyre; i.e., dyed cloth. The French alters Latin *Serum* (Chinese) to *Sirians,* both exotic, although the Latin clearly means "silk." From ancient times, the secretion of the *murex* (a shellfish) was used as a purple dye.

and ful stylle. Ne blod ishad° by egre° hate en hadde nat deyed° yit armures. For wherto° or whych wodness° of enemys wolde fyrst moeven armes whan they say° crwel woundes, ne none meedes° be of blod ishad? "I wolde that owre tymes sholde torne ayein to the olde maneres! But the angwissous° love of havinge brenneth° in folk moore crwely than the fyr of mowntaigne Ethna *(that ay° brenneth).* Allas, what was he that fyrst dalf° up the gobetes° or the weyhtes of gold covered under erthe, and the precyous stoones that wolden han be hydd? He dalf up precyous perils *(that is to seyn, that he that hem fyrst up dalf, dalf up a precyous peril, for-whi for° the precyousnesse of swyche thinge hath many man be in peril).*

Prose 6. Quid autem de dignitatibus.

"But what shal I seye of dignites and of powers the whiche ye men that neyther knowen verray° dignite ne verray power areysen° hem as heye as the hevene? The whiche dignites and powers, yif they comen to any wycked man, they don as grete damages and destruccіouns as doth the flawmbe° of the mountaigne Ethna whan the flawmbe walweth° up; ne no deluge ne doth so° crwel harmes. Certes°, the remenbreth wel, as I trowe°, that thilke° dignite that men clepen° the imperye° of consulers, the whyche that whilom° was byginninge of fredom, yowre eldres coveiteden° to han don away that dignitee for the pride of the consulers. And ryht for the same pride, yowr eldres byforn that tyme hadden don awey owt of the cyte of Rome the kynges name *(that is to seyn, they nolde han no lengere no kynge).*

"But now, yif so be that dignites and powers ben yeven to goode men—the which thing is ful selde°—what agreable thinges is ther in tho dignites or powers but oonly the goodnesse of foolkes that usen hem? And therfor it is thus that honour ne comth nat to vertu for cause° of dignite, but, ayeinward°, honour comth to dignite for cause of vertu. But whiche is thilke yowre dereworthe° power, that is so cleer° and so requerable°? O ye erthelyche bestes°, considere ye nat over which thinge that it semeth that ye han power? Now yif thow saye° a mous amonges other muses°, that chalenged° to himself-ward ryht and power over alle oother muses, how gret scorn woldestow han of hit! *(Glosa. So fareth it by men; the body hath power over the body).* For yif thow looke wel upon the body of a wyht°, what thing shaltow fynde moore freele° than is mankynde—the whiche men wel ofte ben slayn with bytinge of smale flyes, or elles with the entringe of crepinge wormes into the privetes of mannes body? But wher shal man fynden any man that may excercen° or haunten° any ryht upon another man, but oonly on his body, or elles upon thinges that ben lowere than the body, the which I clepe fortunows° possessyouns? Maystow ever have any comaundement over a fre corage°? Maystow remwen° fro the estat of his propre reste a thowht that is clyvinge° togidere in himself by stidefast resoun? As whylom° a tyraunt wende° to confownde a freman of corage, and wende to constreyne him by torment to maken him discoveren and acusen folk that wysten° of a conjuraciourn° *(which I clepe a confederacie)* that was cast ayeins this tyraunt, but this freman boot of° his owne tonge and cast it in the visage° of thilke woode° tyraunt, so that the tormentes that this tyraunt wende to han maked matere of crwelte, this wise man maked it matere of vertu.

23, ishad, *shed,* **egre,** *bitter* **24 deyed,** *dyed,* **wherto,** *why* **25 wodnesse,** *madness* **26 say,** *saw* **27 meedes,** *profits* **29 angwissous,** *anxious* **30 brenneth,** *burns* **32 ay,** *always* **33 dalf,** *dug,* **gobetes,** *nuggets* **37–38** ***for-whi for,*** *as a consequence of* 2 Prose 6. **3 verray,** *true,* **areysen,** *exalt* **7 flawmbe,** *flame* **8 walweth,** *surges* **9 so,** *such,* **Certes,** *surely* **10 trowe,** *believe* **11 thilke,** *that,* **clepen,** *call,* **imperye,** *power* **12 whilom,** *once* **13 coveiteden,** *desired* **22 ful selde,** *very seldom* **26 for cause,** *because,* **ayeinward,** *conversely* **28 dereworthe,** *beloved* **29 cleer,** *bright,* **requerable,** *desirable* **29–30 erthelyche bestes,** *earthly beasts* **32 saye,** *saw* **33 muses,** *mice,* **chalenged,** *claimed* **37 wyht,** *person* **38 freele,** *frail* **43 excercen,** *exercise* **44 haunten,** *practice* **47 fortunous,** *changeable* **48 fre corage,** *free spirit* **49 remwen,** *remove* **50 clyvinge,** *holding* **51 whylom,** *once* **52 wende,** *thought* **55 wysten,** *knew,* **conjuracioun,** *conspiracy* **57 boot of,** *bit off* **58 visage,** *face* **59 thilke woode,** *that mad*

31 mowntaigne Ethna, Mount Etna, a volcano in Sicily. **17 don,** Hn is missing two leaves between here and 2.pr7.75. **35 *Glosa,*** see 1.pr.74–80n. **52–62 tyraunt . . . ,** the tyrant is Nearchus (or Diomedon in some sources); the freeman who bit off his own tongue is the philosopher Zeno; see Diogenes Laertius 9.5.26–27.

"But what thing is it that a man may don to another man, that he ne may receyven the same thinge of oother folkes in himself *(or thus, what may a man don to folk that folkes ne may don him the same)*? I have herd told of Busirides, that was wont° to slen° his gestes that herberweden° in his hows, and he was sleyn himself or° Ercules that was his gest. Regulus hadde taken in batayle many men of Affryke and cast hem into feteres°, but sone after he moste yeve° hys handes to ben bounde with the cheynes of hem that he hadde whylom° overcomen. Wenestow° thanne that he be myhty that hath no power to don a thinge, that oothre ne may don in him that he doth in oothre? And yit mooreover, yif it so were that thise dignites or poweres hadden any propre or natural goodnesse in hemself, never nolden° they comen to shrewes°. For contraryous thinges ne ben nat wont° to ben ifelawshiped° togidere. Nature refuseth that contrarious thinges ben ijoigned. And so, as I am in certein that ryht wycked folk han dignites ofte tyme, than sheweth it wel that dignites and powers ne ben nat goode of her owne kinde°, syn° that they suffren° himself to cleven° or joinen hem to shrewes And certes, the same thing may I moost digneliche° jugen and seyn of alle the yiftes of Fortune that moost plenteuously comen to shrews. Of the which yiftes I trowe that it owhte° ben considered that no man dowteth that he nis strong in whom he seth° strengthe; and in whom that swyftnesse is, soth it is that he is swift. Also musike maketh musiciens, and phisike maketh phisiciens, and rethoryke rethoryens°. For-why° the nature of everything maketh his proprete°, ne it nis nat entremedled° with the effectes of the contraryous thinges; and, as of wil it chaseth owt thinges that to it ben contrarie. But certes, rychesse may not restreyne avarice unstaunched°; ne power ne maketh nat a man myhty over himself, whiche that vicyous lustes holden destreyned° with cheynes that ne mowen° nat be unbownden. And dignites that ben yeven to shrewede° folkes nat oonli ne maketh hem nat digne°, but it sheweth rather al opynly that they ben unworthi and undigne. And why is it thus? Certes, for ye han joye to clepen° thinges with false names that beren hem alle in the contrarye, the which names ben ful ofte reproeved° by the effecte of the same thinges. So that thise ilke° rychesse ne owhten nat by ryht to ben cleped° rychesses; ne swich° power ne owhte nat ben cleped power; ne swich dignite ne owhte nat ben cleped dignite. And at the laste, I may conclude the same thing of alle the yiftes of Fortune, in which ther nis nothinge to ben desired, ne° that hath in himself naturel bownte°, as it is ful wel iseene°. For neyther they ne joignen hem nat alwey to goode men, ne maken hem alwey goode to whom that they ben ijoigned.

Metre 6. Novimus quantas dederit ruinas.

"We han wel knowen how many grete harmes and destruccyouns weren don by the Emperour Nero. He let brennen° the cyte of Rome, and made slen° the senatoures. And he, crwel, whilom slow° his brother. And he was maked moyst° with the blood of his moder *(that is to seyn, he let slen and slitten° the body of his moder, to sen wher he was conseyved)*, and he looked on every halve° upon her colde

68 wont, *accustomed,* **slen,** *slay* **69 herberweden,** *lodged* **70 of,** *by* **72 feteres,** *chains* **73 moste yeve,** *had to give* **74 whylom,** *formerly* **75 Wenestow,** *do you think* **81 never nolden,** *never would,* **shrewes,** *villains* **82 wont,** *accustomed* **83 ifelawshiped,** *joined* **87–88 of her owne kinde,** *by their own nature,* **syn,** *since,* **suffren,** *allow* **89 cleven,** *hold* **90 digneliche,** *fittingly* **93 owhte,** *ought* **95 seth,** *sees* **98 rethoryens,** *rhetoricians* **99 For-whi,** *for this reason* **100 maketh his proprete,** *establishes what is proper to it,* **entremedled,** *intermixed* **104 unstaunched,** *unrestrained* **107 destreyned,** *restrained,* i.e., **mowen,** *may* **109 shrewede,** *evil* **110 digne,** *noble* **112 clepen,** *call* **115 reproeved,** *contradicted* **116 ilke,** *same* **117 cleped,** *called* **118 swich,** *such* **122 ne,** *nor* **123 bownte,** *goodness* **124 iseene,** *seen* **2 Meter 6. 3 let brennen,** *caused to be burned* **4 made slen,** *commanded to be slain* **5 whilom slow,** *once slew* **6 maked moyst,** *dampened* **7 *slitten,*** *slit open* **9 halve,** *side*

68–70 Busirides . . . Ercules, Busiris, legendary king of Egypt, annually sacrificed a guest to Zeus; when he arranged to sacrifice Hercules, the hero broke his bonds and killed the king. Compare *MkT* 7.2103. **70–75 Regulus . . . ,** in Cicero's *Offices* 1.13.39 and 3.26.99–100, the Roman consul Regulus exemplifies fidelity to a promise because, instead of benefiting from an exchange of prisoners, he returned to captivity and death in Carthage. **2 Meter 6.** Chaucer adapted a portion of this poem into verse in *MkT* 7.2479–94. **3ff. Emperour Nero . . . ,** the infamous Roman emperor Nero (37–68 C.E.) was thought responsible for the burning of Rome; he condemned to death his stepbrother, Britannicus, and his mother, Agrippina, among others.

dede body ne no teere ne wette his face, but he was so hard-herted that he myhte ben domesman° or juge of hir dede beaute. And natheles, yit governede this Nero by ceptre alle the poeples that Phebus the sonne may sen°, cominge fram his owtereste° arysinge til he hide his bemes under the wawes° (*that is to seyn, he governed alle the poeples by sceptre inperial that the sonne goth abowte, from est to west*). And ek this Nero governed by ceptre alle the poeples that ben under the colde sterres that hyhten° Sevene Tryones (*this is to seyn, he governede alle the poeples that ben under the party° of the north*). And ek Nero governede alle the poeples that the vyolent wynd Nothus scorkleth°, and baketh the brenning° sandes by his drye hete (*that is to seyn, alle the poeples in the sowth*). But yit ne myhte nat al his hye° power torne° the woodnesse° of this wikked Nero. Allas, it is a grevous fortune, it is, as ofte as wykked swerd is joigned to crwel venym" (*that is to seyn, venimous crwelte to lordshippe*).

Prose 7. Tum ego scis inquam.

Thanne seyde I thus: "Thow wost° wel thyself that the coveytise of mortal thinges ne hadden never lordshipe of me; but I have wel desyred matere of thinges to done° (*as who seyth, I desyred to han matere of governaunce over comunalitees*) for vertu stille° ne sholde nat elden°" (*that is to seyn, that lest° that, or° he wax old his vertu, that lay now ful stylle, ne sholde nat perisse° unexcercised in governaunce of comune, for which men myghten speken or wryten of his goode governement*).

Philosophie. "For sothe°," quod she, "and that is a thing that may drawen to governaunce swiche hertes as ben worthi and noble of hir nature, but natheles hit may nat drawen or tollen swiche° hertes as ben ibrowht° to the fulle perfeccyoun of vertu, that is to seyn, coveytyse of glorye and renoun to han wel admynystred the comune° thinges or don gode desertes° to profyt of the commune. For se now and consydere how lytul° and how voyde of alle prys° is thilke° glorie. Certein thing is°, as thow hast lerned by the demonstracyoun of astronomye, that al the envyroninge° of the erthe abowte ne, halt° but the resoun° of a prikke at regard of° the gretnesse of hevene; that is to seyn, that yif ther were maked comparisoun of the erthe to the gretnesse of hevene, men wolden jugen in al that the erthe ne helde no space. Of the whyche litel regioun of this worlde, the ferthe partye° is enhabited with lyvinge bestes that we knowen, as thou hast thyself ylerned by Tholome that proveth it. And yif thow haddest withdrawen and abated° in thy thowht fro thilke ferthe partye as moche space as the see and the mareys° contenen° and overgoon, and as moche space as the regioun of drowhte overstrechcheth (*that is to seyn, sandes and desertes*) wel unnethe° sholde ther dwellen° a ryht streyt° place to the habitasyoun of men. And ye thanne, that ben envyroned and closed within the leste prykke of thilke prykke, thinken ye to manyfesten yowre renoun and don° yowre name to ben born° forth? But youre glorye, that is so narwh° and so streyte ithrongen° into so lytul bowndes, how mochel coveyteth° it in largesse° and in gret dooinge? And also sette this therto, that many a nacyoun, diverse of tonge and of maneres and ek of resoun° of her lyvinge, ben enhabyted in the clos° of thilke lytul habytacule°. To the whiche naciouns, what for deficulte of weyes, and what for dyversite of langages, and what for

---

12 domesman, *magistrate* **13 ceptre,** *scepter* **15 sen,** *see,* **owtereste,** *furthest* **16 wawes,** *waves* **21 hyhten,** *are called* **23 party,** *region* **24 scorkleth,** *scorches,* **brenning,** *burning* **28 hye,** *high,* **torne,** *change,* **woodnesse,** *madness* **2 Prose 7. 1 wost,** *know* **4 matere of thinges to do,** *reason to do things* **6 stille,** *inactive* **7 elden,** *grow old,* **that lest,** *in order to avoid,* **or,** *before* **9 perisse,** *perish* **12 For sothe,** *truly* **16 tollen swiche,** *lure such,* **ibrowht,** *brought* **19 commune,** *public* **19–20 don gode desertes,** *accomplished good things* **21 lytul,** *little* **22 pris,** *value,* **thilke,** *that* **22–23 Certein thing is,** *it is certain* **24 envyroninge,** *circumference* **25 ne halt,** *holds not,* **resoun,** *equivalent* **26 at regard of,** *in relation to* **31 ferthe partye,** *fourth part* (one quarter) **35 abated,** *reduced* **36 mareys,** *marshes* **37 contenen,** *contain* **39 wel unnethe,** *barely* **40 dwellen,** *remain,* **ryht streyt,** *very narrow* **44 don,** *make* **45 born,** *carried* **46 narwh,** *narrow,* **streyte ithrongen,** *tightly constrained* **47–48 muchel coveyteth,** *much desires* **48 largesse,** *generosity* **51 resoun,** *mode* **52 clos,** *enclosure,* **habytacule,** *habitation*

21 Sevene Tryones, the seven chief stars of Ursa Minor, the Little Dipper. **24 Nothus,** Notus, the south wind. **33 Tholome,** Ptolemy (second century), Greco-Egyptian astronomer and geographer whose *Almagest* was for the Middle Ages the epitome of astrological science. **54 dyversite,** C[2] reads "deficulte."

defawte of unusage° and entrecomuninge° of marchaundise, nat only the names of syngler men ne may nat strecchen, but ek the fame of cytes ne may nat strecchen. At the laste, certes, in the tyme of Marchus Tulius, as himself writ in his book that the renoun of the comune° of Rome ne hadde nat passed ne clowmben over the mountaigne that hyhte° Caucasus, and yit was thilke tyme Roome wel waxen and gretly redowted of° the Parthes, and ek of other folk enhabytinge abowte. Sestow nat° thanne how streyt and how compressed is thilke glorye that ye travaylen° abowte to shewe and to multiplye? May thanne the glorye of a singler Romayne strechchen thyder as° the fame of the name of Rome may nat clymben ne passen? And ek, seystow nat that the maneres of dyverse folk and ek her lawes ben discordaunt among hemself, so that thilke thinge that som men jugen worthy of preysinge, oother folk jugen that it is worthi of torment? And therof comth it that thogh a man delyte him in preysinge of his renoun, he may nat in no wyse bryngen forth ne spreden his name to many maner° peoples. Therefor every manere man owhte to ben apayed of° his glorye that is publysseod° among his owne neighbours. And thilke noble renoun shal ben restreyned within the bowndes of o manere folk. But how many a man that was ful noble in his tyme hath the wrechched and nedy foryetinge of wryteres put owt of mynde and don awey! Al be it so that, certes, thilke° wrytinges profyten lytul, the whyche wrytinges long and derk elde° doth awey, bothe hem and ek her autours. But yow men semeth to geten yow a perdurablete°, whan ye thinken that in tyme tocominge yowre fame shal lasten. But natheles, yif thow wolt maken comparysoun to the endeles spaces of eternite, what thing hast thow by whiche thow mayst rejoysen the° of long lastinge of thy name? For yif ther were maked comparysoun of the abydinge of a moment to ten thowsand wynter, for as mochel as bothe the spaces ben ended, for yit hath the moment som porcyoun of it, althowgh it lytul be. But natheles, thilke selve° nowmbre of yeres, and ek as many yeres as therto may be multyplyed, ne may nat, certes, ben comparysoned to the perdurablyte that is endeles, for of thinges that han ende may be maked comparysoun, but of thinges that ben withowten ende to thinges that han ende may be maked no comparysoun. And forthi° is it that althowgh renoun of as longe tyme as evere the lyst° to thinken were thowt to the regard of° eternite, that is unstaunchable° and infynyt, it ne sholde nat oonly semen lytel, but pleynlyche ryht nawht°. But ye men, certes, ne konne don nothinge aryght, but yif it be for the audience of poeple and for idil rumours, and ye forsaken the grete worthinesse of conscience and of vertu, and ye seken your gerdouns° of the smale wordes of straunge folkes.

"Have° now, her° and understonde, in the lyhtnesse of swych pride and veyne glorye how a man scornede festyvaly° and meryly swych vanite. Whilom° ther was a man that hadde assayed° with stryvinge° wordes another man, the whiche nat for usage° of verray vertu but for prowd veyne glorye had taken upon him falsly the name of a philosophre. This rather° man that I spak of thowhte he wolde assaye wher° he thilke° were a philosophre or no—that is to seyn, yif that he wolde han suffred lyhtly° in pacience the wronges that weren don unto him. This feynede°

---

55 defawte of unusage, *lack of familiarity,* **entrecomuninge,** *exchange* **61 comune,** *republic* **62 hyhte,** *is called* **64 redowted of,** *feared by* **66 Sestow nat,** *don't you see* **67 travaylen,** *labor* **70 thyder as,** *where* **80 maner,** *kinds of* **81 apayed of,** *satisfied by* **82 publyssed,** *made public* **88 thilke,** *these* **90 elde,** *age* **92 a perdurablete,** *immortality* **97 rejoysen the of,** *celebrate yourself for* **103 selve,** *same* **110 forthi,** *for this reason* **112 the lyst,** *you wish* **112–13 to the regard of,** *in comparison with* **113 unstaunchable,** *limitless* **115 pleynlyche ryht nawht,** *clearly nothing at all* **120 gerdouns,** *rewards* **122 Have,** *receive,* **her,** *hear* **124 festyvaly,** *happily* **125 Whilom,** *once* **126 assayed,** *tested,* **stryvinge,** *contentious* **127 usage,** *habit* **130 rather,** *other* **131 wher,** *whether,* **he thilke,** *this one* **133 lyhtly,** *easily* **134 feynede,** *false*

59–65 Marchus Tulius, Cicero. The passage derives from Macrobius's *Commentary* on the dream of Scipio (2.10.3), a portion of Cicero's *Republic* 6.22. **64 Parthes,** Parthians, an ancient people from near the Caspian Sea. **75 oother,** Hn resumes here; see 2pr6.17n. **87 nedy foryetinge of wryteres,** needy forgetting of writers, a mistranslation of Latin *scriptorum inops . . . oblivio* (forgotten for lack of writers). **100 the spaces,** C[1] reads "two spaces." **125–39** No specific source has been found for this anecdote, which suggests that those who seek the name of philosopher disqualify themselves. The association of silence and wisdom is a classical and biblical commonplace.

philosophre took pacience a lytel whyle, and whan he hadde receyved wordes of owtrage, he as in stryvinge ayein° and rejoysinge of himself seyde at the laste ryht thus: 'Understondestow nat that I am a philosophre?' That oother man answerde ayein ful bytingly and seyde: 'I hadde wel understonden it yif thow haddest holden thy tonge stille.' But what is it to thise noble worthi men—for, certes, of swyche foolke speke I—that seken glorye with vertu? What is it?" quod she. "What atteyneth° fame to swyche foolk, whan the body is resolved° by the deth at the laste? For yif it so be that men dyen in al *(that is to seyn, body and sowle),* the whyche thing owre resoun deffendeth° us to byleven, thanne is ther no glorye in no wyse. For what sholde thilke glorye ben whan he of whom thilke glorye is seyd to be nis ryht nawht° in no wyse? And yif the sowle, whyche that hath in itself science° of goode werkes, unbownden fro the prison of the erthe, wendeth° frely to the hevene, despyseth it nat thanne alle erthely occupacioun, and being in hevene rejoyseth that it is exempt fro alle erthely thinges? *(As who seith, thanne rekketh° the sowle of no glorye of renoun of° this world).*

Metre 7. Quicunque solam mente.

"Whoso that with overthrowinge° thowght oonly seketh glorye of fame, and weneth° that it be sovereyn good, lat him looken upon the brode shewinge contreyes of hevene, and upon the streyte° site of this erthe, and he shal ben ashamed of the encres° of his name that may nat fulfylle the litel compas° of the erthe. O what coveyten° prowde folk to lyften up her nekkes in ydel° in the dedly yok of this worlde? For althowgh that renoun ysprad, passinge to ferne° poeples, goth by diverse tonges, and althowgh that grete howses or kynredes° shynen with cler° titles of honours, yit natheles deth despyseth alle heye° glorye of fame, and deth wrappeth togydere the heye hevedes° and the lowe, and maketh egal° and evene the heyeste to the loweste. Wher wonen° now the bones of trewe Fabrycius? What is now Brutus, or stierne° Catoun? The thynne° fame yit lastinge of hir ydel names is marked with a fewe lettrees; but althowgh that we han knowen° the fayre wordes of the fames of hem, it is nat yeven to knowe hem that ben dede and consumpte°. Liggeth° thanne stille, al owtrely° unknowable, ne fame ne maketh yow nat knowe. And yif ye wene° to lyven the longere for wynde° of yowre mortal name, whan o cruwel day shal ravysshe° yow, thanne is the seconde deth dwellinge° unto yow." *(Glose. The fyrst deth he clepeth° heere departinge of the body and the sowle, and the seconde deth he clepeth as heere the stintinge° of the renoun of fame.)*

Prose 8. Set ne me inexorabile.

"But for as mochel as thow shalt nat wenen°," quod she, "that I bere untretable° batayle ayeins Fortune, yit somtyme it byfalleth that she, desseyvable°, desserveth to han ryht good thank of men; and that is whan she hirself opneth° and whan she descovereth° hir frownt°, and sheweth hir maneres. Peraventure° yit understondestow nat that° I shal seye. It is a wonder that I desyre to telle, and forthy unnethe° may I unpleyten° my sentense° with wordes—for I deme that contraryous Fortune profiteth more to men than Fortune debonayre°. For alwey whan Fortune semeth debonayre, than she lyeth falsly in byhetinge the hope of welefulnesse°; but forsothe° contraryous Fortune is alwey

---

137 ayein, *against* **146 atteyneth,** *amounts* **147 resolved,** *dissolved* **150 deffendeth,** *forbids* **153 nis ryht nawht,** *is nothing at all* **155 science,** *awareness* **156 wendeth,** *travels* **160 *thanne rekketh,*** *then cares,* *of, for* 2 Meter 7. **1 overthrowinge,** *overwhelming* **2 weneth,** *thinks* **5 streyte,** *narrow* **6 encres,** *spread* **7 compas,** *circle* **8 what coveyten,** *why crave* **9 in ydel,** *in vain* **11 ferne,** *foreign* **13 kynredes,** *families,* **cler,** *bright* **14 heye,** *high* **16 hevedes,** *heads* **17 egal,** *equal* **18 wonen,** *lie* **19 stierne,** *stern* **20 thynne,** *slender* **22 han knowen,** *have known* **24 consumpte,** *consumed,* **Liggeth,** *lie* **25 owtrely,** *utterly* **27 wene,** *think,* **wynde,** *breath* **28 ravysshe,** *destroy* **29 dwellinge,** *remaining* **30 *clepeth,*** *calls* **32 *stintinge,*** *ceasing* 2 Prose 8. **1 wenen,** *think* **2 untretable,** *irreconcilable* **4 desseyvable,** *able to deceive* **6 hirself opneth,** *opens herself,* **descovereth,** *reveals* **7 frownt,** *face* **8 Peraventure,** *perhaps,* **that,** *what* **10 forthy unnethe,** *therefore scarcely,* **unpleyten,** *unfold* **11 sentense,** *meaning* **13 debonayre,** *beneficial* **15 byhetinge,** *promising,* **welefulness,** *happiness* **16 forsothe,** *truly*

156 erthe, Latin gloss in C^2: "corporis" (body). **157 it,** Latin gloss in C^2: "anima" (soul). **5 site,** C^2 reads "cyte," but the Latin is *situm.* **18 Fabrycius,** Fabricius (third century B.C.E.), a Roman consul known for virtue.

sothfast° whan she sheweth hirself unstable thorw hir chaunginge. The amyable° Fortune desseyveth folk; the contrarye Fortune techeth. The amyable Fortune byndeth with the beaute of false goodes the hertes of folk that usen hem; the contrarye Fortune unbyndeth hem by the knowinge of freele° welefulnesse. The amyable Fortune maystow sen° alwey wyndinge and flowinge, and ever mysknowinge° of hirself; the contrarye Fortune is atempre° and restreyned, and wys thorw excersyse of hir adversitee. At the laste, amyable Fortune with hir flateringes draweth myswandringe° men fro the sovereyne good; the contraryous Fortune ledeth ofte folk ayein to soothfast goodes, and haleth° hem ayein as with an hooke. Wenestow° thanne that thow owhtest to leten° this a lytel thing, that this aspre° and horible Fortune hath discovered° to the the thowhtes of thy trewe frendes? For-why° this ilke Fortune hath departed° and uncovered to the bothe the certeyn° vysages and ek the dowtous° visages of thy felawes. Whan she departed awey fro the, she took awey hir frendes and lafte the thyne frendes. Now whan thow were ryche and weleful°, as the semede°, with how mochel woldestow° han bowht the fulle knowinge of this *(that is to seyn, the knowinge of thy verray° freendes)*? Now pleyne the nat° thanne of rychesse ilorn°, syn° thow hast fownden the moste precyous kynde of rychesses, that is to seyn, thy verray frendes.

Metre 8. Quod mundus stabili fide.

"That the world with stable feith varieth acordable° chaunginges; that the contraryous qualite of elementes holden among hemself aliaunce perdurable°; that Phebus the sonne with his goldene chariet bryngeth forth the rosene° day; that the mone hath commaundement over the nyhtes, whiche nyhtes Hesperus the eve sterre hath browht; that the se, gredy° to flowen, constreyneth with a certeyn ende his floodes, so that it is nat leveful° to strechche his brode termes or bowndes upon the erthes *(that is to seyn, to covere alle the erthe)*—al this acordaunce° of thinges is bownden with Loove, that governeth erthe and see, and hath also comaundementes to the hevenes. And yif this Loove slakede° the brydeles, alle thinges that now loven hem togederes wolden maken a batayle contynuely, and stryven to fordoon° the fasoun° of this worlde, the which they now leden in acordable feith by fayre moevinges. This Loove halt togideres poeples joigned with an hooly bond, and knytteth sacrement of maryages of chaste looves; and Love enditeth° lawes to trewe felawes. O weleful° were mankynde yif thilke° Love that governeth hevene governed yowre corages°!"

Explicit liber secundus.

---

17 sothfast, *truthful* **18 amyable,** *friendly* **23 freele,** *frail* **24–25 maystow sen,** *you may see* **26 mysknowinge,** *ignorant* **27 atempre,** *temperate* **30 myswandringe,** *errant* **33 haleth,** *pulls,* **Wenestow,** *do you think* **34 owhtest to leten,** *ought to consider* **35 aspre,** *bitter* **36 discovered,** *revealed* **37 For-why,** *for this reason* **38 departed,** *differentiated* **39 certeyn,** *reliable,* **dowtous,** *untrustworthy* **43 weleful,** *happy,* **the semede,** (it) *seemed to you* **44 woldestow,** *would you* **45 verray,** *true* **46 pleyne the nat,** *don't lament* **47 ilorn,** *lost,* **syn,** *since* **2 Meter 8. 2 acordable,** *harmonious* **4 perdurable,** *eternal* **6 rosene,** *rosy* **9 gredy,** *eager* **11 leveful,** *permissible* **13 acordaunce,** *harmony* **17 slakede,** *slackened* **19 fordoon,** *destroy* **20 fasoun,** *operation* **25 enditeth,** *composes* **26 weleful,** *happy,* **thilke,** *the same* **27 corages,** *hearts*

19 Brutus . . . Catoun, Lucius Junius Brutus (sixth century B.C.E.), reputed founder of the Roman republic; Marcus Porcius Cato (third–second century B.C.E.), famed as a moralist. **30** ***Glose*, see 1.pr4.74–80. 2 Meter 8.** Chaucer adapts this as a poem in *TC* 3.1744–64. **27a *Explicit liber secundus*,** Here ends Book Two.

BOOK 3

Incipit liber tercius.

Prose 1. Iam cantum illa finierat.

By this she hadde ended hir songe, whan the sweetnesse of hir ditee° hadde thorw-perced me that was desirous of herkninge, and I astoned hadde yit streyhte° myn eres *(that is to seyn, to herkne the bet° what she wolde seye),* so that a litel hereafter I seyde thus: "Oh thow that art sovereyn comfort of angwissous corages°, so thow hast remounted° and norysshed me with the weyhte of thy sentenses° and with delit of thy synginge so that I trowe° nat now that I be unparygal° to the strokes of Fortune *(as who seyth, I dar wel now suffren al the assautes of Fortune, and wel deffende me fro hir).* And tho remedies whyche that thow seydest her-byforn that weren ryht sharpe, nat oonly that I am nat agrysen° of hem now, but I, desirous of heringe, axe° gretely to heren the remedyes."

Than seyde she thus: "That feelede° I ful wel," quod she, "whan that thow, ententyf° and stylle, ravysshedest° my wordes. And I abood° til that thow haddest swych habyte of thy thowght as thow hast now, or elles tyl that I myself had maked to the the same habyt, which that is a moore verray° thing. And certes, the remenaunt of thinges that ben yit to seye ben swyche that fyrst whan men tasten hem they ben bytinge, but whan they ben receyved withinne a whyht°, than ben they swete. But for° thow seyst that thow art so desirous to herkne° hem, with how gret brenninge° woldesthow glowen yif thou wystest° whyder° I wol leden the!"

"Whyder is that?" quod I.

"To thilke verray welefulnesse°," quod she, "of whyche thyn herte dremeth. But for as moche as thy syhte is ocupied and distorbed by imagynasyoun of erthely thinges, thow mayst nat yit sen thilke selve° welefulnesse."

"Do," quod I, "and shewe me what is thilke verray welefulnesse, I preye thee, withowte taryinge."

"That wole I gladly don," quod she, "for the cause of the. But I wol fyrst marken the° by wordes, and I wol enforcen me° to enformen the thilke false cause of blisfulnesse that thow more° knowest, so that whan thow hast fully byholden thilke false goodes and torned thyne eyen to that oother syde, thow mowe° knowe the clernesse of verray blysfulnesse.

Metre 1. Qui serere ingenuum volet agrum.

"Whoso wole sowe a feeld plentiuous, lat him fyrst delyvere it fro thornes and kerve asunder with his hook the bushes and the fern so that the korn may comen hevy of eres and of greynes. Hony is the more swete yif mowthes han fyrst tasted savoures° that ben wyckid. The sterres shynen more agreablely whan the wynd Nothus leteth° his plowngy° blastes; and after that Lucifere the day sterre hath chased awey the dirke nyht, the day the fayrere ledeth the rosene hors° of the sonne. And ryht so thow, byholdinge fyrst the false goodes, bygyn to withdrawen thy nekke fro the yok of erthely affecciouns; and afterward the verray goodes shollen entren into thy corage°."

Prose 2. Tum defixo paululum visu.

Tho fastnede° she a lytul the syhte of hir eyen, and withdrowh hir ryht° as it were into the

<u>3 Prose 1.</u> 2 **ditee,** *poem* 4 **streyhte,** *stretched* 5 ***bet,*** *better* 7 **angwissous corages,** *anguished hearts* 8 **remounted,** *raised again* 9 **sentenses,** *arguments* 10 **trowe,** *believe* 11 **unparygal,** *unequal* 16 **agrysen,** *afraid* 17 **axe,** *ask* 19 **feelede,** *felt* 20 **ententyf,** *attentive* 21 **ravysshedest,** *seized* 22 **abood,** *waited* 25 **verray,** *true* 29 **whyht,** *person* 30 **for,** *because* 31 **herkne,** *listen to* 32 **brenninge,** *burning,* **wystest,** *knew* 33 **whyder,** *where* 35 **thilke verray welefulnesee,** *that true happiness* 40 **selve,** *same* 45 **marken the,** *indicate to you* 46 **enforcen me,** *strive* 48 **more,** *better* 51 **mowe,** *may* <u>3 Meter 1.</u> 6 **savoures,** *tastes* 8 **leteth,** *ceases,* **plowngy,** *stormy* 11 **rosene hors,** *rosy horses* 15 **corage,** *heart* <u>3 Prose 2.</u> 1 **fastnede,** *fixed* 2 **ryht,** *just*

<u>Book 3.</u> ***Incipit liber tercius,*** Here begins Book Three. **36 whyche thyn,** C[2] reads "whyche thynge." **38 erthely,** C[2] reads "herthely." **43 withowte,** C[2] reads "withhowte." <u>3 Meter 1.</u> **ingenuum,** C[2] reads "ingenium." **3 bushes,** C[2] reads "bosses." **8 Nothus,** Notus, the south wind. **9 Lucifere,** Lucifer (light-bringer), another name for Venus, the morning star.

streyte sete° of hir thowht, and bygan to speke ryht thus: "Alle the cures°," quod she, "of mortal foolk, whiche that travaylen hem° in many manere studies, goon certes by diverse weyes, but natheles they enforsen hem° alle to comen oonly to oon° ende of blysfulnesse. And blysfulnesse is swyche a good that whoso that hath geten it, he ne may over that nothing moore desyre. And this thing is forsothe° the sovereyn° good that conteyneth in hymself alle manere goodes, to the whyche good yif ther faylede anything, it myhte nat ben cleped° sovereyn good, for thanne were ther som good, owt of this ilke° sovereyn good, that myhte ben desyred. Now is it clere and certein thanne, that blysfulnesse is a perfyt estat by the congregasyoun of alle goodes; the whyche blysfulnesse, as I have seyd, alle mortal foolk enforsen hem to geten by dyverse weyes. For-why° the coveytise° of verray good is naturelly yplaunted in the hertes of men, but the myswandringe errour mysledeth hem into false goodes. Of the whyche men, som of hem wenen° that sovereyn good be to lyven withowte nede of anything, and travaylen hem to be haboundaunt of rychesses. And som oother men demen° that sovereyn good be for to ben ryht digne° of reverence, and enforcen hem to ben reverenced among hir neyghbours by the honours that they han ygeten. And some folk ther ben that holden that ryht heyh° power be sovereyn good, and enforcen hem for to regnen°, or elles to joignen hem to hem that regnen. And it semeth to some oother foolk that noblesse of renoun be the sovereyn good, and hasten hem to geten gloryous name by the arts of werre and of pees. And many folk mesuren° and gessen that sovereyn good be joye and gladnesse, and wenen° that it be ryht blysful thyng to plowngen hem in voluptuous delit. And ther ben folk that entrechaungen the causes and the endes of thyse forseyde goodes, as they that desyren rychesses to han power and delytes; or elles they desyren power for to han moneye, or for cause of renoun. In thise thinges, and in swyche oothre thynges, is torned alle the entencioun of desyringes and of werkes of men, as thus, noblesse and favoure of poeple, whyche that yeveth to men, as it semeth hem, a manere clernesse° of renoun; and wyf and chyldren, that men desyren for cause of delit and of merynesse. But forsothe°, frendes ne sholden nat be rekned° among the godes of fortune, but of vertu, for yt ys a ful hooly manere° thyng. Alle thise oothre thinges, forsothe, ben taken for cause of power or elles for cause of delit. Certes, now am I redy to referren° the goodes of the body to thise forseyde thinges aboven. For it semeth that strengthe and gretnesse of body yeven power and worthynesse, and that beaute and sweftnesse yeven noblesses and glorye of renoun, and hele° of body semeth yeven delit. In alle thise thinges it semeth oonly that blysfulnesse is desired. For-why° thilke° thing that every man desyreth most over alle thinges, he demeth° that yt be the sovereyn good. But I have deffyned° that blysfulnesse is the sovereyn good, for whych every whyht° demeth that thilke estat that he desyreth over alle thinges that it be blysfulnesse.

"Now hast thow thanne byforn thyn eyen almest al the purposed° forme of the welefulnesse of mankynde, that is to seyn, rychesses, honours, power, and glorye, and delits. The whiche delit oonly consyderede Epicurus, and juged and establysshed that delit is the sovereyn good; for as moche as alle oothre thinges, as him thowhte, byrefte° awey joye and myrthe fram the herte. But I retorne ayein to the studies of men, of whiche men the corage° alwey reherseth° and seketh the sovereyn good, al be it so that it be with

---

3 streyte sete, *deep seat* **4 cures,** *cares* **5 travaylen hem,** *trouble themselves* **7 enforsen hem,** *strive* **8 oon,** *the single* **12 forsothe,** *truly,* **sovereyn,** *ultimate* **15 cleped,** *called* **16 ilke,** *same* **22 For-why,** *consequently,* **coveytise,** *desire* **26 wenen,** *believe* **29 demen,** *judge* **30 ryht digne,** *very worthy* **34 heyh,** *high* **35 regnen,** *reign* **40 mesuren,** *gauge* **42 wenen,** *think* **53 manere clernesse,** *kind of brightness* **56 forsothe,** *truly,* **rekned,** *reckoned* **58 manere,** *kind of* **61 referren,** *relate* **66 hele,** *health* **68 For-why,** *consequently,* **thilke,** *that* **70 demeth,** *thinks* **71 deffyned,** *stated* **72 whyht,** *person* **76 purposed,** *supposed* **82 byrefte,** *deprived* **85 corage,** *heart,* **reherseth,** *returns to*

3 Prose 2. 3 sete, C^2 reads "cyte." **79 Epicurus,** Greek philosopher (c. 341–270 B.C.E.) who argued that pleasure (which he defined as freedom from pain, fear, or worry) was the goal of human life.

a dirked° memorye; but he not° by whiche paath, ryht° as a dronken man not nat° by whiche paath he may retorne him to his hows. Semeth it thanne that foolk foleyen° and erren that enforcen hem to have nede of nothing? Certes, ther nis non oother thyng that may so wel performe° blysfulnesse as an estat plentyous of alle goodes, that ne hath nede of non oother thing, but that it is suffysaunt° of hymself unto hymself. And foleyen swyche folk°, thanne, that wenen° that thilke thing that is ryht good, that it be ek ryht worthy of honour and of reverence? Certes, nay. For that thing nys neyther foul ne worthy to ben despised that welneyh° alle the entencyoun of mortal foolk travaylen° for to geten yt. And powere, owhte° nat that ek to ben rekened amonges goodes? What elles? For it is nat to wene° that thilke thyng that is most worthy of alle thinges be feble and withowte strengthe. And cleernesse of renoun, owhte that to ben despised? Certes, ther may no man forsake that alle thyng that is ryht excellent and noble, that it ne semeth to ben ryht cleer and renomed°. For certes, it nedeth nat to seye that blysfulnesse be nat angwyssous° ne drery, ne subgyd to grevaunces ne to sorwes, syn° that in ryht lytel thynges folk seken to have and to usen that may delyten hem. Certes, thise ben the thinges that men wolen and desyren to geten. And for this cause desyren they rychesses, dignites, regnes, glorye, and delices. For therby wenen they to han suffysaunse°, honour, power, renoun, and gladnesse. Than is it good that men seken thus by so many diverse studies. In whiche desyr it may lyghtly° ben shewed how gret is the strengthe of nature, for how so° that men han diverse sentences° and discordinge, allgates° men acorden alle in lovinge the ende° of good.

Metre 2. Quantas rerum flectat.

"It lyketh me to shewe by subtil song, with slakke° and delitable° soun of strenges°, how that Nature, myhty, enclyneth° and flitteth° the governements of thinges, and by whyche lawes she, purveyable°, kepeth the grete world, and how she, byndinge, restreyneth alle thinges by a bonde that may nat ben unbownde. Al be it so that the lyouns° of the contre of Pene beren the fayre chaynes, and taken metes° of the handes of folk that yeven it hem, and dreden her sturdy° maystres of whiche they ben wont° to suffren betinges. Yif that her horyble mowthes ben bybled° *(that is to seyn, of bestes devowred),* her corage of tyme passed, that hath ben ydel and rested, repeyreth° ayein, and they roren grevously, and remembren on her nature, and slaken° her nekkes fram hir chaynes unbownde; and her mayster, fyrst to-torn° with blody toth, assayeth the wode wrathes of hem *(this is to seyn, they freten° hir mayster).* And the jangelinge° bryd that syngeth on the heye braunches *(that is to seyn, in the wode)* and after is enclosed in a streyht° cage althowh that the pleyinge bysynesse° of men yeveth hem honyede drynkes and large metes° with swete studye, yit natheles yif thylke bryd, skyppinge owt of hir streyte cage, seth° the agreables shadewes of the wodes, she defowleth with hir feet hir metes ishad°, and seketh mowrninge° oonly the wode, and twitereth desyringe the wode with hir swete voys. The yerde° of a tre that is haled° adown by myhty strengthe boweth redyly the crop° adown, but yif that the hand of hym that it bent lat it goon ayein, anon the crop loketh upryht to hevene. The sonne Phebus that falleth at even in the westrene wawes° retorneth ayein eftsones° his carte by pryve° paath

---

87 dirked, *darkened,* **he not,** *they don't know* **88 ryht,** *just,* **not nat,** *knows not* **90 folyen,** *commit folly* **93 performe,** *bring about* **96 suffysaunt,** *sufficient* **97 foleyen swyche folk,** *do such people commit folly,* **wenen,** *think* **101 welneyh,** *nearly* **102 travaylen,** *labor* **103 owhte,** *ought* **105 wene,** *think* **111 renomed,** *renowned* **112 angwyssous,** *anxiety ridden* **114 syn,** *since* **120 suffysaunse,** *self-sufficiency* **123 lyghtly,** *easily* **124 how so,** *even though* **125 sentences,** *opinions* **126 allgates,** *nevertheless* **127 ende,** *goal* 3 Meter 2. **2 slakke,** *soft,* **delitable,** *pleasant,* **strenges,** *strings* **3 enclyneth,** *moves,* **flitteth,** *changes* **5 purveyable,** *able to provide* **8 lyouns,** *lions* **10 taken metes,** *accept food* **11 sturdy,** *stern* **12 wont,** *accustomed* **13 bybled,** *bloodied* **16 repeyreth,** *returns* **17 slaken,** *loosen* **19 to-torn,** *torn apart* **21** ***freten,*** *eat* **22 jangelinge,** *noisy* **24 streyht,** *narrow* **25 pleyinge bysynesse,** *amused attention* **26 large metes,** *generous food* **28 seth,** *sees* **30 metes ishad,** *scattered food* **31 mowrninge,** *yearning* **33 yerde,** *stem,* **haled,** *pulled* **34 crop,** *sapling* **38 wawes,** *waves* **39 eftsones,** *again,* **pryve,** *secret*

87 dirked memorye, it is a Platonic and neo-Platonic commonplace that wisdom is a recollection of the dim or lost memory of truths known to humans before our descent into material existence. See 3.pr3.1–6. **9 Pene,** Carthage, in northern Africa. **25 pleyinge,** C[2] reads "pleynynge." The Latin is *ludens.* **28 owt,** Hn has lost a leaf between here and the beginning of Meter 3.

thereas it is wont° aryse. Alle thinges seken ayein to her propre cours, and alle thinges rejoysen hem of her retorninge ayein to her nature. Ne non ordynaunce° nis bytaken° to thinges but that that hath joyned the endinge to the bygynninge and hath maked the cours of itself stable *(that it chaungeth nat from his propre kynde°).*

Prose 3. Vos quoque o terrena animalia.

"Certes also ye men, that ben erthelyche beestes, dremen alwey yowre bygynninge, althowh it be with a thynne imagynacyoun; and by a maner° thowghte, al be it nat clerly ne perfytly, ye loken fram afer to thylke verray fyn° of blysfulnesse. And therfore naturel entencyoun° ledeth yow to thylke verray good, but many maner errours mystorneth yow therfro°. Considere now yif that by thylke thinges by whiche a man weneth° to geten him blysfulnesse, yif that he may comen to thylke ende that he weneth to come by nature. For yif that moneye or honours or thyse oother forseyde thinges bryngen to men swych a thyng that no good ne fayle hem ne semeth fayle, certes than wole° I graunte that they ben maked blysful by thylke thinges that they han geten. But yif so be that thylke thynges ne mowen° nat performen° that they byheten°, and that ther be defaute° of manye goodes, sheweth it nat thanne clerly that fals beaute° of blysfulnesse is knowen and ataynt° in thylke° thynges? Fyrst and forward thow thyself, that haddest habundaunces of rychesses nat long agoon, I axe° yif that, in the habundaunce of alle thylke richesses, thow were never angwissous° or sory in thy corage° of any wrong or grevaunce that bytydde the° on any syde?"

"Certes," quod I, "it ne remembreth me nat that evere I was so free of my thowht that I ne was alwey in angwyssh of somwhat°."

"And was nat that," quod she, "for that the° lacked somwhat that thow noldest nat han° lacked, or elles thow haddest that thow noldest nat han had?"

"Ryht so is it," quod I.

"Thanne desiredest thow the presence of that oon and the absence of that oother?"

"I graunte wel," quod I.

"Forsothe°," quod she, "than° nedeth ther somwhat that every man desireth?"

"Ye, ther nedeth," quod I.

"Certes," quod she, "and he that hath lacke or nede of awht° nis nat in every wey suffysaunte° to hymself?"

"No," quod I.

"And thow," quod she, "in al the plente of thy rychesses haddest thilke° lacke of suffisaunse?"

"What elles?" quod I.

"Thanne may nat rychesses maken that a man nis nedy°, ne that he be suffisaunt to hymself; and yit that was it that they byhyhten°, as it semeth. And ek certes I trowe that thys be gretly to consydere, that moneye ne hath nat in his° owne kynde° that it ne may ben bynomen of hem° that han it, mawgre° hem."

"I byknowe it wel," quod I.

"Why sholdesthow nat byknowen it," quod she, "whan every day the strengere° folk bynemen it fro the feblere, mawgre hem? For whennes comen elles alle thyse foreyne compleyntes° or quereles of pletynges but for that men axen ayein here° moneye that hath ben bynomen hem by force or by gyle, and alwey mawgre hem?"

"Right so is it," quod I.

"Than," quod she, "hath a man nede to seken him foreyne° help by whyche he may deffende his moneye?"

"Who may sey nay?" quod I.

"Certes," quod she, "and him nedede non help yif he ne hadde no moneye that he myhte lese."

---

40 wont, *accustomed to* **43 non ordynaunce,** *no law,* **bytaken,** *assigned* **47 kynde,** *nature* **3 Prose 3. 4 maner,** *kind of* **6 thylke verray fyn,** *that true goal* **7 entencyoun,** *inclination* **9 therfro,** *from this* **11 weneth,** *thinks* **16 wole,** *will* **19 mowen,** *may,* **performen,** *bring about* **20 byheten,** *promise,* **defaute,** *lack* **22 fals beaute,** *illusion* **23 ataynt,** *attained,* i.e., **thylke,** *those* **24 forward,** *foremost* **25 axe,** *ask* **27 angwissous,** *anxious* **28 corage,** *heart* **29 bytydde the,** *happened to you* **32 somwhat,** *something* **33 for that the,** *because you* **34 noldest nat han,** *wished not to have* **41 Forsothe,** *truly,* **than,** *then* **45 awht,** *anything* **46 suffysaunte,** *sufficient* **49 thilke,** *this* **53 nis nedy,** *is not needy* **54 byhyhten,** *promised* **57 his,** *its,* **kynde,** *nature* **57–58 bynomen of hem,** *taken from them* **58 mawgre,** *in spite of* **61 strengere,** *stronger* **63–64 foreyne compleyntes,** *public appeals* **64 quereles of pletynges,** *contentious pleadings* **65 axen ayein here,** *request the return of their* **70 foreyne,** *external*

3 Prose 3. 6 verray fyn of blysfulnesse, compare *TC* 5.1828–32. **33–35** This idea is echoed in *PF* 90–91.

"That is dowteles," quod I.

"Than is this thing torned into the contrarye," quod she. "For richesses, that men wenen° sholde make suffisaunce, they maken a man rather han nede of foreyne help. Whych is the manere or the gyse°," quod she, "that rychesse may dryve awey nede? Ryche foolk, may they neyther han hunger ne thurst? Thyse ryche men, may they fele no coold on her lymes° on wynter? But thow wolt answeren that ryche men han ynow° wherwith they may staunchen her honger, slaken her thurst, and don awey coold. In thys wyse may nede be counforted by rychesses, but certes nede ne may nat al utrely° ben don awey. For thowgh this nede, that is alwey gapinge and gredy, be fulfyld with rychesses and axe° anything, yit dwelleth thanne a nede that myhte be fulfyld. I holde me stille and telle nat how that lytel thyng suffiseth to nature, but certes to averyce ynowh ne suffiseth nothing°. For syn that° rychesses ne may nat al doon awey nede, but rychesses maken nede, what° may it thanne be that ye wenen that richesses mowen yeven° yow suffisaunce?

Metre 3. Quamvis fluente dives auri gurgite.

"Al were it so that a ryche coveytous man hadde a ryver fletinge° al of gold, yit sholde it never staunchen his coveytyse; and thow° he hadde his nekke ycharged° with precyous stones of the Rede See, and thow he do ere° his feeldes plentyuous with an hundred oxen, never ne shal his bytinge bysynesse° forleten° him whyl he leveth°, ne the lyhte° rychesses ne shol nat beren him compaignie whan he is ded.

Prose 4. Set dignitates honorabilem.

"But dignitees°, to whom they ben comen, maken they him honorable and reverent? Han they nat so gret strengthe that they may putte vertuus in the hertes of foolk that usen the lordshippes of hem? Or elles may they don awey the vyces? Certes, they ne be nat wont° to don awey wykkednesse, but they ben wont rather shewen wykkednesse. And therof comth it that I have ryht gret desdaigne that dignites ben yeven ofte to wykked men. For which thyng Catullus cleped° (*a consul of Rome, that hyhte°)* Nomyus, 'postum°' or 'boch°' *(as who seyth, he cleped him a congregasyoun of vyces in his brest, as a postum is ful of corupsyoun),* al were° this Nomyus set in a chayre of dignite. Sesthow nat° thanne how gret vilenye dignitees don to wykked men? Certes, unworthynesse of wykked men sholde be the lasse° isene° yif they nere renomed° of none honours. Certes, thow thyself ne myhtest nat ben browht with° as manye perils as thou myhtest suffren that thow woldest beren the magestrat° with Decorat *(that is to seyn, that for no peril that myhte befallen the by offense of the Kyng Theodoryke thow noldest nat be felawe° in governaunce with Decorat)* whan thou saye° that he hadde wykked corage° of a lykerous shrewe° and of an acusor°. Ne I ne may nat for swyche honours jugen hem worthy of reverence that I deme° and holde unworthy to han thylke° same honours. Now yif thow saye a man that were fulfild° of wysdom, certes thow ne myhtest nat deme that he were unworthy to the honour or elles to the wysdom of which he is fulfyld?"

"No," quod I.

"Certes, dignites," quod she, "apertienen proprely° to vertu, and vertu transporteth° dignite anon° to thilke man to whych she hirself is conjoigned. And for as moche as honours of poeple ne may nat maken folk digne° of honour, it is wel seyn clerly that they ne han no propre beaute of dignite. And yit men owhten taken mor heed in thys.

78 wenen, *believe* **81 gyse,** *way* **85 lymes** *limbs* **86 ynow,** *enough* **90 utrely,** *utterly* **92 axe,** *ask for* **96 nothing,** *not at all* **96–97 syn that,** *because* **98 what,** *why* **99–100 mowen yeven,** *might give* **3 Meter 3. 2 fletinge,** *flowing* **3 thow,** *though* **4 ycharged,** *loaded* **5 ere,** *plow* **7 bytinge bysynesse,** *gnawing concerns* **8 forleteth,** *leave,* **leveth,** *lives,* i.e., **lyhte,** *unreliable* **3 Prose 4. 1 dignitees,** *public offices* **6 wont,** *accustomed* **11 cleped,** *labeled* **12** ***that hyhte,*** *who is named,* **postum,** *tumor,* **boch,** *ulcer* **14–15 al were,** *even though* **16 Sesthow nat,** *don't you see* **18 lasse,** *less* **19 isene,** *seen,* **renomed,** *renowned* **21 ben browht with,** *have been threatened with* **23 beren the magestrat,** *share the office of magistrate* **26** ***felawe,*** *companion* **27 saye,** *saw,* **corage,** *heart* **28 lykerous shrewe,** *greedy villain,* **acusor,** *informer* **30 deme,** *judge* **31 thylke,** *these* **32 fulfild,** *full* **37–38 apertienen proprely,** *pertain appropriately* **38 transporteth,** *conveys* **39 anon,** *immediately* **42 digne,** *worthy*

97 awey, C[2] reads "alwey." **3 Meter 3. 5 Rede See,** Red Sea, which lies between Africa and Arabia. **3 Prose 4. 11–12 Catullus . . . Nomyus,** in his *Carmen* (Song) 52.2, the Roman poet Catullus mocks Nonius, a Roman official, by calling him a tumor. **23 Decorat,** a Roman magistrate about 508 C.E. **25** ***Kyng Theodoryke,*** see 1.pr4.75n. **44–52** The clauses are rearranged in some of the manuscripts; the reading here from C[2] follows the sequence of the Latin.

For yif it so be that a wykked whyht° be so mochel° the fowlere° and the moore owtcast that he is despised of most folk, so as dignite° ne may nat maken shrewes digne° of reverence, the whych shrewes dignete° sheweth to moche° foolk, thanne maketh dignete shrewes rather so moche more despised than preysed; and forsothe° nat unpunisshed *(that is for to seyn, that shrewes revengen hem ayeinward upon dignetes)*, for they yilden° ayein to dignetes° as gret gerdoun°, whan they byspotten and defowlen dignetes with hire vylenie. And for as mochel as thow mowe° knowe that thilke verray° reverence ne may nat comen by thyse shadwy transitorye dignetes, undyrstond now thus: yif that a man hadde used and had many maner dignitees° of consules, and were comen peraventure° amonges straunge nacyouns, sholde thilke honour maken him worshipful and redowted° of straunge foolk? Certes, yif that honour of poeple were a naturel yift to dignites, it ne myhte never cesen nowher amonges no manere foolk to don his offyce°, ryht as fyre in every contre ne stynteth° nat to eschaufen° and to ben hoot. But for as mochel as for to ben holden honourable or reverent ne cometh nat to foolk of her propre strengthe of nature, but oonly of the false opynioun of foolk *(that is to seyn, that wenen° that dignetes° maken foolk digne° of honour)*, anon° therfore, whan that they comen thereas° folk ne knowen nat thylke dignites, her honours vanesshen awey, and that anon. But that is amonges straunge° folk, maysthow seyn°. Ne° amonges hem ther° they weren born ne duren nat thylke dignitees° alwey? Certes, the dignite of the provostrye° of Rome was whylom° a gret power; now is it nothing but an idel name, and the rente of° the senatorye a gret charge°. And yif a whyht° whylom hadde the office to taken heede to the vytayles° of the poeple, as of corn and oother thynges, he was holden amonges grete. But what thyng is now more owtcast than thylke provostrye°? And as I have seyd a lytel her-byforn°, that thylke thyng that hath no propre beaute of hymself receyveth somtyme prys° and shyninge and somtyme leseth it by the opinioun of usaunces°. Now yif that dignitees° thanne ne mowen° nat maken foolk digne of reverence, and yif that dignites wexen fowle of her wylle by the felthe of shrewes°, and yif that dignites lesen her shyninge by chaunginge of tymes, and yif they wexen fowle by estymacyoun of poeple, what is it that they han in hemself of beaute that owhte ben desyred? *(As who seyth, non)*. Thanne ne mowen they yeven° no beaute of dignete to non oother.

Metre 4. Quamvis se Tyrio superbus ostro.

"Al be it so that the prowde Nero, with alle his woode° luxurie, kembde° him and aparaylede° him with fayre purpres of Tyrye, and with whyte perles, algates° yit throf° he hateful to alle foolk *(this is to seyn, that al was he behated of alle folk, yit this wycked Nero hadde gret lordshippe)*, and yaf° whylom to the reverents senatours the unworshipful setes of dignities. *(Unworshipful setes he clepeth° here, for that Nero, that was so wykked, yaf tho dignetes°.)* Whoso wolde thanne resonably wenen° that blysfulnesse were in swyche honours as ben yeven by vycyous shrewes?

Prose 5. An vero regna.

"But regnes and famyliarites of° kynges, may they maken a man to ben myhty? How elles, whan her blysfulnesse dureth perpetualy? But

45 whyht, *person* **46 sheweth to mochel,** *exposes to much,* **fowlere,** *more foul* **47 so as dignite,** *given that honor* **48 digne,** *worthy* **49 dignete,** *honor,* **moche,** *many* **52 forsothe,** *truly* **54 yilden,** *give back* **54 dignetes,** *public offices* **54–55 as gret gerdoun,** *as great a reward* **57 mowe,** *may,* **thilke verray,** *this true* **61 maner dignitees,** *of the kinds of honors* **62 peraventure,** *perhaps* **64 redowted,** *respected* **67 his offyce,** *its function* **68 stynteth,** *ceases* **69 eschaufen,** *grow hot* **73 wenen,** *think* **74 dignetes,** *public offices,* i.e., **digne,** *worthy,* **anon,** *immediately* **75 thereas,** *where* **78 straunge,** *foreign,* **maysthow seyn,** *you might say,* **Ne,** i.e., is it not true that, **ther,** *where* **80 duren nat thylke dignitees,** (might) *not these honors endure* **81 dignite of the provostrye,** *office of the provost* (city manager) **82 whylom,** *formerly* **83 rente of,** *salary to* **84 charge,** *burden,* **whyht,** *person* **85 vytayles,** *food* **88 thylke provostrye,** *this office of provost* **89 her-byforn,** *before this* **91 prys,** *value* **92–93 opinioun of usaunces,** *current attitudes* **93 dignitees,** *high offices* **94 mowen,** *may* **96 felthe of shrewes,** *stain of wicked men* **101 yeven,** *give* **3 Meter 4. 2 woode,** *insane,* **kembde,** *combed,* **aparayled,** *dressed* **4 algates,** *neverthless,* **throf,** *thrived* **7 yaf,** *gave* **9 clepeth, labels 10 tho dignetes,** *those offices* **11 wenen,** *think* **3 Prose 5. 1 famyliarites of,** *associations with*

89 seyd a lytel her-byforn, see 3.pr4.40–43. **3 Meter 4. 3 purpres of Tyrye,** robes dyed purple in Tyre; imperial purple.

certes, the olde age of tyme passed, and ek of present tyme now, is ful of ensaunpyles how that kynges ben chaunged into wrechchednesse owt of her welefulnesse°. O a noble thing and a cleer° thing is power, that is nat fownden myhty to kepen° itself! And yif that power of reaumes° be auctour° and makere of blysfulnesse, yif thilke power lacketh on any syde amenuseth° it nat thilke blysfulnesse and bryngeth in wrechchednesse? But yit al be it so that the reaumes of mankynde strechchen brode, yit mot° ther nede ben° moche foolk over whyche that every kyng ne hath no lordshipe ne comaundement. And certes, upon thilke side that power fayleth, whych that maketh foolk blysful, ryht on that same syde none-power° entreth undernethe that maketh hem wrechches. In this manere thanne moten° kynges han more porcioun of wrechchednesse than of welefulnesse. A tyraunt, that was kyng of Sysile, that hadde assayed° the peril of his estat shewede by symylitude the dredes of reaumes by gastnesse° of a swerd that heng over the heved° of his famylier°. What thyng is thanne this power, that may nat doon awey the bytinges of bysynesse ne eschue° the prikkes of drede? And certes, yit wolden they lyven in sikernesse°, but they may nat; and yit they gloryfye hem in her power. Holdest thow° thanne that thylke man be myhty that thow seyst that he wolde don that he may nat doon? And holdest thou thanne him a myhty man that hath envyrownede° his sydes with men of armes or serjaunts, and dredeth more hem that he maketh agast° than they dreden him, and that is put in the handes of his servaunts for he sholde seme myhty? But of famylieres or servaunts of kynges what sholde I telle the anything, syn° that I myself have shewed the that reames hemself° ben ful of gret feblesse? The whyche famylieres, certes, the ryal° power of kynges in hool estat and in estat abated° ful ofte throweth adown. Nero constreynede Senek, his famylier and his mayster, to chesen on what deeth he wolde deyen. Antonius comaundede that knyghtes slowen° with her swerdes Papynian his famylier, which Papynian that hadde ben longe tyme ful myghty amonges hem of the court. And yit certes they wolden bothe han renounced her power; of whyche two Senecke enforcede him° to yeven to Nero his richesses, and also to han gon into solytarye exil. But whan the grete weyhte° *(that is to seyn, of lordes power or of fortune)* draweth° hem that sholen falle, neyther of hem ne myhte do that he wolde. What thing is thanne thilke power, that thowh men han it, yit they ben agast°, and whanne thow woldest han it, thow nart nat siker°; and yif thow woldest forleten° it, thow mayst nat eschuen° it? But wheyther° swyche men ben frendes at nede, as ben conseyled by fortune and nat by vertu? Certes, swyche foolk as weleful fortune maketh freendes, contraryous fortune maketh hem enemys. And what pestylence is moore myhty for to anoye a wyht than a famylier enemy?

Metre 5. Qui se volet esse potentem.

"Whoso wole be myhty, he mot daunten° his crwel corage°, ne putte nat his nekke, over-comen, under the fowle reynes of lecherye. For al be it so that thy lordshype strechche so fer that the contre of Ynde° quaketh at thy comaundements or at thy lawes, and that the last ile in the see that hyhte° Tyle be thral° to the, yit yif thou mayst nat putten awey thy fowle dyrke desyrs, and dryven owt fro thee wrechched complayntes, certes, it nis no powere that thow hast.

---

7 welefulnesse, *happiness* **8 cleer,** *shining* **9 kepen,** *protect* **10 reaumes,** *realms,* **auctour,** *author* **12 amenuseth,** *diminishes* **15 mot,** *must* **16 nede ben,** *necessarily be* **20 none-power,** *powerlessness* **22 moten,** *must* **25 assayed,** *experienced* **27 gastnesse,** *terror* **28 heved,** *head,* **famylier,** *subject* **30 eschue,** *avoid* **32 sikernesse,** *security* **33 Holdest thow,** *do you consider* **37 envyrownede,** *surrounded* **39 agast,** *fearful* **43 syn,** *since* **44 reames hemself,** *kingdoms themselves* **46 ryal,** *royal* **47 abated,** *lessened* **51 slowen,** *slay* **55–56 enforcede him,** *strove* **58 weyhte,** *weight* **59 draweth,** *pulls* **62 agast,** *afraid* **63 nart nat siker,** *are not secure* **64 forleten,** *abandon,* **eschuen,** *avoid* **65 wheyther,** (let us consider) *whether* **3 Meter 5. 1 mot daunten,** *must overcome* **2 crwel corage,** *fierce heart* **5 Ynde,** *India* **7 hyhte,** *is called,* **thral,** *subject* **3 Prose 6.**

3 Prose 5. 20 none-power, C^1 reads "noun-power." **24 kyng of Sysile,** Dionysius (the elder), King of Syracuse; when Damocles praised the stability of the king's realm, Dionysius seated Damocles beneath a sword that hung suspended by a single hair, an image of the ruler's peril. **48 Nero . . . Seneca,** see 1.pr3.59n. **50–52 Antonius . . . Papynian,** M. Antoninus Caracalla executed the Roman jurist Aemilius Papianius (c.212) because he supported Caracalla's brother. **66–69 But wheyther . . . ,** i.e., Philosophy asks whether true friends are those who are made by fortune or by virtuous action. **3 Meter 5. 7 the last ile . . . Tyle,** Thule, the name given by the ancients to the northernmost island of Europe; "Ultimate Thule" signifies the outermost edge of the known world.

Prose 6. Gloria vero quam fallax.

"But glorye, how deceyvable° and how fowl is it ofte! For whych thyng nat unskylfully° a tragedyen *(that is to seyn, a makere of ditees° that hyhten° tragedies)* cryde and seyde: 'O glorye, glorye,' quod he, 'thow nart nothing elles to thowsandes of foolkes but a gret swellere of eres°!' For manye han had ful gret renoun by the false opynioun of the poeple, and what thyng may ben thowht fowlere than swyche preysinge? For thylke° foolk that ben preysed falsly, they moten nedes° han shame of her preysinges. And yif that foolk han geten hem thonk° or preysinge by her desertes, what thyng hath thylke prys eched° or encresed to the conscience of wyse folk, that mesuren her good nat by the rumour of the poeple but by the sothfastnesse° of conscience? And yif it seme a fayr thyng a man to han encresed and spred his name, than folweth it that it is demed to ben a fowl thing yif it ne be isprad and encresed. But, as I seyde a lytul her-biforn, that syn° ther mot nedes ben° many foolk to whyche foolk the renoun of a man ne may nat comen, it befalleth that he that thow wenest be° glorious and renomed semeth in the nexte partie° of the erthes to ben withowte glorye and withowte renoun.

"And certes, amonges thyse thynges I ne trowe nat that the prys and grace of the poeple nis neyther worthy to ben remenbred, ne cometh of wyse jugement, ne is ferme perdurably°. But now, of thys name of gentellesse°, what man is it that ne may wel sen how veyn and how flyttinge a thyng it is? For yif the name of gentellesse be refferred to renoun and clernesse° of lynage°, thanne is gentyl name but a foreyne° thyng *(that is to seyn, to hem that gloryfien hem of her lynage)*. For it semeth that gentellesse be a maner° preysinge that comth of the deserte of auncestres. And yif preysinge maketh gentilesse, thanne moten they nedes be° gentyl that ben preysed. For which thing it folueth that yif thow ne have no gentellesse of thyself *(that is to seyn, preyse that comth of thy deserte)*, foreyne gentyllesse ne maketh the nat gentyl. But certes, yif ther be any good in gentyllesse, I trowe° it be aloonly this, that it semeth as that a maner necessitee be inposed to gentel men for that they ne sholden nat owtrayen° or forlyven° fro the vertuus of her noble kynrede.

Metre 6. Omne hominum genus in terris.

"Al the lynage of men that ben in erthe ben of semblable° byrthe. On° allone is fader of thynges. On allone mynystreth° alle thinges. He yaf° to the sonne his beemes, he yaf to the moene hir hornes, he yaf the men to the erthe, he yaf the sterres to the hevene. He encloseth with menbres the sowles that comen fram his hye sete°. Thanne comen alle mortal folk of noble sede. Why noysen ye° or bosten of yowre eldres, for yif thow loke yowr bygynninge, and God yowr auctor and yowre makere, thanne nis ther no forlyved° wyht, but yif° he norysse his corage unto vyces and forlete° his propre burthe.

Prose 7. Quid autem de corporis.

"But what shal I seye of delites of body, of whyche delites the desyringes ben ful of angwyssh, and the fulfyllinges of hem ben ful of penaunce? How gret sykenesse and how gret soruwes unsufferable, ryht as a manere° frut° of wyckednesse, ben thilke delytes wont° to bryngen to the bodyes of foolk that usen hem! Of whyche delytes I not° what joye may ben had of her moevinge. But thys wot I wel, that whosoever wole remenbren him of his luxures°, he shal wel understonde that the yssues° of delites ben sorwful and sorye. And yif

1 deceyvable, *deceptive* **2 nat unskylfully,** *not unreasonably* **3 ditees,** *poems* **4 hyhten,** *are called* **7 eres,** *ears* **10 thylke,** *those* **11 moten nedes,** *necessarily* **13 thonk,** *thanks* **15 thylke prys eched,** *this praise added* **17 sothfastnesse,** *truth* **22 syn,** *since,* **mot nedes ben,** *must necessarily be* **25 wenest be,** *think to be* **26 partie,** *section* **32 ferme perdurably,** *stable eternally* **33 gentellesse,** *gentility* **36 clernesse,** *fame,* **lynage,** *lineage* **37 foreyne,** *external* **39 maner,** *kind of* **42 moten they nedes be,** *they must necessarily be* **47 trowe,** *think* **50 owtrayen,** *deviate,* **forlyven,** *degenerate* **3 Meter 6. 2 semblable,** *similar,* **On,** *one* **3 mynystreth,** *administers* **4 yaf,** *gave* **8 hye sete,** *high throne* **9 noysen ye,** *do you make noise about* **12 forlyved,** *degenerate* **13 but yif,** *unless* **14 forlete,** *abandon* **3 Prose 7. 5 ryht as a manere,** *like a kind of,* **6 frut,** *fruit,* **wont,** *accustomed* **8 not,** *know not* **11 luxures,** *lusts* **12 yssues,** *results*

3 Prose 6. 4–6 O glorye . . . , from Euripedes, *Andromache* 319–20. **22 lytul her-biforn,** see 2.pr7.76–80. **3 Meter 6.** This is echoed in *WBT* 3.1109ff. and in Chaucer's "Moral Balade" (Short Poem 12). **12 wyht,** C[1] reads "wyght or ongentil."

thylke delites mowen° maken folk blysful, than by the same cause moten° thyse bestes° ben cleped° blysful, of whyche bestes al the entencyoun hasteth to fulfylle her bodyly jolite. And the gladnesse° of° wyf and chyldren were an honest thyng, but it hath ben seyd that it is over mochel ayeins kynde° that chyldren han ben fownden tormentours to her fadres—I nat° how manye—of whyche chyldren how bytinge° is every condycioun it nedeth nat to tellen it the that hast or thus° tyme assayed° it, and art yit now angwyssous°. In this approve I the sentence of my disciple Eurydyppys, that seyde that he that hath no chyldren is weleful° by infortune°.

Metre 7. Habet hoc voluptas.

"Every delit hath this, that it anguisseth hem with prikkes that usen° it. It resembleth to thise flyenge flyes that we clepen ben°; that after he hath shad° his agreable honyes, he fleth awey and styngeth the hertes of hem that ben ysmyte with bytinge overlonge holdinge°.

Prose 8. Nihil igitur dubium.

"Now is it no dowte thanne that thise weyes ne ben a manere° mysledinges to blysfulnesse, ne that they ne mowe nat leden folk thyder as they byheten° to leden hem. But with how grete harmes thise forseyde weyes ben enlaced° I shal shewe the shortly. For-why° yif thow enforcest the° to asemble moneye, thow most byreven° him his moneye that hath it. And yif thow wolt shynen with dignetes°, thow most bysechen and supplien° hem that yeven° tho dignitees. And yif thow coveytest° by honour to gon byforn oother folk, thow shal defowle thyself thorw humblesse° of axinge°. Yif thow desyrest power, thow shalt by awaytes° of thy subgits anoyously ben cast under by many peryles. Axestow° glorye? Thow shalt ben so destrat° by aspre° thinges that thou shalt forgoon sykernesse°. And yif thow wolt leden thy lyf in delites, every wyht° shal despisen the and forleten° the, as thow that art thral° to thing that is ryht fowl and brotel° *(that is to seyn, servaunt to thy body).* Now is it thanne wel seen, how lytel and how brotel possessyoun they coveyten that putten the goodes of the body aboven her owne resoun. For maysthow sormounten° thyse olyfaunts° in gretnesse or weyht of body? Or maysthow ben strengere than the bole°? Maysthow ben swyftere than the tygre? Byhold the spaces and the stablenesse and the swyft cours of the hevene, and stynt° somtyme to wondren on fowle thinges. The whych hevene, certes, nis nat rather for thyse thynges to ben wondred upon than for the resoun by whych it is governed. But the shyning of thy forme *(that is to seyn, the beaute of thy body),* how swyftly passinge is it, and how transytorye! Certes, it is more flyttinge than the mutabylytee of flowers of the somer sesoun. For so Arystotle telleth, that yif that men hadden eyen of a beest that hyhte° lynx, so that the lokinge of foolk myghte percen thorw the thynges that withstonden it, whoso loked thanne in the entrayles of the body of Alcidiades, that was ful fayre in superfyce° withowte, it sholde seme ryht fowl. And forthy°, yif thow semest fayr, thy nature maketh nat that, but the desceyvaunce° of the feblesse of the eyen that loken. But preyse the goodes of the body as mochel as ever the list°, so that thow knowe algates° that whatso

13 mowen, *may* **14 moten,** *must,* **bestes,** *beasts* **15 cleped,** *called* **17 gladnesse of,** *joy in* **19 over mochel ayeins kynde,** *a great deal against nature* **21 nat,** *know not* **22 bytinge,** *painful* **23 or thus,** *before this* **24 assayed,** *experienced,* **angwyssous,** *anxiety ridden* **27 weleful,** *happy,* **infortune,** *misfortune* 3 Meter 7. **2 usen,** *enjoy* **3 clepen ben,** *call bees* **4 shad,** *spread* **6 ben ysmyte with bytinge overlonge holdinge,** *are smitten with a pain that lasts too long* 3 Prose 8. **2 manere,** *kind of* **4 byheten,** *promise* **5 enlaced,** *intertwined* **6 For-why,** *because* **6 enforcest the,** *push yourself* **8 byreven,** *deprive* **9 dignetes,** *honors* **10 supplien,** *beg,* **yeven,** *bestow* **11 coveytest,** *desire* (covet) **13 humblesse,** *lowness,* **axinge,** *asking* **14 awaytes,** *snares* **16 Axestow,** *Do you ask for* **17 destrat,** *bothered,* **aspre,** *bitter* **18 sykernesse,** *security* **19 wyht,** *person* **20 forleten,** *abandon,* **thral,** *slave* **21 brotel,** *fragile* **26 sormounten,** *surpass* **olyfaunts,** *elephants* **28 bole,** *bull* **30 stynt,** *cease* **41 hyhte,** *is called* **45 in superfyce,** *on the surface* **46 forthy,** *therefore* **47 desceyvaunce,** *deception* **49–50 the list,** *you wish* **50 algates,** *nevertheless*

3 Prose 7. **26 Eurydyppys,** Greek dramatist, Euripides, *Andromache* 418–20. 3 Prose 8. **39–46 Arystotle . . . Alcidiades . . . ,** no parallel has been found in the extant works of Aristotle, although there is evidence that the account may have been in his lost *Protrepticus.* The Athenian general and statesman, Alcibiades, was known for his physical beauty and political corruption. **41 lynx,** Chaucer capitalizes on the tradition that the lynx has sharp eyes, although in the Latin the reference is to Lynceus, the keen-eyed Argonaut who sailed with Jason seeking the Golden Fleece. **47–48 desceyvaunce of the,** C[2] reads "deceyvable or the."

it be *(that is to seyn, of the godes of thy body)* whych that thow wondrest upon may ben destroyed or dyssolved by the hete of a fevere of thre dayes. Of alle whyche forseyde thinges I may reducen this shortly in somme,° that thyse worldly goodes whyche that ne mowen nat yeven that° if they beheten°, ne ben nat perfyt by congregacioun of alle goodes, that they ne ben nat weyes ne pathes that bryngen man to blysfulnesse, ne maken men to ben blysful.

Metre 8. Eheu! que miseros tramite.

"Alias, whych° folye and whych ygnoraunce mysledeth wandringe wrechches fro the paath of verray° goode! Certes, ye ne seken no gold in grene trees, ne ye ne gaderen° nat precyous stones in the vynes, ne ye ne hyden nat yowre gynnes° in the hye mountaygnes to kachche fyssh of whyche ye may maken ryche festes. And yif yow lyketh to honte to rooes°, ye ne gon nat to the foordes of the water that hyhte° Tyrene. And over this, men knowen wel the crykes° and the cavernes of the see yhyd° in floodes, and knowen ek whych water is most plentyuous of whyte perles, and knowen whych water habowndeth° most of rede purpre *(that is to seyn, of a manere° skellefish with whych men dyen purpre)*, and knowen whych strondes° habownden most with tendre fysshes, or of sharpe fysshes that hyhten° echynnes°. But folk suffren° hemself to ben so blynde that hem ne rechcheth° nat to knowe where thilke godes° ben ihydd° whyche that they coveyten°, but plowngen° hem in erthe and seken there thylke° good that sormounteth° the hevene that bereth the sterres. What preyere may I maken that be digne° to the nyce° thowhtes of men? But I preye that they coveyten rychesse and honours, so that whan they han geten tho false goodes with gret travayle, that therby they mowe knowen the verray° goodes.

Prose 9. Hactenus mendacis formam.

"It suffyseth that I have shewed hyderto the forme of false welefulnesse°, so that yif thow loke now clerly, the order of myn entencyoun requireth from hennesforth to shewen the the verray welefulnesse."

"For sothe," quod I, "I se wel now that suffysaunce° may nat comen by rychesses, ne power by reames°, ne reverence by dignitees, ne gentylesse by glorye, ne joye by delices."

"And hasthow wel knowen the causes," quod she, "why it is?"

"Certes, me semeth," quod I, "that I se hem ryht as thowgh it were thorw a lytel klyfte°. But me were levere° knowen hem more opynly of the."

"Certes," quod she, "the resoun is al redy. For thylke thing that symply is o° thing, withowten any devysyoun, the errour and folye of mankynde departeth° and devydeth it, and mysledeth it, and transporteth from verray and parfyt° good to goodes that ben false and unparfyt. But sey me this: wenesthow° that he that hath nede of power, that him ne lacketh nothing?"

"Nay," quod I.

"Certes," quod she, "thow seyst aryht. For yif so be that ther ys a thing that in any partye° be feblere of power, certes, as in that, it mot nedes ben° nedy of foreyne help."

"Ryht so is it," quod I.

"Suffysaunce and power ben thanne of o kinde°?"

"So semeth it," quod I.

"And demesthow°," quod she, "that a thing that is of this manere *(that is to seyn, suffysaunt and myhty)* owhte ben despyced°, or elles that it be ryht digne° of reverence aboven alle thinges?"

---

55 somme, *summary* **57 that,** *what,* **beheten,** *promise* <u>**3 Meter 8.**</u> **1 whych,** *what* **3 verray,** *true* **4 gaderen,** *gather* **6 gynnes,** *nets* **8 honte to rooes,** *hunt deer* **10 hyhte,** *is called* **11 crykes,** *inlets* **12 yhyd,** *hidden* **14 habowndeth,** *abounds* **15 *manere,*** *kind of* **17 strondes,** *shores* **18 hyhten,** *are called* **19 echynnes,** *sea urchins,* **suffren,** *allow* **20 rechcheth,** *care* **21 thilke godes,** *those goods,* **ben ihydd,** *are hidden* **22 coveyten,** *desire* (covet), **plowngen,** *plunge* **23 thylke,** *those,* **sormounteth,** *surpass* **25 digne,** *worthy* **26 nyce,** *foolish* **30 verray,** *true* <u>**3 Prose 9.**</u> **2 welefulnesse,** *happiness* **7 suffysaunce,** *sufficiency* **8 reames,** *kingdoms* **13 klyfte,** *crack* **14 me were levere,** *I would rather* **17 o,** *one* **19 departeth,** *separates* **21 parfyt,** *perfect* **22 wenesthow,** *do you think* **28 partye,** *portion* **29 mot nedes ben,** *must necessarily be* **31–32 o kinde,** *a single nature* **34 demesthow,** *do you think* **36 despyced,** *despised* **37 digne,** *worthy*

<u>**3 Meter 8.**</u> **10 Tyrene,** Tyrrhenian sea, the waters west of Italy. **14–15 rede purpre,** red-purple; see 2m5.10–11n.

"Certes," quod I, "it nis no dowte that it is ryht worthy to ben reverenced."

"Lat us," quod she, "adden thanne reverence to suffysaunce and to power, so that we demen that thise thre thinges be al o thing."

"Certes," quod I, "lat us adden it, yif we wolen graunten the sothe°."

"What demesthow thanne?" quod she. "Is that a dyrk thing and nat noble *(that is suffisaunt, reverent, and myhty)* or elles that it is ryht noble and ryht cler° by celebryte of renoun? Considere thanne," quod she, "as we han graunted her-byforn, that he that ne hath nede of nothing, and is most myhty and most digne of honour, yif hym nedeth any clernesse° of renoun, whych clernesse he mighte nat graunten of hymself, so that, for lacke of thylke clernesse°, he myghte seme the febelere on any side or the more owtcast." *(Glose. This is to seyn, nay. For whoso that is suffysaunt, myhty, and reverent, clernesse of renoun folweth of the forseyde thinges; he hath it al redy of his suffysaunce.)*

Boece. "I may nat," quod I, "denye it; but I mot graunte as it is, that this thing be ryht celebrable° by clernesse of renoun and noblesse."

"Thanne folweth it," quod she, "that we adden clernesse of renoun to the ther forseyde thinges, so that ther ne be amonges hem no difference?"

"This is a consequens," quod I.

"This thing thanne," quod she, "that ne hath nede of no foreyne° thing, and that may don alle thinges by his strengthes, and that is noble and honorable, nis nat that a mery thing and a joyful?"

Boece. "But whennes°," quod I, "that any sorwe myhte comen to this thing that is swyche°, certes, I may nat thinke."

Philosophie "Than moten we graunte," quod she, "that this thing be ful of gladnesse, yif the forseyde thinges ben sothe°. And certes, also mote we graunten that suffysaunce, power, noblesse, reverence, and gladnesse ben only diverse by names, but her substaunce hath no diversite."

Boece. "It mot nedly ben so," quod I.

Philosophie "Thilke thing thanne," quod she, "that is oon and symple in his nature, the wykkednesse of men departeth° yt and devydeth it; and whan they enforcen hem to geten partye° of a thing that ne hath no part, they ne geten hem neyther thilke partye that nis non, ne the thing all hool that they ne desyre nat."

Boece. "In whych manere?" quod I.

Philosophie "Thilke man," quod she, "that secheth richesses to flen povertee, he ne travayleth him° nat for to gete power, for he hath levere° ben dyrk and vyl° and ek withdraweth from hymself many naturel delites for he nolde lese° the moneye that he hath assembled. But certes, in this manere he ne geteth him nat suffisaunce, that power forleteth°, and that moleste° prykketh, and that fylthe maketh owtcast, and that dyrkenesse hydeth. And certes, he that desireth oonly power, he wasteth and scatereth rychesse, and despyseth delits, and ek honour that is withowte power, ne he ne preyseth glorye nothing. Certes, thus seesthow wel that manye thinges faylen to hym, for he hath somtyme defaute° of many necessytees, and many angwysses byten him. And whan he ne may nat don tho defautes awey°, he forleteth° to ben myhty, and that is the thing that he most desyreth. And ryht thus may I maken semblable resouns° of honours, and of glorye, and of delits. For so as every of thyse forseyde thinges is the same that thise oother thinges ben *(that is to seyn, al oon thing)*, whoso that ever seketh to geten that oon of thise and nat that oothre, he ne geteth nat that° he desireth."

Boece. "What seysthow thanne, yif that a man coveyteth° to geten alle thise thinges togydere?"

Philosophie "Certes," quod she, "I wolde seye that he wolde geten him sovereyn blysfulnesse;

---

45 sothe, *truth* **49 cler,** *famous* **56 thylke clernesse,** *that fame* **64 celebrable,** *worthy of acclaim* **72 foreyne,** *external* **76 whennes,** *from what* **77 swyche,** *such* (as this) **81 sothe,** *true* **89 departeth,** *separates* **91 partye,** *a portion* **98 travayleth him,** *troubles himself* **99 levere,** *rather,* **vyl,** *vile* **101 nolde lese,** *would not lose* **103 forleteth,** *abandons* **104 moleste,** *trouble* **112 defaute,** *lack* **113–14 don tho defautes awey,** *make those lacks* (go) *away* **114 forleteth,** *ceases* **117 semblable resouns,** *similar arguments* **122 that,** *what* **125 coveyteth,** *desires*

51 her-byforn, see 3.pr2.107ff.

but that shal he nat fynde in tho thinges that I have shewed, that ne mowen° nat yeven that they beheten°."

Boece. "Certes, no," quod I.

"Thanne," quod she, "ne sholden men nat by no wey seken blysfulnesse in swyche thinges as men wene° that they ne mowen yeven, but o thing senglely of alle that men seken."

Boece. "I graunte wel," quod I, "ne no sothere° thing ne may ben sayd."

Philosophie "Now hasthow thanne," quod she, "the forme and the causes of false welefulnesse. Now torne and fiitte° the eyen of thy thowght, for there shalthow sen anon thilke verray blysfulnesse that I have byhyht° the."

Boece. "Certes," quod I, "it is cler and open, thowh it were to a blynde man. And that shewedest thow me ful wel a lytel herebiforn, whan thou enforcedest the° to shewe me the causes of the false blysfulnesse. For but yif° I be bygyled, thanne is thilke the verray blysfulnesse parfyt that parfytly maketh a man suffisaunt, myhty, honourable, noble, and ful of gladnesse. And for thow shalt wel knowe that I have wel understonden thyse thinges within my herte, I knowe wel that thilke blysfulnesse that may verrayly yeven° oon of the forseyde thinges, syn they ben al oon, I knowe, dowteles, that thilke thing is the fulle blysfulnesse."

Philosophie "O my norye°," quod she, "by this opinioun I seye that thow art blysful, yif thow putte this therto that° I shal seyn."

"What is that?" quod I.

"Trowesthow° that ther be anything in thise erthely mortal towmbling° thinges that may bryngen this estat?"

"Certes," quod I, "I trowe it nawht; and thow hast shewed me wel that over thilke good ther nis nothing more to ben desired."

Philosophie "Thise thinges thanne," quod she, *(that is to sey, erthely suffisaunce° and power and swyche thinges)* "eyther they semen lyckenesses° of verray good, or elles it semeth that they yeve to mortal foolk a manere° of goodes that ne ben nat parfyt°. But thilke good that is verray and parfyt, that may they nat yeven."

Boece. "I acorde me wel," quod I.

Philosophie "Thanne," quod she, "for as mochel as thow hast knowen which is thilke verray blysfulnesse, and ek whiche thilke thinges ben that lyen falsly° blysfulnesse *(that is to seyn, that by deceite semen verray goodes)*, now byhoveth the° to knowe whennes° and where thow mowe seke° thilke verray blysfulnesse."

"Certes," quod I, "that desire I gretly, and have abyden° longe tyme to herknen° it."

"But for as moche," quod she, "as it liketh to° my dissipule Plato in his book of *in Tymeo*, that in ryht lytel thinges men sholden bysechen the help of God, what jugest thow that be now to done, so that we may deserve to fynde the sete of thilke verray good?"

Boece. "Certes," quod I, "I deme that we shollen clepen° the fader of alle goodes, for withowten him nis ther nothing fownden aryht."

"Thow seyst aryht," quod she, and bygan anon to syngen ryht thus:

Metre 9. O qui perpetua mundum.

"O thow fader, creator of hevene and of erthes, that governest this world by perdurable° resoun, that comaundest the tymes to gon from syn° that age hadde bygynninge; thow that dwellest thyself ay stedefast and stable, and yevest° alle oothre thinges to ben moeved, ne foreyne° causes necesseden the° nevere to compowne° werk of floteringe° matere, but oonly the forme of sovereyn good iset within the withowte envye, that moevede the frely. Thow that art alderfayrest°, beringe the

130 mowen, *may* **131 beheten,** *promise* **135 wene,** *think* **138 sothere,** *truer* **141 flitte,** *change* **144 byhyht,** *promised* **148 enforcedest the,** *strove* **149–50 but yif,** *unless* **156 verrayly yeven,** *truly give* **160 norye,** *pupil* **162 putte this therto that,** *add to this what* **165 Trowesthow,** *do you think* **166 towmbling,** *changeable* **172** ***suffisaunce,*** *sufficiency* **174 lyckenesses,** *imitations* **176 manere,** *kind,* **parfyt,** *perfect* **183 lyen falsly,** *counterfeit* **185 byhoveth the,** *it is necessary for you* **186 whennes,** *from what,* **mowe seke,** *may seek* **189 abyden,** *waited,* i.e., **herknen,** *hear* **191 liketh to,** *pleases* **197 clepen,** *call* (upon) **3 Meter 9. 2 perdurable,** *everlasting* **4 syn,** *the time* **6 yevest,** *grants* **7 foreyne,** *external,* **necesseden the,** *necessitate you* **8 compowne,** *create,* **floteringe,** *changeable* **11 alderfayrest,** *fairest of all*

174 lyckenesses, singular in C[1] and Hn. **192** ***in Tymeo,*** Plato's *Timaeus,* 27c. **3 Meter 9.** A compressed adaptation of Plato's *Timaeus* 27c-42d, influenced by neo-Platonic commentary.

fayre world in thy thowht, formedest this world to the lyknesse semblable of that fayre world in thy thowht. Thow drawest al thing of thy sovereyn ensaumpler°, and comaundest that this world, parfytlyche imaked°, have freely and absolut his parfyt partyes°. Thow byndest the elementes by parfyt nowmbyre porcionables°, that the colde thinges mowen acorden with the hote thinges, and the drye thinges with the moyste thinges; that the fyr, that is purest, ne fle nat over hye°, ne that the hevynesse ne drawen nat adown overlowe the erthes that ben plownged in the wateres. Thow knyttest togydere the mene sowle° of treble kynde°, moevinge alle thinges, and devydest it by menbres° acordinge. And whan it is thus devyded, and it hath asembled a moevinge into two rowndes°, it goth to torne ayein to hymself, and envyrowneth° a ful deep thowht, and torneth the hevene by semblable° ymage. Thow by evene-lyke° causes enhansest° the sowles and the lasse lyves°, and, ablinge hem heye° by lyhte cartes°, thow sowest° hem into hevene and into erthe. And whan they ben converted to the by thy benigne lawe, thow makest hem retorne ayein to the by ayein-ledinge° fyr.

"O fader, yive thow to the thowht to styen° up into the streyte sete°, and graunte him to envirowne° the welle° of good; and the lyhte yfownde°, graunte him to fychen° the clere syhtes of his corage in the. And skatere° thow and to-breke thow the weyhtes and the clowdes of erthely hevynesse, and shyne thow by thy bryhtnesse. For thow art clernesse; thou art peysyble° reste to debonayre° folkes; thow thyself art bygynninge, berere°, ledere, paath, and terme°; to loke on the, that is owre ende.

Prose 10. Quoniam igitur que sit.

"For as moche thanne as thow hast seyn which is the forme of good that nis nat parfyt° and whych is the forme of good that is parfyt, now trowe° I that it were good to shewe in what this perfeccyoun of blysfulnesse is set. And in this thing, I trowe that we sholden fyrst enquere for to wyten° yif that any swyche manere good as thilke good that thow hast dyffynyssed° a lytel heere-biforn *(that is to seyn, sovereyn good)* may ben fownde in the nature of thinges, for that veyn ymagynacyoun of thowght ne deceyve us nat, and putte us owt of the sothfastnesse of thilke thing that is summitted° to us. But it may nat ben deneyed that thilke good ne is, and that it nis ryht as a welle° of alle goodes. For alle thing that is cleped° of inparfyt is proeved inparfyt by the amenusinge° of parfeccioun, or of thing that is parfyt. And therof comth it° that in everything general°, yif that men sen anything that is inparfyt, certes, in thilke general ther mot° ben somthing that is parfyt. For yif so be that perfeccyoun is don awey, men may nat thinke ne seye fro whennes thilke thing is that is cleped inparfyt. For the nature of thinges ne took nat hir begynninge of thinges amenused and inparfyt, but it procedeth of thinges that ben al hoole and absolute°, and dessendeth so down into owtterest° thinges, and into thinges empty and withowten frut. But, as I have ishewed a lytul her-byforn, that yif ther be a blysfulnesse that be freele° and veyn and inparfyt, ther may no man dowte that ther nis som blysfulnesse that is sad°, stydefast, and parfyt."

---

15 ensaumpler, *archetype* **16 parfytlyche imaked,** *perfectly made* **17 partyes,** *portions* **18 nowmbyres porcionables,** *ratios* **22 over hye,** *too high* **25 mene sowle,** *middle soul,* **treble kynde,** *triple nature* **27 menbres,** *portions* **28 rowndes,** *orbits* **30 envyrowneth,** *encircles* **32 semblable,** *similar,* **evene-lyke,** *parallel* **33 enhansest,** *raise,* **lasse lyves,** *lesser beings* **34 ablinge hem heye,** *enabling them to rise,* **lyhte cartes,** *light chariots* **35 sowest,** *plant* **38 ayein-ledinge,** *returning* **40 styen,** *climb,* **streyte sete,** *strict seat* **41 envirowne,** *comprehend / dwell near* **welle,** *source* **42 yfownde,** (having been) *found,* **fychen,** *fix* **43 skatere,** *scatter* **47 peysyble,** *peaceful,* **debonayre,** *good* **48 berere,** *bearer* **49 terme,** *conclusion* **3 Prose 10. 2 parfyt,** *perfect* **4 trowe,** *think* **7 wyten,** *know* **9 dyffynyssed,** *defined* **14 summitted,** *submitted* **16 welle,** *source* **17 cleped,** *called* **18 amenusinge,** *diminishing* **19 comth it,** *it happens* **20 everything general,** *all things universally* **22 mot,** *must* **28 absolut,** *complete* **30 owtterest,** *outermost* **33 freele,** *frail* **35 sad,** *stable*

17 and absolut, omitted in C². **24–27** The cosmology is notoriously dense, but one explanation is that creation came about through the harmonizing of sameness and otherness into existence—so that being is the middle soul of a triune nature—setting in motion the spilling forth into particularities. **25 mene sowle,** Latin gloss in C²: "anima mundi" (spirit of the world). **29 two rowndes,** circles of counter movement characterize the outflow of creation and its concomitant return to its source as well as the operation of the physical universe, visibly in motion in response to an invisible mover. **36 benigne,** C² reads "bygynnynge." **3 Prose 10. 9 heere-biforn,** see 3.pr9.150–53 and 3.pr2.11–22. **32 her-byforn,** see3.pr10.16–19.

Boece. "This is concluded," quod I, "fermely and sothfastly."

Philosophie. "But considere also," quod she, "in wham° this blysfulnesse enhabyteth°. The comune acordaunce and conseite° of the corages° of men proeveth and graunteth that God, prynce of alle thinges, is good. For so as nothing ne may of ben thowht bettre than God, it may nat ben dowted thanne that he that nothing nis bettre, that he nis good. Certes, resoun sheweth that God is so good that it proveth by verray force that parfyt good is in him. For yif God ne is swych°, he ne may nat ben prinse of alle thinges. For certes somthing possessing in itself parfyt good sholde be more worthy than God, and it sholde semen that thilke thing were fyrst and eldere than God. For we han shewed apertly° that alle thinges that ben parfyt ben fyrst or° thinges that ben unparfyt. And for-thy°, for as moche as that my resoun or my processes ne go nat awey withowte an ende, we owen° to graunten that the sovereyn God is ryht ful of sovereyn parfyt good. And we han establysshed that the sovereyn good is verray blysfulnesse: thanne mot it nedes be° that verray blysfulnesse is set in sovereyn God."

Boece. "This take I wel," quod I, "ne this ne may nat ben withseid° in no manere."

"But I preye the," quod she, "see now how thou mayst proeven, holyly° and withowte corupcioun, this that I have seyd, that the sovereyn God is ryht ful of sovereyn good."

"In whych manere?" quod I.

"Wenesthow awht°," quod she, "that this prynce of alle thinges have itake° thilke sovereyn good anywher owt° of himself—of whych sovereyn good men proveth that he is ful—ryht as thow myhtest thinken that God, that hath blysfulnesse in hymself, and thilke blysfulnesse that is in him, weren dyvers° in substaunce? For yif thow wene° that God have receyved thilke good owt of himself, thow mayst wene that he that yaf thilke good to God be more worthy thanne is God. But I am byknowen° and confesse°, and that ryht dignely°, that God is ryht worthy aboven alle thinges. And yif so be that this good be in him by nature, but that it is dyvers fro him by weninge resoun°, syn we speke of God prynce of alle thinges—faigne° whoso feigne may—who was he that hath conjoigned thise diverse thinges togider? And ek, at the laste, se wel that a thing that is divers from anything, that thilke thing nis nat that same thing fro whych it is undyrstonden to ben divers. Thanne folweth it that thilke thing that by his nature is divers fro soverein good, that that thing nis nat sovereyn good, but certes, that were a felonous corsednesse° to thinken that of him that nothing is more. worth For alwey, of alle thinges, the nature of hem ne may nat ben bettre than his bygynning. For whych I may concluden, by ryht verray resoun, that thilke that° is bygynning of alle thinges, thilke same thing is sovereyn good in his substaunce."

Boece. "Thow hast seyd ryhtfully," quod I.

Philosophie. "But we han graunted," quod she, "that the sovereyn good is blysfulnesse."

"And that is soth," quod I.

"Thanne," quod she, "moten° we nedes° graunten and confessen that thilke same sovereyn good be God."

"Certes," quod I, "I ne may nat denye ne withstonde the resouns purposed, and I se wel that it folweth by strengthe of the premysses."

"Loke now," quod she, "yif this be proved yit more fermely thus: that ther ne mowen° nat ben two sovereyn goodes that ben diverse amonge hemself. For certes, the goodes that ben dyverse amonges hemself, that oon nis nat that that othre is; thanne ne mowen neyther of hem ben parfyt, so as

---

39 wham, *whom,* **enhabyteth,** *resides* **40 conseite,** *understanding* **41 corages,** *hearts* **48 ne is swych,** *is not such* **53 apertly,** *openly* **54 or,** *before* **55 for-thy,** *therefore* **57 owen,** *ought* **61 mot it nedes be,** *it necessarily must be* **64 withseid,** *denied* **66 holyly,** *wholly* **70 Wenesthow awht,** *do you think in any way* **71 have itake,** *has taken* **72 owt,** *outside* **77 dyvers,** *different,* **wene,** *think* **81 am byknowen,** *acknowledge,* **confesse,** *declare* **82 dignely,** *fittingly* **85 weninge resoun,** *hypothesis* **86 faigne,** *pretend* **95 corsednesse,** *cursedness* **100 that thilke that,** *that that which* **108 moten,** *must,* **nedes,** *necessarily* **117 mowen,** *may*

52 thing, omitted in C[2] and Hn; the French has *chose.*

eyther of hem lakketh to° other. But that that nis nat parfyt, men may sen apertly° that it is nat sovereyn. The thinges thanne that ben sovereynly goode ne mowen by no wey ben diverse. But I have wel concluded that blysfulnesse and God ben the sovereyn good, for whyche it mot nedes ben that sovereyn blysfulnesse is sovereyn divynyte."

"Nothing," quod I, "nis more sothfast° than this, ne more ferme by resoun; ne a more worthy thing than God may nat ben concluded."

Philosophie. "Upon thise thinges thanne," quod she, "ryht as thyse geometryens,° whan they han shewed her proposiciouns, ben wont° to bryngen in thinges that they clepen porysmes° *(or declaraciouns of forseyde thinges),* ryht so wole I yeve the heere as a corolarye *(or a mede of coroune).* For-why° for as moche as by the getinge of blysfulnesse men ben maked blysful, and blysfulnesse is divinitee, thanne is it manyfest and open that by the getinge of divynitee men ben maked blysful. Ryht° as by the getinge of justice they ben maked just, and by the getinge of sapience° they ben maked wyse: ryht so, nedes°, by the semblable° resoun, whan they han geten devynyte, they ben maked goddes. Thanne is every blysful man god. But certes, by nature ther nis but o God; but by the partycypasioun of devynyte ther ne let° he desturbeth nothing that ther ne ben many goddess."

"This is," quod I, "a fayr thing and a precyous, clepe° it as thow wolt, be it porisme° or corellarye" *(or meede of corowne or declaringes).*

"Certes," quod she,"nothing nis fayrere than is the thing that by resoun sholde ben added to thyse forseyde thinges."

"What thing?" quod I.

"So," quod she, "as it semeth that blysfulnesse conteneth many thinges, it were for to whyten° wheyther that alle this thinges maken or conjoignen as a manere body of blysfulnesse, be diversite of partyes° or of menbres°, or elles yif any of alle thilke thinges be swych that it acomplyse by hymself the substaunce of blysfulnesse, so that alle thise oothre thinges ben refferred° and browht to blysfulnesse" *(that is to seyn, as to the chef of hem).*

"I wolde," quod I, "that thow makedest me clerly to understonde what thow seyst, and that thow recordedest me° the forseyde thinges."

"Have I nat juged," quod she, "that blysfulnesse is good?"

"Yis, forsothe," quod I, "and that sovereyn good."

"Adde thanne," quod she, "thilke° good *(that is maked of blysfulnesse)* to alle the forseyde thinges. For thilke same blysfulnesse that is demed to ben sovereyn suffisaunce°, thilke selve is sovereyn power, sovereyn reverence, sovereyn clernesse° *(or noblesse),* and sovereyn delit. Conclusio. What seyst thow thanne of alle thise thinges, that is to seyn, suffysaunce, power, and this oothre thinges—ben they thanne as menbres of blysfulnesse, or ben they referred° and browht to sovereyn good, ryht as alle thinges that ben browht to the chief of hem?"

Boece. "I undyrstonde wel," quod I, "what thow purposest to seke, but I desire for to herkne° that thow shewe it me."

Philosophie. "Tak now thus the discressioun° of this questyoun," quod she. "Yif alle thise thinges," quod she, "weren menbres to felicite, than weren they diverse that oon from that oother. And swych is the nature of partyes or of menbres that diverse menbres compownen° a body."

"Certes," quod I, "it hath wel ben shewed heere-biforn that alle thise thinges ben alle o thing."

"Thanne ben they none menbres," quod she, "for elles it sholde seme that blysfulnesse

---

122 to, *to* (the) **123 apertly,** *obviously* **130 sothfast,** *truthful* **135 geometryens,** *practitioners of geometry* **137 wont,** *accustomed* **138 clepen porymes,** *call deductions* **140 For-why,** *because* **145 Ryht,** *just* **147 sapience,** *wisdom* **148 nedes,** *necessarily,* **semblable,** *similar* **152 let,** *hinders* **156 clepe,** *call* **157 porisme,** *deduction* **164-165 it were for to whyten,** *it is to be determined* **167 partyes,** *portions,* **168 menbres,** *parts* **171 ben refferred,** *are related* **176 recordedest me,** *remind me of* **182 thilke,** *this* **185 suffisaunce,** *sufficiency* **187 clernesse,** *fame* **192 referred,** *related to* **197 herkne,** *listen* **198 discressioun,** *determination* **204 compownen,** *compose*

140 *mede of coroune,* gift of a garland; a bonus. Middle English *corolarye* (Modern *corollary*) comes from Latin *corolla,* garland; it meant the money paid for a garland of flowers, hence a gratuity. **146 they ben maked just,** this is not in the English; supplied from the French. **183 *of,*** not in the English text; supplied from the French.

were conjoigned al of on menbre allone, but that is a thing that may nat be don."

"This thing," quod I, "nis nat dowtous°; but I abyde to herknen the remnaunt of thy questyoun."

"This is open and cler," quod she, "that alle oothr thinges ben referred and browht to good. For therfore is suffisaunce requered°, for it is demed to ben good; and forthy° is power requered, for men trowen° also that it be good. And this same thing mowen we thinken and conjecten° of reverence, and of noblesse, and of delit. Thanne is sovereyn good the somme and the cause of al that awhte° ben desyred. For-why° thilke thing that withholdeth no good in itself, ne semblaunce of good, it ne may nat wel in no manere be desired ne required. And the contrarye, for thogh that thinges by her nature ne ben nat goode, algates° yif men wene° that they ben goode, yit ben they desyred as thowgh that they weren verraylyche° goode. And therfor is it that men owhten to wene by ryht, that bounte° be the sovereyn fyn° and the cause of alle the thinges that ben to requeren. But certes, thilke that° is cause for which men requeren anything, it semeth that thilke same thing be most desyred. As thus, yif that a wyht° wolde ryden for cause of hele°, he ne desyreth nat so mochel the moevinge to ryden as the effect of his hele. Now thanne, syn that alle thinges ben required for the grace of good, they ne ben nat desyred of alle foolk moore thanne the same good. But we han graunted that blysfulnesse is that thing for whyche that alle thyse oothre thinges ben desyred; thanne is it thus that certes oonly blysfulnesse is requered and desired. By whyche thing it sheweth clerly, that of good and of blysfulnesse is al oon and the same substaunce."

"I se nat," quod I, "wherfore that men myhten discorden° in this."

"And we han shewed that God and verray blysfulnesse is al oo thing."

"That is soth," quod I.

"Thanne mowen° we conclude sikerly° that the substaunce of God is set in thilke same good, and in non oother place.

Metre 10. Huc omnes pariter venite capti.

"O cometh alle togyder now, ye that ben icawht and ibownde with wyckede cheynes° by the decyvable° delyt of erthely thinges enhabytinge in yowre thowht! Her shal ben the reste of yowre labours; her is the havene stable in peysyble° quiete; this allone is the open refut° to wrechches. *(Glosa. This is to seyn, that ye that ben combred° and deceived with worldely affeccyouns, cometh now to this sovereyn good that is God, that is refut to hem that wolen comen to him.)* Textus. Alle the thinges that the ryver Tagus yeveth yow with his goldene gravayles°, or elles alle the thinges that the ryver Herynus yeveth with his rede brynke, or that Indus yeveth that is next the hote party° of the world, that medleth° the grene stones with the whyte, ne sholde nat cleeren the lookinge° of yowre thowht, but hyden rather yowre blynde corages° within her dyrknesse. Al that lyketh° yow heere, and exciteth and moeveth yowre thowhtes, the erthe hath norysshed it in his lowe caves. But the shyning by whyche the hevene is governed and whennes° he hath his strengthe, that eschueth° the dyrke overthrowinge of the sowle, and whoso may knowen thilke lyht of blysfulnesse, he shal wel seyn that the whyte bemes of the sonne ne ben nat cleer."

Prose 11. Assencior inquam.

Boece. "I assente me," quod I, "for alle thise thinges ben strongly bownden with ryht ferme resouns."

---

213 dowtous, *doubtful* **218 requered,** *required* **219 forthy,** *therefore* **220 trowen,** *think* **222 conjecten,** *suppose* **224 awhte,** *ought,* **For-why,** *for this reason* **230 algates,** *nevertheless,* **wene,** *think* **232 verraylyche,** *truly* **233 bounte,** *goodness,* **234 sovereyn fyn,** *ultimate end* **236 thilke that,** *that which* **238 wyht,** *person* **239 cause of hele,** *reasons of health* **252 discorden,** *disagree* **256 mowen,** *may,* **sikerly,** *certainly*
3 Meter 10. **2 cheynes,** *chains* **3 decyvable,** *deceptive* **6 peysyble,** *peaceful* **7 refut,** *refuge* **8 combred,** *encumbered* **12 gravales,** *gravel* **15 hote party,** *hot part* **16 medleth,** *mixes* **17 cleeren the lookinge,** *clear the vision* **19 corages,** *spirits* **20 lyketh,** *pleases* **23 whennes,** *from which* **24 eschueth,** *avoids*

232 they, Hn ends here; the manuscript is incomplete. **7–11** ***Glosa*** **. . . Textus,** see 1.pr4.74–80n. **12 Tagus,** the Tajo, a river in Spain. **13 Herynus,** the Hermus river, now the Gediz in Turkey, also known as the Sarabat. **14 Indus,** river in India.

Philosophie. "How mochel wylthow preysen it," quod she, "yif that thow knowe what thilke good is?"

"I wol preys it," quod I, "by preys withowten ende yif it shal betidde° me to knowe also togydere God that is good."

"Certes," quod she, "that shal I do the° by verray resouns, yif that tho thinges that I have concluded a litel her-byforn dwellen° oonly in her fyrst graunting."

Boece. "They dwellen graunted to the," quod I. *(This is to seyn, as who seyth, I graunte thy forseyde conclusiouns.)*

"Have I nat shewed the," quod she, "that the thinges that ben requered of many folkes ne ben nat verray goodes ne parfyte, for they ben dyverse that oon fro that oothre; and so as ech of hem is lackinge to other, they ne han no power to bryngen a good that is ful and absolut? But thanne at erst° ben they verray good, whan they ben gadered togidere alle in to o° forme and into on° wyrkinge, so that thilke thinge that is suffisaunce, thilke same be power, and reverence, and noblesse, and myrthe. And forsothe, but yif° alle thyse thinges ben alle oon same thing, they ne han nat° wherby that they mowen° ben put in the nowmber of thinges that owhten° ben requered or desyred."

Boece. "It is shewed," quod I, "ne herof may no man dowten."

Philosophie. "The thinges thanne," quod she, "that ne ben no goodes whanne they ben diverse, and whan they bygynnen to ben alle oon thing thanne ben they goodes—ne comth it hem nat thanne by the getinge of unite that they ben maked goodes?"

Boece. "So it semeth," quod I.

"But alle thing that is good," quod she, "grauntesthow that it be good by the participacioun of good, or no?"

"I graunte it," quod I.

"Thanne mosthow° graunten," quod she, "by semblable° resoun, that oon and good be oo same thing. For of thinges of whyche that the effect nis nat naturely diverse°, nedes° the substance mot be oo same thinge."

"I ne may nat denye that," quod I.

"Hasthow nat knowen wel," quod she, "that alle thing that is hath so longe his dwellinge and his substaunce as longe as it is oon, but whan it forleteth° to ben oon yit mot nedes dyen and corumpe° togyder?"

"In which manere?" quod I.

"Ryht as in bestes," quod she, "whan the sowle and the body ben conjoigne in oon and dwellen togydyre, it is cleped° a beest. And whan her unite is destroyed by the desseveraunce that oon from that oother, thanne sheweth it wel that it is a ded thing, and that it nis no lengere no beest. And the body of a whyht°, whil it dwelleth in oo forme by conjunccyoun of menbres, it is wel seyn that it is a figure of mankynde. And yif the partyes of the body ben so devyded and dissevered *(that oon fro that oother)* that they destroyen unite, the body forleteth to ben that° it was byforn. And, who wolde renne° in the same manere by alle thinges, he sholde seen that withowte dowte everything is in his substaunce as longe as it is oon, and whan it forleteth to ben oon it dieth and periseth."

Boece. "Whan I consydere," quod I, "manye thinges, I se non oother."

"Is ther anything thanne," quod she, "that in as moche as it lyveth naturelly, that forleteth the talent° or appetyt of his beinge, and desireth to come to deth and to corupcioun?"

"Yif I consydere," quod I, "the beestes that han any manere nature of wylninge° and of nyllinge°, I ne fynde no beest but yif it ben constreyned fro withowte forth° that forleteth or despiseth the entensyoun to lyven and to duren°, or that wole his thankes° hasten hym to dyen. For every beest travayleth him° to deffende and kepe the savacioun of his lyf, and eschueth° deth and destrucioun. But certes, I dowte me of herbes and of trees *(that is to seyn, that I am in a dowte of swiche things*

---

3 Prose 11. **8 betidde,** *happen to* **10 do the,** *make you* (know) **12 dwellen,** *remain* **23 at erst,** *initially* **25 o,** *one,* **on,** *one* **28 but yif,** *unless* **29 ne han nat,** *have nothing* **30 mowen,** *may* **31 owhten,** *ought* **46 mosthow,** *you must* **47 semblable,** *similar* **49 naturely diverse,** *different in nature,* **nedes,** *necessarily* **55 forleteth,** *ceases* **56 corumpe,** *decay* **60 cleped,** *called* **65 whyht,** *person* **71 that,** *what,* **renne,** *continue* **80 forleteth the talent,** *abandons the desire* **84 wylninge,** *willing* **85 nyllinge,** *not willing* **86 withowte forth,** *outside* **88 duren,** *continue,* **wole his thankes,** *willingly* **89 travayleth him,** *strives* **91 eschueth,** *avoids*

as herbes or trees) that ne han no feelinge sowles *(ne no naturel wyrkinges servinge to appetytes as bestes han)* wheither thei han appetid° to dwellen and to duren."

"Certes," quod she, "ne therof thar° the nat dowte. Now loke upon thise herbes and thise trees. They wexen° first in swyche places as ben covenable° to hem, in whyche places they ne mowen nat sone dyen ne dryen, as longe as her nature may deffenden hem. For som of hem waxen in feeldes, and som in mountaignes, and oothre waxen in marys°, and oothre cleven° on roches, and summe waxen plentyuous in sondes, and yif that any wyht enforce him° to beren hem into oothre places, they wexen drye. For nature yeveth to everything that that° is convenient° to him, and travayleth that they ne dye nat, as longe as they han power to dwellen° and to lyven. What woltow seyn of this, that they drawen alle her noryssinges by her rootes, ryht as they hadden her mowthes iplounged within the erthes, and sheden° by her maryes° her wode and her bark? And what woltow seyn of this, that thilke thing that is ryht softe, as the marye is, that is alwey hidd in the sete al withinne, and that is defended fro withowte by the stidefastnesse of wode, and that the uttereste° bark is put ayeins the destemperaunce° of the hevene as a defendowr myhty to suffren harm? And thus, certes, maystow wel sen how gret is the diligence of nature. For alle thinges renovelen° and puplisshen° hem with seed imultiplyed, ne ther nis no man that ne wot° wel that they ne ben ryht as a foundement° and edyfice for to duren° nat only for a tyme but ryht as° for to duren perdurabely° by generacyoun. And the thinges ek that men wenen° ne haven none sowles, ne desire they nat ech of hem by semblable resoun to kepen that is hers° *(that is to seyn, that is acordinge to her nature in conservacioun of her beinge and enduringe)*? For wherfor elles° bereth lyhtnesse the flaumbes up, and the weyhte presseth the erthe adoun, but for as moche as thilke° places and thilke moevinges ben covenable° to everich of hem? And forsothe everything kepeth thilke that° is acordinge and propre to him, ryht as thinges that ben contraryes and enemys corompen° hem. And yit the harde thinges, as° stoones, clyven° and holden her partyes togyder ryht faste° and harde, and deffenden hem in withstondinge that they ne departe nat lyhtly atwyne°. And the thinges that ben softe and fletinge°, as is water and eyr, they departen° lyhtly and yeven place to hem that breken or devyden hem, but natheles, they retornen sone ayein into the same thinges fro whennes they ben arraced°. But fyr fleeth and refuseth alle devysyoun. Ne I ne trete nat heere now of wilful moevinges of the sowle that is knowinge, but of the naturel entencioun° of thinges, as thus ryht as we swolwe the mete° that we recyven and ne thinke nat on it, and as we drawen owre breth in slepinge that we wite° it nat whil we slepen. For certes, in the beestes the love of her lyvynges ne of her beinges ne comth nat of the wilninges° of the sowle, but of the bygynninges of nature. For certes, thorw constreyninge causes° wil desireth and embraceth ful ofte tyme the deth that nature dredeth. *(That is to seyn as thus, that a man may ben constreyned so by som cause that his wil desireth and taketh the deth which that nature hateth and dredeth ful sore.)* And somtyme we seeth the contrarye, as thus that the wil of a wiht° destorbeth and constreyneth that that° nature desireth and requereth al-wey, that is to seyn, the werk of generacioun°, by the whiche generacioun only dwelleth and is sustened the longe durablete of mortal thinges.

97 appetid, *desire* **98 thar,** *need* **100 wexen,** *grow* **101 covenable,** *suitable* **105 marys,** *marshes* **106 cleven,** *hold* **108 wyht enforce him,** *person strives* **110 that that,** *that which,* **convenient,** *suitable* **112 dwellen,** *remain* **116 sheden,** *spread* **117 maryes,** *fiber* **122 uttereste,** *outermost* **123 destemperaunce,** *disturbance* **126 renovelen,** *renew* **127 puplisshen,** *propagate* **128 wot,** *knows* **129 foundement,** *foundation* **130 duren,** *continue,* **ryht as,** *just as* **131 perdurabely,** *continually* **132 wenen,** *think* **134 that is hers,** *what is theirs* **137 wherfor elles,** *why else* **139 thilke,** *those* **140 covenable,** *suitable* **142 thilke that,** *that which* **144 corompen,** *corrupt* **145 as,** *such as,* **clyven,** *cling* **146 ryht faste,** *very firmly* **148 lyhtly atwyne,** *easily apart* **149 fletinge,** *flowing* **150 departen,** *separate* **153 arraced,** *torn apart* **157 entencioun,** *instinct* **158 mete,** *food* **160 wite,** *know* **163 wilninges,** *willings* **165 constreyninge causes,** *compelling reasons* **172 wiht,** *person,* **that that,** *that which* **174 generacioun,** *propagation*

155 wilful, C[2] reads "weleful." The Latin is *voluntariis.*

"And thus this charite and this love, that everything hath to hymself, ne comth nat of the moevinge of the sowle, but of the entencioun of nature. For the purvyaunce° of God hath yeven to thinges that ben creat of him this that is a ful gret cause to lyven and to duren, for which they desiren naturelly her lyf as longe as ever they mowen°. For whych thow maist nat drede° by no manere that alle the thinges that ben anywhere, that they ne requeren naturelly the ferme stablenesse of perdurable dwellinge, and ek the eschuinge° of destruccyoun."

Boece. "Now confesse I wel," quod I, "that I see now wel certeynly, withowte dowtes, the thinges that whylom° semeden uncerteyn to me."

Philosophie. "But," quod she, "thilke thyng that desireth to be and to dwellen perdurably, he desireth to ben oon, for yif that that oon were destroied, certes, beinge ne shulde ther non dwellen° to no wiht."

"That is soth," quod I.

"Thanne," quod she, "desiren alle thinges oon."

"I assente," quod I.

"And I have shewed," quod she, "that thilke same oon is thilke that° is good?"

Boece. "Ye, for sothe," quod I.

"Alle thinges thanne," quod she, "reqyren good, and thilke good thanne maist thow descryven ryht thus: good is thilke thing that every wyht desireth."

"Ther ne may be thowht," quod I, "no moore verray° thing. For either alle thinges ben referred° and browht to nowht, and floteren° withowte governour, despoiled° of oon as of her propre heved°, or elles, yif ther be anything to which that alle thinges tenden and hyen°, that thing moste ben the sovereyn good of alle goodes."

Philosophie. Thanne seyde she thus: "O my nory°," quod she, "I have gret gladnesse of the, for thow hast fichched° in thyn herte the myddel sothfastnesse°, that is to seyn, the prikke°. But this thing hath ben descovered to the in that° thow seydest that thow wystest° nat a lytel her-byforn°."

"What was that?" quod I.

"That thow ne wystest nat," quod she, "whych was the ende of thinges. And certes, that is the thing that every wiht° desireth. And for as mochel as we han gadered and comprehended that good is thilke thing that is desired of alle, thanne moten we nedes° confessen° that good is the fyn° of alle thinges.

Metre 11. Quisquis profunda mente.

"Whoso that seketh soth° by a deep thoght, and coveyteth nat to ben deceyved by no mysweyes°, lat him rollen and trenden° withinne hymself the lyht of his inward syhte; and lat him gadere ayein, enclyninge into a compas°, the longe moevinges of his thowhtes; and lat him techen his corage° that he° hath enclosed and hyd in his tresors°, al that he° compaseth° or seketh fro withowte. And thanne thilke° thing that the blake cloude of errour whilom° hadde ycovered shal lyhten° more clerly thanne Phebus hymself ne shyneth. *(Glosa, Whoso wole seken the dep grounde of soth in his thowht, and wol nat be deceyved by false proposiciouns that goon amys fro the trouthe, lat him wel examine and rolle withinne hymself the nature and the propretes of the thing; and lat him yit eftsones° examine and rollen his thowhtes by good deliberacioun or° that he deme°; and lat him techen his sowle that it hath, by naturel pryncyples kyndeliche° yhid within itself, alle the trowthe the whiche he ymagyneth to ben in thinges withowte. And thanne alle the dyrknesse of his mysknowinge shal seme more evydently to syhte of his understondinge thanne the sonne ne semeth to syhte withowteforth.)*

"For certes the body, bryngynge the weyhte of foryetinge, ne hath nat chased owt of yowre thowhte al the clernesse of yowre knowing, for certeynly the seed of sooth haldeth and clyveth° within yowre corage, and it is awaked and excited by the wynde and

---

181 purvyaunce, *providence* **185 mowen,** *are able* **186 drede,** *doubt* **189 eschuinge,** *avoiding* **193 whylom,** *formerly* **199 dwellen,** *remain* **205 thilke that,** *that which* **212 verray,** *true* **213 referred,** *related,* **floteren,** *flutter* **214 despoiled,** *deprived* **215 heved,** *head* **217 hyen,** *hasten* **220 nory,** *pupil* **221 fichched,** *fixed* **222 myddel sothfastnesse,** *central truth* **223 prikke,** *pinpoint* **224 in that,** *which,* **wystest,** *knew* **225 her-byforn,** *before this* **229 wiht,** *person* **232 moten we nedes,** *we necessarily must* **233 confessen,** *declare,* **fyn,** *end* **<u>3 Meter 11.</u> 1 soth,** *truth* **3 mysweyes,** *missteps,* **trenden,** *turn* **5–6 enclyninge into a compas,** *gathering into a circle* **7 corage,** *heart,* **he,** *it* **8 his tresors,** *its treasures,* **he,** *it* **9 compaseth,** *encircles* **10 thilke,** *that* **11 whilom,** *formerly* **12 lyhten,** *shine* **18 *eftsones*,** *again* **19 *or*,** *before,* **deme,** *concludes* **21 kyndeliche,** *naturally* **30 clyveth,** *clings*

225 lytel her-byforn, see 1.pr6.40–45. **<u>3 Meter 11.</u> 13 *Glosa*, see 1.pr4.74–80n.**

by the blastes of doctryne. For wherefor° elles demen° ye of yowre owne wyl the ryhtes° whan he ben axed°, but yif so were° that the noryssinges of resoun ne lyvede iplownged in the depthe of yowre herte? *(This is to seyn, how sholden men demen the sooth of anything that were axed, yif ther nere° a roote of sothfastnesse that were yplownged and hyd in the naturel pryncyples, the whiche sothfastnesse lyved within the depnesse of the thowght?)* And yif so be that the Muse and the doctryne of Plato syngeth sooth, al that every whyht lerneth, he ne doth nothing elles thanne but recordeth°, as men recorden thinges that ben foryeten."

Prose 12. Tum ego Platoni inquam.

Thanne seide I thus: "I acorde me gretly to Plato, for thow remenbrest and recordest me thise thinges yit the secounde tyme, that is to seyn, fyrst whan I loste my memorye by the contagyous° conjuncsioun of the body with the sowle, and eftsones° afterward whan I loste it, confownded by the charge° and by the burdene of my sorwe."

And thanne seide she thus: "Yif thow looke," quod she, "fyrst the thinges° that thow hast graunted, it ne shal nat ben ryht fer that thow ne shalt remembren thilke thing that thow seydest that thow nystest nat°."

"What thing?" quod I.

"By which governement," quod she, "that this world is governed."

"Me remenbreth it wel," quod I, "and I confesse wel that I ne wiste° it nawght. But al be it so that I se now from afer what thow purposest, algates° I desire yit to herkene° it of the° more pleynly."

"Thow ne wendest° nat," quod she, "a litel her-byforn that men sholden dowte that this world nis governed by God."

"Certes," quod I, "ne yit ne dowte I it nawht, ne I nel never wene° that it were to dowte *(as who seith, but I wot° wel that God governeth this world)*. And I shal shortly answeren the by what resouns I am browht to this. This world," quod I, "of so manye diverse and contrarious parties, ne myhte never han ben assembled in o forme but yif ther nere oon that conjoignede so manye diverse thinges. And the same diversite of her natures, that so discorden° that oon fro that oother, moste departen° and unjoignen the thinges that ben conjoigned yif ther ne were oon that contenede° that he hath conjoyned and ibownde. Ne the certeyn ordre of nature ne sholde nat brynge forth so ordene° moevinges—by places, by tymes, by dooinges, by spaces, by qualities—yif ther ne were oon that were ay steadfast dwellinge, that ordeynede and disponede° thise diversitees of moevinges. And thilke° thing, whatsoever it be, by which that alle thinges ben maked and ilad°, I clepe° him 'god', that is a word that is used to alle foolk."

Thanne seyde she: "Syn° thow feelest thus thise thinges," quod she, "I trowe° that I have litel moore to done that thow, myhty of welefulnesse°, hool and sounde, ne see eftsones° thy contre. But lat us loken the thinges that we ha purposed° her-byforn. Have I nat nowmbred° and seyd," quod she, "that suffisaunce° is in blesfulnesse, and we han acorded° that God is thilke same blysfulnesse?"

"Yis, forsothe," quod I.

"And that to governe this world," quod she, "ne shal he never han nede of non help fro withowte? For elles, yif he hadde nede of any help, he ne sholde nat have no ful suffisaunce?"

"Yis, thus it mot nedes be," quod I.

"Thanne ordeyneth° he by hymself allone alle thinges?" quod she.

"That may nat be deneyed," quod I.

"And I have shewed that God is the same good?"

"It remembreth me wel," quod I.

---

32 wherefor, *why* **33 demen,** *judge,* **ryhtes,** *truths* **34 axed,** *asked,* **but yif so were,** *unless it were so* **38 nere,** *were not* **44 recordeth,** *remember* <u>3 Prose 12.</u> **5 contagyous,** *contaminating* **6 eftsones,** *again* **7 charge,** *weight* **10 fyrst the thinges,** *at the earlier things* **13 nystest nat,** *did not know* **18 wiste,** *knew* **20 algates,** *nevertheless,* **herkene,** *hear* **21 of the,** *from you* **22 wendest,** *thought* **26 wene,** *think* **27 wot,** *know* **35 discorden,** *severs* **35–36 moste departen,** *must separate* **37 contenede,** *maintained* **40 ordene,** *well-ordered* **43 disponede,** *regulated* **44 thilke,** *this* **46 ilad,** *led,* **clepe,** *call* **48 Syn,** *because* **49 trowe,** *think* **51 welefulnesse,** *happiness* **52 eftsones,** *soon again* **53 ha purposed,** *have proposed* **54 nowmbred,** *tallied* **55 suffisaunce,** *sufficiency* **56 acorded,** *agreed* **65 ordeyneth,** *establishes*

42 doctryne of Plato, Plato's doctrine of remembrance (*anamnesis*) posits that all human learning is recollection of the wisdom that was forgotten when the soul was imprisoned in the body at birth; *Phaedo* 72–76. <u>3 Prose 12.</u> **12–13 thilke thing that thow seydest,** see 1.pr6.33–35. **23 her-byforn,** see 1.pr6.12–18.

"Thanne ordeyneth he alle thinges by thilke good," quod she, "syn he, which that we han acorded to be good, governeth alle thinges by hymself; and he is as a keye and a stiere°, by which that the edifice of this world is ikept stable and withowte coroumpinge°."

"I acorde me gretely," quod I. "And I aperceivede a lytul her-byforn that thow woldest seye thus, al be it so that it were by a thinne suspecyoun."

"I trowe it wel," quod she, "for, as I trowe, thow ledest now moore ententyfly° thyne eyen to loken the verray goodes. But natheles the thing that I shal telle thee yit ne sheweth nat lasse to looken°."

"What is that?" quod I.

"So as men trowen," quod she, "and that ryhtfully, that God governeth alle thinges by the keye of his goodnesse, and alle thise same thinges, as I have tawht the, hasten hem by naturel entencyoun° to comen to good. Ther may no man dowten that they ne ben governed voluntaryely, and that they ne converten hem of her owne wil to the wil of her ordenour°, as they that ben acordinge and enclyninge to her governoure and her kyng."

"It mot nedes be° so," quod I, "for the reaume° ne sholde nat semen blysful yif ther were a yok of mysdrawinges° in diverse partyes, ne the savinge° of obedient thinges ne sholde nat be."

"Thanne is ther nothing," quod she, "that kepeth his nature, that enforceth him° to goon ayein God?"

"No," quod I.

"And yif that anything enforcede him to withstonde God, myhte it avaylen° at the laste° ayeins him that we han graunted to ben almyghty by the ryht of blysfulnesse?"

"Certes," quod I, "al owtrely° it ne myhte nat avaylen him."

"Thanne is ther nothing," quod she, "that eyther wole or may withstonden to this sovereyn good?"

"I trowe nat," quod I.

"Thanne is thilke the sovereyn good," quod she, "that alle thinges governeth strongly, and ordeyneth° hem softely°."

Thanne seyde I thus: "I delite me," quod I, "nat oonly in the endes or in the somme° of the resouns that thow hast concluded and proeved, but thilke° wordes that thow usest deliten me moche moore. So at the laste fooles that sumtyme renden° grete thinges owhten ben ashamed of hemself." *(That is to seyn, that we fooles that reprehenden° wikkedly the thinges that towchen Goddes governaunce, we owhten ben as shamed of owreself, as I, that seyde that God refuseth° oonly the werkes of men, and ne entremeteth° nat of it.)*

Philosophie. "Thow hast wel herd," quod she, "the fables of the poetes, how the gyaunts assayleden the hevene with° the goddes; but forsothe, the debonayre° force of God deposede° hem, as it was worthy° *(that is to seyn, destroyede the giaunts, as it was worthy)*. But wilthow that we joignen togidere thilke same resouns? For peradventure°, of swych conjuncioun may sterten up som fair sparkle of soth°."

"Do," quod I, "as the liste°."

"Wenest thow°," quod she, "that God ne be almyhty? No man is in dowte of it."

"Certes," quod I, "no wyht° ne dowteth it, yif he be in his mynde."

"But he," quod she, "that is almyhty—ther nis nothing that he ne may°?"

"That is soth," quod I.

"May God don yvel?" quod she.

"Nay, forsothe," quod I.

"Thanne is yvel nothing," quod she, "syn that he ne may nat don yvel that may don alle thinges."

---

74 stiere, *rudder* **76 coroumpinge,** *corrupting* **82 ententyfly,** *attentively* **84–85 ne sheweth nat lasse to looken,** *is no less clear* **91 entencyoun,** *instinct* **95 ordenour,** *creator* **98 mote nedes be,** *must necessarily be* **99 reaume,** *realm* **100 mysdrawinges,** *contentions* **101 savinge,** *preservation* **104 enforceth him,** *strives* **108 avaylen,** *accomplish,* **at the laste,** *ultimately* **111 owtrely,** *utterly* **119 ordeyneth,** *establishes,* **softely,** *gently* **121 summe,** *conclusion* **123 thilke,** *those* **125 renden,** *tear down* **127 reprehenden,** *criticize* **130 refuseth,** *rejects* **131 entremeteth,** *involves* (himself) **134 with,** *against* **135 debonayre,** *benign* **136 deposede,** *dealt with,* **worthy,** *fitting* **139 peraventure,** *perhaps* **141 soth,** *truth* **142 the liste,** *pleases you* **143 Wenest thow,** *do you think* **145 wyht,** *person* **148 ne may,** *may not* (do)

74 keye, here and at line 89, Chaucer mistranslates Latin forms of *clavus* (helm) as forms of *clavis* (key). **118–19** Echoes the Vulgate book of Wisdom 8.1. **133 fables of the poetes . . . ,** the titans' unsuccessful attack on the gods, defeated by Jove, is a common figure of chaos assaulting order; see, e.g., Ovid, *Metamorphoses* 1.151ff. It is possible, however, to read this as the titans and the gods collaborating ("with" rather than "against" in line 134). **136 deposede,** C^2 reads "desposede." The Latin is *deposuit.*

"Scornest thow me," quod I, *(or elles pleyesthow or deceivesthow me)* "that hast so woven me with thy resouns the hows of Dydalus, so entrelaced that it is unable to be unlaced? Thow that oother whyle° entrest ther thou issest°, and oother whyle issest ther thow entrest, ne fooldesthow nat togydere *(by replycasioun° of wordes)* a manere° wonderful cercle or envyroninge° of the symplicyte devyne? For certes, a lytel her-byforn, whan thow bygunne at blysfulnesse, thow seydest that it is sovereyn good, and seidest that it is set in sovereyn God, and seydest that God hymself is sovereyn good, and that God is the fulle blysfulnesse. For which thou yave me as a covenable yift°, that is to seyn, that no wyht nis blysful but yif he be good also therwith. And seidest ek that the forme of good is the substaunce of God and of blysfulnesse. And seidest that thilke same oon is thilke same good that is requered and desired of alle the kynde of thinges. And thow proevedest in disputinge that God governeth alle the thinges of the world by the governements of bownte°, and seydest that alle thinges wolen obeyen to him, and seydest that the nature of yvel nis nothing. And thise thinges ne shewedest thow nat with none resouns itaken fro withowte, but by proeves° in cercles and hoomlich knowen°, the whiche proeves drawen to hemself her feith and her acord, everich of hem of oother."

Thanne seyde she thus: "I ne scorne the nat *(ne pleye, ne deceyve the),* but I have shewed the the thing that is grettest over alle thinges by the yift of God that° we whilom° preyeden. For this is the forme of the devyne substaunce, that is swich that it ne slydeth nat into owtterest foreyne° thinges, ne ne resseiveth no straunge thinges in him. But ryht° as Parmanydes seide in Grec of thilke devyne substaunce, he seide thus, that thilke devyne substaunce torneth the world and the moevable cercle of thinges, whil thilke devyne substaunce kepeth itself withowte moevinge. *(That is to seyn, that it ne moeveth nevermo, and yit it moeveth alle oothre thinges.)* But natheles, yif I have styred resouns° that ne ben nat taken fro withowte the compas of thing of which we treten, but resouns that ben bystowed within that compas, ther nis nat why that thow sholdest merveylen, syn thow hast lerned by the sentense of Plato that nedes° the wordes moten° be cosynes to the thinges of which they speken.

Metre 12. Felix qui potuit boni.

"Blysful is that man that may sen the clere welle of good; blysful is he that may unbynden him fro the bondes of the hevy erthe. The poete of Trace *(Orpheus),* that whilom° hadde ryht gret sorwe for the deth of his wyf, after that he hadde maked by his weepply° songes the wodes moevable to rennen°, and hadde maked the ryveres to stonden stylle, and hadde maked the hertes° and the hyndes° to joignen dredeles° her sydes to cruwel° lyouns *(for to herknen his songe),* and hadde maked that the hare was nat agast of the hownde, which that was plesed by his songe; so whan the moste ardent love of his wif brende° the entrayles of his brest, ne the songes that hadden overcomen alle thinges ne myhten nat asswagen° hir lord *(Orpheus),* he pleynede° him of the hevene goddes that weren crwel to him. He wente him to the howses of helle, and there he temprede his blaundysshinge° soonges by resowninge strenges°, and spak and soonge in wepinge al that ever he hadde receyved, and laved owt° of the noble welles of his moder *(Calyope),* the goddesse. And he soonge with as mochel as he myhte of wepinge, and with as moche as love that dowblede his sorwe myhte yeve him and

159 oother whyle, *sometimes* **160 issest,** *exits* **162 replycasioun,** *repetition,* **manere,** *kind of* **163 envyroninge,** *circumference* **170 covenable yift,** *suitable gift* **178 bownte,** *goodness* **183 proeves,** *arguments,* **hoomlich knowen,** *known familiarly* **190 that,** *to whom,* **whilom,** *earlier* **193 owtterest foreyne,** *remote external* **194 ryht,** *just* **202 styred resouns,** *used arguments* **207 nedes,** *necessarily,* **moten,** *must* **<u>3 Meter 12.</u> 4 whilom,** *once* **6 weepply,** *sad* **7 rennen,** *run* **9 hertes,** *male deer,* **hyndes,** *female deer* **10 dredeles,** *fearless,* **cruwel,** *fierce* **14 brende,** *burned* **17 asswagen,** *soothe,* **pleynede,** *lamented* **20 blaundysshinge,** *soothing* **21 by resowninge strenges,** *with resonant strings* **23 laved owt,** *dipped from*

157 woven, C[1] reads "wonnen." **hows of Dydalus,** the Labyrinth, built by Daedalus. **164 a lytel her-byforn,** see 3.pr2.9ff. **190 we whilom preyeden,** Philosophy and Boethius prayed to God at 3.m9. **195 Parmanydes,** Parmenides, Greek philosopher. C[2] reads "Apermanides." **207 sentense of Plato,** the saying of Plato; see Timaeus 29b. Chaucer echoes the notion that words and deeds should be in accord in *CT* 1.742 and 9.208. **<u>3 Meter 12.</u> 3–4ff., poete of Trace,** Orpheus, poet of Thrace, was renowned for the marvelous powers of his songs; he descended into hell in order to seek the release of his wife, Eurydice. See Ovid *Metamorphoses* 10.1f. **24 *Calyope*,** Calliope, the chief Muse.

thechen° him; and he commoevede° the helle, and requerede and bysowhte by swete preyere the lordes of sowles in helle of relesinge *(that is to seyn, to yilden° him his wyf).*

"*(Cerberus)* the porter of helle, with his thre hevedes, was cawht and al abayst° for the newe songe; and the thre goddesses *(Furies)* and vengeresses of felonies that tormenten and agasten° the sowles by anoy° woxen° soruful and sory, and wepen teeres for pite. Tho° no was nat the heved° of Yxion itormented by the overthrowinge wheel; and Tantalus, that was destroyed by the woodnesse° of longe thurst, despiseth the flodes to drynke; the fowl that hihte voltor°, that eteth the stomak or the gyser° of Ticyus, is so fulfyld of his song that it nil eten ne tyren° no more. At the laste the lord and juge of sowles was moeved to misericordes° and cryde, 'We ben overcomen,' quod he. 'Yive° we to Orpheus his wyf to bere him compaignye. He hath wel ibowht hir by his song and his ditee°. But we wol putte a lawe in this, and covenaunt° in the yifte, that is to seyn, that til he be owt of helle, yif he looke byhynde him, that his wyf shal comen ayein unto us.'

"But what is he that may yive° a lawe to loveres? Love is a gretter lawe and a strengere to himself *(than any lawe that men may yeven).* Allas, whan Orpheus and his wyf weren almest at the termes° of the nyht *(that is to seyn, at the laste bowndes of helle),* Orpheus lookede abakward on Erudice his wyf, and loste hir, and was ded. This fable apartieneth to yow alle, whosoever desireth or seketh to lede his thowht into the sovereyn day *(that is to seyn, to clernesse of sovereyn god).* For whoso that ever be so overcomen that he fychche° his eyen into the putte° of helle *(that is to seyn, whoso sette his thowhtes in erthely thinges),* al that evere he hath drawen of° the noble good celestial, he leseth° it whan he loketh the helles," *(that is to seyn, into lowe thinges of the erthe).*

Explicit liber tercius.

BOOK 4

Incipit liber quartus.

Prose 1. Hec dum Philosophia dignitate vultus.

Whan Philosophie hadde songen softely and delitablely the forseyde thinges, kepinge the dignite of hir cheere and the weyhte of hir wordes, I thanne, that° ne hadde nat al owterly foryeten° the wepinge and the mowrninge that was set in myn herte, forbrak° the entencyoun of hir that entendede yit to seyn some oothre thinges. "O," quod I, "thow that art gyderesse° of verrey° lyht, the thinges that thow hast seid me hiderto ben so cleere to me and so shewinge° by the devyne lookinge of hem, and by thy resouns, that they ne mowen° ben overcomen. And

---

28 **thechen,** *teach,* **commoevede,** *moved to pity* 31 **yilden,** *give* 33 **abayst,** *abashed* 36 **agasten,** *frighten,* **anoy,** *torture,* **woxen,** *grew* 37 **Tho,** *then* 38 **heved,** *head* 40 **woodnesse,** *madness* 42 **hihte voltor,** *is called vulture* 43 **gyser,** *liver* 44 **tyren,** *tears* 46 **misericordes,** *pity* 47 **Yive,** *give* 49 **ditee,** *poem* 50 **covenaunt,** *contract* 55 **yive,** *give* 58 **termes,** *boundary* 66 **fychche,** *fix,* **putte,** *pit* 68 **drawen of,** *derived from* 69 **leseth,** *loses* 4 Prose 1. 4 **that,** *who* 5 **owterly foryeten,** *completely forgotten* 7 **forbrak,** *interrupted* 9 **gyderesse,** *guide,* **verrey,** *true* 11 **shewinge,** *evident* 13 **mowen,** *may*

32 ***Cerberus,*** the three-headed watchdog of hell. **38 Yxion,** Ixion was fastened to an ever-turning wheel. **39 Tantalus,** tormented by perpetual thirst. **43 Ticyus,** Tityus, tormented by having his liver torn by two vultures; see *TC* 1.786–88. **54–55 lawe to loveres,** see *CT* 1.1164. **55 gretter,** C^2 reads "gret." The Latin is *maior.* **71a *Explicit liber tercius,*** Here ends Book Three. Book Four. ***Incipit liber quartus,*** Here begins Book Four. Meter 1. **1–10** The description of ascent here matches with details of the geocentric universe, suggesting that through thought humans can join in the vast design of the cosmos. Concentric spheres of air, cloud, and fire (ether) surround the earth within the even higher realm of the firmament, which includes the twelve "houses" or "mansions" of the zodiac.

thilke° thinges that thou toldest me, al be it so that I hadde whilom° foryeten hem for the sorwe of the wrong that hath ben don to me, yit natheles thei ne weren nat al owtrely unknowen to me. But this same is namely a ryht gret cause of my sorwe: that so as° the governoure of thinges is good, yif that yveles mowen ben° by any weyes, or elles yif that yveles passen° withowte punyssinge. The whiche thing oonly° how worthi it is to ben wondred upon, thow considerest it wel thyself certeynly. But yit to this thing ther is yit another thing ijoigned more to be wondred upon. For felonye is imperisse°, and flowreth *(ful of rychesses)*. And vertu nis nat aloonly withowte meedes°, but it is cast under and fortroden° under the feet of felonous foolk, and it abieth° the torments instide° of wikkede felounes. Of alle whiche thinges ther nis no wyht that may merveylen ynowh, ne compleyne that swiche thinges ben doon in the regne of God, that alle thinges woot° and alle thinges may°, and ne wole° nat but oonly good thinges."

Thanne seyde she thus: "Certes," quod she, "that were a gret mervayle, and an enbasshinge° withowten ende, and wel moore horible than al monstres, yif it were as thow wenest°, that is to seyn, that in the ryht ordenee° hows of so mochel° a fader and an ordenoure of meyne°, that the vesseles that ben fowle and vyl° sholden ben honoured and heryed°, and the precyous vesseles sholden ben defowled and vyl. But it nis nat so, for yif tho° thinges that I have concluded a lytel her-byforn ben kept hoole and unraced°, thow shalt wel knowe by the autoryte of God, of the whos regne I speke, that certes the goode foolk ben alwey mighty and shrewes ben alwey owtcast and feble; ne the vices ne ben nevermo withowte peyne°, ne the vertues ne ben nat withowte mede°; and that blysfulnesses comen alwey to goode folk, and infortune° comth alwey to wikked foolk. And thow shalt wel knowe manye thinges of this kynde that shollen cesen° thy pleyntes, and strengthen the with stidefast sadnesse°. And for thow hast seyn the forme of the verray blysfulnesse by me, that have whilom° shewed it the, and thow hast knowen in whom blysfulnesse is iset, alle thinges itreted that I trowe ben necessarye to putten forth, I shal shewe the the wey that shal bryngen the ayein unto thin hows°. And I shal fycchen fetheres in° thi thowht, by whiche it may areysen in hyhte so that, alle tribulacyoun ydon awey, thow by my gydinge and by my paath and by my sledes° shalt mowe° retorne hool and sownd into thi contree.

Metre 1. Sunt etenim penne volucres mihi.

"I have, forsothe, swifte fetheres that surmounten the heyhte of hevene. Whan the swifte thowht hath clothed itself in tho fetheres, it despiseth the hateful erthes, and surmounteth° the rowndnesse of the grete ayr; and it seth° the clowdes byhynde his bak; and passeth the heyghte of the regyon of the fyr, that eschaufeth° by the swifte moevinge of the fyrmament, til that he areyseth hym into the howses that beren the sterres, and joyneth his weyes with the sonne Phebus, and felawshipeth° the wey of the olde colde Saturnis; and he ymaked a knyht of the clere sterre *(that is to seyn, that the thowght is maked goddes knyht by the sekinge of trowthe to comen to the verray knoleche° of God)*. And thilke thoght renneth by the cercle of the sterres, in alle places ther as the shyninge nyht is painted *(that is to seyn, the nyht that is clowdeles, for on nyhtes that ben clowdeles it semeth as the hevene were peynted with diverse ymages of sterres)*. And whanne he hath idoon ther inowh°, he shal forleten° the laste hevene, and he shal pressen° and wynden° on the bak of the swifte firmament, and he shal ben maked parfit of

14 thilke, *those* **15 whilom,** *formerly* **19 so as,** *given that* **21 mowen ben,** *might exist* **22 passen,** *occur* **23 oonly,** *by itself* **27 imperisse,** *empress* **29 meedes,** *rewards* **30 fortroden,** *trampled* **31 abieth,** *suffers,* **instide,** *instead* **35 woot,** *knows* **36 may,** *can do,* **wole,** *wills* **40 embasshinge,** *bewilderment* **42 wenest,** *think,* **ordenee,** *established* **43 mochel,** *great* **43–44 ordenoure of meyne,** *householder* **45 vyl,** *vile,* **heryed,** *praised* **47 tho,** *those* **49 unraced,** *untorn* **53 peyne,** *punishment* **54 mede,** *reward* **56 infortune,** *misfortune* **58 shollen cesen,** *will stop* **60 sadnesse,** *stability* **62 whilom,** *earlier* **66 thin hows,** *your home* **67 fycchen fetheres in,** *affix wings to* **70 sledes,** *vehicles,* **mowe,** *be able to* 4 Meter 1. **5 surmounteth,** *surpasses* **6 seth,** *sees* **8 eschaufeth,** *heats up* **12 felawshipeth,** *accompanies* **16 knoleche,** *knowledge* **22 idoon ther inowh,** *achieved enough there* **23 forleten,** *leave,* **pressen,** *push* **24 wynden,** *advance*

9 areyseth hym, C[1] reads "aryseth." **17 thoght,** C[1] reads "soule."

the worshipful lyht of God. Ther halt° the Lord of Kynges the ceptre of his myht, and atempreth° the governementes of the world, and the shyninge juge of thinges, stable in hymself, governeth the swifte cart or wayn° *(that is to seyn, the circuler moevinge of the sonne).* And yif thy wey ledeth the ayein so that thow be browht thider°, thanne wolthow seye now that that is the contre that thow requerest, of which thow ne haddest no mynde: 'But now it remembreth me wel, her was I born, her wol I fastne my degree° *(heer wole I dwelle)*'. *But* yif the liketh thanne to loken on the dyrknesse of the erthe that thow hast forleten°, thanne shalthow sen that thise felonous tyraunts that the wrecchede people dredeth now shollen ben exiled fro thilke fayre contre."

Prose 2. Tum ego pape inquam.

Than seyde I thus: "Owh, I wondre me that thou bihetest° me so grete thinges; ne I ne dowte nat that thou ne mayst wel performe that thou byhetest°. But I preye the oonly this, that thow ne tarye nat to telle me thilke thinges that thow hast moeved°."

"Fyrst," quod she, "thow moost nedes° knowen that goode folk ben alwey stronge and myhty, and the shrewes ben feeble and desert and naked of alle strengthes. And of thise thinges, certes°, everich° of hem is declared and shewed by other. For so as good and yvel ben two contraries, yif so be that good be stidefast, than sheweth the feblesse of yvel al openly. And yif thou knowe clerly the frelenesse° of yvel, the stidefastnesse of good is knowen. But for as moche as the fey° of my sentence shal be the more ferme and haboundaunt°, I wil gon by that oo wey and by that other; and I wole conferme the thinges that ben purposed°, now on this side and now on that side. Two thinges ther ben in whiche the effect° of alle the dedes of mankynde standeth, that is to seyn, wil and power. And yif that oon of thise two fayleth, ther nis nothing that may be don. For yif that wil lakkit, ther nis no wiht° that undertaketh to don that he wol nat don; and yif power fayleth, the wil nis but in ydel and stant for nawht. And therof comth it that yif thow see a wiht that wolde° geten that he may nat geten, thow mayst nat dowten that power ne fayleth hym to haven that he wolde."

"This is open and cler," quod I; "ne it ne may nat ben deneyed in no manere."

"And yif thou see a wyht," quod she, "that hath doon that he wolde doon, thou nylt nat dowten that he ne hath had power to doon it?"

"No," quod I.

"And in that that° every wyht may°, in that men may holden him myhty *(as who seyth, in so moche as man is myhty to doon a thing, in so mochel men halt him myhty),* and in that that he ne may, in that men demen him to ben feble."

"I confesse it wel," quod I.

"Remenbreth the," quod she, "that I have gaddered and shewed by forseyde resouns that al the entencioun of the wil of mankynde, which that is lad by diverse studies°, hasteth to comen to blisfulnesse."

"It remembreth me wel," quod I, "that it hath ben shewed."

"And recordeth° the nat thanne," quod she, "that blisfulnesse is thilke same good that men requeren°; so that whan blisfulnesse is requered of alle, that good also is requered and desired of alle?"

"It ne recordeth me nat," quod I, "for I have it gretly alwey fichched° in my memorie."

"Alle folk thanne," quod she, "goode and eke badde, enforcen hem° withowte defference of entencioun to comen to good."

"This is a verray consequence," quod I.

"And certein is," quod she, "that by the getinge of good ben men ymaked goode."

"This is certeyn," quod I.

"Thanne geten goode men that° they desiren?"

"So semeth it," quod I.

"But wikkede folk," quod she, "yif they geten the good that they desiren, they ne mowe° nat be wikkede."

26 halt, *holds* **28 atempreth,** *controls* **30 wayn,** *wagon* **33 thider,** *there* **37 fastne my degree,** *fix my steps* **40 forleten,** *left behind* **4 Prose 2. 2 bihetest,** *promise* **4 byhetest,** *promise* **6 moeved,** *raised* **7 moost nedes,** *must necessarily* **11 certes,** *surely,* **everich,** *each* **16 frelenesse,** *frailty* **17 fey,** *truth* **19 haboundaunt,** *abundant* **21 purposed,** *proposed* **23 effect,** *outcome* **27 wiht,** *person* **31 wolde,** *wants to* **41 that that,** *that which,* **may,** *can do* **51 studies,** *ways* **55 recordeth,** *remember* **57 requeren,** *seek* **61 fichched,** *fixed* **64 enforcen hem,** *strive* **70 that,** *what* **74 mowe,** *may*

30 or wayn, omitted in C[1]. **32 thy,** C[2] reads "this." **36 now,** omitted in C[1].

"So is it," quod I.

"Thanne so as that oon and that other," quod she, "desiren good, and the goode foolk geten good, and nat the wikke foolk, thanne nis it no dowte that the goode foolk ne ben myhty and wikkede foolk ben feeble?"

"Whoso that ever," quod I, "dowteth of this, he ne may nat considere the nature of thinges ne the consequence of resouns."

"And over this," quod she, "yif that ther be two thinges that han oo same purpose by kynde°, and that oon of hem pursueth and parformeth thilke same thing by naturel office, and that oother ne may nat doon thilke naturel office, but folweth by other manere thanne is convenable° to nature him that acomplesseth his purpos kyndeli, and yit he ne acomplesseth nat his owne purpos—wheither of thise two demestow for moore myhty?"

"Yif° that I conjecte°," quod I, "that thou wolt seye, algates° yit I desire to herkne° it more pleynly of the."

"Thow nylt nat thanne deneye," quod she, "that the moevement of goinge° nis in men by kynde?"

"No, forsothe," quod I.

"Ne thou ne dowtest nat," quod she, "that thilke naturel office° of goinge ne be the office of feet?"

"I ne dowte it nat," quod I.

"Thanne," quod she, "yif that a wyht be myhty° to moeve and goth upon his feet, and another, to whom thilke naturel office of feet lakketh, enforceth him to goon crepinge upon his handes, which of thise two owhte to ben holden the moore myhty by ryht?"

"Knyt forth the remenaunt°," quod I, "for no wyht ne dowteth that he that may gon by naturel office offeet ne be moore myhty than he that ne may nat."

"But the soveryn good," quod she, "that is eveneliche purposed° to the good foolk and to badde, the goode folk seken it by naturel office of vertuus, and the shrewes enforcen hem to geten it by diverse coveytyse° *(of erthely thinges)*, which that nis no naturel office to geten thilke same soveryen good. Trowestow that it be any other wyse?"

"Nay," quod I, "for the consequence is open and shewinge° of thinges that I have graunted—that nedes° goode folk moten° ben myhty and shrewes feeble and unmyhty."

"Thow rennest aryht° biforn me," quod she, "and this is the jugement *(that is to seyn, I juge of the)*, ryht as thise leches° ben wont° to hopen *(of sike folk)*, whan they aperceyven that nature is redressed° and withstondeth to° the maledye. But for I se the now al redi to the understondinge, I shal shewe the moore thikke° and continuel resouns. For loke° now, how gretly sheweth the feblesse and infirmite of wikkede folk, that ne mowen nat comen to that° her naturel entencioun ledeth hem, and yit almost thilke naturel entencioun constreineth hem. And what *(were to demen° thanne of shrewes)* yif thilke naturel help hadde forleten° hem, the which *(naturel help of intencioun)* goth alwey biforn hem, and is so gret that unnethe° it may ben overcome? Considere thanne how gret deffaute° of power and how gret feblesse ther is in wikkede felonous folk. *(As who seyth, the gretter thing that is coveyted and the desire nat acomplised, of the lasse myht is he that coveyteth it and may nat acomplisse. And forthi° Philosophie seyth thus by sovereyn good:)* Ne shrewes ne requeren° nat lyhte meedes° ne veyn games, whiche they ne may folwen ne holden. But they faylen of thilke somme° and of the heyhte of thinges *(that is to seyn, sovereyn good)*, ne thise wrechches ne comen nat to the effect *(of sovereyn good)* the which they enforcen hem oonly° to geten by nyhtes and by dayes, in the getinge of which good the strengthe of good foolk is ful wel ysene. For ryht so as thow myhtest demen him myhty of goinge that goth on his feet tyl he myhte come to thilke place fro the° whiche place ther ne laye no wey forthere to ben gon, ryht so most thow nedes demen him for ryht myhty that geteth

87 kynde, *nature* **91 covenable,** *suitable* **95 Yif,** (even) *if,* **conjecte,** *do guess* **96 algates,** *nevertheless,* **herkne,** *hear* **99 goinge,** *walking* **104 office,** *function* **107 myhty,** *strong enough* **112 Knyt forth the remenaunt,** i.e., *continue the argument* **117 eveneliche purposed,** *equally intended* **120 coveytyse,** *desire* **125 shewinge,** *evident* **126 nedes,** *necessarily,* **moten,** *must* **128 rennest aryht,** *run properly* **130 leches,** *physicians,* **wont,** *accustomed* **132 redressed,** *restored,* **withstondeth to,** *counteracts* **135 thikke,** *deep,* **loke,** *consider* **138 that,** *what* **141 demen,** *think* **142 forleten,** *left* **144 unnethe,** *scarcely* **145 deffaute,** *lack* **150 *forthi,*** *therefore* **151 requeren,** *seek* **152 lyhte meedes,** *insignificant rewards* **154 thilke somme,** *that sum* **157–58 the which they enforcen hem only,** *for which only they strive* **163 fro the,** *from*

and ateyneth to the ende of alle thinges that ben to desire, byyonde the whiche ende ther nis nothing to desire. Of the which power of good folk men may conclude that the wikked men semen to be bareyne and naked of alle strengthe. For why forleten° they vertuus and folwen vices? Nis it nat for that they ne knowen nat the goodes? But what thing is moore feeble and more caytyf° thanne is the blyndnesse of ignoraunce? Or elles they knowen ful wel whiche thinges that they owhten° folwe, but lecherie and coveytyse overthroweth hem mystorned°, and certes, so doth distemperaunce to feeble men that ne mowen nat wrastlen ayeines the vices. Ne knowen they nat thanne wel that they forleten° the good wilfully and tornen hem wilfully to vyces? And in this wyse they ne forleten nat oonly to ben myhty, but they forleten al owtrely° in any wyse for to ben. For they that forleten the comune fyn° of alle thinges that ben, they forleten also therwithal for to ben.

"And peraventure° it sholde semen to som folk that this were a merveyle to seyen, that shrewes, whiche that contienen° the moore° partye of men, ne ben nat ne han no beinge. But natheles it is so, and thus stant° this thing. For thei that ben shrewes, I deneye nat that they ben shrewes, but I deneye, and seye simpleli and pleynly, that they ne ben nat, ne han no beinge. For ryht as thow myhtest seyen of the carayne° of a man that it were a ded man, but thow ne myhtest nat symplely callen it a man, so graunte I wel forsothe° that visious folk ben wikked, but I ne may nat graunten absolutly and symplely that they ben. For thilke thing that withholdeth° ordre and kepeth nature, thilke thing is, and hath beinge; but what thing that fayleth of that *(that is to seyn, that he forleteth naturel ordre)*, he forleteth thilke beinge that is set in his nature. But thow wolt seyn that shrewes mowen°. Certes, that ne deneye I nat; but certes, her power ne dessendit° nat of strengthe but of feeblesse. For they mowen don wikkednesses, the whiche they ne myhte nat don yif they myhten dwellen in the forme and in the doinge of good folk. And thilke power sheweth ful evidently that they ne mowen ryht nawht. For so as I have gadered, and proeved a litel her-byforn that yvel is nawht, and so as shrewes mowen° oonly but shrewednesses, this conclusioun is al cleer, that shrewes ne mowen ryht nawht, ne han no power. And for as moche as thou understonde which is the strengthe of this power of shrewes, I have difinissed° a litel her-byforn that nothing is so myhty as sovereyn good."

"That is soth," quod I.

"And thilke same sovereyn good may don non yvel?"

"Certes no," quod I.

"Is ther any wyht° thanne," quod she, "that weneth° that men mowen doon alle thinges?"

"No man," quod I, "but he be owt of his witte."

"But, certes, shrewes mowen don yvel?" quod she.

"Ye, wolde God," quod I, "that they myhten don non!"

"Thanne," quod she, "so as he that is myhty to doon only but goode thinges may don alle thinges, and they that ben myhty to don yvele thinges ne mowen nat alle thinges, thanne is it open thing and manifest that they that mowen don yvel ben of lasse power. And yit *(to proeve this conclusioun)* ther helpeth me this, that I have ishewed her-byforn, that alle power is to be nowmbred among thinges that men owhten requere°. And I have shewed that alle thinges that owhten ben desired ben referred° to good, ryht as to a maner heyhte° of her nature. But for to mowen° don yvel and felonye ne may nat ben referred to good. Thanne nis nat yvel of the nowmbyr of thinges that owhte ben desired. But alle power owhte ben desired and requered. Than is it open and cler that the power ne the mowinge° of shrewes nis no power. And of alle

171 forleten, *abandon* **174 caytyf,** *miserable* **177 owhten,** *ought to* **178 mystorned,** *misled* **182 forleten,** *abandon* **185 al owtrely,** *completely* **186 fyn,** *end* **189 peraventure,** *perhaps* **191 contienen,** *include,* **moore,** *greater* **193 stant,** *stands* **198 carayne,** *corpse* **200 forsothe,** *truly* **203 withholdeth,** *maintains* **208 mowen,** *have power* **210 dessendit,** *derives* **218 mowen,** *can do* **223 difinissed,** *explained* **229 wyht,** *person* **230 weneth,** *thinks* **247–48 owhten requere,** *ought to seek* **249 referred,** *related* **250 maner heyhte,** *kind of apex* **251 mowen,** *be able* **257 mowinge,** *ability*

217 her-byforn, see 3.pr12.152–54. **223 her-byforn,** see 3.pr12.113–15. **246 her-byforn,** see 3.pr10.216–23.

thise thinges it sheweth wel that the goode folk ben certeynly myhty, and the shrewes dowteles ben unmyhty. And it is cler and open that thilke sentence of Plato is verray and soth, that seyth that oonly wyse men may doon that they desiren. And shrewes mowen hawnten that° hem liketh°, but that they desiren *(that is to seyn, to comen to sovereygn good),* they ne han no power to accomplissen that. For shrewes don that hem lyst° whan by the thinges in which they deliten, they wenen° to ateyne to thilke good that they desyren, but they ne geten ne ateynen nat therto, for vices ne comen nat to blisfulnesse.

Metre 2. Quos vides sedere celsos.

"Whoso that° the covertoures of her veyn aparayles myhte strepen of° thise prowde kynges, that thou seest sitten on heyh in her chayres, glyteringe in shyninge purpre, envyrowned° with sorwful armures°, manassinge° with crwel mowth, blowinge° by woodnesse° of herte, he sholde seen thanne that thilke° lordes beren withinne her corages° ful streyte° cheynes. For lecherie tormenteth hem in that oon syde with gredy venyms, and trowblable ire that arayseth in him the floodes of trowblinges tormenteth upon that oother side her thowht, or sorwe halt° hem wery and ykawht, or slidinge and deceyvinge hope tormenteth hem. And therfore, syn° thow seest oon heed° *(that is to seyn, oon tyraunt)* beren so manye tyranyes, thanne ne doth thilke tyraunt nat that he desireth, syn he is cast doun with so manye wikkede lordes *(that is to seyn, with so manye vices that han so wikkedly lordshippes over him).*

Prose 3. Videsne igitur quanto.

"Seestow nat thanne in how gret fylthe thise shrewes ben ywrapped, and with which cleernesse thise good foolk shynen? In this sheweth it wel that to goode foolk ne lakketh nevermo her meedes°, ne shrewes lakken nevermo torments. For of alle thinges that ben ydoon°, thilke° thing for which anything is don, it semeth as by ryht that thilke thing be the meede of that—as thus, yif a man renneth in the stadie° *(or in the forlong°)* for the corone°, thanne lyth° the meede in the corone for which he renneth. And I have shewed that blysfulnesse is thilke same good for which that alle thinges ben doon. Thanne is thilke same good purposed to° the workes of mankinde ryht as a comune meede, which meede ne may ben dessyvered° fro good foolk. For no wiht as by ryht fro thennesforth that him lakketh goodnesse ne shal ben cleped° good. For which thing, folk of goode maneres°, her meedes ne forsaken hem nevermo. For al be it so that shrewes wexen° as woode° as hem list° *(ayenes goode folk),* yit neverthelesse the corone of wyse men shal nat fallen ne faaden. For foreyne shrewednesse° ne bynymeth° nat fro the corages of goode foolk her propre honour. But yif that any wyht° rejoyse him of goodnesse that he hadde taken fro withowte *(as who seyth, yif that any wiht hadde his goodnesse of any oother man than of himself),* certes he that yaf° him thilke goodnesse, or elles som oother wyht, myhte benyme it him. But for as moche as to every wyht his owne propre bownte° yeveth him his meede, thanne at erst° shal he faylen of meede whan he forleteth° to ben good. And at the laste so as alle meedes ben requered for° men wenen° that they ben goode, who is he that nolde deme° that he that is ryht myhty of good were partles° of meede? And of what meede shal he be gerdoned°? Certes, of ryht fayre meede and ryht grete aboven alle meedes, Remembre the of thilke noble corolarye that I yaf the a litel her-byforn, and gadere it togider in this manere: so as good hymself is blisfulnesse, thanne is it cleer and

---

264 hawnten that, *continue to do what,* **hem liketh,** *pleases them* **267 hem lyst,** *pleases them* **268 wenen,** *think* **4 Meter 2. 1 Whoso that,** *whoever* **2 of,** *from* **4 envyrowned,** *surrounded* **5 sorwful armures,** *stern soldiers,* **manassinge,** *menacing* **6 blowinge,** *puffing,* **woodenesse,** *madness* **7 thilke,** *these* **8 corages,** *hearts,* **ful streyte,** *very tight* **13 halt,** *holds* **15 syn,** *because* **16 oon heed,** *one head* **4 Prose 3. 5 meedes,** *rewards* **7 ydoon,** *done,* **thilke,** *that* **10 stadie,** *stadium,* **forlong,** *racetrack* **11 corone,** *crown,* **lyth,** *lies* **15 purposed to,** *intended for* **17 dessyvered,** *separated* **20 cleped,** *called* **21 maneres,** *habits* **22 wexen,** *become* **23 woode,** *angry,* **hem list,** (it) *pleases them* **25–26 foreyne shrewednesse,** *external evil* **26 bynymeth,** *deprives* **28 wyht,** *person* **31 yaf,** *gave* **34 bownte,** *goodness* **35 thanne at erst,** *only then* **36 forleteth,** *ceases* **37 ben requered for,** *are sought because* **38 wenen,** *think* **39 nolde deme,** *would not think* **40 partles,** *without a share* **41 gerdoned,** *rewarded*

261–67 sentence of Plato . . . , although the specific statement is not to be found in Plato, much of 4.pr.2–3 adapts his *Gorgias* 466–81, 505–07. **4 Prose 3. 44 her-byforn,** see 3.pr10.139–50.

certeyn that alle good folk ben maked blysful for they ben goode. And thilke folk that ben blysful, it acordeth and is covenable° to ben goddes. Thanne is the meede of goode folk swich that no day shal enpeyren° it, ne no wikkednesse ne shal derken it, ne power of no wyht ne shal nat amenusen° it, that is to seyn, to ben maked goddes.

"And syn it is thus *(that goode men ne faylen nevermo of her meede)*, certes no wys man ne may dowte of undepartable° peyne of the shrewes *(that is to seyn, that the peyne of shrewes ne departeth nat from hemself nevermo).* For so as goode and yvel, and peyne and meedes ben contrarye, it mot nedes° ben that ryht as we seen bytyden° in gerdoun° of goode, that also mot the peyne of yvel answery° by contrarye party° to shrewes. Now thanne, so as bownte° and prowesse ben the meede to goode foolk, also is shrewednesse itself torment to shrewes. Thanne whoso that ever is entechched° and defowled with peyne, he ne dowteth nat that he is entechched and defowled with yvel. Yif shrewes thanne wolen preysen hemself, may it semen to hem that they ben withowten party of° torment, syn they ben swiche that the uttereste wikkednesse *(that is to seyn, wikkede thewes°, which that is the owttereste and the worste kynde of shrewednesse)* ne defowleth ne entechcheth nat hem oonly, but infecteth and envenymeth hem gretly? And also looke on shrewes, that ben the contrarye party of goode men, how gret peyne felawshippeth and folweth hem! For thou hast lerned a lytel her-byforn that alle thing that is and hath beynge is oon, and thilke same oon is good. Thanne is this the consequence that it semeth wel, that alle that is and hath beynge is good *(this is to seyn, as who seyth that beinge and unite and goodnesse is al oon).* And in this manere it folweth thanne that alle thing that fayleth to ben good, it stynteth° for to be and for to han any beinge; wherfore it is that shrewes stynten for to ben that they weren. But thilke oother forme of mankynde, that is to seyn the forme of the body withowte, sheweth yit that thise shrewes weren whilom° men; wherfor whan they ben perverted and torned into malice, certes than han they forlorn° the nature of mankynde. But so as oonly bownte and prowesse° may enhawnsen° every man oover other men, thanne mot it nedes be that shrewes, which that shrewednesse hath cast owt of the condicioun of mankynde, ben put under° the merite and the desert of men. Thanne bytydeth° it that yif thou seest a wyht that be transformed into vices, thow ne mayst nat wene° that he be a man. For yif he be ardaunt in averyce, and that he be a ravaynour° by vyolence of foreyne richesse°, thow shalt seyn that he is lyke to the wolf. And yif he be felonows and withowte reste, and exersise his tonge to chidinges, thou shalt lykkne him to the hownd. And yif he be a prevey awaytour ihidd°, and rejoyseth him to ravysse° by wiles, thou shalt seyn him lyke to the fox-whelpes. And yif he be distempre° and quaketh for ire, men shal wene that he bereth the corage° of a lyoun. And yif he be dredful° and fleinge, and dredeth thinges that ne owhten nat to ben dredd, men shal holden him lyk to the hert°. And yif he be slowh and astoned° and lache°, he lyveth as an asse. And yif he be liht and unstidefast of corage, and chaungeth ay° his studies°, he is lykned to bryddes. And yif he be plownged in fowle and unclene luxuris°, he is withholden° in the fowle delices of the fowle sowe. Thanne folueth it that he that forleteth° bownte and prowesse, he forleteth to ben a man; syn he may nat passen into the condicioun of God, he is torned into a best.

---

49 covenable, *fitting* **51 enpeyren,** *impair* **53 amenusen,** *diminish* **57 dowte of undepartable,** *doubt the inseparable* **61 mot nedes,** *must necessarily* **62 bytyden,** *happen,* **gerdoun,** *reward* **63 answery,** *correspond* **64 contrarye party,** *opposite* **65 bownte,** *goodness* **68 entechched,** *stained* **72 withowten party of,** *have no portion of* **74 thewes,** *habits* **89 stynteth,** *ceases* **94 whilom,** *once* **97 forlorn,** *lost* **98 prowesse,** *virtue,* **enhawnsen,** *raise* **102 under,** *below* **103 bytydeth,** *happens* **105 wene,** *think* **107 ravaynour,** *looter,* **foreyne richesse,** *the riches of others* **112 prevey awaytour ihidd,** *secret hidden lurker* **113 ravysse,** *steal* **114 distrempre,** *intemperate* **116 corage,** *heart* **117 dredful,** *fearful* **119 hert,** *deer* **120 astoned,** *dazed,* **lache,** *lazy* **122 ay,** *constantly,* **studies,** *pursuits* **124 luxuris,** *lusts,* **withholden,** *trapped* **126 forleteth,** *abandons.*

68–70 peyne . . . defowled with, omitted in C²; eyeskip. **81 her-byforn,** at 3.pr11.200–05.

Metre 3. Vela Naricii ducis.

"Eurus° the wynd aryvede° the sayles of Ulixes, duc of the contre of Narice, and his wandringe shippes by the see into the ile ther as° Circes, the fayre goddesse, dowhter of the sonne, dwelleth, that medleth to° hir newe gestes drynkes that ben towched and maked with enchauntements. And after that hir hand, myhty over the herbes, hadde chaunged hir gestes into diverse maneres°, that oon of hem is covered his face with forme of a boere, that oother is chaunged into a lyoun of the contre of Marmorike, and his nayles and his teth wexen°, that oother of hem is neweliche chaunged into a wolf, and howleth whan he wolde wepe, that oother goth debonayrely° in the hows as a tygre of Inde. But al be it so that the godhed of Mercurie, that is cleped° the bryd of Archadie, hath had mercy of° the duc Ulixes, biseged with diverse yveles, and hath unbownden him fro the pestelence of his oostesse°, algates° the roweres and the maryneres° hadden by this idrawen into her mowthes and dronken the wikkede drynkes. They that weren wexen swyn° hadden by this ichaunged her mete° of bred for to eten akkornes° of okes. Non of her lemes° ne dwelleth with hem hool, but they han lost the voyce and the body; oonly her thowht dwelleth with hem stable, that weepeth and byweyleth the monstruous chaunginge that they suffren. O overlyht° hand! *(As who seyth, O feble and lyht is the hand of Circes the enchaunteresse, that chaungeth the bodies of folkes into bestes, to regard and to comparisoun of mutassioun that is maked by vices!)* Ne the herbes of Circes ne ben nat myhty. For al be it so that they may chaungen the lymes of the body, algates yit they may nat chaunge the hertes, for withinne is yhydd the strengthe and vigor of men, in the secre toure° of her hertes *(that is to seyn, the strengthe of resoun)*. But thilke venyms° of vices todrawen a man to hem moore myhtyly than the venym of Circes. For vices ben so cruel° that they percen and thorwpassen the corage withinne; and, thogh they ne anoye nat the body, yit vices wooden° to destroyen men by wownde of thowht."

Prose 4. Tum ego fateor inquam.

Than seyde I thus: "I confesse and am aknowe° it," quod I, "ne I ne se nat that men may sayn, as by ryht that shrewes ne ben chaunged into bestes by the qualyte of her sowles, al be it so that they kepen yit the forme of the body of mankynde. But I nolde nat of° shrewes, of which the thowht crwel woodeth alwey into destruccioun of goode men, that it were leveful° to hem to don that."

"Certes," quod she, "ne it nys nat leveful to hem, as I shal wel shewe the in covenabele° place; but natheles, yif so were that thilke that° men wenen be leveful° to shrewes were bynomen hem° *(so that they ne myhte nat anoyen or doon harm to goode men)*, certes a gret partye of the peyne to shrewes sholde ben allegged° and releved. For al be it so that this ne seme nat credible thing, peraventure°, to some folk, yit moot it nedes be that shrewes ben moore wrechches° and unsely° whan they may doon and performe that they coveyten° than yif they myhte nat complyssen that° they coveyten. For yif so be that it be wrechchednesse to wylne° to don yvel, than is moore wrechchednesse to mowen° doon yvel, withowte whiche mowinge° the wrecched wil sholde languesse withowte effect. Than, syn that everyche° of

---

4 Meter 3. 1 **aryvede,** *pushed ashore* 3 **ile ther as,** *isle where* 5 **medleth to,** *mixes for* 9 **maneres,** *kinds* 13 **wexen,** *grew* 16 **debonayrely,** *tamely* 18 **cleped,** *called* 19 **of,** *on* 21 **oostesse,** *hostess,* **algates,** *nevertheless* 22 **maryneres,** *mariners* 24 **wexen swyn,** *become swine* 25 **mete,** *food* 26 **akkornes,** *acorns* 27 **lemes,** *limbs* 31 **overlyht,** *too feeble* 40 **toure,** *tower* 42 **thilke venyms,** *those venoms* 44 **cruel,** *fierce* 47 **wooden,** *rage* 4 Prose 4. 1–2 **am aknowe,** *acknowledge* 7 **nolde nat,** *wish it were not true* 9 **leveful,** *permitted* 11 **covenable,** *suitable* 12 **that thilke that,** *that that which* 13 **wenen to leveful,** *believe to be permitted* 13–14 **bynomen hem,** *taken from them* 16 **allegged,** *alleviated* 18 **peraventure,** *perhaps* 20 **wrechches,** *miserable,* **unsely,** *unhappy* 21 **coveyten,** *desire* 22 **complyssen that,** *accomplish what* 23 **wylne,** *will* 25 **mowen,** *be able to* 26 **mowinge,** *ability* 27 **syn that everyche,** *because every*

4 Meter 3. 1 **Eurus,** the southeast wind. **2ff. Ulixes . . . ,** Ulysses, leader of the Neritians (the residents of Ithaca, where mount Neritos is located), landed with his men on the isle of Circe, where the enchantress changed the men to beasts; Ovid *Metamorphoses* 14.240ff. 12 **Marmorike,** Marmarica, in Libya. 18 **bryd of Archadie,** bird of Arcadia, i.e., Mercury, the winged messenger of the gods, who was born in Arcadia.

thise thinges hath his wrechchednesse *(that is to seyn, wyl to doon yvel and mowinge to don yvel),* it mot nedes be that they ben constreyned by three unselynesses°, that woolen° and mowen° and performen felonyes and shrewednesses."

"I acorde me," quod I; "but I desire gretly that shrewes losten sone thilke unselynesses, that is to seyn, that shrewes weren despoyled° of mowinge to don yvel."

"So shullen they," quod she, "sonner° peraventure than thow woldest, or sonner than they hemself wene to lakken mowinge to don yvel. For ther nis nothing so late, in so short bowndes of this lyf, that is long to abyde° namelyche, to a corage inmortel, of whiche shrewes the grete hope and the hye compassinges° of shrewednesses is ofte destroyed by a sodeyn ende or° they ben war. And that thing estableth to shrewes the ende of her shrewednesse, For yif that shrewednesse. maketh wrechches, than mot he nedes ben° most wrechched that lengest is a shrewe; the whiche wikked shrewes wolde I demen aldermost unsely° and caytyfs°, yif that her shrewednesse ne were fynyshed at the leste wey by the owttereste° deth. For yif I have concluded soth° the unselynesse of shrewednesse, than sheweth it cleerly that thilke wrechchednesse is withowten ende, the whiche is certeyn to ben perdurable°."

"Certes," quod I, "this conclusioun is hard and wonderful to graunte, but I knowe wel that it acordeth moche to the thinges that I have graunted her-byforn."

"Thou hast", quod she, "the ryht estimacioun of this. But whosoever wene° that it be a hard thing to acorde him to a conclusioun, it is ryht that he shewe that some of the premysses ben false; or elles he moot shewe that the collations° of proposiciouns nis nat spedful° to a necessarye conclusioun. And yif it ne be nat so, but that the premysses ben ygraunted, ther nis not why° he sholde blame the argument. For this thing that I shal telle thee now ne shal nat seme lasse wonderful, but of the thinges that ben taken also it is necessarie" *(as who seyth, it folweth of that which that is purposed byforn).*

"What is that?" quod I.

"Certes," quod she, "that is that thise wikked shrewes ben moore blysful *(or elles lasse wrechches)* that abyen° the torments that they han deserved than yif no peyne of justice ne chastysede hem. Ne this ne seye I nat now for that any man myhte thinke that the maners of shrewes ben coriged° and chastised by venyaunce, and that they ben browht to the ryht wey by the drede of the torment, ne for that they yeven to oother folk ensaumple to flen fro vices; but I understande yit in another manere that shrewes ben moore unsely whan they ne ben nat punyssed, al be it so that ther ne be had no resoun or lawe of correcsioun, ne non ensaumple of lookinge°."

"And what manere shal that ben," quod I, "oother than hath be told her-byforn?"

"Have we nat thanne graunted," quod she, "that goode folk ben blysful, and shrewes ben wrechches?"

"Yis," quod I.

"Thanne," quod she, "yif that any good were added to the wrechchednesse of any wyht°, nis he nat moore weleful° than he that he hath no medlinge° of good in his solitarye wrechchednesse?"

"So semeth it,"quod I.

"And what seystow thanne," quod she, "of thilke wrechche that lakked alle goodes *(so that no good nis medled in his wrechchednesse),* and yit, over al his wykkednesse for which he is a wrechche, that ther be yit another yvel anexed and knytte to him? Shal nat men demen him more unsely than thilke wrechche of whiche the unselynesse is releved by "the partycipacioun of som good?"

"Whi sholde he nat?" quod I.

"Thanne, certes," quod she, "han shrewes, whan they ben punysshed, somwhat of good anexed to her wrechchednesse, that

---

31 unselynesses, *sorrows,* **woolen,** *desire to,* **mowen,** *are able to* **35 despoyled,** *deprived* **37 sonner,** *sooner* **41 abyde,** *wait for* **44 compassinges,** *plans* **45 or,** *before* **48 nedes ben,** *necessarily be* **51 aldermost unsely,** *most of all unhappy,* **caytyfs,** *captives* **53 owttereste,** *final* **54 soth,** *truth* **57 perdurable,** *everlasting* **63 wene,** *thinks* **67 collacions,** *combination* **68 spedful,** *conducive* **70 why,** *reason* **79 abyen,** *receive* **83 coriged,** *corrected* **91–92 ensaumple of lookinge,** *example for others to see* **101 wyht,** *person,* **weleful,** *happy* **102 medlinge,** *mixture*

31 three, C² reads "the." The Latin is *triplici.* **39–40 lakken . . . yvel,** omitted in C².

is to seyn, the same peyne that they suffren which that is good by the resoun of justyce; and whan thilke same shrewes ascapen withowte torment, than han they som what more of yvel yit over the wikkednesse that they han don, that is to seyn, defaute° of peyne, which defaute of peyne, thow hast graunted, is yvel for the deserte of felonye°"

"I ne may nat denye it," quod I.

"Moche moore thanne," quod she, "ben shrewes unsely whan they ben wrongfully delyvered fro peyne than whan they ben punysshed by ryhtful venyaunce. But this is open thyng and cleer, that it is ryht that shrewes ben punysshed, and it is wykkednesse and wrong that they escapen unpunysshed."

"Who myhte deneye that?" quod I.

"But," quod she, "may any man denye that al that is ryht nis good; and also the contrarye, that al that is wrong is wykke?"

"Certes," quod I, "these thinges ben cleere inowh°, and that we han concluded a lytel her-byforn. But I preye the that thow telle me yif thou acordest to leten° no torment to sowles after that the body is ended by the deeth?" *(This is to seyn, understandestow awht that sowles han any torment after the deth of the body?)*

"Certes," quod she, "yee and that ryht gret. Of which sowles," quod she, "I trowe that some ben tormented by asprenesse° of peyne, and some sowles, I trowe, ben exersised by a purginge mekenesse. But my conseyl° nis nat to determenye of thise peynes. But I have travayled° and told yit hiderto for thow sholdest knowe that the mowinge° of shrewes, which mowinge the semeth to ben unworthy, nis no mowinge. And ek of shrewes, of which thou pleynedes° that they ne were nat punysshed, that thou woldest seyn that they ne weren nevermo withowten the torments of her wykkednesse. And of the licence° *(of the mowinge to don yvel)* that thow preydest that it myhte sone ben ended, and that thou woldest fayn° lernen that it ne sholde nat longe dure°. And that shrewes ben moore unsely° yif they were of lengere duringe, and most unsely yif they weren perdurable°. And after this, I have shewed the that moore unsely ben shrewes whan they escapen withowte her ryghtful peyne than whan they ben punyssed by ryhtful venyaunce. And of this sentence folweth it that thanne ben shrewes constreyned at the laste with most grevous torment, whan men wene that they ne be nat punysshed."

"Whan I considere thy resoun," quod I, "I ne trowe nat that men seyn anything moore verayly°. And yif I torne ayeyn to the studyes of men, who is he to whom it sholde seme that he ne sholde nat oonly leven° thise thinges but ek gladly herkne° hem?"

"Certes," quod she, "so it is. But men may nat, for they han her eyen so wont° to the derknesse *(of erthely thinges)* that they ne may nat lyften hem up to the lyht of cleer sothfastnesse°. But they ben lyke to bryddes° of which the nyht lyhtneth° her lokinge and the day blyndeth hem. For whan men looken° nat the ordre of thinges, but her lustes and talents° they wene° that eyther the leve° or the mowinge to don wykkednesse, or elles the scapinge withowte peyne, be weleful°. But considere the jugement of the perdurable lawe. For yif thou conferme thy corage to the beste thinges, thou ne hast no nede of no juge to yeven the prys° or mede°, for thow hast joined thyself to the moost excellent thing. And yif thow have enclyned thy studyes to the wykked thinges, ne sek no foreyne wrekere° owt of thyself. For thow thyself hast thryst° thyself into wikke thinges ryht as° thow myhtest loken° by diverse tymes the fowle erthe and the hevene, and that alle other thinges stynten° fro withowte *(so that thow nere neyther in hevene ne in erthe, ne saye° nothing moore)*. Than it sholde semen to

---

123 defaute, *lack* **125 for the deserte of felonye,** *for what evil deserves* **139 inowh,** *enough* **141 acordest to leten,** *agree to allow for* **147 asprenesse,** *bitterness* **149 conseyl,** *intention* **151 travayled,** *labored* **152 mowinge,** *power* **155 pleynedest,** *complain* **158 licence,** *granting* **161 fayn,** *like to* **162 dure,** *survive,* **unsely,** *unhappy* **164 perdurable,** *everlasting* **175 verayly,** *truly* **177 leven,** *believe* **178 herkne,** *hear* **180 wont,** *accustomed* **183 sothfastnesse,** *truthfulness* **183 bryddes,** *birds* **184 lyhtneth,** *illuminates* **186 looken,** *recognize* **187 talents,** *desires* i.e., **wene,** *think* **188 leve,** *freedom* **189 weleful,** *happy* **193 prys,** *prize,* **mede,** *reward* **197 foreyne wrekere,** *external punisher* **198 thryst,** *thrust* **199 as,** *as if,* **loken,** *look at* **201 stynten,** *cease* **203 saye,** *were to see*

140 her-byforn, see 4.pr3.60–64. **202** ***nere neyther in hevene ne in erthe,*** omitted in C[1], but in the French.

the, as by oonly resoun of lookinge, that thow were now in the sterres and now in the erthe. But the poeple ne looketh nat on thise thinges°. What thanne? Shal we thanne aprochen us to hem that I have shewed that they ben lyk to bestes? And what woltow seyn of this: yif that a man hadde al forlorn° his syhte, and hadde foryeten that he ever sawh, and wende° that nothing ne faylede him of perfeccioun of mankynde—now we that myhten sen the same thinges, wolde we nat wene° that he were blynde? Ne also ne acordeth nat the poeple to that I shal seyn, the which thing is sustened by a stronge fowndement° of resouns, that is to seyn, that moore unsely ben they that don wrong to oothre folk than they that the wrong suffren."

"I wolde heren thilke same resouns," quod I.

"Denyesthow," quod she, "that alle shrewes ne ben worthy to han torment?"

"Nay," quod I.

"But," quod she, "I am certein, by many resouns, that shrewes ben unsely°."

"It acordeth°," quod I.

"Thanne ne dowtestow nat," quod she, "that thilke folk that ben worthi of torment, that they ne ben wrechches?"

"It acordeth wel," quod I.

"Yif thow were thanne yset a juge or a knower of thinges, whether trowestow° that men sholden tormenten° him that hath don the wrong or elles him that hath suffred the wrong?"

"I ne dowte nat," quod I, "that I nolde don suffisaunt satisfaccioun to him that hadden suffred the wrong by the sorwe of him that hadden don the wrong."

"Thanne semeth it," quod she, "that the doere of wrong is moore wrechche than he that suffred wrong?"

"That folweth wel," quod I.

"Than," quod she, "by thise causes, and by othre causes that ben enforced by the same roote, fylthe or synne by the propre° nature of it maketh men wrechches. And it sheweth wel that the wrong that men don nis nat the wrechchednesse of° him that reseyveth the wrong, but the wrechchednesse of him that doth the wrong. But certes," quod she, "thise oratours or advocats° al the contrarye, for they enforcen hem to commoeve° the juges to han pite of hem that han suffred and resseyved the thinges that ben grevous and aspre°, and yit men sholden moore ryhtfully han pite of hem that don the grevaunces and the wronges. The whiche shrewes, it were a moore covenable° thing that the accusours or advocats, nat wroth, but pitous and debonayre°, ledden tho shrewes that han don wrong to the jugement, ryht as men leden syke folk to the leche°, for that they sholden seken owt the maladies of synne by torment. And by this covenaunt, ether the entente of deffendours or advokats° sholde faylen and cesen in al°, or elles yif the office of advocats wolde bettre profyten to men, it sholde ben torned into the habite of accusacioun *(that is to seyn, they sholden accuse shrewes, and nat excuse hem).* And ek the shrewes hemself, yif hit were leveful° to hem to sen at any clyfte° the vertu that they han forleten°, and sawh that they sholden putten adown the felthes of her vices by the torments of peynes, they ne owhte nat, ryht for the recompensacyoun for to geten hem bownte° and prowesse° which that they han lost, demen° ne holden° that thilke peynes weren torments to hem; and ek they wolden refuse the attendaunce° of her advocats, and taken hemself to her juges and to her accusors. For which it bytideth° that as to the wyse folk, ther nis no place ileten° to hate *(that is to seyn, that ne hate hath no place amonges wyse men).* For no wyht nyl haten goode men but yif

---

206–07 thise thinges, i.e., *the stars* **210 ay forlorn,** *completely lost* **212 wende,** *thought* **214 wene,** *think* **217 fowndement,** *foundation* **227 unsely,** *unhappy* **228 acordeth,** *follows* **234 whether trowestow,** *which* (would) *you think* **235 tormenten,** *punish* **248 propre,** *intrinsic* **251 of,** *for* **254 advocats,** *lawyers* **255 enforcen hem to commoeve,** *strive to encourage* **258 aspre,** *bitter* **261 covenable,** *suitable* **262 debonayre,** *gentle* **265 leche,** *physician* **268 advokats,** *defense lawyers,* **in al,** *completely* **273 leveful,** *allowed* **274 clyfte,** *peephole* **275 forleten,** *abandoned* **278 bownte,** *goodness* **279 prowesse,** *virtue* **280 demen,** *think,* **holden,** *maintain* **282 attendaunce,** *service* **284 bytideth,** *happens* **285 ileten,** *allowed*

252–53 but the wrechchednesse . . . the wrong, lacking in C²; eyeskip.

he were over-mochel a fool; and for to haten shrewes, it nis no resoun. For ryht so as langwissinge° is maledye of body, ryht so ben vyces and synne maledye of corage°. And so as we ne deme nat that they that ben syke of her body ben worthy to ben hated, but rather worthy of pyte, wel moore worthi nat to ben hated but for to ben had in pite ben they of whiche the thowhtes ben constreyned by felonows wykkednesse, that is moore cruwel° than any langwyssinge of body.

Metre 4. Quid tantos iuvat excitare motus.

"What deliteth yow° to exciten so grete moevinge of hateredes, and to hasten and bysien° the fatal disposicioun of yowr deth with yowr propre handes? *(That is to seyn, by batayles or by kontek°?)* For yif ye axen° the deth, it hasteth him of his owne wyl; ne deth ne taryeth° nat his swifte hors°. And the men that the serpent and the lyown and the tygre and the bere and the boor seken to slen with her teth, yit thilke° same men seken to slen everych of hem oother° with swerd. Lo, for° her maneres ben diverse and descordaunt, they moeven° unryhtful oostes° and crwel batayles, and wylnen° to perise by entrechaunginges of dartes! But the resoun of crweltee nis nat inowh ryhtful°. Wiltow thanne yelden° a covenable gerdoun° to the desertes of men? Love ryhtfully goode folk, and have pite on shrewes."

Prose 5. Hic ego video inquam.

"Thus se I wel," quod I, "eyther what blysfulnesse or elles what unselynesse° is establyssed in the desertes of goode men and of shrewes. But in this ilke° fortune of poeple I se somwhat of good and somwhat of yvel. For no wyse man hath levere ben° exiled poore and nedy and nameles than for to dwellen in his cyte and flowren of rychesses and be redowtable° by honour and strong of power. For in this wyse more clerly and more witnessefully° is the office° of wyse men itreted°, whan the blysfulnesse and the powste° of governours is, as it were, yshad° amonges poeples that be neighebours and subgits, syn that namely prysoun, lawe, and thise oothre torments° of laweful peynes ben rather owed to felonous citezeins—for the whiche felonous citezeins tho peynes ben° establysshed—than for good folk.

"Thanne I mervayle me gretly," quod I, "why that the thinges ben so mysentrechaunged° that torments of felonyes pressen and confownden goode folk, and shrewes ravysshen° medes° of vertu *(and ben in honours and in gret estats)*. And I desyre ek for to weten° of the what semeth the to ben the resoun of this so wrongful a conclusioun? For I wolde wondre wel the lasse°, yif I trowede° that al thise thinges weren medled° by fortunous happe°. But now hepeth° and encreseth myn astonyenge God, governour of thinges, that so as God yeveth ofte tymes to goode men goodes and myrthes°, and to shrewes yveles and aspre° thinges, and yeveth ayeinward to goode folk hardnesses, and to shrewes he graunteth hem her wyl and that° they desiren. What defference thanne may ther be bytwixen that that° God doth and the happe of fortune, yif men ne knowe nat the cause why that it is?"

"Ne it nis no merveyle," quod she, "thowgh that men wenen° that ther be somewhat folyssh and confuse, whan the resoun of the ordre is unknowe. But althogh that thou ne knowe nat the cause of so gret a disposicioun, natheles for as moche as God, the goode governour, atempreth° and governeth the world, ne dowte the nat that alle thinges ben doon aryht.

---

290 langwissinge, *faintness* **291 corage,** *spirit* **298 cruwel,** *fierce* **4 Meter 4. 1 What deliteth yow,** *why are you pleased* **2 bysien,** *prompt* **5 kontek,** *strife,* **axen,** *ask for* **7 taryeth,** *delays,* **hors,** *horses* **10 thilke,** *these* **11 hem oother,** *those others* **12 for,** *because* **13 moeven,** *incite,* **oostes,** *armies* **14 wylnen,** *seek* **16 inowh ryhtful,** *right enough* **17 yelden,** *give,* **covenable gerdoun,** *suitable reward* **4 Prose 5. 2 unselynesse,** *unhappiness* **4 ilke,** *same* **6 levere ben,** *rather be* **9 redowtable,** *respectable* **11 witnessefully,** *evidently,* **office,** *responsibility* **12 itreted,** *enacted,* **powste,** *power* **13 yshad,** *spread* **16 torments,** *punishments* **18 tho peynes ben,** *those punishments are* **22 mysentrechaunged,** *mistakenly reversed* **23 ravysshen,** *steal* **24 medes,** *rewards* **25 weten,** *know* **28 lasse,** *less,* **trowede,** *believed* **29 medled,** *muddled* **29–30 fortunous happe,** *random chance* **30 hepeth,** *heaps up* **33 myrthes,** *joys* **34 aspre,** *bitter* **36 that,** *what* **38 that that,** *that which* **42 wenen,** *think* **47 atempreth,** *moderates*

Metre 5. Si quis Arcturi sidera.

"Whoso that ne knowe nat the sterres of Arctour itorned neygh° to the sovereyn centre° or poynt *(that is to seyn, itorned neyh to the sovereyn pool° of the fyrmament),* and wot° nat why the sterre Boetes passeth or gadereth° his weynes° and drencheth° his late flambes in the see, and whi that Boetes the sterre unfoldeth his over swifte arysinges, thanne shal he wondren of° he lawe of the heye eyr°. And ek yif that he ne knowe nat why that the hornes of the fulle moone wexen paale and infect° by the bowndes of the derke nyht, and how the moone, dyrk and confuse°, discovereth° the sterres that she hadde icovered by hir cleere visage. The comune erroure moeveth° folk, and maket wery° her basyns° of bras by thikke° strokes. *(That is to seyn, that ther is a manere° of poeple that hihte° Coribandes that wenen° that, whan the moons is in the eclypse, that it be enchaunted, and therfore for to rescowe° the moone, they beten her basyns with thikke strokes.)* Ne no man ne wondreth whan the blastes of the wynd Chorus beten the strondes° of the see by quakinge floodes; ne no man wondreth whan the weyhte of the snowh, iharded by the colde, is resolved by the brenninge hete of Phebus the sonne, for her sen° men redely the causes.

"But the causes ihid *(that is to seyn, in hevene)* trowblen the brestes of men; the moevable° poeple is astoned of alle thinges that comen selde° and sodeynly in owre age. But yif the trowbly erroure of owre ignoraunce departede fro us *(so that we wysten° the causes why that swyche thinges bityden°),* certes they sholden cese to seme wondres."

Prose 6. Ita est inquam.

"Thos° is it," quod I. "But so as thou hast yeven° or byhyht° me to unwrappen the hyd causes of thinges, and to discovere me the resouns covered with dyrknesses, I prey the that thou devyse° and juge me of this matere, and that thou don° me to understonden it; for this meracle or this wonder trowbleth me ryht gretly."

And thanne she, a lytel what smylinge, seyde: "Thou clepest° me," quod she, "to telle thing that is grettest of alle thinges that mowen° ben axed, and to the whiche questioun unnethes° is ther awht inogh to laven° it *(as who seyth, unnethes is ther suffisauntly anything to answere parfytly° to thy questioun).* For the matere of it is swych that whan o dowte is determyned and kut awey, ther wexen° oother dowtes withowte nowmber, ryht as the hevedes° wexen of Ydre *(the serpent that Ercules slowh).* Ne ther ne were no manere ne non ende but yif that a wyht constreynede tho dowtes by a ryht lyfly° and quyk fyre of thowht *(that is to seyn, by vigour and strengths of wit).* For in this matere men weren wont° to maken questions of the simplicite of the purvyaunce° of God, and of the order of destine, and of sodeyn happe°, and of the knowinge and predestinacioun divine, and of the lyberte of fre wille, the whiche thinges thou thyself aperceyvest wel of what weyht° they ben. But for as mochel as the knowinge of thise thinges is a manere porcyoun° of the medicine of the°, al be it so that I have lytel tyme to don it, yit natheles I wol enforcen me° to shewe somwhat of it. But althogh the norysinges of

---

4 Meter 5. 2 **itorned neygh,** *turns near,* **sovereyn centre,** *North Pole* 4 **pool,** *pole,* **wot,** *knows* 5 **gadereth,** *drives* 6 **weynes,** *carts,* **drencheth,** *drowns* 9 **of,** *at,* **heye eyr,** *upper air* 12 **infect,** *dimmed* 13 **confuse,** *obscured,* **discovereth,** *reveals* 15 **moeveth,** *prompts* 16 **maket wery,** *makes weary,* **her basyns,** *their basins* 17 **thikke,** *frequent* 18 ***manere,*** *kind,* ***hihte,*** *are called,* ***wenen,*** *think* 20 ***rescowe,*** *rescue* 23 **strondes,** *shores* 27 **her sen,** *here see* 29 **moevable,** *changeable* 31 **selde,** *seldom* 33 ***wysten,*** *knew* 34 ***bityden,*** *happen* 4 Prose 6. 1 **Thos,** *thus,* **yeven,** *given,* 2 **byhyht,** *promised* 5 **devyse,** *explain* 6 **don,** *make* 10 **clepest,** *call upon* 12 **mowen,** *may* 13 **unnethes,** *scarcely,* **laven,** *moisten* 15 ***parfytly,*** *perfectly* 17 **wexen,** *grow* 18 **hevedes,** *heads* 22 **lyfly,** *lively* 24 **wont,** *accustomed* 25 **purvyaunce,** *providence* 27 **happe,** *chance* 30 **weyht,** *importance* 32 **manere porcyoun,** *a kind of portion* 33 **of the,** *for you* 34 **enforcen me,** *strive*

4 Meter 5. 2 **Arctour,** Arcturus, a very bright star in the constellation Boötes, the Plowman, near the North Pole. **5–9 Boetes . . . ,** Boötes; describes the setting and rapid rising of the constellation. 18 ***Coribandes,*** Corybantes, the followers of the nature goddess Cybele, who accompanied her with the clash of tambourines. Although not associated with the Corybantes in classical tradition, the practice of noise making on the occasion of a lunar eclipse is recorded in a number of places, e.g., Livy, 26.5.9, Tacitus, *Annales* 1.28, and Juvenal, *Satires* 6.441–42. 23 **Chorus,** Caurus, the northwest wind. 4 Prose 6. 19 **Ydre,** Hydra, the dragon-like monster slain by Hercules; when one of its many heads is cut off, it grows two in its place.

dite of musike° deliteth the, thou most suffren arid forberen a litel of thilke delite whyle that I weve to the° resouns yknit by ordre."

"As it lyketh° to the," quod I, "so do."

Tho spak she ryht as by another bygynninge, and seyde thus: "The engendringe° of alle thinges," quod she, "and alle the progressiouns of muable° nature and al that moeveth in any manere taketh his causes, his ordre, and his formes of the stablenesse of the dyvine thowght. And thike devyne thowht, that is yset and put in the towr *(that is to seyn, in the heyhte)* of the symplicite of God, stablyssheth many manere gyses° to thinges that ben to done. The whiche manere, whan that men looken it in thilke pure klennesse of the divyne intelligence, it is ycleped° purvyaunce; but whan thilke maner is referred by men to thinges that it moveth and disponeth°, thanne of olde men it was cleped destyne. The whiche thinges, yif that any wyht looketh wel in his thowht the strengthe of that oon and of that oother, he shal lyhtly° mowen seen° that thise two thinges ben diverse. For purvyaunce is thilke devyne reson that is enstablysshed in the sovereyn prynce of thinges, the whiche purvyaunce disponeth alle thinges. But destine is the disposicioun and ordinaunce clyvinge° to moevable° thinges, by the whiche disposicioun the purvyaunce° knitteth alle thinges in her ordres. For purvyaunce embraceth alle thinges to-hepe°, althogh that they ben diverse, and althowgh they ben infynyte; but destyne departeth° and ordeyneth° alle thinges singulerly, and dyvyded in moevinges, in places, in formes, in tymes. As thus: lat the unfoldinge of temporel ordynaunce, assembled and ooned° in the lookinge of the dyvyne thowt, be cleped° purvyaunce; and thilke same assemblinge and ooninge°, devyded and unfolden by tymes, lat that ben called destyne. And al be it so that thise thinges ben diverse, yit natheles hangeth that oon of° that oother, for-why° the order destynal procedeth of° the symplycite of purvyaunce. For ryht as a werkman that aperceyveth in his thoght the forme of the thing that he wol make, and moeveth the effect of the werk, and ledeth that° he hadde loked byforn in his thowht symplely and presently, by temporel ordinaunce°, certes, ryht so God disponeth° in his purvyaunce, syngulerly and stablely, the thinges that ben to done, but he amynystreth° in many maneres and in dyverse tymes by destine thilke same thynges that he hath desponed.

"Thanne, wheyther that destyne be exercysed owther° by some dyvyne spyrits, servaunts to the devyne purvyaunce, or elles by som sowle, or elles by alle nature servinge to God, or elles by the celestial moevinges of sterres, or elles by the vertu° of angeles, or elles by the diverse subtylyte of develes, or elles by any of hem, or elles by hem alle, the destinal ordynaunce is ywoven and acomplyssed. Certes, it is open° thing that the purvyaunce is an unmoevable and simple forme of thinges to done; and the moveable bond and the temporel ordynaunce of thinges, whiche that the devyne symplycite of purvyaunce hath ordeyned to done, that is destine. For which it is that alle thinges that ben put under destyne ben, certes, subgits to porvyaunce, to whiche purvyaunce destyne itself is subgit and under. But some thinges ben put under purvyaunce that surmownten° the ordynaunce of destyne; and tho ben thilke° that stablely ben yfechched negh° to the fyrste godhed. They surmownten the ordre of destynal moevablete. For ryht° as of cercles that tornen abowte a same centre or abowte a poynte, thilke cercle that is innerest or most withinne joyneth to the simplesse of the myddel, and is, as it were, a centre or a poynt to that oother cercles that tornen

---

36 dite of musike, *poetry* **38 weve to the,** *weave for you* **39 lyketh,** *is pleasing* **42 engendringe,** *generation* **43 muable,** *mutable* **49 gyses,** *ways* **52 ycleped,** *called* **55 disponeth,** *regulates* **58 lyhtly,** *easily* **59 mowen seen,** *be able to see* **64 ordinaunce clyvinge,** *arrangement clinging* **64 moevable,** *changeable* **66 purvyaunce,** *providence* **68 to-hepe,** *together* **70 departeth,** *separates,* **ordeyneth,** *arranges* **74 ooned,** *united* **75 cleped,** *called* **76 ooninge,** *unity* **79 of,** *from* **80 for-why,** *because* **81 of,** *from* **85 ledeth that,** *brings forth what* **87 temporel ordinaunce,** *temporal sequence* **88 disponeth,** *regulates* **90 amynystreth,** *manages* **94 owther,** *either* **98 vertu,** *power* **102 open,** *evident* **112 surmownten,** *surpass* **113 tho ben thilke,** *these are those* **114 yfechched negh,** *fixed near* **116 ryht,** *just*

116 of, omitted in C[1], but in the Latin.

abowten him. And thilke that° is owtterest, compased° by larger envyronninge°, is unfolden° by largere spaces in so moche as it is fertherest fro the myddel simplicite of the poynt. And yif ther be anything that knytteth and felawshippeth himself to thilke myddel poynt, it is constreyned into symplicite *(that is to seyn, into unmoevablete)*, and it ceseth to be shad° and to fleten° diversely. Ryht so, by semblable° resoun, thilke thing that departeth fyrthest fro the fyrst thowht of God, it is unfolden and summytted to grettere bondes of destinye; and in so moche is the thing moore fre and laus fro° destine, as it axeth and holdeth him nere to thilke centre of thinges *(that is to seyn, God)*. And yif the thing clyveth° to the stydefastnesse of the thoght of God, and be withowte moevinge, certes, it sormownteth the necissite of destyne. Thanne ryht swych comparysoun as it is of skylinge° to understondinge, and of thing that is engendred° to thing that is, and of tyme to eternite, and of the cerkle to the centre, ryht so is the ordre of moevable destyne to the stable symplycite of purvyaunce.

"Thilke ordynaunce° moeveth the hevene and the sterres, and atempreth° the elyments togydere amonges hemself, and transformeth hem by entrechaungeable mutasioun°. And thilke same ordre neweth° ayein alle thinges growinge and fallinge adown, by semblable° progressiouns of sedes° and of sexes *(that is to seyn, male and femele)*. And this ilke° ordre constreyneth the fortunes and the dedes of men by a bond of causes nat able to ben unbownde; the whiche destynal causes, whan they passen owt fro the bygynninges of the unmoevable purvyaunce, it mot nedes be° that they ne be nat mutable. And thus ben the thinges ful wel ygoverned, yif that the symplicite dwellinge in the dyvyne thoght sheweth forth the ordre of causes, unable to ben ybowed°; and this ordre constreyneth by his propre stablete the moevable thinges or elles they sholden fleten folyly°. For which it is that alle thinges semen to ben confus and trowble to us men, for we ne mowen nat considere thilke ordynaunce; natheles, the propre manere of everythinge, dressinge° hem to goode, disponeth° hem alle. For ther nis nothing don for cause of yvel; ne thilke thing that is don by wykkede folk nis nat don for yvel. The wheche shrewes, as I have shewed ful plentiuously, seken good, but wikked errour mystorneth° hem, ne the ordre cominge fro the poynt of sovereyn good ne declyneth° nat fro his bygynninge.

But thou mayst seyn, what unreste may ben a worse confusioun than that goode men han somtyme adversite and somtyme prosperite, and shrewes also han now thinges that they desiren, and now thinges that they haten? Wheyther men° lyven now in swych° hoolnesse of thowht *(as who seyth, ben men now so wyse)*, that swyche folk as they demen to ben goode folk or shrewes, that it moste nedes ben that folk ben swyche as they wenen? But in this manere the domes° of men discorden°, that thilke men that some folk demen worthy of mede, oother folk demen hem worthy of torment. But lat us graunt, I pose, that som man may wel demen or knowen the goode folk and the badde; may he thanne knowen and sen thilke inneryste atempraunce° of corages°, as it hath ben wont° to ben seyd of bodies? *(As who seyth, may a man speken and determinen of atempraunces in corages, as men were wont to demen or speken of complexiouns° and atempraunces of bodies?)* Ne it ne is nat an unlyk° myracle to hem that ne knowen it nat *(as who seyth, but it is lyk a merveyle or a myracle to hem that ne knowen it nat)* why that swete thinges ben covenable° to some bodies that ben hoole, and to some bodies bittere

122 thilke that, *that which* **123 compased,** *encompassed,* **envyronninge,** *surrounding,* **unfolden,** *expanded* **130 shad,** *scattered,* **fleten,** *drift* **131 semblable,** *similar* **135 laus fro,** *loose from* **138 clyveth,** *holds* **142 skylinge,** *reasoning* **143 engendred,** *generated* **147 ordynaunce,** *arrangement* **148 atempreth,** *balances* **150 entrechaungeable mutasioun,** *reciprocal changes* **151 neweth,** *renews* **152 semblable,** *similar* **153 sedes,** *seeds* **154 ilke,** *same* **159 mot nedes be,** *is necessary* **164 ybowed,** *turned aside* **166 fleten folyly,** *drift aimlessly* **170 dressinge,** *directing* **171 disponeth,** *regulates* **176 mystorneth,** *misdirects* **177 declyneth,** *turns away* **184 Wheyther men,** *who among men,* **swych,** *such* **189 domes,** *judgments* **189–190 discorden,** *disagree* **196 atempraunce,** *temperament,* **corages,** *hearts,* **wont,** *accustomed* **199** ***complexiouns,*** *humours* **201 unlyk,** *dissimilar* **204 covenable,** *suitable*

thinges ben covenable, and also why that some syke folk ben holpen° with lyhte medicynes, and some folk ben holpen with sharppe medicynes. But natheles, the leche° that knoweth the manere and the atempraunce of hele° and of maledye ne merveyleth of it nothing. But what oother thing semeth hele of corages but bownte° and prowesse°? And what other thing semeth maledye of corage but vices? Who is elles kepere of good or dryvere awey of yvel but God, governour and lechere° of thowhtes? The wheche God, whan he hath byholden from the heye toure of his purveaunce, he knoweth what is covenable to every wyht, and leneth° hem that he wot° that is covenable to hem. Lo, herof comth and herof is don this noble myracle of the ordre destynal, whan God, that al knoweth, doth swyche thing, of which thing that unknowinge folk ben astoned°. But for to constreine° *(as who seyth, but for to comprehende and telle)* a fewe thinges of the devyne depnesse, the whiche that mannes resoun may understonde, thilke man that thou wenest° to ben ryht juste and ryht kepinge of equite, the contrarye of that semeth to the devyne purveaunce that al wot. And Lukan, my famyler°, telleth that the victorious cawse lykede to° the goddes, and the cause overcomen lykede to Catoun. Thanne what so ever thou mayst sen that is don in this world unhoped or unwened°, certes, it is the ryht ordre of thinges, but as to thy wykkede opynyoun, it is a confusioun. But I soppose that som man be so wel ithewed° that the devyne jugement and the jugement of mankynde acorden hem togyder of him, but he is so unstidefast of corage that yif any adversite come to hem, he wol forleten°, paraventure°, to continue innocence, by the whiche he ne may nat withholden° fortune. Thanne the wyse dispensacioun of God spareth him, the whiche man adversite myhte enpeyren°, for that God wol nat suffren° him to travayle°, to whom that travaile nis nat covenable°. Another man is parfyt° in alle vertus, and is an holy man, and negh° to God, so that the purvyaunce of God wolde demen that it were a felonye that he were towched with any adversites, so that he wol nat suffre that swych a man be moeved with any bodyly maledye. But so as seyde a phylosophre, the moore excellent by me° *(he seyde in Grec)* that 'vertuus han edified° the body of the holy man.' And ofte tyme it bytydeth° that the somme° of thinges that ben to done is taken° to governe to goode folk for that the malyce haboundaunt of shrewes sholde ben abated. And God yeveth and departeth° to oothre folk prosperites and adversites ymedled tohepe° after° the qualite of her corages°, and remordeth° some folk by adversitee, for they ne sholde nat wexen prowde by longe welefulnesse°. And oother folk he suffreth to ben travayled with harde thinges for that they sholden confermen the vertus of corages by the usage and exercitacioun of pacience. And oother folk dreden moore than they owhten° the whiche they myhten wel beren; and somme dispyse that° they mowe nat beren. And thilke° folk God ledeth into experience of hymself by aspre° and sorwful thinges. And many oothre folk han bowht honourable renoun of this world by the prys of gloryous deth. And som men that ne mowen° nat ben overcomen by torments han yeven ensaumple to othre folk that vertu may nat ben overcomen by adversites. And of alle thinges ther nis no dowte that they ne ben don ryhtfully and ordenely°, to the profyt of hem to whom we sen thise thinges bytyde.

207 ben holpen, *are helped* **209 leche,** *physician* **211 hele,** *health* **213 bownte,** *goodness,* **prowesse,** *virtue* **217 lechere,** *healer* **220 leneth,** *gives,* i.e., **wot,** *knows* **225 astoned,** *astonished* **226 constreine,** *bring together* **229 wenest,** *think* **233 famyler,** *associate* **233–34 lykede to,** *pleased* **237 unwened,** *unthought* **240 so wel ithewed,** i.e., *of such good habits* **244 forleten,** *cease,* **peraventure,** *perhaps* **246 withholden,** *withstand* **248 enpeyren,** *injure* **249 suffren,** *allow,* **travayle,** *suffer* **250 covenable,** *fitting* **251 parfyt,** *perfect* **252 negh,** *close* **257–58 by me,** *than myself* **258 edified,** *built* **260 bytydeth,** *happens,* **somme,** *totality* **261 taken,** *given* **264 departed,** *divides* **265 ymedled tohepe,** *mixed together,* **after,** *according to* **266 corages,** *hearts,* **remordeth,** *troubles* **268 welefulnesse,** *happiness* **273 owhten,** *ought* **274 that,** *what* **275 thilke,** *these* **276 aspre,** *bitter* **280 mowen,** *may* **284 ordenely,** *as decreed*

208 sharppe, C^2 reads "bittere." **232–35 Lukan . . . Catoun,** Lucan (39–65 C.E.), Roman poet, in his *Pharsalia* 1.128.233 comments in this way on the gods and on Cato (234–149 B.C.E.), Roman statesman and moralist. **257–59 seyde a phylosophre . . . ,** quotation not identified for certain. Probably not Parmenides, although Trivet indicates so in his gloss. **274–75 and somme . . . beren,** lacking in C^2 and C^1, although the clause is there in the Latin; reading from Caxton's edition, c.1478.

For certes, that adversite comth somtyme to shrewes, and somtyme that that° they desiren, it comth of thise forseide cawses. And of sorwful thinges that bytyden to shrewes, certes no man ne wondreth, for alle men wenen° that they han wel deserved it, and that they ben of wykkede meryte. Of whiche shrewes the torment somtyme agasteth° oothre to don° felonies, and somtyme it amendeth° hem that suffren the torments. And the prosperite that is yeven to shrewes sheweth a gret argument to goode folk, what thing they sholden demen° of thilke welefulnesse, the whiche prosperite men sen ofte serven to shrewes. In the which thing I trowe that God dispenseth, for peraventure the nature of som man is so overthrowinge° to yvel, and so uncovenable°, that the nedy poverte of his howshold myhte rather egren° him to don felonyes. And to the maladie of him God putteth remedie, to yeven hym richesses. And som oother man byholdeth his conscience defowled with synnes, and maketh comparisoun of his fortune and of himself, and dredeth peraventure that his blysfulnesse, of which the usage is joyeful to him, that the leesinge° of thilke blysfulnesse ne be nat sorwful to him; and therfor he wol chaunge his maneres, and for he dredeth to leese his fortune, he forleteth° his wykkednesse. To oothre folk is welefulnesse yyeven unworthyly, the wheche overthroweth hem into distruccioun that they han desserved. And to som oothre folk is yeven power to punyssen, for that it shal be cause of contumacioun° and exercysinge to goode folk, and cause of torment to shrewes. For so as ther nis non alyaunce bytwixe goode folk and shrewes, ne shrewes ne mowen° nat acorden amonges hemself. And why nat? For shrewes discorden of hemself by her vices, the whiche vices al torenden° her consciences, and don ofte tyme thinges, the whiche thinges whan they han don hem, they demen that tho thinges ne sholden nat han ben don. For which thing thilke sovereyn purveaunce° hath maked ofte tyme faire myracle, so that shrewes han maked shrewes to ben goode men. For whan that som shrewes sen that they suffren wrongfully felonyes of oothre shrewes, they wexen eschaufet° into hate of hem that anoyeden hem, and retornen to the frut of vertu, whan they studien to ben unlyk to hem that they han hated. Certes, oonly this is the devyne myht, to the wheche myht yveles ben thanne goode whan it useth tho yveles covenably° and draweth owt the effect of any goode *(as who seyth, that yvel is good oonly to the myht of God, for the myht of God ordeyneth thilke yvel to good)*.

"For oon ordre enbraseth° alle thinges, so that what wyht° that departeth fro the resoun of thilke ordre which that is assyngned to him, algates° yit he slydeth into another ordre, so that nothing nis leveful° to folye in the reame of the devyne purvyaunce *(as who seyth, nothing nis withowten ordinaunce in the reame° of the devyne purvyaunce)*; syn that the ryht stronge God governeth alle thinges in this world. For it nis nat leveful to man to comprehenden by wit, ne unfolden° by word, alle the subtyl ordinaunces and disposisiouns of the devyne entente. For oonly it owhte suffise to han looked° that God hymself, makere of alle natures, ordeyneth and dresseth° alle thinges to goode. Whyl that he hasteth to withholden° the thinges that he hath maked into his semblaunce *(that is to seyn, for to withholden thinges into good, for he hymself is good)*, he chaseth owt al yvel fro the bowndes of his communalyte by the ordre of necessite destynable°. For which it folweth that yif thou looke° the purvyaunce ordeyninge the thinges that men wenen ben° outrageous or habowndant° in erthes, thou ne shalt nat sen in no place nothing of yvel. But I se now that thou art charged° with the weyhte of the questyoun, and wery with the lengthe of my resoun, and that thow abydest° som swetnesse of songe. Tak thanne this drawht; and whan thou art wel refresshed and refect°, thow shal be moore stydefast to stye° into heyere questyouns.

---

287 that that, *that which* **290 wenen,** *think* **293 agasteth,** *frightens,* **to don,** *from doing* **294 amendeth,** *corrects* **298 demen,** *judge* **302 overthrowinge,** *overwhelmingly* **303 uncovenable,** *unsuitable* **304 egren,** *incite* **311 leesinge,** *loss* **315 forleten,** *abandons* **320 contumacioun,** *disobedience* **323 mowen,** *may* **326 torenden,** *tear apart* **330 purveaunce,** *providence* **335 wexen eschaufet,** *grow heated* **341 covenably,** *suitably* **345 enbraseth,** *embraces* **346 what wyht,** *whatever person* **348 algates,** *nevertheless* **349 leveful,** *permitted* **350 reame,** *realm* **355 unfolden,** *explain* **358 looked,** *considered* **359 dresseth,** *arranges* **361 withholden,** *maintain* **366 destynable,** *subject to destiny* **367 looke,** *consider* **368 wenen ben,** *think to be* **369 habowndant,** *superfluous* **371 charged,** *burdened* **373 abydest,** *await* **375 refect,** *revived* **376 stye,** *climb*

Metre 6. Si vis celsi iura tonantis.

"If thou, wys°, wilt demen° in thy pure thowht the ryhtes or the lawes of the heye thonderere *(that is to seyn, of God)*, loke thou and byhold the heyhtes of the sovereyn hevene. There kepen the sterres by ryhtful alliaunce of thinges her olde pees°. The sonne, imoeved by his rody° fyr, ne distorbeth nat the colde cercle of the moone. Ne the sterre ycleped° the Bere, that enclyneth his ravysshinge° cours abowten the sovereyn heyhte of the worlde, ne the same sterre Ursa nis nevermo wasshen in the depe westrene see, ne coveyteth° nat to deeyn° his flaumbes in the se of the occian, althogh he se° oothre sterres iplownged in the see. And Hesperus the sterre bodeth° and telleth alwey the late nyhtes; and Lucifer the sterre bringeth ayein the cleere day.

"And thus maketh love entrechaungeable° the perdurable° courses; and thus is discordable batayle iput owt of the contre of the sterres. This acordaunce atempreth° by evenelyk° maneres the elyments, that the moyste thinges stryvinge with the drye thinges yeven place by stowndes°; and the colde thinges joynen hem by feyth to the hote thinges; and that the lyhte fyr aryseth into heyhte; and the hevy erthes avalen° by her weyhtes. By thise same causes the flowry yer yildeth swote° smelles in the fyrste somer sesoun warminge; and the hoote somer dryeth the cornes°; and autumpne comth ayein, hevy of apples; and the fletinge° reyn bydeweth° the wynter. This atempraunce° norisseth and bryngeth forth alle thing that bretheth lyf in this world; and thilke same atempraunce, ravysshinge°, hideth and bynymeth°, and drencheth under the laste deth, alle thinges iborn.

"Amonges thise thinges sitteth the heye makere, kyng and lord, welle° and bygynninge, lawe and wys juge, to don equite; and governeth and enclyneth the brydles of thinges. And tho thinges that he stereth° to gon by moevinge he withdraweth° and aresteth, and affermeth° the moevable or wandringe thinges. For yif that he ne klepede nat ayein° the ryht goinge of thinges, and yif that he ne constreynede hem nat eftsones° into rowndnesses enclynede, the thinges that ben now continued by stable ordinaunce, they sholden departen from her welle *(that is to seyn, from her bygynninge)*, and faylen *(that is to seyn, torne into nowht)*. This is the comune love to alle thinges. And alle thinges axen to ben holden by the fyn° of good, for elles ne myhten they nat lasten, yif they ne come nat eftsones° ayein, by love retorned, to the cause that hath yeven hem beinge *(that is to seyn, to God)*.

Prose 7. Iamne igitur vides.

"Sestow nat thanne what thing folweth alle the thinges that I have seyd?"

"What thing?" quod I.

"Certes," quod she, "al outrely° that alle fortune is good."

"And how may that be?" quod I.

"Now understand," quod she, "so as alle fortune, wheyther so it be joyeful fortune or aspre° fortune, is yeven eyther by cause of gerdoninge° or elles of exersysinge of good folk, or elles by cause to punnysshen or elles chastysen shrewes, thanne is alle fortune good, the whiche fortune is certeyn that it be eyther ryhtful or elles profitable."

"Forsothe, this is a ful verray° resoun," quod I; "and yif I considere the purvyaunce and the destyne that thou tawhtest me a lytel her-byforn, this sentence is sustened by stydefast resouns. But yif it lyke unto the, lat us nowmbren hem amonges thilke thinges of whiche thou seydest a litel her-byforn that they ne were nat able to ben wened to° the poeple."

---

4 Meter 6. 1 **wys,** *wise,* **demen,** *discern* 6 **her olde pees,** *their ancient peace* 7 **rody,** *red* 8 **sterre ycleped,** *constellation called* 9 **ravysshinge,** *violent* 12 **coveyteth,** *desires* 13 **deeyn,** *dye* 14 **se,** *sees* 16 **bodeth,** *announces* 19–20 **love entrechaungeable,** *mutual love* 20 **perdurable,** *everlasting* 22 **atempreth,** *moderates* 23 **evenelyke,** *equal* 25 **by stowndes,** *in proper times* 28 **avalen,** *sink* 30 **swote,** *sweet* 32 **cornes,** *grains* 33 **fletinge,** *pouring* 34 **bydeweth,** *moistens,* **atempraunce,** *balance* 37 **ravysshinge,** *seizing* 38 **bynymeth,** *takes away* 41 **welle,** *source* 44 **stereth,** *stirs* 45 **withdraweth,** *pulls back* 46 **affermeth,** *makes firm* 47–48 **klepede nat ayein,** *did not call back* 49 **eftsones,** *again* 56 **fyn,** *goal* 58 **eftsones,** *in return* 4 Prose 7. 4 **outrely,** *utterly* 8 **aspre,** *bitter* 10 **gerdoninge,** *rewarding* 15 **ful verray,** *completely true* 22–23 **wened to,** *understood by*

9–11 **Bere . . . Ursa,** the Great Bear, Ursa Major, or the Big Dipper, a constellation in the northern hemisphere that never sets. 15 **Hesperus,** the evening star. 17 **Lucifer,** the morning star. 18 **her-byforn,** see 4.pr6.50ff. 21 **her-byforn,** see 4.pr4.179–81 and 4.pr6.225–29.

"Why so?" quod she.

"For that the comune word of men," quod I, "mysuseth this manere speche of fortune, and seyn oftetymes that the fortune of som wyht° is wykkede."

"Wyltow thanne," quod she, "that I aproche a lytel to the wordes of the poeple, so that it seme nat to hem that I be overmoche departed as fro the usage of mankynde?"

"As thou wolt," quod I.

"Demestow° nat," quod she, "that alle thing that profiteth is good?"

"Yis," quod I.

"And certes, thilke thing that exersiseth or coriget°, profiteth?"

"I confesse it wel," quod I.

"Thanne is it good?" quod she.

"Why nat?" quod I.

"But this is the fortune," quod she, "of hem that eyther ben put in vertu and bataylen ayeins aspre thinges, or elles of hem that eschwen° and declynen° fro vices and taken the wey of vertu."

"This ne may I nat denye," quod I.

"But what seystow of the myrye° fortune that is yeven to good folk in gerdoun°? Demeth awht° the poeple that it is wykked?"

"Nay, forsothe°," quod I; "but they demen, as it soth is, that it is ryht good."

"And what seystow of that oother fortune," quod she, "that, althogh that it be aspre°, and restreyneth the shrewes by ryhtful torment, weneth awht the people° that it be good?"

"Nay," quod I, "but the poeple demeth that it is most wrechched of alle thinges that may ben thoght."

"War° now and loke° wel," quod she, "lest that we, in folwinge the opynyoun of the poeple, have confessed° and concluded thing that is unable to ben wened to° the poeple."

"What is that?" quod I.

"Certes," quod she, "it folweth or comth of thinges that ben graunted, that alle fortune, whatsoever it be, of hem that ben eyther in poscessioun of vertu, or in the encres of vertu, or elles in the purchasinge° of vertu, that thilke fortune is good, and that alle fortune is ryht wikkede to hem that dwellen in shrewednesse" *(as who seyth, and thus weneth nat the poeple).*

"That is soth," quod I, "al be it so that no man dar confesse it ne byknowen° it."

"Why so?" quod she. "For ryht as the stronge man ne semeth nat to abayssen° or disdaignen° as ofte tyme as he hereth the noyse of the batayle, ne also it ne semeth nat to the wyse man to beren it grevously, as ofte as he is lad into the stryf of fortune. For bothe to that oon man and ek to that oother, thilke difficulte is the matere: to that oon man of encres of his glorious renoun, and to that other man to confirme his sapience° *(that is to seyn, to the asprenesse° of his estat).* For therfore is it called vertu, for that it susteneth and enforseth by his strengthes that it nis nat overcomen by adversites. Ne certes, thou that art put in the encres or in the heyhte of vertu ne hast nat comen to fleten° with delices°, and for to welken° in bodily luste. Thow sowest or plawntest a ful egre batayle in thy corage ayenes every fortune. For° that the sorwful fortune ne confownde the nat, ne that the merye fortune ne corumpe° the nat, ocupye the mene° by stydefast strengthes. For al that ever is under the mene, or elles al that overpasseth the mene despiseth welefulnesse° *(as who seyth, it is vicious),* and ne hath no meede° of his travaile°. For it is set in yowr hand *(as who seyth, it lyth in yowr powere)* what fortune yow is levest° *(that is to seyn, good or yvel).* For alle fortune that semeth sharp or aspre, yif it ne exersyse nat the good folk ne chastiseth the wykked folk, it punysseth.

Metre 7. Bella bis quinis.

"The wrekere° Attrides *(that is to seyn, Agamenon)* that wrowhte° and continuede the batayles by ten yer, recovered and purgede in wrekinge

28 wyht, *person* **35 Demestow,** *do you think* **38 coriget,** *corrects* **45 eschewen,** *avoid,* **declynen,** *turn away* **48 myrye,** *pleasant* **49 gerdoun,** *reward* **50 awht,** *in any way* **51 forsothe,** *truly* **54 aspre,** *bitter* **56 weneth awht the poeple,** *do the people think in any way* **61 War,** *be aware,* **loke,** *consider* **63 confessed,** *disclosed* **64 wened to,** *thought by* **70 purchasinge,** *acquiring* **76 byknowen,** *acknowledge* **78 abaysen,** *be frightened* **79 disdaignen,** *be disturbed* **86 sapience,** *wisdom* **87 asprenesse,** *bitterness* **92 fleten,** *float* **93 delices,** *delights,* **welken,** *waste* **95 For,** *so* **97 corumpe,** *corrupt* **98 mene,** *middle way* **100 despiseth welefulnesse,** *renounces happiness* **102 meede,** *reward,* **travaile,** *labor* **104 levest,** *most preferred* **4 Meter 7. 1 wrekere,** *avenger* **2 wrowhte,** *made*

1 Attrides, Agamemnon, son of Atreus and leader of the Greek forces in the Trojan War.

by the destrucsyoun of Troye the loste chaumbres of maryaage° of his brother. *(This is to seyn, that he, Agamenon, wan ayein° Eleyne that was Menelaus wyf his brother.)* In the mene while that thilke Agamenon desirede to yeven sayles to the Grekyssh navye°, and bowhte ayein° the wyndes by blod, he unclothede him of pyte of fader°, and the sory preest yeveth in sacryfyinge the wrechched kuttinge of throte of the dowhter. *(That is to seyn, that Agamenon let kutten the throte of his dowhter by the preest to maken allyaunce with his goddes, and for to han wynde with whiche he myhte wenden° to Troye.)*

"Ytakus *(that is to seyn, Ulixes)* bywepte° his felawes ylorn°, the whiche felawes the feerse° Poliphemus, ligginge in his grete cave, hadde freten° and dreynt° in his empty wombe. But natheles Pholiphemus, wood° for his blynde visage, yald° to Ulixes joye by his sorwful teeres. *(This is to seyn, that Ulixes smot owt the eye of Poliphemus that stood in his forehed, for which Ulixes hadde joye, whan he say° Poliphemus wepinge and blynde.)*

Hercules is celebrable° for his harde travayles°. He dawntede° the prowde Centaures *(half hors, half man)*, and he birafte the dispoylinge° from the crwel° lyoun *(that is to seyn, he slowh° the lyoun and rafte° him his skyn)*. He smot° the briddes° *(that hyhten° Arpiis)* with certeyn° arwes. He ravysshede° apples fro the wakinge dragown, and his hand was the moore hevy for the goldene metal. He drowh° Cerberus *(the hownd of helle)* by his treble° cheyne. He, overcomer, as it is seyd, hath put an unmeke° lord foddre° to his crwel hors°. *(This is to seyn, that Hercules slowgh Dyomedes, and make his hors to freten° him.)* And he, Ercules, slowh Idra *(the serpent)* and brende° the venym. And Achelows the flood, defowled° in his forhed, dreynte° his shamefast visage in his strondes° *(This is to seyn, that Achelows koude transfigure himself into diverse lyknesses; and as he fawght with Ercules, at the laste he tornede him into a bole°; and Hercules brak of oon of his hornes, and he, for shame, hidde him in his river.)* And he, Ercules, caste adown Antheus *(the gyaunt)* in the strondes° of Lybye; and Kacus apaysede° the wraththes of Evander. *(This is to seyn, that Hercules slowgh the monstre Kacus, and apaysede with that deth the wraththe of Evander.)* And the brystlede° boor markede with scomes° the shuldres of Herkules, the whiche sholdres the heye cercle of hevene sholde thriste°. And the laste of his labours was that he sustened the hevene upon his nekke unbowed; and he deservede eftsones° the hevene to ben the prys° of his laste travayle.

"Goth now thanne, ye stronge men, theras° the heye wey of the grete ensaumple ledeth yow. O nyce° men, why nake° ye yowre backes? *(As who seyth, O ye slowe and delicat° men, why flee ye adversytes, and ne fyhten nat ayenes hem by vertu, to wynnen the mede° of the hevene?)* For the erthe, overcomen, yeveth° the sterres." *(This is to seyn, that whan that erthely lust is overcomen, a man is maked worthy to the hevene.)*

Explicit liber quartus.

---

5 maryaage, *marriage* **6 *wan ayein,*** *won back* **9 yeven sayles to the Grekyssh navye,** i.e., he wanted the Greek navy to sail **10, bowhte ayein,** *bought back* **11 unclothede him of pyte of fader,** *discarded the pity of fatherhood* **17 *wenden,*** *travel* **18 bywepte,** *wept for* **19 ylorn,** *lost,* **feerse,** *fierce* **21 freten,** *eaten,* **dreynt,** *drowned* **22 wood,** *insane* **23 yald,** *gave* **26 *say,*** *saw* **28 celebrable,** *worthy of praise,* **travayles,** *labors* **29 dawntede,** *tamed* **30 birafte the dispoylinge,** *seized the spoils* **31 crwel,** *fierce* **32 *slowh,*** *slew,* ***rafte,*** *deprived* **smot,** *struck* **33 briddes,** *birds,* ***hyhten,*** *are called,* **certain,** *sure* **34 ravysshede,** *took away* **36 drowh,** *pulled* **37 treble,** *triple* **38 unmeke,** *proud* **39 foddre,** *food,* **hors,** *horses* **41 *freten,*** *eat* **42 brende,** *burned* **43 defowled,** *dishonored* (by the loss of his horns) **44 dreynte,** *drowned,* **strondes,** *banks* **47 *bole,*** *bull* **51 strondes,** *beach,* **apaysede,** *appeased* **55 brystlede,** *bristling,* **scomes,** *foam* **57 sholde thriste,** *was to uphold* **60 eftsones,** *in return* **61 prys,** *reward* **62 theras,** *where* **64 nyce,** *foolish,* **nake,** *make bare* (in flight) **65 *delicat,*** *vulnerable* **67 *mede,*** *reward* **68 yeveth,** *gives*

7 *Eleyne that was Menelaus wyf his brother,* Helen, who was his brother Menelaus's wife, i.e., wife of the brother of Agamemnon. **18 Ytakus,** Ithacus, Ulysses of Ithaca. **22 Pholiphemus,** Polyphemus, the Cyclops (one-eyed giant), trapped in his cave Ulysses's men, later freed when Ulysses stupefied the giant with wine and blinded him. **28–61** The mythological labors of Hercules vary in detail from source to source. **28 travayles,** singular in C^1. **33 *Arpiis,*** the Harpies, woman-headed birds. **42 Idra,** the many-headed Hydra. **43 Achelows,** Achelous, the river-god who could assume many shapes. **50 Antheus,** Antaeus. **51 Kacus,** the giant Cacus. **59 hevene upon his nekke,** Hercules temporarily relieved Atlas of the burden of holding up the heavens. **70a *Explicit liber quartus,*** Here ends Book Four.

BOOK 5

Incipit liber quintus.

Prose 1. Dixerat oracionisque quibus cursum.

She hadde seyd, and torned the cours of hir resoun to some oothre thinges to ben treted and to ben ysped°. Thanne seyde I, "Certes, ryhtful is thin amonestinge° and ful digne° by autorite. But that thou seydest whilom° that the questyoun of the divyne purviaunce is enlaced° with many oother questiouns, I understonde wel and proeve it by the same thing. But I axe yif that thou wenest° that hap° be anything in any weys; and yif thou wenest that hap be anything, what is it?

Thanne quod she, "I haste me to yilden° and assoylen° to the the dette of my byhest°, and to shewen and opnen the wey by which wey thou mayst come ayein to thy contre. But al be it so that the thinges which that thou axest ben ryht profitable to knowe, yit ben they diverse somwhat fro the paath of my purpos. And it is to dowten° that thou ne be maked wery by mysweyes° so that thou ne mayst nat suffice to mesuren the ryht wey."

"Ne dowte the therof nothing," quod I. "For for to knowen thilke thinges togedere, in the whiche thinges I delite me gretly, that shal ben to me instyde of reste, syn it is nat to dowten of the thinges folwinge, whan every syde of thy disputacioun shal han be stydefast to me by undowtous° feith."

"Thanne," seyde she, "that manere wol I don the," and bygan to speken ryht thus: "Certes," quod she, "yif any wyht° deffenisshe° hap in this manere, that is to seyn, 'hap is bytydinge ibrowht forth by foolissh° moevinge and by no knettinge of causes,' I conferme that hap nis ryht nawht° in no wyse; and I deme alowtrely° that hap nis, ne dwelleth but a voyce° *(as who seyth, but an idel word)*, withowten any sygnificacioun of thing submitted to that vois. For what place myhte ben lefte, or dwellinge, to folye and to disordenaunce°, syn that God ledeth and constreyneth alle thinges by ordre? For this sentence is verray and soth°, that 'nothing ne hath his beinge of nawht'. To the whiche sentence none of thise olde folk ne withseyde° never, al be it so that they ne understonden ne meneden° it nawht by God prince and bygynnere of werkinge, but they casten° as a manere fowndement° subject material°, that is to seyn, of the nature of alle resoun. And yif that anything is woxen° or comen of no cawses, thanne shal it seme that thilke thing is comen or woxen of nawht. But yif this ne may nat ben don, thanne is it nat possible that hap be any swych thing as I have diffynisshed a lytel her-biforn."

"How shal it thanne be?" quod I "Nys ther thanne nothing that by ryht may be cleped° eyther 'hap' or elles 'aventure° of fortune'; or is ther awht°, al be it so that it is hidd fro the poeple, to which thise wordes ben convenable°?"

"Myn Arystotulis," quod she, "in the book of his *Phisik* diffynyssheth this thing by short resoun and negh° to the sothe°."

"In which manere?" quod I.

"As ofte," quod she, "as men don anything for grace° of any oother thing, and another thing than thilke° thing that men entenden to don bytydeth° by some causes, it is cleped 'hap.' Ryht as a man dalf° the erthe bycause of tylyinge° of the feeld, and fownde there a

5 Prose 1. **3 ysped,** *accomplished* **4 thin amonestinge,** *your advice,* **digne,** *worthy* **5 whilom,** *formerly* **7 enlaced,** *involved* **9 wenest,** *think* **10 hap,** *chance* **12 yilden,** *give* **13 assoylen,** *fulfill,* **byhest,** *promise* **19 to dowten,** *doubtful* **20 mysweyes,** *bypaths* **28 undowtous,** *certain* **31 wyht,** *person,* **deffenisshe,** *define* **33 foolissh,** *confused* **35 nis ryht nawht,** *does not exist* **36 deme alowtrely,** *conclude absolutely* **37 voyce,** *sound* **40 disordenaunce,** *disorder* **42–43 verray and soth,** *valid and true* **45 withseyde,** *denied* **46 meneden,** *meant* **48 casten,** *considered it,* i.e., the claim that nothing has its being in nothing **48–49 manere fowndement,** *kind of foundation* **49 material,** *matter* **51 is woxen,** *grows* **58 cleped,** *called* **59 aventure,** *accident* **60 awht,** *anything* **62 convenable,** *applicable* **65 negh,** *near,* **sothe,** *truth* **68 grace,** *sake* **69 thilke,** *that* **70 bytydeth,** *comes about* **71 dalf,** *digs* **72 tylyinge,** *tilling*

Book 5. ***Incipit liber quintus,*** Here begins Book Five. **5 seydest whilom,** see 4.pr6.12–18. **6 the divyne,** C^2 reads "thy divyne." **56 her-biforn,** at lines 32–34. **63–64 Arystotulis . . . *Phisik*,** Aristotle's *Physics* 2.4–5.

gobet° of gold bydolven°, thanne wenen° folk that it is byfalle by fortunows bytydinge. But for sothe, it nis nat of nawht, for it hath his° propre causes, of whiche causes the cours unforeseyn and unwar semeth to han maked hap. For yif the tylyere of the feld ne dolve nat in the erthe, and yif the hyder of the gold ne hadde hidde the gold in thilke place, the gold ne hadde nat ben fownde. Thise ben thanne the causes of the abregginge° of fortuit° hap, the which abregginge of fortuit hap comth of causes encowntringe° and flowinge togydere to hemself, and nat by the entencioun of the doere. For neither the hidere of the gold ne the delvere of the feeld ne understonden nat that the gold sholde han ben fownde; but as I sayde, it bytydde and ran togydere that he dalf theras° that oother hadde hyd the gold. Now may I thus dyffynisse° 'hap': hap is an unwar° bytydinge of causes assembled in thinges that ben don for som oother thing. But thilke° ordre, procedinge by an uneschuable° byndinge togydere, which that descendeth fro the welle° of purvyaunce that ordeyneth alle thinges in her places and in her tymes, maketh that the causes rennen and assemblen togydere.

Metre 1. Rupis Achimenie scopulis.

"Tigris and Eufrates resolven° and spryngen of oo welle in the kragges of the roche of the contre of Achemenie, ther as the fleynge batayle° fichcheth° her dartes retorned in the brestes of hem that folwen hem. And soone after tho same ryveres, Tigris and Eufrates, unjoinen and departen° her wateres. And yif they comen togyderes, and ben assembled and cleped° togydere into o cours, thanne moten° thilke thinges fleten togydere which that the water of the entrechaunginge flod bringeth. The shippes and the stokkes arraced° with the flood moten assemblen, and the wateres imedled° wrappeth or implieth° many fortunel° happes or maneres, the whiche wanderinge happes, natheles, thilke° declyninge lownesse of the erthe and the flowinge ordre of the slydinge water governeth. Ryht so Fortune, that semeth as that it fleteth with slaked° or ungovernede brydles, it suffereth° brydles *(that is to seyn, to ben governed)*, and passeth by thilke° lawe" *(that is to seyn, by thilke devyne ordenaunce).*

Prose 2. Animadverto inquam.

"This undirstonde I wel," quod I, "and I me acorde° wel that it is ryht as thou seyst. But I axe yif ther be any liberte of fre wil in this ordre of causes that clyven° thus togidere in hymself; or elles I wolde witen° yif that the destynal cheyne constreyneth the movinges of the corages° of men?"

"Yis," quod she, "ther is liberte of fre wil, ne ther ne was nevere no nature of resoun° that it ne hadde liberte of fre wil. For everything that may natureli usen resoun, it hath doom° by which it decerneth and demeth everything. Thanne knoweth it by itself thinges that ben to fleen and thinges that ben to desiren. And thilke thing that any wyht demeth to ben desired, that axeth or desireth he; and fleeth thilke thing that he troweth° to ben to fleen. Wherfore in alle thinges that resoun is, in hem also is liberte of wyllinge and of nyllinge°. But I ne ordeyne nat *(as who seyth, I ne graunte nat)* that this liberte be evene-lyk° in alle thinges. For-why° in the sovereynes dyvynes substaunces *(that is to seyn, in spirits)* jugement is moore cleere, and wil nat icoromped°, and myht redy to speden° thinges that ben desired. But the sowles of men moten needes be° moore free whan they looken hem in the speculacioun or lookinge of°

73 gobet, *lump,* **bydolven,** *buried,* **wenen,** *think* **76 his,** *its* **82 abregginge,** *connecting* **83 fortuit,** *fortuitous* **84 encowntringe,** *encountering* (each other) **90 theras,** *where* **92 dyffynisse,** *define,* **unwar,** *unplanned* **94 thilke,** *that* **95 uneschuable,** *inevitable* **96 welle,** *source* **5 Meter 1. 1 resolve,** *release* **3 fleynge batayle,** *fleeing troups* **4 fichcheth,** *fix* **7 departen,** *separate* **9 cleped,** *are called,* **moten,** *must* **12 stokkes arraced,** *uprooted tree trunks* **14 imedled,** *mixed,* i.e., **implieth,** *imply* **15 fortunel,** *accidental* **16 thilke,** *that* **20 slaked,** *slack,* **suffereth,** *submits to* **22 thilke,** *the same* **5 Prose 2. 2 acorde,** *agree* **4 clyven,** *hold* **5 witen,** *know* **7 corages,** *hearts* **9 nature of resoun,** *rational nature* **11 doom,** *judgment* **17 troweth,** *thinks* **20 nyllinge,** *not willing* **21 evene-lyk,** *equal* **22 For-why,** *for this reason* **24–25 wil nat icoromped,** *will is not corrupted* **25 speden,** *accomplish* **27 moten needes be,** *are necessarily* **28 looken hem in the speculacioun or lookinge of,** *consider or contemplate*

5 Meter 1. **1–3 Tigris . . . Achemenie,** the Tigris and Euphrates rivers do not actually originate together in the Achaemenian rocks (named after Achaemenius, the grandfather of Cyrus, king of Persia), but the rivers were connected by ancient canals and eventually they flow together in southern Iraq. **4 fleynge batayle,** famed for shooting backward while retreating, the Parthians conquered portions of the Tigris-Euphrates area.

the devyne thoght, and lasse free whan they slyden into the bodies, and yit lasse free whan they ben gadered togidere and comprehended° in erthely membres°. But the laste servage° is whan that they ben yeven to vices, and han yfalle from the possessioun of her propre resoun. For after that they han cast awey her eyen fro the lyht of the sovereyn sothfastnesse° to lowe thinges and derke, anon° they derken by the clowdes of ignoraunce and ben trowbled by felonous talents°; to whiche talents whan they aprochen and asenten, thei hepen and encresen the servage which they han joyned to hemself. And in this manere they ben kaytyfs° fro her propre liberte. The whiche thinges, nathelesse, the lookinge° of the devyne purvyaunce seth°, that alle thinges byholdeth and seth fro eterne, and ordeyneth hem everych in her merites as they ben predestynat. *(And it is seyd in Grek that)* alle thinges he seth and alle thinges he hereth.

Metre 2. Puro clarum lumine.

"Homer with the hony mowth *(that is to seyn, Homer with the swete dites°)* syngeth that the sonne is cleer by pure lyht; natheles yit ne may it nat, by the infirme lyht of his beemes, breken or percen the inwarde entrailes of the erthe or elles of the see. So ne seth nat God, makere of the grete world. To him that looketh alle thinges from an heh° ne withstondeth° no thinges by hevynesse of erthe, ne the nyht ne withstondeth nat to him by the blake klowdes. Thilke God seeth, in oo strokk of thoght, alle thinges that ben, or weren, or sholle comen, and thilke God, for he loketh and seth alle things alone, thow mayst seyn that he is the verray° sonne."

Prose 3. Tum ego en inquam.

Thanne seyde I, "Now am I confownded by a moore hard dowte than I was."

"What dowte is that?" quod she. "For certes, I conjecte° now by whiche thinges thou art trowbled,"

"It semeth," quod I, "to repugnen° and to contraryen gretly that God knoweth byforn alle thinges, and that there is any freedom of liberte. For yif so be that God looketh° alle thinges byforn, ne God ne may nat ben deceyved in no manere, than mot it nedes ben° that alle thinges bytyden° the whiche that the purvyaunce of God hath seyn byforn to comen. For which, yif that God knoweth byforn nat oonly the werkes of men, but also her conseyles and her willes, thanne ne shal ther be no liberte of arbitre°. Ne certes ther ne may be noon oother dede, ne no wil, but thilke which that the devyne purvyaunce, that may nat ben deceyved, hath feeled° byforn. For yif that they myhten wrythen° awey in oothre manere than they ben purveyed, thanne sholde ther be no stydefast prescience° of thing to comen, but rather an uncerteyn opynyoun, the whiche thing to trowen° of God, I deme it felonye and unleveful°. Ne I ne proeve nat thilke° same resoun *(as who seyth, I ne alowe nat, or I ne preyse nat, thilke same resoun)* by which that som men wenen° that they mowen assoylen° and unknytten the knotte of this questioun. For certes, they seyn that thing nis nat to comen for that° the purvyaunce of God hath seyn it byforn that is to comen, but rather the contrarye *(and that is this)*, that for that the thing is to comen, therfore ne may it nat ben hidde fro the purvyaunce of God; and in this manere this necessite slydeth ayein into the contrarye partye°. Ne it ne byhoveth nat°, nedes°, that thinges bytyden

32 comprehended, *contained,* i.e., **membres,** *limbs* **33 laste servage,** *lowest servitude* **37 sothfastnesse,** *truth* **38 anon,** *immediately* **40 talents,** *desires* **43 kaytyfs,** *captives* **45 lookinge** *considering* **46 seth,** *sees* **5 Meter 2.** **dites,** *songs* **8 an heh,** *on high* **9 withstondeth,** *opposes* **15 verray,** *true* **5 Prose 3.** **4 conjecte,** *guess* **6 repugnen,** *be opposed* **9 looketh,** *sees* **11–12 mot it nedes ben,** *it must necessarily be* **12 bytyden,** *occur* **17 arbitre,** *will* **20 feeled,** *perceived* **21 wrythen,** *twist* **23 prescience,** *foreknowledge* **25 trowen,** *believe* **26 unleveful,** *impermissible* **27 thilke,** *that* **29 wenen,** *think* **29–30 mowen assoylen,** *might solve* **32 for that,** *because* **38 contrayre partye,** *opposite side* **38–39 Ne it ne byhoveth nat,** *it need not be,* **nedes,** *necessarily*

49–50 alle thinges he seth and . . . hereth, a Homeric formula used to describe the sun; see *Iliad* 3.277, *Odyssey* 11.109 and 12.323. **5 Meter 2. 1–3** No quotation from Homer has been identified. Evidently, Boethius's original here quoted the Homeric formula that is translated in 5.pr2.49–50.

that ben purvyed, but it byhoveth, nedes, that thinges that ben to comen ben yporveyed°—but as it were ytravayled° (*as who seyth, that thilke answere procedeth ryht as thogh men travayleden or weren bysy)* to enqueren the whiche thing is cause of the whiche thing, as wheyther the prescience is cause of the necessite of thinges to comen, or elles that the necessite of thinges to comen is cause of the purvyaunce. But I ne enforce me° nat now to shewen it, that the bitydinge° of thinges iwist biforn° is necessarie, how so or in what manere that the ordre of causes hath itself; althogh that it ne seme nat that the prescience bringe in necessite of bytydinge to thinges to comen. For certes, yif that any wight° sitteth, it bihoveth° by necessite that the opinioun be soth of him that conjecteth° that he sitteth. And ayeinward° also is it of the contrarye: yif the opynioun be sooth of any wyht for that he sitteth, it byhoveth by necessite that he sitte. Thanne is heere necessite in that oon and in that oother, for in that oon is necessite of sittinge, and certes in that oother is necessite of sooth°. But therfore ne sitteth nat a wight for that° the opynyoun of the sittinge is soth, but the opynioun is rather sooth for that a wyht sitteth byforn. And thus, althogh that the cause of the sooth cometh of that other syde *(as who seith, that althogh the cause of soth comth of the sitting, and nat of the trewe opynyoun)*, algates° yit is there comune necessite in that on and in that oother. Thus sheweth it that I may make semblable skyles° of the purvyaunce° of God and of thinges to comen. For althowh that for° that thinges ben to comen, therfore ben they purveyed, nat certes for they ben purveyed, therfore ne bytyde they nat°. Yit natheles, byhoveth° it by necessite that eyther the thinges to comen ben ypurveyed of God, or elles that the thinges that ben purveyed of God bytyden° *(by necessite)*. And this thing only suffiseth ynowh to destroyen the freedom of owre arbitre *(that is to seyn, of owre free wil)*. But now, certes *(sheweth it wel how fer fro the sothe and)* how up-so-down° is this thing that we seyn, that the bytydinge of temporel thinges is cause of the eterne prescience°. But for to wenen° that God purvyeth the thinges to comen for° they ben to comen, what oother thing is it but for to wene that thilke thinges that bytydden whilom° ben causes of thilke sovereyn purvyaunce *(that is in God)*? And herto° *(I adde yit this thing:)* that ryht as whan that I wot° that a thing is, it byhoveth by necessite that thilke selve thing be; and ek whan I have knowe° that anything shal bytyden, so byhoveth it by necessite that thilke same thing bytyde; so folweth it thanne that the bytydinge of the thing iwist biforn° ne may nat ben eschwed°. And at the laste, yif that any wyht wene a thing to ben oother weyes thanne it is, it is nat oonly unscience°, but it is deceyvable opynyoun ful diverse and fer fro the soothe of science°. Wherfore, yif anything be so to comen, so that the bytydinge of hit ne be nat certeyn ne necessarye, who may weten° byforn that thilke thing is to comen? For ryht as scyence ne may nat ben medled° with falsnesse *(as who seyth, that yif Y wot° a thing, it ne may nat be false that I ne wot it)*, ryht so thilke thing that is conceyved by science ne may nat ben non oother weys thanne as it is conceyved. For that is the cause whi that science wanteth lesing° *(as who seyth, why that wytinge° ne receyveth nat leesinge of that it wot)*. For it byhoveth by necessite that everything be ryht as science comprehendeth it to be. What shal I thanne seyn? In which manere knoweth God byforn the thinges to comen yif they ne be nat certein? For yif that he deme that they ben to comen uneschewably°, and so

42 yporveyed, *foreseen,* **ytravayled,** *attempted* **49 enforce me,** *strive* **50 bitydinge,** *happening* **51 iwist biforn,** *foreknown* **55 wight,** *person* **56 bihoveth,** *must be* **57 conjecteth,** *knows* **58 ayeinward,** *conversely* **64 sooth,** *truth* **64–65 for that,** *because* **70 algates,** *nevertheless* **73 semblable skyles,** *similar arguments,* **purvyaunce,** *foreknowledge* **74 for,** *because* **76–77 nat certes for they ben purveyed, therfore ne bytyde they nat,** *certainly not that they will happen because they are foreknown* **78 byhoveth,** *need be* **81 bytyden,** *happen* **85 up-so-doun,** *upside-down* **87 prescience,** *foreknowledge* **88 for to wenen,** *to think* **89 for,** *because* **91 bytydden whilom,** *happened formerly* **92 herto,** *in addition* **93 wot,** *know* **96 knowe,** *knowledge* **99 iwist biforn,** *foreknown* **100 eschwed,** *avoided* **102 unscience,** *error* **104 science,** *knowledge* **106 weten,** *know* **108 medled,** *mixed* **109 wot,** *know* **114 wanteth lesing,** *lacks falsehood* **115 wytinge,** *knowing* **121 uneschewably,** *inevitably*

42–44 but as it were ytravayled . . . to enqueren, the syntax is very difficult; the Latin suggests something like "as though the problem was to explain." **69–70** ***that althogh the cause of the soth . . . and nat of the,*** in the margin in C[2].

may be that it is possyble that they ne shollen nat comen, God is deceyved. But nat oonly to trowen° that God is deceyved, but for to speke it with mowth, it is a felonous synne. But yif that God wot° that ryht so as thinges ben to comen, so shullen they comen, so that he wite egaly° *(as who seyth, indifferently)* that thinges mowen° ben doon or elles nat ydoon, what is thilke° prescience that ne comprehendeth no certeyn thing ne staable? Or elles what difference is ther bitwixe the prescience and thilke japeworthy dyvyninge° of Tyresye the dyvynour, that seyde, 'Al that I seye,' quod he, 'either it shal be, or elles it ne shal nat be'? Or elles how mochel is worth the dyvyne prescience moore than the opynyoun of mankynde, yif so be that it demeth the thinges uncerteyn, as men doon, of the whiche domes of men the bytydinge nis nat certein? But yif so be that non uncerteyn thing ne may ben in him that is ryht certein welle° of alle thinges, thanne is the bytydinge certeyn of thilke thinges whiche he hath wist byforn fermely to comen. For which hit folweth that the freedom of the conseyles and of the werkes of mankynd nis non°, syn that the thoght of God, that seth alle thinges withowten errowr of falsnesse, byndeth and constreyneth hem to a bitydinge *(by necessite)*. And yif this thing be oones° ygraunted and receyved *(that is to seyn, that ther nis no free wille)* than sheweth it wel how gret destruccyoun and how grete damages ther folwen of thinges of mankynde. For in ydel ben ther thanne purposed° and byhyht° meedes° to goode folk and peynes to badde folk, syn that no moevinge of fre corage voluntarye ne hath nat deserved hem *(that is to seyn, neyther meede ne peyne)*. And it sholde seme thanne that thilke thing is alderworst° which that is now demed for aldermoost just and most ryhtful, that is to seyn, that shrewes ben punysshed, or elles that goode foolk ben ygerdoned°. The whiche foolk, syn that her propre wil ne sent hem nat to that oon ne to that oother *(that is to seyn, neyther to goode ne to harm)*, but constreyneth hem certeyn necessite of thinges to comen, thanne ne shollen ther nevere ben, ne nevere weren, vice ne vertu, but it sholde rather ben confusioun of alle dissertes medled° withowten discrecioun. And yit ther folweth anoother inconvenyent°, of the whiche ther ne may ben thoght no moore felonous ne moore wykke, and that is this: that, so as the ordre of thinges is yled and comth of the purvyaunce of God, ne that nothing nis leveful° to the conseyles of mankynde *(as who seyth, that men han no power to doon nothing, ne wilne nothing)*, than folweth it that owre vices ben referred° to the makere of alle good *(as who seyth, thanne folweth it that God owhte han the blame of owre vices, syn he constreyneth us by necessite to doon vices)*.

"Thanne is ther no resoun to hopen in God, ne for to preyen to God. For what sholde any wyht hopen to God, or why sholde he preyen to God, syn that the ordenaunce of destyne, which that ne may nat ben inclyned°, knytteth and streyneth alle thinges that men may desyren? Thanne sholde ther be doon awey thilke oonly allyaunce bytwixen God and men, that is to seyn, to hopen and to preyen. But by the prys° of rihtwessenesse and of verray mekenesse we desserven the gerdoun of the dyvyne grace, which that is inestymable *(that is to seyn, that it is so gret that it ne may nat ben ful ypreysed°)*. And this is oonly the manere *(that is to seyn, hope and preyeres)* for which it semeth that men mowen° speke with God, and by resoun° of supplicacioun be conjoined to thilke cleernesse that nis nat aproched no rather or that° men beseken it and impetren° it. And yif men wene nat that hope ne preyeres ne han no strengthes by the necessite of thinges to comen yreceyved, what thing is her thanne by whiche we mowen ben conjoined and clyven° to thilke sovereyn prynce of thinges? For which it byhoveth° by

124 trowen, *think* **126 wot,** *knows* **128 wite egaly,** *knows equally* **129 mowen,** *may* **130 thilke,** *that* **133 japeworthy dyvyninge,** *ridiculous prophesying* **143 welle,** *source* **147–48 nis non,** *is nothing* **152 oones,** *once* **156 purposed,** *intended,* **byhyht,** *promised* **157 meedes,** *rewards* **161 alderworst,** *worst of all* **165 ygerdoned,** *rewarded* **172 medled,** *mixed* **173 inconvenyent,** *incongruity* **178 leveful,** *permitted* **181 referred,** *traced* **190 inclyned,** *diverted* **194 prys,** *value* **198** ***ful ypreysed,*** *fully praised* **200 mowen,** *might* **201 resoun,** *means* **202–03 nis nat aproched no rather or that,** *is not approached any sooner than before* **204 impetren,** *ask for* **208 clyven,** *hold* **209 byhoveth,** *need be*

134–36 Tyresye . . . , Tiresias, the blind prophet of Thebes, says this in Horace, *Satires* 2.5.59.

necessitee that the lynage of mankynde, as thou songe a lytel her-byforn, be departed and unjoined from his welle, and faylen *(of his bygynninge, that is to seyn, God).*

Metre 3 Quenam discors.

"What discordable cause hath to-rent° and unjoygned the byndinge or the alliaunce, of thinges *(that is to seyn, the conjunccioun of God and man)*? Whiche God hath establysshed so gret batayle bitwixen thise two soothfast° or verray° thinges *(that is to seyn, bytwixen the purvyaunce of God and fre wil)* that they ben synguler and devyded, ne that they ne wolen nat ben meddeled° ne cowpeled togydere? But ther nis no discord to the verray thinges, but they clyven, certeyn, alwey to hemself. But the thoht of man, confownded and overthrowen by the dirke menbres° of the body, ne may nat by fyr of his derked looking° *(that is to seyn, by the vigour of his insyhte, whyl the sowle is in the body)*, knowe the thinne subtyl knyttinges of thinges. But wherfore eschaufeth° of it so, by so gret love, to fynden thilke notes° of soth icovered. *(That is to seyn, wherfore eschaufeth the thoght of man by so gret desyr to knowen thilke notificasions that ben ihyd under the covertoures of sooth?)* Wot it awht thilke° thing that it, angwyssous°, desireth to knowe? *(As who seyth, nay; for no man travayleth° for to witen° thinges that he wot. And therfore the texte seyth thus:)* But who travayleth to witen thinges yknowe°? And yif that he ne knoweth hem nat, what seketh thilke blynde thoght? What is he that desireth anything of which he not ryht nawht°? *(As who seith, whoso desireth anything, nedes somwhat he knoweth of it, or elles he ne kowde nat desire it)* Or who may folwen thinges that ne ben nat iwist°? And thogh that he seke tho thinges, wher shal he fynde hem? What wyht° that is al unkunninge° and ignoraunt may knowe the forme that is yfownde? But whan the sowle byholdeth and seth the heye thoght *(that is to seyn, God)*, thanne knoweth it togidere the somme and the syngularitees *(that is to seyn, the principules and everych by hymself).*

"But now, whil the sowle is hidde in the clowde and in the derkenesse of the menbres of the bodi, it ne hath nat al foryeten° itself, but it withholdeth° the somme of thinges and leeseth° the syngularites. Thanne whoso that seketh sothnesse, he nis in neyther nother habite°. For he not nat° al, ne he ne hath nat al foryeten, but yit him remembreth the somme of thinges that, he withholdeth, and axeth conseyl, and retreteth° deepliche thinges iseyn byforn *(that is to seyn, the grete somme in his mynde)*, so that he mowe° adden the partyes that he hath foryeten to thilke that he hath withholden."

Prose 4. Tum illa vetus inquit.

Thanne seyde she: "This is," quod she, "the olde questioun of the purvyaunce of God. And Marchus Tullius, whan he devyded the dyvynacIouns *(that is to seyn, in his book that he wroot Of Divinaciouns)*, he moevede gretly this questioun; and thou thyself has isowht it mochel, and owtrely°, and longe. But yit ne hath it nat ben determyned ne isped° fermely and diligently of any of yow. And the cause of this dirkenesse and of this dificulte is for that° the moevinge of the resoun of mankynde ne may nat moeven to *(that is to seyn, applien or joynen to)* the symplicite of the dyvyne prescience°; the whiche *(symplicite of the devyne prescience)* yif that men myhten thinken it in any maner *(that is to seyn, that yif men myhten thinken and comprehenden the thinges as God seth° hem)*, thanne ne sholde ther dwellen owtrely° no dowte: the whiche resoun and cause of difficulte I shal assaye° at the laste to shewe and to speden°, whan I have fyrst yspended°

---

5 Meter 3. 1 **to-rent,** *torn apart* 5 **soothfast,** *truthful* 6 **verray,** *true* 9 **meddeled,** *mixed* 13 **menbres,** *limbs* 14 **fyr of his derked looking,** *light of his darkened sight* 17 **wherfore eschaufeth,** *why burns* 18 **thilke notes,** *these signs* 22 **Wot it awht thilke,** *does it know anything of that* 23 **angwyssous,** *anxious* 24 ***travayleth,*** *struggles* 26 ***witen,*** *understand* 27 **yknowe,** *known* 29–30 **not ryht nawht,** *knows not anything* 33 **iwist,** *known* 35 **wyht,** *person,* **unkunninge,** *unknowing* 44 **al foryeten,** *completely forgotten* 45 **withholden,** *retains* 46 **leeseth,** *loses* 47–48 **neyther nother habite,** *in neither one condition nor the other* 48 **not nat,** *knows not* 51 **retreteth,** *reconsiders* 53 **mowe,** *may* 5 Prose 4. 7 **owtrely,** *thoroughly* 8 **isped,** *completed* 10–11 **for that,** *because* 14 **prescience,** *foreknowledge* 17 ***seth,*** *sees* 18 **owtrely,** *utterly* 20 **assaye,** *try* 21 **speden,** *accomplish,* **yspended,** *dealt with*

211 songe . . . her-byforn, 4m6.47–54. 5 Meter 3. **Marchus Tullius,** Cicero, in *On Divination* 2.8.20ff., explores the value of divination if Fate rules everything; at 2.60, he lists various kinds of divination. **devyded,** C[2] reads "devynede," but the Latin is *distribuit.*

and answered to the resouns by which thou art ymoeved. For I axe why thou wenest° that thilke resouns of hem that assoylen° this questioun ne be nat spedful° ynowh ne sufficient: the whiche solucioun, or the whiche resoun, for that it demeth that the prescience nis nat cause of necessite to thinges to comen, than ne weneth it nat that fredom of wyl be destorbed or ylett° by prescience. For ne drawestow nat arguments from elleswhere of the necessite of thinges tocomen *(as who seyth, any oother wey than thus)* but that thilke thinges that the prescience wot byforn ne mowen nat unbytyde°? *(That is to seyn, that they moten° bytyde.)* But thanne, yif that prescience ne putteth no necessite to thinges to comen, as thow thyself hast confessed it and byknowen a litel her-biforn, what cause or what is it *(as who seyth, ther may no cause be)* by which that the endes voluntarie° of thinges myhten be constreyned to certeyn bytydinge? For by grace of positioun°, so that thou mowe the betere understonde this that folweth, I pose° *(per impossibile)* that ther ne be no prescience°. Thanne axe I," quod she, "in as mochel as apertieneth to that, sholden thanne thinges that comen of fre wyl ben constreyned to bytyden by necessite?"

Boece. "Nay," quod I.

"Thanne ayeinward°," quod she, "I suppose that ther be prescience, but that it ne putteth no necessite to thinges; thanne trowe° I that thilke selve° fredom of wil shal dwellen al hool and absolut and unbownden. But thou wolt seyn that, al be it so that prescience nis nat cause of the necessite of bytydinge to thinges to comen, algates° yit it is a syngne° that the thinges ben to bityden by necessite. By this manere thanne, althogh the prescience ne hadde never iben, yit algate° or at the leeste weye it is certeyn thing that the endes and bytydinges of thinges to comen sholden ben necessarye. For every signe sheweth and signefieth oonly what the thing is, but it ne maketh nat the thing that it signefieth. For which it byhoveth° fyrst to shewen that nothing ne bytydeth° that it ne bytydeth by necessite, so that it may appere that the prescience is syngne of this necessite; or elles yif ther nere no necessite, certes thilke prescience ne myhte nat be syne of thing that nis nat. But certes, it is now certeyn that the proeve of this, ysustened by stydefast resoun, ne shal nat ben lad° ne proeved by syngnes, ne by arguments itaken fro withowte, but by causes covenable° and necessarye. But thou mayst seyn, how may it be that the thinges ne bytyden nat that ben ypurveyed° to comen? But certes, ryht as we trowen that tho thinges which that the purvyance wot° byforn to comen ne ben nat to bytyden. But that ne sholden we nat demen, but rather, althogh that they shal bytyden, yit ne have they no necessite of her kynde° to betyden. And this maystow lihtly° aperceyven by this that I shal seyn. For we sen many thinges whan they ben doon byforn owre eyen, ryht as men sen the kartere° worken in the torninge and atempringe° or adressinge° of his kartes or charietes. And by this manere *(as who seyth, maystow undirstonde)* of alle oother workmen. Is ther thanne any necessite *(as who seyth, in owre lookinge)* that constreyneth or compelleth any of thilke thinges to ben don so?"

Boece. "Nay," quod I, "for in ydel and in veyn were all the effect of craft, yif that alle thinges weren moeved by constreyninge" *(that is to seyn, by constreyninge of owre eyen or of owre syht).*

Philosophie. "The thinges thanne," quod she, "that whan men doon hem ne han no necessite that men doon hem, ek tho° same thinges fyrst or° they ben doon they ben to comen withowte necessite. For-why° ther ben somme thinges to bytyden, of which the endes and the bytydinges of hem ben absolute and qwit of alle necessite. For certes, I ne trowe

23 wenest, *think* **24 assoylen,** *solve* **25 spedful,** *valid* **30 ylett,** *hindered* **35 ne mowen nat unbytyde,** *may not fail to happen* **36 moten,** *must* **41 ends voluntarie,** *voluntary outcomes* **43 grace of positioun,** *sake of argument* **45 pose,** *posit* **46 prescience,** *foreknowledge* **51 ayeinward,** *contrarily* **53 trowe,** *think* **54 thilke selve,** *this same* **58 algates,** *nevertheless* **58 syngne,** *sign* **61 algate,** *nevertheless* **67 byhoveth,** *is necessary* **68 bytydeth,** *happens* **75 lad,** *derived* **77 covenable,** *logical* **80 ypurveyed,** *foreseen* **82 wot,** *knows* **85 of her kynde,** *by their nature* **86 lihtly,** *easily* **89 kartere,** *cart driver* **90 atempringe,** *guiding* **91 adressinge,** *driving* **104 ek tho,** *and those* **105 or,** *before* **106 For-why,** *consequently*

43 positioun, C² and C¹ read "possessioun"; the Latin *positionis.* **69–71 so that . . . necessite,** omitted in C²; eyeskip.

nat that any man wolde seyn this, that tho thinges that men doon now, that they ne weren to bytyden fyrst or they weren idoon; and thilke same thinges, althogh that men hadde ywist° hem byforn, yit they han free bytydinges°. For ryht as science° of thinges present ne bryngeth in no necessite to thinges that men doon, ryht so the prescience of thinges to comen ne bryngeth in no necessite to thinges to betyden. But thou mayst seyn that of thilke same it is idowted, as wheither that of thilke thinges that ne han non issues° and bitidinges necessaries, yif therof may ben any prescience; for certes, they semen to discorden. For thou wenest° that yif that thinges ben iseyn byforn, that necessite folweth hem, and yif necessite fayleth hem, they ne myhten nat ben wyst° byforn; and that nothing ne may ben comprehended by science but certein°, and yif tho thinges that ne han no certeyn bytydinges ben purveyed as certeyn, it sholde ben dirknesse of opynioun, nat soothfastnesse of science°. And thou wenest° that it be diverse fro the hoolnesse of science that any man sholde deme a thing to ben ootherweys thanne it is itself. And the cause of this erroure is that of alle the thinges that every wyht° hath yknowe, they wenen that tho thinges ben iknowe aloonly by the strengthe and by the nature of the thinges that ben iwist° or iknowe; and it is al the contrarye. For al that ever is yknowe, it is rather comprehended and knowen nat after his strengthe and his nature, but after the faculte *(that is to seyn, the power and the nature)* of hem that knowen. And for this thing shal mowen shewen° by a short ensaumple: the same rowndnesse of a body, ootherweys° the sihte of the eye knoweth it, and ootherweyes° the towchinge. The lookinge, bi castinge of his beemes°, waiteth and seth from afer al the body togidere, withowte moevinge of itself; but the towchinge clyveth° and conjoigneth to the rownde body, and moeveth abowte the envyroninge°, and comprehendeth by partyes° the rowndnesse. And the man himself, ootherweys wit° byholdeth him, and ootherweys ymaginacioun, and oother weys resoun, and other weys intelligense. For the wit comprehendeth withowte-forth° the figure of the body of the man that is establyssed in the matere subject, but the ymaginacioun comprehendeth only the figure withowte the matere. Resoun surmounteth ymaginacioun, and comprehendeth by an universal lookinge the comune spece° that is in the singuler peces. But the eye of intelligence is heyere°, for it surmounteth the envyroninge of the universite°, and loketh over that bi pure subtilite of thoght thilke same symple forme *(of man that is perdurably° in the dyvyne thoght).* In whiche this owhte gretly to ben considered, that the heyeste strengthe to comprehenden thinges enbraseth and contieneth° the lowere strengthe; but the lowere strengthe ne aryseth nat in no manere to heyere strengthe. For witte ne may nothing comprehende owt of matere, ne the ymagynacioun ne looketh nat the universels speces, ne resoun taketh nat the symple forme so as intelligence taketh; but intellygence, that looketh al aboven, whan it hath comprehended the forme, it knoweth and demeth alle the thinges that ben under that forme. But she knoweth hem in thilke manere in the whiche it comprehendeth thilke same symple forme that ne may never ben knowen to none of that oother *(that is to seyn to none of tho thre forseyde thinges of the sowle)*. For it knoweth the universite of resoun, and the figure of the ymaginacioun, and the sensible material conceyved bi wit. Ne it ne useth nat nor° of resoun ne of ymagynacioun ne of wit withowte-forth, but it biholdeth alle thinges, so as I shal seye, bi a strok of thoght formely°, withowte discours or collacioun°. Certes, resoun, whan it looketh° anything universel, it ne useth nat of ymaginacioun,

---

114 ywist, *known* **115 bytydinges,** *occurrences,* **science,** *knowledge* **121 issues,** *outcomes* **124 wenest,** *think* **127 wyst,** *known* **129 but certein,** *except (something) certain* **132 soothfastenesse of science,** *truth of knowledge,* **wenest,** *think* **137 wyht,** *person* **139 iwist,** *known* **145 shal mowen shewen,** *may be shown* **147 ootherweys,** *in one way* **148 ootherweyes,** *in another way* **149 beemes,** *beams* **152 clyveth,** *attaches* **154 envyroninge,** *circumference,* **partyes,** *portions* **156 wit,** *sense* **159 withowte-forth,** *from the outside* **165 spece,** *species* **167 heyere,** *higher* **168 universite,** *universal* **170 *perdurably,*** *everlastingly* **173 conteineth,** *contains* **192 nor,** *neither* **195 formely,** *in terms of their simple forms* **195 collacioun,** *comparison* **196 looketh,** *perceives*

149 castinge of his beemes, in classical and medieval optical theory, the eye was thought to project a beam onto the object viewed.

nor of witte, and algates° yit it comprehendeth the thinges ymaginable and sensible. For resoun is she that diffynissheth° the universel of hir conseyte° ryht thus: man is a resonable two-foted beest. And how so that this knowinge is universel, yet nis ther no wyht that ne woot° wel that a man is a thing ymaginable and sensible°. And this same considereth wel resoun; but that nis nat by ymagynacioun nor by wit, but it looketh it by a resonable concepcioun. Also ymaginacioun, al be it so that it taketh of wit the bygynninges to seen° and to formen the figures, algates althogh that wit ne were nat present, yit it envyrowneth and comprehendeth alle thinges sensible, nat by resoun sensible of deeminge°, but bi resoun imaginatif. Sestow nat° thanne that alle the thinges in knowinge usen moore of her faculte or of her power thanne they doon of the faculte or power of thinges that ben iknowe? Ne that nis nat wrong; for so as every jugement is the dede or doinge of him that demeth, it byhoveth that every wyht° performe the werk and his entencioun, nat of foreyne° power, but of his propre power.

Metre 4. Quondam porticus attulit.

"The Porche *(that is to seyn, a gate of the town of Athenes ther as philosophres hadden her congregasioun to desputen)*, thilke° Porche browhte somtyme olde men, ful dirke in her sentenses *(that is to seyn, philosophres that hyhten° Stoyciens)*, that wenden° that ymages and sensibilitees *(that is to seyn, sensible ymaginaciouns, or elles ymagynaciouns of sensible thinges)* weren enpreynted into sowles fro bodies withowteforth *(as who seyth, that thilke Stoyciens wenden that the sowle hadde ben naked of itself, as a myroure or a cleene parchemyn°, so that alle fygures mosten fyrst comen fro thinges fro withowteforth into sowles, and ben aprented into sowles)*, Text, ryht° as we ben wont° somtyme, by a swyfte poyntel°, to ficchen° lettres empreinted in the smothenesse or in the pleynnesse of the table of wex or in parchemin that ne hath no figure ne note in it. *(Glose. But now argueth Boece ayenes that opynyoun, and seyth thus:)* But yif the thryvinge sowle ne unpleyteth° nothing *(that is to seyn, ne dooth nothing)* by his propre moevinges, but suffreth and lith° subgit to tho figures and to tho notes° of bodies withowteforth°, and yildeth ymages ydel and veyn in the manere of a myrour, whennes° thryveth thanne or whennes comth thilke knowinge in oure sowle that descerneth and byholdeth alle thinges? And whennes is thilke strengthe that biholdeth the synguler thinges? Or whennes is the strengthe that devydeth thinges iknowe; and thilke strengthe that gadereth togydere the thinges devyded; and the strengthe that cheseth his entrechawnged° wey? For somtyme it heveth up the heved° *(that is to seyn, that it heveth up the entencioun to ryht° heye thinges)*, and somtyme it dessendeth into ryht lowe thinges. And whan it retorneth into hymself, it reproeveth° and distroyet the false thinges by the trewe thinges. Certes, this strengthe is cause moore efficient, and mochel moore myhty to sen and to knowe thinges, thanne thilke cause that suffreth and receyveth the notes and the figures inpressed in maner of matere. Algates° the passioun *(that is to seyn, the suffraunce° or the wit)* in the qwyke° body goth byforn, excitinge and moevinge the strengthes of the thoght. Ryht so as whan that clernesse° smyteth the eyen and moeveth hem to sen, or ryht so as voys or sown hurteleth to the eeres *and commoeveth hem to herkne*, than is the strengthe of the thoght imoeved and excited, and clepeth° forth to semblable° moevinges the speces that it halt° withinne itself; and addeth tho speces to

198 algates, *nevertheless* **200 diffynissheth,** *defines* **201 conseyte,** *understanding* **204 woot,** *knows* **205 ymaginable and sensible,** *able to be imagined and sensed* **210 seen,** *perceive* **213 deeminge,** *judging* **214 Sestow,** *don't you see* **220 byhoveth,** *is necessary* **221 wyht,** *person* **222 of foreyne,** *by external* **5 Meter 4. 3 thilke,** *that* **5 *hyhten,*** *are called* **6 wenden,** *thought* **12 *parchemyn,*** *parchment* **15 ryht,** *just,* **wont,** *accustomed* **16 poyntel,** *stylus,* **ficchen,** *etch* **21 unpleyteth,** *unfolds* **23 lith,** *lies* **24 notes,** *written marks* **25 withowteforth,** *external* **26 whennes,** *from where* **35 entrechawnged,** *varied* **36 heved,** *head* **37 *ryht,*** *very* **39 reproeveth,** *responds to* **46 Algates,** *nevertheless* **47 *suffraunce,*** *receptivity,* **qwyke,** *alive* **50 clernesse,** *brightness* **54 clepeth,** *calls* **55 semblable,** *similar,* **halt,** *holds*

5 *Stoyciens,* Stoics, a school of Greek philosophers. The name derives from the *Stoa Poikilê* (Painted Porch) in Athens, the site of lectures by Zeno, founder of the Stoics. **15 Text,** indicates the end of the commentary and the return to the text; see 1.pr4.74–80n. **19 *Glose,*** indicates the beginning of an explanation or commentary (gloss); see 1.pr4.74–80n. **52 hurteleth,** C[1] reads ""hurteth."

the notes and to the thinges withowteforth, and medleth° the ymages of thinges withowteforth to tho formes ihidde withinne hymself.

Prose 5. Quod si in corporibus sentiendis.

"But what yif that in bodies to ben feeled° *(that is to seyn, in the takinge of knowelechinge of bodyly thinges)*, and al be it so that° the qualites of bodies that ben objecte° fro withowteforth moeven and entalenten° the instruments of the wittes; and al be it so that the passioun° of the bodi *(that is to seyn, the witte or the suffraunce°)* goth toforn° the strengthe of the workinge corage, the which passioun or suffraunce clepeth° forth the dede of the thoght in himself, and moeveth and exiteth in this menewhile the formes that resten withinneforth°; and yif that in sensibele° bodies, as I have seyd, owre corage nis nat itawht or empreinpted by passioun to knowe thise thinges, but demeth and knoweth of his owne strengthe the passioun or suffraunce subject to the body: moche more thanne° tho thinges that ben absolut and quite fro° alle talents° or affecciouns of bodies *(as God or his aungeles)* ne folwen nat in discerninge thinges object° fro withowteforth, but they accomplyssen and speden° the dede of her thoght. By this resoun thanne ther comen many maner knowinges to diverse and differinge substaunces. For the wit° of the body, the whiche wit is naked and despoyled of alle oother knowinges, thilke wit comth to beestes that ne mowe nat° moeven hemself her and ther, as *(oystres and muscules and other swiche)* shellefyssh of the see that clyven° and ben norysshed to roches. But the ymaginacioun comth to remuable beestes°, that semen to han talent to fleen or to desiren anything. But resoun is aloonly to the lynage of mankynde, ryht as intelligence is oonly to the devyne nature. Of which it folweth that thilke knowinge is moore worth thanne thise othre, syn it knoweth by his propre nature nat oonly his subject *(as who seyth, it ne knoweth nat aloonly that apertieneth° properly to his knowinge)*, but it knoweth the subjects of alle oother knowinges. But how shal it thanne be yif that wit and ymaginacioun stryven ayein resoninge, and seyn that of thilke universels° thinges that resoun weneth° to sen, that it nis ryht nawht? For wit and imaginacioun seyn that that, that is sensible or ymaginable, it ne may nat be universel. Thanne is eyther the jugement of resoun soth° ne that ther nis nothing sensible; or elles, for that° resoun wot° wel that many thinges ben subject to wit and to ymaginacioun, thanne is the concepcioun of resoun veyn and false, which that looketh and comprehendeth that that is sensible and synguler as universel. And yif that resoun wolde answeren ayein to thise two *(that is to seyn, to witte and to ymaginacioun)*, and seyn that soothly she hirself *(that is to seyn, resoun)* loketh and comprehendeth, by resoun of universalite, bothe that that° is sensible and that that is ymaginable; and that thilke two *(that is to seyn, wit and ymaginacioun)* ne mowen nat strechchen ne enhansen° hemself to the knowinge of universalite, for that the knowinge of hem ne may exceden ne surmounte the bodyly figures: certes, of the knowinge of thinges, men owhten rather yeven credence to the moore stidefast and to the moore parfyt jugement. In this manere stryvinge° thanne, we that han strengthe of resoninge and of ymagininge and of wit *(that is to seyn, bi resoun and by ymaginacioun and bi wit)*, we sholde rather preyse the cause of resoun *(as who seyth; than the cause of wit and of ymaginacioun)*.

"Semblable° thing is it that the resoun of mankynde ne weneth° nat that the devyne intelligence biholdeth or knoweth thinges to comen, but ryht as the resoun of mankynde

58 **medleth,** *mixes* 5 Prose 5. 1 **feeled,** *perceived* 3 **al be it so that,** *even though* 4 **objecte,** *tangible* 5 **entalenten,** *stimulate* 6 **passioun,** *sensation* 8 ***suffraunce,*** *response,* **goth toforn,** *precedes* 10 **clepeth,** *calls* 13 **withinneforth,** *internally,* **sensibele,** *corporeal* 19 **thanne,** *then* 20 **quite fro,** *free from,* **talents,** *desires* 22 **object,** *tangible* 23 **speden,** *perform* 26 **wit,** *senses* 29 **ne mowe nat,** *may not* 32 **clyven,** *cling* 33 **remuable beestes,** *animals capable of movement* 41 ***that apertieneth,*** *what pertains* 46 **thilke universals,** *those universal* 47 **weneth,** *thinks* 51 **soth,** *true* 52 **for that,** *because,* **wot,** *knows* 62 **that that,** *that which* 65 **enhansen,** *raise* 71 **manere stryvinge,** *kind of pursuit* 77 **Semblable,** *similar* 78 **weneth,** *thinks*

5 Prose 5. **1 what yif that in bodies to ben feeled,** as the gloss indicates, this is best construed as "if in perceiving corporeal things." The following set of conditional clauses is set in contrast to "muche more" in line 18 below.

knoweth hem. For thou arguest and seyst thus: that yif it ne seme nat to men that some thinges han certeyn and necessarye bytydinges°, they ne mowen° nat ben wyst° byforn certeynly to bytyden. And thanne nist ther no prescience of thilke thinges. And yif we trowe that prescience be in thise thinges, thanne is ther nothing that it ne bitydeth by necessite. But certes, yif we myhten han the jugement of the dyvyne thoght, as we ben parsoneres° of resoun, ryht so as we han demed that it bihoveth° that imaginacioun and wit be bynethe° resoun, ryht so wolde we demen that it were ryhtful thing that mannes resoun owhte to submitten itself and to ben bynethe the dyvyne thoght. For which, yif that we mowen *(as who seyth, that yif we mowen, I conseyle that)* we enhanse us into the heihte° of thilke sovereyn intelligence; for ther shal resoun wel seen that that it ne may nat biholden in itself. And certes that is this, in what maner the prescience of God seth alle thinges certeins° and diffinisshed°, althowh they ne han no certeyn issues or bitidinges. Ne this nis non opinioun, but it is rather the simplicite of the sovereyn science° that nis nat enclosed nor ishet° within none bowndes.

Metre 5. Quam variis terris animalia.

"The beestes passen bi the erthes bi ful diverse figures. For som of hem han her bodies strawght° and crepen in the dust, and drawen after hem a traas° or a forwh ikontynued° *(that is to seyn, as nadres° or snakes)*. And oother beestes, by the wandringe lyhtnesse of her winges, beten the wyndes, and overswymmen the spaces of the longe eyr by moist fleeinge°. And oother bestes gladen° hemself to diggen her traas or her steppes in the erthe with her goings or with her feet, and to gon eyther by the greene feeldes, or elles to walken under the woodes. And al be it so that thou seest that they alle discorden° bi diverse formes, algates° her faces, enclyned°, hevyeth° her dulle wittes. Oonly the lynage of man heveth° heyeste his heye heved°, and stondeth lyht with his upryht body, and byhooldeth the erthes under him. And but yif thou, erthely man, wexest° yvel owt of thy wit, this figure amonesteth the°, that axest the hevene with thy ryhte visage and hast areysed thy foreheved, to beren up aheygh thy corage, so that thy thoght ne be nat ihevyed° ne put lower under foote, syn that thy body is so heye areysed.

Prose 6. Quoniam igitur uti paulo ante.

"Therfore thanne, as I have shewed a litel her-byforn, that alle thing that is iwyst° nis nat knowen by his nature propre but by the nature of hem that comprehenden it, lat us loke now in as mochel as it is leveful° to us *(as who seyth, lat us loke now as we mowen°)* which that the estat is of the devyne substaunce, so that we mowen ek knowen what his science is. The commune jugement of alle creatures resonables thanne is this, that God is eterne. Lat us considere thanne what is eternite; for certes that shal shewen us togidere the devyne nature and the devyne science.

"Eternite, thanne, is parfyt° possessioun and altogidere of lyf intermynable°. And that sheweth moore cleerly bi the comparisoun or the collacioun of temporel thinges. For alle thing that lyveth in tyme, it is present, and procedeth fro preterits° into futures *(that is to seyn, fro tyme passed into tyme cominge)*; ne ther nys nothing establysshed in tyme that may enbracen togider° al the space of his lyf. For certes, yit ne hath it taken the tyme of tomorwe, and it hath lost the tyme of yisterday. And certes, in the lyf of this day ye ne lyven no moore but ryht as in the moevable and transitorye moment. Thanne thilke° thing that suffreth temporel condicioun, althogh that it nevere bygan to be, ne thogh it never cese for to be, as Aristotle demed of the world, and althogh that the

---

83 bytydinges, *happenings* **84 mowen,** *may,* **wyst,** *known* **90 parsoneres,** *partakers* **92 bihoveth,** *is necessary,* **bynethe,** *beneath* **98 heihte,** *height* **103 certeins,** *certain,* **diffinisshed,** *defined* **106 science,** *knowledge* **107 ishet,** *shut* <u>5 Meter 5.</u> **3 strawght,** *stretched out* **4 traas,** *track,* **forwh ikontynued,** *continuous furrow* **5 nadres,** *adders* **8–9 moist fleeinge,** *liquid* (effortless) *flying* **9 gladen,** *please* **14 discorden,** *are different* **15 algates,** *nevertheless,* **enclyned,** *bowed down* **16 hevyeth,** *weigh down* **17 heveth,** *raises* i.e., **heved,** *head* **20 wexest,** *grow* **21 amonesteth the,** *reminds you* **25 ihevyed,** *weighed down* <u>5 Prose 6.</u> **2 iwyst,** *known* **5 leveful,** *permitted* **6 mowen,** *are able* **14 parfyt,** *perfect* **15 intermynable,** *without end* **19 preterits,** *times past* **22 enbracen togider,** *embrace simultaneously* **28 thilke,** *that*

<u>5 Prose 6.</u> **2 her-byforn,** see 5.pr4.140ff. **30–31 as Aristotle deemed of the world,** *De Caelo* (*Concerning the Heavens*) 1.10.279b.

lyf of it be strechched with infinite of tyme, yit algates° nis it no swych thing that men myhten trowen° by ryht that it is eterne. For althogh that it comprehende and embrace the space of lyf infynit, yit algates ne embraseth it nat the space of the lyf altogidere, for it ne hath nat the futures that ne ben nat yit *(ne it ne hath no lengere the preterits that ben idoon or ipassed).* But thilke thing, thanne, that hath and comprehendeth togider al the plente of the lyf intermynable, to whom ther ne fayleth nawht of the future, and to whom ther nis nawht of the preterite escaped nor ipassed, thilke same is iwitnessed and iproeved by ryht to be eterne. And it byhoveth° by necessite that thilke thing be alwey present to hymself, and compotent° *(as who seyth, alwey present to hymself, and so myhly that al be ryht at his plesaunce),* and that he have al present the infynyte of the moevable tyme. Wherfore° som men trowen° wrongfulli that whan they heren that it semede to Plato that this world ne hadde never bygynninge of tyme, ne that it never shal han faylinge, they wenen° in this manere that this world be maked coeterne with his makere. *(As who seyth, they wene that this world and God ben maked togider eterne, and that is a wrongful weninge.)* For oother thing is it° to ben ilad° by lyf intermynable, as Plato graunted to the world, and oother thing is it to enbrace togydere al the present of the lyf intermynable, the whiche thing it is cleer and manyfest that it is propre to° the devyne thoght.

"Ne it ne sholde nat semen to us that God is eldere thanne thinges that ben imaked by quantyte of tyme, but rather by the proprete of his symple nature. For this ilke° infynyt moevinge of temporel thinges folweth° this presentarye estat° of lyf unmoevable; and so as it ne may nat countrefeten it, ne feynen it, ne be evenlyke° to it for the inmoevablete *(that is to seyn, that is in the eternite of God),* it faileth and falleth into moevinge fro the simplicite of the presence of God, and disencreseth° into the infynit quantite of future and of preterit°. And so as it ne may nat han togider al the plente of the lyf, algates° yit for as moche as it ne ceseth nevere for to ben in som manere, it semeth somdel° to us that it folweth and resembleth thilke thing that it ne may nat atayne to ne fulfyllen, and byndeth itself to som manere° presence of this litel and swyfte° moment, the which presence of this lytele and swifte moment, for that it bereth a manere ymage or lyknesse of the ay-dwellinge presence of God, it graunteth to swyche manere thinges as it bitydeth° to that it semeth hem as thise thinges han yben and ben°.

"And for that the presence of swych lytel moment ne may nat dwelle°, therfor it ravysshed° and took the infynyte wey of tyme *(that is to seyn, bi successioun).* And bi this manere is it idoon for that it sholde contynue the lyf in gooinge, of the which lyf it ne myhte nat enbrace the plente in dwellinge. And for-thy°, yif we wollen putten worthi names to thinges, and folwen Plato, lat us seye thanne sothly that God is 'eterne', and the world is 'perpetuel.' Thanne, syn that° every jugement knoweth and comprehendeth by his owne nature thinges that ben subject unto him, ther is sothly° to God alweys an eterne and presentarie estat; and the science of him°, that over-passeth al temporel moevement, dwelleth in the symplycyte of his presence, and embraceth and considereth alle the infynyt spaces of tymes, preterits and futures, and looketh in his symple knowinge alle thinges of preterit ryht as they weren idoon presently ryht now. Yif thou wolt thanne thinken and avyse° the prescience, bi which it knoweth alle thinges, thou ne shalt nat demen it as prescience of thinges to comen, but thou shalt demen it moore ryhtfully that it is science of presence, or of instaunce°, that never ne fayleth. For which it nis nat ycleped

33 algates, *nevertheless* **34 trowen,** *think* **46 byhoveth,** *must be* **48 compotent,** *all-powerful* **51 Wherfore,** *therefore* **52 trowen,** *think* **55 wenen,** *think* **59–60 oother thing is it,** *it is one thing* **60 ilad,** *led* **64 propre to,** *intrinsic to* **69 ilke,** *same* **70 folweth,** *imitates* **71 presentarye estat,** *ever-present condition* **73 evenlyke,** *equal* **76 disencreseth,** *diminishes* **78 preterit,** *past* **79 algates,** *nevertheless* **81 somdel,** *somewhat* **84 manere,** *kind of* **85 swyfte,** *transitory* **89 bitydeth,** *happens* **90–91 han yben and ben,** *have been and are* **93 dwelle,** *remain* **94 ravysshed,** *seized* **98 for-thy,** *therefore* **102 syn that,** *because* **105 sothly,** *truly* **106–07 science of him,** *his knowledge* **114 avyse,** *consider* **118 instaunce,** *present time*

53 Plato, Plato discusses whether the cosmos has a temporal beginning or if it is eternal in *Timaeus* 28–29. **100 Plato,** Plato discusses the world as a temporal extension of eternity in *Timaeus* 37.

'previdence°,' but it sholde rather ben cleped 'purviaunce°,' that is establysshed ful fer fro ryht lowe thinges, and byhooldeth from afer alle thinges, ryht as it were fro the heye heyhte of thinges.

"Why axestow thanne, or why desputestow thanne, that thilke thinges ben doon bi necessite whiche that ben yseyn and knowen bi the devyne syhte, syn that forsothe° men ne maken nat thilke thinges necessarye which that they sen ben idoon in her syhte? For addeth thy bihooldinge° any necessite to thilke thinges that thou bihooldest presente?"

"Nay," quod I.

Philosophie "Certes, thanne, if men mighte maken any digne° comparisoun or collacioun of the presence divine and of the presence of mankynde, ryht so as ye sen some thinges in this temporel present, ryht so seth God alle thinges bi his eterne present. Wherfore this devyne prescience° ne chaungeth nat the nature ne the proprete of thinges, but bihooldeth swyche thinges present to hym-ward as they shullen bityde to yow-ward in tyme to comen. Ne it ne confowndeth nat the jugement of thinges; but bi o° syhte of his thowht, he knoweth the thinges to comen, as wel necessarye as nat necessarye. Ryht so as whan ye seen togidere a man walken on the erthe and the sonne arysen in the hevene, al be it so that ye sen and biholden that oon and that oother togider, yit natheles ye demen and discernen that that oon is voluntarye and that oother necessarie. Ryht so thanne the devyne lookinge, byholdinge alle thinges under him, ne trowbleth nat the qualite of thinges that ben certeynly present to hym-ward; but, as to the condicioun of tyme, forsothe° they ben future. For which it folweth that this nis non opinioun, but rather a stidefast knowinge, istrengthed by sothnesse, that whanne that God knoweth anything to be, he ne unwot nat° that thilke thing wanteth° necessite to be. *(This is to seyn, that whan that God knoweth anything to bityde, he wot wel that it ne hath no necessite to bityde.)*

"And yif thou seyst heere that thilke thing that God seth to bityde, it ne may nat unbityde° *(as who seith, it mot° bityde)*, and thilke thing that ne may nat unbityde, it mot bityde bi necessite. And that thou streyne° me by this name of 'necessite', certes I wol wel confessen° and byknowe° a thing of ful sad° trowthe, but unnethe shal ther any wyht mowe sen it° or come therto but yif° that he be byholder of the devyne thoght. For I wol answeren the thus: that thilke thing that is future, whan it is referred° to the devyne knowinge, thanne is it necessarye; but certes, whan it is understonden in his owne kynde, men sen it is owtrely° fre, and absolut *(fro alle necessite)*.

For certes, ther ben two maneres° of necessite. That oon necessite is symple, as thus: that it bihovetn° bi necessite that alle men be mortal *(or dedly)*. Anoother necessite is condicionel, as thus: yif thou wost° that a man walketh, it bihoveth by necessite that he walke. Thilke° thing thanne that any wyht° hath iknowe° to be, it ne may ben non oother weyes thanne he knoweth it to be. But this condicioun ne draweth nat with hir thilke necessite symple. For certes, this necessite condicionel, the propre nature of it ne maketh it nat, but the adjeccioun° of the condicioun maketh it. For no necessite ne constreyneth a man to gon that goth bi his propre wil, al be it so that whan he goth, that it is necessarie that he goth. Ryht on° this same manere thanne, yif that the purvyaunce of God seeth anything present, than mot° thilke thing ben bi necessite, althogh that it ne have no necessite of his owne nature, But certes, the futures that bityden bi freedom of arbitre°, God seth hem alle togidere present. Thise thinges thanne, yif they ben referred° to the devyne syhte, thanne ben they maked necessarye bi the condicioun of the devyne knowinge. But certes, yif thilke

---

120 previdence, *foreknowing* **121 purviaunce,** *providence* **128 forsothe,** *truly* **131 bihooldinge,** *seeing* **135 digne,** *worthy* **140 prescience,** *foreknowledge* **146 o,** *one* **158 forsothe,** *truly* **163 ne unwot nat,** *does not fail to know,* **wanteth,** *lacks* **169 unbityde,** *fail to happen,* **mot,** *must* **171 streyne,** *constrain* **173 confessen,** *disclose,* **byknowe,** *acknowledge,* **ful sad,** *very firm* **174–75 unnethe shal ther any wyht mowe sen it,** *scarcely may any person be able to see it* **175 but yif,** *unless* **178 referred,** *considered in relation* **181 owtrely,** *utterly* **183 maneres,** *kinds of* **185 bihoveth,** *must be* **187 wost,** *know* **189 Thilke,** *that,* **wyht,** *person* **190 iknowe,** *known* **195 adjeccioun,** *addition* **199 Ryht on,** *just in* **201 mot,** *must* **205 arbitre,** *will* **207 referred to,** *considered in relation*

thinges be considered bi hemself, they ben absolut° of necessite, and ne forleten° nat ne cesen° nat of the liberte of her owne nature. Thanne, certes, withowte dowte alle the thinges shollen ben doon which that God wot° biforn that they ben to comen. But som of hem comen and bityden of free arbitre *(or of free wille)* that, al be it so that they bytyden, yit algates° ne lese they nat her propre nature in beynge, by the which fyrst, or that they weren idoon, they hadden power nat to han bityd."

Boece. "What is this to seyn thanne," quod I, "that thinges ne ben nat necessarye by her propre nature, so as they comen in alle maneres° in the lyknesse of necessite by the condicioun of the devyne science?"

Philosophie "This is the difference," quod she; "that tho thinges that I purposede the a lytel her-byforn, that is to seyn the sonne arysinge and the man walkinge, that ther-whiles° that thilke thinges ben ydoon, they ne myhte nat ben undoon; natheles, that oon of hem or it° was ydoon, it byhoved° by necessite that it was idoon, but nat that oother. Ryht so is hit here that the thinges that God hath present, withowte dowte they shollen ben. But som of hem descendeth of the nature of thinges *(as the sonne arysinge)*, and som descendeth of the powere of the doeres *(as the man walkinge)*. Thanne seyde I no wrong, that yif that these thinges ben referred° to the devyne knowinge, thanne ben they necessarye; and yif they ben considered by hemself, thanne ben they absolut° fro the bond of necessite. Ryht so as alle thinges that apiereth or sheweth to the wittes, yif thou referre it to resoun, it is universel; and yif thou referre it or loke it to itself, than is it singuler. But now yif thou seyst thus, that yif it be in my power to chaunge my purpos, than shal I voyde the purvyaunce of God whan that peraventure° I shal han chaunged the thinges that he knoweth byforn, thanne shal I answere the thus: Certes, thou mayst wel chaungen thy purpos. But for as mochel as the present sothnesse° of the devyne purvyaunce biholdeth that thou mayst chaunge thy purpos, and wheyther thou wolt chaunge it or no, and whyderward° that thou torne it, thou ne mayst nat eschuen° the devyne prescience, ryht as thou ne mayst nat fleen the syhte of the presente eye° althowh that thow torne thyself by thi free wyl into diverse acciouns. But thou mayst seyn ayein, how shal it thanne be? Shal nat the devyne science be chaunged bi my disposicioun, whan that I wol o° thing now, and now anoother? And thilke prescience, ne semeth it nat to entrechaunge stowndes° of knowinge?" *(As who seyth, ne shal it nat seme to us that the devyne prescience° entrechaungeth his diverse stowndes of knowinge, so that it knowe sumtyme o thing and somtyme the contrarie of that thing?)*

"No, forsothe," quod I.

Philosophie. "For the devyne syhte renneth toforn°, and seth° alle futures, and clepeth° hem ayein, and retorneth hem to the presence of his propre knowinge. Ne he ne entrechaungeth nat, so as thou wenest°, the stoundes of forknowinge, as now this, now that; but he ay-dwellinge comth byforn, and embraseth at o strook alle thy mutaciouns. And this presence to comprehenden and to sen alle thinges, God ne hath nat taken it of the bitydinge of thinges to come, but of his propre simplicite. And herbi° is assoyled° thilke thing that thou puttest a litel her-byforn, that is to seyn, that it is unworthy thing to seyn that owr futures yeven cause of the science° of God. For certes, this strengthe of the devyne science, which that embraceth alle thinges bi his presentarye° knowinge, establyssheth maner to alle thinges, and it ne oweth nawht to latter° thinges. And syn that these thinges ben thus *(that is to seyn, syn*

---

211 absolut, *devoid,* **forleten,** *abandon* **212 cesen,** *cease* **214 wot,** *knows* **218 algates,** *nevertheless* **225 maneres,** *ways* **231 ther-whiles,** *when* **233 or,** *before,* **byhoved,** *was necessary* **242 referred,** *considered in relation* **244 absolut,** *free* **252 peraventure,** *perhaps* **256 sothnesse,** *truth* **259 whyderward,** *whichever way* **260 eschuen,** *escape* **262 presente eye,** *eye of the person watching* **267 wol o,** *choose one* **269 entrechaunge stowndes,** *confuse instances* **271 *prescience,*** *foreknowing* **276 toforn,** *before,* **seth,** *sees* **277 clepeth,** *calls to* **279 wenest,** *think* **286 herbi,** *by this,* **assoyled,** *resolved* **289 science,** *knowledge* **292 presentarye,** *ever-present* **294 latter,** *subsequent*

221–26 Boece . . . , the following question is part of Philosophy's speech in Chaucer's source; by posing it as Boethius's question and by introducing the exclamation at line 274, Chaucer turns the end of the work into more of a dialogue. **229 her-byforn,** see 5.pr6.148–54. **274** See 5.pr.6.221–26n. **287 her-byforn,** see 5.pr3.84–87.

that necessite nis nat in thinges by the devyne prescience), than is ther freedom of arbitre° that dwelleth hool and unwemmed° to mortal men. Ne° the lawes ne purposen° nat wykkedly medes° and peynes to the wyllinges° of men that ben unbownden and quite° of alle necessite. And God, byholder and forwitere° of alle thinges, dwelleth above; and the present eternite of his syhte renneth° alwey with the diverse qualite of owre dedes, despensinge and ordeymnge meedes to goode men, and tormentes to wykked men. Ne° in ydel ne in veyn ne ben ther nat put in God hope and preyeres, that ne mowen nat ben unspedful° ne withowte effect, whan they ben ryhtful.

"Withstond° thanne and eschue° thou vices; worshipe and love thou virtuus; areys° thy corage to ryhtful hopes; yilde° thou humble preyeres aheyh°. Gret necessite of prowesse° and vertue is encharged and commaunded to yow, yif ye nyl nat dissimulen°, syn that ye worken and doon *(that is to seyn, yowre dedes or yowre workes)* byforn the eyen of the juge that seth *(and demeth)* alle thinges." *(To whom be glorye and worshipe bi infynyt tymes.* AMEN.)

Explicit Liber Boecii.

---

297 arbitre, *will* **298 unwemmed,** *unqualified* **299 Ne,** *nor do,* **purposen,** *appoint* **300 medes,** *rewards,* **wyllinges,** *decisions* **301 quite,** *free* **302 forwitere,** *foreknower* **304 renneth,** *runs* **307 Ne,** *neither* **310 unspedful,** *futile* **312 Withstond,** *resist,* **eschue,** *avoid* **313 areys,** *raise* **314 yilde,** *give* **315 aheyh,** *on high,* **prowesse,** *strength* **317 dissimulen,** *pretend*

321a ***Explicit Liber Boecii,*** Here ends the book of Boethius.

Treatise on the Astrolabe

Treatise on the Astrolabe

Introduction

An astrolabe is hand-held device used to calculate the relative positions of the sun and the stars as they vary with the passing of time and with the observer's location. It is rather like a global positioning device, although the astrolabe's primary function is to locate positions, not on the surface of the earth, but on the universal or celestial globe projected outward from earth as imagined in Ptolemaic astronomy. Stars can be located for any given time and date, and conversely the time and date of the terrestrial observation can be deduced when the positions of the stars are known. Widely useful before the general availability of maps, calendars, and clocks, the astrolabe can even be used to measure the height of tall terrestrial objects—towers and trees. Furthermore, it was used to determine basic data for astrological reckoning—what we think of rather reductively as personal horoscopes. In the Middle Ages, however, knowing the configuration of the stars helped people to locate themselves in time and space, and such knowledge was thought important to medical diagnosis, military planning, historical analysis, divination, and more. Like a modern calculator or computer, the astrolabe was used in many, many ways.

In manuscript count, the *Treatise on the Astrolabe* is second only to the *Canterbury Tales* among Chaucer's works. Its thirty-three manuscripts (including a fragment described in 2003; see no. 1665) indicate the work's importance in the history of English vernacular science as well as in helping us to understand the impressive range of Chaucer's interests and knowledge. He is the first English author to make use regularly of elaborate astronomical descriptions, and astrological principles underlie a number of his plots and characterizations. Although we cannot be certain to what extent Chaucer accepted the validity of astrological predictions, *Astrolabe* suggests that astronomy was more than a poetic device for him. Like economic and political trend watching are today, the study of the stars was serious business for Chaucer, for his contemporaries, and for many subsequent generations. His treatise is the one of the earliest discussions of a scientific instrument in English, used in and outside the English scientific community for two hundred years—until the time when Copernicus, Galileo, and the telescope changed the way people look at the stars.

The *Treatise on the Astrolabe* is an instructional manual, and evidently one of the reasons that it was so popular is the clarity of its instruction. Fifteenth- and sixteenth-century commentators praise the lucidity of the work, and modern scholars of technical writing commend its various techniques: personal address and tone, use of illustrations, and precision of description. Chaucer addressed the work to his ten-year-old son, Lewis, and wrote in an appropriate pedagogic style—using technical terminology when necessary but otherwise using the simple diction that he calls the "naked wordes in Englissh" (30) and "lihte Englissh" (55), and pausing recurrently for clarification and repetition. Part 1 describes the various components of an astrolabe and Part 2 consists of forty problems or calculations for the instrument. Three more parts were planned but never completed (see Prologue 80–110). Useful, illustrative diagrams accompany the text in some manuscripts, and it is evident that Chaucer intended them to help identify the parts of the astrolabe and how to use it. To clarify his technique, we include twenty-two of them derived from the complete program of illustrations in Cambridge University Library MS Dd.3.53.

The opening or Prologue of the *Astrolabe* is one of the few extant examples of Chaucer's free composition in prose, and the most personal portion of the treatise. It has garnered great praise from critics for style and clarity. Much of Parts 1 and 2 is amplification and rearrangement—some is straightforward translation—of composite Latin materials that circulated together under the title *De Compositione et Operatione Astrolabii.* In turn, these derive from materials attributed to Mâshâ'allâh, a famed eighth-century Jewish astrologer who wrote in Arabic. None of his original works survive, but we follow tradition in referring to Chaucer's source as "Massahalla" in our notes, although some scholars now refer instead to "pseudo-Massahalla." Only one secondary source has been identified (see 1.17.20-21n). Designed for the year 1391, the practical examples or exercises included in the *Astrolabe* are Chaucer's own, evidence that he began to compose the work in that year, even though it is likely that he continued to work on it in an ongoing way. The work is incomplete, and some of the sections at the end seem to have been added late; some manuscripts add further spurious sections (see the notes to Part 2.36 and 39)

If the beginning date of 1391 for the *Astrolabe* is correct, then ten-year-old "Litell Lowys" was born in 1380 or 1381, close to the date of legal accusation of rape, dated May 1, 1380, brought against Chaucer by Cecily Champain. This has led some modern scholars to speculate that Lewis was the son of Cecily rather than Chaucer's wife, Philippa. No corroboration survives, and the accusation of rape itself has been interpreted in different ways (forced coitus or abduction?), leaving us with intriguing possibilities but no certainties. Apart from the reference to Lewis that opens the *Astrolabe* and the sixteenth-century colophon that exists in one manuscript (see the Explicit after 2.40.81), only one record attests to the existence of Lewis at all—a document that mentions him along with Chaucer's better-known son, Thomas, at Carmarthen Castle, Wales, in 1403. What is almost certain is that Chaucer's intended audience included more than just Lewis. The astrolabe that he describes is calibrated for the latitude of Oxford (11), which was the center of mathematical and astronomical study of the day, and the treatise seems addressed to a friend (9) as well as other readers (45). Apparently, Chaucer wrote for Lewis, but with a broader group in mind. The engaging personal style of the opening gives way to denser style as the difficulty of the material develops.

Scholarly study of the *Astrolabe* is summarized in Sigmund Eisner's edition of the treatise for the Chaucer Variorum (2002; no. 63). J. D. North explores most deeply Chaucer's relations with the astral sciences in *Chaucer's Universe* (2d ed. 1990; no. 436). Andrew Cole analyzes the *Astrolabe* as a vernacular translation in "Chaucer's English Lesson" (2002; no. 1663). Marijane Osborn, *Time and the Astrolabe in the Canterbury Tales* (2002; no. 437) reads the presence of astrolabic knowledge in the frame of Chaucer's Canterbury fiction, while Catherine Eagleton offers perspective on the ongoing influence of the work in "'Chaucer's own astrolabe': Text, Image and Object" (2007, no. 1664). For comments on Lewis and on the *Astrolabe* as a didactic treatise, see Seth Lerer, "Chaucer's Sons" (2004; no. 1670). In "History, Technical Style, and Chaucer's *Treatise on the Astrolabe*" (1987; no. 1672), George Ovitt, Jr. argues for the cultural importance of the astrolabe itself, as well as for Chaucer's treatise. See John Hagge, "The First Technical Writer in English: A Challenge to the Hegemony of Chaucer" (1990; no. 1667), for a sobering assessment of Chaucer's place in the development of technical writing in English. He is often claimed to be the first English technical writer, but Hagge shows he participates in a rich and developing tradition.

Treatise on the Astrolabe

PROLOGUE

Litell Lowys my sone, I have perceived well by certeyne evidences thine abilite to lerne sciencez touchinge noumbres and proporciouns; and as wel considere I thy bisi preyere° in special to lerne the Tretis of the Astrelabie. Than for as mechel° as a philosofre seith, "He wrappeth him in° his frend that condescendeth° to the rihtful preiers of his frend," therfor have I geven the a suffisaunt° astralabie as for owre orizonte°, compowned after° the latitude of Oxenford, upon which by mediacion of this litel tretis I purpose to teche the a certein nombre of conclusions° apertenyng to the same instrument. I seye a certein of conclusiouns for thre causes°. The furste cause is this: truste wel that alle the conclusiouns that han ben fownde, or elles possibli myhten be fownde in so noble an instrument as an astralabie, ben unknowe perfitly to any mortal man in this regioun, as I suppose. Another cause is this: that sothly°, in any tretis of the astrelabie that I have seyn there ben some conclusions that wole nat in alle thinges performen hir byhestes°. And some of hem ben to harde to thy tendre age of x yer to conseyve°.

This tretis, divided in 5 parties, wole I shewe the° under ful lihte° rewles and naked° wordes in Englissh, for Latyn ne kanstow° yit but smal, my litel sone. But natheles, suffise to the thise trewe conclusiouns in Englissh, as wel as suffisith to thise noble clerkes Grekes thise same conclusiouns in Grek, and to Arabiens in Arabik, and to Jewes in Ebrew, and to the Latyn folk in Latyn; whiche Latyn folk han hem furst owt of othre diverse langages, and writen in hir owne tonge, that is to sein°, in Latyn. And God wot° that in alle this langages, and in many mo, han thise conclusiouns ben suffisantly lerned and tawht, and yit by diverse rewles, ryht as° diverse pathes leden diverse folk the ryhte wey to Roome. Now wol I prey mekely every discret persone that redith or herith this litel tretis, to have my rewde endytyng for excused°, and my superfluite of wordes, for two causes. The firste cause is for

4–5 bisi preyere, *industrious request* **6 mechel,** *much* **7 wrappeth him in,** *joins himself to* **8 condescendeth,** *agrees* **10 suffisaunt,** *workable,* **owre orizonte,** *our horizon* **11 compowned after,** *constructed for* **14 conclusions,** *calculations* **16 causes,** *reasons* **22 sothly,** *truly* **25–26 performen hir byhestes,** *fulfill their promises* (i.e., calculate correctly) **27 conseyve,** *understand* **29 the,** *you,* **lihte,** *easy* **30 naked,** *plain* **31 ne kanstow,** *you understand not* **39 sein,** *say* **40 wot,** *knows* **43 ryht as,** *just as* **46–47 to have my rewde endytyng for excused,** *to excuse my simple writing* **49 curious enditing,** *complicated writing,* **sentence,** *meaning*

Text based on MS Cambridge Dd.3.53 (Dd[1]), with select corrections and variants from Bodley 619 (Bl[1]), Bodley Rawlinson D.913 (Rl[1]), and Harvard University, Houghton Library, English 920 (Hv). Various titles appear in the manuscripts, attributing the work to Chaucer and identifying its topic; Bl[1] and others read "Brede and Milke for Children." The figures are taken from R. T. Gunther's translation of Dd[1], although we include them for the Prologue and Part 1 only. **1 Litell Lowys my sone,** Lewis Chaucer is listed in 1403 with the better-known Thomas Chaucer, elsewhere documented as a son of Chaucer. Nothing more is known for certain about Lewis, but see the Introduction and the colophon (from Dd[1]) at the end of this work. **have perceived,** Bl[1] reads "aperceyve." For lines 1–2, Hv reads "Certeyne evydences, my lytel sone Lewes, have do me to undertande thyne abylte." **7 philosofre seith,** the source has not been identified. **9 frend,** because the word is not a common form of address from father to son, critics have suggested that the audience of the treatise was not really Chaucer's son. It is quite possible that Chaucer wrote it to his son, but for a larger audience. See 45n. **26–27 to harde . . . conseyve,** Rl[1] and Hv read "to harde to understonde and to conceyve to the tendre age of the." **27 age of x yer,** ten years old. Critics speculate a birth date of about 1380 for Lewis, near the time when Chaucer was accused of the rape of Cecily Champain. As a result, some have inferred that Lewis may have been her son. **38 writen,** Bl[1], Rl[1] and Hv read "wroten hem." **43–44 diverse paths . . . to Rome,** proverbial; compare *TC* 2.36–37. **45 every discrete persone that redith,** another indication that Lewis is not Chaucer's only intended audience; see 9n.

that curious enditing° and hard sentence° is ful hevy° at ones for swich° a child to lerne. And the seconde cause is this, that sothly° me semeth° betre to writen unto a child twies a good sentence than he forgete it ones.

And Lowis, yif so be that I shewe the in my lihte° Englissh as trewe conclusiouns towcheng this matere, and nahwt° only as trewe but as many and as subtil conclusiouns as ben shewed in Latyn in ani commune tretis of the astrelabie, kon° me the more thank; and preye God save the King, that is lord of this langage, and alle that him feyth bereth and obeieth, everech° in his degree, the more and the lasse. But considere wel that I ne usurpe° nat to have fownde° this werk of my labour or of myn engin°. I nam but a lewd° compilatour of the labour of olde astrologens, and have hit translated in myn Englissh only for thi doctrine°. And with this swerd shal I slen envie.

The firste partie° of this tretis shal reherse the figures and the membres of thin astrolabie, by cause° that thow shalt han the grettre knowyng of thine owne instrument.

The second partie shal teche the werken° the verrey practic° of the forseide conclusiouns, as ferforth° and as narwe° as may be shewyd in so smal an instrument portatif aboute°. For wel wot° every astrologien that smalest fraccions ne wol nat ben shewid in so smal an instrument, as in subtil tables calkuled° for a kawse°.

The 3 partie shal contienen diverse tables of longitudes and latitudes of sterres fixe° for the astrolabie, and tables of declinacions° of the sonne, and tables of longitudes of citeez and of townes—and as wel for the governance of a clokke as for to finde the altitude meridian—and many nother notable conclusioun, after the kalendres° of the reverent clerkes°, frere° J. Somer and frere N. Lenne.

The 4 partie shal ben a theorik° to declare the moevinge of the celestial bodies with causes. The whiche ferthe partie in special shal shewen a table of the verray° moeving of the mone from howr to howre, every day and in every signe, after thyn° almenak. Upon which table ther folwith a canon° suffisant to teche as wel the maner of the wyrkyng of that same conclusioun as to knowe in owre orizonte° with which degree of the zodiak that the mone arisith in any latitude, and the arising of any planete after his latitude fro the ecliptik lyne?

The 5 partie shal ben an introductorie after the statutz° of owr doctours°, in which thow maist lerne a gret part of the general rewles of theorik° in astrologie. In which 5 partie shaltow° fynde tables of equacions of howses° aftur the latitude of Oxenford, and tables of dignetes° of planetes, and other noteful thinges, yif God wol vouchesauf°, and his Modur the Mayde, mo° than I behete°, & c.

---

50 **ful hevy,** *very difficult,* **swich,** *such* 51 **sothly,** *truly* 52 **me semeth,** *it seems to me* 55 **lihte,** *easy* 56 **nahwt,** *not* 59 **kon,** *give* 62 **everech,** *each of them* 63 **usurpe,** *claim* 64 **fownde,** *created* 65 **engin,** *ingenuity,* **lewd,** *unlearned* 67 **doctrine,** *learning* 69 **partie,** *part* 71 **by cause,** *for the purpose* 73 **the werken,** *you to work* 74 **verrey practic,** *precise practice* 75 **ferforth,** *far,* **narwe,** *exactly* 76 **portatif aboute,** *portable* 77 **wot,** *knows* 79 **calkuled,** *calculated,* **kawse,** (specific) *purpose* 81 **sterres fixe,** *fixed stars* 82 **declinacions,** *angles* (see n.) 87 **after the kalendres,** *in accord with the tabulations* (see n.) 88 **clerkes,** *scholars,* **frere,** *friar* 89 **a theorik,** *an explanation* 92 **verray,** *exact* 94 **after thyn,** *in accord with your* 95 **a canon,** *instructions* 97 **owre orizonte,** *our horizon* (i.e., the horizon seen in Oxford) 100–01 **ecliptik lyne,** *the path of the sun through the sky dividing the zodiac* 103 **statutz,** *rules* (astronomical) 104 **doctours,** *experts* 105 **theorik,** *principles* 106 **shaltow,** *you will,* **howses,** *sections* (see n.) 108 **dignetes,** *beneficial influences* 109 **vouchesauf,** *grant* 110 **mo,** *more,* **behete,** *promise*

51 **And,** omitted in Bl[1]. **60–61 King . . . lord of this langage,** the earliest known reference to the idea of "the King's English," and perhaps an indication of Chaucer's awareness of the importance of the royal Chancery in establishing an official form of written English. Hv reads "these langagis" **62 obeieth,** Hv reads "obedience." **66 olde astrologens,** ancient astrologers. Chaucer's used as a source *De Compositione et Operatione Astrolabii,* a Latin translation of writings attributed to Massahalla, the eighth-century Jewish-Arabian scientist; no complete source is known because some of Chaucer's material is not found in Massahalla. It is possible that Chaucer compiled the material himself, as he claims in line 65. **68 swerd,** Rl[1] and Hv read "swerd only." **shal I,** Bl[1] reads "I shal. **77 that smalest,** Bl[1] and Hv read "that the smalest." **80 3 partie,** Chaucer's *Astrolabe* includes only Parts 1–2 of the five listed, but the unique manuscript of *Equatorie of the Planetis* includes materials that are similar to some of those mentioned here in Parts 3–5. **82 declinations,** angles of the sun to the equator, which vary daily. **83 sonne,** Dd[1] reads "som." **85–86 altitude meridian,** height above the horizon of a meridian (a line circling the earth passing through the two poles). **87–88 kalendres . . . Somer . . . Lenne,** John Somer and Nicholas Lynne, friars associated with Oxford, both constructed calendars for the location of Oxford that included data for the 1390s. Such calendars tabulated various data—elevations of the sun, phases of the moon, positions of the planets, etc.—specific to a location. Chaucer's astrological information in *MLP* 2.1–14 and *ParsP* 10.4–11 has parallels with that in Lynne's *Kalendarium.* **91 causes,** Bl[1], Rl[1], and Hv read "the causes." **105 theorik,** compare *Equat* 558. **106 howses,** the houses (or mansions) divide the celestial sphere into twelve segments, used for astrological rather than astronomical purposes (which were not clearly distinguished in the Middle Ages).

PART 1

Here byginneth the descripcion of the astrelabie.

1. Thyn astrelabie hath a ring to putten on the thoumbe of thy ryht hand in takyng the heyhte of thynges. And tak kep°, for from hennesforthward I wol clepe° the heyhte of anything that is taken by thy rewle "the altitude" withowte mo wordes°.

2. This ring rennyth in a maner turret°, fast° to the moder° of thyn astrelabie, in so rowm° a space that hit desturbeth nat the instrument to hangen after his rihte° centre. [*Figure 1*]

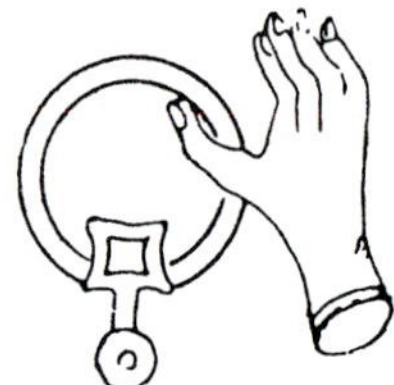

[*Figure 1*]

3. The Moder of thin astrelabie is the thikkeste plate, perced° with a large hole°, that rescevieth in hir wombe° the thynne plates compowned° for diverse clymatz°, and thy riet° shapen in manere of a net or of a webbe of a loppe°. And for the more declaracioun, lo here the figure. [*Figure 2*]

4. This moder is devyded on the bak half° with a lyne that cometh dessendinge fro the ryng down to the nethereste° bordure. The whiche lyne, fro the forseide ryng unto the centre of the large hole amydde°, is cleped° the Sowth Lyne, or elles the Lyne Meridional. And the remenant° of this lyne downe to the bordure is cleped the North Lyne, or elles the Lyne of Midnyht. And for the more declaracioun°, lo here the figure. [*Figure 3*]

[*Figure 2*]

5. Over thwart° this forseide longe lyne, ther crosseth hym another lyne of the same lengthe from est to west. Of the whiche lyne, from a litel croys + in the bordure unto the centre of the large hole, is cleped the Est Lyne, or elles the Lyne Orientale; and the remenant of this lyne, fro the forseide centre unto the bordure, is cleped the West Lyne, or the Lyne Occidentale. Now hastow her the 4 quarters of thyn astrelabie, devyded after the 4 principals plages° or quarters of the firmament. And for the more declaracioun, lo here thi figure. [*Figure 4*]

1.3 tak kep, *pay attention* **1.4 clepe,** *call* **1.6 withowte mo wordes,** *with no more explanation* **2.1 rennyth in a maner truet,** *acts as a kind of swivel,* **fast,** *attached* **2.2 moder,** *mother* (i.e., body), **rowm,** *roomy* **2.4 after his rihte,** *from its exact* **3.2 perced,** *recessed,* **hole,** *cavity* **3.3 wombe,** *central portion* **3.4 compowned,** *constructed,* **diverse clymatz,** *different latitudes* **3.5 riet,** *rete* (technical term; see n.) **3.6 loppe,** *spider* **4.1 bak half,** *reverse side* **4.3 nethereste,** *lowest* **4.5 amydde,** (in the) *middle,* **cleped,** *called* **4.7 remenant,** *remainder* **4.9–10 more declaracioun,** *greater clarity* **5.1 Over thwart,** *horizontally across* **5.11 principals plages,** *principal compass directions*

1.2 of thy, Bl[1] reads "of the." **1.4 wol,** Dd[1] and Rl[1] read "wolde." **1.5 thy,** Bl[1], Rl[1], and Hv read "the." **1.6 altitude,** the angle, measured in degrees, between the horizon and a star or planet. **2.2 thyn,** Hv reads "the." **3.1 thin,** Hv reads "this." **3.5 riet,** the rete is mounted on the body of the astrolabe and can be revolved to indicate the locations of various stars. Unlike the solid plates, it is openwork tracery, with various arms and spokes, flame-shaped star pointers, and circle of the zodiac described in section 21; see figure 2. **3.6–7 And for . . . figure,** generally omitted in all manuscripts except Dd[1], which includes figures and references to them here and at the end of sections below. **5.7 centre,** Dd[1] reads "+"; Bl[1] reads "hool."

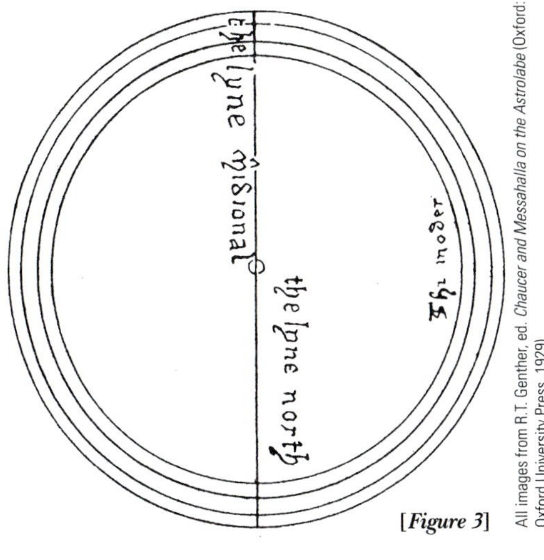

[*Figure 3*]

All images from R.T. Genther, ed. *Chaucer and Messahalla on the Astrolabe* (Oxford: Oxford University Press, 1929)

left side. Forget nat this, lite Lowys. Put the ring of thyn astralabie upon the thowmbe of thy ryht hand, and thanne wole his right syde be toward thy left side, and his left syde wol be toward thy right side. Tak this rewle general, as wel on the bak as on the wombe side°. Upon the ende of this est lyne, as I first seide, is marked a litel +, wher as everemo generaly is considered the entring° of the first degree in which the sonne ariseth. And for the more declaracioun, lo here the figure. [*Figure 5*]

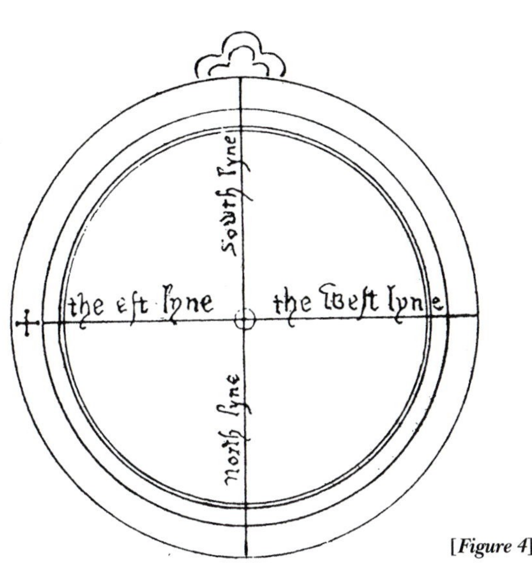

[*Figure 4*]

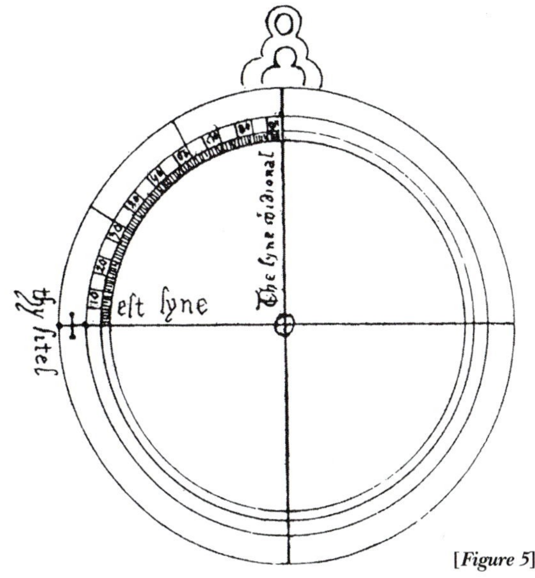

[*Figure 5*]

6. The est side of thin astrelabie is cleped° the riht side, and the west side is cleped the

7. Fro this litel + up to the ende of the lyne meridional under the ring shaltow° fynden the bordure devyded with 90 degres; and by that same proporcioun is every quarter of thine astrolabie devyded. Over the whiche degrees ther ben nowmbres of augrym° that devyden thilke° same degres fro 5 to 5, as shewith by longe strykes° bytwene. Of whyche longe strykes the space bytwene contienith a mile wey°. And every degree of the bordure contieneth 4

6.1 cleped, *called* **6.9 wombe side,** i.e., *front side* (described in 1.3) **6.11 entring,** *beginning* **7.2 shaltow,** *you will* **7.6 nowmbres of augrym,** *Arabic numerals* **7.7 thilke,** *these* **7.8 strykes,** *lines* **7.9 contienith a mile wey,** *contains twenty minutes* (see n.)

6.1 est side, the directions are given from the perspective of someone looking from *behind* the astrolabe. **6.12 first degree,** i.e., the little cross marks the place on the astrolabe that parallels the point in the sky where the sun rises above the horizon and moves through the 24 hours of the day. **which,** here and elsewhere Dd[1] reads "wich." **7.2 shaltow,** Bl[1] reads "shalt." **7.9 mile wey,** an idiomatic expression for a period of time equal to about twenty minutes (the time it takes to walk a mile); on the astrolabe, five degrees.

minutes, that is to seyn, minutes of an howre. And for more declaracioun, lo here the figure. [*Figure 6*]

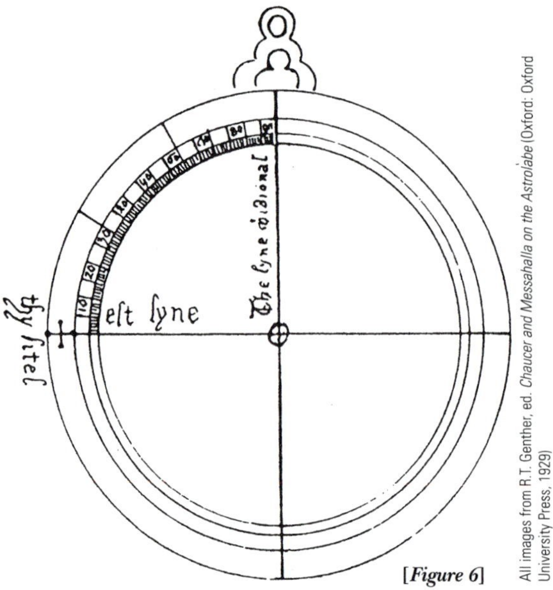

[*Figure 6*]

All images from R.T. Genther, ed. *Chaucer and Messahalla on the Astrolabe* (Oxford: Oxford University Press, 1929)

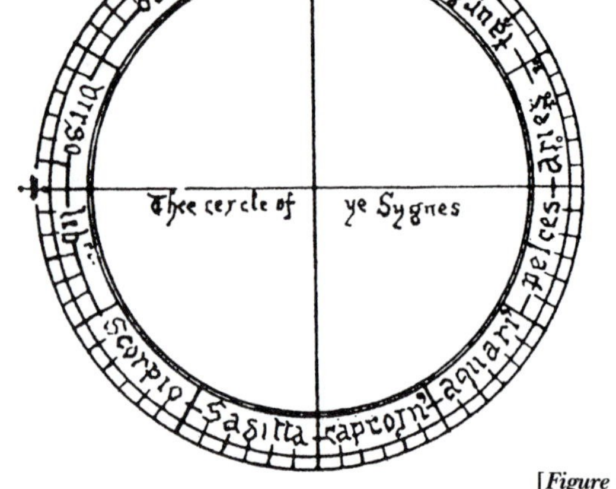

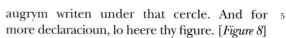

[*Figure 7*]

augrym writen under that cercle. And for more declaracioun, lo heere thy figure. [*Figure 8*]

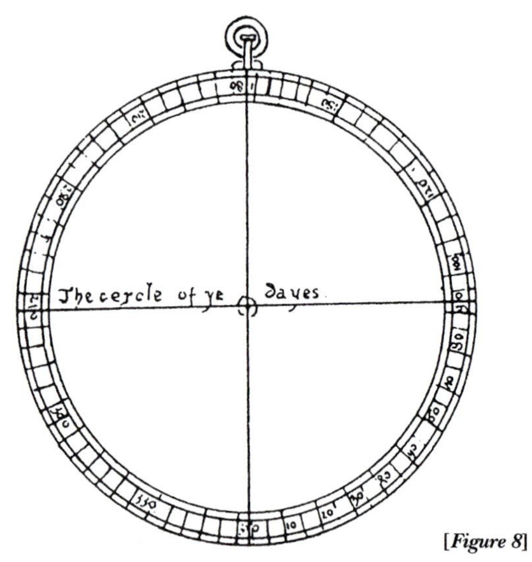

[*Figure 8*]

8. Under the compas° of thilke° degres. ben writen the names of the 12 signes, as Aries, Taurus, Gemini, Cancer, Leo, Virgo, Libra, Scorpio, Sagittarius, Capricornus, Aquarius, Pisces; and the nombres of the degres of tho signes ben writen in augrim° above, and with longe devysiouns, fro 5 to 5, devyded fro tyme that the signe entreth unto the laste ende. But understond wel that thise degrees of signes ben everich of hem considered of 60 mynutes, and every minute of 60 seceondes, and so forth into smale fraccions infinit, as seith Alkabucius. And therfor, know wel that a degree of the bordure contieneth 4 mynutes, and a degre of a signe contieneth 60 mynutes, and have this in mynde. And for the more declaracioun, lo here thy figure. [*Figure 7*]

9. Next this folwyth the Cercle of the Dayes, that ben figured in maner of degrees, that contienen in nowmbre 365, dyvyded also with longe strikes fro 5 to 5, and the nombres in

10. Next the cercle of the dayes folweth the Cercle of the names of the Monthes; that

8.1 Under the compas, *within the circle,* **thilke,** *these* **8.6 augrim,** *Arabic numerals*

7.11 that is to, Bl[1] reads "this is to"; Dd[1] and Rl[1] read "this to." **8.8 unto,** Bl[1] and Hv read "into." **8.11 mynutes,** both minutes of time and angular measurement. As there are sixty minutes in an hour, there are also sixty minutes in each degree of a circle's 360 degrees. **8.13 Alkabucius,** Alcabitius; tenth-century Arabic astronomer, Alî al-Qasîbî, whose treatise was translated into Latin as *Introductorium ad Scientiam Judicialem Astronomie (Introduction to the Art of Astrology).*

is to seyen, Januare, Februare, Marcius, April, Mayus, Juyn, Julius, Augustus, Septembre, October, Novembre, Decembre. The names of thise monthes were cleped° thus, somme for hir propretes, and some by statutz° of lordes Arabyens, some by other lordes of Rome. Ek° of thise monthes, as liked° to Julius Cesar and to Cesar Augustus, some were compowned° of diverse nombres of dayes, as Juyl and August. Thanne hath Januare 31 daies, Februare 28, March 31, Aprill 30, May 31, Junius 30, Julius 31, Augustus 31, September 30, Octobre 31, Novembre 30, December 31. Natheles, althowh that Julius Cesar tok 2 dayes out of Feverer° and put hem in his monith of Juyll, and Augustus Cesar cleped the monyth of August after his name and ordeyned it of 31 daies, yit truste wel that the sonne dwelleth therfor nevere the more ne lesse in on° signe than in another.

11. Than folwen the names of the Halidayes° in the Kalender, and next hem° the lettres of the ABC on which they fallen. And for the more declaracioun, loo here thi figure. [*Figure 9*]

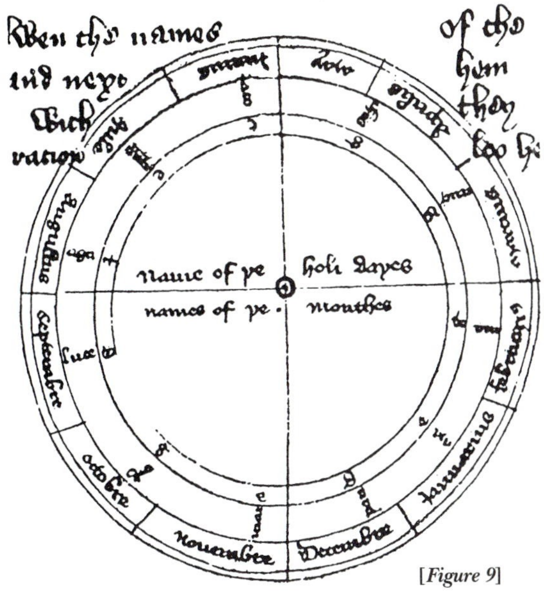

12. Next the forseide Cercle of the ABC under the cros lyne is marked the skale°, in maner of 2 squyres°, or elles in manere of laddres, that serveth by his 12 poyntes and his devisiouns of ful many a subtil conclusioun. Of this forseide skale, fro the croos lyne unto° the verrey angle° is cleped *Umbra Recta,* or elles *Umbra Extensa,* and the nether° partie is cleped the *Umbra Versa.* And for the more declaracioun, lo here the figure. [*Figure 10*]

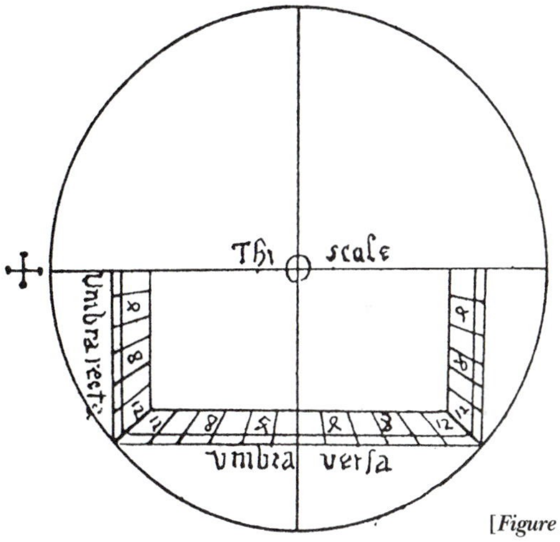

13. Thanne hastow° a brod Rewle° that hath on either ende a squar plate perced with certein holes, some more° and some lesse°, to resseyven the stremes° of the sonne by day, and ek by mediacioun° of thyn eye to knowe the altitude of sterres by nyhte. And for the more declaracioun, lo here thi figure. [*Figure 11*]

[*Figure 9*]

All images from R.T. Genther, ed. *Chaucer and Messahalla on the Astrolabe* (Oxford: Oxford University Press, 1929)

[*Figure 10*]

10.6 cleped, *named* **10.7 statutz,** *proclamations* **10.8 Ek,** *also* **10.9 liked,** *was pleasing* **10.10 compowned,** *composed* **10.17 Feverer,** *February* **10.21 one,** *one* **11.1 Halidayes,** *holy days* **11.2 nexte hem,** *after them* **12.2 skale,** *scale* (see n.) **12.3 squyres,** *squares* (i.e., carpenter's rulers) **12.6 unto,** *down to* **12.7 verrey angle,** *right angle* **12.8 nether,** *lower* **13.1 hastow,** *you have,* **Rewle,** *ruler* **13.3 more,** *large,* **lesse,** *small* **13.4 stremes,** *rays* **13.5 mediacioun,** *means*

10.5–20 The information here is etymologically and historically imprecise at points, even though the description of the Julian calendar is essentially correct. All of the month names are Latin (none Arabic), and as editors have pointed out, Julius Caesar took no days from February, although Augustus Caesar did transfer one from February to August in order to give his name-month as many days as July. **10.6 thus,** Dd[1] reads "in Arabyens." **10.8 Arabyens,** omitted in Dd[1]. **10.20–22 sonne dwelleth . . . more ne lesse in on signe than in another,** not true, as is pointed out in an erudite gloss in Bl[1], copied in other manuscripts. The sun's time in the signs varies somewhat with the season. **11.3 ABC,** the Sunday or Dominical letters (A–G) by which the dates of movable Christian feasts were determined from year to year. **12.2 skale,** the shadow scale, used to calculate the height of terrestrial objects. **12.5–9** The manuscripts, the text here, and figure 10 are all incorrect. The *Umbra Recta* or *Umbra Extensa* (right shadow or extended shadow) is the name for the lower horizontal portion of the scale, while the *Umbra Versa* (left shadow) is its perpendicular vertical portion. **13.1 Rewle,** see fig. 11; the technical name for this sighting bar is *alidade.*

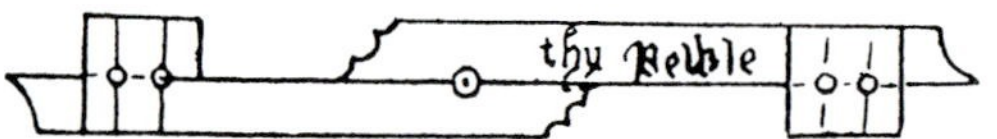

[*Figure 11*]

14. Thanne is ther a large Pyn, in maner of an extre°, that goth thorow the hole, that halt the tables of the clymates° and the riet° in the wombe of the moder, thorw which pyn ther goth a litel wegge which that is cleped the Hors°, that streyneth° alle thise parties to hepe°. This forseide grete pyn in maner of an extre is ymagynd° to be the Pol Artyk° in thin astralabie. And for the more declaracioun, lo here the figure. [*Figure 12*]

[*Figure 12*]

15. The wombe side° of thyne astrelabie is also devyded with a longe croys in 4 quarters from est to west, fro sowth to north, fro riht side to left side, as is the bak side. And for the more declaracioun, lo here thi figure. [*Figure 13*]

16. The bordure of which wombe side is devyded fro the poynt of the est lyne unto the poynt of the south lyne under the ring in 90 degres. And by that same proporcioun is every quarter devyded, as ys the bak syde. That amonteth° 360 degrees. And understond wel that degres of this bordure ben answering and consentrik to the degrees of the Equinoxial°, that is devyded in the same nombre as every othere cercle is in the heie° hevene.

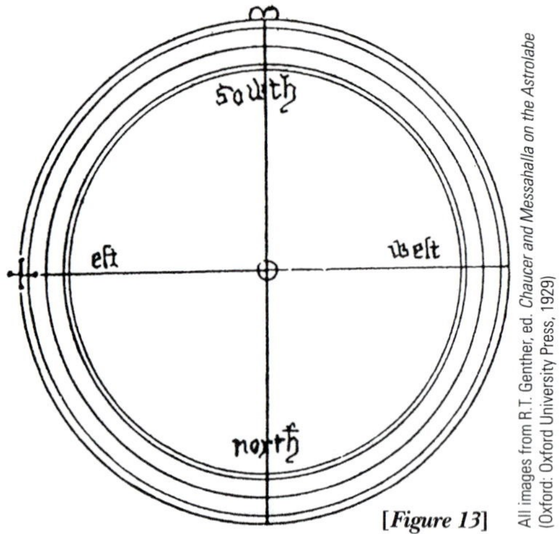

[*Figure 13*]

All images from R.T. Genther, ed. *Chaucer and Messahalla on the Astrolabe* (Oxford: Oxford University Press, 1929)

This same bordure is devyded also with 23 lettres capitals and a smal croys + above the south lyne, that sheweth the 24 howres equals of the clokke. And, as I have said, 5 of thise degrees maken a mile wey°, and 3 mile wey maken an howre. And every degree of this bordure conteneth 4 minutes, and every minut 60 secoundes. Now have I told the twye°. And for the more declaracioun, lo here the figure. [*Figure 14*]

17. The plate under thi riet is descrived° with 3 principal cercles, of whiche the leste° is cleped the Cercle of Cancer, bycause that the heved° of Cancer turneth evermore consentrik upon the same cercle. In this heved of Cancer is the grettest declinacioun northward of the sonne. And therfor is he cleped the Solsticioun of Somer; whiche declinacioun, after° Ptholome, is 23 degrees and 50 minutes as wel in Cancer

14.2 extre, *axle* **14.3 tables of the clymates,** *recordings of the latitudes* (on an incised plate; see 1.3.3–4), **riet,** *rete* (see 1.3.5n) **14.6 Hors,** *horse,* **streyneth,** *holds* **14.7 to-hepe,** *together* **14.8 ymagynd,** *understood,* **Pol Artyk,** *north pole* **15.1 wombe side,** *front side* **16.6 amonteth,** *amounts to* **16.8 Equinoxial,** *celestial equator* (see n.) **16.10 heie,** *high* **16.15 mile wey,** *twenty minutes* (see 1.7.9n) **16.18 twye,** *twice* **17.1 descrived,** *incised* **17.2 leste,** *smallest* **17.3 heved,** *head* **17.8 after,** *according to*

14.4–6 thorw which pyn . . . Hors, a cotter pin; the plates and pointers of the astrolabe are held on the central-axis pin, anchored by a wedge that passes through a hole pierced through the pin. The wedge is called a horse in Latin (*equus*) and in Arabic (*al-Faras*), and may be shaped as or decorated accordingly. **14.4 ther,** Bl[1] reads "that." **16.8 consentrik,** Rl[1] and Hv read "consentynge." **Equinoxial,** the celestial circle that results when the plane of the earth's equator is projected outward onto the sphere of the heavens. **16.11 is devyded also,** Bl[1] reads "also is devyded." **16.11–12 23 lettres capitals and a smal croys,** these 24 divisions, one for each hour of the day, indicate that the basic scale of the astrolabe postulates a day of 24 equal hours, starting with the cross at noon and moving to 1:00 p.m. at A, 2:00 p.m. at B, and so on. Our letters *J, V,* and *W* are omitted from this sequence because these historically variant forms of other letters were not distinctive. **16.12 croys + above,** Hv reads "croys above that is to say begynnid fro." **16.14 as I have said,** see 1.7.9. **16.18 I,** omitted in Dd[1]. **17** In this section Chaucer adds to Massahalla, his primary source. **17.1 thi riet,** Bl[1], Rl[1], and Hv read "the riet." **17.2 principal,** Dd[1] reads "tropical"; Bl[1], "tropik." **17.3–4 heved of Cancer,** one of the pointers on the riet, the head of Cancer represents the point where the sun enters Cancer, and always traces the circle of Cancer on the plate as the riet is revolved. **17.6 declinacioun,** the angle of difference between a celestial object and the equator. **17.8 Ptholome,** Ptolemy, astronomer from Alexandria, whose collected works were called the *Almagest* (*al,* Arabic "the"; *magest,* Greek "greatest"), elsewhere cited by Chaucer in *MilT* 1.3208, *WBT* 3.182–83 and 324–25, and *SumT* 3.2289. **17.9 23 degrees and 50 minutes,** imprecise; 23 degrees, 31 minutes (or about 23.5 degrees) is more accurate.

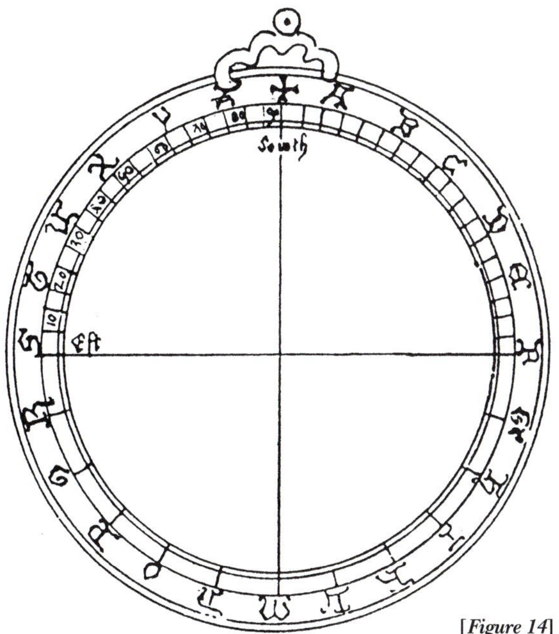

[*Figure 14*]

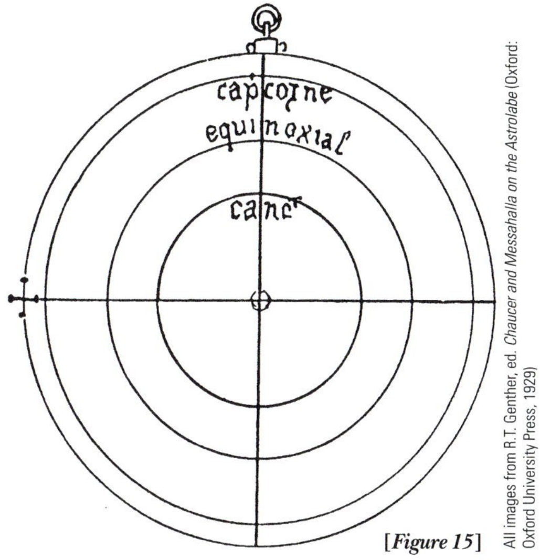

[*Figure 15*]

All images from R.T. Genther, ed. *Chaucer and Messahalla on the Astrolabe* (Oxford: Oxford University Press, 1929)

as in Capricorne. This signe of Cancre is cleped° the Tropik of Somer, of *tropos°*, that is to seyn "agaynward°", for thanne byginneth the sonne to passe fro usward°. And for the more declaracioun, lo here the figure. [*Figure 15*]

The middel cercle in wydnesse of thise 3 is cleped the Cercle Equinoxial, upon whiche turneth evermo the hedes of Aries and Libra. And understond wel that evermo this cercle equinoxial turnyth justly fro verrey est to verrey west as I have shewed the in the spere solide°. This same cercle is cleped also the Weyere° *(equator)* of the day, for whan the sonne is in the hevedes° of Aries and Libra, than ben the daies and the nyhtes illike° of lengthe in al the world. And therfore ben thise two signes called the Equinoxies. And alle that moevyth within the hevedes of thise Aries and Libra, his moeving is cleped northward; and alle that moevyth withoute thise hevedes, his moevyng is clepid sowthward as fro the equinoxial. Tak keep of° thise latitudes north and sowth, and forget it nat. By this cercle equinoxial ben considered the 24 howres of the clokke, for everemo the arisyng° of 15 degrees of the equinoxial maketh an howre equal of the clokke. This equinoxial is cleped the gyrdel° of the firste moevyng, or elles of the *angulus primi motus vel primi mobilis.* And *nota°* that firste moevyng is cleped moevyng of the firste moevable of the 8 spere, whiche moevyng is fro est to west, and eft agayn° into est. Also it is cleped gyrdel of the first moeving, for it departeth° the

17.11 cleped, *called,* **of *tropos,*** *from tropos* (Greek "turning") **17.12 agaynward,** *returning* **17.13 fro usward,** *away from us* **17.21 spere solide,** *globe* (see n.) **17.22 Weyere,** *weigher* (Latin *equator*) **17.23 hevedes,** *heads* **17.24 illike,** *equal* **17.31 Tak keep of,** *pay attention to* **17.35 arisyng,** i.e., the sun's rising **17.37 gyrdel,** *girdle* **17.39 *nota,*** *note* **17.42 eft agayn,** *thereafter back* **17.43 departeth,** *divides*

17.16 Cercle Equinoxial, the celestial equator; this ring on the astrolabe is equivalent to the imagined circle in the heavens where the plane of the world's equator meets the celestial sphere. See 1.16.8n. **17.20–21 as I have shewed the in the spere solide,** Chaucer apparently refers to earlier lessons that included the use of a globe, an armillary sphere, or a treatise on the sphere. Scholars have suggested that it is a reference to the treatise by Johannis de Sacrobosco, *De Sphaera* (*Concerning the Sphere*), to which Chaucer refers at 1.21.83 and which may influenced sections 26 and 39 of Part 2. **17.22 the Weyere *(equator)*,** the manuscripts provide this explanation in various ways. **17.24 nyhtes,** Dd[1] reads "nyht." **17.38–39 *angulus primi motus vel primi mobilis,*** angle of the prime mover or the prime movable. The distinction between prime mover and prime movable is the same as between agent and recipient: one moves, the other is moved. Eisner Variorum 251n reports that *angulus* was a recurrent misconstrual of *cingulus* (cincture or girdle). In place of the Latin phrase, the other manuscripts read "sonne" or "first moevable." **17.41 8 spere,** the sphere of the stars was usually thought to be set into motion by the Prime Mover of the ninth sphere, although more complicated models were suggested in the Middle Ages.

firste moevable, that is to seyn, the spere, in 2 ilike° parties evene distantz° fro the poles of this world.

The wydeste of thise 3 principal cerkles is cleped° the Cercle of Capricorne bycause that the heved° of Capricorne turneth evermo consentrik upon the same cercle. In the heved of this forseide Capricorne is the grettest declinacioun sowthward of the sonne, and therfor is it cleped the Solsticioun of Wynter. This signe of Capricorne is also cleped the Tropik of Wynter, for thanne bygynneth the sonne to come agayn to usward°. And for the more declaracioun, lo here thi figure. [*Figure 16*]

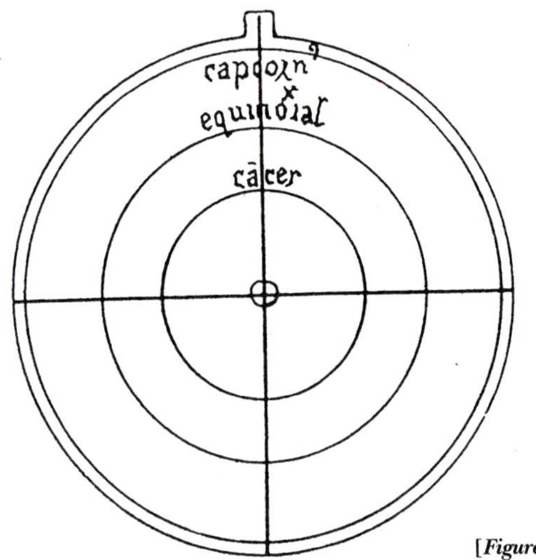

[*Figure 16*]

18. Upon this forseide plate ben compassed° certein cercles that hihten Almicanteras°, of which som of hem semen° perfit cercles, and somme semen inperfit. The centre that standith amiddes the narwest cercle° is cleped the Senith°. And the netherest° cercle, or the firste cercle, is clepid the Orisonte°, that is to seyn, the cercle that devydeth the two emysperies°, that is, the partie° of the hevene above the erthe and the partie benethe. Thise almykanteras ben compowned° by 2 and 2, albeit so that on divers° astrelabies some almykanteras ben devyded by on, and some by two, and somme by 3, after the quantite° of the astrelabie. This forseide cenyth is ymagened to ben the verrey° point over the crowne of thyn heved; and also this senyth is the verrey pool° of the orisonte in every regioun. And for the more declaracioun, lo here thi figure. [*Figure 17*]

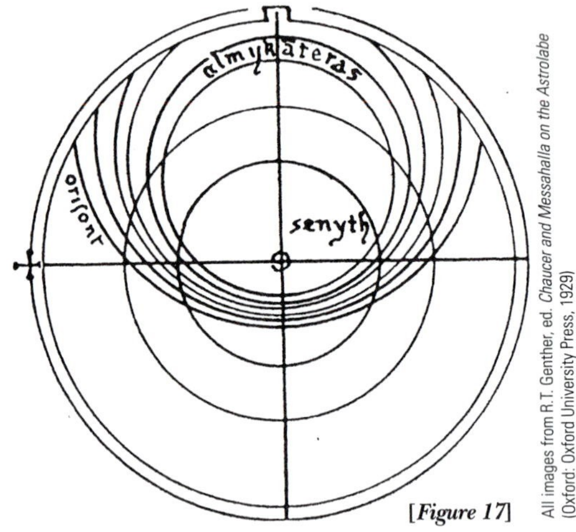

[*Figure 17*]

All images from R.T. Genther, ed. *Chaucer and Messahalla on the Astrolabe* (Oxford: Oxford University Press, 1929)

19. From this senyth, as it semeth, ther come a maner krokede strykes° lyke to the clawes° of a loppe°, or elles like to the werk of a womanes calle°, in kervyng overthwart° the almykanteras. And thise same strykes or divisiouns ben cleped Azymuthz°. And they devyden the orisonte of thin astrelabie in 24 devisiouns.

17.45 ilike, *equal,* **evene distantz,** *equally distant* **17.48 cleped,** *called* **17.49 heved,** *head* **17.56 to usward,** *toward us* **18.1 ben compassed,** *are drawn* **18.2 hihten Almicanteras,** *are called almucantars* (see n.) **18.3 semen,** *seem to be* **18.5 narwest cerle,** *smallest circle* **18.6 Senith,** *zenith,* **netherest,** *lowest* **18.7 Orisonte,** *horizon* **18.9 emysperies,** *celestial hemispheres,* **partie,** *portion* **18.11 compowned,** *constructed* **18.12 divers,** *various* **18.14 quantite,** *size* **18.16 verrey,** *precise* **18.17–18 verrey pool,** *true pole* **19.2 a maner krokede strykes,** *curved lines of a kind,* **clawes,** i.e., *legs* **19.3 loppe,** *spider* **19.4 calle,** *hairnet,* **kervyng overthwart,** *cutting across* **19.6 Azymuthz,** *azimuths* (see n.)

17.49 turneth, Dd[1] and Hv read "turnyd." **17.52 declinacioun,** see 1.17.6n. **18.2 Almicanteras,** almucantars, derived from Arabic: circles (and curved lines) on the astrolabe that measure the altitude of celestial objects. **18.6 Senith,** zenith, the point in the celestial sphere directly over the head of the observer; marked on the astrolabe at the center of the smallest of the almucantars. Should not be confused with the similar word of different meaning at 1.19.10, although the two have been conflated in the modern lexicon. **18.7 Orizonte,** the observer's horizon as it extends outward to the celestial sphere; on the astrolabe, the outermost of the almucantars. **18.11 compowned by 2 and 2,** refers to the fact that the almucantars on Chaucer's astrolabe indicate every two degrees of latitude; larger, more refined astrolabes indicate each degree. The six almucantars in figure 17 are not representative, and the zenith ("senyth") is not located precisely. Compare figure 18 where the "senyth" is more accurately indicated. **19.6 Azymuthz,** azimuths, derived from Arabic: lines on the astrolabe that extend from the zenith to points (or signets) on the horizon to mark where heavenly bodies rise.

And thise azimutz serven to knowe° the costes° of the firmament, and to othre conclusiouns, as for to knowe the cenyth° of the sonne and of every sterre. And for more declaracioun, lo here thi figure. [*Figure 18*]

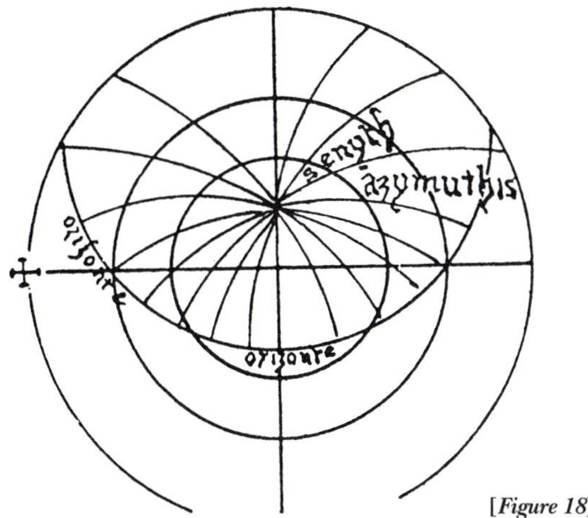

[*Figure 18*]

20. Next thise azymutz, under° the cercle of Cancer, ben ther 12 devysiouns embelif°, moche like to the shap of the azimutes, that shewen the spaces of the howres of planetes. And for mor declaracioun, lo here thi figure. [*Figure 19*]

21. The riet° of thine astrelabie with thy zodiak, shapen in maner of a net or of a lopwebbe° aftur the olde° descripcioun, which thow maist tornen up and doun as thyself liketh, conteneth certein nombre of sterres fixes°, with hir longitudes and latitudes determynat, yif so be that the makere° have nat erred. The names of the sterres ben writen in the margin of the riet ther as they sitte, of whiche sterres the smale poynt is cleped the Centre.

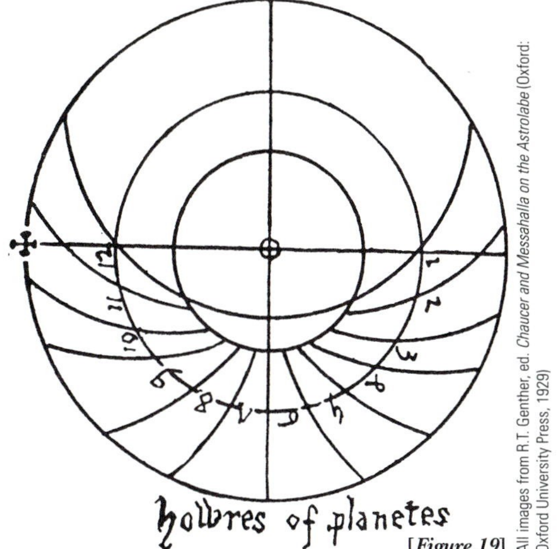

[*Figure 19*]

All images from R.T. Genther, ed. *Chaucer and Messahalla on the Astrolabe* (Oxford: Oxford University Press, 1929)

And understond also that alle sterres sittinge wythin the zodiak of thin astrolabie ben cleped sterres of the north, for they arysen by northe the est lyne. And alle the remenant fixed, out of the zodiak, ben cleped sterres of the sowth—but Y sey nat that they arysen alle by sowthe the est lyne; witnesse on Aldeberan and Algomeysa. Generally understond this rewle, that thilke° sterres that ben cleped sterres of the north arysen rather° than the degree of hir longitude, and alle sterres of the sowth arisen after the degre of hir longitude—this is to seyn, sterres fixed in thin astralabie. The mesure of this longitude of sterres is taken in the lyne eclyptik of hevene, under which lyne, whan that the sonne and the mone ben lyne-riht°, or elles in the superfice of° this lyne, than is the eclips of the sonne or of the mone, as Y shal declare, and ek the cause why. But sothly° the Ecliptik Lyne of thy

19.8 knowe, *locate* **19.9 costes,** *regions or sections* **19.10 cenyth,** *signet; the point on the horizon where a heavenly body rises* (see 1.18.6n and 1.19.6n) **20.1 under,** *below* **20.2 embelif,** *oblique* **21.1 riet,** *rete* (see 1.3.5, 1.14.3 and figure 2) **21.3 lop-webbe,** *spider web,* **olde,** *previous* **21.5 sterres fixes,** *fixed stars* **21.7 makere,** i.e., *maker of the astrolabe* **21.19 thilke,** *these* **21.20 rather,** *earlier* **21.27 lyne-riht,** *exactly in line* **21.27–28 in the superfice of,** *on the surface* (or edge) *of* **21.30 sothly,** *to be precise*

20.4 spaces of the howres of planetes, i.e., the "unequal hours"; see Part 2, section 12. **21.2 zodiak,** the small, circular portion of the rete represents (and is here called) the zodiac, a representation of the band in the celestial sphere within which the planets appear to move. **21.3 olde descripcioun,** see 1.3.5–6 and 1.19.2–3. **21.4 maist tornen,** the rete can be turned on the central axis. **21.8–9 margin of the riet,** not only the rim of the rete, but also the spoke-like arms of its tracery. **21.10 smale poynt,** for each of the stars named, the rete has a flame-shaped tongue of metal (see figure 2); the point of each tongue is called the center, which indicates the position of the star on the plate. **21.18 Aldeberan and Algomeysa,** stars south of the ecliptic but north of the equator. Bl[1] includes reference to three additional stars—"Menker, Algenze, Cor Leonis"—along with a marginal gloss that indicates these five stars were inscribed on the Merton College astrolabe. **21.24 this,** Bl[1] reads "the." **21.29 as Y shal declare,** information on the eclipses and their causes is not included, presumably planned for a later section.

zodiak is the owttereste bordure of thy zodiak, ther° the degrees ben marked.

Thy Zodiak of thine astralabie is shapen as a compas which that contieneth a large brede°, as aftur the quantite° of thine astralabie, in ensample° that the zodiak in hevene is ymagened to ben a superfice° contenyng a latitude of 12 degrees, wheras al the remenant of cercles in the hevene ben ymagined verrey° lynes withowte eny latitude. Amiddes this celestial zodiak is ymagined a lyne which that is cleped the Ecliptik Lyne, undur which lyne is evermo the way of the sonne. Thus ben ther 6 degrees of the zodiak on that on° side of the lyne, and 6 degrees on that other. This zodiak is devided in 12 principal devisiouns, that departen° the 12 signes. And, for the streitnes° of thin astrelabie, than is every smal devisioun in a signe departid by two degrees and two—I mene degrees contenyng 60 minutes. And this foreside hevenissh zodiak is cleped the Cercle of the Signes, or the Cercle of the Bestes, for *zodia* in langage of Grek sownyth° "bestes" in Latyn tonge. And in the zodiak ben the 12 signes that han° names of bestes, or elles for° whan the sonne entreth in any of the signes, he taketh the proprete of swich bestes; or elles for° that the sterres that ben there fixed ben disposed in signes of bestes, or shape like bestes, or elles whan the planetes ben under thilke° signes they causen us by hir influence operaciouns and effectes lik to the operaciouns of bestes.

And understonden also that whan an hot planete comyth into an hot signe, than encresseth his hete; and yif a planete be cold, thanne amenuseth° his coldnesse bycause of the hote signe. And by this conclusioun maystow take ensample in° alle the signes, be they moist or drye, or moeble or fix°, rekenyng the qualite of the planete as I first seide. And everich of thise 12 signes hath respecte to° a certein parcelle° of the body of a man and hath it in governance, as Aries hath thin heved°, and Taurus thy nekke and thy throte, Gemyni thyn armholes and thin armes, and so forth, as shal be shewed more pleyn in the 5 partie of this tretis. This zodiak, which that is part of the 8 spere, overkerveth° the equinoxial. And he overkerveth hym again in evene parties, and that on half declineth sowthward, and that other northward, as pleynly declareth the Tretis of the Spere. And for more declaracioun, lo here thi figure. [*Figure 20*]

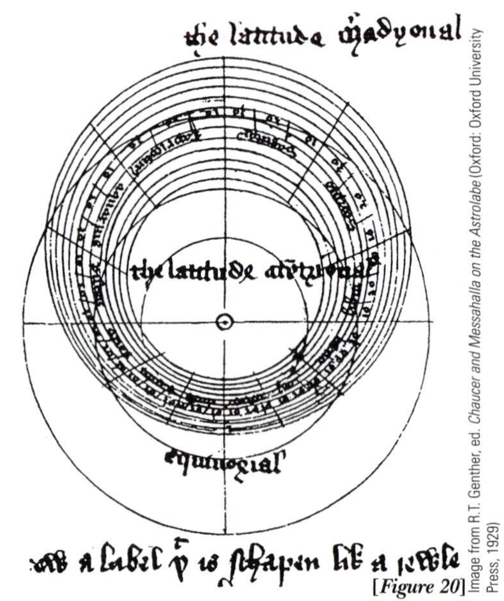

[*Figure 20*]

Image from R.T. Genther, ed. *Chaucer and Messahalla on the Astrolabe* (Oxford: Oxford University Press, 1929)

22. Thanne hastow a Label that is schapen lik a rewle, save that it is streit and hath no

21.32 ther, *where* **21.34 brede,** (circular) *band* **21.35 as aftur the quantite,** *in accord with the size* **21.36 in ensample,** *to represent* **21.37 superfice,** *geometric form* (i.e., a circular band) **21.39 verrey,** *genuine* **21.44 on,** *one* **21.47 departen,** *divide* **21.48 for the streitnes,** *because of the smallness* **21.53 sownyth,** *means* **21.55 han,** *have* **21.56 or elles for,** *either because* **21.58 or elles for,** *or else because* **21.61 thilke,** *these* **21.67 amenuseth,** *lessens* **21.69 ensample in,** *as an example of* **21.70 moeble or fix,** *mobile or fixed* **21.72 respecte to,** *correspondences with* **21.73 parcelle,** *part* **21.74 thin heved,** *your head* **21.79 overkerveth,** *cuts across*

21.33 Zodiak, i.e., the circular band that is part of the rete; see 1.21.2n. The width of this metal band varies with the size of the astrolabe, but in all cases it represents the northern half (6 of 12 degrees) of the celestial belt on which the planets appear to move. The outer edge of the metal band represents the ecliptic line (or path of the sun) that divides the celestial zodiac into two portions of 6 degrees each. **21.34 which,** Dd[1] reads "with." **21.38 wheras,** Dd[1] reads "where." **21.53** ***zodia,*** Latin *zodiacus* and English *zodiac* (by way of French *zodiaque*) derive ultimately from the Greek diminutive *zōidion* (depicted animal) and *kúklos* (circle of). **21.55 names of bestes,** the names of the signs of the zodiac derive (as asserted in 21.58–59) from the constellations with which they once corresponded; because of complex celestial motions, however, the correspondences are no longer apparent even though the names remain. **21.70 moeble or fix,** Eisner, Variorum 350n identifies the movable signs as Aries, Cancer, Libra, and Capricorn; the fixed, as Taurus, Leo, Scorpio, and Aquarius; and the remainder as neither. **21.77–78 the 5 partie of this tretis,** the fifth part of the treatise does not exist; see Prologue.80n. Apparently it would have included commonplace descriptions of correspondences between the zodiac and the human body. **21.83 Tretis of the Spere,** see 1.17.20–21n. **22.1–2 Label . . . lik a rewle,** the sighting bar on the back of the astrolabe, shaped like a ruler; see 1.13.1 and figure 21.

plates on either ende with holes. But with the smale point of the forseide label shaltow kalcule° thyne equaciouns in the bordure of thine astrolabie, as by thine almury. And for the more declaracioun, lo here thy figure. [*Figure 21*]

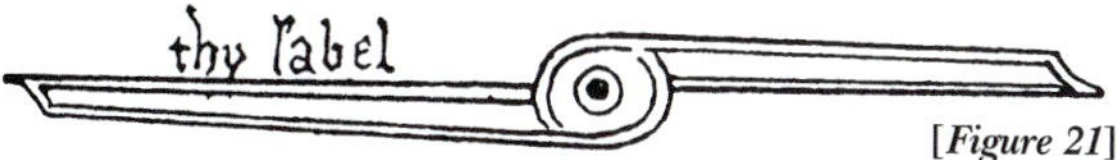

[*Figure 21*]

23. Thine almury is cleped the Denticle° of Capricorne, or elles the Kalculer. This same almury sit fix° in the hed of Capricorne, and it serveth of many a necessarie conclusioun in equaciouns of thynges, as shal be shewed. And for the more declaracioun, lo here thy figure. [*Figure 22*]

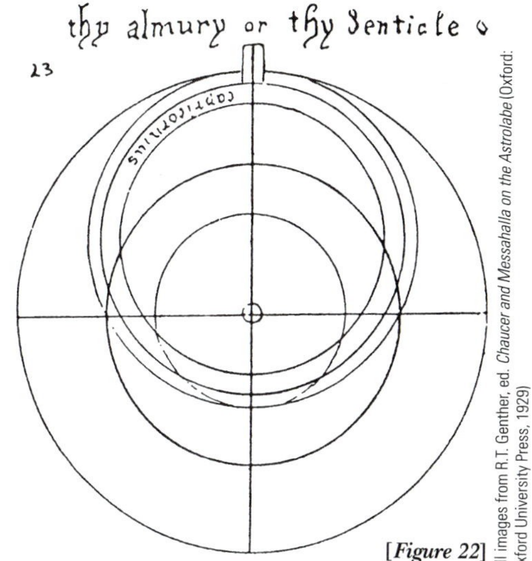

[*Figure 22*]

Her endith the descripcion of the astrelabie.

PART 2

Her bygynnen the conclusions of the astrelabie.

1. To fynde the degree in whych the sonne is day by day, after hir cours abowte.

Rekene° and knowe which is the day of thi monthe, and ley thi reule up° that same day, and thanne wol the verray point of thy rewle sitten in the bordure, upon the degree of thy sonne.

Ensample as thus°: the Yer of Oure Lord 1391, the 12 day of March at midday, I wolde° knowe the degree of the sonne. I sowhte in° the bak half of myn astrelabie and fond the cercle of the daies, the which I knowe by the names of the monthes writen undir the same cercle. Tho° leide I my rewle over this forseide day, and fond the point of my rewle in the bordure upon the firste degree of Aries, a litel within the degree. And thus knowe I this conclusioun.

Another day I wolde knowe the degree of my sonne, and this was at midday in the 13 day of Decembre. I fond the day of the monthe in maner as I seide. Tho leide I my rewle upon this forseide 13 day, and fond the point of my rewle in the bordure upon the first degree of Capricorne, a lite within the degree. And than hadde I of this conclusioun the ful experience. And for the more declaracioun, lo here thy figure.

22.4–5 shaltow kalcule, *you will calculate* **23.1 Denticle,** *tooth* **23.3 sit fixe,** *sits fixed* **Part 2 1.1 Rekene,** *calculate* **1.2 up,** *upon* **1.6 Ensample as thus,** *for example* **1.7 wolde,** *wanted to* **1.8 sowhte in,** *looked on* **1.12 Tho,** *then*

22.6 almury, indicator near the head of Capricorn. **Part 2 1b** ***hir,*** Bl[1], Rl[1], and Hv read *"his."* **1.7 1391, the 12 day of March,** March 12, 1391. The choice of year helps us to date the composition of *Astrolabe.* March 12 was the spring equinox in the Julian calendar (March 20 in the Gregorian calendar introduced into Europe in 1582, into England and its colonies in 1752). This is a basic, demonstrative calculation that positions the rule horizontally across the back of the astrolabe. **1.18–19 13 day of Decembre,** December 13 is the winter solstice in the Julian calendar; the rule is vertical on the back of the astrolabe. **1.26 lo here thy figure,** we have not included illustrations to Part 2 in this edition.

2. To knowe the altitude of the sonne, or of other celestial bodies.

Put the ring of thine astrelabie upon thy riht thowmbe, and turne thi lift side agayn° the light of the sonne, and remeve° thi rewle up and down til that the stremes of the sonne shyne thorgh bothe holes of thi rewle. Loke thanne how many degrees thy rewle is areised fro the litel crois upon thine est line, and take ther the altitude of thi sonne. And in this same wyse maistow° knowe by nyhte the altitude of the mone or of brihte sterres. This chapitre is so general ever in on° that ther nedith no more declaraeion, but forget it nat. And for the more declaracioun, lo here the figure.

3. To knowe every tyme of the day bi liht of the sonne, and every tyme of the nyht by the sterres fixe, and eke to knowe by nyht or by day the degree of any signe that assendeth on the est orisonte°, which that is cleped° communly the assendent, or elles oruscupum°.

Tak the altitude of the sonne whan the list°, as I have said; and set the degree of the sonne, in cas that it be byforn the middel of the day, among thyne almykanteras on the est side of thine astralabie; and yif it be after the middel of the day, set the degree of thy sonne upon the west side —take this manere of settyng for a general rewle, ones for evere°. And whan thow hast set the degree of thy sonne up° as many almykanteras of heyhte as was the altitude of the sonne taken by thi rewle, ley over thi label upon the degree of the sonne. And thanne wol the point of thi label siten in the bordure upon the verrey tid° of the day.

Ensample as thus: the Yer of Oure Lord 1391, the 12 day of March, I wold knowe° the tyd of the day. I tok the altitude of my sonne, and fond that it was 25 degrees and 30 of minutes of heyhte in the bordure on the bak syde. Tho turnede I myn astrelabie, and bycause that it was byforn midday, I turnede my riet and sette the degree of the sonne, that is to seyn, the I degree of Aries, on the right syde of myn astrolabie, upon that, 25 degrees and 30 of minutes of heyhte among myn almikanteras. Tho leide I my label upon the degree of my sonne, and fond the poynte of my label in the bordure upon a capital lettre that is cleped an X. Tho rekened I alle the capitalles lettres fro the lyne of midnyht unto this for seide lettre X, and fond that it was 9 of the clokke of the day. Tho loked I down upon the est orisonte, and fond ther the 20 degree of Gemynis assending, which that I tok for myn assendent. And in this wyse hadde I the experience for evermo in which maner I sholde knowe the tyde of the day, and ek myn assendent.

Tho wolde I wyte° the same nyht folwyng° the howr of nyht, and wrowhte° in this wyse: Among an hep of sterris fixe°, it liked me for to take the altitude of the feire white sterre that is cleped Alhabor°, and fond hir sitting on the west side of the line of midday, 18 degres of heyhte taken by my rewle on the bak syde. Tho sette I the centre of this Alhabor upon 18 degrees among myn almikanteras upon the west side, bycause that she was fonden on the west side. Tho leide I my label over the degree of the sonne that was descended under the weste orizonte, and rikened° alle the lettres capitals fro the lyne of midday unto the point of my label in the bordure; and fond that it was passed 8 of the clokke the

2.2 agayn, *toward* **2.3 remeve,** *move* **2.9 maistow,** *you can* **2.12 general ever in on,** *generally applicable* **3e orisonte,** *horizon,* **cleped,** *called* **3f *oruscupum,*** *horoscope* (see n.) **3.1–2 the list,** *you wish* **3.9 ones for evere,** *once and always* **3.10 up,** *upon* **3.15–16 verrey tid,** *precise time* **3.18 wold knowe,** *would like to know* **3.41 wyte,** *know,* **same nyht folwyng,** *following night* **3.42 wrowhte,** *worked* **3.43 hep of sterris fixe,** *group of fixed stars* **3.45 cleped Alhabor,** *named Sirius* (the Dog Star) **3.53 rikened,** *counted* (reckoned)

2.12 ever, Dd[1] reads "every." **3f *oruscupum,*** horoscope, but not our modern meaning of a star chart; here synonymous with "ascendant." **3.4 almykanteras,** almucantars, described in 1.18.2. **3.31 cleped an X,** called an "X,"one of the letters described in Part 1, section 16. **3.37 assendent,** a technical term; here the ascendant is the degree of the zodiac that is arising in the east at a particular moment. The term can also refer to the configuration of celestial bodies at the moment of a person's birth or a moment otherwise thought to be propitious in a person's life. Defined in 2.4.7–9. **3.40** Bl[1] includes here an additional passage about the locations of celestial bodies; see Eisner Variorum 440n. **3.41–59** Bl[1] gives a different set of readings for using the Dog Star to determine the time and ascendant, although the technique is the same. Some of the readings here from Dd[1] are corrections made on the manuscript. **3.48 centre,** the tip or point of the indicator; see the dog-head indicator of the Dog Star—figure 2, bottom center.

space of 2 degrees. Tho loked I doun upon myn est orisonte, and fond ther 23 degrees of Libra assending, whom I tok for myn assendent. And thus lerned I to knowe ones for ever in which manere I shuld come to the howr of the nyht and to myn assendent, as verreyli° as may be taken by so smal an instrument.

But natheles in general wolde I warne the for evere°, ne mak the nevere bold to have take a just° ascendent by thin astrolabie, or elles to have set justly a clokke, whan any celestial body by which that thow wenest governe thilke thynges ben ney° the sowth lyne. For trust wel, whan that the sonne is ney the meridional lyne, the degre of the sonne rennyth so longe consentrik° upon the almikanteras that sothly thow shalt erre fro the just assendent. The same conclusioun° sey I by° the centre of any sterre fix by nyht; and moreover, by experience I wot wel that in owre orisonte°, from xi of the clokke unto on° of the clokke, in takyng of a just assendent in a portatif° astrelabie, hit is to hard to knowe—I mene from xi of the clokke byforn the howre of noon til on of the clok next folwing. And for the more declaracion, lo here thi figure.

4. Special declaracion of the assendent.

The assendent sothly, as well in alle nativitez° as in questiouns and elecciouns° of tymes, is a thing which that thise astrologiens gretly observen. Wherfore me semeth convenient, sin that° I speke of the assendent, to make of it special declaracioun. The assendent sothly, to take it at the largeste°, is thilke degree that assendeth at any of thise forseide tymes upon the est orisonte. And therefor, yif that any planet assende at that same tyme in thilke forseide degree, than hath he no latitude fro the ecliptic lyne, but he is than in the degree of the ecliptic whiche that is the degree of his longitude. Men seyn that thilke planete is *in horoscopo*. But sothly, the hows° of the assendent, that is to seyn the firste hous or the est angle, is a thing more brod and large. For after the statutz° of astrologiens, what celestial body that is 5 degres above thilk degre that assendeth, or within that nowmbre, that is to seyn, ner the degree that assendeth, yit rikne thei° thilke planet in the assendent. And what planete that is under thilke degree that assendith the space of 15 degrees, yit sein thei° that thilke planete is lyk to him that is in the hows of the assendent. But sothly, yif he passe the bondes of thise forseide spaces, above or bynethe, they seyn that the planete is failling fro the assendent. Yit sein° thise astrologiens that the assendent, and eke the lord of the assendent, may be shapen° for to be fortunat° or infortunat°.

As thus: a fortunat assendent clepen they° whan that no wykkid planete, as Saturne or Mars, or elles the Tail of the Dragoun, is in the hows of the assendent, ne that no wikked planete have non aspecte° of enemyte upon the assendent. But they wol caste° that thei have a fortunat planete in hir assendent, and yit in his felicite°, and than sey they that it is wel.

3.62 verreyli, *accurately* **3.65 for evere,** *once and for all* **3.65–66 ne mak the nevere bold to have take a just,** *don't ever be so rash as to calculate a precise* **3.68–69 by which that thow wenest governe thilke thynges ben ney,** *by which you think to gauge such things is close to* **3.72 consentrik,** *in line with* (see n.) **3.74 conclusioun,** *result,* **by,** *about* **3.77 orisonte,** *horizon* (locale), **on,** *one* **3.79 portatif,** *portable* **4.1 nativitez,** *times of birth* **4.2 eleccioun s,** *selections* **4.5 sin that,** *since* **4.7 largeste,** *most general meaning* **4.17 hows,** *house* **4.19 statutz,** *rules* **4.23 yit rikne thei,** *they still consider* **4.26–27 yit sein thei,** *they say further* **4.31 Yit sein,** *further say* **4.33 shapen,** *ordained,* **fortunat,** *positive influence* **4.34 infortunat,** *negative influence* **4.35 clepen they,** *they call* (it) **4.39 aspecte,** *position* **4.40 caste,** *calculate* **4.42 felicite,** *favorable influence*

3.64 natheles, Bl[1], Rl[1], and Hv read "natheles this rule." **3.72 rennyth so longe consentrik,** when calculating the sun's position near the meridian (near noon; the sun is on the meridian at noon), the edge of the rete and the almucantar lines are so close together on the astrolabe (especially a small one) that measurements are unreliable. **4** This section is not in Massahalla. It pertains to astrology rather than astronomy, although the two were not clearly distinct in the Middle Ages; it describes the method for determining the sign of the zodiac and degree of that sign for any specific moment in time, usually a moment considered important or ominous. **4.7 largeste,** Dd[1] reads "largesse." **4.9 upon,** Dd[1] reads "un." **4.12–15 than hath . . . that is the degree of his longitude,** from Bl[1]; the other manuscripts omit or severely truncate. The ecliptic line (or path of the sun) divides the band of the zodiac in half. **4.16** ***in horoscopo,*** i.e., in the ascendant; see n. to 2.3f above. **4.26 15 degrees,** some editors emend to "25 degrees," although neither can be wholly correct since the number varies with the given astrological house. **4.27 is lyk,** Dd[1] reads "il like." **in,** omitted in most manuscripts; from Hv. **4.30 failling,** Bl[1], Rl[1], and Hv read "falling." **4.32–33 lord of the assendent,** the planet that governs a given "house" or segment of the heavens: the moon in Cancer, Mercury in Gemini and Virgo, Venus in Taurus and Libra, the sun in Leo, Mars in Aries and Scorpio, Jupiter in Sagittarius and Pisces, and Saturn in Capricorn and Aquarius. **4.37 Tail of the Dragoun,** the point where the moon passes the ecliptic descending southward. **4.41 fortunat planete,** Venus or Jupiter; the moon, the sun, and Mercury are neutral. As mentioned in 2.4.35–36, Saturn and Mars are negative.

Fortherover, they seyn that the infortunyng of an assendent is the contrarie of thise forseide thinges. The lord of the assendent sey they that he is fortunat whan he is in god place fro° the assendent as in angle, or in a succedent° whereas he is in his dignite and conforted with frendly aspectes of planetes and wel resceyved. And eke that he may sen the assendent, and that he be nat retrograd ne combust°, ne joigned with no shrewe° in the same signe, ne that he be nat in his descencioun°, ne joigned with no planete in his discencioun, ne have upon him non aspecte infortunat; and than sey they that he is wel.

Natheles, thise ben observauncez of judicial matiere° and rytes of paiens°, in which my spirit ne hath no feith, ne no knowyng of hir *horoscopum.* For they seyn that every signe is departed in 3 evene parties by 10 degrees, and thilke porcioun they clepe° a Face. And althogh that a planete have° a latitude fro the ecliptik, yit sey some folk so that° the planete aryse in that same signe wyth any degree of the forseide face in which his longitude is rekned, that yit is the planete *in horoscopo,* be it° in nativite or in eleccioun, &c. And for the more declaracioun, lo here the figure.

5. To knowe the verrey equacioun of the degree of the sonne, yif so be that it falle bytwixe thyn almikanteras.

For as moche as the almykanteras in thine astrelabie ben compownet° by two and two, whereas some almykanteras in sondry astrelabies ben compowned by on and on, or elles° by 2 and 2, it is necessarie to thy lernyng to teche the first to knowe and worke with thine owne instrument. Wherfor whan that the degree of thy sonne falleth bytwixe two almikanteras, or elles yif thine almykanteras ben graven° with over gret° a point of a compas° (for bothe thise thinges may causen errour as wel in knowyng of the tid° of the day as of the verrey° assendent), thow most werken in this wise: set the degree of thy sonne upon the heyer° almykanteras of bothe, and waite wel wheras° thine almury towcheth the bordure, and set ther a prikke of ynke. Set down agayn the degree of thy sonne upon the nethere° almykanteras of bothe, and set ther another prikke. Remewe° thanne thine almury in the bordure evene amiddes° bothe prikkes, and this wol lede justly° the degree of thi sonne to sitte bytwixe bothe almykanteras in his riht place. Ley thanne thy label over the degree of thy sonne, and find in the bordure the verrey tide° of the day or of the nyht. And as verreyly shaltow finde upon thyn est orisonte thyn assendent. And for more declaracioun, lo here thy figure.

6. To knowe the spring of the dawing° and the ende of the evening, the which ben called the two crepusculis°!

Set the nadir of° thy sonne upon 18 degrees of heihte among thyn almykanteras on the west side, and ley thy label on the degre of thy sonne, and thanne shal the poynt of thi label shewe the spryng° of day. Also set the nadair of thy sonne upon 18 degres of heyhte among thine almykanteras

4.46 god place fro, *good place relative to* **4.47 succedent,** *following* (see n.) **4.51 retrograde ne combust,** *moving neither contrary to nor too close to the sun* **4.52 shrewe,** *evil planet* **4.53 descencioun,** *descending in the zodiac* (losing influence) **4.57–58 judicial matiere,** *predictive matter* **4.58 rytes of paiens,** *practices of pagans* **4.62 clepe,** *call* **4.63 have,** *may have* **4.64 yit sey some folk so that,** *yet some people say that as long as* **4.67 be it,** *whether it is* **5.2 compownet,** *constructed* **5.5 or elles,** *rather than* **5.10 ben graven,** *are engraved* **5.11 over gret,** *too large,* **compas,** *engraving tool* **5.13 tid,** *time* **5.14 verrey,** *precise* **5.16 heyer,** *higher* **5.17 waite wel wheras,** *observe carefully where* **5.20 nethere,** *lower* **5.22 Remeve,** *move* **5.23 evene amiddes,** *halfway between* **5.24 lede justly,** *move precisely* **5.27 verrey tide,** *precise time* **6a** ***spring of the dawing,*** *beginning of the dawn* **6c** ***crepusculis,*** *times of twilight* **6.1 nadir of,** *the point on the ecliptic opposite to* **6.5 spryng,** *beginning*

4.47 angle . . . succedent, technical terms; the angles are the first, fourth, seventh, and tenth of the houses; the succedent are those that follow—the second, fifth, eighth, and eleventh. The other four houses are called "cadent." **4.48 dignite,** technical term; moment of heightened influence. **4.49 wel,** omitted in Dd[1]. **4.56 than,** omitted in Dd[1]. **4.57–60** Chaucer here rejects astrological prediction or fortune telling; the attitude is similar to the one expressed in *FranT* 5.1129–34, but different than those underlying *GP* 1.414–18 and *MLT* 2.295–308. **4.61 10,** omitted in Dd[1]. **4.62 Face,** technical term; one-third (i.e., ten degrees) of any sign of the zodiac. **4.66 his,** Dd[1] reads "is." **4.67 yit is,** Dd[1] reads "yit it is." **4.68 &c,** omitted in Bl[1] and Hv. **5.2 two and two,** an astrolabe with almucanters marked for each degree is more accurate than one marked for every two degrees, as is Lewis's. **5.15 of,** omitted in Dd[1]. **5.17 almury,** see figure 22. **5.26 label,** see figure 21.

on the est side, and ley over thy label upon the degree of the sonne, and with the point of thy label find in the bordure the ende of the evenyng, that is, verrey° nyht. The nadir of the sonne is thilke degree that is opposit to the degree of the sonne, in the 7 signe.

As thus: every degree of Aries bi ordre is nadir to every degree of Libra by ordre; and Taurus to Scorpion; Gemini to Sagittare; Cancer to Capricorne; Leo to Aquarie; Virgo to Pisces; and yif any degree in thi zodiak be dirk, his nadir shal declare him. And for the more declaracioun, lo here thy figure.

7. To knowe the arch° of the day, that some folk kallen the day artificial, from the sonne arising til hit go to reste.

Set the degree of thy sonne upon thine est orisenonte°, and ley thy label on the degree of the sonne, and at the poynt of thy label in the bordure set a prikke°. Turn thanne thy riet aboute til the degree of the sonne sit upon the west orisonte, and ley thy label upon the same degree of the sonne, and at the point of thy label set another prikke. Rekne thanne the quantitee of tyme in the bordure bytwixe bothe prikkes, and tak ther thin ark of the day. The remenant of the bordure under the orisonte is the ark of the nyht. Thus maistow rekne bothe arches, or every porcioun, of wheither° that the liketh°. And by this manere of wyrkyng maistow se how longe that any sterre fix° dwelleth above the erthe, fro tyme that he riseth til he go to reste. But the day natural, this is to seyn 24 houres, is the revolucioun of the equinoxial with as moche partie of the zodiak as the sonne of his propre moevinge passeth in the mene whyle. And for the more declaracioun, lo here thi figure.

8. To turn the howres inequales in° howres equales.

Knowe the nombre of the degrees in the howres inequales, and departe hem by 15, and tak ther thyn howres equales. And for the more declaracioun, lo here thy figure.

9. To knowe the quantite of the day vulgare°, that is to seyen, from spring of the day unto verrey nyht.

Know the quantite of thi crepusculis°, as I have tawht in the chapitre byforn, and adde hem to the arch of thy day artificial; and tak ther the space of alle the hole° day vulgar, unto verrey nyht. The same manere maistow worke to knowe the quantite of the vulgar nyht. And for the more declaracioun, lo here the figure.

10. To knowe the quantite of howres inequales by day.

Understond wel that thise howres inequales ben cleped howres of planetes, and understond wel that somtyme ben thei lengere by day than by nyht, and somtyme the contrarie. But understond wel that evermo generaly the howr inequal of the day with the howre inequal of the nyht contenen 30 degrees of the bordure, whiche bordure is evermo answering to the degrees of the equinoxial. Wherfor departe° the arch of the day artificial in 12, and tak ther the quantite of the howre inequal by day. And yif thow abate° the quantite of the howre inequal by daye owt of 30, than shal the remenant that leveth° performe° the howre inequal by nyht. And for the more declaracioun, lo here the figure.

6.11 verrey, *precise beginning of* **7a arch,** *arc* (see n.) **7.2 orisenonte,** *horizon* **7.4 set a prikke,** *make a mark* **7.14 or wheither,** *whichever* **7.15 the liketh,** *you wish* **7.17 sterre fix,** *fixed star* **8a in,** *into* **9a *vulgare*,** *artificial* (see Part 2, section 7). **9.1 crepusculis,** *times of twilight* **9.4 hole,** *entire* **10.10 departe,** *divide* **10.13 abate,** *subtract* **10.15 leveth,** *remains,* **performe,** *provide*

6.8 est, Dd[1] reads "west." **6.20** Dd[1] reads "is." **his, 7a *arch*,** arc; the length of the day, measured as the distance that the sun travels through the sky as it varies with the season; see section 2.13. This "artificial" day is distinguished from the "natural" day that is composed of 24 equal hours. **8a *houres inequales*,** the unequal hours are the time of daylight or nighttime on any given day divided by 12. **8.2 15,** fifteen degrees on the border of an astrolabe equals one hour on the clock. **9** Section nine is not in Massahalla. **9.2 the chapitre byforn,** i.e., Part 2, section 6. **10.4 than,** Dd[1] reads "&c." **10.6–7 day with the howre inequal of the,** omitted in Dd[1] and Hv by eyeskip. **10.9 answering,** Dd[1] reads "answerint."

11. To knowe the quantite of howres equales.

The quantite of howres equales, that is to seyn, the howres of the clokke, ben departed by 15 degrees alredy in the bordure of thin astralabie, as wel by nyht as by day, generaly for evere°. What nedeth more declaracioun? Wherfor°, whan the list° to know how manye howres of the clokke ben passed, or any part of any of thise howres that ben passed, or elles how many howres or partie of howres ben to come, fro swich a tyme to swych a tyme, by day or by nyhte, knowe the degree of thy sonne, and ley thy label on it. Turne thy riet abowte joyntly with thy label, and with the point of it rekne in the bordure fro the sonne arise unto the same place ther thow desirest, by day as by nyhte. This conclusioun wol I declare in the laste chapitre of the 4 partie of this tretis so openly that ther shal lakke no worde that nedeth to the declaracioun. And for the more declaracioun, lo here the figure.

12. Special declaracioun of the houres of planetes.

Understond wel that everemo fro arysing of the sonne til it go to reste, the nadir of° the sonne shal shewe the howre of the planete. And fro that tyme forward al the nyht til the sonne arise, than shal the verrey degree° of the sonne shewe the howre of the planete.

Ensample as thus: the 13 day of March fil upon a Saterday per aventure°, and at the arising of the sonne I fond the secounde degree of Aries sitting upon myn est orisonte, al be it that it was but lite°. Than fond I the 2 degree of Libra, nadir of my sonne, dessending on my west orisonte. Upon which west orisonte every day generally at the sonne ariste° entreth the howre of any planete, after which planete the day bereth his name, and endeth in the nexte strik of the plate under the forseide west orisonte. And evere, as the sonne clymbeth uppere and uppere, so goth his nadir downere and downere, techyng by swich strikes the howres of planetes by ordre as they sitten in the hevene. The first howre inequal of every Satterday is to Saturne; and the secounde to Jupiter; the 3 to Mars; the 4 to the Sonne; the 5 to Venus; the 6 to Mercurius; the 7 to the Mone; and thanne agayn the 8 is to Saturne; the 9 to Jupiter; the 10 to Mars; the 11 to the Sonne; the 12 to Venus. And now° is my sonne gon to reste as for that Setterday. Thanne sheweth the verrey degree of the sonne the howr of Mercurie entryng under my west orisonte at eve; and next him succedeth the Mone; and so forth by ordre, planete after planete, in howre after howre, al the nyht longe til the sonne arise. Now riseth the sonne that Sonday by the morwe, and the nadir of the sonne, upon the west orizonte, sheweth me the entring of the howre of the forseide sonne. And in this maner succedeth planete under planete, fro Saturne unto the Mone, and fro the Mone up agayn to Saturne, howre after howre generaly. And thus know I this conclusioun. And for the more declaracioun, lo here the figure.

13. To knowe the altitude of the sonne in middes of the day, that is cleped the altitude meridian.

Set the degree of the sonne upon the lyne meridional, and rikene how many degrees of

---

11.5 for evere, *at all times* **11.6 Wherfor,** *therefore,* **the list,** *you wish* **12.2 nadir of,** *the point on the sun's path opposite to* **12.5 verrey degree,** *apex* **12.8 per aventure,** *perhaps* **12.11 lite,** *little* (i.e., somewhat short of two degrees) **12.14 sonne ariste,** *sunrise* **12.29 now,** *at this time*

11.18–19 4 partie of this tretis, part four does not exist although it is described in the Prologue, 88–101. The numeral is omitted in Dd[1]. **11.19 ther,** omitted in Dd[1]. **12** Concerned with the astrological notion that the unequal hours of the day are governed by particular planets, section twelve is not in Massahalla. The planet for which the day is named governs the first unequal hour of the day, and each following unequal hour is dominated by the next planet, counting inward toward earth. In the example, the first unequal hour of Saturday (named for the planet) is dominated by Saturn, the next hour by Jupiter, and so on down to the seventh hour, dominated by the moon. Saturn again dominates the eighth hour, Jupiter the ninth, and so on. The idea is adapted for narrative purposes in *KnT* 1.2217ff., where the particular hours are auspicious times. The hours of the planets are marked on the lower half of the front plate of the astrolabe (see figure 19), so that the position of the sun after it sets below the horizon indicates the unequal hours at night, while its nadir indicates them during the day. **12.2 the sonne til,** Dd[1] omits "the." **12.8 upon a Saterday,** March 13 fell on Saturday in 1389 and again in 1395. **12.12 my sonne,** this idiomatic use of the possessive is used in 2.12.29, 25.39, and 39.9, and in *Equat* 342. **12.17 plate,** Bl[1] reads "planete." **12.31 howr of Mercurie,** in the given case, the thirteenth hour. **13b altitude meridian,** i.e., the highest ascent of the sun (or any star) on a given day. Sections 13–18 follow section 21 in several manuscripts. **13.1–2 lyne meridional,** the line from the top of the astrolabe to its center; it represents a celestial circle that passes through the point over an observer's head and the celestial poles; see 1.4.3–6.

almikanteras ben bytwixe thyn est orisonte and the degree of the sonne. And tak ther thyn altitude meridian, this is to seyne, the heiest of the sonne as for that day. So maistow knowe in the same lyne°, the heiest cours that any sterre fix° clymbeth by nyht; this is to seyn that whan any sterre fix is passed the lyne meridional, than byginneth it to descende, and so doth the sonne. And for the more declaracioun, lo here thy figure.

14. *To knowe the degree of the sonne by thy riet, for a maner curiosite°, &c.*

Sek bysily° with thi rewle the heiest of the sonne in midde of the day. Turne thanne thyn astrelabie, and with a prikke of ynk marke the nombre of that same altitude in the lyne meridional. Turne thanne thy ryet abowte til thow fynde a degree of thi zodiak acording with° the prikke, this is to seyn, sittynge on the prikke. And in soth, thow shalt fynde but 2 degrees in al the zodiak of that condicioun°, and yit thilke 2 degrees ben in diverse signes. Than maistow lyhtly° by the sesoun of the yer knowe the signe in which that is the sonne.

15. *To know which day is lik to which day as of lengthe, &c.*

Loke whiche degrees ben allik fer fro° the hevedes° of Cancer and Capricorn, and lok, whan the sonne is in any of thilke degrees, than ben the dayes ilike° of lengthe. This is to seyn, that as long is that day in that monthe as was swych a day in swich month°; ther varieth but lite. Also, yif yow take 2 daies naturaly in the yer ilike fer fro° eyther pointes of the equinoxial in the opposit parties, than as long is the day artificial of that on day as is the nyht of that othere, and the contrarie. And for the more declaracioun, lo here thi figure.

16. *This chapitre is a maner declaracioun to conclusiouns that folwen.*

Understond wel that thy zodiak is departid in 2 halfe cercles, as fro the heved of Capricorne unto the heved of Cancer, and agaynward fro the heved of Cancer unto the heved of Capricorne. The heved of Capricorne is the lowest point wheras the sonne goth in winter, and the heved of Cancer is the heyest point in whiche the sonne goth in somer. And therfor understond wel that any two degrees that ben ilike fer fro any of thise two hevedes, truste wel that thilke° two degrees ben of ilike declinacioun° be it sowthward or northward, and the daies of hem ben ilike of lengthe, and the nyhtes also, and the shadwes ilike, and the altitudes ilike at midday for evere°. And for more declaracioun, lo here thi figure.

17. *To knowe the verrey degree of any maner sterre straunge° or unstraunge after° his longitude, thow° he be indeterminat in° thine astralabie, sothly to the trowthe, thus he shal be knowe.*

Take the altitude of this sterre whan he is on the est side of the lyne meridional, as ney° as thow maist gesse°; and tak an assendent anon riht by som maner sterre fix which that thow knowest; and forget nat the altitude of the firste sterre, ne thyn assendent. And whan that this is don, espie° diligently whan this same firste sterre passeth anything° the sowth west-ward,

13.7 same lyne, i.e., *line meridian* **13.8 sterre fix,** *fixed star* **14b** ***for a maner curiosite,*** *just for curiosity's sake* **14.1 Sek bysily,** *seek carefully* **14.6–7 acording with,** *aligning with* **14.9 of that condicioun,** i.e., *that align with the reading on the meridian line* **14.11 maistow lyhtly,** *you can easily* **15.1 allik fer fro,** *equally distant from* **15.2 hevedes,** *heads* (i.e., beginnings; see 1.17.3–4n) **15.4 ilike,** *equal* **15.6 swych a day in swich month,** i.e., *the other day in the other month* **15.8 ilike fer fro,** *equally distant from* **16.11 thilke,** *these same* **16.12 declinacioun,** *angular distance from the equator* **16.15 for evere,** *always* **17b,** ***straunge,*** *unknown* (i.e., not shown on the rete), ***after,*** *with respect to* **17c** ***thow,*** *even if,* ***indeterminat in,*** *not plotted on* **17.2 ney,** *close* **17.4 gesse,** *estimate* **17.7 espie,** *watch* **17.8 passeth anything,** *passes to any extent to*

14.1 Sek bysily . . . heiest of the sonne, as is described in section 13. Section 14 reverses the procedure of 13, and editors have explained that it makes possible a check of the precision of the almucantar lines on a given astrolabe. **15.8–10 naturaly . . . artificial,** for the distinction between natural and artificial (applied both to days and to hours), see the note to Part 2.7a *arch.* **16** There is no calculation here, but a statement of information pertinent to sections 13–15; the heading indicates that perhaps it should precede them. **16.4 of Cancer,** Dd[1] reads "of the Cancer." **16.12 ilike,** Dd[1] reads "ilke." **17** As editors have pointed out, the methods here for determining the positions of celestial bodies are erroneous, in part due to a confusion of latitude and declination and in part because the notion of celestial longitude used here is not sufficiently specific; see Eisner Variorum, notes to Conclusion 17. **17.3 tak an assendent,** as described in Part 2.3.

and cacche him anon riht in the same nowmbre of altitude on the west side of this lyne meridional as he was kawht on the est side. And tak a newe assendent anon riht by som maner sterre fixe which that thow knowest; and forget nat this secounde assendent. And whan that this is don, rikne° thanne how manye degrees ben bytwixe the firste assendent and the seconde assendent, and rikne wel the middel degree bytwyne bothe assendentes, and set thilke middel degree upon thin est orisonte. And waite° thanne what degre that sit upon the lyne meridional, and tak ther the verrey degre of the ecliptik in which the sterre stondeth for the tyme. For in the ecliptik is the longitude of a celestial body rekened, evene fro the hed of Aries unto the ende of Pisces. And his latitude is rikned after° the quantite of his declinacion, north or sowth towarde the poles of this world.

As thus: yif it be of the sonne or of any fix sterre, rekene his latitude or his declinacioun fro the equinoxial cercle; and yif it be of a planete, rekne than the quantite of his latitude fro the ecliptik lyne. Al be it so that fro the equinoxial may the declinacion or the latitude of any body celestial be rikned, after the site° north or south, and after the quantite of his declinacion. And riht so may the latitude or the declinacion of any body celestial (save only of the sonne, after his site north or sowth, and after the quantite of his declinacioun) be rekned fro the ecliptik lyne, fro which lyne alle planetes som tyme declinen north or sowth, save only the forseide sonne. And for the more declaracioun, lo here thi figure.

18. To knowe the degrees of the longitudes of fixe sterres after that they ben determinant in thine astrolabie, yif so be that they ben trewly set.

Set the centre° of the sterre upon the lyne meridional, and tak kep of° thi zodiak, and loke° what degree of any signe that sit on the same lyne meridional at that same tyme, and tak the degree in which the sterre standeth; and with that same degree comth that same sterre unto that same lyne° fro the orisonte. And for more declaracioun, lo here thi figure.

19. To knowe with which degree of the zodiak any sterre fixe in thine astrelabie ariseth upon the est orisonte, althey° his dwellyng be in another signe.

Set the centre of the sterre upon the est orisonte, and loke° what degre of any signe that sit upon the same orisonte at that same tyme. And understond wel that with that same degre ariseth that same sterre. And thys merveyllous arising with a strange° degree in another signe is bycause that the latitude of the sterre fix is either north or sowth fro the equinoxial°. But sothly, the latitudes of planetes ben comunly rekned fro the ecliptik°, bicause that non of hem declineth but fewe degrees owt fro the brede° of the zodiak. And tak god kep° of this chapitre of arising of the celestial bodies. For truste wel that neyther mone° ne sterre as in owre embelif° orisonte ariseth with that same degree of his longitude, save in o cas, and that is whan they have no latitude fro the ecliptik lyne. But natheles, som tyme is everiche of thes planetes under the same lyne. And for more declaracioun, lo here thi figure.

20. To knowe the declinacioun° of any degree in the zodiak fro the equinoxial cercle, &c.

Set the degree of any signe upon the lyne meridional, and rikne his altitude in almykanteras fro the est orizonte up to the same degree set in the forseide lyne, and set ther a prikke°. Turne up thanne thy riet, and set the heved of Aries or Libra in the same meridional lyne, and set ther another prikke. And

17.15 rikne, *calculate* **17.20 waite,** *observe* **17.26 after,** *with respect to* **17.36 site,** *position* **18.1 centre,** *pointer* (see n.) **18.2 tak kep of,** *pay attention to,* **loke,** *observe* **18.7 same lyne,** i.e., *the line meridian* **19c** ***althey,*** *although* **19.2 loke,** *observe* **19.6 strange,** *different* **19.9 equinoxial,** *celestial equator* (see 1.16.8n) **19.11 ecliptik,** *path of the sun* **19.12 brede,** *band* **19.13 tak god kep,** *pay good attention* **19.15 mone,** *moon,* **embelif,** *oblique* (i.e., off of the horizontal line that marks the east-west horizon on the astrolabe) **20a declinacioun,** *angle of distance* **20.5 prikke,** *mark*

17.9 cacche, Dd[1] reads "hath." **17.25 hed of Aries unto the ende,** Dd[1] reads "hed of the Aries unto ende." **17.39 save only of the sonne,** because the path of sun *is* the ecliptic, by definition it cannot decline or deviate from it; the declension of the sun is measured from the celestial equator. **18.1 centre,** the end or point of a given star-indicator on the rete; see 1.21.10. **18.3 on,** Dd[1] reads "vn." **19** This section is not in Massahalla.

whan that this is don, considere the altitudes of hem bothe; for sothly the difference of thilke altitudes is the declinacion of thilke degre fro the equinoxial. And yif so be that thilke degree be northward fro the equinoxial, than is his declinacion north; yif it be sowthward, than is it sowth. And for the more declaracioun, lo here thi figure.

21. To knowe for what latitude in any regioun the almikanteras of any table ben compowned°.

Rikne how manye degrees of almikanteras in the meridional lyne be fro the cercle equinoxial unto the senith°, or elles fro the pool artik° unto the north orisonte; and for so gret a latitude or for so smal a latitude is the table° compowned. And for more declaracion, lo here thi figure.

22. To knowe in special the latitude of owre countray°—I mene after the latitude of Oxenford—and the heyhte of owre pol°.

Understond wel that as fer is the heved of Aries or Libra in the equinoxial from owre orisonte° as is the senyth from the pole artik; and as hey° is the pol artik fro the orisonte° as the equinoxial is fer fro the senyth. I prove it thus by the latitude of Oxenford. Understond wel that the heyhte of owre pool artik fro owre north orisonte is 51 degrees and 50 minutes; than is the senyth from owre pool artik 38 degrees and 10 minutes; than is the equinoxial from owre senyth 51 degrees and 50 minutes; than is owre south orisonte from owre equinoxial 38 degrees and 10 minutes. Understond wel this reknyng. Also forget nat that the senyth is 90 degrees of heyhte fro the orisonte, and owre equinoxial is 90 degrees from owre pool artik. Also this shorte rewle is soth°, that the latitude of any place in a regioun is the distance fro the senyth unto the equinoxial. And for more declaracioun, lo here thi figure.

23. To prove evidently° the latitude of any place in a regioun by the preve° of the heyhte of the pol artik in that same place.

In some wynters nyht, whan the firmament is clere and thikke-sterred, waite a tyme til that any sterre fix sit lyne-riht perpendiculer° over the pol artik°, and clepe° that sterre A. And wayte another sterre that sit lyne-riht under A, and under the pol, and clepe that sterre F. And understond wel that F is nat consideret but only° to declare that A sit evene° overe the pool. Take thanne anon riht° the altitude of A from the orisonte, and forget it nat. Lat A and F go farwel° til agayns the dawenyng° a gret while, and come thanne agayn, and abid til° that A is evene under the pol and under F. For sothly, than wole F sitte over the pool, and A wol sit under the pool. Tak than eft sones° the altitude of A from the orisonte, and note as wel his secounde altitude as his firste altitude. And whan that this is don, rikne how manye degrees that the firste altitude of A excedeth his seconde altitude, and tak half thilke porcioun that is exceded, and adde it to his seconde altitude. And tak ther° the elevacioun of thy pool, and eke the latitude of thy regioun. For thise two ben of a nombre°; this is to seyn, as many degrees as thy pool is elevat, so michel° is the latitude of the regioun.

Ensample as thus: par aventure° the altitude of A in the evening is 56 degrees of heyhte. Than wol his seconde altitude or the dawing° be 48; that is 8 lasse than 56, that was his firste altitude at even. Tak thanne the half of 8

21b compowned, *calibrated* **21.3 senith,** *zenith* (see 1.18.6n), **pool artik,** *north pole of the celestial sphere* **21.5 table,** *plate* (see n.) **22b countray,** *region* **22c pol,** *pole* (i.e., the north pole of the celestial sphere) **22.3 orisonte,** (south point of the) *horizon* **22.4 hey,** *high,* **orisonte,** (north point of the) *horizon* **22.18 soth,** *true* **23a evidently,** *unmistakably* **23b preve,** *calculation* **23.3 lyne-riht perpendiculer,** *straight-line directly* **23.3–4 pol artik,** *north celestial pole* **23.4 clepe,** *call* **23.7–8 but only,** *except* **23.8 evene,** *exactly* **23.9 anon riht,** *immediately* **23.10–11 Lat A and F go farwel,** *let A and F do as they will* **23.11 til agayns the dawenyng,** *until the coming of dawn* **23.12 abid til,** *wait until* **23.15 eft sones,** *again* **23.22 tak ther,** *conclude from that* **23.24 ben of a nombre,** i.e., *are equal* **23.26 michel,** *much* **23.27 par aventure,** *perhaps* **23.29 or the dawing,** *before the dawn*

20.12–14 northward . . . sowthward, degrees indicated on the plate by the inside of the circle of signs are north and those outside the circle are south; also recorded as plus (north) and minus (south). **21.5 table,** i.e., the incised plate which displays the equator, almucantars, etc. **22** Sections 22–23 are not in Massahala; sections 22–25 offer different methods of determining the same thing—the altitude of the north celestial pole at a given location (here Oxford), which is equal to the latitude of that location and others that are on the same meridian. **22c *Oxenford,*** Oxford, the location for which Chaucer's astrolabe is constructed; see Prologue 11. **22.4 as hey is,** Dd[1] reads "as hey as." **22.9 38,** here and at 22.13 Bl[1] reads "39." **23.1 wynters nyht,** "The night must be in winter so that a star may be visible at the beginning and end of a twelve-hour interval" (Eisner Variorum 833n). **23.19 that,** Dd[1] reads "that wel." **23.23 latitude,** Bl[1], Dd[1], and Rl[1] read "altitude." **23.30 8,** omitted in Dd[1]; Bl[1] reads "8 degrees."

and adde it to 48, that was his seconde altitude, and than hastow 52. Now hastow the heyhte of thy pol, and the latitude of the regioun. But understond wel that to prove this conclusioun and many another fair conclusioun, thow most have a plomet° hanging on a lyne heyer than thin heved on a perche°, and thilke lyne mot° hange evene perpendiculer° bytwixe the pool and thine eye. And thanne shaltow sen yif A sitte evene over the pool and over F at evene, and also yif F sitte evene over the pool and over A or° day. And for more declaracion, lo here thi figure.

24. Another conclusioun° to prove the heyhte of the pool artik fro the orisonte.

Tak any sterre fixe that nevere dissendeth under the orisonte in thilke regioun, and considere his heiest altitude and his lowest altitude fro the orisonte; and make a nombre of° bothe thise altitudes. Tak thanne and abate° half that nombre, and tak ther° the elevacioun of the pol artik in that same regioun. And for more declaracioun, lo here thi figure.

25. Another conclusioun to prove the latitude of the regioun, &c.

Understond wel that the latitude of any place in a regioun is verreyly° the space° bytwixe the senyth° of hem that dwellen there and the equinoxial cerkle°, north or sowthe, takyng the mesure in the meridional lyne, as sheweth in the almykanteras of thine astrelabie. And thilke space is as moche as the pool artik is hey in the same place fro the orisonte. And than is the depressioun° of the pol antartik°, that is to seyn, than is the pol antartik bynethe the orisonte the same quantite of space, neither more ne lasse. Thanne, yif thow desire to knowe this latitude of the regioun, tak the altitude of the sonne in the middel of the day, whan the sonne is in the hevedes° of Aries or of Libra (for thanne moeveth the sonne in the lyne equinoxial), and abate° the nombre of that same sonnes altitude owt of 90, and thanne is the remenaunt of the noumbre that leveth° the latitude of the regioun.

As thus: I suppose that the sonne is thilke day at noon 38 degrees and 10 minutes of heyhte. Abate thanne thise degrees and minutes owt of 90; so leveth there 51 degrees and 50 minutes, the latitude. I sey nat this but for ensample, for wel I wot° the latitude of Oxenforde is certein minutes lasse, as I myhte prove. Now yif so be that the semeth to long° a taryinge° to abide til° that the sonne be in the hevedes of Aries or of Libra, thanne waite° whan the sonne is in any other degree of the zodiak, and considere the degree of his declinacion fro the equinoxial lyne. And yif it so be that the sonnes declinacion be northward fro the equinoxial°, abate thanne° fro the sonnes altitude at noon the nombre of his declinacion, and thanne hastow the heyhte of the hevedes of Aries and Libra.

As thus: my sonne is par aventure° in the firste degre of Leoun 58 degrees and 10 minutes of heyhte at noon, and his declinacion is almost 20 degrees northward fro the equinoxial. Abate thanne thilke 20 degrees of declinacion owt of the altitude at noon; than leveth thee° 38 degrees and odde° minutes —lo ther the heved of Aries or Libra, and thyn equinoxial in that regioun. Also yif so be that the sonnes declinacioun be sowthward fro the equinoxial, adde thane thilke declinacion to the altitude of the sonne at noon;

23.37 plomet, *weight* **23.38 on a perche,** *from a horizontal rod* **23.39 mot,** *must,* **evene perpendiculer,** *exactly straight* **23.43 or,** *before* **24a conclusioun,** *calculation* **24.4 make a nombre of,** *add together* **24.5 abate,** *subtract* **24.6 tak ther,** *conclude from that* **25.2 verreyly,** *precisely,* **space,** *angular distance* **25.3 senyth,** *point overhead* **25.4 equinoxial cercle,** *celestial equatorial circle* **25.9 depressioun,** *"descent"* (i.e., opposite of altitude), **pol antartik,** *south celestial pole* **25.15 hevedes,** *head* **25.17 abate,** *subtract* **25.19 leveth,** *remains* **25.26 wot,** *know* **25.28 the semeth to,** *it seems to you too long,* **taryinge,** *delay* **25.29 abide til,** *wait until* **25.30 waite,** *observe* **25.35 equinoxial,** *celestial equator,* **abate thanne,** *subtract then* **25.39 par aventure,** *perhaps* **25.45 leveth thee,** *remains to you,* **odde,** *a few leftover*

23.37 plomet hanging on a lyne, the plumb-line enables the observer to gauge when the sample star A is directly above or below the celestial pole, used instead of or in conjunction with star F for alignment. The pole itself cannot be sighted in the sky, so its altitude is here determined by finding the mean between the maximum and minimum altitudes of a star that appears to circle it nearby. **25.3 the,** omitted in Bl[1], Dd[1], and Rl[1]. **25.15 is in the hevedes of Aries or of Libra,** i.e., on the celestial equator. **25.22 and 10 minutes,** Bl[1] reads "and 25 minutes"; omitted in Hv and Rl[1]. **25.27 is certein minutes lasse, as I myhte prove,** the manuscripts vary here, and editors comment on the fact that the latitude of Oxford is actually 51° 45'. **25.40–41 and 10 minutes,** other manuscripts read "and 17 minutes" or omit the numeral.

and tak ther the hevedes of Aries and Libra, and thyn equinoxial. Abate thanne the heyhte of the equinoxial owt of 90 degrees, and thanne leveth there the distans of the pole 51 degrees and 50 minutes of that regioun fro the equinoxial. Or elles, yif the lest°, take the heiest altitude fro the equinoxial of any sterre fix that thow knowest, and tak his nethere elongacioun lengthing° fro the same equinoxial lyne, and wirke in the maner forseid. And for more declaracion, lo here thi figure.

26. *Declaracioun of the assencioun of signes, &c.*

The excellence of the sper solide, amonges other noble conclusiouns, sheweth manifeste the diverse assenciouns of signes in diverse places, as wel° in the rihte cercle as in the embelif cercle°. Thise auctours writen that thilke signe is cleped° of riht ascensioun with which more part of the cercle equinoxial and lasse part of the zodiak ascendeth; and thilke signe assendeth embelif with whiche lasse part of the equinoxial and more part of the zodiak assendeth. Fertherover° they seyn that in thilke cuntrey° where as the senith of hem that dwellen there is in the equinoxial lyne, and her orisonte passing by the two poles of this worlde, thilke folke han this riht cercle and the riht orisonte.

And everemo the arch of the day and the arch of the niht is ther ylike long°, and the sonne twyes every yer passinge thorow the cenyth of her heved; and 2 someres and 2 wynteres in a yer han this forseide poeple. And the almykanteras in her astrolabies ben streyhte as a lyne, so as sheweth in this figure. The utilite to knowe the assenciouns in the rihte cercle is this: truste wel that by mediacioun of thilke assenciouns thise astrologiens by hir tables and hir instrumentz knowen verreyly the assencioun of every degree and mynut° in al the zodiak, as shal be shewed. And *nota* that this forseid rihte orisonte, that is cleped *orison rectum,* divideth the equinoxial into riht angles; and the embelif orisonte, wheras the pol is enhansed° upon the orisonte, overkerveth° the equinoxial in embelif angles, as sheweth in the figure. And for the more declaracioun, lo here the figure.

27. *This is the conclusioun to knowe the assenciouns of signes in the riht cercle, that is, circulus directus, &c.*

Set the heved of what signe the liste° knowe his assending in the riht cercle upon the lyne meridional, and waite° wher thine almury° towcheth the bordure, and set ther a prikke. Turne thanne thy riet westward° til that the ende of the forseide signe sitte upon the meridional lyne, and eft sones° waite wher thin almury towcheth the bordure, and set ther another prikke. Rikne° thanne the nombre of degrees in the bordure bytwyxe bothe prikkes, and tak the assencioun of the signe in the riht cercle°. And thus maystow wyrke with every porcioun of thy zodiak, &c. And for the more declaracioun, lo here thy figure.

28. *To knowe the assencions of signes in the embelif cercle in every regioun, I mene in circulo obliquo.*

Set the heved of the signe which as the list° to knowe his ascensioun upon the est orisonte, and

---

25.56 yif the lest, *if you wish* **25.58–59 nethere elongacioun lengthing,** *angular distance extending downwards* **26.4 as wel,** *both* **26.4–5 rihte cercle . . . embelif cercle,** *right circle* (the equator, i.e., zero latitude) . . . *oblique circle* (i.e., latitudes other than the equator) **26.6 cleped,** *called* **26.11 Fertherover,** *furthermore* **26.12 cuntrey,** *region* (i.e., on the equator) **26.18 is ther ylike long,** *are in that region the same length* **26.28 mynut,** *minute* **26.33 enhansed,** *raised,* **overkerveth,** *intersects* **27.1 the liste,** *you wish* **27.3 waite,** *observe,* **almury,** *pointer* (see 1.23.1) **27.5 westward,** *clockwise* **27.7 eft sones,** *again* **27.9 Rikne,** *count* **27.11–12 riht cercle,** *equator* **28a embelif,** *oblique* **28.1 the list,** *you wish*

25.54 pole 51, Dd[1] reads "pole an that 51." **26** Not in Massahalla, this section develops material found in Part 2, section 4; perhaps developed with reference to Johannis de Sacrobosco; see 1.17.20–21n. **26.1 sper solide,** see 1.17.20–21n. **26.6–11 cleped of riht ascensioun . . . ascendeth,** signs of right (or direct) ascension are those that take a longer time to rise in the east than do the signs of oblique ascension; the length of time varies because, from the observer's point of view, the signs of right ascension ascend more vertically. **26.11–16 Fertherover . . . riht orisonte,** from Bl[1]; omitted in Dd[1], Rl[1], Hv, and most other manuscripts. **26.20 2 someres and 2 wynteres,** this description of the equatorial tropics is essentially accurate in that there are two dry seasons and two wet seasons. Dd[1] reads "2 someres and 2 the wynteres." **26.22 almykanteras in her astrolabies ben streyhte,** i.e, the almucantars on astrolabes constructed for people living on the equator will be straight. Critics agree that the horizon line is straight on such an astrolabe, but point out that the almucantars would be circular. **26.24 assenciouns,** Bl[1], Hv, and Rl[1] read "assenciouns of signes." **26.29 zodiak,** Bl[1], Hv, and Rl[1] read "zodiak in the embelif cercle." **26.30 rihte orisonte,** horizon at the equator. **26.33 enhansed,** Dd[1] reads "enhawsed."

waite° wher thyn almury towcheth the bordure, and set ther a prikke. Turne thanne thy riet upward til that the ende of the same signe sitte upon the est orisonte, and waite eft sones° wher as thine almury towcheth the bordure, and set ther another prikke. Rikne thanne the nowmbre of degrees in the bordure bytwyxe bothe prikkes, and tak ther the assencioun of the signe in the embelif cercle. And understond wel that alle signes in the zodiak, fro the heved of Aries unto the ende of Virgo, ben cleped° signes of the north fro the equinoxial; and these signes arisen bytwyxe the verrey est and the verrey north in owre orisonte° generaly forevere. And alle signes fro the heved of Libra unto the ende of Pisces ben cleped signes of the sowth fro the equinoxial; and thise signes arisen evermo bytwyxe the verrey est and the verrey sowth in owre orisonte. Also every signe bytwixe the heved of Capricorne unto the ende of Geminis ariseth on owre orisonte in lasse than 2 howres equales; and thise same signes, fro the heved of Capricorne unto the ende of Geminis, ben cleped "tortuous° signes" or "kroked° signes," for they arisen embelif° on oure orisonte; and thise krokede signes ben obedient to° the signes that ben of riht assencioun. The signes of riht assencioun ben fro the heved of Cancer to the ende of Sagittare; and thise signes arisen more upriht, and they ben called ek sovereyn signes; and everich of hem ariseth in more space than in to° howres. Of which signes, Gemini obeieth to Cancer; and Taurus to Leo; Aries to Virgo; Pisces to Libra; Aquarius to Scorpioun; and Capricorne to Sagittare. And thus evermo 2 signes that ben ilike fer fro° the heved of Capricorne obeien everich of hem til other. And for more declaracioun, lo here the figure.

29. To knowe justly° the foure quarters of the world, as est, west, north, and sowth.

Tak the altitude of thy sonne whan the list, and note wel the quarter of the world in which the sonne is for the tyme by the azymutz°. Turne the thanne thine° astrolabie, and set the degree of the sonne in the almikanteras of his altitude on thilke° side that the sonne stant°, as is the manere in taking of howres; and ley thy label° on the degree of the sonne, and rikene how many degree of the bordure ben bytwixe the lyne merdional and the point of thy label; and note wel that nowmbre. Turne thanne agayn thyn astralabie, and set the poynt of thy gret rewle°, ther thow takest thyne altitudes, upon as many degrees in his bordure fro his meridional as was the point of thy label fro the lyne meridional on the wombe side°. Tak thanne thyn astrolabie with bothe handes sadly and slely°, and lat the sonne shyne thorow bothe holes of thy rewle; and sleyly in thilke shynynge lat thyn astrelabie kowch adown evene° upon a smothe grond, and thanne wol the verrey lyne merydional of thyn astrolabie lye evene° sowth, and the est lyne wole lye est, and the west lyne west, and north lyne north, so that° thow werke softly and avisely° in the cowching; and thus hastow the 4 quarters of the firmament. And for the more declaracioun, lo here the figure.

30. To knowe the altitude of planetes fro the wey° of the sonne, whether so they be north or sowth fro the forseide wey.

Lok whan that a planete is in the lyne meridional, yif that hir° altitude be of the same heyhte that is the degree° of the sonne for that day, and than is the planete in the verrey wey of the

28.3 waite, *observe* **28.6 eft sones,** *again* **28.14 cleped,** *called* **28.16 orisonte,** *horizon* **28.27 tortuos,** *bent,* **kroked,** *crooked* **28.28 embelif,** *oblique* **28.29 ben obedient to,** *correspond to* (see n.) **28.35 to,** *two* **28.39 ilike fer from,** *equally far from* **29a** ***justly,*** *accurately* **29.3 azymutz,** *azimuths* (see figure 18) **29.3–4 Turne the thanne thine,** *then turn your* **29.6 thilke,** *that* **29.7 stant,** *stands* **29.8 label,** *indicator* (see figure 21) **29.13 rewle,** *sighting bar* (see figure 11) **29.17 wombe side,** *front side* (described in 1.3.1–4) **29.18 sadly and slely,** *steadily and carefully* **29.21 kowch adown evene,** *be laid down flat* **29.23 evene,** *precisely* **29.25 so that,** *as long as* **29.26 avisely,** *deliberately* **30a** ***wey,*** *path* (see n.) **30.2 hir,** *its* **30.3 degree,** *noon-time altitude*

28.4 set ther, from Rl[1]. Dd[1] reads "ther"; Bl[1] and Hv "ther set." **28.15 these,** Bl[1] and Dd[1] read "the." **28.29 ben obedient to,** a metaphoric way of categorizing the oblique signs, used in astrology to describe correspondences between the oblique signs and the "sovereign" or right signs, as in 28.35–41. The distinction has to do with the length of time it takes the signs to rise (less and more than two hours respectively). **28.31–32 Cancer to the ende of Sagittare,** added into Dd[1] in a later hand, with "heed" instead of "ende"; reading from Hv. **29.1 Tak the altitude of thy sonne . . . ,** as instructed in Part 2, sections 2–3, using both sides of the astrolabe. **29.13 thow,** Dd[1] reads "two." **29.19 rewle,** Dd[1] reads "rewles." **30a–b** ***altitude,*** should read "latitude," as in Bl[1] and Hv. ***wey of the sonne,*** as Chaucer explains in lines 14–17, this is not the celestial ecliptic, but the diurnal path, i.e., the sun's apparent path on a given day. When the sun is "low" in the winter sky, its path will appear to be shorter.

sonne, and hath no latitude. And yif the altitude of the planete be heyere than the degree of the sonne, than is the planete north fro the wey of the sonne swych° a quantite of latitude as sheweth by thyn almykanteras. And yif the altitude of the planete be lasse than the degree of the sonne, thanne is the planete sowth fro the wey of the sonne swich a quantite of latitude as sheweth by thine almykanteras—this is to seyn, fro the wey wheras the sonne wente thilke day, but nat from the wey of the sonne in every place of° the zodiak. And for the more declaracioun, lo here the figure.

31. To knowe the senyth° of the arysing of the sonne, this is to seyn, the partie° of the orisonte° in which that the sonne ariseth.

Thow most first considere that the sonne ariseth nat alwey verrey° est, but sometyme by north the est, and somtyme by sowthe the est. Sothly°, the sonne ariseth nevermo verrey est in owere orisonte but he be in the heved of Aries or Libra. Now is thine orisonte departed in 24 parties by thy azymutz°, in significacioun of 24 partiez of the world (al be it so that shipmen rikne thilke partiez in 32). Thanne is ther no more but waite° in which azymutz that thi sonne entreth at his arisyng, and tak ther the senyth of the arysing of the sonne.

The manere of the devisioun of thine astralabie is this—I mene as in this cas: first is it devided in 4 plages° principaly with the lyne that goth from est to west, and than with another lyne that goth fro south to north. Than is it devided in smale partiez of azymutz, as est, and est by sowthe, whereas is the firste azimut above the est lyne; and so forth fro partie to partie til that thow come agayn unto the est lyne. Thus maistow understond also the senyth of any sterre, in which partie he riseth, &c. And for the more declaracion, lo here the figure.

32. To knowe in which partie of the firmament is the conjunccioun°.

Considere the tyme of the conjunccion by thy kalender, as thus: lok how many howres thilke conjunccion is fro the midday of the day precedent, as sheweth by the canoun° of thy kalender. Rikne thanne thilke nombre of howres in the bordure of thyn astralabie, as thow art wont° to do in knowyng of the howres of the day or of the nyht; and ley thy label° over the degree of the sonne; and thanne wol the point of thy label sitte upon the hour of the conjunccion. Loke thanne in which azymut the degree of thy sonne sitteth, and in that partie of the firmament is the conjunccioun. And for the more declaracioun, lo here thy figure.

33. To knowe the senyth of the altitude of the sonne, &c.

This is no more to seyn but any tyme of the day tak the altitude of the sonne; and by the azymut in which he stondeth maistow sen in whiche partie of the firmament he is. And the same wyse maistou sen by° the nyht of any sterre, whether the sterre sitte est or west or north, or any partie bytwene, after the name of the azimut in which is the sterre. And for the more declaracioun lo here the figure.

34. To knowe sothly the degree of the longitude of the mone, or of any planete that hath no latitude for the tyme fro the ecliptik lyne.

Tak the altitude of the mone, and rikne thine altitude up among thyne almykanteras on

30.8 swych, *such* **30.16 in every place of,** *throughout* **31a** ***senyth,*** *point on the horizon* (see n.) **31b** ***partie,*** *part,* **orisonte,** *horizon* **31.2 verrey,** *true* **31.4 Sothly,** *indeed* **31.7 azymutz,** *azimuths* (see figure 18) **31.10 waite,** *observe* **31.16 plages,** *regions* **32b** ***conjunccioun,*** *conjunction* (see n.) **32.4 canoun,** *table* **32.7 wont,** *accustomed* **32.8 label,** *indicator* (see figure 21) **33.5 by,** *during*

30.16 zodiak, other manuscripts add some version of "for on the morowe wyl the sonne be on another degree and norther or souther par aventure." **31a** ***senyth,*** not zenith in its usual sense, but the point of sunrise on the horizon. Several manuscripts read "signet." **31.9 partiez in 32,** the modern compass is divided into 32 parts for more accurate measurement. Evidently this began with navigation; see Eisner Variorum 1055n. **31.20 and est by,** Dd[1] and Hv read "and est and by." **32b** ***conjunccioun,*** the conjunction or proximity of two celestial bodies, here the sun and the moon. Section 32 is not in Massahalla. **32.5 kalendar,** not the modern calendar; see Prologue 87–88n. **32.7 knowyng of the howres,** see Part 2, section 3. **33** This section parallels section 31 in its concern with locating celestial points by direction. **33.3 stondeth,** Dd[1] reads "shal stondith." **33.5 by the,** Bl[1], Rl[1], and Hv read "by." **33.7 north,** Bl[1], Rl[1], and Hv read "north or southe." **33.8 which is the sterre,** Bl[1], Rl[1] and Hv "which the sterre stondith." **34.1 Tak the altitude of the mone,** as in Part 2, section 2.

which side that the mone stande, and set ther a prikke. Tak thanne anon riht° upon the mones side the altitude of any sterre fix° which that thow knowest, and set his centre upon his altitude among thin almykanteras ther the sterre is fownde. Waite° thanne which degree of the zodiak toucheth the prikke of the altitude of the mone, and tak ther the degree in which the mone standeth. This conclusioun is verrey soth° yif the sterres in thine astrolabie stonden after the trowthe°: Of comune°, tretis° of astrolabie ne make non excepcioun° wheyther the mone have latitude or non, ne on wheither° side of the mone the altitude of the sterre fix be taken. And *nota* that yif the mone shewe himself by liht of day, than maistow wyrke this same conclusioun by the sonne, as wel as by the fix sterre. And for the more declaracioun, lo here thy figure.

35. *This is the workinge of the conclusioun to knowe yif that any planete be directe or retrograde°.*

Tak the altitude of any sterre that is cleped a planete, and note it wel. And tak ek anon the altitude of any sterre fix that thow khowest, and note it wel also. Come thane agayn the thridde or the ferthe nyht next folwing, for thanne shaltow aperceyve wel the moeving of a planete, wheither so he moeve forthward or bakward. Awaite° wel thanne whan that thy sterre fix is in the same altitude that she was whan thow toke hir firste altitude; and tak than eftsones° the altitude of the forseide planete, and note it wel. For trust wel, yif so be that the planete be on the riht side of the meridional lyne, so that his seconde altitude be lasse than his firste altitude was, thanne is the planete directe. And yif he be on the west side in that condicion, thanne is he retrograd. And yif so be that this planete be upon the est side whan his altitude is taken, so that his secounde altitude be more than his firste altitude, thanne is he retrograde, and yif he be on the west side, than is he directe. But the contrarie of thise parties° is of the cours of the moone; for sothly, the moone moeveth the contrarie from other planetes as in hir episicle°, but in non other manere. And for the more declaracioun, lo here thy figure.

36. *The conclusiouns of equaciouns of howses°, after the astralabie, &c.*

Set the bygynnyng of the degree that assendeth upon the ende of° the 8 howr inequal°; thanne wol the bygynnyng of the 2 hows sitte upon the lyne of midnyht°. Remeve° thanne the degree that assendeth and set him on the ende of the 10 howr inequal; and thanne wol the bygynnyng of the 3 hows sitte upon the midnyht lyne. Bryng up agayn the same degree that assendeth first, and set him upon the orisonte°; and thanne wol the begynnyng of the hows sitte upon the lyne of midnyht. Tak thanne the nadir of° the degree that first assendeth, and set him on the ende of the 2 howr inequal; and thanne wol the bygynnyng of the 5 hows sitte upon the lyn of midnyht; set thanne the nadir of° the assendent on

34.4 anon riht, *immediately* **34.5 sterre fix,** *fixed star* **34.8 Waite,** *observe* **34.12 verrey soth,** *quite precise* **34.13 stonden after the trowthe,** i.e., *are marked accurately on the astrolabe,* **Of comune,** *generally* **34.14 tretis,** *treatises,* **ne make non excepcioun,** i.e., *ignore minor variations* (see n.) **34.16 wheither,** *which* **35b** ***directe or retrograde,*** *moving in the same direction* (west to east) *or opposite direction* (east to west) *as the sun* **35.8 Awaite,** *observe* **35.11 eftsones,** *again* **35.23 parties,** *sides* **35.25 hir episicle,** *their small circles* (see n.) **36a** ***equaciouns of howses,*** *determining the houses* (see Prologue 106n) **36.2 ende of,** i.e., *the line on the astrolabe that marks,* **8 howr inequal,** *eighth unequal hour* (see the note to Part 2, section 12) **36.4 lyne of midnyht,** see 1.4.9, **Remeve,** *move* **36.10 orisonte,** *horizon* (see figure 18) **36.16 nadir of,** *the point diametrically opposite to*

34.9 toucheth, Dd[1] and Rl[1] read "to whiche"; Bl[1] "towhithe." **34.13 Of,** omitted except in Dd[1]. **34.14** That is, astrolabic authorities ignore minor variations because the moon is never far off of the ecliptic; as a result, it is treated as if it were always on it. **35.22 west side,** Dd[1] reads "west side & yf he be on the east side." **35.24–26 sothly . . . manere,** Dd[1] is garbled; reading from Hv. **35.26 episicle,** an epicycle is a "small circle, having its centre on the circumference of a greater circle" (*OED* 1); the planets in the Ptolemaic system were understood to be carried on small circles (their epicycles) whose centers described the large circles of orbital motion; the positing of epicycles helped to account for the periodic retrograde motion in the planets' apparent orbits. **36** Sections 36 and 37 offer two methods for determining the astrological houses. For the various methods, see Eisner Variorum notes to Conclusions 36 and 37. From this point forward, the manuscripts vary in their sequence of sections, and some manuscripts add as many as six additional ones. **36.1–2 degree that assendeth,** a given point in time indicated on the astrolabe's circle of signs. The user sets the degree for a given time—e.g., any moment for which a horoscope is desired—and reads the results accordingly. **36.8 midnyht lyne,** see *Equat* 184–85.

the ende of the 4 howre; than wol the bygynnyng of the 6 house sitte on the midnyht lyne. The bygynnyng of the 7 hows is nadir of the assendent, and the bygynnyng of the 8 hows is nadir of the 2; and the bygynnyng of the 9 hows is nadir of the 3; and the bygynnyng of the 10 hows is the nadir of the 4; and the bygynnyng of the 11 hows is nader of the 5; and the bygynnyng of the 12 hows is nadir of the 6. And for the mor declaracion, lo here the figure.

37. Another manere of equaciouns of howses by the astralabie.

Tak thine assendent°, and thanne hastow thi 4 angles; for wel thow wost° that the opposit of thin assendent, that is to seyn thy bygynnyng of the 7 hows, sit° upon the west orizonte; and the bygynnyng of the 10 hows sit upon the lyne meridional; and his opposit upon the lyne of mydnyht. Thanne ley thi label° over the degree that assendeth, and rekne fro the point of thy label alle the degrees in the bordure, til thow come to the meridional lyne; and departe° alle thilke degrees in 3 evene parties, and tak the evene equacion of 3. For ley thy label over everich of 3 parties, and than maistow se by thy label in which degree of the zodiak is the bygynnyng of everich of thise same howses fro the assendent: that is to seyn, the begynnyng of the 12 hows next above thine assendent; and thanne the bygynnyng of the 11 hows; and thanne the 10, upon the meridional lyne, as I first seide. The same wyse wyrke thow fro the assendent down to the lyne of midnyht, and thanne thus hastow other 3 howses: that is to seyn, the bygynnyng of the 2 and the 3 and the 4 howses. Thanne is the nader° of thise 3 howses the bygynnyng of the 3 howses that folwen. And for the more declaracioun, lo here thi figure.

38. To fynde the lyne merydional to dwelle fix in any certein place.

Tak a rond plate of metal—for werpinge°, the brodere the bettre—and make therupon a just compas°, a lite within the bordure; and ley this ronde plate upon an evene grond, or on an evene ston, or on an evene stok° fix in the gronde; and ley it even by a level. And in centre of the compas stike an evene° pyn or a wir upriht, the smaller the betere. Set thy pyn by a plom-rewle° evene upryht; and let this pyn be no iengere than a quarter of the diametre of thi compas fro the centre. And waite bisily° aboute 10 or 11 of the clokke and whan the sonne shyneth, whan the shadwe of the pyn entreth anythyng within the cercle of thi plate an her-mele°, and mark ther a prikke with inke. Abide° thanne stille waityng on the sonne after 1 of the clokke, til that the schadwe of the wyr or of the pyn passe onything owt of the cercle of the compas, be it never so lite; and set ther another prikke of ynke. Tak than a compas° and mesure evene° the middel bytwixe bothe prikkes, and set ther a prikke. Take me thanne a rewle, and draw a strike evene alyne° fro the pyn unto the middel prikke; and tak ther thy lyne meridional for evererno, as in that same place°. And yif thow drawe a croslyne° overthwart the compas, justly over° the lyne meridional, than hastow est and west and sowth; and

37.1 assendent, *point of the zodiac rising in the east* (see 2.3.37n) **37.2 wost,** *know* **37.4 sit,** *sits* **37.7 label,** *ruler* (see figure 21) **37.11 departe,** *divide* **37.25 nader,** *diametrical opposite* **38.1 for werpinge,** *to avoid warping* **38.3 just compas,** *perfect circle* **38.5 stok,** *post* **38.7 evene,** *straight* **38.9 plom-rewle,** *plumb line* **38.12 waite bisily,** *observe diligently* **38.15 her-mele,** *hair's breadth* **38.16 Abide,** *wait* **38.21 compas,** *mathematical compass or dividers* (for measuring and making circles) **38.22 evene,** *precisely* **38.24 strike evene alyne,** *straight line-mark* **38.26–27 as in that same place,** *for that location* **39.27 croslyne,** *crossing line* **38.28 justly over,** *perpendicular to*

37.2 4 angles, the four "astrological houses that begin at the four cardinal points: the First, on the east horizon, the ascendant; the Fourth, on the line of midnight, the bottom of heaven; the Seventh, on the west horizon, the descendent, and the Tenth, on the meridian, the mid-heaven" (Eisner Variorum 1158n). See 2.4.47n. **37.8 assendeth,** Dd[1] reads "assendet." **37.14 in which degree of the zodiac is the,** the addition of "is" is Skeat's emendation of Dd[1]; other manuscripts read "in the zodiac the." **37.17 hows,** Dd[1] reads "howses." **37.18 thanne,** omitted in Dd[1]. **37.26 3 howses that folwen,** actually the nadirs of 2, 3, and 4 indicate the beginnings of 8, 9, and 10. **38** Not in Massahalla, this section does not use the astrolabe, but describes a way to determine the true south (the line meridian) of a given location and consequently the other three cardinal points. **38.10 no lengere than . . . ,** scholars have noted that the length of the pin affects when its shadow will reach the border. When conducted at ten or eleven a.m. (see 38.12), and with a pin of the length specified, the experiment works from October to February. **38.23 me,** omitted in Rl[1], Hv, and other manuscripts.

par consequence than° the nadir of the sowth lyne is the north lyne. And for more declaracioun, lo here thi figure.

39. Descripcion of the meridional lyne, of longitudes, and latitudes of citees and townes from on to another, and of clymatz.

This lyne meridional ys but a maner° descripcioun or lyne ymagined, that passeth upon the pooles° of this world and by the cenyth° of owre heved. And hit is cleped° the lyne meridional, for in what place that any maner man is at any tyme of the yer, whan that the sonne, by moeving of the firmament, cometh to his verrey° meridian place, than is hit verrey midday, that we clepen owre noon, as to thilke° man; and therfore is it cleped the lyne of midday.

And *nota* that for evermo of° any 2 citees or of 2 townes, of whiche that o town aprocheth neer° the est than doth that other town, truste wel that thylke townes han diverse° meridians. *Nota* also that the arch of the equinoxial° that is conteyned or bounded bytwixe the 2 meridians ys cleped the longitude of the town. And yif so be that two townes have illike meridian, or on meridian, than is the distance of hem bothe illike fer fro° the est; and the contrarie. And in this manere they chaunge nat her meridian, but sothly they chaungen her almikanteras for the enhansing° of the pool° and the distance of the sonne.

The longitude of a clymat° is a lyne ymagined fro est to west illike distant fro the equinoxial. The latitude of a clymat is a lyne ymagined from north to south the space° of the erthe, fro the bygynnyng of the firste clymat unto the verrey ende of the same climat, evene directe agayns° the poole artik. Thus seyn some auctours, and somme of hem seyn that yif men clepen° the latitude thay mene the arch meridian that is contiened or intercept° bytwixe the cenyth and the equinoxial. Thanne sey they that the distaunces fro the equinoxial unto the ende of a clymat, evene agayns the poole artyk, is the latitude of a climat for sothe°. And for more declaracioun, lo here thi figure.

40. To knowe with which degree of the zodiak that any planete assendith on the orisonte, wheyther so that his latitude be north or sowth.

Knowe be thine almenak the degree of the ecliptik of any signe in which that the planete is rekned for to be, and that is cleped the degree of his longitude; and knowe also the degree of his latitude fro the ecliptik north or sowth. And by this samples folwynge in special maistow wyrke for sothe in every signe of the zodiak. The degree of the longitude, par aventure°, of Venus or of another planete was 6 of Capricorne, and the latitude of him was northward 2 degrees fro the ecliptik lyne. I tok a subtil compas° and cleped that on poynt of my compas A, and that other poynt F. Than tok I the point of A, and set it in the ecliptik line evene in my zodiak, in

38.30 par consequence than, *consequently then* **39.2 a maner,** *a kind of* **39.3 pooles,** *poles,* **cenyth,** *zenith* (point directly overhead) **39.4 cleped,** *called* **39.7 verrey,** *precise* **39.9 as to thilke,** *in relation to that* **39.11 for evermo of,** *always for* **39.13 neer,** *nearer* **39.14 diverse,** *different* **39.16 equinoxial,** *celestial equator* **39.20 illike fer fro,** *equally distant from* **39.23 enhansing,** *elevation* **39.24 pool,** *pole* **39.25 clymat,** *region* (see n.) **39.28 space,** i.e., *surface* **39.31 evene directe agayns,** *aligned in relation to* **39.33 clepen,** *refer to* **39.34 is contiened or intercept,** *is enclosed or cuts* **39.39 for sothe,** *truly* **40.8–9 par aventure,** *perhaps* **40.12 compas,** *mathematical compass* (for measuring and making circles)

39 The readings in Dd[1] and Bl[1] are less reliable from this point forward; the text provided is corrected from Rl[1] as printed by Skeat 3.237. Only a few of the variants are included here as examples. Like 38, sections 39 and 40 are not in Massahalla and are not concerned with the astrolabe itself—perhaps some indication of dissolving focus; 39 may have been developed with reference to Johannis de Sacrobosco; see 1.17.20–21n. **39.2 or lyne,** Dd[1] reads "or the lyne." **39.3 this world,** Dd[1] reads "this the world." **39.4 cleped the,** Dd[1] reads "the same." The etymology of *meridian* in this sentence is essentially correct, from a form of Latin *medius* (middle) and *die* (of the day), evidently derived (as are lines 39.4–21) from Sacrobosco; see 1.17.20–21n. **39.6–7 by moevyng,** Dd[1] reads "shyneth onythinge." **39.11 that for evermo of any 2 citees,** Dd[1] reads "for evermo of any lynes." **39.13 neer,** Dd[1] reads "towarde." **39.16 conteyned,** Dd[1] reads "considered." **39.17 longitude,** modern measurements of longitude use the anchoring point of the prime meridian (at Greenwich) to make them universal rather than relative to a given location. In this section, "longitude" and "latitude" apply to terrestrial measurements rather than those projected out to the celestial sphere—loosely the length and breadth of a given region. **39.25 clymat,** a region on the surface of the earth (somewhat like colloquial use of "the tropics"); *climate* only later came to mean the conditions of weather in such a region. **39.30 same,** Dd[1] reads "sede." **39.31 the poole artik,** Dd[1] and Bl[1] read "from north to south." **39.32 of hem seyn,** Rl[1] reads "clerkis seyn." **39.33 latitude thay mene,** Bl[1] reads "latitude of a cuntrey that is." **39.34 or intercept,** Dd[1] reads "or except"; omitted in Bl[1]. **40.7 sothe,** Dd[1] reads "sonne." **40.10–11 6 of . . . 2 degrees,** the numerical readings from here to the end are from Dd[1] (as emended by Skeat), even though they do not produce accurate results; Bl[1] has different numerals and no numerals were entered in Rl[1]. **40.14 tok,** Dd[1] reads "strikke."

the degree of the longitude of Venus, that is to seyn, in the 6 degree of Capricorne. And thanne sette I the point of F upward in the same signe, bycause that the latitude was north, upon the latitude of Venus, that is to seyn, in the 6 degree fro the heved° of Capricorne. And thus have I 2 degrees bytwixe my two prikkes. Than leide I down softely° my compas, and sette the degree of the longitude upon the orisonte. Tho° tok I and wexede my label° in maner of a peyre tables° to resceyve distintinctly the prikkes of my compas. Tho tok I this forseide label and leide it fix° over the degree of my longitude. Tho tok I up my compas and sette the point of A in the wex on my label, as evene° as I kowde gesse over the ecliptik lyne, in the ende of the longitude; and sette the point of F endlang in my label upon the space of the latitude, inwarde and over the zodiak, that is to seyn, northward fro the ecliptik. Than leide I down my compas and lokede wel in the wey upon the prikke of A and of F. Tho turned I my riet til that the prikke of F sat upon the orisonte. Than saw I wel that the body of Venus in hir latitude of 2 degrees septentrionalis° assended in the ende of the 6 degree in the heved of Capricorne. And *nota* that in the same maner maistow wyrke with any latitude septentrional in alle signes; but sothly° the latitude meridional of a planete in Capricorne may not be take bycause of the litel space bytwixe the ecliptik and the bordure of the astrelabie; but sothly, in alle other signes it may.

Also the degree, par aventure°, of Juppiter or of another planete was in the first degree of Pisces in longitude, and his latitude was 3 degrees meridional. Tho tok I the point of A and sette it in the firste degree of Pisces on the ecliptik, and thanne set I the point of F downward in the same signe, bycause that the latitude was sowth 3 degrees, that is to seyn, fro the heved° of Pisces. And thus have I 3 degrees bytwixe bothe prikkes. Thanne sette I the degree of the longitude upon the orisonte. Tho tok I my label, and leide it fix° upon the degree of the longitude. Tho sette I the point of A on my label, evene over the ecliptik lyne, in the ende evene of the degree of the longitude, and set the point of F endlang in my label the space of 3 degrees of the latitude fro the zodiak, this is to seyn, sowthward fro the ecliptik, toward the bordure; and turned my riet til the prikke of F sat upon the orisonte. Thanne say° I wel that the body of Juppiter in his latitude of 3 degrees meridional ascended with 14 degrees of Pisces *in horoscopo.* And in this maner maistow wyrke with any latitude meridional, as I first seide, save in Capricorne. And yif thow wolt pleie° this craft with the arysing of the mone, loke thow rekne wel her cours howre by howre; for she ne dwelleth nat in a degree of his longitude but a litel while, as thow wel knowest. But natheles, yif thow rekne hir verreye moeving by thy tables howre after howre [breaks off].

Explicit tractatus de Conclusionibus Astrolabii, compilatus per Galfridum Chauciers ad filium suum Lodewicum, scolarem tunc temporis Oxonie, ac sub tutela illius nobilissimi philosophi Magistri N. Strode, etc.

40.21 heved, *beginning* (head) **40.23 softely,** *carefully* **40.25 Tho,** *then,* **wexede my label,** *waxed my indicator* (so that the wax could take an impression) **40.26 peyre tables,** *writing tablet* (see n.) **40.28 leide it fixe,** *fixed it* **40.31 evene,** *precisely* **40.41 septentrionalis,** *northward* **40.45 sothly,** *truly* **40.50 par aventure,** *perhaps* **40.58 heved,** *beginning* **40.61 leide it fix,** *fixed it* **40.70 say,** *saw* **40.75 pleie,** *perform*

40.26 peyre tables, a kind of medieval notebook with an inset wax surface; notes or marks were pressed or scratched into the wax and then smoothed when no longer needed. See, e.g., *SumT* 4.1731. **40.48 signes,** Dd[1] reads "tymes." **40.81** Late manuscripts complete the sentence "thou shalt do wel ynowe"; some add some six more sections that do not appear to be by Chaucer, although there has been considerable disagreement on the point. **40.81a–d Explicit . . . ,** Here ends the treatise concerning the calculations of the astrolabe compiled by Geoffrey Chaucer for his son Lewis, who was a student at the time at Oxford and under the tutelage of that most notable master of philosophy N. Strode, etc. This colophon is in a later hand and appears only in Dd[1]. Ralph Strode was certainly known to Chaucer (see *TC* 5.1857), so the "N." here may be a mistake or an indication of *nomen* (name). Strode, however, left Oxford in 1387.

Equatorie of the Planetis

Equatorie of the Planetis

Introduction

As an instruction manual on the use of an astronomical calculator, *Equatorie of the Planetis* is a companion piece to Chaucer's *Treatise on the Astrolabe.* Someone who knew or knew of Chaucer and shared his interests in astronomy and astrology composed it; perhaps it was written *for* Chaucer, or somewhat more likely, Chaucer himself wrote it. Among their several functions, astrolabes were used to compute the positions of the sun and stars, but the larger and more specialized equatories helped to calculate the relatively complicated positions of the moon and stars, which required greater mathematical sophistication to account for epicycles or apparent changes in the direction of astral movement (195n). Such conclusions could be derived through laborious mathematical calculation, yet the time saved with the instruments was considerable—much as with a modern computer or calculator. Indeed, *calculator* is a fair translation of *Equatorie;* hence we might call it in modern English *Calculator of the Planets.*

The treatise begins with directions on how to construct an equatorie and then offers several exercises in its operation. Three diagrams illustrate the treatise, and we include them here because they clarify the workings of the instrument and because they are similar to those that accompany *Astrolabe* as presented here, encouraging connection between the two works. Not included are the extensive tables of mathematical information referred to in *Equatorie* and necessary to operate the instrument (see, e.g., 110n). These tables accompany the treatise in its sole manuscript, Peterhouse MS 75.I, now in the Cambridge University Library, executed for the most part in the same handwriting that is in the treatise. In a table (folio 5v) constructed to convert a span years into a number of days, under the year 1392, Chaucer's name is used to label a *radix* or basis for calculation: "defferentia Christi et Radix Chaucer" (the difference between [the radix date of the Incarnation of] Christ and the radix of Chaucer). The number of days given is accurate to the end of the year 1392 (508,428; the number is in sexagesimal notation) and the use of Chaucer's name encourages attribution of the work to him.

Supporting the attribution, the calculations in *Equatorie* are keyed to the latitude of London, its dialect is consistent with what has been determined to be Chaucer's, and the date aligns precisely with a time in Chaucer's life when he was engaged deeply with astronomy. Evidence internal to the treatise (see 26–28), the "radix Chaucer" itself, and evidence found elsewhere in the manuscript enable scholars to date *Equatorie* with unusual precision—between December 31, 1392 and September 15, 1393—close on the heels of *Astrolabe* (begun in 1391), although each treatise includes material that was added later. In fact, the incomplete *Astrolabe* promises to include material that is similar to that given in *Equatorie,* while *Equatorie* (also incomplete) evidently refers back to Chaucer's earlier treatise (see 184). *Equatorie* is in no way a continuation of *Astrolabe,* but it is its complement.

The original transcriber and editor of the *Equatorie of the Planetis,* scientific historian Derek J. Price (1955; no. 70), was the first to propose that we attribute the treatise to Chaucer, and he argued further that the handwriting of the Peterhouse manuscript is Chaucer's own. Yet Price wisely cautioned that without established examples of Chaucer's script for comparison, the claim can only be tentative. The number of corrections and erasures in the manuscript strongly indicate ongoing composition, most likely the process of a working translation, but the evidence for Chaucer's own handwriting is slim.

Handwriting aside, efforts to attribute the treatise to Chaucer on the basis of language and prose style began with the analysis of R. M. Wilson that accompanies Price's edition. Confirmation (and denial) of Wilson's tentative support of the attribution have been frustrated by the fact that the treatise translates or adapts an earlier work (or works) in Latin, based on Arabic materials (1n and 191n). Apart from *Astrolabe*, Chaucer's other translations in prose (*Boece*, *Tale of Melibee*, and *Parson's Tale*) differ significantly from *Equatorie* in genre, subject matter, and source material, making attribution by comparative analysis difficult, if not impossible: Chaucer's "translations" are often quite free by modern standards, but it is clear that he adjusted style and vocabulary to those of his source texts. Comparisons with the syntax and vocabulary of *Astrolabe* (which is also rooted in the Arabic-Latin scientific tradition) have been also inconclusive to date because the data samples are small and because the level of scientific expertise varies rather widely between the two texts, presumably because Chaucer addressed *Astrolabe* to ten-year-old Lewis while *Equatorie* is a more advanced work. The most extensive analysis of style and authorship is pointedly inconclusive: Kari Anne Rand Schmidt, *The Authorship of the Equatorie of the Planetis* (1993; no. 1678), transcribes *Equatorie* and three contemporaneous treatises (including a manuscript of *Astrolabe*), presents a more exhaustive list of erasures and corrections than did Price, assesses aspects of style statistically, and considers the case for attribution to be unproven. In "A Case Against Chaucer's Authorship of the *Equatorie of the Planetis*" (2005; no. 1673), Jennifer Arch argues less cautiously that the prose styles of *Equatorie* and *Astrolabe* differ, and she thinks that Chaucer did not have astronomical skills necessary the write *Equatorie*.

J. D. North, however, shows that nothing in *Equatorie* is beyond the moderate level of astronomical expertise evident in many of Chaucer's poems, even though the style and vocabulary of *Equatorie* outpace those in *Astrolabe*. In *Chaucer's Universe* (2d ed. 1990; no. 436), North confirms much of Price's original argument for Chaucer's authorship, sidesteps questions relating to handwriting and holographs, and shows in great detail how deep were Chaucer's astral interest and knowledge. In short, he shows that *Equatorie* certainly connects well with *Treatise on the Astrolabe*, and that they together bear witness to the explosion in vernacular science in late fourteenth-century England. Where others consider the attribution of *Equatorie* to be unproven, North thinks it all but certain. *Equatorie of the Planetis* is not included in other editions of Chaucer's works.

Equatorie of the Planetis

In the name of God pitos° and merciable. Seide [Leyk] the largere that thow makest this instrument, the largere ben thi chef devisiouns. The largere that ben tho° devisiouns, in hem may ben mo° smale fracciouns. And evere the mo of smale fracciouns, the ner° the trowthe of thy conclusiouns.

Tak therfore a plate of metal, or elles a bord that be smothe shave by level°, and evene° polised. Of which, whan it is rownd by compas°, the hole diametre shal contene 72 large enches, or elles 6 fote of mesure. The whiche rownde bord, for° it shal nat werpe ne krooke° the egge° of the circumference, shal be bownde with a plate of yren in maner of a karte whel. This bord, yif the likith°, may be vernissed or elles glewed with perchemyn° for honestyte°.

Tak thanne a cercle° of metal that be 2 enche of brede°, and that the hole° dyametre within this cercle shal contene 68 enches, or 5 fote and 8 enches, and subtili° lat this cercle be nayled upon the circumference of this bord or ellis mak this cercle of glewed perchemyn. This cercle wole I clepe° the Lymbe° of myn equatorie, that was compowned° the Yer of Crist 1392 complet, the laste meridie° of Decembre.

This lymbe shaltow devyde in 4 quarters by 2 diametral lynes° in maner of the lymbe of a comune astrelabye°, and lok° thy croys be trewe proved by geometrical conclusioun°. Tak thanne a large compas° that be trewe, and set the fyx point over the middel of the bord on which middel shal be nayled a plate of metal rownd. The hole diametre of this plate shal contiene 16 enches large, for in this plate shollen ben perced alle the centris of this equatorie, and ek in proces of tyme may this plate be turned abowte after that auges° of planetes ben moeved in the 9 spere°. Thus may thin instrument laste perpetuel.

Tak thanne, as I have seid byforn, the fix fot of thy compas and set it in the middel of this plate, and with the moevable point of thi compas descrive° a cercle in the ferthest circumference of thy lymbe. And *nota* that the middel poynt of this plate wher as the fix fot of thy compas stondith wole I calle Centre Aryn.

---

1 pitos, *compassionate* **4 tho,** *those* **5 mo,** *more* **6 ner,** *nearer* **9 by level,** *verified by level,* **evene,** *evenly* **10–11 by compas,** *verified by a mathematical compass* **13 for,** *so that* **14 krooke,** *bend,* **egge,** *edge* **16 the likith,** *you choose* **17 perchemyn,** *parchment* **18 honestyte,** *precision* **19 cercle,** i.e., *flattened hoop* **20 brede,** *breadth,* **hole** *entire* **22 subtili,** *carefully* **25 clepe,** *call,* **Lymbe,** *border* **26 compowned,** *constructed* (see 26–28n.) **27 meridie,** *meridian* (noon) **30 diametral lynes,** (perpendicular) *lines that pass through the center* **31 astrelabye,** *astrolabe,* **lok,** *make sure* **32 conclusioun,** *calculation* **33 compas,** *mathematical compass* **41 auges,** *apogees* (see n.), **9 spere,** *ninth sphere* **46 descrive,** *mark*

Text based on Peterhouse, Cambridge, MS 75.1, as edited and translated by D. J. Price, compared with the transcription by Kari Anne Rand Schmidt. **1 In the name of . . . ,** the traditional Arabic opening "bismillah" (in the name of Allah) indicates that this work, like the *Treatise on the Astrolabe,* is based on a source ultimately Arabic in origin. **2 Leyk,** this erased word is visible under ultraviolet light, although the reading has been questioned. John of Linères and Nicholas Lynn, famous astronomers, have been suggested as referents; Price notes that the word may be a mistranslation (read from right to left) of the Arabic word *qīla* ("it is said"). Rand Schmidt notes North's suggestion of *leyc* with an abbreviation for *er,* suggesting Robert of "Leycester," a Franciscan astronomer. **10–11 by compas,** interlinear. **12 large enches,** the Saxon inch, equal to 1.1 modern inches. Edward I in 1305 mandated the modern inch, but the traditional inch continued to be used, particularly in trade. Chaucer's experience with weights and measures in the Custom House might have encouraged him to use the popular measure. **19–22 Tak thanne . . . 5 fote and 8 enches,** erased and corrected in the manuscripts. Price notes that the original seems to read: "tak thanne a cercle of metal that be 2 enche of brede & that the hole dyametre contene 72 enches or 6 fote & subtili." The revision removes any ambiguity. Rand Schmidt reports a somewhat more tentative reconstruction. **26–28 compowned the Yer of Crist 1392 complet, the laste meridie of December,** i.e., the instrument was constructed for use after the year that ended on noon, December 31, 1392. The dates used for examples in the treatise (at 678, 697 and 723), however, like those in Chaucer's, are in 1391. **complet,** not counting the year current in which the date is taken (i.e., 1392 complete is 1393 incomplete). **laste meridie,** astronomical years ended and began at noon rather than midnight. **31 comune astrelabye,** see *Astr* 1.5. **38 alle the centris,** the various astronomical centers that pertain to an equatory; see *MED centre* 7. **41 auges,** apogees; in medieval usage, the furthest point from earth in the orbits of the planets, sun, and moon. In each annual revolution, their positions shift slightly relative to the ninth sphere of the fixed stars; adjustment keeps the equatory precise. **50 Aryn,** Arin (or Azin) indicates the center of the habitable world in medieval geography, and here is applied to the center of the equatory to represent the center of the geocentric cosmos; glossed Latin "terre" (earth) at line 346.

Mak thanne a narwer° cercle that be descrived upon° the same centre aryn but litel quantite fro the forthest° forseid° cercle in the lymbe, in whiche space shollen ben devyde° mynutes of the lymbe. Mak thanne a narwere cercle somwhat ferther distaunt fro the laste seid cercle, in which shal be devyded the degres of the same lymbe. Mak yit a narwere cercle somwhat ferthere distaunt fro this laste seid cercle, in which shal ben writen the nombres of degres. Mak yit a narwere cercle somwhat ferther distaunt fro this laste seid cercle, in which shollen ben writen the names of 12 signes. And *nota* that this laste seid cercle wole I calle the Closere of the Signes°.

Now hastow 5 cercles in thy lymbe and alle ben descrived upon centre aryn. And everich of the 4 quarters in thi lymbe shal ben devided in 90 degres, that is to sein, 3 signes. And everi degre shal be devided in 60 minutes. And shortly, thi lymbe is devided in maner of the lymbe in the bak side of an astrelabie.

Devyde thanne thilke lyne that goth fro centre aryn unto the cercle closere of the sygnes in 32 parties equales°, whiche parties ben cleped Degres of the Semydiametre, Marke thise parties dymli°, and *nota* that this diametral lyne devided in 32 parties shal be cleped Lyne Alhudda.

Set thanne the fix point of thy compas upon the ende of the firste devysioun fro centre aryn in lyne alhudda, and the moevable point upon the ende of the 30 devisioun fro the fix poynt of thi compas in the same lyne. So dwelleth ther but 1 devisioun bytwixe thy moevable point and the closere of the signes, and 1 devysioun bitwixe thy fix poynt and the centre aryn. And descryve thus a cercle, and tak° ther the eccentrik cercle of the Sonne. Scrape thanne awey° the devysiouns of lyne alhudda.

Devyde yit dymly oculte the same lyne alhudda fro centre aryn unto the closere of the signes in 60 parties equales. Set thanne the fix poynt of thy compas in centre aryn, and the moevable point in 12 degres and 28 minutes of lyne alhudda, and descrive a cercle. And that is the Centre Defferent of the mone.

Perce° thanne al the circumference of this defferent in 360 subtil° holes, equales of space, and thise spaces bytwixe the holes ben devyded owt of the degres of the lymbe. And *nota* that the Yer of Crist 1392 complet, the aux° of Saturnus was the last meridie° of Decembre at Londone; I seye the aux of Saturne in the 9 spere was 4 dowble signes 12 degres 7 minutes 3.2 etc. The remenaunt of auges sek hem in the table of auges folwynge.

Tak thanne a rewle° and ley that on ende° in centre aryn and that other ende in the lymbe, in the ende of the minut wher as° endith the aux of the planete. And draw ther a lyne with a sharp instrument fro centre aryn unto the closere of the signes, and no ferthere for

---

51 narwer, *smaller* **52 descrived upon,** *marked with reference to* **53 forthest,** *outermost,* **forseid,** *aforementioned* **55 devyde,** *divided* **66 Closere of the Signes,** *encloser* (or enclosure) *of the* (zodiacal) *signs* **77 parties equales,** *equal sections* **79 dymli,** *lightly* **91 tak,** *understand* **92 Scrape . . . awey,** *erase* **101 Perce,** *pierce* **102 subtil,** *careful* **105 aux,** *apogee* (singular of "auges; see 41n) **106 meridie,** *midday* (noon) **111 rewle,** *ruler,* **that on ende,** *one of its ends* **113 wher as,** *wherever*

51 narwer cercle, Price notes that the scale of the concentric bands marked on the limb is left unspecified. No specification is needed, however, as the widths of the bands can vary within the overall two-inch width of the limb. Evidently (as in the marked portions of figures 1 and 2), the bands of minutes and of degrees (both indicated by slash marks) are narrower than those that label the degrees by number and identify the signs by their names. **55 mynutes,** there are sixty minutes in each degree of a circle's 360 degrees. **73–74** see *Astr* 1.4–8. **77 synges:** interlinear Latin gloss "versus finem geminorum" (toward the end of Gemini). This indicates that the line is drawn from the center to the "end" (30°) of Gemini, i.e., the top of the circle. **78 Semydiametre,** semidiameter; *radius,* in modern usage. **79 dymli:** interlinear Latin gloss "ut postea deleantur" (to be deleted later)—the reason that sections are marked lightly. **diametral,** "semidiametral" is intended. **81 Alhudda,** perigee; opposite of apogee (see 41n). The word is from Arabic. **91–92 eccentrik cercle of the sonne,** it was thought that the earth was within the sun's orbit but not at the precise center of that orbit. The orbits of the other planets were also thought to be "eccentric" relative to the earth. **94 dymly oculte,** interlinear. **102 360 subtil holes,** 360 holes (even pin-pricks) evenly distributed around a seven-inch circle are difficult to execute. Price suggests the full number was never pricked and that the instructions are a mathematical ideal. See 168–69 and 503, where an even smaller circle compels the author to admit the limitations of his instrument; also compare *Astr* 1.21.47–51. **105 complet,** interlinear and followed by "ultimo 10.bre in meridie London" (the last mid-day in December London), which is erased; Rand Schmidt questions Price's reading. **106 last,** interlinear. **110 table of auges folwynge,** not included in this edition, a table in the manuscript (folio 6v) gives very precise readings, but precedes the text rather than following it, perhaps indicating that the arrangement of the quires is faulty.

empeiryng° of the lymbe. And fasteby° this lyne, writ the name of the planete. This rewle° is general for alle planetis.

Sek thanne in thi table of centris the distaunce of the centre equant of Satume fro centre aryn, which is 6 degres 50 minutes. Set thanne the fix point of thy compas in centre arin, and the moevable poynt in 6 degres and 50 minutes in lyne alhudda fro centre aryn. Turne than softely° thy compas abowte til that the moevable poynt towche the lyne of the aux of Saturne. And stondinge alwey stille the fix poynt of thy compas in centre aryn, marke with thy moevable poynt in the lyne of the aux of Saturnus a dep prikke, for in that prikke shal be perced a smal hole for the centre equant of Saturnus. And faste by this hole mak an E in signefyeng of equant.

Thanne tak awey thy compas and loke in thi table of centris the distaunce of the centre defferent° of Saturnus, and that is 3 degres and 25 minutes. Set thanne the fix point of thy compas in centre aryn, and thy moevable point in 3 degres and 25 minutes in lyne alhudda, and torne softely thi compas til that the moevable point towche the forseide lyne of the aux of Saturne. And stonding stille thy fix poynt of thi compas in centre aryn, marke with the moevable poynt in the lyne of the aux of Saturne a dep prikke, for therin shal be perced a smal hole for the centre defferent of Saturnus, and fasteby this hole mak an D for defferent.

And *nota* that by this ensample of Saturnus shaltow make the centres defferentes, and ek the equantes, of alle the planetis after hir distaunces fro centre aryn, and prikke hem in the lynes of hir auges.

Thanne shaltow sette the fix point of thy compas in the lyne of the aux of Mercurie, evene° bytwixe the centre E and centre D of Mercurius, and strid° the moevable poynt til it wole towche bothe centre E and ek centre D of Mercurius, and descryve ther a litel cercle. And thanne shaltow se that the lyne of the aux of Mercurie departith° this litel cercle in 2 arkes equals, this is to seye that the lyne kerveth this litel cercle evene amidde°.

This litel cercle shal be perced ful of smale holes *in circumferencia circuli*° by evene proporcioun, as is the centre defferent of the mone in 360 holes yif it be possible, or in 180, or in 90 atte leste. But sothly, the spaces bytwixe the holes ne shal nat be devided owt of the grete lymbe of the instrument, as is the centre defferent of the mone, but owt of the circumference of the same litel cercle it shal be devided by thy compas.

Scrape thanne awey thilke° 60 devysiouns in lyne alhudda, and yit devyde the same lyne alhudda in 5 parties equales by compas° fro centre aryn unto the cercle that is closere of the signes. And everych of thilke 5 parties shal be devided in 60 parties. Thise divisouns ne shal nat ben scraped awey.

Devyde thanne the line that goth fro centre aryn to the hed of Capricone, which lyne is cleped° in the Tretis of the Astrelabie the midnyht line. I seye devyde this midnyht lyne in 9 parties equals fro centre aryn unto the closere of the signes. And everich of thise devysiouns shal be devided by thy compas in

---

116–17 for empeiryng, *to avoid damaging,* **fasteby,** *nearby* **118 rewle,** *technique* **126 softely,** *carefully* **137 centre defferent,** see 121n. **157 evene,** *halfway* **158 strid,** *extend* **162 departith,** *divides* **164 evene amidde,** *evenly in the middle* **166** ***in circumferencia circuli,*** *in the circumference of the circle* **175 Scrape thanne awey thilke,** *then erase those* **177 5 parties equales by compas,** *five equal parts measured by* (mathematical) *compass* **184 cleped,** *called*

118 planete: interlinear Latin gloss "cuius est aux" (whose aux it is). **120 table of centris,** no such table exists in the manuscript as it is now bound, but Price notes that the following value (6° 50′) is used by many writers. Half of this value is used at 137–40. **121 centre equant,** a center point of the orbital Epicycle (see 195n); the similar notion of a "centre defferent" (137) was especially helpful for explaining the orbits of Mercury and the moon, described in 94–100 and 155–74. See Price 99–104 and 169. **128 stille,** interlinear. **137–38 3 degres and 25 minutes,** see 120n. **138 Set thanne,** interlinear gloss: "a centre aryn." **143 forseide,** interlinear. **153 distaunces:** interlinear Latin gloss "in tabulis" (in the table); see 136n. **166** ***in circumferencia circuli,*** (in the circumference of the circle); interlinear. **167–69 centre defferent of the mone . . . 90 atte leste,** see 121n and 102n. **177 by compas,** interlinear. **184 Tretis of the Astrelabie,** evidently a reference to Chaucer's *Astr,* the only English version known to have existed at the time. **185 midnyht line,** see *Astr* 1.4.9 and 2.36.8.

60 parties equales. Thise devysiouns ne shal nat be scraped awey.

Laus Deo vero. Now hastow the visage° of this precios equatorie. *Nota* that thise last seid 9 divisiouns in the midnyht lyne shollen serven for equacioun° of the 8 spere.

Now for the composicioun° of the epicicle for the visage of thyn equatorie, thow shalt make a cercle of metal of the same brede and of the same widnesse in circumference, in diametre, and in alle thinges lik to the lymbe of thin instrument. And in the same manere shal it be devyded in mynutis, in degres, in nombres, in names of signes, and in 5 cercles compased as is the firste seid lymbe, save° that the eccentrik of the sonne ne shal nat be in the epicicle, and also that it be nat filed to ney° to the closere of his signes list° thow perce the hole of thi commune centre defferent amys° or elles list the hole breke. This epicicle mot have suffisaunt thikkenesse to sustene hymself°.

Tak thanne this epicicle and ley it sadly° and evene° upon the visage of thin equatorie so that Aries of thin epicle lie evene upon the hed of Aries in the lymbe of thin equatorie, and Libra upon Libra, and Cancer upon Cancer, and Capricorne upon Capricorne, and every signe upon signe—this is to seyn, the hed of every signe upon hed of every signe.

Tak thanne a renspyndle° or a boydekyn°, and in direct of° the hed of Cancer thow shalt in the cercle that is closere of the signes make a litel hole thorw the epicicle. And thanne shaltow se that yif thow have trewely compased° thy cercles, that the poynt of thy renspindle shal have towched the closere of the signes in direct of the hed of Cancer in thyn equatorie. This litel hole that is no grettere than a smal nedle shal be cleped° the Comune Centre Defferent of Planetes.

Tak thanne a barre of metal of the brede° of a large enche and of suffisaunt thyknesse°. Of the whiche barre, that on ende shal be sowded to the closere of the signes in direct of Aries in this epicicle, and that other ende shal be sowded to the closere of the signes in direct of Libra in the same epicicle. Draw thanne by thi rewle a lyne fro the hed of Aries to the hed of Libra endelong° the barre, and draw swich another lyne overthwart° the barre fro the hed of Cancer to the hed of Capricorne. And in the secci-oun° of this crois is the centre of the epicicle.

Tak thanne a rewle of latoun° that ne be nat ful thykke, and lat it be the brede of an enche, and the lengthe shal be as long as al hol the diametre of the epicicle. This rewle mot° be shape in maner of a label on an astrelabie. The centre of this rewle shal be

191 visage, *face* (body) **194 equacioun,** *calculation or adjustment* (see n.) **195 composicioun,** *construction* **204 save,** *except* **206 filed to ney,** *cut* (with a file) *too near,* **list,** *to avoid the possibility that* **208 amys,** *by mistake* **210 sustene hymself,** *keep its shape* **211 sadly,** *carefully* **212 evene,** *exactly* **219 renspyndle,** *piercing spindle,* **boydekyn,** *awl* **220 in direct of,** *exactly at* **223 compased,** *marked* **228 cleped,** *called* **231 brede,** *width* **231–32 suffisaunt thyknesse,** i.e., *sufficiently thick so that it will not bend* **233 sowded,** *soldered* **238 endelong,** *along the length of* **240 overthwart,** *across* **242 seccioun,** *intersection* **243 rewle of latoun,** *ruler of copper alloy* **247 mot,** *must*

191 Laus Deo vero, "praise be to the true God," another translation of an Arabic commonplace formula; see 1n. **194 equacioun,** the information to enable this calculated adjustment is not included in the work, seemingly due to the author's failure to complete it. Such calculation accounted for minor variations (later "trepidation") in the progress of the eighth sphere, which held the signs of the zodiac. After this line, some four lines of writing space are left blank in the manuscript, clearly observable in Price's facsimile but somewhat cropped in Rand Schmidt's. This blank is especially notable since it occurs at a point of transition, indicated by the formulaic invocation at 191, by the note that begins in 192, and the shift in topic from face (or visage) to epicycle at 195. Perhaps further notes were to be included concerning the midnight line or the equation of the eighth sphere. **195 epicicle,** the ring-shaped part of the equatory (see figure 2), separate from the main disk (called the "visage" or "face"). This epicycle is not to be confused with the small orbital circles of planetary motion, also called "Epicycles," which were hypothesized to explain apparent variation in motion as the planets moved in their large orbits. To distinguish the part of the instrument from the small orbit, the latter is uppercase "Epicicle" in our text (contrary to Price's practice in his translation); spelling varies in the manuscript. **200 lymbe,** see line 25. **204–08 the eccentrik . . . hole breke,** these lines are written at the top of the page and marked for insertion. **206 closere of his signes,** line that defines the band called the "closer of the signs"; see 66. **207 hole:** interlinear Latin gloss "foramen" (hole). **211–12 sadly and,** interlinear. **213 Aries,** interlinear Latin gloss "capud" (head). **217 every,** interlinear. **220–21 thow shalt,** interlinear. **222 make:** interlinear "perce" (pierce). **231 large enche,** see 12n. **240 overthwart,** interlinear. **247–48 label on an astrelabie,** pointer on an astrolabe; see *Astr* 1.22, figure 21.

nayled to the centre of the forseide barre in swich a manere that this label may torne abowte as doth the label of an astrelabie. In middes of this nayl that fastnyth the barre and the label togidere, ther mot be a smal prikke that be dep, which prikke is the centre of thin epicicle.

Tak thanne by thy large compas the distaunce bytwixe centre aryn and the closere of the signes, which distaunce is the lengthe of lyne alhudda. And be it on a long rewle or elles be it on a long percemyn°, marke with thy compas the forseide distaunce, and devyde it in 60 parties equals. And than hastow a newe lyne alhudda.

Sek thanne in thy table of centres the semydiametre of the Epicicle° of Saturnus, and that is 6 degres and 30 minutes of swiche degres as ben 60 in line alhudda. Tak thanne with thy compas the space of 6 degres and 30 minutes of lyne alhudda, and set the fix point of thy compas in the centre of thin epicicle that is the poynt in the hed of the nail. And endelong the label set the moevable poynt of thi compas, and with that moevable poynt mak a marke, a strik° in the label, and fasteby° the strik writ SA for Saturne. This ensample of Saturne techith how to maken in the label alle the semydiametres of Epicicles of alle the planetis. *Nota* that the sonne ne hath non Epicicle, and *nota* that alwey as the label turnyth, so shewith it the Epicicle of every planete.

Laus Deo vero. Now hastow complet thyn equatorie with alle hise membris°. And *nota* that eccentrik of the sonne shal nat be compassed° in this epicicle. Explicit°.

The Face of the Equatorie

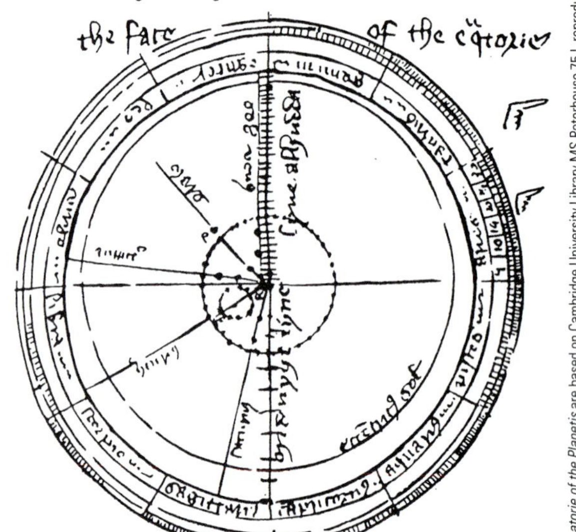

FIGURE 1. The Face of the Equatorie

Nota that every centre mot ben also° smal as a nedle°, and in every equant mot be a silk thred°.

Nota that the eccentrik of the sonne is compaced° on the bord of the instrument and nat on the lymbe for sparing° of metal.

Nota shortly that but so be that° bothe the closeres of the signes ben precisly ilike° of widnesse, and but so be that centre aryn stonde precise° as fer fro his closere of the signes as the centre of thin epicicle stondith fro the comune centre defferent precise, thyn epicicle

260 percemyn, (strip of) *parchment* **265 Epicicle,** *small orbit* (see 195n) **274 strik,** *slash* **275 fasteby,** *near* **283 membris,** *pieces* **284 compassed,** *marked* **285 Explicit,** (this treatise or this section) ends here **286 mot ben also,** *must be as* **287 nedle,** *needle-prick* **287–88 a silk thred,** i.e., a slash as fine as silk thread **290 compaced,** *marked* **291 sparing,** *saving* **292 but so be that,** *unless* **293 ilike,** *alike* **295 precise,** *precisely*

254 prikke: interlinear Latin gloss "id est punctus" (i.e., puncture). **261–62 devyde it in 60 parties,** these measurements were made previously (94–96) and erased (175–76); Price suggests this may indicate bad planning or the desire to complete the construction of the face before beginning the epicycle of the instrument. **271 poynt:** interlinear Latin gloss "punctus." **282 Laus Deo vero,** see 191n. Price suggests that this formula and the explicit at 285 indicate that the source may have ended here, and that another section (or another source) begins again at 343. The intervening summary and illustrations are original, and have similarities with Chaucer's *Astr.* **283–85 And *nota* . . . epicicle,** As Rand Schmidt observes, this is a single line in the manuscript, added before "Explicit" in a small version of the same hand. **284 eccentrik of the sonne,** see 91–92n. As noted in 291–93 and 305–06, the "eccentric" (i.e., somewhat off-center) circle of the sun's apparent path around the earth is marked on the board of the face of the equatory, the sixth circle counting inward. It is labeled "eccentrik sol" in figure 1. **286–342** In the manuscript, the text of these lines is arranged to flank the three figures, and in the case of Figure 1, fill space below it. The two pointing hands of Figure 1 align with the first and second notes in the text, lines 286 and 289 respectively, and a third pointing hand marks the beginning of the third note (292). A pointing hand also indicates the note in 502. After 342 there is a blank page (74v), which leads Price (p. 15) to think that the treatise was continued at a later date. **290–91 the bord . . . nat on the lymbe,** i.e., on the wooden portion of the face rather than on the attached metal limb (which would have to be larger if it were to accommodate more markings).

is fals. But natheles°, yif thow myshappe° in this cas I shal teche the a remedie. Knokke thi centre defferent innere or owtre til it stonde precise upon the closere of the signes in the lymbe of thin equatorie. So wole thanne the centre of thin epicicle precise stonde upon centre aryn.

The sixte cercle is the eccentric of the sonne. And the 5 cercle that is red is the closere of the signes. And the seccioun° of the crois is centre aryn. And that other centre is the centre of the eccentrik of the sonne. And the lyne devyded in 9 is the midnyht lyne (I wot° wel it is figured boistosly°). And the cercle abowte centre aryn is the centre defferent of the mone. The litel cercle is the defferent of mercurie. The smale lynes ben lynes of auges. The prikkes in the lynes ben the centris equantis and defferentis. And alle thise centres save the equant of Mars ben bytwixe centre aryn and the centre defferent of the mone. The owterest space° is mynutis, and the nexte space is degres, and the thridde space is nombres of degres, and the ferthe space is for names of signes. But natheless, the narwere cercle of the signes is cleped the closere of the signes, and it is compased with red.

Nota, file nat to ney° the rede cercle that is closere of the signes list° the commune centre defferent breke. Lat stonde a litel lippe as shewith in direct of° the hed of Cancer.

Nota, I conseile the ne write no names of signes til that thow hast proved that thi

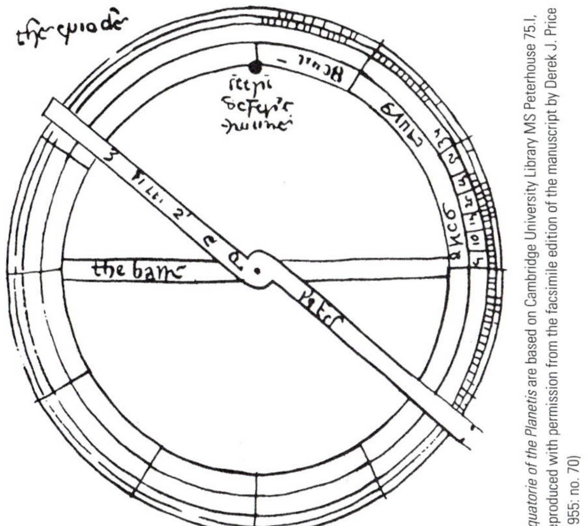

Figure 2. The epicycle.

comune centre defferent is trewli and justli set in direct of the closere of the signes of thin equatorie.

This epicicle is devyded and compased in alle thinges lik to the lymbe of the equatorie, but° it hath non eccentrik of the sonne. The prikke that stant in the closere of the signes in direct of the ende of Geminis is the commune centre defferent.

But natheless thus lith thin instrument whan thow makest equacioun° of thy mone:

Sek medius motus° of Saturnus, Juppiter, Mars, and Venus, and hir mene argumentis in thy tables, and writ hem in thy sklat°. Put thanne a blak thred in centre aryn, and a

298 natheles, *nevertheless,* **myshappe,** *err* **307 seccioun,** *intersection* **311 wot,** *know,* **figured boistosly,** *drawn crudely* **319 owterest space,** i.e., *outermost band* **326 file nat to ney,** *cut* (with a file) *not too near* **327 list,** *to avoid the possibility that* **329 in direct of,** *exactly at* **337 but,** *except that* **342 makest equacioun,** *determine the position* **343 Sek medius motus,** *seek the mean motion* (see n.) **345 sklat,** *slate* **346 centre aryn:** interlinear Latin gloss "terre" (earth).

299–304 Knokke . . . , Price notes that this may indicate the author's practical experience with making such instruments and he reports that modification of the equatory's epicycle does not impair its accuracy because it serves largely as a "sort of protractor for setting the label to its place." Rand Schmidt observes that a single "almost perpendicular stroke" crosses out the lines. **306 cercle that is red,** red ink is used here in the manuscript illustration of figure 1. **311 figured boistosly,** this apology supports the idea that the manuscript, including its diagrams, is the author's original work. **317 equant of Mars,** in his note, Price describes an apparent error in calculating the equant of Mars and marking it in figures 1 and 3. **328–29 litel lippe . . . hed of Cancer,** the head of Cancer coincides with the end of Gemini, the point called the common center defferent of the planets; it is marked on the inner rim of the epicycle of figure 3 with a heavy dot that seems to represent the lip or indicator mentioned. See 228–29 and 339–40. **331 signes:** interlinear Latin gloss "id est in epiciclo" (i.e., on the epicyle). **342 thy mone,** similar usage of the possessive pronoun as an idiom of familiarity recurs at 678; compare *Astr* 2.12.12n. **343ff. Sek medius motus . . . ,** Price (pp. 107–10) explains the technical terms for values used in the calculation of the planetary positions, values tabulated elsewhere in the manuscript. Latin "medius motus" (mean motion) refers to an angle or point in the zodiac posited for the purpose of calculating the position of the center of the Epicycle of a given planet. An "equacioun" is a correction or adjustment to this angle or point; once corrected, the reading of the motus is "verrey" (true, actual). An "argument" is a value or measurement of an arc of a circle or the corresponding angle of the two radii that define the arc. Above the text on fol. 75r (which begins with 343) is a Latin gloss: "pro argumentis trium superiorum minue eorum med' mot' de med' mot' solis et remanet argumentum" (for the arguments of the three superior planets subtract their medium motus from the medium motus of the sun and the argument will remain).

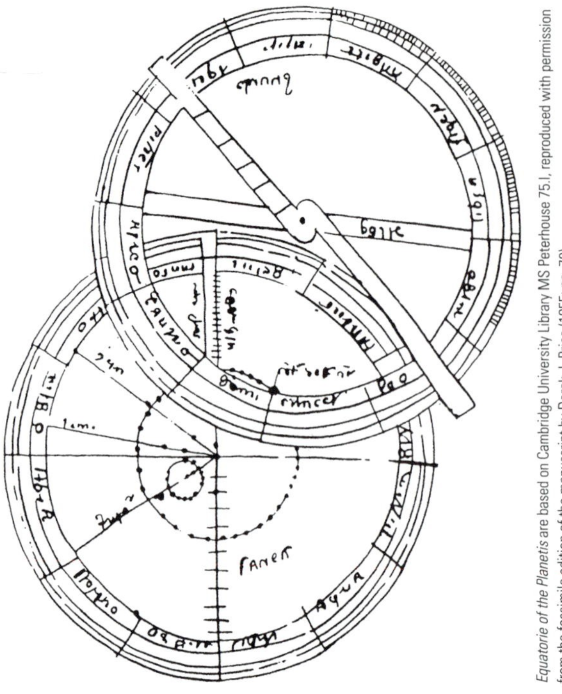

FIGURE 3.

whit thred in centre equant of any planete that the list have of equacion°. And put the comune centre defferent of thyn epicicle upon the centre different in thy plate of thilke planete that thow desirest to have equacioun. I sey that with a nedle thow shalt stike° the comune centre defferent of thin epicicle upon the centre defferent that is perced on thy plate for swich a planete as the list to have of equacioun.

Loke thanne fro° the hed of Aries wher the mene motus of thy planete endith, in the grete lymbe of thy plate, and ley ther thy blake thred. Ley thanne thy white thred equedistant by° the blake thred in the same lymbe, and proeve by a compas that thy thredes lyen equedistant. Under whiche white thred ley the pool° of thyn epicicle, and stondinge° thyn epicicle stille° in this maner—I seye, stondinge the pool of thin epicicle undir thy white thred stille, and the commune centre different fix with thy nedle to the forseide centre defferent of the planete desired—tak than thy blake thred and ley it so that it kerve° the centre of the epicicle and streche° forth up unto upperest part of the same epicicle. And than shal this blake thred shewe bothe the verrey motus of the Epicicle in the grete lymbe, and ek the verrey aux° of the planete in the epicicle. And thanne the ark bytwixe medios motus of the planete and the verrey motus of the Epicicle is cleped° the equation° of his centre in the lymbe, to whom is lik° the equacion of his argument in his epicicle. That is to sein the ark bytwixe his mene aux and his verrey aux. For sothly°, the mene aux is shewed in the epicicle, by the white thred under which thow puttest the pol of the epicicle, and the verrey aux is shewed in the epicicle by the blake thred.

And stondinge stille° thin epicicle in this same disposicioun, ley the ende of thy label that is graven fro° the white thred as many signes, degres, and minutes as shewith the mene

---

348 the list have of equacioun, *you wish to calculate the position of* **352 stike,** *fix* **357 Loke thanne fro,** *find then starting from* **361 equedistant by,** *parallel to* **364 pool,** *pole* (i.e., center), **stondinge,** *holding in place* **365 stille,** *firmly* **371 kerve,** *cuts across,* **streche,** *reaches* **375 verrey aux,** *true apogee* (see 105 and 41n) **378 cleped,** *called,* **equation,** *calculation* **379 to whom is lik,** *which is equal to* **382 sothly,** *truly* **387 stondinge stille,** *holding in place* **388–89 ley the ende of thy label that is graven fro,** *place the marked end of your ruler away from* (see n.)

Figure 3, as Price notes, the complete equatory here shows the common center defferent of the planets (at the head of Cancer) aligned by pin with one of holes in the circle of the center defferent of the moon to determine the ecliptic longitude of the moon. **347 centre equant,** see 121n. The marking of centers equant on the main plate is described in 120ff. **348–49 comune centre defferent of thyn epicicle,** see 340. **350 centre different in thy plate,** see 150–52. *Different* and *defferent* are used interchangeably. **357 Loke thanne:** interlinear Latin gloss "pro successione signorum" (by the succession of signs [i.e., counterclockwise]). **359ff. ley ther thy blake thred . . . ,** for the basics of the uses of threads in this operation, see Price, p. 54, fig. 3. **368 forseide,** reading from Rand Schmidt; Price reads "foreseide." **374 motus:** interlinear Latin gloss "locum" (position). **374–76 Epicicle . . . epicicle,** for the two uses of the word, see 195n. **379 lymbe:** interlinear Latin gloss "zodiacus." **381 That is to sein the ark . . . ,** the equation of the argument of the given planet is determined by the arc on the epicycle that measures the difference between the planet's mean apogee ("aux") and its true apogee. This value is equal to ("is lik" 379) the equation of the center measured on the limb or border of the plate. **388–89 label that is graven,** the marking (or engraving) of the planets on the ruler is described in 264–78.

argument in thy tables for that day of thy planete desired. And rekne this mene argument fro the white thred after successioun of signes° of every planete, save° only of the mone. And ligginge° the marked ende of thy label upon the ende of this mene argument in the epicicle, ley thy blake thred upon the marke of thy planete that is graven in thi label. And wher as° the same blake thred kervyth the lymbe of thy plate, tak ther the verrey place of the planete in the 9 spere. And the ark bytwixe the verrey place of the planete and the verrey place of the Epicicle considered in the lymbe is cleped Equacioun of his Argument.

This maner of equacioun° is for Saturnus, Juppiter, Mars, and Venus, but in the remenaunt of planetes in some thinges it varieth.

Sol

The mene motus of the sonne ben rekned fro the hed of Aries after successioun of signes. The sonne hath non Epicicle, ne non equant, and therfor the pol° of the epicicle mot ben instide° of the body of the sonne in the 9 spere. The white thred that thow puttest in his centre defferent in the plate mot ben instide of the white thred that othre planetes han in hir centres equantis.

The blake thred that evermo stant in centre aryn mot be leid at the ende of his mene motus. Tak thanne his white thred and lei it equedistant in the lymbe by° the blake thred, whiche blake thred shewith the mene motus of the sonne.

Fixe thanne with thy nedle the commune centre defferent of thyn epicicle to centre aryn, and remew° nat thy nedle. And under this white thred ley softely° the pol of the epicicle, and wher as the white thred kervyth the grete lymbe tak ther the verrey place of the sonne in the 9 spere.

The ark of the lymbe bytwixe his aux, that is now in Cancer, and the blake thred, is the argument of the sonne. The ark bytwixe the blake thred and the white in the lymbe is the equacion of the sonne, which ark nis but litel.

The mene motus of the sonne is the ark in the lymbe bytwixe the hed of Aries and the blake thred in the same lymbe. The verrey motus of the sonne is the ark of the lymbe bytwixe the hed of Aries and the blake thred whan it is remewed fro the mene motus and crossith the white thred in the pol of the epicicle. The same verrey motus was shewed erst° by the white thred of the defferent whan it lay equedistant by the blake thred in the limbe.

And *nota* that the markes in thy label descriven the Epicicles of planetes as the label turneth.

Mercurius (this canon is false)

Rekne after succession of signes fro the hed of Aries in the lymbe the mene motus of Mercurius, and considere ek how mochel° in the same lymbe is bytwixe the hed of Aries and the lyne of his aux that yit° is in the lattere ende of Libra. And rekne alwey after successioun of signes.

Withdraw° thanne the quantite° in the lymbe bytwix the hed of Aries and the forseid aux owt of his mene motus and considere how moche is the remnaunt° of his mene motus whan

393 after successioun of signes, *following the sequence of zodiacal signs* (i.e., counterclockwise) **394 save,** *except* **395 ligginge,** *placing* **399 wher as,** *wherever* **405 equacioun,** *calculation* **412 pol,** *center* **412–13 mot ben instide,** *must be used instead* **421 equedistant in the lymbe by,** *on the border parallel to* **426 remew,** *remove* **427 softely,** *carefully* **444 erst,** *before* **452 mochel,** *much* **454 yit,** *still* **457 Withdraw,** *subtract,* **quantite,** *amount* **460 remnaunt,** *remainder*

391 thy tables, the manuscript reads "thy grene tables," with "grene" lined out. Tables of mean arguments for the planets are included in the manuscript; as Price notes, green ink is not used on them although it is used to outline a different table. **399–400 kervyth the lymbe of thy plate,** cuts across the border of the plate. Price gives a useful diagram in his edition (p. 54). **400 place:** interlinear Latin gloss "locum" (position). **402 place:** interlinear Latin gloss "locum" (position). **planete:** interlinear Latin gloss "in limbo" (on the border). **408a** ***Sol,*** sun. Subtitle in the left margin, after a one-line gap in the manuscript. The new section is in the same hand, though smaller. **415 plate:** interlinear Latin gloss "lamina" (plate). **426 nedle,** interlinear. **442 it:** interlinear Latin gloss "id est filium" (that is, the thread). **449a** ***Mercurius (this canon is false),*** atop the page, with "Mercurius" lined out and "this canon is fals" added. **450–506,** a single page, it has been crossed-out with diagonals for excision. Presumably the comment about the false "canon" (rule) was added when the excision marks were made; see also 551a. For much of the page, the punctuation has been marked over in red.

this aux is thus withdrawe owt of al the hoole mene mot. And so mochel° rekne after succession of signes in his litel cercle, fro the lyne of his aux that kervyth the same litel cercle. I seye°, rekne after successioun of signes, from lettere D that is graven in his lytel cercle, and procede in the same litel cercle toward lettere E opposit to D.

I sey rekne thilke° remnaunt of the mene motus that dwelde° whan the quantite of his aux was withdraw owt of his hole mene motus, as I have seid byforn. And wher as° thilk remnaunt forseid endith in the litel cercle, tak ther the verrey centre defferent of Mercurie, as it happith diversely somtyme in on hole and somtyme in an other. For lettere D ne servyth of nothyng ellis but for to shewe the wher thow shalt bygynne thy reknyng in thy litel cercle; ne lettere E ne servyth nat but for to shewe the which wey that thow shalt procede fro lettere D.

Now hastow founde thy defferent and thin equant, in which equant put a whit thred and stike° with a nedle the comune centre defferent upon his centre defferent in the plate. And with thin epicicle wirk and with thy thredes as thow workest with Saturnus, Juppiter, Mars, and Venus.

Nota that yif the aux of Mercurie be fro the hed of Aries more than his mene motus fro the same hed, than shaltow adde 12 signes to his mene motus. Than maistow withdraw his aux owt of his mene motus.

And *nota* generaly that thy nedle ne be nat remewed° whan it is stikyd thorw the commune centre defferent into any centre different on thy plate til thin equacion of the planete be endid, for yif thy commune centre different stirte° fro the centre on thy plate, al thin equacion of thy planete desired is lorn°.

Hic nota that the centre defferent of Mercurie hath but 24 holes as in myn instrment, wherfor I rekne but 2 holes for a signe, as in the gretter cerkle of Mercurie fro the lyne of his aux.

Luna

Rekne after succession of signes fro the hed of Aries in the lymbe the mene motus of the mone, and rekne in the same manere the mene motus of the sonne as fer as it strechcheth. Withdraw thanne the mene motus of the sonne owt of the mene motus of the mone, and considere that difference. And the quantite of that difference, that I clepe° the remenaunt. Rekne it fro the ende of the mene motus of the sonne in the lymbe bakward agayn successioun of signes°, and wheras endith this remenaunt mak a mark in the lymbe.

Draw thanne thy blake thred to this forseide mark, and wher as thy blake thred kervyth the cercle defferent of the mone, in that same hole is the centre defferent of the mone, as it happith. And in the nadyr of° this hole is the centre equant. Put thanne in this centre equant a whit thred. Now hastow thy two centres.

Stike thanne thy commune centre defferent upon the centre defferent of the mone. With thy nedle yit rekne agayn the mene motus of the mone fro the hed of Aries after successioun of signes, and ley ther thy blake thred. And ley thy white thred equedistant by° the blake thred in the lymbe.

Moeve thanne softely° the pool of thyn epicicle under thy blake thred. Tak thanne

462 so mochel, *as much* **464 seye,** *repeat* (say) **469 thilke,** *that* **470 dwelde,** *remained* **472 wher as,** *wherever* **484 stike,** *fix* **495 remewed,** *removed* **499 stirte,** *shifts* **501 lorn,** *lost* **514 clepe,** *call* **516–17 bakward agayn successioun of signes,** *clockwise* **523 nadyr of,** *point opposite to* **532 equedistant by,** *parallel to* **534 softely,** *carefully*

462 mene mot, i.e., "mene motus"; an abbreviation is missing; see note to 343ff. **462–63 after succession of signes,** counterclockwise; an error, reiterated at 465–66. The calculation around the small circle should be clockwise. **469–70 of the mene motus,** added in the margin. **479 E,** interlinear. **480–81 shewe the which wey that thow shalt procede,** another error; letters at either end of a diameter cannot indicate direction. Price notes also that another, more serious theoretical error underlies the instructions here. **486 epicicle,** the manuscript reads "epicle." **502 *Hic nota*,** note this. There is a pointing hand in the margin; see 286–342n. **503 hath but 24 holes as in myn instrment,** see 102n. **506a *Luna*,** moon; written at the top of the page and in the left hand margin alongside the writing space. **510 sonne:** interlinear Latin gloss "a capite arietis" (from the head of Aries). **512 of the moone:** an erroneous claim is cancelled here "and as moche as the mene mot of the mone is more than the mene mot of the sonne." **514 remenaunt,** Price notes that the "modern equivalent" is the "mean elongation of the Moon." **515 ende of the,** interlinear. **535–37 Tak thanne . . . the epicicle,** interlinear.

thy white thred and ley it over the pol of the epicicle, and wheras° thy white thred kervyth° the cercle of the epicicle, tak ther the mene aux in thyn epicicle, and fro this white thred rekne in thyn epicicle bakward agayns successioun of signes thy mene argument.

I seye rekne it in the degres of thin epicicle, and where as endith thy reknynge in the epicicle, ley ther the marked ende of thy label°. And ley thy blake thred upon the mark of the mone in thy label. And wher as this same blake thred kervyth the lymbe, tak ther the verrey place of the mone in the 9 spere.

Nota that the pool of the epicicle ne shal nat ben leyd under the blake thred of non other planete save only of the mone.

(this canon° is fals)

And *nota* that yif the mene motus of the sonne is more than the mene mot of the mone, than shaltow adde 12 signes to the mone mot of the mone, and thanne maistow withdrawe° the mene mot of the sonne owt of the mene motus of the mone.

And shortly for to speken of this theorike, I sey that the centre of hir° *(lune)* Epicicle *in volvella* moevyth equally aboute the centre of the zodiac, that is to sein, aboute the pol° of the epicicle that is thy riet°.

And thy blake thred, whan it first leid thorw° the pol of thyn epicicle, it shewith the verrey aux of the planete, riht as the white thred shewith the mene aux in the same epicicle. Item, whan thow hast rekned the argument° of a planete in thin epicicle, thanne is the body of the planete in thin epicicle at the ende of thyn argument. And whan thy blak thred is leid thorw the marke of a planete in thi label, in maner, forseid, than shewith thy blake thred the verre° place of the planete at regard of° the 9 spere, as shewith in thy lymbe.

And the ark bytwixe the verrey motus and the mene motusof the mone is the equacion of his argument in the lymbe. And the ark bytwixe his mene aux and his verrey aux is the equacion of his argument in the epicicle.

To knowe the latitude of the mone by thyn instrument, loke in thyn almenak the verrey motus of the mone and the verry motus of Caput Draconis Lune° at the same tyme. And yif so be that thy verre mot° of thy mone be lasse than 6 signes fro Caput Draconis, withdraw the verrey motus of Caput owt of the verrey motus of the mone and writ that difference, for that is hir *(i.e., lune)* verrey argument.

And so many signes, degrees, and minutes as thow hast in the verrey argument of hir latitude, rekne hem fro the hed of Aries after successioun of signes° in thy lymbe, and wher as endith thy reknyng, ley that on end° of the thred. And the middle of thy thred shal kerve° the meridional lyne and strechche so forth overthwart al the dyametre of thy plate unto the lymbe.

As thus, I suppose° that on ende of thy thred laye after succession of signes 10 degres fro the hed of Aries; in the lymbe that other ende of thy thred shold lye 20 degres of Virgo in the lymbe. Considere thanne how

---

537 wheras, *wherever,* **kervyth,** *cuts across* **544 label,** *ruler* **551a** ***canon,*** *rule* **555 withdrawe,** *subtract* **558 theorike,** *principle* **559 hir,** *its* **561 pol,** *center* **562 riet,** *upper plate* (see n.) **563 thorw,** *across* **567 argument,** *arc of motion* (see n. to 343ff.) **573 verre,** *true,* **at regard of,** *in relation to* **584 Caput Draconis Lune,** *Head of the Moon Dragon* (see n.) **585 mot,** *motus* (motion) **593–94 after successioun of signes,** *counterclockwise* **595 ley that on end,** *place there one end* **597 kerve,** *intersect* **600 As thus, I suppose,** *for example, if I assume*

547 ther, interlinear. **551a** ***(this canon is fals),*** added atop folio 77r; the page opens with 552–80, which Price and Rand Schmidt report as canceled with crossing diagonals (compare 450–506n). Price finds no serious error in the calculation here. **558 theorike,** a term used to describe the intended treatment of Part 5 of *Astr,* Prologue 105. **559** ***(lune)*****,** moon's; interlinear Latin gloss. **559–60** ***in volvella,*** rotating; interlinear Latin gloss. **562 riet,** a technical term; the rete is one of the parts of an astrolabe, similar to the epicycle of the equatory in that it is read against the main face or plate. See *Astr* 1.3.5n. **565 planete,** interlinear "in epiciclo." **567 hast,** interlinear. **570 thy,** in right margin. **584 Caput Draconis Lune,** the head of the moon dragon is the point where the moon's ascending orbit intersects the sun's apparent path, causing an eclipse; the dragon is the legendary beast that swallows the moon to cause the eclipse. **585 verre mot,** true motion; see note to 343ff. **589** Marginal Latin gloss: "i.e., verum argumentum latitudinis Lune" (that is, the true argument of the latitude of the moon). ***(i.e., lune)*****,** that is, the moon's; interlinear Latin gloss. **590 argument:** interlinear Latin gloss "id est latitudinis" (that is, its latitude). **592 verrey,** interlinear. **592–93 of hir latitude,** interlinear. **597 meridional lyne,** Price notes that this is another name for line alhudda of 175–81, the radius on the face of the equatory that extends from its center to its top.

many degres and minutes that the middel of thy thred lith fro centre aryn° wher as evermo bygynnith° this reknyng—I seye°, considere in the seccions of the meridional lyne how many degres and minutes lith the middel of thy thred fro centre aryn, and tak ther the nombre of the latitude septentrional° of thy mone fro the ecliptik, which latitude ne passith never 5 degres.

And yif the verrey motus of the mone be more than 6 signes fro the verrey mot° of Caput°, than shaltow withdraw the verrey motus of Cauda° owt of the verrey motus of the mone, and bygynne thy reknynge at the hed of Libra and procede bakward agayns successioun of signes°.

As thus, that yif that on ende° of thy thred laye agayn successioun of signes 10 degres fro the hed of Libra, than sholde that other ende lye in the 10 degres fro the hed of Aries after successioun of signes.

Considere thanne in the meridional lyne the quantite meridional° of the latitude of thy mone fro the ecliptik, as I have told byforn, that the quantite of degres and minutes that the middel of thy thred in the meridional lyne lith fro centre aryn, the same quantite of degres and minutes is the latitude of the mone fro the eclyptik, be it north, be it sowth.

And *nota* that generaly evermo° bothe endes of thy thred shollen lyen equedistant fro° thilke diametre that kervyth° the hevedes of Aries and Libra.

Yit quykly° understond this canon°. I sey when the forseide verrey argument of the mone is precisly 90 degres fro the hed of Aries in the lymbe after succession of signes, tak ther the grettest latitude of the mone septentrional. And yif so be that hir verrey argument passe anything 90 degres fro the hed of Aries, styrt° over the meridional lyne into the firste of Cancer, and ley ther that on ende of thy thred and that other ende into the laste of Geminis. And so forth, day by day, shaltow descende in the meridional lyne after that the reknynge of thy verrey argument requerith til thow come agayn to centre aryn, for than hastow mad equacion° of latitudes for 6 signes, as I first seide. And everemo lith thy thred equedistant fro the diametre that kervyth the hevedes of Aries and Libra.

And evermo as many degres and minutes as the midel of thy thred lith in the meridional lyne fro centre aryn, so many degres and minutes is the latitude of the mone fro the ecliptik. And whan thy verrey argument passith 6 signes, wyrk with Cauda as I tawhte the, and ascende upward in the meridional lyne day by day to the laste° of Geminis in° the lymbe. And fro thennes discende agayn, as I have seid byforn.

And *nota* that whan the mone is direct with° Caput or Cauda, she hath no latitude, and whan she passith Caput til she be 3 signes in distance fro Caput she is septentrional ascendinge, and in hir grettest latitude septentrional. And fro the ende of thilke 3 signes she is septentrional descending til she come to the opposit of Caput, that is to seyn Cauda Draconis, and fro Cauda til she come mid wey bytwix Capud and Cauda. And fro thennes is she meridional assending til she come agayn at Capud.

(1391, 17 Decembris) Ensample: my mone was 12 degres 21 minutes of Virgo, and Caput was 4 degres 46 minutes of Aries. Tho drow° I the verrey motus of Caput, that is to seyn 0 in signes 4 degres 46 minutes, owt

606 centre aryn, *center of the equatory, representing earth* (see 50n) **606–07 wher as evermo bygynnith,** *from which this reckoning always begins,* **seye,** *repeat* **611 septentrional,** *northward* **615 mot,** *motus* (motion) **616 Caput,** *head* (of the moon dragon; see 584n) **617 Cauda,** *tail* (of the moon dragon; the point of the descending orbital intersection) **619–20 bakward agayns successioun of signes,** *clockwise* **621 on ende,** *one end* **627 meridional,** *southward* **634 generaly evermo,** *in all cases* **635–36 lyen equedistant fro,** *lie parallel to* **636 kerveyth,** *intersects* **638 quykly,** *clearly,* **canon,** *rule* **645 styrt,** *cross* **652 mad equacion,** *worked out* **663 laste,** *end,* **in,** *on* **666–67 direct with,** *exactly at* **681 Tho drow,** *then subtracted*

608–09 meridional lyne, see 597n. **615 verrey mot,** true motus or motion; see note to 343ff. **642 septentrional,** interlinear Latin gloss "i.e. ab ecliptica" (that is, from the ecliptic [the sun's apparent path]). **644 anything,** interlinear. **669 in distance,** interlinear Latin gloss "pro successionibus signorum" (by procession of signs). **675 mid wey,** interlinear Latin gloss "in medio." **and Cauda,** Price notes that an addition is necessary for sense: "she is meridional descending" (it is southward descending). **678 Ensample,** Price notes that the dates and numbers in the three examples conform to the tables that are included in the manuscript and hence are probably practical illustrations (as contrasted with the theoretical examples in *Astr*). Although there are errors, the calculations are so accurate that they must have been worked out from the tables rather than the instrument. Given here in parentheses, the date for each example is written in the left-hand margin of the manuscript. **my mone,** see 342n.

of the verrey moevyng of the mone, that is to sein owt of 5 signes 12 degres 21 minutes. Tho fond I that the verrey argument of the mone dwelde° 5 signes 7 degres 35 minutes.

Tho rekned I after successioun of signes° fro the hed of Aries in the lymbe the same 5 signes 7 degres 35 minutes, and ther leide I that on ende of my thred, and that other ende lay in 22 degres 35 minutes of Aries. Tho karf° the midel of my thred the meridional lyne, I degre and 54 minutes fro centre aryn, by which I knew that the latitude of my mone was I degre and 54 minutes septentrional° descending fro the ecliptik.

(1391, 19 Februarii) Another ensample: I fond my mone in 8 degres 13 minutes of Virgo, and Caput Draconis in 20 degres and 42 minutes of Aries. Tho drow I the verrey motus of Caput fro the verrey motus of the mone in this manere. I say wel that I myht nat drawe 20 degres owt of 8 degres, ne 42 minutis owt of 13 minutes. Tho added I 30 degres to the forseide 8 degres of Virgo, and 60 minutes to the 13 minutes of the same Virgo. And tho drow I the verrey motus of Caput owt of the verrey motus of the mone. Tho dwelde me the verrey argument of the latitude of the mone, that is to seyn 4 signes 17 degres 31 minutes.

Tho leide I that on ende of my thred 4 signes 17 degres 31 minuta fro the hed of Aries in the lymbe after successioun of signes, and that other ende lay equedistant fro the diametre that passith by the hevedes of Aries and Libra. And tho fond I the middel of my thred karf the meridional lyne at 3 degres and 22 minutes fro the centre of the erthe that is centre aryn. Wherfor I knew wel that my mone was 3 degres 22 minutes in latitude septentrional descendinge fro the ecliptik.

(1391, 23 Februarii) The thridde ensample is this: I fond in myn almenak the verrey motus of the mone was 6 degres 24 minutes of Scorpio, and the verrey motus of Caput was 20 degres 29 minutes of Aries. Tho moste° I wirke with Cauda bycause that verre motus of my mone passed mor than 6 signes. Tho drow I the verrey motus of Cauda owt of the verrey motus of the mone in this maner. I added 30 degres to 6 degres of Scorpio and 60 minutes to 24 minutes of the same Scorpio. Tho dwelde me the verrey argument of latitude of the mone, 0 in signes 15 degres 55 minutes.

Tho leide I that on ende of my thred 0 in signes 15 degres 55 minutes fro the hed of Libra agains succession of signes bycause that I wirke with Cauda. And that other ende of my thred lay equedistant fro the diametre that passith by° the hevedes of Aries and Libra. And tho fond I that the middel of my thred karf the meridional lyne, 1 degre 22 minutes fro centre aryn. Bi which I knew the latitude of my mone was 1 degre 22 minutes fro the ecliptil meridional° discendinge.

Thus shaltow procede day by day upward fro the hed of Libra unto 90 degres agayns succession of signes, that is to seyn unto the firste of Cancer, and thanne stirt over the meridional lyne whan thy verrey argument of thy latitude of the mone passit anything° 90 degres, and ley that on ende of thy thred in Gemini and that other ende in Cancer and so com downward day bi day til thow come agayn at centre aryn. And thanne wink with Caput as I have told byfore.

And *nota* that whan any eclips *(lune)* fallith in Aries, Taurus, Gemini, Cancer, Leo, Virgo, than is the eclips in Caput, and the remenant of the eclipses ben in Cauda.

686 dwelde, *remained* **687 after successioun of signes,** *counterclockwise* **692 karf,** *intersected* **695 septentrional,** *northward* **727 Tho moste,** *then must* **742 passith by,** *goes through* **747 ecliptil meridional,** *ecliptic southward* **753 passit anything,** *exceeds at all*

688 the same, interlinear. **692 the,** interlinear. **697–98 I fond:** interlinear Latin gloss "scilicet in almenak" (namely, in the almanac). Price notes that it would have been unusual to record the true place of the moon with such precision in an almanac; it is more likely that tables would have been used. **710 4 signes,** interlinear. **713 31 minuta,** interlinear. **715 lay,** interlinear. **734–35 of latitude,** interlinear. **739 agains succession of signes,** interlinear. **759–63** Price notes that this is not accurate. **759 *(lune)*,** (of the moon); interlinear Latin gloss.

Chaucer in His Time

Chaucer's Language and Versification

The Text of This Edition

Chaucer in His Time

NOT ONE OF THE 493 records printed and discussed in the *Chaucer Life-Records,* ed. M. M. Crow and C. Olson (1966, no. 146), identifies Chaucer as an author. They chronicle the distinguished career of a courtier, diplomat, and civil servant. This must have been the character in which Chaucer viewed himself. His poetry he must have regarded as a fortunate talent by which he could advance his career in government. Only this can account for the fact that so many of his pieces were never finished and for the fact that, so far as we can tell, no manuscript of his works dates from before his death. Evidently, like Shakespeare, he gave no thought to the "publication" of his writings. The performance satisfied their intention. But this lack of interest in preserving an official canon contrasts with the hints we have of his desire to be remembered as a poet—in the *House of Fame,* at the conclusion of *Troylus and Criseyde,* in the lists of his titles in the *Legend of Good Women,* and the Retraction to the *Canterbury Tales.*

The life-records show Chaucer emerging from the class in society that has produced the most notable writers in England and elsewhere, the prosperous upper middle class that must continue to work for a living, but with cultivation, education, some leisure, and resources to collect and create in the intellectual and aesthetic sphere. Until F. J. Furnivall in 1876 discovered a deed of conveyance of a house on Thames Street in which Chaucer described himself as "me Galfridum Chaucer filium Johannis Chaucer vinetarii Londonie," his specific parentage was not known. But as early as 1598, Thomas Speght, in the biography attached to his edition, had surmised of his parents, "whether they were Merchants, (for in the places where they have dwelled, the Armes of the Merchants of the Staple have been seene in the glasse windowes), or whether they were of other calling, it is not necessary to search; but wealthy no doubt they were, and of good account in the commonwealth, who brought up their Sonne in such sort, that both he was thought fitte for the Court at home, and to be imployed for matters of State in forraine countreyes." This surmise has been largely confirmed by modern scholarship. Chaucer's father and other relatives were wealthy vintners (wine importers and wholesale merchants), who served in the army, furnished provisions for the court, and occupied official positions both for the king and the City of London.

The nature of the first records reveals how fragmentary and fortuitous our knowledge of Chaucer is. These turned up in 1851 on some scraps used as stuffing in the covers of a manuscript now owned by the British Library. They are a list of the expenses and gifts from 1356 to 1359 of the household of Elizabeth, Countess of Ulster and wife of Lionel, second son of Edward III. Her two attendants mentioned most frequently are Philippa Pan' and Galfrido Chaucer. Chaucer's function is not indicated; presumably he was a page. Philippa's identity has been much debated. The most attractive theory is that "Pan'" is a contraction of "Panneto," one form of the name of Sir Paon de Roet, father of Philippa Chaucer and Katherine Swynford, who was mistress and eventually (1396) wife of John of Gaunt, Duke of Lancaster, third son of Edward III. If this surmise is correct, Chaucer married the demoiselle with whom he had served as a young boy.

The date of Chaucer's birth is not known. In the Scrope-Grosvenor trial of 1386, he gave his age as "xl ans et plus armeez par xxvii ans"—forty years and more, having borne arms for twenty-seven years. Efforts have failed to make these terms precise, but the first part sets Chaucer's birth before 1346. The customary age for going to war was sixteen or seventeen, which would move the date back to 1342 or earlier. The twenty-seven years is quite accurate, because in 1359–1360 he served in the French war. In 1360 he was captured and ransomed for sixteen pounds—thirteen shillings fourpence less than for Sir Robert de Clinton's horse, as has been often remarked. Such military experience for Chaucer, as for his father before him, was clearly expected of one who hoped to be accepted by an aristocracy whose business was still war, even though his own ambitions might run in a totally different direction. Chaucer had no doubt been given a good elementary education before he joined the household of the countess. Serving in a noble household and joining Prince Lionel on a military expedition must have been regarded as a continuation of his education.

But the period between the 1360 record of his military service and 1366, when he reappears traveling in Spain, is the longest gap in Chaucer's life-records after their commencement in 1357. Indeed, there are records every year from 1366 until the last one in 1400. The best supposition is that during these six years he was continuing his education in the Inns of Chancery and Inns of Court, which prepared him for an administrative career. In the Inns of Chancery, aspiring clerks were taught, first, the Chancery hand in which all official documents had to be written and, second, the forms and language (in Chaucer's time still Latin and French) in which they were enrolled. Without such training, Chaucer could not have been appointed controller of customs in 1374 with the provision that "rotulos suos dicta officia tangentes manu sua propria scribat"—that he write the rolls touching said office in his own hand. After two or three years in an Inn of Chancery, he could proceed to an Inn of Court, where he would hear lectures on law and government. The only evidence for such education comes much too late. Speght, in the 1598 life already referred to, said that "manye yeres since, master Buckley did see a recorde [of the Inner Temple], where Geffrye Chaucer was fined two shillinges for beatinge a Franciscane fryer in fletestreate." No records from the Inns of Court in Chaucer's day have survived, but Edith Rickert discovered that Master Buckley was keeper of the records of the Inner Temple in Speght's time, and so in a position to see such a record, and the offense and penalty are similar to others listed in the earliest records that do survive.

By 1366 this period was over and Chaucer reappears traveling in Spain, probably in connection with the Black Prince's campaign in support of Don Pedro of Castile, to whose fate Chaucer later alluded in the *Monk's Tale* (*CT* 7.2375ff.), but possibly simply on a pilgrimage to the shrine of St. James of Compostella (*CT* 1.466). In the same year the king granted Philippa Chaucer a life annuity of ten marks as a demoiselle in attendance upon Queen Philippa, and in 1367 the king granted Geoffrey his first annuity of twenty marks. Scholars have debated the timing and the wording of these grants. The facts that Philippa was referred to in her own person rather than as the wife of Geoffrey Chaucer and that she received her grant first make it appear that Chaucer had married above himself and that Philippa's connections in court would do his career no harm. Her father, Sir Paon de Roet, had come from Hainault in northern France in Queen Philippa's personal entourage, and he was Guienne King of Arms—that is, he was charged with recording the genealogies of the noble families in England's valuable territories in southern France.

From 1367 to 1374 Chaucer was "vallectus" (yeoman); in 1368 he was promoted to "armiger" (esquire) in the king's household, but without specific assignment. His status during this period is described in the *Liber Niger* of the household of Edward IV (the household ordinances of Edward III have not survived): "These Esquires of household of old be accustomed, winter and summer, in afternoones and eveninges to drawe to Lordes chambres within court, there to keep honest company after there Cunninge [i.e., skill, knowledge], in talking of Chronicles of Kinges, and of otheres pollicies, or in pipeing or harpeing, songinges, or other actes marcealles, to helpe to occupie the Court, and accompanie estraingers till the time require of departing." We can see how one with a gift for storytelling and poetry would be in demand. ("Chronicles of kings" are specifically referred to in the *Book of the Duchess,* 11. 57–58.) The contacts one made in such a situation would be the foundations for a career.

We see this career developing as Chaucer is assigned to carry messages abroad and serve on diplomatic missions, in 1368 and 1370 to France and in 1372–1373 on a six-month trip to Italy. On this trip he visited Genoa and Florence. Boccaccio was in Florence that winter, lecturing on Dante, and Petrarch was living in Padua, near Venice. There is no evidence that Chaucer met either, but it is hard to believe that one concerned with poetry would have missed the opportunity. Upon his return to England, he began immediately to show the influence of Dante and Boccaccio, and the Clerk (*CT* 4.27) says that he learned his tale from Petrarch in Padua. If Chaucer ever did meet either Boccaccio or Petrarch, it would have had to be at this time, because Petrarch died in 1374 and Boccaccio in 1375, before Chaucer's next trip to Italy in 1378.

Chaucer's extended absence in 1372–1373 involves a domestic situation that has troubled some scholars. One of the problems of Chaucer biography is his relation to Thomas Chaucer, one of the wealthiest men in England in the fifteenth century, whose daughter became Duchess of Suffolk, whose grandson married the sister of Edward IV, and whose great-grandson was declared heir apparent to Richard III, only to be killed in battle. Thomas Chaucer is referred to as the son of Geoffrey Chaucer in contemporary records, but his birth and early years are shrouded in mystery. After using the Chaucer coat of arms for a few years, he shifted to the de Roet arms of his mother. It has been suggested that the reason for his rapid advancement was that he was the illegitimate son of John of Gaunt by Philippa. From Gaunt's illegitimate children by Philippa's sister Katherine (legitimized by Gaunt's marriage to Katherine in 1396) were descended all of the English kings after Henry VI. If there is any truth in the conjecture that Philippa was also Gaunt's mistress—which is not unimportant in view of Chaucer's treatment of women in his writings and in view of the progress of his own career—it depends on the timing of events in 1373–1374.

When Chaucer departed for Italy in December 1372, Philippa was one of the demoiselles-in-waiting upon Gaunt's second wife, Constance of Castile, and Katherine (who that year bore Gaunt John Beaufort) was governess to his children by Blanche of Lancaster. Chaucer returned on May 23, 1373. On July 13 Gaunt went to lead a campaign in France. He returned to England in April 1374, and within two months Chaucer was made financially independent: on April 23 the king granted him a pitcher of wine daily (perhaps eighteen thousand dollars a year at present values); on May 10 he was given the house over Aldgate rent-free; on June 8 he was appointed controller of customs (another ten pounds—fifteen thousand dollars a year); and on June 13 he and Philippa together were granted another life annuity of ten pounds by John of Gaunt. All of this, together with previous grants and subsequent gifts and wardships, made Chaucer a prosperous man.

Philippa continued to receive gifts and payments from Gaunt, always in her own name, and the year before her death in 1387 she was admitted, again without her husband, to the fraternity of Lincoln Cathedral in a ceremony honoring the admission of Gaunt's oldest son, the future Henry IV. Although her annuity was usually drawn at the hand of her husband, warrants transferring payments in 1378–1379 to receivers in Lincolnshire indicate that Philippa did not live with Chaucer over Aldgate the entire period after 1374, a circumstance that may throw light on the wry self portrait in the *House of Fame* (11.641–660). And while we are setting down these personal details, there is the curious business of the legal release granted in May 1380, by Cecily Champain to Geoffrey Chaucer for her "raptus." Despite arguments to the contrary, legal opinion holds that the word means what it says—that Chaucer had been sued for rape and had to seek legal quittance. Since the quittance came after the fact, this episode must have occurred around the time that Philippa was living in Lincolnshire. Scholars have conjectured that "Litell Lowys," to whom the *Treatise on the Astrolabe* is addressed, might have been the consequence of this episode (*Astrolabe,* 1. 27n).

Chaucer's earliest poetry is related to the household of John of Gaunt. Whether or not the *Prier a Nostre Dame* was written for Blanche of Lancaster, the *Book of the Duchess* was certainly composed as an elegy on her death in 1368. Fifteenth-century collector and critic John Shirley asserted that the *Complaint of Mars* was likewise composed at the command of John of Gaunt. So both in documented fact and in undocumented tradition and surmise, Chaucer's literary and personal lives were entangled with the house of Lancaster.

But Chaucer's main career continued to be as esquire to the King. In 1376 and 1377, he was sent three times to France to negotiate for peace. This involved discussion of marriage between ten-year-old Richard (who succeeded his grandfather in 1377) and eleven-year-old Marie, daughter of the king of France, which appears to be satirized in the *Parliament of Fowls.* In 1378, he went again to Italy, leaving his power of attorney with his friends the poet John Gower and Richard Forester. This trip was to negotiate with Barnabo Visconti, ruler of Milan, whose fate is described in the *Monk's Tale* (*CT* 7.2399ff.). On these occasions, he was allowed to appoint a deputy in the office of controller.

In February 1385, Chaucer was given license to appoint a permanent deputy in his office. This represents another crux in his career. By October of that year, he had been appointed a justice of the peace in Kent. In August 1386, he was elected a member of parliament from Kent. In October, the Aldgate residence was leased to Richard Forester. That December, Adam Yardley replaced Chaucer as controller of customs. And in 1388, when the "Merciless Parliament" was investigating all of the grants made by Edward III and Richard II, he transferred his royal annuity to John Scalby. These events are all associated with the coup in the English government by which Thomas of Woodstock, youngest son of Edward III, replaced his brother John of Gaunt as the power behind the throne. All of the members of Richard's and Gaunt's households found themselves under suspicion. Richard's ineptitude, which was part of what led to this development, may be criticized in Alceste's speech to the God of Love in the *Legend of Good Women* (11.342ff.) and in *Lack of Steadfastnesse,* and Chaucer's own discouragement at the situation may be reflected in *Balade de Bon Conseil.* In any case, it may have been the prospect of freedom from administrative responsibility that led Chaucer to lay plans for an extensive work like the *Canterbury Tales.*

However, this period of comparative retirement did not last long. In 1389, Richard declared himself of age, dismissed Thomas of Woodstock from the Council, and took the rule into his own hands. Chaucer was immediately given the heaviest responsibilities of his career: clerkship of the king's works, overseeing the maintenance of Westminster Palace, the Tower of London, and many of the king's other castles, manors, and properties (such as the wool quay). In this capacity he supervised a large staff and handled great sums of money to pay for materials and labor. In connection with the large sums he had to carry about with him, Chaucer was robbed three times in four days in September 1390—at the "Fowle Ok" in Kent, at Hatcham in Surrey, and in Westminster. The beating and injuries mentioned in the inquest concerning these robberies may have been a factor in his giving up the clerkship the next June (1391). Meanwhile, he had been appointed subforester of Petherton Park, Somersetshire (1390). Probably this was a sinecure that allowed him to live near London, although he may have lived for a while in Somerset. Other than this, after his retirement from the clerkship of the king's works, Chaucer appears not to have held an official position.

In 1394, King Richard granted Chaucer a new annuity of twenty pounds, but he evidently had difficulty collecting the money due him. He was sued for debt; he transferred real estate; he borrowed money. Matters appeared to improve when the new king, Henry IV, doubled his annuity in an enrollment dated the day of his coronation, October 13, 1399. But this grant, too, had problems, since it was not actually made until February 1400 and backdated to October. In December 1399 Chaucer signed a fifty-three-year lease for a dwelling in Westminster Close. This may have been simply because he wanted to live in Westminster, but it has been pointed out that Westminster Abbey was a refuge for debtors, and his move there may have been connected with his financial exigency. (The question as to why he signed such a long lease in the last year of his life is explained by the conventions of English land tenure, where it is customary to buy the unexpired term of a long lease rather than to buy freehold.) A final record indicates that he received his last tun of wine on the royal grant before September 29, 1400. But he died before he could collect the money due him from Henry IV's annuity.

The date of Chaucer's death, inscribed on his sixteenth-century tomb in Westminster Abbey, is October 25, 1400. He was buried in the abbey because, as a resident of the close, he was a member of the parish. However, his burial there initiated the "Poets' Corner" in Westminster Abbey.

One gets the impression that Chaucer was most active as a writer when he was busiest as an administrator. Before 1374, he had translated all or part of the *Romaunt of the Rose* and written the *Book of the Duchess* and some other short poems. During his twelve years in the controller's office and in the midst of many trips abroad, he wrote *Parliament of Fowls, House of Fame, Boece, Troylus and Criseyde,* and *Palamon and Arcite* (the Knight's Tale). During his three years out of office he began *Legend of Good Women* and the *Canterbury Tales.* During the three years of the clerkship of the king's works, he no doubt continued work on the *Canterbury Tales* and began one, possibly two, astronomical treatises, *Astrolabe* and *Equalorie.* Except for the revision of the Prologue to *Legend of Good Women,* there is nothing except two "begging" balades that we can assign with assurance to the eight years of his retirement. His *Lenvoy a Scogan* implies that he may have felt his poetic gift was drying up. The *Complaint to His Purse* is a final plea to King Henry.

The "Chaucer Chronology" in the front endpapers of this edition summarize the important dates connected with Chaucer's life. Yet we go out pretty much as we came in. Little in the biographical records throws light on the personality of the poet or the meaning of the poems. Yet the charisma of the poems makes us endlessly curious about the nature of the man.

It is impossible to write a biography of Chaucer in the modern sense because the materials (manuscripts, letters, and observations by intimate contemporaries) are not available before the seventeenth century. Writing materials were too expensive; literacy was not sufficiently widespread. The best available biography is Derek Pearsall's *The Life of Geoffrey Chaucer* (1992, no. 182). Rich with beautiful illustrations of fourteenth-century life, Derek Brewer's *Chaucer and His World* (2d ed. 1992) has been reprinted as *The World of Chaucer* (2000, no. 167). Even more recent is the readable but extravagant set of surmises in *Who Murdered Chaucer? A Medieval Mystery*, by Terry Jones and others (2003, no. 178).

Chaucer's Language and Versification

CHAUCER'S LANGUAGE is important, not only intrinsically as the language of a great poet, but also as an example of the language from which Modern Standard English developed. Chaucer did not create modern written English. That evolved in the fifteenth century when the clerks in the English civil service—Chancery, as it was then called—switched government and parliamentary record-keeping from French and Latin to English. Chaucer did his own writing as a civil servant in French and Latin. But the governing classes by his time were *speaking* English, even though they were still *writing* in French and Latin. So Chaucer took the brave step (which his friend John Gower did not, at first) of writing his poems for the entertainment of the court in the vernacular—the spoken language. Like Chancery Standard, when it developed in the next century, the language that Chaucer and his London companions developed for poetry used a vocabulary more than half French, with many French idioms and expressions (*man of law, playn eleccioun, parfay, entrechaunge*). This was because his literary models were French and because he was writing for an audience still essentially bilingual.

The miracle is that the language of Chaucer's poetry is as close to the idiom of Modern English as it is. This is not true of his prose, or of fifteenth-century Chancery prose, even though the grammatical forms were quickly standardized. The greater facility of Chaucer's poetry illustrates what scholars have so often observed—that verse is the earliest mode of artistic expression in any language. It takes centuries to develop a lucid prose style, and this prose tradition must be passed from one generation to the next. When it ceases to be taught, it disappears, as Latin prose did after the fourth century and as Old English prose did after 1066.

Chaucer's spelling and pronunciation were more different from Modern English than his grammar and vocabulary. This is because of two changes in pronunciation that affected the language between Chaucer's time and Shakespeare's: (1) long vowels all underwent what is called "the great vowel shift"; (2) inflectional endings weakened or disappeared. For convenience, the differences in pronunciation have been listed in the back endpapers of this edition. Here we discuss only the principles that underlie the changes.

1. In Chaucer's time, the difference between the vowels of *fat–fate, met–mete, bit–bite, god–good, but–about* was length, not quality. In the century following Chaucer, length ceased to have phonemic value in English, and the long vowels all shifted in quality, as indicated in the diagram on p. 966. Spelling began to be standardized before this shift in sound was completed. This means that the spelling of the shifted vowels in Modern English is different from the spelling of equivalent sounds in other languages using the Latin alphabet: English *ice*—French *ici*, English *demon*—French *démon*. Hence, the generalization is that the long vowels of Middle English should be pronounced as the same spellings would be in Latin or any modern European language.
2. A second process that has gone on throughout the history of English is contraction of the sort that has led to the reduction of Old English *hlaford* to *lord* and is today leading to the reduction of *probably* to *probly*. Since spelling in the fourteenth century was still largely phonetic, the generalization is that there are no silent letters or syllables in Chaucer's English. The most widespread difference this makes in the pronunciation of Chaucer's English is that the inflectional endings *es* and *ed*, which have now been contracted, were then pronounced as separate syllables: *walkes, walked, stones.* Thus there were many fewer monosyllabic words in Chaucer's English, which has important implications for rhythm and meter.

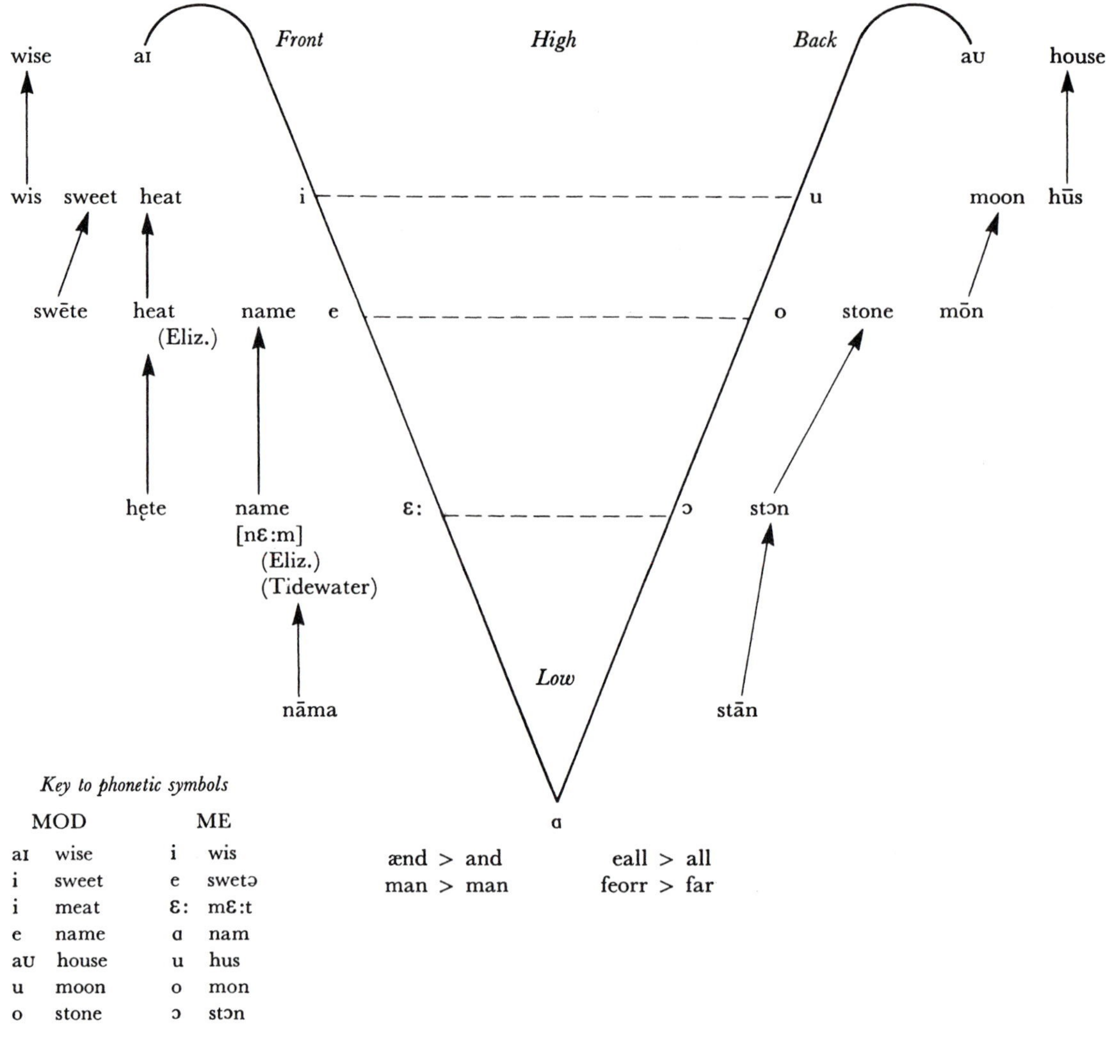

Consonants that have since become silent—*gnaw, folk*—were then pronounced. The spelling *gh* (then often spelled *h*) still had the palatal sound it has in Scots and German: *night* (*niht*), *bought* (*bohte*). When this sound occurred finally, it was already changing to *w*, as indicated by spellings like *bow* and *throwe* (through).

Also, most important, the many French words being introduced into English in Chaucer's time kept their French accent; *licóur, coráge.*

Pronunciation of all letters, Latinate vowels, alternation of French and English accent, and pronunciation of palatals that have since become vocalized or become silent all mean that Chaucer's poetry has to be read more slowly than modern poetry. If it is hurried over, it loses its music. The fact that the differences in Chaucer's pronunciation were not understood in the seventeenth century resulted in his then being considered a rough and crude prosodist, although his "matter" was thought delightful. Most of the principles of his exquisite assonance and rhythm were rediscovered by Thomas Tyrwhitt and nineteenth-century philologists.

Chaucer's most important contribution to English poetry is the iambic pentameter line, for which he had no model in English. Most poetry after the Norman Conquest was either in relaxed alliterative verse or else in tetrameter couplets modeled on the French and Latin octosyllabics. The four-stress line in couplets or quatrains was the favorite form in English poetry from the *Owl and the Nightingale* to the *Pearl* and Gower's *Confessio Amantis.* Chaucer used it for three of his early poems, the

Romaunt of the Rose (whatever part of it may be by him), *Book of the Duchess,* and *House of Fame.* Then he turned to the more sophisticated pentameter line. His models for this have frequently been debated. Since he evidently began to use it only after his trip to Italy, and since more than half his lines have feminine endings (thanks to the final *e*), there appears to have been an influence of the hendecasyllabic (eleven syllables), which Dante called the "most famous" line of the Italian poets. On the other hand, the decasyllabic was a line frequently employed in the French poems which served Chaucer as his earliest models. Chaucer's task was to adapt this Continental syllable-counting meter to English stressed rhythm.

Both the French and Italian lines employed the movable caesura, and the movable caesura is a feature of Chaucer's line. However, in native English alliterative verse he found a fixed caesura with two strong stresses and a varying number of weak stresses in each half line. This has led to the assertion by some critics that Chaucer's rhythm—as distinguished from his meter—was really four-beat, two on each side of the caesura, superimposed on a more or less decasyllabic line (since a good many lines run to eleven syllables, and some have only nine). This scansion works well for the opening lines of the *Canterbury Tales: Whán thăt Aṕrill̆ / wĭth hĭs shóurĕs sóotĕ // Thĕ dróghtĕ of Márch / hat̆h pércĕd tŏ thĕ róotĕ.* Most authorities, however, hold that Chaucer regularly used five stresses in a line: *Whán thăt Aṕrill̆ / wĭth hís shóurĕs sóotĕ // Thĕ dróghtĕ of Maŕch / hat̆h pércĕd tó thĕ róotĕ.* The different levels of stress that were developing in Middle English made it possible for some stresses to be pronounced more heavily than others, so that while the line employed five stresses from a metrical point of view, the audience heard only the four maximal stresses. The chief mark of Chaucer's facility as a prosodist is the "naturalness" of his verse. The metrical stresses fall on the lexical stresses and reinforce the rhetorical emphasis without strain or distortion. When there are inversions either of stress or syntax, they are pleasurable instead of distracting. This is what is meant by "Chaucer's good ear." Keats said, "if poetry comes not as naturally as the leaves on a tree it had better not come at all." Even though Chaucer had no models for the English iambic pentameter, no subsequent poet has used it with more ease and expressiveness than he.

Nouns

In the case of the noun, Old English dative *e* was preserved in some prepositional phrases: *to grounde, in londe.* Some words have an uninflected genitive singular form from OE *e: sonne, fader, lady* (*his lady grace*). There are more plurals in *en* or *n* than in Modern English: *ashen, bosen, doghtren, foon.* Although plurals are usually syllabic *es,* in polysyllabic French words they are sometimes contracted to *s, barouns, conclusions;* when the word ends in *t* this is sometimes represented by *z, advocatz, servantz.*

Nouns appear frequently in apposition to their governing words, *a barrel ale, a manner Latyn corrupt.* The partitive is expressed by *of, Of smale houndes hadde she, Of remedies of love she knew.* Nouns with the possessive ending *es* can be used as modifiers, *lyves creature* (living creature), *shames deth* (shameful death), *I shal nedes have* (I must needs have), *his / hir thankes* (thankfully, willingly). Double possessives continue to be divided as in Old English, *the Seintes Legende of Cupide* (the legend of the saints of Cupid), *the Kyng Priamus sone of Troye* (the son of King Priam of Troy).

Pronouns

The first person pronoun is usually *I;* southern *ich* is used for emphasis and with contractions, *theech* (*thee ich,* may I prosper); northern *ik* is used in the Reeve's Tale. The second person singular is regularly *thou, thyn, thee.* Plural forms *ye, your, you* were already beginning to be used for the singular, generally reflecting formality or respect (e.g., in the Clerk's Tale, *CT* 4.306–50, Walter addresses Janicula with the singular; Janicula addresses Walter with the plural; and Walter addresses Griselda with the plural. Gentles usually address each other with the plural, like the lovers in the Franklin's Tale and *Troylus,* but common folk use the singular, as in the Miller's and Reeve's Tales; Pandarus generally uses singular *thou* forms but addresses Criseyde with the plural *ye* forms as they approach Troylus's bed chamber, *TC* 2.1716ff. Such distinctions provide nuances not available in Modern English.) Interrogative *thou* is often elided, *artow, thynkestow.*

The neuter singular was usually *it,* but the possessive continued to be Old English *his,* which should not be mistaken for personification (as in line 1 of *CT*). The feminine singular forms are *she* and *hir(e)* / *her(e)*, and the third person plural forms, *they, hir(e)* / *her(e)*, *hem.* There is confusion between feminine singular *her(e)* (her), plural *her(e)* (their), adverb *her* (here), and verb *her* / *heren* (to hear). In particular, plural *her* (their) should not be mistaken for singular *her* (her). With or without a final *e,* pronouns are always monosyllabic.

Plural of the demonstrative pronoun *that* is *tho. This,* often with a final *e, thise,* is either singular or plural. *Thilke* (*that ilke,* the same) is likewise either singular or plural. Both *that* and *the are* often elided, *th'estate, the tother.*

The relative pronoun may be omitted as a subject, *With hym ther was dwellynge a poure scoler, /* ***Hadde*** *lerned art.* Relative *that* is used as a collocation with pronouns and adverbs, *whom that* (but never *who that*), *if that, whan that*; it should not be mistaken for a demonstrative (as in line 1 of *CT*). Indefinite *man* is frequently used instead of the passive, *she wept if men smoot it.* The "ethical dative" or "dative of advantage" cannot be translated into Modern English, *To seken* **hym** *a chauntrie, And to the hors he goth* **hym** *faire.* The reflexive pronoun is usually the same as the personal, *To be my wyf and reule* **hire** *after me*; the *self* forms are usually intensive, *Ther walketh now the lymytour* ***hymself.***

Adjectives

Adjectives that do not already end in *e* frequently take *e* when modifying plural nouns and in "weak" positions, i.e., following articles, demonstratives, or prepositions, or with vocatives: *a fair prelat / yven faire wyves: a young Squier / the yong***e** *sonne: an hard thing / with hard***e** *grace: ye be lief / soothly, lev***e** *brother.*

Comparison of adjectives is generally the same as in Modern English except that the Old English mutated vowels of the comparative and superlative are sometimes preserved, *old / elder/ eldest: long / lenger / lengest: strong / strenger / strengest.* The French-influenced *more-most* comparison was usually used with pollysyllabic French words, *Moore delicaat / moore pompous / moost honourable.*

Adverbs

Adverbs are formed by adding *ly* or *liche,* but also by by adding *e* unless the adjective already ends in *e: a clene sheepe / caste him clene out of his lady grace; a lyght gypoun / knokkeden ful lighte.* The *s* forms of the adverb occur more frequently than in Modern English, *while***s***, eftsone***s***, unnethe***s***,* as do the *en* forms, *about***en***, abov***en***, bifo***rn***.* *Very* is never used as an intensive adverb, but always as an adjective, *He was a verray, parfit, gentil knyght.* The intensive is expressed by special idioms like *for the maistrie, for the nones. Ther* and *ther-as* may be used as relatives, *for over al* **ther** *he com. As* is sometimes omitted from comparisons, *His nekke* [as] *whit was as;* and omitted when correlative with *so, Ne was so worldly* [as] *for to have office.*

Prepositions

Prepositions may follow the words they govern, *seyde his maister to, rood hym agayns,* but seldom come at the end of the clause, *That men of yelpe, to shorte with oure weye.* An exception is the preposition *in* which can occur at the end spelled *inne: Hire to delivere of wo that she was inne; Doun into helle, where he yet is inne.*

Verbs

The inflections of verbs are second person (with *thou*) *est* (*st*), and third person *eth* (*th*) usually spelled with thorn; *eth* is variously contracted, *rit* (*rideth*), *worth* (*wortheth*), *halt* (*holdeth*). Very occasionally (BD 73,257, HF 426, as confirmed by the rhymes) we find northern third person *es,* which also marks the dialect of the students in the Reeve's Tale.

The mark of the infinitive and the plural indicative and subjunctive is frequently, but not always, *en: they mak***en***, they slep***en***, He leet the feeste of his nativitee / Doon cry***en***.* A favorite contraction of *haven* is *han.*

The principle parts of the verbs were much as they are in Modern English, but in Chaucer's English there were more strong verbs (verbs that show tense by change of vowel), *delve / dolf / dolven: crepe / crop / cropen: shouve / shoof / shoven.* The past participles of strong verbs normally end in *en,* but the *n* is often dropped: *founden/ founde.* The preterite of *hoten, highte,* has the passive sense "to be named / called." Past participles of both strong and weak verbs may take the prefix *y /i: ydon /* I-*yeven.*

The impersonal *it* of Modern English is often lacking, [it] *Bifil that in that seson,* and especially in idioms like *me thynketh* (it seems to me), *me liketh* (it pleases me), *hire lyste nat* (it did not please her).

One of the chief reasons for the different flavor of Chaucer's language is the scarcity of progressive forms, whose sense is expressed by simple verbs: *Ye goon* [are going] *to Canterbury, fowles maken* [were making] *melodye.* The auxiliary verb for the perfect tenses is usually a form of *be* rather than of *have: At nyght were* [had] *come into that hostelrye, That from the tyme of kyng William were* [had] *yfalle.* Auxiliaries that have fallen out of use are *gan* (began), *what that the day gan sprynge, this noble duc gan ryde,* and *doon* (cause to be done), *he dide doon sleen hem* (he had them killed), *If that ye done us bothe dyen* (if you cause us both to die).

Infinitives frequently lack *to. Come soup***en** and *if yow liketh know***en** are marked by *en,* but *hym liste ride* and *Bidde hym descende* are unmarked, like the infinitives in Modern English subjunctives (I shall go, I would go). The subjunctive is used more frequently than in Modern English: for condition, *if she telle it;* for wishes, *God yelde yow* (may God reward you); for hypotheses, *I trowe he were a geldyng;* for concessions, *Al were he short.*

Negation

The usual sign of negation is *ne* before the verb, *ne wolde,* frequently elided with the verb, *nolde, nas, nath.* This may be reinforced by a following *nat / nought, it ne seme naught,* which can be reduced by omitting *ne, it availeth noght.* But the more negatives loaded into a clause, the more negative it is, *He nevere yet no vileyne ne sayde / In al his lyf unto no maner wight.*

Syntax

The conversational tone of Chaucer's writing is the result of less formal parallelism and subordination that we find in Modern written English. Among the syntax of oral language, we find Chaucer using **ellipsis:** *And* [we] *made forward erly for to ryse, And by his covenant* [he] *yaf rekenynge;* **parataxis:** *An horn he bar, the bawdryk was of grene; Bad nat every wight he sholde go selle,* **anacoluthon** (shift in grammar): *The reule of seint Maure or seint Beneit, / Bycause that it was old and somdel streit, / This ilke monk leet olde thynges pace.*

The Text of This Edition

THE TEXTS INCLUDED in this edition are lightly corrected versions of those published in John H. Fisher's *The Complete Poetry and Prose of Geoffrey Chaucer* (1977; no. 37). Changes to his text are listed with the individual works below. As in Fisher's first edition, the goal here is conservatively emended versions of quality manuscripts (in the case of *Romaunt of the Rose* the early edition), with (1) abbreviations silently expanded and thorn written *th*; (2) capitalization, punctuation, and some paragraphing introduced to ease modern reading; (3) word division regularized to modern conventions; (4) conservative treatment of final *e*; (5) modern distribution of *u* and *v*, *i*, and *j*, and *F* for *ff*; and (5) some silent corrections and inclusion or omission of metrical fillers.

While I have followed Fisher's text, I have rewritten his notes, which, though not exhaustive, include some abbreviated data from manuscript families or groupings as well as corrections and select variants. I have reduced the data to corrections of the base text and variants from a second, high-quality witness (sometimes a third), some readings encouraged by consultation of source material, and indications of other instances where the paired "best" texts are unsatisfactory or particularly questionable. I have eliminated information about manuscript families, seeking to indicate instances where the base text has been changed or where the second text varies from the best, but not attempting to summarize a set of variant options or groupings. Good editions and facsimiles of most of the witnesses to Chaucer's works have been produced since Fisher's text, some with full or extensive collation of witnesses to the texts. Such resources lessen the need to include all variants in a reading text, and I have used the facsimiles and collations to check Fisher, in addition to referring when necessary to the microfilm copies from which he originally worked. Throughout I have consulted the apparatus of other editions, especially that of Walter W. Skeat (1894–97, no. 39) and of the various editors of *The Riverside Chaucer* (1987, no. 36). Whenever possible, I followed the system of sigils that has developed in recent work with Chaucer manuscripts.

Canterbury Tales

The base text of the *Canterbury Tales* in this edition is Ellesmere 26.C.9 in the Huntington Library, San Marino, California (El). Linne Mooney identified the Ellesmere scribe as Adam Pinkhurst (2006; no. 30), who also produced during his long career the Hengwrt manuscript, National Library of Wales, MS Peniarth 392.D (Hg). Pinkhurst produced Hg before El, both before 1410, and it is possible that he completed Hg before Chaucer's death in 1400. El and Hg are the earliest and best manuscripts of the *Canterbury Tales*, requiring sustained correction from other versions only in a few sections (the *Monk's Tale* for example). Because the Ellesmere was produced as a single polished work, its text is more regular in meter and spelling than that of Hengwrt, and yet it is often less careful. On the other hand, it is more complete than Hg (which lacks all of the *Canon's Yeoman's Tale* and has lost much of the *Parson's Tale*), and the El order of the tales is what most scholars today accept as the closest to Chaucer's intention. Where El and Hg agree, the reading is usually taken as authoritative. Where they disagree, context, source material, and the evidence of other manuscripts help determine the reading.

More than eighty manuscripts of the *Canterbury Tales* survive, although many are partial by intent (single tales, for example) and many are fragmentary by damage or omission. Early editions by William Caxton, Richard Pynson, William Thynne, John Stow, and Thomas Speght are also of textual value. Complete collations are available in the 1940 edition of Manly and Rickert (MR, no. 43), and The *Canterbury Tales* Project (no. 3) has since

1996 begun to replace and augment MR with complete facsimiles, transcriptions, and collations. This work goes slowly, but when a *Canterbury Tales* Project e-text is available, it is more thorough and usable than MR. Also very useful, the volumes of the Variorum Chaucer that have been produced so far collate the most important manuscripts and printed editions and provide other valuable information and perspective.

Corrections and adjustments to Fisher:

KnT 1.1323: "to" replaces "do"
RvT 1.4129: dash added
MLT 2.34: "us a" replaces "us as"
MLT 2.107: semicolon replaces comma
MLT 2.471: midline question mark, followed by capital letter
MLT 2.706: colon added
MLT 2.732: closing quotation marks added
SumT 3.1736: "wolde" replaces "wholde"
SumT 3.2217: colon replaces comma
SumT 3.2218: quotation marks deleted
SumT 3.2228: quotation marks added
ClT 4.7: quotation marks deleted
ClT 4.283: semicolon replaces comma
ClT 4.867: "my" replaces "youre"
MerT 4.2218: "ful" deleted
MerT 4.1780: "as" deleted
SqT 5.694: "Where" replaces "There."
ShT 7.432: "oure" replaces "my"
Thop 7.833a: rubric added: "[The Second Fit]"
Thop 7.891a: rubric changed: "[The Third Fit]" for "[The Second Fit]"
Mel 7.1146: "therfore" replaces "therefore"
Mel 7.1851: semicolon replaces comma
CYT 8.638: "thy" replaces "they"
CYT 8.1345: comma replaces period
ParsT 10.755: "Genesis 9" replaces "Genesis 5"
ParsT 10.863: "fyngres" replaces "syngres"

Troylus and Criseyde

The text of *Troylus and Criseyde* is based on MS M.817 (Cl) in the Pierpont Morgan Library in New York, formerly known as the Campsall manuscript. Because it bears on its first page the arms of Henry V when he was Prince of Wales (Shakespeare's Prince Hal), it must have been written between 1399 and 1413, making it the earliest complete manuscript of *Troylus*. The other most important manuscript, and the one most other editions have been based upon, despite its omission of 4.491–532, is Corpus Christi College, Cambridge, MS 61 (Cp). This revision follows Fisher in his effort to record all substantive variants from Cp and to correct Cl from it, but other witnesses are cited only rarely. Fisher followed the theory of R. K. Root (1926, no. 58) that posited several distinguishable stages of authorial revisions in Chaucer's composition of the *Troylus*, but Ralph Hanna III (in Ruggiers 1984, no. 38), Barry Windeatt (1984, no. 59) and Stephen Barney (1993, no. 24) have shown Root's theory to be deeply flawed. So I have opted for much simpler textual apparatus. This produces the illusion of a simple textual tradition—which is certainly not true—but it has the advantage of enabling students to observe readily where the two major manuscripts disagree, similar to the situation found with El and Hg for the *Canterbury Tales.* Windeatt includes complete collations of the sixteen complete or nearly complete manuscripts of *Troylus* and its three early printed editions; he also lists the sixteen known fragments of the poem. Important among the fragments is the so-called "Cecil Fragment," Hatfield House, Box S.1, because Adam Pinkhurst copied it, as he did El, Hg, and more. For facsimiles of the major manuscripts, see nos.19–21.

Corrections and adjustments to Fisher:

1.294: "so fair" replaces "to fair"
1.595: period added within quotation marks
1.606: "sayleth" replaces "fayleth"
1.682: period replaces question mark
2.1298: "yeres" replaces "monthes"
2.1680: "That" replaces "Than"
3.422: "ne" replaces "me"
3.1365 "blynne" replaces "bilynne."
4.58: period deleted
5.948: period and capital added
5.961: comma replaces period midline

Book of the Duchess

Three manuscripts and William Thynne's edition of 1532 (Th) attest to the text of *Book of the Duchess.* The base text here is Bodleian Library, Oxford, Fairfax MS Fairfax 16 (F), although Th is the base for lines 31–96 where the manuscripts are lacking. Th is also used to correct F and provide selected variants. Murray McGillivray, ed., *Book of the Duchess: A Hypertext Edition 2.0* (1999, no. 23) includes facsimiles of the four witnesses, but for collations see Helen Phillips, *The Book of the Duchess* (1993, no. 68).

Corrections to Fisher:

179 "how" replaces "ho"
529 "goodely" replaces "godoely"
916 "now" replaces "not"

Parliament of Fowls

The text of *Parliament of Fowls* is based on Cambridge University Library MS Gg.4.27 (Gg), with corrections and select variants from Bodleian Library, Oxford, MS Fairfax 16 (F). The two are the earliest of fourteen surviving manuscripts, and Caxton's edition of 1477–78 is also considered a valued witness. The unorthodox spelling of Gg bas been normalized in accord with the conventions used elsewhere in this edition. For collations, see D. S. Brewer's *The Parlement of Foulys* (1972, no. 60).

Correction to Fisher: 190 "briddes" replaces "foules"

House of Fame

The text of *House of Fame* is based on Bodleian Library, Oxford, MS Fairfax 16 (F), with corrections and select variants from Magdalene College, Cambridge, MS Pepys 2006 (P) through line 1843 (where P breaks off), and from Caxton's *Book of Fame* of 1483 (Cx) for the remainder of the poem. Bodleian Library, Oxford, MS Bodley 638 and Thynne's edition of 1532 are the only other early witnesses to the text. Cx and Th are used for several omitted or defective lines, indicated in the notes. For collations, see N. R. Havely's edition (1994, no. 64).

Corrections to Fisher:

617 "neviwe" replaces "neviw"
667 "hast" replaces "has"
1491: "this" replaces "his"

Legend of Good Women

Janet Cowen and George Kane (1995, no. 61) collate the twelve manuscripts and Thynne's edition (1532) of *Legend of Good Women*, most of them fragmentary in some way, either through loss of leaves or because they include only a single legend. The two most important manuscripts are Bodleian Library, Oxford, MS Fairfax 16 (F), and Cambridge University Library MS Gg.4.27 (Gg). Although lacking several lines, F has the most complete, high-quality text, and is the base text here. Gg has a unique version of the Prologue to the poem, apparently Chaucer's own revision, which is here presented separately and assigned line numbers G1-G545. The textual notes to the G-Prologue (or Prologue II) record where the two versions differ. Textual notes to the F-Prologue (Prologue I) and the rest of the poem record corrections and variants of F from Gg or from Trinity College, Cambridge University, MS R.3.19 (Tr).

Corrections and adjustments to Fisher:

332: no italics for "Creseyde"
1019: comma replaces semicolon
1126: "honorable" replaces "noble"
1295: "nyght" replaces "myght"
1519: semicolon replaces comma
1520: comma deleted
1528: period replaces dash
1529: colon replaces dash
1531: semicolon replaces period
1551: period replaces comma
1574: "al thoo" replaces "althoo"
2331: "yet" replaces "get"

Short Poems

Fourteen of the twenty-two poems in this edition are included in Part One of *The Minor Poems*, volume five of the Variorum edition of Chaucer's works. That volume, edited by George B. Pace and Alfred David (1982, no. 67), presents manuscript descriptions, collations, discussions of attribution and dating, and extensive commentary on poems numbered 7–20 in this edition, although treated in different order. Part Two of *The Minor Poems* has not been published, but earlier collations for all of the short poems (except 7, 9, and 21) are in John Koch, *Chaucers Kleinere Dichtung* (1928, no. 65). Comprehensive discussions of the authenticity of the poems are included in volume one of Skeat's edition (1894–97, no. 39), Eleanor P. Hammond's *Chaucer: A Bibliographical Manual* (1908; no. 86), Aage Brusendorff, *The Chaucer*

Tradition (1925, no. 1681), and *The Riverside Chaucer* (1987, no. 36). In this edition, substantive changes and selected variants are recorded in the notes. Titles and rubrics of the works vary, often assigned by modern editors.

1. *Prier a Nostre Dame* (also *An ABC*): seventeen manuscripts (including a sixteen-line fragment) and Speght's edition of 1602; text based on Bodleian Library, Oxford, MS Fairfax 16 (F), with corrections and variants from Cambridge University Library MS Ff.5.30 (Ff^2). In F the poem is independent; in Ff^2 it is inserted in an anonymous prose translation of Guillaume Deguileville's *Le Pèlerinage de la Vie Humaine*, the French poem from which Chaucer translated his *ABC*. One correction to Fisher: *ABC* 159 "floure" replaces "floue."
2. *Anelida and Arcite*: twelve manuscripts and Caxton's edition of 1477–78; text based on Bodleian Library, Oxford, MS Fairfax 16 (F), with corrections and variants from Caxton's edition of 1477–78 (Cx) for lines 1–210, and for the rest from Magdalene College, Cambridge University, Pepys 2006 (P).
3. *Complaint of Mars*: seven manuscripts (one with two versions) and early editions by Julian Notary (1499–51) and William Thynne (1532); text based on Bodleian Library, Oxford, MS Fairfax 16 (F), with corrections and variants from the complete version in Magdalene College, Cambridge University, Pepys 2006 (P). One adjustment to Fisher: delete comma in *Mars* 153.
4. *Complaint of Venus*: seven manuscripts (one with two versions) and early editions by Julian Notary (1499–51) and William Thynne (1532); text based on Bodleian Library, Oxford, MS Fairfax 16 (F), with corrections and variants from the complete version in Magdalene College, Cambridge University, MS Pepys 2006 (P).
5. *A Complaint Unto Pity*: nine manuscripts and William Thynne's edition of 1532; text based on Bodleian Library, Oxford, MS Fairfax 16 (F), with substantive variants from British Library MS Harley 78 (H^1).
6. *A Balade of Pity* (also *A Complaint to His Lady*): two manuscripts and John Stowe's edition of 1561; text based on British Library MS Additional 34360 (A^5), with variants from British Library MS Harley 78 (H^1).
7. *Womanly Noblesse*: found only in British Library MS Additional 34360 (A^5).
8. *To Rosemounde*: found only in Bodleian Library, Oxford, MS Rawlinson Poetry 163 (R).
9. *Proverbe of Chaucer*: four manuscripts and John Stowe's edition of 1561; text based on Bodleian Library, Oxford, MS Fairfax 16 (F), with variants from British Library MS Additional 16165 (A^3).
10. *Fortune*: ten manuscripts, Caxton's edition of 1477–78, and Thynne's of 1532; text based on Bodleian Library, Oxford, MS Fairfax 16 (F), with corrections and variants from Cambridge University Library MS Ii.3.21 (C^2) and Bodleian Library, Oxford, MS Ashmole 59 (A).
11. *Balade de Bon Conseil* (also *Truth*): twenty-two manuscripts (two with two versions) and most early editions attest to this popular poem; text based on Huntington Library, San Marino, California, MS Ellesmere 26.C.9 (El), with variants from the first of two versions in Bodleian Library, Oxford, MS Fairfax 16 (F) and from British Library MS Additional 10340 (A^1), which is the only version to include the Envoy (22–28).
12. *Moral Balade of Gentilesse*: ten manuscripts, Caxton's edition of 1477–78, and Thynne's of 1532; text based on British Library MS Cotton Cleopatra D.7 (C), with corrections and variants from Bodleian Library, Oxford, MS Ashmole 59 (A).
13. *The Former Age*: two manuscripts; text based on Cambridge University Library MS Ii.3.21 (C^2) with variants from Cambridge University Library MS Hh.4.12 (Hh).
14. *Lack of Steadfastnesse*: fifteen manuscript copies and Thynne's edition of 1532; text based on British Library MS Cotton Cleopatra D.7 (C), with corrections and variants from British Library Harley 7333 (H^4).
15. *To Adam Scriveyn*: found only in Trinity College, Cambridge University, MS R.3.20.
16. *Lenvoy de Chaucer de Bukton*: text based on Bodleian Library, Oxford, MS Fairfax 16 (F). One other manuscript survives, Coventry, City Record Office, MS Coventry, along with Thynne's edition of 1532.
17. *Lenvoy de Chaucer a Scogan*: three manuscripts, Caxton's edition of 1477–78, and Thynne's of 1532; text based on Bodleian Library, Oxford, MS Fairfax 16 (F), with variants from Magdalene College, Cambridge University, MS Pepys

2006 (P) and Cambridge University Library MS Gg.4.7 (Gg).

18. *Complaint of Chaucer to His Purse*: eleven manuscripts, a transcription from manuscript, Caxton's edition of 1477–78, and Thynne's of 1532; text based on Cambridge University Library MS Ff.1.6 (Ff[1]), with corrections from Bodleian Library, Oxford, MS Fairfax 16 (F).
19. *Merciless Beauté*: text based on Magdalene College, Cambridge University, MS Pepys 2006 (P), not attributed to Chaucer. A seventeenth-century copy of P is in British Library MS Additional 38179.
20. *Against Women Unconstant*: three manuscripts and Stowe's edition of 1561; text based on Bodleian Library, Oxford, MS Fairfax 16 (F), corrected from British Library MS Harley 7578 (H[5]) and British Library MS Cotton Cleopatra D.7 (C). Not attributed to Chaucer in the manuscripts.
21. *A Balade of Complaint*: text found only in British Library MS Additional 16165, not attributed to Chaucer.
22. *An Amorous Complaint Made at Windsor* (also *Complaynt D'Amours*): three manuscripts; text based on Bodleian Library, Oxford, MS Fairfax 16 (F), corrected from British Library MS Harley 7333 (H[4]). Not attributed to Chaucer in the manuscripts. Correction to Fisher: *Comp d'Am* 8: "seyn" replaces "seyen"

Romaunt of the Rose

The base text for this edition is the version printed by William Thynne in 1532 (Th), with variants from University Library, Glasgow, MS Hunter 409 (G). G. J. E. Blodgett (1979, no. 1646) has shown that printer's marks indicate Thynne set his text from the G, but Th is more complete and the printer seems to have had reference to at least one other manuscript. Charles Dahlberg describes both in his Variorum edition (1999, no. 62) and provides comprehensive collation. Since Dahlberg's edition, Simon Horobin (2006, no. 1648) has transcribed a fragment recently found in the National Library of Scotland among the papers of Reverend Joass in the Sutherland Collection. The fragment is witness to a portion lacking in G, and provides evidence that Thynne had reference to more than one manuscript.

Corrections and adjustments to Fisher:

261: "his" added
307: "Nor" replaces "Ner"
1090: terminal period added
1134: "to have" replaces "have"
1222: "thing" deleted
1359: "gret" replaces "great"
1473: period replaces comma
2067: "susprised" replaces "suprised"
2079: "ye" replaces "he"
2085: "that" replaces "than"
2591: comma deleted
2786: "Dothe" replaces "Dother"
2874: comma replaces semicolon
3133: "and" replaces "the"
3164: "So" replaces" "For"
3555: "you" replaces "your"
3774: "with" added
3995: "this" replaces "his"
4096: "me" replaces "men"
4291: "so" deleted
4324: "I see" replaces "If so"
4388: "kepe" replaces "kept"
4439: "Sayde" replaces "Says"
4753: "be" replaces "he"
4842: "than" replaces "that"
4878: "Unto" replaces "Onto"
4881: "all" replaces "a"
4895: "damage" replaces "domage"
4973: "damage" replaces "domage"
5047: "wol" replaces "wal"
5207: "Goddes" replaces "Goodes"
5210: "in" added
5236: "valor" replace "value"
5401: "For" replaces "Ful"
5638: "forth as nought" replaces "frost as hot"
5803: "is" replaces "in"
5990: "shal" replaces "shel"
6054: "ye" replaces "we"
6110: comma replaces period
6179: "morcels" replace "morcets"
6226: "worldly" replaces "wordly"
6418: comma replaces period
6871: "hem" replaces "han"
7146: "that that" replaces "that the"
7178: "that" replaces "to"
7275: "a" deleted
7449: comma replaces period
7594: "was" replaces "is"

Boece

Of the ten manuscripts and two early editions of *Boece,* two are of superior quality. Cambridge University Library MS Ii.3.21 (C^2) is used as a base text here because it is complete, because it is accompanied by a Latin original and commentary that are part of the tradition that influenced Chaucer, and because it includes versions of Chaucer's Boethian poems *Fortune* and *The Former Age* (Short Poems, nos. 10 and 13). The Latin phrases at the beginning of each section derive from the Latin in C^2. Cambridge University Library MS Ii.1.38 (C^1) is also complete and includes a number of readings that accord with the Latin and the French, selectively recorded in the textual notes. The notes also record a number of unusual spellings in C^2 (see, e.g., 1.pr1.3n, 1.pr2.21n, etc.). For support of C^2 over C^1 as a base text, see Tim William Machan, "The Consolation Tradition and the Text of Chaucer's *Boece*" (1997, no. 1655); for full collations, see Machan's *Chaucer's* Boece*: A Critical Edition* (2008, no. 66a).

Estelle Stubbs (2002, no. 35) and Linne R. Mooney (2006, no. 30) both suggest that Adam Pinkhurst was the scribe of the incomplete and damaged National Library of Wales, MS Peniarth 393D (Hn), perhaps even that the corrections in Hn may be in Chaucer's own hand. This gives Hn more interest and, if the suggestion is correct, more authority than it was known to have when Fisher's edition was first published. In this revision, therefore, the notes indicate where Hn is a witness to the text.

Corrections and adjustments to Fisher:

Bo 2.pr4.28 "thow" replaces "how"
Bo 2.pr7.26-27 "comparisoun" replaces "com parisoun"
Bo 3.m9.18 "parfyt" added
Bo 4.pr1.19 colon replaces comma
Bo 4.pr4.9 "it" replaces "if"
Bo 5.pr5.4 comma deleted

Treatise on the Astrolabe

The text in this edition is based on Cambridge University Library MS Dd.3.53 (Dd^1). Sigmund Eisner lists and describes the thirty-two manuscripts and fragments of *Treatise on the Astrolabe* in his Variorum edition of the work (2002, no. 63). Catherine Eagleton identified an additional fragment in 2003 (no. 1665) that was washed incompletely from Royal College of Physicians, London MS 358, and Kari Anne Rand Schmidt describes Dd^1 and transcribes it diplomatically in *Authorship of the Equatorie of the Planetis* (1993, no. 1678); she points out (p. 59) that Dd^1 provides some of the data used in important discussions of Chaucer's spelling and language. It is the only manuscript to include a full program of sixty-two illustrations that Chaucer evidently intended to accompany his text. R. T. Gunther reproduces all but one of the Dd^1 illustrations in volume 5 of his *Early Science in Oxford* (1929; no. 74), revised and abbreviated in *Chaucer on the Astrolabe* (1931); we include the first twenty-two to show how Chaucer clarifies his verbal descriptions with helpful visuals. Dd^1 is here corrected with Bodleian Library, Oxford, MS Bodley 619 (Bl^1) with reference to two other manuscripts: Bodleian Library Rawlinson D.913 (Rl^1), especially useful for calculation 39 where both Dd^1 and Bl^1 are faulty, and, Houghton Library, Harvard University, MS English 920 (Hv). Six spurious calculations (numbered 41–46 in some editions) have not been included here as they do not occur in the best manuscripts and are not in Chaucer's style.

Corrections and adjustments to Fisher:

1.13.2: delete "a"
1.21.35: comma replaces semicolon
2.23.27: delete comma
2.26.14: "two" added
2.26.33: "enhansed" replaces "enhawsed"
2.28.32: "ende" replaces "heed"

Equatorie of the Planetis

The text of *Equatorie* is based, with permission, on Derek J. Price's edition of Cambridge University Library MS Peterhouse 75.I (1955; no. 70), which includes a facsimile as well as a description, transcription, and translation. Capitalization and punctuation have been added, and the three diagrams are included. The text has been compared with the diplomatic transcription and notes in Kari Anne Rand Schmidt, *The Authorship of the Equatorie of the Planetis* (1993, no. 1678), which includes a facsimile, the diagrams, and a concordance to the treatise.

Corrections and adjustments to Fisher:

94: "oculte" added after "dymly"
368: "forseide" replaces "foreseide"
383: delete comma
453: delete comma
551a: italics added to "*this canon is fals*"
589: "*(i.e., lune)*" replaces "*(lune)*"
325a and 349: cap "Epicicle" reduced to "epicicle" (see 195n)
374, 378, 403, and 559: lowercase "epicicle" raised to cap "Epicicle"

About the Illustrations

The frontispiece is a reproduction of the portrait of Chaucer in the margin of Thomas Hoccleve's *Regement of Princes* in British Library MS Harley 4866, folio 88. For discussion of this and other portraits of Chaucer, see the appendix in Derek Pearsall's *The Life of Geoffrey Chaucer* (1992, no. 152).

With two exceptions, the pictures of the Canterbury pilgrims included at the beginnings of the tales in this volume are from drawings made by W. H. Hooper, derived from the illustrations in the Ellesmere manuscript of the Canterbury tales, Huntington Library, San Marino, CA, MS 26.C.9. The drawings accompanied the transcription of *The Ellesmere MS. of the Canterbury Tales*, edited by Frederick J. Furnivall for the Chaucer Society, Series 1 (London: Trübner, 1868–79). The two exceptions are the first and the last in the sequence: the group of pilgrims on page 11 derives from a woodcut published in 1484 (sometimes dated 1482) in William Caxton's second edition of *The Canterbury Tales*; the portrait of Chaucer on page 393 is a detail from the Hoccleve portrait, our frontispiece.

The diagrams accompanying *Treatise on the Astrolabe* derive from Cambridge University Library MS Dd.3.53, as reproduced by R. T. Gunther, *Chaucer and Messahalla* (1929, no. 74). Gunther includes the complete program of sixty-two figures from the manuscript; we include only the first twenty-two that accompany Part 1 to illustrate how the diagrams clarify the text. The three diagrams accompanying *Equatorie of the Planetis* are based on Cambridge University Library MS Peterhouse 75.I, reproduced with permission from the facsimile edition of the manuscript by Derek J. Price (1955; no. 70). The linguistic diagram on page 966 is by John H. Fisher.

Bibliography

Bibliography

Below is a selection of scholarly works and literary criticism that pertain to Chaucer and the literature he wrote. It includes all of the works cited in this volume and other works useful for study of Chaucer and for exploring specific topics in his literature. For these purposes, it is arranged by subject matter rather than critical approach or method. This bibliography emphasizes works written in English that are generally accessible by means of university library services. It focuses on recent works, especially ones published between 1975 and 2007, but also includes some earlier works of enduring influence. Omitted are dissertations, collections of essays (except in cases of particular focus or utility), and works of fewer than five pages. Essays in collections are listed individually. For comprehensive bibliographical coverage, see nos. 1 and 80–86.

In the interest of saving space, some individual entries are truncated: subtitles of books are included only when necessary for clarity; multiple editors are reduced to lead names and editors of collections are not included in the Index of Authors; titles of book series and reprint information are generally not included. The cross referencing at the ends of sections is not exhaustive, so the user is advised to refer to related topics as listed in the Classifications that follow.

Electronic Resources

1. *Chaucer Bibliography Online.* <http://uchaucer.utsa.edu>. Annotated bibliography of Chaucer studies from 1975 to present.
2. *Chaucer Metapage.* <http://englishcomplit.unc.edu/chaucer>. The monitored hub of Chaucer sites on the WWW.
3. *The Canterbury Tales Project.* <http://www.canterburytalesproject.org/>. Transcription and analysis of the manuscripts of *The Canterbury Tales.* See also *The* Canterbury Tales *Project Occasional Papers. Volumes I and II,* edited by Norman Blake and Peter Robinson. Oxford: Office for Humanities Communication, 1993 and 1997.

See also nos. 22, 101.

Manuscript Facsimiles—Compilations and Miscellanies

4. *Bodleian Library Manuscript Fairfax 16.* Intro. John Norton-Smith. London: Scolar, 1979.
5. *Cambridge Library, MS Gg.4.27: A Facsimile.* Intro. Malcolm Parkes and Richard Beadle. 3 vols. Norman, OK: Pilgrim, 1980. [See no. 11]
6. *The Findern Manuscript (Cambridge University Library MS Ff.1.6).* Intro. Richard Beadle and A. E. B. Owen. London: Scolar, 1977.
7. *Magdalene College, Cambridge, MS Pepys 2006: A Facsimile.* Intro. A. S. G. Edwards. Norman, OK: Pilgrim, 1986.
8. *Manuscript Bodley 638: A Facsimile: Bodleian Library, Oxford University.* Intro. Pamela Robinson. Norman, OK: Pilgrim, 1982.
9. *Manuscript Tanner 346: A Facsimile: Bodleian Library, Oxford University.* Intro. Pamela Robinson. Norman, OK: Pilgrim, 1980.
10. *Manuscript Trinity R.3.19: A Facsimile: Trinity College, Cambridge.* Intro. Bradford Y. Fletcher. Norman, OK: Pilgrim, 1987.
11. *Poetical Works: A Facsimile of Cambridge University Library MS Gg.4.27.* 3 vols. Ed. M. B. Parkes and Richard Beadle. Cambridge, UK: Brewer, 1979–80. [See no. 5]
12. *Works of Geoffrey Chaucer and the Kingis Quair: A Facsimile of Bodleian Library, Oxford, MS Arch. Selden B.24.* Intro. Julia Boffey and A. S. G. Edwards. Cambridge, UK: Brewer, 1997.

Manuscript Facsimiles—Canterbury Tales

13. *The Canterbury Tales: A Facsimile and Transcription of the Hengwrt Manuscript, with Variants from the Ellesmere Manuscript.* Ed. Paul G. Ruggiers. Intro. by Donald C. Baker, A. I. Doyle, and M. B. Parkes. Norman: U of Oklahoma P, 1979.
14. *The Canterbury Tales by Geoffrey Chaucer: The New Ellesmere Chaucer Facsimile* (of Huntington Library MS EL 26 C 9). Ed. Daniel Woodward and Martin Stevens. San Marino, CA: Huntington Library; Tokyo: Yushodo, 1995. Monochromatic ed., 1997.
15. *Caxton's Canterbury Tales: The British Library Copies.* Ed. Barbara Bordalejo. Leicester, UK: Scholarly Digital Editions, 2003.
16. *The Ellesmere Manuscript of Chaucer's Canterbury Tales: A Working Facsimile.* Intro. Ralph Hanna, III. Rochester, NY: Boydell & Brewer, 1989.
17. *The Hengwrt Chaucer: Digital Facsimile.* Ed. Estelle Stubbs. Leicester, UK: Scholarly Digital Editions, 2000.
18. *A Six-Text Print of the Canterbury Tales.* Ellesmere, Hengwrt, Cambridge Gg.4.27, Petworth, Corpus, Lansdowne 851. London: Chaucer Society, first ser., nos. 1, 14–15, 25, 30–31, 37, 49, 1869–77.

Manuscript Facsimiles—Troylus and Criseyde

19. *The Pierpont Morgan Library Manuscript M.817.* Intro. Jeanne Krochalis. Norman, OK: Pilgrim, 1986.

20. *St. John's College, Cambridge, Manuscript L.1: A Facsimile.* Intro. Richard Beadle and Jeremy Griffiths. Norman, OK: Pilgrim, 1983.
21. *Troilus and Criseyde: A Facsimile of Corpus Christi College Cambridge MS 61.* Intro. M. B. Parkes and Elizabeth Salter. Cambridge: Brewer, 1978.

Manuscript Facsimiles—Other Works

22. Caie, Graham D. *The Romaunt of the Rose.* <http://www.memss.arts.gla.ac.uk/default.htm>.
23. McGillivray, Murray, ed. *Geoffrey Chaucer's Book of the Duchess: A Hypertext Edition 2.0.* Calgary: U of Calgary P, 1999.

Manuscripts and Textual Studies

24. Barney, Stephen A. *Studies in 'Troilus': Chaucer's Text, Meter, and Diction.* East Lansing, MI: Colleagues, 1993.
25. Blake, N. F. "Geoffrey Chaucer and the Manuscripts of *The Canterbury Tales.*" *JEBS* 1 (1997): 96–122.
26. Doyle, A. I., and M. B. Parkes. "The Production of Copies of the *Canterbury Tales* and the *Confessio Amantis* in the Early Fifteenth Century." In *Essays Presented to N. R. Ker,* edited by M. B. Parkes and A. G. Watson. London: Scolar, 1979.
27. Hanna, Ralph. "Authorial Versions, Rolling Revision, Scribal Error? Or the Truth about *Truth.*" *SAC* 10 (1988): 23–40.
28. ———. *London Literature, 1300–1380.* Cambridge, UK: Cambridge UP, 2005.
29. ———. *Pursuing History: Middle English Manuscripts and Their Texts.* Stanford, CA: UP of Stanford, 1996.
30. Mooney, Linne R. "Chaucer's Scribe." *Speculum* 81 (2006): 97–138.
30a. Mosser, Daniel W. *A Digital Catalogue of the Pre-1500 Manuscripts and Incunables of the Canterbury Tales.* Birmingham, UK: Scholarly Digital Editions, 2010.
31. ———. "Reading and Editing the *Canterbury Tales*: Past, Present, and Future?" *Text* 7 (1994): 201–32.
32. Owen, Charles A., Jr. *The Manuscripts of The Canterbury Tales.* Cambridge, UK: Brewer, 1991.
33. Seymour, M. C. *A Catalogue of Chaucer Manuscripts Tales.* 2 vols. Aldershot, UK: Scolar, 1995–97.
34. Stevens, Martin, and Daniel Woodward, eds. *The Ellesmere Chaucer: Essays in Interpretation.* San Marino, CA: Huntington Library; Tokyo: Yushodo, 1995.
35. Stubbs, Estelle. "A New Manuscript by the Hengwrt / Ellesmere Scribe? Aberystwyth National Library of Wales, MS. Peniarth 393D." *JEBS* 5 (2002): 161–67.

See also nos. 220, 336, 339, 596, 871, 1106, 1108, 1253, 1570, 1646, 1648, 1665-66.

Editions—Complete

36. Benson, Larry D., gen. ed. *The Riverside Chaucer.* Boston: Houghton Mifflin, 1987.
37. Fisher, John H., ed. *The Complete Poetry and Prose of Geoffrey Chaucer.* 1977. 2d ed. Fort Worth, TX: Holt, Rinehart, and Winston, 1989.
38. Ruggiers, Paul, ed. *Editing Chaucer: The Great Tradition.* Norman, OK: Pilgrim, 1984.
39. Skeat, Walter W., ed. *The Complete Works of Geoffrey Chaucer, Edited from Numerous Manuscripts.* 7 vols. Oxford: Clarendon P, 1894–97.
40. *Geoffrey Chaucer: The Works, 1532: With Supplementary Material from the Editions of 1542, 1561, 1598, and 1602.* Intro. D. S. Brewer. London: Scolar, 1969. Rpt. 1976.

Editions—The Canterbury Tales and Individual Tales

41. Blake, N. F., ed. *The Canterbury Tales by Geoffrey Chaucer Edited from the Hengwrt Manuscript.* London: Arnold, 1980.
42. Boenig, Robert, and Andrew Taylor, eds. *The Canterbury Tales.* Buffalo, NY: Broadview, 2008.
43. Manly, John M., and Edith Rickert, eds. *The Text of the Canterbury Tales, Studied on the Basis of all Known Manuscripts.* 8 vols. Chicago: U of Chicago P, 1940.
44. Mann, Jill, ed. *The Canterbury Tales.* New York: Penguin, 2005.
45. *The General Prologue.* Ed. Malcolm Andrew, Daniel J. Ransom, Lynne Hunt Levy, and others. Variorum Chaucer, Vol. 2, Parts 1A and 1B. Norman: U of Oklahoma P, 1993.
46. *The General Prologue on CD-ROM.* Ed. Elizabeth Solopova. Cambridge: Cambridge UP, 2000.
47. *The Manciple's Tale.* Ed. Donald C. Baker. Variorum Chaucer, Vol. 2, Part 10. Norman: U of Oklahoma P, 1984.
48. *The Miller's Tale.* Ed. Thomas W. Ross. Variorum Chaucer, Vol. 2, Part 3. Norman: U of Oklahoma P, 1983.
49. *The Miller's Tale on CD-ROM.* Ed. Peter Robinson. Cambridge: Cambridge UP, 2004.
50. *The Nun's Priest's Tale.* Ed. Derek Pearsall. Variorum Chaucer, Vol. 2, Part 9. Norman: U of Oklahoma P, 1984.
51. *The Nun's Priest's Tale on CD-ROM.* Ed. Paul Thomas. Birmingham, UK: Scholarly Digital Editions, 2006.
52. *The Physician's Tale.* Ed. Helen Storm Corsa. Variorum Chaucer, Vol. 2, Part 17. Norman: U of Oklahoma P, 1987.
53. *The Prioress's Tale.* Ed. Beverly Boyd. Variorum Chaucer, Vol. 2, Part 20. Norman: U of Oklahoma P, 1987.
54. *The Squire's Tale.* Ed. Donald C. Baker. Variorum Chaucer, Vol. 2, Part 12. Norman: U of Oklahoma P, 1990.
55. *The Summoner's Tale.* Ed. John F. Plummer III. Variorum Chaucer, Vol. 2, Part 7. Norman: U of Oklahoma P, 1995.
56. *The Wife of Bath's Prologue on CD-ROM.* Ed. Peter Robinson. Cambridge: Cambridge UP, 1996.

See also no. 852.

Editions—Troylus and Criseyde

57. Barney, Stephen A., ed. *Troilus and Criseyde: With Facing-Page Il Filostrato.* New York: Norton, 2006.

58. Root, Robert Kilburn, ed. *The Book of Troilus and Criseyde.* Princeton, NJ: Princeton UP, 1926.
59. Windeatt, B. A., ed. *Troilus and Criseyde: A New Edition of The Book of Troilus.* New York: Longman, 1984.

Editions—Other Works

60. Brewer, D. S., ed. *The Parlement of Foulys.* 2d ed. New York: Barnes and Noble, 1972.
61. Cowen, Janet, and George Kane, eds. *The Legend of Good Women.* East Lansing, MI: Colleagues P, 1995.
62. Dahlberg, Charles, ed. *The Romaunt of the Rose.* Variorum Chaucer, Vol. 7. Norman: U Oklahoma P, 1999.
63. Eisner, Sigmund, ed. *A Treatise on the Astrolabe.* Variorum Chaucer, Vol. 6, Part One. Norman: U Oklahoma P, 2002.
64. Havely, N. R., ed. *The House of Fame.* Durham: Durham Medieval Texts, 1994.
65. Koch, John, ed. *Chaucers Kleinere Dichtungen.* Heidelberg, Winter, 1928.
66. Lynch, Kathryn L., ed. *Dream Visions and Other Poems.* New York: Norton, 2007.
66a. Machan, Tim William, ed. *Chaucer's* Boece*: A Critical Edition Based on Cambridge University Library, MS Ii.3.21, ff. 9ʳ—180ᵛ.* Heidelberg: Universitätsverlag Winter, 2008.
67. Pace, George B., and Alfred David, eds. *The Minor Poems.* Variorum Chaucer, Vol. 5, Part 1. Norman: U of Oklahoma P, 1982.
68. Phillips, Helen, ed. *Chaucer: The Book of the Duchess.* 2d ed. Durham: Durham Medieval Texts, 1993.
69. ———, and Nick Havely, eds. *Chaucer's Dream Poetry.* New York: Longman, 1997.
70. Price, Derek J., ed. *The Equatorie of the Planetis: Edited from Peterhouse MS. 75.* Cambridge, UK: Cambridge UP, 1955.

Modern English Translations

71. Coghill, Nevill, trans. *The Canterbury Tales.* Harmondsworth: Penguin, 1951. (verse)
72. Dempsey, James, trans. *The Court Poetry of Chaucer: A Facing-Page Translation in Modern English.* Lewiston, NY: Mellen, 2007. (Short Poems, verse)
73. Ecker, Ronald L., and Eugene J. Crook, trans. *The Canterbury Tales by Geoffrey Chaucer.* Palatka, FL: Hodges & Braddock, 1993. (verse)
74. Gunther, R. T., ed. and trans. *Chaucer and Messahalla on the Astrolabe.* Oxford: Oxford UP, 1929.
75. McMillan, Ann, trans. *The Legend of Good Women.* Houston: Rice UP, 1987.
76. Richmond, E. B., trans. *The Parliament of Birds.* London: Hesperus, 2004.
77. Stone, Brian, trans. *Love Visions: The Book of the Duchess, The House of Fame, The Parliament of Fowls, The Legend of Good Women.* New York: Penguin, 1983.
78. Windeatt, Barry, trans. *Troilus and Criseyde: A New Translation.* New York: Oxford UP, 1998. (verse)
79. Wright, David, trans. *The Canterbury Tales.* New York: Random House, 1965. (prose)
See also no. 1650.

Bibliographies—Comprehensive

80. *Studies in the Age of Chaucer.* Annual annotated bibliography, 1979—.
81. Bowers, Bege K., and Mark Allen, eds. *Annotated Chaucer Bibliography, 1986–1996.* Notre Dame, IN: U of Notre Dame P, 2002.
82. Baird-Lange, Lorrayne Y., and Hildegard Schnuttgen. *A Bibliography of Chaucer, 1974–1985.* Hamden, CT: Archon, 1988.
83. Baird, Lorrayne Y. *A Bibliography of Chaucer, 1964–1973.* Boston, MA: Hall, 1977.
84. Crawford, William R. *Bibliography of Chaucer, 1954–63.* Seattle: U of Washington P, 1967.
85. Griffith, Dudley David. *Bibliography of Chaucer, 1908–1953.* Seattle: U of Washington P, 1955.
86. Hammond, Eleanor Prescott. *Chaucer: A Bibliographical Manual.* 1908. Reprint. New York: Peter Smith, 1933.
See also nos. 1, 165, 238.

Bibliographies—Individual Works

87. *Chaucer's General Prologue to the Canterbury Tales: An Annotated Bibliography, 1900–1984.* Caroline D. Eckhardt. Toronto: U of Toronto P, 1990.
88. *Chaucer's Knight's Tale. An Annotated Bibliography, 1900–1985.* Monica McAlpine. Toronto: U of Toronto P, 1991.
89. *Chaucer's Miller's, Reeve's, and Cook's Tales [An Annotated Bibliography: 1900–1992].* Eds. T. L. Burton and Rosemary Greentree. Toronto: U of Toronto P, 1997.
89a. Goodall, Peter, and others, eds. *Chaucer's* Monk's Tale *and* Nun's Priest's Tale*: An Annotated Bibliography 1900-2000.* Toronto: University of Toronto Press, 2009.
90. *Chaucer's Wife of Bath's Prologue and Tale. An Annotated Bibliography, 1900 to 1995,* Eds. Peter G. Beidler and Elizabeth M. Biebel. Toronto: U of Toronto P, 1998.
91. *Chaucer's Pardoner's Prologue and Tale. An Annotated Bibliography, 1900–1995.* Marilyn Sutton. Toronto: U of Toronto P, 2000.
92. *Chaucer's Lyrics and Anelida and Arcite: An Annotated Bibliography, 1900–1980.* Russell A. Peck. Toronto: U of Toronto P, 1984.
93. *Chaucer's Romaunt of the Rose and Boece, Treatise on the Astrolabe, Equatorie of the Planetis, Lost Works, and Chaucerian Apocrypha: An Annotated Bibliography, 1900 to 1985.* Russell A. Peck. Toronto: U of Toronto P, 1988.

Dictionaries and Reference

94. Andrew, Malcolm. *The Palgrave Literary Dictionary of Chaucer.* New York: Palgrave Macmillan, 2006.
95. Benson, Larry D. *A Glossarial Concordance to the Riverside Chaucer.* 2 vols. Hamden, CT: Garland, 1993.
96. Besserman, Lawrence. *Chaucer and the Bible: A Critical Review of Research, Indices, and Bibliography.* New York: Garland, 1988.
97. Davis, Norman, Douglas Gray, Patricia Ingham, and Anne Wallace-Hadrill. *A Chaucer Glossary.* Oxford: Clarendon P, 1979.

98. De Weever, Jacqueline. *Chaucer Name Dictionary: A Guide to Astrological, Biblical, Historical, Literary, and Mythological Names in the Works of Geoffrey Chaucer.* New York: Garland, 1988.
99. Foster, Edward E., and David H. Carey. *Chaucer's Church: A Dictionary of Religious Terms in Chaucer.* Brookfield, VT: Ashgate, 2002.
100. Gray, Douglas, ed. *The Oxford Companion to Chaucer.* Oxford: Oxford UP, 2003.
101. Kurath, Hans, Sherman M. Kuhn, Robert E. Lewis, and others, eds. *The Middle English Dictionary.* Multiple vols. Ann Arbor: U of Michigan P, 1952–2001. <http://quod.lib.umich.edu/m/med/>.
102. Oizumi, Akio. Programmed by Kunihiro Miki. *A Complete Concordance to the Works of Chaucer.* 12 vols. New York: Olms-Weidmann, 1991–94.
103. Rogers, Shannon L. *All Things Chaucer: An Encyclopedia of Chaucer's World. Volume 1: A–J. Volume 2: K–Z.* Westfield, Conn.: Greenwood P, 2007.
104. Rossignol, Rosalyn. *Critical Companion to Chaucer: A Literary Reference to His Life and Work.* New York: Facts On File, 2007.

Handbooks and Introductions

105. Boitani, Piero, and Jill Mann, eds. *The Cambridge Companion to Chaucer.* 2d ed. Cambridge: Cambridge UP, 2003.
106. Brewer, Derek. *An Introduction to Chaucer.* London: Longman, 1984.
107. Brown, Peter, ed. *A Companion to Chaucer.* Oxford: Blackwell, 2000.
108. Dillon, Janette. *Geoffrey Chaucer.* New York: Macmillan, 1993.
109. Ellis, Steve, ed. *Chaucer: An Oxford Guide.* New York: Oxford UP, 2005.
110. Hussey, S. S. *Chaucer: An Introduction.* 2d ed. London: Methuen, 1981.
111. Lerer, Seth, ed. *The Yale Companion to Chaucer.* New Haven, CT: Yale UP, 2006.
112. Norton-Smith, John. *Geoffrey Chaucer.* London: Routledge, 1974.
113. Richmond, Velma Bourgeois. *Geoffrey Chaucer.* New York: Continuum, 1992.
114. Rigby, S. H. *Chaucer in Context: Society, Allegory, and Gender.* Manchester, UK: Manchester UP, 1996.
115. Rowland, Beryl, ed. *Companion to Chaucer Studies.* Rev. ed. New York: Oxford UP, 1979.
116. Rudd, Gillian. *The Complete Critical Guide to Geoffrey Chaucer.* New York: Routledge, 2001.
117. Saunders, Corinne. *Chaucer.* Blackwell Guides to Criticism. Oxford: Blackwell, 2001.
118. Saunders, Corinne, ed. *A Concise Companion to Chaucer.* Malden, MA: Blackwell, 2006.

Reception History

119. Alderson, William L., and Arnold C. Henderson. *Chaucer and Augustan Scholarship.* Berkeley: U of California P, 1970.
120. Barrington, Candace. *American Chaucers.* New York: Palgrave Macmillan, 2007.
121. Boswell, Jackson Campbell, and Sylvia Wallace Holton. *Chaucer's Fame in England: STC Chauceriana 1475–1640.* New York: MLA, 2004.
122. Brewer, Derek, ed. *Geoffrey Chaucer: The Critical Heritage.* 1978. Reprint. 2 vols. London: Routledge, 1995.
123. Cooper, Helen. "Chaucerian Representation." In *New Readings of Chaucer's Poetry,* edited by Robert G. Benson and Susan J. Ridyard. Cambridge, UK: Brewer, 2003. 7–30.
124. Ellis, Steve. *Chaucer at Large: The Poet in the Modern Imagination.* Minneapolis: U of Minnesota P, 2000.
125. Matthews, David. *The Making of Middle English, 1765–1910.* Minneapolis: U of Minnesota P, 1999.
126. Miskimin, Alice S. *The Renaissance Chaucer.* New Haven, CT: Yale UP, 1975.
127. Morse, Charlotte C. "Popularizing Chaucer in the Nineteenth Century." *ChauR* 38 (2003): 99–125.
128. Prendergast, Thomas A., and Barbara Kline, eds. *Rewriting Chaucer: Culture, Authority, and the Idea of the Authentic Text, 1400–1602.* Columbus: Ohio State UP, 1999.
129. Richmond, Velma Bourgeois. *Chaucer as Children's Literature: Retellings from the Victorian and Edwardian Eras.* Jefferson, NC: McFarland, 2004.
130. Spurgeon, Caroline F. E. *Five Hundred Years of Chaucer Criticism and Allusion 1357–1900.* 1908–17. Reprint. 3 vols. Cambridge: Cambridge UP, 1925; New York: Russell & Russell, 1960.
131. Trigg, Stephanie. *Congenial Souls: Reading Chaucer from Medieval to Postmodern.* Minneapolis: U of Minnesota P, 2002.

See also nos. 38, 218.

Early Print Culture

132. Bishop, Laura M. "Father Chaucer and the Vivification of Print." *JEGP* 106 (2007): 336–63.
133. Dane, Joseph A. *The Myth of Print Culture, Essays on Evidence, Textuality, and Bibliographical Method.* Toronto: U of Toronto P, 2003.
134. ———. *Who Is Buried in Chaucer's Tomb? Studies in the Reception of Chaucer's Book.* East Lansing: Michigan State UP, 1998.
135. Edwards, A. S. G. "Chaucer from Manuscript to Print." *Mosaic* 28.4 (1995): 1–12.
136. Gillespie, Alexandra. *Print Culture and the Medieval Author: Chaucer, Lydgate, and Their Books, 1473–1557.* Oxford: Oxford UP, 2006.
137. Hellinga, Lotte, and J. B. Trapp, eds. *The Cambridge History of the Book in Britain. Volume 3: 1400–1557.* Cambridge, UK: Cambridge UP, 1999.
138. Higl, Andrew. "Printing Power: Selling Lydgate, Gower, and Chaucer." *Essays in Medieval Studies* 23 (2006): 57–77.
139. Kuskin, William, ed. *Caxton's Trace: Studies in the History of English Printing.* Notre Dame, IN: U of Notre Dame P, 2006.
140. Rust, Martha Dana. *Imaginary Worlds in Medieval Books.* New York: Palgrave Macmillan, 2007.

141. Schoff, Rebecca L. *Reformations: Three Medieval Authors in Manuscript and Movable Type.* Turnhout, Belgium: Brepols, 2007.

See also no. 335.

Biography and Biographical Contexts

142. Ackroyd, Peter. *Chaucer.* Chatto & Windus, 2004.

143. Bennett, J. A. W. *Chaucer at Oxford and Cambridge.* Toronto: U of Toronto P, 1974.

144. Brewer, Derek. *Chaucer and His World.* 2d ed. 1992. Reprint. *The World of Chaucer.* Rochester, NY: Brewer, 2000.

145. Cannon, Christopher. "*Raptus* in the Chaumpaigne Release and a Newly Discovered Document Concerning the Life of Geoffrey Chaucer." *Speculum* 68 (1993): 74–94.

146. Crow, Martin M., and Clair C. Olson, eds. *Chaucer Life Records. From Materials Compiled by John M. Manly and Edith Rickert, with the Assistance of Lillian Redstone and Others.* Oxford: Clarendon, 1966.

147. Hornsby, Joseph A. "Was Chaucer Educated at the Inns of Court?" *ChauR* 22 (1988): 255–68.

148. Howard, Donald R. *Chaucer: His Life, His World, His Works.* New York: Dutton, 1987. Also pub. as *Chaucer and the Medieval World.* London: Weidenfeld and Nicolson, 1987.

149. Kern, Alfred. *The Ancestry of Chaucer.* 1906. Reprint. [New York: AMS], 1973.

150. Matheson, Lister M. "Chaucer's Ancestry: Historical and Philological Re-Assessments." *ChauR* 25 (1991): 171–89.

151. Pearsall, Derek. "Chaucer's Tomb: The Politics of Reburial." *MAE* 64 (1995): 51–73.

152. ———. *The Life of Geoffrey Chaucer: A Critical Biography.* Oxford: Blackwell, 1992.

153. Rudd, Martin B. *Thomas Chaucer.* Research Publications of the U of Minnesota, 9. Minneapolis, 1926.

154. Serrano-Reyes, Jesús L. "John of Gaunt's Intervention in Spain: Possible Repercussions for Chaucer's Life and Poetry." *SELIM* 6 (1996): 117–45.

See also nos. 343, 526, 672, 1199, 1201, 1223, 1670, 1637.

Language—General

155. Burnley, [John] David. *A Guide to Chaucer's Language.* Norman: U of Oklahoma P, 1983.

156. ———. "French and Frenches in Fourteenth-Century London." In *Language Contact in the History of English,* edited by Dieter Kastovsky and Arthur Mettinger. Frankfurt am Main: Lang, 2001. 17–34.

157. Davis, Norman. "Chaucer and Fifteenth-Century English." In *Geoffrey Chaucer.* Writers and their Background. Edited by D. S. Brewer. London: Bell, 1974. 58–84.

158. Eliason, Norman. *The Language of Chaucer's Poetry: An Appraisal of the Verse, Style, and Structure.* Copenhagen: Rosenkilde, 1972.

159. Elliott, R. W. V. *Chaucer's English.* London: Deutsch, 1974.

160. Fisher, John H. "A Language Policy for Lancastrian England." *PMLA* 107 (1992): 1168–80.

161. Horobin, Simon. *Chaucer's Language.* New York: Palgrave Macmillan, 2007.

162. ———. *The Language of the Chaucer Tradition.* Cambridge: Brewer, 2003.

163. Kerkhof, Jelle. *Studies in the Language of Geoffrey Chaucer.* 2d ed. Leiden: Leiden UP, 1982.

164. Kökeritz, Helge. *A Guide to Chaucer's Pronunciation.* 1954. Reprint. Toronto: U of Toronto P, 1978.

165. Oizumi, Akio, ed. *A Bibliography of Writings on Chaucer's English.* New York: Olms-Weidmann, 1995

166. Roscow, Gregory. *Syntax and Style in Chaucer's Poetry.* Cambridge: Brewer, 1981.

167. Rothwell, W. "The Trilingual England of Geoffrey Chaucer." *SAC* 16 (1994): 45–67.

168. Sandved, Arthur O. *Introduction to Chaucerian English.* Woodbridge: Brewer, 1985.

169. Schaefer, Ursula, ed. *The Beginnings of Standardization: Language and Culture in Fourteenth-Century England.* Frankfurt am Main: Lang, 2006.

170. Smith, Jeremy J. "Chaucer and the Invention of English." *SAC* 24 (2002): 335–46.

Language—Lexicon and Register

171. Baum. Paull F. "Chaucer's Puns." *PMLA* 71 (1956): 225–46. "Chaucer's Puns: A Supplementary List." *PMLA* 73 (1958): 167–70.

172. Benson, Larry D. "The 'Queynte' Punnings of Chaucer's Critics." *SAC Proceedings* 1 (1985): 3–50.

173. Burnley, J. D. *Chaucer's Language and the Philosopher's Tradition.* Cambridge: Brewer, 1979.

174. Cannon, Christopher. *The Making of Chaucer's English: A Study of Words.* Cambridge: Cambridge UP, 1998.

175. DeWeever, Jacqueline. "Chaucerian Onomastics: The Formation of Personal Names in Chaucer's Works." *Names* 28 (1980): 1–31.

176. Jucker, Andreas H. "'Thou art so loothly and so oold also': The Use of *Ye* and *Thou* in Chaucer's *Canterbury Tales.*" *Anglistik* 17.2 (2006): 57–72.

177. Knapp, Peggy A. *Time-Bound Words: Semantic and Social Economies from Chaucer's England to Shakespeare's.* New York: St. Martin's, 2000.

178. Knappe, Gabriele, and Michael Schümann. "*Thou* and *Ye*: A Collocational-Phraseological Approach to Pronoun Change in Chaucer's *Canterbury Tales.*" *SAP* 42 (2006): 213–38.

179. Mazzon, Gabriella. "Social Relations and Form of Address in the Canterbury Tales." In *The History of English in a Social Context,* edited by Dieter Kastovsky and Arthur Mettinger. New York: Gruyter, 2000. 135–68.

180. Mersand, Joseph. *Chaucer's Romance Vocabulary.* 1937. Reprint. Port Washington, NY: Kennikat, 1968.
181. Pakkala-Weckström, Mari. *The Dialogue of Love, Marriage and Maistrie in Chaucer's Canterbury Tales.* Helsinki: Société Néophilologique, 2005.
182. Pearsall, Derek. "*The Franklin's Tale,* Line 1469: Forms of Address in Chaucer." *SAC* 17 (1995): 69–78.
183. Phillips, Susan E. *Transforming Talk: The Problem with Gossip in Late Medieval England.* University Park, Penn.: Pennsylvania State UP, 2007.
184. Ross, Thomas W. *Chaucer's Bawdy.* New York: Dutton, 1972.
185. Rothwell, W. "Chaucer and Stratford atte Bowe." *BJRL* 74 (1992): 3–28.
186. Rudanko, Juhani. "'I Wol Sterve': Negotiating the Issue of a Lady's Consent in Chaucer's Poetry." *Journal of Historical Pragmatics* 5.1 (2004): 137–58.

See also nos. 644, 807, 811, 1677.

Style, Rhetoric, and Rhetorical Tradition

187. Benson, Larry D. "The Beginnings of Chaucer's Style." In *Contradictions: From Beowulf to Chaucer,* edited by Theodore M. Andersson and Stephen A. Barney. Brookfield, VT: Ashgate, 1995. 243–65.
188. Benson, Robert G. *Medieval Body Language: A Study of the Use of Gesture in Chaucer's Poetry.* Copenhagen: Rosenkilde, 1980.
189. Birney, Earle. *Essays on Chaucerian Irony.* Ed. Beryl Rowland. Toronto: U of Toronto P, 1985.
190. Camargo, Martin. "Time as Rhetorical Topos in Chaucer's Poetry." In *Medieval Rhetoric: A Casebook,* edited by Scott D. Troyan. New York: Routledge, 2004. 91–107.
191. Cannon, Christopher. "Chaucer's Style." In Boitani and Mann, no. 105. 233–50.
192. Chickering, Howell. "Unpunctuating Chaucer." *ChauR* 25 (1990): 96–109.
193. Copeland, Rita. "Chaucer and Rhetoric" In Lerer, no. 111. 122–43.
194. Fisher, John H. "Chaucer and the Written Language." In *The Popular Literature of Medieval England,* edited by Thomas J. Heffernan. Knoxville: U of Tennessee P, 1985. 237–51.
195. Gray, Douglas. "'Lat be thyne olde ensaumples': Chaucer and Proverbs." In *Interstices: Studies in Middle English and Anglo-Latin Texts in Honour of A. G. Rigg,* edited by Richard Firth Green and Linne R. Mooney. Toronto: U of Toronto P, 2004. 122–36.
196. Hass, Robin R. "'A Picture of Such Beauty in Their Minds': The Medieval Rhetoricians, Chaucer, and Evocative *Efficio.*" *Exemplaria* 14 (2002): 383–422.
197. McGavin, John J. *Chaucer and Dissimilarity: Literary Comparisons in Chaucer and Other Late-Medieval Writing.* Teaneck, NJ: Fairleigh Dickinson UP, 2000.
198. Murphy, James J. "A New Look at Chaucer and the Rhetoricians." *RES* 15 (1964): 1–20.
199. Muscatine, Charles. *Chaucer and the French Tradition: A Study in Style and Meaning.* Berkeley: U of California P, 1957.
200. Payne, Robert O. "Rhetoric in Chaucer: Chaucer's Realization of Himself as a Rhetor." In *Medieval Eloquence,* edited by James J. Murphy. Berkeley: U of California P, 1978. 270–87.
201. ———. "Chaucer and the Art of Rhetoric." In Rowland, no. 115, 42–64.
202. Reiss, Edmund. "Chaucer and Medieval Irony." *SAC* 1 (1979): 67–82.
203. Woods, Marjorie Curry. "In a Nutshell: 'Verba' and 'Sententia' and Matter and Form in Medieval Composition Theory." In *The Uses of Manuscripts in Literary Studies,* edited by Charlotte Cook Morse and others. Kalamazoo, MI: Medieval Institute, 1992. 19–39.

See also nos. 591, 639–43, 726, 745, 820–21, 912, 971, 1139, 1169, 1264–83, 1406, 1442, 1459.

The Vernacular, Translation, and Textuality

204. Copeland, Rita. *Rhetoric, Hermeutics, and Translation in the Middle Ages: Academic Traditions and Vernaular Texts.* Cambridge: Cambridge UP, 1991.
205. Gellrich, Jesse. *The Idea of the Book in the Middle Ages: Language Theory, Mythology, and Fiction.* Ithaca, NY: Cornell UP, 1985.
206. Kiser, Lisa. *Truth and Textuality in Chaucer's Poetry.* Hanover, NH: UP of New England, 1991.
207. Minnis, Alastair. "'I speke of folk in seculer estaat': Vernacularity and Secularity in the Age of Chaucer." *SAC* 27 (2005): 25–58.
208. Potter, Russell A. "Chaucer and the Authority of Language: The Politics and Poetics of the Vernacular in Late Medieval England." *Assays* 6 (1991): 73–91.
209. Schaefer, Ursula. "Textualizing the Vernacular in Late Medieval England: Suggestions for Some Heuristic Reconsiderations." In *Language and Text: Current Perspectives on English and Germanic Historical Linguistics and Philology,* edited by Andrew James Johnston and others. Heidelberg: Winter, 2006. 269–90.
210. Taylor, Paul Beekman. "Chaucer's Strategies of Translation." *ChauY* 4 (1997): 1–19.

See also nos. 355, 885, 919, 957, 1167, 1647, 1649, 1651, 1657, 1659, 1663.

Prosody and Versification

211. Baum, Paull F. *Chaucer's Verse.* Durham, NC: Duke UP, 1961.
212. Brody, Saul Nathaniel. "Chaucer's Rhyme Royal Tales and the Secularization of the Saint." *ChauR* 20 (1985): 113–31.
213. Cable, Thomas. "Issues for a New History of English Prosody." In *Studies in the History of the English Language: A Millennial Perspective,* edited by Donka

Minkova and Robert Stockwell. Berlin: Mouton de Gruyter, 2002. 125–51.

214. Dauby, Hélène. "Chaucer et l'Allitération." *L'Articulation Langue-Littérature dans les Textes Médiévaux Anglais, II.* GRENDEL, no. 3. Ed. Colette Stévanovitch. Nancy: Publications de l'Association des Médiévistes Anglicistes de l'Enseignement Supérieur, 1999. 133–42.
215. Duffell, Martin J. "'The craft so long to lerne': Chaucer's Invention of Iambic Pentameter." *ChauR* 34 (2000): 269–88.
216. Finnie, Bruce W. "On Chaucer's Stressed Vowel Phonemes." *ChauR* 9 (1975): 337–41.
217. Gaylord, Alan T., ed. *Essays on the Art of Chaucer's Verse.* New York: Routledge, 2001.
218. Groves, Peter. "Water from the Well: The Reception of Chaucer's Metric." *Parergon* 17.1 (2000): 51–73.
219. Knight, Stephen. *Rymyng Craftily: Meaning in Chaucer's Poetry.* Sydney: Angus & Robertson, 1973.
220. Mann, Jill. "Chaucer's Meter and the Myth of the Ellesmere Editor of *The Canterbury Tales. SAC* 23 (2001): 71–107.
221. Masui, Michio, ed. *A New Rime Index to The Canterbury Tales Based on Manly and Rickert's Text of the Canterbury Tales.* Tokyo: Shinozaki Shorin, 1988.
222. Osberg, Richard H. "'I kan nat geeste': Chaucer's Artful Alliteration." In Gaylord, no. 217. 195–227.
223. Putter, Ad. "Chaucer's Verse and Alliterative Poetry: Grammar, Metre, and Some Secrets of the Syllable Count." *PoeticaT* 67 (2007): 19–35.
224. Robinson, Ian. *Chaucer's Prosody: A Study of the Middle English Verse Tradition.* London: Cambridge UP, 1971.
225. Southworth, James G. *Verses of Cadence: An Introduction to the Prosody of Chaucer.* Oxford: Blackwell, 1954.
226. Stevens, Martin. "The Royal Stanza in Early English Literature." *PMLA* 94 (1979): 67–76.
227. Tarlinskaja, Marina G. *English Verse: Theory and History.* The Hague: Mouton, 1976.

See also, nos. 639, 745, 896, 1100, 1279, 1450, 1588.

Prose

228. Bornstein, Diane. "Chaucer's *Tale of Melibee* as an Example of the *Style clergial.*" *ChauR* 12 (1978): 236–54.
229. Chisnell, Robert E. "Chaucer's Neglected Prose." In *Literary and Historical Perspectives of the Middle Ages,* edited by Patricia W. Cummins, Patrick W. Conner, and Charles W. Connell. Morganton: West Virginia UP, 1982. 156–73.
230. Lawler, Traugott. "Chaucer." In *Middle English Prose: A Critical Guide to Major Authors and Genres,* edited by A. S. G. Edwards. New Brunswick, NJ: Rutgers UP, 1984. 291–313.
231. Schlauch, Margaret. "The Art of Chaucer's Prose." In *Chaucer and Chaucerians: Critical Studies in Middle English,* edited by D. S. Brewer. University: U of Alabama P, 1966. 140–63.

See also nos. 1667, 1671–72.

Sources and Analogues—General

232. Benson, Larry D., and Theodore Andersson, eds. *The Literary Context of Chaucer's Fabliaux.* Indianapolis, IN: Bobbs-Merrill, 1971.
233. Bryan, W. F., and Germaine Dempster, eds. *Sources and Analogues of Chaucer's 'Canterbury Tales.'* 1941. Reprint. London: Routledge and Kegan Paul; New York: Humanities P, 1958.
234. Correale, Robert M., and Mary Hamel, eds. *Sources and Analogues of the Canterbury Tales,* 2 vols. Rochester, NY: Brewer, 2002–05.
235. Diekstra, Fran. "Chaucer's Way with His Sources: Accident into Substance and Substance into Accident." *ES* 62 (1981): 215–36.
236. [Diamond, Arlyn, and Nancy Bradbury, eds.] "Colloquium: The Afterlife of Origins." *SAC* 28 (2006): 217–70.
237. Miller, Robert P., ed. *Chaucer: Sources and Backgrounds.* New York: Oxford UP, 1977.
238. Morris, Lynn King. *Chaucer Source and Analogue Criticism: A Cross-Referenced Guide.* New York and London: Garland, 1985.
239. Pratt, Robert A. "Chaucer and the Hand that Fed Him." *Speculum* 41 (1966): 619–42.

See also no. 1405.

Sources and Analogues—Editions

240. Albertano of Brescia. *Albertani Brixiensis Liber Consolationis et Consilii.* Ed. Thor Sundby. London: Chaucer Society, 2d ser., 8, 1873.
241. Boccaccio, Giovanni. *Tutte le Opere di Giovanni Boccaccio.* Gen. ed. Vittore Branca. Rev. ed. Milan: Mondadori, 1964–.
242. ———. *De Casibus Vivorum Illustrium.* In no. 241, vol. 9. Trans. Louis B. Hall, *The Fates of Illustrious Men.* New York: Ungar, 1965.
243. ———. *De Claris Mulieribus.* In no. 241, vol. 10. Trans. Guido A. Guarino, *Concerning Famous Women.* New Brunswick, NY: Rutgers UP, 1963.
244. ———. *Il Decamerone.* In no. 241, vol. 4. Trans. G. H. McWilliam, *The Decameron.* Harmondsworth: Penguin, 1972.
245. ———. *Il Filocolo.* In no. 241, vol 1. Trans. Donald Cheney, with Thomas G. Bergin, *Filocolo.* New York: Garland, 1985, and in Havely, no. 259.
246. ———. *Il Filostrato.* In no. 241, vol. 2. Trans. Robert P. apRoberts and Anna Bruni Seldis, *Il Filostrato.* New York: Garland, 1986, and excerpts in Havely, no. 259.
247. ———. *Il Teseida.* In no. 241, vol. 2. Trans. Bernadette M. McCoy, *The Book of Theseus.* New York: Medieval Text Association, 1974, and in Havely, no. 259.
248. Boethius. *Theological Tractates and The Consolation of Philosophy.* 2nd ed. Trans. H. F. Stewart, E. K. Rand, and S. J. Tester. Cambridge, MA: Harvard UP, 1973.
249. Caecilius Balbus [Pseudo]. *De Nugis Philosophorum, Quae Supersunt.* Ed. Edward Woefflin. Basil: Schweighauser, 1855.

250. Cato, "Dionysius." *Dicta Catonis* [*Disticha Catonis*]. In *Minor Latin Poets*. 2 vols. Rev. ed. Trans. J. Wight Duff and Arnold M. Duff. Cambridge, Mass.: Harvard UP; London: Heinemann, 1935. 1: 585–639.
251. Cicero. *De Senectute, De Amicitia, De Divinatione.* With an English Translation by William Armistead Falconer. Cambridge: Harvard UP; London: Heinemann, 1979.
252. *Claudian, with an English Translation.* Ed. and trans. Maurice Platnauer. Cambridge, MA: Harvard UP, 1922.
253. Dante Alighieri. *Convivio.* Ed. Maria Simonelli. Bologna: Pátron, 1966. Trans. Richard H. Lansing, *Dante's Il Convivio (The Banquet).* New York: Garland, 1990.
254. Froissart, Jean. *Jean Froissart: An Anthology of Narrative & Lyric Poetry.* Ed. and trans. Kristen M. Figg and R. Barton Palmer. New York: Routledge, 2001.
255. Geoffrey of Monmouth. *The Historia Regum Britannie of Geoffrey of Monmouth.* Ed. and trans. Neil Wright. 5 vols. Cambridge: Brewer, 1985–95.
256. Gower, John. *The Complete Works of John Gower.* Ed. G. C. Macauley, 4 vols. EETS. 1899–1902.
257. Guido de Columnis. *Historia Destructionis Troiae.* Ed. Nathaniel Edward Griffin. Cambridge, MA: Medieval Academy, 1936. Trans. Mary Elizabeth Meek, *Historia Destructionis Troiae: Guido delle Colonne.* Bloomington, IN: Indiana UP, 1974.
258. Guillaume de Lorris and Jean de Meun. *Le Roman de la Rose.* Ed. Ernest Langlois. 5 vols. Paris: SATF, 1914–24; Felix Lecoy. 3 vols. Paris: Champion, 1965–70. Trans. Charles Dahlberg, *The Romance of the Rose.* Princeton: Princeton UP, 1983.
259. Havely, N. R., trans. *Boccaccio—Sources of Troilus and the Knight's and Franklin's Tales.* Cambridge, UK: Brewer, 1980.
260. Innocent III, Pope (Lotario dei Segni). *De Miseria Condicionis Humane.* Ed. and trans. Robert E. Lewis. 1978. Reprint. London: Scolar, 1980.
261. Jerome, Saint. *Letter Against Jovininum.* Trans. W. H. Fremantle, *The Principal Works of St. Jerome.* Vol. 6 of *A Select Library of Nicene and Post-Nicene Fathers of the Christian Church,* 2d. ser. Reprint. Grand Rapids, MI: Eerdmans, 1989. Also available in Hanna and Lawler, no. 869.
262. Livy. *Livy, with an English Translation.* Ed. and Trans by B. O. Foster and others. 14 vols. London: Loeb, 1919–59.
263. Machaut, Guillaume de. *The Judgment of the King of Navarre.* Ed. and trans. James I. Wimsatt and William W. Kibler. With music edited by Rebecca A. Baltzer. New York: Garland, 1988.
264. ———. *Le Jugement du roy de Behaigne and Remede de Fortune.* Ed. James I Wimsatt and William W. Kibler. Athens: U of Georgia P, 1988.
265. Macrobius. *Commentary on the Dream of Scipio.* Trans. William Harris Stahl. New York: Columbia UP, 1952.
266. Martianus Dumiensis. *De Moribus.* In no. 274.
267. Nicholas of Lynn. *The Kalendarium of Nicholas of Lynn.* and trans. Sigmund Eisner and Gary Mac Eoin. Athens: U of Georgia P, 1980.
268. Ovid. [*Ars Amatoria.*] *The Art of Love and Other Poems.* Ed. and trans. J. H. Mozley. Rev. ed. G. P. Goold. Cambridge: Harvard UP, 1979.
269. ———. *Fasti.* Ed. and trans. James George Frazier. Cambridge: Harvard UP, 1976.
270. ———. *Heroides and Amores.* Ed. and trans. Grant Showerman. 2d ed. Rev. G. P. Goold. Cambridge: Harvard UP, 1977.
271. ———. *Metamorphoses.* 2 vols. Ed. and trans. F. J. Miller. Rev. ed. G. P. Goold. Cambridge: Harvard UP, 1976–77.
272. Petrarch. *Prose.* Ed. Guido Martellotti. Trans. in part, Aldo S. Bernardo and others, *Letters of Old Age.* Baltimore: Johns Hopkins UP, 1992. (tale of Griselda)
273. Petrus Alphonsus. *The Disciplina Clericalis of Petrus Alphonsi.* Trans. and ed. Eberhard Hermes. Eng. trans. P. R. Quarrie. Berkeley: U of California P, 1970.
274. Publilius Syrus. *Sententiae.* Includes *De Moribus* of Pseudo-Seneca, Martianus Dumiensis. Ed. Edward Woefflin. Leipzig: Tuebner, 1869.
275. Sercambi, Giovanni. *Il Novelliere.* Ed. Luciano Rossi. Rome: Salerno, 1974.
276. Valerius Maximus, *Memorable Doings and Sayings.* 2 vols. Ed. and trans. D. R. Shackleton Bailey. Cambridge: Harvard UP, 2000.

Classical and Continental Relations

277. Battles, Dominique. *The Medieval Tradition of Thebes: History and Narrative in the OF Roman de Thèbes, Boccaccio, Chaucer, and Lydgate.* New York: Routledge, 2004.
278. Battles, Paul. "Chaucer and the Tradition of Dawn-Song." *ChauR* 31 (1997): 317–38.
279. Boitani, Piero, ed. *Chaucer and the Italian Trecento.* Cambridge, UK: Cambridge UP, 1983.
280. Brown, Murray. "Poets, Peace, the Passion, and the Prince: Eustache Deschamps's 'Ballade to Chaucer.'" In *Chaucer's French Contemporaries,* edited by R. Barton Palmer. New York: AMS, 1999. 187–215.
281. Butterfield, Ardis. "Chaucer's French Inheritence." In Boitani and Mann, no. 105. 20–35.
282. Calabrese, Michael A. *Chaucer's Ovidian Arts of Love.* Gainesville: UP of Florida, 1994.
283. Calin, William. "Machaut's Legacy: The Chaucerian Inheritence Reconsidered." In *Chaucer's French Contemporaries,* edited by R. Barton Palmer. New York: AMS, 1999. 29–46.
284. Cooper, Helen. "The Four Last Things in Dante and Chaucer." *NML* 3 (1999): 39–66.
285. Crépin, André. "Chaucer and the French." In *Medieval and Pseudo-Medieval Literature,* edited by Piero Boitani and Anna Torti. Tübingen: Narr, 1984. 55–77.
286. Desmond, Marilynn. *Reading Dido: Gender, Texuality, and the Medieval Aeneid.* Minneapolis: U of Minnesota P, 1994.

287. Edwards, Robert R. *Chaucer and Boccaccio: Antiquity and Modernity.* New York: Palgrave, 2002.

287a. Fansler, Dean Spruill. *Chaucer and the Roman de la Rose.* New York: Columbia UP, 1914. Rpt. Gloucester, Mass.: Peter Smith, 1965.

288. Fyler, John M. *Chaucer and Ovid.* New Haven: Yale UP, 1979.

289. Ginsberg, Warren. *The Cast of Character: The Representation of Personality in Ancient and Medieval Literature.* Toronto: U of Toronto P, 1983.

290. ———. *Chaucer's Italian Tradition.* Ann Arbor: U of Michigan P, 2002.

291. Hagedorn, Suzanne C. *Abandoned Women: Rewriting the Classics in Dante, Boccaccio, & Chaucer.* Ann Arbor: U of Michigan P, 2004.

292. Harbert, Bruce. "Chaucer and the Latin Classics." In *Geoffrey Chaucer.* Writers and their Background. Ed. D. S. Brewer. London: Bell, 1974. 137–53.

293. Hoffman, Richard L. *Ovid and the Canterbury Tales.* Philadelphia: U of Pennsylvania P, 1966.

294. Jefferson, Bernard L. *Chaucer and the Consolation of Philosophy.* 1917. Reprint. New York: Haskell, 1965.

295. Koff, Leonard Michael, and Brenda Deen Schildgen, eds. *The Decameron and the Canterbury Tales: New Essays on an Old Question.* Madison, NJ: Fairleigh Dickinson UP, 2000.

296. Lewis, C. S. *The Discarded Image: An Introduction to Medieval and Renaissance Literature.* Cambridge UP, 1967.

297. McCall, John P. *Chaucer Among the Gods: The Poetics of Classical Myth.* University Park: Pennsylvania State UP, 1979.

298. McTurk, Rory. *Chaucer and the Norse and Celtic Worlds.* Burlington, VT: Ashgate, 2005.

299. Minnis, A. J. *Chaucer and Pagan Antiquity.* Cambridge: Brewer, 1982.

300. Neuse, Richard. *Chaucer's Dante: Allegory and Epic Theater in The Canterbury Tales.* Berkeley: U of California P, 1991.

301. Nolan, Barbara. *Chaucer and the Tradition of the Roman Antique.* Cambridge: Cambridge UP, 1992.

302. Nolan, Edward Peter. "Knocking the Mary Out of the Bones: Chaucer's Ethical Mirrors of Dante." In *Through a Glass Darkly: Specular Images of Seeing and Knowing from Virgil to Chaucer.* Ann Arbor: U of Michigan P, 1990. 193–217.

303. Phillips, Helen. "Fortune and the Lady: Chaucer and the International 'Dit'." *NFS* 38 (1999): 120–36.

304. Shannon, Edgar F. *Chaucer and the Roman Poets.* Cambridge: Harvard UP, 1929.

305. Simpson, James. "Breaking the Vacuum: Ricardian and Henrician Ovidianism." *JMEMSt* 29 (1999): 325–55.

306. ———. "Chaucer as a European Writer." 2007. In Lerer, no. 111. 55–86.

307. Taylor, Karla. *Chaucer Reads "The Divine Comedy".* Stanford, CA: Stanford UP, 1989.

308. ———. Chaucer's Volumes: Toward a New Model of Literary History in the *Canterbury Tales.*" *SAC* 29 (2007): 43–85.

309. Thompson, N. S. *Chaucer, Boccaccio, and the Debate of Love: A Comparative Study of The Decameron and The Canterbury Tales.* Oxford: Clarendon, 1996.

310. Wallace, David. *Chaucer and the Early Writings of Boccaccio.* Cambridge, UK: Brewer, 1985.

311. ———. *Chaucerian Polity: Absolutist Lineages and Associational Forms in England and Italy.* Stanford, CA: Stanford UP, 1997.

312. Wetherbee, Winthrop, III. "Chaucer and the European Tradition." *SAC* 27 (2005): 3–21.

313. Wilson, Grace G. "'Amonges Othere Wordes Wyse': The Medieval Seneca and the *Canterbury Tales.*" *ChauR* 28 (1993): 135–45.

314. Wimsatt, James I. *Chaucer and His French Contemporaries: Natural Music in the Fourteenth Century.* Toronto: U of Toronto P, 1991.

See also nos. 412, 861, 1396, 1439, 1494, 1517, 1526.

English Relations, Contemporary and Later

315. Barr, Helen. *Socioliterary Practice in Late Medieval England.* Oxford: Oxford UP, 2001.

316. Bowers, John M. *Chaucer and Langland: The Antagonistic Tradition.* Notre Dame, IN: U of Notre Dame P, 2007.

317. Burrow, J. A. *Ricardian Poetry: Chaucer, Gower, Langland and the Pearl Poet.* New Haven, CT: Yale UP, 1971.

318. Davenport, W. A. *Chaucer and His English Contemporaries: Prologue and Tale in the Canterbury Tales.* New York: St. Martin's P, 1998.

319. Donaldson, E. Talbot. *The Swan at the Well: Shakespeare Reading Chaucer.* New Haven, CT: Yale UP, 1985.

320. Fisher, John H. *The Importance of Chaucer.* Carbondale: Southern Illinois UP, 1992.

321. ———. *John Gower: Moral Philosopher and Friend of Chaucer.* New York: New York UP, 1964.

322. Hieatt, A. Kent. *Chaucer, Spenser, Milton: Mythopoetic Continuities and Transformations.* Montreal: Mc-Gill-Queen's UP, 1975.

323. Kean, P. M. *Chaucer and the Making of English Poetry.* 2 vols. London: Routledge, 1972.

324. Krier, Theresa M., ed. *Refiguring Chaucer in the Renaissance.* Gainesville: UP of Florida, 1998.

325. Lerer, Seth. "The Chaucerian Critique of Medieval Theatricality." In *The Performance of Medieval Culture,* edited by James J. Paxson and others. Cambridge: Brewer, 1998. 59–76.

326. Lindeboom, B. W. *Venus' Owne Clerk: Chaucer's Debt to the Confessio Amantis.* New York: Rodopi, 2007.

327. Morse, Ruth, and Barry Windeatt, eds. *Chaucer Traditions: Studies in Honour of Derek Brewer.* Cambridge, UK: Cambridge UP, 1990.

328. Pearsall, Derek. "The English Chaucerians." In *Chaucer and Chaucerians,* edited by D. S. Brewer. London: Nelson, 1966. 201–39.

329. Robinson, Ian. *Chaucer and the English Tradition.* Cambridge, UK: Cambridge UP, 1972.

330. Thompson, Ann. *Shakespeare's Chaucer: A Study in Literary Origins.* New York: Barnes & Noble, 1978.

331. Walker, Greg. *Writing Under Tyranny: English Literature and the Henrician Reform.* Oxford: Oxford UP, 2005.
332. Yeager, R. F., ed. *Chaucer and Gower: Difference, Mutability, Exchange.* Victoria, BC: U of Victoria, 1991.
See also nos. 119, 121, 125–26, 130, 837, 1504, 1537.

Idea of the Author

333. De Looze, Lawrence. *Pseudo-Autobiography in the Fourteenth Century: Juan Ruiz, Guillaume de Machaut, Jean Froissart, and Geoffrey Chaucer.* Gainesville: UP of Florida, 1997.
334. Dinshaw, Carolyn. *Chaucer and the Text: Two Views of the Author.* New York: Garland, 1988.
335. Gillespie, Alexandra. *Print Culture and the Medieval Author: Chaucer, Lydgate, and Their Books, 1473–1557.* Oxford: Oxford University Press, 2006.
336. Hanna, Ralph, III. "Presenting Chaucer as Author." In *Medieval Literature: Texts and Interpretations,* edited Tim William Machan. Binghamton, NY: Center for Medieval and Early Reniassance Studies, 1991. 17–39.
337. Kimmelman, Burt. *The Poetics of Authorship in the Late Middle Ages.* New York: Lang, 1996.
338. Lerer, Seth. *Chaucer and His Readers: Imagining the Author in Late-Medieval England.* Princeton, NJ: Princeton UP, 1993.
339. Mayer, Lauryn S. "Caxton, Chaucerian Manuscripts, and the Creation of an *Auctor.*" In *Worlds Made Flesh: Reading Medieval Manuscript Culture.* New York: Routledge, 2004. 121–54.
340. Miller, Jacqueline T. *Poetic License: Authority and Authorship in Medieval and Renaissance Contexts.* New York: Oxford UP, 1986.
341. Minnis, Alastair. "The Author's Two Bodies? Authority and Fallibility in Late-Medieval Textual Theory." In *Of the Making of Books,* edited by Pamela Robinson and Rivkah Zim. Brookfield, VT: Ashgate, 1997. 259–79.
342. ———. *The Medieval Theory of Authorship.* Cambridge,UK: Brewer, 1982.
343. Pask, Kevin. "'England's Olde Ennius': Geoffrey Chaucer." In *The Emergence of the Author: Scripting the Life of the Poet in Early Modern England.* Cambridge,UK: Cambridge UP, 1996. 9–52.
344. Zieman, Katherine. "Chaucer's Voys." *Representations* 60 (1997): 70–91.
See also nos. 478, 1105, 1219–20, 1518.

Audience

345. Amtower, Laurel. *Engaging Words: The Culture of Reading in the Later Middle Ages.* New York: Palgrave, 2000.
346. Coleman, Janet. *Medieval Readers and Writers, 1350–1400.* New York: Columbia UP, 1981.
347. Eade, J. C. "'We ben to lewd or to slowe': Chaucer's Astronomy and Audience Participation." *SAC* 4 (1982): 53–85.
348. Green, D. H. *Women Readers in the Middle Ages.* Cambridge, UK: Cambridge UP, 2007.
349. Mehl, Dieter. "Chaucer's Audience." *LeedsSE* 10 (1978): 58–74.
350. Middleton, Anne. "Chaucer's 'New Men' and the Good of Literature in the *Canterbury Tales.*" In *Literature and Society,* edited by Edward W. Said. Baltimore: Johns Hopkins UP, 1980. 15–56.
351. Pearsall, Derek. "*The Canterbury Tales* and London Club Culture." In Butterfield, no. 502. 95–108.
352. Reiss, Edmund. "Chaucer and His Audience." *ChauR* 14 (1980): 390–402.
353. Strohm, Paul. "Chaucer's Audience(s): Fictional, Implied, Intended, Actual." *ChauR* 18 (1983): 137–45.
354. ———. "Chaucer's Fifteenth-Century Audience and the Narrowing of the 'Chaucer Tradition.'" *SAC* 4 (1982): 3–32.
See also nos. 885, 1287–88, 1542, 1591.

Orality and Performance

355. Andreas, James R. "Chaucer's Defense of the Vulgar Tongue." *Postscript* 9 (1992): 19–30.
356. Axton, Richard. "Chaucer and the Idea of the Theatrical Performance." In *Divers Toyes Mengled: Essays on Medieval and Renaissance Culture in Honour of Andre Lascombes,* edited by Michel Bitot. Tours: Université François Ralelais, 1996. 83–100.
357. Bowden, Betsy. *Chaucer Aloud: The Varieties of Textual Interpretation.* Philadelphia: U of Pennsylvania P, 1987.
358. Coleman, Joyce. "On Beyond Ong: Taking the Paradox Out of 'Oral Literacy' (and 'Literate Orality')." In *Medieval Insular Literature Between the Written and Oral II: Continuity of Transmission,* edited by Hildegard L. C. Tristram. Tübingen: Narr, 1997. 155–76.
359. Ganim, John M. *Chaucerian Theatricality.* Princeton, NJ: Princeton UP, 1990.
360. ———. "Forms of Talk in *The Canterbury Tales.*" *PoeticaT* 34 (1991): 88–100.
361. Grudin, Michaela Paasche. *Chaucer and the Politics of Discourse.* Columbia: U of South Carolina P, 1996.
362. Lindahl, Carl. "The Oral Undertones of Late Medieval Romance." In *Oral Tradition in the Middle Ages,* edited by W. F. H. Nicolaisen. Binghamton, NY: Medieval & Renaissance Texts & Studies, 1995. 59–75.
363. Rosenberg, Bruce. "The Oral Performance of Chaucer's Poetry." *Folklore Forum* 13 (1980): 224–37.
364. Rowland, Beryl. "Pronuntiatio and Its Effect on Chaucer's Audience." *SAC* 4 (1982): 33–51.
365. Volk-Birke, Sabine. *Chaucer and Medieval Preaching: Rhetoric for Listeners in Sermons and Poetry.* Tübingen: Narr, 1991.
See also nos. 164, 977, 1090, 1098, 1397, 1435, 1493, 1521, 1548.

Poetics and Narrative Technique

366. Burlin, Robert B. *Chaucerian Fiction.* Princeton, NJ: Princeton UP, 1977.

367. Davenport, Tony. *Medieval Narrative: An Introduction.* Oxford: Oxford UP, 2004.
368. Davidoff, Judith M. *Beginning Well: Framing Fictions in Late Middle English Poetry.* Rutherford, NJ: Fairleigh Dickinson UP, 1988.
369. Ferster, Judith. *Chaucer and Interpretation.* Cambridge, UK: Cambridge UP, 1985.
370. Fichte, Joerg O. *Chaucer's "Art Poetical": A Study of Chaucerian Poetics.* Tübingen: Narr, 1980.
371. Hanning, Robert W. "And countrefete the speche of every man / He coude, whan he sholde telle a tale': Toward a Lapsarian Poetics for *The Canterbury Tales.*" *SAC* 21 (1999): 29–58.
372. Jordan, Robert O. *Chaucer and the Shape of Creation: The Aesthetic Possibilities of Inorganic Structure.* Cambridge, MA: Harvard UP, 1967.
373. ———. *Chaucer's Poetics and the Modern Reader.* Berkeley: U of California P, 1987.
374. King, Pamela. "Chaucer, Chaucerians, and the Theme of Poetry." In *Chaucer and Fifteenth-Century Poetry,* edited by Julia Boffey and Janet Cowen. London: King's College, 1991. 1–14.
375. Koff, Leonard Michael. *Chaucer and the Art of Storytelling.* Berkeley: U of California P, 1988.
376. Lawton, David. *Chaucer's Narrators.* Cambridge, UK: Brewer, 1985.
377. McGerr, Rosemarie P. *Chaucer's Open Books: Resistence to Closure in Medieval Discourse.* Gainesville: UP of Florida, 1998.
378. Payne, Robert O. *The Key of Remembrance: A Study of Chaucer's Poetics.* New Haven, CT: Yale UP, 1963.
379. Pearsall, Derek. "Towards a Poetics of Chaucerian Narrative." In *Drama, Narrative and Poetry in The Canterbury* Tales, edited by Wendy Harding. Toulouse: Presses Universitaires du Mirail, 2003. 99–112.
380. Scala, Elizabeth. *Absent Narratives, Manuscript Textuality, and Literary Structure in Late Medieval England.* New York: Palgrave Macmillan, 2002.
381. Sklute, Larry. *Virtue of Necessity: Inconclusiveness and Narrative Form in Chaucer's Poetry.* Columbus: Ohio State UP, 1984.
382. Wood, Chauncey. "Affective Stylistics and the Study of Chaucer." *SAC* 6 (1984): 21–40.

See also no. 1562.

Philosophy

383. Blamires, Alcuin. *Chaucer, Ethics, and Gender.* Oxford: Oxford UP, 2006.
384. Dunleavy, Gareth W. "Natural Law as Chaucer's Ethical Absolute." *Transactions of the Wisconsin Academy of Sciences, Arts, and Letters* 52 (1963): 177–87.
385. Fisher, John H. "The New Humanism and Geoffrey Chaucer." *Soundings* 80 (1997): 23–39.
386. Foster, Edward E. *Understanding Chaucer's Intellectual and Interpretative World: Nominalist Fiction.* Lewistown, NY: Mellen, 1999.
387. Grudin, Michaela Paasche. "Credulity and the Rhetoric of Heterodoxy: From Averroes to Chaucer." *ChauR* 35 (2000): 204–22.
388. Keiper, Hugo, Richard Utz, and Cristoph Bode, eds. *Nominalism and Literary Discourse: New Perspectives.* Atlanta, GA: Rodopi, 1997.
389. Myles, Robert. *Chaucerian Realism.* Cambridge, UK: Brewer, 1994.
390. Owen, Charles A., Jr. "The Problem of Free Will in Chaucer's Narratives." *PQ* 46 (1967): 433–56.
391. Patch, Howard. *The Goddess Fortuna in Medieval Literature.* Cambridge, MA: Harvard UP, 1927.
392. ———. *The Tradition of Boethius: A Study of His Importance in Medieval Culture.* New York: Oxford UP, 1935.
393. Peck, Russell A. "Chaucer and the Nominalist Question." *Speculum* 53 (1978): 745-60.
394. Roney, Lois. "The Theme of Protagonists's Intention Versus Actual Outcome." *ES* 64 (1983): 193–200.
395. Ruggiers, Paul G. "Platonic Forms in Chaucer." *ChauR* 17 (1983): 366–81.
396. Shepherd, Geoffrey. "Religion and Philosophy in Chaucer." In *Geoffrey Chaucer,* edited by D. S. Brewer. London: Bell, 1974. 262–89.
397. Utz, Richard, ed. *Literary Nominalism and the Theory of Rereading Late Medieval Texts.* Lewiston, NY: Mellen, 1995.
398. Van Dyke, Carolynn. *Chaucer's Agents: Cause and Representation in Chaucerian Narrative.* Madison, NJ: Fairleigh Dickinson UP, 2005.
399. Watts, William H., and Richard J. Utz. "Nominalist Perspectives on Chaucer's Poetry: A Bibliographical Essay." *M&H* 20 (1994): 147–73.

See also no. 764, 850.

Religion, Ethics, and The Bible

400. Aers, David. *Chaucer, Langland, and the Creative Imagination.* London: Routledge, 1980.
401. ———. *Faith, Ethics, and the Church: Writing in England, 1360-1409.* Cambridge, UK: Brewer, 2000.
402. ———, and Lynn Staley. *The Powers of the Holy: Religion, Politics, and Gender in Late Medieval English Culture.* University Park: Pennsylvania State UP, 1996.
403. Astell, Ann. *Job, Boethius, and Epic Truth.* Ithaca, NY: Cornell UP, 1994.
404. Benson, C. David. "Varieties of Religious Poetry in 'The Canterbury Tales': 'The Man of Law's Tale' and 'The Clerk's Tale'." *SAC Proceedings* 2 (1987): 159–67.
405. ———, and Elizabeth Robertson, eds. *Chaucer's Religious Tales.* Cambridge: Brewer, 1990.
406. Besserman, Lawrence. *Chaucer's Biblical Poetics.* Norman: U of Oklahoma P, 1998.
407. Boenig, Robert. *Chaucer and the Mystics: The Canterbury Tales and the Genre of Devotional Prose.* Lewisburg, PA: Bucknell UP, 1995.
408. Boyd, Beverly. *Chaucer and the Liturgy.* Philadelphia: Dorrance, 1967.
409. David, Alfred. *The Strumpet Muse: Art and Morals in Chaucer's Poetry.* Bloomington: Indiana UP, 1976.
410. Fehrman, Craig T. "Did Chaucer Read the Wycliffite Bible?" *ChauR* 42 (2007): 111–38.

411. Fletcher, Alan J. "Chaucer the Heretic." *SAC* 25 (2003): 53–121.
412. Fyler, John M. *Language and the Declining World in Chaucer, Dante, and Jean de Meun.* New York: Cambridge UP, 2007.
413. Haskell, Ann. *Essays on Chaucer's Saints.* The Hague: Mouton, 1977.
414. Hill, John M. *Chaucerian Belief: The Poetics of Reverence and Delight.* New Haven, CT, Yale UP, 1991.
415. Hudson, Anne. *The Premature Reformation: Wycliffite Texts and Lollard History.* Oxford: Clarendon, 1988.
416. Jeffrey, David Lyle, ed. *Chaucer and Scriptural Tradition.* Ottawa: U of Ottawa P, 1984.
417. Kamowski, William. "Chaucer and Wyclif: God's Miracles Against the Clergy's Magic." *ChauR* 37 (2002): 5–25.
418. Kelly, Henry Ansgar. "Sacraments, Sacramentals, and Lay Piety in Chaucer's England." *ChauR* 28 (1993): 5–22.
419. Kerby-Fulton, Kathryn. *Books Under Suspicion: Censorship and Tolerance of Revelatory Writing in Late Medieval England.* Notre Dame, IN: U of Notre Dame P, 2006.
420. McIlhaney, Anne E. "Sentence and Judgment: The Role of the Fiend in Chaucer's *Canterbury Tales.*" *ChauR* 31 (1996): 173–83.
421. Reed, Teresa P. *Shadows of Mary: Reading the Virgin in Medieval Texts.* Cardiff: U of Wales P, 2003.
422. Rhodes, Jim. *Poetry Does Theology: Chaucer, Grosseteste, and the Pearl-Poet.* Notre Dame, IN: U of Notre Dame P, 2001.
423. Schildgen, Brenda Deen. "Jerome's *Prefatory Epistles* to the Bible and *The Canterbury Tales.*" *SAC* 15 (1993): 111–30.
424. Watson. Nicholas. "Langland and Chaucer." In *The Oxford Handbook of English Literature and Theology,* edited by Andrew Hass, David Jasper, and Elisabeth Jay. New York: Oxford UP, 2007. 363–81.
425. Wenzel, Siegfried. "Chaucer and the Language of Contemporary Preaching." *SP* 73 (1976): 138–61.
425a. Zieman, Katherine. *Singing the New Song: Literacy and Liturgy in Late Medieval England.* Philadelphia: University of Pennsylvania Press, 2008.

See also nos. 96, 99, 854.

Science and Pseudoscience

426. Acker, Paul "The Emergence of an Arithmetical Mentality in Middle English Literature." *ChauR* 28 (1994): 293–302.
427. Brewer, Derek. "Chaucer and Arithmetic." In *Medieval Studies Conference, Aachen 1983,* edited by Wolf-Dietrich Bald and Horst Weinstock. Frankfurt am Main: Lang, 1984. 111–19.
428. Brown, Peter. *Chaucer and the Making of Optical Space.* New York: Lang, 2007.
429. Cartwright, John H. "Medieval Cosmology and European Literature: Dante and Chaucer." In *Literature and Science: Social Impact and Interaction,* edited by John H. Cartwright and Brian Baker. Denver: ABC-CLIO, 2005. 1–29.
430. Curry, Walter C. *Chaucer and Medieval Sciences.* 1926. Enlarged ed. New York: Barnes and Noble, 1960.
431. Holley, Linda Tarte. *Chaucer's Measuring Eye.* Houston: Rice UP, 1990.
432. Lightsey, Scott. *Manmade Marvels in Medieval Culture and Literature.* New York: Palgrave Macmillan, 2007.
433. Linden, Stanton J. *Darke Hierogliphicks: Alchemy in English Literature from Chaucer to the Restoration.* Lexington: U of Kentucky P, 1996.
434. Lionarons, Joyce Tally. "Magic, Machines, and Deception: Technology in the *Canterbury Tales.*" *ChauR* 27 (1993): 377–86.
435. Mooney, Linne R. "Chaucer and Interest in Astronomy at the Court of Richard II." In *Chaucer in Perspective,* edited by Geoffrey Lester. Sheffield: Sheffield Academic P, 1999. 139–60.
436. North, J. D. *Chaucer's Universe.* Rev. ed. Oxford: Clarendon, 1990.
437. Osborn, Marijane. *Time and the Astrolabe in The Canterbury Tales.* Norman: U of Oklahoma P, 2002.
438. Parker, R. H. "Accounting in Chaucer's *Canterbury Tales.*" *Accounting, Auditing, Accountability* 12.1 (1999): 92–112.
439. Wood, Chauncey. *Chaucer and the Country of the Stars: Poetic Uses of Astrological Imagery.* Princeton, NJ: Princeton UP, 1979.

See also nos. 646, 652, 910.

Psychology and Subjectivity

439a. Collette, Carolyn P. *Species, Phantams, and Images: Vision and Medieval Psychology.* Ann Arbor: U of Michigan P, 2001.
440. Fradenburg, L. O. Aranye. *Sacrifice Your Love: Psychoanalysis, Historicism, Chaucer.* Minneapolis: U of Minnesota P, 2002.
441. Ganim, John M. "Chaucer, Boccaccio, Confession, and Subjectivity." In Koff and Schildgen, no. 295. 128–47.
442. Patterson, Lee. *Chaucer and the Subject of History.* Madison: U of Wisconsin P, 1991.

See also nos. 520, 620, 647, 665, 678, 772, 991.

Sex, Love, and Marriage

443. Brewer, Derek. "Some Notes on 'Ennobling' Love and Its Successors in Medieval Romance." In *Cultural Encounters in the Romance of Medieval England,* edited by Corinne Saunders. Cambridge, UK, Brewer, 2005. 117–33.
444. Cannon, Christopher. "Chaucer and Rape: Uncertainty's Certainties." *SAC* 22 (2000): 67–92.
445. Cooney, Helen, ed. *Writings on Love in the English Middle Ages.* New York: Palgrave Macmillan, 2006.
446. Denomy, Alexander J. *The Heresy of Courtly Love.* New York: Macmillan, 1947.

447. Jacobs, Kathryn. *Marriage Contracts from Chaucer to the Renaissance Stage.* Gainesville: UP of Florida, 2001.
448. Kelly, H. A. *Love and Marriage in the Age of Chaucer.* Ithaca, NY: Cornell UP, 1975.
449. ———. "Meanings and Uses of *Raptus* in Chaucer's Time." *SAC* 20 (1998): 101–65.
450. Lewis, C. S. *The Allegory of Love.* 1936. Reprint. Oxford: Oxford UP, 1958.
451. Lipton, Emma. *Affections of the Mind: The Politics of Sacramental Marriage in Late Medieval English Literature.* Notre Dame, IN: U of Notre Dame P, 2007.
452. McCarthy, Conor. *Marriage in Medieval England: Law, Literature, and Practice.* Woodbridge, Suffolk: Boydell, 2004.
453. O'Donoghue, Bernard. *The Courtly Love Tradition.* Manchester: Manchester UP, 1982.
454. Richmond, Velma Bourgeois. "'Pacience in Adversitee': Chaucer's Presentation of Marriage." *Viator* 10 (1979): 323–54.
455. Rose, Christine. "Reading Chaucer Reading Rape." In *Representing Rape in Medieval and Early Modern Literature,* edited by Elizabeth Robertson and Christine Rose. New York: Palgrave, 2001. 21–60.
456. Sadlek, Gregory. *Idleness Working: The Discourse of Love's Labor from Ovid Through Chaucer and Gower.* Washington, DC: Catholic U of America P, 2004.
457. Saunders, Corrine. *Rape and Ravishment in the Literature of Medieval England.* Cambridge, UK: Brewer, 2001.
458. Slaughter, Eugene. *Virtue According to Love in Chaucer.* New York: Bookman, 1957.
459. Spearing, A. C. *The Medieval Poet as Voyeur: Looking and Listening in Medieval Love Narratives.* Cambridge, UK: Cambridge UP, 1993.
460. Taylor, Paul B. *Chaucer's Chain of Love.* Madison, NJ: Fairleigh Dickinson UP, 1996.

See also nos. 487, 549, 586, 942, 955.

Sexualities

461. Burger, Glenn. *Chaucer's Queer Nation.* Minneapolis: U of Minnesota P, 2003.
462. ———. "Shameful Pleasures: Up Close and Dirty with Chaucer, Flesh, and the Word." In *Queering the Middle Ages,* edited by Glenn Burger and Steven Kruger. Minneapolis: U of Minnesota P, 2001. 213–35.
463. Dinshaw, Carolyn. *Getting Medieval: Sexualities and Communities, Pre- and Postmodern.* Durham, NC: Duke UP, 1999.
464. Lochrie, Karma. "Presumptive Sodomy and Its Exclusions." *Textual Practice* 13 (1999): 295–313.
465. ———. *Heterosyncrasies: Female Sexuality When Normal Wasn't.* Minneapolis: U of Minnesota P, 2005.
466. Pugh, Tison. *Queering Medieval Genres.* New York: Palgrave Macmillan, 2003.
467. Tinkle, Theresa. *Medieval Venuses and Cupids: Sexuality, Hermeneutics, and English Poetry.* Stanford CA: Stanford UP, 1996.

See also nos. 471, 796, 901–02, 1055, 1058, 1402.

Women

468. Blamires, Alcuin. *The Case for Women in Medieval Culture.* Oxford: Clarendon P, 1997.
468a. Collette, Carolyn P. *Performing Polity: Women and Agency in the Anglo-French Tradition, 1385–1620.* Turnhout, Belgium: Brepols, 2006.
469. Cox, Catherine S. *Gender and Language in Chaucer.* Gainesville: UP of Florida, 1997.
470. Diamond, Arlyn. "Chaucer's Women and Women's Chaucer." In *The Authority of Experience: Essays in Feminist Criticism,* edited by Arlyn Diamond and Lee R. Edwards. Amherst: U of Massachusetts P, 1977. 60–83.
471. Dinshaw, Carolyn. *Chaucer's Sexual Poetics.* Madison: U of Wisconsin P, 1989.
472. Green, Richard Firth. "Chaucer's Victimized Women." *SAC* 10 (1988): 3–21.
473. Hallissy, Margaret. *Clean Maids, True Wives, Steadfast Widows: Chaucer's Women and Medieval Codes of Conduct.* Westport, CT: Greenwood, 1993,
474. Hansen, Elaine Tuttle. *Chaucer and the Fictions of Gender.* Berkeley: U of California P, 1992.
475. Mann, Jill. *Feminizing Chaucer.* Rochester, NY: Brewer, 2002.
476. Martin, Priscilla. *Chaucer's Women: Nuns, Wives, and Amazons.* Iowa City: U of Iowa P, 1990.
477. Masi, Michael. *Chaucer and Gender.* New York: Lang, 2005.
478. Summit, Jennifer. *Lost Property: The Woman Writer and English Literary History, 1380–1589.* Chicago: U of Chicago P, 2000.
479. Weismann, Hope Phyllis. "Antifeminism and Chaucer's Characterization of Women." In *Geoffrey Chaucer: A Collection of Original Essays,* edited by George D. Economou. New York: McGraw Hill, 1976. 93–110.

See also nos. 622, 632, 636.

Men

480. Beidler, Peter G., ed. *Masculinities in Chaucer: Approaches to Maleness in The Canterbury Tales and Troilus and Criseyde.* Rochester, NY: Brewer, 1998.
481. Crocker, Holly A. *Chaucer's Visions of Manhood.* New York: Palgrave Macmillan, 2007.
482. Davis, Isabel. *Writing Masculinity in the Later Middle Ages.* New York: Cambridge UP, 2007.
483. Mitchell, J. Allan. "Dressing and Redressing the Male Body: Homosocial Poetics in *Troilus and Criseyde.*" *Postscript* 5.2 (2000): 1–19.
484. Pugh, Tison, and Marcia Smith Marzec, eds. *Men and Masculinities in Chaucer's Troilus and Criseyde.* Rochester, NY: Brewer, 2008.
485. Zeikowitz, Richard E. *Homoeroticism and Chivalry: Discourses of Male Same-Sex Desire in the Fourteenth Century.* New York: Palgrave Macmillan, 2003.

See also nos. 723, 727, 804, 1319.

Honor, Chivalry, and Pity

486. Allen, Valerie. "Waxing Red: Shame and the Body, Shame and the Soul." In *The Representation of*

Women's Emotions in Medieval and Early Modern Culture, edited by Lisa Perfetti, Gainesville: UP of Florida, 2005. 191–210.

487. Benson, Larry D. "Courtly Love and Chivalry in the Later Middle Ages." *Fifteenth-Century Studies: Recent Essays*, edited by R. F. Yeager. Hamden, CT: Archon, 1984. 237–57.
488. Brewer, Derek. "Honour in Chaucer." *E&S* 26 (1973): 1–19.
489. Burnley, David. *Courtliness and Literature in Medieval England.* New York: London, 1998.
490. Coghill, Nevill. *Chaucer's Idea of What Is Noble.* London: English Association, 1971.
491. Gray, Douglas. "'Pite for to Here—Pite for to Se': Some Scenes of Pathos in Late Medieval Literature." *PBA* 87 (1995): 67–99.
492. Guerin, Dorothy. "Chaucer's Pathos: Three Variations." *ChauR* 20 (1985): 90–112.
493. Harding, Wendy. "The Function of Pity in Three Canterbury Tales." *ChauR* 32 (1997): 162–74.
494. Meecham-Jones, Simon. "The Invisible Siege—The Depiction of Warfare in the Poetry of Chaucer." In *Writing War: Medieval Literary Responses to Warfare*, edited by Corinne Saunders and others. Cambridge, UK: Brewer, 2004. 147–67.
495. Monz, Dominic. *Gentelesse und Gentils: Der Weltliche Adel und Seine Werte in Geoffrey Chaucer's "Canterbury Tales."* Regensburg: Braun, 2002.
496. Pratt, John H. *Chaucer and War.* Lanham, MD: UP of America, 2000.
497. Saul, Nigel. "Chaucer and Gentility." In *Chaucer's England: Literature in Historical Context*, edited by Barbara A. Hanawalt. Minneapolis: U of Minnesota P, 1991. 41–55.
498. Stugrin, Michael. "Ricardian Poetics and Late Medieval Cultural Pluriformity: The Significance of Pathos in the *Canterbury Tales*." *ChauR* 15 (1980): 155–67.
499. Taylor, Paul Beekman. "The Uncourteous Knights of *The Canterbury Tales*." *ES* 72 (1991): 209–18.

See also nos. 654, 666, 766, 768, 770, 779, 917, 982, 993.

Social Classes and the City

500. Blamires, Alcuin. "Chaucer the Reactionary: Ideology and The General Prologue to *The Canterbury Tales*." *RES* 51 (2000): 523–39.
501. Brewer, Derek. "Class Distinction in Chaucer." *Speculum* 43 (1968): 290–305.
502. Butterfield, Ardis, ed. *Chaucer and the City.* Cambridge, UK: Brewer, 2006.
503. DeVries, David N. "Chaucer and the Idols of the Market." *ChauR* 32 (1998): 391–99.
504. Eaton, R. D. "Gender, Class, and Conscience in Chaucer." *ES* 84 (2003): 205–18.
505. Forkin, Thomas Carney. "'Oure Citee': Illegality and Criminality in Fourteenth-Century London." *EMSt* 24 (2007): 31–41.
506. Ganim, John M. "Chaucer and the Noise of the People." *Exemplaria* 2 (1990): 71–88.
507. Justice, Steven. *Writing and Rebellion: England in 1381.* Berkeley: U of California P, 1994.
508. Knapp, Peggy. *Chaucer and the Social Contest.* New York: Routledge, 1991.
509. Knight, Stephen. "Politics and Chaucer's Poetry." In *The Radical Reader*, edited by Stephen Knight and Michael Wilding. Sydney: Wild and Woolley, 1977. 169–92.
510. Lindahl, Carl. "The Festive Form of the *Canterbury Tales*." *ELH* 52 (1985): 531–74.
511. Patterson, Lee. "'No Man His Reson Herde': Peasant Consciousness, Chaucer's Miller, and the Structure of the *Canterbury Tales*." *SAQ* 86 (1987): 457–95.
512. Raybin, David. "Chaucer as a London Poet: A Review Essay." *EMSt* 24 (2007): 21–29.
513. Strohm, Paul. *Theory and the Premodern Text.* Minneapolis: U of Minnesota P, 2000.
514. Turner, Marion. *Chaucerian Conflict: Languages of Antagonism in Late Fourteenth-Century London.* Oxford: Clarendon, 2007.
515. Wallace, David. "In Flaundres." *SAC* 19 (1997): 63–91.
516. Yager, Susan. "Chaucer's *Peple* and *Folk*." *JEGP* 100 (2001): 211–33.

See also nos. 587, 816–17, 995, 1159, 1315, 1456.

The Court and Patronage

517. Astell, Ann. *Political Allegory in Late-Medieval England.* Ithaca, NY: Cornell UP, 1999.
518. Bowers, John M. *The Politics of Pearl: Court Poetry in the Age of Richard II.* Cambridge, UK: Cambridge UP, 2001.
519. Brewer, Derek. "Chaucer's Anti-Ricardian Poetry." In *The Living Middle Ages: Studies in Mediaeval English Literature and Its Traditions*, edited by Uwe Boker and others. Stuttgart: Belser, 1989. 115–28,
520. Crane, Susan. *The Performance of Self: Ritual, Clothing, and Identity During The Hundred Years War.* Philadelphia: U of Pennsylvania P, 2002.
521. Green, Richard Firth. *Poets and Princepleasers: Literature and the English Court in the Late Middle Ages.* Toronto: U of Toronto P, 1980.
522. Meyer-Lee, Robert J. *Poets and Power from Chaucer to Wyatt.* Cambridge: Cambridge UP, 2007.
523. Staley, Lynn. *Languages of Power in the Age of Richard II.* University Park: Pennsylvania State UP, 2005.
524. Strohm, Paul. "Politics and Poetics: Usk and Chaucer in the 1380's." In *Literary Practice and Social Change in Britain, 1380–1530*, edited by Lee Patterson. Berkeley: U of California P, 1990. 83–112.

See also nos. 693, 1551, 1554, 1590, 1634.

Bureaucracy and The Law

525. Braswell, Mary Flowers. *Chaucer's "Legal Fiction": Reading the Records.* Teaneck, NJ: Fairleigh Dickinson UP, 2001.
526. Carlson, David. *Chaucer's Jobs.* New York: Palgrave Macmillan, 2004.

527. Dobbs, Elizabeth. "Literary, Legal, and Last Judgments in *The Canterbury Tales.*" *SAC* 14 (1992): 31–52.
528. Green, Richard Firth. *A Crisis of Truth: Literature and Law in Ricardian England.* Philadelphia: U of Pennsylvania P, 1999.
529. Hornsby, Joseph Allen. *Chaucer and the Law.* Norman, OK: Pilgrim, 1988.
530. Johnston, Andrew James. *Clerks and Courtiers: Chaucer, Late Middle English Literature, and the State Formation Process.* Heidelberg: Winter, 2001.
531. Mead, Jenna. "Chaucer and the Subject of Bureaucracy." *Exemplaria* 19 (2007): 39–66.
532. Robertson, Kellie. *The Laborer's Two Bodies: Labor and the "Work" of the Text in Medieval Britain, 1350–1500.* New York: Palgrave Macmillan, 2006.
533. Strohm, Paul. *Social Chaucer.* Cambridge, MA: Harvard UP, 1989.

See also nos. 718, 825, 836, 838, 1388.

Nation and Otherness

534. Bowers, John M. "Chaucer After Smithfield: From Postcolonial Writer to Imperialist Writer." In *The Postcolonial Middle Ages,* edited by Jeffrey Jerome Cohen. New York: St. Martin's P, 2000. 53–66.
535. Collette, Carolyn P., and Vincent J. DiMarco. "The Matter of Armenia in the Age of Chaucer." *SAC* 23 (2001): 317–58.
536. Cox, Catherine S. *The Judaic Other in Dante, the "Gawain" Poet, and Chaucer.* Gainesville: UP of Florida, 2005.
537. Delany, Sheila. *Chaucer and the Jews: Sources, Contexts, Meaning.* New York: Routledge, 2002.
538. Dinshaw, Carolyn. "Pale Faces: Race, Religion, and Affect in Chaucer's Texts and Their Readers." *SAC* 23 (2001): 19–41.
539. Heffernan, Carol Falvo. *The Orient in Chaucer and Medieval Romance.* Rochester, NY: Boydell and Brewer, 2003.
540. Heng, Geraldine. *Empire of Magic: Medieval Romance and the Politics of Cultural Fantasy.* New York: Columbia UP, 2003.
541. Kelly, Henry Ansgar. "Jews and Saracens in Chaucer's England: A Review of the Evidence." *SAC* 27 (2005): 129–69.
542. Lampert, Lisa. *Gender and the Jewish Difference from Paul to Shakespeare.* Philadelphia: U of Pennsylvania P, 2004.
543. Lynch, Kathryn L., ed. *Chaucer's Cultural Geography.* New York: Routledge, 2002.
544. Pearsall, Derek. "Chaucer and Englishness." *PBA* 101 (2000): 77–99.
545. Said, Edward W. *Orientalism.* New York: Pantheon, 1978.
546. Schildgen, Brenda Deen, *Pagans, Tartars, Moslems, and Jews in Chaucer's Canterbury Tales.* Gainesville: UP of Florida, 2001.
547. Thomas, Alfred. *A Blessed Shore: England and Bohemia from Chaucer to Shakespeare.* Ithaca, NY: Cornell UP, 2007.

See also no. 965.

Symbol and Allegory

548. Akbari, Suzanne Conklin. *Seeing Through the Veil: Optical Theory and Medieval Allegory.* Toronto: U of Toronto P, 2004.
549. Chance, Jane. *The Mythographic Chaucer: The Fabulation of Sexual Politics.* Minneapolis: U of Minnesota P, 1995.
550. Dean, James. *The World Grown Old in Later Medieval Literature.* Cambridge, MA: Medieval Academy, 1997.
551. Emmerson, Richard K., and Ronald B. Herzman. *The Apocalyptic Imagination in Medieval Literature.* Philadelphia: U of Pennsylvania P, 1992.
552. Hermann, John P., and John J. Burke, Jr., eds. *Signs and Symbols in Chaucer's Poetry.* University: U of Alabama P, 1981.
553. Huppé, Bernard F., and D. W. Robertson, Jr. *Fruyt and Chaf: Studies in Chaucer's Allegories.* Princeton, NJ: Princeton UP, 1963.
554. Justman, Stewart. "Literal and Symbolic in the *Canterbury Tales.*" *ChauR* 14 (1980): 199–214.
555. Klene, Jean, C.S.C. "Chaucer's Contribution to the Popular Topos: The World Upside-Down." *Viator* 11 (1979): 321–34.
556. Robertson, D. W., Jr. *A Preface to Chaucer: Studies in Medieval Perspective.* Princeton, NJ: Princeton UP, 1962.
557. Rowland, Beryl. *Blind Beasts: Chaucer's Animal World.* Kent, OH: Kent State UP, 1971.
558. ———. "The Horse and Rider Figure in Chaucer's Works." *UTQ* 35 (1966): 246–59.

See also no. 565, 694.

Spaces, Landscapes, and Ecology

559. Douglass, Rebecca M. "Ecocriticism in Middle English Literature." *SiM* 10 (1998): 136–63.
560. Haskell, Ann. "Chaucerian Women, Ideal Gardens, and the Wild Woods." In *A Wyf Ther Was: Essays in Honour of Paule Mertens-Fonck,* edited by Juliette Dor. Liége: U of Liége, 1992. 193–98.
561. Heffernan, Carol Falvo. "Wells and Streams in Three Chaucerian Gardens." *PLL* 15 (1979): 339–57.
562. Howes, Laura L. *Chaucer's Gardens and the Language of Convention.* Gainesville: UP of Florida, 1997.
563. Kern-Stähler, Annette. *A Room of One's Own: Reale und mentale Innenräume weiblicher Selbstbestimmung im spätmittelalterlichen England.* Frankfurt am Main: Peter Lang, 2002.
564. Lynch, Kathryn. "Partitioned Fictions: The Meaning and Importance of Walls in Chaucer's Poetry." In *Art and Context in Late Medieval English Narrative,* edited by Robert R. Edwards. Cambridge: Brewer, 1994. 107–25.
565. Robertson, D. W., Jr. "The Doctrine of Charity in Medieval Literary Gardens." *Speculum* 26 (1951): 24–49.
566. Stanbury, Sarah. "EcoChaucer: Green Ethics and Medieval Nature." *ChauR* 39 (2004): 1–16.
566a. ———. "Women's Letters and Private Space." *Exemplaria* 6 (1994): 271–85.

567. Wallace, David. *Premodern Places: Calais to Surinam, Chaucer to Aphra Behn.* Oxford: Blackwell, 2004.

See also nos. 718, 801, 803, 812, 1366, 1477.

The Arts, Illustrations, and Portraits of Chaucer

568. Davis, R. Evan. "The Pendant in the Chaucer Portraits." *ChauR* 17 (1982): 193–95.

569. Finley, William K. and Joseph Rosenblum, eds. *Chaucer Illustrated: Five Hundred Years of the Canterbury Tales in Pictures.* London: British Library, 2003.

570. Fleming, John V. "Chaucer and the Visual Arts of His Time." In *New Perspectives on Chaucer Criticism,* edited by Donald M. Rose. Norman, OK: Pilgrim, 1981. 121–36.

571. Hussey, Maurice, comp. *Chaucer's World: A Pictorial Companion.* Cambridge: Cambridge UP, 1967.

572. Kendrick, Laura. "The Jesting Borders of Chaucer's *Canterbury Tales* and of Late Medieval Manuscript Art." In *Animating the Letter: The Figurative Embodiment of Writing from Late Antiquity to the Renaissance.* Columbus: Ohio State UP, 1999. 217–25.

573. Kolve, V. A. *Chaucer and the Imagery of Narrative: The First Five Canterbury Tales.* Stanford, CA: Stanford UP, 1984.

574. McGregor, James H. "The Iconography of Chaucer in Hoccleve's *De Regimine Principum* and the *Troilus* Frontispiece." *ChauR* 11 (1977): 338–50.

575. Miller, Miriam Youngerman. "Illustrations of the *Canterbury Tales* for Children: A Mirror of Chaucer's World?" *ChauR* 27 (1993): 293–304.

576. Seymour, Michael. "Manuscript Portraits of Chaucer and Hoccleve." *Burlington Magazine* 124 (1982): 618–32.

577. Wilkins, Nigel. *Music in the Age of Chaucer.* Cambridge: Brewer, 1980.

See also nos. 791, 1438, 1497, 1511, 1519.

Canterbury Tales—General

578. Ashton, Gail. *Chaucer's The Canterbury Tales.* Continuum Reader's Guide. New York: Continuum, 2007.

579. Brown, Peter. *Chaucer at Work: The Making of the Canterbury Tales.* New York: Longman, 1994.

580. ———, and Andrew Butcher. *The Age of Saturn: Literature and History in the Canterbury Tales.* Oxford: Blackwell, 1991.

581. Cooper, Helen. *The Canterbury Tales.* Oxford Guides to Chaucer. 2d ed. Oxford: Oxford UP, 1996.

582. Hirsh, John C. *Chaucer and the Canterbury Tales: A Short Introduction.* Oxford: Blackwell, 2003.

583. Howard, Donald R. *The Idea of the Canterbury Tales.* Berkeley: U of California P, 1976.

584. Kendrick, Laura. *Chaucerian Play: Comedy and Control in the "Canterbury Tales."* Berkeley: U of California P, 1988.

585. Lawler, Traugott. *The One and the Many in The Canterbury Tales.* Hamden, CT: Archon, 1980.

586. Miller, Mark. *Philosophical Chaucer: Love, Sex, and Agency in the Canterbury Tales.* Cambridge: Cambridge UP, 2004.

587. Olson, Paul. *The Canterbury Tales and the Good Society.* Princeton, NJ: Princeton UP, 1986.

588. Pearsall, Derek. *The Canterbury Tales.* Unwin Critical Library. London: Allen & Unwin, 1985.

589. Phillips, Helen. *An Introduction to the Canterbury Tales: Reading, Fiction, Context.* New York: St. Martin's, 2000.

590. Ruggiers, Paul. *The Art of the Canterbury Tales.* Madison: U of Wisconsin P, 1965.

591. Russell, J. Stephen. *Chaucer and the Trivium: The Mindsong of the Canterbury Tales.* Gainesville: UP of Florida, 1998.

592. Shoaf, R. A. *Chaucer's Body: The Anxiety of Circulation in the Canterbury Tales.* Gainesville: UP of Florida, 2001.

593. Traversi, Derek. *The "Canterbury Tales": A Reading.* Newark: U of Delaware P, 1983.

594. Wetherbee, Winthrop. *Geoffrey Chaucer: The Canterbury Tales.* 1989. Revised. Cambridge: Cambridge UP, 2004.

CT—Evolution and Order of Canterbury Tales

595. Benson, Larry D. "The Order of *The Canterbury Tales.*" *SAC* 3 (1981): 77–120.

596. Blake, N. F. *The Textual Tradition of the Canterbury Tales.* London: Arnold, 1985.

597. Dempster, Germaine. "The Fifteenth-Century Editions of the *Canterbury Tales* and the Problem of Tale Order." *PMLA* 64 (1949): 1123–42.

598. Furnivall, F. J. A. *A Temporary Preface to the Chaucer Society's Six-Text Edition of Chaucer's Canterbury Tales: Part I, Attempting to Show the Right Order of the Tales, and the Days and Stages of the Pilgrimage.* Chaucer Society, 2d ser., 3. London, 1868.

599. Horobin, Simon. "Additional 35286 and the Order of the *Canterbury Tales.*" *ChauR* 31 (1997): 272–78.

600. Keiser, George. "In Defense of the Bradshaw Shift." *ChauR* 12 (1978): 191–201.

601. Lawton, David. "Chaucer's Two Ways: The Pilgrimage Frame of 'The Canterbury Tales.'" *SAC* 9 (1987): 3–40.

602. Olson, Glending. "The Terrain of Chaucer's Sittingbourne." *SAC* 6 (1984): 222–36.

603. Pearsall, Derek. "Pre-empting Closure in *The Canterbury Tales*: Old Endings, New Beginnings." In *Essays on Ricardian Literature,* edited by A. J. Minnis, and others. Oxford: Clarendon, 1997. 23–38.

604. Pratt, Robert A. "The Order of the *Canterbury Tales.*" *PMLA* 66 (1951): 1141–67.

605. Spencer, Matthew, and others. "Analyzing the Order of Items in Manuscripts of *The Canterbury Tales.*" *ComH* 37 (2003): 97–109.

606. Tatlock, J. S. P. "*The Canterbury Tales* in 1400." *PMLA* 50 (1935): 100–39.

CT—Structure and Frame

607. Allen, Judson Boyce, and Theresa Anne Mortiz. *A Distinction of Stories: The Medieval Unity of Chaucer's Fair Chain of Narratives for Canterbury.* Columbus: Ohio State UP, 1981.
608. Astell, Ann. *Chaucer and the Universe of Learning.* Ithaca, NY: Cornell UP, 1996.
609. Baldwin, Ralph. *The Unity of the Canterbury Tales.* Copenhagen: Rosenkilde & Bagger, 1955.
610. Condren, Edward I. *Chaucer and the Energy of Creation: The Design and Organization of the Canterbury Tales.* Gainesville: UP of Florida, 1999.
611. Cooper, Helen. *The Structure of the Canterbury Tales.* Athens: U of Georgia P, 1984.
612. Dean, James. "Dismantling the Canterbury Book." *PMLA* 100 (1984): 746–62.
613. Frese, Dolores Warwick. *An Ars Legendi for Chaucer's Canterbury Tales.* Gainesville: UP of Florida, 1991.
614. Gittes, Katharine S. *Framing the Canterbury Tales: Chaucer and the Medieval Frame Tradition.* New York: Greenwood, 1991.
615. Mandel, Jerome. *Geoffrey Chaucer: Building the Fragments of the Canterbury Tales.* Cranbury, NJ: Associated U Presses, 1992.
616. Olson, Glending. "Chaucer's Idea of a Canterbury Game." In *The Idea of Medieval Literature,* edited by James M. Dean and Christian Zacher. Newark: U of Delaware P, 1992. 72–90.
617. Rogers, William E. *Upon the Ways: The Structure of the Canterbury Tales.* Victoria, BC: U of Victoria, 1986.
See also no. 368.

CT—Genres

618. Allen, Elizabeth. *False Fables and Exemplary Truth in Later Middle English Literature.* New York: Palgrave, 2005.
619. Andreas, James R. "The Rhetoric of Chaucerian Comedy: The Aristotelian Legacy." *Comparatist* 8 (1984): 56–66.
620. Ashton, Gail. *The Generation of Identity in Late Medieval Hagiography: Speaking the Saint.* New York: Routledge, 2000.
621. Blamires, Alcuin. "Philosophical Sleaze? The 'strok of thoght' in the Miller's Tale and Chaucerian Fabliau." *MLR* 102 (2007): 621–40.
622. Crane, Susan. *Gender and Romance in Chaucer's Canterbury Tales.* Princeton, NJ: Princeton UP, 1994.
623. Davenport, W. A. *Chaucer: Complaint and Narrative.* Cambridge, UK: Brewer, 1988.
624. Finlayson, John. "Definitions of Middle English Romance." Parts I & II. *ChauR* 15 (1980): 44–62, 168–81.
625. Galloway, Andrew. "Middle English Prologues." In *Readings in Medieval Texts: Interpreting Old and Middle English Literature,* edited by David F. Johnson and Elaine Treharne. Oxford: Oxford UP, 2005. 288–305.
626. Hines, John. *The Fabliau in English.* New York: Longman, 1993.
627. Kelly, Henry Ansgar. *Chaucerian Tragedy.* Cambridge: Brewer, 1997.
628. Morse, Ruth. "Absolute Tragedy: Allusions and Avoidances." *PoeticaT* 38 (1993): 1–17.
629. Payne, F. Anne. *Chaucer and Menippean Satire.* Madison: U of Wisconsin P, 1981.
630. Rowland, Beryl. "What Chaucer Did to the Fabliaux." *SN* 51 (1979): 205–13.
631. Salih, Sarah, ed. *A Companion to Middle English Hagiography.* Rochester, NY: Brewer, 2006.
632. Sanok, Catherine. *Her Life Historical: Exemplarity and Female Saints' Lives in Late Medieval England.* Philadelphia: U of Pennsylvania P, 2007.
633. Scanlon, Larry. *Narrative, Authority, and Power: The Medieval Exemplum and the Chaucerian Tradition.* Cambridge, UK: Cambridge UP, 1994.
634. Spencer, H. Leith. *English Preaching in the Late Middle Ages.* Oxford: Clarendon P, 1993.
635. Strohm, Paul. "Some Generic Distinctions in the *Canterbury Tales.*" *MP* 68 (1971): 321–28.
636. Weisl, Angela Jane. *Conquering the Reign of Femeny: Gender and Genre in Chaucer's Romance.* Cambridge, UK: Brewer, 1995.
637. Wetherbee, Winthrop. "Chaucer and the Tragic Vision of Life." *PoeticaT* 55 (2001): 39–53.
638. Wheatley, Edward. *Mastering Aesop: Medieval Education, Chaucer, and His Followers.* Gainesville: UP of Florida, 2000.
See also nos. 656, 780, 795.

CT—Style and Rhetoric

639. Benson, C. David. "The Aesthetic of Chaucer's Religious Tales in Rhyme Royale." In *Religion in the Poetry and Drama of the Late Middle Ages in England,* edited by Piero Boitani and Anna Torti. Cambridge, UK: Brewer, 1990. 101–17.
640. ———. *Chaucer's Drama of Style: Poetic Variety and Contrast in the Canterbury Tales.* Chapel Hill: U of North Carolina P, 1986.
641. Smallwood, T. M. "Chaucer's Distinctive Digressions." *SP* 82 (1985): 437–49.
642. Taavitsainen, Irma. "Personality and Styles of Affect in the Canterbury Tales." In *Chaucer in Perspective,* edited by Geoffrey Lester. Sheffield: Sheffield Academic P, 1999. 18–34.
643. Winick, Stephen D. "Proverbial Strategy and Proverbial Wisdom in *The Canterbury Tales.*" *Proverbium* 11 (1994): 259–81.

CT—Characterization

644. Edwards, A. S. G. "Chaucer and the Poetics of Utterance." In *Poetics: Theory and Practice in Medieval English Literature,* edited by Piero Boitani and Anna Torti. Bury St. Edmunds: Brewer, 1991. 57–67.
645. Engelhardt, George J. "The Ecclesiastical Pilgrims of the *Canterbury Tales*: A Study in Ethnography." *MS* 13 (1983): 41–51.

646. Friedman, John B. "Another Look at Chaucer and the Physiognomists." *SP* 78 (1981): 138–52.
647. Leicester, H. Marshall. *The Disenchanted Self: Representing the Subject in the Canterbury Tales.* Berkeley: U of California P, 1990.
648. Lumiansky, Robert M. *Of Sondry Folk: The Dramatic Principle of the Canterbury Tales.* Austin: U of Texas P, 1955.
649. Manly, John M. *Some New Light on Chaucer.* 1926. Reprint. New York: Peter Smith, 1952.
650. Parr, Roger P. "Chaucer's Art of Portraiture." *SMC* 4 (1974): 428–36.
651. Specht, Henrik. "The Beautiful, the Handsome, and the Ugly: Some Aspects of the Art of Character Portrayal in Medieval Literature." *SN* 56 (1984): 129–46.
652. Wurtele, Douglas. "Some Uses of Physiognomical Lore in Chaucer's Canterbury Tales." *ChauR* 17 (1982): 130–41.

See also nos. 430, 738–39.

CT—Women, Men, and The Marriage Argument

653. Allman, W. W., and D. Thomas Hanks, Jr. "Rough Love: Notes Toward an Erotics of The *Canterbury Tales.*" *ChauR* 38 (2003): 36–65.
654. Baker, Donald C. "Chaucer's Clerk and the Wife of Bath on the Subject of Gentilesse." *SP* 59 (1962): 631–40.
655. Biscoglio, Frances Minetti. *The Wives of "The Canterbury Tales" and the Tradition of the Valiant Women of Proverbs 31:10-31.* San Francisco: Mellen Research UP, 1991.
656. Donnelly, Colleen. "Silence or Shame: How Women's Speech Contributes to Generic Conventionality and Generic Complexity in *The Canterbury Tales.*" *Lang&S* 24 (1991): 433–43.
657. Edwards, Robert R. "Some Pious Talk about Marriage: Two Speeches from the *Canterbury Tales.*" In *Matrons and Marginal Women in Medieval Society,* edited by Robert R. Edwards and Vickie Ziegler. Woodbridge, Suffolk: Boydell, 1995. 111–27.
658. Haahr, Joan G. "Chaucer's 'Marriage Group' Revisited: The Wife of Bath and the Merchant in Debate." In *Homo Carnalis,* edited by Helen R. Lemay. *Acta* 14 (1990): 105–20.
659. Kaske, R. E. "Chaucer's Marriage Group." In *Chaucer the Love Poet,* edited by Jerome Mitchell and William Provost. Athens: U of Georgia P, 1973. 45–66.
660. Kittredge, George Lyman. "Chaucer's Discussion of Marriage." *MP* 9 (1912): 435–67.
661. Laskaya, Anne. *Chaucer's Approach to Gender in the Canterbury Tales.* Cambridge, UK: Brewer, 1995.
662. McCarthy, Conor. "Love, Marriage, and Law: Three Canterbury Tales." *ES* 83 (2002): 504–18.
663. Mandel, Jerome. "Courtly Love in the *Canterbury Tales.*" *ChauR* 19 (1985): 277–89.
664. Nelson, Marie. "'Biheste is dette': Marriage Promises in Chaucer's *Canterbury Tales.*" *PLL* 38 (2002): 167–99.
665. Robertson, Elizabeth. "Marriage, Mutual Consent, and the Affirmation of the Female Subject in the *Knight's Tale,* the *Wife of Bath's Tale,* and the *Franklin's Tale.*" In *Drama, Narrative and Poetry in The Canterbury Tales,* edited by Wendy Harding. Toulouse: Presses Universitaires du Mirail, 2003. 175–93.
666. Silvia, D. S. "Geoffrey Chaucer on the Subject of Men, Women, and Gentillesse." *Revue des Langues Vivants* 33 (1967): 228–36.
667. Straus, Barrie Ruth. "Reframing the Violence of the Father: Reverse Oedipal Fantasies in Chaucer's Clerk's, Man of Law's, and Prioress's Tales." In *Domestic Violence in Medieval Texts,* edited by Eve Salisbury and others. Gainesville: UP of Florida, 2002. 122–38.
668. Weisl, Angela Jane. "'Quiting Eve': Violence Against Women in the *Canterbury Tales.*" In *Violence Against Women in Medieval Texts,* edited by Anna Roberts. Gainesville: UP of Florida, 1998. 115–36.

CT—Voice and the Narrator

669. Burrow, J. A. "Elvish Chaucer." In *The Endless Knot: Essays on Old and Middle English in Honor of Marie Borroff,* edited by M. Teresa Tavormina and R. F. Yeager. Cambridge, UK: Brewer, 1995. 105–11.
670. Donaldson, E. Talbot. "Chaucer the Pilgrim." *PMLA* 69 (1954): 928–36.
671. Harding, Wendy. "Gendering Discourse in the Canterbury Tales." *BAM* 64 (2003): 1–11.
672. Kane, George. *The Autobiographical Fallacy in Chaucer and Langland Studies.* London: Lewis, 1965.
673. Kuczynski, Michael P. "'Don't Blame Me': The Metaethics of A Chaucerian Apology." *ChauR* 37 (2003): 315–28.
674. Leicester, H. Marshall. "The Art of Impersonation: A General Prologue to *The Canterbury Tales.*" *PMLA* 95 (1980): 8–22.
675. Mandel, Jerome. "Other Voices in the *Canterbury Tales.*" *Criticism* 19 (1977): 157–71.
676. Millns, Tony. "Chaucer's Suspended Judgments." *EIC* 27 (1977): 1–19.
677. Nolan, Barbara. "A Poet Ther Was: Chaucer's Voices in the *General Prologue.*" *PMLA* (1986): 154–69.
678. Spearing, A. C. *Textual Subjectivity: The Encoding of Subjectivity in Medieval Narratives and Lyrics.* Oxford: Oxford UP, 2005.

CT—Various Themes

679. Biebel, Elizabeth M. "Pilgrims to Table: Food Consumption in Chaucer's *Canterbury Tales.*" In *Food and Eating in Medieval Europe,* edited by Martha Carlin and Joel T. Rosenthal. Rio Grande, OH: Hambledon P, 1998. 15–26.
680. Blandeau, Agnès. "The Trader's Time and Narrative Time in Chaucer's *Canterbury Tales.*" *BAM* 72 (2007): 21–29.

681. Blodgett, E. D. "Chaucerian *Pryvetee* and the Opposition to Time." *Speculum* 51 (1976): 477–93.
682. Brosamer, Matthew. "The Cook, the Miller, and Alimentary Hell." In *Chaucer and the Challenges of Medievalism*, edited by Donka Minkova and Theresa Tinkle. New York: Lang, 2003. 235–51.
683. Canfield, J. Douglas. *Word as Bond in English Literature from the Middle Ages to the Restoration.* Philadelphia: U of Pennsylvania P, 1989.
684. Costigan, Edward. "'Privetee' in the *Canterbury Tales.*" *SEL* 60 (1983): 217–30.
685. Delasanta, Rodney. "The Theme of Justice in *The Canterbury Tales.*" *MLQ* 31 (1970): 298–307.
686. Fichte, Jorge O. "Konkurrierende und Kontrastierende Zeitmuster in Chaucers *Canterbury Tales.*" In *Zeitkonzeptionen Zeiterfahrung Zeitmessung: Stationen ihres Wandels vom Mittelalter bis zum Moderne*, edited by Trude Ehlert. Paderborn: Schoningh, 1997. 223–41.
687. Goldstein, R. James. "Future Perfect: The Augustinian Theology of Perfection and the *Canterbury Tales.*" *SAC* 29 (2007): 87–140.
688. Hieatt, Constance B. "'to boille the chiknes with the marybones': Hodge's Kitchen Revisited." In *Chaucerian Problems and Perspectives*, edited by Edward Vasta and Zacharias P. Thundy. Notre Dame, IN: U of Notre Dame P, 1979. 139–63.
689. Mann, Jill. "Anger and 'Glosynge' in the Canterbury Tales." *PBA* 76 (1990): 203–23.
690. ———. "Parents and Children in *The Canterbury Tales.*" In *Literature in Fourteenth-Century England*, edited by Piero Boitani and Anna Torti. Cambridge, UK: Brewer, 1983. 165–83.
691. Mertens-Fonke, Paule. "The *Canterbury Tales* and the *via moderna.*" *PoeticaT* 67 (2007): 37–51.
692. Orme, Nicholas. "Chaucer and Education." *ChauR* 16 (1981): 38–59.
693. Quinn, William A. "Chaucer's 'Janglerye.'" *Viator* 18 (1987): 309–20.

CT—The Pilgrimage Motif

694. Allen, Mark. "Moral and Aesthetic Falls on the Canterbury Way." *SCRev* 8 (1991): 36–49.
695. Dyas, Dee. *Pilgrimage in Medieval English Literature, 700–1500.* Cambridge, UK: Brewer, 2001.
696. Eisner, Sigmund. "The Ram Revisited: A Canterbury Conundrum." *ChauR* 28 (1994): 330–43.
697. Georgianna, Linda. "Love So Dearly Bought: The Terms of Redemption in 'The CanterburyTales.'" *SAC* 12 (1990): 85–116.
698. Howard, Donald R. *Writers and Pilgrims: Medieval Pilgrimage Narratives and Their Posterity.* Berkeley: U of California P, 1980.
699. Jonassen, Frederick B. "The Inn, the Cathedral, and the Pilgrimage of *The Canterbury Tales.*" In *Rebels and Rivals: The Contestive Spirit in The Canterbury Tales*, edited by Susanna Fein Greer and others. Kalamazoo, MI: Medieval Institute, 1991. 1–35.
700. Knapp, Daniel. "The Relyk of a Saint: A Gloss on Chaucer's Pilgrimage." *ELH* 39 (1972): 1–26.
701. Morgan, Gerald. "Moral and Social Identity and the Idea of Pilgrimage in the *General Prologue.*" *ChauR* 37 (2003): 285–314.
702. Reiss, Edmund. "The Pilgrimage Narrative and the *Canterbury Tales.*" *SP* 67 (1970): 295–305.
703. Webb, Diana. *Pilgrimage in Medieval England.* New York: Hambledon, 2000.
704. Zacher, Christian. *Curiosity and Pilgrimage.* Baltimore, MD: Johns Hopkins UP, 1976.

CT—Names and Number of Pilgrims; Pilgrims Without Tales

705. Bowers, John M. "Chaucer's Canterbury Tales—Politically Corrected." In Prendergast and Kline, no. 128. 13–44.
706. Brosnahan, Leger. "The Authenticity of 'And Preestes Thre.'" *ChauR* 16 (1982): 293–310.
707. Eckhardt, Caroline D. "The Number of Chaucer's Pilgrims: A Review and Reappraisal." *YES* 5 (1975): 1–18.
708. Eliason, Norman. "Personal Names in the *Canterbury Tales.*" *Names* 21 (1973): 137–52.
709. Gastle, Brian. "Chaucer's 'Shaply' Guildsmen and Mercantile Pretensions." *NM* 99 (1998): 211–16.
710. Harwood, Britton J. "The 'Fraternitee' of Chaucer's Guildsmen." *RES* 39 (1988): 413–17.
711. Kirk, Elizabeth. "Langland's Plowman and the Recreation of Fourteenth-Century Religious Metaphor." *YLS* 2 (1988): 1–21.
712. McColly, William B. "Chaucer's Yeoman and the Rank of His Knight." *ChauR* 20 (1985): 14–27.
713. Rogers, P. Burwell. "The Names of the Canterbury Pilgrims." *Names* 16 (1968): 339–46.
714. Thompson, Kenneth J. "Chaucer's Warrior Bowman: The Roles and Equipment of the Knight's Yeoman." *ChauR* 40 (2006): 386–415.
See also nos. 98.

CT—The Host

715. Allen, Mark. "Mirth and Bourgeois Masculinity in Chaucer's Host." In Beidler, no. 480. 9–21.
716. Carruthers, Leo. "Narrative Voice, Narrative Framework: The Host As 'Author' of *The Canterbury Tales.*" In *Drama, Narrative and Poetry in The Canterbury Tales*, edited by Wendy Harding. Toulouse: Presses Universitaires du Mirail, 2003. 51–67.
717. Gaylord, Alan T. "*Sentence* and *Solaas* in Fragment VII of the *Canterbury Tales*: Harry Bailly as Horseback Editor." *PMLA* (1967): 226–35.
718. Hanawalt, Barbara A. "The Host, the Law, and the Ambiguous Space of Medieval London Taverns." In *Medieval Crime and Social Control*, edited by Barbara A. Hanawalt and David Wallace. Minneapolis: U of Minnesota P, 1999. 204–23.
719. Leitch, L. M. "Sentence and Solaas: The Function of the Hosts in the *Canterbury Tales.*" *ChauR* 17 (1982): 5–20.

720. Page, Barbara. "Concerning the Host." *ChauR* 4 (1970): 1–13.
721. Pichaske, David R., and Laura Sweetland. "Chaucer on the Medieval Monarchy: Harry Bailly in the *Canterbury Tales.*" *ChauR* 11 (1977): 179–200.
722. Plummer, John F. "'Beth fructuous and that in litel space': The Engendering of Harry Bailly." In *New Readings of Chaucer's Poetry*, edited by Robert G. Benson and Susan J. Ridyard. Rochester, NY: Brewer, 2003. 107–18.
723. Pugh, Tison. "Queering Harry Bailly: Gendered Carnival, Social Ideologies, and Masculinity Under Duress in the *Canterbury Tales.*" *ChauR* 41 (2006): 39–69.
724. Scheps, Walter. "'Up roos oure Hoost, and was oure aller cok': Harry Bailly's Tale-Telling Competition." *ChauR* 10 (1975): 113–28.
725. Travis, Peter W. "The Body of the Nun's Priest, or, Chaucer's Disseminal Genius." In *Reading Medieval Culture: Essays in Honor of Robert W. Hanning*, edited by Robert M. Stein and Sandra Pierson Prior. Notre Dame, IN: U of Notre Dame P, 2005. 231–47.

See also nos. 1023, 1039.

CT Part 1

726. Fisher, John H. "The Three Styles of Fragment I of the *Canterbury Tales.*" *ChauR* 8 (1973): 119–27.
727. Jensen, Emily. "Male Competition as a Unifying Motif in Fragment A of the *Canterbury Tales.*" *ChauR* 24 (1990): 320–28.
728. Siegel, Marsha. "What the Debate Is and Why It Founders in Fragment A of the *Canterbury Tales.*" *SP* 82 (1985): 1–24.

See also no. 573.

CT1—The General Prologue

729. Andrew, Malcolm. "Context and Judgment in the 'General Prologue'." *ChauR* 23 (1989): 316–37.
730. Badendyck, J. Lawrence. "Chaucer's Portrait Technique and the Dream Vision Tradition." *English Record* 21 (1970): 113–25.
731. Bowden, Muriel. *A Commentary on the General Prologue to the Canterbury Tales.* New York: Macmillan, 1948.
732. Cooney, Helen. "The Limits of Human Knowledge and the Structure of Chaucer's 'General Prologue.'" *SN* 63 (1991): 147–59.
733. Cooper, Helen. "Langland's and Chaucer's Prologues." *YLS* 1 (1987): 71–81.
734. Cunningham, J. V. "The Literary Form of the Prologue to the *Canterbury Tales.*" *MP* 49 (1952): 172–81.
735. Eberle, Patricia J. "Commercial Language and the Commercial Outlook in the *General Prologue.*" *ChauR* 18 (1983): 161–74.
736. George, Jodi-Anne, ed. *Geoffrey Chaucer: The General Prologue to the Canterbury Tales.* New York: Columbia UP, 2000.
737. Higgs, Elton D. "The Old Order and the 'Newe World' in the General Prologue to the *Canterbury Tales.*" *HLQ* 45 (1982): 155–73.
738. Hodges, Laura. *Chaucer and Costume: The Secular Pilgrims in the General Prologue.* Cambridge, UK: Brewer, 2000.
739. ———. *Chaucer and Clothing: Clerical and Academic Costume in the General Prologue to The Canterbury Tales.* Rochester, NY: Brewer, 2005.
740. Hoffman, Arthur. "Chaucer's Prologue: Two Voices." *ELH* 21 (1954): 1–16.
741. Lambdin, Laura C., and Robert T. Lambdin, eds. *Chaucer's Pilgrims: An Historical Guide to the Pilgrims in* The Canterbury Tales. Westport, CT: Greenwood, 1996.
742. Mann, Jill. *Chaucer and Medieval Estates Satire: The Literature of Social Classes and the General Prologue.* Cambridge: Cambridge UP, 1972.
743. Martin, Loy D. "History and Form in the General Prologue to the *Canterbury Tales.*" *ELH* 45 (1978): 1–17.
744. Morgan, Gerald. "The Design of the General Prologue to the *Canterbury Tales.*" *ES* 58 (1977): 481–93.
745. Owen, Charles A., Jr. "Chaucer's Witty Prosody in 'General Prologue,' Lines 1-42." In *Chaucer's Humor: Critical Essays*, edited by Jean Jost. New York: Garland, 1994. 261–70.
746. Sklute, Larry. "Catalogue Form and Catalogue Style in the General Prologue of the *Canterbury Tales.*" *SN* 52 (1980): 35–46.

See also nos. 45–46, 87, 500, 625, 677.

CT1—The Knight and His Tale

747. Amtower, Laurel. "Mimetic Desire and the Misappropriation of the Ideal in *The Knight's Tale.*" *Exemplaria* 8 (1996): 125–44.
748. Bergan, Brooke. "Surface and Secret in the Knight's Tale." *ChauR* 26 (1991): 1–16.
749. Blake, Kathleen. "Order and the Noble Life in Chaucer's *Knight's Tale.*" *MLQ* 34 (1973): 3–19.
750. Bowers, John M. "Three Readings of *The Knight's Tale*: Sir John Clanvowe, Geoffrey Chaucer, and James I of Scotland." *JMEMSt* 34 (2004): 297–307.
751. Broughton, Laurel. "He Conquered al the Regne of Femenye: What Chaucer's Knight Doesn't Tell About Theseus." In *Speaking in the Medieval World*, edited by Jean E. Godsall-Myers. Boston: Brill, 2003. 43–63.
752. Brown, Emerson, Jr. "Chaucer's Knight: What's Wrong with Being Worthy?" *Mediaevalia* 15 (1993 for 1989): 183–205.
753. Clopper, Lawrence. "The Engaged Spectator: Langland and Chaucer on Civic Spectacle and the *Theatrum.*" *SAC* 22 (2000): 115–39.
754. Cooney, Helen. "Wonder and Boethian Justice in the 'Knight's Tale.'" In *Noble and Joyous Histories: English Romances, 1375–1650*, edited by Eilean Ni Cuilleanain and J. D. Pheifer. Dublin: Irish Academic P, 1993. 27–58.
755. Cowgill, Bruce Kent. "*The Knight's Tale* and the Hundred Years' War." *PQ* 54 (1975): 670–79.

756. Epstein, Robert. "'With many a florin he the hewes boghte': Ekphrasis and Symbolic Violence in the Knight's Tale." *PQ* 85 (2006): 49–68.
757. Fichte, Joerg O. "Man's Free Will and the Poet's Choice: The Creation of Artistic Order in Chaucer's *Knight's Tale*." *Anglia* 93 (1975): 335–60.
758. Finlayson, John. "*The Knight's Tale*: The Dialogue of Romance, Epic, and Philosophy." *ChauR* 27 (1992): 126–49.
759. Fowler, Elizabeth. "The Afterlife of the Civil Dead: Conquest in the *Knight's Tale*." In *Critical Essays on Geoffrey Chaucer*, edited by Thomas Stillinger. New York: Hall, 1987. 59–81.
760. ———. "Chaucer's Hard Cases." In *Medieval Crime and Social Control*, edited by Barbara A. Hanawalt and David Wallace. Minneapolis: U of Minnesota P, 1999. 124–42.
761. Ganim, John. "Chaucerian Ritual and Patriarchal Discourse." *ChauY* 1 (1992): 65–86.
762. Hamaguchi, Keiko. "Domesticating Amazons in *The Knight's Tale*." *SAC* 26 (2004): 331–54.
763. Hanning, Robert W. "'The Struggle Between Noble Design and Chaos': The Literary Tradition of Chaucer's *Knight's Tale*." *LittR* 23 (1980): 519–41.
764. Hazell, Dinah. "Empedocles, Boethius, and Chaucer: Love Binds All." *CarmP* 11 (2002): 43–74.
765. Helterman, Jeffrey. "The Dehumanizing Metamorphosis of *The Knight's Tale*." *ELH* 38 (1971): 493–511.
766. Jones, Terry. *Chaucer's Knight: The Portrait of a Medieval Mercenary*. Baton Rouge: Louisiana State UP, 1980.
767. ———. "The Image of Chaucer's Knight." In *Speaking Images: Essays in Honor of V. A. Kolve*, edited by Robert F. Yeager and Charlotte C. Morse. Asheville, NC: Pegasus P, 2001. 205–36.
768. Keen, Maurice. "Chaucer's Knight, the English Aristocracy and the Crusade." In *English Court Culture*, edited by V. J. Scattergood and L. W. Sherborne. New York: St. Martin's P, 1983. 45–61.
769. Mitchell-Smith, Ilan. "'As Olde Stories Tellen Us': Chivalry, Violence, and Geoffrey Chaucer's Critical Perspective in 'The Knight's Tale.' *FCS* 32 (2007): 83–99.
770. Muscatine, Charles. "Form, Texture, and Meaning in Chaucer's *Knight's Tale*." *PMLA* 65 (1950): 911–29.
770a. Noguchi, Shunichi. "Prayers in Chaucer's 'Knight's Tale'." *PoeticaT* 41 (1994): 45–50.
770b. Rigby, Stephen H. *Wisdom and Chivalry: Chaucer's* Knight's Tale *and Medieval Political Thought*. Boston: Brill, 2009.
771. Robertson, D. W., Jr. "The Probable Date and Purpose of Chaucer's *Knight's Tale*." *SP* 84 (1987): 418–39.
772. Roney, Lois. *Chaucer's "Knight's Tale" and Theories of Scholastic Psychology*. Tampa: U of South Florida P, 1990.
773. Schweitzer, Edward C. "Fate and Freedom in *The Knight's Tale*." *SAC* 3 (1981): 13–45.
774. Sherman, Mark A. "The Politics of Discourse in Chaucer's 'Knight's Tale'." *Exemplaria* 6 (1994): 87–114.
775. Stein, Robert M. "The Conquest of Femenye: Desire, Power, and Narrative in Chaucer's *Knight's Tale*." In *Desiring Discourse: The Literature of Love, Ovid Through Chaucer*, edited by James J. Paxson and Cynthia A. Gravlee. Selinsgrove, PA: Susquehanna UP, 1998. 188–205.
776. Storm, Melvin. "From Knossos to Knight's Tale: The Changing Face of Chaucer's Theseus." In *The Mythographic Art*, edited by Jane Chance. Gainesville: U of Florida P, 1990. 215–31.
777. Stretter, Robert. "Cupid's Wheel: Love and Fortune in *The Knight's Tale*." *M&H* 31 (2005): 59–82.
778. Wasserman, Julian N. "Both Fixed and Free: Language and Destiny in Chaucer's *Knight's Tale* and *Troilus and Criseyde*." In *Sign, Sentence, Discourse: Language in Medieval Thought and Literature*, edited by Julian N. Wasserman and Lois Roney. Syracuse NY: Syracuse UP, 1989. 194–222.
779. Wetherbee, Winthrop. "Chivalry Under Siege in Ricardian Romance." In *The Medieval City Under Siege*, edited by Ivy A. Corfis and Michael Wolf. Woodbridge: Boydell, 1995. 207–23.
780. ———. "Romance and Epic in Chaucer's *Knight's Tale*." *Exemplaria* 2 (1990): 303–28.
See also no. 88, 1039.

CT1—The Miller and His Tale

781. Blum, Martin. "Negotiating Masculinities: Erotic Triangles in the Miller's Tale." In *Masculinities in Chaucer*, edited by Peter G. Beidler. Rochester, NY: Brewer, 1998. 37–52.
782. Bowker, Alvin W. "Comic Illusion and Dark Reality in *The Miller's Tale*." *MLS* 4 (1977): 27–34.
783. Boyd, David Lorenzo. "Seeking 'Goddes Pryvete': Sodomy, Quitting, and Desire in 'The Miller's Tale.'" In *Word and Works*, edited by Peter S. Baker and Nicholas Howe. Toronto: U of Toronto P, 1998. 243–60.
784. Briggs, Frederick M. "Theophany in the 'Miller's Tale.'" *MAE* 65 (1996): 269–79.
785. Bullón-Fernández, María. "Private Practices in Chaucer's *Miller's Tale*." *SAC* 28 (2006): 141–74.
786. Cooper, Geoffrey. "'Sely John' in the 'Legende' of the *Miller's Tale*." *JEGP* 79 (1980): 1–12.
787. Donaldson, E. Talbot. "Idiom of Popular Poetry in the Miller's Tale." 1951. Reprinted in *Speaking of Chaucer*. New York: Norton, 1970. 13–29.
788. Donaldson, Kara Virginia. "Alisoun's Language: Body, Text, and Glossing in Chaucer's *The Miller's Tale*." *PQ* 71 (1992): 139–53.
789. Farrell, Thomas J. "Privacy and the Boundaries of Fabliau in the 'Miller's Tale.'" *ELH* 56 (1989): 773–95.
790. Friedman, John B. "Nicholas's 'Angelus ad Virginem' and the Mocking of Noah." *YES* 2 (1992): 162–80.

791. Gellrich, Jesse. "The Parody of Medieval Music in the *Miller's Tale.*" *JEGP* 72 (1974): 176–88.
792. Heffernan, Carol Falvo. "Chaucer's Miller's Tale, Reeve's Tale, Boccaccio's *Decameron,* and the French Fabliaux." *Italica* 81 (2004): 311–24.
793. Johnston, Andrew James. "The Exegetics of Laughter: Religious Parody in Chaucer's *Miller's Tale.*" In *A History of English Laughter,* edited by Manfred Pfister. New York: Rodopi, 2002. 17–33.
794. Jones, George F. "Chaucer and the Medieval Miller." *MLQ* 16 (1955): 3–15.
795. Lewis, Robert E. "The English Fabliau Tradition and Chaucer's *The Miller's Tale.*" *MP* 79 (1982): 241–55.
796. Lochrie, Karma. "Women's 'Pryvetees' and the Fabliau Politics in the *Miller's Tale.*" *Exemplaria* 6 (1994): 287–304.
797. Parry, Joseph D. "Interpreting Female Agency and Responsibility in *The Miller's Tale* and *The Merchant's Tale.*" *PQ* 80.2 (2001): 133–67.
798. Porter, Gerald. "The Miller in Oral and Written Narrative—An Aspect of Character or of Role? In *English Far and Wide,* edited by Risto Hiltunen and others. Turku: TurunYliopisto, 1993. 59–74.
799. Prior, Sandra Pierson. "Parodying Typology and the Mystery Plays in the *Miller's Tale.*" *JMRS* 16 (1986): 57–73.
800. Silar, Theodore I. "Chaucer's Joly Absolon." *PQ* 69 (1990): 409–17.
801. Woods, William F. "Private and Public Space in the *Miller's Tale.*" *ChauR* 29 (1994): 166–78.
See also nos. 48–49, 89, 511.

CT1—The Reeve and His Tale

802. Arthur, Ross G. "'Why Artow Angry?': The Malice of Chaucer's Reeve." *ESC* 13 (1987): 1–11.
803. Brown, Peter. "The Confinement of Symkyn: The Function of Space in the *Reeve's Tale.*" *ChauR* 14 (1980): 225–36.
804. Crocker, Holly A. "Affective Politics in Chaucer's *Reeve's Tale*: 'Cherl' Masculinity after 1381." *SAC* 29 (2007): 225–58.
805. Ellis, Deborah. "Chaucer's Devilish Reeve." *ChauR* 27 (1992): 150–61.
806. Grennen, Joseph E. "The Calculating Reeve and His Camera Obscura." *JMRS* 14 (1984): 245–59.
807. Horobin, S. C. P. "J. R. R. Tolkien as a Philologist: A Reconsideration of the Northernisms in Chaucer's *Reeve's Tale.*" *ES* 82 (2001): 97–105.
808. Kohanski, Tamarah. "In Search of Malyne." *ChauR* 27 (1993): 228–38.
809. Moore, Bruce. "The Reeve's Rusty Blade." *MAE* 58 (1989): 304–12.
810. Plummer, John F. "'Hooly Chirches Blood': Simony and Patrimony in Chaucer's *Reeve's Tale.*" *ChauR* 18 (1983): 49–60.
811. Tolkien, J. R. R. "Chaucer as Philologist: *The Reeve's Tale.*" In *Transactions of the Philological Society,* 1934, pp. 1–70.
812. Woods, William F. "Symkyn's Place in the *Reeve's Tale.*" *ChauR* 39 (2004): 17–40.
See also nos. 89.

CT1—The Cook and His Tale

813. Bertolet, Craig E. "'Wel Bet Is Token Appul Out of Hoord': Chaucer's Cook, Commerce, and Civic Order." *SP* 99 (2002): 229–46.
814. Partridge, Stephen. "Minding the Gaps: Interpreting the Manuscript Evidence of the Cook's Tale and the Squire's Tale." In *The English Medieval Book: Studies in Memory of Jeremy Griffiths,* edited by A. S. G. Edwards and others. London: British Library, 2000. 51–87.
815. Scattergood, V. J. "Perkyn Revelour and the *Cook's Tale.*" *ChauR* 19 (1984): 14–23.
816. Strohm, Paul. "'Lad with Revel to Newegate': Chaucerian Narrative and Historical Meta-Narrative." In *Art and Context in Late Medieval English Narrative,* edited by Robert R. Edwards. Cambridge: Brewer, 1994. 163–76.
817. Wallace, David. "Chaucer and the Absent City." In *Chaucer's England: Literature in Historical Context,* edited by Barbara A. Hanawalt. Minneapolis: U of Minnesota P, 1991. 59–90.
818. Woods, William. "Society and Nature in the 'Cook's Tale'." *PLL* 32 (1996): 189–205.
See also nos. 89, 505.

CT Part 2

CT2—The Man of Law and His Tale

819. Archibald, Elizabeth. "Contextualizing Chaucer's Constance: Romance Modes and Family Values." In *The Endless Knot: Essays on Old and Middle English in Honor of Marie Borroff,* edited by M. Teresa Tavormina and R. F. Yeager. Cambridge: Brewer, 1995. 161–75.
820. Astell, Ann W. "Apostrophe, Prayer, and the Structure of Satire in The Man of Law's Tale." *SAC* 13 (1991): 81–97.
821. Bestul, Thomas H. "The *Man of Law's Tale* and the Rhetorical Foundations of Chaucerian Pathos." *ChauR* 9 (1975): 216–26.
822. Black, Nancy B. *Medieval Narratives of Accused Queens.* Gainesville: U of Florida, 2003.
823. Block, Edward A. "Originality, Controlling Purpose, and Craftsmanship in Chaucer's *Man of Law's Tale.*" *PMLA* 68 (1953): 572–616.
824. Bloomfield, Morton W. "The *Man of Law's Tale*: A Tragedy of Victimization and Christian Comedy." *PMLA* 87 (1972): 384–90.
825. Bolton, W. F. "Pinchbeck and the Chaucer Circle in Law Reports and Records of 11-13 Richard II." *MP* 84 (1987): 401–06.
826. Caie, Graham. "'This Was a Thrifty Tale for the Nones': Chaucer's Man of Law." In *Chaucer in*

Perspective, edited by Geoffrey Lester. Sheffield: Sheffield Academic P, 1999. 47–60.

827. Clark, Susan L., and Julian N. Wasserman. "Constance as Romance and Folk Heroine in Chaucer's *Man of Law's Tale*." *RUS* 64 (1978): 13–24.
828. Clogan, Paul M. "The Narrative Style of the *Man of Law's Tale*." *M&H* 8 (1977): 217–33.
829. Delany, Sheila. "Womanliness in the *Man of Law's Tale*." *ChauR* 9 (1974): 63–72.
830. Dugas, Don-John. "The Legitimization of Royal Power in Chaucer's *Man of Law's Tale*." *MP* 95 (1997): 27–43.
831. Edwards, A. S. G. "Critical Approaches to the *Man of Law's Tale*." In Benson and Robertson, no. 405, 85-94.
832. Landman, James. "Proving Constant: Torture and *The Man of Law's Tale*." *SAC* 20 (1998): 1–39.
833. Lavezzo, Kathy. "Beyond Rome: Mapping Gender and Justice in *The Man of Law's Tale*." *SAC* 24 (2002): 149–80.
834. Lewis, Robert E. "Chaucer's Artistic Use of Pope Innocent III's *De Miseria Conditionis* in the *Man of Law's Tale*." *PMLA* 81 (1966): 485–92.
835. Lynch, Kathryn. "Storytelling, Exchange, and Constancy: East and West In Chaucer's *Man of Law's Tale*." *ChauR* 33 (1999): 409–22.
836. McKenna, Isobel. "The Making of a Fourteenth-Century Sergeant of the Law." *RUO* 45 (1975): 244–62.
837. Nicholson, Peter. "The *Man of Law's Tale*: What Chaucer Really Owed to Gower." *ChauR* 26 (1991): 153–74.
838. Nolan, Maura. "'Acquiteth Yow Now': Textual Contradiction and Legal Discourse in the Man of Law's Introduction." In *The Letter of the Law: Legal Practice and Literary Production in Medieval England*, edited by Emily Steiner and Candace Barrington. Ithaca, NY: Cornell UP, 2002. 136–53.
839. Paull, Michael R. "The Influence of the Saint's Legend Genre in the *Man of Law's Tale*." *ChauR* 5 (1971): 179–94.
840. Raybin, David. "Custance and History: Woman as Outsider in Chaucer's *Man of Law's Tale*." *SAC* 12 (1990): 65–84.
841. Robertson, Elizabeth. "Nonviolent Christianity and the Strangeness of Female Power in Geoffrey Chaucer's *The Man of Law's Tale*." In *Gender and Difference in the Middle Ages*, edited by Sharon Farmer and Carol Braun Pasternack. Minneapolis: U of Minnesota P, 2003. 322–51.
842. Schibanoff, Susan. "Worlds Apart: Orientalism, Antifeminism, and Heresy in Chaucer's *Man of Law's Tale*." *Exemplaria* 8 (1996): 59–96.
843. Schlauch, Margaret. *Constance and the Accused Queens*. New York: New York UP, 1927.
844. Spearing, A. C. "Narrative Voice: The Case of Chaucer's *Man of Law's Tale*." *NLH* 32 (2001): 715–46. Revised in no. 678.
845. Wood, Marjorie Elizabeth. "The Sultaness, Donegild, and Fourteenth-Century Female Merchants: Intersecting Discourses of Gender, Economy, and Orientalism in Chaucer's *Man of Law's Tale*." *Comitatus* 37 (2006): 65–85.

See also no. 404.

CT Part 3

846. Hanning, Robert W. "Roasting a Friar, Mis-Taking a Wife, and Other Acts of Textual Harrassment in Chaucer's *Canterbury Tales*." *SAC* 7 (1985): 3–21.
847. Kamowski, William. "The Sinner Against the Scoundrels: The Ills of Doctrine and 'Shrift' in the Wife's of Bath's, Friar's, and Summoner's Narratives." *Religion and Literature* 25 (1993): 1–18.
848. Owen, Charles A., Jr. "Fictions Living Fictions: The Poetics of Voice and Genre in Fragment D [3] of the *Canterbury Tales*." In *Poetics: Theory and Practice in Medieval English Literature*, edited by Piero Boitani and Anna Torti. Bury St. Edmunds: Brewer, 1991. 37–55.
849. Szittya, Penn R. "The Green Man as Loathly Lady: The Friar's Parody of the Wife of Bath's Tale." *PMLA* 90 (1975): 386–94.
850. Wasserman, J. N. "The Ideal and the Actual: The Philosophical Unity of *Canterbury Tales* MS. Group III." *Allegorica* 7 (1982): 65–99.

CT3—The Wife of Bath and Her Tale

851. Aguirre Daban, Manuel. "The Riddle of Sovereignty." *MLR* 88 (1992): 273–82.
852. Beidler, Peter G., ed. *Geoffrey Chaucer: "The Wife of Bath": Complete Authoritative Text with Biographical and Historical Contexts, Critical History and Essays from Five Contemporary Critical Perspectives*. New York: Bedford-St. Martin's, 1996.
853. Blamires, Alcuin. "Refiguring the 'Scandalous Excess' of Medieval Women: The Wife of Bath and Liberality." In *Gender in Debate*, edited by Thelma S. Fenster and Clare A. Lees. New York: Palgrave, 2002. 57–78.
854. ———. "Wife of Bath and Lollardy." *MAE* 58 (1989): 224–42.
855. Carruthers, Mary. "The Wife of Bath and the Painting of Lions." *PMLA* 94 (1979): 209–22. Reprinted with an "Afterword" in *Feminist Readings in Middle English Literature*, edited by Ruth Evans and Lesley Johnson. New York: Routledge, 1994. 22–53.
856. Charles, Casey. "Adversus Jerome: Liberation Theology in the *Wife of Bath's Prologue*." *Assays* 6 (1991): 55–71.
857. Colmer, Dorothy. "Character and Class in the *Wife of Bath's Tale*." *JEGP* 72 (1974): 329–39.
858. Cooper, Helen. "The Shape-Shiftings of the Wife of Bath, 1395-1670." In Morse and Windeatt, no. 327, 168–84.
859. Delany, Sheila. "Sexual Economics, Chaucer's Wife of Bath and The Book of Margery Kempe." 1975. Reprinted in *Feminist Readings in Middle*

English Literature, edited by Ruth Evans and Lesley Johnson. New York: Routledge, 1994. 72–87.

860. ———. "Strategies of Silence in the Wife of Bath's Recital." *Exemplaria* 2 (1990): 49–69.
861. Desmond, Marilynn. *Ovid's Art and the Wife of Bath: The Ethics of Erotic Violence.* Ithaca, NY: Cornell UP, 2006.
862. Dickson, Lynne. "Deflection in the Mirror: Feminine Discourse in the *Wife of Bath's Prologue* and *Tale.*" *SAC* 15 (1993): 61–90.
863. Dor, Juliette. "The Wife of Bath's 'Wandrynge by the Weye' and Conduct Literature for Women." In *Drama, Narrative and Poetry in The Canterbury* Tales, edited by Wendy Harding. Toulouse: Presses Universitaires du Mirail, 2003. 139–55.
864. Fleming, John V. "Sacred and Secular Exegesis in the *Wyf of Bath's Tale.*" In *Retelling Tales,* edited by Thomas Hahn and Alan Lupack. Rochester, NY: Brewer, 1997. 73–90.
865. Friedman, John Block. "Alice of Bath's Astral Destiny: A Re-Appraisal." *ChauR* 35 (2000): 66–81.
866. Galloway, Andrew. "Marriage Sermons, Polemical Sermons, and *The Wife of Bath's Prologue.*" *SAC* 14 (1992): 3–30.
867. Gottfried, Barbara. "Conflict and Relationship, Sovereignty and Survival: Parables of Power in the *Wife of Bath's Prologue.*" *ChauR* 19 (1985): 202–24.
868. Hagen, Susan K. "The Wife of Bath: Chaucer's Inchoate Experiment." In *Rebels and Rivals: The Contestive Spirit in The Canterbury Tales,* edited by Susanna Freer Fein and others. Kalamazoo, MI: Medieval Institute, 1991. 105–24.
869. Hanna, Ralph, III, and Traugott Lawler, eds. *Jankyn's Book of Wikked Wyves.* Athens: U of Georgia P, 1997.
870. Ingham, Patricia Clare. "Pastoral Histories: Utopia, Conquest, and the *Wife of Bath's Tale.*" *TSLL* 44 (2002): 34–46.
871. Kennedy, Beverly. "The Rewriting of the Wife of Bath's Prologue in Cambridge Dd.4.24." In Prendergast and Kline, no, 128, 203–33.
872. Longsworth, Robert. "The Wife of Bath and the Samaritan Woman." *ChauR* 34 (2000): 372–87.
873. McCarthy, Conor. "The Position of Widows in the Later Fourteenth-Century English Community and the *Wife of Bath's Prologue.*" In *Authority & Community in the Middle Ages,* edited by Donald Mowbray and others. Phoenix Mill, Gloucestershire: Sutton, 1999. 101–15.
874. McKinley, Kathryn. "The Silenced Knight: Questions of Power and Reciprocity in the *Wife of Bath's Tale.*" *ChauR* 30 (1996): 359–78.
875. Masi, Michael. "Boethius, the Wife of Bath, and the Dialectic of Paradox." In *New Directions in Boethian Studies,* edited by Noel Harold Kaylor, Jr., and Philip Edward Phillips. Kalamazoo, MI: Medieval Institute, 2007. 143–54.
876. Matthews, William. "The Wife of Bath and All Her Sect." *Viator* 7 (1974): 413–43.
877. Minnis, Alastair. "From *Coilles* to *Bel Chose*: Discourses of Obscenity in Jean de Meun and Chaucer." In *Medieval Obscenities,* edited by Nicola McDonald. York, UK: York Medieval P, 2006. 156–78.
878. Morrison, Susan Signe. "Don't Ask; Don't Tell: The Wife of Bath and Vernacular Translations." *Exemplaria* 8 (1996): 97–123.
879. Oberembt, Kenneth J. "Chaucer's Anti-Misogynist Wife of Bath." *ChauR* 10 (1976): 287–302.
880. Passmore, S. Elizabeth, and Susan Carter, eds. *The English "Loathly Lady Tales: Boundaries, Traditions, Motifs.* Kalamazoo, MI: Medieval Institute, 2007.
881. Patterson, Lee. "'For the Wyves Love of Bathe': Feminine Rhetoric and Poetic Resolution in the *Roman de la Rose* and the *Canterbury Tales.*" *Speculum* 58 (1983): 656–95.
882. Puhvel, Martin. "The Death of Alys of Bath's 'Revelour' Husband." *NM* 103 (2002): 328–40.
883. Robertson, D. W., Jr. "The Wife of Bath and Midas." *SAC* 6 (1984): 1–20.
884. Root, Jerry. "'Space to Speke': The Wife of Bath and the Discourse of Confession." *ChauR* 28 (1994): 252–74.
885. Schibanoff, Susan. "The New Reader and Female Textuality in Two Early Commentaries on Chaucer." *SAC* 10 (1988): 71–108.
886. Shapiro, Gloria. "Dame Alice as Deceptive Narrator." *ChauR* 6 (1971): 130–41.
887. Smith, Warren S. "The Wife of Bath Debates Jerome." *ChauR* 32 (1997): 129–45.
888. Strohm, Paul. "Treason in the Household." In *Hochon's Arrow: The Social Imagination of Fourteenth-Century Texts.* Princeton, NJ: Princeton UP, 1992. 121–44.
889. Thundy, Zacharias P. "Matheolus, Chaucer, and the Wife of Bath." In *Chaucerian Problems and Perspectives,* edited by Edward Vasta and Zacharias P. Thundy. Notre Dame, IN: U of Notre Dame P, 1979. 24–58.
890. Wimsatt, James I. "The Wife of Bath, the Franklin, and the Rhetoric of St. Jerome." In *A Wyf Ther Was,* edited by Juliette Dor. Liége: University of Liége, 1992. 275–81.

See also nos. 56, 90, 1044, 1358.

CT3—The Friar and His Tale

891. Berlin, Gail Ivy. "Speaking to the Devil: A New Context for *The Friar's Tale.*" *PQ* 69 (1990): 1–12.
892. Bryant, Brantley L. "'By Extorcions I Lyve': Chaucer's *Friar's Tale* and Corrupt Officials." *ChauR* 42 (2007): 180–95.
893. Geltner, G. "Faux Semblants: Antifraternalism Reconsidered in Jean de Meun and Chaucer." *SP* 101 (2004): 357–80.
894. Hahn, Thomas, and Kaeuper, Richard W. "Text and Context: Chaucer's *Friar's Tale.*" *SAC* 5 (1983): 67–101.
895. Kline, Daniel T. "'Myne by Right': Oath Making and Intent in *The Friar's Tale.*" *PQ* 77 (1998): 271–93.
896. Lenaghan, R. T. "The Irony of the *Friar's Tale.*" *ChauR* 7 (1973): 281–94.

897. Murtaugh, Daniel M. "Riming Justice in the *Friar's Tale.*" *NM* 74 (1973): 107–12.
898. Richardson, Janette. "Friar and Summoner, The Art of Balance." *ChauR* 9 (1975): 227–36.
899. Williams, Arnold. "Chaucer and the Friars." *Speculum* 28 (1953): 499–513.
900. Williams, David. "'From Chaucer's Pan to Logic's Fire: Intentionality in Chaucer's *Friar's Tale.*" In *Literature and Ethics: Essays Presented to A. E. Malloch,* edited by Gary Wihl and David Williams. Montreal: McGill-Queen's UP, 1988. 77–95.

CT3—The Summoner and His Tale

901. Bowers, John M. "Queering the Summoner: Same-Sex Union in Chaucer's *Canterbury Tales.*" In *Speaking Images: Essays in Honor of V. A. Kolve,* edited by R. F. Yeager and Charlotte C. Morse. Asheville, NC: Pegasus, 2001. 301–24.
902. Cox, Catherine S. "'Grope Wel Bihynde': The Subversive Erotics of Chaucer's Summoner." *Exemplaria* 7 (1995): 145–77.
903. Finlayson, John. "Chaucer's *Summoner's Tale*: Flatulence, Blasphemy, and the Emperor's Clothes." *SP* 104 (2007): 455–70.
904. Fleming, John V. "Anticlerical Satire as Theological Essay: Chaucer's *Summoner's Tale.*" *Thalia* 6 (1983): 5–22.
905. Hanks, D. Thomas, Jr., "Chaucer's *Summoner's Tale* and 'the first smel of fartes thre." *ChauY* 4 (1997): 33–43.
906. Haselmayer, L. A. "The Apparitor and Chaucer's Summoner." *Speculum* 12 (1973): 43–57.
907. Hasenfratz, Robert. "The Science of Flatulence: Possible Sources for the *Summoner's Tale.*" *ChauR* 30 (1996): 241–61.
908. Kabir, Ananya Jahanara. "From Twelve Devouring Dragons to the *Develes Ers*: The Medieval History of an Apocryphal Punitive Motif." *Archiv* 238 (2001): 280–98.
909. Lancashire, Ian. "Moses, Elijah and the Back Parts of God: Satiric Scatology in Chaucer's *Summoner's Tale.*" *Mosaic* 14 (1981): 17–30.
910. O'Brien, Timothy D. "'Ars-metrik': Science, Satire, and Chaucer's Summoner." *Mosaic* 23.4 (1990): 1–22.
911. Olson, Glending, "The End of *The Summoner's Tale* and the Uses of Pentecost." *SAC* 21 (1999): 209–45.
912. Shippey, Tom. "Bilingualism and Betrayal in Chaucer's 'Summoner's Tale.'" In *Speaking in the Medieval World,* edited by Jean E. Godsall-Myers. Boston: Brill, 2003. 125–44.
913. Somerset, Fiona. "'As just as is a squyre': The Politics of 'Lewed Translacion' in Chaucer's *Summoner's Tale.*" *SAC* 21 (1999): 187–207.
914. Szittya, Penn R. "The Friar as False Apostle: Antifraternal Exegesis and the *Summoner's Tale.*" *SP* 71 (1974): 19–46.

See also no. 55.

CT Part 4

915. Cherniss, Michael D. "The *Clerk's Tale* and *Envoy,* the Wife of Bath's Purgatory, and the *Merchant's Tale.*" *ChauR* 6 (1972): 235–54.
916. Hardman, Phillipa. "Chaucer's Tyrants of Lombardy." *RES* 31 (1980): 172–78.
917. Levy, Bernard S. "*Gentilesse* in Chaucer's *Clerk's* and *Merchant's* Tales." *ChauR* 11 (1977): 306–18.

CT4—The Clerk and His Tale

918. Bronfman, Judith. *Chaucer's Clerk's Tale: The Griselda Story Received, Rewritten, Illustrated.* New York: Garland, 1994.
919. Campbell, Emma. "Sexual Poetics and the Politics of Translation in the Tale of Griselda." *CL* 55 (2003): 191–216.
920. Carruthers, Mary J. "The Lady, the Swineherd, and Chaucer's Clerk." *ChauR* 17 (1983): 221–34.
921. Chickering, Howell. "Form and Interpretation in the *Envoy* to the *Clerk's Tale.*" *ChauR* 29 (1995): 352–72.
922. Delasanta, Rodney. "Nominalism and the *Clerk's Tale* Revisited." *ChauR* 31 (1997): 209–31.
923. Denny-Brown, Andrea. "*Povre* Griselda and the All-Consuming *Archewyves.*" *SAC* 28 (2006): 77–115.
924. Edden, Valerie. "Sacred and Secular in the *Clerk's Tale.*" *ChauR* 26 (1992): 369–76.
925. Farrell, Thomas J. "The *Envoy de Chaucer* and the *Clerk's Tale.*" *ChauR* 24 (1990): 329–36.
926. Finlayson, John. "Petrarch, Boccaccio, and Chaucer's *Clerk's Tale.*" *SP* 97 (2000): 255–75.
927. Finnegan, Robert Emmett. "'She Should Have Said No to Walter': Griselda's Promise in *The Clerk's Tale.*" *ES* 75 (1994): 302–21.
928. Gilmartin, Kristine. "Array in the *Clerk's Tale.*" *ChauR* 13 (1979): 234–46.
929. Grudin, Michaela Paasche. "Chaucer's *Clerk's Tale* as Political Paradox." *SAC* 11 (1989): 63–92.
930. Harding, Wendy. "The Dynamics of Law in the *Clerk's Tale.*" *ChauY* 4 (1997): 49–59.
931. ———. "Griselda's 'Translation' in the *Clerk's Tale.*" In *Medieval Translator, 6,* edited by Roger Ellis and others. [Turnhout]: Brepols, 1998. 194–210.
932. Heninger, S. K. "The Concept of Order in Chaucer's *Clerk's Tale.*" *JEGP* 56 (1957): 282–95.
933. Lynch, Kathryn L. "Despoiling Griselda: Chaucer's Walter and the Problem of Knowledge in *The Clerk's Tale.*" *SAC* 10 (1988): 41–70.
934. McKinley, Kathryn L. "*The Clerk's Tale*: Hagiography and the Problematics of Lay Sanctity." *ChauR* 33 (1998): 90–111.
935. Mann, Jill. "Satisfaction and Payment in Middle English Literature." *SAC* 5 (1983): 17–48.
936. Morse, Charlotte C. "Critical Approaches to the *Clerk's Tale.*" In Benson and Robertson, no. 405, 71–83.
937. Ramsey, Roger. "Clothing Makes a Queen in *The Clerk's Tale.*" *JNT* 7 (1977): 104–15.

938. Sledd, James. "The *Clerk's Tale*: The Monsters and the Critics." *MP* 51 (1953): 73–82.
939. Stanbury, Sarah. "Regimes of the Visual in Premodern England: Gaze, Body, and Chaucer's *Clerk's Tale*." *NLH* 28 (1997): 261–89.
940. Waugh, Robin. "A Woman in the Mind's Eye (And Not): Narrators and Gazes in Chaucer's *Clerk's Tale* and Two Analogues." *PQ* 79 (2000): 1–18.
941. Williamson, Tara. "'T'assaye in thee thy wommanheede': Griselde Chosen, Translated, and Tried." *SAC* 27 (2005): 93–127.

See also no. 404, 520.

CT4—The Merchant and His Tale

942. Benson, Donald R. "The Marriage 'Encomium' in the *Merchant's Tale*: A Chaucerian Crux." *ChauR* 14 (1979): 48–60.
943. Brown, Emerson, Jr. "Chaucer, the Merchant, and Their Tale: Getting Beyond Old Controversies: Part I." *ChauR* 13 (1978–79): 141–56; "Part II," 247–62.
944. Bugge, John. "Damyan's Wanton *Clyket* and an Ironic New *Twiste* to the Merchant's Tale." *AnM* 14 (1973): 53–62.
945. Burnley, J. D. "The Morality of *The Merchant's Tale*." *YES* 6 (1976): 16–25.
946. Cahn, Kenneth S. "Chaucer's Merchants and the Foreign Exchange: An Introduction to Medieval Finance." *SAC* 2 (1980): 81–119.
947. Dove, Mary. "'Swiche Olde Lewed Wordes': Books About Medieval Love, Medieval Books About Love and the Medieval Book of Love." In *Venus and Mars*, edited by Andrew Lynch and Philippa Maddern. Nedlands: U of Western Australia P, 1995. 11–33.
948. Edwards, A. S. G. "The Merchant's Tale and Moral Chaucer." *MLQ* 51 (1990): 409–26.
949. Edwards, Robert R. "Narration and Doctrine in the *Merchant's Tale*." *Speculum* 66 (1991): 342–67.
950. Field, Rosalind. "January's 'Honeste Thynges': Knighthood and Narrative in the *Merchant's Tale*." *RMS* 20 (1994): 37–49.
951. Heffernan, Carol Falvo. "Contraception and the Pear Tree Episode of Chaucer's *Merchant's Tale*." *JEGP* 94 (1995): 31–41.
952. Jager, Eric. "The Carnal Letters in Chaucer's Earthly Paradise." In *The Tempter's Voice: Language and the Fall in Medieval Literature*. Ithaca, NY: Cornell UP, 1993. 241–98.
953. Jonassen, Frederick B. "Rough Music in Chaucer's *Merchant's Tale*." In *Chaucer's Humor: Critical Essays*, edited by Jean E. Jost. New York: Garland, 1994. 229–58.
954. Kohler, Michelle. "Vision, Logic, and the Comic Production of Reality in the *Merchant's Tale* and Two French Fabliaux." *ChauR* 39 (2004): 137–50.
955. Neuse, Richard. "Marriage and the Question of Allegory in the *Merchant's Tale*." *ChauR* 24 (1989): 115–31.
956. Rose, Christine. "Women's 'Pryvete,' May, and the Privy: Fissures in the Narrative Voice in the *Merchant's Tale*, 1944–86." *ChauY* 4 (1997): 61–77.
957. Sheridan, Christine. "Commodification and Textuality in the Merchant's Tale." *SP* 102 (2005): 27–44.
958. Simmons-O'Neill, Elizabeth. "Love in Hell: The Role of Pluto and Proserpine in Chaucer's *Merchant's Tale*." *MLQ* 51 (1990): 389–407.
959. Stock, Lorraine Kochanske. "Making It in the *Merchant's Tale*: Chaucer's Signs of January's Fall." *Semiotica* 63 (1987): 171–83.
960. Tatlock, J. S. P. "Chaucer's *Merchant's Tale*." *MP* 33 (1935): 367–81.
961. Wentersdorf, Karl P. "Theme and Structure in *The Merchant's Tale*: The Function of the Pluto Episode." *PMLA* 80 (1965): 522–27.

CT Part 5

962. Goodman, Jennifer. "Dorigen and the Falcon: The Element of Despair in Chaucer's *Squire's* and *Franklin's Tales*." In *Feminea Medievalia I*, edited by Bonnie Wheeler. Cambridge: Cambridge Academic P, 1993. 69–90.
963. Lee, Brian S. "The Question of Closure in Fragment V of *The Canterbury Tales*." *YES* 22 (1992): 190–200.
964. Lynch, Kathryn. "East Meets West in Chaucer's Squire's and Franklin's Tales." *Speculum* 70 (1995): 530–51.

CT5—The Squire and His Tale

965. Ambrisco, Alan S. "'It Lyth Nat in My Tonge': Occupatio and Otherness in the *Squire's Tale*." *ChauR* 38 (2004): 205–28.
966. Berry, Craig A. "Flying Sources: Classical Authority in Chaucer's *Squire's Tale*." *ELH* 68 (2001): 287–313.
967. Braddy, Haldeen. "The Genre of Chaucer's *Squire's Tale*." *JEGP* 41 (1942): 279–90.
968. Dane, Joseph A. "'Tyl Mercurius Hous He Flye': Early Printed Texts and Critical Readings of the *Squire's Tale*." *ChauR* 34 (2000): 309–16.
969. Fyler, John M. "Domesticating the Exotic in the *Squire's Tale*." *ELH* 55 (1988): 1–26.
970. Goodman, Jennifer R. "Chaucer's *Squire's Tale* and the Rise of Chivalry." *SAC* 5 (1983): 127–36.
971. Haller, Robert S. "Chaucer's Squire's Tale and the Uses of Rhetoric." *MP* 62 (1965): 285–95.
972. Heffernan, Carol F. "Chaucer's *Squire's Tale*: The Poetics of Interlace or the 'Well of English Undefiled.'" *ChauR* 32 (1997): 32–45.
973. Jones, Lindsey M. "Chaucer's Anxiety of Poetic Craft: The *Squire's Tale*." *Style* 41 (2007): 300–18.

973a. Ingham, Patricia Clare. "Little Nothings: *The Squire's Tale* and the Ambition of Gadgets." *SAC* 31 (2009): 53–80.

974. Kamowski, William. "Trading the 'Knotte' for Loose Ends: The *Squire's Tale* and the Poetics of Chaucerian Fragments." *Style* 31 (1997): 391–412.
975. Neville, Marie. "The Function of the *Squire's Tale* in the Canterbury Scheme." *JEGP* 50 (1951): 167–79.
976. Sharon-Zisser, Shirley. "The *Squire's Tale* and the Limits of Non-Mimetic Fiction." *ChauR* 26 (1992): 377–94.
See also no. 54, 814.

CT5—The Franklin and His Tale

977. Arnovick, Leslie K. "Dorigen's Promise and Scholars' Premises: The Orality of the Speech Act in the *Franklin's Tale*." In *Oral Poetics in Middle English Poetry*, edited by Mark C. Amodio. New York: Garland, 1994. 125–47.
978. Battles, Dominique. "Chaucer's *Franklin's Tale* and Boccaccio's *Filocolo* Reconsidered." *ChauR* 34 (1999): 38–59.
979. Bleeth, Kenneth. "The Rock and the Garden: The Limits of Illusion in Chaucer's *Franklin's Tale*." *ES* 74 (1993): 113–23.
980. Brown, Carole Koepke. "'It Is True to Conceal Art': The Episodic Structure of Chaucer's *Franklin's Tale*." *ChauR* 27 (1992): 162–85.
981. Calabrese, Michael. "Chaucer's Dorigen and Boccaccio's Female Voices." *SAC* 29 (2007): 259–92.
982. Carruthers, Mary J. "The Gentilesse of Chaucer's Franklin." *Criticism* 23 (1981): 283–300.
983. Eaton, R. D. "Narrative Closure in Chaucer's *Franklin's Tale*." *Neophil* 84 (2000): 309–21.
984. Flake, Timothy H. "Love, *Trouthe*, and the Happy Ending of the *Franklin's Tale*." *ES* 77 (1996): 209–26.
985. Greenberg, Nina Manasan. "Dorigen as Enigma: The Production of Meaning and the *Franklin's Tale*." *ChauR* 33 (1999): 329–49.
986. Jonassen, Frederick B. "Carnival Food Imagery in Chaucer's Description of the Franklin." *SAC* 16 (1994): 99–117.
987. Luengo, Anthony E. "Magic and Illusion in *The Franklin's Tale*." *JEGP* 77 (1978): 1–16.
988. McEntire, Sandra J. "Illusions and Interpretation in the *Franklin's Tale*." *ChauR* 31 (1996): 145–63.
989. Morgan, Gerald. "Experience and the Judgment of Poetry: A Reconsideration of *The Franklin's Tale*." *MAE* 70 (2001): 204–25.
990. Pakkala-Weckström, Mari. "'Have Her My Trouthe—Til That Myn Herte Breste': Dorigen and the Difficulty of Keeping Promises in the *Franklin's Tale*." In *Variation Past and Present*, edited by Helena Raumolin-Brunberg and others. Helsinki: Société Néophilologique, 2002. 287–300.
991. Pitcher, John A. "Word and Werk" in Chaucer's *Franklin's Tale*." *L&P* 49 (2003): 77–109.
992. Pulham, Carol A. "Promises, Promises: Dorigen's Dilemma Revisited." *ChauR* 31 (1996): 76–86.
993. Riddy, Felicity. "Engendering Pity in the *Franklin's Tale*." In *Feminist Readings in Middle English Literature*, edited by Ruth Evans and Lesley Johnson. London: Routledge, 1994. 54–71.
994. Ronquist, E. C. "The Franklin, Epicurus, and the Play of Values." In *Chaucer and Language: Essays in Honour of Douglas Wurtele*, edited by Robert Myles and David Williams. Montreal: McGill-Queen's UP, 2001. 44–60.
995. Saul, Nigel. "The Social Status of Chaucer's Franklin: A Reconsideration." *MAE* 52 (1983): 10–26.
996. Schutz, Andrea. "Negotiating the Present: Language and Trouthe in the *Franklin's Tale*." In *Speaking in the Medieval World*, edited by Jean E. Godsall-Myers. Boston: Brill, 2003. 105–24.
997. Seaman, David M. "'As Thynketh Yow': Conflicting Evidence and the Interpretation of *The Franklin's Tale*." *M&H* 17 (1991): 41–58.
998. Smith, Warren S. "Dorigen's Lament and the Resolution of the *Franklin's Tale*." *ChauR* 36 (2002): 374–90.
999. Specht, Henrik. *Chaucer's Franklin in the Canterbury Tales: The Social and Literary Background of a Chaucerian Character*. Copenhagen: Akademisk Forlag, 1981.
1000. Sweeney, Michelle. *Magic in Medieval Romance from Chrétien de Troyes to Geoffrey Chaucer*. Dublin: Four Courts, 2000.
1001. Traversi, Derek. "The Franklin's Tale." In *The Literary Imagination: Studies in Dante, Chaucer, and Shakespeare*. Newark: U of Delaware P, 1982. 87–119.

CT—Part 6

1002. Amoils, E. R. "Fruitfulness and Sterility in the Physician's and Pardoner's Tales." *ESA* 17 (1974): 17–37.
1003. Haines, R. Michael. "Fortune, Nature, and Grace in Fragment C [6]." *ChauR* 10 (1976): 220–35.
1004. Lee, Brian S. "Justice in the *Physician's Tale* and the *Pardoner's Tale*: A Dialogic Contrast." *ChauY* 4 (1997): 21–32.
1005. Lewis, Celia. "Framing Fiction with Death: Chaucer's *Canterbury Tales* and the Plague." In *New Readings of Chaucer's Poetry*, edited by Robert G. Benson and Susan Ridyard. Rochester, NY: Brewer, 2003. 139–64.
1006. Pelen, Marc M. "Murder and Immorality in Fragment VI (C) of the *Canterbury Tales*: Chaucer's Transformation of Theme and Image from the *Roman de la Rose*." *ChauR* 29 (1994): 1–25.
1007. Trower, Katherine B. "Spiritual Sickness in the Physician's and Pardoner's Tales: Thematic Unity in Fragment VI of the *Canterbury Tales*." *ABR* 29 (1978): 67–86.

CT6—The Physician and His Tale

1008. Bloch, R. Howard. "Chaucer's Maiden's Head: *The Physician's Tale* and the Poetics of Virginity." *Representations* 28 (1989): 113–34.
1009. Brown, Emerson. "What is Chaucer Doing with the Physician and His Tale?" *PQ* 60 (1981): 129–49.

1010. Brown, William H. "Chaucer, Livy, and Bersuire: The Roman Materials in *The Physician's Tale.*" In *On Language: Rhetorica, Phonologica, Syntactica,* edited by Caroline Duncan-Rose and Theo Venneman. New York: Routledge, 1988. 39–51.
1011. Crafton, John Micheal. "*The Physician's Tale* and Jephtha's Daughter." *ANQ* 20.1 (2007): 8–13.
1012. Delany, Sheila. "Slaying Python: Marriage and Misogyny in a Chaucerian Text." In *Writing Women: Women Writers and Women in Literature Medieval to Modern.* New York: Schocken, 1983. 47–75.
1013. Harley, Marta Powell. "Last Things First in Chaucer's *Physician's Tale*: Final Judgment and the Worm of Conscience." *JEGP* 91 (1992): 1–16.
1014. Hirsh, John C. "Chaucer's Roman Tales." *ChauR* 31 (1996): 45–57.
1015. Kline, Daniel T. "Wardship and Raptus in the Physician's Tale." In *Essays on Medieval Childhood: Responses to Recent Debates,* edited by Joel T. Rosenthal. Donington, UK: Shaun Tyas, 2007. 108–23.
1016. Mandel, Jerome H. "Governance in the *Physician's Tale.*" *ChauR* 10 (1976): 316–25.
1017. Middleton, Anne. "The *Physician's Tale* and Love's Martyrs: 'Ensamples Mo Than Ten' as a Method in the *Canterbury Tales.*" *ChauR* 8 (1973): 9–32.
1018. Prior, Sandra Pierson. "Virginity and Sacrifice in Chaucer's *Physician's Tale.*" In *Constructions of Widowhood and Virginity in the Middle Ages,* edited by Cindy L. Carlson and Angela Jane Weisl. New York: St. Martin's, 1999. 165–80.
1019. Skerpan, Elizabeth. "Chaucer's Physicians: Their Texts, Contexts, and the *Canterbury Tales.*" *JRMMRA* 5 (1984): 41–56.
1020. Uebel, Michael. "Public Fantasy and Logic of Sacrifice in *The Physician's Tale.*" *ANQ* 15.3 (2002): 30–33.
1021. Ussery, Huling E. *Chaucer's Physician: Medicine and Literature in Fourteenth-Century England.* New Orleans: Tulane U Dept. of English, 1971.

See also no. 52.

CT6—The Pardoner and His Tale

1022. Bishop, Ian. "The Narrative Art of the *Pardoner's Tale.*" *MAE* 36 (1967): 15–24.
1023. Burger, Glenn. "Kissing the Pardoner." *PMLA* 107 (1992): 1143–56.
1024. Calabrese, Michael A. "'Make a Mark That Shows': Orphean Song, Orphean Sexuality, and the Exile of Chaucer's Pardoner." *Viator* 24 (1993): 269–86.
1025. Condren, Edward I. "The Pardoner's Bid for Existence." *Viator* 4 (1973): 177–205.
1026. Delasanta, Rodney. "Sacrament and Sacrifice in the Pardoner's Tale." *AnM* 14 (1973): 43–52.
1027. Dillon, Janette. "Chaucer's Game in the Pardoner's Tale." *EIC* 41 (1991): 208–21.
1028. Dinshaw, Carolyn. "Chaucer's Queer Touches / A Queer Touches Chaucer." *Exemplaria* 7 (1995): 75–92.
1028a. Fletcher, Alan J. "The Topical Hypocrisy of Chaucer's Pardoner." *ChauR* 25 (1990): 110–26.
1029. Fowler, Elizabeth. "Character and Habituation of the Reader: The Pardoner's Thought Experiment." In *Literary Character: The Human Figure in Early English Writing.* Ithaca, NY: Cornell UP, 2003. 32–94.
1030. Frantzen, Allen J. "*The Pardoner's Tale,* the Pervert, and the Price of Order in Chaucer's World." In *Class and Gender in Early English Literature,* edited by Britton J. Harwood and Gillian R. Overing. Bloomington: Indiana UP, 1994. 131–48.
1031. Green, Richard Firth. "Further Evidence for Chaucer's Representation of the Pardoner as a Womanizer." *MAE* 71 (2002): 307–09.
1032. ———. "The Pardoner's Pants (and Why They Matter)." *SAC* 15 (1993): 131–45.
1033. Grigsby, Bryon Lee. *Pestilence in Medieval and Early Modern Literature.* New York: Routledge, 2004.
1034. Gross, Gregory W. "Trade Secrets: Chaucer, the Pardoner, the Critics." *MLS* 25.4 (1995): 1–36.
1035. Halverson, John. "Chaucer's Pardoner and the Progress of Criticism." *ChauR* 4 (1970): 184–202.
1036. Hoerner, Fred. "Church Office, Routine, and Self-Exile in Chaucer's Pardoner." *SAC* 16 (1994): 69–98.
1037. Kellogg, A. L., and L. A. Haselmayer, "Chaucer's Satire on the Pardoner." *PMLA* 66 (1951): 251–77.
1038. Kelly, Henry Ansgar, "The Pardoner's Voice, Disjunctive Narrative, and Modes of Effemination." In *Speaking Images: Essays in Honor of V. A. Kolve,* edited by R. F. Yeager and Charlotte C. Morse. Asheville, NC: Pegasus, 2001. 411–44.
1039. Legassie, Shayne Aaron. "Chaucer's Pardoner and Host—On the Road, in the Alehouse." *SAC* 29 (2007): 183–223.
1040. McAlpine, Monica A. "The Pardoner's Homosexuality and How It Matters." *PMLA* 95 (1980): 8–22.
1041. Matsuda, Takami. "Death, Prudence, and Chaucer's *Pardoner's Tale.*" *JEGP* 91 (1992): 313–24.
1042. Maxfield, David K. "St. Mary Rouncivale, Charing Cross: The Hospital of Chaucer's Pardoner." *ChauR* 28 (1993): 148–63.
1043. Minnis, A[lastair] J. "Chaucer and the Queering Eunuch." *NML* 6 (2003): 107–28.
1044. ———. *Fallible Authors: Chaucer's Pardoner and Wife of Bath.* Philadelphia: U of Pennsylvania P, 2008.
1045. Osborn, Marijane. "Transgressive Word and Image in Chaucer's Enshrined *Coillions* Passage." *ChauR* 37 (2003): 365–84.
1046. Patterson, Lee. "Chaucerian Confession: Penitential Literature and the Pardoner." *M&H* 7 (1976): 153–73.
1047. ———. "Chaucer's Pardoner on the Couch: Psyche and Clio in Medieval Literary Studies." *Speculum* 76 (2001): 638–80.
1048. Purdon, Liam. "The Pardoner's Old Man and the Second Death." *SP* 89 (1992): 334–49.

1049. Richardson, Gudrun. "The Old Man in Chaucer's *Pardoner's Tale*: An Interpretative Study of His Identity and Meaning." *Neophil* 87 (2003): 323–37.

1050. Sedgewick, G. G. "The Progress of Chaucer's Pardoner, 1880-1940." *MLQ* 1 (1940): 431–58.

1051. Shaffern, Robert W. "The Pardoner's Promises: Preaching and Policing Indulgences in the Fourteenth-Century English Church." *Historian* 68.1 (2006): 49–65.

1052. Snell, William. "Chaucer's *Pardoner's Tale* and Pestilence in Late-Medieval Literature." *SIMELL* 10 (1995): 1–16.

1053. Storm, Melvin. "The Pardoner's Invitation: Quaestor's Bag or Becket's Shrine?" *PMLA* 97 (1982): 810–18.

1054. Strohm, Paul. "Chaucer's Lollard Joke: History and the Textual Unconscious." *SAC* 17 (1995): 23–42.

1055. Sturges, Robert S. *Chaucer's Pardoner and Gender Theory: Bodies of Discourse.* New York: St. Martin's P, 2000.

1056. Thomas, Susanne Sara. "Textual Exhibitionism: The Pardoner's Affirmation of Text Over Context." *Mediaevalia* 22 (1998): 13–47.

1057. Williams, David. "'Lo, How I Vanysshe': The Pardoner's War Against Signs." In *Chaucer and Language: Essays in Honour of Douglas Wurtele*, edited by Robert Myles and David Williams. Montreal: McGill-Queen's UP, 2001. 143–73.

1058. Zeikowitz, Richard E. "Silenced but Not Stifled: The Disruptive Queer Power of Chaucer's Pardoner." *DR* 82.1 (2002): 55–73.

See also nos. 91, 1213.

CT Part 7

1059. Astell, Ann. "Chaucer's 'Literature Group' and the Medieval Causes of Books." *ELH* 59 (1992): 269–87.

1060. Gruenler, Curtis. "Desire, Violence and the Passion of Fragment VII of *The Canterbury Tales*: A Girardian Reading." *Renascence* 52 (1999): 35–56.

See also no. 717.

CT7—The Shipman and His Tale

1061. Abraham, David H. "*Cosyn* and *Cosynage*: Pun and Structure in the *Shipman's Tale*." *ChauR* 11 (1977): 319–27.

1062. Adams, Robert. "The Concept of Debt in *The Shipman's Tale*." *SAC* 6 (1984): 85–102.

1963. Buckmaster, Dale, and Elizabeth Buckmaster. "Studies of Accounting and Commerce in Chaucer's *Shipman's Tale*." *Accounting, Auditing, & Accountability* 12.1 (1999): 113–28.

1064. Fulton, Helen. "Mercantile Ideology in Chaucer's *Shipman's Tale*." *ChauR* 36 (2002): 311–28.

1065. Ganim, John M. "Double Entry in Chaucer's *Shipman's Tale*: Chaucer and Bookkeeping Before Pacioli." *ChauR* 30 (1996): 294–305.

1066. Jager, Eric. "*The Shipman's Tale*: Merchant's Time and Church's Time, Secular and Sacred Space." In *Chaucer and the Challenges of Medievalism*, edited by Donka Minkova and Theresa Tinkle. Frankfurt: Lang, 2003. 253–60.

1067. Joseph, Gerhard. "Chaucer's Coinage: Foreign Exchange and the Puns of the *Shipman's Tale*." *ChauR* 17 (1983): 341–57.

1068. Nicholson, Peter. "The Shipman's Tale and the *Fabliaux*." *ELH* 45 (1978): 583–96.

1069. Rogers, William E., and Paul Dower, "Thinking about Money in Chaucer's *Shipman's Tale*." In *New Readings of Chaucer's Poetry*, edited by Robert G. Benson and Susan J. Ridyard. Rochester, NY: Brewer, 2003. 119–38.

1070. Scattergood, V. J. "The Originality of the *Shipman's Tale*." *ChauR* 11 (1977): 210–31.

1071. Sheridan, Christian. "Funny Money: Puns and Currency in the *Shipman's Tale*." In *Medieval English Comedy*, edited by Sandra M. Hordis and Paul Hardwick. Turnhout, Belgium: Brepols, 2007. 111–23.

1072. Silverman, Albert H. "Sex and Money in Chaucer's *Shipman's Tale*" *PQ* 32 (1953): 329–36.

1073. Thormann, Janet. "The Circulation of Desire in *The Shipman's Tale*." *L&P* 39.3 (1993): 1–15.

CT7—The Prioress and Her Tale

1074. Adams, Robert. "Chaucer's 'Newe Rachel' and the Theological Roots of Medieval Anti-Semitism." *BJRL* 77 (1995): 9–18.

1075. Bale, Anthony. *The Jew in the Medieval Book: English Antisemitisms, 1350–1500.* Cambridge,UK: Cambridge UP, 2006.

1076. Bauer, Kate. "'We Thrughoutly Hauen Cnawyng': Ideas of Learning and Knowing in Some Works of Chaucer, Gower, and the Pearl-Poet. In *Satura: Studies in Medieval Literature in Honour of Robert R. Raymo*, edited by Nancy R. Reale and Ruth E. Sternglantz. Donington: Shaun Tyas, 2001. 205–26.

1077. Besserman, Lawrence. "Chaucer, Spain, and the Prioress's Antisemitism." *Viator* 35 (2004): 329–53.

1078. Collette, Carolyn P. "Critical Approaches to the 'Prioress's Tale' and the 'Second Nun's Tale.'" In Benson and Robertson, no. 405, 95–107.

1079. Dahood, Roger. "The Punishment of the Jews, Hugh of Lincoln, and the Question of Satire in Chaucer's *Prioress's Tale*." *Viator* 36 (2005): 465–91.

1080. Delany, Sheila. "Chaucer's Prioress, the Jews, and the Muslims." *Medieval Encounters* 5 (1999): 198–213.

1081. Eaton, R. D. "Sin and Sensibility: The *Conscience* of Chaucer's Prioress." *JEGP* 104 (2005): 495–513.

1082. Ferris, Sumner. "The Mariology of the *Prioress's Tale*." *ABR* 32 (1981): 232–54.

1083. Fradenburg, Louise O. "Criticism, Anti-Semitism, and the *Prioress's Tale.*" *Exemplaria* 1 (1989): 69–115.
1084. Frank, Hardy Long. "Seeing the Prioress Whole." *ChauR* 25 (1991): 229–37.
1085. Frank, Robert Worth, Jr. "Miracles of the Virgin, Medieval Anti-Semitism, and the *Prioress's Tale.* In *The Wisdom of Poetry*, edited by Larry D. Benson and Siegfried Wenzel. Kalamazoo: Western Michigan P, 1982. 177–88.
1086. Gaynor, Stephanie. "He Says, She Says: Subjectivity and the Discourse of the Other in the Prioress's Portrait and Tale." *Medieval Encounters* 5 (1999): 375–90.
1087. Hahn, Thomas. "The Performance of Gender in the Prioress." *ChauY* 1 (1992): 11–34.
1088. Koretsky, Allen C. "Dangerous Innocence: Chaucer's Prioress and Her Tale." In *Jewish Presences in English Literature*, edited by Derek Cohen and Deborah Haller. Montreal: McGill-Queen's UP, 1990. 10–24.
1089. Oliver, Kathleen M. "Singing Bread, Manna, and the Clergeon's *Greyn.*" *ChauR* 31 (1997): 357–64.
1090. Orth, William. "The Problem of the Performative in Chaucer's Prioress Sequence." *ChauR* 42 (2007): 196–210.
1091. Osberg, Richard H. "A Voice for the Prioress: The Context of English Devotional Prose." *SAC* 18 (1996): 25–54.
1092. Power, Eileen. "Madam Eglentyne: Chaucer's Prioress in Real Life." In *Medieval People.* 10th ed. London: Methuen, 1963.
1093. Rambuss, Richard. "Devotion and Defilement: The Blessed Virgin Mary and the Corporeal Hagiographics of Chaucer's *Prioress's Tale.*" In *Textual Bodies*, edited by Lori Hope Lefkovitz. Albany: State U of New York P, 1997. 75–99.
1094. Rex, Richard. *"The Sins of Madame Eglentyne" and Other Essays on Chaucer.* Newark, NJ: U of Delaware P, 1995.
1095. Ridley, Florence. *The Prioress and the Critics.* U of California English Studies 30. Berkeley: U of California P, 1965.
1096. Saito, Isumu. "'Greyn' of Martyrdom in Chaucer's *Prioress's Tale.*" In *Arthurian and Other Studies Presented to Sunichi Noguchi.* Cambridge: Brewer, 1993. 31–38.
1097. Spector, Stephen. "Empathy and Enmity in the Prioress's Tale." In *The Olde Daunce.* Eds. Robert R. Edwards and Stephen Spector. Albany: State U of New York P, 1991. 211–28.
See also nos. 53, 1102, 1161.

CT7—The Tale of Sir Thopas

1098. Børch, Marianne. "Writing Remembering Orality: Geoffrey Chaucer's *Sir Thopas.*" *European Journal of English Studies* 10.2 (2006): 131–48.
1099. Conley, John. "The Peculiar Name *Thopas.*" *SP* 73 (1976): 42–61.
1100. Gaylord, Alan T. "Chaucer's Dainty 'Dogerel': The 'Elvyssh' Prosody of *Sir Thopas.*" *SAC* 1 (1979): 83–104.
1101. ———. "The 'Miracle' of *Sir Thopas.*" *SAC* 6 (1984): 65–84.
1102. Hamel, Mary. "And Now for Something Completely Different: The Relationship Between the *Prioress's Tale* and the *Rime of Sir Thopas.*" *ChauR* 14 (1980): 251–59.
1103. Jones, E. A. "'Loo, Lordes Myne, Heere Is a Fit!: The Structure of Chaucer's *Sir Thopas.*" *RES* 51 (2000): 248–52.
1104. Olson, Glending. "A Reading of the Thopas-Melibee Link." *ChauR* 10 (1975): 147–53.
1105. Patterson, Lee W. "'What Man Artow?': Authorial Self-Definition in *The Tale of Sir Thopas* and *The Tale of Melibee.*" *SAC* 11 (1989): 117–75.
1106. Purdie, Rhiannon. "The Implications of Manuscript Layout in Chaucer's *Tale of Sir Thopas.*" *Forum* 41 (2005): 263–74.
1107. Scattergood, V. J. "Chaucer and the French War: *Sir Thopas* and *Melibee.*" In *Court and Poet*, edited by Glyn S. Burgess and others. Liverpool: Cairns, 1981. 287–96.
1108. Tschann, Judith. "The Layout of *Sir Thopas* in the Ellesmere, Hengwrt, Cambridge Dd.4.24 and Cambridge Gg.4.27 Manuscripts." *ChauR* 20 (1985): 1–13.
1109. Wright, Glenn. "Modern Inconveniences: Rethinking the Parody in *The Tale of Sir Thopas.*" *Genre* 30 (1997): 167–94.

CT7—The Tale of Melibee

1110. Aers, David. "Chaucer's *Tale of Melibee*: Whose Virtues?" In *Medieval Literature and Historical Inquiry.* Cambridge: Brewer, 2000. 68–81.
1111. Dobyns, Ann. "Chaucer and the Rhetoric of Justice." *Disputatio* 4 (1999): 75–89.
1112. Ferster, Judith. "Chaucer's *Tale of Melibee*: Contradictions and Context." In *Inscribing the Hundred Years' War in French and English Cultures*, edited by Denise N. Baker. Albany: State University of New York Press, 2000. 73-89.
1113. Forhan, Kate L. "Poets and Politics: Just War in Geoffrey Chaucer and Christine de Pizan." In *Ethics, Nationalism, and Just War: Medieval and Contemporary Perspectives*, edited by Henrik Syse and Gregory M. Reichberg. Washington, D.C.: Catholic University Press, 2007. 99–116.
1114. Grace, Dominick. "Telling Differences: Chaucer's *Tale of Melibee* and Renaud de Louens' *Livre de Mellibee et Prudence.*" *PQ* 82 (2003): 367–400.
1115. Hoffman, Richard L. "Chaucer's Melibee and Tales of Sondry Folk." *Classica et Medievalia* 30 (1969): 552–77.
1116. Johnson, Lynn Staley. "Inverse Counsel: Contexts for the *Melibee.*" *SP* 87 (1990): 137–55.
1117. Kennedy, Kathleen E. "Maintaining Love Through Accord in the *Tale of Melibee.*" *ChauR* 39 (2004): 165–76.

1118. Mann, Jill. “Newly Identified Quotations in Chaucer’s *Tale of Melibee* and the *Parson’s Tale.*” In *The Medieval Book and a Modern Collector,* edited by Takami Matsuda and others. Cambridge, UK: Brewer, 2004. 61–71.

1119. Moore, Stephen G. “Apply Yourself: Learning While Reading the *Tale of Melibee.*” *ChauR* 38 (2003): 83–97.

1120. Owen, Charles A., Jr. “The *Tale of Melibee.*” *ChauR* 7 (1973): 267–80.

1121. Pakkala-Weckström, Mari. “Prudence and the Power of Persuasion—Language and *Maistrie* in the *Tale of Melibee.*” *ChauR* 35 (2001): 399–412.

1122. Stillwell, Gardner. “The Political Meaning of Chaucer’s *Tale of Melibee.*” *Speculum* 19 (1944): 433–44.

1123. Strohm, Paul. “The Allegory of the *Tale of Melibee.*” *ChauR* 2 (1967): 32–42.

See also nos. 1104-05, 1107.

CT7—The Monk and His Tale

1124. Beichner, Paul E. “Daun Piers, Monk and Business Administrator.” *Speculum* 34 (1959): 611–19.

1125. Delasanta, Rodney. “‘Namoore of this’: Chaucer’s Priest and Monk.” *TSL* 13 (1968): 117–32.

1126. Jensen, Emily. “‘Winkers’ and ‘Janglers’: Teller/Listener/Reader Response in the *Monk’s Tale,* the Link, and the *Nun’s Priest’s Tale.*” *ChauR* 32 (1997): 183–95.

1127. Norsworthy, Scott. “Hard Lords and Bad Food Service in the *Monk’s Tale.*” *JEGP* 100 (2001): 313–32.

1128. Olsson, Kurt. “Grammar, Manhood, and Tears: The Curiosity of Chaucer’s Monk.” *MP* 76 (1978): 1–17.

1129. Pardee, Sheila. “Sympathy for the Monastery: Monks and Their Stereotypes in *The Canterbury Tales.*” *JRMMRA* 14 (1993): 65–79.

1130. Pearsall, Derek. “‘If heaven be on this earth, it is in cloister or in school’: The Monastic Ideal In Later Medieval English Literature.” In *Pragmatic Utopias: Ideals and Communities, 1200-1630,* edited by Rosemary Horrox and Sarah Rees Jones. Cambridge: Cambridge UP, 2001. 11–25.

1131. [Scanlon, Larry, ed.] “Colloquium on *The Monk’s Tale.*” *SAC* 22 (2000): 381–440.

1132. Wenzel, Siegfried. “Why the Monk?” In *Words and Works,* edited by Peter S. Baker and Nicholas Howe. Toronto: U of Toronto P, 1998. 261–69.

1133. White, Robert B., Jr. “Chaucer’s Daun Piers and the Rule of St. Benedict: The Failure of an Ideal.” *JEGP* 70 (1971): 13–30.

1134. Zatta, Jane Dick. “Chaucer’s Monk: *A Mighty Hunter Before the Lord.*” *ChauR* 29 (1994): 111–33.

See also no. 89a.

CT7—The Nun’s Priest and His Tale

1135. Baswell, Christopher. “Aeneas in 1381.” *NML* 5 (2002): 8–58.

1136. Bloomfield, Morton W. “The Wisdom of the Nun’s Priest’s Tale.” In *Chaucerian Problems and Perspectives,* edited by Edward Vasta and Zacharias P. Thundy. Notre Dame, IN: U of Notre Dame P, 1979. 70–82.

1137. Brody, Saul Nathaniel. “Truth and Fiction in the *Nun’s Priest’s Tale.*” *ChauR* 14 (1979): 33–47.

1138. Broes, Arthur T. “Chaucer’s Disgruntled Cleric: The Nun’s Priest’s Tale.” *PMLA* 78 (1963): 156–62.

1139. Camargo, Martin. “Rhetorical Ethos and the *Nun’s Priest’s Tale.*” *Comparative Literature Studies* 33 (1996): 173–86.

1140. Finlayson, John. “Reading Chaucer’s ‘Nun’s Priest’s Tale’: Mixed Genres and Multi-Layered Worlds of Illusion.” *ES* 86 (2005): 493–510.

1141. Gallacher, Patrick. “Food, Laxatives, and the Catharsis in Chaucer’s Nun’s Priest’s Tale.” *Speculum* 51 (1976): 49–68.

1142. Houwen, L. A. J. R. “Fear and Instinct in Chaucer’s *Nun’s Priest Tale.*” In *Fear and Its Representations in the Middle Ages and Renaissance,* edited by Anne Scott and Cynthia Kossos. Turnhout, Belgium: Brepols, 2002. 17–30.

1143. Hoy, Michael. “The Nun’s Priest’s Tale.” In *Chaucer’s Major Tales,* edited by Michael Hoy and Michael Stevens. London: Bailey, 1969. 135–62.

1144. Kaylor, Noel Harold. “*The Nun’s Priest’s Tale* as Chaucer’s *Anti-Tragedy.*” In *The Living Middle Ages: Studies in Mediaeval English Literature and Its Tradition,* edited by Uwe Boker and others. Stuttgart: Belser, 1989. 87–102.

1145. Knight, Stephen. “Form, Content and Context in *The Nun’s Priest’s Tale.*” In *Studies in Chaucer,* edited by G. A. Wilkes and A. P. Reimer. Sydney: U of Sydney, 1981. 64–85.

1146. McAlpine, Monica E. “The Triumph of Fiction in the Nun’s Priest’s Tale.” In *Art and Context in Late Medieval English Narrative,* edited by Robert R. Edwards. Cambridge, UK: Brewer, 1994. 79–92.

1147. Oerlemans, Onno. “The Seriousness of the *Nun’s Priest’s Tale.*” *ChauR* 26 (1992): 317–28.

1148. Pratt, Robert A. “Some Latin Sources of the Nonnes Preest on Dreams.” *Speculum* 52 (1977): 538–70.

1149. ———. “Three Old French Sources of the Nonnes Preestes Tale.” *Speculum* 47 (1972): 422–44, 646–68.

1150. Scanlon, Larry. “The Authority of Fable: Allegory and Irony in the *Nun’s Priest’s Tale.*” *Exemplaria* 1 (1989): 43–68.

1151. Schauber, Ellen, and Ellen Spolsky. “Stalking a Generative Poetics.” *NLH* 12 (1981): 397–413.

1152. Travis, Peter W. “Reading Chaucer *Ob Ovo*: Mock-*Exemplum* in the *Nun’s Priest’s Tale.*” In *The Performance of Medieval Culture,* edited by James J. Paxson and others. Cambridge, UK: Brewer, 1998. 161–81.

See also nos. 51, 89a, 1126.

CT Part 8

1153. Cowgill, Bruce Kent. "Sweetness and Sweat: The Extraordinary Emanations in Fragment Eight of the *Canterbury Tales*." *PQ* 74 (1995): 343–57.
1154. Grennen, Joseph E. "Saint Cecilia's 'Chemical Wedding': The Unity of *Canterbury Tales*, Fragment VIII." *JEGP* 65 (1966): 466–81.
1155. Longsworth, Robert M. "Privileged Knowledge: St. Cecilia and the Alchemist in the *Canterbury Tales*." *ChauR* 27 (1992): 87–96.
1156. Masciandaro, Nicola. *The Voice of the Hammer: The Meaning of Work in Middle English Literature.* Notre Dame, IN: U of Notre Dame P, 2007.
1157. O'Connell, Brendan. "'Ignotum per ignocius': Alchemy, Analogy, and Poetics in Fragment VIII of *The Canterbury Tales*." In *Transmission and Transformation in the Middle* Ages, edited by Kathy Cawsey and Jason Harris. Dublin: Four Courts, 2007. 131–56.
1158. Rosenberg, Bruce A. "The Contrary Tales of the Second Nun and the Canon's Yeoman." *ChauR* 2 (1968): 278–91.
1159. Scattergood, John. "Chaucer in the Suburbs." In *Medieval Literature and Antiquities*, edited by Myra Stokes and T. L. Burton. Cambridge, UK: Brewer, 1987. 145–62.

See also no. 1184.

CT 8—The Second Nun and Her Tale

1160. Børch, Marianne. "Chaucer's *Second Nun's Tale*: Record of a Dying World." *ChauY* 5 (1998): 19–40.
1161. Collette, Carolyn P. "Chaucer's Discourse of Mariology: Gaining the Right to Speak." In *Art and Context in Late Medieval English Narrative*, edited by Robert R. Edwards. Cambridge, UK: Brewer, 1994. 127–47.
1162. Connolly, Thomas. *Mourning Into Joy: Music, Raphael, and Saint Cecilia.* New Haven, CT: Yale UP, 1994.
1163. Filax, Elaine. "A Female I-deal: Chaucer's Second Nun." In *Sovereign Lady: Essays on Women in Middle English Literature*, edited by Muriel Whitaker. New York: Garland, 1995. 133–56.
1164. Hirsh, John C. "The Politics of Spirituality: The Second Nun and the Manciple." *ChauR* 12 (1977): 129–46.
1165. Jankowski, Eileen S. "Chaucer's *Second Nun's Tale* and the Apocalyptic Imagination." *ChauR* 36 (2001): 128–48.
1166. Johnson, Lynn Staley. "Chaucer's Tale of the Second Nun and the Strategies of Dissent." *SP* 89 (1992): 314–33.
1167. Kennedy, Thomas C. "The Translator's Voice in the Second Nun's *Invocacio*: Gender, Influence, and Textuality." *M&H* 22 (1995): 95–110.
1168. Luecke, Janemarie. "Three Faces of Cecilia: Chaucer's Second Nun's Tale." *ABR* 33 (1982): 35–48.
1169. Peck, Russell A. "The Ideas of *Entente* and Translation in Chaucer's *Second Nun's Tale. AnM* 8 (1967): 17–37.
1170. Raybin, David. "Chaucer's Creation and Recreation of the *Lyf of Seynt Cecile*." *ChauR* 32 (1997): 196–212.

See also nos. 632, 1014, 1078.

CT8—The Canon's Yeoman and His Tale

1171. Bishop, Louise M. *Words, Stones, and Herbs: The Healing Word in Medieval and Early Modern England.* Syracuse: Syracuse UP, 2007.
1172. Bruhn, Mark J. "Art, Anxiety, and Alchemy in the *Canon's Yeoman's Tale*." *ChauR* 33 (1999): 288–315.
1173. Campbell, Jackson J. "The Canon's Yeoman as Imperfect Paradigm." *ChauR* 17 (1982): 171–81.
1174. Duncan, Edgar H. "The Literature of Alchemy and Chaucer's Canon's Yeoman's Tale: Framework, Theme and Characters." *Speculum* 43 (1968): 633–56.
1175. Harwood, Britton J. "Chaucer and the Silence of History: Situating the Canon's Yeoman's Tale." *PMLA* 102 (1987): 338–50.
1176. Knapp, Peggy. "The Work of Alchemy." *JMEMSt* 30 (2000): 575–99.
1177. Landman, Mark H. "The Laws of Community, Margery Kempe, and the *Canon's Yeoman's Tale*." *JMEMSt* 28 (1998): 389–425.
1178. McCracken, Samuel "Confessional Prologue and the Topography of the Canon's Yeoman." *MP* 68 (1971): 289–91.
1179. Patterson, Lee. "Perpetual Motion: Alchemy and the Technology of the Self." *SAC* 15 (1993): 25–57.
1180. Raybin, David. "'And Pave It Al of Silver and Gold': The Humane Artistry of *The Canon's Yeoman's Tale*." In *Rebels and Rivals: The Contestive Spirit of The Canterbury Tales*, edited by Susanna Freer Fein and others. Kalamazoo, MI: Medieval Institute, 1991. 189–212.
1181. Staley, Lynn. "The Man in Foul Clothes and a Late Fourteenth-Century Conversation About Sin." *SAC* 24 (2002): 1–47.
1182. Thomas, Susanne Sara. "Representing (Re)production: The Canon's Yeoman's Revelations of Textual Impotence." *Crossings* 1 (1997): 159–73.

See also nos. 433, 482.

CT Part 9

1183. Kealy, J. Kiernan. "Voices of the Tabard: The Last Tales of the Canterbury Tales." In *From Arabye to Engelond*, edited by A. E. Christa Canitz and Gernot R. Wieland. Ottawa: U of Ottawa P, 1999. 113–29.
1184. Weil, Eric. "An Alchemical Freedom Flight: Linking the Manciple's Tale to the Second Nun's and Canon's Yeoman's Tales." *MedPers* 6 (1991): 162–70.

CT9—The Manciple and His Tale

1185. Allen, Mark. "Penitential Sermons, the Manciple, and the End of the *Canterbury Tales.*" *SAC* 9 (1987): 77–96.
1186. Burrow, J. A. "Chaucer's Canterbury Pilgrimage." *EIC* 36 (1986): 97–119.
1186a. Craun, Edwin D. *Lies, Slander, and Obscenity in Medieval English Literature: Pastoral Rhetoric and the Deviant Speaker.* Cambridge, UK: Cambridge UP, 1997.
1187. Dean, James. "The Ending of the *Canterbury Tales,* 1952–1976." *TSLL* 21 (1979): 17–33.
1188. Fradenburg, Louise. "The Manciple's Servant Tongue." *ELH* 52 (1985): 85–118.
1189. Fumo, Jamie C. "Thinking Upon the Crow: The *Manciple's Tale* and Ovidian Mythography." *ChauR* 38 (2004): 355–75.
1190. Ginsberg, Warren. "Chaucer's Canterbury Poetics: Irony, Allegory, and the *Prologue* to *The Manciple's Tale.*" *SAC* 18 (1996): 55–89.
1191. [Grady, Frank]. "Colloquium: *The Manciple's Tale.*" *SAC* 25 (2003): 285–337.
1192. Harwood, Britton J. "Language and the Real: Chaucer's Manciple." *ChauR* 6 (1972): 268–79.
1193. Kensak, Michael. "What Ails Chaucer's Cook? Spiritual Alchemy and the Ending of *The Canterbury Tales.*" *PQ* 80 (2001) (2001): 213–31.
1194. Patton, Celeste A. "False 'Rekenynges': Sharp Practice and the Politics of Language in Chaucer's *Manciple's Tale.*" *PQ* 71 (1992): 399–417.
1195. Pelen, Marc M. "The Manciple's 'Cosyn' to the 'Dede'." *ChauR* 25 (1991): 343–54.
1196. Scattergood, V. J. "The Manciple's Manner of Speaking." *EIC* 24 (1974): 124–46.
1197. Striar, Brian. "The *Manciple's Tale* and Chaucer's Apolline Poetics." *Criticism* 33 (1991): 173–204.
1198. Wood, Chauncey. "Speech, the Principle of Contraries, and Chaucer's Tales of the Manciple and the Parson." *Mediaevalia* 6 (1980): 209–29.

See also nos. 47, 1012, 1164.

CT Part 10

1199. Dean, James. "Chaucer's Repentance: A Likely Story." *ChauR* 24 (1989): 64–76.
1200. Vaughan, Míceál F. "Creating Comfortable Boundaries: Scribes, Editors, and the Invention of the Parson's Tale." In *Rewriting Chaucer,* edited by Prendergast and Kline, no. 128. 45–90.
1201. Wurtele, Douglas. "The Penitence of Geoffrey Chaucer." *Viator* 11 (1980): 355–61.

CT10—The Parson and His Tale

1202. Bestul, Thomas. "Chaucer's *Parson's Tale* and the Late-Medieval Tradition of Religious Meditation." *Speculum* 64 (1989): 600–19.
1203. Brown, Emerson, Jr. "The Poet's Last Words: Text and Meaning at the End of the *Parson's Prologue.*" *ChauR* 10 (1976): 236–42.
1204. Delasanta, Rodney. "Penance and Poetry in the *Canterbury Tales.*" *PMLA* 93 (1978): 240–47.
1205. Finke, Laurie A. "'To Knytte up al this Feeste': The Parson's Rhetoric and the Ending of the *Canterbury Tales.*" *LeedsSE* 15 (1984): 95–107.
1206. Finlayson, John. "The Satiric Mode and the *Parson's Tale.*" *ChauR* 6 (1971): 94–116.
1207. Little, Katherine C. *Confession and Resistance: Defining the Self in Late Medieval England.* Notre Dame, IN: U of Notre Dame P, 2006.
1208. McCormack, Frances. *Chaucer and the Culture of Dissent. The Lollard Context and Subtext of the Parson's Tale.* Dublin: Four Courts, 2007.
1209. Patterson, Lee W. "The *Parson's Tale* and the Quitting of the *Canterbury Tales.*" *Traditio* 34 (1978): 331–80.
1210. Pitard, Derrick G. "Sowing Difficulty: *The Parson's Tale,* Vernacular Commentary, and the Nature of Chaucerian Dissent." *SAC* 26 (2004): 299–330.
1211. Raybin, David, and Linda Tarte Holley, eds. *Closure in The Canterbury Tales: The Role of the Parson's Tale.* Kalamazoo, MI: Medieval Institute, 2000.
1212. Swanson, Robert W. "Chaucer's Parson and Other Priests." *SAC* 13 (1991): 41–80.
1213. Waters, Claire M. "Holy Duplicity: The Preacher's Two Faces." *SAC* 24 (2002): 75–113.
1214. Wenzel, Siegfreid. "Chaucer's Parson's Tale: 'Every Tales Strengthe'." In *Europäische Lehrdictung. Festschrift für Walter Naumann zum 70 Geburtstag,* edited by Hans Gerd Rötzer and Herbert Walz. Darmstadt: Wissenschaftliche Buchgesell, 1981. 86–98.
1215. Wurtele, Douglas J. "The Anti-Lollardry of Chaucer's Parson." *Mediaevalia* (1989): 151–68.

See also nos. 601, 1118, 1198.

CT10—Chaucer's Retraction

1216. Furrow, Melissa. "The Author and Damnation: Chaucer, Writing, and Penitence." *FMLS* 33 (1997): 244–57.
1217. Knapp, Robert. "Penance, Irony, and Chaucer's Retraction." *Assays* 2 (1983): 45–67.
1218. McGerr, Rosemarie Potz. "Retraction and Memory: Retrospective Structure in the *Canterbury Tales.*" *CL* 37 (1985): 97–113.
1219. Obermeier, Anita. *The History and Anatomy of Auctorial Self-Criticism in the European Middle Ages.* Atlanta: Rodopi, 1999.
1220. Pigg, Daniel F. "Figuring Subjectivity in 'Piers Plowman C,' the Parson's 'Tale,' and 'Retraction': Authorial Insertion and Identity Politics." *Style* 31 (1997): 428–39.
1221. Sayce, Olive. "Chaucer's Retractions: The Conclusion of the *Canterbury Tales* and Its Place in Literary Tradition." *MAE* 40 (1971): 230–48.
1222. Travis, Peter W. "Deconstructing Chaucer's Retraction." *Exemplaria* (Special Issue) 3 (1991): 135–58.

1223. Vaughan, Míceál F. "Personal Politics and Thomas Gascoigne's Account of Chaucer's Death." *MÆ* 75 (2006): 103–22.

See also nos. 1653.

Troylus and Criseyde—General Criticism

1224. Benson, C. David. *Chaucer's Troilus and Criseyde.* London: Unwin Hyman, 1991.

1225. Bishop, Ian. *Chaucer's Troilus and Criseyde: A Critical Study.* Bristol: U of Bristol Academic Publications,1981.

1226. Frantzen, Allen J. *Troilus and Criseyde: The Poem and the Frame.* New York: Twayne, 1993.

1227. Gordon, Ida. *The Double Sorrow of Troilus.* Oxford: Oxford UP, 1970.

1228. Kaminsky, Alice R. *Chaucer's Troilus and Criseyde and the Critics.* Athens: Ohio UP, 1980.

1229. Morgan, Gerald. *The Tragic Argument of "Troilus and Criseyde."* 2 vols. Lewiston, NY: Mellen, 2005.

1230. Root, R. K., and H. N. Russell. "A Planetary Date for Chaucer's *Troilus.*" *PMLA* 39 (1924): 48–53.

1231. Spearing, A. C. *Troilus and Criseyde.* London: Edward Arnold, 1976.

1232. Windeatt, Barry. *Troilus and Criseyde.* Oxford Guides to Chaucer. New York: Clarendon, 1992.

1233. Wood, Chauncey. *The Elements of Chaucer's Troilus.* Durham, NC: Duke UP, 1984.

TC—Literary Relations

1234. Anderson, David. "Theban History in Chaucer's *Troilus.*" *SAC* 4 (1982): 109–33.

1235. Benson, C. David. *The History of Troy in Middle English Literature.* Totowa, NJ: Rowman and Littlefield, 1980.

1236. Boitani, Piero, ed. *The European Tragedy of Troilus.* Oxford: Clarendon, 1989.

1237. Clogan, Paul M. "The Theban Scenes in Chaucer's *Troilus.*" *M&H* 12 (1984): 167–85.

1238. Federico, Sylvia. *New Troy: Fantasies of Empire in the Late Middle Ages.* Minneapolis: U of Minnesota P, 2003.

1239. Fleming, John V. *Classical Imitation and Interpretation in Chaucer's Troilus.* Lincoln: U of Nebraska P, 1990.

1240. Gleason, Mark J. "Nicholas Trevet, Boethius, Boccaccio: Contexts of Cosmic Love in *Troilus,* Book III." *M&H* 15 (1987): 161–88.

1241. Hanly, Michael G. *Boccaccio, Beauvau, Chaucer: Troilus and Criseyde: Four Perspectives on Influence.* Norman, OK: Pilgrim Books, 1990.

1242. Lewis, C. S. "What Chaucer Really Did to *Il Filostrato.*" *E&S* 17 (1932): 56–75.

1243. Nolan, Barbara. *Chaucer and the Tradition of the Roman Antique.* New York: Cambridge UP, 1992.

1244. Pratt, Robert A. "Chaucer and *Le Roman de Troyle et de Cresieda.*" *SP* 53 (1956): 509–39.

1245. Stillinger, Thomas C. *The Song of Troilus: Lyric Authority in the Medieval Book.* Philadelphia: U of Pennsylvania P, 1992.

1246. Sudo, Jan. "Chaucer's Imitation and Innovation in *Troilus and Criseyde.*" *PoeticaT* 13 (1982): 50–74.

1247. Wetherbee, Winthrop. *Chaucer and the Poets: An Essay on Troilus and Criseyde.* Ithaca, NY: Cornell UP, 1984.

1248. Young, Karl. *The Origin and Development of the Story of Troilus and Criseyde.* London: Chaucer Society, 2d Series, 40, 1908.

TC—Genres and Structure

1249. Adamson, Jane. "The Unity of *Troilus and Criseyde.*" *Critical Review* 14 (1971): 17–37.

1249a. Bessent, Benjamin R. "The Puzzling Chronology of Chaucer's *Troilus.*" *SN* 41 (1969): 99–111.

1250. Brenner, Gerry. "Narrative Structure in Chaucer's *Troilus and Criseyde.*" In *Chaucer's Troilus: Essays in Criticism,* edited by Stephen A. Barney. Hamden, CT: Archon, 1980. 131–44.

1251. Camargo, Martin. *The Middle English Verse Epistle.* Tubingen: Niemeyer, 1991.

1252. Frantzen, J. Allen. "The 'Joie and Tene' of Dreams in *Troilus and Crieyde.*" In *Chaucer in the Eighties,* edited by Julian N. Wasserman and Robert J. Blanch. Syracuse, NY: Syracuse UP, 1986. 105–19.

1253. Hardman, Phillipa. "Chaucer's Articulation of the Narrative in *Troilus*: The Manuscript Evidence." *ChauR* 30 (1995): 111–33.

1254. Kelly, Henry Ansgar. *Chaucerian Tragedy.* Rochester, NY: Brewer, 1997.

1255. McAlpine, Monica E. *The Genre of Troilus and Criseyde.* Ithaca, NY: Cornell UP, 1978.

1256. McCall, John P. "The Five-Book Structure of Chaucer's *Troilus.*" *MLQ* 23 (1962): 297–308.

1257. Meech, Sanford B. *Design in Chaucer's Troilus.* Syracuse, NY: Syracuse UP, 1959.

1258. Robertson, D. W. Jr. "Chaucerian Tragedy." *ELH* 19 (1952): 1–37.

1259. Rowe, Donald W. *O Love O Charite! Contraries Harmonized in Chaucer's Troilus.* Carbondale, Southern Illinois UP, 1976.

1260. Sigal, Gale. "The Alba Lady, Sex-Roles, and Social Roles: 'Who Peyntede the Leon, Tel Me Who.'" In *Rhetorical Poetics of the Middle Ages,* edited John M. Hill and Deborah M. Sinnreich-Levy. Teaneck, NJ: Fairleigh Dickinson UP. 2000, 221–40.

1261. Stierstorfer, Klaus. "Markers of Transition: Laughter in Chaucer's *Troilus and Criseyde.*" *ChauR* 34 (1999): 18–37.

1262. Torti, Anna. *The Glass of Form: Mirroring Structures from Chaucer to Skelton.* Cambridge, UK: Brewer, 1991.

1263. Windeatt, Barry. "*Troilus* and the Disenchantment of Romance." In *Studies in Medieval English Romances: Some New Approaches,* edited by Derek Brewer. Cambridge, UK: Brewer, 1988. 129–47.

See also nos. 1297, 1299, 1393.

TC—Style and Rhetoric

1264. Bradbury, Nancy Mason. "Gentrification and the *Troilus*." *ChauR* 28 (1994): 305-29.

1264a. Chickering, Howell. "The Poetry of Suffering in Book V of *Troilus*." *ChauR* 34 (2000): 243–68.

1265. Clark, S. L., and Julian N. Wasserman. "The Heart in *Troilus and Criseyde*: The Eye of the Breast, the Mirror of the Mind, the Jewel in Its Setting." *ChauR* 18 (1984): 316–28.

1266. Delany, Sheila. "Techniques of Alienation in *Troilus and Criseyde*." In *The Uses of Criticism*, edited by A. P. Foulkes. Bern: Lang, 1976. 77–95. Rpt. in Shoaf no. 1290, 29–46.

1267. Ganim, John M. *Style and Consciousness in Middle English Narrative*. Princeton, NJ: Princeton UP, 1983.

1268. Hall, Ann C. "Educating the Reader: Chaucer's Use of Proverbs in *Troilus and Criseyde*." *Proverbium* 3 (1986): 47–58.

1269. Hermann, John P. "Gesture and Seduction in *Troilus and Criseyde*." *SAC* 7 (1985): 107–35.

1270. Koretsky, Allen C. "Chaucer's Use of the Apostrophe in *Troilus and Criseyde*." *ChauR* 4 (1970): 242–66.

1271. Lambert, Mark. "Telling the Story in *Troilus and Criseyde*." In Boitani and Mann, no.105, 78–92.

1272. Macey, Samuel L. "The Dramatic Elements in Chaucer's *Troilus*." *TSLL* 12 (1970): 301–23.

1273. Mack, Peter. "Argument and Emotion in *Troilus and Crisede*." In *Medieval Rhetoric: A Casebook*, edited by Scott D. Troyan. New York: Routledge, 2004. 109–26.

1274. Manning, Stephen. "*Troilus*, Book V: Invention and the Poem as Process." *ChauR* 18 (1984): 288–303.

1275. Murray, Molly. "The Value of 'Eschaunge': Ransom and Substitution in *Troilus and Criseyde*." *ELH* 69 (2002): 335–58.

1276. O'Brien, Timothy. "*Sikernesse* and *Fere* in *Troilus and Criseyde*." *ChauR* 38 (2004): 276–93.

1277. Paxson, James J. "The Semiotics of Character, Trope, and Troilus: The Figural Construction of the Self and the Discourse of Desire in Chaucer's *Troilus and Criseyde*." In *Desiring Discourse: The Literature of Love, Ovid Through Chaucer*, edited by James J. Paxon and Cynthia A. Gravlee. Selinsgrove, PA: Susquehanna UP, 1998. 206–26.

1278. Schibanoff, Susan. "Prudence and Artificial Memory in Chaucer's *Troilus*." *ELH* 42 (1975): 507–17.

1279. Stokes, Myra. "Recurring Rhymes in *Troilus and Criseyde*." *SN* 52 (1980): 287–97.

1280. Taylor, Karla. "Proverbs and the Authentication of Convention in *Troilus and Criseyde*." In *Chaucer's Troilus: Essays in Criticism*, edited Stephen A Barney. Hamden, CT: Shoestring, 1980. 277–96.

1281. Wimsatt, James I. "The French Lyric Element in *Troilus and Criseyde*." *YES* 15 (1985): 18–32.

1282. ———. "Medieval and Modern in Chaucer's *Troilus and Criseyde*." *PMLA* 92 (1977): 203–16.

TC—Narrator and Narrative Technique

1283. Fumo, Jamie C. "'Little Troilus': Heroides 5 and Its Ovidian Context in Chaucer's *Troilus and Criseyde*." *SP* 100 (2003): 278–314.

1284. Jordan, Robert O. "Metafiction and Chaucer's *Troilus*." *ChauY* 1 (1992): 135–55.

1285. Kinney, Clare Regan. "Dilation, Design, and Didacticism in *Troilus and Criseyde*." In *Strategies of Poetic Narration*. Cambridge, UK: Cambridge UP, 1992. 31–68.

1286. Liu, Hongying. "As Chaucer's Narrator Says, So Say I." *MedPers* 4–5 (1989–90): 117–24.

1287. Mehl, Dieter. "The Audience of Chaucer's *Troilus and Criseyde*." In *Chaucer and Middle English Studies in Honour of Rossell Hope Robbins*, edited by Beryl Rowland. London: Unwin, 1974. 173–89.

1288. Rowland, Beryl. "Chaucer's Speaking Voice and Its Effect on His Listeners' Perception of Criseyde." *ESC* 7 (1981): 129–40.

1289. Salter, Elizabeth. "*Troilus and Criseyde*: Poet and Narrator." In *Acts of Interpretation . . . Essays in Honor of E. Talbot Donaldson*, edited by Mary J. Carruthers and Elizabeth D. Kirk. Norman, OK: Pilgrim, 1982. 281–91.

1290. Shoaf, R. A., ed. *Chaucer's Troilus and Criseyde: ' Subgit to alle Poesie": Essays in Criticism.* Binghamtom, NY: Medieval & Renaissance Texts & Studies, 1992.

1291. Spearing, A. C. "A Ricardian 'I': The Narrator of *Troilus and Criseyde*." *Essays on Ricardian Literature in Honour of J. A. Burrow*, edited by A. J. Minnis and others. Oxford: Clarendon, 1997. 1–22.

1292. Waswo, Richard. "The Narrator of *Troilus and Criseyde*." *ELH* 50 (1983): 1–25.

See also nos. 459, 678.

TC—Philosophy and Theme

1293. An Sonjae (Brother Anthony). "No Greater Pain: The Ironies of Bliss in Chaucer's *Troilus and Criseyde*." In Noel Harold Kalor, Jr., and Richard Scott Nokes. Kalamazoo, MI: Medieval Institute, 2007. 117–32.

1294. Andretta, Helen Ruth. *Chaucer's Troilus and Criseyde: A Poet's Response to Ockhamism*. New York: Lang, 1997.

1295. apRoberts, Robert P. "The Boethian God and the Audience of the *Troilus*." *JEGP* 69 (1970): 425–36.

1296. Bloomfield, Morton. "Distance and Predestination in *Troilus and Criseyde*." *PMLA* 72 (1957): 14–26.

1297. Clopper, Lawrence. "The Form of Romance and the Resolution of Theological Issues." *M&H* 15 (1987): 119–46.

1298. Eldredge, Laurence. "Boethian Epistemology and Chaucer's Troilus in the Light of Fourteenth Century Thought." *Mediaevalia* 2 (1976): 49–75.

1299. Giancarlo, Matthew. The Structure of Fate and the Devising of History in Chaucer's *Troilus and Criseyde*." *SAC* 26 (2004): 227–66.

1300. Goodman, Jennifer R. "Nature as Destiny in *Troilus and Criseyde.*" *Style* 31 (1997): 413–27.
1301. Grady, Frank. "The Boethian Reader of *Troilus and Criseyde.*" *ChauR* 33 (1999): 230–51.
1302. Grennen, Joseph E. "Aristotelian Ideas in Chaucer's *Troilus*: A Preliminary Study." *M&H* 14 (1986): 125–38.
1303. Hill, T. E. *"She, This in Blak": Vision, Truth, and Will in Geoffrey Chaucer's "Troilus and Criseyde."* New York: Routledge, 2006.
1304. Howard, Donald R. "The Philosophies in Chaucer's *Troilus.*" In *The Wisdom of Potry*, edited by Larry D. Benson and Siegfried Wenzel. Kalamazoo, MI: Western Michigan U, 1982. 151–75.
1305. Klassen, N. "Optical Allusions and Chaucerian Realism: Aspects of Sight in Late Medieval Thought and *Troilus and Criseyde.*" *Stanford Humanities Review* 2.2–3 (1992): 129–46.
1306. Mann, Jill. "Chance and Destiny in *Troilus and Criseyde and the Knight's Tale.*" In Boitani and Mann, no. 105, 93–111.
1307. Martin, Thomas L. "Time and Eternity in Troilus and Criseyde." *Renascence* 51 (1999): 167–99.
1308. Mitchell, J. Allan. "Romancing Ethics in Boethius, Chaucer, and Lévinas: Fortune, Moral Luck, and Erotic Adventure." *CL* 57.2 (2005): 101–16.
1309. Nair, Sashi. "'O brotel wele of mannes joie unstable!': Gender and Philosophy in *Troilus and Criseyde.*" *Parergon* 23.2 (2006): 35–56.
1310. Newman, Barbara. "Feynede Love, and Faith in Trouthe." In *Chaucer's Troilus: Essays in Criticism*, edited by Stephen A. Barney. Hamden, CT: Shoestring, 1980. 257–75.
1311. Reichl, Karl. "Chaucer's *Troilus*: Philosophy and Language." In Boitani, no 1236, 133-52.
1312. Scanlon, Larry. "Sweet Persuasions: The Subject of Fortune in *Troilus and Criseyde.*" In Shoaf, no. 1290, 211–23.
1313. Schaber, Bennet. "*Troilus and Criseyde* and the Order of Translation." In *Ideas of Order in the Middle Ages*, edited by Warren Ginsberg. Binghamton: State U of New York, 1988. 23–43
1314. Stokes, Myra. "'Wordes White': Disingenuity in *Troilus and Criseyde.*" *ES* 64 (1983): 18–29.
1315. Turner, Marion. "*Troilus and Criseyde* and the 'Treasonous Aldermen of 1382'." *SAC* 25 (2003): 225–57.
1316. Urban, Malte. "Chaucer's *Troilus and Criseyde* as a Critique of Medieval Historiography." *CarmP* 12 (2003): 75–90.
1317. ———. "Myth and the Present: Chaucer's *Troilus* as a Mirror for Ricardian England." In *Riddles, Knights and Cross-dressing Saints: Essays on Medieval English Language and Literature*, edited by Thomas Honegger. New York: Lang, 2004. 33–54.
1318. Williams, David. "Distentio, Intentio, Attentio: Intentionality and Chaucer's Third Eye." *Florilegium* 15 (1998): 37–60.

See also no. 1390.

TC—Sex, Love, and Marriage

1319. Aers, David. "Masculine Identity in the Courtly Community: The Self Loving in *Troilus and Criseyde.*" In *Gender, Community, and Individual Identity*. New York: Routledge, 1988. 117–52.
1320. Christmas, Peter. "*Troilus and Criseyde:* The Problems of Love and Necessity." *ChauR* 9 (1975): 285–96.
1321. Dahlberg, Charles. "The Poet of Unlikeness: Chaucer." In *The Literature of Unlikeness*. Hanover, NH: UP of New England, 1988. 125–38.
1322. Davis, Adam Brooke. "The Ends of Fiction: Narrative Boundaries and Chaucer's Attitude Toward Courtly Love." *ChauR* 28 (1993): 54–66.
1323. Gilles, Sealy. "Love and Disease in Chaucer's *Troilus and Criseyde.*" *SAC* 25 (2003): 157–97.
1324. Helterman, Jeffrey. "Masks of Love in *Troilus and Criseyde.*" *CL* 26 (1974): 14–31.
1325. Hill, John. "Aristocratic Friendship in *Troilus and Criseyde*: Pandarus, Courtly Love, and Ciceronian Brotherhood in Troy." In *New Readings of Chaucer's Poetry*, edited by Robert G. Benson and Susan J. Ridyard. Cambridge, UK: Brewer, 2003. 165–82.
1326. Howard, Donald R. "Courtly Love and Lust of the Flesh." In *The Three Temptations: Medieval Man in Search of the World*. Princeton, NJ: Princeton UP, 1966. 76–160.
1327. Liggens, Elizabeth M. "The Lovers' Swoons in *Troilus and Criseyde.*" *Parergon* 3 (1985): 40–60.
1328. Margherita, Gayla. "Historicity, Femininity, and Chaucer's *Troilus.*" *Exemplaria* 6 (1994): 243–69.
1329. Pugh, Tison. "Christian Revelation and the Cruel Game of Courtly Love in *Troilus and Criesyde.*" *ChauR* 39 (2005): 379–401.
1330. Stanbury, Sarah. "The Lover's Gaze in *Troilus and Criseyde.*" In Shoaf, no. 1290, 224–38.
1331. Wack, Mary. "Lovesickness in *Troilus.*" *PCP* 19 (1984): 55–61.
1332. Windeatt, Barry. "'Love That Oughte Ben Secree' in Chaucer's *Troilus.*" *ChauR* 14 (1979): 116–31.

See also nos. 1349-50.

TC—Characterization and Minor Characters

1333. Baswell, Christopher C., and Paul Beekman Taylor. "The 'Faire Queene Eleyne' in Chaucer's *Troilus.*" *Speculum* 63 (1988): 293–311.
1334. Brewer, Derek. "The Ages of Troilus, Criseyde, and Pandarus." *Studies in English Literature* (Tokyo): 1 (1972): 3–13.
1335. Bronson, Larry. "The 'Sodeyn Diomede'—Chaucer's Composite Portrait." *Ball State University Forum* 25 (1984): 14–19.
1336. Fleming, John V. "Deiphoebus Betrayed: Virgilian Decorum, Chaucerian Feminism." *ChauR* 21 (1986): 182–99.
1337. Gasse, Rosanne. "Deiphebus, Hector, and Troilus in Chaucer's *Troilus and Criseyde.*" *ChauR* 32 (1998): 423–39.

1338. Greenfield, Stanley B. "The Role of Calkas in *Troilus and Criseyde*." *MAE* 36 (1967): 141–51.

1339. Johnson, Lynn Staley. " The Medieval Hector: A Double Tradition." *Mediaevalia* 5 (1979): 165–82.

1340. Kiernan, Kevin S. "Hector the Second: The Lost Face of Troilus-tratus." *AnM* 16 (1975): 52–62.

1341. Olson, Alexandra Hennessey. "In Defense of Diomede: 'Moral' Gower and and *Troilus and Criseyde*." *InG* 8 (1987): 1–12.

1342. Sanok, Catherine. "Criseyde, Cassandre, and the *Thebaid*: Women and the Theban Subtext of Chaucer's *Troilus and Criseyde*." *SAC* 20 (1998): 41–71.

1343. Schibanoff, Susan. "Argus and Argyve: Etymology and Characterization in Chaucer's *Troilus*." *Speculum* 51 (1976): 647–58.

1344. Zeitoun, Franck. "The Eagle, the Boar, and the Self: Dreams, Daydreams, and Violence in *Troilus and Criseyde*." *Cercles* 6 (2003): 45–53.

TC—Troylus

1345. Barney, Stephen A. "Troilus Bound." *Speculum* 47 (1972): 445–58.

1346. Carruthers, Mary. "On Affliction and Reading, Weeping and Argument: Chaucer's Lachrymose Troilus in Context." *Representations* 93 (2006): 1–21.

1347. Ciccone, Nancy. "Saving Chaucer's Troilus 'with desir and resoun twight'." *Neophil* 86 (2002): 641–58.

1348. Goldstein, R. James. "Chaucer, Suicide, and the Agencies of Memory: Troilus and the Death Drive." In *Speaking Images: Essays in Honor of V. A. Kolve*, edited by R. F. Yeager and Charlotte C. Morse. Ashville, NC: Pegasus, 2001. 185–304.

1349. Love, Damian. "'Al This Peynted Process': Chaucer and the Psychology of Courtly Love." *ES* 83 (2002): 391–98.

1350. Martin, June Hall. "Troilus." In *Love's Fools: Aucassin, Troilus, Calisto, and the Parody of the Courtly Lover.* London: Támesis, 1972. 37–70.

1351. Masi, Michael. "Troilus: A Medieval Psychoanalysis." *AnM* 11 (1970): 81–88.

1352. Moore, Marilyn Reppa. "Who's Solipsistic Now? The Character of Chaucer's Troilus." *ChauR* 33 (1998): 43–59.

1353. Mann, Jill. "Troilus' Swoon." *ChauR* 14 (1980): 319–35.

1354. Noh, Kyung Lee. "Acedia as a Motive in Troilus' Tragedy." *Medieval and Early Modern English Studies* 15 (2007): 271–87.

1355. Rudat, Wolfgang. "Chaucer's *Troilus and Criseyde:* The Narrator-Reader's Complicity." *American Imago* 40 (1983): 103–13.

1356. Taylor, Davis. "The Terms of Love: A Study of Troilus's Style." *Speculum* 51 (1976): 357-69.

See also nos. 1337, 1340.

TC—Criseyde

1357. Aers, David. "Criseyde: Woman in Medieval Society." *ChauR* 13 (1979): 177–200.

1358. Amtower, Laurel. "Chaucer's Sely Widows." In *The Single Woman in Medieval and Early Modern England: Her Life and Representation*, edited by Laurel Amtower and Dorothea Kehler. Tempe: Arizona Center for Medieval and Renaissance Studies, 2003. 119–32.

1359. apRoberts, Robert P. "Criseyde's Infidelity and the Moral of the *Troilus*." *Speculum* 44 (1969): 383–402.

1360. Behrman, Mary. "Heroic Criseyde." *ChauR* 38 (2004): 314–36.

1361. David, Alfred. "Chaucerian Comedy and Criseyde." In *Essays on Troilus and Criseyde*, edited by Mary Salu. Cambridge, UK: Brewer, 1979. 90–104.

1362. Haahr, Joan G. "Criseyde's Inner Debate: The Dialectic of Enamorment in the *Filostrato* and the *Troilus*." *SP* 89 (1992): 257–71.

1363. Howard, Donald R. "Experience, Language, and Consciousness: *Troilus and Criseyde*, II, 596-931." In *Chaucer's Troilus: Essays in Criticism*, edited by Stephen A. Barney. Hamden, CT: Archon, 1980. 159–80.

1364. Howes, Laura L. "Chaucer's Criseyde: The Betrayer Betrayed." In *Reading Medieval Culture: Essays in Honor of Robert W. Hanning*, edited by Robert M. Stein and Sandra Pierson Prior. Notre Dame IN: U of Notre Dame P, 2005. 321–43.

1365. Kellogg, Laura D. *Boccaccio's and Chaucer's Cressida.* New York: Peter Lang, 1996.

1366. Koster, Josephine A. "*Privitee, Habitus*, and Proximity: Conduct and Domestic Space in Chaucer's *Troilus and Criseyde*." *EMSt* 24 (2007): 79–91.

1367. McAlpine, Monica. "Criseyde's Prudence." *SAC* 25 (2003): 199–224.

1368. Mapstone, Sally. "The Origins of Criseyde." In *Medieval Women: Texts and Contexts in Late Medieval Britain*, edited by Jocelyn Wogan-Browne and others. Turnhout, Belgium: Brepols, 2000. 131–47.

1369. Mieszkowski, Gretchen. *The Reputation of Criseyde, 1155-1500.* Hamden, CT: Archon, 1971.

1370. Milliken, Roberta. "Neither 'Clere Laude' Nor 'Sklaundre': Chaucer's Translation of Criseyde." *Women's Studies* 24 (1995): 191–204.

1371. Pearsall, Derek. "Criseyde's Choices." *SAC, Proceedings* 2 (1986): 17–32.

1372. Sell, Jonathan P. A. "Cousin to Fortune: On Reading Chaucer's Criseyde." *RCEI* 48 (2004): 193–204.

1373. Vitto, Cindy L., and Marcia Smith Marzec, eds. *New Perspectives on Criseyde.* Fairview, NC: Pegasus P, 2004.

1374. Woods, Majorie Curry. "Chaucer the Rhetorician: Criseyde and Her Family." *ChauR* 20 (1985): 28–39.

TC—Pandarus

1375. Camargo, Martin. "The Consolation of Pandarus." *ChauR* 25 (1991): 214–28.

1376. Carton, Evan. "Complicity and Responsibility in Pandarus' Bed and Chaucer's Art." *PMLA* 94 (1979): 47–61.
1377. Fyler, John M. "The Fabrications of Pandarus." *MLQ* 41 (1980): 115–30.
1378. Mieszkowski, Gretchen. *Medieval Go-Betweens and Chaucer's Pandarus.* New York: Palgrave Macmillan, 2006.
1379. Pugh, Tison. "Queer Pandarus: Silence and Sexual Ambiguity in Chaucer's *Troilus and Criseyde.*" *PQ* 80 (2001): 17–35.
1380. Rutherford, Charles S. "Pandarus as a Lover: 'A Joly Wo' or 'Loves Shotes Keene'?" *AnM* 13 (1972): 5–13.
1381. Slocum, Sally K. "How Old is Chaucer's Pandarus?" *PQ* 58 (1979): 16–25.
1382. Stroud, T. A. "The Palinode, the Narrator, and Pandarus's Alleged Incest." *ChauR* 27 (1992): 16–30.
See also nos. 459, 484, 1325, 1355.

TC—The Ending

1383. Farrell, Thomas J. "The 'Fyn' of the *Troilus.*" In *Subjects on the World's Stage,* edited by David G. Allen and Robert A. White. Newark: U of Delaware P, 1995. 38–53.
1384. McGerr, Rosemarie P. "Meaning and Ending in a 'Paynted Proces': Resistence to Closure in *Troilus and Criseyde.*" In Shoaf, no. 1290, 179–98.
1385. Osberg, Richard. "Between the Motion and the Act: Intentions and Ends in Chaucer's *Troilus.*" *ELH* 48 (1981): 257–70.
1386. Papka, Claudia Rattazzi. "Transgression, the End of Troilus, and the Ending of Chaucer's *Troilus and Criseyde.*" *ChauR* 32 (1998): 267–81.
1387. Pulsiano, Phillip. "Redeemed Language and the Ending of *Troilus and Criseyde.*" In *Sign, Sentence, Discourse: Language in Medieval Thought and Literature,* edited by Julian N. Wasserman and Lois Roney. Syracuse, NY: Syracuse UP, 1989. 153–74.
1388. Silar, Theodore I. "An Analysis of the Legal Sense of the Word *Fin (Finalis Concordia)* in *Piers Plowman, Sir Gawain, Pearl,* Chaucer's Works and Especially the Ending of *Troilus and Criseyde. ChauR* 32 (1998): 282–309.
1389. Spearing, A. C. "Narrative Closure: The End of *Troilus and Criseyde.*" In *Readings in Medieval Poetry.* Cambridge, UK: Cambridge UP, 1987. 107–33.
1390. Steadman, John M. *Disembodied Laughter: "Troilus" and the Apotheosis Tradition: A Reexamination of Narrative and Thematic Concerns.* Berkeley: U of California P, 1972.
1391. Yeager, R. F. "'O Moral Gower': Chaucer's Dedication of *Troilus and Criseyde.*" *ChauR* 19 (1984): 87–99.

Dream Visions

1392. Brown, Peter, ed. *Reading Dreams.* Oxford: Oxford UP, 1999.
1393. Condren, Edward I. *Chaucer from Prentice to Poet: The Metaphor of Love in Dream Visions and Troilus and Criseyde.* Gainesville, UP of Florida, 2008.
1394. D'Agata D'Ottavi, Stephania. *Il Sogno e Il Libro: La "Mise en Abyme" nei Poemi Onirici di Chaucer.* Rome: Bulzoni Editore, 1992.
1395. Edwards, Robert R. *The Dream of Chaucer: Representation and Reflection in the Early Narratives.* Durham, NC: Duke UP, 1989.
1396. Heinrichs, Katherine. *The Myths of Love: Classical Lovers in Medieval Literature.* University Park: Pennsylvania State UP, 1990.
1397. Klitgard, Ebbe. "Chaucer as Performer: Narrative Strategies in the Dream Visions." *RCEI* 47 (2003): 101–13.
1398. Kruger, Steven F. *Dreaming in the Middle Ages.* Cambridge, UK: Cambridge UP, 1992.
1399. Lynch, Kathryn L. *Chaucer's Philosophical Visions.* Cambridge, UK: Brewer, 2000.
1400. Minnis, A. J., with V. J. Scattergood, and J. J. Smith. *The Shorter Poems.* Oxford Guides to Chaucer. New York: Oxford UP, 1995.
1401. Russell, J. Stephen. *The English Dream Vision: Anatomy of a Form.* Columbus: Ohio State UP, 1988.
1402. Schibanoff, Susan. *Chaucer's Queer Poetics: Rereading the Dream Trio.* Toronto: U of Toronto P, 2006.
1403. St. John, Michael. *Chaucer's Dream Poems: Courtliness and Individual Identity.* Aldershot, UK: Ashgate, 2000.
1404. Traversi, Derek. *Chaucer: The Earlier Poetry: A Study in Poetic Development.* Newark: U of Delaware P, 1987.
1405. Windeatt, B. A., ed. *Chaucer's Dream Poetry: Sources and Analogues.* Cambridge: Brewer, 1982.
See also no. 730.

Book of the Duchess

1406. Allen, Valerie. "Portrait of a Lady: Blanche and the Descriptive Tradition." *ES* 74 (1993): 324–42.
1407. Anderson, J. J. "The Narrators in the *Book of the Duchess* and the *Parlement of Foules.*" *ChauR* 26 (1992): 219–35.
1408. Bahr, Arthur W. "The Rhetorical Construction of Narrator and Narrative in Chaucer's *The Book of the Duchess.*" *ChauR* 35 (2000): 43–59.
1409. Burrow, J. A. "Politeness and Privacy: Chaucer's *Book of the Duchess.*" In *Studies in Late Medieval and Early Renaissance Texts in Honour of John Scattergood,* edited by Anne Marie D'Arcy and Alan J. Fletcher. Dublin: Four Courts, 2005. 65–75.
1410. Butterfield, Ardis. "Lyric and Elegy in the Book of the Duchess." *MAE* 60 (1991): 33–60.
1411. ———. "Pastoral and Politics in Machaut and Chaucer." *SAC* 16 (1994): 3–27.
1412. Carruthers, Mary. "'The Mystery of the Bed Chamber': Mnemotechnique and Vision in Chaucer's *The Book of the Duchess.*" In *The Rhetorical Poetics of the Middle Ages: Reconstructive Polyphony,* edited

by John M. Hill and Deborah M. Sinnreich-Levi. Teaneck, NJ: Fairleigh Dickinson UP, 2000. 67–87.

1413. Cherniss, Michael D. "The Narrator Asleep and Awake in Chaucer's *Book of the Duchess.*" *PLL* 8 (1972): 115–26.

1414. Condren, Edward I. "The Historical Context of the *Book of the Duchess*: A New Hypothesis." *ChauR* 5 (1971): 195–212.

1415. Crane, Susan. "Froissart's *Dit dou Bleu Chevalier* as a Source for Chaucer's *Book of the Duchess.*" *MAE* 61.1 (1992): 59–74.

1416. Dean, James. "Chaucer's *Book of the Duchess* : A Non-Boethian Interpretation." *MLQ* 46 (1985): 235–49.

1417. Dilorenzo, Raymond D. "'Wonder and Words': Paganism, Christianity, and Consolation in Chaucer's *Book of the Duchess.*" *UTQ* 52 (1982): 20–39.

1418. Donnelly, Coleen. "Challenging the Convention of Dream Vision in *The Book of the Duchess.*" *PQ* 66 (1987): 421–35.

1419. Edwards, Robert. "*The Book of the Duchess* and the Beginning of Chaucer's Narrators." *NLH* 13 (1989): 189–204.

1420. Ellis, Steve. "The Death of *The Book of the Duchess.*" *ChauR* 29 (1995): 249–58.

1421. Ellman, Maud. "Blanche." In *Criticism and Critical Theory*, edited by Jeremy Hawthorn. London: Arnold, 1984. 98–100.

1422. Ferster, Judith. "Intention and Interpretation in the *Book of the Duchess.*" *Criticism* 22 (1980): 1–24.

1423. Hanning, Robert W. "Chaucer's First Ovid: Metamorphosis and Poetic Tradition in *The Book of the Duchess.*" In *Chaucer and the Craft of Fiction*, edited by Leigh A. Arrathoon. Rochester, MI: Solaris, 1986. 121–63.

1424. Hardman, Phillipa. "The *Book of the Duchess* as a Memorial Monument." *ChauR* 28 (1994): 205–15.

1425. Hill, John M. "The *Book of the Duchess*, Melancholy, and That Eight-Year Sickness." *ChauR* 9 (1974): 35–50.

1426. Kensak, Michael. "'My first matere I wil yow telle: Losing (and Finding) Your Place in Chaucer's *Book of the Duchess.*" In *"Seyd in Forme and Reverence": Essays on Chaucer and Chaucerians*, edited by T. L. Burton and John F. Plummer. Provo,UT: Chaucer Studio, 2005. 83–96.

1427. Means, M. H. *The Consolation Genre in Medieval English Literature.* Gainesville: U of Florida P, 1972.

1428. Nolan, Barbara. "The Art of Expropriation: Chaucer's Narrator in *The Book of the Duchess.*" In *New Perspectives in Chaucer Criticism*, edited by Donald M. Rose. Norman, OK: Pilgrim, 1981. 203–22.

1429. Owen, Charles A. "Chaucer: Beginnings." In *The Rhetorical Poetics of the Middle Ages: Reconstructive Polyphony*, edited by John M. Hill and Deborah M. Sinnreich-Levi. Teaneck, NJ: Fairleigh Dickinson UP, 2000. 45–66.

1430. Palmer, J. J. N. "The Historical Context of the *Book of the Duchess*: A Revision." *ChauR* 8 (1974): 253–61.

1431. Pelen, Marc M. "Machaut's Court of Love Narratives and Chaucer's *Book of the Duchess.*" *ChauR* 11 (1976): 128–55.

1432. Phillips, Helen. "*The Book of the Duchess*, Lines 31-96: Are They a Forgery?" *ES* 67 (1986): 113–21.

1433. ———. "Structure and Consolation in the *Book of the Duchess.*" *ChauR* 16 (1981): 107–18.

1434. Prior, Sandra Pierson. "'Routhe' and 'Hert-Hunting' in the *Book of the Duchess.*" *JEGP* 85 (1986): 1–19.

1435. Quinn, William A. "Medieval Dream Visions: Chaucer's Book of the Duchess." In *Readings in Medieval Texts*, edited by David F. Johnson and Elaine Treharne. Oxford: Oxford UP, 2005. 323–36.

1436. Rooney, Anne. "The *Book of the Duchess*: Hunting and the *Ubi Sunt* Motif." *RES* 38 (1987): 299–314.

1437. Ross, Diane M. "The Play of Genres in the *Book of the Duchess.*" *ChauR* 19 (1984): 1–13.

1438. Salda, Michael Norman. "Pages from History: The Medieval Palace of Westminster as a Source for the Dreamer's Chamber in the *Book of the Duchess.*" *ChauR* 27 (1992): 111–25.

1439. Salter, Elizabeth. "Chaucer and Internationalism." *SAC* 2 (1980): 71–79.

1440. Shoaf, R. A. "'Mutatio Amoris': 'Penitentia' and the Form of *The Book of the Duchess.*" *Genre* 14 (1981): 163–89.

1441. Stevenson, Kay Gilliland. "Readers, Poets, and Poems Within the Poem." *ChauR* 24 (1989): 1–19.

1442. Stock, Lorraine Kochanske. "'Peynted . . . text and [visual] glose': Primitivism, Ekphrasis, and Pictorial Intertextuality in the Dreamers' Bedrooms of *Roman de la Rose* and *Book of the Duchess.*" In *"Seyd in Forme and Reverence": Essays on Chaucer and Chaucerians*, edited by T. L. Burton and John F. Plummer. Provo, UT: Chaucer Studio, 2005. 97–114.

1443. Taylor, Mark N. "Chaucer's Knowledge of Chess." *ChauR* 38 (2004): 299–313.

1444. Thompson, Lou. "The Narrator as Mourner and Therapist in Chaucer's *Book of the Duchess.*" *Soundings* 70 (1987): 435–43.

1445. Thundy, Zacharias P. "The Dreme of Chaucer: Boethian Consolation or Political Celebration?" *CarmP* 4 (1995): 91–109.

1446. Tisdale, Charles P. "Boethian 'Hert-Hyntynge': The Elegaic Pattern of the *Book of the Duchess.*" *ABR* 24 (1973): 365–80.

1447. Travis, Peter W. "White." *SAC* 22 (2000): 1–66.

1448. Walker, Denis. "Narrative Inconclusiveness and Consolatory Dialectics in *The Book of the Duchess.*" *ChauR* 18 (1983): 1–17.

1449. Watson, Robert A. "Dialogue and Invention in the Book of the Duchess." *MP* 98 (2001): 543–76.

1450. Wetherbee, Winthrop. "Theme, Prosody, and Mimesis in the *Book of the Duchess.*" In *Essays on the*

Art of Chaucer's Verse, edited by Alan T. Gaylord. New York: Routledge, 2001. 283–95.

1451. Wimsatt, James I. *Chaucer and the French Love Poets: The Literary Background of The Book of the Duchess.* Chapel Hill: U of North Carolina P, 1968.

1452. ———. "The *Book of the Duchess*: Secular Elegy or Religious Vision?" In Hermann and Burke, no. 552, 113–29.

1453. Zimbardo, Rose A. "The *Book of the Duchess* and the Dream of Folly." *ChauR* 18 (1984): 329–46.

See also 1459.

Parliament of Fowls

1454. Bennett, J. A. W., ed. *The Parlement of Foules: An Interpretation.* 2d ed. Oxford: Clarendon, 1969.

1455. Benson, Larry D. "The Occasion of the *Parliament of Fowls.*" In *The Wisdom of Poetry*, edited by Larry D. Benson and Siegfried Wenzel. Kalamazoo, MI: Medieval Institute, 1982. 123–44.

1456. Bertolet, Craig E. "'My Wit Is Sharp: I Love No Taryinge': Urban Poetry in the *Parlement of Foules.*" *SP* 93 (1996): 365–89.

1457. Boyd, David Lorenzo. "Compilation as Commentary: Controlling Chaucer's *Parliament of Fowls.*" *SAQ* 91 (1992): 945–64.

1458. Braddy, Haldeen. *Chaucer's Parlement of Foules in Relation to Contemporary Events.* 2d ed. New York: Octagon, 1969.

1459. Bridges, Margaret. "The Picture in the Text: Ecphrasis as Self-Reflexivity in Chaucer's *Parliament of Fowls, Book of the Duchess,* and *House of Fame.*" *Word & Image* 5 (1989): 151–58.

1460. Brown, Emerson, Jr. "Priapus and the Parlement of Foulys." *SP* 72 (1975): 258–74.

1461. Cadden, Joan. "Trouble in the Earthly Paradise: The Regime of Nature in Late Medieval Christian Culture." In *The Moral Authority of Nature*, edited by Lorraine Daston and Fernando Vidal. Chicago: U of Chicago P, 2004. 207–31.

1462. Cherniss, Michael D. "The Parliament of Fowls." In *Boethian Apocalypse: Studies in Middle English Vision Poetry.* Norman, OK: Pilgrim, 1987. 119–47.

1463. Cooney, Helen. "The *Parlement of Foules*: A Theodicy of Love." *ChauR* 32 (1998): 339–76.

1464. Cowgill, Bruce Kent. "*The Parlement of Foules* and the Body Politic." *JEGP* 74 (1975): 315–35.

1465. Davis, Kathleen. "Hymeneal Logic: Debating Political Community in *The Parliament of Fowls.*" In *Imagining a Medieval English Nation*, edited by Kathy Lavezzo. Minneapolis: U of Minnesota P, 2004. 161–90.

1466. Dean, James. "Artistic Conclusiveness in Chaucer's *Parliament of Fowls.*" *ChauR* 21 (1986): 16–25.

1467. Dubbs, Kathleen E., and Stoddard Malarkey. "The Frame of Chaucer's *Parlement.*" *ChauR* 13 (1978): 16–24.

1468. Eldredge, Laurence. "Poetry and Philosophy in the *Parlement of Foules.*" *RUO* 40 (1970): 441–59.

1469. Fradenburg, Louise Olga. *City, Marriage, Tournament: Arts of Rule in Late Medieval Scotland.* Madison: U of Wisconsin P, 1991.

1470. Giancarlo, Matthew. *Parliament and Literature in Late Medieval England.* Cambridge, UK: Cambridge UP, 2007.

1471. Hewitt, Kathleen. "'Ther It Was First': Dream Poetics in the *Parliament of Fowls.*" *ChauR* 24 (1989): 20–28.

1472. Johnston, Andrew James. "Literary Politics in Debate: Chaucer's *Parliament of Fowls* and Clanvowe's *Book of Cupid.*" In *Proccedings: Anglistentag 2006 Halle*, edited by Sabine Volk-Birke. Trier: Wissenschaftlicher Verlag Trier, 2007. 147–57.

1473. Jordan, Robert O. "The Question of Unity and the *Parlement of Foules.*" *ESC* 3 (1977): 373–85.

1474. Kearney, J. A. "The *Parliament of Fowls*: The Narrator, the 'Certeyn Thyng,' and the 'Commune Profyt'." *Theoria* 45 (1975): 55–71.

1475. Kelley, Michael R. "Antithesis as the Principle of Design in the *Parlement of Foules.*" *ChauR* 14 (1979): 61–73.

1476. Kelly, Henry A. *Chaucer and the Cult of Saint Valentine.* Leiden: Brill, 1986.

1477. Kiser, Lisa. "Chaucer and the Politics of Nature" In *Beyond Nature Writing: Expanding the Boundaries of Ecocriticism. Under the Sign of Nature: Explorations in Ecocriticism*, edited by Karla Armbruster and Kathleen R. Wallace. Charlottesville: U of Virginia P, 2001. 41–56.

1478. McCall, John P. "The Harmony of Chaucer's *Parliament.*" *ChauR* 5 (1970): 22–31.

1479. McDonald, Charles O. "An Interpretation of Chaucer's *Parlement of Foules.*" *Speculum* 30 (1955): 444–57.

1480. Newman, Barbara. "Did Goddesses Empower Women? The Case of Dame Nature." In *Gendering the Master Narrative: Women and Power in the Middle Ages*, edited by Mary C. Erler and Maryanne Kowaleski. Ithaca, NY: Cornell UP, 2003. 135–55.

1481. Olson, Paul A. "The *Parlement of Foules*: Aristotle's *Politics* and the Foundation of Human Society." *SAC* 2 (1980): 53–69.

1482. Oruch, Jack B. "St. Valentine, Chaucer, and Spring in February." *Speculum* 56 (1981): 534–65.

1483. Peck, Russell A. "Love, Politics, and Plot in the *Parlement of Foules.*" *ChauR* 24 (1990): 290–305.

1484. Pinti, Daniel. "Commentary and Comedic Reception: Dante and the Subject of Reading in *The Parliament of Fowls.*" *SAC* 22 (2000): 311–40.

1485. Quilligan, Maureen. "Allegory, Allegoresis, and the Deallegorization of Language: The *Roman de la Rose*, the *De Planctu Naturae*, and the *Parlement of Foules.*" In *Allegory, Myth, and Symbol*, edited Morton W. Bloomfield. Cambridge, MA: Harvard UP, 1981. 163–86.

1486. Reed, Thomas. "Chaucer's *Parlement of Foules*: The Debate Tradition and the Aesthetics of Irresolution." *RUO* 50 (1980): 215–22.

1487. Ruud, Jay. "Realism, Nominalism, and the Inconclusive Ending of the Parliament of Fowls." *InG* 22 (2002): 1–28.
1488. Spearing, A. C. "Al This Mene I Be Love." *SAC Proceedings* 2 (1986): 169–77.
1489. Takada, Yasunari. "Chaucer's Use of Neoplatonic Traditions." In *Platonism and the English Imagination,* edited by Anna Baldwin and Sarah Hutton. Cambridge, UK: Cambridge UP, 1994. 45–51.
1490. Tinkle, Theresa "The Case of the Variable Source: Alan of Lille's 'De planctu Naturae,' Jean de Meun's 'Roman de la Rose,' and Chaucer's 'Parlement of Foules.'" *SAC* 22 (2000): 341–77.
1491. White, Hugh. *Nature, Sex, and Goodness in a Medieval Literary Tradition.* New York: Oxford UP, 2000.
See also no. 1407.

House of Fame

1492. Amtower, Laurel. "Authorizing the Reader in Chaucer's *House of Fame.*" *PQ* 79 (2000): 273–91.
1493. Arnovick, Leslie K. "'In Forme of Speche' is Anxiety: Orality in Chaucer's *House of Fame.*" *Oral Tradition* 11 (1996): 320–45.
1494. Baswell, Christopher. *Virgil and Medieval England.* Cambridge, UK: Cambridge UP, 1995.
1495. Bennett, J. A. W. *Chaucer's Book of Fame: An Exposition of the House of Fame.* Oxford: Clarendon, 1968.
1496. Boitani, Piero. *Chaucer and the Imaginary World of Fame.* New York: Barnes and Noble, 1984.
1497. Braswell, Mary Flowers. "Architectural Portraiture in Chaucer's *House of Fame.*" *JMRS* 11 (1981): 101–12.
1498. Carruthers, Mary. "The Poet as Master Builder: Compositional and Locational Memory in the Middle Ages." *NLH* 24 (1993): 881–904.
1499. Dane, Joseph A. "Chaucer's Eagle's Ovid's Phaethon: A Study in Literary Reception." *JMRS* 11 (1981): 71–82.
1500. Delany, Sheila. *Chaucer's House of Fame: The Poetics of Skeptical Fideism.* Chicago: U of Chicago P. 1972.
1501. Doob, Penelope. "Chaucer's House of Fame." In *The Idea of the Labyrinth from Classical Antiquity Through the Middle Ages.* Ithaca, NY: Cornell UP, 1990. 307–39.
1502. Erzgraber, Willi. "Problems of Oral and Written Transmission as Reflected in Chaucer's *House of Fame.*" In *Historical and Editorial Studies in Medieval and Early Modern English,* edited by Mary-Jo Arn and H. Wirtjes. Groningen: Wolters-Nordhoff, 1985. 113–28.
1503. Evans, Ruth. "Chaucer in Cyberspace: Medieval Technologies of Memory and *The House of Fame.*" *SAC* 23 (2001): 43–69.
1504. Grady, Frank. "Chaucer Reading Langland: *The House of Fame.*" *SAC* 18 (1996): 3–23.
1505. Grennen, Joseph E. "Chaucer and Chalcidius: The Platonic Origins of the *House of Fame.*" *Viator* 15 (1984): 237–62.
1506. Harwood, Britton J. "Building Class and Gender into Chaucer's *House.*" In *Class and Gender in Early English Literature: Intersections,* edited by Britton J. Harwood and Gillian R. Overing. Bloomington: Indiana UP, 1994. 95–111.
1507. Havely, Nicholas R. "Muses and Blacksmiths: Italian Trecento Poetics and the Reception of Dante in *The House of Fame.*" In *Essays on Ricardian Literature in Honour of J. A. Burrow,* edited by A. J. Minnis and others. Oxford: Clarendon, 1997. 61–81.
1508. Irvine, Martin. "Medieval Grammatical Theory and Chaucer's *House of Fame.*" *Speculum* 60 (1985): 850–66.
1509. Jeffrey, David Lyle. "Sacred and Secular Scripture: Authority and Interpretation in *The House of Fame.*" In *Chaucer and the Scriptural Tradition.* Ottawa: U of Ottawa P, 1984. 207–28.
1510. Jimura, Akiyuki. "Chaucer's Use of 'Soth' and 'Fals' in *The House of Fame.*" *Philologia* 23 (1991): 11–35.
1511. Kendrick, Laura. "Chaucer's *House of Fame* and the French Palais de Justice." *SAC* 6 (1984): 121–33.
1512. Kennedy, Thomas C. "Rhetoric and Meaning in *The House of Fame.*" *SN* 68 (1996): 9–24.
1513. Koonce, B. G. *Chaucer and the Tradition of Fame: Symbolism in the House of Fame.* Princeton, NJ: Princeton UP, 1966.
1514. Kordecki, Leslie. "Subversive Voices in Chaucer's *House of Fame.*" *Exemplaria* 11 (1999): 53–77.
1515. Kruger, Steven F. "Imagination and the Complex Movement of Chaucer's *House of Fame.*" *ChauR* 28 (1993): 117–34.
1516. Leyerle, John. "Chaucer's Windy Eagle." *UTQ* 40 (1971): 247–65.
1517. Meecham-Jones, Simon. "'Betwixen Hevene and Erthe and See': Seeing Words in Chaucer's *House of Fame.*" In *Unity and Difference in European Cultures,* edited by Neil Thomas and Françoise Le Saux. Durham, UK: U of Durham, 1998. 155–71.
1518. Miller, Jacqueline T. "The Writing on the Wall: Authority and Authorship in Chaucer's *House of Fame.*" *ChauR* 17 (1982): 95–115.
1519. Minnis, A. J. "Figures of Olde Werk: Chaucer's Poetic Sculptures." In *Secular Sculpture: 1300–1550,* edited Phillip Lindley and Thomas Frangenberg. Stamford, UK: Shaun Tyas, 2000. 124–43.
1520. Pinti, Daniel J. "Translation and the Aesthetics of Synecdoche in Chaucer's *House of Fame.*" *MedPers* 8 (1993): 105–11.
1521. Quinn, William A. "Chaucer's Recital Presence in the *House of Fame* and the Embodiment of Authority." *ChauR* 43 (2008): 171–96.
1522. Rowland, Beryl. "The Art of Memory and the Art of Poetry in the *House of Fame.*" *RUO* 51 (1981): 163–71.
1523. Ruffolo, Lara. "Literary Authority and the Lists of Chaucer's *House of Fame*: Destruction and Definition through Proliferation." *ChauR* 27 (1993): 325–41.
1524. Simpson, James. "Dante's *Astripetam Aquilam* and the Theme of Poetic Discretion in the *House of Fame.*" *E&S* 39 (1987): 1–18.

1525. Steadman, John M. "*The House of Fame*: Tripartite Structure and Occasion." *Connotations* 3 (1993): 1–12.
1526. Steinberg, Glenn. "Chaucer in the Field of Cultural Production: Humanism, Dante, and the *House of Fame*." *ChauR* 35 (2000): 182–203.
1527. Stevenson, Kay. "The Endings of Chaucer's *House of Fame*." *ES* 59 (1978): 10–26.
1528. Watts, Ann C. "*Amor gloriae* in Chaucer's *House of Fame*." *JMRS* 3 (1973): 87–113.
See also nos. 205, 286, 625, 1459.

Legend of Good Women

1529. Allen, Peter L. "Reading Chaucer's Good Women." *ChauR* 21 (1987): 419–34.
1530. Boffey, Julia. "'Twenty Thousand More': Some Fifteenth- and Sixteenth-Century Responses to *The Legend of Good Women*." In *Middle English Texts and Traditions*, edited A. J. Minnis. Rochester, NY: York Medieval P, 2001. 279–97.
1531. Canitz, A. E. Christa. "Courtly Hagiomythography and Chaucer's Tripartite Genre Critique in the *Legend of Good Women*." In *From Arabye to Engelond*, edited by A. E. Christa Canitz and Gernot R. Wieland. Ottawa: U of Ottawa P, 1999. 131–53.
1532. Collette, Carolyn P. *The Legend of Good Women: Context and Reception*. Cambridge, UK: Brewer, 2006.
1533. Cowen, Janet M. "Chaucer's *Legend of Good Women*: Structure and Tone." *SP* 82 (1985): 416–36.
1534. Delany, Sheila. *The Naked Text: Chaucer's Legend of Good Women*. Berkeley: U of California P, 1994.
1535. Edwards, Robert R. "Faithful Translations: Love and the Question of Poetry in Chaucer." In *The Olde Daunce: Love, Friendship, Sex, and Marriage in the Medieval World*, edited by Robert R. Edwards and Stephen Spector. Albany: State U of New York P, 1991. 138–53.
1536. Frank, Robert W., Jr. *Chaucer and the Legend of Good Women*. Cambridge: Harvard UP, 1972.
1537. Galloway, Andrew. "Gower's Quarrel With Chaucer, and the Origins of Bourgeois Didacticism in Fourteenth-Century London Poetry." In *Calliope's Classroom: Studies in Didactic Poetry from Antiquity to the Renaissance*, edited by Annette Harder and others. Dudley, MA: Peeters, 2007. 45–67.
1538. Hansen, Elaine. "The Feminization of Men in Chaucer's *Legend of Good Women*." In *Seeking the Woman in Late Medieval and Renaissance Writings*, edited by Sheila Fisher and Janet E. Halley. Knoxville: U of Tennessee P, 1989. 51–70.
1539. ———. "Irony and the Antifeminist Narrator in Chaucer's *Legend of Good Women*." *JEGP* 82 (1983): 11–31.
1540. Harvey, Elizabeth D. "Speaking of Tongues: The Poetics of Feminine Voice in Chaucer's *Legend of Good Women*." In *New Images of Women*, edited by Edelgard E. DuBruck. Lewiston, NY: Mellen, 1989. 47–60.
1541. Kiser, Lisa. *Telling Classical Tales: Chaucer and the Legend of Good Women*. Ithaca, NY: Cornell UP, 1983.
1542. McDonald, Nicola F. "Chaucer's *Legend of Good Women*, Ladies at Court and the Female Reader." *ChauR* 35 (2000): 22–42.
1543. McLeod, Glenda. "Al of Another Tonne." In *Virtue and Venom: Catalogs of Women from Antiquity to the Renaissance*. Ann Arbor: U of Michigan P, 1991. 81–109.
1544. Moon, Hi Kyung. "'The Legend of False Men'?" Chaucer's Legend of Good Women Re-titled." *Medieval English Studies* (Seoul) 11.1 (2003): 117–30.
1545. Palmer, R. Barton. "Chaucer's *Legend of Good Women*: The Narrator's Tale." In *New Readings of Chaucer's Poetry*, edited by Robert G. Benson and Susan J. Ridyard. Cambridge, UK: Brewer, 2003. 183–94.
1546. Percival, Florence. *Chaucer's Legendary Good Women*. Cambridge: Cambridge UP, 1998.
1547. Phillips, Helen. "Chaucer and Jean Le Fevre." *Archiv* 232 (1995): 23–36.
1548. Quinn, William A. *Chaucer's Rehersynges: The Performability of The Legend of Good Women*. Washington, DC: Catholic U of America P, 1994
1549. Rowe, Donald W. *Through Nature to Eternity: Chaucer's Legend of Good Women*. Lincoln: U of Nebraska P, 1988.
1550. Simpson, James. "Ethics and Interpretation: Reading Wills in Chaucer's *Legend of Good Women*." *SAC* 20 (1998): 73–100.
1551. Taylor, Andrew. "Anne of Bohemia and the Making of Chaucer." *SAC* 19 (1997): 95–119.
1552. Travis, Peter W. "Chaucer's Heliotropes and the Poetics of Metaphor." *Speculum* 72 (1997): 399–427.
See also nos. 205, 291, 632, 1494.

LGW—The Prologue

1553. Blamires, A[lcuin]. "A Chaucer Manifesto." *ChauR* 24 (1989): 29–44.
1554. Coleman, Joyce. "'A bok for king Richardes sake': Royal Patronage, the *Confessio*, and the *Legend of Good Women*." In *On John Gower: Essays at the Millennium*, edited by R. F. Yeager. Kalamazoo, MI: Medieval Insitute, 2007. 104–23.
1555. Eadie, John. "The Author at Work: The Two Versions of the Prologue to the *Legend of Good Women*." *NM* 93 (1992): 135–43.
1556. Fisher, John H. "The Revision of the Prologue to the *Legend of Good Women*: An Occasional Explanation." *South Atlantic Bulletin* 43 (1978): 75–84.
1557. Hanrahan, Michael. "Seduction and Betrayal: Treason in the *Prologue* to the *Legend of Good Women*." *ChauR* 30 (1996): 229–40.
1558. Kimmelman, Burt. "'Thanne Motyn We to Bokys': Writing's Harvest in the Prologue to the *Legend of Good Women*." *JEBS* 3 (2000): 1–35.

1559. Lowes, John L. "The Prologue to the *Legend of Good Women* as Related to the French Marguerite Poems and the *Filostrato*." *PMLA* 19 (1904): 593–683.

1560. Martin, Ellen E. "Chaucer's Ruth: An Exegetical Poetic in the Prologue to the *Legend of Good Women*." *Exemplaria* 3 (1991): 467–90.

1561. Payne, Robert O. "Making His Own Myth: The Prologue to Chaucer's *Legend of Good Women*." *ChauR* 9 (1975): 197–211.

1562. Peck, Russell A. "Chaucerian Poetics and the Prologue of the *Legend of Good Women*." In *Chaucer in the Eighties*, edited by Julian N. Wasserman and Robert J. Blanch. Syracuse: Syracuse UP, 1986. 39–55.

1563. Phillips, Helen. "Literary Allusion in Chaucer's Ballade, 'Hyd, Absalon, thy gilte tresses clere.'" *ChauR* 30 (1995): 134–49.

1564. ———. "Register, Politics, and the *Legend of Good Women*." *ChauR* 37 (2002): 101-28.

1565. Seymour, M. C. "Chaucer's Revision of the Prologue to *The Legend of Good Women*." *MLR* 92 (1997): 832–41.

1566. Strohm, Paul. "Queens as Intercessors." In *Hochon's Arrow: The Social Imagination of Fourteenth-Century Texts*. Princeton, NJ: Princeton UP, 1992. 95–119.

See also 625, 1219.

LGW—The Legends

1567. Aloni, Gila. "A Curious Error? Geoffrey Chaucer's Legend of Hypermnestra." *ChauR* 36 (2001): 73–86.

1568. ———. "What Chaucer's 'Good Women' Dared Not Say." In *Paroles et Silences dans la Littérature Anglaise au Moyen Age*, edited Leo Carruthers and Adrian Paphagi. Paris: Association des Médié vistes Anglicistes de l'Enseignement Supérieur, 2003. 119–34.

1569. Brown, Sarah Annes. "Philomena." *Translation and Literature* 13 (2004): 194–206.

1570. Doyle, Kara A. "Thisbe Out of Context: Chaucer's Female Readers and the Findern Manuscript." *ChauR* 40 (2006): 231–61.

1571. Galloway, Andrew. "Chaucer's *Legend of Lucrece* and the Critique of Ideology in Fourteenth-Century England." *ELH* 60 (1993): 813–32.

1572. Getty, Laura J. "'Other Smale Ymaad Before': Chaucer as Historiographer in the *Legend of Good Women*." *ChauR* 42 (2007): 48–75.

1573. Haas, Renate. "'Kissing the Steppes of Uirgile, Ouide, etc.' and *The Legend of Good Women*." In *Anglistentag 1989 Würzburg: Proceedings*, edited by Rudiger Ahrens. Tübingen: Niemeyer, 1990. 298–309.

1574. Kolve, V. A. "From Cleopatra to Alceste: An Iconographic Study of *The Legend of Good Women*." In Hermann and Burke, no. 552, 130–78.

1575. Laird, Judith. "Good Women and *Bonnes Dames*: Virtuous Females in Chaucer and Christine de Pizan." *ChauR* 30 (1995): 58–70.

1576. McGregor, James H. "The Medieval Art of Imitation and Chaucer's *Legenda Tesbe*." *Mediaevalia* 9 (1986 for 1983): 181–203.

1577. Meale, Carol M. "Legends of Good Women in the European Middle Ages." *Archiv* 229 (1992): 55–70.

1578. Mehl, Dieter. "The Storyteller and His Audience: *The Legend of Good Women*." In *Chaucer: An Introduction to His Narrative Poetry*. Cambridge, UK: Cambridge UP, 1986. 98–119.

1579. Minnis, A. J. "Repainting the Lion: Chaucer's Profeminist Narrative." In *Contexts of the Pre-Novel Narrative*, edited by Roy Ericsen. New York: Gruyter, 1994. 153–83.

1580. Morse, Ruth. *The Medieval Medea*. Cambridge, UK: Brewer, 1996.

1581. Oka, Saburo. "Chaucer's Transformations of *The Legend of Philomela* in *The Legend of Good Women*." *Thought Currents in English* 63 (1990): 79–109.

1582. Ruff, Nancy K. "'Sely Dido': A Good Woman's Fame." *Classical and Modern Literature* 12 (1991): 59–68.

1583. Saunders, Corinne J. "Classical Paradigms of Rape in the Middle Ages: Chaucer's Lucretia and Philomela." In *Rape in Antiquity*, edited by Susan Deacy and Karen F. Pierce. London: Duckworth, 1997, 243–66.

1584. Sylvester, Louise. "Reading Narratives of Rape: The Story of Lucrece in Chaucer, Gower and Christine de Pizan." *LeedsSE* 31 (2000): 115–44.

1585. Taylor, Beverly. "The Medieval Cleopatra: The Classical and Medieval Tradition of Chaucer's *Legend of Cleopatra*." *JMRS* 7 (1977): 249–69.

1586. Warburton, Rachel. "Reading Rape in Chaucer; *or* Are Cecily, Lucretia, and Philomela Good Women?" In *Diversifying the Discourse: The Florence Howe Award for Outstanding Feminist Scholarship, 1990–2004*, edited by Mihoko Suzuki and Roseanna Dufault. New York: MLA, 2006. 270–87.

See also nos. 286, 1494.

Short Poems

1587. Boffey, Julia. "The Reputation and Circulation of Chaucer's Lyrics in the Fifteenth Century." *ChauR* 28 (1993): 23–40.

1588. Davenport, W. A. "Ballades, French and English, and Chaucer's 'Scarcity' of Rhyme." *Parergon* 18.1 (2000): 181–201.

1589. Gray, Douglas. "Middle English Courtly Lyrics: Chaucer to Henry VIII." In *A Companion to the Middle English Lyric*, edited by Thomas G. Duncan. Rochester, NY: Brewer, 2005. 120-49.

1590. Lampe, David. "The Courtly Rhetoric of Chaucer's Advisory." *RMS* 9 (1983): 70–83.

1591. Lenaghan, R. T. "Chaucer's Circle of Gentlemen and Clerks." *ChauR* 18 (1983): 155–60.

1592. Robbins, Rossell Hope. "Chaucer and the Lyric Tradition." *PoeticaT* 15–16 (1983): 107-27.

1593. —. "The Lyrics." In Rowland, no. 115, 380–402.

1594. Ruud, Jay. *"Many a Song and Many a Leccherous Lay": Tradition and Individuality in Chaucer's Lyric Poetry.* New York: Garland, 1992.

1595. Stephens, John."The Uses of Personae and the Art of Obliqueness in Some Chaucer Lyrics." Part I *ChauR* 21 (1987): 360-73; Part II *ChauR* 21 (1987): 459–68; Part III *ChauR* 22 (1987): 41–52.

1596. Wimsatt, James I. *Chaucer and the Poems of "Ch" in University of Pennsylvania MS French 15.* Cambridge, UK: Brewer, 1982. Rev. ed. TEAMS Middle English Texts Series. Kalamazoo: Medieval Institute Publications, Western Michigan University, 2009.

1597. ———. "Guillaume de Machaut and Chaucer's Love Lyrics." *MAE* 47 (1978): 66–87.

See also nos. 27, 67, 92, 314, 469, 1400.

SP—Prier a Nostre Dame (An ABC)

1598. Boitani, Piero. "'His Desir Wol Fle Withouten Wynges': Mary and Love in Fourteenth-Century Poetry." In *The Tragic and the Sublime in Medieval Literature.* Cambridge, UK: Cambridge UP, 1989. 177–222.

1599. Crampton, Georgia Ronan. "Chaucer's Singular Prayer." *MAE* 59 (1990): 191–213.

1600. Donavin, Georgiana. "Alphabets and Rosary Beads in Chaucer's *An ABC.*" In *Medieval Rhetoric: A Casebook,* edited by Scott D. Troyan. New York: Routledge, 2004. 25–39.

1601. Phillips, Helen. "Chaucer and Deguilleville: The *ABC* in Context." *MAE* 62 (1993): 1–19.

1602. Quinn, William A. "Chaucer's Problematic *Priere*: *An ABC* as Artifact and Critical Issue." *SAC* 23 (2001): 109–41.

1603. Thompson, John. "Chaucer's *An ABC* in and out of Context." *PoeticaT* 37 (1993): 38–48.

See also no. 421.

SP—Anelida and Arcite

1604. Edwards, A. S. G. "The Unity and Authenticity of *Anelida and Arcite.*" *SB* 41 (1988): 177–88.

1605. Favier, Dale A. "Anelida and Arcite: Anti-Feminist Allegory, Pro-Feminist Complaint." *ChauR* 26 (1991): 83–94.

1606. Norton-Smith, John. "Chaucer's *Anelida and Arcite.*" In *Medieval Studies for J. A. W. Bennett,* edited by P. L. Heyworth. Oxford: Clarendon P, 1981. 81–99.

1607. Stallcup, Stephen. "With the 'Poynte of Remembraunce': Re-Viewing the Complaint in *Anelida and Arcite.*" In *Feminea Medievalia I,* edited by Bonnie Wheeler. Cambridge: Academia P, 1993. 43–68.

1608. Wimsatt, James I. "*Anelida and Arcite*: A Narrative of Complaint and Comfort." *ChauR* 5 (1970): 1–8.

See also nos. 92, 277, 442.

SP—Complaints

1609. Askins, William R. "A Camp Wedding: The Cultural Context of Chaucer's *Brooch of Thebes.*" In *Place, Space, and Landscape in Medieval Narrative,* edited by Laura Howes. Knoxville, U of Tennessee P, 2007. 27–41.

1610. Chance, Jane. "Anti-Courtly Love in Chaucer's Complaints." *Mediaevalia* 10 (1988 for 1984): 181–97.

1611. Nolan, Charles J. "Structural Sophistication in 'The Complaint Unto Pity'," *ChauR* 13 (1979): 363–72.

1612. Patterson, Lee W. "Writing Amorous Wrongs: Chaucer and the Order of Complaint." In *The Idea of Medieval Literature,* edited by James M. Dean and Christian Zacher. Newark: U of Delaware P, 1992. 55–71.

1613. Phillips, Helen. "*The Complaint of Venus*: Chaucer and de Graunson." In *The Medieval Translator 4,* edited Roger Ellis and Ruth Evans. Binghamton, NY: Medieval & Renaissance Texts & Studies, 1994. 86–1013.

1614. Prendergast, Thomas A. "Politics, Prodigality, and the Reception of Chaucer's *Purse.*" In *Reinventing the Middle Ages and Renaissance,* edited by William F. Gentrup. Turnhout, Belgium: Brepols, 1998. 63–76.

1615. Scase, Wendy. *Literature and Complaint in England: 1272–1553.* New York: Oxford UP, 2007.

1616. Scattergood, John. "Chaucer's *Complaint of Venus* and the *Curiosite* of Graunson." *EIC* 44 (1994): 171–89.

1617. Strohm, Paul. "Saving the Appearances: Chaucer *Purse* and the Fabrication of the Lancaster Claim." In *Hochon's Arrow: The Social Imagination of Fourteenth-Century Texts.* Princeton, NJ: Princeton UP, 1992. 75–94.

1618. Takada, Yasunari. "The Brooch of Thebes and The Girdle of Venus: Courtly Love in an Oppositional Perspective." *PoeticaT* 29-30 (1989): 17-38.

1619. Yeager, R. F. "'Saving the Appearances' II: Another Look as Chaucer's *Complaint ot His Empty Purse.*" In *"Seyd in Forme and Reverence": Essays on Chaucer and Chaucerians,* edited by T. L. Burton and John F. Plummer. Provo: UT: Chaucer Studio, 2005. 151–64.

1620. ———. "Chaucer's 'To His Purse': Begging or Begging Off?" *Viator* 36 (2005): 373–414.

See also 398, 623.

SP—To Rosemounde

1621. Fichte, Joerg O. "*Womanly Noblesse* and "*To Rosemounde*: Point and Counterpoint of Chaucerian Love Lyrics." *SAC, Proceedings* 1 (1984): 181–94.

1622. Stemmler, Theo. "Chaucer Ballade *To Rosemounde*—A Parody?" In *Literature and Religion in the Later Middle Ages,* edited by Richard G. Newhauser and John A. Alford. Binghamton: NY: Medieval & Renaissance Texts & Studies, 1995. 11–23.

1623. Vasta, Edward. "*To Rosemounde*: Chaucer's 'Gentil' Dramatic Monologue." In *Chaucerian Problems and Perspectives*, edited by Edward Vasta and Zacharias P. Thundy. Notre Dame, IN: U of Notre Dame P, 1979. 97–113.

SP—Boethian Balades

1624. Allen, Valerie. "The 'Firste Stok' in Chaucer's *Gentilesse*: Barking Up the Right Tree." *RES* 40 (1989): 531–37.
1625. Chance, Jane. "Chaucerian Irony in the Boethian Short Poems: The Dramatic Tension between Classical and Christian." *ChauR* 20 (1986): 235–45.
1626. Galloway, Andrew. "Chaucer's *Former Age* and the Fourteenth-Century Anthropology of Craft: The Social Logic of a Premodernist Lyric." *ELH* 63 (1996): 535–53.
1627. Gwiazda, Piotr. "Reading the Commonplace: Boethius, Chaucer, and the Myth of the Golden Age." *CarmP* 11 (2002): 75–91.
1628. Hill, Thomas D. "Adam, 'The First Stocke,' and the Political Context of Chaucer's *Gentilesse*." In *"Seyd in Forme and Reverence": Essays on Chaucer and Chaucerians*, edited by T. L. Burton and John F. Plummer. Provo, UT: Chaucer Studio, 2005. 145–50.
1629. Norton-Smith, John. "Textual Tradition, Monarchy, and Chaucer's *Lak of Steadfastnesse*." *RMS* 8 (1982): 3–10.
1630. Purdon, Liam. "Chaucer's *Lak of Stedfastnesse*: A Revalorization of the Word." In *Sign, Sentence, Discourse: Language in Medieval Thought and Literature*, edited by Julian N. Wasserman and Lois Roney. Syracuse: Syracuse UP, 1989. 144–52.
1631. Scattergood, John. "Social and Political Issues in Chaucer: An Approach to *Lak of Steadfastnesse*." *ChauR* 21 (1987): 469–75.
1632. Scattergood, V. J. "Chaucer's Curial Satire: the *Balade de bon Conseyl*." In *Reading the Past: Essays on Medieval and Renaissance Literature*. Dublin: Four Courts, 1996. 199–214.
1633. Schmidt, A. V. C. "Chaucer and the Golden Age." *EIC* 26 (1976): 99–115.
1634. Strohm, Paul. "The Textual Environment of Chaucer's *Lak of Steadfastnesse*." In *The Idea of Medieval Literature*, edited by James M. Dean and Christian Zacher. Newark; U of Delaware P, 1992, 129–48.
1635. Wong, Jennifer. "Chaucer's 'Boethian' Lyrics." *CarmP* 11 (2002): 93–116.

See also nos. 27, 497.

SP—Verse Epistles

1636. Besserman, Lawrence. "Chaucer's Envoy to Bukton and 'Truth' in Biblical Interpretation: Some Medieval and Modern Contexts." *NLH* 22 (1991): 177–97.
1637. Burnley, David. "Scogan, Shirley's Reputation, and Chaucerian Occasional Verse." In *Chaucer in Perspective*, edited by Geoffrey Lester. Sheffield, UK: Sheffield Academic P, 1999. 28–46.
1638. Chance, Jane. "Chaucerian Irony in the Verse Epistles: 'Wordes unto Adam,' 'Lenvoy a Scogan,' and 'Lenvoy a Bukton'." *PLL* 21 (1985): 115–28.
1639. David, Alfred. "Chaucer's Good Counsel to Scogan." *ChauR* 3 (1969): 265–74.
1640. Epstein, Robert. "Chaucer's Scogan and Scogan's Chaucer." *SP* 96 (1999): 1–21.
1641. Horvath, Richard P. "Chaucer's Epistolary Poetic: The Envoys to Bukton and Scogan." *Chaucer Review* 37 (2002): 173–82.
1642. Lenaghan, R. T. "Chaucer's *Envoy to Scogan*: The Uses of Literary Convention." *ChauR* 10 (1975): 46–61.
1643. Mize, Britt. "Adam, and Chaucer's Words unto Him." *ChauR* 35 (2001): 351–77.
1644. Ruud, Jay. "Chaucer and Nominalism: *The Envoy to Bukton*." *Medieavalia* 10 (1988 for 1984): 199–212.
1645. Scattergood, John. "Old Age, Love, and Friendship in Chaucer's Envoy to Scogan." *NMS* 35 (1991): 92–101.

Romaunt of the Rose

1646. Blodgett, James E. "Some Printer's Copy for William Thynne's 1532 Edition of Chaucer." *The Library* 6th ser. 1 (1979): 97–113.
1647. Eckhardt, Caroline D. "The Art of Translation in *The Romaunt of thre Rose*." *SAC* 6 (1984): 41–63.
1648. Horobin, Simon. "A New Fragment of the *Romaunt of the Rose*." *SAC* 28 (2006): 205–15.
1649. Sánchez-Marti, Jordi. "Chaucer's 'Makyng' of the Romaunt of the Rose." *Journal of English Studies* 3 (2001–02): 217–36.
1650. Sutherland, Ronald, ed. *The Romaunt of the Rose and Le Roman de la Rose*. Berkeley: U of California P, 1968.

See also nos. 62, 93.

Boece

1651. Aertsen, Henk. "Chaucer's Boece: A Syntactic and Lexical Analysis." In *History of Englishes: New Methods and Interpretations in Historical Linguistics*, edited by Matti Rissanen and others. New York: Gruyter, 1992. 671–87.
1652. Eckhardt, Caroline D. "The Medieval *Prosimetrum* Genre (from Boethius to *Boece*)." *Genre* 16 (1983): 21–38.
1653. Johnson, Ian. "The Ascending Soul and the Virtue of Hope: The Spiritual Temper of Chaucer's *Boece* and *Retractions*." *ES* 88 (2007): 245–61.
1654. Kaylor, Noel Harold, Jr. *The Medieval Consolation of Philosophy: An Annotated Bibliography*. Garland Medieval Bibliographies. New York: Garland, 1992.

1655. Machan, Tim William. "The Consolation Tradition and the Text of Chaucer's *Boece*." *PBA* 91 (1997): 31–50.
1656. ———. "Scribal Role, Authorial Intention, and Chaucer's *Boece*." *ChauR* 24 (1989): 150–62.
1657. ———. *Techniques of Translation: Chaucer's Boece.* Norman, OK: Pilgrim, 1985.
1658. ———, ed., with A. J. Minnis. *Sources of the Boece.* Athens: U of Georgia P, 2005.
1659. Malaczkov, Szilvia. "Geoffrey Chaucer's Translation Stategies." *Perspectives: Studies in Translatology* 9.1 (2001): 33–44.
1660. Minnis, Alastair J. "Aspects of the French and English Traditions of the *De Consolatione Philosophiae*." In *Boethius: His Life, Thought and Influence,* edited by Margaret Gibson. Oxford: Blackwell, 1981. 312–49.
1661. ———, ed. *Chaucer's "Boece" and the Medieval Tradition of Boethius.* Cambridge, UK: Brewer, 1993.
1662. ———, ed. *The Medieval Boethius: Studies in the Vernacular Translations of "De Consolatione Philosophiae."* Cambridge, UK: Brewer, 1987.
See also no. 93.

Treatise on the Astrolabe

1663. Cole, Andrew. "Chaucer's English Lesson." *Speculum* 77 (2002): 1128–67.
1664. Eagleton, Catherine. "'Chaucer's own astrolabe': Text, Image and Object." *Studies in History and Philosophy of Science* 38 (2007): 303–26.
1665. ———. "A Previously Unnoticed Fragment of Chaucer's Treatise on the Astrolabe." *JEBS* 6 (2003): 161-73.
1666. ———, and Matthew Spencer. "Copying and Conflation in Geoffrey Chaucer's *Treatise on the Astrolabe*: A Stemmatic Analysis Using Phylogenetic Software." *Studies in History and Philosophy of Science* 37 (2006): 237–68.
1667. Hagge, John. "The First Technical Writer in English: A Challenge to the Hegemony of Chaucer." *Journal of Technical Writing and Communication* 20 (1990): 269–89.
1668. Laird, Edgar. "Astrolabes and the Construction of Time in the Late Middle Ages." *Disputatio* 2 (1997): 51–69.
1669. ———. "Chaucer and Friends: The Audience for the *Treatise on the Astrolabe*." *ChauR* 41 (2007): 439–44.
1670. Lerer, Seth. "Chaucer's Sons." *University of Toronto Quarterly* 73 (2004): 906–15.
1671. Lipson, Carol S. "Descriptions and Instructions in Medieval Times: Lessons To Be Learnt From Geoffrey Chaucer's Scientific Instruction Manual." *Journal of Technical Writing and Communication* 12 (1982): 243–56.
1672. Ovitt, George, Jr. "History, Technical Style, and Chaucer's *Treatise on the Astrolabe*." In *Creativity and the Imagination: Case Studies from the Classical Age to the Twentieth Century,* edited by Mark Amsler. Newark: U of Delaware P, 1987. 34–58.
See also nos, 63, 74, 93, 437.

Equatorie of the Planetis

1673. Arch, Jennifer. "A Case Against Chaucer's Authorship of the *Equatorie of the Planetis*." *ChauR* 40 (2005): 59–79.
1674. Benson, Larry. "Chaucer's Spelling Reconsidered." *English Manuscript Studies 1100-1700* 3 (1992): 1–28.
1675. Edwards, A. S. G., and Linne R. Mooney. "Is the *Equatorie of the Planetis* a Chaucer Holograph?" *ChauR* 26 (1991): 31–42.
1676. Krochalis, Jeanne E. "Postscript: The *Equatorie of the Planetis* as a Translator's Manuscript." *ChauR* 26 (1991): 43–47.
1677. Partridge, Stephen. "The Vocabulary of 'The Equatorie of the Planetis'." *English Manuscript Studies 1100–1700* 3 (1992): 29–37.
1678. Rand Schmidt, Kari Anne. *The Authorship of The Equatorie of the Planetis.* Chaucer Studies, no. 19. Cambridge: Brewer, 1993.
1679. Robinson, Pamela. "Geoffrey Chaucer and the Equatorie of the Planetis: The State of the Problem." *ChauR* 26 (1991): 17–30.
See also nos. 70, 93.

Chaucer's Canon, Chronology, and Apocryphal Works

1680. Bonner, Frances W. "The Genesis of the Chaucer Apocrypha." *SP* 48 (1951): 461–81.
1681. Brusendorff, Aage. *The Chaucer Tradition.* London: Oxford UP, 1925.
1682. Costomiris, Robert. "The Yoke of Canon: Chaucerian Aspects of *The Plowman's Tale*." *PQ* 71 (1992): 185–98.
1683. Forni, Kathleen. *The Chaucerian Apocrypha: A Counterfeit Canon.* Gainesville: UP of Florida, 2001.
1684. Lynch, Kathryn L. "Dating Chaucer." *ChauR* 42 (2007): 1–22.
1685. McCarl, Mary Rhinelander, ed. *The Plowman's Tale: The c. 1532 and 1606 Editions of a Spurious Canterbury Tale.* New York: Garland, 1997.
1686. Shippey, T. A. "The Tale of Gamelyn: Class Warfare and the Embarrassments of Genre." In *The Spirit of Medieval Popular Romance,* edited by Ad Putter and Jane Gilbert. New York: Longman, 2000. 78–96.
1687. Skeat, Walter W. *The Chaucerian Canon with a Discussion of the Works Associated with the Name of Geoffrey Chaucer.* Oxford: Oxford UP, 1900.
See also nos. 39 (volume 7), 1230.

Classifications

Electronic Resources 1–3
Manuscript Facsimiles—Compilations and Miscellanies 4–12
Manuscript Facsimiles— *Canterbury Tales* 13–18
Manuscript Facsimiles—*Troylus and Criseyde* 19–21
Manuscript Facsimiles—Other Works 22–23
Manuscripts and Textual Studies 24–35
Editions—Complete 36–40
Editions—*Canterbury Tales* and Individual Tales 41–56
Editions—*Troylus and Criseyde* 57–59
Editions—Other Works 60–70
Modern English Translations 71–79
Bibliographies—Comprehensive 80–86
Bibliographies—Individual Works 87–93
Dictionaries and Reference 94–104
Handbooks and Introductions 105–118
Reception History 119–131
Early Print Culture 132–141
Biography and Biographical Contexts 142–154
Language—General 155–170
Language—Lexicon and Register 171–186
Style, Rhetoric, and Rhetorical Tradition 187–203
The Vernacular, Translation, and Textuality 204–210
Prosody and Versification 211–227
Prose 228–231
Sources and Analogues—General 232–239
Sources and Analogues—Editions 240–276
Classical and Continental Relations 277–314
English Relations, Contemporary and Later 315–332
Idea of the Author 333–344
Audience 345–354
Orality and Performance 355–365
Poetics and Narrative Technique 366–382
Philosophy 383–399
Religion, Ethics, and the Bible 400–425a
Science and Pseudoscience 426–439
Psychology and Subjectivity 439a–442
Sex, Love, and Marriage 443–460
Sexualities 461–467
Women 468–479
Men 480–485
Honor, Chivalry, and Pity 486–499
Social Classes and the City 500–516
The Court and Patronage 517–524
Bureaucracy and the Law 525–533
Nation and Otherness 534–547
Symbol and Allegory 548–558
Spaces, Landscapes, and Ecology 559–567
The Arts, Illustrations, and Portraits of Chaucer 568–577
Canterbury Tales—General 578–594
CT—Evolution and Order of *Canterbury Tales* 595–606
CT—Structure and Frame 607–617
CT—Genres 618–638
CT—Style and Rhetoric 639–643
CT—Characterization 644–652
CT—Women, Men, and Marriage 653–668
CT—Voice and the Narrator 669–678
CT—Various Themes 679–693
CT—The Pilgrimage Motif 694–704
CT—Names and Number of Pilgrims; Pilgrims Without Tales 705–714
CT—The Host 715–725
CT—Part 1 726–728
CT1—The General Prologue 729–746
CT1—The Knight and His Tale 747–780
CT1—The Miller and His Tale 781–801
CT1—The Reeve and His Tale 802–812
CT1—The Cook and His Tale 813–818
CT—Part 2
CT2—The Man of Law and His Tale 819–845
CT—Part 3 846–850
CT3—The Wife of Bath and Her Tale 851–890
CT3—The Friar and His Tale 891–900
CT3—The Summoner and His Tale 901–914
CT—Part 4 915–917
CT4—The Clerk and His Tale 918–941
CT4—The Merchant and His Tale 942–961
CT—Part 5 962–964
CT5—The Squire and His Tale 965–976
CT5—The Franklin and His Tale 977–1001
CT—Part 6 1002–1007
CT6—The Physician and His Tale 1008–1021
CT6—The Pardoner and His Tale 1022–1058
CT—Part 7 1059–1060
CT7—The Shipman and His Tale 1061–1073
CT7—The Prioress and Her Tale 1074–1097
CT7—The Tale of Sir Thopas 1098–1109
CT7—The Tale of Melibee 1110–1123
CT7—The Monk and His Tale 1124–1134
CT7—The Nun's Priest and His Tale 1135–1152
CT—Part 8 1153–1159
CT8—The Second Nun and Her Tale 1160–1170
CT8—The Canon's Yeoman and His Tale 1171–1182
CT—Part 9 1183–1184
CT9—The Manciple and His Tale 1185–1198
CT—Part 10 1199–1201
CT10—The Parson and His Tale 1202–1215
CT10—Chaucer's Retraction 1216–1223

Troylus and Criseyde—General Criticism 1224–1233
TC—Literary Relations 1234–1248
TC—Genres and Structure 1249–1263
TC—Style and Rhetoric 1264–1282
TC—Narrator and Narrative Technique 1283–1292
TC—Philosophy and Theme 1293–1318
TC—Sex, Love, and Marriage 1319–1332
CT—Characterization and Minor Characters 1333–1344
TC—Troylus 1345–1356
TC—Criseyde 1357–1374
TC—Pandarus 1375–1382
TC—The Ending 1383–1391
Dream Visions 1392–1405

Book of the Duchess 1406–1453

Parliament of Fowls 1454–1491

House of Fame 1492–1528

Legend of Good Women 1529–1552
LGW—The Prologue 1553–1566
LGW—The Legends 1567–1586

Short Poems 1587–1597
SP—Prier a Nostre Dame (An ABC) 1598–1603
SP—Anelida and Arcite 1604–1608
SP—Complaints 1609–1620
SP—To Rosemounde 1621–1623
SP—Boethian Balades 1624–1635
SP—Verse Epistles 1636–1645

Romaunt of the Rose 1646–1650

Boece 1651–1662

Treatise on the Astrolabe 1663–1672

Equatorie of the Planetis 1673–1679

Chaucer's Canon, Chronology, and Apocryphal Works 1680–1687

Abbreviations

Chaucer's Works

ABC	*An ABC or Prier a Nostre Dame*
Adam	*Adam Scriveyn*
Anel	*Anelida and Arcite*
Astr	*Treatise on the Astrolabe*
Bal Compl	*A Balade of Complaint*
BD	*Book of the Duchess*
Bo	*Boece*
Buk	*Lenvoy de Chaucer a Bukton*
CkT, CkP	*Cook's Tale, Cook's Prologue*
ClT, ClP	*Clerk's Tale, Clerk's Prologue*
Compl d'Am	*Complaynt d'Amours*
CT	*Canterbury Tales*
CYT, CYP	*Canon's Yeoman's Tale, Canon's Yeoman's Prologue*
Equat	*Equatorie of the Planetis*
For	*Fortune*
Form Age	*The Former Age*
FranT, FranP	*Franklin's Tale, Franklin's Prologue*
FrT, FrP	*Friar's Tale, Friar's Prologue*
Gent	*Gentilesse*
GP	*General Prologue to Canterbury Tales*
HF	*House of Fame*
KnT, KnP	*Knight's Tale, Knight's Prologue*
Lady	*A Complaint to His Lady* or *A Balade of Pity*
LGW, LGWP	*Legend of Good Women, Prologue to Legend of Good Women*
ManT, ManP	*Manciple's Tale, Manciple's Prologue*
Mars	*Complaint of Mars*
Mel, MelP	*Tale of Melibee, Prologue to Tale of Melibee*
MercB	*Merciles Beaute*
MerT, MerP	*Merchant's Tale, Merchant's Prologue*
MilT, MilP	*Miller's Tale, Miller's Prologue*
MkT, MkP	*Monk's Tale, Monk's Prologue*
MLT, MLP	*Man of Law's Tale, Man of Law's Prologue*
NPT, NPP	*Nun's Priest's Tale, Nun's Priest's Prologue*
PardT, PardP	*Pardoner's Tale, Pardoner's Prologue*
ParsT, ParsP	*Parson's Tale, Parson's Prologue*
PF	*Parliament of Fowls*
PhyT	*Physician's Tale*
Pity	*Complaint unto Pity*
Prov	*Proverbs*
PrT, PrP	*Prioress's Tale, Prioress's Prologue*
Purse	*Complaint of Chaucer to His Purse*
Ret	*Chaucer's Retraction*
Rom	*Romaunt of the Rose*
Ros	*To Rosemounde*
RvT, RvP	*Reeve's Tale, Reeve's Prologue*
Scog	*Lenvoy de Chaucer a Scogan*
ShT	*Shipman's Tale*
SNT, SNP	*Second Nun's Tale, Second Nun's Prologue*
SqT, SqP	*Squire's Tale, Squire's Prologue*
Sted	*Lack of Steadfastnesse*
SumT, SumP	*Summoner's Tale, Summoner's Prologue*
TC	*Troilus and Criseyde*
Th, ThP	*Tale of Sir Thopas, Prologue to the Tale of Sir Thopas*
Truth	*Truth or Balade de Bon Conseil*
Ven	*Complaint of Venus*
WBT, WBP	*Wife of Bath's Tale, Wife of Bath's Prologue*
Wom Nob	*Womanly Noblesse*
Wom Unc	*Against Women Unconstant*

Miscellaneous

EETS	Early English Text Society
MED	*Middle English Dictionary.* Ed. Hans Kurath and others. Ann Arbor: U of Michigan P, 1952–2001.
MR	Manly, John M., and Edith Rickert, eds. *The Text of the Canterbury Tales, Studied on the Basis of All Known Manuscripts.* 8 vols. Chicago: U of Chicago P, 1940.
OED	*Oxford English Dictionary.* Ed. J. A. Simpson and E. S. C. Weiner. 2d ed. Oxford: Clarendon, 1989.
PL	Patrologia Latina. *Patrologiae cursus completus, sive biblioteca universalis, integra, uniformis, commoda, oeconomica, omnium SS. Patrum, doctorum scriptorumque ecclesiasticorum . . . .:* [Series Latina . . . .]. Ed. J-P Migne. 221 vols. Paris: Migne, 1844-91.
PP	Langland, William. *Piers Plowman: A Parallel-Text Edition of the A, B, C, and Z Versions.* Volume I: Text. Ed. A. V. C. Schmidt. London: Longman, 1995.
RR	*Roman de la Rose*
SATF	*Société des Anciens Textes Française*

Journals

ABR	*American Benedictine Review*
AnM	*Annuale Medievale*
ANQ	*American Notes and Queries*
Archiv	*Archiv für das Studium der Neueren Sprachen und Literaturen*
BAM	*Bulletin des Anglicistes Médiévistes*
BJRL	*Bulletin of the John Rylands University Library of Manchester*
CarmP	*Carmina Philosophiae*
ChauR	*Chaucer Review*
ChauY	*Chaucer Yearbook*
C&L	*Christianity and Literature*
CL	*Comparative Literature*
CollL	*College Literature*
ComH	*Computers and the Humanities*
DQR	*Dutch Quarterly Review*
DR	*Dalhousie Review*
E&S	*Essays and Studies*
EIC	*Essays in Criticism*
ELH	*ELH: English Literary History*
EMSt	*Essays in Medieval Studies*
ES	*English Studies*
ESA	*English Studies in Africa*
ESC	*English Studies in Canada*
FCS	*Fifteenth-Century Studies*
FMLS	*Forum for Modern Language Study*
HLQ	*Huntington Library Quarterly*
InG	*In Geardagum*
JEBS	*Journal of the Early Book Society*
JEGP	*Journal of English and Germanic Philology*
JEP	*Journal of Evolutionary Psychology*
JMEMSt	*Journal of Medieval and Early Modern Studies*
JMRS	*Journal of Medieval and Renaissance Studies*
JNT	*Journal of Narrative Technique*
JRMMRA	*Journal of the Rocky Mountain Medieval and Renaissance Association*
L&H	*Literature and History*
L&P	*Literature and Psychology*
Lang&S	*Language & Style*
LeedsSE	*Leeds Studies in English*
LittR	*Literary Review (Madison, NJ)*
M&H	*Medievalia et Humanistica*
MAE	*Medium Aevum*
MedPers	*Medieval Perspectives*
MLQ	*Modern Language Quarterly*
MLR	*Modern Language Review*
MLS	*Modern Language Studies*
MP	*Modern Philology*
MS	*Mediaeval Studies*
N&Q	*Notes and Queries*
Neophil	*Neophilologica*
NFS	*Nottingham French Studies*
NLH	*New Literary History*
NM	*Neuphilologische Mitteilungen*
NML	*New Medieval Literatures*
PBA	*Proceedings of the British Academy*
PCP	*Pacific Coast Philology*
PLL	*Papers on Language and Literature*
PMAM	*Publications of the Medieval Association of the Midwest*
PMLA	*PMLA: Publications of the Modern Language Association*
PoeticaT	*Poetica: An International Journal of Linguistic Literary Study* (Tokyo)
PQ	*Philological Quarterly*
RCEI	*Revista Canaria de Estudios Ingleses*
RES	*Review of English Studies*
RMS	*Reading Medieval Studies*
RUO	*Revue de l'Université d'Ottawa*
RUS	*Rice University Studies*
SAC	*Studies in the Age of Chaucer*
SAQ	*South Atlantic Quarterly*
SB	*Studies in Bibliography*
SCRev	*South Central Review*
SEL	*Studies in English Literature, 1500–1900*
SELIM	*SELIM: Journal of the Spanish Society for Mediaeval English Language and Literature*
SiM	*Studies in Medievalism*
SIMELL	*Studies in Medieval English Language and Literature*
SMC	*Studies in Medieval Culture*
SN	*Studia Neophilologica*
SP	*Studies in Philology*
SSF	*Studies in Short Fiction*
TSL	*Tennessee Studies in Literature*
TSLL	*Texas Studies in Language and Literature*
UTQ	*University of Toronto Quarterly*
YES	*Yearbook of English Studies*
YLS	*Yearbook of Langland Studies*
WS	*Women's Studies*

Index of Authors in the Bibliography

Abraham, David H., 1061
Acker, Paul, 426
Ackroyd, Peter, 142
Adams, Robert, 1062, 1074
Adamson, Jane, 1249
Aers, David, 400–02, 1110, 1319, 1357
Aertsen, Henk, 1651
Aguirre Daban, Manuel, 851
Akbari, Suzanne Conklin, 548
Albertano of Brescia, 240
Alderson, William L., 119
Allen, Elizabeth, 618
Allen, Judson Boyce, 607
Allen, Mark, 81, 694, 715, 1185
Allen, Peter L., 1529
Allen, Valerie, 486, 1406, 1624
Allman, W. W., 653
Aloni, Gila, 1567–68
Ambrisco, Alan S., 965
Amoils, E. R., 1002
Amtower, Laurel, 345, 747, 1358, 1492
Anderson, David, 1234
Anderson, J. J., 1407
Andersson, Theodore, 232
Andreas, James R., 355, 619
Andretta, Helen Ruth, 1294
Andrew, Malcolm, 45, 94, 729
An Sonjae (Brother Anthony), 1293
apRoberts, Robert P., 246, 1295, 1359
Arch, Jennifer, 1673
Archibald, Elizabeth, 819
Arnovick, Leslie K., 977, 1493
Arthur, Ross G., 802
Ashton, Gail, 578, 620
Askins, William R., 1609
Astell, Ann W., 403, 517, 608, 820, 1059
Axton, Richard, 356

Badendyck, J. Lawrence, 730
Bahr, Arthur W., 1408
Baird-Lange, Lorrayne Y., 82–3
Baker, Donald C., 13, 47, 54, 654
Baldwin, Ralph, 609
Bale, Anthony, 1075
Barney, Stephen A., 24, 57, 1345
Barr, Helen, 315
Barrington, Candace, 120
Baswell, Christopher [C.], 1135, 1333, 1494
Battles, Dominique, 277, 978
Battles, Paul, 278
Bauer, Kate, 1076
Baum, Paull F., 171, 211
Beadle, Richard, 5–6, 11, 20
Behrman, Mary, 1360
Beichner, Paul E., 1124
Beidler, Peter G., 90, 480, 852
Bennett, J. A. W., 143, 1454, 1495
Benson, C. David, 404–5, 595, 639–40, 1224, 1235
Benson, Donald R., 942
Benson, Larry D., 36, 95, 172, 187, 232, 487, 595, 1455, 1674
Benson, Robert G., 188
Bergen, Brooke, 748
Berlin, Gail Ivy, 891
Berry, Craig A., 966
Bertolet, Craig E., 813, 1456
Bessent, Benjamin R., 1249a
Besserman, Lawrence, 96, 406, 1077, 1636
Bestul, Thomas H., 821, 1202
Biebel, Elizabeth M., 90, 679
Birney, Earle, 189
Biscoglio, Frances Minetti, 655
Bishop, Ian, 1022, 1225
Bishop, Laura M., 132
Bishop, Louise, 1171
Black, Nancy B., 822
Blake, Kathleen, 749
Blake, N. F., 25, 41, 596
Blamires, Alcuin, 383, 468, 500, 621, 853–4, 1553
Blandeau, Agnès, 680
Bleeth, Kenneth, 979
Bloch, R. Howard, 1008
Block, Edward A., 823
Blodgett, E. D., 681
Blodgett, James E., 1646
Bloomfield, Morton W., 824, 1136, 1296
Blum, Martin, 781
Boccaccio, Giovanni, 241–47
Bode, Cristoph, 388
Boenig, Robert, 42, 407
Børch, Marianne, 1098, 1160
Boethius, 248
Boffey, Julia, 12, 1530, 1587
Boitani, Piero, 105, 279, 1236, 1496, 1598
Bolton, W. F., 825
Bonner, Frances W., 1680
Bordalejo, Barbara, 15
Bornstein, Diane, 228
Boswell, Jackson Campbell, 121
Bowden, Betsy, 357
Bowden, Muriel, 731
Bowers, Bege K., 81
Bowers, John M., 316, 518, 534, 705, 750, 901
Bowker, Alvin W., 782
Boyd, Beverly, 53, 408
Boyd, David Lorenzo, 783, 1457
Bradbury, Nancy Mason, 236, 1264
Braddy, Haldeen, 967, 1458
Braswell, Mary Flowers, 525, 1497
Brenner, Gerry, 1250
Brewer, Derek S., 40, 60, 106, 122, 144, 427, 443, 488, 501, 519, 1334
Bridges, Margaret, 1459
Briggs, Frederick M., 784
Brody, Saul Nathaniel, 212, 1137
Broes, Arthur T., 1138
Bronfman, Judith, 918
Bronson, Larry, 1335
Brosamer, Matthew, 682
Brosnahan, Leger, 706
Broughton, Laurel, 751
Brown, Carole Koepke, 980
Brown, Emerson, Jr., 752, 943, 1009, 1203, 1460
Brown, Murray, 280
Brown, Peter, 107, 428, 579–80, 803, 1392
Brown, Sarah Annes, 1569
Brown, William H., 1010
Bruhn, Mark J., 1172
Brusendorff, Aage, 1681
Bryan, W. F., 233
Bryant, Brantley L., 892
Buckmaster, Dale, 1063
Buckmaster, Elizabeth, 1063
Bugge, John, 944
Bullón-Fernández, María, 785
Burger, Glenn, 461–62, 1023
Burke, John J., 552
Burlin, Robert B., 366
Burnley, John David, 155–56, 173, 489, 945, 1637
Burrow, J. A., 317, 669, 1186, 1409
Burton, T. L., 89
Butcher, Andrew, 580
Butterfield, Ardis, 281, 502, 1410–11

Cable, Thomas, 213
Cadden, Joan, 1461
Caecilius Balbus, 249
Cahn, Kenneth S., 946
Caie, Graham D., 22, 826
Calabrese, Michael A., 282, 981, 1024
Calin, William, 283
Camargo, Martin, 190, 1139, 1251, 1375
Campbell, Emma, 919
Campbell, Jackson J., 1173
Canfield, J. Douglas, 683
Canitz, A. E. Christa, 1531
Cannon, Christopher, 145, 174, 191, 444

Carey, David H., 99
Carlson, David, 526
Carruthers, Leo, 716
Carruthers, Mary J., 855, 920, 982, 1346, 1412, 1498
Carter, Susan, 880
Carton, Evan, 1376
Cartwright, John H., 429
Cato, 250
Chance, Jane, 549, 1610, 1625, 1638
Charles, Casey, 856
Cherniss, Michael D., 915, 1413, 1462
Chickering, Howell, 192, 921, 1264a
Chisnell, Robert E., 229
Christmas, Peter, 1320
Ciccone, Nancy, 1347
Cicero, 251
Clark, Susan. L., 827, 1265
Claudian, 252
Clogan, Paul M., 828, 1237
Clopper, Lawrence, 753, 1297
Coghill, Nevill, 71, 490
Cole, Andrew, 1663
Coleman, Janet, 346
Coleman, Joyce, 358, 1554
Collette, Carolyn P., 439a, 468a, 535, 1078, 1161, 1532
Colmer, Dorothy, 857
Condren, Edward I., 610, 1025, 1393, 1414
Conley, John, 1099
Connolly, Thomas, 1162
Cooney, Helen, 445, 732, 754, 1463
Cooper, Geoffrey, 786
Cooper, Helen, 123, 284, 581, 611, 733, 858
Copeland, Rita, 193, 204
Correale, Robert M., 234
Corsa, Helen Storm, 52
Costigan, Edward, 684
Costomiris, Robert, 1682
Cowen, Janet M., 61, 1533
Cowgill, Bruce Kent, 755, 1153, 1464
Cox, Catherine S., 469, 536, 902
Crafton, John Micheal, 1011
Crampton, Georgia Ronan, 1599
Crane, Susan, 520, 622, 1415
Craun, Edwin D., 1186a
Crawford, William R., 84
Crépin, André, 285
Crocker, Holly A., 481, 804
Crook, Eugene J., 73
Crow, Martin M., 146
Cunningham, J. V., 734
Curry, Walter C., 430

D'Agata D'Ottavi, Stephania, 1394
Dahlberg, Charles, 62, 1321
Dahood, Roger, 1079
Dane, Joseph A., 133–34, 968, 1499
Dante Alighieri, 253
Dauby, Hélène, 214
Davenport, Tony, 367
Davenport, W. A., 318, 623, 1588
David, Alfred, 67, 409, 1361, 1639
Davidoff, Judith M., 368
Davis, Adam Brooke, 1322
Davis, Isabel, 482
Davis, Kathleen, 1465
Davis, Norman, 97, 157
Davis, R. Evan, 568
Dean, James, 550, 612, 1187, 1199, 1416, 1466
Delany, Sheila, 537, 829, 859–60, 1012, 1080, 1266, 1500, 1534
Delasanta, Rodney, 685, 922, 1026, 1125, 1204
De Looze, Lawrence, 333
Dempsey, James, 72
Dempster, Germaine, 233, 597
Denny-Brown, Andrea, 923
Denomy, Alexander J., 446
Desmond, Marilynn, 286, 861
DeVries, David N., 503
De Weever, Jacqueline, 98, 175
Diamond, Arlyn, 236, 470
Dickson, Lynne, 862
Diekstra, Fran, 235
Dillon, Janette, 108, 1027
Dilorenzo, Raymond D., 1417
DiMarco, Vincent J., 535
Dinshaw, Carolyn, 334, 463, 471, 538, 1028
Dobbs, Elizabeth, 527
Dobyns, Ann, 1111
Donaldson, E. Talbot, 319, 670, 787
Donaldson, Kara Virginia, 788
Donavin, Georgiana, 1600
Donnelly, Colleen, 656, 1418
Doob, Penelope, 1501
Dor, Juliette, 863
Douglass, Rebecca M., 559
Dove, Mary, 947
Dower, Paul, 1069
Doyle, A. I., 13, 26
Doyle, Kara A., 1570
Dubbs, Kathleen, 1467
Duffell, Martin J., 215
Dugas, Don-John, 830
Duncan, Edgar H., 1174
Dunleavy, Gareth W., 384
Dyas, Dee, 695

Eade, John. C., 347
Eadie, John, 1555
Eagleton, Catherine, 1664–66
Eaton, R. D., 504, 983, 1081
Eberle, Patricia J., 735
Ecker, Ronald L., 73
Eckhardt, Caroline D., 87, 707, 1647, 1652
Edden, Valerie, 924
Edwards, A. S. G., 7, 12, 135, 644, 831, 948, 1604, 1675
Edwards, Robert R., 287, 657, 949, 1395, 1419, 1535
Eisner, Sigmund, 63, 696
Eldredge, Laurence, 1298, 1468
Eliason, Norman, 158, 708
Elliot, R. W. V., 159
Ellis, Deborah, 805
Ellis, Steve, 109, 124, 1420
Ellman, Maud, 1421
Emmerson, Richard K., 551
Engelhardt, George J., 645
Epstein, Robert, 756, 1640
Erzgraber, Willi, 1502
Evans, Ruth, 1503

Farrell, Thomas J., 789, 925, 1383
Favier, Dale A., 1605
Federico, Sylvia, 1238
Fehrman, Craig T., 410
Ferris, Sumner, 1082
Ferster, Judith, 369, 1112, 1422
Fichte, Joerg O., 370, 686, 757, 1621
Field, Rosalind, 950
Filax, Elaine, 1163
Finke, Laurie A., 1205
Finlayson, John, 624, 758, 903, 926, 1140, 1206
Finley, William K., 569
Finnegan, Robert Emmett, 927
Finnie, Bruce W., 216
Fisher, John H., 37, 160, 194, 320–21, 385, 726, 1556
Flake, Timothy H., 984
Fleming, John V., 570, 864, 904, 1239, 1336
Fletcher, Alan J., 411, 1028a
Fletcher, Bradford Y.10
Forhan, Kate L., 1113
Forkin, Thomas Carney, 505
Forni, Kathleen, 1638
Foster, Edward E., 99, 386
Fowler, Elizabeth, 759, 760, 1029
Fradenburg, Louise. Olga Aranye, 440, 1083, 1188, 1469
Frank, Hardy Long, 1084
Frank, Robert Worth, Jr., 1085, 1536
Frantzen, Allen J., 1030, 1226, 1252
Frese, Dolores Warwick, 613
Friedman, John Block, 646, 790, 865
Froissart, Jean, 254
Fulton, Helen, 1064
Fumo, Jamie C., 1189, 1283
Furnivall, F. J. A., 598
Furrow, Melissa, 1216
Fyler, John M., 288, 412, 969, 1377

Gallacher, Patrick, 1141
Galloway, Andrew, 625, 866, 1537, 1571, 1626

Ganim, John M., 359–60, 441, 506, 761, 1065, 1267
Gasse, Rosanne, 1337
Gastle, Brian, 709
Gaylord, Alan T., 217, 717, 1100–01
Gaynor, Stephanie, 1086
Gellrich, Jesse, 205, 791
Geltner, G., 893
Geoffrey of Monmouth, 255
George, Jodi-Anne, 736
Georgianna, Linda, 697
Getty, Laura J., 1572
Giancarlo, Matthew, 1299, 1470
Gilles, Sealy, 1323
Gillespie, Alexandra, 136, 335
Gilmartin, Kristine, 928
Ginsberg, Warren, 289–90, 1190
Gittes, Katherine, 614
Gleason, Mark J., 1240
Goldstein, R. James, 687, 1348
Goodall, Peter, 89a
Goodman, Jennifer R., 962, 970, 1300
Gordon, Ida, 1227
Gottfried, Barbara, 867
Gower, John, 256
Grace, Dominick, 1114
Grady, Frank, 1191, 1301, 1504
Gray, Douglas, 97, 100, 195, 491, 1589
Green, D. H., 348
Green, Richard Firth, 472, 521, 528, 1031–32
Greenberg, Nina Manasan, 985
Greenfield, Stanley B., 1338
Greentree, Rosemary, 89
Grennen, Joseph E., 806, 1154, 1302, 1505
Griffith, Dudley David, 85
Griffiths, Jeremy, 20
Grigsby, Bryon Lee, 1033
Gross, Gregory W., 1034
Groves, Peter, 218
Grudin, Michaela Paasche, 361, 387, 929
Gruenler, Curtis, 1060
Guerin, Dorothy, 492
Guido de Columnis, 257
Guillaume de Lorris, 258
Gunther, R. T., 74
Gwiazda, Piotr, 1627

Haahr, Joan G., 658, 1362
Haas, Renate, 1573
Hagedorn, Suzanne C., 291
Hagen, Susan K., 868
Hagge, John, 1667
Hahn, Thomas, 894, 1087
Haines, R. Michael, 1003
Hall, Ann C., 1268
Haller, Robert S., 971
Hallissy, Margaret, 473
Halverson, John, 1035
Hamaguchi, Keiko, 762
Hamel, Mary, 234, 1102
Hammond, Eleanor Prescott, 86
Hanawalt, Barbara A., 718
Hanks, D. Thomas, Jr., 653, 905
Hanly, Michael G., 1241
Hanna, Ralph, III, 16, 27–29, 336, 869
Hanning, Robert W., 371, 763, 846, 1423
Hanrahan, Michael, 1557
Hansen, Elaine Tuttle, 474, 1538–39
Harbert, Bruce, 292
Harding, Wendy, 493, 671, 930–31
Hardman, Phillipa, 916, 1253, 1424
Harley, Marta Powell, 1013
Harvey, Elizabeth D., 1540
Harwood, Britton J., 710, 1175, 1192, 1506
Haselmayer, L. A., 906, 1037
Hasenfrantz, Robert, 907
Haskell, Ann, 413, 560
Hass, Robin R., 196
Havely, Nicholas.R., 64, 69, 259, 1507
Hazell, Dinah, 764
Heffernan, Carol Falvo, 539, 561, 792, 951, 972
Heinrichs, Katherine, 1396
Hellinga, Lotte, 137
Helterman, Jeffrey, 765, 1324
Henderson, Arnold C., 119
Heng, Geraldine, 540
Heninger, S. K., 932
Hermann, John P., 552, 1269
Herzman, Ronald B., 551
Hewitt, Kathleen, 1471
Hieatt, A. Kent, 322
Hieatt, Constance B., 688
Higgs, Elton D., 737
Higl, Andrew, 138
Hill, John M., 414, 1325, 1425
Hill, T. E., 1303
Hill, Thomas D., 1628
Hines, John, 626
Hirsh, John C., 582, 1014, 1164
Hodges, Laura, 738–39
Hoerner, Fred, 1036
Hoffman, Arthur, 740
Hoffman, Richard L., 293, 1115
Holley, Linda Tarte, 431, 1211
Holton, Sylvia Wallace, 121
Hornsby, Joseph Allen., 147, 529
Horobin, Simon S. C. P., 161–62, 599, 807, 1648
Horvath, Richard P., 1641
Houwen, L. A. J. R., 1142
Howard, Donald R., 148, 583, 698, 1304, 1326, 1363
Howes, Laura L., 562, 1364
Hoy, Michael, 1143
Hudson, Anne, 415
Huppé, Bernard F., 553
Hussey, Maurice, 571
Hussey, S. S., 110

Innocent III, Pope, 260
Ingham, Patricia Clare, 870, 973a
Irvine, Martin, 1508

Jacobs, Kathryn, 447
Jager, Eric, 952, 1066
Jankowski, Eileen S., 1165
Jean de Meun, 258
Jefferson, Bernard L., 294
Jeffrey, David Lyle, 416, 1509
Jenson, Emily, 727, 1126
Jerome, Saint, 261
Jimura, Akiyuki, 1510
Johnson, Ian, 1653
Johnson, Lynn Staley. See Staley, Lynn.
Johnston, Andrew James, 530, 793, 1472
Jonassen, Frederick B., 699, 953, 986
Jones, E. A., 1103
Jones, George F., 794
Jones, Lindsey M., 973
Jones, Terry, 766–67
Jordan, Robert O., 372–73, 1284, 1473
Joseph, Gerhard, 1067
Jucker, Andreas H., 176
Justice, Steven, 507
Justman, Stewart, 554

Kabir, Ananya Jahanara, 908
Kaeuper, Richard W., 893
Kaminsky, Alice R., 1228
Kamowski, William, 417, 847, 974
Kane, George, 672
Kaske, R. E., 659
Kaylor, Noel Harold, 1144, 1654
Kealy, J. Kiernan, 1183
Kean, P. M., 323
Kearney, J. A., 1474
Keen, Maurice, 768
Keiper, Hugo, 388
Keiser, George, 600
Kellogg, A. L., 1037
Kellogg, Laura D., 1365
Kelly, Henry Ansgar, 418, 448–49, 541, 627, 1038, 1254, 1476
Kelley, Michael R., 1475
Kendrick, Laura, 572, 584, 1511
Kennedy, Beverly, 871
Kennedy, Kathleen E., 1117
Kennedy, Thomas C., 1167, 1512
Kensak, Michael, 1193, 1426
Kerby-Fulton, Kathryn, 419

Kerkhof, Jelle, 163
Kern, Alfred, 149
Kern-Stähler, Annette, 563
Kiernan, Kevin S., 1340
Kimmelman, Burt, 337, 1558
Kinney, Clare Regan, 1285
King, Pamela, 374
Kirk, Elizabeth, 711
Kiser, Lisa, 206, 1477, 1541
Kittredge, George Lyman, 660
Klassen, Norman., 1305
Klene, Jean, C. S. C., 555
Kline, Barbara, 128
Kline, Daniel T., 895, 1015
Klitgard, Ebbe, 1397
Koch, John, 65
Koff, Leonard Michael, 295, 375
Kohanski, Tamarah, 808
Kohler, Michelle, 954
Kökeritz, Helge, 164
Kolve, V. A., 573, 1574
Koonce, B. G., 1513
Kordecki, Leslie, 1514
Koretsky, Allen C., 1088, 1270
Koster, Josephine A., 1366
Knapp, Daniel, 700
Knapp, Peggy A., 177, 508, 1176
Knapp, Robert, 1217
Knappe, Gabriele, 178
Knight, Stephen, 219, 509, 1145
Krier, Theresa M., 324
Krochalis, Jeanne, 19, 1676
Kruger, Steven F., 1398, 1515
Kuczynski, Michael, 673
Kuhn, Sherman M., 101
Kurath, Hans, 101
Kuskin, William, 139

Laird, Edgar, 1668–69
Laird, Judith, 1575
Lambdin, Laura C, 741
Lambdin, Robert T., 741
Lambert, Mark, 1271
Lampe, David, 1590
Lampert, Lisa, 542
Lancashire, Ian, 909
Landman, James, 832
Landman, Mark, 1177
Laskaya, Anne, 661
Lavezzo, Kathy, 833
Lawler, Traugott, 230, 585
Lawton, David, 376
Lee, Brian S., 963, 1004
Legassie, Shayne Aaron, 1039
Leicester, H. Marshall, 647, 674
Leitch, L. M., 719
Lenaghan, R. T., 896, 1591, 1642
Lerer, Seth, 111, 325, 338, 1670
Levy, Bernard S., 917
Levy, Lynne Hunt, 54
Lewis, C. S., 296, 450, 1242
Lewis, Celia, 1005
Lewis, Robert E., 101, 795, 834
Leyerle, John, 1516
Liggens, Elizabeth M., 1327
Lightsey, Scott, 432
Lindahl, Carl, 362, 510
Lindeboom, B. W., 326
Linden, Stanton J., 433
Lionarons, Joyce Tally, 434
Lipson, Carol S.1671
Lipton, Emma, 451
Little, Katherine C., 1207
Liu, Hongying, 1286
Livy, 262
Lochrie, Karma, 464–65, 796
Longsworth, Robert M., 872, 1155
Love, Damian, 1349
Lowes, John L., 1559
Luecke, Janemarie, 1168
Luengo, Anthony E., 987
Lumiansky, Robert M., 648
Lynch, Kathryn L., 66, 543, 564, 835, 933, 964, 1399, 1684

McAlpine, Monica A., 88, 1040, 1146, 1255, 1367
McCall, John P., 297, 1256, 1478
McCarl, Mary Rhinelander, 1685
McCarthy, Conor, 452, 662, 873
McColly, William B., 712
McCormack, Frances, 1208
McCracken, Samuel, 1178
McDonald, Charles O., 1479
McDonald, Nicola F., 1542
McEntire, Sandra J., 988
McGavin, John J., 197
McGerr, Rosemarie Potz., 377, 1218, 1384
McGillivray, Murray, 23
McGregor, James H., 574, 1576
McIlhaney, Anne E., 420
Mckenna, Isobel, 836
McKinley, Kathryn L., 874, 934
McLeod, Glenda, 1543
McMillan, Ann, 75
McTurk, Rory, 298
Macey, Samuel L., 1272
Machan, Tim William, 66a, 1655–58
Machaut, Guillaume de, 263–64
Mack, Peter, 1273
Macrobius, 265
Malaczkov, Szilvia, 1659
Malarkey, Stoddard, 1467
Mandel, Jerome H., 615, 663, 675, 1016
Manly, John M., 43, 649
Mann, Jill, 44, 220, 475, 689–90, 742, 935, 1118, 1306, 1353
Manning, Stephen, 1274
Mapstone, Sally, 1368
Margherita, Gayla, 1328
Martianus Dumiensis, 266
Martin, Ellen E., 1560
Martin, June Hall, 1350
Martin, Loy D., 743
Martin, Priscilla, 476
Martin, Thomas L., 1307
Marzec, Marcia Smith, 484, 1373
Masciandaro, Nicola, 1156
Masi, Michael, 477, 875, 1351
Masui, Michio, 221
Matheson, Lister M., 150
Matsuda, Takami, 1041
Matthews, David, 125
Matthews, William, 876
Maxfield, David K., 1042
Mayer, Lauryn S., 339
Mazzon, Gabriella, 179
Mead, Jenna, 531
Meale, Carol M., 1577
Means, M. H., 1427
Meech, Sanford B., 1257
Meecham-Jones, Simon, 494, 1517
Mehl, Dieter, 349, 1287, 1578
Mersand, Joseph, 180
Mertens-Fonke, Paule, 691
Meyer-Lee, Robert J., 522
Middleton, Anne, 350, 1017
Mieszkowski, Gretchen, 1369
Miki, Kunihiro, 102
Miller, Jacqueline T., 340, 1518
Miller, Mark, 586
Miller, Miriam Youngerman, 575
Miller, Robert P., 237
Milliken, Roberta, 1370
Millns, Tony, 676
Minnis, Alastair J., 207, 299, 341–42, 877, 1043–44, 1400, 1519, 1579, 1658, 1660–62
Miskimin, Alice S., 126
Mitchell, J. Allan, 483, 1308
Mitchell-Smith, Ilan, 769
Mize, Britt, 1643
Moon, Hi Kyung, 1544
Mooney, Linne R., 30, 435, 1675
Moore, Bruce, 809
Moore, Marilyn L. Reppa, 1352
Moore, Stephen G., 1119
Monz, Dominic, 495
Morgan, Gerald, 701, 744, 989, 1229
Morris, Lynn King, 238
Morrison, Susan Signe, 878
Morse, Charlotte Cook, 127, 936
Morse, Ruth, 327, 628, 1580
Mortiz, Theresa Anne, 607
Mosser, Daniel W., 30a, 31
Murphy, James J., 198
Murray, Molly, 1275
Murtaugh, Daniel M., 897
Muscatine, Charles, 199, 770
Myles, Robert, 389

Nair, Sashi, 1309
Nelson, Marie, 664
Neuse, Richard, 300, 955
Neville, Marie, 975
Newman, Barbara, 1310, 1480
Nicholas of Lynn, 267
Nicholson, Peter, 837, 1068
Noguchi, Shunichi, 770a
Noh, Kyung Lee, 1353
Nolan, Barbara, 301, 677, 1243, 1428
Nolan, Charles J., 1611
Nolan, Edward Peter, 302
Nolan, Maura, 838
Norsworthy, Scott, 1127
North, J. D., 436
Norton-Smith, John, 4, 112, 1606, 1629

Oberembt, Kenneth J., 879
Obermeier, Anita, 1219
O'Brien, Timothy D., 910, 1276
O'Connell, Brendan, 1157
O'Donoghue, Bernard, 453
Oerlemans, Omo, 1147
Oizumi, Akio, 102, 165
Oka, Saburo, 1581
Oliver, Kathleen M., 1089
Olsen, Clair C., 146
Olson, Alexandra Hennessey, 1341
Olson, Glending, 602, 616, 911, 1104
Olson, Paul A., 587, 1481
Olsson, Kurt, 1128
Orme, Nicholas, 692
Orth, William, 1090
Oruch, Jack B., 1482
Osberg, Richard H., 222, 1091, 1385
Osborn, Marijane, 437, 1045
Ovid, 268–71
Ovitt, George, Jr., 1672
Owen, A. E. B., 6
Owen, Charles A., Jr., 32, 390, 745, 848, 1120, 1429

Pace, George B., 67
Page, Barbara, 720
Pakkala-Weckström, Mari, 181, 990, 1121
Palmer, J. J. N., 1430
Palmer, R. Barton, 1545
Papka, Claudia Rattazi, 1386
Pardee, Sheila, 1129
Parker, R. H., 438
Parkes, Malcolm B., 5, 11, 13, 21, 26
Parr, Roger P., 650
Parry, Joseph D., 797
Partridge, Stephen, 814, 1677
Pask, Kevin, 343
Passmore, S. Elizabeth, 880
Patch, Howard, 391–92
Patterson, Lee W., 442, 511, 881, 1046–47, 1105, 1179, 1209, 1612
Patton, Celeste A., 1194
Paull, Michael R., 839
Payne, F. Anne, 629
Payne, Robert O., 200–01, 378, 561
Paxson, James J., 1277
Pearsall, Derek, 50, 151–52, 182, 328, 351, 379, 544, 588, 603, 1130, 1371
Peck, Russell A., 92–3, 393, 1169, 1483, 1562
Pelen, Marc M., 1006, 1195, 1431
Percival, Florence, 1546
Petrarch, 272
Petrus Alphonsus, 273
Phillips, Helen, 68–9, 303, 589, 1432–33, 1547, 1563–64, 1601, 1613
Phillips, Susan E., 183
Pichaske, David R., 721
Pigg, Daniel F., 1220
Pinti, Daniel, 1484, 1520
Pitcher, John A., 991
Pittard, Derrick G., 1210
Plummer, John F. III, 55, 722, 810
Porter, Gerald, 798
Potter, Russell A., 208
Power, Eileen, 1092
Pratt, John H., 496
Pratt, Robert A., 239, 604, 1148–49, 1244
Prendergast, Thomas A., 128, 1614
Price, Derek J., 70
Prior, Sandra Pierson, 799, 1018, 1434
Publilius Syrus, 274
Pugh, Tison, 466, 484, 723, 1329, 1399
Puhvel, Martin, 882
Pulham, Carol A., 992
Pulsiano, Phillip, 1387
Purdie, Rhiannon, 1106
Purdon, Liam, 1048, 1630
Putter, Ad, 223

Quilligan, Maureen, 1485
Quinn, William A., 693, 1435, 1521, 1548, 1602

Rambuss, Richard, 1093
Ramsey, Roger, 937
Rand Schmidt, Kari Anne, 1678
Ransom, Daniel J., 45
Raybin, David, 512, 840, 1170, 1180, 1211
Reed, Teresa P., 421
Reed, Thomas, 1486
Reichl, Karl, 1311
Reiss, Edmund, 202, 352, 702
Rex, Richard, 1094
Rhodes, Jim, 422
Richardson, Gudrun, 1049
Richardson, Janette, 898
Richmond, E. B., 76
Richmond, Velma Bourgeois, 113, 129, 454
Rickert, Edith, 43
Riddy, Felicity, 993
Ridley, Florence, 1095
Ridyard, Susan J., 123
Rigby, S. H., 114, 770b
Robbins, Rossell Hope, 1592–93
Robertson, D. W., 553, 556, 565, 771, 883, 1258
Robertson, Elizabeth, 405, 665, 841
Robertson, Kellie, 532
Robinson, Ian, 224, 329
Robinson, Pamela, 8, 9, 1679
Robinson, Peter, 49, 56
Rogers, P. Burwell, 713
Rogers, Shannon L., 103
Rogers, William E., 617, 1069
Roney, Lois, 394, 772
Ronquist, E. C., 994
Rooney, Anne, 1436
Root, Jerry, 884
Root, Robert Kilburn, 58, 1230
Roscow, Gregory, 166
Rose, Christine, 455, 956
Rosenberg, Bruce A., 363, 1158
Rosenblum, Joseph, 569
Ross, Diane M., 1437
Ross, Thomas W., 48, 184
Rossignol, Rosalyn, 104
Rothwell, W., 167, 185
Rowe, Donald W., 1259, 1549
Rowland, Beryl, 115, 364, 557–58, 630, 1288, 1522
Rudanko, Juhani, 186
Rudat, Wolfgang, 1355
Rudd, Gillian, 116
Rudd, Martin B., 153
Ruff, Nancy K., 1582
Ruffolo, Lara, 1523
Ruggiers, Paul, 38, 395, 590
Russell, H. N., 1230
Russell, J. Stephen, 591, 1401
Rust, Martha Dana, 140
Rutherford, Charles S., 1380
Ruud, Jay, 1487, 1594, 1644

Sadlek, Gregory, 456
Said, Edward, 545
Saito, Isumu, 1096
Salda, Michael Norman, 1438
Salih, Sarah, 631
Salter, Elizabeth, 21, 1289, 1439
Sánchez-Marti, Jordi, 1649
Sandved, Arthur O., 168
Sanok, Catherine, 632, 1342
Saul, Nigel, 497, 995
Saunders, Corinne J., 117–18, 457, 1583
Sayce, Olive, 1221
Scala, Elizabeth, 380
Scanlon, Larry, 633, 1131, 1150, 1312
Scase, Wendy, 1615

Scattergood, V. John., 815, 1070, 1107, 1159, 1196, 1616, 1631–32, 1645
Schaber, Bennet, 1313
Schaefer, Ursula, 169, 209
Schauber, Ellen, 1151
Scheps, Walter, 724
Schibanoff, Susan, 842, 885, 1278, 1343, 1402
Schildgen, Brenda Deen, 295, 423, 546
Schlauch, Margaret, 231, 843
Schmidt, A. V. C., 1633
Schnuttgen, Hildegard, 82
Schoff, Rebecca L., 141
Schümann, Michael, 178
Schutz, Andrea, 996
Schweitzer, Edward C., 773
Seaman, David M., 997
Sedgewick, G. G., 1050
Sell, Jonathan P. A., 1372
Sercambi, Giovanni, 275
Serrano-Reyes, Jesús L., 154
Seymour, M.C., 33, 1565
Seymour, Michael, 576
Shaffern, Robert W., 1051
Shannon, Edgar F., 304
Shapiro, Gloria, 886
Sharon-Zisser, Shirley, 976
Shepherd, Geoffrey, 396
Sheridan, Christian, 957, 1071
Sherman, Mark A., 774
Shippey, Tom T. A., 912, 1686
Shoaf, R. A., 592, 1290, 1440
Siegel, Marsha, 728
Sigal, Gale, 1260
Silar, Theodore I., 800, 1388
Silverman, Albert H., 1072
Silvia, D. S., 666
Simmons-O'Neill, Elizabeth, 958
Simpson, James, 305–06, 1524, 1550
Skeat, Walter W., 39, 1678
Skerpan, Elizabeth, 1019
Sklute, Larry, 381, 746
Slaughter, Eugene, 458
Sledd, James, 938
Slocum, Sally K., 1381
Smallwood, T. M., 641
Smith, Jeremy. J., 170
Smith, Warren S., 887, 998
Snell, William, 1052
Solopova, Elizabeth, 46
Somerset, Fiona, 913
Southworth, James G., 225
Spearing, A. C., 459, 678, 844, 1231, 1291, 1389, 1488
Specht, Henrik, 651, 999
Spector, Stephen, 1097
Spencer, H. Leith, 634
Spencer, Matthew, 605, 1666
Spolsky, Ellen, 1151
Spurgeon, Caroline F., 130
St. John, Michael, 1403
Staley, Lynn, 402, 523, 1116, 1166, 1181, 1339
Stallcup, Stephen, 1607
Stanbury, Sarah, 566, 566a, 939, 1330
Steadman, John M., 1390, 1525
Stein, Robert M., 775
Steinberg, Glenn, 1526
Stemmler, Theo, 1622
Stephens, John, 1595
Stevens, Martin, 14, 34, 226
Stevenson, Kay Gilliland, 1441, 1527
Stierstorfer, Klaus, 1261
Stillinger, Thomas C., 1245
Stillwell, Gardner, 1122
Stock, Lorraine Kochanske, 959, 1442
Stokes, Myra, 1279, 1314
Stone, Brian, 77
Storm, Melvin, 776, 1053
Straus, Barrie Ruth, 667
Stretter, Robert, 777
Striar, Brian, 1197
Strohm, Paul, 353–54, 513, 524, 533, 816, 888, 1054, 1123, 1566, 1617, 1634
Stroud, T. A., 1382
Stubbs, Estelle, 17, 35
Sturges, Robert S., 1055
Sturgin, Michael, 498
Sudo, Jan, 1246
Summit, Jennifer, 478
Sutherland, Ronald, 1650
Sutton, Marilyn, 91
Swanson, Robert W., 1212
Sweetland, Laura, 721
Sweeney, Michelle, 1000
Sylvester, Louise, 1584
Szittya, Penn R., 849, 914

Taavitsainen, Irma, 642
Takada, Yasunari, 1489, 1618
Tarlinskaja, Marina G., 227
Tatlock, J. S. P., 606, 960
Taylor, Andrew, 42, 1551
Taylor, Beverly, 1585
Taylor, Davis, 1356
Taylor, Karla, 307–08, 1280
Taylor, Mark N., 1443
Taylor, Paul Beekman., 210, 460, 499, 1333
Thomas, Alfred, 547
Thomas, Paul, 51
Thomas, Susanne Sara, 1056, 1182
Thompson, Ann, 330
Thompson, John, 1603
Thompson, Kenneth J., 714
Thompson, Lou, 1444
Thompson, N. S., 309
Thormann, Janet, 1073
Thundy, Zacharias P., 889, 1445
Tinkle, Theresa, 467, 1490
Tisdale, Charles P., 1446
Tolkien, J. R. R., 811
Torti, Anna, 1262
Trapp, J. B., 137
Traversi, Derek, 593, 1001, 1404
Travis, Peter W., 725, 1152, 1222, 1447, 1552
Trigg, Stephanie, 131
Trower, Katherine B., 1007
Tschann, Judith, 1108
Turner, Marion, 514, 1315

Uebel, Michael, 1020
Urban, Malte, 1316–17
Ussery, Huling E., 1021
Utz, Richard J., 388, 397, 399

Valerius Maximus, 276
Van Dyke, Carolynn, 398
Vasta, Edward, 1623
Vaughan, Míceál F., 1200, 1223
Vitto, Cindy L., 1373
Volk-Birke, Sabine, 365

Wack, Mary, 1331
Walker, Denis, 1448
Walker, Greg, 331
Wallace, David, 310–11, 515, 567, 817
Wallace-Hadrill, Anne, 97
Warburton, Rachel, 1586
Wasserman, Julian N. J. N., 778, 827, 850, 1265
Waswo, Richard, 1292
Waters, Claire M., 1213
Watson, Nicholas, 424
Watson, Robert A., 1449
Watts, Ann C., 1528
Watts, William H., 399
Waugh, Robin, 940
Webb, Diana, 703
Weil, Eric, 1184
Weisl, Angela Jane, 636, 668
Weismann, Hope Phyllis, 479
Wentersdorf, Karl P., 961
Wenzel, Siegfried, 425, 1132, 1214
Wetherbee, Winthrop, 312, 594, 637, 779–80, 1247, 1450
Wheatley, Edward, 638
White, Hugh, 1491
White, Robert B., Jr., 1133
Wilkins, Nigel, 577
Williams, Arnold, 899
Williams, David, 900, 1057, 1318
Williamson, Tara, 941
Wilson, Grace G., 313
Wimsatt, James I., 314, 890, 1281–82, 1451–52, 1596–97, 1608
Windeatt, Barry. A., 59, 78, 327, 1232, 1263, 1332, 1405
Winick, Stephen D., 643

Wong, Jennifer, 1635
Wood, Chauncey, 382, 439, 1198, 1233
Wood, Marjorie Elizabeth, 845
Woods, Marjorie Curry, 203, 1374
Woods, William F., 801, 812, 818
Woodward, Daniel, 14, 34
Wright, David, 79
Wright, Glenn, 1109
Wurtele, Douglas J., 652, 1201, 1215

Yager, Susan, 516
Yeager, R. F., 332, 1391, 1619–20
Young, Karl, 1248

Zacher, Christian, 704
Zatta, Jane Dick, 1134
Zeikowitz, Richard E., 485, 1058
Zeitoun, Franck, 1344
Zieman, Katherine, 344, 425a
Zimbardo, Rose A., 1453

Glossary

The most convenient comprehensive glossary to Chaucer—with line numbers and parts of speech—is *A Chaucer Glossary* (1979; no. 97), although it can be supplemented by reference to *A Glossarial Concordance to the Riverside Chaucer* (1993; no. 95) or the glossary in the back of *The Riverside Chaucer* (1987; no. 36). The most authoritative resource is *The Middle English Dictionary* (2001; no. 101), freely available online for everyone's use at <http://quod.lib.umich.edu/m/med/>.

Because substantive words have been glossed on the pages where they occur, the following glossary is composed chiefly of form words: verb forms, adverbs, prepositions, and variant spellings. The great difficulty with creating or using a Middle English glossary, as with reading the texts, is that spellings were not standardized. Each scribe spelled as he thought he heard the words and felt little compunction about spelling the same word differently in contiguous passages. The Chaucer surname was spelled at least six ways in the records: *Chaucer, Chaucere, Chaucey, Chauser, Chausier,* and *Chawceres.* The reader should bear in mind the common variations in orthography: *i* and *y* are interchangeable *(ire, yre); e* and *i* are interchangeable *(be, bi); ee, ie,* and *e* are interchangeable *(leef, lief, lefe); o* and *ou* are interchangeable *(conseil, counseil);* vowels and consonants may be doubled *(brode, brood; unethe, unnethe);* metathesis may occur *(thorp, throp*); and there are other variations (see the essay on Chaucer's Language, esp. pp. 965–66). Imagination, context, and association must be called on to interpret both words and forms.

a, a, one, on
abaissen, to be dismayed
abandoune, to devote
abiden, to wait for, to dwell, to endure
abit, waited for
abite, habit, clothes
abayst, abashed, shy
aboghte, bought, paid for, endured
abood, waited for, delayed
aboute, about, engaged in
abreyden, to awake, to start up
accioun, action, accusation
acorsen, to curse
acoyen, to caress, to soothe
adawen, to awake
adoun, downwards, at the bottom
advertence, attention
afered, afraid
aferen, to frighten
affect, desire *(n)*
aforyeyn, opposite
after, after, for, in accordance with
again, against, toward, compared with, in return, again
agains, instead of, near to, opposite to
agilten, to do wrong, injure
agref, in grief, angry
agreggen, to aggravate
agroos, trembled, was terrified
agrysen, to tremble, to be terrified
acknowen, to acknowledge
alday, continually
alder, of all *(archaic genitive)*
alderbest, best of all
aldernext, nearest of all
algate(s), always, at any rate, nevertheless
alleggen, to allege, to alleviate
allowen, to approve, to applaud
als, also
alther, see *alder*
altherfirst, first of all
alyne, in line
amased, to be amazed
amayen, to dismay
amenusen, to lessen, to diminish
ame(o)ven, to move, to dismay
among, between, among, always
amonges, together, sometimes
amortisen, to kill
anguisshen, to cause pain
anhangen, to hang
anientissen, to annihilate
anon, at once, soon
anonrightes, immediately
anything, at all
apayen, to satisfy, to please
apeiren, to injure, to damage
aperceyven, to perceive, to realize
apert, evident, openly
appetyt, desire
apposen, to question
appreven, to approve, to prove
apyken, to adorn
aquyten, to pay back
aracen, to uproot, to tear out, to erase
areden, to explain, to guess

aretten, to blame, to attribute to
arewe, arowe, in a row
arowe, arrow
arten, to induce
artow, you are, are you
ascaunces, as if
ascry, outcry, alarm *(n)*
aslaken, to satisfy, to diminish
aspre, sharp, bitter
assoilen, to absolve, to pay, to explain
asterten, to escape
ataken, to overtake
auntren, to risk it
availen, to avail, to be useful, to be effective
avalen, to fall down
avauncen, to advance, to be profitable
avaunten, to boast
aventure, luck, fortune
avouterye, adultery
avowen, to proclaim
avys, advice
avysen, to consider
awaiten, to watch for, to ambush
awhapen, to amaze, to frighten
awreken, to avenge
axen, to ask
ay, always
ayein, ayeins, see *again, agains*

bachelere, young man, young knight
bacin, basin
baiten, to feed
bale, suffering
balke, roof beam
bane, death, cause of death
barm, bosom
baude, bawd, pimp
bauderie, mirth, obscenity
baume, balm
beden, to offer, to command
beeth, be *(imperative)*
bekken, to nod
bely, belly, bellows
benden, to bend, to turn
benedicite, bless you
bent, grassy slope
beren, to bear, to carry, to conduct oneself
bespreynt, sprinkled
bet, better
beten, to heal, to mend
beten, to beat
bidden, to ask, to command
biheste, promise, command
biheten, to promise
bihighte, promised
bihoten, to promise
bihoven, to suit, to be necessary
biknowen, to acknowledge
bileve, belief
bileven, to believe, to stay behind
binimen, to take away
bireven, to take away, to deprive
biseyen, to gaze; **wel beseye,** good looking
bishenden, to bring to ruin
bishitten, to shut up
bisi, bisy, active, careful, intense
bisinesse, work, attention
bistad, in trouble
bitraisen, to betray
bityden, to happen
bitymes, early, soon
biwreyen, to reveal
biwryen, to betray
blenden, to make blind
blent, blinded
blinnen, to cease
boden, to proclaim
boistous, crude, plain
bokeler, small shield
bolt-upright, flat on the back
bord, table
borwe, security *(n)*
bo(o)te, benefit, remedy *(n)*
bo(o)telees, without remedy
bour, bedroom
bourde, joke
brede, breadth
breme, furiously, fiercely
brennen, to burn
breste, to break
bretful, full to the brim
breyden, to awake, to start up
brood, broad, large
brotel, brittle, fickle
brouken, to enjoy, to use
burel, rough, ignorant
but if, unless
buxom, obedient
by, concerning, near, during
byden, to wait
byen, to buy, to redeem
byhighte, promised

caas, case, event, chance
caitif, captive, miserable wretch
can, to be able, to know
canstow, do you know, can you
caryene, corpse
cart, cart, chariot
casten, to throw, to calculate
casuelly, accidentally
catel, chattels, property

cause, cause, reason, purpose
certes, certainly, indeed
ceynt, girdle
chacen, to chase, to hunt
chaffaren, to bargain
chaire, chair, throne
chalangen, to claim, to challenge
chapman, merchant
char, chariot
charge, load *(n)*
chaunce, chance, destiny
chep, trade, bargain *(n)*; cheap *(adj)*
che(e)re, face, expression, behavior
cherl, commoner, ruffian
chesen, to choose
child, child, young man
cle(e)r, clear, bright, beautiful, obvious
clene, clean, pure
clepen, to call, to name
cleren, to grow clear, to grow bright
clerk, student, scholar
clippen, to cut, to embrace
clombe, climbed
clos, enclosure
clos, close, secret *(adj)*
clout, rag
cokewold, cuckold, deceived husband
comm(o)even, to persuade
compas, plan, circle *(n)*
compassen, to contrive, to encircle *(v)*
conjecten, to conjecture
connen, to be able, to learn
conning, skill, knowledge
conseil, council, secret
constreinen, to compel, to control
contek, strife
convenient, suitable, appropriate
converten, to change
conveyen, to convey, to accompany
corage, courage, heart, spirit, disposition
corps, cors, body
cosin, cousin, relative
cote armure, coat of arms
couchen, to lie down, to lay down
coude, could, knew
counten, to calculate accounts
counting-bord, accounting office
couthe, could, knew, known
covenable, fitting, suitable
covert, secret
covyne, deceitfulness
coy, quiet
craft, trade, cunning
creaunce, belief *(n)*
creauncen, to borrow on credit
croys, cross
cunnen, to know
cunning, skill
cure, care, treatment, attention
curteis, courteous

daliaunce, small talk, flirting
dan, daun, lord (title of respect, from Lat. *dominus*)
daswen, to be dazed, to dim
daunger, aloofness, disdain, control
daunten, to tame, to subdue
debaat, quarrel
debonair, kind, gentle
deedly, deadly, causing death, subject to death
deel, part
defaut, fault, lack
degre(e), social rank, level, rung
delen, to divide, to have dealings (with)
delicat, dainty, sensitive
delices, delights, pleasures
deliveren, to release
demen, to judge, to decide
departen, to separate, to divide
dereworthe, beloved, valuable
despyt, spite, malice, disdain
destreynen, to constrain, to distress, to keep
devoir, duty
devys, device, discretion
devysen, to devise, to tell, to describe
deynen, to grant, to condescend
deynte, valuable object, delight *(n)*; pleasant, rare *(adj)*
dighten, to prepare, to dress
discoveren, to reveal
discryven, to describe, to make a mark
disese, discomfort, displeasure
dispenden, to spend
dispitous, spiteful, cruel
disponen, to dispose, to arrange
disporten, to play, to amuse
divynen, to guess
doom, judgment, opinion
doon, to do, to cause to be done
douten, to fear, to frighten
drenchen, to drown
dressen, to dress, to address, to direct, to prepare
dreynte, drowned
dreyen, to suffer, to endure
duren, to endure, to last
durren, to dare
durring, daring, courage
dwellen, to remain, to delay

echen, to increase
echoon, each one
eft, again, afterward

eft-sone, immediately, afterward, once again
egre, bitter, fierce
eke, eek, also
elde, old age
elden, to grow old
elles, otherwise, else
emforth, to the extent of
enchaufen, to burn, to grow hot
enchesoun, reason, occasion
endelong, lengthwise, alongside
endyten, to compose, to write
enforce, to strive, to compel, to strengthen
engyn, contrivance, ingenuity
entecchen, to stain, to infect
entenden, to give attention to, to attend, to intend
ententif, diligent, eager
entremetten, to interfere
er(e), before, rather
eren, to plow
erst, first, before
ermen, to feel sad
eschaufen, to burn, to grow hot
eschewen, to escape, to avoid
esily, easily, slowly
espyen, to observe, to perceive, to inquire, to spy upon
estat, rank, condition
estres, interior (of a building)
ethe, easy
eyr, air, heir

facultee, disposition, capacity
fallen, to befall, to happen
falsen, to deceive, to be untrue
fare, conduct, behavior, business
faren, to behave, to travel
faste, firmly, intensely, close by, quickly
fawe, glad, anxious
fayn, gladly, eagerly
fee, reward, compensation
feendly, fiendlike
feet, feat, deed, performance
feffen, to endow, to present
fel, skin
fel, cruel, terrible
felawe, companion
fele, many
felonous, fierce, wicked
ferd, fear *(n);* frightened, feared (past t. *v*); traveled
fere, mate, companion
feren, to frighten, to be afraid
ferforth, as far as
ferly, strange
ferme, income, rent
fermen, to make firm
fern, long ago
ferne, distant
ferre, distant, farther
feste, feast, pleasure
festen, to feast, to please
fet, fette, fetched
fetis, neat, attractive
fey, faith
feynen, to feign, to pretend, to counterfeit
ficchen, to fix
fil, fild, befell, happened
finden, to find, to provide for
fint, finds
fleen, to fly, to flee
fleigh, (it) flies
flemen, to banish
fleten, to float, to drift
fley, flew
flitten, to pass away
flokmele, in a group
flough, flew
flyen, to fly; (they) fled
foisoun, abundance
folily, foolishly
fonden, to try
fongen, to receive
for-, intensifying prefix
for, because
forbrused, badly bruised
fordon, to destroy, to kill
forlesen, to lose
forleten, to forsake, to cease
forlorn, lost
fors, force; **no fors**, no matter
forthy, therefore
forward, promise, agreement
for-why, for what reason
foryaf, forgave
foryeten, to forget
foryeven, to forgive
fot-hoot, hot-footed, immediately, quickly
foul, fowl, bird; dirty, ugly
f(o)undement, foundation, anus
foynen, to thrust, to stab
foyson, abundance
fraynen, freynen, to ask, to beseech
free, generous, bounteous
fremede, foreign, wild
freten, to eat (like an animal), to devour
fro, from
froten, to rub
frounce, wrinkle
ful, very, full, completely, total
furlong, 220 yards
furlong-wey, brief time (time it takes to walk a furlong)
furthren, to help

fyn, end, result *(n);* refined
fynt, (he) finds

gabbe, idle talk, lies
galen, to exclaim, to yell
game, entertainment, pleasure, game, joke
gan, began
gat, got
gaude, toy, trick
gay, dressed up, decorated
geaunt, giant
geeth, goes
gent, refined
gerdoun, reward
gere, equipment, apparel
gery, changeable
geste, tale, story
gif, if
gin, snare, contrivance
ginne, to begin, to try
girle, young person, girl
glede, live coal
glood, glided
glosen, to gloss, to interpret, to lie
gobet, piece
go(o)n, to go, to walk
go(o)st, spirit, soul, ghost
governaunce, management, rule
grace, favor, divine gift, fortune
grame, anger, harm
gras, grace, favor
graven, to engrave, to dig, to bury
gree, favor; rank
gre(e)t, great, principal
greythen, to prepare, to adorn
greven, to harm, to feel unhappy
grint, ground (past t. of *grind)*
grisly, horrible
gropen, to grope, to search, to examine
grucchen, to grumble
gruf, groveling, prostrate
guerdon, reward
gyen, to guide
gylour, beguiler
gyse, manner, way, guise
gyte, dress *(n)*

haf, heaved
habundaunce, abundance
halen, to pull, to attract
halke, corner
halp, helped
hals, neck
halt, held
halten, to limp
halwe, saint, shrine
hap, chance, luck
happed, (it) happened
hardely, boldly
hardy, brave
harm, pain, injury, pity
harwed, harried, despoiled
hastow, hast thou (have you)
hatte, promised, was named
haunten, to engage in, to practice
heet, was named
heigh, high, lofty
hele, health
helen, to conceal
henten, to catch, to seize
her, her, here, their
heren, to hear
herien, to praise
heste, command (*n*)
heten, to promise
hethen, hence
hette, promised, was named
heven, to heave, to lift
heved, head
hevy, heavy, sad
heye, high, aristocratic
hider, hither
highte, promised, was named
hir, her, their
hit, it
holly, wholly
holpe, helped
holt, woodland
holt, (he) holds
honest, creditable, honorable
hongen, to hang
hool, whole
hoten, to command, to promise
housbondrye, domestic management
hoven, to watch, to attend
hy, high
hye, haste
hyen, to hasten

i- (y-), prefix indicating past tense
ich, I
ilike, alike, equally
ilke, same, like
in, inne, dwelling
inned, lodged
inogh, enough
iwis, certainly, indeed

janglen, to chatter
jape, trick, joke

joly, cheerful, amorous, handsome
journee, day's march
juyse, justice

keen, cows *(n)*; sharp, bold *(adj)*
keepen, to care for, to notice
kemben, to comb
kempte, combed, neatly dressed
kene, keen, eager
kepe, care, attention
kinde, nature, lineage, disposition
kindely, naturally
knitten, to join
koude, could, knew, knew how to
kythen, to show, to display

lakken, to blame, to disparage
lappe, flap, edge or hem of a garment
lappen, to enfold
large, large, generous
las, lace, net, snare
laude, praise, honor
launde, grassy clearing
lay, song, law
leef, lief, dear, agreeable, beloved
lemman, sweetheart
lenen, to lend
lere, flesh, skin
leren, lernen, to teach, to learn
lesen, to lose
lesing, untruth
lest, inclination, pleasure *(n)*; for fear that, in case that *(conj)*
leten, to permit, to abandon
letten, to prevent, to hinder
leven, to believe, to allow
lever, rather, preferable
lewed, unlearned, ignorant, immoral
liche, like
liggen, to lie
light, light, joyous, fickle
lightly, easily, quickly
likerous, lecherous
lisse, comfort, solace
list, pleasure, desire; (with dative *me list, you list)* it pleases
lite, little
loos, praise
losen, to praise
loth, hateful, unwilling
lufsom, lovable
lust, desire, pleasure
lyflode, means of living
lyst, lystow, you lie

maistow, you may, may you
maistrye, control, skill, professional competence
make, mate
malgre, in spite of
manere, kind of, method
mat, dejected, defeated
maugre, in spite of
may, maiden
medlen, to mingle, to mix
meed, reward, bribe
mene, middle, mediator
menen, to say, to intend, to mean
mesure, moderation, measurement
meten, to dream, to meet
meynee, household, followers, retinue
misericorde, pity, mercy
misese, trouble, discomfort
mo, more
moeble, moveable property, furniture
moot, mot, mote, must, ought to, shall
moutance, amount
mowen, to be able
muchel, much, many

n-, negative prefix
nadde, had not *(ne had)*
nam, am not
namore, no more
nas, was not
nayten, to refuse
ne, not, nor
neigh, near
nempnen, to name, to say
nere, nearer *(adv)*; were not *(v)*
nether, lower
nevenen, to name, to say
nexte, nearest
nil, will not
niste, knew not
nolde, would not
noot, don't know
nones (for the, with the), on this occasion, in this situation, indeed *(only in phrases)*
nost, don't know
nouthe, now, at present
ny, near
nyce, foolish

or, ere, before
ordinaunce, arrangement, order, command
outrage, excess
owen, to own, to be obligated
owher, anywhere

paas, pas, pace, step
pacen, to pass, to go, to proceed

paramour, sweetheart, love-making *(n)*; for the sake of love *(adj)*
paraventure, perhaps, by accident
pardee, an exclamation (Fr. *par Dieu)*
parfey, an exclamation (Fr. *par fei)*
parfit, perfect
parten, to share, to divide
partye, portion
passen, to surpass, to overcome
payen, to satisfy, to pay *(v)*; pagan *(n)*
perdurable, eternal
peyne, pain, torture
pighte, pitched, fell
plat, flat
plesaunce, pleasure
pleten, to plead, to argue
pleyne, to complain, to lament
plighte, plucked, pulled
plighten, to pledge
port, behavior, carriage
povre, poor
preef, proof, assertion, test
prees, press, crowd, throng
prest, ready, prompt
preven, to prove, to test
preyen, to beseech, to request
priken, to puncture, to urge, to incite
prime, 9:00 a.m.
pris, prize, value, price
privee, secret, intimate
process, process, argument, narrative
propre, one's own, especial, well made
proven, to test
purpre, purple
purveiaunce, foresight, foreseeing, providence
pyne, pain, torture

queynt, strange, curiously contrived *(adj)*; female genitalia *(n)*
quik, alive, lively, quick
quiken, to revive
quod, said
quo(o)k, quaked, trembled
quyten, to repay, to reward, to pay back

rage, anger, passion, grief
rakel, rash *(adj)*
rathe, soon, quickly
rather, earlier, more willingly
ravisshen, to abduct, to carry away
real, royal
recchen, to care about
recorden, to recall, to confirm
reden, to read, to advise
re(e)d, counsel, advice *(n)*; the color red *(adj)*
refut, refuge
regne, realm, dominion over
reckenen, to reckon, to calculate accounts
rekken, to care about
reneyen, to deny, to renounce
rente, income, revenue
repairen, to return, to go back
repreve, reproof, reproach
requeren, to be sought for, to ask, to request
resoun, correct, sensible, an argument
respyt, delay
reven, to rob, to remove
reward, regard, attention
rewde, rude, plain
rewen, to have pity, to sorrow, to regret
rewthe, pity
right, right, just, straight
rihtwis, righteous
rode, cross; complexion
ronne, ran
roof, pierced
ropen, reaped
rote, by heart *(by rote)*
rote, root; fiddle
rounen, to whisper
route, band, company
routen, to roar, to snore
routhe, pity, mercy
rowe, roughly *(adv)*; row, line *(n)*
ryven, to pierce

sad, sober, steadfast
sans, sauns, without
sauf, save, except
sawe, speech, saying
skathe, a pity, misfortune
science, knowledge, science, wisdom
scripture, writing
scrit, writing
sechen, to seek
secree, secret, confidential
see, seat
sein, seyn, to say
sekernes, security
sely, holy, good, innocent, pitiable, foolish
semblable, similar
semblaunt, appearance
semely, attractive, pleasant
sentence, meaning, subject, maxim
sermoun, discourse, sermon
servage, servitude
seurete, security
sewen, to follow, to chase
sey, saw (past t. of *see)*
shaltow, you shall, shall you

shapen, to plan, to contrive, to intend
shenden, to disgrace, to destroy
shene, bright, shining, beautiful
sheten, to shoot
shetten, to shut
shonde, shame, disgrace
shrewe, scoundrel, villain
shrewednesse, wickedness
shrift, confession
siken, to sigh
siker, sure, secure
sith, sithen, since, afterward
sithes, times
skile, reason, cause
skilful, reasonable
slee, to slay
sleighte, trickery
smert, pain
socour, help
sola(a)s, consolation, pleasure, entertainment
somdel, somewhat
sond, sand
sonde, messenger
sort, destiny
so(o)t, sweet
so(o)th, true, truely
sounen, to sound, to incline toward, to accord with
sours, source, rising
sovereyn, supreme, principal
speden, to succeed, to hasten, to finish
spillen, to spill, to destroy
statut, law
stede, horse, place
stenten, to stop, to cease
steren, to stir up
sterten, to start, to move quickly
sterven, to die
stevene, voice
stinten, to leave off, to stop
stounde, hour, time, while
stra(u)nge, foreign, unfamiliar
streit, narrow
streynen, to compress, to constrain
studien, to consider thoughtfully
suffisaunce, sufficiency
surmouten, , to surpass
sweven, dream *(n)*; to dream *(v)*
swich, such
swink, work
swote, sweet
swoune, swoon, faint
swythe, quickly
swyven, have sexual intercourse
syk, sick, sigh
sythe, time

t'-, prefix *to*
t'acord, to accord
talent, wish, appetite
tecches, flaws
tene, vexation, adversity
terme, appointed time
th'-, prefix *the, thee*
th'absence, the absence
th'alight, thee alight
thar, it is necessary
theen, to prosper
theech, theek, I (may) prosper
th'ende, the end
therwith, with that
therwithal, moreover
thewes, habits, morals
thilke, that same, that sort
thinken, to seem; **me thinkes,** it seems to me; **how thinketh you,** how does it seem to you
thirlen, to pierce
tho, those, then
thonke, thank(s)
thorp, village
thral, slave, subject
thresten, to thrust
thridde, third
thrift, welfare, success
thriftily, fittingly
thringen, to crowd, to press
throwe, short time
thryven, to thrive, to prosper
to-, intensifying prefix
tobreken, to break to pieces
todriven, to scatter
tohepe, together
tollen, to take a toll, to attract
toracen, to tear to pieces
tough, tough, strong, troublesome
travaile, labor, suffering
treten, to treat, to behave, to describe
tretys, well-fashioned, neat
triste, trust
trouthe, fidelity, promise
trowen, to believe
tweye, two
twinnen, to separate, to sever
tyden, to befall, to happen

uncouth, strange, curious
uncunninge, ignorant, foolish, unknowing
undern, morning
undertaken, to declare, to undertake
unethe, scarcely, with difficulty
unhap, misfortune
unkinde, unnatural

unlust, disinclination
unmete, unfit
unwar, unexpected, unaware
unwist, unknown
upbreyde, accuse
upright, upright, flat on one's back
usage, usage, custom
usen, to be accustomed, to use

verray, true, genuine, actual, precise
vertu, power, excellence
viage, voyage, trip
vileinye, disgrace, evil, shameful speech, shameful action
vouche sauf, affirm, agree, grant

waden, to wade, to enter upon
waiten, to attend upon
wanten, to be lacking, to be absent
war, prudent, cautious
warien, to curse
warisshen, to cure
warnen, to inform, to warn
wayten, to wait, to expect, to observe
wele, good fortune, success *(n)*; happy *(adj)*
welden, to rule over
welle, spring, source
wenden, to go
wenen, to suppose, to imagine, to think
wenestow, do you suppose
wente, turn, path
werche, work
were, doubt
weren, to wear, to defend
werien, to make weary
wernen, to refuse, to forbid
werreyen, to make war
wexen, to increase, to become, to grow
wey, way, path
weyven, to waive, to turn aside, to neglect
wher, where, whether
whylom, once, formerly
wight, person, living creature *(n)*; active, nimble *(adj)*
wikke, wicked
wilnen, to desire
wilninge, willing
winnen, to win, to gain
wirchen, to work
wissen, to teach
wiste, knew
witen, to know
witestow, did you know
withal, moreover
withseyen, to contradict, to renounce
witing, knowledge
wol, (I) will
wolt, woltow, will you
wolde, would
wone, custom, wont
wonen, to dwell, to inhabit
wood, mad, insane, furious
worship, honor, reputation
worthen, to be, to become
wot, (I) know, (he) knows
wost, wostow, (do) you know
wraw, angry, fretful
wrecche, wretch, unhappy being
wreche, vengeance
wroghte, worked
wryen, to cover, to hide; to turn aside
wrythen, to twist away, to escape
wyten, to blame, to accuse

y-, prefix indicating past tense
yaf, gave
yare, ready
yate, gate
yede, walked
yelden, to give, to yield
yerde, stick, rod, bough
yerne, eager, brisk
yeven, to give
ynogh, enough
yore, long ago, formerly, for a long time
yvel(e), evil
ywis, certainly